D0757616

AMERICAN AUTHORS

1600-1900

THE AUTHORS SERIES

AMERICAN AUTHORS: 1600-1900

BRITISH AUTHORS BEFORE 1800

BRITISH AUTHORS OF THE NINETEENTH CENTURY

EUROPEAN AUTHORS: 1000-1900

TWENTIETH CENTURY AUTHORS

TWENTIETH CENTURY AUTHORS: FIRST SUPPLEMENT

WORLD AUTHORS: 1950-1970

THE JUNIOR BOOK OF AUTHORS

MORE JUNIOR AUTHORS

THIRD BOOK OF JUNIOR AUTHORS

AMERICAN AUTHORS
1600-1900

A Biographical Dictionary of American Literature

Edited by

STANLEY J. KUNITZ

and

HOWARD HAYCRAFT

COMPLETE IN ONE VOLUME WITH
1300 BIOGRAPHIES AND
400 PORTRAITS

NEW YORK
THE H. W. WILSON COMPANY
NINETEEN HUNDRED THIRTY-EIGHT

First Printing 1938

Second Printing 1940

Third Printing 1949

Fourth Printing 1955

Fifth Printing 1960

Sixth Printing 1964

Seventh Printing 1968

Eighth Printing 1977

PRINTED IN THE UNITED STATES OF AMERICA

International Standard Book Number 0-8242-0001-2

Library of Congress Catalog Card Number 38-27938

Preface

IN the growing library of contemporary reference productions this work aims to fill the gap caused by the omission of a handy one-volume biographical dictionary in the field of American literature. No work answering to or even resembling this description is today in print. The *Cyclopaedia of American Literature* by the brothers Duyckinck (2 vols.) and *Allibone's Critical Dictionary of English Literature and British and American Authors* (5 vols.) are essentially products of the mid-nineteenth century and as such no longer commonly available or serviceable. The only other analogous work is O. F. Adams' slight and forgotten *Dictionary of American Authors,* the last edition of which appeared in 1905. Information on the minor American authors in the universal encyclopedias is, when it is found at all, often inadequate and sometimes erroneous. The average student of American literature, in search of ready biographical data, has relied, perforce, almost wholly on the twenty volumes of the great *Dictionary of American Biography* or the even more numerous volumes of the *National Cyclopaedia of American Biography,* to be found only in the larger public and institutional libraries of the country. The editors of the present work, although it is in a single volume prepared mainly for smaller libraries, schools, and individual desk reference, have been able, by virtue of the special nature of the project, to include sketches of many authors of merit and interest who do not appear in any of the larger general works of collective biography. The book has been conceived and executed as a unit, and an earnest effort has been made to coordinate and integrate all the material, particularly the critical judgments.

This volume contains, in all, biographies of almost 1300 authors, of both major and minor significance, who participated in the making of our literary history from the time of the first English settlement at Jamestown in 1607 to the close of the 19th century. No living authors are included. The length of the sketches, ranging from approximately 150 to 2500 words, is roughly proportionate to the importance of the literary contributions of the subjects. Primary emphasis has been on "professional" men and women of letters—poets, novelists, historians, biographers, critics, etc.—as the phrase is generally interpreted; but the reader will find as well many educators, statesmen (with the exception of Presidents of the United States), orators, jurists, clergymen, and the like, whose published works (though no longer "literary" in today's meaning of the term) made up much of our national literature in an earlier day.

Each biographical sketch is followed by a list of the principal works of the author in question, with original dates of publication. A list of biographical and critical sources about each author is also given as a guide to further study.

A feature of the volume of which the editors are—pardonably, we hope—proud is the presence of exactly 400 photolithographically reproduced portraits, many of them rare and hitherto unpublished.

More than 150 of the portraits are from the photographic collection of Frederick H. Meserve of New York City, to whom we owe the privilege of publishing them as a contribution to Americana. Most, though not all, of the Meserve portraits are original and previously unpublished photographs and daguerreotypes by the great pioneer of American photography, Mathew B. Brady, reproduced here for the first time from the original negatives in Mr. Meserve's possession.

In the selection of the 400 portraits no effort was spared to discover authentic and representative portrayals of the subjects. Whenever possible, portraits were chosen which showed the subjects in the prime of their careers, rather than in the sunset years. Where non-photographic portraits are used, the names of the artists and dates of portraits are given whenever known. All the portraits are believed to be authentic and contemporary unless otherwise noted.

In the preparation of this work the editors have been aided by an unusually capable staff of writers, including B. Alsterlund, Eleanor Danysh, Miriam Allen deFord, Dorothy Fletcher, Mary Grahn, K. Ward Hooker, Julia E. Johnsen, Lina Kahn, Marianna Lewis, and Sylvia Spencer. Special acknowledgment is gratefully made to Miss Alsterlund, who has acted so ably as editorial assistant, and to Miss deFord, whose suggestions and contributions have proved of exceptional value. We also wish to express our thanks to the Photostat, Picture, and Reference Information departments of the New York Public Library and to the Manuscript and Periodicals division and the Rare Book room of the Library of Congress for their many acts of unfailing courtesy and helpfulness.

The contents of this book have been checked and re-checked against the best available sources to guarantee their accuracy, but we do not flatter ourselves that in a work of such scope and multiplicity of detail we have been able to eliminate all errors of fact or type. We should appreciate having these brought to our attention so that they may be corrected in future editions.

THE EDITORS
September 1938

American Authors: 1600-1900

ABBEY, HENRY (July 11, 1842-June 7, 1911), poet, was born at Rondout (a part of Kingston), N. Y., the son of Stephen Abbey, a grain merchant, and Caroline (Vail) Abbey. He studied at Kingston Academy and the Hudson River Institute, but family financial reverses kept him from college. When he was twenty his first book appeared—a volume of poems entitled *May Dreams.* After a brief editorship on the Rondout *Courier* and journalistic experience in New York, he became teller in the Rondout bank in 1864, but left shortly to enter his father's business. He married Mary Louise Dubois, of Kingston, in 1865.

Always active in business, Abbey devoted his leisure to poetry. Modest to an extreme, he had a droll wit, a special fondness for children, and a marked antipathy to travel. It was said of him, "It is doubtful if he would know how to make an enemy." He was essentially a minor, but not untalented, writer of pleasant verse. The best of his twelve books were *Ballads of Good Deeds* (1872) and *Poems* (1879). The simple rhythm of his early poetry earned him a wide contemporary reputation, but his later work —didactic and effusively patriotic—was not equally popular. He died in a sanitarium in Tenafly, N. J.

Principal Works: May Dreams, 1862; Ralph and Other Poems, 1866; Stories in Verse, 1869; Ballads of Good Deeds, 1872; Poems, 1879; The City of Success, 1884; Phaethon, 1901; Dream of Love, 1910.

About: Bookman May 1912.

ABBOTT, JACOB (November 14, 1803-October 31, 1879), juvenile writer, clergyman, and educator, was born at Hallowell, Maine, the eldest of seven children of Jacob Abbot, 2d, and Betsey (Abbot) Abbot. (The family name was originally "Abbot"; Jacob and his brother John [*q.v.*] added the second "t" while they were at college.) The father and mother were second cousins, both descended from the same early Puritan ancestor.

The Abbot household was naturally religious and conservative, but it was pious without being narrow, and the elder Jacob had both the inclination and the means to give his sons a thorough classical education. The four of these sons who reached maturity all made names for themselves in education, the ministry, and literature.

Courtesy of Bowdoin College Library
JACOB ABBOTT

The younger Jacob was educated at Hallowell Academy and Bowdoin College, from which he was graduated at seventeen. He then taught a year in Portland Academy, where Henry Wadsworth Longfellow was one of his pupils; studied for the Congregational ministry at Andover Theological Seminary; and was appointed tutor and later (at only twenty-one) professor of mathematics and natural philosophy at Amherst College. All this time he was formulating new theories of teaching. In 1828 he married Harriet Vaughan, of Hallowell, and soon afterwards went to Boston to organize and conduct the Mt. Vernon School for Girls, a pioneer institution where he had his first opportunity to try out his ideas. These were simple and direct, and based on confidence, kindness, and fairness; he believed, for instance, in treating his pupils as equals, trusting them with responsibility, and letting them "learn by doing." (Unlike his contemporary, Bronson Alcott, however, his educational experiments aroused no storms of protest—perhaps because they were confined to *methods* of instruction. His actual teachings were thoroughly conventional and orthodox.)

Abbott's first writing grew out of lectures given at this school; these were collected as *The Young Christian,* and the book was sufficiently popular to become the first of a series. (Indeed, everything he ever wrote was in a series of small volumes, ranging from six to thirty-six.) In 1833 he resigned from the school and became minister of the Eliot Congregational Church, which he had helped to found, in Roxbury, Mass. At about the same time he formed a life-long connection with Harper & Brothers, the publishers, and began to turn out the long list of mildly didactic tales about "everyday" life which made him the most popular juvenile writer of his time. First came the famous "Rollo Books," written in the style of Thomas Day's English *Sandford and Merton*; they eventually reached a total of twenty-eight volumes. Other series followed, in rapid succession. Shortly his literary work began to monopolize all his energy, and he turned over his pulpit to his brother John and retired to his father's farm, now at Farmington, Maine, to devote his full time to writing.

In Farmington, in 1843, Mrs. Abbott died, at the birth of her sixth child. (The best known of these children was Lyman Abbott, 1835-1922, for many years editor of the *Outlook.*) Heartbroken, the widower left his children with their grandparents and went to New York where his three brothers were thinking of starting a school for girls. He joined them in the enterprise and acted as president of the Abbott School for Girls until 1851; Helen Hunt Jackson was one of the pupils. In 1853 he remarried, his second wife being Mary (Dana) Woodbury, a widow. They spent much of their time in travel, visiting Europe many times. After her death, in 1869, Abbott returned to Farmington and lived out the last decade of his life in the placid Maine countryside. He died peacefully two weeks before his seventy-sixth birthday. So highly was he esteemed that an editorial in *Harper's Weekly* compared him (quite inappropriately) with Hans Christian Andersen.

Counting the books he edited, Abbott produced by his own efforts the amazing total of more than 200 volumes, all highly successful in their day but now mostly forgotten. Modern youth would become quickly bored by the stiff little adventures of Rollo and his companions; but it should be remembered that in their own time (the era of the incredible "Parley Books" of S. G. Goodrich [*q.v.*] and his imitators) Abbott's works were infinitely more human and less priggish and prissy than any other writing available to children. Moreover, some of his later books had genuine flavor. The *Franconia Stories,* for example, can be read with pleasure even today. "Still fragrant as dried fern," May Lamberton Becker has said of them.

Abbott was a kindly, devout man, with a gentleness and simplicity that were almost childlike. He had no great talents as a writer except sincerity and industry; these he had in abundance. In his old age, with his short white beard, round cheeks, and old-fashioned spectacles, he was the prototype of the New England grandfather of tradition. It was his delight to quote a homely maxim as his rule in teaching, writing, and living: "When you consent, consent cordially; when you refuse, refuse finally; when you punish, punish good-naturedly; commend often, never scold." In his modest way he typified the Puritan heritage at its simple best—both in his virtues and limitations. His literary significance lies in the fact that he was one of the first Americans to attempt to write for children as human beings; he was an important, if distant, forerunner of modern juvenile literature.

Principal Works: The Young Christian Series, 1832-; The Rollo Books, 1834-; The Makers of History Series; Franconia Stories; Harper's Story Books; Abbott's Fireside Series; Science for the Young Series, 1872-.

About: Abbott, E. H. Being Little in Cambridge; Abbott, J. The Young Christian (see Memoir by E. D. Abbott in 1822 ed.); Abbott, L. Silhouettes of My Contemporaries; Harper's Weekly November 22, 1879.

ABBOTT, JOHN STEVENS CABOT (September 18, 1805-June 17, 1877), biographer, historian, and clergyman, was born in Brunswick, Maine. He was the son of Jacob Abbot, 2d, and Betsey (Abbot) Abbot; younger brother of Jacob Abbott [*q.v.*]; and uncle of Lyman Abbott. With his more famous brother Jacob, he added a "t" to the family name. Graduated from Bowdoin College in the class of 1825 with Nathaniel Hawthorne and Henry Wadsworth Longfellow, he received his theological training at Andover Seminary and was ordained to the Congregational ministry in January 1830. He soon entered upon his first pastorate, at Worcester, Mass., and held subsequent offices in Roxbury and Nantucket in the same state until 1843, when his restless spirit led him to join his three brothers in New York City at their newly-founded seminary for young ladies. Meanwhile, he had married Jane Williams Bourne, of New Bedford, Mass., who was a devoted helpmate, ably assisting in his researches and relieving him of much literary drudgery.

Abbott returned to Brunswick in 1853, and there he wrote his popular life of Napoleon. He praised Bonaparte so lavishly that the book, though successful, greatly antagonized the critics; rumors were even spread that he had been bribed by the French. (Emerson put his finger on a more serious weakness when he said: "It [the biography] seems to teach that Napoleon's great object was to establish in benighted Europe our New England system of Sunday schools.")

In 1861 Abbott returned to the ministry. He spent the declining years of his life in New Haven and Fair Haven, Conn., where he died after a long illness. Indefatigable, systematic, a man of high standards and purpose, Abbott produced fifty-four books on diverse subjects, including European history and juvenile literature. *The Mother at Home,* compiled from lectures before the parish ladies of Worcester, was probably his most popular work after his life of Napoleon. It was published in England and translated into many languages, even the dialects of India and Africa. Although his work was widely read in its time, it had no lasting literary influence.

Principal Works: The Mother at Home, 1833; The History of Napoleon Bonaparte, 1855; The Empire of Austria, 1859; The Empire of Russia, 1860; Italy, 1860; Practical Christianity, 1862; Civil War in America (2 vols.) 1863, 1866; History of Napoleon III, 1868; Romance of Spanish History, 1869; History of Frederick the Great, 1871; Pioneers and Patriots of America (12 vols.) 1873-1876.

About: Ladd, H. O. Memorial of John S. C. Abbott.

ADAIR, JAMES (c.1709-c.1783) was a pioneer Indian trader and author, about whose life there are very few verifiable facts. According to tradition, he was born in County Antrim, Ireland, and came to America about 1735, probably disembarking at Charleston, S. C. In the same year he began trading with the Indians of the Southern colonies, living among them as friend and brother for almost forty years, and studying their manners and customs. His preface to *The History of the American Indians* states that it was written among "our old friendly Chicasaws," with whom he chiefly traded. The writing was accomplished under the greatest difficulties, as he was separated from society and libraries, frequently interrupted by business, and obliged to conceal papers—especially traders' letters—because of the natives' jealousy and suspicion.

It is said that Adair was married, had several children, and that he died soon after the Revolutionary War, in North Carolina. The evident background of scholarship in his book reveals that he was well educated. Despite his attempt to prove that the Indians are descendants of the ancient Jews, his Indian history is a faithful and valuable contribution to the early historical literature of America. It was translated into German as early as 1782.

Principal Work: The History of the American Indians, 1775.

About: Adair, J. B. The Adair History and Genealogy; Logan, J. H. A History of the Upper Country of South Carolina; McCready, E. History of South Carolina Under the Royal Government; Volwile, A. T. George Croghan and the Western Movement: 1741-1782; Nation August 27, 1914.

ADAMS, ABIGAIL (SMITH) (November 11, 1744 [o.s.]-October 28, 1818), letter writer, was the wife of John Adams, second president of the United States, and the mother of John Quincy Adams, sixth president. She was born at Weymouth, Mass., the daughter of the Rev. William Smith, the Congregational minister of the town, and Elizabeth (Quincy) Smith, the descendant of a noteworthy pioneer Massachusetts family.

(There have been three prominent Abigail Adamses in American history, and they are frequently confused. In chronological order, they were: (1) the subject of this sketch, Abigail (Smith) Adams, 1744-1818, wife of John Adams; (2) their daughter, Abigail (Adams) Smith, 1765-1813, wife of Colonel William Stephen Smith; and (3) Abigail (Brooks) Adams, 1808-1889, wife of the diplomat Charles Francis Adams, Sr., and mother of the authors Henry Adams, Charles Francis Adams, Jr., and Brooks Adams [*qq.v.*].)

In childhood Abigail was frail and delicate and was never sent to school. Instead, she spent most of her time with her grandparents, at Braintree (in the portion of that town now known as Quincy). Her grand-

After a portrait by G. Stuart
ABIGAIL ADAMS

mother, a woman of some education, was her only teacher. This separation from her parents and friends was the foundation of her excellence as a letter writer; in those days of slow and hard travel, correspondence was the only way in which she could keep in touch with those she had left behind.

Her health improved, and though she was never pretty she grew into an interesting and attractive young woman, with dark lustrous eyes and black hair. (In later years she became very stout.) She was a bit of a flirt, too, with a keen sense of humor that kept her heart free until she met young John Adams, already a rising lawyer. Her family disapproved of him, since his father was a working farmer and they considered themselves aristocrats. Nevertheless she married him in 1764, and their marriage, in spite of its separations and hardships, was notably happy. They had three sons and a daughter, the oldest of the family being John Quincy Adams.

With the first rumblings of discontent against England, strenuous years began for Abigail Adams. Most of the stirring days preceding and following the Declaration of Independence were spent by her husband in Philadelphia, while she remained in Braintree with their children. She had a farm to run as well as a household, and she had to face, alone, battles too near for comfort, and the hazards of an epidemic of dysentery. But Abigail Adams was always an ardent politician, and she was a staunch rebel from the beginning. To this first separation we owe some of the finest of her letters. In 1778 her husband was sent to France as a member of the American Commission. For six years she managed all his affairs in America. In 1784, after the signing of the treaty of peace, she joined him in Paris. The following year he became the first American minister to England. Mrs. Adams carried off well the onerous duties of a minister's wife, though her letters reveal how bitterly she resented the insults covertly dealt to the representatives of the new republic and late enemy. It was not until 1787 that the family returned to America.

From 1789 to 1797 Adams was vice-president under Washington, and Mrs. Adams made her home with him, first in New York and then in Philadelphia. From 1797 to 1801 he was president, and for the last three months of his term she became the first mistress of the White House. Washington was a dreary, muddy waste, the unfinished White House little more than an unheated barn, where Mrs. Adams dried the family wash in the East Room. After years of courts and sophisticated capitals, the society of the raw town was little to her liking. More Federalist even than her husband, she objected fiercely to the growing power of the Republicans under Jefferson and never forgot or forgave Jefferson's defeat of Adams at the third election. Probably much of the accusation brought against Adams of undue formality and pomp should more justly have been addressed to his wife.

Her health was beginning to fail again, and from 1801 she lived quietly at Quincy, as her old home was now called. The greatest grief of her life was the death in 1813 of her beloved only daughter, Abigail—one of the few Adamses who failed to reach an advanced age. Nevertheless, she retained to her last day the wit, the serenity, and the cheerfulness which so characterize her letters, where, it has been said, she "mixed laughter with learning." She was a violent partisan, and she was most outspoken in her likes and dislikes, but there is in her letters also a fund of apt characterization, vivid comment, and delightful observation. It must be remembered that she never had any idea that her private correspondence would appear in print, and laughed away as too ridiculous for serious comment a suggestion made during her lifetime that selections from the letters be published. She died at Quincy at the age of seventy-four. Her husband outlived her by eight years, dying at ninety-one. It was not until twenty-two years after her death that the first volume of her letters, edited by her grandson Charles Francis Adams, Sr., appeared.

Principal Works: Letters of Mrs. Adams: The Wife of John Adams, 1840; Familiar Letters of John Adams and His Wife during the Revolution, 1876.

About: Adams, J. & A. Familiar Letters (see Memoir by Charles Francis Adams); Bobbé, D. Abigail Adams: The Second First Lady; Bradford, G. Portraits of American Women; Minnegerode, M. Some American Ladies; Richards, L. E. Abigail Adams and Her Times.

ADAMS, BROOKS (June 24, 1848-February 13, 1927), historian, was born at Quincy, Mass. He was the youngest son of Charles Francis Adams, Sr., diplomat, and Abigail (Brooks) Adams and was a brother of Henry Adams and Charles Francis Adams, Jr. [*qq.v.*]. He was educated in England at the time of his father's residence as American minister, and at Harvard College, from which he was graduated in 1870. After attending the law school for a year, he went to Geneva as private secretary to his father when he was arbitrating the "Alabama" claims for the United States, under the Treaty of Washington. Returning to America, he became a member of the bar and practiced law until 1881 when a severe illness caused him to retire. Like his brothers, he turned his attention to literature, and in 1887 published his first and perhaps most important work—*The Emancipation of Massachusetts,* a strong attack on the accepted accounts of early New England history, in which he advanced the opinion that the Colonists were held in religious and political bondage by the clergy and seldom rose above this tyranny. The book was widely discussed in camps of opinion which were divided between approbation and protest. In 1895 he published the *Law of Civilization and Decay,* a study of society.

Adams was married in 1889 to Evelyn, the daughter of Admiral Charles Henry Davis. In 1904 he became a lecturer in the Boston University School of Law, remaining for seven years. He published little original writing in his later years. Overshadowed by his more famous brothers, he was nevertheless a minor historian of genuine, if limited, ability.

Principal Works: The Emancipation of Massachusetts, 1887; Law of Civilization and Decay, 1895; America's Economic Supremacy, 1900; The New Empire, 1902; Theory of Social Revolutions, 1913.

About: Harvard Graduates' Magazine June 1927; Massachusetts Historical Society Proceedings May 1927.

ADAMS, CHARLES FOLLEN (April 21, 1842-March 8, 1918), dialect poet, was a descendant of the Revolutionary patriot Samuel Adams. He was born in Dorchester, Mass., the ninth child of Ira Adams and Mary Elizabeth (Senter) Adams, and received a common school education in Dorchester. Until he was twenty he worked for a firm of dry-goods merchants in Boston. In 1862 he enlisted in the 13th Massachusetts Infantry and served with his regiment from the second battle of Bull Run until he was wounded on the first day of Gettysburg and taken prisoner. (He was released three days later by Union troops.) After the war he returned to Boston and set up his own business as a merchant. In 1870 he married Harriet Louise Mills, of Boston.

Adams wrote for diversion, producing many sentimental poems in the German dialect (known as "scrapple English") used by the Pennsylvania Dutch and German emigrant soldiers in the Union army. Although the pathos of his rhymes brought tears to thousands of eyes in the past, they can now be classified only as "popular verse."

Principal Works: Leedle Yawcob Strauss and Other Poems, 1877; Dialect Ballads, 1888.

About: Rand, J. C. One of a Thousand; New England Magazine February 1906; New York Times March 9, 1918.

ADAMS, CHARLES FRANCIS, JR. (May 27, 1835-March 20, 1915), historian and economist, was a member of the illustrious Adams family of Massachusetts which gave two presidents—his grandfather and his great-grandfather—to the United States. He was the son of Charles Francis Adams, Sr., 1807-1886, Minister to England during the Civil War, and Abigail (Brooks) Adams, and was the slightly older brother of the famous Henry Adams [*q.v.*]. (Charles Francis Adams III, Secretary of the Navy from 1928 to 1932 in the Hoover cabinet, was his nephew and namesake.)

As befitted an Adams, Charles Francis was born in Boston and was graduated from Harvard (1856) and admitted to the bar (1858). The Civil War diverted his career, for he served throughout and was mustered out in July 1865 with the brevet rank of brigadier general of volunteers. A few weeks later he married Mary Hone Ogden of Newport, R.I.

This was the great period of railroad-building, and Adams became a railroad expert. As early as 1869, he was a member of the board of railroad commissioners of Massachusetts; in 1882 he became director, and in 1884 president, of the Union Pacific Railway, serving in this post until his resignation in 1890. His resignation was caused by his desire to devote himself to other interests which were closer to his heart—education, public service, and history. He

CHARLES FRANCIS ADAMS, JR.

had been from 1882 a member of the board of overseers of Harvard (remaining on it until 1906), and was an active power for reform of the musty curriculum of the time, with special reference to the department of English. He was successively vice-president and president of the Massachusetts Historical Society, and edited early American historical manuscripts for the Prince Society, of which he became president in 1895. He also helped to plan the notable park system of Boston. Yet he felt that, compared with those of his ancestors, his life had thus far been a failure (he had his share of the melancholy which plagued his brother Henry), and this feeling was a factor in his resignation from the Union Pacific.

After his resignation, Adams moved from Quincy, Mass. (in whose public school system he had taken a keen interest) to Lincoln, Mass., and then in 1905 to Washington, which was his home thenceforth. The remainder of his life, ten fruitful years, he dedicated to study and writing. He died shortly before his eightieth birthday.

Charles Francis Adams' historical work is by no means negligible, for he had an uncommon talent for clarifying confused and complicated material and reducing it to clear and readable form. Primarily he was a critic, with the forthright spirit of one trained from youth to think of himself as a predestined leader of men; but being an Adams, this spirit was tempered by Puritan caution and reverence for tradition, so that in the end he usually recommended moderation and thus negated some of his own most cogent censures, particularly in the field of education. Nevertheless, he was not the least eminent member of his remarkable family.

In historical research Adams' chief interest was in the history of his own state, and he unearthed a number of forgotten bits of Massachusetts history. His biography of his father was definitive, and is a model of the very delicate art of recounting the life of one with close personal ties to the author. His financial and economic works on railroad questions are now outdated, but were authoritative in their time. Whatever his subject, his style is urbane, flowing, and above all lucid.

Principal Works: Chapters of Erie and Other Essays (with Henry Adams) 1871; Railroads: Their Origin and Problems, 1878; Notes on Railroad Accidents, 1879; Richard Henry Dana, 1890; History of Braintree, 1891; Three Episodes in Massachusetts History, 1892; Columbus and the Spanish Discovery of America (with G. E. Ellis, G. Bradford, A. McKenzie, J. Winsor) 1892; Massachusetts: Its Historians and Its History, 1893; Charles Francis Adams the First, 1900; Lee at Appomattox, 1902; Three Phi Beta Kappa Addresses, 1907; Studies: Military and Diplomatic, 1911; Seward and the Declaration of Paris, 1912; Trans-Atlantic Historical Solidarity, 1913; Autobiography, 1916.

About: Adams, C. F. Autobiography; Nation March 25, 1915; Outlook March 31, 1915; New York Times March 21, 1915.

ADAMS, CHARLES KENDALL (January 24, 1835-July 26, 1902), historian and educator, was born in Derby, Vt., the son of Charles Adams, a farmer, and Maria (Shedd) Adams. After an elementary education, he taught in a district school at seventeen. In 1856 the family moved to Iowa. After some poor training at Denmark Academy, he entered the University of Michigan, very badly prepared, and worked his way through, being graduated in 1861. Andrew D. White, the famous historian and educator, was his professor of history and became his lifelong friend. Through White, he was made instructor of history in 1862, assistant professor in 1863, and professor in 1868. In 1863 he had married Abigail Disbrow Mudge, and with her help and by a leave of absence he spent a year and a half studying in Europe. He introduced the seminar method of university instruction at Michigan. Meanwhile White had become president of Cornell, and Adams had lectured there frequently. In 1885 he succeeded White as president. At Cornell he established the law school, the schools of history and political science, and the departments of agriculture, civil engineering, and archaeology. His wife died in 1889, and the next year he married Mary Mathews Barnes. In 1892 he resigned to devote himself to writing, but at White's request became instead president of the University of Wisconsin. From 1892 to 1895 he edited *Johnson's Universal Cyclopedia.* At Wisconsin he founded his third university library, and did much to improve the graduate school. His health failed in 1900, a trip to Italy and Germany brought no cure, and after a final collapse he resigned as president in 1901 and moved to Redlands, Calif. There he died, two weeks after moving into his new home. He left his entire estate to the University of Wisconsin for graduate work in English, Greek, and history. Adams had leisure for very little writing, but what historical work he had time to do is sound.

Principal Works: Democracy and Monarchy in France, 1874; A Manual of Historical Literature, 1882; Representative British Orations (ed.)

1884; Christopher Columbus: His Life and Work, 1892; A History of the United States (with William P. Trent) 1903.

ABOUT: Smith, C. F. Charles Kendall Adams: A Life Sketch.

ADAMS, HANNAH (October 2, 1755-December 15, 1831), compiler, belonged to a branch of the famous Adams family of Massachusetts, and was born in Medfield. She was the daughter of Thomas Adams, Jr., whose almost greedy appetite for knowledge won him the name "Book Adams," and of Elizabeth (Clark) Adams, and was distantly related to President John Adams. Even as a small child she had her father's insatiable thirst for learning; too frail to go to school, she was taught at home—Latin, Greek, geography, and logic—by student boarders. During the Revolutionary War she earned a little money by tutoring and making lace. It was the reading of Broughton's *Dictionary of Religions* and her subsequent determination to make a compilation of her own that would be more accurate and less biased that resulted in the appearance, in 1784, of an *Alphabetical Compendium of the Various Sects Which Have Appeared From the Beginning of the Christian Era to the Present Day.* But only the publisher benefited from the book's success, and not until seventeen years later when she brought out a second edition was she substantially rewarded.

Miss Adams suffered temporary blindness during the writing of *A Summary History of New England* (1799), and recovered only by complete rest and the constant application of "laudanum and seawater." Her own abridgment (1804) of this book, for school use, had been anticipated by a cheaper edition issued by the Rev. Jedidiah Morse [*q.v.*], a "friend" of the author, who, Miss Adams alleged, had infringed upon her rights. A ten years' controversy ensued, and numerous influential literary figures came to the fore with their comments; in general, Dr. Morse's "defence" was looked upon as pitiably vulnerable. In *The Truth and Excellence of the Christian Religion* (1804) were portraits of eminent laymen who had defended Christianity in their writings, and excerpts from their works. Relying largely on scattered and unmethodical notes, with only a few good sources on which to draw, she prepared a fairly extensive *History of the Jews* (1812); more than a dozen years later came *Letters on the Gospels.*

She had an extraordinarily placid countenance, about which one of her biographers wrote, "No one could see her without feeling she was not of this world." Many legends grew up around the intensity of her mental application—according to one, the librarian at the Boston Athenaeum, unable to disengage her from her book, used to "lock her in," while he went home for lunch. That she was possessed of many New England "peculiarities" is quite likely; but that she was perhaps the first American woman to make writing a profitable profession bears not only likelihood but significance.

After a portrait by C. Harding
HANNAH ADAMS

PRINCIPAL WORKS: Alphabetical Compendium of the Various Sects . . , 1784; A Summary History of New England, 1799; The Truth and Excellence of the Christian Religion, 1804; History of the Jews, 1812; A Narrative of the Controversy Between the Rev. Jedidiah Morse, D.D., and the Author, 1814; Letters on the Gospels, 1826.

ABOUT: Adams, H. A Memoir of Miss Hannah Adams; Brooks, Van W. Flowering of New England; Dedham Historical Register July 1896.

ADAMS, HENRY (February 16, 1838-March 27, 1918), historian and intellectual, was born in Boston, the son of Charles Francis Adams, Sr., and Abigail (Brooks) Adams. As Adams himself remarked in his autobiography: "Probably no child, born in the year, held better cards than he." He was the great-grandson of John Adams, second president of the United States, and grandson of John Quincy Adams, sixth president of the United States. His father was shortly to become a famous diplomat. Three of his brothers also became distinguished, one as a statesman, two as writers and men of affairs.

In a sense, the Adams family at the time of Henry's birth and early years represented the nearest thing to an hereditary political aristocracy to be found in America. But from youth he regarded this condition as a liability rather than an asset; to his way of thinking it was a dead weight of tradition and responsibility which only limited his opportunities. Thus were laid early in the frail, sensitive boy—who had nearly died of fever at the age of three—the foundations of the pessimism which governed his later life and philosophy.

As Henry Adams himself records, his life was one long education. Formally, he was educated at a private school in Boston and at Harvard, from which he was graduated in 1858, without honors, and feeling that college "had taught little, and that little ill." He had, however, learned to speak in public, and his first writings had appeared in the *Harvard Magazine.* For two years he studied civil law in a desultory way at the Universities of Berlin and Dresden, with side trips to Switzerland, Italy (where he had a chance interview with Garibaldi), France, and England. He returned to Boston late in 1860.

His father was then a Congressman, and the son served as his secretary during the term which saw the beginning of the Civil War. In 1861 Charles Francis Adams was appointed Minister to England, and Henry sailed with him as his private secretary. He remained for seven years. It was a difficult time; most English opinion was hostile to the North, and though Henry Adams had entrée to the most brilliant circles, and in many ways this was the pleasantest period of his life, it is not surprising that he became more Bostonian than ever—though all the while disliking and avoiding Boston. In letters to New York and Boston papers he wrote intemperately of the probability of war with England, and came near to causing an "international incident." When, after the war, his function as secretary became largely ornamental, he began to prepare, reluctantly, for an American career. He determined on the press, though his first articles in the *North American Review* already pointed toward his interest in history.

For two years he lived in Washington, writing free lance articles, mostly on finance, for the New York papers. Then, after another brief trip to England, he yielded to family pressure, and against his will became, from 1870 to 1877, assistant professor of history at Harvard. His concept of history—broadly accepted today but almost unique in his time—was based on the operation of fundamental forces and energies, rather than

From a portrait by J. B. Potter
HENRY ADAMS

external events. (He wrote in one of his essays: "The historian's business is to follow the track of energy; to find where it comes from and where it went to; its complex course and shifting channels; its values, equivalents, conversions.") Though a remarkably successful teacher, stimulating and provocative, his heart was not in his classroom, but in the editorship of the *North American Review,* which he conducted simultaneously with his teaching. In 1876 he took a Ph.D. degree at Harvard.

In 1872 he married Marian Hooper, an heiress and a woman of remarkable character. She killed herself in 1885. Adams loved only two women in his life, his sister and his wife, and both died tragically. (His sister died of tetanus, following a carriage accident in Italy, in 1870.) Nowhere in his autobiographical writings does he so much as mention his marriage; the wound was too deep to probe. He commissioned Augustus St. Gaudens to place over Marian Adams' grave in Rock Creek Cemetery, Washington, D.C., an enigmatic statue symbolizing the mystery of death; and when he could no longer endure life in a new home without her, he set out on a restless wandering to escape from his memories.

Before the tragedy, however, Adams had begun to come into his own as an historian. His lives of Gallatin and Randolph had appeared, as well as his anonymous novel, *Democracy,* an intimate picture of official Washington whose authorship was not revealed until after his death. In 1878 he had resigned both his posts, as teacher and editor, and had moved to Washington, spending his summers at Beverly, Mass., and devoting his entire time to writing. Following his wife's death he made a long trip to Japan, returning to Washington to finish his massive and masterly *History of the United States.* The next year he spent again in the Orient, returning by way of Europe. The remainder of his life was spent mostly in Washington, with frequent journeys in America and abroad. He received an honorary LL.D. from Western Reserve University, and became president of the American Historical Association.

By now he was firmly established as an historian. But the work by which his name will live longest was yet to come. For Henry Adams is remembered primarily as the author of two profoundly reflective and intellectually stirring books, *Mont-Saint-Michel and Chartres* and *The Education of Henry Adams*—those elaborate expressions of the dilemma of the genteel mind confronted by our modern industrial civilization. Both were privately printed long before their public appearance. His last work, *The Degradation of the Democratic Dogma,* published posthumously by his brother Brooks Adams, was a less important but interesting attempt to correlate history with statistical science.

Adams lived past his eightieth birthday—carrying out the family tradition of longevity. He died in his sleep at his home in Washington after spending the evening listening to medieval songs, the favorite recreation of his last years, and was buried beside his wife beneath St. Gaudens' brooding statue. His will commanded that no names, dates, or inscriptions should ever be placed over the grave.

Adams' books, with their severe intellectuality, have brought him a not entirely deserved reputation for coolness as a person. Actually, under a reserved exterior, he could be warm and sympathetic, his few close friends have testified. Though he had no children of his own, he always kept toys in his house, and in his later years he was surrounded by a circle of devoted nieces. His drawing room, both during his wife's lifetime and on the rare occasions he chose to open it after her death, was called the most brilliant *salon* in Washington.

No single glib phrase—or number of them—can explain the complex mind and enigmatic character of Henry Adams. Perhaps, however, it may be said that his was one of those troubled intellects at once too early and too late for their era. A medievalist in his emotions and esthetic tastes, he nevertheless foresaw more clearly than any other thinker of his lifetime the intellectual conflicts of the twentieth century.

The actual close relation between these seemingly diverse points of view may best be understood by careful study of *Mont-Saint-Michel* and the *Education*—the two strangely contrasting works which he deliberately undertook in order to express the dilemma of the world as he saw it. To quote his biographer James Truslow Adams: "[He] had established in his mind two forces, which he represented by the Virgin and the dynamo. . As a working hypothesis to try out his theory and see whither it might lead, [he] decided to take two points between which he could trace the operation of force, and so possibly establish a direction and a rate of acceleration. He chose as one point, that from which to start, the point at which, in his opinion, 'man held the highest idea of himself as a unit in a unified universe,' which he located in the twelfth century. The other point was to be, for convenience, *himself,* as a symbol of twentieth century multiplicity."

The sense of failure that dominated Adams' life, despite his enviable inheritance and superior talent, was not so much a private as a public intuition. It is true that, as an Adams, the only "success" that could have meant anything to him was in politics; but what troubled him most and lay at the roots of his defeatism was the realization that he symbolized an outmoded tradition, that the new industrial capitalism rising to ubiquitous power and authority had and would have no use for his type of sensitive mind and scrupulous conscience.

His was a nature essentially seclusive and introverted, burdened with a stultifying sense of responsibility to play a distinguished part in the practical world. His real gift to posterity was the fruit of his seminal mind. He will never be a popular writer, but for thoughtful readers he will always be an immensely influential one.

Principal Works: Chapters of Erie and Other Essays (with Charles Francis Adams, Jr.) 1871; The Life of Albert Gallatin, 1879; Democracy: An American Novel (anonymous) 1880; John Randolph, 1882; Esther: A Novel (by "Frances Snow Compton") 1884; History of the United States of America During the Administrations of Jefferson and Madison, 1885-1891; Historical Essays, 1891; Mont-Saint-Michel and Chartres, 1904 (privately printed; published 1913); The Education of Henry Adams, 1907 (privately printed; published 1918); The Life of George Cabot Lodge, 1911; The Degradation of the Democratic Dogma, 1919; Letters to a Niece and Prayer to the Virgin of Chartres (ed. by Mabel LaFarge) 1920; Letters: 1858-1891 (ed. by W. C. Ford) 1930.

ABOUT: Adams, H. The Education of Henry Adams; Adams, H. Letters: 1858-1891; Adams, Mrs. H. Letters: 1843-1885; Adams, J. T. Henry Adams; Adams, J. T. The Adams Family; Atlantic Monthly October 1918; Yale Review October 1920.

ADAMS, HERBERT BAXTER (March 16, 1850-July 30, 1901), historian and teacher, was born in Shutesbury, Mass., the son of Nathaniel Dickinson Adams, a prosperous lumber merchant, and Harriet (Hastings) Adams. In his early childhood the family moved to Amherst, where the boy attended the public schools, later preparing at Phillips Exeter Academy for Amherst College. He was graduated from Amherst in 1872, at the head of his class, and—Germany being then the world-center for historical research—proceeded to Göttingen and Berlin, finally taking his Ph.D. at Heidelberg, with highest honors, in 1876.

The same year he became a fellow in history at Johns Hopkins University, which had started its own career that very term. In 1878 he was made associate, in 1883 associate professor, and in 1891 full professor. The entire remainder of Adams' life was spent in Baltimore, at Johns Hopkins University; he was inseparable from it and it from him, and he resigned, because of the ravages of a chronic disease, only a few months before his death. He never married, and had practically no personal life. He was not, however, a mere recluse; he left the university on numerous occasions between 1878 and 1881 to lecture at Smith College (itself then only three to six years old), and, rather curiously, was regularly connected with the Chautauqua schools from 1888 to 1891. He then resigned from any formal connection with Chautauqua, but retained a sort of supervisory interest for several years thereafter.

HERBERT BAXTER ADAMS

Primarily Adams was a teacher, and a great teacher. He made Johns Hopkins the Mecca for all serious young students of history in the 'nineties, and half the important American teachers of history in the early part of the twentieth century had been his pupils. He was a stimulator, a cultural enzyme, who fought academic dry rot, pedantry, snobbishness, and stuffiness as the educational devils they are. So much of his energy was given to his teaching that actually his only full-length book was his biography of Jared Sparks. Nevertheless he was a voluminous writer in the more technical aspects of his chosen field (early American and particularly New England history), though nearly all his work appeared in the form of monographs and papers. Most of these were in the *Johns Hopkins University Studies in History and Political Science,* which he founded, of which he was the only editor, and which died with him, its last volume being a collection of tributes to him by his colleagues and pupils. He was also one of the founders of the American Historical Association, and was its secretary from its foundation, in 1884, until 1900, when increasing weakness made it necessary for him to give up all his duties and creep back to Amherst to await his death.

A slight, shy man, with a quiet, dry wit and an immense loyalty to his university and the students who became his disciples, Adams was greatly beloved by those who came under his influence. He is a constituent part, not only of the history of Johns Hopkins, but also of the history of American historical research.

PRINCIPAL WORKS: Maryland's Influence in Founding a National Commonwealth, 1877; The Germanic Origin of New England Towns, 1881; Norman Constables in America, 1883; Saxon Tithing Men in America, 1883; Village Communities of Cape Anne and Salem, 1883; Methods of Historical Study, 1884; Maryland's Influence Upon Land Cessions in the United States, 1885; The College of William and Mary, 1887; Notes on the Literature of Charities, 1887; Seminary Libraries and University Extension, 1887; The Study of History in American Colleges, 1887; Thomas Jefferson and the University of Virginia, 1888; The Encouragement of Higher Education, 1889; The State and Higher Education, 1890; Seminary Notes on Recent Historical Literature (with J. M. Vincent, W. B. Scaife, etc.) 1890; Columbus and His Discovery of America (with H. Wood, M. Kayserling, C. Adler, C. W. Bump) 1892; Life and Writings of Jared Sparks, 1893; Is History Past Politics? 1895; Jared Sparks and Alexis deTocqueville,

1898; State Aid to Higher Education (in symposium) 1898; Public Educational Work in Baltimore, 1899; Public Libraries and Popular Education, 1900.

About: H. B. Adams: Tributes of Friends (*Johns Hopkins University Studies in History and Political Science: Vol. 23*); Vincent, J. M. Herbert Baxter Adams; Outlook October 12, 1901; Review of Reviews September 1901.

ADAMS, JOHN (1704-January 22? 1740), clergyman, poet, and scholar, is believed to have been born in Nova Scotia, the son of John Adams of that locality. He received an excellent elementary schooling for the times and was graduated from Harvard in 1721. Following his ordination in the ministry he was placed in a church at Newport, R.I., as assistant to Rev. Nathaniel Clap, who, resenting Adams' appointment, withdrew for a period of two years, at the end of which time Adams himself was dismissed. He was associated with a church in Philadelphia for a while, and then returned to Cambridge, Mass. Not long afterwards he left the ministry and gave his full time to literary pursuits. He died at the age of thirty-six. At his funeral Harvard fellows acted as pall-bearers, and distinguished members of the faculty were among the procession.

Except for his ordination sermon, which appeared in print in 1728, and his miscellaneous pieces in *A Collection of Poems by Several Hands,* a volume which reverberated with the figures and phrases of Pope, Adams' only published work was *Poems on Several Occasions: Original and Translated,* assembled and issued five years after his death. According to the preface, these bits of "Musick for the Ear, Landskip for the Eye, and rich Repast for the highest Understanding" were written merely as "a sort of pleasing Relaxation from severer studies . . . now given to the Publick from his own original Draughts, without the additional Beauties and Polishings they would doubtless have received, if Heaven had continued him." Included in the book was "Revelation of St. John the Divine, translated" and many of the pieces were strongly reminiscent of the Psalms. Adams' verse was indeed patently imitative. Had he "descended" more often to that stark simplicity which he but rarely achieved, he might have escaped the charge of drowsy conventionalism which is posterity's verdict on his work.

About: Adams, J. Poems on Several Occasions: Original and Translated (see Preface); Tyler, M. C. History of American Literature During Colonial Times; Massachusetts Magazine April 1789.

ADAMS, NEHEMIAH (February 19, 1806-October 6, 1878), theologian and historian, was born in Salem, Mass., son of Nehemiah Adams, Sr., a Congregationalist deacon. He was educated at the Salem Latin School, Harvard, and the Andover Theological Seminary. After being ordained, he became co-pastor of the Shepard Church, in Cambridge, Mass., in 1829. In 1831 the other minister died and he remained as sole pastor to 1834, when he was appointed minister of the Essex Street Congregational Church, in Boston. Here he remained for the rest of his life. In 1832 he had married Martha Hooper, who died in 1848, leaving seven children. In 1850 he married Sarah Williston Brackett, by whom he had two more children. Amherst conferred an honorary D.D. degree on him in 1847.

In 1854 he visited the South, where he was so hospitably received that he became its lifelong friend. He was opposed to the excesses of abolitionism, and was severely criticized for his pro-South writings. After the Civil War he was a foremost worker for reconciliation between the two national factions. In 1869 he suffered a stroke of paralysis, from which he never entirely recovered. During the next year he took a trip around the world in a ship commanded by his son—the source of his best known book, *A Voyage Around the World.* In theology he was orthodox, and firmly opposed to Unitarian tendencies in the Congregational church. His prose style is formal but good, being openly modeled on that of Addison.

Principal Works: Remarks on the Unitarian Belief, 1832; The Life of John Eliot, 1847; The Friends of Christ in the New Testament, 1853; A Southside View of Slavery, 1854; The Communion Sabbath, 1856; The Sable Cloud, 1861; At Eventide, 1871; A Voyage Around the World, 1871 (as Under the Mizzen Mast, 1873).

About: Congregational Year Book, 1879; Congregationalist October 16, 1878; New York Observer October 17, 1878.

ADAMS, SAMUEL (September 27, 1722-October 2, 1803), statesman and polemic writer, was born in Boston, the son of Samuel Adams, a wealthy shipowner, brewer, and member of the colonial House of Representatives, and Mary (Fifield) Adams. He was a cousin of John Adams, second president of the United States. After receiving his B.A. at Harvard in 1740 and his M.A. in 1743, Adams studied law for a while, then worked in a counting house, then was set up by his father in business for himself. He promptly lost the £1000 his father had given him, and became the senior

After a portrait by J. S. Copley
SAMUEL ADAMS

Adams' assistant. The father died in 1748, and the son soon lost his entire fortune. As collector of taxes he owed the city of Boston £8000. In other words, he was a most incompetent business man, always in debt and dependent on his friends for assistance. In public affairs, however, he was thoroughly at home and as efficient as he was disinterested.

From 1747 Adams mixed in politics, beginning with articles in the *Independent Advertiser*. He became the leader of the radicals who advocated separation from England. From 1765 to 1774 he was in the House of Representatives, part of the time as clerk, drafting most of its official papers and contributing to the Boston *Gazette*. He "managed" the Boston Tea Party, signed the Declaration of Independence, served in the first and second Continental Congress, was lieutenant-governor of Massachusetts from 1789 to 1793, and governor from 1794 to 1797. He was twice married, in 1749 to Elizabeth Checkley, who died in 1759 leaving two children, and in 1764 to Elizabeth Wells.

A skilled writer in the field of polemics and controversy, bitter and vindictive, Adams was as influential as he was voluminous. His style was forceful, lucid, epigrammatic. He was a man who flourished in adventure and danger, and functioned least well in times of peace. Jefferson called him "the fountain of our more important measures," and William Bentley, a contemporary, wrote of Adams as "feared by his enemies, too secret to be loved by his friends, . . . the severity of Cato in his manners, the dogmatism of a priest in his religious observances." In spite of his many and obvious defects, Samuel Adams well deserves to be called "the Father of the American Revolution."

PRINCIPAL WORKS: Writings (ed. by H. A. Cushing) 1904-08; Warren-Adams Letters, 1917-25.

ABOUT: Adams, J. James Otis, Samuel Adams, and John Hancock; Guedalla, P. Fathers of the Revolution; Harlow, R. V. Samuel Adams; Hosmer, J. K. Samuel Adams; Miller, J. C. Sam Adams; Wells, W. V. The Life and Public Services of Samuel Adams.

ADAMS, WILLIAM TAYLOR ("Oliver Optic") (July 30, 1822-March 27, 1897), juvenile writer, was born in Medway, Mass., the son of Captain Taban Adams and Catherine (Johnson) Adams. His early education is not known, except that he was not a college graduate. He appeared in Boston at the age of twenty, with a few years' experience as a public school teacher behind him, and immediately secured a position as principal of the grammar school in Dorchester, then a separate village but now a constituent part of the city of Boston. After serving as first usher, then principal, of the Boylston School in Boston, he was transferred at his own request to the Bowditch School. His home remained in Dorchester, and he was for fourteen years a member of the Dorchester school committee. He also served one term in the Massachusetts legislature, but his political career was as undistinguished as it was brief.

Paralleling his professional duties, Adams had, from the early 'fifties, been writing and publishing stories for boys, all in series, and all under his lifelong pseudonym of "Oliver Optic," a name as potent a magnet for young readers in the mid-century as those of Alger or Henty. From about 1850 on, he wrote in all about a thousand stories in magazines and newspapers, as well as some 116 full-length books. Finally in 1865 he resigned his position as principal so as to devote all his time to writing and editing. From 1867 to 1875 he conducted his most popular children's magazine, *Oliver Optic's Magazine for Boys and Girls,* and later was for several years editor successively of *Our Little Ones* and *Student and Schoolmate.* It would be impossible to enumerate all Adams' books by title; there were some fifteen series, each containing half a dozen or more volumes.

"Oliver Optic" did not write adventure stories in the style of Henty, or success fables like Alger. His books were the forerunners of such modern series as *The Rover Boys*—his young heroes traveled much, often in strange ways, and learned geography and natural science as they went; they had experiences in the army and navy, and imbibed heavy doses of patriotism; they were athletic, upright, well-mannered lads who just escaped priggishness in the same way that their creator escaped it—by reason of their vitality. There was always a strong moralistic strain in Adams' books—he was a Sunday School superintendent for all his active life—and no evil-doers ever intruded on his tales. Although he made a half-hearted attempt to write for all young people, he knew very little about girls, who are distinct supernumeraries in his stories, the good little sisters who stay at home until their brothers return to tell them the history of their adventures, and on whose prayers for their safe return the brothers can always rely. Nevertheless, girls as well as boys read the books, and read them devotedly to well within the next generation.

"Oliver Optic's" stories, re-read in the cold light of adulthood, reveal some very careless writing and a good deal of extremely cheap oratory. They were written in haste, and they repeat themselves frequently. His two novels for adults are best forgotten. But the man had a real gift for vivid narrative; he could convey a feeling of excitement and curiosity to his readers: and no critic who once wandered breathlessly in an open boat over the submerged tree-tops of the flooded Amazon basin with

Collection of Frederick H. Meserve
WILLIAM TAYLOR ADAMS
("Oliver Optic")

"Oliver Optic" could ever have the heart to deny him his meed of well-earned praise.

Principal Works: Hatchie: The Guardian Slave, 1853; The Boat Club Series, 1854; Riverdale Story Books, 1858-62; Woodville Series, 1861-67; Army and Navy Series, 1865-94; Young America, 1867-69; Starry Flag Series, 1867-69; The Way of the World (novel) 1867; Lake Shore Series, 1869; Onward and Upward Series, 1870; Yacht Club Series, 1872-1900; Great Western Series, 1875-82; Living Too Fast (novel) 1876; Young America Abroad, 1899.

About: Critic April 3, 1897; Munsey's Magazine October 1886.

"ADELER, MAX." See CLARK, CHARLES HEBER

AGASSIZ, ALEXANDER (December 17, 1835-March 27, 1910), zoologist, oceanographer, and executive, was born at Neuchâtel, Switzerland, the son of the great naturalist Jean Louis Rodolphe Agassiz [*q.v.*] and Cécile (Braun) Agassiz. As a child he had studied and drawn aquatic and other animals; and at the age of fourteen, shortly after his mother's death, he joined his father in America. He attended Cambridge (Mass.) High School, received a B.A. from Harvard in 1855, a B.S. in engineering in 1857, and five years later a B. S. in natural history. While attached to the United States survey of the Washington territory boundaries (1859) he collected marine animals along the southern Pacific coast and in Puget Sound. In the following year he was married to Anna Russell. After his first scientific paper, on butterflies, came the enlightening *North American Acalephae* and *Embryology of the Starfish*, both of which he himself illustrated. During his father's absence, in 1865, he acted as chief of the Harvard Museum, and a year later went to Calumet, Mich., to become superintendent of a then unprofitable copper mine, which under his able management, both actual and absentee, was able, at the time of Agassiz's death, to declare the highest dividends in the history of metal mining.

In 1869 he went abroad; and in 1872 began to publish his *magnum opus* in systematic zoology, *Revision of the Echini*. The death of both his father and his wife in 1873 stifled temporarily his ambition and interest. He sought distraction in travel; and along the west coast of South America made some significant observations of coral reefs which almost convinced him that these phenomena were not mere fringes around sinking volcanoes (he was slowly embracing the anti-Darwinianism of his father). Agassiz' subsequent findings, though many times revised, never became definitive law. In 1874 he became curator of, and later endowed, the University Museum which his father had begun to build.

During the last thirty years of his life, on government and private expeditions in the Gulf Stream, to the Great Barrier Reef of Australia, and in West Indian waters he conducted careful scientific research. His work on the configuration of ocean beds and on the nature of marine fauna was highly original, and not only in the United States but in England, France, and Prussia were his achievements honored. His writings were clear, well-ordered, and exhaustive but belong, obviously, to science rather than to literature.

PRINCIPAL WORKS: North American Acalephae, 1865; Embryology of the Starfish, 1865; Revision of the Echini, 1872; North American Starfishes, 1877.

ABOUT: Agassiz, G. Letters and Recollections of Alexander Agassiz; Bulletin of the Harvard Museum of Comparative Zoology: Vol. 44.

Collection of Frederick H. Meserve
LOUIS AGASSIZ

AGASSIZ, JEAN LOUIS RODOLPHE (May 28, 1807-December 12, 1873), naturalist, commonly known as Louis Agassiz, was born in Motier, Canton Fribourg (one of the French cantons), Switzerland. His father, the Rev. Louis Rodolphe Agassiz, was Protestant pastor of the town, descendant of a long line of ministers driven out of France by the Revocation of the Edict of Nantes; his mother, Rose (Mayor) Agassiz, a physician's daughter, was his first teacher. In 1817 Agassiz was sent to the gymnasium at Bienne (Biel), in Canton Berne, with his brothers. He was already interested in natural science, and in these early days started his famous collection of fishes. From the gymnasium he went to the Academy at Lausanne; in 1823 and 1824 studied medicine at Zurich, then proceeded to Heidelberg and Munich. In Munich in 1829, at the age of twenty-two, he was appointed to classify the Brazilian fishes collected by a scientist who had died soon after his return to Germany. The same year Agassiz received his M.D. degree from Munich, and the next year his Ph.D. from Erlangen.

After a year spent in the Vienna hospitals, he went in 1831 to Paris. There he met Cuvier and Humboldt, the two greatest influences in his career. He became Cuvier's devoted disciple, and assumed as his own the great naturalist's inflexible antagonism to the evolutionary theory. Humboldt was of more practical service—in 1832 he secured for the young naturalist a position as professor of natural history at Neuchâtel, Switzerland. Here Agassiz created a museum, founded a science society, and turned his home into a combined club, school, and laboratory for his students and a publishing house for his own and their writings. In 1833 he married Cécile Braun, sister of a well known botanist, and was chagrined when the care of two daughters and a son gradually made it impossible for her to be much of an assistant to him. The marriage was not very happy, and Agassiz finally sent his wife and children back to her family.

While at Neuchâtel, Agassiz spent his summers in the Alps, studying glaciation. He also did a good deal of work on echinoderms, and went to England to study fossil fish. In 1846 came the turning-point in his life; he went to the United States to deliver two series of lectures and decided to remain permanently. Most of 1847 he spent cruising along the shore of Massachusetts in a Coast Survey ship, studying marine life (he made a similar trip in Florida in 1850 and 1851), and the next year he was made professor of zoology and geology at the Lawrence Scientific School of Harvard University. That year his wife died, and he sent for his children. (His son Alexander [*q.v.*] later became a distinguished scientist.) In 1850 he married Elizabeth Cabot Cary, his devoted helpmate thenceforth and his biographer.

From 1851 to 1854 Agassiz was professor of anatomy and zoology at the Medical College in Charleston, S. C. In 1859 he was enabled to open the museum of comparative zoology of which he had long dreamed. Of this, the noted Agassiz Museum, at Harvard, he was curator until his death. Meanwhile he traveled all over the United States, and also, in 1865, to Brazil. In 1868 he was appointed non-resident professor of natural history at Cornell, which opened its doors that year. In 1871 he went on a warship around Cape Horn to the Pacific Coast for the Coast Survey. And in 1873 he could at last fulfill his other scientific dream, the establishment of the Penikese Island School of Natural History, on Penikese Island, in Buzzard's Bay, Mass., bought for this purpose by John Anderson of New York. The single three-months session of that school was an epoch in the history of American science. It died with its creator, who did not live the year out.

Agassiz' writings on natural history, biology, geology, and marine palaeontology were many, and his command of English was amazing. There is no hint in any of his books that he was writing in a foreign tongue. He himself was no less amazing as a personality—a tall, broad-browed man, a born teacher, generous to a fault (indeed, unwisely extravagant), deeply pious (the real source of his anti-evolutionary views, which he acknowledged privately had become modified toward the end of his life), magnetic, over-sensitive, and irritable, a marvelous stickler for detail, above all a romantic idealist. It was the age of natural historians rather than research biologists, and Agassiz was among the greatest of their breed.

PRINCIPAL WORKS: Recherches sur les Poissons Fossiles, 1833-47; Natural History of the Fresh-Water Fishes of Europe, 1839-40; Études sur les Glaciers, 1840; Études Critiques sur les Mollusques Fossiles, 1840-45; Fossil Fishes of the Devonian System, 1844; Fishes of the London Clay, 1845; Système Glaciare, 1847; Principles of Zoology (with A. A. Gould) 1848; Bibliographia Zoologiae et Geologiae (with H. E. Strickland) 1848-54; Lake Superior, 1850; Classification of Insects, 1851; Structure of Animal Life, 1852; Contributions to the Natural History of the United States of America, 1857-63; Methods of Study in Natural History, 1863; Geological Sketches, 1866-76; A Journal in Brazil (with E. C. Agassiz) 1868.

ABOUT: Agassiz, E. C. Louis Agassiz: His Life and Correspondence; Cooper, L. Louis Agassiz as a Teacher; Husband, J. Americans by Adoption; James, W. Memories and Studies; Marcou, J. Life, Letters, and Works of Louis Agassiz; Paton, L. E. Elizabeth Cary Agassiz; Thayer, W. M. Men Who Win; Walcott, C. D. Louis Agassiz; Independent May 23, 1907; Popular Science Monthly April 1907; July 1907; December 1907.

AGASSIZ, LOUIS. See AGASSIZ, JEAN LOUIS RODOLPHE

"AGATE." See REID, WHITELAW

"AGRICOLA." See CREVECOEUR, MICHEL-GUILLAUME JEAN DE

AIKEN, GEORGE L. (December 19, 1830-April 27, 1876), actor and playwright, was born in Boston, Mass. At the age of eighteen he made his first appearance on the stage, at Providence, R.I. He continued to act, without notable success, for nearly two decades. In 1867 he retired from the stage to devote his time to writing. He died in Jersey City, N.J., at the age of forty-five.

Aiken's sole claim to remembrance is his dramatization of Harriet Beecher Stowe's famous anti-slavery novel, *Uncle Tom's Cabin.* The first performance of the play was given at Troy, N.Y., on September 27, 1852, with Aiken in the cast. From the first it was an astounding success. In Troy it had the unheard-of run of 100 nights. In New York it played almost a year. Traveling companies were sent to all the leading Northern cities. After the Civil War it was even more popular than before. Numberless "tom shows" trouped up and down rural America every summer for decades, pitching their tents nightly and thrilling the natives with the tearful old melodrama. Even today it is frequently revived as a museum piece. It has probably been performed more times than any other play ever written.

As anyone knows who can recall a performance of Aiken's dramatization, it does *not* rank among the literary classics of the stage. It is extravagantly melodramatic and more a loose collection of episodes from the book than a real play. But poorly as it fares by critical standards, it was in its time a powerful force in the crusade against slavery and for that reason is historically important.

PRINCIPAL WORKS: *Plays*—Orion: The Gold Beater, 1851; Uncle Tom's Cabin, 1852; The Old Homestead, 1856; The Emerald Ring, 1858; The Doom of Deville, 1859; Josie, 1870. *Reminiscences*—Leaves From an Actor's Life.

ABOUT: Brown, T. A. History of the American Stage; Wemyss, F. C. Chronology of the American Stage.

AINSLIE, HEW (April 5, 1792-March 11, 1878), poet and brewer, was born at Bargeny Mains, Ayrshire, Scotland. His father, George Ainslie, a farmer employed on a noble estate, gave him a good education with a private tutor and at the best schools of Ballantrae and Ayr. When he was seventeen he was apprenticed to an attorney in Glasgow. Soon dissatisfied, he returned to Roslin, then the family home. He worked as a landscape gardener until 1810 when he went to Edinburgh to become a copyist in the Register House, and serve as amanuensis to Dugald Stewart, the philosopher. In 1812 he married his cousin, Janet Ainslie. His first book was published anonymously in 1822.

Also in 1822, Ainslie came to America. When farming ventures in Hoosick, N.Y., and New Harmony, Ind. (at Robert Owen's colony), failed, he entered the brewing business. His poetry, chiefly in dialect, won recognition in Scotland, and he was extremely proud of the fact that he was permitted to kiss Burns' widow on a visit to Scotland in 1864.

Tall, with tousled hair and beard, he had a sociable manner that brought him many friends. He devoted the last years of his life to gardening, and died in Louisville, Ky., where he lived with his children. His poetry, mostly light and humorous, has little emotional depth.

Principal Works: A Pilgrimage to the Land of Burns, 1822; Scottish Songs, Ballads, and Poems, 1855.

About: Ainslie, H. A Pilgrimage to the Land of Burns (see Memoir by T. C. Latto in 1892 ed.); Ainslie, H. Scottish Songs, etc. (see Notes).

AKERS, ELIZABETH (CHASE) (October 19, 1832-August 7, 1911), poet, was born in Strong, Maine, the daughter of a lawyer named Thomas Chase. Her mother, Mercy (Barton) Chase, died while she was a child, and she lived with relatives at Farmington, Maine. In 1851 she married Marshall S. M. Taylor, but the marriage was unhappy and she was soon divorced. In 1855 she became assistant editor of the Portland *Transcript*, and soon after began contributing verse to the *Atlantic Monthly*. Her first poems, published in 1856, appeared under the pseudonym of "Florence Percy." The volume was sufficiently successful to enable her to travel in Europe, where she met a sculptor from Maine, Benjamin P. Akers, whom she married in 1861. He died the following year. After another period on the staff of the *Transcript*, she married, in 1865, E. M. Allen, a New York merchant. From the close of the Civil War to 1873 they lived in Richmond, Va.; they then returned to Maine and in 1874 she became literary editor of the Portland *Daily Advertiser*, a position she held until 1881. Her last years were spent in Tuckahoe, N.Y., where she died at nearly seventy-nine. By her wish she was cremated, with no religious ceremony.

Mrs. Akers (her later work was all done under this name) was very popular in her time, though her commonplaceness and sentimentality have brought oblivion to her poems today. Her best known poem was "Rock Me to Sleep," written in 1859, and a stand-by of "elocutionists" for many years. She emerged triumphant from a dispute as to its authorship. In fairness, it should be said that many of her poems are more melodious and less sickeningly sweet than this bathetic piece of wish-fulfilment.

Principal Works: Forest Buds From the Woods of Maine, 1856; Poems, 1866-68-69; Queen Catherine's Rose, 1885; The Silver Bridge, 1886; The High-Top Sweeting, 1891; The Proud Lady of Stavoren, 1897; The Ballad of the Bronx, 1901; The Sunset Song and Other Verses, 1902.

About: Willard, F. E. & Livermore, M. A. Prominent American Women; New York Tribune August 12, 1911.

ALCOTT, AMOS BRONSON (November 29, 1799-March 4, 1888), educator, philosopher, and poet, was born in Wolcott, Conn., the son of Joseph Chatfield Alcox and Anna (Bronson) Alcox. (Bronson—as he was known—and his cousin William Andrus Alcott [*q.v.*] joined in changing the spelling of their common surname to "Alcott" when they went to school.)

After a country schooling, he set out, still a boy, for the South, with the intention of becoming a teacher; instead, he found himself with a pack on his back and a position as traveling salesman, or more truly peddler, for a New England firm. No stranger peddler ever lived. Alcott wandered round the South, with Norfolk, Va., as his headquarters, staying for weeks or even months wherever he received an invitation, and charming his hosts by his conversation—but selling no goods. In 1823 he returned home, with a record of having sold less than five dollars' worth of his wares.

By this time he had already formulated his very advanced educational theories—too advanced for their time—and he opened an infant school in Boston. He taught not from text-books, but by conversation (always Alcott's fetish), in a sort of Socratic method adapted to the limits of childish understanding, and he included in the curriculum talks on religion and even mild approaches to sexual instruction: all of which engaged the interest of a few pioneers, more in England than in America, but prepared the way for later disaster in the conventional surroundings of Boston in the 'thirties.

In 1830 Alcott married Abigail (Abba) May, a woman of charm and force, heart and soul with him in his work. Two years later they opened a school in Germantown, Pa., but, in a short time returned to Boston.

Four daughters were born to them, besides a son who died at birth—four little girls who were later to become immortal as Meg, Jo, Beth, and Amy in Louisa May Alcott's [*q.v.*] *Little Women.* But the revived Boston school was near its end. Alcott was denounced for blasphemy and obscenity, after the publication of his *Conversations With Children on the Gospel* had revealed to outraged parents just what their offspring were learning in the way of unorthodoxy. He was besides an open abolitionist, and the climax came when he refused to dismiss a little Negro girl who was one of his pupils. He met imperturbably the threats of violence, but he closed the school and retired to Concord, which was his home thereafter.

The Alcotts lived in the deepest poverty, while the father endeavored to earn their living by giving lectures—or, rather so-called "conversations." One paid one's fifty cents, and if the inspiration descended, Alcott talked interminably, explaining his philosophy, which was a blend of Transcendentalism and reform in dress, food, and living; if it did not descend, he explained that he could speak only when inspired, and that ended the session. In 1842 he was able to make a visit to England, where he found himself hailed as "the American Pestalozzi," and a school near London was named Alcott House in his honor. There also he met Carlyle, and gave rise to one of the dour Scot's most crabbed judgments. He came back with two Englishmen in his tow—Charles Lane and H. G. Wright. Lane bought a hundred acres near Harvard, Mass., and for seven months of 1843 the three, with Lane's son and the Alcott mother and children, struggled with the tragi-comedy of communal life at "Fruitlands." None of them knew how to farm, or was used to manual labor, and their troubles were augmented by Alcott's very peculiar ideas on diet. For example, they were not only strict vegetarians, not even eating milk or eggs, but they were confined also to "aspiring vegetables" that grew above the ground. To cap the climax, Lane was violently opposed to family life, and wanted Alcott to send away his wife and children. This was too much: Alcott was a devoted if irresponsible husband and father, and he refused. The Lanes and Wright then departed, and further attempts to keep alive on the farm were futile. Alcott went to bed and turned his head to the wall, determined to die; but his wife and his oldest daughter finally persuaded him to face life once more.

They went back to Concord, and Alcott became a "peripatetic philosopher," travelling

Collection of Frederick H. Meserve
A. BRONSON ALCOTT

wherever he could secure an engagement to lecture—or "converse"—on diet, race (he was an early proponent of the Nordic superiority creed), or other aspects of his philosophy. Friends, including the Emersons, helped as unobtrusively as they could, in the face of Mrs. Alcott's sensitive pride, and from her earliest girlhood the second daughter, Louisa, became the chief support of the family. Fortunately for Alcott, his entire family adored him, and considered it an honor to be able to labor in his behalf. After his early books on education, Alcott published but little, and most of that was privately; he did, however, contribute many series of his "Orphic Sayings" to the *Dial,* then edited by Margaret Fuller.

In the end, his life was probably not too hard, though his wife died, worn out, in 1877, and the daughter who had had the chief burden survived him by but two days. He died in Boston at more than eighty-eight.

Emerson called Alcott, whom he nevertheless respected and cherished, a "tedious archangel," and that remains his best description. Tall, fair, shy, with the loquacity of the really bashful man; lazy, vain, an invincible optimist, he wandered the roads of New England like some later Don Quixote. He was quite obviously a crank, and frequently a bore. Yet he made his real contribution to American thought. He was a true educational pioneer, and progressive American schools today owe as much to Bronson Alcott as they do to Pestalozzi, Froebel, or Mme. Montessori. After all, he was merely the typical Transcendentalist carried to an extreme degree, and "Fruitlands" was not much more futile and romantic than was "Brook Farm." Nothing that he wrote has any current interest, but he set ideas in motion, and he had the courage of his ideals. He must have been intolerable to live with, but he should be remembered not without gratitude and some measure of admiration.

Odell Shepard is authority for the statement that "not a thousandth part" of Alcott's manuscripts has ever been published. The greater part of this unpublished work—including private journals, drafts of books, and notes of travel and conversation—lay undisturbed for almost half a century in eighty bound volumes on the shelves of a private library in Concord, until it was made available to Professor Shepard, who made use of it in his biography of Alcott, published in 1937.

PRINCIPAL WORKS: Observations on the Principles and Methods of Infant Instruction, 1830; Doctrine and Discipline of Human Culture, 1836; Conversations With Children on the Gospel, 1836-37; Emerson (anonymous) 1863; Tablets, 1868; Concord Days, 1872; Table Talk, 1877; New Connecticut (poetry) 1881; Sonnets and Canzonets (poetry) 1882; Ralph Waldo Emerson, 1882.

ABOUT: Christy, A. The Orient in American Transcendentalism; Higginson, T. W. Contemporaries; Morrow, H. W. The Father of Little Women; O'Brien, H. E. Lost Utopias; Peabody, E. P. A Record of Mr. Alcott's School; Sanborn, F. B. & Harris, W. T. A. Bronson Alcott: His Life and Philosophy; Sears, C. E. Bronson Alcott's Fruitlands; Shepard, O. Pedlar's Progress: The Life of Bronson Alcott; Atlantic Monthly April 1894; Nation March 8, 1888; Saturday Review of Literature March 27, 1937.

ALCOTT, BRONSON. See ALCOTT, AMOS BRONSON

ALCOTT, LOUISA MAY (November 29, 1832-March 6, 1888), novelist, was born in Germantown, then a separate town but now part of Philadelphia, where her father, the educator and philosopher Bronson Alcott [*q.v.*], was then conducting a school. Her mother was Abigail (May) Alcott. Louisa was the second of four sisters. Although she spent a short time in a private school, and was tutored by Thoreau for some time, she received most of her education from her father.

To this unpractical, eccentric father she was devoted from earliest childhood, and suffered agonies because she felt that she was inferior to her sisters in her worship of him. When a mob surrounded his Boston school in 1837, threatening to hang him and burn the building, it was Louisa, aged five, who dispersed them by shaking her little fist and crying: "Go away, bad people!" In 1843 occurred the seven disastrous months of trying to keep alive by farming in a vegetarian community at "Fruitlands" near the town of Harvard, Mass. The four little girls helped their mother do all the cooking and household work, and gained an early experience of hard toil. From the beginning Louisa knew that she, like her mother whom she so much resembled, must be the center and support of their strange family.

She sewed, she taught country schools, she even went into domestic service, but above all, from the age of sixteen, she wrote. Anyone who has read *Little Women* can find in Jo's early experiences the story of Louisa Alcott's painful beginnings as an author. For the most part she wrote melodramatic, unreal stories for newspapers and fugitive magazines, and thought herself lucky if she received five to ten dollars for one. For fifteen years she was as near a complete failure as any writer could be.

Then in 1862, during the Civil War, she went to Washington as a volunteer nurse in the military hospital at Georgetown. The experience wrecked her health, but it made her reputation. From the letters she wrote home she made a book of "hospital sketches," which when published the next year made her name known to the nation—though she received only $200 for all rights. Hopefully she set to work on a novel, *Moods,* which was always her own favorite of her books. It was not very well received, but it made a little money, and in 1866 she was able to make her only trip to Europe, in the hope of regaining her health. She did not do so, but her first long absence from her home in Concord with leisure to think made her receptive to her publisher's suggestion that she write a book for girls based on the life she actually knew. *Little Women* was the result, and even then Miss Alcott was so doubtful of its prospects that she tried to secure a thousand dollars for the rights instead of accepting royalties. It made both her fortune and her fame, so that the slight flurry of her first successful book was lost in the whirlwind of her present popularity. Though meant for the reading of the young, grown men wept over Beth's deathbed (based on the actual bitter loss in 1858 of her own sister of the same name) and laughed aloud over the exploits of Jo and Amy. Miss Alcott's days of poverty and worry were over, though not her days of overwork. She became the sole breadwinner of the family, carried the whole burden without complaint, and only her diary revealed the melancholy behind her outward cheer. The death of her mother in 1877, and

Collection of Frederick H. Meserve
LOUISA MAY ALCOTT

soon after of her beloved younger sister May (a promising artist) in childbirth, clouded her days still further. She was a normal, warm-hearted, affectionate woman, but she had no social graces and no time to acquire them. When she must give Jo a husband she is awkward, and with good reason: Jo in real life never had a suitor or a love-affair—at least that the world knows about.

All her later books (all juveniles except *Work,* founded on her own early trials as a breadwinner when there were no occupations for ladies except sewing or teaching) were immense successes—most of all *Little Men,* based on her own nephews. She took great delight, when publishers clamored for a story, in reaching down into the literal "flour barrel" where she kept rejected manuscripts, and presenting them with something which they had turned down in the days before *Little Women.* Sometimes they were manuscripts which had been wisely rejected: there is evidence in much of her work of haste, of writing for money instead of from the urge to write. She never expressed fully the great talents she possessed; she learned too early that writing is a way to earn a living.

But what richness nevertheless is in her work! If there be an immortal American story, *Little Women* surely has a claim to that title, and *Little Men* and *An Old-Fashioned Girl* are not too far behind it. The tomboy who grew up into the tall girl with chestnut hair and dark, flashing eyes had the spark of genius in her, and all she needed was a happier life, some respite from care and responsibility, to have brought it all out for the world's good. When she wrote of the world she knew and remembered—of Boston and Concord in the mid-century; a whole scheme of existence unique of its kind and now vanished forever—she was superb.

Her life after her first success was uneventful: she lived at home, a loving daughter and sister and aunt; she worked interminably; she lent her voice to the causes of abolition and woman suffrage. She died in Boston on the day her father was buried. With all his pioneer labors in education, she was his greatest contribution to American literature.

Even today, a play and a motion picture have proved the perennial charm of *Little Women.* It is not by accident that Jo is universally acknowledged to be the most vivid person in the book. Miss Alcott knew Jo as she knew no other being on earth; she pitied her and laughed at her and loved her, and she gave her a satisfaction and completion in life which fate had withheld from Jo's prototype and creator.

Principal Works: Flower Fables, 1854; Hospital Sketches, 1863; Moods, 1864; Little Women, 1867; An Old-Fashioned Girl, 1869; Little Men, 1871; Aunt Jo's Scrap-bag, 1871-79; Shawl Straps, 1872; Work, 1873; Eight Cousins, 1874; Rose in Bloom, 1876; Silver Pitchers and Other Stories, 1876; A Modern Mephistopheles, 1877; Under the Lilacs, 1878; Jack and Jill, 1880; Proverb Stories, 1882; Spinning Wheel Stories, 1884; Lulu's Library, 1885-89; Jo's Boys, 1886.

About: Anthony, K. Louisa May Alcott; Cheney, E. D. Louisa May Alcott: Her Life, Letters, and Journals; Holland, R. S. Historic Girlhoods; Kirkland, W. M. Girls Who Became Writers; Meigs, C. L. The Story of the Author of Little Women: Invincible Louisa; Moses, B. Louisa May Alcott: Dreamer and Worker; Atlantic Monthly March 1890; Century Magazine May 1891; New England Magazine March 1892.

ALCOTT, WILLIAM ANDRUS (August 6, 1798-March 29, 1859), educator, physician, and editor, was born in Wolcott, Conn., the son of Obed Alcox and Anna (Andrus) Alcox. He was brought up on his father's farm and attended the district school with his cousin A. Bronson Alcott [*q.v.*], who joined him in changing the family name. He taught school for four years in Litchfield and Hartford Counties, and at twenty-two went South with Bronson Alcott. They planned to teach school in the South, but gave up the idea after walking from Charleston, S.C., to Norfolk, Va. William went into the classroom again in Connecticut and introduced many novel reforms, such as abolishing crude, backless benches for small children and introducing a proper ventilating system.

His untiring work for educational improvements eventually brought on a tubercular infection from which he never fully recovered. Resolving to study medicine in order to advance his teaching methods, he attended the Yale Medical School in New Haven, and was licensed to practice medicine and surgery in 1826. He returned to Wolcott and taught in the Central School, where he put into practice some of his new ideas—adding grammar and geography to the curriculum, and using plants, flowers, and maps in the schoolroom. In 1836, he married Phebe Bronson, daughter of Deacon Irad Bronson, of Bristol, Conn. His health suffered another relapse and he was obliged to give up the school for the outdoor life of itinerant physician in his district. Just as he was about to abandon all idea of teaching, W. C. Woodbridge, a follower of the popular Fellenberg movement, persuaded him to join in establishing at Hartford a miniature school patterned after the famous vocational institution at Hofwye, Switzerland.

At this time he began to write extensively on educational subjects, achieving a wide reputation. In 1831 he went to Boston with Woodbridge to edit the *Annals of Education*, a monthly journal, and *Juvenile Rambles*, the first magazine for children published in America. At the end of two years, S. G. Goodrich ("Peter Parley") invited him to become editor of *Parley's Magazine*, a position he held for four years. By his writings and lectures, Alcott helped the progress of educational reform to a considerable extent. He died at Auburndale, Mass., and his character is epitomized in his dying message to his son, "Tell William to live for others, not himself."

PRINCIPAL WORKS: Confessions of a Schoolmaster, 1839; Lectures for the Fireside, 1852; The Home Book of Life and Health, 1856; Forty Years in the Wilderness of Pills and Powders, 1859.

ABOUT: Alcott, A. B. New Connecticut; Dwight, T. Travels in New England and New York; Orcutt, S. History of Wolcott, Conn.; American Journal of Education, 1857.

ALDEN, HENRY MILLS (November 11, 1836-October 7, 1919), editor and philosophical writer, was born at Mt. Tabor, Vt., in the Green Mountains, the son of Ira Alden and Elizabeth (Moore) Alden. He was ninth in descent from John Alden of the "Mayflower." His father, however, was a poor farmer who in 1842 moved to Hoosick Falls, N.Y., where the child of five went to work as a bobbin boy in a mill from dawn to eight at night. He had hardly any schooling until he was fourteen; then by his own initiative he went to Ball Seminary, working his way by serving as janitor, and in 1853 entered Williams College, being graduated in 1857. The great educator Mark Hopkins was then president of Williams, and exercised a lasting influence on Alden. Part of every year Alden taught in district schools in Vermont and New York, but on his graduation he went, at his mother's wish, to Andover Theological Seminary and was graduated in 1860. He was never ordained, however.

Soon after, he met Harriet Beecher Stowe, who interested herself in him and saw to it that his philosophical essays were published in the *Atlantic Monthly*. In 1861 he went to New York, and after trying vainly to enlist in the Union army, taught in private schools. More of his work appeared in the *Atlantic*, and in 1863 and 1864 he was asked to give the Lowell Institute lectures in Boston. At the same time he started collaborating with Dr. A. H. Guernsey in *Harper's Pictorial History of the Great Rebellion*—the start of his lifelong connection with Harper & Brothers. From 1863 to 1869 he was managing editor of *Harper's Weekly*, and then served as editor of *Harper's Magazine* to his death.

A highly religious man, something of a mystic (though no ascetic), Alden aimed at making *Harper's* a "family magazine"—a process which required the emasculation of Hardy's *Jude the Obscure*. Within these limits, however, he was a great editor. He has been called the last of the old New Eng-

HENRY MILLS ALDEN

land type of writer and thinker. His own writing is a blend of orthodox theology and a mystical worship of nature. At his death he was the dean of magazine editors in America.

Alden was twice married: in 1861 (on an income of $7 a week!) to Susan Frye Foster, who died in 1895, leaving four children; and in 1900 to a Virginian poet, Ada Foster Murray.

PRINCIPAL WORKS: God in His World, 1890; A Study of Death (edited, with W. D. Howells) 1895; The Heart of Childhood, 1906; Magazine Writing and the New Literature, 1908; In After Days: Thoughts on the Future Life (symposium, with others) 1910.

ABOUT: Harper, J. H. The House of Harper; Bookman November-December 1919; Harper's Magazine December 1919; Review of Reviews November 1919.

ALDEN, JOSEPH (January 4, 1807-August 30, 1885), educator, was born in Cairo, N.Y. He was the son of Eliab and Mary (Hathaway) Alden, and traced his ancestry to John Alden of the "Mayflower." He began teaching at the age of fourteen and rose to a high position in the contemporary educational world. Graduated from Union College in 1829, he subsequently studied at Princeton Theological Seminary and was ordained to the Congregational ministry, but he soon left the pulpit to accept a professorship at Williams College, where he remained ten years, teaching English literature, political economy, and history. In 1852 he took the chair of philosophy at Lafayette College, but resigned in 1857 to accept the presidency of Jefferson College, holding the office five years. From 1867 to the end of his life, he was the principal of the State Normal School at Albany, N.Y. He married twice: in 1834, Isabella Livingstone, a clergyman's daughter; and in 1882, Amelia Daly, of Tompkinsville, Staten Island. His numerous books were educational in nature.

Well-poised, of medium height, Alden had a precise manner of speech and diversified interests. His writing was the practical, instructive product of an alert mind.

PRINCIPAL WORKS: The Aged Pilgrim, 1846; Elizabeth Benton: or, Religion in Connection With Fashionable Life, 1846; The Example of Washington Commended to the Young, 1846; The Jewish Washington: or, Lessons in Patriotism and Piety Suggested by the History of Nehemiah, 1846; Alice Gordon: or, The Uses of Orphanage, 1847; The Lawyer's Daughter, 1847; Anecdotes of the Puritans, 1849; Christian Ethics, 1866; Elements of Intellectual Philosophy, 1866; Science of Government, 1866; A Textbook of Ethics, 1867; Introduction to the Uses of the English Language, 1875; Studies in Bryant (with introduction by W. C. Bryant) 1876; Thoughts on the Religious Life (with introduction by W. C. Bryant) 1879; First Principles of Political Economy, 1879; Self-Education: What to Do and How to Do It, 1880.

ABOUT: New York Herald August 31, 1885; New York Observer September 3, 1885; Williams College Biographical Annals 1871.

ALDEN, WILLIAM LIVINGSTONE (October 9, 1837-January 14, 1908), journalist, was born at Williamstown, Mass. He was the son of the educator Joseph Alden [*q.v.*] by his first wife, Isabella (Livingstone) Alden. He attended Lafayette College for three years, but changed to Jefferson College when his father accepted the presidency. Graduated with the class of 1858, he went to New York City to read law, and was admitted to the New York bar in 1860. Five years later he married Agnes M. McClure and gave up his legal practice in order to write. He soon became identified with the literary group known as the Lotos Club. He was assistant editor of the *Citizen* for a short time and later wrote leading articles for the *Times, World, Graphic,* and other papers. During Cleveland's first administration, he was appointed consul-general to Rome, and on his retirement in 1890, he was decorated by King Humbert For the next thirteen years he was leader writer for the Paris edition of the *Herald.* Moving to London, he became literary correspondent to the New York *Times,* and contributed widely to magazines. He died in Buffalo, N.Y.

Extremely fond of outdoor life, especially canoeing, Alden designed a special canoe and took a number of interesting cruises which he described in magazine articles. He wrote a popular life of Columbus during the 'eighties and contributed six volumes to *Harper's Young People's Series.* In his day he was considered a clever writer of humorous articles.

PRINCIPAL WORKS: Domestic Explosives, 1877; Shooting Stars, 1878; The Cruise of the Canoe Club, 1883; Trying to Find Europe, 1889; Among the Freaks, 1896; Cat Tales, 1905.

ABOUT: New York Times January 16, 1908.

ALDRICH, THOMAS BAILEY (November 11, 1836-March 19, 1907), novelist and poet, was born in Portsmouth, N.H., the son of Elias Taft Aldrich and Sarah (Bailey) Aldrich. His father was of a wandering nature, however, and much of the boy's childhood was spent away from New England, in New York and especially in New Orleans. It was while he was back in Portsmouth (the "Rivermouth" of *The Story of a Bad Boy,* as he was its "Tom Bailey") that his father died, in 1849.

Collection of Frederick H. Meserve
THOMAS BAILEY ALDRICH

Aldrich had been preparing to enter Harvard; now, however, he had to end his schooling and go to work. An uncle in New York offered him a position in his counting-house, but already the boy's mind was set on writing, and soon afterwards he began composing graceful verses for the magazines and cultivating what literary company he could discover.

His reward came in 1855, when after the publication of his first book of poems, N. P. Willis made Aldrich junior literary critic of his *Evening Mirror*. Before the year was out the young poet had become assistant editor of Willis' other property, the *Home Journal*. When the Civil War broke out, he did not enlist, but was sent to the front as war correspondent of the *Tribune*. Returning from the front, he became in 1862 managing editor of the *Illustrated News*

The year 1865 was the turning-point of Aldrich's life. In that year he married, most happily, Lilian Woodman of New York, who survived him and their son; and he went to Boston as editor of *Every Saturday*, a position he held until 1874. Boston was the home of Aldrich's heart, temple of the gods—Longfellow, Holmes, Emerson—whom he worshipped; in later years an unkind commentator said that he was "Boston-plated." He began presently to contribute verses to the *Atlantic Monthly*; once, venturing into the editor's office, he saw on his desk some memoranda to "send contract to R.W.E., pay check to O.W.H.," etc., and daringly added: "Don't forget to accept poem by T.B.A."!

Every Saturday expired at the end of 1874. By this time Aldrich had won fame, not only by his most popular poem, "The Ballad of Babie Bell," but also by his most popular short story and novel—*Marjorie Daw* and *The Story of a Bad Boy*, respectively. The latter, a nostalgic gilding of his boyhood in Portsmouth, is still read for its humor and verve. He could afford to take time off from editorial duties, and did so for six years, commencing his vacation by the first of his many trips to Europe with his wife.

In 1881 the fire from heaven descended on him; he took up Elijah's mantle. In other words he was selected to succeed William Dean Howells as editor of the *Atlantic Monthly*, undoubtedly the highest honor Aldrich could ever have conceived—as it was indeed the most definite recognition of merit which literary America had at that time to offer. He remained as editor until 1890, when he retired to devote all his time to his own writing. As an editor, though not quite in the class of Field or Howells, he was competent; he still could draw on many of the great old names for contributions, and he carried on the *Atlantic* tradition religiously. His position gave him much leisure. He was able to make frequent trips abroad, to bring out two volumes of poems and two of non-fiction, and to prepare a stage version of his *Mercedes*, though it was not acted until 1894. Always fond of the theater, Aldrich was a close friend of Edwin Booth, who encouraged him, not too wisely, in dramatizing his essentially non-dramatic verse. Later a version of his *Judith and Holofernes*, renamed *Judith of Bethulia*, was acted by Nance O'Neill.

The remaining seventeen years of Aldrich's life after he left the *Atlantic* were in the main years of happiness, of universal recognition, of great prosperity (his admiration for men of wealth, very much akin to Mark Twain's and with the same basic cause, made him known to carpers as "the Little Brother of the Rich"), and of productive labor. They were saddened, however, by the death from tuberculosis in 1904 of his only child, his son Charles. He and his wife spent the next year in Egypt in a vain attempt to forget their grief. His seventieth birthday was the occasion of a wide celebration in literary circles which attested the great regard in which his fellow-craftsmen held him. The following March he died in Boston, following an unsuccessful operation.

To the last Aldrich was unusually youthful in appearance, with bright blue eyes and a tawny mustache hardly touched with grey. Witty (sometimes caustic), urbane, and serene, he was personally popular and his gregarious nature welcomed a large assembly of friends. He had small interest in non-literary affairs of the day, but was essentially a conservative, with a dislike for reformers, whom he thought cranks, and for Bohemians, whom he thought cheats. He held grudges, and let them influence his judgment: Whitman, for example, was no poet because he still owed Aldrich nine dollars! But the chief impression he gave was of a happy contentment with life, combined with a touchingly juvenile reverence for his great predecessors in the literature of New England.

In spite of the charm of *Marjorie Daw* and some others of his stories, his poetry is much better than his prose. As a poet he has been compared to many others, but is perhaps nearest to the urbanity, grace, and wistfulness of Horace. His workmanship is superb, and he can take the slightest theme and make of it an artistic creation. That, indeed, is just what he did in most of his novels, which have shallow and even trivial themes, hardly worthy of the beautiful treatment he accorded them. All his best work was done before 1881, when he capitulated altogether to the Boston literary orthodoxy. There was indeed something slightly adolescent about Aldrich's work to the end, just as there was about his appearance. But America has produced few writers, and particularly few poets, capable of Aldrich's exquisite craftsmanship at its best. He was a jeweler in words, and if his jewels were not always genuine, the finished ornament was no less a masterpiece of its kind.

Principal Works: *Poetry*—The Bells, 1855; Pompinea, 1861; Cloth of Gold, 1874; Flower and Thorn, 1877; Friar Jerome's Beautiful Book, 1881; Mercedes and Later Lyrics, 1884; Windham Towers, 1890; Judith and Holofernes, 1896. *Fiction*—The Story of a Bad Boy, 1870; Marjorie Daw and Other People, 1873; Prudence Palfrey, 1874; The Queen of Sheba, 1877; A Rivermouth Romance, 1877; The Stillwater Tragedy, 1880; Two Bites at a Cherry, with Other Tales, 1894; A Sea Turn and Other Matters, 1902; Quite So, 1907. *Non-fiction*—From Ponkapog to Pesth, 1883; An Old Town by the Sea, 1893; Ponkapog Papers, 1903.

About: Aldrich, L. W. Crowding Memories; Greenslet, F. Life of Thomas Bailey Aldrich; Winter, W. Old Friends; Atlantic Monthly May 1907, August 1907; Bookman May 1907; Outlook March 30, August 24, 1907.

ALEXANDER, ARCHIBALD (April 17, 1772-October 22, 1851), theologian and educator, was born in Rockbridge County, Va. His parents were William Alexander and Ann (Reid) Alexander, of the Scotch-Irish farming settlement near Lexington. He was brought up in an intellectual, religious atmosphere. At the age of seven he had already begun Latin and knew his shorter catechism, and by the time he reached his teens he was proficient in shooting, swimming, and riding. He matriculated at Liberty Hall (now Washington and Lee University) at an early age, and studied under the Rev. William Graham, who encouraged him to go into the ministry. On November 7, 1794, he was ordained pastor of two small churches in Charlotte County, and in 1796, when he was only twenty-four, he was called to the presidency of Hampden-Sidney College, a position he held for ten years, with the exception of one intervening year when he resigned to make an lengthy trip to New England. On April 5, 1802, he married Janetta Waddel, daughter of Dr. James Waddel, the "Blind Preacher" of Louisa County.

In the spring of 1807 Alexander accepted the important pastorate of the Pine Street Church in Philadelphia. In the same year he was elected moderator of the General Assembly, and he was instrumental in the establishment of the Presbyterian theological seminary at Princeton, N.J., in 1812. He was the first professor, and remained at the seminary until his death, teaching and exerting a wide influence by his scholarship and pious example.

He was small and slight, with dark penetrating eyes and thick hair. Of simple tastes, with a vivacious manner, and a musical voice, he had an extraordinary gift for pulpit oratory. His literary activities included theological essays, reviews, tracts, and sermons.

Principal Works: A Brief Outline of the Evidences of the Christian Religion, 1825; The Canon of the Old and New Testaments, 1826; Suggestions in Vindication of Sunday Schools, 1829; The Lives of the Patriarchs, 1835; Thoughts on Religious Experience, 1841; Biographical Sketches of the Founder and Principal Alumni of the Log College, 1845; History of Colonization on the Western Coast of Africa, 1846; Outlines of Moral Science, 1852.

About: Alexander, J. W. Life of Archibald Alexander; Sprague, W. B. Annals of the American Pulpit: III; Princeton Theological Review October 1905.

ALEXANDER, JOHN HENRY (June 26, 1812-March 2, 1867), scientist and poet, was born in Annapolis, Md., the son of William Alexander, a merchant, and Mary (Stockett) Alexander. He received a B.A. degree from St. John's College, Annapolis, at only fourteen, and for a time studied law.

His interest, however, was always primarily in applied science, and he soon abandoned the law to make a survey for a railroad. (This was the beginning of the great era of railroad building in America.) Before he was twenty-one the Maryland state officials had appointed him to make a complete topographical and geological survey of the state, and in 1834 the office of state topographical engineer was created for him. In 1836 he married Margaret Hammer, by whom he had five sons and a daughter.

Alexander was interested also in coal geology and discovered new fields in Maryland and Pennsylvania, being president of a coal company from 1836 to 1845. Meanwhile he had begun an agitation for standardization of weights and measures, and in 1842 left his former state office to devote himself to this work, continuing his topographical studies, however, as coadjutor of the Coast Survey. His *Universal Dictionary of Weights and Measures* is still a standard work. In 1857 the United States government sent him to Europe to advocate the unification of coinage, and he was about to be appointed director of the mint when he died.

A very versatile man, Alexander also acted as professor of mining and civil engineering at the University of Pennsylvania and professor of natural history at St. John's College, and at his death he was professor of natural philosophy at the University of Maryland. He left books in manuscript dealing with Indian languages, parliamentary procedure, and the history of surnames. A devout and active Episcopalian, he published two volumes of religious poetry. These are inferior, however, to his prose, which is pure and limpid.

Principal Works: *Prose*—Report on Standards of Weight and Measure for the State of Maryland, 1845; A Universal Dictionary of Weights and Measures: Ancient and Modern, 1850. *Poetry*—Introits, 1844; Catena Dominica, 1855.

About: Hilgard, J. E. Memoir of John H. Alexander (*National Biographical Memoirs*); Pinkney, W. Biographical Memoir of John H. Alexander (*Maryland Historical Society*).

ALGER, HORATIO, JR. (January 13, 1834-July 18, 1899), juvenile writer, was born in Revere, Mass., the oldest child of the Rev. Horatio Alger, a Unitarian minister, and Olive (Fenno) Alger. His childhood was a long nightmare: his father, a coming-to-life of the caricature Puritan, allowed the little boy no recreation whatever; only study, discipline, and prayer under his personal supervision. He broke the boy's will and frustrated his life. Finally Horatio was released to Gates Academy, and then to Harvard, from which he was graduated in 1852.

For a while he was a private tutor, with occasional excursions into journalism; then in 1855 he entered the Harvard Divinity School, against his wish. He finished his course there, but when his parents came to his graduation, they found that he had fled with two friends to Paris. Behind this rebellion was a youthful love-affair, ended by his father, which left lifelong marks on the son. In Paris, where he had gone to write, he lived instead *la vie de Bohème* in the true Murger manner. To escape from the lady in whose clutches he had fallen, he returned to America—but she took the same boat! He lost her, however, at the dock, and went back to Massachusetts. Again he tried tutoring, and made several typical tragi-comic efforts to join the Union army. The climax was an illness and his rescue by his father, who finally persuaded him to be ordained. In December 1864 he became minister of the Unitarian congregation at Brewster, Mass.

Two years later he resigned and went to New York, which was to be his home for thirty years. He knew he wanted to be a writer—to write a great book, the nature and subject of which varied with the years, though he died still dreaming of it. Instead, his first publication of any consequence was a boys' story, "Ragged Dick," which appeared in *Student and Schoolmate*, edited by William Taylor Adams ("Oliver Optic"). This came to the attention of Charles O'Connor, superintendent of the Newsboys' Lodging House, who sought Alger out and became his closest friend. Though he had rooms elsewhere (and once even owned a very unsuccessful curio shop!), Alger was thenceforth inseparable from the home; he practically lived there, was its chaplain, its benefactor, its publicizer. The boys worshipped him and he, who never grew up, worshipped them in return. For his first publisher, A. K. Loring, who brought out *Ragged Dick* as a book in 1867, and for other publishers later, he poured out nearly 130 books for boys, in series of eight or ten each, sometimes two or three a year. He had published several bad novels already, but now he found his stride.

The books were so much alike that often characters intruded themselves into the wrong volume. They were endlessly repetitious, and all built on the same model. Probably no one has read them all. But they made Alger, in sheer bulk of readers, perhaps the most popular author who has

HORATIO ALGER
an imaginary portrait

ever lived. He was thought of as an authority, a source of endless information; his fan mail was enormous, his visitors multitudinous. He overflowed in the most prodigal generosity to the worthy and unworthy alike. But he felt himself a failure, and the fat, pale little man with the clouded eyes was the unhappiest creature on earth. His overflowing heart, which had made him, timorous as he was, the effective scourge of the vicious padrone system by which the little Italian street musicians were tortured, found solace in the adoption of a little Chinese boy, Wing: but soon Wing was killed by a wagon. To ease his hurt, Alger made a trip West, which ended in illness and near-insanity. Somehow, on the eastward return, he found himself in Peekskill, N.Y., where—by a grotesque sequence only he could experience—he was arrested (wholly mistakenly) for murder! He was released within a few hours, but out of this mischance grew his acquaintance with Una Garth, a married woman with whom he fell madly in love. She tired of him and fled with her husband and brother to her former home in France; he followed her, and she finally drove him completely insane. With the first return of lucidity, he crept home to Charles O'Connor at the Newsboys' Lodging House.

Then at last O'Connor died, and Alger, with all his clubs and his charities and his fame, was utterly alone. Finally in 1898 he went to his married sister, in Natick, Mass., and there, at sixty-five, he died. He had never had any real happiness in his life. His father had done his work well.

Alger never wrote the book he longed to write, and probably he did not have it in him to become a real writer. His stories were exactly in accord with the temper of his time; they were ready-made for the boys of America of the '70s and '80s, but they can hardly be called literature. His verse was very bad (though the folk-ballad, "John Maynard," has survived in school readers). In other words, he could not write: yet nearly every man alive today in the United States read him avidly as a boy. Mayes in his biography lists 121 of his titles, and in one copy an unknown reader added five more. There were, besides, his early novels and a book of verses, *Grandfather Baldwin's Thanksgiving* (1875). To list them all would be futile: Alger himself could not remember them, and soon they will all be forgotten.

PRINCIPAL WORKS: Bertha's Christmas Vision, 1856; Nothing to Do, 1857; Frank's Campaign, 1864; Paul Preston's Charge, 1865; Helen Ford, 1866; Ragged Dick Series, 1867; Luck and Pluck Series, 1869; Tattered Tom Series, 1871; From Canal Boy to President, 1881; From Farm Boy to Senator, 1882; Abraham Lincoln: The Backwoods Boy, 1883.

ABOUT: Mayes, H. R. Alger: A Biography Without a Hero; New York Tribune January 28, 1917.

ALLEN, ALEXANDER VIETS GRISWOLD (May 14, 1841-July 1, 1908), theologian, was born in Otis, Mass. His father, the Rev. Ethan Allen, was a "low church" Episcopal rector, poverty-stricken, pious, and somewhat bigoted. His mother was Lydia (Burr) Allen. When the child was four the family moved to Nantucket, and when he was fourteen, to Vermont. Meanwhile he had had no schooling except from his father. Yet at eighteen he had prepared himself to enter the sophomore class of Kenyon College, in Ohio, and was graduated at the head of his class in 1862. He then entered the college's theological seminary, Bexley Hall, but the evangelical atmosphere of the school repelled him, and after a period of religious doubt and agonizing, from which he was helped back to faith only by a devout study of the philosophical works of Coleridge, he changed in 1864 to the Andover Theological Seminary, where the prevailing influences were more liberal. He was ordained deacon in 1865, while still a student, and priest in 1866, and became rector of St. John's Church, Lawrence, Mass. The next year he was appointed instructor of church history in the Episcopal Theological School at Cambridge, and in 1869 was made professor, a position he held until his death. In 1872 he married Elizabeth Kent Stone;

she died in 1892, and in 1907 he married Paulina Cony Smith.

Allen's most important work is *The Continuity of Christian Thought.* This, though in some ways original and distinguished, is marred by his adherence to the Greek tradition, and his consequent unfairness to and even ignorance of the Latin fathers. His two-volume life of Phillips Brooks is the definitive biography of that eminent divine.

Principal Works: The Continuity of Christian Thought, 1884; Jonathan Edwards, 1889; Religious Progress, 1894; Christian Institutions, 1897; Life and Letters of Phillips Brooks, 1900; Freedom in the Church, 1907.

About: Slattery, C. L. Alexander V. G. Allen.

ALLEN, ELIZABETH AKERS. See AKERS, ELIZABETH (CHASE)

ALLEN, JAMES LANE (October 21, 1849-February 18, 1925), novelist and short story writer, was born on a farm near Lexington, Ky., in the heart of the Blue Grass country, the son of Richard Allen and Helen (Foster) Allen. The family, descended from early American settlers, was reduced to extreme poverty and underwent much hardship during the Civil War and Reconstruction. With this background it was natural that his heart and memory should go back, when he began to write, to an idealized South before the war.

Allen worked his way through Transylvania Academy and Transylvania College (then known as Kentucky University) and was graduated in 1872. For a year he taught a district school in Kentucky, for another year in a high school in Richmond, Mo., and in 1875 established a private school of his own in Lexington, Mo. A year later he returned to Kentucky and to Transylvania to work for his M.A. degree, which he secured in 1877. The next year he became principal of Transylvania Academy, then from 1880 to 1883 was professor of Latin and English at Bethany College, in West Virginia, which gave him another (honorary) M.A. in 1880. For the next two years he ran another private school, this time in Lexington, Ky.

He was thus very late in beginning as an author, though he had been interested in literature (as well as in natural science) from boyhood, and had already contributed poems, stories, and articles to *Harper's*, the *Atlantic Monthly*, the *Independent*, and other magazines of high standing. In 1885 he gave up teaching forever to devote himself to writing. It was not, however, until the publication of *Flute and Violin* in 1891 that he had any real success. In 1893 he moved to New York City, which was his home thenceforth.

Collection of Frederick H. Meserve

JAMES LANE ALLEN

A Kentucky Cardinal, published in 1894, was Allen's most popular book. After *The Mettle of the Pasture*, in 1903, his work became increasingly mystical and even unintelligible, and his popularity declined sharply. Since he was shy, reticent, and had a horror of publicity, he did nothing to keep himself in the public eye. Warm-hearted and of charming manners in an intimate circle, he was formal, dignified, and extremely sensitive in his relations to the world outside. He never married, and his life after 1893 was uneventful, punctuated only by the appearance of new novels and by several trips to Europe. His scholarly face, with high forehead, drooping mustache, and spectacles, was quite unfamiliar to the vast public which knew and loved his early books.

As a writer, Allen was essentially a romantic, and one of the most strongly regional of writers. His earlier and more successful books, and nearly all the later ones as well, dealt with the Kentucky of his boyhood, idealized and covered with a veil of affectionate nostalgia. (He would never revisit Kentucky in later years, lest he be disillusioned by witnessing some change.) Through all his work there runs a vein of pathos, a quiet, spiritual melancholy. Few writers have had a keener feeling for nature, which is almost as much a character in his novels as are the human beings depicted in them. (Incidentally, the "Kentucky cardinal" is a bird—not a prelate of the church!)

Allen was a conscious stylist, as might have been expected of a Latinist; his prose at its best is pure and sonorous. He is largely forgotten now, but *A Kentucky Cardinal, The Choir Invisible* (an expansion of *John Gray,* published in 1893), and some of the stories in *Flute and Violin* possess a vitality which has outlasted their period and their *genre.* His poems, which have a serious beauty, have never been gathered in a volume.

Principal Works: Flute and Violin, 1891; The Blue Grass Region of Kentucky, and Other Kentucky Articles, 1892; John Gray, 1893; A Kentucky Cardinal, 1894; Aftermath (sequel to A Kentucky Cardinal) 1895; Summer in Arcady, 1896; The Choir Invisible, 1897; Two Gentlemen of Kentucky, 1899; The Reign of Law, 1900; The Mettle of the Pasture, 1903; Bride of the Mistletoe, 1909; The Doctor's Christmas Eve, 1910 (the last two are part of an uncompleted trilogy); The Heroine in Bronze, 1912; The Last Christmas Tree, 1914; The Sword of Youth, 1915; A Cathedral Singer, 1916; The Kentucky Warbler, 1918; The Emblems of Fidelity, 1919; The Alabaster Box, 1923; The Landmark (short stories) 1925.

About: Henneman, J. B. Shakespearian and Other Papers; Knight, G. C. James Lane Allen and the Genteel Tradition; Townsend, J. W. James Lane Allen; Bookman June 1895, June 1897, October 1900.

"ALLEN, JOHN W., Jr." See LESLEY, PETER.

ALLEN, JOSEPH HENRY (August 21, 1820-March 20, 1890), theologian and Latinist, was born in Northboro, Mass., the son of the Rev. Joseph Allen and Lucy (Ware) Allen. He was reared in a devout atmosphere—his father being a minister, and his mother the daughter of the Rev. Henry Ware, radical professor of divinity at Harvard—and was educated in the parsonage school established by his father in Northboro, and at Harvard in the class of 1840. Three years later he was graduated from the Harvard Divinity School. The following October he was ordained minister of the First Congregational Society of Jamaica Plain. He married Anna Minot Weld on May 22, 1845.

Between 1847 and 1857 he took charge of churches in Washington, D.C., and Bangor, Maine, but was so temperamentally unsuited to clerical life that he took up teaching and for several years lectured on ecclesiastical history at the Harvard Divinity School. This began a period of literary activity, and he was a frequent contributor to Unitarian periodicals. During the Civil War he was editor of the *Christian Examiner* and in 1887-91 of the *Unitarian Review.* Although he gave up an active interest in the ministry, he frequently filled pastorless pulpits and ministered to a number of churches from Maine to California. He died in Cambridge, Mass.

Allen had a retiring, meditative nature, and was not a convincing speaker, although he sometimes defended important causes, like the abolition movement, with surprising zeal. His name is chiefly associated with the popular Latin manuals which he prepared in collaboration with Prof. J. B. Greenough, but his writings also include many contributions to Unitarian literature.

Principal Works: Manual of Latin Grammar, 1868; A Latin Reader, 1869; Latin Primer, 1870; Our Liberal Movement in Theology, 1882; Christian History in Its Three Great Periods, 1883; Historical Sketch of the Unitarian Movement, 1894.

About: Christian Register 1902; New York Evening Post March 21, 1898.

ALLEN, PAUL (February 15, 1775-August 18, 1826), poet and editor, was born in Providence, R.I., the son of Paul Allen, Sr., and Polly (Cooke) Allen, and was educated at Rhode Island College (now Brown University). He was graduated in 1793 with a reputation as an orator, several of his orations having been published. He studied law, but was totally unfit to practice it: all his life he was a sort of lesser Hartley Coleridge, childlike, irresponsible, and trusting—always in trouble except when his friends looked after him and cared for him.

He moved to Philadelphia, where he became a contributor to the *United States Gazette* and the *Port Folio,* and supervised the printing of the first history of the Lewis and Clark expedition (1814) by Nicholas Biddle. He then moved permanently to Baltimore, where he contributed to the *Portico* and for a while acted as editor of the *Federal Republican and Baltimore Telegraph.* A period followed when he was imprisoned for a debt of thirty dollars, but he was rescued by friends and fellow-members of the Delphian Club, who started a paper known as the *Journal of the Times* so as to provide for him as editor. From 1818 to 1824 he was editor of the *Morning Chronicle,* then of the *Saturday Evening Herald,* and he also acted as publisher of the *Morning Post.* He seems never to have been married. He had long contemplated writing a history of the American Revolution, but actually very little of the volume published under that title in 1819 was his; he was too irresolute to complete so long a work, and most of the writing was done by his friend John Neal.

A short, dark, near-sighted, ugly man with a disagreeable whining voice, Allen nevertheless won faithful friends by his good nature and simplicity of spirit. His writing is facile and graceful, but too diffuse and highly imitative of English models—chiefly of Cowper.

PRINCIPAL WORKS: Original Poems: Serious and Entertaining, 1801; Noah, 1821.

ABOUT: Neal, J. Randolph; Scharf, T. J. History of Baltimore; Sioussat, A. L. Old Baltimore.

ALLEN, WILLIAM (January 2, 1784-July 16, 1868), clergyman, educator, and historian, was born in Pittsfield, Mass. His father, the Rev. Thomas Allen, was pastor of the First Congregational Church in Pittsfield for forty-six years, and his mother, Elizabeth (Lee) Allen, was a descendant of Governor Bradford of Plymouth. He was graduated from Harvard, studied theology, and received his license to preach in 1804.

During the next six years he was assistant librarian and regent at Harvard, and compiled the first edition of his famous *American Biographical and Historical Dictionary.* Upon his father's death in 1810 he was ordained pastor at Pittsfield. Three years later he married Maria Malleville Wheelock, who died several years afterward. She was the daughter of President Eleazar Wheelock of Dartmouth College, whom Allen succeeded in 1817. He held office during the two years of fruitless legislative effort to alter the college charter to that of a university.

In December 1819 he accepted the presidency of Bowdoin College and entered another tempestuous period. He established the Medical School of Maine, broadened the curriculum, and graduated such prominent students as William Pitt Fessenden, Franklin Pierce, H. W. Longfellow, Jacob and John S. C. Abbott, and Nathaniel Hawthorne. In 1831 he married Sarah Johnson Breed of Norwich, Conn. The following June his trustees ousted him from office by enacting a special state law providing that all college officers be re-elected by the trustees after each commencement. He failed of re-election, appealed to the federal circuit court, and was reinstated after two years of litigation. He held office again for five years but was so unpopular that he was finally forced to resign. Moving to Northampton, Mass., he devoted himself to literary work until his death.

Strict and unyielding, yet impartial and just, Allen made many enemies who failed to understand his contradictory disposition, though he was at all times respected for his scholarship and literary achievement. His *Biographical Dictionary* stands as a notable pioneer among works of its kind.

PRINCIPAL WORKS: American Biographical and Historical Dictionary, 1809; Accounts of Shipwreck and Other Disasters at Sea, 1823; Junius Unmasked: or, Lord George Sackville Proved to be Junius, 1828; Lectures to Young Men, 1830; Psalms and Hymns for Public Worship, 1835; Memoir of John Codman, D.D., 1853; Wunnissoo: or, the Vale of Hoosatunnuk, 1856; A Book of Christian Sonnets, 1860; Poems of Nazareth and the Cross, 1866.

ABOUT: Lord, J. K. History of Dartmouth College; Smith, J. E. A. History of Pittsfield; Sprague, W. B. A Discourse Delivered in the First Congregational Church in Northampton, Mass.; New England Historical and Genealogical Register, 1869.

ALLEN, WILLIAM FRANCIS (September 5, 1830-December 9, 1889), classical scholar, was born at Northboro, Mass., the son of the Rev. Joseph Allen and Lucy (Ware) Allen, and younger brother of Joseph Henry Allen [*q.v.*]. His father, a Unitarian clergyman, prepared him for college in his parsonage school. He was graduated from Harvard in 1851, and, after spending three years tutoring in a private family in New York, traveled extensively in Europe, studying history and antiquity.

Returning to Boston in 1856, he became associate principal of the English and Classical School at West Newton, remaining there seven years. In 1862 he married Mary Tileston Lambert. He spent two years in the South with the Freedmen's and Sanitary Commissions at St. Helena Island, S.C., and Helena, Ark. During this time he collected the Negro songs included in his *Slave Songs of the United States.* He was superintendent of the schools of Charleston, S.C., for several months, professor of ancient languages at Antioch College, Yellow Springs, Ohio, for one year, and taught for a year at Eagleswood Military College, Perth Amboy, N.J. In 1867 he took the chair of ancient languages and history in the University of Wisconsin, remaining there until his death. His wife died in 1865, and in 1868 he married Margaret Loring Andrews, of Newburyport, Mass.

Allen was beloved by all who knew him. Versatile, a tireless worker, he wrote more than 900 articles and reviews on classical, historical, political, and other subjects, and was one of the first to use the examination of original sources and topical study in history instruction.

PRINCIPAL WORKS: Slave Songs of the United States, 1867; A Latin Reader, 1869; Latin Lessons, 1869; Manual of Latin Grammar, 1868; six volumes of Latin texts and selections, with J. B. Greenough and J. H. Allen, known as the *Allen and Greenough Series,* 1873, 1874, 1875; An Introduction to Latin Composition, 1870; The *Germania* and *Agricola* of Tacitus, 1880; The *Annals* of Tacitus: Books 1-4, 1890; Short History of the Roman People, 1890.

About: Butler, J. D. Translations of the Wisconsin Academy, Sciences, Arts and Letters: Vol. 8; Frankenburger, D. B. Essays and Monographs, Memorial Volume, 1890; Smith, C. L. Classical Review: Vol. 4.

ALLIBONE, SAMUEL AUSTIN (April 7, 1816-September 2, 1889), lexicographer and bibliographer, was born in Philadelphia, of French Huguenot and English Quaker descent. His mother's family had come over with Penn. He was privately educated, and for ten years worked as an official of the Insurance Company of North America. His real interest was in literature, however, and he was encouraged by George W. Childs, the publisher, to complete his impressive *Critical Dictionary of English Literature,* published in three volumes from 1858 to 1871, and still useful. (From 1887 to 1892 a two-volume supplement was issued by John Foster Kirk.)

From 1867 to 1873 and again from 1877 to 1879 Allibone was editor of publications and corresponding secretary of the American Sunday School Union. He was a devout and active Episcopalian. In 1879 he moved to New York to act as librarian of the great Lenox Library (now a part of the New York Public Library). He prepared both a descriptive catalog and a card catalog for this collection. In 1886 he was invited to help edit Appleton's *Cyclopedia of American Biography*; he declined the offer but did contribute several articles to it. In 1888 he resigned as librarian to travel and rest, and he died at Lucerne, Switzerland, on the European tour he had commenced soon after his retirement. He was married to Mary Henry, of Philadelphia.

A handsome, gracious-mannered, sweet-spirited, and witty man, Allibone was personally popular in literary circles. His work is sound and scholarly, and some of his collections are still of value to students.

Principal Works: A Critical Dictionary of English Literature and British and American Authors, 1858-71; An Alphabetical Index to the New Testament, 1868; The Union Bible Companion, 1871; Poetical Quotations From Chaucer to Tennyson, 1878; Prose Quotations From Socrates to Macaulay, 1879; Great Authors of All Ages, 1880.

About: McConnell, S. D. In Memory of S. Austin Allibone (Historical Society of Pennsylvania).

ALLSTON, WASHINGTON (November 5, 1779-July 9, 1843), artist and poet, was born at Brook Green Domain, in the district of Waccamaw, S.C., the son of Capt. William Allston and Rachel (Moore) Allston. When he was two years old, his father died. His mother later married Henry C. Flagg, chief of the medical staff of General Nathanael Greene's army in the Revolutionary War.

From a portrait by G. W. Flagg
WASHINGTON ALLSTON
1841

Before the age of six, young Allston evidenced a precocious artistic temperament: he locked himself in his room and began an oil painting of Vesuvius. His stepfather prescribed the more "bracing air" of Newport, R.I., and here the child became attracted to a Mr. King, quadrant maker and portrait painter. Entering Harvard in 1796, where his Beau Brummel habits won him the title of "Count," he exhibited a flare for verse-writing, caricature, and the painting of nudes. A year before his graduation, despite a morbid shyness, he became engaged to Ann, sister of his fellow-student, William Ellery Channing.

On the strength of the sale of his patrimonial estate he sailed for London in May 1801. He had completely abandoned his stepfather's suggestion of a medical career, and during the next seven years studied art in London, Paris, and Rome, making firm friends of Washington Irving and Coleridge. In 1808 Allston returned to America to marry Ann Channing (she died a few years later); he sailed again for Europe in 1810, with his wife and S. F. B. Morse, later the inventor of the telegraph. In England he began to paint in high seriousness. *Dead Man Revived by Touching the Bones of the Prophet Elisha,* perhaps his greatest accomplishment, was followed by his famous portrait of Coleridge, painted during his convalescence from a severe illness. He completed several other canvases before returning to America, in 1818, and settling in Boston.

In ill health, worried by debt, and lacking a real stimulus, he began, in a poorly lighted barn, a painful attempt to round out *Belshazzar's Feast,* a huge painting well-started in England. Following his second marriage, to Martha R. Dana, it was, according to Henry James, "the grim synthetic fact of Cambridgeport," to which the Allstons removed, that brought on the complete dissipation of his artistic achievement. A painter of his school needed Titianesque models, not undiluted metaphysics! Allston worked on the *Feast* six hours before his death, but never finished it.

Besides *Monaldi,* a long tale full of Italian souvenirs, his only literary product was *Sylphs of the Seasons: With Other Poems,* sentimental and satiric, praised by Wordsworth and Southey, and containing his well known "America to Great Britain." As a gentle man of extreme charm Allston was unbelievably idolized; as a painter he had been strangely and pathetically thwarted; and as a man of letters his stature was determined almost entirely by his intimacy with many of the literary lions of his day.

Principal Works: *Poems*—The Sylphs of the Seasons: With Other Poems, 1813. *Novel*—Monaldi, 1841.

About: Brooks, Van W. The Flowering of New England; Flagg, J. B. Life and Letters of Washington Allston.

ALSOP. RICHARD (January 23, 1761-August 20, 1815), poet, was born at Middletown, Conn., the son of Richard Alsop, Sr., and Mary (Wright) Alsop. He spent most of his life at Middletown and at nearby Hartford, where he was one of the group known as the "Hartford Wits." (The most prominent members of this group were Joel Barlow and Timothy Dwight [*qq.v.*]. They lived in Hartford, they were all Yale men, and they had begun their literary careers in college.)

Alsop, the eldest son of a wealthy merchant, had been prepared for Yale by private tutors. He received his M.A. degree in 1798. At that time graduation from Yale or Harvard usually meant a clerical career, but Alsop had no taste for the ministry. He became instead a gentleman farmer, and also what might be called a gentleman merchant, for he had heavy interests in the river trade, and at one time ran a bookstore in Hartford. He was one of the very few American millionaires of his time. Essentially, however, he was an aristocrat, with nothing of the tradesman about him. He had been too young to be actively interested in the Revolution, but his sympathies were strongly anti-democratic. Indeed, though he made a very conventional obeisance in verse to Washington when the great man died, the chief objects of his satirical attacks were the revolutionary leaders, John Hancock and John Adams.

RICHARD ALSOP

Keenly interested in sport, in natural history, and in his business, Alsop nevertheless found plenty of leisure for writing. He was a regular contributor to the first *American Mercury*, edited by his friend Joel Barlow, and to the *Monthly Magazine and American Review*, edited by Charles Brockden Brown. In a period when authors were few and far between in America, and most of these concerned with religious themes, work which might have gone unnoticed in more flourishing times gained much renown, and Alsop's was no exception. *The Political Greenhouse* even gained the honor of a denunciation in Congress, Alsop being accused of trying to embroil Connecticut in a war with France!

Alsop died suddenly of heart failure while on a visit to his seat in Flatbush, N.Y., the original residence of his first American ancestors.

His poetry may be divided into two classes—the serious work, which was pedantic, imitative, and dull; and the satire, which was keen without being caustic, playful but pointed. He had real wit, though the flavor of it is lost now by the obsolescence of his subjects. He was besides a genuine scholar, who translated from half a dozen ancient and modern languages. In his interest in Scandinavian literature he was the first

American precursor of Longfellow. In his own day he was most famous for the "ingenious fancy" of his long poem (unpublished in book form until 1856) which celebrated the charms of that faculty, but which is actually a dreary imitation of Akenside's *Pleasures of the Imagination.* His fictitious "Narrative" is after Defoe: it was his only prose. Today any interest in his writing must be purely historical, though the man himself still retains a reminiscent attraction.

PRINCIPAL WORKS: American Poems, 1793; The Political Greenhouse for the Year 1798, 1799; A Poem: Sacred to the Memory of George Washington, 1800; The Echo (with Timothy Dwight [probably]) 1807; Narrative of the Adventures and Sufferings of John R. Jewitt, 1815; The Charmes of Fancy, 1856.

ABOUT: Alsop, R. The Charmes of Fancy (see biographical sketch by T. Dwight); Beers, H. A. The Connecticut Wits.

"AMERICAN SHIPMASTER." See CODMAN, JOHN

AMES, CHARLES GORDON (October 3, 1828-April 15, 1912), clergyman and editor, was a foundling born in Dorchester, Mass. Thomas and Lucy (Foster) Ames adopted him when he was about three years old and brought him up on their farm, near Canterbury, N.H. In 1842 he was baptized into the Freewill Baptist Church, and the same year he left the farm to enter a printing establishment operated by his denomination at Dover, N.H. Influenced by this religious affiliation, he determined to go into the ministry and was licensed to preach before he was eighteen. He studied at Geauga Seminary near Cleveland and was ordained in 1849. He married Sarah Jane Daniels of Dover, N.H., in 1850, and Julia Frances Baker, of Cincinnati, in 1863.

In 1851 he founded the first Freewill Baptist church in the frontier community of St. Anthony, Minn. He took a great interest in civic affairs, held prominent offices, and was the first editor of the *Minnesota Republican,* predecessor of the Minneapolis *Tribune.*

Dissatisfied with the attitude of his congregation, he withdrew from the ministry for a time, returned to New England in 1859, and became a member of the Unitarian Church of the Disciples in Boston. He organized Unitarian Societies in Bloomington, Ill., Cincinnati, and Albany, N.Y. He enthusiastically supported the North during the Civil War, and when a physical disability excluded him from military service, insisted upon paying for a substitute out of his modest funds. In 1865 one of his plans resulted in one of the first organized charity societies in the United States. After five years as pastor of a church in Germantown, Pa., he resigned to become editor of the *Christian Register.* He returned to the active ministry in 1880 and spent eight years organizing the Spring Garden Church, Philadelphia. He succeeded James Freeman Clarke at the Church of the Disciples, Boston, remaining there as pastor and pastor-emeritus until his death.

His literary work was the natural outcome of his daily thought. Straightforward and simple, he wrote as he spoke and lived.

PRINCIPAL WORKS: George Eliot's Two Marriages, 1885; As Natural as Life, 1894; Poems, 1898; Sermons of Sunrise, 1901; Five Points of Faith, 1903; Living Largely, 1904.

ABOUT: Winter, A. A. Charles Gordon Ames: A Spiritual Autobiography With an Epilogue; Boston Transcript April 16, 1912.

AMES, FISHER (April 9, 1758-July 4, 1808), Federalist, orator, and essayist, was born in Dedham, Mass., the son of Nathaniel Ames [*q.v.*] and Deborah (Fisher) Ames. After his father's death his mother took charge of the family tavern and provided for young Fisher's preparation for Harvard. He entered college at the age of twelve, was an active debater, a ranking scholar and, moreover, a lad of impeccable behavior. After his graduation in 1774 he spent five years teaching school and pursuing independent reading in the classics; then he studied law and was admitted to the bar in 1781.

At the very height of Shay's Rebellion, Ames upheld the spirit of restraint in an article in the Boston *Independent Chronicle.* His three "Camillus" essays of 1787, pleading for a sane popular choice between anarchy and government, precipitated a strong sentiment in favor of a federal convention and brought Ames no uncertain reputation as a publicist. From 1789 to 1797 he was a member of Congress (first through fourth); and he frowned upon the "yawning listlessness" of his colleagues and the contention, of some of them, that the best government governs least. He sympathized with Boston mercantile interests and regarded offensive retaliation in tariff negotiations, on the part of the United States, as a menace to our commerce with England.

From the Anglo-American incidents of 1793-94 sprang the anti-British sentiment that led Madison to his proposals for a "commercial war": Ames exposed the folly of an attempt to "quarrel ourselves into their good will," and contended that it was a far "better policy to feed nations than to starve them." For this speech Ames, with Benedict Arnold and the Devil, was burned in effigy in Charleston, S.C. On April 28, 1796, although not fully recovered from a severe illness, Ames delivered, in Congress, a "most bewitching piece of parliamentary oratory" that secured House execution of Jay's treaty. Ames retired, in 1797, to the village of his birth; and in 1805 was elected to the presidency of Harvard, but declined. On his Dedham estate were a piggery, a dairy, and an orchard, and his house abounded in excellent hospitality. "Squire Ames" was a sympathetic townsman, a gay host, and an inimitable conversationalist. He was married in 1792 to Frances Worthington of Springfield.

As an orator he was without a peer in his own generation. His political formulae, derived from the ancients, had little application to emergent America. But his letters and essays had a brisk clarity that was sustained by the use of a rapid and nervously effective metaphor.

Principal Works: Works of Fisher Ames, 1809 (superseded by the 1854 2-volume ed.); The Influences of Democracy on Liberty, Property, and the Happiness of Society (London) 1835.

About: Moore, W. F. Representative Men of Massachusetts; Class of 1854 Harvard University: Report; Boston Transcript.

AMES, NATHANIEL (July 22, 1708-July 11, 1764), almanac-maker, physician, and inn-keeper, was born at Bridgewater, Mass., the son of Captain Nathaniel Ames and Susannah (Howard) Ames. Nothing is known of his formal learning but it is more than likely that his medical training was hardly more than an apprenticeship to a country doctor. At the age of seventeen he issued (probably with the aid of his father) his first annual almanac. In 1732 he removed to Dedham and three years later was married to Mary, daughter of Captain Joshua Fisher. By her he had one child, Fisher Ames, who died in infancy. After his first wife's death in 1737 he was married to Deborah, daughter of Jeremiah Fisher, by whom he had five children; Fisher Ames, statesman and publicist [*q.v.*], was their third son.

Ames' first almanac (1725) preceded James Franklin's *Rhode Island Almanack* by three years and Benjamin Franklin's *Poor Richard* by eight; in it he reminded his reader that he had exposed himself to the "dangerous and sharp Teeth of envious Detractors, which is a great Hazard . . . in this polished Age, among so many fine and curious Wits. . . ." Ames titled himself "Student in Physick and Astronomy" and on these subjects he exhausted his literary energies in both poetry and prose; in each issue, after a semi-serious calendar in verse came "Interlined Wisdom and Humor," with such entries as:

April—

Poland for Two Kings in Blood are soaking, and are as bad on't as if they'd no king

December—

Now warming pans are better than Fans

There were miscellaneous articles and significant excerpts from the British poets as well. In all, Ames succeeded in rounding out a literary item which in his own day was indispensable to New England households and which has now come to be regarded as an interesting and not-too-plentiful vehicle of early American humor.

About: Ames, F. A Bit of Ames Genealogy; Briggs, S. The Essays, Humor, and Poems of Nathaniel Ames; Kittredge, G. L. The Old Farmer and His Almanac.

ANDREWS, ELISHA BENJAMIN (January 10, 1844-October 30, 1917), historian, economist, and educator, was born in Hinsdale, N.H., the son of the Rev. Erastus Andrews, a Baptist minister, and Almira (Bartlett) Andrews. In his infancy the family moved to Sunderland, Mass., and in 1858 to Suffield, Conn. Here he attended the Connecticut Literary Institute. A year later the Civil War broke out, and Andrews enlisted as a private. He lost an eye at Petersburg, and was discharged in 1864 with the rank of second lieutenant. He immediately returned to school, first at the Powers Institute, Bernardston, Mass., then at the Wesleyan Academy, Wilbraham, Mass. He proceeded to Brown University, where he received his B.A. in 1870 and his M.A. in 1873. In 1912 he obtained a Ph.D. at the University of Nebraska, and he was the recipient of many honorary degrees.

In the course of a busy lifetime crowded with ministries and professorships, Andrews served as president of three universities: Denison (Granville, Ohio) 1875-79; Brown, 1888-98; University of Nebraska, 1900-08. After resigning from Nebraska because of ill-health, he took a two-year trip around the world. In 1912 he moved to Florida, where he died at Interlaken. He was buried on the campus of Denison University.

Andrews was a believer in bimetallism, and was practically forced out of the presidency of Brown for that reason; however, in 1903 he publicly renounced his faith in free silver. His trend of thought was highly ethical, but his chief interest was in economics, and his histories are all economic in character.

PRINCIPAL WORKS: Institutes of Constitutional History, 1884; Institutes of General History, 1885; Institutes of Economics, 1889; An Honest Dollar, 1889; The Economic Law of Monopoly, 1890; The Duty of a Public Spirit, 1892; Wealth and Moral Law, 1894; History of the United States, 1894; History of the Last Quarter Century in the United States, 1896 (expanded as The United States in Our Own Time, 1904); The Sin of Schism, 1896; Cosmology, 1900; The Call of the Land, 1913.

ABOUT: Bronson, W. C. History of Brown University; Meiklejohn, A. Freedom and the Call; Providence Journal October 31, 1917.

"AMGIS." See SARGENT, LUCIUS MANLIUS

ANDREWS, JOHN (April 4, 1746-March 29, 1813), clergyman, scholar, and educator, was born in Cecil County, Md., the son of Moses and Letitia Andrews. He was educated at the neighboring Elk School, a Presbyterian institution, and at the College of Philadelphia, from which he was graduated with honors in 1764. After studying theology under the Rev. Thomas Barton, an Anglican clergyman, he went to London in 1767 for his ordination, after which he was appointed "missionary" to Lewes, Del., by the Society for Propagating the Gospel in Foreign Parts. The local climate was unsuitable to his health and he moved to York, Pa., after three years. In 1772 he married Elizabeth Callender, by whom he had ten children. In order to support his large family, he accepted a position as rector of St. John's in Queen Anne's County, Md., where he remained until after the Declaration of Independence, when he started a classical school at York, Md. In 1782 Andrews became rector of St. Thomas's in Baltimore County, and in 1785 he was chosen principal of the new Episcopal Academy in Philadelphia. Six years later when this institution was absorbed by the University of Pennsylvania, he was elected vice-provost, which appointment included the chairs of moral philosophy and the classics. He was acting provost from 1802 to 1806, and was made provost in 1810, holding office until his death.

In 1798 one of Andrews' children was burned to death and his wife died from shock upon hearing the news. Deeply affected by this double loss, he turned entirely to religion and the classics, becoming outstanding for his scholarship, especially in the classical field. He was tall and portly, with a square face and ruddy complexion.

PRINCIPAL WORKS: A Compend of Logic, 1801; Elements of Rhetorick and Belles Lettres, 1813.

ABOUT: Lippincott, H. M. The University of Pennsylvania; Smith, H. W. Life and Correspondence of the Rev. William Smith; Sprague, W. B. Annals of the American Pulpit; The Port Folio series 3, I.

ANDREWS, STEPHEN PEARL (March 22, 1812-May 21, 1886), economist and philosopher, was born in Templeton, Mass., the youngest of nine children of the Rev. Elisha Andrews and Wealthy (Lathrop) Andrews. He was an uncle of E. Benjamin Andrews, the economist and historian[*q.v.*]. In 1831 he went with his brother to New Orleans, where he studied law and was admitted to the bar. An ardent abolitionist, he proposed manumission of the slaves by purchase. In 1839 he moved to Houston, Texas (then an independent republic), where he became a prominent lawyer, but because of his abolitionist ideas he and his wife, whom he had married in 1835 in New Orleans, were mobbed in 1843 and barely escaped with their lives. Andrews went to England to try to raise money for his manumission scheme. He was unsuccessful, but his meeting with Isaac Pitman in London gave him his second great interest—shorthand. He went to New York in 1847, and for several years was a foremost advocate of shorthand there and in Boston, establishing a school in the latter city.

A remarkable linguist, who knew 32 languages well, Andrews was also a spelling reformer and invented a universal language, precursor of Esperanto, which he called Alwato. He became increasingly interested in philosophy and sociology, and during his latter years perfected his scheme of "Universology," with its ideal state called "Pantarchy," which he had first evolved in New Orleans in his youth. Andrews is frequently spoken of sneeringly as "an eccentric philosopher"; it is true that he is frequently obscure—deliberately so in many cases; but he was simply a religious and economic radical born before his time. Pantarchy was next-door to anarchy, and the anarchists still claim Andrews as their own. Most of his energy in the New York period, however, was given to the cause of Free Thought; he was a prominent member of the Liberal Club and active in the early days of the Rationalist magazine, the *Truth Seeker*. He was a man greatly beloved by his colleagues, simple and sincere and unfailingly optimistic.

PRINCIPAL WORKS: The Comprehensive Phonographic Class Book, 1845; The Phonographic Reader, 1845; The Sovereignty of the Individual,

1851; Cost the Limit of Price, 1851: Discoveries in Chinese, 1854; Primary Grammar of Alwato, 1877; The Basic Outlines of Universology, 1877.

ABOUT: Macdonald, G. E. Fifty Years of Free Thought; Independent February 26, 1903.

ANDREWS, WILLIAM LORING (September 9, 1837-March 19, 1920), bibliophile, direct descendant of William Andrews who first settled the Town of Quinnipac, afterwards called New Haven, was born in New York City. He was the son of Loring Andrews and Caroline (Delamater) Andrews, and attended private schools because of ill health. After completing his education, he entered his father's prosperous leather business in 1855. On October 17, 1860, he married Jane Elizabeth Crane of New York City. He was a director of the Continental Fire Insurance Company, a trustee for the Bank of Savings, and a trustee of New York University.

In 1877 he withdrew from active business to devote himself to private interests. Among other activities, he was a trustee of the Metropolitan Museum (instrumental in establishing its library), and was manager of the House of Refuge on Randall's Island.

Andrews' integrity and keen business ability coupled with his genuine love of fine arts elevated him to a high position in metropolitan circles. Books were his consuming interest and he collected many rarities in English and American literature. In 1855 he entered the publishing field, bringing out his own writings and a few choice works in carefully selected type, paper, illustration, and binding. Using the engravings of E. D. French and S. L. Smith, and employing Walter Gillias and Theodore De Vinne for printing, he issued volumes whose beauty of format command the highest respect of bibliophiles. On February 5, 1884, at Andrews' residence, the name Grolier was chosen for the famous Book Club. He founded the Society of Iconophiles of New York in 1895.

Andrews' miscellaneous writings are distiguished by their scholarly style and competent research.

PRINCIPAL WORKS: Roger Payne and His Art, 1892; Jean Grolier, 1892; Among My Books, 1894; An Essay on the Portraiture of the American Revolutionary War, 1896; A Journey of the Iconophiles Around New York, 1897; New Amsterdam, New Orange, New York, 1897; Gossip About Book-Collecting, 1900; Paul Revere and His Engravings, 1901; New York as Washington Knew It After the Revolution, 1905; An English XIXth Century Sportsman, 1906.

ABOUT: Bonner, W. T. New York: The World's Metropolis; Growall, A. American Book Clubs; Wilson, J. G. Memorial History of the City of New York; Catalogue of William Loring Andrews Collection of Early Books in Yale University; Year Book of the Grolier Club, 1921; New York Times, New York Tribune, March 21, 1920.

ANTHON, CHARLES (November 19, 1797-June 29, 1867), classical scholar, was born in New York City. His father, Dr. George Christian Anthon, was a German; his mother, Genevieve (Jadot) Anthon, of French descent, was from Detroit, then a frontier trappers' post. In 1811 he entered Columbia, where he won so many honors that his name was withdrawn from competition. He then studied law, from 1815 to 1819, with his brother, and was admitted to the bar. His spare time, however, was all given to study and reading in ancient and modern languages, and he never had any intention of practicing law.

In 1820 he was made adjunct professor of Greek and Latin at Columbia, and in 1830, when the departments were divided, he became Jay Professor of Greek, and also headmaster of the grammar school then attached to the college. Unmarried, he lived with his sisters, and left New York only once, in 1831, to visit his mother's birthplace in Detroit, returning by way of Montreal. Very retiring, without social life, he was nevertheless no recluse, but a witty and cheerful man whose nickname in the college was "Bull." His days were strictly divided for work and study, with a solitary walk at night as his only recreation. His health failed, but in spite of this he continued to teach almost to the day of his death. His college pupils liked him, but the grammar school boys feared him, for he was the strictest of disciplinarians.

Anthon introduced German scholarship in the classics into America; he was the first to prepare critical and exegetical editions of the classical authors, beginning with his Horace in 1830. Later he edited Cicero, Tacitus, Caesar, Sallust, Virgil, Juvenal, Xenophon, and Homer, and he made a fortune from his text-books. These editions were so full, with the difficult passages translated, that they have served as "ponies" for every subsequent generation of students—scarcely the result their author anticipated! He was undoubtedly the greatest single influence on classical learning in America of his age.

PRINCIPAL WORKS: A System of Latin Prosody and Metre, 1838; Anthon's Classical Dictionary, 1842 (based on his edition of *Lamprière's Classical Dictionary,* 1833); A System of Ancient and Mediaeval Geography, 1850.

ABOUT: Galaxy (Columbia College) September 1867; New York Times July 30, 1867.

"ANTILON." See DULANY, DANIEL

"ANTIQUARY, THE." See LIVERMORE, GEORGE

APES, WILLIAM (January 31, 1798- ?), missionary and Indian historian, was born in an Indian settlement near Colrain, Mass. His father was a half-breed, and his mother a descendant of King Philip. While his parents engaged in itinerant basket-making, he spent an unhappy childhood with cruel grandparents. During his fifth year, his grandmother broke his arm, and his uncle and a white neighbor removed him from her care, placing him in a white family where he became Christianized. Running away at the age of fifteen, he enlisted in the army and took part in General Hampton's campaign against Canada, General Wilkinson's attack on Montreal, and the battle of Lake Champlain (all in the War of 1812). When he returned from the wars, he attempted to become a Methodist preacher, but was refused his license by the Methodist Episcopal Conference. He then joined the Methodist Society, and was ordained in 1829.

Visiting Cape Cod four years later, he became a leader of the Marshpee Indians who, through the indifference of the white missionary appointed by Harvard College, were subjected to unjust taxation and lack of police protection, educational, and religious advantages. Apes became a member of the tribe, and encouraged them so outspokenly to stand for their rights that he was arrested, charged with inciting a riot, and sentenced to thirty days in jail. At the end of his term he joined the Indian deputation which petitioned the legislature, and it was mainly through his sincere eloquence that laws were passed which placated the Indians. There is no further information about his career after this time. It is known that he married a white woman, but the date and place of his death are not recorded.

Apes' literary activities include four books. While not important in themselves, they are an interesting contribution to the history of the American Indians.

PRINCIPAL WORKS: A Son of the Forest (autobiography) 1829; The Experiences of Five Christian Indians, 1833; Indian Nullification of the Unconstitutional Laws of Massachusetts Relative to the Marshpee Tribe, 1835; Eulogy of King Philip, 1836.

ABOUT: Deyo, S. L. History of Barnstable County, Mass.; Laws of the Commonwealth of Massachusetts Passed by the General Court, 1834.

APPLETON, THOMAS GOLD (March 31, 1812-April 17, 1884), poet and essayist, wit and conversationalist, was born in Boston, the son of Nathan Appleton and Maria (Gold) Appleton. His father, one of the founders of the Lowell, Mass., textile industry, was a Congressman and a wealthy man whose son inherited his fortune. Appleton's sister Frances was Longfellow's second wife. He was brought up in the midst of future celebrities, Wendell Phillips and John Motley being his greatest friends in childhood. In later years he was in the center of the literary coterie of Boston's most brilliant period, intimate with Emerson and Holmes, a founder and prominent member of the famous Saturday Club.

THOMAS GOLD APPLETON

For a year he attended the Boston Latin School, then was sent to the Round Hill School, Northampton, Mass., conducted by George Bancroft, the future historian. To please his father he studied law for a year, after being graduated from Harvard in 1831; but he had no interest in the subject and never practiced that or any other profession. Much of his time was spent in Europe, where he was familiar with every art gallery. A rather talented painter, he was an art collector and one of the greatest benefactors of the Boston Museum of Fine Arts, of which he was a trustee; he was a trustee also of the Athenaeum and the Public Library. He was a lifelong bachelor.

Appleton had literary ambitions and published numerous volumes, but in writing he was never more than an amateur. "Pleasant" is the best way to describe his prose essays, and his verse is formal and stilted. Where he really shone was in the now forgotten art of conversation. His aquiline nose, heavy grey mustache, sensitive mouth, and brilliant eyes were familiar for years at every dinner table in Boston where urbanity and culture were the criteria of acceptance.

One after another of his contemporaries has testified that he was the wittiest man of his time and place—a tribute which meant something when, for example, it was rendered by so acute a critic as the senior Oliver Wendell Holmes. But so evanescent a thing is wit that, although Appleton is remembered chiefly for his *bons mots*, few of the *mots* themselves have survived. He is supposed, though not certainly, to have been the author of the famous saying that "All good Americans, when they die, go to Paris." He certainly said that "America is a splendid exile for the Saxon race." His only other saying which has received permanent form is his remark, on seeing a ship sink below the horizon, that "a chip with a thought in it goes round the world." These do not seem excessively brilliant; undoubtedly his unrecorded sayings had more point—at least on the occasions on which they were uttered.

Free-handed with his inherited wealth, sympathetic and warm-hearted, gregarious and magnetic, "Tom" Appleton, as he was always called, was widely beloved. Because they were fond of him, the best critics of his day praised his trivial essays and travel books and his stiff little poems, for which he himself found the most apt title—*Faded Leaves*. But the chief fascination he held for his friends was the lively fancy which sparkled in his conversation but which he could not fix in print. He was one of those men whom everyone knows while they are alive, but who become only a vaguely familiar name as soon as the last person is dead who remembers their attractive personality. He himself was his only work of art.

Principal Works: *Poetry*—Faded Leaves, 1872; Fresh Leaves, 1874. *Prose*—A Sheaf of Papers, 1875; A Nile Journal, 1876; Syrian Sunshine, 1877; Windfalls, 1878; Chequer Work, 1879.

About: Hale, S. Life and Letters of Thomas Gold Appleton; Atlantic Monthly June 1884; Harper's Weekly May 3, 1884.

APTHORP, WILLIAM FOSTER (October 24, 1848-February 19, 1913), music critic, son of Robert Apthorp and Eliza (Hunt) Apthorp, was born in Boston, Mass. He came of a distinguished New England family of early settlers, among whom was the Rev. East Apthorp, founder of Christ Church, Cambridge. At the age of eight William was taken to Europe to study languages and art, for which he already had marked talent. He attended school in France, Germany, and Italy, and studied drawing and painting under Guglielmi and Garelli. In Florence, he was a fellow student with John Singer Sargent. Returning to Boston in 1860, he prepared for college at E. S. Dixwell's school, and was graduated from Harvard in 1869. During this time he became increasingly interested in music, and gave up painting to study piano, harmony, and counterpoint with Professor John K. Paine and, later, advanced pianoforte under Professor B. J. Lang. He was married on August 17, 1876, to Octavie Loir Iasigi, of Lynn, Mass.

Realizing that he would never become a great painter or musician, he settled down to teaching at the National College of Music in Boston. When it closed, he joined the New England Conservatory, and also held classes in aesthetics and musical history in the College of Music of Boston University until 1886. His career as a music critic began in 1872 when William Dean Howells, founding a music department in the *Atlantic Monthly*, invited him to become music editor. When the department was discontinued, Apthorp served as music critic for the *Sunday Courrier*, the *Traveler*, and the *Transcript*, until 1903, when failing eyesight caused him to retire from active work. He also contributed articles to leading magazines. From 1888 to 1890, in collaboration with John Denson Champlin, Jr., he was critical editor of *Scribner's Cyclopedia of Music and Musicians*. Between 1892 and 1901 he edited the program books of the Boston Symphony Orchestra. He died in Switzerland.

Principal Works: Some of the Wagner Heroes and Heroines, 1889; Musicians and Music Lovers, 1894; By the Way, 1898; The Opera: Past and Present, 1901.

About: Howe, G. L. & Matthews, W. S. B. (ed.). One Hundred Years of Music in America; Boston Herald February 22, 1913; Boston Transcript February 20, 1913.

ARDEN, EDWIN HUNTER PENDLETON (February 4, 1864-October 2, 1918), playwright and actor-manager, was born in St. Louis, Mo., the son of Arden Richard Smith, editorial writer on the old St. Louis *Republican*, and Mary (Hunter) Smith. After attending the public schools, he went West at the age of seventeen, where he worked as mine helper, cowboy, railroad brakeman, clerk, reporter, and theatrical manager. He dropped the name Smith when he entered the theatre.

He first appeared on the stage in Chicago in 1882, in the Shakespearian company of Thomas W. Keene, whose daughter, Agnes Ann, he married the following year. Joining the stock company at the Boston Museum in 1884, he played in *The Rivals,* the plays of Dion Boucicault and Augustin Daly, took Shakespearian roles, and supported such actors as Edwin Booth, D. B. Lester Wallack, William Warren, and John Gilbert. The following year he appeared with Edwin Booth's company in a variety of parts. During this time he wrote several successful plays—*The Eagle's Nest, Raglan's Way,* and *Barred Out.* After starring in these plays for nine seasons under his own management, he joined William H. Crane's company in 1895. Then came a successful period in which he supported Julia Arthur in *A Lady of Quality,* and Maude Adams in Rostand's *L'Aiglon,* his interpretation of Metternich winning much acclaim. After a short vaudeville engagement, he starred in the dramatization of Marah Ellis Ryan's book, *Told In the Hills,* of which he was co-author. He died in New York City. His plays were competent but of no great significance.

Principal Works: The Eagle's Nest; Raglan's Way; Barred Out; Zorah.

About: Brown, T. A. History of the New York Stage; New York Times October 3, 1918.

ARNOLD, GEORGE (June 24, 1834-November 5, 1865), poet and humorist, was born in New York City, the son of a clergyman—presumably the Rev. George B. Arnold. From 1837 to 1849 the family lived in Alton, Ill., then on a farm in Monmouth County, N.J. He was educated at home and from 1852 to 1854 studied with a portrait painter in New York. In later years he used his art training only for the writing of some critical essays and to illustrate his own light verses. After a brief experience on the staff of a magazine, he became a free lance. During the Civil War he served as a private in a fort on Governor's Island. Early in 1865 his health broke and he was discharged from the army, but he died (probably of tuberculosis) before the year was out, at only thirty-one.

Arnold was one of the group with Fitz James O'Brien and other writers of the day who were the center of New York's "Bohemian" colony of the 'fifties, the group which gathered, drank, and talked in Pfaff's Beer Cellar. Versatile—too versatile—and prolific, he frittered away his talents and never fulfilled his real promise. He wrote under many pseudonyms, mostly burlesques in verse and prose, the best known being under the name of "McArone." These were mainly war sketches, such as "The Life and Adventures of Jeff Davis." He never collected any of his scattered writings into a volume, but after his early death his friends brought out two collections of his poems, combined in one in 1886.

Principal Works: Drift: A Sea-Shore Idyl and Others, 1866; Poems Grave and Gay, 1867.

About: Arnold, G. Collected Poems (see Memoir by W. Winter); New York Tribune November 10, 1865.

ARNOLD, ISAAC NEWTON (November 30, 1815-April 24, 1884), lawyer, congressman, and historian, was the son of Dr. George Washington Arnold and his wife, Sophia (Mason) Arnold. He was born at Hartwick, Otsego County, N.Y., and was educated at neighboring schools. At the age of fifteen he taught in a district school, and at the same time studied law in the offices of Richard Cooper and Judge E. B. Morehouse at Cooperstown. He was admitted to the bar in 1835 and after a year's practice went to Chicago, where, with Mahlon D. Ogden, he formed a law partnership which continued for eleven years and became large and important, with cases both criminal and civil. Arnold became prominent in Illinois politics and in 1860 was elected to the 37th Congress. He was violently opposed to slavery and in 1862 moved the amendment abolishing slavery—the first step taken by Congress in favor of the abolition of slavery in the United States. This bill passed both houses on February 1, 1865.

Arnold was married twice; first, to Catherine E. Dorrance of Pittsfield, Mass., and second, to her sister, Harriet Augusta Dorrance. He was one of the founders of the Chicago Historical Society which numbered among its treasures the original manuscript of the emancipation proclamation, given to Arnold by President Lincoln.

A competent writer with a clear, simple style, Arnold is best remembered for his *Life of Abraham Lincoln.* Although it was at one time the finest biography available, it is chiefly valuable today as a source.

Principal Works: The History of Abraham Lincoln and the Overthrow of Slavery, 1866; Life of Benedict Arnold, 1880; Life of Abraham Lincoln, 1884.

About: Palmer, J. M. The Bench and Bar of Illinois.

"ARP, BILL." See SMITH, CHARLES HENRY

ARRINGTON, ALFRED W. (September 17, 1810-December 31, 1867), lawyer, historian, and poet, was born in Iredell County, N.C. His father, H. Archibald Arrington, a Methodist minister, was descended from a former British army officer who had settled on a large plantation in North Carolina, and his mother was a Miss Moore of Scottish extraction. Alfred was given a good education and became exceedingly well-informed at an early age. When he was only nine years old, he traveled to the wilderness of Arkansas with his father, and at the age of eighteen likewise became an itinerant Methodist preacher. His natural eloquence brought him much success and he preached in Arkansas, Indiana, and Missouri for five years, but in 1834 he abandoned religious precepts and took up the study of law. Although he was admitted to the Missouri bar in 1835, he moved to Arkansas where he built up a thriving practice, and became a member of the state legislature. When politics failed to sustain his interest he pulled up stakes again, went to Texas for a time, and later visited the East. Using the pseudonym "Charles Summerfield," he published in 1847 *The Desperadoes of the South West,* a vivid account of the lynch law. Remaining in New York and Boston for two years, he engaged in journalism and wrote an abstruse essay, *The Mathematical Harmonies of the Universe,* which was translated into French and German. In 1849 he returned to Texas and became a judge of the 12th (Rio Grande) district, retaining this position until ill-health forced him to resign. Moving to New York he resumed his writing under the name of "Charles Summerfield" and in 1856 published *The Rangers and Regulators of the Tanaha,* a novel concerning the transitional stage of Southwestern life. A year later he went to Chicago and entered the practice of law again. In his last years, for his own pleasure, he wrote a number of poems which were collected and published posthumously. During this time he turned again to religion and was received into the Catholic faith. He died in Chicago.

Though he was equipped with unusual ability, Arrington's unstable, restless nature obstructed his attainments both in literature and in the legal field, where his exceptional oratorical powers would probably have elevated him to a high position.

Principal Works: The Desperadoes of the South West, 1847; The Rangers and Regulators of the Tanaha, 1856; Poems of Alfred W. Arrington, 1869.

About: Arrington, A. W. Poems (see Preface); Linden, U. F. Reminiscences of the Early Bench and Bar of Illinois; Wilson, J. M. Memorial to Alfred W. Arrington.

ARTHUR, TIMOTHY SHAY (June 6, 1809-March 6, 1885), novelist, was born on a farm in Orange County, N.Y. He was named for his grandfather, Timothy Shay, a Revolutionary officer. In his infancy the family moved to West Point, and in 1817 to Baltimore. Here he went to public school, but was thought so dull that the teacher advised his being taken out and put to work. He was apprenticed to a watchmaker, but the training so injured his sight that he could never practice the trade. Except for a few months at night school, he had no further education. Friends found a place for him in a Baltimore counting house, and he worked as a clerk for several years. In 1836 he married Ellen Alden; five sons and two daughters resulted from the marriage.

Collection of Frederick H. Meserve
T. S. ARTHUR

Gradually Arthur drifted into writing, first as editor of the Baltimore *Athenaeum,* then on various ephemeral local weeklies. Meanwhile he had begun to contribute to *Godey's Ladies' Book,* and in 1841, to be nearer his chief market, he moved to Philadelphia. In 1845 he founded *Arthur's Ladies' Magazine,* which failed in a short time. He had better luck with a weekly started in 1850, *Arthur's Home Gazette,* which in 1853 became a monthly as *Arthur's Home Magazine.* This he was still editing and publishing at the time he died. For a while he also published the *Children's Hour, Once a Month,* and the *Workingman,* but these he sold as soon as they were well established.

In all, Arthur was the author of some seventy books, strongly moral and didactic novels advocating thrift, family life, and religion (he was a prominent Swedenborgian), and inveighing against lotteries, gambling, and, above all, liquor. From his youth he was a strong "temperance man," though he was not a teetotaler and was not in favor of prohibition. He attributed strikes and all the workers' troubles to alcoholism!

All these books, as well as his worthy but dull magazine stories, would long be forgotten had it not been for his one great success, *Ten Nights in a Barroom.* This rivaled *Uncle Tom's Cabin* in popularity in its own time, and has become a sort of sub-classic of American literature, known by name to millions who never read it or saw the play made from it. The sottish father, the pitiful child, the drunken murderer, are its stock figures. Arthur had the knack of combining preaching with sensationalism, and it made him rich and famous. Aside from fiction, he wrote only a series of hack "cabinet histories" of the various states with W. H. Carpenter (1850 to 1856).

Principal Works: Six Nights With the Washingtonians: A Series of Original Temperance Tales, 1842; Married and Single: or, Marriage and Celibacy Contrasted, 1845; The Lady at Home, 1847; The Maiden, 1848; Pride and Prudence: or, The Married Sisters, 1850; Sparing to Spend, 1853; Ten Nights in a Barroom and What I Saw There, 1854; Lights and Shadows of Real Life, 1867; Three Years in a Mantrap, 1872; Cast Adrift, 1873; Woman to the Rescue, 1874; The Strike at Tivoli Mills, 1879.

About: Anon. T. S. Arthur: His Life and Work; Arthur, T. S. Lights and Shadow of Real Life (see Autobiographical Preface).

ASHLEY, MARY. See TOWNSEND, MARY (ASHLEY)

ASTOR, WILLIAM WALDORF (March 31, 1848-October 18, 1919), novelist and publisher, was born in New York City, son of John Jacob Astor, 2d, and Charlotte (Gibbes) Astor. He was the grandson of the first John Jacob Astor, founder of the famous family fortune. He was prepared by private tutors for Columbia Law School, and for a while was a member of a law firm, then became manager of his father's estate. He withdrew from this to enter politics, and in 1877 was a Republican member of the state assembly, and in 1879 of the state senate. He ran twice for Congress but failed of election. In 1878 he married Mary Dahlgren Paul. From 1882 to 1885 he was United States minister to Italy, by appointment of President Arthur.

It was following this period that Astor took to writing, producing in all three historical romances, remarkable only in that they were written by a multi-millionaire. His father died in 1890, and he inherited about a hundred million dollars, twenty million of which he spent before his own death. He built the Waldorf Hotel, later part of the old Waldorf-Astoria, but his American career was nearly over. Political disappointment, his wife's social ambitions, and an alleged fear that his children might be kidnapped, led to his moving permanently to England. In 1893 he bought the daily *Pall Mall Gazette* in London, together with its weekly edition, the *Budget,* and changed them from Liberal to Conservative papers. He established the monthly *Pall Mall Magazine* soon after. But he soon tired of publishing, and though he contributed articles occasionally to the magazine, he was seldom seen at its offices. In 1911 he bought the weekly *Observer,* but three years later he sold all his publications together. In 1916 he was created Baron Astor of Hever Castle (once the residence of Anne Boleyn), and in 1917 Viscount Astor. Lady Astor, the M.P., is his daughter-in-law.

A quarrelsome, crotchety old man, with more enemies than friends, he detested his native country, yet was so sensitive to its opinion that he once sent out a false report of his death in the hope of seeing the American obituaries. As a writer his work does not outdo the performance of any literate person who has traveled in Europe and read some history. He died at Brighton, England, at seventy-one, his older son succeeding to the title.

Principal Works: Valentino: An Historical Romance of the Sixteenth Century in Italy, 1885; Sforza: A Story of Milan, 1889; Pharaoh's Daughter and Others, 1900.

About: London Times October 20, 1919.

"ATALL, PETER, JR." See WALN, ROBERT

ATKINSON, EDWARD (February 10, 1827-December 11, 1905), economist and industrialist, was born in Brookline, Mass., the son of Amos and Anna (Sawyer) Atkinson. Educated at private schools in Brookline and Boston, at the age of fifteen he secured work with a Boston textile commission house where he built fires, swept floors, packed goods, and acted as confidential clerk. He remained for five years, and in 1848 rose to the treasurership of several textile-manufacturing companies. He was married to Mary Caroline Heath in 1855.

His business career now well established, he began to interest himself in factory mutual insurance, and was instrumental in establishing the Boston Manufacturer's Mutual Insurance Company, of which he became the president. It promoted mutual insurance in a restricted field, in which the factor of "exposure" was greatly reduced. These precautions governing construction and use improved the industrial framework of the country considerably, and Atkinson expanded his ideas in a series of articles and pamphlets. As the result of an interest disclosed in *The Science of Nutrition,* 1896, he invented the Aladdin oven, a fully insulated mechanism with heat applied from a common lamp in which kerosene oil replaced the coal burned in the ordinary kitchen range. At one time it amused Atkinson to provide his dinner guests with succulent dishes prepared in their presence on this apparatus.

Atkinson was a large man of dignified bearing. He was obstinate but just, extremely well-informed, and unusually gifted as a public speaker. His published works cover a wide range of subjects including wages, fire loss, banking, nutrition, war and peace, and economic legislation. While these were worthy contributions in their respective fields, they were of little literary importance.

PRINCIPAL WORKS: Cheap Cotton by Free Labor, 1861; Our National Domain, 1879; Labor and Capital Allies Not Enemies, 1880; Railroads of the United States, 1880; Cotton Manufacturers of the United States, 1880; What Is a Bank? 1881; The Railway and the Farmer, 1881; Distribution of Products, 1885; Facts and Figures: The Basis of Economic Science, 1904.

ABOUT: Commercial and Financial Chronicle December 16, 1905; New York Times December 12, 1905.

ATKINSON, GEORGE FRANCIS (January 26, 1854-November 15, 1918), botanist, was born in Raisinville, Monroe County, Mich., the son of Joseph and Josephine (Fish) Atkinson. He attended Olivet College until his junior year when he transferred to Cornell University, where he was graduated in 1885. In the same year he was appointed assistant professor of entomology and zoology in the University of North Carolina, becoming associate professor the following year. In 1888 he went to the University of South Carolina as professor of botany and zoology, and in 1889 was called to the newly established chair of biology and botany at the Alabama Polytechnical Institute, where he found exceptional opportunities for botanical research relative to the agricultural interests of the state and of the South.

In 1892 he accepted the associate professorship of cryptogamic botany at Cornell. In four years he became the head of the department, holding office until his death. Engrossed in the study of the marvelous fungi on the slopes of Mount Rainier, Atkinson imprudently remained there too late into the fall, contracted pneumonia, and expired in a hospital in Tacoma, Wash. In his fatal delirium, he tried to dictate his latest observations to his nurse.

Atkinson was the first president of the American Botanical Society. In 1905 he was a delegate to the International Botanical Congress at Vienna, and in 1910 was a representative at the Brussels meeting.

He wrote the first successful book on the higher fungi—*Studies of American Fungi*; and in a fine natural history study—*Biology of Ferns*—won readers beyond the strictly scientific. Numbering 150, his scientific papers, published in bulletins and botanical journals, enjoyed a wide reputation, both in America and Europe. Through his untiring investigations he ranks as an outstanding mycologist. Vigorous, charming, he possessed a youthful spirit which never left him.

PRINCIPAL WORKS: Biology of Ferns, 1893; First Studies of Plant Life, 1901; Studies of American Fungi, 1911.

ABOUT: Botanical Gazette April 1919; Journal of the New York Botanical Gardens December 1918; Science March 7, 1919, April 18, 1919.

"ATOM, ANN." See WALWORTH, JEANETTE RITCHIE (HADERMANN)

AUDUBON, JOHN JAMES (April 26, 1785-January 27, 1851), artist and naturalist, was born Fougère Rabin—the illegitimate son of Jean Audubon, a French naval officer stationed in Santo Domingo by a Creole woman who was called "Mlle. Rabin." As a small child his father took him and his younger half-sister to France, where the father's wife not only received them kindly, but adopted them and had them legitimized. In 1800 the boy was baptized as Jean Jacques Audubon. His childhood was spent partly in Louisiana and partly in France, with a year in a French military school and another studying painting in Paris (1802-03). He was petted and spoiled by his stepmother, and was an undisciplined, vain, rather lazy youth when he went to live on his father's farm near Philadelphia in 1804. But he worked hard at painting, and he was already a keen natural historian. Both in America and back again in France the next year, Audubon divided his time between art and hunting, being at this period an ardent shooter of birds.

This idle life was ended when his indulgent father lost his money and went bankrupt. The young man had to go to work, but he had been fitted for nothing but a life

Collection of Frederick H. Meserve
JOHN JAMES AUDUBON

of leisure. He came back to America, where he was already engaged to Lucy Bakewell, and with a French partner equally untrained and inexperienced, tried to become a general merchant in the wilderness of Kentucky. Usually his partner stood behind the counter waiting for non-existent customers while Audubon scoured the woods for birds—by this time to study and paint, not to slaughter them. Brave Lucy Bakewell, who had the greatest faith in his genius, married him in 1808 and went back with him to a series of dolorous failures alternating with occasional prosperity. Already he was at work on his great series of *Birds of North America.* Indeed, it is from this period that the long feud with the ornithologist Alexander Wilson dates, a feud which at the time considerably injured his reputation and career.

Finally, in 1819, he became completely bankrupt, was imprisoned for debt, and was obliged to go to Cincinnati to work as a taxidermist. His wife, one of the most admirable women in the history of literature, came to the rescue. She took a position as governess, and for twelve years supported the entire family, including their two sons. Audubon was free to go on with his real work. In 1826 he managed to travel to England and Scotland, and in Edinburgh he obtained his first recognition. Until 1844 he journey continuously between Great Britain and the United States; and when he returned permanently to this country he ranged it from Florida and Texas to Labrador in search of subjects for his paintings. His sons grew up to be his assistants; one, John Woodhouse Audubon, was an early explorer of the California valleys. Both sons married daughters of Dr. John Bachman, who collaborated with Audubon in his later books, as William Macgillivray had done in the earlier. The usual procedure was to publish first the colored plates (the *Birds of North America* alone had 453 hand-colored plates, and 1,065 life-sized figures, representing 489 species—though Audubon was mistaken as to some of these), and then to bring out the text separately. In this the collaborator provided the scientific and classificatory data, while Audubon contributed the personal incidents and the vivid if sentimental narrative.

As his fame increased, Audubon became more of a myth than a man. A dandy in his youth, he dressed now like a frontiersman, with long hair and baggy clothes. He built a home near 158th Street and Riverside Drive, New York, which is now Audubon Park, and there he lived in state when he was not out on exploring and painting trips. In his last years his mind failed, and though he was not yet sixty-six when he died, he had been for some time in a state of senility.

As an artist, Audubon has been condemned as "photographic," but he was the first to paint birds in their natural poses and to display all their beauty in detail. As a writer he is too emotional for scientific verity, and frequently his work is careless and inaccurate. He was capable too of deliberate hoaxing, not through dishonesty but because of a rather adolescent love of practical joking. But his work is vastly readable, and he deserves the unique place he has gained in the literary as well as in the artistic and scientific history of his adopted country.

One of the notable publishing achievements of recent years was a book of reproductions, in color, of Audubon's bird plates, which was issued in 1937, virtually a century after first publication.

Principal Works: The Birds of North America, 1827-38 (octavo form, 1840-44); Ornithological Biography (with William Macgillivray) 1831-39; A Synopsis of the Birds of North America, 1839; The Viviparous Quadrupeds of North America (plates) 1842-45 (text, by J. Bachman) 1846-54; Delineations of American Scenery and Character (ed. by F. H. Herrick) 1926.

About: Arthur, S. C. Audubon: An Intimate Life of the American Woodsman; Audubon, L. B. Life of John James Audubon the Naturalist; Audubon, M. R. Audubon and His Journals; Burroughs, J. John James Audubon; Herrick, F. H. Audubon the Naturalist; Muschamp, E. A. Audacious Audubon; Peattie, D. C. Singing in the Wilderness; Rourke, C. M. Audubon; Harper's Magazine September 1880.

"AUNT FANNY." See GAGE, FRANCES DANA (BARKER)

AUSTIN, JANE (GOODWIN) (February 25, 1831-March 30, 1894), juvenile writer and historical novelist, was born in Worcester, Mass., to which her parents had come from Plymouth. Her father, Isaac Goodwin, was a lawyer, author of legal manuals, and a well known antiquarian and authority on Pilgrim history, while her mother, Elizabeth (Hammatt) Goodwin, was a highly educated woman who achieved a certain reputation in later life for her poems. When her father died during Jane's early childhood, her mother moved to Boston, educating her daughter in private schools. Studious, with a flair for research which manifested itself at an early age, Jane took a great interest in the family genealogy and began to write stories around the lives of her Pilgrim ancestors. These were first written for her own amusement but later for publication. After her marriage to Henry Austin of Boston, at the age of seventeen, she gave up writing to bring up her three children. Thirteen years later she resumed her work and began to send stories to the leading periodicals of the day—*Harper's Magazine*, the *Atlantic Monthly, Putnam's Magazine, Emerson's Magazine,* and the *Galaxy.*

Mrs. Austin lived in Boston most of her life, with the exception of a short residence in Concord, where she formed friendships with Louisa Alcott, Emerson, and the Hawthornes. A woman of great tact, she was always surrounded by an admiring group of "Mayflower" descendants and intellectuals in Boston society. She followed a strict routine, devoting her mornings to writing or the study of Pilgrim history, constantly enlarging her knowledge of the first settlers and carefully verifying every point before putting it on paper. Besides her short stories, Mrs. Austin was the author of more than twenty books, and was at work on another at the time of her death in Roxbury. The atmosphere, customs, and characters of early New England days are admirably set forth in her writings.

JANE GOODWIN AUSTIN

Of her numerous books those which are best remembered today are her "Pilgrim Books" for children: *Standish of Standish, Betty Alden, A Nameless Nobleman,* and *Dr. LeBaron and His Daughters.* They still rank high among American juvenile classics.

Principal Works: Fairy Dreams, 1859; Dora Darling: The Daughter of the Regiment, 1865; The Tailor Boy, 1865; Outpost, 1867; Cipher: A Romance, 1869; The Shadow of Moloch Mountain, 1870; Moonfolk, 1874; Mrs. Beauchamp Brown, 1880; A Nameless Nobleman, 1881; The Desmond Hundred, 1882; Nantucket Scraps, 1883; Standish of Standish, 1889; Dr. LeBaron and His Daughters, 1890; Betty Alden, 1891; It Never Did Run Smooth, 1892; Queen Tempest, 1892; David Alden's Daughter and Other Stories, 1892; The Twelve Great Diamonds, 1892.

About: Stockwell, M. L. Descendants of Francis LeBaron of Plymouth, Mass; Book Buyer May 1894; Literary World April 1894; Boston Transcript March 30, 1894; Boston Herald and Boston Journal March 31, 1894.

AUSTIN, WILLIAM (March 2, 1778-June 27, 1841), story-writer and essayist, was born in Lunenburg, Mass., the son of Nathaniel Austin, a prosperous pewterer, and Margaret (Rand) Austin. The burning of Charlestown at the battle of Bunker Hill had driven his parents from that city, but they returned shortly after William's birth. Young Austin attended the Rev. John Shaw's school, in Haverhill, and was graduated from Harvard in 1798. His admiration for the writings of Rousseau culminated, during his senior year, in his outspoken *Strictures on Harvard University.* Although he later retracted many of his condemnations of that "death-bed of genius," he had been somewhat justified in saying that the extravagant "muse of belles lettres" would "recoil at the sight of our walls." For Harvard of that day was a fine place for sharp-witted lawyers, well-trained merchants, and undemonstrative clergymen, but it had as yet little concern for nebulous creatures called men of genius.

On the United States frigate "Constitution" Austin earned his passage to England by serving as chaplain—the first government

From a portrait by H. C. Pratt
WILLIAM AUSTIN

appointee to this office in the navy—and schoolmaster. He studied law in 1802 and 1803 at Lincoln's Inn, London. He became acquainted, at this time, with the New England artist-author, Washington Allston, and wrote *Letters From London,* which, for their lively descriptions of British barristers and statesmen, became universal reading among American lawyers. When he returned to Charlestown he succeeded in building up a large law practice, and between 1811 and 1834 served five terms in the general court. He also represented the county of Middlesex in the senate from 1821 to 1823.

During all this time he was writing, principally for his own pleasure, but his stories found their way into such periodicals as the *New England Galaxy*, the old *New England Magazine*, and the *American Monthly Magazine*. Best known of his narratives is the classic "Peter Rugg the Missing Man," which appeared in the *Galaxy* for September 10, 1824. Like Irving's earlier "Rip Van Winkle," which it superficially resembled, it was for the times a distinct literary *tour de force*. Set against a background of symbolism and authentic local folk-lore, it remains the best American variation of the "Wandering Jew" theme—this eerie tale of the ghost who spent fifty years asking the way to Boston. It was very popular and widely influenced other writers, among them Hawthorne and Poe. Hawthorne, whose *chiaroscuro* it foreshadowed, used Peter Rugg as a character in *A Virtuoso's Collection*; Louise Imogen Guiney made him the subject of a ballad; and Amy Lowell wrote a prose poem about him. Less well remembered of Austin's tales, but deserving in their own right, were "Martha Gardner," a strong plea for the rights of labor, and "The Man With the Cloaks," drawn from a German fairy-tale.

Austin was first married, June 1806, to Charlotte Williams, who died in 1820, and on October 3, 1822, to Lucy Jones; he was the father of fourteen children. A frank and impulsive radical—his mother had been an ardent Tory and his father a spirited patriot—he had at one time been embroiled in a duel because he had written a blunt and indignant letter flaying one General Simon Elliot for questionable court procedure. His activities as civic leader and commentator left him little time for the exercise of his mystic-moral imagination and his rather well integrated sense of humor in the writing of short stories.

"Peter Rugg," however, has become one of those classics which everyone knows—without being able to name the author.

PRINCIPAL WORKS: Strictures on Harvard University, 1798; Letters From London, 1804; Essay on the Human Character of Jesus Christ, 1807; Literary Papers, 1890.

ABOUT: Austin W[illiam]. Literary Papers (see Biographical Sketch by J. W. Austin); Austin, W[alter]. William Austin.

AVERY, BENJAMIN PARKE (November 11, 1828-November 8, 1875), journalist and diplomat, was born in New York City. He was the son of Samuel Putnam Avery, Sr., and Hannah (Parke) Avery, and a brother of Samuel Putnam Avery, Jr., the well known art connoisseur. His father was a poor hotel keeper who died during the cholera epidemic of 1852, leaving his widow to bring up their six children. Receiving most of his education from reading, Benjamin learned the trade of bank-note engraving in the house of Rawdon, Wright & Hatch, and when he was nineteen set out for California to prospect for gold. He had a hard experience, and was often ill and destitute, but in 1856, with money saved during employment as druggist and general storekeeper, he courageously established at North San Juan the *Hydraulic Press,* a weekly newspaper with a Republican and anti-slavery policy in a hostile community. Four years later he became editor and part proprietor of the *Marysville Appeal,* which grew to be one of the most influential papers in the state. In 1861 he married Mary A. Fuller, of Michigan, and was also elected state printer on the same ticket with Leland Stanford for governor. When his term of office expired, he joined the editorial staff of the San Francisco *Bulletin*, and later took over the editorship of the *Overland Monthly*. In 1874 he was appointed United States Minister to China. He died at Peking, and was interred in San Francisco, with public honors.

PRINCIPAL WORKS: California Pictures in Prose and Verse, 1878.

ABOUT: The Genealogical Record of the Dedham Branch of the Avery Family in America; In Memoriam: Benjamin Parke Avery (pamphlet, 1875); Harper's Weekly May 2, 1874.

BACHMAN, JOHN (February 4, 1790-February 24, 1874), naturalist and Lutheran clergyman, was born in the village of Rhinebeck, Dutchess County, N.Y., of good German and Swiss stock, the son of Jacob Bachman and Eva Bachman. Overcoming family disapproval, young Bachman secretly began studying natural history during his early boyhood and earned enough money to buy necessary textbooks by catching and skinning beavers. He matriculated at Williams College but collapsed from overwork and left before graduation. Regaining his health by out-of-door living, he taught school in Ellwood and Philadelphia, Pa., until 1813 when he was licensed to preach in the Lutheran Church. His first charge was the "Gilead Pastorate" comprising three churches near Rhinebeck. Ordained in December 1814 he accepted a call to St. John's Lutheran Church in Charleston, S.C. and succeeded through tireless efforts in building up a large and devout congregation. Two years after settling in Charleston he married Harriet Martin, daughter of a German Lutheran minister.

Meanwhile, Bachman was fraternizing with prominent scientific men—Alexander Wilson, the ornithologist, Baron Von Humbolt, famous explorer and naturalist, and John James Audubon, with whom he became closely associated. By 1835 Bachman had begun to assist Audubon by collecting southern animals and observing their habits. Besides their famous collaboration upon *The Viviparous Quadrupeds of North America*, the alliance was further cemented by the marriage of two of Audubon's sons to Bachman's daughters.

During the Civil War Bachman remained consistently neutral in viewpoint, but actively attended the sick and dying until he was forced against his will to flee from Charleston before the evacuation. He died of paralysis in Columbia, S.C.

PRINCIPAL WORKS: A Catalogue of the Phaenogamous Plants and Ferns Native and Naturalized Found Growing in the Vicinity of Charleston, S.C., 1834; The Viviparous Quadrupeds of North America (text for J. J. Audubon's plates) 1846-54; The Unity of the Human Race, 1850; A Defense of Luther and the Reformation, 1853.

ABOUT: Bachman, C. & Haskell, J. B. John Bachman; Jacobs, H. E. History of the Evangelical Lutheran Church in the United States.

BACON, DELIA SALTER (February 2, 1811-September 2, 1859), critic and miscellaneous writer, the "first Baconian," was born in a log cabin, the first house in Tallmadge, Ohio. Her father, the Rev. David Bacon, was a Congregationalist missionary who failed in his mission and returned in 1812, heartbroken, to his home in Connecticut, where in 1817 he died. His widow, Alice (Parks) Bacon, and six children were left in abject poverty, and Delia was reared by Mrs. Delia Williams (perhaps an aunt), in Hartford. There she attended the celebrated school of Catharine Beecher, sister of Henry Ward Beecher, until she was fifteen. Then she and a sister tried for four years to establish a private school, in Connecticut, New Jersey, and New York, but they failed for lack of means and because of Delia's frail health. Next she took to lecturing on literature and history, at which she won some success.

All of Delia Bacon's life that matters to history began in 1852, when (perhaps first attracted by the name) she became the first Baconian. In her opinion, however, Bacon alone did not write Shakespeare's plays, but they were produced by Bacon, Raleigh, and Spenser as a means of spreading secretly a liberal philosophy. For a while even Emerson was converted to her theory, and in 1853 he sent her to Carlyle in London. Carlyle welcomed her, but soon dropped her when she refused to study the sources and preferred to rely on her intuition. For four years she lived in destitution in a London garret, enduring disappointments, hunger, and rebuffs with equal indifference. She was rescued by Hawthorne, then American consul at Liverpool, who even secured a publisher for her. In 1865 she became obsessed with the idea that important papers were concealed in Shakespeare's grave and tried desperately to have it opened.

Whatever one may think of the Shakespeare-Bacon controversy, there is no doubt that Delia Bacon was definitely insane. Her book appeared in 1857, but she never knew the ridicule and scorn it elicited, for by this time her mind was quite gone. In 1858 her nephew took her back to America, where she died soon after. Mingled with the incoherence and unreadable diffuseness of her book are a few pages of valuable criticism, but that is all.

PRINCIPAL WORKS: Tales of the Puritans, 1831; The Bride of Fort Edward (play) 1839; Philosophy of the Plays of Shakespeare Unfolded, 1857.

ABOUT: Bacon, T. Delia Bacon: A Biographical Sketch; Hawthorne, N. Our Old Home.

BACON, EDWIN MUNROE (October 20, 1844-February 24, 1916), journalist, was born in Providence, R.I. He was the son of Henry Bacon and Eliza Ann (Munroe) Bacon, who gave him an excellent education in private schools in Providence, Philadelphia, and Boston. At the age of nineteen he became a reporter on the Boston *Daily Advertiser*. He next became associated with the *Illustrated Chicago News* and at the end of its brief career joined the staff of the New York *Times* as assistant night editor, later becoming news editor. In 1873 he was appointed editor of the Boston *Globe* and held the position for five years when a change in policy caused him to resign. Returning to the *Daily Advertiser* he became chief editor in 1883. In 1886 he accepted the editorship of the Boston *Post,* holding it until 1891 when he resigned because of ill health. On October 24, 1867, he was married to Gusta E. Hill, daughter of Ira Hill of Boston.

Upon his retirement, Bacon put his exceptional knowledge of Boston and New England into a series of descriptive books. He died in Cambridge, Mass.

Bacon's journalistic ability was more conscientious than brilliant. He had a full realization of the responsibilities of his various editorships, and his thoroughness and accuracy set a fine example to his associates.

PRINCIPAL WORKS: A Dictionary of Boston, 1886; Boston Illustrated, 1893; Historic Pilgrimages in New England, 1898; Literary Pilgrimages in New England, 1902; Boston: A Guide Book, 1903; The Connecticut River and the Valley of the Connecticut, 1906; Rambles Around Old Boston, 1914.

ABOUT: Boston Transcript, Boston Globe, Boston Herald, February 25, 1916.

BAGBY, GEORGE WILLIAM (August 13, 1828-November 29, 1883), editor and humorist, was born in Buckingham County, Va. He was the son of George Bagby, a Lynchburg merchant, and Virginia (Evans) Bagby, who died when young George was six. He received his early education at a boarding-school at Prince Edward Court House and at Edgehill School at Princeton, N.J. After attending Delaware College for two years he studied medicine at the University of Pennsylvania, being graduated in

GEORGE WILLIAM BAGBY

1849. Returning to Lynchburg, he established an office for a short time but gave it up for literature. He wrote a series of successful articles for the Lynchburg *Virginian,* and eventually purchased, with George Woodville Latham, the Lynchburg *Express* which lived for only two or three years under their management. After newspaper experience in Washington, D.C., in 1860 he succeeded John R. Thompson as editor of the *Southern Literary Messenger* in Richmond.

Bagby joined the Confederate army during the Civil War but was discharged because of ill health. He then returned to the *Messenger,* remaining as editor until January 1864. During this time he was correspondent for papers throughout the South where his faithful reports from the Southern capital were eagerly read.

In 1863 Bagby married Lucy Parke Chamberlayne of Richmond, who bore him ten children. After the war, he went to New York City as a journalist, but defective eyesight forced him to return to Virginia where he turned to lecturing as a means of livelihood.

The year 1867 found Bagby in Orange, Va., where he became editor and part owner of *Native Virginia.* Three years later he was appointed custodian of the state library, a position which he held for three consecutive administrations. Meanwhile he was contributing widely to newspapers and magazines and travelling through Virginia giving his famous lectures "The Old Virginia Gentleman" and "The Virginia Negro."

Bagby was among the earliest to master Negro psychology and dialect in literature and while his reputation as a humorist extended beyond Virginia, his popularity in his native state was such that his name was a household word. His best known piece is "Jud Browning's Account of Rubenstein's Playing." In his serious writing his inclination toward sentimentality was usually relieved by the liveliness of his style. A year after his death in Richmond, his widow collected the first volume of *Selections From the Miscellaneous Writings of Dr. George W. Bagby*, with a biographical sketch by Edward S. Gregory. The second volume appeared the following year and both were printed in limited editions.

PRINCIPAL WORKS: John M. Daniel's Latch Key, 1868; What I Did With My Fifty Millions: By Moses Adams, 1874; Meekins's Twinses, 1877; Canal Reminiscences, 1879; Selections From the Miscellaneous Writings of Dr. George W. Bagby, 1884, 1885.

ABOUT: Chamberlayne, C. G. Library of Southern Literature; King, J. L. Dr. William Bagby: A Study of Virginia Literature; Page, T. N. The Old Virginia Gentleman.

BAILEY, EBENEZER (June 25, 1795-August 5, 1839), educator, was born at West Newbury, Essex County, Mass., the son of Paul Bailey, a farmer, and Emma (Carr) Bailey. After his graduation from Yale in 1813, he became a teacher in a school in New Haven, and at the same time took up the study of law. This heavy schedule was too strenuous and he went to Richmond, Va., as tutor in the family of a Colonel Carter. In a year he returned to Massachusetts and in 1819 opened a private school for young ladies in Newburyport. Four years later he left to become headmaster of the Franklin Grammar School for Boys in Boston. In 1825 he was appointed principal of the Girls' High School of Boston, one of the first high schools for girls in the United States. It was considered a doubtful experiment and in 1827, Josiah Quincy, then Mayor of Boston, attacked it severely, pronouncing it a a complete failure. Supported by many indignant citizens, Bailey wrote a vigorous reply—*Review of the Mayor's Report Upon the High School for Girls*. This was published in 1828, but its influence was not sufficient to keep the school alive. In 1827 Bailey opened the Young Ladies' High School, a private institution, which he conducted with great success until it collapsed in the financial panic of 1837. Undaunted, Bailey then established in 1838 a boys' school in Roxbury, moving the school to Lynn the following year. He died in Lynn from lockjaw brought on by an accident.

Bailey was a man of varied interests. He was one of the founders of the American Institute of Instruction, a member of the Common Council of Boston, and a director of the House of Reformation. He wrote a number of poems and frequently contributed to magazines. His textbooks were his most popular works. As an educator he was highly esteemed and was regarded as among the first of his day.

PRINCIPAL WORKS: The Young Ladies' Class Book, Bakewell's Philosophical Conversations, 1833; First Lessons in Algebra, 1833.

ABOUT: Inglis, A. J. The Rise of the High School in Massachusetts; American Journal of Education June 1863; School Review May 1899.

BAILEY, JAMES MONTGOMERY (September 25, 1841-March 4, 1894), humorist and publisher, was born in Albany, N.Y., son of James Bailey, a carpenter who died from a fall in 1843, and Sarah (Magee) Bailey. In 1846 his mother remarried. He was educated in the public schools and apprenticed to a carpenter. In 1860 he went to Danbury, Conn., where he practiced his trade until 1862. Then he enlisted in the Union army, was captured at Gettysburg, and for two months was a prisoner of war at Belle Isle Prison.

Before this Bailey had already begun to contribute humorous articles to the New York *Sunday Mercury*, and sent comic sketches of army life to a Danbury newspaper throughout his service. At the end of the war, with Timothy Donovan, an army comrade and a printer, he bought the Danbury *Times*. In 1870 this was consolidated with the *Jeffersonian* as the Danbury *News*. From this time on Bailey was best known as "the Danbury *News* man." In nine months he brought the circulation of his weekly paper from 1,920 to 30,000. It was read nationally and even internationally. His humorous sketches were so enjoyed that 33,000 copies of *Life in Danbury* were sold in the first eleven weeks it was out.

In 1866 Bailey married Catharine Douglass Stewart. In 1873 he visited California, in 1874 Europe; and from 1876 he gave occasional lectures. In 1878 Donovan sold out his interest, and in 1883 Bailey began to publish a daily edition of the *News*, which had previously appeared weekly. He felt that his humor was wearing thin, or public taste was changing, and gradually he built up a strong local paper on orthodox lines. He was a civic leader in his town, being president of the Board of Trade, founder of the Danbury Hospital, and president of the Relief Society. Personally he was a moody man, with the melancholy of

Collection of Frederick H. Meserve
JAMES M. BAILEY

most humorists; he was the sort of lavishly generous person who is all his life an "easy mark." He was known everywhere for his harmless eccentricities, such as refusing to wear a necktie, and by his excessive love for dogs. His broad, burlesque humor is out of date now, and there is little in his work to explain to a modern reader why our grandfathers chuckled and guffawed over it. Bailey has, however, the credit of being the first newspaper humorist and the father of all the columnists.

PRINCIPAL WORKS: Danbury News Man's Almanac, 1873; Life in Danbury, 1873; They All Do It, 1877; England From a Back Window, 1878; Mr. Phillips' Goneness, 1879; The Danbury Boom, 1880; History of Danbury (completed by S. B. Hill) 1896.

ABOUT: Bailey, J. M. History of Danbury (see Sketch by S. B. Hill); Munsey's Magazine May 1890.

BAIRD, HENRY MARTIN (January 17, 1832-November 11, 1906), clergyman and historian, leading authority on Huguenot history, was born in Philadelphia. He was the son of Robert Baird, a distinguished Presbyterian minister, and Fermine Amaryllis (Du Buisson) Baird, of Huguenot descent; a brother, Charles Baird, was also an historian. He attended schools in France and Switzerland during his family's residence abroad when his father was sent by the French Association to study the religious conditions of France and other countries. In 1850 he was graduated from the University of the City of New York. An aptitude for linguistic and historical study was already apparent, and he spent the next three years pursuing historical studies in Athens and Rome. He then turned to theology and studied at Union Theological Seminary in New York, but was graduated from the Seminary at Princeton in 1856. He served as tutor in the college during this time and until 1859, when he accepted the chair of Greek language and literature in New York University. Soon after this he married Susan Elizabeth Baldwin. He remained at New York University until 1902, when advanced age necessitated his retirement. He died in Yonkers, N.Y., of apoplexy at the age of seventy-five.

Aside from his pedagogic duties, Baird contributed numerous articles to the reviews on many subjects, although he was chiefly interested in Greek and Huguenot research. Excepting *The Life of the Rev. Robert Baird*, published in 1866, and *Theodore Beza: The Counsellor of the French Reformation* (1899), his best known works are six volumes on the Huguenots, a series on which Baird labored for more than thirty years and which deservedly holds a prominent place in American historical writing upon European subjects. Baird's writings attest his unquestionable scholarship, and if there is a fault to be cited it is that his keen interest in the Huguenots sometimes unduly biased his critical faculties.

PRINCIPAL WORKS: Modern Greece, 1856; The Life of the Rev. Robert Baird, 1866; Theodore Beza: The Counsellor of the French Reformation, 1899; The History of the Rise of the Huguenots of France (2 vols.) 1879; The Huguenots and Henry of Navarre (2 vols.) 1886; The Huguenots and the Revocation of the Edict of Nantes (2 vols.) 1895.

ABOUT: Book Buyer September 1895; Princeton Theological Seminary Necrological Report, 1907; New York Tribune, New York Times November 12, 1906.

BAKER, BENJAMIN A. (April 4, 1818-September 6, 1890), playwright, was born in New York City. After a very brief schooling he was apprenticed to a harness-maker. His early life is obscure, but by 1837 he somehow found himself in Natchez, Miss., and on the stage, in support of Junius Brutus Booth. Two years later he returned to New York as an actor, and soon after began writing plays, the first of which were burlesques. In 1851 he was a theater manager in Washington, and in 1853 in San Francisco, where he managed the Metropolitan Theatre for the divorced wife of Edwin Forrest. In 1856 he was recalled to New York to manage Edwin Booth's stock company, and thenceforth became a theatrical agent. In 1885 he was made assistant secretary of the Actors' Fund (for pensions), and served in this capacity, beloved by his fellow-professionals, who knew him as "Uncle Ben," until his death at seventy-two.

Baker's most successful play, one which established a new theatrical *genre,* was *A Glance at New York,* the only one which has been published. It was written for his own benefit, but at first the manager refused to put it on, as he considered it too vulgar. It was built around the character of Mose, the volunteer fireman, the typical "Bowery boy" of the period. It was an immense success and was widely imitated, and he himself wrote a number of other farces along the same line.

Principal Works (date of production): A Glance at New York, 1848; New York As It Is, 1848; Three Years After, 1849; Mose in China, 1850.

About: Seilhamer, J. An Interviewer's Album; New York Herald September 7 and 11, 1890.

BAKER, WILLIAM MUMFORD June 5, 1825-August 20, 1883), clergyman and miscellaneous writer, was born in Washington, D.C., the son of Daniel Baker and Elizabeth (McRobert) Baker. His father was a scholarly Presbyterian minister who held many pastorates in the Southern states. Young William decided at an early age to follow in his father's footsteps and pursued his education accordingly. He was graduated with honors from Princeton College in 1846 and studied at Princeton Seminary from 1847 to 1848. On April 26, 1848, he was licensed to preach by the Presbytery of New Brunswick, N.J., and was ordained by the Presbytery of Little Rock, Ark., in 1850. The same year, January 5, 1850, he married Susan John Hartman at Raleigh, Tenn. He preached for a short time in Galveston, Texas, and then removed to Austin, where he remained until 1865 reorganizing the First Presbyterian Church.

After the Civil War, Baker moved to the North. From 1866 to 1872 he held a pastorate at Zanesville, Ohio; the next two years found him in Newburyport, Mass., and he was at South Boston between 1874 and 1876.

Baker's literary career began during his years in the South when he published the book for which he is most remembered—*Inside: A Chronicle of Secession,* a thinly disguised account of his experiences during the war, published under the pseudonym "George F. Harrington." His position at that time was difficult inasmuch as he was torn between his deep love for the South and a strong sympathy with the Federal cause. In the years between 1876 and 1881 Baker devoted himself exclusively to writing but accepted a call to the South Church in Philadelphia in 1881, where he remained but two years. Broken in health, he returned to Boston, where he died.

Principal Works: The Life and Labors of Daniel Baker, 1858; Inside: A Chronicle of Secession, 1866; Oak Mot, 1868; The New Timothy, 1870; Mose Evans, 1874; Carter Quarterman, 1876; The Virginians in Texas, 1878; A Year Worth Living, 1878; Colonel Dunwoddie: Millionaire, 1878; His Majesty: Myself, 1880; Blessed Saint Certainty, 1881; The Ten Theophanies, 1883; The Making of a Man, 1884.

About: Boston Transcript August 21, 1883; Princeton Theological Seminary Necrology Report, 1884.

BALDWIN, JOSEPH GLOVER (January?, 1815-September 30, 1864), historian and biographer, was born near Winchester, Va., the son of Joseph Clarke Baldwin and Eliza (Baldwin) Baldwin, who were distant relatives. The family was a good one reduced to poverty, but Baldwin appears to have had no schooling whatever. However, he must somehow have educated himself, for at the age of twelve he was a clerk of the district court, and at seventeen was editor of a Winchester newspaper. It is certain that he was an omnivorous reader, and by private study gave himself a thorough education, including training in the law.

Having decided that he was now competent to practice law, he determined to find an environment where there would be more opportunity than Virginia, with its distinguished attorneys, afforded, and so in 1836 he set out for what was then the Southwestern frontier, in Mississippi. From there he moved to Alabama, where he had considerable success. In 1839 he married Sidney White, daughter of an Alabama judge. Their six children all died in infancy. He went into politics and in 1844 served in the state legislature as a Whig; in 1849, however, when he ran for Congress he was defeated. Disappointed in his political ambitions, and also still feeling the urge to new adventure, he went to San Francisco in 1854. There he played a prominent part in the early days of the city, and in 1858 was made associate justice of the California Supreme Court. In 1862 he retired to private practice—perhaps induced to do so in part by anti-Southern feeling during the Civil War. He died as a result of an operation performed when he was threatened with tetanus after an accident. His last days were saddened by the hardships of his parents in Virginia, when he was unable to communicate with them because of the war.

From his first days in Mississippi and Alabama, Baldwin had kept a commonplace book, giving vivid details of the life and people of his new environment. These eventually grew into his *Flush Times,* a picturesque part of local history. A paper he contributed to the *Southern Literary Messenger* on Jackson and Clay was the nucleus of his useful though dull work on *Party Leaders.* These were his only published works. He is better remembered, especially in California, as a lawyer and politician than as an author.

PRINCIPAL WORKS: The Flush Times of Alabama and Mississippi, 1853; Party Leaders, 1855.

ABOUT: Mellen, G. F. Library of Southern Literature; Owen, T. M. History of Alabama; Field, S. J. Personal Reminiscences of Early Days in California.

BALESTIER, CHARLES WOLCOTT (December 13, 1861-December 6, 1891), publisher and miscellaneous writer, brother-in-law of Rudyard Kipling, was born in Rochester, N.Y. He was the son of Henry Wolcott Balestier and Anna (Smith) Balestier, and a descendant of Oliver Wolcott, signer of the Declaration of Independence. Balestier's father died when he was nine, and his boyhood was spent in Rochester with his grandfather, Erasmus Peshine Smith, educator and international lawyer, who in 1871 became financial advisor to the Mikado of Japan. During Mr. Smith's absence, Wolcott Balestier (as he was known) entered schools in Baltimore, Washington, New York, Denver, and Brattleboro, Vt., the summer home of his paternal grandparents. Graduated from the Rochester Free Academy in 1880, he matriculated at Cornell in 1881, but the following year went West, via the South, and his impressions embody much of his best literary work. In 1884 he was put in charge of the patent collection of the Astor Library, New York City.

As early as his seventeenth year, Balestier had sent small contributions to the *Atlantic Monthly,* and during his Rochester Academy days he was a reporter on the Rochester *Post-Express.* The year 1884 was a productive one in which his first novel, *A Potent Philtre,* appeared in the New York *Tribune. A Fair Device,* a love story, and a campaign life of James G. Blaine were published by James G. Lovell, a connection which was to play an important part in Balestier's future career.

In 1885 he became editor of a weekly miscellany, *Tid-Bits,* which a year later became *Time,* a popular humorous paper. In 1888 Lovell sent Balestier to England to secure original manuscripts for his firm, and, soon after his arrival in London, his rooms in Westminster became the meeting-place of important literary figures. He formed a partnership with William Heinemann, and launched the "English Library" for publishing English and American books on the Continent in competition with the house of Tauchnitz.

Soon after his arrival in England, Balestier met Rudyard Kipling, who married his sister Caroline in 1892. His famous brother-in-law dedicated *Barrack-Room Ballads* to him and the two collaborated on *The Naulahka* (published 1892), Balestier contributing the American chapters. "Naulahka" was also the name Kipling gave the house he built near Brattleboro, Vt., when he came to America after his marriage, and which he abandoned forever after a deep-seated quarrel with Beatty Balestier, Wolcott's brother, made life there unendurable.

During his years of business enterprise Wolcott Balestier worked on the manuscript of *Benefits Forgot,* a novel which was posthumously published in the *Century Magazine,* and in book form in 1894. Three short stories were collected in *The Average Woman,* also published posthumously. He died from typhus in Dresden, Germany, while on a business trip.

Balestier was slender, with dark hair, pallid complexion, and intense blue eyes. He had an unquestioned literary gift, but is chiefly remembered for his prominence in the publishing world and as a friend and brother-in-law of Kipling.

PRINCIPAL WORKS: A Potent Philtre, 1884; A Victorious Defeat, 1886; The Average Woman, 1892; The Naulahka (with Rudyard Kipling) 1892; Benefits Forgot, 1894.

ABOUT: Day, R. E. Dante: A Sonnet Sequence; Van de Water, F. F. Rudyard Kipling's Vermont Feud; Century Magazine April 1892; Cosmopolitan 1892.

BALESTIER, WOLCOTT. See BALESTIER, CHARLES WOLCOTT

BALLOU, ADIN (April 23, 1803-August 5, 1890), Universalist clergyman, propagandist, and founder of the Hopedale Community, was born at Cumberland, R.I., the son of Ariel and Edilda (Tower) Ballou, and was descended from Maturin Ballou, part-owner with Roger Williams of Providence Plantation in 1646. Adin's education began at elementary schools in Cumberland but ceased at the age of seventeen when his father bitterly opposed his entering Brown University. The following year he believed himself called to the ministry. Volunteering to preach the next Sunday at the village church, which he had joined when he was twelve, he thus began a religious career which finally led to acceptance into the fellowship of the Christian Church in 1821. Shortly afterward he was expelled because of pro-Universalist views. He then joined the Universalists and during 1823 preached in Mendon, Bellingham, Medway, and Boston. Between 1824 and 1827 he was in charge of the Universalist society in Milford, Mass., and the Prince Street association in New York City, but 1828 found him again in Milford, participating in the stormy question of universal salvation then dividing the Universalists. Ballou finally withdrew from the denomination and in 1831 formed the "Massachusetts Association of Restorationists," comprising thirty-one ministers. It was dissolved in 1841, but Ballou considerably influenced Universalist and Unitarian thought by expounding his organization's doctrines in the *Independent Messenger.*

In January 1841 he joined thirty-one others in organizing the Hopedale Community, near Milford, a group founded on "brotherly love and the Gospel of Jesus Christ." Ballou became the first president, and the Hopedale Community enlarged its membership and carried on various enterprises, including road-making, farming, building, and the publication of *The Practical Christian,* edited by Ballou. He resigned the presidency in 1853 in order to write *Practical Christian Socialism,* in which he outlined a plan to organize another project, a "Practical Christian Republic."

Ebenezer Draper became president of Hopedale and with his brother George, withdrew their three-fourths of the Community stock, then valued at $40,000, invested it in the Hopedale Manufacturing Company, increased their personal wealth, and gradually transformed the town into a manufacturing center. Unable to survive, in 1868 the Community merged with the Unitarian Hopedale Parish, of which Ballou became pastor until 1880, after which he devoted his time to literature.

Principal Works: Memoir of Adin Augustus Ballou, 1853; Practical Christian Socialism, 1854; Primitive Christianity and Its Corruptions, 1870; History of the Town of Milford, 1882; An Elaborate History and Genealogy of the Ballous in America, 1888; Autobiography, 1896; History of the Hopedale Community, 1897.

About: Staples, C. A. In Memoriam: Rev. Adin Ballou; Arena December 1890; Boston Journal and Boston Herald August 6, 1890; Milford Journal August 5, 1890; New England Magazine April 1891; New World December 1898.

BALLOU, MATURIN MURRAY (April 14, 1820-March 27, 1895), journalist, traveler, and editor, was born in Boston, Mass. He was the youngest son of the Rev. Hosea Ballou, a distinguished Universalist minister, and Ruth (Washburn) Ballou. Educated at the English High School, he passed his entrance examinations for Harvard but decided to give up a college education in order to follow a business career. At the age of nineteen he became a clerk in the Boston Post Office where he remained for five years. Meanwhile he began writing, and contributed frequently to the *Olive Branch,* a small local paper. On September 15, 1839, he was married to Mary Anne Roberts.

Ballou was next appointed deputy navy-agent in the Boston Customs House, but he resigned this position in order to accompany his wife, who was in ill health, on a cruise among the West India Islands. During their travels he wrote descriptive letters home which were published in magazines and later included in his books. Returning to Boston he founded and edited *Gleason's Pictorial,* later *Ballou's Pictorial,* one of the pioneer American illustrated newspapers. In 1872 he became the first editor and business manager of the Boston *Daily Globe,* and during two years of journalism, also engaged in many business and financial enterprises, including the construction of the costly St. James Hotel, later converted into Franklin Square House, a residence for working women and girls.

Ballou traveled extensively from 1870 until his death, which occurred in Cairo, Egypt. He wrote travel books, biography, history, and many plays.

Principal Works: Red Rupert: The American Buccaneer, 1845; The Naval Officer: or, The Pirate's Cave, 1845; The Spanish Musketeer, 1847; The Biography of Rev. Hosea Ballou, 1852; The History of Cuba, 1854; Due West: or, Round the World in Ten Months, 1884; Due South: or, Cuba Past and Present, 1885; Under the Southern Cross: or, Travels in Australia, Tasmania, New Zealand, Samoa and Other Pacific Islands, 1888.

About: Ballou, A. History and Genealogy of the Ballous in America, 1888; Boston Globe March 29, 1895.

BANCROFT GEORGE (October 3, 1800-January 17, 1891), historian, was born in Worcester, Mass., the son of the Reverend Aaron Bancroft, a Unitarian minister and author of a life of Washington, and Lucretia (Chandler) Bancroft, of vigorous New England stock. As a boy he had the *comme il faut* precocity of scholars-to-be, and it is said that at the age of six his father whetted the lad's mind with the most trying questions on Roman history. He attended school a while in Worcester and then went to Phillips Exeter Academy, where he became a friend of Jared Sparks, entering Harvard at the age of thirteen. Bancroft was a graduate (1817) of such abundant promise that after a year at the Divinity School at Cambridge the college sent him abroad to study. In 1820 he received the degree of Doctor of Philosophy and Master of Arts from the University of Göttingen. Like Edward Everett and George Ticknor, who had preceded him in the acquisition of a European "finish," he was among those young Americans for whom "true happiness" lay in the "culture of the intelligence." Gracefully he made the acquaintance of Byron and Lafayette, learned to waltz, and became a horseman of the first order.

He returned to Cambridge in 1822, bursting not only with erudition but with some explosive mannerisms—borrowed from various European *milieus*—that were a little bit too much for cautious Cambridge. Homesick for the culture and *Gemütlichkeit* of Germany, he put in one dreary year as a tutor in Greek at Harvard, published a thin volume of rather youthful poems in 1823, and then took himself off to Northampton, Mass., where he founded, with J. G. Cogswell, the experimental Round Hill school. The project embodied German and Swiss methods which were still too advanced to be practical here, and Bancroft, admittedly a poor teacher, was brazenly caricatured as "the Critter" by his own pupils. In 1831 he sold his interests in the school and returned to Worcester to write book reviews and political articles for the *North American Review*. Jared Sparks, editor of this able journal, coveted Bancroft's contributions, but found his political attitudes and his tortuous style somewhat disconcerting. Bancroft joined the Democratic Party at a time when its star was in the ascendant nationally—but *not* in Boston, where it still required not only condescension but courage to venture the remark that "a Democrat may be honest in his convictions." He went to Washington, and, as he himself put it, drew his chair "close up" to the powers that were. Jackson and Van Buren liked a man who could put eloquence into politics: in 1837 he was appointed Collector of the Port of Boston (and found a niche for Hawthorne in the Custom House); in 1844 he ran—though unsuccessfully—for governor of Massachusetts; and the following year Polk made Bancroft his Secretary of the Navy.

Bancroft's sympathy with the common people was unquestionable, but, like many spokesmen of popular causes, he may have suffered from a little self-deception and sentimentality when he commended General Houston's march into Texas and the seizure of California in order to extend, said he, the "area of freedom." Emerson went so far as to call him a "soldier of fortune" who would "take any side and defend it."

Collection of Frederick H. Meserve
GEORGE BANCROFT

His appointment, in 1846, as United States Minister to Great Britain was much to his liking and put within his grasp the facilities of European research on his *History of the United States*, begun fifteen years before, of which three volumes had been completed. The influences of England and the Continent were, he found, only superficial and he remained "all too American." From London he wrote in 1848, "The world is growing weary . . . of hereditary kings . . . my residence in Europe has confirmed my love for the rule of the people." On his return to the United States in 1849 he made his home in New York City and worked steadily on his *History*, the tenth and last volume of which did not appear until 1874.

During the Civil War Bancroft allied himself with the Northern pro-Union Democrats, and became an active supporter of Lincoln, whom he had, at first, greatly underrated. In 1867 he was sent by Andrew Johnson as Minister to Germany and was retained by Grant until 1874. Göttingen conferred on him an honorary LL.D.; he enjoyed a thorough rebound of his extreme love of German life. At seventy-four he came back to America for good, spending his summers in Newport and his winters in Washington. He remained "more than a passive Unitarian" and grew old with a certain mellowness. With a showy white beard and with a large red rose in his buttonhole he never failed to attract attention in Capital society. In 1827 he had married Sarah H. Dwight, who died ten years later, leaving two sons and a daughter. In 1838 he married a widow, Elizabeth Bliss Davis, by whom he had one daughter. She died in 1886.

Besides his *chef d'œuvre,* the *History,* Bancroft wrote lives of Van Buren and Lincoln, both of which were excessively pompous in parts, and a series of historical short stories, exercises in narrative writing indulged in during the Göttingen days. For his *History* he had delved into the archives of England, France, and Germany and had carried on a limitless correspondence. Like Peter Force [*q.v.*] he collected and preserved invaluable items belonging to the period of the Revolution. Despite his scholarliness he was sometimes guilty of conveying a very misleading impression by quoting mere fragments out of context. His style was "turgid" and often dulled by stereotyped phrases, and only occasionally had it any real impetus. But because Bancroft was a thoroughgoing student, unencumbered by provincialism, and with an enviable experience in diplomacy, his historical writings were far superior to the colorless chronicles and annals of his predecessors.

Principal Works: Poems, 1823; History of the United States From the Discovery of the American Continent, 1834-84; Literary and Historical Miscellanies, 1855; History of the Formation of the Constitution of the United States, 1882; Martin Van Buren to the End of His Public Career.

About: Bassett, J. S. The Middle Group of American Historians; Brooks, V. W. The Flowering of New England; Hittell, T. H. George Bancroft and His Services to California; Howe, M. A. D. Life and Letters of George Bancroft; Long, O. W. Literary Pioneers; Century January 1887; Harper's June 1862; Nation January 22, 1891; Outlook July 5, 1902.

BANDELIER, ADOLPH FRANCIS ALPHONSE (August 6, 1840-March 18, 1914), historian and anthropologist, was born in Berne, Switzerland, the son of a Swiss army officer and criminal judge. He attended the Wengern School in Berne, and sailed, in 1848, for the United States with his mother, joining his father in Illinois. As a boy he began a collection of butterflies, minerals, etc.; he was educated at home and then returned to Switzerland, at fifteen, to study geology at the University of Berne. Back in the United States again, he was married to Josephine Huegy in 1860. Following the publication, 1877-79, of his scholarly findings on the ancient Mexicans (*On the Art of War and Mode of Warfare,* etc.) he engaged in archaeological and historical investigations in New Mexico and in Peru. After the death of his wife, at Lima, he was married to Fanny Ritter in 1893.

With her he spent ten years in Bolivia and Peru, and upon returning to New York, in 1903, became associated with the Museum of Natural History. For the Carnegie Institution of Washington he did preliminary research in New Mexico and was then sent to Spain, where he died in 1914.

In his research Bandelier went always directly to the primary sources and for his anthropological notes collected, whenever possible, legendary data, etc., from the surviving aborigines. He was, therefore, in a position to discredit numerous less authoritative writings and to give to his own historical legacy a scholarly significance.

Principal Works: On the Art of War and Mode of Warfare, 1877; On the Distribution and Tenure of Lands, 1878; Final Report of Investigations Among the Indians . . 1890, 1892; The Islands of Titicaca and Koati, 1910.

About: American Anthropologist April-June 1914.

BANNISTER, NATHANIEL HARRINGTON (January 13-November 2, 1847) was a playwright about whose early life little is known. He was born either in Delaware or Baltimore, Md., and made his first appearance on the stage at the age of sixteen as Young Norval in Home's tragedy, *Douglas,* at the Front Street Theatre in Baltimore. His New York début occurred in 1831 at the Chatham Theatre. His popularity as an actor in the South was never equalled in New York. He sold his most successful play, *Putnam: The Iron Son of '76,* a vigorous melodrama about Israel Putnam, for fifty dollars. It was first produced August 5, 1844, ran for seventy-eight consecutive nights at the Bowery Theatre, New York, and was published in Boston about 1859.

In 1838 Bannister appeared in some of his own plays—*The Syracusen Brothers, The Two Spaniards, Gentleman of Lyons: or, The Marriage Contract,* and others. In *The Maine Question* he acted with his wife, Amelia Greene, widow of John Augustus Stone, actor-playwright, whom Bannister married in 1835.

Although he was one of the most prolific of the early dramatists, he derived little financial benefit from his plays, many of which were unpublished. Bannister was primarily interested in dramatizing American characters and his plays probably owed their popularity more to their subject matter than their dramatic value. He died in New York City.

PRINCIPAL WORKS: Gaulantus, 1836; England's Iron Days, 1837; The Gentleman of Lyons: or, The Marriage Contract, 1838; The Three Brothers, 1840; Putnam: The Iron Son of '76, 1859.

ABOUT: Brown, T. A. History of the New York Stage; Ireland, J. N. Recollections of the New York Stage; Ludlow, N. M. Dramatic Life As I Found It.

BARBER, JOHN WARNER (February 2, 1798-June 22, 1885), historian, traveler, and engraver, was born in East Windsor, Conn., the son of Elijah and Mary (Warner) Barber. Not long after the death of his father in 1812, when the support of the family fell largely on young John, he began a seven-year apprenticeship with Abner Reed, a bank-note engraver. Barber worked a while independently before going to New Haven in 1823 to set up a business of his own. In both wood and copperplate engraving his work was hardly more than mediocre, for his interest was not in the achievement of any artistic excellence but in the strengthening, by means of simple pictures, the argument or gospel of the text in question. He drove his horse about the country, stopping intermittently to draw numerous little sketches from which he afterwards made the engravings for his first book, *Historical Scenes in the United States.*

In August 1853 he sailed for Liverpool and after a sojourn principally in England and Scotland he returned in November of the same year with materials for *European Historical Collections.* For a time he was an illustrator for the *New York Independent,* a religious journal; when a number of the subscribers loudly protested against the manner in which he had drawn angels' wings and saints' faces, he continued to send more of the same kind of work despite his publishers' constant refusal, and then shortly brought suit against them for breach of contract.

After a photograph

JOHN W. BARBER

During the years 1856-61, in association with Henry Howe, the historian, he journeyed through all but three of the existing states collecting historical, geographical, and biographical data for his most exhaustive work, *Our Whole Country. . .* This 1500-page two-volume book contained 600 engravings, two-thirds of which Barber himself executed from his original drawings, and an amazing amount of statistical material. Meanwhile he had issued a number of volumes on various Eastern localities as well as *The Loyal West in the Times of the Rebellion* and religious allegories, emblems, etc., including *The Bible Looking-Glass,* which had a remarkable sale in America and was later published in Germany. Some time after the death of his first wife in 1826 he was married to Ruth Green; he had one child by his first wife and five by his second.

During the Civil War he placed his sympathies with the abolitionists; and one of his aids to the temperance cause was the preparation of some odd and cleverly illustrated charts bearing very obvious propaganda. So sunny and cheerful was Barber's manner that Henry Howe said of him " . . . no crowned monarch hath such peace"; and his gravity and dignity, said George L. Fox, made him "a figure of lost years." His work as an engraver was remarkable only perhaps for its quantity; his writings, which in sum were a kind of tremendous local history, can still be read for their odd bits of information and antiquarian flavor.

PRINCIPAL WORKS: Historical Scenes in the United States, 1827; New England Scenes, 1833; Elements of General History, 1844; The Dance of Death, 1846; European Historical Collections, 1855; The Loyal West in the Time of the Rebellion, 1865; Religious Allegories, 1866; The Picture Preacher, 1880.

ABOUT: Linton, W. J. A History of Wood Engraving in America; Nash, C. C. John Warner Barber and His Books; Stauffer, D. M. American Engravers on Copper and Steel; New Haven Evening Register June 22, 1885.

BARKER, JAMES NELSON (June 17, 1784-March 9, 1858), dramatist, was born in Philadelphia where his father John Barker, a general in the American Revolution, was alderman and mayor. He received, however, only a common school education, and does not seem to have been much of a student. From early youth his twin interests were politics (on the Democratic side) and the stage.

In 1807 his first play, *Tears and Smiles,* a comedy of Philadelphia manners, was produced. *The Embargo* (a political play) followed in 1808, and in the same year *The Indian Princess: or, La Belle Sauvage.* This drama, founded on the story of Pocahontas, was the first American play on an Indian subject, and also the first play, first performed in America, to be acted later in England.

In 1810 Barker went to Washington to make a first-hand study of governmental administration (actually, it appears, to be near the source of political preferment), and this city later became his home. In 1811 he married Mary Rogers, sister of a well known Connecticut painter, against the opposition of his father; they seem, however, to have become reconciled later.

When the War of 1812 broke out, Barker, who had just seen the successful production of his *Marmion,* adapted from Scott's poem (for his growing political interests by no means retarded his dramatic production), enlisted, became a captain in service on the Canadian frontier, and did not return until 1817, by which time he was assistant adjutant general with the rank of major. His dual career immediately recommenced: in 1817 his *Armourer's Escape* appeared for the first time on the stage, and in the same year he succeeded his father as alderman. In 1819 he was elected mayor of Philadelphia, and was noted for his philanthropies while in office.

He continued to write—articles on dramatic criticism, biographies of Jay and Clinton, and more plays. In fact, *Superstition,* produced in 1824, was not only Barker's own best play, but perhaps the best written in America up to that date. It dealt with Puritan days in New England. Meanwhile his undistinguished poems appeared regularly in the then popular annuals.

In 1829 Jackson appointed him Collector of the Port of Philadelphia, and his duties in this position, which he held until 1838, lessened his literary output. Although *The Court of Love* was produced in 1836, it had been written in 1817, as *How to Try a Lover.*

In 1838 Van Buren made Barker Comptroller of the Treasury. He does not seem to have been adequate to the duties of this very important office and soon resigned, but he served in the Treasury as acting comptroller, and then as clerk, to the time of his death twenty years later. During these last years in Washington Barker practically ceased to write, except for a few prologues to other dramatists' plays.

Five of Barker's plays have appeared in printed form, in collections, as well as some adaptations of English and French comedies. His work is now almost forgotten, however, though *Superstition* at least has genuine merit, and *The Indian Princess* possesses at any rate a lasting historical interest.

Principal Works: Tears and Smiles, 1807; The Embargo, 1808; The Indian Princess: or, La Belle Sauvage, 1808; Marmion, 1812; The Armourer's Escape, 1817; Superstition, 1824; The Court of Love, 1836. (The Spanish Rover, published 1804, never produced.)

About: Quinn, A. H. History of the American Drama; Simpson, H. Lives of Eminent Philadelphians.

BARLOW, JOEL (March 24, 1754-December 24, 1812), poet, was born in Reddington, Conn., the son of Samuel Barlow and Esther (Hull) Barlow, and was reared on a farm nearby. After a short period in preparatory school, and two months at Dartmouth College, he went to Yale. From the beginning he was a rebel against the rigid curriculum of the time, and his versatility and appetite for experience were evident in early youth. Though he took time out during his vacations to serve as a soldier in the rather haphazard Revolutionary Army, he secured his B.A. degree in 1778. He settled in Hartford, where with Alsop, Trumbull, and the Dwights, he became one of the group known as "the Hartford wits"; he was indeed the principal contributor to their joint production, the *Anarchiad.* At the same time he taught school, ran a stationery business, published a magazine, and studied for the bar. The magazine was the *American Mercury,* as ebullient a publication for its day as was once its modern namesake. Rather remarkably he served also (though he seems never to have been ordained as a clergyman) as chaplain of the Fourth Massachusetts Brigade.

Meanwhile his grandiose dithyramb in fake Miltonic verse, *The Vision of Columbus,* was coming out, part by part. Literary fame was easy to acquire in America in the late eighteenth century, and Barlow became

After a portrait by R. Fulton
JOEL BARLOW

at least locally renowned. But, though he had been admitted to the bar in 1786, he was a failure as a lawyer, and he could not live by verse. He became an associate of the Ohio Company, formed to encourage foreign and particularly French immigration to Ohio; and in 1788 he went to France as agent of a similar organization, the Scioto Company, which he does not appear to have known to be an arrant fraud. In 1781 he had married Ruth Baldwin, and his wife soon followed him abroad. The company was exposed and disbanded, though no personal blame attached to Barlow. Undaunted, he went to London to live by writing and on his wits.

In England he met and became friendly with Thomas Paine and Joseph Priestley, the great chemist, who was also a Unitarian minister and a radical reformer. Barlow, who had been a natural rebel—though chiefly a cheerful, gregarious egotist—gradually became transformed into a serious and fervent radical in politics and religion. He moved to France, was made a French citizen in 1792, and was active in the early days of the French Revolution. He lived still by writing, often in French as well as in English, and was the first translator of Volney's famous *Ruins of Empire*. He was also the publisher of Paine's *Age of Reason*. Also, he became exceedingly wealthy through judicious investment in French consols.

He returned to America a rich man, and much more of a personality, with his only good poem, *Hasty Pudding*, and some first-rate political prose to his credit. In 1795 he proved himself to be a statesman as well. Sent to Algiers as consul, he secured the freedom of Americans taken prisoner there, and negotiated treaties with Tunis, Algiers, and Tripoli. In 1805 he returned to America once more, with the intention of retiring. He interested himself as always in many things: he was one of the first backers of Robert Fulton's steamboat, and Fulton, an artist by profession, painted his benefactor's portrait in gratitude. He set to work on a history of the United States.

But he was quite uncured of his poetic delusion, and in his leisure hours he proceeded to turn the already inflated *Vision of Columbus* into twice as long and three times as tedious a near-epic, *The Columbiad*. This verse monstrosity—which nevertheless conceals in its turgid depths a few fine lines—appeared in 1807.

Barlow considered his public career closed, but Madison appointed him minister to France in 1811. His primary mission was to negotiate a trade treaty with Napoleon, who was then conducting his Russian campaign. With characteristic energy, he set out in 1812 to interview the emperor in Poland. After waiting in vain for over a month near Cracow, he started to return to Paris, in the midst of winter. He was caught in the disastrous retreat from Moscow, and the day before Christmas he died as a result of hardship and exposure. He was buried in Poland; relatives endeavored to have his body brought back to America, but conditions were too unsettled, and in later years neither individuals nor the United States government have cared enough about Barlow to incur the necessary effort and expense.

Barlow's only readable poem was the light-hearted mock pastoral, *Hasty Pudding*, based on nostalgic memories of New England while he was an exile in France. His serious poetic efforts are execrable. But he wrote a vigorous prose, almost as good as Paine's in the same *genre*; and as a character he was one of the most interesting and likable men of his time.

PRINCIPAL WORKS: *Poetry*—An Elegy on the Late Hon. Titus Homer, Esq., 1782; Dr. Watts' Imitation of the Psalms of David: Corrected and Enlarged, 1785; The Vision of Columbus, 1787; The Conspiracy of Kings, 1792; Hasty Pudding, 1796; The Columbiad, 1807. *Prose*—A Letter to the National Convention of France, 1792; Advice to the Privileged Orders, 1792; A View of the Public Debt . . . of the United States, 1800.

ABOUT: Todd, C. B. Life and Letters of Joel Barlow; Tyler, M. C. Three Men of Letters; Zunder, T. A. The Early Days of Joel Barlow.

BARNARD, HENRY (January 24, 1811-1900), educator and editor, was born in Hartford, Conn., the son of Chauncy and Elizabeth (Andrus) Barnard. He prepared for college at Monson, Mass., and the Hopkins Grammar School in Hartford, and was graduated from Yale with honors in 1830. His interest in educational improvement began during his student days and his literary and oratorical talents were evident. Leaving college, he resolved to devote himself to public service and turned to the legal profession, for which he prepared himself in New York City and Hartford. He was admitted to the bar in 1835, but before establishing a practice, traveled in Europe, where he investigated the Fellenbergh School, discussed education with Lord Brougham, and made the acquaintance of Carlyle, De Quincey, Wordsworth, and Lockhart.

From 1830 to 1842 Barnard was secretary of the board of school commissioners in Connecticut, and from 1842 to 1849 was school commissioner of Rhode Island. Meanwhile his reputation had spread, and his educational reports were read in Europe as well as America. He became a popular speaker and addressed gatherings throughout the United States. On one of his tours he met Josephine Desnoyers of Detroit, whom he married September 6, 1847.

By 1849 Barnard's importance in the educational field was unquestionable. Two colleges offered him professorships, and he declined four school superintendencies in large cities and the presidencies of the then frontier universities of Indiana and Michigan. Connecticut again enlisted his services, and he was elected principal of the Normal School at New Britain and superintendent of the common schools of the state. Resigning in 1855, he founded the *American Journal of Education,* which he continued to edit until 1882.

Collection of Frederick H. Meserve
HENRY BARNARD

From 1858 to 1860 he was chancellor of the University of Wisconsin. In 1866 he accepted the presidency of St. John's College, Annapolis, Md., but resigned to become the first United States Commissioner of Education, an office which he effectively held for three years, after which he retired to Hartford, where he died at the age of eighty-nine.

Unostentatious, generous, ever devoted to his work, in his later years Barnard was a venerable old man with white hair, a long flowing beard, and serene countenance. He was extremely fond of animals and devoted his leisure hours to reading and gardening.

During Barnard's early stay in Rhode Island, he issued the *Rhode Island School Journal,* and during office as secretary of the Connecticut school board founded the *Connecticut Common School Journal.* His greatest contribution to literature, however, was the *American Journal of Education* of which the *Cambridge History of American Literature* says: "No other educational periodical so voluminous and exhaustive has issued from either private or public sources. It will ever constitute a mine of information concerning this and earlier periods in both Europe and America." In the educational development of America, Barnard ranks as a leader and shares honors with Horace Mann.

Principal Works: History of the Legislation of Connecticut Respecting Common Schools, 1853; School Architecture, 1854.

About: Monroe, W. S. Educational Labors of Henry Barnard; National Educational Association Proceedings 1901; U. S. Bureau of Education Bulletin 1919.

BARNES, CHARLOTTE MARY SANFORD (1818-April 14, 1863), actress and playwright, was the daughter of John and Mary (Greenhill) Barnes, English actors, who first appeared at the Park Theatre, New York, in April 1816, where John Barnes was a popular low comedian and Mrs. Barnes was the leading dramatic actress. Charlotte was brought on the stage at the age of three in *The Castle Spectre,* and later made her début in the part of Angelo in the same play at the Tremont Theatre in Boston, and in New York City, March 29, 1834. In the same year she played Juliet to her mother's Romeo, and attempted other ambitious roles. In 1842 she visited England where her interpretation of Hamlet had a good reception. Returning in 1846, she married Edmond S. Connor, a well-known actor manager, and in 1847 became leading lady in his company at the Arch Street Theatre in Philadelphia.

Charlotte Barnes appeared in the title rôle of her first original play—*Octavia Bragaldi: or, The Confession*—at the National Theatre, New York, November 8, 1837. It was a romantic tragedy in blank verse based on a murder which occurred in Frankfort, Ky., when Colonel Jeroboam O. Beauchamp killed Colonel Solomon P. Sharp, solicitor-general of Kentucky, on the discovery that the latter had seduced his wife before her marriage. It was a theme which had interested both T. H. Chivers—*Conrad and Eudora*, 1834—and Edgar Allan Poe in his unfinished tragedy *Politian* (first published 1923), but Charlotte Barnes' play, written at the age of eighteen, was the first to be acted. She transferred the scene to Milan in the fifteenth century and exhibited much skill in surrounding the plot with romantic and glamorous atmosphere. She acted in the play successfully in England and America; it drew large audiences as late as 1854. A long list of adaptations followed.

Because of certain defects in eyes, voice, and figure, Charlotte Barnes never achieved her mother's reputation as an actress, but as a playwright she won a permanent place for herself in early American theatrical history.

PRINCIPAL WORKS: Octavia Bragaldi: or, The Confession; Lafitte, 1838; The Forest Princess: or, Two Centuries Ago, 1848; Plays, Prose, and Poetry, 1848; A Night of Expectations, 1850; Charlotte Corday, 1851.

ABOUT: Quinn, A. H. History of the American Drama; Rees, J. Dramatic Authors of America.

BARR, MRS. AMELIA EDITH (HUDDLESTON) (March 29, 1831-March 10, 1919), novelist, was born in Ulverston, Lancashire, England, the daughter of William Henry Huddleston, a Methodist minister, and his wife Mary. Her schooling was rather desultory, in various small private schools, until at sixteen she was forced by her father's loss of money to become a teacher. After a short time in a country school she went to the High School in Glasgow for further preparation for her profession. There she met a young merchant, Robert Barr, whom she married in 1850 against the opposition of his Scottish family, who resented his marrying an English girl and a poor one at that.

During a visit made to Glasgow by Henry Ward Beecher and his sister, Harriet Beecher Stowe, they met the Barrs and suggested that they emigrate to America. When, a year or so later, Barr became bankrupt, they acted on the suggestion, leaving Scotland permanently in 1853. They settled first in Chicago, but soon went to Texas, where the husband acted as accountant on the financial records of the Texas Republic which antedated the state of Texas. During a yellow fever epidemic in Galveston in 1867, Barr and three of their sons, one of them newborn, died. Of their thirteen children, of whom only nine had lived beyond their first days, there were now left with the widow only three daughters. She tried to support them by running a boarding house, but it was a failure. The next year she arrived in New York with three young children and exactly $5.18.

AMELIA E. BARR
1880

True to his promise, Beecher helped her, encouraging her to write and publishing her first offerings in his paper, the *Christian Union* (later the *Outlook*). Mrs. Barr began her career as a novelist in 1872, but it was not until the publication of *Jan Vedder's Wife*, in 1885, that she achieved popularity or prosperity. The habits formed in these years of heroic struggle persisted, and she continued until her last years to pour out from one to three novels annually. Many of these had historical backgrounds, particularly dealing with English provincial history and that of Texas and of New York City. In all, her books numbered seventy-five or more, and she herself lost count of them. She died at eighty-eight at a daughter's home in New York.

Highly romantic and sentimental, Mrs. Barr's novels were all written in haste and are extremely superficial. She was popular with the mothers of young girls of the '80s and '90s, because her work could be relied on always to be "clean" and "wholesome." She was not only deeply religious, but also had a strong strain of superstition (she believed implicitly in reincarnation, astrology, and palmistry), and this characteristic also appears in her books. But she had a genuine gift for pleasing narrative and apt description, and her real interest in history, especially in the struggle for liberty in America and England, made many of her novels worth reading for the historical matter they contained. None of her many books, however, is destined long to survive her.

PRINCIPAL WORKS: *Novels*—Romance and Reality, 1872; Jan Vedder's Wife, 1885; A Bow of Orange Ribbon, 1886; A Daughter of Fife, 1886; A Border Shepherdess, 1887; Christopher and Other Stories, 1888; Prisoners of Conscience, 1897; Friend Olivia, 1898; Remember the Alamo, 1898; Trinity Bells, 1899; The Maid of Maiden Lane, 1900; A Song of a Single Note, 1902; The Belle of Bowling Green, 1904; The Strawberry Handkerchief, 1908; The Hands of Compulsion, 1909; Playing With Fire, 1914; The Measure of a Man. 1915; The Winning of Lucia, 1915; Christine, 1916; Profit and Loss, 1916; Joan, 1916; An Orkney Maid, 1917; The Paper Cap, 1918. *Non-Fiction*—All the Days of My Life, 1913; Three Score and Ten: A Book for the Aged, 1915; Songs in the Common Chord (poems) 1919.

ABOUT: Barr, A. E. All the Days of My Life; Bookman May 1920; Nation August 14, 1913; Review of Reviews May 1919.

BARTLETT, JOHN (June 14, 1820-December 3, 1905), lexicographer and publisher, was born in Plymouth, Mass., the son of William Bartlett and Susan (Thacher) Bartlett. After a public school education he became an employee in the University Book Store in Cambridge. The access to books, and acquaintance with Harvard professors, made the book store his university. He soon showed the results of his constant study, until the usual reply to any question in the store was "Ask John Bartlett." From a commonplace book he began to keep at this time grew the famous and still invaluable *Familiar Quotations*, known to thousands of students as "Bartlett's."

In 1862 and 1863 Bartlett served as a volunteer paymaster in the South Atlantic Squadron of the Navy. He then entered the employ of Little, Brown & Co., the Boston publishers, became a partner in 1865, and senior partner in 1878. In 1851 he had married Hannah Stanifield Willard, daughter of the professor of Hebrew at Harvard, and she was of the greatest help to him in his work. She died in 1904; they had no

JOHN BARTLETT

children. Bartlett resigned in 1889 to devote himself entirely to editing and writing. After his wife's death he never left his house. In earlier and more active years he had been a keen fisherman, and shared with his friend James Russell Lowell an interest in whist and chess. Though he never entered a college, Bartlett was given an honorary M.A. by Harvard, and was elected to the American Academy of Arts and Sciences.

Bartlett's Shakespeare concordance is still the best and most detailed in existence. His *Familiar Quotations* ran through nine editions in his lifetime and was enlarged and revised in 1914 by Nathan Haskell Dole and again in 1937 by Christopher Morley and Louella D. Everett.

PRINCIPAL WORKS: Familiar Quotations, 1855; New Method of Chess Notation, 1857; Shakespeare Phrase Book, 1882; New and Complete Concordance of Shakespeare, 1894.

ABOUT: Higginson, T. W. Carlyle's Laugh and Other Surprises; American Academy of Arts and Sciences Proceedings 1906; Boston Transcript December 4, 1905.

BARTLETT, JOHN RUSSELL (October 23, 1805-May 28, 1886), antiquarian and bibliographer, was born in Providence, R.I., the son of Smith Bartlett and Nancy (Russell) Bartlett. He was educated in the Canadian cities of Kingston and Montreal, and later attended the academy at Somerville, N.Y. Returning to Providence in 1824 he clerked for a time in his uncle's drygoods store but left to enter a banking house where he remained for nine years. During this time his intellectual pursuits led him to active membership in the Franklin Society, established for the study of natural sciences, the Rhode Island Historical Society, and the Providence Athenaeum, which he was instrumental in founding in 1831.

Bartlett moved to New York City in 1836. After a brief association with a commission house, he opened a bookstore with Charles Welford for the importation and sale of choice foreign works. Both partners were distinguished bibliophiles and their bookstore became the rendezvous of prominent literary men, including Albert Gallatin with whom Bartlett formed the American Ethnological Society. Bartlett not only assisted scholars in important historical research, but began to publish his own writings. His well-known *Dictionary of Americanisms* appeared in 1848, went into four editions, and was published in Dutch and German.

In 1850 President Taylor appointed Bartlett United States Commissioner to determine the boundary line between the United States and Mexico, under the Treaty of Guadalupe Hidalgo. Serving for three years, he made extensive surveys and explorations in the Southwest and in 1854 published his observations in two volumes entitled *Personal Narrative of Explorations and Incidents Connected With the United States and Mexican Boundary Commission.*

Elected secretary of state in Rhode Island in 1855, he held office for seventeen years, served as acting governor for one year, and during his administration arranged and edited a two hundred-year accumulation of state records, causing them to be bound into ninety-two volumes and twenty-eight portfolios.

Bartlett was twice married, first on May 15, 1831, to Eliza Allen Rhodes, who died in 1853; and second, November 12, 1863, to Ellen Eddy. In his later years he aided John Carter Brown in the acquisition of Brown's noted collection of books, and from 1865 to 1882 published the *John Carter Brown Catalogue*, a monumental bibliography of early Americana, in four volumes. It is still regarded as an indispensable guide to students of early American history. In the field of historical and ethnological research, Bartlett contributed works of inestimable value.

Principal Works: Progress of Ethnology, 1847; Dictionary of Americanisms, 1848; Reminiscences of Albert Gallatin, 1849; Personal Narrative of Explorations and Incidents Connected With the United States and Mexican Boundary Commission, 1854.

About: Gammell, W. Life and Services of John Russell Bartlett; Proceedings of the American Antiquarian Society, October 1886; Providence Journal May 29, 1886.

BARTON, BENJAMIN SMITH (February 10, 1766-December 19, 1815), physician and naturalist, was born at Lancaster, Pa., the son of Thomas Barton, an Episcopalian minister, and Esther (Rittenhouse) Barton. His parents died before he was fifteen, leaving him financially secure and with a strong intellectual heritage. He entered an academy at York, Pa., in 1880 and while pursuing classical studies developed an interest in natural history which he stimulated by collecting plants and insects and watching birds in his spare time. He had a talent for drawing which aided him in recording his observations.

After four years at the College of Philadelphia, he studied medicine at Edinburgh and London, where he became a member of the Royal Medical Society and won a Harveian prize. In 1789 he received his M.D. degree at Göttingen. Returning to Philadelphia, he practiced medicine and taught at the College of Philadelphia which was united with the University in 1791. In 1790 he became professor of natural history and botany, later transferring to the chair of theory and practice of medicine.

Barton married Mary Pennington of Philadelphia in 1797. His son, Thomas Pennant Barton, became the first important American collector of Shakespeariana. Benjamin Barton was an indefatigable worker, and his late hours finally impaired his health, causing him to succumb to tuberculosis at the age of forty-nine.

He wrote treatises on natural history and medicine, chief among which are *Collections for an Essay Towards a Materia Medica of the United States*, 1798-1804, and *Elements of Botany*, the first elementary botany written by an American. In his writings he was more concerned with facts than literary style.

Principal Works: Collections for an Essay Towards a Materia Medica of the United States, 1798-1804; Memoir Concerning the Fascinating Faculty Which Has Been Ascribed to the Rattlesnake and Other American Serpents, 1796; New Views of the Origin of the Tribes and Nations of America, 1797; Fragments of the Natural History of Pennsylvania, 1799; Elements of Botany, 1803.

About: Barton, W. P. C. A Biographical Sketch of Professor Barton; Harshberger, J. W. The Botanists of Philadelphia and Their Work; Kelly, H. A. Some American Medical Botanists; Thacher, J. American Medical Biography; Port Folio April 1816.

BARTRAM, JOHN (March 23, 1699-September 22, 1777), naturalist, was born near Darby, Pa., (now a suburb of Philadelphia), of Quaker parents, William Bartram and Elizabeth (Hunt) Bartram. He was largely self-taught, his interest in botany having manifested itself in boyhood. He is said to have hired a tutor to teach him Latin so that he could read Linnaeus. He became a master of general information of a type impossible in modern times; he served at times as physician, pharmacist, and lawyer without any professional qualifications but with marked success; and he was in addition a practical stone mason and builder.

In 1728 he bought a plot of land at Kingsessing, on the Schuylkill River (now contained within the city limits of Philadelphia). Here he remained for the rest of his life and here performed the first hybridizing experiments in America. He built his own stone houses, two of which still stand as part of the city park system. In 1733 he began his long correspondence with the English botanist Peter Collinson, for whom he acted as a collector of American plants and seeds. Bartram's letters to Collinson form a source book for the introduction of European plants into America. His collecting tours took him to every part of the then frontier, first alone, and in later years with his even more celebrated son William [*q.v.*]. On the side, as it were, he also collected shells, birds, insects, fish, and turtles, which William drew. He was besides a pioneer in geology, with surprisingly accurate views of the actual nature of fossils; he was the first advocate of deep-sea soundings; and he suggested to Franklin the exploration which later was carried on, under Jefferson, by Lewis and Clark. Famous scientists came to his little Pennsylvania estate from all over the world; the great Linnaeus, indeed, called him the best "natural botanist" of his time. He was indisputably the first native-born American botanist. In 1743 he became an original member of Franklin's American Philosophical Society.

In 1723 he married Mary Morris, who died in 1727, leaving two sons. Two years later he married Ann Mendenhall, by whom he had four daughters and five sons, one of whom was William. A tall, erect man of great dignity, he had strong convictions, some of which caused him later to be read out of the Friends' Meeting. He detested slavery, and not only freed his own slaves, but had the freedmen eat regularly at his table with his family and guests. In Bartram's Gardens may be seen still the grave of one of these emancipated slaves who spent all their lives in Bartram's service and on his bounty. In 1765 Collinson managed to have Bartram named botanist to the king, with a small pension attached to the office. To celebrate his new dignity he made his farthest journey, to Florida, where he became the first to discover and describe the royal palm. A genus of mosses is named Bartramia in his honor.

It will be seen that Bartram was not primarily a writer, but in his letters and in the two volumes of descriptions of his travels he displays an aptitude for clear and homely narrative that might be expected of one so versatile and yet so sound. A great deal of his writings remains still in manuscript form in various libraries and museums.

PRINCIPAL WORKS: Observations on the Inhabitants, Climate, Soil, etc. . . . From Pensilvania to Lake Ontario, 1751; Description of Eastern Florida, 1769.

ABOUT: Darlington, W. Memorials of John Bartram and Humphrey Marshall; Youmans, W. J. Pioneers of Science in America.

BARTRAM, WILLIAM (February 9, 1739-July 22, 1823), naturalist and travel writer, was the son of John Bartram [*q.v.*], the pioneer American botanist, and his second wife Ann (Mendenhall) Bartram. He was born on his father's estate and experimental farm at Kingsessing, Pa. (now part of Philadelphia). He had a twin sister, and is therefore one of the few twins to become distinguished persons.

Formally Bartram had little education, but a father so well read and so talented as his afforded constant schooling of the best sort. The boy displayed a marked talent for drawing and he was encouraged to develop it, though he had only a few actual lessons. At eighteen he was apprenticed to a merchant, and four years later set up for himself as an independent trader at Cape Fear, N.C. But his mercantile career was brief. By 1765 he had returned to his father's home, and during that year and the next he went on the first of his exploring and collecting tours with the older botanist, up St. John's River. In 1767 he settled on a farm of his own nearby, but this too was a mere interruption to his real career. By 1773 he had started his own explorations, which continued for four years and covered all the Southeastern portion of the country. Bartram was interested not only in plants or even nature, but was keenly alive also (more even than his father had been) to the human beings he met on his journeys. He became the first real student of the American Indians and was accepted by them as one of themselves. The Seminoles knew him always as Puc-puggy, the Flower Hunter.

When the elder Bartram died in 1777, William's brother John inherited the Gardens, and William acted as his partner. His

After a portrait by C. W. Peale
WILLIAM BARTRAM

brother died and left the Gardens to his daughter, with whom William Bartram lived thenceforth. In 1782 the University of Pennsylvania offered to make him its professor of botany, but he declined on the ground of poor health; though he was always frail, and his journeys were miracles of endurance for one of his small and slight physique, the real reason for his refusal was an excruciating shyness. Probably the same trait accounts for his never having married. He was, however, a sweet-natured, affectionate man, much beloved by his family and friends. He was all his life a devout Quaker, retiring and modest and unnoticed except for such harmless eccentricities as his habit of always dressing in leather from head to foot.

Yet this quiet, retiring man was not only one of the foremost botanists of his day, but also one of its greatest literary influences. His botanical work was for the most part contributed to B. S. Barton's *Philadelphia Medical and Physical Journal.* He also compiled a list of 215 native birds, the most extensive one made before the days of Alexander Wilson, who named Bartram's Sandpiper after him in recognition. In 1786 he became a member of the American Philosophical Society, but this seems to have been the only scientific acclaim he received.

His books of travel, however, especially the second and last, were the sources of inspiration for a generation of writers. Men as far apart in literary interest and field as Chateaubriand, Rousseau, Coleridge, and Wordsworth drew from Bartram their descriptions of the American wilderness and its aboriginal inhabitants, and based on his account their whole picture of "the noble savage" and his New World environment. Meanwhile the father of this school of romantic theory continued to live quietly with his niece in his Pennsylvania garden, working humbly at the experiments his father had initiated. One summer day he finished writing the description of a plant and stepped out into the garden; and there on the threshhold the old man of eighty-four dropped dead of heart failure.

Principal Works: Observations on the Creek and Cherokee Indians, 1789; Travels Through North and South Carolina, Georgia, East and West Florida, etc., 1791.

About: Fagin, N. B. William Bartram: Interpreter of the American Landscape.

BASCOM, JOHN (May 1, 1827-October 2, 1911), philosopher, was born in Genoa, N.Y., son of the Rev. John Bascom, a Presbyterian minister who died when Bascom was a small child, and Laura (Woodbridge) Bascom. An elder sister helped him to secure an education, and he was graduated from Williams College in 1849. After a year of teaching at Hoosick Falls, N.Y., he studied law, then in 1851 entered Auburn Theological Seminary. The next year he acted as tutor of rhetoric and oratory at Williams, and married Abbie Burt, who died in 1854. Bascom next entered Andover Theological Seminary, but a year later found him back at Williams as professor of rhetoric and oratory—both of which, and teaching as a whole, were most distasteful to him. In 1856 he married Emma Curtiss.

Bascom stayed at Williams until 1874, alleviating his hatred of his profession by the writing of magazine articles. Then he was elected president of the University of Wisconsin. He remained there until 1887, resigning then because of conflict with the Republican politician who was "boss" of the state and because his advocacy of prohibition was offensive to a community which owed its prosperity largely to brewing. Bad investments had reduced him to poverty, and he was forced to return to lecturing, on sociology this time, at Williams. In 1891 he became professor of political science. He was able to resign in 1903.

In revolt against the extreme Calvinism of his upbringing, Bascom became a quasi-Rationalist. He was not, however, actually a Free Thinker, but a "harmonizer" of science and religion. He has had little influence on philosophical trends, but his clear and attractive style served to popularize his many volumes.

Principal Works: Political Economy, 1859; Aesthetics: or, The Science of Beauty, 1862; Philosophy of Rhetoric, 1866; Principles of Psychology, 1869 (as Science of Mind, 1881); Science, Philosophy, and Religion, 1871; Philosophy of English Literature, 1874; Philosophy of Religion, 1876; Ethics: or, The Science of Duty, 1879; Natural Theology, 1880; Problems in Philosophy, 1885; The New Theology, 1891; Historical Interpretation of Philosophy, 1893; Social Theory, 1895; Evolution and Religion, 1897; Growth of Nationality in the United States, 1899; God and His Goodness, 1901; Things Learned by Living, 1913.

About: Bascom, J. Things Learned by Living; Robinson, S. John Bascom: Prophet.

BATEMAN, MRS. SIDNEY FRANCES (COWELL) (March 29, 1823-January 13, 1881), playwright, actress, and manager, was born Sidney Frances Cowell in an unidentified town in New Jersey. Her mother, Frances (Sheppard) Cowell died shortly after Sidney's birth and she was brought up by her father, Joseph Cowell, an English actor, whose original name was Witchett. She made her first appearance on the stage in New Orleans in 1837 and two years later married Hezekiah Linthicum Bateman, an actor-manager in St. Louis, Mo.

In 1856 Mrs. Bateman anonymously produced *Self,* a social satire, at Bateman's St. Louis Theatre. The play had a long run and was followed by another success: *Geraldine: or, Love's Victory,* produced at Wallack's Theatre, New York City, in 1859. It was later played in London as *Geraldine: or, The Master Passion.* The following year Mrs. Bateman dramatized Longfellow's poem *Evangeline,* and her daughter Kate appeared in the title rôle. In 1863 the Bateman family moved to England where Kate had made an enormous success in *Leah the Forsaken.* With a company which included Henry Irving, Mr. and Mrs. Bateman became joint-managers of the Lyceum Theatre in London in 1871. *Fanchette: or, The Will o'-the Wisp,* Mrs. Bateman's adaptation of *Die Grille,* was produced in the same year. After her husband's death in 1875, she continued to manage the theatre until Irving took over the lease three years later and she rebuilt Sadler's Wells Theatre, managing it with remarkable business acumen and reviving the reputation it had enjoyed under Samuel Phelps. With Joaquin Miller's *The Danites,* in 1880 she presented to an English audience the first entire American company in an American play. Although she appeared on the stage many times, Mrs. Bateman's ability rested in playwriting and stage management rather than acting. Her extensive knowledge of theatrical technique, unflagging energy, and willingness to develop any idea, however ambitious, earned her a small but secure place among nineteenth century dramatists.

Principal Works: Self, 1856; Geraldine: or, Love's Victory, 1859; Evangeline, 1860; Fanchette: or, The Will o'-the Wisp, 1871.

About: Hutton, L. Curiosities of the American Stage; Academy January 22, 1881; London Times January 14, 17, 18, 1881.

BATES, ARLO (December 16, 1850-August 24, 1918), novelist, poet, and teacher, was born in East Machias, Maine, the son of Dr. Niran Bates, a physician who had literary leanings, and Susan (Thaxter) Bates. He was educated at Washington Academy and proceeded to Bowdoin College, securing his B.S. in 1876 and his M.A. in 1879. In 1894 the college conferred an honorary Litt.D. on him.

Bates began writing while he was still in college. On his graduation he went to Boston and for a year lived the classic life of the poor unknown young author—living in a garret, starving, and tutoring or painting china to eke out his living. In 1878 he became, through friends, secretary of a Republican club, and edited its organ, the *Broadside.* For a while also he worked as clerk in a metal works. He was rescued by becoming editor, in 1880, of the Boston *Sunday Courier,* a position he held until 1893. This was the period of most of his creative literary output. In 1882 he married Harriet L. Vose, herself a writer under the pseudonym of

ARLO BATES

"Eleanor Putnam." This happy marriage, marked by one book written in collaboration, was ended four years later by the death of his wife. All his volumes of poetry thereafter were dedicated to her memory.

In 1893 Bates became professor of English at the Massachusetts Institute of Technology. The greater part of his energy which was not given to teaching after this time went to the production of text-books, though he continued to write poetry and even some fiction. He became well known also as a lecturer on literature, having given one series of Lowell Lectures as early as 1895. He resigned in 1915, when he was sixty-five, and died in Boston three years later.

Bates' is now practically a forgotten name, though in his time he had a considerable reputation. His poems and novels were never anything more than urbane and pleasant—with the exception of *Sonnets in Shadow,* a dirge for his dead wife—and they make dull reading now. His text-books, however—though pedestrian—are still useful.

PRINCIPAL WORKS: *Fiction*—Patty's Perversities, 1881; Mr. Jacobs, 1883; The Pagans, 1884; A Wheel of Fire, 1885; A Lad's Love, 1887; Prince Vance (with his wife) 1888; The Philistines, 1889; Albrecht, 1890; A Book o' Nine Tales, 1891; In the Bundle of Time, 1893; The Puritans, 1898; Love in a Cloud, 1900; The Diary of a Saint, 1902; The Intoxicated Ghost, 1908. *Poetry*—Berries of the Brier, 1886; Sonnets in Shadow, 1887; The Poet and His Self, 1891; Told in the Gate, 1892; Under the Beech Tree, 1899; The Torch Bearers, 1894; The Supreme Gift, 1911. *Play*—A Mother's Meeting, 1909. *Text-books*—Talks on the Study of Literature, 1895; Talks on Writing English, 1896 (second series, 1901); Talks on Teaching Literature, 1906.

ABOUT: Literary World June 1904; New England Magazine August 1900; New York Times August 26, 1918.

BAYLOR, FRANCES COURTENAY (January 20, 1848-October 19, 1920), novelist, was born at Fort Smith, Ark., the daughter of James Dawson, an army officer, and Sophie (Baylor) Dawson. Her childhood was spent at various army posts, including San Antonio and New Orleans. About 1865 her mother resumed her maiden name of Baylor (whether the father was dead or his wife left him is uncertain), and took the girl, whose whole education had been from the mother, back to her own early home in Winchester, Va. There, with the other daughter, who had married the Confederate General Walker, they went to England for several years. Returning to America, Miss Baylor, as she was now known, began writing stories for various papers, all under the name of a male relative. Her poems, though never gathered into a volume, were well known in her time; they are nearly all patriotic in nature. In 1896 she married George Sherman Barnum, of Savannah, Ga.; he died soon after, and after a short residence in Lexington, Va., she returned to Winchester, where she spent the rest of her life with her mother and sister and the latter's family. She ceased to write, spending her last quarter century in contemplation of a novel she never even began. She died while reading in the public library.

Imbued with her mother's highly aristocratic and pedantic spirit, Frances Baylor reflected in all her novels (most of them for young people) a combination of earnest bookishness and snobbish superiority. Her principal theme was the common interests and sympathies of the "best people" of America and England. The only exception is *Juan and Juanita,* the most animated but also the most sensational of her books. *Behind the Blue Ridge* is her only novel with an entirely American background.

PRINCIPAL WORKS: On Both Sides, 1885; Behind the Blue Ridge, 1887; Juan and Juanita, 1888; A Shocking Example (short stories) 1889; Claudia Hyde, 1894; Miss Nina Barrow, 1897; The Ladder of Fortune, 1899; A Georgian Bungalow, 1900.

ABOUT: Alderman, E. A. & Harris, J. C. Library of Southern Literature; Gordon, A. C. Jr. Virginian Writers of Fugitive Verse; Critic April 7, 1888.

BEATTY, CHARLES CLINTON (c. 1715-August 13, 1772), Presbyterian clergyman and early writer on Indian affairs, was born in County Antrim, Ireland. His father was a British army officer who died during Charles' childhood. In 1729 his mother brought him to America where, in order to support them both, he became a peddler. While stopping at Log College, Neshaminy, Pa., he was induced by William Tennent, the head master, to study theology, and received his license to preach at Nottingham, Pa., in 1742. The following year he was assigned to the church at Neshaminy, becoming William Tennent's successor as pastor.

Missionary work especially interested him and he enthusiastically supported David Brainerd's attempts to convert the Indians. On June 24, 1746, he married Anne Reading, daughter of the president of the Council of New Jersey and later governor of the province. In 1754 he made a missionary tour to Virginia and North Carolina, and the next year was chaplain to the Pennsylvania troops that defended northwestern Pennsylvania after the massacre of the Moravian missionaries near Lehighton. He was sent to England in 1760 by the synod to solicit funds for the relief of needy Presbyterian ministers and their families, and received a donation from George III. Three years after his return he investigated the condition of the Indian tribes at Duffield. In 1772 he visited the West Indies to raise money for the College of New Jersey, of which he was a trustee. Soon after his arrival in Barbados, he died of yellow fever.

Beatty published the *Journal of a Two Months Tour Among the Frontier Inhabitants of Pennsylvania* in 1768, and other works about Indian affairs. Their importance is mainly historical.

PRINCIPAL WORKS: Double Honour Due to the Laborious Gospel Minister, 1756; Journal of a Two Months Tour Among the Frontier Inhabitants of Pennsylvania, 1768; A Letter to the Rev. John Erskine; Further Remarks Respecting Indian Affairs.

ABOUT: Alexander, A. The Log College; Murphy, T. The Presbytery of the Log College; Smith, J. Old Redstone; Sprague, W. B. Annals of the American Pulpit.

BECK, CHARLES (August 19, 1798-March 19, 1866), classical scholar, was born at Heidelberg, in Baden. His father was a merchant who died when Charles was a child, and his mother married Dr. De Wette, a professor of theology at Heidelberg. Charles enjoyed a happy home-life and absorbed much learning from his kind, intellectual step-father. Studying at the University of Berlin, he majored in the classics and theology, and was ordained at Heidelberg July 7, 1882. The degree of Ph.D. was conferred upon him at Tübingen the following year. A political upheaval caused his step-father to be removed from his professorship and he took his family to Basel where he became associated with the University. After a short service as a lecturer in the same university, Charles Beck sailed to America in 1824 with Dr. Follen, a German political exile, whose radical views Beck shared.

After teaching at the Round Hill School at Northampton, Mass., Beck opened a school in 1830 at Philipstown on the Hudson, opposite West Point, but within two years was elected professor of Latin at Harvard College, where he remained until his retirement eighteen years later.

Beck's personality was well-suited to pedagogic life and he made a place for himself among the distinguished scholars of his generation through his conscientious instruction. Although he was loyal to his adopted country, his enthusiasm for German scholarship considerably influenced American students and led to the popular exodus to German universities. His publications were mainly classical, the best known being a collation and description of the manuscripts of the *Satyricon* of Petronius Arbiter, published in 1863. Beck was married twice: first in 1827 to Louisa A. Henshaw, of Northampton, Mass., who died in 1830 and second to her sister, Mrs. Teresa H. Phillips, in 1831.

PRINCIPAL WORKS: Introduction to the Metres of Horace, 1835; Latin Syntax, 1838; a collation and description of the manuscripts of the *Satyricon* of Petronius Arbiter, 1863.

ABOUT: Peabody, A. P. Harvard Reminiscences; Newell, W. The Christian Citizen: A Discourse Occasioned by the Death of Charles Beck.

"BEDOTT, WIDOW." See WHITCHER, FRANCES MIRIAM (BERRY)

BEECHER, CATHERINE ESTHER (September 6, 1800-May 12, 1878), educator and reformer, was born at East Hampton, Long Island, where her father, the Reverend Lyman Beecher, held the pastorate of the Congregational Church. Of the nine children that her mother, Roxana (Foote) Beecher, bore her husband, three others rose to fame—Henry Ward Beecher, Edward Beecher, and Harriet Beecher Stowe [*qq.v.*]. Catherine was educated at home in a cultured atmosphere until her tenth year when the family moved to Litchfield, Conn., where she attended a private academy for young ladies. Here she was instructed in painting and music, which she later taught in a girls' school in New London, Conn. In 1823 the sudden and tragic death of her fiancé, Professor Alexander Metcalfe Fisher, of Yale College, greatly changed the course of her life. Resolved to find solace in good works, in 1824 she established a small private school for young ladies at Hartford, thereby filling a decided need in the neglected field of education for women. It grew to have 150 pupils and a wide reputation for excellent scholarship. In 1832 she sold her interest and accompanied her father to Cincinnati when he accepted the presidency of Lane Theological Seminary. Here she founded the Western Female Institute, after the pattern of her Hartford school and conducted its affairs until ill health forced her to give it up in 1837.

For the remainder of her life she devoted herself to reform movements for the advancement of women in the educational and professional world and was instrumental in organizing women's colleges in Burlington, Ia., Quincy, Ill., and Milwaukee, Wis. During her long influential career she published a number of books in an effort to bring about much-needed reforms and was a recognized power in the causes she upheld. Although she was a valiant fighter for women's educational rights, she was rigidly opposed to suffrage. She had the crusading character of the Beechers, softened by great personal charm and an infectious wit. Her intelligent leadership is inextricably woven into the history of her era.

PRINCIPAL WORKS: An Essay on Slavery and Abolitionism: With Reference to the Duty of American Females, 1837; A Treatise on Domestic Economy for the Use of Young Ladies at Home and at School, 1841; The Duty of American Women to Their Country, 1845; The Evils Suffered by American Women and American Children: The Causes and the Remedy, 1846; Miss Beecher's Domestic Receipt Book, 1846; Physiology and Calisthenics for Schools and Families, 1856; Woman Suffrage and Woman's Profession, 1871.

ABOUT: Beecher, C. E. Educational Reminiscences and Suggestions; Beecher, L. Autobiography; Stowe, C. E. Life of Harriet Beecher Stowe.

BEECHER, HENRY WARD (June 24, 1813-March 8, 1887), clergyman, orator, editor, and miscellaneous writer, was born in Litchfield, Conn., one of the thirteen children of Lyman Beecher [*q.v.*], the noted divine. His mother was Lyman Beecher's first wife, Roxana (Foote) Beecher, who died when the boy was three. He was sent to various schools, including the one run by his sister Catherine in Hartford, where he was the only boy; but he was considered dull and sluggish until he attended the Mt. Pleasant Classical Institute at Amherst. He was graduated from Amherst College in 1834, and proceeded to Lane Theological Seminary, Cincinnati, of which his father was then president. While he was a divinity student, he wrote for local newspapers and for a time edited the Cincinnati *Journal*, a Presbyterian paper.

In 1837 he was licensed to preach, and was made minister of a small church in Lawrenceburg, Ind., first going East to marry Eunice White Bullard, to whom he had been engaged for several years. They had ten children.

In 1838 Beecher was ordained, and the next year moved to the Second Presbyterian Church, Indianapolis, where he remained until 1847. At the same time he edited the *Western Farmer and Gardener*, being always an enthusiastic gardener. He was gaining a reputation as a pulpit orator, and was twice invited to Boston churches. He liked the West, but finally at his wife's insistence accepted a call to the Plymouth Church (Con-

Collection of Frederick H. Meserve
HENRY WARD BEECHER

gregationalist) in Brooklyn, where he was an immense success. Going to hear Beecher preach was a regular part of visiting New York for most tourists. His sermons were taken down every week—he preached extemporaneously, without notes—and were circulated as printed pamphlets. He also lectured extensively, and was a regular contributor to the *Independent*, of which he was editor from 1861 to 1864. From 1870 to 1881 he edited the *Christian Union*. During the Civil War he toured England in the interest of the North, and is credited with having done much to prevent English allegiance to the Confederate cause. He was never, however, more than a lukewarm abolitionist.

Beecher's prosperous career was halted and permanently marred in 1874 when Theodore Tilton, who had succeeded him as editor of the *Independent*, brought a suit accusing Beecher of adultery with Mrs. Tilton. The scandal rocked Victorian America to its very foundations. The situation was a complicated one, and though the jury disagreed and was dismissed, and Beecher had been previously cleared by his church, the only verdict today can be the Scotch one of "not proven." If he was not guilty of adultery, he was at least guilty of incredible carelessness and foolishness. His reputation never entirely recovered. Moreover, his religious views were not considered sound by other Congregationalists, and in 1882 he withdrew from his denomination's ministerial association.

He died of a cerebral hemorrhage, soon after his return from a second trip to England. It is estimated that 40,000 persons attended his funeral.

Beecher's was primarily an emotional nature, hearty, vital, defiant of convention. His long flowing hair, his ruddy face, his grey-blue eyes under drooping lids, were the indication of the moody, flamboyant, magnetic personality characteristic of the colorful Beecher family. He was not an original thinker, but he was quick-witted and fertile-minded, a man who thought in images, was never at a loss for a phrase, and was embarrassed by the richness of the ideas which came to him. In writing he was graphic, picturesque, and pithy. Even his published sermons were interesting. In spite of his slow start, he was a born orator, and as a writer he imparted life to the dullest subjects.

PRINCIPAL WORKS: Seven Lectures to Young Men, 1844; Star Papers, 1855; New Star Papers, 1859; Plain and Pleasant Talks About Fruits, Flowers and Farming, 1859; Norwood: or, Village Life in New England (fiction) 1867; Life of Jesus the Christ, 1871-91; Yale Lectures on Preaching, 1872-74; Evolution and Religion, 1885.

ABOUT: Abbott, L. Henry Ward Beecher; Barrows, J. H. Henry Ward Beecher: The Shakespeare of the Pulpit; Hibben, P. Henry Ward Beecher: An American Portrait; Rourke, C. M. Trumpets of Jubilee; Stowe, L. B. Saints, Sinners, and Beechers.

BEECHER, LYMAN (October 12, 1775-January 10, 1863), clergyman, was born in New Haven, the son of David Beecher, a blacksmith, and his third wife, Esther (Lyman) Beecher. Lyman Beecher's mother died of tuberculosis when he was two days old, and as his father remarried twice more, he was reared by his uncle in Guilford, Conn. He went to Yale in 1793, where he was much influenced by the famous Timothy Dwight, who was professor of theology as well as president. Later he studied divinity under Dwight, and in 1799 was ordained and became minister of the Presbyterian Church in East Hampton, Long Island. The same year he married Roxana Foote, who died of tuberculosis in 1816, leaving nine children. In 1817 he married Harriet Porter, who died in 1835, leaving four children. His last wife was Mrs. Lydia (Beals) Jackson, who survived him.

In 1810 Beecher was called to the Litchfield, Conn., Presbyterian church. There he became known for his fiery sermons against liquor. He founded and contributed to the *Connecticut Observer*, a Presbyterian publication. In 1826 he went to the Hanover Street Church (Congregationalist) in Boston. A great revival he held there led,

Collection of Frederick H. Meserve

LYMAN BEECHER

through his anti-Catholic sermons, to the sacking of a convent in Charlestown by an enraged mob. In 1832, when Lane Theological Seminary was founded, he was called to be its first president, and also, like Dwight before him, acted as professor of theology. Suspected of heresy, he was tried by the local presbytery and the synod, but was acquitted. The affair, however, led to a schism in the Presbyterian Church in 1837. In 1850 he resigned, and spent the last years of his life with his son Henry Ward Beecher in Brooklyn.

All of Lyman Beecher's sons became ministers. Several of his children attained celebrity; the best known were Henry Ward Beecher and Harriet Beecher Stowe [*qq.v.*].

Like his son Henry after him, Lyman Beecher had a commanding and magnetic personality, and was a person of unconventional tastes and behavior, with a mighty relish for life. His sermons were marked more by eloquence than by discretion or diplomacy—as witness the disastrous episode in Boston. As Constance Rourke says of him, he was "never aware of frustration, never admitting defeat." He was handsome even in old age, with a high intellectual forehead, the wide mouth of the orator, and deep-set eyes above a masterful nose; and even to the last days of his senility in his eighties, his was a vibrant, passionate nature.

Lyman Beecher's sermons and magazine articles were collected and published after his retirement, but he was a better preacher than writer, and they are of small interest to modern readers.

Principal Works: Collected Works, 1852; Autobiography and Correspondence, 1863-64 (ed. by Charles Beecher).

About: Beecher, L. Autobiography and Correspondence; Hayward, E. T. Lyman Beecher; Rourke, C. M. Trumpets of Jubilee; Stowe, L. B. Saints, Sinners, and Beechers; White, J. C. Personal Recollections of Lyman Beecher.

BEERS, ETHEL LYNN (January 13, 1827-October 11, 1879), poet and story writer, was born in Goshen, N.Y. Her maiden name was Ethelinda Eliot. Her father, Horace William Eliot, a druggist, postmaster, and justice of the peace, and a veteran of the War of 1812, was a lineal descendant of John Eliot, the "Apostle to the Indians"; her mother was Keziah (Westcott) Eliot. Her first work was written under the name of "Ethel Lynn," and after her marriage, in 1846, to William H. Beers, of New York, she was known as Ethel Lynn Beers, the "Lynn" being merely a part of her original "Ethelinda."

Mrs. Beers' most famous poem was "All Quiet Along the Potomac," the title and first line of which at least are known to almost every literate American. During the Civil War two Southern writers claimed it as theirs, after a story was printed to the effect that the anonymous verses had been found on the body of a dead Confederate soldier, but she was able to prove that it had been published in *Harper's Magazine*, under the title of "The Picket Guard," in 1861. Certainly neither of the two claimants ever wrote anything else, and Mrs. Beers continued to write verses and stories, principally for the New York *Ledger*. Many of these, unpretentious and sentimental but appealing, became very well known—perhaps the most familiar being "Which Shall It Be?" in which the parents try to choose one of their children to give up for adoption.

Though not given to superstition or melancholy, Mrs. Beers had for years confessed to a premonition that if her poems were ever collected in a volume she would die as soon as they were published. They appeared on October 10, 1879, and the next day she died suddenly—whether as a result of a strange sort of psychological suicide or not will never be known.

Principal Works: General Frankie: A Story for Little Folks, 1863; All Quiet Along the Potomac and Other Poems, 1879.

About: New York Ledger November 8 and 15, 1879; New York Times October 13, 1879.

BEERS, HENRY AUGUSTIN (January 2, 1847-September 7, 1926), educator, the son of George Webster Beers, and Elizabeth Victoria (Clerc) Beers, was born in Buffalo, N.Y., while his parents, natives of Connecticut, were there on a visit. His paternal grandfather was Seth Preston Beers, a prominent Litchfield County lawyer and member of the Connecticut legislature, whose extensive library gave young Beers his first knowledge of New England nature and literature. His mother's parents were both deaf mutes. Educated at the Hartford High School and Yale College, from which he was graduated in 1869, he studied law, and was admitted to the bar in 1870. He had hardly established a practice when he accepted a tutorship in Yale College in 1871, where he remained for the duration of his life as tutor, assistant professor, professor, and professor emeritus. In 1876 he spent a summer and autumn at Heidelberg, studying under Kuno Fischer, and the following year attended Bronson Alcott's School of Philosophy at Concord where he made the acquaintance of Lowell and Emerson.

Beers was excessively modest and refused all honorary degrees, which he justly deserved for his wide knowledge of English literature. He called them "empty honors." He was greatly beloved by the students who regarded him as the personification of Yale tradition.

His writings include poetry, creative prose, and scholarly prose, and he takes his place in American literature with his histories of romanticism in England.

Principal Works: History of English Romanticism in the Eighteenth Century, 1899; History of English Romanticism in the Nineteenth Century, 1901.

About: Osborn, N. G. Men of Mark in Connecticut.

BELKNAP, JEREMY (June 4, 1744-June 20, 1798), historian and clergyman, was born in Boston, where his family had lived since 1637. His given name was Jeremiah, later changed by himself to the more euphonious Jeremy. His father, Josiah Belknap, was a leather dresser and furrier, sufficiently prosperous to send his son to the Boston Latin School and then to Harvard; his mother was Sarah (Byles) Belknap. Jeremy entered college before he was fifteen, being graduated in 1762.

For five years, while he studied for the Congregational ministry, he taught school in Massachusetts and New Hampshire towns, and at the beginning of 1767 he became minister of the church at Dover, N.H. The same year he married Ruth Eliot, daughter

From an old print
JEREMY BELKNAP

of a Boston bookseller. Belknap, with his intellectual interests, was very lonely in Dover; the only congenial companionship he had was with Governor Wentworth, and when the Revolution came that ended, for Wentworth was a Tory. (So were many of the members of Belknap's family; he had two old cousins who used to drink the king's health well into the nineteenth century). He himself sided with the Revolutionists, but his health forbade any active participation, even when he was appointed chaplain of the New Hampshire troops at Cambridge.

For nearly twenty years Belknap struggled with a congregation which begrudged him every penny of his tiny salary, even to firewood. He was so poor he could not send his sons to college, but had to put them out as farm-hands or indenture them to tradesmen. Finally in 1786 he resigned. For a year he preached in various churches, until in 1787 he was called to the Federal Street Church in Boston, where he remained for the rest of his life.

Forced in upon himself, the isolation in Dover made Belknap an historian, though he "had doubts about the propriety of a minister's dabbling in history." His *History of New Hampshire* began to appear in 1784. Once in Boston, he was able to indulge his passion for antiquarianism and the collection of early documents, and he was the leading founder in 1790 of the Antiquarian Society, first of its kind in the United States, which in 1794 was incorporated as the Massachusetts Historical Society, with himself as corresponding secretary. He finished his history; and then published, first in the *Columbian Magazine* of Philadelphia and later in book form, his satirical allegory on the British colonies in America, *The Foresters,* and two volumes of his *American Biography.* This latter work, devoted to the lives of early explorers and leaders, was left unfinished by his sudden death from apoplexy at fifty-four.

Belknap's most important work was the *History of New Hampshire,* which would be more celebrated had it covered a broader field. Even as it was, Bryant said it was the first book "to make American history attractive." It is a complete study to 1789, including the natural history of the region, and is genuinely scholarly, impartial, and written in a style strong, straightforward, and clear. Yet it was a financial failure, and did not even pay its own cost until after the author's death. Belknap, with his friend and classmate Ebenezer Hazard, was also the first collector of original historical papers in America. He wrote a number of theological works of no contemporary interest but evidencing the fact that his history was written in the spare leisure of a busy clergyman. He himself considered the chief honor of his life to have been the conferring on him of a D.D. degree by Harvard in 1792.

PRINCIPAL WORKS: Sermon on Military Duty, 1773; History of New Hampshire, 1784-92; The Foresters, 1792; A Discourse Intended to Commemorate the Discovery of America by Christopher Columbus, 1792; Life of Isaac Watts (anonymous; with Life of Dr. Doddridge, by Andrew Kippis) 1793; American Biography (unfinished) 1794-98; Dissertations on the Character, Death, and Resurrection of Jesus Christ, 1795; Sermon Delivered Before the Convention of the Clergy of Massachusetts, 1796.

ABOUT: Marcou, J. B. Life of Jeremy Belknap; Massachusetts Historical Society Collections: Series 5, Vols. I, II, III; Series 6, Vol. IV; Atlantic Monthly May 1891; Nation May 9, 1878.

BELL, JAMES MADISON (April 3, 1826-1902), Negro poet and lecturer, was born at Gallipolis, Ohio, where he lived until he was sixteen, and then moved to Cincinnati. Making his home with his brother-in-law, George Knight he learned the plasterer's trade. In 1848 he married Louisiana Sanderline, by whom he had several children. Six years later he took his family to Canada to live, remaining until 1860.

Bell was radical in his feeling against slavery, and became the personal friend of John Brown, aiding him in rallying men to participate in the raid of 1859. He went to California in 1860. Here he wrote some of his poems and crusaded against the injustice done the Negroes. In 1865 he settled in Toledo, Ohio, but frequently travelled in the East, encouraging the freedmen and educating them in their civic duties. He was drawn into politics and in 1868 was delegate from Lucas county to the state convention and delegate at large to the national Republican convention that nominated Grant for a second term. He was a gifted speaker and campaigned for Grant on the public platform.

The Poetical Works of James Madison Bell appeared in 1901. His poem "The Day and the War" commemorates John Brown; the style of "The Progress of Liberty" indicates his admiration of Byron. Bell had a pleasing speaking voice and his readings of his own commonplace poems gave them a greater distinction than they actually possessed.

PRINCIPAL WORKS: The Poetical Works of James Madison Bell, 1901.

ABOUT: Bell, J. M. The Poetical Works of James Madison Bell (see Note by B. W. Arnett); Ohio Centennial Anniversary Celebration. . . . Complete Proceedings.

BELLAMY, EDWARD (March 26, 1850-May 22, 1898), novelist and sociologist, was born and lived most of his life in Chicopee Falls (now part of Chicopee, near Springfield), Mass., where his father, Rufus King Bellamy, had been a Baptist minister for thirty-five years; his mother was Maria (Putnam) Bellamy. Most of his education was in the public school of the village, though he spent a few months at Union College, Schenectady, N.Y., as a special student in literature. During all of 1868 he was abroad, for the most part in Germany, and it was the sight of city slums in Europe that first brought before this essentially village-minded man the plight of the economically dispossessed.

Returned to America, he studied law and was admitted to the bar, but never practiced. Then, after a short period on the New York *Evening Post,* he became editor of the Springfield *Union,* and in 1880, with his brother, he founded the Springfield *Daily News.* But his heart was no more in newspaper work than in the law; he longed for a life devoted entirely to literature, and as soon as possible he achieved it. As early as 1873 his first novel, *The Duke of Stockbridge,* began to be serialized in a magazine (it was never finished by him, but was published with an ending by another hand two years after he died); it is concerned with Shay's Rebellion, evidence of his preoccupation already with the social issue. He contributed stories to various magazines, and in 1880 published *Dr. Heidenhoff's Process.* This, with his other early novel, *Mrs. Ludington's Sister,* was concerned with psychic phenomena, in which he had a keen interest, and caused him to be hailed by one reviewer as "a lineal descendant of Hawthorne." Actually, however, he never returned to this theme; his writings became exclusively identified with social problems.

In 1882 he married Emma Sanderson, and at the same time he definitely withdrew from active newspaper work. He devoted himself conscientiously to working out a formulated plan for the remedy of economic evils, and by 1886 had arrived at the solution implicit in his famous *Looking Backward,* which appeared in 1888.

Looking Backward sold over a million copies in its first few years. Bellamy Clubs were formed, leading to formation of a Nationalist Party. Bellamy, the taciturn, reticent, and modest, forced himself into the open as an enthusiastic propagandist for actualization of the theories contained in the book. (At this writing, his widow and daughter are still living and are still speaking and writing for the same cause.) In 1891 he founded the *New Nation,* in Boston, as an organ for his views, but increasing illness forced him finally to give it up. It became apparent that he was suffering from tuberculosis, but he refused to obey medical commands to find a more healthful climate, until he could finish *Equality,* the sequel to *Looking Backward.* This is much more of a tract and less of a novel. Then he went to Colorado, but too late; he was brought back only just in time to die in his native town, at barely forty-eight.

EDWARD BELLAMY

This is not the place to discuss the economic theories of *Looking Backward*; but it should be pointed out that though Bellamy is usually spoken of as a "Utopian Socialist," he was nothing of the kind. His system was a pure state capitalism, a complete nationalization of all industry which has actually much in common with the totalitarian state, now spoken of as Fascism. (Needless to say, however, Bellamy's own attitude would never have permitted him to acquiesce in present-day Fascist methods.) He himself thought of his system as "enlightened self-interest, wholesale common sense." In his day, the chief objection made to his book was that it "glorified materialism," but he presupposed a sort of social change of heart as a preliminary to his economic change. William Dean Howells pointed out that Bellamy's "imagination was intensely democratic"; his system is inherently American, and American of the village or small town, not of the city. To modern readers the chief attraction of *Looking Backward* is the charm of its style, and the fascination of his daring predictions, which included radio, television, and moving pictures—yet his characters still drove about in carriages. His contemporaries compared *Looking Backward* to Henry George's *Progress and Poverty*; except for his disciples, it has descended nowadays to nearer kinship with H. G. Wells' early "scientific" romances, a wonder-story of a dream rather than a model of the future.

Bellamy, a slender, slight, mustached man (in later years he wore a beard) whose bright eyes were his most notable physical characteristic, was a strange mixture of diffidence and ardor. By nature he was a recluse, and his long illness made him still more retiring; but in his zeal for his cause he forced himself into public notice and controversy.

His book has outlived his personality; millions of people know of *Looking Backward* who have scarcely heard of Bellamy. No biography of him has been written. As Heywood Broun has remarked, "It seems that what he wrote was so much more important than what he was."

PRINCIPAL WORKS: Dr. Heidenhoff's Process, 1880; Mrs. Ludington's Sister, 1884; Looking Backward: 2000-1887, 1888; Equality, 1897; The Blind Man's World and Other Stories, 1898; The Duke of Stockbridge, 1900.

ABOUT: Bellamy, E. Equality (see biographical sketch in 1910 ed.); Bellamy, E. The Duke of Stockbridge (see Introduction by F. Bellamy); Tucker, C. Glimpses of Authors; Atlantic Monthly August 1898; Bookman August 1897.

BELLAMY, ELIZABETH WHITFIELD (CROOM) (April 17, 1837-April 13, 1900), novelist and story-writer, was born near Quincy, Fla., the daughter of William Whitfield Croom and Julia (Stephens) Croom. Through her education at the Spingler Institute in New York City, and in Philadelphia, she formed her love of literature and music. In 1858 she married her cousin, Charles E. Bellamy of North Carolina, who served as a surgeon in the Confederate army during the Civil War. He died in 1863, leaving his widow in such straitened circumstances that she began a long career of teaching literature and historical subjects in Mobile, Ala.

In 1867 Mrs. Bellamy published a Southern novel, *The Four Oaks,* under the name of "Kamba Thorpe," which she retained for many years when writing short stories for *Appleton's Journal* and other leading magazines. In 1876 another novel—*The Little Joanna*—appeared, and in 1888 *Old Man Gilbert* was brought out under her own name. This was followed by *Penny Lancaster* in 1889.

Mrs. Bellamy typified the Southern woman of her time. Gracious and thoughtful of others, she also possessed a courageous spirit and a strong will to rise above the difficult problems of Reconstruction days. Aside from her teaching and writing, she found time for private lectures on Shakespeare, in whom she was greatly interested. Her books, while not important as literature, are interesting pictures of Southern life.

PRINCIPAL WORKS: The Four Oaks, 1870; The Little Joanna, 1876; Old Man Gilbert, 1888; Penny Lancaster, 1889.

ABOUT: Owen, T. McA. History of Alabama and Dictionary of Alabama Biography; Mobile Register April 14, 15, 1900.

BENJAMIN, PARK (August 14, 1809-September 12, 1864), poet and editor, was born in Demerara, British Guiana, where his father, Parke Benjamin, a New England sea captain, had business connections; his mother was Mary (Gall) Benjamin, a native of the Barbadoes. At the age of four he was sent to Norwich, Conn., for treatment of a disease which left him a cripple, with shrunken legs. He attended Harvard for two years, then went to Washington (now Trinity) College, in Hartford, Conn., where he was graduated in 1829. Here he founded the first of his papers, the short-lived Norwich *Spectator.* The next year he went to the Harvard Law School, changing in 1832 to the Yale Law School. He was admitted to the bar in Boston, but spent more time in literature than in law. By

1834 he was on the staff of the *New England Magazine,* and became its owner and editor the following year. In 1838 it was merged with the *American Monthly Magazine,* which Benjamin followed to New York, his home thereafter. On the magazine's demise in 1838, he became literary editor of several ephemeral magazines, including Horace Greeley's *New Yorker,* then in 1839 founded two papers, the *Evening Signal,* and the *New World.* The latter he maintained to 1845. The remainder of his life he spent as a literary agent, as a speaker and reader of extemporaneous verse in lyceums, and in various editorial ventures, the least brief of which was a literary weekly in Baltimore. In 1845 he married Mary Brower Western. His son, Park Benjamin (1849-1922), was a writer on applied science and a patent attorney, and became better known than his father.

Benjamin's *New World,* his most famous undertaking, reprinted essays by British writers without recompense to them, thanks to the non-existence of a copyright law. It also issued "extras" containing novels, for which Benjamin secured second-class mailing privileges on the ground that they were part of a magazine. He was a caustic and vituperative critic who was frequently sued for libel; an embittered man who avenged his crippled condition on the world. His poems have never been collected and are now practically forgotten.

Principal Work: The Harbinger (with O. W. Holmes and J. S. Sargent) 1833.

BENJAMIN, SAMUEL GREENE WHEELER (February 13, 1837-July 19, 1914), miscellaneous writer, painter, and diplomat, was born in Argos, Greece, the son of Nathan Benjamin, a distinguished missionary, and Mary Gladding (Wheeler) Benjamin. Living in Greece and the Levant until his eighteenth year, young Benjamin passed a colorful boyhood and absorbed impressions which were later molded into a restless spirit and an intense dislike of routine. He attended school in Smyrna, learned Latin from his father, and easily mastered several other languages. Studying drawing under capable teachers, at the age of seventeen he sent acceptable pictures to the *Illustrated London News* during the Crimean War in 1854. After his father's death from typhus in 1855, Benjamin returned to America, entered Williams College, and was graduated in 1859. Two years later he became assistant in the New York State Library at Albany but he was so incapable of adapting himself to systematic life that his health broke down and he resorted to extensive travel. In 1863 he married Clara Stowell of Brookfield, Mass.

In 1870 he established studios in Boston and New York City successively and became well-known as a marine painter. Literature also occupied his attention and he often dictated while he painted. His first book *Constantinople, The Isle of Pearls, and Other Poems* appeared in 1860 and was followed by others on various subjects, including travel and contemporary art.

A widower for several years, Benjamin married Fannie Nichols Weed in 1882 and shortly afterward went to Persia as first American Minister. His sociable nature and deep understanding of the Oriental mind made him a popular and efficient diplomat. Passionately fond of the sea, he crossed the Atlantic forty-five times in small sailing ships, endured the roughest weather without complaint, drank and smoked to the degree that he sometimes took no water for months, and wrote and painted as he lived, with vigor and enthusiasm. His books never achieved wide acclaim, but in contrast with some of their popular contemporaries, are readable today.

Principal Works: Constantinople, The Isle of Pearls, and Other Poems, 1860; Ode on the Death of Abraham Lincoln, 1865; The Turk and the Greek, 1867; The Choice of Paris: A Romance of the Troad, 1870; Contemporary Art in Europe, 1877; Art in America, 1879; Troy: Its Legend, History, and Literature, 1880; The Cruise of the Alice May, 1884.

About: Benjamin, S. G. W. The Life and Adventures of a Free Lance.

BENNETT, D. M. (December 23, 1818-December 6, 1882), editor and Free Thought writer, was one of the pioneers of Rationalism in America. He was born in Springfield, N.Y., and after learning the printing trade, at the age of fifteen joined the New London Shaker community. He studied medicine and became the community's physician. In 1845 he left the community, since it preached and practiced celibacy, and he and another member of the colony, Mary Wicks, had fallen in love. They were married and Bennett became a drug clerk in St. Louis, then went into business for himself. He owned proprietary medicine, seed, and drug businesses in Rochester, Cincinnati, and Kansas City; at various times he was wealthy, then met with reverses. In 1873, at Paris, Ill., he founded the *Truth Seeker,* a Rationalist magazine still published, and soon after moved it to New York. For years he wrote most of the paper himself, and was also a frequent lecturer on science and Free Thought topics. In 1877 Anthony

Comstock secured his arrest for publication of an article on the propagation of marsupials; the case was dismissed but he was rearrested for selling a pamphlet on birth control and sentenced to thirteen months in the Albany penitentiary. He continued his editorial duties from his cell. In 1881 he made a tour around the world, his letters being published as *An Infidel Abroad.* He died as the result of an attack of hiccoughs, dictating his last article the day before his death. His widow, who had followed her husband into Free Thought and had given the *Truth Seeker* its name, died in 1898.

PRINCIPAL WORK: An Infidel Abroad, 1881.

ABOUT: Macdonald, G. E. Fifty Years of Freethought.

BENNETT, EMERSON (March 16, 1822-May 11, 1905), poet and novelist, was born at Monson, Mass. Receiving his education in the local schools and Monson Academy, at the age of seventeen he went to New York City where he took up a literary career and brought out his first book, *The Brigand,* which the *Knickerbocker Magazine* ridiculed as a "little poeticle pamphlick." In 1843 while in Philadelphia, he wrote a short novel, *The Unknown Countess,* for a newspaper contest. Then setting out for the West by a roundabout route from Baltimore to Pittsburgh, he arrived in Cincinnati in 1844. Two years later he became editor of the *Casket,* a weekly magazine, and contributed widely to other magazines and newspapers, including the *Quarterly Journal and Review.* He married Eliza G. Daly of Philadelphia in 1847.

The year 1850 marked a return to his birthplace for a short time, after which he settled permanently in Philadelphia. Meanwhile he was writing novels as fast as his publishers could print them. Some of them were serialized in the *Saturday Evening Post,* substantially increasing the circulation. In 1856 he was engaged to write exclusively for the *New York Ledger.* He died in Philadelphia after a five-year illness.

Bennett's writing dealt chiefly with adventure and intrigue in the pioneer days of Virginia and the Western frontier. His plots were melodramatic structures only partially concealed by the thin covering of his excessively sentimental style, and though the sales of two of his books reached 100,000 copies, Bennett is virtually a forgotten writer today.

PRINCIPAL WORKS: The Brigand, 1842; The Unknown Countess, 1843; The League of the Miami, 1845; The Bandits of the Osage, 1847; Mike Fink, 1848; The Prairie Flower, 1849.

ABOUT: Bennett, E. Villeta Linden (see Preface); Venable, W. H. Beginnings of Literary Culture in the Ohio Valley.

BENTLEY, WILLIAM (June 22, 1759-December 29, 1819), clergyman, diarist, and antiquarian, was born in Boston, Mass., the son of Joshua and Elizabeth (Paine) Bentley. After graduating from Harvard in 1777 he spent six years teaching school and tutoring in Latin and Greek. He was ordained to the ministry in 1783 and became pastor of the East Church at Salem, remaining until the end of his life.

Bentley's liberal views on theology and politics exercised a broadening influence on contemporary thought and he took a prominent part in New England affairs, from the pulpit and through contributions to the *Salem Register.* Among his manifold interests, he carried on an international correspondence with important men in various fields of activity. One of his correspondents was Thomas Jefferson, who, recognizing Bentley's unusual qualifications, offered him the presidency of the proposed University of Virginia.

Book collecting became Bentley's consuming interest. From a slender purse he acquired a valuable library, and a group of historical and natural curiosities which he bequeathed to the American Antiquarian Society and other institutions. His linguistic ability gave him a fluent command of European languages, and a reading knowledge of Oriental tongues.

A thirty-five year diary, with a Pepysian flair for gossip, was Bentley's most important contribution to American literature. Of special interest to antiquarians and genealogists, it was held by the American Antiquarian Society for many years and finally published by Essex Institute between 1905 and 1914.

PRINCIPAL WORKS: Diary: 1784-1819, 1905-1914.

ABOUT: Batchelor, G. Social Equilibriums and Other Problems; Bentley, W. Diary; Buckingham, J. T. Specimens of Newspaper Literature.

BENTON, JOEL (May 29, 1832-September 15, 1911), journalist and poet, was born at Amenia, Dutchess County, N.Y. He was the son of Simeon Blackman Benton and Deborah (Hallock) Benton, and was educated at Amenia Seminary. On leaving school, he was made editor of the Amenia *Times,* where he remained until 1856 when he retired in order to devote his time to farming, writing, and lecturing. He was active in civic affairs, serving as principal of the Academy, town supervisor, and delegate to political conventions. In 1872 he resumed his editorship in support of Horace Greeley's presidential campaign. Between 1883 and 1885 he did journalistic work in Chicago and St. Paul. Returning east, he settled in Poughkeepsie, where he died. He never married.

Alert, distinguished in appearance, always well-dressed, Benton moved in intellectual circles and delighted to write about his distinguished acquaintances. His style was too forced ever to attain literary distinction.

Principal Works: Emerson as a Poet, 1883; The Truth About Protection, 1892; Greeley on Lincoln, 1893; In the Poe Circle, 1899; Life of P. T. Barnum, 1902; Persons and Places, 1905; Memories of the Twilight Club, 1909; Amenia Seminary Reunion, 1907.

About: Benton, C. E. Caleb Benton and Sarah Bishop: Their Ancestors and Descendants; Benton, C. E. Troutbeck: A Dutchess County Homestead; Poughkeepsie Daily Eagle September 16, 1911.

BERGH, HENRY (August 29, 1811-March 12, 1888), founder of the American Society for the Prevention of Cruelty to Animals, was the son of a prosperous shipbuilder, Christian Bergh and Elizabeth (Ivers) Bergh. Henry attended Columbia College, but preferring to manage his father's business, did not remain to take his degree. Six years later, on the death of Christian Bergh, Henry and his wife, Catherine Matilda Taylor, whom he married in 1836, went to Europe where they spent five years and Bergh was appointed secretary of the legation at St. Petersburg. During this time he became increasingly incensed by the cruelties imposed upon animals, especially horses. After the severe climate of Russia forced his resignation, he visited England to consult the Earl of Harrowby, president of the Royal Society for the Prevention of Cruelty to Animals, with the view to forming a similar organization in America.

Returning to this country after the Civil War, Bergh devoted his energies and a considerable part of his fortune to philanthropic work. On April 10, 1866, the American Society for the Prevention of Cruelty to Animals was officially formed, with Bergh as president. By this time contributions to its support were more frequent, and on one occasion, startling. In 1871 Louis Bonard, a miserly Frenchman, who had lived in squalid obscurity, left a will revealing that $150,000 worth of property and a shabby trunk filled with layers of gold and silver watches, diamonds and other jewels were all bequeathed to the S.P.C.A., thereby greatly aiding its advancement.

Also sensitive to the injustice against children, Bergh was instrumental in founding the Society for the Prevention of Cruelty to Children, in 1875. These two humane societies now have branches in virtually every large city throughout the world, and Bergh rightfully takes his place among the foremost American philanthropists.

Tall and thin, with the deep-set, burning eyes of a crusader, Bergh's appearance attracted as much attention as his activities, and his sharp rebukes to cruel drivers often created exciting little street scenes. Apart from philanthropy, he wrote several plays, *The Streets of New York,* a book of sketches, and *Married Off: A Satirical Poem,* published in 1860. These were chiefly for recreation and merit little literary recognition.

Principal Works: The Streets of New York; Married Off: A Satirical Poem, 1860.

About: McClure's Magazine March 1902; Scribner's Monthly April 1879; New York Herald, New York Times, New York Tribune March 13, 1888.

"BERKLEY, HELEN." See MOWATT, ANNA CORA (OGDEN) RITCHIE

BERNARD, WILLIAM BAYLE (November 27, 1807-August 5, 1875), dramatist and biographer, was born in Boston, Mass. His parents were John Bernard, an English actor, and his third wife, a former Miss Wright, the family governess. After 1819 the Bernards returned to England where Bayle was educated. His stage career was short-lived but he wrote over a hundred successful plays, many of which were acted by Hackett, John Brougham, Lewis Morrison and other actors prominent in England and America. He is said to be the first to popularize the eccentric rural American on the stage. Among his important plays were *The Kentuckian* and an early dramatization of *Rip Van Winkle,* produced in 1832. *His Last Legs,* a farce, was first acted in 1839 and became a great favorite with the public. Aside from playwrighting, he produced a novel—*The Freebooter's Bride,* while serving in the Army Accounts Office between 1826 and 1830, and edited his father's papers, bringing them out in two volumes in 1830 under the title *Retrospections of the Stage.* A collection of his own papers, edited and introduced by Brander Matthews and Laurence Hutton, appeared posthumously in 1887 as *Retrospections of America.*

Bayle was a popular figure in London literary and theatrical circles, and substantially enriched American stage literature with the valuable material comprising his biographical works.

PRINCIPAL WORKS: Retrospections of the Stage (ed.) 1830; The Dumb Belle, 1831; His Last Legs, 1839; Retrospections of America, 1887.

ABOUT: Bernard, W. B. (ed.). Retrospections of the Stage; Retrospections of America; Scott, C. & Howard C. The Life and Times of Edward Leman Blanchard.

BEVERLEY, ROBERT (c.1673-1722), historian of Virginia, was born on a plantation in Middlesex County, Va., the son of Robert Beverley, a Yorkshire "cavalier" gentleman, who emigrated to Virginia in 1663 and within a few years became a prominent political figure. Young Beverley was educated in England, and returning to the United States after the death of his father, he volunteered as a scrivener in the provincial secretary's office. On the strength of his achievements here he was shortly recommended for service as clerk of a legislative committee, and by 1696 he had assumed responsibilities as clerk of the General Court, clerk of the Council, and clerk of the General Assembly. Through connections at the statehouse Beverley became a freeholder, and at various intervals during the years 1699-1706 he qualified as burgess for the capital in the Assemblies.

He went to England in June 1703 to defend his own interests in a matter which was under consideration of the Privy Council, and was obliged to remain a year and a half. He wrote back some very candid letters on "publick affairs," one of which influenced the Assembly in the formulation of an Address to the Crown, preferring what were in effect petty charges against one Robert Quarry, surveyor general of the customs. The reply to this address was a harrowing rebuke to the Assembly and occasioned Beverley's political demise about a year after his return to Virginia. Retiring to his estate in King and Queen County, he presided in the county court, experimented in grape-growing, and plunged into some extensive land speculation. He was married to Ursula Byrd, by whom he had one son, William.

On the *History and Present State of Virginia* rests Beverley's reputation as an historian; it was written as a kind of reaction against John Oldmixon's vapid account of the *British Empire in America,* especially those pages, which Beverley had examined in England, relating to Virginia and Carolina. His own book purported to be an "honest account of the ancientist as well as most profitable Colony" under British sovereignty; it was issued in a revised, though unimproved, edition in 1722, and at the same time appeared his *Abridgement of the Public Laws of Virginia.*

Beverley knew the Indians well, and in the first edition of his *History* he playfully asserted: "I am an Indian, and don't pretend to be exact in my Language. . . . I would ask [the reader] not to criticize too unmercifully my Stile." It is true that he made "not a few errors," yet he had much less to fear from posterity than did many of his contemporaries, for because of his plainness, directness, and freedom from imitation and pedantry, his work has survived two centuries as a significant source.

PRINCIPAL WORKS: History and Present State of Virginia, 1705; The Abridgement of the Public Laws of Virginia, 1722.

ABOUT: Beverley, R. History and Present State of Virginia (see Preface, etc.); Tyler, M. C. History of American Literature During Colonial Times; Virginia Magazine: Vols. 2, 3, 20, 21, 22.

BIDDLE, NICHOLAS (January 8, 1786-February 27, 1844), litterateur, editor, and financier, was born in Philadelphia, the son of Charles Biddle, vice-president of Pennsylvania under the constitution of 1776, and Hannah (Shepard) Biddle of Beaufort, N.C. He entered the University of Pennsylvania at the age of ten, but was denied a degree three years later because of his youth. At the College of New Jersey, at Princeton, he did advanced study, largely in the classics, and was graduated in 1801. He was much attracted by the healthy literary enthusiasm of Joseph Dennie, who that same year founded the *Port Folio*, the first American periodical devoted to the making of a native literature, although it was not until 1806 that Biddle began to write regularly for this journal.

Meanwhile, when Gen. John Armstrong went as minister to France in 1804 he took Biddle as his secretary, and after witnessing Napoleon's self-coronation at Notre Dame, the nineteen-year-old youth was intrusted with the auditing and payment of claims against French privateers by those who had been despoiled during the Napoleonic wars. He studied and did some extensive traveling on the Continent before his appointment as legation secretary at London, and on his visits to Cambridge University is said to have exhibited an astounding brilliancy in his conversations with the dons.

Biddle resumed his study of law on his return to the United States in August 1807, and was admitted to the bar in December 1809. He had become a member of the "Tuesday Club," Dennie's Philadelphia coterie of potential *Folio* contributors, and for several years was a whole-hearted man of letters. At the request of Gen. William Clark he began, in March 1810, the writing of the Louisiana expedition account, and on October 4 of the year following he was married to Jane Craig. Upon the death of his associate Dennie, in 1812, Biddle became the editor of what was, at that time, the foremost periodical in America. His election to the legislature forced him to surrender the last-minute details of his *History of the Expedition of Captains Lewis and Clark* (1814) to one Paul Allen, a journalist. Out of Clark's oral statements and a mass of notes and day-books, Biddle had woven a skilfully coherent narrative. His *Ode to Bogle*, celebrating a locally famous caterer and undertaker, was many times republished and established him as a writer of brilliant light verse as well as prose.

Biddle's life from 1814 on was largely that of a statesman and financier. He aided in getting loans for the War Department, wrote up a remarkable report of the Hartford Convention of January 1814, and as president of the Bank of the United States, weathered, with real diplomacy, the harrowing investigations of government officials and rival financiers.

When he retired to "Andalusia" on the Delaware in March 1839 his home became the haven of many intellectuals, including eminent European exiles whose conversations Biddle ably recorded in his papers. His progressively modern attitude towards socio-economic problems has, in the light of his long career as executive and financier, a special significance. From the literary historian's point of view, however, it is to be regretted that political events swerved him aside from the kind of pursuits that had yielded his expedition narrative and his dexterous verse.

Principal Works: History of the Expedition of Captains Lewis and Clark, 1814; Ode to Bogle, 1829.

About: Biddle, C. Autobiography of Charles Biddle; Catterall, R. C. H. The Second Bank of the United States.

BIERCE, AMBROSE GWINETT (June 24, 1842-1914?), essayist and story writer, was the youngest of nine children of Marcus Aurelius Bierce and Laura (Sherwood) Bierce. His father was a poverty-stricken, pious, eccentric farmer, originally from Connecticut but settled on Horse Cave Creek, Meigs Co., Ohio, in a log cabin on a rough and badly managed farm. Bierce detested all his family except his brother Albert, and with a mixture of sensitiveness and snobbishness tried to throw a fog over his antecedents and early life, but as a matter of fact he had many of the family traits. Like himself and his brother Albert, his father, Marcus Aurelius Bierce, had loathed all *his* family except his brother Lucius Verus (the names are evidence of classical training somewhere in the generation before); and this uncle Lucius, grown into a general, an attorney, and a prominent politician, not only gave Ambrose the only formal education he ever had—a year at the Kentucky Military Institute at seventeen—but also helped to form his literary standards and his style.

AMBROSE BIERCE

Providentially for him, the Civil War offered him release from the hated home to which he had had to return when the military institute burnt down. He enlisted with the 9th Indiana Infantry as a drummer boy, fought bravely all through the war, was wounded at Kenesaw Mountain, and emerged from the war as a lieutenant with the brevet title of major. He was appointed custodian of "captured and abandoned property" at Selma, Ala., and relieved from this post to accompany General Hazen on an inspection tour of army posts from Omaha to San Francisco. In San Francisco his only loved brother was then living, and Bierce secured his discharge from government service to remain there with him. Ambrose was made night watchman at the Sub-treasury, a branch of the Mint; but his active intelligence could not remain long satisfied with the monotony of such a position. He became interested in local politics, and produced for his own amusement a series of cartoons of persons in the daily news. These his brother sent anonymously to both sides of the current political controversy, and one day Bierce found the streets placarded (those were highly disputatious days) with reproductions of his drawings. At once the artist's identity became known, and he was a marked figure in a city always receptive to colorful personalities.

The result of his minor fame, however, was not more drawings, but his emergence as a writer. He began to write political squibs for the *News Letter,* soon was put in charge of its "Town Crier" column, and by 1868 was its editor. In 1871 he turned his hand to fiction, and his first story "The Haunted Valley" was published in the *Overland Magazine.* Bierce was launched. His satirical paragraphs were quoted everywhere; he had found his niche. The San Francisco of the '70s and '80s was made for him, and he for it.

But he did not linger there long. In 1871 he married Mary Ellen Day, daughter of a Nevada mine-owner, a forty-niner; and after a few months in the suburban town of San Rafael they sailed for England. There, fresh from association with Bret Harte and Mark Twain and Joaquin Miller, he fitted easily into the group around Tom Hood, Jr. Soon he was on the staff of Hood's humorous magazine, *Fun,* and contributing also to *Figaro* and *Hood's Comic Annual.* He edited and wrote every word of the two numbers of a magazine called the *Lantern,* founded in the interest of the Empress Eugénie. He might have stayed in London permanently; but his health failed, he was homesick for California, and his mother-in-law came and took home with her his wife and his two little sons. Soon he learned that another child was on the way. He resigned his various assignments and returned to San Francisco in 1876.

For the next ten years he conducted his famous "Prattler" column in the *Argonaut* and wrote for the *Wasp,* of which he became editor in 1880. The next year, sick of journalism, he suddenly rushed to Deadwood, S.D., for a hare-brained mining venture that came to nothing. In a few months he was back on the *Wasp,* and stayed until the paper died in 1886.

In 1887 young William Randolph Hearst took over the moribund *San Francisco Examiner* from his father, Senator George Hearst. Immediately he transferred to it Bierce and his "Prattler" column. Bierce, a lifelong sufferer from asthma, could not live long in the city, but from his home in St. Helena, and later in Auburn, he sent in his daily column. It was the period of his greatest influence and his greatest fertility, when he made and broke reputations at will. He was the literary dictator of the Pacific Coast, at a time when San Francisco was its undisputed cultural center. Outside of the West he was not widely known, and most of his early books had to be privately published. But at home he was supreme; even those whom he lacerated and who hated him acknowledged his power. He befriended many young writers—George Sterling, Herman Scheffauer, Gertrude Atherton, and Rupert Hughes among them. He had his kinder side, and those who loved him; but his name stood for cruel wit, for bitter invective.

Then his decline began. In 1889 his older son, Day, died in a shooting affray with another young man who was also killed, a fight over a worthless girl. In 1891 Mrs. Bierce left her husband, from whom she had long been estranged. (She divorced him just before her own death in 1904.) He was doubtless glad when in 1896 Hearst sent him to Washington to lobby against the railroad refunding bill. In a year he was back, but though his style and viewpoint remained unchanged, the spontaneity had gone out of his work. Times were changing, and he was not changing with them. The next year he left San Francisco and returned to Washington as Washington correspondent of the New York *American,* a position he held until his resignation in 1909, at the same time conducting a department in the *Cosmopolitan* (then not owned by Hearst). His creative days were over. What he wrote thenceforth was mostly repetitious. One more blow was dealt him; in 1901 his other son, Leigh, died, a confirmed alcoholic. He was on good terms with his daughter, he still had his adoring disciples, but he was old and tired, and he had been disillusioned with life and humanity since the Civil War.

In 1913 Ambrose Bierce came back to California for the last time. He spent a few months, mostly seeing old friends, and then left for a trip to Mexico. The rest is silence. The last heard from him was in 1914. The probability is that he was killed by one side or the other in the civil warfare then raging between Villa and Carranza. There are many stories, ranging from suicide, to survival still in some South or Central American country. He has become a legend; but no one really knows how, where, or when Bierce died.

Bierce has been so praised and so attacked, so idolized and so hated, that it is difficult to extricate the man from the myth. The fact is that he was a mass of contradictions. At bottom generous, sensitive, soft-hearted, affectionate, he was capable also of callousness, injustice, and downright cruelty. He called himself a cynic, and yet he was easily aroused to anger, as no true cynic is. He hated religion and he hated the working-class movement, because he hated his family, and they were Puritanical bigots and poor working farmers. Four years of war made his excitable nerves, by over-compensation, entirely indifferent to suffering; the result was his unfeeling, unemotional depictions of horror, his fascination by death. He was an extreme individualist, and also a good deal of a snob. In language he was a purist, with a fanatical devotion to classical traditions of style; yet he could be guilty of atrocious floridity in the worst journalistic mode of his period. His verse was negligible and sometimes cheap. He has been much over-rated in California, and much under-rated elsewhere. The personal journalism that made his power is dead. But there will survive some of his stories of terror, a few of his epigrams, and his superb letters, masterpieces of unpremeditated expression such as few of his dry and artificial narratives ever were.

It may be that Bierce's name will be of more value to the future historian of American literature than the actual worth of his writing merits. He was in the direct tradition of Fitz James O'Brien and Poe in the development of the short story, and like them was a master of brevity in horror. He repeated himself endlessly, for his harp had a single string; but in the history of his *genre* Ambrose Bierce must undoubtedly have a small but secure place.

Principal Works: The Fiend's Delight (under name of Dod Grile) 1872; Nuggets and Dust Panned Out in California (under name of J. Milton Sloluck) 1872; Cobwebs From an Empty Skull, 1874; The Dance of Death (under name of William Herman, with T. A. Harcourt) 1877; The Dance of Life (under name of Mrs. J. Milton Bowers) 1877; Tales of Soldiers and Civilians, 1891 (as In the Midst of Life, 1898); Black Beetles in Amber (verse) 1892; The Monk and the Hangman's Daughter (adapted from a translation by G. A. Danziger from the German of Richard Voss) 1892; Can Such Things Be? 1893; Fantastic Fables, 1899; Shapes of Clay (verse) 1903; The Devil's Dictionary (The Cynic's Word Book) 1906; The Shadow on the Dial and Other Essays, 1909; Write It Right, 1909; Collected Works, 1909.

About: Bierce, A. Letters (ed. by B. C. Pope, with Memoir by G. Sterling); Bierce, A. 21 Letters (ed. by S. Loveman); Boynton, P. H. More Contemporary Americans; Brooks, Van W. Emerson and Others; Cooper, F. T. Some American Story Tellers; DeCastro, A. D. Portrait of Ambrose Bierce; Grattan, C. H. Bitter Bierce; McWilliams, C. Ambrose Bierce: A Biography; Neale, W. Life of Ambrose Bierce; Starrett, V. Ambrose Bierce; Starrett, V. Buried Caesars; American Mercury September 1925, February 1929, September 1929, March 1931; Bookman August 1925, November 1929; Sunset Magazine October 1929.

BIGELOW, JOHN (November 25, 1817-December 19, 1911), historian and biographer, was born in Bristol (now Malden), N.Y., the son of Asa Bigelow and Lucy (Isham) Bigelow. First a student at Washington (Trinity) College, Hartford, Conn., he was graduated from Union College, Schenectady, N.Y., in 1835. He received an honorary LL.D. from Union in 1886, and from the University of the City of New York in 1889. In 1838 he was admitted to the bar. From 1845 to 1848 he was an inspector of Sing Sing Prison. From 1848 to 1861 he was joint proprietor and editor of the New York *Evening Post* with William Cullen Bryant, whose biography he wrote later. His other close connection with a celebrated man was with Samuel J. Tilden, head of the Free Soil Democrats; Bigelow became his biographer and editor of his collected works. In 1850 he married Jane Poultney. An extended trip to Jamaica was the inspiration of a book, as were visits to Haiti and Europe. In 1861 he was United States consul, later consul general at Paris, and in 1865 and 1866 was United States minister to France, where he did valuable work in preventing French and British aid to the Confederacy. He returned to the United States in 1867 and settled in New York. From 1875 to 1877, when Tilden was governor of New York, Bigelow was his secretary of state. He was a devout Swedenborgian, and his philosophical books have a distinctly Swedenborgian tinge.

Bigelow's most important achievement was the editing of the first full edition of Franklin's *Autobiography,* and his biography of Franklin. He was a voluminous writer, but his work was very uneven. The best known of his political works is *France and the Confederate Navy.* He published books on the history of the United States which were translated into both French and Italian. He lived to the age of ninety-four.

A son, Poultney Bigelow (1855-), became a well known author and traveler.

Principal Works: Jamaica in 1850, 1851; Memoir of the Life of John Charles Frémont, 1856; The Proprium, 1867; Life of Benjamin Franklin, 1868; Beaumarchais the Merchant, 1870; France and Hereditary Monarchy, 1871; Wit and Wisdom of the Haytians, 1877; Molinas the Quietest, 1882; France and the Confederate Navy: An International Episode, 1888; The Bible That Was Lost and Is Alive Again, 1893; William Cullen Bryant, 1893; Life of Samuel J. Tilden, 1895; The Mystery of Sleep, 1897; Lest We

Forget, 1905; The Useful Life, 1906; The Panama Canal, 1908; Retrospections of an Active Life, 1906 (two additional volumes edited by his son, 1913); Toleration and Other Essays and Studies, 1926.

ABOUT: Bigelow, J. Retrospections of an Active Life.

"BIGLEY, CANTELL, A." See PECK, GEORGE WASHINGTON

"BILLINGS, JOSH." See SHAW, HENRY WHEELER

BINGHAM, HIRAM (October 30, 1789-November 11, 1869), missionary and translator, was born in Bennington, Vt., the son of Calvin Bingham, a farmer, and Lydia (Denton) Bingham. Educated in the district schools and Middlebury College, from which he was graduated in 1816, he studied at the Andover Theological Seminary and in September 1819 was ordained for the foreign-mission service. At the ordination he met Sybil Moseley, of Westfield, Mass., and married her twelve days later. They sailed from Boston with a large company on the brig "Thaddeus" on October 23, 1819, and took up mission work in Honolulu where they lived in a native hut for more than a year until a frame house could be built. Bingham and others of his party soon acquired a knowledge of the native language and devised an alphabet in order to write exercises with which to teach the people reading. This resulted in the publication in 1822 of Bingham's *Elementary Lessons in Hawaiian.* It was followed by a translation of the New Testament into Hawaiian on which his associates collaborated, and by 1839 they had translated the entire Bible. In 1831 he brought out his *First Book for Children* and the *Scripture Catechism.*

During his many years' residence on the islands, Bingham worked unceasingly to establish Christianity among the natives. Services were first held out-of-doors under the giant hibiscus trees, but a year after the Binghams' arrival, a church was erected. In 1826 Bingham made an extensive preaching tour of the island with Kaahumanu, a pupil and wife of the first great king, who was at that time occupying the throne. She had accepted the Christian faith in 1825 and was endeavoring to convert her subjects. In 1840 Mrs. Bingham's health necessitated their return to America. She died at Easthampton, Mass., in 1848 and Bingham remained in America, preaching and writing. On August 24, 1854, he married Naomi Emma Morse. He died in New Haven, Conn., where he was pastor of the African Church for a time. His best-known work is *Residence of Twenty-one Years in the Sandwich Islands: or, The Civil, Religious, and Political History of Those Islands,* a valuable contribution to the history of the islands.

PRINCIPAL WORKS: Elementary Lessons in Hawaiian, 1822; First Book for Children, 1831; Scripture Catechism, 1831; Residence of Twenty-One Years in the Sandwich Islands, 1847.

ABOUT: Anderson, R. History of the Sandwich Island Mission; Ellis, W. Journal of a Tour Around Hawaii; Hawley, E. C. Introduction of Christianity Into the Hawaiian Islands.

BINGHAM, HIRAM (August 16, 1831-October 25, 1908), translator and missionary, son of Hiram Bingham [*q.v.*] and Sybil (Moseley) Bingham, was born in Honolulu, where his parents were missionaries. Here he attended a missionary school, and coming to America with his family when he was eight, was sent to Williston Academy, in Easthampton Mass., and then entered Yale. For a year following his graduation in 1853 he was principal of the Northampton high school, and then spent a year abroad as a private tutor. Ill health prevented him from completing his studies at Andover Seminary, but he was set upon a missionary career and was, in November 1856, ordained at New Haven, Conn. The same month he was married to Minerva Clarissa Brewster, and in December they sailed from Boston for Honolulu and Micronesia, on the brig "Morning Star." In the Gilbert Islands he endured seven years of disease, scarcity of food, and dealings with unscrupulous traders before returning to the United States, 1865-66, only to embark again in a small two-masted schooner.

After a tour of Micronesia he settled down in Honolulu, in December 1868, and began work on a Gilbertese Bible, completing the New Testament in April 1873; the entire Bible, finished in 1890, went into seven editions before his death. He sailed once more for the Gilbert Islands, preaching, teaching, and working on a Gilbertese dictionary, published in 1908. He also published a hymn and tune book in this same tongue, and his wife wrote *Bible Stories in the Gilbertese.* In the course of his translations and etymological researches Bingham succeeded in expanding the inadequate 4000-word Gilbertese to a language three times its original size.

A son, Hiram Bingham (1875-), was governor of Connecticut and United States senator from that state.

PRINCIPAL WORKS: Gilbertese Translation of the Bible, 1890; Gilbert Islands Bible Dictionary, 1895; Gilbertese Dictionary, 1908.

ABOUT: Gulick, O. H. Pilgrims of Hawaii; Missionary Herald December 1908.

BIRD, ROBERT MONTGOMERY (February 5, 1806-January 23, 1854), dramatist and novelist, was born at New Castle, Del., the son of John Bird and Elizabeth (von Leuvenigh) Bird. His father, a state senator, died suddenly in 1810, and the boy was reared by his uncle, Nicholas van Dyke, "President of the State of Delaware." He was educated at Germantown Academy in Philadelphia, and in 1824 entered the medical school of the University of Pennsylvania, receiving his M.D. in 1827. He had studied medicine merely to please his family, and, always shrinking from contact with financial questions, refused to ask for fees: it is not unnatural that he practiced only one year. His interest in science, however, was genuine and lifelong.

He had no income when he abandoned his profession, and his only equipment for life was a training in half a dozen languages and a talent for writing. His intimate friend was the famous tragedian Edwin Forrest, and he turned to playwrighting for a livelihood. His earlier plays, modern comedies and romances, were never produced and are still in manuscript. Then, in 1830, Forrest bought his *Pelopidas*; but there was no part in it outstanding enough for so celebrated an actor, so the next year he substituted Bird's *The Gladiator* instead. This play, based on the story of Spartacus, became one of Forrest's best known rôles. It earned for Bird in 1836 membership in the English Dramatic Authors' Society, and was the first play written in English ever to achieve a thousand performances during its author's lifetime.

In 1833 Bird started with Forrest for a trip to Mexico and South America. They were halted by cholera at New Orleans, but Bird's interest in the southern continent bore fruit in his best play, *The Broker of Bogota,* dealing with South America in the eighteenth century. His *Oralloossa,* produced in 1832, had had its scene among the Incas of Peru. But his promising career as a dramatist was cut short by Forrest's shabby treatment of him, which led to a permanent break between them. Forrest not only cheated his trusting friend, who had relied on oral contracts with him, but also refused permission for publication of his plays. They were not published until 1917, when it was discovered that the copyright which Forrest claimed had never been entered!

Bird, after a vain trip to England to try to secure some money for his work, turned to novel writing. Fortunately for this high-minded but unpractical man, his novels were a great success. They were for the most part realistic stories of American history;

After a daguerreotype
ROBERT MONTGOMERY BIRD

the best is *The Hawks of Hawk-Hollow,* but the most popular was *Nick of the Woods,* in which he substituted a real savage for the idealized Indian of Fenimore Cooper.

In 1840 Bird's health broke from overwork, and he had to spend several months on a farm on the Eastern Shore of Maryland. He had married, in 1837, Mary Mayer, daughter of a Lutheran minister: their only son, Frederick, became a well-known hymn writer and editor of *Lippincott's Magazine.* Bird recovered for a time, returned to Philadelphia, and from 1841 to 1843 acted as professor of materia medica and medicine at the newly organized Pennsylvania Medical College. In 1847 he bought a part interest in a newspaper, the Philadelphia *North American,* and for a time acted as its literary editor. But his health was permanently weakened, and he died suddenly of cerebral congestion at not quite forty-nine.

Tall, fair, and dignified in appearance, Bird was a man of the highest integrity, idealistic and unsuspecting of evil in anyone. Even his bitter experience with Forrest could not change his trusting nature—or his vague approach to practical problems. He never has had the reputation his work deserved; he was not one to cry his own wares. His novels have been forgotten, and it was not until sixty-three years after his death, when his plays were published, that it became evident that here was one of the finest, as well as one of the earliest, of our native dramatists.

PRINCIPAL WORKS: *Plays*—The Gladiator, 1831; Oralloossa, 1832; The Broker of Bogota, 1834.

Novels—Calavar: or, The Knight of the Conquest, 1834; The Infidel: or, The Fall of Mexico, 1835; The Hawks of Hawk-Hollow, 1835; Sheppard Lee (anonymous) 1836; Nick of the Woods, 1837; The Adventures of Robin Day, 1839; A Belated Revenge (under name of Ipsico Poe; finished by F. M. Bird) 1889. *Miscellaneous*—Peter Pilgrim: or, A Rambler's Recollections, 1838.

ABOUT: Foust, C. E. Life and Dramatic Works of Robert Montgomery Bird; Quinn, A. H. A History of the American Drama From the Beginning to the Civil War; Nation August 3, 1916.

"BLACK, IVORY." See JANVIER, THOMAS ALLIBONE

BLAIR, JAMES (1655-April 18, 1743), founder and first president of William and Mary College, was born in Scotland, and made his first voyage to America at the age of thirty. He had received his Master of Arts degree from the University of Edinburgh in 1673; had been ordained in the Church of England; and for several years had served as rector of the parish of Cranston, exercising "exemplary diligence, care, and gravity." Through employment in the office of the Master of the Rolls in London he met Dr. Henry Compton, Bishop of London, who urged him to go as a missionary to Virginia. Here Blair was extended a rectorship at Varina (afterwards Henrico); and in December 1689 was appointed commissary or deputy to the Bishop of London, in whose diocese Virginia was included.

At the very first of a series of conventions to which he called the clergy of the colony Blair projected his plans for the establishment of a college. The burden of promoting the project fell largely upon his own shoulders: he was selected, in May 1691, to proceed to London to present a memorial, in behalf of the enterprise, to their Majesties King William and Queen Mary. By November he had secured the active interest of the Bishop of London, the Bishop of Worcester, and the Archbishop of Canterbury; and after much solicitation of funds the charter, naming Blair as president "during his natural life," was at last granted on February 8, 1693. From 1694 to 1710 he held a parish in Jamestown, not far from the proposed site (later Williamsburg) of the college; and from 1710 until his death he served Bruton parish in Williamsburg. For almost fifty years Blair was a member of the council, being reinstated, after a little more than a year's suspension by order of the King (who had likewise appointed him); and for six months, 1740-41, he was acting governor of the colony.

Courtesy of College of William & Mary Library
JAMES BLAIR

Blair was several times called to London on college business, and despite a certain amount of rank opposition, considerable indifference, and a destructive fire in 1705, the college was at last established, and at the time of his death there were three substantial buildings.

Blair wrote a series of 117 discourses on *Our Savior's Divine Sermon on the Mount* which were twice published in London and won him high praise. His range of topics was remarkably wide, the thought carefully welded, and the language generally terse and effective. With Henry Hartwell and Edward Chilton he was joint author of *The Present State of Virginia and the College . . . to Which is Added the Charter*; although prepared for the Board of Trade in 1697 it was not published until 1727 (London). It is, however, as an objective educator and organizer, working against the odds of self-seeking politicians, rather than as a writer, that Blair assumes importance in the intellectual history of Virginia.

PRINCIPAL WORKS: Our Savior's Divine Sermon on the Mount, 1722; The Present State of Virginia and the College . . . to Which Is Added the Charter, 1727.

ABOUT: Meade, W. Old Churches, Ministers, and Families of Virginia; Perry, W. S. Papers Relating to the History of the Church in Virginia, 1660-1776; Tyler, L. G. Williamsburg: The Old Colonial Capital; Tyler, L. G. The Cradle of the Republic; Tyler, M. C. History of American Literature During Colonial Times; Johns Hopkins University Studies in History and Political Science: Vol. 19, No. 10.

BLAKE, JOHN LAURIS (December 21, 1788-July 6, 1857), encyclopedist and clergyman, was born in Northwood, N.H., the son of Jonathan and Mary (Dow) Blake. Educated at the district school and Phillips Exeter Academy, he was graduated from Brown University in 1812. Shortly afterward he entered the Congregational ministry, but soon transferred to the Episcopal Church. He was ordained in 1815, when he established St. Paul's parish in Pawtucket, R.I., and served as rector for five years. His subsequent charges included Hopkinton and Concord, N.H., where he founded a girls' school which he moved to Boston in 1822 when he became rector of St. Matthew's Church. At the same time he edited the *Gospel Advocate,* which joined with the *Episcopal Watchman* in 1827. Resigning from the clergy in 1830, he spent a short time in New York, and then moved to Orange, N.J., where he devoted himself to literature for the remainder of his life. He was twice married, first: to Louisa Gray Richmond, who died January 3, 1816, and second: to Mary Howe, December 6, 1816.

Well-informed, an indefatigable worker, Blake published more than forty books on diversified subjects. These were mainly text-books and encyclopedias of useful information. Especially interested in agricultural progress and rural education, he produced in 1853 *A Family Text-Book for the Country*: *or, The Farmer at Home.* Among his other works were *A Family Encyclopedia of Useful Knowledge* and the *General Biographical Dictionary,* which achieved thirteen editions in twenty years and stands as the most important title in a group of books that did not outlive their time.

Principal Works: General Biographical Dictionary, 1835; A Family Encyclopedia of Useful Knowledge, 1852; A Family Text-Book for the Country, 1853.

About: Cogswell, E. C. History of Nottingham, Deerfield, and Northwood, N. H.; Church Review and Ecclesiastical Register October 1857; Historical Catalogue of Brown University 1764-1904.

BLAKE, HARRISON GRAY OTIS (April 10, 1816-1898), literary compiler, was born in Worcester, Mass. He was graduated from Harvard in 1835, two years before Henry Thoreau, but his intimacy with the poet-naturalist did not begin until about thirteen years later when a very long and punctual correspondence sprang up between them. With Theophilus Brown [*q.v.*], the tailor-epigrammatist, who was well established in Worcester in the 'fifties, he made a virtual cult of walking, and together they often journeyed to Concord for a visit with Thoreau.

When the North-South question began to take on the appearance of actual war, Blake assumed comparative indifference, and several years later sailed for Europe. In Dresden, however, he became strangely hypnotized by the military enthusiasm of the Franco-German conflict; and his good friend Brown was writing him, in the midsummer of 1870, advising him against any temptations to enlist and urging his speedy return. From 1881 until 1892 Blake was engaged in the editing of four volumes of selections from Thoreau's manuscript journals—thirty-nine heterogeneous blank-books, boarded up in a strong box, bequeathed to him by Sophia Thoreau. His extensive correspondence with the keeper of the journals put him in a position to pass on many of the details with considerable discrimination. Those letters of Thoreau's which were addressed to Blake himself have been condemned for their strains of moral purity and their "overtones of smugness in which the generosity of thought does not sufficiently impoverish the giver." However true this may be, it is only fair to say that Blake stood high among Thoreau's intellectual comrades, even though he was "so Transcendental," says Van Wyck Brooks, "that Henry had to walk on stilts to please him." Blake was, moreover, exasperatingly conscientious, unceasingly driven by a "merciless sense of duty."

It is to Blake's literary credit that not only was he, as a letter writer, capable of appealing to the philosophical side of Thoreau's nature, but that he himself faithfully and competently edited a portion of Thoreau's journals.

Principal Works: *Edited*—Writings of Henry David Thoreau: Vols. 5-8.

About: Atkinson, J. B. Henry Thoreau the Cosmic Yankee; Brooks, V. W. Flowering of New England; Brown, T. Excerpts From the Letters of Theo. Brown; Scudder, H. E. Writings of Henry David Thoreau: Vol. 11.

BLAKE, LILLIE (DEVEREUX) (August 12, 1835-December 30, 1913), novelist and reformer was born in Raleigh, N.C. Her father George P. Devereux died when Lillie was an infant, and her mother Sarah Elizabeth (Johnson) Devereux took her to New Haven, Conn., where she was educated at Miss Apthorp's school for girls and tutored by Yale University professors. Possessed of beauty, wit and charm, she enjoyed unusual popularity as a young lady. At the age of twenty she married Frank G.Q. Umsted, a Philadelphia lawyer, who died in 1855, leaving her with two children to support.

She took up her pen and within the year published a novel entitled *Southwold.* This was followed by short stories in the leading periodicals, other novels, and newspaper work. *Rockford: or, Sunshine and Storm* appeared in 1863, and she was also a contributor to the *Galaxy,* afterward the *Atlantic Monthly,* under the pseudonym "Tiger Lily."

Upon her marriage to Grenfill Blake in 1866, she moved to New York City where she soon interested herself in women's rights. Through her tireless activities, forceful pen, and frequent lectures, she procured many advantages for women and won them the right to serve as census takers, police station matrons, and physicians in insane asylums. War nurses received pensions through her influence. She was president of the New York State Woman's Suffrage Association for eleven years, and president of the New York City Suffrage League from 1886 until 1900 when she founded the National Legislative League.

Mrs. Blake was primarily occupied with the cause of women's freedom from legal tyranny, and although her style cannot be classified as distinguished, her writings played a useful and important part in the suffragist movement. Her best known book was *Fettered for Life: or, Lord and Master,* published in 1874.

PRINCIPAL WORKS: Southwold, 1859; Rockford, 1863; Fettered for Life, 1874; Woman's Place Today, 1883.

ABOUT: New York Sun, New York Tribune December 31, 1913; New York Tribune December 29, 1913.

BLAKE, MARY ELIZABETH (McGRATH) (September 1, 1840-February 26, 1907), poet, was born in Dungarven, Ireland, the daughter of Patrick and Mary (Murphy) McGrath, who came to America about 1850, settling in Quincy, Mass. Her education was received at the local high school, Emerson's Private School in Boston, and the Academy of the Sacred Heart, Manhattanville. In 1865 she married John G. Blake, a Boston physician, and became the mother of eleven children, of whom five sons were sent to Harvard and one daughter to Radcliffe.

Despite the busy life of rearing a large family, she found time for writing, and contributed prose and verse to the leading newspapers and periodicals, including the *Atlantic Monthly, Scribner's, North American Review,* and others. She also wrote many articles for the *Catholic World,* and held a prominent place among Roman Catholic writers in America. Although she published much prose, her reputation was gained chiefly through her poetry, especially in Boston, where she was invited to write memorials for Wendell Phillips, and other important figures. Her books were principally collections of her verse. *Poems,* containing early lyric attempts, appeared in 1882, and *Verses Along the Way* was published in 1890. Two volumes of poems for children were *The Merry Months All,* 1885, and *Youth in Twelve Centuries,* 1886.

She was fond of travel and made five trips to Europe, adapting herself with ease to the customs of each country, and acquiring an intimate knowledge of their history and geography through walking trips. She died in Boston.

PRINCIPAL WORKS: Poems, 1882; The Merry Months All, 1885; Youth in Twelve Centuries, 1886; Verses Along the Way, 1890; In the Harbour of Hope, 1907.

ABOUT: Blake, M. E. In the Harbour of Hope (see Note by K. E. Conway); Cullen, J. B. Story of the Irish in Boston; Publishers' Weekly March 9, 1907; Boston Globe February 7, 1907.

BLEDSOE, ALBERT TAYLOR (November 9, 1809-December 8, 1877), editor and Confederate historian, was born in Frankfort, Ky., the son of Moses Owsley and Sophia Childress (Taylor) Bledsoe. At West Point he was a fellow student of Jefferson Davis and Robert E. Lee, and was graduated in 1830. After further study and a law practice in Springfield, Ill., in the same courts with Lincoln and Douglas, he taught mathematics at Kenyon College and at the universities of Miami, Mississippi, and Virginia. He was made assistant secretary of war of the Confederacy, and was sent to London by President Jefferson Davis for investigations on the North-South issue. The outcome of his research was: *Is Davis a Traitor? or, Was Secession a Constitutional Right Previous to the War of 1861?* It was published in 1866 and was a boon to Davis' defenders.

In 1867 Bledsoe founded the *Southern Review,* dedicated to the "despised, disfranchised, and down-trodden people of the South," and for ten years he was publisher, editor, and chief contributor. But Southerners were poor and apathetic and the magazine failed. Two religious tracts, *Examination of President Edwards' "Inquiry into the Freedom of the Will"* and *A Theodicy: or, Vindication of the Divine Glory* preceded *Essay on Liberty and Slavery* (1856). He was married to Harriet Coxe in 1836.

Bledsoe was sincere but fanatically biased: he denounced not only democracy but all new thought. It is only as a record of an unadjusted Southerner in the decade after the War that his writings have an historical value.

PRINCIPAL WORKS: Examination of President Edwards' "Inquiry Into the Freedom of the Will," 1845; A Theodicy: or, Vindication of the Divine Glory, 1853; Essay on Liberty and Slavery, 1856; Is Davis a Traitor? or, Was Secession. . ., 1866.

ABOUT: Davidson, J. W. Living Writers of the South.

BLEECKER, ANN ELIZA (October 1752-November 23, 1783), poet, was the posthumous daughter of Brandt Schuyler, a member of the distinguished and wealthy Colonial family, and Margareta (Van Wyck) Schuyler. She was born in New York City, and from her earliest childhood manifested an avid interest in reading and writing. At the age of seventeen she married John J. Bleecker, of New Rochelle. They first lived in Poughkeepsie, and later moved to Tomhanick, a frontier village near Albany where Bleecker owned property and built a comfortable house. In 1777 when Burgoyne's army approached the terrorized community, Bleecker hastened to Albany to find quarters for his wife and two little daughters, but during his absence Mrs. Bleecker, overcome by fear, fled with the children to the nearest safety zone. She had difficulty in obtaining shelter and was forced to sleep on a bare attic floor, before her husband found her. Finally reaching Albany, they remained until Burgoyne's army surrendered, but meanwhile death had claimed Mrs. Bleecker's eldest child, her mother, and her sister.

The Bleeckers found Albany an "unsociable, illiterate, stupid town" and risked their lives to return to their home at Tomhanick, but almost immediately Bleecker departed on militia duty. At this time, to occupy her mind, Mrs. Bleecker read widely in the classics and wrote much light verse, which she afterward destroyed. In 1781 Bleecker was captured by Tories, and despite ill-health, Mrs. Bleecker set out to rescue him. He was soon delivered, but the strain of the experience seriously affected Mrs. Bleecker's health, causing increasing despondency, until she died at Tomhanick.

In her poems, which appeared in the *New York Magazine* and were published in book form after her death under the title *The Posthumous Poems of Ann Eliza Bleecker*, 1793, the technical skill is usually marred by an overtone of extreme melancholy, rendering them unpalatable for present-day taste. Mrs. Bleecker's life was perhaps more interesting than her work, and her fortitude and conjugal devotion were of the highest quality.

PRINCIPAL WORKS: The Posthumous Poems of Ann Eliza Bleecker, 1793.

ABOUT: Bleecker, A. E. The Posthumous Works of Ann Eliza Bleecker; Munsell, J. Annals of Albany: Vol. 2; Schuyler, G. Colonial New York: Vol. 2.

BLOOD, BENJAMIN PAUL (November 21, 1832-January 15, 1919), philosopher, mystic, and poet, was born in Amsterdam, N.Y., the son of John and Mary (Stanton) Blood. Educated at the local schools, Amsterdam Academy, and Union College, he returned to the ancestral farm where he spent the remainder of his life reading and writing the poetry and philosophy which were his consuming interests. Before his twenty-first birthday, he composed *The Bride of the Iconoclast*, a long poem in Spenserian stanzas, and *The Philosophy of Justice*, an undertaking which temporarily changed his atheistic views to an unorthodox Christian outlook. This precocious output was followed, at long intervals, by *Optimism* (1860), an attempted theodicy, and *The Colonnades* (1868), a philosophic epic in blank verse. A mystic experience received from nitrous oxide while in a dentist's chair started him on occult pursuits for the following twenty-seven years and lifted him into prominence in 1874 when he published *The Anaesthetic Revelation and the Gist of Philosophy*, an elucidation of his experiments with the effects of anaesthetics. The book received wide attention and brought Blood into a lively correspondence with J. H. Stirling, Lord Tennyson, and William James. In 1920 *Pluriverse* was published posthumously. It set forth the dynamic and pluralistic philosophic attitude that Blood finally attained, and his ruthless attack on monism.

PRINCIPAL WORKS: The Philosophy of Justice, 1851; The Bride of the Iconoclast, 1854; Optimism, 1860; The Colonnades, 1868; The Anaesthetic Revelation and the Gist of Philosophy, 1874; Pluriverse, 1920.

ABOUT: Blood, B. P. Pluriverse (see Introduction by H. M. Kallen).

"BLY, NELLIE." See SEAMAN, ELIZABETH (COCHRANE)

BOKER, GEORGE HENRY (October 6, 1823-January 2, 1890), poet and dramatist, was born in Philadelphia, the son of Charles Boker, a wealthy banker. In 1842 he was graduated from Princeton (then known as the College of New Jersey), where he had already displayed his talent for writing as a founder of and contributor to the

Nassau Monthly. In 1844 he married Julia Mandeville Riggs, of Georgetown, D.C., and they spent nearly a year in Europe. Boker had been studying law, but he now abandoned this professional career and turned to writing.

His first play, *Calaynos,* was produced in London in 1848—without his permission; it was performed in America the following year. His best, and best known, play, *Francesca da Rimini,* first produced by Lawrence Barrett in 1855, was revived by Otis Skinner as late as 1902. Primarily, Boker was a poet: the only two definitely bad plays he ever wrote were also the only two in prose (*The Bankrupt* and *The World a Mask*): most of his dramas were in blank verse, and based on themes drawn from history or literature.

In 1857 Boker's father died, under a cloud, and his son abandoned poetry to clear his memory. It took him until 1873 to prove definitely that the older man had actually saved, not (as he had been accused of doing) wrecked the Girard Bank. Meanwhile the Civil War also interrupted his immersion in poetry. Although a Democrat, he was strongly pro-Union; he was the founder, in 1862, of the Union League in Philadelphia—the first to be formed in the country, and he served as its secretary and later as its president. His *Poems of the War* bore evidence of his sympathies, though he never joined the army. In 1871 he was appointed minister to Turkey, where he proved himself an able and effective diplomat, though he was handicapped by lack of cooperation at home. In 1875 he was sent as minister plenipotentiary to Russia. Here also he was exceedingly popular, but the Hayes administration disliked him, and in spite of the Czar's protests he was recalled in 1878.

Collection of Frederick H. Meserve
GEORGE HENRY BOKER

He was received in Philadelphia like a conquering hero. Much of his time thereafter was given to the service of his adopted city: in 1886 he headed the Fairmount Park Commission, for the extension and improvement of that largest of city parks; and he was president of the exclusive Philadelphia Club. He was also closely connected with *Lippincott's Magazine,* through which he hoped to restore Philadelphia's lost prestige as a literary center. Always kind to aspiring authors, through the magazine he held out a helping hand not only to Charles Godfrey Leland and Richard Henry Stoddard, but also to Southern poets like Paul Hamilton Hayne and William Gilmore Simms, the former of whom had served in the Confederate Army.

A quiet, reticent man, to whom public duties were purely that and nothing more, and who longed constantly for the opportunity which became ever rarer to devote himself entirely to writing in retirement, Boker was nevertheless exceedingly popular. He was known as "the handsomest man in Philadelphia," and was one of the most distinguished. He died suddenly of heart failure at sixty-seven. Eight years previously he had been able formally to publish his father's vindication, in a work he called *The Book of the Dead.*

As a poet, Boker's best work was in his sonnets, of which he wrote 314 in all. His sonnets on public affairs are forceful and sometimes almost Miltonic, but they are now forgotten with the issues which evoked them. The haunting melody of his love-sonnets, however, has not yet wholly died away. Indeed, his finest sonnet sequence was never published until Boker's biographer, E. S. Bradley, brought it out in 1929. These and his *Francesca da Rimini* occupy a small niche of immortality all their own.

Principal Works: A Lesson of Life, 1848; Francesca da Rimini, 1855; Plays and Poems (including Calaynos, Anne Boleyn, Leonor deGuzman) 1856; Poems of the War, 1864; Königsmark, The Legend of the Hounds, and Other Poems, 1869; Book of the Dead, 1882; Nydia (rewritten as Glaucus, but unfinished) 1929; Sonnets: A Sequence on Profane Love (ed. by E. S. Bradley) 1929. [Also plays produced but never published: The Betrothal, 1850; The World a Mask, 1851; The Bankrupt (anonymous) 1855.]

About: Bradley, E. S. George Henry Boker: Poet and Patriot; American Literature November

1936; Atlantic Monthly March 1890; Lippincott's Magazine June 1890; Scribner's Magazine June 1923.

BOLTON, SARAH (KNOWLES) (September 15, 1841-February 21, 1916), poet and reformer, was born in Farmington, Conn., of old New England stock. The daughter of John Segar Knowles and Elizabeth (Miller) Knowles, she was brought up in the country but moved with her mother to Hartford at the age of eleven when her father died. She began to write at a very early age, even publishing verses before she was fifteen. Graduating from the Hartford Female Seminary in 1860, she taught school in Natchez, Miss., until the outbreak of the Civil War, when she returned to Connecticut to teach in Meriden. In 1864 she published her first volume of poems *Orlean Lamar and Other Poems,* which received back-handed compliments from reviewers. This was followed by a novel *Wellesley* published in the *Literary Recorder* in 1865. A year later she married Charles Edward Bolton of Cleveland, who joined her in taking a prominent part in the temperance crusade in Ohio. Mrs. Bolton wrote a book for the cause which had a total sale of 250 copies, but with undampened enthusiasm pushed on to further efforts. After an editorial affiliation with the *Congregationalist* in Boston, she spent two years in Europe studying higher education and better working conditions for women. Returning to America, she became secretary of the Woman's Christian Association and assisted Frances E. Willard in the Woman's Christian Temperance Union. Despite these offices, Mrs. Bolton devoted considerable time to writing, producing two volumes of poetry as well as a number of fictional works and a successful series of books bearing such titles as *Poor Boys Who Became Famous, Girls Who Became Famous* and others. She had no outstanding literary talent but wrote with the robust style of the reformer. Among the many causes she championed, prevention of pigeon-shooting in Ohio and of cruelty to dogs may be noted.

Principal Works: Orlean Lamar and Other Poems, 1864; From Heart and Nature, 1887; Poor Boys Who Became Famous, 1885; Girls Who Became Famous, 1886; Famous American Statesmen, 1888; Famous Men of Science, 1889; The Inevitable and Other Poems, 1895.

About: Bolton, C. K. The Boltons in Old and New England; Bolton, S. K. Pages From an Intimate Autobiography.

BOLTON, SARAH TITTLE (BARRETT) (December 18, 1814-August 4, 1893), poet, was born in Newport, Ky. Her father Jonathan Belcher Barrett was the son of a Revolutionary army officer, and her mother Esther (Pendleton) Barrett was of a prominent Virginia family closely related to James Madison. Shortly after Sarah's birth her family moved to Jennings County, Ind., later settling in Madison, Ind., where she was educated. She began writing at an early age and contributed verses to newspapers in her own town and Cincinnati. These caught the attention of Nathaniel Bolton, a young newspaper man, whom she married at the age of seventeen. Making their home first in Indianapolis, where Bolton was editor of the *Indiana Democrat,* after a short time they purchased a farm near the city. They turned their house into a tavern, with Mrs. Bolton acting as hostess, cook, and manager of their large adjacent dairy. This successful enterprise became known for miles around and attracted many famous guests.

In 1858 her husband died, and five years later Mrs. Bolton married Judge Addison Reese, of Keokuk, Iowa. After living in Canton, Mo., and Europe, she returned to Indianapolis, where she died at the age of seventy-nine.

Mrs. Bolton took a prominent part in Indiana public and literary life, organizing various reforms—notably property rights for women in the constitutional convention of 1850, and writing patriotic verse. Among her poems "Paddle Your Own Canoe" was the acknowledged favorite. Her *Poems* were published in 1865, and the year preceding her death *Songs of a Life Time* appeared. Edited by John Clark Ridpath, it included preliminary remarks by Lew Wallace and James Whitcomb Riley. Although Mrs. Bolton's works were popular in her day, they were not distinguished by any literary quality.

Principal Works: Poems, 1865; The Life and Poems of Sarah T. Bolton, 1880; Songs of a Life Time, 1892.

About: Dunn, J. P. Greater Indianapolis; Woollen, W. W. Biographical and Historical Sketches of Early Indiana; Indianapolis Sentinel August 5, 1893.

BONER, JOHN HENRY (January 31, 1845-March 6, 1903), poet, was born in Salem, N.C., of Moravian parents, Thomas Jacob and Phoebe Elizabeth Boner. He was a Republican and opposed to secession: during the Civil War he was an obscure printer (a trade to which he had been apprenticed following a few years in a local academy) and thus escaped attention; and with Reconstruction he was one of the few white Southerners to find themselves on the winning side.

JOHN HENRY BONER

By 1868 Boner had already founded two papers, the Salem *Observer* and the Asheville *Pioneer,* both of which were speedy failures. With Carpet-Bag government, he became reading-clerk of the constitutional convention, and then, from 1869 to 1870, chief clerk of the North Carolina House of Representatives. In the latter year he married Lottie Smith.

Soon came the downfall of the Carpet-Baggers and the re-establishment of Democratic government in North Carolina; Boner found himself not only out of a job but without friends in his home town. He succeeded in being appointed a typesetter in the Government Printing Office in Washington, where he remained from 1871 to 1887. Then with the election of Cleveland he was discharged for "offensive partisanship." His verse had attracted the attention of Edmund Clarence Stedman, the banker poet, who invited him to come to New York.

For more than twenty years Boner gravitated between various editorial and hack-writing jobs: with the *Century Dictionary* from 1887 to 1891; the *Library of American Literature* from 1888 to 1890; on the staff of the New York *World* in 1891 and 1892; on the *Standard Dictionary* from 1892 to 1894; and on the *Literary Digest* in 1894 and 1895. A dispute with the editor ended the last position, and at the same time the house he had built on Staten Island was sold for taxes, and his health gave way from the strain. From 1896 to 1899 he worked on *Appleton's Annual Cyclopedia*; in 1900 he was reinstated in the Government Printing Office. He was no longer able to work, however, and went back to his home in North Carolina. His health did not improve, and in 1903 he returned to Washington to die. He was buried in the Congressional Cemetery, but the Boner Association, made up of his admirers, removed his body to his birthplace, where it now lies.

Boner was an ineffectual man whose life was a series of mistakes. He thought of himself as a great poet, a successor of Spenser, Keats, and Poe, his three idols, but actually his verse was sentimental and conventional. He is best in vivid descriptions of life in his boyhood home, and as a conscious artist he progressed, his later work being better than his earlier. But he is now a neglected writer, forgiven but also forgotten by the South that he loved even while he deserted it.

Principal Works: Sparrows in the Snow, 1877; Whispering Pines, 1883; Some New Poems, 1901; Poems, 1903.

About: Southern Atlantic Quarterly April 1904; Charlotte Observer January 6, 1906.

"BONNER, SHERWOOD." See MacDOWELL, KATHERINE SHERWOOD (BONNER)

BOTTA, ANNE CHARLOTTE (LYNCH) (November 11, 1815-March 23, 1891), poet and anthologist, was the daughter of Patrick Lynch, who came to America early in the nineteenth century after four years imprisonment following the Irish Rebellion of 1798. Settling in Bennington, Vt., he married Charlotte Gray, daughter of a Revolutionary officer, and there young Anne was born. She contributed prose and verse to literary periodicals at an early age, and after attending, and subsequently teaching, at the Albany Female Academy, made a home for her widowed mother and herself in Providence, R.I. Besides attracting an interesting group of persons to their home, she continued to teach, and also edited the *Rhode Island Book,* a collection from the writings of state authors. In 1845, a position as teacher in the Brooklyn Academy for Women took her to New York City to live and three years later she published *Poems,* a collection of her own work. Her home in Waverly Place soon became the gathering-place of such famous figures as Edgar Allan Poe, Horace Greeley, Margaret Fuller, Bayard Taylor, and R. H. Stoddard.

In 1851 her financial circumstances were greatly improved by the payment of a government debt for her grandfather's military services, and she passed the year 1853 abroad. In 1855 she married Vincenzo Botta, an eminent scholar, who was at that time occupying the chair of Italian language and literature at the University of the City of New York, and they drew such a distinguished assemblage of authors, artists, and musicians around them that the "Botta evenings" became famous.

Anne C. Lynch Botta possessed all the qualifications to make her hostess of the first important American literary salon—charm, tact, dignity, and facile repartee. Her most important publication, *A Handbook of Universal Literature,* received wide attention and was used as a textbook in many schools. Her poetry was thoroughly conventional and undistinguished.

PRINCIPAL WORKS: Poems, 1848; A Handbook of Universal Literature, 1860.

ABOUT: Botta, V. Memoirs of Anne C. L. Botta With Selections From Her Correspondence and From Her Writings in Prose and Poetry; Allen, H. Israfel: The Life and Times of Edgar Allan Poe; New York Times, New York Tribune March 24, 1891.

BOUCICAULT, DION. See Kunitz & Haycraft (eds.). *British Authors of the Nineteenth Century*

BOUDINOT, ELIAS (c. 1803-June 22, 1839), Indian editor, was born among the Cherokee tribe, near the site of Rome, Ga. His native appellation was Galagina, or "Buck Deer" in the Cherokee language. He was educated at the mission school at Cornwall, Conn., where he adopted the name of the school benefactor, Elias Boudinot.

Returning to Georgia in 1823, Boudinot collaborated with the Rev. Samuel A. Worcester, a medical missionary, in translating the New Testament into Cherokee characters. Five years later the Cherokee National Council invited him to become editor of the *Cherokee Phoenix,* the first newspaper ever printed for the enlightenment of an Indian tribe. It was suppressed in 1835 because of an editorial against the state attitude toward Cherokees. Meanwhile, in 1833 Boudinot had published a book entitled *Poor Sarah: or, The Indian Woman.* He had married in 1826 Harriet Ruggles Gold, by whom he had several children, including Elias Cornelius Boudinot, prominent Indian lawyer. Ten years later, after his first wife's death, Boudinot married Delight Sargent.

Influenced by government agents and his politically ambitious cousin, John Ridge, in 1835 he signed a treaty for removal of the tribal domain to a new reservation west of the Mississippi. Until this act Boudinot had been a powerful force among the Cherokees but opinion quickly turned against him, and he was assassinated soon after his arrival at Park Hill, Indian Territory (now Oklahoma). In importance, Boudinot's literary activities never approached his achievements in Indian leadership.

PRINCIPAL WORK: Poor Sarah: or, The Indian Woman, 1833.

ABOUT: Knight, L. L. Georgia's Landmarks, Memorials, and Legends; Lumpkin, W. The Removal of the Cherokee Indians From Georgia.

BOURKE, JOHN GREGORY (June 23, 1846-June 8, 1896), ethnologist and soldier, was born in Philadelphia of Irish parents, Edward and Anna (Morton) Bourke, who so carefully supervised their son's education that he was already studying Latin, Greek, and Gaelic at the age of eight. Pretending to be two years older, he ran away from home when he was sixteen to enlist in the 15th Pennsylvania Cavalry, and fought with this division until the close of the Civil War, when he entered the United States Military Academy at West Point. Graduated in 1869, he was detailed to the 3d United States Cavalry and spent the next fourteen years in the Southwest where he became interested in the life of the American Indian. In 1884, after making careful notes on the habits and customs of the various tribes, he produced *The Snake Dance of the Moquis of Arizona,* the first publication on this subject. Returning to Washington, D.C., with his wife, Mary F. Horback, of Omaha, Neb., he wrote ten important ethnological papers for the *American Anthropologist,* and between 1886 and 1891 brought out five books based on his Indian observations. He died in Philadelphia.

Of medium height, with irregular features and a strong military physique, Bourke, though not handsome, was a man of impressive appearance. His Irish ancestry was apparent in a keen wit and a story-telling ability that added lively touches to his lighter writings. His historical works are free from pretense and are valuable contributions to the records of the American Indian.

PRINCIPAL WORKS: The Snake Dance of the Moquis of Arizona, 1884; An Apache Campaign, 1886; Mackenzie's Last Fight With the Cheyennes, 1890; On the Border With Crook, 1891; Scatalogic Rites of All Nations, 1892; The Medicine Men of the Apache, 1892.

ABOUT: Cullum, G. W. Biographical Register; American Anthropologist July 1896.

BOURNE, EDWARD GAYLORD (June 24, 1860-February 24, 1908), historian, was born in Strykersville, N.Y., son of the Rev. James Russell Bourne, a Congregational minister, and Isabella (Staples) Bourne. Tuberculosis of the bone, to which he finally succumbed at forty-seven, made him lame from boyhood. He was educated at Norwich Free Academy, where he was head of his class, and received his B.A. from Yale in 1883. He had specialized in the classics, but he fell under the influence of the great economist, William Graham Sumner, and decided to make economic history his lifework. Accordingly he declined a graduate fellowship to the American School in Athens, and remained at Yale to study economics and history.

From 1885 to 1887 he was instructor in mediaeval history at Yale, and from 1886 to 1888 lecturer in political science. Then he became instructor in history and economics at Adelbert College, in Cleveland, being promoted to a professorship in 1890. In 1892 he secured his Ph.D. from Yale, which in 1895 called him back to be professor of history. In the same year he married Annie Thomson Nettleton. At Yale, Bourne taught European history until 1897, and American history thereafter. He was essentially an historical critic, with special reference to the economic aspects of history. Besides his own writing, he edited numerous original documents relating to early American history. He was active in the American Historical Association, was president of the New England History Teachers' Association in 1901, and was about to be made editor of the Massachusetts Historical Association publications when his health failed badly and he found himself unable to serve. He was working on a life of John Motley, the historian, when he died.

Principal Works: The Surplus Revenue of 1837, 1885; Prince Henry: The Navigator, 1894; The Proposed Absorption of Mexico in 1847-48, 1900; Essays in Historical Criticism, 1901; Historical Introduction to the Philippine Islands, 1903; Spain in America, 1904; Discovery, Conquest, and Early History of the Philippine Islands, 1907.

About: Yale Alumni Weekly March 25, 1908.

BOUTON, JOHN BELL (March 15, 1830-November 18, 1902), journalist, was born in Concord, N.H. Of French descent, he was the son of the Rev. Nathaniel Bouton and Mary Anne Persis (Bell) Bouton, daughter of Governor John Bell of New Hampshire. Graduated from Dartmouth College with high honors, John Bell Bouton first studied law, and then turning to journalism, became editor of the Cleveland *Plain Dealer* in 1851. After 1857 he moved to New York where he edited the *New York Journal of Commerce* and *Appleton's Annual Cyclopedia.* He married his cousin, Eliza Nesmith of Lowell, Mass., in 1873.

Bouton retired from active business in 1889, making his home in Cambridge, Mass. Extremely patriotic, deeply interested in public service, he possessed a keen sense of humor and a love of travel. His publications include essays, novels, and travel books, the best known being *Roundabout to Moscow: An Epicurean Journey.* Though lightened by occasional flashes of wit, his writings typify the tedious, involved style of his generation.

Principal Works: Loved and Lost, 1857; Round the Block: An American Novel, 1864; A Memoir of General Louis Bell, 1865; Roundabout to Moscow: An Epicurean Journey, 1887; The Enchanted: An Authentic Account of the Strange Origin of the New Psychical Club, 1891; Uncle Sam's Church: His Creed, Bible, and Hymn-book, 1895.

About: Dartmouth College Catalogue, 1910; Boston Evening Transcript November 18, 1902.

BOUVET, MARIE MARGUERITE (February 14, 1865-May 27, 1915), linguist and author of children's books, was born in New Orleans of French parents, Jean François Bouvet, of noble descent, and Adelphine (Bertrand) Bouvet, the well-educated daughter of a cavalry officer under Charles X of France. After spending her early childhood with paternal grandparents at Lyons, France, she attended Loquet-Leroy Female Institute, New Orleans, and in 1885 was graduated from St. Mary's College, Knoxville, Ill. She then became a French instructress and tried her hand at writing juvenile stories with historic European backgrounds. *Sweet William,* an appealing account of William the Conqueror, with a Mont St. Michel setting, was published in 1890. It was enthusiastically received and still enjoys a certain popularity. Her other works, while pleasant, are excessively sentimental.

Miss Bouvet possessed great charm of manner and a keen Gallic wit. Before her death she lived in Reading, Pa., with an old college friend.

Principal Works: Sweet William, 1890; Little Marjorie's Love Story, 1891; Prince Tip-Top, 1892; My Lady, 1894; A Child of Tuscany, 1895; Pierrette, 1896; A Little House in Pimlico, 1897; Tales of an Old Château, 1899; Fleurs des Poètes et des Prosateurs Français, 1900; Bernardo and Laurette, 1901; The Smile of the Sphinx, 1911.

BOWDITCH, NATHANIEL (March 26, 1773-March 17, 1838), mathematician, astronomer, and authority on navigation, was born at Salem, Mass., the son of Habakkuk Bowditch, a poor cooper, and Mary (Ingersoll) Bowditch. At the age of ten he was obliged to leave school to help in his father's

From a portrait by C. Osgood
NATHANIEL BOWDITCH

shop, but already he showed the makings of a student. For a while he studied bookkeeping, then at twelve became a clerk in a ship chandlery. He studied Latin in order to read Newton and found an error in the famous *Principia.* From 1795 to 1803 he was at sea, first as ship's clerk, then as supercargo, finally as master; and all the time he studied—mathematics, astronomy, languages. Reading J. Hamilton Moore's *Practical Navigator,* the standard work on the subject, he found eight thousand errors, and what started out to be his American edition of the book ended as a practically new work under his own name. He edited every edition of this up to the tenth, in 1837; there have been fifty-six editions since. The work became indispensable, and was probably the first American book to have a wide sale in England.

In 1802 Harvard gave an honorary M.A. to this man who had never seen the inside of a college, following it in 1816 with an LL.D., and thereafter he was known as Dr. Bowditch. In 1806, indeed, Harvard invited him to be its Hollis professor of mathematics, but he declined, as he declined later offers from the University of Virginia and West Point. He was already in a new position—that of president of the Essex Fire and Marine Insurance Company. That his presidency depended more on actuarial services than on executive functions was shown by his acceptance in 1823 of an offer to be actuary of the Massachusetts Hospital Life Insurance Company. This post he held for the remainder of his life. He had in 1809 been elected a Fellow of the American Academy of Arts and Sciences (he was its president from 1829 to his death), and this removal to Boston gave him an opportunity to pursue a long-cherished project—a translation and revision of Laplace's immortal classic of mathematics, the *Mécanique Céleste.* He worked from 1814 to 1827 on this, and the Boston Public Library still shows his original manuscripts, acquired on its foundation in 1852. But he refused all publishing offers; he wished to produce this work in his own way at his own expense. His salary was not large, but most of it he devoted to this aim, with the cooperation of his family, who promised to undergo any sacrifices to see it finished. He had in 1798 married Elizabeth Boardman, who died within six months; in 1800 he married his cousin, and his mother's namesake, Mary Ingersoll, who bore him six sons and two daughters.

While he was working on Laplace, and also performing his actuarial duties, Bowditch found the time to contribute twenty-three papers to the *Memoirs* of the American Academy of Arts and Sciences. The translation when completed was a triumph for American learning; Simon Newcomb, the great astronomer, says that "it made an epoch in American science." *The Practical Navigator,* Van Wyck Brooks remarks, was "as stoutly built as one of the clipper-ships for which Dr. Bowditch had prepared the way." Clear, thorough, and accurate, a sagacious critic, this slight, prematurely grey man with aquiline nose and high forehead, this "little nimble man with burning eyes," was one of the earliest of the great American scholars, a thinker who with as discouraging a start as Franklin had outdone Franklin in the pure power of intellect. He died suddenly of heart failure just before his sixty-fifth birthday.

Principal Works: New American Practical Navigator, 1802; Laplace's *Mécanique Céleste* (trans.) 1829-39; Useful Tables, 1844.

About: Bowditch, H. J. Sketch of the Life and Character of Nathaniel Bowditch; Bowditch, N. I. Memoir of Nathaniel Bowditch; Brooks, Van W. The Flowering of New England; Newcomb, S. Side-lights on Astronomy; Young, A. Discourse on the Life and Character of Nathaniel Bowditch.

BOWEN, FRANCIS (September 8, 1811-January 21, 1890), philosopher and editor, was born at Charlestown, Mass., the son of Dijah and Elizabeth (Flint) Bowen. He attended the Mayhew Grammar School at Boston, Phillips Exeter Academy, and Harvard College, from which he was graduated with honors in 1838. After two years as a mathematics instructor at Exeter, he returned to Harvard as tutor in intellectual philosophy and political economy. In 1839 he resigned from these duties to spend a year of travel and study in Europe. On his return he settled in Cambridge, wrote a number of his well-known books and edited the *North American Review* during the following ten years.

In 1851 when Louis Kossuth visited America in the interests of the Hungarian revolution, Bowen published *Hungary: The Rebellion of the Slavonic, Wallachian, and German Hungarians Against the Magyars,* a sharp protest, which offended public opinion and lost Bowen his appointment as McLean professor of history at Harvard, although the College later elected him to the Alvord professorship of natural religion, moral philosophy, and civil polity, which he held until his resignation thirty-six years later. His wife was Arabella Stuart, daughter of Charles J. and Eliza (Austin) Stuart, whom he married at Portsmouth, N.H., in 1848.

Bowen produced more than fifteen books and contributed numerous articles to periodicals. His *Modern Philosophy: From Descartes to Schopenhauer and Hartmann,* published in 1877, is a valuable contribution to the field of philosophy and is distinguished by a lucid critical power and a concise style. He died at Cambridge, Mass.

PRINCIPAL WORKS: Life of Sir William Phips, 1837; Life of Baron Steuben, 1838; Critical Essays on a Few Subjects Connected With the History and Present Condition of Speculative Philosophy, 1842; Life of James Otis, 1844; Life of Benjamin Lincoln, 1847; Lowell Lectures on the Application of Metaphysical and Ethical Science to the Evidences of Religion, 1849; Hungary: The Rebellion of the Slavonic, Wallachian, and German Hungarians Against the Magyars 1851; Principles of Political Economy, 1856; Treatise on Logic, 1864; American Political Economy, 1870; Modern Philosophy: From Descartes to Schopenhauer and Hartmann, 1877; Gleanings From a Literary Life, 1880; A Layman's Study of the English Bible, 1885.

ABOUT: Eliot, C. W. Harvard Memories; Sawyer, T. T. Old Charlestown; Boston Evening Transcript January 22, 1890; Boston Herald January 22, 23, 1890.

BOWNE, BORDEN PARKER (January 14, 1847-April 1, 1910), philosopher, was born in Leonardville, N.J., the son of Joseph and Margaret (Parker) Bowne. He was sensitive and impressionable, and after attendance at a private school, was entered as a sophomore at the University of the City of New York, from which he was graduated in 1871 with a most distinguished record. He taught for a while, held a short pastorate, and then studied in Europe at Halle and Göttingen, returning in 1875. For the New York *Independent* he was religious editor, and his brilliant criticism of Herbert Spencer's philosophy was published in the *New Englander.* In 1875 he was married to Kate Morrison and the following year he became head of the department of philosophy of Boston University, serving for almost thirty years. In 1905-06 he made a world tour, during which he developed a new respect for Oriental peoples.

Bowne's philosophy had its beginnings in the objective idealism of his German contemporary; Rudolf Hermann Lotze. But by bringing all philosophy and religion to a pragmatic test of life and by laying supreme emphasis on personality, he evolved what he called Personalism. Conservative, in part, he had an allegiance to open-mindedness that once brought him to trial for heresy. His writings include: *Studies in Theism, Metaphysics, The Christian Revelation,* and *Personalism.* With sound philosophy and refreshed religious opinion, they throw considerable light on the ever-changing relationship between metaphysics and theology.

PRINCIPAL WORKS: Philosophy of Herbert Spencer, 1874; Studies in Theism, 1879; The Christian Revelation, 1898; The Immanence of God, 1905; Personalism, 1908; Studies in Christianity, 1909.

ABOUT: Methodist Review May-June 1922.

BOYESEN, HJALMAR HJORTH (September 23, 1848-October 4, 1895), educator and writer of miscellaneous and juvenile works, was the son of a professor of mathematics at the naval academy in Frederiksvärn, Norway, where he was born. As a child, he often visited his maternal grandfather, a judge at Systrand on the Sognefjord, where he heard from the household servants ballads and folk-lore which he incorporated in his writings in later life. He was educated in the Latin School at Drammen, the gymnasium at Christiania, the University of Leipzig, and the University of Christiania, where he received the degree of Ph.D. in 1868. The following year he came to America and became associate editor of a Norwegian newspaper, published in Chicago, called the *Fremad.* Leaving in order to perfect his knowledge of English, he became tutor in Greek and Latin at Urbana University, in Ohio, and it was at this time that a nostalgic memory of his native land led him to write *Gunnar* his best novel, published serially in the *Atlantic Monthly* in 1873. William Dean Howells was the editor, and the two men formed an enduring friendship. After a year of philosophical and linguistic studies at Leipzig,

Boyesen was made professor of German at Cornell University in 1874. Six years later he came to New York with his wife, the former Elizabeth Keen, and entered the German department of Columbia College, where he eventually occupied the chair of Germanic languages and literature

Possessing a remarkable facility for languages, an alert mind, and a Scandinavian determination, Boyesen mastered his adopted tongue sufficiently to write more than twenty-five books on miscellaneous subjects, including essays, history and criticism. In two books for boys—*The Modern Vikings*, 1887; and *Boyhood in Norway*, 1892—his fertile imagination and quiet humor are admirably manifest. His other books, somewhat ponderous in style, maintain a position midway between mediocrity and assured literary merit.

Principal Works: *Novels*—Gunnar, 1874; Falconberg, 1879; Queen Titiania, 1881; Ilka on the Hill-top, 1881; A Daughter of the Philistines, 1883; The Light of Her Countenance, 1889; Against Heavy Odds, 1890; A Fearless Trio, 1890; A Golden Calf, 1892. *Stories*—Tales From Two Hemispheres, 1876; Vagabond Tales, 1889; Norseland Tales, 1894. *Juvenile*—The Modern Vikings, 1887; Boyhood in Norway, 1892. *Miscellaneous*—Goethe and Schiller, 1879; Idyls of Norway, 1882; The Story of Norway, 1886; Commentary on the Writing of Henrik Ibsen, 1894; Literary and Social Silhouettes, 1894; Essays on Scandinavian Literature, 1895.

About: Dial December 1, 1895; Open Court February 13, 1896; Sewanee Review May 1896; Sunday News-Tribune (Detroit) April 8, 1894.

"BOYLESTON, PETER." See CURTIS, GEORGE TICKNOR

BRACKENRIDGE, HENRY MARIE (May 11, 1786-January 18, 1871), lawyer and social historian, was born in Pittsburgh, Pa., the son of Hugh Henry Brackenridge [*q.v.*]. When he was only two his father gave him lessons from the horn-book and at seven he was sent by flatboat to Louisiana to learn French. Returning to Pittsburgh, he was given further instruction by his father and acquired from him a wittiness, a love of reading, and a liberal political philosophy. He was admitted to the bar in 1806 and for the next five years attempted to set up a practice first in Baltimore, then in Somerset, Pa., and finally in St. Louis, where he hit upon some good material for a column in the *Missouri Gazette*. A river log which he kept in 1811 later became the source of Washington Irving's *Astoria*. Miscellaneous articles and new chapters on Louisiana, his home since November 1811, were the contents of his first book, *Views of Louisiana* (1814).

Brackenridge anticipated, in his *South America: A Letter on the Present State . . .* 1817, a foreign policy which, six years afterwards, was incorporated into the Monroe Doctrine. He was made secretary of a commission to study political South America; and in his *Voyage to South America* he glimpsed the weakness of the Spanish American republics. In 1834 came *Recollections of Persons and Places in the West*, a valuable piece of early social history. Brackenridge fell short of any tremendous political or literary eminence, but he was a participant in, and a recorder of, many of the events which mark significant stages in the growth of the nation.

Principal Works: Views of Louisiana, 1814; History of the Late War, 1816; South America: A Letter on the Present State of That Country to James Monroe, 1817; Recollections of Persons and Places in the West, 1834.

About: Brackenridge, H. M. Recollections of Persons and Places in the West; Pittsburgh Daily Gazette January 19, 1871.

BRACKENRIDGE, HUGH HENRY (1748-June 25, 1816), poet and novelist, was born in Campbeltown, Scotland, the son of William Brackenridge, a farmer. His family was so poor that they had to sell all their possessions in order to emigrate to America in 1753. They settled on a farm in York County, Pa., where the boy, a natural student encouraged by an intelligent mother, educated himself by reading, under the guidance of a friendly minister. Like the young Lincoln, he often walked thirty miles to borrow a book. The first school he ever entered was as a teacher, in Maryland, at fifteen. Before he was twenty he had saved enough money to enter Princeton, where he worked his way through by acting as master of the grammar school—a quaint commentary on the nature of Princeton (then the College of New Jersey) in its early years. He was graduated in 1771, writing with his classmate Philip Freneau the Commencement poem, "The Rising Glory of America." While acting as head of an academy in Maryland, he studied divinity, and received his M.A. from Princeton in 1774.

A Whig and an ardent patriot, Brackenridge served as chaplain throughout the Revolution, and also wrote many pamphlets and verses to help the cause of independence. In 1779 he became editor of the *United States Magazine*, in Philadelphia. Religious doubts had impelled him to leave the ministry, and now he studied law with Samuel Chase in Annapolis. In 1781 he moved to Pittsburgh, then a frontier village in the Far West. There he helped to found the

After a portrait by G. Stuart
H. H. BRACKENRIDGE

town's first newpaper (the Pittsburgh *Gazette*), its first bookstore, and its first academy. In 1786 and 1787 he was a member of the state assembly, and he became the chief advocate of the new Federal Constitution in the West—though when he ran for election to the constitutional convention he lost. The Whiskey Rebellion, in 1793, cast a cloud on his reputation: his attitude pleased neither side, and even involved this keen patriot in a charge of disloyalty, from which he was absolved by Alexander Hamilton.

He became a leader in the new Republican (later the Democratic) party, and in 1799 was appointed a justice of the Supreme Court of Pennsylvania. In 1801 he moved from Pittsburgh to Carlisle. He remained in this town, and on the Supreme Court bench, until his death.

The name and date of marriage of his first wife are unknown, but she died in 1788, leaving a son, Henry M. Brackenridge [*q.v.*], who became a well known literary figure. In 1790 Brackenridge married Sabina Wolfe, a farmer's daughter, proposing marriage at their very first meeting. Eccentricity, combined with a certain formidable dignity, were his most prominent characteristics. Added to them was a caustic wit which made him more respected than loved. Of his integrity and the sincerity of his patriotism there can be no doubt.

Brackenridge's prose was better than his verse, which was stilted and pompous. He himself said that his plays were intended only for school or amateur production. Butler's *Hudibras* was the avowed model of his verses, as Swift was his master in prose. His best, and best known, work was the picaresque satirical novel, *Modern Chivalry*. This book, brought out in parts and constantly revised and rewritten to bring it up to date, was the first substantial literary achievement of the new West. Democrat though he was, Brackenridge had a sharp eye for the bombastic, ridiculous, and corrupt in the new democracy of the frontier, and *Modern Chivalry* missed no opportunities for satire. The second part of the novel is inferior, but the first has real point and power, and is still worth reading quite aside from its historical significance.

Principal Works: The Rising Glory of America (with Philip Freneau) 1772; The Battle of Bunker's Hill (verse play) 1776; The Death of General Montgomery (verse play) 1777; Six Political Discourses, 1788; Modern Chivalry: Containing the Adventures of Captain John Farrago and Teague O Regan, His Servant, 1792-1815; Law Miscellanies, 1814.

About: Brackenridge, H. H. Modern Chivalry (see Memoir by H. M. Brackenridge in editions of 1846 and 1856); Brackenridge, H. M. Recollections of Persons and Places in the West; Heartman, C. F. Bibliography of the Writings of Hugh Henry Brackenridge.

BRADFORD, GEORGE PARTRIDGE

(February 16, 1807-January 26, 1890), scholar and reformer, was born in Duxbury, Mass., the son of Captain Gamaliel Bradford, who had fought in the Revolutionary War, and Elizabeth (Hickling) Bradford. His mother died when he was ten and his sister Sarah Ripley guided his preparation for college. In 1825 he was graduated from Harvard, and three years later from the Divinity School, but he preached only occasionally, for he regarded the pulpit as a very inadequate social organ. After dabbling in several educational enterprises in Plymouth and elsewhere, he joined the Brook Farm community at West Roxbury during the early stages of the experiment. George Ripley, one of the Farm's organizers, was editing *Specimens of Standard Foreign Literature* and to this Bradford contributed "Selections From Fénelon." Bradford had fed on Greek and Latin along with his earliest English syllables, and the uncouth spondees and dactyls of the gusty religious titan, Orestes Brownson, who often invaded Brook Farm, are said to have given him more than one sleepless night.

Upon leaving the Community he returned to Plymouth and became a systematic and well-informed gardener, interrupting his simple life for only an occasional journey to Europe. If ever there was such a thing as an out-and-out unrelenting New England conscience, this cautious classicist had it: during one of Webster's open-air addresses, on finding himself being swept to the front of the crowd, he cried out "I have no ticket. . .I have no right to be here!"—and righteously fought his way back to the farthest rim of the circle.

The "Selections," mentioned above, and a chapter on "Philosophic Thought in Boston" for Justin Winsor's *Memorial History of Boston* are the bulk of Bradford's writings. It is as the silver-tongued classicist, the Brook Farm botanist that Bradford "the ever-gentle" played his little part in the New England literary scene.

Principal Works: Selections From Fénelon, (in Ripley, G. *Specimens of Standard Foreign Literature,* 1838 ff.); Philosophic Thought in Boston (in Winsor, J. *Memorial History of Boston,* 1880-81).

About: Brooks, V. W. Flowering of New England; Thoreau, H. D. The Writings of Thoreau; National Encyclopaedia of Biography.

BRADFORD, JOSEPH (October 24, 1843-April 13, 1886), actor, journalist, poet, and playwright, began life as William Randolph Hunter, the son of a wealthy Southern planter. He was born near Nashville, Tenn., and grew up in luxurious surroundings, among many fine books which stimulated his early love of literature. On September 29, 1860, he entered the United States Naval Academy at Annapolis. His scholastic standing was excellent, but an excessive amount of demerits provoked his dismissal on April 14, 1862. Two months later he enlisted in the North Atlantic Blockading Squadron and was attached to the "U.S.S. Minnesota" and the "U.S.S. Putnam." This subordinate service caused such an upheaval in his ultra-conservative family that relations were entirely severed and his patrimony bequeathed to the next of kin.

Assuming the name of Joseph Bradford, his mother's surname, he turned to a theatrical career. Joining a stock company in Baltimore, he played in light comedies and toured in various cities along the Atlantic Coast. While acting in Boston he left the stage to write his own plays. He not only achieved success as a playwright but enjoyed a small reputation as poet and journalist by virtue of his contributions to the Boston *Courier* over the signature of "Jay Bee." His plays were mainly comedies or long musical productions with arresting titles: *In and Out of Bondage,* 1877, *Our Bachelors,* 1877, and *Cherubs,* 1885.

Principal Works: New German, 1872; Law in New York, 1873; 20,000 Leagues Under the Sea, 1874; The Conditional Pardon, 1875; Fritz's Brother, 1875; Out of Bondage, 1876; In and Out of Bondage, 1877; Our Bachelors, 1877; John Mishler, 1882; One of the Finest, 1883; A Wonderful Woman, 1883; Cherubs, 1885; Rose and Coe, 1886.

BRADFORD, WILLIAM (1589/90-May 9/19, 1657—old and new calendar), governor and historian of Plymouth, was born in Austerfield, Yorkshire, the only son of William Bradford, a yeoman who died in 1591, and Alice (Hanson) Bradford. His mother remarried, and the boy was left to the mercy of a harsh grandfather and uncles who gave him no education except training as a farmhand. While still a boy he earned their displeasure by joining the Separatist (Puritan) congregation of William Brewster, at Scrooby, and when the congregation moved for the sake of religious freedom to Holland, in 1609, he went with them, first to Amsterdam and then to Leyden. In 1611, when he came of age, he inherited a "fair estate" from his father's property, but lost it all in unwise investment. He became a citizen of Leyden, and worked there as a weaver of serge and fustian. At the same time he educated himself, belatedly but thoroughly, and laid up for himself an appreciable fund of learning, in Dutch and Latin as well as in English.

Bradford was one of the leaders in the move to emigrate to America, and was one of the "Pilgrim Fathers" (though then a young man) who landed in Plymouth from the "Mayflower" in 1620. He was a member of the first exploring expedition, under Miles Standish, and was from the beginning a

WILLIAM BRADFORD
an imaginary portrait

prominent member of the colony. In 1621 he was elected governor, and was re-elected thirty times—every year until 1656 except for five when "by importunity I gat off." Since he received no salary until 1639, and then only £20, and since the burden and responsibility were most onerous, one can understand the "importunity." Plymouth was always both better governed and more liberal than the Massachusetts Bay Colony, and in both points it was William Bradford who could be thanked for it. He was no dour, long-faced bigot, but a man of deep sincerity, great simplicity, and unassailable integrity, who yet had more than a touch of humor and a fair amount of tolerance—though he did join in the persecution of the Quakers.

In his old age Bradford studied Hebrew, and to the end he was solicitous for the improvement of education in the colony, trying in vain to secure the establishment of a college which should be a Plymouth rival to Harvard. His history of the colony was written, not for publication, but for the edification of his descendants. These, incidentally, were and are very many, and have included some of the most illustrious of American names. In 1613 he had married Dorothy May, in Amsterdam, but she was drowned in Cape Cod Harbor in the winter of 1620, leaving one son. In 1623 he married Alice (Carpenter) Southworth, a widow with two sons, and by her he had two more sons and a daughter.

The manuscript of the history, which had been consulted by early historians of New England but not published, was stolen by British soldiers during the Revolution and taken to England. It was identified in 1855, when it was in possession of the Bishop of London. In 1897 it was returned to America by the British government. (It had already been published in full in 1856, Book I having been published in 1841 from an early copy.) Bradford wrote it from 1630 to 1651, but brought it up to only 1646. Like other writings and letters of Bradford's which have since appeared in print (largely through the Massachusetts Historical Society), it is not primarily the work of a writer, but is the simple account of his own recollections written by a man of affairs. Besides a short series of *Dialogues* summarizing the religious thought of the Colony, Bradford wrote, in Hudibrastic metre, some much-labored descriptive verse, setting forth the material and moral states of his people, contained in the "little book with a black cover" mentioned in his will. Moreover it is believed that he was at least in part responsible for *A Revelation or Journell . . . of the English Plantation* issued in London in 1622. His Plymouth history is not, however, without conscious art, and is obviously the production of a man of wide reading and some culture. It has a vivid and even racy style and is good reading on its own account, as well as an exceedingly important historical source.

Principal Works: A Dialogue Between Some Young Men and Sundry Ancient Men, 1855 (third Dialogue [second lost], ed. by Charles Deane, 1870); History of Plimmoth Plantation, 1856.

About: Blaxland, G. C. "Mayflower" Essays; Mather, C. Magnalia; Plumb, A. H. William Bradford of Plymouth; Shepard, J. Governor William Bradford and His Son; Usher, R. G. The Pilgrims and Their History; Nation April 8, 1897.

BRADSTREET, ANNE (1612?-September 16, 1672), poet, was born in Northampton, England, the daughter of Thomas Dudley, who in her childhood moved to Boston, Lincolnshire, and became steward of the Earl of Lincoln, and Dorothy Dudley. Though both Dudley and the Earl were Puritans, Anne was reared in an atmosphere of wealth and culture and some liberality: she reported that she had "eight tutors" at a time, and that she learned music and dancing as well as languages.

In 1628, when she was about sixteen, she was married to Simon Bradstreet, also in the Earl's service. Though he was considerably her senior, he far outlived her, not dying until 1697, almost a centenarian. Bradstreet's father was a non-conformist minister, who had conformed long enough to enable his son to receive his M.A. degree from Cambridge.

In 1630 the Dudleys and the Bradstreets joined the Winthrop party which settled on Massachusetts Bay. Mrs. Bradstreet, a fastidious, civilized lady and something of a blue-stocking, was wretched in the rough pioneer environment to which she had been transported, first in Cambridge, then in Ipswich, and finally in North Andover. But her deep love for her husband (theirs was an ideal marriage) and a sincere religious conversion helped to soften the misery of her daily life, and she found in poetry a refuge and a sublimation. Gradually as conditions grew easier, she could set up a little replica of her aristocratic home in England, for both her husband and her father served as governors of the Massachusetts Bay colony, and she moved in high administrative circles which had wealth, learning, and influence, if they did not have many of the amenities or graces of life.

Besides her social duties the governor's lady had heavy maternal responsibilities.

From a drawing by E. C. Garrett
ANNE BRADSTREET
an imaginary portrait

She was the mother of eight children and lived to see herself many times a grandmother, Oliver Wendell Holmes, Richard Henry Dana, and Wendell Phillips being among her multitudinous descendants. Somehow in the midst of so busy an existence she managed to write some seven thousand lines of verse. Its publication never entered her mind, but on a trip to England her brother-in-law took her manuscripts with him, and had her poems published without her knowledge. After her death they were republished, with additions, in Boston. Her florid title, "The Tenth Muse, Lately Sprung up in America," was destined to survive her work in the annals of literature.

Mrs. Bradstreet's models were Spenser, Sidney, Raleigh, and above all the didactic Huguenot poet DuBartas, much of whose work she merely paraphrased in English. She never became really skilled in metrics, and her rhythm is very faulty. Her poems are not only obviously derivative, but frequently feeble and narrow as well. Yet when she wrote of matters known to her through experience instead of through reading—as in her poems to her husband or her personal "Contemplations"—when, in other words, she exercised her slender talent for versification instead of trying to imitate writers too far her superior in thought as well as in style, her work is not unpleasing. She has one short poem, "The Author to Her Book," which, though metrically rough, is charmingly whimsical, and gives an indication of a personal attractiveness that induced many contemporaries to exaggerate their admiration of her work. Cotton Mather, for example, turned from the contemplation of hell long enough fairly to wallow in fulsome praise of the divine Mrs. Bradstreet. Perhaps the fact that she was the first woman to write verse in English in America exposed her to adulation which injured her in the eyes of posterity, whatever it did to smooth her path while she lived.

Anne Bradstreet was far from being "the tenth muse" or any kind of muse at all. Her poems for the most part are as dull as they are pedantic. Had she remained in England they would never have seen the light of publication—it was as a curiosity, as the production of an American, and a female American at that, that they excited any interest even in her own time outside of Massachusetts. But merely because she herself was a charming, gentle creature, an exotic figure among the homespun bigots of that seventeenth century middle-class colony, she has retained a certain tenuous reputation entirely unjustified by any intrinsic merit in anything she wrote. Hers was the last echo of "polite letters" in a country to become increasingly provincial for the next two hundred and fifty years.

Principal Works: The Tenth Muse, Lately Sprung up in America, 1650.

About: Campbell, H. Anne Bradstreet and Her Times; Chautauquan January 1912.

BRAINARD, JOHN GARDINER CALKINS (October 21, 1796-September 26, 1828), poet, was born in New London, Conn., the son of Jeremiah G. Brainard, judge of the superior court of Connecticut, and Sarah (Gardiner) Brainard. He was graduated from Yale College in 1815, studied law in the office of his brother, William F. Brainard, and was admitted to the bar in 1819. In Middletown he built up a small practice, but took more interest in the writing of verse for the New Haven *Microscope* than in the pursuit of his legal career, for which he was, indeed, temperamentally ill-suited. In 1822 he was made editor of the (Hartford) *Connecticut Mirror*, disliked the discipline entailed, but took real delight in filling his columns with quantities of poems, later published in volume form as *Occasional Pieces of Poetry*. The critics' approbation of the book should have been something of a stimulus for this rising poet, but a habit of severe procrastination and an inferiority complex prevented him from producing anything beyond the rather unimportant *Fort Braddock Letters* (1827).

Among Brainard's best descriptive poems were "Niagara," supposedly written in twenty minutes, and "Connecticut River"; both were much quoted in their day. His later verses, belonging to the period of his retirement in New London after leaving the *Mirror* in 1827, such as "The Invalid on the East End of Long Island," are a reiteration of his constant dejection; *Fugitive Tales* (1830) was further evidence of this melancholia. In the last months of his life he steeped himself in the doctrines of Christian grace and became a communicant of the First Congregational Church at New London, where he died of consumption in 1828.

He has been described as a "clumsy little man with paddling walk, pale sensitive face, abstracted air, careless dress, and great personal charm." He was a witty conversationalist when not overcome by extreme timidity and self-consciousness. A flowery elegance, a stilted morality, and an adolescent zeal pervaded his verse, but his sensitivity to the details of nature lent a redeeming delicacy to his many descriptive lines.

PRINCIPAL WORKS: Occasional Pieces of Poetry, 1825; Fort Braddock Letters, 1827; Fugitive Tales, 1830.

ABOUT: Dexter, F. B. Biographical Sketches of Graduates of Yale College; Robbins, R. The Poems of John G. C. Brainard; Whittier, J. G. The Literary Remains of John G. C. Brainard.

BRAINERD, DAVID (April 20, 1718-October 9, 1747), missionary to the Indians, was born in Haddam, in the Colony of Connecticut, the son of Hezekiah Brainerd, one of His Majesty's Council, and Dorothy (Hobart) Brainerd. As a child he was hyper-emotional and morbidly introspective and conscientious, and many of his later religious experiences may have had pathological origins. He entered Yale in 1739, but was dismissed three years later for having made some derogatory remarks about the Rector and a tutor.

In July 1742 he was licensed to preach, after studying with the Rev. Jedediah Mills, and was appointed missionary to the Indians by the Correspondents of the Society in Scotland for the Propagation of Christian Knowledge. For five years he labored at Indian settlements scattered throughout the Hudson Valley. He had long been a victim of tuberculosis, and in the spring of 1747 he became physically exhausted and died in October at Northampton, Mass., in the home of Jonathan Edwards, to whose daughter he was engaged.

"Brainerd's Journal," published in two parts as *Mirabilia Dei Inter Indicos* and *Divine Grace Displayed*, records his religious experiences, physical weakness, teachings, travels, etc. The diary spanned but one short, limited, and over-sensitive life, but it stood, until the middle of the nineteenth century, as the dominating stimulus and guide for pioneering missionaries

PRINCIPAL WORKS: Mirabilia Dei Inter Indicos, 1746; Divine Grace Displayed, 1746.

ABOUT: Edwards, J. An Account of the Life of the Late Reverend Mr. David Brainerd.

BRANN, WILLIAM COWPER (January 4, 1855-April 2, 1898), editor, reformer, and "iconoclast," was born in Humboldt, Ill. His mother died when he was less than three and he was placed in the care of one William Hawkins, on whose farm young Brann learned to despise rural life. Ignoring his guardian's kindnesses, he climbed out of his window on a winter night—at thirteen he was seeking complete independence. As bell boy, painter, drummer, and then printer he made enough to live on, and, at the same time, read widely and schooled himself in languages.

Shortly after scoring a small success as a reporter he was married, March 3, 1877, to Carrie Martin, of Rochelle, Ill., and became, subsequently, an editorial writer on the St. Louis *Globe-Democrat.* But domestic misfortunes followed, and the Branns emigrated to Texas, a state of potentially endless opportunities. The Houston *Post* made him chief editorialist, but he was too candidly radical and he withdrew in 1891. At Austin he established the *Iconoclast*, a monthly, which the *Statesman* immediately branded a "veritable roasting mill, a skinning machine, with a full set of knives and a revolution like a drunken buzz-saw." It was first issued in July and suspended a few months later.

Brann readily found another market for his galling philippics—the St. Louis *Globe-Democrat* and the San Antonio *Express.* In the spring of 1894 he had sold his printing press to W. S. Porter ("O. Henry"), of Austin, who had begun to publish a humorous weekly, keeping the name *Iconoclast.* Apparently re-energized by Porter's speculations, Brann retrieved his press, and started again, in Waco, Tex. (Porter happily renamed his own paper the *Rolling Stone.*) Within four years the revived *Iconoclast* reached a circulation of 90,000. In this blatant journal of opinion, Brann strove to "break foolish idols and shatter false ideals. . ." He admitted that a work of destruction is not always "of a high order. Anybody may destroy . . . it requires a genius to build up. . . But destruction is

WILLIAM COWPER BRANN
("Brann, The Iconoclast")

sometimes necessary." Any subject was within his pale; among his best articles were some discerning papers on Carlyle and on Hugo's *Les Miserables* and a very clear-headed projection of what would later have been called anti-Prohibition argument. But when George Washington Cable voiced disapproval of slavery, Brann countered with a flat denunciation of the whole Negro race and let fly a host of inordinately flagrant missiles that could have endeared him to no sane critic.

In an early issue of the *Iconoclast* Brann had struck up a quarrel with Baylor University, a local Baptist college, that proved to be no forgive-and-forget affair: about three years later, in the summer of 1897, a certain G. B. Gerald wrote a defense of Brann, which J. W Harris, editor of the (Waco) *Times-Democrat* refused to publish. In the pistol fracas that ensued, Harris and his brother, W. A. Harris, were killed. The blame fell heavily on Brann. On April 1, 1898, one Capt. T. E. Davis is said to have opened fire on him; both men died the following day. Brann's funeral was attended by many on whom his attack had been most noxious, but in the huge assemblage of mourners there was nothing but complete and wholly sincere sympathy. Of his writings three were published before his death: *Brann's Speeches and Lectures* (1895?); *Potiphar's Wife* (1897), a revision of the Story of Joseph; and *Brann's Scrap-book* (1898). *Brann the Iconoclast* (1903, 2 vols.), selected articles, etc., appeared posthumously.

Brann's fall from fame had been as rapid as his rise: he not only lacked a single and well-defined aim but he treated problems of ethical and personal conduct by methods of virtual violence. He seemed to align himself arbitrarily with the minority and to relish the jaundiced vision of a misanthrope. His subject matter is, moreover, largely "dated." But it is only fair to say that he thought himself sincere. Above all, he was a master of "journalese," with a "gargoylean" vocabulary that would have stamped any ordinary newspaper man as a full-fledged pedant.

Principal Works: Brann's Speeches and Lectures, 1895(?); Potiphar's Wife, 1897; Brann's Scrap-book, 1898; Brann the Iconoclast, 1911.

About: Brann, W. C. Brann the Iconoclast (see Introduction by J. W. Shaw); Brann, W. C. Complete Works (see Preface by M. Hastings); South Atlantic Quarterly January 1915.

"BREITMANN, HANS." See LELAND, CHARLES GODFREY

BREWSTER, WILLIAM (July 5, 1851-July 11, 1919), ornithologist, was born at Wakefield, Mass., the son of John and Rebecca Parker (Noyes) Brewster. He inherited an abundance of New England tradition, spending his boyhood near the Longfellows in Cambridge, where he attended the Washington Brattle Street School that stood opposite the fabled "spreading chestnut tree." Frail health and poor eyesight made his entering Harvard quite inadvisable, and after a year in his father's banking house, he withdrew and interested himself in ornithology. With Daniel Chester French, whose father was an amateur taxidermist, and who, many years later, was to edit Brewster's "Concord Journals," the lad had shared an early enthusiasm for bird lore. At the age of fourteen he began to acquire much skill in the mounting of his specimens; and he enhanced his collection by expeditions to the far South, Colorado, and the British West Indies.

Although Brewster became an authority on the taxonomy of North American birds and wrote some notable papers in this field, his most valuable publications concerned the living bird. He was one of the founders of the Nuttall Ornithological Club (1876), which for a while met regularly at his home, and of the American Ornithologists' Union (1883). As president of the Massachusetts Audubon Society and member of the state Game Commission, Brewster maintained a consistently sensible attitude towards game

WILLIAM BREWSTER

preservation. For eight years he was in charge of the bird and mammal collections of the Boston Society of Natural History, and from 1885 until his death served the Museum of Comparative Zoology.

Brewster was a tall and well-proportioned man with handsome features and a kindly and engaging expression. He spent much of his later life at "October Farm," a 300-acre wild life preserve on the outskirts of Cambridge, just across from Ball's Hill and Walden Pond, where, almost a half century earlier, Thoreau had built his house in the woods. Although Brewster certainly had the poet-naturalist's love of the open and tenderness of feeling towards birds, he regarded them, in the main, with a professional eye and a scientifically objective mind. There is in his notes little or nothing of philosophy, asceticism, or subjectivity; no rediscovery of Thoreau's law of divine respect, of being "suddenly neighbor to the birds; not by having imprisoned one, but by having encaged myself near them. . . ."

Brewster was married to Caroline F. Kettell, of Boston, on February 9, 1878. Largely in the interest of his health he went once to Europe and, three times to England, where he cultivated a friendship with Rudyard Kipling. Amherst conferred an M.A. on Brewster in 1880, and Harvard in 1889.

His major publications include *Descriptions of the First Plumage in Various North American Birds*, *Bird Migration*, and *Birds of the Cambridge Region of Massachusetts*, and over 250 papers for the *Bulletin of the Nuttall Club* and the *Auk*. He was a slow and painstaking writer, with a high regard for accuracy, and sent his work to scientific journals only. His belief that his articles were unworthy of publication in the more widely read periodicals limited their popularity, but his services in the interests of American ornithology were in no wise confined to the printed page.

Modern readers know Brewster best by the belated publication, in 1936 and 1937, of his "Concord Journals," in two volumes entitled *October Farm* and *Concord River*: two books which have given him (not entirely correctly) a reputation as a sort of latter-day Thoreau. The connotation, nevertheless, is accurate insofar as it identifies him with the minds and ideas of the nineteenth century. Despite the fact that he lived well into the present century, he belonged to the end to the Concord of the past—the last of the "old school" naturalists.

PRINCIPAL WORKS: Descriptions of the First Plumage in Various North American Birds, 1878-79; Bird Migration, 1886; Birds of the Cambridge Region of Massachusetts, 1906; Birds of the Lake Umbagog Region, Maine, 1924-25 (unfinished); October Farm (ed. by D. C. French) 1936; Concord River (ed. by S. O. Dexter) 1937.

ABOUT: Brewster, W. October Farm and Concord River; Thoreau, H. D. Writings of Thoreau; The Auk January 1920.

BRIDGE, HORATIO (April 8, 1806-March 20, 1893), naval officer, diarist, and biographer, was born in Augusta, Maine. He was graduated from Bowdoin in the same class (1825) with Hawthorne and Longfellow. After a course of study at the Northampton law school he was admitted to the bar in 1828, practiced a few years, and then embarked on his "great enterprise"—the building of a dam across the Kennebec River. But the cost was tremendous and on completion of the work a new freshet opened up and swept away dam, mills, and mansion, and Bridge was financially ruined. He entered the navy as a paymaster and his assignment to the sloop of war "Saratoga" for a Mediterranean cruise provided the materials for the *Journal of an African Cruiser*. After sixteen years' service he was made Paymaster General, which office he held for fifteen years, including the whole period of the Civil War. In 1873 he retired to his country home, "The Moorings," at Athens, Pa., where he died twenty years later.

For his literary achievements Bridge was heavily indebted to Hawthorne, who edited the popular and generously reviewed *Journal*, and whose long friendship, begun in college, occasioned his *Personal Recollections of Nathaniel Hawthorne*. (Bridge, however, had adequately reciprocated by assisting his old schoolfellow both politically and financially.) The reminiscences, are, on the whole, pleasingly free from the hero-worshipping vein, and, by bringing into focus some of the otherwise hazier portions of Hawthorne's life they represent a valuable though small segment of American biography.

PRINCIPAL WORKS: Journal of an African Cruiser, 1845; Personal Recollections of Nathaniel Hawthorne, 1893.

ABOUT: Bridge, H. Personal Recollections of Nathaniel Hawthorne; Brooks, V. W. Flowering of New England; National Cyclopaedia of American Biography: Vol. 4.

BRIGGS, CHARLES FREDERICK (December 30, 1804-June 20, 1877), novelist and journalist, son of Jonathan C. Briggs and Sally (Coffin) Briggs, was born on the island of Nantucket, Mass. He went to sea at an early age, but after several voyages gave up maritime life to enter business in New York City. In 1839 he published his first novel—*The Adventures of Harry Franco: A Tale of the Great Panic,* based on his sea experiences, and used the name of his hero as a pen-name in several subsequent novels. Five years later he founded the *Broadway Journal.* Edgar Allan Poe contributed to the first issue and eventually became co-editor. Briggs retired from the *Journal* in 1845 because of an inability to adapt himself to Poe's peculiar temperament, and spent the next eight years writing fiction. In 1853 he joined the editorial staff of *Putnam's Magazine,* in association with Parke Godwin and George William Curtis. After three years the magazine suspended publication for ten years and in the interim Briggs edited the New York *Times.* Becoming financial editor of the Brooklyn *Union* in 1870, he remained three years and left to assume the editorship of the *Independent,* which occupied him until his death. He died in Brooklyn and was survived by his widow and one daughter. Among his writings was a sketch of Poe for the *Encyclopaedia Britannica.* His friend James Russell Lowell gave him the copyright privileges of his *Fable for Critics,* in which he included an appreciative portrait of him. Briggs takes his place in American literature more from his association with Edgar Allan Poe and other prominent writers than from the merits of his novels.

PRINCIPAL WORKS: The Adventures of Harry Franco: A Tale of the Great Panic, 1839; The Haunted Merchant, 1843; Working a Passage, 1846; The Trippings of Tom Pepper, 1847.

ABOUT: Allen, H. Isratel: The Life and Times of Edgar Allan Poe; Independent June 28, 1877; New York Times, New York Tribune, New York Herald June 22, 1877.

BRINTON, DANIEL GARRISON (May 13, 1837-July 31, 1899), physician and ethnologist, was born at Thornbury, Pa., the son of Lewis and Ann (Garrison) Brinton. Tutored by the Rev. William E. Moore, he matriculated at Yale College in 1854, where as an undergraduate he greatly distinguished himself in literary activities. After graduation, he entered Jefferson Medical College, receiving his M.D. in 1861. Further studies at Heidelberg and Paris led to his establishing a practice in West Chester, Pa., for a brief period until he joined the Federal army in 1862 as acting assistant surgeon, serving with distinction at many great battles, including Chancellorsville and Gettysburg. A severe sunstroke necessitated his leaving active duty for hospital work.

After leaving the army in 1865, he married Sarah Tillson of Quincy, Ill., and returned to his West Chester practice. In 1867 he became assistant editor of the *Medical and Surgical Reporter* in Philadelphia, and seven years later took the editor's chair.

In 1859 Brinton's *Notes on the Floridian Pensinsula* revealed his interest in anthropology and by 1884 he was holding the professorship of ethnology and archaeology in the Academy of Natural Sciences of Philadelphia, and two years later became professor of American linguistics and archaeology in the University of Pennsylvania. His writings were based on extensive library research rather than field work, and although many of his theories were interesting they were quite often inaccurate. His two most important books are *Notes on the Floridian Pensinsula* and *The American Race* (1891), a systematic classification of aboriginal languages in North and South America. The absence of accuracy in Brinton's work prevented him from taking a foremost place among American anthropologists, but his efforts undeniably paved the way for later important ethnological and archaeological discovery.

PRINCIPAL WORKS: Notes on the Floridian Peninsula, 1859; Library of Aboriginal Literature, 1882; The American Race, 1891.

ABOUT: Stokes, A. P. Memorials of Eminent Yale Men; Biographical Record of Class of Fifty-Eight: Yale University; Philadelphia Public Ledger, Philadelphia Press August 1, 1899.

BRISBANE, ALBERT (August 22, 1809-May 1, 1890), social reformer, was born in Batavia, N. Y., the son of James and

Mary (Stevens) Brisbane. He was sent to a boarding-school on Long Island, and then studied in New York City under private tutors; among whom was John Monesca, whose social theories tempted the lad with the idea of European study. In Paris under Guizot and in Berlin under Hegel he piled up new ideas, but Fourier, with his formula for "dignifying and rendering attractive the manual labors of mankind," had, so Brisbane thought, the makings of the most feasible Utopia.

Poor health on his return to the United States in 1834 dampened his Fourierism campaign, but in 1840 he published *Social Destiny of Man: or, Association and Reorganization of Industry* which some time later strongly interested Horace Greeley, editor of the New York *Tribune*, who joined Brisbane in setting up the *Future*, a journal entirely devoted to this new "Associationism." It was abandoned in two months and Brisbane turned his attention to writing for the *Tribune*, the radical *Plebeian*, and the *Dial*, the Brook Farm organ. His "hasty propaganda" gave birth to numerous experiments in Associationism—Brook Farm among them—the general failure of which caused a waning of interest in the whole movement. In 1876, however, he published *General Introduction to Social Sciences* containing the essence of Fourier's social theory and a translation of his *History of Universal Unity*. Brisbane was twice married, and by his first wife, Sarah White, he had three children, one of whom, Arthur (1864-1937), became a widely known editor and columnist, with views completely antithetical to his father's high-minded idealism; Albert Brisbane's second wife was Redelia Bates.

Brisbane was a highly educated man with a vigorous mind, but he failed as a social reformer because he lacked an ability to lead, as well as a realization of the practical difficulties in the way of a universal panacea for evil. He wrote with comparative ease as well as fervor, but only as object lessons in social reform have his writings survived the movement of which they were a part.

Principal Works: Social Destiny of Man: or, Association and Reorganization of Industry, 1840; General Introduction to Social Sciences, 1876.

About: Brisbane, R. Albert Brisbane: A Mental Biography With a Character Study.

BRISTED, JOHN (October 17, 1778-February 23, 1855), clergyman, lawyer, and miscellaneous writer, was born at Sherborne, Dorsetshire, England. The son of an Anglican clergyman, he was educated at Winchester College, studied medicine in Edinburgh, and afterwards read law for two years in the office of Joseph Chitty, the celebrated editor of Blackstone's *Commentaries*, and became a member of the society of barristers of the Inner Temple. He came to America in 1806 and settled in New York City where he practiced his profession for twenty-three years. Devoting his leisure to literature and lecturing, he published several books which achieved prominence by the caustic critiques they received from Fitz-Greene Halleck. After 1807 Bristed edited the *Monthly Register, Magazine, and Review of the United States*, a periodical founded in 1805 by Stephen Cullen Carpenter of Charleston, S.C. His lecture course included a wide range of subjects—metaphysics, history, political economy, the science of government, and common, statute, and international law. A deep interest in theology led him to take orders in the Episcopal church. Studying divinity under Bishop Griswold of the Eastern diocese, he was ordained in 1828, became Bishop Griswold's assistant at St. Michael's Church, Bristol, R.I., and in the following year succeeded him as rector, remaining until 1843 when failing health caused him to resign. He organized St. Mark's Church, Warren, R.I., and devoted his energies to extending episcopacy in the state.

Bristed's infectious enthusiasm, strong will, and unflagging industry greatly aided him in his clerical and literary life. His most characteristic publication is *A Pedestrian Tour Through Part of the Highlands of Scotland in 1801* (2 vols., 1804).

Principal Works: The Adviser: or, The Moral and Literary Tribunal (4 vols.) 1802; A Pedestrian Tour Through Part of the Highlands of Scotland in 1801 (2 vols.) 1804; Critical and Philosophical Essays, 1804; The Society of Friends Examined, 1805; Edward and Anna, 1806; Hints on the National Bankruptcy of Britain, 1809; The Resources of the British Empire, 1811; Oration on the Utility of Literary Establishments, 1814; The Resources of the United States of America, 1818; Thoughts on the Anglican and Anglo-American Churches, 1823.

About: Kirby, T. F. Winchester Scholars; Providence (R.I.) Daily Post February 27, 1855; Newport (R.I.) Advertiser February 28, 1855.

BRODHEAD, JOHN ROMEYN (January 2, 1814-May 6, 1873), historian, was born in Philadelphia, the son of the Reverend Dr. Jacob Brodhead and Elizabeth (Bleeker) Brodhead, a descendant of Jan Jansen Bleeker, early Dutch settler. Educated at Albany Academy and Rutgers College, he read law and was admitted to the bar in 1835 but abandoned a legal career to become an attaché to the legation at the Hague, under Harmanus Bleeker, a relative. A deep interest in the Dutch aspect of early

New York history led to a state appointment to search foreign archives for important historical data, and after four years he returned to America with eighty volumes of manuscript which was edited by E. B. O'Callahan and B. Fernow and published by the state under the title *Documents Relating to the Colonial History of the State of New York,* Albany, 1856-86.

In 1845, in *Senate Document No. 47,* Brodhead published a report of his activities, and spent the following three years as secretary of the legation in London. In 1853 he published the first volume of his *History of the State of New York,* and in the same year was appointed naval officer of the port of New York. Brodhead's official duties delayed publication of the second volume until 1871. He married Eugenia Bloodgood in 1856 and settled in New York, where he became an active member of the New York Historical Society and the St. Nicholas Society, a trustee of the Astor Library, and a loyal alumnus of Rutgers College, where he founded the Brodhead Prize for proficiency in the classics.

Principal Works: History of the State of New York, 1853-71.

About: Scribner's Monthly February 1877; New York Tribune May 7, 1873.

BROOKS, CHARLES TIMOTHY (June 20, 1813-June 14, 1883), Unitarian minister, translator, and poet, was born in Salem, Mass., the son of Timothy and Mary King (Mason) Brooks. He attended Salem Latin Grammar School, was graduated from Harvard in 1832, and from the Divinity School three years later. After acting as visiting pastor in Boston and New York churches, he began, January 1, 1837, a long and extremely active ministry in Newport, R.I. The year following he was married to Harriet Lyman Hazard.

Brooks began to write for the *North American Review, Harper's,* and the Boston *Transcript,* and in 1837 he published Schiller's *William Tell,* the first of a long series of German translations which was to include two excellent English versions of Jean Paul Richter: *Titan,* highly praised by Thomas Carlyle, and *The Invisible Lodge. Aquidneck and Other Poems* and *Songs of Field and Flood* contain Brooks' original verse, and "Madras in Pictures," occasioned by his journey to India in 1853, appeared in *Harper's.* His own poetry bears a stereotyped sentimentality, but his rare knowledge of Teutonic language and literature and his rhetorical care in transcribing the original thought elevate him to a place of eminence among the translators of German verse.

Principal Works: *Translations*—William Tell, 1837; Faust, 1856; Titan, 1862; Invisible Lodge, 1883. *Original Verse*—Aquidneck and Other Poems, 1848; Songs of Field and Flood, 1853. *Miscellaneous*—The Old Stone Mill Controversy, 1851.

About: Andrews, W. P. Poems: Original and Translated by Charles T. Brooks (see Memoir by Charles W. Wendte).

BROOKS, ELBRIDGE STREETER (April 14, 1846-January 7, 1902), juvenile writer, was born in Lowell, Mass., son of Elbridge Gerry Brooks, a Unitarian minister and prominent abolitionist, and Martha (Monroe) Brooks. In his childhood his father held charges at Bath, Maine; Lynn, Mass.; and New York, at which last-named city Elbridge attended the Free Academy (now the College of the City of New York). He left in his junior year, and in 1864 was a clerk for D. Appleton and Co. He served in a similar capacity with other publishing houses until 1879, when he joined the staff of the *Publishers' Weekly.* From 1883 to 1885 he was dramatic critic and literary editor of the Brooklyn *Daily Times,* and in 1884 he became also associate editor of *St. Nicholas,* the juvenile magazine. In 1887 he became editor of D. Lothrop & Co. and moved to Somerville, Mass., to be near his work in Boston. Except for a period between 1892 and 1895, when the firm was in financial difficulties, he continued in this position for the remainder of his life. From 1891 to 1893 he was editor of *Wide Awake,* another juvenile periodical, as well. In 1870 Brooks had married Hannah Melissa DeBaun, and they had two daughters, one of whom, Geraldine, became a writer.

Brooks wrote over forty books for young people, all of them historical or biographical in character. The reason for his popularity seems hard to find, for his books are wooden and mechanical, baldly written and dull. Nevertheless they all had a good sale, and new editions of many of them have continued to appear.

In person, Brooks was an intellectual looking man, with aquiline nose, keen, deep, spectacled eyes, and, in his later years, white hair and beard.

Principal Works: Historic Boys, 1875; Historic Girls, 1877; The Story of the American Indian, 1887; The Story of the American Sailor, 1888; The Story of New York, 1888; The Story of the American Soldier, 1889; The True Story of Christopher Columbus, 1892; The Century Book for Young Americans, 1894; Boy Life of Napoleon, 1895; The True Story of George Washington, 1895; A Boy of the First Empire, 1895; The True Story of Abraham Lincoln, 1896; Century Book of the American Revolution, 1897; The True

Story of U. S. Grant, 1897; The True Story of the United States, 1897; Chivalric Days, 1898; The Master of the Strong Hearts, 1898; The True Story of Benjamin Franklin, 1898; Historic Americans, 1899; Stories of the Old Bay State, 1899; The Story of the War With Spain, 1899; The True Story of Lafayette, 1899.

ABOUT: Boston Herald January 8, 1902; Boston Transcript January 7, 1902.

BROOKS, JAMES GORDON (September 3, 1801-February 20, 1841), editor and poet, was born either at Red Hook, N.Y., or Claverack-on-the-Hudson, the son of David Brooks, a Revolutionary officer and Congressman. Graduated from Union College in 1818, he read law in Poughkeepsie but gave up the idea of practicing to follow a literary career. By his sixteenth year he was attracting much attention with poems and prose published under the pseudonym "Florio." After 1823 he joined the editorial staff of the *Minerva*, a literary magazine published in New York City, and subsequently edited the *Literary Gazette*, the *American Athenaeum*, and the *Morning Courier*, until 1830. Meanwhile, in 1828 Brooks had married Mary Elizabeth Aiken of Poughkeepsie, who had published poetry under the signature "Norma." In 1829 husband and wife brought out their collected poems as *The Rivals of Este and Other Poems*. Despite the fact that his wife attempted more ambitious subjects, Brooks' poems are of a higher standard.

Removing to Winchester, Va., in 1830, he edited the *Republican* for eight years, and then returned North with Mrs. Brooks to make a home in Albany, N.Y. The Albany *Advertiser* employed him as editor but a disagreement with the owners precipitated his resignation after a year. Before his death in Albany he edited the *New Era* in New York. He achieved a fairly wide reputation as a poet but is chiefly remembered for his long journalistic record.

PRINCIPAL WORKS: The Rivals of Este and Other Poems, 1829.

ABOUT: Griswold, R. W. The Poets and Poetry of America; Hudson, F. Journalism in the U. S.; Albany Daily Argus February 22, 1841; Troy Daily Whig February 22, 1841.

BROOKS, MARIA (GOWEN) (c. 1794-November 11, 1845), poet, was born in Medford, Mass., of Welsh ancestry. Her original name was Abigail Gowen (it was changed by court order in 1819 to Mary Abigail, but she was always known as Maria), and her parents were William Gowen, a goldsmith, and Eleanor (Cutter) Gowen. A precocious child, she began writing verse early. In 1809 her father died, a bankrupt, and her education was taken over

From a portrait by F. Alexander
MARIA GOWEN BROOKS

by her brother-in-law John Brooks, widower of her older sister, a man of nearly fifty with two sons. The next year, when she was not more than sixteen (more likely fourteen or fifteen) he married her. Needless to say, her marriage was most unhappy. The ill-matched couple moved to Portland, Maine, and there her husband became bankrupt. It was during this period, in an endeavor to retrieve the family fortunes, that she published her first volume of poems, "by a lover of the fine arts." Meanwhile she bore two sons, cared devotedly for her two stepsons, and found time to fall deeply in love with a young Canadian officer. In 1823 Brooks died. The widow went to Cuba, where her uncle, a coffee planter, soon after died in turn and left her his estate and his fortune. She proceeded at once, with her brother as chaperon, to Canada, met her officer again, and became engaged to him. But an estrangement followed, twice she attempted suicide without winning him back, and finally in despair she returned to Cuba. Her novel, *Idomen*, gives in fictional form the story of this unhappy affair.

Mrs. Brooks lived in Cuba, writing her poems in a little Grecian temple on her estate, dressed always in white, aloof and mysterious, until her older son was ready for college; then she accompanied him to Hanover, N.H., where he attended Dartmouth. She had long been in correspondence with the English poet, Southey, who admired her work extravagantly and nicknamed her "Maria del Occidente"; and in 1830 she went to England and there, after a short tour in France, settled down for more than a year, becoming practically one of the group of "Lake Poets" living near Grasmere, and including Wordsworth, Coleridge, and Southey. It was here that she completed her epic, *Zóphiël,* the first canto of which had been published in America in 1823. She returned to the United States when her son, later a distinguished army officer, went to West Point, and she lived with him there and wherever he was stationed until 1843. In that year her other son and one of her stepsons died in Cuba of tropical fever, giving rise to perhaps her best known poem, the "Ode to the Departed."

Before the year was out Mrs. Brooks too went back to her Cuban estate, and set to work on a new long poem to be called *Beatriz: The Beloved of Columbus.* But two years later, before the poem was completed, she and her surviving stepson both died of the same fever (probably malaria) which had decimated her family.

Mrs. Brooks in her lifetime was praised beyond all merit, compared to Byron and to Swinburne. Charles Lamb paid her a left-handed compliment by denying that she could have written *Zóphiël*—"as if there ever had been a woman capable of anything so great!" As a matter of fact, her work was lush, syrupy, feminine in the worst meaning of the term—the sort of thing that might well be written, as it was, in a marble temple by a lady garbed in white with passion-flowers in her hair. Nevertheless, this pretty blonde with all her affectations possessed real talent; Van Wyck Brooks speaks of her "bell-like depth of tone" against the "pallid poems of the thirties." Had she written less, more would have survived, and even as it is, there are passages of power and beauty in her work. She may not have been, as Southey called her, "the most impassioned and imaginative of poetesses," but in the New England of the first half of the nineteenth century she was indeed a phenomenon.

PRINCIPAL WORKS: Judith, Esther, and Other Poems, 1820; Zóphiël, 1833; Idomen: or, The Vale of Yumuri (prose) 1843.

ABOUT: Brooks, V. W. The Flowering of New England; Granniss, R. S. An American Friend of Southey; Griswold, R. W. Female Poets of America; American Collector August 1926; Graham's Magazine August 1848; Harper's Magazine January 1879.

BROOKS, MARY ELIZABETH (AIKEN). See BROOKS, JAMES GORDON

BROOKS, NOAH (October 24, 1830-August 16, 1903), journalist and juvenile writer, son of Barker Brooks, a master shipbuilder, and Margaret (Perkins) Brooks, was born in Castine, Maine. Attending the local schools until his eighteenth year, he went to Boston to study painting, but soon abandoned his brushes for a literary career. At twenty-one he joined the editorial staff of the *Atlas,* a Boston daily, and contributed essays and humorous stories to periodicals. Five years later a business partnership took him to Illinois and when it failed he moved to Kansas, and finally to Marysville, Calif., where he and Benjamin P. Avery, afterwards United States Minister to China, became joint-publishers of the *Daily Appeal.* During this time, Brooks' contributions to the *Overland Monthly* led to a friendship with Bret Harte, then editor.

In 1862 Brooks sold out his newspaper interest and returned to the East to become Washington correspondent of the *Sacramento Union.* He soon became an intimate friend of Abraham Lincoln and was invited to serve as his private secretary, but the assassination occurred before he assumed his duties, and luckily a severe cold kept him away from the presidential box on the fatal night. After brief service as naval officer in the San Francisco custom house, Brooks took the managing editorship of the San Francisco *Alta California.* Five years later he moved to New York to serve on the editorial staff of the New York *Times* and the Newark *Daily Advertiser.* In 1892 he retired from journalism and traveled extensively. He died in Pasadena, Calif., having

Collection of Frederick H. Meserve
NOAH BROOKS

survived his wife, Caroline Fellows, of Salem, Mass., whom he married in 1856.

A keen sense of humor and excellent story-telling ability made him a welcome member of any gathering. He belonged to a number of religious and literary organizations and was one of the founders of the Authors Club of New York. Of his numerous works his books for boys have survived and are still read, but his serious writings have been long since forgotten. Such books as *The Boy Emigrants* and *First Across the Continent* came from his personal experience and form a valuable as well as a readable record of the times.

PRINCIPAL WORKS: The Boy Emigrants, 1876; The Fairport Nine, 1880; Our Baseball Club, 1884; The Boy Settlers, 1891; American Statesmen, 1893; Tales of the Maine Coast, 1894; Abraham Lincoln and the Downfall of American Slavery, 1894; How the Republic Is Governed, 1895; Washington in Lincoln's Time, 1896; Short Studies in American Party Politics, 1896; The Story of Marco Polo, 1896; The Mediterranean Trip, 1896; History of the United States, 1896; Henry Knox: A Soldier of the Revolution, 1900; Abraham Lincoln: His Youth and Early Manhood, 1901.

ABOUT: The Lamp September 1903; New York Herald, New York Tribune, New York Times August 18, 1903.

BROUGHAM, JOHN (May 9, 1810-June 7, 1880), actor and playwright, was born in Dublin, Ireland, of Irish-French descent. He studied for a medical career at Trinity College and the Peter Street Hospital until his twentieth year when financial reverses forced him to leave college to earn his own living. He went to London and by 1831 had joined Mme. Vestris' theatrical company at the Olympic, and later at Covent Garden, where, he maintained, he gave Dion Boucicault the idea of *London Assurance.* In 1840 he became manager of the London Lyceum and wrote several plays for its repertoire. He was in America in 1842 taking the part of Felix O'Callahan in *His Last Legs* at the Park Theatre, New York City, and later joined Burton's company at the famous Chambers Street Theatre, where he remained for many years, acting and writing plays and burlesques, including his famous *Columbus.* The year 1850 marked the opening of Brougham's Lyceum in New York City, an unsuccessful enterprise, as the razing of an adjoining building imperilled the walls and public safety. After reviving *King John* at the Bowery, he became a member of Wallack's company and wrote a number of plays, including a dramatization of *Bleak House,* and *Pocahontas,* his best known burlesque. In 1860 he returned to the English stage for five years. For his adaptation of *The Duke's Motto* for Charles Fechter he was rewarded with a box of cigars. He returned to New York permanently in 1865 and four years later again opened Brougham's Theatre on West Twenty-Fourth Street, with *Better Late Than Never* and *The Dramatic Review for 1868,* a presentation similar to the "revues" of the twentieth century, but finally lost the management of the theatre and was eventually reduced to such straitened circumstances that the Academy of Music settled a $10,000 annuity on him.

PRINCIPAL WORKS: *Dramatizations*—Dombey and Son, Bleak House, The Duke's Motto; *Burlesques*—Pocahontas, Columbus; *Reviews*—Better Late Than Never, The Dramatic Review of 1868.

ABOUT: Winter, W. Life, Stories, and Poems of John Brougham; Other Days; New York Times, New York Tribune June 8, 1880.

BROWN, CHARLES BROCKDEN (January 17, 1771-February 22, 1810), novelist and journalist, was born in Philadelphia of a Quaker family which had come to Pennsylvania with William Penn. His father, Elijah Brown, was a fairly prosperous merchant, who passed on his business to Charles' older brothers, and who could afford to give his youngest son a good education at a private school; his mother was Mary (Armitt) Brown. Charles was a prodigy, a frail, precocious child with whom reading was a passion and almost a vice. He wrote early, and while still at school planned three grandiose historical epics in verse. Rather unfortunately for him, his uncritical family and friends proclaimed him a scholar and a genius. He was a bit of the latter, but nothing at all of the former. Surrounded by so much adulation, however, it is not surprising that he became the first American to be a professional literary man, earning his living—for a few years at any rate—solely by his pen.

He did not, of course, take this drastic step immediately; he was first apprenticed to a lawyer, with the idea of combining the law and literature. (His first published work, a prose dithyramb called "The Rhapsodist," had appeared in the *Columbian Magazine* in 1789.) By 1793, appalled at the imminent dull compulsions of a legal career, all afire with romantic notions, he threw up his profession and proclaimed himself a writer and nothing else. Mingled with this determination was a tender shrinking from the worry and responsibility he was casting on his family, who in turn, though strongly disapproving, could deny him nothing and promised to stand by. Both he and they were sure—and were justified in their certainty—that he could not earn an adequate living by such means alone. Even in England the writer without a patron was still rare, and in America in the eighteenth century he was unknown.

A solitary, melancholy youth, "a proud and lonely soul," Brown tried to find some intellectual companionship in the Belles Lettres Club of like-minded young Philadelphians which he founded. But there were not enough of them, and they did not answer the needs of this fiery young disciple of Thomas Jefferson and William Godwin. He began spending more and more time in New York, where his friend Dr. Elihu Hubbard Smith, who was a writer as well as a physician, was living, and where a much more congenial club, the Friendly Society, also welcomed him. From 1798 to 1801 he lived almost entirely with Smith, and acted as chief editor of the Society's *Monthly Magazine and American Review* from 1799 to 1800, when it expired. His feminist dialogue, *Alcuin,* and nearly all his novels were written during these few years, in feverish haste.

Disaster brought a close to this period of Brown's life. Dr. Smith did not believe that yellow fever was contagious. When a great epidemic broke out in New York in 1801, he took into his house a young Italian suffering from the disease. Brown's family, who had fled from Philadelphia in the epidemic of 1793 (which Brown described so vividly in *Arthur Mervyn*) begged him to come to them, but he refused to leave his friend. Both he and Smith contracted the fever; the Italian and Smith died. Brown came back to Philadelphia.

His career as a literary free lance was over. He went into partnership with his brothers as a merchant. The business failed in 1806. Two years previously he had married Elizabeth Linn, sister of a Presbyterian minister, and the first of their four children had now been born. An exemplary husband and father, he was tied to the grindstone for life. He became a small independent trader and eked out his livelihood by hack journalism, translations, and political pamphlets. His novels had gained him a wide reputation—Scott and Godwin admired them, and *Ormond* was a favorite of Shelley who named one of his poems after its heroine, Constantia—but they had brought him no money. He edited and wrote most of the *Literary Magazine and American Register* from 1803 to 1807, and of the new *American Register* from 1807 to his death. Though writing was an absolute need to him, and he was wretched without it, he had leisure aside from his political pamphlets

After a portrait by J. Sharples
CHARLES BROCKDEN BROWN

only for a tragedy, which he burned when told it was unactable, and the prospectus of a *System of General Geography* which he did not live to finish. For by this time he was far gone in tuberculosis, of which he died at thirty-nine.

Under an equable exterior, Brown concealed the "tormented state of mind" in which, in all his novels, he was so much interested. He was an essential romantic, who progressed from making ideal architectural designs and constructing vast Utopias to writing novels which should be "inspirations to the great." Unfortunately these novels display plain marks of both haste and immaturity. Nevertheless, in spite of weakness in plot construction and a tendency to stilted verbosity, they show also remarkable power. He is a master of danger, terror, and suspense, "the next after Hoffmann in the literature of the Weird." Nothing of "the Weird," however, is left unexplained in his novels; he is dealing not with the supernatural but with psychopathology, with "soaring passions and intellectual energy"—the two human characteristics which he conceived to be within his field of treatment. He is, moreover, authentically American; disciple of Godwin though he was, his characters all tread American soil which can be mistaken for no other. (It was in recognition of this fact that he was made, in 1809, an honorary member of the New York Historical Society.) In *Edgar Huntley,* for example, the American Indian is for the first time introduced into fiction.

Lifelong ill health harried him; he left much fragmentary work (sometimes drawing on earlier fragments for material for his later writings) because he had neither time nor strength to complete all that his impatient mind could not keep from planning. Slovenly in dress and careless about money, he had some of the characteristics of the traditional Bohemian; on the other hand he was abstemious and reserved, and a lifelong abstainer from liquor in a heavy-drinking age. Though reared a Quaker, he was read out of meeting for marrying outside the faith and seems to have been a Deist of the type of Franklin, Jefferson, and Paine. Surrounded by a more critical and more congenial environment than his time or his country could provide, he would have realized much more of his potential genius. Even as it is, *Wieland*, his best book, remains a masterpiece of abnormal psychology, and there are scenes and descriptions in *Arthur Mervyn, Ormond,* and *Edgar Huntley* which only the highest talent could have achieved. It is Brown's fate to be fossilized as "the first American novelist," but it is a strange ending for a man who was above all else a passionate dreamer.

Principal Works: Alcuin: A Dialogue, 1798; Wieland: or, The Transformation, 1798; Ormond: or, The Secret Witness, 1799; Edgar Huntley: or, Memoirs of a Sleep-Walker, 1799; Arthur Mervyn: or, Memoirs of the Year 1793, 1799-1800; Clara Howard, 1801; An Address to the Government of the United States on the Cession of Louisiana, 1803; Jane Talbot, 1804; A View of the Soil and Climate of the United States of America (tr. from the French of C. F. S. Volney) 1804; An Address to the Congress of the United States on the British Treaty, 1806; An Address to the Congress of the United States on Restrictions Upon Foreign Commerce, 1809; A Prospectus of a System of General Geography, 1809; Carwin: The Biloquist and Other American Tales and Pieces, 1822.

About: Brown, C. B. Wieland (see Introduction by F. L. Pattee to 1926 ed.); Clark, D. L. A Critical Biography of Charles Brockden Brown; Dunlap, W. Life of Charles Brockden Brown; Erskine, J. Leading American Novelists; Higginson, T. W. Caryle's Laugh and Other Surprises; Marble, A. R. Heralds of American Literature; Prescott, W. H. Life of Charles Brockden Brown (*Sparks' American Biographies: Vol. 7*); Vilas, M. S. Charles Brockden Brown; American Literature November 1936; Dial February 16, 1910; Fortnightly Review September 1, 1878; Nation January 14, 1915.

BROWN, SOLYMAN (November 17, 1790-February 13, 1876), poet, teacher, clergyman, and dentist, was born at Litchfield, Conn., the son of Nathaniel and Thankful (Woodruff) Brown. He prepared for the ministry at Litchfield, and Yale College, graduating in 1812, and, after an additional year of study, received a four-year license to preach in Congregational Church pulpits. It was not renewed, on the grounds that two years of preparation were required. The Rev. Lyman Beecher was Brown's chief opponent in the ensuing controversy, and Brown bitterly attacked his views. These writings failed to advance his clerical ambitions. In 1820 he moved to New York City where he taught the classics in several fashionable private schools until, in 1834, he became a practicing dentist, active in organizing state and national dental associations. He spent four years (1846-50) at Ithaca and Danby, N.Y. preaching in Swedenborgian churches; then returned to New York City where he opened a dental supply depot and published his *Semi-Annual Dental Expositor* for two years.

Various other business enterprises occupied his attention until 1862 when he went back to Danby to preach until his retirement eight years later. He died in Dodge Center, Minn., and was survived by his wife, the former Elizabeth Butler of New York City, and eight children.

Besides possessing considerable literary ability, Brown was talented in sculpture and painting. He was deeply religious and was able through his fine oratory to convey his fervor to others. His numerous publications were chiefly about dentistry, although he contributed much poetry to newspapers and periodicals. His best known work, *Dentologia* (1833), other than being the only dental didactic poem in English, has little distinction, but was so popular in its day and field that one enthusiastic reviewer bestowed upon Brown the title, "The Poet Laureate of the Dental Profession."

Principal Works: An Address to the People of Litchfield County, 1818; Second Address to the People of Litchfield County, 1818; Servile Spirits and Spiritual Masters, 1820; The Birth of Washington: A Poem, 1822; A Comparative View of the Systems of Pestalozzi and Lancaster, 1825; Sermons, 1825; Dentologia, 1833; Llewellen's Dog: A Ballad, 1840; The Importance of Regulating the Teeth of Children, 1841; Cholera King, and Other Poems, 1842.

About: Taylor, J. A. History of Dentistry; Biographical Sketches of Graduates of Yale College: Vol. 6; New Christian Messenger March 10, 1909, April 11, 1917; New Jerusalem Messenger March 1, 1876.

BROWN, THEOPHILUS (September 15, 1811-1879?), Worcester wit and tailor, was born in the sleepy village of Seekonk (then Rehoboth), Mass., the son of a Samuel Brown. His father died when he was very small, and "Theo" went to live in Attleboro, Mass., with one Asa Allen, a Universalist who always received the visiting clergy, on parish call, with a bottle, and whose wife dealt out a "thinness of diet" with tea and coffee that were "strong of water." But Theo passed four happy years in these surroundings, thriving on much Arcadian mischief and a minimum of second-rate schooling.

He was married to Sarah A. Knowlton, July 9, 1845, in Worcester, Mass., and there set up on Main Street a tailor's shop which became the modest rendezvous of Edward Hamilton, a ballad writer, Samuel Jennison, a pianist, John Weiss, who fed upon Greek mythology, and Harrison ("Harry") Blake [*q.v.*] who, like Brown himself, was a disciple of Thoreau and a devout and indefatigable walker. Patronage came without solicitation, and Brown found himself steadily confronted with the task of "cutting a passage through this mountain of woolens." But the "zoom" of his scissors never drowned out a blue-jay battle coming through his East window, or the strains of the flute player, whose undiluted happiness always put a match to Brown's easily combustible optimism. Good music changed his world from an "opaque, muddy tumble-bug's ball" to a "shining sphere, bathed in light, cushioned in air, and whirling off with us amid the stars." With the aid of his friend Chamberlin, he arranged a series of educational lectures given at Brinley Hall. "John Weiss helps us. ." he says in one of his letters. . . "He writes them and delivers them and we do all the rest."

In his last years Brown dabbled frequently in verse, and some of his limericks and *bon mots* appeared in the "Editor's Drawer" of *Harper's*. His loyal admiration for Emerson is best illustrated by his own remark on the occasion of a Phi Beta Kappa lecture by the Concord poet. To a friend who was fretting over the danger of their tardy arrival Brown replied, "If we *are* late, it is better to *miss* hearing Emerson than to *hear* anyone else." He had, indeed, an unaffected love for real life—his own had been a simple, sunny, and satisfying one—and to him "Thoreau's pokeweed, bending over with its rich burden, seemed more juicily and healthily interesting than Dante's dried phantoms." Brown's heaviest lament was the fact that "we are born too young . . . we begin by doing everything we ought not to do too much and everything we ought to do too little, until we find we have made a botch of what might have been a success." Had he written his own epitaph it would doubtless have contained the sentiment of this one, scribbled off in a moment of merriment—

> Under this sod, beneath these trees,
> Lieth the pod of Solomon Pease.

THEOPHILUS BROWN

Brown's writings were only incidental echos of a buzzing era, but the candidness of his slants on certain Concord and Worcester intellectuals and his own uncommon personality were among the forces that brought New England to its full flower.

Principal Works: Excerpts From the Letters of Theo Brown, 1879.

About: Brooks, V. W. Flowering of New England; Brown, T. Excerpts From the Letters of Theo. Brown; Thoreau, H. D. Intimate Letters; Worcester Society of Antiquity Collections: Vol. 12.

BROWN, WILLIAM HILL (1765-September 2,(?) 1793), possible author of "the first American novel," poet, and dramatist, was the son of Gawen Brown, celebrated Boston clockmaker who installed the famous time-piece on Old South Church, and Elizabeth (Hill) Brown. Very little is known about his childhood, but while he still retained a youthful point of view he began to contribute poems to the *Palladium* and set to work on the writing of a romantic tale "Harriot: or, The Domestic Reconciliation" which appeared in the first issue of the *Massachusetts Magazine* (January 1789).

During the same month Isaiah Thomas, printer, author, and bookseller issued anonymously *The Power of Sympathy/or the/ Triumph of Nature/Founded in Truth,* a recital (with fictitious accompaniments) of the scandal involving the immediate family of Mrs. Sarah (Apthorp) Morton [*q.v.*], poetess, (who lived on State Street opposite the Browns), intimating that Mrs. Morton's husband was the seducer of her sister Frances Apthorp who, after bearing a child, took her own life by drinking poison. The book is one of the several claimants to the title "the first American novel." Except for a few objections to its indelicacies, it appears to have occasioned little comment in its time and was perhaps never ascribed—in print—to anyone until Francis Samuel Drake in 1878 (*History of Roxbury*) named Mrs. Morton as its author. Despite the unlikeliness of this ascription, it was not until 1894 when the tale was in serial reprint in the *Bostonian Magazine* that credence was given to the theory of Brown's authorship, advanced by his niece, Mrs. Rebecca Valentine Thompson, in an interview with Arthur W. Brayley, editor of the journal. Interpretations of a few brief press comments and unmistakeable similarities between the *Power of Sympathy* and other writings of William Hill Brown would seem to substantiate Mrs. Thompson's story.

Brown wrote a tragedy on the death of Major André, Revolutionary spy (*West Point Preserved*) which survived twenty-seven performances at the Haymarket Theatre in 1797; *Penelope,* a comedy "in the style of the West-Indies"; the *Yankee* and other essay series; and *Ira and Isabella,* a short novel published posthumously. He went South to study law; and he died in Murfreesborough, N. C., at the age of twenty-eight.

The *Power of Sympathy* has long been an exceedingly rare piece of Americana, not because of any literary excellence (for it is stiflingly sentimental and didactic) but because the Mortons bought up and destroyed all the copies they could lay hands on. Until 1867, when a dozen unopened first editions were found in an old trunk, the book was almost non-existent. The ascription of authorship, then, involves not so much an equitable distribution of credit, as the solution of a minor literary mystery.

PRINCIPAL WORKS: The Power of Sympathy, 1789; West Point Preserved, 1797; Ira and Isabella, 1807.

ABOUT: Brown, W. H. The Power of Sympathy (see bibliographical note by Milton Ellis); Hill, H. A. History of Old South Church; Marble, A. R. From 'Prentice to Patron; Paine, R. T. Works in Verse and Prose (see "A Monody—To the Memory of William Hill Brown"); American Literature January 1933.

BROWN, WILLIAM WELLS (c. 1816-November 6, 1884), Negro reformer and historian, was reputed to be the son of George Higgins, a white slaveholder, and an unidentified woman-slave. Born in Lexington, Ky., he went to St. Louis at an early age and worked first on a steamboat, and later in the printshop of Elijah P. Lovejoy, editor of the St. Louis *Times,* for about a year, when he was again hired out on a steamboat. In 1834, during an attempted escape into Canada, he was harbored by Wells Brown, a Quaker whose name he adopted. Through a position as steward on a Lake Erie steamboat he aided many colored fugitives in escaping to freedom, and soon began to champion the cause of his people publicly in lectures for the Western New York Anti-Slavery Society and the Massachusetts Anti-Slavery Society. He also interested himself in temperance, woman's suffrage, and prison reform, and came in contact with William Lloyd Garrison, Wendell Phillips, and other prominent abolitionists. In 1849, during a trip to Europe as representative to the American Peace Society at the Peace Congress in Paris, he met Victor Hugo, James Haughton, George Thomson, and Richard Cobden.

Having no formal schooling, Brown studied diligently to educate himself and even during busy years as a reformer acquired sufficient medical knowledge to practice, had he wished. He published his first book in 1847 under the title *Narrative of William W. Brown: A Fugitive Slave,* and followed it with a number of others of a historical nature, including *The Black Man: His Antecedents, His Genius, and His Achievements* (1863), which ran into ten editions, and *The Rising Son: or, The Antecedents and the Advancement of the Colored Race* (1874), a volume widely praised by abolitionists. He was married to a free Negress and had two daughters. Today Brown stands as an able historian and pioneer in the field of Negro literature. He died in Chelsea, Mass.

PRINCIPAL WORKS: *Narratives*—Narrative of William W. Brown: A Fugitive Slave, 1847; Three Years in Europe, 1852; Clotel: or, The President's Daughter, 1853. *History*—The Black Man: His Antecedents, His Genius, and His Achievements, 1863; The Negro in the American Rebellion: His Heroism and His Fidelity, 1867; The Rising Son: or, The Antecedents and the Advancement of the Colored Race, 1874.

ABOUT: Brown, J. The Biography of an American Bondman; (see also Brown's autobiographical writings); Boston Transcript November 8, 1884.

BROWNE, CHARLES FARRAR ("Artemus Ward") (April 26, 1834-March 6, 1867), humorist, was born near Waterford, Maine, the son of Levi Brown, a lumber merchant and member of the state legislature, and Caroline (Farrar) Brown. (The family name was Brown; Charles himself added the "e.") He attended the country school till the age of twelve, when his father's death made it necessary to him to earn his living. He was then apprenticed to a printer on a paper at Lancaster, N. H. At fourteen he worked for his older brother, who was editing the Norway (Maine) *Advertiser,* and on other small papers in the neighborhood. He then moved to Boston, where for three years he worked as a printer, and where his first published article, on Cornwallis, was published in the *Carpet Bag* in 1852. He became a wandering journeyman printer, such as were common in those days, working in various parts of the South and West until he became first a reporter on and then city editor of the Cleveland *Plain Dealer* in 1857.

It was in this paper that "Artemus Ward," the pseudonym by which he became better known than by his own name, first appeared, signed to a letter from "the manager of a sideshow." The misspelled words the puns, and the broad humor exactly suited the American taste of the time, and Browne's reputation grew rapidly. In 1859 he went to New York to succeed Charles Godfrey Leland as a member of the staff of *Vanity Fair,* which had been established as an American rival of *Punch.*

It was in 1861 that Browne gave the first of his lectures, the real source of his fame. He soon came under the management of Dr. E. P. Hingston, who remained his friend and companion as well as his manager for the rest of his life. The lectures were enormously popular, and though he continued to write for various periodicals, all his books are lecture transcripts. The Civil War was now on, and though Browne was already tubercular and could never have been a soldier, he was an ardent Union man and donated freely from his lecture profits to the Federal cause. His great admiration for Lincoln was reciprocated; it is a matter of record that Lincoln read aloud to his cabinet a "piece by Artemus Ward" just before he announced to them the writing of the Emancipation Proclamation. The two men had much in common—deep melancholy as well as frontier humor.

In 1863 Browne was invited to give his lectures in the Far West. He spent a year in California (starting in San Francisco)

Collection of Frederick H. Meserve

CHARLES FARRAR BROWNE
("Artemus Ward")

and Nevada, and came back by way of Salt Lake City. It was on this trip that he met Samuel Clemens (the future Mark Twain) and launched the latter's career by sending "The Jumping Frog of Calaveras" to the New York *Mercury.* He fell ill in Utah, and was nursed back to health by a Mormon woman. The Mormons interested him hugely, and thereafter they were the chief topic of his lectures.

In 1866 Browne was invited to lecture in England. He had a premonition that he would never return, and so informed his family. (He was never married.) He was an enormous success with everyone from Queen Victoria to the most illiterate of his hearers; he became a regular contributor to *Punch*; he revivified the Savage Club; he was the lion of the day. And all the while he was dying on his feet. Finally he could no longer continue. With his last strength he traveled to Southampton, for its milder climate, and there he died, six weeks before his thirty-third birthday. A rumor that he had been converted to Roman Catholicism on his death-bed was controverted by Dr. Hingston, who was with him. He was interred in Kensal Green, London, but when it was found that in his will he had asked to be buried at his birthplace, his remains were exhumed and sent to Maine.

Browne's written humor is a dreary thing to read nowadays. We no longer find it funny to misspell words. But even in transcript his lectures give a hint of the reasons for his overwhelming popularity. His humor in them was whimsical, quiet; he was that funniest of all things, a sad man sadly uttering excruciatingly funny statements. Primarily he was a moralist and a critic, a sallow, thin, sandy-haired preacher who happened also to be an incurable humorist. His private jokes were classic; his public jokes were the very best sugar-coating on a medicinal pill. The Artemus Ward who spelt them as "goaks" is dead; the Charles Farrar Browne who was light-heartedly playful on his death-bed has a hold on our affections and memory.

PRINCIPAL WORKS: Artemus Ward: His Book, 1862; Artemus Ward: His Travels, 1865; Artemus Ward in London (ed. by T. W. Robertson) 1867; The Mormons (ed. by E. P. Hingston) 1868; Sandwiches by Artemus Ward, 1868; Artemus Ward's Panorama, 1869; Letters, 1900.

ABOUT: Browne, C. F. Artemus Ward: His Works Complete (see Biographical Sketch by M. D. Landon); Browne, C. F. Selected Works (see Introduction by A. J. Nock to 1924 ed.); Haweis, H. R. American Humorists; Hingston, E. P. The Genial Showman; Rourke, C. M. American Humor; Seitz, D. C. Artemus Ward; Atlantic Monthly September 1934.

BROWNE, FRANCIS FISHER (December 1, 1843-May 11, 1913), editor, was born at South Halifax, Vt., the son of William Goldsmith and Eunice (Fisher) Browne, but the family soon moved to Chicopee, Mass., where Francis attended school and worked in the printing department of his father's newspaper office. During the Civil War he served with the 46th Massachusetts Regiment, and upon leaving the army read law in an office in Rochester, N.Y. He subsequently studied law at the University of Michigan, but gave up a legal career to return to the printing trade. In 1867 he married Susan Seman Brooks and shortly afterward they moved to Chicago where Browne became associated with the *Western Monthly,* a periodical, which he bought within two years and renamed the *Lakeside Monthly.* Securing distinguished contributors, he managed the magazine successfully for six years until ill health forced him to discontinue publication and retire. During his convalescence, he wrote editorials for Chicago newspapers, and served as literary editor of the *Alliance.* In 1880 he launched the *Dial,* a monthly review and index of current literature, which ultimately became the leading journal of literary criticism until it went out of existence after Browne's death in Santa Barbara, Calif.

Equipped with sound literary ability, competent critical judgment, and the determination to overcome ill-health and the privation that besieged his family of nine children, he left behind him an enviable editorial record, several fine anthologies, a collection of his own poems, and an important contribution to Lincolniana—*The Everyday Life of Abraham Lincoln* (1886), drawn from the personal testimony of many of Lincoln's contemporaries.

PRINCIPAL WORKS: *Anthologies*—Golden Poems by British and American Authors, 1881; The Golden Treasury of Poetry and Prose, 1883; Bugle Echoes, 1886; Laurel Crowned Verse, 1891-92. *Verse*—Volunteer Grain, 1895. *Miscellaneous*—The Everyday Life of Abraham Lincoln, 1886.

ABOUT: Book Buyer May 1900; Bookman May 1900; Dial May 1, June 1, 16, 1913; Review of Reviews July 1913.

BROWNELL, HENRY HOWARD (February 6, 1820-October 31, 1872), poet and historian, was born in Providence, R.I., the son of Dr. Pardon Brownell and Lucia (de Wolf) Brownell. His father was a physician, his uncle an Episcopal bishop. He was graduated from Washington (Trinity) College, Hartford, Conn., in 1841, and for a year taught school at Mobile, Ala. He then returned to Connecticut, studied law, and was admitted to the bar in 1844. He never took the law seriously, however, but soon gravitated into literary pursuits. He and his brother were obscure hack writers when the Civil War changed Henry Brownell's whole career. Admiral Farragut, struck by a rhymed version of his orders published in the Hartford *Evening Press,* looked up the writer and had him appointed master mate in the navy, then ensign and his own secretary. Brownell's war poems became famous; Oliver Wendell Holmes called him "our battle laureate." In 1867 he traveled through Europe with Farragut, again as his secretary. He then returned to Hartford, and lived there quietly, unmarried, until he died, of cancer of the face, at fifty-two.

Brownell's earlier poems are tedious, crude, and imitative. His war poems, however, written often in the heat of battle, are vivid, vigorous, and alive with a glowing patriotism. One poem, "Down!" which compares the Union cause to a ship successful in battle with another ship, the Confederacy, is of interest because it contains several phrases and images which appeared later in Walt Whitman's famous "Captain, My Captain," though there is no proof of actual plagiarism.

PRINCIPAL WORKS: *Poetry*—Poems, 1847; Ephemerson, 1855; Lyrics of a Day, 1864; Lines of Battle, 1912; *Prose*—The People's Book of Ancient and Modern History, 1851; The Discoverers, Pioneers, and Settlers of North and South America, 1853.

ABOUT: Brownell, H. H. Lines of Battle (see Introduction by M. A. DeW. Howe); Burton, R. Literary Likings; Atlantic Monthly November 1907; Hartford Courant November 9, 1872.

"BROWNING, HENRY C." See MOWATT, ANNA CORA (OGDEN) RITCHIE

BROWNLOW, WILLIAM GANNAWAY ("Parson Brownlow") (August 29, 1805-April 29, 1877), political and theological writer, was born in Wythe Co., Va., the son of Joseph A. Brownlow and Catharine (Gannaway) Brownlow. When he was five his parents moved to Tennessee, near Knoxville, and six years later they both died, leaving him to be reared by his mother's relatives. He had very little formal education, but spent his spare hours in study while learning carpentry. In 1826 he became a Methodist minister, and for ten years thereafter was an itinerant preacher throughout the South. Politics always interested him, and controversy was his passion. He first came into public notice by opposing nullification in South Carolina in 1828. Though he believed in slavery, he was violently against secession. In 1838 he found an outlet for his opinions in the *Tennessee Whig,* which he edited. From 1839 to 1849 he was editor of the Jonesboro *Whig and Independent,* and in 1849 of the Knoxville *Whig*; all of these seem to have been the same paper, published in different localities. With the start of the Civil War he remained strongly pro-Union, flew the last Union flag in Knoxville, and expressed himself openly in his paper until it was suppressed in 1861. He then fled to the North Carolina mountains, but was captured and returned to Knoxville. In December he was arrested for treason to the Confederacy, but when he incurred typhoid fever in prison was released and kept under surveillance. In a few months he was sent through the Confederate lines into Federal territory. In the North he spent two years lecturing, with a few months out to pen his *Sketches of the Rise, Progress, and Decline of Secession.* Under the better known title of "Parson Brownlow's Book," this fire-eating document became one of the all-time best-sellers; for decades after the Rebellion it was a virtual Bible in countless thousands of Northern homes.

After the war Brownlow returned to Knoxville, and under Reconstruction was made governor of Tennessee by acclamation. His incumbency was marked by the calling of Federal troops against the mayor of Nashville, and by a proclamation of martial law to fight the original Ku Klux Klan. From 1869 to 1875 he was U.S. Senator from Tennessee; then he bought back the *Whig,* which he had sold in 1869, and edited it to his death. He was married, his wife's name being Eliza O'Brien.

Brownlow was a bitter, unscrupulous fighter, a die-hard Federalist of the old school, and more than a little of a demagogue. He had no particular ability as a writer, except a turn for invective, and survives only as part of Civil War history.

PRINCIPAL WORKS: Helps to the Study of Presbyterianism, 1834; A Political Register, . . . With the Life and Public Services of Henry Clay, 1844; Americanism Contrasted to Foreignism, Romanism, and Bogus Democracy, 1856; Ought American Slavery to Be Perpetuated? 1858; Sketches of the Rise, Progress, and Decline of Secession, 1862.

ABOUT: Cutler, E. M. William Gannay Brownlow: Fighting Parson of the Southern Highlands; Putnam's Magazine April 1869; New York Evening Post April 30, 1877.

BROWNSON, ORESTES AUGUSTUS (September 16, 1803-April 17, 1876), philosophical writer, was born in Stockbridge, Vt., the youngest son of Sylvester Augustus and Relief (Metcalfe) Brownson. He had a twin sister, being one of the few twins ever to achieve celebrity. His father died when he was six, and the impoverished widow was forced to leave her youngest children, the twins, to charity. He was reared in the most Spartan school of Puritanism by relatives at Royalton, Vt., doing farm work from early childhood, and except for a brief period at Ballston

After a daguerreotype
ORESTES AUGUSTUS BROWNSON
c. 1843

Academy having no schooling but his own reading. In 1822 he was a Presbyterian, two years later a Universalist, two years later still ordained as a Universalist minister. In 1827 he married Sally Healy, and became an itinerant preacher in Vermont, New Hampshire, and northern New York. In 1829 he was made editor of the *Gospel Advocate,* Auburn, N.Y., but his views became too liberal even for his liberal church, and he developed into a free lance writer and lecturer. He became an associate of those early Socialists, Robert Dale Owen and Fanny Wright; he was corresponding editor of their *Free Enquirer*; in 1828 he helped to organize the Workingmen's Party.

Then in 1832 he fell under William Ellery Channing's influence, and followed him into the Unitarian ministry. He served Unitarian churches in Walpole, N.H., and Canton, Mass., then in 1836 founded his own church in Boston, among the workers. His articles in the *Christian Examiner,* published during this period, gave him an undeserved reputation as a philosopher; actually Brownson was never a profound or original thinker, but a man who, as Van Wyck Brooks remarks, "rushed from one position to another, with a headstrong vehemence, telling the world each time how right he was." In 1838 he founded the *Boston Quarterly Review,* a Democratic organ, nearly all of which he wrote. In 1842 the magazine was merged with the *Democratic Review,* New York, in 1844 resuming its publication in Boston and changing its name to *Brownson's Quarterly Review.* (It died in 1865, was revived in 1873, and published again until 1875.)

By this time the greatest and final change had come to Brownson's variable convictions: he who had sent his son as a colonist to Brook Farm, who had been the associate of Channing, Thoreau, Brancroft, and Ripley, had become a convert to the Roman Catholic Church. In his new incarnation as in his old, Brownson was a vociferous and truculent propagandist. Soon he was suspected by his new colleagues of heresy, thanks to his advocacy of an "American" form of Catholicism; his invitation to become professor of philosophy at Dublin University was withdrawn, and he was investigated and admonished to be more cautious. But this bewhiskered, roaring, clumsy giant knew neither fear nor diplomacy. Wherever he moved—in 1855 to New York, in 1857 to Elizabeth, N.J., in 1875 to Detroit, where he died the next year—he engaged all and sundry in argument and mental combat. "Something more than a journalist, something less than a sage," with his political books called "mental gladiatorial exercises" and his religious work not far behind them, Brownson nevertheless was a potent figure in nineteenth century American culture. His magazine was the first American periodical to be widely circulated in England. His writing, confused and noisy as it is, is nevertheless a valuable index to a typical variety of American mind and personality of its period. His fame spread farther in his lifetime than that of many of his more distinguished contemporaries. And under all his changes of thought there was a coherent, authentically New England character, a sort of living source-book which has left its traces in his published works.

Principal Works: New Views of Christianity, Society, and the Church, 1836; Charles Elwood: or, The Infidel Converted, 1840; The Mediatorial Life of Jesus, 1842; Essays and Reviews, 1852; The Spirit-Rapper: An Autobiography (fiction) 1854; The Convert: or, Leaves From My Experience, 1857; The American Republic: Its Constitution, Tendencies, and Destiny, 1865; Conversation on Liberalism and the Church, 1870.

About: Brooks, V. W. The Flowering of New England; Brownson, H. F. Orestes A. Brownson's Early Life, Middle Life, Later Life; Brownson, O. A. The Convert; Michel, V. G. The Critical Principles of Orestes A. Brownson; Sargent, D. Four Independents.

"BRUTUS." See SIMPSON, STEPHEN

BRYAN, MARY (EDWARDS) (May 17, 1842-June 15, 1913), journalist and popular novelist, was born on a plantation near Tallahassee, Fla., the daughter of Major John D. Edwards and Louisa Critchfield (Houghton) Edwards. Receiving her early education from her mother, an exceptionally cultured woman, she was later sent off to boarding-school at Thomasville, Ga., but left at the age of fifteen to marry I. E. Bryan, a wealthy Louisiana planter.

She had been an omnivorous reader as a child and had published verses and stories even before her 18th birthday, when she became literary editor of the *Literary Crusader,* at Atlanta, Ga. She was correspondent to several other Southern periodicals, and in 1866 took over the editorship of the Natchitoches (La.) *Tri-Weekly.* From 1874 to 1884 she was associate editor of the *Sunny South,* a popular weekly. Meanwhile in 1880 her first novel, *Manch,* deriving its title from the Indian proper name "Comanche" appeared. It was followed by *Wild Work,* based on carpet-bagging and Ku Klux Klan activities in the South. In 1885 she moved to New York where she edited several magazines, among which was *Munroe's Star Recitations for Parlor,*

School, and Exhibitions. Besides being a popular contributor to Street & Smith's early publications, she wrote eight novels and three volumes of verse in her spare time at night.

Returning to Georgia in 1895 she resumed her editorship of the *Sunny South,* which later became *Uncle Remus' Magazine*; eventually she edited the *Half Hour Magazine.* Mrs. Bryan took an active interest in literary societies and through her wit and charm attracted many prominent literary figures to her New York home. Her books, though mediocre, invariably brought out a moral lesson and were sufficiently sensational in style to achieve an ephemeral popularity.

PRINCIPAL WORKS: Manch, 1880; Wild Work, 1881.

ABOUT: Tardy, M. T. The Living Female Writers of the South; Atlanta Constitution June 15, 17, 1913.

BRYANT, WILLIAM CULLEN (November 3, 1794-June 12, 1878), poet, was the son of Dr. Peter Bryant, a physician who was something of a scholar and a prominent member of the state legislature, and Sarah (Snell) Bryant. His mother was a "Mayflower" descendant; his father's ancestors had emigrated to America about 1632. The poet was born in Cummington, Mass., in the beautiful Hampshire Hills in the western part of the state, and the lovely and still primitive scenery of his boyhood became and remained the inevitable background and inspiration of his verse.

After gaining what knowledge the district schools could give him—supplemented by his father's well-selected store of 700 books—the boy was sent for a year to an uncle, a clergyman, for intensive study of Latin, and then to another minister to study Greek. He had been an exceedingly precocious child, who could read at sixteen months; now his progress was such that in two months he was reading the New Testament in Greek, and at fifteen he entered Williams College as a sophomore. He had been, too, a frail child, with an abnormally large head, but a sensible regimen prescribed by his father had made him into a healthy youth who loved to roam the woods and was an enthusiastic if untrained naturalist.

Williams College at that time was little more than a country school, with only four teachers. Bryant's heart was set on Yale; he left Williams at the end of a year and prepared himself at home for the junior year at the larger college; but his father's means could not permit him any further schooling. He was sent instead to read law at the nearby town of Worthington, and he spent three unhappy years there, from 1811 to 1814.

Collection of Frederick H. Meserve
WILLIAM CULLEN BRYANT

Already, however, he was a poet, and a published poet. As a child, he had prayed for the gift of poetry. His father encouraged him; a youthful anti-Jeffersonian satire in verse, *The Embargo,* had already been printed as "by a youth of fifteen" (actually he was thirteen when it was written). In the disappointment of his ambition to enter Yale, and at the decision to apprentice him instead to the hated profession of law, he produced, in the autumn of 1811, his greatest poem, "Thanatopsis"—one of the remarkable achievements of literature when the author's age is considered. This, with his exquisite "To a Waterfowl," and sundry other verses of the time, he made no attempt to publish, but hid them away in a corner of his desk.

In 1815 Bryant was admitted to the bar, in Plainfield, Mass. He started practice in Plainfield, but soon moved to Great Barrington. There he remained, chafing at the requirements of his abhorred profession, until 1825. In 1821 he had married Frances Fairchild, and their first child was born in 1822; dreams of escape from the law seemed forever futile.

But escape was close at hand. In 1817 Bryant's father went to New York, with "Thanatopsis" and "To a Waterfowl" in his valise, and presented the poems, without their author's knowledge, to the *North American Review.* Richard Henry Dana, one of the editors, later Bryant's close and constant friend, at first refused them, on the ground that no one in America could write in such a style, and that Dr. Bryant was either trying to hoax the magazine or had himself been hoaxed. Once he was persuaded they were genuine, he published them with alacrity, and the young man's reputation was made.

In 1821 Bryant read in Boston the Phi Beta Kappa poem of the year, "The Ages," and also published his first volume of poems. His growing fame bore fruit three years later, when he made an arrangement by which he was to supply at least a hundred lines of verse a month to the *United States Literary Gazette,* for $200 a year. He was now recognized as America's leading poet, and in 1825 he was appointed as co-editor of the *New York Review and Athenaeum Magazine,* at $1000 a year. He left his wife and child in Great Barrington and went to New York alone. His fortunes were at low ebb. He soon found that $1000, which was wealth in a country town in Massachusetts, was poverty, even in 1825, in New York, especially since he was thrown now with all the literary lights of the city and had to share their expensive conviviality. Reluctantly at last he applied for a license to practice law in New York State. He was just about to hang out his dreaded shingle again when, in 1826, he was made assistant editor of the *Evening Post.*

Bryant remained with the *Evening Post* for the rest of his life. In 1829 he became full editor, and gradually bought up a third interest in the paper. The staff was small, and it was a time when newspaper editors not only edited, but wrote, reported, and did make-up as well. He had small leisure for poetry in a working day which began at 7 A. M. and lasted till dark. The paper was Jacksonian Democrat in policy, an advocate of free trade, and Bryant threw himself into political affairs with zeal. Under his editorship the *Evening Post* became noted for its literary style; in later years he compiled a famous Index Expurgatorius for the paper's Style Book, in which among other things he condemned such current colloquialisms as "rough" and "rowdy" (as nouns) and "Secesh" (a favorite word of Walt Whitman's).

After 1830 he was able to take things a little more easily; he acquired an exceedingly able assistant, William Leggett, and he had freedom again to do some work of his own. The result was a new volume of poems, which through the offices of Washington Irving was given an English edition and made Bryant's name known abroad. He began also to travel a bit, went to Canada in 1833, and the next year made the first of his six trips to Europe. Indeed, he had every intention of settling permanently in Europe with his family, on the proceeds of his third interest in the prosperous *Evening Post.* But in 1836 Leggett became ill, and alarming reports reached Bryant of the paper's situation.

He returned in haste from Heidelberg, to find the paper practically dying. Leggett was able, but he was also an extreme radical, whose editorial views had alienated most of the subscribers. Bryant severed connections with him, increased his holdings to half ownership, and by indefatigable effort brought the paper back to its feet by 1840. He never abandoned it again, though he left it frequently for short tours abroad.

The slavery dispute ended the Democratic affiliation of both Bryant and his paper. By 1856 he had espoused the new Republican doctrines; he was firmly behind John Brown and Lincoln, favored immediate emancipation, and it was not until the days of Reconstruction that he broke with the radical "Black Republicans" and backed Johnson's (unsuccessful) policy of conciliation. After Grant's inauguration, his active political interests were at an end. In 1865, after 44 years of the greatest happiness, Mrs. Bryant had died, and most of the aging widower's outside interests died with her. To assuage his grief, he made his last trip to Europe, only to find unbearable the scenes they had known together. He came home and buried himself in his translations of Homer.

He was still, however, at the service of innumerable public projects and functions, and one of these at last caused his death. On May 29, 1878, he stood in a broiling sun to give the oration at the unveiling of a statue of Mazzini; on the way home he fell and struck his head, causing concussion of the brain. He lapsed into a coma, and died, still unconscious, two weeks later.

The Bryant of the last years, with patriarchal white beard, is a familiar picture. In earlier life he was slight, with dark hair and the large head still noticeable which had so alarmed his mother. He was wiry, a great believer in outdoor life, and something of an athlete.

Bryant has fittingly been called "the American Wordsworth." The two had much in common, as men and as poets. Bryant, like Wordsworth, was cold, austere, and ultra-dignified, though he had none of the English poet's pomposity. His calmness and chilliness were indeed the result of self-discipline of an originally very heated temper; in his younger days he once cowhided, on a New York street, a man with whom he had had a disagreement! Primarily, like Wordsworth, he was a poet of nature; on his forty-acre estate on Long Island, as half a century earlier in the hills of Massachusetts, he lived close to the soil. Even in extreme old age he delighted in gardening and swimming.

Over half his poetic output—which was relatively small as compared with the prolific verse of most of his contemporaries—deals with natural scenery or the objects of nature. Indeed, one of his chief limitations as a writer is his almost entire lack of human emotion. One tenderly pathetic poem—"The Death of the Flowers"—and one gay poem—"Robert of Lincoln"—make up the sum of his expression of common feeling. Essentially he was a meditative philosopher, though his philosophic range was limited. His poetic interests were narrow, but his art was conscious and exalted. He lacked flexibility and fertility, but few poets have excelled him in close observation coupled with imaginative insight. As a journalist, his influence was chiefly literary; as an occasional prose writer, he is merely competent; but as a poet he stands almost in the first rank.

His supreme achievement, of course, was "Thanatopsis," that "Puritan dirge" which in reality is as much pagan as it is Unitarian. The middle portion, unspoiled by hackneyed over-quotation, is magnificent. Lucretius himself might well have fathered it.

It remains to say that Bryant's translations of Homer are still the best in English verse, and the nearest to the actual spirit of the Greek.

Principal Works: *Poetry*—The Embargo, 1808; Poems 1821; Poems, 1832; The Fountain and Other Poems, 1842; The White-Footed Doe and Other Poems, 1844; A Forest Hymn, 1860; Thirty Poems, 1864; Voices of Nature, 1865; The Iliad of Homer Translated Into English Blank Verse, 1870; The Odyssey of Homer Translated Into English Blank Verse, 1871; The Flood of Years, 1876. *Prose*—Tales of the Glauber Spa (anonymous) 1832; Letters of a Traveller, 1850 (second series, 1859); A Discourse on the Life and Genius of James Fenimore Cooper, 1852; A Discourse on the Life, Character, and Genius of Washington Irving, 1860; Letters From the East, 1869; Some Notices on the Life and Writings of Fitz-Greene Halleck, 1869; A Discourse on the Life, Character, and Work of Gulian Crommelin Verplanck, 1870.

About: Bigelow, J. William Cullent Bryant; Bradley, W. A. William Cullen Bryant; Curtis, G. W. The Life, Character, and Works of William Cullen Bryant; Godwin, P. A. Biography of William Cullen Bryant; Nevins, A. The Evening Post; Stedman, E. C. Poets of America; Sturges, H. C. Chronologies of the Life and Writings of William Cullen Bryant; Symington, A. J. William Cullen Bryant; Wilson, J. G. Bryant and His Friends; Bookman April 1897; New England Magazine March 1892.

BUCKMINSTER, JOSEPH STEVENS (May 26, 1784-June 9, 1812), scholar and Unitarian clergyman, was born in Portsmouth, N.H., the son of the Rev. Joseph Buckminster and Sarah (Stevens) Buckminster. He received his early education at home, learning to read Greek at the age of five, and after attending Phillips Exeter Academy, entered Harvard as a sophomore and was graduated at sixteen. For a while he was an instructor at Exeter, but he suffered from an acute epileptic attack and turned to the less strenuous duties of a tutor, in the home of a relative, Theodore Lyman, of Boston and Waltham. Extensive reading in theology and the influence of an ecclesiastic strain in his ancestry made him easily attracted to the ministry. His associations with Dr. James Freeman caused him to sympathize with the Unitarian movement, and he shortly broke away from his orthodox inheritance. At the end of a year's study he preached his first sermon, in the spring of 1804, at York, Maine, before being ordained and installed in the Brattle Street Church, Boston. After twelve months of brilliant ministry, ill health forced him to withdraw and he sailed for Europe in 1806. He preached occasionally in England, and in Paris he purchased 3000-odd volumes—British essayists and poets, botanical journals, topographical works, and Italian and Spanish dictionaries—which became, in 1807, the nucleus of the Boston Athenaeum. It was from the Anthology Club, a select group of literary Bostonians, whose contributions were subsequently published in the *Monthly Anthology*, that the Athenaeum evolved, and Buckminster was among its founders.

He was awarded the first Dexter Lectureship on Biblical Criticism, at Harvard, established in 1811, and although he died shortly after his appointment, he had succeeded in making some firm predictions of an American intellectual awakening: "You are destined to witness," he said in one of his discourses, "the dawn of our Augustan Age . . . and to contribute to its glory." He had a grace and dignity of bearing, and a freshness and alertness in his critical attitude. His writings are confined to two volumes of sermons, published posthumously in Boston, but they were sturdy ground-work for Biblical scholarship in America.

About: Lee, E. B. Memoirs of Rev. Joseph Buckminster, D.D.

BULFINCH, THOMAS (July 15, 1796-May 27, 1867), historian and popular mythologist, was one of the eleven children of the famous architect Charles Bulfinch and Hannah (Apthorp) Bulfinch. He was born at Newton, Mass., and educated at the Boston Latin School, Phillips Exeter Academy, and Harvard, from which he was graduated in 1814. He taught for a year at the Boston Latin School, then assisted his brother, who owned a store. Another brother became a Unitarian minister and a writer. In 1818 the whole family went to Washington, where the father had been appointed as architect of the Capitol. He remained in business there until 1825, then went to Boston. Bulfinch was an unsuccessful business man who met with frequent failure. In 1837 he became a clerk in the Merchants' Bank of Boston, and there he remained until his death, without initiative, content to hold modest and even humble positions so long as they allowed him leisure for writing and study. He was interested in natural history, and was secretary of the Boston Society of Natural History; he was a mild abolitionist and follower of William Lloyd Garrison; but his main interest was in literature. His year of teaching had also given him a lifelong interest in boys, and he became the benefactor of many poverty-stricken youths.

The best as well as the best known of Bulfinch's works is the *Age of Fable*, a popularization of Greek, Roman, Scandinavian, Celtic, and Oriental mythology, still useful as an elementary reference work. He was writing a book called *Heroes and Sages of Greece and Rome* when he died. A quiet, retiring man who hated controversy, he was devoted to his family; he never married but lived with his brothers and sisters all his life.

Principal Works: Hebrew Lyrical History, 1853; The Age of Fable, 1855; The Age of Chivalry, 1858; The Boy Inventor, 1860; Legends of Charlemagne, 1863; Poetry of the Age of Fable, 1863; Shakespeare Adapted for Reading Classes, 1865; Oregon and Eldorado, 1866.

About: Peabody, A. P. Voices of the Dead; Boston Commonwealth June 1, 1867; Boston Daily Advertiser May 28, 1867.

BUNCE, OLIVER BELL (February 8, 1828-May 15, 1890), essayist and publisher, was born in New York City, of English stock. Educated at Rand's Academy, he clerked in his uncle's stationery store and spent his free time reading other authors' books and trying to write his own. When he was twenty-two, his first play—*The Morning of Life*, a rural comedy—was produced at the Bowery Theatre. Three more plays followed—*Marco Bozzaris*, a modern Greek historical dramatization; *Fate: or, The Prophet*, a romantic tragedy in verse; and *Love in '76*, an outstanding comedy of Revolutionary War days, acted and produced by Laura Keene at her theatre in 1857. All but the last-mentioned have been lost.

From impecunious playwriting, Bunce turned to publishing and established his own firm under the name of Bunce & Brother, a venture which failed to survive the trials of insufficient capital. He next became associated with the publishing house of James C. Gregory, and after a short time with Harper & Brothers. Later he became literary manager of D. Appleton & Company, remaining until he died of tuberculosis. He was an indefatigable worker, and struggled so valiantly to overcome the ill health that besieged him for twenty years that he remained at his desk until a week before the end and actually read manuscripts on his deathbed.

Besides editing *Appleton's Journal* and taking an unusually keen interest in manuscripts submitted to the house, Bunce found time to aid William Cullen Bryant in editing an enormously successful series of lavishly illustrated volumes: *Picturesque America* (1872-74); *Picturesque Europe* (1875-79), and *Picturesque Palestine* (1881-84); as well as publishing seven books of his own. *The Opinions and Disputations of Bachelor Bluff*, a collection of social essays published in 1882, is his best known book, but his reputation was made on his acute editorial taste and judgment.

Principal Works: *Plays*—The Morning of Life, 1848; Marco Bozzaris, 1850; Fate: or, The Prophet, 1856; Love in '76; 1857. *Miscellaneous*—The Romance of the Revolution, 1852; A Bachelor's Story, 1859; Life Before Him, 1860; Bensley, 1863; The Opinions and Disputations of Bachelor Bluff, 1881; My House: An Ideal, 1885; The Adventures of Timias Terrystone, 1885. *Anthology*—Fair Words About Fair Women, 1884.

About: Benjamin, S. G. W. Life and Adventures of a Freelance; Derby, J. C. Fifty Years Among Authors, Books, and Publishers; Quinn, A. H. History of the American Drama; New York Times, New York Tribune, May 16, 1890.

BUNNER, HENRY CUYLER (August 3, 1855-May 11, 1896), poet and story writer, was born in Oswego, N.Y., but moved as a small child to New York City. His parents were Rudolph Bunner and Ruth (Tuckerman) Bunner. He prepared at a private school for entrance to Columbia, but found a college education beyond his parents' means. After a short time as clerk in an importing house, he joined the staff of a magazine called the *Arcadian*. This soon failed, and in 1877, when the humorous magazine *Puck* (the first in America) was

H. C. BUNNER

founded, he became assistant editor, and soon after editor-in-chief. He retained this post for the rest of his life, though contributing stories also to *Century, Scribner's, Harper's,* and other magazines. In the early days of *Puck,* he wrote nearly half of each issue, and even wrote the captions of the drawings. It was he who, in 1884, suggested the famous cartoon of James G. Blaine as the "tattooed man" which helped to elect Grover Cleveland president.

In 1886 Bunner married Alice Learned, of New London, Conn. Of their five children, two died in infancy. Nevertheless, few marriages have been happier. From that time on every one of his books was dedicated to "A.L.B." Incidentally, he himself hated his given names, always signed his work "H.C. Bunner," and even his wife habitually called him "Bunner." It was not until after his death that his friends knew his full name.

A year after his marriage, Bunner moved to Nutley, N.J., which was his home thereafter. There and in New York he was the center of a brilliant social group, its life and leader. His memory was phenomenal, his conversation unfailingly witty, and he was as sympathetic and as loyal to his friends as he was strong in his likes and dislikes. In appearance he was markedly of his period, with a short "spade" beard and moustaches, eye-glasses on a cord, and rather *outré* clothes; but his mind and his personality were timeless in their verve and breadth of sympathy. In later years he scarcely ever wrote a line by hand, dictating even his poems. Never very strong, his health failed at forty (he was probably tubercular), and after a futile trip to California he returned to Nutley to die.

There was something French about Bunner's clear-cut, light, and exquisite talent, and indeed Maupassant was his master in prose. In his *Made in France,* a series of adaptations from Maupassant, he added an original story of his own, and not a single critic spotted the hoax. His inventiveness and adroitness were best suited to the short story—his "stories to be read while the candle burns" may be considered the first of the now popular "short shorts"—and his novels themselves are really expanded short stories. In a sense he is a predecessor of O. Henry, in his ardent devotion to the New York scene; he loved the city passionately and never tired of writing of it.

Bunner's plays, mostly written in collaboration, are undistinguished. He is at his very best as a poet. No one in America has ever excelled him as a writer of light lyrical verse, ranging in tone from Austin Dobson to Herrick and Heine. He was an unequaled parodist, in both prose and verse. Frank Stockton never entirely forgave him for one parody which was a complete take-off on the original author's style and method; and Bunner's parody of "Home, Sweet Home," in the style of various poets from Whitman to Kipling, is superb. There was nothing caustic about his wit; it was as sweet-tempered, as ebullient, and as spirited as the man himself. It is a misfortune that one of the most brilliant of American authors should have died in his prime.

Principal Works: *Poetry*—Airs From Arcady and Elsewhere, 1884; Rowen (Second Crop Songs) 1892; The Poems of H. C. Bunner, 1896; Three Operettas, 1897. *Novels*—A Woman of Honor, 1883; The Midge, 1886; The Story of a New York House, 1887. *Short Stories*—In Partnership: Studies in Story Telling (with Brander Matthews) 1884; Short Sixes: Stories to be Read While the Candle Burns, 1890; Zadoc Pine and Other Stories, 1891; The Runaway Browns, 1892; Made in France: French Tales Retold With a United States Twist, 1893; More Short Sixes, 1894; Love in Old Cloathes, 1896. *Miscellaneous*—Tower of Babel (play) 1883; Jersey Street and Jersey Lane (sketches) 1896.

About: Bunner, H. C. Stories of H. C. Bunner: First Series (see Introductory note by B. Matthews to 1916 ed.); Matthews, B. The Historical Novel and Other Essays; Bookman July 1896, June 1912; Scribner's September 1896.

"BUNTLINE, NED." See JUDSON, EDWARD ZANE CARROLL

BURDETTE, ROBERT JONES (July 30, 1844-November 19, 1914), humorist and clergyman, was born in Greensboro, Pa., the son of Frederick Edwin Burdette and Sophia Eberhart (Jones) Burdette, who brought him up in Cumminsville, Ohio, and Peoria, Ill. He served with the 47th Illinois Regiment during the Civil War and took part in the siege of Vicksburg. At the close of the war, he taught school in Peoria for a short time, worked as a United States railway clerk, and then set out for New York City to study languages, and art at Cooper Institute. In 1869 he returned to Peoria, where work on the Peoria *Daily Transcript* led him to an interview with Horace Greeley. Two years later he founded the Peoria *Review*, an unsuccessful venture of three years' duration. He next became associated with the Burlington (Iowa) *Daily Hawk-Eye*, and built up a nation-wide circulation with his column "Hawkeyetems of Roaming Robert."

Though continuing newspaper work, he became increasingly interested in lecturing, and delivered his first and most famous recitation, "The Rise and Fall of the Moustache," over five thousand times. He next turned to religion and became licensed to preach in Baptist pulpits in 1888. He travelled from Maine to California and considerably increased the membership of several churches through his enthusiastic oratory. He was twice married: on March 4, 1870, to Carrie S. Garrett; and on March 25, 1899, to Mrs. Clara (Bradley) Wheeler-Baker.

Running through his humor was a personal philosophy which won him the phrase "physician of the merry heart." The best known of his numerous publications is *The Rise and Fall of the Moustache and Other Hawkeyetems*, published in 1877. Burdette achieved great fame in his day and occupies a small but permanent place in the annals of American humor.

PRINCIPAL WORKS: *Humor*—The Rise and Fall of the Moustache and Other Hawkeyetems, 1877; Hawk-Eyes, 1879; Schooners That Pass in the Dark, 1894; Chimes From a Jester's Bells, 1897; Old Time and Young Tom, 1912. *Verse*—Smiles Yoked With Sighs, 1900; The Silver Trumpets, 1912. *Miscellaneous*—A Life of William Penn, 1882.

ABOUT: Burdette, C. B. Robert J. Burdette: His Message.

BURK, JOHN DALY (c. 1775-April 11, 1808), dramatist, was born in Ireland. To escape political embroilment, he fled to America in 1796 disguised as a woman, in clothes borrowed from a Miss Daly, whose name he whimsically added to his own as a gesture of gratitude. He first lived in Boston where he established a newspaper, the *Polar Star and Boston Daily Advertiser*, on October 6, 1796. It failed after six months and Burk then went to New York City and published a second unsuccessful paper, the *Time Piece*. Petersburg, Va., was his next stop, and here he remained until he was fatally wounded by a Frenchman named Coquebert, in a duel caused by Burk's hot temper.

Burk published several volumes of a historical nature but is best known as a dramatist. His play *Bunker Hill: or, The Death of General Warren*, first produced at the Haymarket Theatre, Boston, on February 17, 1797, was a pioneer attempt to stage an American battle scene. This play brought him great financial gain and was popular on patriotic holidays for many years. A. H. Quinn calls Burk's second play, *Female Patriotism: or, The Death of Joan d'Arc* (Park Theatre, New York, 1798), "one of the bright spots that reward the reader of our early drama."

Burk's fiery temper and love of freedom found expression in dramatic writing uncertain in quality but of historical interest to students of American drama.

PRINCIPAL WORKS: *Plays*—Bunker Hill: or, The Death of General Warren, 1797; The Death of General Montgomery in Storming the City of Quebec, 1797; Female Patriotism: or, The Death of Joan d'Arc; Bethlem Gabor: Lord of Transylvania, 1807. *History*—A History of the Late War in Ireland, 1799; History of Virginia, 1804-16.

ABOUT: Campbell, C. Some Materials to Serve for a Brief Memoir of John Daly Burk; Wegelin, O. Early American Plays.

BURLEIGH, GEORGE SHEPARD (March 26, 1821-July 20, 1903), poet and reformer, was born at Plainfield, Conn., the son of Rinaldo and Lydia (Bradford) Burleigh, and was brought up on a farm in a poor but intellectual atmosphere where discussions of the religious, educational, and philanthropic topics of the day inculcated reform attitudes in him and his brothers—Charles Calistus, William Henry [*q.v.*], Lucian, and Cyrus. After a common school education, George continued his farmer-life, composed poetry and lectured on slavery to the surrounding countryside. His first book, *Elegiac Poem on the Death of Nathaniel Peabody Rogers*, appeared in 1846, and closely resembles the style of *Lycidas* and *Adonais*. During the following two years he edited the *Charter Oak*, an abolitionist paper at Hartford, Conn. In 1849 he married Ruth Burgess of Little Compton, R.I., and in the same year published *The Maniac and Other Poems*. Among his other works are *Signal Fires on the Trail of the Path-*

finder, 1856, an anonymous poetical campaign tract and tribute to General John C. Frémont; and a translation in 1874 of *Legende des Siècles* by Victor Hugo. His name will be remembered longer in connection with reform movements than literature.

PRINCIPAL WORKS: Elegiac Poem on the Death of Nathaniel Peabody Rogers, 1846; The Maniac and Other Poems, 1849; Signal Fires on the Trail of the Pathfinder, 1856.

ABOUT: Burleigh, C. Genealogy of the Burley or Burleigh Family of America; Providence Journal July 22, 24, 1903.

BURLEIGH, WILLIAM HENRY (February 2, 1812-March 18, 1871), journalist and reformer, was the son of Rinaldo Burleigh and Lydia (Bradford) Burleigh, a descendant of the early Massachusetts governor. Born and brought up on his father's farm at Woodstock, Conn., Burleigh was educated at a local school supervised by his father, and early apprenticed to a clothier and a printer. In his eighteenth year he was employed by the Stonington *Phenix* and soon set up his own articles in type without first writing them. Between 1833 and 1837 he was contributing editor to the Schenectady *Cabinet* (New York), and the *Unionist*, published to encourage Prudence Crandall's colored school. Meanwhile he married Harriet Adelia Frink, of Stonington, Conn.

An ardent reformer, Burleigh began lecturing for the American Anti-Slavery Society, and joined the editorial staff of several papers advocating temperance, peace, and women's suffrage, among them the *Christian Freeman* and the *Prohibitionist*. In 1855 he was appointed harbor master of the port of New York and later port warden, holding the position until 1870. Ten years after his first wife's death in 1864, he married Mrs. Celia Burr of Troy, N.Y., a prominent teacher and suffragist, who became a Unitarian minister. After Burleigh's death from an epileptic attack which occurred in Brooklyn, she collected his poems, first published in 1841, in a new edition.

On a number of occasions, Burleigh's heated attacks on vice subjected him to mob violence, but he was in reality a man of gentle temperament, with kindly, dark eyes and the long white hair generally associated with benevolence. Too busy ever to indulge his love of solitude, he wrote it into his poems, which were undoubtedly read by his friend, John Greenleaf Whittier.

PRINCIPAL WORKS: Poems, 1841, 1871; The Rum Fiend and Other Poems, 1871.

ABOUT: Burleigh, W. H. Poems (1871 edition); New York Times March 19, 1871; New York Tribune March 20, 1871.

BURRITT, ELIHU (December 8, 1810-March 6, 1879), "the learned blacksmith," linguist and reformer, was born in New Britain, Conn., one of the ten children of Elihu Burritt, an eccentric shoemaker who had fought in the American Revolution, and Elizabeth (Hinsdale) Burritt. Almost entirely self-taught, except for one term in his older brother's boarding-school, where his health broke under the double burden of learning and teaching, he was apprenticed to a blacksmith on his father's death in 1828. At the smithy he studied constantly, until he was the master of thirty-two languages, with a slightly lesser command of a dozen more. At the same time he performed prodigies of manual labor, and in the end ruined his health. An attempt at becoming a grocer failed because of his excessive shyness. Then in 1837 he set out for Worcester, with the idea of proceeding later to India to study Sanskrit. Edward Everett, then governor of Massachusetts, heard of him and offered to send him to Harvard, but he was too modest to accept. He stayed in Worcester, went back to the smithy, and in 1839 began publication of a magazine called the *Literary Gemini*, for the teaching of French. In 1841 he first gave his lecture on "Application and Genius," which spread his fame all over New England.

He had meanwhile become an ardent and life-long advocate of peace; from 1844 to 1851 he published the pacifist *Christian Citizen*, and he also edited the *Advocate of Peace and Universal Brotherhood*, and wrote and distributed tracts called "Friendly Ad-

Collection of Frederick H. Meserve

ELIHU BURRITT

dresses." In 1846 he went to England, where he founded the League of Universal Brotherhood and published the *Bond of Brotherhood,* at the same time showering England and France with propaganda leaflets called "Olive Leaves," in which he went so far as to advocate a general strike against war. He remained in Europe, organizing and attending peace conferences, until 1852. In that year he returned to America and edited the *Citizen of the World,* in Philadelphia.

The Crimean War, starting in 1854, put an end to his hopes of peace, and thereafter he campaigned for cheap international postage and for gradual emancipation of the slaves by compensation of their owners. In 1865 Lincoln appointed him consular agent in Birmingham. Five years later he retired to his old home in New Britain, where for the remainder of his life he farmed, wrote, and taught languages. He never married.

Longfellow remarked on the sweetness and simplicity of Burritt's character, saying that "nothing ever came from his pen that was not wholesome and good." No bigot, he had friends who disagreed wholly with his views. His many books are full of homely observation, agricultural wisdom, and noble and single-hearted love for humanity. He was not a great writer, but he was a great man.

PRINCIPAL WORKS: Sparks From the Anvil, 1846; Peace Papers for the People, 1848; Olive Leaves, 1850-53; Miscellaneous Writings, 1850; Thoughts of Things at Home and Abroad, 1854; Hand-Book of the Nations, 1856; Walk From London to John O'Groat's, 1864; Walk From London to Land's End and Back, 1865; The Mission of Great Sufferings, 1867; Walks in the Black Country, 1868; Ten-Minute Talks on All Sorts of Topics (including Autobiography) 1873; Why I Left the Anvil, 1877; Chips From Many Blocks, 1878.

ABOUT: Brooks, Van W. The Flowering of New England; Burritt, E. Ten-Minute Talks; Northend, C. Life of Elihu Burritt; New England Magazine June 1897; Saturday Review of Literature September 4, 1937.

BURROUGHS, JOHN (April 13, 1837-March 29, 1921), essayist, was born near Roxbury, N.Y., the son of Chauncey A. Burroughs, a farmer, and Amy (Kelly) Burroughs. One of his ancestors was a Salem, Mass., minister who was executed as a wizard.

From early childhood Burroughs was a nature lover, but the only way he could see to make a living was by teaching. Therefore at seventeen, after preliminary training in the local schools, he himself set about teaching in just such schools. A term at Ashland Collegiate Institute, then back to teaching, and his first writing—pompous essays, very Johnsonian in style; another term

Collection of Frederick H. Meserve

JOHN BURROUGHS

at Cooperstown Seminary, where he steeped himself in Emerson; then more teaching, this time in Illinois. Finally at twenty, his education finished, he married Ursula North, a year his senior. "If I live," he wrote her (for they were too poor to live together for the first two years of their marriage), "I shall be an author." In 1859 a teaching position in East Orange, N.J., gave him his first opportunity to establish a home.

In 1860 Burroughs published in the *Atlantic Monthly* an article so thoroughly in Emerson's idiom that Lowell, then editor, searched Emerson's works for it, and *Poole's Index* ascribed it to Emerson. Piqued by this, Burroughs began to cultivate a style and a field of his own—both appearing for the first time in his nature essays in the New York *Leader.* In 1864 he went to Washington as a clerk in the Treasury Department, remaining until 1873. Here he met Whitman, the greatest friend of his life and the subject of his first book. In 1865 the *Atlantic* published the first of Burroughs' major essays on nature, which caused Henry James to call him "a sort of reduced Thoreau."

From 1873 to 1884, Burroughs was U.S. Bank Examiner for New York State. He bought a fruit farm near Esopus, and his cabin there ("Slabsides"), his house "Riverby," presided over by his physician and Boswell, Dr. Clara Barrus, and his old home near Roxbury, became the focuses of his life and places of pilgrimage for admiring nature lovers. Edison, Theodore Roosevelt,

Henry Ford, and John Muir were his closest friends. He traveled much, campaigned against "nature fakers," farmed, and wrote indefatigably. Colgate, Yale, and the University of Georgia gave him honorary degrees. All that marred his old age was the World War, which embittered him deeply, disturbing his optimistic calm.

In the winter of 1920-21 he visited southern California, where an abscess developed in his chest. An operation was unsuccessful, and he set out with Dr. Barrus to die at home. But the end came on the train, in eastern Ohio, five days before his eighty-fourth birthday. A heavy-set, burly man with a long beard, Burroughs in old age somewhat resembled Tolstoi. Beginning as a prose poet of nature (he also published one volume of poems, and his early poem, "Waiting," is still familiar), gradually he became more scientific in his outlook, a sort of "detective of nature" and a strong evolutionist. Then in his later years he changed again to a natural mysticism which stemmed from Bergson. Through all his philosophic changes, however, his style remained vivid and idiomatic, with a sure feeling for the felicitous phrase. He established the nature essay in its modern form as a literary *genre* in America.

Principal Works: Notes on Walt Whitman as Poet and Person, 1867; Wake-Robin, 1871; Winter Sunshine, 1875; Birds and Poets, 1877; Locusts and Wild Honey, 1879; Pepacton, 1881; Fresh Fields, 1884; Signs and Seasons, 1886; Indoor Studies, 1889; Riverby, 1894; Whitman: A Study, 1896; Squirrels and Other Fur Bearers, 1900; The Light of Day, 1900; Literary Values, 1904; Far and Near, 1904; Ways of Nature, 1905; Bird and Bough (poems) 1906; Camping and Tramping With Roosevelt, 1907; Leaf and Tendril, 1908; Time and Change, 1912; The Summit of the Years, 1913; The Breath of Life, 1915; Under the Apple Trees, 1916; Field and Study, 1919; My Boyhood, 1922; The Heart of Burroughs' Journals, 1928.

About: Barrus, C. The Life and Letters of John Burroughs, John Burroughs, Boy and Man, Our Friend John Burroughs, Whitman and Burroughs; Burroughs, J. My Boyhood (completed by Julian Burroughs); DeLoach, R. J. H. Rambles With John Burroughs; Haring, H. A. The Slabsides Book of John Burroughs; Johnson, C. John Burroughs Talks: His Reminiscences and Comments; Kennedy, W. S. The Real John Burroughs.

BURTON, WILLIAM EVANS (September 24, 1804-February 10, 1860), actor-manager, editor, publisher, and miscellaneous writer, was born in England. His father, William George Burton, was a London printer, author of *Researches. . .Illustrative of the Sacred Scriptures* (1805), who died while young Burton was attending St. Paul's School to prepare for the Church. Leaving his studies to take charge of the printing business, William Evans Burton soon became interested in amateur theatricals and joined a group of professionals in 1825. During his six years with the company, he developed a decided talent for comedy rôles and in 1831 made his first important appearance at the London Pavilion. The following year he became comedian at the Haymarket and in 1834 accepted an American engagement, spending four years at the Arch Street Theatre, Philadelphia, playing such roles as Sir Peter Teazle, Dogberry, and Bob Acres. In 1848 he published a volume of his collected magazine sketches entitled *Waggeries and Vagaries.* Meanwhile, in 1837 he started the *Gentleman's Magazine,* a monthly publication which was edited for a year by Edgar Allan Poe before Burton sold it to George R. Graham in 1840.

By 1848 William Evans Burton opened Burton's Theatre which became the most popular theatre in New York and was famous throughout the country for its amusing presentations. In 1856 he moved the company to a larger theatre uptown but failed in two years. However, he soon replenished his coffers by a successful tour. Making his last appearance at Mechanics Hall, Hamilton, Canada, in 1859, he returned to New York in poor health and died of heart trouble two months later. Burton first married an actress, from whom he was divorced before he came to America, and second, to Caroline Glessing, of London, on July 18, 1834. His flair for comedy was as evident in private life as it was on the stage and he was said to be greatly beloved—although Poe's letters present a somewhat contrary picture. As an actor-manager, he set a high standard of theatrical excellence which considerably influenced the American theatre. His large personal income enabled him to acquire an extensive library, which included valuable Shakespeariana. His publications were numerous and gained him a small place in literature.

Principal Works: *Humor*—Waggeries and Vagaries, 1848. *Plays*—Ellen Wareham, 1833; *Edited*—The Literary Souvenir, 1838-40; The Cyclopaedia of Wit and Humor, 1858.

About: Brown, T. A. History of the New York Stage; Keese, W. L. William E. Burton: Actor, Author, and Manager; Hutton, L. & Matthews, B. Actors and Actresses of Great Britain and the United States.

BUTLER, WILLIAM ALLEN (February 20, 1825-September 9, 1902), lawyer and miscellaneous writer, was born in Albany, N.Y. He was the son of Benjamin Franklin Butler, attorney-general in President Jackson's cabinet, and Harriet (Allen) Butler.

Young Allen was educated at schools in Georgetown, D.C., and Hudson, N.Y., and the Grammar School of the University of the City of New York, and was graduated from the same institution in 1843. He then read law in his father's office, was admitted to the bar in July 1846, and rapidly established a successful practice. His wide knowledge of admiralty law led indirectly to his marriage with Mary Russell Marshall, daughter of Captain Charles H. Marshall, agent and part-owner of the famous Black Ball line of Liverpool packets.

Aside from his brilliant legal career, Butler had many civic and educational interests, and faithfully served the University of the City of New York in many capacities during the long stretch of years following his graduation. After the death of his uncle, Charles Butler, president, he was appointed to take his place. In 1890 when the Supreme Court of the United States celebrated its hundredth anniversary at the Metropolitan Opera House, New York City, Butler was one of the speakers with Chief Justice Fuller and Justice Field. In his later years, he returned to "Round Oak," his home in Yonkers, and took a considerable interest in the political and religious life of the town. In his busy life he found time for writing and produced several volumes of satirical poems (his *Nothing to Wear* is a minor humorous classic), two unsuccessful novels, a number of legal books, and four biographies, including *Martin Van Buren: Lawyer, Statesman, and Man*, published in 1862.

Principal Works: *Poetry*—Two Millions, 1858; Nothing to Wear: An Episode of City Life, 1857. *Novels*— Mrs. Limber's Raffle: or, A Church Fair and Its Victims, 1876; Domesticus: A Tale of the Imperial City, 1886. *Miscellaneous*—Martin Van Buren: Lawyer, Statesman, and Man, 1862; Memorial of Charles H. Marshall, 1867; Lawyer and Client: Their Relation, Rights, and Duties, 1871; Evert Augustus Duyckinck, 1879; Samuel J. Tilden, 1886; The Revision of the Statutes of the State of New York and the Revisers, 1889; Oberammergau, 1891.

About: Butler, H. A. A Retrospect of Forty Years: 1825-65, 1911; Annual Report Association of the Bar of the City of New York 1904.

BUTTERWORTH, HEZEKIAH (December 22, 1839-September 5, 1905), journalist and juvenile and patriotic writer, was born at Warren, R.I., the son of Gardiner M. and Susan (Ritchie) Butterworth. He attended the town high school and prepared for Brown University under one of the professors, but never matriculated. From earliest childhood he took a keen interest in books and as a youth wrote for the local paper. A series of articles on self-education attracted the notice of the owner and editor of the *Youth's Companion* and he became associated with the magazine from 1870 to 1894, more than doubling the circulation with his popular contributions.

Trips to Europe and South America resulted in seventeen volumes of *Zig Zag Journeys*, and an earnest interest in religion was manifested in lectures and *The Story of the Hymns*, which in 1875 was awarded the George Wood Gold Medal as the most influential book of the year. His writings were too sentimental to attain permanent literary value.

Practicing what he preached, Butterworth's life was marked by kindness and charitableness toward his fellow-men; all the sterling qualities of his character were reflected in the benign expression of his face. He never married.

Principal Works: The Story of the Hymns, 1875; Zig Zag Journeys, 1887-1894.

About: New England Magazine January 1906; Boston Evening Transcript September 6, 1905.

BYLES, MATHER (March 15, 1706/7-July 5, 1788), Congregational clergyman and poet, was the son of Josiah [or Josias] Byles, a saddler, and Elizabeth (Mather) Byles, daughter of Increase Mather [*q.v.*]. After his father's death in 1708 he was brought up by his mother, his maternal grandfather, and his uncle, Cotton Mather [*q.v.*], to whose invaluable library Byles became the heir, many years later. It is likely that he attended the Boston Latin School before entering Harvard, from which he was graduated in 1725. He prepared himself for the ministry; received his M.A. degree in 1728; and from 1732 until the outbreak of the Revolutionary War he served the newly founded Hollis Street Congregational Church in Boston.

Byles was strongly Tory-minded, but kept his politics out of the pulpit. After the British evacuation, however, his own congregation dismissed him, because of his more evident sympathies; he was sentenced to an (un-enforced) banishment; and he spent the rest of his life in relative retirement. Benjamin Franklin was an intimate friend of Byles and maintained a long correspondence with him. He was awarded the degree of S. T. D. from the University of Aberdeen in 1765. Byles was twice married: in 1733 to Mrs. Anna Gale; and three years after her death, in 1744, to Rebacca Tailer.

Much of his verse, in imitation of his English idols, appeared in a variety of periodicals, including the *New England Weekly Journal*; and the best of it was published in *Poems on Several Occasions* and *The Conflagration: Applied to That Grand Period or Catastrophe of Our World.* . . . During the 'thirties and early 'forties he published a number of religious dissertations, one of the more interesting of which was *A Discourse on the Present Vileness of the Body and Its Future Glorious Change by Christ.*

Byles made no distinguished contribution either to theology or to literature. He was an inveterate punster and a conscious cultivator of the art of repartee; and he was probably less interested in the sombre letters of religion than in the execution of impressively clever verse.

PRINCIPAL WORKS: A Discourse on the Present Vileness of the Body and Its Future Glorious Change by Christ: To Which is Added, A Sermon on the Nature and Importance of Conversion, 1732; Affection on Things Above, 1740; The Glories of the Lord of Hosts and the Fortitude of the Religious Hero, 1740; The Flourish of the Annual Spring, 1741; Poems on Several Occasions, 1744; The Conflagration: Applied to That Grand Period or Catastrophe of Our World..., 1755.

ABOUT: Bruce, W. C. Benjamin Franklin Self-Revealed; Eaton, A. W. H. The Famous Mather Byles; Sargent, L. M. Dealings With the Dead; Tudor, W. Life of James Otis; Proceedings of the American Antiquarian Society: Vol. 33.

BYRD, WILLIAM (March 28, 1674-August 26, 1744), travel writer, was born at "Westover," on the James River, Va., the son of William Byrd, planter and president of the Council of State, and Mary (Horsmanden) Byrd. He was sent to school in England at an early age, then traveled in Holland and France, and read law at the Middle Temple. After being admitted to the bar he returned to Virginia in 1692, and was at once elected to the House of Burgesses. He was much in England, usually on business for the colony, and in 1698 was made agent, and in 1706 receiver-general, succeeding his father, who had died in 1704. In 1699 he took in on his estates 300 destitute Huguenot refugees, whose descendants still live in Virginia. From 1709 to his death he was a member of the Council, and in his last year its president. In 1728 he was one of the commissioners who established the dividing line between Virginia and North Carolina—the source of his best known and most entertaining writing. In 1733 he laid out the city of Richmond on land he owned, thus founding Richmond, and Petersburg as well.

Yet in spite of his vast estates, his lordly style of living, and his fine library (of 3500 volumes, in what was still more or less a wilderness frontier), Byrd was constantly in debt and never extricated himself from financial difficulties. As T. J. Wertenbaker says,

From a portrait by G. Kneller

WILLIAM BYRD
1704

he "typified the grace, the charm, the culture, and also the rather lax business methods of the Virginians of the eighteenth century." In 1706 he married Lucy Parke; she died in 1716, leaving two daughters, and he subsequently married Maria or Marion Taylor, by whom he had two sons.

As a statesman, a planter, a man of affairs, and above all a great gentleman, Byrd of course never considered himself an author. His writing was a mere pleasant avocation, like his interest in science which made him a Fellow of the Royal Society, and a close friend of Charles Boyle, Lord Orrery. Indeed, until his privately preserved manuscripts were published nearly a century after his death, if he was known by the general public it was as a figure in early Virginia history, or as father of the lovely Evelyn Byrd whose (apocryphal) love story is part of the folklore of the South. Today he would probably be known, if at all, as one of the ancestors of Admiral Richard Byrd.

Yet this "well-built, haughty man with an aquiline nose" was a born writer. Thackeray read and admired him, and he provided part of the inspiration for *Henry Esmond* and *The Virginians.* His style is delightful—fresh, vivid, full of humor, with a modern ring. His contemporaries lauded his "happy proficiency in polite and varied learning," but colonial America was full of learned men, especially in New England; what it lacked was minds lively, keen, and picturesque. William Byrd supplied that lack. A wit, a bibliophile, an art-lover, equally at home in court circles in London and in the midst of his fields of "that bewitching vegetable, tobacco," he is one of the most attractive figures of early American history, and his works, especially in the well-edited later edition, deserve to be read more widely.

Principal Works: The Westover Manuscripts (History of the Dividing Line Between Virginia and North Carolina, A Journey to the Land of Eden, A Progress to the Mines) 1841; The Writings of Col. William Byrd (ed. by J. S. Bassett) 1901.

About: Beatty, R. C. William Byrd of Westover; Century Magazine June 1891; Scholastic December 18, 1937; Virginia Magazine of History and Biography October 1901, January 1902.

CABLE, GEORGE WASHINGTON (October 12, 1844-January 31, 1925), writer of Creole tales, social crusader, and religious leader, was born in New Orleans, the son of George Washington Cable and Rebecca (Boardman) Cable. His father belonged to an old Virginian family, his mother came of rock-ribbed Puritan stock, and he, by circumstance of birth and early environment, was ostensibly a child of the mellow South. To these facts are traceable the strange paradoxes in Cable's point of view as an author and as a moulder of social thought, during a period of American history when the political vocabulary was filled with uncompromising "isms."

At the age of fourteen, upon the death of his father, he became the chief support of the family which included several children. In 1863 he and his two sisters had fled from New Orleans in fear, had been intimidated into registering as "enemies of the United States," and were again driven back into the Confederacy. The boy George enlisted in the 4th Mississippi Cavalry, was twice wounded, but served to the end of the war, at which time he contracted "breakbone fever."

Collection of Frederick H. Meserve
GEORGE W. CABLE

It was during two years of slow recuperation that he began to write. His first real assay was a column, "Drop Shot," written for the New Orleans *Picayune*; and in 1869 he was added to the staff as a reporter. But his starched parochialism intervened. "I would not violate my conscientious scruples," he later wrote in explanation of his dismissal, "or more strictly, the tenets of my church, by going to a theatre to report a play." He then found employment as accountant and correspondence clerk for A. C. Black & Company, cotton factors. On December 7, 1869, he was married to Louise S. Bartlett.

Financially and domestically he was settled, but intellectually he was incurably restless. His formal learning had been scant. But in keeping with the economizing and discriminating bent of his Puritan mother, he had worked out a system of self-education. Begun at camp during the war, it was now continued in high seriousness; he rose regularly at four in the morning. After conquering French, he began to dig into the city archives. It was in these old records of the Creoles—the French-speaking natives of Louisiana—that he found the subject matter for his finest tales. Edward King, a literary scout who had been sent into the South by Scribner's, procured Cable's short story " 'Sieur George" for *Scribner's Monthly*. Six years later, *Old Creole Days,* a volume of seven tales, appeared. From the point of view of the literary historian, this work contains the best representation of the French dialect spoken by the Creole Negroes of Louisiana. (The word "Creole" is commonly applied to both races.) In general, the South was quite willing to commend Cable's literary artistry, despite the fact that he had delineated a crude and unflattering stratum of society, one that spoke either Negro French or a Creole patois. Only among the higher levels of Creoles was there audible protest. And from the North came nothing but good words.

Cable had now a substantial claim to authorship. He turned to it as a profession when A. C. Black & Company suddenly dissolved. In 1880 came *The Grandissimes*; in this historical romance the Cavalier tang of his Virginian heritage was disciplined by an unbending "conscience" that spoke out against slavery. The critics approved of his descriptive finesse but charged him with having weakened his book by naive, moralistic intrusions. "It was impossible," said Cable, "that a novel written by me then should escape being a study of the fierce struggle going on around me. . ." In 1884 appeared *The Creoles of Louisiana,* an elaboration of what he had written for the United States Census for 1880; here was an historical treatment of a people whom he had been accused of misrepresenting in fiction. *Dr. Sevier,* a narrative of pathos that exposed prison evils, was published in 1885. His social awareness was growing; his first major brief for Negro justice, *The Silent South,* followed. The editor of the Atlanta *Constitution* charged Cable with advocating a mingling of the races, regardless of the fact that the author had plainly referred to such a proposal as a mere "fool's dream," and had given his full support to an equality of rights, a concurrent advancement of the black and white races.

In 1885 he left the South behind him and took a charming house in Northampton, Mass., which remained his home until his death in 1925. With a gift from his friend Andrew Carnegie he established the Home-Culture Clubs, now the Northampton People's Institute. In this project he became completely absorbed. By 1896 the movement had gained sufficient impetus to carry it into thirteen states. His writings during these years reflect not only the reformer but the religious leader (see *The Busy Man's Bible,* 1891). Moreover, he and Mark Twain undertook some extensive tours on which each read from his works. During some of these performances, Cable, after many apologetic prologues, sang from his collection of primitive, drawling Creole melodies.

He was a slight man, with sharp eyes and a finely pointed beard, and perched on his high bicycle he was a familiar figure about Northampton. His seven children—the first son died at the age of four—were ever more than a delight to him. "This world seems to me," he put it, "as definitely for joy as for use or discipline." But he knew sorrow as well. Two years after the death of his first wife in 1904, he had married Eva S. Stevenson, whose broad intellectual interests were a comfort to him, but she, too, preceded him in death. He was again married, at the age of seventy-nine, to Mrs. Hannah Cowing, a Northampton friend of long standing. Together they wintered in Florida, where Cable spent his last hours.

Fundamentally, Cable's wholesome eclecticism was very much alive during his last years. But an inevitable spirit of nostalgia and reminiscence set in; domestic security and literary fatigue caused a relaxation of some of the sturdier purposes behind his "middle" romances. Nor could he duplicate, in the six novels which appeared between 1901 and 1918, the rare tincture of charm of his very early tales, which had made him a major exponent in the "local color episode" in American literature. For he had preserved in literary form an exotic segment of our civilization, which, by constant social change, is fast losing its identity. Yet he is not a figure easily assigned to one particular category. As an author he was both a delicate romanticist and a Dickensian realist. As a social thinker he was an earnest abolitionist—though an ex-Confederate soldier and once a slave-holder—and an equally sincere sympathizer with the misjudged and perplexed South. His only unifying credo, perhaps, was this: ". . that a man *belongs* to the community in which he lives, to whatever extent he can serve it, consistently with the fact of equal moment that he belongs to his nation and the human race to the extent of his power to serve them."

Principal Works: *Historical Romances*—The Grandissimes, 1880; The Creoles of Louisiana, 1884; Dr. Sevier, 1885; Bonaventure, 1888; Strange True Stories of Louisiana, 1889; Strong Hearts, 1889; The Cavalier, 1901; Bylow Hill, 1902; Kincaid's Battery, 1908; Gideon's Band, 1914; The Flower of the Chapdelaines, 1918; Lovers of Louisiana, 1918. *Stories*—Old Creole Days, 1879. *Miscellaneous*—The Silent South, 1885; The Negro Question, 1888 (?); The Busy Man's Bible, 1891; The Amateur Garden, 1914.

About: Bikle, L. L. C. George W. Cable: His Life and Letters; Harkins, E. F. Little Pilgrimages Among Men; Toulmin, H. A., Jr. Social Historians; Bookman June 1931; Century Magazine February 1882 and April 1885.

"CADMUS." See ZACHOS, JOHN CELIVERGOS

CALEF, ROBERT (1648-April 13, 1719), iconoclastic student of witchcraft, cloth merchant, and overseer of the poor, is believed to have been born in England. He settled in Boston in 1688, and five years later, on the heels of the Salem witchcraft trials, he secured a copy of Cotton Mather's account of an attempt to exorcise one Margaret Rule ("Another Brand Pluckt From the Burning") and circulated some distasteful observations on the conduct, during this seance, of both the author and his father Increase Mather. Cotton Mather thereupon accused

Calef of being "a sort of Saducee . . . who makes little Conscience of lying . . ."; Calef was tried for libel, but the case was shortly dropped.

Calef's *More Wonders of the Invisible World,* an analysis of Cotton's book, miscellaneous polemical correspondence, and a well annotated record of the Salem trials of 1692, was ready in 1697, but no Boston publishers would issue it. It appeared in 1700 in England, and its strength as a diatribe against the Mathers was not in the least diminished by physical distance. A contemporary historian stated that Calef was "furnished with materials for his work by Mr. Brattle of Cambridge; and his brother, of Boston; and other gentlemen." (Calef himself was a tithing-man, an assessor, etc., but no scholar; the Brattles, however, were men of learning.) According to a rather slim tradition Increase Mather, then president of Harvard ordered the book to be burned in Harvard Yard.

Actually the controversy between the disciples of the Mathers and the followers of Calef still exists; there is, however, some significance in the fact that Cotton Mather made no reply to that "Libellous Book lately come into this Countrey. . . ." It cannot be denied that Calef was the author of not only a forthright and orderly condemnation of an outmoded view of witchcraft but a real tonic for intellectual inertia.

ABOUT: Boas, R. & L. Cotton Mather: Keeper of Puritan Conscience; Burr, G. L. Narratives of the Witchcraft Cases; Calef, R. More Wonders of the Invisible World; Drake S. G. Annals of the Witchcraft; Granite Monthly May 1907.

CALHOUN, JOHN CALDWELL

(March 18, 1782-March 31, 1850), orator and statesman, was born in the "96 District," near Abbeville, S.C., the son of Patrick and Martha (Caldwell) Calhoun. Both parents were of Presbyterian Irish descent; the father, a surveyor and a member of the South Carolina legislature, had been born in Donegal. He died when Calhoun was a small child.

Calhoun was educated in an academy kept by his brother-in-law, and at Yale, from which he was graduated in 1804. He studied law in Charleston and at a law school in Litchfield, Conn., was admitted to the bar in 1807, and started practice in Abbeville. In 1808 he was elected to the state legislature, and in 1811 to Congress. From 1817 to 1825 he was secretary of war, from 1825 to 1831 vice-president, under Jackson, and in 1831, having resigned the vice-presidency, he was a senator. He resigned from the senate in 1843 to become secretary of state,

Collection of Frederick H. Meserve

JOHN C. CALHOUN

and returned to the senate in 1845. During the last five years of his life he was ill most of the time, and finally died while still in office. In 1811 he had married his cousin, Florida Calhoun, who brought him a considerable fortune and the estate, thenceforth his home, of Fort Hill. They had nine children. Three colleges gave him honorary LL.D. degrees—Hamilton, Yale, and Columbia.

Such was the bare outline of Calhoun's political career. It gives no hint either of his immense influence or of his oratorical genius. The most famous men of his time were quick to recognize his worth. Edward Everett called Clay "the great leader," Webster "the great speaker," and Calhoun "the great thinker." Calhoun was, however, great in all three fields—leadership, oratory, and thought. The doctrine chiefly associated with his name, that of nullification (the right of a state to declare a national law—*e.g.* the tariff—unconstitutional, and thus nullify it) went down to defeat; and his advocacy of slavery (his primary aim being to placate the South and keep it in the Union) also proved to be the losing side; but this does not alter the fact that he was one of the leaders of political thought of his time. With Clay, he did more than anyone else to bring about the War of 1812, yet later he was the dominating power in settling peaceably with England the question of ownership of the Oregon territory.

Daniel Webster, with a neatness of locution worthy of Noah of that name, remarked that Calhoun was "a man of undoubted genius and of commanding talent." He had an unusually analytical mind, acute, subtle, and philosophical, and he relied on logic rather than on emotional appeal. Nevertheless, what Clay quaintly called "the charm and captivating influence of his colloquial powers" was his distinguishing characteristic; he was outstanding as an orator in the great age of oratory. He was a strict constitutionalist, yet bold and daring in his political thinking; though allied with the Whigs, he called himself an independent and felt beholden to no party. His spare figure, with its harsh features and its burning blue eyes, dominated every important debate in the Senate in his time. He wrote little, and the mass of his published work consists of reports of his speeches, lessened in appeal by the lack of the personality of the direct speaker; but the two essays he wrote in his last year, the "Discourse on the Constitution" and the "Disquisition on Government," display his power of analysis and his vigorous and trenchant style.

Principal Works: Speeches, 1843; Address to the People of the South, 1849; Works, 1851-53; Complete Works, 1853-55; Correspondence, 1899.

About: Bradford, G. As God Made Them; Dodd, W. E. Statesmen of the Old South; Hollis, C. The American Heresy; Hunt, G. John C. Calhoun; Meigs, W. M. The Life of John Caldwell Calhoun; Pinckney, G. M. Life of John C. Calhoun; Styron, A. The Cast-Iron Man; von Holst, H. E. John C. Calhoun.

CALKINS, NORMAN ALLISON (September 9, 1822-December 22, 1895), editor and educator, was born in Gainesville, N.Y., the son of Elisha Deming Calkins and Abigail (Lockwood) Calkins, and was descended from an early Plymouth settler. He attended the common schools of the district and then spent several terms at an academy. At the age of eighteen he began to teach, in Castile, N.Y., continuing his own studies during the summer. In the fall of 1846 he resigned a position as county superintendent at Gainesville, N.Y., to become editor of the *Student*, a highly successful family miscellany and school reader published monthly in New York. At the time of its merger with the *Schoolmate*, Calkins withdrew, and in 1861 published his most valuable book, *Primary Object Lessons for a Graduated Course of Development.* In it were projected the Pestalozzian principles of object teaching in which he had long been interested; three more writings in this same category followed between the years 1877 and 1889. Calkins was married to Mary Hoosier in 1854.

In the National Education Association he had held various offices before becoming its president in 1886; and from 1861 until his death he was assistant superintendent of the schools of New York City. His writings underwent numerous editions and several translations, in their day, but educational advancement has caused them to become outmoded.

Principal Works: Primary Object Lessons for a Graduated Course of Development, 1861; Teaching Color, 1877; How to Teach Phonics, 1889.

About: New York Times December 23, 1895; National Education Journal of Proceedings and Addresses, 1896.

CALVERT, GEORGE HENRY (January 2, 1803-May 24, 1889), cosmopolite, essayist, and miscellaneous writer, was born on the family estate near Bladensburg, Md., the eldest son of wealthy parents, George Calvert and Rosalie (Stier) Calvert. His father claimed descent from the Lords Baltimore. His mother, a descendant of Rubens, came to America from Antwerp with her father about the close of the eighteenth century. A brother, Charles Benedict Calvert, became a well known Congressman and champion of agricultural legislation.

On graduation from Harvard in 1823, Calvert sailed for England, visited an uncle's château near Antwerp, and then became one of the first Americans to enroll at Göttingen, where for fifteen months he studied history and philosophy. During 1825-27 he visited Goethe at Weimar, and lived in Edinburgh, Antwerp, and Paris. In 1829 he married

From a portrait by W. Hunt

GEORGE HENRY CALVERT
1859

Elizabeth Steuart of Baltimore (who died when ninety-three, in 1897). Until the middle of 1836 he was an editor of the Baltimore *American.* Abroad again from 1840-43, he visited Wordsworth in August 1840, and later resided in Germany and Italy. On returning, he lived in Newport, R.I., in a rambling house surrounded by firs, until his death at the age of eighty-six. His third and last trip to Europe was in 1851-52. He was chairman of the Newport School Committee for a time, and in 1853-54 was Democratic mayor of that city. His sympathies were with the North in the Civil War.

Calvert's once widely known published works were written over a period of fifty-four years, and aroused divided sentiments. Some of his contemporaries praised his versatility and industry, his sense of beauty, his philosophic caste of mind, his originality, and his pure, scholarly style. Others as sharply criticized his lyric and narrative poems as a dilution of Tennyson's style, or his prolific production of verse as of a sort no reader could mistake for poetry. Poe called him "essentially a feeble and commonplace writer of poetry, although his prose compositions have a certain degree of merit."

His writings on phrenology and the water cure were the first on these subjects to be published in America. He also pioneered in the study of German literature and in interpreting Goethe and Schiller. But, although his motives were to serve the general welfare by practical suggestions fr m the laws of health, philosophy, and art, his writings did not make any lasting impression. Best known in their time among his voluminous works were *The Gentleman,* an essay on manners, and *First Years in Europe* and *Scenes and Thoughts in Europe,* studies of Germany and France in the middle years of the century. His greatest literary usefulness was as a somewhat fragile cultural bridge between the old and new continents.

A friend of Calvert's old age described him as tall, dark, gaunt, stooped, introspective, courteous, dignified, and respected by all.

Principal Works: *Essays*—Illustrations of Phrenology, 1832; Scenes and Thoughts in Europe, 1846, Second Series, 1852; Introduction to Social Science, 1856; Moral Education, 1857; The Gentleman, 1863; First Years in Europe, 1866; Goethe: His Life and Works, 1872; Brief Essays and Brevities, 1874; Essays Aesthetical, 1875. *Biography*—A Volume From the Life of Herbert Barclay, 1833; The Life of Peter Paul Rubens, 1876; Charlotte von Stein: A Memoir, 1877; Wordsworth, 1878; Shakespeare, 1879; Coleridge, 1880; Shelley, 1880; Goethe, 1880. *Poetry*—Cabiro: Cantos I, II, 1840; Miscellany of Verse and Prose, 1840; Poems, 1847; Joan of Arc, 1860; Cabiro: Cantos III and IV, 1864; Anita, etc., 1876; A Nation's Birth, etc., 1876; Ellen, 1867; Life, Death, etc., 1882; Threescore, etc., 1883; Sibyl, 1883; The Nazarine, 1883. *Dramas*—Count Julian: A Tragedy, 1840; Comedies: The Will and the Way, Like Unto Like, 1856; Arnold and Andre: An Historical Drama, 1864; The Maid of Orleans, 1874; Brangomar: A Tragedy, 1883; Mirabeau: An Historical Drama, 1885. *Lectures*—German Literature, 1836; Fortieth Anniversary, Battle of Lake Erie, 1853; Shakespeare, 1886.

About: Payne, W. M. Leading American Essayists; Redwood Library and Athenaeum: Catalog of Books in the Library of G. H. Calvert; Tompkins, H. B. A Bibliography of the Works of George Henry Calvert.

"CAMILLUS." See AMES, FISHER

CAMPBELL, BARTLEY (August 12, 1843-July 30, 1888), writer and producer of melodramas, was born in Pittsburgh, the son of Bartley Campbell, Sr., and Mary (Eckles) Campbell. He attended private school, started to study law, and then turned directly to a newspaper career. From Pittsburgh he went to New Orleans, in 1869, where for a time he edited the *Southern Magazine.* With the appearance of his first play, *Through Fire* (1871), he withdrew from journalism. In 1872 he went to Chicago to write and direct plays for Hooley's Theatre. He took his company, in 1875, to San Francisco, and here he assembled some excellent material for *My Partner,* a straightforward frontier drama with authentic pathos.

Campbell now became his own producer; he staged *The Virginian in England* in 1876, and wrote *A Heroine in Rags,* and *How Women Love* (1877). On his return came *The Galley Slave, The White Slave,* and *Siberia,* a series of extravagant tableaux. *Separation* preceded Campbell's last play *Paquita* (1885).

He was a tall and prepossessing gentleman, with a face strongly resembling that of Artemus Ward, the humorist. In a little more than ten years he made and spent a fortune. His mental and physical energies were sadly dissipated and he was removed to the State Hospital for the Insane at Middletown, N.Y., a year and a half before his death. He left a widow (*née* Williams, of Allegheny City, Pa.) and two sons.

The prestige of the American playwright *per se* was greatly strengthened by Campbell's achievements; and his best piece of work, *My Partner,* was admitted to be "another proof that the American drama can stand on its own legs." Nevertheless he fell short of any real greatness. His plays bear the stamp of the journalist rather than that of the conscious craftsman. Nor are they, with slight exception, aged in the spirit of any particular *milieu,* for Campbell was essentially a roving person, who had a producer's point of view and was mindful of box-office incentives.

PRINCIPAL WORKS: *Plays* (unpublished)—Through Fire, 1871; Peril: or, Love at Long Branch, 1872; Fate, 1872-1873; Risks: or, Insure Your Life, 1873; The Virginian, 1873; On the Rhine, 1875; Bulls and Bears, 1875; Heroine in Rags, 1876; How Women Love, 1877; Clio (in verse) 1878; My Partner, 1879; The Galley Slave, 1879; Fairfax, 1879; The White Slave, 1882; Siberia, 1882; Separation, 1884; Paquita, 1885.

ABOUT: Brown, T. A. A History of the New York Stage; Quinn, A. H. A History of the American Drama; New York Mirror August 4, 1888; New York Times September 17, 1879, July 31, 1888; San Francisco Evening Bulletin November 29, 1882.

CAMPBELL, CHARLES (May 1, 1807-July 11, 1876), editor and historian, was born in Petersburg, Va., the son of John Wilson Campbell, a local bookseller who had published in 1813 a *History of Virginia to 1781.* Young Campbell went to Princeton and upon his graduation in 1825 began to teach, founded his own classical school in Petersburg in 1842, and from 1855 to 1870 was principal of Anderson Academy.

Campbell had an early interest in collecting historical manuscripts and documents, and one of his valuable letters was lent to Bishop William Meade for publication in his *Old Churches and Families of Virginia.* In 1837 Campbell began to contribute regularly to the *Southern Literary Messenger* and was for a time one of the conductors of the "Editor's Table"; he also wrote some articles for the *Virginia Historical Register.* In 1847 appeared his most extensive work, *An Introduction to the History of the Colony and Ancient Dominion of Virginia.* He was editor-author of *Some Materials for a Memoir of John Daly Burk,* and, in 1860 published the *Orderly Book of Gen. Andrew Lewis.*

Because he had a scholar's point of view and much physical energy for ferreting out inaccessible materials, he became, especially in his Old Dominion annals, one of the most exhaustive of writers on state history.

PRINCIPAL WORKS: An Introduction to the History of the Colony and Ancient Dominion of Virginia, 1847; Orderly Book of Gen. Andrew Lewis, 1860; Genealogy of the Spotswood Family, 1868; Materials for a Memoir of John Daly Burk, 1868.

ABOUT: The South in the Building of the Nation: Vol. 11.

CANNON, CHARLES JAMES (November 4, 1800-November 9, 1860), poet, storyteller, and playwright, was born in New York City, the son of an humble but enterprising Irishman. He had the disadvantages of ill health and a lack of education, and he settled down at an early age to a long career as a custom-house clerk. His writings were the product of his leisure hours.

CHARLES J. CANNON
c. 1843

Facts, Feelings, and Fancies (1835), Cannon's first published work, is a miscellany with a dominantly moody tone, broken only by convulsive resentment or quiet gaiety. *The Poet's Quest and Other Poems* followed in 1841, and in addition to the title poem, contains numerous short melancholy verses prompted by the death of friends. The subject of the title poem in *The Crowning Hour* (1843) is Columbus' first sight of land, and the remaining poems are largely religious.

A pleasant little narrative, *Mora Carmodi: or, Woman's Influence* appeared in 1844. One of Cannon's critics, a Catholic, declared the author to be a man "with a bit of genius" but advised such literary upstarts "to invent some method of disposing of their heroines without sending them to a convent." It is presumably the same critic who, a year later, complained that *Father Felix* tended "rather to feed a sickly sentimentalism than to nourish a robust piety."

In the preface of *Poems: Dramatic and Miscellaneous* (1851) the author anticipates leaving the "unprofitable trade of ballad-making." Trow's *Directory* for 1850-51 continues to list Cannon as a clerk, however, and the statement merely forcasts his plunge into the field of the drama. In "The Sculptor's Daughter," a somber piece, the rare flashes of poetry are drowned out by a Doric sternness and a monotony of stock characters. *The Oath of Office* (1854), a tragedy, was "successfully produced" at the Bowery Theatre on March 18, 1850, but enjoyed no long run. It has a certain power, and, although architecturally faulty, is conceded to be Cannon's best work. But the playwright was discouraged and abandoned theatricals. A selection of reminiscent tales called *Ravellings From the Web of Life* appeared in 1855 over the pseudonym "Grandfather Greenway."

Cannon was an unassuming man with a gentle and cautious manner. Except for a brief residence in Brooklyn toward the close of his life, he made his home in and about Greenwich Village. His allegiance to his clerkship as well as a consciousness of his scant literary equipment put a visible stamp upon his writings, and although he made no startling contributions to American letters, his works rank favorably with the passing literature of that day.

Principal Works: *Poetry*—The Poet's Quest, 1841; The Crowning Hour, 1843; Poems: Dramatic and Miscellaneous, 1851. *Tales*—Mora Carmodi: or, Woman's Influence, 1844; Father Felix: A Catholic Story, 1845 (?); Ravellings From the Web of Life, 1855. *Dramas*—Oath of Office, 1854; Dramas, 1857. *Miscellaneous*—Facts, Feelings, and Fancies, 1835; Scenes and Characters From the Comedy of Life, 1847.

About: Brownson's Quarterly Review January 1845, January 1846, October 1857; Spirit of the Times March 23, 1850; *also* Prefaces to the author's various works.

CAPEN, NAHUM (April 1, 1804-January 8, 1886), social historian, was born in Canton, Mass., the son of Andrew and Hannah (Richards) Capen. Given a Latin school education, he read widely in the classics and in the works of Benjamin Franklin, whom he almost idolized. At nineteen he wrote (but did not publish) a simplified or popularized version of *Plutarch's Lives.* He began the study of medicine under his older brother Robert, but was in poor health and accepted, instead, a partnership in the publishing house of March, Capen & Long. He was married to Elizabeth Ann More on October 14, 1830.

Capen had written a good many miscellaneous papers on copyright laws, Free Trade, etc., before the appearance of his first book *The Republic of the United States of America . . . Its Duties to Itself . . .*, an anonymous politico-historical eulogy of James Buchanan, then secretary of state and a likely candidate for the presidency. In 1832 Dr. Johann K. Spurzheim, German physician and one of the founders of phrenology, visited the United States. Capen became his guide and adviser and later wrote *Reminiscences of Dr. Spurzheim and George Combe*, containing the early deliberations of the Boston Phrenological Society of which Capen was the founder. From 1857-61 he was postmaster of Boston, an appointee of President Buchanan.

He had contemplated an extensive *History of Democracy* but only one volume was ever printed (1874). Had Capen's learning been broader and his outlook more cosmopolitan he would doubtless have avoided a strain of naïveté and dogma that prevented him from becoming a ranking political historian.

Principal Works: The Republic of the United States of America . . . Its Duties to Itself, 1848; The History of Democracy in the United States, 1851-52; Reminiscences of Dr. Spurzheim and George Combe, 1881.

About: United States Democratic Review May 1858; Boston Transcript January 9, 1886.

"CAPTAIN JACK." See CRAWFORD, JOHN WALLACE

CAREY, HENRY CHARLES (December 15, 1793-October 13, 1879), economist, was born in Philadelphia. He was the son of the publisher and economist Mathew Carey [*q.v.*] and Bridget (Flahavan) Carey and was his father's chief disciple. The relations between the two were very similar to those between James and John. Stuart Mill, the English father-and-son economists. Like John Stuart Mill, Carey was educated entirely by his father, and never attended a school. At the age of eight, he acted as his father's agent at a book sale in New York, and at ten took charge for a time of a branch office in Baltimore. In 1817 he became a partner in his father's firm, under the title of Carey, Lea, & Carey. (The present successors of this firm are Lea & Febiger, the scientific publishers.) During his father's lifetime Henry Charles Carey became head of the firm, which acted as American publishers for Carlyle, Scott, and Washington Irving. In spite of the nonexistence of a copyright law, he always paid royalties to his British authors—a rare procedure in those days.

Carey was married early to a sister of the well known artist C. R. Leslie, but she died soon after and he never remarried. He did no writing until 1835, when his growing interest in economics found voice in an *Essay on the Rate of Wages.* This interest continued, until in 1838 he retired from business to devote all his time to political econ-

Collection of Frederick H. Meserve
HENRY C. CAREY

omy. From 1849 on, he was a frequent contributor to the New York *Tribune*, then under the editorship of Horace Greeley. After 1860 he wrote only one book, but numerous pamphlets continued to pour from his pen. In 1872 he was a delegate to the Pennsylvania Constitutional Convention, his only public office.

Until 1845 Carey was a free trader; after that he became increasingly an advocate of high tariffs until in the end he was the father of the traditional protectionist policy of the Republican Party. He also became an intense nationalist and an Anglophobe. His works were translated into seven European languages and Japanese, and he was the first American economist to have an international fame. His was an optimistic economic theory, based on the idea that there are natural economic laws which work for the benefit of mankind and spread prosperity among all classes, if they are not interfered with by the perversity or stupidity of man. He denied the Malthusian theory that population growth tends to increase want. He was equally opposed to the "pessimistic" school of classical economists, represented by Ricardo, and the socialistic school, Dühring, the enemy of Marx, was one of his disciples.

Though in his writing Carey was sharp and vehement, he himself was a gentle, kindly man, with a handsome, sensitive countenance. His evening parties, known as "Carey Vespers," constituted the nearest American approach to the French salons. He was above all an original thinker, though his system has solidified into a narrow emphasis on the tariff which he himself would probably have regretted. To European economists of his generation he represented the whole of American economic thought.

Principal Works Essay on the Rate of Wages, 1835; Principles of Political Economy, 1837-40; Commercial Associations in France and England, 1845; Past, Present, and Future, 1848; Harmony of Interests: Manufacturing and Commercial, 1851; The Slave Trade: Domestic and Foreign, 1853; Letters to the President, 1858; Principles of Social Science, 1858-59; Unity of Law, 1872.

About: Elder, W. Memoir of Henry Charles Carey; Kaplan, A. D. H. Henry Charles Carey: A Study in American Economic Thought; Teilhac, E. Pioneers of American Economic Thought in the Nineteenth Century.

CAREY, MATHEW (January 28, 1760-September 26, 1839), publisher and economist, was born in Dublin, Ireland, the son of Christopher Carey, an army contractor. A fall in infancy left him lame for life, and made him a shy, backward boy who had little schooling, but was a natural linguist. Against his father's wishes, he apprenticed himself to a bookseller and printer. His first published article, a plea against dueling, was published in the *Hibernian Journal* in 1777. Two years later an anonymous paper by him, hotly defending the Irish Catholics, led to an inquiry in Parliament, and to the offer of a reward for apprehension of the author by an outraged group of English (and anti-Irish) Catholic conservatives. His family sent him for safety to Paris, where he worked in the printing plant set up by Benjamin Franklin at Passy. In a year it was safe for him to return to Dublin, and there he became editor of the *Freeman's Journal.*

In 1873 his prosperous father, by this time reconciled to the son's choice of a vocation, set him up as proprietor of the *Volunteer's Journal*, which he made into a bitterly anti-English publication. The consequence was that he served a short term in Newgate Prison in 1784. On his release, he decided to emigrate, and escaped from Ireland dressed as a woman. He landed in Philadelphia, where he found Lafayette, whom he had known in Paris. Lafayette insisted on lending him $400, and would not allow him to repay the loan until 1824, when the French patriot had lost his own fortune. With this help, Carey managed to keep going, and in 1785 he founded and edited the *Pennsylvania Herald.* In it he advocated his doctrine of protection for American industries. In spite of his hatred for dueling, the personal flavor of the journalism of the period forced him into a duel, in 1786, with the editor of the *Independent Gazeteer*, in which Carey was badly injured. He launched two magazines, the *Columbian Magazine* and the *American Museum: or, Universal Magazine.* Neither of them paid its way, though both had wide influence, and Carey was extremely poor. Nevertheless in 1791 he married Bridget Flahavan, and they had nine children, one of whom, Henry Charles Carey [*q.v.*], became an economist more noted than his father. Finally Carey was compelled to give up his purse-draining publications, and borrowed money to start as a bookseller, printer, and publisher. This firm prospered, and eventually became Carey, Lea, & Carey.

Carey's public services were many. With Stephen Girard (who was his close friend, though Girard was a Rationalist and Carey a devout Catholic), he served through the yellow fever epidemic of 1793, writing a pamphlet later to describe its horrors. He founded the Hibernian Society, to care for poor Irish immigrants, and in 1796 helped to found the first Sunday School society in America. In 1802 he was a director of the Bank of Pennsylvania. He was a charter member of the Philadelphia Society for the Promotion of National Industry, and wrote most of the society's published statements. He was strongly in favor of universal education, and wrote many pamphlets on the subject. When he died in 1839, his funeral was one of the largest ever seen in Philadelphia.

Though personally he was a friend of peace, Carey frequently descended to vituperation in his writings. He was an ardent protectionist, but not a chauvinist, as his son tended to become: after the War of 1812 he wrote *The Olive Branch* with the object of reconciling the United States and England. Aside from a tendency toward personal abuse of those who disagreed with him, his style was strong and clear, and often eloquent.

From a portrait by J. Neagle
MATHEW CAREY
1825

PRINCIPAL WORKS: The Olive Branch, 1814; Vindiciae Hibernicae, 1819; Essays on Political Economy, 1822; Autobiographical Sketches, 1829; Miscellaneous Essays, 1830.

ABOUT: Bradsher, E. L. Mathew Carey: Editor, Author, and Publisher; Carey, M. Autobiographical Sketches; Rowe, K. W. Mathew Carey.

"CARLETON." See COFFIN, CHARLES CARLETON

CARLETON, HENRY (1785-March 28, 1863), essayist and jurist, whose name was originally Henry Carleton Cox, was a native of Virginia. After two years at the University of Georgia he entered Yale and was graduated in 1806. He removed to New Orleans in 1814, read law in the office of Edward Livingston, the eminent jurist, and shortly built up an excellent practice. The state legislature authorized and provided the funds for his collaboration with Louis Moreau Lislet on a translation of *Las Siete Partidas,* Louisiana's long enforced principal Spanish code. In 1832 he was appointed United States attorney for the eastern district of Louisiana, and, in 1837, judge of the supreme court of that state. His years of public office were trying ones owing to the prolonged critical relations between the United States and Mexico; he resigned in 1839 because of ill health.

On his return from a journey abroad Carleton settled in Philadelphia, where he published, as the harvest of some philosophical speculations, *Liberty and Necessity* and an *Essay on the Will.* He was twice married: on May 29, 1815, to Aglaé D'Avezac de Castera; and after her death, to Mrs. Maria Vanderburgh Wiltbank.

Carleton's metaphysical tracts seem to have had little durability, but his code translation preserved a rather uncommon aspect of legal history and contributed substantially towards "an understanding of the laws of Spain."

PRINCIPAL WORKS: Las Siete Partidas (translation) 1820; Liberty and Necessity, 1857; Essay on the Will, 1863.

ABOUT: Whitaker, E. S. Sketches of Life and Character in Louisiana.

CARLETON, HENRY GUY (June 21, 1856-December 10, 1910), playwright, was born in Fort Union, N.M., the son of General James Henry and Sophie Garland (Wolfe) Carleton. He studied under the Jesuits at Santa Clara College, San Francisco, and was graduated in 1870 as a civil and mining engineer. For a while he served as a cavalry officer in the army; and it was while writing for the *Times* in New Orleans, that he took part in the suppression of the reconstruction government in Louisiana.

When Carleton was only fifteen he had written a play called *The Age of Gold*; and at twenty-five he wrote *Memnon*, a blank verse tragedy laid in Egypt, in which he had observed the dramatic unities; it was later privately "printed, not published." In 1892 he went to New York and in the year following became managing editor of *Life*; for this magazine he wrote the "Thompson Street Poker Club" papers, which in 1884 were published in book form, "affectionately and yet cautiously dedicated" to Robert Cumming Schenck, a famous congressman, soldier, and authority on draw poker. Carleton's rowdy colored protagonists were the Reverend Thankful Smith, Cyanide Whiffles, and Jubilee Anderson, every one of them with a balmy conscience and a loud aversion to interloping "suckahs from Hoboken." *Lectures Before the Thompson Street Poker Club*, a sequel (Rev. Thankful Smith is the supposed expositor), appeared in 1889.

In 1886 Carleton had joined the editorial staff of the New York *World* where he remained for several years. Ever since his arrival in New York he had been turning out rather melancholy plays—about fifteen in all—which found little sale. It was some time after removing to Boston that he wrote for Nat Goodwin, the comedian, *The Gilded Fool*, produced with great success in Providence, R.I., in 1892. Charles Frohman, the New York theatrical manager, saw the play and engaged Carleton to write *The Butterflies* (1893), starring John Drew and creating for Maude Adams a part that established her stage reputation. In 1894 he wrote another play for Nat Goodwin, *Ambition*; after long procrastination over the third act he finally threw it together in great haste. New York critics regarded the piece with apathy, but on tour it drew capacity audiences.

Carleton had an acute stammer but his ever-ready sense of humor seems to have spared him much embarrassment. Like many hard-pressed writers he was guilty of overlooking some of his personal obligations. As a playwright he was, perhaps, more concerned about box office receipts than he was about any purposeful development of an American drama, but his plays are interesting samples of what came between the conventionalism of "stock" and the evolution of a native dramatic conscience.

Courtesy of Syracuse University Library
HENRY GUY CARLETON
1896

PRINCIPAL WORKS: *Plays*—Memnon, 1881; Victor Durand, 1884; The Gilded Fool, 1892; The Butterflies, 1893; Ambition, 1894; Lem Keith, 1894. *Miscellaneous*—The Thompson Street Poker Club, 1884; Lectures Before the Thompson Street Poker Club, 1889.

ABOUT: Goodwin, N. C. Nat Goodwin's Book; prefaces, etc., to Carleton's works.

CARLETON, WILL (October 21, 1845-December 18, 1912), writer of domestic ballads and stories, was born on a farm near Hudson, Mich. He was the son of John Hancock Carleton and Celestia (Smith) Carleton and was christened William McKendree; he never used the full name.

Will was a dreamy child whose fondness for reading and barnyard declamation was frowned upon by his exacting father as the folly of "spoiling a tolerably good farmer to become an intolerably bad orator." His learning was periodically interrupted, and he taught country school before entering Hillsdale College in 1865. Upon graduation he worked first on a Chicago newspaper, then became editor and part owner of the Hillsdale *Standard*, and finally was editor of the *Detroit Weekly Tribune*. It was the reporting of a divorce case (1871) that sug-

WILL CARLETON

gested his first poem, "Betsy and I are Out," which appeared in *Harper's Weekly*. The question of authorship of this ballad gave rise to a petty feud between Carleton and an Eastern authoress who was in need of publicity. When *Farm Ballads* was published in 1873 the sale soon ran to 40,000 copies, for in it were his most famous poem, "Over the Hill to the Poor House," and other verses that had become established favorites. *Farm Legends* (1875) and *Farm Festivals* (1881) completed the cycle.

Carleton met Mark Twain and John Hay in New York in 1872, and on a return journey in 1876 he took tea at Walt Whitman's in Camden, N.J. His own account of this event, however, betrays an unfortunate naïveté in literary discernment. He went to England, Ireland, and Scotland in 1878, and returned after a brief stay in Paris. Boston provided the sentiment for *City Ballads* (1885), *City Legends* (1889), and *City Festivals* (1892). He resided there until 1882, at which time he married Adora Niles Goodell and moved to Brooklyn.

In 1884 Carleton toured Europe extensively and lectured in England. Since 1871 he had been accustomed to reading in public five nights a week, and for this his remuneration had grown from the scant proceeds of parish audiences to a weekly average of about $90. The panic of 1873 had dampened his immediate hopes for the undertaking of a literary publication, but in 1894 he succeeded in founding a monthly called *Every Where*, which contained poems, short stories, and timely topics, and enjoyed a circulation of 50,000. It was issued until several months after his death. A number of short tales, more miscellaneous verse, and some minor plays rounded out Carleton's later formal writings.

He was a tall, willowy man with a sallow complexion and merry eyes. After the death of his wife in 1904, his primary interest lay in the promotion of charities. Fanny Crosby, the blind hymn writer, was but one of the many he aided. He was active almost until the day of his death. When he went back to Michigan for a homecoming in 1907 there was still ample evidence of his popularity among rural folk.

There is nothing in Carleton's works that is imaginative, significant, or sublime. He has, moreover, been accused of inconsistency in his use of colloquialisms. Yet, as a sentimental recorder of domestic farm life in the Middle West and a cheerfully sympathetic observer of the underprivileged, he reflects both an era and an attitude of American life.

Principal Works: *Poetry*—Poems, 1871; Farm Ballads, 1873; Farm Legends, 1875; Farm Festivals, 1881; City Ballads, 1885; City Legends, 1889; City Festivals, 1892; Rhymes of our Planet, 1895; Songs of Two Centuries, 1902; Poems for Young Americans, 1906. *Plays*—The Romance of St. Paul, 1909; Arnold and Talleyrand, 1909; The Burglar-Bracelets.

About: Corning, A. E. Will Carleton; Michigan Historical Collections: Vol. 39; Toledo Blade December 19, 1912.

"CARMEN, FELIX." See SHERMAN, FRANK DEMPSTER

CARRINGTON, HENRY BEEBEE (March 2, 1824-October 26, 1912), lawyer, military organizer, and historian, was born in Wallingford, Conn., the son of Miles M. and Mary (Beebee) Carrington. In his twelfth year he studied classics under special tutors, and acquired an early interest in military affairs. But the frailty of his health prevented his entering West Point; he was graduated from Yale College in 1845, and while teaching in Tarrytown, N.Y., he was encouraged by Washington Irving in some research which later resulted in his *Battles of the American Revolution*. To the narratives themselves he added some interesting points of view on militarism as historical material.

Carrington went to Columbus, Ohio, in 1848 and practiced law with much success. He made many political acquaintances, and in 1857 through an appointment as adjutant general he became active in the organizing and forwarding of troops. When his own military court, in which he had exposed various disloyal orders, was held illegal by the United States Supreme Court, he was mustered out of the service, but continued valuable negotiation of treaties with the Indians and aided in the setting up of new reservations. In 1869 he was detailed as professor of military science at Wabash College, Ind. Carrington was twice married, first to Margaret Irvin Sullivant; and in 1871, to Fanny (Courtney) Grummond.

His writings, largely military-historical, combined the practicality of army life with a semi-scholarly thoroughness of study and careful research, and his *Battles of the American Revolution* still holds a good ranking among our chronicles of war.

Principal Works: American Classics, 1849; Russia Among the Nations, 1851; Battles of the American Revolution, 1876; Crisis Thoughts, 1878; The Six Nations, 1892.

About: Record of the Class of 1845 of Yale College.

CARRYL, CHARLES EDWARD (December 30, 1841-July 3, 1920), juvenile writer and stock broker, was born in New York City, the son of Nathan Taylor Carryl and his wife, a former Miss Lyons. He attended various small day schools in New York before going to Irving Institute at Tarrytown, N.Y., where he was a student until the summer of 1857. His business career began early and with much promise, and in the capacities of officer and director he was actively interested in railroad corporations from 1863 to 1872. In 1874 he became a member of the New York Stock Exchange and retained his seat in that organization until March 1908.

Although Carryl had written a small book, *The Stock Exchange Primer,* in 1882, his first noteworthy publication was a delightful juvenile, *Davy and the Goblin* (1885) for which his highly imaginative children, Guy and Constance, provided strictly fresh inspiration, chapter by chapter. The ridiculous Cockalorum, Ribsy the cab horse, the whale in the waistcoat, etc., artfully combined with familiar Mother Goose personalities, hypnotized his intimate audience. These tales were published serially in *St. Nicholas Magazine* and first appeared in book form in 1885. Seven years afterward came another volume, *The Admiral's Caravan,* brought out as a holiday book following its run as a feature in *St. Nicholas*; it was devoted to the incomparable maneuvers of little wooden figures—Harlequin, the stork-ferryman, etc.

In 1899 with the publication of *The River Syndicate and other Stories* Carryl had turned from juveniles to the conventional short story. The frame-work of these tales was a variety of crime techniques, and, although they were not bad fabrications, they achieved only a limited popularity. No other writings of any importance followed, but Carryl's strong interest, later on, in the working out of ingenious charades prompted the appearance of *Charades of an Idle Man* (1911).

Carryl was a dark-complexioned man of small build, always meticulously groomed. He commonly wore a cutaway coat. His social obligations were, apparently, quite numerous. During a long term as secretary of the Players he enjoyed a real friendship with the actor Edwin Booth. He also had membership in the University, Union, and Century Clubs of New York. After moving to Boston in his sixty-fourth year, he became active in the St. Botolph and Algonquin Clubs of that city. Mary Wetmore, to whom Carryl had been married in 1869, died in 1896. His adored son Guy, who was making his name known as a poet and humorist, died suddenly in 1904. Carryl himself died in Boston in 1920, and was buried in Brooklyn, N.Y.

From the scantiness of Carryl's writings and his own financial independence it is obvious that he wrote to please himself, and, so far as the juveniles are concerned, for the creation of another kind of pleasure for his readers. Of these two motives there is little doubt as to the fulfillment of the former, and Carryl's success as a writer for children is evidence of the achievement of the latter.

Courtesy of Mrs. Constance Carryl Sargent
CHARLES E. CARRYL

Although he wrote less, Carryl's career is interestingly parallel to that of Kenneth Grahame, the English banker-story teller. Both were successful businessmen; both wrote juvenile fantasies in their leisure hours; and both took their inspiration from sons who died prematurely.

Principal Works: *Juveniles*—Davy and the Goblin, 1885; The Admiral's Caravan, 1892. *Stories*—The River Syndicate and Other Stories, 1899. *Miscellaneous*—The Stock Exchange Primer, 1882; Charades by an Idle Man, 1911.

CARTER, ROBERT (February 5, 1819-February 15 1879), editor, was born in Albany, N.Y., of Irish parents. There was little money to spend on young Carter's education, but he was sent, for a while, to the Jesuit College of Chambly in Canada. He was appointed an assistant to his guardian, a librarian, but withdrew at the age of nineteen in order to trade upon his literary ability. In 1841 he went to Boston to prepare some religious pamphlets on Swedenborgianism, and there met James Russell Lowell, with whom he edited the *Pioneer,* a literary monthly which was abandoned after three issues. He was chief clerk in the Cambridge post office in 1845, then literary consultant for several publishers, and in 1848 heartily joined the Free Soilers and became the editor of the Boston *Commonwealth,* their chief organ.

After subsequent editorial posts in Boston, he became Washington correspondent for the New York *Tribune* and then aided George Ripley and Charles A. Dana in bringing out the first edition of the *American Encyclopedia.* For five years he was editor of the Rochester (N.Y.) *Democrat.* In addition to this ceaseless journalistic activity he found time for the writing of two unimpressive novels, *The Armenian's Daughter* and *The Great Tower of Tarudant,* as well as the slightly effusive *Summer Cruise on the Coast of New England. The Hungarian Controversy* contained a vehement defence of the Hungarian revolutionists.

In 1846 he was married to Ann Augusta Gray, a writer of juveniles; and in 1864 Susan Nichols, who had published some handbooks on art, became his second wife. Carter enjoyed friendships with the foremost litterateurs of his generation and could carry a whole calendar of events in his mind. He was, however, inordinately restless and was, by profession, necessarily preoccupied with matters of immediate rather than lasting interest.

Principal Works: The Hungarian Controversy, 1852; A Summer Cruise on the Coast of New England, 1864.

About: Carter, R. A Summer Cruise on the Coast of New England (see Introduction); Boston Transcript February 17, 1879.

CARUTHERS, WILLIAM ALEXANDER (1800?-August 29, 1846), novelist, was born in Virginia, apparently of a good and prosperous family. Very little is known about his life. He was a student at Washington College (now Washington and Lee) in 1819 and 1820, and at some time must have studied medicine, for by 1840 he was a prominent physician in Savannah, Ga. His only known medical achievement was a guerrilla warfare he carried on in the press against the then popular fad of mesmerism. He seems to have written from early youth, his first article, on the climbing of the Natural Bridge of Virginia, having appeared in 1820 in the *Knickerbocker Magazine.* His first book, *The Kentuckian in New York,* written in the form of "letters to the folks back home," was a humorous work which he deprecated, saying that his real interest was in the history of the South, and particularly in the chivalrous traditions of Tidewater Virginia. He does not seem ever to have been in New York himself. His two other novels, though they still contained some dry humor, were high-flown, verbose performances, strongly imitative of Sir Walter Scott. He was a semi-invalid for some time before his death, and died in the hilly country of northern Georgia, in Marietta, where he had gone with his son in a fruitless effort to regain his health.

Principal Works: The Kentuckian in New York, 1834; The Cavaliers of Virginia, 1835; The Knights of the Horseshoe: A Traditionary Tale of the Cocked Hat Gentry in the Old Dominion, 1845.

About: Alderman, E. A. & Harris, J. C. Library of Southern Literature; Johnson, J. G. Southern Fiction Prior to 1860.

CARVER, JONATHAN (April 13, 1710-January 31, 1780), traveler, geographer, and diarist, was born in Weymouth, Mass., the son of David and Hannah (Dyer) Carver. When Jonathan was eight his family moved to Canterbury, Conn., and on his father's death he was put in the care of an uncle who gave him a comparatively good education, which probably included some work in medicine. Carver enlisted as a sergeant in the army in the late 'forties; he was wounded at the siege of Fort William Henry in 1757.

Upon the advice of Major Robert Rogers, who was then in command at Mackinac,

Carver set out, in 1766, on a journey westward by way of the Great Lakes; he crossed and then ascended the Mississippi, entered what is now the Minnesota River and after finally reaching Lake Superior he returned in 1767 to Mackinac, and then proceeded to Boston. Finding no publisher for his volume of travels he sailed for England in February 1769, and there busied himself with miscellaneous literary work for the rest of his life. He was first married (in Connecticut) to Abigail Robbins in 1746; and, apparently without divorce proceedings, he was again married in London in 1774, to Mrs. Mary Harris.

His *Travels in Interior Parts of America,* containing a compilation of notes on Indian culture, first appeared in 1778; and it has since run through many editions and translations. He failed to acknowledge some of his borrowings and was charged with plagiarism. Carver's original manuscript, still extant in the British Museum, is considerably superior to the published book, which appears to have undergone the butchering of some literary hack. Carver was also the author of a *New Universal Geography* and a treatise on tobacco growing, but his travel book, which now has only a historical value, was his most significant piece of writing.

ABOUT: Carver, J. Travels in Interior Parts of America; American Historical Review: Vol. 11; Wisconsin Magazine of History: Vols. 3 and 12.

CARY, ALICE (April 26, 1820-February 12, 1871), poet and novelist, was born on a farm at Mt. Healthy, near Cincinnati, Ohio, the daughter of Robert Cary and Elizabeth (Jessup) Cary. She had practically no schooling, but was educated by a mother who was unusually intelligent. However, the mother died in 1835, and the father soon remarried. Her stepmother was a harsh, unsympathetic woman who discouraged any interests of the nine stepchildren aside from household and farm duties. Alice's first poem appeared in the Cincinnati *Sentinel* (afterwards the *Star of the West*), which long remained her only medium, until she began contributing stories, under the name of "Patty Lee," to the *National Era.*

Publication of the joint poems of her younger sister Phoebe [*q.v.*] and herself raised sufficient money for her to travel to New York and New England, where she met Whittier, who wrote about her the poem called "The Singer." She had suffered also the pain of a broken engagement to marry, and she determined not to return to Ohio,

Collection of Frederick H. Meserve
ALICE CARY

but to settle in New York and live by writing. By indefatigable industry and great thrift she managed to make her way, and soon sent for Phoebe and another sister. She contributed both prose and verse regularly to the leading magazines of the time, the *Atlantic, Harper's, Putnam's,* and the *Independent.* The sisters' home on 20th Street became a sort of gathering place for the literary world of the period. Alice Cary was an invalid for years before her death, but she retained her social charm and her "advanced" and liberal views. She was the first president of the first women's club, Sorosis, and was active in the Universalist church. She also kept on writing to the end, and was working on a new novel, *The Born Thrall,* when she died.

Her work was exceedingly popular, and her prose still has its charm, especially her pictures of life in Ohio in her girlhood. Her verse, though Poe praised it, is less likely to live; it is diffuse and unvaryingly melancholy in tone. It displays, however, much poetic feeling and a genuine love of nature.

PRINCIPAL WORKS: *Poetry*—Poems (with Phoebe Cary) 1849; Lyra and Other Poems, 1852; The Maiden of Tiascala, 1855; Ballads, Lyrics, and Hymns, 1866. *Prose*—Clovernook Papers, 1852; Hagar: A Story of Today, 1852; Clovernook Children, 1854; Married: Not Mated, 1856; Pictures of Country Life, 1859; The Bishop's Son, 1867; Snow-Berry: A Book for Young Folks, 1867; The Lover's Diary, 1868.

ABOUT: Clemmer, M. [Mrs. Ames]. A Study of Alice and Phoebe Cary; Griswold, R. W. Female Poets of America; Parton, J. Eminent Women of the Age.

CARY, PHOEBE (September 4, 1824-July 31, 1871), poet and hymn-writer, was, like her sister Alice [*q.v.*], born at Mt. Healthy, near Cincinnati, one of the nine children of Robert Cary, a pioneer farmer, and Elizabeth (Jessup) Cary. She was only eleven when their mother died, and as she never went to school most of her education was received from the older sister from whom she was inseparable. She was only thirteen when she started to write, and about a third of the poems in *Poems of Alice and Phoebe Cary* are hers.

When Alice Cary had established herself in New York she sent for her younger sister, and thereafter they were always together. They left New York only for occasional visits to the farm in Ohio. As Alice was an invalid for many years, Phoebe took entire charge of their household; and since the sisters were never wealthy, this meant long hours spent in actual housework and cooking. This may in part account for the fact that Phoebe Cary's literary output was much less voluminous than her sister's. Moreover, she published nothing in prose. Her nature was very different from her sister's; she was much less melancholy, was of a buoyant, vigorous temperament, and was noted for her wit. She was, however, deeply religious, and many of her poems are hymns. She is, in fact, chiefly remembered as the author of the famous hymn, "Nearer Home," better known by its opening line: "One sweetly solemn thought comes to me o'er and o'er." With the Rev. Dr. C. F. Deems, Phoebe Cary edited in 1869 a collection of *Hymns for All Christians*, which is still in use.

Collection of Frederick H. Meserve
PHOEBE CARY

Though her health had always been excellent, the strain of her last months of devotion to her sister proved too much for it, and she died, in Newport, R.I., less than six months after Alice Cary. Her last published writing was a memorial of her sister in the *Ladies' Repository*. Her writing was often careless, and she herself thought little of it; but it is really more poetic, in the true sense, than the more popular work of her older sister.

Principal Works: Poems (with Alice Cary) 1849; Poems and Parodies, 1854; Poems of Faith, Hope, and Love, 1868.

About: Clemmer, M. [Mrs. Ames]. A Study of Alice and Phoebe Cary; Griswold, R. W. Female Poets of America; Parton, J. Eminent Women of the Age.

"CASTLEMON, HARRY." See FOSDICK, CHARLES AUSTIN

CATHERWOOD, MARY (HARTWELL) (December 16, 1847-December 26, 1902), historical romanticist and juvenile writer, was born in Luray, Ohio, the daughter of Marcus Hartwell and Phoebe (Thompson) Hartwell. Her father was a physician, and both her parents were well educated—her mother unusually so, for the period. Both father and mother died in 1857. Miss Hartwell was graduated from the Female College (or Seminary), Granville, Ohio, in 1868, and became a teacher, first at Danville, Ill., then at Newburgh, N.Y. At the same time she began writing stories, one of the earliest winning a prize from *Wood's Household Magazine*, in Newburgh.

In 1887 she married James Catherwood, who at the time owned a confectionery store in Indianapolis. Later he moved to Hoopeston, Ill., where he was postmaster in the Cleveland administrations and also acted as a real estate operator. In her later years Mrs. Catherwood was separated from her husband, and spent most of her time in Maine and Canada, though she died in Chicago.

The first real success she had came with *The Romance of Dollard*, in 1889, and this struck the note for all her future work, which consisted almost entirely of historical novels, first dealing with the French, and later with the Anglo-Saxon, colonists in America. She also wrote a number of juvenile books, some of them historical in nature, which are still popular. Her work is sentimental and too "sweetly refined" for modern taste, but she did genuine research in her historical material, and her stories of the French colonials especially are authentic pictures of the times and the people. The great historian Francis Parkman, whose findings she followed implicitly, gave his full approval to the historical details of her novels.

Principal Works: A Woman in Armor, 1875; Cracque-o'-Doom, 1881; Rocky Fork, 1882; Old Caravan Days, 1884; The Secrets of Roseladies, 1888; The Romance of Dollard, 1889; The Story of Tonty, 1890; The Lady of Fort St. John, 1891; Old Kaskaskia, 1893; The White Islander, 1893; The Chase of St. Castin and Other Stories of the French in the New World, 1894; The Spirit of an Illinois Town, 1897; The Days of Jeanne D'Arc, 1897; Heroes of the Middle West: The French, 1898; Spanish Peggy, 1899; The Queen of the Swamp and Other Plain Americans, 1899; Mackinack and Lake Stories, 1899; Lazarre, 1901.

About: Dondore, D. A. The Prairie and the Making of Middle America; Wilson, M. L. Biography of Mary Hartwell Catherwood.

GEORGE CATLIN

CATLIN, GEORGE (July 26, 1796-December 23, 1872), ethnologist and artist, was born in Wilkes-Barre, Pa., the fifth of fourteen children of Putnam Catlin, a soldier in the American Revolution, and Polly (Sutton) Catlin, who as a child had been captured by Indians in the Wyoming Massacre. From the beginning, therefore, he had reason to be unusually interested in the American Indians. He had practically no schooling, but grew up as a sort of white savage who spent most of his time in fishing, hunting, and exploring. Nevertheless in 1817 he went to Litchfield, Conn., to study law, and was admitted to the Pennsylvania bar two years later. He was also beginning his career as an artist, self-taught but extremely talented.

Until 1823 he practiced law at Luzerne, Pa., then moved to Philadelphia, abandoned his profession, and set up as a painter of portraits and miniatures. In 1824 he was made a member of the Pennsylvania Academy of Fine Arts. He then moved to Washington, where he painted Dolly Madison and other celebrities. In 1828 he married Clara B. Gregory, of Albany, N.Y., whom he had met while painting the portrait of Governor Clinton. She proved to be a perfect helpmeet, accompanying him on most of his later extensive tours.

In 1829, after seeing a delegation of Indians in Philadelphia, he resolved to devote the remainder of his life to preserving the appearance and a record of the customs of what he felt was a dying race. Without financial aid of any kind, he set out on this gigantic task. At first he spent his summers among the Indians, learning their languages and living as one of them, and subsidized these visits by painting during the winter. Then he gave all his time to this ethnological mission, from 1832 to 1840 living among the Indians in Florida and the Far West. His life was frequently in danger, as the Indians were fearful of having their portraits painted, and if any misfortune occurred later to the tribe, Catlin was blamed for it. He painted more than 600 portraits of most of the then existent tribes, under the greatest difficulty. From 1837 to 1852 he traveled in South America and Europe, exhibiting his pictures. Then by unwise speculation he became bankrupt, and his collection was taken over as security for a loan by Joseph Harrison, of Philadelphia. Catlin was never able to redeem the pictures, which after being exhibited at the Centennial Exposition in 1876 were given by Harrison's widow to the United States National Museum (Smithsonian Institution). About 200 pictures remained in his possession, and are now owned by his heirs.

In the same manner as Audubon wrote notes for his pictures, Catlin wrote several volumes describing his work and recounting his adventures. Some of these first appeared in the New York *Daily Commercial Advertiser*, between 1830 and 1839. He was also the author of a curious little work on "mal-respiration," which recommended keeping the mouth closed at all times, especially in sleep.

As a writer of literature, Catlin was not important, but his portraits and records of the Indians in the mid-nineteenth century are unique and are among our most valuable historical treasures. He died in Jersey City, N.J., where he had retired in old age.

Principal Works: Letters and Notes on the Manners, Customs, and Condition of the North American Indians, 1841; Catlin's North American Indian Portfolio, 1844; Catlin's Notes of Eight Years' Travels and Residence in Europe, 1848; The Breath of Life: or, Mal-Respiration, 1861; Life Among the Indians, 1867; Last Rambles Amongst the Indians of the Rocky Mountains and the Andes, 1867; O-Kee-Pa: A Religious Ceremony and Other Customs of the Mandans, 1867.

About: Miner, W. H. George Catlin; Youmans, E. L. Pioneers of Science; Nature January 23, 1873; Popular Science Monthly July 1891; Smithsonian Institution, Annual Reports 1885, 1890.

"CAUSTIC, CHRISTOPHER." See FESSENDEN, THOMAS GREEN

"CENTZ, P.C., BARRISTER. See SAGE, BERNARD JANIN

"CERRO GORDO." See KELLY, JONATHAN FALCONBRIDGE

CHAMBERLAIN, MELLEN (June 4, 1821-June 25, 1900), historian, was born in Pembroke, N.H., the son of Moses and Mary (Foster) Chamberlain. He attended the district schools and an academy at Pembroke, and at the Literary Institute at Concord, N.H., he prepared for Dartmouth College, from which he was graduated in 1844. In 1848 he received an LL.B from the Dane Law School (Harvard); during the following year he was admitted to the bar, and on June 6 was married to Martha Ann Putnam.

He settled permanently in Chelsea, Mass., and occupied, successively, several civic and legal offices. In 1878 he was made librarian of the Boston Public Library, resigning after twelve scholarly years of service; and on his death he left this institution the fine collection of manuscripts and autographs that he had begun as a lad of fifteen. For Justin Winsor's *Narrative and Critical History of America* (1888) he wrote a chapter on "The Revolution Impending," and in 1890 Lindsay Swift edited a volume of Chamberlain's writings under the title *John Adams: The Statesman of the American Revolution. . .* The Massachusetts Historical Society published posthumously *A Documentary History of Chelsea* from his incomplete manuscripts, plans, engravings, etc. He was, indeed, a man of taste and scholarship, and his scant writings are filled with invaluable historical minutiae.

Principal Works: The Revolution Impending (in J. Winsor's *Narrative and Critical History...*) 1888; John Adams: The Statesman of the American Revolution. . . . 1890; A Documentary History of Chelsea: 1624-1824 (2 vols.) 1908.

About: Haynes, H. W. Memoir of Mellen Chamberlain (in *Proceedings of the Massachusetts Historical Society,* 2d ser. Vol. 20.)

CHANDLER, ELIZABETH MARGARET (December 24, 1807-November 2, 1834), poet and early anti-slavery writer, was born near Wilmington, Del., the daughter of Thomas and Margaret (Evans) Chandler, who died when Elizabeth was an infant. Under the care of her grandmother, in Philadelphia, she was sent to Friends' schools until she was thirteen. She was a timid child and had, already, become overly serious and reflective. Very shortly she began to write essays and verse for anonymous publication, and the appearance of her best known poem, "The Slave Ship," in the *Casket,* a monthly journal, prompted Benjamin Lundy, the editor of the *Genius of Universal Emancipation* to invite her regular contributions. Among these were "The Wife's Lament," "The Captured Slave," and "The Slave's Appeal"; in 1829 she was put in charge of the "female department" of the journal. "The Brandywine," "Schuylkill," "The Sunset Hour," and "Summer Morning" were unassuming descriptive verses and bore none of the didacticism of her slavery poems.

In 1830 she went to the Midwest and made her home at "Hazelbank," a farm in Lenawee County in the Territory of Michigan. There she continued as a contributor to the *Genius* until she was stricken with a "remittent fever" which resulted in her early death. In 1836 Lundy, who had, in a sense, "discovered" Miss Chandler, published her *Essays: Philanthropic and Moral* and *Poetical Works of Elizabeth Margaret Chandler: With a Memoir of Her Life and Character.* Her prose is patently outmoded and her poetry, though sometimes endowed with a simple and fragile beauty, does not rise above the fleeting verse of her contemporaries.

Principal Works: Essays: Philanthropic and Moral, 1836; Poetical Works of Elizabeth Margaret Chandler: With a Memoir of Her Life and Character, 1836.

About: Griswold, R. W. The Female Poets of America.

CHANNING, EDWARD TYRRELL (December 12, 1790-February 8, 1856), editor and educator, was born in Newport, R.I., the son of William and Lucy (Ellery) Channing, and younger brother of William Ellery Channing the elder [*q.v.*]. He spent part of his childhood in Newport, and entered Harvard at thirteen; because of participation in the student rebellion of 1807 he was denied his degree, but was awarded an

From a portrait by G. P. A. Healy
EDWARD TYRRELL CHANNING

honorary M.A. in 1819. After a study of law under his brother Francis, he was admitted to the bar in 1813, but was, apparently, a rather poorly equipped attorney, and gladly turned to literary pursuits. He belonged to a not-too-serious "reading club" in which all members were free to aim their Latin quips at one another. With President Kirkland of Harvard, Richard Henry Dana, the poet, and others, he had contemplated founding a *New England Magazine and Review,* but transferred his interests to William Tudor's *North American Review,* first issued in May 1815. As its editor from May 1818 to October 1819, Channing kept an eye on the rising *literati* at home and on current literary movements abroad.

In 1819 he became Boylston professor of rhetoric and oratory at Harvard. Among his pupils were Ralph Waldo Emerson and Henry Thoreau, who carefully kept his college themes and who later admitted that it was Channing who had taught him to write; Oliver Wendell Holmes was another "pale student" who

> .... shivering in his shoes,
> Sees from his theme the turgid rhetoric ooze.

For thirty-two purely academic years Channing pursued a consistently ruthless attack on "turgid rhetoric"—literary hombast was sternly frowned upon by Boston men of letters. He retired five years before his death in 1856. During that same year Richard Henry Dana, Jr., the author of *Two Years Before the Mast* edited Channing's *Lectures Read to the Seniors in Harvard College.*

Traditionally, Channing had a "bland, superior look," Puritan strength, and classic literary tastes. He published practically nothing, but the long list of conspicuous authors who owe their achievements to his tutelage is sufficient testimony to his ability as a teacher.

ABOUT: Channing, E. T. Lectures Read to the Seniors at Harvard College (See Memoir by R. H. Dana, Jr.).

CHANNING, WILLIAM ELLERY (the Elder) (April 7, 1780-October 2, 1842), clergyman and publicist, was born in Newport, R.I., the son of William Channing, the attorney-general of the state, and Lucy (Ellery) Channing. He prepared for college with an uncle in New London, Conn., and entered Harvard at only fourteen, being graduated four years later. During his college years he lived with another uncle, Francis Dana, chief justice of Massachusetts, and during his vacations taught school at Lancaster, Mass. From 1798 to 1800 he was a tutor in the household of D. M. Randolph, United States marshal, in Richmond, Va. Previously he had been highly strung but healthy and active; but now overwork and a self-enforced ascetic discipline made him a semi-invalid for the remainder of his life.

After a year and a half at home in Newport, Channing was given the nominal position of regent at Harvard, which meant in practice that he could be supported while he studied at the Harvard Divinity School. In 1803 he was ordained as a Congregationalist minister and installed in the Federal Street Church, in Boston, where he remained as pastor until his death. In 1812 and 1813 he was Dexter lecturer at the Harvard Divinity School, but ill health compelled him to resign. In 1814 he married his cousin, Ruth Gibbs. His son, Dr. W. F. Channing, became a noted inventor.

Channing, a retiring, unworldly man, a natural recluse, shielded by his wife and his close friends from the hurly-burly of life, might have been expected to be the last person in the world to lead a theological revolt. However, from his early days as a debater in college, he had had a keen interest in public questions and in ethical problems, and his conscience did not allow him to remain silent when he became convinced of the fallacies of the Calvinist doctrines of his church. As the inscription on his statue in the Public Gardens in Boston says, "he breathed into theology a human spirit"; he shrank from the implications of

From a portrait by S. Gambardella
WILLIAM ELLERY CHANNING I

Calvinism, and at the ordination of Jared Sparks in 1819 he preached a crucial sermon which resulted in the foundation of Unitarianism as a denomination in America. Inevitably he became the leader of the Unitarian group, much as he hated factionalism and controversy. In 1825 he was a founder of the American Unitarian Association, and from 1821 he was associated with the Unitarian magazine, still the official organ, the *Christian Register.*

In 1822 and 1823, on leave of absence from his church, he traveled in Europe, meeting and strongly impressing Wordsworth and Coleridge. After his return a co-pastor was appointed to relieve him of pastoral duties, in which he had never been very efficient, and from this time on his chief influence was exercised through writing. His essays in the *Christian Examiner* on Milton, Napoleon, and Fénelon, and other essays (including the famous one on "Self Culture") in the *North American Review* and elsewhere, established him as a foremost spokesman in the causes of public education (in which he anticipated Froebel in some particulars) and temperance, labor, pacifism, and anti-slavery—though he shrank from the radicalism of the more extreme abolitionists.

But famous as Channing was as preacher and propagandist, perhaps his greatest service was rendered to American literature. Many of the greatest names of the period among New England writers were in a sense his disciples. Emerson, Longfellow, Lowell, Holmes, Bryant, all acknowledged their debt to him and his effect on their work. In a sense he infused a spirit of broad and liberal religion into American letters. He himself, in what he thought of as a "literary Declaration of Independence," said that literature was "the expression of a nation's mind in writing" (*Remarks on American Literature*), and he labored eloquently to remove the last vestiges of slavish imitation of English models from the writings of Americans.

Outwardly his life was uneventful after his European tour. In 1835 he visited the West Indies, and his early interest in anti-slavery, first excited in Virginia, was renewed. His zeal coupled with his moderation caused him to be attacked by both sides in the controversy, but he was used to that from a similar experience in the early days of Unitarianism, and since he never cared for social contacts and since both ill health and a complete lack of social tact had conspired to separate entirely his public and private life, he was unmoved by the abuse accorded him. A short, slight man with very large eyes and a notably clear voice, he was seldom seen except in the pulpit or on the lecture platform. His sweetness of nature endeared him to a little group of intimates, and he needed no wider association. He died at Bennington, Vt., of a fever contracted while on a journey.

Channing's sermons were described as "fervent and solemn," after he conquered an early tendency to stilted didacticism. As a writer, his style was racy and glowing, simple and graceful, with passages of chaste beauty. More than most writers or most public men, his literary influence lived after him, in its reflection in the work of the many celebrated men who were his younger contemporaries, and several of whom were his parishioners as well.

Principal Work: Remarks on American Literature, 1830; Miscellanies, 1830; Slavery, 1835; The Abolitionist, 1836; Emancipation, 1840; Collected Works, 1841-72; The Duty of the Free States, 1842; The Perfect Life, 1872.

About: Chadwick, J. W. William Ellery Channing: Minister of Religion; Channing, W. H. Life of William Ellery Channing; Eliot, C. W. Four American Leaders; Peabody, E. P. Reminiscences of the Rev. William Ellery Channing; Unitarian Review March 1888.

CHANNING, WILLIAM ELLERY (the Younger) (November 29, 1818-December 23, 1901), poet and essayist, was born in Newport, R.I., the son of the brother of the celebrated divine whose namesake he became. His father, Walter Channing, was a physician and a professor in the Harvard Medical School; his mother was Barbara (Perkins) Channing. The boy was usually known as Ellery Channing, to distinguish him from his famous uncle. His mother died when he was very young, and he spent an unhappy childhood with a great-aunt in Milton, Mass. He attended George Bancroft's Round Hill School, in Northampton, Mass., and the Boston Latin School, and in 1834 entered Harvard. Here, however, his lack of tractability and discipline first asserted itself; in a few months he became bored with chapel, then with college itself, and disappeared. He was found by his family calmly writing poetry in a country retreat, and he refused to return to Harvard The next year his first poem was published, in the *New England Magazine*.

In 1839 he went to Illinois to become a pioneer farmer! In a short time, however, he discovered his unfitness for that career, and next went to Cincinnati to live with a clergyman uncle, his mother's brother; here he tutored, played at reading law, and wrote for the Cincinnati *Gazette*. In 1842 he returned to Massachusetts and married Ellen Fuller, sister of Margaret Fuller. Of their sons, Edward became a well known historian, Walter a noted psychiatrist.

Channing had by this time met Emerson and become closely attached to him. He moved to Concord to be near its "sage," and lived there for most of his life thereafter, though in 1844 he was in New York City, on the staff of the *Tribune*, in 1845 traveled in France and Italy, and from 1855 to 1858 was one of the editors of the New Bedford *Mercury*. In Concord he was an intimate associate not only of Emerson, but of Bronson Alcott and Hawthorne and above all of Thoreau, whose first biographer and literary executor he became. As his seclusiveness and mystical other-worldliness increased, he separated from his family and lived alone, until in old age, a semi-invalid, he was taken in by his devoted disciple, Franklin B. Sanborn, in whose home he died at eighty-three. Most of his writing appeared first in the *Dial*.

Channing was the personification of Transcendentalism pushed to its utmost. He wrote only by "inspiration," and was incapable of revising or amending his work. His mysticism and idealism took the outward form of hazy obscurity. He was an exceedingly careless writer, and Thoreau characterized his style as "sublimo-slipshod." Poe lambasted him unmercifully in *Graham's Magazine* when his first volume of poems appeared, pointing out his numerous sins against metre, syntax, and diction. His work was uneven and undisciplined, and in consequence he received little critical notice during

After a photograph
WILLIAM ELLERY CHANNING II

his lifetime and is seldom read today. Yet, as Sanborn loyally remarked, his poetry displays an occasional "rare and fitful genius," and it is an indigenous product of New England, unmistakably stemming from its physical soil. Rigorous editing might bring together in one volume a sufficient number of poems, particularly nature poems, to establish Channing's right to a place in the galaxy of New England writers of the mid-nineteenth century. No such editor is now likely to arise, however, and he will probably remain practically unknown, except as one of the many superior members of one of the most distinguished of American families.

Principal Works: *Poetry*—Poems, 1843; Poems: Second Series, 1847; The Woodman and Other Poems, 1849; Near Home, 1858; The Wanderer: A Colloquial Poem, 1871; Eliot, 1885; John Brown and the Heroes of Harper's Ferry, 1886; Poems of Sixty-Five Years, 1902. *Prose*—Conversations in Rome Between an Artist, a Catholic, and a Critic, 1847; Thoreau: The Poet-Naturalist, 1873.

About: Channing, W. E. Poems of Sixty-five Years (see Biographical Introduction by F. B. Sanborn); Atlantic Monthly December 1900; Critic February 1902.

CHANNING, WILLIAM HENRY (May 25, 1810-December 23, 1884), clergyman and essayist, was born in Boston, the son of Francis Dana and Susan (Higginson) Channing. He was a nephew of William Ellery Channing the Elder (whose biographer he became) and a cousin of William Ellery Channing the Younger [*qq.v.*]. He was educated at the Boston Latin School and at Harvard, where he was graduated in 1829.

He then attended the Harvard Divinity School, being graduated in 1833. After supplying several near-by churches, he spent 1835 and 1836 in Europe, returning to marry Julia Allen. He then went to New York, where he made an unsuccessful attempt to establish a free church among the working class. In 1837 he was pastor of a Unitarian Church in Cincinnati (though he was not ordained until 1839) and also edited the Unitarian magazine, the *Western Messenger.* Religious doubts caused him to resign in 1841, but he soon regained his faith, if not in God then in "transfigured humanity," and from 1843 to 1845 was leader of an independent religious society in New York. After a few months at the Transcendentalist colony of Brook Farm, and a conversion to the Socialist philosophy of the French economist Fourier, he became, from 1847 to 1850, leader of the (Fourierist) Religious Union of Associationists, in Boston. In 1849 and 1850 he also edited the *Spirit of the Age,* a Fourierist magazine. From 1852 to 1854 he served Unitarian churches in Troy and Rochester, N.Y. He next went to England, and from 1854 to 1857 was minister of the Renfrew Street Chapel in Liverpool, then succeeded the famous James Martineau in the Hope Street Chapel. He returned to the United States in 1861, was minister of the Unitarian Society in Washington, served on the Sanitary Commission during the Civil War, and in 1863 and 1864 was chaplain of the House of Representatives. After the war he returned to England. He died in London, but his remains were brought to Boston for burial. His son became a Member of Parliament; his daughter married the poet, Sir Edwin Arnold.

WILLIAM HENRY CHANNING

Channing was an idealist and a mystic, an extremely undisciplined and unpractical man, but a foremost worker in good causes and a noted preacher. Besides his original writings he translated T. S. Jouffroy's *Introduction to Ethics* from the French, and edited his uncle's sermons as *The Perfect Life.* His biography of his uncle was his principal writing, and is the definitive life.

PRINCIPAL WORKS: The Gospel of Today, 1847; Life of William Ellery Channing, 1848; Memoirs of Margaret Fuller Ossoli (with R. W. Emerson and J. F. Clarke) 1852; Memoirs and Writings of James Handasyd Perkins, 1857; The Civil War in America, 1861; Lessons From the Life of Theodore Parker, 1884.

ABOUT: Frothingham, O. B. Memoir of William Henry Channing; Unitarian Review March 1885.

CHAUNCY, CHARLES (January 1, 1705-February 10, 1787), theologian, was the son of Charles Chauncy, a Boston merchant, and Sarah (Walley) Chauncy. His great-grandfather, also Charles Chauncy, was the second president of Harvard.

He was graduated from Harvard in 1721, received his M.A. in 1724 (in 1742 Edinburgh conferred a D.D. degree on him), and in 1727 was ordained as minister of the First Church (Congregational) in Boston, retaining that position, sometimes alone, sometimes with a co-pastor, all his life. In 1727 also he was married to Elizabeth Hirst. He outlived two of his three wives, marrying Elizabeth Townsend in 1738 and Mary Stoddard in 1760.

Chauncy was the great liberalizing religious power of his era, the chief antagonist of Jonathan Edwards, George Whitefield, and the Revivalists of "the Great Awakening." His writings were all theological, and revolved around Revivalism—which he opposed as a manifestation of abnormal psychology; the British attempt to force bishops on the American church—which he fought as an invasion of Congregationalist independence; and the anti-Calvinist, or at least neo-Calvinist, doctrine of the benevolence of God—of which he was the leading American advocate. During the American Revolution he was a firm patriot, but he took little part in extra-theological affairs. He was essentially intellectual, unemotional, and prosaic; his writing was clear, pedestrian, and logical, but far too intellectualized for the "enthusiasts" (precursors of the Methodists) whom he excoriated.

PRINCIPAL WORKS: Sermon on Enthusiasm, 1742; Seasonable Thoughts on the State of Religion in New England, 1743; Letters to Whitefield, 1744, 1745; Complete View of Episcopacy, 1771; Salvation for All Men (anonymous) 1782; The Benevolence of the Deity, 1784; Five Dissertations on the Fall and Its Consequences, 1785.

ABOUT: Fowler, W. C. Memorials of the Chaunceys; Walker, W. Ten New England Leaders.

CHEETHAM, JAMES (1772-September 19, 1810), journalist, was born probably in or near Manchester, England. He was a young hatter at the time of the first rumblings of the industrial revolution, and as a member of the Constitutional Society of Liberals he was arrested July 23, 1793, on charge of conspiracy to overthrow the government. He was freed the following April and remained in Manchester until the riots of 1798 forced him to set sail for America.

In partnership with D. Denniston, a cousin of DeWitt Clinton, the statesman, he bought a half interest in Greenleaf's (New York) *Argus*, and, issued as the *American Citizen*, it became the spokesman of the Republicans, victors in the political upheaval of 1800. In allegiance to the Clinton factions Cheetham wrote a pretentious and vindictive *View of the Political Conduct of Aaron Burr*, suggesting that Burr had made unscrupulous efforts to win the presidency in 1800. William Coleman, of the *Evening Post*, bitterly opposed Cheetham's stand; both were subsequently arrested.

Cheetham published, in 1809, a contemptful and distorted life of Thomas Paine, the American free-thinker of English birth, with whom he had become acquainted. His limited prestige waned rapidly in the years before his death, and his writings are valuable only as a record of contemporary political opinion.

PRINCIPAL WORKS: A View of the Political Conduct of Aaron Burr, 1802; Life of Thomas Paine, 1809.

ABOUT: Francis, J. W. Old New York; Proceedings of the Massachusetts Historical Society: Ser. 3, Vol. 1.

CHEEVER, EZEKIEL (January 25, 1614-August 21, 1708), classicist and educator, was born in London, the son of humble parents. He was grounded in the classics at Christ's Hospital and at Emmanuel College, Cambridge, which he entered in 1633. In 1637 he sailed for Boston and the year following became master of the public school at New Haven, where he was a man of much prestige and a veritable pillar of the church. Removing to Ipswich, he made the free school there famous, and had a wide intellectual influence on the townspeople. From 1670 to the very end of his life he was in charge of the Boston Latin School, a rigid disciplinarian and a "skillful, painful, faithful schoolmaster." His funeral sermon was delivered by Cotton Mather, one of his pupils, and he was mourned by a distinguished gathering.

Cheever's preserved writings are: *Scripture Prophecies Explained*, three essays on the millennium; and his highly influential *Accidence: A Short Introduction to the Latin Language*, of which twenty editions were issued, for a century New England's textbook of the Latin language. Though meagre in volume, Cheever's literary output stands high in its field.

PRINCIPAL WORKS: Scripture Prophecies Explained, 1757; Accidence: A Short Introduction to the Latin Language, 1785.

ABOUT: Gould, E. P. Ezekiel Cheever: Schoolmaster.

CHENEY, EDNAH DOW (LITTLEHALE) (June 27, 1824-November 19, 1904), social annotater and reformer, was born in Boston, the daughter of Sargent Smith Littlehale and Ednah Parker (Dow) Littlehale. She attended several private schools in succession, and was requested to leave the last because of an undisciplinary attitude.

On May 19, 1853, she married Seth Wells Cheney, a crayon artist and engraver, and with him made a journey to Europe. In 1856 she was left a widow, with an infant daughter, and began to interest herself in various social enterprises—Freedman's Aid, Woman's Rights, and the New England Hospital for Women and Children. At the Concord School of Philosophy she lectured on the history of art, and as a member of Margaret Fuller's conversation classes she had a passing acquaintance with Emerson, the Alcotts, and Theodore Parker. Her writings range from handbooks on citizenship to a *Life of Louisa May Alcott*, and *Gleanings in Fields of Art*. She had a directness of style, but no perceptible brilliance, and it was as an educational and social reformer that she did her most effective work.

PRINCIPAL WORKS: Patience, 1870; Faithful to the Light and Other Tales, 1871; Gleanings in Fields of Art, 1881; Selected Poems From Michelangelo Buonarroti, 1885; Life of Louisa May Alcott, 1888.

ABOUT: Cheney, E. D. Reminiscences; Boston Evening Transcript November 19, 1904.

CHENEY, JOHN VANCE (December 29, 1848-May 1, 1922), poet, essayist, and librarian, was born in Groveland, N.Y., the son of Simeon Pease Cheney, a traveling singing-master, and Christiana (Vance) Cheney, pianist and singer. As a child he had a certain musical talent, but after attendance at private academies he studied law and was admitted to the bar. He disliked the legal profession, and began to contribute poems to periodicals, largely to the *Century*, then under the editorship of Richard Watson Gilder. He was married, in 1876, to his cousin Abbey Perkins; they were divorced six years later.

Cheney went to California in 1876, and for seven years was librarian of the Free Public Library in Sacramento. Among his literary associates at this time were Joaquin Miller and Edwin Markham. From 1894 until 1909 he was librarian of the Newberry Library, Chicago, and in 1903 he was married to Sara Barker Chamberlain.

Thistle-Drift, a volume of verse, appeared in 1887, followed by *Wood Blooms* and *Poems*; his poem, "The Happiest Heart," attained a moderate popularity. *The Golden Guess* and *That Dome in Air*, critical essays, are marked by a good literary discrimination; but his verse, though tasteful and well executed, had no enduring characteristics.

PRINCIPAL WORKS: *Verse*—Thistle-Drift, 1887; Wood Blooms, 1888; Poems, 1905. *Essays*—The Golden Guess, 1892; That Dome in Air, 1895.

CHESEBROUGH, CAROLINE (March 30, 1825-February 16 1873), novelist and story-teller, was born in Canandaigua, N.Y., the daughter of Nicholas Goddard and Betsey (Kimball) Chesebrough. She attended Canandaigua Seminary, and at about the age of twenty-three began to write stories and articles for magazines, soon finding a market with the *Knickerbocker*, *Putnam's* and *Harper's*. Her first book, a volume of tales, *Dream-Land by Daylight* (1852), was followed by numerous novels for children and for adults; the last to appear was *The Foe in the Household*. The scenes are laid chiefly in the East, the plots being slow and tiring, and the sentiments tediously moralizing.

From 1865 until the time of her death she taught English in the Packer Collegiate Institute, Brooklyn, N.Y., where her resourcefulness and her integrated personality made her long-remembered. As a writer she achieved an occasional vividness of description, but her style was full of mediocrities, and her literary reputation was decidedly "on the wing."

PRINCIPAL WORKS: Dream-land by Daylight, 1852; Susan: The Fisherman's Daughter, 1855; Peter Carradine, 1863; The Foe in the Household, 1871.

ABOUT: New York Daily Tribune February 19, 1873.

CHILD, FRANCIS JAMES (February 1, 1825-September 11, 1896), philologist, was born in Boston, the son of Joseph Child, a sailmaker, and Mary (James) Child. As a poor boy who expected to have to learn a trade, he attended the English High School, but the principal of the Boston Latin School, attracted by his ability, had him transferred to his institution and then lent him the money to go to Harvard, from which he was graduated in 1846. Until 1848 he was a tutor in mathematics at Harvard, and for the next year in history and political economy. But his bent was strongly for comparative philology, and from 1849 to 1851 he was able to study at the universities of Berlin and Göttingen, the latter of which gave him an honorary Ph.D. in 1854. Unaware, apparently, of the presence of a great philologist on its faculty, Harvard kept him correcting freshman themes as professor of rhetoric and oratory from 1851 to 1876, when at last he was made professor of English literature. In 1860 he married Elizabeth Ellery Sedgwick; they had four daughters.

Child's special field was middle English. He edited the definitive edition of Spenser, was editor-in-chief of the American edition of *British Poets*, and was an authority on the English of Chaucer and Gower. He is best known, however, for his complete and invaluable edition of English and Scottish popular ballads. This ten-volume work, preceded twenty-five years earlier by a less compendious collection, he left unfinished. His influence on his pupils was very great, and he was a fructifying force in American scholarship. Far from being a dry-as-dust professor, however, he was noted for his impulsiveness, his animation, and his bubbling humor.

PRINCIPAL WORKS (edited): Four Old Plays, 1848; Poetical Works of Edmund Spenser, 1855; English and Scottish Ballads, 1857-58; Observations on the Language of Chaucer and Gower, 1863 (in *Memoirs American Academy of Arts and Sciences*); Poems of Sorrow and Comfort, 1865; English and Scottish Popular Ballads, 1883-98.

ABOUT: Bradford, G. As God Made Them; Howells, W. D. Literary Friends and Acquaintance; Atlantic Monthly December 1896; Nation September 17, 1896.

CHILD, LYDIA MARIA (FRANCIS) (February 11, 1802-October 20, 1880), antislavery writer and agitator, was born in Medford, Mass., the youngest of six children of Convers Francis, a baker, and Susannah (Rand) Francis. She was educated in the village school, but her real education came from her brother, a Unitarian minister and later a professor at the

Collection of Frederick H. Meserve
LYDIA MARIA CHILD

Harvard Divinity School. For a year she both studied and taught at a seminary in Medford, then from 1825 to 1828 conducted a private school at Watertown, Mass. In 1826 she founded the *Juvenile Miscellany,* the first monthly for children in America. In 1828 she married David Lee Child, a lawyer, a member of the Massachusetts legislature, and editor of the *Massachusetts Journal,* but for all that an unpractical visionary, of the true New England type, with whom her life was one of poverty, though of perfect congeniality. Both became ardent abolitionists of the most extreme school, and most of Mrs. Child's energies went to that cause. Her *Appeal in Favor of That Class of Amcricans Called Africans,* the first anti-slavery book, was immensely influential, though it cost her a heavy price of social ostracism and killed the *Juvenile Miscellany.* From 1840 to 1844 she edited the *National Anti-Slavery Standard,* a New York weekly, then turning it over to her husband. In 1852 the Childs inherited a small farm at Wayland, Mass., and this was their home for the remainder of their lives. (David Child died in 1872.) The farm was a station in the Underground Railroad, through which escaping slaves were routed, and Mrs. Child continued to write voluminously. Her offer to nurse John Brown after he was wounded at Harper's Ferry led to a correspondence with the governor of Virginia and with Mrs. Mason, wife of the author of the Fugitive Slave Law, later printed as a pamphlet which had an enormous circulation. Even the Emancipation Proclamation was not sufficiently sweeping for her, and she remained a radical Republican to her death.

Yet in spite of this fanaticism, Mrs. Child was primarily a lover of beauty, a completely self-abnegating personality, selfless and devoted. She was not handsome, and in later life was obese, but she was noted for her bright eyes and her perfect teeth. To many she became a sort of symbol of the abolitionist cause.

As a writer, her creative gifts were small. Her novels are weak in characterization and very didactic. But she was no mere emotional ranter; in general she wrote with logic, clarity, and force. She was "advanced" in many ways, though anti-slavery claimed most of her attention: she was a woman suffragist, a pioneer in sex education, and unorthodox in her religious views, though her writings on religion are marred by a lack of factual background and a semi-spiritistic mysticism which wars with her Rationalist tendencies. The same failure to acknowledge facts not consistent with her theories is the main fault of her best known book, the *Appeal*; for example, she states dogmatically that there is no biological difference at all between whites and Negroes except "the color of the complexion." She was an enzyme in the body politic during one of the most unsettled periods of American history, but as a writer she now belongs only to that history.

Principal Works: *Fiction*—Hobomok, 1824; The Rebels: or, Boston Before the Revolution, 1825; Philothea, 1836; Fact and Fiction, 1846; Autumnal Leaves: Tales and Sketches in Prose and Rhyme, 1857; Miria: A Romance of the Republic, 1867. *Non-Fiction*—The Frugal Housewife, 1829; The Coronal (verse) 1831; The Mother's Book, 1831; An Appeal in Favor of That Class of Americans Called Africans, 1833; The Oasis, 1834; History of the Condition of Women in Various Ages and Nations, 1835; Letters From New York, 1843-45; Isaac T. Hopper, 1853; Progress of Religious Ideas Through Successive Ages, 1855; The Right Way the Safe Way, 1880; Correspondence With Governor Wise and Mrs. Mason of Virginia, 1860; The Freedman's Book, 1865; Aspirations of the World, 1878.

About: Child, L. M. F. Letters (see Biographical Introduction by J. G. Whittier); Higginson, T. W. Contemporaries; Atlantic Monthly December 1882; Harper's Magazine October 1890; Nation January 25, 1883.

CHIPMAN, DANIEL (October 22, 1765-April 23, 1850), biographical historian and lawyer, was born in Salisbury, Conn., the son of Samuel and Hannah (Austin) Chipman. Daniel studied under his elder brother Nathaniel, helped with the farm work, and entered Dartmouth College, from which he was graduated in 1788. He was admitted to the bar in 1790, and four years afterwards began a practice in Middlebury which was to last twenty-five years. In 1796 he was married to Eleutheria Hedge, and until 1822 served, intermittently, as constitutional-convention delegate, state attorney, and member of the governor's council, and was, at the same time, professor of law at Middlebury College from 1806 till 1816. In 1823 he was appointed first reporter of the supreme court of Vermont.

Ill health demanded his retirement in 1829 and in the years that followed he wrote estimable biographies of three political figures, Hon. Nathaniel Chipman, Colonel Seth Warner, and Thomas Chittenden, to which his innately sound judgment and long judicial experience lent authority.

Principal Works: Life of Hon. Nathaniel Chipman, 1846; Life of Colonel Seth Warner, 1848; Memoir of Thomas Chittenden, 1849.

About: Vermont Historical Gazetteer: Vol. I.

CHIVERS, THOMAS HOLLEY (October 18, 1807 or 1809-December 18, 1858), poet, remembered largely for his association and controversies with Edgar Allan Poe, was the oldest of seven children of Col. Robert Chivers, a prosperous plantation owner of Washington, Ga. His mother had been a Miss Digby. He studied medicine at Transylvania University, Lexington, Ky., and received his M.D. with honors in 1830, but there was no economic necessity for him to practice his profession, and he never did so. However, as late as 1856, Oglethorpe University offered him its chair of physiology.

Chivers spent the year after his graduation in western Georgia, among the Cherokee Indians, with whom he was unusually sympathetic. In early youth he had married, the name of his wife being unknown, and had had a daughter. But because she believed scandal told about him, his wife had left him and forbidden him to see their child. (The dates of this episode are uncertain; Chivers, who wrote so much about his most intimate feelings, was always obscure as to dates, and may have deliberately put even the date of his birth two years back, in order to appear to be the senior instead of the junior of Poe.) This Byronesque situation, which gave birth to his first privately published book of poems, *The Path of Sorrow*, was ended by dissolution of the marriage. Chivers' wanderings took him farther and farther North, until in 1834, in Springfield, Mass., he married again, his bride being Harriet Hunt, a sixteen-year-old beauty. In

THOMAS HOLLEY CHIVERS

all, two sons and two daughters were born to them; but the oldest and dearest, Florence Allegra, died in 1842 (her death gave birth to his most famous poem, "The Lost Pleiad," from which he later claimed that Poe plagiarized "The Raven"); and the three others all died within three months of 1848. Later two daughters and a son were born who survived him.

Meanwhile, Chivers' next few years were spent in Philadelphia and New York, where he became the acquaintance, almost the friend, of Poe.

Chivers met Poe only a few times, and in later years Poe ceased to answer his letters—though Chivers had invited him to be his guest for the remainder of his life! It was not until after Poe's death that Chivers began to claim that "The Raven" was stolen from "The Lost Pleiad," and "Ulalume" from another of his poems. It is true that Poe abstracted occasional words, phrases, and ideas from Chivers as from others—it was an age of borrowing—but what he took he individualized; and Chivers in turn took much of Poe's material over wholesale. Until Chivers became half-insane, he bore no rancor over the alleged plagiarism, and even contemplated a biography of Poe to defend him against Griswold's attacks.

Poe published Chivers' poems in the *Southern Literary Messenger* and *Graham's Magazine*, and Chivers busied himself with several verse plays, which, though they had obvious merit, never found production. Two of them were published later—one based on a celebrated Kentucky murder case of the period, the other the first version in modern literature of the Celtic legend of Deirdre, best known to moderns through the play by John Millington Synge. It was not until 1856 that Chivers returned to the South. He died suddenly, at Decatur, Ga.

S. Foster Damon, Chivers' biographer, says very aptly that Chivers had great genius without possessing the least talent. He was utterly uncritical of his own work, and Poe hit him off exactly in the criticism that he was "at the same time one of the best and one of the worst poets in America." Sublimity and absurdity, pathos and bathos, lie down comfortably together in his verse. He was a mystic, a Swedenborgian, at one time a Spiritualist, a Transcendentalist, and an Associationist (one of the group that followed the Socialist ideas of the French economist and philosopher Fourier). It followed, in his own mind, that everything he wrote was inspired and must be regarded with equal awe and lack of discrimination. But he was also a really great and original metrist, whose remarkable experiments in rhythm and in word-coinage influenced not only Poe (as Poe in turn influenced him), but also Swinburne, Rossetti, and even Kipling. Even the Symbolists learned, at third hand, some things from the poems of Chivers.

Unfortunately, his egotism, like his sensitiveness, grew with the years. Kind-hearted and generous he always remained, but his megalomania increased alarmingly. "I," he proclaimed, "am the Southern man who taught Mr. Poe all these things." Wild and half-mad, with the single-minded intensity of genius, he might be, but it should be noted that he was not only a skilled painter, but that he invented a practical machine to shred the fibre from silkworm cocoons; and he must have kept up with the progress of medicine to have been offered a university chair after twenty-six years without practicing his profession. It may be funny when he compares his broken heart to a broken egg, but Chivers could be exalted as well as ridiculous. English and American literature both owe him a great debt, and it is the ingratitude and injustice of posterity which have condemned him to being a "lost Pleiad" of the poetic heavens.

PRINCIPAL WORKS: The Path of Sorrow: or, The Lament of Youth, 1832; Conrad and Eudora: or, The Death of Alonzo, 1834; Nacoochee: or, The Beautiful Star, 1837; The Lost Pleiad and Other Poems, 1845; Search After Truth (prose) 1848; Eonchs of Ruby: A Gift of Love, 1850; Memoralia: or, Phials of Amber Full of the Tears of Love, 1853; Virginalia: or, Songs of My Summer Nights, 1853; Atlanta: or, The True Blessed Island of Poetry, 1853; Birthday Song of Liberty, 1856; The Sons of Usna, 1858.

ABOUT: Bell, L. C. Poe and Chivers; Benton, J. In the Poe Circle; Damon, S. F. Thomas Holley Chivers: Friend of Poe; Huneker, J. Pathos of Distance; Century Magazine January and February 1903; Boston Transcript April 24, 1897.

CHOATE, RUFUS (October 1, 1799-July 13, 1859), lawyer and orator, was born on Hog Island (now part of Essex), Mass., the son of David and Miriam (Foster) Choate. The precocious child, with a marvellously retentive memory, was educated at an academy at New Hampton, N.H., and at Dartmouth, from which he was graduated in 1819 as valedictorian. He tutored at Dartmouth for a year, then studied law in Washington, and was admitted to the bar in 1823, starting practice at Danvers, Mass. During his five years there, he served terms in both houses of the state legislature. In 1830 he was elected to Congress, was re-elected the following term, but resigned, and returned to Boston to practice law. In 1841 he succeeded Webster as senator, but on Webster's return to the Senate refused all further political office, except for a short term as attorney-general of his state in 1853. In 1825 he had married Helen Wolcott; they had seven children. He died at Halifax, N.S., while en route to Europe.

Choate's talent was twofold, for law and oratory. A scholar above all, he devoted part of each day throughout his life to literature, history, and philosophy. He was especially interested in Greek history, and had planned to write a history of Greece, for which he never had leisure; for this purpose he wrote, but never published, a translation of Thucydides. As an orator, he was among the foremost of his time, marked above all by wit, urbanity, and, on occasion, flaming rhetoric. Van Wyck Brooks calls him "a fiery speaker, witty, weighty, plain and grand by turns, an orator for the thinking few." His "weirdly exotic" appearance, his dark, compressed, and twisted countenance, was matched by immense personal magnetism; as a colleague said to him: "You dressed the common and mean things of life with a poetic charm and romance." His published speeches are but a pale reflection of his oratory.

PRINCIPAL WORK: Works, 1862.

ABOUT: Brooks, Van W. The Flowering of New England; Brown, S. G. Memoir of Rufus Choate; Fuess, C. M. Rufus Choate: The Wizard of the Law; Neilson, J. Memories of Rufus Choate; Parker, E. G. Reminiscences of Rufus Choate: The Great American Advocate.

CHOPIN, KATE (O'FLAHERTY) (February 8, 1851-August 22, 1904), novelist and short story writer, portrayer of Creole and Acadian life, was born in St. Louis, the daughter of Thomas O'Flaherty, a prosperous business man who had been an emigrant from County Galway, Ireland, and Eliza (Faris) O'Flaherty, who was of French extraction. Her mother was the second wife, and Kate had a beloved older half-brother who died from typhoid fever caused by his imprisonment in the Civil War as a Confederate soldier. Her father was killed in a train wreck when she was only four.

She was graduated from the Sacred Heart Convent in 1868—she was throughout her life a devout, liberal-minded Catholic—and for two years lived the life of an attractive girl in the "high society" (of French origin) in which her mother moved. Then, in 1870, she married Oscar Chopin of Louisiana, who at that time was working in a St. Louis bank, but who settled as a cotton factor in New Orleans after their European honeymoon. (He was a Creole and pronounced his surname in the French manner—like the composer's.) In 1880, with their five sons (a daughter was born later), they moved to his sister's cotton plantation in Cloutiersville, in Natchitoches Parish, La. To this fortunate move the world owes Mrs. Chopin's charming and penetrating stories of her Creole and "Cajun" neighbors; she was an inspired listener always, and what she heard and saw now she re-created later.

KATE CHOPIN
1870

Oscar Chopin died suddenly of swamp fever in 1882, and after trying for two years to run the plantation single-handed, Kate yielded to her mother's entreaties and returned to St. Louis, her home for the remainder of her life. Here she began to write, and her first work was privately printed, at the solicitation of friends who had enjoyed her vivid letters. Aware of the amateurishness of her work, she gave herself to intensive study of the French models she most admired, with results which have gained her a place in almost the front rank of American story writers. Soon her tales for children began to appear in the *Youth's Companion, Wide Awake,* and *Harper's Young People*; her more ambitious stories for adults were published in *Harper's Magazine* and the *Century.* She also contributed essays and dramatic criticism to the St. Louis newspapers. Her first book was published in 1890, followed by others at three or four year intervals.

But just when success seemed to have arrived, disaster fell from an unforeseen source. In 1899 she wrote a novel, *The Awakening,* about mixed marriage and a wife's love for another man than her husband. Mild as the topic seems today, it aroused the full venom of the unco' guid of the time, and the invective they heaped on the sensitive author froze the creative impulse within her. This beautifully written book—like Hardy's *Jude the Obscure* too far ahead of its time—was her last major work. She continued to write sparingly, both stories and verse, but she was now *persona non grata* to the orthodox publishers and editors; moreover, the hurt she had incurred killed the spontaneous grace and lightness which had made her Louisiana stories things unique of their kind. She was just beginning to take heart again when she died suddenly, of cerebral hemorrhage, after a hot day at the St. Louis Exposition of 1904.

Kate Chopin, with her once black hair prematurely white, her bright brown eyes, her delicate skin, and her graceful figure, was likened by her friends to a great lady of old France. She was quiet and reserved, but alive with sympathy and interest. At no time did she take herself seriously as a "literary personage." Indeed, so great was her aversion to personal publicity that most contemporary readers thought "Kate Chopin" was a pseudonym.

When she wrote she worked rapidly, never revising or rewriting her first draft. Her style is exquisite, poignant, yet restrained, with delicate humor and keen perception of the human—especially the feminine—mind. Her best work has a symmetry and sharpness of outline which inevitably suggests Maupassant. In fact, her best known story, "Désirée's Baby," in *Bayou Folk,* reads as if it might have been written by Maupassant had he, like Kate Chopin, lived in Natchitoches Parish instead of Normandy.

Principal Works: At Fault, 1890; Bayou Folk, 1894; A Night in Acadie, 1897; The Awakening, 1899.

About: Dondore, D. A. The Prairie and the Making of Middle America; Pattee, F. L. The Development of the American Short Story; Rankin, D. S. Kate Chopin and Her Creole Stories; The Writer August 1894.

CHURCH, BENJAMIN (August 24, 1734-1776), essayist, poet, and convicted traitor to the American cause in the Revolution was born at Newport, R.I., grandson of Col. Benjamin Church, a conspicuous soldier of the French and Indian Wars, and a son of Benjamin Church. In his twelfth year he entered the Boston Latin School and in 1754 was graduated from Harvard. He studied medicine and somewhat later went to London where he was married to Hannah Hill of Ross, Herefordshire. Returning to the United States he made his home at Raynham, Mass. Although he appeared to ally himself with the Whigs, through his political essays, etc., it is said that he himself prepared the spirited Tory responses and wrote song parodies that were obvious slurs upon the cause of the colonists. His testimony upon the examination of the body of Crispus Attucks, killed in the Boston Massacre, was incorporated into James Spear Loring's *The Hundred Boston Orators.* He probably wrote for *The Censor,* a Loyalist journal; and on March 5, 1773 he delivered an *Oration to Commemorate the Bloody Tragedy of the Fifth of March 1770.*

Even after Paul Revere had implicitly accused Church of reporting the proceedings of a supposedly secret Whig caucus to the Tories, Church remained within the confidence of the Whigs. In July 1775 he was made director and chief physician of the first Army Hospital (at Cambridge). That same month he sent a cipher letter to a British officer at Newport; it was intercepted; and Church was tried by court martial in October. The letter, which he admitted he had written, was, he asserted, intended only to intimidate the Britishers. The Continental Congress ordered his imprisonment, but because of illness he was paroled within the colony. It is recorded that he was allowed to leave Boston Harbor in May 1776; but his ship was never heard from.

A sample of Church's early verse, *The Choice: A Poem, After the Manner of Pomfret,* written when he was eighteen but not published until 1802, bristled with a self-consciousness and a heavy borrowing from the contemporary English poets:

> Whatever station be for me designed
> May virtue be the mistress of my mind...

In addition to his prose works, mentioned above, Church has been credited with the authorship of a satire upon the Stamp Act, *The Times,* written in the effort to destroy the "notion of arbitrary power heretofore drank in" and dedicated to the "honest Farmer and Citizen." The sentiment of the poem is well illustrated by these lines:

> Art thou persuaded . . .
> Torries are nuisances and Traffick worse,
> And to be blind sagacity of course,
> The Stamp and Land Tax are as blessings meant,
> And opposition is our free consent

Principal Works: The Times, 1765; An Oration . . . to Commemorate the Bloody Tragedy of the Fifth of March, 1770; The Choice: A Poem, After the Manner of Pomfret, 1802.

About: Church, B. The Times (see Preface); Owen, W. O. The Medical Department of the U. S. Army . . . 1776-1886; Sabine, L. Biographical Sketches of the Loyalists of the American Revolution; Toner, J. M. The Medical Men of the Revolution.

"CHURTON, HENRY." See TOURGÉE, ALBION WINEGAR

CLAFLIN, TENNESSEE CELESTE. See WOODHULL, VICTORIA (CLAFLIN)

CLAPP, HENRY, JR. (November 11, 1814-April 2, 1875), humorist, journalist, and "king of the Bohemians," was born on the island of Nantucket, Mass. It is said that he tried a sailor's life for a while; and in his twenties he became secretary to Albert Brisbane and had a ranking responsibility in the publication of *The Social Destiny of Man.* Clapp was fast becoming a reformer-lecturer-writer of boundless energy. Under the leadership of Nathaniel P. Rogers, of New Hampshire, he aroused some effective anti-slavery sentiment, setting up his own organ, the *Essex County Washingtonian* (afterwards the *Pioneer*) published at Lynn, Mass., "independent in everything and neutral in nothing" (the same motto, incidentally, that appeared much later on Joseph Addison Turner's strongly Southern *Countryman,* launched in April 1862). In 1846

Clapp incorporated pieces from his weekly into *The Pioneer: or, Leaves From an Editor's Portfolio.*

Clapp was abroad during the 'fifties; in Paris he sought out Horace Greeley (whom he dubbed "a self-made man who worships his creator"); and both returned with increased interest in the social theories of François Charles Fourier. In October 1858 Clapp founded the *Saturday Press,* engaging Thomas Bailey Aldrich to write book reviews and James O'Brien to cover the theatre; neither remained long, however, but William Winter, who joined the *Press* in 1859, weathered those precarious last weeks which ended in its suspension in 1860. The *Press* was a "satire with no kindness in it," firing mercilessly at political and intellectual humbugs and was, therefore, a veritable invitation to enmity. Clapp wrote for the *New York Leader* for a while, and then revived his old journal, with this characteristic announcement: "This paper was stopped in 1860 for want of means: it is now started again for the same reason." Winter states that Clapp made his second attempt in 1866, but Mark Twain, in his *Autobiography,* says that "Jim Smiley and his Frog" (later *The Celebrated Jumping Frog*) was presented to Clapp by the New York publisher, Carleton, and appeared in the last issue of the *Saturday Press,* November 18, 1865; and it seems likely that Clapp had gotten his "second wind" only a few months before.

Over the signature "Figaro" he wrote innumerable stage critiques, and he dashed off nimble parodies, in verse, seemingly without effort. As a prologue to *Husband Versus Wife,* a domestic lament with a rattling rhythm, he made a burlesque version of Leigh Hunt's "Abou ben Adhem."

There had arisen in New York, during the winter of 1859-60 a literary circle (not self-named), "the Bohemians"—Walt Whitman, Thomas Bailey Aldrich, Charles Dawson Shanly, George Arnold, and others—of which Clapp, "withered, embittered, grotesque . . . a good fighter . . . a kind heart" was "king." The famous "Pfaff's," German restaurant in a basement on lower Broadway, was their rendezvous.

Clapp, however, belongs to literary history not because of his measurable professional accomplishments or his intellectual friendships, but because of his uncommon wit and the strength and subtlety of his own critical perceptions.

Principal Works: The Pioneer: or, Leaves From an Editor's Portfolio, 1846; Husband Versus Wife, 1858.

About: Clapp, H. Jr. The Pioneer (see Introduction); Howe, M. A. deW. Memories of a Hostess; Traubel, H. With Walt Whitman in Camden; Winter, W. Old Friends.

CLAPP, HENRY AUSTIN (July 17, 1841-February 19, 1904), dramatic critic and lawyer, was born in Dorchester, Mass. As a child he was frequently taken to the theatre, and when he entered Dorchester High School, Dr. William J. Rolfe, headmaster, encouraged him in a careful reading of Shakespeare's plays. In 1860 Clapp was graduated from Harvard; he taught a while in Boston Latin School; and his subsequent study in a law office was interrupted by the outbreak of the Civil War. Clapp enlisted as a private in Company F, 44th Massachusetts volunteers, and after about nine months' service, largely in North Carolina, he returned to New England, entered Harvard Law School, and was graduated with honors in 1864. He became managing clerk for Hutchins & Wheeler, and then opened an office of his own. In 1875 he was appointed assistant clerk of the Supreme Judicial Court of Suffolk County; and in 1887 he was made clerk, which post he held until the time of his death.

As book reviewer for the Boston *Daily Advertiser* he made his plunge, in 1862, into journalism; and within six years he had full charge of the dramatic and music departments of this paper. He was a contributor, at the same time, to the *Atlantic, Outing,* and *Every Saturday,* and to the leading New York dailies. He became dramatic critic of the Boston *Herald* in 1902; and that same year his *Reminiscences of a Dramatic Critic,* which had run in the *Atlantic* in 1901, appeared, with revisions and additions, in book form. Despite Frank J. Wilstach's contention that Clapp delighted in harrowing the fledglings of the stage, attempted to force his personal prejudices upon the general public, and gave the impression of being "teased, tired, and tormented" by the theatre, the book contained an abundance of amicable incident and significant biography. Clapp had no professional snobbery: he went regularly to the "third-class houses" in order to give them whatever encouragement they deserved; but he was "a deadly enemy of the dirty farces and plays imported by commercial managers to foul the public morals and stain the stage." Clapp delivered eight courses at the Lowell Institute; and was awarded an honorary master of arts degree from Harvard in 1894. He was survived by his wife, Florence (Clark) Clapp and a son Roger.

Portions of Clapp's critical theory were often severely attacked by contemporary reviewers, but in view of the fact that it was always "after office hours" that he turned to literary pursuits, it is decidedly to his credit that among the dramatic critics of his time he perhaps stood second only to William Winter.

ABOUT: Clapp, H. A. Reminiscences of a Dramatic Critic; Harvard University Class of 1860; Critic July 1902; New York Dramatic Mirror March 5, 1904.

CLARK, CHARLES HEBER ("Max Adeler") (July 11, 1847-August 10, 1915), novelist and humorist, was born in Berlin, Md., the son of William J. Clark, an Episcopal clergyman whose abolitionist sympathies made his stays short in Southern parishes. Charles was educated at a school in Georgetown, D.C., and at the age of fifteen became an office boy in a Philadelphia commission house. He enlisted in the Civil War two years later and was discharged from the Union Army at the close of the war. He then became a reporter on the Philadelphia *Inquirer*, and within two months was promoted to editorial writer. Later he was dramatic and music critic of the *Evening Bulletin*, and an editorial writer on the *North American*. His private interests were economic, and he was a strong advocate of a high tariff. This bias led him to become editor and proprietor of the *Textile Record*, a founder and secretary of the Manufacturers' Club, and editor of its organ, the *Manufacturer*. He became independently wealthy through investments and retired from editorial work to his suburban home at Conshohocken, Pa. He was twice married, his first wife having been Clara Lukens; she died in 1895, and two years later he married Emily K. Clark.

Nearly all of Clark's writing was published under the pseudonym of "Max Adeler." His best known work was *Out of the Hurly Burly*, extremely popular in its time but deadly dull now, with its boisterous, extravagant humor. He hated his own reputation as a humorist in later years and tried to live it down by writing very serious and extremely boring novels, whose only merit is their background, derived from boyhood memories of Maryland and from the beautiful surroundings of the author's home on the Schuylkill.

PRINCIPAL WORKS: Out of the Hurly Burly: or, Life in an Odd Corner, 1874; Elbow Room, 1876; Random Shots, 1879; The Fortunate Island and Other Stories, 1882; Captain Bluitt: A Tale of Old Turkey, 1901; In Happy Hollow, 1903; The Quakeress, 1905; By the Bend in the River, 1914.

ABOUT: Book Buyer September 1902; Book News Monthly January 1916.

CLARK, HENRY JAMES (June 22, 1826-July 1, 1873), zoologist and botanist, was born in Easton, Mass., the son of Henry Porter Clark, life-long friend of the elder Henry James, and Abigail Jackson (Orton) Clark. He attended Brooklyn schools and then the University of the City of New York, graduating in 1848. While a teacher at White Plains he made some unusual botanical observations and was invited, in 1850, to become a private assistant in the Botanic Garden in Cambridge, Mass. In 1854 he was graduated, *summa cum laude*, from Lawrence Scientific School at Harvard, and that same year was married to Mary Young Holbrook, of Boston. At Cambridge he became right hand man to Louis Agassiz, the Swiss naturalist, for whose *Contributions to the Natural History of the United States. . .* Clark did some invaluable work. A quarrel over the authorship of the book led to Clark's publication of *A Claim for Scientific Property*. His lectures at the Lowell Institute in 1864 were published the following year.

He accepted a call to Pennsylvania State College in 1866, and to the University of Kentucky in 1869; he suffered from a severe illness three years later, and died at the age of forty-seven. His wider scientific writings, though extensive and accurate, have, obviously, a ranking which is only subordinate to his scholarly zoological and botanical research.

PRINCIPAL WORKS: Some Remarks on the Use of the Microscope, as Recently Improved . . . , 1859; Mind in Nature: or, The Origin of Life, and the Mode of Development of Animals, 1865.

ABOUT: National Academy of Sciences. Biographical Memoirs: Vol. 9.

CLARK, LEWIS GAYLORD (October 5, 1808-November 3, 1873), editor and miscellaneous writer, twin brother of Willis Gaylord Clark [*q.v.*], Philadelphia poet and journalist, was born and brought up in the rural community of Otisco, N.Y. He was the son of Eliakim Clark, who married the daughter of Lemon Gaylord, a native of Connecticut who had emigrated to Onondaga County, N.Y.

Lewis and Willis Clark were educated at the nearby Onondaga Academy and cultivated a taste for learning through the example of an uncle, Willis Gaylord, locally prominent editor of the *Genesee Farmer and Albany Cultivator*. Lewis went to New York

Collection of Frederick H. Meserve
LEWIS GAYLORD CLARK

City about 1834, where he contributed an article, "A Contrasted Picture," to the *Knickerbocker*. This was the beginning of his long association with the magazine.

In 1834 Clark and his friend Clement M. Edson bought the *Knickerbocker* and reorganized it with Clark as editor. Under his guidance it became a leading periodical and included the writings of many of the leading literary figures of the day, although the financial foundation was always far from secure. Clark, however, served as editor without interruption until December 1860. Several years later he edited a few more issues, but the magazine had outlived its popularity. Clark's position made him a prominent figure in the literary life of New York City. He was secretary of the St. Nicholas Society, a charter member of the Century Club, and a close friend of Dickens, Longfellow, and Irving.

After Clark lost his magazine, he wrote for *Harper's* and *Lippincott's* and for two years he held clerical positions in the New York Custom House. He died from the effects of a paralytic stroke, leaving his wife, Ella Maria Curtis, whom he had married in 1834.

Lewis Gaylord Clark's editorial duties left little time for literary work not connected with his magazine. Among his published works were collections of reminiscences and selections from the *Knickerbocker—The Knickerbocker Sketchbook* and *Knick-Knacks From an Editor's Table.* His style reflected the quiet humor and graceful elegance of his personality. T. B. Thorpe, writing in *Harper's,* described him as ". . . exceedingly popular everywhere—blessed with a handsome person, an expressive face, crowned by a broad forehead, charmingly shaded by a stray curling lock... By his exquisite taste and unvarying good nature he wielded a powerful and healthy influence upon American authorship."

PRINCIPAL WORKS: The Literary Remains of the Late Willis Gaylord Clark (ed.) 1844; The Knickerbocker Sketch-Book, 1845; Knick-Knacks From an Editor's Table, 1852; The Life, Eulogy, and Great Orations of Daniel Webster, 1854.

ABOUT: Bulletin of the New York Public Library June 1938; Harper's New Monthly Magazine March 1874; New York Evening Post November 4, 1873; New York Times, New York Tribune November 5, 1873.

CLARK, WILLIS GAYLORD (October 5, 1808-June 12, 1841), poet and journalist, was born in Otisco, N.Y., the son of a pioneer farmer, Eliakim Clark. He was a twin brother of Lewis Gaylord Clark [*q.v.*], who edited the *Knickerbocker Magazine* for twenty-seven years. His education began at home under a maternal uncle, the Rev. George Colton, and was continued at the old Onondaga Academy, near Syracuse. In young manhood Willis moved to Philadelphia, where for a while he owned and edited a short-lived magazine, and then served on the staffs of several other literary and religious periodicals. Finally he became associated with the venerable Philadelphia *Gazette,* and in 1836 he married the owner's niece, Anne Poyntell Caldcleugh. The marriage was of brief duration; Mrs. Clark soon died of tuberculosis, and it was not long after until Willis realized that he had contracted the disease.

He had, however, a few active years still ahead of him, during which he became editor of the *Gazette* and changed its politics from Jacksonian Democrat to Whig. He served as associate editor on his brother's magazine, conducting a department called "Ollapodianna," and also contributed verse to literary annuals and leading periodicals. In 1833 he brought out a slender volume of poetry, but his complete works were not published until after his death. Aside from his literary merit, he deserves remembrance as the first American to advocate in print the adoption of international copyright.

Clark's prose is mostly humorous, but there is a deep vein of sentiment apparent beneath the surface. His poetry was subdued in tone and often of a religious nature; Poe said of him that he had been the first to "render the poetry of religion attractive."

The "glorious future" which Bulwer-Lytton had predicted for him was cut short by his death from tuberculosis at the age of thirty-three.

PRINCIPAL WORKS: The Spirit of Life and Other Poems, 1833; The Literary Remains of the Late Willis Gaylord Clark, 1844; The Poetical Writings of Willis Gaylord Clark, 1847.

ABOUT: Clark, W. G. Literary Remains (see Memoir by L. G. Clark); Griswold, R. W. Poets and Poetry of America; Bulletin of the New York Public Library June 1938; Knickerbocker Magazine April 1842.

CLARKE, JAMES FREEMAN (April 4, 1810-June 8, 1888), Unitarian clergyman, Transcendalist, and author of religious works, was born in Hanover, N.H., although his parents, Samuel Clarke and Rebecca Parker Hull (Freeman) Clarke, moved shortly thereafter to Newton, Mass., where young Freeman Clarke was brought up under the intellectual guidance of his step-grandfather, Dr. James Freeman, and his maternal grandfather, General William Hull.

He prepared for Harvard at the Boston Latin School, and in 1833 was graduated from the Harvard Divinity School and ordained in Boston. A month later he took the pulpit of the Unitarian Church in Louisville, Ky., remaining seven years. During this time he edited the *Western Messenger* (1836-39), and secured for his publication pieces from his friends William Ellery Channing and Ralph Waldo Emerson. Upon his return to Boston, in 1841, he founded a new Unitarian Church, The Church of the Disciples, and as its pastor stirred Boston by emphasizing the power of the laity and other shocking innovations.

During 1850-54 he absented himself from his church to travel abroad for his health and serve as minister of the Unitarian Church at Meadville, Pa., the native town of his wife, Anna Huidekoper, whom he had married in 1839.

Returning to Boston in 1854, he resumed his pulpit at The Church of the Disciples, maintained during his absence by faithful members of the laity, and took a prominent part in the civic, educational, and religious life of the city. He was a member of the State Board of Education (1863-69); trustee of the Boston Public Library (1879-88); non-resident professor in the Harvard Divinity School (1867-71); and member of the Board of Overseers of Harvard College from 1863 to 1888. He also found time to support such movements as temperance, anti-slavery, and woman suffrage; and to produce a number of books on religious subjects, chiefly *The Ten Great Religions* (1883). *Self-Culture,* published in 1882, mirrored the opinions of the Transcendental Club, whose membership, besides Clarke, included Alcott, Emerson, Margaret Fuller, Miss Peabody, Orestes Brownson, and other notables.

Collection of Frederick H. Meserve
JAMES FREEMAN CLARKE

Dr. Clarke was a man of broad vision, amiable disposition, and unshakeable loyalties, who admirably exemplified in his own life the attributes of Christian behavior. While his writing brought some light into religious literature and influenced contemporary thought, it has never been held with the same high regard as that of his fellow Transcendentalists.

PRINCIPAL WORKS: The Christian Doctrine of Forgiveness of Sin, 1852; The Christian Doctrine of Prayer, 1854; Orthodoxy: Its Truths and Errors, 1866; Common Sense in Religion, 1874; Essentials and Non-Essentials in Religion, 1878; Self-Culture, 1882; The Ten Great Religions, 1871-83; Anti-Slavery Days, 1884; The Problem of the Fourth Gospel, 1886.

ABOUT: Clarke, L. F. Heralds of a Liberal Faith; Hale, E. E. James Freeman Clarke; Massachusetts Historical Society Proceedings March 1889.

CLARKE, MacDONALD (June 18, 1798-March 5, 1842), poet, was born in Bath, Maine. Very little is known about his disordered life; he first came to New York in 1819, and is supposed to have married an actress, though her name and fate have been lost. He was undoubtedly insane (he was known, to himself and others, as "the mad poet"), but how much of his lunacy was real and how much feigned it is hard to tell. Certainly he was able to write coherently at times, and at other times he babbled sheer gibberish. Without visible means of support, he was a familiar figure on Broadway, dressed always in semi-military style, and the avowed admirer of all the ladies, to whom he wrote odes which sometimes annoyed them exceedingly. In a fragment of autobiography, he says that he was "conceived in Jamaica and born in Maine," but even this bit of family history is followed by a flight in which he calls himself "the greatest Poet of the world," and claims that "he ought to have the freedom of the City, the girls of the gentry gratis."

Fitz-Greene Halleck, who had a kind heart, befriended him; and there must have been many others who did so, for he brought out frequent volumes of verse which someone must have paid for. Undoubtedly he lived chiefly by gifts and "borrowings." In spite of his lady killer's pose, he seems to have been harmless, and Halleck declared that "his oddities were all amiable." Every Sunday he turned up at Grace Church, where he was a regular communicant—and from the pious parishioners of which he probably gathered much of his sustenance.

Finally, on a rainy March evening, a policeman picked up the ragged wreck and took him to Blackwell's Island for safekeeping. There the next morning he was found "drowned in water from an open faucet." As this seems a difficult means of accidental death, it must be supposed to have been suicide—though surely by a unique method. He was buried in Greenwood Cemetery, Brooklyn, and Halleck, who without doubt paid the funeral expenses, erected a monument on which was inscribed his memorial verse:

> By friendship's willing hand erected,
> By genius, taste, and art adorned,
> For one too long in life neglected,
> But now in death sincerely mourned.

On another panel of the monument was a verse of Clarke's own, which shows his style in his more lucid moments:

> But what are human plaudits now?
> He never deemed them worth his care,
> Yet Death has twined around his brow
> The wreath he was too proud to wear.

Be that as it may, his better poems display humor, satire, sentiment, and a deep vein of tenderness. Today, however, he survives only by a single couplet, frequently paraphrased:

> Now twilight lets her curtain down
> And pins it with a star.

Principal Works: Review of the Eve of Eternity and Other Poems, 1820; Elixir of Moonshine by the Mad Poet, 1822; The Gossip, 1825; Poetic Sketches, 1826; The Belles of Broadway, 1833; Death in Disguise: A Temperance Poem, 1833; Poems, 1836; Cross and Coronet, 1841.

Collection of Frederick H. Meserve
MacDONALD CLARKE

CLARKE, MARY BAYARD (DEVEREUX) (May 13, 1827-March 30, 1866), poet and editor, was born in New Bern, N.C. The daughter of Thomas Pollock Devereux and Katherine Anne (Johnson) Devereux, she claimed descent from five colonial governors and from Jonathan Edwards and Dr. Samuel Johnson, president of King's College, now Columbia University. When Mary Devereux was a young child, her mother died and her father engaged an English governess who so strictly supervised the child's education that she subjected her to the prescribed academic course at Yale University. The young student thus became widely read, and besides cultivating a graceful literary style, acquainted herself with modern languages. Counterbalanced by a sprightly sense of humor, her scholarly mind was never an obtrusion in social life and she was regarded as one of the rare women in America who, "without being a blue-stocking, was thoroughly educated."

In 1848, six years after her marriage to William J. Clarke, she brought out *Wood Notes*, a collection of North Carolina poetry, including some of her own under the pseudonym, "Tenella." Threatened by tubercular symptoms, she spent the winter of 1854-55 in Havana but soon abandoned the pleasant life there for the more beneficial climate of San Antonio. When the Civil War broke out, her husband joined the Confederate army, and she returned with her four children to North Carolina, where she became a prolific writer of patriotic verse for newspapers. Much of this output was collected in 1866 in *Mosses From a Rolling Stone or Idle Moments of a Busy Woman.* Reduced circumstances caused by the war forced her to earn money and she increased the speed of her pen for the remainder of her life, reviewing books, editing the *Southern Field and Fireside,* and contributing to other magazines. Among other activities she published *Clytie and Zenobia* in 1871, translated a French novel, composed a libretto, *Miskodeed,* and wrote Sunday-school hymns at five dollars apiece. Poverty and depression brought on paralysis, and her life came to an end one month after that of her husband, who had long been an invalid. Although her writing commanded respect in her day, it is now shelved among pleasing but unimportant works.

Principal Works: Wood Notes, 1848; Mosses From a Rolling Stone: or, Idle moments of a Busy Woman; Clytie and Zenobia, 1871.

About: Alderman, E. A. & Harris, J. C. Library of Southern Literature; Clarke, M. B. Poems; Raymond, J. Southland Writers.

CLARKE, REBECCA SOPHIA (February 22, 1833-August 16, 1906), writer of juvenile books under the name "Sophie May," was born in Norridgewock, Maine the daughter of Asa and Sophia (Bates) Clarke. Educated at the Norridgewock Female Academy, and tutored in Greek and Latin, she taught in Evansville, Ind., while living in the home of a married sister, until increasing deafness caused her to return to Norridgewock. When she was twenty-eight, she wrote an article at the suggestion of a friend, for the Memphis, Tenn., *Daily Appeal,* and immediately embarked on a career that later gained for her the title "the Dickens of the Nursery." Using her pen-name, she contributed stories to the *Little Pilgrim,* which were collected as the *Little Prudy* series (1863-65), bringing in the sum of fifty dollars a volume. Of her forty books for children, the best known are in the *Dotty Dimples* series (1867-69). Noted fo- her brunette beauty in her girlhood, Rebecca Clarke took a prominent part in Norridgewock's civic activities during her long residence and left behind her a reputation for kindliness and unselfishness. She died in the white-columned red-brick house where she was born.

Principal Works: *Juvenile*—Little Prudy Stories, 1863-65; Dotty Dimples Stories, 1867-69; Little Prudy's Flyaway Series, 1870-73; Quinnebasset Series, 1871-91; Flaxie Frizzle Stories, 1876-84; Little Prudy's Children Series, 1894-1901. *Novels*—Drone's Honey, 1887; Pauline Wyman, 1897.

About: Boston Transcript August 17, 1906; Kennebec Journal August 18, 1906; Lewiston Journal February 2, 1924; Portland Daily Press August 18, 1906.

"CLAVERS, MRS. MARY." See KIRKLAND, CAROLINE MATHILDA (STANSBURY)

CLAY, HENRY (April 12, 1777-June 29, 1852), statesman and orator, was born in a section of Hanover County, Va., known as "the Slashes," the son of John and Elizabeth (Hudson) Clay. His father, a Baptist minister, died when the boy was four, and his childhood was a struggle with hard work and poverty. His mother remarried and moved to Kentucky, and when Clay was fourteen his stepfather found him a place as clerk in a store in Richmond. Soon afterwards he became errand boy for the clerk of the High Court of Chancery. Chancellor White was struck by his abilities, and made him his copyist, at the same time directing his reading. He studied law, and was admitted to the bar in 1797, going to Lexington, Ky., to practice. There, two years later, he married Lucretia Hart, by whom he had eleven children.

Clay's political career is long and involved; from his first election to the state

Collection of Frederick H. Meserve
HENRY CLAY

legislature in 1803 and to the United States Senate in 1806 (at twenty-six!) he was nearly always in one or the other house of Congress, though constantly "finally retiring." For much of the time he was Speaker of the House; it is said that when he arose in the House the Senate became empty. As a member of the commission to make peace with England after the War of 1812 (precipitated in large part by Calhoun and himself), he signed the Treaty of Ghent, in 1814. In 1824 he was secretary of state under John Quincy Adams; the false accusation of "bargain and corruption" followed him for years, since he had been a candidate for president and had withdrawn in Adams' favor. Partly on this charge he fought three duels, one with the famous John Randolph of Roanoke. In spite of his outstanding position, he was constantly disappointed in his ambition to become president, and was much embittered by his repeated failures.

Clay was "the great conciliator." Though he was not the actual author of the Missouri Compromise, his advocacy and modification of this attempt to solve the slavery problem always associate it with his name. First, last, and all the time, his fundamental aim was the preservation of the Union. To keep the Union he was, like Calhoun, willing to perpetuate slavery, though he had not Calhoun's conviction of its righteousness.

No student, a man of convivial habits, free-spoken and generous, Clay was a great party chieftain rather than a great statesman. As a lawyer it is said that no murderer he defended was ever hanged. His tall figure, his high forehead, grey eyes, and wide mouth, might have stood for the archetype of the orator. Less logical than Calhoun, less witty than Choate, less plausible than Webster, he was nevertheless an orator of fire and distinction. He was often short-tempered, autocratic, and overbearing, and he made many enemies; but even they conceded his magnificent presence, his sonorous voice, and his personal fascination. Theoretically he was a democrat; in practice he had to lead. Highly imaginative, his speeches were not so much reasoned arguments as flights of exaltation. His only published work is the reports of his speeches. As is usually the case, they must have sounded far better than they read. Clay was one of the great oratorical trinity of his time, with Calhoun and Webster, and all of them found their greatest fame in the living voice and presence, and left its memory rather in their effect on their contemporaries than in the printed reflection of their mighty words.

PRINCIPAL WORKS: Speeches, 1842; The Works of Henry Clay, 1857.

ABOUT: Bradford, G. As God Made Them; Colton, C. The Life and Times of Henry Clay; Mayo, B. Henry Clay: Champion of the West; Poage, G. R. Henry Clay and the Whig Party; Rogers, J. M. The True Henry Clay; Schmucker, S. M. The Life and Times of Henry Clay; Schurz, C. Life of Henry Clay.

CLEMENS, JEREMIAH (December 28, 1814-May 21, 1865) historical novelist, senator, and soldier, was born in Huntsville, Ala. His father was James Clemens, a Kentuckian who had migrated to the Tennessee Valley in 1812 when it still belonged to the Mississippi Territory, and his mother was a sister of the Hon. Archie E. Mills, member of the Alabama State Legislature. Young Clemens was educated at La Grange College, and was among the first students to matriculate at the University of Alabama on its opening in 1831 at Tuscaloosa. Preparing for a legal career, he completed a law course in Transylvania College, Lexington, Ky., and returned to Alabama to open an office. Recognized as a promising lawyer, he was appointed to a federal district attorneyship, volunteered for service in a skirmish against the Cherokees, and sat in the state legislature from 1839 to 1844. Once whetted, his appetite for politics and military service influenced him to leave Alabama in 1842 to engage in the war for Texan independence, in which he commanded a company of volunteers. When war was declared against Mexico in 1847, he joined the regular army as major of the 13th United States Infantry, served as chief of the depot of supplies and retired in 1848 with the rank of colonel.

Returning to Alabama, he was elected in 1849 to the United States Senate, where his eloquence as a debater was outstanding. His enthusiastic support of Fillmore for president turned the people of Alabama against him and he retired from politics to write historical novels, publishing one each year from 1856 to 1865. Among these was *The Rivals: A Tale of the Times of Aaron Burr and Alexander Hamilton* (1860). During this time he lived in Memphis, Tenn., and edited the *Memphis Eagle and Enquirer*. Once again he returned to Alabama to take an active part in politics, but Unionist tendencies brought him increasing unpopularity and in 1862 he moved to Philadelphia where he conducted a pamphlet campaign against his native state and advocated the re-election of Lincoln in 1864. He died in Huntsville a few weeks after peace was declared. His erratic temperament dissipated his talents, and it cannot be said that his writings brought any life into American letters.

Principal Works: Bernard Lile: An Historical Romance of the Texan Revolution and the Mexican War, 1856; Mustang Gray: A Romance, 1858; The Rivals: A Tale of the Times of Aaron Burr and Alexander Hamilton, 1860; Tobias Wilson: A Tale of the Great Rebellion.

About: Brewer, W. Alabama; Garrett, W. Reminiscences of Public Men in Alabama; Owen, T. M. History of Alabama.

CLEMENS, SAMUEL LANGHORNE ("Mark Twain") (November 30, 1835-April 21, 1910), novelist, essayist, and travel writer, was born in Florida, Mo., the son of John Marshall Clemens, a visionary lawyer and landowner from Virginia, and Jane (Lampton) Clemens. When he was five, the family, which was always on the move, went to Hannibal, Mo., and in 1847 the father died there. This put an end to the boy's very elementary schooling, and he was apprenticed to his brother Orion, who ran a country paper, the *Missouri Courier.* In 1853 Clemens set out for the East as a journeyman printer, getting as far as New York and Philadelphia, and ending back in Keokuk, Iowa, where Orion was publishing another paper. After an abortive start to South America, he became, in 1857, an apprentice pilot on the Mississippi, and remained on the river, as apprentice and journeyman pilot, until the Civil War.

For about two weeks he was a second lieutenant in the Confederate Army (all the rest of his family being staunch Unionists); but he managed to be mustered out for undescribed "disabilities," and again joined Orion, who had been appointed secretary of the territory of Nevada. Samuel Clemens went along as his brother's secretary, but finding he had neither duties nor salary, he became an unsuccessful prospector, then a reporter in Carson City, the capital of Nevada. By 1862 he was city editor of the Virginia City, Nev., *Enterprise,* and in his work for this paper he first used the familiar pseudonym "Mark Twain," a depth call of the Mississippi pilots. A meeting with Charles Farrar Browne ("Artemus Ward") first aroused his literary ambitions, but his earliest work was the crudest sort of humor, consisting mostly of hoaxes and tall stories.

A farcical duel, arising out of the personal journalism then the style, caused his exit from Nevada. He went to San Francisco in 1864 and joined the staff of the *Morning Call,* though he wrote also for the *Golden Era* and the *Alta California.* More important, he met Bret Harte, the first purely literary figure he had ever known. The next year his story of *The Celebrated Jumping Frog of Calaveras County,* first published in a New York newspaper, made him a nationally famous humorist overnight—though he himself, and justly, did not think highly of it. The Sacramento *Union* sent him to Hawaii (then known as the Sandwich Islands) to write travel sketches, and when he returned the paper assigned him to go around the world and send letters on his journey. Instead, as soon as he reached New York, he joined a party traveling on the "Quaker City" to the Mediterranean and Palestine.

Collection of Frederick H. Meserve

SAMUEL LANGHORNE CLEMENS ("Mark Twain")

This tour was the crucial point in Mark Twain's career. The book which grew from it, *Innocents Abroad,* established him solidly as a writer, and through it he met Olivia Langdon, daughter of a wealthy Elmira, N.Y., family, and fell in love: first with her picture, then with her. They were married in 1870. Clemens had already bought a part interest in the Buffalo *Express,* and edited it from 1869 to 1871, when he moved to Hartford, his home until 1891.

His brain always hot with schemes, he lost the fortune earned by his books in backing an impractical typesetting machine; then in 1884 he invested in the Charles L. Webster Company, a publishing house which made enormous profits from its sales of Grant's *Memoirs,* but gradually failed and went completely bankrupt in 1894, leaving Clemens penniless. Like Scott before him, he dedicated himself to paying his debts and regaining his standing financially. This he triumphantly accomplished by means of a world lecture tour in 1895 and 1896. But it was a bitter victory, for during his absence his best loved child, his daughter Susie, died.

From this time on Mark Twain's life was a strange compound of public glory and private tragedy. He lived abroad most of the time, for several years in a villa in Florence. His adored wife died in 1904, his daughter, Jean in 1909, leaving him (since his only son had died in infancy), but one daughter, Clara, who married the pianist Ossip Gabrilowitsch. Honors were heaped upon him; Yale had given him an M.A. degree in 1888 and followed it with an LL.D. in 1901, the University of Missouri did the same in 1902; but the proudest moment of his life was when Oxford conferred the same degree on him in 1907. He was so proud of his scarlet doctor's gown from Oxford that he wore it at his daughter's wedding. In his last years he built a house, "Stormfield," at Redding, Conn., and there he died of angina pectoris, as he had superstitiously expected, when Halley's Comet—which had heralded his birth—came round again.

Few more complex natures than his have ever lived, or few concerning whom there are so many contradictory opinions. Van Wyck Brooks sees him as the victim of the Puritanism of the East, embodied in his wife, the frustrated pioneer whose rebellion was all subconscious. To Bernard DeVoto he *is* the free, untrammeled pioneer, his very defects turned into virtues as the voice of the liberty-loving and democratic West. As a matter of fact, the truth about Mark Twain seems to be that though his mind grew up, his heart remained always that of a child. Hot-tempered, profane, wreathed in tobacco smoke, enthralled by games and gadgets, extravagant, sentimental, superstitious, chivalrous to the point of the ridiculous—he was all these things. This was Samuel Clemens, the boy who is most of Tom Sawyer; the young roughneck in Nevada and California; the man who shocked the smug Boston hierarchy by his incredible *gaffe* at the dinner to Whittier; the passionate defender of Harriet Shelley and Joan of Arc; the bitter enemy of Christian Science; the man who meekly let his wife edit the life out of his manuscripts; the libertarian who nevertheless chose as his dearest friend a multi-millionaire and the most reactionary of capitalists; the Rationalist whose next dearest friend was a clergyman; the great show-piece of the latter years (a position akin to that of Bernard Shaw later) who reigned like a king in pomp and innocent vanity, whose lightest word was eagerly sought and as eagerly given.

But besides this Samuel Clemens there was Mark Twain, a conscious artist who grew to resent his fame as a humorist, who alternated garrulity with taciturnity, who was as deeply dyed a pessimist as the world has ever seen, an apostle of cynicism and despair as truly as was Swift. Much of the writing in this vein never saw the light until he was near his death, though penned long before; most of it never passed Olivia's hawklike eye. But it must never be forgotten that Clemens, who was so outspoken and aggressive in some ways, had little power of self-criticism and was unusually dependent on guidance and approval to work at all. If his wife had not been his censor, he would have found another. It is true that he made a conscious effort to assimilate himself to the purse-proud "refined" society which was his later environment; he knew very well that he would never be accepted as actually one of the genteel, but he tried. Exceedingly impressionable, he could not help being influenced by those with whom he was thrown, from William Dean Howells, who had undergone something of the same transformation, to the Standard Oil magnate, H. H. Rogers. This being so, how very much more he must inevitably have been influenced by the woman he worshipped—a woman who, without any marked talent of her own, nevertheless loved him and did her best to make him over into the kind of man her family and friends would approve.

This inner struggle—a frustration more of his own making than enforced from the outside—is the root of his nostalgia for the past. We should be grateful for it, for it gave us *Tom Sawyer, Life on the Mississippi*, and *Huckleberry Finn*. If Mark Twain had stayed in the South or the West, he might be classed now with Artemus Ward or Josh Billings, a half-forgotten humorist. As it was, "there was too much virility in him [remarks Edward Wagenknecht] for him to permit himself to be pushed very far from his native bent." And since, to quote his official biographer, Albert Bigelow Paine, he "lived curiously apart from the actualities of life," in a sort of dream world, the nature of his dreams was important to posterity. The *Jumping Frog*, the crude *Roughing It*, the self-righteous *Innocents Abroad*, are hardly readable today, but while the English language lasts, Huck and Nigger Jim will drift down the Mississippi, Tom will cajole the other boys into whitewashing the fence for him. That hawklike figure with the bushy brows, the drooping mustache, the red hair turned to grey curls, garbed all in white as if for the tropics, concealed a lazy genius, a vain genius, often a credulous genius, but always a genius.

A word more must be said on Mark Twain's style. It must be remembered always that for many years he was a lecturer, that he was always a talker. He wrote as he talked, for the ear more than for the eye. His cadence is the cadence of speech. It is a style at its best almost inimitable. It is very like the speaking style of Lincoln, and Howells said more than he knew when he called Clemens "the Lincoln of our literature."

PRINCIPAL WORKS: The Celebrated Jumping Frog of Calaveras County and Other Sketches, 1867; Innocents Abroad, 1869; Roughing It, 1872; The Gilded Age (with C. D. Warner) 1874; Mark Twain's Sketches: New and Old, 1875; The Adventures of Tom Sawyer, 1876; Punch, Brothers, Punch! and Other Sketches, 1878; A Tramp Abroad, 1880; The Stolen White Elephant, 1882; 1601 (privately printed) 1882; The Prince and the Pauper, 1882; Life on the Mississippi, 1883; The Adventures of Huckleberry Finn, 1884; Tom Sawyer Abroad, 1894; A Connecticut Yankee at King Arthur's Court, 1889; The American Claimant, 1891; Merry Tales, 1892; The £1,000,000 Bank Note and Other New Stories, 1893; The Tragedy of Pudd'nhead Wilson, and the Comedy, Those Extraordinary Twins, 1894; In Defense of Harriet Shelley and Other Essays, 1894; Personal Recollections of Joan of Arc, 1896; Tom Sawyer: Detective, 1897; How to Tell a Story and Other Essays, 1897; Following the Equator, 1897; More Tramps Abroad, 1897; The Man That Corrupted Hadleyburg, 1900; A Double Barreled Detective Story, 1902; My Début as a Literary Person: With Other Essays and Stories, 1903; Adam's Diary, 1904; Eve's Diary, 1905; The $30,000 Bequest and Other Stories, 1906; What Is Man?, 1906; Captain Stormfield's Visit to Heaven, 1909; Is Shakespeare Dead? 1909; Mark Twain's Speeches, 1910; The Mysterious Stranger, 1916; Mark Twain's Letters, 1917; Mark Twain's Autobiography, 1924.

ABOUT: Benson, I. Mark Twain's Western Years; Brashear, M. M. Mark Twain: Son of Missouri; Brooks, Van W. The Ordeal of Mark Twain; Clemens, C. My Father: Mark Twain; Clemens, S. L. Mark Twain's Autobiography; DeVoto, B. Mark Twain's America; Henderson, A. Mark Twain; Howells, W. D. My Mark Twain; Lawton, M. A Lifetime with Mark Twain; Leacock, S. B. Mark Twain; Paine, A. B. Mark Twain: A Biography; Wagenknecht, E. C. Mark Twain: The Man and His Work; Bookman June 1910; Catholic World March 1917; Harper's Weekly December 17, 1910; North American Review June 1910, April 1917; Overland Monthly September 1915.

CLEMMER, MARY (May 6, 1839-August 18, 1884), novelist and newspaper woman, was born in Utica, N.Y., the daughter of Abraham and Margaret (Kneale) Clemmer. During her girlhood her parents moved to Westfield, Mass., where she attended the Westfield Academy until decreasing family resources made it no longer possible. At the age of sixteen she married the Rev. Daniel Ames, a Presbyterian minister many years her senior, the marriage terminating in divorce in 1874. She lived in several states prior to a residence in Washington, D.C., and was held as a prisoner at Harper's Ferry in 1862 when the Confederate army entered.

Her earliest literary effort was a poem published in the Springfield *Republican*, and by her twentieth year she was supporting herself and her parents by her contributions to newspapers. Her first novel *Victoire* was published in 1864 and thereafter she produced *Eirene: or, A Woman's Right* (1871), and *His Two Wives* (1874). Other activities between 1866 and 1872 included "A Woman's Letters From Washington," regularly sent to the New York *Independent*, and a daily column for the Brooklyn *Daily Union*.

A runaway accident sustained in 1878 led to chronic ill health and ultimately to the cerebral hemorrhage which caused her death in Washington. Meanwhile she had married Edmund Hudson, editor of the *Army and Navy Register*. In appearance she was fair and blue-eyed, with a slender, graceful figure. Her personality was a mixture of sensitivity and the fearlessness of a crusader for the many radical movements in which she was interested. Her writing reflected the florid sentimentality of her day and deserves no special recognition.

PRINCIPAL WORKS: Victoire, 1864; Eirene: or, A Woman's Right, 1871; Memorial of Alice and Phoebe Cary, 1873; Outlines of Men, Women, and Things, 1873; Ten Years in Washington, 1874; His Two Wives, 1874 .

ABOUT: Hudson, E. A Memorial of Mary Clemmer; Our Famous Women, 1884; Nation August 21, 1884; New York Commercial Advertiser August 19, 1884.

CLEVELAND, HENRY RUSSELL (October 3, 1808-June 12, 1843), educator and literary figure, was born in Lancaster, Mass., the son of Richard J. Cleveland, a wealthy merchant navigator, and his wife, Dorcas (Hiller) Cleveland; and a brother of Horace William Shaler Cleveland, landscape architect and author. Brought up on his father's beautiful estate, he was an unusually quick-minded child who absorbed much learning from his scholarly father, who was instrumental in founding a small academy in Lancaster. Young Cleveland was tutored for college by Jared Sparks, "the patriarch of American history," and was immediately recognized as a brilliant student when he entered Harvard in 1823. Following his graduation at nineteen, he taught at the Livingstone County High School for Boys, Geneseo, N.Y. During a summer vacation in Cambridge he contracted the fever which was a forerunner of the chronic ill health that later besieged him.

After 1829 he lived in Cambridge tutoring private pupils, but went in 1830 with his brother Horace to visit his parents at Havana, where his father was vice-consul of the United States. Greatly benefited by the warm climate, he sailed for Europe in 1831. In Paris he met his former college friend, Ralph Waldo Emerson, and took rooms with him in a private boarding house. During this time Cleveland became private secretary to William Cabell Rives, minister of the United States to the French Court; he also served the American Polish Committee as secretary and in this capacity often met Lafayette. Some of his European impressions appeared in the *New England Magazine* under the title "Scenes in Europe."

Returning to America in 1833, he became proctor at Harvard, and the following year, with his classmate, Edmund L. Cushing, opened a school for boys in Boston, which enjoyed almost immediate success. About this time Cleveland published his *Remarks on the Classical Education of Boys.*

After his marriage to Sarah P. Perkins, of Boston, in 1838, he severed his school connections and resided at his wife's mother's estate, Pine Bank, Roxbury. In the same year he published an edition of Sallust to fill a need for an inexpensive and correct text for school use. Devoting himself to study and writing, he contributed widely to periodicals, lectured in Boston on classic and romantic literature, and acquainted himself with the German, French, Spanish, and Italian languages. He was, in addition, a competent organist. In the spring of 1841, while lecturing on organ music in a draughty auditorium, he contracted a cold from which he never fully recovered. Vainly seeking the once-effective tonic of the Cuban climate, he returned to New Orleans in May 1843. Here his friend Ralph Waldo Emerson met him and they spent several weeks discovering the charms of the old city. Taking the steamboat "Missouri" up the Mississippi to St. Louis, Cleveland took a decided turn for the worse and was carried off the vessel to comfortable quarters in St. Louis, where he died a month later. Throughout this time, he was sustained by Emerson's faithful bedside vigil.

Principal Works: Remarks on the Classical Education of Boys, 1835; A Letter to the Hon. Daniel Webster on the Causes of the Destruction of the Steamer Lexington as Discovered in the Testimony Before the Coroner's Jury in New York, 1840; Life of Hendrik Hudson (in *Library of American Biography,* ed. by J. Sparks) 1854.

About: Brooks, V. W. The Flowering of New England; Hillard, G. S. Selections From the Writings of Henry R. Cleveland: With A Memoir.

CLIFFTON, WILLIAM (?, 1772-December ?, 1799), poet, was the son of a wealthy Philadelphia Quaker, who was probably a shipbuilder. The boy was handsome and intelligent, but frail, and when at nineteen he showed tubercular tendencies and suffered a hemorrhage, no attempt was made to oblige him to pursue any trade or profession. He soon drifted away from the Quaker surroundings of his childhood and spent his time in music and painting, for both of which he had much talent. He was adept, too, at field sports, particularly shooting. This active outdoor life probably prolonged his existence to even the scant twenty-seven years he achieved.

Early interested in politics, Cliffton was a Federalist, an extreme conservative, and an anti-Jacobin, who even favored war with France rather than recognition of the radicals of the French Revolution. He was one of a group known as the Anchor Club that held sessions at which poems and papers were read, and here most of his own poems first were presented to public notice. Nearly all of them were directed against France and the Revolution; one was a pretended translation from Talleyrand, and another, left unfinished at his death, was "The Chimeriad," a satire in the style of Pope's "Dunciad." Some of his verses were published in the *Gazette of the United States* (Philadelphia), and his "Poetical Epistle to William Gifford," the English anti-Jacobin publicist, was prefixed to the American edition of Gifford's works.

Aside from his political verse, Cliffton wrote occasional lyrics for his friends, which were collected in a posthumous volume. He had a genuine lyric gift, the equal of that of any American of his time except Philip Freneau's, and some of his work has a faint premonitory echo of the charm and grace of Joseph Rodman Drake. He died too young, however, for any just estimate to be formed of his actual capabilities. He was not one of the geniuses whose early death cannot hide their greatness, as were Keats and Shelley, for example; but he was one of the few actual poets of an unpoetic time and place.

Principal Works: The Group, 1776; Poems: Chiefly Occasional, 1800.

About: Cliffton, W. Poems: Chiefly Occasional (see Introductory Notes); Oberholtzer, E. P. Literary History of Philadelphia.

CLINCH, CHARLES POWELL (October 20, 1797-December 16, 1880), playwright, critic, and editor, was born in New York City, the son of James Clinch, a well-to-do ship-chandler. Educated in the public schools, he became secretary to Henry Eckford, a prominent marine architect, and father-in-law of Joseph Rodman Drake, the poet, an association that resulted in his moving in a literary circle including Fitz-Greene Halleck and others.

The year 1835 was an important one in his life, for he was then elected a member of the New York State legislature and lost a fortune in insurance stocks as a result of the great fire which swept the city. Eight years later he was appointed inspector in the New York Custom House, and served also as deputy collector and assistant collector until he retired in 1876. He died four years later in New York City.

Despite his active business life, Clinch found time for literary pursuits, including playwrighting, criticism, and editorials. He wrote *The Expelled Collegians* and *The First of May,* both of which were produced at the Broadway Theatre, and dramatized Cooper's *The Spy,* which may never have been produced professionally, although the manuscript bears rehearsal notations.

By copyrighting their verses before they were sent to the New York *Evening Post,* Clinch was active in helping Drake and Halleck to conceal their identity when they published *The Croakers,* their clever series of verse satires. Clinch greatly admired Halleck's poetry but was not above vying with him for the prize address in manuscript form on the occasion of the opening of the Park Theatre in New York in 1821. He will be remembered longer for his connection with literary figures than for his rather second-rate writings.

Principal Works. The Expelled Collegians; The First of May, The Spy, 1822.

About: Mabie, H. W. The Writers of Knickerbocker New York; Wilson, J. G. Life and Letters of Fitz-Greene Halleck; Bryant and His Friends; New York Evening Post December 16, 1880; New York Times, Herald, Tribune, World, Sun, December 17, 1880.

COAN, TITUS (February 1, 1801-December 1, 1882), missionary-author, was born at Killingworth, Conn., the son of Gaylord Coan, a farmer, and Tamza (Nettleton) Coan. Young Coan attended the district schools, was tutored by the Rev. Asa King, and was graduated from the academy at East Guilford (now Madison), Conn. After teaching in Killingworth and neighboring towns, he was received into the fellowship of the Presbyterian Church on March 2, 1828. Influenced by Charles G. Finney, the evangelist, he entered the Auburn Theological Seminary in June 1831. Two years later he was licensed to preach and shortly afterward was ordained by the American Board as a missionary to Patagonia in 1833, an unsuccessful venture from which he soon returned. On November 3, 1834, he married Fidelia Church and sailed from Boston for service in Hilo on the east coast of the island of Hawaii. Coan soon learned the new language and took charge of work in Hilo and Puna, a nearby district. His unceasing work succeeded in drawing such large crowds into Hilo that the scene took on the aspect of a daily revival meeting. He was sympathetic to the natives and lenient in admitting them to membership and in one year witnessed the baptism of 5,244. He spent the major part of his life in the islands, returning only once to America in 1870 because of his wife's ill health. She died two years later on their return to Hilo, and in 1873 he married Lydia, the daughter of Hiram Bingham, the distinguished missionary.

When the elder Charles Nordhoff visited the Sandwich Islands in 1873 he wrote of Coan: "And in Hilo when you go to visit the volcano you will find Dr. Coan, one of the brightest and loveliest spirits of them all, the story of whose life in the Umato island, whose apostle he was, is as wonderful and as touching as that of any of the earlier apostles, and shows what great works unyielding faith and love can do in redeeming a savage people."

Coan's two travel-books *Adventures in Patagonia* and *Life in Hawaii* are admirable testimonies of his keen interest in the natural life of the islands.

Principal Works: Adventures in Patagonia, 1880; Life in Hawaii, 1882.

About: Anderson, R. Sandwich Islands Mission; Blackman, W. F. The Making of Hawaii; Coan, L. B. Titus Coan.

COBB, LYMAN (September 18, 1800-October 26?, 1864), educator and text-book writer, was born in Lenox, Mass., the son of Elijah William and Sally (Whitney) Cobb. It is not known where he was educated but, since he began teaching at the age of sixteen and refers to himself as "Master of Arts" in some of his publications, it is assumed that he was well-grounded. His text-books in spelling, reading, and arithmetic were on virtually every school-house desk, and it is for these that he is remembered, especially his famous *Cobb's Spelling Book,* brought out when he was nineteen. His firm opinions with regard to spelling led to a heated controversy with Noah Webster, and at another time with Charles W. Sanders.

His outstanding book was *The Evil Tendencies of Corporal Punishment,* published in 1847, a work much applauded by Galdaudet, Mann, Russell, and Griscom.

Cobb's strong patriotic spirit led him to include "chiefly American pieces" in *The North American Reader* (1835). His service in the field of education was useful, but as a writer he did not merit any marked attention. He was married in 1822 to Harriet Chambers of Caroline, Tompkins County, N.Y., and his death occurred at Colesburg, Pa.

Principal Works: Cobb's Spelling Book, 1821; The Juvenile Reader No. 1, 1830; North American Reader, 1835; New Sequel or Fourth Reading Book, 1843; The Evil Tendencies of Corporal Punishment, 1847.

About: Allison, C. E. History of Yonkers; Scharf, J. T. History of Westchester County; Ithaca (N.Y.) Journal March 1, 1865.

COBB, SYLVANUS, JR. (June 5, 1823-July 20, 1887), popular story writer, was born in Waterville, Maine, the oldest of nine children of the Rev. Sylvanus Cobb, a Universalist minister with some literary pretensions, and Eunice (Waite) Cobb. Two of his brothers became noted artists and writers on art and music. His boyhood was spent in Malden, Mass. From early childhood he showed a turn for writing, and was so ardent a grammarian that he succeeded in having himself expelled from high school after a dispute with his teacher on a point of parsing! His father then apprenticed him to a printer (a natural choice under the circumstances), but he ran away and enlisted in the navy at eighteen. He was discharged in 1844 and returned home to work on his father's magazine, the *Christian Freeman.* The next year he married Jane Head.

In 1846, with a brother, he founded a magazine called the *Rechabite,* a temperance organ which freely libeled Clay, Webster, President Polk and other notables of the day; it soon expired. For a while Cobb edited the *New England Washingtonian* and the *Waverley Magazine,* and from 1850 to 1856 he was on the staff of two popular story magazines of the day, the *Flag of Our Union* and the *Pictorial Drawing Room.* In 1856 he formed a connection with the New York *Ledger* which lasted for the remainder of his life. To it, in thirty-one years, he contributed 130 novelettes, 834 short stories, and 2,305 brief sketches! (There already lay behind him 36 published novelettes and 200 short stories.) Some of the novelettes were later published in book form, and he also edited his father's autobiography, in 1867, and added an introduction to it. In his early years with the *Ledger* he lived in Maine, but in 1869 he moved to Hyde Park, Mass., a suburb of Boston, where he died.

As a literary figure Cobb hardly exists; but he is of interest as the first American to apply "mass production" methods to writing. His stories were immensely popular, since they were nicely fitted to the viewpoints and opinions of the semi-literate public at which they were aimed: they were at once moral and sensational, romantic and naïve, pious and sentimental. He had real dramatic skill and a certain knack for rough-and-ready characterization, but his enormous output belongs more in the realm of manufacture than in that of literature.

Principal Works: The King's Talisman, 1851; The Patriot Cruiser, 1859; Ben Hamed, 1864.

About: Cobb, E. W. Memoir of Sylvanus Cobb, Jr.

COCHRANE, ELIZABETH. See SEAMAN, ELIZABETH (COCHRANE)

CODMAN, JOHN (October 16, 1814-April 6, 1900), sea captain-author, was born in Dorchester, Mass., the son of the Rev. John Codman, pastor of the Second Parish in Dorchester, and Mary (Wheelwright) Codman. His father's comfortable home was a stopping place for visiting clergymen and amid their theological discussions and the vivid reminiscences of a sea-faring grandfather, young Codman's adolescent mind was molded. He attended Amherst College for two years from 1832 to 1834, and left to sail the seas in a clipper ship, his nautical life taking him many times to the Orient and providing him with such experiences as commanding a troopship plying between Constantinople and the Crimea during the Crimean War, and serving as captain of a transport carrying stores to Port Royal, S.C., during the early part of the Civil War. After 1864 he engaged in coastwise trade between the United States and South America, and was often accompanied by his wife, Anna G. Day, of New York, whom he married in 1847.

John Codman led a full life and enjoyed many interests made possible by the accumulation of a sizable fortune. When on land, he spent much time in Idaho, where he owned a ranch and many horses, and made many trips between Boston and New York on horseback. He published a number of pamphlets favoring free ships and shipbuilders' materials, as opposed to subsidies for the merchant marine. He wrote five books, including *Sailors' Life and Sailors' Yarns* (1847), his outstanding work. His keen sense of humor and inexhaustible store of sea-yarns made him an enjoyable companion at all times, and earned him a small place in marine literature. He sometimes used the pseudonyms "American Shipmaster" and "Captain Ringbolt."

Principal Works: Sailors' Life and Sailors' Yarns, 1847; Ten Months in Brazil, 1867; The Round Trip, 1879; Winter Sketches From the Saddle, 1888; An American Transport in the Crimean War, 1896.

About: Orcutt, W. D. Good Old Dorchester; Amherst College: Alumni Biographical Record; Boston Transcript April 7, 1900.

CHARLES CARLETON COFFIN

COFFIN, CHARLES CARLETON (July 26, 1823-March 2, 1896), war correspondent and historical novelist, was born at Boscawen, N.H., the son of Thomas Coffin, a farmer, and Hannah (Kilburn) Coffin. He was educated at the village school, with one year at a local academy, and taught himself surveying and civil engineering at night. In 1846 he married Sallie Russell Farmer, and with her brother he installed in Boston, in 1852, the first electric fire-alarm system. Previously he had constructed the time telegraph line between Harvard Observatory and Boston.

He had written occasionally for New Hampshire papers, in the intervals of farming and surveying, and from 1851 most of his time was given to newspaper work. He was first with the Boston *Atlas*, then with the *Journal*, for which he was correspondent from 1854 to 1867. For this paper he traveled all over the United States in 1858, then went to Washington. When the Civil War broke out he became the *Journal's* war correspondent, his dispatches being sent in under the name of "Carleton." He was at the front with the Union Army from the Battle of the Wilderness to the Fall of Richmond. In 1866 the *Journal* sent him to report the Prusso-Austrian War, and he returned by way of the Orient and California.

Meanwhile he had begun a long series of highly popular war, patriotic, and historical stories, many of them for boys—a field in which he has seldom been surpassed. In 1870 he received an honorary M.A. from Amherst. He settled in Boston, where he wrote, lectured widely (he delivered more than 2,000 lectures in all), and was elected to the assembly in 1884, and to the state senate in 1890. His leisure hours were spent as organist at the Shawmut Congregational Church. He died at his home in Brookline, Mass., a suburb of Boston, of apoplexy, two weeks after he had celebrated his golden wedding.

Coffin was one of the best war correspondents of his day: vivid, vigorous, highly patriotic and moral, and fearless and audacious in securing his stories. The same qualities went into his tales for boys, the work for which he is best remembered. It is the rare "juvenile" which survives the half-century mark; yet modern boys find the same pleasure in such books as *The Boys of '76* and the *Drum-Beat* series, as did their fathers before them.

Principal Works: My Days and Nights on the Battle-field, 1864; Following the Flag, 1865; Four Years of Fighting, 1866 (as The Boys of '61, 1881); Winning His Way, 1866; Our New Way Round the World, 1869; The Seat of Empire, 1870; Caleb Krinkle, 1875; The Boys of '76, 1876; The Story of Liberty, 1879; Life of General Garfield, 1880; Old Times in the Colonies, 1880; Building the Nation, 1883; Drum-Beat of the Nation (series) 1887-91; Life of Lincoln, 1892; Daughters of the Revolution, 1892; Dan of Millbrook, 1896.

About: Bullard, F. L. Famous War Correspondents; Griffis, W. E. Charles Carleton Coffin: War Correspondent, Traveler, Author, and Statesman.

COGGESHALL, GEORGE (November 2, 1784-August 6, 1861), sea captain-author, was born in Milford, Conn., the son of William and Eunice (Mallet) Coggeshall. Inheriting a love of the sea from his father, a shipmaster, young Coggeshall made his first long voyage to Cadiz as a cabin-boy and at twenty-five received his first command. He served as captain of the privateers "David Porter" and "Leo" in the War of 1812 and cleverly escaped imprisonment after two days incarceration in Gibraltar when the "Leo" was captured off Lisbon by the frigate "Granicus."

Coggeshall served the sea for almost sixty years but during his leisure found time to keep a journal and to read assiduously. In the seventeen years following his retirement from the sea he wrote a number of books, among which his *History of the American Privateers and Letters-of-Marque* is still of value to students of naval history. His years of loneliness, discipline, and alert thinking produced a vigorous style which at its best may be compared to Defoe's. Coggeshall was married twice: his first wife, Sarah, died in 1822, and his second in 1851.

Principal Works: Voyages to Various Parts of the World, 1851 (second series, 1852); Thirty-Six Voyages to Various Parts of the World, 1858; History of the American Privateers and Letters-of-Marque, 1856; An Historical Sketch of Commerce and Navigation From the Birth of the Saviour Down to the Present Date, 1860.

About: Maclay, E. S. A History of American Privateers; Coggeshall's writings.

COGGESHALL, WILLIAM TURNER (September 6, 1824-August 2, 1867), journalist and miscellaneous writer, was born in Lewistown, Pa., the son of William Coggeshall and Eliza (Gratz) Coggeshall. Nothing is known of his education. In 1842 he went to Akron, Ohio, and from 1844 to 1846 was editor and part owner of a temperance paper there. In 1845 he married Mary Maria Carpenter. In 1847 he moved to Cincinnati, and was connected with various papers—chiefly the *Genius of the West,* which he published from 1853 to 1856. When the Hungarian patriot Louis Kossuth toured America, Coggeshall accompanied him and reported his speeches during part of his trip. From 1856 to 1862 he was literary editor of the *Ohio State Journal,* Columbus, and in 1858 and 1859 also edited the *Ohio Educational Monthly.*

In 1861 he was military secretary to Governor Dennison of Ohio, then for a year was owner and editor of the Springfield, Ohio, *Republic.* In 1865 he edited the *Ohio State Journal,* resigning to become private secretary to Governor Cox. Late in 1866 he was appointed United States minister to Ecuador. By this time Coggeshall was far advanced in tuberculosis; nevertheless, he accepted the appointment, taking his daughter Jessie with him as assistant. His chief service during his few months of incumbency was to secure the right of Protestant burial for foreigners dying in Ecuador. He was almost the first beneficiary of this privilege. He died at Quito, Ecuador, the following August, at less than forty-three. His daughter carried on his office for four months, then herself died on the way home.

When a revolution occurred in Ecuador soon after, Coggeshall's body was disinterred from the Protestant cemetery and stored in a warehouse. Eventually it, together with his daughter's remains, was sent back to Ohio at public expense, and buried in Columbus.

Coggeshall had a worthy and full career, but as a writer he is negligible. His essays consisted of conventional moralizing (though when aroused to controversy he could summon a vigorous style), and his novels are awkward and didactic. He has some claim to reputation, however, as an early advocate of regionalism in American literature.

Principal Works: Signs of the Times (Spirit Rapping) 1851; Easy Warren and His Contemporaries, 1854; Oakshaw: or, The Victim of Avarice, 1855; Need and Availability of the Writing and Spelling Reform, 1857; The Protective Policy in Literature, 1859; Home Hits and Hints, 1859; The Poets and Poetry of the West (anthology) 1860; Stories of Frontier Adventure, 1863; The Journeys of Abraham Lincoln, 1865.

About: Venable, W. H. Beginnings of Literary Culture in the Ohio Valley; Ohio State Journal October 19, 1870.

COLDEN, CADWALLADER (February 7, 1688 [n.s.]-September 28, 1776), statesman and scientist, was born in Ireland, but was the son of a Presbyterian minister, Alexander Colden, of Dunse, Scotland. He received his B.A. at the University of Edinburgh in 1705, and proceeded to London to study medicine. In 1708 or 1710 he emigrated to Philadelphia, where he practised medicine and was also a merchant. On a visit to London in 1715 he met Halley and other famous scientists, and married Alice Christie, a Scotswoman. In 1718 he went to New York, where he became surveyor-general of the colony and master in chancery. From 1720 he was on the governor's council, but had to wait until 1761 before receiving the long-promised post of lieutenant-governor. Until his death he acted frequently as governor during that official's absence in England.

After a portrait by J. S. Copley
CADWALLADER COLDEN

A man of universal mind and attainments, Colden wrote on applied mathematics, history, botany, physics, medicine, and philosophy, and was a regular correspondent of Linnaeus, Franklin, and Dr. Johnson. He first introduced the Linnaean system into American botany, and he was the first to suggest the founding of the American Philosophical Society. He compiled astronomical tables for his own use, and is said to have been the real inventor of stereotyping. He was best known in his own day, however, for his Loyalist sympathies and his opposition to the impending Revolution. In his defence of the Stamp Act, he was burned in effigy and his carriages were destroyed. When the Revolution really started, after the Battle of Lexington, he retired to his estate at Flushing, L.I., where he died.

Of his ten children, one daughter became a distinguished botanist, a son was a noted scholar, and a grandson was a famous lawyer and mayor of New York City.

In science, Colden is remembered for his early essays on anti-Newtonian physics, with his own theory of gravitation; in literature, for his *History of the Five Indian Nations*. Though this is dull and sometimes confused, and taken almost wholly from French sources, it is still an authority.

PRINCIPAL WORKS: The History of the Five Indian Nations of Canada Which Are Dependent on the Province of New York, 1727; An Explication of the First Causes of Action in Matter, 1745 (as The Principles of Action in Matter, 1751); Letters on Smith's History of New York, 1768; Letters and Papers of Cadwallader Colden (New York Historical Society) 1918-23.

ABOUT: Keys, A. M. Cadwallader Colden: A Representative Eighteenth Century Official; Riley, L. W. American Philosophy: The Early Schools.

COLLENS, THOMAS WHARTON (June 23, 1812-November 3, 1879), jurist-author, was born in New Orleans, the son of John Wharton Collens and Marie Louise (de Tabiteau) Collens. Training as a printer led to an interest in writing and publication. Considerably influenced by the opinions of Robert Dale Owen and the philosophy of Fourier, he contributed articles on social problems to the local newspapers. Taking up the study of law, he was admitted to the bar in 1833 and rapidly became a noticeable figure in New Orleans courts. From 1834 to 1842 he was successively clerk and reporter of the state senate, chief deputy clerk of the federal circuit court, and district attorney for the Parish of Orleans. In 1842 he was appointed presiding judge of the city court of New Orleans, and later served as judge of the first district court (1856), and was twice elected judge of the seventh district court (1867-73). Though he was opposed to secession he supported the Confederacy.

Collens, despite his busy legal career, published a number of books. A play *The Martyr Patriots: or, Louisiana in 1769* was produced at the old St. Charles Theatre in 1836. His wife, Amenaide Milbrou, presented him with eight children and left him a widower for many years.

Using French as his daily language, elegant in manner and dress, he typified the gallant Louisiana gentleman of his time. His writings never measured up to the distinction of his brilliant legal record.

PRINCIPAL WORKS: The Martyr Patriots: or, Louisiana in 1769, 1836; The Eden of Labor: or, The Christian Utopia, 1876.

ABOUT: McCaleb, T. The Louisiana Book: Selections From the Literature of the State; The South in the Building of the Nation: Vols. 7 and 11; New Orleans Daily Democrat, New Orleans Times November 9, 1879.

COLTON, CALVIN (September 14, 1789-March 13, 1857), journalist and political economist, was born at Longmeadow, Mass. He was the son of Luther Colton, a major in the American army during the Revolution, and his wife, Thankful (Woolworth) Colton, and was a descendant of Roger Wolcott, governor of Connecticut from 1750-54. Educated at Monson Academy and Yale College, from which he was graduated in 1812, he studied divinity at Andover Theological Seminary and later held Presbyterian pastorates in Le Roy and Batavia, N.Y. Bereft of his wife, Abby North (Raymond) Colton, and hampered by an affection of the voice, he gave up the ministry in 1826, although he returned to it ten years later when he took orders in the Episcopal Church and served the following year as rector of the Church of the Messiah in New York City.

In 1831 he went to England to become correspondent for the New York *Observer*, and during his four years' residence brought out three travel books of unusual distinction, *Manual for Emigrants to America, Tour of the American Lakes . . .*, and *Four Years in Great Britain*.

Returning to America he supported Whig policies by writing pamphlets and a series of political essays under the pseudonym "Junius" (probably in imitation of the earlier and more famous "Junius Letters"). He edited the *True Whig* in Washington during 1842-43, and went the following year to Ashland, Ky., to accept the honor of becoming Henry Clay's official biographer and editor of his works.

In 1852 he went to Trinity College, Hartford, Conn., to occupy the chair of Public Economy, which had been established through favorable reaction to his book *Public Economy for the United States.* Remaining until his death, which occurred in Savannah, Ga., he attracted nation-wide attention by his efforts to mold the protective system. In 1850, at the Smithsonian Institution, he delivered *A Lecture on the Railroad to the Pacific* in which he fervently advocated a transcontinental railroad on the ground that it would unite the human family. Colton's writings, while much respected in their day, have now been eclipsed by more advanced works.

PRINCIPAL WORKS: History and Character of American Revivals in Religion, 1832; Manual for Emigrants to America, 1832; The Americans, 1833; Tour of the American Lakes and Among the Indians of the North-West Territory in 1830, 1833; Church and State in America, 1834; Four Years in Great Britain, 1835; A Lecture on the Railroad to the Pacific, 1850; The Genius and Mission of the Protestant Episcopal Church in the United States, 1853. *Pamphlets*—Abolition a Sedition, 1839; Colonization and Abolition Contrasted, 1839; Reply to Webster, 1840; One Presidential Term, 1840; The Crisis of the Country, 1840; The Junius Tracts, 1843-44; Public Economy for the United States, 1848. *On Henry Clay*—The Life and Times of Henry Clay, 1846; The Last Seven Years of the Life of Henry Clay, 1853; The Private Correspondence of Henry Clay, 1855; The Works of Henry Clay, 1856-57.

ABOUT: Dexter, F. B. Biographical Sketches of Graduates of Yale College; International Monthly Magazine August 1851; Longmeadow Centennial, 1884.

COLTON, WALTER (May 9, 1797-January 22, 1851), theologian, journalist, and miscellaneous writer, was born in Rutland County, Vt. He was the son of Deacon Walter Colton, a poor weaver, and Thankful (Cobb) Colton, and a brother of Gardner Quincy Colton, pioneer anaesthetist. He grew up in Georgia, a small village overlooking Lake Champlain, and at an early age was apprenticed to an uncle who was a Hartford cabinet-maker. After joining the church in his nineteenth year, he prepared for college and the ministry at the Hartford Grammar School. Between 1818 and 1822 he attended Yale, afteward studying divinity at Andover Theological Seminary. While there, he wrote a sacred drama, "News Carrier's Address," which won a two-hundred dollar prize from a Boston newspaper. After graduation in 1825, he accepted the chair of moral philosophy and belles-lettres in the Scientific and Military Academy at Middletown, Conn., and also served the students as chaplain. Several articles published in the Middletown *Gazette* led to the editorship of the *American Spectator and Washington City Chronicle*, and during this time Colton occasionally preached at the church attended by Andrew Jackson. Later rewarded by the President's friendship, he was often a guest at the White House, and on January 29, 1831, was given a naval chaplaincy. A three-year cruise in the "Constellation," with Commodore George C. Read, resulted in Colton's first important publications, *Ship and Shore: or, Leaves From the Journal of a Cruise on the Levant* (1835), and *A Visit to Constantinople and Athens* (1836). He was ordered to the naval station at Charlestown, Mass., and for a brief time in 1837 edited the *Colonization Herald*, Washington, D.C. Ill health prevented him from assuming the duties of chaplain and historiographer of the South Sea Surveying and Exploring Squadron to which he was appointed in the same year. In 1838 he went to the naval station at Philadelphia as chaplain and also became co-editor of the *Independent North American.* In 1850 he published *Deck and Port: or, Incidents of a Cruise in the United States Frigate "Congress" to California*, an account of a long cruise in the Pacific Squadron flagship. Meanwhile, in 1846 he was appointed alcade, or chief judge, of Monterey and the neighboring territory, and took a prominent part in early California life by establishing the first California newspaper, the *Californian*, and by building the first school house. In a letter to the Philadelphia *North American and United States Gazette*, he made the first public announcement of the discovery of gold in Sacramento Valley. He died in Philadelphia a year after publication of *Three Years in California: 1846-1849* (1850), a valuable and interesting book. His wife was Cornelia B. Colton, a distant relative, of Philadelphia. Colton's writings hold a secure place in American historical records.

Principal Works: Ship and Shore: or, Leaves From the Journal of a Cruise to the Levant, 1835; A Visit to Constantinople and Athens, 1836; Deck and Port: or, Incidents of a Cruise in the United States Frigate "Congress" to California, 1850; Three Years in California: 1846-1849, 1850; The Sea and the Sailor: Notes on France and Italy and Other Literary Remains, 1851.

About: Colton, W. The Sea and the Sailor; North American and United States Gazette January 23, 1851; Survey April 5, 1913.

CONE, ORELLO (November 16, 1835-June 23, 1905), clergyman, educator, and New Testament commentator, was born in Lincklaen, Chenango County, N.Y., the son of Daniel Newton and Emily (Sadd) Cone. After attending the Academy at New Woodstock, and Cazenovia Seminary in Madison County, N.Y., he taught in private schools and subjected himself to a rigid course of self-instruction. He was both student and teacher at St. Paul's College at Palmyra, Mo., during 1858-61, and in 1864 became a Universalist minister. While holding the pastorate of the Universalist Church of Little Falls, N.Y., he married Mariamne Pepper, on October 4, 1864.

An appointment to the professorship of Biblical Languages and Literature in the Theological School of St. Lawrence University, Canton, N.Y., led to the scholarly pursuits upon which his later reputation was built. He was an active contributor to the *Universalist Quarterly* and edited a progressive volume—*Essays Doctrinal and Practical by Fifteen Clergymen* (1889).

Between the years 1880 and 1897 he served as president and professor of philosophical subjects at Buchtel College, Akron, Ohio (now the Municipal University of Akron). During this time he occupied himself with vast New Testament research in connection with the series of books which increased his reputation as critic and scholar. Among these volumes were *Gospel Criticism and Historical Christianity* and *The Gospel and its Earliest Interpretations*. His well-known and exhaustive monograph, *Paul: The Man, the Missionary, and the Teacher*, was published in 1898 following a year's study in Berlin, Paris, and London.

In the last seven years of his life, he accomplished a prodigious amount of work, in preaching, writing, and teaching. Before taking the Richardson Professorship of Biblical Theology, at the Theological School of St. Lawrence University, he held a brief pastorate at the Unitarian Church of Lawrence, Kans., in 1898-99.

In a day of religious intolerance, Cone's liberal views were often attacked but his unshakeable faith in his own ability to interpret the Scripture admirably weathered the storms of criticism and elevated him to a secure place among nineteenth century New Testament scholars.

Principal Works: Essays Doctrinal and Practical by Fifteen Clergymen, 1889; Gospel Criticism and Historical Christianity, 1891; The Gospel and Its Earliest Interpretations, 1893; Paul: The Man, the Missionary, and the Teacher, 1898; Evolution and Theology and Other Essays, 1900; Rich and Poor in the New Testament, 1902.

About: Cone, W. W. Some Account of the Cone Family in America; Forbes, H. P. The Necrology of St. Lawrence University; Universalist Leader July 1, 1905.

CONGDON, CHARLES TABER (April 7, 1821-January 18, 1891), editor and poet, was born in New Bedford, Mass., the son of Benjamin Taber Congdon and Deborah (Hartt) Congdon, and a relative of William Cullen Bryant. While carrying papers for the New Bedford *Courier*, a weekly newspaper edited by his father, he composed his first poem, "Ode to Commerce." After studying at the village schools, he attended Brown University for three years without graduating (though the honorary degree of M.A. was conferred upon him in 1879). Then followed a period when he served on newspapers in New Bedford and Providence. Meanwhile he married Charlotte M. Bayliss of his native town, who died at the birth of their only child.

In 1854 he went to Boston to edit the *Atlas*, New England's leading Whig organ, remaining until Horace Greeley invited him to join the staff of the New York *Tribune* in 1857. Becoming known as Greeley's most valuable assistant, he contributed valuable editorials to the paper, which were later published as *"Tribune" Essays* in 1869. His newspaper associates said that "Congdon wrote from the head, while Greeley wrote from the heart." His writings appeared in the leading periodicals—*Vanity Fair*, edited by Artemus Ward, *The North American Review*, and the *Knickerbocker Magazine*.

Using the pseudonym "Paul Potter," he acted as New York correspondent of the *Boston Courier*.

Shortly after leaving college in 1840, he published a volume of poetry with the high-flown title *Flowers Plucked by a Traveler on the Journey of Life*, and in 1862 brought out *The Warning of War*, a poem which attracted wide attention. He died of heart failure in the New York hotel where he made his home. Although Congdon was gifted with keen editorial judgment and a powerful style, his words were of no lasting literary value.

PRINCIPAL WORKS: Flowers Plucked by a Traveler on the Journey of Life, 1840; The Warning of War, 1862; "Tribune" Essays, 1869.

ABOUT: Congdon, C. T. Reminiscences of a Journalist; Ellis, L. B. History of New Bedford and Its Vicinity; New York Tribune January 19, 1891.

CONRAD, ROBERT TAYLOR (June 10 1810-June 27, 1858), jurist and dramatist, was born in Philadelphia, the son of John and Eliza Conrad. His father was a publisher, who issued the works (among others) of Joel Barlow and Charles Brockden Brown. Conrad was trained for the law, and admitted to the bar in 1831. His literary interests, however, were strong, and from 1831 to 1834 he was on the staff of the *Daily Commercial Intelligencer*, which later became the Philadelphia *Gazette*. In his spare time he wrote poems and plays, and his first play, *Conrad: King of Naples*, was produced in 1832.

In 1834 he became city recorder, and in 1838 judge of the court of criminal sessions. His literary career continued, paralleling his judicial life, and in 1843 he was chairman of the committee which awarded Poe the prize of $100 for *The Gold Bug*. In 1845 he became associate editor of the *North American*, and in 1848 assistant editor of *Graham's Magazine*. At this time he also edited and revised *Biography of the Signers of the Declaration of Independence*, by John Sanderson and others. In 1854 he was elected the first mayor of "Greater Philadelphia," after the city was consolidated with the county, and in 1856 and 1857 he was judge of the court of quarter sessions. He still wrote plays: *Aylmere*, his best known play under its later title of *Jack Cade*, had been produced as early as 1835, but he continued to rewrite it under various titles until 1841. A play of his later years, *The Heretic*, was produced after his death, in 1863, but has now totally disappeared.

Conrad's reputation was strictly of his own time, when he was rated by some as just a little below Shakespeare. Actually, he was a man of narrow views, a "Know-Nothing" (the party of the 'fifties which approximated the latter-day Ku Klux Klan), and an advocate of "Blue Sunday" and other Puritanical restrictions; a florid orator in the worst style of his era; and a stilted, bombastic writer.

PRINCIPAL WORKS: Aylmere: or, The Bondman of Kent; and Other Poems, 1852; Devotional Poems, 1862.

ABOUT: Conrad, R. T. Devotional Poems (see Introduction by G. H. Boker); Philadelphia Public Ledger June 28, 1858.

CONWAY, MONCURE DANIEL (March 17, 1832-November 15, 1907), biographer and essayist, was born near Falmouth, Va., the son of Walker Peyton Conway and Margaret (Daniel) Conway. It was a good Virginia family, the father being a member of the state legislature, the mother the granddaughter of a signer of the Declaration of Independence. They were strict and fanatical Methodists, but large slave-owners as well. Conway was educated at Fredericksburg Academy, then entered Dickinson College (Carlisle, Pa.) as a sophomore at fifteen, becoming a junior in four months. He was graduated in 1849. It is interesting that 55 years later, when Conway was a Freethinker, this Methodist College named a new building Conway Hall, in exchange for $50,000 from Andrew Carnegie, also a Rationalist and Conway's

Collection of Frederick H. Meserve
MONCURE DANIEL CONWAY

friend! It also conferred an L.H.D. degree on its distinguished graduate.

At this time Conway was a "converted Methodist," and also an ardent advocate of slavery. Both views underwent a change under the influence of Emerson, Carlyle, and Coleridge. He studied law for a while in Warrenton, Va., then joined the Baltimore Methodist Conference and served for two years as a Methodist minister in Virginia. Then, against his family's wishes, he entered the Harvard Divinity School, and was graduated in 1854. He came out of Harvard an outspoken abolitionist, and when he returned home the neighbors drove him away with violence because he had befriended a fugitive slave. He became pastor of the Unitarian Church in Washington, D.C., but was dismissed in 1856 after an anti-slavery sermon. He was called to the First Congregational Church of Cincinnati, and in 1858 he married Ellen Davis Dana of that city, who died in 1897. Some of his father's slaves, who escaped to Ohio, he settled at Yellow Springs, where their descendants still live. He had begun to write for the *Atlantic Monthly*, and in 1860 edited a literary magazine, namesake of the famous *Dial*, to which Emerson and W. D. Howells contributed. In 1862 he moved to Concord, Mass., and edited the *Commonwealth*, a literary and anti-slavery paper of Boston.

In 1863 Conway went to England to lecture on behalf of the North in the Civil War; he was made minister of South Place Chapel, Finsbury, London, which from Unitarian beginnings had become (and still is) practically a Freethought forum, and he remained until 1884. While in England he contributed to *Fraser's Magazine* and the *Fortnightly Review*, and acted as correspondent for New York and Cincinnati papers. Gradually he had become an active Freethinker, was a regular delegate to the International Congress of Freethinkers, and later (after his life of Paine had brought him his greatest celebrity) was president of the New York Freethinkers' Society. He became also a strong advocate of a unicameral government, without a senate or a president, on the plan of Louis Blanc, the French radical economist. He returned to America in 1884, but visited Europe frequently, and from 1892 to 1897 was again minister of South Place Chapel. He died in Paris just as he was about to return to his home in New York.

Besides his original writings, Conway edited the works of Thomas Paine, and prepared an anthology of sacred literature. He was a sound and careful biographer, but his style, though lucid, was rather pedestrian. His work was very popular in his lifetime, but all that is likely to remain of it is his authoritative biography of Paine. His autobiography, however, is valuable for its glimpses of all the great of his day in England and America, most of whom were his close personal acquaintances.

Principal Works: Tracts for Today, 1858; The Rejected Stone, 1861; The Golden Hour, 1862; The Earthward Pilgrimage, 1870; Republican Superstitions, 1872; Idols and Ideals, 1877; Demonology and Devil-lore, 1879; A Necklace of Stories, 1880; The Wandering Jew and the Pound of Flesh, 1881; Thomas Carlyle, 1881; Emerson at Home and Abroad, 1882; Pine and Palm, 1887; Omitted Chapters of History, 1888; George Washington and Mt. Vernon, 1889; Life of Nathaniel Hawthorne, 1890; Prisons of Air, 1891; Life of Thomas Paine, 1892; Centenary History of South Place Chapel, 1895; Solomon and Solomonic Literature, 1899; Autobiography, Memories, and Experiences, 1904; Addresses and Reprints, 1909.

About: Conway, M. D. Autobiography; Macdonald, G. E. Fifty Years of Freethought; Walker, E. C. A Sketch and an Appreciation of Moncure D. Conway; Harper's Weekly September 25, 1875.

COOK, CLARENCE CHATHAM (September 8, 1828-June 2, 1900), art critic, was born in Dorchester, Mass., the son of Zebedee Cook and Caroline (Tuttle) Cook. He received his B.A. at Harvard in 1849, and studied architecture with his brother-in-law in Newburgh, N.Y. He did not become an architect, however, but was a teacher of art until he gradually made a place for himself as a journalist and art critic. In 1853 he married Louisa (DeWindt) Whittemore, widow, a descendant of John Adams. From 1863 to 1869 he conducted a column of art criticism in the New York *Tribune*, under Horace Greeley; in 1869 Greeley sent him to Paris as art correspondent, but the Franco-Prussian War broke out, and after a few months in Italy he returned to New York. He left the *Tribune* after Greeley's death because his space was cut down by the new editor. Besides his original books, he translated Viardot's *Wonders of Sculpture* (1873), adding a chapter on American sculpture; edited the American edition of Lübke's *History of Art* (1878); and supplied the text for Dürer's drawings of the *Life of the Virgin* (1874). For years he was involved in a controversy with the Metropolitan Museum of Art over the authenticity of the Cypriote antiquities; unfortunately he was not an archaeologist and was proved to be in the wrong. From 1884 to 1892 he edited the *Studio*. He died at Fishkill Landing, N.Y., his home during his later years.

Cook was a critic dreaded by most artists—slashing, scathing, and brutal in his comments. He could, however, be graceful and urbane when he was not enraged, and personally he was charming. His cruel and direct attacks on individual artists were actuated by his love of art; he was an early friend of the Impressionists, and one of the first to introduce etching as a means of illustration. He was, all in all, a brilliant pioneer in American art criticism.

Principal Works: The New York Central Park, 1869; The House Beautiful, 1878; What Shall We Do With Our Walls? 1881; Art and Artists of Our Time, 1888.

About: International Studio November 1900; New York Tribune June 3, 1900.

COOK, FLAVIUS JOSEPHUS (Joseph Cook) (January 26, 1838-June 24, 1901), author-lecturer, was born on a farm near Ticonderoga, N.Y., the son of William Henry Cook and Merett (Lamb) Cook. He attended the local schools and further prepared himself for Phillips Academy, Andover, by reading most of the available books in his small community. Entering Yale in 1858 he remained until ill health caused him to leave in 1861. Later transferring to Harvard, he was graduated with honors in 1865, and during the following four years attended Andover Theological Seminary. After two years preaching near Boston and two years of European travel and study at German universities, he settled in Boston, and soon packed the Tremont Temple by his Monday noon prayer-meetings, which were later known as the "Monday Lectures." These intellectual-religious addresses remained popular for twenty years, were delivered in many other states, published in newspaper and book form, and translated into many languages. Cook, orthodox in his own views, nevertheless clarified and explained the new thinking—the relation of science to religion—in a fluent, well-informed manner. Some of his statements were severely attacked by writers who referred to his attitude as "Spread Eagle Philosophy," or "Theological Charlatanism."

A man of impressive stature, with a leonine head of red hair, he was a sensationalist with an exaggerated sense of his own importance, and although his powerful, convincing voice frequently thundered erroneous statements, he was often right and in the main deserved his popularity Lyman Abbott said of him: "Mr. Cook is an electrical machine. He is a surcharged thundercloud. He sparkles all over. His lectures are skies with vivid flashes, sweeping rain, and loud thunder."

Cook lectured in Europe and the Far East with considerable success and was attempting a second tour in 1895 when he suffered a stroke from which he never fully recovered, although he delivered several lectures before his death. He married Georgiana Hemingway of New Haven, Conn., in 1887. Early in his career he dropped "Flavius Josephus" for the less pretentious "Joseph" by which he was known. Of his eleven published lectures, his *Biology* received the greatest acclaim. It was more as lecturer than as writer that he made his reputation.

Principal Work: Biology, 1877; Transcendentalism, 1877; Orthodoxy, 1877; Conscience, 1878; Heredity, 1878; Marriage, 1878; Labor, 1879; Socialism, 1880; Occident, 1884; Orient, 1886; Current Religious Perils, 1888.

About: Congregationalist July 6, 1901; Zion's Herald June 21, 1911; New York Tribune June 26, 1901.

COOK, JOSEPH. See COOK, FLAVIUS JOSEPHUS

COOKE, JOHN ESTEN (November 3, 1830-September 27, 1886), novelist and historian, was born near Winchester, Va., of a distinguished family. His father, John Rogers Cooke, was a noted lawyer; his mother, Maria (Pendleton) Cooke, was descended from Edmund Pendleton, the Revolutionary patriot; and his uncle, Philip St. George Cooke [*q.v.*], was a brigadier-general in the United States Army. Philip Pendleton Cooke [*q.v.*], the author, was an older brother.

John Esten Cooke was reared near Frederick, in the Valley of Virginia, until the family house burnt down in 1839 and they moved to Richmond. He was educated at Charlestown Academy and by a private tutor, but left school at sixteen and studied law in his father's office. His heart, however, was all in writing, and after *Harper's Magazine* and the *Southern Literary Messenger* accepted his early stories he decided on a literary career. An ardent Secessionist, he served in the Confederate Army throughout the Civil War, on the staff of his nephew-by-marriage, General J. E. B. Stuart. After Stuart's death, he was with Lee at Appomattox. He rose from private to the rank of captain, but was known always as "Major Cooke," a promotion recommended by Stuart but not confirmed by the Confederate Senate. After the war he returned on parole to the Valley region of Virginia, married Mary Francis Page in 1867 (a markedly happy marriage till her death in 1878), and settled in "The Briers," in Clarke County, his home henceforth. All

JOHN ESTEN COOKE

his three children became distinguished—his daughter Susan as an educator, one son as a physician, the other as a naval officer. He died of typhoid fever.

Cooke was at once the last of the disciples of Cooper, of the romantic historians of America's past, and the first of the later school (typified by Thomas Nelson Page) of idealizers of the pre-Civil War South. He wrote too much for his own reputation, and he realized before he died that literary history had passed him by—accepting the fact with characteristic kindly humor. He was a poetic romanticist, whose keen sense of drama is overweighed by a rather cloying charm, but his books are well-grounded; he knew his colonial and Revolutionary history, and he knew every foot and every inhabitant of the valley which is the background of most of his novels. This knowledge makes his history of Virginia probably his most lasting work. After his wife died, a deeper note came into his writing, but it lost the dashing spirit which had been one of its chief attractions. His war experiences served him as material for most of his later novels, as well as for most of his historical works. He is old-fashioned and out-moded, but his best novels, such as *The Virginia Comedians* and its sequel, *Henry St. John: Gentleman,* or *Surry of Eagle's Nest* and its sequel, *Mohun,* in which Lee is one of the characters, still are readable and engaging. What Richard Henry Stoddard wrote of him at his death, intended as unalloyed compliment, is today at once a tribute and an indictment: "His books have the charm of elegant comedy, the pathos of pastoral tragedy, sparkles of wit, flashes of humor, and everywhere the amenities of high breeding."

PRINCIPAL WORKS: *Novels*—Leather Stocking and Silk, 1854; The Virginia Comedians, 1854; Ellie, 1855; The Last of the Foresters, 1856; Henry St. John: Gentleman, 1859; Surry of Eagle's Nest, 1866; Mohun, 1868; Fairfax, 1868; Hilt to Hilt, 1869; The Heir of Gaymount, 1870; Dr. Paul Vandike, 1872; Her Majesty the Queen, 1873; Pretty Mrs. Gaston and Other Stories, 1874; Canolles, 1877; Stories of the Old Dominion, 1879; The Maurice Mystery, 1885; My Lady Pocahontas, 1885. *History and Biography*—The Youth of Jefferson, 1854; Stonewall Jackson, 1863; Wearing of the Gray, 1867; Hammer and Rapier, 1870; Life of General Robert E. Lee, 1871; Life of Samuel J. Tilden, 1876; Virginia: A History of the People, 1883.

ABOUT: Beaty, J. O. John Esten Cooke: Virginian; Critic October 16, 1886; Harper's Weekly October 9, 1886.

COOKE, PHILIP PENDLETON (October 26, 1816-January 20, 1850), poet and story writer, was born near Martinsburg, Va. (now W.Va.), the son of John Rogers Cooke, a prominent attorney, and Maria (Pendleton) Cooke. The whole family was distinguished; Edmund Pendleton, the Revolutionary patriot, was his great-uncle; Gen. Philip St. George Cooke [*q.v.*] was his uncle; and his much younger brother, John Esten Cooke [*q.v.*], became a well known novelist. Philip Pendleton Cooke grew up on various of the family plantations near Winchester and in the beautiful Shenandoah Valley. After preparation at the Martinsburg Academy, he was graduated from the College of New Jersey (Princeton) in 1834 at only eighteen and after three years of college; this, however, argues more for the laxity of the curriculum than for his scholarship, for he spent more time reading poetry than in study.

He then read law with his father, and was admitted to the bar in 1836, when not yet twenty. The next year he married Willie Anne Corbin Taylor Burwell (who, however, employed only the second and last of her names). He had written poetry from his college days, and his first verses appeared in the *Knickerbocker Magazine* before he was graduated. Though he wrote constantly, and had serials running frequently in *Graham's,* the *Southern Literary Messenger,* and the *Gentleman's Magazine* (then under the editorship of Poe), Cooke can hardly be considered a professional writer. He was a Southern gentleman of the old school, who practiced law in a desultory way; was a popular figure in society, where his handsome face with its

PHILIP PENDLETON COOKE

bright hazel eyes and curly chestnut hair, his brilliant conversation, and his convivial spirit made him a favorite; and put much of his energy into hunting, which was always his passion. In 1845 he moved to a plantation near Ashby's Gap, Va., where he became known to all the neighborhood as "the Nimrod of the Shenandoah." Keenly alive to beauty, and a true if superficial nature-lover, his aesthetic appreciation bubbled over in poems which have grace and charm but are quite conventional in form. In 1847, at his cousin's suggestion, he published a group of these—ostensibly translations from Froissart but actually original compositions written after Froissart's stories. This was his only published volume, though the unfinished historical novel, *The Chevalier Merlin,* which was running in the *Southern Literary Messenger* at the time of his death, and which Poe greatly admired, was intended to be published in book form when completed.

Cooke died at only thirty-three of tuberculosis, and there attaches to him the pathos of all talent and charm that vanish early. But it is only local patriotism that keeps his name alive today. His best known poem was "Florence Vane," which was set to music and became a parlor favorite, and was translated into several languages. It is excessively sentimental, in the standardized mode of "keepsake" and "annual" verse. His stories were better, being vivid bits of whimsy and satire, with the true romantic touch; but since they were uncollected, they died with him.

Principal Work: Froissart Ballads and Other Poems, 1837.

About: Beaty, J. O. John Esten Cooke: Virginian; Painter, F. V. N. Library of Southern Literature; Southern Literary Messenger October 1851, June 1858.

COOKE, PHILIP ST. GEORGE (June 13, 1809-March 20, 1895), military writer, was born at Leesburg, Va., the son of Dr. Stephen Cooke, an officer in the American Revolution, and Catherine (Esten) Cooke, of English birth. The "Philip" was bestowed upon him at West Point; he was originally named St. George in honor of his mother's country. Two of his brothers were eminent lawyers; two of his nephews (John Esten Cooke and Philip Pendleton Cooke [*qq.v.*]) became well known writers.

He was graduated from West Point in 1827 and commissioned to the 6th Infantry at various Western stations. In 1832 he was in the Black Hawk War. The next year he became first lieutenant of the 1st Dragoons (later the 1st Cavalry), in 1835 captain. For the next ten years he was engaged in Indian fighting and in leading and protecting parties of immigrants and traders en route to Arkansas, Texas, and New Mexico. In the Mexican War he was with General Kearny's Western army, which took over New Mexico (including the present Arizona) and California from Mexican rule. By 1858 he was a colonel, having previously been commissioned major and lieutenant-colonel. He spent 1860 in Europe, observing the war between the Central Powers and Italy. He returned to take charge of a Utah post. When the Civil War broke out, although his brother and his son were Confederate officers, and his daughter had married the famous Confederate general, J. E. B. Stuart, Cooke chose to remain with his country rather than his state. He was in command of the Army of the Potomac during the Peninsular Campaign, and thereafter served as recruiting officer and court martial judge. In 1861 he had been made a brigadier general, in 1865 a major general. After the war he commanded successively the departments of the Platte, Cumberland, and the Lakes, until he retired in 1873. With his wife, who had been Rachel Hertzog, a Philadelphia Jewess, he moved to Detroit, where he died at nearly 86.

Cooke's only two non-technical books are partly autobiographical. His *Conquest of New Mexico and California* is valuable as first-hand history, being for the most part taken from his diary written at the time.

PRINCIPAL WORKS: Scenes and Adventures in the Army, 1857; Cavalry Tactics, 1861; The Conquest of New Mexico and California, 1878.

ABOUT: Cooke, P. St. G. Scenes and Adventures in the Army; Golder, F. A. March of the Mormon Battalion.

COOKE, ROSE (TERRY) (February 17, 1837-July 18, 1892), poet and story writer, was born in West Hartford, Conn., the daughter of Henry Wadsworth Terry, a Congressman, and Anne (Hurlbut) Terry. The family was wealthy, the father's father being a bank president, the mother's father a prosperous shipbuilder. As a small child illness kept her from active play; hence she could read at three, and was her father's companion when he visited his constituents. Already she was storing up pictures of New England scenes and people. In 1833 the family moved to Hartford, where Rose learned to be an accomplished housekeeper. She was graduated from the Hartford Female Seminary in 1843, and for several years she taught in schools in Hartford and Burlington, N.J., and as a governess. She returned home to rear the children of her sister, who had died.

Though she wrote from earliest youth, literature always had to take second place behind her household cares. Much of her time also was given to church work; she was a devout Presbyterian. But her poems, which antedated her stories, gradually made their way into print, first through Charles A. Dana's publication of them in the New York *Tribune*. Her New England stories, which appeared mostly in *Harper's* and the *Atlantic Monthly*, were not collected into volumes until some time after her marriage. In 1873, having reared her sister's family, she was married to Rollin Hillyer Cooke, an iron manufacturer, and went with him to live in Winsted, Conn. In 1887 they moved to Pittsfield, Mass. In 1889 she was very ill with pneumonia, and remained an invalid thereafter, never writing again. Repeated attacks of influenza finally caused her death three years later.

Mrs. Cooke's one novel was her least successful work. Her poems are unstereotyped and show a sensitive feeling for nature and deep religious feeling. But she will be remembered, if at all, for her stories of New England country life, forerunners of Mary Wilkins Freeman's in the same *genre*. They are marked by freshness and spontaneity, and instinct with a keen observant humor. Tall, dark, with deepset eyes and high forehead, Mrs. Terry was rather striking than beautiful. Her nature was as vivid and direct as her appearance.

ROSE TERRY COOKE

She is one of the first of American regional realists, and deserves a better fate than the oblivion which is her lot today. Her stories have historical as well as literary interest; in them a vanished New England countryside lives again. She had a good eye for character, and though perhaps she did not see very far beneath the surface, and took outward placidity for inward content, her intention at least was realistic, and to a considerable extent she accomplished it. She wrote few poems after she turned to fiction, but in later years she published a reprint of the former volume together with all the verse she had composed after 1860.

PRINCIPAL WORKS: Poems, 1860; Happy Dodd: or, She Hath Done What She Could, 1878; Somebody's Neighbors, 1881; Root-Bound and Other Sketches, 1885; The Sphinx's Children and Other People's, 1886; No: A Story for Boys, 1886; Complete Poems, 1888; Steadfast (novel) 1889; Huckleberries Gathered From the New England Hills, 1891.

ABOUT: Pattee, F. L. The Development of the American Short Story; Critic July 23, 1892; Boston Herald July 20, 1892; Boston Transcript July 19, 1892.

COOLBRITH, INA DONNA (March 10, 1842-February 29, 1928), poet, was born near Springfield, Ill. Her parents' given names are not known, but they were from New England. Her father died when she was an infant, and her mother married William Pickett, a St. Louis newspaper man. About 1852 the family emigrated to California, settling first in Plumas County, then in Los Angeles, which was hardly more than a sleepy *pueblo*. The child's only education was in the negligible public schools of the town, but she was an omnivorous reader. In 1865 the Picketts moved again to San Francisco, her home thenceforth. She became a teacher until 1868, when Bret Harte made her co-editor of his recently founded *Overland Monthly.* Miss Coolbrith (who never married), Harte, and Charles Warren Stoddard were familiarly known as "the Golden Gate Trinity"; they formed the nucleus of the interesting literary group which grew up in San Francisco immediately after the Civil War. It was she who gave to Cincinnatus Heine Miller the name of "Joaquin."

In those more lenient days Miss Coolbrith could become not only a teacher without training, but also a librarian. From 1874 to 1893 she was librarian of the Oakland Free Library; from 1897 to 1899 (after four years of illness), of the San Francisco Mercantile Library, and from 1899 to the famous San Francisco fire of 1906, of the Bohemian Club Library. She was the only woman member this famous club of artists, musicians, and writers ever had—the only woman permitted to enter its doors except on New Year's Eve. The fire destroyed the library with its treasures, and also Miss Coolbrith's own possessions, including her manuscripts. She had already, however, published the three volumes of verse which were all she ever produced.

In 1915, at the Panama Pacific International Exposition, Miss Coolbrith convened a World Congress of Authors, and herself was made poet laureate of California by the governor and the legislature. As she grew old she became a sort of living memorial of a great period of the past, the only survivor of the days of Harte, Twain, and Stevenson, and her salons were eagerly attended. Her simple and spontaneous verse had a national as well as a local reputation, much of it appearing in *Scribner's* and the *Century.* She had some lyrical ability and power of sympathetic expression, but she was distinctly a minor regional poet.

INA DONNA COOLBRITH
1895

PRINCIPAL WORKS: A Perfect Day and Other Poems, 1881; The Singer of the Sea, 1894; Songs From the Golden Gate, 1895.

ABOUT: Library Journal March 15, 1928; Overland Monthly November 1915, November 1920, April 1928; Sunset Magazine January 1915; New York Times March 1, 1928; Oakland, Cal., Tribune February 29, 1928.

"COOLIDGE, SUSAN." See WOOLSEY, SARAH CHAUNCY

COOMBE, THOMAS (October 21, 1747-August 15, 1822), clergyman and poet, was born in Philadelphia, and was graduated from the College of Philadelphia (later the University of Pennsylvania) in 1766. While still in college, he translated the Latin poems of John Beveridge, published in Beveridge's *Epistolae Familiares* (1765). He studied divinity, and in 1768 went to England to be ordained, there being at that time no provision for Episcopal ordination in America, since there were no bishops. While there he served as chaplain to the Marquis of Rockingham.

He returned to Philadelphia in 1772, and became assistant rector of the famous Christ's Church in that city, later being transferred to St. Peter's. At that time he was an American patriot whose sermon in 1775 in favor of the Continental Congress appeared in three editions within a single year. When the Declaration of Independence was signed, however, he began to worry about his ordination oath in the event of a revolution, retracted his previous views, and proclaimed himself a Loyalist. With other Tories, he was ordered banished to Staunton, Va., but on the plea of his ill health the deportation order was not carried out, and he left unmolested for England.

There he became chaplain to the Earl of Carlisle, and in 1794 was appointed prebendary of Canterbury and chaplain-in-ordinary to George III. He became a member of the celebrated literary and artistic group that included David Garrick, Sir Joshua Reynolds, and Oliver Goldsmith. For Goldsmith he had a special admiration, and dedicated to him his only memorable work, *The Peasant of Auburn.* Auburn was, of course, the name of Goldsmith's "deserted village," and Coombe's lugubrious verses on the disasters befalling an emigrant to America were intended to be a continuation of Goldsmith's poem.

Coombe received an honorary D.D. from the University of Dublin in 1781. He never returned to America, but died in London.

PRINCIPAL WORK: The Peasant of Auburn: or, The Emigrant, 1783.

ABOUT: Anderson, J. S. M. History of the Church of England in the Colonies . . . of the British Empire; Gentleman's Magazine August 1822.

COOPER, JAMES FENIMORE (September 15, 1789-September 14, 1851), novelist, was born in Burlington, N.J., the eleventh child of William Cooper and Elizabeth (Fenimore) Cooper. The father later became a judge and a member of the New York State legislature. When the child was barely a year old, William Cooper moved his family into what was then the wilderness of Otsego Lake, N.Y., where he took up large land holdings, which grew into the little town of Cooperstown. James Cooper, therefore, from his earliest childhood was surrounded by the woods and intimately acquainted with the Indians who figured so largely in the most famous of his novels. (Incidentally, until after his writing days had begun, he was known simply as James or James Kent Cooper. After his father's death, he tried to have his name legally changed to Fenimore, so as to inherit some property from his mother's family. This was refused, but he wrote his name thereafter James Fenimore Cooper, at first with a hyphen between the two names.)

From the tuition of his older sister, a beautiful and brilliant girl who died young, Cooper was sent to Albany as a private student to the Rev. Thomas Ellison, an English clergyman. In 1802 he became a student at Yale. There he remained only two years, when he was expelled because of some boyish prank. He returned to Cooperstown, and after two years of deliberation, his father decided that the new United States Navy was the best place for his ebullient and by no means bookish son. In preparation, he was signed on as a seaman in a sailing vessel bound from Maine to England. A year later, on his return, he received his commission in the Navy.

After two years, Cooper was assigned to a group of naval officers who were establishing a fresh-water navy in the Great Lakes. He chafed under the dullness of this humdrum assignment, but so long as his father lived there was no means for his livelihood otherwise. Two important events changed his career completely. The first was his father's death at the hand of a political opponent, and his inheritance, together with his brothers', of a large estate, unfortunately soon dissipated by all of them; the second was his marriage on January 1, 1811 to Susan De Lancey.

Cooper was only 21 and his bride was only 18, but she had a will of her own. She had no intention of possessing an absentee husband. The following May he resigned from the Navy. Moreover, after a few months she saw to it that they settled down on a farm of her own at Scarsdale, N.Y. For several years, while their four daughters and the first of their two sons were born (he died in infancy), Cooper settled down as a country squire, his chief outside interest being the part ownership of a whaling boat to Patagonia.

Then came the trifling incident which made of him an author. In 1819, reading aloud to his wife from a new English novel, he exclaimed "I could write you a better book myself." Since he had always disliked writing even letters, his wife laughed at him. Out of obstinacy, he finished the book, which appeared anonymously in 1820 as *Precaution. Precaution* was merely a half humorous imitation of the more lady-

From a daguerreotype by M. B. Brady
JAMES FENIMORE COOPER

like English novel of the period, but Cooper had tasted blood. The next year he produced, again anonymously, what Henry Walcott Boynton calls "the first living American novel," *The Spy*.

By the time Cooper left America in 1826, for his seven years' sojourn abroad, he was the author of six novels and engaged on the seventh. Before this period, however, there were four years spent in New York City, where he became acquainted with the literati of the period and was the mainspring of an informal club of writers and artists known as the Bread and Cheese Club. This was probably the happiest period of Cooper's life. It was ended by the necessity of educating his four daughters in all the accomplishments that he considered desirable. He decided to take his family to France. Before leaving he was appointed United States Consul at Lyons, though he had no intention of being a resident official, and in fact seems never to have visited the town. The first two of his seven years were spent for the most part in England where he became acquainted with Sir Walter Scott—better acquainted, he felt, than Lockhart was willing to acknowledge in his father-in-law's biography. In Paris, where most of his time was spent, his great friend was Lafayette. Unfortunately this friendship, though the old hero never knew it, caused the first warp in Cooper's career which changed him in the end from a high romancer to a bullish, angry litigant. He became involved in an argument being conducted by Lafayette on the subject of French and American taxation and before he got through, he had managed to offend a number of his fellow countrymen. By the time he returned to New York in November 1833, the way was already open for the series of unpleasant criticisms and disputes which marked and marred all Cooper's later years.

Back in Cooperstown he began to quarrel with the neighbors over questions of trespass and property rights. The high-hearted romances of his early period, even the artificial but sincere historical novels, now became overshadowed by heavy-handed satire masquerading as fiction, and containing most unpalatable criticisms of a country which he still loved but which seemed to him to have deteriorated sadly in the years that he was away from it. From this time, also, date the various libel suits which Cooper brought against reviewers of his novels and of his *History of the Navy*.

It would be a mistake, however, to think of Cooper as only a disgruntled old curmudgeon who had turned sour on the world. To begin with, there remained still in the future some of the most vital and rich of the *Leatherstocking Tales*; in the second place, his life was by no means the constant contention sometimes pictured. His home and family were as dear to him as they were peaceful and harmonious, he had close and loyal friends, and even in Cooperstown he was not entirely unpopular. Add to this the fact of his ill health, which had begun in Europe and never again deserted him, and also the plain truth that many of his criticisms were excellently justified and it will be seen that Cooper was something more than a mere peevish inveigher against Yankees, newspapers, Englishmen, and the rest of his long list of objects of hatred.

In view of the practical immortality which has attended the best of Cooper's works, it is interesting to note that though his novels sold fairly well for a time, and brought him at one period an income of about $20 000 per year—almost unprecedented for the early nineteenth century—they did not make him permanently rich. He had a heavy burden of debt, left by his extravagant elder brothers, and he himself loved to live in grand style, in the lavish opulence of his father, the squire and judge. In his later years, therefore, Cooper frequently was hard pressed for money and wrote literally for his bread and butter.

His life after his return to Cooperstown, was without event except for his acrimonious but successful law-suits. He died finally, of sclerosis of the liver, the day before his sixty-second birthday.

It is the fashion to say nowadays that Cooper is good stuff for boys, that his noble Redman never was on land or sea, that he could not write English and was inexcusably clumsy and careless, and that he was outdated even before he died. But these strictures, true as they may be, ignore the immense vitality of his work. Singlehanded, at a time when American literature was almost a thing unborn, Cooper created real and living books in two distinct fields—the sea story and the romantic story of the wilderness. When he wrote *The Pilot* in 1823, it was in face of the criticism that nobody could make the sea interesting, and certainly, as long as America remembers her past, Natty Bumppo and Uncas will not be forgotten.

PRINCIPAL WORKS: Precaution, 1820; The Spy, 1821; The Pioneers, 1823; The Pilot, 1823; Lionel Lincoln, 1825; The Last of the Mohicans, 1826; The Prairie, 1827; The Red Rover, 1828; Notions of the Americans: Picked up by a Traveling Bachelor, 1828; The Wept of Wish-ton-Wish, 1829; The Water-Witch, 1830; The Bravo, 1831; A Letter to His Countrymen, 1834;

The Monikins, 1835; Homeward Bound, 1838; Home as Found, 1838; The History of the Navy of the United States of America, 1839; The Pathfinder, 1840; The Deerslayer, 1841; The Two Admirals, 1842; The Wing-and-Wing, 1842; Wyandotte, 1843; Ned Myers, 1843; Afloat and Ashore, 1834; Satan's Toe, 1845; The Chainbearer, 1846; The Redskins, 1846; The Crater, 1847; The Ways of the Hour, 1850.

About: Boynton, H. W. James Fenimore Cooper; Brownell, W. C. American Prose Masters; Clymer, W. B. S. James Fenimore Cooper; Cooper, J. F. Correspondence; Cooper, S. F. Pages and Pictures From the Writings of James Fenimore Cooper; Erskine, J. Leading American Novelists; Lounsbury, T. R. James Fenimore Cooper; Parrington, V. L. The Romantic Revolution in America; Phillips, M. E. James Fenimore Cooper; Spiller, R. E. James Fenimore Cooper.

COOPER, SUSAN FENIMORE (April 17, 1813-December 31, 1894), naturalist and biographer, was the oldest child of James Fenimore Cooper [*q.v.*], the novelist, and Susan (De Lancey) Cooper. She was born on a farm at Scarsdale, N.Y., and with her sisters was educated in a French School from 1826 to 1833. Her life was uneventful; she never married, but lived at home in Cooperstown, N.Y., devoting herself to numerous charities, rural rambles, and her writing. Her principal charitable interest was an orphan asylum known as The House of the Holy Savior, which she founded in 1873 with five inmates and which grew into a large institution, housing a hundred orphans.

Besides her original writings, she edited the American edition of *Country Rambles* by the English naturalist, John L. Knapp (1853). She is best known for her first work, *Rural Hours,* which has a naïve freshness of observation and a grasp of detail which makes it a sort of minor *White of Selborne.* Although her father had forbidden the publication of a biography, Miss Cooper published many valuable reminiscences of his domestic life and history in her *Pages and Pictures* and in the various prefaces for an edition of James Fenimore Cooper's complete works brought out between 1876 and 1884.

Principal Works: Rural Hours, 1850; Rhyme and Reason of Country Life, 1854; Mt. Vernon: A Letter to the Children of America, 1859; Pages and Pictures From the Writings of James Fenimore Cooper, 1861; William West Skiles: A Sketch of Missionary Life, 1890.

About: Boynton, H. W. James Fenimore Cooper.

COOPER, THOMAS (October 22, 1759-May 11, 1839), educator, scientist, and political economist, was born in London, the son and namesake of Thomas Cooper, a man of apparent standing, and was educated at Oxford. From early youth he was a radical both in politics and religion; his training in medicine and chemistry made him a materialist, his study of law inclined him to the extremes of democratic opinion. Admitted to the bar, he traveled the Northern Circuit, and in Manchester founded a democratic club of which James Watt, the inventor, was an active member. He was also a close friend of Joseph Priestley, the discoverer of oxygen, who possessed similar political views; later he married Priestley's daughter.

After a portrait by C. Ingham
THOMAS COOPER
1829

For some years his radical activities were regarded tolerantly, if not sympathetically. But finally the publication of a pamphlet in reply to Edmund Burke's anti-Jacobin *Reflections on the Revolution in France* brought a threat of prosecution, and, with Watt, Cooper fled to Paris. There he joined the revolutionists, and was even a candidate for the Convention in opposition to the Duc d'Orleans.

In 1795, becoming disgusted with the extremes of "the Terror," Cooper emigrated to the United States, settling in Northumberland, Pa., where his friend Priestley was then living. There he began the practice of law and continued his career as a pamphleteer. In 1799, in the Reading, Pa., *Advertiser,* he published an attack on President John Adams which caused his arrest under the Alien and Sedition Acts. He was imprisoned for six months and fined $400; the fine, however, being repaid many years later, with interest. The affair earned him the friendship of Jefferson, whose cause he had espoused. On his release from prison he was appointed land commissioner, and in 1806 president-judge of the court of common pleas for the fourth district of Pennsylvania, but in 1811 he was impeached by the state senate for "overbearing conduct" and was removed from office. (Most historians agree that the charges—though inspired by political motives—were at least partially justified.)

Cooper's checkered career then turned to pedagogy. After teaching chemistry for a short while at Dickinson College, Carlisle, Pa., and chemistry and mineralogy at the University of Pennsylvania, Jefferson made him professor of natural science and law in the University of Virginia, but such was the opposition of the clergy that he never took the chair. In 1820 he moved to South Carolina. There he became professor of chemistry at South Carolina College (later the University of South Carolina), in Columbia, and in 1821 was elected president. In 1823 he was asked to teach metaphysics, but refused, suggesting the establishment instead of a chair of political economy.

He was a popular teacher and became much interested in education, advocating free tuition all the way up to and including the university. He also continued his interest in politics, but had by this time almost completely reversed his early democratic beliefs. He was now a leading defender of slavery and one of the earliest advocates of nullification! Naturally these—and his religious views—gained him both bitter enemies and staunch friends. In 1832 he was tried before the board of trustees on the charge of holding opinions inimical to the welfare of the college. He was acquitted, but the next year he resigned the presidency, and in 1834 his professorship as well—though just previously the college had given him an honorary LL.D. degree.

The remainder of Cooper's life was spent in codifying and editing the statutes of South Carolina, by appointment of the legislature. He published five volumes of these, besides writing for the *Southern Quarterly* and other magazines, and issuing many pamphlets. His position in South Carolina was almost as influential as was Jefferson's in Virginia. His literary style was vigorous and forthright; he was an enemy of obscurity in writing as well as in philosophic thought. In addition to his original writing, he edited the *Emporium of Arts and Sciences* (1812-14) and Thomson's *System of Chemistry* (1818).

In appearance, Cooper was remarkable for his small body and disproportionately large head. Slender as a youth, in his later years he became stout and waddling. He lived to his eightieth year. Loyal and genial in his personal relationships, he was formidable in controversy. Bitter, brilliant, changeable, he was at the same time one of the most able and contradictory men of his times, and certainly one of the most stimulating figures in the America of the early nineteenth century. The one consistent point in his philosophy was a hatred of tyranny so violent that it frequently mistook its objects.

Principal Works: Letters on the Slave Trade, 1787; Tracts: Ethical, Theological, and Political, 1790; Some Information Respecting America, 1794; Political Essays, 1800; Tracts on Medical Jurisprudence, 1819; Elements of Political Economy, 1819; Lectures on the Elements of Political Economy, 1826; A Treatise on the Law of Libel and the Liberty of the Press, 1830; Manual of Political Economy, 1833.

About: Himes, C. F. The Life and Times of Judge Thomas Cooper; Kelly, M. Additional Chapters on Thomas Cooper; Malone, D. The Public Life of Thomas Cooper; Taylor, R. G. Chapters From the Life of Thomas Cooper; South Atlantic Quarterly 1919, 1920, 1923.

COPPÉE, HENRY (October 13, 1821-March 21, 1895), soldier, educator, and miscellaneous writer, was born in Savannah, Ga., where his parents, Edward and Carolina (DeLavillate) Coppée, had settled after their flight from Santo Domingo during the great slave uprising. His father became a medical practitioner, founded the first Presbyterian Church in Savannah in 1827, and was a charter member of the Georgia Historical Society in 1839.

Henry entered Yale in 1839 but left after two years to study civil engineering. He spent a brief time in survey and construction work for the Georgia Central Railroad, and when he was nineteen entered West Point. After graduation in 1845, he was detailed to duty in Mexico, where his valorous conduct earned him a captaincy.

At the end of the war he returned as professor of French to West Point, where, with the exception of a year's duty at Fort McHenry, he continued to teach in various departments until 1855, when he took the chair of English literature and history at the University of Pennsylvania. At the outbreak of the Civil War, Coppée opposed his native state and zealously supported the Union cause by his numerous writings on military science, among which were *Manual of Batallion Drill, Manual of Evolutions of the Line,* and *Manual of Courts-Martial.*

He edited the *United States Service Magazine*, a new publication which was discontinued two later years later when he gave up the editorship and his chair at the University of Pennsylvania to become the first president of Lehigh University. Resigning the presidency in 1874, he devoted himself to writing and teaching and remained at the university as professor of English literature and international and constitutional law. Upon the death of President Lamberton, he became acting president and continued in that capacity until his death. Other activities included a twenty-one year membership in the general conventions of the Protestant Episcopal Church, and service as a regent of the Smithsonian Institution.

Both in his youth, and in the latter days when his silvery hair and long white beard gave him a patriarchal appearance, he was a handsome man, of unusual charm of manner.

His ornate style was the result of a too-facile pen, but his prolific and varied output is a monument to the extraordinarily wide range of his intellect. His *History of the Conquest of Spain* is his best known work.

Principal Works: Elements of Logic, 1857; Gallery of Famous Poets, 1858; Elements of Rhetoric, 1859; Gallery of Distinguished Poetesses, 1860; Select Academic Speaker, 1861; Manual of Batallion Drill, 1862; Manual of Evolutions of the Line, 1863; Manual of Courts-Martial, 1863; Songs of Praise in the Christian Centuries, 1864; Grant and His Campaigns. A Military Biography, 1866; Lectures in English Literature, 1872; English Literature Considered as an Interpreter of English History, 1873; History of the Conquest of Spain by the Arab Moors, 1881.

About: Biographical Register: 1891; Centennial of the United States Military Academy at West Point.

CORNWALLIS, KINAHAN (December 24, 1839-August 15, 1917), lawyer, editor, and miscellaneous writer, was born in London. His father, William Baxter Kinahan, assumed Cornwallis—the surname of his wife Elizabeth—as a condition of her patrimony. Kinahan Cornwallis was schooled for the ministry in Liverpool under the guidance of the Rev. John B. Williams, but was unable to adapt his radical ideas to the Church and took up the study of medicine at the medical school attached to the Liverpool Infirmary. This failed to engage his attention and he entered the British Colonial Civil Service, spending two years in Melbourne, Australia. During this time and later, he visited the Philippines, Singapore, Ceylon, Suez, Egypt, and various parts of Japan, Africa, South America, and Canada.

The year 1860 found him in New York City on the staff of the New York *Herald*, where he remained nine years as financial editor. In 1860 he received a State Department appointment to accompany the Prince of Wales, afterwards Edward VII, on his travels through America; and in 1863 he was admitted to the New York bar. After leaving the *Herald*, he became editor and proprietor of the *Knickerbocker Magazine* and the *Albion* until 1886, when he took over the *Wall Street Daily Investigator*, later renamed the *Wall Street Daily Investor*. Meanwhile, in addition to his editorial activities, he carried on a successful law practice, and managed to write a prodigious number of varied works until his declining years. Of this *mélange* his novels and travel books were his best efforts, although it cannot be said that they enriched American literature.

Cornwallis was a man of scholarly mind, quiet humor, and dignified bearing. He was married twice: first, to Annie Louise Tisdale of New York; and second, to Elizabeth Chapman of Hartford, Conn. He died in New York City.

Principal Works: *Novels*—Howard Plunkett, 1857; Wreck and Ruin, 1858; Pilgrims of Fashion, 1862; Adrift With a Vengeance, 1865; A Marvelous Coincidence, 1891; Two Strange Adventures, 1897. *Miscellaneous*—An Australian Poem, 1857; The New Eldorado: or, British Columbia, 1858; Two Journeys to Japan, 1859; A Panorama of the New World, 1859; My Life and Adventures, 1860; The Crosstrees, 1859; The Gold Room and the New York Stock Exchange and Clearing House, 1879; The History of Constructive Contempt of Court, 1892; International Law, 1892; Historical Poems, 1892; The Song of America and Columbus, 1892; The Conquest of Mexico and Peru, 1893; The War for the Union, 1899.

About: Cornwallis, K. My Life and Adventures; New York Times August 17, 1917; New York Tribune August 18, 1917.

CORSON, HIRAM (November 6, 1828-June 15, 1911), teacher and critical writer, was born in Philadelphia, the son of Joseph Dickinson Corson and Ann (Hagey) Corson. Attending schools in Montgomery County, he was an outstanding pupil, owing partly to early training in mathematics and classical languages under his parents. During his twenty-fifth year he went to Washington, D.C., where he became a reporter in the Senate, and afterwards served seven years as a librarian in the Smithsonian Institution.

In 1854 he married Caroline Rollins of Boston, who had been educated in Europe and who considerably influenced her husband's literary taste. Between 1859 and 1865 he taught and lectured at Girard College in Philadelphia. He took no part in the Civil War except to publish at its conclusion *A Revised Edition of Jaudon's English Orthographical Expositor* (1866), a volume designed "for the use of the

Southern freedman." In the same year he became professor of rhetoric and literature in St. John's College, Annapolis, remaining until 1870, after which time he taught literature at Cornell. Meanwhile he was producing books in which his scholarship and critical ability were admirably set forth. Among his important works was *Aims of Literary Study,* published in 1895.

A man of progressive ideas and fearless viewpoint, he spoke and wrote freely against slavery, organized religion, and the social effects of concentrated wealth. In his declining years he wholeheartedly embraced spiritualism and decorated a special room in his house with the portraits of deceased loved ones, consoling himself with daily offerings of fresh flowers and the thought that his revered spirits were constantly surrounding him. His posthumous book, *Spirit Messages,* recounts his daily communication with his wife, who had died in 1901 and who was apparently convening with famous and friendly ghosts on the other side.

Corson's interest in Robert Browning's poetry took him to England in 1882 to deliver a lecture before the Browning Society of London, which the poet himself warmly applauded. The Browning Societies which spread throughout America were organized chiefly through Corson's activities and his *Introduction to the Study of Robert Browning's Poetry,* published in 1886, had a wide sale. Among his many distinguished acquaintances was Walt Whitman, whose poetry Corson steadfastly championed in the face of early criticism.

His scholarly writings greatly influenced the literary trend of his time and may be examined with interest today.

PRINCIPAL WORKS: A Revised Edition of Jaudon's English Orthographical Expositor, 1866; An Introduction to the Study of Robert Browning's Poetry, 1886; An Introduction to the Study of Shakespeare, 1889; Primer of English Verse, 1892; Aims of Literary Study, 1895; Spirit Messages, 1911.

ABOUT: Poole, M. E. A Story Historical of Cornell University: With Biographies of Distinguished Cornellians; New York Tribune June 16, 1911.

CORY, CHARLES BARNEY (January 31, 1857-July 29, 1921), ornithologist, was born in Boston, Mass., the son of Barney Cory, of vigorous seafaring stock, and Eliza (Glynn) Cory, of Newport, R.I. As a boy Cory had a penchant for outdoor life, and at sixteen he began a collection of bird skins which undoubtedly fixed his interest in ornithology. He attended Park Latin and William Eayr's schools. In 1876 he entered Lawrence Scientific School of Harvard but did not finish; he began studies at Boston Law School where he remained only a few months. A trip to Florida in 1877 occasioned his first publication, *Southern Rambles,* a kind of nonsense diary. The next four years found him in the Magdalen Islands, the Bahamas, Europe, and the West Indies, collecting specimens and meeting recognized ornithologists. His father's death in 1882 made him virtually a millionaire.

In 1883 Cory married Harriet W. Peterson of Duxbury, Mass., a woman of charm and kindred interests. Their thousand-acre estate near Hyannis included what was perhaps the first bird sanctuary in the United States.

A Naturalist in the Magdalen Islands appeared in 1878 and *Beautiful and Curious Birds* in 1880, but from 1885 to 1900 ornithological publications came thick and fast. *Hypnotism and Mesmerism* (1888) was the outcome of Cory's determination to expose scientific tricksters. In 1891 he dabbled in comic opera, writing a slap-stick on the tortures of "auditioning," etc., called *A Dress Rehearsal. Montezuma's Castle and other Weird Tales,* with a certain imaginative merit, was brought out in 1899. *Vagrant Verses* was published posthumously.

Cory had been "honorary curator" (he so called himself) at the Field Museum, Chicago, for about thirteen years, when, in 1906, the sudden collapse of his entire fortune obliged him to accept a salary. As curator of zoology he worked untiringly until his death in Ashland, Wis. He left his wife and one son, Charles B. Cory, Jr.

As a writer Cory's best work was in his vast ornithological output. His other literary assays, although not without merit, were little more than pleasant outlets for a variety of energies.

PRINCIPAL WORKS: *Ornithological*—Beautiful and Curious Birds of the World, 1880; The Birds Series, 1879-1909; catalogues, lists, etc. *Travel, Scientific*—A Naturalist in the Magdalen Islands, 1878; Southern Rambles, 1881; Hunting and Fishing in Florida, 1896. *Miscellaneous*—Hypnotism and Mesmerism, 1888; A Dress Rehearsal, 1891; Montezuma's Castle and Other Weird Tales, 1899; Vagrant Verses, 1934.

ABOUT: The Auk April 1922; Chicago Tribune January 31, 1921.

COTTON, JOHN (December 4, 1584-December 23, 1652), religious writer and Puritan clergyman, was born in Derby, Derbyshire, England, the son of Roland Cotton, a prosperous lawyer. Upon finishing grammar school he entered Trinity College, Cambridge, at the age of thirteen, transferring to Emmanuel, a college much more sympathetic towards Puritanism. His first claim to distinction was the admirable delivery of a funeral oration for the master of Peter House.

Cotton was innately both religious and scholarly, and his theological aptitude warranted the demand for his services as head lecturer, dean, catechist, and tutor. But when he was about twenty-nine he was asked by the people of Boston, Lincolnshire, to settle there in the ministry, and he returned to Cambridge only to receive the degree of Bachelor of Divinity. He married Elizabeth Horrocks in 1613. Less than three years later Cotton was beginning to nurse some strong convictions about old corruptions left unreformed in the National Church; he could no longer remain a strict conformer. It was not the harmless church ceremony in itself that he resented, but rather its imposition upon those who earnestly disliked it.

For a year, beginning September 1630, Cotton was disabled by a quatern ague, and it was this same illness which shortly cost the life of his wife. He was married a second time to Mrs. Sarah (Hawkridge) Story, in 1632, and by her he had six children, three boys and three girls.

By July 1633 Laud, Archbishop of Canterbury, had cast some scathing remarks on the unpardonable nature of Cotton's nonconformity and Puritanism. That very month Cotton, with his wife, Thomas Hooker, and Samuel Stone, set out for America in the "Griffin," a 300-ton ship carrying 200 passengers. Seven weeks of voyaging, during which occurred the birth of Seaborn Cotton, brought them to New Boston on the third of September. The townspeople had anticipated Cotton's arrival with a season of prayers and fasting. The infant Seaborn was baptized and John Cotton was chosen teacher of the First Church. "Order" was the watchword of the new Congregationalists, with much emphasis on unity, popular rights, and civil liberty. With these principles they reconciled their aristocratic traditions by assuming that "democracy necessarily runs into aristocracy because the executive power must fall into the hands of a few." A minor instance of Cotton's democratic simplicity was his quick abrogation of the requirement for women to wear veils in public worship. Indeed his prestige in the new colony was considerable, and in 1641 he received a letter bearing impressive signatures—Oliver Cromwell's among them—that urged him to return to England with other leaders. Nothing came of this invitation.

JOHN COTTON

Following a tract justifying the formation of the new settlement, *God's Promise to His Plantation*, Cotton wrote *The Keyes of the Kingdom of Heaven* (1644), which served as the standard ecclesiastical guide of the New England Church until the appearance of the *Cambridge Platform* in 1648. Although the fact has escaped most historians, Cotton was the author of Book II of *A Survey of the Summe of Church-Discipline* (London, 1648); Book I was written by Hooker. That year saw also the publication of *The Way of the Congregational Churches Cleared*, in which Cotton identified New England Congregationalism more closely with aristocratic Presbyterianism than with democratic Brownism, the cult of the more radical Nonconformists. But Puritanism's odd mixture of certain conservative and nonconservative attitudes still needed clarification.

The first years of Cotton's ministry were pleasant ones, but trouble soon came with the advent of Antinomianism—a doctrine stating that the dispensation of grace as set forth in the New Testament frees the Christian from the obligations of Old Testament moral law. At first, Cotton, with apparent naïveté, was somewhat misinformed by Anne Hutchinson, a strong protagonist of this movement. He later allied himself with the opposition, but, nevertheless, shielded Anne for a time. She balked at repentance and was eventually banished. In this affair, Cotton's behavior was, on the whole, humane and practical. Years before he had sheltered German refugee divines in his English home.

Cotton Mather, son of Increase Mather and John Cotton's youngest daughter Maria, states that his grandfather had a "clear fair sanguine complexion . . . and a ruddy countenance" and that he was "rather low than tall and rather fat than lean." It is said that the keeper of a Derby inn that John Cotton frequented often "wished that man out of his house for he was not able to swear with him under his roof." This beloved clergyman's hope that he should not outlive his work was fulfilled. For on a ferry crossing to Cambridge, where he was expected for a sermon, Cotton caught a severe cold which developed into a fatal inflammation of the lungs. Life itself, as he had lived it, was remarkable, and his massive writings may be said to comprise the soundest key to Puritan ideals in their middle stage.

Principal Works: *Religious*—God's Promise to His Plantation, 1630; The Keyes of the Kingdom of Heaven, 1644; The Way of the Churches of Christ in New England, 1645; Milk for Babes, 1646; The Way of the Congregational Churches Cleared, 1648; Bk. II of Survey of the Summe of Church-Discipline, 1648.

About: M'Clure, A. W. The Life of John Cotton; Mather, C. Johannes in Eremo; Norton, J. Memoir of John Cotton.

"COUSIN ALICE." See HAVEN, EMILY (BRADLEY) NEAL

"COUSIN VIRGINIA." See JOHNSON, VIRGINIA WALES

"COVENTRY, JOHN." See PALMER, JOHN WILLIAMSON

COX, HENRY HAMILTON (c. 1769-c. 1821), poet, was born in Ireland, the son of Joshua and Mary (Cox) Hamilton. He assumed the name Cox in 1784 under the will of Sir Richard Cox, the second baronet of that name, as a condition of inheriting the estate of Dunmanway, County Cork.

After serving in the British army in India, he came to America about 1799 with his wife, Letitia Elinor, daughter of David Wilson Hutcheson of Dublin. First settling in York, Pa., he moved in 1813 to a large farm in Chester County, near London Grove. Becoming an active member of the Society of Friends, he sometimes preached and was known to address the congregation as "My Lords." He brought his large family of children to the meeting house in a farm cart, "dumping them as if they were a load of potatoes." Although the neighbors raised eyebrows at his eccentricities, they respected his capability and gentlemanly bearing.

In 1817 Cox returned to his estate in Ireland, which had been cleared of debt. Denouncing his Quaker affiliations, he returned to the Anglican Church; this religious experience later was used by Bayard Taylor as a basic plot for "The Strange Friend," a story in his *Beauty and the Beast*.

When he first came to America Cox made a handsome gift to the Library Company of Philadelphia of five volumes of seventeenth-century manuscripts, chiefly consisting of official documents concerning affairs in Ireland. He probably obtained these "Irish State Papers" through legitimate channels, but they were generously returned to the British Government in 1867 by the Library Company to complete a series.

Occupying no special niche in American literature, Cox nevertheless added richness to rural poetry with his well-constructed "Pennsylvania Georgics," which were later included in his *Metrical Sketches: By a Citizen of the World*, published in 1817.

Principal Works: Metrical Sketches: By a Citizen of the World, 1817.

About: Cope, G. & Futhey, J. S. History of Chester County, Pennsylvania; Lewis, J. J. Sketch of the Life of Henry Hamilton Cox (Ms. in the Library of the Historical Society of Pennsylvania).

COX, PALMER (April 28, 1840-July 24, 1924), writer and illustrator of books for children, creator of the famous "Brownies," was born in Granby, Quebec, of Scottish parents, Michael and Sarah (Miller) Cox. He spent an apparently impressionable childhood in this Scottish community, and after finishing at Granby Academy he set out for San Francisco in 1863, working first for a railroad company and then for a shipbuilding concern. He was, at the same time, submitting light verse and drawings to various newspapers, but the reception given his first book, *Squibs of California* (1874), was less than lukewarm.

In 1876 he went to New York and found work on *Wild Oats,* a comic weekly which enjoyed only a feeble five years' existence. At this period he published a kind of ballad-burlesque, called *That Stanley!,* satirizing Sir Henry Morton Stanley's African expedition in search of Livingstone.

Not until Cox was forty did he begin his famous career with *St. Nicholas Magazine*. At first he contributed miscellaneous short poems and drawings of no special distinction. What he needed, he felt, was a productive idea on which to build a continuing

PALMER COX

series of stories and pictures. So from the legends of the Grampian Mountains of Scotland told to him when he was a child, Cox evolved the inexhaustible adventures of the Brownies. "The Brownies' Ride," the first of these tales, appeared in *St. Nicholas,* February 1883, and the earliest publication in book form was *The Brownies: Their Book* (1887).

It is admittedly true that in the folk lore of the ancients were strange creatures similar to these good elfins, and that certain carved figures, kobolds, belonging to medieval Germany, bore a resemblance to them also. But Cox modified his Grampian beings with a deftness that made them live in their own right. There were all kinds of Brownies—Dudes, Cadets, Policemen, Cowboys, etc.—some with corkscrew antennae and some with long beards, but all with round paunches, spindling legs, and tapering feet. Their world is one of no pain, no crime, and all laughter. Moreover Cox insisted that they "do good, just for the sake of doing good, and not for the sake of any reward"; and that they never repeat an activity once performed—which precedent, from the narrator's point of view, was not always easy to maintain. Their clean-fun adventures were loved by two generations of children. The author's studio on Broadway was papered with Brownie mementoes and letters. He himself estimated that he had drawn over a million of these good sprites; and of the thirteen books in the *Brownies* series, all of which are in verse except one, more than a million copies were sold before his death. His pleasant royalties enabled him to go back to the Granby region and to retire in a spacious home, called "Brownie Castle," which he had built on the outskirts of Quebec, and there he died, unmarried, in July 1924.

"It is doubtful," commented the New York *Times,* "whether any fashion in children's literature has ever swept a country so completely as Palmer Cox's Brownies took possession of American childhood in the early 'eighties."

PRINCIPAL WORKS: Squibs of California, 1874; That Stanley! 1878; The Brownie series (13 vols.) 1887-1925.

ABOUT: Current Opinion September 1924; Nation August 6, 1924; St. Nicholas October 1924.

COX, SAMUEL SULLIVAN (September 30, 1824-September 10, 1889), Congressman and political writer, was descended from a distinguished line of early settlers. His grandfather was Gen. James Cox, soldier of the Battles of Brandywine and Germantown, speaker of the New Jersey legislature, friend of Thomas Jefferson, and member of the tenth Congress. His son, the father of Samuel Sullivan Cox, married a daughter of Samuel Sullivan, state treasurer, while editing the *Muskingum Messenger* in Zanesville, Ohio.

After two years at Ohio State University, the youthful Samuel entered Brown University. Graduated with high honors, he returned to Ohio, where he read law and eventually opened an office in Cincinnati. In 1849 he married Julia A. Buckingham of Zanesville. This happy partnership inculcated a taste for literature and travel. As a result of a visit to Europe, in 1852, he published his first book, *A Buckeye Abroad,* which was well received. Giving up law entirely, and turning to journalism, he became editor and proprietor of the *Ohio Statesman* at Columbus. His flowery description of a sunset earned him the soubriquet "Sunset." Politics next engaged his attention and in 1855 President Pierce offered him the post of secretary of the legation in England. He declined in favor of a similar appointment in Peru but was stricken with a local fever en route and never assumed his duties. In 1856, however, restored to health, he was elected to Congress and entered upon a long and influential career of service to his country. Among his outstanding activities he influenced Lincoln's decision to treat Southern seamen as prisoners of war instead of pirates; and he was especially vigorous in opposing privateering.

At the National Democratic Convention in 1884 he seconded McClellan's nomination for the presidency.

Failure to regain reelection resulted in his removal to New York City, where he resumed his law practice and produced his book, *Eight Years in Congress,* in 1865. Three years later he returned to Congress and launched upon another period of powerful activity, especially in connection with the development of the West. In 1885 he was appointed minister to Turkey by President Cleveland, served but one year, and returned to Congress to fill the seat vacated by Joseph Pulitzer. He died after a strenuous trip to the Northwest in 1889.

Despite his Congressional duties, Cox found time to produce many books from his fluent pen, all of which only served to increase his political stature. His forceful career was built upon a strong foundation of deep religious belief, scholarly education, and fearless conduct, and his personality was softened by a ready wit and an ever-present courtesy.

Principal Works: A Buckeye Abroad, 1852; Puritanism in Politics, 1863; Eight Years in Congress, 1865; Why We Laugh, 1876; Free Land and Free Trade, 1880; Arctic Sunbeams, 1882; Orient Sunbeams, 1882; Three Decades of Federal Legislation, 1885.

About: Cox, W. Van Z. Life of Samuel Sullivan Cox; Congressional Record: 51st Congress, 1st Session.

COXE, RICHARD SMITH (January 1792-April 28, 1865), lawyer and legal writer, was born in Burlington, N.J. He was the great-grandson of Colonel Daniel Coxe, Colonial politician, and a son of William Coxe, pomologist, and Rachel (Smith) Coxe. Prepared at the Burlington Academy and with a private tutor, he matriculated at the College of New Jersey (Princeton) in 1805. Graduated in 1808, he read law for three years under the supervision of Judge William Griffith, studied with Horace Binney in Philadelphia, and was admitted to the bar of the supreme court of Pennsylvania, December 11, 1812. His marriage in 1816 to Susan, daughter of Judge Griffith, took him back to Burlington where he established a practice and served as deputy attorney general for Burlington County. In 1822 he moved to Washington, D.C., and was admitted to the bar of the circuit court of the District of Columbia. He pleaded many important cases before the Supreme Court. In 1840 he took as a second wife Mrs. Susan R. Wheeler, daughter of John Warren of New York.

Apart from his professional activities, he sought no public office. Of a retiring nature, he devoted his leisure to writing and scholarly pursuits. His special attention to the English classics resulted in court arguments distinguished by their logical eloquence, and he was often invited to speak on important occasions. His books dealt chiefly with legal subjects. He died in Washington.

Principal Works: A New Critical Pronouncing Dictionary of the English Language Compiled by an American Gentleman, 1813; Reports of Cases Argued and Determined in the Supreme Court of New Jersey . . . , 1816; Digest of Decisions Supreme, Circuit, and District Courts, United States: 1789-1829, 1829; Review of the Relations Between the United States and Mexico, 1846; The Present State of the African Slave-Trade, 1858.

About: Clement, J. Sketches of the First Emigrant Settlers in Newton Township, N.J.; Hageman, J. F. & Woodward, E. M. History of Burlington and Mercer Counties, N.J.; Livingston, J. Biographical Sketches of Eminent American Lawyers; Evening Star (Washington) April 28, 1865.

COZZENS, FREDERICK SWARTWOUT (March 11, 1818-December 23, 1869), humorist, was born in New York City, the son of Frederick Swartwout a prosperous merchant. The father, however, wished his son to become his successor in the wholesale grocery and wine trade, discouraged his literary proclivities, and had him trained for a commercial career. He did succeed his father, built up the business still further, and developed American wine-growing, being the first to introduce and sell wine made in Ohio. His leisure he gave to writing, though it was never more than an avocation with him. Under the pseudonym of "Richard Hayward," the name of an ancestor, he contributed humorous articles to the *Knickerbocker Magazine* and other periodicals, some of which were later published in book form. He also edited a trade journal called the *Wine Press,* in which he conducted a column of essays and sketches. After the Civil War he failed in business and retired to Rahway, N.J. He died suddenly while on a visit to Brooklyn. Cozzens was at one time considered a leading humorist in the broad burlesque style of his era, but his work has long been forgotten.

Principal Works: Yankee Doodle, 1847; Prismatics, 1853; Sparrowgrass Papers, 1856; Acadia: A Sojourn Among the Blue-noses, 1858; Sayings of Dr. Bushwacker and Other Learned Men, 1867; Memorial of Fitz-Greene Halleck, 1868; Sayings: Wise and Otherwise, 1880.

About: Cozzens, F. S. Sayings: Wise and Otherwise; Lippincott's Magazine May 1890; New York Herald December 25, 1869; Putnam's Monthly January 1908.

"CRABSHAW, TIMOTHY." See LONGSTREET, AUGUSTUS BALDWIN

"CRADDOCK, CHARLES EGBERT." See MURFREE, MARY NOAILLES

CRAFTS, WILLIAM (January 24, 1787-September 23, 1826), poet and lawyer, was born in Charleston, S.C., the oldest child of William Crafts and Margaret (Tébout) Crafts. The father was a native of Massachusetts who had settled in the South and married a South Carolinian.

A precocious boy, Crafts was graduated from Harvard at eighteen. He then studied law in Charleston, and after receiving his M.A. from Harvard in 1808 was admitted to the South Carolina bar in 1809. Handsome, witty, and gregarious, Crafts was more or less spoiled by adulation, and wasted his talents in the easy pursuit of local celebrity. He was elected to the lower house of the state legislature in 1810, and later served another term. In 1820 he was elected to the state senate, and was still a senator at the time of his death. He did some good work for public education, but as a lawyer he had so wasted his opportunities that his ignorance of the law was notorious, his chief asset in criminal cases being his eloquence. He was a famous orator, constantly in demand. His verse appeared for the most part, together with essays and dramatic criticism, in the Charleston *Courier*. In 1823 he married his cousin, Carolina Crafts Holmes. He died at Lebanon Springs, N.Y., where he had gone for his health, and was buried in Boston.

Crafts' poems are imitative of Byron, Moore, Pope, and Gray. He had genuine ability, but never developed his gift, since whatever he wrote was received with acclaim by his friends. His work was remembered only until the appearance on the Southern scene of poets of a larger calibre.

Principal Works: The Raciad and Other Occasional Poems, 1810; The Sea Serpent: A Dramatic Jeu d'Esprit, 1819; Sullivan's Island and Other Poems, 1820; A Selection in Prose and Poetry From the Miscellaneous Writings of the Late William Crafts, 1828.

About: Crafts, W. A Selection in Prose and Poetry (see Memoir by S. Gilman); Parrington, V. L. Main Currents of American Thought; Charleston Courier and News July 12, 1903.

CRANCH, CHRISTOPHER PEARSE (March 8, 1813-January 20, 1892), painter, critic, poet, and Unitarian minister, was born in Alexandria, Va., the thirteenth child of William Cranch, jurist, and Anna (Greenleaf) Cranch. His parents were natives of Massachusetts and his grandmother was a sister of Abigail Adams, wife of John Adams, second president of the United States. Graduated from Columbian College, Washington, in 1831, and later attending the Divinity School at Harvard, he preached as a Unitarian minister in Maine, Virginia, Missouri, the District of Columbia, Ohio, and in Louisville, Ky., where he occupied the pulpit vacated by James Freeman Clarke. Becoming editor of the *Western Messenger*, he made use of early drawing instruction and attracted much attention by his comic illustrations for some of Emerson's sentences in the *Essays* which had amused him. In 1840 while he was living and preaching at South Boston, some of his poetry was published by Emerson in the *Dial*, and he was a frequent and sympathetic guest at Brook Farm.

In 1843 he married a cousin, Elizabeth De Windt, of Fishkill, N.Y., whose encouragement led him to take up painting seriously, and after several lean years in New York City, they went in 1846 to Italy with George William Curtis for further study. During their three-year stay, they won the friendship of many distinguished persons, including Robert Browning.

After 1849 they spent several winters in New York and in 1853-63 lived in Paris, where Cranch painted with great industry and became friendly with the Barbizon group of painters. Except for a trip to Europe in 1880, the latter part of his life was spent in Cambridge, Mass. Here his intellectual and artistic gifts were stimulated to production by the scholarly atmosphere of Harvard. His *Translation of the Æneid* is his best known work and is well respected by classical scholars.

Principal Works: Translation of the Æneid, 1872; The Bird and the Bell: With Other Poems, 1875; Ariel and Caliban: With Other Poems, 1887.

About: Codman, J. T. Brook Farm: Historical and Personal Memoirs, 1894; Cooke, G. W. The Poets of Transcendentalism; Scott, L. C. The Life and Letters of Christopher Pearse Cranch; Critic January 30, 1892; Harper's Magazine April 1892; Boston Transcript January 20, 1892.

CRANE, ANNE MONCURE (January 7, 1838-December 10, 1872), novelist, was the daughter of Jasper Crane, one of the founders of New Haven and Newark, and Jean Niven (Daniel) Crane, of Falmouth, Va. She was born in Baltimore, Md., where her father had established a home while engaged in the leather business. First tutored by the Rev. N.A. Morrison, she is said to have been graduated from an unidentified institution in 1855. Her first novel, *Emily Chester*, was written at the age of twenty as a requirement for membership in a small club composed of literary young women and was published anonymously by Boston publishers in 1864. Despite its immature, halting style it achieved wide popularity in America and England, was dramatized, and underwent translation into several languages. Her marriage in 1869 to Augustus Seemüller, a successful New York business man, took her to Manhattan to live, and here she became so affected by the degradation and vice of the city that she produced *Reginald Archer* in 1871, an attack so vehement and outspoken that she even stirred up the indignation of the moralists and was bitterly assailed for her unseemly interest in subjects not examined by the ladies of her era. Ill and persecuted by criticism, she sailed for Europe and soon died at Stuttgart. Her novels were not distinguished by literary merit, but nevertheless set the pace for the popular fiction of the day.

Principal Works: Emily Chester, 1864; Opportunity, 1867; Reginald Archer, 1871.

About: Boyle, E. Biographical Sketches of Distinguished Marylanders; Shepherd, H. E. Representative Authors of Maryland; Galaxy July 15, 1866 and August 1, 1866; Nation January 30, 1873.

CRANE, STEPHEN (November 1, 1871-June 5, 1900), novelist, was born in Newark, N.J., the fourteenth and youngest child of the Rev. Jonathan Townley Crane, a Methodist minister, and Mary Helen (Peck) Crane. The father was a good, unsophisticated, narrow-minded man, the mother entirely wrapped up in piety. The family moved frequently as the father received new charges, finally winding up at Port Jervis, N.Y., where the Rev. Mr. Crane died in 1880. Mrs. Crane made their living thereafter by acting as correspondent for religious papers.

Crane was educated at the Hudson River Institute, Claverack, N.Y., and spent a year each at Lafayette College and Syracuse University. He began his journalistic career early by helping his brother secure items about summer visitors in Asbury Park, N.J., where they lived for a time; and he financed his college attendance by acting as correspondent for the New York *Tribune*. This work and the captaincy of the baseball team seem to have taken up more of his time than did his studies. In 1890 his mother died, and the boy of eighteen had to find a means to make his own way in the world.

He went to New York, like most aspiring young writers, and for five years he starved. He was penniless and ill, and all he saw of the city was its harshest aspects. What little money he had he earned by free lance work for the *Tribune* and the *Herald*. The Bowery was his headquarters, and from the bitter scenes he viewed daily he distilled the earliest of American realistic novels, *Maggie: A Girl of the Streets*. No publisher would touch it, and he borrowed $700 from his brother to have it printed, in paper covers, by a firm ashamed to have its imprint on the book. A hundred copies were sold; most of the rest went to light the fire to keep him warm. But Hamlin Garland read and admired it, and through him William Dean Howells; and better days began for the young man. In 1895 he was able to publish *The Red Badge of Courage*, that remarkable reconstruction of the inmost being of a recruit in his first battle, written by an author who had never smelt powder. It made him famous—but it earned him less than $100.

STEPHEN CRANE

Through his new celebrity, however, he secured a position with a syndicate which sent him to Texas and Mexico to write of his travels. On his return, in 1896, he found himself fated to be a war correspondent; it was by mere accident that war had been the theme of his novel—what he was interested in was the realistic depiction of life and feeling in any milieu—but since it had been, it was inevitable that he should be sent (by the New York *Journal*) to report the Graeco-Turkish war. Back from Greece, he set out to "cover" the filibustering campaigns in Cuba. On the way the ship was wrecked, and Crane spent four days in an open boat before the party was rescued. This experience ruined his health, and planted the seeds of the tuberculosis which killed him; but it also resulted in "The Open Boat," a little masterpiece of naturalism.

In 1898 Crane went to England. In London he married Cora Taylor, whom he had met in Jacksonville, Fla., when he was recovering from the illness caused by the shipwreck. She was a good-looking blonde, older than he, who was madame of a house of assignation when they first met. She loved him devotedly, went to Greece to nurse him through another illness, made him the best of wives; and though it was obvious that she did not belong to his social stratum (the Cranes were an old New Jersey family of Revolutionary descent), no one in England knew her whole story, and she was accepted without comment. It was Crane himself who became the object of malicious, unprincipled, and wholly false gossip. Because he had written a book about a prostitute, he was said to be a seducer; because he was ill and tired easily, the story was spread that he took morphine and that he could not write unless he was drunk. Mrs. Crane felt this slander more than he, but it was effectual in keeping him out of his native land for most of the rest of his short life.

The Cranes settled at Oxted, Surrey, where they met Joseph Conrad, who became Crane's close friend, staunch admirer, and loyal defender. Good-natured to the point of the ridiculous, Crane let his house be overrun with acquaintances who enjoyed his wife's cooking, invaded his privacy, kept him from work, camped on him by the month, and then went away to spread more scandal about him. He was glad, when the Spanish-American War started, to be sent to Cuba by the New York *World*. It was his last assignment; he returned to New York very ill, to find the same old ill-willed gossip raging everywhere he went. Disgusted, he set sail for England permanently. He took a house at Brede, Sussex, and there his health grew alarmingly worse. Yet he was writing regularly through all this, and some of his best work was the superhuman effort of an exhausted man. Plans were made for him to go to the warm climate of St. Helena for the London *Morning Post*, but a series of hemorrhages made further work impossible. He was rushed to Badenweiler, Germany, in the Black Forest, where he died. He was buried in Elizabeth, N.J., and his birthplace in Newark has been made a memorial museum by the city.

At twenty-eight and a half, when he died, Stephen Crane had made for himself a permanent place in the literature of the English language. Howells called "The Open Boat" "the finest short story in English." Edward Garnett believed him to be "the chief impressionist of the age." Of the *Whilomville Stories,* Booth Tarkington exclaimed (in a letter to Alexander Woollcott), "beautifully, beautifully done"; and Woollcott calls "The Blue Hotel" "a superb Hemingway story written before Hemingway was born." *Maggie,* that waif privately printed by the pseudonymous "Johnston Smith" (for Crane did not dare, if he hoped to work as a newspaper reporter in 1892, to sign his own name), has its crudities, but with Gissing it prepared the way for Dreiser. "The Monster" is one of the most heart-breaking pieces of irony ever written, full of what Richard Watson Gilder, who refused to publish his work in the *Century,* called Crane's "grim flippancy." His masterpiece, however, remains *The Red Badge of Courage*, written at twenty-three. It illustrates better than any of his works what Thomas Beer points out, that Crane's "search in aesthetic was governed by terror." No one since Poe has so unerringly evoked that emotion.

In his two books of unrhymed poems, openly inspired by his passion for the relatively few poems then published of Emily Dickinson, Crane was as anticipatory as in his stories. They have the gnomic severity, the clipped and cryptic excitement, of what we are pleased to call modernist poetry.

Conrad remarked that Crane "had no surface"—he was all interior. Extraordinarily sensitive, he reminds one of those tropical amphibians that change color at the slightest alteration in their temperature. It is no wonder that evil gossip was spread about him for he was utterly careless of appearance in his direct and honest dealing with the world. Pompous Elbert Hubbard, who thought wearing a Windsor tie made him a Bohemian, wailed that Crane "had no sense of propriety." He had none, he wanted none. Although typically American in appearance, "long and spare," with steady, penetrating blue eyes, Crane did not belong in the provincial America of the 'nineties; he could not fit, like Richard Harding Davis, into the dashing, elegant rôle of war correspondent. Had he not burnt his life out febrilely so soon, he might have found a more agreeable climate, a more congenial and stimulating society, in the twentieth century.

PRINCIPAL WORKS: Maggie: A Girl of the Streets, 1892; The Red Badge of Courage, 1895; The Black Riders and Other Lines (poetry) 1895; George's Mother, 1896; The Little Regiment, and Other Episodes of the Civil War, 1896; The Third Violet, 1897; The Open Boat, and Other Tales of Adventure, 1898; Active Service, 1899; The Monster, and Other Stories, 1899; War Is

Kind (poetry) 1899; Wounds in the Rain, 1900; Whilomville Stories, 1900; The O'Ruddy (with Robert Barr) 1903; Men, Women, and Boats, 1921.

About: Beer, T. Stephen Crane: A Study in American Letters; Conrad, J. Notes on Life and Letters; Follett, W. The Second Twenty-Eight years: A Note on Stephen Crane; Ford, F. M. Portraits From Life; Garnett, E. Friday Nights; Loggins, V. I Hear America; Raymond, T. L. Stephen Crane; Starrett, V. Bibliography of Stephen Crane; Bookman May 1895, July 1900, April 1926; North American Review August 1900; Saturday Review of Literature October 23, 1937; Yale Review April 1914.

CRAWFORD, FRANCIS MARION (August 2, 1854-April 9, 1909), novelist, was born at Bagni di Lucca, Italy, the son of Thomas Crawford, an American sculptor of Irish descent, and of Louisa (Ward) Crawford, a sister of Julia Ward Howe. His father died while he was still a small child, and his mother married an American artist, Luther Terry. Crawford was named for Gen. Francis Marion, a collateral ancestor.

He was educated partly in America, at St. Paul's School, Concord, Mass., and at Harvard; but for the most part in Europe: at Trinity College, Cambridge, the University of Heidelberg, and the University of Rome. Though he never gave up his American citizenship, and always spoke of America as "home," Crawford was really a deracinated European, a multilingual cosmopolitan. He had a great gift for languages, and to further his study of Sanskrit, with a view to teaching it, went to India in 1879. There for two years he edited a paper in Allahabad. From India he brought the fixation of a lifelong interest in the occult (he had besides a strong vein of superstition); a conversion to the Roman Catholic Church, of which he was thenceforth a devout adherent; and the plot and characters of his first novel, *Mr. Isaacs.* This, however, was not published until 1882, after a year or more of hack writing and reviewing in New York and Boston. In 1883 he returned to Italy, which was his home ever after; though in his last years as a successful novelist he generally spent the winter months in New York. In 1898 he toured the entire United States, lecturing and reading—and incurred a pulmonary disease which eventually led to his death at fifty-four.

F. MARION CRAWFORD

In 1884, at Constantinople, Crawford married Elizabeth Berdan, daughter of a Civil War general. They had two sons and two daughters. Essentially domestic, he was happiest in his own home (for most of his married life the beautiful Villa Crawford in Sorrento), surrounded by his adoring relatives, mostly feminine. High society was his birthright, but he disliked it; he was at once self-confident and shy, and though, with his imitations and songs (he had a fine tenor robusto voice, and once thought of singing professionally), he was the life of an intimate group, he used his knowledge of wider circles only to give authentic background to his novels. His books were popular and remunerative from the first, but his extravagance, his generosity and need to live grandly, kept him hard at work turning out 5000 words a day, two or more novels a year. He worked almost up to the moment of his death. Physically, he was markedly handsome, six feet two, well formed, with golden hair in youth and an innocent delight in his own appearance. He knew half a dozen arts and trades, from fencing to silver-smithing; he could turn his hand to everything and do it well. He loved the theater and rejoiced in the dramatization of some of his novels.

Crawford was primarily a romanticist and a romancer. His novels depended largely on the complications of plot, but it is their vivid characterizations and the rich detail of their setting which give them continued life. His cousin, Maud Howe Elliott, says rightly that he "was like a chameleon; he took the color of his surroundings and made them his own." Hugh Walpole called him "first, last, and all the time a story teller." "Ouida" (Louise de la Ramée), perhaps the most penetrating of his critics, unconsciously put her finger on his weakness as well as on his strength when she said that he was "ever present in his books." Not one of them lacks some picture of the author. His cousin remarks: "Crawford's black sheep are very black, his heroes are in the grand style. . . . That was the way he saw people. In real life he either loved or hated passionately. His mind was like a mirror. In it he saw oftenest his own face."

He wrote too profusely to give opportunity for the full and mature expression of his really fine talents. Charm, vividness, picturesqueness are there, but the underlying philosophy often seems very shallow. His is a fashion in fiction which has passed. Perhaps it has passed only for a time, and our grandchildren will read again with avidity the novels which our grandparents loved. His best works are the novels laid in Italy, which he knew so well—*Saracinesca, Sant' Ilario*, and *Don Orsino*. The most popular, however, was the posthumous (and inferior) *White Sister*.

Principal Works: *Novels*—Mr. Isaacs, 1882; Dr. Claudius, 1884; To Leeward, 1884; Zoroaster, 1885; Children of the King, 1885; A Tale of a Lonely Parish, 1886; Saracinesca, 1887; Marzio's Crucifix, 1887; Paul Patoff, 1887; With the Immortals, 1888; Greifenstein, 1889; Sant' Ilario, 1889; A Cigarette Maker's Romance, 1890; Khaled, 1891; The Witch of Prague, 1891; The Three Fates, 1891; Don Orsino, 1892; Pietro Ghisleri, 1893; A Roman Singer, 1894; Casa Braccio, 1894; Katharine Lauderdale, 1894; The Upper Berth, 1894; Taquisara, 1896; A Rose of Yesterday, 1897; Corleone, 1898; Via Crucis, 1899; In the Palace of the King, 1900; Marietta, 1901; Cecilia, 1902; Man Overboard, 1903; Whosoever Shall Offend, 1904; Fair Margaret, 1905; A Lady of Rome, 1906; The Little City of Hope, 1907; The Primadonna, 1908; The White Sister, 1909; Wandering Ghosts, 1911. *Non-Fiction*—The Novel: What Is It? 1893; Constantinople, 1895; Bar Harbor, 1896; Ave Roma Immortalis, 1898; Rulers of the South, 1900 (as Sicily, Calabria, and Malta, 1904); Francesca da Rimini (play), 1902; The Life of Pope Leo XIII, 1904; Salve Venetia, 1905.

About: Cooper, F. J. Some American Story Tellers; Elliott, M. H. My Cousin: F. Marion Crawford; Harkins, E. F. Little Pilgrimages Among the Men Who Have Written Famous Books; Collier's Weekly April 3, 1910; Edinburgh Review July 1906; Forum May 1909; McClure's Magazine March 1895.

CRAWFORD, JOHN WALLACE ("Captain Jack") (March 4, 1847-February 28, 1917), frontier scout and writer, was born in County Donegal, Ireland. His parents were John Austin Crawford, a Glasgow tailor, whose revolutionary speeches forced him to flee from Scotland, and Susie (Wallace) Crawford, a descendant of William Wallace, the Scottish chieftain.

Young Crawford was brought to America at the age of eleven to join his father who had emigrated in 1854 and settled in Minersville, Pa., as a coal miner. The lad, who had only a month's schooling in his life, went to work in the mines and busied himself there until the Civil War when he served with the 48th Pennsylvania Volunteers. He was wounded at Spottsylvania, May 12, 1864, and while convalescing in the Saterlee Hospital in West Philadelphia learned to read and write through the interest of a sister of charity. A return to the front resulted in fresh wounds at Petersburg, April 2, 1865. Four years later he married Anna M. Stokes of Numidia, Pa., and eventually they set out for the West, where he worked at various odd jobs.

Collection of Frederick H. Meserve
"CAPTAIN JACK" CRAWFORD

He was among the original seven men who settled the Black Hills region after the Custer expedition in 1874, was a member of the board of trustees of Custer City, and chief of scouts for a volunteer organization known as the Black Hills Rangers. During the Sioux War he served as a scout and messenger for both Merritt and Crook. He succeeded "Buffalo Bill" Cody as Merritt's chief of scouts, and later served as a scout in the Apache skirmishes. Post trading at Fort Craig, N.M., and the position of special agent of the Indian Bureau occupied him for a time. In 1886 he acquired a ranch near San Marcial, on the Rio Grande, where he lived, with the exception of brief occupancies of his home in Brooklyn.

By reciting his own verses and relating weird and witty stories of scout life he gained a wide reputation, and by 1879 his first book, *The Poet Scout*, appeared. It was enlarged and reprinted in 1886 and was followed by three others. He wrote several plays in which he took the principal rôles and was the author of more than a hundred short stories.

Tall, sensitive, with nervous gestures, Crawford fancied himself as "the poet scout" and built up the part in his dress, wearing his hair and beard in the style of his friend "Buffalo Bill." Fundamentally of modest tastes, he spoke of himself as "simple Jack Crawford." A pledge to his mother on her deathbed caused him to refrain from alcohol throughout his life. He died in Brooklyn, leaving no writings of more than ephemeral interest.

PRINCIPAL WORKS: The Poet Scout, 1879; Camp Fire Sparks, 1893; Lariattes, 1904; The Broncho Book, 1908.

ABOUT: Crawford, J. W. The Poet Scout and Lariattes (see Introductions); Smith, J. E. A Famous Battery and Its Campaigns; Brooklyn Eagle February 28, 1917.

CRÈVECOEUR, MICHEL-GUILLAUME JEAN DE (commonly called St. John de Crèvecoeur) (January 31, 1735-November 12, 1813), agricultural and travel writer, was born near Caen, Normandy, France, the son of Guillaume Jean de Crèvecoeur and Marie-Anne-Thérèse (Blouet) de Crèvecoeur. In later years he claimed that de Crèvecoeur was merely the name of an estate, and that the correct family name was St. Jean, or even St. John, for he alleged a connection with the famous English family of that name. In America he dropped his baptismal name and frequently called himself J. Hector St. John.

All of de Crèvecoeur's early life is obscure. It is thought that he was sent to England for schooling as a child, and that he lived there until 1754, when he went to America because of the death of his fiancée; that he served under Montcalm in Canada, perhaps as a mapmaker, and for some years thereafter as a surveyor in Pennsylvania, and explored the Great Lakes and the Ohio River. *Some* de Crèvecoeur certainly did all these things, and it was probably Michel-Guillaume, who in later years found it politically expedient not to be too confiding about his past connections. But all that is certainly known is that in 1764 he was naturalized (as a British subject, of course); that he bought and worked a farm called "Pine Hill," in Orange County, N.Y.; and that in 1769 he married Mehitable Tippet, daughter of a merchant in Yonkers.

From a portrait by Vallière
ST. JOHN DE CRÈVECOEUR
1786

It was from this farm that he wrote his delightful *Letters From an American Farmer,* as well as numerous articles and essays (some of them not collected until 1925) signed "Agricola." Certainly he had been educated in England, for he wrote English far better than he did French. He also introduced into America the cultivation of alfalfa, vetches, and other crops, as later on he introduced the potato into Normandy. He was a practical farmer and knew his subject well.

When the colonies revolted, de Crèvecoeur, who by birth was one of the future allies of America, remained a loyalist. Inevitably he found it more comfortable to leave the country; in 1780 he went to New York, then occupied by British troops, to sail for France. Instead he was arrested as a spy; and it was over a year before he was able to leave. In 1783 he returned, to find disaster. The Indians (Orange County being then the frontier) had burned his home, his wife was dead, his two surviving children were lost. Eventually he found them; a kind Bostonian had taken them to rear with his own family, and their father recovered them and made a home for them. His Tory views seem to have been forgiven him, especially as he returned with an appointment as French consul in New York; in later years Washington, Franklin, and Jefferson were among his friends. Bowing to accomplished fact, he labored faithfully to improve the commercial relations of his adopted and his native country. The *Letters* had been published in England in 1782, and by the patronage and assistance of the Duc de Rochefoucauld he had been enabled to translate the book into French.

The *Letters* were immensely popular, but they had rather an unfortunate effect. So laudatory and idyllic a picture of American farm life did de Crèvecoeur paint (though he indicted slavery and enlarged on the danger of Indian attacks on the frontier) that more than five hundred families left France to settle on the Ohio River, where most of them perished from hunger and malaria. Yet this was hardly the author's fault, nor could he have anticipated it. He himself was pleasingly modest about his production, saying, "There is something truly ridiculous in a farmer quitting his plow and his axe, and then flying to his pen." He praised the climate and the fertility of the new country, but (though he had plenty of practical experience of his own) he omitted to warn his readers of the impossibility of success for untrained, unequipped, and inexperienced immigrants in the wilds of what was then the extreme West.

A lover of his fellow-beings, a benevolent, warm-hearted man, he had the common touch which makes his principal work the most delightful American writing of the colonial period. He could be bitterly angry—as witness his diatribe against slavery and his description of the lynching of a Negro—but he excelled in homely pathos and bits of humor. He had real descriptive power, coupled with keen observation, and he makes one fairly see the scenes and people of his narrative. It is unfortunate that so many readers, instead of enjoying the story, decided without due preparation to make it their own.

De Crèvecoeur's health failed under the heavy duties of his consulship, as might be expected of a farmer compelled to live and work in a city, and from 1785 to 1787 he was in France on leave of absence. He began another leave in 1790, and this time he never returned. He resigned and stayed in Europe, for the most part at Rouen, though for a time he was at Altona, near Hamburg, where his daughter's husband (her name was America-Francès, and Jefferson had attended her wedding) was in the American diplomatic service. He died finally at Sarcelles, near Paris, without seeing America again.

So much of colonial literature is concerned primarily with philosophy and religion, that de Crèvecoeur's work is almost all that survives which busies itself with the details of daily physical life. He had oddities of style, his syntax was sometimes weak, and his grammar uncertain; but in general his writing is simple and trenchant. The manuscripts he (or his publisher) suppressed in 1782, perhaps as unduly lengthening the book, were discovered in 1922 and published three years later, and they were very much worth publishing. His work in French on his travels in America is dull, and has a perfunctory atmosphere, but whenever he touched on the life and observations of an American farmer he was at his happiest, and can be read with enjoyment and profit today.

Principal Works: Letters From an American Farmer, 1782; La Culture des Pommes de Terre, 1795; Voyage Dans la Haute Pennsylvanie et Dans l'État de New-York, 1801; Sketches of Eighteenth Century America (ed. by H. L. Bourdin, R. G. Gabriel, & S. T. Williams) 1925.

About: de Crèvecoeur, R. Saint John de Crèvecoeur: Sa Vie et Ses Ouvrages; Mitchell, J. P. St. Jean de Crèvecoeur; Nation September 23, 1925; North American Review September 1925.

CRÈVECOEUR. ST. JOHN. See CRÈVECOEUR, MICHEL-GUILLAUME JEAN DE

"CREYTON, PAUL." See TROWBRIDGE, JOHN TOWNSEND

CROLY, DAVID GOODMAN (November 3, 1829-April 29, 1889), journalist and writer on philosophy, was born in County Cork, Ireland, the son of Patrick and Elizabeth Croly. With his parents he came to America when a small boy and, with brief interruptions, lived the rest of his life in New York City. In 1854 he was graduated from New York University and immediately afterwards became a reporter on the New York *Evening Post*. Later he became an editor on the *Herald*, managing editor of the *World*, and editor-in-chief of the *Daily Graphic*, an early picture-paper. In 1878 failing health and disputes with the proprietors caused his resignation. At one time he founded and edited a magazine called *The Modern Thinker*; it had only a brief life. His wife Jane (Cunningham) Croly [*q.v.*] was also a well known journalist. They were married in 1857.

Croly's main personal interest was in philosophy, particularly in Positivism (the rationalistic system of the French thinker Auguste Comte) and most of his original writings dealt with the Comtist philosophy and its implications. He was the coiner of the word "miscegenation." In his authorship, as in his journalism, he was independent and iconoclastic.

PRINCIPAL WORKS: Miscegenation, 1864; Seymour and Blair: Their Lives and Services, 1868; A Primer of Positivism, 1871; Glimpses of the Future, 1888.

ABOUT: New York Times April 30, 1889.

CROLY, JANE (CUNNINGHAM) ("Jenny June") (December 19, 1829-December 23, 1901), journalist, often called "the first American newspaper woman," was born in Market Harborough, Leicestershire, England, the daughter of the Rev. Joseph H. and Jane Cunningham. When she was twelve years old her father brought her to America and joined his son in supervising her education. They lived in Poughkeepsie and New York City, and for a short while young Jane Cunningham attended school at Southbridge, Mass., where her literary ability came to light in editorial and dramatic writing for school publications. Hiding behind the pseudonym "Jenny June," taken from a book of verse by Benjamin F. Taylor, she became at twenty-six a feature writer on women's fashions and was a pioneer in syndicating her articles.

In 1857 she married David Goodman Croly [*q.v.*], an enterprising New York journalist, and became the mother of five children whose upbringing did not conflict with her journalistic activities. She became virtually the first woman reporter and gathered and wrote her material so systematically that an editor was moved to say, "Why, you go on so naturally and make so little fuss about your work that I sometimes forget that you are a woman."

JANE CUNNINGHAM CROLY
("Jennie June")
c. 1869

In a period when there was little in newspapers to interest feminine readers, she pioneered in raising the standard of the woman's department, established the first shopping column, and introduced chatty articles about fashions and news of interest to housewives.

During her career she edited *Demorest's Illustrated Monthly*, and the *Home-Maker*, and was part-owner of the famous *Godey's Lady's Book*. Becoming the first woman correspondent for out-of-town papers, she sent her articles to Boston, Chicago, New Orleans, Richmond, Baltimore, and other cities. Her various other New York editorial connections were with the New York *World*, *Graphic Daily Times*, and the New York *Times*, and for five years she served as dramatic critic and assistant editor of the *Messenger*.

"Jenny June" Croly's fashion articles became the talk of America, as she advanced her progressive ideas. Stressing simplicity in an ornate age, she loudly decried foreign frills and furbelows and urged her readers to modify elaborate housekeeping.

She founded the Sorosis, the first important woman's club; was the first president of the New York State Federation of Women's Clubs; and founded the Women's Press Club in 1889. She was the author of a number of books, among which *The History of the Woman's Club Movement in America* is best known.

Small, blue-eyed, brown-haired, "Jenny June" was always in advance of her time and ardently championed the struggle for women's rights. Through her wit and charm she attracted the important men and women of arts and letters to her Grove Street, and later, 71st Street salons.

After a serious accident in 1898 she lived mainly in England but died in New York City. Of herself she said, "I have never done anything that was not helpful to women, so far as it lay in my power."

PRINCIPAL WORKS: Jenny June's American Cookery Book, 1866; For Better or Worse: A Book for Some Men and All Women, 1875; The History of the Woman's Club Movement in America, 1898.

ABOUT: Cunningham, J. Jane Cunningham Croly: "Jenny June"; Ross, I. Ladies of the Press; Harper's Bazaar March 3, 1900; Woman's Journal January 4, 1902; Critic March 1904; New York Times December 24, 1901.

CUMMINS, MARIA SUSANNA (April 9, 1827-October 1, 1866), novelist, was the daughter of Judge David Cummins and Mehitable Cummins, of Middleton, Mass. Born in Salem, she was a true daughter of

New England and could trace her ancestry to the earliest settlers of Ipswich. She was tutored at home by her father who encouraged her literary talent, and was later a pupil at Mrs. Charles Sedgwick's fashionable school at Lenox. After publishing stories in the *Atlantic Monthly* and other periodicals, in 1854 she produced her first novel, *The Lamplighter.* This pious but dramatic love-story achieved instant success and was translated into French and German. Subsequent novels were received with less enthusiasm. After the death of her father, Miss Cummins moved to Dorchester, where she led a quiet life in an old house surrounded by spacious gardens and an orchard. Apart from her writing she divided her time between home and church. Her genuine gift for characterization was marred by a tedious style and excessive moralizing. She died in Dorchester.

Principal Works: The Lamplighter, 1854; Mabel Vaughan, 1857; El Fureidis, 1860; Haunted Hearts, 1864.

About: Hall, N. Sermon Preached in the First Church, Dorchester, on the Sunday (October 8, 1866) Following the Decease of Maria S. Cummins; Orcutt, W. D. Good Old Dorchester; Boston Daily Advertiser October 2, 1866.

CURTIN, JEREMIAH (September 16, 1840?-December 14, 1906), philologist and comparative mythologist, was born in Greenfield, Wis., in either 1838 or 1840, the son of David Curtin and Ellen (Furlong) Curtin. His parents could give him only a common school education, but from the German, Polish, and Scandinavian settlers in the neighborhood he gained his first interest and training in linguistics. By his own labor he managed to earn his way through Carroll College (Waukesha, Wis.), Phillips Exeter Academy, and Harvard, where he received his B.A. degree in 1863. On the invitation of the officers of a Russian fleet which visited the United States in 1864, he went to St. Petersburg (Leningrad), where he worked as a translator until he became assistant secretary of the American Legation. From 1870 he traveled throughout eastern Europe and western Asia, apparently in the service of the Czarist government, studying Slavonic languages, then spent a year in the British Isles collecting folklore. He returned to America and became connected with the Bureau of American Ethnology, from 1883 to 1891, doing research in Indian languages and customs. In 1872 he had married Alma M. Cordelle, of Vermont.

Curtin was an early translator of Tolstoy, Sienkiewicz, and other Russian and Polish authors. His ethnological work covered the Slavonic, Celtic, Mongolian, and American Indian peoples. He is said to have been familiar with seventy languages and dialects. A turn for romanticism and mysticism saved his work from the dryness of much of such specialized study. Many of his researches were published posthumously.

Principal Works: Myths and Folk Tales of the Russians, Western Slavs, and Magyars, 1890; Myths and Folklore of Ireland, 1890; Hero Tales of Ireland, 1894; Tales of the Fairies and of the Ghost World, 1895; Creation Myths of Primitive America, 1898; The Mongols in Russia, 1908; The Mongols: A History, 1908; A Journey in Southern Siberia, 1909; Myths of the Modocs, 1912; Fairy Tales of Eastern Europe, 1915; Introduction to Seneca Fiction, Legends, and Myths (with J. N. B. Hewitt) 1919; Wonder Tales From Russia, 1921; Seneca Indian Myths, 1923.

About: Critic May 1900; Harvard Graduates Magazine March 1907; London Times December 29, 1906; New York Tribune December 15, 1906.

CURTIS, GEORGE TICKNOR (November 28, 1812-March 28, 1894), lawyer, novelist, and author of legal treatises, was born at Watertown, Mass., the son of Benjamin and Lois (Robbins) Curtis. His middle name was derived from his paternal stepgrandfather, whose son, George Ticknor, the critic, was one of his friends. His brother, Benjamin R. Curtis, was a justice of the United States Supreme Court.

Graduating from Harvard in 1832, he taught school, and studied law at the Harvard Law School and in the Boston office of a relative, C. P. Curtis. Admitted to the bar in 1836, he practiced for a short time in Worcester and in 1837 returned to Boston. In 1862 he moved to New York City, where he pursued his legal career for the next twenty-four years. Since a large amount of his practice was before the United States Supreme Court, he kept an office at Washington, D.C., and rose to prominence as a patent lawyer. Among his distinguished clients were Goodyear, Morse, Thomas Blanchard, Cyrus McCormick, and many other inventors of note.

Meanwhile the took an active part in politics, and as a Whig and friend of Daniel Webster, served the Massachusetts House from 1840 to 1843, declining reelection. He also refused the ministry to Great Britain, offered to him by Webster when he was secretary of state under President Tyler.

As a United States Commissioner, in 1852, he managed the return to slavery of Thomas Sims, under the Fugitive Slave Act of 1850, thereby incurring the wrath of the Abolitionists. Following the example of many of the Webster "Cotton" Whigs, he became a Democrat. During the Civil War his sympathies were Unionist, but he did not hesitate to criticize the administration when occasion prompted. In New York City, where he was associated with Tammany Hall, he refused a judgeship. Although he never held office, his influence was keenly felt, many of his opinions being set forth in pamphlets and magazine articles. Outstanding among these was an argument favoring state indemnity for the proprietors of the Ursuline Convent at Charlestown, Mass., which was burned by a mob.

Curtis was a man of retiring nature who divided his time between his office, his study, and his family. He published many books and achieved a certain reputation for scholarship, but his laborious style prevented him from rising to greater distinction. His *Life of James Buchanan* (1883) and the series of volumes which comprised his rambling *Constitutional History of the United States* . . . (1889-96), are his chief works. In his late years he wrote a novel, *John Charaxes: A Tale of Civil War,* under the pen-name "Peter Boyleston."

He was twice married: first in 1844, to Mary Oliver Story, daughter of Justice Joseph Story; and, after her death, to Louise A. Nystrom, in 1851. He died at Washington, D.C.

PRINCIPAL WORKS: Digest of Cases Adjudicated in the Courts of Admiralty of the United States and in the High Court of Admiralty in England, 1839; Treatise on the Rights and Duties of Merchant Seamen, 1841; A Treatise on the Law of Copyright, 1847; A Treatise on the Law of Patents, 1849; Equity Precedents, 1850; Commentaries on the Jurisdiction, Practice, and Peculiar Jurisprudence of the Courts of the United States, 1854-58. *Biography*—Life of Daniel Webster, 1870; Memoir of Benjamin Robbins Curtis, 1879; Life of James Buchanan, 1883. *History*—Constitutional History of the United States From Their Declaration of Independence to the Close of the Civil War, 1889-1896. *Novel*—John Charaxes: A Tale of the Civil War, 1889.

ABOUT: Harvard Graduates Magazine June 1894; New York Times, Boston Transcript March 29, 1894.

CURTIS, GEORGE WILLIAM (February 24, 1824-August 31, 1892), essayist, editor, and orator, was born in Providence, R.I., the son of George and Mary Elizabeth (Burrill) Curtis. His mother, the daughter of a senator and chief justice of Rhode Island, died in 1826. The boy was sent with his older brother, James Burrill Curtis, to school in Jamaica Plains, Mass., until 1835, when the father remarried and they returned to Providence. In 1839 the family moved to New York City, and after a few months with private tutors Curtis ended his formal education and went to work for a year as clerk in a counting house.

This, however, was so irksome an occupation that in 1842 he went with his brother (the greatest influence on his early life) to Brook Farm, the Transcendentalist colony, where they remained for eighteen months; George William Curtis' job there was to trim and clean the lamps. For eighteen months more the boys farmed near Concord, in close contact with Emerson, who became the guiding light of the younger brother's mind. In 1845 he returned to New York and joined the staff of the *Tribune,* and for this paper he traveled for four years, from 1846 to 1850, to Europe, Egypt, and Syria, sending home letters which made up the contents of his first three books. In 1853 he became co-editor of *Putnam's Monthly,* and the next year started to write the "Editor's Easy Chair" department in *Harper's,* a lifelong connection which made him one of the most influential authors in America. In 1856 he married Anna Shaw.

Putnam's was sold to Dix, Edwards, & Co., and Curtis bought an interest in the firm, though he had no financial responsibility for its affairs. It failed, with the magazine, in 1857, and Curtis assumed its liabilities, without any legal compulsion. It took him to 1873 to pay off the debt. Meanwhile he had become editor of *Harper's Weekly,* in 1863, and also contributed regularly to *Harper's Bazaar.*

Though he continued to write throughout his life, Curtis's career may be divided into two sections, the first literary, the second as a publicist. He was always in demand as an orator, and his lecture on "Political Infidelity" especially was given many times. In 1860 and 1864 he was a delegate to the Republican National Convention, and in 1868 was a presidential elector. He refused an offer of the ministry to England because he felt it his duty to continue his social interests at home. He had been an active abolitionist; now he was a worker for many good causes—woman suffrage, conciliation between capital and labor, above all civil service reform. He was from 1880 president of the New York Civil Service Reform Association. He had broken with the Republicans over Blaine's nomination, and supported Cleveland in both his campaigns. In 1869 he had lectured on English literature at Cornell, and from 1890 to his death he was chancellor of the University of the State of New York. He was vice-president of the American Unitarian Association. There were few aspects of American thought in

Collection of Frederick H. Meserve
GEORGE WILLIAM CURTIS

which George William Curtis was not a gently guiding figure. His sad, kindly face, framed with "Burnside" whiskers, was familiar on every serious platform. Three universities had honored him with an M.A. degree, three with an LL.D., Columbia with an L.H.D. He should have died a painless death, as gentle as himself, but he became a victim of cancer of the stomach, which killed him at sixty-eight.

A sort of Cavalier Puritan, high-minded yet gallant, an idealist to the point of sentimentalism, yet with strong convictions and the courage to stand by them, a compound of charm and tender satire and fortrightness—that was George William Curtis both as man and as author. He is little read today, and his style seems "soft" to moderns, but America has had few nobler sons. He was Emerson's "American scholar" turning his intellect to the concerns of daily life.

Principal Works: Nile Notes of a Howadji, 1851; The Howadji in Syria, 1851; Lotus Eating, 1852; Potiphar Papers, 1853; Prue and I, 1857; Trumps: A Novel, 1861; Charles Sumner, 1874; William Cullen Bryant, 1879; Robert Burns, 1880; Washington Irving, 1891; James Russell Lowell: An Address, 1892; Essays From the Easy Chair, 1892-97; Orations and Addresses (ed. by C. E. Norton) 1893-94.

About: Cary, E. George William Curtis; Chadwick, J. W. George William Curtis; Godwin, P. Commemorative Addresses; Merrill, E. B. A Tribute to the Life and Public Service of George William Curtis; Payne, W. M. Leading American Essayists; Winter, W. George William Curtis: A Eulogy; Atlantic Monthly January 1893; Cosmopolitan October 1894; Harper's Monthly February 1893, December 1897; McClure's Magazine October 1904; Nation September 18, 1892; Review of Reviews October 1892.

CURTIS, HARRIOT. See FARLEY, HARRIET

CUSHING, CALEB (January 17, 1800-January 2, 1879), statesman and miscellaneous writer, was born in Salisbury, Essex County, Mass., of fine old New England stock, many of his ancestors having been Colonial clergymen or judges. He was the son of John Newmarch Cushing, wealthy merchant and ship-owner, and Lydia (Dow) Cushing, of Seabrook, N.H., who died when Caleb was ten years old. In 1802 the Cushing family moved to Newburyport, where Caleb grew up to be one of the leading citizens. His prodigious intellect enabled him to enter Harvard in his thirteenth year. Graduated with honors in 1817, after a year at the Harvard Law School, he read law in Newburyport and was admitted to the bar in 1821. Meanwhile, during the previous year, he had tutored in mathematics at Harvard, and translated Robert J. Pothier's treatise, *On Maritime Contracts of Letting to Hire.* While practicing law in Newburyport, he edited the local newspaper, delivered many public addresses, mastered at least four modern languages, and entered politics, representing the Massachusetts General Court in 1824 and serving as state senator in 1826.

Cushing married Elizabeth Wilde, daughter of Judge Samuel Sumner Wilde, of the supreme judicial court, 1824. She died a few years later and he never remarried.

After a European trip in 1829-32, Cushing re-entered the political arena and won a Whig election to Congress in 1834. Serving for four consecutive terms, he was a leading figure in anti-slavery agitation. By 1840 his position was so secure that it was generally assumed that he was the logical political successor to Everett and Webster, but Cushing made the unfortunate step of involving himself in a political duel raging between Henry Clay and President John Tyler, with the result that his support of Democratic principles so outraged the Whigs that they forced his retirement from Congress on March 3, 1843, and he suffered the humiliation of having Tyler's three attempts to name him Secretary of the Treasury rebuffed by the Senate. But his wounded pride was soon eased by the soothing ointment of an important appointment as commissioner to China where he negotiated the difficult Treaty of Wang Hiya, which

CALEB CUSHING

broadened merchant trading between China and America. On his return from this highly successful mission, he toured the Northwest, and then made a triumphant entry into the Massachusetts General Court.

During the Mexican hostilities he used his personal fortune to organize a regiment, and served as Colonel and Brigadier-General.

Cushing became a member of the state legislature for the fifth time in 1850, was mayor of Newburyport in 1851-52, and served Franklin Pierce as Attorney-General. From 1857-60 he was once again in the Massachusetts legislature.

During the Civil War he executed confidential missions for Lincoln. In 1866 he went to Bogota to negotiate a treaty with the Columbian Government, regarding the proposed Panama Canal, and was counsel for the United States at the Geneva conference in 1872 to settle the "Alabama" claims. In 1874 he was appointed minister to Spain where he remained until 1877 when he was succeeded by James Russell Lowell. He died in Newburyport. Emerson considered him the foremost scholar of his time and Wendell Phillips once said, "I regard Mr. Cushing as the most learned man now living." His vast intellect embraced a knowledge of subjects so varied that it was said there was almost no subject with which he was not familiar. A man of tireless energy, he seldom allowed himself more than five hours sleep, and it was thus, amid his busy political life, that he found time to publish his books.

Principal Works: On Maritime Contracts of Letting to Hire, 1821; A History of Newburyport, 1826; A Review Historical and Political of the Late Revolution in France, 1833; Reminiscences in Spain, 1833.

About: Fuess, C. M. Biography of Caleb Cushing; A Memorial of Caleb Cushing From the City of Newburyport, 1879.

CUSHING, FRANK HAMILTON (July 22, 1857-April 10, 1900), ethnologist and archaeologist, was born at Northeast, Pa., the son of Thomas Cushing and Sarah (Crittenden) Cushing. When he was thirteen the family moved to Medina, N.Y. This country was rich in Indian remains, and soon engaged the boy's archaeological interest. When he was only fifteen he drew the attention of ethnologists by his discovery of the process of making Indian arrow-heads. He went to Cornell University in 1875, but spent most of his time there in making a collection of aboriginal material for the Centennial Exposition in Philadelphia. He became curator of the collection, and was invited to become curator of the ethnological department of the National Museum, in Washington. In 1879 he was assistant ethnologist of an expedition to the Zuñi country in New Mexico. He remained behind when the expedition left, and for two years lived with the Zuñis as one of them, being adopted into the tribe. In 1882 he conducted a party of Zuñis on a religious pilgrimage to the Atlantic Ocean. Two of them stayed in Washington to help Cushing write up his researches. During this trip East, Cushing married Emily Tennyson Magill. Later he returned to the Pueblo and stayed till 1884, when because of ill health he had to leave. With him he brought back three of his adopted brothers.

From 1886 to 1888 he conducted archaeological explorations in Arizona, exhuming the "lost cities" of the Pueblos. His next exploration discovered the fabled "Seven Cities of Cibola." His health had been ruined, however, by the hardships he had undergone, and he was an invalid thereafter. Nevertheless, he continued to write of his finds for the Bureau of American Ethnology, and in 1896, on a visit to Florida, he discovered the remains of lake-dwellings in the Florida Keys—the relics of a hitherto unknown people. Most of his writings consisted of reports and pamphlets for the Bureau of Ethnology.

Principal Works: Zuñi Fetiches, 1881; Myths of Creation, 1882; Adventures in Zuñi, 1883; Studies of Ancient Pueblo Ceramic Art, 1885; Manual Concepts, 1892; Primitive Copper

Working, 1894; The Arrow, 1895; Outlines of Zuñi Creation Myths, 1896; Primitive Motherhood, 1897; Zuñi Folk Tales, 1901.

ABOUT: Annual Report Bureau of American Ethnology 1901; New York Times April 11, 1900.

CUSHING, LUTHER STEARNS (June 22, 1803-June 22, 1856), jurist and author of legal treatises, was born in Lunenberg, Worcester County, Mass., the son of Edmund and Mary (Stearns) Cushing. His father held prominent positions in Massachusetts politics for forty years as representative in the Massachusetts General Court, state senator, and member of the governor's council. Young Luther attended the neighborhood schools, read law in a Lunenberg office, and was graduated from Harvard in 1826 with the distinction of being the only member of his class to receive the degree of LL.B. After leaving Harvard he joined Charles Sumner and George S. Hilliard in editing the *American Jurist and Law Magazine*, a Boston publication. From 1832 to 1844 he was clerk of the Massachusetts House of Representatives. After a brief service in the Massachusetts House of Representatives, he was appointed judge of the city court of common pleas, but resigned in 1848 to become official reporter of the decisions of the supreme court of the commonwealth. During 1848-49 and 1850-51 he lectured on Roman Law in the Harvard Law School, and was offered a professorship in 1851, but ill health forced him to decline the honor. Five years later he died in Boston on his birthday. He was married twice: first, in 1840 to Mary Otis Lincoln, a lineal descendant of the patriot, James Otis; and after several years as a widower, to Elizabeth Dutton Cooper, in 1853.

Despite his busy life, he produced a number of books on legal subjects and was the author of *A Manual of Parliamentary Practice: or, Rules of Proceedings and Debate in Deliberative Assemblies* (1844). This pocket-sized volume met instant approval and was adopted as a guide to all organized assemblies. It was revised after Cushing's death by his brother, Judge Edmund Lambert Cushing, chief justice of the supreme court of New Hampshire, and is still used by legislative bodies.

Of Cushing's other works, his translations of legal treatises are outstanding and his name not only enjoys a high reputation in legal literature, but is synonomous with painstaking research and deep knowledge of fine legal points.

PRINCIPAL WORKS: *Translations*—Law of Possession (Savigny) 1838; Treatise on the Contract of Sale (Pothier) 1839; Effects of Drunkeness on Criminal Responsibility (Mattermaier) 1841; *Original Works*—A Manual of Parliamentary Practice, 1844; A Practical Treatise on the Trustee Process, 1853; Reports of Controverted Election Cases in the House of Representatives of the Commonwealth of Massachusetts From 1780 to 1852, 1853; An Introduction to the Study of Roman Law, 1854; Elements of the Law and Practice of Legislative Assemblies in the United States, 1856.

ABOUT: Cushing, J. The Genealogy of the Cushing Family; Boston Advertiser June 23, 1856.

"CUSHMAN, CLARA." See HAVEN, EMILY (BRADLEY) NEAL

CUSTIS, GEORGE WASHINGTON PARKE (April 30, 1781-October 10, 1857), playwright, was born at George Washington's home, Mt. Vernon, Va., his father, John Parke Custis, being Martha Washington's son by her first marriage. His mother was Eleanor Calvert, a descendant of Lord Baltimore, the founder of Maryland. His father having died early, he was reared by his grandmother at Mt. Vernon, moving to Arlington on her death in 1802. He attended Princeton (then the College of New Jersey), but was not graduated, leaving in 1799 to become aide-de-camp to Gen. Charles Pinckney, with the rank of colonel. In 1804 he married Mary Lee Fitzhugh; their daughter, Mary, became the wife of Gen. Robert E. Lee. Custis served in the defense of the city of Washington during the War of 1812.

His first published writing was a series of "Conversations With Lafayette," in the Alexandria, Va., *Gazette*, in 1824. In 1826 he began serializing in two papers his memories of George Washington, which were not published until 1860. His first play, *The Indian Prophecy*, was produced in Philadelphia in 1827. *Pocahontas: or, The Settlers of Virginia*, his most successful play, was the only one published. A wealthy country gentleman in the old Southern tradition, Custis considered his plays mere divertissements and kindnesses to "the poor rogues of actors," and never thought of himself as a professional dramatist. His plays are all historical in nature, though very far from being historically accurate. The others include *The Railroad* (produced 1830, in Philadelphia), *North Point: or, Baltimore Defended* (Baltimore, 1833), and *The Eighth of January* (New York, 1834).

PRINCIPAL WORKS: Pocahontas: or, The Settlers of Virginia, 1830; Recollections and Private Memoirs of Washington by His Adopted Son, 1860.

ABOUT: Custis, G. W. P. Recollections and Private Memoirs of Washington (see Memoir by M. C. Lee); Quinn, A. H. History of the American Drama From the Beginning to the Civil War.

CUTLER, LIZZIE (PETIT) (?, 1831-January 16, 1902), novelist, was born in Milton, Va. in a fairly prosperous farming family named Petit. Her mother died when the child was still an infant, and she was reared by an aunt and a great-aunt, in and near Charlottesville. What little education she received came as a result of contact with those connected with the University of Virginia, situated in this town.

Her first novel, *Light and Darkness,* was published, with thinly veiled anonymity, in 1855, and was attacked as "a tale of guilty love." Overcome by the denunciation, she fled to New York, and thereafter was careful to make her heroes and heroines entirely virtuous, according to the novelistic canons of the time. In 1858 she gave public readings, and decided to go on the stage; instead, she married Peter G. Cutler, a New York attorney, and until his death in 1870 was wholly absorbed in domesticity and social life. The fortune he left her was soon lost in unwise investments, and the widow returned to Charlottesville. Her last thirty years were pathetic ones; she wrote industriously and eagerly, preserving the strictest rectitude in her stories, but fashions had changed and no one wanted her contributions. She died alone and forgotten in a Richmond boarding-house, a beneficiary of the charity of a few old friends who remembered her past. Her novels are of no importance; she was a very minor figure among the host of sentimental women, North and South, who scribbled verses and stories in the mid-nineteenth century.

PRINCIPAL WORKS: Light and Darkness: A Story of Fashionable Life, 1855; Household Mysteries: A Romance of Southern Life, 1856; The Stars of the Crowd: or, Men and Women of the Day, 1858.

ABOUT: Freeman, J. D. ("Mary Forrest"). Women of the South; Johnson, J. G. Southern Fiction Prior to 1860; Raymond, I. Southland Writers.

CUTTER, GEORGE WASHINGTON (1801-December 25, 1865), poet, was born in Quebec, Canada, where he received a rather insubstantial early education and then began the study of law. Upon removal to Terre Haute, Ind., he served a term there in the lower house of the state legislature (1838-39). While practicing law in Covington, Ky., he was strongly excited by some of the first skirmishes of the Mexican War and set about recruiting a part of the 2d Kentucky Regiment. Cutter's actions in the battle in which Col. Clay lost his life were entirely heroic and the ensuing victory was the inspiration of "Buena Vista," the best known of his military poems.

At the close of the War, he became a zealous Whig, stumped in various social and political causes, and served a clerkship in Washington until 1853. He was divorced from his first wife. Mrs. Frances Ann Drake, an actress, and was married a second time in the West.

Of Cutter's four volumes of verse, *The Song of Steam and Other Poems* was, perhaps, the most vigorous in sentiment, bearing a little of the unconventionality which characterizes poets of a much later day; "Song of Lightning" in *Poems and Fugitive Pieces* achieves a kind of momentum by an artful use of action-filled words. But Cutter's verse, for the most part, has been largely eclipsed by the vast number of Civil War poems that sprang up after his death.

PRINCIPAL WORKS: Buena Vista and Other Poems, 1848; The Song of Steam and Other Poems, 1857; Poems and Fugitive Pieces, 1857; Poems: National and Patriotic, 1857.

ABOUT: Coggeshall, W. T. Poets and Poetry of the West; Evening Star (Washington) December 27, 1865.

DABNEY, RICHARD (?, 1787-November 25, 1825), poet, was born on a plantation in Louisa County, Va., the son of Samuel Dabney and Jane (Meriwether) Dabney. Meriwether Lewis, the explorer, was his first cousin. Though the family was a distinguished one, there were twelve children, and the father was far from wealthy. The boy, however, was able to attend a classical school in Richmond, and was so good a student that by the time he was seventeen he was teaching Latin and Greek at a Richmond academy. About 1812 he moved to Philadelphia and entered the employ of Mathew Cary, one of the best known publishers of the time. Unfortunately, Dabney, though brilliant, was also weak; he was a confirmed drunkard, and following an injury received in a theatre fire in Richmond in 1811, he became an opium addict also. Cary was finally obliged to discharge him, and he returned to his father's plantation. There he taught a country school for a while, but for most of his remaining years was incapacitated for any steady employment. He never married, but died on the plantation at thirty-eight, an unhappy, embittered failure. His only volume of poems, published by himself in Richmond in 1812, and reissued by Cary in 1815, fell completely flat both times, though it gained him sufficient local reputation for the incorrect ascription to him of a popular anonymous poem of the time, "Rhododaphne." Nearly half the volume consists of correct but unpoetic translations from the Latin, Greek, Italian, and French; the original verses are amateurish, imitative of all the better known English poets of the time, and heavily didactic.

PRINCIPAL WORK: Poems: Original and Translated, 1812, 1815.

ABOUT: Duyckinck, E. A. & G. L. Cyclopaedia of American Literature.

DABNEY, VIRGINIUS (February 15, 1835-June 2, 1894), novelist and teacher, was born in Gloucester County, Va., the son of Thomas Smith Gregory Dabney, a cavalier Southerner, and Sophia (Hill) Dabney. He spent his childhood in Mississippi, was educated by tutors, and attended the University of Virginia. Before his marriage, in 1858, to Ellen Maria Heath, he traveled in Europe; returning to Virginia, he became a captain in the Confederate Army. He established, in succession, three private schools, and then made literary connections in New York City where he lived until his death in 1894.

The Story of Don Miff (1886) is a novel with a jaunty and yet rather foresighted comment on the social order evolving from the post-war period; *Gold That Did Not Glitter* (1889) was less successful. Superficially, he was slightly progressive; but fundamentally, he was the counterpart of the highly unpractical aristocracy of the Old South.

PRINCIPAL WORKS: The Story of Don Miff, 1886; Gold That Did Not Glitter, 1889.

ABOUT: Bruce, P. A. History of the University of Virginia; Dabney, W. H. The Dabneys of Virginia; Richmond Times June 3, 1894.

DAHLGREN, SARAH MADELEINE (VINTON) (July 13, 1825-May 28, 1898), miscellaneous writer, was born in Gallipolis, Ohio, the daughter of Samuel Finley Vinton, for twenty years United States Congressman, and Romain Madeleine (Bureau) Vinton, who died in 1831. She went to school in the East, and became hostess for her father in Washington. Her surroundings occasioned *A Washington Winter* and *The Woodley Lane Ghost and Other Stories.* In *Thoughts on Female Suffrage* she sharply opposed women in politics.

Three years after the death of her first husband, Daniel C. Goddard, she was married to Rear Admiral John Adolphus Dahlgren, who died in 1870. Mrs. Dahlgren's Catholic missionary activities and literary "salon" occupied her late years. She was a versatile and careful writer, but neither highly original nor profound.

PRINCIPAL WORKS: Idealities, 1859; Thoughts on Female Suffrage, 1871; Etiquette of Social Life in Washington, 1873; South Mountain Magic, 1882; A Washington Winter, 1883; The Lost Name, 1886; The Woodley Lane Ghost and Other Stories, 1899.

ABOUT: Vinton, J. A. The Vinton Memorial; Washington Post May 29, 1898; Evening Star May 30, 1898.

DALY, AUGUSTIN. See DALY, JOHN AUGUSTIN

DALY, CHARLES PATRICK (October 31, 1816-September 19, 1899), jurist and legal writer, was born in New York City, of Irish emigrant parents. After a scant education he worked as a clerk, cabin boy on a trading vessel, and carpenter's apprentice. He studied law, and was admitted to the bar in 1839. Five years later he was made a judge of the court of common pleas of the City of New York, and became, later, chief justice, serving until 1885; his *Reports* ("Daly's Cases") cover the years 1859-91. He distinguished himself at the time of the Astor Place Riots in 1849 and, during the Civil War, gave sane and unprejudiced advice to President Lincoln and Secretary Seward.

He had a scholarly love for the drama and for many years was president of the American Geographical Society. His technical writings form an astute contribution to legal literature.

PRINCIPAL WORKS: Julius C. Verplanck: His Ancestry, Life, and Character, 1870; Barratry: Its Origin, History, and Meaning in the Maritime Laws, 1872; First Theatre in America: When Was the Drama First Introduced in America? 1896; Birthday Verses, 1897.

ABOUT: Kohler, M. J. Chas. P. Daly: A Tribute to His Memory; Green Bag November 1894; New York Times September 20, 1899.

DALY, JOHN AUGUSTIN (July 20, 1838-June 7, 1899), playwright and theatrical producer, was born in Plymouth, N.C., the elder son of Capt. Denis Daly, a sea captain and shipowner from Limerick, Ireland, and Elizabeth (Duffrey) Daly, born in the West Indies of Irish descent. Captain Daly died in 1841, and the widow, with two small sons, moved first to Norfolk, Va., and then in a few years to New York City, where she supported her children by sewing. Augustin (he never used his first name), attended the public schools, but as soon as possible transferred to night school and went to work as a clerk to help his mother. It was largely by his efforts that his brother (later his biographer) was enabled to stay in school and to become a lawyer.

From boyhood Daly had been interested in the stage, not as actor, but as producer, and he had taken part in numerous amateur juvenile productions. In 1856 he ventured to put on a whole performance in Brooklyn. Three years later he became dramatic critic of the *Sunday Courier*, doing free lance criticism for several other papers as well. He continued this work for ten years, long after he had secured some standing both as manager and as playwright.

His first play, *Leah the Forsaken*, was produced in 1862; it was an adaptation of a German play. Many of his early dramas were adaptations from the French or German, or dramatizations of popular novels, chiefly by Dickens and Charles Reade (*Griffith Gaunt, Pickwick Papers*, etc.). His first, and immensely popular, original play, *Under the Gaslight*, was performed in 1867. Before this, during the Civil War, he had been manager of a theatrical troupe playing the Southern cities under Federal control—his own Southern birth being relied on to make him acceptable to the inhabitants. This was the forerunner of a lifetime of tours throughout this country and in Europe.

In 1869 Daly married Mary Duff, daughter of a theatre proprietor. Their two sons both died of diphtheria on one day in 1884. From this tragedy dated his lifelong love of and charity to poor and unhappy children.

Daly found the star system in full swing on the American stage: most theatres had resident stock companies to which the stars paid periodical visits. He resolved to substitute a repertory company, each member of which should be of high rank. In this manner he developed the talents of such actors and actresses as John Drew, Fanny Davenport, Ada Rehan, Otis Skinner, and

AUGUSTIN DALY
1875

Clara Morris. He helped also to bring forth the work of native playwrights, of whom Bronson Howard was the chief; he himself ceased writing original plays after 1879, and was always reluctant to have his dramas published. His first theatre was the Fifth Avenue, which was destroyed by fire in 1873. He immediately leased another theatre and gave it the same name, with his own added. At one time he was lessee of three New York theatres, and later added one in London. It was while on a business trip to the latter in 1899 that he died, on a side jaunt to Paris, of pneumonia with cardiac complications. Always a practicing Roman Catholic, he was buried from St. Patrick's Cathedral in New York.

Daly was a tall, strikingly handsome man, with abundant dark hair and flashing eyes, who would have made a good actor had not his taste been for other phases of the theatrical profession. Though he was an autocrat to his company, his kindness, his generosity, and the purity and simplicity of his life made him widely beloved. Without being a prig, he was in strong contrast to the raffish Bohemianism of much of the stage in his time—for example, he never in his life either smoked or drank.

He himself did not think very highly of his plays, and the best of them (*Divorce, Pique, Horizon*) were never published. Probably the most creditable of those appearing in printed form is *Frou Frou*. They were frequently melodramatic, and they all belong to an earlier fashion of play writing. His greatest achievement was as a producer; the theater was his whole life, and his pride was that he more than any other one man had won for the acting profession a respect that had largely been lacking when his efforts began.

Principal Works (published): Under the Gaslight, 1867; Griffith Gaunt, 1868; Frou Frou, 1870; Woffington: A Tribute to the Actress and the Woman (biography) 1888; Seven-Twenty-Eight, 1897; A Night Off, 1897.

About: Daly, J. F. The Life of Augustin Daly; Skinner, O. Footlights and Spotlights; Century Magazine June 1898; McClure's Magazine January 1901; Scribner's Magazine March 1901.

DANA, CHARLES ANDERSON (August 8, 1819-October 17, 1897), editor, was born at Hinsdale, N.H., the son of Anderson Dana and Ann (Denison) Dana. His mother died when he was nine. The father, in spite of good ancestry, was a ne'er-do-well, and the children were parceled out to various relatives. Charles was sent to an uncle's farm, and then, at twelve, to another uncle in Buffalo, in whose general store he became a clerk. His remarkable facility in languages displayed itself early, and by study after business hours he prepared himself for college. The store failed in the panic of 1837, and two years later Dana was able to matriculate at Harvard, supporting himself by teaching. In his junior year his eyes failed from over-study. He was never again able to read by artificial light. He was obliged to leave Harvard, but in 1861 the college conferred an honorary B.A. on him as of the class of 1843.

Dana at this time was an enthusiastic young radical; and when Brook Farm, the idealistic community of Transcendentalist philosophers and primitive communists, was formed at Roxbury, Mass., he became one of the first colonists, being employed as teacher of Greek and German. He remained until the colony failed in 1846. The day before the fire which caused its final collapse, he had married Eunice Macdaniel, whom he had met at Brook Farm. The actress, Ruth Draper, is their granddaughter.

Faced with the need of earning a living for his bride and himself, Dana first became assistant editor of the *Daily Chronotype*, a Congregationalist paper in Boston, at four dollars a week. The next year Horace Greeley, with whom he had become acquainted through their common interest in Brook Farm, brought him to New York as city editor of the *Tribune*. In spite of marked differences of opinion with Greeley, he remained with the *Tribune* for fifteen years. In 1848 he took leave of absence for a year in Europe, reporting "the year of revolution" for several papers. From this first-hand experience with the grim actualities of revolution dates Dana's gradual apostacy from his earlier views, and the birth of the reactionary attitude of his later years.

With the approach of the Civil War, Dana and Greeley became more discordant than before. During Greeley's absences in Washington and elsewhere, Dana acted as editor, and their antagonism grew still more acute. Finally, by a rather shabby maneuver, Greeley forced his resignation in 1862. It was the luckiest thing that ever happened to Dana.

Until 1865, he was in the employ of the War Department, part of the time as Assistant Secretary. He was a devoted henchman of Secretary Edwin Stanton, who kept him in the field as "the eyes of the department." Otto Eisenschimml, in *Who Murdered Lincoln?*, implies that he was little better than a spy for Stanton on Grant and Sherman.

Collection of Frederick H. Meserve

CHARLES A. DANA

He resigned at the end of the war, and after a year in Chicago as editor of the *Republican*, which failed, he secured enough capital to buy the New York *Sun*. From this time on, Dana's history is the history of the *Sun*. He was pre-eminent among the great personal editors who used their papers as organs for their own opinions and prejudices. He fought Grant, Hayes, Cleveland, and Blaine with equal relentlessness; he fought labor unions and the civil service; he hated Chicago, where he had failed; he hated Henry Ward Beecher and William Jennings Bryan; and where Dana hated, his newspaper became a means of bitter personal attack.

At the same time, he made the *Sun* a really great paper, live, witty, and sparkling. It was called "the newspaper man's newspaper," and was a model of journalistic style and news coverage. His staff adored him, and he attracted to himself and developed many of the best known journalists and publicists of their time, among them Richard Harding Davis, David Graham Phillips, Jacob Riis, and E. P. Mitchell.

His only interests outside the paper were his family, to which he was devoted, and the study and teaching of foreign languages. When he died, the *Sun*, at his express order, printed no obituary; it merely announced, under the masthead, "Charles Anderson Dana, editor of the *Sun*, died yesterday afternoon."

In youth, Dana was markedly handsome, tall, with piercing blue eyes, and blond hair and beard. In age, he grew bald, and his long white beard gave him a patriarchal appearance. His editorial duties left him little time for writing, but what he did write was noted for conciseness, clarity, and force. He edited (with George Ripley) the *New American Cyclopaedia,* in 1857-63, and the *Household Book of Poetry* in 1857.

PRINCIPAL WORKS: The Art of Newspaper Making, 1895; Recollections of the Civil War, 1898; Eastern Journeys, 1898.

ABOUT: O'Brien, F. M. The Story of the Sun; Rosebault, C. J. When Dana Was the Sun; Stone, C. Dana and the Sun; Villard, O. G. Some Newspapers and Newspapermen; Wilson, J. H. The Life of Charles A. Dana.

DANA, JAMES DWIGHT (February 12, 1813-April 14, 1895), geologist and zoologist, was born in Utica, N.Y., the son of James Dana, of New England lineage, and Harriet (Dwight) Dana. He had an extraordinary aptitude for sciences, was entered at Yale, but left in 1833 to become a naval instructor. In 1837 he was appointed geologist and mineralogist on a South Seas exploring expedition, finished the reports in 1855, and then became professor of natural history at Yale. He was married in 1844 to Frances Silliman, by whom he had four children.

On his South Seas observations he wrote three technical volumes, and, following a journey to the Hawaiian Islands, *Characteristics of Volcanoes.* He had great mental and physical energies, and despite a nervous breakdown and chronic illness he continued to teach until 1890. Honorary scientific societies, both here and abroad, acknowledged the excellence of his investigations and writings.

PRINCIPAL WORKS: Zoophytes, 1846; Geology, 1849; Crustacea, 1852-54; Corals and Coral Islands, 1872; Characteristics of Volcanoes, 1890.

ABOUT: Gilman, D. C. The Life of James Dwight Dana; American Journal of Science, 1895.

DANA, RICHARD HENRY, SR. (November 15, 1787-February 2, 1879), poet and essayist, was born in Cambridge, Mass., and lived most of his long life in that state. He was the son of Francis Dana, governor, congressman, and diplomat, and of Elizabeth (Ellery) Dana, daughter of a signer of the Declaration of Independence. Though he was a frail and delicate child, who was hardly expected to survive, he lived to be ninety-one.

He entered Harvard in 1804, but was suspended because of a student "mutiny," and refused to return. Long afterwards he received his B.A. as of the class of 1808. He studied law with prominent attorneys, as the custom then was, in Boston, Baltimore, and Newport, and was admitted to the Massachusetts bar in 1811. He seems, however, to have practiced very little if at all. Though in later years he served one term in the state legislature, his primary interest was always in literature.

Collection of Frederick H. Meserve
RICHARD HENRY DANA, SR.

From the founding of the *North American Review* in 1815, he was a contributor, and in 1818 he became associate editor; it was he who accepted the young Bryant's *Thanatopsis.* About a year later he went to New York, where for six months in 1821 he conducted a magazine called *The Idle Man,* along the lines of Washington Irving's famous *Salmagundi.* On the decease of this periodical he returned to Boston. He contributed poems and essays to most of the periodicals of the time, including the *New York Review,* then edited by Bryant, whose first publisher he himself had been. In 1839 and 1840 he gave a course of literary lectures in New York, Boston, Philadelphia, and elsewhere, in which he espoused the theory, then still debatable, that Shakespeare was a greater poet than Pope.

However, Dana was too academic, too withdrawn from interest in social and political affairs, ever to be popular; and from about 1840 on, he went into studious retirement. In dignified seclusion he read and studied, but he no longer wrote for publication. His only outside interest was in religion; in the split in the Congregational Church, 1825-35, which resulted in the rise of Unitarianism, he remained with the Trinitarians, and in later life he was a prominent Episcopalian.

In 1813 Dana had married Ruth Charlotte Smith. They had four children. The oldest son, and his namesake [*q.v.*], became a better known writer than the father had ever been.

Dana's best known poem is *The Buccaneer,* a powerful narrative in verse with strong supernatural elements. Though it is undoubtedly original in conception, the style owes something to both Wordsworth and Coleridge. Perhaps his chief importance in American literature is the fact that he was one of the first writers in this country to emphasize simplicity and directness of expression, and to avoid the rococo sentimentality which marred so much writing of the period.

PRINCIPAL WORKS: The Buccaneer and Other Poems, 1827; Poems and Prose Writings, 1833.

ABOUT: Wilson, J. G. Bryant and His Friends; Harper's Magazine April 1879; Harper's Weekly February 22, 1879; Boston Transcript February 3, 1879.

DANA, RICHARD HENRY, JR. (August 1, 1815-January 6, 1882), travel writer, was the oldest son of Richard Henry Dana, Sr., the poet and essayist, and Ruth Charlotte (Smith) Dana. He was born in Cambridge, Mass. He entered Harvard in 1831, but in his junior year suffered from a severe attack of measles, which so weakened his sight that he was obliged to leave college. To regain his health, he decided to ship as an ordinary sailor before the mast, and in August 1834 he sailed on the brig "Pilgrim" around Cape Horn to California.

It was this voyage which not only restored Dana to health but also gave him his permanent place in literature. He kept a minute diary of the voyage, which in 1840 was published as *Two Years Before the Mast.* Meanwhile he had re-entered Harvard in 1836, and the following year was graduated at the head of his class. He was admitted to the bar in 1840, having, during the previous year, been instructor in elocution at Harvard, and from the beginning took an active interest in politics. He was one of the founders of the Free Soil Party, which preceded the Republican Party, and though he was not an abolitionist, he acted as attorney in several celebrated cases of fugitive slaves. From 1861 to 1866 he was United States Attorney for Massachusetts, and the following year he was one of the counsel for the Federal government in the trial of Jefferson Davis for treason. During the same year he was a member of the Massachusetts Legislature. From 1866 to 1868 he lectured at the Harvard Law School. His political ambitions, however, remained unsatisfied, largely because of his aloofness and a certain arrogance of manner. He lost to Benjamin F. Butler in the Congressional election of 1868, and when in 1876 Grant named him as minister to England, the Senate failed to confirm the appointment.

However remote and dignified his manner, Dana never forgot his experiences on the "Pilgrim." The brutal treatment of sailors which he witnessed aroused his lifelong indignation and sympathy. Until, in his later years, he became the great American authority on international law, his specialty was admiralty law, and his book, *The Seaman's Friend,* a manual on this subject, became a standard authority in both America and England.

In 1841 Dana married Sarah Watson. They had six children, whose education he himself conducted. His great passion was for travel, and as often as his duties permitted he made extended trips abroad. In 1859 and 1860 he journeyed around the world. In 1878 he retired from his legal partnership and went to Europe for what he intended to be several years of study, culminating in a comprehensive work on international law. While living in Rome in 1882, before the contemplated book had been begun, he was attacked by pneumonia and succumbed in a few days. He is buried in the Protestant cemetery in Rome, near the graves of Shelley and Keats.

Dana's literary reputation rests on *Two Years Before the Mast,* one of the most

Collection of Frederick H. Meserve
RICHARD HENRY DANA, JR.

delightful books ever written. It aroused public interest not only in the condition of seamen, but also in California, then a Spanish colony. The book was translated into French anonymously, perhaps by James Fenimore Cooper. Dana's keen eye and ready pen noted everything he saw, on the "Pilgrim" on the voyage out on the "Alert" on his return voyage, and in southern California during his months there while the ship cruised the coast collecting hides and tallow. As Edward Larocque Tinker says: "No more vigorous and unbiased account of a sailor's life, psychology, and superstitions, seen from the fo'castle point of view, has ever been written, for Dana was an observant, articulate boy, curious about every detail." The words are equally true of the descriptions of Spanish California and its earliest Yankee settlers.

Principal Works: Two Years Before the Mast, 1840; The Seaman's Friend, 1841; To Cuba and Back, 1859.

About: Adams, C. F., Jr. Richard Henry Dana: A Biography; Dana, R. H. Jr. Two Years Before the Mast (see biographical introduction by J. D. Hart to 1937 edition); Cambridge Historical Society Publications 1917.

DARBY, WILLIAM (August 14, 1775-October 9, 1854), compiler and geographer, was born in Lancaster County, Pa., the son of Patrick and Mary (Rice) Darby, Irish settlers in Pennsylvania, who shortly migrated to Ohio. He was denied an education, but read indefatigably, and began to teach at eighteen. In 1799 he suffered reverses as a cotton planter, and accepted a position as deputy surveyor for the United States. For his *Geographical Description of the State of Louisiana* . . . he amassed much valuable data, and received only slight compensation forty years later. He made three revisions of Brookes' (London, 1762) *General Gazetteer*; in 1832 he was writing for the first American edition of the *Edinburgh Encyclopaedia.* Two years after the death of his first wife, formerly Mrs. Boardman, in 1844, Darby was married to Elizabeth Tanner. In 1829 Darby published *Mnemonika: or, The Tablet of Memory* purporting to be a "Register of Events From the Earliest Period to the Year 1829," but obviously too cursory, in its 300-odd meagre pages, to be of much value. Nevertheless, as a recorder of historical, geographical, and statistical material he was authoritative and methodical.

Principal Works: A Geological Description of the State of Louisiana, 1816 and 1817; View of the United States: Historical, Geographical, and Statistical, 1828; Mnemonika: or, The Tablet of Memory, 1829.

About: Egle, W. H. The Dixons of Dixon's Ford; Daily Globe October 10, 1854; Daily National Intelligencer October 10, 1854; Historical Magazine October 1867.

DAVIDSON, JAMES WOOD (March 9, 1829-June 15?, 1905), miscellaneous writer, was born on a farm in Newberry Co., S.C., his parents being Alexander and Sarah Davidson. The family was very poor, but the boy worked his way through South Carolina College (later the University of South Carolina), being graduated in 1852. He then taught Greek at various institutions in the state until the Civil War, when he served under Stonewall Jackson in Virginia. After the war, he was so poverty-stricken that he had no clothing except his old Confederate uniform.

Entering journalism, Davis worked for two years in Washington before joining the staff of the New York *Evening Post,* where he remained for ten years. In 1884 he married a widow, Josephine Allen, who had an independent income. They settled at Lake Worth, Fla., and Davidson became a member of the constitutional convention and of the state legislature. Later he returned to Washington and for a long time was a clerk in the Treasury.

Except for *The Poetry of the Future,* a perspicacious and even prophetic work of criticism, Davidson's writing was all in the nature of compilations. When he died he was at work on a dictionary of Southern writers, which was never finished or published.

Principal Works: A School History of South Carolina, 1869; Living Writers of the South, 1869; The Correspondent, 1886; The Poetry of the Future, 1888; Florida of Today, 1889.

About: Alderman, E. A. & Harris, J. C. Library of Southern Literature; Wauchope, G. A. Writers of South Carolina; Columbia (S.C.) State July 3, 1905.

DAVIDSON, THOMAS (October 25, 1840-September 14, 1900), philosopher and educator, was born in Aberdeenshire, Scotland, the son of Thomas Davidson, a poor farmer, and Mary (Warrender) Davidson, a pious peasant woman. His avidity for learning attracted the attention of the parish schoolmaster, Robert Wilson, who took him into his own home and prepared him for college, in return for his teaching of the younger pupils. In 1856 he entered King's College, Aberdeen, on a scholarship, being graduated in 1860 with high classical honors and prizes. Until 1863 he was rector of Old Aberdeen Grammar School; then he taught Latin and Greek at Tunbridge Wells and Wimbledon, England. In 1866 he went to

THOMAS DAVIDSON

Canada to teach in the Collegiate Institution at London, Ontario. The next year he went to Boston, then to St. Louis, where he became principal of a branch high school and edited the *Western Educational Review.*

Davidson had by this time lost his early piety and had become a Positivist (following the French Rationalist philosopher Auguste Comte) and something of a radical. In St. Louis he came into contact with a group of ardent disciples of the great German philosopher Hegel, who encouraged him in the study of Greek and German philosophy. In 1875 he returned to Boston, and from that time on became a sort of wandering scholar, tutoring, lecturing, writing, and always on the move. From 1878 to 1884 he lived mostly in Greece and Italy, leading a hermit's existence, and at one time almost joining the Roman Catholic Church. Back in London in 1883 for a brief stay, he founded the Fellowship of the New Life, which later developed into the famous Fabian Socialist Society. He returned to America and founded a branch of the Fellowship in New York, with a "Summer School for the Cultural Sciences," held first in New Jersey, then in Connecticut, and finally on a farm he bought at Keene, N.H. The great interest of his later years was the Breadwinners' College, founded in association with the People's Institute and the Educational Alliance of New York.

A short, stumpy man with a full brown beard, Davidson had a magnetic personality, which with his exuberant good humor won him friends wherever he went. He never married. He was a noted linguist, with a remarkable memory, prodigious learning, and lofty idealism, united with unusual modesty. His writing was original and scholarly, though the nature of his subjects is not conducive to easy reading. He was the pure type of wandering scholar, a species almost unique in America.

Principal Works: The Parthenon Frieze and Other Essays, 1882; The Place of Art in Education, 1886; Prolegomena to *In Memoriam,* 1889; Aristotle and Ancient Educational Ideals, 1892; The Education of the Greek People and Its Influence on Civilization, 1894; Rousseau and Education According to Nature, 1898; A History of Education, 1900; The Education of the Wage Earner, 1905.

About: James, W. Memories and Studies; Knight, W. Memorials of Thomas Davidson.

DAVIS, CHARLES HENRY STANLEY (March 2, 1840-November 7, 1917), Orientalist and physician, was born in Goshen, Conn., the son of Timothy Fisher Davis and Moriva (Hatch) Davis. His father was a physician, and he was educated to follow in the same profession. He studied medicine at the University of Maryland and the University of the City of New York, receiving his M.D. at the latter institution in 1866, and then doing post-graduate work in Boston, New York, London, and Paris. In 1867 and 1868 he published the *Boston Medical Register.* In 1869 he married Caroline Elizabeth Harris, and settled in Meriden, Conn., where most of his boyhood had been spent. Aside from his practice his interests were many; he was three times a member of the state legislature between 1873 and 1886, and began his publications in philology, particularly Oriental philology, as early as 1878. From this same year to 1881 he issued an *Index of Periodical Literature,* one of the several predecessors of the more famous *Poole's.* From 1886 to 1898 he was physician for the Curtis Home for Orphans, and from 1895 to 1900 for the State School for Boys. He was mayor of Meriden in 1887-88, president of the board of education from 1898 to 1908, and clerk of the county medical society from 1870 to his death. In addition to all this, he published widely in such disparate fields as medicine, history, philosophy, and antiquarianism, as well as in philology. From 1887 he was editor of *Biblia,* later merged with the *American and Antiquarian and Oriental Journal.* This crowded career was ended at seventy-seven by an unsuccessful operation for duodenal ulcer.

Principal Works: History of Wallingford and Meriden, Connecticut, 1870; Grammar of the Old Persian Language, 1878; The Voice as a

Musical Instrument, 1879; Classification, Education, and Training of Feeble-Minded, Imbecilic, and Idiotic Children, 1883; The Egyptian Book of the Dead, 1894; History of Egypt in the Light of Modern Discoveries, 1896; Greek and Roman Stoicism, 1903; The Self-Cure of Consumption Without Medicine, 1904; How to Be Successful as a Physician, 1905; Grammar of the Modern Irish Language, 1909; Some of Life's Problems, 1914.

ABOUT: Atkinson, W. B. The Physicians and Surgeons of the United States; American Medical Association Journal November 24, 1917.

DAVIS, MARY EVELYN (MOORE) (April 12, 1852-January 1, 1909), miscellaneous writer, was born in Talladega, Ala., the daughter of John Moore and Marian Lucy (Crutchfield) Moore. At the age of nine, on a Texas plantation she began to write war poems for Southern dailies. *Minding the Gap,* her collected verse, appeared in 1867. She was married in 1874 to Thomas Edward Davis, editor of the Houston *Telegraph.* They went to New Orleans in 1879, where their home in the French quarter became the modest rendezvous of *literati. In War Times at La Rose Blanche* and *Jaconeta* bear interesting reminiscences; her only novel, *The Little Chevalier,* appeared in 1903.

Despite an extraordinary circle of friends, Mrs. Davis spent her late life in comparative misery. Her scant and miscellaneous writings did not long outlive her.

PRINCIPAL WORKS: Minding the Gap, 1867; In War Times at La Rose Blanche, 1888; Under Six Flags: The Story of Texas, 1897; Jaconeta, 1901; The Little Chevalier, 1903.

ABOUT: Davidson, J. W. Living Writers of the South; Smith, W. B. Library of Southern Literature; Daily Picayune January 2, 1909.

DAVIS, REBECCA BLAINE (HARDING) (June 24, 1831-September 29, 1910), novelist, was born in Washington, Pa., the daughter of Richard Harding and Rachel Leet (Wilson) Harding. When she was a small child her parents moved first to Alabama, later to Wheeling, W.Va. (then Va.). She was educated at home, mostly by her own reading. She began to write very early, and had some small success with stories in magazines, but it was not until 1861 that she gained any wide attention to her work, when she began to appear in the *Atlantic Monthly.* In 1863 she married L. Clarke Davis, a Philadelphia journalist, and Philadelphia was her home thenceforth. She had a large family—one of her sons was the author Richard Harding Davis—but she continued her literary work. From 1869 to the mid-'seventies she was associate editor of the New York *Tribune.* She died at Mt. Kisco, N.Y., at seventy-nine.

Mrs. Davis's earlier novels, particularly *Margaret Howth,* her first big success and probably her best book, were grimly realistic, belonging to the "naturalistic" school of Zola. She was consciously pioneering in this field in America, thirty years before Stephen Crane, forty years before Theodore Dreiser. But her work was crude and often careless, and gradually became more conventional and orthodox. At her worst, she was superior in profundity and feeling to the best produced by her much more celebrated son.

PRINCIPAL WORKS: Margaret Howth, 1862; Dallas Galbraith, 1868; Berrytown, 1872; John Andross, 1874; A Law Unto Herself, 1878; Natasqua, 1886; Kent Hampden, 1892; Doctor Warrick's Daughters, 1896; Frances Waldeaux, 1897; Bits of Gossip, 1904.

ABOUT: Davis, R. B. H. Bits of Gossip; New York Times September 30, 1910.

DEANE, SAMUEL (July 10, 1733-November 12, 1814), clergyman and agricultural writer, was born in Dedham, Mass., the son of Samuel Deane, a blacksmith and inn-keeper, and Rachel (Dwight) Deane. His father's occupation was no bar to his education in the democratic New England of the 18th century, and he was graduated from Harvard in 1760. While at college he wrote a poem for a volume of congratulatory addresses to George III on his accession to the throne. For three years he remained at Harvard as tutor and librarian, then was ordained in the Congregational Church and became co-pastor in Portland, Maine. He remained as minister of this church until his death fifty years later. In 1775, however, the British fleet bombarded and burnt Portland, and Deane moved to a farm in Gorham, going to Portland to preach but devoting the rest of his time to farming. This experience gave rise to his only important book, a complete encyclopedia of agriculture, the first to be published in America. He returned to Portland in 1782. In 1776 he had married Eunice Pearson, six years his senior, who died in 1812; they had no children. Deane received an M.A. degree from Harvard and a D.D. from Brown University. From 1794 to 1813 he was vice-president of Bowdoin College.

PRINCIPAL WORKS: The New England Farmer or Georgical Dictionary, 1790; Pitchwood Hill (verse) 1795.

ABOUT: Goold, W. Portland in the Past; McLellan, H. C. History of Gorham, Maine.

DE CLEYRE, VOLTAIRINE (November 17, 1866-June 6, 1912), poet and essayist, was born in Leslie, Mich., the daughter of

Auguste and Eliza de Cleyre. The father, then a Free Thinker, named her for Voltaire. When she was a year old her parents moved to St. John's, Mich., where she finished grammar school at twelve. By this time her father, who had returned to the Catholic Church, sent her to a convent in Canada, in the hope that she would become a nun. She was graduated from the convent school in 1882, but had lost her religious faith and was soon launched on her career as a Free Thought lecturer. The Haymarket bombing case converted her to Anarchism. From 1892 she lived in Philadelphia, teaching languages and conducting classes for workers, chiefly among the Jewish immigrants. In 1897 she visited England and Scotland, in 1902 she went to Norway. In 1901 an insane man named Helcher shot her and wounded her seriously, but she refused to prosecute him. She wrote widely for the *Open Court*, the *Twentieth Century*, and the *Independent*, as well as for Rationalist and radical magazines, and translated the works of Jean Grave and Louise Michel from the French and a number of poems from the Yiddish. At her death she left an uncompleted novel written in collaboration with her teacher and "companion," the well known Anarchist Dyer D. Lum (died 1903). Miss de Cleyre's essays and sketches were strong and aptly phrased, though emotional and sometimes sentimental; she is at her best in her poetry, which has both melody and fire.

PRINCIPAL WORK: Selected Works (ed. by H. Havel) 1913.

ABOUT: Macdonald, G. E. Fifty Years of Freethought; Symes, L. & Clement, T. Rebel America.

DEERING, NATHANIEL (June 25, 1791-March 25, 1881), dramatist and editor, was born in Portland, Maine, the son of Nathaniel and Almira (Ilsley) Deering. He was graduated from Harvard College in 1810, studied law, and was admitted to the bar in 1815. But his real interests were literary: he became editor of the *Independent Statesman* and continued to write breezy prose and verse for local dailies. In 1824 he married Anna Margaret Holwell, by whom he had nine children.

Deering was always financially independent; declining William Cullen Bryant's offer to join the New York *Evening Post,* he began play-writing. In 1830 he finished *Carabasset: or, The Last of the* have had some influence on Howells' writing. in pseudo-Miltonic style; *The Clairvoyants,* confusions of a gentleman in a "mesmeric state," was produced in 1844; and *Bozzaris,* a tragedy based on the Greek Revolution of 1821 and his most elaborate attempt at sustained blank verse, was published in 1851. Deering was a man of much personal charm and a writer by inclination only, whose works, reflecting largely his own predilections, would doubtless have risen in value had they been subjected to constant and healthful criticism.

PRINCIPAL WORKS: Carabasset: or, The Last of the Norridgewoks, 1830; The Clairvoyants, 1844; Bozzaris, 1851.

ABOUT: Chaplin, L. B. Life and Works of Nathaniel Deering (University of Maine Studies, ser. 2; nos. 32-34, 1934-35).

DE FONTAINE, FELIX GREGORY (1834-December 11, 1896), journalist and compiler, was born in Boston, Mass., the son of Louis Antoine De Fontaine, a French nobleman. Felix was taught by private tutors, and at twenty-five became a reporter in Washington, D.C. Soon afterwards he was married to Georgia Vigneron Moore of Charleston, S.C., and founded in Columbia, S.C., the *Daily South Carolinian.* For the New York *Herald* he wrote pithy articles on the slavery question and made some valuable war "scoops." In the early 'seventies he became first the *Herald's* financial editor and then its art and dramatic editor, serving until the end of his life.

His ponderous *Cyclopaedia of the Best Thoughts of Charles Dickens* appeared in 1873 (second edition as *The Fireside Dickens,* 1883). *Birds of a Feather Flock Together* (1878) was a collection of E. H. Sothern's reminiscences. In *Army Letters of Personne,* begun in 1896 as a serial publication, he wrote intimate observations of the old Confederate front. De Fontaine had a knack for uncovering good material, but his literary reputation, in sum, was both limited and fleeting.

PRINCIPAL WORKS: A History of American Abolitionism: Together With a History of the Southern Confederacy, 1861; Marginalia, 1864; Cyclopaedia of the Best Thoughts of Charles Dickens, 1873; Birds of a Feather Flock Together, 1878.

ABOUT: Snowden, Y. History of South Carolina; Charleston News and Courier December 12, 1896.

DE FOREST, JOHN WILLIAM (May 31, 1826-July 17, 1906), novelist and miscellaneous writer, was born in Humphreysville (now Seymour), Conn., his parents being John Hancock DeForest and Dotha (Woodward) DeForest. His father was a cotton manufacturer and merchant, who died when the son was thirteen. He did not attend college, but spent some years abroad, in Florence, Paris, and Beirut, Syria, where his brother conducted a missionary school. He returned to America in 1856, and married Harriet Silliman Shepard, a brilliant classical scholar. In 1859 Yale conferred an honorary M.A. on him, in recognition of his historical and travel books. He returned from another European trip to serve as captain in the Union army throughout the Civil War, not being mustered out of the service until 1868. The remainder of his life was spent in New Haven.

DeForest was best known as a novelist, his work being realistic but without distinction of style, and not so popular as it may have deserved. W. D. Howells was one of its warm admirers, and DeForest seems to have had some influence on Howell's writing.

PRINCIPAL WORKS: *Novels*—Witching Times, 1856; Seacliff, 1859; Miss Ravenel's Conversion From Secession to Loyalty, 1867; Kate Beaumont, 1872; The Wetherel Affair, 1873; Honest John Vane, 1875; Playing the Mischief, 1876; Irene the Missionary, 1879; The Bloody Chasm, 1881; A Lover's Revolt, 1898. *Non-Fiction*—History of the Indians of Connecticut, 1851; Oriental Acquaintance, 1856; European Acquaintance, 1858; The Downing Legends (verse) 1901; Poems: Medley and Palestina, 1902.

ABOUT: New Haven Evening Register July 18, 1906.

DELANO, ALONZO (July 2, 1806 [or 1802]-September 9, 1874), humorist, social historian, and Argonaut, whose *nom de guerre* was "Old Block," was born in Aurora, N.Y., the son of Dr. Frederick and Joanna (Doty) Delano. He—and likewise his third cousin twice removed, Franklin Delano Roosevelt—had among his ancestors a royal "Pilgrim father," Phillippe de la Noye, who, "to the everlasting regret of his descendants . . . just missed the Mayflower and had to wait for the next boat. . ." Young Delano attended public schools and Aurora Academy and from his fifteenth year until he set out for California he lived almost entirely in the Middle West. At South Bend, Ind., he was a dealer in dry goods, staples, etc. He married Mary Burt at Aurora in 1830, and by her had one child, Harriet.

On April 19, 1849, he set out with a small party from St. Joseph, Mo., on a 2000-mile trek through the wilderness, going, in general, "as the crow flies," and encountering cholera outbreaks, food shortages, and skirmishes with the Indians. By mid-September they were in Shasta County, Calif., and not with his "pan" but with his pen Delano earned his bread and butter. The New Orleans *True Delta* had solicited his "scoops" from the mining districts, and hence came the earliest "Old Block" humor. He became a regular contributor to the *Pacific News*, and his sketches were picked up by the New York *Times* and many Western papers.

Meanwhile Delano had established, in San Francisco, a thriving produce business, and when the fire of May 4, 1851, "cooked his cabbages on Long Wharf" he set out for Grass Valley and "went to quartz." Delano & Company operated until late fall, when he sold out, made a journey home to the Middle West, and returned to find "diggings" still consistently poor. On Main Street, Grass Valley, he built up a banking business, and during the panic of 1855 dared to invite depositors to come in and get their money "as long as it lasts," while on his desk lay a wire saying, "Close the bank and seal the safe." Following the death of his first wife in 1871, Delano married Marie Harmon, of Warren, Ohio.

When *Pen Knife Sketches: or, Chips of the Old Block* appeared in 1853, Delano already had a large audience. *The Miner's Progress,* a pun-filled parody, published anonymously, has been widely attributed to Delano. His excellent *Life on the Plains and Among the Diggings,* chronicle of his westward trek (reprinted in 1936 with a slight title change), was followed by *Old Block's Sketch Book,* a kind of Davy Crockett almanac, and *A Live Woman in the Mines,* a play that was revived in 1935. In *A Sojourn With Royalty* were meaty selections from his published articles.

He was a stocky gentleman with a conservative adaptation of a Cyrano nose. With boisterous "John Phoenix" (George Horatio Derby), Delano may be said to have founded the traditional California humor that oscillated between absurdity and pathos and was soon to become the *pièce de résistance* of Bret Harte and Mark Twain.

PRINCIPAL WORKS: *Prose*—Pen Knife Sketches: or, Chips of the Old Block, 1853; Life on the Plains and Among the Diggings, 1854; Old Block's Sketch Book, 1856. *Verse*—The Miner's Progress, 1853. *Play*—A Live Woman in the Mines, 1857.

ABOUT: Delano, A. Life on the Plains and Among the Diggings; personal information from Edmund G. Kinyon, Grass Valley, Calif., see also Forewords to A Sojourn with Royalty (1936 ed.) and to Pen Knife Sketches (1934 ed.).

DELANY, MARTIN ROBINSON (May 6, 1812-January 24, 1885), Negro author and civic leader, was born in Charles Town, W. Va., the son of Samuel Delany, whose father had belonged to the Golah tribe, and Pati Delany, daughter of a Mandingo prince. As a small boy he was taught by book-peddlers, and in 1831 he went to Pittsburgh and became interested in medicine. In 1843 he was married to Kate A. Richards, and founded the *Mystery,* a small but effective paper. His book on *The Condition, Elevation, Emigration, and Destiny of the Colored People of the United States, Politically Considered* (1852) made him a kind of harbinger of Booker T. Washington. *Principia of Ethnology: The Origin of Races and Color, etc.,* appeared in 1879.

Delany was the first Negro major in the United States army. His extensive activities in civic and racial movements left a deeper mark than did his concurrent writings.

PRINCIPAL WORKS: The Condition, Elevation, Emigration, and Destiny of the Colored People of the United States, Politically Considered, 1852; Principia of Ethnology: The Origin of Races and Color, 1879.

ABOUT: Holly, J. T. In Memoriam (A. M. E. Church Review October 1886); Rollin, A. Life and Public Services of Martin R. Delany; News and Courier (Charleston, S. C.) October 2 and 3, 1874.

DE LEON, THOMAS COOPER (May 21, 1839-March 19, 1914) playwright and social historian, was born in Columbia, S.C., the son of Mardici Heinrich De Leon and Rebecca (Lopez-y-Nunez) De Leon, both of whom were descended from emigrants from the Spanish West Indies. He attended Georgetown University in Washington, D.C., and then became a topographical clerk. His life in the Confederate army, from 1861 to 1865, was well recorded in *Four Years in Rebel Capitals* (1890); and *Belles, Beaux, and Brains of the '60's* (1907) threw a gay and gossipy slant on social life in the post-war South.

De Leon's burlesque, *Hamlet ye Dismal Prince,* had a phenomenal run in the Spring of 1870, opening the same night as Edwin Booth's stately début in the real *Hamlet,* and was, in the opinion of the critic William Winter, one of the funniest things in the world. In the years that followed De Leon wrote two travesties and two local-color novels. His interests were constantly shifting and almost limitless. In his writings there was an occasional but not a lasting brilliance.

PRINCIPAL WORKS: *Autobiographical*—Four Years in Rebel Capitals, 1890; Belles, Beaux, and Brains of the '60's, 1907. *Drama*—Hamlet ye Dismal Prince, 1870. *Novels*—Creole and Puritan, 1889; Crag-Nest, 1897.

ABOUT: De Leon, T. C. Four Years in Rebel Capitals (see sketch of the author in 1892 ed.); Mobile Register March 20, 1914.

"DEMBRY, R. EMMETT." See MURFREE, MARY NOAILLES

DE MILLE, HENRY CHURCHILL (September 17, 1853-February 10, 1893), playwright, was born in Washington, N.C., the son of William Edward and Margaret Blount (Hoyt) De Mille. He remained a while on his father's farm, then went to New York, entered Columbia College, and in 1875 received B.A. and M.A. degrees. The following year he married Mathilde Beatrice Samuel. He was for a short time an actor, then an instructor in dramatic art, and finally a reader and writer of plays. With David Belasco, of the Madison Square Theatre, he wrote *The Wife, Lord Chumley, The Charity Ball,* and *Men and Women.*

It was only by stock engagements that his plays, of the popular gold-leaf variety, briefly outlived their hey-day on Broadway.

PRINCIPAL WORKS: The Wife, 1887; Lord Chumley, 1888; The Charity Ball, 1889; Men and Women, 1890.

ABOUT: Brown, T. A. A History of the New York Stage; Winter, W. Life of David Belasco; Theatre November 24, 1888.

DENNIE, JOSEPH (August 30, 1768-January 7, 1812), journalist, was born in Boston, the only child of Joseph Dennie and Mary (Green) Dennie. His maternal grandfather had been publisher of the *Boston News-Letter.* When he was seven, during the American Revolution, his parents moved to Lexington, where he first attended school. His childhood was clouded by his father's recurrent attacks of insanity. Though the boy early showed literary talent, it was felt that he must earn his living as soon as possible, so he was sent to commercial school and then put in a counting-house. However, he proved his unfitness for a business career, and was reluctantly allowed to prepare for Harvard. His career there was broken by illness and by suspension following conflict with the authorities, but he was graduated in 1790. He disliked the college and attacked it constantly in his writings.

After reading law for three years in New Hampshire, Dennie was admitted to the Massachusetts bar in 1794. His career as a lawyer was brief. In his very first case he was lectured by the judge for "using fine language," and practiced exceedingly little thereafter. Instead he and another young man, Royall Tyler, began writing a series of essays, in the Addisonian style, most of which were published in New Hampshire papers or in a short-lived periodical of Dennie's editing called the *Tablet.* In 1796 he moved to Walpole, N.H., where he became the center of a coterie called the Literary Club, the members being all lawyers and all Federalists. He began contributing essays, under the pseudonym of "Lay Preacher," to the *New Hampshire Journal and Farmer's Museums,* and soon after became its editor.

JOSEPH DENNIE

The essays had wide popularity and influence, but the paper did not prosper, and in 1799 he left Walpole and went to Philadelphia, then the literary capital of the nation.

For a few months he was personal secretary to the then Secretary of State, Timothy Pickering, and also was on the staff of *Fenno's Gazette of the United States*. Neither position lasted long, and an attempt to publish his "Lay Preacher" essays as a book also failed. Dennie persuaded a Philadelphia bookseller to finance a magazine, the *Port Folio* which came out under his editorship in 1802. This position he retained to his death, but his literary output was small, owing to ill health, constant financial difficulties which used up his energies, and his taste for social amusements. The influence of the magazine was very wide, both in America and in England; Dennie became a nationally and even internationally known figure, more through his personality than through his writings. Such writers as Thomas Moore, Leigh Hunt, and Thomas Campbell sent him their poems to publish from manuscript—the first American editor to be so honored by English writers. When Moore came to America he visited Dennie and wrote a poem in his honor.

Dennie as the "American Addison" was soon out-rivaled by Washington Irving, and the fact that only a few of his essays were brought out in book form, in a very slim volume, made it easy to forget him after his death. His essays in the *Port Folio*, signed "Oliver Oldschool," were never reprinted. But he was the first professional litterateur in America, with the possible exception of Charles Brockden Brown, and certainly the first American Bohemian. His slight figure, his dandified dress and elegant speech, were the outward sign of a born aristocrat, a true *redactor temporis acti*, who hated democracy and loved only the "remembrance of times past." Over his grave in Philadelphia the ambiguous tribute is carved that he "contributed to chasten the morals and to refine the taste of the nation."

PRINCIPAL WORK: The Lay Preacher, 1796.

ABOUT: Clapp, W. W., Jr. Joseph Dennie; Ellis, H. M. Joseph Dennie and His Circle; New England Magazine August 1896.

DENTON, DANIEL (fl. 1670), publicist, was born at Hempstead, Long Island, N.Y., the eldest son of the Rev. Richard Denton. His exact dates are unknown, but he seems to have been born about 1640 and to have died about 1700. Long Island being then mostly open country, Denton became, after a private education, a gentleman farmer or "planter," near Jamaica. In this town he also served as town clerk and held other similar minor public offices. The only date certainly known for him is that of publication of his only book, 1670. This, *A Brief Description of New-York* (the newly English province, not the city, which until six years previously had been New Amsterdam), is the first separate work in English on its subject. It was written and published while Denton was in London on public or private business. He stayed in England too long for his own good; on his return he found that his wife had been unfaithful to him, and he divorced her. To avoid this disgrace (a very real one in his time), he moved to New Jersey, in which colony he also held public office. Several years later he remarried, and, the scandal having died down, returned with his second wife to his farm near Jamaica, where he spent the remainder of his life.

PRINCIPAL WORK: A Brief Description of New-York, 1670.

ABOUT: Denton, D. A Brief Description of New-York (see Bibliographical Note by V. H. Palstits in 1937 edition).

DE PEYSTER, JOHN WATTS (March 9, 1821-May 4, 1907), soldier and biographer, was born in New York City, the son of Frederick and Mary Justina (Watts) de Peyster. After instruction by tutors, wide reading, and travel, he entered Columbia College; but ill health forced him to leave. He was married, in 1841, to Estelle Livingston, and in 1845 entered military activity, rising to the rank of brigadier-general, with a major-general brevet.

De Peyster's works were largely historical-biographical; of these the first was *The History of the Life of Leonard Torstenson* (1855); *Practical Strategy . . .*, based on the achievements of the Austrian Field Marshal Traun, appeared in 1863; and *Napoleone di Buonaparte* (1896) was the last of a long list. He himself was an excellent military organizer and could apply his own technical knowledge to the subject matter of his writings. The Royal Historical Society of Great Britain made him one of its members, but his books, in sum, lack distinction of style, and have only a moderate biographical value.

Principal Works: The History of the Life of Leonard Torstenson, 1855; The Ancient, Medieval, and Modern Netherlanders, 1859; An Inquiry Into the Career and Character of Mary Stuart, 1883; Napoleone di Buonaparte, 1896.

About: Allaben, F. John Watts de Peyster; New York Times May 6, 1907.

From a portrait by F. B. Carpenter
GEORGE HORATIO DERBY
("John Phoenix")

DERBY, GEORGE HORATIO ("John Phoenix") (April 3, 1823-May 15, 1861), humorist, was born in Dedham, Mass., the son of John Barton Derby and Mary (Townsend) Derby. From the father the son inherited a literary bent and also a turn for practical joking and eccentric humor. After an elementary schooling he moved to Concord, Mass., and worked in a store. He was enrolled in West Point (the United States Military Academy) in 1842, and was graduated high in his class in 1846. Almost immediately he was assigned to the Topographical Engineers, with which branch of the army he was associated throughout the remainder of his career.

He served through the Mexican War and was wounded severely in the battle of Cerro Gordo. In 1849 he was sent to California, and except for a brief period in Texas in 1852, remained on the Pacific Coast until 1856. He commanded three exploring expeditions, to the Mother Lode country, the San Joaquin Valley, and the Colorado River. His transfer is said to have been made in punishment for flippancy in an official report, but if so he did not repent, for the same touch of humor appears in his reports of these explorations.

In 1853 Derby was on duty in San Diego. He had been writing for several years, and when a friend who edited the San Diego *Herald* left town temporarily he put Derby in charge. He transformed the paper into a riotous burlesque, incidentally changing its politics from Democratic to Whig, and found himself also transformed overnight, from a slightly censured army officer to a famous humorist. His humorous essays began to appear in the *Pioneer: or, Monthly California Magazine*, of San Francisco, under the names of "John Phoenix" and "Squibob." Collections appeared in book form under both titles. Meanwhile he continued in the army, writing as an avocation. During this period also he married Mary Ann Coons.

In 1856 he was transferred to the east. In 1859, when he was serving in Florida, he suffered a sunstroke, which affected his mind. He was on sick leave thereafter, though he was promoted to the rank of captain in 1860. He never recovered, but died in New York soon after the outbreak of the Civil War.

Derby's humor was of the burlesque, boisterous, "Western" type once so overwhelmingly popular, and now so deadly dull. His natural eccentricity made it easy for him to express himself in this form, characterized by punning, exaggeration, mock-heroics, and grotesque misspellings. Such as the form is, he was a master of it, and in his time was, certainly in the West, and probably throughout America, the acknowledged king of humor. His influence may be traced readily in the early works of Mark Twain and Bret Harte. He was the eponymous focus of humorous myth and legend, and California history is full of (largely apocryphal) accounts of his jokes and stories attributed to him.

Principal Works: Phoenixiana: or, Sketches and Burlesques, 1855; The Squibob Papers, 1859.

About: Derby, G. H. Phoenixiana (see preface by J. V. Cheney to 1897 edition); Stewart, G. R. John Phoenix, Esq.: A Life of Captain George H. Derby, U.S.A.; Century Magazine November 1901; Harper's Weekly May 17, 1913.

DE VINNE, THEODORE LOW (December 25, 1828-February 16, 1914), typographer, was born in Stamford, Conn., the son of Daniel and Joanna Augusta (Low) De Vinne. He was taught by his father and in nearby schools, and was then apprenticed to a printer. In 1848 he went to New York, and became, eventually, the manager of Theo. L. De Vinne & Company, printers (later The De Vinne Press). The excellence of his work in engravings and half-tones was unequaled; on *Scribner's* and *St. Nicholas* as well as the *Century* his craftsmanship was far in advance of that of his contemporaries. De Vinne was a founder, in 1884, of the Grolier Club, an association of lovers of beautiful books, for which he printed some of its finest volumes.

Among De Vinne's own valuable technical writings are: *The Invention of Printing, Historic Printing Types,* and *Notable Printers of Italy During the Fifteenth Century,* incorporating the commercial and artistic phases of the art. He himself had a strong preference for the so-called "masculine" type—strong, firm, and black—with a Gothic influence.

De Vinne was married, in 1850, to Grace Brockbank of New York City. He was civic-minded and widely admired, and was an unfaltering idealist in his profession. His achievements as a writer and artisan form a very significant portion of the history of American typography.

Principal Works: The Invention of Printing, 1876; Historic Printing Types, 1886; Notable Printers of the Fifteenth Century, 1910.

About: Theodore Low De Vinne (privately printed); New York Evening Post January 20, 1923 (Lit. Rev. Sec.); New York Herald February 17, 1914.

DEXTER, FRANKLIN BOWDITCH (September 11, 1842-August 13, 1920), historian and antiquarian, was born in Fairhaven, Mass., the son of Rodolphus Williams Dexter and May (Taber) Dexter. He was educated at Williston Seminary and at Yale, from which he was graduated in 1861 with high honors. He did not participate in the Civil War, but taught for two years in the Collegiate and Commercial Institute, in New Haven. He then returned to Yale, and remained in its service for the remainder of his long life. He had little existence outside the university, though he was married, his wife having been Theodosia Wheeler of New York City. Dexter was successively tutor in mathematics and Greek, assistant librarian, assistant treasurer, registrar, secretary of the Yale Corporation, and Larned Professor of American History. Many of these offices he held concurrently. His special field was the history of Yale itself, and he was essentially an antiquarian. His most important work was a series of biographies and annals of Yale graduates. He personally cataloged the university library and smaller Yale libraries.

Principal Works: Biographical Sketches of the Graduates of Yale College With Annals of the College History, 1885-1912; Sketch of the History of Yale University, 1887; Literary Diary of Ezra Stiles, 1901; Documentary History of Yale University: 1701-1745, 1916; New Haven Town Records: 1649-1684, 1917-19; Jared Ingersoll Papers, 1918; A Selection From the Miscellaneous Historical Papers of Fifty Years, 1919.

About: Yale Alumni Weekly October 15, 1920.

DEXTER, TIMOTHY (self-styled "Lord Timothy Dexter") (January 22, 1747-October 23, 1806), eccentric speller and punctuator, philosopher-wit, and merchant, was born in Malden, Mass., the son of Nathan and Esther (Brintnall) Dexter. His parents were poor and inconspicuous and he had only a minimum of learning. "Clear Nature," he said much later in life, "has been my schoolmaster." After working about seven years as a farm hand he went to Charleston, S.C., where he served a short apprenticeship to a leather dresser. Returning north, he set up shop "at the Sign of the Glove," in Newburyport, Mass., and in May 1770 he married Elizabeth (Lord) Frothingham, a widow, with four children of her own, by whom he had a son and a daughter. Mrs. Dexter contributed to the family income by establishing a huckster's business on the premises.

While Dexter's friends were getting small booty from the plunder of British ships during the early months of the Revolution, he himself was quietly and shrewdly buying up depreciated Continental currency; and with the adoption of Hamilton's policy of funding and assumption in 1791, he fell into sudden and incredible weath. Dexter moved his family into a pretentious mansion, got himself flashy carriages and handsome horses, hired a coachman, and with the purchase of two elaborate ships, the "Mehitabel" and the "Congress," began an extensive overseas trade. What part is fact and what part fiction in his subsequent enterprises is quite unanswerable: it is said that he sold 42,000 warming pans to Cubans who believed them

From an old print
"LORD" TIMOTHY DEXTER

to be cooking utensils; got his "oan pris" on the purchase of 340 tons of whalebone by professing to need it as "stay stuff" for ship rigging and promptly revolutionized the corset industry; and sold crated cats to warehouse owners in the tropics for keeping down rodents.

Dexter's obsession of self-importance was manifest in many forms. He rode post-haste from Boston with the news of the death of Louis XVI, and then bribed the Newburyport deacons to ring the churchbells in order to lend a little drama to his announcement; and after his removal to Chester, N.H., he slipped gracefully into the title of "Lord Timothy Dexter."

On Dexter's return to Newburyport, following a quarrel in Chester, Jonathan Plummer [*q.v.*], once a wheelbarrow vendor of fresh haddock, declared himself now "Poet Lauriet to his Lordship." After the appearance of "Dexter's Chatchize," strategically labeled "For Men and Not for Children," in the *Newburyport Impartial Herald*, came an unsigned metaphysical squib, "Wonder of Wonders," which Oliver Wendell Holmes attributed to Dexter. And it was a long time before the *Herald* editors could refrain from embellishing these "scratchings" with punctuation! *A Pickle for the Knowing Ones* (1802), Dexter's sole volume, ran the whole gamut of personal observations and philosophies; the first edition was entirely without punctuation marks, but the second had a page of "stops" and instructions to his readers to "peper and solt it as they plese." He remained an eccentric to the very end, setting up his effigy in his own front-yard gallery of notables and conducting a successfully solemn mock funeral. Machiavellian *parvenu* and avowed toper that he was, he had become a kind of stylist in his own right, and moreover, in legendary dimensions, an incomparable literary figure.

ABOUT: Knapp, S. L. Life of Timothy Dexter; Marquand, J. P. Lord Timothy Dexter; Seitz, D. C. Uncommon Americans; Bulletin of the New York Public Library February 1922.

DIAZ, ABBY (MORTON) (?, 1821-April 1, 1904), novelist and essayist, was born in Plymouth, Mass., the only daughter of Ichabod Morton and Patty (Weston) Morton. Her father, an early abolitionist, was a trustee of Brook Farm, the famous Transcendentalist colony to which so many of the best known of the New England thinkers of the '40s belonged and for several years from 1842 on, she lived there, for most of the time as teacher of the infant school. She married Emanuel Diaz, of Portuguese descent, but he died within a few years, leaving her with two small sons to support. She taught school in Plymouth until 1861, when, her first story having appeared in the *Atlantic Monthly*, she resolved to devote all her time to writing. Thereafter she wrote juvenile stories, adult novels, and works of non-fiction, her principal interests being feminism, pacifism, and a rather vague mysticism. Her best known book was the humorous juvenile series known as *The William Henry Letters*, which was exceedingly popular and later was dramatized. From 1880 to her death she lived at Belmont, Mass.

PRINCIPAL WORKS: The William Henry Letters, 1870; Neighborhood Talks, 1876; Domestic Problems, 1884; Only a Flock of Women, 1893.

ABOUT: Swift, L. Brook Farm; Boston Transcript, April 1 and 2, 1904.

DICKINSON, EMILY ELIZABETH (December 10, 1830-May 15, 1886), poet, was born, lived, and died in Amherst, Mass. Her father, Edward Dickinson, of an old Massachusetts family, was the leading lawyer of the town, served a term in Congress as a Whig, and was treasurer of Amherst College, which his father had founded. Her mother, whose personality and influence amounted to practically nothing, was Emily Norcross.

Emily attended Amherst Academy; spent one year (1847-48) at South Hadley Female Seminary (ancestress of Mt. Holyoke College); visited Washington and Philadelphia for a few weeks in the spring of 1854, while her father was in Congress; spent part of 1864 and 1865 in Boston to be treated for eye trouble, and died at fifty-

EMILY DICKINSON
as a young girl *

five of Bright's disease. That is the entire record of her outward life. It is the least important thing about her.

To account for Emily Dickinson the recluse, who for twenty years never went farther than her garden gate, who saw no one but her family and a very few chosen friends, who dressed always in white and wrote her poems secretly on scraps of paper, rolled and tied with a thread and thrust into bureau drawers, one need not imagine any strange mysteries of love and renunciation. Certainly Emily loved an unknown man, loved him deeply and unceasingly, but could not or would not marry him, though he loved her in return. Whether his name were Gould or Hunt or Wadsworth does not matter in the least. So far as that goes, she undoubtedly loved before him the young Leonard Humphrey who died at twenty-six, the teacher who first told her she was to be a poet. What concerns us is not the name of the man whom Emily Dickinson loved, or the rationalization she invented for her sacrifice of that love and her withdrawal from the world, but the actual emotional fixation which made both renunciation and seclusion inevitable. That was plainly to be found in her relations to her father.

She had the same sort of demanding, tyrannical, autocratic, and possessive father as did Elizabeth Barrett; and she did not escape. Probably Elizabeth Barrett would not have escaped either, had Robert Browning been less vital and compelling than he was. Emily's lover was not strong enough to overcome the terrific attachment, half love, half fear, that tied her to Edward Dickinson. Her father had set and molded her outward existence. America and England in her day were full of such fathers and such daughters; in most cases the inner life of the daughter, too, became a mere pallid echo of the father's will. The difference was that Edward Dickinson's elder daughter (the younger, Lavinia, was completely crushed) happened to be a genius. She was not strong enough to break loose from him in body; even in mind her father was inextricably mingled and confused with God: but she had the unbreakable arrogance of all true genius. Her hermit life, driven into and upon herself, was her answer to the tyranny which turned an ardent, gay, witty girl into a shy and withered spinster, with plain pale face under red-brown hair—a small ghost-like creature with a high, "surprised" voice and "sherry-colored" eyes.

Emily, the quintessence and distillation of the Puritan spirit, poured out her pure nectar in rare and precious drops. She wrote little until the early 'sixties; the shock and chaos of the Civil War may well have been the precipitating cause. In 1862 she sent four poems to Thomas Wentworth Higginson for confirmation of her innate knowledge that she was authentically a poet; her selection of him was inspired by an article of his in the *Atlantic Monthly*. She was too much for Higginson, the friend of young aspiring writers; he was kindly, he patronized her, he understood her not at all. He gave her solemn advice on correctness of rhyme and meter, and undertook clumsily to pare away the facets of her diamonds. She kept him as a friend, but she never made the same mistake again. In all her lifetime only two of her poems were published, and those without her consent. She asked that her manuscripts be burned after her death; Lavinia, appalled by the piles and piles of them—some 1500 poems in all—could not bring herself to complete the task of destruction which she had begun. All Emily Dickinson's published volumes were posthumous, and there still may be in possession of her secretive family some poems which have never seen print.

There is no use in trying to compare Emily; to compare her is to limit her. She is different and separate from any; she is herself. Her fragments of spirit are like no other poems in English. Samuel G. Ward, Julia Ward Howe's brother, F. Mar-

* Reproduced, by special permission, from *The Letters of Emily Dickinson*, edited by Mabel Loomis Todd (Harper & Bros., 1931). Copyright. Photographed from an original daguerreotype. The only authentic portrait of Emily Dickinson later than childhood.

ion Crawford's beloved "Uncle Sam," who was one of the best amateur critics of his day, hit Emily Dickinson off patly when he said, "she was the articulate inarticulate." Her irregularities, her half-rhymes, her strange, brief, broken sentences, are a necessary constituent of her poetry—as Higginson never learned.

The quatrain in iambic trimeter which she made her prevailing form is as much hers as the quatrain in iambic tetrameter associates itself in one's mind with Housman. She is most herself in that brief and severe form. But what distinguishes her most is the utter freshness and daring of her imagery. It is as if language had come newly minted to Emily.

If that were all, it would be enough and over-enough. But it is not all. Emily's rôle, says Genevieve Taggard, "was that of the sceptic; she was God's critic. Without God she would have been nothing." But her God was not the New England God of Calvin; he was a private creation, which wore largely the features of Edward Dickinson. "And then finally Emily pardoned God." Another writer, Cora Jarrett, sums her up by saying: "She speaks the language of those who take life hard."

When the time comes for final summing up, something of Emily Dickinson's will surely be among the salvage of posterity.

Principal Works: Poems, 1890; Poems: Second Series, 1891; Letters of Emily Dickinson, 1894; Poems: Third Series, 1896; The Single Hound, 1914; Complete Poems, 1924; Further Poems, 1929; Complete Letters, 1931.

About: Bianchi, M. D. Emily Dickinson Face to Face; Life and Letters of Emily Dickinson; Bradford, G. Portraits of American Women; Dickinson, E. Selected Poems (see Preface by Conrad Aiken to 1924 edition); Higginson, T. W. Carlyle's Laugh; Jenkins, M. Emily Dickinson: Friend and Neighbor; Pollitt, J. Emily Dickinson: The Human Background of Her Poetry; Taggard, G. The Life and Mind of Emily Dickinson; Atlantic Monthly October 1891, January 1915, June 1927; Catholic World October 1931; Harper's Magazine March 1930; Sewanee Review April 1937.

DICKINSON, JOHN (November 8, 1732-February 14, 1808), pamphleteer, was born in Talbot County, Md., the son of Samuel Dickinson and his second wife, Mary (Cadwalader) Dickinson. When he was eight years old the family moved to Dover, Del. There he was educated at home by tutors until 1750, when he went to Philadelphia to study law. In 1753 he went to London and was entered in the Middle Temple, being admitted to the bar in 1757. He returned to America and started the practice of law in 1760. However, it was the political and historical aspects of his profession which most interested him, and as these interests grew he gradually abandoned the law altogether.

Pennsylvania and Delaware were at that time under the same government and proprietorship, and Dickinson was a member of the legislatures of both colonies—of Delaware in 1760 (being elected speaker of the Assembly) and of Pennsylvania in 1762. Although he was fundamentally a conservative, his first published work was a pamphlet against the Stamp Acts, in 1765. His attitude at this time, however, was very mild, and he opposed all overt opposition to the acts. At the end of 1767 he began publishing in the *Pennsylvania Chronicle* the series of articles on British policy toward the American colonies which later, in book form, was called *Letters From a Farmer in Pennsylvania to the Inhabitants of the British Colonies.* These, though conciliatory, showed such command of the subject that they gained him wide renown; he was publicly thanked at a meeting in Boston, and was given an honorary LL.D. by the College of New Jersey (Princeton). In 1770 he was again elected to the Pennsylvania Legislature, and drafted its *Petition to the King*, as he had earlier drafted the *Declaration of Rights* of the Stamp Act Congress (1765). His career as "the penman of the Revolution" had begun in earnest. Gradually he was forced to alter his conciliatory and pacific methods. He was a member of the First Continental Congress for only a week,

From a portrait by C. W. Peale
JOHN DICKINSON
1791

but served throughout the Second, and continued to draft most of its principal messages and publications.

Dickinson was at this time still hopeful of avoiding open rupture with England, and voted against the Declaration of Independence. Yet when the Continental Army was formed, he was one of two Congress members to serve. He had been colonel of the first Philadelphia battalion, but resigned his commission, and later served as a private in the Battle of Brandywine.

After refusing one election to Congress from Delaware, he accepted and served in 1779; and in 1781 he was president of the Supreme Executive Council of Delaware. He was a member of the convention which framed the Federal Constitution, and advocated its adoption in a series of vigorous letters signed by the pseudonym of "Fabius." He retired from public life after adoption of the Constitution, and lived quietly on his estate in Delaware, with his wife, Mary Norris, whom he had married in 1770. His time was given to collection of his publications in book form, but he retained his keen interest in public affairs, and was frequently consulted as an adviser. He was a founder of Dickinson College (Carlisle, Pa.), which was named for him. He died in Wilmington at seventy, and was buried in the Friends' Cemetery there; he was a lifelong Quaker, in spite of his military service.

Dickinson's writings were always calm, persuasive, and mild in tone, but distinguished for their thorough grasp of detail and the extent of the economic and historical information that they revealed.

Principal Works: Letters From a Farmer in Pennsylvania to the Inhabitants of the British Colonies, 1768; The Political Writings of John Dickinson, Esq., 1801.

About: Stillé, C. J. The Life and Times of John Dickinson; Harper's Magazine July 1901.

DIDIER, EUGENE LEMOINE (December 22, 1838-September 8, 1913), popularizer, was born in Baltimore, the son of Franklin James and Julia (LeMoine) Didier. He attended Loyola College, and in 1867-68 was the editor of *Southern Society*, a journal of Southern writings. His high admiration for Poe occasioned the rather mawkish and very popular *Life of Edgar Allan Poe* (1879) and *Poe Cult* (1909), a collection of magazine articles. In the early 'eighties he began a series of ten-cent *Primers for the People*, popularizing Literature, Matrimony, etc.

Didier had, fortunately, no financial cares; but an obvious literary vanity in no wise enhanced his meagre fame as a writer.

Principal Works: The Life and Poems of Edgar Allan Poe, 1877; American Publishers and English Authors, 1879; Political Adventures of James G. Blaine, 1884.

About: Shepherd, H. E. Representative Authors of Maryland; Baltimore Evening Sun September 9, 1913.

DIMAN, JEREMIAH LEWIS (May 1, 1831-February 3, 1881), clergyman and historian, was born in Bristol, R.I., the son of Byron and Abby Alden (Wight) Diman. He attended public schools, was graduated from Brown University in 1851, and from Andover Theological Seminary in 1856. During pastorates in Fall River and Brookline he refused offers from larger churches, and in 1864 accepted a professorship at Brown. He contributed to the *Nation*, the *North American Review*, and to the Providence *Journal*. His Lowell Lectures, in Boston, were published in 1881, as *The Theistic Argument as Affected by Recent Theories*; he had read the exponents of the most recent philosophical thought and had arrived at sound and tolerant conclusions as to which religious corollaries should be rightly replaced and which should be maintained.

In 1861 he was married to Emily G. Stimson. Diman was a scholarly clergyman, and in the classroom was a wise and witty lecturer; had he written more, he might have become an enviable literary figure.

Principal Works: The Theistic Argument as Affected by Recent Theories, 1881.

About: Hazard, C. Memoirs of the Rev. J. Lewis Diman, D. D.; Providence Journal February 4, 1881.

DINSMOOR, ROBERT (October 7, 1757-March 16, 1836), poet, was born on a farm near Windham, N.H., the son of William Dinsmoor, of northern Irish descent, and Elizabeth (Cochran) Dinsmoor. The little schooling he secured came in the interims of farm labor. He enlisted in the American Revolution and served throughout, later returning to his father's farm. Though a layman, he was active in the Presbyterian Church, being deacon and clerk of the session. His first wife, Mary Park, died after the birth of two sons and nine daughters, and soon afterward he married Mary Davidson Anderson. He wrote verse, mostly in the Scottish Lowland dialect common among the "Scotch Irish" of the neighborhood. Written mostly for the edification of his family and friends, his poems privately printed in 1828, but it was not until long after his death that they were collected into a published volume. The poet Whittier was his friend, and did much to popularize his homely ballads, the subjects of which were taken largely from domestic incidents of his rural neighborhood.

PRINCIPAL WORK: Poems of Robert Dinsmoor: The Rustic Bard, 1898.

ABOUT: Dinsmoor, R. Poems (see Introduction by J. Dinsmoor); Whittier, J. G. Old Portraits and Modern Sketches.

"DIOGENES." See POWELL, THOMAS

DITHMAR, EDWARD AUGUSTUS (May 22, 1854-October 16, 1917), critic and editor, was born in New York City, the son of Henry and Anna B. Dithmar. He was educated in the grammar schools of that city, and at the age of twenty-three he joined the staff of the New York *Times*. Within five years he was made night editor, and in 1884 he became dramatic editor, at which post he may be said to have "arrived" as a literary commentator. Two years earlier he had married Ella B. Knapp, of New Rochelle, N.Y. In 1901 he was appointed London correspondent of the *Times*, and his intelligent interpretations soon won him the confidence of the leaders of British political thought. Returning to the United States he took over the editorship of the *New York Times Saturday Review of Books*.

By an astute appraisal of the theatre Dithmar had saved the literary lives of many a deserving upstart playwright; it was he who had persuaded Richard Mansfield, the actor, to employ Clyde Fitch to write *Beau Brummel*, sparing young Fitch from what would probably have been complete discouragement. In collaboration with William Winter, Brander Matthews, and Laurence Hutton, Dithmar prepared biographical sketches of several theatrical lions. As a critic he belonged to the so-called "impressionistic" school (as opposed to the "classical" or "didactic"), and judged the play *per se* and on its own immediate impression, regardless of preconceived criteria. He published relatively little, but his knowledge of the theatre did much to fix the course of American drama during the 'eighties and 'nineties.

PRINCIPAL WORKS: Theatrical Miscellany, 1884-86; Record of the New York Theatres (11 vols.) 1884-1900; Memories of Daly's Theatres, 1897; John Drew, 1900.

ABOUT: New York Times October 17-21, 1917.

DIX, DOROTHEA LYNDE (April 4, 1802-July 17, 1887), philanthropist and miscellaneous writer, was born in Hampden, Maine, the daughter of Joseph Dix and Mary (Bigelow) Dix. Her father was a religious bigot, and her childhood home was most unhappy; at the age of ten she left it voluntarily to live with her maternal grandparents in Boston, where her grandfather was a well known physician. She was educated privately, and at sixteen was teaching in Worcester, Mass. In 1821 she opened a private school in her grandparents' house in Boston, and continued to conduct it, so far as her frail health would permit, until 1834. This school laid special stress on moral training; and at the same time she wrote a number of ethical works and semi-tracts, some of them for the Unitarian Church, in which she was active. Finally her ill health forced her to abandon her school, and she spent several years with friends near Liverpool, England, returning to America in 1838.

After a daguerreotype

DOROTHEA LYNDE DIX
c. 1858

In 1841 came the event which changed her life and made her famous. She started a Sunday School class in the East Cambridge House of Correction, and was horrified by the conditions she found there. For fifty years thereafter Dorothea Dix was an avenging angel in the cause of the wretched inmates of prisons, almshouses, and particularly insane asylums. In an age when women never appeared on public platforms or before legislatures, her indomitable pity carried her frail body inexorably on its mission. She toured all the country, investigating the horrible conditions of the poor and lunatic, and securing, in eleven states, establishment of state hospitals for the insane, based on the humane methods of the French psychiatrist Pinel. After turning her attention to Canada, she toured England in the same cause, from 1854 to 1857. When the Civil War started, she organized and superintended the woman nurses in the Union forces. After the war, she continued her administrative work in the founding and supervision of insane asylums, finally retiring at eighty to the first state hospital her efforts had organized, at Trenton, N.J. There she died at eighty-five, still conducting her vast philanthropic enterprise from an invalid's bed.

Though Miss Dix's *Conversations on Common Things* reached a 60th edition, it is not as a writer that she has been and will be remembered. She was the great pioneer in America of decent, humanitarian treatment of the mentally ill and defective. Her *Memorial to the Legislature of Massachusetts* was the first of a series of burning documents addressed to state legislatures and to Congress exposing almost unbelievable horrors in the care of the insane. She found a torture chamber and she left a laboratory.

PRINCIPAL WORKS: Conversations on Common Things, 1824; Evening Hours, 1825; Meditations for Private Hours, 1828; The Garland of Flora, 1829; Ten Short Stories for Children, 1827-28 (as American Moral Tales for Young Persons, 1832); Memorial to the Legislature of Massachusetts, 1843.

ABOUT: Bromberg, W. The Mind of Man; Deutsch, A. The Mentally Ill in America; Marshall, H. E. Dorothea Dix: Forgotten Samaritan; Menninger, K. A. The Human Mind; Roe, A. S. Dorothea Lynde Dix; Tiffany, F. Life of Dorothea Lynde Dix.

DODDRIDGE, JOSEPH (October 14, 1769-November 9, 1826), clergyman and frontiersman, was born near Bedford, Pa., the son of John and Mary (Wells) Doddridge. He grew up in the wilderness of Washington County and gained an intimacy with Indians and pioneers that later enriched his *Notes on the Settlement and Indian Wars*. . . . First an itinerant Methodist minister, he shortly transferred his allegiance to the Episcopal Church and took a parish in Wellsburg, W. Va., traveling on horseback in missionary interests.

He married Jemima Bukey in 1795, studied medicine, and successfully combined this with the ministry. Beyond his *Notes*, a good piece of colonial history, his literary achievements were negligible.

PRINCIPAL WORKS: Treatise on the Culture of Bees, 1813; Notes on the Settlement and Indian Wars of the Western Parts of Virginia and Pennsylvania . . . , 1824.

ABOUT: Doddridge, N. Notes, etc. (see Memoir in 1876 and 1912 eds.); Doddridge, S. E. The Doddridges of Devon.

DODGE, MARY ABIGAIL (March 31, 1833-August 17, 1896), essayist, was born in Hamilton, Mass., the daughter of James Brown Dodge and Hannah (Stanwood) Dodge. She was very precocious, writing in almost mature style at the age of six. She was graduated from the Ipswich (Mass.) Female Seminary in 1850, and after two and a half years at home became an English teacher in a Hartford, Conn., high school. In 1858 she went to Washington, D.C., as governess to the children of Gamaliel Bailey, editor of the *National Era*, an anti-slavery magazine. Under the pseudonym of "Gail Hamilton," which she used for all her writing, Miss Dodge began to contribute articles to this magazine, her first published work. In 1860 she returned to Massachusetts to care for her mother, an invalid, until the latter's death in 1868. From 1865 to 1867, she edited, with J. T. Trowbridge and Lucy Larcom, a juvenile magazine called *Our Young Folks*, later merged with *St. Nicholas*. At this period also she published numerous volumes of essays. In 1871 she returned to Washington, her home thenceforth, though she traveled much abroad and frequently visited her birthplace. In 1872 and 1873 she was editor, with S. S. Wood, of *Wood's Household Magazine*. Although interested and active in politics (she was related by marriage to the well-known Maine politician, James G. Blaine, who almost became president in 1884), she was a stout foe of woman's suffrage. This stand was contrary to her general attitude, which was liberal and rationalistic. Her essays reflect her vigor of mind and her ready wit.

PRINCIPAL WORKS: Country Living and Country Thinking, 1862; A New Atmosphere, 1865; Woman's Wrongs: A Counter-Irritant, 1868; The Battle of the Books, 1870; Woman's Worth and Worthlessness, 1872; Our Common School System, 1880; A Washington Bible Class, 1891; Biography of James G. Blaine, 1895; X Rays, 1896; Gail Hamilton's Life in Letters, 1901.

ABOUT: Dodge, M. A. Gail Hamilton's Life in Letters; Arena December 1896; Critic August 22, 1896; Dial September 16, 1901; Independent November 14, 1901.

DODGE, MARY ELIZABETH (MAPES) (January 26, 1831-August 21, 1905), juvenile writer and editor, was born in New York City, the daughter of James Jay Mapes and Sophia (Furman) Mapes. Her father was a scientist and an intimate of many celebrities, and she grew up in a circle which included many of the best known figures of the period, among them William Cullen Bryant and Horace Greeley. She was educated at home by her father and by private tutors.

Collection of Frederick H. Meserve
MARY MAPES DODGE

In 1851, at twenty, she married William Dodge, an attorney, and they had two sons. Mr. Dodge died in 1858, and his widow found herself obliged to support her two small children. Her father had moved to Newark, N.J., and she returned to his home with her boys and set about earning a living by writing. Her first book appeared in 1864. She was successful from the first; she knew her *forte* and her limitations and confined herself almost entirely to stories for children, such as those she had told her own sons. In a period when most juvenile fiction was didactic, moralizing, and dreary, her freshness and verve were immediately popular. Her few adult stories appeared in the *Atlantic Monthly, Harper's Magazine,* and the *Century.*

In 1870 she became associate editor of *Hearth and Home,* and in 1873, when the juvenile magazine, *St. Nicholas,* was founded, she was made its first editor. She remained in this position until her death, thirty-two years later, and under her management the magazine became a leader, and even unique, in its class.

Mrs. Dodge was recognized for many years as the foremost American writer of juvenile stories of her time. Her greatest success was with her story of Dutch children, *Hans Brinker,* published in 1865, the same year as *Alice in Wonderland.* Though she had never visited Holland, she put so much research into this book that it was accepted as authentic by the Dutch themselves. Like all her books, it is distinguished by keen humor, originality, and a quality which is not so much sympathy with the child mind as identification with it. A handsome woman, there was always something soft and childlike about her face, and she could romp and play with young people as if she were still their own age.

There was nothing immature about her mind, however; she was a good executive, had excellent judgment, and if her lifelong acquaintance with famous writers was of assistance to her at first in getting *St. Nicholas* started, it was unneeded in later years, when her high standards attracted to its pages writers whose names meant something to the world at large, many of whom did their only juvenile writing for her. Bryant, Longfellow, and Whittier, her friends, wrote for *St. Nicholas,* as did Rudyard Kipling, who had read the magazine as a child. Frances Hodgson Burnett's *Little Lord Fauntleroy,* the most popular story of its day, ran serially in *St. Nicholas.*

In her later life Mrs. Dodge gradually withdrew from active management of *St. Nicholas,* and during her last seventeen years she spent long summers at Onteora Park, in the Catskill Mountains of New York, where her cottage, "Yarrow," to which she added a wing or bay window every year, was a gathering place for such friends and neighbors as Mark Twain, Brander Matthews, John Burroughs, and Maude Adams. It was there she died, at the age of seventy-four. Her funeral procession was made up spontaneously by the children of the community, who had loved her as a friend and almost as one of themselves.

Hans Brinker has become a standard children's classic, almost to the same degree as has Louisa Alcott's *Little Women* (which it preceded by two years); and *Donald and Dorothy* is also still enjoyed. Mrs. Dodge also wrote three volumes of verse, two of them for children, which, though not great poetry or perhaps even poetry at all, are delightful for their quaint humor and original expressions.

Principal Works: *Prose*—Irvington Stories, 1864; Hans Brinker: or, The Silver Skates, 1865; A Few Friends and How They Amused Themselves, 1869; Theophilus and Others, 1876; Donald and Dorothy, 1883; Baby World, 1884; The Land of Pluck, 1894. *Verse*—Rhymes and Jingles, 1874; Along the Way, 1879; When Life Is Young, 1894.

About: Century November 1905; Critic October 1905; Current Literature October 1905; St. Nicholas Magazine October 1905; New York Times August 22, 1905.

DODGE, THEODORE AYRAULT (May 28, 1842-October 25, 1909), historian, was born in Pittsfield, Mass., the son of Nathaniel S. Dodge and Emily (Pomeroy) Dodge. He was taken to Europe in childhood, received his early schooling in Berlin, and attended the University of Heidelberg and University College, London. He returned to the United States in 1862 and enlisted in the Union army. He was wounded at Gettysburg, losing his right leg, and served through the remainder of the Civil War in the Provost Marshal's office in Washington, being mustered out in 1866 with the rank of major. He had meanwhile studied law and received an LL.B. degree from Columbian (now George Washington) University. He was appointed to the regular army before his retirement as a volunteer, and served as superintendent of the War Department buildings until 1870, when further disabilities from his wound forced him to retire from active service. He was then a brevet lieutenant-colonel, but in 1904 was breveted major, the same rank he had held as a volunteer.

Dodge moved to Cambridge, Mass., and entered business with the avowed intention of making a sufficient fortune to retire and devote himself to writing. Unlike most persons who conceive such a plan, he succeeded, though he did not retire until 1900. In the meantime he had written most of his books, and had crossed the Atlantic some 80 times in pursuit of historical information. From 1880 he was president of a company which had almost a monopoly of the manufacture of rubber hose in America. After his retirement, he moved to Paris, died in France, and was brought home to be buried in the Arlington National Cemetery. In 1865 he had married Jane Marshall Neil, and after her death he married, in 1892, Clara Isabel Bowden.

Though he wrote essays, verse, and books on horsemanship, Dodge is known for his military histories, based on thorough research and actual inspection of the scenes of great battles of the past.

PRINCIPAL WORKS: The Campaign of Chancellorsville, 1881; A Bird's-eye View of Our Civil War, 1883; Patroclus and Penelope, 1885; Great Captains, 1889; Alexander, 1890; Hannibal, 1891; Caesar, 1892; Riders of Many Lands, 1894; Gustavus Adolphus, 1895; Napoleon (4 vols.) 1904-07.

ABOUT: Massachusetts Historical Society Proceedings 1909-10.

"DOESTICKS, Q.K. PHILANDER." See THOMSON, MORTIMER NEAL

"DOGBERRY." See MULFORD, PRENTICE

DONNELLY, IGNATIUS (November 3, 1831-January 1, 1901), novelist, essayist, and politician, was born in Philadelphia, the son of Philip Carroll Donnelly, a physician of Irish birth, and Catherine Frances (Gavin) Donnelly. His younger sister, Eleanor Cecilia, became known as a writer of religious verse. Donnelly was graduated from the Central High School, the oldest high school in Philadelphia, in 1849, and then read law with Benjamin Harris Brewster, later atadmitted to the bar in 1852, and in 1855, at only 24, declined a Democratic nomination to the legislature. The same year he married Katharine McCaffrey; and the next year he moved to Hastings, Minn. There he practiced law, acquired several farms, and (having become a Republican), twice ran unsuccessfully for the territorial senate. Minnesota became a state in 1858, and the next year Donnelly was elected lieutenant governor. He was re-elected in 1861, and having served for a time as acting governor, was thereafter known as "Governor" Donnelly. In 1862 he was elected for the first of three terms as congressman. He distinguished himself as a reformer, the "farmer's friend," and it was probably at this time that he did the wide reading which formed the background of his later books. His congressional career was ended by a factional dispute, but from 1873 to 1878 he served in the Minnesota state senate. Through various transitions he finally emerged as a Populist (**a**

Collection of Frederick H. Meserve
IGNATIUS DONNELLY

member of the People's Party). He ran again for Congress in 1884, served in the legislature in 1887 as a leader of the Farmers' Alliance, and when he died was the Populist candidate for vice-president. He edited several political papers, chiefly the *Anti-Monopolist* and the *Representative,* made one trip to Europe, and, his wife having died, married (1896) Marian Hansen, over forty-five years his junior. He settled in Minneapolis, and died there, at his new father-in-law's house, of heart failure, during a party to welcome in the twentieth century.

His death was appropriate: Donnelly was an epitome of the nineteenth century. He was a reformer, not a radical (as *Caesar's Column* testifies); his mind was quick, versatile, and often brilliant, but shallow and illogical. Whether he was expounding the arguments for the lost Atlantis (an eccentric theory of the cause of the Ice Ages), the writing of Shakespeare's plays by Bacon, the future of labor, or the Populist theory of currency: he was always interesting, always provocative—and nearly always unsound. There was a touch of the faker about him, a bit of the pioneer, a good deal of the earnest liberal, even a little of the enthusiast and the scholar. Few more authentically American writers have ever lived. He deserves rehabilitation, if only as a museum piece.

Principal Works: Atlantis: The Antediluvian World, 1882; Ragnarok: The Age of Fire and Gravel, 1883; The Great Cryptogram, 1888; Caesar's Column: A Story of the Twentieth Century, 1891; The American People's Money, 1895; The Cipher in the Plays and on the Tombstone, 1899.

About: American Parade January-March 1929; Minnesota Historical Society Collections 1915; Mississippi Valley Historical Review 1921.

DORR, JULIA CAROLINE (RIPLEY) (February 13, 1825-January 18, 1913), poet and novelist, was born in Charleston, S.C., the daughter of William Young Ripley and Zulma DeLacy (Thomas) Ripley. She spent most of her life in Vermont, where, after a rather haphazard schooling, she settled down to a leisurely existence writing novels, books of travel, and much verse. In 1847 she was married to Seneca M. Dorr, who joined her father in the marble industry.

Her first three books, all novels, were published under the name "Caroline Thomas"; her poems, especially the later ones, drew small compliments from Oliver Wendell Holmes and E. C. Stedman, and Emerson included a specimen of her verse in his *Parnassus.* The lilt of her stanza was unimpeded and its meter not obviously forced, but she slipped frequently into conventional treatments and hero-worshiping sentimentality.

Principal Works: *Novels*—Farmingdale, 1854; Lanmere, 1856; Sybil Huntington, 1869. *Travel*—Bermuda, 1884; A Cathedral Pilgrimage, 1896. *Verse*—Poems, 1872; Last Poems, 1913.

About: Harper's Weekly February 1, 1913; Rutland Herald January 20, 1913.

DORSEY, ANNA HANSON (McKENNEY) (December 12, 1815-December 25, 1896), novelist, was born in Georgetown, D.C., the daughter of William and Chloe Ann (Lanigan) McKenney. She was educated at home and her early verse found publication in several magazines. In 1837 she was married to Lorenzo Dorsey; influenced by the Catholic revival in England, they both became converted to that faith. *The Student of Blenheim Forest,* a novel, is somewhat redolent of this change of religious point of view. *Woodreve Manor,* appearing five years later, is full of comment on her own *milieu*; and *Palms* eulogizes the light of the Church in terms of its early Roman interpretations.

Mrs. Dorsey disliked publicity, and was certainly not vain in her self-criticism. She was the author, in all, of about thirty books, of which many were pervaded with a strongly Catholic point of view. They were somewhat overrun with a monotonous nostalgia and a sentimental didacticism, and, though highly popular in their day, have not endured.

Principal Works: The Student of Blenheim Forest, 1847; Oriental Pearl: or, The Catholic Emigrants, 1848; Woodreve Manor, 1852; Tangled Paths, 1885; Palms, 1887.

About: Ave Maria January 16, 1897; Evening Star (Washington) December 26, 1896.

DORSEY, SARAH ANNE (ELLIS) (February 16, 1829-July 4, 1879), romancer and editor, daughter of Thomas and Mary (Routh) Ellis, was born on a plantation near Natchez, Miss. She was educated in languages and the fine arts, traveled in Europe, and in 1853 was married to Samuel W. Dorsey. She began to write for the *Churchman. Recollections of Henry Watkins Allen* (1866), a slightly tedious life of the Confederate governor of Louisiana, was followed by *Lucia Dare* (1867), a Civil War romance.

Shortly before her death she was editing the writings and recollections of Jefferson Davis, whose wife had long been her friend. As an author, she drew intelligently upon her immediate surroundings, but her literary reputation was decidedly fleeting.

PRINCIPAL WORKS: Recollections of Henry Watkins Allen, 1866; Lucia Dare, 1867; Agnes Graham, 1869; Panola: A Tale of Louisiana, 1870.

ABOUT: Davidson, J. W. Living Writers of the South; New Orleans Times July 5, 1879; Natchez Democrat July 6, 1879.

DOUGLAS, AMANDA MINNIE (July 14, 1831-July 18, 1916), writer of juveniles, was born in New York City, the daughter of John N. and Elizabeth (Horton) Douglas. She studied at the City Institute and under private tutors. After 1853 she lived in Newark, N.J., wrote stories for various weeklies, and became a member of the Ray Palmer literary club for women and the New Jersey Women's Press Club. *In Trust,* her first book, appeared in 1866, and after *Larry* (1893), a novel winning the *Youth's Companion* award, came much juvenile fiction—the Kathie Series, the Little Girl Series, and the Helen Grant Series.

Miss Douglas was a close friend of Louisa M. Alcott, of whose works hers are slightly reminiscent. Her books, though simply and even at times vivaciously written, are now almost wholly forgotten.

PRINCIPAL WORKS: In Trust, 1866; Larry, 1893; Red House Children at Grafton, 1913.

ABOUT: Douglas, C. J. G. A Collection of Family Records; Newark Evening News July 18, 1916; New York Times July 19, 1916.

DOUGLASS, FREDERICK (February, 1817?-February 20, 1895), abolitionist and journalist, was born at Tuckahoe, Md., the son of a Negro slave, Harriet Bailey, who had some Indian blood, and of an unknown white father. He was originally known as Frederick Augustus Washington Bailey, but took the name of Douglass (from Scott's *Lady of the Lake*) on his escape from slavery. He was reared to the age of eight by his maternal grandmother; then he was sent to Baltimore to live with the family of Hugh Auld, a relative by marriags of his master, Capt. Aaron Anthony. Mrs. Auld taught him to read and write. When Captain Anthony died, in 1833, he was returned to Mr. Auld's brother, who hired him out to two successive masters. He attempted unsuccessfully to escape in 1836. He was arrested, released for lack of evidence, and sent back to Hugh Auld, who apprenticed him to a ship caulker. In 1838, disguised as a sailor, he escaped to New York. There he married a free colored woman, Anna Murray, and they went to New Bedford, Mass., where he worked as a laborer. In 1841 he made his first

Collection of Frederick H. Meserve
FREDERICK DOUGLASS

speech before the Massachusetts Anti-Slavery Society, and was made its agent.

For four years he worked for the society, traveling and speaking in the face of persecution and danger. In 1845 he wrote a frank autobiography, and fearing lest it should lead to his recapture, he went to England for two years. He returned to America in 1847, and until 1860 conducted the *North Star* (later called *Frederick Douglass's Paper*) at Rochester, N.Y., also lecturing frequently. From 1851 he was allied with the conservative wing of the abolitionists, and opposed John Brown's raid at Harper's Ferry. Two of his sons served in the Negro regiment he recruited during the Civil War. In 1871 he was appointed by Grant assistant secretary of the Santo Domingo Commission; from 1877 to 1881 was marshal of the District of Columbia; from 1881 to 1886 was recorder of the District; and from 1889 to 1891 was American minister-resident and consul general in Haiti. He died at Anacostia Heights, D.C. In 1884, his wife having died, he married Helen Pitts, a white woman. He was noted as an orator and was long active in the woman suffrage movement. His writings, which displayed an easy command of vigorous English, were all autobiographical.

PRINCIPAL WORKS: The Narrative of the Life of Frederick Douglass: An American Slave, 1845; My Bondage and My Freedom, 1855; Life and Times of Frederick Douglass, 1881.

ABOUT: Chesnutt, C. W. Frederick Douglass; deFord, M. A. Love Children; Douglas, F. The Narrative of the Life of Frederick Douglass; My Bondage and My Freedom; Life and Times of Frederick Douglass; Holland, F. M. Frederick Douglass: The Colored Orator; Washington, B. T. Frederick Douglass.

DOUGLASS, WILLIAM (c.1691-October 21, 1752), physician, maker of almanacs, and economist, was born in the village of Gifford, Haddington County, Scotland, the son of George Douglass. He was schooled in the classics and in modern languages; studied medicine at Edinburgh, Leyden, and Paris; and in Scotland came somewhat under the influence of the eminent physician, Archibald Pitcairne. Douglass made a journey to the West Indies and then settled in Boston in 1718. At the outbreak of a severe small-pox epidemic, in 1721, he won a considerable following with his seemingly authoritative objections to the use of inoculation, which, he held, spread rather than checked the disease. He issued four pamphlets on this subject, three of which were anonymous. There was, at this time, a popular tendency to undervalue the practice of medicine; Douglass, in a letter dated February 20, 1720/21, stated that "we [in Boston] abound with Practitioners though no other graduate than myself."

In 1736 Douglass published the first thorough and clinical description of scarlet fever, *The Practical History of a New Epidemical Eruptive Miliary Fever . . . in Boston New England in the years 1735 and 1736,* which antedates the treatise of John Fothergill, the English physician, by twelve years. Douglass not only fully described the nature of the eruption, etc., but discussed the conditions of greatest susceptibility. Moreover, he became, in time, completely though unwillingly convinced of the value of small-pox inoculation.

Douglass was seriously interested in meteorology and botany and in 1743, over the signature "William Nadir" he issued *Mercurius Nov-Anglicanus,* a highly personal, jaunty, and informational almanac. For his *Summary: Historical and Political, of the First Planting, Progressive Improvements, and Present State of the British Settlements in North America* he had access to very few authoritative sources; but he succeeded in assembling a mass of miscellaneous material which he seasoned with a generous measure of forthright opinions; and unlike similar documents of the period it was supplied with a fairly adequate index. He also prepared *A Discourse Concerning the Currencies of the British Plantations,* in which he had a non-parochial grasp of the fundamentals of exchange, reaffirming his belief in colonial adherence to the "universal commercial medium."

Douglass had, it appears, more than one professional enemy, and in the fact that he was "always positive and sometimes accurate" may lie a part of the explanation. His combined medical and literary achievements still make good supplementary reading in colonial history.

Principal Works: The Practical History of a New Epidemical Eruptive Miliary Fever . . . in Boston New England in the Years 1735 and 1736, 1736; A Discourse Concerning the Currencies of the British Plantations in America, etc., 1739; Mercurius Nov-Anglicanus, 1743; A Summary: Historical and Political, of the First Planting, Progressive Improvements, and Present State of the British Settlements in North America, 1755.

About: Boas, R. & L. Cotton Mather: Keeper of the Puritan Conscience; Douglass, W. Summary: Historical and Political . . . ; Green, S. A. Notes on a Copy of Dr. William Douglass' Almanach for 1743, Touching on the Subject of Medicine in Massachusetts; Kelly, H. A. & Burrage, W. L. American Medical Biographies.

DOWNING, ANDREW JACKSON (October 30, 1815-July 28, 1852), horticulturist and landscape architect, was born in Newburgh, N.Y., the son of Samuel and Eunice (Bridge) Downing. He attended an academy at Montgomery, N.Y., and several years afterward, aided his brother in the operation of a nursery, established before the death of his father. In 1838 he was married to Carolina Elizabeth DeWint; and, strongly influenced by the best landscape design of the surrounding Hudson estates, he began his popular *Treatise on the Theory and Practice of Landscape Gardening. Fruits and Fruit Trees of America,* in 1846, became a second classic, and from that year until his death he was the editor of the *Horticulturist.* Downing plotted the grounds of the Capitol, the White House, and the Smithsonian Institution in Washington, but he was drowned, in 1852, when the "Henry Clay" caught fire on the Hudson, before the work was completed.

The accuracy and clarity of Downing's writings greatly enhanced his reputation as the foremost American authority on landscape gardening and as a brilliant horticulturist.

Principal Works: A Treatise on the Theory and Practice of Landscape Gardening, 1841; Cottage Residences, 1842; The Fruits and Fruit Trees of America, 1845; Architecture of Country Houses, 1850.

About: Horticulturist September, October, November 1852; New York Times July 28, 1852.

"DOWNING, MAJOR JACK." See SMITH, SEBA

DRAKE, BENJAMIN (1795-April 1, 1841), historian and editor, was born in Mays Lick, Ky., the son of Isaac and Elizabeth (Shotwell) Drake. His schooling was scant, and after clerking at a drug store in Cincinnati he studied law and had a good though brief practice. Drake aided in the founding of the *Cincinnati Chronicle* and edited it for seven years. *Tales and Sketches From the Queen City,* imaginary yarns about Cincinnati, was published in 1838.

His concise accounts of the Sac and Fox, Black Hawk, and Shawanoe Indians, appearing 1838-41, are the work of a careful collector of obscure facts and form a small but important historical document.

PRINCIPAL WORKS: Cincinnati in 1826, 1827; Tales and Sketches From the Queen City, 1838; The Life and Adventures of Black Hawk: With Sketches of Keokuk, the Sac and Fox Indians, and the Late Black Hawk War, 1838; Life of Tecumseh and His Brother . . . With an Historical Sketch of the Shawanoe Indians, 1841.

ABOUT: Mansfield, E. D. Memoirs of the Life and Services of Daniel Drake; Cincinnati Gazette April 2, 1841.

DRAKE, FRANCIS SAMUEL (February 22, 1828-February 22, 1885), historian, was born in Northwood, N.H., the son of Samuel Gardner Drake [*q.v.*], Boston bookseller and author, and Louisa (Elmes) Drake. His childhood was passed in Boston, and at twenty he was a lieutenant in the Boston Light Guards. In 1856 he was married to E. M. Valentine, lived in Kansas a while, and served in the Civil War. Returning to Boston, he published, in 1872, *A Dictionary of American Biography Containing Nearly Ten Thousand Notices,* in which he attempted a comprehensive and non-regional selection. *The Town of Roxbury* was published in 1878; *Indian History for Young Folks* (1885) has maintained a limited popularity.

Drake's point of view was quite provincial and his influence as a historiographer is decidedly restricted.

PRINCIPAL WORKS: Dictionary of American Biography Containing Nearly Ten Thousand Notices, 1872; Life and Correspondence of Henry Knox, 1873; Town of Roxbury, 1878; Tea Leaves . . , 1884.

ABOUT: Drake, S. G. Genealogical and Biographical Account of the Family of Drake; Washington Post February 23, 1885.

DRAKE, JOSEPH RODMAN (August 7, 1795-September 21, 1820), poet, was born in New York City, the son of Jonathan Drake and Hannah (Lawrence)) Drake. When he was a small child his father died, and his mother remarried and moved with her new husband and her three daughters to New Orleans, leaving the boy in the charge of relatives in what was then a country town, but is now a part of New York City. At eighteen the boy was a student of medicine at a private school, and it was there that he first met Fitz-Greene Halleck, the poet, who became his intimate friend and his collaborator.

In 1816 he was graduated in medicine, at the head of his class, but he did not practise at once. In the same year he married Sarah Eckford, daughter and heiress of a wealthy ship-builder, and with her he made an extensive honeymoon tour of Europe. Drake's friends, including Halleck, were very dubious about this marriage, fearing its effect on his career and his personality, but it seems to have been reasonably happy and it certainly never made a snob of Drake or dried up his poetic vein.

In 1819 Dr. Drake, as he was then known, opened a drugstore, a natural thing for a physician to do in those days when medicine and pharmacy were practically the same profession. Already, however, the first symptoms of tuberculosis were evident in the young doctor, as he himself was only too well aware. Overwork in his store completed the damage. Only a few months later, he went to New Orleans to visit his mother, in the hope that the warmer climate might benefit him. It was too late, and he returned to New York and to his wife only to die. His grave in the private burying ground of his cousins, the Hunt family, of "Hunt's Point," is now a protected landmark of the city of New York. It was of his death that Halleck wrote the well known and touching lines:

Green be the turf above thee,
Friend of my better days!
None knew thee but to love thee;
None named thee but to praise.

This, which would be hyperbole when spoken of most persons, seems to have been literally true of Drake. He was an engaging and winning person, a warm and eager friend, and so modest about his poetic gift that when he copied his own favorites among his poems in a notebook in 1817 he called them "Trifles in Rhyme," and on his deathbed he asked his wife to destroy all his unpublished verses. Fortunately she disobeyed him, and in 1835 some of them, including his most famous poem, "The Culprit Fay," were published by his daughter. His complete works were not published until 1936.

Indeed, the only writing of Drake's which saw print during his short lifetime was the series of satirical topical verses called *The Croaker Papers* which he and Halleck

After a portrait by J. Paradise
JOSEPH RODMAN DRAKE

wrote together and published in the *Evening Post* as by "Croaker, Sr., Croaker, Jr., and Croaker & Co." These attracted immense comment, though the excitement over the identity of the authors can be explained largely by the fact that American literature in 1819 was still in its swaddling clothes and that, like Dr. Johnson's poodle, the wonder was not that it was done well but that it was done at all. Something of the same significance attaches to "The Culprit Fay," which was written in three days with the avowed intention of showing that American rivers, as well as British, were worthy of celebration. Yet it is a charming thing in its own right, airy as gossamer, and with something of magic in it.

An interesting parallel may be drawn between the lives of Drake and Keats. Their dates were almost synchronous, their professions similar, and the cause of their deaths the same. Keats is of course infinitely the greater poet—Drake, whatever his potentialities, never revealed more than minor talent—but the American shared with his great fellow-poet a sensitivity to nature and a dreamy sensuousness. He was through and through a romantic, even though a lesser member of that rich school of poetry.

Like many tubercular persons, Drake was extremely handsome, with clear skin, bright blue eyes, and thick golden hair—"the handsomest man in New York," Halleck called him. Coleman, the editor of the *Post*, said of him: "Drake looked the poet; you saw the stamp of genius in every feature." He was as lovable as he was brilliant, and his premature death may have been as great a loss to American literature as it was a lasting blow to his adoring friends.

Principal Works: The Culprit Fay and Other Poems, 1835; Life and Works (ed. by F. L. Pleadwell), 1936.

About: Drake, J. R. Life and Works (see Memoir by F. L. Pleadwell); Bookman June 1897; Century Magazine July 1910; Harper's Magazine June 1874; New York Times Book Review November 22, 1936.

DRAKE, SAMUEL ADAMS (December 19, 1833-December 4, 1905), historian, was born in Boston, the son of Samuel Gardner Drake [*q.v.*] and Louisa (Elmes) Drake. He was educated in the public schools, and following his marriage to Isabella G. Mayhew in 1858, he did newspaper work in Kansas and served in the Civil War. On the death of his first wife, he was married to Olive N. Grant in 1866. Drake dedicated *Nooks and Corners of the New England Coast* (1875) to Longfellow, and *The Heart of the White Mountains* (1882) to Whittier.

Except for a children's book about California and several Middlewest accounts, Drake's works were limited to New England subjects. Within their scope they bear a strong fidelity to sentiment and tradition.

Principal Works: Nooks and Corners of the New England Coast, 1875; The Heart of the White Mountains, 1882; The Making of the Ohio Valley States, 1894; The Young Vigilantes: A Story of California Life in the Fifties, 1904.

About: Drake, S. G. Genealogical and Biographical Account of the Family of Drake; New York Times December 5, 1905.

DRAKE, SAMUEL GARDNER (October 11, 1798-June 14, 1875), historian and antiquarian, was born in Pittsfield, N.H., the son of Simeon and Love Muchmore (Tucke) Drake. He attended village schools, and then worked in Boston and Baltimore; on returning to Pittsfield he studied law and took charge of a school. From 1828-30 he was a book-auctioneer, and shortly set up his own shop in Boston. *Indian Biography* (1832) went through numerous editions and appeared as *Book of the Indians* in 1842. He was one of the founders of the New-England Historic Genealogical Society and edited fifteen volumes of its *Register*. On a contemplated history of New England he did considerable research abroad, during the years 1858-60.

Francis Samuel and Samuel Adams Drake [*qq.v.*] were sons by his first wife, Louisa Elmes, whom he had married in 1825; after her death, Sarah Jane Drake, a relative, became his second wife. As antiquarian and publisher he did much to preserve portions of early New England history.

PRINCIPAL WORKS: Indian Biography, 1832; Old Indian Chronicle, 1836; Indian Captivities, 1839; The History and Antiquities of Boston, 1856; The Witchcraft Delusion in New England (3 Vols.) 1866.

ABOUT: Drake, S. G. Genealogical and Biographical Account of the Family of Drake; Potter's American Monthly October 1875.

DRAPER, JOHN WILLIAM (May 5, 1811-January 4, 1882), scientist and historian, was born near Liverpool, England, the son of the Rev. John Christopher Draper and Sarah (Ripley) Draper. The father's name was an assumed one; he had come of a wealthy Roman Catholic family, but was disowned when he was converted to Methodism by John Wesley, and changed his name, his real name being unknown. He was a Methodist minister, and the son was educated at a Methodist school called Woodhouse Grove, and at London University. In 1830, while only nineteen and still a student, he married Antonia Pereira Gardner, whose father was physician at the court of Dom Pedro I of Brazil.

In 1832 Draper's father died, and the entire family emigrated to America, settling in Christiansville, Va., where they had cousins, descendants of an American branch. Draper had already published some geological papers, and now set up a laboratory, his first published work being on experiments he was conducting in capillary attraction. In 1835, by the help of his devoted sister, an artist, he went to the University of Pennsylvania, and the next year received a medical degree. That autumn he became professor of chemistry and natural philosophy at Hampden-Sidney College, and two years later undergraduate professor of chemistry at the University of the City of New York. He remained at this institution during the rest of his life; in 1839 he helped to organize its medical school, of which he became president in 1850. He did much to establish New York as a medical center; his zeal was undaunted by a disastrous fire in 1865 which destroyed the medical school and all his library, notes, and apparatus.

Meanwhile he continued to do important work in scientific research, his name being connected with early experiments in photography, radiant energy, and the electric telegraph. (Among other pioneer achievements, he is credited with making the first photographic portrait of the human face, in 1839). This double career would have been enough for most men, but Draper added a third. He is chiefly remembered as an historian.

Collection of Frederick H. Meserve
JOHN WILLIAM DRAPER

In his own words, his aim was to present "history seen through the medium of physiology," since he held that "social advancement is as completely under the control of natural law as is bodily growth." His *Intellectual Development of Europe* is a classic, and his *History of the Conflict Between Religion and Science* has been complemented, not superseded, by Andrew D. White's later *History of the Warfare of Science With Theology in Christendom.* Personally, Draper was a deist of the eighteenth century type, and strongly influenced also by the rationalistic Arabic philosophers of the Middle Ages.

He died, still in harness, at seventy-one; on the very day of his death the university officials had re-assigned his classes to him—for in addition to writing, research, and administrative duties he continued to teach. His death took place at his home at Hastings-on-Hudson, which he had bought in 1840.

Draper was very short in stature, burly, with side-burns, white in his later years. He spoke with a strong North-of-England accent. Fearless, thorough, original in mind and persuasive in speech, he was one of the great fighters for the liberation of the human mind. His son Henry became a noted spectroscopist and was also an analytical chemist, and both other sons were teachers of science. The Hastings estate, including the Draper Observatory, was presented by his daughter to the American Scenic and Historic Society, which conducts the observatory as a memorial to him.

Principal Works: A Treatise on the Forces Which Produce the Organization of Plants, 1844; Treatise on Chemistry, 1846; Treatise on Natural History, 1849; Human Physiology: Statical and Dynamical, 1856; History of the Intellectual Development of Europe, 1863; Thoughts on the Future Civil Policy of America, 1865; History of the American Civil War, 1867-70; Contributions to Chemistry, 1874; History of the Conflict Between Religion and Science, 1874; Scientific Memoirs, 1878.

About: American Journal of Science 1882; Harper's Weekly February 11, 1882; National Academy of Sciences: Biographical Memoirs 1886; Proceedings American Philosophical Society January-June 1882.

DRAPER, LYMAN COPELAND (September 4, 1815-August 26, 1891), historian and collector, was born in Erie County, N.Y., the son of Luke and Harriet (Hoisington) Draper. He attended the village school in Lockport, N.Y., worked in a store, entered a college in Granville, Ohio, and finished at the Hudson River Seminary. Lyman read widely in frontier history, and at twenty-three resolved to become a biographer of those Western heroes whom historians had neglected. With subordinate money-making interests—journalism, potato-growing, etc.,—he spent most of his life in the Ohio Valley and deep South, draining truthful reminiscences from the pioneer survivors, and recording them verbatim. In 1852 he moved to Madison, Wis., and as secretary of the Wisconsin State Historical Society began the publication of the valuable *Wisconsin Historical Collections*, of which he edited ten.

Draper contributed to *Appleton's Cyclopaedia*, and wrote *King's Mountain and Its Heroes* (1891). In 1853 he married his cousin, Lydia Chadwick, who died in 1888; the following year he married Catherine T. Hoyt. In manuscripts and miscellaneous papers Draper tirelessly amassed a fund of significant historical material.

Principal Works: Wisconsin Historical Collections (ed., 10 vols.); King's Mountain and Its Heroes, 1881.

About: Draper, T. W.-M. The Drapers in America; Madison Democrat August 27, 1891.

DRAYTON, JOHN (June 22, 1766-November 27, 1822), governor of South Carolina and social historian, was born near Charleston, S.C., the son of William Henry Drayton, himself an author in slight degree, and Dorothy (Golightly) Drayton. He attended Nassau Grammar School, at Princeton, N.J., and the College of New Jersey, finishing his studies in England. Returning to Charleston, he was married, in 1794, to Hester Rose, and entered upon an active political career, culminating in the governorship, 1800-02 and 1808-10 and a judiciary appointment by President Madison in 1812.

Letters Written During a Tour Through the Northern and Eastern States of America appeared in 1794; into *A View of South Carolina. . .* (1802) he wrote some acute observations; and from notes left by his father he prepared *Memoirs of the American Revolution. . .*, in two significant volumes (1821). His reputation, however, rests not so much on his writings as on his achievements in public affairs.

Principal Works: Letters Written During a Tour Through the Northern and Eastern States of America, 1794; A View of South Carolina as Respects Her Natural and Civil Concerns, 1802; Memoirs of the American Revolution: From Its Commencement to the Year 1776 . . . , 1821.

About: Taylor, E. H. D. The Draytons of South Carolina and Philadelphia (Pubs. Geneal. Soc. Pa., VIII, 1923); Charleston Courier November 29, 1822.

DRESSER, JULIUS A. (1838-1893), metaphysical writer and founder of New Thought, was the son of Asa and Nancy (Smart) Dresser, and was born in Maine. In 1860 he visited, for treatment of "a nervous disorder," the celebrated Phineas P. Quimby [*q.v.*], the mental healer, among whose other patients or pupils at about the same time were Mary Baker Eddy and Warren Felt Evans [*qq.v.*]. He became interested in Quimby's methods, and was given access to Quimby's still unpublished manuscripts. He did not, however, become a healer himself until 1882, when he moved to Boston with his wife, who had been Annetta G. Seabury, and who was also a mental healer. Dresser was a founder of and constant contributor to the monthly, *Mental Healing*. Gradually he modified Quimby's system until he had evolved a new theory of disease and a philosophy which became known as "New Thought." He is generally considered the originator of this school of philosophy, one of whose chief exponents was his son, Horatio Willis Dresser. Julius Dresser did not deny the existence of the natural universe, but considered that "the Omnipresent Wisdom" held all nature in its control, and that by yielding to this "Wisdom" man could not help obtaining health, happiness, and even prosperity; "right thinking" ("in tune with the universe," as a later New Thought writer, Ralph Waldo Trine, put it) being the foundation of all good in the temporal world.

Very little is known of the details of Dresser's life. His wife survived him, and as late as 1914 was a healer and teacher in

Boston. He wrote little, and his claim to distinction rests largely upon his priority in what has become a widespread and popular school of teaching.

PRINCIPAL WORK: The True History of Mental Science, 1899.

ABOUT: Dresser, H. W. A History of the New Thought Movement; Dresser, H. W. Health and the Inner Life.

DU CHAILLU, PAUL BELLONI (July 31, 1835-April 30, 1903), explorer and travel writer, was probably born in Paris, and almost certainly in France, though according to some accounts his birthplace was New Orleans. His father, whose given name is unknown, was in the African trade, at Gaboon, on the west coast. It seems fairly well established that the son spent his boyhood there and was educated at the Jesuit Mission school. From the beginning he showed an aptitude for natural history, and also acquired a firm foundation in the various native languages of the region—both excellent groundwork for a career as an explorer.

He appears to have come to America about 1852, and soon afterwards succeeded in securing the support of the Philadelphia Academy of Natural Sciences for an exploration of central Africa, undertaken in 1856, when he was only twenty-one. The trip lasted four years, and Du Chaillu was probably the first white man to see living anthropoid apes. He returned to the United States at the end of 1859, and two years later published his *Explorations and Adventures in Equatorial Africa.* For the most part this earned him more notoriety than fame, and more ridicule than praise. While controversy still raged over his reported discoveries, he undertook another expedition, from 1863 to 1865, which resulted in his *Journey to Ashangoland.* Again his accounts of pygmy tribes excited the same disbelief as had his former stories of chimpanzees and gorillas. Du Chaillu was an explorer, not a scientist, and he had a tendency to heighten the colors of his narrative. However, in the main his observations were accurate, and subsequent explorations by others vindicated many of his most bitterly disputed statements.

PAUL B. DU CHAILLU

After several years in New York, writing and lecturing, Du Chaillu turned his attention to another quarter of the globe. In 1871 he travelled to Sweden, Norway, and Lapland, and returned with material for two more books. In 1901, at sixty-six, he journeyed to Russia with the intention of describing it as he had done the Scandinavian countries. This trip, however, was never finished, for the traveler died suddenly in St. Petersburg (Leningrad), after having published only a few "Letters From Russia" as the beginning of his contemplated book.

Du Chaillu was never married. He was something of a solitary, best at home in the wilds, and he resented keenly the abuse and ridicule heaped on his African books. He was a trifle too much given to posing in heroic attitudes, but he had good grounds for his self-confidence and assurance. The fact is that his was the fatal gift of vivid writing; he could not help being interesting and exciting, and these are attributes which are seldom forgiven by the pompous Dr. Dryasdusts. His chief scientific error, perhaps, was his insistence on the ferocity of the timid gorilla; but after all Du Chaillu could not be expected to know that the huge beast crashing through the underbrush was more alarmed than vicious, and that perhaps the gorilla was as frightened by the explorer's saturnine countenance and bald head as the explorer was by the gorilla's hairy bulk!

PRINCIPAL WORKS: Explorations and Adventures in Equatorial Africa, 1861; A Journey to Ashangoland, 1867; Stories of the Gorilla Country, 1868; Wild Life Under the Equator, 1869; Lost in the Jungle, 1869; My Apingi Kingdom, 1870; The Country of the Dwarfs, 1871; The Land of the Midnight Sun, 1881; The Viking Age, 1889.

ABOUT: Vaucaire, M. (translated by E. P. Watts). Paul Du Chaillu: Gorilla Hunter; Harper's Magazine June 1861, April 1868; Harper's Weekly May 16, 1903; Independent May 14, 1903; Scientific American May 9, 1903.

DUCHÉ, JACOB (January 31, 1737/38-January 3, 1798), theological and miscellaneous writer, was born in Philadelphia, the son of Col. Jacob Duché, formerly mayor of the city, and Mary (Spence) Duché. He was graduated in the first class of the College of Philadelphia (the University of Pennsylvania), in 1757, and then studied for a year at Cambridge University, England, and was ordained deacon. He returned to Philadelphia in 1759 and became assistant rector of Christ's and St. Peter's Churches and teacher of oratory at his alma mater. In the same year he married Elizabeth Hopkinson, sister of Francis Hopkinson, one of the signers of the Declaration of Independence. Duché at first was chaplain of the Continental Congress, and published two patriotic sermons, but after the Declaration he turned Tory. A letter he wrote to Washington urging Congress to recall the Declaration caused such execration that in 1777 he left for England. The Pennsylvania Assembly proscribed him and confiscated his property, but allowed his family to join him. He was made secretary and chaplain of a London orphan asylum. He repented his recantation bitterly, and poured out letters of appeal for his return to America, which was not granted until 1792, when he was an invalid from a paralytic stroke. He lived six years longer, a convert to Swedenborgianism and eccentric to the point of insanity.

Duché in his earlier years was a popular preacher and was always a prolific writer. His writing, however, is platitudinous and bombastic.

PRINCIPAL WORKS: Pennsylvania: A Poem, 1756; An Exercise (verse) 1762; The Life and Death of the Righteous, 1763; Human Life: A Pilgrimage, 1771; Observations on a Variety of Subjects: Literary, Moral, and Religious, 1774; The Duty of Standing Fast in Our Spiritual and Temporal Liberties, 1775; Discourses on Various Subjects, 1779; Sermons Preached in America, 1788; A Sermon: For the Benefit of the Humane Society, 1791.

ABOUT: Sabine, L. Biographical Sketches of Loyalists of the American Revolution; Pennsylvania Magazine of History and Biography 1878.

DUFFIELD, SAMUEL AUGUSTUS WILLOUGHBY (September 24, 1843-May 12, 1887), hymnologist and clergyman, was born in Brooklyn, N.Y., the son of the Rev. George Duffield and Anna Augusta (Willoughby) Duffield. He studied under William FewSmith, at Philadelphia and was graduated from Yale in 1863. His father instructed him in theology, and he held, successively, between the years 1867 and 1886, six pastorates in the Middlewest and in the East. In 1867 he married Hattie S. Haywood.

Duffield's *Warp and Woof* evidences a certain poetic gift; and as a hymnologist he contributed to Charles Seymour Robinson's *Laudes Domini* and compiled *English Hymns: Their Authors and History,* a valuable and exhaustive survey. *The Latin Hymn Writers and Their Hymns,* unfinished at the time of his death, was published in 1889. His literary province was obviously small, and his early death restricted the volume of his work.

PRINCIPAL WORKS: Warp and Woof, 1870; English Hymns: Their Authors and History, 1886; The Latin Hymn Writers and Their Hymns, 1889.

ABOUT: Duffield, S. A. W. The Latin Hymn Writers (see Preface); Presbyterian May 21, 1887.

DUGANNE, AUGUSTINE JOSEPH HICKEY (?, 1823-October 20, 1884), poet, novelist, and miscellaneous writer, was born in Boston. Nothing is known of his parentage or education. In 1845 he moved to Philadelphia and supported himself by writing cheap paper-backed novels. He also did a large amount of hack compilation in popular history and economics. His tragedy, *The Lydian Queen,* was produced in 1848. Soon after, he went to New York and added book reviewing to his other forms of literary and semi-literary activity. He became connected as an orator with the Know-Nothing Party, and was a member of the New York Assembly in 1855. In 1862 he joined the Union army as lieutenant-colonel of the New York Volunteers. A few months later he was taken prisoner in Louisiana and was in Southern prison camps for nearly two years. He was then paroled and was mustered out for disability. During his later years he lived in New York, and was on the staff of the *Tribune* and of the *Sunday Dispatch,* a Masonic paper. He died of tuberculosis, from which he had suffered ever since the Civil War.

Duganne managed to be both sensational and dull in his writing, and none of his work long survived his death.

PRINCIPAL WORKS: Massachusetts (verse) 1843; Home Poems, 1844; Parnassus in Pillary (verse) 1851; Art's True Mission in America, 1853; Poetical Works, 1855; Camps and Prisons, 1865; Ballads of the War, 1865; Fighting Quakers, 1866; Governments of the World, 1882; Injuresoul (satirical verse) 1884.

ABOUT: New York Tribune October 22, 1884; New York Sunday Dispatch October 26, 1884.

DULANY, DANIEL (June 28, 1722-March 17, 1797), lawyer, statesman, and pamphleteer, was born in Annapolis, Md., the son of Daniel Dulany and Rebecca (Smith) Dulany. He was sent to school in

England and after attending Eton College and Clare Hall (Cambridge University) he studied law at the Middle Temple; he was admitted to the Maryland bar at the age of twenty-five. In 1749 he was married to Rebecca Tasker. Two years later he was elected a member of the Maryland Legislative Assembly, where for three years he defended the government against the popular faction; and after his appointment to the Governors' Council in 1757 he continued to promulgate the same policies.

Not long after the passage by the British Parliament of the famous stamp-tax act Dulany issued, in pamphlet form, some sound *Considerations on the Propriety of Imposing Taxes on the British Colonies for the Purpose of Raising a Revenue, by Act of Parliament,* citing taxation without representation as a violation of English common law; and to portions of Dulany's briefs William Pitt later made numerous references in his speeches for repeal. The *Considerations* also contained a plea for the freedom of the press, without which, he contended, "the prediction that the 'Constitution of the British Government was too excellent to be permanent' will appear to have some weight." In 1766 he published another historically significant pamphlet on The *Right to the Tonnage, the Duty of the Twelve Pence per Hogshead on all Exported Tobacco, and the Fines and Forfeitures in the Province of Maryland.*

Dulany's popularity ran high until 1773 when he plunged himself, via the columns of the *Maryland Gazette,* into what became a rather galling controversy: over the signature "Antilon" he defended the governor's rights to fix the amounts of officers' fees; and Charles Carroll, the Revolutionary leader, as "First Citizen" held that the fees should be fixed by Assembly legislation. Dulany's long-nourished antipathy for radical factions sent him, at the outbreak of the Revolutionary War, into retirement at Hunting Ridge, Md. Dr. Alexander Hamilton [*q.v.*], physician and author of the *Itinerarium,* was a brother-in-law.

Dulany was not, it would seem, overburdened by professional scruples; yet even though certain allowances must be made in the testimony of one of his contemporaries that he was "indisputably the best lawyer on this continent," it is certainly true that in his writings and in his extensive legal activities he noticeably influenced the judicial and diplomatic sentiment of the period.

PRINCIPAL WORKS: Considerations on the Propriety of Imposing Taxes in the British Colonies for the Purpose of Raising a Revenue, by Act of Parliament, 1765; The Right to the Tonnage, the Duty of Twelve Pence per Hogshead on all Exported Tobacco, and the Fines and Forfeitures in the Province of Maryland, 1766.

ABOUT: Riley, E. S. Correspondence of "First Citizen" Charles Carroll, and "Antilon" Daniel Dulany, Jr.; Maryland Archives (scattered); Maryland Historical Magazine: Vol. 13; Maryland Gazette.

DUMMER, JEREMIAH (c. 1679-May 19, 1739), historian and colonial agent, was born in Boston, the son of Jeremiah and Anna (Atwater) Dummer. He was graduated from Harvard in 1699, and from Utrecht received the degree of Doctor of Philosophy in 1703. After returning to Boston for a while, he settled down permanently in England. By 1710 he had an eminent legal practice and good social connections, and was appointed Massachusetts colonial agent. Through negotiations with a wealthy Mr. Yale, who had held a governorship in India, Dummer effected the financial beginnings of Yale College. He had, meanwhile, been appointed colonial agent for Connecticut.

In *A Letter to a Noble Lord: Concerning the Late Expedition to Canada* he vindicated Massachusetts in its unfortunate Canadian enterprise; and he drew up a strong *Defence of the New England Charters* that was twice reprinted. Political complications resulted in his dismissal from both agencies nine years before his death. His writings are shrewd and uninhibited, and his extensive labors in New England's behalf had a far-reaching effect.

PRINCIPAL WORKS: A Letter to a Noble Lord . . . , 1712; Defence of the New England Charters, 1721.

ABOUT: Dexter, F. B. Biographical Sketches of the Graduates of Yale College: Vol. I; and scattered sources.

DUNBAR, PAUL LAURENCE (June 27, 1872-February 9, 1906), poet and story writer, was born in Dayton, Ohio. His father, Joshua Dunbar, and his mother, Matilda Murphy, had both been slaves in Kentucky, but had escaped to the North. Paul, their only child, was educated in the public schools of Dayton and at the Steele High School, where he was the only Negro student, but was editor of the student magazine and wrote the class song on his graduation in 1891. He wanted to be a lawyer, but lacked the means, and was obliged to take a job running an elevator, at four dollars a week. His early poems appeared in local newspapers, and in 1893 he published a small volume at his own expense, paying the publishers, a religious publication house, by selling the books personally to passengers on his elevator.

Soon after this he was employed, through the influence of Frederick Douglass, at the Haiti Building in the Chicago World's Fair. When this was over he returned to Dayton and to utter discouragement. He still kept on writing, however, and his work showed greater originality; he was finding his *métier* in the songs of his own people. A few influential white men befriended him, and helped him to publish his second thin volume; and in 1896 William Dean Howells gave him a full-page review in *Harper's Weekly* which constituted his first national recognition. The same year his *Lyrics of Lowly Life* appeared, his first collection to receive genuine publication. He rapidly became very popular and something of a fashion; he was asked to lecture, which he did reluctantly and without much success, and he visited England and read his own poems there in 1897. In 1897 and 1898, on his return from England, he served as assistant in the Library of Congress, the position being secured for him by Robert G. Ingersoll. In 1898 he married Alice Ruth Moore, herself a writer.

All this intensive travel, work, and excitement were too much for a naturally frail body, and by 1899 Dunbar was far gone in tuberculosis. He spent the next winter in Colorado, but without benefit to his health. He returned to Dayton and kept on writing, though he was no longer able to speak publicly or to engage in any other occupation. Gradually he lost his courageous struggle against disease, dying at the age of thirty-four.

Dunbar's portrait shows a slender, sensitive young man, of "medium brown" complexion. He is one of the few Negro writers who have been acclaimed by their own race as well as by the whites; he is still remembered by them with warm affection and sympathy, and numerous societies and a Washington high school have been named for him. Yet though he felt himself to be one in spirit with his co-racialists, he himself preferred his work in literary English, and regretted that the public chose his dialect verses. The public in this case was a better critic than the author; Dunbar's writing, either prose or verse, in ordinary English shows little more than the average talent possessed by thousands of literary-minded young writers, whereas his dialect songs and stories have seldom been exceeded for simplicity, tenderness, and lyric sweetness. His poems are essentially singable, and many of them have been set to music, perhaps, the best known being "When Malindy Sings." His short stories of Negro life are rich in pathos and unforced humor. His novels are too ambitious and too much given to backgrounds unfamiliar to the author to be very successful. His was essentially a lyric gift, which implies condensation; and though he chafed under the restrictions put upon him by the very nature of his talent, he must in the end have been content to realize in himself the sweetest singer his race had yet brought forth in America.

PAUL LAURENCE DUNBAR

Principal Works: *Poetry*—Oak and Ivy, 1893; Majors and Minors, 1895; Lyrics of Lowly Life, 1896; Complete Poems, 1913. *Fiction*—The Uncalled, 1896; The Love of Landry, 1900; The Fanatics, 1901; The Sport of the Gods, 1902; Best Stories of Paul Laurence Dunbar (ed. by B. Brawley) 1938.

About: Brawley, B. Paul Laurence Dunbar: Poet of His People; Dunbar, A. R. & others. Paul Laurence Dunbar: Poet Laureate of the Negro Race; Wiggins, L. K. The Life and Works of Paul Laurence Dunbar; Chicago Times-Herald October 14, 1900.

DUNIWAY, ABIGAIL JANE (SCOTT) (October 22, 1834-October 11, 1915), suffragist and social historian, was born near Groveland, Ill., the daughter of John Tucker and Ann (Roelofson) Scott. When she was eighteen her family began a long trek by ox-team wagon to the Oregon country. Her mother and brother died en route, and the following winter, after arrival at Lafayette, Ore., Abigail taught in a district school. In 1853 she married Benjamin Charles Duniway, and after nine years of "backwoods" life was left a widow with six children to support. It was as a millinery retailer, in contact with many women, that she became aware of the real need for a champion of women's rights. For sixteen years she worked unceasingly as lecturer, lobbyist, and manager of her own *New Northwest,* a weekly, founded in 1871. Both Idaho and Oregon finally adopted woman suffrage; and she published a history of the cause in 1914.

Mrs. Duniway was the author of *Captain Gray's Company: or, Crossing the Plains and Living in Oregon* and *From the West to the West,* both novels; and *David and Anna Matson,* a long narrative poem dedicated to Whittier, whose tale of domestic grief had inspired it. Her prose lacked brilliance, and her verse was often forced and ordinary: as a crusader rather than as a writer she exerted her greatest influence.

PRINCIPAL WORKS: Captain Gray's Company: or, Crossing the Plains and Living in Oregon, 1859; David and Anna Matson, 1876; From the West to the West, 1905; Path Breaking: An Autobiographical History of the Equal Suffrage Movement in Pacific Coast States, 1914.

ABOUT: Scott, Harvey W. History of the Oregon Country; Morning Oregonian (Portland) October 12, 1915.

DUNLAP, WILLIAM (February 19, 1766-September 28, 1839), artist, playwright, and historian, was born at Perth Amboy, N.J., the only child of Samuel Dunlap, an Irish soldier turned storekeeper, and Margaret (Sargeant) Dunlap. In 1777 the family, which was Loyalist in its sympathy, found it safer to move to New York. There, the following year, the boy's education was brought to an end by an accident which destroyed the sight of one eye. In spite of this, the twelve-year-old boy determined to develop his considerable artistic talent, studied art, and at sixteen set up as a portrait painter. He made pastels of both George and Martha Washington. In 1784 the father, who had become a wealthy importer, sent him to London to study with Benjamin West. He remained three years, but it was the temporary end of his career as a painter. Instead of studying, he spent most of his time at the theater, and became completely enamored of the stage.

On his return to America he ceased to be an artist and set out to make a career as a playwright. His first comedy failed of acceptance, but his second, *The Father* (later published under the title *The Father of an Only Child*), was produced with some success in 1789. In the same year he married Elizabeth Woolsey.

But plays, which he continued to write, and poems, which he also essayed, were not a sufficient means of income, so his father made him a partner in his china importing business. However, Dunlap's heart still

From a portrait by C. Ingham
WILLIAM DUNLAP

yearned for the theater. In 1796 he began a third career (or a fourth, if his business partnership be included), this time as a theatrical manager. He bought a quarter interest in the only theater in New York, the Old American Company. Unfortunately, this venture was doomed from the beginning by irresponsible partners, at enmity with each other, by his own lack of business ability, by a long illness from yellow fever, and by the changing taste of the public. Finding that his own plays were an insufficient drawing card, he translated French and German dramas and presented them, but still the theater languished, until in 1805 he was obliged to declare himself bankrupt and to lose all his holdings.

By this time Dunlap had a wife and two children to support. Undaunted, he went back to his painting, and for a year became an itinerant miniaturist, though he had had no training in painting miniatures. By 1806 he was glad to accept a position as assistant to one of his own actors who had become a manager. This position lasted until 1811, when he again abandoned the stage and turned once more to his brushes. The War of 1812 made painting an unnecessary luxury, so the indefatigable Dunlap decided to publish and edit a magazine, the *Monthly Recorder*. This died after five issues, and Dunlap was once more adrift. From 1814 to 1816 he acted as assistant paymaster general to the New York State Militia. The remainder of his life was spent chiefly as a painter and as a miscellaneous writer, often hardly more than a literary hack.

His interest in art, however often he deserted it, was genuine, and he was one of the founders of the National Academy of Design, in 1826, and served as its vice-president and its professor of historical painting. Frequently ill and always overworked and overburdened by anxiety, Dunlap succumbed to a paralytic stroke and died in New York, in the midst of writing his last volume.

Modest, courageous, generous, and abstemious, Dunlap had relatively small talent, and was always competent rather than highly gifted. However, he was a forerunner and something of a pioneer, his romantic plays being the first of their kind in America. His remarkable versatility was perhaps his chief drawback, but it enabled him to leave his mark on several departments of his country's art, drama, and literature. Only one of his plays was published in his lifetime, *The Father of an Only Child.*

PRINCIPAL WORKS: Memoir of George Fred. Cooke, 1813; Life of Charles Brockden Brown, 1815; History of the American Theater, 1832; History of the Rise and Progress of the Arts of Design in the United States, 1834; Thirty Years Ago: or, The Memoirs of a Water-Drinker (novel) 1836; A History of New York, for Schools, 1837; History of the New Netherlands, 1839-41.

ABOUT: Coad, O. S. William Dunlap; Odell, C. D. Annals of the New York Stage; Yale Review July 1914.

DU PONCEAU, PIERRE ÉTIENNE (PETER STEPHEN) (June 3, 1760-April 1, 1844), historian and philologist, was born at St. Martin, Île de Ré, France, the son of an army officer. He learned English and Italian in childhood from soldiers stationed at St. Martin. He was educated at the Benedictine College of St. Jean Angely and the episcopal college at Bessuire, with the intention of entering the church. But in 1775 he abandoned this career and went to Paris, where he became secretary to the philologist, Count de Gebelin. In 1777 he went to America as secretary to Baron Steuben, the Prussian general who was on Washington's staff. He was appointed captain in the Continental army the next year, and became Steuben's aide-de-camp. He was obliged to leave the army in 1780 because of tuberculosis. He became an American citizen in 1781, and for two years was under-secretary to Robert R. Livingston, the Secretary for Foreign Affairs. He then studied law and was admitted to the Pennsylvania bar in 1785, the next year becoming an attorney of the supreme court. In 1788 he married Anne Perry. He became a noted authority on international law and wrote widely on this subject. In old age he was deaf and almost blind, but his mentality remained unimpaired; at 78 he won a $2000 prize from the French Institute for a philological work in French. He was president of the American Philosophical Society in 1828.

PRINCIPAL WORKS: English Phonology, 1817; A Discourse on the Early History of Pennsylvania, 1821; A Brief View of the Constitution of the United States, 1834; Dissertation on the Nature and Character of the Chinese System of Writing, 1838.

ABOUT: American Law Magazine April 1845.

DUPUY, ELIZA ANN (1814-January 15, 1881), novelist, was born in Petersburg, Va., the daughter of a ship-owner and merchant. She was largely self-educated, and, following the publication of her first novel, *Merton: A Tale of the Revolution,* she became a governess in Natchez, Miss., and here wrote her popular *Conspirator,* a novel based upon Aaron Burr's life and conceded by many to be her best work. She spent her entire life in the South, teaching and writing; *The Huguenot Exiles,* an historical narrative with ancestral reminiscences, and *The Planter's Daughter,* reeking with murder, madness, and tears, were among the most widely read of her novels. Despite Miss Dupuy's firmly Southern point of view, her articles and short stories were accepted by Northern journals during the years of the Civil War. She wrote numerous long tales, 1860-68, for the New York *Ledger* under the pen name "Annie Young."

She was a facile writer and systematic worker, but the sensationalism and melodrama that invaded her novels gave them an early-waning popularity.

PRINCIPAL WORKS: The Conspirator, 1850; The Huguenot Exiles, 1856; All for Love, 1873; The Discarded Wife, 1875.

ABOUT: Davidson, J. W. Living Writers of the South; Raymond, I. Southland Writers.

DURFEE, JOB (September 20, 1790-July 26, 1847), jurist and philosophical historian, was born in Tiverton, R.I., the son of Thomas and Mary (Lowden) Durfee. He was educated at home and in the public schools and was graduated from Brown University with high honors in 1813. In 1817 he was admitted to the bar, having studied law under his father, and after two terms in the state legislature, he was elected speaker of the House in 1827. From 1835 until his death he was chief justice of the supreme court of Rhode Island, and was especially distinguished for his dignity, impartiality, and strong common sense.

Durfee's largest single production was *The Panidèa: or, An Omnipresent Reason*

Considered as the Creative and Sustaining Logos by Theoptes, a cumbersome and pedantic philosophical tract which, obviously, had a very slight appeal. His addresses to various societies include: *Aboriginal History; The Idea of the Supernatural Among the Indians; Progress of Ideas;* and *The Rhode Island Idea of Government.* Durfee was a jurist of repute, but his writings found a very limited number of readers.

PRINCIPAL WORKS: Aboriginal History, 1838; The Idea of the Supernatural Among the Indians, 1839; The Progress of Ideas, 1843; The Panidèa: or, An Omnipresent Reason Considered as the Creative and Sustaining Logos by Theoptes, 1846.

ABOUT: Reno, C. Memoirs of the Judiciary and the Bar of New England: Vol. 2; Historical Catalogue Brown University 1764-1914.

DURIVAGE, FRANCIS ALEXANDER (1814-February 1, 1881), journalist and playwright, was born in Boston, the son of Francis and Lucy (Everett) Durivage, and nephew of Edward Everett [*q.v.*]. He attended school in Boston and then embarked upon a career in journalism. As a foreign correspondent of several American newspapers he went to Paris and in 1859-60 he met Steele MacKaye, the American dramatist and inventor, who was conducting classes in the new Delsarte system of stage calisthenics. Upon returning to the United States he aided in popularizing the Delsartean doctrines of expression and collaborated with MacKaye on an article for the *Atlantic* and on *Monaldi,* one of Durivage's several failures in playwriting, produced in New York in January 1872. His reputation as a columnist was best established by a series of humorous articles appearing in numerous journals over the signature "Old Un," and for a while he edited *Ballou's Pictorial Drawing-Room Companion.* He was married to Almira Alderworth.

Durivage was one of the first literary commentators to practice a thoroughly "candid criticism." But his writings were miscellaneous, scattered, and too frail to endure.

PRINCIPAL WORKS: *Collaborations*—Stray Subjects Arrested and Bound Over . . . , 1848; Monaldi, 1872. *Compilations*—Popular Cyclopaedia of History, 1845; Life Scenes From the World Around Us, 1853.

ABOUT: Adams, O. F. Dictionary of American Authors; Winter, W. Old Friends.

DURRETT, REUBEN THOMAS (January 22, 1824-September 16, 1913), historian and collector, was born in Henry County, Ky., the son of William and Elizabeth (Rawlings) Durrett. He attended Georgetown (Ky.) College, in 1849 received an A. B. degree from Brown University, and after a year at the law school of the University of Louisville, he began a long legal practice. In 1852 he was married to Elizabeth H. Bates, and five years later he became editor and part owner of the Louisville *Courier,* then an ambitious rival of the better known *Journal.* His outspoken championing of secession, in 1862, cost him a short military imprisonment.

Durrett gave up his practice in 1880 and directed his untiring energies to the collecting of all kinds of Ohio Valley literature, aiding numerous students of Western history in their researches. In 1884 he was founder of the Filson Club, which published his *Southern Bivouac* contributions in volume form, as well as *John Filson: The First Historian of Kentucky* and *Traditions of the Earliest Visits of Foreigners to North America.* Durrett was a painstaking and thorough recorder, but it was as a collector of over fifty thousand books, besides manuscripts and old newspaper files, that he rendered inestimable service to the advancement of Western letters.

PRINCIPAL WORKS: John Filson: The First Historian of Kentucky, 1884; Traditions of the Earliest Visits of Foreigners to North America, 1908.

ABOUT: Library of Southern Literature; Louisville Courier-Journal September 17, 1913.

DUYCKINCK, EVERT AUGUSTUS (November 23, 1816-August 13, 1878), editor and biographer, was born in New York City, the son of Evert Duyckinck, a descendant of the founders of New Amsterdam, and Harriet (June) Duyckinck. His father was, for forty years, a most reputable New York publisher, and he and his brother, George Long Duyckinck, acquired a taste for good books. In 1835 he was graduated from Columbia College, studied law, and two years later was admitted to the bar. He did not practice, and after a year in Europe, 1838-39, he returned to New York and was married to Margaret Wolfe Panton in April of the following year. Their home at 20 Clinton Place attracted many who were soon to become eminent men of letters—Washington Irving, James Fenimore Cooper, Fitz-Greene Halleck, William Cullen Bryant, and Charles King.

He had been an occasional contributor of literary criticisms to the *New York Review,* and from 1840-42 he was co-editor of *Arcturus: A Journal of Books and Opinion.* From February 6 to April 24, 1847, he edited the *Literary World: A Journal of American and Foreign Literature, Science, and Art,* and then severed connections with this weekly until October 1848, when he and his broth-

EVERT AUGUSTUS DUYCKINCK

er took it over and edited it, jointly, until December 31, 1853. As a literary journal it was top-notch, but although it reached a large audience, it was a failure as a commercial enterprise.

The two brothers then set to work on the research and editing of a *Cyclopaedia of American Literature*, personal and critical notices of American authors, from the Colonial period on, first appearing in 1855 and later revised and enlarged. In 1852 Evert Duyckinck edited the first edition in book form of Thackeray's *Confessions of Fitz-Boodle,* as well as the first American edition of his *Yellowplush Papers. Irvingiana*, a compilation of Irving anecdotes, appeared in 1859, and a year later he prepared the notes and wrote the preface for *Salmagundi Papers* (1860). During the next ten years he contributed the text for some highly popular subscription works, among which were *National Portrait Gallery of Eminent Americans* and *Lives and Portraits of the Presidents of the United States.* He also wrote short memorials of John Allan, Francis L. Hawks, Henry T. Tuckerman, and Fitz-Greene Halleck.

Duyckinck lived at a time when the "old" was noticeably receding and the "new" was being strongly championed by dashing and influential writers. But he, as well as his brother George, whose special interest lay in the biographical literature of the Protestant Episcopal Church, was cautious and discriminating in his acceptance of modernisms, and spent his energy in the recording of the lives and philosophies of his distinguished predecessors and contemporaries.

PRINCIPAL WORKS: *Edited*—Confessions of Fitz-Boodle, 1852; Yellowplush Papers, 1852; Cyclopaedia of American Literature (2 vols.) 1855; Salmagundi Papers, 1860. *Memorials*—John Allan, 1864; Francis L. Hawks, 1871; Henry T. Tuckerman, 1872; Fitz-Greene Halleck, 1877. *Miscellaneous*—National Portrait Gallery of Eminent Americans (2 vols.) 1861-62; Lives and Portraits of the Presidents of the United States, 1865.

DUYCKINCK, GEORGE LONG. See DUYCKINCK, EVERT AUGUSTUS

DWIGHT, JOHN SULLIVAN (May 13, 1813-September 5, 1893), music critic and editor, was born in Boston, the son of Dr. John Dwight, physician and freethinker, and Mary (Corey) Dwight. He was an affectionate and sensitive lad with a strong love of music. After preparing at the Boston Latin School he went to Harvard, was graduated in 1832, and entered the Harvard Divinity School, where he formed a lasting friendship with Theodore Parker. On May 20, 1840 he was ordained and installed in the Unitarian church at Northampton, Mass., and two of his sermons were printed in the *Dial,* literary organ of the Transcendentalists, edited by Margaret Fuller.

But the ministry soon became "no longer congenial" to him, he quietly resigned, and in November 1841 joined the Brook Farm community of Transcendentalists. His mind had long been occupied with Mozart and Haydn (a rumored cause of his "want of fluency in prayer"!) and he shortly began to organize the Mass Clubs to sing the famous songs of the old masters. Abiding by one rule only, i.e., to "follow one's attractions," he conducted numerous elective courses at the Farm—highly practical botany and geology, etc. Dwight was a constant contributor to, and for some time editor of, the *Harbinger*, the Brook Farm journal which survived the community itself.

From 1847 to 1851 Dwight wrote reviews and musical criticisms for various Boston and New York periodicals, and for the first half of the year 1851 he was musical editor of the Boston *Commonwealth.* He married Mary Bullard, a member of his choir, in 1851. The following year he established *Dwight's Journal of Music: A Paper of Literature and Art,* of which he was editor and chief contributor, until 1881, and, prior to 1858, publisher as well. Through his columns of European news, short biographies of musicians, and analyses of numerous original compositions, he became the musical dictator of Boston. He lectured

JOHN SULLIVAN DWIGHT

frequently, wrote a chapter on music for Justin Winsor's *Memorial History of Boston,* and from 1885 to 1890 aided in the revision of musical definitions for *Webster's International Dictionary.* His scholarly work on *Select Minor Poems Translated From the German of Goethe and Schiller* had appeared in 1839.

Dwight was a slender and beaming little man, with a bashful air and a delight in simple and aesthetic pleasures. His miscellaneous writings exerted a far-flung influence on the musical tastes of his day.

PRINCIPAL WORKS: Select Minor Poems Translated From the German of Goethe and Schiller, 1839; The History of the Handel and Haydn Society of Boston, Mass.: Vol. 1, 1883.

ABOUT: Cooke, G. W. John Sullivan Dwight: Brook-Farmer, Editor, and Critic of Music; Boston Advertiser September 6, 1893.

DWIGHT, MARIANNE. See ORVIS, MARIANNE (DWIGHT)

DWIGHT, THEODORE (December 15, 1764-June 12, 1846), lawyer and editor, was born in Northampton, Mass., the son of Major Timothy and Mary (Edwards) Dwight and brother of Timothy Dwight [*q.v.*]. When the lad was thirteen his father died, and his mother brought him up on a nearby farm. He studied law with his uncle Pierpont Edwards, of New Haven, and was admitted to the bar in 1787. In Haddam he set up his practice, and was married, in 1792, to Abigail Alsop, sister of Richard Alsop, the poet.

Dwight entertained a far-sighted opposition to slavery; and for the *Connecticut Courant* and *Connecticut Mirror* he wrote ultra-Federalist articles. He became a widely-known pamphleteer, and in 1814 acted as secretary of the Hartford Convention, editing its journal in 1833. He had founded the Albany *Daily Advertiser* in 1815, and two years later, the New York *Daily Advertiser,* which he managed until his retirement in 1836. Three years later appeared his highly controversial *Character of Thomas Jefferson as Exhibited in His Own Writings.*

His journalism, characterized by the accepted outspokenness of his day, was not especially arresting. But as one of that select body, the "Hartford Wits," he temporarily "laughed away the popular taste for bombast" and aided in cultivating "a vigorous interest in poetry."

PRINCIPAL WORK: Character of Thomas Jefferson as Exhibited in His Own Writings, 1839.

ABOUT: Dwight, B. W. History of the Descendants of John Dwight; New York Tribune June 13, 1846.

DWIGHT, THEODORE (March 3, 1796-October 16, 1866), educator and traveler, was born in Hartford, Conn., the son of Theodore [*q.v.*] and Abigail (Alsop) Dwight. He studied under his much revered uncle Timothy at Yale, from which he was graduated in 1814. Poor health barred him from the study of theology, and he went abroad in 1818 and again in 1820. From 1833 until his death he lived in Brooklyn and New York, teaching, working on his father's New York *Advertiser,* and engaging in civic enterprises. He made some English-Spanish translations, and in 1845 founded *Dwight's American Magazine and Family Newspaper,* which he continued until 1852. He was married to Eleanor Boyd, of New York, in 1827.

The most famous of the numerous political exiles whom Dwight sheltered was Garibaldi, and he published, in the United States, the autobiography of this Italian patriot. Dwight was the author of numerous travel books, instructive juveniles, and historical and philological tracts which demanded a wide knowledge of languages. His writings, useful and careful commentaries in themselves, have, however, no unusual merit or significance.

PRINCIPAL WORKS: Things as They Are, 1834; Dictionary of Roots and Derivations, 1837; History of Connecticut, 1840; Life of General Garibaldi: Translated From His Private Papers, 1861.

ABOUT: Dexter, F. B. Biographical Sketches Graduates Yale College (Vol. 6); Dwight, B. W. The History of the Descendants of John Dwight...

DWIGHT, THEODORE WILLIAM (July 18, 1822-June 29, 1892), jurist and educator, was born at Catskill, N.Y., the grandson of Timothy Dwight [*q.v.*] and son of Dr. Benjamin Woolsey Dwight and Sophia Woodbridge (Strong) Dwight. As a child he was an ardent reader and had a very retentive memory. He was graduated from Hamilton College in 1846, and entered Yale Law School in 1841. The following year he became a tutor at Hamilton and was not admitted to the New York bar until 1845. In twelve years' professorship at Hamilton, beginning in 1846, he systematized and extended the law school, enabling it to become a regular department of law in 1853. Dwight believed in the prime importance of principles and formulae, to which cases were only subordinate material. In 1858 the Columbia Law School was established, and Dwight became its professorial mainstay, pursuing his "Socratic, illustrative, and expository" method. With the adoption (1891) of the "case system," i.e., whereby a principle is regarded as evolving from decided cases, Dwight resigned from Columbia and widened his activities in state and civic reforms.

Dwight was for a time, associate editor of the *American Law Register*. As a teacher and expositor of legal principles his influence was considerably greater than as a judicial historian.

PRINCIPAL WORKS: Report on the Prisons and Reformatories of the United States and Canada, 1866; James Harrington and his Influence Upon American Political Institutions and Political Thought, 1887.

ABOUT: In Memoriam Theodore William Dwight (n.d.); New York Times June 30, 1892.

DWIGHT, TIMOTHY (May 14, 1752-January 11, 1817), educator, theologian, and poet, was born in Northampton, Mass., the son of Major Timothy Dwight, a prosperous merchant, and of Mary (Edwards) Dwight, daughter of the famous theologian and philosopher Jonathan Edwards. He was the oldest of thirteen children.

A remarkably apt and precocious child, he was educated chiefly by his mother, and he entered Yale at thirteen, ready for his junior year; in fact, it is said that he was practically prepared for college by the age of eight. He remained for the full four years, however, being graduated with the highest honors in 1769.

From 1769 to 1771 Dwight was principal of the Hopkins Grammar School, in New Haven, and then returned to Yale, where he was a tutor until 1777. An extreme ascetic, who injured his eyes and his general health by his austerity, he was converted at fifteen,

After a portrait by J. Trumbull
TIMOTHY DWIGHT

and was licensed to preach by the Congregational church in 1776. In 1777 he married Mary Woolsey, and resigned from the college to become a chaplain with the Continental Army. He was an enthusiastic patriot, and wrote several martial songs which were popular among the soldiers.

In 1779 he resigned from the army and settled in Northampton, where he preached occasionally, ran a school, worked two farms, and served in the Massachusetts legislature, in 1781 and 1782. In 1783 he became minister of a church at Greenfield Hill, Conn., and was ordained.

Dwight remained in Greenfield Hill until 1795, continuing his almost superhuman activities in many fields. He established another successful school, and now began to write in earnest. From his student days he had had literary interests; he was one of the group later known as "the Hartford wits," and one of its most prolific versifiers. He now poured forth a series of epic and narrative poems, interspersed with published sermons. But his greatest distinction was still before him. In 1705 he declined an offer of the presidency of Union College, and was rewarded shortly thereafter by election to follow Ezra Stiles as president of Yale. This was the greater honor in that Stiles had cordially disliked him and only his unexpected death caused the selection of Dwight.

For the remainder of his life Dwight was Yale's president, acting also as professor of theology and, according to his wont, in half a dozen other capacities. His eagerness to take upon himself all possible duties and responsibilities caused him to be dubbed "Pope Dwight" by those who resented his pervasive leadership. Certainly he was one of the most important men of his time.

In truth, Dwight was a strange mixture of the most opposite qualities—vain, ambitious, bigoted, intolerant, yet at the same time high-minded, hard-working, persevering under the handicap of partial blindness, and strongly self-disciplined. He was not brilliant, but he was highly intellectual; he had a remarkable memory and a keen and well-trained mind. His books, whether long-winded poems or dogmatic sermons, are unreadable now, but they had an enormous influence on their contemporary readers. He was a great teacher and a great executive. He typified in the extreme the best and worst of what we mean when we speak of the Puritans of New England.

In person, Dwight was tall and bald, with piercing black eyes behind spectacles. His voice is said to have been at the same time harmonious and penetrating. He carried with him an air of authority and command which were the outward cloak of a dominating personality. He had a large family, of whom two sons were distinguished ministers and educators, and his grandson and namesake followed him as president of Yale from 1886 to 1899.

Principal Works: *Poetry*—The Conquest of Canaan, 1785; Greenfield Hill, 1794; The Triumph of Infidelity, 1788. *Prose*—A Discourse on the Genuineness and Authenticity of the New Testament, 1794; The Nature, and Danger, of Infidel Philosophy, 1798; The Duty of Americans, at the Present Crisis, 1798; Discourse on the Character of George Washington, 1800; Theology Explained and Defended, 1818-19; Travels in New England and New York, 1821-22.

About: Howe, M. A. DeW. Classic Shades; Sprague, W. B. Life of Timothy Dwight; Tyler, M. C. Three Men of Letters.

DYER, LOUIS (September 30, 1851-July 20, 1908), classical scholar and lecturer, the son of Charles Volney Dyer, M.D., and Louisa Maria (Gifford) Dyer, was born in Chicago, Ill. He received his early education under private tutors abroad and then attended, successively, the University of Chicago, the University of Munich, and Harvard, from which he was graduated in 1874. He pursued further studies at Balliol College, Oxford, returned to the United States in 1877, and became tutor and then professor of Greek at Harvard. *The Greek Question and Answer* and a scholarly edition of Plato's *Apology and Crito* belong to this period.

After 1887 Dyer spent most of his life at Oxford; having been made master of arts in 1893, he was appointed lecturer and examiner. In 1889, however, he delivered the Lowell Institute lectures in Boston (*Studies of the Gods in Greece at Certain Sanctuaries Recently Excavated*), and in 1900 the Hearst Lectures on Greek art at the University of California. *Oxford as It Is* became an indispensable guide for Rhodes scholars; his reviews and articles appeared in numerous intellectual journals of the day.

He was married in 1889 to Margaret Anne, daughter of Alexander Macmillan, the publisher. His Sunbury Lodge became the haven of Oxfordians, old and young. He was a sound classical scholar, with a broad knowledge of modern tongues and an astute appreciation of the literatures of the ancients.

Principal Works: The Greek Question and Answer, 1884; Apology and Crito, 1886; Studies of the Gods in Greece at Certain Sanctuaries Recently Excavated, 1891; Oxford as It Is, 1902; Machiavelli and the Modern State, 1904.

About: Educational Review September 1908; Nation (N.Y.) July 23, October 15, 1908; London Times July 21, 1908.

EASTBURN, JAMES WALLIS (September 26, 1797-December 2, 1819), poet and clergyman, was born in London, England, the son of James Eastburn, who, with his family, emigrated to America in 1803. While a student at Columbia College he established a literary friendship, of life-long duration, with Robert Charles Sands, two years his junior; together they set up, in succession, two campus periodicals. Some time after his graduation in 1816 he and Sands formed a "Literary Confederacy" (limited to four members) which aided in the writing and circulating of a journal called the *Aeronaut*; and for the New York *Daily Advertiser* they wrote (1817) an essay series called "The Neologist," as well as "The Amphilogist" for the *Commercial Advertiser* (1819).

Meanwhile Eastburn had gone to Bristol, R.I., to study theology under Bishop Griswold; was ordained deacon in October 1818; and was shortly made rector of St. George's Church, in Accomac County, Virginia. With Sands he had begun, in 1817, *Yamoyden,* a long narrative of King Philip, the sachem of the Wampanoags and the theme of poetic romance. Their research consisted of hardly more than a glance at William Hubbard's *Narrative of the Troubles With the Indians in New England*; "we began," said Sands, "to meddle with the charge before we had blazoned the field." By the summer of 1818 the piece was virtually completed. Eastburn, in very poor health, undertook a rest voyage to the Canary Islands, in the early winter of 1819-20, carrying the manuscript with him for final draft. But he died on the fourth day out. And in the year following Sands corrected the poem's obvious errors, added a little new material, avoiding any change in plot or any destruction of his "deceased friend's poetical identity," and published it.

In the course of an extremely short life Eastburn is said to have written a mass of verse—most of which never reached publication. He maintains some significance in literary history, not so much, perhaps, for the passing merits of *Yamoyden* as for his apparently remarkable poetic promise.

ABOUT: Allen, W. American Biographical Dictionary; Eastburn, J. W. & Sands, R. C. Yamoyden (see Introduction): Griswold, R. W. Poets and Poetry of America.

"E. D. M." See MANSFIELD, EDWARD DEERING

EDDY, MARY MORSE (BAKER) (July 16, 1821-December 3, 1910), metaphysical writer and founder of Christian Science, was born at Bow, N.H., the daughter of Mark Baker, a fairly prosperous farmer and justice of the peace, and Abigail (Ambrose) Baker. She was a frail child and was educated mostly at home. At the age of twenty-two she married George Washington Glover, a New Englander residing in Charleston, S.C., where he was a contractor and builder. She accompanied her husband south, where he died a few months later. Left destitute and expecting motherhood, the young widow was sent home to New Hampshire by the Masonic Lodge. In 1844 her only child was born and was named for his father. So far as her health would permit, Mrs. Glover then taught private pupils to support herself. In 1853 she married a relative of her stepmother, Dr. Daniel Patterson, an itinerant dentist and homoeopathic physician. The marriage was unhappy from the first; in 1873 she divorced him for cause and resumed the name of Glover.

In the meantime an event had occurred which changed the course of her life. Always frail, her health became so bad in 1862 that she despaired of ever recovering. At length she journeyed to Portland, Maine, to be treated by Phineas P. Quimby [*q.v.*], the founder of mental healing in America. She came away declaring herself cured. She became Quimby's ardent disciple and enthusiastically began teaching his system to others, adding more and more of her own ideas as time went on. In 1875 she published the first edition of *Science and Health,* the book on which the religion known as Christian Science is based. Briefly, the chief tenets of this sect (as summarized by its founder in another book) are: "Eternal mind is the source of all being; there is no matter; sin, sickness, and death are illusions; and this was revealed to the world by Jesus Christ."

In 1876 Mrs. Glover founded the first Christian Scientists' Association in Lynn, Mass. The next year she married one of her chief disciples, Asa Gilbert Eddy. He died in 1882—the victim, Mrs. Eddy believed, of "malicious animal magnetism" (injury by thought). Mrs. Eddy then moved to Boston, where she founded the Massachusetts Metaphysical College. In 1883 she founded the *Christian Science Journal,* as a monthly. The *Quarterly* followed in 1890; the *Sentinel,* a weekly, in 1898; and the *Monitor,* a daily, in 1908. In all of these and in the organization and government of the sect—which had grown to an estimated membership of a hundred thousand by the time of her death—Mrs. Eddy took a controlling part.

The history of few religious movements is free from internal controversies, and Christian Science was no exception. But Mrs. Eddy always emerged victorious and with increased prestige in the eyes of her followers. Eventually, however, the strain began to tell on her. In 1889 she retired to Concord, N.H., and for the next two decades directed the affairs of her church

Collection of Frederick H. Meserve
MARY BAKER EDDY

in absentia, as "pastor emeritus." Except for rare public appearances she lived in strict seclusion, invisible to all save a few carefully chosen personal associates: virtually a legend in her own lifetime. In 1908, eighty-seven and feeble, she returned from Concord to Chestnut Hills, a suburb of Boston. There she died two years later at nearly ninety and was buried in Mt. Auburn Cemetery. She left an estate appraised at two and a half million dollars.

Though she seldom appeared in public after 1890, Mrs. Eddy was often photographed, and her followers were all familiar with her spare figure, deep-set grey eyes, and masses of chestnut hair, white in old age. Her face showed sensitiveness, coupled with indomitable will.

Many books, friendly and unfriendly, have been written about Mary Baker Eddy and the religion she founded. She has been portrayed as a saint and messiah, and as a fanatic and charlatan. Each new biography arouses fresh storms of controversy. It may still be some years before she can be seen in true historical perspective. In the meantime, the non-partisan reader can only study what has been written on both sides and weigh the evidence for himself.

Few books ever written have had wider influence than Mrs. Eddy's own *Science and Health,* and for this reason she must be accorded a place in any history of literature; yet she cannot be called a really literary figure. As a writer she was untrained and even unacquainted with the rules of composition. (Professor Allen Johnson, editor of the *Dictionary of American Biography,* spoke of her "literary helplessness.") Much of her later work was professionally edited.

Viewed purely as a religious leader, however, she was—whatever one's feelings regarding her—a figure virtually unique in modern times. As Stephen Zweig says, "With her frail lever she moved the world."

Principal Works: (dates of first publication): Science and Health, 1875; The Science of Man, 1876; Christian Healing, 1886; The People's Idea of God, 1886; Unity of Good, 1887; Historical Sketch of Christian Science Healing, 1888; Retrospection and Introspection, 1891; No and Yes, 1891; Rudimental Divine Science, 1891; Christ and Christmas: A Poem, 1893; Poems, c.1894; Manual of the Mother Church, 1895; Miscellaneous Writings, 1896; Christian Science Versus Pantheism, 1898; also articles, hymns, etc., collected and uncollected.

About: Bates, E. S. & Dittemore, J. Mary Baker Eddy: The Truth and the Tradition; Dakin, E. F. Mrs. Eddy: The Biography of a Virginal Mind; Powell, L. P. Christian Science: The Faith and Its Founder; Powell, L. P. Mary Baker Eddy: A Life Size Portrait; Ramsay, E. M. Christian Science and Its Discoverer; Springer, F. C. According to the Flesh: A Biography of Mary Baker Eddy; Wilbur, S. Life of Mary Baker Eddy; McClure's Magazine January 1907-June 1908.

EDGARTON, SARAH CARTER (March 17, 1819-July 9, 1848), poet and writer of juveniles, was born in the village of Shirley, Mass., the daughter of a fairly prosperous manufacturer. She attended village schools and, for one short term, an academy in Westford, Mass., but she was uncomfortably shy and made few friends. At twelve she was writing simple poetic descriptions, which she showed no one, and elaborate acrostics. Her first appearance in print came in September 1836 when she began several years of occasional writing for the *Ladies' Repository.* In 1839 she edited the first issue of the *Rose of Sharon,* one of the many then-popular "annuals" which, quite unlike "perennials," were neither hardy nor of spontaneous regeneration; nine more volumes of the *Rose* were prepared under her direction. *The Palfreys,* tales for children, and its sequel, less of a juvenile, *Ellen Clifford,* belonged to these earlier years. *The Flower Vase* (1844), "Containing the Language of Flowers and Their Poetic Sentiments," with botanical classifications and moral emblems, was a companion-book to *Fables of Flora,* which placed a little more emphasis on poetry content.

Following her marriage, on July 28, 1846, to Amory Dwight Mayo she lived in Gloucester, Mass., where her husband was pastor of the Independent Christian Society. Less than two years later she was taken seriously ill and died within a few days at twenty-nine.

As a child Sarah Edgarton had acquired simple devotional habits, and although she later became strongly religious she was in no sense a fanatic. At all times she avoided theological disputations. Of her literary methods she said: "The time that many spend in revision I occupy in the original moulding of my thoughts." But it was brilliance and rejuvenation—not patient rewriting or long "moulding"—that she and many of her female contemporaries needed in order to win more than a mere mention in the early records of New England literature.

Principal Works: The Flower Vase, 1844; Fables of Flora, 1844; The Palfreys; Ellen Clifford; The Poetry of Woman; Spring Flowers; Memoir and Poems of Mrs. Julia H. Scott.

About: Griswold, R. W. The Female Poets of America; Mayo, A. D. Selections From the Writings of Mrs. Sarah Carter Edgarton Mayo: With a Memoir by Her Husband.

EDWARDS, JONATHAN (October 5, 1703-March 22, 1758), theological writer, was born at East Windsor, Conn., the son of the Rev. Timothy Edwards and Esther (Stoddard) Edwards. He was the only boy among eleven children. His maternal grandfather, the Rev. Solomon Stoddard, was pastor of the church in Northampton, Mass., where he himself later served.

An exceedingly precocious child, his interest both in philosophy and in natural science awoke very early. He was taught at home by his mother, and before he was thirteen was ready for college. Yale was then in the process of organization, with groups of students in various Connecticut towns; Edwards was among those who insisted on remaining in Wethersfield, but in his sophomore year the college was finally established at New Haven. At Yale he met the writings of Locke and Newton, which impressed him deeply and permanently, and began the "notes on the scriptures" which, in his beautifully clear hand or in his original system of shorthand, he kept up throughout his life. He was graduated in 1720, but remained in New Haven studying theology.

In 1721 the crucial event of Edwards' development took place; he experienced conversion, which with him was a quasi-mystical experience shaking his whole mental and emotional being. At this time his views were undoubtedly heretical, being practically equivalent to pantheism but by an effort of will he overcame his early rebellion against Calvinist doctrine and reconciled the two opposing opinions by making an acute "realization of Divine Grace," similar to his own, the criterion for all Christians.

In 1722 and 1723 Edwards was minister of a Presbyterian church in New York, which failed for lack of financial support. He returned to Yale as a tutor, but was obliged to resign because of ill health—all his life he was very frail, frequently a semi-invalid. In 1726 he became his grandfather's colleague at Northampton. The next year he married Sarah Pierpoint, a girl of seventeen.

Stoddard died in 1729, and Edwards became sole pastor of the church. His doctrine of "justification by faith" led him to oppose his grandfather's free offering of communion to all convinced Christians; he insisted that only those in "a state of grace" might partake. Opposition and trouble began early, led by Elisha Williams; but for the present it was overwhelmed by the series of revivals and the epidemic of hysterical conversions

After a portrait by C. W. Peale
JONATHAN EDWARDS

which began in 1734. Instead of stopping these manifestations, Edwards encouraged them, until his sermons on predestination and eternal damnation frightened some of his parishioners into attempted suicide. In 1740 a new wave of apocalyptic revivalism broke on the church, with the "Great Awakening" inspired by the English evangelist George Whitefield, which spread throughout New England. From this time on, Edwards' church was divided between the adorers and slaves of his doctrine and the rebels who finally secured his dismissal in 1750 and forbade his preaching in Northampton.

He was sent into practical exile, as minister and missionary to the Indians in Stockbridge, Mass. It was a time for Edwards not only of defeat and humiliation, but also of extreme poverty, so that his wife and daughters had to sell their embroidery and painted fans in the Boston market. Nevertheless he continued, undaunted, to pour forth polemical writings and sermons. One of his daughters had married the Rev. Aaron Burr, president of the College of New Jersey (Princeton). Burr died in 1757 (leaving an infant son, better known than his namesake and father), and Edwards was chosen to take his son-in-law's place. He hesitated, largely because of lack of experience in teaching, but his mission in Stockbridge was a failure, and so in January 1758 he went to Princeton. Two months later he died of complications following inoculation (not vaccination) for smallpox, which was epidemic at the time.

Tall, slender, frail, with delicate features, piercing eyes, and a low, quiet voice, Edwards was loved only by his worshiping family and a very few intimate friends. He had no social graces, as he himself confessed; he was absent-minded, deeply absorbed and introspective, and an extreme ascetic. His home life—he, like his father, had eleven children, founders of the famous family so beloved by eugenists—was most happy, a little heaven on earth whose head preached hell in the hereafter.

It is difficult for us today to do justice to Jonathan Edwards. We remember his *Sinners in the Hands of an Angry God,* we see him rejoicing in the pitiful terror of a four-year-old baby in dread of hell, we see his arrogance, his delight in battle, his aloofness from the ordinary human sympathies. Yet his was a first-rate intellect—F. A. Christie calls him "the first great philosophic intelligence in American history." Perhaps only a mystic can comprehend this man who believed so fanatically that we are saved only at the arbitrary will of a wrathful God, that the very violence of his asseverations makes modern students suspect a deep unconscious mutiny within himself. He was the founder and the fountain-head of what we call "New England theology," or American Puritanism. He formulated its four doctrines, enumerated by H. B. Parkes as the belief that conversion must be an emotional convulsion, with physical concomitants; that goodness itself is lovely and to be loved; that Christian conscience is a sufficient guide to conduct; and that Christian faith results in moral behavior. Although none but the second of his theses has proved invulnerable, the man himself remains, as "God-intoxicated" as was Spinoza.

As a writer, Edwards was more set on winning arguments than on putting forth his views in pleasing style. He himself, who once in a while descended to novel-reading, said when he read Richardson's *Pamela* that it made him regret his "inattention to the graces of good writing." Paul Elmer More remarked: "In his service to a particular dogma of religion Edwards deliberately threw away the opportunity of making for himself, despite the laxness of his style, one of the very great names in literature." His description of his early pantheistic emotions, and the fervor and intellectual power of his major works on freedom of the will and original sin, are a constituent part of the American literary tradition.

Principal Works: God Glorified in the Work of Redemption, 1731; A Devine and Supernatural Light, 1734; A Faithful Narrative of the Surprising Work of God, 1737; Discourses on Various Important Subjects, 1738; Sinners in the Hands of an Angry God, 1741; The Distinguishing Marks of a Work of the Spirit of God, 1741; Some Thoughts Concerning the Present Revival of Religion in New England, 1742; A Treatise Concerning Religious Affections, 1746; An Humble Inquiry Into the Rules of the Word of God, 1749; Misrepresentations Corrected and Truth Vindicated, 1752; A Careful and Strict Enquiry Into . . . Freedom of the Will, 1754; The Great Christian Doctrine of Original Sin Defended, 1758; Two Dissertations, 1765; A History of the Work of Redemption (unfinished) 1774.

About: Allen, A. V. G. Jonathan Edwards; DeWitt, J. Jonathan Edwards: A Study; Dwight, S. E. The Life of President Edwards; Hopkins, S. The Life and Character of the Late Rev. Jonathan Edwards (revised by J. Hawksley as Memories of the Rev. Jonathan Edwards, A.M.); McGiffert, A. C., Jr. Jonathan Edwards; Miller, S. Life of Jonathan Edwards; Parkes, H. B. Jonathan Edwards: The Fiery Puritan; Turpie, D. Jonathan Edwards; Congregationalist October 3, 1903; Harper's Magazine November 1871; Harper's Weekly June 23, 1900; Independent October 1, 1903; Living Age January 24, 1874; New England Magazine April 1890; World's Work October 1903.

EGGLESTON, EDWARD (December 10, 1837-September 2, 1902), novelist and historian, was born in Vevay, Ind., the son of Joseph Cary Eggleston and Mary Jane (Craig) Eggleston. The father, who died when the boy was nine, was of a good Virginia family, and a graduate of William and Mary College. The son's formal education, however, was slight. His mother was remarried, to a Methodist minister, in 1850, and moved with her children from one small Indiana town to another—an excellent experience for the future novelist of Hoosier life. He read widely, and a teacher who was also a writer, Mrs. Julia Dumont, encouraged his early productions; but his health was frail, and he could not take advantage of a scholarship his father had provided at Indiana Asbury University (now DePauw). One year of his boyhood, 1854, was spent near his father's old home, at Amelia Academy, Va., where he received impressions which turned him violently against slavery.

Brought up in the narrowest and strictest form of Methodism, Eggleston's early religiosity warred with his literary ambitions. On his return to Indiana in 1854 he became a Bible agent, but his health broke down completely, and in 1856 he went to Minnesota, where he worked for surveyors and on farms and made an abortive attempt to go to Kansas to help the "Free Soil" advocates. Ordained as a Methodist minister, though without attendance at any seminary, he became a circuit rider in his former home, only to break down once more. He returned to Minnesota, and from 1858 to 1866 was first a Bible agent, then a minister in various small towns there. In 1866 he moved to Evanston, Ill., and became associate editor of a juvenile magazine, *Little Corporal.* The next year he became editor of the *National Sunday School Teacher.* In 1870 he went to New York to join the staff of the *Independent,* whose western correspondent he had been, remaining also as corresponding editor of the *National Sunday School Teacher* until 1873. In 1871 he left the *Independent* to edit *Hearth and Home,* where his first adult novels (he had already begun to publish books for children) appeared serially. He lived in Brooklyn and from 1874 to 1879 was pastor of the Church of Christian Endeavor in that city; for gradually he had outgrown the narrow theology of his youth and had become practically a Unitarian.

Always interested in history, and regarding his novels as in essence historical records, Eggleston began to abandon fiction for actual history after a trip to Europe in 1879. He had as his aim the writing of history which should be, not political or statistical, but a depiction of the ordinary life of the common people of the given time and place. He had found his forte, but he failed to complete even a small part of the vast historical projects he had in mind. He retired to his country home at Lake George, N.Y., coming to New York only occasionally, but the sporadic and fragmentary character of his education made the necessary research for his historical writing a long and laborious process; he had besides to keep on writing fiction and especially juveniles in order to earn his living.

Collection of Frederick H. Meserve
EDWARD EGGLESTON

Eggleston was twice married, in 1858 to Lizzie Snider, who died in 1889; and in 1891 to Frances Goode. His always delicate health continued to betray him whenever he overworked, which was frequently; his father had died of tuberculosis and he anticipated the same end, though actually he was never tubercular, but suffered from malaria in youth and from nervous disorders in later life. In 1899 he had a stroke of apoplexy; he recovered partially, but a second stroke in August 1902 led to his death a month later.

Eggleston looked like his most famous character—the "Hoosier Schoolmaster." His thick hair and long shaggy beard, white in his old age, gave him a patriarchal appearance. He was always a born teacher; as an anonymous critic in the *Independent* put it, he was "just a little bit too fond of imparting elementary information in a stentorian voice." However, he was as kindly as he was moralistic and didactic. In spite of his strong anti-slavery views, he was never bitter toward the South and never forgot that he himself was half a Southerner; his younger brother, George Cary Eggleston [*q.v.*], fought throughout the Civil War as a Confederate, but the two were the best of friends and co-workers as soon as the war was over.

His novels are very uneven, with little plot, but they are invaluable as records of a swiftly changing locale and its inhabitants. Indiana in his boyhood was a frontier; by the time he started to write about it, it was a settled, civilized community. Eggleston's gift for languages stood him in good stead in catching the dialect of the Scotch-Irish pioneers who were the original "Hoosiers," and he portrayed their *mores* with a candid conviction which bears the stamp of accuracy. *The Hoosier Schoolmaster* and *Roxy* are the best of his novels, though *The Graysons* is interesting as being one of the first novels to include Lincoln as a character. His style was concise and clear, if undistinguished, and the earlier books are unmarred by the self-conscious "literary" touch which appears in the later ones. Carl Van Doren calls him "the earliest American realist whose work is still remembered." The same critic speaks of his historical works as "erudite, humane, and graceful." His juvenile stories are too sentimental for modern taste.

PRINCIPAL WORKS: *Novels*—The Hoosier Schoolmaster, 1871; The End of the World, 1872; The Mystery of Metropolisville, 1873; The Circuit Rider, 1874; Roxy, 1878; The Graysons, 1888; The Faith Doctor, 1891; Duffels (short stories) 1893. *Juveniles*—Mr. Blake's Walking Stick, 1870; Tecumseh and the Shawnee Prophet, 1878; Pocahontas and Powhatan, 1879; Montezuma, 1880; The Hoosier Schoolboy, 1883; Queer Stories for Boys and Girls, 1884; Home History of the United States, 1889. *History*—A History of the United States and Its People, 1888; The Beginners of a Nation, 1896; The Transit of Civilization From England to America, 1901; New Centennial History of the United States, 1904.

ABOUT: Eggleston, F. Edward Eggleston; Eggleston, G. C. The First of the Hoosiers; Nicholson, M. The Hoosiers; Atlantic Monthly December 1902; Forum August 1887, November 1890; Independent May 12-19, 1870; Review of Reviews October 1902.

EGGLESTON, GEORGE CARY (November 26, 1839-April 14, 1911), novelist, journalist, and juvenile writer, was born at Vevay, Ind., the son of Joseph Cary Eggleston and Mary Jane (Craig) Eggleston. He was the younger brother of Edward Eggleston [*q.v.*],the novelist and historian. He spent a year at Indiana Asbury University (now DePauw), but left at the age of sixteen and became a school teacher—perhaps the original of his brother's famous "Hoosier Schoolmaster." The next year, 1856, he inherited the plantation in Amelia County, Va., which had belonged to his father's family, and moved to the South. Edward Eggleston's experience in Virginia had made him an abolitionist; but George Eggleston fell romantically in love with the South and though he opposed secession considered himself henceforth a loyal Virginian.

He studied law at Richmond College, but the Civil War interrupted his studies. He enlisted in the Confederate army, first in the cavalry and then in the artillery, and served throughout the war, as an officer, with a younger brother, Joseph, as his aide. In 1867 he moved to Cairo, Ill., where he was connected with a bank and a steamboat company. The next year he married Marion Craggs, and started to practice law in Mississippi. He disliked the law, however, and aspired to journalism; in 1870 he moved to New York and became a reporter on the Brooklyn *Daily Union*. He then joined his brother on the staff of *Hearth and Home*, and succeeded him as editor. After a period of free lance writing, in 1875 he became literary editor of the New York *Evening Post* under William Cullen Bryant; in 1881 a reader for Harper & Brothers; in 1885 literary editor and then editor-in-chief of the *Commercial Advertiser*, and in 1889 an editorial writer on the *World*, where he remained until his death.

Someone has said that Edward Eggleston was an "author" and George Cary Eggleston merely a "writer." This is hardly fair, but it is true that his novels are lushly sentimental—Southern romances carried to the extravagant extreme of sweetness and light. He deserves credit, however, for his energetic defence of the American scene for American novelists. His autobiographical works, particularly *A Rebel's Recollections*, are interesting and valuable human documents.

PRINCIPAL WORKS: *Novels*—A Man of Honor, 1873; Juggernaut (with D. Marbourg) 1891; Dorothy South, 1902; Evelyn Byrd, 1904. *Juveniles*—Big Brother Series, 1875-1882; Strange Stories From History, 1886. *Miscellaneous*—A Rebel's Recollections, 1874; The First of the Hoosiers: Reminiscences of Edward Eggleston, 1903; Recollections of a Varied Life, 1910; The History of the Confederate War, 1910.

ABOUT: Eggleston, G. C. A Rebel's Recollections; Recollections of a Varied Life; Bookman May 1912; Outlook April 29, 1911; New York Evening Post April 15, 1911.

ELDER, SUSAN (BLANCHARD) (April 19, 1835-November 3, 1923), historian, poet, and miscellaneous writer, was born at Fort Jessup, La., where her father, Albert Gallatin Blanchard, later a brigadier-general in the Confederate army, was stationed as a United States army captain. Her mother, Susan (Thompson) Blanchard, died when she was a small child. She was sent North to live with her mother's relatives in Masachusetts, but soon returned to Louisiana, and attended the Girls' High School, New Orleans, and St. Michael's Convent of the Sacred Heart. From the age of sixteen she contributed poems and stories to Southern newspapers under the pseudonym of "Hermine." In 1855, at twenty, she was married to Charles D. Elder, brother of the Roman Catholic Archbishop of Cincinnati, and became a convert to the Catholic Church. After the capture of New Orleans during the Civil War, the Elders moved to Selma, Ala., where their home was converted into a military hospital. After the war they returned to New Orleans, where Mrs. Elder acted as teacher of natural science and mathematics in the Picard Institute and the New Orleans High School from 1878 to 1884, and was on the staff of the *Morning Star* from 1882 to 1890. Her husband died in 1890, and she spent her last years in Cincinnati with her only surviving child.

Besides a negligible novel, Mrs. Elder wrote literary criticisms, plays for Catholic schools and colleges, biography, history, and verse. Her verse, which is her best work, conveys her twin attachments, to her religion and to the cause of the Confederacy. It is melancholy and emotional, but stilted and without originality.

PRINCIPAL WORKS: James the Second, 1874; Savonarola, 1875; Ellen Fitzgerald: A Southern Tale, 1876; The Leos of the Papacy, 1879; Elder Flowers (poems) 1912; Life of Abbé Adrien Rouquette, 1913; A Mosaic in Blue and Gray, 1914.

ABOUT: Davidson, J. W. The Living Writers of the South; Tardy, M. T. The Living Female Writers of the South; Cincinnati Enquirer November 4, 1923.

"ELIOT, ALICE." See JEWETT, SARAH ORNE

ELIOT, CHARLES WILLIAM (March 20, 1834-August 22, 1926), educator, was born in Boston, the son of Samuel Atkins Eliot, mayor and congressman, and Mary (Lyman) Eliot. He was educated at the Boston Latin School and at Harvard, receiving his B.A. in 1853, second in his class, and his M.A. in 1856. From 1853 to 1858 he acted first as tutor in mathematics and then as assistant professor of mathematics and chemistry. He resigned in 1863 and spent two years in Europe, returning in 1865 as professor of analytical chemistry at the newly organized Massachusetts Institute of Technology. From this post, which he held for four years, though abroad again in 1867 and 1868, he was elected president of Harvard.

In 1858 Eliot had married Ellen Derby Peabody, by whom he had four sons, of whom only two grew up and only one—a prominent Unitarian clergyman—survived him. Mrs. Eliot died of tuberculosis in 1869, the same month her husband was elected president of Harvard. In 1877 he married Grace Hopkinson, who died in 1924.

In the forty years he presided over Harvard, Eliot became undoubtedly the most influential educator in the United States. His forty annual reports are a record of what he accomplished, from the days when (according to his own story) the boys called him "Charlie" to those when he was referred to as "old Eliot." Eliot planned for a university of graduate schools centering around Harvard College, for undergraduates, preparatory to all professional study. He established the elective system, written examinations, Sabbatical leave for the faculty, exchange professorships, the Harvard Annex (later Radcliffe College), the summer school, the bestowal of the M.D.Sc. and Ph.D. degrees, and the curriculum with emphasis on "modern" subjects as opposed to

Collection of Frederick H. Meserve
CHARLES WILLIAM ELIOT

the classics and mathematics—in other words, he made Harvard what it is today, though his long opposition to football bore no fruit. When he retired at 75, and became professor emeritus, he remained as energetic as ever, as speaker, writer, and public figure. In 1911-12 he made a world tour in the interest of peace. From 1910 he began editing the Harvard Classics (the "five-foot book shelf"), and most of his books were published at an age when most people have ceased to function.

The germ of Eliot's educational theories is in his articles on "The New Education," in the *Atlantic Monthly* in 1869. He was primarily not a teacher, but an administrator with exceptionally high executive abilities. Honors and degrees were heaped upon him, and in his extreme old age he became a sort of symbol of the old-fashioned New England individualist, who thought and called himself a liberal because he believed in a system of optimistic *laissez-faire*. Exceedingly cold and reserved in manner, wearing thick glasses for his short sight, and his face disfigured by a large birthmark, Eliot nevertheless commanded respect by his dignity and devotion to his own standards, and a small, close circle found him warmhearted and affectionate as well. He had a certain dry humor, a facility in the apt and telling phrase, and a clarity and simplicity of style which made models of his books on subjects usually heavily and turgidly treated. His mind was active to the day of his death, at 92; a few days before, he announced that he would die on Saturday, as the Sunday trains (he died at his summer home, Mt. Desert, Maine) would be most convenient; and he did actually die early Sunday morning. It was a perfect example of the self-possession and self-control of this last of "the Puritan liberals."

PRINCIPAL WORKS: Manual of Inorganic Chemistry (with F. H. Storer) 1867; Compendious Manual of Qualitative Chemical Analysis (with F. H. Storer) 1869; The Happy Life, 1896; American Contributions to Civilization, and Other Essays, 1897; Educational Reform, 1898; John Gilley: Farmer and Fisherman, 1899; Charles Eliot: Landscape Gardener, 1902; More Money for the Public Schools, 1903; Four American Leaders, 1906; University Administration, 1908; The Religion of the Future, 1909; Education for Efficiency, 1909; The Durable Satisfactions of Life, 1910; The Conflict Between Individualism and Collectivism in a Democracy, 1910; The Future of Trades Unionism and Capitalism in a Democracy, 1910; The Road Toward Peace, 1915; The Training for an Effective Life, 1915; A Late Harvest (ed. by M. A. DeW. Howe) 1924; Charles W. Eliot: The Man and his Beliefs (ed. by W. A. Neilson) 1926.

ABOUT: Cotton, E. H. The Life of Charles W. Eliot; Howe, M. A. DeW. Classic Shades; James, H. Charles W. Eliot; Saunderson, H. H. Charles W. Eliot: Liberal Puritan; Atlantic Monthly March 1899, November 1929; Bostonian (Boston University Alumni Magazine) April 1931; Outlook August 6, 1904; Boston Transcript August 22, 1926.

ELIOT, JARED (November 7, 1685-April 22, 1763), clergyman, physician, and natural scientist, was born in Guilford, Conn., the son of Joseph and Mary (Wyllys) Eliot, and grandson of John Eliot [*q.v.*], missionary to the Indians. He was graduated from the Collegiate School of Connecticut (Yale College) in 1706, and after teaching school for a short time accepted a permanent pastorate at Killingworth (now Clinton), Conn., where for forty years he preached at least once every Sunday. At the same time he pursued his interests in the natural sciences, and became the ranking physician in the New England colonies. Moreover, he succeeded in smelting the black sand which often covers the sea beaches and thereby extracting iron; his *Essay on the Invention, or Art of Making Very Good, If Not the Best Iron, From Black Sea Sand* (1762) won an award from the Royal Society of London. In his *Essay on Field Husbandry in New England*, published in six parts, between 1748 and 1759, he worked out some of the rudiments of agricultural science. Eliot is credited with having made the first bequest for a permanent endowment of the Yale Library. He married Hannah Smithson in 1710.

His writings are only a partial record of his pioneering in applied science, but the relative "newness" of their content made them not only valuable tracts in their own day but fragments of particular interest to later historians.

PRINCIPAL WORKS: Essay on Field Husbandry in New England, 1748-59; Essay on the Invention, or Art of Making Very Good, If Not the Best Iron, From Black Sea Sand, 1762.

ABOUT: Dexter, F. B. Biographical Sketches of the Graduates of Yale College: 1701-1745; Sprague, W. B. Annals of the American Pulpit.

ELIOT, JOHN (July or August, 1604-May 21, 1690), theological writer, known as "the Apostle to the Indians," was born at Widford, Hertfordshire, England; or at all events was baptized there on August 5, 1604. He was the son of Bennett and Lettice (Aggar) Eliot, his father being a yeoman and small landowner. He received his B.A. at Jesus College, Cambridge, in 1622, and was probably ordained, though this is not definitely known. He became an usher in a grammar school at Little Baddow, Essex, whose headmaster, the Rev. Thomas Hooker [*q.v.*], was a Puritan and influenced Eliot sufficiently to cause him to leave the Established Church. When Hooker with others emigrated to New England in 1631, Eliot accompanied them. For a short time he settled in Boston, but in 1632 followed Hooker's group to Roxbury, where he became a "teacher" in the church. He was connected with this church for sixty years, being sole pastor for more than forty. In 1632 also he married Hanna or Ann Mumford (also sometimes given as Mulford or Mountfort), to whom he had been engaged in England and who followed him to America. They had six children, of whom only one survived his parents. Mrs. Eliot died in 1687.

Eliot took an active part in the activities of the Puritan community, and in 1637 helped to banish Ann Hutchinson, accused of heresy. His chief interest, however, was in the conversion of the Indians, and he is known to posterity as "the Apostle to the Indians." A good linguist, he set about learning the Massachusetts Indian language, though his first sermons to the natives, in 1646 at Dorchester Mills, were in English, which few of them understood. By the next year he was speaking their own tongue fluently.

In 1649, at Eliot's instigation, an association was formed in England known as the Society for Propagation of the Gospel in New-England, which financed Eliot's missionary work. He set about translating the Bible, publishing the New Testament in 1661 and the Old Testament (the first book printed in North America) in 1663. He also

After a family portrait

JOHN ELIOT

founded an Indian college to train native ministers, but this was a failure, its only graduate dying at twenty, and the plant became his printing office. Though in many ways Eliot was innocent of the limitations and natures of his converts, translating works on logic and metaphysics for untutored savages, he did realize that the Indians must have their own separate communities. He founded his first Indian town at Natick in 1651, as a "self-governing" community controlled only by his own laws, which rivaled in severity the famous Connecticut "Blue Laws." By 1675 there were fourteen such villages, with about 1,100 converts, twenty-four of whom had become preachers. Then King Philip's War, an Indian uprising, scattered and ruined the settlements—indeed, the native who had helped him print the Old Testament was one of the leaders of the massacres. Gradually the whole scheme came to nothing, though four villages still existed at his death; so that in a sense Eliot's mission was a failure.

Eliot was the founder of the Roxbury Latin School, still in existence. Besides his Indian translations he wrote several theological works in English. His *Christian Commonwealth,* republican in sentiment, was the first American book to be suppressed; it was condemned in 1661 and Eliot had to make a public retraction. He outlived this quasi-disgrace, as well as the partial defeat of his mission, and died in his sleep, still an active minister, at the age of eighty-six.

Principal Works: A Primer or Catechism in the Massachusetts Indian Language, 1654; The Christian Commonwealth, 1659; Up-Bookum Psalmes, 1663; The Communion of Churches, 1665; Indian Grammar Begun, 1666; Indian Dialogues, 1671; Indian Logick Primer, 1672; The Harmony of the Gospels, 1678; Dying Speeches of Several Indians, 1680.

About: Fiske, J. The Beginnings of New England; Francis C. Life of John Eliot; Mather, C. Magnalia; Walker, W. Ten New England Leaders; American Society of Church History Papers 1897.

ELIOT, SAMUEL (December 22, 1821-September 14, 1898), historian and philanthropist, was born in Boston, the son of William Harvard Eliot and Margaret Boies (Bradford) Eliot. At his graduation from Harvard in 1839 he stood first in his class, and after two dull years in a counting house went abroad for his health. In Rome he began a history of liberty, of which he finished only four of the contemplated twelve volumes. Following his return he married Emily Marshall Otis of Boston, in 1853, and moved to Brookline, where he gave free instruction to workingmen's children. Through his Episcopalian connections he was made professor of history at Trinity College, Hartford, in 1856, and became president of this institution in 1860.

In 1864 he returned to Boston and devoted the rest of his life to the service of religious, educational, and charitable organizations, in the capacity of headmaster, trustee, chairman of boards, etc. Eliot's writings include, besides the history mentioned above, translations from the Spanish poet José Zorilla; *Selections From American Authors,* containing a part of Franklin's autobiography, familiar letters of John and Abigail Adams, and pleasant fiction—all designed for the development of a "love of reading"; and *Poetry for Children,* a collection of American and British rhymes. Eliot was a devout Episcopalian and a disinterested provider for the underprivileged; his literary pursuits were, therefore, seemingly subordinate to his many philanthropic activities, and his influence among men of letters was necessarily slight.

Principal Works: Passages From the History of Liberty, 1847; The Liberty of Rome (2 vols.) 1849 (later re-published in 4 vols., with title change); Selections From American Authors, 1879; Poetry for Children, 1879.

About: Proceedings of the Massachusetts Historical Society, 1901; Boston Transcript September 15, 17, 1898.

ELLET, CHARLES (January 1, 1810-June 21, 1862), civil engineer and technical writer, was born in Bucks County, Pa., the son of Charles Ellet, a Quaker farmer, and

Mary (Israel) Ellet, daughter of the high sheriff of Philadelphia. His mother sympathized with the lad's early determination to study engineering, but his father opposed it. Ellet left home at seventeen, working first as a rodman and then as an assistant engineer. He studied in France at l'École Polytechnique in 1830, and on foot made a tour of European engineering plants. His treatise on rate-making, *Essay on the Laws of Trade,* was published in 1839.

At Fairmount, Pa., Ellet built, over the Schuylkill, the first important suspension bridge in the United States, and seven years later he completed (1849) a span of 1,010 feet over the Ohio at Wheeling, W.Va., which was destroyed by fire in 1854. Following the publication of his *Physical Geography of the Mississippi Valley,* he made an extensive study for the War Department, and in *The Mississippi and Ohio Rivers* recommended the construction of upland reservoirs for the retention of surplus waters. Legislation to effect his plans failed, but his reports were reissued in 1927-28 for the Committee on Flood Control.

With his visit to Europe during the Crimean War he began to popularize "ramboats" as tools of naval warfare; they were used in June 1862 at the surrender of Memphis, during which Ellet was the only Union man wounded. He died two weeks later, and his wife, Elvira Daniel, whom he had married in 1837, survived him only eight days.

He wrote prolifically for technical and popular journals, and published some forty-odd books, written in a readable expository style and representing a substantial advancement over the technological thought of his day.

PRINCIPAL WORKS: Essay on the Laws of Trade, 1839; Physical Geography of the Mississippi Valley, 1849; The Mississippi and Ohio Rivers, 1853; Coast and Harbor Defences, 1855; Military Incapacity and What it Costs the Country, 1862.

ABOUT: Stuart, C. B. Lives and Works of Civil and Military Engineers of America; Harper's February 1866; Evening Star (Washington) June 23, 1862.

ELLET, ELIZABETH FRIES (LUMMIS) (October 1818-June 3, 1877), translator and chronicler of the accomplishments of American women, was born at Sodus Point, Lake Ontario, N.Y., the daughter of Dr. William N. and Sarah (Maxwell) Lummis. She attended the Female Seminary in Aurora, N.Y., and at sixteen published a translation of Silvio Pellico's tragedy *Euphemio of Messina.* A year later came a tragedy and original poems under the title of *Teresa Contarini.* Following her marriage to Dr. William H. Ellet she lived in Columbia, S.C., where her husband held a professorship at South Carolina College. In 1849 they returned to New York where she continued to live after Dr. Ellet's death in 1859.

She made translations from the German, French, and Italian, prepared criticisms, and adapted foreign legends: *The Characters of Schiller*; the semi-historical *Scenes in the Life of Joanna of Sicily*; and a book of obscure German legendary fragments, *Evenings at Woodlawn.* In her comprehensive *Women of the American Revolution,* as well as in *Pioneer Women of the West* and *Queens of American Society,* her approach to American history was, obviously, that of a feminist. Among her miscellaneous writings were: *Ramblings About the Country, Watching Spirits, Family Pictures From the Bible,* etc. Her poetry was stereotyped in sentiment and slightly halting in metre, but her prose, though diluted by an excess of gossip, won her recognition which today is somewhat hard to account for.

PRINCIPAL WORKS: Teresa Contarini, 1835; The Characters of Schiller, 1839; Rambles About the Country, 1840; Women of the American Revolution, 1848; Evenings at Woodlawn, 1849; Family Pictures From the Bible, 1849; Novelettes of the Musicians, 1852; Pioneer Women of the West, 1852.

ABOUT: Griswold, R. W. Female Poets of America; New York Times June 4, 1877.

ELLIOT, JONATHAN (1784-March 12, 1846), editor and publicist, was born in Carlisle, England. His parentage and education are unknown, and much of his career and character are also without record. It is known that he emigrated to New York in 1802 and worked as a printer; that in 1810 he went to South America to fight as a volunteer under Simon Bolivar, the great liberator; and it is supposed that he served on the American side in the War of 1812.

In December, 1813, with two other men, he published the first daily evening paper in Washington, the *Washington Evening Gazette.* Suspended when the British captured the city, the paper reappeared in 1815 as the *Washington City Weekly Gazette*; in 1817 it became a daily again. Elliot sold it in 1826. As a printer, he also handled all the government's printing and became very prosperous; naturally, as a Federalist beneficiary, he was strongly anti-Jacksonian, and in 1828 edited a paper against Jackson and the Democrats called *We, The People.* He was active in politics, but apparently always with a mercenary aim in view, and though he has been termed by contemporaries generous and kindly in private life, he does not seem to have been a very admirable person in all his public dealings. He was married and had two children, but the details of his private life are unknown. He died in Washington at sixty.

Elliot's chief claim to remembrance is as the editor and publisher of the debates of the Constitutional Congress, a very valuable source-book, the first volume of which was issued in 1827, the fifth and last in 1836. In 1827 he also published the first formulated Diplomatic Code of the United States, and in 1845 he edited the papers of President Madison.

PRINCIPAL WORKS: Debates, Resolutions, and Other Proceedings in Convention on the Adoption of the Federal Constitution, 1827-36; Diplomatic Code of the United States of America, 1827 (as American Diplomatic Code, 1834); Historical Sketches of the Ten Miles Square Forming the District of Columbia, 1830; The Funding System of the United States and Great Britain, 1845.

ABOUT: Washington Daily National Intelligencer March 13, 1846; Washington Daily Union March 14, 1846.

ELLIOTT, SARAH BARNWELL (1848-August 30, 1928), woman suffragist and novelist, was born in Georgia, the daughter of Stephen Elliott, the first Protestant Episcopal bishop of Georgia, and Charlotte Bull (Barnwell) Elliott. From the early 'seventies until her death, except during residence abroad and in New York, she lived on the Cumberland Plateau, in Sewanee, Tenn. In her own home and from special tutors she received her early education, and in 1886 studied at Johns Hopkins.

Three of her earliest novels, *The Felmeres, A Simple Heart,* and *John Paget,* were directly inspired by a highly religious environment. For *Jerry,* however, which appeared serially in *Scribner's Magazine* during 1891 and 1892, she turned to Tennessee mountain life, and wrote, from the vantage point of familiarity and sympathy, a tragic tale that became, almost immediately, not only national but international literary property. Two subsequent novels and a biography, *Sam Houston,* failed to reach the level of *Jerry.*

She lived in New York from 1895 until 1902; on her return to Sewanee she spent much of her time in suffragist activities, and in patriotic and literary circles. she was a frequent and widely popular hostess. As a writer her fame rests almost entirely on *Jerry,* and through its publication she not only became one of the first to assert the need of rural industrial schools in the South but made a much-needed escape from the sentimentality of ante-bellum letters.

PRINCIPAL WORKS: The Felmeres, 1879; A Simple Heart, 1889; John Paget, 1893; An Incident and Other Happenings, 1899; The Durket Sperret, 1898; The Making of Jane, 1901; Sam Houston, 1900.

ABOUT: Library of Southern Literature: Vol. 4; Sewanee Purple October 21, 1928.

ELLIS, EDWARD SYLVESTER (April 11, 1840-June 20, 1916), historian and juvenile series writer, was born at Geneva, Ohio, the son of Sylvester and Mary (Alberty) Ellis. He was educated at the State Normal School of New Jersey, at Trenton, and received an honorary M.A. from Princeton in 1887. He began his career as a teacher in Trenton, and from 1875 to 1886 was successively principal, school trustee, and superintendent of schools. In 1874 and 1875 he edited *Public Opinion,* a Trenton daily, and from 1878 to 1881 was editor of *Golden Days,* a juvenile magazine in Philadelphia. After 1881 his entire time was devoted to writing. In 1862 he married Anna M. Deane, by whom he had one son, who became a teacher of philosophy at West Point; after her death, in 1900, he married Clara Spalding Brown, of Los Angeles. His home was in Upper Montclair, N.J., but he died while on a vacation trip to Cliff Island, Maine.

Ellis' books, of which there were "torrents," are about equally divided between stories for boys and history for children and adults. His *Seth Jones* was one of the earliest of the "dime novels" and sold 600,000 copies. He was the author of several long series of such works, including the *Deerfoot Series,* the *Young Pioneer Series,* and the *Log Cabin Series.* As he wrote under seven pseudonyms (mostly the names of army officers) and had eight publishers scattered through the country, no real bibliography is possible. He was a bit of an eccentric, who thought everyone could live to be a centenarian by refraining from tobacco and liquor and indulging in athletics (though he himself died at seventy-six); he was highly patriotic and moral, and to modern readers his work is exceedingly dull.

PRINCIPAL WORKS (non-fiction): Continental Primary Physiology, 1885; Eclectic Primary History of the United States, 1885; Youth's History of the United States, 1887; School History of the United States, 1892; History of Our Country 1896; People's Standard History of the United States, 1898; The Story of South Africa, 1899; From Tent to White House, 1899; School History of the State of New York, 1899.

ABOUT: New York Times June 21 1916.

ELSON, LOUIS CHARLES (April 17, 1848-February 14, 1920), music critic, lecturer, and teacher, was born in Boston, the son of Julius and Rosalie (Schnell) Elson. He attended public schools and received his first piano lessons from his mother, afterwards studying under Leipzig masters. He edited *Vox Humana* and was music critic for the Boston *Courier* before joining (1886) the Boston *Advertiser*, with which he was connected until the time of his death. His free public lectures on the history and appreciation of music became a Boston institution and won him no mean reputation. In 1873 he was married to Bertha Lissner, by whom he had one child, Arthur. For forty years he directed the theory department of the New England Conservatory of Music, presenting a thorough analysis of form, supplemented by two sets of lectures, one on instrumentation and the other on musical history.

Elson was, moreover, the author of a long list of books ranging from the standard textbook, such as *Theory of Music*, to volumes like *Shakespeare in Music*, a scholarly etymological study in which he identified many puzzling musical allusions in the plays. His highly valuable *History of American Music* predicted an era of promising native development. As a scholarly author, a candid but gentle critic and a popular lecturer, Elson furthered the progress of musical enlightenment in the United States.

Principal Works: Curiosities of Music, 1880; German Songs and Song Writers, 1882; The Theory of Music, 1890; The National Music of America, 1899; History of German Song, 1903; The History of American Music, 1904; Women in Music, 1918; University Musical Encyclopaedia, 1912.

About: Mathews, W. S. B. A Hundred Years of Music in America.

EMBURY, EMMA CATHERINE (c. 1806-February 10, 1863), poet and writer of tales, was born in New York, the daughter of Dr. James R. Manley, a physician of note, and Elizabeth (Post) Manley. She cultivated an early taste for good reading and at about the age of twenty she became a regular, though unremunerated, contributor of juvenile verse and stories to the New York *Mirror*. On May 10, 1828, she married Daniel Embury, a Brooklyn banker with intellectual tendencies, and was shortly the central figure of a modest salon. Although she was sought out by numerous magazine editors she appears to have written for pure pleasure and not for money. Among her many better known published tales were *Guido: A Tale* and *Constance Latimer: or, The Blind Girl.* Selections from her prose, as well as *Poems of Emma C. Embury*, were published posthumously. In 1848 Mrs. Embury was stricken with a chronic illness, and for two years before her death in 1863 she was a complete invalid.

Her verse, patently conventional and filled with far-fetched imagery was greatly overrated by contemporary critics. A word in praise of her prose was, perhaps, more justifiable. Poe, however was doubtless misled by Mrs. Embury's personal charm when he paid her stories almost lavish tribute: her writings are hardly more than fair specimens of that literature which sprang up during the heyday of the "female poet" in America.

Principal Works: Guido: A Tale, 1828; Constance Latimer: or, The Blind Girl, 1838; American Wild Flowers in Their Native Haunts, 1845; Glimpses of Home Life: or, Causes and Consequences, 1848; The Waldorf Family: or, Grandfather's Legend; Poems of Emma C. Embury, 1869; Prose Writings of Mrs. Emma C. Embury, 1893.

About: May, C. Female Poets; Read, T. B. Female Poets of America (7th ed.); Godey's Magazine and Lady's Book August 1846; New York Times February 14, 1863.

EMERSON, RALPH WALDO (May 25, 1803-April 27, 1882), essayist and poet, was born in Boston of what has been called the "Brahmin" caste—descendants of the Puritan worthies of the seventeenth century. His father was William Emerson, a Unitarian minister and chaplain during the Revolution; his mother, Ruth (Haskins) Emerson. The father died in 1811, leaving six small children. Of these, three brothers besides Ralph (who preferred to be called Waldo), were highly intellectual, but another brother was mentally defective; and of the two brothers who died young, one was insane for a time. The mother was obliged to take in boarders to support her family, and not she, but the paternal aunt, Mary Moody Emerson, was the great formative influence in the boy's early life. Miss Emerson was an eccentric to the point of lunacy, but also the possessor of a strange gnomic genius whose gift for succinct phrasing descended to her nephew.

Emerson attended the Boston Latin School, and entered Harvard in 1817, earning his way as messenger and waiter. He received his B.A. in 1820, and for three years taught in his oldest brother's private school for girls, a task he disliked and to which he felt himself inadequate. On his aunt's advice, he turned to the ministry, the seventh of his family in line to adopt that profession. His studies at the Harvard Divinity School were interrupted by incipient tuberculosis, which sent him to Florida and Georgia in search of a warmer climate; however, he was "approbated to preach" in 1826, and in 1829 became pastor of the Second Church (Unitarian) in Boston. In the same year he married Ellen Louisa Tucker, a beautiful girl of seventeen, already doomed to tuberculosis. She died seventeen months later.

Van Wyck Brooks, in *The Flowering of New England,* describes Emerson as he appeared in those days—"tall, excessively thin, . . . pale, with a tomahawk nose, blond, with blue eyes and smiling, curved lips." The "majestic dignity" to be his later had not yet developed. Slow to mature, palpably a misfit in the conventional pulpit, and wretched over his wife's death, Emerson became more and more at odds with his congregation, until finally in 1832 he broke with the church on the issue of the rite of communion. He continued to preach sporadically until 1847, but after 1838 at least he was obviously heterodox, and he never served as a regular minister again. Instead, at the end of 1832, he sailed for Europe. There he met the three men whose work and ideas meant most to him, Coleridge, Wordsworth, and Carlyle—with whom he formed the beginning of a lifelong friendship, marked by forty years of correspondence. Plato and the neo-Platonists, the Indian philosophers, the German idealists, and above all Swedenborg, were the other sources of Emerson's slowly emerging *Weltanschauung.* He went to Europe a "lonely wayfaring man," as Carlyle called him, a seeker; he returned with his life-attitude and life-work clearly set before him.

In 1834 he settled in Concord, the home of some of his ancestors, in a house which was his home until 1872, when it burnt and was exactly replaced by a fund raised by his friends. In 1835 he married Lydia Jackson (whose brother was chief claimant to the discovery of ether anaesthesia), who changed her name to "Lidian" at his request for the sake of euphony. They had two sons and two daughters, but the oldest and best-loved, Waldo, died in 1841. Around Emerson in Concord gathered the group which came to be known as "the Concord school"— Bronson Alcott, Thoreau (who lived with the Emersons for long periods as a sort of housekeeper), Hawthorne (always a bit aloof), and Margaret Fuller. These were the Transcendentalists, the idealists who would reform the world from within out, who relied on intuition and the perfectibility of mankind. Emerson disclaimed their label, but he was their inspiration and the

Collection of Frederick H. Meserve
RALPH WALDO EMERSON

core of their association. To them, as finally to America, he typified "Man Thinking," the ideal scholar who would in the end, as in Plato's Republic, be the world's ideal king. Two lectures, the Phi Beta Kappa address at Harvard in 1837, on "The American Scholar," and the address to the Harvard Divinity School in 1838 which laid bare the pretensions of orthodox theology and alienated Harvard for thirty years, were the battle-calls and clarions of this group and of its fringes in Boston and elsewhere in New England.

Meanwhile, Emerson had to live and to support his family; and (since he allowed his literary agent to defraud him for most of his life, and when he was most famous received no more than $600 a year from his books) his only way to do this was by lecturing. Every year he made a lecture tour, extending annually farther and farther west; and these lectures were the source of most of his essays, as the lectures in turn came from the detailed journal he had kept ever since 1820. When he was not on a tour, he lived very quietly, studying and reading, drinking in new inspiration from the few of his like-minded friends. He regarded with benevolence such experimental colonies as Brook Farm and Alcott's Fruitlands, but he stood aside from active participation in these or other public movements, until slavery got under his skin and made him, through the '50s, an ardent abolitionist, who even rejoiced in the coming of civil war. On the whole, as the years passed, he tended to lose most of his early radicalism, and abandoned many of the beliefs which had fired younger thinkers when he too was young. (It is recorded that he once visited Thoreau, who was serving a jail term as a protest against unjust taxation. Emerson was greatly distressed. "Why are you here?" he asked in anguish. "Why are you *not* here?" demanded the doughtier Thoreau.)

After sixty he wrote and thought nothing really new; he had developed slowly, and he sank early into senescence. Honors were heaped upon him; Harvard gave him forgivingly an honorary LL.D. and made him a trustee; the great of the world flocked to his Concord doorstep; he traveled like a king to California and then again to Europe (his last farewell to Carlyle) and to Egypt; and he came back a white-haired man afflicted with a strange aphasia. He whose whole life had been service to words as the expression of thought forgot most of his words; he could describe objects, but could not name them, and he forgot the names of his oldest friends. He was nearly eighty when he died, quickly and quietly, of pneumonia.

Emerson's aquiline face was oddly asymmetrical. From one view it was "angelic," as Mark Van Doren calls it; from another, it had the aspect of a shrewd New England farmer. In the man himself there was this same dualism; he was a dreamer who soared high but who renewed his strength like Antaeus by contact with the earth. His tall slender form, his burning blue eyes, his low, thrilling voice bespoke the poet and the prophet; but there was salt on his tongue and ordinary common sense in his judgments. The extremism and fanaticism of many of the abstract New England thinkers, saints slightly run to seed like Alcott and Margaret Fuller, were not for him. He retained a large sanity not often coupled with subjective idealism so strong as his. The combination made him, in Paul Elmer More's words, "a kind of lay preacher to the world." John Van der Zee Sears, last survivor of Brook Farm, remembered him in his youth as characteristically "happy but not joyful."

As of himself, so also of his writing. As a poet he was most uneven, capable of bare, bad verse and a kind of archaic obscurity. Yet his dozen great poems possess, as Van Wyck Brooks remarks, "a nervous, intellectual style, swift, clear, and cold as a mountain stream." His essays are full of phrases which from epigrams have become household words. His prose style, pieced together from notes and journal entries, was gnomic, cumulative, fresh thought piled on thought. He is the most quotable and, with Shakespeare and Pope, among the most quoted of authors, the fragments of his wisdom frequently outshining the works in which they are embedded. To hear him lecture in his best days must have been a rare experience, for he required much of his audiences in concentration and understanding—more than many of the pioneer communities, seeking "culture," were willing or able to give.

Every constituent part of Emerson's philosophy may be found elsewhere, either in the European and Oriental sources where he found his inspiration, or in writings of others of the New England group influencing and influenced by him. Compensation—the nice balancing of good and evil in nature and in fate—self-reliance, the "oversoul" (akin to the modern subconscious)—each has its advocates elsewhere. It was Emerson's function to synthesize these scattered concepts, and to weave them into a fabric stout enough to serve as a sail against the winds of opposing doctrine. Brook Farm; the *Dial*, that Transcendentalist magazine of which he was part editor; the Saturday Club, the group of literary Brahmins to which he belonged from its beginning—all these are gone; but the spirit that informed them is permanently part of the American heritage: and that spirit primarily is Emerson's.

"The purpose of life seems to be to acquaint man with himself," he wrote in his journal in 1833. "We need not fear that we can lose anything by the progress of the soul," he said in his essay on *Love*. And again: "Nothing can bring you peace but yourself." This is the quintessence of individualism, a kind of dignified anarchy not unlike Thoreau's. But it still has meaning—by that law of compensation Emerson celebrated—to our more mutually dependent time. Emerson entered Harvard as a messenger—and as a messenger he left—and remains in—the world.

Principal Works: Nature, 1836; The American Scholar, 1837; Address Before the Senior Class in Divinity College, Cambridge, 1838; Essays: First Series, 1841, Second Series, 1844; Poems, 1847; Miscellanies, 1849; Representative Men, 1850; English Traits, 1856; The Conduct of Life, 1860; May Day and Other Pieces (poems) 1867; Society and Solitude, 1870; Letters and Social Aims, 1876; Complete Works, 1884; Journals, 1909-14; Uncollected Writings, 1912.

About: Brooks, Van W. Emerson and Others; Brooks, Van W. The Life of Emerson; Cabot, J. E. A Memoir of Ralph Waldo Emerson; Carpenter, F. I. Emerson and Asia; Dillaway, N. Prophet of America; Emerson, E. W. Emerson in Concord; Firkins, O. W. Ralph Waldo Emerson; Barnett, R. Life of Ralph Waldo Emerson; Gray, R. M. Emerson: A Study of the Poet as Seer; Holmes, O. W. Ralph Waldo Emerson; McGiffert, A. C. (ed.). Young Emerson Speaks; Michaud, R. (translated by G. Boas) Emerson: The Enraptured Yankee; Perry, B. Emerson Today; Russell, P. Emerson: The Wisest American; Sanborn, F. B. Ralph Waldo Emerson; Scudder, T. The Lonely Wayfaring Man; Woodberry, G. E. Ralph Waldo Emerson; American Scholar May 1935, January and March 1936; Atlantic Monthly January and February 1897, June 1903; Century Magazine April 1883; Independent May 21, 1903; North American Review May 1903; Overland Monthly October 1884; Scribner's Magazine November 1909.

EMMETT, DANIEL DECATUR (October 29, 1815-June 28, 1904), song-writer, minstrel, and professed author of "Dixie," was born in Mount Vernon, Ohio, the son of Abraham Emmett, blacksmith and soldier of the War of 1812, and Sarah (Zerick) Emmett. After a very scant schooling he went to work in his father's shop; then learned to read and to write, and was apprenticed to a printer. At thirteen he found employment with the *Huron Reflector* (Norwalk, Ohio); later transferred to the *Western Aurora* (Mount Vernon) and in his eighteenth year joined the army as a fifer, serving first at Newport, Ky., and afterwards at Jefferson Barracks, near St. Louis. He had written "Old Dan Tucker" when he was only fifteen or sixteen, and now at camp he carried on a little desultory study of music.

In 1835 he was discharged from the army, and during the year following he traveled with a circus troupe. In the winter of 1842-43 he organized the "Virginia Minstrels."

Collection of Frederick H. Meserve
"DAN" EMMETT

Decked out in "white ducks," glaring calico shirts, and blue swallow-tails (Emmett was his own fashion creator), they reached, in a New York run of almost three weeks, a new high in an almost untried variety of vaudeville. Their performances on tour in America were riotously received; but their English audiences were completely discouraging.

In 1857 Emmett joined the Bryant Minstrels; and two years later, according to one version of the "Who-wrote-Dixie" account, when Bryant sent him a "rush" request for a "walk-around" (that part of a song which is without words and which gives the singer a chance to strut a little, twirl his cane, etc.), he struck off a melody that was afterwards adopted with infinite variations in the lines, as the war-song of the Confederacy. During these years Emmett composed a number of songs, among which were: "The Road to Richmond," "Walk Along, John," and "Here We Are: or, Cross Ober Jordan." And for the first twelve or thirteen years after the close of the War he traveled with his own troupe. After several years' residence in Chicago he retired to a little farm outside Mount Vernon, and for the comforts of his late life he received a stipend from the Actor's Fund of New York City.

As early as 1828 one Thomas D. Rice had popularized a "Jim Crow" act, borrowed from a Negro stable-boy who used to do a shuffle step and a little jump that set his "heel-a-rickin'." But the actual minstrel troupe was Emmett's own innovation. There was "lightning in his heels and patter in his voice," and his name would certainly have been preserved by the theatrical historian even if it had never been associated with the authorship—his claims to which, incidentally, have recently been rather substantially contested—of the long-popular "Dixie."

ABOUT: Galbreath, C. B. Daniel Decatur Emmett: Author of "Dixie"; Odell, G. H. Annals of the New York Stage; Street, J. H. Look Away! A Dixie Notebook; Etude December 1936; Harper's June 1889.

ENGLISH, GEORGE BETHUNE (March 7, 1787-September 20, 1828), soldier and diplomat, was born in Cambridge, Mass., the son of Thomas and Penelope (Bethune) English. He was graduated from Harvard in 1807, studied law for a short time, and then sought a commission in the army. He received an M. A. from the Harvard Divinity School, but was a failure in the pulpit. On the basis of his Hebrew studies he wrote *The Grounds of Christianity Examined by*

Comparing the New Testament With the Old, to which Edward Everett replied with *A Defense of Christianity Against the Work of G. B. English,* accusing him of plagiarism. Shortly after his removal to the West, he secured an appointment as lieutenant of the marines and cruised the Mediterranean. At Alexandria he resigned his commission, embraced Mohammedanism, and as an officer in the Egyptian army accompanied the Pasha of Egypt on a military expedition to the Sudan. On his return to the United States he published *A Narrative of the Expedition to Dongola and Senaar* (London, 1822; Boston, 1823), white man's first description of this region; and *Five Pebbles From the Brook,* a rejoinder to Everett, prepared several years earlier.

As a secret agent to sound out the possibilities of opening the Black Sea to American trade, English went to Constantinople. Intricate diplomatic entanglements and the fact that he was suspected of espionage hastened his return to Washington. He departed again for the Levant in 1825 as an interpreter, and sailed for home in 1827. English was an excellent linguist and, moreover, was possessed of considerable versatility. But a lack of scruples, intellectually, and a general fickleness not only blighted his diplomatic career but lessened the historical value of his scant writings.

PRINCIPAL WORKS: The Grounds of Christianity Examined by Comparing the New Testament With the Old, 1813; A Narrative of the Expedition to Dongola and Senaar, 1822 and 1823; Five Pebbles From the Brook, 1824.

ABOUT: Knapp, S. L. American Biography; Daily National Intelligencer September 22, 1828.

ENGLISH, THOMAS DUNN (June 29, 1819-April 1, 1902), poet and playwright, was born in Philadelphia. His father's name was probably Robert English; the family were Irish Quakers, whose name was originally Angelos. He was educated at Wilson's Academy, Philadelphia; the Friends' Academy, Burlington, N.J.; and the medical school of the University of Pennsylvania, before this serving for a short time on the Pennsylvania Geological Survey. He received his M.D. degree in 1839, his thesis being a defense of phrenology. After this he read law, and was admitted to the bar in 1842. But literature attracted him more than did either law or medicine.

From 1839 on, he was a frequent contributor to *Burton's Gentleman's Magazine,* one of whose editors was Poe. From an intimate friend, he became one of Poe's worst enemies; the publisher of the *Evening Mirror* lost a libel suit brought by Poe in consequence of a charge of forgery brought against Poe by English.

THOMAS DUNN ENGLISH

In 1844 English moved to New York, where he edited an anti-Tyler paper called *Aurora,* which like all his other publishing ventures soon expired. For a short time he was weigher at the Port of New York. The next year he edited the *Aristidean,* which also soon failed, and then, after six months in Washington, he returned to Philadelphia, where he was publisher of a weekly humorous magazine called *John Donkey.* This died under the weight of libel suits; English had an irrepressible tendency to bad temper and scurrility.

In 1849 he married Annie Maxwell Meade, who died in 1899, leaving four children. From 1852 to 1856 he practiced both law and medicine at Lawnsville (now Logan), Va., and was the first mayor of the town. After another year in New York, he settled in 1858 in New Jersey, his home thereafter. He was a member of the New Jersey legislature in 1863 and 1864, as a "Copperhead" (Southern sympathizer). In 1870 he published the *Old Guard,* which also failed after a few numbers. In 1876 he received an honorary LL.D. from William and Mary College. During 1878 he was on the staff of the Newark *Sunday Call.* He served in Congress as a Democrat from 1891 to 1895. In his old age he was practically blind.

English acknowledged that he wrote only for money. His several novels (mostly written under pseudonyms) and his twenty or more plays were all verbose and facile. Only *The Mormons* had any considerable success. He is remembered solely as one of Poe's enemies, and as the author of "Ben Bolt," the song, published in 1843, which Du Maurier made famous by incorporating it in *Trilby*.

Principal Works: Walter Woolfe, 1842; MDCCCXLIV: or, The Power of the S.F., 1845; Poems, 1855; The Mormons: or, Life at Salt Lake, 1858; Ambrose Fecit: or, The Peer and the Painter, 1869; American Ballads, 1880; Boy's Book of Battle Lyrics, 1885; Jacob Schuyler's Millions, 1886; Select Poems of Dr. Thomas Dunn English, 1894; Fairy Stories and Wonder Tales, 1897; The Ballad of Brave Bill Anthony, 1898.

About: Midland Monthly January 1897; New York Times April 2, 1902.

"ERRATIC ENRIQUE." See LUKENS, HENRY CLAY

"ESEK, UNCLE." See SHAW, HENRY WHEELER

EVANS, AUGUSTA JANE (May 8, 1835-May 9, 1909), novelist, was born in Columbus, Ga., the daughter of Matthew Ryan Evans and Sarah Skrine (Howard) Evans. She spent her early childhood in Texas and after moving to Alabama wrote, during her fifteenth or sixteenth year, *Inez: A Tale of the Alamo*, a somewhat soggy mixture of war, love, and religious prejudice. It was published anonymously in 1855, but made little stir. Four years later came *Beulah*, pretentious and pedantic, of which 21,000 copies were sold in a year. *Macaria: or, Altars of Sacrifice* was burdened with mythological and philosophical allusions and long Latin quotations. Two years later came *St. Elmo*, a sentimental brief for righteousness, less sodden with "learning" and far more sanguine than *Macaria*, despite its obvious pathos. Some critics enthusiastically praised it; others bitterly condemned it; and William Webb pleasantly parodied it with *St. Twel'mo*. Publicity was rampant and its sale was phenomenal; it became one of the inexplicable "popular classics" of all time. Whole generations have laughed and cried over its obvious melodramatics.

Like many female authors of her era she seemed to write with almost too much ease, and in a consistently sentimental and moralistic strain. *St. Elmo* has been called "the most praised, best abused novel ever written."

Between 1875 and 1887 she wrote a love chronicle and a mystery tale; her last two books were *A Speckled Bird*, built upon post-war developments, and *Devota*, published in 1907, scornful of various current social trends. In December 1868 she was married to a wealthy widower, Lorenzo Madison Wilson, whom she survived almost twenty years.

Principal Works: Inez: A Tale of the Alamo, 1855; Beulah, 1859; Macaria: or, Altars of Sacrifice, 1864; St. Elmo, 1866; Vashti, 1869; Infelice, 1875; At the Mercy of Tiberius, 1887; A Speckled Bird, 1902; Devota, 1907.

About: Derby, J. C. Fifty Years Among Authors; Raymond, I. Southland Writers; Mobile Register May 10, 1909.

EVANS, NATHANIEL (June 8, 1742-October 29, 1767), poet, was born in Philadelphia, the son of Edward Evans, a merchant. He was educated at the Philadelphia Academy (afterwards the University of Pennsylvania). He was then put in a counting house, but was so unhappy that his father allowed him to return to the Academy when his apprenticeship was over. Though he never was graduated, he was so brilliant a student that the Academy gave him an M.A. degree in 1765. He then went to England, where he was ordained as a clergyman and returned to America under the auspices of the Society for Propagating the Gospel in Foreign Parts, as a missionary to Gloucester County, N.J., and chaplain to the Irish Viscount Kilmorey. By this time, however, he was advanced in tuberculosis, and less than a year later he died, at twenty-five, at Haddonfield, N.J. He was buried in Christ Church, Philadelphia.

Evans was one of the literary coterie that gathered around Francis Hopkinson, in Philadelphia. In 1767, just before his death, he edited the poems and plays of Thomas Godfrey, another of the group. His own poems were closely imitative of Milton, Gray, Collins, and other English poets, but they showed considerable natural grace and melody. His early death cut short a career of real promise.

Principal Works: An Ode on the Late Glorious Successes of His Majesty's Arms, 1762; The Love of the World Incompatible With the Love of God (prose) 1766; Poems on Several Occasions: With Some Other Compositions, 1772.

About: Jackson, M. K. Outlines of the Literary History of Colonial Pennsylvania; Oberholtzer, E. P. The Literary History of Philadelphia.

EVANS, WARREN FELT (December 23, 1817-September 4, 1889), metaphysical writer, was born at Rockingham, Vt., the son of Eli and Sarah (Edson) Evans. He was educated at Chester Academy, Middlebury College and Dartmouth, but left the latter institution without taking a degree. In 1840 he married Charlotte Tinker, by whom he had three children. In 1844 he was ordained as a Methodist minister, and during the next twenty years held eleven charges in various parts of New England. He then withdrew from the Methodist Conference and joined the Church of the New Jerusalem (Swedenborgian). A year before this, he had gone to Portland, Maine, to be treated by Dr. Phineas P. Quimby [*q.v.*], the mental healer, among whose other pupils were Mary Baker Eddy and Julius Dresser [*qq.v.*]. Evans became Quimby's disciple, though modifying Quimby's rather vague beliefs into a formula affected by his own philosophical studies. In the end his system held that disease is "an abnormal mental condition," to be cured by mental suggestion; there are elements in his exposition of the philosophy of Fichte, Hegel, and Bishop Berkeley. All this had close affiliation with the "Oversoul" of the Transcendentalists, and also bears evidence of connection with the modern theories of New Thought and Christian Science.

Evans established in Salisbury, Mass., in 1870, a sort of mental sanitarium known as the Evans Home, where he also taught pupils. Though he certainly never studied medicine, he assumed the title of "M.D." and was known as "Dr." Evans. A kindly, high-minded man of great integrity, he had no concern for financial profit, and believed sincerely in the system he had evolved from Quimby. His books were all written as instructions for non-resident pupils, and were highly popular in their time.

Principal Works: The Mental-Cure, 1869; Mental Medicine, 1872; Soul and Body, 1876; The Divine Law of Cure, 1884; The Primitive Mind Cure, 1885; Esoteric Christianity and Mental Therapeutics, 1886.

About: Leonard, W. J. The Pioneer Apostle of Mental Science: A Sketch of the Life and Works of the Rev. W. F. Evans, M.D.

EVE, JOSEPH (May 24, 1760-November 14, 1835), inventor and poet, was born in Philadelphia, the son of Oswald (or Oswell) and Anna (Moore) Eve. When the lad was about fourteen his family settled in the British West Indies, and as early as 1787 his own invention of a "machine for the separating of seed from cotton" was in use on the islands. Several years later he returned to Charleston, S.C., and his gin, subsequently adapted to animal or water power, brought a price of $250.

In 1810 Eve moved to Georgia, built "The Cottage" near Augusta, and carried on various experiments in gunpowder and steam. He was also indulging himself in verse-writing at this time, and the local dailies published his short poems and excerpts from two longer ones, "Projector" and "Better to Be," a rambling response to Hamlet's soliloquy. Eve was married to Hannah Singeltary, of Charleston County, S.C., and their son, Joseph Adams Eve, became a distinguished physician.

Joseph Eve was a most likable and well-informed gentleman and a friend of Benjamin Franklin. Five years before the appearance of Eli Whitney's first workable cotton gin, Eve's model was in use on the Bahama Islands, and he was the originator of several other substantial devices; but his contribution to American letters was both slight and incidental.

About: Jones, C. C. Jr. Memorial History of Augusta, Ga.; Augusta Chronicle, April 14, May 29, July 3, 17, 1824 and July 14, 1912.

EVERETT, ALEXANDER HILL March 19, 1790-June 29, 1847), editor and diplomat, was born in Boston, the son of the Rev. Oliver Everett, minister of the South Church, and Lucy (Hill) Everett, and older brother of Edward Everett [*q.v.*]. After his graduation from Harvard in 1806 he taught, for a while, at Phillips Exeter Academy, where Edward was enrolled, and then read law in the office of John Quincy Adams, to whom he was private secretary, 1809-10, during Adams' term as Minister to Russia. He was, subsequently, secretary of the American legation at The Hague, then chargé d'affaires, and from 1825 until 1829 acted as minister to Spain during a period of much inter-continental communication on state matters. In *Europe* (1822) and *America* (1827) he recorded his extensive diplomatic experience, and proffered a few conjectures on the future of national strength. At the time of President Kirkland's resignation from Harvard (1828), Everett and his brother Edward were both likely candidates, but Josiah Quincy was chosen.

Everett had, at one time, been a member of a very select "hasty pudding" reading club—Edward Everett, Edward Tyrrel Channing, George Ticknor, *et al.*—which observed a minimum of formality and devoted itself to the writing of Latin jibes. And his activities in the Anthology Club had included a brief editorship of its *Monthly Anthology*. When he returned from Europe in 1830, therefore, he readily became one of the literary mainstays of the *North American Review*, that highly capable spokesman for the New England "renaissance." He succeeded Jared Sparks as its editor, and contributed enlightening essays on the South American republics, European-American relations, including translations into German, French, and Spanish, and literary papers on Voltaire, Madame de Sevigné, Chinese man-

ALEXANDER HILL EVERETT
c. 1842

ners, etc.; his passages from *Brahma Purana* were among the first American transcriptions from the Oriental.

In the five years that followed, however, the *Review* lost ground financially, and it was the substantial assistance of one Peter C. Brooks that saved Everett and his brother Edward, whose aid he had summoned, from worse plight. A small breach was beginning to open between these two brothers, and it was widened by Alexander's transfer of allegiance from the Whigs, who had supported him through several terms in the legislature, to the Democrats. And when he openly opposed his brother's (Whig) re-election to the governorship, in 1839, the gulf became considerably wider—especially when it transpired that Edward had lost by a single vote! Little by little Alexander's social and political ties with Massachusetts became less firm. He was president of Jefferson College in Louisiana, but resigned because of poor health; and somewhat later illness obliged him to turn back on his journey to China (1845), where he had been sent as United States minister. He set out again, and died in Canton shortly after his arrival.

Everett's knowing and witty articles for the *Review* were published in book form as *Critical and Miscellaneous Essays* (1846-47). He is credited with having had a sprightly and vigorous mind, and a literary career was within reach. But fraternal and political disturbances not only affected his diplomatic career, but slowly consumed his zest for the pursuit of letters.

PRINCIPAL WORKS: Europe, 1822; New Ideas on Population: With Remarks on the Theories of Malthus and Godwin, 1823; America, 1827; Critical and Miscellaneous Essays, 1846-47.

ABOUT: Brooks, V. W. The Flowering of New England; Frothingham, P. R. Life of Edward Everett; Christian Examiner January 1848.

EVERETT, DAVID (March 29, 1770-December 21, 1813), poet and journalist, was born in Princeton, Mass., the son of David Everett, a soldier in the American Revolution, and Susannah (Rolfe) Everett. He was a second cousin of Edward Everett, the orator [*q.v.*]. After being graduated from the Academy at New Ipswich, N.H., he taught grammar school there. He then went to Dartmouth College, and received his B.A. in 1795, as valedictorian of his class. He read law, was admitted to the bar, and practiced in Boston. In 1799 he married Dorothy Appleton; they had no children.

From 1802 to 1807 he was a lawyer in Amherst, N.H., then returned to Boston. There in 1809 he founded the Boston *Patriot,* a Democratic paper. In 1811 he was register of probate for Suffolk County, Mass., and from 1810 to 1812 clerk of the Massachusetts House of Representatives. In 1812 he became editor of the *Pilot.* But he had developed tuberculosis, and in 1813 was obliged to seek a milder climate. He went to Marietta, Ohio, where he founded the *American Friend*; but a few months later he died.

An ardent patriot, Everett was a conciliator, opposed to political factionalism. He wrote voluminously, producing essays on ethics and economics, plays, and poems. One play, *Daranzel,* had some success. But of all his work nothing is remembered now save a little verse he wrote for a pupil in New Ipswich, which begins:

> You'd scarce expect one of my age
> To speak in public on the stage.

PRINCIPAL WORKS: Common Sense in Dishabille, 1799; Daranzel: or, The Persian Patriot, 1800; Slaves in Barbary (play) 1810.

ABOUT: Chapman, G. T. Sketches of the Alumni of Dartmouth College; Proceedings American Antiquarian Society 1890.

EVERETT, EDWARD (April 11, 1794-January 15, 1865), orator and essayist, was born at Dorchester, Mass., the fourth of eight children of the Rev. Oliver Everett, a Unitarian clergyman who died in 1802, and Lucy (Hill) Everett. He received his B.A. at Harvard in 1811, as the youngest and the most brilliant member of his class, and for three years thereafter he served as tutor at the college while he studied divinity.

In 1814 he received his M.A., and immediately, though he was not yet twenty, he was elected minister of the Brattle Street Church (Unitarian) in Boston; already he had a reputation as a public speaker of genius. John Adams called him "our most celebrated youth," and he was as handsome as he was gifted. Indeed, President Kirkland of Harvard compared him not unfavorably with Apollo.

In 1815 he was appointed professor of Greek literature at Harvard, and to prepare for this post was given a leave of absence in Europe, which stretched to four years, during which he became the first American to receive a Ph.D. from Göttingen. He returned to America in 1819, and until 1826 served as professor at Harvard. Emerson was among his pupils. At the same time, from 1820 to 1824, he edited the *North American Review,* and contributed many articles to it. In 1822 he married Charlotte Gray Brook, of a wealthy Boston family; they had six children.

Everett's Phi Beta Kappa address at Harvard in 1824, delivered in the presence of Lafayette, was an impressive performance which established him as one of the greatest orators in a time of great oratory. It secured his election to Congress, in which he served four terms, from 1825 to 1835. At the same time Yale gave him an honorary LL.D. in 1833, and Harvard (of which he was a trustee) in 1835. Between 1836 and 1839 he served four terms as governor of Massachusetts, being defeated the fifth time by only one vote. (His brother Alexander [*q.v.*] had voted against him!) He then went abroad for a rest, but President Harrison appointed him minister to England, and he served in this post from 1841 to 1845. While he was abroad he received an honorary D.C.L. from Oxford, and an LL.D. from Cambridge and Dublin. From 1846 to 1849 he was president of Harvard, but he found this appointment little to his liking, and resigned. For four months in 1853 he was Secretary of State, under Fillmore. He then served as senator from Massachusetts from 1853 to 1854, but resigned, ostensibly because of poor health, actually because his absence when the Kansas-Nebraska bill, involving the slavery question, came to vote, caused him to be accused of timidity.

At this time Everett became very much interested in the restoration of Mt. Vernon as a national monument, and from 1853 to 1859 he toured the country, devoting the proceeds of his speeches to this cause. He

Collection of Frederick H. Meserve
EDWARD EVERETT

was by this time the foremost orator of America. We have lost our taste for oratory nowadays, especially for florid rhetoric, but in Everett's day it was the great American art, and he was supreme in it. It was he who delivered the official, the "great" address on the battlefield of Gettysburg in 1863—Lincoln's few words were a mere formal afterthought!

In 1860 Everett allowed himself to be nominated for vice-president by the Constitutional Union Party, an offshoot of the formerly powerful Whigs. The ticket was badly defeated, and Everett's name was last on the list.

It was the end of his public career, but he continued to speak indefatigably, traveling through the nation during the Civil War and defending the cause of the Union. His death was the direct result of fatigue from a speech made in behalf of the starving people of Savannah, Ga.; for he was always a conciliator and had no hatred for the South. He was working on a book on international law at the time of his death, but it was never completed. In fact, he had time to write very little, and most of his published work consists of his speeches in written form.

Emerson wrote of Everett in his journal: "Webster has done him incalculable harm by Everett's too much admiration of his iron nature; warped him from his true bias all these twenty years, and sent him cloud-hunting at Washington and London, to the ruin of his solid scholarship, and fatal diversion from the pursuit of his right prizes."

Everett was highly ambitious and not overly courageous, a little spoiled and vain; but these defects were counterbalanced by immense erudition, personal magnetism, and a sincerely tolerant viewpoint. His work loses by being read instead of heard, but there is no doubt that he was one of the greatest orators America ever produced.

Principal Works: Orations and Speeches on Various Occasions, 1836-58; Life and Works of Daniel Webster, 1852; Mount Vernon Papers, 1859; Life of Washington, 1860.

About: Frothingham, P. R. Edward Everett: Orator and Statesman; Long, O. W. Literary Pioneers; Brooks, Van W. The Flowering of New England; Boston Daily Advertiser January 16, 1865; London Quarterly Review December 1840.

EYTINGE, ROSE (November 21, 1835 (?)-December 20, 1911), actress and memoir writer, was the daughter of David and Rebecca Eytinge. She was educated at home and acquired an early liking for the theatre; after an amateur success at the age of eighteen she joined Geary Hough's stock company, playing the lead in *The Old Guard* for seven dollars a week. From the Green Street Theatre (Albany, N.Y.), managed by David Barnes, who later became her husband, she went to New York to support Booth in *The Fool's Revenge* and *Richelieu*; then came *Oliver Twist* and some time afterwards she was the creator of Laura Courtland in *Under the Gaslight.* Divorced in 1862 from her first husband, she was married a second time to Colonel George H. Butler, and in 1869 accompanied him to Egypt, where he was sent as consul-general. Following a second divorce she returned to the stage for *The Geneva Cross* and *Led Astray. Antony and Cleopatra,* produced in New York in 1877, was, perhaps, the high point in her career: she was artistically and physically well equipped to play the queen, and her sojourn in Egypt had provided her with an unchallengeable interpretation.

Three years later she entered a short engagement in London, winning the compliments of Dickens, Gladstone, Charles Reade, and others. During her late years she conducted schools of acting, wrote *Golden Chains,* a play which found no very wide audience; a romance called *It Happened This Way*; and *Memories of Rose Eytinge,* informative and pleasant but laden with self-indulgence. It is, of course, in her histrionic rather than her literary achievements that her chief claim to fame lies.

Principal Works: It Happened This Way, 1890; Memories of Rose Eytinge, 1905.

About: Eytinge, R. Memories of Rose Eytinge; Trumble, A. Great Artists of the American Stage; New York Times December 21, 1911.

"FABIUS." See DICKINSON, JOHN

FAIRFIELD, SUMNER LINCOLN (June 25, 1803-March 6, 1844), poet, was born at Warwick, Mass., the son of Dr. Abner Fairfield and Lucy (Lincoln) Fairfield. His father died when he was young, leaving the family in straitened circumstances. For several years he lived with his grandfather, but he was so unhappy there that his mother finally took him away and sent him to grammar school in Hadley, Mass. From 1818-20 he studied at Brown University but was forced to leave because of lack of funds. He then taught in Georgia and later in South Carolina. In 1825 he spent four months in England. Upon his return he married Jane Frazee. Shortly after his marriage all his household furnishings were seized for debt. With bad luck dogging his footsteps he spent the next few years moving from New York to Boston, back to New York, then to Virginia, Philadelphia, and back to New York again. During this time he was acting on the stage and teaching.

In 1831 Fairfield finished his masterpiece *The Last Night of Pompeii*; he later claimed that Bulwer Lytton plagiarized it in his *Last Days of Pompeii.* From 1832-38 he published and edited the *North American Magazine.* He died in New Orleans in 1843.

Fairfield was subject to spells of insanity and all his poetry shows the effect of his morbidity and bitterness. His verse was of the Puritan school, showing the influence of Milton. As an editor his slogan was truth, regardless of results. He had few friends, and his poetry, at times reaching a high level in early American literature, is now little read.

Principal Works: The Siege of Constantinople, 1822; Poems, 1823; Lays of Melpomene, 1824; Mina, 1825; The Passage of the Sea, 1826; The Cities of the Plain, 1827; The Heir of the World, 1829; Abaddon, 1830; The Last Night of Pompeii, 1832; Poems and Prose Writings of Sumner Lincoln Fairfield, 1841.

About: Fairfield, J. The Life of Sumner Lincoln Fairfield; Patterson, M. R. Sumner Lincoln Fairfield.

FARLEY, HARRIET (February 18, 1817-November 12, 1907), editor and miscellaneous writer, was born in Claremont, N.H., where her father was pastor of the Congregational church. Of an old New England family, she was the daughter of the Rev.

HARRIET FARLEY

Stephen Farley and Lucy (Saunders) Farley. When she was six the family moved to Atkinson, N.H. There she received thorough training in common-school subjects, French, drawing, and needlework.

Because the family was a large one and money scarce, Harriet was forced, at the tender age of fourteen, to support herself. She said afterward that she had "plaited palm-leaf straw, bound shoes, taught school, and worked at tailoring." She had been educated to teach but the idea was distasteful to her. She preferred to become a mill-hand in Lowell, Mass.—a trade attracting many daughters of rural families—and managed not only to support herself but to contribute to the family's income.

It was an era of lofty paternalism. For the cultural benefit of the mill hands, various "improvement circles" were started about this time in Lowell. The outcome of one of these was the periodical, *Lowell Offering*, which eventually brought Harriet fame both at home and abroad. It began in 1841 and consisted solely of the contributions of the girl mill workers. In 1842 Harriet Farley and Harriot Curtis, one of her co-workers, took over its publication. Because it was solely a mill-hand publication it attracted wide-spread interest in this country and in England, where it came to the notice of Harriet Martineau and Charles Knight. It was discontinued in 1845 but started again by Harriet in 1847 under the new title, *The New England Offering*, with limited success. She herself did practically all the work involved in its publication, including even the sewing and cutting of the pages on occasion.

Harriet married John Intaglio Donlevy in 1854 and moved to New York. She lived to the age of ninety. Among her published works the most outstanding are *Happy Nights at Hazel Nook* and *Shells From the Strand of the Sea of Genius*, both of which are collections of articles and essays, many of which had appeared in the *Lowell Offering*. Except for their topical and historical value, her writings cannot be regarded as important literature.

Principal Works: Mind Amongst the Spindles. 1844; Shells From the Strand of the Sea of Genius, 1847; Happy Nights at Hazel Nook, 1852; Fancy's Frolics: or, Christmas Stories Told in a Happy Home in New England, 1880.

About: Becker, M. L. (ed.). Golden Tales of New England; Coburn, F. W. History of Lowell and Its People; Larcom, L. A New England Girlhood; Robinson, H. H. Loom and Spindle; Athenaeum August 28, 1841; August 17, 1844; Atlantic Monthly November 1881; Lowell Offering July, August 1845; Review of Reviews December 1907.

"FARMAN, ELLA." See PRATT, ELIZA ANNA (FARMAN)

FARMER, JOHN (June 12, 1789-August 13, 1838), antiquarian and genealogist, was born in Chelmsford, Mass. There he attended a private school until 1803, when his family moved to New Hampshire. Shortly afterward he started to work in a store, going to school when business was slack. He studied medicine but, because of his frail health, never practiced. In 1810 he started teaching, keeping it up for a few years with unusual success. But his greatest interest was in genealogy and local history. His first writing was a genealogy of his own family, published in 1813.

In 1821, Farmer moved to Concord, N.H., where he opened an apothecary store. In his spare time he continued his study of New Hampshire annals and New England genealogy, and his labors soon produced a number of books which won him considerable recognition among scholars. Dartmouth College gave him an honorary M.A. in 1822. The last year or two of his life he spent in examining, arranging, and indexing the state papers at Concord. Of his several works, *A Genealogical Register of the First Settlers of New England* is the most important.

Principal Works: An Ecclesiastical Register of New Hampshire, 1821; The New Military Guide, 1822; The New Hampshire Annual Register, 1822-38; Collections: Historical and Miscellaneous, 1822-24; A Gazetteer of the State of New Hampshire, 1823; A Genealogical Register of the First Settlers of New England, 1829; A Catechism of the History of New Hampshire, 1829; History of New Hampshire, 1831.

ABOUT: Le Bosquet, J. A Memorial . . . of John Farmer; American Quarterly Register February 1839; New-England Historical and Genealogical Register January 1847; Aegis August 22, 1838.

FARNHAM, ELIZA WOODSON (BURHANS) (November 17, 1815-December 15, 1864), philanthropist and miscellaneous writer, was born in Rensselaerville, N.Y. She was the daughter of Cornelius and Mary (Wood) Burhans. Mrs. Burhans died when Eliza was six, and the child was sent to live with an aunt. There she spent an unhappy childhood, and because of this, even at that early age, determined to try to decrease the misery in the world.

In 1835 she moved to Illinois, and a year later married Thomas Jefferson Farnham [*q.v.*]. In 1837 the Farnhams moved to New York, and in 1844, after four years of visiting prisons and lecturing to women, Mrs. Farnham received an appointment as matron of the female department of the state prison at Sing Sing. She stayed there till 1848, successfully proving her theory that prisoners respond to kindness. It was about this time that she published her first book, *Life in Prairie Land,* a book of travel and life in the West.

In 1849 she went to California after attempting to organize a group of women emigrants to accompany her. Although her project failed, it was favored by Horace Greeley, Henry Ward Beecher, and others. She spent several years in California trying to better the conditions of needy women.

Soon after her first husband's death in 1848, she married William Fitzpatrick, but retained the name of Farnham. She returned to New York in 1856, studied medicine for two years, and in 1859 founded a society to help indigent women to establish a home in the West. She personally conducted several groups to their new home.

She is best known for *Woman and Her Era,* in which she intelligently discussed vocations and intellectual interests for women. She also wrote two novels, popular in their time.

PRINCIPAL WORKS: Travel—Life in Prairie Land, 1846; California: Indoors and Out, 1856. *Essays*—Woman and Her Era, 1864. *Novels*—Eliza Woodson: or, The Early Days of One of the World's Workers, 1864; The Ideal Attained, 1865.

ABOUT: Burhans, S., Jr. Burhans Genealogy; New York Tribune December 16, 1864: New York Times December 18, 1864.

FARNHAM, THOMAS JEFFERSON (1804-September 13, 1848), lawyer and travel writer, was a native of Maine. Little is known of his antecedents or early life. He practised law in Peoria, Ill., for several years. In 1839, inspired by an Indian boy, he started West at the head of a group of nineteen men. With only four men still faithful, he crossed the Colorado Mountains and finally reached Fort Vancouver. He then visited the settlers on the Willamette, taking home with him a petition from them asking that Oregon be taken under United States protection. From there he went, via the Sandwich Islands, to California where he was instrumental in securing the release of English and American prisoners from the Mexican government. He returned to Illinois by way of Mexico and the Mississippi.

Following this trip he lived for a time in New York, but in 1846 or '47 moved to San Francisco, where he practiced law till his death.

His only claim to recognition as an author lay in his contributions to Far West geography. His most important book was *Travels in the Great Western Prairies, the Anahuac and Rocky Mountains, and in the Oregon Territory.* As a writer he was facile and interesting; as a man he had a forceful and charming personality. Eliza Woodson (Burhans) Farnham [*q.v.*] was his wife.

PRINCIPAL WORKS: Travels in the Great Western Prairies, the Anahuac and Rocky Mountains, and in the Oregon Territory, 1841; Life and Adventures in California, 1846.

ABOUT: Clarke, S. A. Pioneer Days of Oregon History; Thwaites, R. G. Early Western Travels; Californian September 16, 1848.

FARQUHARSON, MARTHA. See FINLEY, MARTHA FARQUHARSON

FAWCETT, EDGAR (May 26, 1847-May 2, 1904), poet, novelist, and playwright, was born in New York. His father, Frederick Fawcett, was an Englishman and a wealthy merchant; his mother was Sarah (Lawrence) Fawcett, an American. Fawcett began in early childhood to write prose and poetry, some of which was published. He attended Columbia College, and, although he made no mark there as a student, he acquired a reputation as a man of letters. He was a member of the Philolexian literary society and through it was known for his undergraduate literary activities. Three years after his graduation, in 1870, Columbia conferred on him an honorary M.A. degree.

Being financially independent, Fawcett devoted himself to writing. He proved to be very prolific and produced poetry, essays, novels and dramas. He had little talent as a poet, his work being too much influenced by the Victorian mode. A few short nature poems are among his best.

Fawcett produced an abundance of works in the field of fiction, his novels numbering about thirty-five. All of them, beginning with *Purple and Fine Linen* in 1873, aim to ridicule New York society, of which he had inside knowledge. His satire was to the point, but his plots were so amateurish, his characters so lifeless, his subjects so dull that they caused Henry Stoddard to remark, "Won't somebody please turn this Fawcett off?"

Fawcett filled his plays with the same social satire. Several of them, including *A False Friend,* were produced, meeting with everything from failure to moderate success. His gayest bit of writing was *The Buntling Ball,* a satirical verse play not intended for the stage.

Fawcett left this country when he was fifty, taking up his residence abroad. The last years of his life were spent in London, and it was there he died.

PRINCIPAL WORKS: *Poetry*—Fantasy and Passion, 1878; Song and Story, 1884; Romance and Revery, 1886; Songs of Doubt and Dream, 1891. *Novels*—Purple and Fine Linen, 1873; Tinkling Cymbals, 1884; The Adventures of a Widow, 1884; An Ambitious Woman, 1884; Rutherford, 1884; A Demoralizing Marriage, 1889; New York, 1898. *Essays*—Agnoticism and Other Essays, 1889. *Plays*—A False Friend, 1880; Our First Families, 1880; Americans Abroad, 1881; Sixes and Sevens, 1881; The Buntling Ball, 1884; The New King Arthur, 1885; The Earl, 1887.

ABOUT: Brown, T. A. A History of the New York Stage; Quinn, A. H. A History of the American Drama from the Civil War to the Present Day; New York Times January 22, 1880, October 6, 1881, May 3, 1904; New York World May 3, 1904; The Times (London) May 3, 1904.

FAY, THEODORE SEDGWICK (February 10, 1807-November 24, 1898), diplomat, poet, and miscellaneous writer, was born in New York, the son of Joseph Dewey Fay and Caroline (Broome) Fay. His father had studied law in the office of Alexander Hamilton and was a successful lawyer, who believed in doing away with imprisonment for debt. Theodore became a clerk in his father's office and was admitted to the bar in 1828. The same year, however, he became an editor, associated with G. P. Morris and N. P. Willis, of the New York *Mirror,* continuing a series of light essays, called "The Little Genius," which his father had started. These early *Mirror* articles were collected in *Dreams of Reveries of a Quiet Man.*

In 1833 he married Laura Gardenier and spent the next three years traveling in foreign countries. During this time he kept the *Mirror* supplied with sprightly travel sketches. His first novel, *Norman Leslie: A Tale of the Present Times,* published in 1835, was received with great applause by his literary friends in New York but was severely criticized by Edgar Allan Poe in the *Southern Literary Messenger.*

Fay spent the rest of his life in Europe, at first holding various diplomatic positions in London and Berlin. In 1853 he was made resident minister to Switzerland. Upon his retirement in 1861 he returned to Germany where he later died at ninety-one. He wrote until after he was eighty, turning his hand to both poetry and school books.

PRINCIPAL WORKS: *Novels*—Norman Leslie: A Tale of the Present Times, 1835; Sydney Clifton, 1839; The Countess Ida, 1840; Hoboken: A Romance, 1843. *Essays*—Dreams and Reveries of a Quiet Man, 1832. *Poetry*—Ulric: or, The Voices, 1851. *Miscellaneous*—A Great Outline of Geography, 1867; First Steps in Geography, 1873; Die Sklavenmacht: Blicke in die Geschichte der Vereinigten Staaten von Amerika, 1865; Die Alabama-Frage, 1872; The Three Germanys, 1889.

ABOUT: Beers, H. A. Nathaniel Parker Willis; Fay, O. P. Fay Genealogy; Fay, T. S. Statement and Account of the Death of His Wife; Griswold, R. W. Prose Writers of America, and Poets and Poetry of America; Mott, F. L. History of American Magazines 1741-1850; New York Evening Post November 25, 1898.

FELT, JOSEPH BARLOW (December 22, 1789-September 8, 1869), antiquarian, was born in Salem, Mass., the son of John Felt, a shipmaster, and Elizabeth (Curtis) Felt. After his father's death in 1802 Joseph went to work for a merchant. Reading biography in his spare time imbued him with the ambition for a college education, and, finally, in 1813, he was graduated from Dartmouth. He first taught and then studied for the ministry. In 1833, however, ill health forced him to retire after his second charge at Hamilton, Mass. While there he had acquired a reputation as an antiquarian and local historian. In 1834 he moved to Boston where, for three years, commissioned by the governor, he classified and arranged old state papers. He was a member and librarian of the Massachusetts Historical Society, and president, 1850-53, of the New England Historic Genealogical Society. In 1857 Dartmouth conferred on him the honorary degree of LL.D. His most outstanding work was an *Ecclesiastical History of New England.* He was married twice. A simple, pious man, his writings were distinguished more for careful research than for any facility of expression.

Principal Works: The Annals of Salem, 1827; History of Ipswich, Essex, and Hamilton, 1834; Historical Account of Massachusetts Currency, 1839; A Memoir, or Defense of Hugh Peters, 1851; Ecclesiastical History of New England, 1851 and 1862; The Customs of New England, 1853.

About: New-England Historical and Genealogical Register January 1870; Proceedings Massachusetts Historical Society 1876.

FELTON, CORNELIUS CONWAY (November 6, 1807-February 26, 1862), classical scholar and college president, was the son of Cornelius Conway Felton, Sr., and Anna (Morse) Felton of Newbury, Mass. He early showed an appetite for learning. Receiving his preliminary education in North Andover, he entered Harvard, graduating from there in 1827. Because of his meager means he was forced to teach while an undergraduate and continued teaching afterward. Beginning at Harvard as tutor in Latin, he rose to be Eliot professor of Greek literature, and finally, in 1860, was unanimously elected president of the college. Unfortunately he was in ill health when he accepted the presidency and lived only a little over a year afterward.

His principal service to literature was in editing classical texts and selections from Greek writers. He studied extensively in Greece. He was interested in modern as well as classical Greek. His two outstanding works—*Greece: Ancient and Modern* and *Familiar Letters From Europe*—were both published several years after his death. The former was his most popular work, consisting of four courses of lectures given before the Lowell Institute in Boston. Noted for his breadth of intellectual interests, he kept a keen eye on all aspects of student life and acted always with great tact. He was a gifted and eloquent orator.

Principal Works: Familiar Letters From Europe, 1866; Greece: Ancient and Modern, 1867.

About: Felton, C[yrus]. A Genealogical History of the Felton Family.

FENNELL, JAMES (December 11, 1766-June 13, 1816), actor and playwright, was born in London. His father, John Fennell, was connected with the navy; his mother was formerly a Miss Brady. He attended Eton and later Trinity College, Cambridge. After gay student days he took up law. Soon afterward, however, he contracted heavy gambling debts and decided to try his luck on the stage. His first rôle, in Edinburgh in 1787, was that of Othello, a part which he played many times during his career.

In 1792 he married Miss B. H. Porter and in 1793 signed a contract with Thomas Wignell to play at the Chestnut Street Theatre in Philadelphia. There he was cordially received, both as an actor and by the social world. He soon discovered he was living beyond his income, and to recoup his fortunes he undertook a wild scheme to manufacture salt from ocean water. This project soon failed and he returned to the stage. In 1797, Fennell made his first appearance—and a very successful one—in New York. He played there most of the time between 1800 and 1806. Finally, worn out from dissipation, he said good-bye to the stage in 1814 in Philadelphia.

Fennell was at one time one of the best known tragedians in America, and had he seriously cultivated his histrionic talents he might have risen to the top of his profession. He was always popular as an actor and could count on playing to large audiences. As a writer he is best known for his five-act comedy, *Lindor and Clara: or, The British Officer,* and for *Apology,* a curious record of his life.

Principal Works: Lindor and Clara: or, the British Officer, 1791; A Review of the Proceedings at Paris During the Last Summer, 1792; An Apology for the Life of James Fennell, 1814.

About: Baker, D. E. & others. Biographia Dramatica; Bernard, J. Retrospections of America; Clapp, W. W. A Record of the Boston Stage; Dunlap, W. A History of the American Theatre; Fennell, J. An Apology for the Life of James Fennell; Odell, G. C. D. Annals of the N. Y. Stage; Wood, W. B. Personal Recollections of the Stage.

FENOLLOSA, ERNEST FRANCISCO (February 18, 1853-September 21, 1908), poet and student of oriental art, was born in Salem, Mass., the son of Manuel Francisco Ciriaco Fenollosa, a versatile Spanish musician, and Mary (Silsbee) Fenollosa, of Colonial (Massachusetts) ancestry. He attended Hacker Grammar School and Salem High School before entering Harvard, from which he was graduated in 1874 with "higher honors" in philosophy. Becoming interested in the new "art movement" at the Boston Museum, he left the Divinity School at Cambridge, and, in 1878 was sent to the University of Tokio to teach political economy, philosophy, and logic.

Fenollosa became increasingly absorbed in the study of Japanese art in relation to its people, and by 1885 his recommendation that "purely Japanese art, with use of Japanese ink, brush, and paper, be re-introduced into all schools" was approved by a special board. In July 1886, a month after his fifth consecutive reappointment to the Chair of Philosophy, in the University, he was sent as a Fine Arts Commissioner to Europe to study contemporary trends. He returned to the United States in 1890 to become curator of oriental art at the Boston Museum, in 1892 began an extensive lecture series on oriental history, literature, and art, and the following year published *East and West: The Discovery of America and Other Poems.* From 1897-1900 he lived in Tokio; returning to the United States, he continued his lectures and wrote a rough draft of *Epochs of Chinese and Japanese Art,* which was edited by his wife after his death. It is an exhaustive and illuminating account, but necessarily inaccurate, for many identifications, etc., were known only to its author.

Ezra Pound, the poet, was named Fenollosa's literary executor and wrote his *Cathay* (1915), poetic translations, from the notes of Fenollosa. He also edited Fenollosa's *Certain Noble Plays of Japan*; *Noh: or, Accomplishment: A Study of the Classical Stage of Japan*; and *The Chinese Written Character as a Medium for Poetry.* They are rare remnants of Japanese culture, and though sometimes unintelligible to Occidentals, are, on the whole, scholarly and lucid.

In the Western world Fenollosa's *Epochs* made him an authoritative exponent of oriental art; he was thrice decorated by the Mikado, and of his influence on Eastern civilization itself Pound says: "It may be an exaggeration to say that he had saved Japanese art for Japan, but it is certain that he had done as much as any one man could have to set the native art in its rightful preeminence and to stop the aping of Europe."

E. F. FENOLLOSA

PRINCIPAL WORKS: *Poetry*—East and West: The Discovery of America and Other Poems, 1893. *Critical studies* (edited by Ezra Pound)—Certain Noble Plays of Japan, 1916; Noh: or, Accomplishment . . . , 1916; The Chinese Written Character as a Medium for Poetry, 1920; (compiled by Mary Fenollosa) Epochs of Chinese and Japanese Art, 1912.

ABOUT: Fenollosa, E. F. Epochs of Chinese and Japanese Art (see Preface); Pound's introductions and notes, in the works.

"FERN, FANNY." See PARTON, SARAH PAYSON (WILLIS)

FERNOW, BERTHOLD (November 28, 1837-March 3, 1908), historian, archivist, and editor, was born in Inowrazlaw, Posen, Germany, son of Edward F. Fernow and Bertha (von Jackmann) Fernow. He was privately tutored, and later studied at the gymnasiums at Magdeburg and Bromberg. He was tremendously interested in agriculture and finally emigrated to America where he bought a farm in Iowa. He served in the Civil War on the Union side and was later, for ten years, engaged in commerce in New York and Berlin. In 1874 he again bought a farm, this time in New Jersey. A year later he was appointed keeper of historical records for New York state and from then on led a scholarly life. From 1882-89 he was connected with the University of the State of New York, and it was during this time that he wrote *Albany and Its Place in the History of the United States.* After 1889 he devoted himself to private research. He never married.

PRINCIPAL WORKS: Documents Relating to the Colonial History of the State of New York 1877-83; Albany and Its Place in the History of the United States, 1886; The Ohio Valley in Colonial Days, 1890; New Amsterdam Family Names and Their Origin, 1898.

FESSENDEN, THOMAS GREEN (April 22, 1771-November 11, 1837), journalist and poet, was born at Walpole, N.H., the son of the Rev. Thomas Fessenden, himself an author in a small way, and of Elizabeth (Kendall) Fessenden. He was educated at Dartmouth, where he earned his way by teaching and by conducting singing schools. He was graduated, as valedictorian of his class, in 1796. Already he had contributed satirical verse, under his lifelong pseudonym of "Dr. Caustic," to college and general magazines.

He studied law, was admitted to the bar and began practice at Rutland, Vt. In 1801 however, he left his profession to go to

THOMAS G. FESSENDEN

England in search of patent rights for a hydraulic machine which was a failure and, apparently, fraudulent. Fessenden remained in England to exploit other inventions, but succeeded only in bankrupting himself. One of his interests was Elisha Perkins' "metallic tractors," a quack extension of mesmerism, which inspired his *Terrible Tractoration.*

Finally he returned to America, and after a short stay in Philadelphia, became editor (1806-07) of a Federalist magazine, the *Weekly Inspector,* in New York. The next year he moved to Brattleboro, Vt., where he returned to the law and also edited the Brattleboro *Reporter* in 1815 and 1816, and the Bellows Falls *Intelligencer* from 1817 to 1822. In 1813 he had married Lydia Tuttle.

In 1822 Fessenden went to Boston, his home thenceforth, and for the remainder of his life was editor of the *New England Farmer* and of two other agricultural journals, much of his spare time being given to the introduction of silk culture in New England. His old interest in invention also revived, his principal invention being a portable hot water stove. In 1835 and 1836 he was Whig representative from Boston in the Massachusetts General Court. In his last years Hawthorne was a lodger in his house, and a member of Fessenden's family is supposed to have been the original of Hester Pyncheon in *The House of the Seven Gables.*

Fessenden was called by his fellow-countrymen "the American Butler" (the allusion being to Samuel Butler, author of *Hudibras*); but actually he was constantly guilty of a coarseness and scurrility which Butler would have scorned. *Democracy Unveiled,* his principal satirical work, consists largely of libelous attacks on the private lives of Jefferson and other leaders among the Democrats. Outside of satire, his best known poem is "Jonathan's Courtship," which provided the inspiration for Lowell's well known poem, "The Courtin'." For lack of a better candidate, he has been hailed as the chief American satirist between Freneau and Lowell; but he is quite inferior to either of them. Fessenden's ardently Federalist verse has no good humor about it, but is bitter, angry, and intolerant.

PRINCIPAL WORKS: *Poetry*—Terrible Tractoration, 1803; Original Poems, 1804; Democracy Unveiled, 1805; Pills: Poetical, Political and Philosophical, 1809. *Prose*—Essay on the Law of Patents, 1810; American Clerk's Companion, 1815; Miniature Bible, 1816; The Ladies' Monitor, 1818; Laws of Patents for New Inventions, 1822.

ABOUT: Hawthorne, N. Fanshawe and Other Pieces; Perrin, P. G. Life and Works of Thomas Green Fessenden; Boston Advertiser November 13, 1837.

FIELD, EUGENE (September 2, 1850-November 4, 1895), poet, humorist, and story writer, was born in St. Louis. Field himself gave his birthday as September 3, but a family Bible discovered in 1937 gives the correct date. His parents, both Vermonters, were Roswell Martin Field, a lawyer, and Frances (Reed) Field. The mother died in 1856, and Eugene and his older brother Roswell [*q.v.*] were sent to her cousin in Amherst, Mass. There he was educated at a private school in Monson, Mass., and for two years, 1868 and 1869, studied at Williams College. In the latter year his father died, and he went with his guardian to Knox College, Galesburg, Ill. The next year he followed his brother to the University of Missouri, and thereafter always considered himself a Westerner—born and bred.

Field did not finish college, but after an abortive attempt to be an actor took all of his $8000 inheritance from his parents that was available, and spent it in a tour of southern Europe, in 1872. On his return, in 1873, he married Julia Sutherland Comstock, to whom he had become engaged in 1871, when she was only fourteen. The remainder of his patrimony he spent on his honeymoon; money always slipped lightly from his hands. In spite of the bride's youth, she made an excellent wife, bore five sons and three daughters, and survived to 1936.

Collection of Frederick H. Meserve
EUGENE FIELD

His money gone, Field went to work on the editorial staff of various newspapers—the St. Joseph *Gazette* in 1875-76; the St. Louis *Journal* and *Times-Journal* from 1876 to 1880; the Kansas City *Times* in 1880 and 1881; and the Denver *Tribune* from 1881 to 1883. In 1883 he went to the Chicago *Morning News,* re-named the *Record* after 1890, and here he remained for the rest of his life. Even in 1889 and 1890, when he was obliged to travel in Europe to regain his failing health, he sent in his copy regularly. He was one of the earliest of the columnists, and his "Sharps and Flats" department was nationally famous. He lived in Buena Park, a suburb of Chicago, where he built his house, called the "Sabine Farm" in memory of his beloved Horace. There he died in his sleep, from heart failure, at forty-five.

Old time Chicago newspaper men still remember Field's tall, reedy form, his pale face, his bald head, and his deep-set blue eyes. They also remember his inveterate practical jokes, not always funny to the victim, and his eccentricities of speech, dress, and conduct. Beneath this boisterous exterior, however, there was a genuine if slight poet, capable of sentiment without sentimentality, whimsical and subtle humor true pathos, and no small amount of erudition. His hobbies were Horace and book-collecting, and he rode both of them in the pages of "Sharps and Flats." He seemed to have a sort of embarrassment before his serious work, and many of his best poems were published by him as the work of palpably unlikely celebrities whom he admired. His stories were less successful than his verse, sometimes crossing the border-line between fancy and silliness. Another of his literary faults was the affected use of real and artificial dialects, especially of a kind of seventeenth century English never actually heard on any living tongue.

But much may be forgiven the man who wrote "Wynken, Blynken, and Nod" and "Little Boy Blue," the latter one of the most affecting child poems in the language. While people still love children, he has a firm memorial in their responsive hearts.

Principal Works: *Poetry*—Tribune Primer, 1882; Culture's Garland, 1887; A Little Book of Western Verse, 1889; Echoes From the Sabine Farm (with R. M. Field) 1892; With Trumpet and Drum, 1892; Second Book of Verse, 1892; Love Songs of Children, 1894; Lullaby Land, 1897. *Stories*—A Little Book of Profitable Tales, 1890; The Holy Cross and Other Tales, 1893; Dibdin's Ghost, 1893; Second Book of Tales, 1896; Love Affairs of a Bibliomaniac, 1896. *Miscellaneous*—Facts, Confessions, and Observations, 1894; Auto-Analysis, 1896.

About: Dennis, C. H. Eugene Field's Creative Years; Field, E. Auto-Analysis; Field, E. Writings in Prose and Verse (see Introduction by R. M. Field to 1911 ed.); Thompson, S. Eugene Field: A Study in Heredity and Contradictions; Thompson, S. Life of Eugene Field; Wilson, F. The Eugene Field I Knew.

FIELD, MAUNSELL BRADHURST (March 26, 1822-January 24, 1875), lawyer, poet, and miscellaneous writer, was born in Peekskill, N.Y., the son of Moses Field and Susan Kittredge (Osgood) Field. He entered Yale in 1837, graduating in 1841 with honors. Because of ill health he set out in 1843 for a tour of Europe, Asia Minor, and Egypt. Upon his return he studied law, and was admitted to the bar in 1848, but, being financially independent, he soon gave it up and returned to Europe in 1854. While there he acted in various diplomatic capacities, and was the first American to receive the Cross of the Legion of Honor from Napoleon.

In 1861 Field became deputy assistant treasurer of the United States in New York, and was later promoted to be assistant secretary of the Treasury at Washington He resigned from this position in 1865 because of ill health, was then appointed collector of internal revenue for the district of New York, and in 1873 was made a judge in New York. He had a keen legal mind unusual financial abilities, and in his various civil capacities enjoyed a reputation of great efficiency. He also possessed marked literary ability and collaborated with the English novelist G. P. R. James in writing *Adrian, or, The Clouds of the Mind.* He is best known, however, for his reminiscences, *Memories of Many Men and of Some Women,* which are written in a gay, delightful style. He had great tact and natural charm of manner, and was a brilliant speaker.

PRINCIPAL WORKS: Adrian: or, The Clouds of the Mind, 1852; Les Hommes Rouges de l'Amérique du Nord, 1855; Memories of Many Men and of Some Women, 1874.

ABOUT: Alexander, De A. S. A Political History of the State of N.Y.; Field, M. B. Memories of Many Men and of Some Women; McAdam, D. & others. History of the Bench and Bar of N.Y.; Pierce, F. C. Field Genealogy; Semi-Centennial Historical and Biographical Record of the Class of 1841 in Yale University.

FIELD, ROSWELL MARTIN (September 1, 1851-January 10, 1919), novelist and journalist, brother of Eugene Field [*q.v.*], was born in St. Louis, of New England descent, his parents being Roswell Martin Field and Frances (Reed) Field. He was educated at Phillips Exeter Academy and the University of Missouri, and later studied law with his uncle in Vermont. Oliver Cromwell was his hero from early youth and his serious views greatly influenced Field thoughout life. In fact, he was so serious-minded that, despite his great affection for his brother, Eugene, he felt forced to criticize him for his perpetual humor.

In 1869, on the death of his father, Field acquired an independent income and soon after took up journalism, working on papers in San Francisco, Kansas City, St. Louis, Chicago, and New York. For about fourteen years he wrote a column called "Lights and Shadows" for the New York *Post,* retiring about six years before his death.

In 1891 he began publishing books, some in collaboration with his brother and wife, including stories, plays for children, and novelettes. He was best known for *In Sunflower Land, Stories of God's Own Country,* a series of sketches about Missouri and Kansas, and for *The Bondage of Ballinger,* a conventional novelette. Some contemporary critics preferred his work to his brother's; but the writings of Eugene Field live today, while those of Roswell Martin Field are all but forgotten.

PRINCIPAL WORKS: In Sunflower Land, Stories of God's Own Country, 1892; A Little Book of Western Verse, 1896; The Muses Up to Date, 1897; The Romance of an Old Fool, 1902; The Bondage of Bullinger, 1903; Little Miss Dee, 1904; Madeline, 1906.

ABOUT: Field, C. K. Genealogical History of the Family of the Late General Martin Field; Thompson, S. Life of Eugene Field; New York Times January 11, 1919.

FIELD, THOMAS WARREN (1821-November 25, 1881), essayist, was born at Onondaga Hill, N.Y. His father was a small tradesman and Thomas received only an elementary education. Starting as a teacher, however, he had a long varied career. In 1844 he moved to New York and became an engineer. He was subsequently florist, surveyor, and teacher in rapid succession, and in 1849 was made principal of a public school in Brooklyn. Soon afterward, having become financially independent through fortunate real estate investments, he retired and took up the cultivation of fruit. He was an assessor from 1865 to 1873, and from then till his death was superintendent of public instruction in Brooklyn. He was a member of the Board of Education for twenty-one years.

In 1848 he published his first work—a small volume of verse, *The Minstrel Pilgrim*—which shows the romantic influence. He edited and wrote many other works, including *The Schoolmistress in History, Poetry, and Romance.* He possessed a valuable library on American Indians which he was finally forced to sell because of financial reverses. He was married four times, his last wife surviving him.

PRINCIPAL WORKS: The Minstrel Pilgrim, 1848; Pear Culture, 1858; Historic and Antiquarian Scenes in Brooklyn and Its Vicinity, 1868; Relation of Alvar Nuñez Cabeça de Vaca, 1871; An Essay Towards an Indian Bibliography, 1873; The Schoolmistress in History, Poetry and Romance, 1874.

ABOUT: American Bibliopolist June 1875; New York Times November 26, 1881; New York Tribune May 24, 26, 1875 and November 26, 1881.

FIELDS, ANNIE (ADAMS) (June 6, 1834-January 5, 1915), poet, diarist-biographer, and literary hostess, was born in Boston, the daughter of Zabdiel Boylston Adams, a prominent physician, and Sarah May (Holland) Adams. She was carefully educated at home and at George B. Emerson's school. At the age of twenty she married James T. Fields [*q.v.*], the distinguished publisher, seventeen years her senior. During their sojourn in Europe, 1859-60, Mrs. Fields kept a diary, but it was not until 1863, when she became strongly aware of the wealth of inimitable personalities who were being drawn to her casual Charles Street salon, that she began to keep a full journal. "What a strange history this literary life in America . . . would make," she wrote in the first pages of her "blue-books." "An editor and publisher at once . . . stands at a confluence of tides where all humanity seems to surge up in little waves. . ." Dr. Oliver Wendell Holmes had taken a house on the same street, and Thomas Bailey Aldrich, for a time, lived just across the way. Not only Hawthorne, Whittier, and Lowell, but Dickens, whose second American journey (1867-68) was the result of Mr. Fields' efforts, and Bret Harte, whose "strong language of the West" and whose Argonaut sympathies she could take in good spirit, valued the hospitality of this gay and intellectual hostess.

Her husband, jovial and invariably Scotch-tweeded, a veritable manufacturer of literary reputations, exchanged his influential publishing business, in 1871, for the more sedentary life of a writer and occasional lecturer. His health was fast failing and he died in April 1881. Shortly afterwards Mrs. Fields set about the preparation of *James T. Fields: Biographical Notes and Personal Sketches,* and in this labor filled many grievously emptied hours. She continued her active part in the establishment of coffee houses for the poor, and worked unstintingly for the Associated Charities.

Sarah Orne Jewett [*q.v.*], already the author of four books, had come to Boston from a Maine village of dignified tradition, and her friendship with Mrs. Fields was deeply founded on the most compatible of intellectual tastes. In 1882 they went abroad together, and they were companions for the remainder of their lives.

Mrs. Fields' writings fall, in the main, into two classes: several volumes of verse—*Under the Olive, The Singing Shepherd and Other Poems,* and *Orpheus: A Masque*—most of which bore strong traces of a Grecian spirit; and prose works which are direct amplifications of the pages of her sprightly journals. M. A. DeWolfe Howe edited an excellent selection from the less familiar passages of her blue-books, under the title *Memories of a Hostess* (1922).

ANNIE ADAMS FIELDS

Her life and the pre-war era of "museum pieces" drew to a close together. Henry James best placed her in the literary scene when he said: "All her implications were gay, since no one so finely sentimental could be noted as so humorous; just as no feminine humor was perhaps ever so unmistakingly directed, and no state of amusement . . . ever so merciful."

Principal Works: *Verse*—Under the Olive, 1880; The Singing Shepherd and Other Poems, 1895; Orpheus: A Masque, 1900. *Prose*—James T. Fields: Biographical Notes and Personal Sketches, 1881; Whittier: Notes of His Life and of His Friendship, 1893; A Shelf of Old Books, 1894; Authors and Friends, 1896; Life and Letters of Harriet Beecher Stowe, 1897; Nathaniel Hawthorne (in Beacon Biographies), 1899; Charles Dudley Warner, 1909; Letters of Sarah Orne Jewett, 1911.

About: Brooks, Van W. The Flowering of New England; Howe, M. A. DeW. Memories of a Hostess: A Chronicle of Eminent Friendships Drawn Chiefly From the Diaries of Mrs. James T. Fields; Boston Transcript January 5, 6, 1915.

FIELDS, JAMES THOMAS (December 31, 1817-April 24, 1881), publisher, biographer, and poet, was born in Portsmouth, N.H. His father, a shipmaster, was lost at sea when the boy was four. He was graduated from the Portsmouth High School in 1830, when he was only twelve, and at sixteen set out for Boston to earn his living and help his widowed mother. He secured work in a book store and publishing house, starting at the same time to write for the local newspapers. By 1839, when he was twenty-one, he was made a junior partner, and the firm's name was changed from Ticknor & Reed to Ticknor, Reed & Fields. After 1854 the name of Reed was dropped. Gradually Fields, who became senior partner and in time the entire firm, built it up into the foremost publishing house of its day, analogous to Murray's in England. Fields was the presiding genius of the famous "Old Corner Bookstore" in Boston, across whose threshhold passed the footsteps of all the most famous New England writers of the great age.

Ticknor and Fields published the works of most of the best known American and English authors of the period. In 1859 the firm acquired the *Atlantic Monthly,* and in 1861 Fields succeeded Lowell as editor, serving until 1870, when he retired from business.

Collection of Frederick H. Meserve
JAMES T. FIELDS

Fields' European, and especially his English, connections were many and close. Between 1847 and 1869 he made four trips to Europe, and he was on intimate terms with most of the literary figures of Great Britain and the Continent. His bearded, smiling face and his stocky figure were familiar wherever writers gathered. Yet actually he was a shy man, reluctant to meet strangers. He had, however, a great gift for friendship, and marked personal charm. He was an early member of the famous Saturday Club, to which Emerson, Hawthorne, Lowell, Longfellow, and Holmes belonged. After his retirement from business, he became a popular reader and lecturer on literary topics.

Fields had been engaged to Mary Willard, who died. In 1850 he married her younger sister, Eliza Josephine, whose life ended soon afterwards. In 1854 he married her cousin, Annie Adams [*q.v.*], who survived him; they conducted the first real American salon. Van Wyck Brooks has given a vivid picture of the Fields ménage in *The Flowering of New England*; to their drawing-room came every local and visiting celebrity, writers chiefly but men and women famed in other fields as well. After Fields died his widow continued her receptions until her own death in 1915. Her husband, who was much her senior, had predeceased her by thirty-four years; he died of angina pectoris after a long illness.

In addition to his original writing, Fields edited, with E. P. Whipple, the *Family Library of British Poetry*. He was a publisher of rare discrimination, and as an editor he was fully as competent as his famous predecessor, keeping the *Atlantic Monthly* up to the high standards set by Lowell. His verse was competent but undistinguished. His volumes of biography and reminiscence are valuable because of his close acquaintance with his subjects. But primarily he was an enzyme in the social body, a focusing point for all that was best in contemporary American culture, and a true "educator of the public."

PRINCIPAL WORKS: *Poetry*—Poems, 1849; A Few Verses for a Few Friends, 1858; Underbrush, 1877; Ballads and Other Verses, 1881. *Prose*—Yesterdays With Authors, 1872; Hawthorne, 1876; In and Out of Doors With Charles Dickens, 1876.

ABOUT: Brooks, Van W. The Flowering of New England; Fields, A. A. James Thomas Fields: Biographical Notes and Personal Sketches; McCabe, J. D., Jr. Great Fortunes and How They Were Made; Atlantic Monthly August 1881, July 1915; Boston Transcript April 25, 1881.

"FIGARO." See CLAPP, HENRY, JR.

FILSON, JOHN (c.1747-October 1788), explorer, cartographer, and historian, was born in East Fallowfield in southwestern Pennsylvania. The date of his birth is unknown, but he was the son of Davison Filson and the grandson of John Filson, an English immigrant. Little is known of him before his arrival in Kentucky in 1783 where he went for the purpose of taking up land. Not long after his arrival he acquired several thousand acres of land and because of that he wrote *Discovery, Settlement, and Present State of Kentucke* with the apparent purpose of attracting settlers to Kentucky in order to increase the value of property. This famous book, the first history of Kentucky, is written in a vivid, colorful style, but many of its historieal facts are fallacious. "The Adventures of Col. Daniel Boon" is found in an appendix to the book. Although written in the first person, it is apparent from its pedantic style that Filson, not Boone, wrote it. It was this account that first made Boone famous in Western history. The volume also included the first map of Kentucky, which is remarkably accurate and for which Filson is chiefly famous. Because there were no printing presses in Kentucky, Filson was forced to go to Wilmington, Del., and have his book published there. It was later translated into French and also published in England. Few copies are still in existence, and they are extremely valuable.

During the next four years Filson did some fur trading, surveyed in Illinois, and made several trips east to Pennsylvania. Finally in 1788, while surveying on the Little Miami, he was killed by an Indian.

PRINCIPAL WORKS: Discovery, Settlement, and Present State of Kentucke, 1784.

ABOUT: Durrett, R. T. John Filson: The First Historian of Kentucky; Phillips, P. L. The First Map of Kentucky.

FINCH, FRANCIS MILES (June 9, 1827-July 31, 1907), jurist and poet, was born in Ithaca, N.Y., the son of Miles and Tryphena (Farling) Finch. He was educated at Ithaca Academy, and received his B.A. at Yale in 1849, having been class poet and editor of the *Yale Magazine*. He received an honorary LL.D. from Hamilton College in 1880, and from Yale in 1889. After his graduation he studied law in Ithaca and practiced there. In 1853 he married Eliza Brooke, who died in 1892. In 1869 he was internal revenue collector of New York, and from 1880 to 1896 associate judge of the New York Court of Appeals. A close friend of Ezra Cornell, when Cornell University was founded by Andrew D. White in 1868, he became much interested in it, and, from the foundation of its College of Law, in 1887, was non-resident lecturer. He became dean of the College of Law in 1892, and was also professor of the history and evolution of law from 1896 to 1903. In 1899 he was president of the New York State Bar Association.

His legal and judicial career competed with his interest in and aptitude for poetry; he was, indeed, invited to teach rhetoric and literature at Cornell but felt that he was unfitted by his years of absorption in the law. His verses he called "only incidents along the line of a busy and laborious life." They were not published until after his death. The best known, besides many college songs still sung, are "Nathan Hale," and above all "The Blue and the Gray," first published in the *Atlantic Monthly* in 1867, and inspired by his hearing that the women of Corinth, Miss., were decorating the graves of both Union and Confederate soldiers. The poem immediately became very popular, and now constitutes Finch's chief claim to celebrity.

PRINCIPAL WORK: The Blue and the Gray and Other Verses, 1909.

ABOUT: Finch, F. M. The Blue and the Gray (see Preliminary Word by A. D. White); New York Evening Post July 31, 1907; New York Times August 1, 1907.

FINLEY, MARTHA FARQUHARSON ("Martha Farquharson") (April 26, 1828-January 30, 1909), novelist and juvenile writer, the creator of "Elsie Dinsmore," was born at Chillicothe, Ohio, the daughter of Dr. James Brown Finley and Maria Theresa (Brown) Finley, who were first cousins. When she was a baby her parents moved to Circleville, Ohio, and when she was six to South Bend, Ind. She was educated in private schools there and in Philadelphia. From 1851 to 1853 she taught school in Indiana country towns, and in the latter year taught in Phoenixville, Pa. She then returned to Philadelphia, where she became connected with the Presbyterian Publication Committee, and began an interminable series of Sunday School books for them. In 1876 she bought a home in Elkton, Md., where the remainder of her life was passed. Nearly all her books were written under the name of "Martha Farquharson"; "Farquharson" being the Gaelic for "Finley."

It will be seen that Martha Finley's life was even less eventful than that of her best-known heroine, Elsie Dinsmore, for Elsie at least became a mother and a grandmother. The private life of Elsie's creator was one of extreme inconspicuousness, devoted entirely to writing, quiet domesticity, and church activities. Her novels for adult readers had small success in their own time, and have long been forgotten. Mildred, her other juvenile subject, never mustered more than a modicum of Elsie's devotees. Miss Finley as a writer must stand or fall with Elsie Dinsmore.

A doctorate in psychology might be earned by a thesis on the Elsie books. It is difficult to understand how even Victorian children could be persuaded to swallow this compound of sentimentality and masochism and clamor for more, up to twenty-eight volumes. Obedience, piety, and smugness are the keynotes of the whole twenty-eight, and Elsie, eternally "bursting into tears," would seem to a present-day child what she is, a nauseous little prig; her dear papa a tyrant of the type of Mrs. Browning's father, with trimmings that make him the silliest sort of caricature of the stock "Southern gentleman"; while Mr. Travilla, who plays "stooge" to Mr. Dinsmore in the earlier volumes and obligingly marries Elsie, fathers her children, and then even more obligingly dies so that she can be reunited with her adored—and converted—father, is a mere cardboard shadow of a man. A breath of fresh air would have blown the whole lot down. Elsie cannot even be compared to Ellen of Susan Warner's *The Wide, Wide*

MARTHA FINLEY

World; for Ellen, though also a pious prig, has charm and life, and the homely detail of Miss Warner's book enthralls the literal mind of the child.

There seems, indeed, to have been no excuse for the immense and long-continuing sale of the Elsie books or of Miss Finley's other juvenile stories; no reason why, forty years after their inception, they should still have outsold any other juveniles except Louisa May Alcott's (which are, of course, in a different category)—and yet that was the case. It is only within the present century that children have stopped reading about Elsie, weeping over her, and perhaps praying for her. The secret of her success lay hidden within the mind of the quiet little old lady with spectacles, a rather grim mouth, and soft, primly arranged white hair. One wonders if after all it was the children who made Elsie's and, in lesser degree, Mildred's, public. Could it have been the parents who chose and insinuated the books, as inculcations of a Victorian ideal? Certainly when the children exposed to Elsie grew up to be parents themselves, confronted with a clear-eyed and realistic brood of youngsters hungry for stronger stuff, the sale of the Elsie books slumped suddenly, never again to be revived.

Principal Works: *Juveniles*—Cassella: or, The Children of the Valleys, 1867; The Elsie Books (28 vols.) 1868-1905; An Old Fashioned Boy, 1870; Our Fred: or, Seminary Life at Thurston, 1874; The Mildred Books (7 vols.) 1878-1894; Twiddletewit: A Fairy Tale, 1898. *Novels*—Wanted: A Pedigree, 1870; Signing the Contract and What It Cost, 1878; The Thorn in the Nest, 1880; The Tragedy of Wild River Valley, 1893.

About: Rutherford, M. American Authors; Willard, F. E. & Livermore, M. A. American Women; Bookman October 1927; Baltimore Sun January 31, 1909.

FINN, HENRY JAMES WILLIAM (June 17, 1787-January 13, 1840), actor and playwright, was born in Sydney, Nova Scotia, but grew up in New York City. He was the son of George Finn, a retired British naval officer, and of Elizabeth Finn. He was educated at Traphagen's Academy, Hackensack, N.J., and Finley's Latin School, Newark, and later studied law in New York. After that he went to England where he joined a band of strolling players, finally playing small parts at the Haymarket Theatre, London, in 1811 and 1812. His first recorded appearance in America was in Philadelphia in 1817. The next year he played in New York, the first of many appearances there. From 1818 to 1821 he acted in Savannah, but, becoming restless, he returned to England where he did miniature painting and acting, finally securing a leading rôle at the Surrey Theatre, London. In 1822 he became connected with the Federal Street Theatre, Boston. It was at this time that he turned to eccentric comedy, in which he was extremely successful. In 1825 he wrote a play, *Montgomery: or, The Falls of Montmorency*. This was produced in Boston, and, although very poor as a play, it gave its author an opportunity to show his skill at comic acting. He remained with the Boston company until his death, but made many trips playing throughout the country, especially in the South, where he was very popular. He died on his way home from a Southern trip when the steamboat "Lexington" burnt in Long Island Sound.

Principal Works: Montgomery: or, The Falls of Montmorency, 1825; Removing the Deposits, 1835; Casper Hauser: or, The Down Easter, 1835.

About: Clapp, W. W. A Record of the Boston Stage; Ireland, J. N. Records of N. Y. Stage; Ludlow, N. M. Dramatic Life as I Found It; Smith, S. F. Theatrical Management in the West and South; Wood, W. B. Personal Recollections of the Stage.

FISHER, GEORGE PARK (August 10, 1827-December 20, 1909), theologian and historian, was born in Wrentham, Mass., the son of Lewis Whiting Fisher and Nancy (Fisher) Fisher. After his graduation from Brown University in 1847 he studied at Yale Divinity School, Auburn Theological Seminary, and—most unusual for students at that time—in Germany for two years, 1852-54.

In 1854 he accepted a position at Yale as Livingston professor of divinity and pastor of the college church. In 1860 he married Adelina Louisa Forbes, by whom he had three children, and in 1861 accepted a professorship of ecclesiastical history in the Divinity School. He taught there for forty years, holding the position of dean, as well, for several years; from 1901 until his death he was associated with the school as emeritus professor. He was honored with the degree of D.D. by Brown University in 1886, by Princeton in 1897, and by Harvard and the University of Edinburgh in 1886; an LL.D. was conferred on him by Princeton in 1879. His published sermons, essays, and histories—among them, *Outlines of Universal History*—all bespeak a broad-minded and liberal viewpoint and an impartial judgment, though none of his writing had lasting value.

Principal Works: History of the Church in Yale College, 1858; National Faults, 1860; Thoughts Pertinent to the Present Crisis, 1861; Essays on the Supernatural Origin of Christianity, 1865; Life of Benjamin Silliman, 1866; The Reformation, 1873; The Beginnings of Christianity, 1877; Faith and Rationalism, 1879; Discussions in History and Theology, 1880; The Christian Religion, 1882; The Grounds of Theistic and Christian Belief, 1883; Outlines of Universal History, 1885; History of the Christian Church, 1887; Manual of Christian Evidences, 1890; The Colonial Era, 1892; A Brief History of the Nations, 1896; History of Christian Doctrine, 1896; An Unpublished Essay of Edwards on the Trinity, 1903.

About: Fisher, P. A. The Fisher Genealogy; Brown Alumni Monthly June 1902, January 1910; Nation December 23, 1909; Outlook January 1, 1910; Yale Divinity Quarterly January 1910; Hartford Daily Courant December 22, 1909.

FISKE, JOHN (March 30, 1842-July 4, 1901), philosopher and historian, was originally named Edmund Fisk Green. He was born at Hartford, Conn., the only child of Edmund Brewster Green and Mary Fisk (Bound) Green. The parents' marriage does not seem to have been very happy; the father, a newspaper editor, finally died in Panama in 1852. The boy was reared by his grandparents, as his mother was busy teaching in New York and Newark; when she remarried, he remained with her parents and in 1855 he legally adopted the name of his great-grandfather, John Fisk. The "e" he added five years later.

He was a very precocious child, who by the time he was eight had read some two hundred serious works, some in Spanish, and by the time he was twenty had a good reading knowledge of eight languages and was more or less familiar with ten others. He attended the Betts Academy, in Stamford, Conn., and entered Harvard as a sophomore

Collection of Frederick H. Meserve

JOHN FISKE

in 1860. His ardent espousal of the findings of evolution, and his discipleship of Herbert Spencer, caused him to be so suspect to the authorities that he was threatened with expulsion, especially after his articles on evolution in the *National Quarterly Review* in 1861 and in the *North American Review* in 1862; however, he was finally given his B.A. in 1864, and his LL.B. from the Harvard Law School the year after. In the year of his graduation from Harvard he had been admitted to the Suffolk County (Mass.) bar, and had married Abby M. Brooks. The six children who resulted from this marriage were the primary reason for Fiske's prolificness as a writer; for years he wrote incessantly to earn a living for his large family.

When Dr. Charles W. Eliot became president of Harvard, it began to be a more comfortable place for evolutionists. Eliot invited Fiske to lecture on philosophy (he had been trying half-heartedly to practice law to eke out the returns from articles), and he remained as lecturer from 1869 to 1871. He was assistant librarian from 1872 to 1879, and a member of the board of overseers from 1879 to 1881. In 1873 he received a year's leave of absence, and by the kindness of a friend who gave him $1000 spent the year in Europe. In England he met Spencer, Darwin, Huxley—all the great pioneer evolutionists whose chief protagonist he was to be in America. From 1879 he became a lecturer at large, perhaps the most popular lecturer on history America has ever known. His audiences included the students of University College, London, and the Royal Institute.

About 1886 he turned from his former chief preoccupation, philosophy, to writing on history. From 1881 he was non-resident lecturer on history at Washington University, St. Louis, and after 1885 its professor of American history; but he continued to reside in Cambridge, Mass. From 1887 to 1889 he edited, with J. G. Wilson, *Appletons' Cyclopaedia of American Biography.* In 1894 the University of Pennsylvania gave him an honorary Litt. D., and Harvard an LL.D., but he never achieved the Harvard professorship for which he longed; when he ceased to be an outlaw because of his evolutionary views, he was looked upon by historians as unsound and superficial.

Indeed, as an historian he is merely a popularizer. Even in his own field of evolutionary philosophy he was "an intellectual middleman," with no or little profundity or originality, but with great brilliance and courage. He performed the same function for Spencer in America that Huxley performed for Darwin in England—that of being his "watch dog." His one important contribution to scientific thought is his explanation of human as compared with animal achievement by the long childhood of the human race—and in this, though he did not realize it, he was anticipated by the Greek philosopher Anaximander. He never entirely shed his early religious conditioning, and wasted much energy in trying to "reconcile" the disparate provinces of science and religion.

Fiske has been called "the largest author in America." He weighed over 300 pounds, and was truly a formidable figure, with flowing mustache, beard, and side whiskers, thick spectacles, and an aggressive nose—the type of the German professor in spite of his English and Irish ancestry. He died at Gloucester, Mass., as a direct result of heat prostration combined with overwork, and was buried at Petersham, where he had a country home.

A middleman Fiske may have been, but the most lucid, charming, and persuasive of middlemen. His easy, flowing style at times became almost musical, music being his passion—he sang, played, and composed. His historical works may be superseded, but his philosophical volumes still retain their delightful clarity and their pointed force.

Principal Works: Myths and Myth-Makers, 1872; The Outlines of Cosmic Philosophy, 1874; The Unseen World, 1876; Darwinism and Other Essays, 1879; Excursions of an Evolutionist, 1884; The Destiny of Man Viewed in the Light of his Origin, 1884; American Political Ideas Viewed From the Standpoint of Universal History, 1885; The Idea of God as Affected by Modern Knowledge, 1886; The Critical Period of American History, 1783-89, 1888; The Beginnings of New England, 1889; The War of Independence, 1889; Civil Government in the United States, 1890; The American Revolution, 1891; The Discovery of America, 1892; A History of the United States for Schools, 1894; Old Virginia and Her Neighbors, 1897; Dutch and Quaker Colonies, 1899; The Origin of Evil, 1899; A Century of Science and Other Essays, 1899; Through Nature to God, 1899; Life Everlasting, 1901; The Mississippi Valley in the Civil War, 1900; Essays: Historical and Literary, 1902; New France and New England, 1902; How the United States Became a Nation, 1904.

About: Abbott, L. Silhouettes of My Contemporaries; Clark, J. S. The Life and Letters of John Fiske; Perry, T. S. John Fiske; Critic August 1901; Harper's Weekly July 20, 1901; Nation January 24, 1918; North American Review July 1901; Unpopular Review July 9, 1918.

FISKE, STEPHEN RYDER (November 22, 1840-April 27, 1916), journalist and theatrical manager, was born in New Brunswick, N.J., the son of William Henry Fiske and Sarah Ann (Blakeney) Fiske. He started his literary career early, being paid for articles before he was twelve and editing a small paper when he was fourteen. He entered Rutgers in 1858 but was asked to leave two years later because of a novel satirizing the faculty. He then went to New York where he started working for the *Herald* as editorial writer, special correspondent, and war correspondent. In 1862 he was made dramatic critic of the *Herald,* which position he held till 1866 when he sailed for England in the first trans-Atlantic yacht race. Chance soon took him to Italy to be with Garibaldi at Rome during the revolution. From there he went to London where he was manager of St. James' Theatre and the Royal English Opera Company. In 1873 he produced his own version of Sardou's play, *Rabagas.* He returned to New York a few years later and in 1877 took over the management of the Fifth Avenue Theatre. He retired in 1879 and founded the New York *Dramatic Mirror.* After giving that up he wrote plays for several years, and was connected with *The Sports of the Times.* In addition to his plays—*Corporal Cartouche* being one of the better known ones—he wrote sketches and stories, including *Holiday Stories.* Fiske was recognized as one of the ablest dramatic critics of his time but was less successful in his original writings.

Principal Works: English Photography: By An American, 1869; Robert Rabagas, 1873; Off-hand Portraits of Prominent New Yorkers, 1884; Holiday Stories, 1891; Paddy From Cork and Other Stories, 1891; Corporal Cartouche; Martin Chuzzlewit; My Noble Son-in-law.

ABOUT: Pierce, F. C. Fiske and Fisk Family; New York Times April 28, 1916; New York Dramatic News May 6, 1916.

FITCH, CLYDE. See FITCH, WILLIAM CLYDE

FITCH, WILLIAM CLYDE (May 2, 1865-September 4, 1909), playwright and man-about-the-theatre, was born in Elmira N.Y., the son of Capt. William Goodwin Fitch of Hartford, Conn., and Alice (Clark) Fitch of Hagerstown, Md. When young Fitch was four his family settled in Schenectady, N.Y., and following high school in Hartford he was sent to Holderness, a New Hampshire boarding-school for boys. He was entered in the class of 1886 at Amherst, and here the cleverness of his literary audacities was applauded, while their questionableness was, in general, overlooked. He staged a bonfire of geometry texts, "The Funeral of Anna Lit," and played other college pranks. In undergraduate theatricals he played several major rôles. Already the theatre had a grip on him.

In the fall after graduation Fitch went to New York with a few notes of introduction. His father had visualized an architect's career for him, but young Fitch knew his own mind. Writing for *Life*, the *Churchman*, etc., was not very lucrative, and—as he put it—"with my college tailor bill still sword-of-Damoclesing over me, I became a tutor."

CLYDE FITCH

Fitch went abroad in May 1888, and the spirit of Paris was old wine to him. Nothing was wanting for the satisfying of his intellectual and aesthetic hungers, and his physical strength seemed to be almost self-generating. In London, where the aesthetic movement was in progress, he found another, though less complete, stimulus.

Back in New York again, he had the good fortune, through recommendations from a friend, E. A. Dithmar, dramatic editor of the New York *Times*, to write a play for Richard Mansfield. It was no easy task for Fitch to bring into the same plane his own dramatic convictions and the histrionic dogmas of the star for whom it was written. But on May 17, 1890, at the Madison Square Theatre, *Beau Brummel* became the first of a long procession of triumphs.

Like other playwrights who were sounding out Broadway at the turn of the century, Fitch was not leaning upon Victorian blank-verse heroics or sentimental adaptations when he could produce a candid picture of American manners. *A Modern Match*, opening on the road and coming to New York in March 1892, is a case in point. Fitch allowed his mind to become saturated with countless observations, large and small, and these were the raw materials of the "Fitchian detail." His plays were scrupulous not only in script but in stage sets as well. "Technique alone," said Fitch, "is machinery," and yet he was well aware of its importance. It figured largely in the success of *Barbara Frietchie*, with Julia Marlowe (1899); the convincing replica of New York's old Hotel Brevoort, the ballet rehearsals, and the dancing master all contributed to the success of *Captain Jinks of the Horse Marines*; and the pitching-steamer effect created by stage carpentry for *The Stubbornness of Geraldine* (1902) only brought the gentle satire into clearer relief.

Fitch has been accused of abusing this literary virtue—effective detail—by overusing it. In *The Girl with the Green Eyes* (1902), a serious character study, he heaped up detail, but the circumstances resulting were largely external to the dramatic impact of the play. *Glad of It* (1903) was a failure, but Fitch had made a worthy attempt to reproduce the interior of a department store. That *The Truth* (1906) won only lukewarm comment from the critics was a shocking setback to the playwright, for despite the fact that he had superimposed caricature on a mood of gravity, the play was a good one. American critics were rather late with their greetings, but the piece had high success abroad the following year. The attitude of the domestic press towards Fitch's plays seemed inordinately hostile. The critics took him lightly and allowed the frivolity and showmanship of Fitch the man to eclipse the earnest purposes of Fitch the dramatist. In his lecture "The Play and the Public" he held it the duty of audiences and critics to accept each play "for what it is, to criticize it where it fails by being untrue to its own pretensions but not to criticize it for not being what, perhaps, they wish it were, but what it never pretended to be."

Very early in his career Fitch went periodically to Europe to keep abreast of Continental stage trends. With long-failing health he sailed on June 25, 1909, and at the very beginning of a lonely journey through the Tyrol he died, on September 4, at Châlons-sur-Marne. *The City,* his last and most virile play, opened December 21, stirring a capacity Lyric audience to tremendous enthusiasm.

Fitch had intellectual sophistication—in the best sense of the word—and, too, a sincere zest for simple pleasures. His dark and lively eyes befitted his "bottled-lightning mind," and although his interests were generous and diverse, they revolved essentially about the stage. Walter Prichard Eaton says of Fitch: "Because he respected the actual theatre too much to give it less than reality . . . or . . . to withdraw contemptuously from its verdicts, he made the actual theatre a better place. . . ."

PRINCIPAL WORKS: *Plays*—Beau Brummel, 1890; Frederick Lemaître, 1891; A Modern Match, 1892; The Masked Ball, 1892; His Grace de Grammont, 1894; The Moth and the Flame, 1898; Nathan Hale, 1899; Barbara Frietchie, 1899; The Climbers, 1901; Captain Jinks of the Horse Marines, 1901; Lovers' Lane, 1901; The Stubbornness of Geraldine, 1902; The Girl with the Green Eyes, 1902; Her Own Way, 1903; The Woman in the Case, 1905; Her Great Match, 1905; The House of Mirth, 1906; The Girl Who Has Everything, 1906; The Straight Road, 1907; The Truth, 1907; Girls, 1908; The Blue Mouse, 1908; A Happy Marriage, 1909; The City, 1909. *Novel*—A Wave of Life, 1891. *Miscellaneous*—Some Correspondence and Six Conversations, 1896; The Smart Set, 1897.

ABOUT: Eaton, W. P. At the New Theatre and Others; Moses & Gerson, Clyde Fitch and His Letters; Moses & Gerson, The Plays of Clyde Fitch.

FITZGERALD, THOMAS (December 22, 1819-June 25, 1891), editor, publisher, and playwright, was born in New York, but when very young moved to New Brunswick, N.J. There he worked on the town's only newspaper, the *Fredonian,* and after acquiring journalistic experience, reported for the *Commercial Advertiser* in New York. Soon afterward he went to Tallahassee, Fla., where he became editor of the *Tallahassean.* In 1847 he moved to Philadelphia where he eventually bought several newspapers which he combined and published as an afternoon daily called the *Evening City Item.* This paper was said to have a circulation of 90,000 and it was through its columns that Fitzgerald advocated many civic reforms, all of which were finally realized. It was the first paper, and for a long while the only one, that reported on baseball, which was only then becoming popular.

Fitzgerald was tremendously interested in music, art, and drama. He was in favor of the Academy of Music as a home for grand opera, and had a noteworthy collection of paintings. He wrote and produced several successful plays, including *Light at Last, Who Shall Win,* and *Perils of the Night.* On one of his annual trips to Europe Fitzgerald was taken ill in London and died there.

PRINCIPAL WORKS: Light at Last, 1867; Patrice: or, The White Lady of Wicklow; Wolves at Bay; Tangled Threads; The Regent; Who Shall Win; Perils of the Night; Bound to the Rock.

ABOUT: Philadelphia Public Ledger June 26, 1891; Proof-Sheet September 1870.

"FITZNOODLE." See VALLENTINE, BENJAMIN BENNATON

"FLACCUS." See WARD, THOMAS

FLAGG, EDMUND (November 24, 1815-November 1, 1890), miscellaneous writer and diplomat, was born in Wiscasset, Maine, the son of Edmund and Harriet (Payson) Flagg. After graduation with honors from Bowdoin College in 1835, he went with his widowed mother and sister to Louisville, Ky. There he began a connection with the *Daily Journal* that lasted until 1861. During 1838-39 he read law in St. Louis, published his first work, *The Far West,* and wrote articles for the *Daily Commercial Bulletin.* In 1839 he returned to Louisville and helped to publish the *Literary News Letter.* He later went to Vicksburg for his health; there he was wounded in a duel. After editing the *Weekly Gazette* in Marietta, Ohio, in 1842-43, he returned to St. Louis where he edited the *Evening Gazette,* acted as court reporter, and wrote books and plays.

In 1849 Flagg went to Europe as secretary to the American minister in Berlin, and during his two year sojourn there traveled extensively. Upon his return to America he was appointed consul to Venice, but after two years he went back to St. Louis where he edited the *Democratic Times* and wrote his best known book, *Venice: The City of the Sea*. In 1854 he went to Washington where he held civil service positions for many years, most of the time as statistician in the Department of State. After 1871 he lived on a farm near Falls Church, Va.

PRINCIPAL WORKS: The Far West, 1838; Mary Tudor, 1844; Ruy Blas, 1845; Mutual Insurance, 1846; Catherine Howard, 1847; Edmond Dantes, 1849; Venice: The City of the Sea, 1853; Report of the Commercial Relations of the United States With All Foreign Nations, 1856-57; De Molai, 1888.

ABOUT: Coggeshall, W. T. The Poets and Poetry of the West; Flagg, C. A. Descendants of Josiah Flagg; Flagg, N. G. & L. C. S. Family Records of the Descendants of Gershom Flagg; Griffith, G. B. Poets of Maine; Lancey, S. H. Native Poets of Maine.

FLAGG, THOMAS WILSON (November 5, 1805-May 6, 1884), naturalist, was born in Beverly, Mass., the son of Isaac and Elizabeth Frances (Wilson) Flagg. In later years he dropped the name of Thomas.

He was graduated from Phillips Andover Academy in 1821, spent three months in Harvard in 1823, and then studied medicine, first at Harvard Medical School in 1824 and 1825, and then with a Beverly physician; however, he never practiced. Soon after this he took a solitary walking trip to Tennessee and Virginia, the first evidence of his turn for natural history. In 1840 he married Caroline Eveleth; they had two sons, one of whom became professor of Greek at Cornell. Flagg served as an insurance agent in Boston, and then as a customs house clerk from 1844 to 1848. His first literary ventures were in the field of politics, and mostly in verse, though he was one of the earliest contributors of essays to the *Atlantic Monthly*. From 1840 he wrote steadily for the *Magazine of Horticulture*, and from this time on he was known primarily as a naturalist. He led an exceedingly retired life, with no interests or connections outside his family circle, but by his own account it was also a singularly happy one. In 1856 he moved to Cambridge, where he died.

PRINCIPAL WORKS: Analysis of Female Beauty, 1834; The Tailor's Shop (verse) 1844; Studies in the Field and Forest, 1857; A Prize Essay on Agricultural Education, 1858; Mount Auburn: Its Scenes, Its Beauties, and Its Lessons (with others) 1861; The Woods and By-Ways of New England, 1872; The Birds and Seasons of New England, 1875.

ABOUT: Essex Institute Historical Collections January-March 1885; Boston Transcript May 7, 1884.

FLAGG, WILSON. See FLAGG, THOMAS WILSON

FLINT, TIMOTHY (July 11, 1780-August 16 or 18, 1840), novelist and historian, was born near North Reading, Mass., the son of William Flint and Martha (Kimball) Flint. He was educated at Phillips Andover Academy and at Harvard, where he was graduated in 1800. The next year he taught school at Cohasset, Mass., then became a preacher at Marblehead, where he married Abigail Hubbard; one of their sons became a minor poet. From 1802 to 1814 Flint was minister of the (Congregationalist) church at Lunenburg, Mass., then part of Fitchburg. He was always keenly interested in natural science, and his chemical experiments gave rise to a slanderous accusation of counterfeiting. The subsequent suits made his position so uncomfortable that he resigned, and after a year of missionary work in New Hampshire, set out for the West under the auspices of the Missionary Society of Connecticut.

From 1815 to 1825 he traveled through the Mississippi Valley, being the first Protestant minister to administer the communion in St. Louis. He then went to New Orleans, where he preached and lectured, and next became principal of a seminary at Alexandria, La. A long illness, from which he never really recovered, sent him North again, and from this time on his sole activity was writing and editing. From 1827 to 1830 he edited the *Western Monthly Review*, in Cincinnati and for a short time in 1833 edited the *Knickerbocker* in New York. Besides his original writings he translated from the French and in 1831 edited the *Personal Narrative* of James O. Pattie, an early explorer. He returned to Louisiana, traveling much in search of benefit to his health, which finally became so bad that he started to return to his old home in Reading. En route he was buried under the ruins of a house destroyed by a tornado at Natchez, Miss., and the effects of this on his already ruined health caused his death in Reading the following August. He was buried in Salem.

Flint was a romanticist, whose writings are all attempts at psychological escape from the disillusioning present to the idealized melodrama of other times and places. A contemporary critic condemned his history as "too interesting for reference," which should recommend it to modern readers.

PRINCIPAL WORKS: Recollections of the Last Ten Years: Passed in the Valley of the Mississippi, 1826; Francis Berrian: or, The Mexican Patriot, 1826; The Life and Adventures of Arthur Clenning, 1828; A Condensed Geography and History of the Western States, 1828 (as The History and Geography of the Mississippi Valley,

1832); George Mason: The Young Backwoodsman, 1829; The Shoshonee Valley, 1830; Indian Wars of the West, 1833; The Biographical Memoir of Daniel Boone, 1834.

ABOUT: Flint, T. Recollections of the Last Ten Years (see also Introduction to 1932 edition, by C. H. Grattan); Kirkpatrick, J. E. Timothy Flint.

"FLORENCE." See OSGOOD, FRANCES SARGENT (LOCKE)

FOLGER, PETER (1617-1690) [exact dates unknown], pioneer and verse-writer, was born in Norwich, England, the son of John and Mirriba (or Maribell) (Gibbs) Folger. He emigrated to Massachusetts with his parents in 1635, and settled first at Watertown. Trained as a surveyor, he went to Martha's Vineyard in 1642 to assist the Rev. Thomas Mayhew, Jr., in that capacity and also as schoolmaster and missionary to the Indians. In 1844 he married Mary Morrils (or Morrell), an indentured servant whom he purchased from her master for £20. Their daughter Abiah became the mother of Benjamin Franklin.

In 1659 Folger went with Tristram Coffin as surveyor and interpreter to Nantucket, which Coffin and his associates owned by grant. So successful and useful was he that in 1663 Coffin offered him half a share of land to settle there. Folger was a universal factotum—teacher, interpreter, town and court clerk, miller, and weaver. In spite of this, he participated in an insurrection of the "half share men" against the large proprietors, and spent some time in jail; but he recovered from this experience with undiminished reputation. About 1675 he had become a Baptist, and occasionally he immersed an Indian convert.

His only book is a piece of homespun verse, a plea for tolerance to all religious sects, couched in what his famous grandson described as "decent plainness and manly freedom." Such tolerance of heresy was highly disapproved by the Puritan leaders of Massachusetts, and it was fortunate for Folger that when he wrote his book he was living on the island of Nantucket, which then belonged not, as now, to Massachusetts, but to the province of New York. Cotton Mather seems in any case to have been ignorant of or to have ignored Folger's unseemly tolerance, for he praised Folger highly in the *Magnalia* for his learning and piety.

PRINCIPAL WORK: A Looking-Glass for the Times: or, The Former Spirit of New England Revived in This Generation, 1676.

ABOUT: Franklin, B. Autobiography; Starbuck, A. The History of Nantucket.

FOLLEN, ELIZA LEE (CABOT) (August 15, 1787-January 26, 1860), abolitionist and miscellaneous writer, was born in Boston, one of thirteen children of Samuel and Sarah (Barrett) Cabot. She received a thorough education and early showed marked intellectual ability. Because of her distinguished family connections she came in contact with the leading people of Boston, and was an outstanding figure in literary and religious circles.

In 1828 Miss Cabot was married to Dr. Charles Follen, a German liberal refugee nine years her junior. Two years later a son was born to them.

Mrs. Follen's great interest in the Sunday School movement and in child education influenced her literary life. For two years she edited the *Christian Teacher's Manual,* and later the *Child's Friend.* Her books for children were well known, *The Well-Spent Hour* (1827) being probably the most popular. In addition to her literary activities she was an ardent member of various anti-slavery societies, serving on committees and writing tracts and poems on slavery. She was considered a very cultivated and brilliant woman and an outstanding figure in Boston. J. Peter Lesley, however, has said of her that she was "one of those enthusiastic, partisan souls, who can see no faults in friends nor virtues in enemies."

PRINCIPAL WORKS: The Well-Spent Hour, 1827; The Skeptic, 1835; Sketches of Married Life, 1838; Poems, 1839.

ABOUT: Briggs, L. V. History and Genealogy of the Cabot Family; Cooke, G. W. Unitarianism in America; Dewey, M. E. Life and Letters of Catharine M. Sedgwick; Annual Report American Anti-Slavery Society, 1860; Liberator January, February 1860.

FORCE, PETER (November 26, 1790-January 23, 1868), historian and archivist, was born near Passaic Falls, N.J., the son of William Force, Revolutionary War veteran, and Sarah (Ferguson) Force. When Peter was three his family moved to New York City, where he attended school until, in his tenth year, he was made an apprentice to William A. Davis, printer. It was one of young Force's duties to carry proof-sheets between the print-shop and the author's residence, and it may have been some of the tastier squibs from the pages of Irving's *Knickerbocker History* that gave him an early fondness for historical anecdotes and records. He learned his craft quickly and solidly and when only twenty-two was elected president of the New York Typographical Society. He served with the army in the War of 1812. In 1815 he went with

PETER FORCE
c. 1860

Davis, who had obtained some government printing contracts, to Washington. Force was inescapably drawn into politics, and although his rôle in public administration in time took on serious and constructive proportions, it was during his first years in the Capital that he mocked Uncle Sam's comic frailties with such doggerel as this printer's oath of political allegiance, addressed to the Senate and the House:

> For if a man was a foe, why I made him an ass,
> If a friend why I scribbled him up to the skies,
> Thus in spite of my conscience have I labored, alas,
> And (*though seldom*) sometimes told confounded big lies.

Following membership in the common council and the board of aldermen, Force was elected mayor of Washington, in 1836, on the Whig ticket. He was re-elected in 1838, and in four trying years effected remarkable reforms.

His surest claim to distinction, however, was his scholarly contribution to historical research. He published the *National Calendar and Annals of the United States* from 1820-24 and from 1828-36, and at the same time set up a semi-weekly newspaper, independent politically, and fairly conservative, the *National Journal*. This became a daily in 1824 and was printed until 1831. Four octavo volumes of reprints from rare pamphlets on early America, called Historical Tracts, appeared at intervals from 1836 to 1846. The *American Archives* series, Force's monumental work, published by means of special appropriation from Congress, was brought out between 1837 and 1853. The nine handsome volumes comprised "a documentary history of the origin and progress of the North American Colonies" down to 1776, and was to have proceeded chronologically to 1789. But Secretary of State Marcy witheld his approval of the contents of certain books, disregarded the contract whereby the Government had become Force's patron, and brought the work to an arbitrary halt in 1853. The blow staggered the careful compiler, but thirteen years afterwards, with certain misgivings, he accepted an offer, tendered by the Librarian of Congress, of $100,000 for the series. For early Americana research, the *Archives* series is invaluable. Force was, moreover, quite well informed on Arctic cartography and on astronomy, and was the first scholar to establish, by contemporary evidence, the correct date of the "Mecklenburg Declaration of Independence."

With a build far from spindling, a well chiseled face, a mass of curly hair, and a darting eye, Force was easily singled out in public places. Despite the limitations of his formal education he became a thoroughgoing intellectual, but never a snob, and he had an outspoken hatred for social bores. He was a zealous collector of all things literary and although his astuteness netted him some unbelievable values for relatively trifling sums, he had no qualms about paying out a small fortune if necessary. Force's death came in his seventy-eighth year, following a digestive disorder, and he was buried in Rock Creek Cemetery, Washington.

PRINCIPAL WORKS: *Historical*—Documentary History of the Revolution, 1843 (?); Tracts and Other Papers, 1836-46; American Archives, 1837-53. *Miscellaneous*—Grinnell Land: Remarks on English Maps of Arctic Discoveries, 1852; Record of Auroral Phenomena, 1856.

ABOUT: American Historical Record January 1874; Records of Columbian Historical Society: Vol. 2; unpublished miscellaneous papers of Peter Force in the Manuscript Division, Library of Congress.

FORD, PATRICK (April 12, 1835-September 23, 1913), journalist, was born in Galway, Ireland. His parents, Edward and Anne (Ford) Ford, died when he was a child and he was then brought to Boston by friends. There he attended public schools and the Latin School. After working as a youth in the newspaper office of William Lloyd Garrison he began his journalist career in 1855, and from 1859 to 1860 was editor and publisher of the Boston

Sunday Times. He served in a Massachusetts regiment during the Civil War, was married in 1863, and from 1864 to 1866 edited the Charleston *Gazette*. In 1870 he moved to New York where he founded the *Irish World*. Extremely interested in Irish independence he spent most of the rest of his life championing the cause. He was one of the founders of the Greenback Labor Party, organized 2500 branches of the Irish Land League in the United States, and succeeded in raising and sending to Ireland for its support over $600,000. To support his strong views on the Irish question Ford published in 1881 *A Criminal History of the British Empire*, and, in 1885, *The Irish Question and American Statesmen*. His methods of championing the cause were explosive, dramatic, and high handed, but in a way effective.

PRINCIPAL WORKS: A Criminal History of the British Empire, 1881; The Irish Question and American Statesmen, 1885.

ABOUT: Bagenal, P. H. The American Irish; New York Times September 24, 1913.

FORD, PAUL LEICESTER (March 23, 1865-May 8, 1902), novelist bibliographer, and historian, was born in Brooklyn, N.Y., the son of Gordon Lester Ford, a lawyer and book collector, and Emily Ellsworth (Fowler) Ford. He was a hunchback, and his delicacy prevented his ever going to school; he was educated by private tutors, and by browsing in his father's magnificent library, now part of the New York Public Library. He was a precocious bibliographer; when only eleven, with an amateur printing outfit he printed an edition of the *Webster Genealogy*, Noah Webster having been his great-grandfather. With his father and his brother Worthington he formed the Historical Printing Club, which issued many reprints of historical documents and bibliographies, chief of which was *Winnowings in American History* (fifteen volumes, 1890-91). At the request of the Historical Society of Pennsylvania, he edited the writings of John Dickinson (1895); he had already edited the works of Jefferson (1892-99) and of Columbus (1892). For this work he consulted original documents in the great European libraries, and his edition of Jefferson is still the best.

In 1894 he published his first novel, *The Honorable Peter Stirling*, based on his abortive efforts to enter politics in Brooklyn; its success was largely due to the erroneous rumor that the chief character was based on Grover Cleveland. Though he brought out other novels—principally *Janice Meredith*, in 1899—he continued his

PAUL LEICESTER FORD

bibliographical work, which grew into the production of notable biographical and historical volumes. From 1890 to 1893 he was also the editor of the *Library Journal*. In 1896 Charles Frohman produced a comedy by Ford, *Honors Are Easy*; both *Peter Stirling* and *Janice Meredith* were also dramatized, the latter having a long run. Old-timers may still remember the fashion of the "Janice Meredith curl," to which it gave rise.

In 1900 he married Mary Grace Kidwell; they had one daughter. On his marriage he moved to Manhattan, where he bought a house. Here, at only thirty-seven, he was shot and killed by a disinherited brother, Malcolm Webster Ford, a famous amateur athlete and a magazine writer, who blamed Paul for his financial difficulties. Malcolm Ford killed himself immediately afterwards.

Ford's novels may be considered merely the diversions of an historian. *Janice Meredith* is the best of them; it was the first of the really "big sellers," selling 200,000 copies in three months. It has historical accuracy and vivid portraiture, but is sentimental and poorly constructed. The semi-realistic *Peter Stirling* is of value as a picture of petty politics in America in the '90s, but is open to the same charges of lack of form and artificiality of sentiment. His other novels are purely trivial. His historical work was both sound and brilliant; his *True George Washington* was the first biography of Washington to present him as an actual human being. His similar study of Franklin, however, has been superseded by more modern treatments. Undoubtedly Ford's sudden and tragic death removed from American history one of its most fertile and valuable representatives.

PRINCIPAL WORKS: *Novels*—The Honorable Peter Stirling and What People Thought of Him, 1894; The Great K. and A. Train Robbery, 1897; The Story of an Untold Love, 1897; Tattle Tales of Cupid, 1898; Janice Meredith: A Story of the American Revolution, 1899; Wanted: A Match-Maker, 1900; Wanted: A Chaperone, 1902. *History and Biography*—Essays on the Constitution, 1892; The True George Washington, 1896; The New England Primer: A History of its Origin and Development, 1897; The Many-Sided Franklin, 1899.

ABOUT: Bookman February 1900; Critic November 1898; Outlook May 7, 1902; New York Evening Post May 9, 1902.

"FORESTER, FRANK." See HERBERT, HENRY WILLIAM

FORNEY, JOHN WIEN (September 30, 1817-December 9, 1891), journalist, politician, and miscellaneous writer, was born in Lancaster, Pa., the son of Peter and Margaret (Wien) Forney. At thirteen he began working in a store, and at sixteen he became an apprentice in the office of the Lancaster *Journal.* Four years later he was editor of the *Intelligencer,* which, after two years he joined with the *Journal.* A Democrat and interested in politics, he early began backing James Buchanan. When the latter became Secretary of State, Forney was made deputy surveyor of the port of Philadelphia. After moving there he became co-proprietor and editor of the *Pennsylvanian.* After the Democrats were defeated in 1848 he tried to become clerk of the House of Representatives but did not succeed until 1851. He took active part in the campaign of 1852, became an editorial writer for the Washington *Daily Union,* and two years later was made a partner in its ownership. After becoming involved in political controversies he left journalism in 1856 and worked strenuously for the nomination and election of Buchanan as president.

Not receiving the expected rewards for his services to Buchanan, Forney finally turned Republican in 1860, and returned to his old position as clerk of the House. From 1861 to 1868 he was secretary of the Senate. In 1861 Forney founded the *Sunday Morning Chronicle,* and a year later, supposedly at the suggestion of Lincoln, he published a daily edition. Through his paper Forney supported Lincoln and, for a while, Johnson, but in 1870 he sold out the paper and returned to Philadelphia. The remaining years of his life he spent writing, traveling, and lecturing. Again becoming a Democrat, he wrote *The Life and Military Career of Winfield Scott Hancock* and also *Anecdotes of Public Men.*

PRINCIPAL WORKS: Anecdotes of Public Men, 1873-81; The Life and Military Career of Winfield Scott Hancock, 1880; The New Nobility, 1881.

ABOUT: Forty Years of American Journalism: Retirement of Mr. J. W. Forney from the Philadelphia "Press"; Harris, A. Biographical History of Lancaster County; Philadelphia Press December 10, 12, 13, 1881; Philadelphia Public Ledger December 10, 1881; Philadelphia Record December 10, 1881; Washington Sunday Chronicle December 11, 1881.

"FORT, PAUL." See STOCKTON, FRANK RICHARD

"FORTH, GEORGE." See FREDERIC, HAROLD

FOSDICK, CHARLES AUSTIN ("Harry Castlemon") (September 16, 1842-August 22, 1915), juvenile series writer, was born in Randolph, N.Y., the son of John Spencer Fosdick and Eunice (Andrews) Fosdick. When he was a baby the family moved to Buffalo, where the father was principal of a public school, and he attended the Central High School there. At the outbreak of the Civil War he went to Cairo, Ill., and enlisted in the Mississippi Squadron, being present at the siege of Vicksburg. Gradually he rose to be superintendent of coal for the squadron. After the war he became a clerk in a store at Villa Ridge, Ill., near

Courtesy of the Library of Congres
CHARLES A. FOSDICK
("Harry Castlemon")

Cairo. In 1867 he married Sarah Stoddard. From 1875 he lived in Westfield, N.Y., near his birthplace. His wife died in 1904, and as she had been his copyist and proofreader, he gave up writing entirely. After traveling around a bit, he settled with a son at Hamburg, N.Y., where he died.

By the time of his death Fosdick was almost forgotten, but he had once been the most popular of all writers for boys, the successful rival of Alger, Henty, and "Oliver Optic." All his books were written under the pseudonym of "Harry Castlemon." The first, *Frank: The Young Naturalist* (1864), introduced the character of Frank Nelson who was himself as a boy; and his Civil War experiences gave rise to many of the earlier books. His stories were realistic, with no sentimentality, briskly written, straightforward, and unadorned. He never made much money on them, for they were sold to the publisher for a lump sum, with no royalties. They were written in series of three to six around a central theme. There were 58 volumes in all.

Fosdick was the uncle of Harry Emerson Fosdick, the liberal clergyman, and Raymond B. Fosdick, the publicist.

PRINCIPAL WORKS: Gunboat, Rocky Mountain, Sportsman's Club, Boy Trapper, Roughing It, Rod and Gun, War, Afloat and Ashore, Pony Express series. [No individual dates are obtainable for these; they ran from 1864 to 1904.]

ABOUT: Buffalo Express August 23, 1915; New York Evening Post August 28, 1915.

FOSDICK, WILLIAM WHITEMAN (January 28, 1825-March 8, 1862), poet and novelist was born in Cincinnati, the son of Thomas Fosdick, a banker and Julia (Drake) Fosdick, an actress. As a youth he attended Cincinnati College and Transylvania University and later studied law in Louisville. He practised in Cincinnati, where, in 1851, he published his historical romance, *Malmiztic the Toltec, and the Cavaliers of the Cross.* In 1852 he moved to New York, where he presumably practiced law but actually did some writing. In 1855 he published *Ariel and Other Poems.* A man of charming personality, he was described by W. H. Venable as a "born poet, a true wit, a boon companion of artists and literary men, a courteous gentleman, loved and admired by every man, woman, and child who knew him." His early death terminated a promising career.

PRINCIPAL WORKS: Malmiztic the Toltec, and the Cavaliers of the Cross, 1851; Ariel and Other Poems, 1855.

ABOUT: Coggeshall, W. T. Poets and Poetry of the West; Venable, W. H. Beginnings of Literary Culture in the Ohio Valley; Cincinnati Daily Commercial March 10, 1862.

FOSS, SAM WALTER (June 19, 1858-February 26, 1911), verse writer, was born in Candia, N.H., the son of Dyer Foss, a farmer, and Polly (Hardy) Foss. His mother died when he was four, and his father remarried and moved to Portsmouth, N.H. Before this the boy had worked on the farm in summer, and gone to school in winter. Now he was graduated (as class poet) from the Portsmouth High School, then attended Tilton Seminary, and proceeded to Brown University, where he received his B.A. in 1882. After a year as a book agent, he bought with a friend the Lynn, Mass., *Union,* changing its name to the *Saturday Union.* From 1884 he was sole editor and proprietor. Obliged to fill in a humorous column one day, he found he had a gift for dialect verse, and thereafter composed the column himself. *Puck, Judge,* and other magazines soon published his verses regularly. From 1887 to 1892 he was editor of the *Yankee Blade,* Boston, and also editorial writer for the Boston *Globe.* In 1887 he married Carrie Maria Conant. He resigned from his newspaper work to do free lance writing, during 1893 and 1894 writing a "poem" a day for a syndicate. In 1898 he was elected librarian of the Somerville Public Library, and retained this position to his death. Though without technical training, he was a successful librarian, and in 1904 was president of the

SAM WALTER FOSS

Massachusetts Library Club. From 1909 until he died he wrote the "Library Alcove" for the *Christian Science Monitor.*

Foss as a writer belongs in the class of Robert Service and Edgar Guest. His imperturbable optimism and his "homespun philosophy" are typical of his time and place. However, he had genuine humor and a good command of dialect. Occasionally, in more serious pieces, he showed some competency as a genuine lyrist; the best of his poems is "Trumpets," which he wrote when he was facing the operation which proved fatal. To the average reader, however, he is best known as the author of "A House by the Side of the Road."

PRINCIPAL WORKS: Back Country Poems, 1892; Whiffs From Wild Meadows, 1895; Dreams in Homespun, 1897; Songs of War and Peace, 1899; The Song of the Library Staff, 1906; Songs of the Average Man, 1907 (with additions, 1911).

ABOUT: Woodward, M. S. Sam Walter Foss: Librarian and Friend to Man; Boston Globe February 27, 1911; Providence Journal June 11, 1922.

FOSTER, HANNAH (WEBSTER) 1759-April 17, 1840), novelist and essayist, was born in Boston, the daughter of a prosperous merchant, Grant Webster. Her mother's name, her education, and her early life are all unknown; probably she was educated at home, though in her writings she showed a keen interest in girls' schools which may have argued some experience with them. She began to write while quite young, principally political articles for local newspapers; these attracted the attention of the Rev. John Foster, of Brighton, Mass., who made her acquaintance in consequence, and in 1785 was married to her. They had two daughters, both of whom became essayists, and after Foster's death she went to live with them in Montreal, where she died.

Mrs. Foster's principal work was one of the earliest American novels, *The Coquette.* Founded on an actual scandal in Massachusetts society, it was immensely popular going into thirteen editions in forty years. She was accused of having too vivid an imagination, but she was sufficiently realistic to give the actual names of all concerned in this drama of seduction, except that of the victim—even the seducer's. Her other book was a dull homily. Carl Van Doren remarks that Mrs. Foster's method of novel-writing "gave to fiction something of the saga element by stealing, in the company of facts, upon a community that winced at fiction."

PRINCIPAL WORKS: The Coquette: or, The History of Eliza Wharton. By a Lady of Massachusetts, 1797; The Boarding School: or, Lessons of a Preceptress to Her Pupils, 1798.

ABOUT: Dall, C. H. The Romance of the Association; Foster, H. W. The Coquette (see Memoir by J. E. Locke in 1855 ed.).

FOSTER, STEPHEN COLLINS (July 4, 1826-July 13, 1864), song writer, was born in Pittsburgh, the son of William Barclay Foster, a merchant, later mayor and member of the legislature, and Eliza Clayland (Tomlinson) Foster. He was educated at schools in Towanda and Athens, Pa., and spent a few months at Jefferson College, Canonsburg, Pa., but most of his real education came from tutors in French, German, painting, and music. Though he played several instruments, he was never a trained musician; nevertheless, he was a born composer. His first song was written at thirteen; "Open Thy Lattice, Love," was published at sixteen, while he was a clerk in a store in Cincinnati. His parents, however, considered music no career for any son of theirs, and sent him to Cincinnati again in 1846 to act as bookkeeper for his brother. However, when his *Songs of the Sable Harmonists* came out in 1848 (though of the songs contained in it, "Uncle Ned" had been given away free, and he had received only $100 for "O Susanna," which with a change of words became the "theme song" of the California '49ers), they relented, and he was allowed to return to Allegheny, where they were then living, and devote himself to composition.

Foster's early Negro songs, including "Nelly Was a Lady," "Old Folks at Home," "Massa's in de Cold, Cold Ground," "My Old Kentucky Home," and "Old Black Joe," were written for the minstrels. In 1851 he sold to Edwin P. Christy, the best known minstrel of the day, the privilege of singing his songs before publication and of having his name as composer on the printed song. It was not until later, when most of his best songs were written, that Foster acknowledged them publicly. He received good royalties on them, however—$15,000 on "Old Folks at Home." It is interesting to note that the author of all these Southern songs saw the South only twice—on a short visit to New Orleans in 1852 and on another across the Ohio River into Kentucky.

In 1850 Foster had married Jane Denny McDowell, and they had one daughter. Just what happened to him about 1860 is still a mystery. But he moved to New York, his wife left him, he took to drink, he turned out potboilers feverishly—poor work, for which for the first time he no longer wrote

STEPHEN FOSTER
c. 1859

his own words—and he finally died in the charity ward of Bellevue Hospital as the result of a drunken accident, when he fell on a glass and cut his throat. His whole property consisted of the clothes he wore, thirty-eight cents, and a scrap of paper bearing the words, "Dear friends and gentle hearts"—which may or may not have been part of a projected song. He was always a gentle, timid, melancholy man, absent-minded and seclusive, and the years only intensified these native traits.

The words of Foster's songs are inseparable from the music; as a writer in the *Atlantic Monthly* put it in 1867, "he thought in tune as he traced in rhyme." His dialect songs were the first outside of their own spirituals to portray the Negroes as human beings, not caricatures; they are sentimental, but they are also tender, simple, and authentically poetic. The non-dialect ballads are a bit saccharine for modern taste, but "Jeannie With the Light Brown Hair" and "Come Where My Love Lies Dreaming" still hold their places in concert repertoire—more, however, for their music, limited but sweet like all that Foster wrote, than for their words. Foster was a genius of the folk-song, one of those rare men who can create something that seems to have grown from a people's heart. Of his 175-odd songs, at least a dozen are immortal. He who died a pauper, a little, frail, brown-eyed man familiar to all the Bowery, now has a half million dollar memorial at the University of Pittsburgh, and his birthplace has been transferred by Henry Ford to make part of Greenfield Village, Mich. He was born on the day Jefferson and John Adams died; he died in the midst of the Civil War; in himself he epitomizes the emotional history of our early years as a nation.

PRINCIPAL WORKS: Songs of the Sable Harmonists, 1848; Ethiopian Melodies. [Innumerable editions of the songs, separately and in groups.]

ABOUT: Foster, M. Biography, Songs, and Musical Compositions of Stephen C. Foster; My Brother Stephen; Howard, J. T. Stephen Foster: America's Troubadour; MacGowan, R. The Significance of Stephen Collins Foster; Milligan, H. V. Stephen Collins Foster: A Biography of America's Folk-Song Composer; Walters, R. Stephen Foster: Youth's Golden Gleam; Atlantic Monthly November 1867; Etude October 1927, August 1937; Literary Digest July 24, 1926, June 19, 1937; Musical America July 2, 1921, April 25, 1929; Musical Courier January 11, 1923, March 22 and 29, 1930; Musical Observer July 1, 1926.

"FRANCO, HARRY." See BRIGGS, CHARLES FREDERICK

"FRANK." See WHITCHER, FRANCES MIRIAM (BERRY)

FRANKLIN, BENJAMIN (January 6 [o.s.], 1706-April 17, 1790), scientist, diplomat, and pamphleteer, was born in Boston, the son of Josiah Franklin, a tallow-maker, and of his second wife, Abiah Folger, daughter of the Nantucket pioneer Peter Folger [*q.v.*]. At eight Franklin was sent to the Boston Grammar School, then, as this was too expensive transferred to Brownell's School for Writing and Arithmetic. At ten his schooling was over; he was apprenticed to his father, but so disliked the trade that at twelve he was sent to his half-brother James, a printer. The boy, who had been talking of running away to sea, settled down in this more congenial atmosphere; however, he and James did not get on well together, and several times he was on the point of breaking his apprenticeship. In 1721 James Franklin founded the *New England Courant,* and as the paper was sensational and frequently in trouble with the authorities, Benjamin for a while became its nominal editor. His first writing, the "Dogood Papers," in imitation of the *Spectator* of Addison and Steele, appeared here.

The friction between the brothers came to a head in 1723; Franklin left Boston and arrived, penniless, in Philadelphia. Here he became a printer in the plant of a man named Keimer. William Keith, the governor of Pennsylvania, admired his thrift and intelligence (by this time bolstered by much private reading), and offered to set him up for himself. Believing Keith's promises of assistance, Franklin sailed for England in 1724, only to find that Keith had fulfilled none of his expectations. Franklin was stranded, and for nearly two years was obliged to work as a printer in London before he could return to Philadelphia. For a few months thereafter he was a clerk in a store; then both he and his employer fell ill, and the employer died. Franklin went back to Keimer, but the next year he and a fellow-worker named Hugh Meredith started in business for themselves.

Franklin was a printer for ten years. In 1728 he bought the *Philadelphia Gazette,* and transformed it from a dull sheet to a lively, sparkling paper—the direct ancestor of the present *Saturday Evening Post.* In 1732 he published the first volume of his famous *Poor Richard's Almanack.* Its aphorisms were largely cribbed from Bacon, Rabelais, and la Rochefoucauld, but colored by his own homely and pungent style. It formed the foundation of its editor's fame and wealth. In 1730 he became public printer for the province.

In the same year he married Deborah Read, whom he had met on his first day in Philadelphia in 1723, courted tepidly, and forgotten while he was in England. Meanwhile she had married a man named Rogers who had deserted her and was never heard from again. As she was never divorced, there is grave doubt whether Franklin's marriage was legal, or his children legitimate. (They had a son who died at four, and a daughter, Sarah, who married Richard Bache.) This would not have troubled Franklin however, for he was already the father of a son, William, whose mother is unknown, but whom he reared in his own home and later made his secretary. In his latter years his companion and amanuensis in France was William's own illegitimate son, William Temple Franklin.

Franklin's multifarious activities at this period extended to every aspect of public life. He was the father of the Pennsylvania Hospital, of the Academy which later became the University of Pennsylvania, of the first free library in America, of the first fire company in Philadelphia, and of the famous club, the Junto, where he reported his first scientific experiments. His research into the nature of electricity is well known, and so are many of his inventions, the chief of which was the Franklin stove. He never patented or sold his inventions, considering that they should be at the service of all mankind. He was grand master of the

From a portrait by J. S. Duplessis
BENJAMIN FRANKLIN
1778

Pennsylvania Grand Lodge of Masons, clerk of the Pennsylvania Assembly, and deputy postmaster, besides establishing printing companies in New York, South Carolina, and Jamaica.

His political career began in 1748, as a member of the city council. For fourteen years from 1750 he was a delegate to the Pennsylvania Assembly. He was a commissioner to deal with the Indians during the French and Indian Wars. Finally, in 1757, he was sent to London to endeavor to obtain concessions from the Penn family, proprietors of the province, in respect to taxation of their holdings. He remained until 1774, as agent for Massachusetts and Georgia as well as for Pennsylvania. Honors were heaped upon him, his fame grew, but his final mission was a failure and he returned under a cloud; the break between the mother country and the colonies was nearing, and he had waged a losing battle for conciliation.

In America he was soon rehabilitated. He became postmaster-general, a member of the Continental Congress, and a commissioner from Congress to Canada. He was one of the committee that framed the Declaration of Independence, and was naturally a signer. In 1776 he was sent to France to attempt to gain French assistance in the struggle which had already begun. He was by this time a widower, Deborah Franklin having died in 1774, while he was in London.

In spite of the machinations of jealous fellow-commissioners, he did secure the aid which won the American Revolution. He remained in France until 1785, being one of the signers of the (first) Treaty of Versailles. When he left he was one of the most honored and the most popular men in all France. He was an old man, but still at the service of his country. His last years were spent in Philadelphia, as president of the Commonwealth of Pennsylvania and a member of the Constitutional Convention. He continued his scientific interests, built three houses, and worked on his autobiography, which was never finished. It had been intended for his beloved son, who rewarded his father's devotion by turning Tory and abandoning the American cause. At eighty-four his strong body gave way, and he died of gallstones, complicated by pleurisy. He is buried, with many members of his family, in Philadelphia.

Franklin's appearance is familiar to all Americans—the bulky body, the high, rounded forehead, the slightly protruding eyes with drooping lids. He was by nature conciliatory, non-combative, shrewd, with a strong feminine element in his make-up, a well-rounded and markedly extroverted man. He seldom practiced what, as "Poor Richard," he preached, and though doubtless his amours were no more in number than those of other men, his candor in confessing them made this aspect of his nature very apparent. He has been called "half peasant, half man of the world," though in his later years the man of the world predominated. He maligns himself in his autobiography—he was far from the mere canny tradesman he there makes himself out to be. In religion he was a deist, in politics a democrat of the school of Jefferson.

There is no doubt, however, that prudence and moderation were Franklin's philosophical foundations, and prudence is neither a very high aim nor a very strong safeguard in the building of character. The idealist may sometimes have his head in the clouds so that his feet stumble, but at least he sees the stars. In a sense we may say that the American genius has had two natures and two poles—the one idealistic, metaphysical, living in abstraction and pure reason, the other shrewd, homespun, self-centered and self-seeking, and that these antitheses were incarnated in the dominant figures of Emerson and Franklin respectively.

As a writer, clarity and precision are Franklin's main characteristics. He was an apt disciple of such writers as Addison, Swift, Defoe, and Bunyan. His ironical wit, with its "dash of genial cynicism," the homely sententiousness of his style, combined with a classical purity of language, make him a model of clearness and flexibility. Yet he was primarily no writer; he never finished a single full-length book. In actuality he was a pamphleteer—the best of the pamphleteers of his era. He was at once too versatile and too slothful, as McMaster remarks, to consider himself seriously as an author. He himself said: "That is well wrote which is best adapted for obtaining the end of the writer." And he obeyed his own precept to the letter.

Principal Works: A Dissertation on Liberty, Necessity, Pleasure, and Pain, 1725; Articles of Belief and Acts of Religion, 1728; Reflection on Courtship and Marriage, 1746; Plain Truth: or, Serious Considerations on the Present State of the City of Philadelphia and Province of Pennsylvania, 1747; Experiments and Observations on Electricity, 1751-54; Poor Richard Improved, 1757; The Interest of Great Britain Considered With Regard to Her Colonies, 1760; Cool Thoughts on the Present Situation of Our Public Affairs, 1764; The True Sentiments of America, 1768; Political, Miscellaneous, and Philosophical Pieces, 1779; Autobiography, 1791-1828 (first published in full, 1868); Complete Works, 1806 (best later editions 1850, 1889, 1905-07).

About: Abbott, J. S. C. Benjamin Franklin; Bruce, W. C. Benjamin Franklin Self-Revealed; Crane, V. W. Benjamin Franklin: Englishman and American; Dudley, E. L. Benjamin Franklin; Faÿ, B. Franklin: The Apostle of Modern Times; Fisher, S. G. The True Benjamin Franklin; Ford, P. L. The Many-Sided Franklin; Franklin, B. Autobiography; Franklin, W. T. Memoirs of the Life and Writings of Benjamin Franklin; McMaster, J. B. Benjamin Franklin as a Man of Letters; More, P. E. Benjamin Franklin; Parton, J. Life and Times of Benjamin Franklin; Russell, P. Benjamin Franklin: The First Civilized American; Smythe, J. H. The Amazing Benjamin Franklin; Weems, M. L. The Life of Benjamin Franklin; Atlantic Monthly September 1887; McClure's Magazine January 1897; North American Review October 1856.

FREDERIC, HAROLD (August 19, 1856-October 19, 1898), novelist, was born in Utica, N.Y., the son of Henry DeMotte Frederic, a railroad employee who was killed in a wreck at the beginning of 1858. His widow supported herself and her child by conducting a dairy, in which, as soon as he was old enough, the boy had to work hard from four o'clock in the morning to school time, then trudge to school to be jeered at and ostracized by other children because of his shabby appearance. At fourteen he left school and worked at various jobs, with a dentist, a druggist, a confectioner, and as office boy on the Utica *Observer*. It was in this position that he first thought of writing, but it did not yet become his profession. He taught himself photographic retouching, and in 1873 went to Boston to work at this trade; but the strain injured his eyes and the next year he had to return to Utica. Unable for a time to take any regular job, he started to write stories which were published in local newspapers. Then after a period of farm labor he became a reporter, in 1876, on the Utica *Herald*. His salary was $9 a week, and on this stipend he rushed into an early, imprudent, and very unhappy marriage.

By 1880 he was associate editor of the paper, and in 1882 he left it to become editor of the Albany *Evening Journal*. Though this was a leading Republican paper, Frederic was a close friend of Grover Cleveland, then Democratic governor of New York. The paper became bankrupt and failed in 1884, a fortunate event for Frederic, for he immediately secured a post as London correspondent of the New York *Times*, a position he retained for the remainder of his life. He sailed for England at once and never returned to the United States. Extending his province beyond London, he toured France and Italy during a cholera epidemic, and in 1891 went to Russia to investigate the persecution of the Jews. His stories of pogroms barred him from the Czar's territory thereafter.

In 1898 Frederic suffered a stroke of paralysis which proved fatal—though he continued to send his stories in to the *Times* up to a week before he died. A devout Christian Scientist, he refused to have medical attention, and a coroner's inquest was therefore ordered on his death, at which his daughter (evidence of his estranged and miserable family life) testified that her father was insane. The jury's verdict, however, was that he was merely "strong-minded, obstinate, and self-opinionated."

HAROLD FREDERIC

Frederic was indeed all these things, in his writings as well as in his personality. As a journalist, he insisted on expressing his views freely and was disliked by his European colleagues because of his "American" brashness and arrogance; but his newspaper found him indefatigably industrious and thoroughly trustworthy. His appearance indicated his nature—he had the long nose and narrow eyes of the fanatic, coupled with full, sensuous lips, until his last years concealed by a heavy beard.

Frederic was no stylist. He was a careless writer, who produced at great speed, and sent his manuscripts unrevised to the printer, with no concern for their appearance or accuracy. It needed much natural talent to overcome these disadvantages, but this, in his earlier years at least, he had.

His first novels were laid in his native Mohawk Valley, and were *genre* stories, among the earliest of contributions to the American "local color" school. A romantic nostalgia breathes through them and gives them a lasting charm. He turned next to historical novels, accurate in detail and, as Carl Van Doren remarks, "lucid and energetic." In still a third mood, he wrote his masterpiece, *The Damnation of Theron Ware,* a study of the spiritual degeneration of a minister, a fine piece of work and a pioneer among realistic psychological novels in English. It attracted as much attention as had Mrs. Humphry Ward's *Robert Elsmere,* another analysis of the ministerial mind, eight years before.

Frederic never did so well again. His last three novels, with English backgrounds with which he had only a superficial acquaintance, were written when his health and spirit were broken, and are negligible performances.

PRINCIPAL WORKS: *Novels*—Seth's Brother's Wife, 1887; The Lawton Girl, 1890; In the Valley, 1890; Brother Sebastian's Friendship, 1891; The Return of the O'Mahony, 1892; The Copperhead, 1893; Marsena and Other Stories, 1894; The Damnation of Theron Ware, 1896 (first published in England as Illumination); March Hares, 1896; Gloria Mundi, 1898; The Market Place, 1899. *Non-Fiction*—The Young Emperor William II of Germany, 1891; The New Exodus: A Study of Israel in Russia, 1892.

ABOUT: Frederic, H. The Damnation of Theron Ware (see Introduction by R. M. Lovett to 1924 ed.); Book Buyer January 1899; Dial November 1, 1898; Saturday Review (London) October 22, November 12, 1898; New York Times October 20, 1898.

FREEMAN, JAMES EDWARDS (1808-November 21, 1884) *genre* painter and writer of memoirs was born in New Brunswick, Canada, of American parents, Joshua Edwards Freeman and Eliza (Morgan) Freeman. A few years later the family returned to the United States and settled in Otsego County, N.Y. With a passion for studying art, Freeman became a student in 1826 at the National Academy of Design in New York. There his ability and industrious application caused him to be beloved and encouraged by older artists, and, in 1833, he was elected a member of the Academy. In 1836 he went to Italy where he remained until he died. From 1840 to 1849 he was consul to Ancona, a position he considered both unimportant and expensive to hold.

Freeman's better known pictures include "The Beggars," "The Flower Girl," "Young Italy," and "The Bad Shoe," all of which are rich in color and very sentimental. "Mother and Child" was his last exhibited picture, and his self portrait hangs in the National Academy rooms.

He published his first volume of memoirs, *Gatherings From An Artist's Portfolio,* in 1877, and his second, *Gatherings From An Artist's Portfolio in Rome,* in 1883. They showed an ability for storywriting, depicting a gay bohemian life—but they are of little literary value.

Principal Works: Gatherings From An Artist's Portfolio, 1877; Gatherings From An Artist's Portfolio in Rome, 1883.

About: Clement, C. E. & Hutton, L. Artists of the Nineteenth Century; Dunlap, W. History of the Rise and Progress of the Arts of Design in the United States; Freeman, F. Freeman Genealogy; Gillespie, W. M. Rome: As Seen by a New Yorker; Tuckerman, H. T. Book of the Artists; American Art Annual 1911; N.Y. Tribune November 30, 1884.

FRÉMONT, JESSIE (BENTON) (May 31, 1824-December 27, 1902), miscellaneous writer, was born near Lexington, Va., the daughter of Senator Thomas Hart Benton and Elizabeth (McDowell) Benton. On her grandfather's Virginia estate, in St. Louis, and in Washington she passed an eventful childhood, and her father's position appears to have pitched her into the swirl of Capital society. When only sixteen she was married to the debonair John Charles Frémont [*q.v.*], who had returned to Washington from an expedition with the Topographical Corps. The Missouri senator was a bit scornful of the match at first, but approved when young Frémont began to evidence real promise as an explorer.

When her husband returned from his first expedition of note, Jessie worked constantly with him on the writing of a lively report (1842-43). In 1849 Frémont was in San Francisco. Jessie weathered a succession of scourges—banditti attacks, tropical fever, and vampire bats—during her journey there by way of the Isthmus (*A Year of American Travel,* 1878).

She returned to Washington as the wife of the first senator from California and went abroad in 1852. During a stay in San Francisco following another European trip she aided in "discovering" Bret Harte, then a newspaper groundling. Soon afterward came the Civil War, and into *The Story of the Guard: A Chronicle of the War* (1863) she incorporated her sentiments.

In the 'seventies the Frémonts suffered a financial loss. Jessie began to contribute regularly to periodicals, and some of her articles appeared in volume form: *Souvenirs of My Time,* 1887; *Far West Sketches,* 1890; and *The Will and the Way Stories,* 1891. She did much of the work on her husband's memoirs. Mrs. Frémont died December 27, 1902, leaving two daughters and a son.

Her activities ranged from presentation at Court, early in Victoria's reign, to anti-slavery "stumping," and her writings, though sometimes nostalgic and self-indulgent, form a lively record of an important era.

Principal Works: The Story of the Guard: A Chronicle of the War, 1863; A Year of American Travel, 1878; Souvenirs of My Time, 1887; Far West Sketches, 1890; The Will and the Way Stories, 1891.

About: Frémont, J. B. Souvenirs of My Time; Frémont, J. B. A Year of American Travel; Frémont, J. C. Memoirs; Phillips, C. C. Jessie Benton Frémont: A Woman Who Made History; Los Angeles Times December 28 and 31, 1902.

FRÉMONT, JOHN CHARLES (January 21, 1813-July 13, 1890), explorer-historian and military leader, was born in Savannah, Ga., son of Jean Charles Frémont, a dashing French emigré, and Anne (Pryor) Frémont, of one of Tidewater Virginia's best families. He was an agile, quick-witted lad. After attendance at Dr. Robertton's school, he entered Charleston College, but was dismissed for irregularity and negligence. Frémont entertained a feeling of insouciance and tremendous release—a foreshadowing of an incurable restlessness.

When young Frémont returned from a long navy cruise, Secretary of War Poinsett became his staunch patron. He was commissioned a second lieutenant in the Topographical Corps, surveying in the Caro-

Collection of Frederick H. Meserve
JOHN C. FRÉMONT

lina mountains, the Georgia Cherokee country, and, with J. N. Nicollet, able scientist, in the upper Mississippi plateaus. Back in Washington in 1840, they drew up their reports, and through Poinsett it was Frémont's good fortune to meet Thomas Hart Benton, senator from Missouri, who strongly upheld Western expansion. Benton's daughter Jessie, a beaming, active, and charming girl of fifteen, and the erect, handsome and promising young Frémont fell madly in love with each other. With the Senator's whole-hearted disapproval they were secretly married October 19, 1841.

In 1842 Frémont made a geographical trek along the Oregon Trail, through South Pass. In St. Louis, Kit Carson, an ingrained adventurer who had long been apprenticed to a rough backwoods saddler, consented to act as guide for $100 a month. Carson was candid and temperate and although at thirty-three he was unable to read or write his own name, he spoke fluently in Spanish, French, and several Indian tongues. In the Wind River range Frémont scaled what he, in error, thought was the Rockies' highest peak (Frémont's Peak, 13,730 feet). He returned to Washington in October, and Jessie helped him draft an exciting account (*Report of the Exploring Expedition to the Rocky Mountains*).

His bold expedition of 1843 took him through Oregon, across the Sierra, and southward beyond Pueblo. War with Mexico was plainly imminent, and a third expedition was arranged. By February 1846 he had set up for the United States a small though hardy force in California—the beginnings of his participation in the conquest of that state. Following the capture of Los Angeles, August 13, a counteracting revolt set in and a recapture occurred in January 1847, despite Frémont's coming to the aid of Stockton and Kearny. Ambiguous instructions and petty bickerings over precedence, on the part of Frémont's superiors, finally resulted in his court martial. Frémont was charged with "mutiny, disobedience of orders, and conduct prejudicial to good order and discipline." Despite his own admirable defence the panel found him guilty. President Polk withdrew the penalty, but Frémont resigned from the service.

Late in 1848 he set out on a private expedition in search of a western rail route. It was a disastrous venture. Eleven men died of cold and starvation. Shortly after his return, Frémont heard of the discovery of gold and purchased property in the Sierras which brought him a fortune. He served a short term as senator from California, December 1850 to March 1851, and in 1856 was defeated by Buchanan for the presidency.

Frémont procured European capital for the working of the quartz deposits on the Mariposa. He was appointed major-general in the U. S. Army in 1861, accepted two commands, and then resigned in 1864. Thereafter not only his military but his political and financial relations fell into swift reverse. His wife's literary energy aided him in the writing of his *Memoirs* (1887). This and a retirement annuity spared him from poverty at his death.

It has been aptly observed that Frémont's impulses were essentially kinetic. Had it not been for his innate rashness and lack of practical judgment his later career might never have turned anti-climactic. But he was an excellent surveyor and mathematician and his forging into the West was enlightening, bold, and disinterested. His "charmed life" makes unforgettable history.

PRINCIPAL WORKS: Report of the Exploring Expedition to the Rocky Mountains, 1843; Defence of Lieut. Col. J. C. Frémont, 1848; Geographical Memoir Upon Upper California, 1849; Daring Adventures of Kit Carson and Frémont, 1878; Memoirs, 1887.

ABOUT: Frémont, J. C. Daring Adventures; Memoirs; Defence; Grierson, F. Valley of Shadows; Nevins, A. Frémont: The West's Greatest Adventurer; New York Tribune July 14, 1890.

FRENCH, ALICE ("Octave Thanet") (March 19, 1850-January 9, 1934), novelist and short story writer, was born in Andover, Mass., the daughter of the Hon. George Henry French, a manufacturer of farm machinery who had held some political offices, and Frances (Morton) French, daughter of a governor of Massachusetts. Before the Civil War the father moved to Arkansas, and though Miss French was educated at Abbott Academy, in Andover, all her adult years were spent in the South and West. From 1882 her winters were spent in the canebrake country of Arkansas, her summers in Davenport, Iowa. She never married, and her chief interest aside from her writing was club work; she was president of the Iowa Society of Colonial Dames, and an active member of half a dozen other patriotic and cultural organizations. She started writing for the literary magazines of the East in the early 1880's, and continued to publish books and stories until she was nearly seventy, when she ceased to write. The State University of Iowa conferred an honorary Litt. D. on her in 1911.

All Miss French's novels and stories were published under the pseudonym of "Octave Thanet." She shrank from publicity and received very little of it; though her novels were popular, her readers knew nothing of her, many of them not knowing even that she was a woman. Though her chosen scene was nearly always the villages of rural Arkansas, she was interested also in English history of the sixteenth century, and to a certain extent in labor problems of her own time; she was an advocate of co-operatives as opposed to labor unions. She was an industrious rather than a gifted writer, determinedly cheerful and full of common sense and brisk sympathy. Her style she modeled on the simplicity and clarity of Maupassant, and her writing is nearly always clear and simple. Her books are hardly worth the reading today, but with a few others, like Kate Chopin and "Charles Egbert Craddock," she helped to found regional fiction in America.

ALICE FRENCH
("Octave Thanet")

PRINCIPAL WORKS: Knitters in the Sun, 1887; We All, 1888; Expiation, 1890; Otto the Knight, 1891; Stories of a Western Town, 1893; An Adventure in Photography, 1893; A Captured Dream and Other Stories, 1897; Missionary Sheriff, 1897; A Book of True Lovers, 1897; The Heart of Toil, 1898; A Slave to Duty and Other Women, 1898; Man of the Hour, 1905; The Lion's Share, 1907; By Inheritance, 1910; Stories That End Well, 1911; A Step on the Stair, 1913; And the Captain Answered, 1917.

ABOUT: Publishers' Weekly January 27, 1934; New York Times January 1 and 10, 1934.

FRENCH, LUCY VIRGINIA (SMITH) (March 16, 1825-March 31, 1881), poet and novelist, was born in Accomac County, Va., of a wealthy and cultured family. Her father, Mease W. Smith, was an educator and lawyer, and her mother, Elizabeth (Parker) Smith, the daughter of a wealthy merchant. After her mother's death, Virginia was sent to Mrs. Hannah's School in Washington, Pa. After graduating with high honors, she and her sister, not being happy at home after their father's remarriage, went to Memphis, Tenn., where they became teachers. Virginia also did some writing for the Louisville *Journal* under the name "L'Inconnue" and in 1852 became editor of the *Southern Ladies' Book.* In 1853 she married Colonel Johns Hopkins French who, after reading one of her poems, "One or Two," determined to meet her and propose to her. After her marriage Mrs. French continued her literary career, editing several newspapers and magazines, and publishing poetry, a five-act tragedy, and two novels, *My Roses* and *Darlingtonia.* She had a sense of the dramatic, liked the romantic and heroic, and did perhaps her best work in poetry. She died at McMinnville, Tenn., where she had spent the twenty-eight years of her married life.

PRINCIPAL WORKS: Wind Whispers, 1856; Istalilxo: The Lady of Tula, 1856; Legends of the South, 1867; My Roses, 1872; Darlingtonia, 1879.

ABOUT: Davidson, J. W. The Living Writers of the South; Tardy, M. T. The Living Female Writers of the South; American Illustrated Methodist Magazine July 1900; Nashville Daily American April 3, 1881.

FRENEAU, PHILIP MORIN (January 2, 1752-December 19, 1832), poet, was born in New York City, the son of Pierre Freneau (the name was originally Fresneau), a wealthy wine importer of Huguenot descent, and Agnes (Watson) Freneau. He was educated at home by private tutors, so well that when he entered the College of New Jersey (now Princeton) as a sophomore at the age of fifteen, the president wrote his mother a letter of congratulation on his preparation. He was graduated in 1771, as a classmate of James Madison, his lifelong friend. Already he was both a poet and an ardent Whig.

For a short time, and very reluctantly, he taught in a seminary in Maryland. In 1776 he went as secretary to a planter in Santa Cruz, Danish West Indies; from the wild and beautiful surroundings of this place came the inspiration for the best of his lyric poetry. He had already to his credit a number of satiric poems, hotly anti-Tory and bitter with invective. On his return to New York in 1778 (a voyage marked by capture by the British and on this occasion a prompt release), he began writing for the *United States Magazine.* It is a curious fact that the "poet of the Revolution" never fought in it. Instead, in 1780, he went as supercargo on a brig plying between New York and the Azores. His capture by a British man-of-war led to imprisonment in the prison-ship "Scorpion," in New York Harbor, with transfer to the hospital ship "Hunter." Starvation and brutality almost cost him his life, but before it was too late he was exchanged and went to regain his health at his family's country home—later his own home—in New Jersey.

Freneau next went to work in the Philadelphia post office, but most of his time was given to writing for and helping to edit the *Freeman's Journal.* He could not remain sedentary; by 1784 he was at sea again, and for five years was master of a brig of his own. He knew shipwrecks and hurricanes, and he learned to know the sea as no other American poet has done. His marriage in 1789 to Eleanor Forman ended his wanderings for ten years; he became editor of the New York *Daily Advertiser,* and then in 1791 went to Philadelphia (then the national capital) to act as clerk of foreign languages for the Secretary of

PHILIP FRENEAU

State. His more important function was as editor and publisher of the *National Gazette,* a Jeffersonian organ in opposition to John Fenno's Federalist *Gazette of the United States.* Supported by Jefferson and Madison, he voiced the feelings of the democrats against the aristocrats, and earned from Washington the epithet of "rascal." In 1793 the paper was suspended because of a yellow fever epidemic, and at the same time Jefferson's retirement lost him his government position. He went to his estate in New Jersey, where he edited (and printed) a small magazine called the *Jersey Chronicle.* In 1795 he was editor of the New York *Time-Piece.*

This ended his editorial career, and soon afterward he returned to sea. Until 1807 he alternated between farming and voyages as a sea captain. All the time he continued to write poetry, and to bring out new collections of his writings. In 1807 he retired to "Mt. Pleasant," his New Jersey home, for the remainder of his life. He was then fifty-five, with a quarter century still before him. He published nothing after 1815, and wrote little. He died in a snowstorm on a winter night, when, returning home after a gathering in the near-by village of Freehold, he lost his way, fell in a bog, and was found dead of exposure the next morning. He was almost eighty-one.

Freneau was the major American poet before Bryant. His humorous and satirical verse, passionately partisan and sometimes coarsely violent, made his contemporary reputation; but his permanent fame rests on his lyrics. He himself knew where his genius lay, and lamented the neglect of what he felt was his best work. He was the first of the romanticists: he had an eye for nature that was keen as well as idealizing; he was our earliest writer to treat the Indians as serious subjects for romantic verse; and above all he was the poet of the sea, both in his descriptive lyrics and in his narrative naval ballads, like the "Battle of Eutaw." In "The House of Night" he anticipated the supernaturalism and macabre Gothicism of Poe. "The Wild Honeysuckle," "The Indian Burying Ground," and others of his lyrics show him at his best. Constantly revising his verse, he frequently injured it; and he always wrote too voluminously and uncritically; but in the midst of crudity and prolixity one comes upon sudden felicities which prove Freneau indubitably a poet, and a poet of more than mediocre rank.

Principal Works: A Poem on the Rising Glory of America, 1771; A Voyage to Boston, 1774; General Gage's Soliloquy, 1775; General Gage's Confession, 1775; The British Prison-Ship, 1781; Poems of Philip Freneau, 1786; A Journey From Philadelphia to New York, by Richard Slender, Stocking Weaver, 1787; Miscellaneous Works of Mr. Philip Freneau: Containing His Essays and Additional Poems, 1788; The Village Merchant, 1794; Poems Written Between the Years 1768 and 1794, 1795; Letters on Various Interesting and Important Subjects, by Richard Slender (prose) 1805; Poems Written and Published During the American Revolutionary War, 1809; A Collection of Poems, on American Affairs, 1815.

About: Austin, M. S. Philip Freneau: The Poet of the Revolution; Forman, S. E. The Political Activities of Philip Freneau; More, P. E. Shelburne Essays; Pattee, F. L. Sidelights on American Literature.

FROTHINGHAM, OCTAVIUS BROOKS (November 26, 1822-November 27, 1895), clergyman and biographer, was born in Boston, Mass., the second child of Nathaniel Langdon Frothingham and Ann Gorham (Brooks) Frothingham. He was graduated from Harvard College in 1843 and from the Divinity School in 1846, and was ordained as pastor of the North Church of Salem in 1847. In 1855, after breaking with his church on the question of slavery, he moved to Jersey City where he became pastor of a new Unitarian society. He soon became widely known as an extraordinarily spiritual man, and admirers of his, who wished his power increased, organized in New York the Third Congregational Unitarian Society, a group which attracted adherents of all faiths. During this twenty-year pastorate, Frothingham was at the height of his intellectual career. Realizing that he held unorthodox views on religion, he founded in Boston in 1867 the Free Religious Association, and served as president until 1878. In 1879 his health failed and, despite a year's rest in France, he never regained it. He retired to Boston, where he finally died, and was cremated at his special request.

Between 1863 and 1891 he wrote many books, the two outstanding ones being *The Safest Creed,* and *Gerrit Smith: A Biography.* Many of his earlier works, written under the stress of a busy life, are full of mistakes and omissions, but in his later books, written at leisure, he was a conscientious and sympathetic biographer.

Principal Works: The Religion of Humanity, 1872; The Safest Creed, 1874; Theodore Parker: A Biography, 1874; Transcendentalism in New England: A History, 1876; Gerrit Smith: A Biography, 1877; George Ripley, 1882; Memoir of William Henry Channing, 1886; Boston Unitarianism, 1820-1850: A Study of the Life and Work of Nathaniel Langdon Frothingham, 1890; Recollections and Impressions, 1822-1890, 1891.

About: Eliot, S. A. Heralds of a Liberal Faith; Frothingham, O. B. Recollections and Impressions: 1822-1890; Proceedings of Massachusetts Historical Society March 1896.

FROTHINGHAM, RICHARD (January 31, 1812-January 29, 1880), historian, was born in Charlestown, Mass., the son of Richard and Mary Thompson Frothingham. After attending public and private schools in Boston, he entered business at the age of eighteen. He was a clerk for a short time in one or two concerns, and in 1834 joined the Middlesex Canal Company where he remained till 1860, rising to the position of treasurer. From 1852 to 1865 he was managing editor of the Boston *Post,* to which paper he had long been a contributor.

An ardent Democrat and greatly interested in politics, he was a delegate to the national convention, member of the state legislature, mayor of Charlestown, and member of the school board. Although never holding a prominent political position, he was essentially public spirited, and associated with many of the most outstanding figures of his day. He is best known as a historian, his works including, among others, *History of the Siege of Boston* and *The Rise of the Republic,* and for his one biography, *Life and Times of Joseph Warren.* His works, though limited in scope, show such careful attention to details and extensive research that little is left for the student in his particular field. Edward Everett called him the "accurate and judicious historian of Charlestown," and valued his historical contributions as important and impartial monographs.

PRINCIPAL WORKS: The History of Charlestown, Massachusetts, 1845-1849; History of the Siege of Boston, 1849; The Command in the Battle of Bunker Hill, 1850; Life and Times of Joseph Warren, 1865; The Rise of the Republic, 1872.

ABOUT: New England Historical and Genealogical Register October 1883; Proceedings Massachusetts Historical Society February 1885.

FULLER, FRANCES. See VICTOR, METTA VICTORIA (FULLER)

FULLER, MARGARET. See FULLER, SARAH MARGARET

FULLER, SARAH MARGARET (Marchesa Ossoli) (May 23, 1810-June 19, 1850), critic and feminist, was born in Cambridgeport, Mass., the oldest child of Timothy Fuller, a Congressman and lawyer, and Margaret (Crane) Fuller. Margaret was her father's special charge, and he forced the mind of the precocious little girl until at six she was reading Latin and by fifteen was familiar also with Greek, French, and Italian, and widely read in English. The harsh regimen ruined her health and made her a prey to nightmares and headaches, but it also made a scholar of her. Her father died suddenly in 1835, and she vowed to educate her brothers and sisters at whatever cost to her own ambitions. She taught in Bronson Alcott's school in Boston, gave private lessons in languages, and from 1837 to 1839 was principal teacher of a school in Providence.

From a daguerreotype
MARGARET FULLER

In 1839 she moved to Boston, where she met Emerson and became closely identified with the school of Transcendentalist philosophers. She published German translations and instituted her series of "conversations," continued to 1844—a sort of forerunner of women's clubs, in the form of gatherings of earnest ladies whom she instructed in social and philosophical subjects. In 1840, with Emerson and George Ripley, she became chief editor of the *Dial,* being obliged also to be its principal contributor. Her removal to New York proved to be the death of the magazine, which had always had an existence as perilous as its influence was wide.

This removal to New York was at the instance of Horace Greeley, who made her literary critic of the *Tribune*. She wrote for him also articles on social questions, based on first-hand investigations of prisons and slums. She lived with the Greeley family, and it was during this period that she fell in love with a Jewish business man named James Nathan (later James Gotendorf), an affair which remained on the sentimentally idealistic plane and finally died of inanition.

By 1846 she had saved enough money to go to Europe, where she met her literary idols—Carlyle, Wordsworth, George Sand, the Brownings. The next year she settled in Rome; she had already become acquainted with the Italian patriot and liberator, Mazzini, and was drawn into his circle. There she met Giovanni Angelo, Marquis Ossoli, ten years her junior. They became lovers soon after, and in 1848 she bore him a son. It seems probable that they were married in 1849, though there is no record of the ceremony. For long periods she was separated from the child, who was left in Rieti, in the Abruzzis, while she and Ossoli worked for Italian liberation in Rome. When the French besieged the city and captured it in June 1849, they fled to Rieti; Ossoli had taken part in the fighting while she worked in the hospitals with the wounded. From Rieti they went to Florence, and then to Leghorn, from which they sailed for America in May 1850. During the voyage the captain died of smallpox; the Ossoli child contracted it, and barely recovered. Almost within sight of New York, the ship was wrecked on Fire Island, and everyone on board perished. The baby's body was washed up on shore, but neither Margaret Fuller nor her husband was ever found. Her manuscript of a complete history of the Roman Revolution, which she was bringing home for publication, was also lost.

In its earlier phases, there is a curious parallelism between Margaret Fuller's career and that of George Eliot, in the days before the Englishwoman became a novelist. It may have been well for the American writer, with her complex nature and economic difficulties, that a life which always bordered on tragedy met with a sharp and sudden end; the future of the little family was dark and uncertain, and Miss Fuller always had as many enemies as she had ardent partisans. One may hear that she was a pedant, a bluestocking, arrogant, hysterical, and affected, loquacious and pretentious; one may hear also that she was a noble, magnetic woman, generous, socially-minded, erudite, and highly gifted in personality as well as in mind. It is quite probable that both versions of her character are true. She was undoubtedly an eccentric, and many who later became her best friends—Emerson, for example—were repelled at first by her nasal voice, her plainness, her peculiar mannerisms, and her aggressiveness; on the other hand no one can study her life or her letters without realizing that essentially she was a woman of remarkable mind, great talents which never came to real fruition, and warm, affectionate nature. She was a pioneer of feminism, and she was a critic of unusual acumen and philosophical breadth. If her life-story is sad and thwarted, as it was, it is largely because she was born out of time and place; a century later, or across the Atlantic Ocean, the world would have known better how to make use of the bounty she had to give it.

Principal Works: Summer on the Lakes, 1844; Woman in the Nineteenth Century, 1845; Papers on Literature and Art, 1846; At Home and Abroad (ed. by A. Fuller) 1856; Life Without and Life Within (ed. by A. Fuller) 1859.

About: Anthony, K. S. Margaret Fuller: A Psychological Biography; Brooks, Van W. The Flowering of New England; Clemmer, M. Men, Women, and Things; Higginson, T. W. Margaret Fuller Ossoli; Howe, J. W. Margaret Fuller (Marchesa Ossoli); Macphail, A. Essays in Puritanism; Outlook June 4, 1910.

FURNESS, WILLIAM HENRY (April 20, 1802-January 30, 1896), clergyman and religious writer, was born in Boston, Mass., the son of William and Rebekah (Thwing) Furness. He attended a "dame's school" and the Latin School, was graduated from Harvard in 1820 and from the Divinity School in 1823. In 1825, he was ordained and installed as the first minister of the Unitarian Church in Philadelphia. The congregation grew rapidly under his leadership, and, in 1875, he was made emeritus pastor, still continuing to preach until his death. In 1847 Harvard honored him with the degree of D.D., and in 1887 Columbia conferred an LL.D. on him.

His two main interests were anti-slavery, which he championed until after the Civil War, and the study of the life of Christ. He did a great deal of research on the latter, publishing several books of which two of the best known are *Jesus and His Biographers* and *The Veil Partly Lifted*.

In addition to these two interests, Furness was one of the first Americans to translate German literature, his most important translation being David Schenkel's *Character of Jesus Portrayed*. He was also a hymn writer, and a lover and promoter of art.

Principal Works: Remarks on the Four Gospels, 1836; Jesus and His Biographers, 1838; A History of Jesus, 1850; Thoughts on the Life and Character of Jesus of Nazareth, 1859; The Veil Partly Lifted, 1864.

About: Eliot, S. A. Heralds of a Liberal Faith; Jordan, J. W. A History of Delaware County, Pennsylvania; Athenaeum February 8, 1896; Christian Register February 6, 1896; Critic February 8, 1896; Nation February 6, 1896; Unitarian Review February 1875.

GAGE, FRANCES DANA (BARKER) (October 12, 1808-November 10, 1884), reformer and miscellaneous writer, was born in Marietta, Ohio, the daughter of Colonel Joseph Barker, one of the original settlers there, and of Elizabeth (Dana) Barker. There she received such education as the frontier village offered, and when she was twenty married James L. Gage, a lawyer of McConnelsville, Ohio. Despite the fact that her home and family, consisting of eight children, made great demands on her, she found time to pursue her reading, writing, and speaking. Mrs. Gage was greatly interested in the slavery question, women's rights, and prohibition. After the family moved to St. Louis in 1853, she was branded an abolitionist and her articles were forbidden to be published. Misfortune dogged their steps in St. Louis, and after three disastrous fires, probably incendiary, and the failure of her husband's health, Mrs. Gage accepted a position as assistant editor of an agricultural paper in Columbus, Ohio During the war she served in various capacities, but her active war work was brought to a stop in 1864 when she was thrown from her carriage and badly injured. After the war she lectured on temperance, but an attack of paralysis in 1867 caused her to give up speaking and devote her time to writing. She became well known for children's stories, under the signature of "Aunt Fanny," sketches of social life, and poems. A temperance tale, *Elsie Magoon: or, The Old Still-House in the Hollow,* was one of her better known works.

PRINCIPAL WORKS: Elsie Magoon: or, The Old Still-House in the Hollow, 1867; Poems, 1867; Gertie's Sacrifice, 1869; Steps Upward, 1870.

ABOUT: Barker, E. F. Barker Genealogy; Brockett, L. P. & Vaughan, M. C. Woman's Work in the Civil War; Stanton, E. C. Eminent Women of the Age; Stanton, E. C., Anthony, S. B. & Gage, M. J. History of Woman Suffrage; New York Tribune November 13, 1884.

GALLAGHER, WILLIAM DAVIS (August 21, 1808-June 27, 1894), editor, poet, and government official, was born in Philadelphia, Pa., the son of Bernard Gallagher, an Irish refugee, and Abigail (Davis) Gallagher, whose father had died in the service of Washington's army at Valley Forge. He spent his boyhood in Southern Ohio, and after attending elementary schools was sent to a seminary in Lancaster. When he was sixteen the *Literary Gazette* published some of his verse, and two years afterwards he entered on a succession of editorial duties on various Ohio literary journals, of which the *Hesperian* was, perhaps, the most significant.

In 1839 Charles Hammond, editor of the Cincinnati *Gazette,* made Gallagher his assistant, and except for a brief break to take over the editorship of the *Daily Message,* an abolitionist newspaper, Gallagher stayed with the *Gazette* until 1850, when he became private secretary to Thomas Corwin, Secretary of the Treasury. Preceding a second secretarial appointment, he was editor of the Louisville *Daily Courier* and the *Western Farmer's Journal*; and President Lincoln afterwards made him special collector of customs and commercial agent in the Mississippi Valley.

Gallagher published three volumes of poems, *Erato No. I, Erato No. II,* and *Erato No. III,* between 1835 and 1837, and edited *Selections From the Poetical Literature of the West* in 1841. Many years later came *Miami Woods, A Golden Wedding, and Other Poems,* which celebated, in Wordsworthian blank verse, the natural charm of the Ohio forests. His lyrics appeared in newspapers and magazines, and, set to music, were often used in theatricals. At a time when Middle West poetry was in a decidedly formative stage Gallagher's verse rang at least as true as that of any of his Ohio contemporaries.

PRINCIPAL WORKS: Erato No. I, 1835; Erato No. II, 1835; Erato No. III, 1837; Selections From the Poetical Literature of the West, 1841; Miami Woods, A Golden Wedding, and Other Poems, 1881.

ABOUT: Venable, E. Poets of Ohio; Louisville Commercial and Louisville Times June 28, 1894.

GALLOWAY, JOSEPH (c.1731-August 29, 1803,), colonial statesman and Loyalist, was born at West River, Maine, the son of Peter Bines Galloway, merchant and owner of several large estates, and Elizabeth Rigbie (or Rigby) Galloway. After the death of his father, Joseph removed with his family to Philadelphia, where he studied law and, in time, acquired a most successful practice. In October 1753 he was married to Grace, daughter of the wealthy Lawrency Growden.

From 1756 to 1776 (except the year 1764-65 when with Benjamin Franklin he petitioned that Crown control replace proprietary government) he held a seat as an assemblyman, and during his political leadership was roundly commended; he supported the War with France, but advanced the aristocratic interests of his own class whenever possible; and although he was mindful of the problems of the empire he kept a sharp eye on the self-governing rights of the colonies, holding that parliament, although legalistically supreme, was at times overstepping constitutionality.

Galloway's ire over the rejection, by the First Continental Congress, of his plan for imperial legislature occasioned *A Candid Examination of the Mutual Claims of Great Britain and the Colonies* and hastened the wane of his popularity. As the war storm broke he escaped to the country, thinking he might remain neutral, but finally fled to the British ranks—for he believed, fundamentally, that the American cause was unjust—and when the Continental forces seized Philadelphia in 1778 Galloway sailed for England. As American Loyalist spokesman and pamphleteer he issued *Letters to a Nobleman* . . . and *A Letter to the Right Honourable Viscount H——e*. . . . With the confiscation of his estates in America he leaned heavily on his British pension. His last years were spent in religious study and he published a number of ecclesiastical tracts. More important to historians, however, were his miscellaneous observations, letters, etc., which aid in explaining a few of the contradictions in the political history of the colonial period.

PRINCIPAL WORKS: A Candid Examination of the Mutual Claims of Great Britain and the Colonies, 1775; Letters to a Nobleman, on the

Conduct of the War in the Middle Colonies, 1779; A Letter to the Right Honourable Viscount H—e, on his Naval Conduct in the American War, 1779; Historical and Political Reflections on the Rise and Progress of the American Rebellion, 1780; Brief Commentaries Upon Such Parts of the Revelation and Other Prophecies as Immediately Refer to the Present Times, 1802.

ABOUT: Keith, C. P. The Provincial Councillors of Pennsylvania; Seibert, W. H. The Loyalists of Pennsylvania; Tyler, M. C. The Literary History of the American Revolution; Pennsylvania Magazine of History and Biography July-December 1902.

GARDEN, ALEXANDER (1685-September 27, 1756), Episcopal clergyman and early champion of Negro rights, was born in Scotland. He was educated there and came to America in 1719, the year in which the Proprietary Government was overthrown. Garden was shortly elected to the rectorship of St. Phillip's and for the greater part of his life served also as commissary of the Bishop of London for the Carolinas, Georgia, and the Bahama Islands. On October 20, 1731, he instituted the "annual meetings of the clergy," the need for which had been occasioned by the rapid growth of the Anglican church. Four years later he made a rest journey into the northern provinces.

In 1738 the Reverend George Whitefield, a fellow-clergyman (*i.e.*, Episcopalian), who had come to America to aid James Edward Oglethorpe in the settlement of Georgia, was favorably received as a guest preacher in the St. Philip's pulpit. He embarked shortly for England, where the unanimity of approval in the various parishes gave him, on his return to the United States in 1740, an excess of confidence. Garden frowned upon Whitefield's newly acquired disregard for canonical obligations—the making of extempore prayers, complete reversal of the order of service, etc.—and in his *Six Lectures to the Reverend George Whitefield* flatly outlined his objections, following up with *Two Sermons: Lately Preached* . . . In 1742 Garden issued a little book on the *Doctrine of Justification . . . in a Letter to Mr. A. Croswell of Groton, in New England.*

He was genuinely interested in the welfare of the Negro; and in 1743 on behalf of the Negro school in Charleston, he secured funds and services from the society for the propagation of the gospel; in this and other fields for social improvement he made decided progress.

Garden resigned from his parish in the Spring of 1854. In his long service to the church he had "neither taken nor granted any relaxation from the letter of the ecclesiastical law." And there had been many odds working against him, for in a letter, dated 1843, he asserted that the state of religion was

> bad enough, God knows. Rome and the Devil have contrived to crucify her twixt two thieves—Infidelity and Enthusiasm . . .

His opinions were fearless and well defined; and although some critics labeled his writings "a medley of truth and falsehood, sense and nonsense, served up with pride and virulence . . . ," he had many intellectual admirers and exerted, it would seem, considerable influence upon the churchmen of his day.

PRINCIPAL WORKS: Six Letters to the Reverend Mr. George Whitefield, 1740; Two Sermons: Lately Preached in the Parish Church of St. Philip, Charles-Town, in South-Carolina, 1740; The Doctrine of Justification: According to the Scriptures and Articles and Homilies of the Church of England . . . in a Letter to Mr. A. Croswell of Groton, in New England, 1742; A Brief Account of the Deluded Dutartres: Extracted From a Sermon . . . , 1762.

ABOUT: McCrady, E. An Historic Church: The Westminster Abbey of South Carolina; Tyler, M. C. A History of American Literature; prefaces to the works.

GARRISON, WILLIAM LLOYD (December 10, 1805-May 24, 1879), reformer and editor, was born in Newburyport, Mass., the son of Abijah and Frances Maria (Fanny) (Lloyd) Garrison. Both parents were from Nova Scotia. The father, a drunken sea captain, deserted his family in 1807. The child was reared by a farmer, and received very little schooling. At nine he was apprenticed to a shoemaker, then to a cabinet maker. The mother studied nursing and moved to Baltimore

Collection of Frederick H. Meserve
WILLIAM LLOYD GARRISON

in 1815; he went with her but became so homesick he returned to Massachusetts and in 1818 was apprenticed to the editor of the Newburyport *Herald*. In 1826, a full-fledged journeyman printer, he published the Newburyport *Free Press,* which printed Whittier's first poems, but which soon failed. He then went to Boston as a printer, and in 1828, with N. H. White, published a reform organ called the *National Philanthropist.*

Garrison was won to the cause of abolition by Benjamin Lundy, a Quaker. For a short time he went to Bennington, Vt., to edit an anti-Jackson paper, but in 1829 he made his first anti-slavery speech in Boston, and from then until the Civil War he gave himself unceasingly to this crusade. He went to Baltimore and with Lundy edited the weekly *Genius of Universal Emancipation,* which cost him seven weeks in prison on a libel charge. After a few months as a lecturer, he started his famous paper, the *Liberator,* in Boston, with Isaac Knapp, in 1830. It became the spearhead of the extremist wing of the abolitionist movement; at one time Georgia offered $5000 for his arrest and conviction. In 1831 he founded the New England Anti-Slavery Society, and in 1833, after his first visit to England, the American Anti-Slavery Society, of which he served twenty-two terms as president. In 1834 he married Helen Eliza Benson; they had seven children.

In 1835 occurred the episode when Garrison was mobbed and dragged through the streets of Boston with a rope around his neck. He was hated not only by advocates of slavery; he antagonized his own supporters, and his uncompromising attitude caused a split in the abolitionist ranks. In 1854 he denounced the Constitution as "a covenant with death and an agreement with hell," and publicly burned a copy. High-handed and violent as he was, he was a non-resistant, practically an anarchist, and never voted but once in his life.

With the Emancipation Proclamation the work of the *Liberator* was over, and Garrison killed it at the end of 1865. His wife had been paralyzed from 1863, and he himself was now in poor health, though he managed one more triumphant visit to England in 1867. The next year his friends raised a fund of $30,000 for his support. He died in his daughter's home in New York City.

Garrison's was a most contradictory nature. Bald and bespectacled, he did not look the part of the bigot he undoubtedly was. Lowell spoke of

> "his features very
> Benign for an incendiary."

But there is no denying that he was a fanatic, an arrogant, self-righteous autocrat, and so gullible and credulous an enthusiast that he swallowed every variety of reform—or, as a contemporary put it, "every infidel fanaticism afloat." (Among them, of course, were some worthy causes.) At the same time he was single-minded, selfless, absolutely without fear, and whole-heartedly devoted to his causes almost to the point of insanity. His editorial style was intense, incisive, and powerful. Though no temperament could seem less poetic than his, he wrote a good deal of verse, highly moralistic, but displaying much imaginative force.

PRINCIPAL WORKS: Thoughts on African Colonization, 1832; Sonnets and Other Poems, 1843; Selections From Writings and Speeches, 1852.

ABOUT: Chapman, J. J. William Lloyd Garrison; Garrison, W. P. William Lloyd Garrison: The Story of His Life Told by His Children; Grimké, A. H. William Lloyd Garrison: The Abolitionist; Higginson, T. W. Contemporaries; Johnson, O. Garrison: An Outline of His Life; Johnson, O. William Lloyd Garrison and His Times; Smith, G. The Moral Crusader: William Lloyd Garrison; Swift, L. William Lloyd Garrison; Villard, O. G. Some Newspapers and Newspaper Men.

GAY, SYDNEY HOWARD (May 22, 1814-June 25, 1888), journalist and abolitionist, was born in Hingham, Mass. His parents were Ebenezer and Mary Alleyne (Otis) Gay, both of Colonial stock. He entered Harvard in 1829, and, although he had to leave because of ill health, the degree of B.A. was conferred on him in 1833. After working in a counting house and traveling in the West, he took up law in his father's office. He soon gave it up, however, because of his intense hatred for slavery and a feeling that he couldn't take an oath to support a constitution which upheld that institution. He then went to Boston where he joined a group of abolitionists headed by Garrison. In 1843 he became editor of the *American Anti-Slavery Standard* in New York, and two years later married Elizabeth Neall. At this time he was an active agent in the "underground railroad." In 1857 he joined the New York *Tribune* staff and from 1862 to 1865 was managing editor, resigning then because of ill health. He became managing editor of the Chicago *Tribune* in 1867 and in 1871 returned to New York where he was a member of the editorial staff of the

Evening Post under William Cullen Bryant. In association with Bryant, Gay undertook a history of the United States. Bryant died soon after the work was started, but the publishers attributed it to him. Though lacking proportion, the history was very readable. In 1884 Gay published his *James Madison* and was working on a life of Edmund Quincy when he died of paralysis.

PRINCIPAL WORK: James Madison, 1884.

ABOUT: Gay, F. L. John Gay of Dedham, Mass., and Some of His Descendants; Lincoln, G. History of the Town of Hingham, Mass.; Boston Post June 27, 1888; Critic June 30, 1888; New York Tribune June 27, 1888.

GAYARRÉ, CHARLES ÉTIENNE ARTHUR (January 9, 1805-February 11, 1895), historian, was born, of Spanish-French aristocracy, on a sugar plantation near New Orleans, the son of Don Carlos and Marie Elizabeth (de Boré) de Gayarré. After graduation from the College of Orleans, he studied law and was admitted to the Philadelphia bar. He returned to New Orleans and published an abridged translation of Martin's *History of Louisiana,* called *Essai Historique sur la Louisiane* (1830). After holding several public offices he was elected to the United States Senate in 1835, but resigned because of ill health.

He went abroad to get medical care and to gather material from the archives of Paris and Madrid. Two drab volumes, in French, *Histoire de la Louisiane,* appeared in 1846 and 1847. His most exhaustive work, *The History of Louisiana,* (1851-66), was published in four volumes with varying subtitles.

Gayarré was denied a political come-back in 1853, and in explanation he wrote *Address to the People of the State on the Late Frauds Perpetrated at the Elections* (1853). In 1854 came *School for Politics,* a kind of closet drama of political intrigue. After the war Gayarré's finances were at low ebb; his farm, "Roncal," just out of New Orleans, was a failure. He now consciously wrote for money. *Fernando de Lemos* was a loose-knit fictional autobiography, with an inferior sequel, *Aubert Dubayet.* An indelible aristocratic pride lay behind *The Creoles of History and the Creoles of Romance,* in which he attacked George Washington Cable's *Grandissimes.* His wife, Mrs. Annie Sullivan Buchanan, whom he had married in 1843, died without issue in 1914.

Gayarré had "the courtesy of the old school of gentlemen," and that cavalier spirit pervaded his writings. As a recorder he was, therefore, too discursive, but he

CHARLES E. GAYARRÉ

was distinctly a leader in the "literary efflorescence of Louisiana."

PRINCIPAL WORKS: *Historical and Biographical*—Essai Historique sur La Louisiane, 1830; History of Louisiana (4 vols.) 1851-66; Philip II of Spain, 1866; Fernando de Lemos, 1872; Aubert Dubayet: or, The Two Sister Republics, 1882; The Creoles of History and the Creoles of Romance, 1885. *Dramatic*—Dr. Bluff in Russia: or, The Emperor Nicholas and the American Doctor, 1865.

ABOUT: Gayarré, C. E. A. The Creoles of History and the Creoles of Romance; Saucier, E. N. Charles Gayarré: The Creole Historian: New Orleans Times-Democrat February 11, 1895.

GAYLER, CHARLES (April 1, 1820-May 28, 1892) playwright and journalist, was born in New York City, the son of C. J. Gayler, a hardware dealer. He was still a law student under Alexander Bradford, in New York, when his first play *The Heir of Glen Avon* was produced in 1839. Two years later he went west, campaigned for Clay, and then secured a post on the Cincinnati *Evening Dispatch.* During these years he wrote some local pieces, a burlesque and an operetta, for the comedian Josh Selsbee. In 1846 he was married to Grace Christian, and in 1850, following a production of *The Buckeye Gold Hunters* (1849), he returned to New York and worked for the *Courier,* the *Express,* and the *Day-Book.*

But play-writing had just begun. *Taking the Chances* (1856), a piece which lifted the Yankee from the comic-strip level, starred McVicker, the well-known Chicago actor; and *The Female American Cousin,* with Julia Daly, saw 120 nights at the London Adelphi. Gayler was scoring veritable "hits" but, by and large, he was "not popular in the press." He therefore had *The Magic Marriage* (about 1861) brought out anonymously. Praise was rampant. But during the second week the author was announced and Gayler was accused of libel. *Bull Run* (1861) prospered for ten weeks at a time of public depression. *The Connie Soogah,* an Irish melodrama, was revamped for production in 1881.

Lights and Shadows of New York and *Fritz: Our Cousin-German* were the last and perhaps best of Gayler's plays. He lived in retirement in Brooklyn for several years before his death.

Gayler was a large man with sunny manners and had friendships without number. At a time when theatrical managers leaned upon foreign successes and shunned domestic pieces, he wrote "upward of 150 plays," largely on the American scene. The veteran critic, William Winter, found in Gayler "a fertility of invention, a breadth of humor, a lively play of fancy, and . . . hearty good feeling."

Principal Works: *Plays*—Heir of Glen Avon, 1839; The Buckeye Gold Hunters, 1849; The Clement County Snake; Taking the Chances, 1856; Olympiana; Love of a Prince; The Sun of the Night (an adaptation from Sejour); The Robbers of the Rhine; The Female American Cousin; The Magic Marriage, 1861 (?); Bull Run: or, The Sacking of Fairfax Courthouse, 1861; Aurora Floyd; Inflation, 1876; The Connie Soogah, 1881; The Bohemian, 1885; Master of Arts; Lights and Shadows of New York, 1888; Fritz: Our Cousin-German, 1888.

About: New York Herald May 29, 1892; New York Times May 29, 1892; New York Tribune October 13, 1875; November 20, 1879; October 4, 1881; December 5, 1881; January 8, 1886; May 29, 1892; June 5, 1892.

GEORGE, HENRY (September 2, 1839-October 29, 1897), economist and reformer, champion of the Single Tax, was born in Philadelphia, the second of ten children of Richard Samuel Henry George, a publisher of religious books, and his second wife, Catherine Pratt (Vallance) George, who had conducted a private school. After five months of high school, George persuaded his father to let him go to work at thirteen. After serving as an errand boy and a clerk, in 1855 he shipped as foremast boy for Melbourne and Calcutta, remaining away a year. On his return he became an apprentice printer. Of a mettlesome disposition, he quarreled with his employers and changed positions often. Finally in 1857 he sailed as a steward to San Francisco; some cousins living there secured his dismissal from the ship, and after an unsuccessful attempt to make his way to the mines he became a printer in San Francisco. By 1860 he was a foreman printer, then with some fellow workmen founded a paper, the *Evening Journal,* which failed for lack of wire connections.

In 1860, against her family's wishes, out of a job and penniless, he married Annie Corsina Fox, Australian-born daughter of a British army officer, and a Roman Catholic. Though George, reared an Episcopalian, had become a Methodist, they were married by a priest and his relations with the Catholic church were always friendly, his chief disciple later being Father McGlynn, who was excommunicated for his adherence to the Single Tax.

The young couple spent several years in the deepest poverty, near to starvation, while their four children were born. George did every sort of work, in Sacramento and San Francisco. In the former city he was converted to free trade. Finally in 1866 he became a printer, then a reporter, on the San Francisco *Times,* rising by 1868 to managing editor. He had started writing in 1865, and his first article anticipating his economic theory was published in the *Overland Magazine* in 1868. After a trip to New York he became editor of the Oakland *Transcript,* but his Single Tax theory (one tax, on land values only, the root of economic inequality being, according to this system, the artificial increase in value of unimproved property) was gradually evolving, and most of his later life was given to writing and speaking in its advocacy. From 1872 to 1875 he was one of the owners of the *Daily Evening Post,* and from 1876 to 1879 inspector of gas meters.

Progress and Poverty, the "Single Tax Bible," was privately printed at the author's expense in 1879 and officially published the next year. In 1880 George moved to New York. In 1881 he visited Ireland as correspondent of the New York *Irish World,* and between 1883 and 1886 made two lecture tours in England for the Land Reform Union. In 1886 he ran second for mayor of New York, being defeated by A. S. Hewitt but outrunning Theodore Roosevelt. From 1886 to 1892 he edited a weekly in support of his theory, the *Standard,* and established at the same time a Land Reform group which grew into the Single Tax Association. In 1888 and 1889 he was in Great Britain again, and in 1890 in Australia. The latter was also the year of the first national Single Tax conference. Overwork brought on an attack of aphasia, from which he recuperated in

Collection of Frederick H. Meserve
HENRY GEORGE

Bermuda. Unwarned by this illness, he continued to work too hard, and in 1897 ran again for mayor of New York as an independent Democrat. The strain killed him; he died of apoplexy three days before election. At his public funeral 100,000 persons passed before his bier.

George's bald head and full red beard, and his unexplained "English accent" were familiar to all serious-minded audiences of the 'nineties. He was the respectable "middle-class radical" typical of his times—a cigar was even named after him! Around the central reform of the Single Tax he gathered numerous minor reform measures, and he was the only American who ever founded an economic theory with a world-wide following. The Single Tax is still a living issue, with thousands of earnest disciples. Though its central idea was not actually original with George, his simplification and clarification of it made it peculiarly his. No economist has ever written in more lucid and severely simple style, and his books are a model of logical presentation and persuasiveness.

Principal Works: Our Land and Land Policy, 1871; Progress and Poverty, 1879; The Irish Land Question, 1881; Social Problems, 1883; Protection or Free Trade, 1886; An Open Letter to Pope Leo XIII, 1891; A Perplexed Philosopher, 1892; The Science of Political Economy, 1897.

About: Geiger, G. R. The Philosophy of Henry George; George, H., Jr. The Life of Henry George; Post, L. F. The Prophet of San Francisco; Sawyer, R. A. Henry George and the Single Tax; Teilhac, E. (transl. by E. A. J. Johnson) Pioneers of American Economic Thought in the Nineteenth Century.

GIBBONS, JAMES SLOAN (July 1, 1810-October 17, 1892), abolitionist and miscellaneous writer, was born in Wilmington, Del., the son of Dr. William and Rebecca (Donaldson) Gibbons. After attending a Friends' school he became a prosperous merchant in Philadelphia, and there married, in 1833, Abigail Hopper, the daughter of a Quaker philanthropist. Moving to New York in 1835, he became one of the organizers of the Ocean Bank and of the Broadway Bank, being cashier of the former for years. He wrote for many newspapers and magazines on the subject of banking and finance but as an author is known chiefly for his war song, "We Are Coming, Father Abraham, Three Hundred Thousand Strong."

Gibbons, always an ardent abolitionist, was much interested in the work of the American Anti-Slavery Society and at one time mortgaged his furniture to preserve the paper, *National Anti-Slavery Standard,* of which he was assistant editor. Because of his connection with this paper he was disowned by the Friends in 1842, but continued to attend their meetings. During the draft riots in 1863, because of his anti-slavery sympathies, he had his home sacked, his papers destroyed, and his life endangered.

Gibbons was widely known for his philanthropies. His wife, who was nine years his senior and survived him, always shared in these interests. Gibbons started the movement to preserve forests that resulted in the national observance of Arbor Day.

Principal Works: The Banks of New York: Their Dealers, the Clearing House, and the Panic of 1857, 1859; Organization of the Public Debt and a Plan for the Relief of the Treasury, 1863; Courtship and Matrimony: With Other Sketches From Scenes and Experiences in Social Life, 1879.

About: Emerson, S. H. Life of Abby Hopper Gibbons; Garrison, W. P. & F. J. William Lloyd Garrison; Friends' Intelligencer Journal October 29, 1892; New York Daily Tribune October 19, 1892; New York Evening Post October 18, 1892.

GIBSON, WILLIAM HAMILTON (October 5, 1850-July 16, 1896), artist and naturalist, was the son of Edmund Trowbridge Hastings and Elizabeth Charlotte (Sanford) Gibson. Born in Newtown, Conn., he was educated at the Gunnery school at Washington, Conn., and Brooklyn Polytechnic Institute. Bored with the general curriculum, he showed great skill in drawing and an ardent love for nature study. His father's death in 1868, however, forced him to find some means of livelihood. He opened an insurance office in Brooklyn, but his early ambition was soon aroused and he set himself up as an artist. Inexperienced as he was, he achieved a surprising success. Some of his early drawings were published with accompanying sketches that he had written. He also did work for various lithographers. His first real chance came in 1872 when he was sent by Appleton's to sketch the Connecticut countryside, these drawings to be later published in William Cullen Bryant's *Picturesque America.* In 1873 he married Emma Ludlor Blanchard.

Gibson became well known as an author and illustrator of nature articles which appeared in the leading magazines. Some of these were reprinted later in his books. Although by no means a scholar, he won a name for himself as a popularizer of nature. His success was largely due to his acute powers of observation and his charming and informal method of presenting his ideas.

Principal Works: Pastoral Days: or, Memories of a New England Year, 1881; Highways and Byways: or, Saunterings in New England, 1883; Strolls by Starlight and Sunshine, 1891; Sharp Eyes, 1892; Our Edible Toadstools and Mushrooms, 1895; Eye Spy, 1897; My Studio Neighbors, 1898; Blossom Hosts and Insect Guests, 1901; Our Native Orchids, 1905.

About: Adams, J. C. William Hamilton Gibson: Artist-Naturalist-Author; Wilson, M. C. C. John Gibson of Cambridge, Mass., and His Descendants; New England Magazine February, 1897; Critic July 25, 1896; New York Tribune July 17, 1896.

GILDER, RICHARD WATSON (February 8, 1844-November 18, 1909), poet, editor, and civic leader, was born at Belle Vue, Bordentown, N.J., the son of William Henry Gilder, a Methodist minister, and Jane (Nutt) Gilder, daughter of a major in the War of 1812. His schooling was scattered, but his aptitude for writing came early. When twelve or thirteen he co-edited, and set the type for, the *St. Thomas Register.* During the Civil War, "Watsey," with his mother's misgivings, joined the 1st Philadelphia Artillery, and his short service in this volunteer company later won him membership in the Grand Army of the Republic.

As paymaster on the Camden and Amboy Railroad he weathered several potential catastrophes and was glad to find an opening on the Newark *Daily Advertiser* as a reporter. He assisted in the founding of the *Morning Register* and at the same time (1869-70) began writing for *Hours at Home,* which in November 1870 was merged with *Scribner's Monthly.* Gilder became managing editor, conducted the "Old Cabinet" column of reminiscences and contemporary comment, and directed the art features. About a year later he met a beautiful young student-artist, Helena de Kay, granddaughter of Joseph Rodman Drake, the poet, and she became the direct inspiration for the delicate love sonnets which he later incorporated into *The New Day.* Through her copy of Omar Khayyám's *Rubaiyat,* Gilder became one of the first American writers to be interested in the Persian poet. Obviously the sensitive young Gilder and the art-loving Helena de Kay had strong mutual attractions. They were married June 3, 1874, and their home, The Studio, on Fifteenth Street, became the casual mecca of many artists and litterateurs—St. Gaudens, La Farge, Joseph Jefferson, Madame Modjeska, the Charles Dudley Warners, and at a time when public sentiment was viciously turned against him, Walt Whitman.

With the publication of a second volume of poems in 1878, *The Poet and His Master,* Gilder had a literary leg to stand on when he met Browning, Austin Dobson, and Edmund Gosse during his stay abroad in 1879. The editorship of *Scribner's* was passed on to Gilder in October 1881, a month before the death of Dr. Holland who had long served as its editor. Under a new name, the *Century,* this organ began its influence in the shaping of contemporary American thought in history, letters, and

Collection of Frederick H. Meserve

RICHARD WATSON GILDER

art. Gilder was an active reformer. In 1883 he aided in the organization of the American Copyright League to back the Dorsheimer International Copyright Bill—the first gun in the final enactment. He was holding office in numerous civic organizations but found time to write considerable verse, which came to him as "a note from an inner pain or happiness." Moreover he was opposing Tammany and was advocating Civil Service Reform, and in 1894 became chairman of the Tenement House Commission.

Overwork began to leave a mark on him. He went abroad in 1894 and revived his "insatiable appetite for the old world." On returning he participated constantly in significant functions. In all Gilder received honorary degrees from the colleges and universities of Harvard, Yale, Princeton, Wesleyan, and Dickinson. His last books were his honest and intimate account, *Grover Cleveland: A Record of Friendship,* and *Lincoln's Genius for Expression.* Gilder's health failed rapidly, but his mind remained alert to the very end.

The severity of Gilder's self-criticism prevented him from writing more than he did. His verse has a well-proportioned cadence with a moderation of sentiment: it is the mellifluous production of a gentleman-poet, without sufficient vitality or passion to be long remembered.

Principal Works: *Poetry*—The New Day, 1875; The Poet and His Master, 1878; Lyrics and Other Poems, 1885; The Celestial Passion, 1887; Two Worlds, 1891; The Great Remembrance and Other Poems, 1893; Poems and Inscriptions, 1901; A Book of Music, 1906; The Fire Divine, 1907. *Prose*—Lincoln the Leader; and Lincoln's Genius for Expression, 1909; Grover Cleveland: A Record of Friendship, 1910.

About: Gilder, R. W. Grover Cleveland: A Record of Friendship; Gilder, R. Letters of Richard Watson Gilder; Century February 1910; Nation November 25, 1909; New York Times November 19, 1909; New York Evening Post November 19, 1909; North American Review January 1910.

GILDERSLEEVE, BASIL LANNEAU (October 23, 1831-January 9, 1924), philologist, scholar, editor, and text book writer, was born in Charleston, S.C. His father was Benjamin Gildersleeve, of English descent, whose family had been in America since about 1635. His mother, Emma Louisa (Lanneau) Gildersleeve was the daughter of an Acadian. An extremely precocious child, Gildersleeve received no formal education until he was thirteen. He could, however, read at four, and knew Latin, Greek, and French before he even went to school. He attended the College of Charleston and Jefferson College, and was graduated from Princeton in 1849 at the age of seventeen. While there, because of his brilliance in Latin and Greek, he could devote a great deal of time to reading Spanish, French, Italian, German, and English literature. He did not, however, neglect his other studies, and was graduated with high honors. The following year he taught in Richmond, and then sailed for three years of study in Europe at the Universities of Berlin, Bonn, and Göttingen. He received his Ph.D. at Göttingen in 1853. After returning to America, he spent three years studying philology, writing articles and a novel, and even tutoring. In 1856 he became professor of Greek at the University of Virginia, and from 1861 to 1866 was also professor of Latin. He enlisted in the Confederate cavalry, spending his summers with the army, and in 1864 received a severe wound that left him with a slight limp. In 1866 he married Eliza Fisher Colston of Virginia, by whom he had a son and daughter.

When Johns Hopkins University was founded in 1876, Gildersleeve became professor of Greek holding the position until 1915 when he became emeritus professor. In 1880 he founded the *American Journal of Philology,* which he edited for forty years, filling it with his personality and wit, his brilliant satire and fearless criticism.

Many universities honored Gildersleeve with degrees. His writings, although scholarly in nature, carried the indications of his wit, his *esprit,* and intellectual energy.

Principal Works: Latin Grammar, 1867; Latin Primer, Latin Reader, and Latin Exercise-Book, 1875; Justin Martyr, 1877; Pindar: Olympian and Pythian Odes, 1885; Essays and Studies, 1890; Syntax of Classical Greek (two parts) 1900, 1911.

About: The Abridged Compendium of American Genealogy; Gildersleeve, W. H. The Gildersleeves of Gildersleeve, Connecticut; The Hopkinsian 1893; New England Magazine February 1893; Princeton Alumni Weekly January 26, 1916.

GILPIN, WILLIAM (October 4, 1813 (?) January 20, 1894), first territorial governor of Colorado, eccentric, and miscellaneous writer, was born in Brandywine, Pa., the son of Joshua and Mary (Dilworth) Gilpin. He received his early instruction from his father in their Quaker home, and then went to England for two years' study at a Yorkshire academy. On his return he entered the University of Pennsylvania from which he was graduated in 1833. He entered West Point in July 1834, learning the following February to read law in Philadelphia. The action and chance-taking of a soldier's life continued to appeal to him, and until 1838, when he became editor of the St. Louis *Missouri Argus,* he performed various services in the army. After a government appointment and a taste of a quiet law practice in Independence, Mo., he set out for the Northwest, joining for about a month the party headed by John Charles Frémont and then proceeding boldly to Oregon City. He returned to Missouri in 1844 and in the spring of 1845 went to Washington, then a "large Virginia village," seeking he said, not public office but the dominion of the West.

In 1861 Gilpin accompanied President-elect Lincoln on his much-heralded journey to Washington, and was shortly appointed territorial governor of Colorado. When he arrived in Denver the Secession flag was flying; in his struggle to preserve that district for the Union he made many harmful enemies, and was finally recalled in 1862. Gilpin went back to Denver, however, and settled there permanently as a landowner and prospector. He was married on February 12, 1874, to Mrs. Julia Pratte Dickerson, of St. Louis, by whom he had three children.

Gilpin wrote a grandiose handbook on natural resources and a conspectus of democracy called *The Central Gold Region,* glorifying Denver and the Mississippi Valley. His *Cosmopolitan Railway* (1890) proposed that the United States become the hub of an international rail system by connecting America with Asia at the Bering Strait; possibly the book was suggested by Hinton Rowan Helper's equally fantastic *Three Americas Railway,* published in 1881. As soldier, editor, politician, and explorer, Gilpin's interests lay in the immediate and the active, yet as a writer he appears to have been only a quaint visionary. Above all, he was an unforgettable figure in early Rocky Mountain history.

PRINCIPAL WORKS: The Central Gold Region, 1860 (reissued in 1873 as The Mission of the North American People); The Cosmopolitan Railway, 1890.

ABOUT: Bancroft, H. H. History of the Life of William Gilpin; Simpson, H. The Lives of Eminent Philadelphians; Denver Republican January 21, 1894.

"GLYNDON, HOWARD." See SEARING, LAURA CATHERINE (REDDEN)

GODEY, LOUIS ANTOINE (June 6, 1804-November 29, 1878), editor and publisher, was born in New York City, the son of Louis and Margaret (Carel) Godey, French Royalists who had fled to America

LOUIS A. GODEY
c. 1850

during the French Revolution. He had little schooling, but at fifteen began running a news-stand and circulating library in New York, educating himself by reading his own wares. He then moved to Philadelphia, his home thenceforth, and for two years was a clerk and editorial assistant on the *Daily Chronicle.* With its editor, Charles Alexander, he started the *Lady's Book* (the first periodical exclusively for women) in 1830. He soon became its sole owner, and in 1837 he bought the *Ladies' Magazine,* of Boston, employed its editor, Mrs. Sarah Josepha Hale, and merged the two magazines as *Godey's Lady's Book.* Though Godey published and edited many other magazines—the *Saturday News and Literary Gazette* (1836), the *Young People's Book* (1841), the *Lady's Music Library* (1842), the *Lady's Dollar Newspaper,* and *Arthur's Home Magazine* (1852-67)—these were short-lived, and it is with the *Lady's Book* that his name is always associated.

From 1837 Godey paid for contributions, a great innovation in those days; and among his contributors were Poe, Longfellow, and Holmes. In 1845 he copyrighted the magazine, a startling departure; previous to that he had, like other American publishers of the era, pirated English writing without compensation. Godey's was famous for its lavish illustrations, its fashion plates, and its high literary standard. Godey's own department, the "Arm Chair," constituted all that he ever wrote; it was given over mostly to "puffs" of the magazine. He boasted that not one "impure" or profane word had ever sullied its pages. He conducted the magazine until 1877, when because of his failing health it was sold to a stock company. It had made him a millionaire.

In 1833 Godey had married Maria Catherine Duke; they had five children. For several years he had been obliged to spend his winters in St. Augustine, Fla., for his health; however he died, suddenly, in Philadelphia. He had known most of the authors of his time, and he was well liked by them; Poe said he had more friends and fewer enemies than any man he had ever known.

ABOUT: Finley, R. E. The Lady of Godey's: Sarah Josepha Hale; Mott, F. L. History of American Magazines; American Mercury August 1924; Philadelphia Public Ledger November 30, 1878.

GODFREY, THOMAS (December 4, 1736-August 3, 1763), poet and dramatist, was born in Philadelphia, son of Thomas Godfrey, inventor of the sea-quadrant. Upon the death of his father, Thomas was apprenticed to a watchmaker, but whenever "he could be absent from his business he was employed in reading or writing." He had an uncommon talent for verse and his "Temple of Fame" appeared anonymously in a city newspaper. William Smith, provost of the College, Academy and Charitable School of Philadelphia, where Thomas was presumably enrolled, recognized the lad's ability, secured his release from the craftshop, and in May 1758 had him commissioned as an ensign in the Pennsylvania militia. Godfrey saw a short and rather inactive service in the campaign against Fort Dusquesne, and from the barracks he wrote a poetic epistle, dated August 10, which caught some of the gloom of his surroundings.

In September the *American Magazine*, edited by Provost Smith, printed a rather commonplace "Ode to Wine," which had been "sent . . . by an unknown hand." "The Invitation" and "Ode on Friendship" (also Godfrey's) had appeared in the *American* earlier in the year.

During the Fort Dusquesne episode Godfrey had met several famous North Carolina rangers, and in 1759 he agreed to go as a factor to Wilmington, a Colonial haven for intellectuals. The county records for July 1760 list Godfrey as one of the "defaulters" in a minor civic duty, but at large, he was "highly esteemed for his many good qualities." Late that summer (1759) Godfrey, knowing that Douglass' American Company was to close its Philadelphia engagement in December, was rushing his tragedy, *The Prince of Parthia,* to a convenient finish—but at the price of dramatic excellence. The play, however, never got into rehearsal until four years after Godfrey's death. Whether it *was* actually produced April 24, 1767, at the New Theatre in Philadelphia is an enigma to theatrical historians. It was duly announced in the Philadelphia weeklies, but no critical estimates of it have been unearthed. Moreover, the *Pennsylvania Gazette* (April 30) affixed to the end of the advertisement for the week following a kind of theatrical rain-check to make amends for the implied withdrawal of "the preceding plays."

The Court of Fancy, admittedly modeled on Chaucer's *House of Fame,* was published in 1762, and in 1763 Godfrey wrote his last poem, "Victory," which his boon companion, Nathaniel Evans, called "a nervous and noble song of triumph." Godfrey returned to Philadelphia, and after a journey to the island of New Providence, went back again to Wilmington. From a long run on horseback, in sweltering heat, he contracted a fever, and died in his twenty-eighth year.

He was "of a corpulent habit of body," and had "an amiable disposition . . . engaging modesty, and diffidence of manner." If we accept Benjamin Franklin's description of Godfrey's mathematical father—"not a pleasing companion . . . for ever denying or distinguishing upon trifles . . ."—the young poet was indeed the more likable.

Besides being the author of the first drama written by a native American for production on the professional stage, Godfrey was the first audible protagonist of what might be called the "art for art's sake" movement within the Colonies. Although his *Prince of Parthia,* placing authentic historical figures in a newly-invented plot, betrays much confusion of tenses and is not easily adapted to present-day histrionics, it is a fresh recapture of the Shakespearian tempo. Had Godfrey lived beyond his twenty-eighth year, he might have sustained that spirit with inestimable skill.

PRINCIPAL WORKS: *Poems*—The Invitation, 1758; Ode on Friendship, 1758; Ode to Wine, 1758; The Court of Fancy, 1762; Victory, 1763; Juvenile Poems on Various Subjects, with The Prince of Parthia: A Tragedy, 1765.

ABOUT: Galt, J. The Life and Studies of Benjamin West; Godfrey, T. The Prince of Parthia (see Introductions by N. Evans to 1765 edition and A. Henderson to 1917 edition); Tyler, M. C. A History of American Literature

During the Colonial Time; American Magazine September 1758; Pennsylvania Gazette April 1767; Pennsylvania Magazine of History and Biography April 1893.

GODKIN, EDWIN LAWRENCE (October 2, 1831-May 21, 1902), editor and publicist, was born in Moyne, County Wicklow, Ireland, but of English ancestry on both sides. His father was the Rev. James Godkin, dissenting minister, editor, and Home Ruler; his mother, Sarah (Lawrence) Godkin. He was educated at Silcoates School, near Leeds, England, and at Queen's College, Belfast, from which he was graduated in 1851. He went to London to read law at Lincoln's Inn, but before long was sub-editor of *Cassell's Illustrated Family Paper.* From 1853 to 1855 he was Crimean War correspondent of the London *Daily News.* He then joined the staff of the Belfast *Northern Whig,* and was offered the editorship, but instead resigned and sailed for America in November 1856. In New York he studied law with the famous David Dudley Field, and was admitted to the bar in 1858, but practiced little. Instead, throughout the Civil War, he was correspondent for the *Daily News.* In 1869 he married Frances Elizabeth Foote, of New Haven. They had two sons and a daughter, of whom only one son survived them. Mrs. Godkin never recovered from their daughter's death in 1873, and herself died in 1875.

In 1865 Godkin became the first editor of the newly founded *Nation,* and the next year took over its ownership. In 1881 the magazine became the weekly edition of Henry Villard's New York *Evening Post,* and Godkin, in addition to continuing his editorship of the magazine, was also associate editor of the newspaper. From 1883 to 1899 he was its editor-in-chief. Following his wife's death he lived for two years in Cambridge, Mass., though continuing his editorial work in New York. In 1884 he married Katherine Sands.

EDWIN LAWRENCE GODKIN
1870

In 1900 he resigned because of ill health, and the next year retired to England. He died of cerebral hemorrhage in Brixham, and was buried at Northampton. He had been honored by an honorary M.A. from Harvard in 1872, and a D.C.L. from Oxford in 1897. Both in America and in England he was the close associate of the best known writers and thinkers of the day, Viscount Bryce being his most intimate friend. Bryce's obituary notice characterized Godkin well as being the possessor of "penetrating intellect and singular powers of expression." He was the foremost liberal of his period, independent, brilliant, sometimes dogmatic, with a pungent style which more than once involved him in libel suits. He made of the *Evening Post* a fighting liberal paper, and of the *Nation* (which is still an independently published review.) the first and principal exponent of progressive thought in America. He was succeeded as editor of the *Nation* by Oswald Garrison Villard, Henry Villard's son.

James Russell Lowell summed up Godkin's career as an editor as a compound of "ability, information, and unflinching integrity." With his associates, the German-born Henry Villard and Carl Schurz, this Irish-born Englishman was one of the great names in the history of American journalism.

PRINCIPAL WORKS: The History of Hungary and the Magyars, 1853; Government (American Science Series) 1871; Reflections and Comments, 1895; Problems of Modern Democracy, 1896; Unforeseen Tendencies of Democracy, 1898; Retrospect of Forty Years, 1899.

ABOUT: Bryce, J. Studies in Contemporary Biography; Godkin, E. L. Retrospect of Forty Years; Ogden, R. Life and Letters of Edwin Lawrence Godkin; Atlantic Monthly September 1908; Nation May 22, 1902, July 8, 1915; New York Evening Post May 21, 1902, December 30, 1909.

GODWIN, PARKE (February 25, 1816-January 7, 1904), editor, was born in Paterson, N.J., where his family had been of some importance for generations. His parents were Abraham and Martha (Parke) Godwin. After graduating from Prince-

Collection of Frederick H. Meserve
PARKE GODWIN

ton in 1834, he read law at Paterson and later went to Louisville, Ky., to open a practice. However, being upset over the presence of slavery, he soon left and went to New York. There, in a boarding house in 1836, he met William Cullen Bryant who offered him a position on the New York *Evening Post.* He was associated with this paper most of the time for the next forty-five years. In 1842, he married Bryant's eldest daughter, Fanny.

Godwin was greatly interested in the social movements of the early 1840's in New England, especially Brook Farm, which he heartily favored. In this connection he later edited *Harbinger,* organ of the disciples of Fourier, and published, in 1844, *Democracy: Constructive and Pacific,* and *A Popular View of the Doctrines of Fourier.* He retained this early idealism all his life. In politics, he was first a Free-Soil Democrat and later a Republican.

In 1853 Godwin became associated with the short-lived *Putnam's Monthly Magazine,* and it was of his contributions to it that his *Political Essays* (1856) consisted. Among his other achievements he edited William Cullen Bryant's works, started a history of France, spoke on many memorial occasions, and translated and published various books. In 1860 he acquired a financial interest in the New York *Evening Post,* becoming editor-in-chief after Bryant's death in 1878. In 1881, however, because of serious controversies with the business manager and half owner, he severed his connection with the *Post,* and soon afterward became editor of the *Commercial Advertiser,* holding this position until he retired.

Godwin was a distinguished figure in his day. The number of his books and journalistic writings is large, but they are of scant importance today.

PRINCIPAL WORKS: Democracy: Constructive and Pacific, 1844; A Popular View of the Doctrines of Fourier, 1844; Vala: A Mythological Tale, 1851; The Cyclopaedia of Biography, 1866, 1878; Out of the Past, 1870; A New Study of the Sonnets of Shakespeare, 1900.

ABOUT: Clayton, W. W. History of Bergen and Passaic Counties, New Jersey; Nelson, W. & Schriner, C. A. History of Paterson and Its Environs; Nevins, A. The Evening Post: A Century of Journalism; Galaxy February 1869; New York Evening Post January 7, 1904.

GOODRICH, CHARLES AUGUSTUS (August 19, 1790-June 4, 1862), clergyman and miscellaneous writer, was born in Ridgefield, Conn. The fourth of ten children, he was the son of the Rev. Samuel and Elizabeth (Ely) Goodrich, and the elder brother of Samuel Griswold Goodrich [*q.v.*]. Showing an early inclination for the ministry, he was sent, at considerable financial sacrifice, to Yale, his father's college. After reading theology, he became, in 1816, a colleague in the First Congregational Church of Worcester, Mass. A protest, started by someone outside the congregation, against Goodrich's political and religious beliefs grew into violent controversy. After a long struggle an ecclesiastical court cleared him of all charges, but Goodrich was so worn out by the controversy that in 1820 he asked to be dismissed. For the next twenty-eight years he lived in Berlin, in his native county, and after that, until his death, in Hartford. He still continued to do some preaching and engaged in politics, being state senator in 1838, but his main occupation was writing.

Goodrich is known chiefly for his children's books and for his *History of the United States of America* (1822) which, frequently revised, went through 150 editions. Another popular book was *A Child's History of the United States.* No list of all his books and their various editions has been compiled. Goodrich married Sarah Upson in 1818 and had seven children.

PRINCIPAL WORKS: History of the United States of America, 1822; Cabinet of Curiosities: Natural, Artificial, and Historical, 1822; Outlines of Modern Geography on a New Plan, 1827; Pictorial and Descriptive View of All Religions; Stories on the History of Connecticut, 1829; Lives of the Signers of the Declaration of Independence, 1829; The Universal Traveller, 1837; A Child's History of the United States, 1846; The Family Tourist, 1848.

About: Case, L. W. The Goodrich Family in America; Dexter, F. B. Biographical Sketches of Graduates of Yale College; Lincoln, W. History of Worcester, Mass.; Rockwell, G. L. History of Ridgefield, Conn.

GOODRICH, FRANK BOOTT (December 14, 1826-March 15, 1894), playwright and miscellaneous writer, was born in Hartford, Conn., the son of Samuel Griswold Goodrich [*q.v.*], author and publisher better known as "Peter Parley," and of his second wife, Mary (Boott) Goodrich. He was graduated from Harvard in 1845, and in 1851, when his father was appointed United States consul at Paris, he accompanied the family there. His letters on the accession of Napoleon III, sent to the New York *Times* under the pseudonym of "Dick Tinto," were later published as *Tricolored Sketches in Paris*. In 1855 he returned to New York, and for several years collaborated with various playwrights in producing original plays and adaptations; the best known was *The Poor of New York*, with Dion Boucicault. In 1859 he married Ella Schmidt; they had no children. In 1860 he started a series of translations of Balzac's novels, which, however, were not carried beyond the second volume and were completed a quarter century later by another hand. After 1865 his sight failed, and having an independent fortune he spent most of his time in travel and merely brought some of his earlier works up to date. A brilliant conversationalist, with a clear, easy style in writing, Goodrich nevertheless was superficial and hasty in his work, and many of his productions are mere pot-boilers.

Principal Works: *Plays*—Fascination (with F. L. Warden) 1857; The Dark Hour Before Dawn (with J. Brougham) 1859. *Miscellaneous*—Tricolored Sketches in Paris, 1855; The Court of Napoleon III, 1857; Man Upon the Sea, 1858 (as Remarkable Voyages, 1873); Women of Beauty and Heroism, 1859 (as World Famous Women, 1871); The Tribute Book, 1865.

About: New York Times March 22, 1894.

GOODRICH, SAMUEL GRISWOLD (August 19, 1793-May 9, 1860), author and publisher of didactic juvenile literature, originator and principal American user of the pseudonym "Peter Parley," was born in Ridgefield, Conn., the son of the Rev. Samuel Goodrich, a Congregational minister, and Elizabeth (Ely) Goodrich. He was schooled at West Lane and at Master Stebbins' seminary, and his first exposure to "pleasurable" reading excited in him "the most painful impressions." This early dislike was apparently the substance, years later, of his point of view in the writing of the Peter Parley tales—"to feed the young mind upon things wholesome and pure instead of things monstrous, false, and pestilent."

Collection of Frederick H. Meserve
SAMUEL GRISWOLD GOODRICH
("Peter Parley")

During the winter of 1808-09 he worked for his brother-in-law, a merchant in Danbury. Two years later he went to Hartford. He served six months in the War of 1812; letters of uncontrolled sympathy and packages filled with small luxuries came regularly from his family.

In 1818 Goodrich was married to Adeline Gratia, daughter of Senator Stephen Rowe Bradley of Vermont; she died June 24, 1822. He had pursued bookselling and publishing in Hartford for four years before his first trip abroad in November 1823. From a conversation with Hannah More, in Edinburgh, he gleaned some ideas for a literary vehicle: the presentation of "useful" material in the chatty manner of an elderly man who speaks to a group of avid youngsters at his knee. In 1827 appeared his "first adventure in authorship," the *Tales of Peter Parley About America*, beginning with the life of Wampum, an Indian of the Connecticut Valley, tracing the Colonial settlements and enumerating the wars, and closing with a bluntly rimed summary:

> Some Dutch, from Holland, settled pat on
> An island which they called Manhattan...

Following his marriage to Mary Boott, in 1826, Goodrich moved to Boston and began to edit *The Token,* a gift-book annual of conservative format, which he continued, except for the year 1829, through 1842. Its pages gave first encouragement to many literary fledgelings, Hawthorne being one of its most successful "finds": this indirect assistance to the Muse may well have been Goodrich's most important contribution to literature. His own *Outcast and Other Poems* appeared in 1836; *Parley's Magazine,* for children, was established in 1833 and sold in 1834; and in 1841 he founded *Merry's Museum* and was its editor until 1850.

Goodrich was elected to the Massachusetts legislature in 1837 and was appointed U.S. Consul at Paris in 1851. He wrote some fairly acute observations on political France during the years 1848-52. When his *Recollections of a Lifetime: or, Men and Things I Have Seen* appeared in 1856 he claimed to be already the "author and editor of about 170 volumes, 116 bearing the name of Peter Parley."

Only the most charitably inclined reader today can discern anything resembling merit in the prissy and priggish "Parley" books—heavy-footed, moralistic "instruction" thinly disguised as fiction. Yet for a brief time they were incredibly popular—perhaps because when they began there simply was no other juvenile literature worth the name; perhaps because their smug righteousness was thoroughly in key with the spirit of the age. Imitators sprang up on both sides of the Atlantic, and Goodrich himself undoubtedly employed hack-writers to turn out many of the titles which he issued over his own imprint. The total sales of the various Parleys ran into millions of copies, with Goodrich receiving the lion's share of the proceeds.

With a shapely nose, thin lips, and a high forehead, Goodrich had "the elegance of classic features." From the age of twenty-five to forty he was threatened with blindness: a fact which makes almost a physical impossibility of his claims of authorship. Opinion of him as a man is divided. He was undoubtedly both pompous and pious, a veritable encyclopedia of platitudes. Some of his contemporaries, moreover, believed him to be activated solely by mercenary motives. On the other hand there are the records of his numerous deeds of kindness to struggling authors and others in need. Van Wyck Brooks calls him "the good Peter Parley" and "an honest, courageous, simple-minded man."

Whichever view is correct, he is chiefly remembered today as a faintly ludicrous symbol of his age rather than for anything he actually contributed to literature.

Principal Works: The Tales of Peter Parley, 1827-1857; The Outcast and Other Poems, 1836; Peter Parley's Historical Compendium, 1837-1853; Fireside Education, 1838; Sketches From a Student's Window, 1841; Peter Parley's Miscellanies, 1844-45; Poems, 1851; History of All Nations, 1855; Recollections of a Lifetime, 1856; A Thousand and One Stories, 1858; Illustrated Natural History of the Animal Kingdom, 1859.

About: Brooks, Van W. The Flowering of New England; Darton, F. J. H. Children's Books in England; Goodrich, S. G. Recollections of a Lifetime; Cornhill Magazine November 1932; International Magazine January 1851; Littell's Living Age April-June 1860; New York Evening Post May 11, 1860.

GOODYEAR, WILLIAM HENRY (April 21, 1846-February 19, 1923), archaeologist, curator, and writer on art, was born in New Haven, Conn., the son of Charles Goodyear, the inventor, and Clarissa (Beecher) Goodyear. While a boy he lived for six years in France and England, later entering Yale, where he specialized in history. After graduating in 1867 he continued his studies at Heidelberg and Berlin. Ill health sent him to Italy and it was there that he became interested in Roman and medieval antiquities. Returning to Berlin he studied under Karl Friederichs, a well known archaeologist, whom in 1869 he accompanied to Cyprus. Returning by way of Syria, Greece, and Italy to study the monuments, he made some discoveries at Pisa that influenced his choice of a life work. After much research in 1874 he published an article, "A Lost Art," in *Scribner's Monthly,* which advanced the theory that mathematical regularity in the great buildings of the past was an exception to the rule—not the rule.

Unable for twenty years to pursue his investigations because of the lack of funds, Goodyear taught, wrote, and lectured. In 1882 he was made curator at the Metropolitan Museum and eight years later he became head of the department of fine arts at the Museum of the Brooklyn Institute of Arts and Sciences. He was instrumental in the founding of the Children's Museum of the Brooklyn Institute and also of the American Anthropological Association. He was married three times. In 1895 he was at last able to undertake a long-desired survey of European architecture. He devoted the next nineteen years to this project with interesting and valuable results. His discovery of the fundamental principle of irregularity had an important effect on the development of modern architecture.

Principal Works: A History of Art, 1888; Grammar of the Lotus, 1891; Roman and Medieval Art, 1893; Renaissance and Modern Art, 1894; Greek Refinements, 1912.

About: Brooklyn Museum Quarterly July 1923; Brooklyn Daily Eagle February 19 and 20, 1923; New York Times February 20, 1923; Yale University Obituary Record 1923.

GOOKIN, DANIEL (1612-1686/7), historian, colonist, and defender of the Indians, is believed to have been born either in Kent, England or in County Cork, Ireland, the son of Daniel Gookin and Mary (Byrd) Gookin. His father became a colonial speculator. Daniel, after spending his later boyhood on a plantation near Newport News, Va., was presented with a huge strip of land on the south bank of the James River.

Gookin sailed for England, and in 1639 was married to Mary Dolling; two years later he returned to Virginia (Nansemond plantation) with his wife and infant son. He was made a burgess and held, successively, a number of public offices.

Gookin was a staunch Puritan, and when the Act of Conformity became a law (1642/43), he migrated first to Maryland and then in 1644 to Massachusetts; he settled in Roxbury, where he aided in the founding of a free grammar school and engaged in coasting trade. A few years later he made his home in Cambridge. In 1649 Gookin began about thirty-five years' service as deputy to the General Court, during which time he made three journeys to England: in 1661; in 1665, when he unwillingly accepted a diplomatic charge from Cromwell; and again in 1658. Returning to Cambridge he assumed several public trusts, and his accomplishments in the interests of the Indians were second only to those of John Eliot.

Only two of the three books which Gookin wrote were published: *An Historical Account of the Doings and Sufferings of the Christian Indians of New England* (in the American Antiquarian Society transactions); and *Historical Collections of the Indians in New England* (in the collections of the Massachusetts Historical Society. The third, an unfinished history of New England, believed to have been destroyed, would doubtless have been a most enlightening document, for Gookin's point of view was far from parochial and he was in a strategic position, diplomatically, for a close observation of the colonial scene.

Principal Works: Historical Collections of the Indians in New England (see Massachusetts Historical Society Collections: Vol. 1, 1792); An Historical Account of the Doings and Sufferings of the Christian Indians of New England (see Transactions and Collections of the American Antiquarian Society: Vol. 2, 1836).

About: Gookin, F. W. Daniel Gookin; Johnson, E. Johnson's Wonderland (ed. by J. F. Jameson); New England Historical and Genealogical Register October 1847 and April 1848.

GORDIN, JACOB (May 1, 1853-June 11, 1909), dramatist, was born in Mirgorod, Poltava, Russia, the son of Michael and Ida Gordin. His parents were wealthy and cultured and were able to provide him with a good private school education, rare among Russian Jews of that period. He became a teacher, dramatic critic, and journalist at Odessa and St. Petersburg (Leningrad). In 1891 his advanced social views (though he belonged to no political party) got him in trouble with the Czarist government, and he was obliged to leave Russia. His previous writing had been in Russian, but on his arrival in New York he became interested in play writing for the East Side Jews who spoke and read only Yiddish. His first play, *Siberia* (1892), was also his first piece of Yiddish writing. He wrote in all about 35 original plays and 43 adaptations from the best contemporary European dramatists, many of them for Bertha Kalich and Jacob Adler; his adaptation of Tolstoy's *Kreutzer Sonata* was translated into English by Langdon Mitchell and produced by Harrison Grey Fiske in 1907. For a short time after his arrival in New York he published and edited a Russian paper, and he continued to write stories, essays, and articles for the *Arbeiter Zeitung*. In 1872 he married Anna Istkowitz; they had eleven children. Not an orthodox Jew, he had, in 1888, founded in Russia the Brotherhood, an association to combine Jewish and Christian ethics; and in New York he organized the Educational League, with similar cultural and ethical aims. Known as "the Shakespeare of the Ghetto," he was a noted figure in New York Jewry, dignified and revered. He died in Brooklyn at fifty-six.

Gordin's plays displayed a stark realism which sometimes was so exaggerated as to seem burlesque, but which had great power. His literary viewpoint was always more Russian than Jewish; he himself said: "I am not a Jewish writer; I am merely a writer writing for Jews." The best known of his plays were *Mirele Efros, Siberia, The Jewish King Lear, God, Man, and the Devil, The Slaughter,* and *The Wild Man.*

Principal Work: Collected Works (in Yiddish) 1910.

About: Hapgood, H. The Spirit of the Ghetto; American Hebrew June 18, 1909; Literary Digest July 3, 1909; Theatre Magazine July 1909.

GOUGE, WILLIAM M. (November 10, 1796-July 14, 1863), financial writer, was born in Philadelphia. In 1833 he published *A Short History of Money and Banking in the United States: Including an Account of the Provincial and Continental Paper Money to Which Is Prefixed an Inquiry into the Principles of the System With Considerations of Its Effects on Morals and Happiness*, which was reprinted in London under the title, *The Curse of Paper-Money and Banking*. Although he was a "crank" on the subject of banks, paper money, and corporations, this book is of value because it shows in detail the organization and abuses of state banks in the early years of the nineteenth century. Between 1834 and 1841, he was clerk in the Treasury Department, and in 1841 edited the *Journal of Banking* in which his contributions showed slightly modified feelings towards banks. In 1854 he was appointed by the Secretary of the Treasury as special examiner. For one year, 1857-58, he served as accountant of the state banks of Arkansas. He died in Trenton, N.J.

PRINCIPAL WORKS: A Short History of Money and Banking in the United States . . . , 1833; An Inquiry Into the Expediency of Dispensing With Bank Agency and Bank Paper in Fiscal Concerns of the United States, 1837; Fiscal History of Texas . . . , 1852; Report of the Accountants of the State Bank of Arkansas, 1858.

ABOUT: Palgrave, R. H. I. Dictionary of Political Economy; Bankers' Magazine and Statistical Register September 1863; Philadelphia Inquirer July 16, 1863; Trenton Daily State Gazette July 16, 1863.

GOUGH, JOHN BARTHOLOMEW (August 22, 1817-February 18, 1886), temperance lecturer and writer, was born at Sandgate, Kent, England, the son of John Gough, a veteran of the Peninsular War living on his pension, and Jane Gough, the village schoolmistress. He was educated at a seminary in Folkestone, where he taught while he was still a student, and in 1829, at only twelve, was sent by his parents to America, where for two years he was a bound boy on a farm in Oneida County, New York. At fourteen he went to New York City and learned the trade of bookbinding. When he was earning $3 a week he sent for his mother and sister, who arrived in 1833. He lost his job, and his mother died as a result of hardship and poverty. Gough in his despair took to drink. For several years he made his way as a comedian in cheap stock companies in New York and Boston, then in 1839 set up as a bookbinder in Newburyport, Mass. He married Lucretia Fowler, who with their infant child died from neglect during one of his drinking bouts. By the time he was twenty-five he was a hopeless drunkard and wastrel. Then in 1842 a slight kindness from a Quaker temperance orator on a Worcester street brought about his redemption. He signed the pledge, and almost immediately, with his natural gift for oratory, became a temperance lecturer. Twice during the first three years he relapsed into debauchery, but each time made a public confession and continued his fight. In 1843 he had married Mary Whitcomb. The remainder of his life was spent in constant lecture tours; his subject was usually temperance, but after 1870 he branched occasionally into other social topics. In 1853, 1857-60, and 1878 he lectured in England. He estimated that in all he had given over 9,600 lectures to nine million hearers, and had collected 140,000 temperance pledges personally and 215,179 through his meetings. Amherst College conferred an honorary M.A. on him in 1863. He died while on tour, in Frankford, Philadelphia, of apoplexy.

With an emotional appeal, touches of humor, and dramatic presentation, Gough wrote as he spoke. He was not an advocate of prohibition laws, but depended on personal and individual reformation.

PRINCIPAL WORKS: Autobiography, 1845 (with A Continuation to the Present Time, 1859; with Personal Recollections, 1869); Orations Delivered on Various Occasions, 1854; Temperance Addresses, 1870; Temperance Lectures, 1879; Sunlight and Shadow: or, Gleanings From My Life Work, 1880; Platform Echoes, 1885.

ABOUT: Gough, J. Autobiography (1869 edition); Sunlight and Shadow; Martyn, C. John B. Gough: The Apostle of Cold Water; Morrow, H. W. Tiger! Tiger! The Life Story of John B. Gough; Boston Transcript February 19, 1886.

GOULD, EDWARD SHERMAN (May 11, 1805-February 21, 1885), miscellaneous writer, was the son of Judge James Gould and Sally McCurdy (Tracy) Gould. He was born in Litchfield, Conn., where his father was at one time head of the Litchfield Law School as well as member of the State Supreme Court. He was graduated from the Litchfield Academy in 1818 and for years made his living by his pen in New York.

For years Gould led a varied life of writing in New York, his works including novels, sketches, comedies, and translations.

In 1843 he published a short novel of adventure, *The Sleep-Rider: or, The Old Boy in the Omnibus*; and in 1862, *John Doe and Richard Roe: or, Episodes of Life in New York,* a series of sketches depicting metropolitan life. In 1867, in an attempt to correct errors in style and philology, he published *Good English: or, Popular Errors in Language.* Gould was considered an authority on philological questions in America and in his critical works tried to raise the standards of American writing. He was married, but was deserted by his wife and two sons.

PRINCIPAL WORKS: Lectures Delivered Before the Mercantile Library Association, 1836; The Sleep-Rider: or, The Old Boy in the Omnibus, 1843; The Very Age! 1850; John Doe and Richard Roe: or, Episodes of Life in New York, 1862; Good English: or, Popular Errors in Language, 1867.

ABOUT: New Haven Evening Register February 23, 1885; New York Times February 22, 1885.

GOULD, HANNAH FLAGG (September 3, 1789-September 5, 1865), poet, was born in Lancaster, Mass., daughter of Benjamin and Griselda Apthorp (Flagg) Gould. In 1808, she moved with her family to Newburyport where she lived a contented, uneventful life until her death fifty-seven years later. It was not till she was in her middle thirties that she began writing. After she had made various contributions to magazines and annuals, her friends collected her writings and in 1832 presented her with her first published work, *Poems.* It was surprisingly successful and was republished in 1833 and 1835, and also in 1836 when a second volume was added. Miss Gould continued to be a popular writer for the next twenty years. She wrote on patriotic and religious subjects as well as nature and child life. She possessed genuine poetic qualities and her poems, always short, were full of humor, a gay fancifulness, and a marked simplicity. Her verses for children were her best, some of them being republished in school readers. Miss Gould was tall and slightly masculine in appearance. She was known alike for her wit and charity.

PRINCIPAL WORKS: Poems, 1832; The Golden Vase: A Gift for the Young, 1843, 1844; Gathered Leaves, 1846; New Poems, 1850; The Diosma: A Perennial, 1851; The Mother's Dream and Other Poems, 1853; Hymns and Other Poems for Children, 1854; Poems for Little Ones, 1863.

ABOUT: Currier, J. J. History of Newburyport, Massachusetts; Gould, B. A. The Family of Zaccheus Gould of Topsfield; Perley, S. The Poets of Essex County, Massachusetts; American Monthly Review July 1832; Baltimore Literary Monument November 1838; New England Magazine May 1832 and April 1833; North American Review October 1835; Southern Literary Messenger January 1836.

GRADY, HENRY WOODFIN (May 24, 1850-December 23, 1889), journalist and orator, was born at Athens, Ga., the son of Col. William S. Grady, a Confederate officer who was later killed at Petersburg, and Anne Elizabeth (Gartrell) Grady. In 1868 he was graduated from the University of Georgia, then until 1870 studied law at the University of Virginia. In 1871 he married Julia King; they had one son and one daughter.

While still a student, Grady had contributed to the Atlanta *Constitution,* and instead of practicing law he became editor of the Rome, Ga., *Courier.* Forbidden to write a story exposing corruption, he bought the two other papers in the town and merged them, but they failed quickly. In 1872 he went to Atlanta, where with two partners he founded the *Herald,* which also collapsed before long, leaving him to support himself and his family by free lance writing for the *Constitution* and the Augusta *Chronicle.* In 1876 almost penniless, he went to New York and secured a post as Georgia correspondent of the New York *Herald.* He held this position until 1879, when Cyrus W. Field, inventor of the trans-Atlantic cable, lent him the money to buy a quarter interest in the *Constitution.* His son succeeded him as its editor.

Grady had meanwhile been gaining fame as an orator. His famous speech on "The New South" was first given in 1886, and thereafter he was in constant demand for talks on the Southern question. He died in direct consequence of a trip to Boston in winter to make one of these speeches, incurring pneumonia which proved fatal. A hospital and a monument were erected in Atlanta as memorials to him.

Grady was "the national pacificator." He believed that the South must cease "waving the bloody shirt," must acknowledge defeat in the Civil War and bend its energies to constructive endeavor. One of his listeners compared his oratorical style to "a cannon ball in full flight, fringed with ribbons," and it is true that he was sentimental, pious, conventional, and given to lush metaphor, but at the same time his sunny sweetness of nature made him universally beloved. He was a brilliant and graphic journalist, aggressive and daring. He shunned public office, but at the time of his premature death was about to be sent to the Senate.

PRINCIPAL WORKS: The New South and Other Addresses, 1904; Complete Orations and Speeches, 1910.

ABOUT: Crawford, T. R. Life and Labors of Henry W. Grady; Graves, J. T. Henry W. Grady; Harris, J. C. Life and Speeches of Henry

W. Grady; Lee, J. W. H. Henry Woodfin Grady; Richardson, F. H. A Fruitful Life; Atlanta Constitution December 23 and 24, 1889, October 21, 1891.

GRAHAM, GEORGE REX (June 18, 1813-July 13, 1894), editor and publisher, was born in Philadelphia. His father, a shipping merchant, died when he was fifteen. In 1832 he was apprenticed to a cabinetmaker, and read law while working full time at his trade. In 1839 he was admitted to the bar, but two months later had abandoned the law to act as assistant editor of the *Saturday Evening Post,* then a struggling weekly of negligible circulation. A few months later he bought *Atkinson's Casket.* The same year he married Elizabeth Fry, who died in 1871. In 1840 Graham bought *Burton's Gentleman's Magazine,* and combined his two properties the next year as *Graham's Magazine.* Poe, Bayard Taylor, and R. W. Griswold were among his associate editors, and Bryant, Cooper, and Longfellow were contributors. As a magazine appealing to the sophisticated, adult mind, *Graham's* became exceedingly popular, and its owner grew rich. He lived in the most extravagant and lavish style, entertaining in a princely manner. In 1846 he bought the Philadelphia *North American,* the next year merging the *United States Gazette* with it, and he purchased an interest in the *Evening Bulletin.* Then unwise speculation ruined him; he took to drink, became bankrupt, and had to assign *Graham's.* He bought it back in 1850 but its success was over, and he sold it in 1853. In 1870 he was completely beggared by a stock swindle. Friends found him a job on the Newark *Daily Journal,* but he was no longer able to do efficient work, and gradually he became blind. For years he lived as a pensioner on the charity of those who had known him in better days. In 1887 he entered the Orange, N.J., Memorial Hospital, where, a senile invalid, he loved to ramble on about his former wealth and his friendships with the great. But in his good years he was a brilliant editor, and he deserves eternal gratitude for his loyal devotion to Poe and his defence of the poet against Griswold and his other maligners.

After a portrait by T. B. Read
GEORGE R. GRAHAM

ABOUT: Sartain, J. The Reminiscences of a Very Old Man; Graham's Magazine July 1850; New York Times July 14, 1894; Philadelphia Evening Bulletin July 16, 1894.

"GRANT, ALLEN." See WILSON, JAMES GRANT

GRAY, ASA (November 18, 1810-January 30 1888), botanist, was born at Paris, N.Y., the oldest of eight children of Moses Gray, a tanner and farmer, and Roxana (Howard) Gray. In 1825, at Fairfield Academy, his interest in natural science was first aroused, and the next year he began his career as a botanist. He was graduated from Fairfield Medical School in 1831 with an M.D. degree, but never practised medicine. From 1832 to 1835 he taught science at Bartlett's High School, Utica. His summers from 1832 to 1842 were spent on collecting trips, in the first of which he met John Torrey, pioneer American botanist, whose assistant he became in 1835. In 1834 he had started issuing his first arrangements of botanical specimens, and had read his first scientific papers before the New York Lyceum of Natural History, whose curator he became in 1836. Appointed professor of botany at the new University of Michigan, he sailed for Europe in 1838 to purchase its botanical library; he remained a year and then resigned without ever going to Michigan. In 1842 he was made Fisher professor of natural history at Harvard, a post he held the remainder of his life, creating the botanical department, contributing his herbarium to it in 1864, and acting as director of its Botanical Garden. In 1873 some of his active duties were delegated to others, but he was still teaching and writing when he died of a stroke at seventy-eight.

Gray was the chief exponent of Darwinism in America, and undoubtedly the country's greatest botanist in his time. Honorary degrees were heaped upon him from Amer-

Collection of Frederick H. Meserve
ASA GRAY

ican and European universities; he was a founder of the National Academy of Sciences, from 1863 to 1873 president of the American Academy of Arts and Sciences, in 1872 president of the American Association for the Advancement of Science, and from 1874 to his death a regent of the Smithsonian Institution. He traveled widely, and found time to be a constant contributor to the *American Journal of Science* (which he helped to edit) and the *Nation*. In 1848 he had married Jane Lathrop Loring, who was his constant co-worker and edited his letters after his death.

Gray's writing is a model of scientific presentation—clear, accurate, succinct, precise, with the saving grace of dry humor.

PRINCIPAL WORKS: Elements of Botany, 1836; Flora of North America (with J Torrey) 1838-43; Botanical Text Book, 1842 (as Structural Botany, 1879); First Lessons in Botany and Vegetable Physiology, 1857; How Plants Grow, 1858; Manual of the Botany of the Northern United States, 1848-67; Field, Forest, and Garden Botany, 1868; How Plants Behave, 1872; Darwiniana, 1876; Natural Science and Religion, 1880; Elements of Botany (new) 1887; Scientific Papers (ed. by C. S. Sargent) 1888.

ABOUT: Bradford, G. As God Made Them; Dana, J. D. A Memoir of Asa Gray; Farlow, W. G. Memoir of Asa Gray; Goodale, G. L. A Century of Science in America; Nation February 2, 1888; Science July 17, 1925.

GREELEY, HORACE (February 3, 1811-November 29, 1872), editor, was born at Amherst, N.H., the son of Zaccheus Greeley, a farmer and day-laborer, and Mary (Woodburn) Greeley, who was noted for her remarkable physical strength. A very precocious child, who read before he was three, Greeley nevertheless had very little schooling, and that in country schools in New Hampshire, Vermont, and Pennsylvania, scenes of his father's fruitless efforts to earn a living for his family. At fourteen he was apprenticed as a printer to the editor of the *Northern Spectator*, Poultney, Vt., which suspended in 1830. After a few months as a tramp printer, he arrived in New York City and by indefatigable labor reached the point where in 1833 he became partner in a printing business whose main job was the printing of lottery sheets. An attempt to establish the city's first cheap paper, the *Morning Post*, had proved abortive, but he was writing articles for the newspapers and looking ahead to establishing another paper of his own. This he did in 1834 with his brother-in-law, Jonas Winchester, the paper being a weekly, the *New Yorker* (first of that name). In 1836 he married Mary Youngs Cheney; of their seven children, five died in infancy, and his wife became a nervous invalid who made their home anything but comfortable.

In 1838 Greeley edited the *Jeffersonian* for a year for the Whigs, and in 1840 another Whig paper, the *Log Cabin*. This with the *New Yorker*, was in 1841 merged with the *Tribune*, first a weekly, then a daily. From then on Greeley's history and that of the *Tribune* are inseparable. He made it one of the country's most influential papers, and he called to its service such persons as Margaret Fuller, Charles A. Dana, Bayard Taylor, George Ripley and George William Curtis. An enthusiast sometimes a faddist, he used the paper as a medium for all his vagaries, from Fourierist Socialism (combined with advocacy of a high tariff!) to temperance, from anti capital punishment to attacks on the theatres. Practically the only progressive cause he did not champion was woman suffrage. A strong abolitionist, he was nevertheless conciliatory and endeavored vainly to bring the Civil War to a close by compromise. His furnishing of bail for Jefferson Davis after the war brought a storm of abuse upon him and killed the sale of his book, *The American Conflict*. He was suspicious of Lincoln and later hurt his paper by his attacks on Grant, but no one doubted his courage or his sincerity.

Though the paper's life was his, he found time for two trips to Europe and one to California ("Go West, young man!" became his motto after the latter journey); and he lectured constantly before clubs and ly

Collection of Frederick H. Meserve
HORACE GREELEY

ceums. His political ambition was his undoing. He had served three months in Congress in 1848-49, and thereafter ran for Congress, the Senate, and the Lieutenant-Governorship of New York without success. In 1872 he was nominated by a coalition of liberal Republicans and Democrats to run against Grant for president. The campaign was an orgy of vilification and libel, and Greeley wore himself out in electioneering. Meanwhile he spent every spare minute at the side of his wife, who died on October 30. He was terribly beaten, carrying only six states. He returned to the *Tribune* to find himself editor in name only; Whitelaw Reid had taken over active conduct of the paper. It was the last blow. He ceased to sleep, brain fever set in, and he died, out of his mind, before the end of November. His funeral was one of the largest ever held in America.

It is easy to see a comic figure in the little man with the round pink face, the abundant chin-whiskers, and the whining voice. He was all his life eccentric and sloppy in dress, and he wrote an execrable hand. He was a good deal of a crank. Yet he was one of the country's foremost editors, a mighty publicist, and a man of unsullied reputation for uprightness and integrity. His style is clear, nervous, and concise, a model of journalistic writing.

PRINCIPAL WORKS: Hints Toward Reforms, 1850; Glances at Europe, 1851; History of the Struggle for Slavery Extension or Restriction, 1856; An Overland Journey From New York to San Francisco, 1860; The American Conflict, 1866; Recollections of a Busy Life, 1868; Essays on Political Economy, 1870; What I Know of Farming, 1871.

ABOUT: Bradford, G. As God Made Them; Greeley, H. Recollections of a Busy Life; Ingersoll, L. D. The Life of Horace Greeley; Linn, W. A. Horace Greeley; Parton, J. Life of Horace Greeley; Rourke, C. M. Trumpets of Jubilee; Seitz, D. C. Horace Greeley: Founder of the New York Tribune; Sotheran, C. Horace Greeley and Other Pioneers of American Socialism; Zabriskie, F. N. Horace Greeley: The Editor; New York Sun November 30, 1872.

GREEN, ASA (February 11, 1789-c. 1839), novelist, was born in Ashby, Mass., one of the nine children of Oliver and Dorothy (Hildreth) Green. He received his B.A. degree from Williams College in 1813 and his M.D. from Brown University in 1822 and from the Berkshire Medical Institution in 1827. He was therefore thirty-eight before he began to practice medicine. He does not seem to have been very successful, for he moved within two years from Lunenburg, Mass., to Townsend, and from Townsend to North Adams; and at the same time he edited two weekly papers, the *Berkshire American* in 1827 and the *Socialist* (which title does not seem to have carried its present implication) in 1828. Both papers failed, and in 1829 he went to New York City, where he abandoned medicine and started a bookstore. At the same time he edited the *Evening Transcript* and began to write novels, producing six within the next eight years. The exact date of his death is unknown, but he died in New York at some time in 1839.

Green was one of the earliest American satirists. All his novels except *The Perils of Pearl Street*, which is partly autobiographical and deals realistically with economic problems, are humorous, and some of them are frankly burlesque. *A Yankee Among the Nullifiers* commemorates a visit to North Carolina in 1832. Green's work should be better known; it is an invaluable source for material concerning professional and middle class life in America in the 1830's.

PRINCIPAL WORKS: The Life and Adventures of Dr. Dodimus Duckworth, A.N.Q., 1833; A Yankee Among the Nullifiers, 1833; The Perils of Pearl Street, 1834; Travels in America by George Fibbleton, Exbarber to His Majesty the King of Great Britain, 1835; A Glance at New York, 1837; The Debtors' Prison, 1837.

GREEN, FRANCES HARRIET (WHIPPLE) (September 1805-June 10, 1878), reformer and miscellaneous writer, was born in Smithfield, R.I., the daughter of George Whipple. By the time she was twenty-five, she was known for various poetic contributions. From 1830 on she was definitely interested in all kinds of reform. In 1841 she published a novel, *The Mechanic,* which showed her interest in the laboring class. *Memoirs of Elleanor Eldridge,* a true story of a Negress hurt by legal injustice, was probably her most popular work. She also published a book on botany and contributed articles and verses to periodicals. In 1842 she married Charles C. Green, an artist, but five years later the marriage ended in divorce. About 1860 she moved to California, where she married William C. McDougall. She published her last work, *Beyond the Veil,* the year of her death.

Principal Works: Elleanor Eldridge, 1838; Elleanor's Second Book, 1839; The Mechanic, 1841; Might and Right: By a Rhode Islander, 1844; Beyond the Veil, 1878.

About: Rider, S. S. Bibliographical Memoirs of Three Rhode Island Authors; Boston Banner of Light August 24, 1878; San Francisco Chronicle June 11, 1878.

GREEN, JOSEPH (1706-December 11, 1780), merchant and poet, was born sometime during 1706, presumably in Boston where it is probable that he attended the South Grammar School. He was graduated from Harvard in 1726 and shortly after became a merchant. Connected by marriage with prominent Bostonian families, he was well known in society and belonged to the Fire Club and a French Club. On the eve of the Revolution he declared himself a Loyalist, and in 1774 joined in a protest to the Governor against the patriots and against suspending British trade. The same year he was appointed counsellor of the province, but in 1775, after patriots had damaged his home, he refused the appointment and sailed to safety in London. It was there he died five years later.

A ready wit and poet, Green's writings, mostly satirical, compared favorably with those of his contemporaries. It is likely that he contributed to the *New-England Weekly Journal,* and the writings that are known to be his include "The Poet's Lamentation for the Loss of His Cat, Which He Used to Call His Muse," a parody on a hymn by Mather Byles; "The Grand Arcanum Detected," 1755; and lines on a picture of John Checkley. Many other works have been dubiously credited to him.

About: Curwen, S. Journals and Letters; Eliot, J. Biographical Dictionary; Ford, W. C. Broadsides and Ballads Printed in Massachusetts: 1639-1800; Griswold, R. W. Poets and Poetry of America; Hutchinson, T. Diary and Letters; Stark, J. H. Loyalists of Massachusetts; Tyler, M. C. A History of American Literature; Gentleman's Magazine (London) December 1780.

GREEN, WILLIAM HENRY (January 27, 1825-February 10, 1900), Hebrew scholar and religious writer, was born in Groveville, N.J., his parents being George Smith Green and Sarah (Kennedy) Green. He was of a religious family, many of his ancestors having been connected in some capacity with the church. After graduating from Lafayette College in 1840, he stayed there as tutor for two years. The following year he attended Princeton Theological Seminary, then returned to Lafayette for another year's teaching, and finally was graduated from the Seminary in 1846. From 1849 to 1851 he was pastor of the Central Presbyterian Church in Philadelphia. For the rest of his life he was connected with Princeton Theological Seminary, first as professor of Oriental and Old Testament literature; as senior member of the faculty, he was for seventeen years president of the Seminary. In 1852 he married Mary Colwell, and six years later he married a second time, his wife being Elizabeth Hayes.

Accurate and precise in his teaching of Hebrew, Green was an outstanding success as professor. In 1861 he published *Grammar of the Hebrew Language,* a practical work marked by its clearness and conciseness of statement. This was followed by numerous religious writings, all of which were extremely conservative and attacked radical criticism.

Principal Works: Grammar of the Hebrew Language, 1861; The Pentateuch Vindicated From the Aspersions of Bishop Colenso, 1863; Moses and the Prophets, 1882; The Hebrew Feasts, 1885; The Higher Criticism of the Pentateuch, 1895; The Unity of the Book of Genesis, 1895; General Introduction to the Old Testament, 1898.

About: Stonecipher, J. F. Biographical Catalog of Lafayette College, 1832-1912; Professor William Henry Green's Semi-Centennial Celebration, 1846-96; Biblical World, June 1900; Presbyterian and Reformed Review, July 1900; New York Observer April 30, 1896; Philadelphia Press May 6, 1896.

GREENE, ALBERT GORTON (February 10, 1802-January 3, 1868), poet and jurist, was born in Providence, R.I., of an old New England family, the son of John Holden Greene, an architect, and Elizabeth (Beverly) Greene. He was graduated from Brown University in 1820, studied law, and was admitted to the bar in 1823. He married, in 1824, Mary Ann Clifford, whose brother, John Henry Clifford, later became governor of Massachusetts. In 1832 Greene dropped his law practice so that he might have time for municipal affairs. In this connection he was clerk of the city council, 1832-67, clerk of the municipal court, 1832-57, and justice of that court, 1858-67.

Although connected for years with public affairs, Greene was essentially a man of letters, more at home in his study than elsewhere. Feeling that he was by no means an outstanding poet he never published a collection of his verses, but his various contributions include "To the Weathercock on Our Steeple," "The Baron's Last Banquet," "Old Grimes," "Stanzas," "Song of the Windmill Spirits," "Adelheid," and his favorite poem, "Ode on the Death of the Rev. Dr. William E. Channing."

Greene was also much interested in industrial art, painting, and sculpture and was a collector of note.

ABOUT: Arnold, S. G. Greene-Staples-Parsons: An Address Delivered Before the R.I. Historical Society; Gorton, A. Life and Times of Samuel Gorton; Greene, G. S. & Clarke, L. B. The Greenes of Rhode Island; Stockbridge, J. C. Catalog of the Harris Collection of American Poetry; Catalog of the Private Library of the late Hon. Albert G. Greene; Historical Catalog of Brown University, 1764-1904; Harper's Magazine November 1868.

GREENE, EDWARD LEE (August 20, 1843-November 10, 1915), botanist, was born in Hopkinton, R.I., the son of William and Abby (Crandall) Greene. He attended Albion Academy but left to serve for three years in the 13th Wisconsin Infantry. His regiment being on garrison, guard, and picket duty, Greene was able to botanize through several southern states. In 1866 he received a Ph.B. from Albion (although the Academy was not of college rank), and, after teaching for a few years, went in 1870 to Colorado to collect plants for Asa Gray and George Engelmann. Shortly afterward he entered an Episcopal Seminary and after his ordination did missionary work through the West. In 1885 he resigned as rector of St. Mark's in Berkeley to become a Catholic layman. He was associated with the University of California for the next ten years, as instructor in botany, assistant professor, and professor. From 1895 to 1904 he was professor at George Washington University, and an associate of the Smithsonian Institute from 1904 to 1914. In return for a small annuity he moved his herbarium and valuable botanical library to Notre Dame University, where he planned to spend his remaining years. Before he was able to carry out his plans he became ill in Washington, where he finally died after a long period of invalidism.

PRINCIPAL WORKS: Pittonia: A Series of Papers Relating to Botany and Botanists, 1887 to 1905; West American Oaks, 1889, 1890; Flora Franciscana, 1891-97; Manual of the Botany of the Region of San Francisco Bay, 1894; Plantae Bakerianae, 1901; Leaflets of Botanical Observation, 1903-09; Landmarks of Botanical History, 1909.

ABOUT: Curtis, G. P. (ed.). Some Roads to Rome in America; Nieuwland, J. A. American Midland Naturalist; Botanical Gazette January 1916; Newman Hall Review 1918; Torreya July 1916.

GREENE, FRANCIS VINTON (June 27, 1850-May 15, 1921), military historian, was born in Providence, R.I., the youngest son of George Sears Greene and Martha Barrett (Dana) Greene. He attended Trinity School in New York and Burlington College, and in 1870 was graduated from West Point at the head of his class. In 1877 he was sent abroad to report on the Russo-Turkish war and for a year and a half was with the Russian headquarters in the field. His report, published in 1879 under the title of *The Russian Army and Its Campaigns in Turkey in 1877-1878,* is his outstanding work, and a standard work for that period, consulted by both foreign and American armies. For the next twenty years he held a variety of positions, and in 1898 entered the Spanish-American war as a colonel, a few days later being appointed brigadier-general of volunteers in charge of the second expedition to the Philippines. Three months later he was made major-general of volunteers, and shortly afterward was sent to Havana as governor of the city. He declined the governorship, but presented a valuable and comprehensive report of the city which was later used in rehabilitating it. After resigning from the army he became managing director of the New Trinidad Lake Asphalt Company, and from 1903 to 1904 was police commissioner of New York—one of the best the city ever had. For the next ten years he was president of the Niagara, Lockport & Ontario Power Company in Buffalo. Retiring in 1915, he returned to New York where he spent the rest of his life. Although he is known as a writer and military historian chiefly because of his work on the Russo-Turkish war, he published in addition many short articles and several books, including a biography entitled *General Greene.*

PRINCIPAL WORKS: The Russian Army and Its Campaigns in Turkey in 1877-78, 1879; Sketches of Army Life in Russia, 1880; The Mississippi, 1882; General Greene, 1893; The Revolutionary War and the Military Policy of the United States, 1911; Our First Year in the Great War, 1918.

ABOUT: Greene, G. C. & Clarke, L. B. The Greenes of Rhode Island; Army and Navy Journal May 21, 1921; New York Times May 16 and 17, 1921; New York Tribune May 16, 1921.

GREENE, GEORGE WASHINGTON (April 8, 1811-February 2, 1883), educator, the son of Nathanael Ray Greene and Anna Maria (Clarke) Greene and the grandson of General Nathanael Greene, was born in East Greenwich, R.I. When he was fourteen he entered Brown University, but, because of ill health, left in 1827 and went to Europe. He spent all but one year of the next twenty abroad, serving from 1837 to 1845 as United States consul at Rome. By chance in southern France he met Henry Wadsworth Longfellow, and he soon became his intimate friend. The famous poet greatly influenced his career and from that time on Greene considered literature his vocation.

His first essays appeared in the *North American Review* in 1835, and while in Rome he wrote a one-volume *Life of Nathanael Greene* (1846). In 1848 he became instructor of modern languages at Brown University, and soon published several textbooks and, in 1850, *Historical Essays.* In 1853 he married Catherine Van Buren Porter, of an old New England family. After his marriage he moved to New York and devoted his time to lecturing and writing. In 1871 he lectured in American history at Cornell University, holding the first chair on that subject established in the United States.

Greene cherished from early youth the ambition to write a complete biography of his distinguished grandfather. He finally published the first volume of *Life of Nathanael Greene* in 1867, the second and third, 1871. Although great labor and an infinite amount of research had gone into this work, it suffered from its author's hero-worship.

PRINCIPAL WORKS: Biographical Studies, 1860; Historical View of the American Revolution, 1865; Life of Nathanael Greene, 1867 and 1871; German Element in the War of Independence, 1876; A Short History of Rhode Island, 1877.

ABOUT: Greene, G. S. & Clarke, L. B. The Greenes of Rhode Island; Longfellow, S. (ed.). Life of Henry Wadsworth Longfellow; Selkreg, J. H. (ed.). Landmarks of Tompkins County, N.Y.; Historical Catalog of Brown University 1764-1904; New York Times February 3, 1883; Providence Journal February 3, 1883.

GREENHOW, ROBERT (1800-March 27, 1854), physician, and miscellaneous writer, was born in Richmond, Va. His parents were Robert Greenhow and Mary Ann (Willis) Greenhow who died in the Richmond theatre fire in 1811. Greenhow was graduated from the College of William and Mary in 1816, and later received his M.D. degree from the College of Physicians and Surgeons in New York. He went to Paris for further study and while in Europe made the acquaintance of many famous men. From 1825 to 1828 he practised medicine in New York and then was appointed translator to the Department of State in Washington. He stayed there till 1850, when he moved to California. Two years later he was appointed law officer to the United States land commission in California, but in 1854 he was badly injured in a fall, from which he never recovered.

It was while Greenhow was connected with the Department of State as translator that he wrote *The History and Present Condition of Tripoli.* It is, however, *The History of Oregon and California,* published in 1844, that gives Greenhow a place among historians.

PRINCIPAL WORKS: History and Present Condition of Tripoli, 1835; History of Oregon and California, 1844.

ABOUT: Alta California March 28, 1854.

GREENLEAF, MOSES (October 17, 1777-March 20, 1834), map maker, was born in Newburyport, Mass., the son of Moses and Lydia (Parsons) Greenleaf. After running an unsuccessful general store in Maine from 1799 to 1806, he took up real estate. Because of a partnership with a man who owned a township in Maine later called Williamsburg, he started in 1810 to make a settlement of the town, and promptly moved his family there. The rest of his life was spent in trying to encourage and develop the settlement of interior Maine. He was thoroughly acquainted with the whole district, and conveyed his knowledge to the general public by his various publications. From 1812 to 1816 he was justice of the peace for Hancock County, and a year later was appointed justice of the court of common pleas for Piscataquis County.

Greenleaf is chiefly noted for his maps of Maine, and for a few of his books, one of which influenced the separation of Maine from Massachusetts: *A Survey of the State of Maine: In Reference to Its Geographical Features, Statistics, and Political Economy.*

PRINCIPAL WORKS: Map of the District of Maine From the Latest and Best Authorities, 1815; A Statistical View of the District of Maine, 1816; Map of the State of Maine With the Province of New Brunswick, 1829; A Survey of the State of Maine, 1829.

ABOUT: Greenleaf, J. E. Genealogy of the Greenleaf Family; Smith, E. C. Moses Greenleaf: Maine's First Map-Maker; North American Review September 1816; Eastern Argus March 26, 1834.

GREENOUGH, HORATIO (September 6, 1805-December 18, 1852), sculptor and writer on art, was born in Boston, the son of David Greenough, a prosperous merchant, and Betsey, or Elisabeth (Bender) Greenough. He displayed early his talent for art, but had no regular instruction until after his graduation from Harvard in 1825. At college he had become the friend of the painter Washington Allston, and had designed a monument for Bunker Hill. Before commencement day he was on his way to Europe, and his diploma was sent after him. In Rome he studied art with Thorwaldsen and started work as a sculptor. The next year, however, malaria obliged him to return home. In 1828 he was in Italy again, and in 1831 he visited Paris to make a portrait bust of Lafayette. Others of his busts were portraits of John Adams, John Quincy Adams, Henry Clay, and James Fenimore Cooper. Making his headquarters in Florence, he worked for ten years on America's first colossal marble group, a statue of Washington designed for the interior of the White House, but so heavy it had to be placed outdoors. It was completed in 1843. In 1837 he had married Louisa Gore, of Boston. The increasing political disturbances in Italy, plus his desire to see his statue properly set in Washington, brought him back to America in 1851. He settled in Newport, and gave a course of lectures on art, part of a book he was planning to write. His theory of functional art was new and exciting, and his influence on the thinking of such of his friends as Emerson was very great. But he was doomed to an early death; he fell ill of brain fever and died at forty-seven at Somerville, Mass., where he had gone for treatment.

Emerson spoke of Greenough's conversation as "both brilliant and deep," and these characteristics are repeated in his vivid, epigrammatic writing, marred only by invective against those who opposed his views. His verse, never collected, was also highly praised. He did not live to complete his book, but parts of it are incorporated in H. T. Tuckerman's *Memoir*.

PRINCIPAL WORKS: Aesthetics in Washington, 1851; Essays on Art (in Memoir by H. T. Tuckerman) 1853; Letters of Horatio Greenough to His Brother Henry Greenough (ed. by F. B. Greenough) 1887.

ABOUT: Brooks, Van W. The Flowering of New England; Tuckerman, H. T. A Memoir of Horatio Greenough; Putnam's Monthly March 1853.

"GREENWAY, GRANDFATHER." See CANNON, CHARLES JAMES

"GREENWOOD, GRACE." See LIPPINCOTT, SARA JANE (CLARKE)

GREGG, JOSIAH (July 19, 1806-February 25, 1850), travel writer, was born in Overton County, Tenn., the son of Harmon and Susannah (Schmelzer) Gregg. The family moved to Illinois in 1809 and to Missouri in 1812. Gregg was reared in this frontier atmosphere, apparently without formal schooling, though somehow he learned some mathematics and astronomy, enough Spanish to be able to read the Mexican archives, and a smattering of medicine which caused him to be called "Dr. Gregg," though he never practiced or claimed the title. To benefit his health, he went in 1831 as a trader to Santa Fé, then owned by Mexico, and until 1840 he traveled back and forth between Mexico and Missouri. In 1844 he went to New York City and succeeded in finding a publisher for the book he had made of his experiences. It was immensely successful, and ran through several editions within a short time.

In 1846 Gregg rode 1,200 miles on horseback to join Col. W. A. Doniphan's expedition from San Antonio, acting as a government agent and also as a newspaper correspondent. His last visit to Santa Fé was in 1849. Then he proceeded to California as a government surveyor, going to the Trinity Mines. The next winter he

From a portrait by C. Batchelor
JOSIAH GREGG

commanded an exploring party over the Coast Range to the Pacific, a terrible ordeal. On the return trip to Trinity, worn out by hardship and exposure, he fell from his horse and died, at Clear Lake, Calif.

Gregg was never married, and little is known of his personal life except that he was widely known in his time and greatly respected. On the whole his book is accurate, and it is a recognized classic of early Western literature. At his death he left the manuscript of a book entitled *Rovings Abroad,* but it was lost and never recovered.

Principal Work: Commerce of the Prairies: or, The Journal of a Santa Fé Trader, 1844.

About: Coy, O. C. Josiah Gregg in California (in *New Spain and the Anglo-American West,* ed. by W. C. Binkley, L. Goodwin, & J. F. Rippy); Mississippi Valley Historical Review March 1930; Proceedings Mississippi Valley Historical Assn. X, 1920; Publications Historical Society of New Mexico 26, 1924.

GRIFFIS, WILLIAM ELLIOT (September 17, 1843-February 5, 1928), educator and clergyman, was born in Philadelphia, the son of Captain John Limeburner Griffis and Anna Maria (Hess) Griffis. He was a mixture of nationalities—his father being of Welsh descent and his mother, German-Swiss. His early education was obtained in a dame and public school. He was with the 44th Pennsylvania regiment for three months during the Civil War, and in 1869 was graduated from Rutgers College. In 1870 he was chosen by Rutgers to fill Japan's request for someone "to organize schools on the American principle and teach the natural sciences" in Fukui. In Fukui he equipped the first chemical laboratory in Japan. The old feudal system was abolished while he was there, and he claimed to have been the only foreigner really to have known feudal Japan. From 1872 to 1874 he taught at what is now the Imperial University at Tokio. He then returned to the United States and for the rest of his life tried to familiarize Americans with Japan and its customs. Two years after his return he published *The Mikado's Empire,* which went into twelve editions and offered a wealth of information on Japan.

Griffis then took up the ministry, being graduated from Union Theological Seminary in 1877. Despite the fact that, until 1903 he held several pastorates, he continued to write. After 1903 he devoted himself entirely to lecturing and writing.

Principal Works: The Mikado's Empire, 1876; Corea: The Hermit Nation, 1882; Matthew Calbraith Perry: A Typical American Naval Officer, 1887; Japan in History, Folk-lore, and Art, 1892; The Religions of Japan From the Dawn of History to the Era of Meiji, 1895; Townsend Harris: First American Envoy to Japan, 1895; America in the East, 1899; Verbeck of Japan, 1900; A Maker of the New Orient: Samuel Robbins Brown, 1902; The Japanese Nation in Evolution, 1907; A Modern Pioneer in Korea: The Life Story of Henry G. Appenzeller, 1912; Hepburn of Japan, 1913; The Mikado—Institution and Person, 1915.

About: Griffis, W. E. The Mikado's Empire, and Sunny Memories of Three Pastorates; Congregationalist May 10, 1928; Korea Mission Field April 1928; New York Times February 6, 1928.

GRIGSBY, HUGH BLAIR (November 22, 1806-April 28, 1881), historian and biographer, was born in Norfolk, Va., the son of the Rev. Benjamin Porter Grigsby and Elizabeth (McPherson) Grigsby. Because of his delicate health he was privately instructed, later spending two years at Yale where he distinguished himself particularly in law. He was admitted to the Norfolk bar, but soon gave up his practice because of increasing deafness. Then, as owner and editor of the Norfolk *American Beacon,* he started a successful journalistic career. From 1828 to 1830 he represented Norfolk in the House of Delegates and was a member of the Virginia Constitutional Convention. Unfortunately, after only six years, ill health forced him to give up his newspaper. He had, however, been operating it so efficiently that he was able to retire with a competency.

From his youth Grigsby had shown a definite talent for biography and many of his later writings are in this field. As the acknowledged historian of Virginia in his day he published several works all of which show thoroughness and a keen knowledge of the facts.

Principal Works: The Virginia Convention of 1829-30, 1854; The Virginia Convention of 1776, 1855; Discourse on the Life and Character of the Honorable Littleton Waller Tazewell, 1860; The History of the Virginia Federal Convention of 1788, 1890-91; The Founders of Washington College, 1890; Discourse on the Lives and Characters of the Early Presidents and Trustees of Hampden-Sidney College, 1913.

About: Grigsby, W. H. Genealogy of the Grigsby Family; New England Historical and Genealogical Register July 1881; State and Richmond Daily Dispatch April 30, 1881; Virginia Historical Society Collections: Vol. 9.

GRIMES, JAMES STANLEY (May 10, 1807-September 27, 1903), philosophical and pseudo-scientific writer, was born in Boston. His exact parentage is not known; two sisters appear to have married two brothers, and he was the son either of Andrew and Polly (Robbins) Grimes or of Joseph and Sally (Robbins) Grimes. His entire life is obscure; it is not known where he was educated, but he practiced law in Boston and New York, and was on terms of familiarity with Webster, Choate, and Clay. Later he was professor of medical jurisprudence at Castleton Medical College and taught at Willard Institute, which claimed to be the first American college for women. Both of these institutions were in Illinois, and from the middle of the century his home was in Evanston, then a pioneer village. He died there at the advanced age of ninety-six. His last public appearance in the East was in a series of debates on spiritualism in Boston in 1860.

From 1832 Grimes had been an exponent of phrenology, but he modified this pseudoscience with theories of his own, and was considered and attacked as a heretic by the orthodox phrenologists. Though it was his writings which first turned the attention of Andrew Jackson Davis, the noted medium and writer on spiritualism, to this subject, Grimes himself was strongly opposed to the spiritualistic hypothesis. He had a receptive, original mind, and the courage of his convictions; and it must be remembered that both phrenology and mesmerism, which he also advocated, were respectable supposedly scientific theories in his day. He was one of the earliest American defenders of the theory of evolution. In later years he grew increasingly erratic, ending with a bizarre hypothesis on the formation of the solar system. He was given to coining words to describe his invented systems, and in general wrote in a high-flown manner which makes him unreadable today. Nevertheless, he was a staunch foe of superstition, and in a more favorable period might well have been a scientific and philosophical thinker of distinction.

Principal Works: A New System of Phrenology, 1839; Etherology, 1845; Phreno-Geology, 1851; Outlines of Geonomy, 1858; Phreno-Physiology, 1893.

About: Riley, W. American Thought From Puritanism to Pragmatism; Chicago Tribune September 29, 1903.

"GRINGO, HARRY." See WISE, HENRY AUGUSTUS

GRISWOLD, RUFUS WILMOT (February 15, 1815-August 27, 1857), editor and anthologist, was born in Benson, Vt., the son of Rufus Griswold, a poor farmer and tanner, and Deborah (Waas) Griswold. His personal history is obscure; it is probable that he had only an elementary education, and at the age of fifteen he was already employed by a newspaper in Albany. He

RUFUS W. GRISWOLD

then became an itinerant printer, and may have been a sailor; he claimed to have traveled widely in both America and Europe, but there is no evidence of this. In 1837 he married Caroline Searles, who died in 1842, leaving two daughters. In the year of his marriage he was licensed to preach as a Baptist minister, but no one seems to know of any pulpit he filled; he also assumed the degrees of D.D. and LL.D., but whence obtained he did not say. In 1838 and 1839, he edited the Vergennes *Vermonter,* devoting himself largely to diatribes against the Roman Catholics, on one hand, and Jefferson and Paine on the other. For the next few months he worked for Greeley on the *New Yorker*; the nature of his position may be inferred from Greeley's statement that he was "the most expert and judicious thief that ever handled scissors." Then he went to Philadelphia, first with the *Daily Standard,* then with the *Gazette.* It was at this time that he met Poe, whose nemesis and traducer he was to become. In 1842 he succeeded Poe as assistant editor of *Graham's Magazine*; in 1843 he was dismissed for dishonesty.

In all Griswold was connected with almost twenty papers and magazines, and wrote, compiled and edited about forty volumes, mostly ephemeral. Some of the titles he claimed for himself have never been seen between covers; he was a really monumental liar—Constance Rourke characterizes him as "able to talk longer with a small capital of truth than any man in existence." He edited the poems of W. M. Praed and Milton's prose, and translated Béranger.

Gradually, largely through the publicity he was able to give both his protégés and his enemies in his anthologies, this pious fraud became the wealthy dean and arbiter of American letters. From 1850 to 1852 he edited the *International Monthly Magazine,* and the following year Barnum's *Illustrated News.* There is some evidence that he was the "ghost writer" of the first edition of Barnum's autobiography; it is known that he did a great deal of hack work of this sort.

Even a mysterious scandal failed to disturb Griswold's position. In 1845, apparently under compulsion, he had secretly married Charlotte Myers, a Charleston (S.C.) Jewess. The marriage was never consummated, and in 1852 he divorced her for desertion. In the same year he married Harriet Stanley McCrillis, by whom he had one son, William McCrillis Griswold [*q.v.*]. In 1856 an effort was made to have the divorce decree set aside, which would have invalidated the later marriage. Griswold was by this time dying of tuberculosis, from which he had long suffered. He defended himself in a public statement, but the matter was still unresolved when he died the following summer. At the time of his death he was engaged on a life of Washington and a biographical dictionary. The latter project probably accounts for his savage review, in the New York *Herald* in 1856, of Duyckincks' *Cyclopaedia of American Literature,* which had forestalled him; it is commonly considered the most destructive book review ever written by an American.

Griswold, however, is best known as the enemy and maligner of Poe. Poe thought him his friend and made him his literary executor. The poet was hardly cold in death before Griswold appeared with a hastily written obituary notice, signed "Ludwig," in the New York *Tribune.* Accused of having perpetrated a mass of malicious slander, he justified himself by an uncalled for "memoir" in the *International Monthly Magazine,* reprinted in his edition of Poe's works (1850), which is a masterpiece of misstatement, but which obscured Poe's real history and character until after Griswold's death.

About the only favorable thing that can be said of Griswold is that he was an advocate of "Americanism" in American literature; yet even this was evidence of a narrow chauvinism. Lowell said of him: "The Reverend Mr. Griswold is an ass, and what's more, a knave." Constance Rourke calls him "this small, smooth, slippery critic." He would be long ago forgotten had he not set himself on record as the enemy of Poe. Erratic, supersensitive, and vindictive, "destitute alike of talent and of integrity" (J. A. T. Lloyd), Griswold is one of the least attractive figures in the whole history of literature.

Principal Works: Poems, 1841; The Poets and Poetry of America, 1842; The Poets and Poetry of England in the Nineteenth Century, 1844; Christian Ballads and Other Poems, 1844; The Prose Writers of America, 1847; The Female Poets of America, 1848; Sacred Poets of England and America, 1848; The Republican Court: or, American Society in the Days of Washington, 1855; Passages From the Correspondence and Other Papers of Rufus W. Griswold (ed. by W. M. Griswold) 1898.

About: Campbell, K. The Poe-Griswold Controversy; Griswold, W. McC. Passages From the Correspondence . . . of Rufus W. Griswold; Griswold, R. W. A Statement; Lloyd, J. A. T. The Murder of Edgar Allan Poe; Rourke, C. M. Trumpets of Jubilee.

GRISWOLD, WILLIAM McCRILLIS (October 9, 1853-August 3, 1899), bibliographer, was born at Bangor, Maine, the son of Rufus Wilmot Griswold [*q.v.*] and Harriet Stanley (McCrillis) Griswold. His father died before the boy was three, leaving a substantial estate. He prepared at Phillips Exeter Academy for Harvard, from which he was graduated in 1875. For the next few years he studied abroad, carefully disciplining himself by making long translations from French and German periodicals until he gained a real proficiency in these languages. At this time he was also contributing letters regularly to the Sunday issues of Boston papers and the literary journals. Returning to the United States, he wrote anonymously for several periodicals, chiefly the *Nation.* He served briefly in the copyright division of the Library of Congress and for a while held a position in the State Department. He was married to Anne Deering Merrill at Bangor, Maine, in 1882, and by her had four children. He died in his forty-sixth year at Seal Harbor, Maine.

Griswold's financial independence allowed him to indulge his "indexical passion" without the necessity of economic profit. The first of his many bibliographical aids was *A General Index to the Nation,* followed by similar guides for the *Contemporary Review,* the *Fortnightly,* and the *Revue des Deux Mondes*; in pamphlet form he issued *A Directory of Writers for the Literary Press* and *A Directory of Authors.* From 1882 to 1885 he issued the *"Q. P."* [Quarterly Periodical] *Index Annual,* and from 1891 to 1895 he issued a series of descriptive lists of "books for the young," "international novels," "novels and tales dealing with ancient history," etc. His *Switzerland* was a collection of abridged travel discourses borrowed from a variety of English and American magazines; and *Mt. Desert Early and Late* was a compilation of articles on Maine summer colonies.

In 1898 came his most important work. From his father's literary remains he selected and published *Passages From the Correspondence and Other Papers of Rufus W. Griswold.* The volume did not attempt to justify the elder Griswold's notorious attack on the memory of Poe, but embodied a frank and valuable treatment of the entire Poe-Griswold controversy. It was the younger Griswold's last and best literary stroke, for although his bibliographical achievements were a potential boon to students and researchers, they employed unwieldy abbreviations and phonetics and could scarcely be said to have influenced American letters to any appreciable extent. Nevertheless, William McCrillis Griswold was in every way a far more estimable and useful citizen than his better known parent.

PRINCIPAL WORKS: General Index to the Nation, 1880; General Index to the Contemporary Review, 1882-85; Directory of Writers for the Literary Press, 1884; Directory of Authors, 1886; A Descriptive List . . . (series) 1891-95; Switzerland, 1892; Mt. Desert Early and Late, 1896; Passages From the Correspondence and Other Papers of Rufus W. Griswold, 1898.

ABOUT: Harvard College Class of 1875: Secretary's Report No. 8; Nation (N.Y.) August 31, 1891; Library Journal September 1899.

"GUARD, THEODORE DE LA." See WARD, NATHANIEL

GUNTER, ARCHIBALD CLAVERING (October 25, 1847-February 24, 1907), novelist, was born in Liverpool, England, the son of Henry and Elizabeth Agnes (Sharpless) Gunter. But his family brought him at the age of six to New York and shortly afterward to San Francisco. There he attended the public schools and the school of mines at the state university. Between 1868 and 1879 he held various positions in San Francisco and Utah as civil engineer, chemist, mine superintendent, and broker. From 1879 on he lived in New York. In 1886 he married Esther Lisbeth Burns, the niece of the curator of paintings in the Metropolitan Museum of Art.

In 1887 Gunter's first novel, *Mr. Barnes of New York,* appeared. To publish it he organized his own company, after the book had been turned down by all the large publishing houses in New York. The book proved to be a sensational success: one of those "popular classics" which appear inexplicably from time to time. More than a million copies sold in the United States alone. For the next few years Gunter was the most widely read American novelist, and, although his sales gradually fell off, he continued to write until his death. His work had little merit and is almost completely forgotten today.

PRINCIPAL WORKS: Found the True Vein, 1872; Mr. Barnes of New York, 1887; Mr. Potter of Texas, 1888; That Frenchman! 1889; Miss Nobody of Nowhere, 1890; Miss Dividends, 1892; Baron Montez of Panama and Paris, 1893; The King's Stockbroker, 1894; A Princess of Paris, 1894.

ABOUT: Bookman October 1902, May 1907; Publishers' Weekly March 2, 1907; Putnam's Monthly April 1907; New York Times February 26, 1907; San Francisco Chronicle February 25, 1907.

"H.H." See JACKSON, HELEN MARIA (FISKE) HUNT

HABBERTON, JOHN (February 24, 1842-February 24, 1921), humorist and editor, was born in Brooklyn, N.Y. After the death of his father, Job John Habberton, in 1848, the boy was reared and educated in Illinois by an uncle. At the age of sixteen he came to New York to learn the publishing business; and after two years as a printer's apprentice and three years of service with the Union army during the Civil War, he finally secured a responsible position with the firm of Harper & Brothers in 1865. His outstanding success in this work encouraged him to try his own hand at publishing in 1872, but within six months he went into bankruptcy. During the rest of his life Habberton wrote and edited for other publishers; between 1874 and 1900 he served on the editorial staffs of the *Christian Union,* the *Outlook,* the New York *Herald, Godey's Magazine,* and *Collier's Magazine.* He married, in 1868, Alice Lawrence Hastings, and resided during most of his later life at New Rochelle, N.Y.

Habberton's first literary success came in 1876, when the Boston publisher Loring accepted his novel *Helen's Babies,* one of the humorous classics of its time. The author was unwilling to put his name to this undignified performance, which he described as a day's record of "the antics of a couple of lively little boys"; yet it found a sale of 250,000 copies in the United States and was almost equally successful abroad. To this rich vein of infantile deviltry Habberton returned again and again in his subsequent writings, but never with the same success. "From book writing," he confessed, "I drifted into journalism." His later work includes a humorous life of George Washington (1884), a very popular play, *Deacon Crankett* (1880), and such exercises in "writing up" current themes as *The Barton Experiment* (1877). He died in 1921 at Glen Ridge, N.J. His literary career had virtually ended at the turn of the century.

PRINCIPAL WORKS: *Novels*—Helen's Babies, 1876; The Jericho Road, 1877; The Scripture Club of Valley Rest, 1877; Other People's Children, 1877; The Barton Experiment, 1877; The Worst Boy in Town, 1880; The Bowsham Puzzle, 1884; Some Boys' Doings, 1901; Caleb Wright: A Story of the West, 1901. *Short Stories*—Some Folks, 1877. *Drama*—Deacon Crankett, 1880. *Miscellaneous*—Life of George Washington, 1884.

ABOUT: Lippincott's Magazine December 1886; New York Times February 26, 1921; New York Tribune February 26, 1921.

"HADERMAN, JANET H." See WALWORTH, JEANETTE RITCHIE (HADERMAN)

HALE, EDWARD EVERETT (April 3, 1822-June 10, 1909), story teller, poet, and Unitarian minister, was born in Boston, the son of Nathan Hale, nephew of the classic Revolutionary figure of the same name, and Sarah Preston (Everett) Hale, sister of Edward Everett [*q.v.*]. When scarcely two years old he was sent to Miss Whitney's dame school, then to Mr. Dowe's school and afterwards to the Public Latin school where he prepared for Harvard, entering at thirteen. Although he made a normal adjustment to college life, he had a constant hankering after the social and intellectual delights of his home.

He was graduated from Harvard in 1839, continued to report the proceedings of the state legislature for the Boston *Daily Advertiser,* a task begun during his senior year in college, and taught for two years at the Boston Latin School. His mother urged him to enter the ministry, and he pursued an independent study of theology. Hale had, at this time, a strange craving for "literary quiet and repose." But four years after his first sermon he was ordained, April 29, 1846, as minister over the Church of Unity at Worcester, and already he was beginning to conceive of the church as a social factor, although his approach was still theoretical.

Hale grew up in a family in which writing for publication was commonplace. His father was editor of the *Advertiser*; his brothers Nathan and Charles and his sister Lucretia [*q.v.*] were all engaged in literary ventures. Edward Hale combined his delight in verbal cleverness with his faith in the efficacy of good didactic writing. "My Double and How He Outdid Me" (1859) and "The Man Without a Country" (1863),

Collection of Frederick H. Meserve
EDWARD EVERETT HALE

an admittedly fictionalized account of the Philip Nolan who had been murdered on an expedition into Texas, are engaging narratives with significant argument. (The latter has become almost an American myth.) These two stories, together with "The Children of the Public" (1863), written for a *Leslie's Illustrated Weekly* competition, appeared later in *If, Yes, and Perhaps* (1868).

In 1852 Hale married Emily Perkins of Hartford, Conn., and in 1856 he accepted a call to the South Congregational Church of Boston. He went abroad with his uncle, Edward Everett, in 1859, and recorded his journey in *Ninety Days' Worth of Europe.* On his return he wrote regularly to Charles, then abroad, and these letters, during the early years of the Civil War, formed an excellent digest of contrary opinions; it was not so much the institution of slavery, *per se,* but rather the social evils evolving from it that he himself bitterly disliked.

The first issue of Hale's monthly, *Old and New,* of which the pervading tone was "as pure religion as we know of," appeared in December 1869. For it he wrote "Ten Times One is Ten," a story of individual unselfishness, which marked the beginning of the widespread "Lend a Hand" movement. Hale went abroad again in 1873, and late that summer moved his family to their country haven at Matunuck, R.I. On a journey through Texas and Louisiana in 1876 he "discovered" the genuineness of what he had supposed was only hearsay hospitality. In the late 'seventies he wrote numerous short stories and several chapters of a *History of the United States* edited by William Cullen Bryant and Sidney Gay.

During the years 1882 to 1892 Hale began to give up some of his routine obligations in Boston. He was called to Washington in February 1882 to vouch for the validity of the Franklin Papers which had been offered for Government purchase, and which he later used as source material for *Franklin in France* (1887-1888). During that same year he went with his sister Susan and daughter Ellen to Spain. Nine years later, on an otherwise glorious outing in California, Hale suffered a leg injury which lamed him for life. His last trip to Europe and the publication of *A New England Boyhood* occurred in 1892. He was much interested in the preservation of peace, and attended the Washington Arbitration Conference, establishing a Permanent Committee, in 1896. Not until May 1899 did he resign from the ministry of the South Congregational Church. In 1903 he was elected Chaplain of the U. S. Senate, and during his stay in the Capital acquired a coterie of good friends. He returned to Boston shortly before his death.

Hale was a man of large, angular frame and well-lined features, with a generous heart, a keen and ingenious mind, and a judicious sense of humor. He had no exalted literary ambitions; to put his ideas down on paper was his prime objective. Much sermon-writing gave him a smooth and instructive style, and his preaching was said to have been like a beautiful "sphere . . . of which every part demands every other part." As a critic of his literary contemporaries he was not always astute. "Emerson's stock of startling phrases concerning soul and mind are [*sic*] getting exhausted" was his remark as a lad of sixteen, and he never overcame his coolness towards the seer of Concord. Hale had been a conservative in his youth and almost a liberal in his later years; above all, he was a realist in that he believed his age to be "a time of protest against untruth."

Principal Works: *Stories*—If, Yes, and Perhaps; Four Possibilities and Six Exaggerations, 1868; Back to Back, 1878; East and West, 1892. *Autobiographical*—Ninety Days' Worth of Europe, 1861; A New England Boyhood, 1892; Memories of a Hundred Years, 1904. *Miscellaneous and Poetry*—Kansas and Nebraska, 1854; The Ingham Papers, 1869; Franklin in France, 1887-88; Poems and Fancies, 1901.

About: Hale, E. E., Jr. The Life of Edward Everett Hale; Hale, E. E. Personal Recollections of Eminent American Poets; Atkinson, C. P. Letters of Susan Hale; Leslie's Illustrated Weekly January 1863.

HALE, LUCRETIA PEABODY (September 2, 1820-June 12, 1900), juvenile and miscellaneous writer, was born in Boston, the daughter of Nathan Hale and Sarah Preston (Everett) Hale. She received her formal learning at Elizabeth Peabody's and George B. Emerson's schools, and was instructed at an early age in dancing, music, and other gentle arts. At thirteen she helped her brother Edward [*q.v.*] make a French translation which marked the beginning of his long literary career. In 1840 she made her first journey to New York; ten years later appeared her *Margaret Percival in America,* a collaboration in which she and Edward presented an up-to-date picture of the church in America.

Miss Hale's literary name was established, however, by the amusing Peterkin series, first printed in *Our Young Folks* and the *St. Nicholas Magazine,* and appearing in book form as *The Peterkin Papers* (1880) and *The Last of the Peterkins with Others of Their Kin* (1886). In April 1871 her sister Susan set up a literary daily called the *Balloon-Post,* the official organ of the French Fair, then in progress in Boston. Only "light freight" was accepted, and among its contributors were Howells, Henry James, and Bret Harte. For this journal Lucretia Hale wrote some matchless parodies of contemporary gems.

During the last twenty years of her life Miss Hale had a growing interest in the public affairs of women; she advocated "morals and sewing" for public school curricula, established correspondence schools, and was active on various educational committees to which women had never had admission. She loved hilarity in its place, but let nothing interfere with her religious obligations. She was always unfailingly kind and when blindness threatened and her mind became somewhat impaired, countless friends did their utmost for her happiness.

It is perhaps in association with the literary activities concurrent in her own family that Miss Hale's writings have a ranking. Nevertheless, her juveniles possess a pleasantly illogical lightness, and her works as a whole are valuably loaded with minutiae of contemporary life.

Principal Works: *Novels*—Six of One by Half a Dozen of the Other, 1872; The Wolf at the Door, 1877. *Juveniles*—The Peterkin Papers, 1880; The Last of the Peterkins with Others of Their Kind, 1886. *Books of Devotion*—The Struggle for Life, 1861; The Service of Sorrow, 1867. *Miscellaneous*—Designs in Outline for Art-Needlework, 1879; Faggots for the Fireside, 1888.

ABOUT: Atkinson, C. P. Letters of Susan Hale; Hale, E. E., Jr. Life of Edward Everett Hale; Hale, E. E. A New England Boyhood; Balloon-Post April 1871; Bookman June 1925; Boston Transcript June 12, 1900.

HALE, SARAH JOSEPHA (BUELL) (October 24, 1788-April 30, 1879), editor and feminist, was born in Newport, N.H., the daughter of Gordon Buell, an officer of four years' service in the War of the Revolution, and Martha (Whittlesey) Buell, a lady of cultural endowments of Saybrook, Conn. There were no good schools in Newport, during Sarah's childhood, and she was taught Latin, mathematics and philosophy by her mother and her brother, Horatio, a law student at Dartmouth. She read the Bible and *Pilgrim's Progress,* and after portions of Milton, Shakespeare, and Cowper, she became absorbed in Mrs. Radcliffe's *The Mysteries of Udolpho,* and was intrigued by the fact that it was written by a woman. She started a small school for children in 1806 and for seven years instructed them in the art of intelligent reading.

In October 1813 she married David Hale, a lawyer of decided ability. The two of them studied together each evening, absorbing French, "general literature," and new sciences. It is recorded that in the fall of 1818 Mrs. Hale was cured of "quick consumption" by a six weeks' trip through the mountains in a gig, with a diet of almost nothing but wild "frost grapes," which hung ripe at the roadside.

After a portrait by W. B. Chambers
SARAH JOSEPHA HALE

Mr. Hale died in 1822, leaving his widow little money for the care of five small children. To Mrs. Hale writing looked like a possible expedient, and with the aid of the Free Masons she published *The Genius of Oblivion and Other Original Poems* (1823), verses of forced rhyme and overworked subject matter. *Northwood: A Tale of New England* (1827), a novel, received a Boston newspaper award. The following year John L. Blake, an Episcopal clergyman, invited her to come to Boston to take charge of the *Ladies' Magazine,* which in 1837 was bought out by Louis A. Godey, and Mrs. Hale became the editor of the new *Lady's Book.* Godey's publicity stratagems and Mrs. Hale's sense of literary propriety made it a flourishing venture, and for it she wrote many things besides editorial comment. *The Judge: A Drama of American Life* appeared during the first half of the year 1851; written in blank verse, it was an unfortunate attempt at a Shakespearean turn of phrase with cumbersome moralizing. In 1837 she compiled *The Ladies' Wreath,* a "gift-book for all seasons." This selection from the "female poetic writings of England and America," admitted only those authors "whose air was upward and onward," and whose style had some "peculiar stamp of individuality which marked their genius as original." Her target was a bit vague, in the first requirement, and slightly high, in the second, but the book had a wide sale. She edited two annuals, *The Opal,* for the years 1845 and 1848, and *The Crocus* for 1849.

The most valuable of her works, however, is *Woman's Record: or, Sketches of All Distinguished Women From the Beginning Till A. D. 1850* (1854). It is strongly flavored with superlatives but constitutes an orderly assemblage of valuable biographical data. In 1856 Mrs. Hale published *The Letters of Madame de Sévigné to Her Daughter and Friends,* and *The Letters of Lady Mary Wortley Montague.*

With a delicately fair skin, hazel eyes, and dark brown side-curls, as well as a superb taste in dress, Mrs. Hale was indeed the ideal "lady of Godey's." Her influence, however, penetrated diverse fields. She founded the Seaman's Aid Society, and was instrumental in the completion of the Bunker Hill Monument and in the establishing of Thanksgiving as a national holiday.

Mrs. Hale earned the distinction of being the first woman editor of a magazine, and she was, moreover, an acknowledged master of "fine English." She remains an admirable representative of intellectual Victorianism.

PRINCIPAL WORKS: *Poetry*—The Genius of Oblivion and Other Original Poems, 1823. *Novel*—Northwood: A Tale of New England, 1827. *Compilations*—Ladies' Wreath, 1837; Opal, 1845 and 1848; Crocus, 1849; Complete Dictionary of Poetical Quotations, 1852; Woman's Record, 1854; Letters of Madame de Sévigné to Her Daughter and Friends, 1856; Letters of Lady Mary Wortley Montague, 1856.

ABOUT: Finley, R. E. The Lady of Godey's; Hale, S. J. B. The Ladies' Wreath; Hale, S. J. B. Woman's Record; Wheeler, E. History of Newport, N. H.; Godey's Lady's Book December 1850-May 1851.

HALE, SUSAN (December 5, 1833-September 1910), painter, letter-writer, and traveler, was born in Boston, Mass., the daughter of Nathan and Sarah Preston (Everett) Hale, and younger sister of Edward Everett Hale and Lucretia Peabody Hale [*qq.v.*]. She attended George B. Emerson's school and was instructed in drawing by one Mr. Fette. In 1867 she and her sister Lucretia went to Egypt, where their brother Charles had been sent as consul general; the high light of their journey was a voyage down the Nile.

On her return Susan took rooms on Boylston Street and conducted classes in painting. She spent the winter of 1872-73 in Paris and at Weimar, studying water-color techniques with Copley Fielding, Henri Harpignies, and several other masters. Returning again, she settled down at the Arts Club, outlined a few books, painted, and wrote travel letters for newspapers. Several times a week she would read to William Amory and to Thomas Gold Appleton, one of Boston's most brilliant conversationalists, whose life she afterwards wrote. Her summers were spent in Matunuck, R.I., the vacation mecca of many of the Hales, and her winters passed in a variety of travel—in Mexico and in Europe. During the winters of 1908 and 1909 Miss Hale sampled some of Washington's social extravagances, and she lived the last winter of her life in Cannes, France.

Besides *The Life and Letters of Thomas Gold Appleton* and a volume on eighteenth century *mores,* she wrote, in collaboration with her brother Edward, two accounts of Spain and the *Family Flight* series, travel narratives covering Egypt, Mexico, and a group of European countries, as well as contemporary and historical Boston. All the nimble limericks which Mrs. William G. Weld had collected into *Nonsense Book* were illustrated by Susan Hale's gay pen-and-ink drawings. For the French Fair, in April 1871, she edited the *Balloon-Post,* a daily that carried only light (but delectable) literary cargo.

Susan Hale had grown up in a home in which the virtues and vices of writing were almost a matter of daily ritual, and she, too, in a gentle and charming manner, sustained the literary tradition.

PRINCIPAL WORKS: A Family Flight Over Egypt, 1882; A Family Flight Through France, Germany, Norway, and Switzerland, 1882; A Family Flight Around Home, 1885; Life and Letters of Thomas Gold Appleton, 1885; A Family Flight Through Mexico, 1886; The Story of Mexico, 1889; The Story of Spain, 1892; Men and Manners of the Eighteenth Century, 1898; Spain, 1907.

ABOUT: Atkinson, C. P. Letters of Susan Hale; Hale, E. E., Jr. The Life of Edward Everett Hale.

HALIBURTON, THOMAS CHANDLER. See KUNITZ & HAYCRAFT (eds.). *British Authors of the 19th Century*

HALL, FITZEDWARD (March 21, 1825-February 1, 1901), American-Anglo philologist, was born at Troy, N.Y., the eldest son of a well-to-do lawyer. After early schooling at Walpole, N.H., and Poughkeepsie, N.Y., he took a civil engineer's degree at Rensselaer Polytechnic Institute in 1842, and entered Harvard. Just before graduation in 1846 he was sent by his father to India, to find a brother who had run away to sea. Detained there, first by shipwreck but later by his own inclination, Hall made his home in Calcutta and began a career of teaching and of studying dialects—his chief interest from the age of fifteen. Appointed tutor, and later (1853) professor of Sanskrit and English at the government college at Benares, he achieved considerable prominence for his scholarly editing of Sanskrit and Hindu texts. In 1854 he married Amy, daughter of Lieutenant-Colonel Arthur Shuldham, at Delhi.

After 1862, when he was made professor of Sanskrit in King's College, London, Hall became almost as great an authority on English philology as on Sanskrit. A caustic and even virulent controversialist, he opposed all projects for regulating or purifying the language, and with his inexhaustible store of examples from English literature he often discomfited less scholarly opponents. In 1869 he retired to Marlesford, Suffolk, to edit Wilson's translation of the *Vishńupuráńá,* and he later rendered valuable assistance to Dr. Murray in preparing the *New English Dictionary.* He died at Marlesford in 1901, leaving a valuable collection of Oriental manuscripts to Harvard University.

Hall was a prolific writer and editor, but his immense philological erudition seems to have hindered rather than benefited his English style.

PRINCIPAL WORKS: Benares Ancient and Medieval, 1868; Recent Exemplifications of False Philology, 1872; Modern English, 1873; On English Adjectives in -able, 1877; Doctor Indoctus, 1880; numerous editions and translations.

ABOUT: Nation March 21, 1895, February 14, 1901; Modern Language Notes March 1901.

HALL, JAMES (August 19, 1793-July 5, 1868), jurist, banker, editor, and miscellaneous writer, was born at Philadelphia, the son of John Hall, a Revolutionary soldier of Maryland planter ancestry and Sarah (Ewing) Hall. His maternal grandfather was provost of the University of Pennsylvania. His education was largely through his mother, who imparted her literary ability to three brothers and himself.

After serving in the War of 1812, Hall entered the legal profession at Shawneetown, Ill., becoming a judge. Later he was appointed State Treasurer at Vandalia. From 1833 to the end of his life he engaged in banking at Cincinnati. Throughout this period of varied public service his literary activity was constant. He edited such publications as the *Illinois Gazette,* the *Illinois Intelligencer,* the *Illinois Monthly Magazine,* which he founded, and the *Western Monthly Magazine,* contributing much of their contents himself. He had previously contributed to the Philadelphia *Port Folio,* and his letters to that journal formed the basis of his first book *Letters From the West,* published in London in 1828. Various other works followed, reflecting his keen interest in the West and his desire to preserve in records its spirit, history, legends and other aspects of life. Several of his titles were published in many editions.

PRINCIPAL WORKS: Letters From the West, 1828; Legends of the West, 1832; The Soldier's Bride and Other Tales, 1833; Sketches of History, Life, and Manners in the West, 1834; History of the Indian Tribes of North America (in collaboration with Thomas L. McKenney) 1836.

ABOUT: McKenney, T. L. & Hall, J. Indian Tribes of North America (see Introduction by F. W. Hodge to 1933 edition); Venable, W. H. Beginnings of Literary Culture in the Ohio Valley; Colophon February 1936; Journal of the Illinois State Historical Society October 1929, April 1930; Ohio Archaeological and Historical Society Publication October 1909.

HALL, SARAH (EWING) (October 30, 1761-April 8, 1830), author of *Conversations on the Bible,* was born in Philadelphia, the daughter of the Rev. John Ewing, for many years provost of the University of Pennsylvania, and Hannah (Sargeant) Ewing. Sarah had no formal education, but read much in history and *belles lettres,* listened to the Latin and Greek recitations of her brothers, and imbibed considerable intellectuality from her father's learned circle. In 1782 she was married to John Hall, son of a wealthy Maryland planter, at whose farm on the Susquehanna they made their home. They moved to Philadelphia in 1790, and Mr. Hall became Secretary of the Land Office and U. S. Marshal for the Pennsylvania district.

Philadelphia was considered, at that time, the "Athens of America," and Mrs. Hall became associated with a group of intellectuals among whom was Dennie, who established the *Port Folio,* a literary journal of promise, in 1800. Mrs. Hall contributed criticisms, verses, and dissertations on the defence of women, on friendship, on discipline, etc.

In 1805 the Halls suffered a financial collapse, and returned from Lamberton, N.J., where they had been for four years, to the Maryland estate. From this time on Mr. Hall's ill health threw the burden of support upon his wife. Their eldest child, John Elihu, became editor of the *Port Folio* in 1816 and Mrs. Hall wrote regularly for its columns during the ten years following.

Her *Conversations on the Bible* (1818) went into four editions here and one in London. In the preparation of this book Mrs. Hall had studied Hebrew and had conducted exhaustive research. It is written in dialogue form and designed not "for mere children," she said, "but rather for young persons somewhat advanced." Five of Mrs. Hall's eleven children preceded her in death; her son Harrison published selections from her writings, with a memoir of her life.

Mrs. Hall's *Conversations* became a literary stand-by; her essays and letters furnish additional proof of the lucidity of her style. She was an attractive and discriminating woman who wanted to see her sex intelligently judged; her vindications were strong but not boisterous, candid but not bitter.

PRINCIPAL WORK: Conversations on the Bible, 1818.

ABOUT: Hall, H. Selections From the Writings of Mrs. Sarah Hall; Hall, S. E. Conversations on the Bible; Mott, F. L. History of American Magazines 1741-1850; Smyth, A. H. Philadelphia Magazines and Their Contributors.

HALLECK, FITZ-GREENE (July 8, 1790-November 19, 1867), poet, was born in Guilford, Conn., the son of Israel Halleck, an English gentleman of Cavalier gallantries, and Mary (Eliot) Halleck, a devout conformer in the Puritan tradition. When he was only three, some drunken militia men, wanting to astonish the youngster, discharged their guns near the lad's head and caused a permanent deafness in his left ear. He was a precocious boy and almost model student. At fifteen he was employed in a country store but found time to dabble in verse-writing; these early lines show a strong influence of his mother's Biblical instruction.

In July 1811 he accepted a position in New York with a banker named Jacob Barker. Halleck became acquainted with the young literati and was elected poet laureate of the "Ugly Club," a fun-poking coterie advocating ugliness "in all its forms." The year following he joined a volunteer military company "The Iron Grays," which disbanded soon afterward.

Joseph Rodman Drake [*q.v.*], the poet, was attracted by young Halleck's poetic leanings; together they wrote a series of satiric poems over the signature of "The Croakers" which appeared in the *Evening Post* and the *National Advocate*. New Yorkers received this lampooning with much relish and even the more discriminating critics were given to hyperbole. The poems were obviously overrated but they constitute an interesting episode in the history of American journalism. In the same vein was *Fanny* (1819), a burlesque on the *nouveaux riches*, which Halleck wrote in imitation of Byron's "Beppo."

The "dark hour," he declared, was upon him in July 1822, and to lift his gloom he went abroad. "Alnwick Castle" was written on his visit to Percy Castle in Alnwick, England. By 1824 Halleck had become a firm friend of James Fenimore Cooper, already the author of four novels, who was founding the "Bread and Cheese Lunch," an exclusive professional fraternity which admitted its members on ballots of "bread" and "cheese" to indicate "yes" or "no." Bryant, De Kay, Verplanck, and King were active in this society, but it lost its vigor some time before 1830.

Following *Marco Bozzaris* (1825), a tribute to patriotic martyrdom, Halleck wrote very little besides *Connecticut*, printed in the *New York Review and Athenaeum* (March 1826), and some indignant articles defending his patron Barker against false charges of unscrupulous action. The first collected edition of Halleck's poems included the lines on "Burns" and "Wyoming" and was issued in February 1827. With the collapse of Barker's business in 1828, Halleck began to write for various gift-book annuals. In 1832 he became confidential secretary to John

Collection of Fredrick H. Meserve
FITZ-GREENE HALLECK

Jacob Astor, and put in long hours at his desk in Astor's Hell Gate home. Halleck's fear of arousing adverse criticism kept him from literary pursuits. In 1837 Columbia College awarded him an honorary Master of Arts degree and the Author's Club made him its vice-president. A second edition of his works came out in 1845 and a handsomely illustrated volume in 1847.

Astor died March 29, 1848, and Halleck received an "annuity of $200" to which the financier's son added a gift of $10,000. The poet left the Astor firm about a year later to retire at Guilford. The death of many friends and a rather meagre income denied him the éclat of his earlier life. Halleck's social prestige, to which he was quite indifferent, had been almost phenomenal; and although he loved a bachelor's independence, he had been engaged in two spirited romances. He enjoyed an enviable friendship with Joseph and Louis Napoleon, and with Dickens, whom he considered "a thorough good fellow with nothing of the author about him but the reputation."

Halleck was of medium stature with slightly stiff and angular features, and in the best of weather he carried a green cotton umbrella under his arm. Many of his tastes were those of an earlier generation; he was a monarchist who looked down upon the "solecisms in manners" and the "vulgar assumptions" of democratic rule.

In "Burns" and in his tribute to Joseph Rodman Drake Halleck achieved a certain vividness and a tasteful simplicity; and his fragile and somewhat clever stanzas, the

"Croaker Poems" and "Fanny," gained a wide though passing popularity. Indeed Halleck considered himself merely a "literary amateur," but his artful versification entitles him to a fair ranking among the casual and satiric poets of the last century.

PRINCIPAL WORKS: *Poems*—Alnwick Castle, with Other Poems, 1827; Selections From British Poets, 1840; Poetical Works of Fitz-Greene Halleck, 1847; Connecticut (second part) 1852; Young America, 1864.

ABOUT: Adkins, N. F. Fitz-Greene Halleck: An Early Knickerbocker Wit and Poet; Wilson, J. C. Poetical Writings of Fitz-Greene Halleck; Lippincott's Magazine February 1868; Putnam's Magazine February 1868; Southern Literary Messenger April 1836.

HALLOCK, CHARLES (March 13, 1834-December 2, 1917), journalist and scientist, was born in New York City, the son of Gerard Hallock and Eliza (Allen) Hallock. He was educated at Yale and at Amherst College, and shortly afterwards became associated with the *Journal of Commerce,* which his father edited for thirty-six years. After journalistic and brokerage activity in Canada he returned to New York and became financial editor of *Harper's Weekly.* Later he founded *Forest and Stream,* which he edited for seven years. He also edited other publications, particularly along lines of nature and sport.

Hallock's first book, *The Recluse of the Oconee,* was published when he was twenty. He was a prolific and versatile writer for over fifty years, his reputation resting mainly on his experience with outdoor life, including natural history, sport, and travel. He identified himself with various movements for game preservation and the conservation of natural resources, pursued collecting and field work for the Smithsonian Institution, and in his last years contributed to antiquarian and metaphysical magazines. He died at Washington, D.C. at eighty-four.

PRINCIPAL WORKS: The Recluse of the Oconee, 1854; A Complete Biographical Sketch of Stonewall Jackson, 1863; Sportsman's Gazeteer, 1877.

ABOUT: Amherst College Biographical Record; Hallock, C. An Angler's Reminiscences; Hallock, C. The Hallock-Holyoke Pedigree; Outing February 1904.

HALPINE, CHARLES GRAHAM ("Miles O'Reilly") (November 20, 1829-August 3, 1868), journalist, poet and miscellaneous writer, was born at Oldcastle, County Meath, Ireland, the son of Nicholas John Halpine, a brilliant Episcopal clergyman who had given up orders and become editor of the *Dublin Evening Mail,* and Anne (Grehan) Halpine. He gave early promise of unusual ability and at seventeen graduated with distinction from Trinity College, Dublin. He took up the study of medicine and of law, but soon abandoned both to enter into journalism in Dublin and in London. Coming to the United States in 1851, after a preliminary period in Boston during which he gained a local reputation as a wit and satirist through the columns of the Boston *Post* and the *Carpet-Bag,* a humorous weekly of which he became co-editor, he removed to New York City where he contributed to its more important journals, including the New York *Herald* and the New York *Tribune,* and became an associate editor of the New York *Times.* In 1857 he acquired an interest in and became principal editor of the *Leader,* his contributions greatly enhancing its popularity and influence.

Collection of Frederick H. Meserve

CHARLES G. HALPINE
("Miles O'Reilly")

From his Dublin period Halpine associated himself with political activity. As a private secretary to Stephen A. Douglas he found himself in close contact with events in the United States, and as a member of the general committee of Tammany Hall he fought its corrupt leadership. When he retired into private life after the Civil War he once more interested himself in municipal reform and became editor and later owner of a reform organ, the *Citizen.* Among the political offices he held was that of register of the County and City of New York.

A volume of his poems collected from newspaper writings was published anonymously in 1854 as *Lyrics of the Letter H.* A later volume of his poetry was edited and published posthumously by Robert

Barnwell Roosevelt. The background for his greatest popularity, however, was presented by the Civil War, from which he emerged a brigadier-general. Under the pseudonym "Miles O'Reilly" he made humorous contributions to the press which attracted national attention. These were published in 1864 as *The Life and Adventures, Songs, Services, and Speeches of Private Miles O'Reilly*. Another volume *Baked Meats of the Funeral* soon followed, which included recollections of the war and other essays. One of his poems, "Sambo's Right to be Kilt" was instrumental in facilitating the enlistment of a Negro regiment for which he prepared first orders.

As a writer Halpine was voluminous and versatile, but he lacked the painstaking qualities essential to style and finish, rarely reading his productions except to correct proof. His power of invention was such that he once caused great public excitement by a long account, written under a wager, of the imaginary resuscitation of a pirate shortly after execution. His unremitting toil made him subject to insomnia from which he was led to find relief in opiates. An accidental overdose of chloroform cut short his career at thirty-nine.

Principal Works: Lyrics of the Letter H, 1854; The Life and Adventures, Songs, Services and Speeches of Private Miles O'Reilly, 1864; Baked Meats of the Funeral, 1866; Poetical Works (ed. by R. B. Roosevelt) 1869.

About: Halpine, C. G. Poetical Works (see Biographical Sketch by R. B. Roosevelt); Read, C. A. Cabinet of Irish Literature; Independent February 12, 1903.

HALSTEAD, MURAT (September 2, 1829-July 2, 1908), journalist and historian, was born in Ross Township, Butler County, Ohio, the son of Griffin Halstead and Clarissa (Willets) Halstead. He was educated at Farmers' College near Cincinnati, contributing to journals while still in college. In 1853 he joined the Cincinnati *Commercial* with which he was associated to the end of his life, early acquiring an interest in it and becoming editor-in-chief when it merged with the Cincinnati *Daily Gazette*. He also edited the Brooklyn *Standard-Union* for a time. In his latter years he turned to the writing of books, producing more than a score, largely of an historical nature, which were sold by subscription.

Halstead early established a reputation as a brilliant war correspondent. He was a prominent figure at Republican national conventions for over fifty years. As a vigorous, independent, and energetic journalist, whose writings are estimated to have averaged a million words a year for forty years, he made the *Commercial* one of the most notable political and literary influences in the country. In 1889 the President nominated him minister to Germany but the Senate refused confirmation owing to his earlier attacks on corruption in senatorial elections. Four of his seven sons entered journalism. He died in Cincinnati at seventy-nine.

Principal Works: Our Country in War and Relations With All Nations, 1898; History of the War with Spain, 1899; Briton and Boer in South Africa, 1900; Galveston, 1901.

About: Merriam, G. S. The Life and Times of Samuel Bowles; American Review of Reviews April 1896, August 1908.

HAMILTON, DR. ALEXANDER (1712-May 11, 1756), diarist, essayist, and physician, was born in the vicinity of Edinburgh, Scotland, the son of William Hamilton, professor of divinity and principal of Edinburgh University, and Mary (Robertson) Hamilton. Alexander was one of thirteen children, most of whom attained eminence in the ministry, medicine, or merchandizing. His father had been installed as principal only three months before his death, November 12, 1732. Young Hamilton "learnt pharmacy of David Knox," an Edinburgh surgeon, and came to America, establishing a medical practice in Annapolis, Md., in the winter of 1738-39. He was preceptor of Dr. Thomas Bond, who in 1752 became the founder of the Pennsylvania Hospital in Philadelphia.

In 1743 Hamilton acknowledged himself to be a "valetudinarian" and in order to regain his health, set out, May 30, 1744, on a journey northward which occasioned his Pepysian *Itinerarium,* dedicated to Onorio Razolini, and presented to him in manuscript form in November 1744. (This copy remained in Razolini's family over a century and a half, when a London publisher purchased it from an Italian bookseller.) Hamilton traveled like a gentleman, with two horses, one of which carried his Negro Dromio. He went to New York by way of Wilmington, Chester, and Perth Amboy, and after six days in the metropolis, which bore a "more urban appearance than Philadelphia" he proceeded in a sloop to Albany. Here he was little impressed but noted the "generality of women to be remarkably ugly." In Boston, however, he encountered many handsome women and although he thought Bostonians, as a whole, "to a degree disingenuous and dissembling," he appraised them to be a very "civilized" folk. All along the route Hamilton was obliged to tolerate howling, drunken inn-keepers and their

From a contemporary caricature
DR. ALEXANDER HAMILTON

abominable fare. He complained of an occasional headache, and on the Susquehanna ferry "was taken with a vapourish qualm," but in sum, the journey had a very salutary effect, and he returned to Annapolis on September 27.

Hamilton was married in 1747 to Margaret Dulany, "a well accomplished and agreeable young lady, with a handsome fortune," daughter of Hon. Daniel Dulany, an eminent lawyer of Annapolis. Not only professionally but socially Hamilton maintained his place among the aristacracy. The "Tuesday Club," which he and Jonas Green, editor of the *Maryland Gazette,* had founded in 1745, attracted "the most distinguished and influential men of the ancient Capital and wits of the first order." All members kept "high jinks," but preserved a modicum of restraint by requiring that "offensive topics of conversation be dealt with by the 'gelastic' method and laughed off the floor." The host was to provide "a gammon of bacon, or any other vittles, and no more." Hamilton, *alias* "Loquacious Scribble, Esq.," was their historiographer, and in a record of "Sederunt 247, November 18, 1755," he notes a shameful literary decadence among the members: ". . . the Poet Laureate's . . . bays are blasted, withered and mildewed with certain fogs, damps, and mists which have intervened between him and the diverse rays of Parnassus." He therefore delegates himself to deliver a series of orations on purely "clubical" subjects, the first to be on "Absurdity."

In the last entry of minutes, dated February 11, 1756, Hamilton, an absentee, addresses a letter to Charles Cole, the president, surrendering the archives of the society. It is doubtful whether there was any subsequent meeting. Dr. Upton Scott, a long-standing member who later received the records from Hamilton's widow and only heir, stated that, in all events, the group certainly never assembled after Hamilton's death.

Fortunately Hamilton enjoyed a certain financial freedom, for he found his profession, in general, to be "in a low state." He was, nevertheless, an astute observer of developments in medicine and related fields. In 1744 he had said that he knew of no way of curing cancer "except by . . . cutting it out," and had made this "Darwinian" comment: "Nature . . . seems by one connecting gradation to pass from one species of creation to another, without any visible gap, interval, or discontinuance in her works." In matters of religious tastes he was highly eclectic, a Presbyterian in Scotland, an Anglican in Maryland, and a visitor to the Jewish synagogue.

A Defense of Dr. Thomson's Discourse (1752) and a medical dissertation published posthumously with Smellie's *Anatomical Tables* (1784) are rather minor pieces. His Tuesday Club Papers, however, are a good close-up of the coffee-house spirit among Colonial intellectuals; and his *Itinerarium,* a jaunty document too candid in personal comment to be intended for publication, is one of the few authoritative accounts of the social life of that period.

PRINCIPAL WORKS: *Autobiographical*—Itinerarium, 1744. *Technical*—A Defense of Dr. Thomson's Discourse, 1752.

ABOUT: Hamilton, G. History of the House of Hamilton; Hart, A. B. Introduction to Itinerarium; Richardson, H. D. Sidelights on Maryland History; Riley, E. S. The Ancient City; Scott, H. Fasti Ecclesiae Scoticani.

HAMILTON, ALEXANDER (January 11, 1757-July 12, 1804), statesman, was born on the island of Nevis, British West Indies, the illegitimate child of James Hamilton, a Scottish merchant, and Rachel (Fawcett) Levine, who was separated from her Danish-Jewish husband. She died in 1768, leaving Alexander and another son by Hamilton; and he, distraught by her death and a weakling by nature, merely absconded and left the boys to their fate. At eleven Alexander was a clerk in a general store; when he was thirteen his employer went to Europe and left him in charge! An account he wrote of a hurricane excited the admiration of some of his other acquaintances, who paid his passage to New York, where he might have better prospects. After a year of study, living with a kindly family in New Jersey, he entered King's College (Columbia). He was never graduated, for the Revolution intervened and he formed an artillery company of which he was made captain. Already, at seventeen, he had written anonymous political pamphlets which were attributed to John Jay, so powerful was their reasoning and so mature their form.

Hamilton became secretary and aide-de-camp to Washington in 1777. In spite of a temporary rupture due to his fanatical pride, they continued friends to Washington's death; in 1799, when war threatened, Washington refused to act as commander-in-chief of the proposed national army unless Hamilton were made second in command. There is almost indisputable evidence that Hamilton actually wrote Washington's famous Farewell Address.

After the war Hamilton, who had married Elizabeth Schuyler, daughter of a general and of a fine old Dutch family, in 1780, retired to New York, studied law for five months, and was admitted to the bar. He was a member of the first Continental Congress, of the New York Legislature, and of the Constitutional Convention, being the only signatory for New York and forcing the Constitution through the Legislature. Already he was a pronounced Federalist, and ripe for his later enmity to Jefferson and Monroe. On behalf of the Constitution, he, Madison, and Jay wrote the eighty-five numbers of the *Federalist,* sixty-three being entirely Hamilton's, and nine more partly his. They are his greatest achievement as a writer, "incomparably superior, whether in content or in form, . . . to all the other political writing of the period" (William MacDonald).

When Washington became president, he made Hamilton his Secretary of the Treasury; in this post, which he held from 1789 to 1795, he accomplished financial miracles, but also made himself insufferable, on the assumption that he was the "prime minister" of the United States and Washington's right-hand man. Two years later came the great disgrace of his career—an accusation of peculation from which he could free himself only by confessing a sordid sexual intrigue. His wife stood by him loyally; and in spite of this strange episode he was deeply devoted to her and to their eight children. In another indiscretion, he wrote a letter attacking John Adams which fell into the hands of Aaron Burr (his nemesis from the earliest years) and was used against him.

From a portrait by J. Trumbull
ALEXANDER HAMILTON

In retaliation Hamilton voted for his enemy Jefferson against Burr in 1801, breaking the deadlock and making Jefferson president.

Though retired from public life—his chief occupations outside of his large law practice were the founding of the New York *Evening Post* and the building of his beautiful home, which Mrs. Hamilton lost when he died penniless—Hamilton still felt himself to be a public character. It was because of this that Burr finally hounded him into accepting a challenge to a duel. Hamilton had cause to hate dueling; his eldest son, a brilliant, handsome boy of nineteen, had been killed in 1801 in a senseless duel in which he refused to fire; and his eldest daughter had gone insane from the shock. Hamilton too refused to fire; Burr's first bullet penetrated his liver, and the next day he died.

Hamilton, who was half French in descent, was wholly Scotch in appearance and personality—a short, wiry, reddish-haired man with deep blue eyes. His immense industry, his remarkable mentality, his great charm, were offset by pride, vanity, and narrow intolerance. In his writing, he is all brain, with no imagination, no humor, no feeling, but with both analytical and synthesizing power and with remarkable talent for abstract thought lucidly expressed.

Principal Works: Works (various compilations of state papers, pamphlets, etc.) 1850, 1885, 1904.

About: Bailey, R. E. An American Colossus; Bowers, C. G. Jefferson and Hamilton; deFord, M. A. Love Children: A Book of Illustrious Illegitimates; Ford; H. J. Alexander Hamilton; Hamilton, A. McL. The Intimate Life of Alexander Hamilton; Hamilton, J. C. The Life of Alexander Hamilton; Hicks, H. H. Alexander Hamilton; Lodge, H. C. Alexander Hamilton; Oliver, F. S. Alexander Hamilton; Riethmüller, C. ilton; Smertenko, J. J. Alexander Hamilton; Shea, G. The Life and Epoch of Alexander Ham- J. The Life and Times of Alexander Hamilton: Vandenberg, A. H. The Greatest American: Alexander Hamilton; Warshaw, R. I. Alexander Hamilton: First American Business Man.

HAMILTON, EDWARD JOHN (November 29, 1834-November 21, 1918), philosopher, was born in Belfast, Ireland, the eldest son of the Rev. William Hamilton, headmaster of the Royal Belfast Institution, and Anna (Patterson) Hamilton. His parents came to America when Hamilton was nine years of age, and soon settled at Cincinnati. His early interest in philosophy was fostered by his father. After attending several institutions of higher education, including Hanover College and Princeton Theological Seminary, he graduated from the latter at twenty-four and spent the next ten years in pastorates and as chaplain of the 7th New Jersey Volunteers. For nearly thirty years he taught at various colleges and universities, including Hanover College, Hamilton College, the University of Washington and a year at Princeton University. During this period he worked on his philosophical books, his first, *A New Analysis in Fundamental Morals* being issued in 1870. He also worked for three years on the *Standard Dictionary.* At sixty-five he went to Plainfield, N.J., where he passed the remainder of his life in literary work.

Hamilton published numerous books and articles on ethics, logic, epistemology, and other philosophical subjects. In order to convey his doctrines to the Germans without misinterpretation, he made two trips to Germany and produced some volumes of his philosophy in that language. He died at Buffalo, N.Y., in his eighty-fourth year.

Principal Works: A New Analysis in Fundamental Morals, 1870; The Human Mind, 1883; The Modalist, 1891; The Perceptionalist, 1899; The Moral Law, 1902; Rational Orthodoxy, 1917.

About: Princeton Theological Seminary Necrological Report August 1919.

"HAMILTON, GAIL." See DODGE, MARY ABIGAIL

HAMMETT, SAMUEL ADAMS (February 4, 1816-December 24, 1865), novelist, was born at New London, Conn., the only child of Augustus and Mary (Dwight) Hammett. After graduating from the University of the City of New York he sought adventure in the Southwest for some ten or twelve years. Returning to New York City in 1848 he established himself as a flour merchant, meanwhile contributing to various magazines articles which he later reworked for his books. His first book, *A Stray Yankee in Texas,* based on his experiences in that state, was published in 1853 under the pseudonym "Philip Paxton." His following volumes appeared as "By the Author of *A Stray Yankee in Texas.*"

Hammett found keen personal enjoyment in the rough outdoor life of the Western frontier, and translated its atmosphere with unusual veracity, freely incorporating Western and Yankee dialect. He died in Brooklyn of pneumonia at forty-nine.

Principal Works: A Stray Yankee in Texas, 1853; The Wonderful Adventures of Captain Priest, 1855; Piney Woods Tavern, 1858.

HAMMON, JUPITER (c. 1720-c. 1800), poet, was an African slave in the family of Henry Lloyd of Lloyd's Neck, Long Island. Little is known of him and the first definite statement referring to him was in the year 1730. In 1761, with the aid of the Lloyd family, a poem by him "An Evening Thought. Salvation by Christ, With Penetential Cries," was published in New York as a broadside of twenty-two quatrains. This preceded the verse of Phillis Wheatley [*q.v.*] by six or more years.

"A Poetical Address to Miss Phillis Wheatley," likewise a broadsheet of which only one known copy is in existence, next appeared in 1778, published in Hartford, Conn., where he lived with his next master, Joseph Lloyd, during the war. A few other productions followed, including "An Essay on the Ten Virgins," "A Winter Piece," and "An Evening's Improvement," which included a poetical dialogue called "The Kind Master and Dutiful Servant." His most important work, however, was in prose, "An Address to the Negroes of the State of New York," which went through three editions.

Hammon's poems were deeply religious in tone. He was apparently highly regarded. Although deeply loyal himself, and in his "Address" exhorting Negroes to be true to their masters, he disapproved of the system of slavery and urged the manumission of younger slaves. His last master, John Lloyd Jr., directed in his will in 1795 that certain of his slaves be freed on reaching the age of twenty-eight. The last known reference to Hammon was in the year 1790.

Principal Works: An Evening's Thought, 1761; An Address to Miss Phillis Wheatley, 1778; An Essay on the Ten Virgins, 1779; A Winter Piece, 1782; An Evening's Improvement: An Address to the Negroes of the State of New York, 1787.

About: Brawley, B. G. The Negro Genius; Wegelin, O. Jupiter Hammon.

HAMMOND, JABEZ DELANO (August 2, 1778-August 18, 1855), historian, politician, and jurist, was born in New Bedford, Mass., the son of Jabez Hammond, a descendent of Colonial settlers, and of Priscilla (Delano) Hammond. Turning from a common school education to teaching, he later practiced medicine at Reading, Vt., and in 1805 was admitted to the New York bar and settled at Cherry Valley, N.Y. He interested himself in politics and served in a number of public capacities, including a term in Congress and a term in the New York Senate, where he gathered impressions that were later to appear in his important work, *The History of Politics in the State of New York,* the first two volumes of which appeared in 1842. This impartial work upon which his reputation as an author rests, recorded a half century of politics best known to him. It was enthusiastically received and passed through four editions. The third volume brought out in 1838, included a biography of Governor Silas Wright.

Hammond became county judge, and after studying educational systems in Europe, served a term as county superintendent of schools. He received the degree of LL.D. from Hamilton College in 1845 and in the same year was appointed a regent of the University of the State of New York. He was twice married, and died at Cherry Valley at the age of seventy-seven.

Principal Work: The History of Political Parties in the State of New York, 1842.

About: Beard, L. Reminiscences; Hammond, R. A History and Genealogy of the Descendants of William Hammond of London, England; Sawyer, J. History of Cherry Valley.

HARBAUGH, HENRY (October 28, 1817-December 28, 1867), religious writer and clergyman, was born on a farm near Waynesboro, Pa., the son of George Harbaugh, a descendant of an early Swiss emigrant, and Anna (Snyder) Harbaugh, of Boonsboro, Md. At eighteen his inordinately practical father put him to work in a mill. But in less than a year, with almost no money, he set out for eastern Ohio. He found a job with a builder, gave singing lessons, taught school and wrote a story for an Ohio weekly. Harbaugh was writing much mediocre verse, at this age, and formed the habit of locking himself in a bolting chest every evening to pore over his books.

Following a course at the academy in New Hagerstown, he entered Marshall College, Mercersburg, dividing the last two of his three years between the college and the seminary. He preached his first sermon in the "Little Cove," near Mercersburg, and returned home to preach in "Harbaugh's Valley," a spot in Frederick County, Md., settled by three sons of Yost Harbaugh. He took his first charge, in December 1843, of two congregations, one in Lewisburg, Pa., and the other six miles out into the country. That same month he was married to Louisa Goodrich, who died September 26, 1847. In November of the following year he was married to Maria Louisa Linn.

Harbaugh was ordained in January 1844 and began, in 1850, a busy ten years' pastorate at the Reformed Church of Lancaster, as well as the editorship of the *Guardian: A Family Magazine,* "devoted to the cause of female education and Christian principles." Between 1848 and 1853 he wrote a three-volume work on the future state; his *Life of Michael Schlatter* appeared in 1857; a small book of *Poems* in 1860; and *The Religious Character of Washington,* sent out to the Civil War soldiers, in 1863. He became the editor of the *Mercersburg Review* in 1867, and was, moreover, the author of several well-known hymns.

Small dissension on matters of the liturgy, etc., precipitated the close of his ministry at Lancaster; and for four years he served the St. John Reformed Church at Lebanon, leaving this post to become professor of theology at Mercersburg. He died in 1867 following a lingering fever.

Despite his heavy build and florid face, Harbaugh was not physically strong. He was "free-spoken and had very little of cant about him" and did much to advance the "Mercersburg theology." *The Fathers of the Reformed Church* was published posthumously, as was his collected verse, *Harbaugh's Harfe* (1870), through which he came to be known as "the father and founder of Pennsylvania dialect writings."

Principal Works: The Heidelberg Catechism, 1849; The Sainted Dead, 1848; Heavenly Recognition, 1851; The Heavenly Home, 1853; Union With the Church, 1853; Birds of the Bible, 1854; Life of Michael Schlatter, 1857; Fathers of the German Reformed Church in Europe and America (2 vols.) 1857-1858; Poems, 1860; Hymns and Chants, 1861; Youth in Earnest, 1867.

About: Harbaugh, L. Life of Henry Harbaugh; Heilman, U. H. The Genesis of der Pihwie; Schaff, D. S. Life of Philip Schaff; Mercersburg Review 1856.

HARLAND, HENRY (March 1, 1861-December 20, 1905), American-Anglo novelist, short story writer, and editor, was born in Russia, at St. Petersburg (now Leningrad). But his parents were Americans of English descent, his father, Thomas Harland, an attorney of Norwich, Conn. The older Harland considered himself heir to a Suffolk baronetcy, allowed to lapse in 1848 because to claim it would, by Connecticut law, have cost him his American property. The Harlands traveled a great deal, and Henry, their only child, was reared mainly in Rome. He studied for a while at the University of Paris and then at Harvard, but was graduated from neither.

After Harvard he returned for a year to Rome, where he acted as correspondent of the New York *Tribune*. Then, back in America, he found a position in the Surrogate's Office in New York.

In 1885 his first novel, *As It Was Written,* appeared under the pseudonym of "Sidney Luska," and for four years he continued to write under this name, his pseudonymous personality purporting to be an immigrant Jew—a strange conceit for a young man of Harland's origin and background. But early in the 'nineties he grew dissatisfied with the cheap success of this sensational fiction, and determined to abandon everything else and to devote himself to the study of style and to the development of the talents which he knew he possessed, but which his early work rather obscured than exemplified.

Collection of Frederick H. Meserve
HENRY HARLAND

Making a clean break with everything in his past he went to England. Most of his life thereafter was spent in London, and he became so closely a part of the London literary group that he is not frequently thought of as an American writer. He came under the influence of Henry James, and the great expatriate became the model of the lesser one. At first the novels published under his own name seem little different, except for increased psychological acumen, from the earlier ones of "Sidney Luska"; but slowly and gradually the writer of sensational realism became an aesthete, an exponent of light and polished comedy in fiction, a literary impressionist.

In 1894 Harland founded that famous quarterly, *The Yellow Book,* which gave its name to an age. He remained its literary editor throughout the three years of its life. This was his own great period. Outside of it he devoted himself entirely to the production of novels and short stories; the first book to bring him general renown was *The Cardinal's Snuff Box.* The only other literary work Harland did was a translation of Matilde Serao's *Fantasia,* and an introduction to Octave Feuillet's *Le Roman d'un Jeune Homme Pauvre.*

Harland married Aline Merriam, a lady of French extraction, who did some work as a translator from the Italian. The marriage was childless. His outer life became increasingly uneventful; gradually his health failed, and he went to Italy with his wife in the search for a kindlier climate. There, at San Remo, he died.

"Sidney Luska's" novels are hardly worth appraisal; they have a rough power and crude promise, but are primarily pot-boilers full of a dated sensationalism. Henry Harland's fiction in his own name, the later work at least, is delicate and witty—if decadent—the work of a slighter, less subtle, and simpler James. It may be doubted if much of it will live, though perhaps *The Cardinal's Snuff Box* and *The Lady Paramount* will survive for students of the period.

But Harland is of importance chiefly as father of *The Yellow Book,* the magazine which first opened the way to public acclaim of most of the literary youngsters of the 'nineties in London. The list of its contributors is a dictionary of the coming writers of the day; and since Aubrey Beardsley was its first art editor, it drew to itself also the best and most characteristic of the illustrators of the *fin de siècle* group. The three years during which it existed were the most meaningful of Harland's life, so far as his effect on English literature and the permanency of his reputation are concerned.

WORKS: (As Sidney Luska)—As It Was Written: A Jewish Musician's Story, 1885; Mrs. Pexeida, 1886; The Yoke of the Thorah, 1888; My Uncle Florimond, 1888; A Latin Quarter Courtship and Other Stories, 1890; Grandison Mather, 1890.

WORKS: (As Henry Harland)—Two Women or One? 1890; Mea Culpa: A Woman's Last Word, 1891; Mademoiselle Miss and Other Stories, 1893; Grey Roses, 1895; Comedies and Errors, 1898; The Cardinal's Snuff Box, 1900; The Lady Paramount, 1902; My Friend Prospero, 1904; The Royal End, 1909.

ABOUT: Burdett, O. The Beardsley Period; Jackson, H. The Eighteen Nineties.

"HARLAND, MARION." See TERHUNE, MARY VIRGINIA (HAWES)

HARRIGAN, EDWARD ("Ned" Harrigan) (October 26, 1845-June 6, 1911), playwright, actor, and producer, was born in New York City, the son of William Harrigan, a Newfoundland sea captain and shipbuilder, and Helen (Rogers) Harrigan, of Charlestown, Mass. He attended the Monroe St. public school, served a short apprenticeship in boat-repairing, and then went West. In San Francisco Harrigan worked into theatricals, playing in farces and melodramas.

With Sam Rickey he came East again, and at the Globe in New York, November 21, 1870, produced *A Little Fraud,* the success of which turned Rickey's head; Harrigan then formed a partnership with "Tony" Hart (Anthony Cannon). Together they went on the road for a while, before establishing themselves in New York, December 2, 1872, at the Theatre Comique. They took over the management in 1876 and two years later launched the hilarious Mulligan Guard cycle, which began with *The Mulligan Guard Picnic,* September 23, 1878, and ran through *Mulligan's Silver Wedding,* opening February 21, 1881, all romping Irish satires from Harrigan's pen. Most of them played more than a hundred nights to capacity houses of highly cosmopolitan folk. For a time they worked against the odds of a stage "not so large as a back parlor." Harrigan and Hart took the leads and "Dave" Braham, the "American Offenbach," whose daughter Harrigan had married in 1870, wrote the music for such catchy lyrics as "John Reilly's Always Dry" and "The Babies on our Block." To the Mulligan series belong also *Cordelia's Aspirations* (1883) and *Dan's Tribulations* (1884), both successes.

From mere vaudeville sketches—about eighty in all—Harrigan had advanced to regular comedies that were loaded with puns

Collection of Frederick H. Meserve

"NED" HARRIGAN & "TONY" HART

and joke-book yarns. Following the "McSorley" group, early in 1883, came a lone theatrical "mistake"—*The Muddy Day*—which the audience left before its finish. Harrigan continued to act after parting company with Hart, and made his last formal appearance at Wallack's Theatre, October 6, 1908 in *His Wife's Family.* His only novel, *The Mulligans.* was published in 1901.

Slim and handsome "Ned" Harrigan seems never to have been spoiled by the onslaught of theatrical success and always enjoyed simple and democratic pleasures. He was a shrewd innovator of the American "type" drama—the Italian, the Irishman, the Negro, etc., in political and social New York. Howells said of him: "Mr. Harrigan accurately realizes . . . the actual life of this city . . . it is what we call low life, though whether it is essentially lower than fashionable life is another question." Harrigan's work had a considerable influence on the life of the American theatre.

PRINCIPAL WORKS: *Plays*—Old Lavender, 1877; The Lorgaire: or, The Murder of the Black Rock, 1878; The Mulligan Guard Picnic, 1878; The Mulligan Guard Ball, 1879; The Mulligan Guard Chowder, 1879; The Mulligan Guard Christmas, 1879; The Mulligan Guard Surprise, 1880; The Mulligan Guard Nominee, 1880; Mulligan's Silver Wedding, 1881; Squatter Sovereignty, 1882; The Blackbird, 1882; Cordelia's Aspirations, 1883; Dan's Tribulations, 1884; The O'Reagans, 1886; Reilly and the Four Hundred, 1890; The Last of the Hogans, 1891. *Novel*—The Mulligans, 1901.

ABOUT: Hornblow, A. History of the Theatre in America; Moses, M. J. The American Dramatist; Quinn, A. H. A History of the American

Drama From Civil War to the Present Day; New York Times June 7, 1911; New York Tribune December 13, 1891; Spirit of the Times, 1879-83; The Sportsman January 25, 1879.

HARRIGAN, "NED." See HARRIGAN, EDWARD

"HARRINGTON, GEORGE F." See BAKER, WILLIAM MUMFORD

HARRIS, BENJAMIN (fl. 1673-1716), author, bookseller, and publisher of the first American newspaper, began his career in London in 1673 with the issue of various Anabaptist pamphlets and broadsides. His *Domestick Intelligence; or, News Both From City and Country,* begun July 7, 1679, was suppressed April 15, 1681. Meanwhile Harris had printed and sold *An Appeal From the Country to the City,* in 1678, and was tried for libel. A "deed of darkness" it was called, upon testimony from the printer's devil that he had "worked at the book at night." Harris was sentenced to stand on the pillory, where his "Wife (like a kind Rib) stood by him," to defend him. Unable to pay a £500 fine he was sent to prison, but won an early release.

Following the publication of more seditious tracts, Harris, looking for a freer field, sailed for New England in 1686. With his son Vavasour, he opened a book and "Coffee, Tee and Chucaletto Shop" in Boston, supervised the printing and sale of *Tulley's Almanack* for 1687, and returned to England on July 12 of that year. He was in London again late in 1688, and, on his return, published, some time before 1690, *The New England Primer,* modeled after his *Protestant Tutor* (London, 1679), a far more propagandistic "speller." The *Primer,* for which Harris wrote the rhymed alphabet, had a phenomenal popularity. *Publick Occurrences Both Forreign and Domestick,* issued by Harris September 25, 1690, was, in three small printed pages the first American newspaper. But because it "contained Reflections of a very high nature" and was unlicensed, it was suppressed before a second issue. A bold insertion of "The French King's Nativity" in the 1694 *Almanack* ended Harris' professional relations with John Tulley. He did, however print the 1695 issue before returning to England, where, despite apparent prosperity, he begged to be "allowed (now) to print the votes of the present parliament to support self and family and pay his debts." In May 1695 came the first issue of *Intelligence Domestick and Forreign*; and *The Holy Bible in Verse* (1701?) went into at least five subsequent editions.

Harris is said to have been a "fair-conditioned . . . peacable man"; his conversation was never "impertinent . . . and his Wit pliable to all Inventions." But he became an inveterate and caustic wag, embroiled in endless literary quarrels. The dates of his birth and death are unknown, but a reference to him, in 1686, as one who "advances in years" suggests that he began his career rather late and that he probably did not live long after 1716, the date of his last publication. His literary influence was, perhaps, less direct in Old England than in New England, where his *Public Occurrences,* though short-lived, marks the beginning of American newspaper history.

Principal Works: Protestant Tutor, 1679; New England Primer, 1689 (?); Holy Bible in Verse 1701 (?).

About: Dunton, J. Life and Errors of John Dunton; Dunton, J. The Living Elegy; Ford, P. L. New England Primer; Littlefield, G. E. Early Massachusetts Press; Page, A. B. John Tulley's Almanacks; Tutchin, J. The Bloody Assizes; A Short But Just Account of the Trial of Benjamin Harris; Letter-Book of Samuel Sewall; Tulley's Almanacks 1687-95.

HARRIS, GEORGE WASHINGTON (March 20, 1814-December 11, 1869), story teller and humorist, was born near Pittsburgh, Pa. At the age of four his family moved to Knoxville, Tenn., and George was apprenticed to a jeweler and learned the silversmith's trade. With unusual mechanical ingenuity, he worked out a model of the first steamboat launched on the Tennessee River, and thereby won the attention of an influential Mr. Swain who later made him a river captain. Young Harris began to contribute technical articles to the *Scientific American,* and during the Whig campaign of 1839 wrote some lively political tracts for southern journals. He slipped easily into the sporting-letter vein and wrote for the New York *Spirit of the Times,* which by 1845 was seeking out his full-length stories; his pseudonym was "Sugartail." In 1857 Harris was appointed postmaster of Knoxville, pursued interests in a foundry and glass factory, and after the Civil War turned to railroad engineering.

With his succession of varied interests and his natural inclination for the freedom of the Smokies and the plebeianism of river trafficking, Harris was obviously absorbed in life *per se* and had no temptation to transcend it, as did his literary contemporaries of New England. The Rabelaisian *Sut Lovingood Yarns* (1867), his only published volume, were dedicated "To the man ur oman huever they be what don't read this yere book" and at the end of the preface was a very significant "Notey Beney"—"Evil be to him that evil thinks." For Sut is a lazy Tennessee yokel, totally unacquainted with moral scruples, having "nary a soul, nothing but a whisky proof gizzard," an innate delight in predatory pranks, and an endless supply of boisterous badinage.

Harris was married September 3, 1835, to Mary Emeline Nance, of Knoxville, by whom he had six children; and very late in his life, Jane E. Pride of Decatur, Ala., became his second wife. He made a journey in December 1869 to Richmond and Lynchburg to arrange for some further publications, but was taken with a stroke of apoplexy on his return to Knoxville. It is believed by some authorities that his widow suppressed the tales which he had in preparation at the time of his death.

The *Yarns* have remained in print five decades, and comprise Harris' sole literary legacy. A-moral, picaresque, and unique in themselves, they are no longer either hastily condemned or ignored by squeamish critics who refuse to acknowledge them as literature. But rather, along with the Davy Crockett extravaganzas and the Mike Fink legends, they are aptly cited as influential precursors of the "Mark Twain humor" which was to come into full flower a few years later.

PRINCIPAL WORK: Sut Lovingood Yarns, 1867.

ABOUT: Blair, W. Native American Humor; Brown, T. J. Library of Southern Literature; Harris, G. W Sut Lovingood Yarns; Meine, F. J. Tall Tales of the Southwest; Davy Crockett's Almanacks, 1835-40; Saturday Review of Literature November 7, November 28, 1936; Scientific American 1866; Spirit of the Times June 24, 1848.

HARRIS, JOEL CHANDLER (December 9, 1848-July 3, 1908) humorist, story teller, and editor, was born near the sleepy town of Eatonton, Ga., the son of Mary Harris, of a good Southern family, and a fun-loving and unambitious Irish day-laborer who deserted his wife shortly before the birth of her child. With the aid of a wealthy Mr. Andrew Reid, Joel was sent for a short time to Miss Davidson's school and to a local academy. But rabbit hunts and "Gully Minstrels" were, to this agile and freckle-faced youngster, infinitely more essential than drab learning. He had, however, great consideration for his devoted mother, and, in answer to a want ad, secured a typesetter apprenticeship with Joseph Addison Turner, editor of the popular *Countryman*, probably the only newspaper ever printed on a Southern plantation. Here, at "Turnwold" Joel became immersed in the old régime—crooning Negroes, yams in the ashes, etc.,—and, from a chimney nook in the slave quarters, he listened to African legends of animal lore. Moreover, in Mr. Turner's well-stocked library there was much to Joel's liking. When Turner caught the lad smuggling into the *Countryman* a few articles "from the case" he began to encourage his protégé. Joel's letter to Lincoln, written about this time, warning him to leave Washington faster "than a sheep can skin a 'simmon tree," and signed "Obediah Skinflint," was doubtless his first attempt at Cracker dialect. At sixteen he had denounced Lincoln, but a little later he had nothing but admiration for him.

Young Harris saw many of his friends leave for the War. When Lee's surrender came in 1865, Joel's rabbit-trapping earnings, in an old trunk under the bed, were now a mere bundle of Confederate paper. Fortunately he found work first in the composing-room of the *Macon Telegraph* and then, in New Orleans, as private secretary to the editor of the *Crescent Monthly*. In the Creole City he made a slight acquaintance with Lafacdio Hearn, but cosmopolitan life had little appeal for him. He returned to Eatonton in 1867 to "nurse a novel," but soon accepted a position with the *Monroe Advertiser*. Here he did some brilliant "paragraphing," composing all his copy at the case, and signing nothing. In 1870 the Savannah *Morning News* offered him an associate editorship. During his stay in Savannah he met Esther LaRose whom he

JOEL CHANDLER HARRIS
c. 1897

married, April 21, 1873, and by her had, in all, nine children. To escape a yellow fever epidemic, in 1876, he went up to "the high country," Atlanta, registering at Kimball House as: "J. C. Harris, one wife, two bow-legged children and a bilious nurse."

The editor of the *Atlanta Constitution* asked Harris to carry on a column which had been featuring a Negro character "Uncle Si,"—whence came the beginning, though a cautious one, of the Uncle Remus tales. Of these, the Tar Baby story, which has even undergone translation into Bengali and African dialects, is perhaps the best loved. To Irwin Russell, a young Texan who had produced authentic and artistic Negro dialect in his *Christmas Night in the Quarters,* Harris acknowledged his indebtedness. In the wake of *Uncle Remus: His Songs and Sayings,* 1880, came innumerable demands from magazine editors for stories. Harris, at this time, would have joined Mark Twain and George Washington Cable on a lecture tour, had it not been for a slight impediment of speech, exaggerated in the company of strangers, which he never succeeded in overcoming.

Harris made an extended visit to New York in June 1882. He contemplated writing a life of Jefferson but feared that "a human treatment of so serious a matter would put the politicians after him"; nor were his plans for a collaboration with Richard Malcolm Johnston on a Southern drama ever executed. In 1892 came *Uncle Remus and His Friends* and the story of his life at "Turnwold": *On the Plantation,* which had first appeared in a McClure syndication. In mid-November of the following year, with Daniel Smith, an illustrator, Harris traced the path of the Sea Island hurricane, going south from Savannah by steam launch and tug-boat. *Scribner's Magazine* published the vigorous account which he succeeded in tapping from the insular Negroes who had witnessed the disaster.

Twenty-four years of invaluable work on the *Constitution* ended when Harris signed a publishing contract with the McClure Phillips Company, late in 1900. Seven years afterwards, this veteran contributor to numerous periodicals, with his son Julian, established his own *Uncle Remus's Magazine.* Don Marquis was an associate editor and Ludwig Lewisohn wrote some of its first articles. After its consolidation with the *Home Magazine,* Harris continued to write essays and new Uncle Remus stories. Theodore Roosevelt's active interest in the welfare of this journal even after the death of Joel Chandler Harris, when Julian was in charge, is one of the many testimonies to the Rough Rider President's fondness for "Uncle Remus."

Harris was a mine of energy, rather short, compact, and broad of shoulder. He was almost pathologically shy—Pennsylvania University wanted to honor him with a degree but he could not bring himself to appear in person for its acceptance. His intimate friendships, James Whitcomb Riley's among them, were invaluable to him; children found in "Uncle Remus" an incomparable affection. His health failed slowly after 1902, but his bounding gaiety never left him. "Humor," he had once said, "is a great thing to live by, and other things being equal, it is a profitable thing to die by."

To Harris, truth was "more important than sectionalism." With an uncanny incongruity of animal-human expressionism and the ability to "think" in the dialect of the Southern Negro, he produced a veritable social document and an unmatched humor.

PRINCIPAL WORKS: *Stories*—Uncle Remus series, 1880-1918; Mingo and Other Sketches in Black and White, 1884; Free Joe and Other Georgian Sketches, 1887; Balaam and His Master, 1891; Tales of the Home Folks in Peace and War, 1898; Chronicles of Aunt Minerva Ann, 1899; On the Wing of Occasions, 1900; The Making of a Statesman, 1902. *Novels*—Sister Jane: Her Friends and Acquaintances, 1896; Gabriel Tolliver: A Story of Reconstruction, 1902.

ABOUT: Baskerville, W. Southern Writers; Blair, W. Native American Humor; Davidson, J. W. Living Writers of the South; Harris, J. Collier. Life and Letters of J. C. Harris; Toulmin, H. A. Social Historians; Scribner's February and March 1894; Uncle Remus's Magazine 1907-08.

HARRIS, MIRIAM (COLES) (July 7, 1834-January 23, 1925), novelist, was born on the island of Dosoris near Glen Cove, Long Island, N.Y. The daughter of Butler Coles and Julia Anne (Weeks) Coles, she numbered among her forebears a Robert Coles who came to Boston in 1630, General Nathaniel Coles of the Revolutionary army, and the Rev. Francis Doughty, the first patroon of Newtown and Flushing, and the first man to preach in English on Manhattan. She was educated at St. Mary's Hall, Burlington, N.J., and at Madame Canda's exclusive school in New York City, and soon began contributing to periodicals. At twenty-six she published anonymously her first novel, *Routledge,* a sentimental romance of a type popular at that period, which remains her best known work. This, as well as her many other novels and books, enjoyed great vogue and passed through many editions.

In 1884 she married Sidney S. Harris, a New York lawyer, and had two children.

After the death of her husband in 1892 she passed much of her time abroad, producing in this period a book on her travels in Spain. She died at her home in Pau, France, at the age of ninety-one.

PRINCIPAL WORKS: Routledge, 1860; The Sutherlands, 1862; Richard Vandermarck, 1871; Missy, 1880; Phoebe, 1884; A Corner in Spain, 1898.

ABOUT: Cole, F. T. The Early Genealogies of the Cole families in America; New York Times January 25, 1925.

HARRIS, THOMAS LAKE (May 15, 1823-March 23, 1906), poet and mystic, was born at Fenny Stratford, England, and was brought to this country in 1827. His father, Thomas Harris, went into business as a grocer and auctioneer at Utica, N.Y.

Left motherless at the age of nine, and mistreated by his step-mother, the boy gradually estranged himself from his family and finally entered the houschold of a Universalist minister of Utica who had befriended him. Harris showed poetic ability early in life: before the age of twenty he had contributed to the Universalist journals, and when in 1843 he pledged full allegiance to Universalism, the church soon found use for his eloquence. After a year's experience as pastor at Minden, N.Y., where he married Mary Ann Arnum in 1845, he was made pastor of the Fourth Universalist Society in New York City. But Universalism could not long satisfy the mind or fill the imagination of this religious adventurer; within two years he became a believer in spiritualism, and in 1848 he started an "Independent Christian Organization" of his own in New York. This society, to which Harris' eloquent preaching attracted many prominent members, lasted only two years, for in 1850 Harris' wife died, and he joined a religious community at Mountain Grove, W.Va.

In this obscure retreat Harris began dictating long poems which embodied his visions of the spiritual regeneration of humanity. The smooth cadence of these verses suggests a certain amount of literary labor, yet Harris claimed that he acted only as a medium or "mouthpiece" through which divine wisdom made itself manifest. Such was the fascination of these poems, especially when recited by a poet and lecturer "whose eyes," so Laurence Oliphant tells us, "were like revolving lights in two dark caverns," that Harris had no difficulty in attracting a considerable following to his own new religion, "The Brotherhood of the New Life," after 1860. Lecturing in Great Britain and Europe (1858-1860 and in 1866), Harris recruited several prominent

From an engraving by J. C. Buttre
THOMAS LAKE HARRIS
c. 1856

Orientals and the brilliant English writer Laurence Oliphant to his movement. The "Brotherhood" settled first at Wassaic, N.Y., then moved about 1863 to Amenia, N.Y., and about 1867 to Portland, near Dunkirk, N.Y., where it occupied for eight years an estate of 1600 acres. Harris controlled the properties of the entire group, yet it was essentially a communistic enterprise, governed wholly by religious motives. Its goal was complete self-surrender to the divine "Use" or purpose, and among its characteristic features were "interior respiration," a concentration-and-breathing-exercise, and "counterpartal marriage," defined as "the indwelling of eternal mate with eternal mate." Harris had two "eternal mates" after his first wife; in 1855 he married Emily Isabella Waters, and after her death in 1883 he married his secretary Jane Lee Waring. In 1875 Oliphant bought out the property at Portland, and Harris led his disciples to Fountain Grove, Calif. After 1892 he retired and lived in New York City.

Harris' poems have considerable beauty of form and imagery, but they are too long and obscure. However lofty and inspiring these visions may have seemed to the poet himself and to his immediate followers, it cannot be said that he truly communicated them to posterity.

PRINCIPAL WORKS: *Poetry*—The Epic of the Starry Heaven, 1854; A Lyric of the Morning Land, 1855; A Lyric of the Golden Age, 1856; The Wisdom of the Adepts, 1884; The New Republic, 1891; The Song of Theos, 1903. *Prose*—The Brotherhood of the New Life, 1891.

About: Austin, A. The Poetry of the Period; Cuthbert, A. A. The Life and World-Work of T. L. Harris; Oliphant, L. Masollam; Swainson, W. P. T. L. Harris and His Occult Teaching; Harper's Magazine February 1892; Occult Review February-March 1923.

HARRIS, WILLIAM TORREY (September 10, 1835-November 5, 1909), philosopher and educator, was born near Killingly, Conn., the son of William and Zilpah (Torrey) Harris. He attended country school, and after a succession of academies he did his first serious studying at Phillips Exeter in Andover, Mass. He entered Yale in 1854, but was acutely restless and left in the middle of his junior year. A variety of iconoclastic literature in which he was steeping himself at this time gave him the "exhilaration of a reformer," and believing the spirit of the borderland to be constructive, not critical and reflective, he went to St. Louis in 1857. The following year he married Sarah T. Bugbee, and by her had two children, Theodore and Edith. From his first teaching position he rose rapidly, becoming Superintendent of Schools in St. Louis within ten years.

The city at that time, with its descendants of French nobility, aristocratic Southerners, energetic New Englanders, and Teutonic radicals, was considered very cosmopolitan, and was good soil for hardy intellectual shoots to take root in. Theodore Parker's essay on German literature had whipped Harris into a determination to master German philosophy. About this time he met Henry Conrad Brokmeyer, a German freethinker and contemplative, who had gone West to build his own cabin and live there alone with his dog. With Brokmeyer and D. J. Snider, Harris founded the so-called "St. Louis school" of idealism, which established the first systematic study of German thought in America. It was Kant's *Critique of Pure Reason* that gave Harris his first insight into this new idealism: an attack against the assumption that we cannot conceive the infinite. That assumption, Harris believed, confused the processes of conception and imagination. Bronson Alcott, the "priest of Neo-Platonic transcendentalism," came to St. Louis to lecture at the school. Harris himself was deep in Hegel, at this time, and wrote an article for the *North American Review*; its rejection no doubt precipitated his founding, in 1867, of the *Journal of Speculative Philosophy,* the first quarterly in English devoted exclusively to philosophy. In it appeared some of the first writings of Charles Peirce, John Dewey, and William James.

Collection of Frederick H. Meserve
WILLIAM TORREY HARRIS

From theory Harris proceeded to application. His *Annual Reports* (1868-80) are highly idealistic, in sympathy with free-will tendencies, and embody the historical method of Hegel, the studying of small data in order to discover large trends. In 1875 Harris was made president of the National Education Association, and in 1880 he attended the International Congress of Education in Brussels. On his return he took the old Alcott home, "Orchard House," in Concord, Mass., and there founded the Concord School of Philosophy and Literature. He had anticipated a recapture of the Emersonian momentum—the Sage was then in his seventy-eighth year—but although Harris' fervor won recognition abroad, the movement lacked the natural genesis and the impelling personalities of the earlier Transcendentalism.

In September 1889 Harris was appointed United States Commissioner of Education and published his *Introduction to the Study of Philosophy* and *The Spiritual Sense of Dante's Divina Commedia,* a strongly Hegelian interpretation. With the appearance of *Hegel's Logic: A Book on the Genesis of the Categories of the Mind* (1890) Harris became the chief American authority on the German idealist. Eight years after *Psychologic Foundations of Education* (1898), he resigned from government service. His health was in decline, and improved only slightly by a stay in the Adirondacks a year before his death.

Harris was of medium build, with dark kindly eyes and a subdued manner. He had a "directive force" which enabled him to publish almost 500 titles, large and small. Moreover, he edited a revised edition of *Webster's New International Dictionary* and wrote prefaces to fifty-eight volumes of the International Education Series. He did indeed bring German thought within the pale of the American mind. Although recent scientific and sociological advancement has lowered the value of his pedagogic findings, he was, nevertheless, an astute educator, and, if not a profound, certainly an orderly, expositor of philosophic theory.

PRINCIPAL WORKS: *Philosophy*—Introduction to the Study of Philosophy, 1889; The Spiritual Sense of Dante's Divina Commedia, 1889; Hegel's Logic: A Book on the Genesis of the Categories of the Mind, 1890; *Education*—The Psychologic Foundations of Education, 1898.

ABOUT: Riley, I. W. American Thought; Roberts, J. S. William Torrey Harris; Education June 1888; Forum April 1887; Providence Journal November 6, 1909.

HARRISON, CONSTANCE (CARY) (April 25, 1843-November 21, 1920), novelist, was born in Fairfax County, Va. Her parents came of distinguished families, her father Archibald Cary of Carysbrook being related to Thomas Jefferson. Both her father and mother were accomplished writers. Her mother Monimia (Fairfax) Cary was the youngest daughter of Thomas, ninth Lord Fairfax. The maternal grandmother's home Vaucluse, near Arlington, Va., where her mother returned with her three children after the early death of her husband, was destroyed during the Civil War. The war period, spent among the exciting scenes of Richmond, Va., where she busied herself in part with nursing and contributing to magazines under the name of "Refugitta," left an indelible impression on her. A visit to Europe with her mother followed, and the following year, 1867, she married Burton Norvell Harrison, a New York lawyer who had been private secretary to Jefferson Davis, the marriage taking place at Morrisania, N.Y., the home of her uncle Gouverneur Morris.

A short story "A Little Centennial Lady" published in *Scribner's Monthly* in 1876, written from the diary and letters of her quaint aunt, Sally Fairfax, first established her popularity. Her novels, by which she is best known, deal largely with New York society and Virginia life, but she was widely traveled and skilled in depicting local color of other places also. Her chapters on English society in *Sweet Bells Out of Tune* were said by Mrs. Thackeray-Ritchie to be the best light work ever done by an alien writer. Her *Anglomaniac* attracted widespread attention. She had a graceful, polished style, and much charm of expression. All her novels were republished in England and several were translated into other languages. She also produced some stories for children and adapted some plays from the French, directing their production. An autobiographical work *Recollections Grave and Gay* was published in 1911. She died at her home at Washington, D.C., at the age of seventy-seven, leaving two sons.

PRINCIPAL WORKS: Belhaven Tales, 1892; Sweet Bells Out of Tune, 1892; A Bachelor Maid, 1894; The Anglomaniac, 1899; Recollections Grave and Gay, 1911.

ABOUT: Harrison, C. C. Recollections Grave and Gay; Book Buyer January 1891.

HARRISON, GESSNER (June 26, 1807-April 7, 1862), teacher and classicist, named after the Swiss poet Salomon Gessner, was born at Harrisonburg, Va. He was the second son of a widely esteemed physician, Peachy Harrison, and of Mary (Stuart) Harrison. A precocious child, at four he commenced his schooling, and at eight had completed the rudiments of Latin. He read continually. It was thought he would follow his father's footsteps in medicine, but as soon as he was graduated from his classical and medical studies at the University of Virginia, at the age of twenty-one, his teacher, Professor George Long, recommended Harrison as his successor in teaching ancient languages, and in spite of vigorous opposition on account of his youth, he was appointed. He remained on the faculty for thirty-one years, retiring in 1859 to open a private classical school for boys in Nelson County, Virginia. The Civil War, however, brought difficulties and anxieties that terminated in his death at fifty-five.

A small, slight man, inclined to be timid, Harrison nevertheless served for twelve years as faculty chairman and was an important influence in helping to curb the turbulence that then animated the student body. He married the daughter of his colleague, Professor George Tucher, and had nine children.

Harrison applied his deep scholarship to the fundamentals of his classical teaching. He was the first American college teacher to interest himself in comparative grammar. He published pamphlets dealing with Greek and Latin prepositions, and one dealing with the geography of ancient Italy and Greece which became a standard text in many universities. His major work, however, was

An Exposition of Some of the Laws of the Latin Grammar, 1852. This was the product of an immense amount of painstaking labor.

PRINCIPAL WORKS: The Geography of Ancient Italy and Southern Greece, 1834; An Exposition of Some of the Laws of the Latin Grammar, 1852.

ABOUT: Bruce, P. A. History of the University of Virginia.

HARRISON, JAMES ALBERT (August 21, 1848-January 31, 1911), philologist, was born at Pass Christian, Miss. He came from literary stock and families distinguished on both sides, his father James P. Harrison, a wealthy planter, being descended from two presidents and a signer of the Declaration of Independence, and the antecedents of his mother, Mary (Thurston) Harrison, being prominent in colonial history. At an early age he was brought to New Orleans and educated there, at the University of Virginia, and in Germany. At twenty-three he accepted a professorship in Latin and modern languages at Randolph-Macon College. Five years later he was called to Washington and Lee University, and in 1895 to the University of Virginia where he remained until the last two years of his life. He married Elizabeth Letcher, the daughter of the war governor of Virginia.

While still a student in Virginia, Harrison commenced to contribute to publications and, when he entered upon teaching, his literary and editorial work became constant. He spent his vacations in unremitting travel, his first book *A Group of Poets and Their Haunts,* 1874, and books on Greece and Spain, written in moments of leisure, being the products of such contacts. He also produced a book of Creole tales and one on George Washington, both of a popular nature. His works were marked by insight and descriptive power.

Harrison's more serious work was linked with his teaching and philological studies. In addition to contributing to more than a dozen periodicals, he served for many years as an editor of the *Century* and *Standard,* edited French and German classics for the classroom, and collaborated in editing an Old-English volume *Beowulf,* and *A Dictionary of Anglo-Saxon Poetry.* His most exhaustive work was the editing of the seventeen-volume edition of Edgar Allan Poe's works, the first volume of which, a biography, was written by him. At the last, his health and sight failing, his wife and only son gave assistance in his more onerous duties. His last two years were spent in retirement at Charlottesville, Va., in almost total blindness.

PRINCIPAL WORKS: A Group of Poets and Their Haunts, 1874; Greek Vignettes, 1877; Spain in Profile, 1879; A History of Spain, 1883; The Story of Greece, 1885; Autrefois: A Collection of Creole Tales, 1885; George Washington: Patriot, Soldier, Statesman, 1906.

ABOUT: Critic May 8, 1886.

HARTE, BRET. See HARTE, FRANCIS BRETT

HARTE, FRANCIS BRETT (BRET HARTE) (August 25, 1836-May 5, 1902), humorist, story teller, and poet, was born in Albany, N.Y., the son of Henry Harte and Elizabeth Rebecca (Ostrander) Harte, and grandson of Bernard Hart, a prosperous Jewish merchant of New York City. "Bret Harte" is, in part, a *nom de guerre,* assumed at the beginning of his literary career. His father was an instructor in the Albany Female Academy from 1833 to 1834, and from that time until his death in 1850 he was constantly moving about, never seeming to obtain any material success. Young Bret exhibited the traditional precocity of authors-to-be by burlesquing, at the age of five, the drab language of his primer, and, at six, by consuming much Shakespeare. He was only eleven when the *New York Sunday Atlas* printed his poem, "Autumnal Musings," but family criticisms were justly and frankly scorching. He left school two years later and worked first in a lawyer's office and then in a counting house. In 1854 Bret set out from Brooklyn to join his mother, recently married to Colonel Andrew Williams, in San Francisco.

It has been said that in the California of the 'fifties was Americanism in its extreme form—"the quintessence of energy and democracy": services of all kinds were at a premium, energies were easily convertible, and because money was almost omnipresent, an "Argonaut" was judged "by his conduct, not by his bank account." Into this novel civilization stepped Bret Harte. He tutored a while; became an express messenger on a hazardous, much looted mountain road; and at Union, north of San Francisco, learned the printer's trade in the office of the *Humboldt Times.* After a little school teaching, drug-store clerking, and probably a fling at mining he ended his two years' roaming with the assistant-editorship of the *Northern California.* But he was shortly released when he wrote an article condemning the casual murder of Indians—a fashionable diversion in Argonaut society.

In 1857 he returned to San Francisco and set type for the *Golden Era.* The editor, spotting Bret's ability, offered him a dollar a column, and hence came "In a Balcony," "Sidewalkings," and "M'liss," one of his finest short stories. Two years after his marriage to Anna Griswold, August 11, 1862, he was appointed Secretary of the California Mint, a veritable sinecure, which he held until his return East. Among his close friends at this time were the Rev. Thomas Starr King, Protestant minister and brilliant lecturer, and Jessie Benton Frémont, by whose intervention Harte's "Legend of Monte del Diablo" (1863) found its way into the *Atlantic Monthly.* In May 1864 appeared the first issue of a literary weekly, the *Californian,* containing Bret Harte's "Neighborhoods I Have Moved From—By a Hypochondriac." At about this time he met Mark Twain; and according to some authorities it was he who induced Twain to put his famous *Jumping Frog of Calaveras* on paper.

In 1867 Harte's first collection of poems, *The Lost Galleon and Other Tales, Condensed Novels,* and the *Bohemian Papers* were published. In July of the following year the *Overland Monthly* was founded by Anton Roman, a bookseller. Bret Harte named the magazine, became its first editor, and in the second issue, under publisher's protest, appeared his "Luck of Roaring Camp." The religious press called it "immoral," California papers thought it "singular," but Eastern critics went headlong into eulogies. Harte prudently refrained from biting again too hastily, and six months elapsed before "The Outcasts of Poker Flat" went to press.

At a time when the Chinese problem was becoming apparent in California, Harte wrote a poem for the *Overland* (September 1870) called "Plain Language From Truthful James" (better known as "The Heathen Chinee"). James W. Gillis, a pocket miner of literary tastes who lived at Jackass Flat, near Tuttletown, where Harte had taught school, was the "James" of the rime. Again the East was the source of good report. But Harte did not rest too heavily on laurels so easily won. He had been made professor of recent literature at the University of California, retained his place at the mint, and had become a successful editor of the *Overland.*

From a professional point of view, Bret Harte was certainly in the ascendant; but small discords were becoming audible: the new publisher of the *Overland* was less pliable than Roman had been; Harte's editorial policies, even when admirably founded, were often undiplomatically executed; and "without cause or provocation" he had broken his long friendship with Mark Twain. (This breach was later mended, but for a short time only.) Moreover, Harte was deeply in debt. In April 1871, with tempting offers in the East, he made a fantastically heralded journey across the continent. At Chicago, the arrangements whereby he was to have become editor of the *Lakeside Monthly* were somewhat garbled, and, in the end, fell through. With his wife and two children Harte spent a week in Cambridge with William Dean Howells. The remark of a member of the famous Saturday Club of wits and intellectuals is rather typical of New England's reaction to this Argonaut, with his lack of profundity and discrimination: "He made it [the meeting] less a feast of reason than a flow of soul." A few days later, however, Harte signed a contract with the James R. Osgood Company, publishers of the *Atlantic,* for $10,000, and in return he contributed, July 1871 through June 1872, four stories and five poems.

Collection of Frederick H. Meserve
BRET HARTE

Harte spent the next seven years, for the most part, in New York City, and then moved to Morristown, N.J., where, with malicious glee, it was rumored that he paid his butcher's bills with the postage stamps enclosed in autograph requests. He had submitted to several arduous lecture tours, but with only meagre financial gain. In 1876 *Scribner's* published his novel *Gabriel Conroy*; the response, unfortunately, was anything but favorable. Moreover, his dramatic collaboration with Mark Twain, *Ah Sin,* opening in Washington, May 5, 1877, received merely a condescending praise.

Obviously, then, Harte could scarcely afford to refuse an appointment as United States Consul at Crefeld, Prussia. In June 1878 he sailed for England, little suspecting that he would never return. He executed his diplomatic duties in a business-like manner, during his two years at Crefeld, made several visits to England, and wrote "A Legend of Sammstandt" and "Views From a German Spion"; "Unser Karl" appeared somewhat later.

In 1880 Harte was transferred to the more lucrative consulship at Glasgow, and his "Young Robin Gray," a tale of Scottish life, is reminiscent of these years. He was removed from office in 1885, and made his home in London, living entirely by his pen. He sent money regularly to his wife, who, in 1898, came to Brighton to live with their son Francis. In 1901 Harte's health failed rapidly and early in the following year he went to Camberley, in Surrey, to stay with Madame Van de Velde, a charming French noblewoman, of long acquaintance. At the end of a cold and sunless spring, he died of cancer of the throat. False notices of his death had been issued in advance, and to press representatives Harte is said to have repeated Mark Twain's statement that "the report was grossly exaggerated."

Bret Harte was of medium height and slight build, and his face, though somewhat pitted by small-pox scars, was handsomely oval and well set off by a thin nose and an aristocratic mustache. Harte had been guilty of flouting his major social obligations, ignoring the letters of his American friends, and appearing to regard his numerous debts as a kind of concomitant of the artistic tradition. The tragic retard, therefore, of his earlier literary momentum has failed to wring much sympathy from his biographers. He himself said, in 1895 ". . much as I love my country, it does not love *me* sufficiently to enable me to support myself there by my pen." Nevertheless, it was the California back-drop that occasioned his best works, and lacking a better one, he reverted to it again and again. But, obviously, writing from old formulae and dissipated sources he could not match the earlier tales. It was the Bret Harte who had written "Luck," "The Outcasts" and "M'liss" of whom Mark Twain said (1871): "[He] trimmed and trained and schooled me patiently . . . changed me from an awkward utterer of coarse grotesqueness. . ."

Harte was no "pot-boiler" author; he was plodding and laborious, never gambling on the possible merits of what he had written. Unable to disclose and develop his characters with an artistic logic, he was no novelist. An ability to observe and retain, a good narrative sense, and a palatable humor are responsible for his continued prestige in the field of very real American literature.

Principal Works: *Tales*—Bohemian Papers, 1867; Condensed Novels, 1867; Mrs. Skagg's Husbands, 1873; Tales of the Argonauts, 1875. *Poetry*—The Lost Galleon and Other Tales, 1867. *Plays*—Ah Sin, 1877; Sue, 1896. *Novel*—Gabriel Conroy, 1876.

About: Blair, W. Native American Humor; DeVoto, B. Mark Twain's America; Greenslet, F. Life of Thomas Bailey Aldrich; Harte, G. B. Letters of Bret Harte; Merwin, H. C. Life of Bret Harte; Pemberton, T. E. Life of Bret Harte; Californian April 22, 1865.

"HAVEN, ALICE B." See HAVEN, EMILY (BRADLEY) NEAL

HAVEN, EMILY (BRADLEY) NEAL

("Alice G. Lee," "Cousin Alice," "Clara Cushman," "Alice B. Haven") (September 13, 1827-August 23, 1863), editor, was born at Hudson, N.Y., the daughter of George Bradley, connected with a line of sea captains, who died on her third birthday, and Sarah (Brown) Bradley. At the age of six her uncle, the Rev. J. Newton Brown, adopted her. Her schooling in Boston and New Hampshire was handicapped by a serious eye affliction which at one time caused blindness for several months; its effects were somewhat mitigated by an unusual memory and a vivid imagination. Under a challenge while at boarding school she sent a story "The First Declaration" to *Neal's Saturday Gazette* of Philadelphia, using the name "Alice G. Lee," its publication being attended with editorial comment. She was married to its editor, Joseph G. Neal, in December 1846, but in six months she was widowed and left to carry on the editorial responsibilities of the *Gazette* and other obligations that entailed much self-denial and determination. In 1853 she married Samuel L. Haven, a New York broker, and they made their home at Mamaroneck, N.Y., where she devoted herself to her home, her five children, her charities, friends and writings so charmingly as to win the admiration of those around her. Her last years were spent in the "Closet Hall" of James Fenimore Cooper, renamed "The Willows." She died in her thirty-fifth year of tuberculosis and was buried at Rye, N.Y.

She retained her adopted name "Alice" all her life. As "Cousin Alice" she wrote several popular books for children; and as "Alice B. Haven" she contributed to the *Lady's Book* and to *Harper's*. She also ran a column for a time in the *Gazette* under the name "Clara Cushman." She produced at least ten more mature books, among which were *Helen Morton's Trial,* 1849; and *All's Not Gold That Glitters,* 1852. On her last work, *The Good Report,* she spent four years but it was not published until after her death. Her work exemplified her strongly Christian nature and reflected the pleasant side of life.

PRINCIPAL WORKS: Helen Morton's Trial, 1849; All's Not Gold That Glitters, 1853; The Good Report, 1867.

ABOUT: Richards, C. B. Cousin Alice; Godey's Lady's Book January 1864.

HAWKS, FRANCIS LISTER (June 10, 1798-September 27, 1866), historian and clergyman, was born in New Bern, N.C., the son of Francis Hawks, whose father, John Hawks, came to North Carolina with Governor Tryon in 1764, and Julia (Stephens) Hawks, of Irish parentage. At seventeen he was graduated from the University of North Carolina, and at his father's wish he began the study of law. He attended the famous school of Judges Reeve and Gould at Litchfield, Conn., and was admitted to the North Carolina Bar in 1819. From 1820 to 1826 he served as reporter of the Supreme Court of that state, and then had one term in the legislature, where, apparently, his eloquence was unmatched. An enviable legal career was within easy reach when he had a sudden reversion to his earlier inclination: he prepared at New Bern for the Episcopalian ministry and was ordained in 1827. Hawks assisted in Philadelphia and New Haven churches and later became rector of St. Stephen's in New York City, and then St. Thomas'.

Publication of his court *Reports* (1823-28) was followed by *Contributions to the Ecclesiastical History of the United States* in two volumes, one devoted to Virginia in 1836 and the second, in 1839, devoted to Maryland. In 1837 he was co-founder and editor of the *New York Review,* contributing church commentaries and biographical notes. In 1842 he edited one volume of the Hamilton Papers from manuscript; Hamilton's son, with appropriations from Congress, completed the work.

When the financial failure of his church school, St. Thomas' Hall, in Flushing, L.I., interfered with his assumption of a new bishopric, Hawks, in 1843, went South. He became rector of Christ Church, New Orleans, and first president of the University of Louisiana. In 1849 he accepted a flattering offer from Calvary Church, New York City, and with it a gift of $30,000 for the discharge of his debts at Flushing. For certain Romanists dissatisfied with the modern Catholic system he founded Eglesia de Santiago, in New York, and conducted services in Spanish. Save for a brief stay in Baltimore, he remained at Calvary Church until the time of his death. During these years he wrote much on church and secular history; his *Poems Hitherto Uncollected* (1873) were published posthumously.

Hawks had an arresting physiognomy and a well-tempered voice. Quick to take anger, and, at times, dangerously impractical, he had, nevertheless, much personal charm. He was twice married: in 1823, to Emily Kirby, who died four years afterward; and later, to Mrs. Olivia Trowbridge Hunt, who survived him. His literary style was unaffected and clear, but his writings now command only a very limited audience.

PRINCIPAL WORKS: *Religious*—Contributions to the Ecclesiastical History of the U. S., 1836 and 1839; Documentary History of the Protestant Episcopal Church (2 vols.) 1863-64. *Historical*—Early History of the Southern States, 1832; The Mecklenburg Declaration of Independence, 1836; History of North Carolina (2 vols.) 1857-58. *Miscellaneous*—Monuments of Egypt, 1850; Peruvian Antiquities, 1853; Romance of Biography, 1855; Poems Hitherto Uncollected, 1873.

ABOUT: Duyckinck, E. A. Memorial; Richardson, N. S. In Memoriam; Trent, W. P. Southern Writers; New York Times September 28, 1866; Putnam's Magazine January 1868.

HAWTHORNE, NATHANIEL (July 4, 1804-May 19, 1864), novelist and short-story writer, was born in Salem, Mass., the son of Nathaniel Hathorne and Elizabeth Clarke (Manning) Hathorne. Both his father and his mother came from a line of lean-jawed Puritans. On board the same ship that brought the charter of the Massachusetts Bay Colony from England was one Major William Hathorne; his son, a witchcraft judge, was the grandfather of Capt. Nathaniel Hathorne, (the father of the novelist), who was lost at sea when young Nathaniel was only four. Capt. Hathorne's widow, whose forebears were prosperous stage-coach pioneers, became a grief-stricken recluse, stifled any predilection for maritime adventure that her child might have had, and, instead, encouraged him in his reading—*The Faerie Queene, The Castle of Indolence, Pilgrim's Progress,* etc. At the age of nine the lad injured his leg in baseball, and sedentary pursuits became a delectable necessity. Three years later he was taken up into the Maine woods and was there exposed to normal, boyish life. So Arcadian was he, for a time, that at the mention of college, he wrote, "Oh! no . . . I was not born to vegetate forever . . . to live and die as calm and tranquil as—a puddle of water." Nevertheless, after a brief siege of bookkeeping in his Uncle Richard Manning's coach office, his protests paled, and he was enrolled in the class of 1825 at Bowdoin. He appears to have shared very little campus life with Longfellow, three years his junior, but, rather, to have sought the confidences of Horatio Bridge and Franklin Pierce, who inhabited a breezy, practical, and hilarious world.

Despite these friendships, four years at Bowdoin made Nathaniel only more apprehensive of any terrestrial plunge. After paying a fine to avoid taking part in commencement, he returned to sleepy Salem, and, changing the spelling of his name to Hawthorne, half-consciously resigned himself to a career of letters. He read voraciously in arid histories and books of obscure travels, took long walks along Salem Neck, and occasionally climbed the steeple of Christ Church to peer down on the town beneath him. It was doubtless during his last year at Bowdoin that he had worked on "Seven Tales of My Native Land"—and then burned the manuscript. The following year he wrote *Fanshawe* (1828), and had it published anonymously and at his own expense ($100). But this ill-starred first novel projected neither the cold actualities of college life nor an idealistic illusion of such. Deeply chagrined, Hawthorne recalled what he could of the score or more sold copies, and pulled down the blinds of his "chamber under the eaves." However, Samuel Griswold Goodrich, a Boston publisher and literary speculator, had perused a copy of *Fanshawe,* and in his 1830 issue of the *Token,* printed the new author's "Young Provincial." Hawthorne was for several years an anonymous contributor to this annual. It was through Goodrich, too, that Hawthorne became the editor (1836) of *The American Magazine of Useful and Entertaining Knowledge,* a mushroom periodical; after four months of filler-writing, proof-reading, and professional haggling he drew a pay check for twenty dollars. In March 1837 appeared the first series of *Twice Told Tales,* over the imprint of the American Stationers' Company to whom his old schoolfellow, Horatio Bridge, had given a guaranty of $250. Of this selection from his magazine contributions Hawthorne later said: "They are not the talk of a secluded man with his own mind and heart . . . but his attempts to open an intercourse with the world." The volume created little stir, but it was no such failure as *Fanshawe.*

Collection of Frederick H. Meserve
NATHANIEL HAWTHORNE

During July and August he visited his good friend Bridge, in Maine, and into his notebook went "hints for characters" and "remarkables," observed from the banks of the Kennebec, where immigrant laborers, encamped in shanties with their families, were at work on a milldam. Unfortunately, these studious portraits never emerged from the journals.

The market for short stories, at this time, was fairly accessible, but Hawthorne was still financially insecure. Through the intervention of a friend he was appointed "measurer of salt, coal, etc." at the Boston Custom House, in January 1839. He tried to regard this earthy and briny occupation as healthful discipline, but at the end of two years he voluntarily resigned. Over in West Roxbury the Transcendentalists were setting up their social community at Brook Farm, in the attempt to establish a happy liaison between sheer intellectualism and the humblest of manual labors. He joined the Brook Farm Institute in April 1841 and made his final withdrawal in November, eventually retrieving the amount due him on his $1000 purchase of stock. Within one year Hawthorne had made two conscious efforts to sound out the current of life, and had recoiled from both with impressions that were far from favorable.

For some time Hawthorne had been writing letters of endearment to Sophia Peabody, whose charm he had admired at the semi-intellectual "Saturday evenings at Miss Burley's." On July 9, 1842, he and Sophia were married, and, taking the Old Manse, which for a century had been the Concord home of the Emersons and Ripleys, they retreated to a decidedly unearthy existence, living on simple fare and receiving their rare callers with an unpropitious frigidity and eeriness. Emerson, whom Hawthorne considered a mere mystic, shared a little of this "molluscan habit," but only Henry Thoreau, at Walden, could match it.

In the early 'forties Hawthorne was writing—largely for the *Democratic Review*—familiar essays and short stories that fell from an allegorical mould, his best means of creating real people in imaginary oppositions. "The Celestial Road" (a parody of *Pilgrim's Progress*), "The New Adam and Eve," and "The Procession of Life," all plausible pieces, were not ultimately convincing.

When the Samuel Ripleys returned to Concord in 1845, the Hawthornes were obliged to surrender the Manse and move to Salem. After refusing an appointment in the Charlestown Navy Yard, Hawthorne accepted the surveyorship at the Salem Custom House in the spring of 1846. Among ladings of pepper from Sumatra, wool from Nova Scotia, etc., he was slightly happier than he had been at Long Wharf a few years before, but the dread of a slow hypnotism of apathy and an inability to write anything worthwhile made him regard his removal, in June 1849, as an ill wind with a good mission. Of this he said, long afterward: "God bless my enemies, say I! If it had not been for their kind services, I might have been in the Surveyor's room this day." Late in the year he moved his family—Una was now five and Julian three—to Lenox, in the western part of the state. The following April saw the publication of *The Scarlet Letter*. Since 1837, when he had written "Endicott and the Red Cross" he had often been tormented by a symbol—a scarlet "A," worn by an adulteress in that tale—which had, at last, worked its way into a full-length book. To offset the dolor of the piece, for which Hawthorne believed the reading public would have little appetite, he wrote a "familiar" prefatory essay on the Custom House. Two thousand copies of *The Scarlet Letter* were lapped up in ten days—his fretting had been quite unnecessary!

Not far from Lenox lived Fanny Kemble, the actress, and Oliver Wendell Holmes, who was summering in Pittsfield. But it was Herman Melville, at Arrowhead, who spoke Hawthorne's language and who actually became an almost frequent caller. During that winter, 1850-51, Hawthorne was hard at work on *The House of Seven Gables.* He believed that "in writing a romance, a man is always . . . careening on the utmost verge of a precipitous absurdity and the skill lies in coming as close as possible, without actually tumbling over." And he avoided "tumbling over," but the book had a milder popularity, at first, than *The Scarlet Letter.*

The following November the Hawthornes left Lenox and took the Horace Mann house in West Newton, where *The Blithedale Romance,* the literary proceeds of the Brook Farm experience, was written. There was nothing epoch-making about the book—it was merely all that could be expected from ingredients that were thin ink for the pen of a romancer. Late in the spring of '52 Hawthorne bought Bronson Alcott's "Hillside" in Concord, rechristened it the "Wayside," and there disciplined himself to the writing of a campaign biography of his old friend, now General Franklin Pierce, the Democratic dark-horse nominee for the Presidency. The little volume could not have made many proselytes, but Pierce won by a large electoral plurality over his opponent. and Hawthorne accepted the lucrative consulship at Liverpool. In July 1853 he and his family sailed from Boston on the "Niagara," saluted by guns on Castle Island. Just under fifty, he was, manifestly, in no literary decline, but for the fixing of his status among writers of imaginative fiction. virtually all the evidence was in.

Quite naturally, Hawthorne disliked the pent-up consular routine, and very shortly was writing, "I am sick of it . . . and long for my hillside—and—my pen." In the summer of 1857 he submitted his resignation and declared himself "no longer a servant." Nevertheless, he had an abhorrence of returning to Concord. In the course of a leisurely tour of England, he reinforced his rather bigoted impressions of the British, "sodden in strong beer," whose conversation he declared was "something like a plum-pudding, as heavy, but seldom so rich." Early in 1858 he left for the Continent, spent ten days in France, and then proceeded to Rome. Italy, "a sort of poetic fairy precinct," was the inevitable source of *The Marble Faun.* He returned to England, remaining until the summer of 1860, when he sailed for the United States and made his home at the Wayside.

In 1862 Hawthorne journeyed to Washington and the following year saw the publication of *Our Old Home,* a collection of

Atlantic articles which had been culled from the fertile and well-turned passages of his English journals. That Hawthorne insisted upon dedicating the book to Pierce, whose Southern sympathies were anathema to countless potential buyers, is high testimony of his devotion to an old friend. He started for New York and Philadelphia with William Ticknor, in March 1864, but the trip was brought to a close by the untimely death of his companion. In the second week of May he set out with Pierce for New Hampshire and the rejuvenating air of the White Mountains. They took lodgings at Pemigewasset House, near Plymouth, and here Hawthorne died in sleep, early in the morning of May 19. Emerson, who was among the pallbearers at the funeral, wrote in his journal on the day following, ". . .there was a tragic element . . . in the painful solitude of the man, which, I suppose, could not longer be endured, and he died of it."

That "painful solitude" had indeed been "endured"—in fact, nourished—since Hawthorne was a boy and it had gotten a hardy growth in his earliest surroundings. As the years went on, it was heightened by his own awareness of it and the harrowing effects of his own efforts to emerge from it and to identify himself with any of the main currents of life. In England and on the Continent he was, perhaps, even more of a spiritual alien, an onlooker, and when he returned to Concord that same sense of isolation became a pathological timidity. "Mr. Hawthorne," wrote Sophia to Pierce in the spring of '64, "intended to make a covenant with you . . . that you will not introduce him to any persons, especially not to any ladies during his absence. . ." Things real and kinetic, such as the awful events of the Civil War, made him fearful and bewildered. In one of his letters to Pierce, dated December 3, 1861, he said, "But perhaps I am as much too despondent as he [a common friend] is too sanguine . . . we are all . . . as happy as the times will permit."

There was something dusky and slightly foreign about Hawthorne's physiognomy—black, brilliant eyes, massive head, and well-cut features. His voice was full and rather caustic and he walked with the lunging gait of a sailor. High devotion to his contemplative cult did not prevent him from being a somewhat idolatrous father, and in his journal he faithfully recorded the everyday activities of his children, rounded off with light and hypothetical fragments of philosophy. Of Sophia he spoke in only endearing terms and his affection was, apparently, wholly returned. Moreover, after Hawthorne's death, Sophia published his *Passages From the American Note-books* and *Passages From the English Note-books.* Unfortunately, her reverence for the socially proper influenced her to revamp many phrases and passages—especially those disclosing any gloom, rusticity, or fondness for low company—leaving them much emasculated and often changed in meaning; her excessive modesty compelled her to lift out numerous vigorously candid expressions. Nevertheless, the note-books are invaluable autobiography, for the author's habits were hardly the kind to encourage any Boswellian satellite. Hawthorne was, moreover, one of the so-called literary exiles, who, once uprooted intellectually, could not survive transplanting: and this mental atrophy only aggravated his social isolation. The finest that he wrote was the noble enactment of his own tragic pride, a suave adjustment of unbending and confusing facts to a formula of half-real and sometimes grim enchantment. With polished intonations, Hawthorne, like Poe, translated the morbid aspect of the American spirit.

Principal Works: *Novels*—Fanshawe, 1828; The Scarlet Letter, 1850; The House of Seven Gables, 1851; The Blithedale Romance, 1852; The Marble Faun, 1860. *Tales*—Twice-Told Tales, 1842; Mosses From an Old Manse, 1846; The Snow Image and Other Twice-Told Tales, 1851. *Juveniles*—A Wonder-Book for Girls and Boys, 1852; Tanglewood Tales for Girls and Boys, 1853. *Biography*—The Life of Franklin Pierce, 1852. *Autobiographical*—Our Old Home, 1863; Passages From the American Note-books, 1868; Passages From the English Note-books, 1870; Passages From the French and Italian Note-books, 1871.

About: Arvin, N. Hawthorne; Bridge, H. Personal Recollections of Nathaniel Hawthorne; Brooks, V. W. Flowering of New England; Goodrich, S. G. Recollections of a Life-Time; Hawthorne, H. Romantic Rebel; Hawthorne, J. Memoirs; James, H. Hawthorne; Democratic Review 1843-44; Pierce Papers, Manuscript Division Library of Congress.

HAY, JOHN MILTON (October 8, 1838-July 1, 1905), diplomat, journalist, historian, and poet, was born at Salem, Ind., the third son of Charles Hay, a frontier doctor, and Helen (Leonard) Hay.

Dr. Hay moved his family to Warsaw, Ill., in 1841, and John was educated in that state until the age of sixteen, when he entered Brown University. The boy earned such distinction at college, particularly in letters, that after graduation he yearned for a career of authorship; however, he entered his uncle's office at Springfield, Ill., in 1859, to study law. During his two years of training there Hay came in contact with Lincoln, J. G. Nicolay, and other Western political leaders, whom he served so well that in 1861,

Collection of Frederick H. Meserve
JOHN HAY

after his admission to the bar, he was made assistant private secretary to the new President. Thus began a distinguished career in diplomacy: after Lincoln's death in 1865 Hay served as secretary of legation at Paris (1865-1867), at Vienna (1867-1868), and at Madrid (1869-1870). His sparkling reminiscences and impressions of this last place, published in 1871 under the title *Castilian Days,* brought him considerable literary fame, which was greatly increased soon afterwards by the appearance of his *Pike County Ballads and Other Pieces.* Two of the ballads, "Jim Bludso" and "Little Breeches," pathetic stories told in the racy idiom of the frontier, were read with enthusiasm throughout the United States.

Hay followed up this first literary success with five years (1870-1875) of editorial writing for the New York *Tribune.* According to Howells, he preferred the impersonality of journalism to the "irksome personal notoriety" which attends the poet or novelist; it is certainly true that he deprecated the "absurd vogue" of his doggerel ballads, expressing the hope that they would be forgotten in a year or two, and that he published his next piece of imaginative writing, *The Breadwinners,* anonymously. This novel, written in defense of capitalism after the Unionist riots of 1877, strongly appealed to conservative sentiment for a while, but soon lost its timeliness.

Soon after his marriage in 1874 to Clara, daughter of the Cleveland financier Amasa Stone, Hay gave up journalism and moved to Cleveland. In 1878 he was appointed assistant secretary of state and moved to Washington, where he settled permanently next door to Henry Adams, his closest friend. During the next ten years, Hay and J. G. Nicolay [*q.v*] worked incessantly on their multi-volume life of Lincoln. Though partisan in its approach, this monumental work was notable for its thoroughness and accuracy, and remains even today a primary source on Lincoln and the Civil War period.

Under President McKinley Hay served as Ambassador to Great Britain (1897-1898) and then as Secretary of State, which office he held until his death at Newburg, N.H., in 1905.

In literature Hay was "jack of all trades, master of none." There are sparkling and memorable passages in all his books, yet he must be considered essentially an occasional writer, a gifted orator and statesman who strayed into literature.

Principal Works: *Poetry*—Pike County Ballads and Other Pieces, 1871; Poems, 1890. *Novel*—The Breadwinners, 1883. *History*—Abraham Lincoln: A History (with John G. Nicolay) 1890. *Miscellaneous*—Castilian Days, 1871, Addresses, 1906.

About: Dennett, T. John Hay; Kreymborg, A. Our Singing Strength; Sears, L. John Hay: Author and Statesman; Thayer, W. R. John Hay; North American Review September 1905; The Nation August 10, 1916.

"HAYES, HENRY." See KIRK, JOHN FOSTER

HAYNE, PAUL HAMILTON (January 1, 1830-July 6, 1886), poet and biographer, was born in Charleston, S.C., the son of Lieut. Paul Hamilton Hayne, U. S. N., a descendant of prominent English gentry, and Emily (McElhenny) Hayne. Because of his father's early death, young Hayne grew up in the home of his illustrious uncle, Robert Y. Hayne, statesman and aristocrat, and enjoyed every advantage that the heyday of ante-bellum Charleston could provide. From preparatory school, where he formed an enduring friendship with Henry Timrod, the poet, Hayne went to Charleston College, was graduated at twenty, and began the study of law. But his early dabblings in verse and his love of the classics made a literary career almost inevitable. He contributed to the *Southern Literary Messenger* and was soon given an editorial post on the *Southern Literary Gazette.* His *Poems* (1855) won the compliments of reputable Northern critics who had been consistently apathetic to Southern writers. Into the legend of the longest of these verses, "The Temptation of Venus," Hayne wrote a

PAUL HAMILTON HAYNE

"deeper moral significance . . . that in the maelstrom of the passions virtue and happiness are sure to go down together." In 1857 came another volume, and a third in 1860.

With a coterie of literary fledgelings who gathered in the "inner sanctum" of John Russell's bookstore in Charleston, Hayne founded (1857) and edited *Russell's Magazine,* designed to "give utterance . . . to the doctrines . . . of the educated minds of the South" and to promote a literature "free from party shackles." The first issue of this creditable monthly appeared April 1857, but the rumblings of the War brought it to an unwarranted end in 1860. Hayne's meagre health permitted only a brief military service as staff officer at Fort Sumter; out of this period came "My Motherland," "Beyond the Potomac," and "The Battle of Charleston." During General Sherman's "march to the sea" the stately Hayne mansion was completely destroyed by fire. A small patrimony, in the pines of upper Georgia, remained to the poet. And on a bushy knoll, sixteen miles from Augusta, he built a rude shack, "Copse Hill," and with his wife, formerly Mary Middleton Michel, daughter of an eminent French physician, and his only child, William, he withstood "rough fare and rickety quarters" and here made his living by his pen alone. Mrs. Hayne, a woman of no mean intellectual tastes, was his invaluable adviser and amanuensis. Pacing up and down in front of his desk, a rough-hewn work bench, or sauntering on horseback over a piny knob, Hayne wrote verse that found its way into the *Atlantic,* the *Century, Harper's,* and the *Southern Bivouac.* Late in 1867 he was literary editor of the *Southern Opinion,* a Richmond weekly, writing reviews and conducting a column of solicited "Reminiscences and Anecdotes of the Late War."

In 1872 appeared *Legends and Lyrics,* perhaps his most mature poems, among which are "Fire Pictures," containing some effective onomatopoeia, and the deftly phrased "Wife of Brittany." For an edition of Timrod's poems (1873) Hayne wrote an introduction that was discerning and tender in sentiment.

Of slight build, with a slenderly oval face, shapely nose, and an Oriental tilt of the eyes, his appearance was decidedly prepossessing. Having never enjoyed more than mediocre health, he was unable to rally from an illness which came early in the summer of 1886. His funeral was held in St. Paul's Episcopal Church, Augusta, and the Hayne Literary Circle paid him special honor.

In his youth Hayne had possessed a kind of exuberant and liberal tolerance. But the harrowing effects of the War naturally engendered in him a certain bitterness, visible, however, only in his prose writings. New England became, to him, an "infectious locality," and he staunchly condemned a brilliant Northern monthly for not letting "our poor, wretched, undone South alone. . . In God's name have we not suffered sufficiently!" In retreat at "Copse Hill" he adhered, in a humble way, to the genteel tradition into which he had been born, detesting "pestilent political writings," and remaining so completely "above the battle" that he regarded Walt Whitman, with his *Leaves of Grass* and *Drum Taps,* as a "moral *sans culotte.*" Hayne stands as a link between two able Southern poets, William Gilmore Simms, whom the War had left "a giant, a Samson, shorn, and helpless," and Sidney Lanier, whose gifts Hayne had been one of the first to recognize. Despite the tunefulness and fragile beauty of much of Hayne's verse, the best of his poems are familiar only to literary inquirers. His writings seem to have passed with the cavalier aristocracy of which he was once a part.

Principal Works: *Verse*—Poems, 1855, 1857, 1860; Legends and Lyrics, 1872; Mountain of the Lovers, 1875.

About: Lanier, S. Music and Poetry; Link, S. A. Pioneers of Southern Literature; Library of Southern Literature; Charleston News and Courier July 8, 1886; Critic April 1901; Russell's Magazine August 1859; Miscellaneous Letters of P. H. Hayne in Manuscript Division of Library of Congress.

HAYS, WILLIAM SHAKESPEARE (July 19, 1837-July 23, 1907), journalist and ballad-writer, best known as Col. Will S. Hays, was born in Louisville, Ky., the son of Hugh Hays, a plow and wagon manufacturer, who had moved to the South from Pittsburgh, and Martha (Richardson) Hays, of Louisville. Young Will was sent to Miss Yubank's private school, and, following a year at Hanover College, in Indiana, he entered Georgetown (Ky.) College. He had done some early literary dabbling, and in 1858 he became a mailing clerk and then a local editor in the office of the *Louisville Democrat.* Here Hays fell in with numerous rivermen, and after earning a master's license, he became, alternately, columnist and captain for the rest of his life. During the 'eighties and 'nineties he was marine editor of the *Louisville Courier Journal,* centering his levee tales around "Old Ike," a racy Negro.

From early childhood Hays had played several musical instruments—with almost no formal instruction—and, being a facile rhymer, set about ballad-making. In Cleveland he succeeded in getting a walk-on in one of Skiff and Gaylor's old-time minstrels, in which he sang his "Evangeline," of very impromptu origin; when published, the song sold 150,000 copies. During the early months of the Civil War he was imprisoned at New Orleans for the writing of a song that nettled General Butler. Hays sold "Mollie Darling" for a pittance, and gave the money to charity; its subsequent popularity would have made him wealthy. He died of a long illness following an apoplectic stroke, and was survived by his widow, Belle McCullough Hays, and their two children.

Hays, in his late years, wore a trim goatee, and his merry eyes disclosed a frail and sentimental sense of humor that pervaded his verse. That he wrote some of the first catchy words for *Dixie* is quite probable; that he did not write the music itself is almost certain,—recent investigations indicate that the basic melody had a remote origin in English folk-song. Three very modest volumes of his poems were published. As a writer of popular songs—300-odd, in all—his influence has been somewhat sustained, but as a poet his reputation was decidedly fugitive.

PRINCIPAL WORKS: *Verse*—The Modern Meetin' House and Other Poems, 1874; Will S. Hays' Songs and Poems, 1886; Poems and Songs, 1895.

ABOUT: Firth, T. J. The Origin of Dixie; Howe, G. L. A Hundred Years of Music in America; History of Kentucky: Vol. IV; Musician October 1906; Louisville Courier Journal July 24, 1907; Louisville Evening Post July 24, 1907.

"HAYWARD, RICHARD." See COZZENS, FREDERICK SWARTWOUT

HEADLEY, JOEL TYLER (December 30, 1813-January 16, 1897), popular biographer and historian, was born at Walton, Delaware County, N.Y., the son of the Rev. Isaac Headley, Congregational minister, and Irene (Benedict) Headley. He was an older brother of Phineas Camp Headley [*q.v.*]. Expecting to follow his father in the ministry, he studied at the Auburn Theological Seminary, but his efforts in the ministry at Stockbridge, Mass., and later in journalism as associate editor of the New York *Tribune* under Horace Greeley led to breakdowns that sent him first to Italy and the Continent, and later to the Adirondacks to regain his health. The reception of his first book, *Italy and the Italians,* 1844, a collection of letters sent from Italy to New York newspapers, persuaded him to follow a literary career. *The Adirondack,* 1849, gave one of the earliest descriptive introductions to what was then a wild and little-known region. Prior to this he had produced two-volume works on both Napoleon and Washington.

Headley was a prolific writer for more than fifty years, producing more than thirtv biographies, histories, and books of travel. His books reached an enormous sale, *Napoleon and His Marshals,* 1846, going into a fiftieth edition in its eighth year. They were, however, more on the order of compilations than works of scholarship.

PRINCIPAL WORKS: Italy and the Italians, 1844; Napoleon and His Marshals, 1845; The Sacred Mountains, 1847; Washington and His Generals, 1847; The Adirondack, 1849.

ABOUT: Benedict, H. M. The Genealogy of the Benedicts in America; Fretz, A. J. A Genealogical Record of the Descendants of Leonard Headley; Headley, J. T. The Miscellaneous Works of the Rev. J. T. Headley (see Biographical Sketch).

HEADLEY, PHINEAS CAMP (June 24, 1819-January 5, 1903), clergyman and popular biographer, son of the Rev. Isaac Headley and Irene (Benedict) Headley was, like his older brother Joel Tyler Headley [*q.v.*], born at Walton, N.Y. Despite educational restrictions, he read law and secured admission to the bar at twenty-eight, but his mother's wish and his own inclination led him to study at the Auburn Theological Seminary and following his graduation in 1850, he held pastorates in Adams, N.Y., and in Massachusetts at West Sandwich, Greenfield, and Plymouth. From the beginning of his ministry he wrote assiduously for publication, and after 1861 he gave himself almost wholly to writing, residing at Boston, and later at Lexington, Mass., where he died. He received an M.A. degree from Amherst College in 1859. He married Dora C. Bartlett and had four children.

Headley's acknowledged aim was to write historical biography in a popular way. Although not scholarly he read widely, and he wrote in a clear and, at times, a picturesque style. His first two books, both published in 1850, were *Historical and Descriptive Sketches of the Women of the Bible,* and *The Life of the Empress Josephine.* Among his many other works were lives of Grant, Napoleon, Lafayette, Kossuth, Mary Queen of Scots, and volumes on Massachusetts in the Civil War. An inspirational and patriotic series for young folk on heroes of the war included such names as Grant, Sherman, Sheridan, Mitchell, Farragut, and John Ericsson. He contributed also to newspapers and magazines.

Principal Works: Historical and Descriptive Sketches of the Women of the Bible, 1850; The Life of the Empress Josephine, 1850; The Life of General Lafayette, 1851; The Life of Napoleon Bonaparte, 1859; Massachusetts in the Rebellion, 1866; The Island of Fire, 1875.

About: Auburn Theological Seminary Biographical Catalogue, 1818-1918; Fretz, A. J. A Genealogical Record of the Descendants of Leonard Headley.

HEALD, HENRY (1779- ?), traveler, letter-writer, and surveyor, was the son of Samuel and Margaret (Gregg) Heald. His birthplace is not known, but he spent his boyhood in New Castle and Chester Counties, Del. He taught school for a while in the village of Hockessin, and with his brothers Samuel and Harmon operated several plants for the manufacture of a spinning-wheel which he himself had invented.

In 1819, encouraged by the prospects of securing a contract for the survey of public lands in Ohio, he and two others set out from Wilmington in a "Dearborn" (a light four-wheeled carriage), going as far west as Illinois. Heald kept only a scanty journal, and when afterwards prevailed upon to publish an account of his journey he issued, about 1819, a selection from his travel letters, written largely to his brothers, under the title *A Western Tour in a Series of Letters,* to which he affixed an apologetic epilogue: " . . . as the price of the entertainment would not admit of a full meal on each dish, I have spread my table like that of a Western hotel—full of dishes and a slice on each."

The *Tour* contains frequent observations on the topography of the country, records the success of his own invention, a "Landometer," for the purpose of determining the soil's richness, etc., but the more significant portions are those which are devoted to a consideration of the cultural levels of the Midwest and the South: He finds a certain lack of refinement in the people of Indiana and Illinois, but slavery, "human nature's blackest foulest blot," he alleged, was inviting an awful decadence in Southern life and thought. With almost uncanny awareness he ventured to say that "there wants but one head amongst the slaves, at any moment, in which will center foresight, cunning and desperate resolution, and a heart inured to cruelty—to devise and execute a plan that will involve thousands, perhaps millions in utter ruin, and shake the union of these states to the centre! . . . "

For some time after his return to Wilmington, Heald was in charge of the New Castle County Poor House. The *Tour* was his only published writing, but it has remained an intelligent contribution to the literature that recaptures frontier society during the decades preceding the Gold Rush era.

About: Heald, H. A Western Tour in a Series of Letters; information from William H. Heald, Wilmington, Del.

HEARN, LAFCADIO (June 27, 1850-September 26, 1904), exotic, editor, translator, and traveler, was born on the Ionian Island of Santa Maura, the son of Charles Bush Hearn, a surgeon-major in the British army, with gypsy ancestry and Don Juan habits, and his lovely Greek wife, Rosa (Tessima) Hearn. Lafcadio (who was christened Patricio Lafcadio Tessima Carlos) was only six when he embarked with his mother for Dublin; but he never forgot the fact that he had been born on an island that was once the haunt of Sappho. He was entrusted to the care of his father's aunt, Mrs. Brenane, a zealous Catholic, who sent him to various parochial schools and then to St. Cuthbert's College in Yorkshire, England, where, at play, occurred an accident that cost the child the sight of his left eye. Constant reading overtaxed the right eye and, in time, greatly enlarged it. To the pious Jesuit fathers Lafcadio announced one day that he had become a Pantheist: he was dismissed, shipped to a school in France near Rouen, and then escaped to Paris—and the Quartier Latin!

Mrs. Brenane was beginning to despair. For a time she put him in the care of an ex-parlor maid, who lived near the docks in London. Finally, under the influence of a co-religionist, she closed the books by sending the lad off to America. He was to go direct to Cincinnati, where money would be forwarded to him. But young Hearn was loth to accept any more "courtesy" benevolence. After two years of semi-starvation and over-powering discouragement in New York, he set out for Cincinnati, where a slim welcome and an even slimmer sum of money awaited him. He ran messages and peddled mirrors until Harry Watkins, a printer, in whose shop Hearn used to sleep, taught him to set type and to read proof. He got a job on a trade paper, but spent most of his time writing grotesque tales in order to keep his mind from mildewing. Then the *Enquirer* took him on as a reporter.

Suddenly Hearn's reputation was on the upgrade. When the horrible "Tan Yard Case" (1874), in which a murderer had attempted to burn the corpse of his victim, was no longer "news," Hearn went over to see the half-charred body and wrote a description so galling in its details that it became the sensation-piece of the whole episode and made his professional claims almost indisputable. He was becoming drugged by an obsession for the macabre; it was only some strange emotional experience—such as scaling St. Patrick's steeple or concealing himself behind a curtain to watch a painter of nudes—that ignited Hearn's imagination. The immediate failure of his attempt, at this time, to set up a weekly, *Ye Giglampz,* devoted to "art, literature, and satire," was, at best, fair warning to Hearn that he was no humorist!

To eye strain, poor food, and long hours of night work he added still another curse by getting himself into an entanglement with a Negress, Althea Foley. The *Enquirer* frowned on the affair and released him. The *Commercial* hired him (at a lower salary) and eventually sent him to New Orleans to report the Hayes-Tilden campaign sentiments, which, to the editor's disquietude, took the form of exotic, impressionistic letters on Creole life. There was no paycheck forthcoming. Through one Major Robinson he was made assistant editor of Marc Bigney's *Item,* for which he wrote everything from the philosophy of imaginative art to colored women's discourses on superstitions. At a time when the paper was tottering financially, Hearn did a series of front page wood-cuts that actually put the *Item* back on its feet again. By moving from the American Section to the Vieux Carré he managed to save $100 and this he spent on setting up a five-cent restaurant, "The Hard Times." It opened on the second of March (1879) and closed for ever on the twenty-third.

He was eager to learn Ghombo (Louisiana Negro) French, and would try out his accent on his charwoman. George Washington Cable supplied him with the scores for the Creole songs. In May 1880, while still performing a galaxy of duties for the *Item,* he prepared his first column of tidbits from foreign literatures for the *Democrat,* which was subsequently merged with the *Times.* Page Baker, editor-in-chief of the new paper, forbade anyone to change even a comma in Hearn's copy; and for five years "The Foreign Press" had a steady appeal.

A little volume of translations from Gautier, appearing in 1882, was Hearn's first book. Into *Stray Leaves From Strange Literatures* (1884) he incorporated the most quixotic of literary fragments; and for *Ghombo Zhèbes,* a little volume of Creole proverbs, he found a publisher only by "throwing in" his culinary editing, *La Cuisine Creole.* A series of brilliantly polished but static sketches, appearing first in *Harper's,* was issued in 1887 as *Some Chinese Ghosts.*

The musty decadence of the Vieux Carré had forced Hearn, in 1881, back to the American Quarter. He took his meals with one Mrs. Courtney, a motherly Irishwoman who saved him goodies and darned his socks. All women, in Hearn's mind, seemed to fall into two classes: gentlewomen, to whom he

LAFCADIO HEARN
1888

felt himself repulsive because of his protruding eye; and women socially and intellectually beneath him but in whom he found a strange attraction—and to this class belonged Mrs. Courtney, Althea Foley, the octoroon dancers, etc.

During the summer of 1884 Hearn went, for a rest, to Grande Ile in the Gulf of the Mississippi, and there witnessed a tidal disaster that gave him the outline of *Chita: A Story of Last Island.* He had caught the beautiful terror of the sea, but a little journalese obtruded here and there. Early in June, three years later, he left New Orleans never to return. He went to New York, and was twice commissioned to the tropics by *Harper's.* His *Two Years in the French West Indies* (1890) was written with a finesse that marked his unconditional release from any literary apprenticeship.

Before his first journey to the tropics Hearn had made an injudicious stay, in New York, with Henry Krehbiel, friend of his Cincinnati days, who now was music critic of the New York *Tribune.* Hearn's uncommon habits were too much for Mrs. Krehbiel. The same chilliness developed during his visit with Dr. George Milbry Gould, a literary Philadelphia oculist, whose friendship had begun with a letter in praise of one of Hearn's early writings and ended in a rancorous misunderstanding over the disposition of his (Hearn's) library.

For some time Hearn had been toying with the idea of going to Japan, a country of untapped exoticisms. He secured a rather ambiguous contract from *Harper's* for articles on Japan, and after completing, post-haste, a translation of Anatole France's *Le Crime de Sylvestre Bonnard*—his finances were in a sorry state—he left New York early in March 1890. Even before his arrival in Japan, a dispute with his publishers was in full swing. By August, however, he was able to ignore his literary commission, having been appointed a teacher in a school at Matsue. *Glimpses of Unfamiliar Japan* was drawn from the two years that followed. In January 1891 he was married to Setsu Koizumi, a twenty-two-year-old Japanese of high Samurai rank. Hearn taught at a government college at Kumato, but left in 1894 to join the Kōbe *Chronicle. Kokoro* and *Gleanings in Buddha-Fields* belong to this period. He was subsequently appointed to the chair of English Literature at the Imperial University of Tokio, which he held until 1903. *Japan: An Attempt at Interpretation* was Hearn's excellent study prepared for a Cornell lecture series which never materialized.

In order to mitigate legal technicalities he had become a Japanese citizen and had taken the name of Koizumi Yakumo. In these last years of his life he came nearest to finding a complete happiness. Hearn was of slight but strong build, with an olive skin and a handsome profile, and possessed an uncanny sensitivity to odors that was emphasized by an habitual quivering of his nostrils. He died following a heart attack in September 1904, and to Kazuo, the eldest of his four children, he had said: "Put my bones in a jar worth about three sen and bury me in some temple on a hill."

Critics have sometimes tried to bridge the many discrepancies in this strange life by merely superimposing Hearn the myope upon Hearn the author. Biologically, Hearn had no stereoscopic vision. But he himself once said: ". . . the possession of a very good eyesight may be a hindrance to those very feelings of sublimity . . . on which depends . . . the predominance of mass over detail" and which "exalt the imagination." Of the East and the West he left a vast legacy of finished and intricate beauty, and whether it was so highly polished as to take on a transparency and a fragility that will not age is a question that will write its own answer.

Principal Works: *Tales*—Chita: A Story of Last Island, 1886; Some Chinese Ghosts, 1887; Two Years in the French West Indies, 1890. *Translations*—One of Cleopatra's Nights, 1882; Stray Leaves From Strange Literatures, 1884. *Miscellaneous*—Gombo Zhèbes, 1885; La Cuisine Creole, 1885; Glimpses of Unfamiliar Japan, 1894; Japan: An Attempt at Interpretation, 1904.

About: Bisland, E. Life and Letters of Lafcadio Hearn; Edwards, O. Some Unpublished Letters of Lafcadio Hearn; Gould, G. M. Concerning Lafcadio Hearn; Kennard, N. H. Lafcadio Hearn; Koizumi, K. Father and I; Ichikawa, S. Some New Letters and Writings of Lafcadio Hearn; Temple, J. Blue Ghost: A Study of Lafcadio Hearn; Tinker, E. L. Lafcadio Hearn's American Days.

HEATH, JAMES EWELL (July 8, 1792-June 28, 1862), occasional writer and state official, was a native of Virginia, his birthplace being probably Northumberland County. He was the son of John Heath, twice a member of Congress and the first president of Phi Beta Kappa, and of Sarah (Ewell) Heath. He passed most of his life in the public service, entering upon a three-term service in the state legislature when he was twenty-two, acting as state auditor for thirty years and holding the office of commissioner of pensions for three years under President Fillmore. He interested himself in educational and religious institutions, and was an officer of the Virginia State Historical and Philosophical Society. He was twice married.

A charming writer to whom Poe referred in 1841 as "almost the only person of any literary distinction" residing in Richmond, Heath's literary production was of the occasional order. His first book, *Edge-Hill: or, The Family of the Fitzroyals,* a story of Virginia plantation life and scenes, although praised by Poe and George Tucker, was not a financial success. Eleven years later his only other published book appeared, a three-act comedy *Whigs and Democrats: or, Love of No Politics,* a satire on rural election practices. Although it was published anonymously, Democratic resentment at this political attack is supposed to have been the cause of his removal from the state auditorship in 1849. Heath gave editorial advice and assistance to Thomas W. White, publisher of the *Southern Literary Messenger,* in the first nine months or more of its establishment.

Principal Works: Edge-Hill: or, The Family of the Fitzroyals, 1828; Whigs and Democrats: or, Love of No Politics, 1839.

About: Hayden, H. Virginia Genealogies; Minor, B. B. The Southern Literary Messenger.

"HEDBROOKE, ANDREW." See SILL, EDWARD ROWLAND

HEDGE, FREDERICK HENRY (December 12, 1805-August 21, 1890), Unitarian clergyman and German scholar, was born at Cambridge, Mass., the son of Levi Hedge [*q.v.*], professor of logic at Harvard, and Mary (Kneeland) Hedge, a granddaughter of President Edward Holyoke of Harvard. Four years of study in Germany, where he was sent at the age of thirteen with George Bancroft, the historian, then eighteen, gave him a thorough grounding in the language and philosophy of that country. Completing his studies at Harvard and the Divinity School, where he made the acquaintance of Emerson, he held, over a period of forty-two years, pastorates in Massachusetts, Maine, and Rhode Island. He served four years as editor of the *Christian Examiner,* was for nineteen years a professor of ecclesiastical history at the Harvard Divinity School, and for twelve years professor of German at Harvard. With Emerson he had attended the first meetings of the "Transcendental Club," which subscribed to no orthodox code of Transcendentalism and was far from being a club. (It was often referred to as the "Hedge Club," for its sessions were occasioned by his journeys to Boston from

FREDERICK H. HEDGE

Bangor, Maine, where he preached to the lumber merchants, intellectual lawyers, and politicians.) For twenty-nine years he was a member of the famous Saturday Club.

Hedge had been class poet and Phi Beta Kappa poet in 1828, and his later verse took the form of hymns and lyrical translations. He had a remarkable memory and could complete a narrative poem of several hundred lines before setting it down on paper; many of his longest sermons were delivered entirely without notes and often without preparation. Hedge's *Prose Writers of Germany* (1848), a collection of translations with critical introductions, first established his position as a German scholar, and he became perhaps the best qualified of the "German party" in the Transcendental movement. In addition to constant contributions to periodicals, he published at least a dozen volumes largely religious, philosophical, and German-inspired. He was sometimes given to bold speculation, and of his condemnation of "Anti-Supernaturalism in the Pulpit," a sermon preached during the Civil War era, it is said that almost nothing since Theodore Parker's "Transient and Permanent" made such a stir. As a critic he was candid and free—when informed that Edmund Gosse proposed to head a list of American poets with Poe, he wrote, "I consider 'Thanatopsis' our greatest *poem*; Emerson our greatest *poet*; Poe *nowhere*." He was well known as an essayist, orator, and exponent and translator of German thought; but from first to last he was a Unitarian minister and conservative ecclesiastic who kept his faith in an independent way.

Principal Works: Prose Writers of Germany, 1846; Reason in Religion, 1865; Ways of the Spirit and Other Essays, 1877; Hours With German Classics, 1886.

About: Brooks, Van W. The Flowering of New England; Chadwick, J. W. Frederick Henry Hedge; Emerson, E. W. The Early Years of the Saturday Club; Nation August 28, 1890; Unitarian Review October 1890.

HEDGE, LEVI (April 19, 1766-January 3, 1844), philosopher, the father of Frederic Henry Hedge [*q.v.*], was born at Warwick, Mass. The second of six sons of Lemuel Hedge, a Congregational clergyman, and Sarah (White) Hedge, daughter of a clergyman, custom and the slender family resources gave the opportunity of a college education to the elder son and Levi was apprenticed to a mason. Later he worked his own way through Harvard, graduating in 1792. In 1795 he was appointed tutor in philosophy at Harvard, the tutorship being made permanent in 1800, and in 1810 giving place to a professorship in logic and metaphysics. In 1801 he married Mary Kneeland, daughter of Dr. William Kneeland and granddaughter of President Holyoke of Harvard. He taught at Harvard for thirty-seven years, resigning in 1832 because of an attack of paralysis, and spending his last twelve years in retirement, enriched with his books and friends.

While teaching Hedge prepared his *Elements of Logic: or, A Summary of the General Principles and Different Modes of Reasoning,* 1816, for his classes. He expected the students to be able to recite his book verbatim. He is rumored to have remarked, "It took me fourteen years, with the assistance of the adult members of my family, to write this book, and I am sure you cannot do better than to employ the precise words of the learned author." The volume was an outstandingly clear and practical work, which went through many editions and was translated into German. His last work was to edit a two-volume manuscript *Treatise on the Philosophy of the Human Mind,* by Thomas Brown of Edinburgh.

Principal Works: Elements of Logic: or, A Summary of the General Principles and Different Modes of Reasoning, 1816.

About: Harvard Graduates Magazine September 1928.

HEILPRIN, ANGELO (March 31, 1853-July 17, 1907), geologist, paleontologist, and explorer, came from a talented line of Hebrew scholars. His father, Michael Heilprin, was a scholarly writer and encyclopedist. His mother was Henrietta (Silver) Heilprin. Born at Sátaralja-Ujhely, Hungary, he was brought to America when three and educated in Brooklyn and Yonkers, N.Y. Among his earliest work was the contributing of several important articles to the *New American Cyclopaedia,* of which his father was associate editor.

After three years abroad in scientific studies under Huxley, Ethridge, and Judd, he became associated in 1890 with the Academy of Natural Sciences and the Wagner Free Institute of Science, Philadelphia, as professor and curator, resigning in 1892. His greatest prominence came from his writings growing out of his travels and explorations, these covering a considerable part of the world. He headed the scientists on the Robert Peary Arctic expedition in 1891 and the relief expedition the following year. During the eruption on Mont Pelée in 1902 he ascended the crater taking observations and photographs in such close proximity as to endanger his life. In 1906 he ascended the Orinoco River, British Guiana, contracting a fever which contributed to his untimely death from heart disease the following year at fifty-four.

Among his other scientific associations and activities Heilprin was a founder and first president of the Geographical Club of Philadelphia and one of the founders of the Alpine Club, limited to mountain climbers. He was lecturer at the Sheffield Scientific School, Yale University in 1904, chief editor of *Lippincott's Gazetteer* in 1905, and for a time editor of a periodical called *Around the World.* He was also an accomplished musician and painter, his pictures appearing at several exhibitions; he received two patents for inventions and was awarded the medal of the Franklin Institute in 1897.

Principal Works: Contributions to the Tertiary Geology and Paleontology of the United States, 1884; Town Geology, 1885; Explorations on the West Coast of Florida, 1887; The Geographical and Geological Distribution of Animals, 1887; The Animal Life of Our Seashore, 1888; The Geological Evidences of Evolution, 1888; The Bermuda Islands, 1889; Principles of Geology, 1890; The Arctic Problem and Narrative of the Peary Relief Expedition, 1893; The Earth and Its Story, 1896; Alaska and the Klondike, 1899, Mont Pelée and the Tragedy of Martinique, 1903; The Tower of Pelée, 1904.

Sources: Morais, H. S. The Jews of Philadelphia; Pollak, G. Michael Heilprin and His Sons; Bulletin of the American Geographical Society November 1907; Bulletin of the Geographical Society of Philadelphia January 1908; Franklin Institute Journal November 1907.

HELPER, HINTON ROWAN (December 27, 1829-March 8, 1909), social historian, was born in Davie County, N.C., the son of Daniel and Sarah (Brown) Helper. At his father's death—Hinton was then a year old—his mother was left with the care of seven children and the management of a small farm. From neighborhood schools he was sent to Mocksville Academy, and then, for several years, worked for a merchant in nearby Salisbury.

In the interests of a local book dealer he went to New York in 1849, but shortly joined the exodus to California. There he spent three years mustering impressions for *The Land of Gold* (1855), from which his Baltimore publisher removed those passages in praise of free labor. Helper, nettled by this episode, returned to North Carolina, made a thorough study of slavery, and in June 1856 set out for the North with *The Impending Crisis of the South* in manuscript. With the author's security against loss, A. B. Burdick, a New York book agent, finally agreed to issue it. Scores of books treating slavery from the Negro's point of view had been published, but Helper's was the first to approach the question from the economic angle and appealed strongly to the non-slave-holding whites. The Southern Democrats who dared to read it called it "incendiary" and its author a "recreant"; Republican leaders of the North distributed 100,000 copies of a *Compendium of the Impending Crisis*; and the resulting furor amplified the rumblings of civil war.

Collection of Frederick H. Meserve
HINTON ROWAN HELPER

In 1861 Lincoln appointed Helper United States Consul at Buenos Aires. While in the Argentine he was married to Maria Luisa Rodriguez, in 1863, and at the end of five drab years in the consulate, he returned to the United States. Three books in maniacal denunciation of the Negro, whose freedom he had championed only in the interest of strengthening white labor, appeared shortly.

With a snowy beard, florid face, and a dignified bearing, Helper, in his late life, became a classic figure in Washington. For more than twenty-five years before his death he had been engrossed in a project for the construction of a railway connecting the three Americas. But his consistently overwhelming failure at last occasioned a bitterness that made him take his own life, in a Washington rooming-house. The rampant popularity (and censure) of Helper's *Impending Crisis* had made him a social economist of note, but his subsequent writings had little force or durability.

Principal Works: *Historical and Political*—Land of Gold: Reality Versus Fiction, 1855; The Impending Crisis of the South: How to Meet It, 1857; Nojoque: A Question for a Continent, 1867; The Negroes in Negroland. . . . , 1868; Noonday Exigencies, 1871; The Three Americas Railway, 1881.

About: Basset, J. S. Anti-Slavery Leaders of North Carolina (in Johns Hopkins University Studies in Historical and Political Science, 16 ser., no. 6, 1898); Americana August 1911; Charlotte Observer April 18, 1909; Nation March 18, 1909; Washington Times March 9, 1909; Miscellaneous Helper Letters, Manuscript Division, Library of Congress; Prefaces to the works.

HENDERSON, DANIEL McINTYRE (July 10, 1851-September 8, 1906), bookseller and poet, was born in Glasgow, Scotland, the son of Thomas Henderson and Margaret Henderson. As a youth his long walks between Blackhill Locks, where his parents moved in 1861, to the parish school and other social and cultural centers of Glasgow gave him ample opportunity for reflective thought and for early poetical effort. After some experience in a draper's shop and as a bookkeeper he came to America in 1873 and spent the remainder of his life in Baltimore, making a trip to Scotland in 1876 to marry Alice M. Ashcroft. They had ten children.

When leaving Scotland Henderson's considerable number of early poems were destroyed and he resolved to write no more verse, being convinced he was no poet. His resolve was soon disregarded, and in 1874 he had an exquisite lyrical piece, "Flowers Frae Hame," set to music by Archibald Johnson of New York. It soon achieved popularity, and other poems began to appear:

simple, spontaneous lyrics, hymns used in churches, verses of delicate thought and feeling, many in dialect. After his early years in Baltimore as bookkeeper he had become proprietor of the University Book Store near Johns Hopkins University, where in a quiet way he was able to indulge a taste for wide reading and for deep and broad contact with poetry. His two books of verse, *Poems: Scottish and American* and *A Bit Bookie of Verse,* appeared in 1888 and 1906 respectively, and brought some recognition from the public and from contemporary poets.

Principal Works: Poems: Scottish and American, 1888; A Bit Bookie of Verse, 1906.

About: Ross, J. D. Scottish Poets in America.

HENNINGSEN, CHARLES FREDERICK (February 21, 1815-June 14, 1877), soldier and miscellaneous writer, was born in Brussels, Belgium, of Scandinavian descent but early established in British citizenship, and accompanied his parents to England in 1830 for residence.

His father's consent to a military career not being obtainable, Henningsen showed his adventurous nature at nineteen by secretly joining the Carlists in Spain under General Zumalacarregui, obtaining a captaincy of the lancers and being knighted in 1835. He also took part in a campaign in the Caucasus and distinguished himself with the Hungarians as commander at Comorn. Refusing a commission in the Russian guards offered by the Czar Nicholas, he joined the Hungarian revolutionary leader Kossuth, and came to America with him in 1851, serving as his confidential secretary. Here he married a widow, Mrs. Connelly, niece of Senator Berrien of Georgia, and settled in the South. He accompanied the expedition of the filibuster William Walker to Nicaragua in 1856, serving as brigadier-general and contributing considerable stores and munitions. During the Civil War he served in the Confederate forces with the rank of Colonel. He spent his last years in needy circumstances in Washington, D.C., where he died suddenly and was buried in the Congressional Cemetery.

Before nineteen, Henningsen had written at least two noteworthy poems, "The Siege of Missalonghi," and "The Last of the Sophis." An accomplished linguist and scholar, he also did some translating of poetry, but the bulk of his literary work was in prose—records, sometimes in two or more volumes, of his experiences and observations among peoples and nations, of a social, cultural, historical, military and political nature. They were written in a direct, forceful style. Some appeared in several editions and in other languages. Prominent among them were accounts of Russian, Polish, and Finnish literature and an exposé of conditions in Russia.

Principal Works: Scenes From the Belgian Revolution, 1832; The Most Striking Events of a Twelvemonth's Campaign With Zumalacarregui (2 vols.) 1836; Revelations of Russia (2 vols.) 1844; The White Slave: or, The Russian Peasant Girl, 1845; Eastern Europe and the Emperor Nicholas (3 vols.) 1846; Sixty Years Hence, 1847; Analogies and Contrasts (2 vols.) 1848; Kossuth and The Times, 1851; The Past and Future of Hungary, 1852.

About: Roche, J. J. The Story of the Filibusters; Scroogs, W. O. Filibusters and Financiers; Walker, W. The War in Nicaragua.

"HENRY, DANIEL, JR." See HOLMES, HENRY DANIEL

HENRY, PATRICK (May 29, 1736-June 6, 1799), orator and statesman, was born in Hanover County, Va., the son of John Henry, a planter of Scottish birth, and Sarah (Winston) (Syme) Henry, for whom this was the second marriage. Such education as he secured was from tutoring by his father, who had had considerable schooling. At fifteen he was a clerk in a store, and the next year, with his brother as partner, was conducting a general store of his own, which failed. In 1754, at eighteen, he married Sarah Shelton, who died in 1775. In 1757 his house burnt down, and a second venture in storekeeping also ended in failure and a burden of debt. Henry decided to try a new occupation, and after reading law was admitted to the bar in 1760. Here he was a distinct success, and soon became widely known as an orator and politician.

In 1765 he was elected to the House of Burgesses, and after his famous campaign against the stamp tax he became the most prominent figure in public life in Virginia. He was an outstanding member of the first Virginia Convention and of the First and Second Continental Congresses, and gained the distinction of being outlawed by the royal governor, Lord Dunmore. When the Revolution broke out, he was for a time colonel of militia, but resigned, and in 1776 succeeded in office the governor who had outlawed him. His wife having died, in 1777 he married Dorothea Dandridge.

He then retired to his new home in the Blue Ridge Mountains, to practice law, but was recalled to the public service and in 1781 was a member of the Virginia Assembly. Jefferson, hitherto his friend and deputy, was censored by this session of the As-

From a portrait ascribed to T. Sully
PATRICK HENRY

sembly, and Henry joined in the censure; henceforth the two were bitter enemies. Gradually Henry (largely out of his fear of the influence of the Northern states) had become a conservative, opposed to the democratic views of Jefferson and Madison. He was governor again in 1784, and was one of the chief opponents of the Federal Constitution, though it was not until 1798 that he definitely declared himself a member of the Federalist Party. Meanwhile he made repeated efforts to retire, and declined successive offers to be secretary of state, chief justice, senator, and minister to France. Emerging from his western home in 1798, the old man stood once more for election to the Assembly, but before it convened he was dead. On his grave stands the incontrovertible statement, "His fame his best epitaph."

Strictly speaking, Patrick Henry was not a writer, his only published works being transcriptions of his speeches, but it must be remembered that oratory was distinctly a form of literature in the first century of the American republic. Jefferson in the early days said of him: "He appeared to me to speak as Homer wrote"; and there is no doubt that he was one of the greatest orators this country has ever known. In appearance, as in temperament, he was the canny Scotsman—shrewd, courageous, and headstrong. Because his most thrilling phrases have become clichés from over-quotation, we must not forget that they were new and exciting when they were first spoken. "As for me, give me liberty or give me death"—"if this be treason, make the most of it"—such succinct utterances prove that whatever else Patrick Henry may have been, he was certainly a great phrase-maker.

Principal Work: Correspondence and Speeches (ed. by W. W. Henry) 1891.

About: Carlton, M. M. Patrick Henry: Orator of the Revolution; Henry, W. W. Patrick Henry: Life, Correspondence, and Speeches; Morgan, G. The True Patrick Henry; Tyler, M. C. Patrick Henry; Wirt, W. Sketches of the Life and Character of Patrick Henry.

HENRY, WILLIAM WIRT (February 14, 1831-December 5, 1900), lawyer and historian, was born at Red Hill, Charlotte County, Va., the home and burial place of his eminent grandfather, Patrick Henry [*q.v.*]. His father, John Henry, was the youngest son of that statesman and orator, and his mother, Elvira Bruce (McClelland) Henry, noted for beauty and charming character, was a granddaughter of Colonel William Cabell of "Union Hill." He received his M.A. degree at the University of Virginia in 1850 and in 1853 entered upon the practice of law, attaining a high reputation and acting for a number of years as commonwealth attorney. After service in the Civil War he became a leading member of the bar in Richmond, Va., practicing before the state supreme court, and a widely esteemed public figure, serving politically for a few years in the House of Delegates and the state Senate. He married Lucy Gray Marshall, daughter of Colonel James P. Marshall, and had four children.

Henry's outstanding work was the life of his grandfather, *Patrick Henry: Life, Correspondence, and Speeches,* published in 1891 in three volumes, which won an important place in biographical and political history. A number of other historical writings, and addresses before historical and patriotic societies contributed to his eminence. His historical writings, mainly Virginiana, included among other subjects Captain John Smith, the George Rogers Clark expedition, the early history of Virginia, the Scotch-Irish in the South, and Sir Walter Raleigh. He was for years vice-president and later president of the Virginia Historical Society, and also a member of several other historical societies.

Principal Work: Patrick Henry: Life, Correspondence and Speeches. (3 vols.) 1891.

About: Eminent and Representative Men of Virginia; Virginia Magazine of History and Biography January 1901.

HENSON, JOSIAH (June 15, 1789-May 5, 1883), escaped Negro slave and clergyman, the best authenticated prototype of "Uncle Tom" in *Uncle Tom's Cabin,* was born a slave on a farm in Charles County, Md. His father and mother both suffered during his early years from the brutality of the slavery system, and he himself later had both shoulder blades and his arm broken by a neighboring overseer as an outcome of defending his master, Riley, in a drunken brawl. Becoming overseer of the farm, he doubled its yield. Later, when his incompetent owner faced ruin, he conducted twenty slaves to Riley's brother in Kentucky, withstanding strong urgings to escape. Frustrated in attempts to purchase freedom, and on the verge of being sold in New Orleans, he finally escaped with his family to Canada, where he settled in Dresden, Ont. Taught to read by his eldest son, and having a natural gift for oratory, he became a Methodist preacher. Thereafter he worked for the welfare of his race, assisted others to escape, encouraged thrift, and endeavored to found a community and industrial school.

Henson was twice married and had twelve children by his first wife. He made three trips to England in the interests of his race, lecturing and preaching, met many people of eminence, and on his last visit was presented by Queen Victoria with her portrait in a gold frame and honored by thousands at a farewell meeting.

Henson's story of his life, as dictated, was first published as a pamphlet of seventy-six pages in 1849 under the title *The Life of Josiah Henson: Formerly a Slave, Now an Inhabitant of Canada, As Narrated by Himself.* It attracted the attention of Harriet Beecher Stowe who personally heard his story and later referred to him in her *Key to Uncle Tom's Cabin.* Later it appeared in enlarged editions, in 1858 as *Truth Stranger Than Fiction: Father Henson's Story of His Own Life* with an introduction by Mrs. Stowe, and in 1870 with a preface by her and an introductory note by the abolitionist and reformer, Wendell Phillips.

PRINCIPAL WORK: The Life of Josiah Henson, 1849.

ABOUT: Brawley, B. G. Early American Negro Writers; Henson, J. The Life of Josiah Henson; Canadian Magazine November 1907; Journal of Negro History January 1918.

HENTZ, CAROLINE LEE WHITING (June 1, 1800-February 11, 1856), miscellaneous writer, was born at Lancaster, Mass., the youngest of eight children of General John Whitney and Orpah (Whiting) Whitney. Three of her brothers as well as her father were officers in the United States Army. In 1824 she married Nicholas Marcellus Hentz a talented French gentleman, a miniature painter and entomologist, at that time associated with the historian George Bancroft as a teacher in Round Hill School, Northampton. Later he taught and headed various academies throughout the South.

At thirteen Mrs. Hentz was author of a poem, a novel, and a tragedy in five acts. In 1831 she was awarded a prize of $500 for a play *De Lara: or, The Moorish Bride,* based on the Moorish conquest of Spain. This was performed in Philadelphia and Boston, and published in 1843. Two other plays quickly followed, both performed in 1852. In the midst of home making, raising a family of four, and assisting her husband with teaching, she produced stories and poems for magazines, her facility being such that she could turn to writing at any time, undisturbed by conditions or people around her. A popular collection of short stories, *Aunt Patty's Scrap Bag,* appeared in 1846. In 1849 her husband became an invalid and they were compelled to close their school. For the rest of her life Mrs. Hentz became the main support, producing a series of highly popular novels and tales, from one to four volumes being published each year from 1850 until her death. She died at Marianna, Fla., from pneumonia, her strength depleted by long attendance on her husband.

PRINCIPAL WORKS: De Lara: or, The Moorish Bride, 1843; Aunt Patty's Scrap Bag, 1846; Linda: or, The Young Pilot of the Belle Creole, 1850; Rena: or, The Snow Bird, 1851; The Planter's Northern Bride (2 vols.) 1854; Ernest Linwood, 1856; The Banished Son and Other Stories of the Heart, 1856.

ABOUT: Hart, J. S. Female Prose Writers of America; West, G. M. St. Andrews, Florida; Whiting, W. Memoir of Rev. Samuel Whiting.

HERBERT, HENRY WILLIAM ("Frank Forester") (April 7, 1807-May 17, 1858), writer of sporting literature, scholar, and poet, was born in London, the son of the Rev. William Herbert, Dean of Manchester, and grandson of the first Earl of Carnarvan. As a small boy he acquired a real skill in riding and hunting. He attended Eton and was graduated from Cambridge in 1830 with an enviable record in the classics; and in the following year he sailed for the United States.

For about eight years he was Latin and Greek preceptor in the Rev. R. Townsend Huddart's school in New York City, and at the same time he edited the *American Monthly Magazine,* 1833-35, and wrote a series of articles for the *American Turf Register* over the signature "Frank Forester," reserving his own name for more strictly literary efforts. The *Turf* columns were the beginning of his sporting writings, which have maintained a much sturdier reputation than his historical romances, such as *The Brothers: A Tale of the Fronde,* or the purely historical *Knights of England, France and Scotland,* or even his scholarly achievement in the classical vein, *Prometheus and Agamemnon of Aeschylus: Translated Into English Verse.* The "Forester" articles were published as *The Warwick Woodlands: or, Things as They Were There Ten Years Ago* (1845), and a second edition, with the author's illustrations, appeared in 1851. He also wrote a number of sporting novels, among which were *My Shooting Box* and *The Deerstalkers.*

In 1852 came *The Quorndon Hounds: or, A Virginian at Melton Mowbray* and five years later the extensive and still authoritative *Frank Forester's Horse and Horsemanship of the United States and British Provinces of North America,* in two volumes. Moreover he was the author of some very creditable verse and executed numerous pen-and-ink drawings and wood-cuts that were by no means amateurish.

Herbert was twice married: in 1839 to Sarah Barker, by whom he had a son, William George; and fourteen years after her death in 1844, to Adela R. Budlong. Shortly after his second wife left him, he took his own life in the Stevens House in New York.

Talented and ambitious, Herbert leaned heavily on the remnants of his English "aristocracy." He often appeared in sporting dress, with cavalier boots and massive King Charles' spurs. His miscellaneous writings under his own name brought him moderate recognition, but it is as "Frank Forester" that he still lives wherever sporting literature is read.

From a portrait by R. S. Boyer
HENRY WILLIAM HERBERT
("Frank Forester")

Principal Works: The Brothers: A Tale of the Fronde, 1835; The Warwick Woodlands...., 1845; My Shooting Box, 1846; The Deerstalkers, 1849; Prometheus and Agamemnon of Aeschylus: Translated Into English Verse, 1849; Frank Forester's Field Sports of the United States and Brit-Translated Into English Verse, 1849; Frank Forester's Fish and Fishing of the United States and British Provinces of North America (London) 1849 (New York) 1850; The Quorndon Hounds . . . , 1852; Frank Forester's Horse and Horsemanship of the United States and British Provinces of North America (2 vols.) 1857.

About: Hunt, W. S. Frank Forester (Henry William Herbert): A Tragedy in Exile; Judd, D. W. Life and Writings of Frank Forester; see also memoirs in works.

"HERMINE." See ELDER, SUSAN (BLANCHARD)

HERNE, JAMES A. (February 1, 1839-June 2, 1901), actor and playwright, was born James Ahern in Cohoes, N.Y., the son of Patrick Ahern, a narrow and irascible Irishman of Dutch Reformed faith, and Ann (Temple) Ahern, a devout Catholic of dignity and affection. Young James wanted to be a sailor but was taken from school at thirteen and made first an errand boy in his father's hardware store, and then an apprentice in a brush factory. His brother Charles took him to the Albany Museum to see his first play, and as James put it, his "destiny was sealed." In seven years he saved a hundred and sixty-five dollars and lost it all in a barnstorming company. Shortly afterwards he made his first regular appearance at the Adelphi Theatre in Troy, playing in *Uncle Tom's Cabin* for six dollars a week. But this "summit of earthly bliss" became a virtual fiasco, and after changing his name to James A. Herne, he returned to the brush factory.

Following a stock run at the Gayety Theatre in Albany, he signed with John T. Ford, prosperous Washington and Baltimore manager. It was Ford who begged him to make the most of his talents. But Herne, supporting Forrest, the Booths, and other titans, was professionally complacent. In 1866 he married Helen Western; they were soon divorced.

In the middle 'seventies Herne went to San Francisco to become stage director of Thomas Maguire's Baldwin Theatre. Here

JAMES A. HERNE

two influences opened up a new level of achievement: his marriage April 2, 1878, to Katharine Corcoran, a dark-eyed, animated Irish lass, Herne's own dramatic "find," and his acquaintance with David Belasco, then stage manager at the Baldwin, who invited Herne to collaborate with him on *Hearts of Oak.* This piece was the epitome of naturalness, uncluttered by the stock villain and other outworn trappings long in vogue. The Hernes played the leads, and it was a triumph.

The Minute Men (1886) had a kind of conventional and comic glamour, and was a financial set-back. A Boston performance of *Drifting Apart,* which had opened in New York in May 1888, moved Hamlin Garland to introduce Herne to the humanitarian Henry George and a companion group of idealistic intellectuals, among whom was William Dean Howells. With these "radicals" Herne concurred on many points, and having dipped into Ibsen, Tolstoi, and Sudermann, he was beginning to shape his own concept of the social drama in his writing of *Shore Acres* (1888). But before he could get this play produced, he finished *Margaret Fleming,* a tale of marital infidelity, which saw a few nights at the village of Lynn, Mass., and was then buffeted about from manager to manager for about a year. With Garland's aid the Hernes produced it May 4, 1891, in Boston. The *Advertiser* condemned its outspokenness, praised its strong truth, and summing it up as "photography," added, ". . . there is a far higher art—portrait painting. . ." *Margaret Fleming* got a New York hearing in December 1891, but the audience was apathetic. Herne was obliged to take a third-rate managership and then a few small parts in order to make ends meet.

In February 1893 the tide turned sharply. *Shore Acres,* a charming play but not without social comment, opened at the Boston Museum and plunged into a five-year success. William Archer, that scholar of the drama, called *Griffith Davenport* (1899) "original American art," but like *Sag Harbor* (1899), which evolved from an effort to re-vamp *Shore Acres,* it left its audience quite indifferent. Herne turned to campaigning for Bryan, and, broken in health, went back to Long Island a short while before his death.

It is said that Herne had, at times, an expression of tremendous sadness, but there was a latent Irish humor in his eyes, and to his four children he was a maker of good fun. If there is a "low" side to his comic creations, it is a remnant of his old "stock days" and has, in all, a kindly flavor. Herne's critics abhorred "that realism that drenches everything with the commonplace," without recognizing it as the harbinger of a new and strong social drama. Herne saw beyond his contemporaries when he said, "We must not condemn an art or institution because a corrupt civilization has affected it . . . the province of the theatre is not to preach objectively but to teach subjectively." The best of the American playwrights at the beginning of this century are heavily indebted to Herne.

Principal Works: (with David Belasco) Hearts of Oak, 1879; Minute Men, 1886; Drifting Apart, 1888; Shore Acres, 1888; Margaret Fleming, 1891; My Colleen, 1891; Sag Harbor, 1899; Griffith Davenport, 1899.

About: Garland, H. Son of the Middle Border; Hapgood, N. The Stage in America; Herne, J. A. Shore Acres (see Introduction); Moses, M. J. The American Dramatist; Boston Daily Advertiser May 5, 1891; Arena September 1892; New York Tribune June 3, 1901.

HEWITT, JOHN HILL (July 11, 1801-October 7, 1890), journalist, musician, and poet, was born in Maiden Lane, New York City, the eldest son of James Hewitt, a violinist and composer of British birth, and his second wife, Eliza (King) Hewitt, daughter of Sir John King of the Royal British Army. Apprenticed after a common school education to a sign painter he ran away. Later he entered the West Point Military Academy, where he studied music under the bandmaster. Resigning, he entered upon a varied and versatile career in a number of Southern cities, including a brief membership in a theatrical company organized by his father and the study of law

Mainly, however, his efforts were given to teaching music and to journalism, in the course of which he edited the *Republican* in Greenville, S.C., the *Minerva,* the *Visitor,* and the *Clipper* in Baltimore, and the *Capitol* in Washington, D.C., two of which he established. He was twice married, had eleven children, and spent his last years in Baltimore, where he died at eighty-nine as the result of a fall.

Hewitt composed over three hundred songs, among which were "Rock Me to Sleep, Mother," and "Carry Me Back to the Sweet Sunny South," and he wrote the music for many. He has sometimes been called the "father of the American ballad." One of his earliest ballads, "The Minstrel's Return from the War," 1825, won him sudden popularity, but the failure of his brother James, who published it, to consider it worth copyright lost them substantial returns. He also wrote many oratorios, of which "Jephtha" was outstanding, cantatas, operas and plays. Some of his work was produced under the pseudonyms "Eugene Ramon," "Col. Marcus Kennedy," and "Jenks."

He was a contemporary of Edgar Allan Poe, and his "The Song of the Wind" won first prize in a contest over Poe's "The Coliseum" since Poe had already been awarded the prose prize in the same contest and the judges were reluctant to give him both. There was a long-standing dislike between the two men.

Principal Works: Miscellaneous Poems, 1838; Shadows on the Wall: or, Glimpses of the Past, 1877.

About: Howard, J. T. Our American Music; Perine, G. C. The Poets and Verse-Writers of Maryland; Scharf, J. T. History of Baltimore City and County; Musical Quarterly January 1931.

HICKOK, LAURENS PERSEUS (December 29, 1798-May 6, 1888), clergyman and philosopher, was born in Bethel, Conn., the son of Ebenezer Hickok and Polly (Benedict) Hickok. Brought up on a farm, he was graduated from Union College and served for thirteen years in pastorates in Kent and Litchfield, Conn., and eight years each in Western Reserve College and Auburn Theological Seminary as professor of theology. In 1852 he entered Union College as vice-president and professor of mental and moral philosophy, succeeding President Nott in that office in 1866. Two years later he resigned to spend his remaining years in retirement at Amherst, Mass., with his literary pursuits. He died in his ninetieth year, and was buried at his birthplace, Bethel.

Strongly influenced by Kant, Hickok brought a powerful and original mind to the exposition of his system of philosophy, in his earliest and most important work *Rational Psychology,* 1849, analyzing the entire process of knowledge and uniting philosophic reasoning with the broadest theological concepts. Later he applied his reasoning to similar expositions of ethics, cosmology, and man. *The Cambridge History of American Literature* says of him "For sheer intellectual power . . . and for comprehensive grasp of technical philosophy Hickok is easily the foremost figure in American philosophy between the time of Jonathan Edwards and the period of the Civil War." Despite this estimate, his work has long been superseded. In addition to his leading works Hickok also published some sermons and addresses.

Principal Works: Rational Psychology, 1849; A System of Moral Science, 1853; Empirical Psychology, 1854; Rational Cosmology, 1858; Creator and Creation, 1872; Humanity Immortal, 1872; The Logic of Reason, 1875.

About: Bailey, J. M. History of Danbury, Conn.; Congregational Year Book, 1889; American Journal of Psychology July 1908.

HIGGINSON, JOHN (August 6, 1616-December 9, 1708), clergyman, was born at Claybrooke, Leicestershire, England, the son of the Rev. Francis Higginson, a Cambridge graduate, who in 1629 transferred his ministerial services to Salem, Mass., and Anna (Herbert) Higginson. His father died the following year and the fourteen-year old boy, sobered by his responsibility as eldest of eight children, was assisted in his education by Governor Winthrop, Cotton Mather, and others. Among other things he acquired a knowledge of the French and Indian languages, and shorthand. Admitted as freeman at nineteen, he passed more than twenty years in Connecticut, four as chaplain at Saybrook Fort, and after some sojourn at Hartford and New Haven he became a "teacher" and later pastor in the Church of the Rev. Henry Whitfield of Guilford, whose daughter he married. In 1659 he sailed for England, but the ship being driven back to Salem, Mass., by a storm, he remained there instead, and the following year was ordained over the same church his father had founded. He served the community for nearly half a century and rose to one of the leading places among the clergy.

Higginson, whose prominence has been attributed more to his high position and learning than to special ability, prepared nearly two hundred of Thomas Hooker's sermons for the press, and his prefaces appear in a few of Cotton Mather's works.

His own printed works numbered about a dozen and were mostly brief. He held aloof from the witchcraft trials, his own daughter being one of the accused. Of his seven children by his first marriage, a son, Nathaniel, attained prominence as Governor of Fort Saint George, India.

PRINCIPAL WORKS: Our Dying Saviour's Legacy of Peace to His Disciples in a Troublesome World, 1686.

ABOUT: Higginson, J. Our Dying Saviour's Legacy of Peace to His Disciples in a Troublesome World (see Preface); Higginson, T. W. Descendents of the Rev. Francis Higginson; Massachusetts Historical Society Proceedings: 2nd series, Vol. 16, 1902.

HIGGINSON, THOMAS WENTWORTH (December 22, 1823-May 9, 1911), New England "man of letters," was born and grew up in Cambridge, Mass. His father, Stephen Higginson, steward of Harvard College, and his mother, Louisa (Storrow) Higginson, reared him in the cultural traditions of the best New England families. At seventeen he was graduated from Harvard, taught for two years, returned as a graduate student, and in 1847 was graduated with the senior class of the divinity school.

In the same year he married Mary Channing and became pastor of the First Religious Society of Newburyport, Mass. Within two years he had to give up his work because of his radical ideas, foremost of which was his devotion to the anti-slavery cause. He was one of the leaders of the extreme abolition movement, pledged to use whatever means were in his power to promote the dissolution of the Union.

He was called to the "Free Church" in Worcester in 1852. The anti-slavery movement became more pressing with each year and on one occasion Higginson was violently engaged on behalf of the fugitive slaves. In letters to the New York *Tribune* he told of his journey to Kansas for the cause in 1856.

In November 1862, already captain of a fine company of his own raising, he was offered the command of the First Regiment of South Carolina Volunteers, the "first slave regiment mustered into the service of the United States in the Civil War." His book *Army Life in a Black Regiment* is a fascinating account of his adventures with these freed slaves who responded splendidly to his sympathetic training and played an unspectacular though not unimportant part in the war.

Wounded and invalided home, he resigned from the army in 1864 and went with his wife to Newport, R.I. They lived quietly there for thirteen years until her death. During that period he wrote continuously, producing his one novel *Malbone,* in which his wife appears as Aunt Jane, his *Army Life,* two volumes of Harvard Memorial Biographies, *Young Folks History of the United States,* and *Oldport Days,* a delightful collection of sketches inspired by his life in Newport. The versatility of the man was one of his strongest characteristics.

Collection of Frederick H. Meserve
THOMAS WENTWORTH HIGGINSON

After the death of his wife, Higginson went abroad. On his return he settled in Cambridge and in 1879 he married Mary Potter Thacher of Newton, Mass., who gave him two daughters and later wrote the story of his life. This latter period was as busy and even more productive than the former. His friendships with the prominent literary men of his day and his encouragement of younger writers gave color to these years. He served a term in the Massachusetts Legislature (1880-1881), wrote the biography of Margaret Fuller Ossoli, onetime editor of the *Dial,* who had influenced him more than anyone except Emerson, and numerous books and articles. A full bibliography of his writings occupies twenty-six pages in Mary Higginson's biography.

A remarkable combination of the courageous man of action and the true scholar, Higginson in his life and work exemplified his own high ideals. He had a fine critical capacity (though he failed utterly to comprehend Emily Dickinson's poetry!), abundant sympathy, and a delightful sense of humor.

His style is graceful and pleasant but lacks fire. His essays are his best work.

PRINCIPAL WORKS: *Autobiography*—Army Life in a Black Regiment, 1870; Cheerful Yesterdays, 1898. *Biography*—Harvard Memorial Biographies (2 vols.) 1866; Margaret Fuller Ossoli, 1884; Life of Francis Higginson: First Minister in the Massachusetts Bay Colony, 1891; Henry Wadsworth Longfellow (in *American Men of Letters Series*) 1902; John Greenleaf Whittier (in *English Men of Letters Series*) 1902; Life and Times of Stephen Higginson, 1907. *Essays*—Atlantic Essays, 1871; Carlyle's Laugh and Other Surprises, 1909; Oldport Days, 1873. *History*—Young Folks History of the United States, 1875; Larger History of the United States, 1885; A Reader's History of American Literature, 1903. *Letters*—Letters and Journals of Thomas Wentworth Higginson, 1921. *Novel*—Malbone, 1869. *Collected Works*—Writings of Thomas Wentworth Higginson (7 vols.) 1900.

ABOUT: Higginson, M. T. Thomas Wentworth Higginson: The Story of His Life.

HILDRETH, RICHARD (June 28, 1807-July 11, 1865), historian and miscellaneous writer, was born in Deerfield, Mass., the son of the Rev. Hosea Hildreth, professor of mathematics at Phillips Exeter Academy, and of Sarah (McLeod) Hildreth. He was graduated from Phillips Exeter in 1822, and from Harvard in 1826. He then read law, and was admitted to the bar in 1830. For two years he practised in Boston and Newburyport, then became co-editor of the Boston *Daily Atlas*. At the same time he contributed articles to the *Ladies' Magazine*, the *American Monthly Magazine*, and the *New England Magazine*. In 1834 he became part owner of the *Atlas*, but was soon bought out by Caleb Cushing, a prominent politician. For two years thereafter his health obliged him to live in Florida, during which period he wrote his now unreadable, but once widely read novel, *The Slave*, which anticipated the popularity of *Uncle Tom's Cabin*.

On his return north he continued to write editorials for the *Atlas*, and acted as its Washington correspondent in 1837 and 1838. He finally left the paper, through which he had opposed the annexation of Texas and fought for abolition of slavery, because it did not share his zeal for prohibition of liquor.

From 1840 to 1843 Hildreth lived in Demarara, British Guiana (again for reasons of health), and edited two anti-slavery papers there, the *Guiana Chronicle* and the *Royal Gazette*. In 1844 he returned to the United States and married Caroline Neagus.

He then projected a series of books on every phase of life treated from the purely inductive scientific viewpoint; but the first two were so badly received that he abandoned the idea and turned to his history of the United States, which was issued from 1849 to 1852. Van Wyck Brooks (in *The Flowering of New England*) describes him at this time as "a tall, thin, aging man in black, deaf, absorbed, sitting at his table in one of the alcoves [of the Boston Athenaeum], with his books and papers before him, rising from his chair only to consult some work of reference."

The history finished, he went to New York, and from 1855 to 1861 worked on the *Tribune*, harbor of so many of Horace Greeley's New England acquaintances. In 1861 Lincoln appointed him United States consul at Trieste. He resigned, because of illness, in 1864, and the following year died at Florence, where he is buried in the Protestant cemetery.

Besides his books, Hildreth wrote many controversial pamphlets, and translated from the French Dumont's version of Bentham's work on legislation. He was also the author of two campaign biographies of William Henry Harrison.

Hildreth's work was as solid as it was dull. The *Athenaeum* (London) in 1853 characterized him for all time as "solid, level, monotonous, pre-eminently respectable." His history could not be more dry, and it is markedly prejudiced in favor of the Federalists (it was carried only to 1821); but it is valuable because of its careful accuracy. He himself was like his writing, though more vehement and caustic in speech than he ever was in print—"very decided," loved by a few friends because he bore no malice, but

RICHARD HILDRETH

hated by many enemies because he never shirked a controversy. He had absolutely no originality, but he was a highly competent and therefore a useful historian.

PRINCIPAL WORKS: The Slave: or, Memoirs of Archy Moore (novel) 1836 (as The White Slave, 1852; as Archy Moore, 1855); History of Banks, 1837; Banks, Banking, and Paper Currencies, 1840; Despotism in America, 1840; Theory of Morals, 1844; History of the United States, 1849-52; Theory of Politics, 1853; Japan as It Was and Is, 1855.

ABOUT: Watt, F. L. A History of American Magazines; Athenaeum November 12, 1853; Harper's Monthly October 1895.

HILL, FREDERIC STANHOPE (1805-April 7, 1851), actor and playwright, was born in Boston, a descendant of Samuel Hill, an early English settler at Machias, Maine. At twenty-two he inherited a small fortune from his father but quickly lost it when, abandoning the study of law, he engaged in publishing the Boston *Lyceum* and the *Galaxy*. Turning to the stage in 1832 he played Shakespearean and other roles in New York and Boston, also holding the position of stage manager of the Warren Theatre, Boston. In 1828 his health caused his retirement and he acted only occasionally thereafter. His only child, Frederic Stanhope Hill, became a naval officer and author.

Hill manifested an early talent for verse and published a small volume, *The Harvest Festival and Other Poems,* at twenty-one. While acting he wrote two plays, *The Six Degrees of Crime: or, Wine, Women, Gambling, Theft, Murder and the Scaffold,* and *The Shoemaker of Toulouse: or, The Avenger of Humble Life,* both melodramas, which were stock pieces in the theatre for nearly two decades. When the latter was first produced, he played the leading rôle of the profligate, Julio Dormilly. He was also considered an accomplished critic and essayist.

PRINCIPAL WORKS: The Harvest Festival and Other Poems, 1826; The Six Degrees of Crime, 1834; The Shoemaker of Toulouse, 1834.

ABOUT: Brown, T. A. History of the American Theatre; Boston Transcript April 7, 1898.

HILLARD, GEORGE STILLMAN (September 22, 1808-January 21, 1879), editor and miscellaneous writer, was born in Machias, Maine, the son of John and Sarah (Stillman) Hillard. He was instructed by private tutors and attended Derby Academy and the Boston Latin School before entering Harvard, from which he was graduated in 1828 with first honors. While a law student in Northampton, Mass., he taught at George Bancroft's Round Hill School; and after receiving an LL.B. from the Dane Law School in Cambridge he entered a Boston law office and was shortly admitted to the bar. He edited the *Christian Register,* set up a law partnership with Charles Sumner, which was to last over twenty-five years, and began to edit the *Jurist.* In 1835 he was elected to membership in the Massachusetts House of Representatives and the same year was married to Susan Tracy Howe, by whom he had one child.

In 1847 he resigned from membership on the city council and went to Europe. Ten years later he became owner and editor-in-chief of the Boston *Courier*; and at the termination of his appointment as United States Attorney, in 1871, he became a member of the firm of Hillard, Hyde, & Dickinson. Hillard died at Longwood, Mass., following a paralytic stroke.

"The Relation of the Poet to His Age" was Hillard's Phi Beta Kappa oration at Harvard in 1843, and in 1839 he had published his own editing of *The Poetical Works of Edmund Spenser,* winning highly favorable criticism. In 1853 came *Six Months in Italy,* informative and discriminating, occasioned by his European journey of 1847; three years later he began the publication of a series of graded readers, which were subjected to picayune quibbles, as well as to larger and more justifiable charges of unwise selection, etc. He did not live to complete his life of George Ticknor.

Professionally Hillard was a lawyer, but by inclination he was an unpretending man of letters, with a real talent for oratory and an enviable breadth of intellectual friendships.

PRINCIPAL WORKS: Poetical Works of Edmund Spenser, 1839; Six Months in Italy, 1853; school reader series, 1856-.

ABOUT: Brooks, Van W. The Flowering of New England; Howe, M. A. DeW. Memories of a Hostess; Palfrey, F. W. Memoir of the Honorable George S. Hillard, LL.D.

HILLHOUSE, JAMES ABRAHAM (September 26, 1789-January 4, 1841), poet, was born in New Haven, Conn., the eldest son of James Hillhouse of Irish ancestry, who was for nearly twenty years a member of Congress, and for fifty years treasurer of Yale University, and of Rebecca (Woolsey) Hillhouse. Graduated from Yale in 1808, he received his Master's degree in 1811, delivering an oration of such excellence on the "Education of a Poet" that the following year the Phi Beta Kappa society invited him to read a poem at its anniversary. He responded with "The Judgment," a vision of final retribution, which was published in 1821. Two dramas in verse followed, *Demetria,* a romantic tragedy of intrigue written in 1813 but not published until 1839, and *Percy's Masque,* which was inspired by Bishop Percy's ballad, "The Hermit of Warkworth." This was published in London in 1819, and in the United States the following year.

After a visit to England in 1819, Hillhouse entered upon a mercantile career in New York and married Cornelia Lawrence, the eldest daughter of a wealthy merchant of that city. The following year, 1823, he returned to New Haven, where he made his home in a beautiful park-like estate known as Sachem's Wood. Of great culture and refinement, a lover of learning and the fine arts, he gave himself to pursuits of leisure and literature. Among his subsequent literary productions were *Hadad,* a five-act blank verse dramatic poem, his longest and most pretentious; "Sachem's Wood," a short poem; and two orations, one being on Lafayette. In 1839 most of his work was republished in two slender volumes entitled *Dramas, Discourses, and Other Pieces.*

The work of Hillhouse received great praise from critics of his day. Although conventional, it was marked by beauty, sustained dignity, and cloquence, and in *Demetria,* in particular, there was notable purity of style.

Principal Works: Percy's Masque, 1819; The Judgment, 1821; Hadad, 1825; Sachem's Wood, 1838; Demetria, 1839.

About: Everest, C. W. The Poets of Connecticut; Hillhouse, J. A. Sachem's Wood (see Notes); Hillhouse, M. P. Historical and Genealogical Collections Relating to the Descendents of Rev. James Hillhouse.

HIRST, HENRY BECK (August 23, 1813-March 30, 1874), poet and lawyer, was born and passed his life in Philadelphia. He was the son of Thomas Hirst, a merchant of some prominence, and Emma (Beck) Hirst. A half-brother, William L. Hirst, took him into his law office at thirteen, but a merchandising venture and other interruptions delayed his admittance to the bar until 1843. He gave his leisure time to literature, contributing frequent poems to the *Ladies' Companion,* the *Southern Literary Messenger,* and *Graham's,* some of these being signed "Anna Maria Hirst." He also served on the staff of two Philadelphia newspapers.

An early interest in ornithology and other natural history led to his publication in 1843 of *The Book of Caged Birds,* a small volume intended to be of practical use to bird lovers and including, in addition to a few quoted poems, three of his own. His first collection

From a daguerreotype

HENRY BECK HIRST

of poems, *The Coming of the Mammoth,* was published in 1845, and three years later *Endymion* appeared, an ambitious effort in four cantos based upon the Greek legend, and produced, according to his declaration, before his perusal of Keats' poem. In 1849 *The Penance of Roland,* a poetical romance with a proem dedicated to his wife, appeared.

Hirst's poems were in their day highly popular and widely copied. He was for a time one of the close companions of Edgar Allan Poe and there have been attempts to ascribe to him some of Poe's poems. He himself always claimed the authorship of Poe's "The Raven." His use of absinthe and other dissipations soon clouded his genius; a contemporary wrote of him that by 1852 he showed marked signs of decay in his faculties. His inordinate self-esteem gave way to the illusions of insanity and made him an object of pity in the streets of his native city. He was finally confined in the Blockley Almshouse, where he died at the age of sixty.

Principal Works: The Book of Caged Birds, 1843; The Coming of the Mammoth, 1845; Endymion, 1848; The Penance of Roland, 1849.

About: Oberholtzer, E. P. The Literary History of Philadelphia; Sartain, J. The Reminiscences of a Very Old Man; Watts, H. L. The Life and Writings of Henry Beck Hirst (Master's thesis, Columbia Univ. 1926).

HITCHCOCK, ETHAN ALLEN (May 18, 1798-August 5, 1870), soldier and miscellaneous writer, was born at Vergennes, Vt., the son of Samuel Hitchcock, a United States Circuit Judge, and Lucy Caroline

(Allen) Hitchcock, daughter of the Revolutionary patriot Ethan Allen. Graduating from West Point Military Academy in 1817, he remained for many years as instructor, in 1829 becoming commander of cadets. In 1841 the War Department assigned him to investigate widespread frauds under the Indian Removal Act of 1830, resulting in so trenchant a report that it was suppressed. He served in the Florida and Mexican wars, and as commander of the Pacific Division he broke up William Walker's filibustering expedition into Mexico. In 1855 he resigned, retiring to St. Louis, but again offered his services during the Civil War, and as major general of volunteers and in other high capacities he gave such important assistance to the Government at Washington that he was one of the last to be mustered out. He married Martha Rinds Nicholls in 1868 and died two years later in the South.

Hitchcock was a man of high scholarly attainments, as well as of sterling character. He wrote extensively and vigorously on many matters, professional, controversial, official, and biographical. He entered deeply into philosophical study, also, and published his first book *The Doctrines of Spinoza and Swedenborg Identified* in 1846, followed in 1847 by *Remarks Upon Alchemy and the Alchemists,* and by further volumes upon Swedenborg, Shakespeare, Spencer, and Dante. He kept a journal during his entire life, and these records were the source of two more recently published volumes, *Fifty Years in Camp and Field,* 1909, and *A Traveler in Indian Territory,* 1930.

Principal Works: The Doctrines of Spinoza and Swedenborg Identified, 1846; Swedenborg: A Hermetic Philosopher, 1858; Remarks on the Sonnets of Shakespeare, 1865; Spencer's Poem Entitled "Colin Clouts Come Home Againe" Explained, 1865; Notes on the "Vita Nuova" and Minor Poems of Dante, 1866; Fifty Years in Camp and Field, 1909; A Traveler in Indian Territory, 1930.

About: Hitchcock, E. H. Fifty Years in Camp and Field (see Biographical notes); Hitchcock, E. H. A Traveler in Indian Territory (see Introduction); Hitchcock, M. L. J. The Genealogy of the Hitchcock Family; The Association of Graduates of the United States Military Academy: Annual Reunion, 1871.

HITCHCOCK, W. See MURDOCH, FRANK HITCHCOCK

HITTELL, JOHN SHERTZER (December 25, 1825-March 8, 1901), journalist and statistician, was the son of Dr. Jacob Hittell, for thirty-four years a practictioner in Hamilton, Ohio, and Catherine (Shertzer) Hittell, and was the older brother of Theodore Henry Hittell [*q.v.*]. He was born in Jonestown, Lebanon County, Pa. Graduated from Miami University in 1843, he studied law, and in 1849 joined the gold rush to California, walking some 1200 miles of the way. After a few years he made his permanent home in San Francisco, in 1853 entering upon a journalistic career of nearly thirty years on the *Alta California.* He never married.

In addition to extensive work as a statistician, on guide books and almanacs, and in connection with the resources of California, which he studied at first hand, he wrote *A History of the City of San Francisco, and Incidentally of the State of California,* noted, as were all his historical writings, for its accuracy. For many years he was historian of the Society of California Pioneers. Among his other writings, marked by unorthodoxy and independent thought, were *The Evidences Against Christianity, A History of the Mental Growth of Mankind,* and *Reform or Revolution.*

Principal Works: The Evidences Against Christianity (2 vols.) 1856; The Resources of California, 1863; The Commerce and Industries of the Pacific Coast, 1882; A History of the Mental Growth of Mankind (4 vols.) 1889-93, A History of the City of San Francisco, and Incidentally of the State of California, 1878; Reform or Revolution, 1900.

About: General Catalogue of the Graduates and Former Students of Miami University, 1899-1909; Overland April 1901; Quarterly of the Society of California Pioneers March 31, 1925.

HITTELL, THEODORE HENRY (April 5, 1830-February 23, 1917), lawyer and historian, was the son of Dr. Jacob Hittell, a descendent of Peter Hittell who came from Bavaria in 1720, and Catherine (Shertzer) Hittell. He was born in Marietta, Pa., but was brought up in Hamilton, Ohio, where his father moved the following year. Entering Miami University (Oxford, Ohio) in 1845, he completed his collegiate courses at Yale in 1849. After a few years of law practice he joined his older brother John Shertzer Hittell [*q.v.*] in San Francisco in 1855. Six years of journalistic work on the San Francisco *Bulletin* and the *Daily Times* followed, the reporting of law news being one of his features; later he became editor. In 1862 he entered on the practice of civil law, acquiring both honor and a large fortune. His last twenty years were given mostly to literary work, his vigor of mind and body being retained to the end. Among the four children born of his marriage in 1858 to Elise Christine Wiehe was the artist, Charles J. Hittell.

For over half a century Hittell carried on the literary work that he loved. His first book *The Adventures of James Capen Adams,* resulted from the narrative told him by a grizzly bear hunter of that name whose acquaintance he had made through his interest in an animal show. He wrote many law pamphlets and four legal works, *The General Laws of California,* being most widely known. His major work, however, was the *History of California* in four volumes, on which he spent about twenty-five years, searching and copying for this purpose many priceless documents in the California archives, which were afterwards burned in the fire of 1906.

PRINCIPAL WORKS: The Adventures of James Capen Adams, 1860; The General Laws of California, 1865; Supplement to the Codes and Statutes of the State of California, 1880; History of California (4 vols.) 1885-97.

ABOUT: In Memoriam: Theodore Henry Hittell (California Academy of Sciences, 1918); Record of the Graduate Members of the Class of 1849 of Yale College; Sunset February 1914.

HODGE, CHARLES (December 27, 1797-June 19, 1878), theologian, was a grandson of Peter Hodge who emigrated from Ireland about 1730, and the son of Hugh Hodge, a prominent physician and a surgeon in the Revolution. He was born in Philadelphia. His mother, the beautiful Mary (Blanchard) Hodge from Boston, of Huguenot descent, was left a widow with the six-months old infant and his two-year old brother Hugh Lenox Hodge, who later became an eminent surgeon. Despite financial difficulties she succeeded in putting both of the boys through college, Charles graduating from Princeton College in 1815 and from the Theological Seminary in 1819. Early marked out by Dr. Archibald Alexander of the seminary for a professional position, he was engaged the next year as an assistant and with the exception of two years spent in Europe passed the remainder of his life there, first as professor of Oriental and Biblical literature, and from 1840 as professor of theology. He was twice married, his first wife being Sarah Bache, a great-granddaughter of Benjamin Franklin, by whom he had eight children.

Hodge was an uncompromising theologian of the Calvinistic type and his doctrines, setting the distinguishing mark for Princeton theology, long stood at the head of contemporaneous theological and ecclesiastical thought. He was an outstanding influence in the Presbyterian Church, and held in honor abroad, particularly among the theologians of Scotland. In personality he was one of the kindliest of men, "loving little children so well that he made a special chink in his logic to save them from the general damnation."

The influence of Hodge was greatly extended by his voluminous writings for the *Biblical Repertory,* later known as the *Biblical Repertory and Princeton Review,* which he founded in 1825 and edited for more than forty years. His first book *A Commentary on the Epistle to the Romans* was published in 1835 and went through nineteen editions by 1880. The most outstanding of his works was *Systematic Theology,* published in three volumes in 1872-73. His exposition in writing and in the classroom was distinguished by exceptional clearness, and he showed remarkable consistency in maintaining the same doctrines unchanged throughout his life; this he carried to the extreme length of being judged almost impervious to newness. A son, Dr. Archibald Hodge, entered the seminary as associate to his father in 1877, succeeding him at his death as professor of theology.

PRINCIPAL WORKS: A Commentary on the Epistle to the Romans, 1835; The Constitutional History of the Presbyterian Church in the United States (2 vols.) 1839-40; The Way of Life, 1841; Essays and Reviews (selected from the Princeton Review) 1867; Systematic Theology (3 vols.) 1872-73; Discussions on Church Polity, 1878; Conference Papers, 1879.

ABOUT: Discourses Commemorative of the Life and Work of Charles Hodge (Princeton Theological Seminary); Hodge, A. A. The Life of Charles Hodge; Proceedings Connected With the Semi-Centennial Commemoration of the Professorship of Rev. Charles Hodge; Salmond, C. A. Princetonia: Charles and A. A. Hodge; Nation November 25, 1880.

HOFFMAN, CHARLES FENNO (February 7, 1806-June 7, 1884), poet, novelist, and editor, was born in New York City, the son of Josiah Ogden Hoffman and his second wife, Maria (Fenno) Hoffman. His father was a noted lawyer, and his half-brothers became distinguished in the same profession. As a child Hoffman was sent to an academy at Poughkeepsie, from which he ran away because of brutal treatment; after this he was taught at home. When he was eleven an accident caused the amputation of his right leg. By over-compensation he trained himself as an athlete, and indeed when he went to Columbia in 1821 he paid so much more attention to sports than to his studies that he was "flunked out" in 1824. He was sent to Albany to study law, and was admitted to the bar in 1827, but his practice of his profession was merely perfunctory, and he spent most of his time writing for the newspapers. In 1830 he abandoned the law altogether, and with Charles King became co-editor of the New York *American,* to which he had been a contributor.

For a few months in 1833 he was editor of the newly founded *Knickerbocker Magazine.* He left to go on a long journey by horseback in the Northwest Territory, the sketches he wrote for the *American* being published later as his first book. From 1835 to 1837 he edited the *American Monthly Magazine,* in which his unfinished novel, *Vanderlyn,* appeared. In 1837 Columbia gave him an honorary M.A. degree. He then edited the New York *Mirror,* and for a short time was with Horace Greeley on the first *New Yorker.* In 1841 he became chief clerk to the surveyor of customs of the Port of New York, and in 1843 and 1844 was deputy surveyor, but lost his job for political reasons. Reverting to journalism, he joined the staff of the *Evening Gazette,* and in 1847 was editor of the *Literary World.*

But his career was near its close. In 1848 he suffered an attack of mental illness, and though he was discharged as cured and went to work as a clerk in the consular bureau of the State Department, he soon relapsed. In 1850 he was committed to the State Hospital in Harrisburg, Pa., where he lived for thirty-four years more: happy, amiable, and sociable, but completely insane.

Poe, who was not given to glowing praise of his literary contemporaries, called Hoffman chivalric, affable, and "a gentleman by birth, education, and instinct." His gentle face, framed in whiskers, with mild eyes peering behind spectacles, was an index of his cordial yet dignified personality while he was in his right mind. As a writer, his great success was his novel, *Greyslaer,* based on a "triangle" murder case in Kentucky. Another novel, *The Red Spur of Ramapo,* was accidentally burnt by a servant and never rewritten. His verse is light and musical, full of a naïve love of nature. Unkind critics called him an imitator of Thomas Moore—a remark which he took goodnaturedly by entitling his next book of poems *The Echo: or, Borrowed Notes for Home Circulation.* Since he lost his mind in early middle age, it is quite possible that under happier circumstances he would have followed up the highly successful novel which first brought him fame, but as it is, he is now practically forgotten.

After a portrait by H. Inman
CHARLES FENNO HOFFMAN
1834

PRINCIPAL WORKS: A Winter in the West, 1835; Wild Scenes in the Forest and Prairie, 1839; Greyslaer: A Romance of the Mohawk, 1839; The Vigil of Faith and Other Poems, 1842; The Echo: or, Borrowed Notes for Home Circulation, 1844; Love's Calendar, Lays of the Hudson, and Other Poems, 1847; The Pioneers of New York, 1848; Poems (ed. by E. F. Hoffman) 1873.

ABOUT: Burns, H. F. Charles Fenno Hoffman; Hoffman, C. F. Poems (see Sketch by W. C. Bryant in 1873 ed.); Godey's Magazine May to November 1846; Magazine of American History August 1884; New York Herald June 9, 1884.

HOGAN, JOHN (January 2, 1805-February 5, 1892), miscellaneous writer, was the son of Thomas and Mary (Field) Hogan. Born at Mallow, County Cork, Ireland, his mother died when he was ten and the following year his father brought him to Baltimore, Md., where he was apprenticed to a shoemaker. In his early twenties he spent several years as an itinerant Methodist preacher, but later engaged in merchandising in Illinois, becoming bank president and land commissioner, and serving in the state legislature. Removing to St. Louis in 1845, he entered into partnership in the grocery business. In 1857 he was appointed postmaster, and in 1864 was elected to Congress.

A series of articles on the resources of St. Louis published in the *Missouri Republican* became the basis of his book *Thoughts About the City of St. Louis: Its Commerce and Manufactures, Railroads, &c.,* 1854. Its great popularity led to its circulation abroad, and it was at least partially responsible for the large Irish and German immigration to that city. In 1860 he published in the

Christian Advocate a series of sketches entitled "History of Methodism in the West."

PRINCIPAL WORK: Thoughts About the City of St. Louis, 1854.

ABOUT: Boogher, S. H. Recollections of John Hogan by His Daughter; Hyde, W. & Conard, H. L. Encyclopedia of the History of St. Louis.

HOLBROOK, JOSIAH (1788-June 17, 1854), educator and lecturer, was born in Derby, Conn., the son of Col. Daniel Holbrook, a prosperous farmer, and Anne (Hitchcock) Holbrook. He was graduated from Yale College in 1810; shortly afterwards conducted a private school in Derby; and in May 1815 was married to Lucy Swift. About four years later he established a not-too-successful industrial school on his father's farm, and then an agricultural seminary, likewise shortly abandoned. His lectures on geology, natural history, etc., in which he urged his village audiences to start their own little collections, were the modest beginnings of the American lyceum. He outlined the aims of this institution, in the *American Journal of Education* for October 1826: mutual intellectual improvement for adults, advanced training for teachers in service, and the establishment of museums and libraries.

Holbrook designed and supervised the manufacture of many of the illustrative devices used in the lyceums; in 1830 he began to publish his *Scientific Tracts Designed for Instruction and Entertainment and Adapted to Schools, Lyceums, and Families*; and in 1832 he set up a short-lived weekly, the *Family Lyceum.* His Lyceum Village established at Berea, Ohio, was, in the end, a failure, and his plans for a similar experiment in the East were never put to a test. Holbrook's scant writings were largely practical educational aids which provided some of the initial impetus for the democratic and multiform lecture movement that was to furrow the intellectual landscape for the next fifty years.

PRINCIPAL WORKS: Scientific Tracts. . . , 1830-; A Familiar Treatise on the Fine Arts: Painting, Sculpture and Music, 1833.

ABOUT: Brooks, Van W. Flowering of New England; Dexter, F. B. Biographical Sketches of the Graduates of Yale College: Vol. 6; National Intelligencer (Washington, D.C.) June 23, 1854.

HOLLAND, EDWIN CLIFFORD (c.1794-September 11, 1824), verse writer, was born in Charleston, S.C., his father John Holland having come there from Wilmington, N.C. His mother, Jane (Hogan) Holland, was the widow of Abraham Marshall of East Florida. After studying law he entered journalism, becoming editor of the Charleston *Times.*

Holland found expression for some of his early efforts in writing in the *Port Folio,* and in articles in local papers signed "Orlando." His volume *Odes, Naval Songs, and Other Occasional Poems,* 1813, marked the beginning of Romantic poetry in South Carolina. As one of the group of Charleston dramatists characterizing the period he contributed a dramatization of Byron's *Corsair,* a melodrama skillfully rendered in blank verse, which was produced in Charleston in 1818. The authorship of Benjamin Elliott's *Refutation of the Calumnies Circulated Against the Southern and Western States Respecting the Institution and Existence of Slavery,* published anonymously in 1822, was wrongly attributed to him for a time.

PRINCIPAL WORKS: Odes, Naval Songs, and Other Occasional Poems, 1813; Corsair, 1818.

ABOUT: Quinn, A. H. History of the American Drama From the Beginning to the Civil War.

HOLLAND, JOSIAH GILBERT (July 24, 1819-October 12, 1881), editor and miscellaneous writer, was born in Belchertown, Mass., the son of Harrison and Anna (Gilbert) Holland. The father was a mechanic and inventor, always poor and shiftless. The family moved around to various towns, in 1820 settling in Northampton, where the boy, who had already worked in factories, went to high school, but broke down and had to leave under the strain of studying and earning his living. For a while he did all sorts of odd jobs, took daguerreotypes, taught, ran a writing school, and finally in 1840 started to study medicine in a doctor's office. He received his M.D. degree in 1843 at the Berkshire Medical College, Pittsfield, Mass., but nature had never intended him to be a physician, and his attempts to secure a practice in Springfield failed completely.

In 1845 he married Elizabeth Luna Chapman, by whom he had one son and two daughters. He eked out his practically nonexistent medical income by writing for the *Knickerbocker Magazine,* and founded the *Bay State Weekly Courier,* which failed in six months. He then gave up any attempt to practice medicine and taught school in Richmond, Va. In 1848 he became superintendent of schools in Vicksburg, Miss., and completely reorganized the public school system there. But by 1850 he was back in Massachusetts, as co-editor with Samuel Bowles of the Springfield *Republican.* At various times he was sole editor, and he never completely deserted the paper, but in

Collection of Frederick H. Meserve
J. G. HOLLAND

1857 he sold out his financial interest. By this time he was both wealthy and famous in consequence of his "human interest" writings on the *Republican,* later collected into books. He was also very much in demand as a lyceum lecturer.

In 1868 and 1869 he traveled in Europe, and on his return became co-editor and co-founder of *Scribner's Monthly,* which in 1881 became the *Century Magazine.* He was to have been sole editor thereafter, but died just before the first number appeared under the new name. From 1870 Holland lived in New York, and for a long time was president of the Board of Education.

Few men have been so popular in their lifetime and so completely forgotten immediately after their death. His compound of sentimentality and didacticism was exactly suited to his period. His facile and most undistinguished verse won him another large public. It is no wonder that many of his readers took it for granted that he was a minister. His early work was published under the pseudonym of "Timothy Titcomb," which somehow seems to fit him better than does his own name. He was a sort of combination of Frank Crane and Lloyd C. Douglas, with overtones of Edgar Guest. The full flavor of J. G. Holland, both in style and subject, may be seen from a single verse from one of his best-known poems:

> Heaven is not gained at a single bound,
> But we build the ladder by which we rise
> From the lowly earth to the vaulted skies,
> And we mount to its summit round by round.

PRINCIPAL WORKS: History of Western Massachusetts, 1855; The Bay-Path: A Tale of Colonial Life, 1857; Timothy Titcomb's Letters to Young People: Single and Married, 1858; Bitter Sweet: A Poem in Dramatic Form, 1858; Gold Foil Hammered From Popular Proverbs, 1859; Miss Gilbert's Career, 1860; Lessons in Life, 1861; Talks to the Joneses, 1863; Plain Talks on Familiar Subjects, 1865; Life of Abraham Lincoln, 1866; Katrinka: Her Life and Mine in a Poem, 1867; The Marble Prophecy and Other Poems, 1872; Arthur Bonnicastle, 1873; Garnered Sheaves (poems) 1873; The Mistress of the Manse (poem) 1874; Sevenoaks, 1875; Every-Day Topics, 1876 and 1882; Nicholas Minturn, 1877; The Puritan's Guest and Other Poems, 1881.

ABOUT: Plunkett, H. M. Josiah Gilbert Holland; Century Magazine December 1881; New York Tribune October 13, 1881; Springfield Republican October 13, 1881.

HOLLEY, MARIETTA ("Josiah Allen's Wife") (July 16, 1836-March 1, 1926), humorist and essayist, was born near Adams, in Jefferson County, N.Y., the daughter of John Milton Holley and Mary (Taber) Holley. Over the signature "Jemyma" she wrote some rather adolescent verse for an Adams newspaper; and, later, articles for the *Christian Union* and the *Independent.*

Her first book, *My Opinions and Betsy Bobbet's: By Josiah Allen's Wife* (1873), was commissioned by the American Book Company after the appearance of a dialect sketch in *Peterson's Magazine.* In this first volume "Josiah Allen's Wife" set the tone that was to be sustained through the whole Samantha series—at the Philadelphia Centennial, the Chicago World's Fair, the Saratoga races, and round the world—the imperturbable and practical Samantha and the acquiescent Josiah, under a thin and inviting gloss of homely humor, make an avowed attempt to better the conditions of society. Both Susan B. Anthony and Frances E. Willard valued Miss Holley's pleasant propaganda in the cause of woman's suffrage and temperance. Other incidental volumes which appeared during her forty years of writing for print were: *Miss Jones' Quilting, Tirzah Ann's Summer Trip, The Widder Doodle's Love Affair,* and an illustrated poem, *The Mormon Wife.*

Miss Holley died in her ninety-first year at her home in Jefferson County, N.Y., where she had spent the greater part of her life. The crude vernacular of her writings has lost some of the tang which her contemporaries found in it; and the pious passages must always have been dull; yet in fairness to her literary position it should be observed that her books went into numerous European translations and that the *Critic* ventured to state that she "has entertained as large an audience . . . as has been entertained by the humor of Mark Twain."

PRINCIPAL WORKS: My Opinions and Betsy Bobbet's: By Josiah Allen's Wife, 1873; Josiah Allen's Wife: Samantha at the Centennial, 1877; My Wayward Partner, 1880; Sweet Cicely: or, Josiah Allen as a Politician, 1885; Samantha at Saratoga, 1887; Miss Jones' Quilting, 1887; Samantha Among the Brethren, 1890; Samantha on the Race Problem, 1892; Tirzah Ann's Summer Trip, 1892; Samantha at the World's Fair, 1893; The Widder Doodle's Love Affair, 1893; Josiah's Alarm, 1893; Samantha in Europe, 1895; Round the World With Josiah Allen's Wife, 1899; Josiah Allen on the Woman Question, 1914.

ABOUT: Child, H. Gazetteer of Jefferson County, N. Y.; Critic January 1905; Outlook March 10, 1926; New York Times March 2, 1926.

HOLLEY, MARY (AUSTIN) (October 30, 1784-August 2, 1846), traveler and author of the first book published on Texas, was born in New Haven, Conn., the daughter of Elijah Austin, hero of Bunker Hill and prominent merchant, and Esther (Phelps) Austin. She attended New Haven schools. In 1805 she was married to the Rev. Horace Holley, who, after serving almost ten years at the Hollis Street Church, Boston, became president of Transylvania University at Lexington, Ky. By 1824, however, Dr. Holley's hard-thinking liberalism was very audibly opposed, and after a stay in Louisiana, he and his wife left the "ever-smelling, violet-scented South, alluring but to destroy," and set sail for New York. He was stricken with yellow fever and died during the voyage.

Amost immediately Mrs. Holley began the writing of *A Discourse on the Genius and Character of the Reverend Horace Holley, LL.D.: President of Transylvania University;* and she journeyed to Washington to secure subscribers to the volume. Becoming bored by another taste of New Orleans' "lazy luxuriance," she set out, in the fall of 1831, on a three-day voyage to a Texas colony which had been founded by Stephen Austin, a distant relative. The communal unit, the personalities, and the surrounding countryside all immeasurably interested her and became the ingredients of her letters published under the title *Texas: Observations, Historical, Geographical, and Descriptive* . . . , the very earliest book on this subject.

Mrs. Holley lobbied in Washington for annexation of the new state, made subsequent journeys to Austin's colony; and wrote, in addition to an unfinished biography of Stephen Austin, a further account of *Texas,* more systematic and more extensive than her earlier volume. These first-hand observations on a frontier that was about to make startling history have a very obvious literary value.

PRINCIPAL WORKS: A Discourse on the Genius and Character of the Reverend Horace Holley . . . , 1828; Texas: Observations, Historical, Geographical . . . , 1833; Texas, 1835.

ABOUT: Hatcher, M. A. Mary Austin Holley: Her Life and Her Works; prefaces to the works.

HOLLISTER, GIDEON HIRAM (December 14, 1817-March 24, 1881), lawyer and historian, was born at Washington, Conn., the son of Gideon Hollister and Harriet (Jackson) Hollister, of Colonial stock. At Yale College, from which he was graduated in 1840, he was class poet and editor of the *Yale Literary Magazine.* He entered upon the practice of law in which he excelled in cross examination, residing variously at Woodbury, Bridgeport, and Litchfield. He attained some political influence in the state, and held office as clerk of the county court, in the state senate, and as minister to Haiti in 1868-69.

Hollister's first book, *Mount Hope: or, Philip, King of the Wamapanoags,* an historical romance of Connecticut, of which his maturer judgment disapproved as too florid in style, was published in 1851. A two-volume *History of Connecticut* . . . , 1855, brought him favorable notice and stands as authoritative and valuable, despite certain shortcomings. Among his other works was *Thomas à Becket,* a tragic poem dramatized and played by Edwin Booth, which was published in 1866 together with a poem "Andersonville," of Civil War popularity, and other verse. His most successful work was a posthumously published historical and autobiographical novel *Kinley Hollow,* aimed at New England Puritanism.

PRINCIPAL WORKS: Mount Hope, 1851; History of Connecticut, 1855; Thomas à Becket, 1866; Kinley Hollow, 1882.

ABOUT: Case, L. W. Hollister Family in America; Kilbourn, D. C. Bench and Bar of Litchfield County, Conn.; (Yale College) Historical Record of the Class of 1840.

"HOLM, SAXE." See JACKSON, HELEN MARIA (FISKE) HUNT

HOLMES, ABIEL (December 24, 1763-June 4, 1837), Congregational clergyman and historian, father of Oliver Wendell Holmes [*q.v.*], was born at Woodstock, Conn., the son of David and Temperance (Bishop) Holmes. He was graduated from Yale College in 1783; two years later he was ordained, but his ministry in the Congregational Church in Midway, Ga., interrupted by a period of tutoring at Yale, ended in June 1791. The following year he was installed in the First Church in Cambridge; and in 1795 came the death of both his wife, Mary Stiles Holmes, to whom he had been married only five years, and her father, Ezra Stiles, president of Yale College, who bequeathed to Holmes forty volumes of priceless manuscripts, which Dr. Stiles had collected with infinite diligence. These papers were excellent material for his *Life of Ezra Stiles, D.D., LL.D.*, and the core of his most significant literary achievement, *American Annals: or, A Chronological History of America From Its Discovery in MCCCCXCII to MDCCCVI.* In two volumes Holmes had made the first systematic attempt at a comprehensive American history; it was an accumulation of bald facts but its archival importance was obvious. His other writings—addresses, sermons, and possibly a group of poems signed "Myron" and included in *A Family Tablet* (1796)—were of only passing interest.

In 1801 Holmes was married to Sarah Wendell, and the fourth of their five children was Oliver Wendell Holmes. Abiel Holmes was a member of historical and learned societies, and for his authorship of the *Annals* might easily be called America's first substantial historiographer.

Principal Works: The Life of Ezra Stiles, D.D., LL. D., 1798; American Annals: or, A Chronological History of America. . . , 1805.

About: Brooks, Van W. Flowering of New England; Collections of the Massachusetts Historical Society: Ser. 3, Vol. 7; Boston Daily Advertiser June 6, 1837.

HOLMES, DANIEL HENRY (July 16, 1851-December 15, 1908), poet, was born in New York City, but was the son of a New Orleans merchant, Daniel Henry Holmes, and of his English wife Eliza Maria (Kerrison) Holmes. From 1852 the family spent their summers at Holmesdale, near Covington, Ky.; but in 1857 the father, a strong Southern sympathizer through an Indianan by birth, feeling a national rupture near, sent his sons to school in France. Henry was educated at Tours and Paris, and then sent to Manchester to be trained for his father's business. In 1869 he went to New Orleans for that purpose, but finding himself unsuited to a mercantile career, and the family being well off, he was permitted instead to go to Cincinnati to study law. He was admitted to the bar in 1872, but devoted far more time to music and literature than to legal matters. In 1883 he married Rachel Gaff, and spent the next year in Europe with her. In 1890 his father gave Holmesdale to him, but until 1904 he spent most of his time abroad. He died suddenly, at Hot Springs, Va., where he had gone for the Christmas holidays, and was buried in Cincinnati.

Holmes's first and most important volume was published under the name of "Daniel Henry, Jun.," and it was the Portland, Maine, publisher, Thomas B. Mosher, who discovered the real identity of the author and made the poems known to the public. These lyrics are written on the theme of twenty-four familiar nursery rhymes, and are marked by originality and quaintness. He never refound their charm in his later verses.

Principal Works: Under a Fool's Cap, 1884; A Pedlar's Pack, 1906; Hempen Homespun Songs, 1906.

About: Holmes, D. H. Under a Fool's Cap (see Foreword by T. B. Mosher and Critical Essay by N. Roe in 1910 ed.); Townsend, J. W. Kentucky in American Letters; Bibelot May 1910; Century Magazine February 1914; Cincinnati Enquirer December 16, 1908.

HOLMES, MARY JANE (HAWES) (April 5, 1825-October 6, 1907), novelist, was born at Brookfield, Mass. Her father Preston Hawes, and her uncle Rev. Joel Hawes, were men of high intellect. Her mother, Fanny (Olds) Hawes, imparted to her a love of poetry, romance, and the beautiful. She was a precocious, imaginative child, fond of her own companionship and of creative fancies. At three she attended school and at six studied grammar. She taught school at thirteen and at fifteen saw her first productions in print. In 1849 she married Daniel Holmes, a lawyer of Brockton, N.Y. They were childless, and she spent much of her time in extensive travel and in writing. She died at Brockton after a few days' illness.

Mrs. Holmes' novels covered over a half century of writing, from *Tempest and Sunshine,* 1854, to *The Abandoned Farm and Connie's Mistake,* published in 1905. During this time thirty-nine novels were published, many in paper covers, the sales aggregating over two million copies. Although one of the most popular novelists of her period, her books possessed no literary merit, but they had wide appeal through such intrinsic qualities as sincerity, naturalness, sympathy, high ideals, and moral tone.

Principal Works: Tempest and Sunshine, 1854; The English Orphans, 1855; The Homestead on the Hillside, 1856; Lena Rivers, 1856; Dora Deane, 1858; Hugh Worthington, 1865; Ethelyn's Mistake, 1869; Daisy Thornton, 1878; Queenie Hetherton, 1883; Mrs. Hallam's Companion, 1894; Dr. Hathern's Daughter, 1895; The Tracy Diamonds, 1899; Rena's Experiment, 1904; The Abandoned Farm and Connie's Mistake, 1905.

ABOUT: Willard, F. E. & Livermore, M. A. A Woman of the Century; Nation October 10, 1907.

HOLMES, OLIVER WENDELL (August 29, 1809-October 7, 1894), essayist, poet, teacher, and physician, was born at Cambridge, Mass., the eldest son of the Rev. Abiel Holmes [*q.v.*], Congregational minister, and Sarah (Wendell) Holmes, daughter of a Boston merchant. The boy grew up in an atmosphere of gentility, moderate wealth, and broad culture, coming in contact with many books and many cultivated people.

After preliminary schooling at Cambridge, Holmes attended Phillips Academy at Andover for a year, and then entered Harvard College in 1825. There is some evidence that his father hoped the boy would enter the ministry, but Holmes' natural inclinations did not lead that way, and the strong Unitarian influence of Harvard nurtured in him a spirit of revolt against his father's Calvinistic orthodoxy. At college he turned naturally to the study of classical literature and languages. From an early age he had admired the English poets Pope and Goldsmith, and had tried to match their dexterity in verse; it was inevitable then, that Harvard's rich classical curriculum should have much to offer him.

After graduation Holmes studied at the Dane Law School for a year—a year which was "less profitable than it should have been," so he tells us, because of "the seductions of verse-writing." Perhaps the most valuable discovery he made during that year is contained in his rueful admission: "The labor which produces an insignificant poem would be enough to master a solid chapter of law. . . ." Yet one of his "insignificant" attempts made at this time served to attract the attention of the whole nation to the young poet. This was "Old Ironsides," a spirited protest in memorable verse against the proposed destruction of the ship "Constitution." The poem, published in the Boston *Daily Advertiser* (September 16, 1830) over the initial "H" and reprinted all over the country, was enthusiastically echoed by hundreds of patriotic Americans, and the Government decided not to confiscate the ship.

In 1831 Holmes gave up his law studies and entered the private medical school of Dr. James Jackson, with the intention of preparing himself for the M.D. degree at Harvard. After attending lectures at this

Collection of Frederick H. Meserve
OLIVER WENDELL HOLMES

school and at Harvard for two years, he went abroad in the spring of 1833 to complete his training in the hospitals and lecture-rooms of Paris. During the two years spent there he seems to have ventured but rarely out of the medical student's beaten track; and in later years he regretted having neglected to "lay up a store of memories which would have been precious to me." However, he traveled widely during the vacations, and made enough progress in his chosen profession so that shortly after his return to Cambridge in 1835 he received the M.D. degree from Harvard.

Beginning as a general practitioner at Cambridge in 1836, Holmes built up a fair practice, but never achieved any great success. It is believed—and acknowledged by Holmes himself—that this was partly due to his reputation as a wit and a poet; certainly the volume of poems which he published in this very same first year of his medical career was more noted for its exuberant jollity than for its soberness. The gay and seemingly frivolous poet managed to obscure the really competent and painstaking physician. In subsequent years Holmes turned more and more to the academic side of his profession; for three seasons he worked at the Massachusetts General Hospital, and from 1838 to 1840 he lectured as Professor of Anatomy at Dartmouth, devoting much of his time to research and competing successfully for medical essay prizes in 1836 and 1837. In June, 1840, he married Amelia Lee Jackson, the daughter of a justice of the

Massachusetts Supreme Court. They had two sons, Oliver Wendell Holmes Jr. (1841-1935), for many years a Justice of the United States Supreme Court, famous for the vigorous liberalism of his dissenting opinions, and Edward Jackson Holmes, a Boston lawyer; and one daughter, Amelia Jackson Holmes (Mrs. Turner Sargent).

From 1840 to 1856 Holmes was known chiefly as a teacher and scientific writer. A vigorous and persistent opponent of homeopathy, he was also an authority on fevers, and his published lectures caused a good deal of controversy and discussion during the 1840's. In 1847 he was appointed Parkman Professor of Anatomy at Harvard Medical School, a position which he held until 1882. In his lectures Holmes was accurate, descriptive, amusing; his wealth of illustrative simile and his ability to be witty, serious, or pathetic so appealed to the students that they were sent to him at the end of the day because he alone could keep them awake.

The Holmeses led an uneventful life in Boston, broken only by occasional lyceum tours and by restful summer vacations at Pittsfield, Mass., and later at the Beverly Farms home of their married daughter, near Boston. Holmes gained the friendship of Longfellow, Lowell, Howells and other prominent Boston literary men, and became an ardent devotee of their "Saturday Club." His domestic life was happy and peaceful; Annie Fields recorded that during the years of his later fame Holmes was "carefully guarded" by his wife from unwelcome instrusions.

Holmes' second appearance in the literary world came about in 1857 and was largely due to the efforts of his friend James Russell Lowell, who had just become editor of the newly created *Atlantic Monthly.* Holmes remarked that "Lowell woke me from a kind of literary lethargy in which I was half slumbering, to call me to active service." The result of this re-awakening was *The Autocrat of the Breakfast-Table,* a series of conversational essays contributed to the early numbers of the *Atlantic*; and Holmes' "service" to the new monthly was considerable, for his bright and universally popular essays are said to have brought it through the financial depression of 1857. From this time forward Holmes' literary activity rarely slackened; the *Autocrat* was followed by three other series of the same kind; in the 1860's he wrote two novels which were widely read and discussed, and between 1862 and 1887 four new collections of his poems appeared. He became a sort of unofficial poet-laureate of Boston, and was called upon to produce appropriate verses for countless occasions, convivial and otherwise—all of which he did with surprising grace. In 1886 he made a second trip to Europe, and was lionized in London as well as in Boston. His last years were spent in retirement in Boston, and he died there in his eighty-fifth year.

In characterizing Holmes most of his contemporaries emphasized his extraordinary charm and vivacity in conversation. Ungainly, short of stature, and illfavored, this man nevertheless made himself "king of the New England dinner-tables." Howells observed, "He could not be with you a moment without shedding upon you the light of his flashing wit, his radiant humor, and he shone equally upon the rich and poor in mind." The "Autocrat" was so generous and good-humored by nature, that he had eventually to learn to hold himself in reserve. Howells noticed that, "He wished to know the character of the person who made overtures to his acquaintance, for he was aware that his friendship lay close to it."

Although Holmes wished to be known primarily as a poet, he is most affectionately remembered today as the Autocrat of the Breakfast-Table. Those twelve sketches contributed to the *Atlantic* in 1857 observed no unity, achieved little coherence; they were in fact only samples "dipped," as he said, "from the running stream of my thoughts." Yet they exhibit the most endearing characteristics of the eloquent Doctor—his pointed wit, his universal interest, his homely wisdom, his conversational skill. As Professor Brander Matthews justly observed, in these papers Holmes' talk is "excellent merely as talk. It has the flavor of the spoken word; it is absolutely unacademic and totally devoid of pedantry." In his next series of essays, *The Professor at the Breakfast-Table,* Holmes was more serious but less entertaining; the last two series—*The Poet at the Breakfast-Table* and *Over the Teacups*—likewise fell below the first in popular appeal if not in intrinsic merit. The Doctor himself explained this decrease in interest by saying that "continuations almost always sag a little."

Holmes' novels also fell below the level of *The Autocrat* in popularity. Somehow the doctor and anatomist never created a real flesh-and-blood character, and never threw himself into the telling of a story for its own sake. *Elsie Venner,* his most widely-discussed work of fiction, was a thesis-novel attacking Calvinism. Its heroine, as the author confessed, "found her origin not in fable or romance, but in a physiological conception, fertilized by a theological dogma." Moreover its style was not that of a novel but that of *The Autocrat*: Holmes the essayist appeared too often, and spent too much time reflecting upon the philosophical details of the book. These digressions were interesting—indeed, Holmes never wrote anything that was not interesting—but most readers felt that they obstructed the progress of the story. In *The Guardian Angel* it is Holmes the anatomist who guides the pen; the novel betrays too much interest in the scientific aspects of heredity, not enough in the characters as human beings. And his last novel, *A Mortal Antipathy,* aroused even less interest than its predecessors. Holmes' prose works also include two biographies, *John Lothrop Motley* and *Ralph Waldo Emerson,* and *Our Hundred Days in Europe,* a colorful account of his last tour abroad.

If posterity has preferred Holmes' *Autocrat* to his poems, it is not because the poems are inferior to others of their kind. Indeed, in the special field of *vers d'occasion* Holmes is often ranked the foremost poet of his time. But the poet himself admitted that many of his "lesser poems were written for meetings more or less convivial, and must of course show something like the fire-work frames on the morning of July 5th." It is the transitory nature of his subjects that has made most of Holmes' verse seem out-of-date. Many of his finer poems have lost their charm with their timeliness: "Old Ironsides" now seems agreeable but not stirring; "The Broomstick Train," written to celebrate the first trolley-cars, loses much of its point as we see the trolley-cars giving way to busses today; even the "Wonderful 'One-Hoss Shay'" becomes unintelligible, and sounds like the forlorn echo of an ancient language in this day of motor-cars. Yet occasionally, as in "The Last Leaf" and 'The Chambered Nautilus," Holmes gave expression to thoughts and emotions that will always haunt men's minds, and these unassuming verses must be counted among the permanent treasures of American poetry.

PRINCIPAL WORKS: *Essays*—The Autocrat of the Breakfast-Table, 1857; The Professor at the Breakfast-Table, 1860; The Poet at the Breakfast-Table, 1872; Pages From an Old Volume of Life, 1883; Over the Teacups, 1890. *Poetry*—Poems, 1836; Songs in Many Keys, 1862; Songs of Many Seasons, 1875; The Iron Gate and Other Poems, 1880; Before the Curfew and Other Poems, 1887. *Novels*—Elsie Venner, 1861; The Guardian Angel, 1867; A Mortal Antipathy, 1884-85. *Biographies*—John Lothrop Motley, 1879; Ralph Waldo Emerson, 1885. *Travel*—Our Hundred Days in Europe, 1887.

ABOUT: Emerson, R. W. Early Years of the Saturday Club; Howells, W. D. Literary Friends and Acquaintances; Lang, A. Adventures Among Books; Lowell, J. R. A Fable for Critics; Morse, J. T., Jr. Life and Letters of Oliver Wendell Holmes; Motley, J. L. Correspondence; The Critic December 1, 1894; National Review July 1896.

HOOKER, THOMAS (1586-July 7, 1647), Congregational clergyman, often called "the first democrat," was born at Marfield, Leicestershire, England, the son of Thomas Hooker, yeoman. He was educated by means of scholarships, first at Market Bosworth, and after 1604 at Cambridge. After taking his B.A. and M.A. degrees at Emmanuel College in 1608 and 1611, Hooker remained there as Dixie fellow until 1618.

Emmanuel College, at that time a "nursery of Puritanism" and Nonconformity, directed Hooker's thought into dangerous channels, and brought him into opposition with Archbishop Laud and the official Church of England. After a quiet rectorship at Esher, Surrey, where in 1621 he married Susan Garbrand, a "waiting-woman" to the wife of his patron, Hooker became lecturer at St. Mary's Church, Chelmsford, in 1626, and his vigorous preaching soon attracted the unfavorable notice of neighboring Conformist clergymen. Some of these complained to Laud that Hooker made too much of the common people, and "blew the

From a statue by C. H. Neihaus
THOMAS HOOKER

bellows of their sedition"; their protest ended with the words, "If my lord tender his own future peace, let him connive at Mr. Hooker's departure." Laud had no difficulty in bringing this about: Hooker was soon obliged to resign the Chelmsford lectureship, and in 1630 was cited to appear before the High Commission Court at London. Rather than deliver himself up to eternal silence, he fled to Holland and remained there in retirement for the next three years.

Meanwhile a group of his English parishioners, known as "Mr. Hooker's company," had migrated to Newtown, Mass., with the understanding that he was to follow. Accordingly, Hooker set sail from Holland in 1633, arriving at Boston aboard the "Griffin" on September 4.

The sermons of this "Saint of God and Son of Thunder" seem to have had much the same effect in the New as in the Old England. "After Mr. Hooker's coming over," wrote Hubbard, "it was observed that many of the freemen grew to be very jealous of their liberties." Within three years of his induction as pastor at Newtown his congregation, which had long been showing signs of political dissatisfaction and land-hunger, migrated under Hooker's leadership to Hartford, Conn. Hooker's correspondence with Governor Winthrop, who opposed the migration, reveals the fundamental cause of this separation: it was a conflict between aristocratic oligarchy and democracy. Winthrop was conducting the Massachusetts Bay colony as a magisterial autocracy; Hooker founded the colony at Hartford as a democratic commonwealth, abolishing both property qualifications and religious tests as limits to the franchise.

Hooker served also as the bulwark of democracy in the church. The "Congregational Way" was being subjected to much criticism and to much Presbyterianizing influence from England in the 1630's; and Hooker was delegated by his fellow clergymen to defend the Church against those who wished to centralize authority. The last great work of his life, his *Survey of the Summe of Church Discipline* (1648), asserted the right of the individual to deal directly with God, through no temporal vicegerent or authority.

Hooker's sermons have come down to us indirectly, from shorthand notes taken by other men; and it may be said that they had little influence beyond the circle of their immediate hearers. Yet his political ideas had a far-reaching effect on American government. For in one sermon, delivered before the General Court at Hartford on May 31, 1638, Hooker elaborated the thesis that "the foundation of authority is laid, firstly, in the free consent of the people"; and in the following year he succeeded in planting this idea in the "Fundamental Orders" of Connecticut, which has been justly called "the first written constitution of modern democracy." He died at Hartford.

Principal Works: *Tracts*—A Survey of the Summe of Church Discipline, 1648. *Sermons*—The Soules Preparation for Christ, 1632; The Soules Humiliation, 1637; The Soules Possession of Christ, 1638; The Danger of Desertion, 1641.

About: Adams, J. T. The Founding of New England; Mather, C. Magnalia Christi Americana; Parrington, V. L. The Colonial Mind; Walker, G. L. Thomas Hooker: Preacher, Founder, Democrat.

HOOPER, ELLEN H. (STURGIS)

(1812?-November 3, 1848), poet, was the daughter of the Hon. William Sturgis, a wealthy Boston merchant, and Elizabeth M. (Davis) Sturgis. Ellen enjoyed the customary advantages of children of well-to-do Bostonians, and as a young lady gave promise of considerable poetic talent. Her pieces, appearing in the *Dial,* Brook Farm's literary organ, interested Emerson and Thomas Wentworth Higginson, both of whom are said to have expressed real hope in her "poetic genius." For the *Disciples' Hymn-Book,* compiled by Rev. J. F. Clarke, she wrote ten hymns, and several of her verses were included in John M. Forbes' *Old Scrap Book.* She was married to Dr. Robert Hooper, a physician; their son, Edward William, who over a period of almost thirty years held major administrative offices at Harvard, was responsible for the private printing of a posthumous collection of Mrs. Hooper's verse.

George Willis Cooke, writing in the *Journal of Speculative Philosophy* (July 1885) stated that Mrs. Hooper's poems were so suffused with very intimately personal feelings that "her family has been very reluctant to have anything written about her" and that this has tended to "keep her from the reputation which she deserves." In her little stanza beginning,

> I slept and dreamed that life was Beauty
> I woke and found that life was Duty. . .

or in another that opens with the line

> She stood outside the gates of Heaven and saw them coming in

there must have been, it would seem, some fragile charm which delighted a few of her more discerning contemporaries, but it is difficult to explain the more extravagant assertion of Margaret Fuller, who wrote from Rome: "I have seen no woman more gifted by nature than she."

ABOUT: Loring, C. G. Memoir of William Sturgis; Journal of Speculative Philosophy July 1885 (see "The Dial: An Historical and Biographical Introduction . . . "); Harvard Alumni Register; New England Historical and Genealogical Register: Vol 3.

HOOPER, JOHNSON JONES (June 9, 1815-June 7, 1862), humorist, was born in Wilmington, N.C. His father, Archibald McLaine Hooper, related to the most prominent families of the state and to William Hooper, signer of the Declaration of Independence, was a journalist. His mother, Charlotte (De Berniere) Hooper, daughter of an English army officer, was a descendant of Jeremy Taylor, English poet and divine.

With a good, though not a college education, Hooper started at fifteen to write for Charleston papers. At twenty he was adrift, journeying in the gulf states and living by his wits, but by 1840 he was reading law under his brother at Lafayette, Ala. Journalism, however, proved a final attraction, and as a Whig he exercised his talent on several papers, the Dadeville *Banner,* the Wetumpka *Whig,* and the Montgomery *Journal.* His greatest success was achieved on the Montgomery *Mail,* which he established in the early '50's and edited until 1861, giving it a national reputation.

In the course of his journalistic work, which attracted attention to his humor, Hooper invented the character of Simon Suggs, an unprincipled sharper embodying many traits of the early Southern frontier type. Some of these chronicles were reprinted in the New York *Spirit of the Times,* and in 1846 most of them were published in book form under the title *Some Adventures of Captain Simon Suggs: Late of the Tallapoosa Volunteers.* The sketches, which attained wide popularity, were, according to the *Cambridge History of American Literature,* "presented with rare irony by an author who had perhaps the most delicate touch of his time and section." In 1851 another book in a similar vein was published, *The Widow Rugby's Husband, A Night at the Ugly Man's, and Other Tales of Alabama.*

Although classed with the foremost Southern humorists and praised by Thackeray, Hooper came to rue the reputation his humor brought him. He felt it prevented men from taking him at a serious and higher valuation, and that it was responsible for his failure to gain higher office. He had served as solicitor of the Ninth Alabama circuit, and was secretary of the Provisional Congress of the Southern States in 1861. A sense of defeat and convivial habits are thought to have hastened the termination of his life, which occurred at Richmond, Va.

PRINCIPAL WORKS: Some Adventures of Captain Simon Suggs, 1846; The Widow Rugby's Husband, 1851.

ABOUT: Garrett, W. Reminiscences of Public Men in Alabama; Owen, T. M. History of Alabama and Dictionary of Alabama Biography; Tandy, J. Crackerbox Philosophers; Watterson, H. Oddities in Southern Life and Character.

HOOPER, LUCY HAMILTON (JONES) (January 20, 1835-August 31, 1893), poet, editor, and journalist, was born at Philadelphia, the daughter of a wholesale grocer, Bataile Muse Jones. Until ten years after her marriage to Robert M. Hooper, a merchant of substance, she partook of the social life of the city, dabbling a little in music and art, and writing occasional poetry. During this period she published a small volume of verse, *Poems With Translations From the German of Geibel and Others,* 1864. Another and complete volume of her poems was published in 1871.

Her husband's failure led her to take a position as an assistant editor in 1868 on the newly established *Lippincott's Magazine,* where her stories, poems, and other articles won recognition. Her husband becoming consul-general at Paris in 1874, she removed there with him and her two children. There she entered actively into social duties, gathered literary and artistic groups around her, and took a keen interest in the cultural and other aspects of Parisian life. Up to two days before her death she acted as a regular correspondent and contributor to American journals, sending articles to papers in Philadelphia, Baltimore, and St. Louis, and to *Lippincott's* and *Appletons' Journal.*

Among her additional published works were two novels, *Under the Tricolor: or, The American Colony in Paris* and *The Tsar's Window.* She also wrote an original play *Helen's Inheritance,* in the production of which her daughter Nettie took the leading part, and collaborated with the French dramatist, Laurencin, in another, *Her Living Image.* A translation by her of Alphonse Daudet's novel *The Nabob,* was published in 1878.

PRINCIPAL WORKS: Poems, 1864, 1871; Under the Tricolor, 1880; The Tsar's Window, 1881; Helen's Inheritance.

ABOUT: Scharf, J. T & Westcott, T. History of Philadelphia; Willard, F. E. & Livermore, M. A. A Woman of the Century.

"HOOSIER POET, THE." See RILEY, JAMES WHITCOMB

HOPE, JAMES BARRON (March 23, 1829-September 15, 1887), journalist and poet, was born in the home of his grandfather, Commodore James Barron, at the Navy Yard, Norfolk, Va. His father Wilton Hope, a handsome, gifted man, was a landed proprietor at Hampton, Va. His mother was Jane A. (Barron) Hope.

Graduating in 1847 from William and Mary College, he entered upon the practice of law at Hampton, but interrupted it to become secretary for three years to his uncle Commodore Samuel Barron, remaining to accompany him, after a duel which was nearly fatal to both participants, on a long cruise in the West Indies. Resuming his practice at Hampton, he became commonwealth's attorney in 1856, and the following year married Anne Beverly Whiting.

After serving as captain and quartermaster in the Civil War, he was left penniless and broken in health. He turned to journalism, associating himself with the Norfolk *Day Book*, and later with the *Virginian*. In 1873 he established the Norfolk *Landmark*, which he edited until his death, making it one of the most influential Southern journals. The additional honor of superintendence of the Norfolk schools came to him in 1885.

Hope's literary ability was prominent even as a boy, and his earliest published poems appeared over the signature "The Late Henry Ellen, Esq." A stirring poem "The Charge at Balaklava" written at twenty-eight was greatly admired and was published in his first volume of verse *Leoni di Monota and Other Poems*, 1857. Two years later his second volume, *A Collection of Poems*, appeared.

A gifted and prominent public speaker, Hope was frequently called upon for renditions at public anniversaries, and came to be styled "Virginia's Laureate." Invited by Congress to be the official poet in 1881 at the Yorktown celebration of Cornwallis' surrender, he prepared and read the long poem "Arms and the Man." A few days before a heart attack suddenly terminated his life he had completed a poem to be read at an unveiling at Richmond.

Hope has been described as a tall, slender, graceful man, with a pale face and rather light hair, a thin, full beard, with a refined Southern manner, charm, and force of character.

PRINCIPAL WORKS: Leoni di Monota and Other Poems, 1857; A Collection of Poems, 1859; Little Stories for Little People, 1874; Under the Empire, 1878; Arms and the Man, 1882.

ABOUT: Davidson, J. W. Living Writers of the South; Hubner, C. W. Representative Southern Poets; Trent, W. P. Southern Writers; Conservative Review March 1900.

"HOPKINS, JEREMIAH." See NOTT, HENRY JUNIUS

HOPKINS, JOHN HENRY (January 30, 1792-January 9, 1868), theologian, first Protestant Episcopal bishop of Vermont, was the only child of Thomas Hopkins, a descendant of the Hopkins family of Coventry, England, and the beautiful and accomplished Elizabeth (Fitzakerly) Hopkins, daughter of a Fellow of Trinity College. Born in Dublin, Ireland, where his father was a merchant, he was brought to America in his eighth year, where his mother later established a successful school for girls at Trenton, N.J. From the time she realized the unusual gifts of the precocious, beautiful boy, she spared no pains to give him the best education through her own efforts and private schools. After an early business venture as superintendent of iron works near Pittsburgh, he read law in spare moments while teaching school, was admitted to the bar, and rapidly rose to the top of his profession. In 1816 he married Melusina Müller of French-German descent.

While a young man Hopkins read widely along free thought lines, becoming familiar with all the principal arguments against Christianity. Asked to serve as organist in the small Trinity Church at Pittsburgh, he soon made his services so valuable that, although a layman, he was offered the rectorship, and gave up his professional salary of $5,000 a year for $800 a year with the church. In 1831 he answered a call to Boston, and the following year went to Vermont as bishop and rector of St. Paul's church, Burlington. There he was enabled to develop a long cherished plan for a church seminary. The panic of 1837 left him to struggle for seventeen years with onerous debt, and a large family to support. Finally he developed a home and school of outstanding beauty at Rock Point, later ceded to the Diocese of Vermont. He attended the Lambeth Conference for bishops at London in 1867; shortly after his return, exposure led to pneumonia and his death. He was interred at Rock Point.

Hopkins was an extraordinarily versatile and talented man, artist, musician, scholar, teacher, and lawyer. He composed nearly all the music for his first church, was so expert in church architecture that many parishes sent to him for plans, and was a recognized authority on the theology of the Church

Fathers which he studied for eighteen years. From 1820 he wrote constantly, publishing more than fifty books and pamphlets, in addition to many contributions to current publications, and written sermons. He was a logical, forceful writer, and a powerful controversialist. His most ambitious work, a commentary on the entire Bible, commenced in 1848, was never finished.

Principal Works: Christianity Vindicated, 1833; The Primitive Creed, 1834; The Primitive Church, 1835; The Church of Rome in Her Primitive Purity Compared With the Church of Rome at the Present Day, 1837; Sixteen Lectures on the Causes, Principles, and Results of the British Reformation, 1844; History of the Confessional, 1850; Slavery: Its Religious Sanction, Its Political Dangers, and the Best Mode of Doing It Away, 1851; The End of Controversy, Controverted (2 vols.), 1854; A Scriptural, Ecclesiastical, and Historical View of Slavery, 1864; The Law of Ritualism, 1866.

About: Carleton, H. Genealogical and Family History of the State of Vermont; Hopkins, J. H., Jr. The Life of the Late Rt. Rev. John Henry Hopkins; Historical Magazine of the Protestant Episcopal Church June 1937.

HOPKINS, LEMUEL (June 19, 1750-April 14, 1801), physician and satirist, was born at Waterbury, Conn., the son of a farmer, Stephen Hopkins, and his second wife, Dorothy (Talmadge) Hopkins. He was a descendant of a John Hopkins who settled in Cambridge, Mass., in 1634. A predisposition to tuberculosis influenced him to study medicine under Dr. Jared Potter of Wallingford, and Dr. Seth Bird of Litchfield, and about 1776 he began to practice at Litchfield, removing to Hartford in 1784. As a physician he was in advance of his time, an original and indefatigable worker. He rose to the top of his profession and was one of the founders of the Medical Society of Connecticut. Yale accorded him the honorary degree of M.A. in 1784.

In Hartford Hopkins was in close association with the eminent group known as the "Hartford Wits," which included Timothy Dwight, John Trumbull, Joel Barlow, David Humphries, and Theodore Dwight. With these and others the greatest part of his work was written and published anonymously. Among the more noteworthy works on which he collaborated were *The Anarchiad: A New England Poem,* first published in 1786, a mock heroic satire suggested by the *Rolliad,* a satire of English Tory politics; *The Echo,* a series of papers published between 1791 and 1805; and *The Political Greenhouse for the Year 1798,* published 1799. He is credited with writing *The Democratiad: A Poem in Retaliation,* 1795; *The Guillotina: or, A Democratic Dirge,* a New Year's poem, 1796; an "Epitaph on a Patient Killed By a Cancer Quack," "The Hypocrite's Hope," and "Verses to General Ethan Allen." He left some unpublished medical manuscripts.

Hopkins was a man of extensive knowledge and reading, with an uncommon memory and powers of abstraction, and a high moral nature. In manner he was singular and eccentric, in appearance, tall, lean, and uncouth. His verse excelled in pungent and humorous satire.

Principal Works: The Anarchiad, 1786; The Democratiad, 1795; The Guillotina, 1796.

About: Barber, J. W. Connecticut Historical Collections; Everest, C. W. The Poets of Connecticut; Thacher, J. American Medical Biography.

HOPKINS, MARK (February 4, 1802-June 17, 1887), educator and philosopher, was born in Stockbridge, Mass., the son of Archibald Hopkins, a poor farmer but of good family connections, and Mary (Curtis) Hopkins. After a desultory schooling in several academies and under a private tutor, he entered Williams College, which had been founded by one of his relatives. He had already had some experience as a teacher, and entered college in the sophomore year, receiving his B.A. in 1824, as valedictorian, and his M.A. in 1827. He then went to the Berkshire Medical College, at Pittsfield, to study medicine, but the next year was called back to Williams and tutored there for two years. Returning to medical college, he obtained his M.D. degree in 1829 and began

Collection of Frederick H. Meserve

MARK HOPKINS

practice, first in New York City and then with a partner in Binghamton, N.Y.

His medical career was brief, however; in 1830 a vacancy caused by a death brought him back to Williams as professor of moral philosophy and rhetoric. He maintained his association with the college for the remainder of his life: as professor of moral and intellectual philosophy from 1836, as professor of Christian theology from 1858, as president from 1836 to 1872, and as pastor of the college church from 1836 to 1883. For, though he never studied theology, Hopkins was licensed as a Congregational preacher in 1833, ordained in 1836, and given D.D. degrees by Dartmouth in 1837 and by Harvard in 1841.

In 1832 he married Mary Hubble, who bore him ten children. One of his sons succeeded him as president of Williams in 1902. He was president of the American Board of Commissioners for Foreign Missions from 1857 to his death.

It was President Garfield who first, at a dinner of Williams alumni, defined a university as "Mark Hopkins on one end of a log and a student on the other." He was undoubtedly a great teacher, who emphasized the individual development of the student, and, as Lyman Abbott puts it, was "companion rather than master of the student's mind." His method, both as teacher and philosopher, was largely Socratic, and he did much to awaken intellectual interest which often led the learner far afield from his master's views. As a philosopher, or more accurately a theologian, he holds by no means so high a place. He had neither profound erudition nor originality of thought. His philosophy, once highly popular but now fallen into neglect, was based on the theory that the world must be rational, because God is rational; that Christianity is true because it declares as "the chief end of man" exactly what is man's own constitution. Actually an emergent evolutionist, he was bitterly opposed to Darwinian evolution. His style, like his theories, frequently seems labored, artificial, and mechanical, and he himself boasted that he needed no dependence on books or libraries, that his philosophy came to him by intuition only.

Those who knew him testified to his sunny charm, the "southern exposure" of his intellect, a characteristic which would not be suspected from a glance at his grim mouth, beaked nose, and aggressive whiskers. To Western readers, it may be well to point out that he was neither identical with nor related to the pioneer California capitalist of the same name.

Principal Works: Lectures on the Evidences of Christianity, 1846; Miscellaneous Essays and Discourses, 1847; Lectures on Moral Science, 1862; Baccalaureate Sermons and Occasional Discourses, 1862; The Law of Love and Love as a Law: or, Christian Ethics, 1869; An Outline Study of Man, 1873; Strength and Beauty, 1874; The Scriptural Idea of Man, 1883; Teachings and Counsels, 1884.

About: Carter, F. Mark Hopkins; Denison, J. H. Mark Hopkins: A Biography; Howe, M. A. DeW. Classic Shades; Spring, L. W. Mark Hopkins: Teacher; Outlook March 1, 1902; Springfield Republican June 18, 1887.

HOPKINS, SAMUEL (September 17, 1721-December 20, 1803), theologian, was born in Waterbury, Conn., the son of Timothy and Mary (Judd) Hopkins. He was reared on his father's farm, but well tutored in preparation for college. He received his B.A. at Yale in 1741 and his M.A. in 1744. In 1742 he was licensed as a Congregational minister, having studied divinity with Jonathan Edwards, with whom he continued to live until 1744. Then he was appointed to a church at Housatonic (now Great Barrington), Mass., which had only five members, with thirty families in the parish. In 1748 he married one of his five parishioners, Joanna Ingersol, by whom he had five sons and three daughters.

Even this small congregation grew restive under the minister's severity and dullness, and in 1769 he was dismissed. For eighteen of his years there, from 1751 on, he had been in close communication with Edwards, who was situated at Stockbridge, nearby. Now, largely through Edwards' influence, he secured the charge of the First Congregational Church at Newport, R.I., where he served from 1770 until his death. In 1776 the British captured Newport, and for four years Hopkins, who was obliged to flee with his family, preached in churches in Newburyport, Mass., and Canterbury and Stamford, Conn. He returned to find his church, which had been used as barracks, in ruins, his home burned down, and his congregation in such poverty that it could no longer pay him a salary. Refusing an offer from a prosperous church in Massachusetts, he elected to remain and to live on whatever his parishioners could contribute. For years he and his whole family lived on less than $200 a year.

An abstemious man by nature, who spent fourteen hours daily at his desk and never took exercise, Hopkins lived almost entirely in the realm of the mind. He was one of the worst preachers who ever lived, with a markedly unpleasant voice. His doctrine, expounded in his books and known as "Hopkinsianism," is repellent to the modern mind.

From an engraving by H. W. Smith
SAMUEL HOPKINS

Yet he had both nobility of thought and courage. In Newport, where pro-slavery feeling was prevalent and most people were slave-owners, he not only freed his own slaves but denounced slavery openly, one of the first clergymen to do so. His reputation grew, and he was coupled with Edwards as the greatest American theologian of his time. In 1790 Brown University recognized his fame by an honorary D.D. degree.

In 1794, at seventy-three, he remarried, his first wife having died the year before. His bride was Elizabeth Mott, principal of a Newport boarding school. In 1799 he became paralyzed, and though he recovered sufficiently to preach, he never walked or wrote again.

Hopkins' doctrine was that God does all for His own glory and for the greatest good of all; that sin and evil are also of His making and a means to this end—though the sinner has free will and is no less to be condemned for choosing evil. Man should be glad to take his place in the divine plan, even should "be willing to be damned." He was also a millenarian, holding that the world would come to an end within the next two hundred years.

William Ellery Channing, who was of his Newport congregation, spoke of his "high relish for truth," and said that he "lived in a world of thought above all earthly passions." His mind was subtle and profound, but he had no power of impressing the general hearer or expressing himself adequately. His writing was heavy and lifeless, and has long ago been forgotten with his now grotesque theology.

Principal Works: Sin, Thro' Divine Interposition, an Advantage to the Universe, 1759; An Enquiry Concerning the Promises of the Gospel, 1765; The True State and Character of the Unregenerate, 1769; Concerning the Nature of True Virtue, 1771; An Inquiry Into the Nature of True Holiness, 1773; A Dialogue Concerning the Slavery of the Africans, 1776; A Discourse Upon the Slave Trade, 1793; A System of Doctrines Contained in Divine Revelation, Explained and Defended, 1793; A Treatise on the Millennium, 1793; Life and Character of Jonathan Edwards, 1799.

About: Ferguson, J. Memoir of the Life and Character of the Rev. Samuel Hopkins, D.D.; Hopkins, S. Works (see Memoir in 1852 ed. by E. A. Park); Patten, W. A. Reminiscences of Samuel Hopkins; Walker, W. Ten New England Leaders; West, S. Sketches of the Life of the Late Samuel Hopkins (containing Autobiography).

HOPKINSON, FRANCIS (October 2, 1737-May 9, 1791), poet-essayist-composer-artist, was born in Philadelphia, the son of Judge Thomas Hopkinson and Mary (Johnson) Hopkinson. Both parents were English by birth and well connected in England. Hopkinson was the first student and the first graduate of the Academy of Philadelphia (the University of Pennsylvania), receiving his B.A. in 1757 and his M.A. in 1760. He studied law under Benjamin Chew, attorney general of the province, and was admitted to practice in the Supreme Court in 1761. From 1761 to 1763 and again from 1771 to 1773 he was secretary of the Philadelphia Library Company. In 1763 he was appointed collector of the customs at Salem, N.J., and in 1766 he sailed for England, with an appointment as commissioner of customs in mind. But neither his relatives Lord North and the Bishop of Worcester, nor his father's friends Benjamin Franklin and Benjamin West, could secure the post for him, so he returned to America.

In 1768 he opened a drygoods store, and in the same year he married Ann Borden, daughter of the founder of Bordentown, N.J. They had three daughters and two sons, one of whom, Joseph, became famous as the author of "Hail, Columbia." From 1772 to 1776 Hopkins was collector of customs at Newcastle, Del. (then under the same government as New Jersey and Pennsylvania). He was removed for disloyalty when he declared for the patriots at the beginning of the Revolution. He moved to Bordentown and returned to the law; in 1774 he was a member of the governor's council, he was a delegate to the First Continental Congress, and a signer of the Declaration of Independence. In 1779 he was

After a portrait by R. E. Pine
FRANCIS HOPKINSON

made judge of admiralty for Pennsylvania, a position his father had held before him; although he was once impeached, he was acquitted and held the post until 1789. In that year he was secretary of the convention which established the Episcopal Church in America. In the same year Washington appointed him first judge of the United States Court in Pennsylvania. He died suddenly of apoplexy at fifty-four, while still holding this office.

Hopkinson was a notably versatile man. A skilled musician and harpsichord performer, he wrote much, including "My Days Have Been So Wondrous Free" (1758), the first song published in America. He was also an artist, who designed the seals of New Jersey, the University of Pennsylvania, and the American Philosophical Society, and helped to design the American flag. He is best known, however, as a writer. As a satirist, chiefly on political subjects, Dr. Benjamin Rush compared him to Swift, and though the comparison is unwarranted, he did have marked satirical powers. Many of his poems also (particularly *The Battle of the Kegs,* the most celebrated) are satirical, but he wrote, as well, numerous lyrics and religious poems. He was a steady contributor to all the magazines of his period, much of his work in them, signed by initials or pseudonyms, being still uncollected. He was perhaps too versatile, and too distinguished in too many fields, for he surpassed in no separate one, and in a sense frittered away his possible achievement. He was undoubtedly, however, one of the most interesting figures in the literary and cultural life of the early Republic.

Principal Works: The Treaty, 1761; Science, 1762; A Pretty Story, 1774; The Prophecy, 1776; The Battle of the Kegs, 1779; The Temple of Minerva, 1781; Seven Songs, 1788; Miscellaneous Essays and Occasional Writings, 1792.

About: Hastings, G. E. The Life and Works of Francis Hopkinson; Sonneck, O. G. T. Francis Hopkinson: The First American Poet-Composer.

"HORNBOOK, ADAM." See COOPER, THOMAS

HOSMER, HEZEKIAH LORD (December 10, 1814-October 31, 1893), miscellaneous writer and politician, was born at Hudson, Columbia County, N.Y., the son of Hezekiah Lord Hosmer and Susan (Throop) Hosmer, of Connecticut lineage. After an academic education he studied law with a kinsman, John W. Allen, of Cleveland, Ohio, and set up practice, riding circuit for a time and residing variously in Willoughby, Painesville, Maumee City, Perrysburg, and Toledo. During the years 1844 to 1855 he edited the Toledo *Daily Blade,* of which he became part proprietor.

Hoping for appointment as Congressional librarian in return for political services, he went to Washington, D.C., in 1860, but instead was made secretary of the House Committee on Territories. In 1864 he obtained appointment as chief supreme court justice of the newly organized territory of Montana, setting up his first court in the dining hall of the Planters' House in Virginia City. The law of that frontier was unformed and the community not wholly sympathetic to his efforts. When his term expired he spent a few years as postmaster, and from 1872 held positions in the custom house and state mining bureau at San Francisco. He was married three times.

Hosmer was early attracted to literary work and as a lawyer in Ohio divided his time between the law and writing. The Irish-American playwright Dion Boucicault is said to have taken part of his plot for a drama from Hosmer's story *Adela: The Octoroon.* In one of his latter works he upheld the Baconian theory of Shakespeare.

Principal Works: Early History of the Maumee Valley, 1858; Adela: The Octoroon, 1860; Bacon and Shakespeare in the Sonnets, 1887.

About: Historical Society of Montana. Contributions. Vol. 3; Raymer, R. G. Montana: the Land and the People. Vol. 1.

HOSMER, JAMES KENDALL (January 29, 1834-May 11, 1927), librarian and historian, was born in Northfield, Mass., where his father, the Rev. George Washington Hosmer, a descendant of James Hosmer who came to Cambridge, Mass., from England in 1635, was minister. His mother was Hanna Poor (Kendall) Hosmer, daughter of the Rev. James Kendall of Plymouth. He was graduated from Harvard and the theological school at Cambridge, and became Unitarian pastor at Deerfield in 1860, but remained in the ministry only until 1866. During the next twenty-six years he was a professor, first at Antioch College, and later at the University of Missouri and Washington University, St. Louis, teaching English literature, rhetoric, history, and German literature. In 1892 he became librarian of the Minneapolis Public Library, taking the title *emeritus* when he resigned in 1904 to give his remaining years to literary work. In 1902 he as president of the American Library Association. He was a genial man, of attractive personality and broad outlook. He was twice married, and died at Minneapolis at ninety-three.

Hosmer's published work was voluminous, scholarly, and widely read. His first book, *The Color Guard,* was based on his Civil War journal. A large part of his writing was historical, but he also published three biographies, two novels, a book of reminiscences, *The Last Leaf,* edited works on the Lewis and Clark expedition and Governor Winthrop's journal, and made many contributions to periodicals and newspapers.

Principal Works: *Biography*—Samuel Adams, 1885; The Life of Young Sir Henry Vane, 1888; The Life of Thomas Hutchinson, 1896. *History*—A Short History of German Literature, 1878; The Story of the Jews, 1885; A Short History of Anglo-Saxon Freedom, 1890; A Short History of the Mississippi Valley, 1901; The History of the Louisiana Purchase, 1902; The Appeal to Arms, 1861-63, 1907; Outcome of the Civil War, 1863-65, 1907. *Journal*—The Color Guard. *Novels*—The Thinking Bayonet, 1865; How Thankful Was Bewitched, 1894. *Reminiscences*—The Last Leaf, 1912.

About: Pocumtuck Valley Memorial Association (Deerfield, Mass.) History and Proceedings: Vol. 7; Proceedings of the American Antiquarian Society: n.s. Vol. 37; New England Historical and Genealogical Register October 1928; Public Libraries March 1924.

HOSMER, WILLIAM HOWE CUYLER (May 25, 1814-May 23, 1877), poet, was born at Avon, N.Y. He was the son of George Hosmer, a distinguished lawyer, and Elizabeth (Berry) Hosmer, and traced his descent from a Thomas Hosmer of Hawkhurst, Kent, England, who came to Massachusetts before 1632. He was graduated from Geneva (now Hobart) College in 1837 and became a law partner of his father at Avon, where he spent most of his life and where he died. He was in the New York custom house from 1854 to 1858, and in the Civil War, during which period his wife and two sons died. He received the honorary degree of M.A. from Hamilton College, the University of Vermont, and his *alma mater*.

Hosmer showed ability as a poet while still a student. His early years had brought him into the closest contact with the Indians, his mother teaching him several Indian tongues, and he "sat by their campfires and in their councils" gaining familiarity with their customs legends, character, and traditions. Besides studying the Indians of the western part of his state, he made a sojourn among those of Wisconsin and Florida as well. The resulting sympathy and understanding he embodied in the many Indian themes of his poems. He was particularly strong in nature descriptions, and at his best in *Bird Notes* and *The Months.*

Principal Works: The Pioneers of Western New York, 1838; The Prospects of the Age, 1841; The Themes of Song, 1842; Yonnondido: or, Warriors of the Genesee, 1844; The Months, 1847; Bird Notes, 1850; Legends of the Senecas, 1850; Indian Traditions and Songs, 1850; The Poetical Works of William H. C. Hosmer, 1854; Later Lays and Lyrics, 1873.

About: Griswold, R. W. The Poets and Poetry of America.

HOUSE, EDWARD HOWARD (September 5, 1836-December 17, 1901), journalist, was the son of Timothy House, a banknote engraver of Boston, where he was born, and of Ellen Maria (Childs) House. After a few years spent in the study of orchestral composition, he joined the Boston *Courier* in 1854 as music and dramatic critic, in 1858 transferring to the New York *Tribune* in the same capacity and as special correspondent. A strong attraction for Japan resulted in his going there in 1870 as a teacher of English. There he devoted his leisure to writing and after a few years resumed journalistic work as a special correspondent to Formosa. In 1883 while in London he was incapacitated by a stroke. The Japanese government awarded him a pension for the rest of his life and a decoration. He returned to Tokio where he died, his last years being given to training the Imperial Band. He aided also in founding the Meiji Musical Society which later became the Imperial Conservatory of Music.

House wrote largely on Japanese affairs, the Mikado's treasury appreciatively providing him with a subsidy in 1877 for the support of the Tokio *Times,* which he founded. After a year the subsidy was withdrawn and given to a more tactful publicist, Captain Brinkley, of the Tokio *Mail*. Captain Brinkley credited House with being the most brilliant writer ever connected with journalism in the Far East. House's novel *Yone Santo* was directed against the missionaries whom he disliked. He had strong dramatic interests and collaborated with Dion Boucicault in his *Colleen Baun*. He was also for five years lessee of the St. James Theatre, London.

PRINCIPAL WORKS: The Kagoshima Affair, 1874; The Shimonoseki Affair, 1875; The Japanese Expedition to Formosa, 1875; Japanese Episodes, 1881; Yone Santo, 1889; Midnight Warning and Other Stories, 1892.

ABOUT: Wildes, H. E. Social Currents in Japan; Nation November 3, 1881.

HOVEY, RICHARD (May 4, 1864-February 24, 1900), poet, was born in Normal, Ill., where his father, Maj. Gen. Charles Edward Hovey, was president of the Normal University. His mother, Harriette Farnham (Spofford) Hovey, was also a well known educator. After the Civil War, in which the father was an officer, the family moved to Washington, where the boy attended Hunt's School. At the age of sixteen he wrote, printed, and published his first book of poems. He was graduated from Dartmouth College in 1885, as class poet and editor of the college magazine; he wrote many of the songs still sung at Dartmouth, and they are conceded to be far superior, as literary productions, to the songs of most other colleges. In 1899 Dartmouth conferred an honorary Litt. D. on him.

After leaving college, Hovey studied art for a year in Washington. Then for a year he was a student in the General Theological Seminary of the Episcopal Church, in New York, serving at the same time as lay assistant in the Church of St. Mary the Virgin. However, he abandoned his plan of entering the clergy, and went to Boston, where he became a newspaper reporter. It was at this time that he met Bliss Carman, with whom so many of his poems were written. Next he became an actor for several years, saying afterwards that he had gone on the stage in order to get practical experience as a playwright. In 1891 and 1892 he was in England and France, and during this visit he came strongly under the influence of the Symbolist poets, Verlaine, Mallarmé, and Maeterlinck, later translating the plays of the last named writer into English, in 1894 and 1896.

In 1894 Hovey married Mrs. Henrietta Russell, the chief exponent in America of the Delsarte system of "eurhythmics"; they had one son. The first two years of their marriage were spent in Europe. On his return Hovey became a lecturer on English literature at Columbia, and professor of the same subject at Barnard College. He had long suffered from an intestinal disturbance, and in 1900, during a slight operation for its relief, he died suddenly of heart failure, at only thirty-five.

RICHARD HOVEY

Because of his association with Bliss Carman, who was a Canadian, Hovey used to be classed with the "Canadian school" of poets; he had, however, no affiliations with Canada. It is hard to say, in view of his early death and the incompletion of his planned work, just how high he should rank as a poet. As Henry Leffert remarks, his promise was greater than his achievement, but he was a versatile, subtle, philosophical writer, with much richness of fancy and masculine strength. His most ambitious project was a series of three trilogies dealing with Launcelot and Guinevere. It was never finished, though four volumes of it appeared before and after his death, under various titles, the last volumes being edited by his widow. But in his lifetime he was better known for the three volumes of *Songs of Vagabondia,* written with Carman. With the *Rubaiyat,* these were the Bible of literary-minded college students in the '90's and the early twentieth century, though their gay flouting of convention and their celebration of the joys of the romantic road seem more than a little *fin de siècle* today. That Hovey, for all his "poetic" appearance, including a dark, flowing beard, was actually alive to the realities of life, is rather unfortunately evidenced by the wild chauvinism of the poems he wrote during the Spanish-American war. He is definitely a minor poet, but a minor poet who might have grown in stature if fate had granted him a longer life.

PRINCIPAL WORKS: The Laurel, 1889; Launcelot and Guinevere, 1891, 1895, 1898, 1907; Seaward: An Elegy, 1893; Songs of Vagabondia (with Bliss Carman) 1891; Taliesin: A Masque, 1896; More Songs of Vagabondia (with Bliss Carman) 1898; Last Songs of Vagabondia (with Bliss Carman) 1901; To the End of the Trail, 1908.

ABOUT: Archer, W. Poets of the Younger Generation; Boynton, P. H. American Poetry; Cappon, J. Bliss Carman; Rittenhouse, J. B. The Younger American Poets; Bookman December 1898, April 1900.

"HOWADJI." See CURTIS, GEORGE WILLIAM

HOWARD, BLANCHE WILLIS (July 21, 1847-October 7, 1898), was the daughter of Daniel Mosely Howard, a descendant of John Howard who came from England to Massachusetts in 1643, and of Eliza Anne (Hudson) Howard. She was born and received a high school education at Bangor, Maine, followed by boarding school at New York City. She commenced to write before her teens. Following the publication of her first book *One Summer* she went to Germany the same year, taking with her a commission from the Boston *Transcript*. At Stuttgart she took into her home and chaperoned American young women students, continuing her own writing and from 1886 editing a magazine in English. A happy but childless marriage in 1890 with Dr. Julius von Teuffel, court physician, followed, which brought her wealth and social standing. She died at Munich two years after her husband.

The Baroness von Teuffel continued to write under her maiden name, Blanche Willis Howard, to the end of her life. She was an able pianist, a keen student, active in charities, caring for several nieces and nephews and maintaining a healthy interest in outdoor activity. Her novels showed idealism and sympathetic characterization and went through translations and large editions, holding their popularity for more than two decades. Among her best liked books were *Guenn,* and *Dionysius the Weaver's Heart's Dearest.*

PRINCIPAL WORKS: One Summer, 1875; One Year Abroad, 1877; Aunt Serena, 1881; Guenn: A Wave on the Breton Coast, 1883; Aulnay Tower, 1885; Tony the Maid, 1887; The Open Door, 1889; A Battle and a Boy, 1892; A Fellowe and His Wife (with William Sharp) 1892; No Heroes, 1893; Seven on the Highway, 1897; Dionysius the Weaver's Heart's Dearest, 1899; The Garden of Eden, 1900; The Humming Top (tr. from Theobald Gross) 1903.

ABOUT: Howard, H. The Howard Genealogy; Willard, F. E. & Livermore, M. A. American Women.

HOWARD, BRONSON CROCKER (October 7, 1842-August 4, 1908), playwright, was born in Detroit, the son of the mayor of the city, Charles Howard, and of Margaret Elizabeth (Vosburgh) Howard. He was prepared for Yale at Russell's Institute, New Haven, but his sight failed (he wore heavy lenses for the remainder of his life), and he was unable to continue his education further. Instead he went to work on the Detroit *Free Press.* It was in Detroit that his first play, *Fantine* (derived from Hugo's *Les Miserables*), was produced in 1864. The next year he went to New York, his home thenceforth; and for five years worked as a reporter on the *Tribune,* the *Evening Mail,* and the *Evening Post,* and as New York correspondent of the *Pall Mall Gazette* (London).

Howard's journalistic days were ended by the enormous success of *Saratoga* in 1870. The play, which deals with the fashionable race-course and watering-place of the mid-century, had an equally long run in England under the title of *Brighton.* All of Howard's hit-plays were as popular in England as in America, and he spent increasingly more time abroad, in his later years having a house in London as well as in New York. In 1880, in London, he married Alice Wyndham, sister of Sir Charles Wyndham, the comedian.

BRONSON HOWARD
1897

Though about forty titles are listed of Howard's acted plays, many of them were adaptations or revisions. Actually only thirteen were original plays. The best known of these were, besides *Saratoga, The Banker's Daughter* (produced 1878), *The Young Mrs. Winthrop* (1882), *One of Our Girls* (dealing with international marriage) (1885), *The Henrietta* (1887), *and Shenandoah* (a Civil War play) (1888). All these had extended runs and held the stage for many years, though it has been many years since the last performance of *Shenandoah,* the longest lived of them.

Howard became in a sense the dean of playwrights in the United States. He was the founder and first president of the American Dramatists' Club (now the Society of American Dramatists and Composers), to which on his death he left his large dramatic library. He was vice-president of the Copyright League, and worked indefatigably for revision of the American laws on international copyright. His eyeglasses, his bald head (he was already hairless at twenty-five), his heavy mustache, and in old age his white beard, were familiar to first-nighters and diners-out in New York and London all through the last quarter of the nineteenth century. He died of heart failure, superinduced by heat prostration.

"A dramatist," Howard himself said, "is a man who writes plays." That expresses exactly his practical and utilitarian attitude toward his profession. He did not like to have his plays published, and few of them have appeared in print. He took the unformed taste of middle-class New York audiences as his criterion and arbiter, aiming deliberately at popularity. In consequence his plays are sprightly and effective, highly ethical, and essentially naïve. They are not art or literature, and none of them will ever become a classic. Nevertheless, he was a pioneer in the dramatic depiction of American manners, and his plays are a complete index to the contemporary culture of his period.

Principal Works: *Plays (published)*—Saratoga, 1870; Old Love Letters, 1878; The Young Mrs. Winthrop, 1882; The Henrietta, 1887; Shenandoah, 1889; Kate, 1906. *Miscellaneous*—Scars on the Southern Seas, 1907; The Autobiography of a Play, 1914.

About: In Memoriam: Bronson Howard (Society of American Dramatists); Mathews, J. B. Gateways to Literature and Other Essays; Moses, M. J. The American Dramatist; Bookman September 1908; North American Review October 1908; New York Times August 5, 1908.

HOWE, HENRY (October 11, 1816-October 14, 1893), historian, was born in New Haven, the son of Gen. Hezekiah Howe and Sarah (Townsend) Howe. His father kept a bookstore and was also a publisher; as the publisher of the first edition of Webster's dictionary, he was a personal acquaintance of Noah Webster and of practically everyone else with literary pretensions in the town, and the boy grew up among books and the conversation of Yale professors. He seems to have had little formal schooling, but to have read omnivorously and listened attentively, and thus to have educated himself. Happening upon J. W. Barber's *Historical Collections of Connecticut,* he was fired by a desire to do similar work. His father in 1839, with a view to securing for him a better financial future than history seemed to offer, placed him in a position in Wall Street, but he rebelled, and by the next year he was at work on a New York historical record, in collaboration with Barber. His method was to go from place to place, collecting material and making sketches. After exhausting the resources of New York, New Jersey, and Virginia, in 1847 he moved to Cincinnati, where he lived and worked until 1878. The year he went West he had married Frances Tuttle.

He continued his historical research in Ohio, and branched out into other semi-historical works, which he sold by subscription. *Our Whole Country,* written with Barber, came at an unfortunate time, when the outbreak of the Civil War made readers very reluctant to consider the country as a whole; it was a complete failure and bankrupted him but he assigned all his property to his creditors and continued his labors. From 1878 to 1885 he lived in New Hampshire; then he returned to Cincinnati and toiled at bringing his book on Ohio down to date. His son F. H. Howe, who was his assistant, finally induced the state legislature to give $20,000 for the copyright and plates of the Centennial edition (1890-91) of the *Historical Collections of Ohio,* but by that time the old historian had died of a paralytic stroke, impoverished by his lifelong labor.

Howe's books are superficial, but full of picturesque detail, and invaluable because he had first-hand knowledge of a way of living and a phase of culture which had no other contemporary historians.

Principal Works: Eminent Mechanics, 1839; Historical Collections of the State of New York (with J. W. Barber) 1841; Memoir of the Most Eminent American Mechanics, 1843; Historical Collections of the State of New Jersey (with J. W. Barber) 1844; Historical Collections of Virginia,

1845; Historical Collections of Ohio, 1847; Historical Collections of the Great West, 1851; The Travels and Adventures of Celebrated Travelers, 1853; Life and Death on the Ocean, 1855; Adventures and Achievements of Americans, 1859; Our Whole Country (with J. W. Barber) 1861 (in part, as All the Western States and Territories, 1867); The Times of the Rebellion in the West, 1867; Over the World, 1883.

ABOUT: Ohio Archaeological and Historical Society Publications IV, 1895; Cincinnati Enquirer October 15, 1893.

HOWE, JULIA (WARD) (May 27, 1819-October 17, 1910), poet, biographer, and reformer, was born in New York City, the daughter of Samuel Ward, a prominent banker, and Julia Rush (Cutler) Ward. Her mother, who wrote but never published verses, died in 1824, and the girl was reared by her father in a home of unusual culture, and educated by governesses and in private schools. She wrote—chiefly verse—from earliest girlhood. Her father died when she was an attractive débutante of twenty, gay and light-hearted, but serious-minded and ambitious. In 1843 she married Dr. Samuel Gridley Howe [*q.v.*], eighteen years her senior, a champion of the underdog in every province, from the slaves to the blind and the feeble-minded. She always called him "Chevalier" and he called her "Diva"—nicknames which characterized them both.

After a year in Europe they settled in Boston, and there, though she bore in quick succession four daughters and two sons (one son died at three), she began to write in earnest, and to take part in her husband's reform activities. With him she edited the *Commonwealth,* an abolitionist paper, and their home became an abolitionist stronghold. She was strongly attracted to the stage at this period, and wrote two plays in verse; one, *Hippolytus,* written for Edwin Booth, never saw production, and the other, *The World's Own,* though it was produced in 1855, was a flat failure. She turned to other fields of literature.

Mrs. Howe burst into national fame in one day, with publication of "The Battle-Hymn of the Republic" in the *Atlantic Monthly* in 1862. As with Mrs. Stowe and *Uncle Tom's Cabin,* she had seized the psychological moment and exactly matched the public temper. Her poem, which was written at night in the dark of a tent near beleaguered Washington at the beginning of the Civil War, brought her only $4, but it also brought her universal acclaim. Largely on the strength of its authorship, she was the first woman to be elected to the American Academy of Arts and Letters.

JULIA WARD HOWE
c. 1865

Her marriage, a true partnership, was broken by Dr. Howe's death in 1876. Stricken to the heart, his widow nevertheless carried on for the sake of her children, and lost her grief in the service of humanity. Her multiple activities from this time on are bewildering to follow. The interests she espoused read like a roster of American social causes. With slavery out of the way, she became engrossed in the feminist movement, was president of the New England Woman Suffrage Association, and was for many years associate editor of the *Woman's Journal,* founded by Alice Stone Blackwell. She was president also of the New England Woman's Club and of the Association for the Advancement of Women. Though she was never ordained, she preached frequently in Unitarian churches, and occasionally in those of other denominations. She lectured all over the country, chiefly on German philosophy. In 1871 she was president of the American branch of the Women's International Peace Association, and in 1872 was sent to London as delegate to a prison reform congress. In 1873 she edited a symposium on *Sex and Education.* These activities had preceded Dr. Howe's death, but as the years went on she only enlarged the scope of her interests.

Gradually she became a true matriarch. Every one of her children became distinguished in literature or some other field, the two best known being her daughters, Laura E. Richards and Maud Howe Elliott, both of them authors. F. Marion Crawford, the novelist, was her nephew. She became the center of half a dozen cultural and literary groups which looked to her as their leader. Living to the age of ninety-one, she retained her mental alertness to the last. Only a few months before her death from pneumonia she journeyed to Smith College to receive an honorary LL.D. In New York in the winter, and in Newport in the summer, she made her home a salon long after she was unable to continue her lecture tours abroad.

It is unfair to judge Mrs. Howe by a single poem, in a style which seems a bit florid to our modern ears. Her verse, though it showed simplicity and feeling, was not of a particularly high order; but her prose is able and distinguished. Her best work is in her biographies, especially in that of Margaret Fuller, whom she knew intimately. To her writing she brought a trained intellect and a discriminating critical power. Two disparate attributes characterize it—a deep religious feeling, and an equally deep and delicate humor. She herself summed up her own career in saying, in her old age, that the aim of life was "to learn, to teach, to serve, to enjoy."

Principal Works: *Poetry*—Passion Flowers. 1854; Words for the Hour, 1857; The World's Own (play) 1857; Later Lyrics, 1868; From Sunset Ridge: Poems Old and New, 1898. *Prose*—A Trip to Cuba, 1860; From the Oak to the Olive, 1868; Memoir of Dr. Samuel Gridley Howe, 1876; Modern Society, 1881; Margaret Fuller, 1883; Is Polite Society Polite? 1895; Reminiscences, 1899; Sketches of Representative New England Women, 1905; At Sunset, 1910.

About: Adams, E. C. & Foster, W. D. Heroines of Modern Progress; Elliott, M. H. The Eleventh Hour in the Life of Julia Ward Howe; Howe, J. W. Reminiscences; At Sunset; Richards, L. E. & Elliott, M. H. Julia Ward Howe.

HOWE, SAMUEL GRIDLEY (November 10, 1801-January 9, 1876), educator and reformer, was born in Boston the son of Joseph Neals Howe, a manufacturer and shipowner, and Patty (Gridley) Howe. He was graduated from Brown University in 1821 (in 1868 the college gave him an honorary LL.D.) and from Harvard Medical School in 1824. He proceeded immediately to Greece, where he was regarded as "the Lafayette of the Greek Revolution," being surgeon of the Greek fleet from 1827 to 1830. Illness forced him back to America, and he was appointed to open the first American school for the blind. He went back to Europe to visit similar institutions there, and while aiding Polish refugees in Prussia was sentenced to six weeks in prison. In 1832 he started the school in his father's house; it grew into the Perkins Institute for the Blind, of which he was head all his life. He himself printed books for the use of his pupils in the so-called Boston Line or Howe raised type. Perhaps his greatest fame came from his training of the blind-deaf girl Laura Bridgman, predecessor of Helen Keller. Howe was also deeply interested in the training of the deaf and the imbecilic (from 1848 to 1875 he was superintendent of the Massachusetts School for Idiotic and Feeble-Minded Youth, a pioneer institution), and the treatment of the insane, prisoners, and ex-convicts. Early in the '40s he became an abolitionist, and after his marriage in 1843 to Julia Ward [*q.v.*], they edited together an anti-slavery paper, the *Commonwealth*. During the Civil War he was active in the Sanitary Commission. From 1865 to 1874 he was chairman of the Massachusetts Board of State Charities, the first in the United States. The struggling Cretans next engaged his attention; he went to Greece in their behalf in 1866, and from 1868 to 1871 edited a magazine devoted to their freedom, the *Cretan*. In 1871 he was one of the commissioners who advised the annexation of Santo Domingo as a means of civilizing the inhabitants.

A modest, retiring man, though of strong feelings, Dr. Howe's writing was always subservient to his philanthropic activities. But Edward E. Allen calls his annual reports on charities "philosophic commonsense put into clear and forcible language";

Collection of Frederick H. Meserve

SAMUEL GRIDLEY HOWE

and Van Wyck Brooks, in *The Flowering of New England,* describes his *Historical Sketch of the Greek Revolution* as "a vigorous and memorable book."

PRINCIPAL WORK: : Historical Sketch of the Greek Revolution, 1828; Reader for the Blind (in raised type) 1839; Letters and Journals (ed. by L. E. Richards) 1906-09.

ABOUT: Faris, J. T. Men Who Conquered; Higginson, T. W. Contemporaries; Howe, J. W. Memoir of Dr. Samuel Gridley Howe; Richards, L. E. Samuel Gridley Howe; Richards, L. E. Two Noble Lives; Sanborn, F. B. Samuel Gridley Howe, the Philanthropist; Stearns, F. P. Chevalier Howe; Hibbert Journal October 1909; Boston Transcript January 10, 1876.

HOWELLS, WILLIAM DEAN (March 1, 1837-May 11, 1920), novelist, poet, and essayist, was born in Martin's Ferry, Ohio, the son of William Cooper Howells, a Welsh printer and journalist, abolitionist and Quaker-turned-Swedenborgian, and of Mary (Dean) Howells, of Irish and German descent. He had very little formal schooling, but at the age of nine was already at work setting type in his father's office. He read indefatigably, poetry chiefly at first, studied languages alone, and thoroughly educated himself, so that the boy who never entered a high school became the man who received honorary degrees from six universities, including Oxford, and was offered (and refused) professorships of literature at Harvard, Yale, and Johns Hopkins.

The father's anti-slavery views kept the family constantly on the move from one Ohio town to another all during his boyhood. They stayed longest in Columbus where from 1856 to 1860 Howells worked on the *Ohio State Journal,* both as compositor and as reporter. In 1860 he wrote a campaign biography of Lincoln, which netted him $160, spent on his first visit to New England, where he met Lowell, Emerson, and Hawthorne, and laid the foundations of his loving reverence for New England writers, writing, and life. He never became "Boston-plated," like Aldrich, but the weight and authority of the Massachusetts milieu affected him almost as profoundly as it did Mark Twain.

The Lincoln biography did even more for him; Lincoln appointed him United States consul in Venice, and he spent four years there, from 1861 to 1865. In 1862, in Paris, he married Elinor Gertrude Mead, of Vermont, who died in 1910 after a markedly happy marriage which resulted in the birth of one son and two daughters (one of whom died young).

In 1865 Howells returned to America, and after a few months of a simultaneous connection with the New York *Times* and the

Collection of Frederick H. Meserve
WILLIAM DEAN HOWELLS

Nation, he went to Boston to become subeditor of the *Atlantic Monthly* under James T. Fields. In 1872 he became editor-in-chief, and he remained with the magazine until 1881. A few years followed during which he took no editorial position, but devoted himself to creative writing. With *A Modern Instance,* in 1882, he had moved into the first rank of American novelists.

In 1891, however, he moved from his beloved Cambridge to New York, his home thenceforth. Since 1886 he had been conducting the "Editor's Study" department of *Harper's Monthly*; but now he left *Harper's* temporarily and for a year was editor of the *Cosmopolitan.* In 1900 he returned to *Harper's* and revived George William Curtis' "Editor's Easy Chair," a piece of furniture he continued to fill until his death.

The remainder of his life was an uneventful series of honors and of fruitful labor. He edited a series of autobiographies, an anthology of short stories, and a "library of adventure," and he wrote voluminously and indefatigably. He was first president of the American Academy of Arts and Letters, from its founding until he died. In 1915 he was awarded the gold medal of the National Institute of Arts and Letters. His seventy-fifth birthday, in 1912, was the occasion of a large commemorative dinner. He had long been recognized (with a play on his middle name) as Dean of American Letters.

In appearance Howells was more the prosperous merchant than the artist—burly, with a square jaw and a "walrus" mustache. He himself was an example of that glorification of the commonplace which he so loved. He began his literary life as a poet, a very negligible one; then in later life he returned to poetry, and showed that he had grown in originality and power of feeling. His first novel to be widely read, *Their Wedding Journey,* was little more than a travel book, and he wrote other travel books, open or disguised, throughout his life. But gradually he was finding himself as a novelist, the change to a modest realism becoming apparent after 1890. Under the influence of Tolstoy's works, his natural humanitarianism also grew until he might (especially in his two utopian novels, *A Traveler From Altruria* and *Through the Eye of the Needle*) have been described as a sort of unorthodox Socialist.

His faults were timidity, superficiality, and squeamishness, which made him shrink from following out the implications of his themes. Yet consciously he was a realist; very early he wrote: "Ah! poor Real Life! Can I make others share the delight I find in thy foolish and insipid face?" His is what Carl Van Doren calls "selective realism." Originally he was a gentle, playful humorist, but his observation of social and economic forces drew a cloud over his sunny sky. He scorned "romance" as he feared and hated superstition. If today he seems too conciliatory and passive, we are largely in his debt for our more realistic approach to life in literature.

For there is no doubt that Howells, as Henry Seidel Canby says, "was responsible for giving the American novel form," and "taught American writers to avoid rhetoric and to write simply, clearly, and straightforwardly." As Oscar Firkins put it: "the rare had taught him to esteem the commonplace, and the exquisite had been his tutor in the virtues of rusticity." And Canby again sums him up well by saying: "His mind was neither very powerful nor startlingly original, but his perceptions were sure, his integrity was absolute, and his craftsmanship as good as any in our literature." He was unmistakably American in treatment as in theme; and what he lost in virility he gained in clarity. His best novels—*A Modern Instance, The Rise of Silas Lapham, A Hazard of New Fortunes, The Leatherwood God*—are solidly built, and without being spectacular go well beneath the surface. As an essayist he had the sure, light touch; and few autobiographies possess more nostalgic charm than *Years of My Youth* and the semi-fictional *A Boy's Town.* It is to be regretted that he died with his later autobiographical work, *Years of My Middle Life,* still unfinished. Like Mark Twain (of whom he wrote one of the best brief lives), he knew all the major literary figures of his period, and he was far more thoroughly accepted by them than Mark Twain ever was. They did some harm to the fresh mind of the young Westerner, but they also did him good, and he had at the core too much artistic and intellectual integrity not to slough off all influences (barring the central influence of Tolstoy) and in the end to express himself as a clear-sighted and warm-hearted individual.

Principal Works: *Novels*—No Love Lost, 1869; Their Wedding Journey, 1872; A Chance Acquaintance, 1873; A Foregone Conclusion, 1875; The Lady of the Aroostook, 1879; The Undiscovered Country, 1880; Dr. Breen's Practice, 1881; A Fearful Responsibility, 1881; A Modern Instance, 1882; A Woman's Reason, 1883; The Rise of Silas Lapham, 1885; Indian Summer, 1886; The Minister's Charge, 1887; April Hopes, 1888; Annie Kilburn, 1889; A Hazard of New Fortunes, 1890; The Shadow of a Dream, 1890; A Boy's Town, 1890; The Quality of Mercy, 1892; An Imperative Duty, 1893; The World of Chance, 1893; The Coast of Bohemia, 1893; A Traveler From Altruria, 1894; The Landlord at Lion's Head, 1897; The Story of a Play, 1898; Ragged Lady, 1899; Their Silver Wedding Journey, 1899; The Kentons, 1902; Questionable Shapes (short stories) 1903; Letters Home, 1903; The Son of Royal Langbrith, 1904; Miss Ballard's Inspiration, 1905; Through the Eye of the Needle, 1907; Fennel and Rue, 1908; New Leaf Mills, 1913; The Leatherwood God, 1916; A Daughter of the Storage (short stories) 1916; The Vacation of the Kelwyns, 1920; Mrs. Farrell, 1921. *Non-fiction*—Poems of Two Friends (with J. J. Piatt) 1860; Venetian Life, 1866; Suburban Sketches, 1871; Poems, 1873; Out of the Question and A Counterfeit Presentment (plays) 1877; Modern Italian Poets, 1887; Criticism and Fiction, 1891; My Literary Passions, 1895; Stops of Various Quills (poetry) 1895; Impressions and Experiences, 1896; Literary Friends and Acquaintances, 1900; Heroines of Fiction, 1901; Literature and Life, 1902; Seven English Cities, 1909; The Mother and the Father (poetry) 1909; Imaginary Interviews, 1910; My Mark Twain, 1910; Familiar Spanish Travels, 1913; Years of My Youth, 1916.

About: Cooke, D. G. William Dean Howells; Firkins, O. W. William Dean Howells; Harvey, A. William Dean Howells; Howells, M. William Dean Howells: Life in Letters; Howells, W. D. Years of My Youth; Phelps, W. L. Essays on Modern Novelists; Atlantic Monthly November 1907; Bookman March 1917, July 1919; Forum January 1902; Harper's July 1920; North American Review January 1912; New Republic June 30, 1937; Saturday Review of Literature March 13, 1937.

HOYT, CHARLES HALE (July 26, 1860-November 20, 1900), playwright, was born in Concord, N.H., the son of George W. Hoyt; his mother's maiden name is not known. He attended the Boston Latin School, and for a short time studied law.

He then became a newspaper reporter in St. Albans, Vt., and from there went to the Boston *Post,* where for five years he was dramatic and musical critic, sports editor, and columnist, all at once. His interest in the drama was first aroused by his newspaper criticisms. His first plays were romantic comedies, and were not very successful, though a few of them were produced. He found himself, however, when he began to write farces, and for years he was the foremost writer of farces in America. Usually plotless, these plays—once overwhelmingly popular and bringing fame and wealth to their author—are satirical and topical in nature, and are now badly "dated." The greatest of his successes was *A Trip to Chinatown,* which earned him half a million dollars in its first four years, and with its 650 performances held a world's record until 1918.

After he left the *Post,* Hoyt moved to Charlestown, N.H. From 1893 to 1897 he was a Democratic member of the New Hampshire Legislature. He was twice married, in 1887 to Flora Walsh, who died in 1892; and in 1894 to Caroline Scales Miskel, a beautiful and talented actress who played leading rôles in all his plays. Her death in 1898 caused his mental collapse; he became insane and was removed to an asylum early in 1900. Released in the custody of friends, he died before the year was out.

Besides writing his plays, Hoyt acted as his own manager and producer, and with a partner was lessee of two New York theatres. The only one of his farces ever to be published was *A Texas Steer,* which appears in *Representative American Dramas* (1925), edited by M. J. Moses.

Principal Works: (date of production): A Bunch of Keys, 1882; A Parlor Match, 1884; A Tin Soldier, 1886; A Hole in the Ground, 1887; A Midnight Bell, 1889; A Texas Steer, 1890; A Trip to Chinatown, 1891; A Temperance Town, 1893; A Milk White Flag, 1893; A Contented Woman, 1897; A Stranger in New York, 1897; A Day and a Night in New York, 1898.

About: Brown, T. A. History of the New York Stage; New York Times November 21, 1900.

HUBBARD, WILLIAM (?, 1621-September 14, 1704), theologian and historian, was born in Ipswich, Suffolk, England. In either 1630 or 1635 (the date is variously given) he emigrated with his father to Massachusetts, where the older Hubbard helped to found a new Ipswich. The son was graduated from Harvard in its first class, that of 1642, and received his M.A. in 1645. The next year he married Margaret Rogers, by whom he had three children. In 1656 he decided to enter the ministry, and was ordained in 1658; from 1665 to 1703 he was minister of the Ipswich (Congregational) Church. Very orthodox in his theology, he was among the leaders in opposition to taxing the churches. In 1684 he substituted for a while as president of Harvard, and in 1688 took Increase Mather's place as rector while he was in England. In one respect he was progressive; he opposed the persecution of witches and protected several of the victims. His wife died about 1700 and the old man scandalized his congregation by marrying his housekeeper, Mrs. Mary Pearce, a widow. Because of criticism of his actions and probably because of increasing senility he resigned in 1703.

Hubbard's principal work is his *General History of New England,* which was financed by the General Court and used as a source book by Cotton Mather and others, but was not published until the Massachusetts Historical Society printed it in 1815. "The work abounds in errors," Dr. John Spencer Bassett points out; and he adds that the early part was taken bodily from Morton's *Memorial* and Winthrop's *Journal,* and that the later portion is "meager and inaccurate."

Principal Works: Narrative of the Troubles With the Indians in New-England, 1677; Sermons, 1684: A Testimony to the Order of the Gospel, in the Churches of New-England (with J. Higginson) 1701; A General History of New England From the Discovery to 1680, 1815.

About: Day, E. W. 1000 Years of Hubbard History; Waters, T. F. Ipswich in the Massachusetts Bay Colony.

HUBNER, CHARLES WILLIAM (January 16, 1835-January 3, 1929), poet, was born at Baltimore Md., his parents, John Adam Hubner and Margaret (Semmilroch) Hubner, having emigrated there from Bavaria. He studied for six years in Germany, and on his return taught music in the Tennessee Female Academy at Fayetteville. After the Civil War in which he served in the Confederate forces he went to Atlanta, Ga., where he was associated editorially with a number of newspapers. In 1896 he became assistant librarian of the Carnegie Library, remaining there for twenty years. He died in Atlanta at ninety-three.

Hubner began writing at the age of ten, his first poem being published at thirteen. His journalistic work gave him an easy facility and a wide range of subject. He published more than a half dozen volumes of verse, including a few dramas. Among his other works was an anthology and a critical volume on Southern poets. The

Poetry Society of his section in 1928 proclaimed him poet-laureate of the South.

Principal Works: Historical Souvenirs of Martin Luther, 1873; Wild Flowers, 1877; Cinderella: or, The Silver Slipper, 1879; Modern Communism, 1880; Poems and Essays, 1881; The Wonder Stone, 1883; War Poets of the South, 1896; Poems, 1906; Representative Southern Poets, 1906; A Sheaf of Sonnets, 1917; Poems of Faith and Consolation, 1927.

About: Jacobs, T. The Oglethorpe Book of Georgia Verse; Rutherford, M. L. The South in History and Literature.

HUDSON, CHARLES (November 14, 1795-May 4, 1881), clergyman, journalist, and politician, was born at Marlboro, Mass., the son of Stephen Hudson and Louisa (Williams) Hudson, and a descendant of Daniel Hudson of England who came to New England about 1639. He became a Unitarian minister at Westminster, Mass., in 1824, and participated in setting up the new denominational Massachusetts Society of Universal Restorationists. From 1828 he engaged in four decades of varied public activity, which included membership in the state legislature, the United States Congress, and the state board of education. He also served as naval officer of the Port of Boston and United States assessor of internal revenue. In public life his ability, industry, and integrity were of the highest. His home was in Lexington from 1849, where he was a leading citizen. He was twice married.

Hudson was editor of the Boston *Daily Atlas,* a Whig newspaper, and a voluminous writer of sermons, public speeches, and other papers. As a member for twenty-one years of the Massachusetts Historical Society he was a frequent contributor of historical memoirs and reports, and his more prominent publications are historical. The town of Hudson, Mass., was named for him.

Principal Works: A Series of Letters Addressed to Rev. Hosea Ballou of Boston, 1827; A Reply to Mr. Balfour's Essays, 1829; A History of the Town of Westminster, 1832; Doubts Concerning the Battle of Bunker Hill, 1857; History of the Town of Marlborough, 1862; History of the Town of Lexington, 1868.

About: Proceedings of the Massachusetts Historical Society: Vol. 18; Memorial Biographies of the New England Historic Genealogical Society: Vol. 8.

HUDSON, HENRY NORMAN (January 28, 1814-January 16, 1886), Shakespearian scholar, was born in Cornwall, Vt. While apprenticed to a coachmaker he prepared himself for Middlebury College, graduating at twenty-six. While teaching in the South, he gave some public lectures on Shakespeare, which, from their popular, romantic presentation, attracted so much appreciative response that he extended them to other cities, including Boston. He became a Protestant Episcopal minister in 1849 and edited for a time the *Churchman* and the *American Church Monthly.* During the Civil War he served as a chaplain and wrote a bitter arraignment of General B. F. Butler in *A Chaplain's Campaign With General Butler,* eliciting an equally bitter reply.

In 1865 Hudson moved to Cambridge, Mass., where he taught, lectured, edited, and wrote on Shakespeare and other English authors. His writings were of high scholarly excellence; his style was pure and dignified. Among his other work he edited the Harvard edition of Shakespeare's complete works, and separate plays with introductions. A bronze tablet was erected to him at Middlebury College in 1927.

Principal Works: Lectures on Shakespeare, 1848; A Chaplain's Campaign With General Butler, 1865; Shakespeare: His Life, Art, and Characters (2 vols.) 1872; Sermons, 1874; Textbook of Poetry, 1880; English in Schools: A Series of Essays, 1881; Studies in Wordsworth, 1884. *Edited*—The Complete Works of William Shakespeare (20 vols.) 1880-81.

About: Hudson, H. N. Essays in English studies (see Introduction by A. J. George); Wright, C. B. The Place in Letters of Henry Norman Hudson; Education March 1886.

HUDSON, THOMSON JAY (February 22, 1834-May 26, 1903), journalist and lecturer, son of John Hudson and Ruth (Pulsifer) Hudson, was born at Windham, Ohio, where he spent his early life on a farm and attended a neighboring academy, supplemented by some private tutoring. He was admitted to the Cleveland bar at twenty-three, but after some eight years of practice in Ohio and Michigan abandoned it for journalism, and edited successively the Port Huron *Commercial Daily,* the Detroit *Daily Union* and the Detroit *Evening News.* In 1877 he went to Washington as correspondent for the Scripps Syndicate. For thirteen years from 1880 he was examiner in the United States Patent Office. In his latter years he was connected with the *Medico-Legal Journal.* He died at Detroit.

The publication of his first book, *The Law of Psychic Phenomena,* an outcome of his interest in psychology and psychical studies, brought him so widespread a reputation that he resigned from the Patent Office and turned to lecturing and writing. The book had an immense sale, eventually passing into its forty-seventh edition. In his third book, *The Divine Pedigree of Man,* he brought in the evolutionary theory, which did not prove so popular. After his death his son, Charles

B. Hudson, collected a final volume of papers that had appeared in various journals.

PRINCIPAL WORKS: The Law of Psychic Phenomena, 1893; A Scientific Demonstration of the Future Life, 1895; The Divine Pedigree of Man, 1899; The Law of Mental Medicine, 1903; The Evolution of the Soul and Other Essays, 1904.

ABOUT: Hudson, T. J. The Evolution of the Soul and Other Essays (see Sketch by C. B. Hudson).

HUGHES, ROBERT WILLIAM (January 16, 1821-December 10, 1901), editor and jurist, was born in Powhatan County, Va., of early Virginia Huguenot descent. His parents, Jesse Hughes and Elizabeth Woodson (Morton) Hughes both died the year following his birth and he was reared by Mrs. General Carrington of Halifax County. At twenty-two he entered upon the practice of law but after some ten years abandoned it when writing proved a superior attraction. For the greater part of twenty years he was associated editorially with Southern papers, the *Examiner, Republic,* and *State Journal of Richmond,* and the Washington *Union.* Under the Grant administration he was made federal district attorney, and failing of election to Congress and as governor, he became judge of the eastern district federal court from 1874 to 1898. He died at his home near Abingdon.

PRINCIPAL WORKS: A Popular Treatise on the Currency Question Written From a Southern Point of View, 1879; A Chapter of Personal and Political History, 1881; Reports of Cases Decided in the Circuit Court of the United States for the Fourth Circuit: 1792-1883 (9 vol.) 1837-1883: The American Dollar, 1885; Editors of the Past, 1897.

ABOUT: Tyler, L. G. Encyclopedia of Virginia Biography.

HUMPHREYS, DAVID (July 10, 1752-February 21, 1818), poet and miscellaneous writer, was born in Derby, Conn., the son of the Rev. Daniel Humphrey and Sarah (Riggs) (Bowers) Humphrey; he himself added the "s" to his name. He was graduated from Yale in 1774 and after two years as a teacher enlisted in the Connecticut militia in 1776. He was on the staff of General Putnam, and, a brilliant soldier, advanced by the end of the Revolution to the rank of lieutenant colonel and aide-de-camp to Washington, to whom he was exceedingly devoted. In 1784 he was sent to Paris as secretary of the negotiating committee for peace, and remained for two years. From 1786 to 1789 he served in the Connecticut Assembly. He was abroad again from 1790 to 1802 first as a special secret agent, then as the first United States minister to Portugal, then as sole commissioner to Algeria, and finally as minister plenipotentiary to Spain, from which office he was recalled by Jefferson. In 1797 he married Ann Frances Bulkeley, daughter of an English banker in Lisbon. On his return to America Humphreys introduced the merino sheep in Connecticut and went into the woolen business at Humphreysville, near Derby. In 1806 and 1807 he was in Europe again in the interest of his cloth factory. During the War of 1812 he served as captain-general of the Veteran Volunteers.

Though he is grouped with the "Hartford wits," Humphreys' verse is very pedestrian, with no lightness or humor. He was "a journeyman in verse," the conscious imitator and unconscious parodist of Pope and Addison. All his writing mirrors his calm assurance, his pomposity and uncritical patriotic fervor, and his "grandiose altruism."

PRINCIPAL WORKS: A Poem Addressed to the Armies of the United States of America, 1780; A Poem on the Happiness of America: Addressed to the Citizens of the United States of America, 1786: Essay on the Life of the Hon. Major General Israel Putnam, 1788; Miscellaneous works of Colonel Humphreys, 1790-1804; Dissertation on the Breed of Spanish Sheep Called Merino, 1802; Oration on the Political Situation of the United States of America in 1759, 1803

ABOUT: Beers, H. A. The Connecticut Wits; Fellows, J. The Veil Removed; Humphreys, F. L. Life and Times of David Humphreys: Soldier—Statesman—Poet, "Belov'd of Washington"; New England Magazine February 1804.

"HUMPHRIES, JACK." See KELLY, JONATHAN FALCONBRIDGE

HUNT, HELEN MARIA (FISKE). See JACKSON, HELEN MARIA (FISKE) HUNT

HUNT, ISAAC (c. 1742-1809), political writer, was born in Bridgetown, Barbados, the son of the Rev. Isaac Hunt, the local rector, and his wife, who had been a Miss Bryan or O'Brien. His chief claim to remembrance is that he became the father of Leigh Hunt, the English poet and critic. He was educated at the Philadelphia Academy (now the University of Pennsylvania), being graduated in 1763, and for three months thereafter was a tutor in English. His anonymous *Letter From a Gentleman in Transilvania,* directed against the proprietors of the colony and published in 1764, attracted some attention, but when the next year he followed this with a series of satires issuing from "Scurrility Hall," the college refused him his M.A. degree in 1766. He received it, however, in 1771. In 1767 he married Mary Shewell. He studied law and was admitted to the bar; but his Loyalist

Political Family and his other Tory activities made his position in America difficult if not dangerous, and after he had been threatened with tar and feathers and actually "carted" out of town he bribed officials and escaped first to Barbados and then to England. There he took holy orders and after serving as curate in Paddington became minister of Bentwick Chapel. Later he was tutor to the nephew of the Duke of Chandos, after whom he named the son who was to become a far more famous author. He was dismissed in consequence of his activities in favor of the American artist John Trumbull, who had been arrested as a spy; and thenceforward his life was a dreary succession of debts and imprisonments for debt. In his later years he was a Unitarian. He died in obscurity in London. An unpractical visionary, he would long ago be forgotten had he not happened to father a noted writer.

Principal Works: The Political Family, 1775; The Rights of Englishmen: an Antidote to the Poison Now Vending by . . . Thomas Paine, 1791.

About: Hunt, L. Autobiography; Trumbull, J. Autobiography.

HUNTER, WILLIAM C. (1812-June 25, 1891), China merchant and miscellaneous writer was born in Kentucky. Before he was thirteen he went to China as a mercantile apprentice, within a few years being associated with the firm of Russell & Company of which he later became a member. He became part owner of the first American steamship which arrived in 1845 to ply in Chinese waters. Soon after the Treaty of Nanking, 1842, abolished the "factories"—the residential and trading section of Canton to which foreigners were exclusively confined—Hunter retired to Macao on the southern coast of China. He died at Nice, France.

Throughout his stay in the "factories" Hunter devoted himself to the study of the Chinese language and made occasional contributions to such English-language journals as the *Canton Register* and the *Chinese Repository*. The first of his two volumes, *The "Fan Kwae"* ["foreign devils"] *at Canton Before Treaty Days: 1825-1844,* was published nearly four decades after the period of which he gives such intimate glimpses. This, as well as the later volume, was written in a spirit of unusual detachment and impartiality.

Principal Works: The "Fan Kwae" at Canton Before Treaty Days: 1825-1844, 1882; Bits of Old China, 1885.

About: Couling, S. Encyclopaedia Sinica.

HUNTINGTON, JEDEDIAH VINCENT (January 20, 1815-March 10, 1862), novelist and editor, was born in New York City, the son of Benjamin Huntington, a stock broker, and Faith Trumbull (Huntington) Huntington, granddaughter of a Revolutionary general, and distantly related to her husband. He was educated at an Episcopal private school, at Yale, and at the University of the City of New York (New York University), from which he received his B.A. in 1835 and his M.A. in 1838. Meanwhile he studied theology at Union Theological Seminary in 1836 and 1837, then proceeded to the University of Pennsylvania, where he received an M.D. degree in 1838, though he never practised medicine. Instead, after three years as teacher of "mental philosophy" at St. Paul's School, Flushing, Long Island, he was ordained deacon in the Episcopal church in 1841 and priest in 1842, and became rector of St. Stephen's Church, Middlebury, Vt. In 1842 he married his first cousin, Mary Huntington; they had no children. He was beginning to write poetry, and his sonnets in *Blackwood's Magazine* were more highly praised in England than in America—a fact which remained true of all his later writing. Becoming increasingly "high church," he finally resigned his charge in 1846 and went to England, then to Rome, where his brother Daniel, a painter, was settled. In 1849 he and his wife both became Roman Catholics. Returning to the United States, he interested himself in the advocacy of an international copyright law, then in 1853 and 1854 edited the *Metropolitan Magazine,* Baltimore, a Catholic periodical which failed by being too "highbrow." In 1857 he founded and edited the St. Louis *Leader,* also a Catholic paper, first a weekly, then a daily, which also failed in 1857, partly because he antagonized readers by denouncing slavery. Until 1861 he lived in New York as a free lance writer, then went to France, where he died, at Pau, of tuberculosis. Besides his original writing he did some French translations. His novels were mere propaganda tracts, partly autobiographical, but his verse was justly described as "classic and Wordsworthian."

Principal Works: The Northern Dawn and Other Poems, 1843; Lady Alice, 1849; Alban: or, The History of a Young Puritan, 1851; The Forest (sequel) 1852; The Pretty Plate (juvenile) 1852; St. Vincent de Paul and the Fruits of His Life, 1852; America Discovered: A Poem, 1852; Blonde and Brunette, 1859; Rosemary, 1860.

About: American Catholic Historical Society Records: September and December 1905; New York Times March 29, 1862.

HUNTLEY, LYDIA HOWARD. See SIGOURNEY, LYDIA HOWARD (HUNTLEY)

HURLBERT, WILLIAM HENRY (July 3, 1827-September 4, 1895), journalist, was the son of Martin Luther Hurlbut, a teacher and Unitarian minister, and Margaret Ashburner (Morford) Hurlbut, and a half brother of Congressman Stephen Augustus Hurlbut. The changed spelling "Hurlbert" was due to an engraver's error, but being liked was thereafter retained. He was graduated from Harvard in 1847, from its Divinity School in 1849, and spent a year in its Law School. He traveled widely throughout Europe and the southern parts of America. After 1883 he lived abroad most of the time, and in 1891 left England after a breach of promise suit. He died at Cadenabbia, Italy.

During an early but brief period in the Unitarian ministry, Hurlbert wrote hymns which were long in use. He started his journalistic work on *Putnam's Magazine* and the *Albion* in 1855. Later he was associated with the New York *Times,* and after the Civil War with the New York *World,* becoming editor-in-chief from 1876 to 1883. He was a brilliant, original, and rapid writer, able, it was said, to write two or three editorials at the same time, alternating the pages. A contemporary referred to him as "the only artist among American journalists" and "the prince of *persifleurs.*" He wrote many poems and, in his latter years, many essays and articles for British and American periodicals.

PRINCIPAL WORKS: Gan-Eden or Pictures of Cuba, 1854; Americans in Paris (play) 1858; General McClellan and the Conduct of the War, 1864; Ireland Under Coercion (2 vols.) 1888; France and the Republic, 1890; England Under Coercion, 1893.

ABOUT: Hurlbut, H. H. The Hurlbut Genealogy; Galaxy January 1869.

HUTCHINSON, THOMAS (September 9, 1711-June 3, 1780), statesman and historian, was born in Boston, the son of Thomas Hutchinson, a merchant, and Sarah (Foster) Hutchinson. He was a lineal descendant of Anne Hutchinson, exiled to Rhode Island in 1637 for heresy. At twelve he went from the North Grammar School to Harvard, where he received his B.A. in 1727, his M.A. in 1730. He then entered his father's business, and being thrifty and money-minded, by the time he was twenty-one he possessed £500 and was part owner of a ship. In 1734 he married Margaret Sanford, the beautiful daughter of the governor of Rhode Island. They had three

From a portrait by J. S. Copley
THOMAS HUTCHINSON

sons and two daughters. When she died in 1753 he was inconsolable and he never remarried.

Hutchinson became a selectman of Boston in 1737, a member of the colonial General Court a few weeks later. He served from 1737 to 1749, except for 1739, and was speaker from 1746 to 1748. In 1740 he went to England as representative of Massachusetts in a dispute with New Hampshire, and stayed until the next year. A brilliant financier, he was strongly opposed to paper money and to the wild-cat banking schemes of the time—a course which earned him the lasting enmity of the Adamses, Otis and Hancock. He was a member of the Council from 1749 to 1766, and in 1752 became judge of probate and justice of common pleas in Suffolk County. In 1754 he represented Massachusetts at the Albany Congress. In 1758 he became lieutenant-governor, in 1760 chief justice, in 1769 acting governor, and in 1771 governor. Most of these offices he held simultaneously. In 1764 he went to England again, against his will, to protest against the sugar tax. Although he opposed the irksome taxes as unwise, he felt strongly that Parliament had the legal right to impose whatever taxes it pleased. This view he advocated openly, and in consequence, during the stamp riots of 1765, his house was twice sacked, and all his furniture and his valuable library containing priceless documents in American history were destroyed. He was later indemnified in the sum of £3000, but American historical sources are the poorer for the looting.

Gradually Hutchinson, always a conservative, became an embittered reactionary, "more Tory than the ministers." It was his sons who owned the tea that was dumped in Boston Harbor. The bringing from England by Franklin of his Loyalist *Letters* made things still more unpleasant for him. He left for England in 1774, always hoping and expecting to return, but never doing so; his property was confiscated, and he lived on a royal pension (he declined a baronetcy but accepted a D.C.L. degree from Oxford) until he died in Brompton, now part of London, before the end of the Revolution.

Hutchinson was an Englishman before he was an American, and though he sincerely loved Massachusetts he wanted the colonies to be more English than England. His history, his principal work as an author, was written mostly in London during his two earlier visits, and was finally brought up to 1803 by his grandson. It is accurate, balanced, and acute, and written with considerable grace. Born fifty years earlier or later, he would undoubtedly have been one of the great men in American history.

Principal Works: A Brief Statement of the Claims of the Colonies, 1764; History of the Colony of Massachusetts Bay, 1764-1828; Collection of Original Papers Relative to the History of the Colony of Massachusetts Bay, 1769; Copy of Letters Sent to Great-Britain, 1773; Strictures Upon the Declaration of the Congress at Philadelphia, 1776; The Witchcraft Delusion of 1692, 1870; Diary and Letters: With an Account of His Administration, 1884.

About: Fiske, J. Essays Historical and Literary; Hosmer, J. K. The Life of Thomas Hutchinson; Hutchinson, P. O. The Diary and Letters of Thomas Hutchinson; Jones, E. A. The Loyalists of Massachusetts; Tyler, M. C. Literary History of the American Revolution.

HUTTON, LAURENCE (August 8, 1843-June 10, 1904), editor and essayist, was born in New York City, the son of John Hutton, a Scotsman, and Eliza Ann (Scott) Hutton. In his childhood he sat on the knee of Thackeray, who gave him his blessing, without much effect. For he was so dull in the private school to which he was sent that at eighteen his father refused to pay for more schooling, and he went to work. From 1861 to 1874 he was in the hop business; after the firm failed, a legacy from his father and his growing literary success enabled him to devote all his time to writing. He was drama critic of the New York *Mail* from 1872, but spent much time abroad, summering always in London. He was a noted collector of books, autographs, and portrait masks. In 1885 he married Eleanor Varnum Mitchell. From 1886 to 1898 he was literary editor of *Harper's Magazine,* conducting the department of "Literary Notes." He received an honorary M.A. from Yale in 1892 and from Princeton in 1897, and from 1901 to his death was a lecturer on English at the latter university. He was a charter member of the Players, the Authors' Club, and the American Copyright League.

In all, Hutton wrote forty-eight books. All of them were gossipy, trivial and superficial. He was neither critic nor creator in a real sense, but merely the possessor of a lively curiosity about people and things. He was distinctly a child of the 'eighties and 'nineties, to which his most active life belongs. Nothing he penned has survived except his charmingly written autobiographical books.

Principal Works: Plays and Players, 1875; Artists of the Nineteenth Century (with C. E. C. Waters) 1879; Literary Landmarks of London, 1885; Actors. . . of Great Britain and the United States From the Days of David Garrick to the Present Time (with Brander Matthews) 1886; Opening Addresses of the American Stage (with William Carey) 1887; Occasional Addresses (with William Carey) 1890; Curiosities of the American Stage, 1891; Literary Landmarks of Edinburgh, 1891; Edwin Booth, 1893; Portraits in Plaster, 1894; Other Times and Other Seasons, 1895; Literary Landmarks of Jerusalem, 1895; Literary Landmarks of Venice, 1896; Literary Landmarks of Rome, 1897; Literary Landmarks of Florence, 1897; A Boy I Knew, 1898; Literary Landmarks of Oxford, 1903; Literary Landmarks of the Scottish Universities, 1904; Talks in a Library, 1905.

About: Critic September 1904 to March 1905; Outlook June 18, 1904.

IMLAY, GILBERT (c. 1754-November 20, 1828), travel writer and novelist, was born probably in Monmouth County, N.J. Very little is definitely known about his life. He was a first lieutenant in the American Revolution, and may possibly have become a captain; at least he was afterwards known by that title. About 1783 he turned up in Kentucky, then a pioneer wilderness. He had bought considerable land there, and was appointed deputy surveyor. He soon got into financial and legal difficulties, and when he was sought by the court for a civil suit in 1785, it was found that he had left Kentucky and probably left the country. In any event he was in London in 1792. From there he went to Paris, where he was involved in a scheme to seize Louisiana from the Spanish. He wrote two French memoirs on this subject. The plan failed, and Imlay turned to some sort of commercial transactions, the nature of which is mysterious, and the legality of which may be doubted, for he was a thoroughly unscrupulous adventurer.

He would have been lost forever in the crowd of similar American fortune-hunters of those troubled times had he not, in 1793, become the lover of Mary Wollstonecraft, and the next year the father of her daughter Fanny. His relations with her were as self-seeking and callous as all his other activities; he neglected her, more than once deserted her, bore unmoved the knowledge that he had twice driven her to attempted suicide, and, while he was living with another woman in London, exploited her by sending her as his agent for his mysterious business affairs in Scandinavia. He saw her for the last time in 1796, just before her marriage to Godwin, the birth of Mary Godwin (Shelley's second wife), and her death. In 1828 a Gilbert Imlay was buried at St. Brelade's, in the island of Jersey. That was probably the last record of one of the least pleasant characters in history, and it is as ambiguous as was his entire earlier career.

His *Topographical Description* of Kentucky, and his novel dealing with the same territory, he claimed to have brought with him from America, but they were probably written in London. Neither of them displays any particular talent for authorship, but they have some historical value.

PRINCIPAL WORKS: A Topographical Description of the Western Territory of North America, 1792; The Emigrants: or, The History of an Exiled Family, 1793.

ABOUT: Godwin, W. Memoirs of the Author of A Vindication of the Rights of Women; Wollstonecraft, M. Letters to Imlay; Indiana University Studies March 1923; Publications of the Modern Language Association of America June 1924.

"INCONNUE, L'" See FRENCH, LUCY VIRGINIA (SMITH)

INGERSOLL, CHARLES JARED (October 3, 1782-May 14, 1862), dramatist and historian, was born in Philadelphia, the son of Jared Ingersoll, Jr., a noted lawyer, and Elizabeth (Pettit) Ingersoll. He was educated at Princeton, but left in 1799, in his junior year, and continued his studies privately with tutors. In 1801 his poetic tragedy, *Edwy and Elgiva,* was produced in Philadelphia with some success. He read law and was admitted to the bar in 1802, at only twenty. Before practicing he toured Europe with Rufus King, the American minister to England. In 1804 he married Mary Wilcocks. In contrast to his Tory grandfather and his Federalist father, he became increasingly anti-British and pro-French, and ended as a Jacksonian Democrat. From 1813 to 1815 he served in Congress, then returned to Philadelphia and the law; from 1815 to 1829 he was United States district attorney. In 1830 and 1831 he was a member of the state assembly, in 1837 secretary of the legation in Berlin, and from 1840 to 1849, after two defeats, once again in Congress. A middle-of-the-roader, advocating conciliation of the South and favoring the annexation of Texas, he won the enmity of John Quincy Adams and Daniel Webster, and when Polk appointed him minister to France the Senate, led by Webster, refused to confirm the appointment. His leisure had all along been given to poetry and history, and in 1849 he retired to give all his time to literary pursuits. Unfortunately, though he was a distinguished lawyer and orator, he was too much of a politician for literature and too much of a literary man for politics. His two works on the history of the War of 1812 are, however, soundly documented; his verse is too bombastic for the modern ear. In addition to his creative writing, he translated much from the French. He was working on a history of the territorial acquisitions of the United States when he died.

PRINCIPAL WORKS: Edwy and Elgiva, 1831; View of the Rights and Wrongs, Power and Policy, of the United States of America, 1808; Inchiquin: The Jesuit's Letters, 1810; Julian: A Tragedy, 1831; Historical Sketch of the Second War Between the United States of America and Great Britain, 1845-49; History of the Second War Between the United States of America and Great Britain, 1852; Recollections, 1861.

ABOUT: Ingersoll, C. J. Recollections; Meigs, W. M. Life of Charles Jared Ingersoll; Philadelphia Daily News May 16, 1862.

INGERSOLL, ROBERT GREEN (August 11, 1833-July 21, 1899), orator, agnostic, and Rationalist writer, was born in Dresden, N.Y., the son of the Rev. John Ingersoll a Presbyterian and Congregationalist minister, and of Mary (Livingston) Ingersoll, daughter of a judge. His mother died when he was an infant, and the father moved to churches in various towns of Ohio, Wisconsin, and Illinois, where the boy got such schooling as he could. For a while he himself taught school in Tennessee. In 1821, having read law with his older brother, Ebon Clark Ingersoll (later a Congressman, and the subject of Robert G. Ingersoll's celebrated funeral address), he was admitted to the bar in Shawneetown, Ill. The brothers became law partners, moving in 1857 to Peoria. Ingersoll ran for Congress in 1860 as a Democrat, but the Civil War turned him into a Republican. He enlisted in 1861 as colonel of an Illinois cavalry regiment, was captured by General Forrest in Tennessee, was paroled, and (since he had no hope

ROBERT G. INGERSOLL
1877

of exchange) was discharged from the army in 1863. From 1867 to 1869 he was attorney general of Illinois, and he would probably have been governor if he had not already begun his series of lectures on behalf of Free Thought.

In 1876, in nominating James G. Blaine for the presidency, he first came to national attention as an orator—and incidentally fastened on Blaine forever the epithet of "the plumed knight"—a bit of hyperbole that Blaine never lived up to. In 1877 he refused Hayes' appointment as minister to Germany. Two years later he moved to Washington, where he practised in the federal courts, and won several noted cases. In 1885 he moved again to New York, his home thenceforth. Besides a large law practice, he lectured indefatigably, earning an average of $100,000 a year, most of which went to charity. He spoke frequently, in addition to his Free Thought addresses, on Burns, Shakespeare, and Lincoln.

In 1862 Ingersoll had married Eva Amelia Parker, and they had two daughters. Few men have had a happier home life than he; in his latter years, surrounded by his children and grandchildren, he was something of a patriarch. His wife, daughters, and sons-in-law all sympathized with and aided him in his anti-religious campaign. In 1896 his health broke down from overwork, and three years later he died of heart disease at his daughter's home in Dobbs Ferry, N.Y. Apcryphal stories are still in circulation that Ingersoll regretted his agnostic views and died "in the faith," but his own family, who were the only ones present, are the best evidence of the falsity of the legend.

Ingersoll had the face of the born orator—burning dark eyes, a wide mouth, and flaring nostrils; even when he had lost most of his hair and what remained was white, he was a markedly handsome man. His most bitter enemies could never deny that he led the most exemplary of lives, that he was upright, courageous, charitable and generous to excess, patriotic a loyal friend, and a faithful and tender father and husband. For the sake of his principles he ruined a political career that might have led to the highest office.

He never composed a book, all his publications being transcripts of his lectures. His style as an orator belongs to his time—florid and emotional, frequently sentimental, and far too embroidered for our modern taste. He was primarily a feeler, not a thinker, and even to some Rationalist critics he seemed to dwell unduly on aspects of Biblical criticism which were already outmoded. His agnosticism stemmed from resentment of the harsh theology of his childhood. Nevertheless, he continues to stand as the mightiest of American Free Thinkers, the giant of an age when religious argument was divorced from economics, and a "pure" and now untenable Rationalism was possible.

Principal Works: The Gods, 1872; Some Mistakes of Moses, 1879; What Must We Do to Be Saved? 1880; About the Holy Bible, 1894; Why I Am an Agnostic, 1896; Superstition, 1898; The Devil, 1899; Lectures Complete, 1883; Prose Poems and Selections, 1884; Collected Works, 1900.

About: Gorham, C. T. Robert G. Ingersoll; Kittredge, H. E. Ingersoll: A Biographical Appreciation; Macdonald, G. E. Fifty Years of Free Thought; Rogers, C. Col. Bob Ingersoll; Bookman September 1899; Outlook July 29, 1899; Review of Reviews September 1899; New York Times July 22, 1899; Chicago Tribune July 22, 1899.

INGRAHAM, JOSEPH HOLT (January 25 or 26, 1809-December 18, 1860), traveller, romanticist, Episcopal clergyman, and prolific writer of fiction, was born in Portland, Maine. The son of James Milk Ingraham and Elizabeth (Thurston) Ingraham, he was named for his grandfather, a prominent citizen and wealthy shipbuilder. Young Ingraham went to sea before his seventeenth year and was in South America during the excitement of several revolutions. He is said to have been a student at Bowdoin College and to have graduated at the age of twenty-four, although there are no substantiating records. He began writing for newspapers prior to his twenty-first birthday and in

1832 was professor of languages at Jefferson College, Washington, Miss., subsequently adding the title "professor" to his name on his multitudinous publications. These appeared with such amazing rapidity that there is no accurate account of all his works. Henry Wadsworth Longfellow gives a vivid picture of the industrious Ingraham in his journal entry for April 6, 1846: "In the afternoon Ingraham the novelist called. A young, dark man with a soft voice. He says he has written eighty novels, and of these twenty during the last year; till it has grown to be merely mechanical with him. These novels are published in the newspapers. They pay him something more than three thousand dollars a year."

Ingraham travelled much between the North and South, but seems to have settled in the Southern states after his marriage to Mary Brooks, the daughter of a prosperous Mississippi planter. He was confirmed in the Protestant Episcopal Church in 1847, and while living in Nashville, Tenn., two years later, established a school for young ladies. From 1852 to 1858 he was connected with churches at Aberdeen, Miss., Mobile, Ala., and Riverside, Tenn. In 1859 an appointment to the pulpit of Christ Church took him to Holly Springs, Miss., where he also became principal of St. Thomas' Hall, a local school for boys. In the same year there emerged from his fertile brain a book of denunciation aptly called *The Pillar of Fire.* This was, and is, his best known work. It is written in the easy style of the letter-form, and is far better than other modern, semi-Biblical works, because into and between the lines of it, Joseph Holt Ingraham wove his varied beliefs and interests. During his clerical career, he produced other religious romances, all immensely popular, and was at work on *St. Paul: The Roman Citizen,* at the time of his death. He used the royalties from these to procure and destroy the copyrights of his first flimsy and embarrassing efforts.

His stories of land and sea adventure included *Lafitte: or, The Pirate of the Gulf,* an elaborate tale which is still in print. He interpreted many topics between the awkward writing of his early novel, *The American Lounger* (1839), and his untimely death at fifty-one.

Ingraham's little known literary enterprises combine the romanticism of the eighteenth century, which he barely missed, and the practical gusto of the nineteenth. Eager for living, observant, he had a range of interest equal and similar to some of his contemporaries. His writing was at once a necessity and an escape from the mold of life in which he found himself placed. In his writing there is, to a greater than usual extent, a clue to the man who left meagre material for biographers. His "notes" are lacking but the influences of Jeremy Taylor and John Donne are evident. It is not beyond credence that Edgar Allan Poe had the benefit of Ingraham's research into the macabre.

Leaving behind him no small amount of writing, Ingraham died in the vestry-room of Christ Church, Holly Springs, from wounds from the accidental discharge of his own gun. Though his writing suffered from overproduction, his religious fiction freed the American novel from the contemporary prejudice which was impeding its progress.

Principal Works: The South-West, by a Yankee, 1835; Lafitte: or, The Pirate of the Gulf, 1836; Burton: or, The Sieges, 1838; The American Lounger, 1839; Quadroone: or, St. Michael's Day, 1841; Frank Rivers: or, The Dangers of the Town, 1843; Rafael: or, The Twice Condemned, 1845; Scarlet Feather: or, The Young Chief of the Albenaquies, 1845; Ringold Griffitt: or, The Raftsman of the Susequehannah, 1847; The Prince of the House of David: or, Three Years in the Holy City, 1855; The Pillar of Fire: or, Israel in Bondage, 1859; The Throne of David: From the Consecration of the Shepherd of Bethlehem to the Rebellion of Prince Absalom, 1860.

About: Library of Southern Literature: Vol. 6; American Quarterly Church Review April 1861; also Ingraham's works.

INMAN, HENRY (July 30, 1837-November 13, 1899), social historian, was born in New York City, the son of the famous portrait and *genre* painter Henry Inman, and of Jane Riker (O'Brien) Inman. His father died when he was eight. He received his education at the Athenian Institute, Rahway, N.J., and with private tutors, and at twenty joined the army, rising at thirty-one to the rank of lieutenant-colonel. Cashiered from the army in 1872, he was subsequently connected with various newspapers in Kansas. He died at Topeka, his last years being spent apart from his family.

Service in Indian campaigns had given him extensive familiarity with the West, and his first sketches of frontier life being widely publicized by the Santa Fé Railroad, he was encouraged to extend them. In some of his efforts he had the cooperation of W. F. Cody (Buffalo Bill). His eccentricities led to the squandering of the large royalties of his last two years. His work, although popular and valuable for its details of pioneer days, was not always historically veracious.

PRINCIPAL WORKS: Stories of the Old Santa Fé Trail, 1881; In the Van of Empire, 1889; The Old Santa Fé Trail: The Story of a Great Highway, 1897; Tales of the Trail, 1898; The Ranche on the Oxhide, 1898; A Pioneer From Kentucky, 1898; The Great Salt Lake Trail (with W. F. Cody) 1898; The Delahoydes, 1899; Buffalo Jones' Forty Years of Adventure, 1899.

ABOUT: Heitman, F. B. History and Register and Directory of the United States Army.

IOOR, WILLIAM (fl. 1780-1830), one of the group of Charleston playwrights of the early nineteenth century, was born in St. George's Parish, Dorchester, S.C., the son of John Ioor, descended from a Hollander settling in that state in 1714.

Ioor, who was described as "a cheery, humorous old gentleman," is credited with two comedies. The first, *Independence: or, Which Do You Like Best, the Peer or the Farmer,* an adaptation of an English novel, *The Independent,* was one of the earliest examples of social comedy in America, and was produced at the Charleston Theatre in 1805. His other, *The Battle of Eutaw Springs and Evacuation of Charleston,* a patriotic play of the American Revolution, was known to have been played in Philadelphia in 1813 and at the Charleston Theatre in 1818.

PRINCIPAL WORKS: Independence: or, Which Do You Like Best, the Peer or the Farmer, 1805; The Battle of Eutaw Springs, 1807.

ABOUT: Quinn, A. H. A History of the American Drama From the Beginning to the Civil War; Snowden, Y. South Carolina Plays and Playwrights.

IRELAND, JOSEPH NORTON (April 24, 1817-December 29, 1898), historian of the New York stage, came of good merchant stock which, with the exception of William Henry Ireland, perpetrator of the notorious Shakespeare forgeries, was undistinguished for literary productivity.

Joseph Norton Ireland's parents were Joseph and Sophia (Jones) Ireland, who moved from their home on Long Island into New York City, where their son was born. He received a common-school education and entered his father's business at an early age, retiring in 1855. Ten years earlier he had married Mary Amelia, the daughter of Walter and Mary (Van Nostrand) Titus, and adopted daughter of John S. and Amelia (Titus) Avery.

After 1857 Ireland lived in Bridgeport, Conn., although his love of the theatre often took him to New York, where he mingled on friendly terms with theatrical people and enjoyed honorary membership in the Players Club and the Dunlap Society.

He began his exhaustive collection of theatrical data as a hobby which later developed into his *Records of the New York Stage From 1750 to 1860.* With the exception of William Dunlap's previous record, *History of the American Theatre,* 1832, Ireland's book was the first reliable history of the New York stage and was used freely by such later theatrical chroniclers as Quinn and Odell.

Ireland claimed no literary place for himself although he wrote two ponderous biographies of actors, *Mrs. Duff,* and *A Memoir of the Professional Life of Thomas Abthorpe Cooper.* He contributed articles on outstanding personalities to *Actors and Actresses of Great Britain and the United States,* edited by Brander Matthews and Laurence Hutton, and contributed a letter to Lawrence Barrett's *Charlotte Cushman,* listing the parts played by the famous actress.

His genial personality and profound interest in the theatre made him the logical historian of the stage, and his personal fortune afforded him the means and leisure to carry on his patient research during his long life. He died at Bridgeport.

PRINCIPAL WORKS: Records of the New York Stage From 1750 to 1860 (2 vols.) 1866-67; Mrs. Duff, 1882; A Memoir of the Professional Life of Thomas Abthorpe Cooper, 1888.

ABOUT: Quinn, A. H. A History of the American Drama From the Beginning to the Civil War; New York Herald, New York Tribune December 30, 1898.

"IRONQUILL." See WARE, EUGENE FITCH

IRVING, JOHN TREAT (December 2, 1812-February 27, 1906), novelist and essayist, was the son of Judge John Treat Irving, one of Washington Irving's brothers, and of Abby Spicer (Furman) Irving. He was born, lived, and died (at the advanced age of ninety-three) in New York City. He was graduated from Columbia in 1828. In 1833 he accompanied Henry W. Ellsworth in a journey to make treaties with the Pawnee Indians, this being the source of his *Indian Sketches* and *Hunters of the Prairie*. On his return to New York he studied law but before settling down to his profession he traveled, from 1835 to 1837, in Europe. In 1838 he married Helen Schermerhorn. In addition to the law he engaged in the brokerage and real estate businesses. He retired in 1887 to devote himself to social and philanthropic activities (he was long president of the Institute for the Blind).

and to writing. He contributed essays to the *Knickerbocker* and other magazines, and wrote several novels under the pseudonym of "John Quod." His Indian books have been cited as examples of the contemporary "gentlemanly and urban concern for the frontier," and he was essentially a very minor litterateur, simply following in the expected tradition of his family, class, and time.

PRINCIPAL WORKS: Indian Sketches, 1835 and 1888: The Hunters of the Prairie: or, The Hawk Chief, 1837; The Quod Correspondence: or, The Attorney, 1842; Harry Harson; or, The Benevolent Bachelor, 1844; The Van Gelder Papers and Other Sketches, 1887 and 1895.

ABOUT: Irving, P. M. Life and Letters of Washington Irving; Columbia University Quarterly June 1906; New York Times February 28, 1906.

IRVING, PETER (October 30, 1771-June 27, 1838), miscellaneous writer, was born in New York City, the son of William Irving and Sarah (Sanders) Irving and brother of Washington Irving [*q.v.*]. He was educated in private schools and received a degree in medicine at Columbia. He was early attracted to literature and, with his brothers William and Washington, was a member of the early literary group, the Calliopean Society, and one of the wits who assembled in Gouverneur Kemble's "Cockloft Hall." In 1802 he established, and edited until 1805, a four-page daily paper, the *Morning Chronicle,* to which his younger brother made early contributions. In 1810 he joined his brother Ebenezer in founding the firm of P. & E. Irving. On its failure in 1818 while he and Washington were with the Liverpool branch, he turned to literature and wrote his one novel, *Giovanni Sbogarro,* a stirring Venetian tale of piratical adventure taken from the French, probably by Charles Nodier. It was not, however, a financial success.

Peter Irving was deeply devoted to his more famous brother Washington, and was the younger's constant literary adviser and guide, and for a considerable time his companion. He never married. After 1815 he was a semi-invalid. He spent about twenty-seven of his years abroad, returning two years before his death in New York.

WORK: Giovanni Sbogarro, 1820.

ABOUT: Duyckinck, E. A. & G. L. Cyclopaedia of American Literature; Irving, P. M. (ed.). The Life and Letters of Washington Irving; Williams, S. T. ed.). The Journals of Washington Irving; Franco-American Review Spring 1937.

IRVING, WASHINGTON (April 3, 1783-November 28, 1859), essayist, biographer, and historian, was born in New York City, the youngest of the eleven children of William Irving, a Scotch merchant from an Orkney family originally named Irvine, and Sarah (Sanders) Irving, granddaughter of an English rector. The father, emigrating to America after his marriage, had fought in the Revolution and named his last-born after his commander-in-chief, who, meeting the child in 1789 when he came to New York to be inaugurated as the first president, bestowed on the boy his blessing. Irving grew up the petted favorite of his much older brothers and sisters, little oppressed by his father's stern Presbyterianism, escaping over roofs to theatres and dancing-school, and even, with his mother's connivance, getting himself confirmed in the Episcopal church. His education was desultory, consisting of attendance at half a dozen private schools, none very good; but he was a great reader, and only delicate health kept him from following his brothers to college at Columbia.

In 1798 he began to read law in the offices of a local attorney, but he was an indifferent student, and spent most of his time in contributing to his brother Peter's *Morning Chronicle.* In 1803 he accompanied an expedition to Montreal through northern New York; and he gave more attention to social pleasures than to either study or writing. In 1804 he was threatened with tuberculosis, and his brothers sent him abroad, where he remained for two years; in Rome,

Collection of Frederick H. Meserve
WASHINGTON IRVING

Washington Allston almost persuaded him to be a painter. When he returned, in 1806, he was admitted to the bar, largely thanks to his winning manner rather than to his knowledge of the law, and he practiced after a fashion until 1810; the only considerable case he was concerned in was Aaron Burr's trial for treason in 1807, and he had a very minor part in that. In 1807, with his brother William and James Kirk Paulding, he began producing the series of sketches known as *Salmagundi,* a sort of aftermath of Addison and forerunner of *Pickwick,* and his first real bid for literary fame.

Meanwhile he had fallen in love with Matilda Hoffman, Judge Hoffman's daughter, who died of tuberculosis at seventeen, during their engagement. There is no doubt this was a lasting sorrow to him; but his nephew's sentimental insistence that he never again was interested in a woman is pure nonsense; he certainly tried to marry Emily Foster in 1822, and he showed varying degrees of attachment for at least half a dozen others. As a matter of fact, like many youngest children of large families, he was a predestined bachelor. He buried his grief in the task of writing his first full-length book, the comic *Knickerbocker's History of New York,* the earliest American humorous work of literary pretensions, and he occupied himself also in politics and business in Washington, where he became a great friend of Dolly Madison, the president's wife. On his retirement from the law he had become a silent partner in his brothers' mercantile firm, with a fifth interest. In 1810 he edited the works of Thomas Campbell, the poet, and wrote a biographical sketch for the volume, and in the War of 1812 he was *aide-de-camp* to Gov. Daniel Tompkins. In 1813 and 1814 he edited the *Analectic Magazine,* in Philadelphia. The next year his brothers sent him to Liverpool to manage their branch there. He expected to return in a year or two, but he stayed seventeen years. His father had died in 1810; in 1817 his mother followed, and the same year the business failed. For the first time Irving was faced with the necessity of writing in order to support himself. *Knickerbocker* and his social connections had earned him the friendship of Scott, Moore, and Byron, and now Scott interested him in German literature and romantic history, and fostered his natural bent toward the picturesque. *The Sketch Book,* published in 1819 and 1820, and containing those immortal tales, "Rip Van Winkle" and "The Legend of Sleepy Hollow," made him actually famous. His head a little turned, he spent a gay year in Paris, then, in 1822, spent a winter in Dresden. In both places, he neglected his own work sadly, though he collaborated on several anonymous farces with John Howard Payne.

His reputation far from helped by the negligible *Tales of a Traveller,* a sort of rewarming of the remains of better material, he spent two unhappy years, partly in France, partly in England. To this period belongs the strange episode with Mary Godwin Shelley, who seems to have been in love with him while Payne, who acted as go-between, was in love with her. Irving finally dropped all his perplexities behind him, when in 1826 he went to Madrid, under semi-official auspices, to write his *Life of Columbus.* On this book he really worked, and it remains the best of his biographical and historical productions. He was recalled to London as secretary of the United States Legation in 1829, and in 1832 he returned to America, to find himself greeted as a triumphal hero. There were voices to say that he was an Anglophile and an arch-conservative—both of which charges were more or less true—but they were drowned out by evidences of Irving's indisputable patriotism (he refused, later, to write for the *Quarterly Review* because it was anti-American), his charm, and his services as a literary ambassador from America to Europe.

He soon wearied of the adulation, and in 1832 accompanied an expedition to the Osage and Pawnee Indian tribes. From this grew *Astoria* and other minor Western works, and also his friendship with John Jacob Astor, as a result of which he became one of the founders of the Astor Library (now part of the New York Public Library). On his return he bought an estate near Tarrytown, known as "Sunnyside," though he preferred its old name of "Wolfert's Roost," and settled there with two of his brothers and several nieces. In 1838 he began a history of the conquest of Mexico, but finding that Prescott had already started such a work, graciously relinquished it. From 1839, just when financial affairs were beginning to be straitened again, he was guaranteed $2000 a year in exchange for monthly contributions to the *Knickerbocker Magazine*. In 1842, after he had declined offers of the mayoralty of New York, a seat in Congress, and the secretaryship of the navy under Van Buren, Tyler appointed him minister to Spain. He accepted, and served for four years, though his preoccupation with political problems tarnished the charm of the early days that had produced not only *Columbus,* but also the *Conquest of Granada* and the *Alhambra,* and he wrote little. Indeed, his writing days were nearing their close, and on his return to "Sunnyside" in 1846 he undertook only two more important works—the pedestrian *Mahomet* and the *Life of Washington,* begun in enthusiasm, ended in exhaustion. The effort probably killed him; he died suddenly of a heart attack at seventy-six.

The word that is always used of Washington Irving is "charm." He was one of the most magnetic and sweetest-natured of men, with his bright dark grey eyes, his stoutish figure, his delightful smile, his head (on which in latter years a wig replaced the vanished hair) held a little to one side. He was modest, kindly, a romantic to his finger-tips, sentimental over old things—old scenes, old stories, old customs, old friends—the soul of courtesy. And as he was, so he wrote. Van Wyck Brooks speaks of his shaping, "in charming prose," the legends of the Hudson River; Richard Garnett remarks on his "easy narrative," his "pellucid style," and calls him "exquisite in all things." These are not the phrases in which one evaluates the greatest literary work, and indisputably he was a minor writer. But he was a minor writer of the foremost rank. He actually established, in *Columbus* and *The Companions of Columbus,* an American school of history. The dry, quiet humor of *Knickerbocker* has genetic relationship with the boisterous humor soon to arise in the Western frontier; both are essentially American.

To paraphrase George Haven Putnam (son of the publisher to whom Irving was faithful even through bankruptcy), Irving's lasting fame arises through the coincidence of marked, if limited talents, and of essential sweetness of character, with the formative years of nineteenth century America. The giants about to arise or in their earliest glory—Poe, Emerson, Hawthorne, Whitman—the New England pundits—Longfellow, Lowell, Holmes—all overtopped him: but he was first. In New York, with no better rivals than Bryant and Halleck and Willis, he seemed even greater than he was. But before Emerson and Lowell, he married American literature to the literature of the world. He has every right to retain the title enthusiastically bestowed upon him, of "Father of American Literature." And if all else were lost, Rip Van Winkle and Ichabod Crane will live forever.

Principal Works: Salmagundi: or, The Whim-Whams and Opinions of Lancelot Langstaff, Esq. (with J. K. Paulding and W. Irving) 1807-08; A History of New-York, by Diedrich Knickerbocker, 1809; The Sketch Book of Geoffrey Crayon, Gent., 1819-20; Bracebridge Hall: or, The Humourists, 1822; Letters of Jonathan Oldstyle, Gent., 1824; Tales of a Traveller, 1824; History of the Life and Voyages of Christopher Columbus, 1828; Chronicles of the Conquest of Granada, 1829; Voyages and Discoveries of the Companions of Columbus, 1831; Tales of the Alhambra, 1832; Crayon Miscellanies, 1835; Legends of the Conquest of Spain, 1835; A Tour on the Prairies, 1835; Astoria, 1836; The Rocky Mountains: or, The Adventures of Captain Bonneville, U.S.A., 1837; Life of Oliver Goldsmith, 1849; Mahomet and His Successors, 1849-50; Wolfert's Roost and Other Papers, 1855; Life of Washington, 1855-59; Spanish Papers and Other Miscellanies (ed. by P. M. Irving) 1868; Journals (ed. by W. P. Trend & G. S. Hellman) 1919; (ed. by S. T. Williams) 1931; Diary (ed. by C. L. Penney) 1926; Letters (ed. by S. T. Williams) 1928.

About: Boynton, H. W. Washington Irving; Hellman, G. S. Washington Irving, Esq.: Ambassador at Large; Irving, P. M. Life and Letters of Washington Irving; Payne, W. M. Leading American Essayists; Warner, C. D. Washington Irving; Williams, S. T. The Life of Washington Irving.

IRVING, WILLIAM (August 15, 1766-November 9, 1821), poet, merchant and politician, was born in New York City, the third and eldest surviving son of William Irving and Sarah (Sanders) Irving. Sixteen years older than his famous brother Washington Irving [*q.v.*], he showed much devotion to the interests of the younger man who referred to him once as "the man I loved most on earth." As a young man he engaged in Indian trading, but soon settled down to a prominent part in the mercantile and political life in New York City. He served in Congress from 1814 to 1819 and died in New York.

Like his brothers Peter and Washington, William Irving brought his wit and talent for literature to enliven the genius of the gatherings at Gouverneur Kemble's "Cockloft Hall." He was one of the trio which included his brother-in-law, the author James K. Paulding, and his brother Washington, who contributed to the humorous and satirical *Salmagundi,* the twenty numbers of which were issued in 1807. The three collaborators wrote anonymously, but William's son Pierre Munro Irving, who was biographer and aide to Washington Irving, has attributed to his father the poetry of these booklets, and two of the Mustapha letters, the fifth and fourteenth.

Principal Works: Salmagundi (contributor) 1807.

About: Biographical Congressional Directory; Duyckinck, E. A. & G. L. Cyclopaedia of American

Literature; Irving, P. M. (ed.). The Life and Letters of Washington Irving; Williams, S. T. (ed.). The Journals of Washington Irving.

"ISABEL." See MOWATT, ANNA CORA (OGDEN) RITCHIE

"ITHACUS." See SHAW, JOHN

JACKSON, HELEN MARIA (FISKE) HUNT (October 15, 1830-August 12, 1885), novelist, poet, and essayist, was born in Amherst, Mass., the daughter of Nathan Welby Fiske, professor of Greek and philosophy at Amherst College, and of Deborah (Vinal) Fiske, who died in 1844. The orphan girl was reared by her aunt. She was educated at Ipswich Female Academy, where she became the lifelong friend of Emily Dickinson, and at a private school in New York. In 1852 she married Captain (later Major) Edward Bissell Hunt, one of the many possibilities as Emily Dickinson's mysterious renounced love. The Hunts lived at various military posts until 1863, when Major Hunt was killed by a submarine gun of his own invention. One of their sons had died in infancy; the other died in 1865. Utterly bereaved, and thinking her life nearly over, the widow moved to Newport. Aside from some childish verses, she had as yet written nothing, and she was already thirty-five.

In Newport she met Thomas Wentworth Higginson, the editor and essayist, who encouraged her to forget her grief by writing. Her first poems appeared in the *Nation,* her first articles in the *Independent.* From 1868 to 1870 she was abroad, and in 1872 she went to California. In 1873 she went to Colorado for relief from hay fever, stayed a year, and met William Sharpless Jackson, a wealthy banker whom she married in 1875. Her home thereafter—the first real home she had known since childhood—was in Colorado Springs. However, any return to domesticity was frustrated by her growing indignation at the treatment of the American Indians by the whites. She went to New York and worked herself into an illness gathering data on the subjects for *A Century of Dishonor,* which she sent at her own expense to every member of Congress. Meanwhile she herself was recuperating in Norway from the exhaustion caused by her labors.

Some slight result of her protest was seen in 1882, when, with Abbott Kinney, of Los Angeles, Mrs. Jackson was appointed special commissioner to investigate the condition of the Mission Indians. Her report was issued

Collection of Frederick H. Meserv[e]

HELEN HUNT JACKSON

in 1883, but secured no amelioration of th[e] situation; so, burning with righteous anger she wrote *Ramona,* intended to fictioniz[e] in vivid form the Indians' plight. It wa[s] immensely popular, but hundreds read i[t] for its picturesque scenes of Spanish day[s] in California to one who became intereste[d] in the Indians. The old Estudillo estate, i[n] San Diego, is now shown to tourists a[s] "Ramona's Marriage Place," and visitors ar[e] encouraged to believe Ramona and Alessandro were actual persons.

Soon after publication of the book, Mrs Jackson, who had become very stout in late[r] years, fell and broke her leg. She did no[t] recover, and it was discovered that she ha[d] cancer. The next summer she was take[n] to Los Angeles and San Francisco for treatment, and in the latter city she died, th[e] following August. By her request, she wa[s] buried beneath a cairn on the top o[f] Cheyenne Mountain, near Colorado Springs but later it proved necessary to remove he[r] remains to a cemetery, to avoid the vandalism of thoughtless tourists.

Few women in American literary histor[y] have had personalities equal in charm an[d] individuality to Helen Hunt Jackson's. Adventurous, witty, unconventional, highl[y] emotional, a good lover and a good hater she was yet the author of philosophical ode[s] which aroused the intense admiration o[f] Emerson. She was no beauty, with he[r] heavy chin, her snub nose, and her narro[w] grey eyes, but her winning smile made u[p] for her lack of regular features, and thi[s] heavy, faded blonde woman evoked the ardent affection of nearly all, men or women, who came under her spell. With all this, she was a shrewd business woman, who made a fortune from her work and knew how to keep it.

Her poems run from domestic verses to passionate love sonnets, and from celebrations of the nature she loved to the odes which Emerson carried around in his pocket. Revolt from the narrow Calvinism of her childhood made her a Rationalist by conviction, though her second husband was a Quaker and she married him according to the rite of that faith.

Except for *Ramona,* her novels are rather sentimental, and for the most part were written with young girl readers in mind. *Ramona,* though it missed its purpose, became her masterpiece through the feeling she put into it. As Ina Coolbrith wrote:

> For her the clamorous today
> The dreamful yesterday became.

A very rapid writer, she yet had a great respect for accuracy, and there was much research behind her apparently easy writing. Higginson remarked that she had "a natural instinct for literary structure." Because of her great aversion to publicity, which made most of her work anonymous (it is still not certain whether the "Saxe Holm" stories, for example, are hers or not), many things she wrote have been lost. What is left, however is enough to assure her a modest immortality.

PRINCIPAL WORKS: In the White Mountains, 1866; Verses, 1870; Bits of Travel, 1872; Bits of Talk About Home Matters, 1873; Saxe Holm's Stories (?) 1874-78; The Story of Boon (verse) 1874; Mercy Philbrick's Choice, 1876; Hetty's Strange History, 1877; Nelly's Silver Mine, 1878; Bits of Travel at Home, 1878; A Century of Dishonor, 1881; The Training of Children, 1882; Ramona, 1884; Glimpses of California and the Missions, 1885; Zeph, 1885; Glimpses of Three Coasts, 1886; Sonnets and Lyrics, 1886; Between Whiles, 1887.

ABOUT: Davis, C. C. & Alderson, W. A. The True Story of Ramona; Higginson, T. W. Contemporaries; James, G. W. Through Ramona's Country; Century Magazine December 1885; Publishers' Weekly October 10, 1931; New York Tribune August 14, 1885.

JACKSON, HENRY ROOTES (June 24, 1820-May 23, 1898), poet, had a distinguished career as judge, general, and diplomat. He was born in Athens, Ga., his father, Henry Jackson, a physician, being professor of mathematics at the University of Georgia; an uncle, James, was once governor of Georgia. He was graduated with high honors from Yale in 1839, studied law, practiced in Savannah, and at twenty-three was assistant United States district attorney. He served through the Mexican War as a colonel. In 1848 he bought the Savannah *Georgian,* and for a year was one of its editors. From 1849 to 1852 he was judge of the superior court, from 1853 to 1858 minister resident in Vienna. On his return he refused the offer of chancellorship of the University of Georgia. On secession of the state, he became a brigadier general in the Confederate Army. He was captured near Nashville in 1864 and was in prison until the end of the Civil War. He then returned to his legal practice. In 1885 he was for a few months the minister to Mexico. He was president of the Georgia Historical Society and the Telford Art Academy, and received M.A. and LL.D. degrees from the state university. He was twice married and had four children.

Jackson was a melodious and facile versifier of the classic nineteenth century school, his verse occasionally rising to genuine poetry. He is best known for "The Red Old Hills of Georgia," written during the Mexican War.

PRINCIPAL WORK: Tallulah and Other Poems, 1850.

ABOUT: Knight, L. L. Reminiscences of Famous Georgians; Northen, W. J. Men of Mark in Georgia; Weber, W. L. Selections From the Southern Poets.

JAMES, HENRY, SR. (June 3, 1811-December 18, 1882), philosopher and theologian, father of Henry James, Jr., and William James [*qq.v.*], was born in Albany, N.Y., the son of William James a prosperous merchant who had emigrated from Ulster, and Catharine (Barber) James, his third wife. When he was no more than fifteen one of his legs was amputated at the thigh, following severe burns. This episode, combined with the discipline of an exacting father, obliged an essentially free-spirited child to adjust himself to a sedentary urban life; and in his intellectual pursuits he was guided, at this time, by Joseph Henry, the most distinguished professor at Albany Academy. Henry James was graduated from Union College in 1830, played with the idea of becoming a lawyer, and then entered Princeton Theological Seminary in 1835; his opposition to Presbyterian orthodoxy was, two years later, quite irreconcilable, and he left without explanation.

In 1837 he sailed for England and in the doctrines of Robert Sandeman, founder of the Sandemanians or Glasites a sect which had originated in Scotland as a reaction against the Presbyterian Church, he found

HENRY JAMES, SR.

his first real substitute for Calvinism. On his return to the United States he edited Sandeman's *Letters on Theron and Aspasio.* But James soon replaced the literal Biblical interpretations of the Sandemanians with the mysticism and symbolism of the Swedenborgians, to which he adhered, though only in part, for the rest of his life. In 1869 James published *The Secret of Swedenborg* . . . but as Howells remarked, "he kept it." However, the book was a clear statement of James' own opinion of that "unaffectedly genial, wise, and good man."

During the 'forties and 'fifties James vacillated between New York—the home of Mary Robertson Walsh, who became his wife in 1840, and the birthplace of his two oldest and most famous children, William and Henry, Jr.—and various cities in Europe. He finally retired to Cambridge. Early in 1882 his wife died; he survived her less than a year.

James' writings were largely defenses of his own religious doctrines. He was a frequent lecturer on Carlyle, Emerson, etc., and religious subjects, avoiding, when possible, a parlor audience, for whom his thoughts were "all too grave and serious." The strength of James' style lay in his use of "outlawed" words, his habit of overstatement (the only real strategy, he believed, for the indolent and less impressionable readers), and a humor that was usually grotesque but sometimes quietly charming. An "unregarded sage" he may have been, yet there is certainly significance, from the literary point of view, in the suggestion that the style of Henry James, Jr., was an elaboration of his father's and that of William James a simplification.

Principal Works: Remarks on the Apostolic Age, 1840; What Is the State? 1846; Letter to a Swedenborgian, 1847; Moralism and Christianity, 1850; Lectures and Miscellanies, 1852; The Church of Christ Not an Ecclesiasticism, 1854; The Nature of Evil Considered, 1855; Christianity the Logic of Creation, 1857; Substance and Shadow, 1863; The Secret of Swedenborg: Being an Elucidation of His Doctrine of the Divine Natural Humanity, 1869; Society of the Redeemed Form of Man, 1879; The Philosophy of Henry James: A Digest, 1883; Literary Remains of the Late Henry James (ed. by William James) 1885.

About: Grattan, C. H. The Three Jameses; Howe, M. A. DeW. Memories of a Hostess; Warren, A. The Elder Henry James.

JAMES, HENRY, JR. (April 15, 1843-February 28, 1916), novelist, was born in New York City, the son of Henry James, Sr. [*q.v.*], philosopher-theologian, and Mary Robertson (Walsh) James, and younger brother of William James [*q.v.*]. He was, in effect, "born with a nostalgia for that far-away paradise" that was Europe: when scarcely a year old he, as well as his brother William, was taken abroad. The Jameses returned to the United States in 1845—but only nominally; in their back-parlor on Fourteenth Street hung the bust of the Bacchante and the vast "Prospect of Florence"; there was an abundance of dark-plum claret and *Punch* arrived regularly; Dickens made his pilgrimage and so did Thackeray. It was not at all strange, then, that Henry James, Sr., as early as 1849, contemplated taking his "four stout boys" (Garth Wilkinson and Robertson were the youngest) to Europe, that they might "absorb French and German and get such a sensuous education as they cannot get here."

It was 1855 when they actually sailed, and in Geneva, London, Paris, Boulogne, and Bonn, young James imbibed, in four years, something of that ever-amorphous—though more imminent—culture. When he entered Harvard in 1862 he knew that what he "'wanted to want' to be was, all intimately, just literary." Charles Eliot Norton, and several years later, William Dean Howells abetted this inclination.

When Lincoln issued his call for Northern volunteers Henry James was eighteen and was suffering from an ailment in his back. Like Henry Adams, Mark Twain, and Thomas Bailey Aldrich, he slipped into the shoes of the much-condemned "spectator" and, at almost the same time, into the "incredibility of print." The *Atlantic,* the *North American Review,* and the first issu of the *Nation* solicited James' critiques and short stories. Hawthorne, Balzac, and George Eliot, whom he himself had "discovered," were his early models. It was during his journey abroad in 1869 that he became aware of the fact that the most adept literary artists were drawing their subject matter from their own *milieux*. This fact must have given him no little concern, for until 1875 James straddled two continents, all the while hesitating to lift his foot very high off American ground. But in the end the "denser, richer, warmer European spectacle" with its "accumulation of history and custom . . . complexity of manners and types" looked like a better "fund of suggestion for a novelist." And it was as a novelist that Henry James was emerging: *Roderick Hudson* had been appearing serially in the *Atlantic* when he began his *annus mirabilis* in Paris. He was invited to musicales and soirées given by the intellectuals, and what was more important, he supped often with Turgenev, from whom he learned a most valuable literary technique—the art of subordinating the plot to an interacting fluctuation of the destinies of the characters.

James went to London in 1876 and took rooms near Piccadilly; the best of his harvest during the four years that followed was *A Portrait of a Lady,* serialized simultaneously (1880) in the United States and England. It was a piece of well-bred writing but it sprang from a still insecure concept of English life. *The Bostonians* (1886) was a thinly wrought piece; *The Tragic Muse* (1890) a deft projection of the histrionic temperament; and *The Princess Casamassima,* for which James' perception of a "grossly materialistic English upper class that wanted blood-letting" was prophetically good, was, in final execution, a mingling of understanding and misunderstanding. *The Spoils of Poynton,* a parade of inheritance quarrels and grievances, was followed by the whitecap of James' quietly consistent, ironic and too frequently ignored humor, *The Awkward Age* (1899).

Meanwhile James had removed to Rye, in Sussex, where, as Mrs. James Fields remarked after her visit there in 1898, he maintained an "impenetrable respectability." Having made a humiliating inroad into the art of playwriting (*The American* and *Guy Domville* were disastrously produced) James seemed to apply himself even more diligently than ever to the perfection of the novel, a form in which he had already achieved a structural excellence. The finest

HENRY JAMES, JR.

of his later writings was *The Ambassadors,* a novel so astutely autobiographical, in part, and so psychologically exhaustive that many have labeled it James' masterpiece. Second to it, perhaps, was *The Wings of the Dove* (1902) or *The Golden Bowl* (1904). *The Ivory Tower* and *The Sense of the Past* remained unfinished at the time of his death.

By 1905 James' mental and physical health seems to have been dissipated by a succession of overdone regrets—he fretted over his expatriation, his choice of a career, his bachelordom, etc., and the panacea for this was to be an American tour which took him into the Deep South and out to the Far West. He saw in America what he believed was an unfortunate gregariousness and a peculiar "dauntless power," about the source of which he had little curiosity. Patently, his observations were thickly prejudiced. He returned to Rye, and, following a complete breakdown in health, he made another journey to America, sailing again for England in August 1911 after the death of his brother William. In 1915 the awful aspect of the World War began to prey upon him; on July 26, despairing of hope that he might bring the United States to the side of England, and as a testimony of the "force of his attachment and devotion to England and to the cause for which she is fighting," he became a British subject. Early the following year he suffered from a stroke from which he never recovered. By direction of his will, James' ashes were laid in Cambridge, Mass. Shortly before his death the King had conferred the Order of Merit on him, and Oxford and Harvard had awarded him honorary doctorates. James was described as being a "small, pale, noticeable man, with large, piercingly observant eyes and hesitant speech."

His critics have assembled an array of esoteric interpretations, which are, in part, the outcome of an episode of speculation over his "Figure in the Carpet" (1896). The "figure," design, or message, instead of defining itself, remained annoyingly obscure. But the air was full of volunteer solutions, contradictory enough to satisfy all. James was, these critics contend, coldly scientific and entirely emotion-swept; an artistic fabricator with no moral substance and a stern-headed moralist; a discerning reporter of life and a hermit in complete isolation from living currents; a worshipper of obscurity and a disciple of clarity and precision. . .

What needs to be kept in mind is that James was at his professional apex during the early years of pre-War crest-of-the-wave civilization, and it was not unnatural that he should have epitomized it. Nor was it odd that he did so from the point of view of upper-class society, be it English or American, to which he himself belonged. Marcel Proust is the only other novelist who so thoroughly incarnated the aristocracy; his treatment of it became, in its most high-spun form, a kind of tenuous but sinewy satire. Was it not wiser for James to avoid going "east of Temple Bar" or "lower than Fourteenth Street" and to achieve relative architectonic perfection, than to penetrate "Whitechapel" or "the lower East Side" and emerge with a clumsy distortion? (*The Princess Casamassima* is a mild case in point.) To St. John Ervine's objection that James seemed to spend "half a lifetime saying 'Boo' to a goose," one might reply: James was not trying to write kinetic fiction—the successful *Turn of the Screw* was perhaps his only serious attempt at a "suspense" tale—he was bent on achieving an accumulation of psychological forces, a *progression d'effet*. He may have had no actual dislike for popularity, but he certainly did not propose to buy it at the cost of what to him were the artistic verities. The success of his early *Daisy Miller*, the most widely read of his novelettes, did not lure him away from his absorbing experimentation in the more extensive and difficult medium, the long novel.

James, ascetically preoccupied with form, may be said to have established in American fiction an excellent *thesis* which, during the immediate post-War decade, became (in the hands of his imitators) an *antithesis* of self-indulgent impressionism; and from which, in *synthesis*, may perhaps evolve an American novel of unique and distinguished character.

PRINCIPAL WORKS: *Novels, Novelettes, and Short Stories*—The Story of a Year, 1865; Watch and Ward, 1871; Transatlantic Sketches, 1875; A Passionate Pilgrim and Other Tales, 1875; Roderick Hudson, 1875; Madame de Mauves, 1875; The Madonna of the Future, 1875; The American, 1877; Daisy Miller, 1878; The Europeans, 1878; A Bundle of Letters, 1879; An International Episode, 1879; The Pension Beaurepas, 1879; Confidence, 1879; Washington Square, 1880; The Diary of a Man of Fifty, 1880; The Portrait of a Lady, 1881; The Point of View, 1882; The Siege of London, 1883; Tales of Three Cities, 1884; Lady Barbarine, 1884; Four Meetings, 1884; Pandora, 1884; The Author of Beltraffio, 1885; The Bostonians, 1886; The Aspern Papers, 1888; The Reverberator, 1888; Louisa Pallant, 1888; A London Life, 1889; The Liar, 1889; The Patagonia, 1889; The Tragic Muse, 1890; The Princess Casamassima, 1890; The Lessons of the Master and Other Stories, 1891; Sir Edmund Orme, 1891; The Marriages, 1891; Brooksmith, 1891; The Real Thing and Other Tales, 1893; The Chaperon, 1893; Greville Fane, 1893; The Private Life, 1893; Owen Wingrave, 1893; The Altar of the Dead, 1895; The Death of the Lion, 1895; The Coxon Fund, 1895; The Middle Years, 1895; Terminations, 1896; The Next Time, 1896; The Figure in the Carpet, 1896; The Friends of the Friends, 1896; The Spoils of Poynton, 1897; What Maisie Knew, 1897; In the Cage, 1898; The Pupil, 1898; The Two Magics, 1898; The Turn of the Screw, 1898; The Awkward Age, 1899; The Soft Side, 1900; The Tree of Knowledge, 1900; The Abasement of the Northmores, 1900; The Great Good Place 1900; Paste, 1900; Europe, 1900; Miss Gunton of Poughkeepsie, 1900; The Real Right Thing, 1900; The Sacred Fount, 1901; The Wings of the Dove, 1902; The Better Sort, 1903; The Ambassadors 1903; The Two Faces, 1903; The Broken Wings, 1903; The Beast in the Jungle, 1903; The Birthplace, 1903; The Beldonald Holbein, 1903; The Story In It, 1903; Flickerbridge, 1903; Mrs. Medwin, 1903; The Golden Bowl, 1904; The Finer Grain, 1910; The Outcry, 1911; The Ivory Tower (unfinished) 1917; The Sense of the Past (unfinished) 1917. *Plays*—Daisy Miller, 1883; The American, 1891; Guy Domville, 1895; The Album 1895; The Reprobate, 1895; The High Bid, 1908 *Travel Sketches*—Portraits of Places, 1883; A Little Tour in France, 1884; English Hours, 1905 The American Scene, 1906; Italian Hours, 1909 *Literary and Art Studies*—French Poets and Novelists, 1878; Hawthorne, 1879; The Art of Fiction 1884; Partial Portraits, 1888; Picture and Text 1893; Essays in London and Elsewhere, 1893; William Wetmore Story and His Friends, 1894; The Lesson of Balzac, 1905; The Question of Our Speech, 1905; Views and Reviews, 1908; Notes on Novelists, 1914; The Art of the Novel: Critical Prefaces, 1934. *Autobiography*—A Small Boy and Others, 1913; Notes of a Son and Brother, 1914 The Middle Years, 1917.

ABOUT: Bosanquet, T. Henry James at Work Brooks, Van W. The Pilgrimage of Henry James Edgar, P. Henry James: Man and Author; Ford F. M. Portraits From Life; Ford, F. M. (as Ford Madox Hueffer) Henry James: A Critical Study Grattan, C. H. The Three Jameses; Herrick, R "Henry James" (in Macy, J. *American Writers o*

American Literature); James, H. A Small Boy and Others; Notes of a Son and Brother; The Middle Years; The Art of the Novel; Roberts, M. Henry James' Criticism; West, R. Henry James.

JAMES, WILLIAM (January 11, 1842-August 26, 1910), psychologist and philosopher, was born in New York City, the eldest child of the theologian Henry James, Sr. [*q.v.*], and Mary Robertson (Walsh) James, and the elder brother of Henry James, Jr. [*q.v.*], the novelist. Like his brothers and sisters, he was reared by a system which included at least a dozen schools in various parts of Europe, and numerous private teachers in Albany and New York. In his earlier years he was divided between art and science, and in 1860 he went to Newport to study painting with William H. Hunt. The next year, however, found him in the Lawrence Scientific School at Harvard. At first his specialties were chemistry, comparative anatomy, and physiology. In 1864 he entered the Harvard Medical School, and in 1865 and 1866 he went with the Thayer Expedition, headed by Agassiz, to Brazil. He returned, first to the Massachusetts General Hospital, then to the Harvard Medical School, and then spent eighteen months in Dresden and Berlin. This was a period of the intensest mental depression, amounting to suicidal melancholia, and the relief he found in philosophy was the starting point of his twofold interest in psychology and in the philosophy of religion. He received his M.D. from Harvard in 1869, but it was three years more before he found himself. His health was too frail and his sight too poor for laboratory work, and he had never intended to practice medicine.

In 1872 he was appointed instructor in physiology in Harvard, and his connection with the university did not cease until 1907, when he became professor emeritus of philosophy. As instructor, assistant professor, and professor, he had taught physiology, psychology, and philosophy. He inaugurated the course on the philosophy of evolution; his was the first course in America on the relation of psychology to physiology; and in 1876 he established the first American psychological laboratory, in which Stanley Hall was one of the early students.

In 1878 James married Alice Howe Gibbons, a markedly happy and companionable union which resulted in five children, of whom four survived him. His years at Harvard were punctuated with many European trips, all of 1882 and 1883 being spent abroad. In 1878 he was commissioned to write his famous *Principles of Psychology,* which appeared in the form of articles in technical journals until its publication as a book in 1890. As early as 1884 he enunciated the theory of visceral emotions (we do not laugh because we are happy, we are happy because we laugh), known as the James-Lange theory.

A lover of unpopular causes, James joined the Society for Psychical Research in 1882 and its American branch in 1884, serving as president of the parent organization in 1894 and 1895. In the same spirit of tolerance and open-mindedness he defended faith healers and opposed the Spanish-American War. In 1896 and 1898 lecture tours took him all over the country for the first time; he grew especially attached to the West, and lectured at both the University of California and Stanford. Invited to give the Gifford Lectures at the University of Edinburgh, he sailed for Europe in 1899. An unwise amount of exercise had badly strained his heart, and all year he was very ill; however, he prepared and gave the lectures, the groundwork of his celebrated *Varieties of Religious Experience,* and was able to return to teach at Harvard, and to give a second course of lectures at Edinburgh in 1902.

By this time James was the most famous living American philosopher, with an international reputation evidenced by doctorates from Edinburgh, Padua, Geneva, and Oxford. In 1906 he was visiting professor at Stanford University, an engagement cut

WILLIAM JAMES
c. 1885

short by the disastrous California earthquake. The next year he retired from active work at Harvard, though he delivered the Hibbert Lectures at Oxford in 1908. In 1910, when his brother Henry was ill, William James and his wife went to him in England; they returned to America together, but the older brother was barely able to reach his beloved country home, at Chocorua, N.H., before another heart attack proved fatal.

William James is generally conceded to be, with Emerson, the greatest philosophic mind which has yet emerged in America. His theory of Pragmatism, an advanced empiricist philosophy (empiricism being the doctrine that truth is based on experience and observation), has been badly understood and has been degraded by some who considered themselves his disciples. To him, it was *pragmatic* that "a thing is what is experienced" and that the way a thing "works" is the best available criterion of the truth of a human cognition. The relations between things are as important as the things themselves, and things with their relations—"things" including beliefs and thoughts—together account for all that exists, with no need for a mysterious "unknowable" or "first cause" behind them. Many doctrines avowedly based on James, however, are mere travesties of his theory.

By his own definitions, James himself was both "tough-minded" and "tender-minded." His nature was a compound of gallantry and sympathy; he was a moody, sensitive, vibrant, deeply ethical human being, with the geniality and humor—and also the neurasthenia—of his Celtic forebears. To look at his portrait—the long, pointed nose, the thinker's forehead and deep-set eyes, the retreating chin beneath the straggly beard—is to realize that here was a man for whom life would be either heaven or hell, who by the accident of fate might construct a world's philosophies or sink into the darkness of introspective melancholy. He was not the least remarkable of a very remarkable family—all neurotic, all brilliant, but none of them so grounded in actuality as he.

Into both psychology and philosophy, William James the author broke like a bombshell. He was incapable of dull or stodgy writing; he had a genius for the concrete and vivid phrase, the telling word. It was activity that most interested him, and he could make the dullest and most abstruse of theories at once clear and vivacious. He was profoundly an individual, an enzyme in the blood of philosophic thought, actuating all who came under his influence, though never sufficiently dogmatic, always too much his unique self, to found any frozen school. He was a biological sport, a variation, and he brought new life into the dying bones of aged philosophy, just as he breathed force and direction into the sturdy youngster, experiental and functional psychology. His world, "so various, so beautiful, so new," was the world of the future, and, as Professor Kallen remarks, "his positive work still is prophetic."

Principal Works: Principles of Psychology, 1890; Psychology: Briefer Course, 1892; The Will to Believe, and Other Essays in Popular Philosophy, 1897; Talks to Teachers on Psychology and to Students on Some of Life's Ideals, 1899; The Varieties of Religious Experience, 1902; Pragmatism, 1907; A Pluralistic Universe, 1908; The Energies of Men, 1908; The Meaning of Truth, 1909; Memories and Studies, 1911; Some Problems of Philosophy, 1911;. Essays in Radical Empiricism, 1912. Letters (ed. by H. James) 1920.

About: Boutroux, E. E. M. William James; Flournoy, T. The Philosophy of William James; Grattan, C. H. The Three Jameses; James, H. A Small Boy and Others, Notes of a Son and Brother; Kallen, H. M. The Philosophy of William James; Perry, R. B. In the Spirit of William James; Royce, J. William James and Other Essays; Sabin, E. E. William James and Pragmatism.

JAMISON, CECILIA VIETS (DAKIN)

(1837?-April 11, 1909), artist and novelist, was born in Yarmouth, N.S., the daughter of Viets and Elizabeth (Bruce) Dakin; the family were descendants of Tories who had fled to Canada during the American Revolution. She was educated in private schools in Canada, New York, Boston, and Paris, and settled with her parents in Boston in her mid-teens. No dates are obtainable regarding her early life, as she herself, with unnecessary coyness, sometimes gave her birth-date as 1848; this however, would have had her married in childhood, for it was about 1860, while she was studying art in Boston, that she married George Hamilton. What became of him, whether he died or she was divorced from him, is unknown; soon after she went to Rome for three years as an art student. There she met Longfellow, who read some of her manuscripts and praised them highly. Thereafter she divided her career between painting and fiction; she had studios in New York and Boston and specialized in portraiture, her best known pictures being of Longfellow and Agassiz. In 1878 she married Samuel Jamison, a New Orleans lawyer, and until 1887 they lived on his plantation near Thibodeaux, La., then moving to New Orleans; most of the summers she spent at Nahant.

Mass. Mr. Jamison died in 1902, and the widow returned to Massachusetts, dying of heart disease at Roxbury, a suburb of Boston.

Mrs. Jamison was best known as a juvenile writer; many of her stories appeared in *St. Nicholas,* and she was noted for the charm with which she portrayed child life. In her novels for adults (*The Story of an Enthusiast* was her own favorite) the story was subordinate to the local backgrounds; she was one of the "regional" genre writers who flourished in America during the late nineteenth century. Many of her novels appeared first in serial form in *Harper's* and *Scribner's.* Her work is badly "dated," and she is little read today.

PRINCIPAL WORKS: Something to Do, 1871; Woven of Many Threads, 1872; A Crown From the Spear, 1872; Ropes of Sand and Other Stories, 1873; My Bonnie Lass, 1877; Lilly of San Miniato, 1878; The Story of an Enthusiast, 1888; Lady Jane, 1891; Toinette's Philip, 1894; Seraph: The Little Violiniste, 1896; Thistledown, 1903; The Penhallow Family, 1905.

ABOUT: St. Nicholas April 1894; Boston Transcript April 13, 1909; New Orleans Daily Picayune April 13, 1909.

JAMISON, DAVID FLAVEL (December 14, 1810-September 14, 1864), historian, was born in Orangeburg District, S.C., the son of a wealthy physician and planter, Van de Vastine Jamison, and of Elizabeth (Rumph) Jamison. After some attendance at South Carolina College he practiced law for a few years, then settled down as a cotton planter and became a leader in public life. Possessing two thousand acres of land and some seventy Negroes, he was strongly pro-slavery, became president of the secession Congress, and was devoted to the end of his life to the civil affairs of the state and of the Confederacy. He married his cousin Elizabeth Ann Carmichael Rumph. In his last years he lived in Barnwell District. He died of yellow fever at Charleston.

Jamison was a man of scholarly attainments to whom historical studies were an especial attraction, and he was a frequent contributor to the *Southern Quarterly* and other southern periodicals. His extended study of the French hero and warrior of the fourteenth century, Bertrand du Guesclin, was completed in the early years of the Civil War and published in England, regardless of the blockade existing both when it was sent out and returned.

PRINCIPAL WORK: The Life and Times of Bertrand du Guesclin (2 vols.) 1864.

ABOUT: Jameson, E. O. The Jamesons in America; Harper's Weekly February 2, 1861.

JANES, LEWIS GEORGE (February 19, 1844-September 4, 1901), educator and lecturer, was born at Providence, R.I., his father being Alphonso Richards Janes, merchant and anti-slavery pioneer, and his mother Sophia (Taft) Janes. He was of Scotch and German lineage, a Scot ancestor, William Janes, having come to New Haven Colony in 1637. On his mother's side he was descended from Peregrine White of the Mayflower. He studied medicine in New York, but became attached to philosophical, religious, ethical and other studies and remained in Brooklyn as teacher and lecturer, acting from 1885 to 1896 as president of the Brooklyn Ethical Association, lecturing in the School of Political Science of the Brooklyn Institute of Arts and Sciences, and teaching history for a year at Adelphi College. Removing to Cambridge, Mass., he was from 1896 director of the Cambridge Conferences for the study of ethics, philosophy, sociology, and religion and the Monsalvat school summer conferences at Eliot, Maine, which attracted distinguished scholars for the study of comparative religion. From 1899 he was also president of the Free Religious Association.

An evolutionist, an earnest seeker after truth, and of wide scholarship, Dr. Janes wrote numerous pamphlets and articles on a variety of subjects for various reviews. His last and most popular work *Health and a Day* was published in his last year. He died suddenly, following the close of a summer conference at Eliot.

PRINCIPAL WORKS: A Study of Primitive Christianity, 1886; Samuell Gorton: A Forgotten Founder of Our Liberties, 1896; Health and a Day, 1901.

ABOUT: Lewis, G. Janes: Philosopher, Patriot, Lover of Man.

JANNEY, SAMUEL McPHERSON (January 11, 1801-April 30, 1880), Quaker minister and miscellaneous writer, was a native of Loudoun County, Virginia. His parents, Abijah and Jane (McPherson) Janney, and some of his ancestors were Friends. His mother died early and he was sent to an uncle's counting house in Alexandria. There he proceeded to educate himself, attending night school, reading avidly, organizing a scientific and literary society. He became partner in a cotton factory which after nine years failed and left him deeply in debt. This he undertook to discharge by opening a boarding school for girls and by writing. After fifteen years he retired to devote himself to his ministry, philanthropy, and literary pursuits, spending a few years as superintendent of Indian Affairs.

He wrote verse early, but after his first book of poetry appeared he gradually lost interest and turned to prose. He was especially the historian and biographer of his denomination. Belonging to the Hicksite sect, of strong anti-slavery sentiment but ministering to both sides in the Civil War, he gained wide eminence and influence. His *Memoirs* written exclusively for his own children, were published posthumously.

PRINCIPAL WORKS: The Last of the Lenape and Other Poems, 1839; The Life of William Penn, 1852; The Life of George Fox, 1853; Conversations on Religious Subjects, and Familiar Dialogues, 1860; History of the Religious Society of Friends: From Its Rise to the Year 1828 (4 vols.) 1860-67; Memoirs, 1881.

ABOUT: Library of Southern Literature Vol. 6; Janney, S. M. Memoirs; Friends' Intelligencer May 29, 1880.

JANVIER, MARGARET THOMSON (February 1844-February 1913), was born in New Orleans, La., in a literary family. Her father, Francis de Haes Janvier, a descendent of a Huguenot refugee of 1683, was the author of some books of poetry and verse, and her mother, Emma (Newbold) Janvier, was a writer of stories for children. A brother, Thomas Allibone Janvier [*q.v.*], also became a writer. She received a common school education. Most of her life was lived at Moorestown, N.J., where she died after an illness of nearly three years.

Miss Janvier commenced early to write stories and verse, mostly juvenile using the pen name "Margaret Vandegrift." Her stories were of a quiet, simple, sentimental and moral nature. Among the magazines in which her work appeared were *St. Nicholas, Harper's Young People,* the *Youth's Companion, Wide Awake,* the *Century,* and the *Atlantic.*

PRINCIPAL WORKS: Clover Beach, 1880; Under the Dog Star, 1881; Holidays at Home, 1882; The Queen's Body Guard, 1883; Doris and Theodora, 1884; Little Bell and Other Stories, 1884; The Absent-Minded Fairy, 1884; Rose Raymond's Wards, 1885; Ways and Means, 1886; Little Helpers, 1889; The Dead Doll and Other Verses, 1889; Umbrella to Mend, 1905.

ABOUT: Adams, O. A Dictionary of American Authors.

JANVIER, THOMAS ALLIBONE (July 16, 1849-June 18, 1913), journalist, was born in Philadelphia, where he was educated in the common schools. His father and mother, Francis de Haes Janvier and Emma (Newbold) Janvier, were both persons of literary ability, and his sister was the author Margaret Thomson Janvier [*q.v.*]. The years 1871-1880 were spent as a journalist in Philadelphia with the *Times,* the *Evening Bulletin,* and the *Press,* following which he made a three years' visit in the same capacity to Colorado, New Mexico, and Mexico, with his wife, the author and painter Catharine Ann Drinker, whom he married in 1879. Later they lived in the Greenwich section of New York City, and made an extended stay from 1893 to 1900 in southern France and England. He died at Moorestown, N.J.

Janvier drew much of his materials from the old and quaint, on which he wrote with sympathetic charm and humor. His diction was exact and graceful. His stories of the art colony of New York, written under the pen name "Ivory Black" became the basis of his first book *Color Studies.* He had a winning personality and polished manners. His warm sympathy for Provence won him honorary membership in the Society of Felibrige.

PRINCIPAL WORKS: Color Studies, 1885; The Mexican Guide, 1886; The Aztec Treasure House, 1890; Stories of Old New Spain, 1891; The Uncle of an Angel and Other Stories, 1891; Embassy to Provence, 1893; In Old New York, 1894; In the Sargasso Sea, 1898; In Great Waters, 1901; The Christmas Kalends of Provence, 1902; The Dutch Founding of New York, 1903; Henry Hudson, 1909; Legends of the City of Mexico, 1910; From the South of France, 1912; At the Casa Napoleon, 1914.

ABOUT: Harper, J. H. The House of Harper; Janvier, T. A. At the Casa Napoleon (see Preface by R. Hitchcock); Outlook June 28, 1913.

JARVES, JAMES JACKSON (August 20, 1818-June 28, 1888), art collector, historian, and miscellaneous writer, was born in Boston, the son of Deming Jarves, a pioneer glass maker, and Anna Smith (Stutson) Jarves. Some authorities give his birthdate as 1820. He was educated at Chauncy Hall School, but ill health and failing sight forced him to give up his plans for Harvard, and ended his formal schooling at fifteen. Soon after, he began extensive travels to California, Mexico, and Hawaii. He seems to have returned to Boston, but by 1840 he was in Honolulu again as founder and editor of the *Polynesian,* the first newspaper published in Hawaii. In 1844 he was made director of the Hawaiian government press and his paper became the official organ of the government. In 1848 Jarves was sent by Kamehameha III as commissioner to negotiate commercial treaties with the United States, Great Britain, and France. He sailed for Europe in 1851, and became so enamored with Florence that he gave up his post and settled there for the remainder of his life. From 1879 to 1882 he served as United

States vice-consul, since he had never abandoned his American citizenship.

An ardent art-lover and art-collector from boyhood, Jarves devoted his entire fortune to making the first important collection of Italian masters of painting to be taken to this country. Unfortunately, he met with little response. He received offers for individual paintings, but refused to break the collection, which finally, in a rather irregular manner, was acquired by Yale. Other paintings from his collection went later to the Cleveland Museum of Art. In 1881, in memory of his father, he gave his Venetian glass collection to the Metropolitan Museum, practically impoverishing himself in consequence. His collection of embroideries, laces, and Renaissance fabrics is in Wellesley College. Jarves exhausted his patrimony in educating Americans in aesthetic taste and knowledge of Italian art, and he had been dead a generation before any appreciable effects of his crusade were seen.

In 1838 he married Elizabeth Russell Swain, and after her death he married, in 1862, Isabel Kast Hayden. She also predeceased him, as did four of his six children, his *Pepero* being a tribute to his son, a highly talented artist who died at fifteen. A modest, retiring man, Jarves received little recognition in his lifetime, though he was given the Order of Kamehameha I by Hawaii and made a Chevalier of the Order of the Crown of Italy by Humbert I in reward for his services in the Florentine exhibit in Boston. He died at Terasp, Switzerland, in the Engadine, and was buried in the English Protestant Cemetery at Rome. Van Wyck Brooks speaks of him as "a lively, shrewd, unworldly, honest soul, with a rare aesthetic taste." His history and his travel books are amateurish, but valuable as sources.

Principal Works: Scenes and Scenery in the Sandwich Islands, and a Trip Through Central America, 1843; History of the Hawaiian or Sandwich Islands, 1843-47; Scenes and Scenery in California, 1844; Parisian Sights and French Principles Seen Through American Spectacles, 1852; Art-Hints: Architecture, Sculpture, and Painting, 1855; Italian Sights and Papal Principles Seen Through American Spectacles, 1856; Kiana: A Tradition of Hawaii, 1857; Why and What Am I? The Confessions of an Inquirer, 1857; Art Studies: The "Old Masters" of Italy, 1861; The Art Idea, 1866; Art Thoughts: The Experiences and Observations of an Amateur in Europe, 1869; A Glimpse at the Art of Japan, 1876; Italian Rambles, 1883; Pepero, the Boy Artist: A Brief Memoir of James Jackson Jarves, Jr., 1891.

About: Judd, L. F. Honolulu . . . From 1828 to 1861; Boston Daily Advertiser July 2, 1888.

"JAY BEE." See BRADFORD, JOSEPH

JAY, WILLIAM (June 16, 1789-October 14, 1858), jurist and reformer, was the second son of the first United States Supreme Court Justice, John Jay, and of Sarah Van Brugh (Livingston) Jay, and a brother of the eminent lawyer Peter Augustus Jay. Born in New York City, he was graduated from Yale in 1807 and, prevented by poor sight from practicing law, he turned to the management of the family estate at Bedford, later his own. With one interruption he was judge in Westchester County, New York, for the twenty-five year period, 1818-1843, his anti-slavery views finally causing his retirement. He died at Bedford.

An Episcopalian, Jay was one of the founders of the American Bible Society, which gave rise to some ecclesiastical controversy. He was a life director of the American Tract Society, and for ten years president of the American Peace Society. In relation to these interests and other humanitarian causes he wrote extensive polemical and other literature, letters, essays, addresses, tracts and pamphlets. Much of his literary effort was directed against slavery. In this and in the advocacy of arbitration in settlement of international disputes he was well in advance of his time.

Principal Works: The Life of John Jay (2 vols.) 1833; An Inquiry Into the Character of the American Colonization, and American Anti-Slavery Societies, 1835; War and Peace, 1842; A Review of the Causes and Consequences of the Mexican War 1849; Miscellaneous Writings on Slavery, 1853

About: Cheever, G. B. The True Christian Patriot; Douglass, F. Eulogy of the Late Hon. William Jay; Tuckerman, B. William Jay and the Constitutional Movement for the Abolition of Slavery.

JEFFREY, ROSA (GRIFFITH) VERTNER JOHNSON (1828-October 6, 1894), poet and novelist, was born at Natchez, Miss. Her father, John Y. Griffith, was a writer of considerable reputation. Her mother, daughter of the Rev. James Abercrombie, a Philadelphia clergyman, died when she was nine months old and she was adopted by a maternal aunt of means whose name, Vertner, she received, and in whose home her life unfolded happily. Her education at the Episcopal Seminary at Lexington, Kentucky, was of the best the times afforded for girls. She was one of the most beautiful women of Kentucky. At seventeen she married Claude M. Johnson of Louisiana who brought her wealth and social leadership. After his death she married, in 1863, Alexander Jeffrey of Edinburgh, Scotland. She died at Lexington at sixty-six. One of her six children, Claude M. Johnson, was for a time mayor of Lexington.

A poem "The Legend of the Opal" was written when she was fifteen, and at twenty-two she was contributing under the pen name "Rosa" to the Louisville *Journal.* Her poetry, for which she had natural talent, brought her recognition throughout the United States. She also published a few novels and wrote several dramas which were never published.

Principal Works: Novels—Woodburn, 1864; Marah, 1884. *Poetry*—Poems, 1857; Daisy Dare and Baby Power, 1871; The Crimson Hand, 1881.

About: Tardy, M. T. Southland Writers; Townsend, J. W. Kentucky in American Letters 1784-1912; Kentucky State Historical Society Register January 1911.

JENKINS, JOHN STILWELL (February 15, 1818-September 20, 1852), lawyer, editor, and popular historian, was born at Albany, N.Y., the son of Ira Jenkins, a merchant and banker, and of Rebecca (Van Heusen) Jenkins. After a year at Hamilton College he studied law, practicing in Jordan, Weedsport, Auburn, and Sennett, in Onondaga and Cayuga counties. Attracted to journalism, he established the *Cayuga Tocsin,* editing this and contributing to its successor the *Cayuga New Era.* He died at Syracuse at thirty-four after an operation.

The works of Jenkins, averaging more than two a year from 1846 to 1851, were mostly popular historical and biographical compilations. His *History of Political Parties in the State of New York* was an abridgment of a two-volume work by Jabez D. Hammond; and his *United States Exploring Expedition* a compilation from a five-volume work by Charles Wilkes and of a book by William Francis Lynch. His *History of the War Between the United States and Mexico,* however, purported to be a first account based on official reports. A novelette "Alice Howard" was published in a Philadelphia journal in 1846.

Principal Works: The New Clerk's Assistant, 1846; History of Political Parties in the State of New York, 1846; The Lives of Patriots and Heroes Distinguished in the Battles for American Freedom, 1847; The Life of Silas Wright, 1847; The Life of General Andrew Jackson, 1847; The History of the War Between the United States and Mexico, 1848; The Generals of the Last War With Great Britain, 1849; The Life of John Caldwell Calhoun, 1850; James Knox Polk, 1850; The Heroines of History, 1851; United States Exploring Expeditions, 1851; Lives of the Governors of the State of New York, 1851.

About: Cayuga County Historical Collections Vol. 7.

JEWETT, SARAH ORNE (September 3, 1849-June 24, 1909), novelist and short story writer, was born in South Berwick, Maine—"Deephaven" in her stories. Her father was Dr. Theodore Herman Jewett, a distinguished physician who had taught obstetrics and the diseases of women at Bowdoin College, and was long president of the Medical Society of Maine; her mother was Caroline Frances (Perry) Jewett, who was partly of French blood.

The child was very delicate, and her schooling was much interrupted. Intermittently she attended the Berwick Academy, and occasionally studied at home with tutors, but her real education and culture—and they *were* real—came from her father's library, and even more from the long trips she took with him as he drove to see his patients in the country districts around the town. These journeys resulted in an intimate knowledge of the Maine countryside and its people, and an attachment to her father which was so strong that it precluded any emotional relation to any other man. A beautiful woman, slender, with dark hair and eyes, she never fell in love or inspired love, though she had many men friends. She did not live in the days of modern psychology, so she never knew the cause of her feeling that "marriage would only be a hindrance," or realized how much of life had unconsciously been taken from her by the father she adored; and in view of just her special type of work it is perhaps well for literature that Sarah Orne Jewett was robbed of the chance to live. She became a true "New England nun," dedicated to the depiction of a life that was even then about to die, and would never again yield to the pen of a first-hand observer.

Encouraged by an older sister, she sent her first story—preceded only by verses for children—to a juvenile magazine, *Riverside.* under the pseudonym of "Alice C. Eliot." It was accepted, and, emboldened, she sent her stories next to the *Atlantic Monthly,* still without her own name. In 1869 the *Atlantic* published the first of a long series, later collected as *Deephaven.*

This book was an immediate success; it came at just the right moment, when the rage for *genre* regional studies of America was at its height and when fiction in general was at a low ebb. It made her famous at a bound; it sent her to Boston and New York and Philadelphia; it made her a friend of the "Boston circle," particularly of Howells, Lowell, Whittier, and Thomas Bailey Aldrich.

In 1878 the beloved father died. Her grief may be imagined, but by this time she had learned to sublimate her emotions by constant work, and her stories continued to be written and published. A deep friendship with another and very remarkable woman—Annie Adams Fields [*q.v.*], the widow of James T. Fields, the publisher, and the hostess of the famous Fields salon in Boston—took the place of all other close personal intimacies. With Mrs. Fields she traveled to the West Indies and to Europe, where she met Tennyson, Arnold, Henry James; but she could write only in South Berwick, and returned to her family home there to bury herself in her stories. She was often ill, and gradually, one by one, all her nearest relatives died except one sister. Outwardly her life was most uneventful; she was still drawing on her memories, "nibbling all around her stories like a mouse," in her own words. The *Century* and *Harper's* now vied with the *Atlantic* for the first publication of most of her tales.

In 1901 Bowdoin conferred on her an honorary Litt. D. degree, the first ever given a woman. Her joy was heightened by the memory that her father had been graduated from the same college in 1834. Her life, like her talent, was at its peak. A few months later she had been condemned to semi-invalidism for the rest of her years, and was never to have strength again to write more than a letter. A fall from a carriage caused spinal injuries from which she never recovered. She gradually faded away during nearly eight years more, but nothing more of hers was published.

Collection of Frederick H. Meserve
SARAH ORNE JEWETT

Miss Jewett grew up in Maine at a time when the great trade with the Orient, which had brought China into every seacoast town of the state, was already menaced by the rise of steamships and the end of the famous old clipper ships. The Civil War rung down the curtain on the era. Abandoned ports and forsaken farms were the commonest of sights around her; and meanwhile her father, on their long country drives, told her stories of earlier and happier days. She knew intimately the old people who were his patients; and they too talked, and she caught their very accent. (She was sparing of dialect, however; Lowell praised her use of it "for flavor, but not so oppressively as to suggest garlic.") She herself said: "My local attachments are stronger than any cat's that ever mewed." Dr. Jewett had written much himself, though only for professional journals, and he formed his daughter's style as well as her personality. Flaubert was one of her models; from him she learned an "almost French clarity and precision."

Immersed in her background as she was, she nevertheless grew with the years. Her biographer, Matthiessen, remarks how she gradually matured from observation of life to life itself. *The Country of the Pointed Firs* is immensely finer than *Deephaven*, though obviously they are literary kin. Her accurate, close studies—"narrow in compass," Lowell said, "like a gem-cutter's"—are easily the best work of their sort that has come out of New England; and since the New England they depicted is dead, they will always be the best. These idylls in prose, marked by what Edward Garnett called "a poetic realism," are in their minor field outstanding.

But Miss Jewett was no universal genius; she was intensely of her own time and place. She has the defects of her era; she is too mild, too gentle. She could not feel passion and so she could not describe it; her love scenes are so stiff as to be funny. It is in describing the old, the odd, the eccentric—of whom her Maine was so full—that she surpasses all other writers in her *genre*. Above all, her work is characterized by a beautiful serenity, like the soft warmth of an autumn sunset. She was ideally the person for just exactly the work she had to do, born in exactly the right place for doing it.

Principal Works: Deephaven, 1877; Play Days (juvenile) 1878; Old Friends and New, 1879; Country By-Ways, 1881; The Mate of the Daylight and Friends Ashore, 1883; A Country Doctor, 1884; A Marsh Island, 1885; A White Heron and Other Stories, 1886; The Story of the Normans (non-fiction) 1887; The King of Folly Island and Other People, 1888; Betty Leicester (juvenile) 1889; Strangers and Wayfarers, 1890; A Native of Winby and Other Tales, 1893; The Life of Nancy, 1895; The Country of the Pointed Firs, 1896; Betty Leicester's English Christmas (juvenile) 1897; The Queen's Twin and Other Stories, 1899; The Tory Lover, 1901; Letters (ed. by A. A. Fields) 1911; Verses (privately printed) 1916.

About: Garnett, E. Friday Nights; Jewett, S. O. Best Stories (see Preface by Willa Cather to 1925 ed.); Matthiessen, F. O. Sarah Orne Jewett; Youth's Companion January 7, 1892; Boston Transcript June 25, 1909, May 16, 1925.

"JOHNSON, BENJAMIN F." See RILEY, JAMES WHITCOMB

JOHNSON, EDWARD (September 1598-April 23, 1672), colonial chronicler, was born at Canterbury, England, where his father, William Johnson, was clerk of St. George's Parish. His mother was Susan (Porredge) Johnson. A joiner by trade, he emigrated to Boston in 1630, shortly after bringing over his wife, Susan (Munnter) Johnson, seven children, and three servants. He was one of the founders of Woburn, Mass., in 1640, and active in almost every responsible office at the disposal of the colony.

His one volume, first published anonymously in England, dealing with the twenty-three years from the founding of Salem in 1628 to the time of Governor John Winthrop, 1651, is of outstanding value as the first published history of New England and an eye-witness narrative recording the essential spirit of the colony with homely detail neglected by other chroniclers. It is an example of intrinsic Puritan thought, and is interspersed with doggerel verse.

Principal Work: Wonder-Working Providence of Sion's Saviour in New England, 1654.

About: Johnson, A. History and Genealogy of One Line of Descent From Capt. Edward Johnson; Johnson, E. Wonder-Working Providence (see Introduction by J. F. Jameson); Tyler, M. C. A History of American Literature.

JOHNSON, HELEN LOUISE (KENDRICK) (January 4, 1844-January 3, 1917), miscellaneous writer and editor, was born at Hamilton, N.Y., the daughter of Asahel Clark Kendrick, college professor of Greek, and of Ann (Hopkins) Kendrick. Her mother died when she was seven and she was sent to a boarding school at Rochester, and later attended Oread Institute, Worcester, Mass. In 1869 she married Rossiter Johnson, an editor and author. They lived first in Concord, N.H., and later in New York City, where in addition to writing she was active in club and social work. Of her four children, only one survived. She died in New York.

A short story "A Night in Atlanta," and stories and Bible sketches for her husband's paper, the *New Hampshire Statesman,* initiated her writing career. Her first publications, the Roddy books, were for children and a compilation, *Tears for the Little Ones,* was prompted by the loss of one of her own. Among her publications was one novel, *Raleigh Westgate,* and a number of compilations. For two years, 1894-1896, she was editor of the *American Woman's Journal,* and she contributed many articles to other journals and to *Appleton's Annual Cyclopaedia.* Her anti-suffrage book, *Woman and the Republic,* was the outcome of her active working against the feminist cause.

Principal Works: Roddy's Romance, 1874; Our Familiar Songs and Those Who Made Them, 1881; Raleigh Westgate: or, Epimenides in Maine, 1889; Woman and the Republic, 1897. *Compiler*—Tears for the Little Ones, 1874; Illustrated Poems and Songs for Young People, 1884; The Nutshell Series, 1884; A Dictionary of Terms, Phrases, and Quotations (with Henry Percy Smith) 1895.

About: Johnson, R. Helen Kendrick Johnson.

JOHNSON, SAMUEL (October 14, 1696-January 6, 1772), philosopher and theologian, first president of King's College, was born in Guilford, Conn., the son of Samuel and Mary (Sage) Johnson. He was graduated from the Collegiate School (later Yale), then at Saybrook, in 1714, and after teaching for a year, became a tutor at the Collegiate School, which had meanwhile moved to New Haven. In 1720 he was ordained and became pastor of the Congregational Church at West Haven. But he was inclining more and more toward the Church of England, and in 1722 he, with some friends similarly situated, went to England and was ordained. In 1724 he returned as a missionary to Stratford, Conn., where he established the first Episcopal church in Connecticut. In 1725 he married a widow, Charity (Floyd) Nicoll. When Bishop Berkeley lived in Newport from 1729 to 1732, Johnson became his friend and disciple. In 1743 Oxford conferred a D.D. degree on him. After having declined offers of the presidency of the new Pennsylvania Academy (later the University of Pennsylvania) and the rectorship of Trinity Church, Newport, he accepted in 1753 an urgent invitation to become the first president of King's College (now Columbia). He set actively to work organizing the new college,

SAMUEL JOHNSON
(1696-1772)

but was constantly interrupted by smallpox epidemics, during one of which his wife, his son, and his stepdaughter died. In 1761 he married Sarah (Hull) Beach, whose daughter had married his son. She also died of smallpox two years later. It is no wonder that Johnson had a deadly fear of this disease. He resigned his office and retired to his old church at Stratford, where he died eleven years later.

Cheerful, benevolent, and tolerant—though a doughty fighter for American bishops—Johnson is ranked with Jonathan Edwards in philosophical acumen, and was certainly a more pleasant character. He never had much influence, however, since he was mainly a follower of Berkeley, and Berkeley's views did not become popular in America in his lifetime.

PRINCIPAL WORKS: Introduction to the Study of Philosophy, 1731; Elements Ethica: or, The First Principals of Moral Philosophy, 1746; Elementa Philosophica, 1752; English and Hebrew Grammar, 1767.

ABOUT: Beardsley, E. E. Life and Correspondence of Samuel Johnson; Chandler, T. B. The Life of Samuel Johnson, D.D.; Riley, I. W. American Philosophy: The Early Schools; Schneider, H. & C. Samuel Johnson: President of King's College.

JOHNSON, SAMUEL (October 10, 1822-February 19, 1882), hymnologist, was born in Salem, Mass., the son of a prominent physician, Dr. Samuel Johnson, and of Anna (Dodge) Johnson. He was in line of descent from Timothy Johnson who lived in Andover in 1674. He was graduated from Harvard in 1842 and from its theological school in 1846. His first pastorate, Unitarian, at Dorchester, lasted only about a year by reason of his liberal views. In 1853 he formed a free church among liberals at Lynn where he preached until 1870. A Transcendentalist, evolutionist, exponent of natural religion, and humanitarian, he preferred to keep himself free from affiliation with any denomination, reform society, or association. Remaining a bachelor, he lived in Salem until his father's death and thereafter on an ancestral farm in West Andover.

An intimate friend for forty years of Samuel Longfellow, brother of the poet Henry Wadsworth Longfellow, Johnson collaborated with him on three books of hymns. The last of these volumes was prepared while the two friends were on an extended European trip together in 1860. Johnson's major work was one of research into Oriental religions, on which he prepared three bulky volumes dealing with India, China, and Persia, the last being left unfinished and published posthumously.

PRINCIPAL WORKS: A Book of Hymns (with S. Longfellow) 1846; Hymns of the Spirit (with S. Longfellow) 1864; Oriental Religions and Their Relation to Universal Religion (3 vols.) 1872-1885; Lectures, Essays, Sermons (ed. by S. Longfellow) 1883.

ABOUT: Johnson, S. Lectures, Essays, Sermons (see Memoir by S. Longfellōw); Julian, J. A Dictionary of Hymnology; Atlantic Monthly June 1883.

JOHNSON, VIRGINIA WALES (December 28, 1849-January 16, 1916), juvenile and miscellaneous writer, was born in Brooklyn, N.Y., the daughter of M. Augustus Johnson and Sarah (Benson) Johnson, both Bostonians. She was descended from the same Judge Samuel Sewall from whom the poet Longfellow traced descent. A trip abroad with her mother and sister taken when she was twenty-six resulted in her remaining there the rest of her life, living mostly in Italy, for which she had an intense love. She never married.

She began writing very young as a pastime and at fifteen had won recognition with her Kettle Drum Series, juvenile stories which, with her Doll's Club Series, were published under the pen name "Cousin Virginia." Most of her more serious work, fiction for adults, travel and popular history, was written abroad.

PRINCIPAL WORKS: The Kettle Club Series (written 1860-1870); The Doll's Club Series, 1870; Travels of an American Owl, 1870; Joseph the Jew, 1873; A Sack of Gold, 1874; The Calderwood Secret, 1875; The Catskill Fairies, 1876; Miss Nancy's Pilgrimage, 1876; A Foreign Marriage, 1880; The Neptune Vase, 1881; Two Old Cats,

1882; An English Daisy Miller, 1882; The Fainalls of Tipton, 1884; Tulip Place, 1886; The House of the Musician, 1887; The Terra-Cotta Bust, 1887; The Treasure Tower, 1892; A Bermuda Lily, 1912; A Lift on the Road, 1913. *Travel and Popular History*—The Lily of the Arno, 1891; Genoa the Superb, 1892; America's Godfather, the Florentine Gentleman, 1894; A World's Shrine, 1902; Many Years of a Florentine Balcony, 1911; Summer Days at Vallombrosa, 1911; Two Quaint Republics: Andorra and San Marino, 1913.

About: Literary World June 3, 1882.

JOHNSTON, ALEXANDER (April 29, 1849-July 20, 1889), historian and educator, was born in Brooklyn, N.Y., of Scotch extraction on both sides, although his father, Samuel G. Johnston, resided in County Antrim, Ireland, before coming to America. Graduated in 1870 from Rutgers College with the highest honors, he was admitted to the New Jersey bar in 1875, but the following year abandoned law for teaching at Rutgers College Grammar School, and some years later founded a classical school at Norwalk, Conn. In 1883 he was called to the chair of jurisprudence and political science at the College of New Jersey (Princeton) where he remained until his death. He was genial, attractive, and highly esteemed, and of such intellectual ability that he seemed to master a subject merely by reading it.

His literary activity, covering a period of ten years, commenced with his realization of the need for a more adequate work on American political history, and he set about supplying this lack with his *History of American Politics.* The high standard of this won for him the offer to prepare articles for J. J. Lalor's *Cyclopaedia of Political Science,* and after some initial diffidence he furnished about a fourth of the material for the three volumes of this work. These contributions were later edited and reprinted by James A. Woodburn in two volumes as *American Political History.* For the *Encyclopaedia Britannica* he prepared articles of outstanding value, concerning which James A. Bryce, who acknowledged the extent to which he had drawn upon Johnston's writings for his *American Commonwealth,* is reported to have said that Johnston was asked to write them "because he was the only man in America who could do it."

Principal Works: History of American Politics, 1879; The Genesis of a New England State (Connecticut) 1883; A History of the United States for Schools, 1885; Connecticut, 1887; The United States: Its History and Constitution, 1889; American Political History (ed. by J. A. Woodburn, 2 vols.) 1905; *Editor*—Representative American Orations to Illustrate American Political History (3 vols.) 1884.

About: Dougherty, J. H. Alexander Johnston and His Contributions to Political History; Century Magazine October 1889; Critic August 3, 1889; Princeton College Bulletin November 1889.

JOHNSTON, RICHARD MALCOLM (March 8, 1822-September 23, 1898), novelist and miscellaneous writer, was born near Powelton, Ga., the son of Malcolm Johnston, a planter and Baptist minister, and Catherine (Davenport) Johnston. He was graduated from Mercer University in 1841, and after a year as a teacher read law in Augusta and was admitted to the bar. In 1844 he married Mary Frances Mansfield. Until 1857, with two intervals of teaching, he practiced law. In that year he was offered an appointment as judge of the northern circuit court of Georgia, the presidency of Mercer, and a professorship of rhetoric and belles-lettres at the University of Georgia. He chose the third, and remained in Athens, the university seat, until 1861. During the Civil War he was on the staff of Governor Brown, and received the courtesy title of colonel. From 1862 to 1867 he conducted a school for boys at Rockby, near Sparta, Ga., which became famous for its substitution of the honor system for the old-time floggings. Sherman's march through Georgia and the further devastation of Reconstruction ruined his school, so that he moved it to Chestnut Hill, near Baltimore, where as the Pen Lucy School he kept it going until 1882. The poet Sidney Lanier encouraged him to write stories of Georgia, most of which appeared first in the *Southern Magazine.* In 1875 he became a Roman Catholic (one of his sons became a priest), and thereafter he lectured at St. Mary's College, Baltimore, which gave him an LL.D. degree in 1895. He never made much from his writing or lecturing, and from 1896 to his death was a clerk in the Bureau of Education in Washington.

Johnston's stories are almost plotless, without action, but loving, nostalgic studies of the country and the people for whom he was homesick ever after he left them. All together they do not equal in value the study of early educational life in Middle Georgia he prepared for the Commissioner of Education in 1895.

Principal Works: The English Classics, 1860; Georgia Sketches, 1864; Dukesborough Tales, 1871; Historical Studies of English Literature, 1872; Life of Alexander H. Stephens (with W. H. Browne) 1878; Old Mark Langston, 1884; Two Gray Tourists, 1885; Mr. Absoalom Billingslea and Other Georgia Folk, 1888; Ogeechee Cross-Firings, 1889; Widow Guthrie, 1890; Studies: Literary and Social, 1892 and 1893; Mr. Fortner's Marital Claims and Other Stories, 1892; Little Ike Templin and Other Stories, 1894; Old Times in Middle Georgia, 1897; Pearce Amerson's Will, 1898; Autobiography, 1900.

ABOUT: Johnston, R. M. Autobiography; Stedman, E. C. & Weeks, S. B. Literary Estimate and Bibliography: Richard Malcolm Johnston; Washington Evening Star September 23, 1898; Baltimore Sun September 24, 1898.

JOHNSTON, WILLIAM PRESTON (January 5, 1831-July 16, 1899), lawyer, soldier, and educator, was born in Louisville, Ky., the son of General Albert Sidney Johnston and Henrietta (Preston) Johnston. His mother died when he was four, and he was brought up by General William Preston and a maternal relative. After interrupted studies at Centre College and Western Military Institute he was graduated from Yale in 1852, studied law at the University of Louisville, and engaged in practice in that city. He served in the Confederate army, rising to the rank of colonel as aide-de-camp to President Jefferson Davis.

In 1867 Johnston was offered the chair of history and English literature at Washington and Lee University by its president, General Robert E. Lee. While there he published a biography of his father, his first and most popular book. In 1880 he became president of Louisiana State University at Baton Rouge, but resigned three years later to become first president of Tulane University of Louisiana on the mergence in 1884, of Tulane and the University of Louisiana at New Orleans. During this period his subsequent important work was published, including three volumes of poems and extensive contributions to periodicals, public addresses, and lectures. He was a regent of Smithsonian Institution and a member of many learned societies. He died at Lexington, Va. He was twice married; his second wife and four of the six children by his first marriage survived him.

PRINCIPAL WORKS: The Life of Gen. Albert Sidney Johnston, 1878; Prototype of Hamlet and Other Shakespearian Problems, 1890; My Garden Walk (poems) 1894; Pictures of the Patriarchs and Other Poems, 1895; The Johnstons of Salisbury, 1897; Seekers After Gold: Sonnets, 1898.

ABOUT: Johnston, W. P. The Johnstons of Salisbury; Memorial Service in Honor of William Preston Johnston; Yale University Obituary Record of Graduates.

JONES, AMANDA THEODOSIA (October 19, 1835-March 31, 1914), poet and inventor, was born in East Bloomfield, N.Y., the fourth of twelve children of Henry and Mary Alma (Mott) Jones. Her ancestry, long established in Massachusetts, included Puritan, Quaker, Huguenot, and Methodist elements. She began to teach after attending the State Normal School at East Aurora, but on the success of her first poems abandoned it for writing. She was a Spiritualist and subject to psychic experiences. A number of inventions, including a vacuum process of canning and liquid fuel, resulted in her acquiring six patents and spending some time developing business interests, but later she returned to writing. A philanthropic interest in unhappy girls and women led to her founding a home for them near Buffalo. In the early 'eighties she settled in Junction City, Kans., where she died. She never married.

Her poetry and other writings appeared from about 1854 in the *Methodist Ladies' Repository* and later in about a dozen other periodicals. She successively edited a reform journal, the *Universe,* and a juvenile periodical, *Bright Eyes.* She was also literary editor of the *Western Rural.* During the Civil War she wrote war poems. She also contributed a series of articles on liquid fuel to *Steam Engineering* and the *Engineer.* Her books, largely poetry, include also some children's stories, one or more novels, and an autobiography.

PRINCIPAL WORKS: Ulah and Other Poems, 1861; Poems, 1867; A Prairie Idyll, 1882; Flowers and a Weed, 1899; Rubáiyát of Solomon and Other Poems, 1905; Poems 1854-1906, 1906; A Mother of Pioneers, 1908; A Psychic Autobiography, 1910.

ABOUT: Jones, A. T. A Psychic Autobiography; Willard, F. E. & Livermore, M. A. A Woman of the Century; Critic November 1905.

JONES, CHARLES COLCOCK, JR. (October 28, 1831-July 19, 1893), historian, was born in Savannah, Ga., the son of the Rev. Charles Colcock Jones, a Presbyterian minister and professor of ecclesiastical history, who devoted his later life to evangelizing the slaves. His mother was Mary (Anderson) Jones—though one authority says her maiden name also was Jones and that she was her husband's cousin. His brother Joseph became a well known physician and sanitary expert.

Jones was educated at South Carolina College, the College of New Jersey (Princeton), and the Harvard Law School, from which he was graduated in 1855. He was admitted to the Georgia bar and practiced in Savannah. In 1858 he married Ruth Berrien Whitehead; she died soon after, and in 1863 he married her niece, Eva Berrien Eve. In 1860 he was mayor of Savannah.

With the Civil War he became a colonel of artillery and served throughout the war, declining the offer of a commission as brigadier-general, He surrendered in 1865, and at the end of the year moved to New York, where he practiced law until 1876.

He had meanwhile already written much on historical topics, particularly in relation to Georgia, and now he retired and moved to Augusta to devote the remainder of his life to history and archaeology. In 1880 he received an honorary LL.D. from the University of the City of New York, in 1882 from Oxford University (now Emory). In addition to his own writings, he edited an ecclesiastical history by his father and several legal works, and was a frequent public speaker. He founded, in 1879, and was president of the Confederate Survivors' Association of Augusta.

Jones' writing, of which his two-volume *History of Georgia* is the most important example, is careful, exhaustive, dignified—and very dull. Most of his historical works extend only through the eighteenth century. He was a rapid and industrious worker, whose output was as voluminous as it was solid and detailed. Bancroft called him "the Macaulay of the South," but he had neither the prejudices nor the brilliance of Macaulay.

Principal Works: Monumental Remains of Georgia, 1861; Historical Sketch of Tomo-Chi-Chi: Mico of the Yarnacraws, 1868; Antiquities of the Southern Indians, 1873; The Siege of Savannah in 1779, 1874; Dead Towns of Georgia, 1878; Hernando de Soto and His March Through Georgia, 1880; History of Georgia, 1883; The English Colonization of Georgia, 1887; Memorial History of Augusta, 1890; History of Savannah, 1890; Nine Annual Addresses, 1893.

About: Jones, C. E. In Memoriam: Col. Charles C. Jones, Jr.; Northen, W. L. Men of Mark in Georgia; Rutherford, M. L. The South in History and Literature; Atlanta Constitution July 20, 1893.

JONES, HUGH (c. 1670-September 8, 1760), clergyman and miscellaneous writer, was a graduate of Cambridge University, England, who came to Virginia in 1716. The following year he began to teach mathematics at the College of William and Mary, serving also as chaplain of the House of Burgesses, "lecturer" of Bruton Church, and minister of Jamestown. In 1721 he revisited England, after which he resumed parochial work first in King and Queen County, Va., and later in Charles and Cecil counties, Md., in the former of which he also taught school. He remained in St. Stephen's Parish, Cecil County, from 1731 to a few years before his death at ninety. He was a man of vigorous intellect, aristocratic leanings, and advanced ideas in education.

Before his long absence in England Jones wrote "An Accidence to Christianity" and "An Accidence to the Mathematicks," and while in London he published a short English grammar, *An Accidence to the English Tongue,* the first English grammar written in America, and *The Present State of Virginia,* an historical monograph including sketches of Maryland and North Carolina, which has been considered the fullest and best contemporary account of early eighteenth century life in the colony.

Principal Works: A Short English Grammar: An Accidence to the English Tongue, 1724; The Present State of Virginia, 1724.

About: Adams, H. B. The College of William and Mary; Sprague, W. B. Annals of the American Pulpit.

JONES, JOHN BEAUCHAMP (March 6, 1810-February 4, 1866), novelist, was born in Baltimore. Very little is known about his early life, except that part of it was spent in Kentucky and Missouri, then pioneer wildernesses, and the background of many of his later novels. In 1840 he married Frances T. Custis. The next year found him in Baltimore, editing the *Sunday Visiter* (*sic*). His first novel, *Wild Western Scenes,* found no publisher, and was issued at his own expense; it was his only real success, selling 100,000 copies in his lifetime. In 1842 he edited the *Madisonian,* the organ of President Tyler. Polk offered him a post as *chargé d'affaires* at Naples, which he declined, but he did spend several months in Europe. In 1858 he established the *Southern Monitor,* in Philadelphia. At the outbreak of the Civil War he went to Montgomery, Ala., then the Confederate capital, as a clerk in the Confederate War Department. He was outspoken in his criticism of President Davis' government, and in consequence became most unpopular in the South. As soon as the war was over, he went North, and died in Burlington, N.J., while seeing his *Rebel War Clerk's Diary* through the press. He died as he had lived—industrious, optimistic, but a foreordained failure. Little notice was taken of his death, and there is no published biographical material.

Jones' novels are sentimental and florid. His most valuable work is the *Diary,* which, though marred by captiousness and prejudice, gives a clear picture of conditions within the Confederacy during the war.

Principal Works: Wild Western Scenes, 1841; Books of Visions, 1847; Rural Sports: A Poem, 1849; The Western Merchant, 1849; The Spanglers and Tingles (The Rival Belles) 1852; Adventures of Col. Gracchus Vanderbomb, 1852; The Monarchist, 1853; The Life and Adventures of a Country Merchant, 1854; Freaks of Fortune: or, The History of Ned Lorn, 1854; The War Path, 1858; Wild Southern Scenes, 1859 (as Secession, Coercion, and Civil War, 1861); A Rebel War Clerk's Diary at the Confederate States Capital, 1866.

About: American Mercury December 1925.

JONES, JOSEPH STEVENS (September 28, 1809-December 29, 1877), dramatist, was born in Boston, the son of Abraham Jones, a sea captain, and Mary (Stevens) Jones. Appropriately, his birthplace is now the site of a theatre. His father was killed by savages during a voyage in 1819, and he had to end his public school education early and go to work. At eighteen he was an actor. For fifteen years he played regularly in Boston companies, was manager of two theatres, and wrote numerous ephemeral plays for quick production. Meanwhile he had been studying medicine, and in 1841 he retired from the stage. In 1843 he received his M.D. from Harvard. He practiced, lectured on anatomy and physiology, and for a long time was city physician of Boston, but he continued to write plays. He was married, though his wife's maiden name is not known, and had three sons, one of whom became an actor.

Jones' most popular play was *The Silver Spoon,* from which later he wrote his novel, *The Life of Jefferson S. Batkins.* Only a few of his 200 plays were published, but several of them held the stage for years, the longest lived being *The Carpenter of Rouen, The People's Lawyer,* and *The Liberty Tree.* He wrote in every *genre*—historical plays, melodramas, comedies, and farces—but though he had authentic humor and a knowledge of playcraft, none of his dramas has any literary standing, nor has any of them survived to the present.

Principal Works: The Silver Spoon: or, Our Own Folks, 1852; Life of Jefferson S. Batkins: Member for Cranberry Center, 1871; Paul Revere and the Sons of Liberty, 1875.

About: Quinn, A. H. A History of the American Drama From the Beginning to the Civil War; Winter, W. The Wallet of Time; Boston Transcript December 31, 1877 and December 30, 1910.

"JONES, MAJOR." See THOMPSON, WILLIAM TAPPAN

JONES, WILLIAM ALFRED (June 26, 1817-May 6, 1900), critic and essayist, was born in New York City. His father, David Samuel Jones, of Irish lineage, was the first judge of Queen's County. His mother was Margaret (Jones) Jones, a granddaughter of Philip Livingston, signer of the Declaration of Independence. After graduation from Columbia in 1836 he studied law, but found literary work more to his taste. From 1861 to 1865 he was librarian of Columbia College, and two years later, at fifty, he retired to Norwichtown, Conn., where he passed the more than thirty remaining years of his life, marrying a second time after the death of his first wife. He was disappointed in his expectation of an inheritance, and, despite his early promise, the last period of his life was unproductive and somewhat eccentric.

During his early literary activity he contributed frequent essays and literary criticisms to such periodicals as the *American Monthly Magazine, Arcturus,* and the *Broadway Journal.* His published books are mostly reprints of these his *Characters and Criticisms* containing most of the material in his previous volumes. He was editorially connected with the *Church Record,* the *Literary World,* and with the *Churchman* under his brother-in-law, the Rev. Samuel Seabury. Pride in his ancestry led him to prepare a genealogy of his family in the *Memorial* of his father. He was a friend and correspondent of many literary men of his day and his work was highly praised by Irving, Bryant, Poe, and others.

Principal Works: The Analyst, 1840; Literary Studies, 1847; Essays Upon Authors and Books, 1849; Memorial of the Late Hon. David S. Jones, 1849; Characters and Criticisms (2 vols.) 1857.

About: Jones, J. H. The Jones Family of Long Island; Mott, F. L. A History of American Magazines.

"JOSIAH ALLEN'S WIFE." See HOLLEY, MARIETTA

JOYCE, JOHN ALEXANDER (July 4, 1842-?), versifier and essayist, was born in Ireland, his father and mother being respectively eighteen and fifteen at his birth. They brought him to the United States in 1846 and settled first in New York State, then in Kentucky, and finally in Virginia (now West Virginia). He attended the Roman Catholic schools until 1854, when he ran away and for two years was a tramp, part of the time a Mississippi River pilot. In 1856 he returned to Kentucky and went to school there until 1859. In 1860 he was certified as insane, and spent three months in the Kentucky State Asylum. Recovering his senses, he enlisted in the Union Army and served through the Civil War with the Kentucky infantry, being mustered out in 1865 as lieutenant colonel. He became a teacher in Iowa, then a tax collector, then studied law in Dubuque, being admitted to the bar in 1866. After three years as a clerk of the Internal Revenue office in Washington, he was transferred to St. Louis as supervisor. In 1874 he made a trip to the Pacific Coast, his account of which in his autobiography gives interesting data concerning the West at this period. In 1875 he was convicted of conspiracy in a whiskey fraud and served two years in the Missouri State Penitentiary, being pardoned in 1877. He claimed to have been the victim of anti-Grant politicians, and this may have been true, since throughout his term he acted as deputy warden!

His later years were spent in Washington, and the date of his death is unknown. Joyce was a writer of voluminous very bad verse, and would long ago have been forgotten had he not made claim to authorship of "Laugh, and the World Laughs with You" written by Ella Wheeler Wilcox. He declined to accept any proof to the contrary, and doubtless quite sincerely believed Mrs. Wilcox had stolen the verses from him.

Principal Works: A Checkered Life (including Poetic Waifs) 1883; Peculiar Poems, 1885; Personal Recollections of Shakspere, 1895; Truth (2 vols.) 1908-09; Robert Burns, 1909.

About: Joyce, J. A. A Checkered Life.

JUDAH, SAMUEL BENJAMIN HELBERT (1799?-July 21, 1876), playwright was born in New York City, the son of Benjamin S. Judah, a merchant bankrupted by the War of 1812, and his wife Elizabeth. They belonged to one of the old Sephardic Jewish families resident in America from early Colonial times. Little is known of Judah's early years, except that he was educated in the public schools, had some knowledge of French, Latin, and Greek, and from boyhood had an inordinate desire to win fame as a dramatist. Unfortunately his talents were not equal to his ambition. His plays, which he boasted took him only from two to four days to write, were hardly worth the time spent on them. They were all inflated bombast; only the first three were produced, and they were howled down by the critics, one of whom called them "an attempt to pour sour European wine into American bottles." Embittered by his failure, Judah then produced his *Gotham and the Gothamites,* an invective which named names and provoked a suit for libel, as a consequence of which he was fined $400 and imprisoned, though he was pardoned by the governor after five weeks because of the state of his health. *The Buccaneers* was in the same vein, but before its publication Judah was persuaded to cut out of the preface its more libelous passages. In 1825, having studied law, he was admitted to the bar, and practiced law in New York for the remainder of his life; his reputation for reliability was not good, but he was a shrewd and clever lawyer, and was financially successful. He never married. An essentially superficial and absurdly vain person, Judah was a negligible writer, whose plays were just not quite bad enough to be funny.

Principal Works: The Mountain Torrent, 1820; The Rose of Arragon: or, The Vigil of St Mark, 1822; Odafriede: The Outcast, 1822; A Tale of Lexington, 1823; Gotham and the Gothamites, 1823; The Buccaneers: A Romance of Our Own Country, 1827; The Maid of Midian, 1833.

About: Daly, C. P. The Settlement of the Jews in New York; Quinn, A. H. A History of the American Drama From the Beginning to the Civil War.

JUDD, SYLVESTER (July 23, 1813-January 26, 1853), novelist and miscellaneous writer, was born in Westampton, Mass., the son of Sylvester Judd, a locally noted antiquarian, and Apphia (Hall) Judd. From 1822 the family lived in Northampton, where the father was editor of a paper. With the interruption of a year as a merchant's clerk at sixteen, Judd was educated at Westfield and Hopkins Academies, and at Yale, from which he was graduated in 1836, meanwhile earning his living by teaching in New Haven. For a year he taught at Templeton, Mass. He declined a professorship at Miami Col lege, in Ohio, for he had been converted to Unitarianism, and Miami was a Presbyterian college. Instead he went to the Harvard Divinity School, where he received his B.D. in 1840, and was ordained as minister of the East Parish (later Christ Church), in Augusta, Maine. Next year he married Elizabeth Williams, daughter of a senator, by whom he had three children. He spent the remainder of his short life in Augusta, though he traveled frequently as a lyceum lecturer. For a while he was chaplain of the Maine legislature, but was deposed in 1842 because of his pacifist views. A "hypersensitive, humble, shrinking soul," as Van Wyck Brooks called him, Judd yet had the courage of his convictions; he continued to oppose war, slavery, and intemperance, though he was more opposed to violence on behalf of his causes. His chief theological theory was the "birthright church," the view that all human beings belong by birth to a universal religious body, and should share in its communion. Eccentric, visionary, and over-scrupulous, Judd nevertheless had much influence. His chief book, the novel *Margaret,* though it is confused and fantastic, is remarkable for its close fidelity to the natural life of New England, its loving observation and description of country sights and sounds. Besides his messianic *Philo,* he left another unpublished piece of verse *The White Hills: An American Tragedy.* Brooks calls him "Hawthornesque," and on several counts he deserves the word.

PRINICPAL WORKS: A Young Man's Account of His Conversion From Calvinism, 1843; Margaret: A Tale of the Real and the Ideal, 1845; Richard Edney and the Governor's Family, 1850; Philo: An Evangeliad, 1850; The Church in a Series of Discourses, 1854.

ABOUT: Brooks, Van W. The Flowering of New England; Hall, A. Life and Character of the Rev. Sylvester Judd; North American Review January 1846, April 1850, April 1851, April 1855.

JUDGE, WILLIAM QUAN (April 13, 1851-March 21, 1896), Theosophist, was born in Dublin, Ireland, one of seven children of Frederick H. Judge, a prominent Freemason, and Alice Mary (Quan) Judge. An illness at the age of seven, supposed to be fatal, fundamentally changed him, and from his recovery in his eighth year he is said to have become deeply enamoured of religious and occult subjects. When he was thirteen, his mother having died, the family came to Brooklyn, N.Y., where Judge eventually practiced law, making a reputation for his thoroughness. In 1875 he came into contact with Mme. H. P. Blavatsky and Col. Henry Steel Olcott, co-founders of the Theosophical Society, of which he was one of the charter members, and after their departure for India he remained the most prominent American representative of it. In 1893 he gave up his law practice to devote himself to the movement, and shortly after, the founders having died, a controversy over his authority arose, leading to the secession of most of the American membership from the international organization then centered at Adyar, India, which came under the presidency of Mrs. Annie Besant. Judge headed the American independent society until his early death at forty-five. He married Ella M. Smith of Brooklyn in 1874 and had one daughter who died young.

Judge wrote and lectured continually in behalf of the movement to which he was devoted, published lectures and pamphlets, and edited the theosophical monthly the *Path* from 1889 until his death. His published books are all of a theosophical nature.

PRINCIPAL WORKS: Yoga Aphorisms of Patanjali, 1889; Echoes From the Orient, 1890; The Ocean of Theosophy, 1893; Notes on the Bhagavad-Gita, 1918.

ABOUT: Green, T. & Niemand, J. (comps.). Letters That Have Helped Me; Irish Theosophist April 1896; Theosophical Quarterly 1931-1932; Theosophy May 1896.

JUDSON, ADONIRAM (August 9, 1788-April 12, 1850), Baptist missionary, was born at Malden, Mass., the son of a Congregational minister, Adoniram Judson, one of whose progenitors, Joseph Judson, came over at an early period from Yorkshire, England. His mother, Abigail (Brown) Judson taught him to read at three. He attained the highest honors at Brown University, from which he was graduated in 1807, and after a period of teaching during which he manifested great skepticism concerning religious matters, he finally matriculated at Andover Theological Seminary. There he helped in the formation of the American Board of Commissioners of Foreign Missions. In 1812 he set sail for the foreign mission field, adopting Baptism before his arrival. At Burmah he found immense difficulties and discouragements, partly by reason of the language, and passed three years without a single convert, but he persisted in spite of hardships, sorrows which included the loss of two of his wives and five of his twelve children, and intense sufferings endured in an eleven-month imprisonment, sometimes in imminent danger of death. His last wife was the writer, Emily (Chubbuck) Judson [*q.v.*], who survived him. He died four days out from

Maulmain, Burmah, on a voyage taken in the hope of benefiting his health, and was buried at sea.

Before entering on his theological studies Judson had published two school text books. His major work, however, was the translation of the Bible into Burmese, and the preparation of an English-Burmese dictionary, the Burmese-English part being left unfinished and later completed by his colleague, Edward A. Stevens.

PRINCIPAL WORKS: Elements of English Grammar, 1808; The Young Lady's Arithmetic, 1808; The Holy Bible: Containing the Old and New Testaments Translated Into the Burmese, 1834; Dictionary: English and Burmese, 1849.

ABOUT: American Baptists Foreign Missionary Society. The Judson Centennial; Heroes of the Free Churches: No. 3; Judson, E. Life of Adoniram Judson; Wayland, F. Memoir of the Life and Labors of Rev. Adoniram Judson.

JUDSON, EDWARD ZANE CARROLL

("Ned Buntline"), (March 20, 1823 [or August 16, 1822]-July 16, 1886), novelist and ruffian, was born, either at Stamford, N.Y., or in Philadelphia, the son of Levi Carroll Judson, an attorney; his mother's maiden name is unknown. Much of his life is obscure, usually through his own fabrications and concealments. He ran away to sea as a small boy, then became an apprentice in the navy, and won a midshipman's commission by heroism in a drowning in the East River in 1838. His skit "The Captain's Pig" was his entrée into the *Knickerbocker Magazine* the same year. He resigned from the navy in 1842, and, after possible participation in the Seminole War and a trip to the Yellowstone for a fur company, in 1844 he founded *Ned Buntline's Magazine,* which soon failed. Then, with Lucius A. Hine, he edited the *Western Literary Journal and Monthly Magazine.* When failure seemed near he deserted, leaving his partner to pay the debts.

He was next heard of in Eddyville, Ky., in 1845, when he won a $600 bounty for capturing two murderers single-handed. He moved to Nashville, where he founded *Ned Buntline's Own,* an enterprise ended in 1846 in a sensational manner. He killed in a duel the husband of his mistress; while he was on trial the dead man's brother fired at him; he jumped from the window, was recaptured, and that night was taken out by a mob and actually lynched. But he was rescued and the rope cut before life was extinct, and he revived. The grand jury refused to indict him, and he was free.

Collection of Frederick H. Meserve

EDWARD Z. C. JUDSON
("Ned Buntline")

He moved to New York, where he resumed *Ned Buntline's Own,* and he claimed to have been in the Mexican War, though there is no record of it. A friend of Edwin Forrest, the tragedian, he incited and led the mob against Forrest's English rival, William Charles Macready, resulting in the Astor Place riot in 1849. He was convicted, paid a fine of $250, and spent a year on Blackwell's Island, from which he was welcomed home as a hero by his friends. In 1852 he appeared in St. Louis, where he was indicted because of an election riot, and jumped his bail. He was one of the organizers of the anti-foreign, anti-labor "Know Nothing" Party, and gave it its name, though he could not run for office because of his prison record. When the party came to an end in 1856 he bought an estate in the Adirondacks (he was always well supplied with cash) and spent his time in hunting and fishing. In 1862 he enlisted in the Union Army, was reduced to the ranks from a sergeantcy, and in 1864 was dishonorably discharged; he announced that he had been "Chief of Indian Scouts" and thereafter called himself "Colonel." About this time he met William F. Cody, gave him the sobriquet of "Buffalo Bill," and engaged him to act in a play written by himself; they parted enemies, however, over the division of profits. He returned to Stamford and finally died there of heart disease. He was four times married; two wives died, one divorced him and secured custody of their child; the last, Anna Fuller, whom he married in 1871, survived him with two children.

Judson's life reads like one of his own 400 or more serials and sensational novels, and indeed he was frequently his own hero. He was the real father of the dime novel. Cheap, boisterous, rowdy, chauvinistic, an incorrigible liar and a generally bad egg, he nevertheless prided himself on his piety (he wrote hymns among other verses), and lectured indefatigably in favor of temperance. His writing was all trash and he himself a rascal of the first order, but he has his place in the history of American eccentrics and the development of American fiction.

PRINCIPAL WORKS: Mysteries and Miseries of New York, 1848; Ned Buntline's Life Yarn, 1848; Stella Delorme: or, The Comanche's Dream, 1860; The Rattlesnake: or, The Rebel Privateer, 1863; Life in the Saddle: or, The Cavalry Scout, 1865; Quaker Saul: The Idiot Spy, 1869; Red Ralph: The Ranger, 1870; The Scouts of the Plains, 1872; Buffalo Bill, 1881.

ABOUT: Pond, F. E. Life and Adventures of "Ned Buntline"; New York Herald July 18, 1886; New York Times April 1, 1873; St. Louis Globe December 27, 28, 1872.

JUDSON, EMILY (CHUBBUCK) (August 22, 1817-June 1, 1854), missionary, was born at Eaton, N.Y., near Hamilton, the fifth child of Charles Chubbuck, of Americanized Welsh lineage, and Lavinia (Richards) Chubbuck. Her childhood was passed in poverty and after eight years of teaching she was enabled to enter the Utica Female Seminary, where she remained to teach English. She met the recently widowed Burmese missionary Adoniram Judson [*q.v.*], then on a visit to America, and accompanied him back to his mission field as his third wife in 1846. Her husband died four years later, and her ill health being almost constant, she returned to America in 1851, purchased a home at Hamilton, and, realizing that her days were limited, made provision for her parents, child, and stepchildren, writing to the end and leaving unfinished an abridged memoir of her husband.

Her early writings, inclined to be light and humorous were published in a Hamilton paper and later in the New York *Mirror*. While at Utica Seminary she published four Sunday School books. After her marriage, at the request of her husband, she wrote a memoir of his second wife, Sarah (Hall) Boardman Judson. Her later volumes were published after her return to America.

PRINCIPAL WORKS: Charles Linn, 1841; The Great Secret, 1842; Allen Lucas, 1842; John Frink, 1843; Trippings in Author-Land, 1846; Alderbrook, 1847; Memoir of Sarah B. Judson, 1848; An Olio of Domestic Verses, 1852; The Kathayan Slave, 1853; My Two Sisters, 1854.

ABOUT: Judson, E. The Life of Adoniram Judson; Kendrick, A. C. The Life and Letters of Mrs. Emily C. Judson; Willson, Mrs. A. M. Lives of the Three Mrs. Judsons.

"JUNE, JENNIE." See CROLY, JANE (CUNNINGHAM)

KANE, ELISHA KENT (February 3, 1820-February 16, 1857), explorer and travel writer, was born in Philadelphia, the son of John Kintzing Kent, an eminent jurist, and Jane Duval (Leiper) Kane. At the University of Virginia, 1837 to 1839, where he was studying to be a civil engineer, an attack of rheumatic fever left his heart permanently injured and obliged him to change his profession. He was graduated from the medical department of the University of Pennsylvania in 1842, and became assistant surgeon in the United States Navy. He spent eighteen months in naval service in the Orient, Africa, and Europe and again was sent to Mexican waters, but twice was invalided home. In 1850 he joined the United States Coast Survey. In the first Grinnell Expedition to search for the lost Arctic explorer, Sir John Franklin, Kane was senior medical officer; in the second, in 1853, he was in command. The second expedition, which secured much valuable geographical and ethnological information, was frozen in, and in 1855 made an epic journey of 1200 miles in the Arctic in 83 days, before it was found by a govern-

Collection of Frederick H. Meserve
ELISHA KENT KANE

mental relief expedition. On Kane's return he sailed to England, where he met Lady Franklin, and then proceeded to Cuba to try to recover his impaired health. He died in Havana, at only thirty-seven. His body lay in state in cities from New Orleans to Philadelphia, and his funeral was a solemn pageant.

After Kane's death an anonymous book charged that he was secretly married to Margaret Fox, one of the sisters who founded American Spiritualism by their alleged mediumship. Letters seem to substantiate this, or at least to indicate that she was his wife-in-fact, if not legally.

Kane's two books on his two expeditions are, with a few scientific papers, all he ever wrote. The second was a grueling task, and he wrote his publisher (only too prophetically) that it had been his "coffin." The books show a real flair for descriptive writing, and the second especially was enormously popular—one of the most universally read books ever published in the United States.

Principal Works: The U. S. Grinnell Expedition in Search of Sir John Franklin, 1853 (as Adrift in the Arctic Ice Pack, 1915); Arctic Explorations, 1856.

About: Anon. The Love Life of Dr. Kane; Elder, W. Biography of Elisha Kent Kane; Greely, A. W. Explorers and Travellers; Rich, E. G. Hans: The Eskimo; Smucker, S. M. Life of Elisha Kent Kane and Other American Explorers.

KEATING, JOHN McLEOD (June 12, 1830-August 15, 1906), editor and historian, was born in Kings County, Ireland, of a North of Ireland family. His parentage and early life are unknown, except that he went to school first in Scotland, then in Dublin, and at thirteen became an apprentice printer. By 1848 he was foreman printer on the Dublin *World*, and active in the Young Ireland Club, the failure of whose rebellion in that year sent him to America. He worked as a printer in New York, New Orleans, Baton Rouge, and Nashville, where he was foreman of the composing room of the Methodist Publishing House. Again in Baton Rouge, he became superintendent of state printing. He had meanwhile been studying for the Episcopal priesthood, but in 1859, when he was prepared for ordination, he found that he could no longer accept the creed. In 1856 he married Josephine Esselman Smith; they had one son and one daughter.

Once more in Nashville, Keating moved from the composing to the editorial room, and became managing editor of the *Daily News*. In 1859, in Memphis, his home thenceforth for many years, he was city editor of the *Daily Morning Bulletin*. He enlisted in the Confederate Army and was for a time private secretary on the staff of Gen. Leonidas Polk. Then he became city editor of the *Daily Argus*. In 1865 he established the *Daily Commercial*, which in 1866 was combined with the *Argus*. A close friend of President Johnson's, he spent 1867 and 1868 in Washington and Johnson appointed him postmaster of Memphis, but the Senate refused to confirm the appointment. In 1868 he bought a half interest in the *Appeal* (now combined with the *Commercial*), and edited it until 1891, when he moved to Washington.

Though Keating wrote much and ably against the carpetbaggers, in favor of conciliation with the North (he had been opposed to slavery), and in advocacy of woman's suffrage, he is known chiefly for his valiant battle for sanitation to end the series of yellow fever epidemics which wasted Memphis from 1867 to 1879. During the worst of these, in 1878, he and one compositor were the only members of the staff not stricken, and got out the paper alone.

Principal Works: History of the Yellow Fever, 1879; History of the City of Memphis and Shelby Co., Tenn., 1888; The Southern Question, 1889; Dirt, Disease, and Degeneration, 1890.

About: Speer, W. S. Sketches of Prominent Tennesseeans; Memphis Commercial-Appeal August 18, 1906.

KEIMER, SAMUEL (February 11, 1688-c.1739), printer and associate of Benjamin Franklin, was born in St. Thomas' parish, Southwark, London. When he was eleven he entered Merchant Taylor's School and was afterwards apprenticed to Robert Tookey, a printer. In 1713 he set up a printing house and with its bankruptcy two years later he was commissioned to the Fleet. By 1717 he was printing again, and for the countenancing of some objectionable passages in the *Weekly Journal* Keimer served fifteen weeks in jail. In 1718 he wrote *A Brand Pluck'd From the Burning: Exemplify'd in the Unparallel'd Case of Samuel Keimer*, a sorrowful exposure of the French Prophets, a sect of emotional fanatics to which he had once belonged; and *The Platonick Courtship*, a piece of doggerel on the allegorical wooing of a "virgin soul."

In 1721 Keimer left his wife and set sail for the United States; and in the summer of 1723, with Benjamin Franklin as his factotum and nothing but a set of worn type and a broken press to work with, he opened his print shop in Philadelphia. *Elegy on the Much Lamented Death of the Ingenious and Well-Behaved Aquila Rose,* from his own pen, was his first imprint.

Keimer had acknowledged a certain kinship with the faith of the Quakers, but when he published a *Parable* (1723) written in a bogus version of the Friends' language, he was, for a time, disowned by them. The breach must have been mended, however, before he printed, at their request, Sewel's *History of the People Called Quakers.*

On Franklin's return from a journey to London he aided Keimer in the printing of some paper money, during 1727 or 1728. After issue of a spurious edition of Jacob Taylor's *Almanac* for 1726 and a professional quarrel with William Bradford, Keimer established, in December 1728, his own *Universal Instructor in All Arts and Sciences and Pennsylvania Gazette,* which weathered thirty-nine issues and was then turned over to Benjamin Franklin and his partner Hugh Meredith. Competition had worked its havoc; he set out for Bridgetown, Barbados, and there revived his trade in 1731 with the founding of the *Barbados Gazette,* the first newspaper in the Caribbean. It is believed that Keimer died shortly after the demise of this journal in 1738.

The only records of Keimer supply us with a picture of a thoroughly pathetic creature, slovenly of manner, incoherent of thought, and floundering of purpose, who would have been easily forgotten, had not Franklin in his *Autobiography* created for him a lively and almost fictional rôle.

PRINCIPAL WORKS: A Brand Pluck'd From the Burning: Exemplify'd in the Unparallel'd Case of Samuel Keimer, 1718; The Platonick Courtship, 1718; Elegy on the Much Lamented Death of the Ingenious and Well-Behaved Aquila Rose, 1723; Parable, 1723.

ABOUT: Hildeburn, C. R. A Century of Printing: The Issues of the Press in Pennsylvania, 1685-1784; The Friend: Vol. 17 (see Kite, N. "Antiquarian Researches Among the Early Printers and Publishers of Friends' Books"); Pennsylvania Magazine of History and Biography July 1930.

KELLEY, JAMES DOUGLAS JERROLD (December 25, 1847-April 30, 1922), naval officer and writer, was born in New York City, the son of Manus Kelley and Annie (Barry) Kelley, and a great grandnephew of Commodore John Barry. He was graduated from Seton Hall College, New Jersey, and in 1868 from the Naval Academy to which he had been appointed by President Lincoln. Serving thirty-three years in various capacities in the Navy, he rose to the rank of commander in 1899 and was retired in 1901. In the World War he was again on the active list as censor of the wireless and in the Office of Naval Intelligence.

Kelley was prize essayist and gold medalist of the Naval Institute in 1881. His books were largely related to the navy, ships, and yachting. Several volumes were produced in collaboration with others, and some were elaborately illustrated in water colors by F. S. Cozzens. After his retirement, Kelley became naval editor of the New York *Herald* until its sale in 1920, for some years being on its board of control and a managing director.

PRINCIPAL WORKS: The Question of Ships, 1884; American Yachts (with F. S. Cozzens) 1884; Typical American Yachts, 1886; A Desperate Chance (novel) 1886; Our Navy, 1892; The Ship's Company and Other Sea People, 1897; Our Country's Defensive Forces in War and Peace (with Col. A. L. Wagner) 1899; The Navy of the United States: 1775-1899, 1900.

ABOUT: Army and Navy Journal May 6, 1922.

KELLOGG, EDWARD (October 18, 1790-April 29, 1858), financial and industrial reformer, was born in Norwalk, Conn., the son of James Kellogg, a well established farmer, and Lydia (Nash) Kellogg. In Dutchess County, N.Y., where his family had removed in 1793, young Kellogg received a scattered education; in 1802 they moved to Northfield, Conn., and here he engaged in a small business and was married, in 1817, to Esther Fenn Warner.

Three years later he established himself in New York City as a wholesale drygoods merchant, under the firm name of Edward Kellogg & Company. He had been doing some wide reading in theology and morals and had begun to reconstruct his own code of business ethics when the panic of 1837 undermined the financial world: Kellogg lost almost every cent he had but was determined not to lose himself as well. He had witnessed the paradox of ample assets and business paralysis and he set about to detect the evils of the monetary system: money, a public medium of exchange, he said, should be under government issue.

By 1843 he had accumulated enough property to retire. He was bitter towards the extortions of usurers and published *Usury: The Evil and the Remedy,* first issued in newspaper form and then, with slight change of title, as a pamphlet *Currency: The Evil and the Remedy.* To his friends protesting against its circulation, warning him that it was strongly opposed to his own interest, he replied that his interest was not in his own pocketbook but in "the human family." He spent five years on the preparation of *Labor and Other Capital: The Rights of Each Secured and the Wrongs of Both Eradicated,* a brief for government issue of notes on land or other "real value" securities, at 1 per cent interest. The book attracted very little immediate attention, but during the Civil War a form of this "interconvertible bond plan of financial reform" was actually adopted. After Kellogg's death in 1858 his daughter, Mary Kellogg Putnam, circularized a pamphlet edition of the little volume, and he became known as the father of Greenbackism, a doctrine effecting a low interest rate, and having, therefore, a strong appeal to laborers and farmers.

Kellogg not only advanced political economy by the introduction of legal-tender paper currency, but as the American prototype of the contemporary radical social philosophers of Europe he gave some of the earliest impetus to the formulation of a National Labor Party and, in the large, to a potential industrial awakening.

Principal Works: Usury: The Evil and the Remedy, 1843 (reissued as Currency: The Evil and the Remedy, 1843); Labor and Other Capital: The Rights of Each. . . . , 1849 (re-edited by Mary Kellogg Putnam as Labor and Capital: A New Monetary System, 1858).

About: Putnam, E. Labor and Capital: A New Monetary System (see Biographical Sketches by M. K. Putnam in 1883 ed.); New York Daily Tribune April 30, 1858.

KELLOGG, ELIJAH (May 20, 1813-March 17, 1901), Congregational clergyman and writer of juvenile stories, was born in Portland, Maine, son of the Rev. Elijah and Eunice (McLellan) Kellogg. He spent his early childhood in Portland and then served a kind of apprenticeship on a farm followed by three years at sea before entering Bowdoin College, from which he was graduated in 1840. At the end of a three year course at Andover Theological Seminary he was ordained pastor of the Congregational church there. An innate devoutness and an intimate understanding of his farm and sea-faring parishioners, with their wholesome and simple pleasures, won him universal affection among the villagers. He had, moreover, a psychological skill in the handling of children and college youths, and often became a most valuable liaison officer between "unmanageables" and the Bowdoin executives.

On June 3, 1855, he was married to Hannah Pearson Pomeroy of Syracuse, N.Y., by whom he had two children. Following a service of twelve years as pastor of the Mariners' Church and chaplain of the Sailors' Home, he settled himself to a modest career of letters, which he had dimly contemplated when as a seminary student he had written "Spartacus to the Gladiators," a piece that was included in the *School Reader* in 1846 and is still a stock declamation-piece. Kellogg's first substantial tale, *Good Old Times,* appearing in 1867 in *Our Young Folks* and issued in volume form several years later, was a re-telling of his grandfather's struggles as a Maine backwoodsman. Its immediate popularity was ample encouragement to this literary probationer and almost thirty books followed. Among them were: *Lion Ben, The Young Ship-Builders of Elm Island, The Sophomores of Radcliffe, A Strong Arm and a Mother's Blessing.* The shores of Casco Bay, the western Pennsylvania frontier with its Scotch-Irish settlers, and the Bowdoin campus provided the back-drops for these stories and the *dramatis personae* were, for the most part, fairly normal, hardy boys, able, self-sufficient, and uncowardly. Kellogg's style bore much evidence of haste, but he employed an idiom which was authentically quaint, and which, from a local-colorist's point of view, has raised the value of his writings.

Principal Works: Good Old Times, 1867 and 1878; Lion Ben, 1869; The Young Ship-Builders of Elm Island, 1870; The Sophomores of Radcliffe, 1872; The Mission of Black Rifle, 1876; A Strong Arm and a Mother's Blessing, 1881.

About: Mitchell, W. B. Elijah Kellogg: The Man and His Work; Daily Eastern Argus (Portland) March 18, 1901.

KELLY, JONATHAN FALCONBRIDGE (August 14, 1817-July 21, 1855?), editor and humorist, most of whose writings appeared over the signature "Falconbridge" was born in Philadelphia. He was provided with the rudiments of a good English education, but was put to work at an early age first for a grocer and then for a perfumer. Yielding to a chronic restlessness and a longing for personal independence he set out alone for the West in 1837. Going most of the way on foot he arrived at Chillicothe, Ohio, without serious mishap. But here he suffered from a severe attack of pleurisy; one John A. Harris, a farmer, and his kindly wife took young Jonathan in, nursed him back to health and then kept him two years as an extra "hand." He returned to Philadelphia, stayed a while with his family, and then traveled with a theatrical company through the middle-Atlantic states and

Pennsylvania; in Pittsburgh he left the players to make a brief and sorry try at the managing of a hotel. Turning again to the stage he toured the South with another troupe of thespians, and then, resorting to a supposedly more lucrative profession, made two attempts, in Pittsburgh and in Cincinnati, at a newspaper partnership.

Soon afterwards he went to New York and with J. W. Taylor set up the *Archer,* devoted to theatrical and musical criticism and intelligence; it was a decided failure—possibly because his newly established book and periodical store began to demand too much attention. During 1845 and 1846 his sketches in the New York *Spirit of the Times* were netting him good prices and the flattery of widespread imitation. Kelly controlled the *Bostonian* for two years, and when this paper ceased publication in 1847 he had become a regular contributor to a number of reputable periodicals, signing his pieces "Jack Humphries," "O.K.," "Cerro Gordo," etc. He remained in Boston and founded the *Aurora Borealis,* a witty journal, of costly and handsome format, that failed financially after a few months. In 1851 he undertook the management of the Waltham (Mass.) *Advocate,* and it, too, was blasted—half a year later. While considering General Sam Houston's suggestion that he make a professional try in Texas, Kelly served four months as editor of the *New York Dutchman* and then went to Cincinnati to conduct the *Great West.* Leaving this paper he accepted a grandiose offer made by the American Party for the launching of its *American Platform,* which survived only two issues. His intellectual vigor had been dissipated by continual business failures and domestic griefs had worked a real hardship on him. He died in Cincinnati following an attack of Asiatic cholera.

A collection of his longer articles and his spirited squibs, reprinted from a variety of periodicals, appeared posthumously under the title *The Humors of Falconbridge* (1856). His reminiscent biography of *Dan Marble* (1851), the actor-wit, was a veritable bundle of tasty theatre gossip. Kelly's professional weakness lay in his tendency to anticipate complete failure at the very first glimmer of misfortune: he seems to have wandered from what might have been a brilliant literary career into a series of vacillating, dissatisfied, and sometimes half-hearted journalistic efforts.

Principal Works: Dan Marble, 1851; Humors of Falconbridge, 1856.

About: Blair, W. Native American Humor; Kelly, J. F. Humors of Falconbridge (see Biographical Sketch); Kelly, J. F. Dan Marble (see prefatory notes).

KEMBLE, FANNY. See KEMBLE, FRANCES ANNE

KEMBLE, FRANCES ANNE (Fanny Kemble) (November 27, 1809-January 15, 1893), actress and theatrical historian, was born in London, the daughter of Charles Kemble and Maria Theresa (De Camp) Kemble. She was educated in France and made her stage début in 1829 at Covent Garden, where her father was proprietor. With an early flair for acting she was not unmindful of the fact that her uncle, John Philip Kemble, and her aunt, Sarah Siddons, were blue-bloods of the British stage. She came to America with her father in 1832 and began two years of unquestionable successes with an engagement in New York in *Hamlet* and then *Fazio.* Although her father was fifty-seven, she played Juliet to his Romeo, and as Julia in *The Hunchback* she was an unfailing favorite. Two weeks before her retirement from the stage in June 1834, she was married to Pierce Butler, a wealthy heir, by whom she had two daughters, one of whom became the mother of Owen Wister, the novelist.

In her candid two-volume *Journal of a Residence in America* (1835) she criticized American life and although her tone was in no way bitter many of her subjects were hotly resentful. During the winter of 1838-39, spent with her husband on his Southern

From a portrait by T. Sully
FANNY KEMBLE

estate, she was repulsed by some of the awful machinery of slavery; her day-book was not published until 1863 (*Journal of a Residence on a Georgian Plantation*). In temperament she had never had much in common with her husband; in taste she was beginning to have even less. She spent most of her summers in the North, went alone to England in 1841, and five years later returned independently to the London stage. During her stay in Italy she wrote *A Year of Consolation.* Her husband, on charge of abandonment, was granted a divorce in 1849. Meanwhile Fanny had sailed again for America and had begun her public readings from Shakespeare, for which, here and in England, there was a maximum demand.

Fanny Kemble was the author of five inconsequential plays; a volume of verse published in 1844; *Far Away and Long Ago,* a meandering novel of the Berkshires; *Notes Upon Some of Shakespeare's Plays*; and the autobiographical *Records of Later Life and Further Records,* which ably account for the resourcefulness of her acting. For though she was not conventionally beautiful she had an undeniable strength of charm on the stage: Longfellow addressed a sonnet to her; and Justice Story, still in the shadow of New England Puritanism, found himself saying "I only thank God I'm alive in the same era with such a woman." Yet she actually had little genuine liking for her profession; she loathed the "strutting" that is often an actor's obligation. Her theatrical interpretations, varying with her moods-of-the-moment and in no wise founded on any set of histrionic dogma, were best when they sprang from mere forgetfulness. And from her pen came some of the liveliest memoirs of the early American stage.

Principal Works: Journal of a Residence in America, 1835; A Year of Consolation, 1847; Journal of a Residence on a Georgian Plantation, 1863; Records of Later Life, 1882; Notes Upon Some of Shakespeare's Plays, 1882; Far Away and Long Ago, 1889; Further Records, 1891.

About: Armstrong, M. Fanny Kemble: A Passionate Victorian; Bobbé, D. Fanny Kemble; Matthews, B. & Hutton, L. Actors and Actresses of Great Britain and the United States; Mail (London) January 18, 1893.

KENDALL, GEORGE WILKINS (August 22, 1809-October 21, 1867), journalist and soldier of fortune, was born in Mount Vernon, N.H., the son of Thaddeus and Abigail (Wilkins) Kendall. After a scant education he learned the printer's trade in Burlington, Vt., and then found employment in Washington on the *National Intelligencer* and the *Telegraph,* and then in New York on Horace Greeley's *Tribune.* He went to Mobile, Ala., in 1832 and for a year was connected with the *Alabama Register.* One John Gibson gave him a job in New Orleans, and in 1837, with Francis A. Lumsden, a Northern acquaintance and fellow-printer, Kendall published the first five-cent paper in that city, naming it after the coin, the *Picayune.* This four-page folio sheet was a simple and bold reflection of the editor's fondness for epigrammatic banter and soon found its audience.

Kendall had not only the journalist's news-sense but the adventurer's restlessness, and in 1841, with the *Picayune* on good footing, he joined a harrowing expedition into Mexico, sleeping in "another Black Hole of Calcutta," suffering detention in a leper prison, and enduring all the hardships that poverty of equipment can effect. *Narrative of the Texan Santa Fé Expedition* (1844) was written on his return.

In the columns of his paper, during the next three years, he made what case he could for "war with Mexico," and then struck out for the Rio Grande rode with the Rangers, and, volunteering as an aide on General Worth's staff, witnessed a large share of the warfare and was himself wounded in the knee. The *Picayune's* coverage of the Mexico conflict made Kendall and his partner veritable originators of the art of war correspondence. Despatches from the front were met at points on the lower Mississippi or Gulf coast by steamers equipped with type cases, often out-speeding the government couriers. The *Picayune* office stood literally mid-channel in the dissemination of war bulletins.

After this journalistic success Kendall spent several years abroad, devoting part of his time to *The War Between the United States and Mexico,* published in 1851, and in Paris was married to Mlle. Adeline de Valcourt. He spent his last years in sheep-raising on a large ranch in what is now Kendall County, Texas.

Kendall's Santa Fé narrative is no literary document, but abounds in human interest and maintains a brisk narrative tempo. His war chronicle recounts graphically the important battles from Vera Cruz to Chapultepec and contains Carl Nebel's excellent folio-sized illustrations. Not only as historian of parts but as a pioneer in modern journalistic methods, Kendall commands recognition among literary figures of the Southwest.

Principal Works: Narrative of the Texan Santa Fé Expedition (2 vols.) 1844; The War Between the United States and Mexico, 1851.

About: Bullard, F. L. Famous War Correspondents; Thompson, W. Recollections of Mexico; Louisiana Historical Quarterly April 1928.

KENNEDY, JOHN PENDLETON (October 25, 1795-August 18, 1870), novelist and biographer, was born in Baltimore, the son of John and Nancy Clayton (Pendleton) Kennedy. He was graduated in 1812 from Baltimore College (now the University of Maryland), and after a brief service in the War of 1812 studied law and was admitted to the bar in 1816. During 1818 and 1819 he and Peter H. Cruse edited a satirical magazine called the *Red Book.* From 1821 to 1823 he was a member of the Maryland House of Delegates—law, politics, and literature having equal holds on his interest.

In 1824 he married Mary Tennant. She died within a year, and in 1829 he married Elizabeth Gray. About this time a legacy from an uncle enabled him to withdraw from the practice of law. His interest in politics remained, however; he served three terms, between 1838 and 1844, as a Whig Member of Congress, where he helped to secure an appropriation for testing Morse's telegraph. In 1846 he returned to the House of Delegates, and was elected speaker. In 1852 Fillmore appointed him Secretary of the Navy. He was the organizer of Perry's expedition to Japan and of Elisha Kent Kane's second expedition to the Arctic. In the Civil War he stood by the Union, though on his mother's side he belonged to a prominent Virginia family, and he voted for Lincoln in 1864 and later for Grant. A public-spirited man, he served for many years as provost of the University of Maryland and as president of the Board of Trustees of Peabody Institute, Baltimore.

Meanwhile his literary life, which was always an avocation, continued. Besides articles on politics in the *National Intelligencer* and elsewhere, he wrote several satirical novels. Though the first (like his early magazine) was largely imitative of his friend Irving, and later ones of Cooper, they remain his chief claim to celebrity. After the Civil War he made three trips to Europe in a vain search for health, during which he became a close friend of Thackeray, and actually wrote one chapter of *The Virginians,* descriptive of a country he knew well and Thackeray not at all.

Collection of Frederick H. Meserve
JOHN PENDLETON KENNEDY

Kennedy also figures in the tragic life of Poe; he was one of the judges who awarded Poe first prize for the *Manuscript Found in a Bottle,* and afterwards befriended him on several occasions, though it is painful to read of his pompous beneficence and Poe's harried gratitude; it was impossible for a prosperous, well fed, commonplace man like Kennedy to understand or really sympathize with a frenzied and tortured genius.

Kennedy's principal work of non-fiction, his biography of William Wirt, Carl Van Doren calls "substantial," and nothing more. His satire Van Doren labels as "tolerable." However, his novels, which were published under the pseudonym of "Mark Littleton," deserve higher praise; though they are imitative, they illustrate his excellent power of romanticizing and enriching fact—for all of them were founded on actual scenes and persons.

Kennedy died at Newport, R.I., after a long and painful illness, an estimable, capable writer and an altruistic and tolerant man, who is remembered chiefly because he knew Thackeray and Poe.

Principal Works: Swallow Barn, 1832; Horse-Shoe Robinson, 1835; Rob of the Bowl, 1838; The Annals of Quodlibet, 1840; Memoirs of the Life of William Wirt, 1842; A Defense of the Whigs, 1844; The Blackwater Chronicle, 1853; Narrative of an Expedition of Five Americans Into a Land of Wild Animals, 1854; Mr. Ambrose's Letters on the Rebellion, 1865; At Home and Abroad, 1872.

About: Gwathmey, E. M. John Pendleton Kennedy; Tuckerman, H. T. The Life of John P. Kennedy.

KENT, JAMES (July 31, 1763-December 12, 1847), "the American Blackstone," jurist and writer on legal subjects, was born in Fredericksburgh, N.Y., the son of Moss and Hannah (Rogers) Kent, his father being an attorney. He received his B.A. at Yale in 1781, his M.A. in 1784, his course of studies being much interrupted by the Revolution, which caused frequent closing of all colleges. He then studied law and was admitted to the bar in 1785. In the same year he married Elizabeth Bailey. He practiced in Poughkeepsie, N.Y., until 1793, when, disappointed at a political defeat by his own brother-in-law, he moved to New York City. A strong Federalist, and a conservative to the point of reaction, he served three terms, between 1790 and 1796, in the New York Assembly. In the latter year he was made Master in Chancery, and while still holding this office served, in 1797, as recorder of the City of New York. In 1798 he was appointed to the New York Supreme Court, and in 1804 became chief justice. Ten years later he was Chancellor of the New York Court of Chancery.

Kent was the first professor of law at Columbia, from 1793 to 1798, but so few students took his courses that he resigned. The lectures, however, formed the groundwork for his famous *Commentaries,* which made him "the American Blackstone" and the father of equity law in America. In 1823 he was retired as Chancellor, since he was sixty, but he was in the prime of mental and physical vigor, and much resented his despotism. For two years from this date he was once more professor of law at Columbia, with exactly the same result. He then finally retired from public life and gave himself to the writing and re-editing of his *Commentaries,* six editions of which appeared before his death (and eight since, besides separate publication of various portions). He received honorary LL.D. degrees from Columbia, Harvard, Dartmouth, and the University of Pennsylvania.

From an engraving by T. Doney
JAMES KENT

Though Kent wrote little except on legal subjects, he was a thorough classical scholar, a great reader who built up a valuable library, part of which he willed to Columbia. His memory was phenomenal, and he is said never to have forgotten anything he learned. He was an individualist, almost anarchistic in his dislike of governmental control, a strange mixture with his extreme Federalism which made him the outstanding advocate of property qualifications for the electorate.

PRINCIPAL WORKS: Commentaries on American Law, 1826-1830; On the Charter of the City of New York, 1836; A Course of Reading, 1840.

ABOUT: Curtis, W. J. James Kent: The Father of American Jurisprudence; Duer, J. A Discourse on the Life, Character, and Public Service of James Kent; Hicks, F. Men and Books Famous in the Law; Kent, W. Memoirs and Letters of James Kent, LL.D.; American Law School Review Spring 1911.

"KERR, ORPHEUS C." See NEWELL, ROBERT HENRY

KEY, FRANCIS SCOTT (August 1, 1779-January 11, 1843), lawyer and poet, was born in Carroll County, Md., the son of John Ross Key and Ann Phoebe (Charlton) Key. He was graduated from St. John's College, Annapolis, in 1798, read law, and was admitted to the bar in 1801. He started practice at Frederick with Roger B. Taney, later chief justice of the United States Supreme Court and Key's brother-in-law. In 1802 he married Mary Tayloe Lloyd, by whom he had six sons and five daughters. He moved to Georgetown and went into practice with his uncle, the eminent Philip Barton Key. He was United States Attorney for the District of Columbia from 1809 to 1817 and from 1833 to 1841. In 1830 he moved to Washington (Georgetown then being a separate city). He died in his daughter's home in Baltimore, of pleurisy, at sixty-three.

Key's fame as a poet rests on a single but immortal poem—the words to "The Star-Spangled Banner," written in 1814 and designed by himself to be sung to the tune

FRANCIS SCOTT KEY

of the popular English drinking-song, "To Anacreon in Heaven." He had gone under a flag of truce to the British fleet, during the War of 1812, to effect the release of a captured friend; he was detained on board ship off Fort McHenry all night, during the bombardment of Baltimore, lest he reveal information he had obtained; and in his relief and patriotic ardor at seeing the American flag still flying in the morning he scribbled the poem on the back of an envelope. Later, in a hotel, he copied it (the copy is now in the Walters Gallery, Baltimore), and his wife took it to the Baltimore *American,* where it appeared at once. The rest of its history every American knows—though not, perhaps, that it has never been legally certified as our national anthem.

The remainder of Key's verses is merely the formal pastime of a cultured man of his period. Many of them are on religious themes, for he was very devout was a lay reader in the Episcopal Church, and for many years a delegate to its general conventions. He wrote the words of the hymn, still in use, "Lord, With Glowing Heart I'd Praise Thee." He never took his verse writing seriously or thought of himself as a literary figure.

PRINCIPAL WORKS: The Power of Literature and Its Connection With Religion, 1834; Poems of the Late Francis Scott Key, 1857.

ABOUT: Smith, F. S. K. Francis Scott Key; Weybright, V. Spangled Banner: The Story of Francis Scott Key; Current History May 1930; Modern Culture November 1900; Baltimore Sun January 13, 1843.

KIDDER, FREDERIC (April 16, 1804-December 19, 1885), merchant and antiquarian, was born in New Ipswich, N.H., the eldest son of Isaiah Kidder, a cotton manufacturer who died when he was seven, and Hepsey (Jones) Kidder. After two years in preparatory school for Dartmouth College, family affairs led him to take a clerkship in a wholesale grocery in Boston. His health failing after four years, he stocked a small schooner with goods and with his brother Edward set up a store in Wilmington, N.C. Eight years later he returned to Boston, engaging in business on India Street. His final years in Melrose, where he lived from 1869, were clouded by the five-year illness of his wife ending in her death in 1875, and his own decline.

Antiquarian interests led Kidder to pursue historical studies in intervals of leisure. These were characterized by the most paintaking and laborious research. With his friend, the physician and naturalist Augustus Addison Gould, he published a history of their native town New Ipswich.

PRINCIPAL WORKS: A History of New Ipswich (with A. A. Gould) 1852; The Expeditions of Capt John Lovewell and His Encounters With the Indians, 1856; The Popham Colony, 1866; Military Operations in Eastern Maine and Nova Scotia During the Revolution, 1867; History of the Boston Massacre, 1870; The Swedes on the Delaware and Their Intercourse With New England, 1874; The Discovery of North America by John Cabot, 1878.

ABOUT: Dean, J. W. Sketch of the Life of Frederic Kidder; Kidder, F. E. A History of the Kidder Family; New England Historical and Genealogical Register April 1887.

KILTY, WILLIAM (1757-October 10, 1821), army surgeon, jurist, and miscellaneous writer, was born in London, England, and educated at the College of St. Omer, France. His parents, John and Ellen (Ahearn) Kilty, brought him to Annapolis, Md., shortly before the Revolution. There he studied medicine and became successively surgeon's mate and surgeon of the Fourth Maryland Regiment, until taken prisoner in the Battle of Camden. After the war he turned to law. For about five years he was chief justice of the circuit court of the District of Columbia. He was chancellor of the state of Maryland from 1806 until his death.

In 1798 the Maryland legislature authorized him to compile the statutes of the state. About eighteen years after their completion the two original volumes were expanded into four with the collaboration of Thomas Harris and John N. Watkins.

Kilty wrote poetry as a pastime, and a satirical historical poem, *The Vision of Don Crocker,* has been attributed to him. He also produced a manuscript poem, "A Burlesque Translation of Homer's Iliad: The Second Part," a sequel to a work of the same name published by Thomas Bridges in England in 1764. Kilty's verses are an adaptation from Pope or Cowper.

PRINCIPAL WORKS: The Laws of Maryland (2 vcls.) 1799-1800; A Report on All Such English Statutes as Existed at the Time of the Frst Emigration of the People of Maryland . . . , 1811; The Vision of Don Crocker, 1813.

ABOUT: Kelly, H. A. & Burrage, W. L. American Medical Biographies.

KIMBALL, RICHARD BURLEIGH (October 11, 1816-December 28, 1892), lawyer, traveler, and social historian, was born in Plainfield N.H., the son of Richard and Mary (Marsh) Kimball. He spent his boyhood in Lebanon, N.H., and at the age of eleven had fulfilled the entrance requirements for Dartmouth, but was not admitted until two years later, and was graduated at seventeen. He studied law, passed his bar examinations in 1836, and that same year went to Paris where he read law with André Dupin, a noted French advocate and statesman. After a brief practice at Waterford, N.Y., he was made master in chancery, and went eventually to New York to become a partner of his brother Elijah H. Kimball in Wall Street. Shortly afterward he set up his own office and maintained a practice until 1854, when he became interested in the history of the Southwest and began some extensive travels in that region. He founded the town of Kimball, Tex., built a portion of the first railroad in that state, and was its president for six years. Kimball was married, in 1844 to Julia Carolina Tomlinson, by whom he had two sons and three daughters.

Kimball's first sizable literary venture was a metaphysical novel, *St. Leger: or, The Threads of Life,* which appeared (1848-49) in the *Knickerbocker* magazine and went immediately into French and Dutch translations. The rest of his writings were largely observations of a business man and day-book comments of an habitual traveler: *Cuba and the Cubans, Romance of Student Life Abroad, Undercurrents of Wall Street, Today in New York,* etc. On one of his numerous Atlantic crossings he made the acquaintance of Washington Irving, from whom he culled some spicy anecdotes which he afterwards published. In November 1867 he was a fellow-passenger with Dickens, and in his Boston welcoming address he gently chided the Englishman for the manner in which he had acknowledged the courtesies extended him during his first American sojourn; and Dickens was forced to admit, at the very select (Delmonico's) press banquet given in his honor, that Kimball's complaint had been well founded! During his last two years Kimball wrote, for the New York *Times,* a series of intimate sketches of his contemporaries intending to publish them in book form as "Half a Century of Recollections." It was, perhaps, Kimball's associations with many eminent statesmen and men of letters, rather than the influence of his writings *per se,* that gave him his literary stature.

PRINCIPAL WORKS: Cuba and the Cubans, 1850; Romance of Student Life Abroad, 1853; Undercurrents of Wall Street, 1862; Was He Successful? 1864; Henry Powers, Banker, 1868; To-day in New York, 1870.

ABOUT: Chapman, G. T. Sketches of the Alumni of Dartmouth College; New York Times December 29, 1892.

KING, CLARENCE (January 6, 1842-December 24, 1901), geologist and explorer, was born in Newport, R.I., the son of James Rives King and Florence (Little) King. He attended Hopkins Grammar School in Hartford, Conn., and at seventeen entered Yale Scientific School, from which he received a B. S. degree in 1862. In May of the year following, with a fellow-geologist, James T. Gardiner, he struck out on horseback for the Far West. An emigrant family joined them at St. Joseph, Mo., and continued with them as far as the Comstock Lode (Nevada). Here, after making a study of the region, King and his companion lost all of their equipment in a fire and were forced to go to work in the mines for a while in order to finance the next leg of their journey. Crossing the Sierras on foot, they went by boat down the Sacramento. Shortly afterwards King volunteered his services as explorer and for almost three years remained with a party making a geological survey of California; during the same period he acted as scientific aid in a desert exploration in Southern California.

On his return east King secured Congressional appropriations for a survey of the Cordilleran ranges between the eastern boundaries of Colorado and California. The project was officially completed in 1877; and the six-volume *Report of the Geological Exploration of the Fortieth Parallel* (1870-80) set perhaps an unequalled precedent among government publications. The first volume, "Systematic Geology," was King's own masterly stroke, reviewing the whole growth of the Cordilleran region; a large portion of the work, however, was prepared by others under King's direction. In it were relatively new scientific data, and the third volume, "Mining Industry," prepared by James Duncan Hague, has survived as a classic in its field. King was appointed director of the United States Geological Survey, which was established in 1878 in order to obviate the needless overlapping that existed among the numerous independent government-supervised parties for Western survey. After putting the organization into form he voluntarily resigned in 1881.

King wrote very little. In addition to his contributions to the *Report* he wrote scientific articles for the *American Naturalist*; "Helmet of Mambrino" in the form of a sprightly letter, for the *Century*; and a series of pleasant sketches, afterward published in book form as *Mountaineering in the Sierra Nevada,* for the *Atlantic Monthly*; William Dean Howells, who became editor in chief of the *Atlantic* in 1871, was a close friend of the scientist. King is said to have been a conversationalist of marked originality, and it has often been regretted that his accomplishments as a geologist were so completely preoccupying as to leave him little inclination for more strictly literary pursuits.

Principal Works: Vol. I, Report of the Geological Exploration of the Fortieth Parallel, 1870-80; Mountaineering in the Sierra Nevada, 1872.

About: American Journal of Science March 1902; National Academy of Science Biographical Memoirs: Vol. 6.

KING, EDWARD SMITH (September 8, 1848-March 27, 1896), journalist and poet, was born in Middlefield, Mass., the son of Edward and Lorinda (Smith) King. His father disappeared during an ocean voyage when young King was only three; his stepfather, a clergyman who left the ministry to become a teacher and millworker, provided him with a scant education. After working a while in a factory King left home, at sixteen, went to Springfield, Mass., and there became associated first with the *Daily Union* and then the *Republican.* He covered the Paris exposition in 1867, and wrote the naïvely romantic *My Paris* on the strength of his impressions. Joining the Boston *Morning Journal* in 1870 he returned to France to report the events of the Franco-Prussian War and the Commune, was twice arrested as a spy by the Germans, volunteered as an emergency nurse, and salvaged many of the bodies of Americans who had been killed in the street. These adventures were the materials for *Kentucky's Love,* dealing with a group of war correspondents, and *Under the Red Flag,* a juvenile.

At the suggestion of Josiah Gilbert Holland, editor of *Scribner's Monthly,* King went South as a literary scout and collector of data for articles on the social and economic effects of the Civil War; the articles were later collected into book form under the title *The Great South* (1875), twice reprinted in England (*The Southern States of North America*) within the year. King made the acquaintance of George Washington Cable, in New Orleans, and was responsible for the subsequent publication of many of Cable's stories in *Scribner's.*

He returned to Europe as correspondent for the *Boston Morning Journal,* with headquarters at Paris, covering the Carlist Wars in Spain and the Russo-Turkish War (1877-78) in the Balkans. Between 1876 and 1887 King published two volumes of verse, *Echoes from the Orient,* lyrics and descriptive snatches of Balkan life, and the narrative *Venetian Lover,* in ornate blank verse; two novels; and the rather grandiose *Europe in Storm and Calm.*

Coming back to America in 1888 he wrote editorials for the New York *Morning Journal* and *Collier's Once a Week,* compiled a guide-book, and did some miscellaneous editing. Three years before his death he wrote his best novel, *Joseph Zalmonah,* an *exposé* of New York's slums and sweatshops. Because King was essentially a journalist and because he regarded authorship as a means of livelihood he made an almost capricious exploitation of a variety of subjects, but although he seldom plumbed their surfaces very deeply, he left a good list of timely writings.

Principal Works: Kentucky's Love, 1873; The Great South, 1875; Echoes From the Orient, 1880; The Gentle Savage, 1883; Europe in Storm and Calm, 1885; The Golden Spike, 1886; A Venetian Lover, 1887; Joseph Zalmonah, 1893.

About: Evening Post (New York) March 28, 1896; Springfield Republican March 29, 1896.

"KINGSBURY, VERNON L." See LUKENS, HENRY CLAY

KINNEY, ELIZABETH CLEMENTINE (DODGE) STEDMAN (December 18, 1810-November 19, 1889), essayist and poet, was born in New York City, the daughter of an eminent merchant, David Low Dodge, and Sarah (Cleveland) Dodge. She was a granddaughter of the colonial poet Aaron Cleveland, and mother of the poet and critic Edmund Clarence Stedman [*q.v.*]. At nineteen she was married to Colonel Edmund Burke Stedman and lived in Hartford, Conn., until his death in 1835. In 1841 she married William Burnett Kinney, editor of the Newark *Daily Advertiser*. He was appointed chargé d'affaires at Sardinia in 1850, and for three years they lived in Turin, and later remained in Florence, Italy, for more than ten years, moving among such eminent persons as the Brownings and Tennysons.

After the death of her first husband Mrs. Kinney made contributions to numerous magazines from "Cedar Brook," her father's country home near Plainfield, N.J. Some of her best poems and critical essays were contributed to her husband's paper, the *Advertiser,* in the ten years following her second marriage. After their return to Newark her verses were collected and published as *Poems.* She also produced two Italian romances in verse, the first, *Felicita,* being based on an incident in Italian history.

PRINCIPAL WORKS: Felicita, 1855; Poems, 1867; Bianca Cappello, 1873.

ABOUT: Hart, J. S. The Female Prose Writers of America; Read, T. B. The Female Poets of America.

KIRK, JOHN FOSTER (March 22, 1824-September 21, 1904), historian and editor, was born at Fredericton, New Brunswick, the son of Abdiel and Mary Kirk. He lived in Halifax for a while and studied under an Oxford graduate at Truro, Nova Scotia; following a short stay in Quebec he went to Boston, continued his studies, and, after rejecting the actor William Charles Macready's suggestion that he try the stage, he succeeded his friend Robert Carter as secretary to William H. Prescott, the historian. Kirk had a real facility for languages, unlimited energy for research, and a varied intellectual background, and made himself indispensable to Prescott, who was always generous in his prefatory acknowledgments.

In May 1850 he went to England with Prescott, and, after a tour on the Continent, returned to the United States in the autumn. He carried on independent research in Prescott's excellent library and contributed critical and historical articles to the *North American Review.* Two volumes of his *History of Charles the Bold: Duke of Burgundy,* for which he owed his inspiration to Barante's *Histoire des Ducs de Bourgogne . . . ,* appeared in 1864; four years later, after a careful examination of French and Swiss manuscript sources and actual observations of the scene of Charles' defeat, came the third and last volume. *Charles the Bold* was obviously a scholarly achievement; but the biographical narrative, though rationally developed, was dissociated from the historical background, and the book as a whole bore certain unhappy extravagances of style.

Kirk became editor of *Lippincott's Magazine* in 1870, and shortly afterwards set to work on a new edition of Prescott's historical writings, the last of which was published in 1902. He was married in 1879 to Ellen Warner Olney, author of numerous popular novels who wrote under the pen-name "Henry Hayes." From 1885 until 1888 he lectured on European history at the University of Pennsylvania. With his resignation from *Lippincott's* he began, in 1886, the painstaking editing of a two-volume *Supplement to Allibone's Critical Dictionary of English Literature*; and somewhat later the preparation of *Lippincott's New Dictionary.* Only a very lenient critic would perhaps still maintain that the author of *Charles the Bold* belonged to "the small band of real historians"; but Kirk's biography, shorter papers, and extensive editings, appraised as a whole, do represent, certainly, an orderly and constructive literary achievement.

PRINCIPAL WORKS: *Biography*—History of Charles the Bold: Duke of Burgundy (3 vols.) 1864-68. *Edited*—Supplement to Allibone's Critical Dictionary of English Literature, 1891; and Lippincott's New Dictionary.

ABOUT: Freeman, E. A. Historical Essays; Lippincott's Monthly Magazine November 1902.

KIRKLAND, CAROLINE MATILDA (STANSBURY) (January 12, 1801-April 6, 1864), early emigrant to the Midwest, social historian, and mother of Joseph Kirkland [*q.v.*], was born in New York City, daughter of Samuel Stansbury, bookseller and publisher, and Elizabeth (Alexander) Stansbury. She probably received her early schooling at home; and on the death of her father she and her mother removed to the western part of the state. Here, in her late twenties, she was married to William Kirkland, grand-nephew of Samuel Kirkland, missionary to the Indians. The Kirklands conducted seminaries in Geneva, N.Y., and then in Detroit before their emigration to the frontier village of Pinckney, Mich. The types of people with whom she soon became acquainted and the crudeness of her domestic surroundings quickly dissolved her comfortable illusions about pioneer life and prompted her to put down her impressions in no timid language: under the pseudonym of "Mrs. Mary Clavers" she wrote *A New Home—Who'll Follow* (1839), published in England as *Montacute,* and reprinted in 1874, with illustrations, as *Our New Home in the West: or, Glimpses of Life Among Early Settlers.* It was a sour and yet amusing analysis of the graft, coarseness, and shallowness that typified the borderland communities. The essay-like *Forest Life* (1842) and the somewhat thin tales of *Western Clearings* were written in a similar vein. But after 1843, when she went back to New York to live, she was unable to maintain that earlier dash of candor and humor, even though she continued, in *The Evening Book: or, Fireside Talks on Morals and Manners* and *A Book for the Home Circle,* to draw upon her Western experience.

After her husband's death in 1846, writing became almost the only means of support for herself and her children. From 1847 to 1851 she filled an editorial post with the *Union Magazine* (later called *Sartain's Magazine of Literature and Art*). She utilized her own personal impressions, gathered from a variety of "pleasure reading," in *Spenser and the Faëry Queen* and in two anthologies, *Garden Walks With the Poets* and *The School-Girl's Garland.* In 1849 she published two volumes of rather bromidic travel letters, *Holidays Abroad*; and in 1857 a drably conventional biography, *Memoirs of Washington.* During her last years she was identified with numerous organizations for social welfare. She died very suddenly, and among the pall-bearers at her funeral were William Cullen Bryant and Nathaniel Parker Willis.

Writing for *Godey's Lady's Book* in 1846, Edgar Allan Poe, too often lavish in his appraisal of women, described Mrs. Kirkland as "brilliantly witty and now and then not a little sarcastic"; had she invested her later writings with more of that semi-comic banter she might have outranked a much larger proportion of the rather nondescript female authors of her day.

Principal Works: A New Home—Who'll Follow, 1839; Forest Life, 1842; Western Clearings, 1845; Spenser and the Faëry Queen, 1847; Holidays Abroad, 1849; The Evening Book. . . , 1851; A Book for the Home Circle, 1852; Garden Walks With the Poets, 1852; Memoirs of Washington, 1857; The School-Girl's Garland, 1864.

About: Duyckinck, E. A. & G. L. Cyclopaedia of American Literature; Hart, J. S. The Female Prose Writers of America; Powell, T. The Living Authors of America; Evening Post (New York) April 6, 7, 11, 1864.

KIRKLAND, JOSEPH (January 7, 1830-April 29, 1894), novelist, journalist, and lawyer, was born in Geneva, N.Y., the son of William Kirkland and Caroline Matilda (Stansbury) Kirkland [*q.v.*], chronicler of frontier life. He spent his early boyhood in "backwoods" Michigan and his later youth in the Illinois pioneer country. His formal education was negligible, but he was ably instructed at home, and after a minor position with Putnam's *Monthly* in his early twenties, he went to Chicago and became associated with the Illinois Central Railroad. From 1875 to 1880, when he was admitted to the Illinois bar, he was in the United States revenue service. For about ten years he was a practicing attorney, at the end of which time he became special correspondent, reviewer, and literary editor of the Chicago *Tribune.* In 1863 he was married to Theodosia Burr Wilkinson, of Syracuse, N.Y.

Kirkland's literary career, roughly coincident with the period of his active law practice, did not begin until he was over fifty, and its best fruit was his novel *Zury: The Meanest Man in Spring County.* A mature reflection of a grim youthful experience, it recapitulated all the niggardliness of frontier life in a full-length portrait of a struggling Illinois settler who, by thrift, shrewdness, and a hard-headed acquisitive battle against the forces of nature, made his way up from the mere dregs to relative prosperity and emerged an actually lovable old man. The chief merit of *The McVeys,* Kirkland's second book, was its depiction—significant though weak—of the mining districts of the upper Mississippi; the tale as a whole bore much less narrative logic and unity of tempo than its predecessor. With *The Captain of Company K,* a Civil War chronicle founded on his two years' service as private and officer, Kirkland won an award offered by the *Detroit Free Press*; it appeared serially in 1890 and in book form the next year. Two ordinary pieces of local history, *The Chicago Massacre of 1812* and *The Story of Chicago,* the latter finished after his death by his daughter Caroline, and some inconspicuous magazine articles were the sum of his last achievements.

In a letter to Hamlin Garland, Kirkland had written: "You're the first actual farmer in American fiction—now tell the truth about it." And it was Hamlin Garland who brought to full flower the seedling of middle-border realism that was Kirkland's *Zury,* "an attempt," said its author, "to reproduce . . . life down in actual contact with the soil itself."

PRINCIPAL WORKS: Zury. . , 1887; The McVeys, 1888; The Captain of Company K, 1891; The Story of Chicago (2 vols.) 1892-94; The Chicago Massacre of 1812, 1893.

ABOUT: Parrington, V. L. Main Currents in American Thought; Chicago Daily Tribune April 30, 1894.

KLIPSTEIN, LOUIS FREDERICK (January 2, 1813-August 20, 1878), philologist, was a native of Winchester, Va., the son of Peter Klipstein, whose father came to America as a surgeon with Hessian troops and later settled at Winchester, and of Frances (Kimmelmyer) Klipstein of Baltimore. He studied at Hampden-Sidney College, the Union Theological Seminary, and received a degree from the University of Giessen, Germany, in 1845. While tutor in a wealthy family at Santee, S.C., where he had gone for his health, he married the daughter of the household, Allston Cahusac Jerman, and turned his attention to the preparation of a series of works on Anglo-Saxon. Heavy losses resulting from their publication affected his wife's inheritance, and his remaining years were clouded by separation, drink, and destitution. In 1878 he wandered to Florida where he died.

In 1844 Klipstein started a monthly publication, the *Polyglott,* devoted to the study of French, Italian, Spanish, Portuguese, German and English. It was soon discontinued but the material was used in his first book, *The Study of Modern Languages.* His texts were probably the first in Anglo-Saxon published in American and were much used. His *Grammar* and *Analecta Anglo-Saxonica* went through several editions. He reprinted *Tha Halgan Godspel on Englise* edited by Benjamin Thorpe, wrote or edited a few other works, and announced six additional titles as being in preparation, which were never completed.

PRINCIPAL WORKS: The Study of Modern Languages; A Grammar of the Anglo-Saxon Language, 1848; Natale Sancti Gregorii Papae: Aelfric's Anglo-Saxon Homily on the Birthday of St. Gregory, 1848; Analecta Anglo-Saxonica: Selections in Prose and Verse From the Anglo-Saxon Literature (2 vols.) 1849.

ABOUT: Englische Studien (Leipsic): Vol. 62; Modern Language Association Publications: Vol. 8.

KNAPP, SAMUEL LORENZO (January 19, 1783-July 8, 1838), lawyer and editor, was born in Newburyport, Mass., the son of Isaac Knapp, sea captain, and Susanna (Newman) Knapp. In 1804 he was graduated from Dartmouth College; later he received an honorary degree in Paris. He practiced law in his native town and in Boston, served in the state legislature, and commanded a regiment of militia in coast defense. Finding law not to his taste he finally deviated into literature. His last three years were spent in failing health in Hopkinton, Mass.

For his first two books Knapp adopted the pseudonyms "Shahcoolen" and "Marshall Soult," and his *Sketches of Public Characters* appeared over the name "Ignatius Loyola Robertson." His second book was written in the Newburyport jail while under imprisonment for debt. At various times he took charge of the Masonic section of the *New England Galaxy and Masonic Magazine,* edited the Boston *Gazette* and the Washington *National Journal,* established and edited the *Boston Monthly Magazine* and the *National Republican,* and was connected with the New York *Commercial Advertiser.* He was a popular orator, with a flowing, graceful, easy style, and among his miscellaneous published works are included a number of orations. His main writing, however, was as a biographer. In this he was laudatory and patriotic, but not trustworthy.

PRINCIPAL WORKS: Letters of Shahcoolen, 1802; Extracts From the Journal of Marshall Soult, 1817; Biographical Sketches of Eminent Lawyers, Statesmen, and Men of Letters, 1821; Memoirs of General Lafayette, 1824; A Discourse on the Life and Character of DeWitt Clinton, 1828; The Genius of Masonry, 1828; Lectures on American Literature, 1829; Sketches of Public Characters, 1830; A Memoir of the Life of Daniel Webster, 1831; Advice in the Pursuits of Literature, 1832; American Biography, 1833; Life of Thomas Eddy, 1834; Tales of the Garden of Kosciuszko, 1834; Female Biography, 1834; The Life of Aaron Burr, 1835; The Bachelors and Other Tales, 1836; Life of Timothy Dexter, 1838.

ABOUT: Buckingham, J. T. Personal Memoirs; Chapman, G. T. Sketches of the Alumni of Dartmouth College; Runnels, M. T. History of Sanbornton, N. H.

KNIGHT, HENRY COGSWELL (January 29, 1789-January 10, 1835), poet and Episcopal clergyman, was born probably in Newburyport, Mass., the son of Joseph and Elizabeth (Cogswell) Knight. Henry was three when Elizabeth Knight died, and his father, who had meanwhile married Mary Treadwell, died six years later. Henry and a younger brother lived for a while with their maternal grandfather Dr. Nathaniel Cogswell, in Rowley, Mass.; and from Dummer Academy, Henry was sent to Phillips Academy, Andover, entering

Harvard in 1808. He disliked even the slightest academic regimentation, devoted much of his time to independent reading, and during his sophomore year published *The Cypriad,* a collection of admittedly imitative poems. One of these, "The Little Sweep," appears to have been almost a duplicate of two verses in Blake's *Songs of Innocence and Experience,* although Knight's access, in 1809, to a copy of this work seems unaccountable. Several of his conventionally classical poems appeared in the *Monthly Anthology.* In 1811 Knight left Harvard and enrolled at Brown University, from which he received B. A. and M. A. degrees the year following.

He was in Philadelphia for a while in 1814, and from here he set out on an extensive journey, of which the only record is his collection of witty and informative *Letters From the South and West: By Arthur Singleton, Esq.* (1824). In *The Broken Harp* (1815), a more romantic assortment than his first volume, there is another startling and equally puzzling resemblance—this time between his "Earl Kandorf and Rosabelle" and Coleridge's unpublished "Christabel."

Knight spent some time in Washington and Richmond before going inland to Kentucky and then down the Ohio and Mississippi to New Orleans, arriving on July 4, 1818. Leaving the Far South in 1819 he returned to Massachusetts by boat. His pamphlet *Fights of Faith,* which appeared anonymously in 1821, was included in his *Poems* ("Second Edition") published the same year. In 1826 the *New England Galaxy* printed a number of his articles.

On May 6, 1827, he was ordained a deacon of the Protestant Episcopal Church and two years later he became rector of Prince George's and St. Bartholomew's parishes in Montgomery County, Md. Returning to New England he published two volumes of *Lectures and Sermons* (1831) and spent the rest of his life near Boston. He died of scarlet fever, at Rowley, Mass., survived by his brother Frederick and his half-brother Antonio. An agile versifier he was, certainly, but his poems seldom emerged from a kind of stilted and imitative vein, and his nimble *Letters from the South . . .* have become his most valuable literary remains.

Principal Works: The Cypriad, 1809; The Broken Harp, 1815; Poems, 1821; Fights of Faith, 1821; Letters From the South and West: By Arthur Singleton, Esq., 1824; Lectures and Sermons, 1831.

About: Buckingham, J. T. Personal Memoirs; Duyckinck, E. A. & G. L. Cyclopaedia of American Literature.

KNIGHT, SARAH (KEMBLE) (April 19, 1666-September 25, 1727), diarist, was born in Boston, Mass., the daughter of Thomas Kemble, a merchant and one of Oliver Cromwell's agents, and Elizabeth (Trerice) Kemble. According to tradition, Sarah's father was put in the stocks for the "lewd and unseemly" act of kissing his wife on the Sabbath. Some time before his death in 1689 Sarah was married to Capt. Richard Knight, a widower, who died in London in about the year 1706, during a prolonged sojourn there. Madam Knight —so called in deference to her professional accomplishments and her social esteem—took over many of her father's responsibilities; was adviser to several relatives; and in the capacity of witness was the signer of numerous public documents. Moreover, she conducted a writing-school where Benjamin Franklin is said to have been a pupil.

Following the death of a wealthy cousin, Caleb Trowbridge, of New Haven, Conn., there was an unaccountable delay in the settlement of the estate. In the face of much intimidating opposition Madam Knight decided to go herself to New York, and, with the aid of the father of the deceased, to expedite the legal proceedings. She set out in October 1704, traveling on horseback with a precariously elusive guide, who, posting along at night, cast a shadow that resembled "a Globe on a Gate post. . . ." Instead of filling her notebook with long and splenetic rantings on the miseries that characterized the average New England inn—an abundance of refractory meats and breads and a dearth of heat and mattresses —she recorded these discomforts with a robust humor that occasionally broke into a brilliant mock-heroic stanza. And there were other features in this mode of travel that could hardly be called pleasurable, *e.g.,* the crossing of a fierce little river in a fragile, narrow, and heavily packed canoe—"I dared not so much as lodge my tongue a hair's breadth more on one side of my mouth than tother, nor so much as think on Lott's wife . . . ," wrote Madam Knight. She remained in New Haven until the sixth of December and then proceeded to New York ". . . a well compacted place, . . . not so strict in keeping the Sabbath as . . . Boston," and seeming to deal, in money matters, "with a great exactness." When her mission was accomplished she returned northward with Thomas Trowbridge and reached home on December 21. She sold her Boston home some time before 1714 and removed to Connecticut, where she prospered in land speculation and in the keeping of a shop and entertainment house.

Her diary was first published in 1825 by Theodore Dwight, of New York; the fact that the handwriting of the "neatly copied" manuscript has never been identified as that of Madam Knight, has suggested that she may have included, by means of her own system of shorthand, much that has not been preserved. Five subsequent editions have appeared, the last of which was issued in 1920. It is a small document, but in it are many witty anecdotes and candidly pithy observations, and among early American travel journals it has no peer.

ABOUT: Historical Magazine August 1858, March 1865; prefaces to the various editions of her diary.

KNOX, THOMAS WALLACE (June 26, 1835-January 6, 1896), traveler, journalist, and inventor, was born in Pembroke, N.Y. His father, a shoemaker, said to be a descendent of the Scotch reformer John Knox, and his mother Jane Wallace (Critchet) Knox, both died before he was six. He worked on a farm at the age of ten, and at twenty-two was principal of an academy at Kingston, N.H. The gold rush drew him in 1860 to Denver, Colo., where he soon became editor of the *Daily News.* After the Civil War, in which he was commissioned lieutenant-colonel on the staff of the Governor of California, he joined the New York *Herald,* as correspondent taking the first of his world travels across Siberia with an American telegraph company. His method of transmitting battlefield plans was patented by him. He died suddenly in New York City.

His Civil War dispatches, published as his first book, *Camp-Fire and Cotton-Field,* enjoyed some popularity. A prolific writer, for eighteen years he turned out two books a year. He was most distinctive as a writer of travel books for boys, his journeys taking him over a wider area than almost any American of his time. His second of the fifteen volumes of the *Boy Traveler* series brought him, in 1881, the distinction of receiving from the King of Siam the Order of the White Elephant, the first ever accorded to an American.

PRINCIPAL WORKS: Camp-Fire and Cotton-Field, 1865; Overland Through Asia, 1870; The Underground World, 1880; The Boy Travelers in the Far East, 1881; How to Travel, 1881; The Pocket-Guide for Europe, 1882; The Lives of James G. Blaine and John A. Logan, 1884; Adventures of Two Youths in the Open Polar Sea, 1885; The Life of Robert Fulton, 1886; Life and Work of Henry Ward Beecher, 1887; Decisive Battles Since Waterloo, 1887; The Republican Party and Its Leaders, 1892.

ABOUT: Carter, N. F. History of Pembroke, N. H.; Book News Monthly February 1892.

LACY, ERNEST (September 19, 1863-June 17, 1916), poet and dramatist, was born in Warren, Pa., the son of Barnet W. Lacy, an attorney, and Martha M. (MacLean) Lacy. His father became bankrupt and died early, leaving Ernest and his brilliant older brother William to make their own way. They attended Hastings Academy, Philadelphia, until 1878, and then studied law, both being ready for the bar before they were twenty-one. Together they themselves printed William's *Examination Into the Philosophy of the Unknowable as Expounded by Herbert Spencer* (1883), a remarkable piece of work for a boy in his early twenties.

Meanwhile Ernest Lacy made his living by preparing students for the bar examinations. His real love, however, was for the theatre, and at the first opportunity he gave up the law and became a theatrical press agent and play reviser, later acting as manager of two Philadelphia theatres and of the Paris Winter Circus. In 1892 he went to London, where he worked as a dramatic coach. He was recalled to Philadelphia to teach public speaking at the venerable Central High School, then the only high school for boys in the city. He remained with the school for the rest of his life, being made assistant professor of English in 1896, professor in 1900, and head of

ERNEST LACY

the department in 1907. In 1903 the Board of Public Education of Philadelphia conferred an honorary Litt.D. upon him. Lacy was an inspiring teacher, with a real love for literature (he was especially devoted to Chatterton) and a keen critical faculty. He did much to develop public debating in the schools. Unfortunately, he put all of his energy into his work, and wrote little. When he died half a dozen poetic dramas were found unfinished in his desk.

In 1885 Lacy married Harriet C. Dugan; they had no children. Only three of his plays were produced, though others exist in manuscript. Julia Marlowe put on *Chatterton* in 1895, and the next year his *Rinaldo* was performed by Joseph Haworth. In 1899 his only popular success, *The Ragged Earl,* was produced; this was an Irish prose comedy, a *genre* in which he excelled, though none of his other plays of this type saw the stage. His last poetic play, *The Bard of Mary Redcliffe,* has never been performed, though Christian Gauss considered it "the greatest poetic drama written in the United States."

Lacy was in appearance a "typical actor" of the old fashioned sort, though actually he was never on the stage—clean-shaven, with deep set eyes, a most melodious voice, and immense dignity. Although he was probably overrated by his associates, he did have great talent, and his plays and poems are full of a rich beauty. Some of his sonnets have been widely reprinted, the one on "Melancholy" being the best known.

Neither Irish comedies nor historic dramas in verse have much appeal today, but Lacy was something more than a mere local celebrity, and some passages in his plays are at least as fine as the best of the plays of similar nature by Stephen Phillips.

Principal Works: Plays and Sonnets, 1900; The Bard of Mary Redcliffe, 1910.

About: Edmonds, F. S. History of the Central High School of Philadelphia; Quinn, A. H. A History of the American Drama From the Civil War to the Present Day; New York Times June 18, 1916.

LADD, JOSEPH BROWN (July 7, 1764-November 2, 1786), poet, was born in Newport, the son of William Ladd, a farmer, Revolutionary soldier, and member of the Rhode Island Legislature, and Sarah (Gardner) Ladd. He was educated privately, and was placed at an early age with a merchant; however, he rebelled against a commercial career, and his father then apprenticed him to a printer. From the age of ten he had written verses, and a satirical ballad he wrote against the eminent theologian, Dr. Samuel Hopkins, so offended Hopkins that he forced Ladd's father to remove the boy from his apprenticeship. Ladd then studied medicine with a local physician who besides taught him the classics and directed his writing, and in 1783 he was licensed to practise. About the same time he fell in love with an orphan, an heiress, and she with him, but her guardian forbade the match. It is from this circumstance that his more serious poems all arose. At the advice of Gen. Nathanael Greene, he went, to forget his grief, to Charleston, S.C., where he set up as a physician. At the same time he continued to write prose and verse on literary, scientific, and political topics. A controversy arising from the last-named caused his death; he was challenged to a duel, fired in the air, and was killed by his opponent. He was only twenty-two.

Ladd's poems are now quite unreadable, consisting mostly of sentimental languishings over his "Amanda." However, he has a place in literary history as one of the first American poets to experiment with new verse forms and to abandon the iambic pentameter couplets which were the hallmark of the eighteenth century. He was alive to new feeling in literature, and showed the influence of the Ossianic poems, Chatterton, and Goethe. He had undoubted talent, and might have gone much farther had he not died so young.

Principal Works: The Poems of Arouet, 1786; Literary Remains of Joseph Brown Ladd, M.D. (ed. by E. L. Haskins) 1832.

About: Ladd, J. B. Literary Remains (see Biographical Sketch by W. B. Chittenden).

LA FARGE, JOHN (March 31, 1835-November 14, 1910), artist and writer on art, was born in New York City, the son of Lieutenant Jean-Frédéric de la Farge, of the French navy, who became a landowner in America, and Louisa (de Saint-Victor) de la Farge. The father later Anglicized his name to La Farge. John La Farge was educated at St. John's College (now affiliated with Fordham University) and Mt. St. Mary's College in Maryland, from which he was graduated in 1853. His early interest in art was desultory, and he began to study law. In 1856 he went to Paris to visit his mother's family, studying painting merely as an accomplishment, and returned to his legal studies in 1858. In 1860 he married Margaret Mason Perry, granddaughter of Commodore Perry and great-granddaughter of Franklin; they had nine children. La Farge moved to Newport on his marriage, and there, through the influence of the artist William M. Hunt, he decided to devote himself entirely to painting. When the Civil War broke out he tried to enlist, but was refused for nearsightedness. His history thenceforth is primarily that of an artist, a landscapist, muralist, and inventor of the "American" method of producing stained glass. However, he also lectured widely and wrote much on the history and nature of art, most of his books being printed versions of his lectures. From 1880 on, he made several trips to Japan and the South Seas, all of which eventuated in books. A man of aloof personality, and all his long life a semi-invalid, he was yet an indefatigable worker, in the end the dean of American artists, honored both in this country and abroad. As a writer, he is colorful and eloquent, his work marked by the same intellectuality and sensitiveness which characterized his painting. He did much to acquaint the American public with Japan in its early days of westernization.

La Farge's grandson, Oliver La Farge, won the 1929 Pulitzer Prize for literature with his novel *Laughing Boy.*

Principal Works: Considerations on Painting, 1895; Hokūsai, 1807; An Artist's Letters From Japan, 1897; Great Masters, 1903; The Higher Life in Art, 1908; One Hundred Masterpieces of Painting, 1912; Reminiscences of the South Seas, 1912; The Gospel Story in Art, 1913.

About: Cortissoz, R. John LaFarge: A Memoir and a Study; Waern, C. John LaFarge: Artist and Writer; Historical Records and Studies U.S. Catholic Historical Society March 1928.

LAMAR, MIRABEAU BUONAPARTE (August 16, 1798-December 19, 1859), statesman and poet, was born in Louisville, Ga., the son of John and Rebecca Lamar, his parents being first cousins. The strange names given him and other members of his family were the work of an eccentric uncle with historical and classical tastes. After an elementary education, Lamar became a merchant in Alabama, but failed. For a while thereafter he was private secretary to Governor Troup, of Georgia. In 1826 he married Tabitha B. Jordan, who died in 1833, leaving one daughter.

In 1828 Lamar founded the Columbus, Ga., *Independent,* and in 1833 became editor of the *Enquirer,* in the same city. After being defeated for Congress, he went to Texas in 1835. He joined Houston's army, was at the battle of San Jacinto, and was breveted major-general. In 1836 he was elected vice-president of the new Republic of Texas, and from 1838 to 1841 was its second president. His administration was a disastrous one, marked by extravagance and by the capture by the Mexican government of 320 men he had sent to Santa Fé to try to win the inhabitants from their allegiance to Mexico. He did, however, found the State University, in 1840, and changed the capital to Austin. He was violently opposed to annexation of Texas to the United States, but in 1844 changed his mind completely and advocated annexation in order to preserve slavery. He served through the Mexican War as a lieutenant-colonel, and afterwards served one term in the new Texas State Legislature.

In 1851, nearly twenty years after the death of his first wife, he married Henrietta Maffitt. He was appointed minister to the Argentine, but never took office. From 1857 to 1859 he was minister to Nicaragua and Costa Rica, but was recalled because he could not secure signing of a treaty. Soon afterwards he died at his plantation at Richmond, Texas. Lamar County, Texas, is named after him.

Lamar's was a contradictory nature: personally he was gentle, honest, and generous; yet he was exceedingly cruel and ruthless to the Indians, and bitterly opposed Houston's policy of leniency. He was a dreamer and visionary, with grandiose plans which never came to fruition. His verse is smooth and flowing, but markedly "dated"; he is a sort of minor Byron of the Southwest.

Principal Works: Verse Memorials, 1857; Papers of M. B. Lamar, 1920-27.

About: Christian, A. K. Mirabeau Buonaparte Lamar; Weber, W. L. The Southern Poets.

LAMB, MARTHA JOANNA READE (NASH) (August 13, 1829-January 2, 1893), editor and social historian, was born in Plainfield, Mass., the daughter of Arvin and Lucinda (Vinton) Nash. Her father had an uncompromising bitterness towards the press, and her early dabblings in the art of writing, as "letters to the Editor," were necessarily submitted without a signature. Not until she was about forty, however, did she do much writing. For some time she occupied an important chair of mathematics in a polytechnic institute and was invited to revise and edit a book on higher mathematics. Her article on "The Coast Survey," appearing in *Harper's New Monthly Magazine,* March 1879, was a clear and simple translation of a few of the mysteries of mathematics into the language of the layman.

After her marriage in 1852 to Charles A. Lamb she lived for several years in Chicago, and there began the writing of juveniles, and, a little later, a novel *Spicy,* which was not without its sentimentality and round-about phraseology. She had long been interested in historical research, and following her removal to New York she began the examination of a mine of source materials which had been almost untouched by earlier historians of the city. Mrs. Lamb sifted colonial documents, old newspapers, and manuscripts and produced a *History of the City of New York: Its Origin, Rise, and Progress* (2 vols. 1871-1881), then reputed to be "the most complete history ever published of any city in the world."

In May 1883 she became editor of the *Magazine of American History,* the only periodical devoted to this subject. The last ten years of her life were spent in the soliciting of articles from brilliant contributors and in the writing of her own, many of which were later published in book form under the titles, *Wall Street in History* and *Unpublished Washington Portraits.* She was elected to membership in twenty-six historical and learned societies in this country and in Europe, and both in Chicago and in New York was very active in charitable enterprises, the establishment of orphan asylums, etc., holding, at the same time, a ranking position in social and literary circles. The obvious merit of her writings and the fact that they were the accomplishments of a female author in an age when women were writing a quantity of pallid, third-rate books excited her critics into frequent superlatives.

Principal Works: Spicy, 1873; A History of the City of New York: Its Origin, Rise, and Progress (2 vols.) 1877-81; Wall Street in History, 1883; Unpublished Washington Portraits, 1888.

About: Willard, F. E. & Livermore, M. A. A Woman of the Century; Proceedings of the New Jersey Historical Society: 2d ser. Vol. 10; Publisher's Weekly January 7, 1893; New York Herald January 4, 1893.

LANDON, MELVILLE DE LANCEY (September 7, 1839-December 16, 1910), humorist and lecturer, whose pen name was "Eli Perkins," was born on a farm in Madison County, N.Y., the son of John and Nancy (Marsh) Landon. He was sent to the district school and local academy and then to Madison (later Colgate) University and Union College, from which he was graduated in 1861. During the Civil War he was a Treasury clerk in Washington and enjoyed a casual acquaintance with such front-page figures as Charles Sumner and William H. Seward. Landon served in Cassius M. Clay's battalion for the defense of the Capital, and after rising to the rank of major he resigned by request and went South to grow cotton in Louisiana and Arkansas with free labor. His subsequent travels abroad included journeys to Paris, Rome, and Athens, and in St. Petersburg he was secretary to his former commander, Clay, then minister to Russia.

The Franco-Prussian War in a Nut-Shell was written on his return, and a lucky plunge into journalism followed. For the (N.Y.) *Commercial Advertiser* he wrote some (then) bubbling columns over the signature "Lan" or "Eli Perkins" published in 1872 as *Saratoga in 1901*; three years later came *Eli Perkins: His Sayings and Doings.* He conducted a lecture tour for "Josh Billings" and then found a field for himself in platform humor, and of his "thousand lectures" many were delivered in colleges and universities. During one tour he made quite a stay at "wicked Cheyenne" and the letters he wrote back to the New York *Sun* so completely delighted the ranchers that they collaborated in the writing and production of a play called "Eli Among the Cowboys."

Like many of the humorists of his day, Landon relied greatly on deformities of sentence, word, logic, etc., and that redoubtable device, the anti-climax; his undistorted, purely anecdotal wit was often palpably thin: not only his three collections, *Wit*

Collection of Frederick H. Meserve

MELVILLE DE LANCEY LANDON

and Humor of the Age; Wise, Witty, Eloquent Kings of the Platform and Pulpit; and *Thirty Years of Wit,* which appeared under varying titles, but his innumerable lectures are evidence of this. His writings, moreover, are underlaid with an obtrusive "philosophical" analysis of the nature of wit, satire, ridicule, and humor, and the sweeping categorical distinctions which he makes often apply only (if then!) to the particular example cited. He edited *The Complete Works of Artemus Ward* (1879) and wrote a campaign brief against free silver: *Money: Gold, Silver, or Bimetalism* (1895). Landon was president of the New York News Association, and during his late years made several journeys to Europe and the Orient, sending back travel letters to the metropolitan dailies. He was married in 1875 to Emily Louise Smith.

With "Artemus Ward," "Petroleum V. Nasby," "Josh Billings," and other celebrated wits Landon passed many an hour in a literary rendezvous under the Fifth Avenue Hotel, the establishment of G. W. Carleton, who was responsible for putting into print many of the bon mots of the 'eighties and 'nineties. Although Eli Perkins was hilariously received as one of the most successful wags of his day, from the literary point of view he has not worn so well as his contemporaries, and falls among the humorists of more fugitive brilliance.

PRINCIPAL WORKS: The Franco-Prussian War in a Nut-Shell, 1871; Saratoga in 1901, 1872; Eli Perkins at Large: His Sayings and Doings, 1875; Complete Works of Artemus Ward, 1879; Wit and Humor of the Age, 1883; Wise, Witty, Eloquent Kings of the Platform and Pulpit, 1890; Thirty Years of Wit, 1891; Money: Gold, Silver, or Bimetalism, 1895.

ABOUT: Blair, W. Native American Humor; New York Times December 17, 1910.

LANE, GEORGE MARTIN (December 24, 1823-June 30, 1897), classicist, was born in Charlestown, Mass., the son of Martin and Lucretia (Swan) Lane. He attended George J. Abbott's school; and it was probably Charles Stearns Wheeler, later an instructor at Harvard, who gave young Lane his first encouragement in classical scholarship. He was graduated from Harvard in 1846 with high distinction, and in Professor Karl Beck's absence took over his Latin classes at the college. In the Harvard tradition, Lane went abroad to study the year following—at Berlin, Bonn, Heidelberg—and, for a dissertation on the city of Smyrna which is still historical authority, received his Ph.D. at Göttingen in 1851. At Harvard he was appointed directly to a full professorship (Latin) the same year, and in 1869 became Pope Professor of Latin. At his resignation in 1894 he was made professor emeritus, having completed forty-three years of the ablest teaching; he was a stickler for scrupulous accuracy and a scholar with a temperament that could provoke a high intellectual response from his students. Lane was twice married: to Frances Eliza Gardiner in 1857, and, two years after her death in 1876, to Mrs. Fanny (Bradford) Clark.

Lane was preeminently a teacher, but he was also the author of a few influential books. It is said that his *Latin Pronunciation* (1871) "worked a revolution in exterminating the English pronunciation of Latin in this country. . ." He aided Charlton T. Lewis in the compilation of *Harper's Latin Dictionary* and made valuable contributions to the original and almost infallible *School Lexicon.* His *Latin Grammar for Schools and Colleges,* published posthumously and representing incidental philological gleanings of almost thirty years, has, with not too much extravagance, been referred to as a "monument of literary art and sympathetic interpretation." It contains a carefully devised syntax that provides for a masterly idiomatic interpretation of the original.

Lane was a courtly gentleman with an enviable sense of humor that was very much in evidence in his "burlesque Harvard Commencement," presented at the Newport Town and Country Club; in his breezy little *Jonah: or, The Black Whale at Ascalon,* an adaptation of a German student song; and his much quoted ballad of "The Lone Fishball," inspired by a meal in a second-rate Boston restaurant.

The soundness and brilliance of Lane's teaching are fairly proverbial; a facility of expression and an admirable literary taste enhanced the value of his few but significant publications.

PRINCIPAL WORKS: Latin Pronunciation, 1871; Latin Grammar For Schools and Colleges, 1898.

ABOUT: Chamberlain, J. L. Harvard University; Harvard Studies in Classical Philology: Vols. 7 & 9; Nation (N.Y.) July 8, 1897.

"LANGDON, MARY." See PIKE, MARY HAYDEN (GREEN)

LANGFORD, NATHANIEL PITT (August 9, 1832-October 18, 1911), explorer and vigilante, a native of Westmoreland, N.Y., was the twelfth child of George Langford II, bank cashier and descendant of John Langford who settled at Salem, Mass., about 1660, and of Chloe (Sweeting) Langford. Journeying westward in 1854, he became bank cashier in St. Paul, Minn., and in 1862 joined Capt. James L. Fiske's Northern Overland Expedition bound for the gold fields. At a distant outpost, Bannack, Mont., Langford was prominent in organizing a vigilante committee to enforce law and order. He held various public offices in Montana until after his return to St. Paul in 1876, among them that of Collector of Internal Revenue. In 1868 he was appointed governor by President Johnson, but was not confirmed by the Senate.

Langford's first book was an account of his vigilante days. As a member of the Montana and Minnesota Historical Societies he made many contributions to their publications. He accompanied the earliest organized party to explore the Yellowstone Park district, and through his articles and lectures was influential in its being made a national park in 1872, he himself serving for five years as its first superintendent, without compensation.

Principal Works: Vigilante Days and Ways (2 vols.) 1890; Diary of the Washburn Expedition to the Yellowstone and Fire Hole Rivers in the Year 1870, 1905.

About: Dimsdale, T. J. Vigilantes of Montana; Langford, N. P. The Discovery of Yellowstone Park 1870; Minnesota Historical Society Collections: Vol. 15.

"LANGSTAFF, TRISTRAM." See LORD, WILLIAM WILBERFORCE.

LANIER, SIDNEY (February 3, 1842-September 7, 1881), poet, was born in Macon, Ga., of Huguenot French descent on the paternal side, Scotch on the maternal. His father was a lawyer, Robert Sampson Lanier, descendant of a long line of musicians, his mother Mary Jane (Anderson) Lanier. The family was strictly and rigidly Presbyterian, but the poet's home was a cultered one, full of books and pictures, and he could not remember when he could not read or when he could not play a musical instrument. He was educated at the Bibb County Academy and entered Oglethorpe University in 1857 as a sophomore. The great influence on him there was Prof. James Woodrow, who taught science and who was later one of the earliest martyrs to be expelled from American colleges for the teaching of evolution. Lanier's college career was interrupted by a year as a post office clerk at Macon, but he was graduated in 1860, and for a year tutored in English at Oglethorpe.

At the beginning of the Civil War he enlisted in the Confederate Army, was in the seven days' fighting around Richmond, and later, with his younger brother, was a signal officer on a blockade runner. In 1864 his

Collection of Frederick H. Meserve
SIDNEY LANIER

ship was captured, and he spent four months in Point Lookout Prison, in Maryland. Discipline was not too severe; he played his flute and he wrote poetry, but physically he underwent such hardship that in this prison were planted the seeds of tuberculosis (fatal to both sides of his family) which finally killed him at thirty-nine. His only novel, *Tiger-Lilies,* written in three weeks, was based on his prison experiences, and is an impassioned outcry against war.

Discharged and paroled, Lanier returned to Macon, ill, poor, and desperate, just in time to see his mother die of tuberculosis. From 1865 to 1867 he was a hotel clerk in Montgomery, Ala.; then, after various attempts at teaching, for the most part as principal of the Prattville, Ala., Academy, he entered his father's office to read law and act as his father's law clerk. Though he never seems to have been admitted to the bar, for years he practiced law in the lower courts of Georgia. In 1867 he married Mary Day, a notably happy union, in spite of poverty, ill health, the burden of rearing four small sons, and a profound religious difference between husband and wife—Mrs. Lanier remaining an orthodox Presbyterian, while her husband had gradually become a sort of mystical pantheist in religion, as he became a left-wing agrarian liberal in economics and politics. All his life Lanier was romantically in love with his wife, and poured out poems to her which are tragic in their conflict between his longing to give her everything and his inability to give her anything but hard work, worry, and despair.

For by this time his fatal disease had fastened itself firmly upon him; he had his first hemorrhage during their honeymoon. Moreover, though poetry and music were the twin springs of his being, neither of them could earn a living for him and his household. He spent his strength in books for children and other hack writing, and he was obliged to travel constantly all over the South and as far north as Pennsylvania, trying to find a climate where he could be well enough to work. Texas was found unsuitable; so was Florida, where he earned his way by writing one of the earliest "booster" books. Baltimore, though its climate was bad for him, offered the best economic opportunity; he became first flautist in the new Peabody Orchestra, on an uncertain tenure, at $60 a month. His published career as a poet began in *Lippincott's Magazine* in 1875, with the beautiful "Corn." This won for him the assignment to write the words for the official cantata of the Centennial Exposition in Philadelphia in 1876; but the critics, forgetting that he was writing words to be sung, covered him with ridicule, and his subsequent lectures, in which he expounded his theory of the identity of poetic and musical rules, only added to the opprobrium. His long, irregular, rhythmic lines shared with Whitman's not only their general form but also the universal scorn with which they were attacked by more conventional writers.

Meanwhile Lanier was becoming deeply interested in Elizabethan versification, on which he was writing and also lecturing privately. In 1879, on his birthday, his reward for years of study and struggle came with an appointment as lecturer on English literature at Johns Hopkins—the first assured income he had had since his marriage. But by this time the poet was a dying man. Somehow he managed to give two courses, on verse and the novel, which later appeared as books edited by his wife; and during this period of constant pain and weakness he was most prolific as a poet—not so much in prophecy of the short time before him as in conscious knowledge that he had few days left in which to speak or sing.

At last he was forced to give up and find a place in which to die. He went to the mountains of North Carolina, and there, at Lyon, he died. He was buried in Greenmount Cemetery, in Baltimore; over his grave is a boulder from Georgia, on which are inscribed words from his fine poem, "Sunrise"—one of the uncompleted series of marsh poems—"I am lit with the sun."

Sidney Lanier was truly "lit with the sun"—intoxicated with nature: too much so, in fact, for he was "blinded by excess of light." His nature worship occasionally extended to bathos, to a self-identification unjustified by its expression. There lingered with him also the glaring fault of all the earlier Southern poets except Poe—a fondness for extravagant conceits and fantastic straining for effect. Nevertheless, he remains one of the few major poets produced in America, and he came near to greatness. The critics who (reversing the storm of denunciation which met and saddened him in life) link him with Poe and Whitman go too far, though there are grounds for the bond with Poe in his melody and with Whitman in his freedom from conventional meter. As a matter of fact, he disliked Whitman's "barbaric yawp" and had no cult for Poe. Intellectually he was the equal of either, and in some ways their superior; he never lost Woodrow's early teachings, and a passion for exactness mingled with his enthusiasm for beauty and his ardent altruism. Lanier's poems, in spite of external appearances, are no "native wood notes wild"; his muse is carefully trained and taught to sing along theoretical lines laid down for her by her master. Indeed, Lanier's defects are the result of his very theories, which he carried too far in practice.

It is doubtful whether a longer life would have altered Lanier's poetic output in any way except to add to it. Though the *Spectator* might lament that he died "in the bud of his genius," he outlived the life-span of Keats and Shelley, and was as complete in his smaller way as they in their greater. He should be taken for what he was, not for what he might have been. And what he was primarily was a musician, some of whose music came out in words. His fine face, with its aquiline features and luminous eyes, is a musician's face; the baby who played a reed flute almost before he could walk became a man who thought and spoke in terms of rhythmic song. It is not in more orthodox verses like "My Springs" or even the rather too celebrated "Song of the Cattahoochie" that the real Lanier may be seen, but in those supreme achievements, "Sunrise" and, above all, the incomparable "Marshes of Glynn."

Principal Works: Tiger-Lilies, 1867; Florida: Its Scenery, Climate, and History, 1875; Poems, 1877; Some Highways and Byways of American Travel, 1878; The Boy's Froissart, 1879; The Boy's King Arthur, 1880; The Science of English Verse, 1880; The Boy's Mabinogion, 1881; The

Boy's Percy, 1882; The English Novel and the Principle of Its Development, 1883; Poems, 1884; Music and Poetry, 1898; Letters, 1899; Retrospects and Prospects, 1899; Shakespeare and His Forerunners, 1902; Bob: The Story of Our Mocking Bird, 1910.

ABOUT: Boykin, L. N. A Study of Sidney Lanier; Higginson, T. W. Contemporaries; Lanier, S. Poems (see Memoir by W. H. Ward in 1884 ed.); Lorenz, L. The Life of Sidney Lanier; Mims, E. Sidney Lanier; Starke, A. H. Sidney Lanier; Century Magazine April 1884; Independent June 12, 1884, June 21 and 28, 1894; Lippincott's Magazine March 1905; Nation November 17, 1881; South Atlantic Quarterly April 1905.

LANMAN, CHARLES (June 14, 1819-March 4, 1895), explorer and artist, was born in Monroe, Mich., the son of Charles James Lanman, a lawyer of English descent from Norwich, Conn., and of Marie Jeanne (Guie) Lanman, of French-Indian blood. After ten years in a New York East India mercantile house, and a few years in an editorial capacity with the Monroe (Mich.) *Gazette,* the Cincinnati *Chronicle,* and the New York *Express,* he went to Washington, D.C., in 1849. There he filled many public offices, including that of head of the Interior Department returns office, assistant assessor, and librarian to the War and the Interior departments, the House of Representatives, and the city library. He was also private secretary to Daniel Webster, and for eleven years secretary of the Japanese legation.

From his earlier years Lanman was an enthusiast in vacation exploration in the United States and Canada, frequently using a canoe. His resulting writings were published in a number of periodicals and later in books, of which he issued thirty-two. As an artist, elected an associate of the National Academy of Design in 1846, he also painted more than a thousand landscapes. His sketches led Washington Irving to refer to him as "the picturesque explorer of our country." For a number of years he received a royalty of a dollar a copy from the government for his *Dictionary of the United States Congress,* but was later deprived of it.

PRINCIPAL WORKS: Essays for Summer Hours, 1842; Letters From a Landscape Painter, 1845; A Summer in the Wilderness, 1847; A Tour to the River Saguenay, 1848; Letters From the Alleghany Mountains, 1849; How-ho-noo: or, Records of a Tourist, 1850; Private Life of Daniel Webster, 1852; Adventures in the Wilds of America, 1854; Dictionary of the United States Congress, 1859; Life of William Woodbridge, 1867; Red Book of Michigan, 1871; *Editor*—Journal of Alfred Ely, 1862; The Japanese in America, 1872.

ABOUT: American Ancestry: Vol. 3; Living Age January 18, 1851.

LARCOM, LUCY (March 5, 1824-April 17, 1893), poet, story writer, and essayist, was born in Beverly (then Beverly Farms), Mass., one of the nine children of Benjamin Larcom, a retired sea captain, and Lois (Barrett) Larcom. She was a precocious child, who could read when she was two, and who wrote and illustrated a volume of juvenile poems at seven. Her father died in 1835 and the mother moved to Lowell, where she opened a boarding house for mill operatives. This was the famous period when the mill girls were daughters of good New England families, full of idealism and literary ambition, considering themselves harbingers of a new day on their munificent wages of three dollars a week. Lucy became a doffer, then a spinner, then bookkeeper in the cloth room. One of her sisters edited the celebrated little magazine, the *Operative's Offering* (which, in 1842, became, with the *Lowell Offering,* the *Lowell Offering and Magazine*); and the girl contributed to it frequently. Through her writing she became acquainted with John G. Whittier, who remained her constant friend and occasionally was her collaborator.

In 1846, with a married sister, she went to Illinois, then frontier country, and for three years taught in pioneer rural schools, where she had to take oath that she was sufficiently familiar with the "three R's" to teach them, her reward being $40 every three months. In 1849 she went to Monticello Seminary, near Alton, Ill., where until 1852 she completed her education and also acted as teacher. She was homesick for

Collection of Frederick H. Meserve
LUCY LARCOM

New England, and returned to Massachusetts, where from 1854 to 1862 she taught English at Wheaton Seminary (now Wheaton College) at Norton. A strong abolitionist, she won the essay prize of the New England Emigrant Aid Company in 1855. Meanwhile her poems were attracting wide attention, though it was not until 1884 that the most popular of them were collected into a definitive edition. From 1865 to 1873 she was on the staff of *Our Young Folks* (predecessor of *St. Nicholas*), and besides her original writing she edited a number of anthologies, some for children, on religion and nature; some of these she did alone, others with Whittier. She finally retired because of ill health, but almost until her death she continued to lecture occasionally on literature at various Massachusetts schools. For a while she lived in Connecticut and in Wisconsin, but she always returned to her old home, and finally died in Boston.

A motherly-looking, absent-minded, talkative, rather self-centered body, Lucy Larcom became the center of a cult which elevated her beyond her deserts. As she grew older she became increasingly mystical; already she had exchanged her early Congregationalist faith for Episcopalianism, and in the end religion was her main topic. Her verse is homely and simple, commonplace in rhyme and meter, but full of honest details of the New England environment she knew so well. Probably the poem which has lingered longest in anthologies is "Hannah Binding Shoes," which is a good example of her moralistic verse. On the whole she may be described as a lesser Whittier, and since Whittier himself has fallen (undeservedly) into desuetude, Lucy Larcom has been almost completely forgotten. Perhaps the best writing she did was the least didactic—her pleasant and historically valuable autobiography, *A New England Girlhood*.

Principal Works: Similitudes From Ocean and Prairie, 1854; Ships in the Mist, 1859; The Sunbeam and Other Stories, 1860; Leila Among the Mountains, 1861; Poems, 1869; Childhood Songs, 1873; Collected Poems, 1884; Easter Gleams, 1890; As It Is in Heaven, 1891; The Unseen Friend, 1892; At the Beautiful Gate and Other Songs of Faith, 1892.

About: Addison, D. D. Lucy Larcom: Life, Letters, and Diary; Larcom, L. A New England Girlhood; New York Tribune April 19, 1893.

LATHROP, GEORGE PARSONS (August 25, 1851-April 19, 1898), editor, playwright, and poet, was born near Honolulu, Oahu, Hawaiian Islands, the son of Dr. George Alfred and Frances Maria (Smith) Lathrop. He attended private school in New York and while studying in Dresden, Germany, from 1867 to 1870, he met Nathaniel Hawthorne's daughter Rose, whom he married in London in 1871 after a return visit to New York and a brief plunge into law at Columbia.

During William Dean Howells' editorship of the *Atlantic Monthly* Lathrop became associate editor (1875), leaving in 1877 to edit the Boston Sunday *Courier* for two years. Lathrop and his wife went abroad in 1881, following the death of their only child Francis Hawthorne Lathrop. For *Harper's Monthly* he wrote *Spanish Vistas*, a series of travel essays which appeared later in book form. During the 'eighties he served as literary editor of the New York *Star*; and in 1887 his dramatization (in collaboration with Henry Edwards) of Tennyson's poem "Elaine," was produced at the Madison Square Theatre in New York, and afterwards in Boston and Chicago.

From 1883 when he organized the American Copyright League until the passage, seven years later, of the international copyright law, substantially his original draft, Lathrop had conducted a resolute campaign. In 1891 he and his wife were converted to Roman Catholicism, and soon afterwards he lent his support to the founding of the Catholic Summer School of America, at New London, Conn., and the institution of the so-called Apostolate of the Press. Some time after Lathrop's death his widow became a nun, Mother Alphonsa, and organized the Servants of Relief for Incurable Cancer Patients, functioning in New York City.

Besides *Spanish Vistas* Lathrop's most important books were *Rose and Roof-tree*, a collection of poems, and *A Study of Hawthorne*. Moreover, he edited *A Masque of Poets* and the Riverside edition (1883) of Hawthorne's works, supplying introductory notes and a biographical sketch of the novelist. He adapted Hawthorne's tale for Walter Damrosch's opera, *The Scarlet Letter*, produced successfully in 1896.

Lathrop traversed a considerable field of letters, pursuing nothing very exhaustively. Yet his editings and miscellaneous writings have retained a portion of their value.

Principal Works: Rose and Roof-tree, 1875; A Study of Hawthorne, 1876; Spanish Vistas, 1883; A Masque of Poets (ed.) 1883; Riverside Edition of Hawthorne's Works (ed.) 1883; A Story of Courage (collaboration with Rose Hawthorne Lathrop) 1894.

About: Catholic Reading Circle Review April-September, 1898; Theatre December 12, 1887; New York Tribune April 29, May 1, 1887, April 20, 1898.

LATHROP, JOHN (January 13, 1772-January 30, 1820), lawyer and poet, an uncle of the historian John Lothrop Motley, was born in Boston, Mass. His father, the Rev. John Lathrop, descended from John Lothropp, the first minister of Scituate, was minister of the Second Church of Boston. His mother was Mary (Wheatley) Lathrop. He delivered a poem at the commencement exercises on his graduation from Harvard in 1792, and attained a reputation as a poet during his subsequent law practice in Dedham and Boston. For ten years from 1799 he conducted a school in Calcutta, India, and contributed to local papers, and on his return he was active in Boston, Washington, and Georgetown, D.C. where he taught school, lectured and wrote, finally obtaining a postoffice position. He was married three times, and died in Georgetown.

Lathrop's writing was never collected, and his poem *The Speech of Canonicus: An Indian Tradition,* published in Calcutta and Boston, remains his best known work. His hope to establish a journal on his return from India was not realized. He edited a periodical, the *Nightingale,* in 1796, and published in the Boston *Polyanthos* in 1812-1814 a series of papers on "The Moral Censor" and lectures on natural philosophy delivered previously in Calcutta and Boston.

Principal Works: An Oration Pronounced July 4, 1796, 1796; An Oration Pronounced on the 4th Day of July, 1798, 1798; The Speech of Canonicus, 1802; The Gentleman's Pocket Register and Free-Mason's Anthology for 1813, 1813.

About: Bridgman, T. The Pilgrims of Boston; Knapp, S. L. Sketches of Eminent Lawyers, Statesmen, and Men of Letters.

LATIMER, MARY ELIZABETH (WORMELEY) (July 26, 1822-January 4, 1904), traveler, translator, and writer of popular histories, was born in London, England, the daughter of Rear Admiral Ralph Randolph Wormeley of the British navy, who had been taken to England in his childhood and had become a British citizen, and Carolina (Preble) Wormeley, the daughter of a Boston East-India merchant. During her childhood her family lived in London, Paris, Boston, Newport, and Virginia, and her education was desultory, conducted largely by tutors. But it was far from monotonous: she attended the funeral of William IV, saw Queen Victoria in coronation regalia, and witnessed the funeral of Napoleon. She made the acquaintance in Paris of a young man named William Makepeace Thackeray and was herself introduced to society at Louis Philippe's balls.

Spending the winter of 1842 in Boston, she met George Ticknor, William H. Prescott, and Julia Ward Howe, all of whom urged her to try her hand at writing. The first of her sallies was a translation of a Mexican poem for the appendix of Prescott's *History of the Conquest of Mexico.* Four years after the appearance of her first novel, *Amabel* (1852) she published *Our Cousin Veronica*; and that same year she was married to Randolph Latimer of Baltimore. After twenty years' devotion to her domestic duties, during which time she gave much of her energy to the care of soldiers injured in the Civil War, she resumed writing with much spirit, and between 1880 and 1903 produced a large amount of work.

Far superior to her rather nondescript stories were her numerous popular histories: nineteenth century chronicles of several countries, *My Scrap Book of the French Revolution, Judea From Cyrus to Titus...,* and *The Last Years of the Nineteenth Century.* There is evidence, in their making, of much serious study, an adequate understanding of world affairs, and a brisk literary style that incorporated a mass of anecdotes without burdening the text. Her history of nineteenth century Germany remained unfinished. She published several translations from French and Italian. Although her writings had little to do with the American scene, she must be credited with having left an able record of impressions gathered from a variegated life.

Principal Works: France in the Nineteenth Century, 1892; Russia and Turkey. . , 1893; England . . . , 1894; Italy in the Nineteenth Century and the Making of Austro-Hungary and Germany, 1896; My Scrap Book of the French Revolution, 1898; Judea From Cyrus to Titus; 537 B.C.-70 A.D., 1899; The Last Years of the Nineteenth Century, 1900. *Translations*—A History of the People of Israel (in collaboration with J. H. Allen) 1888-96; The Steel Hammer, 1888; For Fifteen Years, 1888; Nanon, 1890; The Italian Republics, 1901; The Love Letters of Victor Hugo: 1820-22, 1901; Talks of Napoleon at St. Helena. . ,1903.

About: The Dial February 1, 1904; The Sun (Baltimore) January 4, 5, 1904.

LAWRENCE, WILLIAM BEACH (October 23, 1800-March 26, 1881), jurist, public official, and political economist, was born in a wealthy and influential family in New York City, his father, Isaac Lawrence, being of early English-American descent. His mother, Cornelia (Beach) Lawrence, was the daughter of a rector of Trinity Church. He was graduated from Columbia College in 1818, studied law in Litchfield, Conn., and in Paris, and engaged in practice for twenty-three years in New York City. From 1850 he lived in Newport, R.I., where he became lieutenant- and acting-governor. Among his many services were those of secretary and chargé d' affaires at the London legation, and member of a commission to compile a code of international law.

Lawrence early developed an outstanding interest in international law and his various writings on the subject were of the highest intellectual order. His second annotated edition of his friend Henry Wheaton's *Elements of International Law* was followed by a successful lawsuit brought by him against Richard Henry Dana, Jr. who issued a similar work at the same time, Lawrence holding that many of the notes in the Dana edition infringed his rights.

PRINCIPAL WORKS: Two Lectures on Political Economy, 1831; The Origin and Nature of the Representative and Federative Institutions of the United States, 1832; A History of the Negotiations in Reference to the Eastern and Northeastern Boundaries of the United States, 1841; Visitation and Search, 1858; Disabilities of American Women Married Abroad, 1866; Commentaire sur les Eléments du Droit International (4 vols.) 1868-1880; The Treaty of Washington, 1871; Letters From Hon. William Beach Lawrence, 1871; Belligerent and Sovereign Rights as Regards Neutrals During the War of Secession, 1873.

ABOUT: Hart, C. A. A Discourse Commemorative of the Life and Services of the Late William Beach Lawrence; Columbia University Quarterly September 1935; New York Genealogical and Biographical Record April, July 1895.

LAWSON, JAMES (November 9, 1799-March 24, 1880), editor, insurance expert, and miscellaneous writer, born in Edinburgh, Scotland, and educated at its university, was the eldest son of James Lawson, a merchant. At sixteen he came to New York, becoming successively accountant and partner in the firm of his uncle, Alexander Thomson. Its failure in 1826 turned him to editorial work in connection with the *Morning Courier,* and the *Mercantile Advertiser.* After 1833 he became widely known in marine insurance. His last years were spent in retirement in Yonkers, N.Y.

Lawson's first literary project was the selection, at the age of twenty-two, of American authors for representation in the English *Literary Coronal,* edited by John Mennon. His occasional verse and articles appeared in many magazines. He was a friend of the actor Edwin Forrest, whom he helped professionally with his criticism, and of Edgar Allan Poe, William Gilmore Simms, and other men of letters. He served on a committee which brought the prize play *Metamora* to Forrest in 1829, and on another which selected James K. Paulding's play *The Lion of the West* for James Henry Hackett in 1831. His own drama *Giordano* was a failure, however, at the Park Theatre in 1828. To his first book, *Ontwa,* a poetical narrative based on the Erie Indians, he brought spirit and eloquence. His *Tales and Sketches* have, however, been referred to as sentimental, stilted, and formal. His books were all published anonymously.

PRINCIPAL WORKS: *Drama*—Giordano, 1832; Liddesdale: or, The Border Chief, 1874; The Maiden's Oath, 1877. *Poetry*—Ontwa: The Son of the Forest, 1822; Poems: Gleanings From Spare Hours of a Business Life, 1857. *Stories*—Tales and Sketches, by a Cosmopolite, 1830.

ABOUT: MacBean, W. M. Biographical Register of St. Andrews Society of the State of New York; Wilson, J. G. The Poets and Poetry of Scotland.

LAWSON, JOHN (d. 1711), Carolinian explorer and social historian, is believed to have been of Yorkshire descent, but of his parentage and early years nothing is known. In 1700, having been amply advised of the attractiveness of "Carolina," he set sail for America. He spent a fortnight in New York, impressed by the enterprising Dutch, the harbors, and the sturdy fortifications; then, putting out from Sandy Hook, he arrived two weeks later in Charleston, S.C., a "thriving colony . . . of more advantage to the crown of Great Britain than any of the other more northerly plantations (Virginia and Maryland excepted)." In the company of four Indians, who were shortly dismissed, and six Englishmen he set out in December for the colony farther north. He plunged through Carolina wilderness, following Indian trails and, as far as Hillsboro, N.C., the famous Georgia-to-Virginia Trading Path. Here Lawson spent several years, and in 1705 aided in securing the incorporation of the town of Bath.

Lawson's only book, *A New Voyage to Carolina: Containing the Exact Description and Natural History of That Country . . .* (1709), appeared first as the second volume of John Steven's *New Collection of Voyages and Travels*; was twice republished under the title of *History of Carolina . . .*; and went into two editions in Germany. It was a candid account of one variety of frontier life, and included not only excellent observations on Indian culture but a brief dictionary of the commonest Indian tongues. Lawson himself returned to England to witness its publication.

Before setting sail again he was recommended, in a petition drawn up by the North Carolina Assembly and directed to the lords proprietors, who were quite aware of his activities, for the office of surveyor-general of North Carolina. With Christopher de Graffenried, a Swiss adventurer, whom he had met in London, he supervised the migration of 600-odd Palatines to found the city of New Bern, N.C. The new settlement provoked suspicion and fear among the Indians, and in September these two colonizers were seized by the Tuscaroras. De Graffenried won his release, but Lawson was put to death.

In the preface to his *History* Lawson lamented the fact that most British travelers who came to America were of mean intelligence and "slender education." His own account, therefore, was projected in the hope of attracting to the colonies superior Englishmen—who might compete more favorably with the French in cultural and material values. Moreover Lawson firmly believed that the marriage of Christians of "mean blood" with the Indians was a "more reasonable way of converting the Indians than to set up our Christian banner in a field of blood." His book was not only a pleasing and authoritative narrative but a very real chapter in early American social history.

ABOUT: Lawson, J. History of Carolina. . . ; Annual Report of the American Historical Association: 1895.

"LAY PREACHER, THE." See DENNIE, JOSEPH

LAZARUS, EMMA (July 22, 1849-November 19, 1887), poet, was born in New York City, of pure Sephardic (Spanish Jewish) stock. Her father was Moses Lazarus, her mother Esther (Nathan) Lazarus. The family was wealthy and cultured, and the girl was educated entirely at home by private tutors. Probably in consequence of this, she was painfully shy; books were her world, and she would always rather write than talk. Her winters were spent in New York, her summers at the seashore, but no matter where she was, she was alone except for her family, to which she was devoted. So attached was she to her father in particular that she never seems to have had any interest in any other man.

Steeped in the classics and the study of languages, she was a prolific writer of verse in her early teens, and her first volume, privately printed the year before its publication in 1867, consisted of poems written between fourteen and sixteen. The chief characteristic of these poems is melancholy—a melancholy deeper than the romantic grief of all young writers. It is not necessary to look into her racial origins to account for this; her life was sufficiently circumscribed and lonely to make her feel unconsciously a prisoner. Emerson opened the prison

EMMA LAZARUS

doors; her work interested him, he invited her to spend a week in Concord, and she dedicated her second book to him. Later, in England, friendship with Browning supplemented this early but lifelong influence.

Up to 1882 there was no Jewish strain in Miss Lazarus' work. She was wholly a child of her century and her native land. The persecution of the Jews by Czarist Russia changed her entire outlook. An article in the *Century Magazine* defending the Russian pogroms roused her not only to hot indignation but to a new study of Judaic history. Thenceforth, nearly all her work was devoted to her new cause. She had long ago lost her orthodox faith, but she became now the voice of protest and encouragement for the Jews as a people. She did more than write; she organized relief for the Russian Jewish refugees, and formulated an educational program for them.

Otherwise her life was almost without events. In 1883 she went to Europe, where she was acclaimed as a poet by other poets; her mother died, then her adored father, and in 1885 she returned to Europe to bury her grief. Her increasing ill health she ignored, even when it was apparent that she was suffering from cancer. Finally she became too ill to go on, and she was brought back to New York barely in time to die, at only thirty-eight.

Emma Lazarus is a noble poet, impassioned and yet exquisite, and it is strange that she is now so little read. Her best work is her verse drama of the 12th Century Thuringian Jews, "The Dance to

Death." But all her writing is interesting, and much of it far more than that. Her translations of Heine have rarely been bettered, and she was a competent translator also of numerous mediaeval Jewish authors. An ardent patriot, she wrote the sonnet which is carved on the base of the Statue of Liberty, the verse in which America was first called "Mother of Exiles," in the old days of free immigration. Modest and diffident to excess, she had courage for any effort when she had found her cause. Her thin, ascetic face, with its brooding eyes, illustrates well the remark of an editorial writer in the *Century* that "the story of her life is the story of a mind."

Principal Works: Poems and Translations, 1867; Admetus and Other Poems, 1871; Alide: An Episode in Goethe's Life, 1874; The Spagnoletto: A Drama in Verse, 1876; Poems and Ballads of Heinrich Heine, 1881; Songs of a Semite (including "The Dance to Death") 1882; By the Waters of Babylon, 1887; Poems, 1889.

About: Stedman, E. C. Genius and Other Essays; American Hebrew November 25 and December 9, 1887, July 5, 1929; Century October 1888; Critic December 10, 1887; Forum March 1912; Poet-Lore June-July 1893; Reform Advocate September 24, 1927.

LEA, HENRY CHARLES (September 19, 1825-October 24, 1909), historian and publisher, was born, lived all his life, and died in Philadelphia. He had a curious ancestry—his father, Isaac Lea [*q.v.*], was an English Quaker, his mother, Frances Anne (Carey) Lea, of Irish Catholic descent. He himself was a lifelong Unitarian.

The older Lea was widely known as a conchologist, the mother was an amateur botanist. Another son, Matthew Carey Lea, became a celebrated chemist. The father was also a publisher, a partner in his father-in-law's firm.

The precocious boy learned Greek at six, and at seven was in school in Paris. His early interests were divided between the classics and science; from the age of sixteen he published articles in scientific journals. In 1843 he entered his father's business, giving his evenings to study and writing, and appearing in many magazines on an unusual variety of topics from fossil shells to Tennyson. Under this overwork his already frail health broke, and in 1847 he had to take a leave of absence for rest and travel. In 1850 he married his first cousin, Anna Caroline Jaudon, by whom he had three sons (two of whom followed him in the publishing business) and a daughter. Two years later his brother married his wife's sister.

From a portrait by R. W. Vonnoh
HENRY CHARLES LEA

The reading of Froissart in 1849 first interested him in history—in the beginning, in the history of jurisprudence, then for the rest of his life in church history. His first historical article was published in the *North American Review* in 1859. Lea approached history from the standpoint of a scientist; he is the most objective of writers—a virtue which became a major error in the eyes of some critics, notably the German Baumgartner. He was an indefatigable worker, whose method was (since he could not leave his business to do his own research) to keep copyists at work in every large European library. Before he wrote a book he prepared an intensive index, and an immense volume of notes and quotations, and he rewrote constantly in his effort to obtain absolute accuracy. He learned German at sixty and Dutch at eighty to supplement his other languages and to prepare himself better for his work.

Meanwhile, he was not only conducting the publishing house, as sole owner after 1865, but he was also extremely active in civic affairs. After the Civil War he was bounty commissioner; he was a prominent Republican and a founder of the Union League Club. But in 1870 the revelations of some of Philadelphia's notorious municipal graft turned him into a reformer; he organized the Municipal Reform Association and served as its president, and he resigned from the Union League Club when it would not follow him in his advocacy of Civil Service reform. He was also the author of the Chace Copyright Act, in 1891. In 1880 he had retired from active participation in business, though he remained a nominal partner till his sons took over in 1885. Once more he broke down from overwork. Dr. S. Weir Mitchell formulated a schedule for his daily living, and by its aid he remained alive and useful to eighty-four. At his death he was working on a history of witchcraft, which was almost completed and may some day be published. Only four days before he died of pneumonia he was at work in his library. This library he willed to the University of Pennsylvania, where it is set up, room, furniture, and books, as a memorial to him. Among his many other benefactions to the university was a hygiene building, and he was most generous also to Jefferson Medical College and other educational institutions.

Though Lea received honorary degrees from the University of Pennsylvania, Princeton, and Harvard, and was long president of the American Historical Association, he was really better known abroad than at home. The Universities of Giessen and Moscow honored him, Bryce asked his help with *The American Commonwealth,* Acton with the *Cambridge Modern History.* Acton, a Roman Catholic, praised his fairness; and indeed it is impossible to tell his own religious views from his scrupulous and unbiased accounts, as accurate as they are comprehensive. With all his honors, he remained a modest, retiring, kindly, humorous little man, frail of body and fine-featured, his thin face framed in snowy hair and beard. Few men have been more loved and honored by all who knew them, few have left behind them a greater or more solid volume of achievement.

PRINCIPAL WORKS: Superstition and Force, 1866; An Historical Sketch of Sacerdotal Celibacy, 1867; Studies in Church History, 1869; Translations and Other Rhymes, 1882; A History of the Inquisition in the Middle Ages, 1888; Chapters from the Religious History of Spain Connected With the Inquisition, 1890; A History of Auricular Confession and Indulgences, 1896; The Moriscos of Spain: Their Conversion and Expulsion, 1901; A History of the Inquisition of Spain, 1906-7; The Inquisition in the Spanish Dependencies, 1908.

ABOUT: Baumgarten, P. M. Henry Charles Lea's Historical Writings; Bradley, E. S. Henry Charles Lea; Lea, A. H. Henry Charles Lea (privately printed); American Historical Review January 1910; Proceedings American Philosophical Society January-April 1911; Proceedings Massachusetts Historical Society December 1909.

LEA, ISAAC (March 4, 1792-December 8, 1886), zoologist and publisher, the son of James and Elizabeth (Gibson) Lea, of Quaker lineage, was born in Wilmington, Del., where his great-great-grandfather, John Lea, had settled in 1699. He was fifteen when his family moved to Philadelphia, and here he joined his brother in the wholesale and importing business. His friendship with Lardner Vanuxem began about this time; together they started a collection of rock and mineral specimens and became early members (1815) of the Academy of Natural Sciences of Philadelphia. Lea forfeited his birthright in the Society of Friends when he joined a volunteer rifle company in 1814, but he saw no active service. In 1821 he was married to Frances Anné Carey, daughter of Mathew Carey, ranking publisher of his day, and for thirty years Lea was a member of the firm of M. Carey & Sons and its various successors.

"An Account of the Minerals at Present Known to Exist in the Vicinity of Philadelphia," appearing in December 1818, was the first of 270-odd technical articles which he contributed, over a period of fifty-eight years, to scientific journals. He was especially interested in the study of fresh-water mollusks and became, in that field, an acknowledged authority. Within his range of subjects were, also: the Northwest Passage, halos with parhelia, fossils, and land and marine Mollusca. The *Proceedings* or *Transactions* of the American Philosophical Society published a large share of his writings and his papers on mollusks were republished intermittently in *Observations on the Genus Unio,* which he issued in thirteen quarto volumes, 1827-74. These contained lithograph illustrations and covered, in all, over 1800 species. When Lea was 84 he prepared his *Catalogue of the Published Works of Isaac Lea, LL.D. . . .* (1876).

Because he was an authority on Mollusca, collectors from all parts of the world sent him specimens for classification, and he thereby not only acquired many new species but enlarged his established series, the whole of which was bequeathed to the United States National Museum. Learned societies here and abroad honored Lea; he was president of the American Association for the Advancement of Science (1860) and of the Academy of Natural Sciences of Philadelphia (1858-63). He is said to have been admittedly self-confident and he did not look kindly upon the activities of his professional competitors. But his publications, written in a style that was direct and unencumbered, were comprehensive and authoritative and represent a considerable achievement in a then youthful science.

Principal Works: Observations on the Genus Unio, 1827-74; Catalogue of the Published Works of Isaac Lea, LL.D. From 1817 to 1876, 1876.

About: Lea, I. Catalogue of the Published Works of Isaac Lea. . . ; Science December 17, 1886; Press (Philadelphia) December 9, 1886.

LEDYARD, JOHN (1751-January 10, 1789), explorer, was born in Groton, Conn., the son of John and Abigail (Hempstead) Ledyard. He attended grammar school in Hartford and then studied law for a while before entering Dartmouth in 1772, at the invitation of its founder, Rev. Eleazar Wheelock. Disliking college discipline and losing interest in his earlier intention of becoming a missionary to the Indians, he took "French leave" before the end of his freshman year, and paddled down the Connecticut to Hartford in a canoe of his own making. He shipped as a sailor for the Mediterranean, returning to New London after he had deserted, and then shipped for London, where, as corporal of marines, he joined Captain James Cook's expedition in search of a Northwest passage between Asia and America. In the 600-ton "Revolution" and the 300-ton "Discovery" they made a voyage lasting over four years and three months, touching the Cape of Good Hope, Tasmania, New Zealand, the Tonga and Society Islands, "rediscovering" the Hawaiian or Sandwich Islands, and proceeding through the Bering Straits to Icy Cape. They sailed back to Hawaii and here Cook was killed in an altercation with the natives, almost two years before their final return to England in October 1780.

Nearly everyone on board had kept his own journal and both ships had issued a weekly newspaper—but all of these were surrendered by order of the commander at the end of the voyage. Two years later, Ledyard, who had meanwhile returned to the United States, wrote his *Journal of Captain Cook's Last Voyage to the Pacific Ocean* (1783); except for dates, distances, and courses of the vessels, he relied entirely upon his own memory. Nathaniel Patten, a Hartford publisher, paid him twenty guineas for the manuscript.

In June 1784 Ledyard sailed for Spain, but although he gained sympathetic attention from Thomas Jefferson and Commodore John Paul Jones in France, his expeditionary projects flatly failed. Nevertheless his spirits were still buoyant, and by way of Norway, Sweden, and Lapland, he made his way to St. Petersburg, but at Yakutsk he was arrested by officials and brought back to the Polish boundary. In July 1788 he left London on an exploring expedition into the interior of Africa. But violent rage over a long caravan delay at Cairo resulted in an illness from which Ledyard never recovered.

To some he was merely the "mad, romantic, dreaming Ledyard," but his visions of opening up trade with the Pacific Northwest became actualities soon after his death; and his *Journal* was seasoned with a naturalness, candor, and occasional *éclat* of comedy that were not to be found in the more extensive and official accounts.

About: Sparks, J. Life of John Ledyard; New York Genealogical and Biographical Record January 1876.

"LEE, ALICE G." See HAVEN, EMILY (BRADLEY) NEAL

LEE, ARTHUR (December 21, 1740-December 12, 1792), diplomatist, was born at "Stratford," in Westmoreland County Va., the son of Thomas and Hannah (Lud-well) Lee, and great-grandson of Richar Lee, the first of the famous Lees of Vir-ginia. Young Lee's father died when he wa about ten years old, and under the guardian-ship of his eldest brother he was sent t Eton. He proceeded to the University o Edinburgh, studying science, polite litera-ture, and medicine, and receiving an M.D degree in 1764. Returning to Virginia, h began to practice medicine (1766) in Wil-liamsburg, and then sailed again for London studied at Lincoln's Inn and Middle Temple and in the spring of 1775 was admitted t the bar.

In imitation of the currently issue "Farmer's Letters" Lee had prepared, i 1768, a series of "Monitor's Letters" fo Rind's *Virginia Gazette*. In London, wher political figures were gaping at the implica-tions of the famous "Junius Letters," h found a lively market for his sarcastic pole-mics on American affairs which he wrot over the signature "Junius Americanus"; o these the best perhaps was his *Appeal to th Justice and Interests of the People of Grea Britain* (1774), followed by a *Second Ap-peal* in 1775. American political leader were delighted with these railleries and ap-pointed Lee as agent of Massachusetts i London.

Lee, who was politically ambitious, s audibly championed the cause of Englishme that for a while his hopes ran high for seat in Parliament. In November 1775 h became a confidential London corresponde for the Continental Congress, and with characteristic lack of diplomacy, made n effort to conceal his suspicions of some o the very men who had selected him. Th following October he was appointed to assist in negotiating a treaty with France and in soliciting her aid. Arriving in Paris in December, he almost immediately began to sluice the ears of his friends in Congress with the most violent and largely ill-founded charges against his colleagues Silas Deane and Benjamin Franklin.

The Lee-Deane controversy effected a sharp split in Congress. Deane was recalled in 1777, and in 1779 Lee too was superseded. Franklin alone emerged with an unblemished record.

Back in America in September 1780, Lee served in several political capacities, but enjoyed little more than a thwarting of his own proposals. His published writings are negligible, but he had a hand in some significant correspondence and state papers belonging to a critical period in American history.

ABOUT: Lee, R. H. Life of Arthur Lee; Wharton, F. The Revolutionary Diplomatic Correspondence of the U. S. North American Review April 1830.

LEE, CHARLES (1731-October 2, 1782), soldier of fortune, Revolutionary general, and a "candidate" for the authorship of the famous *Letters of Junius,* was born in Dernhall, Cheshire, England, the son of John and Isabella (Bunbury) Lee. He attended a free grammar school at Bury St. Edmunds and later an academy in Switzerland. That he received a commission in the army at the age of eleven is not too improbable, in a day when "ensigns and cornets were duly enrolled, and drew their quarterly stipends before leaving the nursery." In May 1751, shortly after his father's death, he was commissioned lieutenant of the 44th regiment, which, three years later, was ordered to America and under Thomas Gage formed the advance of Braddock's army at the battle of Monongahela. Lee was adopted into a Mohawk tribe under an alleged Indian name, "Ounewaterika" ("boiling water"), but took for his bride the daughter of White Thunder, a Seneca chief After serving intermittently in the British regiment until late in the year 1760 he returned to England; feasted on military adventure in Spain, Poland, and Turkey; wrote some noisy criticism of the English government; and in 1773 sailed again for America.

With his *Strictures on a Pamphlet Entitled "A Friendly Address to All Reasonable Americans"* (1774), a thrust at Dr. Myles Cooper's conciliatory approaches, Lee fed the blaze of controversy that preceded the Revolution. In June of the year following, five days before renouncing his half-pay in the British army, he obtained an appointment as second major-general of the Continental Army. He was a glory-seeker and a none-too-brilliant strategist, and was himself captured by Colonel Harcourt's British dragoons on December 13, 1776. During a year's imprisonment he wrote "Mr. Lee's Plan, 29th March 1777," supplying the enemy with inside information; but historians have been hesitant in labeling Lee an outright traitor. His inglorious army career came to an end in 1778 when for his unseemly conduct towards Washington in the battle of Monmouth, a court martial found him guilty of disobedience of orders, unnecessary retreat, and gross disrespect for the Commander-in-Chief. Lee lived in Virginia a while, and then removed to Philadelphia, where he died in 1782. He was buried in Christ Church graveyard, despite his own request: "I desire that I may not be buried in any church or church-yard . . . for since I have resided in this country I have kept such bad company when living that I do not wish to continue it when dead."

From a caricature by B. Rashbrooke
CHARLES LEE

The Lee Papers (published in the *Collections of the New York Historical Society*). preserve some of the éclat of his military career. His bitterness towards the British government in the decade preceding the War of Independence, his frequent rhetorical brazenness, similarities in spelling, etc., between some of his political epistles and the *Letters of Junius,* and his own breezy ambiguities led some critics to identify him as Junius. But Lee's absence from England and his noticeable tendency to assume credit for the achievements of others weaken the case considerably. He was, moreover, an extraordinary mixture of acquisitiveness and extreme generosity, of malice and sincere kindness, and he remains one of the most equivocal figures in American history.

PRINCIPAL WORKS: Strictures on a Pamphlet Entitled "A Friendly Address to All Reasonable Americans," 1774; Lee Papers, 1872-75.

ABOUT: Fiske, J. Essays Historical and Literary; Langworthy, E. Memoirs of the Life of the Late Charles Lee; Sparks, J. Lives of Charles Lee and Joseph Reed.

LEE, ELIZA (BUCKMINSTER) (c.1788-June 22, 1864), was born at Portsmouth, N.H., the daughter of the Rev. Joseph Buckminster and Sarah (Stevens) Buckminster, both descendants of the Puritan poet, Anne Bradstreet. The influence of her father and her brother, Joseph Stevens Buckminster, one of the first and most prominent Unitarian ministers of New England, encouraged the development of her own considerable intellectual powers, and her marriage in 1827 to a wealthy Brookline, Mass., resident gave her further opportunity to cultivate them through study and literary pursuits.

She produced many translations from Jean Paul Richter and other German authors, and her translation of Richter's biography brought her considerable success. Her memoir of her father and brother was praised by Carlyle. As late as the 'seventies, fifteen of her volumes were included in a popular series.

PRINCIPAL WORKS: Sketches of a New England Village, 1838; Life of Jean Paul F. Richter (tr.) 1842; Naomi: or, Boston Two Hundred Years Ago, 1848; Memoirs of Rev. Joseph Buckminster, D.D., and of His Son, Rev. Joseph Stevens Buckminster, 1849; Florence: The Parish Orphan, 1852; Parthenia: or, The Last Days of Paganism, 1858.

ABOUT: Lee, W. John Leigh of Agawan (Ipswich) Mass.; Brownson's Quarterly Review October 1849; North American Review October 1849.

LEE, HANNAH FARNHAM (SAWYER) (1780-December 27, 1865), was born in Newburyport, Mass., the daughter of a physician, Dr. Micajah Sawyer. She became in 1807 the second wife of George Gardner Lee, a naval officer who died nine years later and left her with three daughters.

Her literary work was commenced at the age of fifty-two when she published an appreciation of Hannah Adams, appended to Joseph Tuckerman's *Memoir* of this eighteenth century compiler. Practically all copies of her first story, *Grace Seymour,* were destroyed by fire after being printed, and it was never republished. The panic of 1837 brought particular timeliness to her *Three Experiments of Living,* discussing living within, under, and over one's income, and brought her her greatest success. It went through thirty American and ten English editions, the later editions including some of her other writings. She was a graceful and effective writer, widely read but of ephemeral influence. Her own name was not attached to her writings, many of her books being published as "By the Author of the Three Experiments of Living," which itself was published anonymously, its author not being known for a long time.

PRINCIPAL WORKS: Grace Seymour, 1835; Three Experiments of Living, 1837; Historical Sketches of Old Painters, 1838; Rosanna: or, Scenes in Boston, 1839; The Life and Times of Martin Luther, 1839; The Life and Times of Thomas Cranmer, 1841; The Huguenots in France and America, 1843; The Log Cabin: or, The World Before You, 1844; Sketches and Stories From Life, 1850; Memoir of Pierre Toussaint, 1853; Familiar Sketches of Sculpture and Sculptors, 1854.

ABOUT: Currier, J. J. History of Newburyport, Mass.; Hale, S. J. Woman's Record; New England Historical and Genealogical Register April 1866.

LEE, HENRY (May 28, 1787-January 30, 1837), biographer and historian, the son of the Revolutionary soldier "Light-Horse Harry" Lee, and his first wife, Matilda (Lee) Lee, was born at "Stratford," Westmoreland County, Va. His half-brother was Gen. Robert E. Lee. He was graduated from William and Mary College in 1808, served in the Virginia legislature, became a major in the 39th Infantry, and entered into political writing for the statesman, John C. Calhoun, and for Andrew Jackson during his presidential campaign, helping also to write his inaugural address. Jackson rewarded him by a consular appointment to Algeria, the Senate refusing confirmation after he had reached his post. His remaining seven years were spent abroad, mainly in Paris, where he died.

He was a brilliant conversationalist, with precocious literary talent, but his works were marred by a controversial tone. His first two books were written in defense of his father against unfavorable allusions in the writings of William Johnson and Thomas Jefferson. In his life of Napoleon, whom he greatly admired, he adopted a similarly controversial tone against Walter Scott. The material prepared for an unfinished second volume of Napoleon was after his death incorporated with the first, in a new edition.

PRINCIPAL WORKS: The Campaign of 1781 in the Carolinas, 1824; Observations on the Writings of Thomas Jefferson, 1832; The Life of the Emperor Napoleon, 1835 (republished in 1837 with new material).

ABOUT: Lee, E. J. Lee of Virginia: 1642-1892; Madison, J. Letters and Other Writings; Wise, H. A. Seven Decades of the Union.

"LEE, PATTY." See CARY, ALICE

LEGGETT, WILLIAM (April 30, 1801-May 29, 1839), journalist, descended from a Westchester County settler of English origin in the seventeenth century, was born in New York City, the son of Abraham Leggett, an officer in the Revolution, and his second wife, Catherine (Wylie) Leggett, of New Rochelle. He became a midshipman in the navy at twenty-one, but resigned after more than three years. He had already published his first volume of verses written while at sea. He now began contributing to periodicals and in 1828 established a weekly, the *Critic,* for which he wrote most of the contents for the ten months of its existence.

Leggett was associated as editor with William Cullen Bryant on the New York *Evening Post* for seven years from 1829, and was chief editor during the year of Bryant's visit abroad. His independence was pronounced, and he warred strenuously against political and economic abuses, his radicalism leading to his defeat for Congress and alienating Tammany. Appointed diplomatic agent to Guatemala, he died before sailing. His political writings were published posthumously and a monument in his honor was erected at New Rochelle.

PRINCIPAL WORKS: *Poetry*—Leisure Hours at Sea, 1825; Journals of the Ocean, 1826; *Stories*—Tales and Sketches, by a Country Schoolmaster, 1829; *Political Writings*—A Collection of the Political Writings of William Leggett (2 vols.) 1840.

ABOUT: Leggett, T. A. Early Settlers of West Farms, Westchester County, N.Y.; Wilson, J. G. Byant and His Friends; United States Magazine and Democratic Review July 1839.

LELAND, CHARLES GODFREY (August 15, 1824-March 20, 1903), poet and miscellaneous writer, was born in Philadelphia, the son of Charles Leland, a commission merchant, and Charlotte Frost (Godfrey) Leland, both parents being of New England descent. He was educated at private schools in Jamaica Plains, Mass., and Germantown, Philadelphia (where Bronson Alcott was his teacher), and was graduated from the College of New Jersey (Princeton) in 1845. In 1867 Harvard gave him an honorary M.A., through the influence of Lowell. After leaving college he went to Germany for two years of study at the Universities of Heidelberg and Munich, becoming thoroughly German in his sympathies. He then proceeded to Paris to study at the Sorbonne, but seems to have spent most of his time there in helping man the barricades during the Revolution of 1848.

Returning to Philadelphia, he studied law, was admitted to the bar, and practiced from 1851 to 1853. Already, however, he was more interested in writing, and had had an article on art in the *Union Magazine* in 1849. For the next few years he abandoned the law for journalism, doing editorial work with R. W. Griswold on Barnum's *Illustrated News* (New York) from 1853 to 1855, then for three years on the Philadelphia *Evening Bulletin,* and for three more on *Vanity Fair.* In 1856 he married Eliza Bella Fisher. For a few months between the Philadelphia paper and *Vanity Fair,* he was editor of *Graham's Magazine,* where appeared the first of his famous German-American dialect poems, "Hans Breitmann's Barty."

In 1861 he was editor of the *Knickerbocker Magazine,* and in 1862 founded and edited the *Continental Monthly,* in Boston, the object of which was to aid the Union cause; he claimed to have coined for this magazine the word "emancipation," to take the place of the rather unrespectable "abolition." The next year he enlisted in a Philadelphia artillery company, but saw very little

CHARLES GODFREY LELAND

service. At the end of the war he went west to prospect for coal and oil, and from 1866 to 1869 he edited the Philadelphia *Press*. That was the end of his formal journalistic career; his father died and left him independently wealthy. He went abroad at once and remained there, mostly in London, until 1880. While in England he became much interested in the teaching of industrial arts, and he returned to Philadelphia to inaugurate this course in the public schools, besides writing several textbooks on the subject. In 1884 he returned to London, where in 1889 he was one of the founders of the Folk Lore Congress, his other chief interest at the time being folk lore and obscure languages. A natural linguist, he became as expert in Romany legends and the Romany tongue as George Borrow; he was proudest of his discovery of Shelta, a Welsh and Irish gypsy dialect which he believed to be the lost artificial language of the ancient Irish bards. It earned him the honor of being made an honorary Fellow of the Royal Society of Literature. Toward the end of his life absorption in the mystic and occult obscured all his other enthusiasms. He lived abroad entirely after 1884, mostly in Italy and southern Germany; he died in Florence, but was brought home to be buried in Laurel Hill Cemetery, Philadelphia.

A big, burly, bearded man, with a huge appetite for food and drink, loud-voiced and jovial, Leland was in appearance and manner the very prototype of his "Hans Breitmann." Yet these richly humorous verses, full of wit and parody, which are his real title to fame, he himself discounted apologetically; he far preferred to be known as a philologist, an occultist, or an advocate of "the minor arts." His work was extraordinarily varied in nature, and his versatility impeded its excellence. He was never a real scholar, though he engaged in scholarly pursuits—translated Heine, and contributed many articles to Appletons' and Johnson's encyclopaedias. Fundamentally he was a man with an enormous zest for life and an easy flow of language. He is no longer much read, and even the once celebrated "Hans Breitmann" would awaken few echoes in modern memories; but he has not deserved so much neglect, and some at least of his many volumes would still reward the not too gullible or too critical reader.

Principal Works: Meister Karl's Sketch Book, 1855; The Poetry and Mystery of Dreams, 1855; Sunshine in Thought, 1862; Mother Pitcher's Poems, 1863; Legends of Birds, 1864; The Breitmann Ballads, 1871; The Music Lesson of Confucius and Other Poems, 1872; The English Gypsies and Their Language, 1873; Egyptian Sketch Book, 1873; Pidgin-English Sing-Song, 1876; Life of Abraham Lincoln, 1879; The Minor Arts, 1880; The Gypsies, 1882; Industrial Education, 1883; The Algonquin Legends of New England, 1884; A Dictionary of Slang (with Albert Barrerre) 1889; Gypsy Sorcery and Fortune Telling, 1891; Etruscan-Roman Remains in Popular Tradition, 1892; Memoirs, 1893; Hans Breitmann in Tyrol, 1894; Legends of Florence, 1895-96; Songs of the Sea and Lays of the Land, 1899; The Unpublished Legends of Virgil, 1901; Hans Breitmann's Ballads, 1914.

About: Jackson, J. A Bibliography of the Works of Charles Godfrey Leland; Leland, C. G. Memoirs; Pennell, E. R. Charles Godfrey Leland: A Biography; Pennsylvania Magazine April 1925; Philadelphia Press March 21, 1903.

LEONARD, DANIEL (May 18, 1740-June 27, 1829), Loyalist propagandist, lawyer, and chief justice of Bermuda, was born in Norton, Mass., the son of Ephraim and Judith (Perkins) Leonard. He was descended from emigrant Welshmen who made a fortune in the iron industry, and as a child Daniel enjoyed all the prerogatives of provincial aristocracy. After his graduation from Harvard in 1760, at which he delivered the salutatory address (in Latin), he began the practice of law at Taunton under Samuel White, speaker of the Massachusetts Assembly, whom he succeeded, in 1769, as King's attorney for Bristol County. With his election to the General Court in the year following he became a zealous young opponent of the Crown. But Governor Hutchinson was well aware of Leonard's professional talents and social prestige, and, under what has become traditionally known as the "Tory pear tree," he is said to have converted this upstart lawyer-dandy to the Royalist point of view. Leonard's infuriated Whig neighbors opened fire on his home at Taunton Green; he himself fled to Boston, and entered the British ranks as solicitor to customs commissioners.

On December 12, 1774 appeared the first of a series of weekly letters which Leonard, over the signature "Massachusettensis," wrote for the *Massachusetts Gazette*. Addressed "To the Inhabitants of the Province of Massachusetts-Bay," they were occasioned by the conviction that "ever since the origin of our controversy with Great Britain the press in its tone has been much devoted to the partizans of liberty . . . little has been published on the part of the government." Allegiance to the crown was as popular in England as unpopular in New England, he reiterated, adding that "we have bid their [Parliament's] defiance, . . . the longest sword must carry it unless we change our measures. . . ." The last of the series (April 8, 1775), lacking none of the characteristic gloss of logic, contained a prophetic threat which shortly became nothing more than a piece of British military self-appraisal:

Nothing short of a miracle could give you [the colonists] one battle, but could you destroy all the British . . . troups, . . . [etc.] it would be but the beginning of sorrow . . . one campaign would ruin you. . . .

John Adams, over the signature "Novanglus" challenged much of this political dogma. Leonard's earlier letters were published in New York in 1775 as *The Origin of the American Contest With Great Britain: Massachusettensis,* issued in Boston during the same year, covered the entire series.

It is said that when Leonard heard that Robert Treat Paine was a signer of the Declaration of Independence "he pictured him the rebel, swinging from the gallows," and that very shortly Paine, as attorney-general, was empowered "to prepare such a reception for Leonard should he return to Massachusetts." For Leonard was shortly exiled, his property confiscated, and by way of Halifax he returned to England. He was admitted to the bar and became chief justice of Bermuda and a ranking English barrister. He was twice married: in 1767 to Anna White, who died in the year following; and in 1770 to Sarah Hammock. He had one child by his first marriage and three by his second.

Leonard's papers have been considered the best American exposition of Royalist doctrines, and they constitute, therefore, a significant piece of colonial archives.

ABOUT: Davol, R. Two Men of Taunton; Jones, E. A. The Loyalists of Massachusetts; Leonard, D. Massachusettensis; Tyler, C. C. The Literary History of the American Revolution; Boston Transcript April 15, 18, 1851.

LEONARD, ZENAS (March 19, 1809-July 14, 1857), trapper and narrator, was the son of Abraham Leonard and Elizabeth (Armstrong) Leonard. He was born near Clearfield, Pa., and worked on his father's farm until he was twenty-one, then entered the store of an uncle in Pittsburgh. Determining to become a trapper, he soon went to St. Louis and in the capacity of a clerk joined an expedition setting out for the Rocky Mountains. He journeyed as far west as California, undergoing many adventures and dangers, part of the time becoming a free trapper with no means of subsistence save his gun and traps, and from 1833 a member of the expedition led by the French-American, Captain Benjamin Louis E. de Bonneville, then exploring the fur country. After more than five years' absence from home, having long been mourned as lost, he reappeared, and so intense was the interest in his story that he wrote an account of his travels that was published in part in the Clearfield *Republican,* and later in book form. The theft of part of his journal by hostile Indians left a gap which he filled in by consulting the journal of the expedition's leader. He later established himself as an Indian and Santa Fé trader on the site of Old Fort Osage, Sibley, Mo., where he died. He left two children. His book, which is highly valued as a narrative of its particular period and field, was issued in a limited edition in 1904 edited by W. F. Wagner, and as a Lakeside Classic in 1934 edited by M. M. Quaife.

PRINCIPAL WORK: Narrative of the Adventures of Zenas Leonard, 1839.

LESLEY, "J.P." See LESLEY, PETER

LESLEY, PETER ("J. P." Lesley) (September 17, 1819-June 1, 1903), geologist, was born in Philadelphia, the son of Peter and Elizabeth Oswald (Allen) Lesley. He attended private school and at fifteen entered the University of Pennsylvania, from which he was graduated in 1838. He was in poor health, however, and sought an appointment to an outdoor position with the state geological survey; his achievements won the high compliments of Henry Darwin Rogers, the director. When the survey was discontinued in 1841, Leslie began three years' study at the Theological Seminary at Princeton, assisting Rogers during vacations in the making of maps and the editing of reports of their geological expeditions. In 1844 he was licensed as a preacher by the Philadelphia Presbytery and then went abroad, dividing his time between study at Halle and travel.

When he returned to Philadelphia in May 1845 he became a colporteur for the American Tract Society; but unable to stand the physical strain he again (1846) joined Rogers, now in Boston, in the preparation of the survey records. Late the following year he took a Congregational pastorate at Milton, Mass., and in 1849 was married to Susan Inches Lyman. His wife's Unitarian affiliations and his own religious liberalism caused considerable friction within the parish and in 1852 he left the ministry and devoted full time to geology. After surveying coal and iron fields for sundry corporations and acting as secretary (1856-64) of the American Iron Association, he became successively professor of mining (1859) at the University of Pennsylvania, dean of the science department, and then dean of the

Towne Scientific School. He was sent abroad by the Pennsylvania Railroad in 1863 to study rail manufacture and the Bessemer steel process. From 1869 to 1873 he edited the *United States Railroad and Mining Register* and then began thirteen years' service as state geologist. During this period the survey published eighty octavo volumes of excellent reports, thirty-three atlases, and a "Grand Atlas." Another physical breakdown prevented Lesley from completing the summary and final issues.

Among his earlier books were the technical *Manual of Coal and Its Topography* and *The Iron Manufacturer's Guide.* Leslie was also a philologist, wrote a little verse, and in Boston delivered a series of the famous Lowell Lectures (1865-66), published as *Man's Origin and Destiny*; over the signature "John W. Allen, Jr." he wrote an account of a pleasure journey called *Paul Dreifuss: His Holiday Abroad.* Although sections of his geological reports bore the marks of legislative pressure, their style, on the whole, had a severity of emphasis and an effective terseness that set them quite apart from most of the literature of this kind.

Principal Works: A Manual of Coal and Its Topography, 1856; The Iron Manufacturer's Guide, 1859; Man's Origin and Destiny, 1868; Paul Dreifuss: His Holiday Abroad, 1882; Reports of the Second Geological Survey of Pennsylvania: 1874-87, 1892, 1895.

About: Ames, M. L. Life and Letters of Peter and Susan Lesley; Merrill, G. P. The First One Hundred Years of American Geology; Philadelphia Inquirer June 3, 1903.

LESLIE, ELIZA (November 15, 1787-January 1, 1858), writer of short stories, juveniles, and books on domestic economy, was born in Philadelphia, the daughter of Robert and Lydia (Baker) Leslie. Her father, whose self-taught accomplishments had won him election to the American Philosophical Society where he became a friend of Thomas Jefferson and Benjamin Franklin, took his family to England for a six years' stay when Eliza was only five. She was instructed at home, given private lessons in French and music, and for three months attended a London school of needlework. During her early years she wrote some negligible, hero-worshiping verse; but her first book, *Seventy-Five Receipts for Pastry, Cakes, and Sweetmeats,* did not appear until 1827. The recipes had been culled from a course at Mrs. Goodfellow's cooking school in Philadelphia. At the suggestion of her publisher she began to write stories for children, and these progressed as the Mirror Series.

Among the four magazines from which Miss Leslie received short-story awards was *Godey's Lady's Book* (for "Mrs. Washington Potts"), and for this tremendously popular journal she wrote (November 1845) an account of her hazardous journey from Philadelphia to Niagara Falls, by boat from New York to Albany and onward by train at the sinister speed of "twenty-one miles an hour!" She contributed to *Graham's Magazine* and edited *The Gift,* an annual, and *The Violet,* a juvenile "souvenir." *Amelia: or, A Young Lady's Vicissitudes* was her only novel and appeared first in the *Lady's Book.* It was her domestic arts publications, such as *The American Girl's Book, The Domestic Cookery Book, The House Book, The Behaviour Book,* etc., that enjoyed a real popularity and brought the best financial returns. Her biography of John Fitch, inventor and friend of her father, remained unfinished at the time of her death.

Miss Leslie's frequent pursuit of a somewhat satirical vein appears to have won her little praise from her critics; and although her stories unfolded easily and her descriptions had a certain convincing accuracy, it is, perhaps, only to the literature of household economy that she made any appreciable contribution.

Principal Works: Seventy-Five Receipts for Pastry, Cakes, and Sweetmeats, 1827; The American Girl's Book, 1831; Pencil Sketches, 1833, 1835, 1837; Domestic Cookery Book, 1837; The House-Book, 1840; The Young Revolutionists, 1845; The Lady's Receipt Book, 1846; Amelia: or A Young Lady's Vicissitudes, 1848; The Dennings and Their Beaux, 1851; The Behaviour Book, 1853.

About: Finley, R. E. The Lady of Godey's; Griswold, R. W. The Prose Writers of America; Hart, J. S. Female Prose Writers of America; New York Times January 4, 1858.

LESLIE, MIRIAM FLORENCE (FOLLINE) ("Miriam F. Squier") (c. 1836-September 18, 1914), editor, was born in New Orleans, La., her father Charles Follin, of French birth, being a one-time large commission merchant who met with various business reverses, and her mother being Susan (Danforth) Follin. By her own statement she had "a pinched and starved little childhood," but she managed to secure a good education which included French, Spanish, and Italian. She had remarkable beauty and charm, and was married four times: in 1854 to David Charles Peacock; about 1856 to Ephraim George Squier, an archaeologist and diplomat, later with the Frank Leslie publications; in 1873 to the publisher Frank Leslie; and in 1891 to the English art and dramatic critic William C.

Kingsbury Wilde, brother of Oscar Wilde. All culminated in divorce except that with Leslie which she characterized as her "one happy matrimonial experience." She had no children.

As "Miriam F. Squier" she was editing *Frank Leslie's Lady's Journal* in 1871. A few years after her marriage to Leslie they took a trip on a sumptuous scale with friends and servants to California. The journey is described in *California: A Pleasure Trip From Gotham to the Golden Gate*. Some unfortunate remarks relative to Virginia City, Nev., led the *Territorial Enterprise* of that city to issue a highly derogatry extra concerning them, dated July 14, 1878. Lavishness and adversity saddled her with a debt of $300,000 on Leslie's death (1880), but by her able management of the estate she was soon able to rebuild a substantial fortune, amounting at her death to over two million dollars. The bulk of this, although greatly reduced by litigation, was left to the cause of woman suffrage.

PRINCIPAL WORKS: California: A Pleasure Trip From Gotham to the Golden Gate, 1877; Rents in Our Robes, 1888; Beautiful Women of Twelve Epochs, 1890; Are Men Gay Deceivers? 1893; A Social Mirage, 1899; *Translations*—Travels in Central America, 1871.

ABOUT: Young, R. The Record of the Leslie Woman Suffrage Commission, Inc.: 1917-1929; Frank Leslie's Popular Monthly November 1898.

LESTER, CHARLES EDWARDS (July 15, 1815-January 29, 1890), biographer and social historian, was born at Griswold, Conn., son of Moses Lester and Sarah (Woodbridge) Lester and great-grandson of Jonathan Edwards. He went to school in New England and at the age of nineteen set out for the Midwest, journeyed down the Mississippi to Natchez, Miss., where he studied law under Robert J. Walker, who afterwards became Polk's secretary of the treasury. Returning north he enrolled at Auburn (N.Y.) Theological Seminary. On August 8, 1837, he was married to Ellen Brown by whom he had one child. Lester accepted several charges in the Presbyterian ministry, but the tax upon his health was too great, and in 1840 he sailed for London as a delegate to the World Anti-Slavery Convention at Exeter Hall, making the acquaintance of several English writers, including Dickens.

Returning to the United States he wrote an exposé of English mine and factory conditions, *The Glory and Shame of England* (1841), and countered a British defense with *The Condition and Fate of England*, an equally effective attack on the evils of the new industrial era. Previously he had published *Chains and Freedom*, a tale of a runaway slave.

He served a five-year consulship at Genoa (1842-47) during which time he made a number of translations from Machiavelli, Ceba, Alfieri, and Azeglio, all appearing in 1845; *My Consulship*, a chronicle of his diplomatic years, was not published until 1853. On his return he became New York correspondent of the London *Times* and in the last thirty years of his life wrote twenty-odd books, among the more popular of which were *Artists of America*, *Our First Hundred Years*, and biographies of Sam Houston, Charles Sumner, Tilden and Hendricks, and Peter Cooper. *The Life and Voyages of Americus Vespucius*, a result of his collaboration with Andrew Foster and his own extensive researches in Italy, first appeared in 1846 and went through numerous subsequent editions. *The Light and Dark of the Rebellion* recorded the misery he witnessed in Washington hospitals during his services there at the time of the Civil War. The manuscript of "The Great Explorers," on which he worked during a chronic illness preceding his death, was never completed.

Lester had a variety of talents and interests and was an intimate friend of such public figures as Webster, Sumner, Frémont, Greeley, and Tilden. His writings were timely rather than polished, with a lively style and a clear liberal point of view.

PRINCIPAL WORKS: Chains and Freedom, 1839; The Glory and the Shame of England (2 vols.) 1841; The Condition and Fate of England, 1842; Artists of America, 1846; The Napoleonic Dynasty, 1852 (collaboration with Edwin Williams); My Consulship, 1853; Our First Hundred Years, 1874-75; America's Advancement, 1876; Sam Houston, 1855; Charles Sumner, 1874; Tilden and Hendricks, 1876; Peter Cooper, 1883.

ABOUT: Lester, C. E. Our First Hundred Years; North American Review April 1846; Southern Quarterly Review January 1854; Detroit Free Press January 30, 1890.

LEWIS, CHARLES BERTRAND ("M. Quad"), (February 15, 1842-August 21, 1924), humorist, one of the very last "crackerbox philosophers" of the "Bill" Nye school, was born in Liverpool, Ohio, the son of a builder and contractor. At fourteen he began to learn the printer's trade in the office of the Pontiac (Mich.) *Jacksonian*, continuing his apprenticeship on Lansing newspapers. Meanwhile he had attended Michigan State Agricultural College for a short time and had seen service as a private in the Union army during the Civil War. He had just accepted the offer of a newspaper editorship in Jonesboro, Tenn., when, on board the "Magnolia," a steamer that had plied the Ohio for fifty years, he was injured in a boiler explosion, and after a long recuperation in Cincinnati he returned to his old post in Lansing. It was his thunderously funny account of this river disaster, "How It Feels to be Blown Up," that gave him his first real introduction to a laugh-loving American public.

In the capacity of legislative reporter Lewis was added to the staff of the Detroit *Free Press* in 1869, and after five years of reportorial work supplemented by an occasional fun-poking paragraph Lewis soon began to make a place for himself among such columinist-wits as James M. Bailey ("Danbury News Man") in Connecticut and Robert J. Burdette ("Burlington Hawkeye Man") in Iowa. One of Lewis' most profitable inventions was the Lime-Kiln Club, over which Brother Gardner, a braggart and "Socratic" Negro, presided (*Brother Gardner's Lime-Kiln Club*); another successful creation was the Bowsers, from whose unending domestic difficulties "M. Quad" drained a familiar but not ineffective brand of humor (*Trials and Troubles of the Bowser Family*).

At the end of twenty-two years with the *Free Press* he went to New York, and for the *World* and *Evening World* he turned out six columns of humor weekly, largely in the same vein that had characterized his earliest essays at comedy. One of his few plays, *Yakie,* was produced in 1884. Lewis was, indeed, almost a front-ranker during an episode in the history of American journalism when the popular demand for caricatures, burlesques, and extravagant word-play were fully exploited.

Principal Works: Quad's Odds, 1875; Goaks and Tears, 1875; Bessie Bane: or, The Mormon's Victim, 1880; The Comic Biography of James A. Garfield, 1881 (?); Brother Gardner's Lime-Kiln Club, 1882; Sawed-Off Sketches, 1884; Sparks of Wit and Humor, 1887; Trials and Troubles of the Bowser Family, 1889.

About: Blair, W. Native American Humor; Who's Who in America, 1920-21; New York Times August 23, 1924; Detroit Free Press August 23, 24, 1924.

LEWIS, CHARLTON THOMAS (February 25, 1834-May 26, 1904), classicist, editor, and lawyer, was born in West Chester, Pa., the son of John J. Lewis and Mary (Miner) Lewis. He attended school in West Chester and was graduated from Yale in 1853, excelling in mathematics and the classics. During the year following he studied law; and in 1856, after previous admission on trial, he became a Methodist Episcopal minister in full standing. His religious duties were interrupted between 1857 and 1862 by professorships at the (Bloomington) Normal University of Illinois and at Troy (N.Y.) University; they were resumed in Cincinnati, Ohio, but very shortly he accepted a post as deputy commissioner under his father, whom President Lincoln had made commissioner of internal revenue.

Lewis settled down permanently to a legal career in New York in 1864; he was, however, editor of the New York *Evening Post* from 1868 to 1871. Politics had a certain fascination for him and in 1896 he was a delegate to the convention of Gold Democrats at Indianapolis, Ind., and aided in the construction of a platform. To organized charities and prison reform he gave generously of his energies, holding major offices in prison associations, attending the International Prison Congress at Paris in 1895, and publicizing the cause in articles and pamphlets. Lewis was twice married: to Nancy D. McKeen in 1861; and two years after her death in 1883, to Margaret P. Sherrard.

Except for a number of authoritative technical tracts on the law of insurance, his writings were chiefly classical in subject.

Principal Works: John Albert Bengel's Gnomon of the Greek Testament (2 vols.) 1860-62; A History of Germany From the Earliest Times, 1874; Harper's Latin Dictionary, 1879; A Latin Dictionary for Schools, 1889; An Elementary Latin Dictionary, 1891.

About: Supplementary History of the Yale Class of 1853; Fifty-Ninth Annual Report of the Prison Association of New York, for the Year 1903; Evening Post (N.Y.) May 27, 1904.

LEWIS, "ESTELLE." See LEWIS, SARAH ANNA (ROBINSON)

LEWIS, SARAH ANNA (ROBINSON) (April 1824-November 24, 1880), poet, was born near Baltimore, Md., the daughter of John N. Robinson, a wealthy and cultured gentleman of Anglo-Spanish descent. She was sent to Emma Willard's Female Seminary at Troy, N.Y., and at an early age began to make translations from the Latin into English verse. Following a long sojourn in Cuba, Sarah was married, in 1841, to Sylvanus D. Lewis, a practicing attorney in Brooklyn, N.Y.; and here they lived until they were divorced, about 1858, and Mrs. Lewis established residence abroad.

Her adolescent poem, "Forsaken," appearing in a magazine in the early 'forties, attracted the attention of Edgar Allan Poe, whose appraisal of a woman's literary ability was too often little more than a measure of her feminine charm. To him she was, henceforth, "Estelle." And above the bust of Pallas in her Brooklyn studio she placed a stuffed raven! Poe not only hailed her as "perhaps the most informed, even the most accomplished" of women authors in America (*Democratic Review,* August 1848), but over the sketch of Mrs. Lewis which had been prepared for Griswold's *Female Poets of America* he scattered gilded superlatives. It is said that the Lewises paid Poe well for this.

Besides verse Mrs. Lewis wrote stories, translations, and travel articles for the *Democratic Review, Graham's Magazine, Godey's Lady's Book,* the *Literary World,* etc. The title poem of her *Child of the Sea and Other Poems* was a frank borrowing from Byron. Her poetic drama, *Sappho,* was translated into modern Greek and staged in Athens. Poe, on the occasion of his farewell call in June 1849, had requested Mrs. Lewis to write his life; but she never felt capable of the task. She spent much of her late life abroad and died in England; her body was brought back to the United States for burial.

Her poetry expressed some of her emotional vagaries, but it lacked musical cadence and was riddled with sentimentality. Her fame, like that of many of her female contemporaries, was borne aloft on the wings of Poe's restless adulation; at the later approach of more objective critics, it was forced into an abrupt descent.

PRINCIPAL WORKS: Records of the Heart, 1844; Child of the Sea and Other Poems, 1848; Myths of the Minstrel, 1852; Sappho, 1868; The King's Stratagem: or, The Pearl of Poland, 1869.

ABOUT: Allen, H. Israfel; Hale, S. J. Biography of Distinguished Women; Lauvriere, E. The Strange Life and Strange Loves of Edgar Allan Poe; Democratic Review August 1848; Southern Literary Messenger September 1848; London Daily News November 26, 1880.

LINN, JOHN BLAIR (March 14, 1777-August 30, 1804), poet, was born in Shippensburg, Pa., the son of the Rev. William Linn, a Presbyterian minister, and Rebecca (Blair) Linn, whose father, brother, and uncle were also ministers. In 1786 the family moved to New York, where in 1795 Linn was graduated from Columbia College. He received his M.A. from Columbia in 1797, and in the same year an honorary M.A. from Union College. In 1803 the University of Pennsylvania gave him an honorary D.D.

In spite of his clerical background, Linn did not turn at once to the ministry. He read law with Alexander Hamilton, and meanwhile amused himself by writing plays. *Bourville Castle: or, The Gallic Orphan,* was produced in New York in 1797, but it was a failure, and was never printed. Meanwhile the young dramatist was in Schenectady, studying theology with a Dutch Re-

From a silhouette by B. Tanner
JOHN BLAIR LINN

formed minister. At the same time he wrote for the Schenectady newspapers. He was licensed to preach in 1798, and was called at once as associate pastor of the First Presbyterian Church, in Philadelphia. In 1799 he married Hester Bailey; they had three sons.

In 1802 he suffered a bad attack of heat prostration, and never fully recovered. He was still able to write, and used most of his waning energy in trying to refute the Unitarian tracts of the famous Dr. Joseph Priestley. He was at work on a long poem when he died at only twenty-seven. The poem, *Valerian,* was published posthumously, though Linn had left it unfinished.

Linn's mind was unoriginal, and much of his work is consciously imitative of English models, chiefly Shenstone and Akenside. His elegy on Washington he frankly labeled an imitation of Ossian—a fantastically inappropriate conjunction of style and subject. He was highly thought of by his contemporaries, largely because of his youth and because of the paucity of rivals in eighteenth century America, but today he is both unread and unreadable. The best his editor and brother-in-law, the celebrated Charles Brockden Brown, could find to say of him was that his poems were "preludes to future exertions and indications of future excellence." In other words, he was one of those writers of whom one says that they showed great promise, and politely trusts that only death kept the promise unfulfilled. The sole value attached to his only finished play is that it was one of the earliest performed in America and written by an American.

Principal Works: Miscellaneous Works: Prose and Poetical, 1795; The Poetical Wanderer, 1796; The Death of George Washington: A Poem in Imitation of the Manner of Ossian, 1800; The Powers of Genius, 1801; A Discourse Occasioned by the Death of the Rev. Jong Ewing, 1802; Valerian, 1805.

About: Linn, J. B. Valerian (see Sketch by C. B. Brown); Simpson, H. The Lives of Eminent Philadelphians.

LIPPARD, GEORGE (April 10, 1822-February 9, 1854), eccentric novelist, unheralded writer for the proletariat, and founder of the "Brotherhood of the Union," was born on a farm in West Nantmeal township, Chester County, Pa. He grew up in Philadelphia, attended public school there, and at the Classical Academy, Rhinebeck, N.Y., he was to prepare for the Methodist ministry; but finding a "contradiction between theory and practice" of Christianity, he switched to the study of law. This too he left, four years later, because it was incompatible with his own beliefs about human justice.

At nineteen he began to cover police-court hearings for the Philadelphia *Spirit of the Times,* a lively and almost daring Democratic daily. He wrote with a fetching mixture of humor and pathos, and under title of "Our Talisman" prepared a series reminiscent of some of the "Sketches by Boz"; these were followed by "Bread Crust Papers," in a similar vein. When Dickens visited Philadelphia in 1842 Lippard wrote an account of the memorable ovation extended him.

From a woodcut by J. R. Telfer
GEORGE LIPPARD
c. 1854

His health began to fail. He withdrew from journalism, and the *Saturday Evening Post* (July 9, 1842) published his first story, "Philippe de Agramont"; a little later came a romance, in serial form, "Herbert Tracy: or, The Legend of the Black Rangers." Early in the year following he contributed a number of tales to the newly founded *Citizen Soldier.* In 1844 *The Monks of Monk Hall* (later called *The Quaker City*), an exposé of Philadelphia's vice, was first issued bi-monthly and afterwards supplemented and reprinted with a tremendous sale; it was also published in England and Germany. Lippard dramatized the book and wrote another play, *Coro: The Priest Robber,* included in the posthumous *Legends of Florence.*

His career as a lecturer began in 1844 with his popular "legends" of the Revolution and the publication of some of these chronicles in the *Saturday Courier* won him a fast-increasing public. Historical narratives and sensational novels flowed from his pen. His quarterly, *The White Banner,* survived (1851) only one issue.

Standing on "Mom Rinker's Rock" in Philadelphia's romantic Wissahickon park, he was married, by moonlight, to Rose Newman in 1847. More significant illustrations of his non-conformity, however, were: the founding of a decidedly "Marxian" theory which could have been only slightly—if at all—influenced by the German socialist; and the organization of the Brotherhood of the Union (later the Brotherhood of America). Poe, whom Lippard probably met through Henry B. Hirst, a versifier and unwilling student of law, gave Lippard much of the credit for rescuing him from the streets on several occasions. Lippard too was regarded as a kind of literary madcap, a "young petrel who swooped, gyrated and cut his circles over the roofs and chimney tops of Philadelphia, sailing up the Wissahickon and down the Brandywine, now scouting its romantic history and now its foolishness and vice. . ." Scattered through Lippard's novels are a few passages of deftly poetic prose but his writings on the whole are more remarkable for quantity than for quality.

Principal Works: The Quaker City, 1845; The Nazarene, 1846; Blanche of Brandywine, 1846; Legends of Mexico, 1847; Washington and His Generals. . , 1847; Paul Ardenheim, 1848; Bel of Prairie Eden, 1848; Washington and His Men: Second Series of Legends of the Revolution, 1850; Adonai: The Pilgrim of Eternity, 1851; Mysteries of the Pulpit, 1852; The Man With the Mask, 1852; The Empire City, 1853; New York: Its Upper-Ten and Lower Million,

1854; Eleanor: or, Slave Catching in Philadelphia, 1854; Legends of Florence, 1864.

ABOUT: Allen, H. Israfel; Lippard, G. Thomas Paine: Author-Soldier of the Revolution (see sketch by J. B. Elliott); Oberholtzer, E. P. The Literary History of Philadelphia; The Brotherhood December 1900; Pennsylvania Magazine of History and Biography April-October 1930; Saturday Courier (Philadelphia) January 15, 1848.

LIPPINCOTT, SARA JANE (CLARKE) ("Grace Greenwood") (September 23, 1823-April 20, 1904), poet and journalist, was born in Pompey, N.Y., one of eleven children of a prominent physician, Dr. Thaddeus Clarke, and Deborah Clarke, both of New England descent. She was educated in Rochester, and when she was nineteen the family moved to New Brighton, Pa., where she wrote her first books. An extended European trip was followed by her marriage in 1853 to Leander K. Lippincott of Philadelphia. Thereafter she wrote constantly. She died at New Rochelle, N.Y., at the home of her only daughter with whom she passed her last four years.

Her writing began as a child with verse published over her own name; when she began to publish her prose writings, she adopted the pen name "Grace Greenwood." She edited with her husband a juvenile monthly, the *Little Pilgrim,* and in addition to producing about a score of books she wrote extensively for various journals. She was one of the earliest regular women newspaper correspondents, her contributions being sent to leading New York, Chicago, and California papers from Washington and Europe. *Greenwood Leaves* and *Haps and Mishaps in Europe* were her most popular books, although the latter was criticized adversely by the London *Athenaeum.* Her writings were light and sentimental.

PRINCIPAL WORKS: Greenwood Leaves, 1850, 1852; Poems, 1851; Recollections of My Childhood and Other Stories, 1852; Haps and Mishaps of a Tour in Europe, 1854; Merrie England, 1855; A Forest Tragedy and other Tales, 1856; Stories From Famous Ballads, 1860; Bonnie Scotland, 1861; Stories and Sights of France and Italy, 1867; New Life in New Lands, 1873; Queen Victoria, 1883; Stories and Sketches, 1892.

ABOUT: Hart, J. S. The Female Prose Writers of America; Oberholtzer, E. P. The Literary History of Philadelphia; Willard, F. E. & Livermore, M. A. A Woman of the Century.

LITTELL, WILLIAM (1768-September 26, 1824), satirist and legal historian, was a native of New Jersey and during his early childhood removed with his family to Pennsylvania. Here he probably remained until about the year 1801 when he settled in Kentucky, practiced medicine (he had studied "Physics and Divinity"), and then began to apply himself to law. At Frankfort, Ky., in 1806, he published *Epistles of William, Surnamed Littell, to the People of the Realm of Kentucky,* largely essays which satirized certain dignitaries of the day; *A Narrative of the Settlement of Kentucky;* and the more valuable and better-known *Political Transactions in and Concerning Kentucky.* His *Statute Law of Kentucky* (1809-19), for which he had contracted with the State in 1805, appeared in five volumes. It was followed by other books on the statute and common law of Kentucky.

After the death of his first wife, Martha Irwin McCracken, to whom he was married in 1816, Eliza P. Hickman, a widow, became (1823) his second wife.

Littell twice departed from the heaviness of his legal tracts, and in addition to his heckling *Epistles. . .* wrote *Festooons of Fancy. . .* which opens with "The Author's Account of Himself (In answer to an invitation to tea, sent by some young ladies)"

> . . .It is a fact I was by nature
> A most unfascinating creature
> . . .through ambition to be wise
> I have almost read out my eyes,
> Immersed in sciences abstruse
> Half out of date and out of use
> Who could assume an easy air
> And intermingle with the fair?

The testimony of his contemporaries defines him as an unmistakable eccentric, but evidence of his reputed disregard for morals and his professional mediocrity is scant and circumstantial.

Littell's personal peculiarities are, of course, of only incidental biographical interest, and his more substantial claims to recognition are his numerous publications in the field of law.

PRINCIPAL WORKS: Epistles of William, Surnamed Littell, to the People of the Realm of Kentucky, 1806; A Narrative of the Settlement of Kentucky, 1806; Political Transactions in and Concerning Kentucky, 1806; Statute Law of Kentucky, 1809-1819; Festoons of Fancy: Consisting of Compositions Amatory, Sentimental, and Humorous in Verse and Prose, 1814; Digest of the Statute Law of Kentucky, 1822; Reports of Cases at Common Law and in Chancery, Decided by the Court of Appeals of the Commonwealth of Kentucky, 1823-24; Cases Selected From the Decisions of the Court of Appeals of Kentucky Not Hitherto Reported, 1824.

ABOUT: Littell, W. Festoons of Fancy; Littell, W. Political Transactions (Filson Club Publications, No. 31).

"LITTLETON, MARK." See KENNEDY, JOHN PENDLETON

LIVERMORE, GEORGE (July 10, 1809-August 30, 1865), antiquarian, the son of Deacon Nathaniel Livermore and Elizabeth (Gleason) Livermore, and a descendant of John Livermore, a Massachusetts settler from Ipswich, England, in 1634, was born in Cambridge, Mass. Denied a college education because of frailty of constitution, he entered a store in the employ of two brothers at fourteen, and by 1834 he had established himself in the shoe and leather business in Boston, and four years later as a wool merchant. From the beginning he spent his spare time in reading and study and his spare money in the purchase of books. He acquired a large and rare library of Bibles and Biblical literature, a subject on which he became an authority, and rare editions of other works. He died at Cambridge, leaving a wife and three sons.

From his early years he wrote verses and Sunday School hymns. In 1849 eight articles published in the *Cambridge Chronicle* over the pen name "The Antiquary" and later republished as *The Origin, History, and Character of the New-England Primer* attracted considerable attention. His highly sensitive nature was intensely affected by the Civil War, in which he gave such help as he could, and when the issue of the use of colored soldiers arose he produced *An Historical Research Respecting the Opinions of the Founders of the Republic, on Negroes as Slaves, as Citizens, and as Soldiers.* President Lincoln is said to have consulted it in writing his *Emancipation Proclamation,* and to have presented to Livermore the pen with which he signed that document. His writing was noted for scholarship and accuracy.

Principal Works: The Origin, History, and Character of the New-England Primer, 1849; An Historical Research Respecting the Opinions of the Founders of the Republic, on Negroes as Slaves, as Citizens, and as Soldiers, 1862.

About: Deane, C. Memoir of George Livermore; Thwing, W. E. The Livermore Family of America; Tribute of the Massachusetts Historical Society to the Memory of George Livermore.

LIVERMORE, MARY ASHTON (RICE) (December 19, 1820-May 23, 1905), reformer, and woman suffragist, was born in Boston, the daughter of Timothy Rice and Zebiah Vose Glover (Ashton) Rice. Her father, a man of strong character, was of New England descent from Wales. Her mother was the daughter of an English captain. Before the end of her first year at the Female Seminary in Charlestown she was engaged as a student-teacher. Later she taught nearly three years on a Virginia plantation, and in the high school at Duxbury, Mass. In 1845 she married a Unitarian minister, the Rev. Daniel Parker Livermore, and after several pastorates in Massachusetts and Connecticut they lived in Chicago during the years 1857 to 1869 where he conducted a church periodical, the *New Covenant.* During the Civil War she became widely known for her efforts in behalf of the Northwestern branch of the Sanitary Commission. From 1869 the Livermores lived in Melrose, Mass., where she died. They had two children.

Mrs. Livermore published her first work, a temperance story, shortly after her marriage. She helped her husband edit the *New Covenant* and did much miscellaneous writing. After the Civil War she became active in woman suffrage and established the *Agitator,* which she merged within a few months with the *Woman's Journal* of Boston, editing this also. From 1872 she attained distinction on the public platform, speaking on various social questions, politics, history, biography and education. Among other writings she published two autobiographical works, contributed a chapter on "Massachusetts Women in the Civil War" to Thomas Wentworth Higginson's *Massachusetts in the Army and Navy During the War of 1861-65,* and was joint editor with Frances E. Willard, the reformer, of a biographical compilation, *A Woman of the Century,* later published as *American Women.*

Principal Works: Pen Pictures, 1865; Thirty Years Too Late, a True Story, 1878; What Shall We Do With Our Daughters, 1883; My Story of the War: A Woman's Narrative of Four Years Personal Experience, 1888; The Story of My Life, 1897; *Joint Editor*—A Woman of the Century, 1893.

About: Logan, Mrs. J. A. The Part Taken by Women in American History; Phelps, E. S. Our Famous Women; Thwing, W. E. The Livermore Family of America; Woman's Journal May 27, 1905.

LIVINGSTON, EDWARD (May 28, 1764-May 23, 1836), juridical writer, was born at "Clermont," the family estate in Columbia County, N.Y., the son of Judge Robert R. Livingston and Margaret (Beekman) Livingston. His grandfather, father, and brother Robert were all distinguished in law and public affairs. The father died in 1775. Livingston was educated at private schools in Albany and Esopus (now Kingston), N.Y., and received his B.A. from the College of New Jersey (Princeton) in 1781, his M.A. in 1784. After studying languages at home for a year with tutors, he read law in Albany, with Hamilton and Burr as his fellow-students, and was admitted to the

After a portrait by J. B. Longacre
EDWARD LIVINGSTON

New York bar in 1785. In 1788 he married Mary McEvers; they had three children, all of whom died young; she herself died in 1801.

Livingston was a member of Congress from 1795 to 1801, a Jeffersonian through pique at neglect of his family by Washington. Already his chief interest was revision of the penal code. He was appointed U.S. District Attorney for the New York District in 1801, and at the same time mayor of New York, filling both offices simultaneously. He recovered from an attack of yellow fever in 1803 to find himself heavily in debt to the government because of an absconding agent. He turned over his whole fortune in repayment, but was so poor a business man that various complications left him still in debt until 1826. He went to New Orleans and began life over again, overwhelmingly in debt privately as well as publicly. There his troubles increased, first from unjust accusation of involvement in Burr's conspiracy, then in a series of suits over land claims in Louisiana. In 1805 he married Louise (d'Azevac de Castera) Moureau de Lassy, a widow of Santo Domingan birth, by whom he had one daughter. During the War of 1812 he was Jackson's right-hand man, and became his lifelong friend. In 1820 he was elected to the Louisiana legislature, and the next year revised the state's penal code, emphasizing prevention of crime. From 1823 to 1829 he represented Louisiana in the House of Representatives, and from 1829 to 1831 in the Senate. For the next two years he was Secretary of State under Jackson, and in 1833 minister to France, where he negotiated payment of American claims from the Napoleonic wars. He resigned in protest against governmental disapproval of his policy.

His sister died and left him her estate in Tarrytown, where he spent his last years, at last free of debt and with leisure to edit and codify his writings. There he died of "bilious colic" just before his sixty-second birthday. He was buried at "Clermont."

Sir Henry Maine called Livingston "the first legal genius of modern times." His works are of course not meant for reading, and belong rather to the law than to literature. He was very advanced in his criminological views, and almost abreast with the most modern penology.

Principal Works: Reports of the Plan of the Penal Code, 1822; System of Penal Law for the State of Louisiana, 1826; System of Penal Law for the United States, 1828; Complete Works on Criminal Jurisprudence, 1873.

About: d'Azevac, A. Recollections of Edward Livingston; Hunt, C. H. Life of Edward Livingston; Louisiana Historical Quarterly January-October 1920; Proceedings Louisiana Bar Assn. 1903.

LIVINGSTON, WILLIAM (November 1723-July 25, 1790), first governor of the state of New Jersey, columnist, and lawyer, was born in Albany, N.Y., son of Philip and Catharine (Van Brugh) Livingston. At the age of fourteen he was sent, with a missionary, to live, for a year among the congenial Mohawks. During his undergraduate years at Yale he became far more interested in law than in mercantilism—the profession originally prescribed for him—and after his graduation in 1741 he entered the New York law office of James Alexander. His preceptors aided in shaping his political philosophy, which was becoming noticeably liberal.

He was admitted to the bar in 1748. Three years later, in a controversy over the establishment of a college in the colony, he set up a rigid opposition to the domination of the Presbyterians by the Episcopalians. In the *Independent Reflector,* an organ founded in 1752 "to oppose superstition, bigotry, priestcraft, tyranny. . . ," and in the *New York Mercury's* "Watch Tower" column he aired his views. Moreover, the Livingston faction, battening on its opposition to the followers of Lieutenant-Governor James De Lancey, succeeded, in 1758, in gaining control of the Assembly. His clear disapproval of Parliamentary interference in provincial affairs did not, however, overcome the difficulty in reconciling certain patrician and plebeian groups. A renewal of his Anglican attack, *Letter to the Right Reverend Father in God, John, Lord Bishop of Landaff,* proved to be no escape from the dilemma; and after the harrowing elections of 1769 he had only to console himself with the writing of the satiric *Soliloquy,* a subtle thrust at provincial representation of British authority.

He retired to his country estate near Elizabethtown, N.J., where he entered not upon the rural quiet for which he had longed in *Philosophic Solitude,* but upon a more brilliant public life: he was a delegate to the First (and Second) Continental Congress, and, by the legislature, was elected first governor of the state. Through a trying. period of war and reorganization his judgment, on the whole, remained diplomatically sound and his energy inexhaustible. His writings, often deftly satiric and neatly developed, were, with a few exceptions, hardly more than by-products of his political career.

Principal Works: Philosophic Solitude, 1747; Letter to the Right Reverend Father in God, John, Lord Bishop of Landaff, 1768; A Soliloquy, 1770.

About: Becker, C. L. History of Political Parties in the Province of New York; Livingston, E. B. Livingstons of Livingston Manor; Sedgwick, T. Jr. A Memoir of the Life of William Livingston; Tyler, M. C. Literary History of the American Revolution.

LLOYD, HENRY DEMAREST (May 1, 1847-September 28, 1903), journalist, industrial reformer, and organizer, was born in New York City, the son of Aaron Lloyd, a Dutch Reformed minister, and Maria Christie (Demarest) Lloyd. Among his ancestors were many dissenters, and he in turn was to rebel against the rigid Calvinism to which he was subjected as a child. In 1869 he received an M.A. degree from Columbia College and was admitted to the New York bar. During three years of optimistic reform activity he contributed (1871) to the defeat of Tammany Hall, and in 1872, supporting free trade, he opposed Greeley's nomination by the Liberal Republicans. But, on the whole, disappointed in the political front, he transferred his interests to journalism, and accepting an offer from the Chicago *Tribune,* launched, in the financial and editorial columns of this paper, his long crusade against monopolies. In 1881, William Dean Howells published in the *Atlantic Monthly* Lloyd's "Story of a Great Monopoly," an exposé of the railroads and Standard Oil Company which ran that (March) issue into seven editions.

Leaving the *Tribune* in 1885 he went abroad, and returned to Chicago with a first-hand knowledge of the English politico-industrial scene. Although an enemy of violence, Lloyd worked to secure the removal of two death sentences placed upon anarchists who had participated in the Haymarket "massacre" of 1886—one of the crises of a growing industrial unrest. Between the publication of *A Strike of Millionaires Against Miners* (1890), an appeal for industrial justice, and *Wealth Against Commonwealth* (1894), a fully documented malediction upon monopolies, Lloyd had unofficially organized the Milwaukee street-car workers and had defended the conduct of Eugene Victor Debs, Socialist advocate, who led the Pullman Strike of 1894. His second book was widely read but provoked a much milder kind of social indignation than he had hoped for.

In 1894 he accepted nomination, on the ticket of the National People's Party, for a seat in Congress; was badly defeated; and with the subsequent weakening and compromising of this party's platform he withdrew entirely. He went abroad again (1897-1901) and from his many observations of social experiment he wrote *Labour Copartnership* and *Newest England,* both on the English scheme; *A Country Without Strikes,* on New Zealand's policy of compulsory arbitration of industrial disputes; and *A Sovereign People,* an account of Switzerland's faith in the initiative and referendum. Lloyd was married in 1873 to Jessie Bross.

He was one of the earliest and most intelligently effective "muckrakers" in the history of American industrial reform, and his writings are an able record of the development and application of his social philosophy.

Principal Works: A Strike of Millionaires Against Miners, 1890; Wealth Against Commonwealth, 1894; Labour Copartnership, 1898; Newest England; A Country Without Strikes, 1900; Man: The Social Creator, 1906; A Sovereign People, 1907.

About: Lloyd, C. Henry Demarest Lloyd; Arena December 1903; Chicago Daily Tribune September 29, 1903.

LOCKE, DAVID ROSS ("Petroleum V. Nasby") (September 20, 1833-February 15, 1888), humorist, was born in Vestal, N.Y., the son of Nathaniel Reed Locke, a Revolutionary soldier, and Hester (Ross) Locke. His schooling ended at ten, and he was apprenticed to the Cortland, N.Y. *Democrat.* In 1850 he began two years traveling over the country as an itinerant printer. From 1832 to 1856, with J. G. Robinson, he conducted the Plymouth, Ohio, *Advertiser,* going on from there to other small Ohio towns, and ending with the Findlay *Jeffersonian,* where the first of his "Nasby" letters appeared. In 1855 he married Martha H. Bodine; they had three sons.

"Petroleum Vesuvius Nasby" was depicted as a "Copperhead" (Southern sympathizer), an illiterate, bombastic, hypocritical preacher through whom his creator poured his anti-slavery and anti-Democratic sentiments. The letters became immensely popular all through the North, especially after the great cartoonist Thomas Nast illustrated them. They made Locke rich as well as famous; in 1865 he was editor of the Toledo *Blade* and was soon able to buy a controlling interest in it. In 1871 he went to New York as managing editor of the *Evening Mail,* and two years later, with a partner, he founded a newspaper advertising agency; but he continued his ownership of the *Blade* and soon returned to Toledo for the remainder of his life.

Though Locke was a constant lecturer and wrote numerous humorous and satirical books, "Nasby" remained his chief creation and the letters continued to appear, the last being written only two months before his death. After the war, "Nasby" became the spokesman (by satirical indirection) of the prohibition forces. Both Lincoln and Grant were great admirers of Locke; Lincoln once postponed a cabinet meeting to read a "Nasby" letter aloud, and Grant called him "the fourth arm of the service" in the Civil War. Both offered him various political offices, all of which he declined; his only political ambition was to be alderman from the third ward of Toledo, and this, after several defeats, he finally achieved, holding the post until his death.

Collection of Frederick H. Meserve
DAVID ROSS LOCKE
("Petroleum V. Nasby")

He was the strongest satirist of his day, but his work is now as dead as are the issues that inspired it. Its use of misspelling and highfaluting words for humorous effect was founded in the first place on "Artemus Ward," but "Ward" had broader interests and more real sense of the comic. Locke himself, as "Nasby," wrote: "Wat posterity will say I don't know; neither do I care. It's this generashen I'm going for." He captured his "generashen," by appeal to strictly contemporary and local emotions and opinions, with the natural result that to succeeding "generashens" he became nothing but a name whose luster had dimmed, or been tarnished, almost to the point of invisibility.

PRINCIPAL WORKS: The Nasby Papers, 1864; Divers Views, Opinions, and Prophecies of Yours Truly, 1865; Swingin' Round the Cirkle, 1866; Ekkoes From Kentucky, 1867; The Moral History of America's Life Struggle, 1872; The Struggles of Petroleum Vesuvius Nasby, 1873; The Morals of Abou ben Adhem, 1875; A Paper City, 1878; Hannah Jane, 1882; Nasby in Exile, 1882; The Demagogue 1891.

ABOUT: Clemens, C. Petroleum Vesuvius Nasby; Ford, R. American Humorists, Recent and Living; The Nasby Letters; New York Herald February 16, 1888; Toledo Blade, February 15, 1888.

LOCKE, RICHARD ADAMS (September 22, 1800-February 16, 1871), journalist, was born at East Brent, Somersetshire, England, son of Richard Locke, a surveyor, and Anne (Adams) Locke. He attended Cambridge and shortly afterwards founded first the democratic London *Republican* and then the *Cornucopia*; both journals failed. In 1832 with his wife, Esther Bowering Locke, and his infant daughter Adelaide he sailed for New York. After serving as a reporter on the *Courier and Inquirer,* he accepted a post, at twelve dollars a week, with the *Sun*—New York's first penny paper—which appeared to be cultivating a peculiarly American variety of sensational journalism. For the *Sun* (August 1835) Locke wrote his celebrated "Moon Hoax," which, in the guise of a reprint from the (then defunct), Edinburgh *Journal of Science,* purported to bare John Herschel's discovery, at the Cape of Good Hope, of the higher forms of animal life on the moon: winged humans, biped beavers occupying well heated houses, etc. Locke clothed the highly questionable with the consistently plausible, and with a subtle scattering of astronomical terms actually brought down from Yale a delegation of inquirers who wanted to see the original Edinburgh article. The *Sun's* circulation jumped to more than 90,000, which was at that time the record for any daily. (Edgar Allan Poe, whose "Hans Pfaall" had, in substance, been anticipated by the appearance of Locke's "Hoax," perpetrated his own "Balloon Hoax" nine years later, issuing a *Sun* "extra" to cover Mr. Monck Mason's fictitious three-day trans-Atlantic balloon flight.)

Locke left the *Sun* in 1836, and with Joseph Price set up another penny daily, the *New Era,* and in it he ventured "The Lost Manuscript of Mungo Park," which, supposedly, disclosed the strange new adventures of the Scottish explorer. But the public was less gullible this time. With the early failure of the *New Era,* Locke became the editorial writer on the Brooklyn *Daily Eagle,* and for a while held a customs-house post.

He had, according to Poe, a forehead that was "truly beautiful in its intellectuality" and a "calm, clear luminousness" about his eyes. His reputation as a journalist rests virtually on a single episode in the history of the American newspaper, and yet it has sustained itself, in a limited way, for over a century.

About: Allen, H. Israfel; O'Brien, F. M. Story of the Sun; Poe, E. A. The Literati; New York Herald February 18, 1871.

LOCKWOOD, RALPH INGERSOLL (July 8, 1798-April 12, 1858?), novelist and lawyer, was born at Greenwich, Conn., the son of Stephen and Sarah (Ingersoll) Lockwood. He spent his boyhood in Greenwich and in 1821 his family removed to Mount Pleasant (now Ossining), N.Y., and purchased a 100-acre farm. Ralph studied law, was admitted to the bar, and went eventually to New York City where he built up a life-long practice, gaining a substantial reputation for wit and eloquence. At the age of twenty-seven he published an *Essay on a National Bankrupt Law* (1825), an analysis of the problems which Congress would face under the proposed legislation and of the breadth of the law's jurisdiction.

Lockwood believed that there were many "faults and absurdities" in English common law, and, concentrating much of his energy on equity, he became an outstanding chancery lawyer; his lack of any false reverence for the courts lent vigor and fearlessness to his criticism of his own profession.

In 1848 he published *Analytical and Practical Synopses of All the Cases Argued and Reversed. . . .*; in 1850 he edited a two-volume American edition of J. E. Bright's *Treatise on the Law of Husband and Wife.* Following a temporary departure from New York during a cholera plague, Lockwood had allowed himself the indulgence of fiction-writing: *Rosine Laval,* under the pseudonym "Mr. Smith," and *The Insurgents,* which appeared anonymously. The plot of the first novel was devised in half an hour and the book itself was completed in six weeks; it is vitiated by a sadly outworn humor, on the one hand, and a succession of unconvincingly harrowing passages, on the other. The second book, although a somewhat more serious piece of writing, was, in general, open to the same criticism.

Lockwood had a natural fondness for good reading, and was, moreover, an accomplished French scholar. He not only lived in France during two brief intervals, but acted as counsel, over a period of several years, for eminent Frenchmen who resided in New York.

Principal Works: Rosine Laval, 1833; The Insurgents, 1835; Analytical and Practical Synopses of All the Cases Argued and Reversed. . . 1848; Treatise on the Law of Husband and Wife, 1850.

About: Holden, F. A. & Lockwood, E. D. Descendants of Robert Lockwood. . . ; biographical material from his works.

LODGE, HENRY CABOT (May 12, 1850-November 9, 1924), historian and biographer, was born in Boston, the son of John Ellerton Lodge, a prosperous merchant, and Anna (Cabot) Lodge. He was educated at Harvard, being graduated in 1871. The same year he married his cousin, Anna Cabot Davis; they had two sons and a daughter. After a year in Europe, he entered the Harvard Law School, receiving his LL.B. in 1875 and being admitted to the bar in 1876. At first, however, literature rather than law or politics seemed destined to be his career; he edited the *North American Review* with Henry Adams from 1873 to 1876, and was associate editor of the *International Review* from 1879 to 1881. In 1876 he received the first Ph.D. from Harvard in political science and lectured on American history at Harvard for the next three years and at the Lowell Institute in 1880. In 1876, also, his first book was published—his *Essays in Anglo-Saxon Law.*

His political career began in the Massachusetts House of Representatives in 1880. Numerous attempts at higher offices failed except for election as delegate to successive Republican national conventions, until in 1887 he was elected to Congress. He served until 1893, when he became a senator. At his death he was the ranking Republican in the Senate, and chairman of the important For-

HENRY CABOT LODGE

eign Affairs committee. "The scholar in politics," as he was called before Woodrow Wilson, his arch-enemy, wrested the phrase from him, was as great a disappointment in one way as Wilson in another; except for advocacy of civil service reform, he was the prime advocate and friend of every reactionary measure; bitter, vindictive, and querulous. He did more than any one man to keep America isolated after the World War and thus to pave the way for future international complications. A close friend of Theodore Roosevelt's, he did not follow him out of the party, but remained a lifelong Republican of the extreme conservative faction.

In addition to his numerous original writings, Lodge edited the works of Alexander Hamilton and *The Education of Henry Adams*. His historical and biographical works display his acute intelligence, untiring industry, and remarkable memory, but are marred by excessive partisanship and the intrusion of personal grudges. A man of real literary skill, distinguished in style and often eloquent, he was also a sophist on occasion and a bitter die-hard to the end, so that he must always be read with caution and allowance for his prejudices.

PRINCIPAL WORKS: Essays in Anglo-Saxon Law, 1876; Life and Letters of George Cabot, 1877; A Short History of the English Colonies in America, 1881; Alexander Hamilton, 1882; Daniel Webster, 1883; Studies in History, 1886; George Washington, 1889; Historical and Political Essays, 1892; Certain Accepted Heroes and Other Essays, 1897; The Story of the Revolution, 1898; Story of the Spanish War, 1899; A Frontier Town and Other Essays, 1906; Early Memories, 1913; The Democracy of the Constitution and Other Essays, 1915; The Senate of the United States, 1921.

ABOUT: Groves, C. S. Henry Cabot Lodge: The Statesman; Lawrence, W. Henry Cabot Lodge; Lodge, H. C. Early Memories; Outlook November 19, December 10, 1924; New York Times November 10, 11, 16, 1924.

LOGAN, CORNELIUS AMBROSIUS (May 4, 1806-February 22, 1853), actor, dramatist, and manager, was born in Baltimore, Md., the son of an Irish farmer. As a child he sang in a church choir, and began, somewhat later, to study for the priesthood at St. Mary's College. For a while he was employed in a shipping house; after several trans-Atlantic voyages as sailor and supercargo, he turned landlubber and began to dabble in New York journalism. With his removal to Philadelphia he became actively interested in the theatre and made his own first appearance at the Tivoli Garden, July 1825, in Maturin's tragedy *Bertram*; several other engagements followed. In 1826 he was in New York playing in *The Road to Ruin, Much Ado About Nothing,* and *The School for Scandal.* With his family he went to Pittsburgh and there became a theatrical manager, touring the Midwest, acting occasionally, and suffering from the customary financial instability of his profession. His rôles of Sir Peter Teazle in *The School for Scandal* and Peter Simpson in *Simpson & Co.* became almost classic, and many of his closest friends believed Peter Logan to be his real name. He was married to Eliza Akeley, by whom he had three daughters, all actresses, and one son, a physician and writer.

Logan was, however, more than an actor-manager. He was the author of a sizable list of farces, most of which exploited Yankee eccentricities. In one of the earliest of these, *Yankee Land,* he introduced a semi-enlightened wiseacre, "Lot Sap Sago"; *The Wag of Maine* and *The Vermont Wool Dealer,* in which "Deuteronomy Dutiful" embodies not only the usual Yankeeisms but many of the marks of the stock villain as well, sustained this somewhat maudlin hilarity. It was in the *Wool Dealer* that Dan Marble, American comedian, made a very successful début before a London audience: the *Court Journal* hailed Logan's yarns as "new, full of drollery, and capitally told." His *Celestial Empire* and *Yankee Land* were billed a little later in Marble's engagement. On a return to New York after a long absence in Ohio and upper New York state, Logan took the part of Aminadab Slocum in his own *Chloroform: or, New York a*

Hundred Years Hence, produced at the Chambers Street Theatre May 24, 1849.

Logan had spent a good share of his life in the "wings" of a theatre; and his domestic environments had been almost everything *but* New England. He had, therefore a combination of what might be called professional sympathy and geographical detachment that allowed him to lampoon the Yankee with a sometimes disarming but always unembittered sense of humor.

Principal Works: Yankee Land: or, The Foundling of the Apple Orchard, 1834; The Wag of Maine, 1835; The Vermont Wool Dealer, 1840; Chloroform: or, New York a Hundred Years Hence, 1849.

About: Brown, T. A. History of the N. Y. Stage: Vol. 3; Kelley, J. F. Dan Marble; Moses, M. J. The American Dramatist; Quinn, A. H. History of the American Drama From the Beginning to the Civil War; Cincinnati Daily Enquirer February 25, 1853.

LOGAN, OLIVE (April 22, 1839-April 27, 1909), actress, journalist, and lecturer, was born at Elmira, N.Y., the daughter of Cornelius Ambrosius Logan and Eliza (Akeley) Logan. She was a sister of the actress Eliza Logan, and the physician Cornelius Ambrose Logan. Her father, a noted comedian, dramatist, and manager of Irish parentage, brought her into contact with the stage from childhood. She made her debut as Mrs. Bobtail in *Bobtail and Wagtail* in Philadelphia in 1854, but her stage career was short, lasting only until 1857, and for a return period of 1865 to 1867. She went abroad in 1857 and thereafter spent considerable time in Europe. The humorist "Artemus Ward" is credited with having influenced her to take up public speaking, and her platform work on social and political topics is said to have brought her $15,000 a year. She was married three times, to Henry A. Delille, or De Lille, in 1857, a divorce following twelve years later; to William Wirt Sikes, member of the American consulate at Cardiff, Wales, in 1872; and some time after Sikes' death in 1883 to a James O'Neill, twenty years her junior. Poverty and insanity clouded her last years and she died in an asylum at Banstead, England.

She contributed successfully to French, English, and American journals writing for a time over the pseudonym "Chroniqueuse." Two dramas written by her were produced in New York, *Surf,* a comedy, by Augustin Daly in 1870, and *Newport* in 1879. She also dramatized Wilkie Collins' novel, *Armadale.* Among her books, several of which pertain to the theatre, were two novels, *Château Frissac* and *They Met by Chance*. Her work is now all but forgotten.

Principal Works: Photographs of Paris Life, 1862; Apropos of Women and Theatres, 1869; Before the Footlights and Behind the Scenes, 1870; The Mimic World, 1871. *Novels:* Château Frissac, 1865; They Met By Chance, 1873.

About: Brown, T. A. History of the American Stage; Daly, J. F. The Life of Augustin Daly.

LONGFELLOW, HENRY WADSWORTH (February 27, 1807-March 24, 1882), poet, was born in Portland, Maine, the second child of Stephen Longfellow, attorney, member of Congress, president of the Maine Historical Society, and a trustee of Bowdoin College in Brunswick; and of Zilpah (Wadsworth) Longfellow, a typical Victorian lady—though pre-Victorian in time—given to admiration of music, poetry, and painting, and to chronic neurasthenia.

Except for a few months in a public school, Longfellow was educated privately, for the most part at the Portland Academy from 1813 to 1821. He then entered Bowdoin as a sophomore, and was graduated fourth in his class, in 1825. He was already published, his first poem having appeared in the Portland *Gazette of Maine* in 1820, followed by many others during his college years. As a senior he wrote to his father "I most eagerly aspire after future eminence in literature"; his exact course was consciously mapped from the beginning. It was a little deflected when he was offered a projected chair in modern languages at Bowdoin if he would first study in Europe. He spent 1826 to 1829 in France, Spain, Italy and Germany, eagerly absorbing the culture which was to mould his style and the life which was to influence his subjects. He returned to find himself offered a meager instructorship instead of the promised position as professor; this he indignantly declined and the chair was finally created for him at $900 a year, with an additional $100 for serving as librarian.

Longfellow remained at Bowdoin until 1835. He prepared text-books in languages and translated the texts; he contributed essays and sketches to the newly founded *North American Review*; but it was not until his last year in Brunswick that his first book of poems, *Voices of the Night,* appeared. In 1831 he married Mary Storer Potter, a Portland beauty. Then came the offer which was to establish him permanently as an American institution; George Ticknor had resigned as Smith professor of modern languages and belles-lettres at Harvard, and Longfellow was appointed as his successor.

He went abroad again at once to improve his knowledge of German and the Scandinavian tongues; and at Rotterdam his wife died in childbirth. The bereaved widower buried himself in his studies, and in Switzerland a further alleviation of his grief came with his first meeting with Frances Elizabeth Appleton, a statuesque American girl of culture and charm, the heroine of his novel *Hyperion* and destined to be his second wife. By the end of 1836 he had returned to America and was teaching in Harvard.

In 1842 and 1843 he was abroad again, and in the latter year he and Miss Appleton were married. Her father bought as their wedding present Craigie House, in Cambridge, once Washington's headquarters, where Longfellow had been living. Their summers they spent in Nahant. Two sons (later an army officer and a painter respectively) and three daughters ("grave Alice, and laughing [Annie] Allegra, and Edith with golden hair") were born to them. Gradually, as Longfellow's fame grew, he became the close associate of all the famous New Englanders of the time, Lowell and Hawthorne being perhaps the nearest to him. He wrote prolifically, and his poems were making him rich—the gamut runs from $15 for "The Skeleton in Armor" to $3000 for "The Hanging of the Crane," a far inferior poem. It was a gracious, full, contented life, utterly unlike the painful existences of most poets.

Longfellow was a conscientious teacher, and the necessary withdrawal of his time and strength from writing to teaching grew onerous. In 1854 he resigned in favor of Lowell. And then, in 1861, the placidity was shattered by a shocking tragedy; his wife, in using a match to melt sealing-wax, set fire to her flimsy dress and was burned to death. He himself was badly burned in trying to rescue her. There is no doubt that the agony of this appalling loss never entirely deserted his heart, though little of its passion entered his work. With five small motherless children to care for, he tried for a while to lose himself in the more mechanical pursuit of translation. His conscientious, though too stiff and literal, version of Dante's *Divine Comedy* was the fruit of the first bitter years after 1861.

The more than two decades remaining to him were only a story of ever-growing fame, which had become world-wide. In 1868 he made his last trip to Europe and was honored by an LL.D. from Cambridge and a D.C.L. from Oxford. Every English and Continental celebrity was delighted to be his acquaintance. His poems were translated

Collection of Frederick H. Meserve
HENRY WADSWORTH LONGFELLOW
in middle life

into a score of languages. Within, he grew more and more lonely, but outwardly his calm cheerfulness was unruffled. What was happening to his real self, however, became apparent when in 1881 he was attacked by vertigo, followed by nervous prostration from which he never really recovered. His death, which was sudden, was caused by peritonitis. He was buried in Mt. Auburn Cemetery in Cambridge. It was at his funeral that the failing Emerson murmured his classic epitaph: "This gentleman was a sweet, beautiful soul, but I have entirely forgotten his name." (Gamaliel Bradford remarks of the incident that, though Emerson's memory was faulty, "his spiritual insight was as keen as ever.") Two years later his bust was placed in the Poets' Corner at Westminster Abbey; he is the only American ever to have been thus honored.

This life, save for its one horror and the few softer griefs which touch all humanity, was of singular and almost unmatched prosperity, the perfect expression of the finest flower of its age and place. The Longfellow cult rose with the years; his friends outvied one another in almost fulsome adulation. Gentle, sweet, pure, benign—these are the adjectives always coupled with his name; the patriarchal white beard, the face which Kingsley called "the mirror of his harmonious and lovely mind," were as well known to all literate Americans as the face of Washington or Lincoln. Yet under all this sweetness and modesty—which were quite actual—was the son of the neurasthenic Zilpah Longfellow, whose nervous sensitivity was so acute that beauty roused in him an almost pathological excitement, and he shrank like a mimosa from a touch of harsh reality. Only slavery aroused his public interest, and that thinly and without emotion. He was a Cambridge Unitarian of the mid-nineteenth century, with all that that implies; but inside the carefully modeled, rosy wax figure was a romantic and a sensitive who never found his own voice. He could be severe and stern on occasion, too, but only rarely, for it took much provocation to arouse passions so thoroughly buried. It seems extreme and perhaps ridiculous to think of Longfellow as a frustrated poet, but that he really was, thanks to the ease of his life's pathway and the swaddling-clothes provided by his highly articulate and adoring friends. Only two dissenting voices cut the unvarying paean of praise in his lifetime—and who would pay attention to the acid comments of that sour blue-stocking, Margaret Fuller, or the rapier-nicks of that dissolute, needy failure, Edgar Allan Poe?

Instead, to Bryant, Longfellow was all "exquisite music" and "creative power"; to Motley he was "musical as is Apollo's lute"; to Prescott his were "the best imaginative poems since *The Ancient Mariner*." English critics swelled the strain with words and phrases like "melody," "feeling," "pathos," "exquisite simplicity of expression," "sweet and limpid purity," "thoroughly original conception and treatment." It would have taken a wilder and sterner genius than Longfellow's to have withstood such folds upon folds of adulatory cotton wadding.

Not that he did not deserve some of these encomiums, though others are absurdly out of place. He did have melody and sweetness and a pure clarity of expression; he had genuine dramatic power in his ballads, deep sympathy, a charm in his purely sensuous images that resembles Keats diluted by Goldsmith. His sonnets are very fine, and have never been rightly appreciated because those who could have found most in them have been repelled from reading him by his other poems. He has been done a great disservice by being thrust down the throats of reluctant American school children, and he himself was so poor a self-critic that he thought his sugary *Evangeline* his greatest work. With his chivalrous Indians like so many knights of a Tennysonian King Arthur, his Chateaubriandish Hiawatha, his Miles Standish a picturesque soldier surrounded by charmingly tinted Puritans, all his characters in the narrative poems, pleasing as they are, suspiciously resemble Longfellow as Indian, Longfellow as Pilgrim Father, Longfellow as Village Blacksmith, as captain of the "Hesperus," and as Spanish Student. Decorum, excessive moderation, and a bald didacticism that sometimes descends into downright foolish bathos; a lack of imaginative passion or the instinct of rebellion: all these have reduced him, in much of his writing, from a true poet to a cultural influence. Herbert Gorman is unfair as well as unkind in calling him "not, perhaps, an American Tennyson, but, in some ways, an American Victoria." As a matter of fact, in his best work he does resemble Tennyson, since both of them were Keats seen through a Victorian veil.

His prose, except for its antiquarian interest, is unimportant. Primarily Longfellow was a poet, and it is as a poet that he must be judged. Van Wyck Brooks compared his soul to a lake, clear, calm, and cool, with buried cities in its depths. Perhaps shrewd, sonorous old Walt Whitman said the last word on him: "He is the poet of the mellow twilight of the past; . . . poet of all sympathetic gentleness, and universal poet of . . . young people."

PRINCIPAL WORKS: Outre-Mer (essays) 1835; Hyperion: A Romance, 1839; Voices of the Night, 1839; Ballads and Other Poems, 1842; Poems on Slavery, 1842; The Spanish Student: A Play in Three Acts, 1843; Poems, 1845; The Belfry of Bruges and Other Poems, 1846; The Poets and Poetry of Europe, 1846; Evangeline, 1847; Kavanagh: A Tale, 1849; The Seaside and the Fireside, 1850; The Golden Legend, 1851; The Song of Hiawatha, 1855; Prose Works, 1857; The Courtship of Miles Standish and Other Poems, 1858; The New England Tragedy (prose) 1860; Tales of a Wayside Inn, 1863; The Divine Comedy of Dante Alighieri (translated) 1865-67; Flower-de-Luce, 1867; The New England Tragedies (verse) 1868; The Divine Tragedy, 1871 (with The Golden Legend and The New England Tragedies as Christus: A Mystery, 1872); Three Books of Song, 1872; Aftermath, 1873; The Hanging of the Crane, 1874; The Masque of Pandora and Other Poems, 1875; Keramos and Other Poems, 1878; Ultima Thule, 1880; In the Harbor: Ultima Thule: Part II, 1882; Michael Angelo, 1883.

ABOUT: Austin, G. L. Henry Wadsworth Longfellow: His Life, His Works, His Friendships; Brooks, Van W. The Flowering of New England; Carpenter, G. F. Henry Wadsworth Longfellow; Gorman, H. S. A Victorian American: Henry Wadsworth Longfellow; Hatfield, J. T. New Light on Longfellow; Higginson, T. W. Henry Wadsworth Longfellow; Livingston, L. S. Bibliography of the Writings of Henry Wadsworth Longfellow; Long, O. W. Literary Pioneers; Longfellow, E. W. Random Memories; Longfellow, S. Life of Henry Wadsworth Longfellow; Robertson, E. S. Life and Writings of Henry Wadsworth Longfellow; Saintsbury, G. E. B. Prefaces and Essays; Skinner, H. C. D. An Echo From Parnassus; Smeaton, W. H. O. Longfellow and His Poetry; Trent, W. P. Longfellow and Other Essays; Underwood, F. H. Lif of Henry Wadsworth Longfellow; Winter, W. Old Friends; Atlantic Monthly January 1859, June 1882, March 1907; Harper's Magazine February and April 1903; North American Review March 1907.

LONGFELLOW, SAMUEL (June 18, 1819-October 3, 1892), clergyman, poet, and philosopher, was born in Portland, Maine, son of Stephen and Zilpah (Wadsworth) Longfellow and much younger brother of Henry Wadsworth Longfellow [*q.v.*]. As a child he read a number of imaginative books and spent much of his time sketching and botanizing the beauty of his seashore home. From Portland Academy he went to Harvard in 1835. Four years later he taught for a while in Elkridge, Md., and, returning to Cambridge, became a college proctor and tutored boys for college entrance.

He entered Harvard Divinity School in 1842. With O. B. Frothingham, T. W. Higginson, and others, he became absorbed in Transcendentalism: from the pulpit of Theodore Parker, from the blackboard of Convers Francis, and from the books of Emerson, Carlyle, and Victor Cousins. After a year's absence—for his health—in the Azores, he returned (1844) to the Divinity School and clarified and strengthened his dogma-free theistic convictions. He had temporary charges at West Cambridge and at Washington, D.C., and was ordained Unitarian minister in Fall River, Mass., in 1848. Despite apparent success he withdrew in 1851 and after a year in France and England as companion and tutor he accepted a call, in 1853, from the Second Unitarian Church in Brooklyn, N.Y. Here he exalted the ceremony of worship and made several innovations in the orders of service: he firmly believed that the Church should have social and cultural functions and objectives as well as the more obvious religious ones. Poor health and a murmuring protest against some of his "radical" points of view hastened his resignation in June 1860. He traveled in Europe two years, returned to Cambridge to preach to Theodore Parker's congregation, made two trips abroad and then took a Unitarian pastorate (1878) in Germantown, Pa. In 1882 he retired to Cambridge to write.

Longfellow edited two books of hymns, one of which was a collaboration; a third anthology was published posthumously. With T. W. Higginson he prepared a volume of verse, *Thalatta: A Book for the Seaside*; and in 1886 came his two-volume biography of his brother, *Life of Henry Wadsworth Longfellow,* with a sequel *Final Memorials of Henry Wadsworth Longfellow,* a year later. He had the logic and the discrimination of a clear thinker, and was, perhaps, one of the most systematic of the Transcendentalists; his hymns have retained a certain amount of their original freshness and strength.

Principal Works: Thalatta: A Book for the Seaside, 1853; A Book of Hymns and Tunes, 1860; Hymns of the Spirit, 1864; Life of Henry Wadsworth Longfellow, 1886; Final Memorials of Henry Wadsworth Longfellow.

About: Frothingham, O. B. Transcendentalism in New England: A History; May, J. Samuel Longfellow: Memoir and Letters; New England Magazine October 1894; Daily Eastern Argus (Portland) October 4, 1892.

LONGSTREET, AUGUSTUS BALDWIN (September 22, 1790-July 9, 1870), July 9, 1870), humorist, jurist, and educator, who sometimes wrote over the signature "Timothy Crabshaw," was born in Augusta, Ga., the son of William Longstreet, an inventor, and Hannah (Randolph) Longstreet. As a small boy he disliked study in any form, but in his late teens while a student at Dr. Moses Waddel's academy in Willington, S.C., he became more friendly towards his books and in 1811 entered Yale. Finishing his course there in 1813, he enrolled in the Litchfield (Conn.) Law School. Late in the following year he returned to Georgia and about two years afterwards married Frances Eliza Parke, a wealthy young lady from Greensboro, where Longstreet had acquired an enviable law practice. He served in the state legislature (1821) and from 1822-25 was judge of the superior court.

From an engraving by J. C. Buttre
AUGUSTUS B. LONGSTREET

The death of his eldest child not only converted him from a vague skepticism to a devout Methodism but temporarily sapped his political ambition.

In 1827 he returned to Augusta and there began his "Georgia Scenes," which appeared first in the Milledgeville (Ga.) *Southern Recorder* and then in his own paper, the Augusta *State Rights Sentinel*; but not until their second publication in book form, in 1840, were they issued under the author's real name. Longstreet stated in the preface that the design of the book had been "wholly misapprehended," that they were not "a mere collection of fancy sketches with no higher object than . . . entertainment" but that they were intended to supply "a chasm in history which has been overlooked—the manners, customs . . wit, dialect, as they appear in all grades of society . . . there is scarcely one word which is not strictly *Georgian*. . ." The book was extremely well received and was perhaps never equaled by either his later sketches or by his novel *Master William Mitten*.

In the *State Rights Sentinel*, which he established in 1834 and edited until 1836, he strongly advocated nullification; but with the disappearance of all hope in this regard he became a Methodist minister and was made president of the newly-founded Emory College, in Oxford, Ga. His *Letters on the Epistle of Paul to Philemon: or, The Connection of Apostolic Christianity With Slavery* was the outcome of a disagreement, within the Methodist denomination, as to the propriety of slave ownership among its bishops; Longstreet upheld the traditionally Southern point of view, that of the secessionist-to-be. On the same subject was *A Voice From the South*, published two years later. Longstreet withdrew (but only briefly) from public life when his *Letters From President Longstreet to the Know-Nothing Preachers of the Methodist Church South* (1855) occasioned very uncomfortable protests. He was elected successively to the presidency of Centenary College in 1849; the University of Mississippi that same year; and the University of South Carolina in 1857.

Like J. J. Hooper, Sol Smith, and other "funny fellows" of the Southwest, Longstreet had been a lawyer, and, riding the circuit, he had collected an astounding stock of frenzied "tall tales." However, he was the first of the group and, naturally, sought out some kind of model—the *Georgia Scenes* are full of Addisonian techniques and plainly belong in the *Spectator* tradition. He had a very noticeable influence on his direct successors, and innumerable passages in the writings of Mark Twain bear an astonishing likeness to portions of the earlier "Cracker" wit.

Principal Works: Georgia Scenes, 1835; Letters on the Epistle of Paul to Philemon: or, The Connection of Apostolic Christianity With Slavery, 1845; A Voice From the South, 1847; Letters From President Longstreet to the Know-Nothing Preachers of the Methodist Church South, 1855.

About: Blair, W. Native American Humor; Wade, J. D. Augustus Baldwin Longstreet; Nineteenth Century (Charleston) February, August, October 1870.

LORD, JOHN (December 27, 1810-December 15, 1894), historical lecturer, was born in Portsmouth, N.H., the son of John Perkins Lord and Sophia (Ladd) Lord, and a descendant of the English Nathan Lord who settled at Kittery, Maine, in 1652. He was graduated in 1833 from Dartmouth College, where his uncle, Nathan Lord [*q.v.*], was president, and from Andover Theological Seminary four years later, supporting himself by teaching during part of his schooling. He married twice, both of his wives being English. About 1854 he established his home in Stamford, Conn., where he died.

His first public speaking was a self-initiated lecture tour in New York State on the subject the "Dark Ages" during his Andover student days. The tour lasted several months, with varying success. A trial of the ministry at New Marlboro, Mass., and Utica, N.Y., convinced him that he was unsuited to that work, and from 1840 he cast his lot as an historical lecturer. Two speaking tours abroad, from 1843 to 1846 and from 1852 to 1854 helped to establish his increasing popularity and success. Altogether he delivered some six thousand lectures. His eccentricities put him at a disadvantage in single lectures and he preferred to deliver courses. A professor once told him that "he succeeded by neglecting all the rhetorical rules, and that if he had followed them he would have been a failure." His books, some of which were used as textbooks in schools and colleges, were widely read. His major published work, *Beacon Lights of History*, in eight volumes, was largely a rewriting of his lectures and other works.

Principal Works: A Modern History From the Time of Luther to the Fall of Napoleon, 1849; A New History of the United States of America for the Use of Schools, 1858; The Old Roman World, 1867; Ancient States and Empires, 1869; The Life of Emma Willard, 1873; Points of History for Schools and Colleges, 1881; Beacon Lights of History (8 vols.) 1883-1896.

About: Andover Theological Seminary Necrology; Twombly, A. S. The Life of John Lord.

LORD, NATHAN (November 28, 1792-September 9, 1870), Congregational clergyman and college president, was born in South Berwick, Maine, son of John Lord and Mehitabel (Perkins) Lord. Like his nephew, John Lord [*q.v.*], the historical lecturer, he was descended from the early Maine settler, Nathan Lord. He was graduated from Bowdoin College in 1809, taught two years at Phillips Exeter Academy, and in 1815 was graduated from the Andover Theological Seminary, beginning, in the following year, a twelve year pastorate at the Amherst, N.H., Congregational Church. With strong, natural gifts of oratory, he became one of the prominent preachers of the state. In 1821 he was made a trustee of Dartmouth College, and in 1828 became its sixth president. Here he was successful as administrator, executive, and educator, and exercised a deep influence on the student body. He received the degrees of D.D. from Bowdoin College in 1828 and of LL.D. from Dartmouth in 1864.

He wrote numerous sermons, essays, and letters. Strong pro-slavery views, set forth in several published "Letters," led to opposition, and he resigned in 1863 in consequence of a vote of the trustees following the presentation of resolutions presented by a Conference of Congregational Churches. He spent his remaining years in Hanover, an annuity being provided him in recognition of his long service.

Principal Works: A Eulogy on the Honorable John Quincy Adams, 1848; Letter of Inquiry to Ministers of the Gospel of All Denominations on Slavery, 1854; A Northern Presbyter's Second Letter, 1855; A Letter to J. M. Conrad, Esq., on Slavery, 1859; A True Picture of Abolition, 1863; The Cherubim and the Flaming Sword, 1864; A Letter to the Alumni of Dartmouth College on Its Hundredth Anniversary, 1869.

About: Lord, C. C. A History of the Descendants of Nathan Lord of Kittery, Me.; Secomb, D. F. History of the Town of Amherst, N.H.; Proceedings of the New Hampshire Historical Society 1903.

LORD, WILLIAM WILBERFORCE (October 28, 1819-April 22, 1917), poet, Civil War chaplain, and Episcopalian clergyman, was born in Madison County, N.Y., the son of the Rev. John Way Lord, a Presbyterian clergyman, and Sarah Bryant (Chase) Lord, first cousin of Chief Justice Salmon P. Chase. From Geneseo (N.Y.) High School he entered the University of Western New York, where he is said to have been graduated in 1837.

W. W. LORD

According to Rufus W. Griswold, poet and literary historian, Lord's health failed him about this time and he was given cabin passage on a whale ship; after three boring months he made his way into forecastle, became a wiry seaman, and is believed to have been captured by cannibals off the African coast and rescued by the very same man-of-war in which Richard Henry Dana, Jr., served his "two years before the mast."

In 1841 Lord entered Auburn (N.Y.) Theological Seminary; two years later he transferred to Princeton Theological Seminary, from which he was graduated in 1845. He was beginning to contribute to *Godey's Lady's Book* and to one or more annuals, over the signature "Tristram Langstaff"; in 1845 also appeared his first book of *Poems*. Press extravaganzas heralded him as "the American Milton," etc., and Wordsworth wrote, in a letter to Bishop Doane,

> I have to thank you for several specimens of the abilities of a young poet, which seem to me of high promise. They are full of deep emotion, and not wanting in vigorous and harmonious expression.

Among Lord's sponsors were several gentlemen who were partisans of the *Knickerbocker Magazine,* which was, at that time, professionally hostile toward Edgar Allan Poe, whose *Raven* Lord had glibly burlesqued ("New Castalia"). Poe unwisely accused Lord of plagiarism and closed his review in the *Broadway Journal* (May 24, 1845) with "Good Lord, deliver us." In all, Poe said much that was unpleasant about Lord, but Lord's only remark about Poe was:

"Poe tried to prove I was not a great poet. It was really a compliment."

During 1845-46 Lord was a fellow at the College of New Jersey and afterwards became a tutor in mental and moral sciences at Amherst. There is conflicting evidence regarding his award of a D.D. degree from the University of Alabama. In 1848 Lord was ordained deacon in the Protestant Episcopal Church and, in 1850, priest. After serving a parish in Somerset County, Md., he went to St. Peter's in Baltimore. He was married February 18, 1851, to Margaret Stockton, by whom he had six children.

Lord was an assistant at St. Ann's in Annapolis before he was made rector (1854) of Christ's Church in Vicksburg, Miss. At the outbreak of the Civil War he retained his pastorate and became also a tireless and able chaplain of the 1st Mississippi brigade of the Confederate army. Much of his property—including an excellent library—was ruined during the siege of Vicksburg. Shortly after the War he became rector of St. Paul's Church, in Charleston, S.C., and in 1871, returning to Vicksburg, he founded the Church of the Holy Trinity. His last years were spent in Cooperstown, N.Y., and he died in New York City in his ninety-eighth year.

It would seem that Lord, after the publication of his first *Poems,* had only occasional literary inclinations. *Christ in Hades,* a religious epic, illustrating "the triumph of moral power over all physical and inferior spiritual force, in the descent of Christ into hell," was "a mythical, heroic, and Christian poem." *André,* an historical narrative in blank verse, in which he allowed himself "only slight poetic freedom," was somewhat thin in dramatic element. *Man, and the Record of his Origin,* one of several of his prose sermons which were separately published, made a strange companion-piece to his serio-comic poem, *The Great Ascidian,* in the same volume.

Lord was decidedly modest, and in 1846, knowing that Griswold was contemplating a sketch of him in the forthcoming *Poets and Poetry of America,* he asked that it be short, for—

> It is not the least among the misfortunes in a young author that while it is still doubtful whether he can make good his title to fame he loses his right to obscurity.

Lord was rescued, at least temporarily, from oblivion by the appearance of *The Complete Poetical Works of W. W. Lord* in 1938, twenty-one years after his death.

Principal Works: Poems, 1845; Christ in Hades, 1851; André, 1856; The Limits of Ritualism in the Protestant Episcopal Church, 1872; Man and the Record of His Origin, 1881; The Complete Poetical Works of W. W. Lord, 1938.

About: Allen, H. Israfel; Lord, W. W. The Complete Poetical Works of W. W. Lord (see Introduction by Thomas Ollive Mabbott); Harper's Magazine December 1908; Harper's Magazine February 1910.

LORING, FREDERICK WADSWORTH (December 12, 1848-November 5, 1871), journalist, was born in Boston, Mass., the son of David Loring, a cabinet maker descended from the Deacon Thomas Loring who came from Devonshire, England, to Massachusetts in 1654. His mother, Mary Hall (Stodder) Loring, to whom he was strongly attached, died when he was eleven. At Harvard, which he entered in 1866, he was enriched by the friendship of Prof. Elbridge J. Cutler and the poet James Russell Lowell. He was only twenty-two when he was asked to join, as the representative of *Appleton's Journal,* the United States expedition under Lieut. George M. Wheeler, which was about to explore Arizona. After undergoing many dangers and privations, he was finally homeward bound when the stage coach was attacked by Apache Indians about ten miles from Wickenburg, Ariz. Loring and all but two of his companions were massacred.

Loring early showed unusual literary talent, and the English novelist Charles Reade is said to have remarked that Loring seemed to him the most promising of the young authors of America. At college he contributed to the *Harvard Advocate,* wrote verse, and completed a drama, *Wild Rose,* which was successfully produced in Boston by George Selwyn. After graduating he was editorially connected with the *Saturday Evening Gazette,* and later with the Boston *Daily Advertiser* and *Every Saturday,* at the same time contributing short stories and verses to the *Atlantic Monthly,* the *Independent, Appleton's Journal,* and the New York *World. Old and New* first carried as a serial his story *Two College Friends.* On his last expedition he sent back light, humorous, and entertaining reports of his experiences, among the titles of which were "Je Horge," touching the Chinese at San Francisco, "A Council of War," "A Glimpse of Mormonism," "Silver Mining in Nevada," and "The Valley of Death."

Principal Works: Wild Rose; Cotton Cultivation in the South (with C. F. Atkinson) 1869; The Boston Dip and Other Verses, 1871.

About: Farish, T. E. History of Arizona; Appleton's Journal December 9, 1871.

LOSSING, BENSON JOHN (February 12, 1813-June 3, 1891), historian, editor, and wood-engraver, was born at Beekman, Dutchess County, N.Y., son of John Lossing, a farmer, and Miriam (Dorland) Lossing. He was descended from Pietre Pieterse Lassingh, a Dutchman who settled in Albany about 1658. Benson's father and mother died when he was a child, and his formal education was limited to three years at a district school. During his apprenticeship to a watchmaker at Poughkeepsie he read a number of history books, and over a period of several years pursued an independent study. At the age of twenty-two he was made joint editor and proprietor of the Poughkeepsie *Telegraph,* Dutchess County's official Democratic journal; and when he became joint editor of the Poughkeepsie *Casket,* a literary fortnightly, he began to learn the art of engraving on wood from J. A. Adams, illustrator for this paper.

He went to New York in 1838 and in 1839 began two years of editing and illustrating for J. S. Redfield's *Family Magazine.* His *Outline History of the Fine Arts,* prepared largely during spare moments, was published in 1840 as one of Harper's Family Library. For the *Pictorial Field Book of the American Revolution* (1850-52) Lossing traveled more than eight thousand miles in the United States and Canada, collecting information and dashing off hasty sketches from which he afterwards made block drawings for engravings. Harper & Bros. had advanced him the funds for this enterprise; the book was issued first in parts and later in two large octavo volumes. During the thirty-five years that followed, Lossing published prolifically, and in all was either author or editor of more than forty titles. Among them were two more of the pictorial series, covering the War of 1812 and the Civil War. From 1872 to 1874 he was an able editor of the *American Historical Record and Repertory of Notes and Queries.* Lossing was twice married: in June 1833 to Alice Barritt; and during the year after her death, to Helen Sweet.

The fact that Lossing's *Pictorial Field Book of the American Revolution* is still interesting to the layman and authoritatively valuable to the antiquarian would seem to make its author more than a mere popularizer of American history.

Principal Works: Outline History of the Fine Arts, 1840; Pictorial Field Book of the Revolution, 1850-52; Our Countrymen. . ., 1855; Pictorial Field Book of the War of 1812, 1868; Pictorial History of the Civil War, 1866-68; A Memorial of Alexander Anderson, M. D., 1872; Biography of James A. Garfield, 1822.

About: Proceedings of the Worcester Society of Antiquity, 1891; American Ancestry: Vol. 3; New York Daily Tribune June 4, 1891.

"LOTHROP, AMY." See WARNER, ANNA BARTLETT

LOTHROP, HARRIETT MULFORD (STONE) ("Margaret Sidney") (June 22, 1844-August 2, 1924), writer of stories for children, was born in New Haven, Conn., the daughter of Sidney Mason Stone, one of the city's first architects, and Harriett (Mulford) Stone. She was graduated from the Grove Hall School in New Haven, and although she appeared to have considerable talent as a writer she failed to attract any attention until 1878, when she became a contributor to *Wide Awake.* Two years later this magazine began the serial publication of that perennial children's favorite, *Five Little Peppers and How They Grew,* of which more than two million copies had been sold at the time of her death. Several books unfolding the narrative of the Pepper family were issued subsequently, but although they were written with the same ease, simplicity, and happy sympathy they never achieved the popularity of the first book.

In 1881 she was married to Daniel Lothrop, publisher, who had taken a strong fancy to some of her early works, and whose firm, D. Lothrop & Company, was obviously strengthened in its own specialty, children's

Harris & Ewing

HARRIETT MULFORD LOTHROP
("Margaret Sidney")

books, by the publication both in book and magazine form of her countless poems and tales.

From 1882 until Mr. Lothrop's death in 1892 they lived at "Wayside," Hawthorne's old home in Concord. Mrs. Lothrop afterwards bought a neighboring estate and during her last years she wrote a few more books for boys and girls. Becoming very much interested in patriotic societies, she founded the Old Concord chapter of the Daughters of the American Revolution and the Old North Bridge Society of the Children of the American Revolution, of which she was active president until 1901.

Although her books were overstocked with didacticism and bore evidence of worked-over materials, the pleasant simplicity of their homely narrative places them in that rather undefined province of "children's classics."

Principal Works: Five Little Peppers, 1881; So As By Fire, 1881; The Pettibone Name: A New England Story, 1882; Hester and Other New England Stories, 1886; A New Departure for Girls, 1886; Dilly and the Captain, 1887; How Tom and Dorothy Made and Kept a Christian Home, 1888; Rob: A Story for Boys, 1891; A Little Maid of Concord Town, 1898; The Judges' Cave, 1900; Sally, Mrs. Tubbs, 1903; A Little Maid From Boston Town, 1910.

About: Swayne, J. L. The Story of Concord Told by Concord Writers; Daughters of the American Revolution Magazine September 1924; Publishers' Weekly August 9, 1924; Boston Transcript August 4, 1924.

LOUNSBURY, THOMAS RAYNESFORD (January 1, 1838-April 9, 1915), scholar and critic, was born in Ovid, N.Y., the son of the Rev. Thomas Lounsbury, a Presbyterian minister, and Mary Janette (Woodward) Lounsbury, daughter of a major in the American Revolution. He was prepared at Ovid Academy for Yale, from which he received his B.A. in 1859 (M.A. 1877). During his undergraduate years he received numerous prizes for English composition and was one of the editors of the *Yale Literary Magazine*. After a brief period in his father's rural home, he went to New York, where he was engaged on the staff of *Appletons' Cyclopaedia*.

The Civil War tore him from this peaceful occupation. He enlisted in 1862 as first lieutenant in the 126th New York Volunteers, was one of the soldiers surrendered to "Stonewall" Jackson at Harper's Ferry, was exchanged, went through the battle of Gettysburg, and in 1863 was stationed at Elmira, N.Y., as adjutant-general of the draft rendezvous. Here he remained until mustered out at the end of the war.

THOMAS RAYNESFORD LOUNSBURY

He then for the first time turned to teaching, first in Lespinasse's French Institute in New York, where he taught Latin and Greek, then as a private tutor in Milburn, N.J. It was during this period that Lounsbury became a serious student of Early and Middle English, his special subjects in later years. In 1870 Yale called him to the newly established Sheffield Scientific School as instructor of English; the next year he became professor of the English language and literature, and so remained until 1906, when he retired and was made professor emeritus. He was also librarian of the Sheffield Scientific School from 1873 to 1896.

In 1871 Lounsbury married, his wife being Jennie D. Folwell. They had one son. His history thereafter was entirely that of a conscientious teacher, scholar, and writer. He was one of the original members of the American Academy of Arts and Letters, and a fellow of the American Academy of Arts and Sciences. He received LL.D. degrees from Yale, Harvard, and Aberdeen, and L.H.D.'s from Princeton and Lafayette. From 1907 he was president of the Simplified Spelling Board. Besides his original works of research he edited Chaucer's minor poems and the works of Charles Dudley Warner; in 1912 he edited an anthology, the *Yale Book of American Verse*. He was still writing and lecturing, if no longer teaching, when he died suddenly, a cigar between his fingers, as he was chatting with a friend.

Lounsbury was a really great scholar—"one of the rarest of his generation," Burton J. Hendrick calls him—but he was no pedant.

A burly, vigorous man with sandy hair and full beard, the tennis champion of the university, he suggested the old soldier rather than the professor. His style was copious, pungent, and as vigorous as himself; even his textbooks were interesting, particularly his *History of the English Language,* which Brander Matthews called with justice "a little masterpiece." His book on Tennyson was left unfinished at his death, and was later completed and edited by Wilbur L. Cross.

PRINCIPAL WORKS: History of the English Language, 1879; James Fenimore Cooper, 1882; Studies in Chaucer (3 vols.) 1891; Shakespeare as a Dramatic Artist, 1901; Shakespeare and Voltaire, 1902; The Standard of Pronunciation in English, 1904; The Text of Shakespeare, 1906; The Standard of Usage in English, 1908; English Spelling and Spelling Reform, 1909; The Early Literary Career of Robert Browning, 1911; The Life and Times of Tennyson From 1809 to 1850, 1915.

ABOUT: Century Magazine February 1898; Critic March 1903; Proceedings American Academy of Arts and Letters 1916; Proceedings American Academy of Arts and Sciences September 1918; Yale Alumni Weekly April 30, 1915; New York Times April 10, 1915.

LOVEJOY, ELIJAH PARISH (November 9, 1802-November 7, 1837), editor and "martyr abolitionist," was born at Albion, Maine, son of a clergyman, Rev. Daniel Lovejoy, and Elizabeth (Pattee) Lovejoy. After his graduation from Colby (then Waterville) College in 1826 he taught school, set out for Missouri, and became editor of a Whig journal in St. Louis. In 1832 he returned to the East to study for the ministry; he was licensed to preach; in 1833 he went back to St. Louis as editor of the St. Louis *Observer,* a Presbyterian weekly. His war against "popery" and intemperance was well supported, but public protest against his abolitionist sentiment shortly became bedlam, and Lovejoy soon went twenty-five miles up the river to the prosperous city of Alton, Ill., and there set up the Alton *Observer.*

Already Lovejoy was becoming less sympathetic with the doctrine of gradual emancipation, which the Altonians upheld, than with a more immediate program, *i.e.,* complete "abolitionism." The dumping of his press, which had been left unguarded on the wharf over the Sabbath, was only the first of a long series of such episodes; each time, however, the Ohio Anti-Slavery Society provided him with another. By November 7, 1838 the situation had become crucial. Following the arrival of a new press, which had been placed in a warehouse under armed guard, Lovejoy, having announced himself quite ready for martyrdom, rushed out to prevent one of a mob from setting fire to the building, and was shot dead.

Lovejoy appeared to regard his *Observer* as essentially a religious organ, but he could not keep from expressing his political and social philosophy in its columns, in editorials, in proposed resolutions, and in citations from the letters of fellow agitators. Not an "author" in today's meaning of the word, Lovejoy nevertheless symbolizes a phase of American journalism that was a definite part of the "literature" of its time.

ABOUT: Beecher, E. Narrative of the Riots at Alton; Lovejoy, J. C. and Owen Memoir of the Rev. Elijah P. Lovejoy; Tanner, H. The Alton Trials; Alton Observer 1836-1837; Philanthropist 1836-1838.

LOWELL, EDWARD JACKSON (October 18, 1845-May 11, 1894), historian, was born in Boston, the son of Francis Cabot Lowell and Mary Lowell (Gardner) Lowell. At the age of nine he was taken abroad to attend Sillig's school at Bellerive, Switzerland; from E. S. Dixwell's (Boston) Latin school he went to Harvard, and was graduated in 1867. The following year he was married to Mary Wolcott Goodrich, daughter of Samuel Griswold Goodrich, better known as "Peter Parley." Lowell made an assay at business, and then studied law; he was admitted to the bar in 1872 and with Brooks Adams practiced law until the time of his wife's death in 1874, when he turned his complete attention to his children and to study. Three years later he was married to Elizabeth Gilbert Jones, daughter of George Jones, one of the founders of the New York *Times.*

He went abroad in 1879 and gathered materials from the German archives for a series of letters on German mercenaries used by Great Britain during the Revolution; these appeared first in the New York *Times,* 1880-81, and were afterwards incorporated into *The Hessians and the Other German Auxiliaries of Great Britain in the Revolutionary War.* For Justin Winsor's *Narrative and Critical History of America* Lowell wrote the chapter on "The United States of America, 1775-1782: Their Political Struggles and Relations with Europe." He abandoned work on a biography of Lafayette in order to concentrate on the preparation of his open-minded, socio-historical *Eve of the French Revolution,* of which his brief was: the uprising came not from France's want of social prosperity but from her consciousness "that her government did not correspond to her degree of civilization." He made a later study of the influence of the French revolution on other countries; this was never completed.

Lowell was for several years treasurer of the American School of Classical Studies at Athens. He has been accredited with "strong social instincts" and a "quick and comprehensive sympathy." His achievements as an historian were neither extensive nor extraordinary but have an obvious value within their limited fields.

Principal Works: The Hessians and the Other German Auxiliaries of Great Britain in the Revolutionary War, 1884; The Eve of the French Revolution, 1892.

About: Proceedings of the Massachusetts Historical Society: 2 ser., Vol. 9; Harvard College Class of 1867: Secretary's Report No. 10; Boston Transcript May 12 and 15, 1894.

LOWELL, JAMES RUSSELL (February 22, 1819-August 12, 1891), poet and critic, was born in "Elmwood," on the outskirts of Cambridge, Mass., the youngest of the five children of the Rev. Charles Lowell, pastor of the West Unitarian Church of Boston, and Harriet Brackett (Spence) Lowell, a poetic, mystically minded woman whose last years were spent in mental aberration. It was from his first cousin that Amy Lowell the poet and Percival Lowell the astronomer were directly descended.

After preparation at a boarding school, Lowell entered Harvard, from which he received his B.A. in 1838, LL.B. 1840, and M.A. 1841. His career, however, was not so distinguished as these degrees might indicate; as a matter of fact, he was "rusticated" to Concord in his senior year because of inattention to his studies and a little undue hilarity in chapel, and in consequence could not read his own class poem. In 1837 and 1838 he had edited *Harvardiana* and contributed some poems to it. At first, however, he intended to be an attorney and was admitted to the bar; but a year in an office without clients brought a close to that. It was an unhappy period for the young man; an unrequited love affair even brought him near to suicide; an attempt at establishing, with Robert Carter, a magazine—*The Pioneer*—resulted in failure after two numbers, though such distinguished names as those of Hawthorne, Whittier, Poe, and the future Mrs. Browning were on his contributors' list.

In 1844 his youthful sorrows came to an end with his marriage to Maria White, one of Margaret Fuller's disciples, herself a poet and an ardent abolitionist. In his class poem Lowell had ridiculed abolition along with all other progressive movements; but now, with his quick impressionability, he wrote fervidly against slavery in the *Liberty Bell* and the *Pennsylvania Freeman,* and became corresponding editor of the New York *Anti-Slavery Standard.* The logical climax of this phase of his career was the appearance in the Boston *Courier* of the first of the famous *Biglow Papers,* those keen, ardent, bitter satires on the Southern slave-holders and their British sympathizers, couched in Yankee dialect.

They appeared in book form in 1848, the year in which he produced four volumes, including the anonymous *Fable for Critics* and *The Vision of Sir Launfal.* Meanwhile he was pouring out prose and verse for the *Dial,* the *Democratic Review,* the *Massachusetts Quarterly,* and *Putnam's.* In 1851 and 1852 he traveled in Europe, chiefly for the health of his wife, long an invalid after the birth of four children and the death in infancy of three of them. The trip was of no avail; she died in 1853.

In 1854 Lowell was offered the Smith professorship of modern languages and belles lettres at Harvard, just vacated by Longfellow. His acceptance was predicated on another European journey to perfect his linguistic knowledge. Nominally he was professor until 1886, and thereafter was professor emeritus, but actually he did little teaching after 1876, when his political career began. In 1863 and 1864 he served also as university lecturer.

While he was abroad this second time, Lowell had left his daughter, his only surviving child, in the care of a governess, Frances Dunlap, who was a niece of the governor of Maine. In 1857 he and Miss Dunlap were married. There were no children from this second marriage. She died in 1885, in London, while he was minister to the Court of St. James.

In addition to his duties as professor, and his constant production as a writer, Lowell now became an editor as well. When the *Atlantic Monthly* was founded in 1857 he became its first editor, and it was under his aegis that it gained the high position which made it a New England institution, a position some shadow of which still remains. In 1862 he resigned, but two years later he was associated with Charles Eliot Norton as editor of the *North American Review,* and this office he held until 1872.

Since 1852 Lowell had been an active Republican, and though he sought no political office he was a presidential elector in 1876. There he stood firm for Hayes against Tilden, and when Hayes became president, in 1877, he rewarded Lowell by appointment as minister to Spain. Unexpectedly, Lowell

Collection of Frederick H. Meserve
JAMES RUSSELL LOWELL

turned out to have diplomatic gifts, and he carried on not unworthily the tradition of Washington Irving in Madrid. In 1880 he was transferred to London—a rather delicate appointment in view of some of his earlier pronouncements against the English. However, Lowell was by now not so much ashamed of Hosea Biglow as embarrassed by his memory; his radical phase had been entirely a reflection of his first wife's influence, and he had long ago reverted to his natural conservatism. He was popular and successful; he was the orator when Coleridge's bust was unveiled at Westminster Abbey, and in 1884 he was made rector of the University of St. Andrew's, in Edinburgh—an honorary absentee office. When the Democrats came back into power, Cleveland recalled him.

Lowell's health had long been precarious, and his most active days were over. He lectured at the Lowell Institute in 1887 on the English dramatists, but for the most part he kept to his study at "Elmwood," or visited his daughter, now Mrs. Burnett, in Southboro. Occasionally he still lectured at Harvard, and he made four more trips to England, where he had left warm friends. Honorary degrees poured in upon him; during his ministry Oxford had conferred a D.C.L. on him and Cambridge an LL.D., and the latter degree came to him also from St. Andrew's, Bologna, and his own Harvard. He was an overseer of Harvard from 1887 to his death, and a member of numerous learned and cultural societies. He edited a series of British poets, writing a brief life of Keats as an introduction to one volume, and he was engaged on a biography of Hawthorne at the time of his death. Prose was now his chief medium; he wrote little poetry, and that little far from his best. He died in "Elmwood," part of which estate was purchased in 1898 by the Lowell Memorial Park Fund and turned into a memorial of its most famous owner.

The keynote to Lowell's character is unsureness and self-consciousness. He was (barring *The Biglow Papers* and his other early anti-slavery poems, fruit of his first marriage) primarily the voice of cultured, conservative, highly literate Cambridge. As derivative and Europeanized as Longfellow, he lacked Longfellow's placid urbanity; he never got over a suspicion of inferiority which placed a perpetual chip on his shoulder. As both critic and poet, though he was no poseur, he posed constantly, following first this model, then that. Yet he had a rich fund of natural talent, if no creative ability. Margaret Fuller, who so often and so unpleasantly (but so accurately) put her finger on her contemporaries' weak spots, spoke of his want of vitality, his stereotyped style, "a copious stream of pleasant sound." Foerster damns him with the faint praise of "accomplished versatility"—he was too spread out, over too many fields, to excel in any one. It is curious to reflect that he never wrote a full book; all his many volumes are made up of collected poems, essays, or lectures. Greenslet remarks that his poetry is at its best when least subjective; it is, in other words, a poetry which echoes other men's voices. He himself was aware of another of his defects; in including himself in the anonymous *Fable for Critics,* he notes that he will never reach the heights unless he "learns the distinction 'twixt singing and preaching."

Yet in one sense Lowell was our first professional man of letters, and certainly he and Poe were our first real critics. He married literature to officialdom, linked poetry and politics, and the match, though not a happy one, produced interesting offspring. In a self-revelatory comment, he says that he had thought of his writing as a "fencing stick," and was surprised to find that it could be used as a weapon. It was so used only in the eager days of his first youth and the accidental radicalism of his first marriage.

Without Tennyson and Byron, without Bryant and even Longfellow, Lowell would scarcely have been a poet. He was clever, intelligent, even scholarly when he settled down to it; he was remarkably facile, and he was truly "accomplished" in the old-fashioned meaning of that word. His most pleasing traits are his robustness (superficial, it is true) and the freshness of his phrasing, though his sentiment is apt to degenerate into sentimentality. He did have a direct feeling for nature—New England nature; he himself burgeoned with the spring and bloomed with the summer, though even in this province he lacked taste.

Lowell was an inveterate punster, occasionally a brilliant one; he could scintillate. Both *The Biglow Papers* and the *Fable for Critics* prove that. Unfortunately his wit sometimes simmered down to a mere jocosity; he treated it as he did the stone columns in the Harvard Yard; when he could not leap one instantly he tried until he could, meanwhile remarking shamefacedly, "I commonly do that the first time." In later years he fancied himself as a pundit; he grew a garrulous bore.

But all this is not to deny that he was an actual force in American letters and a cultural influence of real importance. As Van Wyck Brooks points out, Lowell was "a complicated soul, . . . compact of incongruities." He was rated too highly in his lifetime, but it would be unjust to give him too low a rating now. His earliest work, which he himself came to deprecate, now constitutes, together with the noble *Harvard Commemoration Ode,* his claim on a modest immortality.

Principal Works: *Poetry*—Class Poem, 1838; A Year's Life, 1841; Poems, 1844; A Legend of Brittany and Other Miscellaneous Poems and Sonnets, 1844; Poems; 2d Series, 1848; The Vision of Sir Launfal, 1848; The Biglow Papers, 1848 (2d Series, 1867); A Fable for Critics, 1848; Poems, 1849; Poems, 1854; Ode: Recited at the Commemoration of the Living and Dead Soldiers of Harvard University, 1865; Under the Willows and Other Poems, 1869; The Cathedral, 1870; The Courtin', 1874; Three Memorial Poems, 1877; Heartsease and Rue, 1888; Last Poems, 1895; Four Poems, 1906. *Prose*—Conversations on Some of the Old Poets, 1845; Fireside Travels, 1864; Among My Books, 1870 (2d Series, 1876); My Study Windows, 1871; Democracy and Other Addresses, 1887; Political Essays, 1888; Latest Literary Essays and Addresses, 1891; The Old English Dramatists, 1892; Letters (ed. by C. E. Norton) 1893; Lectures on English Poets, 1897; New Letters (ed. by M. A. DeW. Howe) 1932.

About: Brooks, V. W. The Flowering of New England; Brownell, W. C. American Prose Masters; Foerster, N. American Criticism; Greenslet, F. James Russell Lowell: His Life and Work; Hale, E. E., Jr. James Russell Lowell; Higginson, T. W. Old Cambridge; Hudson, W. H. Lowell and His Poetry; Parrington, V. L. The Romantic Revolution in America; Pollak, G. International Perspective in Criticism; Reilly, J. J. James Russell Lowell as a Critic; Scudder, H. E. James Russell Lowell; Underwood, F. H. The Poet and the Man; Literary World (Boston) June 27, 1885; North American Review February 1919.

LOWELL, ROBERT TRAILL SPENCE (October 8, 1816-September 12, 1891), Protestant Episcopal clergyman and writer of poems and stories, was born in Boston, son of the Rev. Charles Lowell, distinguished Unitarian minister, and Harriet Brackett (Spence) Lowell, and older brother of the poet James Russell Lowell [*q.v.*]. He received his earliest instruction at the Round Hill School in Northampton, Mass., founded by Joseph Green Cogswell, to whom Lowell, many years later, dedicated a book of poems with "love and reverence." After his graduation from Harvard in 1833 he began a medical course but left this to enter a business partnership with his eldest brother. Three years later, however, he went to Schenectady, N.Y., to study for holy orders under Dr. Alonzo Potter, former rector of St. Paul's in Boston.

In 1842 Lowell sailed for Bermuda and, during the year following, was ordained priest and made a domestic chaplain to the bishop. Some time later, at his own request he was transferred to Newfoundland, and at Bay Roberts he served as representative of the English Society for the Propagation of the Gospel. On a journey home he was married (1845) to Mary Ann Duane, by whom he had seven children. After returning again to Newfoundland he came back to the United States in broken health, but worked for the establishment of a mission in a very poor section of Newark, N.J. In Duanesburg, N.Y., he became rector of Christ Church. Nine years later he refused a professorship at Racine (Wis.) College, but the year afterward (1869) he accepted the headmastership of St. Mark's School, Southboro, Mass., and still later he became a professor at Union College, in Schenectady.

Lowell had not only a robust energy for religious enterprises, but a literary sensitivity. The merits of his *New Priest in Conception Bay,* a tale which incorporated some vivid Newfoundland pictures, have, according to some critics, been grossly understated. From his experience as headmaster at St. Mark's came a book for boys, *Antony Brade: A Story of a School*; and from his Schenectady days, *A Story or Two From an Old Dutch Town.* He also wrote *Fresh Hearts That Failed Three Thousand Years Ago: With Other Things*; a volume of *Poems*; short stories, addresses, and sermons. The "Relief of Lucknow," best known of his poems, appeared in the *Atlantic Monthly* for February 1858. Lowell's contribution to the field of letters won for him a small but enviable distinction

PRINCIPAL WORKS: The New Priest in Conception Bay, 1858; Fresh Hearts That Failed Three Thousand Years Ago: With Other Things, 1860; Poems, 1864; Antony Brade: A Story of a School, 1874; A Story or Two From an Old Dutch Town, 1878.

ABOUT: Scudder, H. C. James Russell Lowell: A Biography; Memorials of the Class of 1833 of Harvard College; The Churchman September 19, 1891; Boston Transcript September 14, 1891.

LUCAS, DANIEL BEDINGER (March 16, 1836-July 28, 1909), "poet of the Shenandoah Valley" and jurist, was born at "Rion Hall," near Charles Town in what is now West Virginia. During infancy he had suffered a spinal injury which prevented him from enjoying a normally active boyhood. He read extensively in his father's fine library and was instructed privately by tutors. As a student at the University of Virginia he gained a considerable reputation as an orator; finishing his courses there in 1854 he went to Judge John W. Brockenbrough's law school, Lexington, Va., and was graduated with honors. He set up practice first in Charles Town and then in Richmond. Lucas was physically incapable of serving to the end of the Civil War, but during the last months of the fighting he ran the blockade in defense of John Yates Beall, a classmate, who had been accused of espionage; he was held in the North and at the time of Lee's surrender Lucas published, in Canada, his best-known poem, "The Land Where We Were Dreaming" (also the title of a posthumous collection of his verse).

By temporary statute Lucas was denied resumption of law practice until after 1870; he tried journalism, became co-editor of the Baltimore *Southern Metropolis*, and found a new audience for a few of his own poems. He was married, in 1865, to Lena Tucker Brooke. In 1871 he returned to law, became one of West Virginia's most distinguished practitioners, and enjoyed almost twenty years of moderate political prominence; his last appointment was to the presidency of the Supreme Court of Appeals.

Lucas found some time, however, for writing. *The Wreath of Eglantine*, a volume of poems on which his sister had collaborated, and *Ballads and Madrigals* are perhaps superior to his blank-verse Civil War dramas: *The Maid of Northumberland* (1884), believed to be the first play written in America on this subject; and *Hildebrand* and *Kate McDonald*, both published posthumously. Through them ran his own military experiences, a few spirited speeches, some excellent descriptions of nature, and numerous Shakespearean echoes. His verse was obviously reminiscent of Keats, Tennyson, and Poe, drawing upon nature, love, and the South-and-the-War for its subject matter. Among his prose works were: *The Memoir of John Yates Beall, Nicaragua: War of the Filibusters,* and an unfinished biography of Lincoln.

To Lucas writing was not a profession but a delight, and like many others, he wrote largely on the impetus of an early (though slight) literary triumph and a growing fund of war sentiments.

PRINCIPAL WORKS: The Memoir of John Yates Beall, 1865; The Wreath of Eglantine, 1869; Ballads and Madrigals, 1884; The Maid of Northumberland, 1884; Nicaragua: War of the Filibusters, 1896; The Land Where We Were Dreaming, 1913; Dramatic Works of Daniel Bedinger Lucas, 1913.

ABOUT: Atkinson, G. W. & Gibbens, A. F. Prominent Men of West Virginia; Norris, J. E. History of the Lower Shenandoah Valley.

LUDLOW, FITZ HUGH (September 11, 1836-September 12, 1870), critic and writer of short stories, was born in New York City, son of the Rev. Henry G. Ludlow, a prominent abolitionist, and Abby (Wills) Ludlow. His father supervised most of his early study, and after entering the college of New Jersey as a junior in 1854, he transferred, after the burning of Nassau Hall, to Union College. Ludlow had, for some time been addicted to the narcotic, hashish, and during his senior year *Putnam's Magazine* accepted "The Apocalypse of Hasheesh." He was graduated in 1856 and the year following he published *The Hasheesh Eater,* incorporating much of his earlier account. It was plainly DeQuincey-colored, but endowed with an imaginativeness of his own creation. He taught school for a year; then studied law in New York under William Curtis Noyes, and was admitted to the bar in 1859 but never practiced.

Ludlow joined the staff of the *World,* and later the *Commercial Advertiser*; in 1861 "The Primpenny Family" appeared serially in *Vanity Fair.* During the 'sixties he prepared dramatic, art, and music criticisms for the *Evening Post* and *Home Journal* and contributed to three Harper publications: for the *Monthly* he wrote a very powerful treatise on the opium habit, "What Shall They Do to be Saved?"; for the *Weekly,* "The New Partner in Clingham and Co., Bankers"; and for *Harper's Bazaar,* "The Household Angel," which, in contrast to the otherwise "vapid temperance literature" of the day, was regarded by one critic as "a real work of genius."

In 1863 Ludlow went West, sending back an occasional descriptive article to the *Atlantic Monthly*; these re-appeared later in *The Heart of the Continent*. In San Francisco, at a famous rendezvous of the literati, the office of California's first literary publication, the *Golden Era,* he met Mark Twain, Joaquin Miller, Charles Warren Stoddard, and Artemus Ward. At a time when Mark Twain's reputation was still local and floundering Ludlow wrote, for a San Francisco journal, a discerning "high encomium" upon this author-in-the-making. In 1864 he dramatized *Cinderella* and three years later published a collection of stories under the title *Little Brother and Other Genre-Pictures.* His first marriage, to Rosalie H. Osborne in 1859, ended unhappily; and in 1867 he married Maria O. Milliken, widow of Judge Milliken of Augusta, Maine.

The *Hasheesh Eater* was Ludlow's first and best book. From the time he wrote it until his early death at the age of thirty-four the drug habit slowly destroyed what might have been a brilliant literary talent.

Principal Works: The Hasheesh Eater, 1857; Little Brother and Other Genre-Pictures, 1867; The Heart of the Continent, 1870.

About: Atlantic Monthly July 1870; Harper's New Monthly Magazine December 1870; Medical Journal and Record January 7, 1925.

"LUDWIG." See GRISWOLD, RUFUS WILMOT

LUKENS, HENRY CLAY (August 18[?], 1838-1900[?]), journalist and parodist, was born in Philadelphia, and was educated in the public schools of that city. At the age of fifteen he was a contributor to daily and weekly newspapers, and after acting as associate editor of *The School Journal,* an amateur periodical, for about a year, 1858-59, he resigned himself to the less congenial but more practical world of trade.

During 1874-75 he visited the Atlantic ports of South America, witnessing the Varela usurpation of the presidency of Uruguay and the bloody episode at Montevideo, which he described in detail for a prominent London illustrated weekly. He returned to the United States, re-established his mercantile connections, and in 1877 settled in New York to devote his full time to writing. Much of his wit, good and bad, over the signature "Erratic Enrique," appeared in his "Gotham Gleanings" column in the Danbury (Conn.) *News.* Very little of his badinage escaped the metropolitan editors, and in September 1877 he joined the staff of the New York *Daily News*; his obvious "epigrams" ("bromides" would be more accurate) became everyday pass-words—"Pretty girls at masquerade balls are blessings in disguise" . . . "An excellent way to avoid paying the butcher is never to buy meat . . ." etc. In May 1886 he was made co-editor, with Allan Forman, of the *Journalist,* a weekly issued in Brooklyn. The year following he and Forman compiled an anniversary volume, *The Journalist: A Souvenir,* containing several specimens of Lukens' light verse.

In 1870 Lukens published his "Lean 'Nora /a/Supernatural, though Sub-pathetic/Ballad /A Good Long Way/(almost ninety-seven years)/after/The German/of/G o t t f r i e d August Burger/by/Henrich Yalc Snekul/." He stated in the preface that "far from implying disparaging derision, a parody generally indicates sudden, deserved . . . lasting popularity." Longfellow confessed "rather a dislike to it . . . in fact the better they [the parodies] are done the worse they are in their effects; for one cannot get rid of them." But John Godfrey Saxe put "this excellent travesty" among his "treasures of light literature." That same year *Don't Give It Away,* "an exhaustive compendium of American humor, bathos, and philosophy and spirited vignettes," edited by Lukens under the pen-name "Vernon L. Kingsbury," appears to have gone to press; but if it ever reached the public it would seem to have been ignored. *Jets and Flashes,* a small book of lampoons, appeared in 1883, and in the late 'eighties Lukens was compiling records of the New York Press Club. For *Harper's,* April 1890, he wrote a somewhat comprehensive but uncritical account of "American Literary Comedians."

Lukens spent his late years in Jersey City, N.J., keeping only slightly in touch with New York publishers. A contemporary described him as "compactly built, of medium height, careless alike of his carriage and carfare and both in face and beauty light complexioned." He prided himself in being "always patient and forbearing when insulted by a man double his size." Because he created nothing distinctly original in American humor he has often been completely overlooked, yet he must be credited with having turned out enough breezy badinage to win him a considerable contemporary following.

Principal Works: Lean 'Nora, 1870; Don't Give It Away, 1870(?); Jets and Flashes, 1883; Journalist: A Souvenir, 1887.

About: Blair, W. Native American Humor; Correspondence in N. Y. P. L. Manuscript Division; Harper's April 1890; Jersey City Directory 1900.

LUNT, GEORGE (December 31, 1803-May 16, 1885), poet and historian, was born in Newburyport, Mass., the son of Abel Lunt, a sea-captain, and Phoebe (Tilton) Lunt. He was sent to Phillips Academy at Exeter, N.H., and then to Harvard, where he was graduated in 1824. He studied law, represented the town in its General Court (1830), was admitted to the bar the following year, and during the late 'thirties served several terms in the state senate and lower house. From 1849 to 1853 he was United States attorney for the district of Massachusetts, gaining considerable reputation as a political speaker. He resumed private practice and a few years later undertook the editorship of the Boston *Daily Courier*, the city's foremost Democratic organ. In it he opposed those policies which threatened estrangement of the South and was rather ambiguously charged with defending "slavery and its attendant evils." He retired in 1865 to devote his time to independent writing.

His first volume of verse had been published in 1826 (*The Grave of Byron: With Other Poems*); then came *Poems*, in 1839; and four years later another collection under title of *The Age of Gold and Other Poems*, the title poem of which was regarded by a contemporary critic as the "vigorous" verse of one who had "mastered well the fine movement of . . . the good old heroic couplet." He made several translations from Virgil and Horace, and classical allusions run through much of his verse. During the 'fifties he published three additional volumes and still another in 1884. In prose he wrote several books on New England life; a piece of military history called *Origin of the Late War*, and a pamphlet entitled *Review of McClellan's Campaigns as Commander of the Army of the Potomac.* He made an occasional contribution to *Harper's* and other magazines. During his last years he worked in the interests of harbor improvement at Scituate, Mass. Lunt was married three times: in 1834 to Sarah Miles Greenwood; in 1845 to Emily Ashton; and in 1864 to Adeline Parsons, sister of the author Thomas William Parsons.

Lunt produced a considerable amount of verse which was moderately well executed but which lacked any durable distinction.

Principal Works: The Grave of Byron: With Other Poems, 1826; Poems, 1839; The Age of Gold and Other Poems, 1843; The Dove and the Eagle, 1851; Lyric Poems, Sonnets, and Miscellanies, 1854; Julia: A Poem, 1855; Eastford: or, Household Sketches, 1855; Three Eras of New England and Other Addresses, 1857; The Union, 1860; Review of McClellan's Campaigns as Commander of the Army of the Potomac, 1863; The Origin of the Late War, 1866; Old New England Traits, 1873; Poems, 1884.

About: Currier, J. J. History of Newburyport; Lunt, T. S. A History of the Lunt Family in America; Boston Daily Advertiser May 18, 1885; Boston Daily Courier May 24, 1885; Newburyport Herald May 19, 1885.

"LUSKA, SIDNEY." See HARLAND, HENRY

LUTHER, SETH (fl. 1817-1846), pamphleteer, one of the earliest of American labor reformers, was born near the end of the eighteenth century, presumably in Providence, R.I. It is possible that he was a descendant of the Welsh Luthers who in 1650 came to Rhode Island and there founded the first Baptist church in America. As he himself stated, he had "no advantages but those of a common school and that of a far inferior kind to those of the present day. . . I am indebted for what little I do know to newspapers and books and to a constant habit of observation." His travels through about fourteen states, north to the "frontiers of Upper Canada" and south to Florida, included a journey down the Ohio River from Pittsburgh to Cincinnati. At the end of these roamings he settled down as a carpenter in a New England milling town, and according to his own story, he spent years "among cotton mills, worked in them, traveled among them."

He had learned to admire the democratic spirit of the frontier and he set about to improve some of the many abuses which resulted from the class distinctions of the industrial East, writing several plain-language pamphlets and making speeches in towns and cities. "You cannot raise one part of the community above another," he asserted, "unless you stand on the bodies of the poor." In his first pamphlet, *An Address to the Working-men of New England* (1832), he attacked the toleration of 12-to-15-hour days for child laborers and unspeakable physical maltreatment and argued that "the whole system of labor in New England, more especially in cotton mills, is a cruel system of exaction on the bodies and minds of the producing classes, destroying the energies of both." Luther's account was, it would seem, quite sound, for although political leaders and the press were unsympathetic, the first American child labor law was passed in Massachusetts in 1842.

The year following the appearance of his first pamphlet Luther published *An Address on the Right of Free Suffrage*; and in 1834, *An Address on the Origin and Progress of Avarice*, a firm condemnation of religious, economic, and political oppression. His constructive program of reform included: a fairer distribution of educational resources by the establishment of public-financed manual labor schools; abolition of licensed monopolies, capital punishment, and imprisonment for debt; complete revision (or abolition) of the militia set-up; a program of economy for the administration of justice, etc. In 1834 he was chosen secretary of the General Trades Convention in Boston, and in 1835 he helped draw up the *Boston Circular,* a manifesto advocating the ten-hour day; this, reprinted in Philadelphia, was said to have encouraged a general strike.

Indomitable sincerity, plain forcefulness, and grim irony were the marks of Luther's style; his information was almost entirely first-hand. In the early literature of the labor movement in America his writings occupy an honored niche.

PRINCIPAL WORKS: An Address to the Working-men of New England, 1832; An Address on the Right of Free Suffrage, 1833; An Address on the Origin and Progress of Avarice, 1834.

ABOUT: Commons, J. R. History of Labour in the United States; Ely, R. T. The Labor Movement in America; American Journal of Sociology July 1908.

LYNCH, JAMES DANIEL (January 6, 1836-July 19, 1903), miscellaneous writer, was born in Boydton, Mecklenburg County, Va. He was connected with the well-known family which gave its name to the city of Lynchburg but lost his father in infancy and was adopted by his wealthy maternal grandfather, Charles W. Baird. After three years in the University of North Carolina he became, in 1860, instructor in Latin and Greek in Franklin Academy, Columbus, Miss., where his cousin, William C. Carter, was principal. During the Civil War he served first as a private, and later organized a company of cavalry. At its close he unsuccessfully tried farming for several years, then entered the practice of law in Columbus, Miss., but impairment of hearing due to war injuries soon turned him to the profession of letters. In his latter years he settled with two sons in Sulphur Springs, Tex., where he died.

Lynch undertook his *Kemper County Vindicated* at the request of prominent citizens of the county. Later he published a biographical volume of jurists of Mississippi which suffered somewhat from his giving unequal notice to the prominent ones. He was nevertheless invited by the governor and chief justice of Texas to prepare a similar work for that state, residing in Austin while engaged in that most important of his prose works. In his poetry, undertaken as recreation, his poem "The Siege of Alamo" brought him his first recognition. A copy of this was hung, printed on parchment, in the old historic fortress at San Antonio. "The Birth of Christ" won him a prize from the *Christian Herald.* His outstanding success was, however, his "Columbia Saluting the Nations," a stately poem of seventy rhythmical couplets, which was adopted by the commissioners of the World's Fair in Chicago in 1893 as the national salutation and which received wide publicity.

PRINCIPAL WORKS: Kemper County Vindicated: A Peep at Radical Rule in Mississippi, 1879; The Bench and Bar in Mississippi, 1881; The Bench and Bar of Texas, 1885.

ABOUT: Mississippi Historical Society Publications: Vol. 3; Tyler, L. G. Encyclopaedia of Virginia Biography.

LYNN, ETHEL. See BEERS, ETHEL (LYNN)

"McARONE." See ARNOLD, GEORGE

McCARROLL, JAMES (August 3, 1814-April 10, 1892), journalist, poet, dramatist, and inventor, born in Lanesboro, County Longford, Ireland, came to Canada at seventeen, locating in or near Toronto, and later in Cobourg, Ont., and elsewhere. He engaged in writing for newspapers and periodicals, soon became influential in politics and literature, and at thirty-one was editing his own paper, the Peterborough *Chronicle.* Appointments in the customs service at Cobourg and Niagara and as surveyor of the port of Toronto were tendered him in recognition of his services. He was also an accomplished musician, taught music and often went on tour, and was for a time music critic of the Toronto *Leader* and the Toronto *Colonist.* As an inventor he was best known for an improved elevator and fireproof wire gauze.

Little of the considerable writing of McCarroll appeared in book form. Among the best so published was the *Terry Finnegan Letters,* a series of humorous Irish dialect sketches. A collected volume of his whimsical, sentimental verse appeared in 1889. His two dramas were modeled on the French romantic school of Dumas and Augustin Scribe. After varied journalistic experience in northern New York State he became associated in New York City with the *People's Cyclopaedia of Universal Knowledge* and the *American Cyclopaedia.* He also served on the editorial staff of *Humanity and Health,* and contributed scientific articles to *Belford's Magazine.*

Principal Works: Terry Finnegan Letters, 1864; The Adventures of a Night (drama) 1865; Almost a Tragedy: A Comedy, 1874; Madeline and Other Poems, 1889.

About: Belford's Monthly June 1892.

McCONNEL, JOHN LUDLUM (November 11, 1826-January 17, 1862), novelist, born in Morgan County, now Scott County, Ill., was the eldest son of Murray McConnel, prominent lawyer, state legislator, and an auditor of the United States Treasury, and of Mary (Mapes) McConnel. The study of law, commenced under his father, was completed by his graduation from the Transylvania Law School in 1843. He took part in the war with Mexico, rose to the rank of captain, and at its conclusion took over the law practice of his father at Jacksonville. He died at thirty-six.

McConnel's literary interest found early expression in overdrawn melodramatic writing, such as his novel *Grahame.* In subsequent work he introduced valuable elements of descriptive and historical interest, as of Mexico in the story of the Mexican war, *Talbot and Vernon*; the frontier life of Texas in *The Glenns*; and picturesque frontier characterization in *Western Characters.* At the time of his death he was engaged on a history of early exploration in America, in which he planned special reference to the early Roman Catholic missionaries.

Principal Works: Grahame: or, Youth and Manhood, 1850; Talbot and Vernon, 1850; The Glenns: A Family History, 1851; Western Characters: or, Types of Border Life in the Western States, 1853.

About: Eames, C. M. Historic Morgan and Classic Jacksonville; Journal of the Illinois State Historical Society April 1925.

McCORD, LOUISA SUSANNA (CHEVES) (December 3, 1810-November 23, 1879), poet and essayist, was born in Charleston, S.C., of Scotch, Irish, and Huguenot ancestry, the daughter of Langdon Cheves, distinguished jurist and statesman, and Mary Elizabeth (Dulles) Cheves. She was carefully educated at Grimshaw's School in Philadelphia, and under private tutors. After her marriage in 1840 to the editor and congressman, David James McCord, she spent much of her time until his death in 1855 on her plantation "Lang Syne" near Fort Motte, S.C., devoting her time personally to its care and to the welfare of its several hundred Negroes. During the Civil War she gave unsparingly of her strength to alleviate the conditions of the soldiers of the Confederacy, and at its close, in reduced circumstances, she retired to Charleston. She had three children. She died at Charleston.

The vigorous intellectual environment in which she was reared had its effect in giving her an early grasp of political and economic problems, and she found time to contribute essays, reviews, and poems to Southern journals, particularly the *Southern Quarterly Review,* her discussions on social questions being clear and conservative, her attitude characteristically that of the Southern aristocracy. In the *Review* under date of January 1853 she essayed a criticism of Harriet Beecher Stowe's *Uncle Tom's Cabin,* but weakened her arguments by attempting to justify slavery as a humanitarian institution. Her translation of Bastiat's *Sophismes Economiques* was expertly done; her single volume of verse, however, showed unevenness of thought. Her five-act tragedy, *Caius Gracchus,* was of the closet drama type.

Principal Works: My Dreams (poems) 1848; Caius Gracchus (drama) 1851. *Translation*—Sophisms of the Protective Policy (from Frederic Bastiat) 1848.

About: Fraser, J. M. Louisa C. McCord; Wauchope, G. A. The Writers of South Carolina.

McCOSH, JAMES (April 1, 1811-November 16, 1894), clergyman, philosopher, and college president, was born in Scotland near the river Doon, the son of Andrew and Jean (Carson) McCosh. He entered Glasgow University at the age of thirteen, made an excellent record there and proceeded to

Collection of Frederick H. Meserve

JAMES McCOSH

Edinburgh University, where he secured his Master of Arts degree in March 1833. Becoming a licensed preacher of the Established Church of Scotland he took charges first at Arbroath and then at Brechin—where arose a lively controversy between the conservatives and the liberals. McCosh, protesting against the technical restrictions, etc., imposed by the State upon the Church, allied himself with the liberals. This group, withdrawing from the Established Church, even in face of financial desolation, founded the Free Church of Scotland.

At Edinburgh, the Intuitionism of William Hamilton was McCosh's earliest stimulus in philosophical thought, but soon finding this too full of negations he shifted to the so-called Scottish school, which vested the human mind with a constitutionality that determines the nature of its experiences and guarantees a supreme authority for its most fundamental beliefs. Believing that Mill's *System of Logic* completely excluded this (to him) all-vital element of the supernatural, McCosh prepared a refutation, *The Method of the Divine Government: Physical and Moral,* which brought him to the immediate attention of several eminent contemporaries; he was appointed to the chair of logic and metaphysics at Queen's College, Belfast, which he held from 1852 until 1868.

Among the books on philosophical processes and interpretations which emerged from McCosh's pen during these years were: *The Intuitions of the Mind Inductively Investigated,* setting forth the doctrines of the Scottish school and tracing the evolution of intuitions from simple cognition to universal principles; and *An Examination of Mr. J. S. Mill's Philosophy,* condemning his sensational psychology, religious skepticism, etc. McCosh's name reached America, and at President John Maclean's resignation (1868) from the College of New Jersey (later Princeton) he was called to assume the office. During an administration of twenty years he succeeded in attracting superior teachers, broadening the curriculum, improving the equipment, buildings, etc.; and he himself conducted courses in psychology and the history of philosophy. He was married in 1845 to Isabella Guthrie, daughter of an eminent Scottish physician.

He published half a dozen more religious and philosophical books—largely extensions of his earlier writings—during his Princeton years. He was one of the first theologians to accept the doctrine of evolution, which he considered in no sense a denial of God. Although his most memorable achievements were in the executive-educational field, his writings have served to clarify a significant portion of nineteenth century philosophy.

Principal Works: The Method of the Divine Government: Physical and Moral, 1850; Typical Forms and Special Ends in Creation, 1855; The Supernatural in Relation to the Natural, 1862; An Examination of Mr. J. S. Mill's Philosophy: Being a Defence of Fundamental Truth, 1866; Christianity and Positivism, 1871; The Scottish Philosophy: Biographical, Expository, Critical, From Hutcheson to Hamilton, 1875; Realistic Philosophy Defended in a Philosophic Series (2 vols.) 1887; First and Fundamental Truths, 1889.

About: Howe, M. A. DeW. Classic Shades; Sloane, W. M. The Life of James McCosh; Nation October 8, 1896; New York Times November 17, 1894.

MacDOWELL, KATHERINE SHERWOOD (BONNER) (February 26, 1849-July 22, 1883), novelist and short-story writer, whose pen name was "Sherwood Bonner," was born in Holly Springs, Miss., daughter of Dr. Charles Bonner, an Irish immigrant, and Mary (Wilson) MacDowell, a Southerner. She was sent first to a private school in Holly Springs and then to a boarding school in Montgomery, Ala. The year 1863 left some very firm impressions on her youthful mind—the siege of Vicksburg, Johnston's army tramping through Holly Springs, and nearby military skirmishes.

When she was only fifteen Nahum Capen, editor of the *Massachusetts Ploughman,* published her first story and offered her some very sane and encouraging advice. She was married in 1871 to Edward MacDowell, and by him had one child; but her temperamentalism and literary ambitions were at odds with a quiet domesticity and she separated from her husband, put her daughter in the hands of a relative, and went to Boston. Here she became secretary to Nahum Capen, and acted as amanuensis to Longfellow; moreover she was constantly writing verse and miscellaneous articles for the Boston *Times,* the Memphis *Avalanche,* and other journals. Many of her magazine contributions, largely reenactments of the Southern scene, were later published in book form as *Dialect Tales* and *Suwanee River Tales.* Meanwhile she had written an autobiographical novel of the Civil War and reconstruction era, *Like Unto Like,* which she dedicated to Longfellow. Then came dialect yarns of the Tennessee Mountain life and of the so-called "Egypt" district in Illinois: yellow-fever tragedies and a variety of human miseries lent a gloomier kind of realism to these later tales. In fact "The Volcanic Interlude," appearing in *Lippincott's Magazine* (April 1880), is said to have caused many readers to withdraw their subscriptions.

Sherwood Bonner perhaps exerted no literary influence of her own, but the best of her tales place her among those early local-colorists whose materials effected a later and more significant American realism.

PRINCIPAL WORKS: Like Unto Like, 1878; Dialect Tales, 1883; Suwanee River Tales, 1884.

ABOUT: Drake, B. M. Southern Writers; Gilligan, D. L. "Life and Works of Sherwood Bonner" (MS. in George Washington University Library); Rutherford, M. L. The South in History and Literature; Harper's Weekly August 11, 1883.

MacGAHAN, JANUARIUS ALOYSIUS (June 12, 1844-June 9, 1878), war correspondent, was born on a farm in Perry County, Ohio, the son of James and Esther (Dempsey) MacGahan. After working for a time as a bookkeeper he went abroad, living in Brussels, Paris, and Germany. The languages he acquired, combined with the influence of his cousin, General Sherman, secured him a position as correspondent on the Franco-Prussian war for the New York *Herald*. Finding the work eminently suited to his talents, he continued it—in Geneva, Cuba, the Pyrenees, the Arctic, and the deserts of Central Asia. Books resulting from these exploits were *Campaigning on the Oxus and the Fall of Khiva* and *Under the Northern Lights*.

He married a Russian woman in 1872. They had one son. In 1876 the London *Daily News* sent him to investigate the Bulgarian situation. This led to his book, *The Turkish Atrocities in Bulgaria*. His reports were instrumental in precipitating the Russo-Turkish war, out of which came Bulgaria's independence, and for this reason Bulgarian envoys at Washington sometimes visit his grave near New Lexington. The articles were among those collected in *War Correspondence of the Daily News*.

He was a favorite among his associates. Death came as a result of typhus contracted in Constantinople while nursing a friend through typhoid. His body was brought to the United States six years later.

PRINCIPAL WORKS: Campaigning on the Oxus and the Fall of Khiva, 1874; Under the Northern Lights, 1876; The Turkish Atrocities in Bulgaria, 1876; articles in War Correspondence of the Daily News, 1877-78.

ABOUT: Bullard, F. L. Famous War Correspondents; London Daily News June 11, 12, 1878; Ohio Archaeological and Historical Quarterly April-July 1912.

"MacGROM, JOHN." See McMASTER, GUY HUMPHRIES

McGUFFEY, ALEXANDER HAMILTON. See McGUFFEY, WILLIAM HOLMES

McGUFFEY, WILLIAM HOLMES (September 23, 1800-May 4, 1873), textbook compiler, was born in Washington County, Pa., near what is today the village of Claysville, the son of Alexander and Anna (Holmes) McGuffey. When he was two his parents moved to Ohio, near Youngstown, then a pioneer wilderness. There he lived until he was eighteen, securing such schooling as he could from his mother, from an occasional session at a rural school, and from the Presbyterian minister in Youngstown, who taught him Latin. He was gifted with a prodigious memory, including the ability to recite whole books of the Bible; in after years he said he had preached 3000 sermons but never wrote one—and he could recall and re-deliver any of them at will!

In 1818 McGuffey went to Old Stone (or Greersburg) Academy, Darlington, Pa., and thence to Washington College, from which he was graduated with honors in 1826. His college life had been interspersed with seasons of teaching. He was immediately made professor of Latin, Greek, and Hebrew at Miami University, Oxford, Ohio, and he remained there for ten years, after 1832 being head of the department of "mental philosophy, philology, and general criticism." In 1827 he married Harriet Speninty (according to some authorities, Spinning), by whom he had three sons and two

WILLIAM HOLMES McGUFFEY

daughters. None of the sons survived him.

In 1829 McGuffey was licensed to preach in the Presbyterian church, though he was never ordained or had a regular ministerial charge. Washington College gave him a D.D. in 1842. All the time he was at Miami he preached every Sunday in a nearby town, and all his life he was a popular lecturer on the Bible and on ethics.

In 1836 he became president of Cincinnati College, and did much to obtain the law granting public schools to Ohio. Later, in Virginia, he performed the same service for his new state. Meanwhile, in 1839, he had become president of Ohio University, at Athens, but in 1843 the university was temporarily quashed through a dispute with the state legislature, and McGuffey went back to Cincinnati, where he taught in Woodward College (really a secondary school). In 1845 he was appointed professor of moral philosophy at the University of Virginia, and held this post for the remainder of his life, teaching up to a few weeks before his death. A Northerner, he went through the Civil War in Virginia with the respect of all his colleagues, notedly generous and friendly to his neighbors both black and white. His wife died in 1853, and in 1857 he married Laura Howard, daughter of the dean of the university; their only daughter died in infancy. He died at Charlottesville, Va., in his seventy-third year.

Up to the present point this might be the life-story of any other estimable but minor American educator of the same period. Yet William Holmes McGuffey is remembered today when men of far greater reputation in his own time are forgotten; not for any of his achievements chronicled above, but for the famous series of public school "Readers" that bears his name. Through these, thousands who never heard of the educator as an individual came to use his name as a household word. (In fact, a prominent American statesman is supposed to have remarked innocently: "Was McGuffey a man? I thought it was a book!")

The McGuffey Readers are, indeed, so familiar to most Americans that it seems hardly necessary to describe them except to the newest generation. In their time they literally served as the whole libraries of millions of young people in rural and small town communities—as truly symbolical of an era in American life as log cabins or rail fences. Their greatest merit, as Katharine Woods points out, was that "they were Readers. They taught children the English language; they gave adventurous, questing youths a rich vocabulary of words." Didactic and moralistic they may have been, yet they were a vast improvement on anything that preceded them. They were repositories of real literature, a sort of condensed course in the English classics; they were wholesome, sensible, and above all, interesting.

The McGuffey series began in 1836 with the *First* and *Second Readers*; in 1837 came the *Primer* and *Third* and *Fourth Readers*; in 1838, the *Speller*; in 1844, the *Fifth Reader*; in 1857 the *Sixth Reader*. Associated with McGuffey in the preparation of the series was his younger brother, Alexander Hamilton McGuffey. Besides his general assistance, Alexander was probably the sole compiler of the *Speller* and the *Fifth Reader*. Numerous revisions were made of the entire series, and from time to time supplementary units were added—charts, elocution texts, high school readers, and the like. New editions appeared as late as 1920. In all—it is estimated—more than 122,000,000 copies have been sold. At the time of this writing, McGuffey Readers are reported still in use in some parts of the country.

In recent years a veritable cult has grown up around McGuffey and his Readers. A McGuffey Museum has been established at Miami University; McGuffey clubs flourish in all sections of the country, with officers, meetings, and programs; Henry Ford has reconstructed, in his "museum village" at Greenfield, Mich., the log cabin in which the educator was born; collectors pay fabulous prices for McGuffey "firsts"; trees which McGuffey planted are guarded almost as shrines. To the uninitiated much of this adulation seems excessive; yet few will dispute Hugh Fullerton when he says: "From 1836 until near the close of the century, Professor McGuffey exerted the greatest influence, culturally, of any person in American history."

About: Minnich, H. C. William Holmes McGuffey and His Readers; McGuffey, W. H. Old Favorites From the McGuffey Readers (see Introduction); Sullivan, M. Our Times: Vol. 2; Tope, M. A. A Biography of William Holmes McGuffey; Vail, H. H. A History of the McGuffey Readers; Time August 3, 1936; Christian Science Monitor September 18, 1935; New York Times Book Review January 3, 1937.

McHENRY, JAMES (December 20, 1775-July 21, 1845), poet and novelist, was born in Larne, County Antrim, Ireland. He studied for the Presbyterian ministry, but because he was a hunchback he felt ill at ease at the pulpit and shortly became a medical student, first at Belfast and then at Glasgow. Sensitive and introspective, he found a distinct pleasure in the writing of poetry; most of his verse was inspired by the simple grace of the Larne valley and the Scottish hills. For several years he was a practicing physician in Larne and Belfast; and in 1817, with his wife and infant son, he sailed for the United States, settling finally in Philadelphia, where as a doctor, draper, politician, and man of letters he remained eighteen years.

Before coming to Philadelphia McHenry had published a volume of verse, *The Pleasures of Friendship,* which he followed with *Waltham,* a poetic chronicle of the Revolutionary period, and his first novel, *The Wilderness: or, The Youthful Days of Washington,* a chronicle of the Protestant Ulstermen in America, written over the signature "Solomon Secondsight" and issued in London. In 1824 he founded and edited the *American Monthly Magazine,* a literary journal (not to be confused with N. P. Willis' *American Monthly Magazine* for which Poe wrote) that failed financially within its first year. Three more books preceded his first assay at play-writing: *The Usurper,* a rather long-drawn-out blank verse tragedy with a Druidical back-drop, which opened at the Chestnut Street Theatre in December 1830. It represented the first attempt to adapt Irish history to the American stage, but its reception was cool. McHenry returned to the novel, and wrote the semi-historic *Meredith: or, The Mystery of Meschianza* and *The Betrothed of Wyoming.*

Meanwhile *The Pleasures of Friendship* had reached a seventh edition and McHenry felt sufficient confidence to venture some (almost hysterical) criticism, in the *American Quarterly Review,* of Wordsworth, Scott, Byron, and other romanticists. *Blackwood's Edinburgh Magazine* and the *Athenaeum* were sufficiently annoyed to blast his critical foundations, as well as his reputation as a critic. McHenry began the writing of a blank-verse epic, *Antediluvians: or, the World Destroyed,* a tale of the Flood—to which Blackwood's critic added vitriol!

McHenry was appointed to the consulate in Londonderry in 1843, and he died in Larne two years later. His small literary stronghold was in the Irish lyric and the portraiture of his Ulster countrymen.

Principal Works: The Pleasures of Friendship, 1822; The Wilderness: or, The Youthful Days of Washington, 1823; The Spectre of the Forest, 1823; O'Halloran: or, The Insurgent Chief, 1824; The Hearts of Steel, 1825; The Usurper, 1827; The Betrothed of Wyoming, 1830; Meredith: or, The Mystery of Meschianza, 1831; Antediluvians: or, The World Destroyed, 1839.

About: Mott, F. L. A History of American Magazines: 1741-1850; Oberholtzer, E. P., The Literary History of Philadelphia; Quinn, A. H. A History of the American Drama From the Beginning to the Civil War; Knickerbocker July 1834, April 1859; Public Ledger (Philadelphia) August 12, 1845.

MacKAYE, JAMES MORRISON STEELE (June 6, 1842-February 25, 1894), dramatist, was born in Buffalo, the son of Col. James Morrison McKay (later changed by him to the Scottish ancestral form of MacKaye), a prominent attorney, and Emily Venton (Steele) McKay. From the beginning, the boy, who was always known as Steele MacKaye, displayed his lifelong characteristics—ardor, wilfulness, improvidence, and indefatigability in whatever really appealed to him. He ran away from school more than once, until he was allowed to study art. At sixteen he was in Paris at the École des Beaux-Arts, painting being his first enthusiasm. In 1859 he returned to New York, where his family had moved, and at the outbreak of the Civil War he enlisted. He was breveted major before he was discharged on account of rheumatic fever. While in the army he first appeared on the stage in a regimental play, as Horatio in *Hamlet.*

For the next few years he was busy finding himself. In 1862 he married Jennie Spring, but they were soon amicably divorced. In 1865 he married Mary Keith Medbery, a descendant of Roger Williams, and a great friend of his first wife, whose son she helped to rear. She had five sons and a daughter of her own, including Percy MacKaye, the playwright. Meanwhile MacKaye was painting, trying to be an art dealer, and exploiting an invention known as "photo-sculpture." In 1864 he was on the stage of the Bowery Theatre. Utterly without money sense, he was always in debt, always prodigally generous, always being cheated. In 1869 he returned to Paris, where he became a disciple of Delsarte and his art of dramatic expression. Returning to New York, he established a school of Delsartian acting, and in 1872 appeared with his pupils in *Monaldi,* a play adapted by him from the French. Another year abroad followed, during which he played *Hamlet* in French in Paris and in English in London—the first American to do so. In 1874 he opened his "School of Expression" in New York. His plays, original and adapted, attracted good audiences; *Rose Michel,* for example, played for 122 performances in 1875. In 1879 he rebuilt the Madison Square

Theatre, the first playhouse to have a double elevated stage, indirect lighting, and artificial ventilation. In all, Mackaye patented over a hundred inventions, mostly for the improvement of theatrical equipment; they included the disappearing orchestra pit and folding chairs.

It was at this theatre that, in 1880, his *Hazel Kirke* began its run of 500 performances, a record for that time. Any other man would have made a fortune by it, but MacKaye, with his genius for making bad contracts, was forced out of his own theatre. Undaunted, he built the Lyceum Theatre, the first to be lighted entirely by electricity, and established the Lyceum Theatre School, first dramatic school in America (later the American Academy of Dramatic Art). The culmination of his ambitions came with the Chicago World's Fair in 1893, for which he planned a huge amphitheatre called a Spectatorium, a revolutionary piece of stagecraft for which he wrote *The World Finder,* dealing with Columbus; Dvorak wrote his *New World Symphony* as musical setting to this play. But MacKaye's financial incompetence ruined him again; all that ever came of his grandiose scheme was a working model produced in 1894. The whole affair literally killed him; he died of nervous exhaustion on a train near Timpas, Colo., while en route to San Diego.

In all, MacKaye wrote over twenty plays, seven of them in collaboration with Tom Taylor and Charles Reade. They are now the most negligible of his remains, being (including *Hazel Kirke*) outmoded sentimental melodramas. The best of his legacy is in his revolutionary technical inventions and ideas for the stage, his belief in the social value of the drama, and his elevating influence on acting and actors. A tall, slender man, who looked uncannily like Poe, he was a fanatical, humorless idealist and propagandist, yet beloved for his charm and his heedless generosity. All he needed was a business manager, but that he never had.

Collection of Frederick H. Meserve
STEELE MacKAYE

PRINCIPAL WORKS (date of production): Won at Last, 1877; Through the Dark (later altered as A Noble Rogue, and as Money Mad) 1879; Hazel Kirke, 1880; A Fool's Errand, 1881; Dakolar, 1885; Paul Kauvar: or, Anarchy, 1887; An Arrant Knave, 1889; Colonel Tom, 1890.

ABOUT: MacKaye, P. Epoch: The Life of Steele MacKaye; The Drama November 1911, February 1912; Chicago Tribune February 26, 1894.

MacKAYE, STEELE. See MacKAYE, JAMES MORRISON STEELE

MacKELLAR, THOMAS (August 12, 1812-December 29, 1899), printer, typefounder, and poet was born in New York City, the son of Archibald and Harriet (Andrews) MacKellar. His schooling ended at fourteen, when the family fortunes changed and he went to work. He set type and read proof for Harper's, and when he was twenty left New York for a position in the type foundry of Johnson and Smith in Philadelphia, of which he became a partner in 1845, and which he brought to a position of eminence among the foundries in this country. In 1866 he wrote *The American Printer,* a work on typography which by 1893 had run into eighteen editions.

In 1844 a first book of his poems appeared, called *Droppings From the Heart.* He was concerned mainly with family, friendship, and religion—the latter especially in *Hymns and a Few Metrical Psalms.* He married Eliza Ross in 1834. They had two sons and eight daughters.

PRINCIPAL WORKS: Droppings From the Heart, 1844; Tam's Fortnight Ramble and Other Poems, 1847; The American Printer, 1866; Rhymes Atween-Times, 1873; Hymns and a Few Metrical Psalms, 1883; Faith, Hope, Love: These Three, 1893.

ABOUT: Griswold, R. W. The Poets and Poetry of America; One Hundred Years: MacKellar Smiths and Jordan Foundry; Ringwalt, J. L. American Encyclopedia of Printing.

MacKENZIE, ROBERT SHELTON (June 22, 1809-November 21, 1881), journalist and biographer, was born at Drew's Court, County Limerick, Ireland, son of Capt. Kenneth Mackenzie of the Kaithness

Fencibles regiment, and Marie (Shelton) Mackenzie. He received his early instruction at Fermoy and taught school there in 1825. But he was shortly offered the editorship of a country journal at Hanley, Staffordshire, England, which was the beginning of a life-long newspaper career. He wrote numerous biographies for the *Georgian Era,* 1830-31; conducted the Derbyshire *Courier* for two years; then assumed the editorship of the Liverpool *Journal*; and in 1834 he became, it is believed, the first paid European correspondent of an American paper and supplied the New York *Evening Star* with a series of letters on literature, politics, and gossip. At the same time he was associated with the Liverpool *Mail,* and a little later, with the (Shrewsbury) *Salopian Journal.* It is uncertain whether or not he received a degree of D.C.L. from Oxford in 1844 and equally ambiguous are the facts relating to his subsequent associations with a London railway firm. In the columns of the London *Sun* and *Weekly Times* he sought publicity for Lord Brougham's Law Amendment Society and was awarded with a brief appointment as official assignee of the Manchester bankruptcy court. He married Georgina Dickinson in 1851; by her he had one child.

Mackenzie came to New York after his wife's death in 1852, held several miscellaneous editorial posts, and in 1857 went to Philadelphia, where for twenty years he was literary and foreign editor and dramatic critic for the *Press.* In 1858 he was married to Adelheid Zwissler, author, by whom he had three children. He aided in organizing the Philadelphia Dental College and during his last years was literary editor of the Philadelphia *Evening News.*

After his *Lays of Palestine* (1828) he published nothing of importance until 1843, the date of his three-volume novel, *Titian: A Romance of Venice,* followed by another multi-volumned piece; a collection of stories, *Bits of Blarney;* the semi-autobiographical *Tressilian and His Friends;* and lives of Charles Dickens and Sir Walter Scott. His editing, in five volumes, of the first orderly and well-documented edition of *Noctes Ambrosianae,* Christopher North's brilliant contributions to *Blackwood's Magazine* during the years 1822 to 1835, was his most constructive literary effort and spared him from the stigma of obvious mediocrity.

Principal Works: Lays of Palestine, 1828; Titian: A Romance of Venice, 1843; Mornings at Matlock, 1850; Bits of Blarney, 1854; Christopher North's Noctes Ambrosianae (ed.) 1854; Tressilian and His Friends, 1859; Life of Charles Dickens, 1870; Walter Scott: The Story of His Life, 1871.

About: Boase, F. Modern English Biography; Ballou's Pictorial Drawing-Room Companion January 12, 1856; Public Ledger (Philadelphia) November 22, 1881.

McKINLEY, CARL. See McKINLEY, CARLYLE

McKINLEY, CARLYLE (November 22, 1847-August 24, 1904), poet, editor, and essayist, often called Carl McKinley, was born in Newnan, Ga., the son of Charles G. and Frances (Jackson) McKinley. He joined a student company, in the Confederate army, and saw considerable active service in the environs of Atlanta. For a while, after the War, he was a cotton broker in Augusta; took a post in the United States marshal's office in Savannah; and then enrolled at Columbia Theological Seminary, Columbia, S. C., being graduated in 1874. Shortly afterward he was married to Elizabeth H. Bryce and, abandoning the ministry altogether, became a teacher in Hugh S. Thompson's school at Columbia. During the years that followed he gradually turned to writing; after serving as a correspondent for the Charleston *News and Courier,* he was sent to Washington to "cover" the Capitol and in 1881, to Charleston to become associate editor.

McKinley was the author of several vigorous monographs, including "An Appeal to Pharaoh," a tonic and intelligent analysis of the Negro question; "The August Cyclone . . .of 1885" and "A Descriptive Narrative of the Earthquake. . .of 1886," published in the *Year Book. . .City of Charleston* (1885 and 1886). Some of his subjective and reflective verses are to be found in *Selections From the Poems of Carlyle McKinley.* He had a sensitivity to word-colors and values and, in pursuit of the romantic and satiric, an obvious literary discrimination: he was, therefore outstanding among the Reconstruction poets and one of the most successful in his effort to preserve the faith and optimism of the New South.

Principal Works: An Appeal to Pharoah, 1889; Selections From the Poems of Carlyle McKinley, 1904.

About: Alderman, E. A. & Harris, J. C. The Library of Southern Literature; Wauchope, G. A. The Writers of South Carolina; News and Courier (Charleston) August 25, 1904.

MACLAY, EDGAR STANTON (April 18, 1863-November 2, 1919), historian, was the son of Robert Samuel Maclay, a missionary, and Henrietta (Sperry) Maclay. He spent his childhood in China and Japan, and in 1881 went to Syracuse College, from which he obtained the B.A. and M.A. degrees. He wrote and edited two books about the Maclay family and several dealing, albeit somewhat inaccurately, with the history of the United States Navy. He worked on the staffs of various New York newspapers. In 1893 he married Katherine Koerber. They had four sons.

A statement criticizing Admiral Schley in the third volume of his *History of the United States Navy* led to his dismissal in 1901 from a minor post in the New York navy yard, after which he had great difficulty in making a living. He wrote little except three biographies of naval officers, and these were scarcely noticed by the public. In 1904 he secured a position on a Brooklyn paper, and shortly before his death he obtained some research work in Washington, D.C.

Principal Works: The Maclays of Lurgan, 1889; A History of the United States Navy (3 vols.) 1894-1901; Reminiscences of the Old Navy, 1898; A History of American Privateers, 1899.

About: Maclay, E. S. The Maclays of Lurgan; Washington Evening Star December 21-26, 1901, November 4, 1919.

McLELLAN, ISAAC (May 21, 1806-August 20, 1899), sportsman and poet, was born in Portland, Maine, the son of Isaac and Eliza (Hull) McLellan. The family moved to Boston, and Isaac attended Phillips Academy and Bowdoin College, from which he was graduated in 1826.

In Boston again, he first engaged in law and journalism, but after a two years' visit in Europe he devoted himself to sport and to writing poems about sport which were published in *Turf Field and Farm, Forest and Stream, American Angler, Amateur Sportsman,* and *Gameland*. In 1886 the first collection of the poems in book form appeared, *Poems of the Rod and Gun,* and in 1896 the last, *Haunts of Wild Game*.

Though the verses could not always be dignified by the name of real poetry, they gave an extensive description of the natural history of this country and others. From 1851 until his death he lived quietly at Greenport, Long Island.

Principal Works: Poems of the Rod and Gun, 1886; Haunts of Wild Game, 1896.

About: Griffith, G. B. The Poets of Maine; Griswold, R. W. The Poets and Poetry of America.

McMAHON, JOHN VAN LEAR (October 18, 1800-June 15, 1871), lawyer and historian, was born in Cumberland, Md., his father an Irish farmer and his mother of a prominent Maryland family. He won highest honors at the College of New Jersey, now Princeton, and was graduated at seventeen. An arrogant mien and rough manner caused him to give up law after about a year of practice in Baltimore, but after some studies in medicine and theology he opened a law office in his birthplace.

Through his powers of observation and of voice he became a popular speaker and was elected to the Maryland House of Delegates in 1823. He appeared there dressed as a huntsman, pleaded eloquently for removal of the political disabilities of the Jews and for state aid to the Chesapeake and Ohio Canal, and became the recognized leader of the House. At this time he began a treatise on the institutions of his state which was published in 1851 as an *Historical View of the Government of Maryland*. The work was trustworthy, enlightened, and written in a good style.

After serving two terms he returned to practice in Baltimore, becoming the most important figure of the Maryland bar, and returning to the House for two more terms, at the conclusion of which he declined to run for office again. He likewise refused a post in President Harrison's cabinet and the attorney-generalship under Tyler. Impairment of sight led to the termination of his career in 1863.

There is no record of his marriage, but he was known to have a son, John A. McMahon, also a distinguished lawyer, who gave his mother's name as Elizabeth (Gougher) McMahon.

Principal Work: Historical View of the Government of Maryland, 1831.

About: Mason, J. T. Life of John Van Lear McMahon; Powell, H. F. Tercentenary History of Maryland.

McMASTER, GUY HUMPHREYS (January 31, 1829-September 13, 1887), jurist and poet, was born in Clyde, N. Y., the son of David and Adeline (Humphreys) McMaster, who removed to Bath when Guy was about a year old. From Franklin Academy at Prattsburg, N. Y., young McMaster went to Hamilton College, where he became acquainted with Charles Dudley Warner and Joseph R. Hawley. He was graduated in 1847 and began the study of law, breaking the routine of his preliminary courses with several literary experiments: the lyric "Carmen Bellicosum," in the *Knickerbocker* (February 1849) over the signature "John MacGrom," and in 1851 a poem "The Northern Lights" and some prose essays for the *American Whig Review*. Two years later he was married to Amanda Church, by whom he had four children.

Meanwhile McMaster had been admitted to the bar; later he formed a partnership with his son-in-law, John F. Parkhurst, which was maintained until the death of the senior member. McMaster was county judge and surrogate and both as lawyer and judge was admired for his legal astuteness and equitable temper.

During the Civil War his "Dream of Thanksgiving Eve," a poem of mingled patriotism and humor, was published in the Hartford *Courant;* and in 1880 "The Professor's Guest Chamber," verse of another variety, appeared in the Utica *Herald.* For the Steuben *Courier* he wrote "Pacific Letters" during a trip to the West Coast in 1877, and "Other Side Letters" at the time of his European journey in 1885. But his literary reputation rests solely on "Carmen Bellicosum," whose well-turned stanzas celebrate the valor of the Continental soldiers. It has appeared in numerous anthologies, including the *Oxford Book of American Verse.* McMaster must be credited with having written a small amount of relatively strong and valid verse at a time when many American poets were completely preoccupied with the flavorless and the sentimental.

ABOUT: Clayton, W. W. History of Steuben County, N.Y.; Hakes, H. Landmarks of Steuben County; Critic October 22, 1887; Galaxy January 1869 (see Stedman, E. C. "A Belt of Asteroids"); Hamilton Literary Monthly October 1887.

McPHERSON, EDWARD (July 31, 1830-December 14, 1895), editor and political writer, was born in Gettysburg, Pa., the son of John Bayard McPherson and Katharine (Lenhart) McPherson. After college and a few years' law study he became editor of the Harrisburg *American,* and he was thereafter connected with Pennsylvania newspapers in various cities. For fifteen years before his death he was owner and editor of the Gettysburg *Star and Sentinel.*

He was elected to Congress in 1859, and remained two terms. He was Clerk of the House from 1863 to 1875, from 1881 to 1883, and from 1889 to 1891, his early legal studies contributing to his success. Other factors were his habit of proceeding calmly through disturbances and objections when calling the roll of recognized members, and his encyclopedic political information. The latter he also put to use in writing his *Political History of the United States of America During the Great Rebellion* and *Political History of the United States of America During the Period of Reconstruction,* which provide a valuable record of the political activities of those periods. He edited a number of political handbooks of a statistical nature. He married Anne Dods Crawford in 1862.

PRINCIPAL WORKS: Political History of the United States of America During the Great Rebellion, 1864; Political History of the United States of America During the Period of Reconstruction, 1871.

ABOUT: Biographical Directory of the American Congress; Blaine, J. G. Twenty Years of Congress; Oberholtzer, E. P. A History of the United States Since the Civil War.

McVICKAR, JOHN (August 10, 1787-October 29, 1868), Protestant Episcopal clergyman and economist, was born in New York City, the son of John McVickar, an Irish emigrant who later became a wealthy maritime merchant, and Anna (Moore) McVickar, of Newtown, Long Island. He was first sent to a "select school established by a few gentlemen for the benefit of their sons," then tutored by a learned Scotch clergyman, and finally enrolled at Columbia College, from which he was graduated as ranking scholar of his class at the age of seventeen. In 1805 he went abroad with his father and on his return began theological studies with the Rev. (later Bishop) Henry Hobart, by whom he was ordained first deacon and then priest and whose biography he was afterward to write. He was married in 1809, to Eliza, daughter of Dr. Samuel Bard, who had been physician to George Washington; and two years later he became rector of the Church of St. James, Hyde Park, N.Y. He remained there until 1817 at which time he became professor of moral philosophy at Columbia College—where the president, three professors, and one adjunct professor were dealing out genteel, aristocratic, and classic-grounded culture to one hundred young men. His pedagogical titles embraced "rhetoric," "belles-lettres," "ancient history," "history of philosophy," and "political economy"—but only loosely and arbitrarily—over a period of years; and at the age of seventy he was appointed to the chair of the "evidences of religion, natural and revealed."

McVickar twice failed, by narrow margins, in election to the presidency of the college—"there was something in his personality which repelled rather than attracted popular approval, an excessive correctness and frigidity, a certain removal from human sympathy." He was essentially a churchman and a moralist. Teaching was, for him, a kind of "ministerial activity." Some of his political and economic writings are hardly more than technically breezy dissertations with over-obvious social and moral argument. His *Outline of Political Economy* and *Interest Made*

Equity were re-drafts of John Ramsay McCulloch's articles in the *Encyclopaedia Britannica* to which he had added explanatory and prefatory notes. A series of letters which he wrote during a second European sojourn in 1830—from England, Scotland, and the Low Countries, Switzerland, and France, are, from the literary point of view, perhaps his best work. His biography of Hobart appeared first in two parts and was republished in 1838 as *The Early Life and Professional Years of Bishop Hobart;* his life of Samuel Bard was issued in 1822. On the subject of banking he wrote several books and a series of unsigned articles for the *New York Review,* 1837-42.

McVickar belonged to a small and highly privileged class and to him the word "democratic" carried inevitable associations of "baseness" and "vice." He gave form to no new ideas, but in the field of moralistic and semi-philosophic literature he was capable of being both supple and clear.

PRINCIPAL WORKS: A Domestic Narrative of the Life of Samuel Bard, M.D., LL.D., 1822; Hints on Banking, 1827; Considerations Upon the Expediency of Abolishing Damages on Protested Bills of Exchange, and the Effect of Establishing a Reciprocal Exchange With Europe, 1829; The Early Life and Professional Years of Bishop Hobart, 1838 (first published as: The Early Years of the Late Bishop Hobart, 1834, and The Professional Years of John Henry Hobart, 1836); A National Bank: Its Necessity and Most Desirable Form, 1841.

ABOUT: McVickar, W. A. The Life of Rev. John McVickar, S.T.D.; Columbia University Quarterly December 1931 (see Dorfman, J. & Tugwell, R. G. "The Rev. John McVickar, Christian Teacher and Economist"); New York Times October 31, 1868.

MACY, JESSE (June 21, 1842-November 3, 1919), frontier philosopher and student of government organization, was born near Knightstown, Henry County, Ind., son of Quaker parents, William and Phoebe (Hiatt) Macy, who in 1818 had migrated from South Carolina to a non-slave state and had built their home in the midst of an unbroken forest. As a small boy Jesse listened to the stories of fugitive slaves who had taken refuge in the Macy home. When he was fourteen his family moved on by covered wagon to Poweshiek County in central Iowa; and at a school in Grinnell and at Friends' Institute near Oskaloosa this "tall gangling figure in a butternut suit" prepared for college. But in the fall of 1864 he was drafted into the army and with Sherman's hospital corps he made the famous march to the sea. At the end of the war he was determined to devote his energies to some form of political reconstruction. He entered Iowa (now Grinnell) College in 1866 and before his graduation in 1870 he had become absorbed in the revelations of Darwin's theory of evolution and began to see many things in a new, clearer, and more rational light: one of his surest beliefs was that science and democracy had come into being at the same time and that the administration of a righteous government would be effected, for the most part, only by intelligent application of the principles of the scientific method.

For forty-two years he taught political science at his alma mater, participating, at the same time, in local politics, and writing articles on the tariff, the gold standard, public utilities, woman's suffrage, etc., for the *Yale Review,* the *Review of Reviews, American Journal of Sociology,* and numerous dailies. In 1872 he was married to Mary Maude Little.

Macy's authorship (and reputation as an original thinker) began in this way: he had, with repeated failure, been trying to rouse his history students to a little genuine interest in early classic life. Closing the text on his table, he pushed it from him and said, "You may take the town of Grinnell for your next lesson." And they did. This experiment was the substance of a new procedure ,in the teaching of government: "a direct, first-hand observation of the elementary forms of local government"; a sifting of basic principles from a mere collection of facts; and then an application of these fundamentals to the various forms of government. *Our Government*.....was his first important analysis of this method. For a work on *The English Constitution* he had received valuable aid during a sojourn abroad; in *Politics and Political Parties, 1846-61,* he held that the institution of slavery could have been destroyed without resort to arms; and *Party Organization and Machinery,* based on considerable Washington research, reviewed political mechanisms and the influences of party personalities. Both literally, as a child of the frontier, and figuratively, as a shaper of new political and educational approaches, Macy was a significant pioneer.

PRINCIPAL WORKS: Civil Government in Iowa, 1881; Institutional Beginnings in a Western State, 1884; Our Government: What it Does and How It Does It, 1886; The English Constitution, 1897; Political Parties in the United States, 1846-61, 1900; Party Organization and Machinery, 1904; Comparative Free Government, 1915;

ABOUT: Macy, K. M. (ed.). Jesse Macy: An Autobiography; Grinnell Review November 1919; Iowa Journal of History and Politics January 1920.

MAGRUDER, JULIA (September 14, 1854-June 9, 1907), novelist and writer of short stories and juveniles, was born in Charlottesville, Va., the daughter of Allen Bowie Magruder, a man of distinction in both law and letters, and Sarah Magruder. When she was three her family removed to Washington; there she was taught by governesses and acquired a strong desire to write. At the age of seventeen she won the Baltimore *Sun* competition for the best serial story. After careful and thoughtful reading in some of the best American and English letters and the arrival at a firm decision to retain the traditions of the Old South and, at the same time, to stamp out sectional prejudices, she began work on a novel *Across the Chasm.* It was published anonymously in 1885 and although it had a small share of clever comedy to neutralize its higher seriousness, it came too closely on the heels of the North-South conflict to get even relatively impartial criticism from either side. There followed about half a dozen rather ordinary novels for all of which she made only one draft; they were written largely on either side of the "eternal triangle" or the lovers-surmount-obstacles pattern.

In 1895 came what has been considered by many her worthiest literary achievement, *Princess Sonia,* written in eighteen days (three hours a day) during a stay in Paris. Richard Watson Gilder, then editor of the *Century,* gave it special mention. The best of her juveniles was *Child-Sketches From George Eliot.* For outstanding periodicals of the day she wrote articles on the change in the social status of women and on child labor; a collection of stories which she had contributed to these same journals was afterward published under the title *Miss Ayr of Virginia.* During her last illness she continued work on *Her Husband,* published posthumously. Not long before her death the French Academy awarded her the Order of the Palm—a literary honor rarely paid to Americans.

Much of Miss Magruder's life was spent abroad, in Scotland, France, and Italy; but her writings were an outgrowth of an earlier *milieu* about which she had no temporary, indirect, or adopted points of view, but rather the beliefs that emerge from one's sense of belonging to a particular environment. Yet although she succeeded in catching something of the social and domestic maladies of the Reconstruction period, she used, for the most part, very ordinary literary vehicles to convey equally ordinary theses, and fell short of achieving any vigor of impression or strength of reality.

Principal Works: Across the Chasm, 1885; A Magnificant Plebeian, 1888; Princess Sonia, 1895; Child-Sketches From George Eliot, 1895; A Realized Ideal, 1898; A Beautiful Alien, 1900; A Manifest Destiny, 1900.

About: Rutherford, M. L. The South in History and Literature; Library of Southern Literature; monograph on Julia Magruder by Alice Archer Graham, in library of George Washington University; Book News March 1897.

MAHAN, ALFRED THAYER (September 27, 1840-December 1, 1914), naval historian and theorist, was born at West Point, the son of Dennis Hart Mahan, professor of military engineering at the Military Academy, and Mary Helena (Okill) Mahan. His younger brother became a commodore in the navy. He himself from his childhood was attracted to the naval service, and after a private school at Hagerstown, Md., and two years at Columbia, he was appointed to Annapolis at sixteen. He was graduated an ensign in 1859, a tall, handsome, blonde youth (in later years bald and bearded), who already displayed his future tendencies, for he was shy, reserved, thoughtful, devout, and a bit of a prig—he spent his last year in Coventry for reporting a classmate for delinquencies of deportment.

After serving with the Brazil squadron, he was commissioned lieutenant in 1861, and spent most of the Civil War in blockade duty. In 1865 he was commissioned lieutenant commander. From 1867 to 1869 he took part in a cruise to Japan, India, and South Africa, laying the foundations of his observations on international, and particularly British, naval strategy. Six months' leave was spent in

ALFRED THAYER MAHAN

Europe in studying the same problem. In 1872 he married Ellen Lyle Evans; they had a son and two daughters.

The first writing Mahan ever did was a small book on the navy in the Civil War, in 1883. His real work did not begin until, having been made captain in 1885 and appointed lecturer on tactics and naval history at the Newport War College the next year, he prepared and published the lectures which became the first of his famous books. He was president of the War College also from 1886 to 1893, with the exception of a year when he was ordered to select a site for a navy yard in the Northwest. This post he desired to retain so as to have leisure for study and writing; but instead, in 1893, he was made commander of the cruiser "Chicago," flagship of the European squadron. It was an embarrassing position; Mahan's recognition came first from England, and Admiral Erben, his superior, did not enjoy having a subordinate who was receiving degrees from Oxford and Cambridge and being hailed and fêted wherever they went. In 1896 he ended the problem by retiring, but during the Spanish War he was called back from Italy, where he was living, to officiate on the board of strategy directing naval operations. In 1899 he was a delegate to the first Hague Peace Conference. In 1902-03 he was president of the American Historical Association, and in 1906 received the rank of rear admiral, retired. He died in Washington, suddenly, of heart failure.

Mahan has been called "the first philosopher of sea power." An expansionist and imperialist, he had great influence on Theodore Roosevelt and Henry Cabot Lodge and their policies. He was always an advocate of closer affiliation between the English-speaking nations, and may properly be called an Anglophile; he opposed arbitration for peace; his general views were conservative in the extreme. His style, except in his memoirs, is elaborate and heavy. Yet he was a pioneer in his field, and no later work on naval history or naval strategy can be written without reference to Mahan's volumes.

Principal Works: The Gulf and Inland Waters (The Navy in the Civil War) 1883; The Influence of Sea Power Upon History 1660-1783; 1890; The Influence of Sea Power Upon the French Revolution and Empire, 1892; Admiral Farragut, 1892; The Interest of America in Sea Power: Present and Future, 1897; The Life of Nelson, 1897; Lessons of the Spanish War, 1899; The Problem of Asia, 1900; Types of Naval Officers, 1901; Retrospect and Prospect, 1902; Sea Power in Its Relations to the War of 1812, 1905; From Sail to Steam: Recollections of Naval Life, 1907; Some Neglected Aspects of War, 1907; Naval Administration and Warfare, 1908; The Harvest Within, 1909; The Interest of America in International Conditions, 1910; Naval Strategy, 1911; Armaments and Arbitration, 1912; The Major Operations of the Navies in the War of American Independence, 1913.

About: Kirkham, G. K. The Books and Articles of Rear Admiral A. T. Mahan, U.S.N.; Mahan, A. T. From Sail to Steam; Taylor, C. C. The Life of Admiral Mahan; Outlook December 9, 1914, January 13, 1915; New York Times December 2, 1914.

"MALACK, MULEY." See NOAH, MORDECAI MANUEL

MALCOLM, JAMES PELLER (August 1767-April 5, 1815), line-engraver and social historian, who during his earlier career spelled his name "Malcom," was born in Philadelphia, the son of Moses and Mary (Peller) Malcom. He attended Friends' School, and just before the first open-fire skirmishes of the Revolutionary War he was taken to Pottstown and placed in school there. After the war he returned to Philadelphia and then began to study art, advancing from simple-line drawing to engraving. His first published specimen, technically weak, but showing considerable promise, was the frontispiece for Col. John Parke's *Lyric Works of Horace.* Under the patronage of two Philadelphians he went to England for three years' study in the schools of the Royal Academy.

Malcolm became an illustrator for the *Gentleman's Magazine* and other British periodicals; and for Daniel Lyson's four volumes of *Environs of London* he engraved seventy-nine plates. It is believed that he returned to America for a brief visit in 1792 or 1793 but his autobiography in the *Gentleman's Magazine* (May 1815) contains no mention of it. His last years were darkened by both illness and poverty.

He was the author and illustrator of two volumes of the history of London society: the sales success of *Anecdotes of the Manners and Customs of London During the Eighteenth Century* (1807) encouraged him in the preparation of the complementary *Anecdotes of . . . London From the Roman Invasion to the Year 1700,* which appeared four years later. When the earlier volume went into a second edition in 1810 Malcolm answered the somewhat hostile remarks of the *European Magazine and London Review* critic with the statement that the famous John Nichols collection had provided the sources of his text as well as the patterns for his illustrations. He also wrote *An Historical Sketch of the Art of Caricaturing* and a kind of travel book on Kent, Gloucester, Hereford, Monmouth, and Somerset counties. Like his engravings, Malcolm's writings were executed with a very obvious technical cautiousness; they represent tireless effort, but they are almost completely lacking in genuine inspiration.

PRINCIPAL WORKS: London Redivivum (4 vols.) 1803-07; Anecdotes of the Manners and Customs of London During the Eighteenth Century, 1807; Excursions in the County of Kent, Gloucester, Hereford, Monmouth, and Somerset, 1807; Anecdotes of the Manners and Customs of London From the Roman Invasion to the Year 1700, 1811; An Historical Sketch of the Art of Caricaturing, 1813.

ABOUT: Stauffer, D. M. American Engravers Upon Copper and Steel; Gentleman's Magazine May 1815; Philadelphia Monthly Magazine April 1829.

MALONE, WALTER (February 10, 1866-May 18, 1915), jurist and poet, was born near Pleasant Hill, Miss., the son of Dr. Franklin Jefferson Malone, a member of the Mississippi constitutional convention of 1868, and Mary Louisa (Hardin) Malone. It is said that he wrote political articles for the Louisville *Courier-Journal* at the age of thirteen; and when he was sixteen he published *Claribel and Other Poems*. During three of his undergraduate years at the University of Mississippi he edited the university magazine, and while he was still a junior he found a publisher for *The Outcast and Other Poems.* He was graduated in 1887 and spent the next ten years in law practice with his brother James H. Malone in Memphis. During 1888 he acted as city editor of the *Public Ledger*; and after experimenting with a variety of literary ventures in New York, 1897-1900, returned to Memphis to re-establish the firm of Malone & Malone. Five years later he was appointed judge of the second division of the Shelby County Circuit Court, which post he held with universal respect until the time of his death.

The first volume of verse to follow his obviously adolescent beginnings was *Narcissus and Other Poems,* and then came two more drab little books (*Songs of Dusk and Dawn* and *Songs of December and June*), abounding in stiff phrases and wandering imagery. *The Coming of the King,* a volume of short stories, appeared the year of his removal to New York; and another book of verse was issued the year in which he returned to Memphis. This was *Songs of North and South,* containing some well-turned seasonal poems and some descriptive pieces of the Southern scene which, although founded on an obviously exuberant affection, constitute his best work.

The year after the publication of *Poems* (1904), revised and completed to date, he struck a popular response with "Opportunity," a verse which in the end brought him what he considered a rather unflattering kind of acclaim. His experiments with playwriting came to almost nothing; and not long after the appearance of *Songs of East and West,* travel poems, he began the long task of shaping an ambitious narrative poem *Hernando de Soto,* which was finally published the year before his death. To the travels, conquests, and death of De Soto, the spell of the Mississippi, and the skirmishes of the Spaniards and Indians, Malone attempted to give epic dignity. But this, like his less pretentious verse, bore the ear-marks of serious literary application and a proportionate lack of brilliant execution.

PRINCIPAL WORKS: Claribel and Other Poems, 1882; The Outcast and Other Poems, 1886; Narcissus and Other Poems, 1892; Songs of Dusk and Dawn, 1894; Songs of December and June, 1896; The Coming of the King, 1897; Songs of North and South, 1900; Poems, 1904; Songs of East and West, 1906; Hernando de Soto, 1914.

ABOUT: Malone, W. Selected Poems (see Sketch by Frazer Hood); Library of Southern Literature; Munsey's Magazine March 1905; (Memphis) Commercial Appeal May 19, 1915.

MANN, HORACE (May 4, 1796-August 2, 1859), educator, was born near Franklin, Mass., the son of a poor farmer named Thomas Mann, who died in 1809 of tuberculosis, and of Rebecca (Stanley) Mann. His childhood was a hell of poverty, drudgery, and religious terror, and he grew up a frail, tubercular lad who at sixteen had spent only a few weeks yearly in bad elementary schools. Then in six months an erratic itinerant teacher prepared him to enter the sophomore class at Brown University, from which he was graduated with the highest honors in 1819. After a few months spent in studying law he returned to Brown as librarian and tutor in Latin and Greek, then in 1821 went to the law school at Litchfield, Conn., and was admitted to the bar in 1823. He practised at Dedham and Boston until 1837, when his legal and political career ended and his educational mission began. Meanwhile he had been a state representative from 1827 to 1833, state senator from 1833 to 1837, and president of the state senate during the last year. In 1830 he had married Charlotte Messer, daughter of the president of Brown, but she died, childless, two years later, leaving him to ten years of incessant grief.

In 1837 Horace Mann, as president of the Massachusetts senate, signed the education bill for which he had fought. He was on his way to renown and wealth as a lawyer and politician. But he gave his future away for the sake of public education. "Let the next

From a daguerreotype

HORACE MANN

generation be my client," he said. He became secretary of the state board of education, and in twelve years, fighting every opposing force from intellectual snobbery to religious bigotry, he revolutionized the schools of the state and laid the foundation for progressive public education in the entire nation. He established the first three normal schools in the United States, started and from 1838 to 1848 edited the semi-monthly *Common School Journal,* averted the restoration of sectarian teaching in the schools, professionalized the occupation of teaching, and produced twelve annual reports which are landmarks in the history of education.

In 1842 he married Mary Tyler Peabody, one of the famous Peabody sisters of Boston, and with her toured Europe for five months studying public education abroad. In 1848 he was elected to Congress; there he quarreled with Daniel Webster on the slavery issue, but was re-elected as an independent when Webster prevented his renomination as a Whig. In 1852 he ran for governor on the Free Soil ticket and was badly defeated; but on the very same day he was appointed president of Antioch College, Yellow Springs, Ohio. There he taught as well—political economy, intellectual and moral philosophy, natural theology. But the seven years he spent there were his death. Antioch, now one of the most advanced of American colleges, was in a chaotic, disorganized condition; in 1859 it was actually sold for debt. Mann labored valiantly to reorganize it and start it going again. He succeeded, but it killed him; he retired, worn out, and a few weeks later he was dead.

"A Puritan without theology," Mann had in him much of the fanaticism which seems inseparable from tireless service in an idealistic cause. He campaigned for care of the insane, for abolition, for religious freedom—but also against the pleasures of life. He was dogmatic, self-willed, stubborn, utterly without humor. Few persons could have loved him very warmly. But he was the father of a common school education in America, a great libertarian, a great educator a great democrat, and a great man. In his last speech to his students at Antioch he uttered his credo: "Be ashamed to die until you have won some victory for humanity."

Principal Works: Twelve Annual Reports (in Life and Works, by M. T. Mann) 1837-1849 Lectures on Education, 1845; A Few Thoughts for a Young Man, 1850; Slavery: Letters and Speeches, 1852; Lectures on Intemperance, 1852 Powers and Duties of Women, 1853; Sermons 1861.

About: Brooks, Van W. The Flowering of New England; Compayré, G. Horace Mann and the Public School in the United States; Culver, T Horace Mann and Religion in the Massachusetts Public Schools; Hinsdale, B. A. Horace Mann and the Common School Revival in the United States; Hubbell, G. A. Horace Mann; Mann, M. T., Life and Works of Horace Mann; Smith, P. Winship, A. E. & Harris, W. T. Horace Mann and Our Schools; Williams, E. I. F. Horace Mann Educational Statesman.

MANN, MARY TYLER (PEABODY)

(November 16, 1806-February 11, 1887), educator and miscellaneous writer, was the second child of Nathaniel and Elizabeth (Palmer) Peabody [*q.v.*]. The father was a physician and dentist; the mother taught her seven children along with others in a school which she conducted.

A bookstore which the family opened in Boston in 1832 was a meeting place for the Transcendentalists. Mary's younger sister married Nathaniel Hawthorne in 1842. The year after, Mary and Horace Mann [*q.v.*] were married. She had been devoted to him for years, but grief over the death of his first wife kept him from thinking of marriage for a decade. It was a happy union for they were perfectly suited to each other intellectually. She helped him much in his work and bore him three sons.

She wrote one book, *The Flower People*, before her marriage, and another in 1857 called *Christianity in the Kitchen: A Physiological Cook Book,* which in spite of its strange title was founded on the science of nutrition as far as it was known in that day.

After her husband died in 1859 she began work on a biography of him and the editing of his writings. *The Life and Works of Horace Mann* appeared in three volumes. (Later an expanded edition of five volumes was published, edited by G. C. Mann.) Besides engaging in philanthropic work, she assisted in her sister Elizabeth's kindergarten, writing an essay on "Moral Culture of Infancy." At the age of eighty she wrote *Juanita: A Romance of Real Life in Cuba Fifty Years Ago* which was published after her death.

PRINCIPAL WORKS: The Flower People, 1838 (rev. ed. 1875); Life and Works of Horace Mann, 1865-68.

ABOUT: Peabody, S. H. & Pope, C. H. Peabody Genealogy; Tupper, F. & Brown, H. T. (eds.). Grandmother Tyler's Book: The Recollections of Mary Palmer Tyler; Boston Transcript February 12, 15, 1887.

MANSFIELD, EDWARD DEERING (August 17, 1801-October 27, 1880), editor, biographer, and social historian, was born in New Haven, Conn., the son of Jared Mansfield, mathematician and physicist, and Elizabeth (Phipps) Mansfield. He passed his early boyhood in Ohio, was afterward sent to school in Connecticut, and then entered the Military Academy at West Point, from which he was graduated in 1819. At the College of New Jersey he began the study of law, was graduated in 1822, continued his studies at the Litchfield Law School, and three years later was admitted to the Connecticut bar. In Cincinnati, Ohio, he set up a practice but it became only a secondary interest to him; and in 1826 with Benjamin Drake, editor and historian, he made an exhaustive study of that city, by house-to-house canvass, for the purpose of stimulating immigration. With a seventy-five dollar grant from the city council they published *Cincinnati in 1826*, a most enlightening study of governmental organization and social and economic needs of the locality; it went into a British edition and a German translation.

Shortly after the founding of the Cincinnati *Chronicle* in 1826 Mansfield became its editor, and through its merger with the *Mirror*, its later re-establishment under its original name, and its subsequent consolidations with the *Atlas* and the *Daily Gazette*, he served intermittently in this capacity. During his editorship of the *Atlas* and *Gazette* he introduced to his readers a number of young writers, including Harriet Beecher Stowe, who later became well known. Mansfield edited the *Railroad Record*, 1853-1871, and during the Civil War decade, over the signature "Veteran Observer," wrote some vigorous pieces for the New York *Times;* his *Gazette* columns were signed "E. D. M." He was an active worker on William Henry Harrison's committee for the promotion of a railroad running from Cincinnati to the South; he prepared *Railroad From the Banks of the Ohio River to the Tide Waters of the Carolinas and Georgia* in pamphlet form. Mansfield was twice married: to Mary Wallace Peck, by whom he had two children; and in 1839, to Margaret Worthington, by whom he had four children.

His *Political Grammar* (later *Political Manual*) was first issued in 1834; *The Utility of Mathematics* appeared the same year. He wrote biographies of General Winfield Scott, Daniel Drake, and Ulysses S. Grant, and in the year before his death he published *Personal Memories: Social, Political, and Literary. . .* Mansfield was an alert and enterprising newspaperman, and his biographical and historical commentaries reflect his reportorial ability.

PRINCIPAL WORKS: The Political Grammar, 1826; The Utility of Mathematics, 1834; Railroad From the Banks of the Ohio River to the Tide Waters of the Carolinas and Georgia, 1835; The Legal Rights, Liabilities, and Duties of Women, 1845; The Life of General Winfield Scott, 1846; The Mexican War, 1848; American Education, 1850; Memoirs of the Life and Services of Daniel Drake, 1855; A Popular and Authentic Life of Ulysses S. Grant, 1868; Personal Memories: Social, Political, and Literary. . ., 1879.

ABOUT: Mansfield, E. D. Personal Memories; Venable, W. H. Beginnings of Literary Culture in the Ohio Valley; Cincinnati Daily Gazette October 28, 1880.

MARCH, FRANCIS ANDREW (October 25, 1825-September 8, 1911), philologist, was born in Sutton (now Millbury), Mass., the son of Andrew Patch March and Nancy (Parker) March. When he was only three his family moved to Worcester, Mass., where he was given an excellent public-school training before entering Amherst College, from which he was graduated in 1845. He found considerable intellectual stimulus at Amherst in Noah Webster's lectures and in the class-room work with Professor William C. Fowler; this was to have a strong influence in the shaping of his career. He taught school and tutored in New England for six years in all, and then decided to begin the study of law, which he pursued under Francis H. Dewey, a Worcester attorney. In 1849 he went to New York to read law in the office of Barney & Butler and in the year following was admitted to the bar. He had practiced for only two years when he was obliged to go South for his health, and secured a teaching position in

Fredericksburg, Va. Two years afterward he was called to Lafayette College at Easton, Pa., and from the duties of tutor he advanced, within two years, to the chair of English language and comparative philology, the first office of its kind either here or in England; he occupied it almost half a century.

At various times March conducted classes in French, German, Latin, Greek, law, political economy, philosophy, and even botany, but his outstanding pedagogical achievement was his elevation of the study of English from a desultory lecture-series status to the dignity of intellectual discipline, entailing a careful explanation of the language and thought of the work under consideration. This exegetical method influenced a number of America's foremost educators.

March spent nearly ten years in research on his exhaustive *Comparative Grammar of the Anglo-Saxon Language . . .*, a detailed analysis of the relationship between the English language and the other tongues of the Indo-European group. He also published a book on philological methods; a class-room *Introduction to Anglo-Saxon. . .*; directed the American staff in the preparation of the *Oxford English Dictionary;* and was the consulting editor of the *Standard Dictionary.* He edited four volumes of Latin and Greek classics, and in the interest of the revision of English orthography he published *The Spelling Reform,* which went into several editions.

March was awarded several honorary degrees and was elected to membership in a number of learned societies. But his *Comparative Grammar* alone was sufficiently comprehensive and astute to attract the attention of European scholars and to assure its author of a place among significant grammarians.

Principal Works: Method of Philological Study of the English Language, 1865; A Comparative Grammar of the Anglo-Saxon Language. . ., 1870; Introduction to Anglo-Saxon: An Anglo-Saxon Reader, 1870; Latin Hymns, 1874; Eusebius, 1874; The Select Work of Tertullian, 1875; Athenagoras, 1876; The Spelling Reform, 1881.

About: Addresses. . . in Honor of Prof. Francis A. March, . . .at Lafayette College, October 24, 1895; Hart, R. N. Francis Andrew March: A Sketch; Skillman, D. A. A Biography of a College; Publications of the Modern Language Association March 1914 (see article by J. W. Bright).

MARKOE, PETER (c. 1752-January 30, 1792), poet and dramatist, was born on the island of Santa Cruz (or St. Croix) in the Danish West Indies, the son of Abraham Markoe, patriot and wealthy plantation owner, and his first wife Elizabeth (Kenny) Rogers. He matriculated at Pembroke College, Oxford, in February 1767; and whether he continued later at Trinity College, Dublin, seems very doubtful, but on May 29, 1775, he was admitted to Lincoln's Inn. During that same year he is listed as a captain of Light Horse in the Philadelphia City Militia, but records of his activities are scant. It is likely that he made several return journeys to Santa Cruz, after his father's removal to Philadelphia, for the purpose of business transactions. In 1785 Peter Markoe received a lottery warrant for 500 acres of Northumberland County (Pa.) land; and from 1786 to 1789 he was listed in the muster roll of the Philadelphia militia. He died in Philadelphia at the age of forty.

Among Markoe's earliest writings were verses addressed to various celebrities, on the occasion of their birthdays, their arrival in Santa Cruz, etc. His *Patriot Chief* (1784), a tragedy laid in Lydia, was rejected by Lewis Hallam's American Company; it was perhaps never produced but it prompted Col. John Parke's epistle "to Mr. Peter Markoe on His Excellent Tragedy Called the Patriot Chief," urging Markoe to utilize native subject matter. *Miscellaneous Poems,* many of which were admittedly written when he was very young, were published by subscription in 1787, and in January of the following year came *The Times,* the satire of which was so local and so personal that it soon became meaningless; nevertheless, one of the critics placed him, at this time, among "the first poetic geniuses in America."

Three years after the establishment, in 1787, of America's first "opera-house" (the Southwark Theatre, Philadelphia) the Old American Company accepted (but never produced) Peter Markoe's *Reconciliation: or, The Triumph of Nature,* one of the first native comic operas. In 1787 he had published *The Algerine Spy in Pennsylvania. . .,* purporting to be letters written "by a native of Algiers on the affairs of the United States"; in 1788, *The Storm,* a description of a recent Southern "tempest," issued with William Falconer's *The Shipwreck.*

Markoe had, for his day, considerable literary versatility, but his writings retain only an historical significance.

Principal Works: The Patriot Chief, 1784; Miscellaneous Poems, 1787; The Algerine Spy in Pennsylvania: or, Letters Written by a Native of Algiers on the Affairs of the United States in America. . ., 1787; Miscellaneous Poems, 1787; The Storm: A Poem Descriptive of the Late Tempest, 1788; The Reconciliation: or, the Triumph of Nature, 1790.

MARSH, GEORGE PERKINS (March 15, 1801-July 23, 1882), philologist, diplomat, and miscellaneous writer, was born in Woodstock, Vt., the son of Charles Marsh, a Congressman and prominent attorney, and Susan (Perkins) (Arnold) Marsh. His first cousin was James Marsh, philosopher and president of the University of Vermont [*q.v.*].

Though Marsh lived to be eighty-one, he was a frail, precocious child who ruined his eyes by too much reading, so that most of his education had to be obtained by ear. He spent only a few months at Phillips Andover Academy, but when he entered Dartmouth he was the most brilliant member of his class, who learned half a dozen languages in his leisure hours. He was graduated in 1820, and for a miserable year taught at the Military Academy in Norwich, Vt. He hated teaching, and later refused an offered chair at Harvard. He was glad to return to Woodstock to study law in his father's office, and in 1825 he was admitted to the bar and started practice in Burlington, Vt. On the side he learned the Scandinavian tongues.

In 1828 he married Harriet Buell, by whom he had two sons. She died in 1833, a few days after the death of her older son. Marsh was not remarried until 1839, his second wife being Caroline Crane, a writer and translator from the German.

In 1835 Marsh became a member of the supreme executive council, which then took the place of a state senate in Vermont. In 1843 he entered Congress as a Whig, and served until 1843, when President Taylor made him minister to Turkey. On being recalled in 1854, he returned to Vermont, where he acted as railroad commissioner from 1857 to 1859. His wool business had failed and he was $10,000 in debt. Meanwhile his fame as a philologist was spreading, and he lectured at Columbia in 1858 and 1859, and at the Lowell Institute, Boston, in 1859 and 1860. Having become a Republican, he was appointed by Lincoln as our first minister to the new kingdom of Italy in 1861, and he served until his death, ending as the dean of the diplomatic corps, with the longest incumbency of any American minister. He died at Vallambrosa, near Florence, and was buried in the Protestant Cemetery in Rome.

Marsh was a sort of universal genius. Among the subjects on which he was an erudite authority were philology, etymology, the study of reptiles, engravings, music, the artificial propagation of fish, comparative grammar, physiognomy, and geography! He was, as Lewis Mumford says, "the fountain-

Collection of Frederick H. Meserve
GEORGE P. MARSH

head of the conservation movement"; he was an early proponent of the "Nordic superiority" myth (though he would hardly have approved of its present forms); he wrote learnedly on the potentialities of the camel as an American domestic beast; he was a connoisseur of bird songs; he was master of thirteen languages; and in addition to his original writings he translated and edited Rask's *Icelandic Grammar,* edited the American edition of Wedgwood's *Dictionary of English Etymology,* and was one of the earliest editors of the *Oxford Dictionary.* Most of his work is now outdated, but it was admirable in its time. His style is a bit dry, and marred rather than adorned by a somewhat ponderous wit. His interest to modern readers is historical, not literary or scientific. He was, however, one of the most typical and most significant examples of the nineteenth century New England mind in action.

PRINCIPAL WORKS: The Goths in New England, 1843; The Camel: His Organization, Habits, and Uses, 1856; Lectures on the English Language, 1860; The Origin and History of the English Language, 1862; Man and Nature, 1864 (as The Earth as Modified by Human Action, 1874); Mediaeval and Modern Saints and Miracles, 1876.

ABOUT: Brooks, Van W. The Flowering of New England; Brown, S. G. A Discourse Commemorative of the Hon. George Perkins Marsh; Koopman, H. L. Bibliography of George Perkins Marsh; Marsh, C. C. Life and Letters of George Perkins Marsh; Mencken, H. L. The American Language; Nation July 27, August 3, October 12, 1882, September 13, 1888; New England Magazine March 1898; New York Times July 25, 1882.

MARSH, JAMES (July 19, 1794-July 3, 1842), compiler, clergyman, and president of the University of Vermont, was born on a farm at Hartford, Vt., the son of Daniel and Marion (Harper) Marsh. He appeared to have been destined for agricultural life until eighteen when he received preparation from one William Nutting, schoolmaster, for entrance to Dartmouth College. As an undergraduate he read widely, especially in the classics and in the literature of the Cambridge Platonists. During a revival in 1815 he was converted, and following his Dartmouth Commencement he spent a year at Andover Theological Seminary; returned to Dartmouth as a tutor, 1818-1820; and went back again to Andover in 1822. He prepared an article on "Ancient and Modern Poetry" for the *North American Review* and assisted in the translation of J. J. Bellerman's *Geography of the Scriptures;* after a year of inactivity he became a teacher at the college and theological school at Hampden-Sidney, Va. In 1824 he became professor of Oriental languages; that same year he was ordained in the Congregational ministry, at Hanover, N. H., and was married to Lucia Wheelock, niece of Dartmouth's president. Two years later Marsh was appointed president of the University of Vermont.

In a seven-year administration he evolved an educational policy that allowed the students considerably increased personal and academic freedom; his inaugural address, *An Exposition of the Course of Instruction and Discipline in the University of Vermont,* set forth his pedagogic thesis. With an increase in emphasis on the "business" side of his office he withdrew from the presidency in 1833 and became professor of philosophy; after the death of his first wife in 1828 he married her sister.

In 1829 Marsh edited and wrote an introductory essay for Coleridge's *Aids to Reflections;* his admiration for English and German romanticism threw him into opposition to the philosophy of Locke and the Scottish School that had taken hold in New England. Coleridge's distinction between reason and the understanding appeared to give Marsh something that would "satisfy the heart as well as the head." His edition caused no small intellectual stir, won the interest of Emerson, and had some influence on the course of Transcendentalism.

Principal Works: An Address Delivered in Burlington Upon the Inauguration of the Author to the Office of President of the University of Vermont, November 28, 1826, 1827; An Exposition in the Course of Instruction and Discipline in the University of Vermont, 1829; Coleridge's Aids to Reflection (ed.) 1829; Selections From the Old English Writers on Practical Theology, 1830.

About: Cheever, G. B. Characteristics of the Christian Philosopher; Torrey, J. The Remains of the Rev. James Marsh:. . .With a Memoir of his Life; Philosophical Review January 1925; Vermont Chronicle July 6. 1842.

MARSHALL, CHRISTOPHER (November 6, 1709-May 4, 1797), diarist, pharmacist, and Revolutionary patriot, is believed to have been born in Dublin, Ireland. After an English classical education he set sail for America at the age of eighteen. In Philadelphia he became a ranking pharmacist, operating a large shop at the sign of the Golden Ball. In 1774 he transferred his business to his three sons and from the very early days of the Revolution completely embraced the American cause: as a member of the Philadelphia committee of inspection and observation he aided in the enforcement of war-time laws, in army habilitation and provisions, in the identification of suspects, etc. He became manager of a textile factory established in 1775; was a delegate to the provincial conference (Philadelphia) which laid the ground-work for new state government and in December 1776 he aided in finding shelter and care for sick and wounded soldiers.

Because of ill health and the threat of a British invasion, Marshall removed to Lancaster in 1777; served on the Council of Safety early that winter, headed the price-fixing committee; and continued his efforts in the procurement of food and clothing for the troops.

The journal which Marshall kept during the war was first edited and published by William Duane in 1839 (*Passages From the Remembrancer of Christopher Marshall*); supplemented by another year's entry, Duane re-issued it in 1849 (*Passages From the Diary of Christopher Marshall*); and in 1877 he released the more comprehensive *Extracts From the Diary of Christopher Marshall: Kept in Philadelphia and Lancaster, During the American Revolution, 1774-1781.* It is slightly Pepysian in its devotion to domestic detail and abounds in miscellaneous personal intelligence that is of obvious interest to military historians; the reader is easily convinced that Marshall was a man of unfailing charitable impulse—illustrated by anything from the mere purchase of a pair of breeches for the son of a needy soldier to his patient supervision of the "part curing of Mary's scalded head." Because of his support of the Revolution Marshall was read out of the Society of Friends, but he maintained an independent adherence to Quaker principles. His factful *Diary* has a very definite place among the significant literature of the War of Independence.

ABOUT: Marshall, C. Extracts From the Diary of Christopher Marshall. . .; Simpson, H. The Lives of Eminent Philadelphians Now Deceased; American Daily Advertiser May 6, 1797.

MARSHALL, JOHN (September 24, 1755-July 6, 1835), biographer and juridical writer, was born near Germantown (now Midland), Va., the oldest of the fifteen children of Thomas and Mary Isham (Keith) Marshall. Through his mother's family he was related to the Randolphs and the Lees, and also to Thomas Jefferson, later his greatest opponent. Though his early life was spent under frontier conditions, his father, to whom he was very close, was a man of culture and standing in the community, and the boy was tutored by him as well as by neighboring clergymen. He first entered the larger world through the American Revolution, serving all through it, including the famous winter at Valley Forge, and being finally mustered out in 1781 with the rank of captain. In 1780, while he was awaiting further orders for service, he studied law at the College of William and Mary and was admitted to the bar.

He was a born orator and debater, and from the beginning made his mark as an attorney, though he retained all his life the easy manners and slipshod dress of the frontiersman, and was looked down upon in consequence by his more aristocratic colleagues. In 1783 he married Mary Willis Ambler, who became the mother of ten children, four of whom died, and who for years before her death in 1831 was a nervous invalid. Marshall was a notably domestic and tender husband, a very human person who enjoyed conviviality and loved the leisurely life of the prosperous planter. He declined numerous appointments to important posts in order to lead the comfortable existence he most enjoyed.

From a portrait by H. Inman
JOHN MARSHALL
1832

However, his rise in politics was inevitable, especially after he became a strong Federalist, Washington's and Adams' friend and Jefferson's enemy. He did much to secure Virginia's ratification of the Constitution (later he kept manhood suffrage out of the constitution of the state itself), he served several terms in the House of Burgesses, and he was one of a commission to France in 1797. From 1799 to 1800 he was in Congress, he was secretary of state under John Adams, and in 1801 he accepted the president's appointment as chief justice of the Supreme Court, a position he held until his death. We are accustomed to think of Marshall as the greatest chief justice in our history; in his own time, however, his appointment was "not greeted with applause from any quarter" (Beveridge), since the Republicans (i.e., the future Democrats) rightly felt he was being foisted on them at the end of a defeated Federalist administration, and his own party considered him too independent and hence not trustworthy.

Marshall was the father of the vital and fundamental theory that the Supreme Court can pass on the constitutionality of laws made by the states. A strict Constitutionalist, he had many times actually to construct the law on given points not clearly covered, and this was his most famous and far-reaching construction.

As an author, except for his published decisions, his only work is his biography of Washington. He wrote it avowedly to make money—though his income was large his needs were always larger—and he was much disappointed when Jefferson spiked his plan of selling it through postmasters all over the country! It is hastily written and badly arranged, and by no means expresses the real intellect of a man of whom Rufus King said that "his head is one of the best organized of anyone I have known." In his juridical writings, on the other hand, his style is clarity itself, simple and masterly. This tall, thin, swarthy man, with the brilliant black eyes and the careless attire, had one of the finest minds ever put at the service of the United States of America—even though some of his decisions may have led to catastrophes as great as the Civil War, and may still complicate the political and economic life of America. He was never ill a day until he was seventy-five, and then he survived one of the brutal operations of his era, and lived five years more before a stage coach injury caused his death from a ruptured liver. He died in Philadelphia and was buried in Richmond, his home for many years.

PRINCIPAL WORKS: The Life of George Washington, 1804-07 (Vol. 1, as A History of the American Colonies, 1824); The Writings of John Marshall Upon the Federal Constitution, 1839.

ABOUT: Beveridge, A. J. The Life of John Marshall; Corwin, E. S. John Marshall and the Constitution; Craigmyle, T. S. John Marshall in Diplomacy and in Law; Dillon, J. F. John Marshall; Farley, J. A. John Marshall; Magruder, A. B. John Marshall; Marshall, J. Autobiographical Sketch; Oster, J. E. The Political and Economic Doctrines of John Marshall; Platt, H. G. John Marshall and Other Addresses; Story, J. A Discourse on the Life, Character, and Services of the Hon. John Marshall; Atlantic Monthly March 1901.

MARTIN, FRANÇOIS-XAVIER (March 17, 1762-December 10, 1846), jurist and historian, a native of Marseilles, France, came to North Carolina as a youth. He lived at first by teaching French, and when he had learned English he got work as a typesetter. Although he had had no previous experience in printing he eventually became the owner of the shop. He published many of his own translations from the French, along with schoolbooks and novels.

Meanwhile he studied law, and at twenty-six was admitted to the bar. He made a number of collections, reprints, and translations of laws and legal works, and was employed by the legislature to make a "revisal" of the *Laws of the State of North Carolina.*

Though a quiet and unassuming lawyer, he soon possessed a thorough knowledge of English, French, and Roman law. In 1809 President Madison appointed him a judge for the Mississippi Territory, from which he was transferred to the Territory of Orleans. When the state of Louisiana was formed, he became its first attorney-general, and from 1815 a justice of the state supreme court. Here his knowledge of French and of law were of inestimable value in creating an orderly system out of the mixture of French, Spanish, and English law then in use. The *Louisiana Reports* contain volumes of his opinions, and from 1811 to 1830 he himself published reports of cases decided by the courts.

His *History of Louisiana and History of North Carolina* are well-documented factual records, but written in a dry and lifeless style. As a speaker he was dull, and his personal life was miserly and without diversion. He never married, and at his death left nearly half a million dollars to a younger brother.

PRINCIPAL WORKS: History of Louisiana, 1827; History of North Carolina, 1829.

ABOUT: Ashe, S. A. Biographical History of North Carolina; State Records of North Carolina; The Jeffersonian December 12, 1846.

MARTYN, SARAH TOWNE (SMITH) (August 15, 1805-November 22, 1879), journalist, juvenile and historical writer, was born in Hopkinton, N.H. Her parents, Ethan and Bathsheba (Sanford) Smith were of old New England families. Her father taught her Greek, Hebrew, and modern languages, and she received some general and musical training at a school in New York City.

From her father she also learned her devotion to temperance and abolitionism, in which movements she was active all her life. She edited a number of magazines, particularly religious and women's journals. She wrote juvenile and historical pieces for the American Tract Society, among the latter being *Margaret: The Pearl of Navarre, The English Exile, Daughters of the Cross,* and *Women of the Bible.*

Her husband was a clergyman, John H. Martyn, who was also her brother-in-law. Their oldest son, William Carlos, became a clergyman and writer. There were two other sons and a daughter. Mrs. Martyn gained a reputation as a hostess to many writers and reformers. She died in New York City.

PRINCIPAL WORKS: Margaret: The Pearl of Navarre, 1867; The English Exile: or, William Tyndale at Home and Abroad, 1867; Daughters of the Cross, 1868; Women of the Bible, 1868.

ABOUT: Hart, J. S. A Manual of American Literature; files of the Ladies' Wreath and the Advocate of Moral Reform.

"MARVELL, IK." See MITCHELL, DONALD GRANT

MASON, JOHN (c.1600-January 30, 1672), soldier, historian, and magistrate, was born in England and came to the United States when he was about thirty-three. He was captain of militia for Dorchester and shortly afterwards aided in the founding of Windsor, Conn.

By May 1637 the powerful Pequot tribes had become so aggressive that the Connecticut authorities dispatched Mason with eighty white men and a hundred Indians. He proceeded to Saybrook Fort, and then, disregarding official orders, he advanced on the Pequots by a roundabout course, took them by complete surprise, and virtually wiped them out, with a slaughter of more than six hundred. The success of Mason's strategy won him promotion to the rank of Major, and the General Court (October 1656) requested that he write a history of the Pequot War. Increase Mather included Mason's narrative in his *A Relation of the Troubles That Have Happened in New England,* assuming John Allyn, then secretary of the Connecticut Colony, to be the author. Rev. Thomas Prince, to whom Mason's grandson had given the original draft, expounded, in an introductory note, the actual facts about the authorship of *A Brief History of the Pequot War: Especially of the Memorable Taking of Their Fort at Mistick in Connecticut,* 1736. It would seem that Mason ignored few details in his account; and he dwelt at some length on the "Special Providences" in which

> John Dier and Thomas Stiles were . . . shot in the nots of their handkerchiefs being about their necks, and received no hurt. . . Lieut. Seeley was shot in the eyebrew with a flat headed arrow, the point turning downwards. . . Lieut. Bull had an arrow shot into a hard piece of cheese. . . etc.

Until the year of his death Mason was an active public official; moreover he was one of the founders of Norwich, Conn., where he passed his last years. After the death of his first wife he was married, in 1639, to Anne Peck; he had one child by his first wife and seven by his second.

"I shall not climb after applause," said Mason in his preface, "nor do I much fear censure"—he was in a position (and he knew it) to summon most of the facts of the Pequot skirmish: and he recorded them with sufficient "plainness and faithfulness" to give them a *per se* historical value.

ABOUT: Hubbard, W. A. Narrative of the Troubles With the Indians in New England; Mason, J. A Brief History of the Pequot War (see Introduction); Sparks, J. Library of American Biography; Underhill, J. Newes From America; Vincent P. A True Relation of the Late Battell Fought in New-England Between the English and the Pequet Salvages.

MASON, LOWELL (January 8, 1792-August 11, 1872), musical educator, compiler, and hymnologist, was born in Medfield, Mass., the son of Johnson Mason, manufacturer and member of the state legislature, and Catharine (Hartshorn) Mason. He was, according to his own account, "a wayward, unpromising boy," but his father, a good 'cellist taught him to play "all manner of musical instruments that came within his reach." At the age of twenty he went to Savannah, Ga., as a bank clerk and he remained there until 1827 when he was called back to Boston for the supervision of music at three Boston churches.

Meanwhile, with the aid of William Gardiner's *Sacred Melodies* he had made a collection of psalm tunes, published as *The Boston Handel and Haydn Society's Collection of Church Music.* He was president of the Handel and Haydn Society from 1827 to 1832 and in 1833 he organized the Boston Academy of Music which aided in placing musical instruction in the public schools. Mason prepared a *Manual of Instruction,* based on the system of Pestalozzi, by which the teaching of singing preceded the instruction in musical symbols. He studied the Continental methods and returning from Europe in 1837 was eventually appointed to teach in all Boston schools. In 1851 he went to New York, and three years later to Orange, N.J. The later years of his life were spent in the activities of musical societies and in the enlargement of his vast library, which, after his death, was presented to Yale.

Mason's own compositions were largely adaptations from the melodies of Handel, Haydn, and Mozart; among his more familiar tunes are "From Greenland's Icy Mountains" and "Nearer, My God, to Thee." But it was as a compiler of music—over fifty books in all—and as a pioneer in systematic musical instruction that he exerted his greatest influence.

PRINCIPAL WORKS: The Boston Handel and Haydn Society's Collection of Church Music, 1822; The Juvenile Psalmist, 1829; Lyra Sacra, 1832; Manual of Instruction, 1834; The Psaltery, 1845; The Song Garden, 1864-65.

ABOUT: Mason, W. Memories of a Musical Life; Seward, T. F. The Educational Work of Dr. Lowell Mason; Dwight's Journal of Music November 22, December 6. 1879; Musician, November 1911; New York Times August 13, 1872.

MASQUERIER, LEWIS (March 14, 1802-?), social reformer and pioneer in phonetic spelling, was born in Paris, Ky., the son of Lewis Masquerier, a French Huguenot emigrant, and Sarah (Hicklin) Masquerier. As a boy his work on the farm was broken only by a rather inadequate frontier schooling and a little reading in the family library. After the death of his father his mother married again, and for a while they lived at the Boonslick settlement on the Missouri River. Young Lewis, however, returned to Paris; worked in a print shop; studied law; and set up an office in Quincy, Ill. His incurable shyness and his dislike for office routine were fatal to his profession, and after a little successful speculation in land he became completely absorbed in the subject of phonetic spelling. As early as 1830 Masquerier had devised a new alphabet—eleven vowels and twenty-two consonants—and following the publication of a preliminary pamphlet he went to New York to popularize his project. A revised font of letters was cast and specimen dictionaries were printed. But the East exposed him to a variety of new interests and his pioneering document, *The Phonotypic Spelling and Reading Manual,* did not appear until 1867. He was married, about 1840, to Anna Taber of Bradford, Vt.

Masquerier acquired an absorbing interest in various proposals for social reform, his chief enthusiasm being Henry George Evans' theory of individualism. Pursuing it to its rational limits he developed, from the "natural and inalienable rights of agrarianism," a variety of anarchism which abolished not only organized government but organized religion and provided for the division of the entire surface of the earth into six-mile-square townships, these in turn to be subdivided into forty-acre homesteads. By means of lectures, booklets, etc., he succeeded in publicizing his Utopia, but the only substantial victory for agrarianism was the adoption (Homestead Act of 1862) of the principle of the distribution of public domain to bona fide settlers.

In his earlier social reform efforts Masquerier had been active in the National Reform Association, and had found kindred interests, during the middle 'forties, among William Henry Channing, Albert Brisbane, and other associationists.

Sociology: or, The Reconstruction of Society, Government, and Property, a collection of his newspaper articles, pamphlets, and miscellaneous poetry, was followed, seven years later, by *An Appendix to Sociology.* Masquerier will, however, probably be longer remembered as an experimentalist in phonetic spelling than as a sociologist, for his theories of agrarianism were in general too loosely visualized and sweepingly impractical.

Principal Works: The Phonetic Spelling and Reading Manual, 1867; Sociology: or, The Reconstruction of Society, Government, and Property, 1877; An Appendix to Sociology, 1884.

About: Commons, J. R. History of Labor; Masquerier, L. Sociology; Masquerier. L. Appendix to Sociology; Randall, G. L. Taber Genealogy.

"MASSACHUSETTENSIS." See LEONARD, DANIEL

MATHER, COTTON (February 12, 1662/3-February 13, 1727/8), theologian, the oldest son of the Puritan divine Increase Mather [*q.v.*], and his first wife, Maria (Cotton) Mather, was born in Boston, where his father was minister of the Second (Old North) Church. His paternal grandfather, Richard Mather, and his maternal grandfather, John Cotton, were also noted Puritan ministers [*qq.v.*]. His precociousness in study and religion, and the awed admiration of all around him, made of the neurotic, sensitive boy a prodigy, a prig, a fanatic, and a tyrant. He entered Harvard at twelve, the youngest student ever to qualify, and was graduated in 1678. Although he felt himself "appointed to carry on the family tradition of leadership," he stuttered badly, and so he resigned himself to studying medicine (his interest in science being early and genuine) instead of divinity. But by 1680 he had schooled himself to speak plainly, and he became his father's assistant at "Old North," refusing a call to New Haven. In 1681 he received his M.A. from Harvard and in 1685 he was ordained. He stayed at the Second Church all his life, until 1723 as his father's colleague, and during the latter's absence in England as his substitute.

In 1686 Mather married Abigail Phillips. She died in 1702 and the next year he married a widow, Elizabeth (Clark) Hubbard, who died in 1713. In 1715 he married another widow, Lydia (Lee) George, who outlived him but was hopelessly insane after the first few years of their marriage. Of his fifteen children by his three wives, nine died in early childhood and only two survived him—and though one of these was a minister, Samuel Mather, the other was a ne'er-do-well and wastrel.

Cotton Mather was so close to his father, as long as Increase Mather lived, that their fortunes rose and fell together. He too was involved in the rebellion against Governor Andros, and was affected by the unpopularity of the charter and governor secured by his father. And he too was deeply implicated in the witchcraft persecutions of 1692. It is probable that neither man was directly responsible, though both of them stimulated the trials by their belief in witchcraft and by their writings. Cotton Mather, however, thought obsession could be cured by prayer and fasting, and disapproved the executions; nevertheless, he was present at one without condemning it, and his later retraction of the extremist viewpoint was half-hearted. Yet against this blot on his career must be set the fact that he had a

After a portrait by P. Pelham
COTTON MATHER
1727

real flair for science. In 1713 he became the first American to be a Fellow of the Royal Society. He helped to introduce inoculation for smallpox into America; he was an advocate of peace; he believed in education for women and slaves. Like his father, with age he grew a bit less dogmatic and more tolerant. But by this time his influence had declined; he had overreached himself, tried in vain to remove Governor Dudley in 1702 because he could not rule him, tried likewise in vain to succeed his father as president of Harvard. He gave up, in pique, the fellowship to which he had been appointed in 1690, and pinned his hopes on Yale. That presidency he was offered in 1721, but he had no desire to leave Boston and his church, or the power of his sermons over his terrorized congregation.

Mather was the prime example of the neurotic in a position of authority. His heavy face, with its high forehead, bulbous nose, and sulky mouth, bears a curious resemblance to Swift's. V. L. Parrington sums him up well: "Self-centered and self-righteous, the victim of strange asceticisms and morbid spiritual debauches, . . . the insularity of his thought and judgment grew into a disease." Celebrated for his learning, he was a pedant rather than a student. He wrote, in seven languages, the astounding number of 470 books, all but one of which have perished except for special students—the only exemption from this fate being the *Magnalia,* valuable as an historical source-book. In their own day, two others of his books had wide popularity—*The Wonders of the Invisible World,* a defense of the Salem witchcraft trials, and *Bonifacius* (*Essays to Do Good*), to which Franklin ascribed "all my usefulness and eminence." The *Magnalia,* the most elaborate biography then written in America, combined with a fragmentary "church history of New England," was, Van Wyck Brooks remarks, "a curious jumble of fact and fiction and personal prejudice," which fired its readers with the thought that "the very ground they trod on was consecrated by Providence."

He had his own theory of style and lived up to it, admiring and achieving an almost unreadable mélange of quotations and allusions; it is no wonder that a contemporary, overcome by this ornate manner, spoke of Mather's writing as "singular but emphatical." To quote Parrington again, "a man of incredible industry, unrestrained by any critical sense and infatuated with printer's ink, he flung together a jumble of old saws and modern instances and called the result a book." In his time he was considered the most remarkable man of his age; today he is of interest chiefly to researchers into psychopathology.

Principal Works: A Poem to the Memory of Mr. Urian Oakes, 1682; Declaration of the Gentlemen, Merchants, and Inhabitants of Boston (Andros Tracts) 1689; Memorable Providences: Relating to Witchcrafts and Possessions, 1689; The Present State of New-England, 1690: Wonders of the Invisible World, 1693; Pietas in Patrian (Life of Sir William Phips) 1697; Eleutheria: or, An Idea of the Reformation in England, 1698; Pastoral Letter to the English Captives in Africa, 1698; A Family Well-Ordered, 1699; Reasonable Religion, 1700; Magnalia Christi Americana: or, The Ecclesiastical History of New-England From Its First Planting, 1702; A Faithful Man: Michael Wigglesworth, 1705; The Negro Christianized, 1706; Corderius Americanus: or, The Good Education of Children, 1708; Bonifacius (Essays to Do Good) 1710; Brethren Dwelling Together in Unity, 1718; Sentiments of the Small Pox Inoculated, 1721; The Christian Philosopher, 1721; The Angel of Bethsada, 1722; Parentator (Life of Increase Mather) 1724; Ratio Disciplinae, 1726; Manductio ad Ministerium, 1726; Diary (ed. by W. C. Ford) 1911-12.

About: Boas, R. P. Cotton Mather: Keeper of the Puritan Conscience; Marvin, A. P. Life and Times of Cotton Mather; Mather, C. Diary; Mather, S. The Life of the Very Reverend and Learned Cotton Mather; Murdock, K. B. Increase Mather; Parrington, V. L. Main Currents in American Thought; Peabody, W. B. O. Life of Cotton Mather; Wendell, B. Cotton Mather: The Puritan Priest.

MATHER, INCREASE (June 21, 1639-August 23, 1723), theologian, was the youngest son of the Rev. Richard Mather [*q.v.*] and his first wife, Katherine (Holt) Mather, and was born in Dorchester, Mass. He was educated at home and in the free school in Boston, and in 1651 entered Harvard, but during his entire course lived in Ipswich or Boston with his tutor. He received his B.A. in 1656, and the next year left for England, where two of his older brothers had preceded him. Going to Ireland, he entered Trinity College, Dublin, and received his M.A. in 1658. He was offered a position at Trinity, but disliked the Irish climate and went instead to Devonshire, where one of Cromwell's chaplains secured his services as a temporary substitute at Great Torrington. In 1659 he was chaplain of the garrison at Guernsey. He preached next at Gloucester, but when it became apparent that the Republic was about to end he returned to Guernsey, in 1660. The next year he served in Weymouth and Dorset, but he refused to conform to the Church of England, and so, though he would have preferred to remain permanently in England, there was no way out but to return to his native land.

In 1661, therefore, Mather found himself back in Massachusetts. Refusing several offers, he stayed in Dorchester as his father's colleague, where he busied himself chiefly first with attacking and then with defending the "half-way covenant," a burning question of the time, which dealt with the right of baptism of children of non-communicant church members. In 1662 he was delegate from Dorchester to the ecclesiastical synod which finally wrestled with this problem.

From a portrait by Van der Spriett
INCREASE MATHER
1688

The same year Mather married his new stepsister, Maria Cotton, daughter of his father's second wife. They had three sons and seven daughters; the oldest son was Increase Mather's celebrated child, Cotton Mather [*q.v.*].

In 1664 Mather was called as "teacher" of the Second (North) Church in Boston, with which his name is always associated. Ten years later he was appointed licenser of the press and at the same time became a fellow of Harvard. He presided at the great "Reforming Synod" of 1679-80, and his was the most influential voice in the fixing of New England Congregationalism into a strictly Calvinistic mold. In 1681 he was offered the presidency of Harvard; he took over the post temporarily but declined the actual office because it would require his living in Cambridge and he would not desert his Boston congregation. (Cambridge is now only a quarter of an hour from Boston; the journey then took half a day.) Four years later he tried a compromise, calling himself president or rector but really being little more than college chaplain, and leaving the conduct of the college to others. Eventually this was used as an excuse by his enemies to force him out.

The loss of Increase Mather's control over New England's theocratic government came from his greatest triumph. The charter of Massachusetts had been revoked, and the citizens were in revolt against Governor Andros. Having just been acquitted of charges of libel arising from a forged letter, Mather was sent in 1688 to appeal to James II; the Andros party was sufficiently strong to oblige him to leave in disguise. James II died soon after, and from his successors, William and Mary, Mather secured a new charter and a new governor of his own choosing, his disciple Sir William Phips. He returned in 1692, and the same year he obtained a charter for Harvard, with the right to grant degrees. That, unfortunately, was also the year of the great witch hunt in Salem, and in the revulsion that followed Mather was accused, not unjustly, of being its chief instigator—though afterward he repudiated it. All these charges, dissatisfaction with the new charter, and Mather's overbearing temper, combined to force him out of public life in 1701. Thenceforth he was merely the teacher of the Second Church, the student, and the writer. He was also America's first Doctor of Divinity; Harvard gave him the degree in 1692, its first honorary degree and its only doctorate until 1771. In 1714 his wife died and the next year he married his nephew's widow, Ann (Lake) Cotton.

"By nature," says V. L. Parrington of Increase Mather, "he was a politician and a statesman rather than a minister. . . . He labored faithfully but never learned to write well." He was of the breed of Wolsey and Richelieu, and Massachusetts was too small for him. His long, narrow head and deep-set eyes betrayed the bigot. He was a fanatical believer in theocracy, with himself as the chief theocrat. Within that frame he could be tolerant and even advanced—but only within it. Mellowed by old age, he displayed, said one enthusiast, "the face of an angel." He was a curious mixture, a man who studied sixteen hours a day, who with his son advocated inoculation for smallpox and established a society in Boston for scientific discussion, yet was a great believer in signs and omens. In a word, he was typical of the New England Puritan of the seventeenth century. As a writer (he fathered 136 books in all), his style was direct and simple, unimaginative and pedestrian, bearing evidence of an uncreative but powerful intellect; modern readers, were there such, would prefer it to the fantastic, barren pedantry of his son's writing, just as they would prefer his straightforward Puritanism to Cotton Mather's hysteria and vanity.

Principal Works: Life and Death of That Reverend Man of God, Mr. Richard Mather, 1670; Important Truths About Conversion, 1674; A Discourse Concerning Baptism and the Consecration of Churches, 1675; A Brief History of the Warr With the Indians, 1676; A Relation of the Troubles Which Have Hapned in New-England by Reason of the Indians There, 1677; Cometographia: or, A Discourse Concerning Comets, 1683; Essay for the Recording of Illustrious Providences, 1684; Several Papers Relating to the State of New-England, 1690; Cases of Conscience Concerning Evil Spirits, 1693; The Great Blessing, of Primitive Counsellours, 1693; The Surest Way to the Greatest Honour, 1699; The Dying Pastor's Legacy, 1722.

About: Calamy, E. Memoirs of the Life of Increase Mather; Holmes, T. J. Increase Mather: His Works (see Introduction by G. P. Winship); Mather, C. Parentator; Mather, C. A Father Departing; Murdock, K. B. Increase Mather: The Foremost American Puritan; Parrington, V. L. Main Currents in American Thought; Pond, E. The Lives of Increase Mather and Sir William Phips; Whitmore, W. H. Memoirs of the Rev. Increase Mather.

MATHER, RICHARD (?, 1596-April 22, 1669), theologian, was born in Lowton, Lancashire, England, the son of Thomas and Margaret (Abrams?) Mather, both members of families of the yeoman class which had fallen into poverty. He was educated at a severe but thorough school in Winwick, near Lowton, and in 1611, at only fifteen, became a master in the grammar school at Toxteth Park, now part of Liverpool. He was converted to the Puritan or Separatist creed in 1614. The next year he left Toxteth Park and returned to Lowton, and by 1618 was able to enter Brasenose College, Oxford; however, after only six months he was called back to Toxteth Park to act as preacher in the chapel there. In spite of his lack of a degree and his Puritan tendencies, he was ordained in the Church of England, though his dissent soon got him into trouble. In 1633 he was suspended for three months, and again in 1634, and he resolved to emigrate. With his wife, Katharine Holt, whom he had married in 1624, he went to Massachusetts in 1635. He settled in Dorchester, from which most of the congregation had migrated to Connecticut, and built up the church there of which he remained minister, or "teacher" as the Congregationalists put it, until his death. He was the original drafter of the Cambridge Platform (1646), which became the basic rule of the New England churches. He was also one of three ministers to translate and write the *Bay Psalm Book*, the first book printed in America. Of his six sons, all but one, who died early, became ministers; the youngest was Increase Mather, father of Cotton Mather [*qq.v.*]. His wife died in 1655 and he remarried, Sarah (Hawkridge) (Story) Cotton, whose second husband had been the famous pioneer minister, John Cotton [*q.v.*]. A bearded,

After an old print

RICHARD MATHER

loud-voiced, domineering man, Mather was well fitted to be the first of the celebrated "Mather dynasty" of Puritan divines.

PRINCIPAL WORKS: The Whole Book of Psalmes (Bay Psalm Book) (with T. Welde and J. Eliot) 1640; Church-Government and Church-Covenant Discussed, 1643; Apologie of the Churches in New-England for Church Covenant, 1643; A Platform of Church Discipline, 1649; A Catechism, 1650; The Summe of Certain Sermons, 1652; A Farewell-Exhortation, 1657; A Disputation Concerning Church-Members, 1659; Journal, 1850.

ABOUT: Mather, C. Magnalia; Mather, I. Life and Death of That Reverend Man of God, Mr. Richard Mather; Mather, R. Journal (with Life and Death of That Reverend Man of God, Mr. dock, K. B. Increase Mather; Walker, W. Ten New England Leaders.

MATHEWS, ALBERT (September 8, 1820-September 9, 1903), miscellaneous writer, was the son of well-to-do parents, Oliver and Mary (Field) Mathews. He was graduated from Yale College and attended Harvard Law School, being admitted to the bar in 1845. He was a contributor to periodicals, and a short while before his second marriage he began to write books. The first, published in 1860 under his pen-name, "Paul Siogvolk," was *Walter Ashwood, A Love Story,* a conventional and artificial novel.

His essays were in better literary style but appealed to only a small public, and now seem old-fashioned. From 1879 to the end of his life he published miscellaneous books fairly often, being at the same time an active participant in the affairs of the New York city and state bar associations.

Though his writings were serious and his bearing stately, he had a genial way with judges and juries, and his friends found him pleasant company. He died at Lake Mohonk, N.Y.

PRINCIPAL WORKS: A Bundle of Papers, 1879; Thoughts on Codification of the Common Law, 1881; Memorial of Bernard Roelker, 1889; Ruminations, 1893; A Few Verses, 1896.

ABOUT: Biographical Record of the Class of 1842 of Yale College; New York State Bar Association Reports: Vol. 5; New York Times September 10, 12, 1903.

MATHEWS, CORNELIUS (October 28, 1817-March 25, 1889), dramatist, editor, and poet, was born in Port Chester, N.Y., the son of Abijah and Catherine (Van Cott) Mathews. He was an underclassman at Columbia College (1830-32) before enrolling at the newly formed University of the City of New York (now New York University), and received his B.A. degree in 1834 at its first commencement. Mathews studied law—at his father's request—and was admitted to the bar in 1837 but shortly turned his entire attention to literary work, which had begun in 1836 with contributions of poetry and light prose to the *American Monthly Magazine* and the *New York Review.* He published a rather ingenious romance called *Behemoth: A Legend of the Mound Builders,* and in 1840, with Evert A. Duyckinck, he founded and edited a monthly, *Arcturus: A Journal of Books and Opinions*; Mathews' novel on the New York political scene, "The Career of Puffer Hopkins" appeared in its columns from June 1841 to May 1842. Lowell's kindly criticism of Mathews' *Poems on Man in his Various Aspects* lent the strongest support to the young poet's reputation.

Politics provided a back-drop for three of his plays: *The Politicians,* a comedy, theatrically unwieldy but enlightening in its exposure of New York electioneering rackets; *Jacob Leisler,* which opened in Philadelphia and continued only briefly in New York; and *False Pretenses: or, Both Sides of Good Society,* a tragedy which attempted a contrast between sincerity and insincerity, but which lacked any very profound sense of social values. *Witchcraft: or, The Martyrs of Salem,* a tragic chronicle of human intolerance, flared up at times into exciting drama; Murdoch opened it at the Walnut Street Theatre in Philadelphia in 1846, and after good runs in the East it proceeded to the Midwest and Far West.

During 1846 and 1847 Mathews published *Yankee Doodle,* a six-cent weekly, very *Punch*-like in its lay-out, dedicated to the "propagation of true genuine Yankee-Doodleism . . . and the utter extirpation of old Fudgeism . . . in art, literature . . . the drama . . ."; but the contemplated dizzying hilarity never emerged. During the last six years of his life he was contributing editor of the New York *Dramatic Mirror.*

PRINCIPAL WORKS: Behemoth: A Legend of the Mound Builders, 1839; The Politicians, 1840; Poems on Man in His Various Aspects under the American Republic, 1843; Witchcraft: or, The Martyrs of Salem, 1846; Jacob Leisler, 1848; False Pretenses: or, Both Sides of Good Society, 1855.

ABOUT: Quinn, A. H. A History of the American Drama From the Beginning to the Civil War; New York Dramatic Mirror, April 6, 1889; New York Times March 27, 1889.

MATHEWS, WILLIAM (July 28, 1818-February 14, 1909), journalist and teacher, was the eldest son of Simeon and Clymena (Esty) Mathews. He was born in Waterville, Maine, attended various preparatory schools in that state, and when only seventeen received the B.A. degree from Waterville (now Colby) College.

He began law practice in 1841 and in the same year started a weekly, the *Watervillonian.* When its demands caused him to abandon his law practice he moved the paper to Gardiner, Maine, calling it the *Yankee Blade.* Still later he moved it to Boston and in 1856 sold it there, to be merged with the *Port Folio.*

After a few years of editing, lecturing, and librarianship, he was made professor of rhetoric and English at the University of Chicago. In 1873 he published *Getting On in the World,* a collection of essays which he had written for the Chicago *Daily Tribune.* The success of this and a second book, *The Great Conversers and Other Essays,* led him, in 1875, to give up teaching for authorship.

From 1880 he lived in Boston. He was married three times.

Principal Work: Getting On in the World, 1873; The Great Conversers and Other Essays, 1874; Hours With Men and Books, 1877; Oratory and Orators, 1879; Literary Style and Other Essays, 1881; Men, Places, and Things, 1887; Nugae Litterariae, 1896.

About: Whittemore, E. C. Centennial History of Waterville, Kennebec County, Maine; Boston Globe January 24, 1909; Boston Herald February 15, 1909; Saturday Review of Literature December 25, 1937.

MATTHEWS, BRANDER. See MATTHEWS, JAMES BRANDER

MATTHEWS, JAMES BRANDER (February 21, 1852-March 31, 1929), novelist, essayist, critic, and playwright, was born in New Orleans, though his father, Edward Matthews, was of New England descent; his mother, Virginia (Brander) Matthews, was from the state of which she was a namesake. The father was wealthy, and the family traveled much; the boy had been twice to Europe before he was fourteen. For the most part they lived in New York, his lifelong home after childhood. He was graduated from Columbia in 1871 as class poet, then studied at the Columbia Law School, being admitted to the bar in 1873. He never practiced law, but started his literary career immediately; at the same time he continued his studies and received his M.A. in 1874. The father lost his fortune in the Jay Cooke Panic, and what had been the son's avocation became his profession, especially as he now had the responsibilities of a husband. In 1873 he had married Ada S. Smith, an English actress known on the stage as Ada Harland.

Matthews, who at this period dropped his first name and was thenceforth known as Brander Matthews, contributed to many

BRANDER MATTHEWS
c. 1894

magazines, including *Scribner's,* the *Nation,* the *Critic,* and *Appleton's*; under the pseudonym of "Arthur Penn" he edited the *Rhymester* and wrote for the *Home Library*; with Laurence Hutton he edited *Actors and Actresses of Great Britain From the Days of David Garrick* (1886); but his chief interest at this time was in play writing. Several of his plays were produced—*Margery's Lovers* in 1884, *This Picture and That* and *A Gold Mine* (written with G. H. Jessop) in 1887, *On Probation* (also with Jessop) in 1889, *The Decision of the Court* in 1893. The titles of some of these show the only use to which he ever put his legal knowledge.

A substitute lectureship in Columbia in 1891 led to his appointment the next year as professor of English. In 1900 he became professor of dramatic literature, the first chair of its kind in America. He taught until 1924, when ill health and the loss of his wife (their only daughter had died previously) caused his resignation. A conspicuous "joiner," he helped to found the Authors' Club, the American Copyright League (later the Authors' League), and the Players; in 1910 he was president of the Modern Language Association, from 1913 to 1914 of the National Institute of Arts and Letters, and from 1922 to 1924 chancellor of its subsidiary, the American Academy of Arts and Letters. He was also the first chairman of the Simplified Spelling Board. In 1907 he was elected to the French Legion of Honor, and was made an officer of the Legion in

1922. He lectured in New York, Boston, and London, and was for a long time, drama critic of the New York *Times*.

Though he lived well into the new century, Matthews was peculiarly of the late nineteenth century, his fastidious, "gentlemanly" style as typical as his side-whiskers and pince-nez. His advocacy of the "well-made play" had much influence on the progress of American drama; he was at home in half a dozen departments of literature and language and wrote authoritatively of them all. His own plays, his novels and stories, have failed to survive their period, but his essays, including his brilliant and witty studies of his beloved New York, and his critical writings are a constituent part of their era and have their place in the history of polite literature in the United States.

Principal Works: *Fiction*—In Partnership (short stories, with H. C. Bunner) 1884; The Last Meeting, 1885; A Secret of the Sea and Other Stories, 1886; A Family Tree and Other Stories, 1889; Tom Paulding (juvenile) 1892; His Father's Son: A Novel of New York, 1895; A Confident Tomorrow, 1899; The Action and the Word, 1900. *Non-Fiction*—The Theaters of Paris, 1880; French Dramatists of the Nineteenth Century, 1881; Pen and Ink, 1885; Americanisms and Briticisms, 1892; Vignettes of Manhattan, 1894; Studies of the Stage, 1894; Aspects of Fiction, 1896; American Literature, 1896; Outlines in Local Color, 1897; The Historical Novel, 1901; Parts of Speech, 1901; The Development of the Drama. 1903; Inquiries and Opinions. 1907; Molière: His Life and His Works, 1910; A Study of the Drama, 1910; A Study of Versification, 1911; Vistas of New York, 1912; Gateways to Literature, 1912; Shakspere as a Playwright, 1913; A Book About the Theater, 1916; These Many Years (autobiography) 1917; The Principles of Playmaking, 1919; Essays on English, 1921; The Tocsin of Revolt, 1922; Playwrights on Playmaking, 1923; Rip Van Winkle Goes to the Play, 1926.

About: Matthews, B. These Many Years; Commonweal April 17, 1929; Review of Reviews June 1929; Scribner's Magazine July 1929.

"MAY, SOPHIE." See CLARKE, REBECCA SOPHIA

MAYER, BRANTZ (September 27, 1809-February 23, 1879), lawyer, journalist, and social historian, was born in Baltimore, the son of Christian Mayer, German emigrant who later became consul-general of Würtemburg in the United States, and Anna Katerina (Baum) Mayer, of Kutztown, Pa. Young Mayer attended Baltimore schools and St. Mary's College, but the larger share of his instruction was in the hands of a private tutor. At eighteen he went to China and India, studying law during the course of his travels; he continued law, on his return, at the University of Maryland; and in 1832 he was admitted to the bar and then went abroad.

Back from his European journey, he practiced law until 1841 when he was appointed secretary of the United States legation in Mexico; he remained there three years. As executor of the will of John McDonogh, former Baltimore merchant and philanthropist, Mayer went from Baltimore to Louisiana in 1851 and again in 1855—the year in which he withdrew from practice and devoted his time to writing. His conciliatory diplomacy as chairman of the Maryland Union Central Committee at the outbreak of the Civil War was not soon forgotten. He was made brigadier-general of the Maryland volunteers in 1862; aided in the recruiting of troops; and retired from the pay department of the army in 1875 with the rank of colonel. Brantz was twice married: in 1835, to Mary Griswold, by whom he had five daughters; and several years after her death in 1845, to Cornelia Poor, who added three daughters to his store.

Mayer's writings were the harvest of his scholarly interest in history. *Mexico as It Was and as It Is,* appearing on the very eve of the Mexican War, survived three editions, despite its highly polemical treatment of the Catholic Church. The Maryland Historical Society, which Mayer had been instrumental in founding in 1844, published, the year following, his edition of the historically significant *Journal of Charles Carroll of Carrollton: During His Visit to Canada in 1776.* His defense of Michael Cresap against the charge of murdering the family of James Logan, a Mingo leader (*Tah-Gah-Jute: or, Logan and Captain Michael Cresap*) was an interesting piece of psychology, but it has been substantially challenged by later historians. Mayer edited the journal of *Captain Canot: or, Twenty Years of an African Slaver*; he was given the captain's copious memoranda by one Dr. James Hall. Mayer's book has long been considered an excellent account of slavery on the west coast of Africa; it was republished in 1928 with an introduction by Malcolm Cowley, and was the direct source of a considerable portion of the "African section" of Hervey Allen's *Anthony Adverse*.

For a while Mayer was editor of the Baltimore *American,* and among his later volumes were annals of Mexico, biographies, and memoirs. His local histories often pretentious and dependent on unreliable statistical sources, are still regarded in part, as valuable records.

Principal Works: Mexico as It Was and as It Is, 1844; Journal of Charles Carroll of Carrollton: During His Visit to Canada in 1776 (ed.) 1845; Tah-Gah-Jute: or, Logan and Captain Michael Cresap, 1851; Mexico: Aztec, Spanish, and Republican (2 vols.) 1851; Calvert and Penn, 1852; Captain Canot: or, Twenty Years of an African Slaver, 1854; Memoir of Jared Sparks, 1867; Baltimore: Past and Present, 1871.

About: Bigelow, J. Retrospections of an Active Life; Mayer, B. Baltimore: Past and Present; Mayer, B. Captain Canot: or, Twenty Years of an African Slaver; Maryland Historical Magazine March 1910; Saturday Review of Literature January 13, 1934; Baltimore American February 24, 1879.

MAYHEW, EXPERIENCE (February 5, 1673-November 29, 1758), missionary, translator of the Indian dialects, and local historian, was born at Chilmark, Martha's Vineyard, Mass., the son of John and Elizabeth (Hilliard) Mayhew. Without any formal education young Mayhew arrived at an independent mastery of the Indian dialect of the Vineyard, and at about the age of twenty he began to preach to the Indians. From the time of his appointment as "teacher" of the English church in Tisbury, he worked unceasingly in the Society for the Propagation of the Gospel in New England. Cotton Mather affirmed that "in the evangelical service among the Indians there is no man that exceeds Mr. Mayhew, if there be any that equals him."

In 1707 Mayhew translated into the Indian tongue Cotton Mather's lecture "The Day Which the Lord Hath Made." About two years later appeared his new Indian translation of the Psalms of David and the Gospel of St. John; in collateral columns of Indian and English it was "next to Eliot's Indian Bible . . . the most important monument of the Massachuset Language." In his "Brief Journal of My Visitation to the Pequot and Mohegin Indians 1713-1714" Mayhew recorded his sojourn among the mainland tribes. His *Indiane Primer,* the "first book by which children may know truely to read the Indian language," was issued in 1720; it contained a rudimentary vocabulary, a few idioms, and numerous specime translations from the Bible. The preface to *Indian Converts: or, Some Account of the Lives and Dying Speeches of a Considerable Number of the Christianized Indians of Martha's Vineyard* explained the author's first-hand knowledge of many of the subjects and assured the reader that "the things reported are worthy of credit"; it was a kind of balance sheet of missionary achievements among the Indians.

Grace Defended, his most important theological piece, embodied a Calvinism that was not orthodox, preserving a measure of free will as against the doctrine of total depravity.

Mayhew was tendered the degree of Master of Arts at Harvard, excused himself from acceptance, and when the college "saw cause to over-rule his modesty" it was conferred upon him in July 1723. In 1695 he was married to Thankful Hinckley of Barnstable; and in 1711 to Remember Bourne of Sandwich, Jonathan Mayhew [q.v.] being a son of the second marriage. He was a man of boundless humanitarian energy and "irreproachable fidelity." His notations on Indian culture and dialects at Martha's Vineyard are of obvious value to the historian and the ethnologist.

Principal Works: Indiane Primer, 1720; Indian Converts, 1727; Grace Defended 1744.

About: Banks, C. E. The History of Martha's Vineyard; Mayhew, E. Indian Converts (see account by Thomas Prince).

MAYHEW, JONATHAN (October 8, 1720-July 9, 1766), clergyman, lecturer, and political philosopher, was born at Chilmark, Martha's Vineyard, the son of Experience Mayhew [q.v.] and Remember (Bourne) Mayhew. He was graduated with honors from Harvard in 1744, and three years later he began a lifelong ministry at the West Church in Boston. Mayhew's Christianity was rational and practical and its source was not Calvinism but the Scriptures, championing the right of individual judgment, rejecting the Trinitarian view, and strengthening the free-will doctrine. His strong dislike of ecclesiastical formalities was the substance of a sermon, delivered during his Dudleian Lectureship at Harvard, on "Popish Idolatry." He prepared three discourses in defense of his objections to a popular suggestion for the introduction of an American episcopate; one of these was a reply to a pamphlet by Archbishop Secker. Several aspects of Mayhew's theology were attacked by members of his profession; to one he answered ("A Letter of Reproof to Mr. John Cleaveland") so bluntly that a century and a half has not devitalized it.

From Milton, Locke, Sidney, and the Bible, Mayhew had drawn some liberal theories of government, condemning arbitrary rule and staunchly supporting civil liberty: his *Discourse Concerning Unlimited Submission and Non-Resistance to the Higher Powers* was a defence of popular disobedience under reasonably warrantable circumstances. *The Snare Broken,* a sermon delivered after the repeal of the Stamp Act, contained a brief for combined law observance and the preservation of individual rights. It was dedicated to William Pitt, but its author dared to assert that "it may be justifiable for private men, at certain extraordinary conjunctures, to take the administration of government in some respects into their own hands." During that same year Mayhew had proposed the circulation of a letter by the Massachusetts lower house, advising a firmer brotherhood among the colonies for a better defence of their liberties. He was married in 1756 to Elizabeth Clarke, who, with his two daughters, survived him.

Mayhew had been granted a degree of D.D. from Aberdeen when the publication (1749) of a volume of sermons was winning him recognition abroad; and the distinguished Londoner, Thomas Hollis, advocate of civil and religious liberty, sought his friendship. His remarkable vigor had, in the championing of noble causes, a kind of harshness and vanity; yet it easily eclipsed his personal weaknesses. He had a ready and sturdy pen for the exposition of his social code and religious creed.

Principal Works: Discourse Concerning Unlimited Submission and Non-Resistance to the Higher Powers, 1750; A Letter of Reproof to Mr. John Cleaveland, 1764; The Snare Broken, 1766.

About: Baldwin, A. M. The New England Clergy and the American Revolution; Banks, C. E. The History of Martha's Vineyard; Blackburne, F. Memoirs of Thomas Hollis; Bradford, A. Memoir of the Life and Writings of Rev. Jonathan Mayhew, D.D.

MAYO, SARAH CARTER (EDGARTON). See EDGARTON, SARAH CARTER

MAYO, WILLIAM STARBUCK (April 15, 1811-November 22, 1895), novelist, was born in Ogdensburg, N. Y., but was of New England ancestry on both sides, being in direct line of paternal descent from the first minister of the Second (Old North) Church in Boston. His father, Obed Mayo, had been in the merchant marine, like most his ancestors before him, but at the wish of his wife, Elizabeth (Starbuck) Mayo, he had come ashore and settled inland as a boatbuilder for the canal and lake trade. He died in 1819.

Mayo studied at the Academy at Potsdam, N. Y., near Ogdensburg, and after a year each in the offices of two local physicians, went to the College of Physicians and Surgeons in New York, from which he received his M.D. in 1832. He set up in practice in Ogdensburg, but after a few years was obliged to leave his profession and travel for the sake of his health. His journeys, which lasted for several years, took him to Spain and northern Africa, and he planned

WILLIAM STARBUCK MAYO

also an expedition to the then unknown center of Africa, but was unable to undertake it. It was during these years that he gained the local color which characterized his principal writings.

On returning to America, he settled in New York and resumed practice, being connected for many years with Blackwell's (now Welfare) Island. In 1851 he married Helen Stuyvesant, of the Dutch pioneer family of New York. At the same time he began to write for the magazines, encouraged by the success of his two novels, *Kaloolah* and *The Berber*. Both—the first especially—were immensely popular; but once he had exhausted this vein, he never recaptured his early public, and in later years he practically ceased writing. Although he had been frail as a child and a young man, he lived to be eighty-four.

Kaloolah was often compared to Melville's *Typee,* which it resembles in form if not in locale, but Mayo always claimed that it had been written before Melville's book was published. It has little plot, but is a loosely autobiographical tale, the life of one "Jonathan Romer" who strongly resembles Mayo himself. It is an uneven mixture of romance adventure, geographical description, and slapstick comedy. *The Berber,* which followed has a well constructed plot and shows some ability in novel-writing, though it again relies heavily on Mayo's memories of his travels. His other novel, *Never Again* (a prophetic title), is a satire of contemporar New York. Besides his novels, Mayo wrot a volume of semi-fiction based on history and two books expressing his interest in science—one on natural history and another, in the form of a letter to Lincoln's Secretary of the Navy, on improvements in the construction of battleships. None of Mayo's books is read today; he had a good eye for detail and some power of vivid description, but was too diffuse and melodramatic for his work to have much survival value.

PRINCIPAL WORKS: Kaloolah: or, Journeyings to the Djebel Kumri, 1849; The Berber. or, The Mountaineer of the Atlas, 1850; Illustrations of Natural Philosophy, 1850; Romance Dust From the Historic Placer, 1851 (as Flood and Field: or, Tales of Battles on Sea and Land, 1855); Letter to the Hon. Gideon Welles, 1862; Never Again, 1873.

ABOUT: New York Tribune November 23, 1895.

MAYO-SMITH, RICHMOND (February 9, 1854-November 11, 1901), statistician and economist, was born in Troy, Ohio, the son of Preserved and Lucy Richards (Mayo) Smith. He studied at Amherst, where Prof. John W. Burgess awoke his interest in economic subjects; at Berlin, and at Heidelberg. He returned to the United States in 1877 and was connected thereafter with Columbia University. He was an able teacher, and his statistics course in the graduate School of Political Science, probably the first ever given in an American university, produced many fine statisticians.

He helped to make an active organization of the American Statistical Association and became one of its vice-presidents in 1889. In the same year he was elected to the International Statistical Institute, and a year later was honored with membership in the National Academy of Sciences and an honorary fellowship in the Royal Statistical Society.

The first volume of his *Science of Statistics, Statistics and Sociology,* was published in 1895, and the second, *Statistics and Economics,* in 1899.

In the economic field he published *Emigration and Immigration* in 1890, in which he set up American political ideals as a standard. He was a member of the first editorial board of the *Political Science Quarterly.*

He married Mabel Percy Ford in 1884. They had four children.

PRINCIPAL WORKS: Emigration and Immigration, 1890; Science of Statistics (2 vols.) 1895-99.

ABOUT: Political Science Quarterly September 1914.

MEEHAN, THOMAS (March 21, 1826-November 19, 1901), botanist, was the son of Edward and Sarah (Denham) Meehan. His father was a gardener on the Isle of Wight.

Thomas came to America in 1848 and was employed by Robert Buist of Philadelphia for about a year. Then he became superintendant of Bartram's Garden, the trees of which he cataloged. This work was amplified and published in 1853 as *The American Handbook of Ornamental Trees.*

He established nurseries of his own, edited the *Gardener's Monthly* and other agricultural papers, and in 1891 founded *Meehan's Monthly.* He was a member of the Academy of Natural Sciences of Philadelphia and a fellow of the American Association for the Advancement of Science. From 1877 he was Pennsylvania state botanist. His most important work is *The Native Flowers and Ferns of the United States.*

As a member of the Philadelphia Common Council he did much to establish small parks throughout the city. In 1852 he married Catherine Colflesh.

PRINCIPAL WORKS: The American Handbook of Ornamental Trees, 1853; The Native Flowers and Ferns of the United States (4 vols.) 1878-80.

ABOUTS: Harshberger, J. W. The Botanists of Philadelphia and Their Work; Meehan's Monthly January 1902.

MEEK, ALEXANDER BEAUFORT (July 17, 1814-November 1, 1865), lawyer, poet, and chronicler of the Southwest, was born in Columbia, S. C., the son of Samuel Mills Meek, a physician and Methodist clergyman, and Anna (McDowell) Meek. Alexander was about five when the Meeks moved to Tuscaloosa, Ala., where he was instructed through the best available means. Two years after his graduation from the University of Alabama in 1833, he was admitted to the bar and established a practice in Tuscaloosa. He served in the Indian war in Florida (1836), first as a non-comsioned officer and later by formal appointment. In 1842 he filled out a term as probate judge in Tuscaloosa County; and for his support of Polk for the presidency he acquired a treasury-department post. He was afterward made federal attorney for the Southern district of Alabama and for several years lived in Mobile. Here he pursued a very pleasant literary life, and by means of his entry into the state legislature in 1853 he became a leader in the establishment of a public school system for Alabama. In 1859 he returned to the legislature and became speaker of the House. He was a conservative Democrat, and a Secessionist—but an unwilling one. From 1862 to 1864 he was a trustee of the University of Alabama. His first wife, Emma (Donaldson) Slatter, died in 1863, seven years after their marriage;

and in 1864 he was married to Mrs. Eliza Jane Cannon, widow of William R. Cannon.

Except for his *Supplement to Aiken's Digest of the Laws of Alabama,* Meek's literary achievements were chiefly two pioneer volumes on Alabama history: *The Southwest* and *Romantic Passages in Southwestern History;* and an abundance of lyrics, the best of which were incorporated into *Songs and Poems of the South.* His two best known poems were "Red Eagle," a study of Weatherford, an Indian whose Saxon or non-aboriginal characteristics provide the chief interest of the piece, and the story of the charge (Crimean War) at Balaklava, which, in Meek's own opinion, was his best verse. In 1849 Meek became associate editor of the Mobile *Daily Register* and he afterward served both the *Flag of the Union* and the *Southron* in an editorial capacity. His success as a pioneer educator in Alabama has, with slight exceptions, measusably outlived any of his rather scant writings.

Principal Works: The Southwest, 1840; A Supplement to Aiken's Digest of the Laws of Alabama, 1841; Romantic Passages in Southwestern History, 1857; Songs and Poems of the South, 1857.

About: Alderman, E. A. Library of Southern Literature; Garrett, W. Reminiscences of Public Men in Alabama; Nixon, H. C. Alexander Beaufort Meek; Advertiser and State Gazette (Montgomery) March 25, 1852.

MELLEN, GRENVILLE (June 19, 1799-September 5, 1841), poet, story-teller, and journalist, was born in Biddeford, Mass. (now Maine), the son of Prentiss Mellen, United States Senator from Massachusetts, and later chief justice of the Supreme Court of Maine, and Sarah (Hudson) Mellen. When he was a boy his parents moved to Portland; he attended Portland Academy and then entered Harvard. He delighted in verse-writing and oratory, and was class poet at his graduation in 1818. After two years at the Harvard Law School and one in his father's law office, he was admitted to the Maine bar, practicing first in Thomaston before settling in North Yarmouth, where he was married, in 1824, to Mary King Southgate.

Mellen's first literary wares were "occasion" poems, celebrating memorable anniversaries in New England's history. With Henry Wadsworth Longfellow, also of North Yarmouth, he wrote verse and prose pieces for the *United States Literary Gazette* and for the *Atlantic Souvenir* and the *Legendary,* gift annuals. In 1827 he published a satirical reminiscence, in verse, under title of *Our Chronicle of '26,* describing the winning of a seat in Congress as

The splendid consummation of the mind,
The soaring climax of whatever is,
The peerless immortality of wind!

and lamenting the sorry state of letters, reflecting that

Fair ladies write our novels—and alas!
They should have pensions for their desperation. . .

His collected *Sad Tales and Glad Tales,* published over the signature "Reginald Reverie," were somewhat diffuse and sentimental, but in their eerie wistfulness were suggestive of Washington Irving.

After the deaths of his infant daughter in September 1828 and his wife in the following May, Mellen spent several restless years, largely in Boston, during which time his only sizable publication was *The Martyr's Triumph. . .and Other Poems,* which, despite an occasional finesse of melody, was highly conventional. For a short while he was editor of the Portland *Advertiser,* and in 1830 he delivered the Harvard Phi Beta Kappa poem, "The Age of Print."

The best of his last four years was spent in the home of Samuel Colman, the painter; and for a portion of this time he was co-editor of the *Monthly Miscellany. A Book of the United States,* an historical volume with abundant statistics, was issued the year before his death; and his "General View of the American Continent" remained in manuscript. Mellen doubtless enjoyed during his own lifetime a literary reputation which his delicate and dreamy writings, almost completely preoccupied with the virtues of life and lacking in both humor and passion, have been unable to sustain.

Principal Works: Our Chronicle of '26, 1827; Sad Tales and Glad Tales, 1828; The Martyr's Triumph . . . and Other Poems, 1833; A Book of the United States, 1838.

About: Chapman, L. B. Monograph on the Southgate Family of Scarborough, Maine; Nevens, J. L. "Grenville Mellen: A Study of His Life and Works" (University of Maine master's thesis); New York Tribune September 6, 1841.

MELVILLE, HERMAN (August 1, 1819-September 28, 1891), novelist, was born in New York City, one of eight children of Allan Melville, a merchant of Scottish descent, and Maria (Gansevoort) Melville, of a Dutch "patroon" family. The father was from Massachusetts, his father being Major Thomas Melville, one of the "Boston tea party" and the "last leaf" of Oliver Wendell Holmes' poem. The mother's father was also a Revolutionary officer—a general. But all this ancestry—Mrs. Melville especially was a fanatic on the subject—did not alter the fact that Allan Melville died bankrupt in 1832, leaving his widow and children without funds. Part of Herman's childhood was spent with his Gansevoort relatives on their prosperous farm—the happiest part, for he declared in later years that his mother hated him, and certainly her coldness drove him from home before he was seventeen. He was a quiet, backward boy who loved to browse in his father's well chosen library better than to prepare his lessons at the Albany Academy, which he attended from eleven to fifteen. By 1834 he was a bank clerk; he tried farming and teaching; and then in 1837 his destiny caught up with him and he shipped as a cabin boy on a freighter to Liverpool. He returned and became a teacher again at Pittsfield and East Albany, but the seawater was in his blood, and by 1841 he was aboard the "Acushnet" bound for the South Seas. It was a momentous voyage; out of its experiences grew all his greatest books, from *Typee* to *Moby Dick*.

The cruelty Melville experienced aboard the "Acushnet" drove him and a companion to jump ship in the Marquesas. Here for four months he was held in a friendly but determined captivity by the then cannibalistic Polynesians. He escaped finally aboard an Australian whaler, not without having had to kill his man. The whaler itself was no paradise, and Melville jumped ship again in Papeete, living and working there for a while as a field hand. 1843 found him in Hawaii, from which he shipped as an ordinary seaman on a United States naval vessel. He was discharged the next year in Boston, and proceeded to his brother's home in Lansingburg, N. Y., full to bursting with experiences and adventures such as had never befallen any American before.

The immediate results were *Typee* and *Omoo*. They were an immense success, went through frequent editions, and made Melville famous as "the man who had lived among cannibals." They also built up for him a strong and savage set of enemies—the missionaries and their allies; for Melville saw the South Seas as the home of "strong, wicked, beautiful men" doomed to ruin by the narrow stupidity of the early missions. Melville's greatest work was still to come, but he had planted the seeds of disaster. In another way also he had dug his own future; in 1847 he married Elizabeth Shaw, daughter of the chief justice of Massachusetts. It was a marriage marked by the utmost loyalty on both sides, and complete lack of understanding. Neither, probably, was ever really happy, but to neither did it

HERMAN MELVILLE
1868

occur to do anything other than stand by. Moreover, in times to come it was only by the generosity of his father-in-law that Melville was able to live and support his family. They had two boys, who died in childhood, and two girls, one of whom survived both parents.

But Melville's long eclipse was still before him. In the early days of his marriage he lived in New York, then after a trip to England to see his British publishers, he moved to a farm, "Arrowhead," near Pittsfield. This was his home until 1863. Hawthorne was living near by, in Lenox, in 1850, and the two men became such friends as was possible where one was a middle-aged recluse, the other a young admirer, still ardent but ready with a little more disillusionment to become a completely pessimistic philosopher. The collapse of his idealistic friendship with Hawthorne was for Melville that last disappointment.

It was in "Arrowhead" that Melville's masterpiece was written. He himself said *Moby Dick* was "broiled in hell fire," and he was on the broiler with it. The super-labor of that enormous catharsis, the spiritual evulsion implied in its writing, killed the essential Melville, though a man lived in his body and wrote books in his name for forty years more. Certainly it was then that misfortune began to dog him. *Moby Dick* was hailed with no acclaim; the reviews were ludicrous in their lack of comprehension, and it was that very year that his publishers refused him any further advance, since he had already had $700 and was unlikely to earn so much in the future! Two years later their plant burnt down and the plates of his books and most of the unsold copies were destroyed. In 1856, in bad physical and nervous health, Melville managed to finance a journey, a sort of pilgrimage to Palestine *via* Constantinople and Liverpool, where Hawthorne was then consul. He was becoming increasingly absorbed in a profound mysticism that was half melancholia, and from which he roused himself only to fruitless efforts to support his household. Twice he appealed in vain for a consular position. He turned lecturer, on the South Seas and "the statuary of Rome," in 1860 going as far as San Francisco. The things he was thinking and feeling grew increasingly difficult of expression. He said: "What I feel most moved to write, that is banned—it will not pay. Yet, altogether, write the *other* way I cannot." In 1863 he moved to New York, the last change of residence. He brought out a few volumes of strangely conventional poetry (*Clarel,* the exception, was written long before), and at the end of his life he wrote again of the sea in a book not published until long after his death. But actually he had ceased to be a writer. "His literary life," Van Wyck Brooks says, "died of inanition, overstrain, and excessive subjectivity, as well as of neglect." But neglect is the greatest culprit. Melville might say he was "reconciled to annihilation," but he could no longer speak when once he realized there were no ears to hear. A few admirers remained in England, but in his own country he was so completely forgotten that when he died there was no mention of the event in the current press. It was not until his centenary, in 1919, that discerning critics opened the eyes of the reading public to the most neglected of all American geniuses.

The man who has written the only American novel worthy to stand on the pinnacle with *Wuthering Heights,* the man who might be called the American Blake, spent his life from 1866 to 1886 as a customs inspector on a wharf at the foot of—ironically—Gansevoort Street. No one knew him, he had no friends, he saw no one. Aloof, pale, hollow-eyed; and heavily bearded, he went about his work and spoke little. At home he sank deeper and deeper into the mazes of a mystical philosopy which had now grown too involved for utterance. At sixty-seven he resigned, his health completely broken. His wife had inherited a small fortune, and his services were no longer necessary. He spent his last years in trying to reconstruct, in *Billy Budd,* the carefree days as a United States sailor already celebrated in *White-Jacket.*

Few authors are so difficult to describe or evaluate as Melville. His earliest books, the two on the South Seas, are pure romance, fresh, exuberant, exciting. They are extroverted Melville. So are the other books of the sea, *Redburn* and *White-Jacket.* With *Mardi,* that strange blend of Rabelais and Thomas Moore (Van Wyck Brooks' interpretation), the intense introvert who was the true Melville has begun to appear. In *Pierre* he has arrived. *Pierre* is the nearest to autobiography of any of Melville's books, a strange, emotional self-probing which to the Philistine readers of its day seemed next door to insanity. After *Moby Dick* most of Melville's novels and tales may be called hackwork and mercifully forgotten, though *Israel Potter* has energy and some lifelike reconstructions of worthies of the days of '76. One or two of the short stories—"Benito Cereno" for instance—display the sombre, almost morbid power which was Melville's hallmark at his best; a few of his poems have a certain rough music. The rest is silence.

There remains *Moby Dick,* and it will remain while English is a known tongue. "To read *Moby Dick* and absorb it," says Viola Meynell, "is the crown of one's reading life." Its contemporaries objected to the technical information on whaling, called it a hodgepodge of nautical adventure and philosophy, doubted Melville's long since authenticated facts of natural history. Now, in the adjusted light of time, when its imaginative truth and greatness are no longer questionable, it is a book that challenges the spirit, for to each the Great White Whale will have a different meaning. Is he evil, is he the soul, is he the subconscious as D. H. Lawrence thought, is he genius, is he the devil, is he God? There are as many answers as there are readers. But for every reader there are the wild beauty, the tragic energy, the splendor, and the depth. *Moby Dick* is one of the books that may well become a man's *vade mecum* and see him through life and death, read more times than memory serves but offering some new richness with every eager reading. It is America's contribution, so far, to the world-novel.

Principal Works: Typee: A Peep at Polynesian Life, 1846; Omoo: A Narrative of Adventures in the South Seas, 1847; Mardi and a Voyage Thither, 1849; Redburn, 1849; White-Jacket: or, The World in a Man-of-War, 1850; Moby Dick: or, The White Whale, 1851; Pierre: or, The Ambiguities, 1852; Israel Potter: His Fifty Years of Exile, 1855; Piazza Tales, 1856; The Confidence Man: His Masquerade, 1857; Battle-Pieces and Aspects of the War (poems) 1866; Clarel: A

Poem and a Pilgrimage to the Holy Land, 1876; John Marr and Other Sailors (poems) 1888; Timoleon and Other Poems, 1891; The Apple-Tree Table and Other Sketches, 1922; Billy Budd, 1924.

ABOUT: Brooks, Van W. Emerson and Others; Freeman, J. Herman Melville; Lawrence, D. H. Studies in Classic American Literature; Minnigerode, M. Some Personal Letters of Herman Melville and a Bibliography; Mumford, L. Herman Melville; Sundermann, von K. H. Herman Melvilles Gedankengut; Weaver, R. M. Herman Melville; American Literature November 1929, November 1930, May 1931; Century Magazine August 1925; Freeman August 23 and 30, 1922; London Mercury December 1920; New Republic August 27, 1919.

MENKEN, ADAH ISAACS (June 15, 1835?-August 10, 1868), actress and poet, was born, it is believed, in Milneburg, a suburb of New Orleans. Her father was probably surnamed Theodore, and she was almost certainly of Jewish birth and named Adah Bertha. Her father died when she was two and her mother soon remarried, the stepfather's name probably being Joseph. All this uncertainty arises from her habit of romancing about herself and her origin. She obtained somehow a rather good education, with a knowledge of languages and of various arts, though the statement that she ever taught French and Latin in a girls' school is probably apocryphal. More likely is the story that she and her putative stepsister danced in Havana as the Theodore sisters. The first sure date in her history is 1856, when she married Alexander Isaacs Menken, a Jewish musician. From 1857 on, she appeared frequently throughout the South as an actress, with her husband as manager, and from the same date her poems began to appear, chiefly in the Cincinnati *Israelite* and in the New York *Sunday Mercury*. In 1859, after her New York début, she left her husband (though she retained his name all her life), and married John C. Heenan, the prizefighter. When this bigamous marriage became known, there ensued a scandal, a divorce by Menken, and a desertion by Heenan. Their son had been born and had died in the interim. In 1861 she appeared for the first time in her famous rôle of Mazeppa, and in the same year she married Robert H. Newell. During this momentous year she announced herself a "secessionist" in Baltimore, was arrested, and released on parole. In 1863 she and Newell went to San Francisco, where Bret Harte and Joaquin Miller became her admirers; the next year she went to London, scene of her greatest triumphs, where Charles Reade, Dickens, D. G. Rossetti, and, above all, Swinburne were conquered by her beauty and her charm. In 1865 she divorced Newell, and the next year she married James Barkley—apparently merely to legitimize their child, for she left him in three days and went to Paris, where her son was born and had George Sand for his godmother. Here she created a furore, and became the last passion of Alexandre Dumas *père*. But she was marked for death; a neglected abscess killed her, in Paris, three months after her last stage appearance. She was buried in the Jewish sector of Père Lachaise Cemetery, and in 1869 her body was moved to Montparnasse.

ADAH MENKEN
1867

Adah Isaacs Menken's assumed first volume of poems may be imaginary; the second, delayed until after her death, was named *Infelicia,* and infelicity is its keynote, as it was her own. She was a bad actress, but a brilliant, impulsive, generous-minded woman, a romantic melancholiac; and her verse, strongly influenced in form by Whitman, has in spite of its exaggerated Byronism some evidence of genuine talent as well as of strong feeling.

PRINCIPAL WORKS: Memories, by Indigena, 1856?; Infelicia, 1868.

ABOUT: Falk, B. The Naked Lady: or, Storm over Adah; Northcott, R. Adah Isaacs Menken; Wyndham, H. Victorian Sensations; New York Illustrated News March 17-April 14, 1860; New York Times August 12, 1868.

MILES, GEORGE HENRY (July 31, 1824-July 24, 1871), poet, playwright, and teacher, was born in Baltimore, the son of William Miles, merchant and former commercial agent of the United States to Haiti, and Sarah (Mickle) Miles, daughter of a

Scotch emigrant. He was graduated from Mount Saint Mary's College, Emmitsburg, Md., in 1843, studied law, and was admitted to the bar. But he found little to his liking in this profession and finally withdrew entirely; shortly after his marriage in 1859 to Adaline Tiers he was appointed professor of English literature at Mount Saint Mary's College. Here he continued his literary labors which he had begun about fifteen years earlier, and in 1867 he retired to his nearby country place, "Thornbrook."

His optimistic energy for writing was perhaps traceable to his early good fortune. He wrote a tragedy *Michael di Lando: Gonfalonier of Florence* when he was twenty; his novel, *The Truce of God,* appeared anonymously in 1847 in the *United States Catholic Magazine;* and *Mohammed: The Arabian Prophet,* with better-than-ordinary blank verse, an effective action sequence, and some well-drawn characters, won a thousand-dollar award offered in 1849 by Edwin Forrest, the actor, for the best original tragedy in five acts. The donor did not use the play himself, but it was produced on October 27, 1851, at the Lyceum Theatre in New York. For the actor James E. Murdock, Miles wrote *Hernando de Soto,* which, although the Indian-play vogue was already in an obvious wane, was decidedly no fiasco when it opened at the Chestnut Theatre in Philadelphia in April 1852. *Señor Valiente,* a comedy, the outcome of a request by John T. Ford, owner of Ford's Theatre in Baltimore, enjoyed subsequent runs both in that city and in New York. *Mary's Birthday: or, The Cynic,* a somewhat successful type-character comedy laid in a suburban estate, was on the boards in 1857.

Brownson's Quarterly Review (October 1856) published Miles' "Inkerman," a poem describing a battle of the Crimean War, and in 1866 he won an *Ave Maria* competition for a poem on the Blessed Virgin. His collected verse bore the title *Christine, A Troubadour's Song, and Other Poems;* and his significantly detailed study of *Hamlet*—one of a contemplated series of critiques—was accepted by the *Southern Review* in 1870. Miles wrote nothing brilliant, scholarly, or ingenious; he was, however, a facile rhymer and his plays were popular with some of the ranking actors of the pre-Civil War era.

Principal Works: Michael di Lando: Gonfalonier of Florence, 1844; The Truce of God, 1847; Mohammed: The Arabian Prophet, 1851; Hernando de Soto, 1852; Señor Valiente, 1859; Christine, A Troubadour's Song, and Other Poems, 1866.

About: Boyle, E. Biographical Sketches of Distinguished Marylanders; Cox, T. E. Gems From George H. Miles; Quinn, A. H. History of the American Drama From the Beginning to the Civil War; Current Literature January 1898; The Magnificat May, June 1908; January 1933.

MILLER, CINCINNATUS HEINE (or HINER) ("Joaquin" Miller) (March 10, 1839 or November 10, 1841-February 17, 1913), poet, novelist, and dramatist, was born in Liberty, Ind., the son of Hulings Miller, a Quaker schoolteacher and preacher, and Margaret (Witt or DeWitt) Miller. Miller's own accounts of his career are so utterly untrustworthy that one must grope for such ordinary data as his actual birthdate or the spelling of his middle name. As a boy he was known as "Nat." The name of "Joaquin," which he finally adopted regularly, was given him after a written defense by him of the California bandit, Joaquin Murietta.

The Miller family was at the time of his birth gradually moving westward, having started in Ohio. By 1852 (he says 1850), they had settled in Oregon, near the present university town of Eugene, where the boy attended what poor schools were at hand. In 1855 he and another lad ran away to the California gold mines. Here he cooked in a mining camp until he came down with scurvy induced by his own cooking. It has been definitely established that Miller was not even in the Castle Rocks battle with the Modocs, where he claimed to have been shot through the right wrist by an arrow. (This was his explanation for his atrocious handwriting.) It is true, however, that he and "Mountain Joe" De Bloney ran a roadhouse at the base of Mt. Shasta, in which Miller was again cook. By 1857 he was living with the Digger Indians, had married a squaw with some kind of ceremony, and had a daughter, Cali-Shasta. The Diggers were notorious horse thieves, and Miller joined in their exploits. In 1859 he was captured, but a friend sawed the bars of his cell that night and he escaped. He lingered in the neighborhood until the Pit River massacre made white sympathizers with the Indians unpopular; then he returned to Oregon with tales of having been one of the William Walker's Filibusters, a "Sachem." and a *vaquero* (cowboy).

At home again, he attended the newly founded Columbia College in Eugene (he says he was graduated, as valedictorian, in 1858, when he was certainly in California), taught for a while in Washington (then a territory), read law, and was admitted to the bar in Portland in 1860 or 1861. Instead

Collection of Frederick H. Meserve
"JOAQUIN" MILLER

of practicing, he went to Idaho to try his luck at mining; failing in this he and Isaac Mossman established a pony express between the two territories. With his profits he bought, in 1863, the *Democratic Register,* in Eugene, which was finally suppressed as pro-Confederate in tone. Meanwhile he had met and married, with no thought for his Indian ties, Minnie Theresa ("Minnie Myrtle") Dyer, who admired his verses; she bore him two children and left him in 1867. Moving to Canyon City, Ore., Miller led a party against the hostile Indians, and as reward was made judge of Grant County court. In 1870 he went to San Francisco, where he became an intimate of Bret Harte, Charles Warren Stoddard, and Ina Coolbrith. The next year he sailed for England. A romantic figure in beard and sombrero, an expert self-advertiser, he gained the patronage of W. M. Rossetti and others, and his first book of poems to be published in England, *Songs of the Sierras,* won him wide acclaim. It is impossible to trace Miller's career exactly in the next few years; he was in Hawaii, South America, Europe, and perhaps the Near East, then in New York, Boston, and Washington. In 1883, apparently without the formality of a divorce, be married Abbie Leland, who survived him, together with his daughter by Minnie Dyer; both in fact, still live (at present writing) at "The Hights" (Miller's spelling), the curious estate near Oakland, Calif., which he purchased in 1886 and which was his home thenceforth. Here his mother, his daughter, and his wife and he each had a cottage; he built a statue to Frémont, a pyramid to Moses, and his own funeral pyre (never used), and planted eucalyptus seedlings which are now a forest. He left it in 1897 to become correspondent for the New York *Journal* in the Klondike, and it is possible, though not certain, that he was present in Pekin during the Boxer Rebellion in 1900. He died at "The Hights," and according to his wishes his ashes were cast to the winds in the High Sierras.

Miller was all his life a splendid poseur, with his expensive boots which he said he wore because he could not afford shoes, his diamond ring (given him "by a duchess") worn in a cabin where the door was always open so tramps could sleep on the floor, his gallon jug of wine, his synthetic rain pattering from pipes on the roof to "inspire" him, his skin covering for his bed, his tales of impossible adventure and high prowess. But he was an authentic part of the old West, his aim, as Ernest Sutherland Bates says, being "to celebrate on an heroic scale the freedom and beauty" of its pioneer days. Banal, half-literate, and imitative as much of his writing was, he told the simple truth when he said to an acquaintance that he wrote neither for fame nor for money, "but because I can't help it." His novels and plays are dead, and most of his poetry, but he himself will long remain a living tradition in the annals of Western literature.

Principal Works: Specimens, 1868; Joaquin et al, 1869; Songs of the Sierras, 1871; Songs of the Sunlands, 1873; Life Amongst the Modocs, 1873; The Ship in the Desert, 1875; The Danites in the Sierras, 1881; The Baroness of New York, 1877; Songs of Italy, 1878; '49: or, The Gold Seekers, 1880; Shadows of Shasta, 1881; Memorie and Rime, 1884; The Destruction of Gotham, 1886; An Illustrated History of Montana, 1894; The Building of the City Beautiful, 1897; Chants for the Boer, 1900; True Bear Stories, 1900; Light, 1907; Overland in a Covered Wagon, 1930.

About: Allen, M. P. Joaquin Miller: Frontier Poet; Miller, C. H. Memorie and Rime, Overland in a Covered Wagon; Peterson, M. S. Joaquin Miller: Literary Frontiersman; Wagner, H. Joaquin Miller and His Other Self; American Mercury February 1926; Frontier May 1931, January-May 1932; Overland Monthly June 1920; Sunset Magazine June 1913; San Francisco Examiner February 18, 1913.

MILLER, EMILY CLARK (HUNTINGTON) (October 22, 1833-November 2, 1913), juvenile writer, editor, and educator, was born in Brooklyn, Conn. Her father, a physician and clergyman, was Thomas Huntington, her mother, Paulina (Clark) Huntington. In 1857 she was graduated from Oberlin College and three years later was married to John Edwin Miller, a teacher. Mrs. Miller helped her husband in his various Sunday school and Y.M.C.A.

activities and also assisted him in the publication of a juvenile magazine, the *Little Corporal,* which in 1875 was merged into *St. Nicholas.* In 1871 she helped to secure the charter for Evanston College for Ladies and, after it became part of Northwestern University in 1873, served as trustee until 1885. She also served as dean of women and assistant professor of English literature from 1891 to 1898.

Mrs. Miller started writing while still in school and, despite her domestic responsibilities—she was the mother of three sons, a daughter having died in infancy—and her many outside interests and activities, continued with her literary career. Her stories always had bits of humor, some good description, natural conversation, and an inevitable moral lesson. Her poetry, while not outstanding, possessed lyrical value, some imagination, and was usually of a spiritual nature. She was at one time associate editor of the *Ladies' Home Journal,* and made many contributions to periodicals of the day.

Principal Works: The Royal Road to Fortune, 1869; The Parish of Fair Haven, 1876; Kathie's Experience, 1886; Thorn Apples, 1887; The King's Messengers, 1891; For the Beloved, 1892; Home Talks About the World, 1894; From Avalon, 1896.

About: Willard, F. E. Women and Temperance; Willard, Frances E. & Livermore, M. A. American Women; New York Times November 5, 1913; St. Paul Pioneer Press November 3, 1913.

MILLER, HARRIET (MANN) ("Olive Thorne Miller") (June 25, 1831-December 25, 1918), juvenile writer and naturalist, was born in Auburn, N.Y. Her parents, Seth Hunt Mann and Mary Field (Holbrook) Mann, moved to Ohio while she was a child, and it was there that she was educated in private schools. In 1854 she married Watts Todd Miller. When her four children were nearly grown she started writing juvenile stories under the pseudonym of "Olive Thorne Miller." She devoted much time to the study of birds and it was about them that her best books were written. She observed them in summer in their natural habitat and in winter she watched them in an aviary in her home. Her stories about them are written with animation and with such lively details that children thoroughly enjoy them. Although they are written entirely as the result of her own observations they contain few scientific mistakes and are entertaining as well as instructive. She spent the first twenty years of her married life in Chicago, then lived in Brooklyn, and, after her husband's death, moved to Los Angeles where she died fourteen years later at the age of eighty-seven.

Principal Works: Little Folks in Feathers and Fur and Others in Neither, 1875; Queer Pets at Marcy's, 1880; Bird-Ways, 1885; In Nesting Time, 1888; A Bird-Lover in the West, 1894; The First Book of Birds, 1899; The Second Book of Birds, 1901; True Bird Stories from my Notebook, 1903; With the Birds in Maine, 1904; Children's Book of Birds, 1915.

About: Mann, G. S. Genealogy of the Descendants of Richard Mann of Scituate, Massachusetts; Willard, F. E. & Livermore, M. A. American Women; Los Angeles Times December 26, 1918; New York Times December 27, 1918.

MILLER, "JOAQUIN." See MILLER, CINCINNATUS HEINE

"MILLER, JOE, JR." See WESTCOTT, THOMPSON

MILLER, OLIVE THORNE. See MILLER, HARRIET (MANN)

MILLET, FRANCIS DAVIS (November 3, 1846-April 15, 1912), war correspondent, painter, and illustrator, was born in Mattapoisett, Mass., the son of Dr. Asa Millet and Huldah A. (Byram) Millet. At eighteen young Millet served about four months as a drummer in the 60th Massachusetts Militia Infantry; he entered Harvard and received (1869) an M.A. degree in modern languages and literature. He was employed by the Boston *Advertiser*; learned something about lithography; and in 1871 went to the Royal Academy, in Antwerp, where he won an astonishing number of prizes and was decorated by the King. In 1873 he was made secretary of the Massachusetts commission to the Vienna exposition, toured the Near East, studied painting a while, and returned to act as Boston *Advertiser* correspondent at the Philadelphia Centennial.

In 1877 he was sent abroad by the New York *Herald* to cover the war between Russia and Turkey, later becoming Archibald Forbes' successor on the London *Daily News* and artist for the London *Graphic.* By a bold breach of military etiquette Millet passed on to some Russian officers a piece of advice on the route of attack, and for this he received the crosses of St. Stanislaus and St. Anne; advancing to Adrianople with his friend, General Gurko, he was presented with the Iron Cross of Rumania. He was a member of the fine arts jury at the Paris exposition (1878) and an exhibitor in its Salon.

Five years after his marriage to Elizabeth Greely Merrill in 1879 he aided in founding a Bohemian colony at Broadway, England;

and it was after his removal to Broadway that his few published works were issued. He was awarded several noteworthy art commissions and traveled extensively. In the execution of his duties as director of the American Academy at Rome Millet booked a passage on the "Titanic"; he went down with the ship.

Most of his tales in *The Capillary Crime and Other Stories,* a collection of magazine contributions, were suggested by life in the Latin Quarter. The title piece concerned the mysterious death of a young artist by discharge of a fire-arm through force of capillary attraction and had a very strange parallel with an actual tragedy reported in a Western newspaper; *From the Black Forest to the Black Sea,* a series of narratives for which *Harper's Magazine* had sent him 1700 miles down the Danube, appeared serially between February and May 1892. Into *The Expedition to the Philippines,* published the year following Dewey's victory at Manila, he incorporated his war correspondence.

Millet is credited with having been the creative spirit of the American Federation of Arts and of the National Commission of Fine Arts; among the best known of his own productions are his decorations in Trinity Church, Boston, and his portrait of Mark Twain. He had, doubtless, more influence on art than on letters; Henry James said of him that he made "pictures without words and words without pictures."

PRINCIPAL WORKS: The Capillary Crime and Other Stories, 1892; From the Black Forest to the Black Sea, 1893; The Expedition to the Philippines, 1899.

ABOUT: Francis Davis Millet: Memorial Meeting (pub. by the American Federation of Arts); Harvard Graduates' Magazine September 1909; World's Work December 1909; American Art News April 20, 1912; New York Times April 16, 1912

MILLS, LAWRENCE HEYWORTH (1837-January 29, 1918), churchman and Iranian scholar, born in New York City, was the son of Philo L. Mills, descendant of a seventeenth century emigrant from Amsterdam to Windsor, Conn., Peter van der Meulen, who changed his name to Mills, and of Caroline (Kane) Mills. He was educated at the University of the City of New York, receiving his B.A. degree in 1858 and M.A. in 1863, and studied for the ministry at the Protestant Theological Seminary in Virginia. From 1861 to 1877 he was engaged in ecclesiastical duties, in Brooklyn and Hartford, Conn., and from 1873 in the American Episcopal Church in Florence, Italy. His absorption in the Avestas, the sacred books of the Parsees, was an outcome of his removal to Germany in 1877, where he engaged in the study of Vedic and Iranian. By 1883 his reputation induced the Orientalist, Prof. Max Müller, to request him to complete translations of the *Sacred Books of the East* left unfinished by James Darmesteter, and he accordingly undertook Volume 31, considered one of the most difficult of the books. He settled in Oxford, England, in 1887, and ten years later became professor of Zend Philology at the University, the chair being especially created for and held by him until his death.

With great erudition and industry Mills wrote numerous articles for leading Orientalist and philological reviews, as well as nearly a dozen books. His work was mainly restricted to the Yasna, the principal liturgical books of the Avestas, and more particularly to that portion known as the Gāthās, metrical and archaic discourses ascribed to Zoroaster. In this field he produced critical reviews, translations, commentaries, and collations of all available texts with their Sanskrit and other equivalents. He also occupied himself in tracing the theological relationship between the Avestas and the New Testament, a comparative interpretation that in some quarters was received doubtfully, and, together with his obscure, involved style, tended somewhat to detract from the otherwise high estimation of his work.

PRINCIPAL WORKS: A Study of the Five Zarathushtrian (Zoroastrian) Gāthās, 1894; The Gāthās of Zarathustra (Zoroaster) in Metre and Rhythm, 1900; Zaraûstra, Philo, the Achaemenids, and Israel, 1905-1906; Avesta Eschatology Compared With the Books of Daniel and Revelations, 1908; The Yasna of the Avesta:. . . A Study of Yasna I, 1910; Our Own Religion in Ancient Persia, 1913; A Dictionary of the Gāthic Language of the Zend Avesta, 1913; An Exposition of the Lore of the Avesta in Catechetical Dialogue, 1916; The Creed of Zarathushtra, 1916; The Fundamental and Dominant Presence of Zoroastrian Thought in the Jewish Exilic, Christian, and Muhammadan Religious and in the Greek and Gnostic Philosophies With Their Modern Successors, 1917. *Editor*—The Ancient Manuscript of the Yasna: With Its Pahlavi Translation (A.D. 1323) Generally Quoted as J 2, Reproduced in Facsimile, 1893. *Translator*—The Sacred Books of the East: Vol. 31, 1887.

ABOUT: Monist April 1918; Open Court August 1905; Journal of the Royal Asiatic Society January 1919.

MINOT, GEORGE RICHARDS (December 22, 1758-January 2, 1802), historian and jurist, was born in Boston, the son of Stephen Minot, a merchant, and Sarah (Clark) Minot. At the age of nine he entered the South Latin School (Boston), where his high seriousness and his youthful charm made him a favorite with his school master John Lovell; and when he matriculated at Harvard in 1774 not only his fondness for reading but his graciousness of manner won him the admiration of his much respected tutor, John Wadsworth, for whom Minot, twenty years later, delivered a memorable funeral oration. He received his B.A. degree in 1778, and entered the law office of William Tudor, judge-advocate on General Washington's staff, who succeeded in getting him an appointment, somewhat later, as clerk of the Massachusetts House of Representatives. After notable achievement both in this capacity and as secretary of the convention called to consider the ratification of the Federal Constitution, he was made probate judge for the County of Suffolk in 1792. Minot was a fellow of the American Academy of Arts and Sciences; in 1791 he aided in the founding of the Massachusetts Historical Society, and was for two years its treasurer and for three years its librarian. It is said that he was a man of distinguished appearance, one whose greatest personal weakness was "a temper by nature irascible." He was married to Mary Speakman, by whom he had two children.

Minot was not a prolific historiographer. His chronicle of Shay's Rebellion, *The History of the Insurrection in Massachusetts . . .* first published in 1788 and reissued more than twenty years later, received sufficient praise to spur him on in his continuation of Thomas Hutchinson's valuable and exhaustive *History of the Colony of Massachusetts Bay,* which Minot issued under the title *Continuation of the History of the Province of Massachusetts Bay From the Year 1748.* He prefaced his first volume with a four-chapter survey extending from 1630 to the Treaty of Aix la Chapelle; his second volume, bringing the narrative down to 1765, was published the year after his death. He prepared several brilliant orations, on the death of Washington, on the anniversary of the Boston Massacre, etc; and he wrote a few miscellaneous pieces for periodicals. His historical works are now outdated.

Principal Works: The History of the Insurrection in Massachusetts in the Year Seventeen Hundred and Eighty-Six and the Rebellion Consequent Thereon, 1788; Continuation of the History of the Province of Massachusetts Bay: From the Year 1748, 1798.

About: Massachusetts Historical Society Collections: Vol. 8; Polyanthos (Boston) March 1806; Boston Gazette January 4, 7, 1802.

MITCHELL, DONALD GRANT ("Ik Marvel") (April 12, 1822-December 15, 1908), essayist, was born in Norwich, Conn., the son of the Rev. Alfred Mitchell, a Congregationalist minister, and Lucretia Mumford (Woodbridge) Mitchell. The father died in 1831, the mother, of tuberculosis, in 1839, and the tubercular tendency in her family caused the death of six of the nine children by 1846. It is not surprising, therefore, that Donald Mitchell had frequent periods of ill health and finally died of a lung hemorrhage—though at the ripe age of eighty-six.

He was educated at Judge Hall's School, in Ellington, Conn., and at Yale, from which he was graduated in 1841; he had been editor of the *Yale Literary Magazine* in his senior year. After graduation he retired to the ancestral farm in Salem Township, New London County, Conn. All his life Mitchell considered his agricultural achievements far more important than his literary productions. He was proud of a medal from the New York Agricultural Society in 1843 for plans for farm buildings, and of his appointment as correspondent of the *Albany Cultivator* (later the *Country Gentleman*). In 1844 he tore himself loose from his beloved rural life to become clerk to the United States consul at Liverpool. A few months of city existence brought on a recurrence of symptoms of tuberculosis; he resigned and went first to the island of Jersey, then on a year's tramping tour of

Collection of Frederick H. Meserve

DONALD GRANT MITCHELL
("Ik Marvel")

the Continent, with the result that his health was restored.

Returning to America, he became Washington correspondent of the New York *Morning Courier and Enquirer,* a connection in which he first employed his usual pseudonym of "Ik Marvel." Next he read law in a desultory way in New York, then in 1848 went to Paris as correspondent to cover the revolution of that year. Back in New York in 1850, he edited a magazine satirizing "society," named the *Lorgnette,* the twelve issues of which he published later as a book, under the pseudonym of "John Timon."

It was in this year, 1850, that Mitchell suddenly leapt into fame with publication of *Reveries of a Bachelor,* which sold 14,000 copies in a year (a large figure in America in 1850 for a non-fiction book), and of *Dream Life* a year later. In 1853 the bachelor deserted his standard to marry Mary Frances Pringle, of Charleston, S.C., and went to Venice as United States consul, appointed by Pierce. He resigned in 1854, and after a year in Paris, where the first of their twelve children was born, returned to America permanently. In 1855 he bought a 360-acre estate near New Haven, which he named "Edgewood." For years he struggled with debt to obtain full ownership of what he made into a model farm, both agriculturally and aesthetically. In 1904 he received a silver cup from the New England Association of Park Superintendents on the basis of what he had accomplished at "Edgewood" and of his writings about it.

Yet his life was not only that of a gentleman farmer. Since his wife was a Southerner, the Civil War was a period of great stress and difficulty for the family, especially as their oldest child, a daughter, died in Charleston, during the war, in her grandparents' home. Continued financial pressure forced Mitchell into the lecture field, which with his reserve and diffidence he disliked heartily. From 1865 he was a trustee of the Yale Art School, and in 1884 and 1885 he lectured at Yale on English literature. The university gave him an honorary LL.D. in 1878. In 1868 and 1869 he edited the *Atlantic Almanac* with Dr. Oliver Wendell Holmes, and in the latter year he was editor of *Hearth and Home.* He designed the Connecticut Building for the Centennial Exposition in 1876, and was United States commissioner to the Paris Exposition in 1878. His last years—his wife died in 1901—were spent in retirement at "Edgewood," cared for by his three unmarried daughters.

Striking in appearance, with deep-set blue eyes, delicate features, and thick, wavy hair, Mitchell was modest and self-depreciatory to a fault. He had few intimates, but those few and his family knew his bubbling humor and his charm. Essentially a "middle-of-the-roader," he was also a praiser of old things; his mind, as Van Wyck Brooks remarks, had a "slightly archaic flavor." His style was limpid, simple, "gently bookish"; he appealed to the shamed sentimentality which is masked by so much ruthlessness in the American temperament. As some unknown critic put it, his two most famous books "are to American literature what a wood fire is to a lonely man on a dreary day." Mitchell is frequently compared to the English writer of sentimental and humorous *trivia,* Jerome K. Jerome.

PRINCIPAL WORKS: Fresh Gleanings, 1847; The Battle Summer, 1850; The Lorgnette, 1850; Reveries of a Bachelor: or, A Book of the Heart, 1850; Dream Life: A Fable of the Seasons, 1851; Fudge Doings, 1855; My Farm of Edgewood, 1863; Seven Stories With Basement and Attic, 1864; Wet Days at Edgewood, 1865; Dr. Johns (novel) 1866; Rural Studies, 1867 (as Out-of-Town Places, 1884); Pictures of Edgewood, 1860; About Old Story Tellers, 1877; Daniel Tyler, 1883; Bound Together, 1884; English Lands, Letters, and Kings, 1889-1897; American Lands and Letters, 1897-1899.

ABOUT: Dunn, W H. The Life of Donald G. Mitchell: Ik Marvel; More, P. E. Shelburne Essays.

MITCHELL, ISAAC (c. 1759-November 26, 1812), novelist, journalist, and victim of literary forgery, was born near Albany, N.Y. The earliest record of his newspaper career reports his founding, in January 1799, of the *American Farmer and Dutchess County Advertiser.* After about two years as editor of this Poughkeepsie journal he joined a rival publication, the *Guardian*; purchased an interest in it; and in June of the following year re-named it the *Political Barometer.* In 1806 Mitchell became editor of the (Albany) *Republican Crisis*; several years later he returned to Poughkeepsie to issue the *Republican Herald,* and, shortly, the *Northern Politician.* He died of typhus fever a few months afterward.

When Mitchell's bizarre "Alonzo and Melissa: A Tale" appeared in serial form in the *Political Barometer* (June-October, 1804) no significant imitation followed. But after its appearance in 1811, under title *The Asylum: or, Alonzo and Melissa* (2 vols.), Daniel Jackson, a twenty-one-year-old teacher at Plattsburg Academy, issued a one-volume novel called *Alonzo and Melissa: or, The Unfeeling Father,* which, except for a few slight verbal substitutions, was identical with Mitchell's story as it had appeared in the *Barometer*. Before 1876 Jackson's "version" was reprinted at least eleven times, with variations in extent of prefatory material, etc., and became an undeniable "best seller." The 1836 edition purported to contain "no indecorous stimulants," pledged itself "not unfriendly to religious virtue," and stated, as its primary thesis, that "a firm reliance on Providence . . . is the only source of consolation in the gloomy hours of affliction." For this out-and-out plagiarism copyright claims would surely have been brought against Jackson, but the deaths (the dates of which have only recently been determined) of Joseph Nelson, proprietor of the *Political Barometer* and of the copyright of Mitchell's novel, and of Isaac Mitchell himself occurred in the year following.

Jackson's forgery has, in the hands of literary historians, doubtless glorified Mitchell's literary importance, but the original tale remains, however, a good illustration of unconscious humor and of the influence of Mrs. Radcliffe and the school of Gothic Romance on some of the early American novelists.

ABOUT: Loshe, L. D. The Early American Novel; New York Times Saturday Review of Books June 4, 11, September 3, 17, 1904; Northern Politician (Poughkeepsie) December 2, 1812.

MITCHELL, JOHN AMES (January 17, 1845-June 29, 1918), editor, novelist, and artist, was born in New York City, the son of Asa and Harriet (Ames) Mitchell. He had an early aptitude for drawing and following his attendance at Phillips Exeter Academy and the Lawrence Scientific School (Harvard) he studied architecture in Boston and, in 1867, began three years' continuation at the École des Beaux-Arts in Paris. At the end of a few years of professional practice in Boston Mitchell returned to Paris and took art courses at the Atelier Julien, acquiring considerable skill in studies in black and white. Several of his etchings appeared in *L'Art*.

When he returned to New York in 1880 the zinc process for black-and-white reproductions was a very new development. Knowing, moreover, that the field for the American etcher was still very small and relatively unturned, he used a ten-thousand-dollar legacy to found the humorous weekly *Life*. Edward S. Martin was literary editor, and the first issue emerged January 4, 1883. Francis Gilbert Attwood of the *Harvard Lampoon,* Oliver Herford, and Charles Dana Gibson were shortly added to the staff.

Mitchell was in a position not only to formulate his own uncompromising opinions but to express them in no timid terms. One of his favorite targets, by volley of editorial or caricature, was modern medicine: he condemned the use of serum, opposed subjecting dogs to vivisection, etc. And he was usually the winner of suits brought against him, including that of Klaw & Erlanger, theatrical producers, who charged him with the publication of a cartoon which they considered objectionable. Mitchell was, in fact, one of the most intimidating political cartoonists of that day.

His novels, produced incidentally, include *Amos Judd* and *The Pines of Lory,* perhaps his two best known books; *The Silent War,* a tale of revolt, with an abundance of killing, blackmailing, etc.; *Gloria Victis,* later published as *Dr. Thorne's Idea,* the study of a criminal's son's gradual emancipation from the hereditary taint; and *Pandora's Box* the story of a young and democratic American architect, who, with delightful frankness, sets out to shatter some of the insular arrogance of an English girl. During the writing of these books Mitchell retained a controlling interest in *Life*. He died of apoplexy, and was survived by his wife, Mary Mott Mitchell.

Not as a novelist, but as an editor-illustrator who could and did anticipate popular tastes and produce humor that was timely and brisk, Mitchell enriched American literary history.

PRINCIPAL WORKS: A Romance of the Moon, 1886; The Last American, 1889; Amos Judd, 1895; That First Affair, 1896; Gloria Victis, 1897; The Pines of Lory, 1891; The Villa Claudia, 1904; The Silent War, 1906; Pandora's Box, 1911.

ABOUT: American Magazine June 1911; Book News Monthly March 1912; Life January 1893, July 18, 1918; New York Times June 30, 1918.

MITCHELL, SILAS WEIR (February 15, 1829-January 4, 1914), medical writer, poet, and novelist, was born, lived, and died in Philadelphia. His father was John Kearsley Mitchell, professor of the practice of medicine at Jefferson Medical College; his mother Sarah Matilda (Henry) Mitchell. He was educated at the University of Pennsylvania, but was obliged to withdraw because of illness in his senior year; in 1906 he received his B.A. degree as of the class of 1848. In 1850 he secured his M.D. from Jefferson, and then studied in Paris for a year, chiefly with Claude Bernard, the great physiologist. On his return he became assistant to his father, whose health was failing and who died a few years later. Though he specialized in neurology, and became

Collection of Frederick H. Meserve
S. WEIR MITCHELL

famous for his "rest cure" for nervous breakdowns, he wrote important papers also on pharmacology, physiology, and toxicology: he was the first to discover, before Noguchi, that the rattlesnake's venom is a double poison. He acted as professor at the Polyclinic, a graduate medical school, and for years was connected with the Orthopaedic Hospital, where among other advancements he furthered the proper training of nurses.

But all this time—and he continued to practice until shortly before his death—half of Weir Mitchell belonged to literature. Dr. Oliver Wendell Holmes had advised him not to do any serious literary work until he was established in his profession, and therefore, although he had published anonymous poems from 1846 onward, and children's stories from the time of the Civil War (in the intervals of acting as assistant surgeon at the Turner's Lane Hospital), his first book of adult fiction was not published until 1880. From that time on, his name appeared more frequently on volumes of poetry and fiction than on medical treatises.

In 1858 Mitchell married Mary Middleton Elwyn, who died in 1862, leaving two sons, one of whom succeeded his father professionally; the other was Langdon Mitchell, the playwright. In 1875 he married Mary Cadwalader, and they had one daughter, whose death at twenty-two was the greatest grief of his life; it was to her that his best poem, "Ode on a Lycian Tomb," was written. Diphtheria, in those pre-anti-toxin days, was Weir Mitchell's curse; it killed his beloved younger brother, his first wife, and his daughter. His second wife survived his death by only nine days.

Mitchell shunned public office, though he was a trustee of the University of Pennsylvania from 1875 to his death, and the first president of Franklin Inn, the celebrated club of writers. He received an honorary M.D. from Bologna University, and LL.D.s from Edinburgh, Harvard, Princeton, and Toronto. His later years, indeed, were passed in what his wife called a "warm bath" of adulation, and the result was a rather lovable vanity, frank and innocent. This tall, slender, bearded man had the softest and most generous of hearts, though in every field outside science he was conservative to the point of reaction.

The best selling of his novels was *Hugh Wynne,* a story of colonial Philadelphia, but his own favorite was the picaresque *Adventures of François.* His novels are about equally divided between historical romances and psychological studies, such as *The Autobiography of a Quack.* In his short story, "The Case of George Dedlow" (though it was written as a sort of hoax on spiritualists), he antedated by thirty years (in magazine, not book, form) the psychological study of a boy in his first battle which has made Crane's *Red Badge of Courage* immortal. His poems are less rewarding to a modern reader than his novels; they sound old-fashioned, whereas Weir Mitchell's sober, careful historical tales and his psychological analyses, based on the physician's intimate knowledge, are almost as fresh as on the day they were written.

PRINCIPAL WORKS: *Medical Works*—Researches Upon the Venom of the Rattlesnake, 1860; Gunshot Wounds and Other Injuries of Nerves (with G. R. Moorehouse & W. W. Keen) 1864 (as Injuries of Nerves and Their Consequences, 1872); Reflex Paralysis (with G. R. Moorehouse & W. W. Keen) 1864; Wear and Tear, 1871; Rest in the Treatment of Disease, 1875; Fat and Blood, 1877; Doctor and Patient, 1888; Nurses and Their Education, 1902. *Poetry*—The Hill of Stones, 1882; The Masque and Other Poems, 1886; Cup of Youth and Other Poems, 1889; A Psalm of Death, François Villon and Other Poems, 1890; The Mother and Other Poems, 1893; Francis Drake and Other Poems, 1893; The Wager, 1900. *Fiction*—Hepzibah Guinness and Other Stories, 1880; In War Time, 1885; Roland Blake, 1886; Prince Littleboy and Other Tales out of Fairyland (juvenile) 1888; Far in the Forest, 1889; Characteristics, 1891; When All the Woods Are Green, 1894; Philip Vernon: A Tale in Prose and Verse, 1895; Hugh Wynne: Free Quaker, 1898; The Adventures of Francois, 1899; Dr. North and His Friends, 1900; The Autobiography of a Quack, 1900; Circumstance, 1901; Little Stories, 1903; Constance Trescott, 1905; The Red City, 1907; The Comfort of the Hills, 1909; John Sherwood: Iron Master, 1911; Westways, 1913. *Biography*—The Youth of Washington, 1904.

ABOUT: Burr, A. R. Weir Mitchell: His Life and Letters; Burr, C. W. S. Weir Mitchell: Physician, Man of Science, Man of Letters; Tucker, B. R. S. Weir Mitchell; Century Magazine January 1930; Philadelphia Public Ledger January 5, 1914.

MITCHELL, WALTER (January 22, 1826-April 15, 1908), clergyman, poet, and novelist, was born at Nantucket, Mass. He was graduated from Harvard in 1846, receiving an honorary M.A. degree from Trinity College, Hartford, Conn., in 1868. After practicing law in Massachusetts for several years, he became a student at the Berkeley Divinity School, Middletown, Conn. Ordained in 1858, he filled ministries in New York and New England; from 1866 to 1872 he was lecturer at the Berkeley Divinity School; in 1900 he became chaplain at Kenyon College, Gambier, Ohio. In his latter years he was a resident of Poughkeepsie and New York City. He died at Poughkeepsie at eighty-two.

Mitchell's best known poem, "Tacking Ship Off Shore," which was a favorite of the English writer of sea stories, William Clark Russell, was widely known among fishermen, and appeared in many anthologies. He was a contributor to magazines, including the *Atlantic Monthly,* and worked at one time on the staff of the *Churchman.* His religious novel of New England life, *Bryan Maurice,* which was well received, was a veiled portrait of Bishop John Williams, dean of the Berkeley Divinity School, and of the life at that institution.

PRINCIPAL WORKS: Bryan Maurice (novel) 1867; "The Mocking Bird" (poem) (in Scribner's Monthly, December 1875; Two Strings to His Bow (novel) 1894.

ABOUT: Adams, O. F. A Dictionary of American Authors; Stedman, E. C. & Hutchinson, E. M. A Library of American Literature; Churchman April 25, 1908.

MITCHILL, SAMUEL LATHAM (August 20, 1764-September 7, 1831), physician, U.S. Senator, and research promoter, was born at North Hempstead, Long Island, the son of Quaker parents, Robert and Mary (Latham) Mitchill. He was instructed in elementary medicine by an uncle, Dr. Samuel Latham, and after three years' study with Dr. Samuel Bard, eminent New York physician and author of medical tracts, he was sent to Edinburgh and received his M.D. degree from the University in 1786. He returned to New York, was licensed to practice medicine, and then began the study of law. Mitchill served as land-purchase commissioner in 1788 and as a member of the state legislature in 1791 (and again in 1798).

In 1792 he became professor of natural history, chemistry, and agriculture at Columbia College. His adherence to the so-called antiphlogistic principles of Lavoiser's new chemistry threw him into a long professional quarrel with Joseph Priestley, the English scientist who came to America to live in 1794 and who with other phlogistic chemists appeared to overlook the quantitative interpretation. Mitchill's *Explanation of the Synopsis of Chemical Nomenclature and Arrangement* appeared in 1801. To the development of industrial chemistry Mitchill contributed experiments with gunpowder, soap, and disinfectants. At the turn of the century he was preparing papers on nitric acid, soda, magnesia, lime, etc.; collecting specimens for class-room displays; and analyzing farm fertilizers.

He aided in the founding of the Society for the Promotion of Agriculture, Arts and Manufacturing, and carried on some pioneer geological research along the Hudson River. Two years after his marriage, in 1799, to the moderately wealthy Catherine (Akerly) Cock, he resigned from the Columbia faculty; he maintained a seat in Congress from 1801 to 1809 and from 1810 to 1813. Among the causes in which he was strongly interested were the enactment of quarantine laws and a thorough exploration of the Louisiana Purchase.

For his own vigorous journal, the *Medical Repository,* which Edward Miller and Elihu H. Smith had aided him in establishing in 1797, as well as for other scientific magazines, he wrote numerous articles: on the fishes of New York, botanical history of North and South America, Indian poetry and antiquities, etc. He delivered a number of excellent addresses and published an exposé of political mythology called *Life, Exploits, and Precepts of Tammany, the Famous Indian Chief* and a biographical *Discourse on the Character and Services of Thomas Jefferson. . .*

Mitchill is said to have had a "chaos of knowledge" that was both envied and decried by his contemporaries. Nevertheless the extent of his learning and the purposefulness of his laboratory inquiry were visible in his writings, and he may be said to have popularized the application of scientific principles to every-day thought and activity.

PRINCIPAL WORKS: The Life, Precepts, and Exploits of Tammany, the Famous Indian Chief 1795; Explanation of the Synopsis of Chemical Nomenclature and Arrangement, 1801; A Discourse on the Character and Services of Thomas Jefferson: More Especially as a Promoter of Natural and Physical Science, 1826.

ABOUT: Mitchill, S. L. Some of the Memorable Events and Occurrences in the Life of Samuel L. Mitchill, of New York, From 1786 to 1821; Pascalis-Ouvière, F. Eulogy on the Life and Character of the Honorable Samuel Latham Mitchill; Smith, E. F. Samuel Latham Mitchill; Youmans, W. J. Pioneers of Science in America; Harper's Magazine April 1879; Journal of Chemical Education March 1928.

MOÏSE, PENINA (April 23, 1797-September 13, 1880), poet, was the youngest of nine children of Abraham Moïse, an Alsatian Jew who had attained wealth in Santo Domingo but was forced to abandon it and flee with his family to the United States during the Negro uprising of 1791, and of Sarah Moïse. She was born in Charleston, S.C. Her father's death when she was twelve compelled her to leave school and assist in the support of the family; thereafter she made use of every available opportunity for self-education and for the cultivation of her literary aptitude. Her life, passed in poverty and hardship, was given to self-sacrificing home and community duties. Although handicapped for twenty years or more by failing eyesight and finally total blindness, she conducted in her latter years, with her sister and niece, a small but exceptionally fine school for young girls. She died at eighty-three.

In her early thirties she published her first book of verse and was contributing extensively to the *Occident and American Jewish Advocate, Godey's Lady's Book,* the *Home Journal, Heriot's Magazine,* and Boston, Washington, New Orleans, and Charleston papers. Her best loved work, a book of hymns published twenty-three years later, was commenced for the use of the Beth Elohim congregation, of which she was at one time Sunday School superintendent. Many of these hymns, characterized as beautiful and stately, and as reminiscent of the verse of Cowper, Addison, and other eighteenth century poets, have been incorporated into other collections, usually without acknowledgment. Some of her best poems were devoted to the emancipation of her own people.

PRINCIPAL WORKS: Fancy's Sketch Book, 1833; Hymns Written for the Use of Hebrew Congregations, 1856.

ABOUT: Elzas, B. A. The Jews of South Carolina; Secular and Religious Works of Penina Moïse, With a Brief Sketch of Her Life, compiled by the Charleston Section, Council of Jewish Women; Critic December 28, 1889.

MONETTE, JOHN WESLEY (April 5, 1803-March 1, 1851), physician and historian, was born near Staunton, Va., the son of Samuel Monett (it was John Wesley who added the "e" to the name), an early French Huguenot settler, and Mary (Wayland) Monett. He passed his boyhood in Chillicothe, Ohio, and received his schooling at the local Academy. With his decision to become a doctor and the removal of his family to Washington, Miss., in 1821, young Monette entered Transylvania University at Lexington, Ky. He made an excellent record in literature and the sciences and received his M.D. degree in 1825. Returning to Washington, he established himself as a physician, and in time earned an estimable reputation. He was married, in 1828, to Cornelia Jane Newman, by whom he had ten children, only four of whom survived childhood.

By lucky investment of capital Monette became financially independent and devoted much of his time to his writings, the earlier portion of which was mainly reports of medical experiments and crudely independent (but amazing) ethnological observations. At the age of twenty-one he projected an essay "on the Causes of the Variety of the Complexion and the Form of the Human Species" which was never completed.

During the 'twenties yellow-fever epidemics wiped out whole communities in the Southwest. But Monette's insistence upon quarantine enforcement completely saved the city of Natchez during the scourge of 1841. Meanwhile he had resumed his interest in racial-biological study and although most of his scientific findings remained unpublished, it has been conceded that hypothetically he anticipated, by thirty-five years, the principles of Darwin's *Origin of Species*; and that his classification of the peoples of the earth into climatic zones or belts was actually a rudimentary form of modern ecology. He was a frequent contributor to the *Western Medical and Physical Journal,* and, in the 'forties and 'fifties, to the *Commercial Review of the South and West* and *De Bow's Review.*

Monette's historical writings appear to have been the outgrowth of a rather early interest in the physical geography of the Mississippi Valley, the subject of his *magnum opus: History of the Discovery and Settlement of the Valley of the Mississippi by the Three Great European Powers . . . and the Subsequent Occupation . . . Until the Year 1846.* For a correlation of the growth of the French, Spanish, and English colonies he was largely dependent upon secondary sources—the archives of foreign governments held the first-hand material—but his pages were amply documented, his story well shaped, and his style relatively supple.

American biographers cannot afford to overlook the results of either his scientific or historical research.

PRINCIPAL WORKS: The Epidemic Yellow Fevers of Natchez, 1838; Observations on the Epidemic Yellow Fever of Natchez and of the Southwest, 1842; History of the Discovery and Settlement of the Valley of the Mississippi by the Three Great European Powers: Spain, France, and Great Britain, and the Subsequent Occupation, Settlement, and Extension of Civil Government by the United States until the Year 1846 (2 vols.) 1846.

ABOUT: Kelly, H. A. & Burrage, W. L. American Medical Biographies; Mississippi Historical Society Publications: Vols. 5, 9; De Bow's Review July 1851.

MONTGOMERY, DAVID HENRY April 7, 1837-May 28, 1928), textbook writer, the only child of David Montgomery, prominent lawyer, and Sarah (Prescott) Montgomery, was born in Syracuse, N.Y. Orphaned at seven, he was brought up by relatives, and attended Brown University and the Harvard Divinity School, from which he was graduated in 1863. A few Massachusetts pastorates convinced him that he was not fitted for church administration, and in 1880 he went to England, returning four years later in impoverished circumstances. The writing of his textbooks finally gained for him success and affluence. He had one son. He died in Cambridge at the age of ninety-one, leaving generous bequests to Harvard, the Cambridge Hospital, and the Boston Athenaeum.

His first textbook, *The Leading Facts of English History,* was written for the grandchildren of John J. May of Boston in gratitude for desk space given at his office. This and similar works on French and American history, which brought out the national narratives in interesting and bold relief, were immediately popular. Several thousand copies of the history of France were said to have been read by American soldiers during the World War. *The Student's American History,* an enlargement of *The Leading Facts of American History,* was widely adopted as one of the best textbooks of its period. In his constant revision of texts he would sometimes spend weeks to effect a minor change. Over nine million copies of his works were sold. He also edited several classics for school use, including *Marmion* and *The Vicar of Wakefield.*

PRINCIPAL WORKS: The Leading Facts of English History, 1886; The Leading Facts of French History, 1889; The Leading Facts of American History, 1890; The Beginner's American History, 1892; The Student's American History, 1897; An Elementary American History, 1904. *Editor*—Benjamin Franklin: His Life, 1888; Heroic Ballads: With Poems of War and Patriotism, 1890; Marmion, 1894; The Vicar of Wakefield, 1904.

ABOUT: Boston Athenaeum: Report of Librarian for the Year 1930.

MOORE, CLEMENT CLARKE (July 15, 1779-July 10, 1863), scholar and poet, best known as the author of " 'Twas the night before Christmas," was born in New York City, the son of the Rev. Benjamin Moore, afterward president of Columbia University and second Episcopal Bishop of New York, and Charity (Clarke) Moore, daughter of a British major. He was tutored by his father and received his B.A. at Columbia in 1798 (M.A. 1801, LL.D. 1829). Though he did not take orders, he was always exceedingly religious, and was probably the author of an anonymous tract (1804) directed against Jefferson's free-thinking views. Hebrew became his specialty and the subject of his teaching in later years.

In 1813 he married Catharine Elizabeth Taylor. On his father's death, in 1816, he inherited a large amount of New York property (Major Clarke's estate of "Chelsea"), which in 1819 he gave for the establishment of the General Theological Seminary. In 1821 he became professor of Biblical learning and the Interpretation of Scripture at the Diocesan Seminary. In 1823 this was merged with the General Theological Seminary, and from 1823 to 1850 Moore was professor of Oriental and Greek Literature at the combined institution, and professor emeritus thereafter.

CLEMENT CLARKE MOORE

On his retirement he moved to Newport, R.I., his home for the rest of his life. From 1813 to 1857 he was a trustee of Columbia, and clerk of the Board of Trustees from 1815 to 1850. He wrote occasionally for the *Port Folio* and the New York *Evening Post,* edited a volume of his father's sermons, and condensed and rewrote Jacques Lavardin's *George Castriot.* His fame, however, rests not on these volumes, on his Hebrew lexicon (though it was long a standard authority), or even on the carefully composed volume of homely and sentimental poems, but on a trifle which he wrote for his children's Christmas celebration in 1822 and which was published in the Troy *Sentinel* in 1823. It was the immortal *Visit of St. Nicholas,* beginning: " 'Twas the night before Christmas, and all through the house Not a creature was stirring, not even a mouse." Moore's prose was oritund and pompous, heavily dignified; most of his verse was, by his own account, a labored exercise; but while American children still celebrate Christmas, Moore's verses about Santa Claus seem likely to be immortal.

Principal Works: A Compendious Lexicon of the Hebrew Language, 1809; Poems, 1844; George Castriot, Surnamed Scanderbeg, King of Albania, 1850.

About: Pelletreau, W. S. The Visit of Saint Nicholas:, . . With Life of the Author; Century Magazine December 1897; Publishers' Weekly December 4, 1937; New York Times July 14, 1863.

MOORE, FRANK (December 17, 1828-August 10, 1904), editor, whose baptismal name was Horatio Franklin Moore but who was known only as Frank Moore, was born in Concord, N.H., the son of Jacob Bailey Moore, journalist, and Mary Adams (Hill) Moore, sister of a governor of the state, Isaac Hill. He was a younger brother of the historian and librarian George Henry Moore [*q.v.*]. When he was eleven, financial reverses brought his father to New York City, and two years later to Washington, D.C. At the age of twenty-seven Moore was contributing to the *New York Criterion,* and from the following year, 1856, when he joined the New York Historical Society, of which his brother was then librarian, he was active in writing and editing, including valuable compilations of the Revolutionary and Civil War periods, and anthologies of war songs of the North and South. From 1867 to 1872 he was attached to the American legation at Paris. He married Laura M. Bailey of Dorchester, Mass. They had no children. He died at Waverly, Mass.

Principal Works: Songs and Ballads of the American Revolution, 1856; American Eloquence: A Collection of Speeches and Addresses, 1857; Diary of the American Revolution From Newspaper and Original Documents, 1859-60; Materials for History, 1861; Heroes and Martyrs, 1862; Songs of the Soldiers, 1864; Lyrics of Loyalty, 1864; Personal and Political Ballads of the War, 1864; Rebel Rhymes and Rhapsodies, 1864; Speeches of Andrew Johnson, 1865; Women of the War, 1866; Anecdotes, Poetry and Incidents of the War, 1866; Record of the Year, 1876; Songs and Ballads of the Southern People, 1886.

About: Stearns, E. S. Genealogical and Family History of the State of New Hampshire.

MOORE, GEORGE HENRY (April 20, 1823-May 5, 1892), librarian, historian, and bibliographer, was the son of Jacob Bailey Moore and Mary Adams (Hill) Moore, and a brother of the editor Frank Moore [*q.v.*]. He was born in Concord, N.H., and educated at Dartmouth College and the University of the City of New York, from which he was graduated in 1842 with the highest honors. From 1841 he was associated with the New York Historical Society, succeeding his father as librarian in 1849. He was a friend and adviser of James Lenox, founder of the Lenox Library, New York, and in 1872 was made its superintendent and a trustee, serving until his death.

Moore was a public speaker of high excellence, and contributed to New York newspapers over the signature E.Y.E. He was also a noted collector of valuable books. He used his exceptional opportunities to engage in extensive research, particularly in American colonial and revolutionary history, and published some twenty-five books and pamphlets. An early pamphlet which attracted considerable attention at the time was one based on new documentary evidence of the character of the Revolutionary general Charles Lee.

Principal Works: The Treason of Charles Lee, 1860; Historial Notes on the Employment of Negroes in the American Army of the Revolution, 1862; Notes on the History of Slavery in Massachusetts, 1866; History of the Jurisprudence of New York, 1872; Notes on the History of Witchcraft in Massachusetts, 1883-85; Washington as an Angler, 1887; Typographiae Neo-eboracensis Primitiae, 1888; Libels on Washington, 1889; The First Folio of the Cambridge Press, 1889; John Dickinson: The Author of the Declaration on Taking Up Arms in 1775, 1890.

About: Lydenberg, H. M. History of the New York Public Library; Stearns, E. S. Genealogical and Family History of the State of New Hampshire; Historical Magazine January 1870; Library Journal May 1892.

"MOORE, MOLLIE E." See DAVIS, MARY EVELYN (MOORE)

MORAN, BENJAMIN (August 1, 1820-June 20, 1886), diplomat, was of English parentage, his father, William Moran, having established himself as a manufacturer of cotton and woolen goods at Doe Run, Pa. Moran was born in West Marlboro Township, Chester County, Pa., and after a common school education entered the printing trade in Philadelphia. When thirty-one he made an extended foot tour of the British Isles, part of his recorded impressions being sent to American periodicals. In 1853 he made a second trip to England, never again returning to his native country. Entering the American legation at London, he became successively clerk, private secretary to James Buchanan who was then minister, assistant secretary to the legation, and from 1864 its secretary, a person popular in British circles, intensely loyal to the Union, and with an exceptional knowledge of the archives. In 1874 he became minister resident to Portugal and shortly afterward chargé d'affaires at Lisbon, where he remained until creeping paralysis compelled his resignation in 1882. His last four years were spent in Braintree, Essex County, England, where he died.

Moran's published work consisted in the main of his British tour sketches which appeared in book form under the title *The Footpath and Highway,* and a sixty-eight page survey of American literature published in *Trübner's Bibliographical Guide to American Literature.* He kept a voluminous daily journal from 1857 to 1874 of his London embassy years, and some extracts from it were published in the *Proceedings of the Massachusetts Historical Society* for March 1915. In spite of an exaggerated sense of the author's importance, it is a valuable source of material for the period covered.

Principal Works: The Footpath and Highway or, Wanderings of an American in Great Britain in 1851 and '52, 1853; "Contributions Towards a History of American Literature," in Trübner's *Bibliographical Guide to American Literature,* 1859.

About: Proceedings of the Massachusetts Historical Society March 1915.

MORFORD, HENRY (March 10, 1823-August 4, 1881), journalist, poet, novelist, and guidebook writer, was born in New Monmouth, N.J., the second of four children of William Morford, a storekeeper of English descent, and Elizabeth (Willett) Morford. The son spent some years in his native village as storekeeper and as postmaster, and at twenty-nine he established at Matawan and edited for a few years the *New Jersey Standard.* Removing to New York he engaged in further editorial work, among his connections being the New York *Atlas* and, from January 1880 to March 1881, the *Brooklyn New Monthly Magazine.* He held an appointment as clerk of the court of common pleas from 1862 to 1868. In his last five years he maintained a bookstore and travel office at 52 Broadway.

Morford's initial literary efforts were in poetry, his verse being contributed at the age of sixteen to the old *New Yorker* and the *Saturday Evening Post.* Of his poetic volumes *The Rest of Don Juan,* imitative of the poet Byron, is the best. The literary quality of his work was variable, and his novels, the three earliest of which were written against the background of the Civil War, are labored productions. He became best known for his guidebooks, his interest in this class of writing being aroused by his early trips abroad, and in his bookstore he made a specialty of them. Among his dramas were "The Merchant's Honor," and "The Bells of Shandon," the latter written in collaboration with John Brougham and produced in New York in 1867.

Principal Works: *Guidebooks*—Morford's Short-Trip Guide to Europe, 1868; Morford's Short-Trip Guide to America, 1872; The Practical Guide to New York City and Brooklyn, 1877; The Travelers' Insurance Company's Hand-Book for Going to Paris, 1878. *Humor*—Sprees and Splashes, 1863. *Novels*—Shoulder Straps, 1863; The Days of Shoddy, 1863; The Coward, 1864; Utterly Wrecked, 1866; Only a Commoner, 1871; The Spur of Monmouth, 1876. *Poetry*—Music of the Spheres, 1840; The Rest of Don Juan, 1846; Rhymes of Twenty Years, 1859; Rhymes of an Editor, 1873. *Stories*—Turned From the Door: A Christmas Story, 1869. *Travel*—Over-Sea, 1867; Paris in '67, 1867; Morford's Scenery and Sensation Hand-Book of the Pacific Railroads and California, 1878; Paris and Half-Europe in '78, 1879. *Miscellaneous*—Red-Tape and Pigeon-Hole Generals as Seen From the Ranks During a Campaign in the Army of the Potomac, 1864.

About: Ellis, F. History of Monmouth County, N. J.; Bibliographer July 1883.

MORGAN, LEWIS HENRY (November 21, 1818-December 17, 1881), ethnologist, was born near Aurora, N.Y., the son of the Hon. Jedediah Morgan and Harriet (Steele) Morgan. He was graduated from Union College, Schenectady, in 1840 (the college gave him an honorary LL.D. in 1873), and after studying law for four years was admitted to the bar and began practice in Rochester. In 1851 he married his cousin, Mary Elizabeth Steele. From 1855 he was attorney for a railroad in the Lake Superior iron region, invested in iron company stock, and became wealthy. First as a Whig, then as a Republican, he served in the New York Assembly from 1861 to 1868, and in the State Senate in 1868-69.

Morgan's interest in the Indians, which led him to ethnology, was aroused in college; later he became leader of a secret society called "The Grand Order of the Iroquois" which aimed at sympathetic study of Indian life. The society sent him to Washington to secure abrogation of an unfair treaty affecting the Senecas, who in 1847 adopted him as a member of the Hawk clan. His articles in 1847 in the *American Review,* "Letters on the Iroquois, by Skenandoah," attracted national attention. In 1849 the State of New York made him curator of its Indian collections, to which he added his own, and his annual reports became organs of his ethnological theories. His book on the Iroquois, in 1851, was the first scientific study of Indian life. After 1859 he abandoned the law and became an active professional ethnologist. From 1859 to 1862 he traveled in Kansas, Nebraska, and as far as the Hudson Bay Territory, studying Indian kinship systems, under the auspices of the Smithsonian Institution. Much of this later work was published in the *North American Review* between 1869 and 1876. Morgan organized the anthropological section of the American Association for the Advancement of Science, was its first chairman in 1875, and in 1879 was president of the Association itself. He left all his property to found a College for Women at the University of Rochester.

Though Morgan's theory that all mankind has progressed from savagery through barbarism to civilization, and especially his family system based on a primitive promiscuity, are now outmoded and discredited, he was extremely influential in his day, and has been called the "Father of American Anthropology." In his last years one of his chief interests was the southwestern Indian Pueblos, and his early work on the beaver was long an authority.

Principal Works: League of the Ho-dé-no-sau-nee, or Iroquois, 1851; Laws of Consanguinity and Descent of the Iroquois, 1858; The American Beaver and His Works, 1868; Systems of Consanguinity and Affinity of the Human Family, 1871; Ancient Society: or, Researches in the Lines of Human Progress from Savagery Through Barbarism to Civilization, 1877; Houses and House-Life of the American Aborigines, 1881.

About: Holmes, W. H. Biographical Memoir of L. H. Morgan; McIlvaine, J. H. The Life and Works of Lewis Henry Morgan; Stern, B. J. Lewis Henry Morgan: Social Evolutionist; Popular Science Monthly November 1880; Science February 14, 1919; New York Tribune December 18, 1881.

MORRIS, GEORGE POPE (October 10, 1802-July 6, 1864), editor and poet, was born in Philadelphia, but spent his early youth in New York, and here, somewhat later, he found employment in a printing office and began to write miscellaneous verse for metropolitan dailies. When he was twenty-one, he founded the *New York Mirror and Ladies' Literary Gazette,* and for a year Samuel Woodworth, a man of numerous literary connections, edited it. On Woodworth's departure Morris assumed complete responsibility, and opened his columns to William Cullen Bryant, James K. Paulding, Nathaniel P. Willis, and Fitz-Greene Halleck while they were, professionally, hardly more than fledgelings.

Brier Cliff, Morris' play based on scenes from the American Revolution, had a relatively long New York run in 1826, and is said to have yielded its author $3,500. It was, however, a burdensome quest for humor, and its starched, flat, and unconversational dialogue was sprinkled with cumbersome "asides." The humor of his volume of prose sketches, *The Little Frenchman and His Water Lots,* published more than ten years later, was far from subtle, but it greatly outdistanced that of *Brier Cliff.*

In the year following the New York *Mirror's* decease, Morris, with the aid of Nathaniel P. Willis, set up the *New Mirror,* the literary level of which lay somewhere between that of the cheap magazine and the penny-paper. A much contested "interpretation of the postage laws" precipitated the end of this journal, but during the same year Morris and Willis began to issue the *Evening Mirror,* remembered chiefly for its publication, in February 1845, of Poe's

Collection of Frederick H. Meserve
GEORGE POPE MORRIS

Raven. Morris sold this paper when the *National Press,* which he had established independently, began to rise in popularity. Willis shortly resumed his associations with Morris, the new publication's title was changed to the *Home Journal,* and Morris remained its highly capable editor until a few months before his death.

Except for an occasional strain of simple beauty or quiet pathos, Morris' *Poems* were plainly spiritless and sentimental; but many of his lyrics were flatteringly received and some were set to music by reputable composers. "Woodman Spare That Tree" and "Near the Lake" brought no mere "faint praise" from most of his critics. But his provision of an outlet, through the columns of his paper, for the early Knickerbocker school, was his most significant literary accomplishment.

PRINCIPAL WORKS: Brier Cliff, 1826; The Deserted Bride and Other Poems, 1838; The Little Frenchman and His Water Lots, 1839; Poems, 1840.

ABOUT: Mott, F. L. A History of American Magazines; Wallace, H. B. Literary Criticisms and Other Papers; Wilson, J. G. Bryant and His Friends; North American Review July 1858; Southern Literary Messenger October 1838; New York Times July 8, 1864.

MORRIS, CAPTAIN THOMAS (fl. 1806), song-writer, man of affairs, and soldier, was born in Carlisle, England, son of Captain Thomas Morris and brother of Charles Morris, the "bard" of the very select "Beefsteak Society." Thomas Morris entered Winchester College in 1741; and while in Ireland in 1748 he joined His Majesty's 17th regiment of infantry. For over a year he studied French in Paris. In 1758 he sailed for America as a lieutenant; he saw immediate service and in 1759 was with Jeffrey Amherst at Lake Champlain. Appointed to a captaincy in 1761 he was garrisoned at Fort Henry in the Mohawk Valley, and it was doubtless here that he got his knowledge of the Indian temperament which became invaluable to him later on.

Volunteering to head an expedition inland for the purpose of winning over some of the Midwest Indians from French to British allegiance, Morris set out on August 26, 1764, from Cedar Point, Ohio; Godefroi, a Frenchman who knew the Indian languages and who was to have been hanged for treason, was released to accompany him. Near the Maumee Rapids they encountered an Indian chief who traded his volume of Shakespeare (!) for a little of Captain Morris' gunpowder. A week later the Captain's escorts were assailed by an overpowering tribe, determined to kill "the Englishman"—who escaped because he had stayed in his canoe to read *Antony and Cleopatra*! (This must surely have been one of the few copies of the plays in the new world, for the first American edition of Shakespeare did not appear until 1795.)

Captain Morris penetrated as far as Ft. Wayne, Ind., but, constantly threatened and maltreated, he fled eastward, making what was perhaps the first white man's trail between that city and Detroit, where he arrived on September 17. "The Villains have nipped my fairest hopes in the bud," he wrote to General Bradstreet. Morris returned to England with his regiment in 1767, and two years afterward was married to a Miss Chubb, by whom he had six children.

Politically, the mission had been a failure. But his official notes, dressed up and inserted into *Miscellanies in Prose and Verse* (1791) under title of "The Journal of Captain Morris"—a single episode revolving around repeated escapes from torture and death told by the chief participant, who was at heart a veritable literary dandy—were not lacking in drama. Morris also published *The Bee: A Collection of Songs; A Life of Rev. David Williams*; *Quashy*: *or, The Coal-Black Maid,* a light tale in couplets; and *Songs Political and Convivial.*

Captain Morris spent, in all, less than ten years in the United States. But his *Journal,* exposing the deep-seated nature of native hostility to British sovereignty, the paramount influence of Pontiac, and the general attitude of the West at a critical period, has become not only an exceedingly rare but a very meaningful piece of Americana.

Principal Works The Bee: A Collection of Songs, 1790; Miscellanies in Prose and Verse, 1791; A Life of Rev. David Williams, 1792; Quashy: or, The Coal-Black Maid, 1796; Songs Political and Convivial, 1802.

About: Morris, T. Miscellanies in Prose and Verse; Parkman, F. Francis Parkman's Works: Vols. 10, 11; American Antiquarian January 1881; Dictionary of National Biography.

MORSE, JEDIDIAH (August 23, 1761-June 9, 1826), geographer, was born in Woodstock, Conn., the son of Jedidiah Morse, a member of the legislature, and Sarah (Child) Morse. He was educated at Woodstock Academy and at Yale, where he received his B.A. in 1783, his M.A. in 1786. He was drafted for service in the Revolution, but was excused because of frail health. While studying theology at Yale, he first became interested in geography, and his *Geography Made Easy* was the first book on the subject to be published in America. He also taught in various Connecticut towns and founded a school for girls in New Haven. He was licensed to preach in 1785, was a tutor at Yale in 1786-87, was ordained in 1786, and in 1787 went to Midway, Ga., as pastor of the Congregational Church. He preached in New York in 1788, and in 1789 became pastor of the church at Charlestown, Mass., where he remained for thirty years. In the same year he married Elizabeth Ann Breese. They had eleven children, of whom only three sons survived; their eldest child was Samuel Finley Breese Morse, artist and inventor of the electric telegraph.

Morse was an orthodox Calvinist in religion, a strong Federalist in politics. His tactics in defense of orthodoxy as overseer of Harvard, and his paper, the *Panoplist* (later the *Missionary Herald*), which he published from 1805 to 1810, did more than anything else to drive the Unitarians out of the Congregational Church. Finally his own church split on this issue, and in 1819 he asked to be dismissed. He retired to New Haven, and spent most of his remaining years studying the condition of the Indians at the request of the Federal government.

He was founder and leader of most of the religious organizations of his day—the New England Tract Society, the American Bible Society, the American Board for Foreign Missions, the Society for Propagating the Gospel Among the Indians, the Charlestown Association for the Reformation of Morals. He was chaplain of the State Prison at Charlestown, and a founder and trustee of

From a portrait by S. F. B. Morse
JEDIDIAH MORSE
1826

Andover Theological Seminary (1808). What would be called today a "Red-baiter," he almost embroiled this country in a war with France by his sensational writings in his paper, the *Mercury and New England Palladium,* against the revolution there and his alleged "discovery" of radical sympathizers here. Yet he is described as sweet-natured, lovable, impulsive, and sensitive, as well as handsome and venerable.

Though his sermons were published, and he wrote for the *Encyclopaedia Britannica,* it is only as a geographer that Morse merits remembrance. His *Geography Made Easy* went through twenty-five editions in his lifetime, and he had practically a monopoly in American schools. Essentially a compiler in his geographical volumes, he nevertheless embodied the best that was known on the subject in his time, and he was undoubtedly the first man in America to consider geography a science worthy of serious consideration. His fame was more than national, as is evidenced by his being asked to contribute to the *Britannica,* and to the bestowal on him of an S.T.D. degree by the University of Edinburgh in 1794, only ten years after the American Revolution.

Principal Works: Geography Made Easy, 1784; The American Geography (later American Universal Geography) 1789; Elements of Geography, 1795; The American Gazetteer, 1797; A New Gazetteer of the Eastern Continent (with Elijah Parish) 1802; A Compendious History of New England (with Elijah Parish) 1804; American Unitarianism, 1815; Annals of the American Revolution, 1824.

About: Morse, E. L. Samuel F. B. Morse; Sprague, W. B. The Life of Jedidiah Morse; World Review November 1927.

MORSE, SIDNEY EDWARDS (February 7, 1794-December 23, 1871), inventor and writer of geographical textbooks, was the son of Jedidiah Morse [*q.v.*], Congregational clergyman and the so-called "father of American geography," and of Elizabeth Ann (Breese) Morse, who was a granddaughter of President Samuel Finley of Princeton University. His elder brother was Samuel Finley Breese Morse, distinguished portrait painter and inventor of the Morse telegraph. Morse was born in Charlestown, Mass. He was graduated from Yale in 1811, studied law at Litchfield, Conn., and later, from 1817 to 1820, attended the Andover Theological Seminary. In 1816 he edited in Boston for about a year the *Recorder,* the first religious newspaper in the United States. (After his death a controversy arose as to whether he or Nathaniel Willis deserved the credit for establishing it.) Some years later, in 1823, he established in New York, with his younger brother, Richard Cary Morse, a similar paper which he edited for thirty-five years. With his brother Samuel he took out a patent for a flexible piston pump, and in his latter years, with his son, a patent for a bathometer for exploring the ocean depths; but his outstanding invention was a process which he called "cerography," by means of which he was enabled to print maps in connection with type, greatly cheapening their production, the first example of such map appearing in 1839. He died of paralysis in his seventy-eighth year.

Morse's literary activity first found expression in a series of articles published in the *Columbian Centinel,* later republished as *The New States: or, A Comparison of the Wealth, Strength, and Opulence of the Northern and Southern States,* and a defence of his father against the charge of plagiarism made by Hannah Adams on the appearance of *A Compendious History of New England.* He soon associated himself with his father in masterly revision and editing of geographical works, and in the production of geographies and atlases of his own. His maps produced by the "cerographic" process so greatly popularized them as to contribute to their immense circulation. They remained in general use beyond the middle of the nineteenth century, as long as he could continue to edit them.

Principal Works: The New States, 1813; Remarks on the Controversy Between Dr. Morse and Miss Adams, 1814; An Atlas of the United States, 1823; A Geographical View of Greece and an Historical Sketch of the Recent Revolution in That Country, 1824; North American Atlas, 1842; The Cerographic Atlas of the United States, 1842-45; The Cerographic Bible Atlas, 1844; A System of Geography for the Use of Schools, 1844; The Cerographic Missionary Atlas, 1848; A Geographical, Statistical, and Ethical View of the American Slaveholders' Rebellion, 1863; Memorabilia in the Life of Jedidiah Morse. *Editor*—A New System of Modern Geography (with Jedidiah Morse).

About: Morse, R. C. My Life With Young Men; Morse, S. E. Memorabilia in the Life of Jedidiah Morse; Obituary Records of the Graduates of Yale College.

MORTON, NATHANIEL (1613-June 29, 1685, o. s.), "Pilgrim father" and Colonial historian, was born at Leyden, in the Netherlands, son of George Morton, once Pilgrim agent in London who afterward sailed for America on the "Anne," and Juliana (Carpenter) Morton, whose sister Alice's second marriage was to Gov. William Bradford. The parents settled at Plymouth when Nathaniel was ten, and he was placed under the tutelage of Bradford, Brewster, Standish, and Fuller. At twenty-one he became not only his uncle's clerk and amanuensis but assumed many of the responsibilities of agent, and remained in very close association with Bradford for over twenty years.

From 1647 to 1685 he was secretary of the colony, dispatching the routine work of government and bearing his trusts with much care and fidelity. It is believed that he drafted most of the colony's laws; and he provided officers and judges living in outlying villages with copies of the statutes. Except for a possible sojourn at Duxbury for a while, he doubtless made Plymouth his permanent home: he was collector, assessor, member of land-survey committees, town clerk in 1674 and 1679, and aided in laying out roads and settling disputes. Probably in return for his various civic services, he was granted several marketable pieces of land; and in his later life he appears to have acquired considerable wealth. In 1671 he became member and secretary of the council of war to conduct the campaign against King Philip and remained active in this organization over a period of years. Morton was married to Lydia Cooper in 1635; and in the year following her death, in 1673, Ann (Pritchard) Templar became his wife.

Having been made custodian of Bradford's writings, Morton was at a real vantage point for the preparation of a Pilgrim history, and at the request of many, including the commissioners of the four colonies, he wrote

New Englands Memoriall. It was printed in Cambridge in 1669 and eventually re-written and enlarged in 1680, after the burning of the first revision. Morton acknowledged his indebtedness to Bradford for records of the years 1620 to 1646, and also to Edward Winslow. The value of his book as authority on the early history of the colony almost disappeared with the recovery, in 1855, of Bradford's valuable *History of the Plimouth Plantation*; it remains, however, the original source for the facts relating to the Compact of 1620, the name of the "Speedwell," and a number of episodes during the years following 1646. Morton's historical achievement emerged from an entirely practical design and was in no sense an attempt at studied literary excellence: "I have," he said, ". . . more solicitously followed the truth of things (many of which I also assert on my own knowledge) than I have studied quaintness in expressions."

ABOUT: Allen, J. K. George Morton of Plymouth Colony and Some of His Descendants; Goodwin, J. A. The Pilgrim Republic; Morton, N. New England's Memorial (see 1903 facsimile edition with Introduction by Arthur Lord), Mayflower Descendant April 1922, April 1924.

MORTON, SARAH WENTWORTH (APTHORP), 1759-May 14, 1846), poet, was born in Boston, the daughter of James and Sarah (Wentworth) Apthorp or Apthorpe. She was baptized on August 29, 1759, so was probably born about the middle of August. In her infancy her parents moved to Braintree, Mass., where she was reared. She was taught entirely at home, but given a wider culture than was common in those days in educating girls. In 1781 she was married to Perez Morton, a Boston attorney, later attorney general of Massachusetts, and they had five children.

From its start in 1789, Mrs. Morton contributed, under her pseudonym of "Philenia," to the *Massachusetts Magazine,* and she had poems published also in the Boston *Columbian Centinel,* the *New York Magazine,* and the *Tablet.* Her *Ouâbi* furnished an English writer, James Bacon, with the plot for his play, *The American Indian.* For some years her verse was widely admired; Robert Treat Paine, Jr., eulogized her as "the American Sappho"; Whittier was among her partisans. Her marked beauty and charm helped to contribute to this high opinion, and so did the fact that few women in America were writing verse at all.

Mrs. Morton's rhymed history of the American Revolution was never finished; *Beacon Hill* and *The Virtues of Society* constitute its two completed portions. The only other book she published was a miscellany of poems combined with some prose autobiography. Her later verses appeared as broadsides or in the *Port Folio* and the *Monthly Anthology,* but her fame gradually decreased until few of the younger generation had heard of her. Until her husband's death in 1837, she lived in Boston or its suburbs, in close association with the Adams and other distinguished families; then she returned to her family home in Braintree (by that time within the city limits of Quincy), where she died at eighty-seven, having survived all her children and all her near relatives.

Mrs. Morton's fate has been a strange one. Her stilted couplets, a sort of imitation of Pope with echoes of Chateaubriand in the subject matter, would long ago have been forgotten, and she herself with them, had she not had erroneously ascribed to her the authorship of "the first American novel" (one of the many claimants to the title), *The Power of Sympathy.* As a matter of fact, she would have been the last person to write this book, even anonymously, since it was based on a scandal affecting her husband and her sister. The actual author was William Hill Brown [*q.v.*]. This, however, was not fully established until 1894, so that meanwhile her name lingered as an important one historically in the record of American literature. It had already been many years since anyone had read her pompous, moralizing verse.

From a portrait by G. Stuart
SARAH WENTWORTH MORTON

If a literary mistake accounts for her posthumous fame, her celebrity in her younger days may, as indicated, be partly accredited to the fact that she was a noted beauty, with much charm of manner. In 1802 she visited Philadelphia and Washington and was the belle of the season, whom the great artist Gilbert Stuart was glad to paint three times—though she was then forty-three and the mother of five. Her life was not a very happy one, and it is pleasing to think that she would have rejoiced in her long celebrity, even though it was based on something she did not do.

PRINCIPAL WORKS: Ouâbi: or, The Virtues of Nature, An Indian Tale, 1790; Beacon Hill: A Local Poem, Historical and Descriptive, 1797; The Virtues of Society, 1799; My Mind and Its Thoughts, 1823.

ABOUT: Morton, S. W. A. My Mind and Its Thoughts; Pendleton, E. & Ellis, M. Philenia: The Life and Works of Sarah Wentworth Morton; American Literature January 1933; Bostonian October 1894-June 1895.

MORTON, THOMAS (fl. 1622-1647), English fur-trader and "playboy," who signed himself "of Clifford's Inn, gent.," and who was schooled in law and in the familiar Latin authors and was recorded as an attorney in the "west countries," first came to America in 1622, with Andrew Weston's party. Of this earlier sojourn Morton afterwards wrote, ". . . while our houses were building I did endeavor to take a survey of the country"; about three months later he returned to England.

On his second voyage Morton settled in what is now Quincy, Mass. He had all the symptoms of a very shady past, and the Pilgrims, whom he regarded as pretty poor company indeed, believed his home at "Merry Mount" to be, so far as temperance and morality are concerned, "by no means a commendable place." According to legend, his Puritan neighbors ruthlessly sacked an elaborate May-pole which Morton, with much care and effort, had erected in his yard: this story was the basis of Hawthorne's "Maypole of Merry Mount," and achieved a modern version in Richard L. Stokes' and Howard Hanson's opera *Merry Mount*, which was produced in New York by the Metropolitan Opera Company in 1932.

Morton staunchly disapproved of trafficking in liquor with the Indians, but he was not sentimental in his own profession—that of fur-trading—and he had utterly no scruples against taking a fat fortune in skins for a relatively worthless gun. He was several times fined and imprisoned for disturbances within the colony and was twice deported to England, suffering confiscation of goods on his second banishment. He succeeded in making his way back to the America, however; and he died in Boston two years after his release from a winter's term in jail.

His only literary legacy, *The New English Canaan* (or, *New Canaan*), published in England in 1637, was a book of verse and prose, with a title intended to suggest "land of plenty." This meaty stock of geographical, historical, political, and literary observations was "written upon tenne yeares knowledge and experiment of the country" (by one who was, nevertheless, dangerously inaccurate and violently prejudiced!). The work was "composed in three bookes": the first, "containing the origin of the natives . . . together with the tractable nature and love towards the English"; the second, the "natural endowments of the country"; and third, "what people are planted there." Morton's frivolous verse, some of which is preserved in the *New Canaan*, was flatly condemned by colonial New Englanders, for its "lasciviousness"—

> She was too good for earth, too bad
> for heaven,
> Why then for hell the match is some-
> what even. . .

but modern critics are more intolerant of its frequent unintelligibility and dullness than its "scandal." Morton's remark that "it is a thing to be admired . . . that a Nation yet uncivilized should more respect age than some nations civilized" was doubtless founded on a piece of his own bitter experience in England. Part of his favorable testimony—some of it was decidedly adverse—concerning New England was that

> No man living there was ever knowne to be troubled with a cold, a cough, or a murre; but many men, coming sick out of Virginea to New Canaan have instantly recovered with the help of the purity of that aire. . .

but this could hardly be taken more literally than a florid mountain-inn advertisement. Despite its many small factual discrepancies, the *New Canaan* is still an enlightening piece of colonial chronicle, and literary historians who have succeeded in sifting the comedy from the uncolored chronicle of events have credited Morton with the authorship of the first book of American humor.

ABOUT: Adams, C. F., Jr. Three Episodes of Massachusetts History; Morton, T. The New English Canaan (see Introduction by C. F. Adams Jr.).

MOTLEY, JOHN LOTHROP (April 15 1814-May 29, 1877), historian, was born in Dorchester (now part of Boston), the son of Thomas Motley, a prosperous merchant and amateur author, and Anna (Lothrop) Motley, a daughter of the minister of Old North Church. They were called "the handsomest pair in Boston," and their son inherited their good looks. In after years Lady Byron said he reminded her more of her husband than any man she had ever seen.

He inherited also a brilliant mind, a flair for the romantic and adventurous, a gift for languages, and a good deal of wilfulness and hauteur. After preparation at private schools, including Bancroft's Round Hill School in Northampton, he entered Harvard at thirteen. There he read novels and refused to study, until he was suspended; nevertheless he was graduated at seventeen, in 1831, with a Phi Beta Kappa key. He proceeded to Berlin and Göttingen, at which latter university he secured his Ph.D. and also gained the lifelong friendship of Bismarck. He returned to America in 1835, and set about the nominal study of law; the next year he was admitted to the bar, but law never held any interest for him and his ambitions were all literary.

In 1837 Motley married Mary Benjamin, sister of the well known journalist Park Benjamin. It was a notably happy marriage, blessed by three daughters and a son who died in infancy; and Mrs. Motley's death in 1874 broke her husband's heart and hastened his death. His father built a house for the young couple on his large estate near Boston, and they settled down to a pleasant life of study, writing and leisure. Motley wrote two novels, contributed articles defending realism in fiction to the *North American Review,* and in 1841 allowed himself to be appointed secretary of the legation at St. Petersburg. He stayed only a few months, disliking the post, the climate, and the loneliness; but his brief experience flowered in his first historical essay, on Peter the Great, in the *North American Review* in 1845.

He had found his *métier*; he would be an historian. By 1847 he had also found his field—the struggle of Holland against Spain. To him, and to his readers later on, there was a distinct analogy between the beginnings of the Dutch Republic and our own; both marked the rise of the middle class man to political power. Unfortunately Prescott, he discovered, was also contemplating work in the same field, and Motley offered to give up his plans. Prescott was generosity itself, offered his notes, and spread the word of Motley's researches. The great work was begun, interrupted only by a year in the Massachusetts House of Representatives in 1849.

Collection of Frederick H. Meserve
JOHN LOTHROP MOTLEY

Very soon Motley found that America in his time did not possess the proper source material for a definitive history. In 1851 he took his family and went abroad, first to Dresden, then to the Hague and Brussels. He studied the original documents, then unpublished, and worked like a drayhorse for five years until he had finished *The Rise of the Dutch Republic.* The English publication, which was first, he paid for himself; but the book was an immediate success, with new editions and translations following fast. In 1856 he returned to New York to see the book through the American press; two years later he was in Europe again, but at the outbreak of the Civil War he hurried home to see if he could be of service. Lincoln appointed him minister to Austria.

From 1861 to 1867 Motley was in Vienna, working on his history as well as keeping his finger on the pulse of European reaction to the Civil War, and guarding United States interests in the Austrian backing of Maximilian's adventure in Mexico. Meanwhile Lincoln had been succeeded by Johnson. A person unknown to Motley informed Johnson that American diplomats, and Motley most of all, were openly his enemies and despised and attacked him. The inquiry sent by Johnson infuriated Motley; his denial carried his resignation as well.

He spent 1868 in America; then in 1869 Grant made him minister to Great Britain. Again his diplomatic career was stormy; Seward was his friend and Grant's enemy, and in consequence Motley was involved in the quarrel and recalled. He refused to leave, and was peremptorily and brutally told that his successor was on the way. It was a hard blow, for Motley, despite his earnest labor as an historian, dearly loved the pomp of office and hobnobbing with celebrities. "Motley might have been another Gibbon, he could certainly have been another Prescott," remarks Brooks, "if, instead of spending years floating about in drawing-rooms, breaking his heart because he had lost his post, he had buried himself in his own mind."

As it was, he never finished his great work, though the third part appeared in 1874; and the remainder of his life was of importance only to himself. He had a slight stroke in 1873, the next year his wife died, and after a last visit to Boston in 1875 he retired to the home of his daughter, Lady Harcourt (all his daughters had married in England), in Dorsetshire. There he died of another attack of apoplexy at sixty-three, and after a funeral that called forth all the notables of London, and at which Dean Stanley preached the sermon, he was buried in Kensal Green.

Motley's story is therefore in some sort one of disappointment, of wasted opportunities, in spite of the universal acclaim, the membership in honorary societies, the degrees bestowed on him by Oxford and Cambridge, Harvard, and Leyden. His work was incomplete, and he failed in the other thing he wanted most to do. Nevertheless, though he did not attain the heights which the favoring conditions of his youth indicated for him, he remains a noteworthy figure in literature. His first novel is a mere adolescent daydream, but his second, *Merry Mount,* has the four-dimensional solidity which continued to appear in his non-fiction. He had a genuine gift for the picturesque, for drama, for apt characterization. He really loved liberty intensely, and put that love into his story of its attainment in Holland.

His work has many defects; in spite of its careful documentation, it is often one-sided, full of Motley's boyish prejudices as well as his boyish enthusiasms. It is injured also by its exclusive preoccupation, especially in the later volumes, with politics and religion, its ignoring of art and science and the life of the people themselves. But it is vivid and it is thorough; and anything that has been written later on the same place and period has had to take Motley's groundwork into account.

Principal Works: Morton's Hope: or, The Memoirs of a Young Provincial, 1839; Merry-Mount: A Romance of the Massachusetts Colony, 1849; The Rise of the Dutch Republic, 1856; History of the United Netherlands, 1860-67; Democracy the Climax of Political Progress, 1869; The Life and Death of John of Barneveld: Advocate of Holland, 1874; Correspondence (ed. by G. W. Curtis) 1889.

About: Bassett, J. S. The Middle Group of American Historians; Brooks, V. W. The Flowering of New England; Holmes, O. W. Ralph Waldo Emerson, John Lothrop Motley: Two Memoirs; Long, O. W. Literary Pioneers; Mildmay, S. St. J. & St. John, H. John Lothrop Motley and His Family; Motley, J. L. Correspondence; Rise of the Dutch Republic (see Biographical Introduction by M. D. Conway in 1896 ed.); Nation April 16, 1914; Boston Transcript May 30, 31, 1877.

MOULTON, ELLEN LOUISE (CHANDLER) (April 10, 1835-August 10, 1908), poet, and juvenile writer, was the only surviving child of Lucius Lemuel Chandler and Louisa Rebecca (Clark) Chandler, both of English ancestry and rigid Calvinists. She was born at Pomfret, Conn., and educated in that village, where one of her schoolmates was the artist, James McNeill Whistler, and at Mrs. Willard's Seminary in Troy, N.Y., where she was class poet at commencement. A few weeks after her graduation in 1855 she was married to the journalist and publisher, William U. Moulton, and for the rest of her life made her home in Boston. Both at home and abroad, where she spent nearly every summer during her last thirty-two years, she was prominent in literary and cultural circles and greatly loved. She died in Boston after a long illness, leaving an only daughter.

From the age of seven she wrote creditable verse, her first published work appearing in magazines when she was about fifteen. Her first book *This, That, and the Other,* a collection of sketches and poems published when she was eighteen, sold exceptionally well. An anonymous novel, *Juno Clifford* followed. She was a prolific writer, contributing to the best newspapers and magazines, acting as literary correspondent to the New York *Tribune* from 1870 to 1876, supplying regular letters on books to the Boston *Sunday Herald* from 1886 to 1892 and publishing some twenty books. Her children's stories won instant success. Her poetry, frequently marked by a strain of melancholy, brought her the highest recognition of her published works, her sonnets being unusually competent. Several volumes edited by her, including two containing the work of the blind poet Philip Bourke Marston, included biographies written by her; her life of Stephen Phillips appeared in 190[illegible] in *Recent English Dramatists.*

Principal Works: *Juvenile Stories*—Bedtime Stories, 1873; More Bedtime Stories, 1874; New

Bedtime Stories, 1880; Firelight Stories, 1883; Stories Told at Twilight, 1890. *Novels*—Juno Clifford, 1855. *Poetry*—Poems, 1877; Swallow Flights, 1878; In the Garden, 1889; At the Wind's Will, 1899; The Poems and Sonnets of Louise Chandler Moulton, 1909. *Stories*—My Third Book, 1859; Some Women's Hearts, 1874; Miss Eyre From Boston, and Others, 1889. *Travel*—Random Rambles, 1881; Lazy Tours in Spain and Elsewhere, 1896. *Miscellaneous*—This, That and the Other, 1854; Ourselves and Our Neighbors: Short Chats on Social Topics, 1897. *Editor*—A Last Harvest, 1891; The Collected Poems of Philip Bourke Marston, 1893; Arthur O'Shaughnessy: His Life and His Work, 1894; Stephen Phillips (in Recent English Dramatists) 1901.

ABOUT: Moulton, L. C. The Poems and Sonnets of Louise Chandler Moulton (see introductory Biography by H. P. Spofford); Whiting, L. Louise Chandler Moulton: Poet and Friend; Bookman February 1909; Poet-Lore, Winter 1908.

MOWATT, ANNA CORA (OGDEN) RITCHIE (March 5, 1819-July 21, 1870), playwright and novelist, best remembered as author of the play *Fashion,* was born in Bordeaux, France, where her father, Samuel Gouverneur Ogden, a New York merchant, was living temporarily. Her mother was Eliza (Lewis) Ogden, granddaughter of a signer of the Declaration of Independence. Anna was the tenth of seventeen children. In 1826 the family returned to New York, and she was educated at private schools in that city and in New Rochelle, and also at home. From her early childhood she wrote verses and loved to act. In 1834, when she was only fifteen, a wealthy New York lawyer, James Mowatt, eloped with her, married her, and continued to educate her. They had no children, and he was more like a doting father than a husband; in return, she stood by him nobly when poverty and ill health came upon him.

Collection of Frederick H. Meserve
ANNA CORA MOWATT

The Mowatts lived in Flatbush (now part of Brooklyn). Mrs. Mowatt published her first book, a romantic tale in verse, at seventeen, under the pseudonym of "Isabel," and followed it the next year with a spirited attack on her critics, in true Byronic style. Pronounced tubercular, she took a sea voyage to Europe to restore her health. By 1840 her husband had become bankrupt, and Mrs. Mowatt instituted a series of public readings, which were a great success. But she was still frail, and her health broke down again. The illness seems to have been psychological rather than physical, for she was "cured by mesmerism." She took to hack writing—stories, as "Helen Berkley," for *Godey's Ladies' Book* and *Graham's Magazine;* a life of Goethe, as "Henry C. Browning"; an edition of the *Memoirs* of Madame d'Arblay; compilations on etiquette, cookery, and what not. Her novel, *The Fortune Hunter,* won the New York *World's* prize of $100; the same paper had previously published her verse play, *Gulzara: or, The Persian Slave.* She worked hard, and she was able to keep the household going.

But real success did not come until 1845, when her play *Fashion* was produced in New York. The five-act farce was immediately popular, and continued to hold the stage for years. (In 1924 it was revived in Provincetown in burlesque style, its exaggerated sentiment and conventional plot disguising its really sprightly humor and sharp characterization.)

One thing it did for its author was to make her an actress. She made her début in New York in 1845, and remained on the stage until 1854, appearing in Shakespearean and other rôles—including those of her own plays. She seems to have been acceptable, and her slender figure, auburn hair, dulcet voice, and charming smile were much admired. In 1847 her *Armand* was produced in New York; two years later she appeared in it in London. These years were full of renewed anxiety; she had brain fever in 1850; her husband lost a second fortune; and after a long illness he died in London in 1851.

In 1854 Mrs. Mowatt retired from the stage to marry William F. Ritchie, a Virginia newspaperman. She lived in Richmond and was active in the movement to buy Mount Vernon for the nation. But in 1861 she left her husband on the issue of secession and never returned to him. She spent the writing romantic novels. She died near London at fifty-one.

Mrs. Mowatt's writing is badly "dated"; it was always facile and superficial; but she possessed wit and vivacity as well as a strong strain of idealism, and she was among the best of the "authoresses" of her time and place. Her autobiography is still worth reading; in many ways she, if not her works, was in advance of her era.

PRINCIPAL WORKS: Pelayo: or, The Cavern of Covadonga, 1836; Reviewers Reviewed, 1837; The Fortune Hunter: or, the Adventures of a Man-about-Town, 1842; Evelyn, 1845; Fashion: or, Life in New York, 1850; Armand or, The Peer and the Peasant, 1849; Autobiography of an Actress, 1854; Mimic Life: or, Before and Behind the Curtain, 1856; Twin Roses, 1857; Fairy Fingers, 1865; The Mute Singer, 1866; The Clergyman's Wife and Other Sketches, 1867; Italian Life and Legends, 1870.

ABOUT: Hutton, L. Curiosities of the American Stage; Mowatt, A. C. O. Autobiography of an Actress; Quinn, A. H. A History of the American Drama From the Beginning to the Civil War; Freeman February 20, 1924; Nation February 20, 1924; New Republic February 13, 1924; New York Times June 7, 1854, July 30, 1870.

MULFORD, PRENTICE (April 5, 1834-c. May 27, 1891), journalist and philosopher, was born at Sag Harbor, Long Island, the son of Ezekiel and Julia (Prentice) Mulford. He was christened Amos Prentice Mulford, but appears to have disregarded his first name. At sixteen he worked in his father's hotel; and after a few months at the state normal school gave up all thoughts of teaching. For a year he was a clerk in New York City, then worked in Illinois for a while, and returning to Sag Harbor shipped for San Francisco on the "Wizard" in 1855. Discharged on the grounds that he was not "cut out for a sailor," he stayed in the city a while and then proceeded down the coast on the schooner "Henry"; after some worthless prospecting on the Tuolumne River, he taught school in a mining camp. (Much later he was to satirize the sentimentality that began to settle over the tobacco-chewing, unshaven miners in "The Life and Adventures of Barney McBrian the Shootist.")

During the "copper fever" of 1862-63 Mulford sank some fruitless shafts on his gold claim, and by the time the silver epidemic swept along he was trying altogether new ventures at Sonora, Calif., as a comic lecturer and as a contributor of essays and verse (over the signature "Dogberry") to the *Union Democrat.* His "cashless reputation" for these fugitive pieces reached the ears of Joseph Lawrence of the *Golden Era,* the Western weekly for which Mark Twain and Bret Harte were making literary history, and Mulford was called to San Francisco. He wrote for several papers, the *Dramatic Chronicle* among them, and for a while edited a Democratic campaign organ, the Stockton *Gazette.*

Financed by San Francisco business men, Mulford sailed for Europe in 1872 to publicize the "good and glory of California." He wrote letters from London to the San Francisco *Bulletin*; reported the Vienna world's fair; and returned to New York in 1873 with his English bride, from whom he was separated a few years later. After a short lecture engagement and then six years as a columnist ("The History of a Day") for the (New York) *Daily Graphic,* he built himself a small cabin in the woods near Passaic, N. J. In *The Swamp Angel* he breezily recorded this Thoreauvian venture; and in the year following came *Prentice Mulford's Story* of his life as sea-cook, prospector, haunter of Red Mountain Bar, lecturer, etc., carried up to the time of his departure from California. Meanwhile he had been issuing monthly pamphlets (the White Cross Library) afterward collected under the title *Your Forces and How to Use Them*: philosophical essays on "The Art of Study," "The Slavery of Fear," etc., written in a graceless but sometimes forceful style, embodying a system of philosophy which came to be known as "New Thought."

Late in May 1891 Mulford set out alone in a dory, for a cruise along the south shore of Long Island, and was found dead in his boat six days later. His common-sense theories of self-edification place him among the writers of what is now regarded as "inspiration literature," but his earlier associations, in California, with the *Golden Era* and the *Overland Monthly* brought him at least within the shadow of men who were, even then, taking on the stature of literary giants.

PRINCIPAL WORKS: The Swamp Angel, 1888; Prentice Mulford's Story, 1889; Your Forces and How to Use Them, 1888.

ABOUT: Mulford, P. About Prentice Mulford; Mulford, P. Prentice Mulford's Story; Occult Review March 1910; New York Times June 1, 1891.

MUNFORD, ROBERT (d. 1784), Revolutionary soldier and dramatist, a member of the Virginia gentry, was born at "Whitehall," Prince George County, Va., his parents being Robert Munford (2d) and Anna (Bland) Munford. He was educated in Wakefield, Yorkshire, England. In the French and Indian War he served as captain of the Second Virginia Regiment, and in the

Revolutionary War attained to the rank of major. Nearly a score of years, from 1765 until his death, were passed as county-lieutenant for Mecklenburg County, some twelve of these being simultaneously served in the House of Burgesses and the General Assembly. He married a first cousin, Anne Beverley of "Blandfield," Essex County. Their only son, William Munford, followed his father's footsteps both in extended political service and as a poet and dramatist.

Munford left a single volume, *A Collection of Plays and Poems,* published posthumously by his son. This includes two prose dramas, *The Candidates,* a three-act satire on country election practices in which probably the earliest Negro character in the American drama, Ralpho, appears; *The Patriots,* a dramatic contrast of real and pseudo-patriotism expressing a hatred of war; an unfinished, scholarly translation in rhyme of Ovid's *Metamorphoses;* and some ten poems of lesser quality. The work is entertaining, and shows shrewd observation, humor and satire.

PRINCIPAL WORKS: A Collection of Plays and Poems, 1798.

ABOUT: Campbell, C. (ed.). The Bland Papers; Painter, F. V. N. Poets of Virginia; Tyler's Quarterly Historical and Genealogical Magazine January 1922; Virginia Magazine of History and Biography January, April 1928.

MUNGER, THEODORE THORNTON (March 5, 1830-January 11, 1910), Congregational clergyman and essayist, was born in Bainbridge, N. Y., the son of Dr. Ebenezer Munger, descended from early English emigrants, and Cynthia (Selden) Munger. He was graduated from Yale in 1851; from the (Yale) Divinity School in 1855; and spent a term at Andover Theological Seminary. "All I hope," he wrote at this time, "is to find some small country congregation whose wants I can supply as a teacher of God's word." He was ordained at the village church (Congregational) of Dorchester, Mass., and filled successively a half-dozen pastorates before becoming minister of the United Church, New Haven. Here he remained until he was seventy and at his resignation was made pastor emeritus. He was twice married: to Elizabeth Kinsman Duncan, and three years after her death in 1886 to Harriet King Osgood.

Munger's literary talent was slow in maturing—he was fifty when his first book, *On the Threshold,* was published. It was a series of sermons to young people, and sold more than 25,000 copies before being reissued as a Cambridge Classic. A companion volume for still younger readers, *Lamps and Paths,* appeared in 1883. In the same year came his most enlightening and most characteristic writing, *The Freedom of Faith,* a discursive monograph on the New Theology, which, he maintained, was more closely related to the older (Greek) theology than to later systems. He believed that it consisted not so much in new doctrines as in new attitudes; he renounced not logic *per se* but over-reliance upon it; recognized the significant development of natural science; and placed "mystery," "sentiment," and "hope" within the sphere of truth.

Munger had been greatly influenced by Horace Bushnell, New England theologian who was a leader in this revolt against dry rationalism, as well as by F. D. Maurice and Frederick W. Robertson, English proponents of this new approach. Indeed he borrowed directly from Robertson these thought methods: the pursuit of positive truth instead of the negative destruction of error; the interpretation of truth as a synthesis of two opposing propositions; the suggestive, rather than the dogmatic, approach in the teaching of spiritual truth. *The Appeal to Life,* a book of sermons, preceded what was perhaps his second most important book, a very adequate account of the life of *Horace Bushnell: Preacher and Theologian.* In his seventy-fourth year he published *Essays for the Day,* some of which had appeared in the *Century Magazine* and the *Outlook.*

Although Munger was actually very sincere in his devotion to his pastorate he was never a tremendously popular clergyman; his wider reputation sprang from his deviation from the traditional heaviness of theological letters and his development of a purer, more rapid, and more finished religious prose.

PRINCIPAL WORKS: On the Threshold, 1880; Lamps and Paths, 1883; The Freedom of Faith, 1883; The Appeal to Life, 1887; Character Through Inspiration, 1897; Horace Bushnell: Preacher and Theologian, 1899.

MURDOCH, FRANK HITCHCOCK (March 11, 1843-November 13, 1872), actor and playwright, was born at Chelsea, Mass., the son of George Frank Hitchcock and Mary (Murdoch) Hitchcock. When he was eighteen his actor-uncle, James Edward Murdoch whose name he adopted, helped him to find work at the Arch Street Theatre, Philadelphia. Here with modesty and a serious ambition not only to improve his acting but to become a first-rate playwright, he took juvenile and light comedy parts in Louisa Lane Drew's company. His early death, at the age of twenty-nine, came from an attack of meningitis.

Only four plays have been accredited to Murdoch. About the production of *The Keepers of Lighthouse Cliff,* from which, according to William Winter, James A. Herne drew the climax of his own *Shore Acres,* almost nothing is known. *Only a Jew,* produced at the Globe Theatre, Boston, early in the year following Murdoch's death, was a fragile melodramatic comedy of parted lovers, of which the saving merits were some novel pawnshop scenes and a very amiable characterization of the *deus ex machina* of the play. The piece for which Murdoch is best remembered was *Davy Crockett,* which opened at the Opera House in Rochester, N. Y., on September 23, 1872, and veritably established Frank Mayo as an actor. With little adherence to the original chronicle of the Tennessee trapper and hero of the Alamo, but with obvious indebtedness to Walter Scott's ballad of Lochinvar and to James Fenimore Cooper's *Deerslayer* and a climaxing scene in which Davy keeps the savage wolves out of the cabin by using his arm as a kind of door-bolt, it met the current demand for a subdued variety of theatrical swashbuckling. His *Bohemia: or, The Lottery of Art* began the customary week's run at the Arch Street Theatre on October 28, 1872, with Murdoch himself very adeptly handling the role of Bob Tangent, a "sensation writer." But this would-be satire on the knavery of dramatic critics was a flat confusion of much personal resentment and little genuine humor; and the local reviewers, on the day following, released their own counter-blast of personal indignation.

Murdoch founded no new school of playwriting. His melodrama is a significant illustration of the theatrical poverty that preceded the emergence of an even semi-indigenous American drama.

Principal Works: The Keepers of Lighthouse Cliff; Davy Crockett, 1872; Bohemia: or, The Lottery of Art, 1872; Only a Jew, 1873.

About: Quinn, A. H. A History of the American Drama From the Civil War to the Present Day; Philadelphia Inquirer and Public Ledger November 14, 1872.

MURFREE, MARY NOAILLES ("Charles Egbert Craddock") (January 24, 1850-July 31, 1922), novelist, was born in Murfreesboro, Tenn., named for her great-grandfather, a Revolutionary officer. Her father was William Law Murfree, a prominent attorney, her mother Fanny Priscilla (Dickinson) Murfree. In early childhood Mary Murfree suffered a fever in conse-

Collection of Frederick H. Meserv

MARY NOAILLES MURFREE
("Charles Egbert Craddock")

quence of which she was a partially paralyzed cripple. Her lameness prevented her from having any active life, either in youth or in later life, and diverted her alert intelligence to study and writing. She attended schools in Nashville, where the family moved in 1856, and in Philadelphia; she was more than an average pianist, and she read law with her father. Her summers she spent at Beersheba, in the Cumberland Mountains, where her close acquaintance with the mountaineers gave her the material for her best known books.

Outwardly her life was quite uneventful. She lived always with her family, who lost their fortune in the Civil War. In 187[illegible] they returned to Murfreesboro from Nashville, in 1881 went to St. Louis for a while and then East, and in 1890 returned permanently to Murfreesboro, where she lived until her death at seventy-two. She never married, and her writing was her whole existence. Even this failed in later years when she became almost blind.

Contrasting with this featureless chronicle, her inner life was sharp and varied. Her first stories appeared in *Lippincott's Magazine* in 1874, under the pseudonym of "R. Emmet Dembry," writing under her own name being thought unsuitable for a Southern "lady." When she began to appear in the *Atlantic Monthly* in 1878, she first took the pseudonym of "Charles Egbert Craddock," after a character in an early story. For some time not even editors and publishers knew she was not a man; Thomas Bailey Aldrich then editor of the *Atlantic,* was astonished when he first met her. He had thought of her, from her style and subject-matter, as a particularly robust and virile male, anything but a small crippled woman. Blonde, with prominent features, large mouth, and deep-set grey eyes, she was not physically attractive, but her mind and personality had charm as well as strength. She had a passion for accuracy, a judicial temperament, a vivacious and witty aptitude in conversation.

Miss Murfree was the first to present the Southern mountaineers in literature. She knew them thoroughly and caught their dialect and mannerisms perfectly. Her stories had pathos and beauty, though when she wrote in her own right she was given to pedantry and bombast, tedious descriptions of landscapes, and weakness of plot. Her people are alive, however, and it is through them that her stories have lived. Gradually her style improved, but at the expense of her early naïve spontaneity. In this later period her best work was in her historical novels of the South in colonial days and during the Civil War. At her death she left an unfinished novel, *The Erskine Honeymoon,* which was later serialized in the Nashville *Banner* but never published in book form.

Principal Works: In the Tennessee Mountains, 1884; Where the Battle Was Fought, 1884; Down the Ravine, 1885; The Prophet of the Great Smoky Mountains, 1885; In the Clouds, 1887; The Story of Keedon Bluffs, 1888; The Despot of Broomsedge Cove, 1889; In the "Stranger People's" Country, 1891; His Vanished Star, 1894; The Phantoms of the Foot-Bridge and Other Stories, 1895; The Mystery of Witch-Face Mountain and Other Stories, 1895; The Juggler, 1897; The Young Mountaineers, 1897; The Bushwhackers and Other Stories, 1899; The Story of Old Fort Loudon, 1899; The Champion (juvenile) 1902; The Frontiersmen, 1904; The Storm Centre, 1905; The Amulet, 1906; The Fair Mississippian, 1908; The Raid of the Guerilla and Other Stories, 1912; The Ordeal, 1912; The Story of Duciehurst, 1914.

About: Baskervil, W. M. Southern Writers; Fiske, H. S. Provincial Types in American Fiction; Rutherford, M. L. The South in History and Literature; Atlantic Monthly July 1884; Outlook August 16, 1922; Nashville Banner August 1, 1922.

MURPHY, HENRY CRUSE (July 5, 1810-December 1, 1882), lawyer and historical writer, was of Irish-Dutch descent, the eldest son of John Garrison Murphy, a native of Monmouth County, N.J., and Clarissa (Runyon) Murphy. His father, a millwright, rose to prominence in Brooklyn, N.Y., where Henry was born. Murphy was graduated from Columbia in 1830, became a member of the politically influential law firm Lott, Murphy & Vanderbilt, and filled a number of prominent offices, including that of mayor of Brooklyn in 1842. He spent two terms as representative in the United States Congress and six terms in the state Senate and was minister to the Netherlands from 1857 to 1861. He narrowly missed being Democratic candidate for president in 1852. His influence was strongly exerted for the building of Brooklyn Bridge; he became president of the private company first authorized to construct it, and later president of the board of trustees when it became a public undertaking. He died in Brooklyn.

Murphy's years in Holland gave him a unique opportunity to pursue in the Dutch archives studies previously commenced in the history of New Amsterdam, and his library of Americana, which became one of the largest and most valuable in the country, further facilitated such investigations. In addition to his own writings on early American history he made valuable translations of a number of Dutch works, including the rare volume *From Holland to America,* by D. P. deVries, and an anthology of early Dutch poets of New York. His *Voyage of Verrazzano,* in which he discounted the claims of that navigator, was to have been part of an unfinished greater work on early maritime discovery in America. He was a contributor to the *North American Review,* the *Democratic Review,* and the *Historical Magazine,* and was the first to issue the *Brooklyn Eagle* in 1841, editing that Democratic newspaper for approximately a year.

Principal Works: The First Minister of the Dutch Reformed Church in the United States, 1857; Henry Hudson in Holland, 1859; Jacob Steendam, Noch Vaster: A Memoir of the First Poet in New Netherland, 1861; The Voyage of Verrazzano, 1875. *Translator and Editor*—The Representation of New Netherland (by A. van der Donck); Voyages From Holland to America, A. D. 1632 to 1644 (by D. P. deVries) 1853; Anthology of New Netherland, 1865; Journal of a Voyage to New York and a Tour of the American Colonies in 1679-80 (by J. Dankers & P. Sluyter) 1867.

About: Brooklyn Daily Eagle December 2, 1882; New York Genealogical and Biographical Record January 1883; United States Magazine and Democratic Review July 1847.

"MURRAY, LIEUT." See BALLOU, MATURIN MURRAY

MURRAY, LINDLEY (June 7, 1745-January 16, 1826), grammarian and writer of religious tracts, was born at Swatara, near Lancaster, Pa., the son of Robert Murray, humble Scotch emigrant who afterward became a wealthy New York merchant, and Mary (Lindley) Murray. His earliest schooling was at the academy in Philadelphia, and during his family's brief sojourn in North Carolina he enjoyed a wilful freedom from all variety of study. Soon afterward he was put in his father's counting-house, but ran away and enrolled in a school in Burlington, N.J. Obliged to return home, he was given a private tutor, under whom he acquired a real interest in literature and law. From Benjamin Kissam he got his legal training; was admitted to the bar; and enjoyed a short but gainful practice among the Quakers. He made a journey to England, 1770-71, before his retirement, at the outbreak of the Revolution, to Islip, Long Island. Returning to New York in 1779, he set himself up as a merchant, and after a few fat years, withdrew to his estate "Bellevue," now the site of Bellevue Hospital. In the year following he set out for England again, and never returned. He lived in relative seclusion, during his last years, at Holgate, just outside York, cultivating his famous garden and devoting considerable time to writing. He was married, in 1767, to Hannah Dobson, who survived him seven years.

Of Murray's text-books the best known by far was his *English Grammar,* a complete revision of which appeared in 1818; it has been conservatively estimated that in the United States and abroad about 2,000,000 copies had been sold before 1850, despite the fact that rival grammarians were constantly exposing Murray's minor discrepancies in syntax. Of his religious writings *The Power of Religion on the Mind in Retirement, Sickness, and Death,* first privately printed, eventually found the widest public; in *The Sentiments of Several Eminent Persons on the Tendency of Dramatic Entertainments* . . . he begged, in a characteristically Quaker vein, that plays—"those powerful and disturbing engines of dissipation, profaneness, and corruption"—be flatly discouraged; and his *Compendium of Religious Faith and Practice,* largely extracts from the Scriptures, was prefaced by some very general moral advice to youth in the Society of Friends. He wrote two biographical studies, and projected, but never completed, a "purified edition of the British poets."

Murray was cautious, gentle, and somewhat priggish. His religious tracts lacked thoroughness of treatment and independence of thought, but his *English Grammar* kept its authority for almost half a century.

Principal Works: The Power of Religion on the Mind in Retirement, Sickness, and Death, 1787; The Sentiments of Several Eminent Persons on the Tendency of Dramatic Entertainments and Other Amusements: With A Few Reflections on the Same Subject Subjoined, c. 1789; Some Account of the Life and Religious Labours of Sarah Grubb, 1792; English Grammar, 1795; Lecteur Francois, 1802; A Biographical Sketch of Henry Tuke, 1815; A Compendium of Religious Faith and Practice, 1815.

"MYRON." See HOLMES, ABIEL

NACK, JAMES M. (January 4, 1809-September 23, 1879), poet, was born and brought up in New York. As a result of his father's financial reverses he was unable to go to school and was taught by his sister, learning to read before he was four and early showing an interest in poetry. When he was nine, he lost his hearing as the result of a fall down stairs under the weight of a heavy fire screen. Eventually the power of speech also failed him. For five years, from 1818 to 1823, he was at the New York Deaf and Dumb Asylum, where he showed great precocity and far outstripped his classmates. At twelve he wrote a tragedy, at fifteen a second, but he destroyed them both. A poem, "The Blue-Eyed Maid," interested Abraham Asten, clerk of the city and county of New York. He finally employed Nack as an assistant and introduced him to the literary lights of the day.

In 1827 he published his first volume, *The Legend of the Rocks and Other Poems.* This proved to be a sensational success and the author was described as an intellectual wonder, a second Byron. He followed this with other books of poems, many of which were reprinted from the earlier works. His verses were popular and often quoted. In 1838 he married a childhood friend, Martha W. Simon, and their marriage seems to have been a happy one.

Although considered a successful poet of his day, Nack wrote nothing of permanent value and is remarkable chiefly for his fortitude in overcoming his physical handicaps. His style was easy, fluent, and melodious but well below the level of the great poets he admired and zealously imitated.

Principal Works: The Legend of the Rocks and Other Poems, 1827; Ode on the Proclamation of President Jackson, 1833; Earl Rupert and Other Tales and Poems, 1839; The Immortal: A Dramatic Romance, 1850; The Romance of the Ring and Other Poems, 1859.

About: Knapp, S. L. Sketches of Public Characters; New York Tribune September 25 1879; see also Memoirs in Nack's works.

NADAL, EHRMAN SYME (February 13, 1843-July 26, 1922), essayist, was born in Greenbrier County, Va. (now W.Va.)

His father was Bernard Harrison Nadal, a distinguished Methodist minister, later a professor, and, when he died, acting president of Drew Theological Seminary; his mother was Jane (Mays) Nadal. After attending various elementary and secondary schools, he entered Columbia College in 1860 but transferred to Yale, from which he was graduated in 1864. After three years of teaching in Pennsylvania, New York, and Kansas, and three more as federal employee in the Philadelphia mint and the dead-letter office in Washington, he became a secretary of legation in London. From 1872 to 1877 he contributed articles to various periodicals and worked for the New York *Evening Post.* From 1877 until November 1883 he was second secretary to the London legation. Returning to the United States, he acted as secretary to the three New York City boards of civil service examiners, contributed to periodicals and the *Evening Post,* and lectured at Columbia University. Although he kept up his writing, after 1900 his main interest was dealing in saddle horses.

Nadal started his literary career when he was in the civil service, and in 1875 published his first volume, *Impressions of London Social Life.* This collection of essays depicts the English life of that time so well that it is still of some value today. Nadal never wrote brilliantly but his works, especially his descriptions of social customs, had a pleasing simplicity that made them popular in their day.

Principal Works: Impressions of London Social Life, 1875; Essays at Home and Elsewhere, 1882; Notes of a Professional Exile, 1895; A Virginian Village, 1917.

About: Nadal, E. S. A Virginian Village; Yale College: Decennial Record of the Class of 1864; Yale University: Obituary Record 1923; New York Times July 28, 1922.

"NADIR, WILLIAM." See DOUGLASS, WILLIAM

"NASBY, PETROLEUM V." See LOCKE, DAVID ROSS

NEAL, JOHN (August 25, 1793-June 20, 1876), novelist and miscellaneous writer, was born in Falmouth (now part of Portland), Maine, the son of John Neal, a Quaker schoolteacher, and Rachel (Hall) Neal. The father died the next month, leaving two month-old infants, John and his twin sister Rachel. After very little schooling the boy became a clerk, an itinerant teacher of penmanship and drawing, and a drygoods merchant. In 1815, in Baltimore, his drygoods business there with John Pierpont having failed, he read law and was admitted to the Maryland bar in 1819. For short periods he edited the Baltimore *Telegraph* and a magazine called the *Portico.* He compiled, in 1819, a history of the American Revolution credited to Paul Allen. In the interim he practiced law. In 1818 he was dismissed from the Society of Friends, one charge being that he had "made a tragedy" (*Otho*). When his novel *Randolph* appeared, the son of William Pinkney, who thought his father libeled in the book, challenged Neal to a duel, but Neal refused and was posted.

Collection of Frederick H. Meserve
JOHN NEAL

In 1823 he went to England, and was the first American to contribute regularly to English periodicals. He wrote on American subjects, and reviewed American authors, including himself! He became the secretary of Jeremy Bentham, the economist, and on his return to America in 1827 became Bentham's chief disciple in this country, translating the French edition of Bentham's *Principles of Legislation* in 1830.

After a brief time in New York, Neal settled in Portland for the rest of his life. In 1828 he married his cousin, Eleanor Hall; they had five children. The same year he became editor of the *Yankee,* and remained nominally its editor till his death. Among other editorial positions he was for a time in charge of the *New England Galaxy* (Boston) and *Brother Jonathan* (New York).

Neal was what is called a "character," a typical Yankee Figaro. He taught fencing, established the first American gymnasiums, practiced law, sold real estate, owned granite quarries, edited magazines, lectured on Bentham, and wrote constantly. He had talent, but he frittered it away. He was a careless and hasty writer, without humor or taste, loquacious and opinionated; yet he had much originality and some power. A true enthusiast, among the earliest of advocates of women's rights and of opponents of capital punishment, kindly but quick-tempered, generous and friendly, remarkable for his strength and agility even in old age, he might have accomplished a great deal in any one of several fields had he not been too busy always in half a dozen others. He was the first editor to encourage Poe; he gave Whittier his earliest hearing; he was Longfellow's lifelong friend. Yet today he is practically unknown, and largely by his own faults as a writer. Professedly he was an imitator of Cooper; actually, especially in his melodramatic verse, his work is modeled after Byron, even though most of it was prose and based on American historical subject matter. He wrote three "dime novels" for the famous Beadle series, and much of his other work really belonged in the same category. His rambling autobiography (whose title, *Wandering Recollections of a Somewhat Busy Life,* might be the description and epitaph of all his writing) is probably the only one of his numerous volumes worth reading today, though *Seventy-Six* is considered the best of his novels.

Principal Works: Keep Cool, 1817; The Battle of Niagara: A Poem Without Notes, 1818; Goldau: or, The Maniac Harper (by "Jehu O'Cataract") 1818; Otho (verse tragedy) 1819; Logan: A Family History, 1822; Errata: or, The Works of Will Adams, 1823; Seventy-Six, 1823; Randolph, 1823; Brother Jonathan, 1825; Rachel Dyer, 1828; Authorship: A Tale, 1830; The Down-Easters, 1833; One Word More (non-fiction) 1854; True Womanhood: A Tale, 1859; The White Faced Pacer, 1863; The Moose Hunter, 1864; Little Moccasin: or, Along the Madawaska, 1865; Wandering Recollections of a Somewhat Busy Life, 1869; Great Mysteries and Little Plagues (non-fiction) 1870; Portland Illustrated, 1874.

About: Brooks, Van W. The Flowering of New England; Daggett, W. P. A Down East Yankee From the District of Maine; Mott, F. L. A History of American Magazines: 1741-1850; Neal, J. Wandering Recollections of a Somewhat Busy Life; Daily Eastern Argus (Portland, Maine) June 21, 1876.

NEAL, JOSEPH CLAY (February 3, 1807-July 17, 1847), journalist and humorist, was born in Greenland, N.H., the son of the Rev. James A. Neal and Christina (Palmer) Neal. Two years later his father died and his mother took her young son back to Philadelphia, their former home. After he was grown, Neal spent some time on the recently discovered coal fields near Pottsville, but at twenty-four he was doing newspaper work, again in Philadelphia. He soon became the editor of the *Pennsylvanian,* a daily founded in 1832; with Morton McMichael and Louis A. Godey he started, in 1836, the *Saturday News and Literary Gazette.* It was later called *Neal's Saturday Gazette and Lady's Literary Museum,* and was edited by Neal until his death. In search of better health he spent 1841-42 in Europe and Africa. In 1846 he married Emily Bradley of Hudson, N.Y., who had contributed to the *Saturday Gazette* under the pen name of "Alice G. Lee." Neal died suddenly only six months after their marriage.

Although the author of many political writings, it is for his humorous sketches that Neal is chiefly known. The first of these were published in the *Pennsylvanian* under the series title of "City Worthies," and showed the foibles of the fashionable and would-be fashionable. The sketches won immediate popularity and were much reprinted. He published a collection of them in 1838 as *Charcoal Sketches: or, Scenes in a Metropolis,* and followed these with other collections, several of which were not published till after his death. Mildly satirical, yet good humored and kindly, the sketches show a definite likeness to Dickens' early work. But unfortunately Neal created no characters that lived or phrases that lasted, and his humor lacked originality and depth.

Principal Works: Charcoal Sketches: or, Scenes in a Metropolis, 1838; In Town and About, 1843; Peter Ploddy and Other Oddities, 1844; Charcoal Sketches: Second Series, 1848; The Misfortunes of Peter Faber and Other Sketches, 1856; Charcoal Sketches: Three Books Complete in One, 1865.

About: Griswold, R. W. The Prose Writers of America; Simpson, H. The Lives of Eminent Philadelphians Now Deceased; Smyth, A. H. The Philadelphia Magazines and Their Contributors; Philadelphia North American July 20, 1847; Pennsylvanian July 19, 1847; Philadelphia Public Ledger July 19, 1847.

NEEF, FRANCIS JOSEPH NICHOLAS (December 6, 1770-April 6, 1854), educator, was born in Soultz, Alsace, the son of Francis Joseph and Anastasia (Ackerman) Neef. Against his father's wishes, he joined the French army under Napoleon when he was twenty-one. He received several promotions but after being severely wounded in 1796 resigned his commission, and three years later became a teacher of languages and gymnastics in the famous Pestalozzian school at Burgdorf in Switzerland. In 1803 he married Eloisa Buss, one of his pupils, and the same year was recommended by Pestalozzi to start a school in Paris along similiar lines. Neef executed this undertaking so well that two years later Pestalozzi again recommended him, this time to a wealthy American, William Maclure, who was interested in having a similar school founded in Philadelphia. Maclure interviewed Neef in Paris and interested him in the project, giving him two years to learn English. Neef arrived in Philadelphia in 1806, and two years later had so mastered the language that he was able to publish his first book, *Sketch of a Plan and Method of Education. . . .* This was called "the first strictly pedagogical work published in the English language in this country." He founded the first Pestalozzian school in America at the Falls of the Schuylkill in 1808 or 1809 and in 1813 moved it to Village Green in Delaware County. From 1814 to 1826 he kept a school in Louisville, Ky., from there going to New Harmony, Ind., at the invitation of Robert Owen, to take charge, with his wife, of the educational program in this experimental community. The experiment failed, and two years later Neef went to Cincinnati and then to Steubenville. He returned to New Harmony, however, in 1834 and lived there for the rest of his life. Neef was known slightly as a naturalist as well as an educator.

PRINCIPAL WORKS: Sketch of a Plan and Method of Education . . . , 1808; The Logic of Condillac (trans.) 1809; Method of Instructing Children Rationally in the Arts of Writing and Reading, 1813.

ABOUT: Boone, R. G. A History of Education in Indiana; Lockwood, G. B. The New Harmony Movement; Monroe, P. A Cyclopedia of Education; Monroe, W. S. History of the Pestalozzian Movement in America; Owen, R. D. Threading My Way; Snedeker, C. D. The Town of the Fearless; American Journal of Education December 1862; Education April 1894; Galaxy August 1867; Indiana School Journal November 1892; Popular Scientific Monthly July 1894.

NEILL, EDWARD DUFFIELD (August 9, 1823-September 26, 1893), clergyman, educator, and historian, was born in Philadelphia, the son of Dr. Henry and Martha R. (Duffield) Neill. He attended the University of Pennsylvania for two years, then transferred to Amherst, from which he was graduated in 1842. After studying theology at Andover Theological Seminary and in Philadelphia, he preached for a year in Galena, Ill., and then became founder and pastor of the First Presbyterian Church in St. Paul, Minnesota Territory. There his interests were wide. He was secretary of the Minnesota Historical Society for twelve years, helped found public schools, was the first superintendent of instruction for Minnesota Territory, was president of the Baldwin School and the College of St. Paul, both of which he founded, and from 1858 to 1861 was chancellor of the state university, which had, as yet, no students. During this period he also published his *History of Minnesota*.

The next ten years Neill spent away from Minnesota. He served as chaplain in the war from 1861 to 1864, from 1864 to 1869 was assistant secretary to Presidents Lincoln and Johnson and for the next two years was consul in Dublin. He did historical research during this period that helped him to produce his most important literary works. After his return to Minnesota he busied himself once more in the educational field. In 1874 he founded and became president of Macalester College, which was first located in Minneapolis and later moved to St. Paul. After ten years he resigned as president but served until his death as professor of history, English literature, and political economy and for several years acted as librarian as well.

Although Neill was not so successful as administrator, he was an aggressive organizer, capable of promoting one project, then another, with equal zeal, enthusiasm, and faith in himself. His writings are valuable to historians for the documentary material he unearthed.

PRINCIPAL WORKS: History of Minnesota, 1858; Terra Mariae: or, Threads of Maryland Colonial History, 1867; History of the Virginia Company of London, 1869; The English Colonization of America During the 17th Century, 1871.

ABOUT: Folwell, W. W. A History of Minnesota; Funk, H. D. A History of Macalester College; Neill, E. D. John Neill of Lewes, Delaware, 1739, and His Descendants; Minnesota Historical Bulletin August 1916.

NELL, WILLIAM COOPER (December 20, 1816-May 25, 1874), Negro miscellaneous writer, was born in Boston, the son of William G. and Louisa M. Nell. He attended a primary school for Negroes, and was later graduated with honors from the Smith School. There, because of his color, he was unable to receive the prizes he had earned. This experience made him champion the cause of equal school rights for Negro children until a law was finally passed in 1855 abolishing separate schools.

He studied law under William I. Bowditch, but Wendell Phillips persuaded him not to seek admission to the bar because it would have meant an oath to protect a constitution which permitted slavery. Instead, he became an active organizer of anti-slavery meetings, and also took up journalism and writing. In 1851 he helped Frederick Douglass to publish the *North Star,* in Rochester, N.Y., and got out a pamphlet called *Services of Colored Americans in the Wars of 1776 and 1812.* A few years later he published *The Colored Patriots of the American Revolution* in which he extolled Crispus Attucks, the first martyr of the Revolution, and attacked the injustice of allowing only white men to hold federal positions. In 1861, when John G. Palfrey became postmaster of Boston, he gave Nell a clerkship. Nell thus was the first Negro to hold a position under the federal government; he remained at this post the rest of his life. He was a man of great mental ability and was much respected by both races.

PRINCIPAL WORKS: Services of Colored Americans in the Wars of 1776 and 1812, 1851; The Colored Patriots of the American Revolution, 1855.

ABOUT: Brown, W. W. The Rising Sun; Woodson, C. G. The Mind of the Negro as Reflected in Letters Written During the Crisis 1800-1860; Boston Daily Globe May 26, 1874; Boston Transcript May 26, 29, 1874.

NELSON, HENRY LOOMIS (January 5, 1846-February 29, 1908), author, editor, and teacher, was born in New York City, the son of Theophilus and Catherine (Lyons) Nelson. In 1867 he was graduated from Williams College where he had acquired a reputation as a charming companion and an independent thinker. After receiving his LL.B. from Columbia in 1869, he was admitted to the New York bar and started to practice. From 1874 to 1876 he was in Kalamazoo, Mich., on business, and it was during these two years that, because of his interest in public affairs, he began writing letters to newspapers, which finally resulted in his giving up law for journalism. In 1876 he became owner and editor of the *Franklin County Times,* in Greenfield, Mass., and two years later he was in Washington as correspondent of the Boston *Post.* In 1885 he became editor of the *Post,* but was removed by a change in the ownership after a year. For the next eight years he did editorial work in New York for the *Star,* the *Mail and Express,* and the *World.* From 1894 to 1898 he edited *Harper's Weekly,* making the paper a real force in shaping political thought. After four years of freelance writing he became, in 1902, the David A. Wells professor of political science at Williams College. He taught well, and kept his interest in the world outside, continuing his writing. He held this position until his sudden death in New York from angina pectoris. In 1874 he had married Ida Frances Wyman.

Nelson was a man of shrewd, energetic, forceful personality and of keen political judgment. A Cleveland Democrat, he had firm and outspoken convictions.

PRINCIPAL WORKS: Our Unjust Tariff Laws, 1884; John Rantoul, 1885; The Money We Need, 1895.

ABOUT: Harper's Weekly March 14, 1908; New York Daily Tribune December 20, 1894; New York Times March 1, 1908; Springfield Republican March 1, 1908.

NEWBERRY, JULIA ROSA (December 28, 1853-April 4, 1876), diarist, was born in Chicago, the daughter of Walter Loomis Newberry, a wealthy capitalist, and Julia Butler (Clapp) Newberry. The story of her brief life is quickly told. Her father died in 1868, leaving half his fortune to found the Newberry Library in the city where he had been one of the pioneer real estate men. Her only sister, to whom she was devoted, died in 1874. She herself was frail and apparently tubercular, and died of a throat infection, at twenty-three.

But in those few years Julia Newberry lived vividly. She was a true child of the lusty young city, just beginning to feel its coming strength and power. Her training and traditions were of the cultured East, but her heart was in the raw prairie town. She was educated as all young girls of wealth were educated in her time, her principal school being Mlle. Pelet's in Geneva. Europe was familiar to her from early childhood; her father indeed was drowned while on a return trip from France. But she was always homesick for Chicago, and her diary is full of it. The family home was burned in the great fire, and with it most of the girl's journals. Julia Newberry survives only in a diary of 1870, discovered in 1932, and in the reminiscences of her younger cousin, Minnie Clapp Mygatt. This diary, and her sketch book, however, are precious documents; for they revive a period and a society all other documentation of which went up in flames in 1871. Merely as a source book of Chicago social history, Julia Newberry is important.

But she is important in herself as well. Her year at home in 1870 was her last. She sailed again for Europe with her tubercular sister, who died at Pau; she herself died in Rome. Almost her last words were: "I want to go home!" She was no scholar and no genius; she was a bright, unaffected

JULIA NEWBERRY

girl, with an observant eye, a keen wit, and an apt felicity of phrasing. Some of the charm of her writing is the charm of the quaint, the unexpected, the involuntarily amusing. But some of it is the charm of the born writer. Julia Newberry with a stronger body might have lived to be the earliest of our realistic regional novelists. In 1872 she set down in her note book her "rules" for "My Book that is to be"—the book that was never written. "At the present moment," she wrote, "I could write an amusing book, twice as readable as some that I get hold of, but I wish to be something more than amusing!" She aspired "not to a moderate success but to a great one."

"Sound, witty, trenchant, or incredibly naïve . . . in any case, alive," Tracy D. Mygatt says of these "rules." "Insight and terse economy of words," is the characterization of Margaret Ayer Barnes and Janet Ayer Fairbank, who see in the diary "a possible indication that with Julia Newberry a mute, inglorious Jane Austen died." Rather, she was a lesser Marie Bashkirtseff—younger, less intense, less gifted, less vain, but of the same pathetic company of beings dowered with talent, magnetism, and vitality, and doomed to death in early youth.

Principal Work: Julia Newberry's Diary, 1933.

About: Mygatt, T. D. Julia Newberry's Sketch Book; Newberry, J. R. Julia Newberry's Diary (see Introduction by Margaret Ayer Barnes and Janet Ayer Fairbank).

NEWCOMB, CHARLES KING (1820-1894), New England "mystic" and philosopher-poet, spent his early years in Providence, R.I., and was graduated from Brown University in 1837. Retaining little of his youthful interest in study for the ministry, he enrolled, several years later, as a "full boarder," (i.e., not a working member) at George Ripley's experimental Brook Farm, on the outskirts of West Roxbury. Newcomb was attracted to this community not because he was bent upon the uplifting of mankind, but because it seemed to offer a seclusion and a simplicity that would invite the contemplative spirit. For Newcomb was submerged in mysticism, "hated intellect with the ferocity of a Swedenborg," and loved the ritual of Catholicism (although he could not tolerate its beliefs!). If, during a Sunday morning skate down the river Newcomb detected a church spire not too far from the shore, he would strike out in that direction, enter the church with his skates in hand, kneel a moment at the altar, and then hurry back to the ice. He regularly chanted the litany or recited Greek in the middle of the night, kept portraits of Loyola and Xavier on the walls of his room, and steeped himself in the writings of St. Augustine.

For the *Dial* (July 1842), the Farm's literary organ, Newcomb wrote a metaphysical-mystical allegory called "Dolon," and Emerson assured Margaret Fuller, the editor, that to send forth its sentences was "worth the printing of the *Dial*." Indeed Emerson believed, at that time, that Newcomb's subtlety of mind was a real mark of genius; but less than ten years later he was much more conservative in his appraisal. According to Hawthorne's journal, April 8, 1843, a caller from the Farm believed that the young dreamer was "passing through a new moral phasis . . . silent and impressive," and some thought him to be "passing into permanent eclipse."

He left West Roxbury in December 1845, returned to Providence, and in 1862 served three months in the Tenth Rhode Island Volunteer Infantry. He was abroad in the 'fifties and in 1870 went to Europe for the remainder of his life. His death came suddenly in 1894 during residence in Paris. It is believed that during his later years he wrote considerably more than a long (unpublished) journal, but no records remain.

A lack of physical vigor, an uncertainty of carriage, a severe nose, dark unkempt hair, and strange musing eyes—these were the merely physical accessories of his undefinable "peculiarity." Even at Brook Farm (where idiosyncrasies were carefully nourished!) he was often the source of a kind of controlled alarm. But he had an unusually gifted mind and his superior abilities, it would seem, had been only lightly tapped.

ABOUT: Arvin, N. The Heart of Hawthorne's Journals; Dwight, M. Letters From Brook Farm; Kirby, G. B. Years of Experience; Sears, J. V. D. Z. My Friends at Brook Farm; Swift, L. Brook Farm; Thoreau, H. D. Works: Vol. 7; Dial July 1842.

NEWCOMB, SIMON (March 12, 1835-July 11, 1909), astronomer, was born in Wallace, N. S., the son of John Burton Newcomb, an itinerant schoolteacher, and Emily (Prince) Newcomb. The family was of New England descent, but had lived in Canada since 1761. After a schooling in which his father was his only teacher, the boy was apprenticed in 1851 to a quack doctor. He ran away, disgusted, two years later, and with difficulty made his way to the United States. From 1854 to 1856 he was a country schoolteacher in Maryland. Joseph Henry, secretary of the Smithsonian Institution, became interested in him, and secured his appointment as a computer in the Nautical Almanac Office, then located at Harvard. This was in 1857; Newcomb attended the Lawrence Scientific School of Harvard in his spare hours, and secured his B.Sc. degree in 1858. He published his first research results in 1860. The next year he became professor of mathematics in the United States Navy, stationed at the Naval Observatory and the Nautical Almanac Office (whose removal to Washington he effected). He was retired for age, with the rank of captain in 1897; in 1906 he was promoted to rear admiral, retired. From 1884 to 1886 he was nominal professor of mathematics at Columbian College (now George Washington University), and from 1884 to 1894 professor of mathematics and astronomy at Johns Hopkins; in 1885 he declined the presidency of the University of California. Newcomb's principal work as an astronomer was in the motion of the moon; he completely reformed the tables of motions of the stars, planets, and moon used by astronomers and navigators. Honors were heaped upon him—degrees from all over the world, membership in and presidency of innumerable learned societies. He was the first American made an associate of the Institute of France since Franklin, received the gold medal of the Royal Astronomical Society, and was awarded the first Huygens medal of the Astronomical Society of the Pacific, given only every twenty years. In 1863 he married Mary Caroline Hassler, daughter of a naval surgeon and granddaughter of the founder of the Coast Survey; they had three daughters.

SIMON NEWCOMB

Outside of technical papers and textbooks, Newcomb as a writer produced books not only on astronomy (his popular astronomy is one of the best, though outdated), but also on political economy, his avocation; and he even wrote a novel. His many-sidedness is also indicated by the fact that he was the first president of the American Society for Psychical Research. He was president of the American Association for the Advancement of Science in 1877.

PRINCIPAL WORKS: A Critical Examination of Our Political Policy During the Rebellion, 1865; Researches on the Motions of the Moon, 1876; The A B C of Finance, 1877; Popular Astronomy, 1878; Calculus, 1884; A Plain Man's Talk on the Labor Question, 1886; Principles of Political Economy, 1886; Elements of Astronomy, 1900; His Wisdom: The Defender (novel) 1900; The Stars, 1901; Astronomy for Everybody, 1902; Reminiscences of an Astronomer, 1903; Spherical Astronomy, 1906; Side Lights of Astronomy, 1906.

ABOUT: Archibald, R. C. Simon Newcomb; Bibliography of Simon Newcomb; Campbell, W. W. Biographical Memoir of Simon Newcomb; Newcomb, S. Reminiscences of an Astronomer; Stone, O. Simon Newcomb; Economic Journal (London) December 1909; Science September 17, 1909, December 22, 1916.

NEWELL, ROBERT HENRY (December 13, 1836-July 1901), humorist and poet, who wrote over the signature "Orpheus C. Kerr," was born in New York City, the son of Robert Newell, an inventor, and Ann (Lawrence) Newell. He was sent to a pri-

Collection of Frederick H. Meserve
R. H. NEWELL
("Orpheus C. Kerr")

vate academy, but after the death of his father his family could not afford to send him to college.

By writing fugitive pieces for the New York press he made a little necessary money and attracted a little editorial attention. For the New York *Sunday Mercury,* of which he became the assistant editor in 1858, he wrote an abundance of timely, but otherwise negligible, miscellanies.

At the outbreak of the Civil War he acted as Washington correspondent for the *Mercury* and began a series of papers which he signed "Orpheus C. Kerr," a conscious corruption of "office seeker," that target of political lampooners—the wave of "spoils" applicants was at crest—when President Buchanan went out and Lincoln came in. These dispatches were "grand battle" takeoffs, flamboyant records of the absurd adventures of the "Mackerel Brigade," parodies of peace terms, war letters, etc. Letter No. 8 (new series) surveyed the harvest of an imaginary competition for the lines of a new national anthem. Entries from Emerson, Holmes, Whittier, Everett, Longfellow, Aldrich, Stoddard, and Willis were printed in full—each one a fairly subtle caricature of the poet's style—accompanied by the judges' rejection analysis: Holmes' anthem, they contended, "could only be sung by a college of surgeons or a Beacon Street tea-party"; and the mock-sublimity of Emerson's sixteen-letter words was labeled "too childish simplicity."

The *Orpheus C. Kerr Papers,* teeming with preposterous exaggeration, mangled spelling, and bold specimens of anti-climax, had some of the flavor of Western journalism and were afterward printed in book form. His two volumes of verse, *The Palace Beautiful and Other Poems* and *Versatilities,* illustrating many moods and containing some Irish extravaganzas, as well as a romance, *There Was Once a Man,* an attempt to satirize the still unthinkably amoral Darwinian theory of the descent of man, have remained relatively obscure. In the early 'seventies he published his own solution of Charles Dickens' *Mystery of Edwin Drood* under the title *The Cloven Foot;* and *The Walking Doll: or, The Asters and Disasters of Society,* a novel of Manhattan life

Though his pathos often thinned to sentimentality and his banter often ran to drivel, "Orpheus C. Kerr," like "Petroleum V. Nasby," "Major Jack" Downing, and "Bill" Arp, gave a tremendous impetus to a native American newspaper humor.

Principal Works: The Orpheus C. Kerr Papers, 1862-65; The Palace Beautiful and Other Poems, 1865; Avery Glibun: or, Between Two Fires, 1867; The Cloven Foot, 1870; The Walking Doll: or, The Asters and Disasters of Society, 1872; There Was Once a Man, 1884.

About: Blair, W. Native American Humor; Tandy, J. Crackerbox Philosophers in American Humor and Satire; New York Daily Tribune July 13, 14, 1901; Brooklyn Daily Eagle, July 12, 13, 28, 1901.

NEWELL, WILLIAM WELLS (January 24, 1839-January 21, 1907), folklorist, editor, and translator, was born in Cambridge, Mass., son of the Rev. William Newell, a clergyman, and Frances Boott (Wells) Newell. From both sides of his family he inherited a taste for the classics, and after preparation at the Cambridge High School and at E. S. Dixwell's school in Boston, he entered Harvard and was graduated in 1859; four years later he received his degree from the Harvard Divinity School. His assistantship to the Rev. Edward Everett Hale at the South Congregational Church (Boston) came to an end shortly when he joined the Sanitary Service of the War Department in Washington. At the close of the Civil War he served the Unitarian Church in Germantown, Pa., and some time later, feeling that he was not altogether suited to the ministry, he gave up his religious duties and from 1868 to 1870 he was a tutor in philosophy at Harvard.

He afterward established his own very successful school in New York, abandoning it in the early 'eighties in order to pursue a few independent scholarly interests. A year or two of travel preceded his withdrawal to Cambridge, where he advanced his study in the fields of fine arts and literature.

Newell's writings fall into two classes: the purely literary, and those which are the results of his research in folk-lore. He translated into English verse the *Sonnets and Madrigals of Michelangelo,* supplementing his version with able annotations. He had already issued *King Oedipus: Oedipus Tyrannus of Sophocles Rendered Into English Verse* in 1881. Newell was the author of a small book of original verse, *Words for Music,* as well as the commonly sung English version of *Adeste Fidelis.*

From the publication of *Games and Songs of American Children* until the time of his death, when he had in preparation *Isolt's Return* (published posthumously), he was constantly studying the literary materials that underlie the ceremonies and belief of the Negro, the American Indian, and the legendary figures of the medieval period. He had aided in the founding, in 1888, of the American Folk-Lore Society and was its permanent secretary; he edited the *Journal of American Folk-Lore* and contributed papers on a variety of subjects. *King Arthur and the Table Round* was perhaps his best known book; and *The Legends of the Holy Grail and the Perceval of Crestien of Troyes* represented a portion of his *Journal* articles.

Newell was a private scholar who did not allow his enthusiasm for facts to eclipse the purpose which his newly discovered data were to serve. His small contribution to the interpretation of classical poetry has become less significant than his historical and broadly humanitarian approach to folk-lore and his success in preserving its more vigorous elements.

Principal Works: King Oedipus: The Oedipus Tyrannus of Sophocles Rendered Into English Verse, 1881; Games and Songs of American Children, 1883; Words for Music, 1895; King Arthur and the Table Round, 1897; The Legend of the Holy Grail and the Perceval of Crestien of Troyes, 1902; Isolt's Return, 1907.

About: Harvard Graduates' Magazine March 1907; Journal of American Folk-Lore January-March 1907; Boston Evening Transcript January 23, 1907.

NEWMAN, HENRY (November 20, 1670-June 26, 1743), philanthropist and miscellaneous writer, was born in Rehoboth, Mass. His parents, the Rev. Noah and Joanna (Flynt) Newman, died when he was very young, and he was brought up by his grandmother. He was graduated from Harvard in 1687, and three years later was awarded an M.A. degree. He had thought of entering the Congregational ministry but his interest in mathematics and liking for the Anglican church changed his mind, and for the next thirteen years he followed numerous pursuits, from librarian at Harvard to merchant in St. John's, Newfoundland. It was indicative of his fondness for mathematics and astronomy that he prepared and published two almanacs, *Harvard's Ephemeris* in 1690, and a year later *News from the Stars.*

In 1703 he sailed for London, where he lived for the rest of his life. There he was connected with various philanthropic organizations, the most important of which was the Society for Promoting Christian Knowledge. He was secretary of this society for nearly forty years and participated in all its varied activities. He always felt that he belonged to New England. Newman served at different times as colonial agent in London and as an agent for Harvard College. He was a man of earnest piety, of unselfish devotion to the cause of others, and of great sympathy with the humanitarian efforts of his day.

Principal Works: Harvard's Ephemeris, 1690; News From the Stars, 1691.

About: Sibley, J. L. Biographical Sketches of Graduates of Harvard University.

NEWMAN, SAMUEL PHILLIPS (June 6, 1797-February 10, 1842), clergyman, rhetorician, and teacher, was born in Andover, Mass., the son of the Rev. Mark Newman, principal of Phillips Academy, and Sarah (Phillips) Newman. From Phillips Academy he went to Harvard and was graduated with honors in 1816. He spent a year in Lexington, Ky., as a private instructor; returned for a year's study at Andover Theological Seminary; and then accepted an appointment as tutor at Bowdoin College, continuing his theological studies at the same time. In 1820 he was licensed to preach as a Congregationalist (although he was believed to have had certain Unitarian leanings) but only rarely did he ever appear in a pulpit.

He was advanced to a professorship in Greek and Latin, and in 1824 he was transferred to the chair of rhetoric and oratory. Over a period of fifteen years he was also lecturer on civil polity and political economy. During the absence of President Allen, 1830-33, Newman was acting president of the college, exhibiting a business sense and an administrative acuteness that equaled his skill as a teacher. Bowdoin, during the 'twenties and 'thirties, was turning out with indubitable success "Congregational ministers, professors of modern languages, senators and governors, allopathic physicians, and presidents," and was not too warmly disposed toward sensitive literary youths. But Newman took the pains to encourage young Nathaniel Hawthorne and to praise his excellent English prose; and it is said that he habitually read Hawthorne's themes aloud to his family. After twenty-one years at Bowdoin Newman became head of the newly established State Normal School at Barre, Mass., but two years later he suffered a rapid breakdown in health from which he never recovered.

Newman's long and indispensable *Practical System of Rhetoric or the Principles and Rules of Style,* which went into more than sixty editions in the United States and was republished in England, was somewhat more abstract and philosophic than modern rhetorics but had, nevertheless, a necessary clarity. In an address before the American Institute of Instruction (Boston) in 1850 on "A Practical Method of Teaching Rhetoric," he emphasized, among other things, the value of individual conferences. The chief merit of his *Elements of Political Economy,* hardly more than well-defined elaborations on some of Adam Smith's writings, lay in the fact that it dealt with a relatively new science; and his *magnum opus*—the *Rhetoric*—has, from a philosophical point of view, become largely an historical item.

PRINCIPAL WORKS: A Practical System of Rhetoric or the Principles and Rules of Style, 1827; Elements of Political Economy, 1835.

ABOUT: Arvin, N. Hawthorne; Cleaveland, N. & Packard, A. S. History of Bowdoin College: With Biographical Sketches of its Graduates; Bowdoin Alumnus June 1931; Portland Evening Advertiser March 7, 1842.

NEWTON, HEBER. See NEWTON, RICHARD HEBER

NEWTON, RICHARD HEBER (October 31, 1840-December 19, 1914), Protestant Episcopal clergyman and theologian, better known as Heber Newton, was born in Philadelphia, the son of the Rev. Richard and Lydia (Greatorex) Newton. He attended school in the city, and after two years at the University of Pennsylvania left college because of poor health; he was afterward granted a B.A. degree as of the class of 1861. Two years later he was graduated from the Divinity School of the Protestant Episcopal Church, and by Alonzo Potter was ordained priest in 1866. He was assistant minister at St. Paul's Church in Philadelphia, 1862-63, and after serving a charge in Sharon Springs, N. Y., he returned to St. Paul's to become its rector. In 1869 he began his real career in the pulpit when he accepted a call to All Souls' Church (Anthon Memorial) in New York City, where, during thirty years' ministry, he gained a reputation as the outstanding liberal of his denomination. On his resignation in 1902 Newton went to California and served as resident preacher at the Leland Stanford, Jr., University; his sympathy with the interests of his students and his theological and moral candor made him exceedingly popular. During his last years he lived in retirement at East Hampton, Long Island.

One of Newton's primary theological interests was the modern critical and historical approach to the Bible. He laid no claims to original research, but he disseminated the results of his investigations of this "Higher Criticism" in *The Right and Wrong Uses of the Bible.* Attempts to bring Newton to trial for a few of his mild iconoclasms only strengthened the position of the religious liberals who shared his point of view. He was interested in the intellectual and ethical aspects of the so-called New Theology that was beginning to assert itself, but he lacked the mysticism and religious fervor that were integral forces in its actual advancement. Newton was a serious student of evolutionary science, and of psychic research; he was, in part, a civic leader and laborite, contributing *Philistinism* and *Social Studies* to this particular field. Newton had no mean knowledge of music, and in addition to a volume on *Parsifal* he wrote *The Mysticism of Music* (published posthumously) which embodied his belief that music "expresses, outside of the Church, the highest principles of religion and morality as they influence the sentiments and actions of men." Newton made no substantial contribution to the literature of theology but to its long-accepted corollaries he directed the interests of a wide and intelligent public.

PRINCIPAL WORKS: The Morals of Trade, 1876; Studies of Jesus, 1880; Book of the Beginnings, 1884; Philistinism, 1885; Social Studies, 1887; Church and Creed, 1891; Christian Science, 1898; Parsifal, 1904; The Mysticism of Music, 1915.

ABOUT: Barratt, N. S. Outline of the History of Old St. Paul's Church, Philadelphia; A Service to Honor the Memory of the Rev. R. Heber Newton, D. D; Churchman January 23, 1915; New York Times December 20, 1914.

NEWTON, WILLIAM WILBERFORCE (November 4, 1843-June 25, 1914), clergyman and miscellaneous writer, was the son of the Rev. Richard Newton and Lydia (Greatorex) Newton, and brother of

Richard Heber Newton [*q.v.*]. He was born and educated in Philadelphia, being graduated from the University of Pennsylvania in 1865 and the Divinity School of the Protestant Episcopal Church in 1868. In 1870 he married Emily Stevenson Cooke, of Philadelphia, who became the mother of one son. For the next thirty years he served as rector at various churches, but in 1900 a serious throat infection so affected his voice that he was forced to give up the ministry.

During this time Newtòn had published many books, including sermons for children, essays, a biography, novels and a book on travel. His best known works, besides his sermons for children, were *Essays of Today: Religious and Theological* and *Dr. Muhlenberg.* Although he wrote well, his writings have no lasting merit as literature. He had a genial countenance and an amiable personality, and in his early years was a compelling speaker.

Principal Works: The Gate of the Temple: or, Prayers for Children, 1876; Essays of Today: Religious and Theological, 1879; The Priest and the Man: or, Abelard and Heloisa, 1883; The Vine Out of Egypt, 1887; Dr. Muhlenberg, 1890; A Run Through Russia, 1894; The Child and the Bishop, 1894; Philip MacGregor, 1895.

About: Boston Transcript June 26, 1914.

NICHOLS, GEORGE WARD (June 21, 1831-September 15, 1885), educator and miscellaneous writer, was born in Tremont, Mount Desert, Me. His father, a sea captain, was John Nichols, his mother, Esther Todd (Ward) Nichols. When George was four the family moved to Boston. There he attended public school and later took up journalism. After spending some time in Kansas he went to Europe in 1859 where he studied under Thomas Couture in Paris. After his return he was art editor for the New York *Evening Post,* and in 1862 joined the Union army as captain. After serving in various capacities he became in 1864 an aide-de-camp of General Sherman, participating in the march to the sea. From notes in his diary, kept during the war, he published in 1865 *The Story of the Great March.* Sixty thousand copies of it were sold within a year and it was translated into several languages. Its success, however, was due rather to its subject matter than its literary skill. *The Sanctuary,* a novel on the same subject, awakened no response.

Soon after the war he moved to Cincinnati, where in 1868 he married Maria Longworth, aunt of Nicholas Longworth (Speaker of the House of Representatives, 1925-1930). He soon made a place for himself in this city. He helped found the School of Design, was interested in art in its relation to industry, was president of the Harmonic Society, and organized the May Festival Association. In 1879, with the aid of Reuben R. Springer, he founded the College of Music of Cincinnati, holding the position of president for the rest of his life. Nichols was essentially a "promoter." He had great organizing and executive energy and was persistent and self-confident. It was largely as the result of his efforts that Cincinnati became a center for music.

Principal Works: The Story of the Great March, 1865; The Sanctuary, 1866; Art Education Applied to Industry, 1877; Pottery: How It Is Made: Its Shape, and Decoration, 1878.

About: Cox, J. D. Memorial Services in Honor of George Ward Nichols . . . March 4, 1887; Harper's Weekly September 26, 1885; Cincinnati Enquirer September 16, 1885.

NICHOLS, MARY SARGEANT (NEAL) (August 10, 1810-May 30, 1884), reformer, was born in Goffstown, N. H., the daughter of William and Rebecca Neal. She received little school instruction, but educated herself by wide reading, being particularly interested in books on anatomy and physiology. She taught for a while in a district school and in 1831 married Hiram Gove. The marriage was unhappy and eventually ended in a divorce. After the birth of her daughter she began seriously to study books on health. In 1837 they moved to Lynn, Mass., where she began to teach anatomy and physiology to young women. In 1840 she was separated from her husband, and, although worried by ill-health and the difficulty of obtaining the custody of her child, by 1844 she had become a water-cure physician in New York. For several years she contributed to the New York *Water-Cure Journal* and published several works. She became known as an advocate of spiritualism, mesmerism, Fourierism, temperance, and dress reform. In 1848 she married Thomas Low Nichols [*q.v.*], by whom she had one child. From 1851 to 1853 they conducted a school in New York to train water-cure physicians, and wrote and talked for nearly all the radical causes of the time. In 1853 they began editing *Nichols' Journal* and two years later Mrs. Nichols published the autobiographical *Mary Lyndon: or, Revelations of a Life.*

When the Civil War started, the Nicholses left for England where they lived for the rest of their lives. Mrs. Nichols contributed to the London *Herald of Health* and became well known in English vegetarian and spiritualistic circles. She was a person of determined courage, and ardently supported many unpopular causes.

Principal Works: Lectures to Women on Anatomy and Physiology, 1846; Experience in Water-Cure, 1849; Mary Lyndon: or, Revelations of a Life, 1855.

About: Hale, S. J. Biographies of Distinguished Women; Nichols' Health Manual; Nichols, M. S. N. Mary Lyndon: or, Revelations of a Life; Poe, E. A. The Literati; Dietetic Reformer and Vegetarian Messenger July 1884.

NICHOLS, THOMAS LOW (1815-1901), social historian, editor, dietitian, and hydrotherapist, came from a family of early English emigrants, and spent his boyhood in Orford, N.H. He studied medicine at Dartmouth; withdrew from college to try journalism; and after completing several apprenticeships he became editor and part owner of the *Buffalonian,* a political organ for which he wielded a fearless pen. In his twenty-fifth year he served a four-month imprisonment for libel; and his first book, *Journal in Jail,* a condensation of his self-indulgent but spirited diary, was published in 1840. He was married to Mary Sargeant Neal Gove, a water-cure physician, in 1848. Two years later he received an M.D. degree from the University of the City of New York; and with his wife founded a school for water-cure practitioners.

Until denounced as a "radical," Nichols was a frequent contributor to the *American Vegetarian and Health Journal* and the *Water-Cure Journal.* In 1853 he and his wife founded *Nichols' Journal of Health, Water-Cure, and Human Progress,* for the promulgation of individual liberty, health reform, spiritualism, etc.; and after their removal to Cincinnati this became *Nichols' Monthly.* At Yellow Springs, Ohio, the home of Antioch College, they set up their "School of Life," known as Memnonia Institute. Horace Mann, Antioch's president, resented the instrusion of this "free-love colony" and almost succeeded in thwarting its establishment. When completely organized, however, the community was much more deeply intrenched in religious asceticism than in free love or in the outgrowth of any other Associationist doctrine: in 1857 the Nichols and other members of the Institute were converted to Catholicism.

Because Nichols could not subscribe to a "brotherhood by force," as he termed the Civil War, he and his wife, in 1861, became voluntary exiles from the United States. America, he said, was a "prison," and Secretary Seward (who had ordered that no citizen leave without a passport) was its "keeper." England received them willingly, and with their Catholic connections they became readily established as journalists.

In addition to his earlier socio-biological books published in America he issued in London, during the 'eighties, several additional tracts on dietary ailments and food reform. His most significant book, however, was *Forty Years of American Life,* which received little attention at the time of its publication; the fact that it was published in England three years after Nichols emigrated from the United States accounts for a certain amount of neglect by American reviewers. It was a source-book of emergent personalities, social movements, and sectional cultures from bucolic New England in the time of his youth to cosmopolitan New York in the sophisticated heydey of the Knickerbocker literati. Nichols' personal judgments, however, were often quite vulnerable. He assailed political demagogy, the American love of sensation, and Abolitionist sentimentalism; but he praised our social democracy and our provision for educational opportunity. With republication in 1937, *Forty Years* has come into its own as an excellent piece of autobiography and social history.

Principal Works: Esoteric Anthropology, 1853; Marriage: Its History, Character, and Results (with M. S. N. G. Nichols) 1854; Forty Years of American Life, 1864; How to Live on Sixpence a Day, 1871; Eating to Live, 1881; Dyspepsia, 1884; Nichols' Health Manual, 1887.

About: Nichols, T. L. Journal in Jail; Nichols, T. L. Forty Years of American Life; files of the (New York) Water-Cure Journal and Nichols' Monthly; Saturday Review of Literature September 11, 1937; New York Herald Tribune Books September 12, 1937.

NICHOLSON, ELIZA JANE (POITEVENT) HOLBROOK (March 11, 1849-February 15, 1896), newspaper proprietor and poet, was born in Hancock County, Miss., the daughter of William J. Poitevent and Mary A. (Russ) Poitevent. She was brought up by an aunt because her mother was an invalid, and in 1867 was graduated from the Amite (La.) Female Seminary. She began writing verses, under the name of "Pearl Rivers," when she was very young, her first contributions being published in the *South,* whose editor encouraged her. She also sent verses to New Orleans papers, the *Home Journal,* and the New York *Ledger.* Colonel A. M. Holbrook, editor of the New Orleans *Picayune,* was impressed with her poems and in 1870 made them a feature in the Sunday paper. She later became literary editor, and married Holbrook in 1872. Earlier in the same year Holbrook had sold the paper and in 1873 his wife published a volume of verse, *Lyrics by Pearl Rivers,* which was well received. In 1874 Holbrook again controlled the *Picayune,* but his death two years later came before he could put it on a sound financial basis, and Mrs. Holbrook was left with an $80,000 debt. About six months later George Nicholson, an Englishman, acquired an interest in the paper and in 1878 he and Mrs. Holbrook were married. From then on the *Picayune* became more successful. Mrs. Nicholson took a great interest in the paper, introducing a society column and supporting many public movements. She was the first Southern woman to be proprietor of an important newspaper.

Though Mrs. Nicholson's appearance was not prepossessing, she had a vivid personality. Her best poems deal with country life. She died in an influenza epidemic ten days after her husband; two sons survived her.

Principal Works: Lyrics by Pearl Rivers, 1873.

About: Harrison, J. H. Pearl Rivers: Publisher of the Picayune; Louisiana Historical Quarterly October 1923; Daily Picayune (New Orleans) February 16, 1896; New Orleans Times-Democrat February 16, 1896.

NICOLAY, JOHN GEORGE (February 26, 1832-September 26, 1901), historian and biographer, was born in Essingen, Bavaria, his parents being John Jacob and Helena Nicolay. In 1838 the family emigrated to America, living successively in New Orleans, Cincinnati, St. Louis, and Pike County, Illinois, where the father ran a flour mill and the son acted as business manager and interpreter. Previously he had had a year's schooling in Cincinnati and another in St. Louis, in German-English schools. This was all his formal education.

On his father's death, he became a clerk in a store in White Hall, Ill., then printer's devil on the Pittsfield (Ill.) *Free Press.* Here he learned typesetting and continued up the ladder until by 1854 he was editor and proprietor.

It was in 1851 that he first met John Hay, who was to be his lifelong friend and collaborator. In 1856 Nicolay sold the paper and became clerk to the secretary of state of Illinois. He was an ardent Republican from the foundation of the party, and 1860 found him private secretary to Lincoln, a post he held until Lincoln's assassination. He also secured the appointment of Hay as his assistant. It was from the intimate association the two young men enjoyed with Lincoln that their ten-volume "history" of him grew, projected from 1861 with Lincoln's approval and completed by aid of family papers furnished them by Robert Lincoln.

Collection of Frederick H. Meserve
JOHN G. NICOLAY

In 1865 Nicolay married Therena Bates, who died in 1885, leaving one daughter, Helena, also a writer; a son had died in infancy. From 1865 to 1869 Nicolay was United States consul in Paris, and from 1872 to 1887 marshal of the United States Supreme Court. The bulk of the work on the great biography was done with Hay between 1875 and 1890, when it appeared. Though he contributed to magazines and wrote the article on Lincoln for the *Encyclopaedia Britannica,* and that on the Civil War for the *Cambridge Modern History,* Nicolay was not a prolific author and published only two other volumes, one an abridgment of the Lincoln biography. Indeed, he had little leisure for writing, with his public offices, his interest in music, drawing, and poetry, and his turn for mechanics which resulted in numerous patents for inventions. With Hay he edited Lincoln's own writings, the two volumes appearing in 1894, and then expanded the work to twelve volumes, which were published posthumously in 1905. After his wife died, he lived with his daughter in Washington until his death.

A frail, slight little man, bearded and spectacled, he concealed a natural fund of humor under a solemn exterior. His interest in history was genuine; he was a life member of the American Historical Society and a founder of the Columbia Historical Society, in Washington, as well as of the Washington Literary Society. His principal contribution is the massive life of Lincoln in which his and Hay's work are so intermingled that it is impossible to tell the author of any one part. As a matter of fact, each author wrote about half. The work is undiscriminating and partisan; it portrays a perfect Lincoln surrounded by noble friends and vile enemies. It has by no means the seasoned judgment of Herndon's estimate or the solid scholarship of Sandburg's or Beveridge's later biographies. It is, however, the authorized life, and its thoroughness and inclusion of detail make it an invaluable source-book.

PRINCIPAL WORKS: The Outbreak of Rebellion, 1881; Abraham Lincoln: A History (10 vols.; with John Hay) 1890; A Short Life of Abraham Lincoln, 1902.

ABOUT: Dennett, T. John Hay; Thayer, W. L. Life and Letters of John Hay; Century Magazine October 1886; Washington Post September 27, 1901.

NILES, HEZEKIAH (October 10, 1777-April 2, 1839), editor and poetical pamphleteer, was born at Jefferis' Ford, Chester County, Pa., the son of Hezekiah Niles, a plane-maker, and Mary (Way) Niles. His parents had left Wilmington, Del., and taken refuge here just before the battle of Brandywine. It is probable that young Niles attended the Friends' School in Wilmington, and at the age of seventeen he was apprenticed to Benjamin Johnson, a Philadelphia printer, whose lack of funds, three years later, forced him to release the boy.

As early as 1797 Niles' essays favoring economic protection found their way into Philadelphia newspapers. Three years later he returned to Wilmington; assisted in the publishing of an almanac; became a job printer; and then formed a partnership with Vincent Bonsal which was dissolved after a serious financial loss. Following the fiasco of his literary journal, the *Apollo,* Niles removed to Baltimore in 1805 and became editor of the strongly Jeffersonian *Evening Post,* which was sold six years later. Immediately he set up his *Weekly Register* (later *Niles' Weekly Register*) which he edited and published for a quarter of a century. It became an organ for economic nationalism in the form of union, internal improvements, protection to industry, and the gradual abolition of slavery; and its editor was always armed with an abundance of statistical evidence. With more than ten thousand dollars of subscription money outstanding, the *Register,* at the end of its second year, was in a precarious position. But with a settlement of these financial obligations and a continued rise in circulation, it soon became a gainful venture.

Niles was intimately associated with Mathew Carey and Henry Clay; and he was the prime mover behind the protectionist conventions of 1827 and 1831, serving in the capacities of speaker, chief secretary, etc. He considered the recharter of the first Bank of the United States (1811) unconstitutional and monopolistic, but the second, he affirmed, was an economic necessity. About the year 1816 or 1817 Niles abandoned Jeffersonianism and became a no-party man; and about ten years later turned Whig. He was twice married: in 1798 to Ann Ogden, by whom he had twelve children; and two years after her death in 1824, to Sally Ann Warner, by whom he had eight children.

Niles spoke in a high key, was "addicted to snuff," and had a "keen gray eye, that lighted up a plain face with shrewd expression." *Principles and Acts of the Revolution in America* and a number of pamphlets were his only published writings; but he made his *Register* so valuable a repository of contemporary data that it has been called "a chief reliance of the historiographer for the first half of the nineteenth century."

ABOUT: Stanwood, E. American Tariff Controversies in the Nineteenth Century; Stone, B. G. Hezekiah Niles as an Economist; Niles' National Register April 6, 13, 1839; (Philadelphia) North American April 4, 1839.

NILES, JOHN MILTON (August 20, 1787-May 31, 1856), editor and political figure, was born in Windsor, Conn. His parents, Moses and Naomi (Marshall) Niles, were in very moderate circumstances, and, with a large family, found it impossible to give John more than an elementary education. He, however, was ambitious, did a great deal of reading, and was admitted to the Hartford bar in 1817. The same year he founded the Hartford *Weekly Times,* a liberal paper which advocated political reforms. From 1821 to 1829 he was a judge of the Hartford County court and in 1829 became postmaster of Hartford. By that time he was a leader of the Jacksonian party, and in 1835 was appointed by the governor to fill a vacancy in the Senate. He served as senator until 1839, ran unsuccessfully for governor in the elections of 1839 and 1840, and from 1840 to 1841 was postmaster general under Van Buren. He again became senator in 1843, continuing to hold office until he retired in 1849. He died of cancer in Hartford in 1856. He was twice married, his first wife being Sarah Robinson, widow of Lewis Howe, and his second, Jane Pratt.

Niles was a man of independence, and moral integrity. He had minor literary talent, and was either author or part author of *A Gazetteer of the States of Connecticut and Rhode-Island,* 1819; *The Life of Oliver Hazard Perry,* 1820; *The Connecticut Civil Officer,* 1823; *A View of South America and Mexico,* 1825; and *History of South America and Mexico,* 1838. He bequeathed his private library to the Connecticut Historical Society and a large sum to the city of Hartford for charities.

About: Biographical Directory of the Amercan Congress; Green's Connecticut Register.

NOAH, MORDECAI MANUEL (July 19, 1785-March 22, 1851), playwright and essayist, was born in Philadelphia, the son of Manuel M. Noah, a Revolutionary soldier, and Zipporah (Phillips) Noah. He was of Sephardic (Spanish Jewish) descent on both sides. His childhood was spent in Charleston, S.C., his father's home, but on his mother's death in 1795 he was sent to her father, a Philadelphia merchant. After a few more years at school the grandfather apprenticed the boy to a carver and gilder. He soon extricated himself from this trade and became clerk in the auditor's office of the United States Treasury. But on removal of the national capital to Washington in 1800 Noah lost his job. He then became a reporter of the sessions of the Pennsylvania legislature in Harrisburg.

On attaining his majority he returned to Charleston, and lived there for several years, writing patriotic articles for the papers under the name of "Muley Malack" (he was an ardent supporter of the War of 1812), and dabbling in play writing, the drama having been his passion from childhood. In 1813 he was appointed United States consul at Tunis; on the way he was captured by the British, but was released after two months in England. He secured the freeing of Americans held by the Algerian pirates, but in 1815 President Monroe recalled him because of some obscure dissatisfaction; in 1817 the State Department vindicated him of all charges.

Noah had returned to America in 1816 and settled in New York. He became a professional journalist, founding and editing a number of papers, first Jacksonian, then Whig, in politics; the last was *Noah's Times and Weekly Messenger,* which he conducted successfully from 1842 to his death. He was sheriff of New York in 1822, in 1823 was admitted to the bar, from 1829 to 1833 was surveyor of the Port of New York, and in 1841 was judge of the New York court

From a portrait by J. W. Jarvi
MORDECAI M. NOAH

of sessions. In 1825 he attempted to estab-lish a Zionist colony, Ararat, at Granc Island, in the Niagara River, but it neve went beyond a monument and a speech. Ir 1826 he married Rebecca Esther Jackson they had six sons and one daughter. H died in New York of an apoplectic stroke

Major Noah, as he was always knowr (he was a major in the New York Militia) was a generous, easy-going, genial mar whose twin idols were the United States anc the theatre. His plays combine the two they are all patriotic paeans. Remarkably versatile, with a racy, lively style, he is ye of more interest today as a personality thar as a writer.

Principal Works: Travels in England, France Spain, and the Barbary States, 1819; She Would B a Soldier, 1819; Marion: or, The Hero of Lak George, 1821; The Grecian Captive, 1822; Gleanings From a Gathered Harvest, 1845.

About: Allen, L. F. The Story of the Table of the City of Ararat; Goldberg, I. Major Noah American Jewish Pioneer; Wolf, S. Mordeca Manuel Noah; Lippincott's Magazine June 1868 New York Tribune March 24, 1851.

"NOCH VASTER." See STEENDAM JACOB

NORDHOFF, CHARLES (August 31 1830-July 14, 1901), journalist, sociologist and adventurer, was born in Erwitte, Westphalia, in the Kingdom of Prussia, and a the age of five came to the United State with his parents, Adelheid (Platé) Nordhoff and Charles Nordhoff. His father wa a fur-trader in Chicago when Fort Dearborn was hardly more than a frontier post.

Charles went to school in Cincinnati and in his fourteenth year was apprenticed to a printer; but believing himself constitutionally unfit for this kind of work, he went east and spent his hard-saved twenty-five dollars in an attempt to ship on a southbound vessel. After repeated discouragements he took another print-shop job, and a year later succeeded in getting passage (and eight dollars a month) aboard the U. S. Receiving Ship "Experiment," lying off the Navy Yard in Philadelphia. At the end of three years he had been around the world, had witnessed maniacal brawls of drunken crews, and had listened to hundreds of yarns of opium smugglers, etc; and when he gave up seafaring and became a newspaper reporter he published, 1855-56, three books on salt-water vagabonding, afterward collected under the title *Nine Years a Sailor.*

In 1857 he became an editor for Harper & Brothers; but in the year following went over to the New York *Evening Post,* and in its columns, as well as in *Secession is Rebellion* and *The Freedom of South Carolina,* he championed the Union cause.

Nordhoff left the *Post* in 1871; spent two years in California and Hawaii; and not long after his return he became a highly successful Washington correspondent for the New York *Herald,* a post which he retained until his retirement sixteen years later. He was not only one of the few political writers in whom public men confided, but one of

CHARLES NORDHOFF

still fewer whom they consulted." On the strength of his own observations of various social communities he wrote *Communistic Societies in the United States*; and prepared a non-partisan and non-sectional survey of political and economic controversies, *The Cotton States in the Spring and Summer of 1875. Politics for Young Americans,* which became a somewhat popular text book, and *God and the Future Life* disclosed the decidedly moral and religious coloration of his thought. The delicate health of his wife, Lida (Letford) Nordhoff, necessitated his spending the last years of his life in California. Charles Bernard Nordhoff, co-author of the famous "Bounty" trilogy, is a grandson.

A sharp reportorial eye, an ideal newsgetter's diplomacy, and an effectively simple literary style not only made Nordhoff's journalistic observations historically significant but invested them with a still untarnished readability.

Principal Works: Man-of-War Life, 1855; The Merchant Vessel, 1855; Whaling and Fishing, 1856; (three foregoing collected in Nine Years a Sailor, 1857); Stories of the Island World, 1857; Secession Is Rebellion, 1860; The Freedom of South Carolina, 1863; America for Free Working Men, 1865; Communistic Societies in the United States, 1875; Politics for Young Americans, 1875; The Cotton States in the Spring and Summer of 1875, 1876; God and the Future Life, 1883.

About: Nordhoff, C. Nine Years a Sailor; Harper's Weekly, July 27, 1901.

NORRIS, MARY HARRIOTT (March 16, 1848-September 14, 1919), educator, novelist, and juvenile writer, was born in Boonton, N.J. Her parents, Charles Bryan and Mary Lyon (Kerr) Norris, sent her to a private school for her preparatory work. There she was the only girl who studied Latin. In 1870 she was graduated from Vassar; industrious and frugal years there are portrayed in her *Golden Age of Vassar* published in 1915. In 1872 she delivered the commencement address at Vassar, and a year later published her first novel, *Fräulein Mina: or, Life in a North American German Family.* This proved to be such a success that she continued to write, her work showing some talent for description and storytelling.

She founded a private school in New York in 1880, and acted as principal of it for the next sixteen years. In 1898 she became dean of women and assistant professor of English at Northwestern University, but, anxious to return to her literary pursuits and other activities, held these positions for only a year. Her influence, however, during the year was great and she was made an honorary member of the class of 1899. She spent the last years of her life at Morristown, N.J. In addition to her original works, she edited a number of schoolroom classics.

PRINCIPAL WORKS: Fräulein Mina: or, Life in North American German Family, 1873; School Life of Ben and Bentie, 1874; Dorothy Delafield, 1886; The Gray House of the Quarries, 1898; The Golden Age of Vassar, 1915.

ABOUT: Norris, M. H. The Golden Age of Vassar.

NORTON, ANDREWS (December 31, 1786-September 18, 1853), Biblical scholar, professor, and editor, was born in Hingham, Mass., the son of Samuel and Jane (Andrews) Norton. After his graduation from Harvard he pursued four years of advanced study; served a short ministry in Augusta, Maine; taught for a year at Bowdoin College; and at the end of a tutorship at Cambridge became Harvard librarian and lecturer on the Bible. From 1819 until 1830 he was Dexter Professor of Sacred Literature in the Harvard Divinity School; on his resignation he remained in Cambridge to continue his literary and theological pursuits. He was married, in 1821, to Catharine Eliot, daughter of Samuel Eliot, wealthy merchant. Their retreat at "Shady Hill" afterward became the home of their son, Charles Eliot Norton [*q.v.*], distinguished scholar, and was long the rendezvous of men of art and letters.

Norton's most commanding work was his treatise on *The Evidences of the Genuineness of the Gospels,* "which proved," says Van Wyck Brooks, "to the satisfaction of honest men . . . that Matthew, Mark, Luke, and John had really written the books that bore their names, a demonstration as clear as Hedge's *Logic.*" It was one of the earliest attempts, in America, at the new critical approach to Biblical literature. In 1852 he published a collection of essays, *Tracts on Christianity*; another book of critiques, *Internal Evidences of the Genuineness of the Gospels,* was issued posthumously. He edited the poems of Mrs. Hemans, his English friend, and, with Charles Folsom, librarian and compiler, four volumes of *The Select Journal of Foreign Periodical Literature.* His own *Verses,* cautious, starched, and formal, appeared in the year of his death.

In January 1812 Norton launched the short-lived *General Repository and Review*; and for a time he edited the *North American Review.* The title of his address, in 1839, *On the Latest Form of Infidelity,* commonly construed as a reply to Emerson's Divinity School Address of 1838, has, unhappily, often been remembered to the exclusion of Norton's more substantial accomplishments.

Norton was a conservative Unitarian who had "put the Calvinists to rout by sheer force of reasoning" (his ability as a logician was uncontested). He rejected any "vulgar" appeal to the "feelings," such as the Pantheistic "soul's sense of things divine" and disregard of the letter of the Scriptures. Norton's petulance and vanity may have justified Emerson's rather extravagant epithet, "the tyrant of the Cambridge Parnassus" or Carlyle's "Unitarian Pope."

PRINCIPAL WORKS: The Evidences of the Genuineness of the Gospels, 1837; On the Latest Form of Infidelity, 1839; Tracts on Christianity, 1852; Verses, 1853; Internal Evidences of the Genuineness of the Gospels, 1855.

ABOUT: Brooks, Van W. The Flowering of New England; Norton, S. & Howe, M. A. De W. Letters of Charles Eliot Norton; Peabody, A. P. Harvard Reminiscences.

NORTON, CHARLES ELIOT (November 16, 1827-October 21, 1908), teacher, scholar and miscellaneous writer, was bor[n] and died in Cambridge, Mass. He was th[e] son of Andrews Norton, professor of sacre[d] history at Harvard, and Catharine (Eliot) Norton. On one side or the other he wa[s] related to half the distinguished Bostonian[s] of his time, and the rest became his clos[e] friends. He was graduated from Harvar[d] in 1846 (M.A. 1849), and for three year[s] worked for his maternal uncles, who wer[e] Boston importers; his spare time he spe[nt] in founding night schools for workingme[n] and in helping Francis Parkman, who wa[s] almost blind, in his work on *The Orego[n] Trail.*

In 1849 Norton shipped for India a[s] supercargo on a ship belonging to his uncle[s] and for two years traveled in Egypt, Ital[y,] France, and England. On his return to Ame[r]ica he went into the East India trade on h[is] own, and at the same time lectured o[n] French literature in Harvard. In 1855 h[e] was ordered abroad again for his healt[h] and this ended his business career. Whe[n] he returned once more in 1857, he ha[d] definitely turned his face toward literatur[e]. He contributed to the early *Atlantic Monthl[y]*; he edited the *North American Review* (wi[th] Lowell) from 1864 to 1868; he was one o[f] the founders of the *Nation,* in 1865; an[d] throughout the Civil War he edited th[e] broadsides of the Loyal Publication Societ[y].

An apostle of culture through art, Norto[n] was the first to teach the history of art [at] Harvard. He lectured there in 1863 an[d] 1864; then in 1874, on his return from fi[ve] years more in Europe, he was regular

Collection of Frederick H. Meserve
CHARLES ELIOT NORTON

appointed as lecturer on art; in 1875 he became professor of the history of art, and after his retirement in 1898, professor emeritus. His other specialty was Dante; he translated the *Vita Nuova* and worked with Longfellow on the latter's version of the *Divina Commedia*.

But Norton's real genius was for friendship. Carlyle, Ruskin, Rossetti, Clough, Lowell, Emerson, were among his intimates. He edited the works or letters of them all. His influence on American culture was incalculable. Two of his pupils, H. B. Brown and W. H. Wiggin, took down his lectures and published them as *A History of Ancient Art*. He was president of the Dante Society, first president of the Archaeological Institute of America, a grand officer of the Order of the Crown of Italy, an original member of the American Academy of Arts and Letters, recipient of honorary degrees from Cambridge, Oxford, Harvard, Yale, and Columbia. "As a teacher, a sage, a moralist, an expounder of manners, a master in the art of discrimination," says Van Wyck Brooks, "he was the most potent of the Brahmins."

Yet, as Brooks also points out, he was limited in aesthetic feeling, a born conservative, one who "had scarcely felt the inner fire." Bound and parochial he may seem now, but in his own time and place he was a social enzyme, stimulating a whole generation to find goodness in beauty and to go beyond their teacher by finding beauty where he could not.

Norton was married in 1862 to Susan Ridley Sedgwick, who died while they were abroad in 1872, leaving three sons and three daughters. He never remarried. He lived to be nearly eighty-one, dying in the same urbane house, "Shady Hill," where he was born. He was primarily a teacher and an editor; his published books were few and are now outmoded. But the history of New England in the cultural life of America would be incomplete without him.

Principal Works: Considerations of Some Recent Social Theories, 1853; Notes of Travel and Study in Italy, 1860; Historical Studies of Church-Building in the Middle Ages, 1880.

About: Brooks, V. W. The Flowering of New England; Emerson, E. W. & Harris, W. F. Charles Eliot Norton; Higginson, T. W. Carlyle's Laugh and Other Essays; Norton, S. & Howe, M. A. De W. Letters of Charles Eliot Norton With Biographical Comment; Atlantic Monthly January 1909; Current Literature December 1908; Dial November 1, 1908; Harper's Weekly October 31, 1908; Harvard Graduates Magazine December 1908; Nation October 29, 1908; North American Review December 1913; Outlook October 31, 1908; Boston Evening Transcript October 20, 21, 22, 1908.

NORTON, JOHN (May 6, 1606-April 5, 1663), Puritan clergyman and theologian, was born in Hertfordshire, England, the son of William and Alice (Browest) Norton. At fourteen he entered Cambridge, from which he received his B.A. in 1623-24 and his M.A. in 1627. A few years later he determined, because of his Puritan leanings, to sail with his wife for New England. Forced back by a severe storm the first time, he made a successful second attempt and arrived in Plymouth in 1635. Shortly afterward he settled in the Massachusetts Bay colony where he was ordained pastor at Ipswich in 1638. He soon became known as one of the colony's leaders and interested himself in the important happenings of the day. Suggested by John Cotton on his death-bed as his successor as pastor of the first church of Boston, Norton, after considerable controversy with the Ipswich pastorate, was finally ordained as such in 1656. Norton was violently opposed to the Quakers and stubbornly advocated the death penalty. In 1662 he and Simon Bradstreet were sent as the colony's agents to lay a petition before Charles II. This mission failed miserably, largely because of the reaction to the Quaker persecution, and Norton lost much of his popularity. Although well-taught, Norton was prejudiced and despotic, completely lacking in a broad and sympathetic understanding. He wrote prolifically, most of his works dealing with theological subjects. His second marriage took place on the day of his installation in Boston.

PRINCIPAL WORKS: A Discussion of That Great Point in Divinity, The Sufferings of Christ, 1653; The Orthodox Evangelist, 1654; Abel Being Dead Yet Speaketh: or, The Life and Death of . . . John Cotton, 1658; The Heart of N- England Rent at the Blasphemies of the Present Generation, 1659.

ABOUT: McClure, A. W. The Lives of John Wilson, John Norton, and John Davenport; Whitmore, W. H. A Genealogy of the Norton Family.

NOTT, ELIPHALET (June 25, 1773-January 29, 1866), college president, clergyman, and inventor, was born in Ashford, Conn. His father, Stephen Nott, was a failure, but his mother, Deborah (Selden) Nott, gave him his primary instruction. He prepared for college under his brother, Samuel, taught school when he was sixteen, and after attending Rhode Island College for less than a year was awarded an M.A. The next year he was licensed to preach, and, sent out by the Domestic Missionary Society of Connecticut, became pastor of the Presbyterian Church in Cherry Valley in upper New York state. In 1798 he was installed as pastor of the First Presbyterian Church in Albany, where he soon won a reputation as one of the most eloquent preachers in the country. Showing a strong interest in education, he became president of Union College in Schenectady in 1804 and continued to hold that position until his death sixty-two years later. Through his untiring efforts and winning personality he was able to put the college, which had been sadly in debt, on a sound financial basis with a secure endowment fund, and to give it a strong faculty. In addition to his educational interests, Nott did considerable investigating with the properties of heat, his research resulting in about thirty patents. He was a man of outstanding executive ability, and was an ardent advocate of temperance and of the abolition of slavery. He was married three times.

PRINCIPAL WORKS: Miscellaneous Works, 1810; Counsels to Young Men on the Formation of Character, 1840; Ten Lectures on the Use of Intoxicating Liquors, 1846; Lectures on Temperance, 1847; Lectures on Biblical Temperance, 1863.

ABOUT: Backus, J. T. Address at the Funeral of the Rev. Dr. Nott; Schmidt, G. P. The Old Time College President; Van Santwood, C. & Lewis, T. Memoirs of Eliphalet Nott; Albany Evening Journal January 29, 1866.

NOTT, HENRY JUNIUS (November 4, 1797-October 9, 1837), humorist and educator, was born in Union District, S.C., the son of Abraham Nott, jurist and Congressman, and Angelica (Mitchell) Nott. From Columbia Academy he entered South Carolina College, at the age of thirteen. Following his graduation in 1814 he studied law with William Harper and was admitted to the bar four years later. The most significant result of his partnership with David J. McCord (they enjoyed only a meager practice) was the publication of two volumes of law reports, on cases running through November 1820.

In 1821 Nott was in poor health, and sailed for Europe, where he spent three years, largely in France and Holland, and devoted much of his time to study. Following his return to the United States, he was appointed by South Carolina College, late in 1824, to the chair of criticism, logic, and the philosophy of language, a professorship that he filled successfully for thirteen years. Nott was on board the steamer "Home" which left New York on October 7, 1837, and was wrecked off the coast of North Carolina; both he and his wife were drowned.

Nott appears to have had an innate enthusiasm for letters, but in addition to occasional contributions to the *Southern Review* he was the author of only one sizable piece of writing: *Novellettes of a Traveller: or, Odds and Ends From the Knapsack of Thomas Singularity, Journeyman Printer.* About one-half of the book consists of a biographical account of the protagonist, a descendant of the slightly earlier picaresque hero of the frontier; and the rest is a collection of tales that includes "The Andalusian Rope-Dancer," "The Solitary," the "Dwarf's Duel," etc. In the preface is an apologia:

> A few terms savouring of a *slight* acquaintance with the "vulgar" tongue it has been found necessary to retain, as they are peculiarly expressive of either American habits or things, which, it is hoped, as they occur but seldom will not be deemed offensive to "ears polite."

In 1835 the *Sketch of the Life of Thomas Singularity, Journeyman Printer* was issued in London as prefatory material for the tales, under the pseudonym of "Jeremiah Hopkins," alleged fellow-apprentice of Singularity. Nott's humor has, naturally, suffered a descent from the "full of fun" level on which his contemporaries placed it; but it achieved an occasional subtlety that has allowed it to compare favorably with much of American wit during the 'thirties and 'forties.

ABOUT: O'Neall, J. B. Biographical Sketches of the Bench and Bar of South Carolina; Scott, E. J. Random Recollections of a Long Life; Wauchope, G. A. The Writers of South Carolina; Charleston Courier October 13-20, 1837; Morning Herald (New York) October 18, 19, 1837.

NOYES, JOHN HUMPHREY (September 3, 1811-April 13, 1886), social reformer and founder of the Oneida Community, was born in Brattleboro, Vt., the son of John Noyes, whose agnosticism had driven him from the study of theology, and Polly (Hayes) Noyes, aunt of Rutherford B. Hayes and a firmly religious woman. He was a pensive child, occasionally subject to outbursts of violence. He entered Dartmouth at fifteen and was graduated with high honors in 1830. In the course of a year's legal study with Larkin G. Mead, in Chesterfield, N.H., he found himself caught up in New England's "religious awakening," was "converted," and gave up law to prepare for the ministry. At Andover Theological Seminary he was the leader of a group of enthusiasts who took oath to be "young converts forever"; but he soon found a want of religious zeal and erudition there and enrolled in Yale Theological Seminary. He was shortly to arrive at the very firm conviction that perfection of human action here on this earth (and not alternate sin and repentance) was the primary thesis of Christ's teachings—all of which was a sharp reaction against several varieties of "perfervid theological doctrinism." From this belief, combined with much of the adventist faith, Noyes deduced a kind of religious sanction for his eventual experiments in communal living. Meanwhile the independence of his thought was winning him a tremendous following in the New Haven Free Church. His license to preach was afterward cancelled, but deliberately ignoring this fact he devoted about fifteen years to the spread of his beliefs and became, in the eyes of the orthodox clergy, a powerful menace. He was married, in 1838, to Harriet A. Holton.

JOHN H. NOYES
1867

From a small Bible-class nucleus which was organized in Putney, Vt., in 1839 there emerged, in 1846, the Putney Community, with its cult of free love, clearly anticipated in Noyes' famous "Battleaxe Letter" of 1837. The unit was shortly dissolved and Noyes was driven out of town. Late in 1847 he founded the Oneida Community, in central New York State. An extensive farm was, of course, a necessity; and the manufacture of steel traps (Hudson's Bay Company used them almost exclusively for about seventy years) provided substantial income from the "outside." Within four years the Community numbered 205 members.

Believing that men's possession of women was one of the strongest incentives to self-seeking, Noyes instituted—long before the word "eugenics" was invented—a system of selective mating and birth control. Not until August 1879, after serious threats of "secession," was the family system ("a first step backward, away from Communism") adopted. This was the beginning of the end.

After reorganization under an unsuccessful joint-stock company which occasioned "a jealous inexperienced insistence upon property," Noyes withdrew to Niagara Falls, Ontario, and lived there, in a small settlement, until the time of his death. His son, Pierrepont Noyes, has reproduced, in *My Father's House* (1937), the religious and social philosophy of this brilliant iconoclast.

John Humphrey Noyes' writings included *The Berean,* an early interpretation of perfectionism, *Bible Communism,* and *Male Continence.* His most thorough study of communistic experiment, *History of American Socialisms,* did not appear until 1870. In the 'thirties and 'forties he published the *Perfectionist,* the *Witness,* and the *Spiritual Magazine*; and during the existence of the Oneida Community, the *Oneida Circular* and the *American Socialist.*

He was the founder of what was admittedly the most successful of American Utopias, one which abided by "nonpolitical and noncontentious" communism and encouraged its members to "live the unselfish lives ordained by Jesus Christ." Of him his son has said: "I knew him to be a man of God . . . I tried to decide whether religious fanaticism had led him astray or he had been . . . 'ahead of his time'. . . . I think . . . if I actually reached any conclusion that it was a little of both."

PRINCIPAL WORKS: The Berean, 1847; Bible Communism, 1848; Male Continence, 1848; History of American Socialisms, 1870; Scientific Propagation, c. 1873; Home Talks, 1875.

ABOUT: Noyes, G. W. (ed.). Religious Experience of John Humphrey Noyes; Noyes, G. W. (ed.). John Humphrey Noyes: The Putney Community; Noyes, P. My Father's House; Seldes, G. The Stammering Century; Bibliotheca Sacra January-October 1921.

NOYES, NICHOLAS (December 22, 1647-December 13, 1717), clergyman and poet, was born in Newbury, Mass., the son of Nicholas Noyes the elder. He was educated at the expense of his uncle, Thomas Parker, pioneer emigrant clergyman whose memoir, written by Noyes many years later, was included in Cotton Mather's ecclesiastical history of New England, *Magnalia Christi Americana*; and at his graduation from Harvard in 1667 young Noyes received first honors. For thirteen years he preached at Haddam, Conn., and then went to Salem Mass., was ordained, and began a long service as colleague of the Reverend John Higginson. Here Noyes wrote a somewhat waggish (yet in no wise scurrilous) elegy on the death of this beloved associate, who

For Rich aray, car'd not a Figg
And wore Elisha's perriwigg. . .
. . . .
Young to the pulpit he did get
And seventy-two years in it did sweat. . .

In 1698 Noyes published a sermon, *New England's Duty and Interest/To be a/Habitation of Justice/and Mountain of Holiness* . . . which he had delivered in May of that year at the General Assembly of the Province of the Massachusetts Bay. It was "something of the prophetical and something didactical," question-and-answer analyses, outlines of doctrines, Biblical citations, etc. For Mather's *Magnalia* Noyes also wrote "A Prefatory Poem," in which he ventured his opinion that

The *stuff* is true, the Trimming neat and spruce,
The *Workman's* good, the Work of publick use;
Most piously designed, a publick store,
And well deserves the public Thanks, and more. . .

With Cotton and Increase Mather and other New England clergymen Noyes aided in promoting the Salem witchcraft trials of 1692—for all of which he afterward publicly confessed his error. It is recorded that during one of the sessions Goody Good, an accused, screamed to Noyes, "and if you hang me God will give you blood to drink!" This threat was believed to have been "fulfilled" a quarter of a century later when Noyes died of apoplexy. (Hawthorne capitalized upon these incidents in his *House of Seven Gables.*)

Noyes' stature was doubtless heightened by the personal glory of some of his brilliant social and professional acquaintances. He was "entertaining and useful in conversation" and was possessed of "eminent sanctity and virtue"; but his ecclesiastical and literary achievements were not, in themselves, highly significant.

ABOUT: Allen, W. American Biographical Dictionary; Boas, R. & L. Cotton Mather: Keeper of the Puritan Conscience; Mather, C. Magnalia Christi Americana; Noyes, N. New England's Duty and Interest.

NUTTALL, THOMAS (January 5, 1786-September 10, 1859), botanist and ornithologist, was born in Settle, England, the son of Jonas Nuttall. His parents lived very humbly, and he was apprenticed at an early age to a printer. He spent his odd moments in the study of natural history, Latin, and Greek; and after several very unexciting years in the print shop he set out for London, failed to find any substantial employment, and in his twenty-third year sailed for America and settled in Philadelphia. Here Benjamin Smith Barton, a botanist, interested him seriously in the study of plants and encouraged him in the collection of native flora. He made numerous excursions along the Atlantic coast; and from 1809 to 1811, with John Bradbury, a Scotch naturalist, he collected extensively

After a portrait by Dert
THOMAS NUTTALL

in Arkansas, Louisiana, and Indian Territory. During the next few years he spent his winters in Philadelphia and made short botanical excursions during the summers.

In 1822 he accepted an appointment as curator of the Botanical Garden of Harvard University, lecturing and experimenting in the culture of rare plants. On his resignation he joined the Wyeth Expedition (1834-35) to the mouth of the Columbia River; proceeded independently to the Sandwich Islands; and then embarked on the same vessel on which Dana was serving his famous "two years before the mast."

Nuttall's earlier publications were almost entirely botanical: *The Genera of North American Plants,* for which he himself set most of the type, and a three-volume continuation of *North American Sylva,* by F. A. Michaux, were outstanding. His "Observations on the Geological Structure of the Valley of the Mississippi," antedated by nearly fifteen years a recognized "pioneer" study in American paleontology by Samuel George Morton. For the *Journal of the Academy of Natural Sciences,* the *Transactions of the American Philosophical Society,* and Silliman's *American Journal of Science* he described new species and drafted reports of his expeditions. During his years at Cambridge he had shifted his interests somewhat to the study of ornithology, and in 1832 he issued a well written *Manual of the Ornithology of the United States and Canada,* a unique feature of which was its recording of bird songs by a syllabic method. His researches made him an innovator and an authority in his field.

He was described by his contemporaries as "disorderly in his dress" and "rough and abrupt" in manner. He spent the last seventeen years of his life in England on an estate bequeathed him by an uncle.

Principal Works: The Genera of North American Plants and a Catalogue of the Species. . . , 1818; A Journal of Travels Into the Arkansas Territory. . . , 1821; An Introduction to Systematic and Physiological Botany, 1827; A Manual of the Ornithology of the United States and Canada, 1832.

About: Harshberger, J. W. The Botanists of Philadelphia; Auk July 1917; Proceedings of the American Philosophical Society: Vol. 7; Plant World April 1907.

NYE, "BILL." See NYE, EDGAR WILSON

NYE, EDGAR WILSON ("Bill Nye") (August 25, 1850-February 22, 1896), humorist, was born in Shirley, Maine, the son of Franklin Nye, a poor farmer, and Eliza-

Collection of Frederick H. Meserve

"BILL" NYE

beth Mitchell (Loring) Nye. In 1852 the family moved to St. Croix County, in Wisconsin, which had just become a state. There the boy grew up in a log cabin in the wilderness, with little schooling except a few terms at the academy in River Falls, Wis., interspersed with periods of work. He then worked and studied in a law office in Chippewa Falls, and for two weeks edited a small paper there.

In 1876 he went to Wyoming and settled near Laramie. With scant formality, he was admitted to the bar by a tolerant committee, and immediately made justice of the peace and known as "Judge Nye," though all his salary was in fees. His living he made through a position on the Laramie *Daily Sentinel* and articles for the Cheyenne *Sun* and the Denver *Tribune.* In 1877 he married Clara Frances Smith; they had two sons and two daughters.

In 1881, with Judge Jacob Blair, Nye founded the Laramie *Boomerang,* and was its editor to 1885. His humorous sketches in this paper, signed "Bill Nye," won him his first considerable reputation. Meanwhile he acted also as postmaster of the town, superintendent of schools, a member of the territorial legislature, and United States Commissioner. His first books were made of selections from his *Boomerang* sketches.

An attack of meningitis (from which he never fully recovered and which eventually caused his death) ended this period of Nye's career. Advised to seek a lower altitude, he went first to Greeley, Colo., then to Hudson, Wis. By 1886 he was in New York; a steady connection with the New York *World* from 1887, and the syndicating of his articles by this paper, insured his national celebrity. From 1885 also he was a constant lyceum lecturer, from 1886 to 1890 lecturing together with his very close friend, James Whitcomb Riley, who supplied the pathos and sentiment while Nye provided the humor and satire. In 1889 he was abroad, reporting the Paris Exposition for the *World.* The next year he moved to Arden, N.C., near Asheville, where he died. In addition to his books, Nye wrote two plays; one, *The Cadi* (1891), was successfully produced in New York; the other, *The Stag Party,* written with Paul Potter in 1895 when he was practically a dying man, was a flat failure.

A bald, spectacled, smooth-shaven man, Nye looked more like a lawyer than a humorist. He was a hard worker, turning out 30,000 words a week at some times. Personally he was quiet and reserved, with few intimates, but innately kindly. He never relied on slang or misspellings as did other humorists of his period; and hasty and superficial as much of his journalistic writing inevitably was, John Dewey was not amiss in calling him "a great satirist." "Few Americans have done more," Dewey added, "to expose pretense and superstition."

In 1938, more than forty years after his death, Nye's fellow-citizens in his birthplace, Shirley, Maine, dedicated a tablet to his memory. Press dispatches at the time called Nye "the Will Rogers of his day," and the comparison is not inept.

Principal Works: Bill Nye and Boomerang, 1881; Forty Liars and Other Lies, 1882; Baled Hay, 1884; Bill Nye's Blossom Rock, 1885; Thinks and Remarks by Bill Nye, 1886; Nye and Riley's Railway Guide (with J. W. Riley) 1888; Bill Nye's Chestnuts Old and New, 1889; Fun, Wit, and Poetry (with J. W. Riley) 1891; Bill Nye's History of the United States, 1894; Bill Nye's History of England From the Druids to the Reign of Henry VIII, 1896; The Guest at Ludlow, 1896.

About: Nye, F. W. Bill Nye: His Own Life Story; Pond, J. B. Eccentricities of Genius; Searight, F. R. The American Press Humorists' Book; Century Magazine November 1891; November 1892; Harper's Magazine March 1919; Munsey's Magazine July 1901; Publisher's Weekly October 2, 1937; New York Times February 23, 1896.

OAKES, URIAN (c.1631-July 25, 1681), poet, clergyman, and Harvard president, was of English birth, the son of Edward and Jane Oakes who emigrated to Cambridge, Mass., in about the year 1640. He was graduated from Harvard in 1649, and in the year following was listed as a fellow of the college. One of his early literary enterprises was the preparation of the Cambridge almanac for 1650, and into some of its emptier pages Oakes worked a skeleton history of the world. For three years he tutored students at the college, and then returning to England he became minister of Tichfield, Hants. After being silenced by the Act of Uniformity (1662) he became headmaster in a grammar school; when the air was again cleared he founded a Congregational church at Tichfield; and then in 1671 accepted a call to the Church of Cambridge, Mass. For a while he served as one of the censors of the Massachusetts press.

On the death of Charles Chauncy, president of Harvard, Oakes had, apparently, unwarrantably high hopes of becoming his successor; and in 1673, with high resentment he conspired to thwart the newly elected Leonard Hoar by urging the undergraduates, according to Cotton Mather's account, "to *Travestie* whatever he [Hoar] *did* and *said.*" Hoar was so harrassed by the whole affair that even after the Board of Overseers, etc. had examined the charges and had sustained him, he withdrew from office. Twice Oakes refused the appointment; but for five years he was "acting president" (he continued his duties at the Cambridge Church) of a disorganized, puzzled, and fast diminishing student body. He did, however, succeed in erecting the first and much-needed Harvard Hall. On February 9, 1679/80, he was again elected president, consented to a formal installation, but died before he was able to do anything very constructive.

Oakes' poetic ability perhaps reached its high point in the verse for which he is best remembered, the *Elegie* on Thomas Shepard, one of the real gems of the colonial era. The energy of his prose was visible in several very effective public orations. In 1673 appeared his *New England Pleaded With*—"faithful advice to the people of God . . . musingly to ponder . . . what will be . . .the sad Issue of sundry and unchristian and crooked ways which too many have been turned aside into." Despite his sojourn in England, Oakes had retained his strong support of early New England principles; and he lamented the existence of the strong personal jealousies which were bringing about a political decadence wherein "men of worth will be lothe to appear on the Stage of Government." Oakes' literary reputation was decidedly limited, but as a classicist of parts and as an educator-organizer, he undoubtedly influenced early New England intellectualism.

About: Mather, C. Magnalia Christi Americana; Nichols, C. L. A Collection of Photographic Reproductions of Massachusetts Almanacs; Quincy, J. The History of Harvard University; Sibley, J. L. Biographical Sketches of the Graduates of Harvard University; Tyler, M. C. A History of American Literature During the Colonial Time.

"OAKSMITH, ELIZABETH." See SMITH, ELIZABETH OAKES (PRINCE)

OBERHOLTZER, SARA LOUISA (VICKERS) (May 20, 1841-February 2, 1930), miscellaneous writer, was born in Uwchlan, Chester County, Pa., the daughter of Paxson and Ann (Lewis) Vickers. Of Quaker ancestry on her father's side, she attended the Friends' Boarding School and later the Millerville State Normal School. In 1862 she married John Oberholtzer, a Philadelphia merchant. She was much interested in social and philanthropic activities, especially in the idea of school savings banks. In this cause she wrote many letters, articles, and pamphlets, and lectured on the subject in almost every state. Before her death over fifteen thousand schools in forty-six states were using the system. In this connection she also edited *School Savings* for many years.

When she was still very young Mrs. Oberholtzer showed marked literary ability. She contributed articles to many magazines and published letters of travel, hymns, a number of volumes of verse, and a novel of Quaker life called *Hope's Heart Bells.* She wrote many commemorative poems and was a close friend of John Greenleaf Whittier. She died in Philadelphia, leaving two sons.

Principal Works: Violet Lee, 1873; Come for Arbutus, 1882; Hope's Heart Bells, 1884; Daisies of Verse, 1886; Souvenirs of Occasions, 1892.

About: Albig, W. E. A History of School Savings Banking; New York Times February 4, 1930.

O'BRIEN, FITZ-JAMES (1828?-April 6, 1862), poet and story writer, was born in County Limerick, Ireland, the son of James O'Brien, an attorney, and Eliza (O'Driscoll) O'Brien. Thanks to his own habit of romanticizing his history, neither his exact birth-date nor his education is known; he claimed to be a graduate of Trinity College, Dublin, but this has been definitely disproved. About 1849 he went to London, and in two years there and two subsequent years in Paris he wasted his entire inheritance, about £8000. Already he had written for various magazines in England and Ireland, and may possibly have had an editorial position on a London paper in 1851.

FITZ-JAMES O'BRIEN

In 1852 O'Brien appeared in New York, a penniless journalist with a few letters from influential friends. He became a habitué of the Bohemia which centered around Pfaff's, haunt of writers as diverse as Walt Whitman and Adah Isaacs Menken. He made his way by his pen in any fashion for which he could find a market: did editorial writing for the *Times;* wrote essays and poems and stories for nearly all the prominent magazines, with *Harper's* as his chief avenue of approach; adapted plays for James Wallack (*A Gentleman from Ireland* was the most successful); and traveled with the Matilda Heron theatrical group as literary assistant to the manager, H. L. Bateman. When he was in funds he lived a life of luxury, in bed by sunrise every morning, and breakfasting promptly at 2 P.M.; when the funds gave out he dodged creditors and camped in the rooms of his friends. As Fred Lewis Pattee says, he had "a gentleman's taste and a hack writer's income." His florid face, his heavy brown mustache, his profile which retreated from a broad brow above deep blue eyes to a tiny pointed chin, were familiar sights in every New York theater barroom where literary folk gathered.

This pleasant if precarious life was interrupted by the Civil War. O'Brien enlisted at once in the New York National Guard. In 1862 he was appointed to the staff of General Frederick Lander, with the rank of lieutenant. Just after he had received special mention for gallantry at the Battle of Bloomery Gap, he was wounded, and six weeks later died of tetanus, at Cumberland, Va. His body was brought back to New York and buried in Greenwood Cemetery.

Facile and spirited, clever and versatile, but utterly undisciplined and rankly careless, O'Brien had talent without mental maturity. His story is the pattern of those of all irresponsible Bohemians, with a tragic accident at its close. His best work was in his stories of the weird and uncanny—"The Diamond Lens," "Wondersmith," and "What Was It?". He wrote realistically of the unreal and because of this Pattee speaks of his adding "a sense of actuality to Poe's unlocalized romance." In truth, he seems much more a sort of minor Bierce, without Bierce's passion or bitterness. His verse is for the most part mere tinkle, and over his work, as over his personality, lies a slight tarnish of the shabby genteel.

Principal Works: Ballads of Ireland, 1856; Collected Poems and Stories, 1881; A Gentleman From Ireland, 1895; Collected Stories, 1925.

About: O'Brien, F.-J. Collected Poems and Stories (see Sketch by W. Winter); Collected Stories (see Introduction by E. J. O'Brien); Parry, A. Garrets and Pretenders; Critic February 26, 1881; South Atlantic Quarterly January 1931; New York Times April 7, 9, 10, 1862.

O'CALLAGHAN, EDMUND BAILEY (February 28, 1797-May 29, 1880), physician and historiographer, was born in southern Ireland, at Mallow, County Cork. In his twenty-fourth year he went to Paris to study medicine, and three years later he sailed for Quebec, where he was admitted to practice and established himself as a physician. In 1834 his literary ability was put to a test in the editing of the *Vindicator,* official organ of the National Patriotic Movement; he was elected a member of the Provincial Parliament; and became secretary and ardent promoter of "The Friends of Ireland." After the Doric Club, a Tory circle strongly opposed to O'Callaghan's activities, destroyed the type, presses, and miscellaneous material in the *Vindicator* office, O'Callaghan fled from Canada, with a high-treason charge against him, and after short residence at Saratoga resumed his medical practice in Albany, N.Y.

At the time of the anti-rent agitation O'Callaghan began a study of the Dutch land grants and acquired some scattered impressions of early New York history from which he prepared some historical papers, during the early 'forties, for the *Northern Light,* a popular monthly. He mastered the Dutch language, and as keeper of the historical manuscripts in the office of the (N.Y.) Secretary of State (1848-70), he had access to the dusty annals of the early settlements. After the publication of his two-volume *History of New Netherland,* he devoted full time, at the request of the State of New York, to the editing of old records, from which emerged the invaluable source books *The Documentary History of the State of New York* and *Documents Relative to the Colonial History of the State of New York.* He also translated some of the minutes of the New Amsterdam burgomasters.

In 1870 O'Callaghan removed to New York City, and within two years completed the editing of its common council minutes, the publication of which was halted by a reform measure introduced following the "Tweed ring" corruption. In addition to an abundance of further siftings from historical records O'Callaghan prepared a *List of Editions of the Holy Scriptures, and Parts Thereof, Printed in America Previous to 1860* and *Jesuit Relations: A Bibliographical Account.*

Six years after the death of his first wife, Charlotte Augustina Crampe, in 1835, he was married to Ellen Hawe, who survived him. His two children, one by each marriage, died in infancy. O'Callaghan's achievements in the medical profession were only ordinary, but the publications resulting from his Knickerbocker researches have remained widely authoritative.

Principal Works: Jesuit Relations: A Bibliographical Account, 1847; The Documentary History of the State of New York (4 vols.) 1849-51; Documents Relative to the Colonial History of the State of New York (11 vols.) 1853-61; A List of Editions of the Holy Scriptures, and Parts Thereof, Printed in America Previous to 1860, 1861; The Register of New Netherland: 1626 to 1674, 1865; Calendar of Historical Manuscripts in the Office of the Secretary of State, Albany (2 vols.) 1865-66.

About: Kelly, H. A. & Burrage, W. L. American Medical Biographies; Records of the American Catholic Historical Society March 1905; Magazine of American History July 1880.

"O'CATARACT, JEHU." See NEAL, JOHN

O'CONNOR, WILLIAM DOUGLAS (January 2, 1832-May 9, 1889), journalist, civil servant, friend and literary champion of Walt Whitman, was born in Boston, of Scotch-Irish descent. As a youth he read extensively, and after contemplating a career in art he was attracted, at the age of twenty-one, by an offer from the Boston *Commonwealth*; in the year following she went over to the (Philadelphia) *Saturday Evening Post.* He was dismissed from the *Post* for the writing of a sympathetic account of John Brown of Osawatomie; and he shortly prepared a vehement Abolitionist rejoinder, *Harrington,* which Walt Whitman called a "fiery and eloquent novel" (despite the fact that he held O'Connor's "extremist" tendencies as his gravest error). From 1860 on O'Connor lived in Washington, filling a succession of government posts with the Light House Board, the Treasury Department, the Revenue Marine Division, and the Life Saving Service, for which he drafted annual reports that bore an uncommon literary excellence and from which Sumner Increase Kimball later published a book of extracts called *Heroes of the Storm.*

O'Connor first met Whitman in Boston in 1860, at the office of Thayer & Eldridge, publishers; and when the poet came to Washington two years later O'Connor secured him an appointment and extended him infinite hospitality. After Whitman's dismissal from a clerkship in the Interior Department O'Connor wrote *The Good Gray Poet,* a kind of diatribe against Secretary James Harlan. For *Putnam's Magazine* (January 1868) he wrote "The Carpenter," an implicit tribute to Whitman's spiritual magnetism. Whitman, commenting upon a remark that the "Carpenter portrait" was "prevailingly sad," said, "It is open to such a suspicion, it must be touched with what is tragic—the minor key: the idea has been exploited before. . . " *Hamlet's Notebook* and *Mr. Donnelly's Reviewers* were the result of O'Connor's ardent Baconian research. And three of his stories were published posthumously with a preface by Whitman. O'Connor was married in 1856 to Ellen M. Tarr of Boston.

It is true that O'Connor was responsible for the origin of a kind of Whitman hero-worship, but the intellectual stimulus of their friendship was more reciprocal than has been generally acknowledged. For Whitman not only regarded O'Connor as his "dear, dear friend and stanch (probably my stanchest) literary believer and champion from the first throughout . . . " but often remarked on O'Connor's cleverness as a phraseologist and even went so far as to say that he (O'C.) was not the "only one of his sort but he certainly is way, way the greatest of his sort."

Principal Works: Harrington, 1860; The Good Gray Poet, 1866; Hamlet's Notebook, 1886; Mr. Donnelly's Reviewers, 1889; Three Tales: The Ghost, The Brazen Android, The Carpenter, 1892; Heroes of the Storm (ed. by S. I. Kimball) 1904.

About: Barrus, C. Whitman and Burroughs; Glicksburg, C. I. Walt Whitman and the Civil War; Traubel, H. With Walt Whitman in Camden; Whitman, W. Letters Written by Walt Whitman to His Mother; Evening Star (Washington) May 10, 1889.

ODELL, JONATHAN (September 25, 1737-November 25, 1818), Loyalist, satirist, missionary, and physician, was born in Newark, N.J., the son of John Odell, descendant of early Massachusetts settlers, and Temperance (Dickinson) Odell. He was graduated from the College of New Jersey (now Princeton) in 1759, studied medicine, and became a surgeon in the British army. During a commission in the West Indies he left the service and went to England to prepare himself for the ministry. He was made a deacon in December 1766 and was ordained priest in the year following. On his return to the United States he was inducted into the office of missionary to St. Ann's Church, in Burlington, N.J., and he served in a similar capacity at Mount Holly. In 1771 he was obliged to find more lucrative employment, and he began the practice of medicine, in Burlington. Odell was married, in May 1772, to Anne De Cou.

From the very beginning of the Revolution he was, admittedly, on the side of the Crown; and in July 1776 for the writing of some verses assailing the American position which were sung by British prisoners he was placed on parole—he escaped, in December, to Governor Franklin's house; and then proceeded to New York City. Charges of treason were afterward brought against him.

Odell remained on the British side throughout; he assumed a large responsibility in the negotiations between Benedict Arnold and British headquarters; and in 1779 was a skillful go-between for André. With André's poem *Cow-Chace,* published only a few weeks before André was hanged, was bound *The American Times,* a series of caricatures of Revolutionary figures, by "Camillo Querno, Poet Laureat to the Congress," which has now been almost conclusively ascribed to Odell. The author believed that because the American Revolution had been "weighed in the balance and found wanting. . . . Ridicule [may] be lawfully employed in the service of Virtue." Much of Odell's verse was in the "Rule, Britannia" vein, appearing in Rivington's *Royal Gazette* and other journals; and Joel Munsell, in 1860, published *The Loyal Verses of Joseph Stansbury and Doctor Jonathan Odell.* Many public men were the victims of his satire, and he was indeed a better lampooner than prophet in his epitaph on Benjamin Franklin, who, he asserted, had kindled little but the "blaze of sedition."

Let Candor then write on his Urn
Here lies the renowned inventor
Whose flames to the skies ought to burn,
But, inverted, descend to the center.

Odell went to England in 1783 as assistant secretary to Sir Guy Carleton, commander-in-chief of the British forces; and in the year following he settled in the Loyalist province of New Brunswick, Canada. He was a man of many talents, and although he published very little it is plainly evident that he wrote with a skilled and trenchant pen.

PRINCIPAL WORKS: The American Times, 1780; The Loyal Verses of Joseph Stansbury and Dr. Jonathan Odell, 1860.

ABOUT: Hills, G. M. History of the Church in Burlington; Odell, J. The American Times; Tyler, M. C. The Literary History of the American Revolution; New England Historical and Genealogical Register January 1892.

O'HARA, THEODORE (February 11, 1820-June 6, 1867), poet and soldier, was born in Danville, Ky. His father was Kane (or Kean) O'Hara, an Irish political exile and a well known teacher. Theodore O'Hara was graduated from St. Joseph's College, Bardstown, Ky., in 1839, having acted as professor of Greek during his senior year. He then read law, and was admitted to the bar in 1842. After an irksome experience as a clerk in the Treasury Department, in Washington, he became assistant editor on the *Kentucky Yeoman,* Frankfort. He served through the Mexican War, becoming a major, then returned to the *Yeoman.* He left once more in 1849 to join Lopez's filibustering expedition to Cuba, but was shot immediately on his arrival and returned home. Contrary to repeated statements, he was never associated with Capt. William Walker, the filibuster.

In 1852 O'Hara became one of six editors of the Louisville *Times,* an aggressive organ of the anti-"Know Nothing" party. He also edited the Louisville *Sun* for a while. The *Times* died in 1855 and for a year he was a captain in the United States Cavalry. Then he edited the Mobile *Register* until the Civil War, when he enlisted in the Alabama Infantry. He saw much service and at the end of the war was a colonel in the Confederate Army. He then set up as a cotton merchant in Columbus, Ga., but fire completely destroyed his property, and he moved to the plantation of a friend in Guerryton, Ala., where he died of malaria the next year. Kentucky had his remains exhumed and reburied in the State Military Cemetery, with a monument. He was never married.

O'Hara had the Irish charm, militancy, and loquaciousness that matched his black hair and hazel eyes and his general appearance of the typical Irish gentleman. He wrote little, but his ready stream of grandiloquent oratory was taken at face value as evidence of talent. His best known poems are "A Dirge for the Brave Old Pioneer" and "The Bivouac of the Dead." The latter, written of the American soldiers killed in the Mexican War, has been quoted on soldiers' monuments and military cemeteries throughout the country. It exists in two versions, the earlier and longer being the better. O'Hara's writings have never been collected.

ABOUT: Ranck, G. W. O'Hara and His Elegies; "The Bivouac of the Dead" and Its Author; Townsend, J. W. Kentucky in American Letters; Century Magazine May 1890; Nation June 29, 1876; Southern Bivouac January and March 1887; Louisville Daily Democrat June 14, 1867.

"O.K." See KELLY, JONATHAN FALCONBRIDGE

"OLD BLOCK." See DELANO, ALONZO

"OLD LINE WHIG." See WILLIAMS, JAMES

"OLDSCHOOL, OLIVER." See DENNIE, JOSEPH

"OLD UN." See DURIVAGE, FRANCIS ALEXANDER

OLIVER, PETER (March 26, 1713-October 1791), Loyalist, jurist, and student of Colonial history, was born in Boston, Mass., the son of Daniel and Elizabeth (Belcher) Oliver. Peter's behavior record at Harvard was blackened by the stealing of a turkey and a goose, but he stood high scholastically at the time of his graduation in 1730. Three years later he was married to Mary Clarke, by whom he had six children. In 1747 when he was appointed judge of the inferior court of common pleas of Plymouth County he entered upon a long service on the bench. In the early 'seventies his Loyalist sympathies began to aggravate the difficulties between England and the Colonies, and there was much resentment over the salary increases which the British government granted members of the judiciary. After attempts at impeachment proceedings against him and the refusal of two grand juries to serve under him, Oliver fled to Halifax and then continued on to England.

The King received him graciously and Oxford awarded him a D.C.L. degree; under government pension he lived at Birmingham until his death. His unpublished "Origin and Progress of the American War to 1776" was patently biased but despite its lack of authenticity is of considerable historical interest. In 1750 he published *A Speech . . . After the Death of Isaac Lothrop*; in 1757, *A Poem Sacred to the Memory of the Honorable Josiah Willard*; and his *Scripture Lexicon* (1787) was adopted as an Oxford textbook. From the historian's point of view Oliver's judicial activities and meagre writings have become hardly more than a lively portion of the Loyalist "swan-song."

PRINCIPAL WORKS: A Speech . . . After the Death of Isaac Lothrop, 1750; A Poem Sacred to the Memory of the Honorable Josiah Willard, 1757; Scripture Lexicon, 1787.

ABOUT: New England Historical and Genealogical Register April 1865, July-October 1886; Proceedings of the Massachusetts Historical Society: Vol. 14.

OLMSTED, FREDERICK LAW (April 26, 1822-August 28, 1903), landscape architect and travel writer, was born in Hartford, Conn., the son of John Olmsted, a merchant, and Charlotte Law (Hull) Olmsted. His mother died in 1826, but from 1827 he was reared by a good stepmother. The family were great travelers, and by the time he was sixteen he had made four thousand-mile trips through New York, New England, and Canada. Eye trouble forced him to study engineering privately instead of going to Yale, though later he took courses there. After two years as a mercantile clerk, a voyage before the mast to China in 1843, and six years as a farmer, he was sent by the New York *Times* to travel through the South and observe conditions there. This assignment grew out of his first book, an account of a walking tour in England with his brother in 1850. Editorial work on *Putnam's Monthly* followed, then a disastrous publishing venture with G. W. Curtis. It was not until 1857, in partnership with Calvert Vaux, that he began his career as the first and still one of the greatest of landscape architects. The rest of his life, except for general secretaryship of the Sanitary Commission during the Civil War, was given to this profession. He was long architect-in-chief of Central Park, New York City, which he created; he was first commissioner of Yosemite; and among his other achievements were the grounds of the University of California and Stanford University; Prospect Park, Brooklyn; the great Boston Park System; the Capitol Grounds in Washington; and the Chicago World's Fair of 1893. In 1859 he married his brother's widow, who had been Mary Cleveland Perkins; he fathered her three children, his nephews; of his own children a son and a daughter survived infancy. After 1878 he resided mostly in Brookline, and he died at Waverly, Mass.

Olmsted's travel books on the South were accurate, unbiased, and a sincere attempt to observe the slave states calmly and reasonably and preserve the tolerance which might have insured peace. In his profession, he "gave definition to the terminology of landscape art."

PRINCIPAL WORKS: Walks and Talks of an American Farmer in England, 1852; A Journey in the Seaboard Slave States, 1856; A Journey Through Texas, 1857; A Journey in the Back Country, 1860 (the previous three as The Cotton Kingdom, 1861; Public Parks and the Enlargement of Towns, 1871; A Consideration of the Justifying Value of a Public Park, 1881; Frederick Law Olmsted, professional papers (ed. by F. L. Olmsted, Jr. and Theodora Kimball) 1922.

ABOUT: Mitchell, B. Frederick Law Olmsted; A Critic of the Old South; Olmsted, F. L. jr. Frederick Law Olmsted: Landscape Architect; Century Magazine October 1893; House and Garden February-July 1906; New York Times August 29, 1903.

ONDERDONK, HENRY (June 11, 1804-June 22, 1886), local historian and educator, was born at Manhasset, in North Hempstead, N.Y., the son of Joseph Onderdonck (*sic*) and Dorothy (Monfoort) Onderdonck. He was graduated from Columbia in 1827 and in November of the following year was married to his cousin Maria Hegeman Onderdonk. During thirty years' service as principal and instructor in the classics at an academy in Jamaica he constantly strengthened his "recreational" interest in Long Island antiquities, and on retirement he became wholly engaged in these studies.

In the preface of one of his earliest volumes he defined his purpose as that of "collecting and arranging in chronological order, the scattered and fragmentary notices of the events that occurred on Long Island, during our Revolutionary struggle." From back newspapers, military records, political broadsides, church records and from actual conversation with the older townspeople he gathered his facts. Two of his first publications contributed new details to the annals of the War of Independence: *Documents and Letters Intended to Illustrate the Revolutionary Incidents of Queens County* and *Revolutionary Incidents of Suffolk and Kings Counties;* and among those for which he had drawn heavily upon church records were: *Antiquities of the Parish Church, Jamaica . . .* and *Antiquities of the Parish Church, Hempstead. . . .* By his early spade-work in church and military genealogy he prepared the ground for some of the host of local historians who were to compile and publish so voluminously a few decades later.

PRINCIPAL WORKS: Documents and Letters Intended to Illustrate the Revolutionary Incidents of Queens County, 1846; Revolutionary Incidents of Suffolk and Kings Counties, 1849; Queens County in Olden Times, 1865; Antiquities of the Parish Church, Jamaica (including Newtown and Flushing) 1880; Antiquities of the Parish Church, Hempstead, including Oysterbay and the Churches of Suffolk County, 1880.

ABOUT: New York Daily Tribune June 24, 1886.

"OPTIC, OLIVER." See ADAMS, WILLIAM TAYLOR

O'REILLY, JOHN BOYLE (June 28, 1844-August 10, 1890), poet and miscellaneous writer, was born near Drogheda, County Louth, Ireland, the son of William David O'Reilly, a mathematician and schoolmaster, and Eliza (Boyle) O'Reilly. He was educated in his father's Nettleville Institute, but at eleven was apprenticed as a printer to the Drogheda *Argus,* to take the place of his brother, who was ill. From 1855 to 1862 he served as printer and reporter on the Preston *Guardian,* in England. Meanwhile, he had become a Fenian, and for the purpose of propaganda he enlisted in the 10th Hussars in 1863 and was stationed in Ireland. He was most rash in his exposure of his views, and it was inevitable that he should be discovered, and only surprising that he was not arrested until 1866. He was court martialed and sentenced to death, but his sentence was commuted first to life, then to twenty years' imprisonment. After solitary confinement in Millbank Prison, hard labor at Chatham, and a term at Dartmoor, he was in 1867 transported to West Australia. There, with the assistance of a priest, he escaped in 1869 on an American whaling vessel, and after hair-trigger escapes and breathless adventures reached Philadelphia in November 1869. The day after his arrival he took out his first naturalization papers.

O'Reilly soon found his way to Boston. By 1870 he was on the staff of the *Pilot,* the most influential Roman Catholic paper in America, and in 1876 he bought a part-interest in it from Archbishop Williams, its proprietor. He remained as manager and editor-in-chief to his death. A prolific writer, a fluent speaker, an ardent patriot

Collection of Frederick H. Meserve
JOHN BOYLE O'REILLY

for both his native and his adopted lands, and a devout Catholic, O'Reilly was very much in demand as a speaker on public occasions, and his facile pen was equally called upon. He had little leisure in which to develop a genuine talent. His life, if full, was happy; in 1872 he married Mary Murphy, who wrote stories under the name of "Agnes Smiley," and with her and their four daughters he lived in Charlestown, Mass. (now part of Boston) in winter, and in summer at Hull, Mass., in one of the oldest houses in Massachusetts, built in 1644 and still standing. It was here that he died, of an accidental overdose of chloral taken for insomnia.

O'Reilly, who loved to be called "the poet," was a social being, friendly and genial, who enjoyed the honors heaped upon him. Notre Dame gave him an LL.D. in 1881, Georgetown University in 1889, and Dartmouth made him an honorary Phi Beta Kappa. After his death a memorial was erected to him in Boston by popular subscription. His ballad-like verses have vigor and still possess a somewhat faded charm. A few phrases from them still linger—for example, "Organized charity, scrimped and iced; in the name of a cautious, statistical Christ." His only novel (except a "composite" with three other writers) was a powerful story of Australian convict life; he himself did his part in helping to end the system of which it treats by securing freedom for all Irish military political prisoners in West Australia in 1876. In addition to his original writing and his journalism, he edited an anthology of Irish poetry. One of his daughters, Mary Boyle O'Reilly, also became a well known writer.

PRINCIPAL WORKS: Songs From Southern Seas, 1873; Songs, Legends, and Ballads, 1878; Moondyne (novel) 1879; The Statues in the Block, 1881; The King's Men (with R. Grant, F. J. Stimson, and J. T. Wheelwright) 1884; In Bohemia, 1886; Ethics of Boxing and Manly Sport, 1888; Poems and Speeches, 1891.

ABOUT: McCarthy, J. Reminiscences; Roche, J. J. Life of John Boyle O'Reilly; Boston Transcript August 11, 1890.

"O'REILLY, MILES." See HALPINE, CHARLES GRAHAM

"ORLANDO." See HOLLAND, EDWIN CLIFFORD

ORVIS, MARIANNE (DWIGHT) (April 4, 1816-December 12, 1901), "Brook Farmer" and letter-writer, was born in Boston, daughter of Dr. John Dwight, religious free-thinker and physician, and Mary (Corey) Dwight. Her brother, John Sullivan Dwight [*q.v.*], had joined George Ripley's Brook Farm Association while it was still in embryo and two years later (1843) she herself became a member. In addition to agriculture, the community operated a number of one-man industries—tailoring, sash-and-blind making, tin-blocking, printing, etc.—and Marianne shortly abandoned most of her duties as Latin instructor and household assistant and gave full time to the painting of a series of water sketches (about 100) of the wild flowers of the district.

The occasion of her marriage to John Orvis, December 24, 1846, at the Farm, was recorded as a "symbol of universal unity"; William Henry Channing, nephew of William Ellery Channing, the poet, delivered a sermon of exactly five words. The Orvises had two children, Christel and Helen; Marianne survived her husband by more than four years and both were buried in Forest Hills Cemetery in Boston.

Her *Letters From Brook Farm, 1844-1847* (1928), edited by Amy Louise Reed and purporting to be the "only considerable body of letters now in existence which were written on the spot by a member of the Brook Farm Community," is perhaps one of the least distorted accounts of the "highs" and "lows" in the morale of the association. On May 11, 1844, she wrote: ". . . we love Brook Farm more than ever . . . are patient in its imperfections and wait for the perfect day." Two years later, when criticism from without had grown increasingly severe: ". . . I have not felt for a moment that we should dare think of abandoning it. . . ." And in March 1847: 'Tho' our state here for some months . . . has . . . been very disagreeable, yet life is more rich to me at this very time than ever. . . " There are, perhaps, few Brook Farm historians who would have observed that "W. H. C. [William Henry Channing] dances with much grace and vivacity," or who, looking out over the burnt ruins of the half-built Phalanstery, would have written; ". . . the immense heavy column of smoke . . . ascended almost perpendicularly . . . spangled with fiery sparks, tinged with glowing colors, ever-rolling and wreathing, solemnly and gracefully, up—up. . ."

ABOUT: Cooke, G. W. John Sullivan Dwight; Orvis, M. D. Letters From Brook Farm, 1844-1847; Swift, L. Brook Farm.

OSBORN, LAUGHTON (c. 1809-December 13, 1878), poet and dramatist, was born in New York City, where his father was a prominent physician. Graduated from Columbia University in 1827, he travelled abroad for a year, and then returned to New York to spend the remainder of his life. Although he was said to be popular during his college days, his disposition underwent a radical change after the death of a favorite sister, and was further soured by unfavorable criticism of the books that he turned out with feverish intensity. These were often published at his own expense, without his name, and included such titles as *The Dream of Alla-Ad-Deen: The Confessions of a Poet*; *The Vision of Rubeta: An Epic Story of the Island of Manhattan: With Illustrations Done on Stone*. The latter was pointed at William Leete Stone, a rival journalist, and also contained a vitrolic attack on Wordsworth.

Fancying himself as a playwright of high intellectual caliber, he wrote a number of tragedies and comedies among which were *The Heart's Sacrifice; Matilda of Denmark; Bianco Capello*; and *Mariamne: A Tragedy of Jewish History,* none of which was ever produced.

The fluency of Osborn's literary style sprang more from pent-up bitterness than a genuine gift, and he was never recognized as a fine writer, even in his day. His eccentricities tried the patience of his contemporaries to the extent that he had almost no friends. Edgar Allan Poe has described him as ". . . chivalrous in every respect, but unhappily, carrying his ideas of chivalry, or rather of independence, to the point of Quixotism, if not of absolute insanity. He has no doubt been misapprehended, and therefore wronged, by the world; but he should not fail to remember that the source of the wrong lay in his own idiosyncrasy—one altogether unintelligible and unappreciable by the mass of mankind."

Osborn was a gifted musician, spoke several languages fluently, and painted moderately well. In 1845 he wrote a *Handbook of Young Artists and Amateurs in Oil Painting.* His two-volume first book, *Sixty Years of the Life of Jeremy Levis* is remembered more because it incited Osborne's life-long crusade against his critics than for any literary merit.

PRINCIPAL WORKS: Sixty Years of the Life of Jeremy Levis, 1831; The Dream of Alla-Ad-Deen: The Confessions of a Poet, 1835; The Vision of Rubeta: An Epic Story of the Island of Manhattan: With Illustrations Done on Stone, 1838; Arthur Carryl, 1841.

ABOUT: Poe, E. A. The Literati; Wilson, J. G. Bryant and His Friends; New York World December 14, 1878.

OSBORN, SELLECK (1782-October 1 (?), 1826), journalist, poet, and cavalry officer, was born in Trumbull, Conn., the son of Nathaniel Osborn. As a boy he served an apprenticeship to a printer, and from June 1802 until January 1803 he edited the *Suffolk County Herald* at Sag Harbor, N. Y. In 1805 he became a co-editor, with Timothy Ashley, of the (Litchfield) *Witness,* and in its columns he buoyed up the village's Democratic minority by providing the local Federalist celebrities with fearless and incriminating nicknames. One "Crowbar Justice" Deming sued the editors for libel. Found guilty by the county court in April 1806, Ashley complied with the orders of the court, but partner Osborn, from his cell, continued as the sole and redoubtable editor of the *Witness.* "Dispassionate men" were said to have admired him for this "persecution of federalism" and he became a kind of politico-literary martyr.

He was released within a reasonable period and on July 8, 1808, was commissioned first lieutenant of light dragoons in the United States army, became a captain, and after service in the War of 1812 was honorably discharged. Returning to journalism, he edited first a paper in Bennington, Vt., then the *American Watchman* (Wilmington, Del.), and the New York *Patriot.* He later removed to Philadelphia where he died shortly afterward.

It was tradition, with Osborn, to maintain in his paper a "poet's corner," for which he never wrote, so he said, without "a strong pressure of moral sentiment." A small collection of these fugitive pieces, nicely versified but quite unoriginal, was published in 1823 as *Poems, Moral, Sentimental, and Satirical.* Like that of many early American newspapermen Osborn's literary significance is traceable to some professionally heretical episode rather than to the achievement of consistent journalistic excellence.

ABOUT: Duyckinck, E. A. & G. L. Cyclopaedia of American Literature; Litchfield Monitor August 13, 1806; National Intelligencer (Washington, D.C.) October 30, 1826.

OSGOOD, FRANCES SARGENT (LOCKE) (June 18, 1811-May 12, 1850), poet, was born in Boston, the daughter of Joseph Locke and Mary (Ingersoll) Foster Locke. Most of her childhood was spent in Hingham, Mass., and her literary talent was apparent at an early age with the publication of her first poems in the *Juvenile Miscellany* under the signature "Florence." In 1835 she married Samuel Stillman Osgood, a painter, whom she had met the previous year, and who had painted a fine portrait of her. They soon sailed for England where they attained considerable success in art and literary circles. In addition to a play which was never staged, and several volumes of poems, Mrs. Osgood contributed to the English magazines during their four-year stay.

The Osgoods returned to America in 1839 and settled in New York, where she was to live until her death. Mrs. Osgood contined her writing, publishing among other works, *The Poetry of Flowers and the Flowers of Poetry,* and *The Cries of New York.*

It was in March 1845 that she met Edgar Allan Poe and formed the deep friendship that is her chief claim to fame. Poe evidently found in Mrs. Osgood a charm and magnetism that distracted his critical sense, for he overpraised rather extravagantly her slight, well-bred talent. Their friendly attachment continued for about two years, and from this brief association Mrs. Osgood achieved more distinction than from a lifetime of gentle Victorian verse.

PRINCIPAL WORKS: A Wreath of Wild Flowers From New England, 1838; The Casket of Fate, 1840; The Poetry of Flowers and the Flowers of Poetry, 1841; The Snowdrop: A New Year Gift for Children, 1842; The Rose: Sketches in Verse, 1842; Puss in Boots, 1844; The Cries of New York, 1846; The Flower Alphabet (Boston, n.d.); Poems, 1846; A Letter About the Lions, 1849.

ABOUT: Griswold, W. M. (ed.). Passages From the Correspondence of and Other Papers of Rufus W. Griswold; Locke, J. G. Book of the Lockes; New York Daily Tribune May 13, 14, 1850; New York Herald May 13, 1850.

OSSOLI, SARAH MARGARET (FULLER), MARCHESA D'. See FULLER, SARAH MARGARET

OTIS, HARRISON GRAY (October 8, 1765-October 28, 1848), statesman, was born in Boston, the son of Samuel Allyne and Elizabeth (Gray) Otis. He attended the Boston Latin School, was graduated from Harvard in 1783, and after reading law was admitted to the Boston bar in 1786. In 1790 he was married to Sally Foster, by whom he had eleven children.

During the inflation-speculation era of the 1790's Otis had, financially, an iron in every fire, and, moreover, was fast becoming a brilliant lawyer. His eloquent Federalist oratory at Boston town meetings indirectly won him, from President Washington, an appointment as district attorney for Massachusetts; he resigned for a seat in Congress (1797-1801), where he was only mildly active, having little taste for the Capital. Nor did he stand for re-election in 1800.

He settled down in Boston but was shortly drawn into politics again. In the course of fifteen years' service (1802-17) in the state legislature he became speaker of the house and, later, president of the senate. Otis led in the preliminary arrangements for the Hartford Convention and was an influential figure at the sessions themselves (December 15, 1814-January 5, 1815). In 1817 he was elected to the United States Senate, but the Washington atmosphere was still unfriendly and he resigned in 1822. Three times, 1829-31, he was elected mayor of Boston.

Except for a number of memorial addresses, *Eulogy on Gen. Alexander Hamilton,* etc., Otis' writings were chiefly political. He was often capable of producing boldly satirical figures of speech. In defense of the Hartford Convention he wrote, in 1824, ". . . men of fair minds . . . are humiliated in discovering . . . that what they have regarded as a 'Blue Light' was a mere *ignis fatuus* and that the Pandemonium was as harmless as a Quaker meeting." Besides his *Letters in Defense of the Hartford Convention* he published *Letters Developing the Character and Views of the Hartford Convention,* and engaged in a bitter pamphlet controversy with J. Q. Adams, who had been loathe to acknowledge him as a political rival.

Although in his youth Otis had been enough of an upstart to make the old Federalists a little wary, he was, fundamentally, a real conservative, and there is a slight suggestion of this fact in his observation that "our own peculiarities are rendered tolerable by habit—a wooden leg is a lead article, and yet a man who has limped on one for forty years can do better with it than with one of cork." It is chronicled that he "breakfasted on goose-livers, and lived gaily and goutily to a good age." Otis had, indeed, a fairly facile pen, but his legal and political activities left little time for purely literary pursuits.

PRINCIPAL WORKS: Proceedings of a Convention of Delegates . . . at Hartford, 1815; Letters Developing the Character and Views of the Hartford Convention, 1820; Otis' Letters in Defense of the Hartford Convention, 1824; Correspondence Between John Quincy Adams . . . and Several Citizens of Massachusetts Concerning the Charge of a Design to Dissolve the Union, 1829.

ABOUT: Morison, S. E. The Life and Letters of Harrison Gray Otis, Federalist; Otis, W. A. A Genealogical and Historical Memoir of the Otis Family in America; Miscellaneous Papers, Manuscript Division, New York Public Library.

OTIS, JAMES (February 5, 1725-May 23, 1783), patriot, political writer, and publicist, was born in West Barnstable, Mass., the son of James Otis and Mary (Allyne) Otis. Prepared for college by the Rev. Jonathan Russell of Barnstable, he attended Harvard, class of 1743; and after studying law under Jeremiah Gridley was admitted to the bar in 1748. In 1750 he moved to Boston, where his eloquence, integrity, and talents soon earned him a place at the head of his profession. In 1755 he married Ruth Cunningham, the daughter of a Boston merchant.

After a portrait by J. D. Blackburn
JAMES OTIS
1755

In 1761 Otis began his activities as a defender of colonial rights, when he resigned the office of advocate general to plead the cause of the colonists in the writs of assistance action. He lost the case, but his speech was delivered with such fire and eloquence, and his arguments were so logical and reasoned as to supply the colonies with effective weapons. A few months later, Otis was elected representative of the Massachusetts legislature. He took a leading part in the Stamp Act Congress at New York in 1764, serving on the committee which drafted the address to Parliament.

In 1769, in consequence of a newspaper controversy with the customs officials, Otis was attacked and severely beaten. Already showing signs of mental instability, he grew worse after the altercation until he became insane and with the exception of a few lucid intervals he never regained his mental balance. He joined the forces at Bunker Hill and took part in the battle, returning home unharmed. He died at Andover, struck by lightning as he stood chatting in the doorway of a friend's house.

Otis wrote many pamphlets, speeches, and treatises, but there are few now extant. His fame rests chiefly on his celebrated speech of 1761, and his powerful and masterly expression of the viewpoint of his countrymen in *The Rights of the British Colonies.*

Principal Works: The Rudiments of Latin Prosody . . . and the Principles of Harmony in Poetic and Prosaic Composition, 1760; A Vindication of the Conduct of the House of Representatives, 1762; The Rights of the British Colonies Assisted and Proved, 1764; Considerations on Behalf of the Colonists, in a Letter to a Noble Lord, 1765; A Vindication of the British Colonies, 1765; Brief Remarks on the Defence of the Halifax Libel on the British-American Colonies, 1765.

About: Adams, C. F. The Works of John Adams; Frothingham, I. R. The Rise of the Republic; Hosmer, J. K. The Life of Thomas Hutchinson; Tudor, W. The Life of James Otis; Wright, B. F. Jr. American Interpretations of Natural Law; The University of Missouri Studies July, October 1929; American Law Review July 1869.

OTIS, MERCY. See WARREN, MERCY (OTIS)

"OUR TALISMAN." See LIPPARD, GEORGE

OWEN, ROBERT DALE (November 9, 1801-June 24, 1877), social reformer and miscellaneous writer, was born in Glasgow, Scotland, the son of Robert Owen, famous social philanthropist, and Ann Caroline (Dale) Owen, and elder brother of David Dale Owen, prominent geologist. After private tutoring, and three years at Emanuel von Fellenberg's school at Hofwyl, near Berne, Switzerland, he came to America to assist his father in establishing a colony devoted to social reform at New Harmony, Ind., where his duties included school teaching and the editorship of the New Harmony *Gazette.* In 1827 he left to join Frances Wright, in an unsuccessful attempt to build up a community interested in emancipation at Nashoba, Tenn. When this, like New Harmony, failed to provide an outlet for his reform enthusiasms, he went to Europe for a time, but soon returned to the United States. Following a brief stay at New Harmony, where he again edited the *Gazette* he moved the paper to New York City changing the name to the *Free Enquirer* and the policy to the advancement of socialistic ideas and religious freedom. He was assisted by Frances Wright, and the journa was published until 1832, when he returne to New Harmony, soon to begin an activ life in Indiana politics. He was elected t the legislature in 1836, served three term until 1838, and rendered valuable servic to the public school system by securing extr funds from the state for its progress. Dur ing 1843-47 he was a member of Congres and among many other activities sponsore the bill in 1845 establishing the Smithsonia Institution, also serving on the organizatio and building committees, and publishing a this time his book *Hints on Public Architec ture.*

While serving as United States ministe at Naples, 1855-58, he delved deeply int spiritualism and wrote two books to exploi his theories. On his return to America h occupied himself chiefly with the cause o emancipation, and wrote several importan pamphlets and books on this subject. H produced one novel, *Beyond the Breaker.* and an autobiography, *Threading My Wa* but his reputation rests on his valuable p litical pamphleteering. He died at his sum mer retreat on Lake George, N.Y. His tw wives were Mary Jane Robinson, whom h married in 1832, and Lottie Walton Kellog who became his wife five years after hi first wife's death in 1871.

Principal Works: *Political*—The Policy Emancipation, 1863; The Wrong of Slave 1864. *Miscellaneous*—An Outline of the Syste of Education at New Lanark, 1824; Pocahonta An Historical Drama, 1837; Hints on Public Arch tecture, 1849; Divorce: Being a Corresponden Between Horace Greeley and Robert Dale Owe

1860; Footfalls on the Boundary of Another World, 1860; The Debatable Land Between This World and the Next, 1872; Threading My Way, 1874. *Novel*—Beyond the Breakers, 1870.

PAGE, DAVID PERKINS July 4, 1810-January 1, 1848), educator and textbook writer, was born in Epping, N.H., the son of a prosperous but bigoted farmer who, opposing an academy education for his son, kept him on the farm until his sixteenth year, when the boy finally won his consent to attend Hampton Academy in New Hampshire. Leaving there he taught in the local school at Epping, and in Newbury, Mass. By his nineteenth year, he was so imbued with the idea of becoming an educator that he opened a private school in Newburyport. Starting with five pupils, he was swamped with more applicants than he could accomodate by the end of the first term. Two years later he was appointed associate principal of the Newburyport High School, where he remained twelve years. Shortly after his appointment in 1832, he married Susan Maria Lunt.

In 1843, following recommendations of Horace Mann and others prominent in the educational field, he was chosen to fill the position of first principal of the new normal school at Albany, N.Y. Assuming his duties amid the confused circumstances of an unfinished building, he soon organized the school and made a great success of his three years' service, attracting many pupils through his unflagging interest in travelling round the state visiting teachers' institutes and lecturing.

This activity established the school on a firm foundation but so lowered Page's vitality that he succumbed to pneumonia after a brief illness. He contributed one valuable book to the educational field, *The Theory and Practice of Teaching: or, The Motives and Methods of Good School-Keeping* (1847), and prepared a "Normal Chart of Elementary Sounds" for classroom use.

Highly esteemed in the educational world, he rightly takes his place among those educators whose efforts to advance American scholarship earned an enduring reputation. Had he lived longer, Page would undoubtedly have produced other and more important educational works. Rising above the handicap of his scanty early training he not only became a remarkably well-educated man, but molded his character into one which was loved and respected by friends and students.

PRINCIPAL WORKS: The Theory and Practice of Teaching: or, The Motives and Methods of Good School-Keeping, 1847.

ABOUT: Greenwood, J. M. The Life and Work of David P. Page; Huntington, E. A. A Funeral Discourse on David Perkins Page; Phelps, W. F. David P. Page: His Life and Teachings; Daily Albany Argus January 4, 1848.

PAGE, THOMAS NELSON (April 23, 1853-November 1, 1922), story writer and essayist, was born at "Oakland," his ancestral plantation in Hanover County, Va., the son of Major John Page, a planter, an attorney, and later a Confederate officer, and Elizabeth Burwell (Nelson) Page. Two of his great-grandfathers were governors of Virginia, and one was a signer of the Declaration of Independence. His parents were related to each other, and both of them were related to most of the aristocratic families of tidewater Virginia. The Civil War and Reconstruction, however, ruined them financially. It was from this double circumstance of his childhood and youth that Page drew the chief sources of his writing—the romantic glamour of a sentimentalized pre-war South, and the gallantly borne misfortunes of the post-war period.

At Washington College (Washington and Lee University), 1869 to 1872, Robert E. Lee, the president, interested himself personally in young Page, who served as editor of the college magazine. Page then read law at home for a year with his father, and for another year acted as tutor in a family living near Louisville, Ky. He next entered the University of Virginia, received his LL.B. degree in 1874, and settled in Richmond as an attorney. Literature already

Collection of Frederick H. Meserve
THOMAS NELSON PAGE

was a rival of the law; he published dialect verses in *Scribner's Monthly* (later the *Century*) as early as 1877, though it was not until 1884 that the *Century* published his first story, "Marse Chan," which made his reputation.

In 1886 he married Anne Seddon Bruce, who died in 1888. In 1893 he remarried, his second wife being Florence (Lathrop) Field, widow of a Chicagoan but a Virginian by birth. Both marriages were childless. The second Mrs. Page died in 1921.

In 1893 also he definitely abandoned the law for writing, and moved to Washington. Here he lived quietly, lecturing and writing, with occasional trips to Europe, until 1913, when President Wilson appointed him Ambassador to Italy. Page's natural tact and diplomacy did much to bring the United States safely through some very delicate situations in Rome during and after the World War. He became deeply interested in the people and literature of Italy, published an elementary work on Dante, and wrote a life of Jefferson in Italian. He resigned in 1919 and returned to America. His health was failing, and his wife's death two years later was a blow from which he never recovered. He died at the plantation in Virginia where he was born, but was buried in Rock Creek Cemetery in Washington. He had been the recipient of honorary degrees from his two *almae matres* and also from William and Mary, Tulane, Harvard, and Yale, and had received the Grand Cordon of the Italian order of Saints Maurizio and Lazzaro in 1921. He was not, contrary to the popular impression, in any way related to that other author, diplomat, and Southerner, Walter Hines Page.

Thomas Nelson Page was a typical Virginia aristocrat of the old school—in everything but appearance, since he was a chubby, stocky man, with pug nose and "cavalryman's" mustache, looking like a prosperous traveling salesman. Mentally and emotionally, however, as well as by inheritance, he was what his brother's biography calls him —a Virginia gentleman. Quite sincerely, he believed that Virginia before the War was a paradise of benevolent feudalism, with happy, loyal slaves and gallant, kindly masters living in perfect amity. His avowed aim in his writing, especially in his stories, was to heal the breach between North and South by presenting a sympathetic picture of the past, and his success is proved by his enormous contemporary popularity.

Unfortunately, though he was a born writer of romance, his amiable superficiality doomed his work to early forgetting, and it has not lasted. A few of his stories may well become classics of their kind—notably "Marse Chan," "Meh Lady," and "Polly." He is at his best in dialect stories, for he had a keen ear and caught the subtle differences of dialect in various parts of the South and even in various parts of Virginia. His juvenile stories, much prized in their day, have not survived, though *Two Little Confederates* contains much valuable autobiographical material. His non-fiction, including his two sketchy lives of Lee, is outdated, and his poems are unremembered. But he was one of the foremost of the *genre* writers of the South who helped bring about a revival of regionalism in our literature, and undoubtedly he did much to heal the wounds on both sides that followed the Civil War.

Principal Works: *Fiction*—In Ole Virginia, Marse Chan, and Other Stories, 1887; Two Little Confederates (juvenile) 1888; Among the Camps (juvenile 1891; On Newfound River, 1891; Elsket and Other Stories, 1892; Pastime Stories (juvenile) 1894; The Burial of the Guns, 1894; The Old Gentleman of the Black Stock, 1896; Two Prisoners, 1897; Red Rock, 1898; Santa Claus' Partner, 1899; A Captured Santa Claus, 1902; Gordon Keith, 1903; Bred in the Bone, 1905; Under the Crust, 1907; John Marvel, Assistant, 1909; The Red Riders (completed by Rosewell Page) 1924. *Non-Fiction*—Befo' de War (verse, with Armistead Churchill Gordon) 1888; The Old South; Essays Social and Historical, 1892; Social Life in Old Virginia, 1897; The Negro—The Southerner's Problem, 1904; The Coast of Bohemia (verse) 1906; Robert E. Lee: The Southerner, 1908; The Old Dominion—Her Making and Her Manners, 1908; Robert E. Lee: Man and Soldier, 1911; The Land of the Spirit, 1913; Italy and the World War; 1920; Dante and His Influence, 1922.

About: Gordon, A. C. Virginian Portraits; Moses, M. J. The Literature of the South; Page, R. Thomas Nelson Page; Toulmin, H. A. Social Historians; Forum January 1923; Outlook November 15, 1922; Scribner's Magazine January 1923.

PAINE, ROBERT TREAT, JR. (December 9, 1773-November 13, 1811), poet and critic, was born in Taunton, Mass., the second son of Robert Treat Paine, signer of the Declaration of Independence and later attorney-general and justice of the Massachusetts Supreme Court, and Sally (Cobb) Paine, sister of the Revolutionary general, David Cobb. Christened Thomas, he grew to dislike a name identical with that of "The Atheist," and after the death of his elder brother he was in 1801 legally renamed.

The family moved to Boston in 1780, and the boy attended the Latin School, where he led his class. At Harvard, from which he was graduated in 1792, he was dis-

After a portrait by G. Stuart
ROBERT TREAT PAINE, JR.

tinguished for his work in Greek, Latin, and composition, and was appointed to read the valedictory and commencement poems. At once established as a poet, in spite of the disfavor into which he soon fell because of his irregular life, he was thereafter in constant demand on a wide variety of occasions for poems and speeches.

Directly after graduation he found work as a clerk, but neglected business for literary pursuits and the theatre. In October 1794, having given up his clerkship, he edited the *Federal Orrery,* a political paper, but his indolence and lack of judgment, together with his marriage, in February 1795, to an actress, Eliza Baker, soon estranged him from his father and most of his conservative friends. At this time, too, he began to drink and run into debt, but was nevertheless asked, on receiving his second degree from Harvard in June 1795, to read the commencement poem, and in 1797 the Phi Beta Kappa poem. He had meanwhile been employed as master of ceremonies at the Boston Theatre.

In 1798 he was reconciled with his father and was persuaded to study law. For several years all went well. In 1798 his poem, "Adams and Liberty," won nation-wide popularity, and in 1799 a speech on a political occasion brought commendatory letters from Washington and President Adams. In 1801 he received his new name, and in 1802 was admitted to the bar and showed great promise. In the fall of 1803, however, his native weaknesses of character brought about a relapse. He abandoned his practice and all regular occupation. In 1805 he was ill and seemed to lack both moral and physical stamina to recover. He could not complete original literary projects, and despite increasing poverty, though he was paid as much as five dollars a line for his verse, wrote carelessly and only at the last moment material requested for occasions. Some theatrical criticism of 1808 alone shows capacity. With his wife and three children already cared for by relatives, he died, not quite thirty-eight, in his father's attic. The great of Boston came to his funeral; Gilbert Stuart, his eminent contemporary, painted his portrait from a death mask; and the next year his works were brought out with reverence.

The regard in which he was held as a poet was partly due to his eccentricities, interpreted by the uncertain taste of the time as the sign of genius. Though his earlier work showed occasional vigor and evident scholarship, it was imitative and in an outmoded literary fashion; his later work revealed lack of real imagination. His dramatic criticism, for its devotion to the theatre, its care and its definiteness, places him easily in the forefront of the few contemporary critics. The time was not yet ripe, however, to nourish either a cultivated man of the theatre or a poet.

Principal Works: The Works in Verse and Prose of the Late Robert Treat Paine, Jr., 1812.

About: Paine, R. J., Jr. The Works in Verse and Prose of Robert Treat Paine, Jr. (see Introduction by C. Prentiss). Massachusetts Historical Society Proceedings 1925-26.

PAINE, THOMAS (January 29, 1737-June 8, 1809), political and theological writer, was born in Thetford, Norfolk County, England, the son of a Quaker corset maker, Joseph Paine, and his wife Frances (Cocke) Paine, an Anglican, his social superior, eleven years his senior, and "of a sour temper and eccentric character." The boy attended the local grammar school until he was twelve, then was apprenticed to his father's trade of stay or corset making. Five years of this were too much for the adventurous boy, and he ran away to sea, enlisting on the "King of Prussia," a privateer. After one year's voyage, however, he returned to Thetford, and for the next seventeen years led an inconspicuous life in Thetford, Sandwich, Dover, and Lewes. In 1759 he married Mary Lambert, an orphan servant girl, who died the following year. He worked as a stay maker, a teacher, a dissenting preacher, a tobacconist, a grocer. For several years he was an exciseman, like Burns; was

After a portrait by G. Romney
THOMAS PAINE

discharged, reinstated, and discharged again, the ostensible reason being negligence, the actual one leadership in a petition to Parliament to raise the excisemen's meager wages. In 1771 he married Elizabeth Ollive, for what he called "prudential reasons"; whatever these were, the marriage was never consummated, and he and his wife separated, amicably but permanently, in 1774, though she lived to 1808.

This was also the year of Paine's final discharge from the customs service, which forced him into bankruptcy. In London he came to the attention of Benjamin Franklin, then in England on his fruitless errand of trying to persuade the government to yield to growing American demands. Though Paine's formal education had been so slight, he had been a lifelong student, with special interest in science, and it was this which won Franklin's approval of "this ingenious worthy young man." Franklin sent the penniless Paine to Philadelphia, with a letter of recommendation to his son-in-law, Richard Bache.

In America Paine found himself at once. He became editor of the *Pennsylvania Magazine,* and a contributor to its rival, the *Pennsylvania Journal.* In 1776 the first portion of *Common Sense,* to be followed by *The Crisis* with its challenging words to "the Summer soldier and the sunshine patriot," burst on a receptive audience, heartened Washington's despondent army, and anticipated the substance and much of the phrasing of the Declaration of Independence. Moreover, he himself enlisted, and served until in 1777 he was appointed secretary of the Congressional committee on foreign affairs.

Paine seems to have had a genius for bringing disaster on himself by rashness and lack of diplomacy. In the controversy between Congress and Silas Deane, commissioner to France,. he rushed to the defense of Congress and revealed secrets known to him because of his post—which he promptly lost. However, he was soon made clerk of the Pennsylvania Assembly, though he forfeited his much needed salary by going to France in 1781 with John Laurens in a successful mission to secure supplies from France. At the end of the Revolution, he was awarded a farm in New Rochelle by New York and £500 by Pennsylvania, and he settled down in Bordentown, N.J., where he occupied himself chiefly in inventing an iron bridge.

In the interest of this bridge he went abroad in 1787, to find himself very soon embroiled again in politics, this time French instead of American. When Burke attacked the French Revolution, Paine came to its defense with *The Rights of Man.* Mild liberal as he would be considered today, the result was his arrest for treason. William Blake smuggled him out of England before he came to trial, and he went to Paris, where he was promptly declared a French citizen (though he never learned to speak or read French) and where four departments elected him as delegate to the Convention. His friends and his views were Girondist—the reformist, conciliatory, middle-of-the-road party. He voted for exile instead of death for the king. Consequently when the more extreme factions came into power, though he had ceased to attend the Assembly after 1793, his citizenship and Parliamentary immunity were revoked, and he was thrown into Luxembourg Prison. It was there that he wrote the first part of his deistical work, *The Age of Reason.* Gouverneur Morris, American minister to France, refused to help him; Washington, once his grateful friend, neglected him. Finally he was rescued by Monroe and Jefferson. He did not return to America until Jefferson was president.

His last years were passed in poverty, neglect, and contumely. His *Age of Reason* firmly deistic as it was, nevertheless neatly dissected the Bible, to the horror of the pious; his bitter letter to Washington and his friendship with Jefferson made him the target of the Federalists; his befriending of the family of his French friend Gen de Bonneville led to libelous attacks; his carelessness of money, his not unnaturally outraged self-esteem, and a bit of intemperance in his disillusioned old age, exposed him to the vilest assaults upon his character. He died a disappointed outcast, expending his last strength to make sure he was never left alone, lest his enemies spread false stories of his death-bed conversion. Few men have ever been treated so shabbily by those who owe them heavy debts as Thomas Paine was treated by America.

Slowly he is coming into his own, as a man and as a writer. Both politically and religiously, his viewpoint is now so old-fashioned that what once seemed wild rebellion now appears mild reaction. Even his face—long nose, deep eyes, humorous mouth—is the face of another era. But the pungency, force, directness, and clarity of his unadorned style assure him his meed of immortality. Occasionally shrillness creeps in; but the greater part of Paine's writing is in the very best mode of the eighteenth century, and it is free from the pomposity which is that mode's chief defect. Essentially he was an inspired journalist before the days of true journalism. Like Defoe before him, he was a really great newspaper man born before his time; and to the factual persuasiveness of Defoe he adds what Defoe lacked—wit and a turn for the apt phrase. As R. L. Duffus says of him: "He represents in many ways the highest idealism, the deepest faith of the eighteenth century, translated brilliantly into journalistic terms and sustained by a character as unselfish as Washington's own."

Principal Works: The Case of the Officers of Excise, 1772; Common Sense, 1776; The Crisis, 1776-1780; Public Good, 1780; Dissertations on Government, the Affairs of the Bank, and Paper-Money, 1786; The Rights of Man, 1791-1792; The Age of Reason, 1794-1796; Dissertation on First Principles of Government, 1795; Letter to George Washington, 1796; Agrarian Justice, 1797.

About: Best, M. A. Thomas Paine: Prophet and Martyr of Democracy; Bradford, G. Damaged Souls; Conway, M. D. The Life of Thomas Paine; Creel, G. Tom Paine—Liberty Bell; Gould, F. J. Thomas Paine; Pearson, H. Thomas Paine: Friend of Mankind; Remsburg, J. E. Six Historic Americans; Rickman, T. C. Life of Thomas Paine; Sedgwick, E. Thomas Paine; Sherman, A. O. Thomas Paine the Patriot; Smith, F. Thomas Paine: Liberator; Vale, G. Life of Thomas Paine; American Literature January and November 1930, May 1933; Christian Century January 27, 1937; Freeman November 7, 1923; Nation January 30, 1937, February 6, 1937; New York Times Magazine January 24, 1937; Virginia Quarterly Review October 1927.

PALFREY, JOHN GORHAM (May 2, 1796-April 26, 1881), historian, was born in Boston, the son of John Palfrey, a ship chandler who later moved to Louisiana, and Mary (Gorham) Palfrey. His paternal grandfather had been paymaster of the American army during the Revolution. He was educated at Phillips Exeter Academy and Harvard, where he received his B.A. in 1815 and his M.A. in 1818. He was then ordained as a Unitarian minister and succeeded Edward Everett as pastor of Brattle Square Church. He resigned in 1831 to become Dexter Professor of Sacred Literature and dean of the theological faculty at Harvard until 1839. At the same time he began contributing to the *North American Review,* acted as editor in 1825 when Jared Sparks, then editor and his Harvard classmate, was abroad, and in 1835 bought the magazine and conducted it until 1843. In all he contributed 31 articles to it between 1817 and 1859.

Palfrey's versatile mind then turned to politics. In 1842 and 1843 he was in the Massachusetts legislature, from 1844 to 1847 secretary of state of Massachusetts, then in Congress for two years (as an abolitionist), and from 1861 to 1867 postmaster of Boston by Lincoln's appointment. He also lectured widely, and in 1851 edited the *Commonwealth.* In 1823 he had married Mary Ann Hammond, and they had six children, of whom two sons were Union generals in the Civil War; one daughter became a writer. He received honorary degrees from Harvard and from St. Andrew's College, Scotland; he was a member of the American Antiquarian Society, and was twice elected to and twice resigned from the Massachusetts Historical Society—the obscure controversy which caused this being now forgotten.

Palfrey wrote a good deal on theology, but his important work was his history of New England, one of the earliest to give a contemporary social background. It was thorough but dull; partisan toward Massachusetts, the clergy, and the American side in the Revolution; disproportionately political, and quite provincial. Nevertheless it was based on solid research and is still a source-book. Van Wyck Brooks summed Palfrey up well by calling him "a Christian lawyer in theology, and a theologian in literature."

Principal Works: Sermons on Duties Belonging to Some of the Conditions of Private Life, 1834; Elements of Chaldee, Syriac, Samaritan, and Rabbinical Grammar, 1835; Academical Lectures on the Jewish Scriptures and Antiquities, 1838-52; Lowell Lectures on the Evidences of

Christianity, 1843; The Relation Between Judaism and Christianity, 1854; History of New England, 1858-1875 (5th volume 1890).

ABOUT: Brooks, Van W. The Flowering of New England; Proceedings American Antiquarian Society: Vol. 1 (1882); Boston Transcript April 27, 1881.

PALMER, ELIHU (August 7, 1764-April 7, 1806), clergyman and writer of philosophical tracts, was born on a farm at Canterbury, Conn., the son of Elihu and Lois (Foster) Palmer. After his graduation from Dartmouth in 1787 and some subsequent courses in divinity, he wavered between the Presbyterian and Universalist ministries, found his radical deism too much for either, and after a study of law was admitted to the bar in 1793. Shortly afterward his wife died of yellow fever and he himself went blind. He became an independent deistic preacher, settling permanently in New York where he founded a society for the promulgation of his creed, last known as the Society of the Columbian Illuminati; its official organ was the *Temple of Reason,* edited by Dennis Driscol, which was suspended in New York but lasted almost two years in Philadelphia. In December 1803 Palmer, with the aid of his second wife, Mary Powell, set up another weekly, the *Prospect: or, View of the Moral World.*

Politically, he was strongly influenced by the French revolutionists, and he hotly opposed all tyranny in the Federalist-Republican conflict. His religious liberalism was far more embittered and extreme, denouncing all the accepted religions and their founders and condemning the Bible for qualities that "shock all common sense and common honesty."

Besides his textbook of deism, *Principles of Nature: or, A Developement of the Moral Causes of Happiness and Misery Among the Human Species,* he published, anonymously, *The Examiners Examined: Being a Defence of the Age of Reason,* and was the author of numerous articles and orations. He made a small contribution to free thought, but his methods and writings were too confused and fantastic to be permanently effective.

PRINCIPAL WORKS: The Examiners Examined: Being a Defense of the Age of Reason, 1794; An Enquiry Relative to the Moral & Political Improvement of the Human Species, 1797; Principles of Nature: or, A Developement of the Moral Causes of Happiness and Misery Among the Human Species.

ABOUT: Leavitt, E. W. Palmer Groups: Posthumous Pieces . . . to Which are Prefixed a Memoir of Mr. Palmer by His Friend Mr. John Fellows . . . and Mr. Palmer's Principles of the Deistical Society of the State of New York.

PALMER, JOEL (October 4, 1810-June 9, 1881), pioneer and diarist, was born in Ontario, Canada, during a brief residence there of his Quaker parents, Ephraim and Hannah (Phelps) Palmer. They returned to New York State at the commencement of the War of 1812 and young Joel was brought up in Lewis and Jefferson Counties until his sixteenth year when he went to Bucks County, Pa., where he worked on canals and other public projects.

In 1830 he married Catherine Caffee, who soon died, and in 1836 he took as a second wife, Sarah Ann Derbyshire. In the same year he went to Indiana as a contractor for the Whitewater canal. Settling at Laurel, in Franklin County, he soon made a place for himself in local politics, serving as representative in the state legislature from 1843 to 1845.

In 1845 he trekked to Oregon across the plains, keeping a journal of his impressions, which was published in 1847 under the title *Journal of Travels Over the Rocky Mountains,* a book which is still recognized as the only complete written record of pioneering along the old Oregon trail.

After returning to Indiana, in 1847, he made a second trip to Oregon, where he served as commissary-general of the volunteer forces in the Cayuse War and was a member of a commission to persuade neighboring tribes not to join the Cayuse.

Among other activities he laid out the town of Dayton on his property in what is now Yamhill County, built a grist mill, and settled down to improve his fortunes. In the year 1853 he became superintendent of Indian affairs for the Oregon Territory, judiciously obtaining land from the Indians without causing uprisings, and negotiating many treaties of cession. Resenting his consideration for the Indians in carrying out his reservation policy, the settlers caused him to be removed from office in 1857, after which time he was active in state politics, serving as speaker of the house of representatives in 1862 and member of the state senate from 1864 to 1866. In 1870 he unsuccessfully ran for governor on the Republican ticket.

Palmer's other interests included the development of routes to British Columbia gold mines, and promotion of the Clackamas Railroad Company and the Oregon Central Railroad Company. At one time he was president of the Oregon City Manufacturing Company. He died in Dayton.

Although his life was chiefly devoted to business pursuits, and he published but one book, his *Journal* occupies an important place in Americana.

PRINCIPAL WORKS: Journal of Travels Over the Rocky Mountains, 1847.

ABOUT: Lang, H. O. History of the Willamette Valley; Scott, H. W. History of the Oregon Country; Oregon Historical Society Quarterly September 1907, March 1922, September 1930, September 1931; Morning Oregonian (Portland) June 10, 1881.

PALMER, JOHN WILLIAMSON (April 4, 1825-February 26, 1906), editor and miscellaneous writer, was born in Baltimore, Md., the son of Edward and Catherine (Croxall) Palmer and brother of James Croxall Palmer, naval surgeon and writer. After completing a medical course at the University of Maryland in 1846, he joined the gold rush of '49. Arriving in San Francisco in that year entirely without funds, he became the city's first physician and said of himself that he was "introduced to more of the pathos and tragedy . . . than any other person on the spot." After a year's practice he went to Hawaii, and later to the Far East where he served as surgeon in the small East India steamer "Phlegethon" through the second Burmese War, 1851-52.

After a few more years of travel in China and India, he returned to America, settling in New York City. Abandoning medicine, he soon established himself as a writer by frequent contributions to *Harper's, Putnam's,* and the *Atlantic Monthly.* In 1856 his first book, *The Golden Dagon: or, Up and Down the Irrawaddi,* a collection of travel sketches in two volumes, was published, and was quickly followed by others which were well received. Turning to drama, he wrote *The Queen's Heart,* a play which was successfully acted by James E. Owens; and several years later translated Jules Michelet's comedies *L'Amour,* and *La Femme,* and also Ernest Legouvé's *Histoire Morale des Femmes.* Meanwhile, in 1855, he married Henrietta Lee, by whom he had one son.

At the outbreak of the Civil War he was on the staff of the New York *Times.* Sympathizing with the Southern cause, he proposed a series of letters on Southern conditions which the *Times* failed to accept, though the New York *Tribune* later engaged him as correspondent. Taking an active part in the war, he served the Confederate army on the staff of Gen. J. C. Breckinridge, and attracted considerable notice with his ballad, "Stonewall Jackson's Way."

Returning to New York after the war he became much occupied with literary work, serving on the editorial staffs of the *Century* and *Standard* dictionaries, reviewing books for the *Literary Digest,* and writing a number of volumes, including a novel, *After His Kind,* which he published under the pseudonym "John Coventry" in 1886.

His collected verse appeared in 1901 under the title *For Charlie's Sake and Other Lyrics and Ballads.* He died in Baltimore, where he lived after 1904. He was greatly beloved through his exceedingly charming manner. His writings on the South were among his best and mark him as an especially sensitive interpreter of Southern life.

PRINCIPAL WORKS: The Golden Dagon: or, Up and Down the Irrawaddi, 1856; Folk Songs, 1856; The Queen's Heart, 1858; The New and the Old: or, California and India in Romantic Aspects, 1859; Epidemic Cholera, 1866; The Poetry of Compliment and Courtship, 1868; Beauties and Curiosities of Engraving, 1878-79; For Charlie's Sake and Other Lyrics and Ballads, 1901.

ABOUT: Burrage, W. L. & Kelly, H. A. American Medical Biographies; Old Maryland March 1906; Baltimore Sun February 27, 1906.

PALMER, RAY (November 12, 1808-March 29, 1887), Congregational clergyman and hymnologist, was born at Little Compton, R.I., the son of Judge Thomas Palmer and Susanna (Palmer) Palmer. He attended Phillips Academy, Andover, and Yale, graduating in 1830, and for several years taught in New York City and New Haven. Licensed to preach in 1832, he was ordained three years later and settled in Maine, where he officiated at the Congregational Church at Bath from 1835 to 1850, when he moved to Albany. After serving as pastor of the First Congregational Church there for the next sixteen years, he became secretary of the American Congregational Union, a post which he held until 1878.

Besides numerous pamphlets and contributions to religious periodicals, Palmer wrote many prose works of a religious nature, among them *Closet Hours.* He is best known, however, as a hymnologist and stands in the front rank of American writers of that class. The most famous of his hymns was "My Faith Looks Up to Thee," which was translated into many languages.

He died in Newark, where he had lived since 1870 and was occupied with his work in the Bellevue Avenue Church until a paralytic stroke caused his retirement in 1884. Here he was much beloved for his noble character, good works, and benevolence. He had married in 1832 Ann Maria Waud, of Newark.

PRINCIPAL WORKS: *Prose*—Spiritual Improvement: or, Aids to Growth in Grace, 1839 (reprinted as Closet Hours, 1851); Doctrinal Text-Book, 1839; Hints on the Formation of Religious Opinions, 1860; Remember Me, 1865; Earnest Words on True Success in Life, 1873; *Poems*—Home: or, The Unlost Paradise, 1872. *Hymns*—Hymns and Sacred Pieces, 1865; Hymns of My Holy Hours, 1867; The Poetical Works of Ray Palmer, 1876; Voices of Hope and Gladness, 1881.

About: Duffield, S. W. English Hymns: Their Authors and History; Hatfield, E. F. Poets of the Church; Ninde, E. S. The Story of the American Hymn; The Congregational Year Book: 1888; Record of the Graduates of Yale University: 1880-90; The Independent April 7, 14, 1887.

PARK, EDWARDS AMASA (December 29, 1808-June 4, 1900) theologian, was born in Providence, R.I., the son of Calvin and Abigail (Ware) Park. His father was a professor in Brown University and a Congregational minister; and Park, a brilliant student, followed the same calling after his graduation from Brown in 1826 and Andover Theological Seminary in 1831. Ordained the year of his graduation, he became pastor of the Congregational church at Braintree, Mass.

He accepted the chair of philosophy and of Hebrew literature at Amherst College in 1835 and the next year that of Sacred Rhetoric in Andover Seminary. He was made professor of Christian theology in 1847, continuing to teach until 1881, when he was retired as emeritus professor. He was married to Ann Maria Edwards, in 1836.

Park began to contribute to periodicals in 1828 and wrote numerous articles and reviews for Biblical and theological encyclopedias and journals. He became co-editor of the *Bibliotheca Sacra* in 1844; was later editor-in-chief, and remained connected with it until his death. He was associated with Dr. Phelps and Lowell Mason in the compilation of *The Sabbath Hymn Book* and published his *Discourses on Some Theological Doctrines* in 1885. It was during this latter part of his lifetime that Dr. Park was saddened by the controversy over the "new theology" which he opposed.

Dr. Park with his austere good looks, his fine speaking voice, and his vigorous oratory had been accustomed to leadership in the pulpit and classroom; but as a stout adherent of the modified form of Calvinism known as the "New England Theology" he lost much of his influence in his later years. He spent the years after his retirement in Andover, where he died at the age of ninety-two.

In his time Dr. Park exerted a great influence. His sermons were both powerful and polished, and he was a source of inspiration to his pupils; but his works are of slight value today, for his dogmatic theology was old-fashioned even before his death.

Principal Works: Selections From German Literature, 1839; The Theology of the Intellect and of the Feelings, 1850; The Indebtedness of the State to the Clergy, 1851; The Sabbath Hymn Book, 1858; The Atonement: Discourses and Treatises by Edwards, Smalley, Maxcy, Emmons, Griffin, Burge, and Weeks, 1859; Discourses on Some Theological Doctrines, 1885; Memorial Collection of Sermons, 1902.

About: Foster, F. H. A Genetic History of the New England Theology; Mackenzie, A. Memoir of Professor E. A. Park; Parks, F. S. Genealogy of the Parke Families; Storrs, R. S. Memorial Address.

PARKE, JOHN (April 7, 1754-December 11, 1789), poet and soldier, was born at Dover, Del., the son of Thomas and Ann Parke. He was educated at Newark College, and later attended the College of Philadelphia, graduating in 1771. He joined the Continental Army at the beginning of the Revolutionary War and, serving in the quartermaster's department, attained the rank of lieutenant-colonel. Resigning from the army in 1778, he retired to his estate in Delaware where he lived until his death. It is believed that Parke was not married.

His best known book, which he published under the signature, "A Native of America," is *The Lyric Works of Horace . . . to Which Are Added A Number of Original Poems.* The work, in rhymed verse, was a paraphrase substituting American notables for the Roman characters of Horace, and applying the descriptions and allusions of the Roman scene to current American events. The ode celebrating the triumph of the Emperor Augustus for example, was applied to Washington's victorious return to Virginia.

Other than his own work the volume contained poems by some of his friends, among which were some translations by David French from Anacreon's *Odes* and Ovid's *Elegies.* Further works by Parke have been lost and his reputation rests solely on this patriotic adaptation.

Principal Work: The Lyric Works of Horace . . . to Which Are Added A Number of Original Poems, 1786.

About: Ryden, G. H. Letters to and from Caesar Rodney; Scharf, J. T. History of Delaware; Magazine of History: Extra No. 91, 1923.

PARKER, JANE (MARSH) (June 16, 1836-March 13, 1913), columnist and novelist, was born in Milan, N.Y., the daughter of Joseph and Sarah (Adams) Marsh. When she was eight years old she was living in Rochester, N.Y., where she later attended several private schools. Her father, at this time, was the editor of various publications of the Adventist or "Millerite" movement, the fanaticism of which left a morbidly fatalistic strain in the child that did not disappear until she accepted Episcopalian orthodoxy. During her eighteenth year she contributed over twenty-five articles, poems, and tales to the popular periodicals of the day, including the *Waverley* and the *Knickerbocker.*

On August 26, 1856, she was married to George Tann Parker, a Rochester lawyer, and in the ten years that followed she wrote numerous juveniles, the most noteworthy of which was the autobiographical *Barley Wood,* an account of a girl's conversion from sectarianism. In *The Midnight Cry,* however, she drew upon episodes in the Millerite delusion, but failed to utilize some of the materials most familiar to her. She wrote a series of articles on Haiti, following her visit there in 1889, ran the "Spectator" column of the *Atlantic* and the "Contributor's Club" in the *Outlook,* and sent numerous pieces to *Harper's.* Mrs. Parker was active in reform, patriotic, and religious activities. Her literary reputation rests largely on the casual papers that she prepared for the *Outlook* and the *Atlantic.*

PRINCIPAL WORKS: Barley Wood, 1860; The Midnight Cry, 1886.

ABOUT: LeMénager, M. The Life and Works of Jane Marsh Parker: 1836-1913 (monograph in George Washington University library); Los Angeles Times March 14, 1913.

PARKER, SAMUEL (April 23, 1779-March 21, 1866), Congregational clergyman, missionary, and author of the *Journal of an Exploring Tour Beyond the Rocky Mountains,* was born at Ashfield, Mass. He was the son of Elisha Parker and Thankful (Marchant) Parker. Graduated from Williams College in 1806 and from Andover Theological Seminary in 1810, he became a missionary in western New York and subsequently preached in New York and Massachusetts.

His work as a missionary for the American Board of Commissioners for Foreign Missions in Oregon helped to establish the claims of the United States to that territory and furthered the settlement of that egion. The American Board, although anxious to establish missions for the Indians in Oregon, was not too ready at first to accept Parker, who they felt was neither young nor vigorous enough to accept such an arduous commission. They feared, too, that Parker, with his lack of tact in handling others, might, despite his sincerity and capability, arouse antagonism.

In 1835, however, with Dr. Marcus Whitman as companion, he went to Liberty, Mo., where the two joined the American Fur Company caravan, traveling as far as the agreed meeting place with the tribes on the Green River. Here Parker set out with his Indian guides, and Whitman returned to enlist more missionaries.

Parker explored the country and shrewdly chose the bases for the missions. His relations with the Indians were friendly and his estimation of the possibilities of Oregon helped advance the colonization of that territory. In September 1836 he left Oregon, visited the Hawaiian Islands and sailed around the Horn to New London, arriving May 1837. The following year his only book, a valuable record of missionary pioneering, was published.

He was married twice: first to Miss N. Sears, and later, in 1815, to Jerusha Lord, a niece of Noah Webster.

PRINCIPAL WORK: Journal of an Exploring Tour Beyond the Rocky Mountains, 1838.

ABOUT: Eells, M. Marcus Whitman: Pathfinder and Patriot; Smith, C. W. A Contribution Toward a Bibliography of Marcus Whitman; The Church At Home and Abroad March 1895.

PARKER, THEODORE (August 24, 1810-May 10, 1860), preacher and reformer, was born in Lexington, Mass., eleventh child of John Parker, farmer and mechanic, and Hannah (Stearns) Parker; his grandfather was John Parker, commander of the minute men at Lexington. The boy was precocious and fun-loving, but kept busy at the farm, his formal education amounting to less than forty months. At seventeen he began teaching, and at twenty enrolled at Harvard, passing all examinations without attendance. Entering Harvard Divinity School in 1834, he was graduated in 1836, and in 1837 was ordained pastor of the Unitarian congregation of West Roxbury, near Boston. In the same year he married Lydia Cabot, a woman whose intellect did not match his, but whose affections did.

The young man who, in his voracious reading, had already felt the influence of Transcendental philosophy, soon joined the Transcendental Club, contributing to its organ, the *Dial,* 1840-44. In the controversy between the liberal and conservative Unitarian ministers of the time, Parker's clear, fearless, and often harsh assertions earned him cordial hate. Of simple, direct religious faith, he delivered a series of lectures in

Collection of Frederick H. Meserve
THEODORE PARKER

Boston, 1841-42, that make up the remarkable *Discourse of Matters Pertaining to Religion.*

Refusing to resign from the Boston Association of Ministers and only confirmed in his faith in his mission by a year's travel abroad, 1843-44, he welcomed in 1845 the opportunity to preach an enlightened liberalism in Boston to the newly organized Twenty-Eighth Congregational Society, which eventually reached a membership of 7,000. Here Parker, who believed a Christian church should be active in reforming the world, discussed social and political questions as well as theology and religion—war, prisons, divorce, education, American statesmen, poverty, and, inevitably, slavery.

Fully aroused by the passage of the Fugitive Slave Law in 1850, he gave up his plan to write a book, "The Development of Religion," and became chairman of the Executive Committee of the Vigilance Committee; hid slaves in his own house; was arrested, with Wendell Phillips and others, for complicity in assisting the slave Anthony Burns; dispatched emigrants to Kansas; was on a secret committee that aided John Brown; wrote hundreds of letters to political leaders; and meanwhile lectured, for he had further extended his audience by giving lyceum talks, preached, and attended to his many pastoral duties.

Such activity, combined with a tendency to tuberculosis, brought on illness, first in 1857, then a severe hemorrhage in January 1859. In February, with his wife and a few friends, he sailed for Vera Cruz, and in June for Europe. He died in Florence at forty-nine and is buried there.

"The most honest, the most sensible, and the most courageous preacher the American pulpit has ever had," Parker exerted a many-sided influence. As a theologian he prepared the way for later liberal criticism, and his "radical" views were eventually accepted by his church. As a reformer his accomplishments in the anti-slavery struggle rank high. His library of 16,000 books, bequeathed to the Boston Public Library, testifies to the background of his scholarship. As a preacher his influence was perhaps greatest. His sermons, written to be heard, are too redundant and exuberant to stand the test of literature, but nevertheless display an admirable massing of facts, a power of copious illustration, a constant homely appreciation of beauty and joy of life, and for "the high contagion of a faith so pure and bold" are still of interest to students of religion.

Principal Works: Theodore Parker's Works (14 vols.) 1863-70 (centenary edition, 15 vols. 1907-11).

About: Chadwick, J. W. Theodore Parker: Preacher and Reformer; Commager, H. S. Theodore Parker; Weiss, J. Life and Correspondence of Theodore Parker; American Mercury January 1927.

PARKMAN, FRANCIS (September 16, 1823-November 8, 1893), historian, was the oldest of the six children of the Rev. Francis Parkman, a Unitarian minister, and Caroline (Hall) Parkman. An inheritance from his paternal grandfather, a merchant, enabled him to devote his life to literature. He was a frail child and spent part of his early years with his maternal grandfather in Medford; at twelve he returned to Boston and prepared for Harvard at the advanced (for the times) Chauncy-Hall School. His college career was interrupted by illness and a consequent trip to Europe, but he secured his B.A. in 1844 and his LL.B. in 1846. He never intended to practice law, however, and was never admitted to the bar. Already he was interested in the Indians, and had mapped out his scheme to write "the history of the American forest." But his first published writing was a series of sketches on his European tour, in the *Knickerbocker Magazine* in 1845.

In 1846 Parkman made his famous journey on the Oregon Trail, living for months with and in the manner of the Indians. He brought back all the material for his first and what many consider his greatest work. It is usual also to say that this journey was the root of the invalidism which wasted his entire later life. It probably had nothing to do with it; the trouble seems to have been more a neurosis than a functional disorder. He was unable to bear light, could open his eyes only in darkness, and exhibited half a dozen other highly suggestive symptoms. Freud not yet having been born, the doctors did the best they could with Parkman, which was nothing at all. He himself, with undaunted courage, invented a machine to write legibly without sight, dictated most of his work, and at the rate of six lines a day, completed, by 1851, his *Conspiracy of Pontiac,* first of the series of books intended to depict the struggle between the French and English in America, including the part played by the Indians. The series was gradually written in sequence, except that *Montcalm and Wolfe* anticipated its chronological order because Parkman wanted to write this climax, and was afraid he might die before he got to it.

Meanwhile, able to write only under such difficulties, he developed a new profession; he became a horticulturist in West Roxbury, raised flowers, made new varieties, for a year was partner in a flower-selling business which failed, and in 1871 and 1872 was professor of horticulture at the Bussey Institution, Harvard. His book on roses was long a standard text; he was president of the Massachusetts Horticultural Society, and as proud of that honor as of his vice presidency of the Massachusetts Historical Society or his fellowship in the American Academy of Arts and Sciences or membership in the Royal Historical Society of Great Britain. As a matter of fact, his books sold very badly, in spite of their spreading reputation, and he was obliged, even with a private fortune, to find other means of adding to his income. In 1850 he had married Catherine Scollay Bigelow, who died in 1858, together with their son, leaving two small daughters. He supported them, but sent them to Mrs. Parkman's relatives, while he lived with his own. It was at this time, in the severest of his mental and nervous crises, that Parkman went to Paris to consult the famous Brown-Sèquard, and was told that he might live six months. He lived thirty-five years, and continued to write until a few months before his death. He finally died, not of his nervous disorder, but of peritonitis.

Parkman was condemned by his constitution and the state of medical science in his day to live as a semi-invalid, but he was never a recluse. He was overseer of Harvard from 1868 to 1871 and from 1874 to

FRANCIS PARKMAN
1882

1876, a fellow of the corporation of Harvard from 1875 to 1888, and one of the founders of the Archaeological Institute of America in 1879. Besides his books, he wrote frequent magazine articles, mostly for the *Atlantic* or the *North American Review.* He even wrote a novel, though not a very good one, as he himself realized. There was plenty of the spirit left of the boy who had been an athlete, the young man who had eaten and slept and hunted with the Sioux. Behind his queer lopsided face, with its jutting chin, long nose, and deep-set little eyes, there was the soul of an artist. For Parkman more than most historians was essentially a producer of literature. He had wanted "to paint the forest and its tenants in true and vivid colors," to "imbue himself with the life and spirit of the time," and though he was one of the earliest writers of American history to undertake the critical use of original sources and documents, he never lost sight of the living quality in his subject. It is easy to find minor fault with Parkman—his neglect of the economic background, the episodic, fragmentary character of his treatment; but he laid a grand foundation, and it is hard to think of any history of the Northwest that does not depend on *The Oregon Trail,* or of Canada and the French Middlewest that does not have behind it the volumes from *The Conspiracy of Pontiac* to *A Half Century of Conflict.* And he has one other glory: he was the first American writer not to glorify or romanticize the Indians, but actually to understand them and describe them as they were. He accomplished the purpose of his boyhood plans.

Principal Works: The California and Oregon Trail, 1849; History of the Conspiracy of Pontiac and the Indian War of Conquest in Canada, 1851; Vassall Morton (novel) 1856; Pioneers of France in the New World, 1865; The Book of Roses, 1866; The Jesuits in North America in the 17th Century, 1867; The Discovery of the Great West, 1869 (as LaSalle and the Discovery, etc., 1879); The Old Régime in Canada, 1874; Count Frontenac and New France Under Louis XIV, 1877; Montcalm and Wolfe, 1884; A Half Century of Conflict, 1892.

About: Brooks, Van W. The Flowering of New England; Farnham, C. H. A Life of Francis Parkman; Sedgwick, H. D. Francis Parkman; Atlantic Monthly May 1894; Bookman July 1897; Century Magazine November 1892; Nation October 10, 1923; North American Review October 1923; Boston Transcript November 9, 1893.

"PARLEY, PETER." See GOODRICH SAMUEL GRISWOLD

PARSONS, THOMAS WILLIAM (August 18, 1819-September 3, 1892), poet, was born in Boston, the son of Thomas William Parsons, M.D., who acted as a dentist as well as a physician, and Asenath (Read) Parsons. He was educated at the Boston Latin School, but was not graduated. After a tour to Europe in 1836, most of it spent in Italy, where he first conceived his lifelong passion for Dante, he entered Harvard Medical School. He never received a degree, but was always called "Dr. Parsons" and for years practiced dentistry in Boston and, in the early 'fifties, in London. He may possibly have taken some dental courses at some unknown school in Boston in 1844, professional requirements being much more lax at that time than now. In 1857 he married Hannah or Anna M. Allen; he had by this time returned permanently to America, and divided his time among Boston, Wayland, and Scituate. After 1872 he ceased to practice, and spent all his time in writing. He died at his sister's home in Scituate, having suffered a stroke of apoplexy and fallen in a well; his body was discovered hours later, the actual cause of death being drowning.

THOMAS WILLIAM PARSONS

Parsons, the original of the "Poet" in Longfellow's *Tales of a Wayside Inn,* was a strange, melancholy creature, sensitive and shy to the point of morbidity, a solitary by nature, yet capable of witty topical verse for such occasions as the opening of a theatre, and much in demand among the very few who knew him. His poetry was nearly all religious—he was a devout Episcopalian of the High Church faction—and as Van Wyck Brooks says, was "graceful and correct, . . . written in taste but quite devoid of magic." It has a certain facile felicity and a rather hollow nobility, best savored in such excerpts as "On a Bust of Dante" and "The Shadow of the Obelisk."

But it was as the worshipper and translator of Dante that Parsons was destined to live, if at all. He was actually the first American translator of any of the *Divine Comedy,* his translation of the first ten cantos of the *Inferno* appearing in 1843, twenty-four years before Longfellow's. He learned the entire *Inferno, Purgatorio,* and *Paradiso* by heart—a task that makes the head reel—and translated them from memory. But his way of work was so peculiar—he wrote and rewrote with infinite care, constantly altering words or changing stanzas even after publication, but was utterly careless as to where his work appeared, and scattered it in newspapers, obscure magazines, badly printed pamphlets, or books whose printing was paid for by himself—that he never received recognition for his really pioneer work. His translation of Dante is uninspired, but it is faithful, and it is an expression of a devotion such as few authors have received. Indeed, in Parsons' long, lean figure, in his long head and deep eyes and aquiline nose, one may almost fancy, in spite of the shaggy eyebrows and the wispy mustache, a certain physical resemblance to his idol. Certainly they were akin in nature—of the same type, however far apart in degree. Anyone less fitted than

Parsons for that most extroverted of professions, dentistry, it is hard to imagine. In feeling, if not in ability, he was born to be what his friend Longfellow named him—"the Poet."

PRINCIPAL WORKS: *Translations*—first ten Cantos of the Inferno, 1843; The Inferno, 1867; The Divine Comedy, 1893. *Poetry*—Poems, 1854; Ghetto di Roma, 1854; The Magnolia, 1866; The Shadow of the Obelisk, 1872; The Willey House and Sonnets, 1875; Poems, 1893.

ABOUT: Parsons, T. W. Poems, 1893 (see Introductions by I. Guiney and E. C. Stedman); Atlantic Monthly February 1893, June 1894; Century July 1894, October 1901; Critic September 10, 17, 1892; Boston Transcript September 6, 1892.

"PARTINGTON, MRS." See SHILLABER, BENJAMIN PENHALLOW

PARTON, JAMES (February 9, 1822-October 17, 1891), biographer and miscellaneous writer, was born at Canterbury, England, the son of James and Ann (Leach) Parton. Brought to the United States in 1827, James received his education in the New York City schools and attended an academy in White Plains, N.Y. He taught there and in Philadelphia for several years, until in 1848 he became an underpaid assistant to Nathaniel Parker Willis, editor of the New York *Home Journal* and brother of Sara Payson Willis [*q.v.*], "Fanny Fern" the journalist, whom Parton was to marry in 1856.

His first published work was the result of a remark to the Mason brothers, publishers, that the life of Horace Greeley would make an interesting story. When asked why he did not do it himself, Parton cited the time and money needed for such an undertaking. The publishers offered to advance the funds, and after eleven months of intensive work the book appeared. It was so well received and the monetary returns were so satisfactory that Parton devoted himself assiduously to writing from that time on, turning out an enormous number of works, among them his famous biographies of Burr, Jackson, and Franklin. That Parton's tastes were catholic is evident in the subjects of his other books, ranging from *Le Parnasse Français,* a book of French poetry, and a work on *Caricature and Other Comic Art* to his articles on smoking and drinking, habits which he strongly deplored.

In 1875, three years after the death of his first wife, Parton moved to Newburyport, where on February 3, 1876, he was married to his step-daughter, Ellen Willis

Collection of Frederick H. Meserve
JAMES PARTON

Eldredge. He lived here until his death, a popular and influential member of the community.

Parton's biographies, the most important of his works, were the result of painstaking research into every possible source of information. He was a courageous biographer, always unprejudiced, and did not unduly minimize the faults or extol the virtues of his heroes. If he did not probe deeply into the characters of his subjects, he at least made them come alive.

PRINCIPAL WORKS: The Life of Horace Greeley, 1855; The Humorous Poetry of the English Language From Chaucer to Saxe, 1856; The Life and Times of Aaron Burr, 1857; Life of Andrew Jackson, 1859-60; General Butler in New Orleans, 1863; Life and Times of Benjamin Franklin, 1864; Life of John Jacob Astor, 1865; Manual for the Instruction of "Rings": Railroad and Political, 1866; How New York is Governed, 1866; Famous Americans of Recent Times, 1867; People's Book of Biography, 1868; Smoking and Drinking, 1868; The Danish Islands: Are we Bound in Honor to Pay for Them? 1869; Topics of the Time, 1871; Triumphs of Enterprise, Ingenuity, and Public Spirit, 1871; Words of Washington, 1872; Fanny Fern: A Memorial Volume, 1873; Life of Thomas Jefferson, 1874; Caricature and Other Comic Art in All Times and Many Lands, 1877; Le Parnasse Français, 1877; Life of Voltaire, 1881; Noted Women of Europe and America, 1883; Captains of Industry, 1884; Some Noted Princes, Authors, and Statesmen of Our Time, 1885.

ABOUT: Beers, H. A. Nathaniel Parker Willis; Currier, J. J. Ould Newbury; McClure's Magazine, June 1893; New England Magazine, January 1893; Outlook, September 16, 1911; Writer, November 1891; Boston Transcript, October 20, 1891; Critic, October 24, 1891; New York Tribune, October 18, 1891.

PARTON, SARA PAYSON (WILLIS) ("Fanny Fern") (July 9, 1811-October 10, 1872), essayist and writer of juvenile literature, was born in Portland, Maine, the daughter of Nathaniel Willis, an anti-Federalist editor, and Hannah (Parker) Willis, and sister of Nathaniel Parker Willis [*q.v.*]. Her family settled in Boston when she was a small child, and after attendance at Catharine Beecher's school in Hartford, where she impressed her superiors with a wilfulness and a complete lack of academic application, Sara wrote a few pieces for the *Youth's Companion,* of which her father was the publisher. In 1837 she was married to Charles H. Eldredge, who died about nine years afterward. She now began to write in earnest—for the support of her two children. "The Model Minister," signed by "Fanny Fern," was published in a Boston home magazine, bringing her only fifty cents in money but opening up a lively market for her essays.

In 1849 she was married to Samuel P. Farrington, from whom she was probably divorced; in 1856 she married James Parton [*q.v.*], a member of the *Home Journal* (New York) staff, who, incidentally, was later one of the first Easterners to make himself audible concerning "an author named Mark Twain." Three years earlier, with the publication of *Fern Leaves From Fanny's Portfolio,* she had "arrived" as a writer of light essays. For the last fifteen years of her life she was connected with the New York *Ledger,* and, at the same time, contributed to several other papers. Her every-day subject matter for these essays was flavored with common sense, sentiment, and justifiable satire, and ably filled the demands of the "man in the street." Besides *Ruth Hall,* a novel with a very unflattering portrait of her brother, and another novel, *Rose Clark,* she wrote several juveniles and *Caper-Sauce: A Volume of Chit-Chat About Men, Women, and Things.* The strength of her writings lay largely in their timeliness, and it is only as casual and often unimportant comment on society that they retain any value.

PRINCIPAL WORKS: Fern Leaves From Fanny's Portfolio: first and second series, 1853 and 1854; Ruth Hall, 1855; Rose Clark, 1856; Fresh Leaves, 1857; A New Story Book for Children, 1864; Folly as it Flies, 1868; Caper-Sauce: A Volume of Chit-Chat About Men, Women, and Things, 1872.

ABOUT: Parton, J. Fanny Fern: A Memorial Volume; New York Daily Tribune October 11, 1872.

"PASQUIN, ANTHONY." See WILLIAMS, JOHN

PASTORIUS, FRANCIS DANIEL (September 26, 1651-c. January 1, 1720), lawyer, poet, and miscellaneous writer, founder of Germantown, Pa., was born in Sommerhausen, Franconia, Germany, the son of Melchior Adam Pastorius and his wife Magdalena Dietz. Pastorius was educated at the Windsheim Gymnasium and the University of Altdorf, where he majored in law and philosophy. He also attended the universities of Strassburg, Basel, and Jena, returning to Altdorf to take the degree of J.D. in 1676. He entered upon the practice of law at Windsheim but after three years moved to Frankfort where he acquired his first knowledge of the Society of Friends. Deeply religious and very much attracted by the ideas of the sect, Pastorius left for America in 1683 as agent for a group of Frankfort Quakers, to buy land in Pennsylvania for a colony. Arriving in Philadelphia on August 20 of that same year, Pastorius bought from William Penn about 15,000 acres and in October began to lay out Germantown.

Pastorius married Ennecke Klostermanns in 1688. He was a man of great influence among the colonists and held many positions of importance until his death. He was the first mayor of Germantown, a member of the Assembly in 1687 and 1691, and taught for many years in Germantown and Philadelphia. He was a prolific writer and although he published only six books, he left several volumes in manuscript, containing poems, philosophical reflections, and notes on theological, medical, and legal subjects.

Pastorius was a renowned scholar and linguist, and was not only adept in seven languages but versed as well in science, medicine, and the law. His book *A New Primmer or Methodical Directions to Attain the True Spelling, Reading & Writing of English* was probably the first textbook of Pennsylvania schools. He published a pamphlet containing a description of the commonwealth and its government, and advice to emigrants, which is his most important work. His contributions as a pioneer and founder of Germantown were of more importance than his slender literary output.

PRINCIPAL WORKS: Four Boasting Disputers of This World Briefly Rebuked, 1697; Umständige Georgraphische Beschreibung Der zu Allerletzt erfundenen Provintz Pensylvaniae (Frankfort and Leipzig) 1700; A New Primmer or Methodical Directions to Attain the True Spelling, Reading, & Writing of English.

ABOUT: Learned, M. D. The Life of Francis Daniel Pastorius (in German American Annals, 1907-08); Pennypacker, S. W. The Settlement of Germantown (Proceedings of the Pennsylvania-

German Society, 1899); Seidensticker, O. The First Century of German Printing in America: 1728-1830.

PATTEN, SIMON NELSON (May 1, 1852-July 24, 1922), economist and miscellaneous writer, was born at Sandwich, De Kalb County, Ill., the son of William and Elizabeth Nelson (Pratt) Patten. He was educated in the local school and at Jennings Seminary, Aurora, graduating in 1874. The following year he entered Northwestern University, but soon left for Germany where he attended the University of Halle and received his degree of Ph. D. in 1878.

After his return to America, he taught in the public schools of Illinois and Iowa until the publication of his work, *The Premises of Political Economy,* in 1885. Three years later, owing to the reputation gained through his book, Patten was appointed to the chair of political economy at the University of Pennsylvania; a position which he held until 1917, five years before his death at Brown's-Mills-in-the-Pines, N.J. He was married to Charlotte Kimball, in 1903, and divorced six years later.

Patten, who retained all of his life the awkwardness and gaucherie of his provincial upbringing, was transformed when in the class-room into a powerful and brilliant teacher. A man of intense personal magnetism, he was an enormous influence in the rapidly increasing interest in political economy. Besides his books on that subject, Patten wrote some verse and a novel, *Mud Hollow,* but the impetus that he gave to the study of economic problems was his most important contribution to his country.

Principal Works: The Premises of Political Economy, 1885; The Development of English Thought, 1899; The New Basis of Civilization, 1907; Folk Love, 1919; Mud Hollow, 1922; Essays in Economic Theory, 1924.

About: Nearing, S. Educational Frontiers; American Economic Review March 1923 Supplement; Annuals American Academy of Political and Social Sciences May 1923; Public Ledger (Phila.) April 6, 1917; Philadelphia Record, July 25, 1922.

PATTIE, JAMES OHIO (1804-1850?), trapper and diarist, was born in Bracken County, Ky., the son of Sylvester Pattie. The younger Pattie's sole publication, *Personal Narrative* (1831), is the only sizable biographical source. According to this, his family removed to Missouri when he was eight years old, and in July 1824 he and his father joined Silvestre Pratte's Santa Fé expedition, which reached its destination on November 5. The two Patties spent several years trapping, and in 1828, with six others, proceeded to Santa Catalina Mission; they were arrested, taken to San Francisco, and were subjected to extreme maltreatment, climaxed by the elder Pattie's death in prison on April 24. The son was released, and made his way first to Mexico City and then to Cincinnati (August 1830).

Of his last years there is only a scant and hypothetical record, suggesting that he attended Augusta College (Ohio), made his home in nearby Dover for a while, and in 1849 joined the Argonauts, and spent some time in San Diego.

Personal Narrative was later plagiarized under the title of *Hunters of Kentucky* (1847), professing to be a record of one B. Bilson. Pattie's book was edited (and possibly largely written) by Timothy Flint; it is highly inaccurate in many important details and misleading in its implications; but regarded as a semi-fictional record of an era in American history which is filled with paradoxes and discrepancies, it is a rousing piece of frontier literature.

About: Cleland, R. G. A History of California: The American Period; Wagner, H. R. The Plains and the Rockies; California Historical Society Quarterly April 1923.

"PAUL, JOHN." See WEBB, CHARLES HENRY

PAULDING, JAMES KIRKE (August 22, 1778-April 6, 1860), novelist, poet, and miscellaneous writer, was born at Great Nine Partners, Dutchess (now Putnam) County, N.Y., the eighth of nine children of William and Catharine (Ogden) Paulding. His father, a Tarrytown merchant, was ruined by pledging his entire fortune to the Revolution, and his mother supported the family by sewing. She also gave them all the education they had except what they themselves acquired in later life by reading. James Paulding had practically no schooling, but in 1824 Columbia gave him an honorary M.A.

In 1797 the boy went to New York. His sister had married William Irving, Washington Irving's brother, and the Irvings became his closest friends. While he worked in an office, he collaborated with them on the famous satirical *Salmagundi,* in 1807 and 1808, and also contributed to Peter Irving's *Morning Chronicle,* and wrote sketches of naval commanders of the War of 1812 for the *Analectic Magazine.* In 1815 his *The United States and England,* a riposte to a savage British review of his verse satire, *The Lay of the Scottish Fiddle,* came to the attention of President Madison,

Collection of Frederick H. Meserve
JAMES KIRKE PAULDING

who appointed him secretary of the Board of Navy Commissioners. From 1815 to 1823, while he held this post, he lived in Washington. In 1818 he married Gertrude Kemble.

In 1824 President Monroe appointed Paulding navy agent for New York, and he served until 1838, when, a good deal against his will, he became Secretary of the Navy in Van Buren's cabinet. He was meanwhile writing steadily, and in 1831 his play, *The Lion of the West,* won a prize offered by James Hackett for an American comedy. At the end of Van Buren's term, in 1841, he traveled through the West with the ex-president, his close friend. Mrs. Paulding had died a few months previously and he was in poor health as well. He retired permanently to Hyde Park, where he lived with his children to a ripe and comfortable old age. After 1849 he ceased even to write except for letters and casual sketches, but he retained his faculties to the last. He was buried in Greenwood Cemetery, Brooklyn. A tall, dark man, in later life completely bald, Paulding was a striking figure, and in youth a handsome one as well.

Today he is forgotten as a writer, though he was almost the father of realistic fiction in America. What he called "rational fiction" was his aim in all his later novels, and he detested the bombast and inflated rhetoric which were the vice of the early nineteenth century. His best work was in his *genre* pictures of the Dutch of New Amsterdam, though he ranged widely over the American landscape and American history. An aggressive patriotism which amounted to Anglophobia was his other most distinguishing characteristic; all his life he rejoiced in twisting the lion's tail, and he had none of the urbanity of his friend Irving. He fancied himself as a poet, but even in his lifetime his friends tried to dissuade him from wasting his talents for fiction on inferior verse. He was a hasty and too prolific writer, yet at his best he had wit, genuine humor, and a natural, simple style. A writer who was praised by Poe, who influenced Hawthorne, and whom Cooper regarded as a rival, is not to be dismissed as negligible, even if his work has long ago been superseded. He helped to create an autochthonous literature in this country, and left his mark on posterity through others if not through his own work. Until Irving wrote his biography of Washington, Paulding's was the standard work. His *Dutchman's Fireside* and *Koningsmarke* are first-rate historical novels and were translated into several languages. Those interested in the *curiosa* of literature may want to know that in the latter novel occurs the celebrated tongue-twister, "Peter Piper picked a peck of pickled peppers," etc.

PRINCIPAL WORKS: The Diverting History of John Bull and Brother Jonathan, 1812; The Lay of the Scottish Fiddle: A Tale of Havre de Grace (verse) 1813; The United States and England, 1815; Letters From the South: By a Northern Man, 1817; The Backwoodsman (verse) 1818; A Sketch of Old England: By a New England Man, 1822; Koningsmarke: or, The Long Finne, 1823; John Bull in America: or, The New Munchausen, 1825; The Merry Tales of the Three Wise Men of Gotham, 1826; New Mirrors for Travelers, 1828; Tales of the Good Woman, 1829; The Dumb Girl, 1830; Chronicles of the City of Gotham, 1830; The Dutchman's Fireside, 1831; Westward Ho! 1832; Life of Washington, 1835; Slavery in the United States, 1836; The Book of St. Nicholas, 1837; A Gift from Fairy Land, 1838; The Old Continental: or, The Price of Liberty, 1846; The Puritan and His Daughter, 1849.

ABOUT: Herold, A. L. James Kirke Paulding, Versatile American; Irving, P. M. Life and Letters of Washington Irving; Parrington, V. L. Main Currents in American Literature; Paulding, W. I. Literary Life of James Kirke Paulding.

"PAXTON, PHILIP." See HAMMETT, SAMUEL ADAMS

PAYNE, JOHN HOWARD (June 9, 1791-April 9, 1852), actor, playwright, and editor, best remembered as the author of "Home Sweet Home," was born in New York City, the sixth of nine children of William Payne, a schoolmaster, and Sarah (Isaacs) Payne. He was precocious, at fourteen, while employed as a clerk, editin in his spare hours the *Thespian Mirror,* a weekly dramatic paper of such merit that friends raised money to send him to Union College. After two terms he left, using the bankruptcy of his father as an excuse to turn to his first love, acting, in 1809 making a tremendous sensation as Young Norval in Home's tragedy, *Douglas.* His later acting career in this country was not successful, and in 1813, with the financial help of friends, he sailed for England. There he won moderate esteem over a period of several years.

He had already written two plays, produced in this country, and in 1814, while waiting for acting engagements, translated a French melodrama that saw successful production at the Covent Garden Theatre. In 1818-19 his adaptation *Brutus,* a history, at the Drury Lane, re-established the fortunes of Edmund Kean the actor, and made the reputation, if not the fortune, of Payne. In 1820 he leased the Sadler's Wells Theatre, went to prison for debts incurred, and wrote himself free with another adaptation, *Thérèse,* a highly successful melodrama. Thereafter, except for the editing of a literary and dramatic weekly, the *Opera Glass,* 1826-27, discontinued because of an illness, Payne devoted himself to the routine of translating and adapting, frequently living in Paris as scout for current productions and to escape creditors in London. During a comparatively prosperous period in Paris, in 1823, he wrote "Home Sweet Home," as the theme song of the opera *Clari,* prepared for Charles Kemble the actor, then manager of the Covent Garden. Since Payne always sold his plays outright, he realized no additional profit from the popularity of his soon world-famous song. The same summer he worked with his lifelong friend, Washington Irving, the outstanding result of their collaboration being the popular *Charles II,* a comedy. At about this time Payne courted, unsuccessfully, Mary Wollstonecraft Shelley, widow of the poet.

In 1832, discouraged by small financial returns after years of hard work—he had written more than sixty plays since 1814—Payne sailed for home. Here he was fêted, and close to $10,000 was raised for him in benefits. His subsequent literary work was a number of articles and projects for books and an international literary magazine. Play writing he did not continue, since American managers could get English plays for nothing, the international copyright not then existing.

Through the influence of friends, among them Daniel Webster, then Secretary of State, he was appointed consul at Tunis in 1842, but lost the post in 1845 with a change of administration. He was re-appointed in 1851, and the following year died in Morocco and was buried there. In 1883 his remains were brought home and reinterred in Oak Hill Cemetery, Washington, D.C.

Collection of Frederick H. Meserve
JOHN HOWARD PAYNE

Payne is important as one of the first American writers to win recognition abroad. Not an original playwright, as a reshaper of other men's work he was extremely competent, his plays showing sound knowledge of the theatre, with well-built scenes, rapid action and easy dialogue. He consciously wrote to sell, for the moment, yet several of his plays held the boards for decades. His journalistic and critical work, characterized by the charm that endeared him to many, is of interest only historically. "Home Sweet Home," set to the air which Payne himself suggested to the composer, Sir Henry Bishop, will probably continue to live.

Principal Works: *Plays*—Brutus: or, The Fall of Tarquin, 1818; Thérèse: The Orphan of Geneva, 1821; Clari: or, The Maid of Milan, 1823; Charles II: or, The Merry Monarch, 1824; Richelieu: A Domestic Tragedy, 1826.

About: Chiles, R. P. John Howard Payne; Harrison, G. Life and Writings of John Howard Payne; Moses, M. J. Representative American Plays; Quinn, A. H. A History of the American Drama From the Beginning to the Civil War.

PEABODY, ANDREW PRESTON (March 19, 1811-March 10, 1893), Unitarian clergyman, editor, and professor, was born in Beverly, Mass., the son of Andrew and Mary (Rantoul) Peabody. He could read at the age of three, was graduated from Harvard when he was fifteen, and two years later became principal of an academy at Portsmouth, N.H. In 1832 he was graduated from Harvard Divinity School and in October of the following year was ordained, first assisting Dr. Nathan Parker, pastor of the South Parish Unitarian church in Portsmouth. On Parker's death, a few weeks later, Peabody assumed full charge and served the parish for twenty-seven years, executing the duties of a conservative clergyman and carrying on literary activities with the *Whig Review* and *North American Review,* of which he was editor and proprietor for half a decade. On September 12, 1836, he was married to Catherine Whipple Roberts.

In 1860 Peabody was appointed Plummer Professor of Christian Morals at Harvard, and, for two short intervals, was acting president of the college. Not for his pulpit eloquence nor for his pedagogical inspiration but for his beneficent counsel and friendship he was popularly titled the "College Saint." He was either author or editor of 190 books and pamphlets—on conversation, travel, morals, etc.; yet the best of his writings were perhaps among the 1600 pages of his *North American Review* papers. Peabody appears to have made no substantial contribution to scholarship, but for many years his unsentimentally moral influence on youthful Cambridge intellectuals was prodigious.

PRINCIPAL WORKS: Conversation: Its Faults and Graces, 1856; Reminiscences of European Travel, 1868; A Manual of Moral Philosophy, 1873; Christian Belief and Life, 1875; Building a Character, 1886.

ABOUT: Young, E. J. Andrew P. Peabody; Unitarian April 1893.

PEABODY, ELIZABETH PALMER (May 16, 1804-January 3, 1894), educator, was born at Billerica, Massachusetts, the daughter of Nathaniel Peabody, a physician, and Elizabeth (Palmer) Peabody, a teacher. Eldest of six children, in girlhood she assisted in her mother's private school, and before she was twenty conducted two private schools of her own and taught for two years as a governess. In 1825 she opened a private school in Boston that she conducted until 1834, in her spare time acting as secretary to the Unitarian clergyman, William Ellery Channing. For two years, 1834-36, she was assistant to Bronson Alcott, poet, philosopher, and educator, at his famous Temple School in Boston, but, disagreeing with him on some of his methods, returned to her parents' home in Salem. Here she maintained her Boston contacts, joined the Transcendental Club in 1836, and visited frequently

ELIZABETH PALMER PEABODY

in the home of Emerson at Concord. Discovering that the anonymous author of several stories in the *New England Magazine* was Nathaniel Hawthorne, a childhood playmate, she tactfully brought him out of his solitude, introduced him to her sister Sophia, whom he married in 1842, and to her Transcendental and literary friends.

In 1839 she moved her family to Boston and opened a unique book store on West Street. The only book store in Boston to carry publications in foreign languages, with an owner extremely hospitable to the discussion of ideas, it immediately became the rendezvous of Harvard professors, liberal clergymen, writers and thinkers interested in the Transcendental movement. Plans for the famous Brook Farm community were made there, and in 1842-3 its organ, *The Dial,* to which Miss Peabody contributed several articles, was printed on a small press in the rear. The store was a success financially only during its first year, and she gave it up about 1844, from then on devoting herself to her life interest, teaching. She advocated reforms in the teaching of history in the public schools, writing several texts to illustrate her methods, and with her sister Mary, who had married Horace Mann the educator in 1843, wrote a book on the training of young children. Already familiar with the work of Froebel, after talking with one of his pupils, Mrs. Carl Schurz, she opened in Boston in 1860 the first kindergarten in the United States. In 1867 she went abroad to study Froebel's methods returning to this country she lectured, pub lished a magazine, the *Kindergarten Messenger,* 1873-5, and wrote several books on kindergarten methods and the training of kindergarten teachers. From 1879 to 1884 she lectured at Alcott's School of Philosophy in Concord. Her reminiscences of men of former days and her prowess in conversation made her much sought after. Almost ninety, she died at her home in Jamaica Plain, and was buried in Concord near Emerson and Hawthorne.

Primarily a student, her works reflect an earnest and well-informed mind and are not particularly distinguished for originality or literary quality. She herself was more important than her writing, and the impact of her vitality, her enthusiasm for worthy causes, her intellectual keenness, her ready generosity, was felt by all who came in contact with her. She made real contributions to education, and was the first in this country to write on kindergartens and to work for their introduction.

PRINCIPAL WORKS: *Text books*—Chronological History of the United States, 1856; Lectures in the Training Schools for Kindergartens, 1888. *Miscellany*—Reminiscences of the Rev. William Ellery Channing, D. D., 1880.

ABOUT: Brooks, Van W. The Flowering of New England; McCart, D. L. Elizabeth Peabody: A Biographical Study.

PECK, GEORGE WASHINGTON (December 4, 1817-June 6, 1859), music critic and journalist, who was born in Rehoboth, Mass., son of George Washington Peck and his second wife, Hannah Bliss (Carpenter) Peck. Following his graduation from Brown University in 1837 he worked for a while in the Middle West and then returned East to study law under Richard Henry Dana, Jr., author of *Two Years Before the Mast.* Admitted to the bar in 1843, he was for several years, at least nominally, a "counsellor." He began, at this time, to write for the Boston *Post,* and in 1845 founded the *Boston Musical Review,* which survived only a few issues.

Two years later he went to New York to join the *Morning Courier and New York Enquirer* staff, and in 1847 his articles on "Music in New York" were printed in the influential but short-lived *American Whig Review.* His contributions during the years 1848 to 1859 included reviews of Longfellow's *Evangeline* and Emily Brontë's *Wuthering Heights,* discussions of new letters in England, some rather macabre speculations on hanging, and forty sonnets. Under the pseudonym "Cantell A. Bigly" he published *Aurifodina* (1849), adventures in gold-intoxicated California. On his journey to Australia in 1853 he sent back travel letters to the New York *Times,* and in 1854 published *Melbourne and the Chincha Islands: With Sketches of Lima, and a Voyage Round the World.*

Peck was neither a prolific nor a profound writer, but he had considerable intellectual energy, and his literary achievements are evidence of a real versatility.

PRINCIPAL WORKS: Aurifodina, 1849; Melbourne and the Chincha Islands . . . , 1854.

ABOUT: Historical Catalogue of Brown University: 1764-1904; autobiographical material in the works.

PECK, GEORGE WILBUR (September 28, 1840-April 16, 1916), humorist, journalist, and governor of Wisconsin, creator of "Peck's Bad Boy," was born at Henderson, N.Y., the son of David B. and Alzina Peck. When he was about three years old the family moved to Wisconsin and settled in the town of Whitewater, where Peck received a public school education. Before he was fifteen he entered the printing office of the Whitewater *Register,* and afterward became part-owner of the *Jefferson County Republican,* on which he worked until 1863, when he enlisted in the Union Army.

After the war Peck started the Ripon *Representative* in which the first of his humorous works "Terence McGrant" appeared. These articles brought him an offer from Marcus M. Pomeroy, publisher, to join the editorial staff of his paper the *Democrat* in New York City, where he remained three years, until removing to La Crosse, Wis., to edit another of Pomeroy's

Collection of Frederick H. Meserve

GEORGE WILBUR PECK

journals, the La Crosse *Democrat.* In 1874 he started his own paper, the *Sun,* taking it four years later to Milwaukee, where it proved a great success, achieving within ten years a circulation of 80,000. Meanwhile, in 1860, he married Francena Rowley of Delavan, Wis.

It was in the *Sun* that Peck's stories of the "Bad Boy" appeared, and the Boy became one of the most famous characters in American humor. He was a boy whose boisterous and rather crude sense of humor expressed itself in a series of sadistic practical jokes at his father's expense, but the stories were so original, fresh, and entertaining, that the whole country was soon in uproarious laughter.

In 1890 Peck was elected mayor of Milwaukee on the Democratic ticket, later that year receiving the nomination for Governor. The election took place in November 1890 and he was re-elected two years later, but on running a third time was defeated and spent the remainder of his life in Milwaukee, making only occasional appearances as lecturer and after-dinner speaker. With pince-nez, goatee, and inevitable red carnation in his button-hole, he was a handsome and distinguished figure, and through his charm and effervescent humor was always a great favorite. Peck, by his creation of the "Bad Boy," placed himself among the foremost American humorists of the nineteenth century, and the famous title has become a synonym for juvenile pranksters.

Principal Works: Adventures of One Terence McGrant, 1871; Peck's Bad Boy and His Pa, 1883; The Grocery Man and Peck's Bad Boy, 1883; How Private Geo. W. Peck Put Down the Rebellion, 1887; Peck's Uncle Ike and the Red Headed Boy, 1889; Sunbeams: Humor, Sarcasm, and Sense, 1900; Peck's Bad Boy With the Circus, 1906; Peck's Bad Boy With the Cowboys, 1907.

About: Aikens, A. J. & Proctor, L. A. Men of Progress; Titus, W. A. Wisconsin Writers; Evening Wisconsin (Milwaukee) April 17, 1916.

PECK, HARRY THURSTON (November 24, 1856-March 23, 1914), editor, classicist, poet, and miscellaneous writer, was born in Stamford, Conn., the son of Harry Peck, a well known educator, and Harriet Elizabeth (Thurston) Peck. He received his B.A. at Columbia in 1881, M.A. 1882, then studied classical philology in Paris, Berlin, and Rome. In 1882 he married Cornelia (Nellie) MacKay Dawbarn, from whom he was divorced in 1908; they had two daughters. In 1883 he secured his Ph.D., rather curiously, at the obscure Cumberland University in Tennessee; in 1884 his L.H.D. from Columbia.

From 1882 to 1886 he was a tutor in Latin at Columbia, from 1886 to 1888 of Latin and Semitic languages, from 1888 to 1904 professor of Latin language and literature, and from 1904 to 1910 Anthon professor of the same subjects. He published many translations and philological studies (his translation of "Trimalchio's Dinner," from the *Satyricon* of Petronius, is the best in English), besides original works on literature and history, juvenile stories, and a volume of poems. He edited Harper's *Dictionary of Classical Literature and Antiquities* in 1897, the Dodd, Mead *International Encyclopedia* in 1892, and with Frank M. Colby and Daniel Coit Gilman edited the *New International Encyclopedia* from 1900 to 1903. From 1897 to 1901 he was literary editor of the New York *Commercial Advertiser,* he was on the staff of *Munsey's* from 1907 to 1911, and above all he was editor of the *Bookman* from its start in 1895 to 1902, and contributing editor to 1907, conducting its famous correspondence department. After his divorce, in 1909, he married Elizabeth Hickman DuBois.

This is the Peck—one of the most brilliant men American teaching and American literature have ever known—whom those who knew him would prefer to remember. There is no doubt that Peck's mind was deranged in later years. In 1910 a breach of promise suit and publication of his letters caused his complete disgrace—loss of his position, his wife, and all his possessions. His first wife came to his rescue, but it was too late. He committed suicide in the cheap room where

Collection of Frederick H. Meserv
HARRY THURSTON PECK

he had been trying to exist by writing articles for the encyclopedia he once edited. Involved in Peck's tragedy was the fate of his half dozen books for the general public. Our less censorious age might well look them up and realize anew the keen wit and the exquisite style of this unhappy man.

PRINCIPAL WORKS: The Semitic Theory of Creation, 1886; Latin Pronunciation, 1890; The Adventures of Mabel, 1896; The Personal Equation, 1897; Greystone and Porphyry (verse) 1899; What Is Good English? and Other Essays, 1899; William Hickling Prescott, 1905; Twenty Years of the Republic, 1906; Hilda and the Wishes, 1907; Literature, 1908; Studies in Several Literatures, 1909; The New Baedeker, 1910.

ABOUT: Beer, T. The Mauve Decade; American Mercury September 1933, January 1934; Critic October 1903; Publishers' Weekly March 28, 1914.

PECK, JOHN MASON (October 31, 1789-March 14, 1858), Baptist preacher and local historian, was born in Litchfield Conn., the son of Asa and Hannah (Farnum) Peck. He made himself useful on his father's farm, schooling being often a secondary consideration. In 1809 he was married to Sarah Paine, and several years afterward he left the Congregational for the Baptist church, in which denomination he was ordained in 1813. Following several New York pastorates, he went to the Middle West, and from the year 1817 his major interests lay in the establishment of missions, Bible societies, and Sunday schools. He was a tireless worker, traveling on horseback among his struggling religious communities. In 1827 he aided in the establishment of Rock Spring Seminary, later Shurtleff College, for the training of teachers and ministers. Here, in Rock Spring, Ill., Peck founded in 1829 the *Pioneer*, a religious journal, merged ten years later with the *Baptist Banner* (Louisville, Ky.). During the 'thirties he compiled a *Guide for Emigrants*, a *Gazetteer of Illinois*, and *The Traveller's Directory for Illinois*; his *Life of Daniel Boone* appeared in 1847 and his revision of James H. Perkins' *Annals of the West* in 1850.

An unsuccessful candidacy for the Illinois constitutional convention (1847-48) was the sum of Peck's political dabbling. He frowned upon the extreme abolitionists and favored enforcement of the Fugitive Slave Law. During his late years he was active in religious publication societies and held, successively, two additional pastorates. His miscellaneous writings for religious journals were of passing interest only, but his geographical-historical notes and registries formed a small contribution to the annals of the early Illinois settlers.

PRINCIPAL WORKS: Guide for Emigrants, 1831; Gazetteer of Illinois, 1834; The Traveller's Directory for Illinois, 1840; Life of Daniel Boone, 1847; Father Clark: or, The Pioneer Preacher, 1855.

ABOUT: Babcock, R. Forty Years of Pioneer Life: Memoir of John Mason Peck . . . ; Hayne, C. Vanguard of the Caravans.

PEFFER, WILLIAM ALFRED (September 10, 1831-October 6, 1912), journalist and U.S. Senator from Kansas, was born in Cumberland County, Pa., the son of John and Elizabeth (Souder) Peffer. He enjoyed a few educational advantages, and at the age of fifteen became a teacher. With the gold prospectors he went to California, but returned shortly to Pennsylvania and was married to Sarah Jane Barber, by whom he had ten children. Peffer lived successively in Indiana, Missouri, and Illinois, and in August 1862 began army service which lasted until June 1865.

He read law, and after being admitted to the Tennessee bar, he practiced in Clarksville for about four years and then removed to Kansas, where he set up an office in Fredonia. Very shortly he bought his own printing plant and began to publish the Fredonia *Journal*; in 1875 he moved to Coffeyville and edited its *Journal;* and in 1881 he became the editor of the subtly Republican *Kansas Farmer,* the strongest agricultural organ in the state. He heralded the appearance of the Farmer's Alliance (1888-89) and urged farmer solidarity. Although he transferred his allegiance from the Republican to the new and more radical People's party he retained sufficient conservatism to win a seat (1890) in the United States Senate on the ticket of his old party. His incessant introduction of new bills and his rambling and confused speeches, with perpetual beard-stroking, made him an easy victim of caricature. Peffer's credo was well-intentioned but inconsistent and poorly founded and it was to the detriment of the Populists, whose platform incorporated many then radical remedies which have since become orthodox policies, that he was mistaken for a member of that group. In 1888 he had issued his pocket-size *Peffer's Tariff Manual*; and in 1891 came *The Farmer's Side*; and in 1900 he reasserted his Republicanism in *Americanism and the Philippines.* Neither his reforms nor his miscellaneous writings appreciably survived him and he has become little more than a minor political figure.

PRINCIPAL WORKS: Peffer's Tariff Manual, 1888; The Farmer's Side, 1891; Americanism and the Philippines, 1900.

ABOUT: History of Montgomery County, Kansas; Topeka State Journal October 7, 1912.

PEIRCE, BENJAMIN (April 4, 1809-October 6, 1880), astronomer, mathematician, and scientific writer, was born in Salem, Mass., the son of Benjamin Peirce, a librarian of Harvard College and author of a history of that institution. His mother was Lydia Ropes (Nichols) Peirce. Young Peirce attended the Salem Private Grammar School and Harvard, from which he was graduated in 1829. After teaching for two years at Round Hill School, Northampton, Mass., Pierce was appointed tutor in mathematics at Harvard, and in 1833, university professor of mathematics and astronomy. In 1842 he was appointed Perkins professor of mathematics and astronomy, a position which he held until his death.

He became eminent in many departments of science, particularly physics, astronomy, mechanics and navigation, and published many textbooks on scientific subjects. His lectures on astronomy, when the interest in Encke's comet was at its height, were a great factor in the establishment of Harvard Observatory. When the *American Nautical Almanac* was established in 1849, Peirce was made consulting astronomer, serving until 1867. From 1852 to 1867 he had charge of the longitude determinations of the United States Coast Survey, and in 1867 became superintendent, holding the office for seven years. Peirce was one of the founders of the National Academy of Sciences, was a member of the American Philosophical Society, an associate of the Royal Astronomical Society, London, and received numerous scholarly honors.

He wrote many books and papers, among them *A System of Analytic Mechanics* and his valuable work, *Linear Associative Algebra,* but his greatest contributions to mathematical progress were through his personal influence rather than his publications. His appealing personality, humor, and dramatic warmth made him an inspiring lecturer, and through his lifelong services as a teacher he became a leader of scientific men of America. He was married in 1833 to Sarah Hunt Mills. His three sons also became eminent—the eldest James, was a mathematician; the second, Charles [*q.v.*], a scientist and philosopher; and the youngest, Herbert, a diplomat.

PRINCIPAL WORKS: An Elementary Treatise on Sound, 1836; An Elementary Treatise on Algebra, 1837; An Elementary Treatise on Plane and Solid Geometry, 1837; An Elementary Treatise on Plane and Spherical Trigonometry . . . , 1840; An Elementary Treatise on Curves, Functions, and Forces, 1841-46; Tables of the Moon, 1853; A System of Analytic Mechanics, 1855; Tables of the Moon's Parallax, 1856; Linear Associative Algebra, 1870; Ideality in the Physical Sciences, 1881.

ABOUT: A History of the First Half-Century of the National Academy of Sciences: 1863-1913; Archibald, R. C. Benjamin Peirce: 1809-1880; Lodge, H. C. Early Memories; Peabody, A. P. Harvard Reminiscences; American Journal of Science September 1881; Popular Astronomy October 1895.

PEIRCE, CHARLES (SANTIAGO) SANDERS (September 10, 1839-April 19, 1914), philosopher, was born in Cambridge, Mass., the son of Benjamin Pierce [*q.v.*], the foremost mathematician of his time in America, and Sarah Hunt (Mills) Peirce, daughter of a senator. One of his brothers became a celebrated mathematician, another a diplomat. He himself said he "grew up in a laboratory"; his father's intensive training reminds one of the relations of James to John Stuart Mill. He was a chemist at eight, a mathematician at ten. Yet when he received his B.A. at Harvard in 1859 he was among the lowest in his class; the conventional teaching of a college was not for him. He fitted better into graduate study, and his M.A. in 1862 and Sc.B. in 1863 were awarded for brilliant work.

Although he was already attracted toward philosophy, Peirce saw no means of livelihood except through science; in 1861 he joined the United States Coast Survey and for thirty years philosophy was merely his avocation, though he lectured at Harvard on the subject in 1864 and 1865 and again in 1869 and 1870. From 1869 to 1875 he was an assistant at the Harvard Observatory, working in photometry (the measurement of light). In 1875 he was the first American delegate to the International Geodetic Conference. At various times he was in charge of weights and measures for the Coast Survey and special assistant in gravity research. He was the first to use the wave-length of a light-ray as a standard unit of measurement.

His real life-work, however, was in logic He taught seldom; except for the Harvard lectures already noted, and the Lowell Institute lectures in 1903 and 1904, his only formal teaching was at Johns Hopkins from 1879 to 1884 (in 1883 he edited the Hopkins

CHARLES SANDERS PEIRCE

Studies in Logic), and a course at Bryn Mawr during the same period. But from 1867 to 1885 he contributed hundreds of important technical papers to the professional journals. He was the real father of pragmatism, the empiricist philosophy; though the later pragmatism of his friend William James so widely differed from his original theory promulgated in 1878 that he changed the name of his own system to "pragmaticism."

Though Peirce's formal connection with the Coast Survey did not end until 1891, he retired in 1887 to Milford, Pa., and ceased receiving any income from the government. He was one of the editors of the *Century Dictionary,* 1889-91, and of *Baldwin's Dictionary of Philosophy and Psychology,* 1901-05. A man of extreme versatility of learning, he wrote articles and reviews, chiefly for the *Nation* and the *Monist,* on subjects as disparate as Egyptology, criminology, philology, and psychology. But he was totally without money sense, utterly unable to manage his practical affairs, and his last years were spent in extreme poverty. He had had domestic difficulties as well; in 1862 he had married Harriet Melusina Fay, a social reformer, his senior in age, whom he divorced in 1883. He claimed to have married thereafter Juliette Froissy, a Frenchwoman, who survived him; but there is no evidence of the marriage. Peirce, always a "queer creature," as James called him, became increasingly eccentric. He suffered for years from cancer, but continued his unwearying labors—a dark little bearded man, like a gnome, with burning dark eyes, half crazy from pain and the morphia taken to deaden it, living in the midst of an inextricable tangle of manuscripts, neglected, destitute, forgotten; but "the most original thinker of his generation" (William James).

Peirce's writings are not for the general reader. He had a certain fierce snobbishness which made him deliberately obscure to fend off all but the chosen intellectual few. He was a great seminal force, a great fructifier, with what Morris Cohen calls "the beautiful but capricious originality of genius." In his lifetime he published only one book, and that on physics. After his death Harvard bought his mass of manuscripts and notes from his widow, and finally reduced them to order by 1931. In 1923 his published papers had been collected in a volume. All philosophical theory must take him into account; he was the greatest logician this country has yet produced; but he is a "philosopher's philosopher," to be taken "straight" only by those trained in the technical verbiage of his subject.

PRINCIPAL WORKS: Photometric Researches, 1878; Chance, Love, and Logic, 1923; Collected Papers, 1931-34.

ABOUT: Peirce, C. S. S. Chance, Love, and Logic (see Introduction by M. R. Cohen); Current History March 1935; Journal of Philosophy, Psychology, and Scientific Methods December 21, 1916; Monist July 1914; Nation May 14, 1914; New Republic February 3, 1937; Science November 16, 1934; Boston Evening Transcript April 21, 1914.

PENHALLOW, SAMUEL (July 2, 1665-December 2, 1726), merchant, judge, and historian, was born at St. Mabyn, Cornwall, England, the son of Chamond and Ann (Tamlyn) Penhallow. When he was eighteen he entered a famous school at Newington-Green, conducted by his father's friend, the Rev. Charles Morton. When the school was closed in 1685, Penhallow was among a small group of pupils who joined Morton in emigrating to America.

Landing at Charlestown, Mass., in July 1686, he soon became prominent in colony activities and was considered an acceptable suitor for the hand of Mary Cutt, daughter of John Cutt, president of the Province of New Hampshire. The marriage was solemnized in 1687 and placed Penhallow in an advantageous position to enter the business and political life of the colonies. Among the positions he held were those of justice of the peace, speaker of the general assembly, recorder, privy councillor, justice and chief justice in the superior court. With a year's exception, from 1699 to his death he was treasurer of the province.

He is named among American writers for his remarkably faithful account of the Indian Wars between 1702-25: *The History of the Wars of New-England with the Eastern Indians: or, a Narrative of Their Continued Perfidy and Cruelty From the 10th of August 1703 to the Peace Renewed the 13th of July 1713, and From the 25th of July 1722 to Their Submission 15 December 1725.* This was published in 1726 from accurate records kept by Penhallow.

Penhallow's first wife died in 1713, leaving him thirteen children and a large fortune. The year following he married the twice-widowed Abigail Atkinson, who bore him one son.

PRINCIPAL WORK: See above.

ABOUT: Bouton, N. Provincial Papers, Documents, and Records Relating to the Province of New Hampshire: Vols. I-IV; Penhallow, P. W. Penhallow Family; Penhallow, S. Diary (in Massachusetts Historical Sociey Collections); New Hampshire Historical Society Collections: Ser. 1, Vol. I (1824).

"PENN, ARTHUR." See MATTHEWS, JAMES BRANDER

"PEPPERPOD, PIP." See STODDARD, CHARLES WARREN

PERCIVAL, JAMES GATES (September 15, 1795-May 21, 1856), poet, was born in Berlin, Conn., the son of James Percival, M.D., and Elizabeth (Hart) Percival. From his mother he inherited his melancholy, from his father, who died in 1807, his sickly constitution. In school his chief interest was geography, and at fourteen he wrote a geographical epic called *The Commerciad.* He was graduated from Yale in 1815 with a brilliant record, but immediately his unfortunate versatility caused him difficulties. After vacillating among various professions, he went to Philadelphia, where he taught school and also entered the medical department of the University of Pennsylvania. In 1819 he transferred to the Medical Institution of Yale, where he received his M.D. in 1820. He began practice in his native town, was a flat failure, is supposed also to have been rejected by a girl with whom he was in love, and attempted suicide.

Unsuccessful even in this, and rather cheered by the publication of his poems in the *Microscope* (New Haven), he moved to Charleston, S.C., and for a few years lived there by journalism. He returned to Connecticut, and for brief periods edited the *Connecticut Herald,* taught chemistry at

After a portrait by F. Alexander
JAMES GATES PERCIVAL

West Point, acted as examining surgeon in a recruiting office in Boston ,and edited the *American Athenaeum* in New York. He always resigned because of "injustice and persecution," since he was a typical paranoic. He studied linguistics, became a real authority on languages, translated from the Slavonic tongues, Greek and Sanskrit—all of which he spoke besides half a dozen less unusual languages. In 1827 and 1828 he assisted Noah Webster in preparation of his famous dictionary.

Meanwhile he taught himself geology, and from 1835 to 1842 was state geologist of Connecticut, resigning because the state would not furnish funds for his comprehensive survey of the natural history of the region. With a half-conscious knowledge of his mental state, he became a voluntary resident of the State Hospital in New Haven, emerging occasionally to do surveying. He built himself a little house without doors or windows in front, where he might live in solitude with his books, but neither he nor his books ever entered it. Instead, in 1854, he was made state geologist of Wisconsin; his leisure time he gave to a new theory of music. He died in Hazel Green, Wis.—"lonely, shy, unmarried, disappointed, poor and dirty," as William Ellery Leonard describes him. Tall, thin, haggard, "with a wild glitter in his eye, startled at the approach of a fellow creature," he roamed the Wisconsin woods as once he had roamed those of Connecticut. Van Wyck Brooks calls him a "rhymester-vagrant," Leonard a "self-constituted, self-conscious poetic genius." He had indeed all the traditional qualities of genius without the genius. Actually one of the most learned man of his time and place, he aspired to immortality as a poet without having more than a modicum of poetic talent. He poured forth endless reams of darkly melancholy verses, fluent and hollow, with only an occasional gleam of graceful beauty to justify the wasted paper and the wasted life. As a "character," he deserves a place in American history; as a poet, he has long ceased to exist, and indeed in any real sense of the term never existed at all.

PRINCIPAL WORKS: Poems, 1821; Clio: Parts I, II, III, 1822-1827; Prometheus: Part II, (with other poems) 1822; The New Haven Whig Song Book, 1840; Report on the Geology of the State of Connecticut, 1842; The Dream of a Day and Other Poems, 1843.

ABOUT: Brooks, Van W. The Flowering of New England; Cogswell, F. H. James Gates Percival and His Friends; Legler, H. E. James Gates Percival; Percival, J. G. Poetical Works (see Biographical Sketch by L. W. Fitch in 1859 ed.); Ward, J. H. Life and Letters of James Gates Percival; Atlantic Monthly July 1859; New Englander April 1867; North American Review April 1867.

"PERCY, FLORENCE." See AKERS, ELIZABETH (CHASE)

"PERKINS, ELI." See LANDON, MELVILLE DE LANCEY

PERKINS, FREDERIC BEECHER (September 27, 1828-January 27, 1899), editor and librarian, was born in Hartford, Conn., the son of Thomas Clap Perkins and Mary Foote (Beecher) Perkins. He entered Yale with the class of 1850 but left in the autumn of 1848 to study law in his father's office. (In 1860 he received an M.A. degree from Yale.) Perkins was admitted to the bar in 1851, but attempted almost no practice, and after a period of teaching he found some editorial work and was subsequently made one of the editors of the New York *Tribune*. He returned to Hartford to edit Henry Barnard's *American Journal of Education*, and for four years was librarian of the Connecticut Historical Society. The publications with which he was connected during the decade that followed included the *Galaxy*, the *Independent*, the *Christian Union*, on which he assisted his uncle Henry Ward Beecher, and from 1870 to 1873 aided his brother-in-law Edward Everett Hale in the editing of the *Old and New*.

Perkins worked in the Boston Public Library prior to his appointment as chief librarian of the San Francisco Public Library, which post he held for the first half of his stay in California; at the completion of miscellaneous editorial work there he returned East, and died in Morristown, N. J., after a chronic illness.

He wrote a portion of *Public Libraries in the United States of America: Their History, Condition, and Management*, and from 1877 to 1880 was an associate editor of the *Library Journal*. Besides many anonymous and rather obscure writings he published *Charles Dickens*, a biography; a novel called *Scrope: or, The Lost Library*; and *Devil Puzzlers and Other Studies*, the title story of which Brander Matthews included among the ten best American short stories. Perkins possessed a vast amount of miscellaneous information and many literary potentialities, but he was professionally restless and all too willing to scatter his intellectual interests.

PRINCIPAL WORKS: Charles Dickens, 1870; The Best Reading, 1872; Scrope: or, The Lost Library, 1874; Check List for American Local History, 1876; Public Libraries in the United States of America: Their History, Condition, and Management, 1876; Devil-Puzzlers and Other Studies, 1877.

ABOUT: Library Journal February 1899; New York Tribune February 4, 1899.

"PERLEY." See POORE, BENJAMIN PERLEY

PERRY, ARTHUR LATHAM (February 27, 1830-July 9, 1905), economist, was born at Lyme, N.H., the son of the Rev. Baxter Perry and Lydia (Gray) Perry. A posthumous child, he grew up in extreme poverty, but after attending the village school he managed to secure several part-terms at the nearby Thetford (Vt.) Academy. For two years he served as a school teacher, until, encouraged by President Mark Hopkins, he entered Williams College in the autumn of 1848. During his sophomore year strong intellectual convictions, rooted in John Stuart Mill's *System of Logic*, were beginning to take form. He was graduated in 1852, taught in Washington, D.C., for a year, and was then called to Williams to become first a tutor and then a professor of political economy, history, and German; he later concentrated on economy only, and was retired in 1891. He was married, August 7, 1856, to Mary Brown Smedley.

Perry had been teaching at Williamstown about ten years when he found, in Frederic Bastiat's *Harmonies of Political Economy*, a strangely unifying, clean-edged, and somewhat new set of economic concepts, which, in practical application, became a code of free trade. His *Elements of Political Economy*, one of the first documents of its kind in America, appeared in 1865 and was followed by *An Introduction to Political Economy* and *Principles of Political Economy.* In the Springfield *Republican* and in the New York *Evening Post* he attacked the proponents of economic protection. Out of his incidental researches on the history of western Massachusetts came *Origins in Williamstown* and its continuation in *Williamstown and Williams College.* But his significant achievement, of course, was his valuable spade-work in the systematizing of political economy in America at a time when the ground was almost unbroken.

Principal Works: Elements of Political Economy, 1865; An Introduction to Political Economy, 1877; Principles of Political Economy, 1891; Origins in Williamstown, 1894; Williamstown and Williams College, 1899.

About: Perry, C. A Professor of Life; Free Trade Broadside: Vol. 1., No. 3; Williams College Bulletin April 1906.

PERRY, BENJAMIN FRANKLIN (November 20, 1805-December 3, 1886), journalist and office-holder, was born in Pendleton District, S. C., the son of Benjamin Perry, a Revolutionary soldier, and Anne (Foster) Perry of Virginia. His early boyhood was spent on a farm, and until he went to a preparatory academy in Asheville, N.C., at the age of sixteen, his schooling had been much interrupted. In Greenville, S.C., he studied law, was admitted to the bar in 1827, and set up a law practice.

In 1832 he began to edit the *Greenville Mountaineer,* a Union party newspaper, and the same year entered on a long political career. For about twenty-five years he was intermittently a member in the state legislature, where he vehemently defended slavery but opposed secession as "madness and folly." Nevertheless he followed his state out of the Union, and under its confederacy was district attorney in 1863, district judge in 1864, and, finally, provisional governor of South Carolina the year following. Perry declined to run for governor, was elected to the United States Senate, but, denied his seat (as a bitter opponent of Reconstruction), he continued his law practice and executed several political commissions. In 1837 he was married to Elizabeth Frances McCall.

He had established, in 1850, the *Southern Patriot,* the only Union paper in the state, and had edited it against great odds. Perry published two volumes of contemporary sketches, *Reminiscences of Public Men* and *Biographical Sketches of Eminent American Statesmen,* both of which brought into better relief many otherwise unidentifiable figures of an obviously important political era.

Principal Works: Reminiscences of Public Men, 1883 and 1889; Biographical Sketches of Eminent American Statesmen, 1887.

About: Perry, H. M. Letters of My Father to My Mother; Reynolds, J. S. Reconstruction in South Carolina; News and Courier (Charleston) December 4, 1886.

PERRY, NORA (1831-May 13, 1896), poet, journalist, and writer of juvenile literature, was the daughter of Harvey and Sarah (Benson) Perry of Dudley, Mass. She spent her childhood in Providence, R.I., and was educated in her own home and in private schools. At the age of eight she wrote a sensational romance, "The Shipwreck," and at eighteen she was contributing to magazines. After removing to Boston she became correspondent for the Chicago *Tribune* and the Providence *Journal.* Her best known poem, "After the Ball" (or "Maud and Madge") was published in 1859 in the *Atlantic Monthly.* It was painfully sentimental, but tremendously popular. Her serial "Rosalind Newcomb" appeared in *Harper's* during 1859 and 1860.

Nora Perry's later writings were, almost without exception, stories for girls: *A Flock of Girls, The Youngest Miss Lorton and Other Stories, Ju Ju's Christmas Party,* etc. To portray rather conventional character and to maintain a simple plot were, apparently, her fundamental by-rules of procedure, and beyond them she attained nothing that could outlive its own age.

Principal Works: After the Ball and Other Poems, 1875; The Tragedy of the Unexpected and Other Stories, 1880; For a Woman: A Novel, 1885; A Flock of Girls, 1887; Brave Girls, 1889; Cottage Neighbors, 1899; Ju Ju's Christmas Party, 1901.

About: Willard, F. E. & Livermore, M. A. American Women, 1897; Critic May 23, 1896; Boston Daily Advertiser May 15, 1896.

PERRY, THOMAS SERGEANT (January 23, 1845-May 7, 1928), scholarly writer and educator, was born at Newport, R.I., the son of Christopher Grant Perry and Frances (Sergeant) Perry. He was directly descended from Oliver Hazard Perry and Benjamin Franklin. Educated at private schools until his seventeenth year, he attended Harvard College, was graduated in 1866, and spent several years of study in Europe in preparation for a tutorship in French and German at Harvard, which he held from 1868 to 1872.

During the next five years he was affiliated with the *North American Review* and in 1877 joined the English Department of Harvard. After 1882 he spent the majority of his time in Europe, devoting himself to the scholarly reading and writing that drew from Oliver Wendell Holmes the tribute that Perry was the best read man he had ever known. As his life progressed he became increasingly interested in languages and was at home in Sanskrit and Russian literature.

In 1874 he married Lilla Cabot of Boston, who became a prominent American painter and also earned a local reputation for her poetry. Between 1898 and 1901 Perry was professor of English at the University of Keiogijiku in Japan, afterward returning to Boston to spend the remainder of his life in intellectual pursuits, and to enhance the city's most cultured circle by his brilliant mind and courtly manners. Less tolerant than his ancestor, Benjamin Franklin, he bore a marked resemblance to him. Perry's death, occurring at Boston, not only removed a brilliant man of letters but one of the last of the type for which Boston was noted in the nineteenth century.

The product of generations of culture, Perry's mind was so sharpened by his own profound studies that he had the faculty to produce writings of a high and stable standard. Among his best known works are: *The Evolution of the Snob* and a comprehensive *History of Greek Literature*.

Principal Works: The Life and Letters of Francis Lieber, 1882; English Literature of the Eighteenth Century, 1883; From Opitz to Lessing, 1885; The Evolution of a Snob, 1887; History of Greek Literature, 1890.

About: Perry, C. B. The Perrys of R.I. and Silver Creek; Morse, J. T. Jr. Thomas Sergeant Perry: A Memoir; Robinson, E. A. Selections From the Letters of Thomas Sergeant Perry; Boston Transcript May 7, 1928.

PETERS, RICHARD (c. 1704-July 10, 1776), clergyman and colonial official, was born in Liverpool, England, the son of Ralph and Esther (Preeson) Peters. He attended Westminster School, and before finishing, at the age of fifteen, he had secretly married one of the servant maids. After three years of study at Leyden, he unwillingly spent five years at the Inner Temple. For some time he had desired to take holy orders; he abandoned the study of law and became deacon, and then priest, in the Church of England. But when it was revealed that his second marriage, to one Miss Stanley, was bigamous, a storm of criticism led him to embark for Philadelphia. Here at Christ Church he assisted Rev. Archibald Cummings, but quarreled openly with him and shortly withdrew. Peters published his self-defending discourses, *The Two Last Sermons Preached at Christ's-Church in Philadelphia, July 3, 1737,* later that same year.

His first secular post was the secretaryship of the provincial land office, and, with additional commissions, he held it until 1760, visiting the Indians and stifling any semblance of harmful "Quaker plots." Eventually, however, he acquired a very healthy tolerance of Quaker thought. Upon retiring as secretary and clerk of the council in 1762 he returned to the ministry and spiritually and materially advanced Christ's and St. Peter's churches. With failing health he resigned September 23, 1775. Peters was the author of *A Sermon on Education* and *A Sermon Preached in the New Lutheran Church of Zion, in the City of Philadelphia, 1769*. He was modestly pious and extremely scholarly—Oxford had conferred on him the degree of D.D. in 1770—and he regarded a universal classical education as the best means of correcting social evils. His writings were almost negligible, but his diplomatic and ecclesiastic functions have become a real part of the history of Philadelphia during the last years of British domination.

Principal Works: The Two Last Sermons Preached at Christ's-Church in Philadelphia, July 3, 1737; A Sermon on Education, 1751; A Sermon Preached in the New Lutheran Church of Zion, in the City of Philadelphia, 1769.

About: Keith, C. P. The Provincial Councillors of Pennsylvania; Pennsylvania Magazine of History and Biography October 1886, July 1899, October 1905; April and October 1907, October 1914.

PETERS, SAMUEL ANDREW (November 20, 1735-April 19, 1826), clergyman, Loyalist, and historian, was born at Hebron, Conn., the son of John and Mary (Marks) Peters. From Yale he received the degrees of bachelor of arts in 1757 and master of arts in 1760; and he was awarded an M.A. from King's College in 1761; but his claims to that of LL.D. appear to have been so questionable that he was openly accused of having "invented" this degree.

Peters sailed for England in 1758; was ordained deacon and priest and appointed missionary by the Society for the Propagation of the Gospel in Foreign Parts; and from 1760 to 1774 he was rector of the Anglican church at Hebron where he constantly deplored "so much liberty instead of Law and Gospel." As the British-Colonial controversy thickened in 1774, Peters was forbidden, by the Sons of Liberty, to write to England. After constant threat and public humiliation he fled to Boston; and in October sailed for England where the Crown provided him with a meagre pension. He preached an occasional sermon in the churches of London and wrote for British magazines.

In 1781, for the avowed purpose of bringing to light some long-concealed truths, he published *A General History of Connecticut.* "Dr. Mather and Mr. Neal," he said, "were popular writers, but they suppressed what are called in New England *unnecessary truths.*" It was, in general, a most unflattering account of the colony and embodied a much contested dissertation on its "blue laws," citing such specimens as "A wife shall be deemed good evidence against her husband," etc. James Hammond Trumbull, a former college mate of Peters, accused him of gross misrepresentation, etc. Four years later Peters published *A Letter to the Reverend John Tyler, A.M.: Concerning the Possibility of Eternal Punishments . . .* ; and in 1807 *A History of the Reverend Hugh Peters* (his claim that Hugh Peter, clergyman, prominent in the early Massachusetts Bay Colony, was his great-grand-uncle has, however, been disproved).

Peters was elected bishop of Vermont in 1794 by a convention which met at Rutland, but the Archbishop of Canterbury, supposedly because of some necessary action of Parliament, was unable to consecrate him. In 1805, however, he returned to America to advance the land-tract claims of the heirs of Jonathan Carver, English explorer. He finally bought the rights himself, and in 1817 made a journey to the region in question Prairie du Chien, on the upper Mississippi) but the claim, in 1826, was disallowed by Congress.

Peters was married three times: in 1760 to Hannah Owen; four years after her death in 1765, to Abigail Gilbert, who died less than a month after their marriage; and in 1773 to Mary Birdseye, who died in June of the year following. His *General History* was his primary literary achievement, but his letters to England during the years 1763 to 1774 form an interesting footnote to a study of the growing friction between Great Britain and the Colonies.

Principal Works: A General History of Connecticut, 1781; A Letter to the Rev. John Tyler, A.M.: Concerning the Possibility of Eternal Punishments, and the Improbability of Universal Salvation, 1785.

About: Force, P. (ed.). American Archives; Perry, W. S. The History of the American Episcopal Church; Peters, E. F. & E. B. Peters of New England; Trumbull, J. H. The Reverend Samuel Peters: His Defenders and Apologists; Churchman May 26 and June 2, 1877.

PETERSON, CHARLES JACOBS (July 20, 1819, March 4, 1887), editor, publisher, and historian, was born in Philadelphia, the son of Thomas P. and Elizabeth Snelling (Jacobs) Peterson. He attended the University of Pennsylvania, studied law, and was admitted to the bar; but he did not practice. At the age of twenty he became an editorial associate of George R. Graham, recent purchaser of *Atkinson's Casket* (afterward re-named *Graham's Magazine*). The following year he bought an interest in the *Saturday Evening Post* and founded his own *Lady's World* (later the *Ladies' National Magazine* and then *Peterson's Magazine*). Ann Sophia Stephens was his chief contributor and valuable assistant. During the 'seventies, by working up a tremendous circulation, *Peterson's* actually overshadowed its highly popular prototype, *Godey's Lady's Book.*

While editing his own magazine, Peterson wrote for the *Saturday Gazette,* the Philadelphia *Bulletin,* and the *Public Ledger.* He was, moreover the author of chronicles of the War of Independence, the War of 1812, and the Mexican War; a group of rather unimpressive historical novels; and the historically valuable *Naval Heroes of the United States,* later enlarged under the titles *A History of the United States Navy* and *The American Navy: Being an Authentic History.* Both professionally and socially Peterson belonged to that coterie of littérateurs who were, in part, responsible for the intellectual revival in Philadelphia during the middle nineteenth century.

Principal Works: Military Heroes of the Revolution: With a Narrative of the War of Independence, 1848; Grace Dudley: or, Arnold at Saratoga, 1849; The Naval Heroes of the United States, 1850; A History of the United States Navy, 1852; Kate Aylesford: A Story of the Refugees, 1855; The American Navy: Being an Authentic History, 1856; The Old Stone Mansion, 1859.

About: Smyth, A. H. The Philadelphia Magazines and Their Contributors; Press (Philadelphia) March 6, 1887; Peterson's Magazine May 1887.

PETERSON, HENRY (December 7, 1818-October 10, 1891), editor, publisher, and poet, was born in Philadelphia, the son of George and Jane (Evans) Peterson, and cousin of the littérateur Charles Jacobs Peterson [*q.v.*]. Put to work at an early age, he was largely self-educated, and at twenty-one he and Edmund Deacon began to publish pamphlets, reprints, etc. For a while he was associated with the *Saturday Gazette,* and in 1846 he became editor of the *Saturday Evening Post.* Two years later he and Deacon bought out the controlling interests and for a quarter of a century the *Post* was, from a literary point of view, Peterson's own product, becoming less of a news-sheet and more of a fiction journal.

Peterson was the author of considerable verse, including *Poems,* published in 1863, *The Modern Job,* a piece of long-drawn free-verse philosophy, and the historical *Faire-Mount* in couplets. Among his novels are: *Pemberton, Confessions of a Minister,* and *Bessie's Lovers.* In 1842 he was married to Sarah Webb, who from 1864 to 1874 was the editor of the *Lady's Friend,* another of the many fashion magazines for which *Godey's Lady's Book* had set the accepted pace. Not as poet or novelist but as editor of a vastly popular weekly Peterson exerted his strongest literary influence.

Principal Works: Poems, 1863; The Modern Job, 1869; Pemberton, 1873; Faire-Mount, 1874; Confessions of a Minister, 1874; Helen: or, One Hundred Years Ago, 1876; Bessie's Lovers, 1877; Columbus, 1893.

About: Jordan, J. W. Encyclopaedia of Pennsylvania Biography; Public Ledger (Philadelphia) October 12, 1891.

PHELPS, ELIZABETH STUART. See WARD, ELIZABETH STUART (PHELPS)

PHELPS, ELIZABETH (STUART), (August 13, 1815-November 30, 1852), novelist and writer of juvenile fiction, daughter of Moses Stuart, Hebrew scholar and one of New England's most formidable theologians, and Abigail (Clark) Stuart, spent her childhood in Andover, Mass. The Stuarts maintained an enviable hospitality and among their frequent guests was Austin Phelps, a resident licentiate in Andover, son of the Rev. Eliakim Phelps who was notorious for his strange and prolonged psychic experience referred to as "house possession." In September 1842 Elizabeth Stuart was married to young Phelps and for six years they lived in Boston, where he was pastor of Pine Street Church; they returned to Andover when he became a professor of sacred rhetoric and homiletics at the Theological Seminary.

Elizabeth Stuart Phelps was in her middle thirties before she ever contemplated writing as a profession. The boundless sale of her *Sunny Side: or, The Country Minister's Wife* almost demanded, during the year following, *The Angel Over the Right Shoulder* and *A Peep at Number Five,* two further pieces of slightly fictional autobiography strongly underlined with domestic pathos. Her juveniles included *Little Mary: or, Talks and Tales for Children* and the four-volume Kitty Brown series. She was heir to a sturdy intellect but was physically frail and of nervous temperament, and, weakened by the strain of constant literary labors, she died at the age of thirty-seven. Her daughter, Elizabeth Stuart (Phelps) Ward [*q.v.*], who at her mother's death was only eight, later embarked upon a successful career in letters. Mrs. Phelps wrote with a facile naturalness, and almost entirely in the popular religious vein; her humor, though now admittedly pale, was, in its day, nicely tempered and pleasant.

Principal Works: The Sunny Side: or, The Country Minister's Wife, 1851; A Peep at Number Five: or, A Chapter in the Life of a City Pastor, 1852; The Angel Over the Right Shoulder: or, The Beginning of a New Year, 1852; The Tell-Tale: or, Home Secrets Told by Old Travelers, 1853; Little Mary: or, Talks and Tales for Children, 1854.

About: Ward, E. S. P. Austin Phelps; Ward, E. S. P. Chapters From a Life.

"PHILENIA." See MORTON, SARAH WENTWORTH (APTHORP)

PHILLIPS, WENDELL (November 29, 1811-February 2, 1884), orator and reformer, was born in Boston, the eighth child of John and Sarah (Walley) Phillips. He attended Harvard, from which he was graduated in 1831, and Harvard Law School. In 1834 he was admitted to the bar, his great gifts of person, character, and mind (along with the prestige of his family, his social position, and wealth) promising much. Success came at once, but he felt little aptitude for the law, and as early as 1836 began his lyceum lectures on subjects in history, the arts, and men, with increasing attention to reform questions, that were to continue almost to his death.

In 1835 the dragging of William Lloyd Garrison through the streets of Boston by a mob stirred Phillips deeply, but he did not declare his allegiance to the abolitionist cause until March 1837. Meanwhile he had met Ann Terry Greene, daughter of a wealthy Boston merchant, herself an ardent abolitionist, whom he married in October, 1837. At a meeting in Faneuil Hall December 8, 1837, following the murder in Illinois of the abolitionist editor, Elijah Lovejoy, Phillips' passionate plea for freedom of speech publicly opened his career. From then on, as champion of a cause hated by the respectable and wealthy, he risked his life often at the hands of mobs, and sacrificed both friends and honors. His wife encouraged him, and he was sustained

Collection of Frederick H. Meserve
WENDELL PHILLIPS

by unusual moral earnestness. Of obvious value to the cause, he set to work as organizer for the Massachusetts Anti-Slavery Society, continued his lyceum lectures, and while abroad for the health of his wife, who had become an invalid, was delegate in 1840 to the World's Anti-Slavery Convention in London.

In the 'forties he opposed the annexation of Texas and the war with Mexico, and in the 'fifties his opposition to the compromises with slavery led him to declare for dissolution of the Union. He criticized much of Lincoln's administration and opposed his reelection. After the war he succeeded Garrison as president of the American Anti-Slavery Society and worked for Negro enfranchisement. In 1870, with the passage of the Fifteenth Amendment, the society disbanded, and Phillips, now an inveterate reformer of almost thirty-five years' standing, went on, a pioneer fighter in the cause of labor, seeing in labor's problems the same economic causes that had nourished slavery. Candidate of the Prohibitionists and the Labor Reform Party for governor of Massachusetts in 1870, he polled 20,000 votes, and in 1871 presided at the Labor Reform Convention, which adopted a forward-looking platform on questions of labor, capital, and finance. He had for a long time espoused such causes as women's suffrage, prison reform, temperance, and Indian rights.

His fortune depleted by private charities and publication of the *Standard,* successor to Garrison's *Liberator,* he went on lecturing. Belatedly, in 1881, Harvard invited him to deliver the annual Phi Beta Kappa address, and, characteristically, Phillips' notable "Scholar in a Republic" inveighed against academic aloofness from the masses. It was one of his last addresses, for in 1884 he died, after a brief illness, of angina pectoris, his wife surviving him by several years.

Phillips was one of the outstanding orators in an age of orators, but his approach to his speeches was not literary. He did not like to write, his preparation being of facts and not of presentation. Emerson said of him that his mind fed upon his audience. There is universal testimony to the power of his voice and presence. Scholarly and cultivated, he nevertheless used a colloquial and easy style. What was extreme and harsh detracts from the permanent value of his thought, but Phillips was an agitator, not an administrator, and he fought grave social wrongs.

PRINCIPAL WORKS: Speeches, Lectures, and Letters: Vol. 1, 1863, Vol. 2, 1891.

ABOUT: Austin, G. L. Life and Times of Wendell Phillips; Martyn, C. Wendell Phillips; Russell, C. E. Story of Wendell Phillips; Sears, L. Wendell Phillips; Sewanee Review July 1913.

PHILLIPS, WILLIAM ADDISON (January 14, 1824-November 30, 1893), soldier, congressman from Kansas, and journalist, was born in Paisley, Scotland, the son of John Phillips. He was about fourteen when his parents came to the United States and settled in Illinois, and in Randolph County young Phillips attended the public schools. At a rather early age he edited a newspaper in Chester, Ill., and after a study of law he was admitted to the bar. As correspondent of the New York *Tribune* he went to Kansas in 1855, entered the political arena as a radical anti-slavery leader, was elected to the state legislature, and at the outbreak of the Civil War was made an officer in the Union Army. He was mustered out in June 1865 and returned to law, politics, and an "advanced" variety of economics, outlined in *Labor, Land, and Law: A Search for the Missing Wealth of the Working People* (1886). In it he opposed Henry George's single-tax theory and advocated a system of graduated taxes, as well as postal savings, government lease of public lands, etc. Phillips served three terms as congressman (Republican) from Kansas, maintaining a strategic balance between party principles and personal convictions.

Upon retirement he became a practicing attorney in Washington, D.C. His mass of anonymous verse, essays, and political tracts remains almost unidentified; several of his articles, however, can be found in the 1885-87 files of the *North American Review.* He was twice married; in 1859 to Carrie Spillman; and two years after her death in 1883, to Anna B. Stapler.

Principal Works: The Conquest of Kansas by Missouri and Her Allies, 1856; Labor, Land, and Law: A Search for the Missing Wealth of the Working People, 1886.

About: Britton, W. Memoirs of the Rebellion on the Border; Kansas Historical Society Collections: vol. 5; Daily Republican (Salina, Kan.) December 1, 1893.

"PHILODICAIOS." See YOUNG, THOMAS

"PHOENIX, JOHN." See DERBY, GEORGE HORATIO

PIATT, JOHN JAMES (March 1, 1835-February 16, 1917), poet and journalist, was born at James' Mills, Ind., the son of John Bear Piatt and Emily (Scott) Piatt. Young Piatt spent most of his youth near Columbus, Ohio, and after attendance at Capital University and Kenyon College he was apprenticed to the publisher of the *Ohio State Journal*; on its staff was William Dean Howells, who was one of the first to recognize Piatt's poetic facility, and who, in 1860, collaborated with him in the publication of *Poems of Two Friends.* Piatt was associated with the Louisville *Journal* and contributed to the *Atlantic*; in 1861, the year of his marriage to Sarah Morgan Bryan, he removed to Washington, where during a six-year government clerkship he became a friend of Walt Whitman. In 1867 he joined the staff of the Cincinnati *Chronicle*; and while serving as assistant clerk (1870) and then librarian (1871-75) of the United States House of Representatives acted as literary editor and correspondent of the Cincinnati *Commercial.*

In 1893 Piatt completed eleven years as United States Consul at Cork (Ireland) and at Dublin. He returned to North Bend, Ohio, and prepared miscellaneous items for newspapers and magazines. Between 1866 and 1897 he wrote and published numerous books of verse and a little prose: *Poems in Sunshine and Firelight, Landmarks and Other Poems, Pencilled Fly-Leaves: A Book of Essays in Town and Country,* etc. There was an occasional strain of vivid realism, of which his best-known poem, "The Morning Street," is a likely example; "The Western Pioneer," a piece of family chronicle, and "At Kilcolman Castle," a fanciful excursion, are representative of some of his other veins. Piatt was no inventor of new forms, but the subject matter of his poems was relatively original and he often succeeded in transcending the sentimentality of many of his contemporaries.

Principcal Works: Poems of Two Friends (in collaboration with William Dean Howells) 1860; Poems in Sunshine and Firelight, 1866; Landmarks and Other Poems, 1872; Pencilled Fly-Leaves: A Book of Essays in Town and Country, 1880; A Book of Gold and Other Sonnets, 1889; Odes in Ohio, and Other Poems, 1897.

About: Coggeshall, W. T. The Poets and Poetry of the West; Duyckinck, E. A. & G. L. The Cyclopaedia of American Literature; Cincinnati Enquirer February 17, 1917.

PIATT, SARAH MORGAN (BRYAN) (August 11, 1836-December 22, 1919), poet, was born in Lexington, Ky., the daughter of Talbot Nelson Bryan, whose father had gone from North Carolina to Kentucky with Daniel Boone's party, and Mary (Spiers) Bryan. Sarah was graduated from Henry Female College at New Castle, Ky., read the English Romantic poets with extreme devotion, and became herself a youthful writer of verse. The Galveston *News* printed some of her first products and George D. Prentice of the Louisville *Journal* even ventured to suggest that she would, in time, be the ranking female poet in America.

Following her marriage, June 18, 1861, to John James Piatt [*q.v.*], she lived in Washington, D.C., and then in North Bend, Ohio; and during her husband's consulship in Ireland she became acquainted with Austin Dobson, Edmund Gosse, Alice Meynell, and other literary folk.

Sarah Piatt published fifteen volumes of her own verse and two collaborations with her husband. Her life in Cork and Dublin provided materials for *An Irish Wild-Flower* and *An Enchanted Castle, and Other Poems: Pictures, Portraits, and People in Ireland.* The British likened her to Elizabeth Barrett Browning, and her later works were published in either London or Edinburgh as well as the United States. Her verse, though tastefully feminine and relatively free of the conventionality and self-indulgence that characterized the poetry of her female contemporaries, is today forgotten.

Principal Works: (collaborations with her husband) The Nests at Washington and Other Poems, 1864; The Children Out-of-Doors: A Book of Verses by Two in One House, 1885 (alone): Selected Poems, 1886; Child's World Ballads, 1887; An Irish Wild-Flower, 1891; An Enchanted Castle and Other Poems: Pictures,

Portraits, and People in Ireland, 1893; Complete Poems, 1894.

ABOUT: Willard, F. E. & Livermore, M. A. American Women; New York Times December 24, 1919.

PICKERING, JOHN (February 7, 1777-May 5, 1846), philologist and lawyer, was born at Salem, Mass., the son of Timothy Pickering, eminent New England statesman, and Jane Rebecca (White) Pickering. While he was a student at Harvard College, from which he was graduated in 1796, his cousin, John Clark, addressed to him his illuminating *Letters to a Student in the University*... (1796). Pickering began a law course in Philadelphia, but in July 1797 he sailed for Lisbon to become secretary to William Smith, American minister to Portugal; in 1799 he went to London, where he served Rufus King, United States minister plenipotentiary to Great Britain, in a similar capacity.

When Pickering returned to Boston in 1801 he had done some extensive studying in languages and had absorbed a certain amount of Continental culture. In 1804 he was admitted to the bar and a year later was married to Sarah White, a relative. He occupied several local political offices, and in 1833 drew up his *Part First: Of the Internal Administration of the Government.* As a lawyer he was not highly popular but his colleagues acknowledged his fundamental astuteness, and the *American Jurist* published many of his brilliant discourses.

From his early years, when he had learned Arabic while traveling with his father, Pickering had a growing appetite for languages. He refused the chairs of Greek and Hebrew at Harvard, and among the twenty tongues which he mastered were the principal European and Semitic languages and several Chinese dialects. His *Comprehensive Lexicon of the Greek Language* was long the official Greek-English dictionary; and his *Vocabulary or Collection of Words Which Have Been Supposed to be Peculiar to the United States of America* was, with varying degrees of authenticity, the first book of Americanisms. Pickering's philological delvings, including his research on North American Indian tongues, were significant contributions to American cultural history.

PRINCIPAL WORKS: Vocabulary or Collection of Words and Phrases Which Have Been Supposed to be Peculiar to the United States of America, 1816; Comprehensive Lexicon of the Greek Language, 1826.

ABOUT: Brooks, Van W. Flowering of New England; Pickering, M. O. Life of John Pickering; White, D. A. Eulogy on John Pickering.

PICKETT, ALBERT JAMES (August 13, 1810-October 28, 1858), historian, was born in Anson County, N.C., the son of Frances (Dickson) and William Raiford Pickett. He spent his boyhood in Alabama, and in his father's country store learned much from the Indian traders; his formal education was admittedly weak. At eighteen he went by horseback and stage to Middletown, Conn., where he was to have enrolled in a military school, but instead, went on to Cambridge, Mass. After two years of study here and in Stafford County, Va., he returned to Alabama and studied law briefly. In 1832 he married Sarah Smith Harris, by whom he had twelve children.

Pickett's interest in agricultural experiments prompted his articles for the *Southern Cultivator;* newspapers accepted his economic and historical essays. He was only passively interested in politics, and he staunchly refused a proposal for gubernatorial nomination in 1853. Of Andrew Jackson, however, he was an ardent admirer. His only substantial literary achievement was the *History of Alabama and Incidentally of Georgia and Mississippi From the Earliest Period* (1851). Pickett effected no purposeful unity in the book, and his style was awkward; but his treatment of territorial Alabama and his first-hand knowledge of this and related historical movements, supplemented by manuscripts, old records, and verbal accounts, invested the document with a certain permanency among Southern archives.

ABOUT: Jackson, C. M. A Brief Biographical Sketch of the Late Colonel Albert James Pickett; Transactions of the Alabama Historical Society: Vol. 4.

PICTON, THOMAS (May 16, 1822-February 20, 1891), journalist and soldier of fortune, was born Thomas Picton Milner, the son of Jane Milner, "widow," of New York City. There is no record of his father. He attended Columbia College and then the University of the City of New York, from which he was graduated in 1840; he was admitted to the bar in 1843, but sailed for Europe and joined the French army under Louis Philippe. A second military adventure began several years after his return when he allied himself with Narciso Lopez's band for a march against Cuba, returned to New York for a little journalism, and then became paymaster in "General" William ("Filibuster") Walker's army for the invasion of Nicaragua.

Thomas Picton (he dropped his last name) had first plunged into journalism in 1850 when with William Herbert ("Frank Forester") he edited a magazine called the *Era*

As a participant in the Native American movement he edited the *Sachem* and later founded the *True American*; and he began to write, sometimes under the pseudonym "Paul Preston," for the *True National Democrat,* the *Sunday Dispatch,* and the *Sunday Mercury. Paul Preston's Book of Gymnastics: or, Sports for Youth* appeared in 1870. During his late years he wrote copiously for the *Clipper*; *Turf, Field, and Farm*; and the *Spirit of the Times,* and the latter published his social and historical "Reminiscences of a Sporting Journalist." Into *Rose Street: Its Past, Present, and Future* went his fondness for the "then and now" of New York. His two breezy plays, *A Tempest in a Teapot* and *There's No Smoke Without Fire* seem to have merited little attention.

PRINCIPAL WORKS: The Fireside Magician, 1870; A Tempest in a Teapot, 1871; There's No Smoke Without Fire, 1872; Rose Street: Its Past, Present and Future, 1873; Paul Preston's Book of Gymnastics: or, Sports for Youth.

ABOUT: New York Tribune February 22, 1891; Spirit of the Times February 28, 1891; Masonic Chronicle and Official Bulletin March 1891.

PIERCE, GILBERT ASHVILLE (January 11, 1839-February 15, 1901), journalist, novelist, governor of Dakota Territory, and first U.S. senator from North Dakota, was born in East Otto, N.Y., the son of Sylvester and Mary Olive (Treat) Pierce. He attended grade school and at fifteen, after his family's removal to Indiana, clerked in his father's general store. Four years later he was married to Anne Maria Bartholomew; he read law in Valparaiso; and after two years at the old University of Chicago was admitted to practice in Indiana.

At the outbreak of the Civil War he enlisted as a volunteer, and rose to the rank of colonel before his retirement in 1865. Pierce was a correspondent for several major dailies during his secretaryship to Oliver P. Morton, the governor of Indiana, through whom he made some influential connections. In 1871 he resigned from a government clerkship in Washington, and in 1872 joined the staff of the Chicago *Inter Ocean,* becoming its managing editor before going over to the *Chicago Daily News.* By 1884 Pierce had gathered considerable prestige and was named governor of the Dakota Territory. When this territory was divided five years later Pierce was elected U.S. senator from North Dakota; he served the two-year short term but was not re-elected in 1891. During his last years he was connected with the Minneapolis *Daily Pioneer Press* and the *Tribune.* Ill health forced him to decline his appointment (January 1893) as minister to Portugal, and he died in Chicago following a long illness.

His *Dickens Dictionary* has become a permanent portion of "the complete Dickens," and his two novels, *Zachariah: The Congressman* and *A Dangerous Woman* drew praise from the critics. *One Hundred Wives,* perhaps his best play, enjoyed an enviable two-year success. Pierce published very little, in all, but evidenced considerably more literary ability than most of the politician-journalists of his time.

PRINCIPAL WORKS: The Dickens Dictionary, 1872; Zachariah: The Congressman, 1876; One Hundred Wives, 1880; A Dangerous Woman, 1883.

ABOUT: Biographical Encyclopaedia of Illinois; Minneapolis Tribune February 16, 1901.

PIERPONT, JOHN (April 6, 1785-August 27, 1866), Unitarian clergyman, reformer, and poet, was born in Litchfield, Conn., the great-grandson of James Pierpont, one of the founders of Yale college, and the son of James and Elizabeth (Collins) Pierpont. He attended Yale, graduating in 1804, and taught for a short time in an academy at Bethlehem, Conn.; leaving to go to South Carolina as tutor in the family of Colonel William Alston. On his return North he studied law in the Litchfield Law School and was admitted to the bar in 1812. After two years of unremunerative practice in Newburyport, Mass., he entered the mercantile world, and at this time his first poems, *Airs of Palestine,* were published and instantly acclaimed as the work of an unusual talent. His business venture proving unsuccessful, he attended the Harvard Divinity School and was ordained pastor of the Hollis Street Church, Boston, in 1819.

He was a prohibitionist and a crusader for abolition; but his ardor for these causes was not shared by his parishioners, and after a seven year struggle ending in Pierpont's exoneration by the ecclesiastical council, he resigned in 1845. He was subsequently pastor of the First Unitarian Society of Troy, N.Y.; and later of the First Congregational (Unitarian) Church of West Medford, Mass. At the beginning of the Civil War he became chaplain of a Massachusetts regiment, but his strength being unequal to the task, he soon resigned and was appointed to a clerkship in the Treasury Department in Washington, a position which he held until his death in Medford, Mass. Pierpont was married twice, first to Mary Sheldon Lord who died in 1855; and in 1857 to Harriet Louise (Campbell) Fowler.

Pierpont's poems, especially *Airs of Palestine,* are the graceful and facile work of an original and understanding temperament.

PRINCIPAL WORKS: The Portrait, 1812; Airs of Palestine, 1816; Airs of Palestine and Other Poems, 1840; The Anti-Slavery Poems of John Pierpont, 1843; The American First Class Book, 1823; The National Reader, 1827.

ABOUT: Dix, J. R. Pulpit Portraits; Ford, A. A. John Pierpont: A Biographical Sketch; Lothrop, S. K. Proceedings of an Ecclesiastical Council in the Case of the Proprietors of Hollis-Street Meeting-House and the Rev. John Pierpont; Boston Transcript August 27, 1866.

PIKE, ALBERT (December 29, 1809-April 2, 1891), poet, editor, lawyer, soldier, and Masonic writer, was born in Boston, the son of Benjamin Pike, a farmer and shoemaker, and Sarah (Andrews) Pike. He was brought up in Byfield and other Massachusetts towns. In 1825 he passed the freshman and in 1826 the junior class examinations at Harvard, but being unable to meet the tuition charges, he could not attend. Already at fifteen supporting himself by teaching, he went on teaching, studying, and writing until 1831, when, irked by the narrowness of New England life, he went West, and for two years was a member of hunting and trapping expeditions in the Southwest territory.

In 1833 he settled in Arkansas, and first taught, then worked as associate editor of the Little Rock *Arkansas Advocate* and as assistant clerk of the territorial legislature. In 1834 the record of his recent adventures and hardships, *Prose Sketches and Poems Written in the Western Country,* was published in Boston, and thereafter, though he continued to write, his poetry became more and more incidental to other work and he made no attempt to publish.

Collection of Frederick H. Meserve
ALBERT PIKE

From 1835 to 1837 Pike was owner-editor of the *Advocate,* and at about the same time was licensed to practice law. Widely read, a hard worker, of commanding physical presence and great vitality, he rapidly won eminence. From 1836 to 1845 he supervised publication of thirteen volumes of reports of law cases and of the *Revised Statutes of Arkansas.* During the Mexican War he served with distinction as captain of a cavalry troop. Admitted to practice before the United States Supreme Court, he subsequently prosecuted many Indian claims. From 1853 to 1857 he lived in New Orleans.

At the outbreak of the Civil War, though opposed to slavery and secession, he supported the Confederate cause. Appointed to negotiate treaties with the Indians, he was later made brigadier-general of the department of Indian Territory, but resenting invasions of what he deemed an independent command, he resigned after considerable controversy and went into retirement. After the War he was suspect both in the North and South, and for a while took refuge in Canada, returning, through the intervention of friends, in the autumn of 1865. Until 1868 he lived in Memphis, and then in Washington, where he practiced until his retirement in 1879. Increasingly devoting himself to Freemasonry—he had become a Mason in 1850—he revised over a period of years the rituals of the Scottish Rite order and contributed heavily to its literature through his research and writings, the most important and extensive of these works being the *Morals and Dogma.* He had been elected Grand Commander of the Supreme Grand Council, Southern Jurisdiction of the United States, in 1859, and held the post for thirty-two years, known and honored by Masons throughout the world.

Pike had married in 1834 Mary Ann Hamilton, of Arkansas, who died in 1876. Of their five children who reached maturity, three survived him. Attended by his daughter, Pike died in his eighty-second year at the house of the Scottish Rite Temple, Washington, and was buried in Oak Hill Cemetery.

Pike has a place in American literature as an early poet of the Southwest. Usually vigorous in expression and occasionally showing real imagination and power of observation, especially when writing of the life about him, he nevertheless lacked opportunity for development, the atmosphere of a young active community being unfavorable to literary growth. What talent he had as poet and man of letters was gradually directed to research and editing, first in the law and then in Freemasonry, and in both fields he produced work of outstanding value.

Principal Works: Prose Sketches and Poems Written in the Western Country, 1834; Morals and Dogma of the Ancient and Accepted Scottish Rite of Freemasonry, 1872.

About: Allsopp, F. W. Albert Pike: A Biography; Thomas, D. Y. Arkansas and Its People; Independent November 17, 1898.

PIKE, JAMES SHEPHERD (September 8, 1811-November 29, 1882), journalist, political writer, was born in Calais, Maine, the son of William and Hannah (Shepherd) Pike. He attended the district school until the age of fourteen, leaving to go into the business world. Several years later he entered journalism as correspondent for the Portland *Advertiser* and the Boston *Courier*. He was the Washington correspondent and associate editor of the *New York Tribune* from 1850 to 1860; during which time he covered the political situation in the capital and gave in his letters a graphic account of those volcanic years.

From 1861 to 1866 Pike was United States minister to the Netherlands. He was a supporter of Horace Greeley for the presidency in 1872, and about that time visited South Carolina for material for his work *The Prostrate State,* a picture of that section under carpet-bag rule. During the latter years of his life he was engaged in the collection and publication of his earlier works, which had appeared in various papers, notably the *Tribune*.

Pike died in his birthplace, Calais, while on a trip from his summer home in Robbinston, Maine. His first wife was Charlotte Grosvenor, whom he married in 1837; his second marriage was with Elizabeth Ellicott of Avondale, Pa.

Pike was a vigorous and aggressive writer, and his books, based on careful observation of the economic and political situations of his time, are able, unbiased commentaries on his contemporaries and their problems.

Principal Works: The Financial Crisis: Its Evils and Their Remedy, 1867; The Restoration of the Currency, 1868; Horace Greeley in 1872, (1873); Chief Justice Chase, 1873; The Prostrate State: South Carolina Under Negro Government, 1874; Contributions to the Financial Discussion: 1874-1875 (1875); The New Puritan, 1879; First Blows of the Civil War, 1879.

About: Evans, C. W. Biographical and Historical Accounts of the Fox, Ellicott, and Evans Families; Griffin, J. History of the Press of Maine; Knowlton, I. C. Annals of Calais, Maine, and St. Stephen, New Brunswick; Boston Courier November 30, 1882; Sun (New York) November 30, 1882; Portland Advertiser November 29, 1882.

PIKE, MARY HAYDEN (GREEN) (November 30, 1824-January 15, 1908), novelist, was born in Eastport, Maine, the daughter of Deacon Elijah Dix Green and Hannah Claflin (Hayden) Green. She attended school at Calais, Maine, and at the age of twelve demonstrated her religious convictions by undergoing baptism in an icy stream. At the Charlestown (Mass.) Female Seminary, from which she was graduated in 1843, her religious faith was still further reinforced. Three years later she was married to Frederick Augustus Pike, who, during the Civil War, was a member of Congress. They lived in Washington from 1861 to 1869; made a journey to Europe; and on their return lived in Calais until Mr. Pike's death in 1886. Her last years were occupied with landscape painting and religious activities.

Two of her most popular writings sprang from her spirited Abolitionist sentiments: *Ida May,* appearing over the signature "Mary Langdon," a thoroughly melodramatic treatment of the fate of a wealthy child who was sold into slavery; and *Caste,* a novel written under the pseudonym "Sydney A. Story, Jr.," hurling its arguments against race discrimination. In *Agnes* she combined a portrait of the American Indian with a chronicle of the Revolutionary War. Like many female novelists of her day, Mrs. Pike basked in the warmth of a popularity that became, at times, almost intense, and then cooled with a speed that left little hope for any real literary permanence.

Principal Works: Ida May, 1854; Caste, 1856; Agnes, 1858.

About: Boston Transcript January 12, 1889; Sun (Baltimore) January 16, 1908.

PINKNEY, EDWARD COOTE (October 1, 1802-April 11, 1828), poet and editor, was born in London, England, during his parents' residence there when his father, William Pinkney of Annapolis, Md., was one of the United States Commissioners to adjust claims under the Jay Treaty. Also a native of Maryland, his mother was Ann Maria (Rodgers) Pinkney, a sister of Commodore John Rodgers of the United States Navy.

As a baby Edward spent two years in Baltimore but was taken back to England in 1807 when his father served as minister to the Court of St. James. Edward received his schooling in London and Baltimore and in 1815 joined the United States Navy, serving mostly in Mediterranean waters until 1824 when he resigned his commission. In the same year he married Georgiana McCausland, an Irish girl from Baltimore.

After leaving the Navy, Pinkney practiced law in Baltimore and became well-known as a poet through his publications: *Look Out Upon the Stars, My Love: A Serenade Written by a Gentleman of Baltimore,* brought out with a musical setting in 1823; and *Rodolph: A Fragment,* which attracted the attention of the *North American Review* and is said to have influenced Poe in writing "Al Aaraaf."

Pinkney edited for one year the bi-weekly *The Marylander,* retiring because of his fast-ebbing health.

In appearance he looked the part of a "Gentleman of Baltimore," and was a romantic figure in the social life of the city, his dauntless code of honor often stirring up sensational challenges to duel. Little known today, his five lyrics, particularly "A Health" and "Serenade," were highly praised by Poe and other contemporary critics, who believed him to be a lyric poet of unusual merit.

PRINCIPAL WORKS: Look Out Upon the Stars, My Love: A Serenade Written by a Gentleman of Baltimore, 1823; Rodolph: A Fragment, 1823.

ABOUT: Boyle, E. Biographical Sketches of Distinguished Marylanders; Hubner, C. W. Representative Southern Poets; Mabbott, T. O. & Pleadwell, F. L. The Life and Works of Edward Coote Pinkney; Baltimore Patriot April 17, 1828; Marylander April 16, 1828; New York Mirror April 26, 1828.

PITKIN, TIMOTHY (January 21, 1766-December 18, 1847), statesman and political economist, was born at Farmington, Conn., the son of the Rev. Timothy Pitkin and Temperance (Clap) Pitkin. He prepared for college under his father and brother-in-law; and after graduating from Yale in 1785 he taught Latin and Greek at Plainfield Academy and then studied law. In 1788 he was admitted to the bar and some time afterward began an extensive political career; he became a member of Congress in 1805. Josiah Quincy, leader of a staunch Federalist group, was a close friend of Pitkin's and the materials for Quincy's speeches against the Embargo and Non-Intercourse acts were reinforced by Pitkin's statistical research. After the defeat of the Federalists in 1819 Pitkin was elected to the Connecticut legislature, where he remained until 1830 and then turned his attention to writing, largely on historical and economic subjects. He was married in 1801 to Elizabeth Hubbard, by whom he had six children.

Pitkin's earlier *Statistical View of the Commerce of the United States of America* (1816), revised and enlarged in 1835, still has considerable value as a reference on economic history. For his *Political and Civil History of the United States* Pitkin had done exhaustive and discriminating research; its style was somewhat stodgy but it contained a vast amount of helpful data. The Société Française de Statistique Universelle awarded him a medal, in 1837, for his scholarly work in statistics. Pitkin's writings were, all in all, highly significant contributions to the then poorly documented science of political economy.

PRINCIPAL WORKS: A Statistical View of the Commerce of the United States . . . , 1816; A Political and Civil History of the United States, 1828.

ABOUT: Memorial Biographies . . . New-England Historical Genealogical Society: Vol. 1; Columbian Register (New Haven) December 25, 1847.

PLUMMER, JONATHAN (July 13, 1761-September 13, 1819), ballad-monger, "poet laureate" to "Lord" Timothy Dexter, [*q.v.*], was born in Newbury, Mass., the son of Jonathan Plummer, a wealthy cordwainer, and Abigail (Greenleaf) Plummer. He was thought to be too "peculiar" to benefit much by schooling, and at an early age was put to peddling halibut from a wheelbarrow. There was little genuine boyishness in his temperament, and his remarkable memory and love for books encouraged quiet and introspective habits. "Allan Ramsay's tuneful works," he says, "ravished my soul with . . . transporting joys," and he was immediately set on becoming a poet.

But it was first as an itinerant preacher and then as a trader that he tried to make a fortune. In both he failed, and at twenty-six considered the advisability of marrying for money. Within two months he was suitor to nine "vigorous and antiquated virgins" but found no escape from bachelordom. He was, for a while, pawnbroker, stuffer of underbeds, and writer of love letters.

In 1795 he succeeded in getting himself a little welcome notoriety by exploiting Timothy Dexter's uncommon genius with the issue of a broadside announcing himself "Lord" Dexter's "poet laureate." After his patron's death he was reduced again to the peddling of sermons, poems, and notions in Market Square.

Plummer's literary organ was the broadside, which usually consisted of a short "ode" and a didactic and often autobiographical discourse illustrated by a crude, moral-pointing wood-cut. His subjects ran from private scandals and "small-pox by inoculation" to interpretations of the "acts of God." In three-part pamphlet form he issued his *Sketch of the History of the Life of Jonathan Plummer* (c. 1797). A riotous and yet pathetic mixture of sycophant and egotist, Plummer has become, like Dexter, an almost legendary figure in literary history.

PRINCIPAL WORKS: History of the Life of Jonathan Plummer (c. 1797). *Broadsides*—The Author's Congratulatory Address to Citizen Timothy Dexter on His Attaining an Independent Fortune, 1793; Parson Pidgin: or, Holy Kissing . . . Occasioned by a Report that Parson Pidgin Had Kissed a Young Woman, 1807.

ABOUT: Ford, W. C. Broadsides, Ballads, Etc., Printed in Massachusetts . . . ; Marquand, J. P. Lord Timothy Dexter of Newburyport; Plummer, J. Sketch of . . . Jonathan Plummer.

From the "Whitman" daguerreotype*
EDGAR ALLAN POE
1848

POE, EDGAR ALLAN (January 19, 1809-October 7, 1849), poet, story writer, and essayist, was born in Boston, but though his first volume of poems was published as by "a Bostonian," and his mother loved the city, he had not a drop of New England blood in his veins. His father was David Poe, Jr. (son of a Revolutionary "general" from Maryland), who had abandoned a law practice in Augusta, Ga., to become an actor, and had married an English actress, a widow, Elizabeth (Arnold) Hopkins. Edgar was the second of three children, all born while the parents migrated from one stock company to another. Both parents were tubercular, and died in the same year, 1811, in Richmond. The children were separated, and Edgar was taken in (though never formally adopted) by John Allan, a wealthy Scotch merchant, whose name he incorporated with his own.

During Allan's first marriage, Poe was the petted child of a prosperous family, Mrs. Allan proving a real mother to him. From 1815 to 1820 the Allans lived in England, where Poe went to school at Stoke Newington, the scene of "William Wilson." He was a handsome, brilliant youngster, equally distinguished in the study of languages and in athletics. All his life he was a noted swimmer, broad jumper, and boxer, in spite of his slight build. On their return to America, the Allans put him under private tutors to prepare him for the University of Virginia, which he entered in 1826.

Up to this time, except for the misfortune of his early orphaning and separation from his brother and sister, the boy's life had been a happy one. From now on, it is a dreary chronicle of misery and misfortune. Every boy in the University of Virginia then —and for a long time after—did a certain amount of drinking, gambling, and running-up of tradesmen's debts; it was a sort of traditional sowing of wild oats by these high-spirited lads of the old Southern ruling class. But if Poe had thought himself one of them, he was soon disillusioned. His foster-father refused to allow him to return after the winter term, and announced that he would put him in a mercantile office. Few boys would have been less fitted for such drudgery. This boy promptly ran away, enlisting as a private in the army, in Boston, in May 1827, as Edgar A. Perry. Three months later he published his first volume of poems, *Tamerlane*.

In 1830 Mrs. Allan lay dying, and almost with her last breath begged her husband to find and rescue the lad she loved as her own son. He did so, grudgingly; he bought him out of the army and procured a commission for him at West Point—a solution as grotesque as the subsequent cadetship of James McNeill Whistler. Poe deliberately refused to obey rules or to study, so as to get himself expelled, which he accomplished in short order. Meanwhile Allan had remarried, and soon his second wife, who in any case hated and was jealous of the handsome son of the strolling actors, bore a son of her own. That was the end of any real relations between Poe and Allan, though before Allan finally threw Poe out of his house he had gone to the trouble of breaking off the poet's first boyish but deep love affair with Elmira Royster. When he died, he left

* Used by special permission of Brown University Library

not a cent to the boy who had been reared in the expectation of being his heir.

In 1831 Poe was thus cast on the world, utterly untrained for any profession, hypersensitive, destitute with no experience in poverty, the author of three volumes of poems which nobody had read. There was only one recourse open to him, and that was journalism. He went to Baltimore, where he discovered an aunt, his father's sister, Maria Clemm, who had a little girl, Virginia. Poe, the perpetual seeker of the mother-image, immediately attached himself to Mrs. Clemm ("You, who have been more than mother unto me") and to her dying day "Muddy" adored her "Eddie." His only bit of luck in the next few years was the winning of a $50 prize offered by the *Baltimore Saturday Visiter* [*sic*] for a story, which he won with "A Ms. Found in a Bottle." He would have won the poetry prize, too, had it not been discovered that both prize manuscripts were by the same author.

Finally, at the end of 1835, he was offered a staff position on the *Southern Literary Messenger,* published in Richmond, then one of the leading magazines. Before going to Richmond he married his cousin Virginia Clemm, who was not yet fourteen. Volumes have been written on this marriage, in which may lie the key to Poe's puzzling personality. Suffice it to say that when Virginia died at twenty-four she still looked like a child and was in all probability a virgin.

In 1837 Poe left the *Messenger* and went to New York. Mrs. Clemm and Virginia, of course, accompanied him in all his wanderings. Failing to find a suitable connection there, he moved to Philadelphia, where he lived for six years, most of the time in a little house now restored as a Poe memorial. It was there that Virginia suffered the first of her hemorrhages which proved her marked for early death. It was there too that the family was in such abject poverty that the sick girl had to warm herself by training the cat to lie on her breast, while her distracted husband, wrapping her in his overcoat, chafed her icy feet. There were periods when Mrs. Clemm went from editor to editor, begging for a few dollars due, a bit of work on order, for her Eddie; when nearly all the family belongings were in the pawnshop; when Poe, the atrociously proud, had to borrow pitiful sums he had no chance of repaying. It is easy to say that it was by his own fault that he was dismissed first from *Burton's Gentleman Magazine,* then from *Graham's,* both of which made enormous strides in circulation under his editorship. But what is a man's fault? There was no international copyright law; $4 was considered a fair price for an article, $15 for a story, and it might be paid six months after publication. Never was there a harder worker than Poe; never one more misunderstood. Certainly there were times when he was disabled by drink; he was a congenital alcoholic, whom one glass sent into a frenzy. He was despairing, his wife dying, the fear of insanity hanging over him, the actuality of want upon him. It would take the hard heart of a Griswold to feel anything for Poe but aching pity.

In 1844 he tried New York again. He worked for a while on N. P. Willis' *Evening Mirror,* then on the *Broadway Journal,* of which he eventually became owner, only to have to suspend for lack of funds. Poe's dream always was to own a magazine, an organ of his own; it is half of the reason behind his strange multiple courtship of wealthy literary-minded widows after Virginia's death. The other half was deep in his agonized subconscious.

Virginia died at the beginning of 1847, in the little house at Fordham, now part of New York City, then far out in the country. The remaining two-and-a-half years of Poe's tormented life may be passed over quickly. The critic, the poet, the writer of "ratiocinative" stories gradually became enmeshed in the wild, half-intellectual mysticism which culminated in "Eureka." He found his lost Elmira—perhaps his "lost Lenore"—now Mrs. Shelton, and a widow. He became engaged to her, he became engaged to Mrs. Sarah Helen Whitman, he became quasi-engaged to at least two other women. At the very time of his death he was making arrangements for his marriage. The painful details of that death need not be dwelt on; in an alcholic daze, half or more insane, he was picked up by election thugs in Baltimore, dragged from poll to poll as a repeater, finally left to die in a gutter, and taken at last to a hospital, where a few days later the end came. "I wish to God somebody would blow my damned brains out," he cried in a moment of awful surcease from delirium. He was buried in Westminster churchyard in Baltimore, where now Mrs. Clemm and Virginia lie beside him. He named as his literary executor Rufus Griswold, who repaid the trust by writing the most scurrilous biography on record, for half a century poisoning the minds of the whole reading public as to what Poe really was and how he really lived.

Poe was the founder of the modern detective story—what Edmond de Goncourt called "the creation of a fable by a+b, . . .

the novel of the future, bound to concern itself more with the story of what happens in the brain of humanity than in its heart." He was also, despite his aberrations of enthusiasm, the ablest critic of his time in America. In verse he achieved incomparable melodic effects, though much that he wrote is shallow and jejune. His influence has been incalculable in both verse and prose on later writers—on Baudelaire, for example, and the whole Symbolist tradition that underlies modern poetry. "This finest of finest of artists," Bernard Shaw has called him. His work was essentially aristocratic; in the America of the 1830's and 1840's it is a pure miracle.

But the man behind this glittering façade, this slender man with the wavy brown hair and the tragic grey eyes, what was he? He was a typically schizoid personality: "I dwelt alone in a world of moan" is his keyword. Those ice-palaces, his short stories; or his essays, equally divided between hack journalism and rather incoherent efforts to express the inexpressible, are the voice of the exterior man, the conscious mind vainly struggling to function in an alien and hostile world. The inner man, the tortured subconscious mind which perceived only too fatally how hopeless was the struggle, appears in those haunted melodies out of time and place which are his poems.

Poe's whole existence from childhood might have been constructed as the ideal hell for such a person as he was. He sought continually for some balance to hold him above the abyss of insanity; he is his own victim of "The Pit and the Pendulum," with the pendulum of necessity beating above him and the black pit threatening below. Alcohol was not a sedative to him, but an exaggerated stimulant. The final refuge was poetry. It was because he felt so profoundly that in his poetry his hidden and proudly defended self was revealed that he endeavored to draw the wool over the eyes of a stupid world in the famous mechanical explanations of "The Poetic Principle." In his poems, under the adroit cover of the specious mechanism he had constructed, Poe could unveil his inner, introverted self before a callous extroverted public. There he could occupy himself incessantly with his core-preoccupation, that death-yearning which was his inmost secret, that longing for the peace which he had never known.

Principal Works: Tamerlane and Other Poems, 1827; Al Aaraaf, Tamerlane, and Minor Poems, 1829; Poems, 1831; The Narrative of Arthur Gordon Pym, 1838; The Conchologist's First Book, 1839; Tales of the Grotesque and Arabesque, 1840; The Prose Romances of Edgar Allan Poe, 1843; Tales, 1845; The Raven and Other Poems, 1845; Eureka: A Prose Poem, 1848.

About: Allen, H. Israfel; Baudelaire, C. Edgar Poe: Sa Vie et ses Oeuvres; Benton, J. In the Poe Circle; Bonaparte, M. Edgar Poe: Étude Psychoanalytique; Brownell, W. C. American Prose Masters; Campbell, K. The Mind of Poe; Dow, D. Dark Glory; Evers, H. H. Edgar Allan Poe; Gill, W. F. The Life of Edgar Allan Poe; Harrison, J. A. New Glimpses of Poe; Harrison, J. A. Poe and His Friends; Ingram, J. H. Edgar Allan Poe; Jackson, D. K. Poe and the Southern Literary Messenger; Kissling, D. & Nethercot, A. H. (eds.). Muse Anthology: Poe Memorial Edition; Krutch, J. W. Edgar Allan Poe; Leigh, O. Edgar Allan Poe; Lloyd, J. A. T. The Murder of Edgar Allan Poe; Macy, J. A. Edgar Allan Poe; Marks, J. A. Genius and Disaster; Moran, J. J. A Defense of Edgar Allan Poe; Phillips, M. E. Edgar Allan Poe: The Man; Pope-Hennessy, U. Edgar Allan Poe; Ransome, A. Edgar Allan Poe; Robertson, J. W. Edgar Allan Poe; Shanks, E. Edgar Allan Poe; Stedman, E. C. Edgar Allan Poe; Ticknor, C. Poe's Helen; Whitman, S. H. Edgar Poe and His Critics; Whitty, J. H. Poeana; Woodberry, G. E. Edgar Allan Poe; American Mercury August 1933; Atlantic Monthly April 1896, December 1899, December 1908; Bookman July 1901, September 1916, October 1927; Century Magazine January 1909, October 1909, December 1910; Dial January 16, 1899; February 16, 1903, November 16, 1909; Harper's Magazine November 1867, September 1872, March 1899; Saturday Review of Literature September 23, 1933; Scribner's Magazine October 1875, April 1876, September 1907; Southern Atlantic Quarterly January 1909, July 1911, January 1912, April 1913, October 1915.

POLLARD, EDWARD ALFRED (February 27, 1831-December 16, 1872), journalist and historical writer, was born at "Alta Vista," Albemarle County, Va., the son of Richard and Paulina Cabell (Rives) Pollard. After Hampden-Sidney College, he attended the University of Virginia from 1847 to 1849 and began the study of law at William and Mary College, completing the course in Baltimore. He spent a number of years in California; and on his return became clerk of the judiciary committee in the House of Representatives during President Buchanan's administration. Influenced by his friend Bishop Meade, he studied for the Episcopal ministry, but turned to journalism instead, and from 1861 to 1867 he was editor of the *Daily Richmond Examiner*. In his paper, Pollard, an intense advocate of the Confederacy, unmercifully attacked Jefferson Davis, whom he accused of inefficiency.

In 1864 he sailed for England to further the sale of his books, but was captured in the blockade and imprisoned at Fort Warren and Fortress Monroe, until exchanged, January 12, 1865, when he returned to Richmond. In 1867, he began the publication of *Southern Opinion,* and the next year *The*

Political Pamphlet, neither of which lasted more than two years. He then moved to New York where he lived for several years, turning out a large number of works. The name of his first wife is not known; but he was married a second time after the war to Marie Antoinette Nathalie Granier. The subject matter of most of Pollard's work is the Civil War, from the viewpoint of the South, and while at times he wrote with ability and penetration, he was often guilty of the jaundiced eye and biased hatred of the fanatic.

Principal Works: The Southern Spy: or, Curiosities of Negro Slavery in the South, 1859; Black Diamonds Gathered in the Darkey Homes of the South; 1859; Black Aaron: A Christmas Story, 1859; Letters of the Southern Spy in Washington and Elsewhere, 1861; The Second Battle of Manassas, 1862; The First Year of the War, 1862; The Second Year of the War, 1863, 1864; The Rival Administrations: Richmond and Washington in December 1863, 1864; The Two Nations: A Key to the History of the American War, 1864; The War in America, 1863-64, 1865; The Third Year of the War, 1865; A Letter on the State of the War, 1865; Observations in the North: Eight Months in Prison and on Parole, 1865; The Last Year of the War, 1866; Southern History of the War, 1866; The Lost Cause: A New Southern History of the War of the Confederates, 1866; Lee and His Lieutenants, 1867; The Lost Cause Regained, 1868; Life of Jefferson Davis: With a Secret History of the Southern Confederacy, 1869; Memoir of the Assassination of Henry Rives Pollard, 1869; The Virginia Tourist, 1870; A Southern Historian's Appeal for Horace Greeley, 1872.

About: Brown, A. The Cabells and Their Kin; Childs, J. R. Reliques of the Rives; Richmond Enquirer and Richmond Dispatch December 18, 1872.

POMEROY, "BRICK." See POMEROY, MARCUS MILLS

POMEROY, MARCUS MILLS (December 25, 1833-May 30, 1896), journalist, printer, and politician, best known as "Brick" Pomeroy, was born in Elmira, N.Y., the son of Hunt Pomeroy, a watchmaker, and Orlina Rebecca (White) Pomeroy. His mother died when he was only two and he was brought up on his uncle's modest farm, helping with the chores, working in the village smithy, and learning all the by-laws of rigid economy. At the age of seventeen he went hobo-fashion to Corning, N.Y., where he served an apprenticeship on the *Journal*; and there a few years later set up his first paper, the *Sun*. In March 1857 he set out for Wisconsin, and founded the Horicon *Argus*. After a succession of printing jobs in various cities he returned to Wisconsin and established the La Crosse *Democrat,* which weathered the bitterest of prejudice and misfortune (1860-66) and then in 1868 reached a circulation of 100,000.

That same year he published the daily New York *Democrat,* with only a fleeting popularity, and *Pomeroy's Democrat,* a weekly which he continued in Chicago five years later. Back in La Crosse again, Pomeroy witnessed reverses in his paper, and left shortly for Colorado where he organized and promoted the highly successful Atlantic-Pacific Railway Tunnel; he became its president in 1890, with offices in New York. In conjunction with the publication of his news monthly, *Advance Thought,* he issued a variety of pamphlets and books. Pomeroy was three times married: divorced from his first wife, Anna Amelia Wheeler, he was married to Mrs. Louise M. Thomas; his third wife, Emma Stimson, survived him.

Pomeroy's most significant books were the miscellaneous collections of his newspaper writings—humorous, sentimental, and sometimes stiffly didactic—among which were *Sense* and *Nonsense,* both published in 1868, *Brick-Dust,* etc. It was his rather sensational personalism and independence and his belligerent crusading for the "underdog" that won him a wide, though fugitive, reputation as a journalist.

Principal Works: Sense, 1868; Nonsense, 1868; Gold-Dust, 1871; Brick-Dust, 1871; Home Harmonies, 1876.

About: Pomeroy, M. M. Journey of Life: Reminiscences and Recollections of "Brick" Pomeroy; Brooklyn Daily Eagle May 30, 1896.

POOL, MARIA LOUISE (August 20, 1841-May 19, 1898), writer of tales, was born in Rockland, Mass., the daughter of Elias and Lydia (Lane) Pool. She was educated in the public schools and in an adequate but simple New England home passed a very ordinary childhood. She was encouraged by her father in the reading of good books. After a period of teaching she began to give her full attention to letters, living first on a farm at Wrentham, Mass., then in Brooklyn, N.Y., and for the last years of her life returned to Rockland. The vogue for local-color stories was still young when she began to write sketches of New England life for Boston and New York papers.

During her very modest travels she gathered materials for *A Golden Sorrow,* a tale with a Florida back-drop; and *Dally, Against Human Nature,* and *In Buncombe County,* all of which were inspired by a single journey into the North Carolina mountain districts. It was familiar territory, however, that she handled most deftly: *Roweny in Boston, In a Dike Shanty,* and

Boss and Other Dogs, although defective in plot and lacking in any very distinctive style, succeeded in capturing the essential spirit of New England life in town and country. Two books, unfinished at the time of her death, were published posthumously. Within her own unpretentious field her literary achievements were ably executed.

PRINCIPAL WORKS: Dally, 1891; Roweny in Boston, 1892; Against Human Nature, 1895; In Buncombe County, 1896; In a Dike Shanty, 1896; Boss and Other Dogs, 1896; A Golden Sorrow, 1898.

ABOUT: Pool, M. L. A Widower and Some Spinsters (see Introduction); New York Tribune May 20, 1898; Boston Transcript May 20, 1898.

POOLE, WILLIAM FREDERICK (December 24, 1821-March 1, 1894), librarian and historian, pioneer of periodical indexing, was born in Peabody (then Salem), Mass., the son of Ward Poole, a tanner, and Eliza (Wilder) Poole. Poverty interrupted his schooling at ten, and he worked until seventeen as a jeweler and a tanner, then entered Leicester Academy, teaching to earn his way. He entered Yale in 1842, but because of taking three years' leave to teach, he did not receive his B.A. until 1849 (M.A. 1852). While in Yale he was librarian of a literary society, and prepared for it his first periodical index. This led to publication of his *Alphabetical Index,* in 1848, which was an immediate success, so much so that on graduation he went to Boston to prepare an enlarged edition. In 1851 he became assistant librarian of the Boston Athenaeum, from 1852 to 1856 was librarian

WILLIAM FREDERICK POOLE

of the Boston Mercantile Library Association, and from 1856 to 1869 was back at the Athenaeum as librarian. For both libraries he compiled extensive catalogs. In 1854 he married Fanny M. Gleason; they had seven children, of whom four survived.

In 1869 Poole resigned from the Athenaeum, and for three years acted as an expert in organizing new libraries, including that of the Naval Academy at Annapolis. From 1871 to 1873 he was librarian of the Cincinnati Public Library, from 1874 to 1887 first librarian of the Chicago Public Library, which he made the then largest in the country, and from 1887 to his death librarian of the newly organized Newberry Library in Chicago. In 1874 and 1875 he edited a literary monthly, the *Owl.* He was an organizer of the American Library Association and its president from 1885 to 1887, vice-president of the International Conference of Librarians, in London, in 1877, and president of the American Historical Association in 1888.

Besides his pioneer work in indexing, Poole wrote historical criticism as an avocation, in a pungent, controversial style quite unlike the dry-as-dust mode expected in his time. His *Index to Periodical Literature* (universally known simply as *Poole's*) is still an essential reference work for its period and was the precursor of the present *Readers' Guide to Periodical Literature.* His last years were spent in Evanston, Ill., where Northwestern University gave him an LL.D. in 1882.

PRINCIPAL WORKS: An Alphabetical Index to Subjects Treated in the Reviews and Other Periodicals to Which No Indexes Have Been Published, 1848 (later editions as Poole's Index to Periodical Literature); The Battle of the Dictionaries, 1856; Websterian Orthography, 1857; The Popham Colony, 1866; Cotton Mather and Salem Witchcraft, 1869; Anti-Slavery Opinions before 1800, 1872; The Ordinance of 1787, 1876; Columbus and the Finding of the New World, 1892; The University Library and the University Curriculum, 1894.

ABOUT: Dial March 16, 1894; Library Journal March and December 1894; Nation July 7 and 28, 1898; Chicago Tribune March 2, 1894.

POORE, BENJAMIN PERLEY (November 2, 1820-May 29, 1887), newspaper correspondent, editor, and miscellaneous writer, was born at "Indian Hill Farm," near Newburyport, Mass., the son of Benjamin and Mary Perley (Dodge) Poore. In 1827 Benjamin accompanied his parents to Washington, D.C., and four years later the family took him abroad. On their return they entered the boy at Dummer Academy, South Byfield, Mass., intending to send him later to West Point. However, Benjamin ran away from Dummer, worked for a time in a printing shop at Worcester, Mass., and later edited the Athens (Ga.) *Southern Whig,* which his father purchased for him.

In 1841 he went to Belgium as attaché to the American legation, and from 1844 to 1848, acting as agent for the Massachusetts government, he collected in Paris copies of important documents bearing on American history. During these years he contributed to the Boston *Atlas,* and on his return to America in 1848 edited the Boston *Daily Bee* and later the Philadelphia *American Sentinel.* About this time he began to write biographies, one of which, a *Life of General Zachary Taylor,* attained wide popularity.

Poore started to write in Washington as a newspaper correspondent in 1854, and during the next thirty years his letters to the Boston *Journal* over the signature "Perley" became an institution. He earned an enviable reputation for accurate and authoritative reporting. During the Civil War he served for a short time as major, but returned in 1861 to Washington where he worked as secretary to the U. S. Society of Agriculture and editor of its *Journal,* as editor of the *Congressional Directory* in 1869, and as clerk of the Senate committee on printing records.

Poore's avocation was his home at "Indian Hill," which housed his collection of colonial art and historical relics; but the greater part of his time was spent in Washington, where he was a great favorite, much in demand as an after dinner speaker. His best writing is to be found in his newspaper correspondence, and his reputation rests upon these letters rather than upon his now somewhat dated biographies. He was married to Virginia Dodge in 1849, and died in Washington, D.C.

Collection of Frederick H. Meserve
BENJAMIN PERLEY POORE

PRINCIPAL WORKS: The Rise and Fall of Louis Philippe, 1848; Life of General Zachary Taylor, 1848; The Early Life and First Campaigns of Napoleon Bonaparte, 1851; The Life and Public Services of John Sherman, 1880; The Life and Public Services of Ambrose E. Burnside: Soldier-Citizen-Statesman, 1882; Life of Ulysses S. Grant, 1885; Sketches of the Life and Public Services of Frederick Smyth of New Hampshire, 1885; Perley's Reminiscences of Sixty Years in the National Metropolis, 1886.

ABOUT: Currier, J. J. History of Newburyport, Mass.; Hurd, D. H. History of Essex County, Mass.; Boston Post, Boston Transcript, Evening Star (Washington, D.C.), and Springfield Republican May 30, 1887.

PORTER, NOAH (December 14, 1811-March 4, 1892), Congregational clergyman, professor, and president of Yale College, was born in Farmington, Conn., the son of Noah and Mehetabel (Meigs) Porter. At the Farmington Academy he prepared for Yale, from which he was graduated in 1831. While serving as a tutor at Yale he studied at the divinity school. He was ordained a Congregational minister in April 1836 and took a parish first in New Milford, Conn., and then in Springfield, Mass. In 1846 he became Clark professor of moral philosophy and metaphysics at Yale, where his personal prestige and his genuine scholarliness, rather than his pedagogical methods, brought him into particular esteem. For fifteen years he was president of Yale; he resigned with failing health, but retained his professorship. He was married to Mary Taylor April 13, 1836.

Porter's chief and most widely-read work, the philosophical-psychological *Human Intellect* (1868), was praised as a "thesaurus of its subject" and was many times reissued. During his college presidency he published four books in a somewhat similar vein. Upon the death of Chauncey A. Goodrich, Porter undertook the editorship of the 1864 edition of Noah Webster's *American Dictionary of the English Language*; he also prepared *Webster's International Dictionary of the English Language,* issued in 1890.

Porter was a frail man with a "rugged old-time Roundhead face, severe and yet serene." As an educator and a theologian he was a thoroughgoing conservative, fair but unyielding to his professional opponents. The University of Edinburgh conferred on him the degree of D.D. in 1886. His thought and writings have become inevitably outdated, but his contribution to the intellectual growth of Yale has not been overlooked.

PRINCIPAL WORKS: The Human Intellect, 1868; The Sciences of Nature Versus the Science of Man, 1871; Science and Sentiment, 1882; The Elements of Moral Science, Theoretical and Practical, 1885; Kant's Ethics, 1886; Fifteen Years in the Chapel of Yale College: 1871-1886, 1888.

ABOUT: Dwight, T. Noah Porter, D.D., LL.D.: Address Delivered at the Funeral Service; Stokes, A. P. Memorials of Yale Men; New Haven Register March 4, 1892.

PORY, JOHN (1572-September 1635), geographer, navigator, and colonial secretary and adviser, was born at Thompston, Norfolk, England, son of William Pory of Butters Hall. From Gonville and Caius College, Cambridge, he received the degrees of B.A. (1591-92) and M.A. (1595); and then learned "cosmographie and forren histories" from Richard Hakluyt, whose *Principal Navigations* (2d ed.) contained an acknowledgment of Pory's industrious talent, and whose encouragement expedited his translation and editing of *A Geographical Historie of Africa: Written in Arabicke and Italian by John Leo, a More.* The signature "I. Pory" was either written in ink or stamped in beneath the dedication of *An Epitome of Ortelius: His Theatre of the World* (1602-03?), "wherein the principle regions of the earth are described in small Mappes . . . done in more exact manner then [*sic*] the lyke declarations in Latin, French or other languages. . . ." It is presumed that Pory contributed in some way to the preparation of this English edition of the work of Abraham Ortelius, renowned geographer.

After five years in Parliament he traveled extensively, 1611-18, holding several embassy posts and writing numerous long and chatty letters, which have had a considerable miscellaneous yield for the "intimate" biographer.

Pory first touched the shores of Virginia on April 19, 1619. Through the influence of relatives he had been appointed secretary of state for the colony by the London Council; and at the new world's first legislative assembly he was elected speaker. He not only ably executed his parliamentary and secretarial duties but also supervised several voyages of exploration and discovery. By 1620 Pory was suspected of splitting his allegiance between two political factions, and probably for this reason his commission as secretary was not renewed. In the summer of 1622 he went aboard the "Discovery" for a voyage along the New England coast. Governor William Bradford (1622) recorded Pory's visit to Plymouth Colony: "There was in this ship [the "Discovery"] a gentleman by name Mr. Iohn Poory . . . and him selfe after his return [to England] did this poore-plantation [of Plymouth] much credite, amongst those of no mean ranck." *Plymouth: John Pory's Lost Description* (edited by Champlin Burrage) remains—and without sectarian bias—a highly flattering account of some of the achievements of the Pilgrims. Shortly after this sojourn in the northern colony the "Discovery" was beaten off its course and wrecked on the Azores; Pory was captured by the Spaniards and, presumably, was threatened with hanging. But he finally succeeded in making his way back to England, where he held several offices of state, and was apparently influential in effecting the recall of the letters patent of the London Company and the resumption of control by the crown. He retired to Sutton St. Edmund four years before his death.

ABOUT: Birch, T. The Court and Times of James the Frst; Burrage, C. (ed.) John Pory's Lost Description of Plymouth Colony; Neill, E. D. History of the Virginia Company of London; Venn, J. Biographical History of Gonville and Caius College; Yardley, J. H. R. Before the "Mayflower."

POSTL, KARL ANTON. See SEALSFIELD, CHARLES

"POTTER PAUL." See CONGDON, CHARLES TABER

POTTER, PAUL MEREDITH (June 3, 1853-March 7, 1921), dramatist, was born in Brighton, England, the reputed son of Arthur John Macleane, editor of *Bibliotheca Classica,* and at one time headmaster of King Edward's School at Bath. Little is known of his early life, but at the age of twenty-three Potter was serving the New York *Herald* as foreign editor, and in 1883 he became London correspondent to the same paper. After further experience, as dramatic critic, Potter went in 1888 to Chicago to write for the *Tribune,* and while there began to write and rewrite plays. This turned out to be his real *métier,* and by 1890 he had begun to achieve real success and wide popularity as a dramatist.

The Ugly Duckling, played in 1890 by Mrs. Leslie Carter, was Potter's first triumph, and it was quickly followed by two more: *The American Minister,* played by William H. Crane, and *Sheridan: or, The Maid of Bath,* in which E. H. Sothern appeared. Potter was most successful in

PAUL MEREDITH POTTER

adapting stories and novels to the stage, hand-tailored to suit the personality of some particular star (a practice which in the opinion of many has been the ruination of the American stage). His most famous work of this kind was the dramatization of George Du Maurier's *Trilby,* given its première at the Park Theatre in Boston, March 11, 1895.

Other tremendously popular dramatizations were *Under Two Flags,* from the novel of Ouida; *Arsène Lupin*; and *The Honor of the Family.* The list of actors who appeared in Potter's plays reads like a theatrical "Who's Who," including such luminaries as Wilton Lackaye, Blanche Bates, Beerbohm Tree, and Otis Skinner.

As a dramatist Potter was a journeyman, not a master craftsman. Extremely adept at bringing the imaginative works of other minds into conformity with a public taste that was at no time of his life high, and was usually eager for sensation and sentimentality, Potter knew thoroughly the stock of theatrical devices of his day, and had a wide reputation in his time, but added nothing of permanent value to the American drama.

Principal Works: The City Directory, 1889; The Ugly Duckling, 1890; The American Minister, 1892; Sheridan: or, The Maid of Bath, 1893; The Victoria Cross, 1894; Trilby, 1895; The Conquerors, 1898; Under Two Flags, 1901; Nancy Stair, 1905; The Honor of the Family, 1907; Arsène Lupin, 1909; The Queen of the Moulin Rouge; The Girl From Rector's.

About: Brown, T. A. History of the New York Stage; Marcosson, I. F. & Frohman, D. Charles Frohman; The Times (London) March 18, 1921; Boston Transcript March 7, Boston Transcript March 7, 1921; New York Herald and New York Times March 8, 1921.

POWELL, THOMAS (September 3, 1809-January 14, 1887), poet, dramatist, and journalist, was born in London and resided for a time in Dulwich before emigrating to the United States in 1849. His English publications included a collaboration, with Wordsworth, Leigh Hunt, Richard Henry Horne, and others, on the editing of *The Poems of Geoffrey Chaucer Modernized* (1841); and more than a dozen books of poems and plays, among which were *The Wife's Revenge, Marguerite, Love's Rescue,* etc.

On his arrival in New York he became connected with the Frank Leslie publishing house, and was the first editor of *Frank Leslie's Illustrated Newspaper* and *Frank Leslie's New Family Magazine*; he wrote intermittently for the *Lantern, Figaro,* the New York *Reveille,* over various signatures —"Diogenes," "Pierce Pungent," "Ernest Trevor," etc. He published several volumes of short biographies that included both English and American contemporary literati: during the first year of his residence in America came *The Living Authors of England,* followed by *The Living Authors of America, Pictures of Living Authors of Great Britain, Chit Chat by Pierce Pungent,* and a retrospect of literary life of the London of the 'thirties called *Leaves From My Life.* Powell was a lively "John Bull" member of the coterie of "lions" that gathered at the famous Pfaff's. His writings—whether they took the form of a journalistic dithyramb or a fairly conventional biographical profile—aided in sustaining the literary tone of the mid-nineteenth century.

Principal Works: The Poems of Geoffrey Chaucer Modernized, 1841 (collaboration); The Wife's Revenge, 1842; Marguerite, 1846; True at Last 1848; Love's Rescue, 1848; The Living Authors of England, 1849; The Living Authors of America, 1850; Pictures of Living Authors of Great Britain, 1851; Chit Chat by Pierce Pungent, 1857; Leaves From My Life.

About: Appleton's Annual Cyclopaedia: 1887; New York Herald January 15, 1887.

PRATT, MINOT (January 8, 1805-March 29, 1878), printer, botanist, and charter member of the famous Brook Farm community, was born in Concord, Mass., the third child of Bela Pratt, a builder and contractor of Weymouth, and Sophia Western (Lyon) Pratt, of Halifax. He appears to have spent a very normal boyhood and had a particular fondness for the study of various forms of outdoor life. On March

22, 1829, he was married to Maria Jones Bridge; and for eight years was a printer, leaving his post as foreman in the office of the *Christian Register* (Boston) to take up his residence at the "Brook Farm Institute of Agriculture and Education." Mrs. Pratt and their three children had been living at the Farm since April and Pratt himself arrived just in time to become one of the signers of the original Articles of Association.

With George Ripley, the founder of the community, and William B. Allen he managed the "General Direction" and aided also in the "Direction of Agriculture." During their four years' residence the Pratts occupied the cottage known as the "Hive"; Theodore Parker Pratt, their youngest son, was the first child born at the Farm. In addition to his administrative charges and his homely domestic chores, Pratt conducted regular classes in botany, indulging his scientific and aesthetic passion for this subject without the slightest inhibition.

It was Albert Brisbane's conversion of many of the Brook Farm members to the Fourieristic theories of sharp divisional grouping that caused Minot Pratt to become a little skeptical of the direction in which the organization was moving; and in April 1845 he and his family left West Roxbury to take possession of a Concord farm which he afterward purchased. Here he spent the rest of his life, farming, continuing his studies in botany, writing his "Flora of Concord," (manuscript of which is in the Concord Library), and contributing an occasional article to local papers. Pratt was of a large and prepossessing build, with strong features and a modest and seemly manner. Compared with many of the inhabitants of Brook Farm, Pratt would seem to fall among the "inarticulate brotherhood"; yet his friends often insisted that there was something of the "temperament of a poet in his fine appreciations."

About: Curtis, G. W. Early Letters to John Sullivan Dwight; Dwight, M. Letters From Brook Farm; Pratt, F. G. The Pratt Family; Sears, J. V. D. Z. My Friends at Brook Farm; Swift, L. Brook Farm; Thoreau, H. D. Works: Vol 7.

PRENTICE, GEORGE DENNISON (December 18, 1802-January 22, 1870), journalist and poet, was born at Preston, Conn., the son of Rufus and Sarah (Stanton) Prentice. He was graduated from Brown University in 1823, then studied law and was admitted to the bar in 1829, although he never established a practice. Meanwhile he had entered the newspaper field in 1825 by editing the *Connecticut Mirror*, and in 1828 became the first editor of the *New England Review*, an anti-Federalist weekly, with a good literary department, published in Hartford. John Greenleaf Whittier was among the early contributors and succeeded Prentice as editor.

By 1830 Prentice had begun to display an unusual understanding of the political situation and was sent to Kentucky to collect material for a campaign life of Henry Clay, which appeared in 1831, under the title *Biography of Henry Clay*. Kentucky politicians, recognizing his keen political insight, invited him to edit an anti-Jackson sheet, the Louisville *Daily Journal*, which first appeared in 1830 and continued under Prentice's fearless guidance until 1868 when it became the Louisville *Courier-Journal*. His editorial ability was sufficient to manage the most powerful Whig paper in the Southwest, and his unwavering support of the Union, despite tempting offers to support the South during the Civil War, considerably influenced Kentucky's refusal to secede.

Honesty and intelligence, combined with humor and generosity, made Prentice an able editor and a popular friend. His poetry has been included in several anthologies of Kentucky and Western literature and was collected in book-form in *The Poems of George D. Prentice* (1876, 1883). Selections from his pungent editorial paragraphs, *Prenticeana*, were brought out in 1860.

Prentice's two sons—he had married Henrietta Benham of Ohio in 1835—fought with the Confederate Army despite their father's strong Northern views.

Principal Works: Prenticeana, 1860, 1870; The Poems of George D. Prentice, 1876, 1883.

About: Prentice, G. D. The Poems of George D. Prentice; Taylor, B. Critical Essays; Watterson, H. George Dennison Prentice: A Memorial Address; Lippincott's Magazine November 1869.

PRESCOTT, WILLIAM HICKLING (May 14, 1796-January 28, 1859), historian, was born in Salem, Mass., the son of Judge William Prescott and Catherine Greene (Hickling) Prescott. In 1808 the family moved to Boston, where the boy was put under a tutor to prepare for Harvard. His mind, however, was far more full of sport and romance than of study; it was misfortune which made a scholar and a writer out of Prescott. In his early years, even in college, he was noted for his horsemanship, his charm, his wit, but never for his studiousness.

It was in his junior year that a skylarking classmate in the dining hall threw a hard bread crust which struck Prescott directly in the left eye. The injury totally and permanently paralyzed the optic nerve. He was graduated in 1814 (M.A. 1817), and started to read law, but very soon the uninjured right eye became inflamed. Alarmed, his father sent him to his maternal grandfather, American consul at St. Michael's in the Azores. This was Prescott's sole experience in his lifetime of a semi-tropical country, its sights and sounds and smells; it served him nobly in later years, when it was hard to believe from his books that he had never beheld either Spain or Mexico or Peru. His eye grew worse, and he went to Europe for a medical opinion, which was disheartening—or would have been to one of less ebullient nature than this handsome, happy-spirited young man. Never again was he able to use his one seeing eye for more than ten minutes at a time, and that seldom; to all practical purposes he was blind, though no one would have guessed it from his outward appearance. In London he found an instrument which was inseparable from him thereafter—a noctograph, a device for writing with a stylus on carbon paper against brass lines.

In 1817 Prescott came home. The law was impossible for him. He could not endure the thought of mere idle invalidism, especially as he was distinctly not an invalid, but an athletic, sociable, convivial lad who enjoyed life to the utmost. In some ways Prescott was very fortunate. He had wealth always, and could buy the services of trained workers and secure any possible alleviations of his handicap; he was surrounded by sympathetic friends, chief of whom was George Ticknor, and by an understanding family; and in 1820 he married the ideal wife for him, Susan Amory, who quietly saw to it that his existence was as normal as it could be. Incidentally, Susan Amory's grandfather had as a British naval captain bombarded the American troops on Breed's (Bunker) Hill commanded by Prescott's grandfather! Their crossed swords, over the Prescott fireplace, gave Thackeray his inspiration for *The Virginians.*

Young Prescott, then, balked of other careers, decided to be a writer. He had never shown much aptitude, but he was fond of history, and after hesitating over literary criticism and biography, he determined he would be an historian. Ticknor first drew his attention to Spain, but his first book, *Ferdinand and Isabella,* took nine years to write, with eight years before that of preliminary research. He could not dictate, but wrote with his noctograph; he could not read handwriting, so had his manuscript printed in large letters for reading before

Collection of Frederick H. Meserve
WILLIAM HICKLING PRESCOTT

revision; he taught himself French, Italian, and Spanish, then trained a reader to pronounce the Spanish words, and did his source work in this laborious fashion. No one of his friends suspected he was writing a book until it was finished; only a week before its publication someone reproached him for not engaging in any serious work. The book, about which he had been so diffident and modest that he had feared to publish it at all, sold out its first edition in five weeks; more importantly, it received instant recognition from the historical authorities of the world.

Prescott had now found a mode of working; his books on Mexico and Peru were written very quickly. Irving, who had been contemplating a work on Mexico, generously gave up the plan as soon as he knew Prescott's intention—just as later on Prescott curtailed his work on Philip II so as not to interfere with Motley's writing on the Dutch Republic. Honors flooded in—LL.D. degrees from Columbia, William and Mary, South Carolina, Harvard; he was made a member of the French Institute, a corresponding member of the Royal Society of Berlin. In 1850 he was persuaded to visit England, where Oxford conferred a D.C.L. degree on him. But travel was too exhausting for him. When, in consequence of the lack of an international copyright, his work was pirated in England just as English work was pirated here, and an English publisher offered to pay him $30,000 and his expenses if he would come to England and do part of the work there to protect his rights

Prescott answered that his expenses would be a million dollars—in other words, he could not contemplate another trip.

So his last years, while he worked on *Philip II* and took time out to edit Robertson's *History of the Reign of Charles V* and add a chapter on Charles after his abdication, were spent quietly in Boston, in Nahant, or (to his greatest pleasure) in the ancestral farm at Pepperell. He remained as he had been always—tall, fair, handsome, remarkably youthful in appearance, with the same sunny disposition, the same modesty, the same generosity which made him give away a tenth of his income in charity. Yet he was no spendthrift, but had a distinct gift for shrewd business dealing. His gayety and his charm were what his friends best remembered of him. In 1858 his active literary career, which had begun with an article in the *North American Review* in 1821, came to an end. After a slight apoplectic stroke he was no longer able to do any sustained work. Yet he seemed quite well on the day when after a cheerful conversation with his wife he went to his bedroom and died suddenly of another attack of apoplexy.

Prescott as a writer has had a curious after-career. He himself conceived of history as narrative, and he was a great narrator. The exciting, the thrilling, the colorful, were what attracted him. He is at his best in such vivid passages, and is apt to grow long-winded and pedantic when he is away from them and expounding duller events. But so thorough was his documentation, with every fact accounted for by a source-notation, that today he is read chiefly by professional historians, while the public he desired to entertain has turned to more modern entertainers.

Utterly unspoiled as he was by fame and adulation, Prescott would have been highly amused by the development. He knew himself for what he was—a "great amateur." He was always a little awed at being taken into the councils of the great, remembering his heedless youth, and the long, arduous road by which he had schooled his memory until he could carry seventy-two pages of text in his mind and remodel a chapter sixteen times before it was ever set on paper. He lived always a little detached from the actual contemporary world about him—removed by his wealth, his blindness, and his preoccupation with other times and places. As Van Wyck Brooks says of him, he was "a first-rate human being, . . . an artist-cavalier, . . . a charming, virile, and romantic boy, with a scholar's conscience and an artist's genius." He was reproached in his lifetime for having no philosophy of history, for ignoring abstract theory. But that was not what he set out to do. What he did undertake, he did magnificently.

Principal Works: Life of Charles Brockden Brown, 1834; The History of the Reign of Ferdinand and Isabella the Catholic, 1838; History of the Conquest of Mexico, 1843; Biographical and Critical Miscellanies, 1845; History of the Conquest of Peru, 1847; History of the Reign of Philip II, 1855-58; Correspondence (ed. by Roger Wolcott) 1925.

About: Bassett, J. S. The Middle Group of American Historians; Brooks, Van W. The Flowering of New England; Howe, M. A. DeW. American Bookmen; Ogden, R. William Hickling Prescott; Peck, H. T. William Hickling Prescott; Ticknor, G. Life of William Hickling Prescott; Harper's Magazine December 1863; Proceedings Massachusetts Historical Society: Vol. IV.

PRESTON, HARRIET WATERS (August 6, 1836-May 14, 1911), translator, bibliographer, and novelist, was born in Danvers, Mass., the daughter of Samuel and Lydia (Proctor) Preston. She was educated at home and afterward lived in England and on the Continent for many years. Before the appearance of her notable translation of Sainte-Beuve's *Portraits of Celebrated Women* she had been a contributor to the *Atlantic* and other magazines. For Charles Dudley Warner's *Library of the World's Best Literature* she wrote critical articles and translations. With Martha Le Baron Goddard she edited the *Complete Poetical Works of Elizabeth Barrett Browning* (Cambridge Edition, 1900); and compiled *Sea and Shore: A Collection of Poems.* Through her translation of Frédéric Mistral's *Mirèio* and her publication of *Troubadours and Trouvères: New and Old* she became a recognized authority on Provençal literature, and she contributed on the subject to Warner's *Library.*

She was a genuine and thorough linguist; and her original writings—*Aspendale, Is That All?,* a New England novel called *A Year in Eden,* etc.—suffer by contrast with her translations. Among the longer of these were Saint-Beuve's *Memoirs of Madame Desbordes-Valmore* and Paul de Musset's *Biography of Alfred de Musset.* In her critical pieces she maintained a relatively unbiased point of view and a simple and readable essay style. Yet despite her achievements as a student of foreign literatures and her miscellaneous pieces she remains among the more obscure authors of the late nineteenth century.

Principal Works: Aspendale, 1871; Love in the Nineteenth Century: A Fragment, 1873; Is That All? 1876; A Year in Eden, 1887; The Guardians, 1888; Sea and Shore: A Collection of

Poems (joint-ed.) 1874; Complete Poetical Works of Elizabeth Barrett Browning (joint-ed.) 1900; Translations: Portraits of Celebrated Women, 1868; The Writings of Madame Swetchine, 1870; Mirèio, 1872; Memoirs of Madame Desbordes-Valmore. . .1873; Biography of Alfred de Musset, 1877; The Georgics of Virgil, 1881.

ABOUT: Boston Transcript May 15, 1911.

PRESTON, MARGARET (JUNKIN) (May 19, 1820-March 28, 1897), an outstanding Confederate woman-poet and prose-writer, was born at Milton, Pa., the eldest daughter of Julia Rush (Miller) Junkin and the Rev. George Junkin, a minister of the Associate Reformed Church, who eventually became president of three colleges: Lafayette College, Miami University at Oxford, Ohio, and Washington College (now Washington and Lee University) at Lexington, Va.

From her father Margaret learned Latin and Greek and formed a taste for good literature. Voracious reading and excessive application to her favorite needlework seriously affected her eyesight as she grew into womanhood, but this affliction, instead of curbing her creative ability, spurred her on to write prose pieces of unusually high merit. Her first book, a prose work entitled *Silverwood: A Book of Memories,* published in 1856, appeared anonymously. In 1865, at the end of the Civil War, she wrote an account of the conflict in narrative verse: *Beechenbrook: A Rhyme of the War,* an edition now extremely rare as most of the copies published in Richmond were burned during the evacuation of the city. It was reprinted in Baltimore in 1866. This book, while recounting the struggles of warfare, was perhaps a reflection of the battle within the poet's inner self. In 1857 she had married a widower with several children, Major John T. L. Preston, a professor of Latin at the Virginia Military Institute, who joined the Confederate forces and ultimately became adjutant-general on the staff of his brother-in-law, General "Stonewall" Jackson. Mrs. Jackson, Margaret's sister Eleanor, joined her father in holding Northern sympathies and left Lexington, where Margaret, torn by family love but loyal to her husband's cause, remained to look after her two small sons.

After the close of the war Preston returned to his professorship while Margaret again enjoyed the quiet life of the beautiful little college town in the Blue Ridge Mountains and took up her pen to write two new volumes of poetry, *Old Song and New* and *Cartoons,* which is considered her best book.

Petite, with auburn hair and aristocratic features, she was a woman of great charm and sensitivity to the feelings of others. In her large circle of friends she was much beloved; her literary gift was highly respected. Southerners regard her as one of their notable nineteenth century poets.

PRINCIPAL WORKS: Silverwood: A Book of Memories, 1856; Beechenbrook: A Rhyme of the War, 1865; Old Song and New, 1870; Cartoons, 1875.

ABOUT: Allan, E. P. Life and Letters of Margaret Junkin Preston; Preston, W. B. The Preston Genealogy; American (Philadelphia) June 3, 1882; Sun (Baltimore) March 29, 1897.

"PRESTON, PAUL." See PICTON, THOMAS

PRICE, WILLIAM THOMPSON (December 17, 1846-May 3, 1920), critic and playwright, was born in Jefferson County, Ky., the son of Joseph Crocket and Susan (Meade) Price. He ran away from school, joined the Confederate army during the Civil War, and after several escapades with cavalry raiders was imprisoned at Rock Island, Ill.; he escaped and in 1867 his parents sent him to Germany for three years' study at Berlin and Leipzig. Returning to the United States, he began to prepare himself for the bar at his father's wish; but he had firm literary inclinations and joined the Louisville *Courier-Journal,* acquiring a lasting friendship with its famous editor Henry Watterson. During his five years as dramatic critic for this daily he wrote a play, *The Old Kentucky Home,* never produced by professionals, and a brief psychological study of a locally famous evangelist in the mountain regions, called *Without Scrip or Purse.*

In 1881 he went to New York, served the *Star* as dramatic critic, 1885-86, and then read plays first for A. M. Palmer, manager of the highly successful stock companies of the Union Square and Madison Square theatres, and later for Harrison Grey Fiske, editor of the *New York Dramatic Mirror* and theatrical manager. At the same time he was writing *The Technique of the Drama* (1892), which made him somewhat of an authority on dramatic architectonics, and biographies of William Charles Macready and Charlotte Cushman. He founded the American School of Playwriting, published three more books on dramatic analysis, and from 1912 to 1915 he conducted *The American Playwright,* a magazine devoted to discussions of this same subject.

Price became, during his late years, a kind of "play doctor," revamping and polishing copy for some of the outstanding playwrights of his day—and without formal recognition. His influence, therefore, on the course of the theatre was undoubtedly considerable, although its real extent cannot be accurately measured.

PRINCIPAL WORKS: Without Scrip or Purse, 1883; The Technique of the Drama, 1892; A Life of William Charles Macready, 1894; A Life of Charlotte Cushman, 1894; The Analysis of Play Construction and Dramatic Principle, 1908.

ABOUT: New York Times May 4, 1920 and May 9, 1920.

PRINCE, LeBARON BRADFORD (July 3, 1840-December 8, 1922), jurist and territorial governor of New Mexico, was born in Flushing, Long Island, the son of William Robert Prince and Charlotte Goodwin (Collins) Prince. At eighteen he founded the Flushing Library and somewhat later launched several extensive civic organizations. He studied law at Columbia, receiving an LL.B. degree in 1866, and the year following published *E Pluribus Unum: The Articles of Confederation vs. the Constitution,* which marked his start in Republican politics. He declined President Hayes' offer of the governorship of the territory of Idaho, but accepted the chief justiceship, in 1879, of the territory of New Mexico.

Covering an extensive circuit on a Spanish-speaking frontier he performed tireless service, and published, during this period, *The General Laws in New Mexico. . .* He resigned from the bench in 1882 and during the next five years spent his time on law, historical research, government, journalism, horticulture, mining, and finance; and in 1883 he was elected president of the New Mexico Historical Society. From 1889 to 1893 he was governor of New Mexico, by Presidential appointment, and during his tenure of office he secured the establishment of the University of New Mexico and other state institutions. He wrote his *New Mexico's Struggle for Statehood* after the victory of a cause which he had so faithfully championed. A firm interest in New Mexican antiquities underlay many of his published works: *Historical Sketches of New Mexico, The Stone Lions of Cochiti, Spanish Mission Churches of New Mexico,* etc. Prime was twice married: in 1879 to Hattie E. Childs, who died less than three months later, and in 1881 to Mary C. Beardsley. From his political vantage point Prince improved the social and intellectual conditions of the frontier, and his unassuming publications were a sizable contribution to New Mexico state records.

PRINCIPAL WORKS: E Pluribus Unum. . .1867; The General Laws of New Mexico. . ., 1880; A Nation or a League, 1880; Historical Sketches of New Mexico, 1883; The Stone Lions of Cochiti, 1903; New Mexico's Struggle for Statehood, 1910; Old Fort Marcy, 1911; A Concise History of New Mexico, 1912; Spanish Mission Churches of New Mexico, 1915; Abraham Lincoln: The Man, 1917.

ABOUT: Twitchell, R. E. The Leading Facts of New Mexican History; Living Church December 30, 1922; Santa Fe New Mexican December 9, 1922.

PRINCE, THOMAS (May 15, 1687-October 22, 1758), theologian and scholar, was born in Sandwich, Mass., the son of Samuel Prince and his second wife, Mercy (Hinckley) Prince. He was graduated from Harvard in 1709, and received his M.A. degree in 1710 *in absentia,* since immediately after graduation he left Massachusetts to spend two years between the British West Indies and England, making several trips back and forth. Finally he settled in England, where, after taking courses in law, medicine, and theology at Gresham College, he preached in the Congregationalist chapel in Coombs, Suffolk. He had been inclined to theology from his college days, being one of Increase Mather's approved "praying students." Homesickness for America overcame him, and in 1717 he returned to Massachusetts, bringing with him his future wife, Deborah Denny, whom he married in 1719. He was ordained and became copastor with Joseph Sewall at Old South

From an old print

THOMAS PRINCE

Church, Boston, where he remained for the rest of his life.

In some ways Prince was typical of the New England clergymen of his day, though a bit more credulous and more enthusiastic than many of them—for example, when the evangelist George Whitefield arrived from England, Prince became his advocate against the more conservative of his colleagues. On the other hand, he was an ardent patriot, and a hot defender of civil liberties, who would almost certainly have been in favor of the Revolution had he lived to see it. But beneath and beyond all this he was essentially a scholar and bibliophile. He began collecting his private library in 1703, even before he entered Harvard, and at his death it was one of the largest and best libraries in America. Some of his books are in the Boston Public Library now. His collection was especially valuable as source history. He published twenty-nine sermons, many of them funeral sermons; but the work which preserves his name is his *Chronological History of New England*, a piece of accurate and carefully documented research which was never properly valued until the development of scientific historical writing. It is in strange contrast to the complete unrealism of his theological works.

PRINCIPAL WORKS: An Account of a Strange Appearance in the Heavens, 1719; Earthquakes the Works of God, 1727; A Sermon on the Death of Cotton Mather, 1728; A Vade Mecum for America: A Companion for Traders and Travelers, 1732; A Chronological History of New England in the Form of Annals, 1736.

ABOUT: Drake, S. G. Some Memoirs of the Life and Writings of the Rev. Thomas Prince; Sewall, J. The Duty, Character, and Reward of Christ's Faithful Servants: A Sermon Preached After the Funeral of Thomas Prince; New England Magazine April 1886; North American Review October 1860.

PROUD, ROBERT (May 10, 1728-July 5, 1813), historian and educator, was born on a farm in Yorkshire, England, the son of William and Ann Proud. He attended a boarding school kept by one David Hall, a preacher in the Society of Friends and a writer of parts. At twenty-two he went to London, and through his relative, Dr. John Fothergill, an eminent Yorkshire physician, became preceptor to the sons of Timothy Bevan, the scientist. His intellectual and physical surroundings were in every way pleasant, but late in 1758 he left England and arrived at Philadelphia on January 3, 1759. In September 1761, after superintending his own academy for a while, he became master of the Friends Public School, resigning in 1779 to try a mercantile venture. His sympathies were firmly Loyalist during the Revolutionary War, and his financial losses were heavy; yet he was sufficiently interested in the United States to bring together an excellent collection of early source materials for his extensive *History of Pennsylvania . . . From . . . 1681 . . . Till After the Year 1742* (1797-98).

Meanwhile he had resumed, in 1780, his position as master of the Friends School; he withdrew in 1790 to give full time to his book. For its publication he had received generous loans, and John Adams and Thomas Jefferson were among its subscribers; but it was a financial failure, and Proud turned to translating and the writing of poems, some of which were well above the average. His last years were passed in poverty and relative obscurity. "Dominie" Proud had, nevertheless, a commanding figure and "most impending brows." In his *History* there was little attempt at literary style, but the book remained for a long time the only authentic record of Pennsylvania's early years.

ABOUT: Memoirs of the Historical Society of Pennsylvania: Vol. 1; Poulson's American Daily Advertiser July 6, 1813.

"PUNGENT, PIERCE." See POWELL, THOMAS

"PUTNAM, ELEANOR." See BATES, ARLO

PYLE, HOWARD (March 5, 1853-November 9, 1911), illustrator and author of children's books, was born in Wilmington, Del., the son of William Pyle and Margaret Churchman (Painter) Pyle. He was educated at the Friends' School, Wilmington, and later at Thomas Clarkson Taylor's private school, but the intellectual life at home and the training and encouragement of his parents were the greatest influence in moulding his career. Inspired by his mother who recognized his artistic talent, he studied art at a private school in Philadelphia, and at the Art Students' League in New York. Returning to Wilmington, he was sidetracked into his father's leather business until a fortunate visit to Virginia provided Pyle with material for an article which he submitted to *Scribner's Monthly*. Stimulated by the appreciation of the owners of the magazine, Pyle came to New York in 1876 and after a year's struggle and constant study sold his first picture, "The Wreck in the Offing," to *Harper's Weekly*. From the sale of this work his fortune improved rapidly and his illustrations appeared in all of the important periodicals.

Collection of Frederick H. Meserve
HOWARD PYLE

He returned to Wilmington in 1880, and the following year was married to Anne Poole. His output of work, his versatility, were remarkable. Colonial days, the period of chivalry, and adventure at sea were his best subjects, but his work as an illustrator of poems and allegory, though not so well known, is unusually fine and reveals his extreme sensitivity.

Pyle's influence as teacher at the Drexel Institute in Philadelphia, from 1894 to 1900, while antagonizing the academicians, was an important influence in the training of several young artists, including Maxfield Parrish.

In 1900 Pyle started his own school in Wilmington, where N. C. Wyeth, Frank Schoonover, and others, were pupils. At the age of fifty-three, Pyle, an indefatigable and serious artist, turned to murals, but feeling that his knowledge was inadequate, went to Italy in 1910 for further study. He was taken ill in Florence and died there the following year.

He was one of the best of American illustrators, with his keen and observant mind, his unerring sense of design and his proficiency in pen and ink, water colors and oils. But it was as author and illustrator of children's books that he won his greatest fame. Stories of chivalry, adventure, and sea tales—particuarly pirate romances retold in Pyle's vigorous prose and illustrated with his bold and beautifully executed pictures stand at the top of American juvenile literature.

PRINCIPAL WORKS: The Merry Adventures of Robin Hood, 1883; Pepper and Salt, 1886; The Wonder Clock, 1888; Otto of the Silver Hand, 1888; Twilight Land, 1895; *Miscellaneous*—Men of Iron, 1892; A Modern Aladdin, 1892; The Story of Jack Ballister's Fortunes, 1895; Rejected of Men, 1903. *Pirate Stories*—Within the Capes, 1885; The Rose of Paradise, 1888; The Ghost of Captain Brand, 1896; The Price of Blood, 1899; Stolen Treasure, 1907; The Ruby of Kishmoor, 1908; Howard Pyle's Book of Pirates, 1921.

ABOUT: Abbott, C. D. Howard Pyle: A Chronicle; Morse, W. S. & Brincklé, G. Howard Pyle: A Record of His Illustrations and Writings; Woman's Home Companion April 1912.

"QUAD, M." See LEWIS, CHARLES BERTRAND

"QUERNO, CAMILLO." See ODELL, JONATHAN

QUIMBY, PHINEAS PARKHURST (February 16, 1802-January 16, 1866), metaphysicist, founder of mental healing in America, was born in Lebanon, N.H., the son of Jonathan Quimby, a blacksmith, and Susannah (White) Quimby. When he was two the family moved to Belfast, Maine, his principal home thereafter. He had only six weeks of schooling in all, but read avidly and gave himself a fair education. He was apprenticed to a clockmaker and practiced the trade for some time; he had a good deal of inventive genius, was one of the early daguerreotype artists, and invented a number of useful tools, including a bandsaw and a boat-steering apparatus. He married Susannah B. Haraden, by whom he had three sons and a daughter.

In 1838 Quimby attended an exhibition of mesmerism (hypnotism) which aroused his deep interest. He experimented and found he himself had mesmeric powers. He began giving exhibits of his own, with a "subject" named Lucius Burkmar, and was so successful that he gave up his trade and took to professional lecturing. During 1845 he made a trip through New England and New Brunswick with Burkmar, during which Burkmar, while in hypnotic trance, gave advice which apparently cured the sick who appealed to them. Finally Quimby came to believe that the cures arose, not from Burkmar's advice, but from the patients' faith. He believed also that he had cured himself of tuberculosis by mental methods.

In 1847 he gave up mesmerism and started mental healing. In 1859 he moved to Portland, where he had a large practice. Among the patients who came to him were Mary Baker Eddy (then Mrs. Patterson), Julius A. Dresser, and the Rev. Warren Felt Evans [*qq.v.*]. To all three he showed his unpublished manuscripts, outlining his rather

PHINEAS P. QUIMBY

nebulous theory, and all three became his disciples. Dresser later founded the New Thought movement and Mrs. Eddy Christian Science. Evans founded no cult but wrote influentially on mental healing. There is still dispute on how much Christian Science owes to Quimby. (He used the term "Christian Science" in 1863.)

Long suffering from an abdominal tumor which did not yield to mental treatment, Quimby was obliged to give up his practice in 1865 and return to Belfast. There he busied himself with revising his manuscripts until his death the next January. The manuscripts were not published until 1921.

Utterly without personal ambition, generous beyond his means, high-minded and scrupulous, Quimby's was an attractive—and an easily exploited—nature. His theory was a sort of modernized Gnosticism: there is no reality but God; disease is a purely mental concept which can be removed only through the mind; "The Truth" is the cure. As diffused through his disciples, his ideas have widely influenced American religious thought.

PRINCIPAL WORKS: The Quimby Manuscripts (ed. by H. W. Dresser).

ABOUT: Bates, E. S. & Dittemore, J. V. Mary Baker Eddy; Dakin, E. F. Mrs. Eddy; Dresser, A. G. The Philosophy of Phineas P. Quimby; Dresser, J. A. The True History of Mental Science; New England Magazine March 1888; Boston Post February 8, 19, 24, March 9, 1883.

"QUINCE, PETER." See STORY, ISAAC

QUINCY, EDMUND (February 1, 1808-May 17, 1877), reformer and miscellaneous writer, was born in Boston, the son of Josiah Quincy [*q.v.*], Member of Congress, mayor of Boston, and president of Harvard, and of Eliza Susan (Morton) Quincy. He was educated at Phillips Academy, Andover, Mass., and Harvard College, and received the degrees of B.A. in 1827 and M.A. in 1830.

After the murder of Elijah P. Lovejoy by a mob at Alton, Ill., in 1837, Quincy became an ardent and radical abolitionist, and was vice-president for several years of the American Anti-Slavery Society. With William Lloyd Garrison and Mrs. Maria Chapman he issued the *Non-Resistant,* an anti-slavery paper, and wrote many articles and pamphlets on the slavery question.

Besides working for the anti-slavery movement, he wrote several works of fiction and a biography of his father. He served as recording secretary of the Massachusetts Historical Society and was a member of the board of overseers of Harvard.

Quincy was married to Lucilla P. Parker in 1833. His many penetrating articles on the slavery question were not collected, but his books, especially his story *Wensley,* with its picture of Colonial days, and the biography of his father, *The Life of Josiah Quincy,* on which he collaborated with his sister Eliza, are the works of a fastidious and well ordered mind.

PRINCIPAL WORKS: Wensley: A Story Without A Moral, 1854; Life of Josiah Quincy, 1867; The Haunted Adjutant and Other Stories, 1885.

ABOUT: Garrison, W. P. & F. J. William Lloyd Garrison; Howe, M. A. DeW. Later Years of the Saturday Club; Wilson, H. History of the Rise and Fall of the Slave Power in America; Boston Transcript May 18, 1887; Nation May 24, 31, 1877.

QUINCY, JOSIAH (February 23, 1744-April 26, 1775), jurist and patriot, usually referred to as Josiah Quincy, Jr., was born in Boston, Mass., the son of Josiah Quincy, a prosperous merchant, and Hannah (Sturgis) Quincy. (The famous Adams family of Massachusetts traced its descent from the same early Colonial ancestry.) He was taught by Joseph Marsh, of Braintree, Mass., was graduated from Harvard in 1763, and received his master's degree in 1766. At the death of Oxenbridge Thacher, under whom he had studied law, Quincy ably absorbed his instructor's gainful practice, and prepared his own reports of *Cases . . . in the Superior Court of Judicature . . . . .*

During 1770 it was Quincy "the Patriot" who upheld the non-importation agreement in "An Address of the Merchants, Traders, and Freeholders of the Town of Boston" in the columns of the Boston *Gazette* and in a recapitulation of committee reports. But despite his intense Americanism, his sense of fairness impelled him to undertake, with John Adams, the defense of the British soldiers involved in the "Boston Massacre." His own brother, Samuel Quincy, was one of the prosecuting attorneys. This act, though disapproved even by his father, has been called the greatest of his life.

Early in 1773 Quincy went to Charleston, S.C., for his health, returning in May, and the "journal" of his trip northward contained some interesting reflections on life in the middle-seaboard states. In May of the following year he published his extensive *Observations of the Act of Parliament Commonly Called the Boston Port-Bill: With Thoughts on Civil Society and Standing Armies,* an astute piece of Colonial opposition to the tract in question. Quincy was now a brilliant patriot leader, though only thirty, and an orator of no mean ability, and on September 28, 1774, he quietly set sail for England, where he was to bring the colonies' point of view to the attention of the British court. The journal of his crossing was filled with significant detail, but the results of his diplomatic interviews in London, which he had contemplated delivering orally on his return, have never been disclosed, for he died—at only thirty-one—a few hours before the ship reached Gloucester. Quincy was married to Abigail Phillips, October 26, 1769; their son Josiah [*q.v.*] became a statesman-reformer and president of Harvard.

During an extraordinarily short life, Quincy, as writer of parts, lawyer and statesman, had become an influential force in a lively and crucial period of Colonial America.

Principal Works: Observations of the Act of Parliament Commonly Called the Boston Port-Bill . . . ,1774; Reports of Cases. . .in the Superior Court of Judicature of the Province of Massachusetts Bay Between 1761 and 1772, 1865; Report of the Record Commissioners. . .Containing the Boston Town Records: 1770-1777. 1887.

About: Quincy, J. Memoir of the Life of Josiah Quincy, Jr.

QUINCY, JOSIAH (February 4, 1772-July 1, 1864), historian and biographer, was born in Braintree, Mass., in a portion of the town named Quincy twenty years later in honor of his family. His father was the pre-Revolutionary patriot known as Josiah Quincy, Jr. [*q.v.*]; his mother Abigail (Phillips) Quincy, sister of the lieutenant-governor of Massachusetts. His father died in

Collection of Frederick H. Meserve

JOSIAH QUINCY
(1772-1864)

1775, leaving a large fortune, but the boy was brought up in the most Spartan manner. From the age of six he was educated at Phillips Andover Academy; received his B.A. at Harvard in 1790, first in his class (M.A. 1793), and then studied law, being admitted to the bar but seldom practicing. In 1797 he married Eliza Susan Morton, a New York beauty; they had two sons and five daughters.

Quincy was the quintessence of the New England aristocrat, born a little too late, in an age already becoming democratic. His life was modeled on that of the Romans of the Republic; he conceived of public office as a duty, owed more to his class than to his country. He first came to public attention through political satires from the Federalist viewpoint, published in the *Port Folio* and the *Monthly Anthology.* In 1804 he was elected to the State Senate, then from 1805 to 1813 served in Congress, becoming the minority leader. He was one of the few to foresee even then the violent outcome of the struggle between the free and the slave states. His opposition to the War of 1812 lost him his seat, and he retired to his Boston mansion and his model farm at Quincy, but not for long. Soon elected to the State Senate again, he served to 1820, then in the lower house as speaker, for another year, resigning to become a municipal judge in Boston. From 1823 to 1827 he was mayor of Boston, a reform mayor who physically transformed the city, modernizing everything from the fire department to the sewage. In 1829 he was elected president of Harvard, and served until 1845; he was an active, progressive president, under whose régime the law school, the library, and the astronomical observatory prospered, but he was unpopular with the authorities because of his aggressive religious liberalism (he was a Unitarian), and with the students because of his fruitless attempts to control their high spirits.

At seventy-three he retired again to his farm, emerging occasionally to receive the respectful admiration of Boston—a classic, conservative figure, with a fine long Roman head; a gentleman urbane, self-assured, his life formed on the principle of *noblesse oblige.* The Massachusetts Historical Society, the American Academy of Arts and Sciences, the Athenaeum, the Massachusetts General Hospital, all knew his guiding hand. In his last years he became a politician again, making his last public speech at ninety-one, for Lincoln and the Union cause. His histories and biographies were the reflection of the man—calm, correct, and a little pompous. The only exception is the *History of Harvard University,* which was written to confute the orthodox Congregationalists, and is full of the ardor of battle. Quincy's reputation was greater than his powers; his mere name elected his son and then his great-grandson mayor of Boston in later years, and it is still a name to reckon with among the close Brahmin circles of the Massachusetts aristocracy.

Principal Works: Memoir of the Life of Josiah Quincy, Jr., of Massachusetts, 1825; The History of Harvard University, 1840; The History of the Boston Athenaeum, 1851; A Municipal History of the Town and City of Boston, 1852; Essay on the Soiling of Cattle, 1852; Memoir of the Life of John Quincy Adams, 1858.

About: Brooks, Van W. The Flowering of New England; Chamberlain, M. John Adams: With Other Essays and Addresses; Massachusetts Historical Society: Tribute to the Memory of Josiah Quincy; Quincy, E. Life of Josiah Quincy.

QUINCY, JOSIAH PHILLIPS (November 28, 1829-October 31, 1910), historian and poet, was born in Boston, the son of Josiah Quincy, mayor of Boston (1845-49), and Mary Jane (Miller) Quincy; grandson of Josiah Quincy, president of Harvard [*q.v.*]; and great-grandson of Josiah Quincy, "the Patriot" [*q.v.*]. He attended Bronson Alcott's school, the Boston Latin School, and Stephen Weld's academy; was graduated from Harvard in 1850, and in 1853 received his master's degree. Returning from a stay in Europe he studied at Harvard Law School and was admitted to the bar in 1854, but soon relinquished law for letters and during the same year published *Lyteria,* a dramatic poem that provoked genuinely cheerful criticism.

Putnam's Magazine published many of Quincy's short stories, as did the *Atlantic,* in which he lengthily but gently lampooned contemporary literati with his *Peckster Professorship,* appearing in book form in 1888. During the Civil War he contributed to the *Anti-Slavery Standard,* wrote numerous discourses for the Boston press, and in 1876 published a miscellany of educational and political tracts under the title *The Protection of Majorities.* To his father's preparation of *Figures of the Past* he gave encouragement and aid. On December 23, 1858, he was married to Helen Fanny Huntington, and made Quincy, Mass., his home for about thirty-five years.

After the appearance of his dramatic poem *Charicles* in 1856, Quincy had given more attention to New England local history and less to verse and when, in 1867, he delivered the Phi Beta Kappa poem at Cambridge he was merely "poet for the day," wrote Mrs. James T. Fields, "for he is apt to disclaim this title usually." With broad and lively intellectual interests and a friendly democratic manner he rightfully belonged among Boston's "good brave men."

Principal Works: Lyteria, 1854; Charicles, 1856; The Protection of Majorities, 1876; The Peckster Professorship, 1888.

About: Howe, M. A. DeW. Memories of a Hostess; Proceedings of the Massachusetts Historical Society: Vol. 45; Boston Transcript November 1, 1910.

"QUOD, JOHN." See IRVING, JOHN TREAT

RAE, JOHN (June 1, 1796-July 14, 1872), economist, was born at Footdee, a suburb of Aberdeen, Scotland, the son of a ship builder or broker of the same name and of Margaret (Cuthbert) Rae. He attended the University of Edinburgh, his unorthodox views leading him to stop just short of receiving his doctor's degree. A change of fortune and a hasty marriage dispelled his expectation of a leisurely, scholarly life, and he emigrated in 1821 to the backwoods of Canada where he taught the children of Hudson's Bay Company traders and later became headmaster of the Gore District Grammar School at Hamilton. Dismissed in 1848, apparently because of his advanced views, and losing his wife soon after, he sailed for California as a ship's physician during the gold rush and finally proceeded to the Sandwich Islands where he became medical agent and later district justice on the island of Maui. After twenty years he returned to Staten Island, N.Y., as guest of a former pupil, Sir Roderick Cameron, and died there within a year. Rae has sometimes been confused with his son, Dr. John Rae, physician and distinguished Arctic explorer in the employ of the Hudson's Bay Company, who was born in the Orkneys in 1813.

His *Statement of Some New Principles on the Subject of Political Economy,* a work of originality, many-sided and abstruse, defending protectionist principles and refuting some of the theories in Adam Smith's *Wealth of Nations,* failed to attract much attention at the time or to bring adequate financial reward. It was nearly thirty years before he learned that John Stuart Mill had noticed it in his *Principles of Political Economy.* Rae published some minor writings while at Hana, Maui, of a sociological and philological nature. An able essay, the "Polynesian Language," first appearing in 1862, was republished in Sir Richard Paget's volume *Human Speech.*

Principal Works: Statement of Some New Principles on the Subject of Political Economy, 1834.

About: Rae, J. The Sociological Theory of Capital (see Biographical Sketch by C. W. Mixter); Quarterly Journal of Economics January 1897, May 1902.

RALPH, JAMES (c.1695-January 24, 1762), political writer, was probably born in New Jersey and spent some of his early life in Philadelphia. He married Rebekah Ogden of Elizabethtown, but deserted her and his daughter of less than a year in 1724 and accompanied Benjamin Franklin to London, remaining abroad the rest of his life. There he turned to teaching and other means of support, writing considerable poetry that failed to attract attention until he was apparently dissuaded from it by a couplet which Alexander Pope inserted in the second edition of his *Dunciad* in retaliation for an attack on him in Ralph's *Sawney.* Some years of dramatic aspiration, writing, and association with Henry Fielding in his Haymarket productions then followed. Although his dramas likewise met with small success, *The Fashionable Lady,* a ballad-opera, is noted as being the first play by an American to be produced on the London stage. From 1839 he became a political writer and pamphleteer, first as assistant editor of Fielding's *Champion* and later in the employ of George Bubb Dodington (Lord Melcombe) and in the interests of Frederick, Prince of Wales. His influence became of such weight that he was finally employed and pensioned by the opposition. He died at Chiswick, England.

Ralph also contributed to the *Prompter* and the *Universal Spectator,* and was associated editorially with the political journals *Old England, The Remembrancer,* the *Protester,* which he established, and as political and historical critic with the *Monthly Review.* Among the work of his latter years was *The Case of Authors by Profession,* a reflection of his Grub Street days and experience. In 1759 he assisted Franklin in *An Historical Review of the Constitution and Government of Pennsylvania.* His most notable, though politically biased, work was his two-volume *History of England,* covering the Restoration through the reign of William III.

Principal Works: *Dramas*—The Fashionable Lady, 1730; Fall of the Earl of Essex, 1731; The Lawyer's Feast, 1744; The Astrologer, 1744. *History*—The History of England, 1744, 1746. *Poetry*—The Muse's Address to the King, 1728; The Tempest, 1728; Sawney, 1728; Night, 1728; Clarinda, 1729; Zeuma, 1729. *Political Pamphlets*—The Groans of Germany, 1734. *Miscellaneous*—The Touchstone, 1728; The Other Side of the Question, 1742; Of the Use and Abuse of Parliament, 1744; The Case of Authors By Profession, 1758.

About: Cross, W. L. History of Henry Fielding; Franklin, B. Life of Benjamin Franklin; Davies, T. Memoirs of the Life of David Garrick; Graham, W. J. English Literary Periodicals.

RAMSAY, DAVID (April 2, 1749-May 8, 1815), physician and historian, was born near Lancaster, Pa., the son of James and Jane (Montgomery) Ramsay. He was graduated from the College of New Jersey in 1765 and after an interval of teaching attended the medical school of the College of Pennsylvania, receiving his degree in 1772. He settled in Charleston where he achieved success as a physician and prominence as an ardent supporter of colonial rights. He was a member of the South Carolina legislature from 1776 until the end of the Revolution and served as army surgeon at the siege of Savannah. On the capture of Charleston, in May 1780, Ramsay with other members of the council of safety was imprisoned in St. Augustine for about a year. In 1782 and 1785 he was a delegate to the Continental Congress and he was long a member of the South Carolina legislature, serving as president of the Senate for three terms.

Ramsay was busy during the war collecting materials for his *History of the American Revolution* and *History of the Revolution of South Carolina* and his sense of discrimination, his retentive memory, and his acquaintance with many of the colonial leaders resulted in works that still have a historical value.

He continued his practice in Charleston from 1786 until his assassination by a maniac in his sixty-sixth year. He wielded great influence, was in constant demand as a speaker, and was distinguished for his philanthropy and benevolence. Ramsay married three times: in 1775 he wed Sabina Ellis who died the next year; his second wife was Frances Witherspoon, whom he married in 1783; and his third marriage was in 1787 to Martha Laurens.

PRINCIPAL WORKS: History of the Revolution of South Carolina, 1785; History of the American Revolution, 1789; Life of George Washington, 1807; Memoirs of the Life of Martha Laurens Ramsay, 1812; Eulogium Upon Benjamin Rush, M.D., 1813; History of the United States, 1816-17; Universal History Americanized, 1819.

ABOUT: Collins, V. L. President Witherspoon: A Biograhphy; American Historical Review July 1902.

RANDALL, JAMES RYDER (January 1, 1839-January 14, 1908), poet, song-writer, and journalist, best remembered as the author of "Maryland, My Maryland," was born in Baltimore, the son of John K. Randall, a wealthy merchant, and Ruth M. (Hooper) Randall. He was tutored by Joseph H. Clarke, who had taught Poe in Richmond; and he entered Georgetown College at the age of ten. Illness forced him to leave school and after a voyage to Brazil and to the West Indies, which occasioned a handful of youthful verse, he returned to Baltimore to work for a firm of printers and typefounders and was afterward employed as a shipbroker's clerk in New Orleans.

In 1860 Randall became a teacher at the then flourishing Poydras College, Pointe Coupée, La. In April of the following year, in the early days of the Civil War, he got news of a clash in the streets of his native Baltimore and of the death of an old school friend; he was unable to sleep, and, rising at midnight he wrote, by the flame of a "sputtering candle," the lines of "Maryland, My Maryland" which was soon to become the "Marseillaise of the Confederate cause." Firm in his belief that the North had been a heartless aggressor, Randall enlisted with the Southern army but was immediately mustered out because of a lung ailment.

He was married to Katherine Hammond in 1866; and after a tedious associate-editorship of the Augusta (Ga.) *Constitutionalist* he went to Washington to act as congressional secretary and at the same time as Washington correspondent for the Augusta *Chronicle*. He also wrote occasional

JAMES RYDER RANDALL

articles for the Baltimore *Catholic Mirror* and the New Orleans *Morning Star*. A collection of his poems, with biographical memoir, was published posthumously.

"Maryland, My Maryland" has retained substantially the same verse form which it had when Randall first read it to his English class and then forwarded it to the editor of the New Orleans *Delta*. Randall acknowledged his indebtedness to James Clarence Mangan, the Irish poet, whose "Karamanian Exile," he said "solved the meter." The Misses Jennie and Hetty Cary of Baltimore adapted it to the tune of "Lauriger Horatius," and Charles Ellerbrock, a young German music teacher and Southern sympathizer, set it to the measure of "Tannenbaum, O Tannenbaum," in which form it has remained. In the year before Randall's death the State of Maryland, at the Jamestown Exposition, and the City of Baltimore, during its Homecoming Week, formally recognized him as the author of the best known of state songs.

ABOUT: Andrews, M. P. The Poems of James Ryder Randall; Perine, G. C. The Poets and Verse-Writers of Maryland; Sun (Baltimore) January 15, 1908.

RANKIN, JEREMIAH EAMES (January 2, 1828-November 28, 1904), hymnologist, poet, and university president, was born in Thornton, N.H., the son of the Rev. Andrew Rankin and Lois (Eames) Rankin, of early New England Scottish and English ancestry. He was graduated from Middlebury College in 1848 (D.D. 1869, LL.D. 1889), and taught school for a few years.

Completing a course at the Andover Theological Seminary with the class of 1854 he was ordained a Congregational minister, and held various pastorates in New England and the East. At Washington, D.C., for fifteen years, from 1869, he attracted large and distinguished audiences of public men to the First Congregational Church. He subsequently served in Orange, N.J., and, having manifested an interest in the Negro race, about 1889 he received a call to the presidency of Howard University, Washington, remaining there for more than thirteen years. He died at Cleveland, Ohio.

Rankin was of somewhat austere appearance, with bushy eyebrows and sideburns. He spoke with rapid intensity and a lush, musical voice, drawing upon poetic imagery and often closing his sermons with an original poem. His pride in his ancestry was shown by his poems in Scottish dialect. He was most widely known as the author of the hymn "God Be With You Till We Meet Again." Besides his poems and hymns, a translated volume of German-English lyrics, and a small journal purported to have been written by Esther Burr, daughter and wife respectively of Presidents Edwards and Burr of Princeton, his published works are largely sermons. He also contributed to several religious papers, including the *Independent.*

PRINCIPAL WORKS: *Compilations*—Gems for the Bridal Ring, 1867. *Hymns*—Hymns Pro Patria, 1889. *Poetry*—The Auld Scotch Mither and Other Poems, 1873; Romano More: or, Ye Old Pilgrims, 1886; Ingleside Rhaims, 1887. *Translator*—German-English Lyrics (2nd ed.) 1898. *Miscellaneous*—Subduing Kingdoms, 1881; The Function of Great Men, 1881; The Tuition of Free Institutions, 1881; Blessedness Among Nations, 1882; The Hotel of God, 1882; Atheism of the Heart, 1886; Christ His Own Interpreter, 1886; Broken Cadences, 1889; The Law of Elective Affinity, 1899; Commodore Philip Inch, 1898; Esther Burr's Journal, 1903.

ABOUT: Congregational Year-Book, 1905; Howard University Medical Department: Historical, Biographical, and Statistical Souvenir; Congregationalist May 16, 1903.

RAUCH, FREDERICK AUGUSTUS (July 27, 1806-March 2, 1841), educator, philosopher, and religious writer, was born in Kirchbracht, Prussia, the son of Heinrich and Friederike (Haderman) Rauch. He was graduated from the University of Marburg in 1827 and subsequently studied at the Universities of Giessen and Heidelberg. Incurring the displeasure of the government because of his advanced opinions and radical beliefs, Rauch had to abandon his promising career, and emigrated to the United States in 1831.

He settled first in Easton, Pa., where he learned English and supported himself by giving piano lessons. He taught German at Lafayette College for a time and was appointed principal of the Academy established by the authorities of the German Reformed Church at York, Pa. Later he was ordained and became professor of Biblical literature in the theological seminary at York, still retaining charge of the Academy, which was moved to Mercersburg in 1835.

Under his guidance the Academy grew into Marshall College, established in 1836, with Dr. Rauch as first president and occupant of the chair of Biblical literature. Twelve years after his death at Mercersburg, the college that he fostered became Franklin and Marshall College at Lancaster, Pa., and still acknowledges the influence of its founder.

Dr. Rauch was married two years after his arrival in America to Phebe Bathiah Moore of Morristown, N.J. He was a profound scholar and left many works of value. In Germany he had written a commentary on *Faust* which Goethe himself praised. His numerous lectures, sermons and articles were of great spiritual inspiration to his students and followers. He was one of the leaders of "Mercersburg theology," an important contribution to American religion, and in his *Psychology or a View of the Human Soul,* he left a treatise on philosophy that was long used in colleges and schools.

PRINCIPAL WORKS: Vorlesungen über Göthe's Faust, 1830; Psychology or a View of the Human Soul: Including Anthropology, 1840; The Inner Life of the Christian, 1856.

ABOUT: Dubbs, J. H. History of Franklin and Marshall College; Nevin, J. W. Life and Character of Frederick Augustus Rauch; Reformed Church Review October 1906; Weekly Messenger of the German Reformed Church March 10, 1841.

RAYMOND, DANIEL (1786-1849?), lawyer and economic writer, was descended from an ancestor of the same name who died at Lyme, Conn., in 1696. He was born in or near New Haven, studied law at Litchfield, and in 1814 was admitted to the bar at Baltimore, Md. He married Eliza Amos of Baltimore, and later Delia Matlock of Virginia, and was the father of six sons and two daughters. Some time after 1840 he probably resided in Cincinnati.

Raymond's *Thoughts on Political Economy,* a work of much originality, which is still read and which constitutes his chief claim to remembrance, broke with foreign economic theories and the dominant thought propounded by the school of Adam Smith. Basing his reasoning on the American economic environment, he opposed the philosophy of individualism, favored governmental regulation, attacked the banks and paper money, and stood for a protective system. His thought had much in common with that of the economists, John Rae and Georg Friedrich List, who were probably influenced by his work. His strong defense of the protective tariff induced the protectionist, Mathew Carey, to offer substantial financial support for a chair of political economy at the University of Maryland, providing Raymond were invited to occupy it. This offer was not accepted by the university. Four editions of his work were issued by 1840, and it was warmly commended in some quarters, although his earlier anti-slavery pamphlet, *The Missouri Question,* had prejudiced the South against him, and his views did not arouse enthusiasm among most contemporary economists and bankers. The fourth edition included a new discourse, *Elements of Constitutional Law,* which was later, in 1845, published separately.

PRINCIPAL WORKS: The Missouri Question, 1819; Thoughts on Political Economy, 1820; The American System, 1828; Elements of Constitutional Law, 1845.

ABOUT: Raymond, S. Genealogies of the Raymond Families of New England; Teilhac, E. Pioneers of American Economic Thought in the Nineteenth Century; Johns Hopkins Studies in Historical and Political Science June 1897.

RAYMOND, GEORGE LANSING (September 3, 1839-July 11, 1929), educator, poet, and writer on aesthetics, was born in Chicago, the son of a merchant, Benjamin Wright Raymond, and Amelia (Porter) Raymond, both of New England descent. He was educated at Williams College (B.A. 1862, M.A. 1865) and Princeton Theological Seminary, from which he was graduated in 1865, and studied art for three years in Europe. The honorary degree LL.D. was conferred on him by Rutgers College in 1883, L.H.D. by Williams College in 1889, and M.A. by Princeton in 1896. After a four-year Presbyterian pastorate at Darby, Pa., he went to Williams College in 1874 as a professor of English literature, aesthetics, oratory, and elocution. The success of his classes in winning prizes year after year in intercollegiate contests led to his call, in 1880, to the chair of oratory and aesthetics at Princeton, which he held for twenty-five years, the last twelve years teaching only aesthetics. From 1905 to 1912 he taught aesthetics at George Washington University.

Raymond wrote one novel, *Modern Fishers of Men,* a humorous, realistic story in the setting of an American suburban town; a few dramas; some textbooks, among which *The Orator's Manual* still remains a standard work; and a large body of competent but unexciting verse; but it is his aesthetic studies that constitute the bulk of his writing, and represent his most valuable contribution. In these studies, marked by some originality and insight, he endeavored to analyze and correlate the fundamental principles of all the arts. A condensation of his teachings has been given in two volumes of classified extracts compiled by Dr. Marion Mills Miller in *A Poet's Cabinet* and *An Art Philosopher's Cabinet.* In 1909 eight volumes of his aesthetic studies were republished in a series entitled *Comparative Aesthetics.*

PRINCIPAL WORKS: *Drama*—The Aztec God and Other Dramas, 1900. *Novels*—Modern Fishers of Men, 1879. *Poetry*—A Poet's Cabinet (comp. by M. M. Miller) 1914. *Textbooks*—The Orator's Manual, 1870. *Miscellaneous*—Poetry as a Representative Art, 1886; The Genesis of Art Form, 1893; Art in Theory, 1894; Painting, Sculpture, and Architecture as Representative Arts, 1895; Rhythm and Harmony in Poetry and Music, 1895; Proportion and Harmony of Line and Color in Painting, Sculpture and Architecture, 1889; The Representative Significance of Form, 1900; The Essentials of Aesthetics, 1906; An Art Philosopher's Cabinet (comp. by M. M. Miller) 1915; Ethics and Natural Law, 1920.

ABOUT: Raymond, G. L. An Art Philosopher's Cabinet (see Preface); American Magazine October 1888.

RAYMOND, HENRY JARVIS (January 24, 1820-June 18, 1869), editor, politician, and historian, founder of the New York *Times,* was born at Lima, N.Y., the son of Jarvis and Lavinia (Brockway) Raymond. He attended Genesee Wesleyan Seminary and was graduated from the University of Vermont in 1840. He had taught school, but disliked it; and eager to get into the newspaper world he set out for New York, where he supported himself as a free-lance writer until he found an opening with Horace Greeley's weekly, the *New Yorker.* When Greeley founded the New York *Tribune* in 1841 he made Raymond his chief assistant; but temperamental differences between the two men led to a break, and in 1843 Raymond joined James Watson Webb's *Morning Courier and New-York Enquirer.* Here he remained until 1851 when his alignment with the Free-Soilers, which had begun after his election to the state assembly in 1849, forced his withdrawal from Webb's paper.

Meanwhile he had become managing editor of *Harper's New Monthly Magazine,* but found little time for this venture when, with George Jones, an ex-*Tribune* acquaint-

Collection of Frederick H. Meserve
HENRY JARVIS RAYMOND

ance, he set up the New York *Daily Times* in September 1851. It became one of the most powerful journals of the country and in only four years had more than twice the circulation of its rival, Greeley's daily.

Raymond's chairmanship of the Republican National Committee in 1866 climaxed more than fifteen years' activity in the party, and his declining of a re-nomination for Congress during that same year virtually ended it. He was married to Juliette Weaver in 1843.

His published works are, unfortunately, poor gauges of his literary finesse: *Disunion and Slavery,* an attack on secession in a series of open letters to W. L. Yancey of Alabama; and a *History of the Administration of President Lincoln,* a hastily prepared campaign document which after Lincoln's death was enlarged and re-titled *The Life and Public Services of Abraham Lincoln,* and was to have been again pruned and more exhaustively treated but was necessarily set aside. Many of his legislative and patriotic speeches appeared in pamphlet form, as did *Association Discussed: or, The Socialism of the Tribune Examined,* the original draft of which was a newspaper controversy with Greeley.

In an age of bitter partisanship Raymond's unyielding moderation and his dislike for personal invective denied him, as an editor, the brilliant political force of Greeley; but with his allegiance to decency and his productive speed and accuracy as a reporter, the integrity of the successful *Times* was an obvious illustration of the victory of good taste over hysteria.

PRINCIPAL WORKS: Disunion and Slavery, 1860; History of the Administration of President Lincoln, 1864.

ABOUT: Alexander, D. S. A Political History of the State of New York; Bigelow, J. Retrospections of an Active Life; Davis, E. History of the New York Times: 1851-1921; Maverick, A. Henry J. Raymond and the New York Press; Scribner's Monthly November 1879, January, March, June, 1880; New York Times, New York Tribune June 19, 1869.

READ, THOMAS BUCHANAN (March 12, 1822-May 11, 1872), poet and painter, was born on a farm in Chester County, Pennsylvania, of Scotch-Irish and English ancestry. As a child he showed ability in drawing and verse making, cultivating both through an orphaned boyhood while earning his living as grocer's helper and cigar maker in Philadelphia, and in Cincinnati. As painter of canal boats and signs and as itinerant portrait painter, finally with a studio of his own in Cincinnati, he numbered among his sitters General William Henry Harrison, then candidate for the presidency.

Believing that opportunity lay in the East, in 1841 the slight youth—Read was five feet tall and seldom weighed more than a hundred pounds—painted his way to Boston, where he set up a studio, and, being competent, soon throve. At night he wrote, receiving encouragement from Longfellow, one of his sitters. Presently his verses began to appear in the Boston *Courier*. In 1843 he married Mary J. Pratt, of Gambier, Ohio, just completing her studies at a Massachusetts seminary.

He moved to Philadelphia in 1846, where he opened a studio, and though he lived later for brief periods in New York, Boston, and Cincinnati and made extensive stays abroad, he was identified with that city and its group of poets. In 1847 a collection, *Poems,* was published, rapidly followed by other work. His portrait painting, by which he made his living, prospered, and in 1850 he made his first trip abroad, where his reputation as a poet had preceded him. Then and later he made many friends, among them painting Thackeray and Browning. In 1853 he settled in Florence, Italy, to paint and to write, but the tragic death of his wife and a small daughter in a cholera epidemic, 1855, brought him back to this country. In 1856 he married Harriet Denison Butler, of Northampton, Mass.

When the Civil War broke out he was abroad again; an ardent supporter of the Union, however, he promptly returned. A member of the staff of General Lew Wallace

Collection of Frederick H. Meserve
THOMAS BUCHANAN READ

during the siege of Cincinnati in 1863, his greater service lay in his tours of the country with the tragedian, James Edward Murdoch. The poet lectured and the actor recited patriotic poems, many of them Read's, among them excerpts from a long narrative poem of pre-Revolutionary days, the *Wagoner of the Alleghanies,* the short "Oath," a favorite with Lincoln, and "Sheridan's Ride," written the afternoon of the day Murdoch read it. Much money was raised for the wounded, and though Read received nothing, his reputation was extended. In 1866, *Poetical Works,* a collection, in three volumes, was published. His subsequent production was small.

He returned to Italy in 1866, his health weakened by war work and fatally weakened in 1871 by an accident. The next year he returned to this country, dying in New York City a few days after his arrival. He is buried in Laurel Hill Cemetery, Philadelphia. His wife but none of his children survived him.

Almost forgotten now except for several short poems, Read was regarded during his life as one of the foremost of American poets and was highly esteemed in England. Some contemporary criticism, however, and most later, has pointed out his too great ease and rapidity of production, his lack of originality and vigor, his reliance on verbal deftness rather than on imagination, on fancy rather than on feeling. Hawthorne said that his pictures were poems and his poems pictures, and time has not been kind to either.

Principal Works: Poems, 1847; Lays and Ballads, 1849; The New Pastoral, 1855; The Wagoner of the Alleghanies, 1862; A Summer Story, Sheridan's Ride, and Other Poems, 1865; Poetical Works (3 vols.) 1866.

About: Harley, L. R. Confessions of a Schoolmaster; Oberholtzer, E. P. Literary History of Philadelphia; Stoddard, R. H. Recollections Personal and Literary; Townsend, H. C. & others. A Memoir of T. Buchanan Read.

REALF, RICHARD (June 14, 1834-October 28, 1878), poet, was born in Framfield, near Leeds, Sussex, England, one of the nine children of Richard Realf or Relfe (the name is pronounced "Relf"), a market gardener turned rural constable, and Martha (Highland) Realf. He had practically no schooling, but was very precocious, turing out verses from early childhood. At ten he was sent to a sister at Brighton, a maid to an aunt of Parnell. The literary set of the town—Harriet Martineau, Samuel Rogers, Lady Byron—made a pet of the boy, who had become half-page, half-clerk. In 1852 they paid for publication of a volume of his poems. Lady Byron then sent him to her nephew in Leicestershire, to be trained as a factor. Disaster followed swiftly; he had an affair with a girl of his master's family, was terribly beaten, and set adrift. He wandered about for weeks, half-insane, was found by his father, a barefoot beggar, and sent to another sister in Maryland.

He got no farther than New York, where he did semi-missionary work from 1854 to 1856 in the Five Points House of Industry. The Abolitionist cause claimed him next; he became heavily involved with John Brown, went to Kansas, was a delegate to Brown's "convention" in Canada in 1858, and was to have been "secretary of state" in Brown's projected commonwealth. Brown sent him to England to secure funds, and the attack on Harper's Ferry occurred in his absence. Realf returned to New Orleans to be arrested for complicity. He was accused, but in all probability falsely, of having betrayed his comrades to save himself.

At the beginning of the Civil War he enlisted in an Illinois regiment, and served to the end, later being stationed in the South as head of a Nego regiment. In 1865 he married Sophia Emery Graves, a Maine school teacher. She went back north, but he never followed her; he claimed to have heard she was dead. They were never divorced, and she kept their secret to his death. In 1867, while drunk (he alternated between alcoholism and lecturing on temperance), he married a woman named

RICHARD REALF
c. 1864

Catherine Cassidy, who became his nemesis. He divorced her—the marriage was, of course, bigamous—but she had the decree set aside. Meanwhile he contracted a third marriage with a woman he loved and who loved him, by whom he had four children, three of them triplets. From 1872 to 1877 he was in Pittsburgh, doing newspaper work on the *Commercial,* lecturing, and trying to support an invalid wife, four children, and numerous members of his own family. He became almost blind, and he was desperately poor; perhaps in his despair he was not always scrupulous about money matters—certainly he sold and re-sold his own poems to various magazines. Everywhere Catherine Cassidy pursued him and tried to ruin him.

Finally his friend Col. R. J. Hinton paid his passage to San Francisco, where he worked as a laborer and then secured a small position in the Mint. And then Catherine appeared again. It was too much. He went to a hotel in Oakland and took poison. He left three sonnets explaining his deed and himself, among the finest of his work.

Ambrose Bierce admired Realf's poetry immensely, but it has not stood the test of time. It is passionate and melancholy, and it has superb lines, but it is full of clichés and bombast. The man himself is more interesting than anything he ever wrote.

Principal Works: Guesses at the Beautiful, 1852; Poems, 1898.

About: Realf, R. Poems. See Memoir by R. J. Hinton; Lippincott's Magazine March 1879; Midland Monthly August 1895; San Francisco Chronicle October 30, 1878.

REDPATH, JAMES (1833-February 10, 1891), journalist, editor, and lecture promoter, was of Scotch birth, born in Berwick-on-Tweed, his father, of the same name, being a native of that country and his mother, Marie Ninian (Davidson) Redpath, an Englishwoman. At seventeen he emigrated with his parents to a farm in Michigan, but soon entered a printing office in Kalamazoo, twenty miles distant. Shortly after, while in Detroit, his writing attracted the attention of Horace Greeley, and he was engaged on the New York *Tribune,* a connection which lasted intermittently for thirty years. He made trips of observation in 1854 and succeeding years to Kansas, through the South, and to Haiti, his zealous anti-slavery crusading sometimes endangering his life. The Haitian government made him Haitian commissioner of emigration in the United States in 1859, and later Haitian consul at Philadelphia. He acted as a correspondent during the Civil War, and at its close became superintendent of schools at Charleston, S.C. Becoming interested in the booking of lecturers, he established in 1868 the Boston Lyceum Bureau, later called by his own name and extended to include other modes of platform entertainment. His partisanship found new expression when in 1879 and later he visited Ireland and became a vigorous denouncer of English rule. In February 1891 he was run over by a street car in New York City and died five days later.

When sixteen, Redpath collaborated with his father on a small volume entitled *Tales and Traditions of the Border.* The pre-war period was productive of several volumes based on his first-hand contacts with slavery; in one, *The Roving Editor,* he recorded personal viewpoints of the slaves. He also wrote sympathetically of John Brown, whom he had interviewed before his arrest and execution and whom he greatly admired. His *Talks About Ireland* contained journalistic letters written during his advocacy of the Irish cause. In 1886 he was an editor of the *North American Review,* but an attack of paralysis caused him to resign the following year.

Principal Works: Tales and Traditions of the Border, 1849; The Roving Editor: or, Talks With Slaves in the Southern States, 1859; A Handbook to Kansas Territory and the Rocky Mountains' Gold Region (with R. J. Hinton) 1859; Echoes of Harper's Ferry, 1860; The Public Life òf Captain John Brown, 1860; A Guide to Hayti, 1860; Talks About Ireland, 1881.

About: Horner, C. F. The Life of James Redpath and the Development of the Modern Lyceum; Proceedings at a Farewell Dinner Given by the

Land League of New York to James Redpath Prior to His Departure for Ireland, at Delmonico's, June 1, 1881.

REED, SAMPSON (June 10, 1800-July 8, 1880), Swedenborgian writer, born in West Bridgewater, Mass., was the youngest of eight children of the Rev. John Reed, for over fifty years pastor of the First Church (Unitarian) of that place, and of his first wife, Hannah (Simpson) Reed. He was graduated from Harvard in the class of 1818 and remained to study theology in its Divinity School; after being converted to Swedenborgianism by Thomas Worcester, his friend and roommate, he abandoned theology and became a druggist. Eventually he built up one of the largest wholesale drug businesses in New England. One of the four children of his marriage with Catharine Clark of Waltham, James Reed, became a Swedenborgian minister. He died in Boston at eighty, after some years of blindness.

Reed is credited with having brought Swedenborgian philosophy to the serious attention of Ralph Waldo Emerson in his *Observations on the Growth of the Mind,* a small volume not naming Swedenborg but based on his doctrine. This, together with an oration on "Genius" delivered by Reed at Harvard on receiving his master's degree in 1821, made a deep impression on Emerson, who held Reed in high esteem. The doctrine of correspondences which had particularly appealed to Emerson was many years later amplified by Reed in another publication, *The Correspondence of the Sun, Heat, and Light.* In addition to his other writings Reed was a leading contributor to the *New Jerusalem Magazine,* edited by his brother Caleb, becoming himself one of its editors in 1854; and in 1843 he founded and edited the *New Church Magazine for Children,* later the *Children's New-Church Magazine.*

Principal Works: Observations on the Growth of the Mind, 1826; The Correspondence of the Sun, Heat, and Light, 1862; A Biographical Sketch of Thomas Worcester, D.D., 1880.

About: Block, M. B. The New Church in the New World; Reed, J. L. The Reed Genealogy; Illinois University Studies in Language and Literature February 1923; New England Quarterly April 1929.

"REFUGITTA." See HARRISON, CONSTANCE (CARY)

REID, WHITELAW (October 27, 1837-December 15, 1912), journalist, diplomat, and historian, was born on a farm near Xenia, Ohio, the son of Robert Charlton Reid and Marion Whitelaw (Ronalds) Reid. He attended the district school and Xenia Academy and was graduated from Miami University at Oxford, Ohio, where he was well grounded in the classics and in modern languages, in 1856. For two years he edited the Xenia *News,* a weekly; and he stumped for Frémont and for Lincoln during their political campaigns.

Early in 1861 Reid was sent to Columbus by the Cincinnati *Times* to report the legislative sessions; he was, at the same time, political correspondent for the Cleveland *Herald,* and the energy and independence of the dispatches which he wrote for the Cincinnati *Gazette* over the signature "Agate," marked the real beginning of his newspaper career. His reports from the battlefields as aide-de-camp of General Rosecrans and his account of the city of Richmond immediately after its fall and of Lincoln's funeral were masterpieces of reporting that won him instant recognition as a front-rank journalist. The day-book of his subsequent tour through the South was incorporated into a volume called *After the War.* Following a short interval as cotton planter in Louisiana and Alabama, he returned to the North and finished his history of *Ohio in the War,* which he published in 1868. For the *Gazette,* from which he had never completely separated, he wrote editorials and covered major political crises.

Collection of Frederick H. Meserve

WHITELAW REID

Later that year he joined the New York *Tribune,* and as managing editor was influential in encouraging contributions of Bret Harte, Mark Twain, and Richard Henry Stoddard. During Greeley's presidential campaign (1872) Reid took charge of the *Tribune,* and with an "aggressive" campaign policy made the paper an effective Greeley organ. On the death of Greeley, Reid retained the editorship, and through unremitting labor, well-considered editorial policies, and the aid of an exceptionally strong staff, made the *Tribune* one of the most vigorous and successful papers in the country.

After his marriage to Elizabeth Mills, in 1881, Reid took a European trip, leaving John Hay in charge of the paper; and on his return began to give less time to journalism and more to politics. He was minister to France under Harrison, and on his ticket (for re-election) Reid ran for vice- president. Five years after their political fiasco, Reid was sent to England as special ambassador to the Queen's jubilee; and in 1902, to the coronation of King Edward VII. He was appointed ambassador to Great Britain three years later, and served until his death.

Besides his *Ohio in the War,* which remains one of the most important state histories of the Civil War, and his reportorial *After the War* papers, he wrote three books on diplomatic policy and foreign relations. These books and his allegiance to a sane and intelligent variety of journalism in his capacity as a metropolitan editor have earned him a substantial ranking among conservative American newspapermen.

PRINCIPAL WORKS: After the War, 1866; Ohio in the War, 1868; Some Consequences of the Last Treaty of Paris, 1899; Our New Duties, 1899; Problems of Expansion, 1900; American and English Studies, 1913.

ABOUT: Cortissoz, R. The Life of Whitelaw Reid; Dennett, T. John Hay; Olcott, C. S. The Life of William McKinley; Seitz, D. C. Horace Greeley; New York Tribune December 16, 1912.

REMINGTON, FREDERIC (October 4, 1861-December 26, 1909), illustrator, painter, sculptor, and adventure writer, was born in Canton, N.Y., the son of Seth Pierre and Clara (Sackrider) Remington. Frederic was a strapping youth who loved the out-of-doors. He attended the Vermont Episcopal Institute, Burlington, and Yale School of Fine Arts (1878-80), where he was a more promising athlete than scholar; and after the death of his father he went west. A sharper soon got all his money, and he made his living as storekeeper, sheep-herder, ranch-cook, cow puncher, and finally, stockman.

Collection of Frederick H. Meserve
FREDERIC REMINGTON

All the while he was filling his portfolio with sketches.

He returned to New York; interested the editor of *Harper's Weekly* in one of his drawings; and when he suggested to the *Century* editor that someone should be sent out to write an Indian story for him to illustrate, he was told to do it himself. He did, and unwittingly began a long career as author and illustrator. He learned to work with oils and watercolors at the Art Students' League in New York, and his famous drawings for Theodore Roosevelt's *Ranch Life and Hunting Trails* insured him of a real following. He went to Germany, slipped into Russia but was shortly expelled, sojourned a while in North Africa, and during the Spanish-American War was a war correspondent in Cuba, where he made the rough sketches for his well-known painting of the "Charge up San Juan Hill." He was married, in 1883, to Eva Adele Caten, and made his home first in New Rochelle and then in Ridgefield, Conn.

Remington's books were, admittedly, little more than a kind of justification for the publication of his drawings—*Pony Tracks, Crooked Trails, Sundown Leflare,* etc.—not literary bonanzas but fresh journalistic accounts of life in the West. That same devotion to minute detail was the distinguishing characteristic of his paintings and bronze pieces (his New Rochelle studio was papered with Indian and cowboy trappings), and no doubt the work of Eadweard Muybridge, pioneer in motion photography, influenced

Remington in the execution of his famous horses-in-action canvases.

He was a member of the American Academy of Arts and Letters, the Society of Illustrators, and the National Academy of Design. A large collection of his work and an accumulation of frontier relics are housed in the Remington Art Memorial at Ogdensburg; four of his statutes are in the Metropolitan Museum of Art; and his magnificent "The Cowboy" stands in Fairmont Park, Philadelphia. Some of his oils now bring $20,000 and more, and it is said that there are probably more forgeries of his works on the market today than of any other American painter. By picture and by narrative he became an "authoritative chronicler of the whole Western land from Assiniboine to Mexico and of all men and beasts dwelling therein."

PRINCIPAL WORKS: Pony Tracks, 1895; Drawings, 1897; Crooked Trails, 1898; Sundown Leflare, 1899; Stories of Peace and War, 1899; Men With the Bark On, 1900; Done in the Open, 1902; John Ermine of Yellowstone, 1902; The Way of an Indian, 1906.

ABOUT: Cortissoz, R. American Artists; Pennell, J. Pen Drawing and Pen Draughtsmen; Smith, F. H. American Illustrators; Vail, R. W. G. Frederic Remington: Chronicler of the Vanished West; Craftsman March 1909; Pearson's Magazine October 1907; American Art News January 1, 1910; Outlook January 8, 1910.

REQUIER, AUGUSTUS JULIAN (May 27, 1825-March 19, 1887), poet, dramatist, and jurist, born in Charleston, S.C., was of French descent, his father being a native of Marseilles, and his mother the daughter of a Haitian planter who had fled to the United States in the slave uprising of 1791. Admitted to the bar at nineteen, he practiced successively at Charleston, Marion, S.C., and Mobile, Ala., where in 1853 he became United States district attorney for Alabama, and later judge of the superior court. In the Spring of 1861 President Davis appointed him district attorney for the Confederacy. Requier later established a successful practice in New York City, remaining there until his sudden death at sixty-one of heart disease. He was twice married.

At Marion, Requier served for a time as editor of the Marion *Star,* and at approximately that time published a short pre-Revolutionary romance of South Carolina, *The Old Sanctuary.* His work also included a number of essays in periodicals. His most noteworthy writing, however, was his lyrical and martial poetry and blank-verse drama. The play *The Spanish Exile,* published at the early age of seventeen, first gave him popularity and was successfully acted. He wrote a tragedy, in 1859, on the oft-used theme of Marco Bozzaris, the Greek patriot; and in the year following he published his *Poems.* His long and pretentious "Crystalline" was somewhat Swedenborgian; and *The Legend of Tremaine* (London) was a sample of his best romanticism. Among his other poems were: "Ashes of Glory," a reply to "The Conquered Banner" by Father Abram J. Ryan, "Clouds in the West," an "Ode to Victory," and "Baby Zulma's Christmas Carol."

PRINCIPAL WORKS: The Spanish Exile, 1842; The Old Sanctuary: A Romance of the Ashley, 1846; Poems, 1860; Ode to Shakespeare, 1862; The Legend of Tremaine, 1864.

ABOUT: Davidson, J. L. The Living Writers of the South; Duyckinck, A. E., and G. L. Cyclopaedia of American Literature; Library of Southern Literature: Vol. 10.

"REVERIE, REGINALD." See MELLEN, GRENVILLE

REYNOLDS, JOHN (February 26, 1788-May 8, 1865), historian, governor of Illinois and member of Congress, was born in Montgomery County, Pa., the son of Irish Protestant parents, Robert Reynolds and Margaret (Moore) Reynolds, who came to the United States in 1785. He passed his boyhood near Knoxville, Tenn., where his parents moved in his first year, and from the age of twelve lived near Kaskaskia and Edwardsville, Ill., returning to Knoxville to study some of the branches of higher knowledge and read law. He began to practice at Cahokia, Ill., in 1814. Although never a brilliant lawyer, he became an associate justice of the Illinois supreme court. He served two terms in the general assembly before his election, in 1830, to the governorship. Moreover, he sat in the United States Congress; and later returned to the state legislature. He was a highly original character, took pains to conceal such education as he had by the adoption of the crude speech of his constituency, whose support he retained through his adroit qualities as a politician and his knowledge of human nature, and "astonished Congress to the utmost by his home-spun pathos and his amusing sallies of humor." A large man, with long furrowed face, he had a statesmanlike and gentlemanly appearance, but a shambling gait and uncultured manners. In 1817 he married a beautiful French Creole, Madame Catherine (Dubuque) LaCroix Manegle, in honor of whose father Dubuque, Iowa, was named; and after her death married Sarah Wilson, a cultured lady of Maryland. He had no children. He was a strong pro-slavery man and an opponent of President Lincoln. He died at Belleville, Ill.

The Pioneer History of Illinois is described by a contemporary as having been written in pencil, paper resting on his knee, no word being revised or altered. It was an unpretentious work with technical defects, but nonetheless an original and valuable historical record, and in the main reliable. Under the thin guise of a romance, *The Life and Adventures of John Kelly,* he issued a collection of his own unappreciated scientific lectures. Among his other work was some ephemeral literature of a political nature, including *The Balm of Gilead,* a tract on slavery, and a colorful autobiography, *My Own Times.* He was one of the editors of the *Star of Egypt,* a campaign paper published in Belleville in 1858-59.

Principal Works: The Pioneer History of Illinois, 1852; The Life and Adventures of John Kelly, 1853; Sketches of the Country on the Northern Route From Belleville, Ill., to New York, 1854; My Own Times, 1855; A Sketch of the Life of Gen. George Rogers Clark, 1856; The Balm of Gilead, 1860.

About: Koerner, G. P. Memoirs of Gustave Koerner; Parrish, R. Historic Illinois; Pease, T. C. The Frontier State; Snyder, J. F. Adam W. Snyder; Illinois State Historical Society Journal April 1913.

RICHARDS, THOMAS ADDISON (December 3, 1820-June 28, 1900), landscape painter, illustrator, art teacher, and author of stories and travel books, was born in London, England, the son of William Richards, a Baptist minister, and Anne (Gardner) Richards. His family came to America when he was eleven, and shortly after made their home in Georgia. He entered the National Academy of Design, New York City, in 1845, becoming an associate three years later and an Academician in 1851, serving also as corresponding secretary for forty years. In 1858 he supervised the first class in the Cooper Union School of Design for Women, and in 1867 he entered the University of the City of New York, now New York University, as professor of art, retiring after twenty years as professor emeritus. He was a member of various art associations and an annual exhibitor in the National Academy of Design for over half a century. His brother was the poet and scientist, Prof. William C. Richards, and his sister the Southern poetess, Mrs. Kate A. DuBose. In 1857 he married Mary Anthony of Providence, R.I., a writer of juvenile stories; they had no children. He died in his eightieth year at Annapolis, Md., and was buried at Providence.

When only twelve Richards wrote and illustrated a manuscript of 150 pages representing his voyage from England. At eighteen his first published book, *The American Artist,* appeared, an illustrated holiday volume on flower painting; and a few years later *Georgia Illustrated,* containing steel engravings with texts written by himself and others. He contributed constantly to *Harper's Magazine,* the *Southern Literary Gazette,* the *Knickerbocker,* and *Orion,* supplying both illustrations and articles, novelties, and tales. Some of his early stories were published as *Tallulah and Jocassee,* appearing the following year under the title *Summer Stories of the South.* Another work of fiction, *American Scenery,* illustrated with steel engravings of American landscapes, appeared later as *The Romance of American Scenery.* His *Pictures and Paintings* was a costly volume of steel engravings with descriptive and biographical texts. His guide books were works of accuracy, *Appleton's Illustrated Handbook of American Travel* being the first complete guide of its kind for the United States and Canada. In his illustrations he particularly specialized in the landscapes of the United States and Europe.

Principal Works: The American Artist, 1838; Georgia Illustrated, 1842; Tallulah and Jocassee, 1852; American Scenery, 1854; Appleton's Illustrated Hand-Book of American Travel, 1857; Appleton's Companion Hand-Book of Travel, 1864; Guide to the Central Park, 1866; Pictures and Painters, 1869.

About: American Art Annual 1900-1901; Tuckerman, H. T. Book of the Artists.

RICHARDSON, ALBERT DEANE (October 6, 1833-December 2, 1869), journalist, was born in Franklin, Mass., the son of Elisha Richardson, a farmer, by his second wife Harriet (Blake) Richardson. His brother, Charles Addison Richardson, was for many years editor of the Boston *Congregationalist.* Educated at the Holliston academy, he taught, school for a time, and at eighteen went to Pittsburgh where he taught, wrote farces for the actor, Barney Williams, appeared a few times on the stage, and entered journalism, a profession that he followed for the remainder of his life, from 1852 in Cincinnati, and from 1857 in Kansas and elsewhere. He was a correspondent for the Boston *Journal,* and from 1859 until his death he was connected with the New York *Daily Tribune.* Before the Civil War he undertook a dangerous secret mission as correspondent to New Orleans, and during the war attempted to run the Confederate blockade at Vicksburg. Taken prisoner, he was held for some eighteen months before escaping with a companion. His wife, Mary Louise Pease, of Cincinnati, and their youngest child having died during his imprisonment, he established himself in New York City. As a result of his engagement to marry Mrs. Abby (Sage) McFarland, who had recently divorced her husband, he was shot by Mr. McFarland in the *Tribune* office and died a week later. On his deathbed he was married to Mrs. McFarland.

Richardson's two early volumes, *The Secret Service* and *Beyond the Mississippi*, based on his newspaper correspondence and written in a popular vein, were sold on subscription and were an immense success. The first covered his Civil War experiences; the latter, his best known and most widely read production, was a copiously illustrated work on the West as it was before the completion of the Union Pacific railroad in 1869. In *Our New States and Territories* he incorporated notes of an observation tour through eight of the Western states. His widow, herself an author, collected and published posthumously a number of his stray writings under the title *Garnered Sheaves*.

Principal Works: The Secret Service, the Field, the Dungeon, and the Escape, 1865; Beyond the Mississippi, 1866; Our New States and Territories, 1866; A Personal History of Ulysses S. Grant, 1868; Garnered Sheaves, 1871.

About: Richardson, A. D. Garnered Sheaves (see Biographical Sketch by A. S. Richardson); The Richardson-McFarland Tragedy; Vinton, J. A. The Richardson Memorial; Nation December 9, 1869.

RICHARDSON, CHARLES FRANCIS (May 29, 1851-October 8, 1913), teacher, editor, and miscellaneous writer, was born in Hallowell, Maine, the son of Moses Charles Richardson, a physician, and his second wife, Mary Savary (Wingate) Richardson, both of old New England stock. Graduated from Dartmouth College in the class of 1871 (M.A. Dartmouth 1874; honorary Ph.D. Union College 1895, and Litt.D. Dartmouth 1911) he taught for a short time in the South Berkshire Institute, New Marlborough, Mass., and from 1872 to 1878 was associated with the New York *Independent*. He edited the Philadelphia *Sunday School Times* from 1878 to 1880, and founded the New York *Good Literature*, which he edited from 1880 to 1882. In 1882 he became Winkley Professor of Anglo-Saxon and English Language and Literature at Dartmouth, establishing a reputation for exceptional ability. He retired as professor emeritus in 1911 and died two years later, at sixty-two, at his summer home in Sugar Hill, N.H.

The College Book, prepared by Richardson in collaboration with H. A. Clark, was a handsome illustrated volume on American colleges. *The Choice of Books*, an inspirational volume which was reissued in England and Russia, received wide approval, as did *A Primer of American Literature*. His one novel, *The End of the Beginning*, suggestive of Hawthorne, was published anonymously. *American Literature 1607-1885*, in two volumes, his most ambitious work, was, despite some serious shortcomings, a popular text for more than a decade. Richardson also contributed to contemporary periodicals and was associate editor of the *International Cyclopedia*.

Principal Works: A Primer of American Literature, 1878; The Cross (poems) 1879; The Choice of Books, 1881; American Literature: 1607-1885, 1887, 1888; The End of the Beginning (novel) 1896; A Study of English Rhyme, 1909. *Editor*—The College Book (with H. A. Clark) 1878; The Last of the Mohicans (by J. F. Cooper) 1897; Poe's Complete Works, 1902; Daniel Webster for Young Americans, 1903.

About: Wingate, C. E. L. History of the Wingate Family; Dartmouth Alumni Magazine November 1913, April 1914.

RICKETSON, DANIEL (July 30, 1813-July 16, 1898), historian and poet, son of Joseph and Anna (Thornton) Ricketson, was born in New Bedford, Mass., where he lived all of his life and published two books on its history which added to his literary reputation. There is little information concerning his early education except that he studied law and gave up the idea of entering the profession to enjoy the literary and political pursuits made possible by the security of his personal fortune. His home, "Brooklawn," on the outskirts of New Bedford, provided him with ample opportunity to study nature, to write the poems which brought him a slight amount of fame, and to entertain the distinguished personages of the day—Emerson, Bronson Alcott, George William Curtis, and others. Thoreau was a frequent visitor and penned his last letter to Ricketson, whom he admired greatly, calling him "a man of very simple tastes, notwithstanding his wealth; a lover of nature; but above all, singularly frank and plain-spoken."

His first wife, Maria Louisa Sampson, to whom he was married in 1834, died in 1877; four children were born of this marriage. In 1880 Angeline Standish Gidley became his second wife.

Friendship with Thoreau and with two generations of the Alcott family has given Ricketson a more prominent place in American literature than his local histories—*The History of New Bedford,* and a posthumous volume, *New Bedford of the Past*—or his poetry. Fortunate in his own circumstances, he was genuinely affected by the problems of working people and wrote much of his deep-rooted feeling into *The Factory Bell and Other Poems,* published in 1873. Biographers of his eminent contemporaries will find much of value in two posthumous collections of his miscellaneous papers—*Daniel Ricketson and His Friends* and *Daniel Ricketson: Autobiographic and Miscellaneous.*

PRINCIPAL WORKS: *History*—The History of New Bedford, 1858; New Bedford of the Past, 1903. *Poetry*—The Autumn Sheaf: A Collection of Miscellaneous Poems, 1869; The Factory Bell and Other Poems, 1873. *Miscellaneous*—Daniel Ricketson and His Friends, 1902; Daniel Ricketson: Autobiographic and Miscellaneous, 1910.

ABOUT: Ricketson, D. Daniel Ricketson and His Friends; Daniel Ricketson: Autobiographic and Miscellaneous; Salt, H. S. The Life of Henry David Thoreau; Sanborn, F. B. Henry D. Thoreau; The Writings of Henry D. Thoreau; Boston Transcript July 18, 1898.

RIDEING, WILLIAM HENRY (February 17, 1853-August 22, 1918), editor and miscellaneous writer, was born in Liverpool, England, the son of William Watkins Rideing, an official of the Cunard Line, and of Emily (Richards) Rideing. An uncle was a rear-admiral in the Royal Navy. He was highly imaginative and while still a boy published some fiction in a Liverpool newspaper. An orphan at sixteen, he came in 1869 to the United States where he was associated as private secretary with Samuel Bowles of the Springfield (Mass.) *Republican,* and later with Whitelaw Reid on the New York *Tribune.* In 1881 he joined the staff of the *Youth's Companion,* remaining with it until his death. During part of these years, 1888-1889, he was also connected as associate and managing editor with the *North American Review.* He married Margaret Elinor Bockus of Boston. He died in Brookline, Mass.

Rideing's published works included some fifteen volumes, largely travel observations, biography, reminiscence and fiction; he also contributed to other journals and periodicals, including *Harper's,* the *Century, and Scribner's.* His *A-Saddle in the Far West* was based upon his experiences in accompanying, as special correspondent for the New York *Times,* the government exploring expedition under Lieutenant Wheeler to the Southwest, during which he traveled on horseback some four thousand miles. His interest in personalities found expression in several of his volumes, particularly in his *Many Celebrities and a Few Others,* which is also revealing in connection with his own life.

PRINCIPAL WORKS: *Biography*—The Boyhood of Living Authors, 1887; George Washington, 1916. *Fiction*—Boys in the Mountains and on the Plains, 1882; A Little Upstart, 1885; The Captured Cunarder, 1896. *Reminiscences*—Many Celebrities and a Few Others, 1912. *Compilations*—Stray Moments With Thackeray: His Humor, Satire, and Characters, 1880. *Miscellaneous*—Scenery of the Pacific Railways, and Colorado, 1878; A-Saddle in the Wild West, 1879; The Alpenstock, 1880; Thackeray's London, 1885; In the Land of Lorna Doone, and Other Pleasurable Excursions in England, 1895; At Hawarden With Mr. Gladstone, and Other Transatlantic Experiences, 1896.

ABOUT: Rideing, W. H. Many Celebrities and a Few Others; Critic March 1904.

RIDPATH, JOHN CLARK (April 26, 1840-July 31, 1900), educator and popular historian, was the son of Abraham Ridpath, of English descent, and of Sally (Matthews) Ridpath who traced her lineage through Governor Samuel Matthews of Virginia. Both were people of culture, and supplemented with their personal instruction the frontier education of their son, who was born on a farm in Putnam County, Ind. He was graduated from Indiana Asbury University, Greencastle, in 1863 (M.A. 1866), and was awarded an honorary LL.D. from Syracuse University in 1880. After holding several minor educational posts he was called, in 1869, to Indiana Asbury where, with various changes in title, he served as professor of belles-lettres, history, and political philosophy, and for six years was vice-president of the University. He was instrumental in securing generous financial aid from the wealthy Washington C. De Pauw, whose name was subsequently given to the university. Ridpath withdrew entirely in 1885 and devoted his time to literary pursuits. He was married, in 1862, to Hannah R. Smythe, by whom he had five children.

As a college student Ridpath had performed phenomenal academic feats, but he was never a pedant; his personality was not easily forgotten and on the occasion of his fiftieth birthday he was honored at a tremendous county celebration.

His exceptional vitality, memory, and capacity for sustained mental effort enabled him to produce an enormous quantity of work. Disregarding the more exacting phases of scholarship, he wrote for the popular taste, with a clear, direct, and sometimes dramatic style, becoming the most widely read historian of his time. His works had an enormous sale. In addition to his published books he was a contributor to periodicals, the author of many articles, poems, and lectures, and editor of the *Arena* in 1897-98. Among the most noteworthy of the works which he edited or wrote were *The Ridpath Library of Universal Literature* in twenty-five volumes, of which he was editor-in-chief, *The Standard American Encyclopedia of Arts, Sciences, History, Geography, Statistics and General Knowledge,* in ten volumes, which he supervised, the *Cyclopedia of Universal History* in four volumes, and numerous other historical references.

PRINCIPAL WORKS: *Biography*—The Life and Work of James A. Garfield, 1882; Life and Work of James G. Blaine (with S. Connor & others) 1893; Life and Memoirs of Bishop William Taylor, 1894, 1895; Napoleon Bonaparte, 1895; James Otis: The Pre-Revolutionist, 1898; Life and Times of William E. Gladstone, 1898. *Editor*—Famous Paintings of the World, 1894; The Ridpath Library of Universal Literature, 1898; The Standard American Encyclopedia of Arts, Sciences, History, Geography, Statistics, and General Knowledge, 1900. *Miscellaneous*—History of the United States: Prepared Especially for Schools, 1875; A Popular History of the United States of America, 1876; Cyclopedia of Universal History, 1880-85; Great Races of Mankind, 1884-94; Columbus and Columbia: A Pictorial History of the Man and the Nation (with J. G. Blaine, J. W. Buel, and B. Butterworth) 1892; Notable Events of the Nineteenth Century, 1896; History of the United States, 1900; Ridpath's Universal History, 1894-99; The New Complete History of the United States, 1895-1907.

ABOUT: A Biographical History of Eminent and Self-Made Men of the State of Indiana; De Pauw University Alumnal Register; American Review of Reviews March 1895.

RILEY, JAMES WHITCOMB (October ber 7, 1849-July 22, 1916), "The Hoosier Poet," creator of "Little Orphant Annie" and other famous American literary characters, was born in Greenfield, a small Indiana town. From his lawyer father, Reuben A. Riley, of Pennsylvania Dutch ancestry, he inherited his oratorical ability; his taste for poetry stemmed from his mother, Elizabeth (Marine) Riley. He was educated chiefly at the small local school, where he took little interest in any of his books except *McGuffey's Reader.* Outside the schoolroom the observant, slender, blue-eyed youth made frequent visits to the courthouse with his father and absorbed much of the town gossip and Indiana dialect which he used to advantage in later years. Although he left school at sixteen, his talents as verse-writer, amateur musician, and painter were already manifest. Ambitious and active, for two summers he traveled around Indiana with a small group of boys who called themselves "The Graphics," decorating country barns and fences with gaudy advertisements. After further excursions as a wandering musician with a patent-medicine company, he returned to Greenfield and joined the staff of the local newspaper. Meanwhile he had begun to contribute verse to other journals and when his brief employment with the Greenfield paper ended, he became associated with the Anderson *Democrat.* Here he perpetrated his famous "Leonainie" hoax in an attempt to prove that a poem could cause a sensation if it purported to be the newly-discovered work of "a genius known to fame." This carefully constructed work led prominent critics to attribute the poem to Poe, and booksellers and scholars wrote to the newspaper in which it appeared, the Kokomo *Dispatch,* requesting an opportunity to see the original manuscript. Displeased that Riley allowed the joke to be printed in a rival paper, his own journal asked him to resign, and the episode caused Riley unwelcome and longstanding publicity. He soon became affiliated with the Indianapolis *Journal* (1877-85) and during this period used the pen-name "Benjamin F. Johnson of Boone," supposedly a county farmer, in writing and publishing one of his most famous poems and subsequent recitations, "When the Frost is on the Punkin." In 1883 his first book was issued —a fifty-page collection of his early poems, *The Old Swimmin' Hole and 'Leven Other Poems.* Bobbs-Merrill & Company became his publishers and during his long career as a writer brought out the popular volumes *Old-Fashioned Roses, Rhymes of Childhood, Green Fields and Running Brooks,* and others.

JAMES WHITCOMB RILEY

Riley settled in Indianapolis, where he lived with close friends until his death. Despite acute stage fright (which he never conquered) he became one of the most popular lecturers in the country and sometimes gave rollicking programs with Bill Nye, the humorist. He seldom ventured into social life, preferring the quietude of his vine-covered home, where he cordially received the homage of a steady stream of visitors. He made almost daily calls at his publishers and was a familiar figure in Indianapolis. Meticulously groomed, dignified, with gold-headed walking stick and white carnation boutonnière, he often incongruously stopped to play games with his beloved neighborhood children and might sometimes be seen throwing snowballs or riding a broomstick with small, congenial colleagues.

Modest to an extreme, he minimized his ability and once remarked, "My work did itself. I'm only the willer bark through which the whistle comes." But behind him were many moments of literary drudgery—many notebooks filled with Hoosier colloquiallisms. At another time he said, "I could not resist the inclination to write. It was what I most enjoyed doing. And so I wrote, laboriously ever, more often using the rubber end of the pencil than the point." He was a born mimic; his flexible voice could assume the precise diction of the lecturer, or lapse into the Midwestern drawl of his popular characters.

In his declining years he became repetitious, and his work failed to measure up to his earlier standard. Though he attempted formal verse, he was most at home in his unaffected homespun rhymes, which Hamlin Garland aptly called "a humble crop gathered from the corners of rail fences, from the vines which clamber upon the porches of small villages, and from the weedy side-walks of quiet towns far from the great markets of the world."

Principal Works: The Old Swimmin' Hole, 1883; Afterwhiles, 1887; Pipes O' Pan at Zekesbury, 1888; Old-Fashioned Roses (London) 1888; Rhymes of Childhood, 1890; Green Fields and Running Brooks, 1892; Poems Here at Home, 1893; Riley Child Rhymes, 1899; Book of Joyous Children, 1902.

About: Dickey, M. The Youth of James Whitcomb Riley; Garland, H. Commemorative Tribute to James Whitcomb Riley; Laughlin, C. Reminiscences of James Whitcomb Riley; Nicholson, M. The Hoosiers; Phelps, W. L. Letters of James Whitcomb Riley.

"RINGBOLT, CAPTAIN." See CODMAN, JOHN

RIPLEY, EZRA (May 1, 1751-September 21, 1841), clergyman and historian, was born in Woodstock, Conn., the fifth of the nineteen children of Noah and Lydia (Kent) Ripley. During his childhood the family moved to a farm at Barre, Mass., where young Ezra grew up with sound agricultural knowledge. He attended Harvard College, was graduated in 1776, and after studying theology under the Rev. Jason Haven at Dedham was ordained in 1778 and put in charge of the First Church in Concord, Mass., where he remained for sixty-three years, delivering his last sermon on the day after his ninetieth birthday.

Despite his domineering personality and his natural inclination to hold the reins both in civic and social life, he was popular in Concord. Caring little for fashion trends, he dressed to suit his own taste in outmoded styles and was so dignified in his bearing that he was ridiculed neither for this nor for his extremely small stature. Among his many activities, he was a member of the school committee, drew up the constitution of the Concord Library, was the organizer of the first temperance society in America, and donated the land on which the Concord Battle Monument was erected.

As a minor historian, he contributed two books of value to America—*History of the Fight at Concord;* and *Half Century Discourse Delivered Nov. 16, 1828.* His only other publications were his collected sermons.

He married Mrs. Phebe (Bliss) Emerson, of Concord, the widow of the Rev. William Emerson, who preceded him in the pastorate at Concord. He had two sons and one daughter, and became the step-grandfather of Ralph Waldo Emerson.

Principal Works: History of the Fight at Concord, 1827; Half Century Discourse Delivered Nov. 16, 1828, 1828.

About: Eliot, S. A. Heralds of a Liberal Faith; Frost, B. & Francis, C. Two Sermons on the Death of Rev. Ezra Ripley; Harper's New Monthly Magazine June 1875; Christian Register October 9, 16, 1841; Christian Examiner January 1842; Boston Daily Advertiser September 22, 1841.

RIPLEY, GEORGE (October 3, 1802-July 4, 1880), clergyman, reformer, editor, literary critic, and "Brook Farmer," was born in Greenfield, Mass., the ninth of ten children of Jerome Ripley, a merchant, and Sarah (Franklin) Ripley. At Harvard, from which he was graduated in 1823 at the head of his class, he realized his usefulness lay "in some retired literary situation" requiring a "fondness for books," but nevertheless entered the Harvard Divinity School, class of 1826, and was ordained pastor of a Unitarian congregation in Boston. He married, in 1827, Sophia Willard Dana, of the Cambridge Dana family, a woman of great cultivation, charm, and courage.

After a photograph

GEORGE RIPLEY

The young clergyman edited for a while the Unitarian weekly, the *Christian Register,* and up to 1840 contributed ten articles to the Unitarian quarterly, the *Christian Examiner.* The Transcendental Club first met at his house, September 1836, and the same year he began editing the fourteen-volume *Specimens of Foreign Standard Literature,* translations of great documents of Transcendental philosophy, published 1838 to 1852. In the controversy between liberals and conservatives in the Unitarian church of the time, Ripley's dignified, balanced, but fully aroused *Letters on the Latest Form of Infidelity,* published 1840, was a notable defence of freedom of thought and tolerance in religion.

In 1841 he resigned from the ministry, convinced of his lack of vocation, and for the next six years directed the famous Brook Farm experiment at West Roxbury, nine miles from Boston, where Transcendental interpretations of Christian ideals were applied to daily social living. It was doomed to fail, for the farm was poor, markets were inadequate, and capital was scarce; in 1844 a shift was made to the more mechanical organization of a Fourier phalanx, but following the destruction by fire of a new building the end came in 1847. Ripley and his wife moved to New York, and after more years of poverty he finally established himself in his "literary situation."

Assistant editor of the *Dial,* organ of the Transcendentalists, in 1840, and editor of its successor, the *Harbinger,* organ of the Fourierists, 1845-49, he was in 1849 hired as literary editor of Greeley's *Tribune,* and for the remainder of his life conducted the first daily literary criticism in an American newspaper. For this pioneer task his sound scholarship and natural critical acumen admirably fitted him. To augment an at first extremely meagre income, he wrote for other journals and in 1850 helped to organize *Harper's New Monthly Magazine,* of which he was literary editor for years, later becoming reader for the house. In 1852, with Bayard Taylor, he edited a handbook on the arts; then, with his former Brook Farm associate, Charles A. Dana, managing editor of the *Tribune* and later owner of the *Sun,* he edited the *New American Cyclopedia,* published 1858 to 1863, a second edition being brought out 1873-76. The work helped him endure his wife's painful illness and death in 1861 and eventually released him from poverty and the debts of Brook Farm, which he had assumed. In 1865 he married a young German widow, Mrs. Louisa A. Schlossberger, with whom he had a happy life of enlarged social contacts. Twice they went abroad, in 1866 and 1869-70, where Ripley was warmly received by contemporary scholars. From Greeley's death in 1872 to his own in 1880 he was president of the Tribune Association. He died in his chair in his library after a brief illness, working almost to the last.

"Too humble to collect the clear and scholarly essays he wrote for his paper"—to quote Van Wyck Brooks—nevertheless "with him literature was a high calling, on a line with the ministry," as O. B. Frothingham has said. He was instrumental in changing the prevailing sentimental tone of criticism to one of reason, and in his kindliness and devotion to high ideals he "did much to make our literature worthy of our hopes" (George Willis Cooke). He is remembered, less for his published works which were negligible, than for his personal influence on the literary life and personalities of his time.

ABOUT: Frothingham, O. B. George Ripley; Swift, L. Brook Farm: Its Members, Scholars, and Visitors.

RITCHIE, ANNA CORA (OGDEN) MOWATT. See MOWATT, ANNA CORA (OGDEN)

"RIVERS, PEARL." See NICHOLSON, ELIZA JANE (POITEVENT) HOLBROOK

"ROBERTSON, IGNATIUS LOYOLA." See KNAPP, SAMUEL LORENZO

ROBINSON, EDWARD (April 10, 1794-January 27, 1863), philologist, geographer, and professor of Biblical literature, was of old New England ancestry, the son of the Rev. William Robinson, for forty-one years pastor in Southington, Conn., where Edward was born, and of his fourth wife, Elisabeth (Norton) Robinson. He was graduated from Hamilton College, Clinton, N.Y., read law, and taught mathematics and Greek. After the early death of his wife, Eliza Kirkland, his editing of some books of the Iliad brought him under the influence of Moses Stuart of Andover Theological Seminary, and he devoted himself assiduously to the study of Hebrew, followed by four years of travel and study abroad. While there he married the brilliant and accomplished Therese Albertine Louise von Jakob, daughter of a Halle professor. He was professor extraordinary of Biblical literature and librarian at Andover from 1830 until 1833 when he resigned and professor of Biblical literature at Union Theological Seminary from 1837 until his death. Before taking over the duties of the latter chair he was given leave of absence to visit the Holy Land, accompanied by the missionary, the Rev. Eli Smith. He remained abroad to prepare the resulting three-volume work of his explorations for publication. In 1852 he made another trip to Palestine, going still farther afield. He died in New York City.

The importance and high scholarship of Robinson's contributions to Biblical science and literature were widely recognized, and his reputation has been enhanced by time. In addition to his *Researches in Palestine* and *Later Researches in Palestine,* which most contributed to his distinction, he also produced several scholarly translations of works and dictionaries of Biblical literature. He founded the *American Biblical Repository* in 1831, contributing nearly half of all the material to the first four volumes, and in 1843 he founded the *Bibliotheca Sacra,* which he edited for nearly a year.

Principal Works: A Dictionary of the Holy Bible for the Use of Schools and Young Persons, 1833; Biblical Researches in Palestine, Mount Sinai, and Arabic Petraea, 1841; Later Biblical Researches in Palestine and the Adjacent Regions, 1856; A Dictionary of the Holy Bible, for General Use in the Study of the Scriptures, 1859; Memoir of the Rev. William Robinson, 1859; Physical Geography of the Holy Land, 1865. *Editor*—Iliadio Libri Novem Priores Librique XVIII et XXII, 1822; Calmet's Dictionary of the Holy Bible, 1832; A Harmony of the Gospels in Greek, 1832. *Translator*—A Greek Grammar of the New Testament (with Moses Stuart) (from the German of G. B. Winer) 1825; A Greek and English Lexicon of the New Testament (from C. A. Wahl's Clavis Philologica Novi Testamenti) 1825, 1836; A Greek Grammar (from the German of P. Buttmann) 1833; A Hebrew and English Lexicon of the Old Testament (from the German of H. F. W. Gesenius) 1836.

ROBINSON, ROWLAND EVANS (May 14, 1833-October 15, 1900), writer of sporting and nature books, was born in the same room in which he died on his grandfather's farm at Ferrisburg, Addison County, Vt. His Quaker parents, Rowland Thomas Robinson and Rachel (Gilpin) Robinson, brought him up in strict accordance with their religious beliefs and kept him so sheltered from worldly contact that the dreamy, lonely young boy began to express himself through his talent for drawing, frequently decorating marketable buttertubs with original political cartoons. He attended the local schools and Ferrisburg Academy, but acquired most of his education through voracious reading, especially the works of Sir Walter Scott.

Soon after his twenty-first year, Robinson went to New York City to work in a draftsman's shop for a brief and unsuccessful period. He returned to rural Vermont life, and though he took a great interest in farming, he went again to New York in 1866, this time to gain success through wood-engraving, fashion-plates, cartoons, and catalogue work for the periodicals and newspapers of Orange Judd and Frank Leslie. Strenuous night work so seriously impaired his eyesight that he returned to Ferrisburg in 1873 to settle permanently. Four years later he began his literary career with an article on "Fox-Hunting in New England" which was published in *Scribner's Monthly* and led him to become a contributor to other leading magazines and to serve on the editorial staff of *Forest and Stream.* In 1893 he was afflicted with total blindness, but continued to write essays, novels, and sporting books which he had begun to publish in 1886 with the appearance of *Forest and Stream Fables.* His wife, Anna Stevens of East Montpelier, whom he married in 1870, served as his amanuensis. Like John Burroughs, he had an intimate knowledge and great love of nature and a facility for interpreting bucolic life in a simple, appealing style. Among Vermont writers he holds a prominent place through his humorous characterizations of the country folk.

Principal Works: Forest and Stream, 1886; Uncle Lisha's Shop: Life in a Corner of Yankeeland, 1887 (centennial edition, Rutland 1933); Sam Lovel's Camps: Uncle Lisha's Friends Under Bark and Canvas, 1889; Vermont: A Study of Independence, 1892; Danvis Folks, 1894; In New England Fields and Woods, 1896; Uncle Lisha s Outing, 1897; A Hero of Ticonderoga, 1898; In the Green

Wood, 1899; A Danvis Pioneer, 1900; Sam Lovel's Boy, 1901; Hunting Without a Gun and Other Papers, 1905; Out of Bondage and Other Stories, 1905; Silver Fields and Other Sketches of a Farmer-Sportsman, 1921.

About: Crockett, W. H. Vermonters; Hazard, T. R. Recollections of Olden Times: Rowland Robinson of Narragansett; Robinson, R. Hunting Without a Gun; Atlantic Monthly January 1901, July 1901; New England Magazine December 1900; Vermonter December 1900; Burlington Free Press and Times October 16, 1900.

ROBINSON, SOLON (October 21, 1803-November 3, 1880), agricultural journalist and novelist, was born in Tolland, Conn., the fourth son of Jacob and Salinda (Ladd) Robinson, and through his father a descendant of the Rev. John Robinson, pastor of the Pilgrims at Leyden. Orphaned at ten, he shortly afterward commenced to make his own way, variously occupied as carpenter's apprentice, peddler, theatre cashier in Cincinnati, and promotor of real estate near North Vernon, Ind. In 1834 he opened a general store in the wilderness of northern Indiana, after 1837 holding such offices as county clerk, justice of the peace, register of claims, and postmaster. His great interest was agriculture. In the years following 1841 he visited practically every state of the union, reporting his observations in agricultural journals; he was active in the formation of the United States Agricultural Society in 1852 and at one time conducted an experimental farm in Westchester County, N.Y. He was twice married: to Mariah Evans of Bucks County, Pa., by whom he had five children; and in 1872 to Mary Johnson of Barton, Vt. From 1868 he lived and wrote in Jacksonville, Fla.

About 1830 Robinson was writing for the local press of Madison, Ind.; from 1837 he contributed to such agricultural journals as the Albany *Cultivator,* the *Prairie Farmer,* and the *American Agriculturist.* He published the *Plow* in New York City in 1852, and became agricultural editor of the New York *Tribune* in 1853, attracting a large following by his homely, humorous writing. Later he published the *Florida Republican* at Jacksonville. He also produced some novels, short stories, and poetry. His volume *Hot Corn-Life Scenes in New York,* sentimental tales of the slums, won an instant popularity and sold to the extent of 50,000 copies in six months. His *Facts for Farmers,* sold by subscription, had almost equal success.

Principal Works: The Will: A Tale of the Lake of the Red Cedars and Shabbona, 1841; Guano: A Treatise of Practical Information for Farmers, 1852; Hot Corn-Life Scenes in New York, 1854; Facts for Farmers, 1864; Me-won-i-toc: A Tale of Frontier Life and Indian Character, 1867; How to Live: Saving and Wasting: or, Domestic Economy Illustrated by the Life of Two Families of Opposite Character (novel) 1873; Selected Writings (ed. by H. A. Kellar) 1936.

About: Ball, T. H. (ed.). Encyclopedia of Genealogy and Biography of Lake County, Indiana; Bungay, G. W. Off-Hand Takings; Robinson, S. Selected Writings (see Introduction by H. A. Kellar).

ROCHE, JAMES JEFFREY (May 31, 1847-April 3, 1908), journalist and poet, was born at Mountmellick, Queens County, Ireland, and at an early age was brought to Charlottetown, Prince Edward Island, by his parents, Edward and Mary Margaret (Doyle) Roche. Receiving his primary schooling from his father, who became a schoolteacher and librarian on the island, James later attended St. Dunstan's College, and in 1866 went to Boston. By 1883 he had made a name for himself in journalism and was serving as assistant editor of the leading American Irish-Catholic journal, the Boston *Pilot,* where he remained seven years until he took over the editorship formerly held by John Boyle O'Reilly.

In 1904 his health showed signs of breaking under the strain of routine business life and he accepted an appointment as consul to Genoa by President Theodore Roosevelt, and afterward acted as consul at Berne, Switzerland, where he died.

Apart from his editorial work in Boston, he was a popular contributor to the leading periodicals—*Atlantic, Century,* and *Harper's.* His first novel, an adventurous story entitled *The Story of the Filibusters,* was published in 1891 and translated into Spanish seventeen years later. A re-issue appeared in 1901 under the title *By-Ways of War: The Story of the Filibusters* and was highly lauded by Richard Harding Davis. Besides writing a number of miscellaneous books, he assisted Lady Gregory, Douglas Hyde, and others in preparing the ten-volume *Irish Literature,* issued in 1904. As a poet he was most at home in the ballad form and composed meritorious pieces in the satirical and humorous vein.

His first wife, Mary Halloran, died in 1885, and he married Mrs. Elizabeth Vaughan Okie in 1904. While his writing reflected to some extent his many-faceted personality, it failed to achieve the same popularity in literature that Roche captured his social life.

Principal Works: *Miscellaneous*—The Story of the Filibusters, 1891 (re-issued as By-Ways of War: The Story of the Filibusters, 1901); Life of John Boyle O'Reilly, 1891. *Poetry*—Songs and Satires, 1886; Ballads of Blue Water and Other

Poems, 1895; Her Majesty the King: A Romance of the Harem, 1898; The V-a-s-e and Other Bric-a-Brac, 1900; The Sorrows of Sap'ed, 1904.

ABOUT: Cullen, J. B. The Story of the Irish in Boston; James Jeffrey Roche: A Memorial and Appreciation, 1908; Boston Transcript April 3, May 3, 1908; Boston Globe April 4, 1908.

ROE, EDWARD PAYSON (March 7, 1838-July 19, 1888), clergyman and novelist, was born in New Windsor, N.Y., where his father, Peter Roe, had retired after a successful business career as a merchant in New York City. Susan (Williams) Roe, the mother of six children of whom Edward was the fourth, was for the most part an invalid, but she seems to have exerted an influence on the literary tastes of her young son.

After attending elementary and secondary schools at Manchester, Vt., Edward entered Williams College. There he suffered from severe eye strain, and, on the advice of President Mark Hopkins, limited his college career to a special two year course. After a year at the Auburn Theological Seminary, he was ordained in 1862 at Somers, N.Y., and became a chaplain during the Civil War. For the next eight years he served as pastor of the Highland Falls (N.Y.) Prebyterian Church.

Absorbed in his ministry, Roe had apparently given little thought to a literary career until 1871, when the catastrophic event of the great Chicago fire served to turn him from his career of country clergyman to that of a popular novelist. Drawn by compassionate curiosity, he visited the city, wandering among the smoky ruins, and returned to write *Barriers Burned Away,* a novel which achieved instant and lasting popularity. Published first as a magazine serial in the *Evangelist,* this story of a stricken Chicago appeared in book form in 1872, became the best-seller of its day, and continued to sell widely throughout the next decade. When his second novel, *Opening A Chestnut Burr,* proved likewise a success, Roe resigned from his pastorate and retired to an estate at Cornwall on the Hudson, where he continued to write for an income averaging $15,000 a year.

He was criticized by some for thus forsaking the ministry, but from statements made to his sister, Mary Roe, it appears that he was profoundly sincere in believing that he could carry on his mission better by the pen than by the pulpit. He was a painstaking and methodical worker, writing a long series of novels, as well as several books on the beauties of nature and on horticulture, which became his avocation.

Collection of Frederick H. Meserve

E. P. ROE

Roe was not, however, always free of financial worries. In 1882 he was forced into bankruptcy by the default of his brother whose notes he had endorsed. As was characteristic of his decent and kindly nature, he sold the copyrights of his books at auction, paying his brother's creditors in full, with no word of complaint.

Married to Anna Paulina Sands, and the father of five children, he spent his later years at the Cornwall estate as a modest but generous host to his many literary friends. It was there he died suddenly of a heart attack at the age of fifty, after an evening reading aloud to his family.

By endowing American fiction with a moral purpose Roe not only strengthened the novel against a kind of chronic popular prejudice, but actually brought it into considerable favor. Although his friends often cited him as Thackeray's equal, Roe appears to have had no delusions about his own status. Writing to a formula, he based his novels on real incidents of topical interest drawn from personal observation or the newspapers, and spiced them to the public taste with romance and pious sentiment. His plots, according to Carl Van Doren, were concerned with the "simultaneous pursuit of wives, fortunes, and salvation."

PRINCIPAL WORKS: *Novels*—Barriers Burned Away, 1872; What Can She Do, 1873; Opening A Chestnut Burr, 1874; From Jest to Earnest, 1875; Near to Nature's Heart, 1876; A Knight of the Nineteenth Century, 1877; A Face Illumined, 1878; A Day of Fate, 1880; Without A Home, 1881; His Sombre Rivals, 1883; A Young Girl's Wooing, 1884; An Original Belle, 1885; Driven Back to

Eden, 1885; He Fell In Love With His Wife, 1886; The Earth Trembled, 1887; Miss Lou, 1888; Found Yet Lost, 1888; The Hornet's Nest, 1892. *Nature*—Play and Profit in My Garden, 1873; A Manual on the Culture of Small Fruits, 1876; Success With Small Fruits, 1880; Nature's Serial Story, 1885; The Home Acre, 1889.

ABOUT: Van Doren, C. The American Novel; Roe, M. A. E. P. Roe: Reminiscences of His Life.

ROGERS, JOHN (December 1, 1648-October 17, 1721), founder of the Rogerene religious sect, was born in Milford, Conn., the third son of James Rogers, who acquired wealth in New London, and Elizabeth (Rowland) Rogers. Converted in 1674 by the Seventh-Day Baptists of Newport, R.I., he soon after developed his own doctrines, including opposition to civil dictation in religious matters, to formal prayers, meeting houses, and salaried clergy, and upholding obedience to conscience, principles of peace and non-resistance, and lawfulness of labor on the Sabbath. He converted his own family and disseminated his principles in New England. Although the Rogerenes suffered constant persecution from state and ecclesiastical authorities and Rogers is said to have been imprisoned with sentences aggregating fifteen years and publicly whipped, he appears to have held the sympathy of his neighbors and was elected to various public offices. His son John Rogers, Jr. (by his marriage with Elizabeth Griswold, who divorced him soon after his conversion) succeeded him in leadership, the sect finally dying out in the nineteenth century. Rogers took a second wife without formal marriage in 1699, and after this union was dissolved he married, in 1714, a Quaker widow, Sarah Cole. He died of smallpox at New London.

Rogers manifested remarkable steadfastness and courage in adhering to his convictions and in his endeavor to obtain greater personal freedom in religion. He propagated his views in thirteen pamphlets written in a plain and concise style. The most notable of these was *The Book of the Revelation of Jesus Christ* (1720).

ABOUT: Bolles, J. R. & Williams, A. B. The Rogerenes; Caulkins, F. M. History of New London; Rogers, J. S. James Rogers of New London, Connecticut, and His Descendants.

ROGERS, ROBERT (November 7, 1731 o.s.-May 18, 1795), colonial ranger and miscellaneous writer, was born in Methuen, Mass., the son of James and Mary Rogers. He led the life of a typical pioneer boy and in 1755 entered the military service, where his exceptional ability as a scout, his daring, and his intelligence soon earned him promotion. The following year he recruited and commanded a corps of fighters known as "Rogers' Rangers," whose recklessness and boisterous bravery soon made them the most colorful group in the service. In 1759 at Crown Point, Rogers and his men wiped out the Saint Francis Indians in a swift and daringly executed attack, a battle vividly described in Kenneth Roberts' popular novel *Northwest Passage*. Later they took possession of Detroit and other Western posts that were ceded by the French after the fall of Quebec.

From an old print

MAJOR ROBERT ROGERS

In 1761 Rogers married Elizabeth Browne, and feeling that he was unappreciated in America, visited England where he published his *Journals* and a play *Ponteach*. He received praise and acclaim from the English people and the post of governor of Mackinaw, Mich., from their king. While holding this office he was accused of plotting with the French but was acquitted for lack of evidence. He revisited England in 1769, but was soon imprisoned for debt. Returning to America in 1775, Rogers was suspected by his countrymen and was arrested as a spy. He was released on parole but accepted a commission in the British army, raising a corps, the Queen's Rangers, with which he joined Howe in Westchester. Defeated and almost captured during a battle near White Plains, Rogers was removed from command. In 1778 his wife sued for divorce, which the New Hampshire legislature granted, and two years later he went to England, where he lived for fifteen years, until his death in a cheap London lodging house.

Rogers' *Journal* is an account of his early years as a ranger and is interesting as the biography of one of the most fascinating characters in early American history. But Rogers was more at ease as soldier than author and his other works are of little interest today.

PRINCIPAL WORKS: A Concise Account of North America, 1865; Journals, 1865; Ponteach: or, The Savages of America, 1766.

ABOUT: Pound, A. Native Stock; Burton Historical Collections Leaflet September 1928; Quarterly of Oregon Historical Society March 1922; Vital Records of Methuen, Mass., 1909.

ROLFE, WILLIAM JAMES (December 10, 1827-July 7, 1910), teacher, philologist, and editor of English classics, was born in Newburyport, Mass. He was the eldest son of John Rolfe, a hatter, and Lydia Davis (Moulton) Rolfe, and traced his descent from Henry Rolfe, a Newbury settler of 1635. He attended Amherst College for three years in the class of 1849, subsequently receiving the honorary degrees M.A. Harvard 1859, Amherst 1865, and LL.D Amherst 1887. For the next twenty years he taught classes, four years as principal and sole teacher of Day's Academy, Wrentham, and from 1852 he was headmaster of high schools in Dorchester, Lawrence, Salem, and Cambridge. He was the first to introduce regular instruction in English literature into the school curriculum. From 1868 he resided in Cambridge, engaged in editing and writing, serving as president of Martha's Vineyard Summer Institute from 1882 to 1888, and of the Emerson College of Oratory, Boston, from 1903 to 1908. He died at Martha's Vineyard at eighty-two. He was married to Eliza Jane Carew in 1856; one of their three sons, John Carew Rolfe, was professor at the universities of Michigan and Pennsylvania.

Rolfe's outstanding work was the editing of school texts and English classics. His edited and written works numbered 144 volumes; in addition he contributed extensively to periodicals and newspapers, was for twenty years an editor of the *Boston Journal of Chemistry* and its successor *Popular Science News,* and for nearly the same length of time had charge of "Shakespeariana" in the *Literary World* and *Critic.* Among his more important edited works were the plays of Shakespeare in forty volumes, the complete works of Alfred Tennyson in twelve volumes, and editions of Walter Scott and Robert Browning. His "Satchel Guide" to Europe, the original work by which he was best known, was annually revised until 1909. He also collaborated with J. A. Gillet in a series of science textbooks. His work, of a popular nature, was marked by accuracy, scholarship, and thoroughness.

PRINCIPAL WORKS: Cambridge Course of Physics (with J. A. Gillet) 1868-72; Satchel Guide to Europe, 1872; Tales From Scottish History, 1891; Shakespeare the Boy, 1896; Elementary Study of English, 1896; Life of Shakespeare, 1902; Shakespeare Proverbs, 1909. *Editor*—A Handbook of Latin Poetry (with J. H. Hanson) 1866; Shakespeare, 1871-84; Select Poems of Robert Browning, 1887; Select Dramas of Robert Browning, 1888; The Poetical Works of Sir Walter Scott, 1888; The Poetic and Dramatic Works of Alfred, Lord Tennyson, 1898.

ABOUT: Obituary Record of the Graduates of Amherst College for the Academic Year Ending June 28, 1911; Amherst Graduates Quarterly January 1912; Emerson College Magazine November 1910; Nation July 14, 1910.

ROPES, JOHN CODMAN (April 28, 1836-October 28, 1899), military historian and lawyer, son of William and Mary Anne (Codman) Ropes, was born in St. Petersburg, Russia, where his father, a Salem merchant, had lived for some time. The family returned to Boston in 1842 and young Ropes attended Harvard College, being graduated in 1857. He studied law at Harvard Law School and on his graduation in 1861 began to practice. He was one of the editors of the *American Law Review* from 1866 to 1869.

An old spinal injury barred Ropes from participation in the Civil War, but, always an assiduous student of things military and historical, he studied the movements and campaigns of the conflict with careful attention. In 1876 he founded the Military Historical Society of Massachusetts for the collection of facts regarding the Civil War.

His greatest work was his unfinished *Story of the Civil War* to which he devoted most of his later years. It was completed in 1913 by his friend William Livermore. Another work on the Civil War, *The Army Under Pope,* a detailed account of the Virginia campaign of August-September 1862, greatly influenced popular thought to a vindication of General Fitz John Porter.

His books, which gained him international fame as an historian, were the result of careful and diligent research. In his Civil War works he gives a fair and unbiased view of both sides and presents a clear panorama of the conflict.

PRINCIPAL WORKS: The Army Under Pope, 1881; The First Napoleon, 1885; The Campaign of Waterloo, 1892; An Atlas of the Campaign, 1893; Story of Civil War, 1894-98.

About: A Memoir of the Life of John Codman Ropes; Daily Evening Transcript (Boston) October 29, 1899.

"ROSA." See JEFFREY, ROSA (GRIFFITH) VERTNER JOHNSON

ROSE, AQUILA (c. 1696-1723), poet, was born in London, England. There is little detailed information on his early life or education except that given in the rhyme prefixed to his posthumous published poems. It is known that he was educated in England, where he lived until unrequited love drove him from the country and that he worked as a common sailor, subjected to such hardships that on his arrival in Philadelphia he was so ill he had to leave the ship. He practiced the trade of printer, married, and settled in Philadelphia, where has was made clerk of the provincial senate and secretary of the assembly. After establishing a ferry over the Schuylkill river, he contracted a fatal cold while trying to rescue one of the boats during a storm.

Rose's poems never appeared during his lifetime but after his death they were collected and published by his son, Joseph Rose. They are splendid examples of the verse of that period when every young gentleman tried to be something of a poetaster, but they have slight value beyond their archaic charm.

Rose was greatly admired and beloved during his career in America. In his *Autobiography* Benjamin Franklin described him as an "ingenious young man of excellent character, much respected in the town, secretary to the assembly, and a pretty poet." Upon his death, Samuel Keimer and Elias Bockett both composed poems in memoriam, and he was given a most elaborate funeral, with preachers, printers, shopkeepers, and the keeper of the seal walking behind the hearse.

Principal Works: Poems on Several Occasions, by Aquila Rose, To Which Are Prefixed Some Other Pieces Writ to Him, and to His Memory after His Decease, 1740.

About: Jackson, M. K. Outlines of the Literary History of Colonial Pennsylvania; Memoirs of the Historical Society of Pennsylvania; Scharf, J. T. & Wescott, H. History of Philadelphia.

ROSS, ALEXANDER (May 9, 1783-October 23, 1856), fur trader and explorer, was born in Nairnshire, Scotland, the son of a farmer of the same name. Emigrating to Canada at twenty-one, he first taught school, and in 1810 joined the Pacific Fur Co. as a clerk. Proceeding to what is now Oregon he helped to establish Fort Astoria, and after its downfall he was in the successive employ of the North West Co. and Hudson's Bay Co. He remained in the Pacific Northwest fifteen years, several times being in charge of Fort Okanogan, and for five years of Fort Nez Percés, otherwise Fort Walla Walla. In 1824 he led an independent expedition to the Snake River country from Montana, and the following year settled with his wife, an Okinagan Indian, and children in the Red River colony, Canada, remaining there for the rest of his life. He was a man of influence and ability, much esteemed, and served as the first sheriff of that colony.

In his latter years he published two valuable first-hand contributions to the history of the fur trade and country: *Adventures of the First Settlers of the Oregon or Columbia River,* narrating the story of expedition establishing the Pacific Fur Co., together with an account of the Indian tribes of the Pacific Coast; and *The Fur Hunters of the Far West,* in two volumes, recounting adventures in the Oregon and Rocky Mountains. In his other published volume *The Red River: Its Rise, Progress and Present State,* he also included an account of the Indians of that section. Some letters by him were published in the 1903 *Transactions of the Historical and Scientific Society of Manitoba,* and the "Journal of Alexander Ross—Snake River Expedition," edited by T. C. Elliott, appeared in the December 1913 *Quarterly of the Oregon Historical Society.*

Principal Works: Adventures of the First Settlers on the Oregon or Columbia River, 1849; The Fur Hunters of the Far West, 1855; The Red River Settlement, 1856.

About: Chittenden, H. M. The American Fur Trade of the Far West; Scott, H. W. History of the Oregon Country; Canadian Magazine June 1917; Queen's Quarterly July 1903.

ROWLANDSON, MARY (WHITE) (c. 1635-c. 1678), Indian captive and writer of a famous autobiography, was the daughter of John White of Lancaster, Mass., and became (about 1656) the wife of Joseph Rowlandson, first minister of Lancaster.

During King Philip's War, on February 10, 1676, Lancaster was attacked and destroyed by the Indians and Mrs. Rowlandson and her three children were captured and carried away to be held for ransom. The youngest child died of exposure, and as the Indians changed camp constantly to evade pursuit, Mrs. Rowlandson endured severe hardship. Accommodations were crude, food scarce, and the uncertainty of the fate in store for herself and her children must have put to the strongest test Mrs. Rowlandson's pioneer fortitude. On May 2, 1676, after about eleven weeks in captivity, she was ransomed, on the payment of twenty pounds, and the restoration of her children soon followed.

After her return home, Mrs. Rowlandson wrote a narrative of her captivity, published in Cambridge in 1682. Her ordeal had evidently not dulled her powers of observation, for her book presents a graphic picture of primitive squalor and cruelty, and exhibits penetrating insight into the ferocity, stoicism, and sometimes casual kindness of the Indian character.

Principal Works: The Soveraignty and Goodness of God: Together With the Faithfulness of His Promises Displayed; Being a Narrative of the Captivity and Restauration of Mrs. Mary Rowlandson, 1682.

About: Drake, S. G. The Old Indian Chronicle, 1867; Nourse, H. S. & Thayer, J. E. The Narrative of the Captivity and Restoration of Mrs. Mary Rowlandson; Stiles, H. R. & Adams, S. W. The History of Ancient Wethersfield; Willard, J. Narrative of the Captivity and Removes of Mrs. Mary Rowlandson.

ROWSON, SUSANNA (HASWELL) (c. 1762-March 2, 1824), novelist, actress, and educator, was born in Portsmouth, England, the daughter of Lieutenant William Haswell and his wife, Susanna Musgrave (or Musgrove). She was brought to America at the age of five and remained until 1778 when the whole family returned to England. Her first novel, *Victoria,* was published in 1786 and was well received. Succeeding books were of no particular note until the novel, *Charlotte, a Tale of Truth* (1791) appeared and established her as a great favorite, especially in America. In three years 20,000 copies were sold and more than 160 editions were printed.

Her husband, William Rowson, a charming and ineffectual man, became bankrupt, and they turned to the stage, first appearing in England and afterward in America between 1793 and 1796. The Rowsons acted chiefly in plays of Mrs. Rowson's authorship, among them *The Volunteers* (January 21, 1795); *Americans in England* (1796), and others. These years were further enlivened by an amusing feud with her English compatriot, William Cobbett, who was objecting to the rabid Americanism of her dramas, wrote a vitriolic attack, *A Kick for a Bite* (1795), and drew from her a vicious retaliation in the preface to *Trials of the Human Heart,* wherein she referred to him as a "kind of loathsome reptile."

On leaving the stage in 1797, she opened a school for girls in Boston, which she conducted successfully until 1822. At the same time she was constantly writing and brought out such works as *Reuben and Rachel* (1798), an historical novel, and *Miscellaneous Poems* (1804), a book designed for young ladies. Other activities included editing the *Boston Weekly Magazine,* and writing for such periodicals as the *Boston Magazine, The Monthly Anthology and Boston Review,* and the *New England Galaxy.*

She died in Boston, having earned the gratitude of this country, not only by her extensive charitable work but by her contributions to education for women and her own example as a woman of exceptional character.

Principal Works: *Novels*—Victoria, 1786; The Inquisitor: or, Invisible Rambler, 1788; Mary: or, The Test of Honour, 1789; Charlotte: A Tale of Truth, 1791; Rebecca: or, The Fille de Chambre, 1792; Reuben and Rachel, 1798. *Essays and Poems*—Poems on Various Subjects, 1788; A Trip to Parnassus, 1788; Miscellaneous Poems, 1804. *Plays*—Slaves in Algiers, 1794; The Volunteers, 1795; The Female Patriot (adapted from Massinger's The Bondman), 1795; Americans in England, 1786.

About: Vail, R. W. G. Susanna Haswell Rowson; Nason, E. A Memoir of Mrs. Susanna Rowson; Cobbett, W. A Kick for a Bite.

ROYALL, ANNE (NEWPORT) (June 11, 1769-October 1, 1854), traveler and editor, was born in Maryland, the daughter of William Newport, of Tory sympathies. From the age of three to thirteen she lived on the frontier of Pennsylvania. On her father's death her mother returned to Virginia and became a menial in the household of Capt. William Royall, a gentleman of wealth and high family, who gave Anne many educational advantages and in 1797 married her. Widowed after sixteen years, she became impoverished when a decade of litigation ended in the award of the property to another heir. Failing to obtain a pension as the widow of a Revolutionary soldier, she traveled extensively during the years 1824 to 1831, recording her impressions and observations in ten volumes of travel. From 1831 to within a few weeks of her death she published in Washington, D.C., two successive independent newspapers, *Paul Pry,* and *The Huntress.* Her last years were often marked by poverty. She died in her home in Washington on the site of what is now part of the grounds of the Library of Congress.

Her books of travel, the outcome of visits to every city, town and village of importance in the country, contain pen-sketches of many of the great and near-great, and still possess sociological interest and historical value. Accurate, clear, and often humorous, they suffer nevertheless from faults of execution and indulgence in personalities.

Anne Royall was also the author of *The Tennessean,* a novel of no merit, and a play, *The Cabinet: or, Large Parties in Washington,* which was acted once in the Masonic Hall in Washington but no longer survives. For thirty years she was a character at the national capital, ruthlessly exposing fraud and graft in high places, suffering injustice, villification, ridicule; often a pathetic figure, but also admirable, independent, charitable, and honest.

PRINCIPAL WORKS: Sketches of History, Life, and Manners in the United States, 1826; The Tennessean (novel) 1827; The Black Book: or, A Continuation of Travels in the United States, 1828-29; Mrs. Royall's Pennsylvania, 1829; Mrs. Royall's Southern Tour, 1830-31; Letters From Alabama, 1830.

ABOUT: Porter, S. H. The Life and Times of Anne Royall; Wright, R. L. Forgotten Ladies; American Mercury September 1927.

RUSH, BENJAMIN (December 24, 1745-April 19, 1813), physician, patriot, and miscellaneous writer, was born in Byberry township, near Philadelphia, the son of John and Susanna (Hall) Rush. His uncle Samuel Finley prepared him for the College of New Jersey, from which he was graduated in 1760. He studied medicine under Dr. John Redman and at the University of Edinburgh, receiving his degree in 1768; and attended medical lectures in London where he enjoyed the friendship of Benjamin Franklin. In 1769 he returned to Philadelphia and began practice, at the same time accepting the chair of chemistry at the College of Philadelphia. He published essays on temperance, hygiene, and slavery within the next few years and wrote constantly for the press on Colonial rights. Rush was married in January 1776 to Julia Stockton, whose father was a member of the Continental Congress; and in June of the same year he was himself elected to that body, and thereby was a signer of the Declaration of Independence.

From 1777 to 1778 Rush was surgeon-general in the armies of the Middle Department; he then returned to Philadelphia and resumed his practice and duties as professor. He was a surgeon in the Pennsylvania Hospital from 1783 until his death; he established the first free clinic in the country in 1786; and he was a founder of Dickinson College. Rush was a member of the Pennsylvania convention that ratified the constitution of the United States in 1787, and also of that for the state constitution. The College of Philadelphia was absorbed by the University of Pennsylvania in 1791, and he became professor of the institutes of medicine and clinical practice; later of theory and practice.

During the yellow-fever epidemic he worked tirelessly and with great zeal, but was attacked by William Cobbett as contributing to the high death rate with his "system" of extreme blood-letting. His book on the disease, in reply to his critics added luster to Dr. Rush's reputation and left an enlightening account of medical practices of that time. He was a member of nearly every medical, literary, and humanitarian movement of his day, and some of his books, notably *Diseases of the Mind,* exemplify the pioneer work of Rush in his profession.

PRINCIPAL WORKS: A Syllabus of a Course of Lectures on Chemistry, 1770; Sermons to Gentlemen Upon Temperance and Exercise, 1772; An Address to the Inhabitants of the British Settlements in America Upon Slave-keeping, 1773; Essays: Literary, Moral and Philosophical, 1798; Medical Inquiries and Observations, 1789; An Account of the Bilious Remitting Yellow Fever as it Appeared in the City of Philadelphia, 1794; Medical Inquiries and Observations Upon the Diseases of the Mind, 1812.

ABOUT: Good, H. G. Benjamin Rush and His Services to American Education; Goodman, N. G. Benjamin Rush: Physician and Citizen; Ramsay, D. An Eulogium Upon Benjamin Rush, M.D.; Poulson's American Daily Advertiser April 21, 1813.

RUSH, JAMES (March 15, 1786-May 26, 1869), physician, psychologist, and miscellaneous writer, was born in Philadelphia, the son of Benjamin and Julia (Stockton) Rush. He attended the College of New Jersey, class of 1805, and the University of Pennsylvania, receiving his degree of M.D. in 1809. Following two years of study in Edinburgh, he returned to Philadelphia, where for several years he practiced medicine. He was married in 1819 to Phoebe Anne Ridgway, an heiress, owner of one of the finest houses in that city, and a brilliant and popular member of society.

Rush gradually gave up his practice and social duties, and allowed psychological researches to claim his entire time. His first book, *The Philosophy of the Human Voice,* covered a field then new and achieved great popularity. His most ambitious work, *Brief Outline of an Analysis of the Human Intellect,* was one of the earliest books on the study of psychology, and while diffuse and of slight interest today, was of value in stimulating interest in that relatively new subject. In his later years Rush lived chiefly in his study, and in his *Rhymes of Contrast on Wisdom and Folly* castigated the younger generation with the acridity of a lonely old man. He died in Philadelphia, leaving most of his estate to the city library, on certain conditions, among which were the reissue five times within the next fifty years of his books (500 copies each), to be sold at cost; the exclusion of all newspapers; and the building of the Ridgway branch of the library.

PRINCIPAL WORKS: The Philosophy of the Human Voice, 1827; Hamlet: A Dramatic Prelude, in Five Acts, 1834; Brief Outline of an Analysis of the Human Intellect, 1865; Rhymes of Contrast on Wisdom and Folly, 1869.

ABOUT: Provisions of the Last Will and Testament of Dr. James Rush: Relating to the Library Company of Philadelphia; A Memorial . . . of Dr. Benjamin Rush. . . . Written by Himself; MSS. in the Ridgway Branch, Library Company of Philadelphia; Public Ledger (Philadelphia) May 28, 1869.

RUSSELL, IRWIN (June 3, 1853-December 23, 1879), poet, the son of Dr. William McNab Russell and Elizabeth (Allen) Russell, was born in Port Gibson, Miss. He attended St. Louis University, being graduated in 1869, when he returned to Port Gibson to study law. He was admitted to the bar in his nineteenth year.

But the precocious Irwin, who had read Milton at the age of six, found literature and adventure more to his taste than attorney's briefs. He had taken several vacations from the law, to go on exciting trips to New Orleans and Texas, and the life on the Mississippi with its fascinating characters had challenged his imagination. His first poem, "A Chinese Tale," appeared in 1869 and he contributed frequently to such magazines as *Puck, Appletons' Journal,* and *St. Nicholas,* often under pseudonyms. His best poems were in Negro dialect and one of the earliest of these, "Uncle Cap Interviewed," appeared in 1876 in *Scribner's Monthly.*

In 1878 there was a yellow fever epidemic in Port Gibson, and Irwin with his father, Dr. Russell, expended almost superhuman energy to relieve the suffering. Irwin went to New York in December of that same year, but after the death of his father, discouraged and ill, worked his passage back to New Orleans. He secured a position on the New Orleans *Times,* but worn out by his terrific labor during the epidemic and the hardships of the journey south, he died in December in a cheap lodging house.

Joel Chandler Harris, who wrote the introduction to Russell's *Poems,* credited him with drawing, in dialect, the first accurate and artistic portrait of the Southern Negro. "No man the South has produced," Harris added, "gave higher evidence of genius in a period so short . . . Had he been spared to letters, all the rest of us would have taken back seats so far as representation of life in the South was concerned."

PRINCIPAL WORKS: Poems by Irwin Russell, 1888 (republished as Christmas Night in the Quarters and Other Poems, 1917).

ABOUT: Baskerville, W. M. Southern Writers: Biographical and Critical Studies; Critic October 27 and November 3, 1888; Texas Review October 1916; Daily Picayune, (New Orleans) June 2, 1907; New Orleans Times December 24, 1879: prefaces to works.

RYAN, ABRAM JOSEPH (February 5, 1838-April 22, 1886), Catholic priest and poet, was born at Hagerstown, Md., the son of Matthew and Mary (Coughlin) Ryan, Irish emigrants. The boy accompanied his parents to St. Louis, Mo., where he attended the Christian Brothers' School, and then went to Niagara University, Niagara Falls, N.Y., to prepare himself for the priesthood. Ordained in 1856, he completed his theological studies and remained to teach at Niagara University for a time, then taught in Missouri. In 1862 he returned to his native South and joined the Confederate Army as a chaplain.

His services to the Confederate cause are still affectionately remembered in the South. Picturesque, kindly, and a man of great personal courage, he devoted himself to humanitarian tasks that nobody else would attempt, and endeared himself to many a suffering war victim. But he served the Confederacy even more effectively with the pen. The final defeat of the Confederate Army, and his own grief at the loss of his younger brother in battle, inspired him to

Collection of Frederick H. Meserve
FATHER RYAN

write such verses as "In Memoriam," "The Conquered Banner," and "The Sword of Robert E. Lee," which struck a responsive note in every true Confederate's heart, and continued to be very popular long after the war was over. Called "the poet of the Lost Cause," Ryan wrote verses tinged with a peculiar, haunting pathos; they were also rhymed to the popular taste and easy to sing.

After the war Ryan wandered about the Southland, serving as priest in Augusta, Ga., New Orleans, Biloxi, Miss., Nashville, Knoxville, and Clarksville, Tenn., Macon, Ga., and, for the longest consecutive period, at Mobile, Ala., where he was pastor of St. Mary's Church from 1870 to 1883. He made occasional trips through the North and West during this period, lecturing in behalf of charitable projects for Southern victims of the war. C. W. Hubner, who met the poet late in life, says that he made a vivid impression on his audiences, having a "remarkably massive head, . . . a pale face, sad and somewhat austere, . . . and a strong passionate nature, but subdued and held in check by a mighty inward purpose." Besides lecturing, Ryan edited for short periods several Southern journals, the *Pacificator* and *The Banner of the South* in Augusta, Ga., and the Catholic weekly *The Star* in New Orleans.

Ryan's songs and poems are said to have passed through twelve editions. Collected and published in 1879, they were for a long time household favorites; several of them were set to music and used extensively in the Southern schools. In 1882 he produced a book of religious verse, *A Crown for Our Queen,* which contains the beautiful and well-loved poem "When." His last literary project was a life of Christ, to which he devoted a great deal of time and labor but which remained unfinished at his death. Ryan was often interrupted in his work by ill health, and he finally retired to a Franciscan monastery in Louisville.

PRINCIPAL WORKS: Father Ryan's Poems, 1879; A Crown for Our Queen, 1882.

ABOUT: Hubner, C. W. Representative Southern Poets; Rutherford, M. C. The South in History and Literature; America December 3, 1927; Commonweal September 18, 1929; Literary Digest May 31, 1913; Southern Bivouac August 1886.

SABIN, JOSEPH, (December 6? 1821-June 5, 1881), bibliographer and bibliophile, was born in England, presumably at the village of Braunston, in Northamptonshire. He was educated at the neighborhood schools and at the grammar schools of Oxford,

JOSEPH SABIN

where in his fifteenth year, Charles Richards, a bookdealer, took him into his shop to teach him bookbinding. The ambitious boy was soon promoted to the salesroom and in three years not only rose to be general manager but had acquired such a vast knowledge of books that his advice was increasingly sought by Richards' patrons. In 1842 he established a bookselling and auctioneering business with a young man named Winterborn, whose sister he later married. The business continued for six years, after which time Sabin, his wife and two sons, came to America. They made a brief stay in New York City, and eventually settled in Philadelphia on a farm on Chestnut Hill.

Sabin worked for a time with the firm of George S. Appleton, where his knowledge of bookbinding was put to valuable use, especially his introduction to America of the hitherto unknown half-binding in calf and morocco. During the year 1850 he was associated with Cooley & Kesse, book auctioneers, and continued with their successors, Lyman & Rawdon, in preparing sales and auction catalogs, a work which was later to make him one of the outstanding American bibliophiles. His first effort in this line was a catalog of Samuel Farmar Jarvis' collection in 1851. In the subsequent five years Sabin worked with Bangs & Company, cataloging important libraries.

Interest in the sale of E. B. Corwin's valuable library of Americana led Sabin to begin his monumental *Dictionary of Books Relating to America: From Its Discovery to the Present Time* (also known as *Bibliotheca Americana*). Begun in 1868, it was not really completed until 1937—more than half a century after Sabin's death. Parts 1 to 82 were edited by Sabin himself; the work was continued by Wilberforce Eames and completed by R. W. G. Vail.

Sabin started a second-hand book store on Canal Street, New York City, in 1856, but moved after a year to Philadelphia, where he soon built up a flourishing business until the outbreak of the Civil War stopped his active and remunerative dealing with the South.

After 1861 he returned to New York, engaged in several business pursuits devoted to rare books and prints, and continued his compilation of *Bibliotheca Americana.* He also published *Sabin & Sons' American Bibliopolist* and the *Sabin's Reprints.* In 1879 he retired from active business to give his entire time to his *Dictionary,* a labor of love which drained him of his fortune. *Bibliotheca Americana* was an invaluable contribution to Americana; through its comprehensive references to American material it placed Sabin at the top of nineteenth century bibliophiles.

Principal Works: The Thirty-Nine Articles of the Church of England: With Scripture Proof and References, 1844; Dictionary of Books Relating to America: From Its Discovery to the Present Time (14 vols.), 1868-84.

About: Allibone, S. A. A Critical Dictionary of English Literature; Publishers' Weekly June 11, 1881; New York Commercial Advertiser, New York Times, New York Tribune June 6, 1881.

SABINE, LORENZO (July 28, 1803-April 14, 1877), historian, was born in Lisbon, N.H., the son of Elijah R. and Ann (or Harriet) Clark Sabin. (Lorenzo later added the "e.") When he was fifteen his father died, and from that time on he supported himself and sometimes contributed toward the expenses of his brothers and sisters. In 1821 he set out for Maine, settling in Eastport where he spent the next twenty years in a variety of pursuits. He later wrote that during that time he "built and owned vessels, fitted out fishermen, and was a petty dealer in codfish and molasses." Around 1848 he moved to Framingham. Mass. Sabine was an intensive reader and a student. While he was at Eastport, with the Canadian border nearby, he met many descendants of American Loyalists. Becoming interested in them he wrote an important historical work, *The American Loyalists: or, Biographical Sketches of Adherents to the British Crown in the War of the Revolution.* He contributed to the *North American Review* articles on the Maine forests and Northeast fisheries. After these appeared he was called to Washington to work for a year in connection wtih the fisheries. He later served for a short time in the House of Representatives and for ten years from 1857 was secretary of the Boston board of trade. The Boston *Evening Transcript* wrote of Sabine: "Probably no man living has so accurate and general knowledge of the individual history of the period of the Revolution as Mr. Sabine has acquired." He was thorough in his research and retained an interest in the personal factors of history. He was married three times.

Principal Works: The American Loyalists: or, Biographical Sketches of Adherents to the British Crown in the War of the Revolution, 1847; Report on the Principal Fisheries of the American Seas, 1853; Notes on Duels and Duelling: . . . With a Preliminary Historical Essay, 1855; Biographical Sketches of Loyalists, 1864.

About: New England Historical and Genealogical Register October 1878; Massachusetts Historical Society Proceedings: 1880; Boston Daily Evening Transcript April 16, 1877.

ST. JOHN, HECTOR. See CRÈVECOEUR, MICHEL-GUILLAUME JEAN DE

SANBORN, FRANKLIN BENJAMIN (December 15, 1831-February 24, 1917), biographer, editor, and journalist, was born at Hampton Falls, N.H., the second son of Aaron and Lydia (Leavitt) Sanborn. A precocious student, and keenly interested in national politics at a very early age, Sanborn prepared himself for Harvard by wide reading in local libraries and finally in 1851 by more formal studies at Phillips Exeter Academy.

Even at Harvard Sanborn would not resign the direction of his studies to college routine; in his *Recollections* he attributes his literary development during the years 1852 to 1855 to his contacts with Emerson, Alcott, Theodore Parker, and to his correspondence with his fiancée, Ariana Smith Walker of Peterborough, N.H., whom he married in 1854 only eight days before her death. Even before his graduation in 1855 Sanborn had started a small school at Concord, at the invitation of Emerson.

Inasmuch as he had the children of Emerson, Hawthorne, Henry James, Horace Mann, and John Brown as pupils, and adopted Alcott's nature-study methods in his teaching, it is small wonder that Sanborn's school soon became a firmly entrenched Concord institution. But there were many interruptions in the routine of his work.

Sanborn's interest in national politics had increased while he was at Harvard, and after 1854 his strong advocacy of the aboli-

FRANKLIN B. SANBORN

tionist cause brought him into practical political work. As agent for the Massachusetts State Kansas Committee, he toured the West in the summer of 1856, reporting on the progress of the Free-Soil agitation. In 1857 he met the abolitionist martyr John Brown; he brought Brown to Concord, raised money for him, and knew of his proposed attack at Harper's Ferry. Because of this knowledge, Sanborn was ordered to testify before a Senate committee during the Brown trial; upon his refusal he was arrested and an attempt was made to seize him. Sanborn resisted; the citizens of Concord protested vigorously, and finally Sanborn was discharged by the Massachusetts Supreme Court.

This incident, the most dramatic one in Sanborn's life, must not be thought typical of his activities. "He was," observes Van Wyck Brooks, "a born antiquarian," and most of his life after 1857 was devoted to collecting biographical data about the great men of Concord. Lodging at Ellery Channing's house, taking his meals at Mrs. Thoreau's, walking and conversing with Emerson and his friends, Sanborn had an unequaled opportunity to learn at first hand the details of Thoreau's, Emerson's, Hawthorne's and Alcott's lives. He learned, according to Mr. Brooks, "more about the Concord people than most of them had ever known themselves;" and these researches bore fruit in a series of biographies, *Henry D. Thoreau, Life and Letters of John Brown, A. Bronson Alcott: His Life and Philosophy, Ralph Waldo Emerson,* and *Hawthorne and His Friends* (the last two in collaboration with W. T. Harris), which remain today invaluable source-books and authoritative biographical works. They are sympathetic studies, for Sanborn was a hero-worshipper, yet they are intelligent and not blindly eulogistic.

In 1862 Sanborn married his cousin Louisa Leavitt, by whom he had three sons. In addition to his biographical work, he edited the *Boston Commonwealth* from 1863 until 1867, wrote for the Springfield *Republican* for many years, and published many controversial articles. In later life his political interests were manifested in vigorous criticisms of New England politicians. He devoted much time and energy to the organization and inspection of charities in Massachusetts, and was active in many of the early projects for social legislation. He died at eighty-five at Plainfield, N.J.

Principal Works: *Biography*—Henry D. Thoreau, 1882; Life and Letters of John Brown, 1885; Dr. S. G. Howe: The Philanthropist, 1891; A. Bronson Alcott: His Life and Philosophy, 1893; (with William Torrey Harris) Ralph Waldo Emerson, 1901; Hawthorne and His Friends, 1908.

About: Sanborn, F. B. Recollections of Seventy Years; Survey March 10, 1917; Century Magazine April 1922.

SANDERSON, JOHN (1783-April 5, 1844), miscellaneous writer and teacher, was the son of William Sanderson, a farmer and Revolutionary soldier, and his wife, Agnes McClellan (Buchanan) Sanderson. He was born in the neighborhood of Carlisle, Pa., and was educated by private tutoring until 1806 when he went to Philadelphia to study for a legal career. Instead he became a teacher and assistant principal in the Clermont Academy, where he also met his future wife, Sophie Carée, the daughter of the headmaster.

His first publication appeared in 1820 when he collaborated with his brother in editing the first two volumes of the *Biography of the Signers of the Declaration of Independence,* later completed in seven volumes by Richard Waln, and others. In 1822 he bought an interest in the *Aurora,* a popular publication which he edited until he sold his rights in 1823 to Richard Penn Smith. At this time he had begun to take an interest in classical and modern languages, and was among the first to insist that classical training should be part of the public school curriculum.

A trip to Europe in 1835 resulted in a series of articles later published in book-form under the title *Sketches of Paris . . . ,* a charming volume replete with anecdotes, descriptions of prominent personalities, well-spiced by a lively sense of humor and a light style. It was published in England and translated into French by Jules Janin (1843). Sanderson's short visit to England provided material for a sequel, "The American in London," partly published in the *Knickerbocker*.

Returning to America in 1836, Sanderson threw himself into state educational work and four years later accepted the invitation of a former pupil, Dr. Alexander Dallas Bache, of Philadelphia, a great-grandson of Benjamin Franklin, to join the staff of the newly opened Central High School of Philadelphia, where Bache was principal. Here Sanderson served as professor of Greek and Latin and assisted in the department of English and belles-lettres until his death.

Sanderson's great charm of manner, delightful sense of humor and original teaching methods did much to dissociate the classics from dryness in the minds of his students, who revered him as a friend and teacher. He was the idealistic pedagogue, unconcerned with the accumulation of wealth, and he never fully developed gifts that would have given him a more prominent place in American letters.

PRINCIPAL WORKS: Biography of the Signers of the Declaration of Independence (first two vols.) 1823-27; Sketches of Paris. . . , 1838

ABOUT: Edmonds, F. S. History of the Central High School of Philadelphia; Griswold, R. W. The Prose Writers of America; Philadelphia Public Ledger April 6, 1844.

SANDS, ROBERT CHARLES (May 11, 1799-December 16, 1832), journalist and miscellaneous writer, was born in New York City. His parents, Comfort Sands, Revolutionary patriot, and Cornelia (Lott) Sands, provided him with such excellent early schooling that he entered the sophomore class of Columbia College at the age of thirteen. Here he joined a fellow-undergraduate, James Wallis Eastburn, in editing two college periodicals, *The Moralist* (one issue), and *Academic Recreations*. After his graduation in 1815, he studied law under David B. Ogden, and in his free time wrote extensively for the *Aeronaut,* a manuscript periodical circulated by a group including Eastburn, who called themselves the "Literary Confederacy," and collaborated on a series of fine essays—"The Neologist" (1817) for the New-York *Daily Advertiser,* and "The Amphilogist" (1819) for the *Commercial Advertiser,* which he edited from 1827 until his death.

With Eastburn he began a translation of the Psalms of David; and a poem, *Yamoyden,* founded on the life of the Indian King Philip. Eastburn died during the collaboration and Sands completed and published the work in 1820.

A growing interest in literature resulted in Sands' giving up his legal practice to join the editorial staff of *St. Tammany's Magazine,* published by the "Literary Confederacy," during 1823-24. He started the *Atlantic Magazine* in 1824 and when it was absorbed by the *New York Review* in 1825, assisted William Cullen Bryant in editing it for two years. With Bryant and Gulian C. Verplanck he published an annual, *The Talisman* (1828-30), in which appears some of his best work.

Sands was a prominent figure in the social and literary life of early New York where he was highly esteemed by a large group of distinguished friends. He died, a bachelor, at Hoboken, N.J., then a rural village which he used as a background for many of his writings.

Though his name is inextricably woven into the history of early Knickerbocker publications, his works have few readers today. At the beginning of his career, he was influenced by Sir Walter Scott, especially in his metrical romance, *The Bridal of Vaumond,* dedicated to Washington Irving, and *Yamoyden.* His studies of Spanish language and history resulted in several publications, including his finest prose work, "Boyuca" in *Tales of Glauber-Spa.*

PRINCIPAL WORKS: The Bridal of Vaumond, 1817; Yamoyden, 1820; Historia de Mejico, 1828; The Life and Correspondence of John Paul Jones, 1830; "Boyuca" (in Tales of Glauber-Spa) 1832.

ABOUT: Verplanck, G. C. The Writings of Robert C. Sands in Prose and Verse; Knickerbocker January 1833; New York Mirror December 29, 1832; New York American December 17, 1832; New York Daily Advertiser December 18, 1832; New York Commercial Advertiser December 17, 1832.

SANGSTER, MARGARET ELIZABETH (MUNSON) (February 22, 1838-June 4, 1912), miscellaneous writer and editor, was born in New Rochelle, N.Y., the daughter of John Munson and Margaret (Chisholm) Munson. Taught by her mother, Margaret could read at the age of four. She later attended schools in Paterson, N.J., and Brooklyn, N.Y. About 1855 she wrote *Little Janey,* which was bought and printed by the Presbyterian Board of Publication. She was then commissioned by the board to write a hundred other juvenile stories. In 1858 she married George Sangster of Scotland; they had one son. After the Civil War they moved to Norfolk, Va., and in 1870 to Brooklyn, where George Sangster died a year later.

Mrs. Sangster contributed prose and verse to many magazines, was assistant editor of *Hearth and Home,* edited the family page of the *Christian Intelligencer,* and from 1889 to 1899 was editor of *Harper's Bazaar.* Although she wrote several novels, most of her works were compilations from her prose and poetical contributions to magazines. She wrote in a cheery, sentimental, and decidedly religious tone, and in a style that was simple, lucid, and straightforward. Although she was blind for several years before her death, she carried on her work with the help of secretaries.

PRINCIPAL WORKS: Poems of the Household, 1882; Little Knights and Ladies, 1895; Home Life Made Beautiful in Story, Song, Sketch, and Picture, 1897; Cheerful To-days and Trustful To-days and Trustful To-morrows, 1899; Winsome Womanhood, 1900; Lyrics of Love, of Hearth and Home, and Field and Garden, 1901; Janet Ward: A Daughter of the Manse, 1902; Eleanor Lee, 1903; Good Manners for All Occasions, 1904; What Shall a Young Girl Read? 1905; Fairest Girlhood, 1906; An Autobiography: From My Youth Up; Personal Reminiscences, 1909; Ideal Home Life, 1910; Eastover Parish, 1912; My Garden of Hearts, 1913.

ABOUT: Sangster, M. E. Autobiography: From My Youth Up; Personal Reminiscences; Willard, F. E. & Livermore, M. A. A Woman of the Century; Christian Herald June 19, 1912; New York Times June 5, 1912.

SARGENT, EPES (September 27, 1813-December 30, 1880), poet, dramatist, editor, and journalist, was born in Gloucester, Mass., son of Epes Sargent and Hannah Dane Coffin, and brother of John Osborne Sargent. He attended the Boston Latin School from 1823 to 1829. His first literary effort was a series of letters published in the school journal that he sent back from Russia during a trip with his father during these years. After finishing school, he was connected with the Boston *Daily Advertiser* and the Boston *Daily Atlas.* In an interlude from newspaper work, he wrote several plays, among them *Velasco* (1837), which was produced in Boston, with Ellen Tree in the leading rôle.

In 1839 he moved to New York where he remained eight years working on the New York *Mirror,* the *New World,* and his own journal, *Sargent's New Monthly Magazine* (January-June 1843). In 1847 he returned to Boston where he edited the Boston *Transcript* for several years, retiring from that paper to devote himself to the authorship of plays, poetry, and educational works. His series of text-books and readers for schools was widely used. With the publication of numerous books of verse, novels, adventure, and other miscellaneous work, together with his editorial duties, Sargent enjoyed a pleasant and well-earned fame. He married Elizabeth W. Weld of Roxbury, Mass., in 1848.

A member of a distinguished family, descended from Gov. John Winthrop and Gov. Joseph Dudley, Sargent was in appearance the perfect aristocrat, exquisitely groomed and meticulous in his every habit. Respected and admired by those with whom he came in contact in his editorial capacity, he numbered among his friends Henry Clay, Daniel Webster, and John C. Calhoun. Though some of his work is of little permanent value, he was a force for good and a leader of education in his own day.

PRINCIPAL WORKS: *Plays*—The Bride of Genoa, 1837; Velasco, 1839; Change Makes Change, 1854; The Priestess, 1854. *Poems*—Songs of the Sea With Other Poems, 1847; The Woman Who Dared, 1870; Harper's Cyclopaedia of British and American Poetry, 1881. *Works on spiritualism*—Planchette: or, The Despair of Science, 1869; The Proof Palpable of Immortality, 1875; The Scientific Basis of Spiritualism, 1880. *Fiction*—Fleetwood: or, The Stain of Birth, 1845; Peculiar: A Tale of the Great Transition, 1864. *Miscellaneous*—American Adventure by Land and Sea, 1841; Life and Services of Henry Clay, 1842; The Emerald, 1866; The Sapphire, 1867.

ABOUT: Dole, N. H. The Complete Works of Edgar Allan Poe; Sargent, E. W. & C. S. Epes Sargent of Gloucester and His Descendants; Boston Transcript December 31, 1880.

SARGENT, LUCIUS MANLIUS (June 25, 1786-June 2, 1867), miscellaneous writer, antiquarian, and temperance advocate, was the seventh child of Daniel and Mary (Turner) Sargent. He was born in Boston, where his father was a wealthy merchant dealing in fishermen's supplies. Young Lucius prepared for college at Phillips Exeter Academy and entered Harvard in 1804. The publication of his criticism of the college cuisine in a pamphlet entitled *No. 1 of the New Milk Cheese* (1807) led to his resignation. Although he subsequently studied law and passed his bar examination, he turned from a legal career to literature when an inheritance afforded him financial independence.

In 1807 he also published *The Culex of Virgil . . .* and a collection of Latin riddles. A volume of poems, *Hubert and Ellen,* appeared in 1812, and three years later, at the Boston peace celebration, he had the honor of hearing his "Wreaths for a Chieftain" sung.

From this time on, he wrote voluminously for newspapers and took up the standard for temperance reform, speaking and writing so vigorously that he became outstanding in the movement. From this interest came his book, *The Temperance Tales.* Besides his ardent crusade against liquor he was an enthusiastic antiquarian, and wrote a series of weekly articles for the Boston *Evening Transcript,* which was published in book form as *Dealings With the Dead.* He contributed articles to other publications under such pseudonyms as "Sigma," "Amgis," and others, and attacked the coolie trade of the British India, and criticized Macaulay for derogatory statements about William Penn.

The whole of Sargent's life was spent in the turmoil stirred up by his argumentative and prejudiced nature. Even at seventy-five he was moved to pen a vituperative abuse against Emerson and other opponents of slavery. (*The Ballad of the Abolition Blunder-buss*).

Despite his hot-headedness, he is said to have been popular in social life. In 1842 Harvard conferred a degree upon him, thereby pardoning his early impulsiveness and adding further recognition to his valuable public services in temperance and antiquarian fields. As a writer he never rose to a high position despite a pleasing style and a natural ability to gather historical data.

He was twice married: first, to Mary Binney of Philadelphia, in 1816; second, to Sarah Cutler Dunn, in 1825.

PRINCIPAL WORKS: No. 1 of the New Milk Cheese, 1807; The Culex of Virgil. . . , 1807; Hubert and Ellen, 1812; The Temperance Tales, 1848; Dealings With the Dead, 1856; The Ballad of the Abolition Blunder-buss, 1861.

ABOUT: Sargent, E. W. & C. S. Epes Sargent of Gloucester and His Descendants; Shephard, J. H. Reminiscences of Lucius Manlius Sargent; Boston Post and Daily Advertiser June 4, 1867.

SARGENT, NATHAN (May 5, 1794-February 2, 1875), journalist, was born in Putney, Vt., the seventh of eleven children of Samuel and Mary (Washburn) Sargent. He was educated in his home town and later studied law. As soon as he was admitted to the bar he moved to Cahawba, Ala., where he lived for some time practicing law and serving as judge of the county and probate courts. In 1821 he married Rosina (Hodgkinson) Lewis by whom he had four children, only one surviving infancy. In 1826 ill health caused him to move to Buffalo, and four years later he gave up practicing law and started a Whig newspaper in Philadelphia called the *Commercial Herald.* This was not a financial success and about 1842 he became a correspondent of the *United States Gazette.* Writing his letters under the name of "Oliver Oldschool" he showed unusual ability and soon won a nation-wide reputation. He was a staunch Whig and later a Republican, faithful to his party, and a firm supporter of Lincoln. He moved to Washington and wrote about Congress and other Capital news. His style of writing was colorful and mocking; he loved to make fun of the Democrats and their editorial supporters. He was, however, of a kindly disposition and his letters, although biting, were never cruel. In addition to his journalistic work he served as sergeant-at-arms of the House of Representatives, as register-general of the United States Land Office, and as commissioner of customs.

PRINCIPAL WORKS: Brief Outline of the Life of Henry Clay, 1844; Some Public Men and Events (2 vols.) 1875.

ABOUT: Sargent, J. S. & A. Sargent Genealogy; New England Historical and Genealogical Register July 1875; Washington National Republican February 3, 1875.

SAUNDERS, WILLIAM LAURENCE (July 30, 1835-April 2, 1891), editor and historian, was born in Raleigh, N.C., the son of the Rev. Joseph Hubbard Saunders and his wife, Laura (Baker) Saunders. Prepared for college at the Raleigh Academy, he attended the University of North Carolina and was graduated in 1854. He then trained for a legal career under Judge William H. Battle, received his license in 1856, and established a practice in Salisbury, where he also edited the Salisbury *Banner.* When the Civil War broke out, he joined the Confederate forces as a private and eventually rose to command of the 46th North Carolina Regiment at the Battle of Appomatox. The effects of wounds received in service troubled him for the duration of his life.

In 1864 he married Florida Cotten, daughter of John W. Cotten of Edgecombe County, N.C. She died a year later and Saunders moved to Chapel Hill, where he resumed his newspaper work, contributing articles to journals and editing the Wilmington *Journal* between 1872 and 1876. Meanwhile he took an active interest in the Ku Klux Klan, although he never officially joined. Summoned before a congressional investigation committee at Washington, he stubbornly refused to divulge information concerning the Klan and was finally released.

After 1876 he settled again in Raleigh, where he established and edited the *Observer,* from which he resigned after a short time in order to become Secretary of State of North Carolina. This entrance into politics gave him sufficient opportunity to exercise his natural bent for leadership, and he became a power in the Democratic party through his carefully planned campaigns and well-written party handbooks. He was also influential in reopening the University of North Carolina, which had been closed for economic reasons after the Civil War.

A man of keen judgment and quick mind, Saunders takes his place in the American literary scene through his extremely capable editing of the ten-volume series, *The Colonial Records of North Carolina* (1886-90), an undertaking enthusiastically supported by Governor T. J. Jarvis.

PRINCIPAL WORKS: The Colonial Records of North Carolina, 1886-90.

ABOUT: Wadell, A. M. The Life and Character of William L. Saunders; Alumni History of the University of North Carolina (second ed., 1924); Trinity Archive June 1896; Raleigh News and Observer April 2, 1891.

SAVAGE, JOHN (December 13, 1828-October 9, 1888), journalist and miscellaneous writer, was born in Dublin, Ireland, and was educated at the Harold's Cross Monastery and the art school of the Royal Dublin Society, where he completed the regular course and took several prizes. He became active in the revolutionary movement, established two journals which were suppressed by the British government, and took part in the insurrection in the south of Ireland. In November 1848, after this unsuccessful revolt, Savage fled to New York, where he was engaged as proof reader for the New York *Tribune*. He soon took up his own pen and contributed articles on art and literary criticism to the New York papers. In 1854 he became literary editor of the *Citizen*, and in the same year married Louise Gouverneur. He published his *'98 and '48: The Modern Revolutionary History and Literature of Ireland* in 1856. The following year he moved to Washington, where he was the leading editorial writer for the *States*, the paper of Stephen A. Douglas, which Savage eventually bought. He served with the 69th regiment in the Civil War, and wrote a number of popular war songs, the best known, *"The Starry Flag,"* being written on board the U.S. transport "Marion" as she sailed up the Potomac under enemy gunfire. These war-inspired ballads, published in 1863, went into a second edition immediately.

In 1867 Savage assumed the office of chief executive of Fenian Brotherhood in America and toured the United States lecturing and organizing societies for the benefit of the cause. In 1868 he wrote *Fenian Heroes and Martyrs.*

He died at his summer home at Laurelside, near Spragueville, Pa., having spent his latter years as a lecturer for Catholic societies and colleges. His writings were of value at the period as patriotic contributions.

PRINCIPAL WORKS: '98 and '48: The Modern Revolutionary History and Literature of Ireland, 1856; Our Living Representative Men, 1860; The Life and Public Services of Andrew Johnson, 1866; Fenian Heroes and Martyrs, 1868. *Play*—Sybil, 1858. *Verse*—Faith and Fancy, 1864; Poems, 1867.

ABOUT: O'Donaghue, D. J. The Poets of Ireland; The Irish Cause on the Pacific: John Savage in California; New York Tribune, New York Times October 11, 1888.

SAWYER, LEMUEL (1777-January 9, 1852), miscellaneous writer and congressman, was born in Camden City, N.C., son of Lemuel Sawyer and Mary (Taylor) Sawyer. He was educated in the local schools, at Flatbush Academy, L.I., and the University of North Carolina. After studying law for three years he was admitted to the bar, but instead of pursuing a legal profession chose politics as a career.

He was in the legislature from 1800 to 1801, was a presidential elector in 1804, and a member of Congress during 1807-13, 1817-23, and 1825-29. Starting out as an ardent Republican, he ended his very often inconsistent career as a Democrat. Although an adherent of governmental economy, Sawyer advocated an increased navy during the War of 1812. His economical and prudent political views were not carried over into his private life, for his habitual extravagance, his dissipation, his love of gay company and his lavishness, together with incompetence in business affairs brought him almost to poverty in his closing years. He had failed to manage successfully his farm in Camden City, and despite his election to Congress three different times because of great personal popularity, he was too unstable to make a brilliant record there.

Sawyer's first wife was Mary Snowden of Camden City. After her death he married Camillia Wertz of Washington, D.C., who died six years later. In 1828 he married Mrs. Diana Fisher of Brooklyn, N.Y., a wealthy widow, whose money Sawyer characteristically squandered. His declining years were spent as a minor clerk in a government department.

During one of his interludes from Congress, he wrote a play *Blackbeard: A Comedy in Four Acts* (Washington, 1824). After his third marriage and his retirement from Congress, he wrote another play, *The Wreck of Honor: A Tragedy in Five Acts* (1826?) and several books, among them his autobiography. Sawyer's plays are indicative of the theatrical taste of the time, and his other writings, especially his autobiography, have no permanent value other than as a picture of contemporary life.

PRINCIPAL WORKS: *Plays*—Blackbeard: A Comedy in Four Acts, 1824; The Wreck of Honor: A Tragedy in Five Acts, 1826(?); *Fiction*—Printz Hall; A Record of New Sweden, 1839: *Biography*—A Biography of John Randolph of Roanoke: With a Selection from His Speeches, 1844; Autobiography of Lemuel Sawyer, 1844.

ABOUT: Wheeler, J. H. Reminiscences and Memoirs of North Carolina and Eminent North Carolinians, 1844; Quinn, A. H. A History of the American Drama From the Beginning to the Civil War; Raleigh Register and North Carolina State Gazette December 2, 1805; Raleigh Register and North Carolina Gazette January 12, 1821, November 25, 1828.

SAXE, JOHN GODFREY (June 2, 1816-March 31, 1887), poet, and humorist, was born in Highgate (then Saxe's Mills), Vt., his father being Peter Saxe, a mill owner and local politician, and his mother Elizabeth (Jewett) Saxe. He was educated at St. Albans Academy, Wesleyan University, and Middlebury College, where he received his B.A. degree in 1839 (M.A. in 1842, honorary LL.D. 1860). He read law at Lockport, N.Y., and St. Albans, and was admitted to the bar in 1843. In 1841 he had married Sophia Newell Sollace, by whom he had six children.

Saxe was superintendent of schools in Chittenden County, Vt., in 1847-48, state's attorney for the county in 1850-51, deputy U.S. collector of customs in 1856, and attorney general of Vermont from 1856 to 1859. He ran twice, without success, for governor as a Democrat, in 1859 and 1860. He took both law and politics lightly, his real interest being in writing. From 1850 to 1856 he owned and edited the Burlington, Vt., *Sentinel,* and he published his humorous verses in *Harper's,* the *Atlantic Monthly,* and the *Knickerbocker Magazine.* He had a wide reputation as a topical and occasional versifier and as a humorous lecturer. In 1860 he moved to New York, then to Albany, where he was on the staff of the *Journal.* From there he went to Brooklyn, but in 1875 returned to Albany and lived with his son; it was there that he died, of a heart attack.

This wit and good fellow in the public eye, who made fun of his extreme height, in private was, like so many wits, seclusive, introverted, and melancholy. His last years, during which he ceased to write and saw no one but his son, were pure tragedy. In 1874 his favorite daughter died of tuberculosis; the next year he was badly injured in a train wreck, and his mind was permanently affected; by the time of his death his wife

Collection of Frederick H. Meserve
JOHN GODFREY SAXE

and all his children but one son (and he was an unusually domestic and affectionate man) had died before him, and the *bon-vivant* and after-dinner speaker had for years been a victim of melancholia, which grew increasingly blacker with advancing age.

E. C. Stedman called Saxe a "college-society, lecture-room, dinner-table rhymster," and this describes him very well. Thomas Hood and Oliver Wendell Holmes were his models, but his light verse is a faint shadow of theirs, seldom attaining its felicitous wit. His vivacity has a hollow sound. At his best, however, he has real point and a disarming charm. His serious verse is very dull and bad. But he was unpretentious, and never claimed to be anything more than he was, dedicating his books humbly to those he knew were his betters in his particular *genre.* Some of his poems still survive in anthologies, though they are little read elsewhere.

In his own day he was exceedingly popular, and long after he had retired into the private hell of the melancholiac, magazines and clubs continued to besiege Saxe for verses and lectures, though he could no longer either write or speak.

PRINCIPAL WORKS: Progress: A Satirical Poem, 1846; Humorous and Satirical Poems, 1850; The Money-King and Other Poems, 1860; Complete Poems, 1861; The Fly-ing Dutchman: or, The Wrath of Herr Vonstoppelnoze, 1862; Clever Stories of Many Nations Rendered in Rhyme, 1865; The Times, the Telegraph, and Other Poems, 1865; The Masquerade and Other Poems, 1866;

Fables and Legends of Many Countries Rendered in Rhyme, 1872; Leisure-Day Rhymes, 1875.

About: Taft, R. W. John Godfrey Saxe; Bookman June 1916; Critic April 9, 1887; National Magazine May 1853; New York Tribune April 1, 1887; Albany Evening Journal April 1, 1887.

"SCAEVA." See STUART, ISAAC WILLIAM

SCHAFF, PHILIP (January 1, 1819-October 20, 1893), Church historian, was born at Chur, the capital of the canton of Grisons, Switzerland. Receiving his early education in his native town, at the Academy of Kornthal, Württemberg, and the gymnasium at Stuttgart, he decided upon a theological career, and pursued his studies at the Universities of Tübingen, Halle, and Berlin (1837-41), and was awarded his degree of licentiate (bachelor) of theology in the latter year.

His plans for remaining in Germany were changed when he was elected by the German Reformed Synod to succeed Dr. F. A. Rauch as professor of church history and literature at the theological seminary at Mercersburg, Pa. He was ordained at Elberfield in April 1844 and in July of that year came to America to assume his duties. His inaugural address, written in German and later expanded and translated into English, *The Principle of Protestantism* (1845), because of its tolerance, its broad and penetrating picture of the Protestant Church as a link in the chain of development and not the final form of Christian doctrine, drew upon him a charge of heresy. He was tried by the Synod but was acquitted in 1845. In the same year he married Mary Elizabeth Schley.

During his years at Mercersburg, Prof. Schaff, often a storm-center because of his broad-minded views, published many works of great value to theology, particularly, *What is Church History: A Vindication of the Idea of Historical Development*. He edited the first German theological periodical in America, *Der Deutsche Kirchenfreund* between 1846 and 1854, and lectured in nearly all departments of theology.

After a two years' leave of absence in 1863, he resigned from Mercersburg, and took up his residence in New York City where he was secretary of the New York Sabbath Committee and a teacher of church history at Union Theological Seminary.

Until his death he was actively engaged in countless works for the good of mankind. His writings, especially those on church history, including his most important publication, *The History of the Christian Church,* were a worthy addition to ecclesiastical literature.

Principal Works: The Principle of Protestantism, 1845; What Is Church History? A Vindication of the Idea of Historical Development, 1846; A Liturgy: or, Order of Christian Worship for the German Reformed Church, 1857; Bibliotheca Symbolica Ecclesiae Universalis: The Creed of Christendom, 1877; History of the Christian Church, 1882-92; Theological Propaedeutic, 1893; A Companion to the Greek Testament and the English Version, 1896. *Edited*—Der Deutsche Kirchenfreund, 1846-54; A Commentary on the Holy Scriptures, 1865-80; Religious Encyclopaedia, 1891.

About: Schaff, D. S. The Life of Philip Schaff. 1897; Good, J. I. History of the Reformed Church in the United States in the Nineteenth Century; General Catalogue of the Union Theological Seminary: 1836-1918; New York Times October 21, 1893.

SCHARF, JOHN THOMAS (May 1, 1843-February 28, 1898), historian and collector of Americana, was born in Baltimore, Md., the son of Thomas G. and Anna Maria (McNulty) Scharf. After attending school at St. Peter's parish and Calvert Hall, he entered his father's lumber business. He soon left it, however, to serve in the Confederate army and navy. He was captured on a dangerous commission to Canada, but fortunately the end of the war prevented his trial as a spy. In 1869 he married Mary McDougall of Baltimore who became the mother of three children. He worked for a while in his father's lumber business, practiced law for four years, served in various editorial capacities on Baltimore papers, and held several official positions. Appointed special inspector of Chinese immigration at the Port of New York, he moved there in 1893.

In the meantime he had written prolifically on local history and had acquired a reputation as an authority on Maryland history. Most of his writings, unfortunately, included biographies of living men and other puffs to make them sell. His *History of Maryland* was an exception to this and, although biased, was comprehensive and is still consulted as a source of information. In addition to his writing he had amassed large and valuable collections of Americana, including pamphlets, newspapers, letters, broadsides, and official Maryland records.

Principal Works: The Chronicles of Baltimore, 1874; History of Maryland, (1879); History of the Confederate States Navy, 1887.

About: Sketch of J. Thomas Scharf; Maryland Historical Magazine September 1926; Baltimore Sun March 1, 1898.

SCHOOLCRAFT, HENRY ROWE (March 28, 1793-December 10, 1864), explorer and ethnologist, was born in Albany

County, N.Y., the son of Lawrence and Margaret Anne Barbara (Rowe) Schoolcraft. He entered Union College at fifteen and later attended Middlebury College. He was especially interested in geology and mineralogy and studied glass-making, starting a book on the subject in 1817. The same year he began exploring in southern Missouri and Arkansas, and, in 1819, published a report, *A View of the Lead Mines of Missouri.* He knew and understood the Indians and consequently in 1822, he was appointed Indian agent for the Lake Superior tribes, and a year later married a quarter-blood Chippewa girl who had been educated in Europe. Much interested in Indians he did extensive research on the subject and urged wider study of Indian ethnology, here and abroad. During 1836-41 he was superintendent of Indian affairs for Michigan, negotiating several important treaties. His writings on Indian subjects were prolific and authoritative and included narratives of his explorations, descriptive of Indian manners and customs, and tales and legends. His ethnological reputation rests chiefly on *Historical and Statistical Information Respecting the History, Condition, and Prospects of the Indian Tribes of the United States,* a work of six folio volumes, containing good illustrations and much material of value on Indians. He was a widely travelled man and well liked by his contemporaries. His second wife, Mary (Howard) Schoolcraft, whom he married in 1847, survived him.

PRINCIPAL WORKS: A View of the Lead Mines of Missouri, 1819; Narrative Journal of Travels Through the Northwestern Regions of the United States . . . to the Sources of the Mississippi River, 1834; Algic Researches (2 vols.) 1839; Oneota, 1844-45; Notes on the Iroquois, 1847; Personal Memories of . . . Thirty Years with the Indian Tribes, 1851; Historical and Statistical Information Respecting the History, Condition, and Prospects of the Indian Tribes of the United States (6 vols.) 1851-7.

ABOUT: Samson, G. W. Henry R. Schoolcraft; Minnesota Historical Society Collections 1893.

SCHURZ, CARL (March 2, 1829-May 14, 1906), statesman and biographer, was born in Liblar, near Cologne, Germany, the son of Christian Schurz, a village schoolmaster turned storekeeper, and Marianne (Jüssen) Schurz. He was educated at the Gymnasium in Cologne from 1839 to 1846, then went to the University of Bonn. There he was caught up in the revolutionary movement of 1848-49, helped Professor Gottfried Kinkel edit a radical paper, and acted as lieutenant in the revolutionary army. He was forced to flee, and escaped to Switzerland, but twice returned secretly to Germany and rescued Professor Kinkel from prison. He then went to England and thence to France as a newspaper correspondent, but was expelled from France in 1850 and returned to England, where he married Margarethe Mayer, of Hamburg. She died in 1876, leaving two sons and two daughters.

Soon after his marriage Schurz came to America with his wife and settled in Philadelphia until 1855, when he bought a farm at Watertown, Wis. Strongly anti-slavery in sentiment he campaigned for Frémont, making German speeches, and in 1857 was nominated for lieutenant-governor of Wisconsin though not yet a citizen! In 1858 he was admitted to the bar and started in practice in Milwaukee. He was delegated to the national Republican convention in 1860, by which time he was a valuable campaign speaker in fluent English. In 1861 Lincoln named him as minister to Spain, but he resigned the next year and enlisted. He was a brigadier-general in charge of a division, served throughout the war, and resigned, as major-general, immediately after Lee's surrender. For the next year he was Washington corrspondent of the New York *Tribune.* He then founded the Detroit *Post* and edited it for a year, and from Detroit went to St. Louis as editor and part owner of the *Westliche Post,* his last connection with German journalism.

From 1869 to 1875 Schurz was senator from Missouri, and was a founder of the Liberal Republican party. He was Secretary of the Interior in Hayes' cabinet from 1877

Collection of Frederick H. Meserve
CARL SCHURZ

to 1881. He then went to New York as co-editor of the New York *Post* and the *Nation* for three years. From 1892 to 1898 he succeeded George William Curtis as editorial writer on *Harper's Weekly*. The remainder of his life was devoted to lecturing and writing as a liberal politician, and to active work for civil service reform. He received LL.D. degrees from Harvard, Columbia, and the University of Missouri. He died in New York at seventy-five. Carl Schurz Park in the heart of "Yorkville" (New York City's German section) is named in his honor.

Schurz was a born liberal, and one of those men who retain the ardor and resiliency of youth in their old age. Tall, lean, and lanky, with a long beard and spectacles, he was not a dashing figure, but he was a highly popular orator in an age of oratory, largely because he could communicate to others his enthusiasm, his unaffected altruism, and his naturally cheerful and amiable disposition. Unfortunately what made him a good orator made him a poor writer. Though he has some very fine and stirring passages in the published speeches and editorials which constitute the main body of his written work, he is inclined to be diffuse and bombastic. He was one of America's most useful citizens, but he would have been the last to claim any distinction as a writer.

Principal Works: Speeches, 1865; The New South, 1885; Life of Henry Clay, 1887; Abraham Lincoln: An Essay, 1889; Reminiscences, 1907-08; Speeches, Correspondence, and Political Papers (ed. by Frederic Bancroft) 1913.

About: Easum, C. V. The Americanization of Carl Schurz; Fuess, C. M. Carl Schurz: Reformer; Husband, J. Americans by Adoption; Schafer, J. Carl Schurz: Militant Liberal; Schurz, C. Reminiscences (see Sketch by Bancroft and W. A. Dunning); Harper's Weekly May 26, 1906; Nation May 17, 1906; New York Times May 15, 1906.

SCHUYLER, EUGENE (February 26, 1840-July 16, 1890), diplomat, scholar, and miscellaneous writer, was born in Ithaca, N.Y., into a family long prominent in New York State social and political affairs. His parents, George Washington and Matilda (Scribner) Schuyler, reared him in a comfortable, cultured background and provided him with every educational advantage. After graduation from Yale College in 1859, he spent two additional years doing graduate work in philosophy and languages, receiving the degree of Ph.D. in 1861. Then followed two years at the Columbia Law School. Graduated in 1863, he passed his bar examination and began to practice in New York City.

During this time he continued to interest himself in languages and in 1865 filed application for a diplomatic post, which resulted in an appointment as consul at Moscow. Serving from 1867 to 1869, he was later consul at Revel, secretary of legation at Saint Petersburg, and secretary of legation and consul general at Constantinople. There, in 1876, he published a report on Turkish atrocities in Bulgaria that attracted international attention and was said to have influenced England more than any other document of the Russo-Turkish war.

In 1880 he became the first American diplomatic representative to the principality of Rumania, and two years later became minister resident and consul general to Greece, Rumania, and Serbia. After two years at Athens he returned to the United States to lecture at Johns Hopkins and Cornell, but went back to Europe in 1886, settling at Alassio. During the year 1889, Blaine, then Secretary of State, nominated him for an assistant secretaryship but the appointment was blocked by a Senate committee on foreign relations that disliked the views expressed in his *American Diplomacy and the Furtherance of Commerce*. He next proceeded to Cairo, occupied a post for a few weeks, was taken desperately ill, and died in Italy.

As early as 1868 Schuyler began a literary career which extended throughout his life. He first edited John A. Porter's *Selections From the Kalevala* (1868) and the next year brought out a translation of Turgeniev's *Father and Sons*, following it with other translations from the Russian. *Peter the Great*, an extensive study in two volumes, was his most important work.

To his diplomatic career Schuyler brought great personal charm and a wide knowledge of foreign affairs, while to his writing he gave the best of his scholarly mind and a marked but unfulfilled literary talent.

Principal Works: Selections From the Kalevala (ed.) 1868; Fathers and Sons, 1867; The Cossacks, 1878; Turkistan: Notes of a Journey in Russian Turkistan, Khokand, Bukhara, and Kuldja, 1876; Peter the Great, 1884; American Diplomacy and the Furtherance of Commerce, 1886.

About: Schaeffer, E. S. Eugene Schuyler: Selected Essays With a Memoir; Obituary Record of Graduates of Yale University 1890-1900; Papers Relating to the Foreign Relations of the United States: 1881, 1883; New York Tribune July 19, 1890.

SCHWATKA, FREDERICK (September 29, 1849-November 2, 1892), explorer, was born in Galena, Ill., the son of Frederick

Schwatka. When he was ten the family moved to Salem, Ore., where he later worked at printing and studied at Willamette University. After graduation from West Point in 1871 he held army posts, while studying medicine and law. In 1875 he was admitted to the Nebraska bar; in 1876 he got a degree from Bellevue Hospital Medical College. He became interested in exploration, however, and it was in that field that he won his fame. He induced the American Geographical Society to back a new attempt to discover the fate of the famous expedition of Sir John Franklin of thirty years earlier. This new expedition, commanded by Schwatka and William Henry Gilder, left New York in 1878, returning two years later after a successful and thrilling trip. From then on Schwatka spent his time exploring, writing, and lecturing. He published several books on expeditions to Alaska and Mexico, including *Along Alaska's Great River* and *In the Land of Cave and Cliff Dwellers.* His adventurous undertakings were of little scientific value although they did prove that white men could carry on scientific work in the Arctic.

PRINCIPAL WORKS: Along Alaska's Great River, 1885; Nimrod in the North, 1885; The Children of the Cold, 1886; In the Land of Cave and Cliff Dweller, 1893.

ABOUT: Bateman, N. & Selby, P. Historical Encyclopedia of Illinois; Cullum, G. W. Biographical Register . . . Officers and Graduates U.S. Military Academy; Gilder, W. H. Schwatka's Search; New York Times November 3, 1892; New York Tribune November 3, 1892.

SCIDMORE, ELIZA RUHAMAH (October 14, 1856-November 3, 1928), writer of guide and travel books, was born in Madison, Wis., the daughter of George Bolles Scidmore and Eliza Catherine (Sweeney) Scidmore. After an education in private schools and a year at Oberlin College (1873-74) she settled in Washington, D.C., and entered the newspaper field through a series of society letters to the New York *Times* and the St. Louis *Globe-Democrat.* This activity led to a trip to Alaska from which point she sent back the newspaper articles later collected in her first book, *Alaska: Its Southern Coast and the Sitkan Archipelago* (1885).

Now well grounded in journalistic experience and confident of her ability to write much-needed guidebooks on Oriental countries, she spent the major part of her time traveling in Japan, India, China, Java, and the Philipines, and produced works containing valuable and interesting information. Among these were *Jinriksha Days in Japan* (1891) and *Appletons' Guide-Book to Alaska and the Northwest Coast* (1893).

Apart from traveling and writing, she became widely known as a lecturer and was a frequent contributor to the leading magazines. An article in the *Century* (March 10, 1910) explains her efforts to have the now-famous Japanese cherry trees planted in Washington. Especially outstanding was her writing for the *National Geographic Magazine,* in which she took a deep interest, having been associated with the National Geographic Society from its earliest beginnings. During her long membership, she served the Society as corresponding secretary, associate editor, foreign secretary, and member of the board of managers, an honor never conferred before on a woman.

Among other activities, she served as one of the secretaries of the Oriental Congress held in Rome in 1897, and was again a delegate when the Congress met in Hamburg in 1902. In 1907 she brought out *As the Hague Ordains,* in which she praised the Japanese treatment of prisoners during the Russo-Japanese War and revealed a keen insight into existing political conditions. This book found great favor with the Japanese Emperor, who conferred a decoration upon her. Additional recognition of her value as an ambassador of good-will was a request by the Japanese Government that her ashes be interred in Yokohama. This mission was carried out by the Japanese minister to Switzerland, after her death in Geneva.

Eliza Scidmore's pioneer writings in the field of Far-Eastern guidebooks are illuminated by a thorough understanding of the history and customs of their subject.

PRINCIPAL WORKS: Alaska: Its Southern Coast and the Sitkan Archipelago, 1885; Jinriksha Days in Japan, 1891; Appletons' Guide-Book to Alaska and the Northwest Coast, 1893; Java: The Garden of the East, 1897; China: The Long-Lived Empire, 1900; Winter India, 1903; As the Hague Ordains, 1907.

ABOUT: Cameron, M. W. The Biographical Encyclopaedia of Women; Hawley, E. C. A Genealogical and Biographical Record of the Pioneer Thomas Scidmore; Washington Evening Star November 3, 1928; New York Times November 4, 1928.

SCOVILLE, JOSEPH ALFRED (January 30, 1815-June 25, 1864), journalist and novelist was born in Woodbury, Conn., the son of Joseph and Caroline (Preston) Scoville. At twenty-two he was a merchant in New York, but soon turned to journalism and politics. He succeeded in finding a publisher for *The Life of John C. Calhoun,* presumably by his friend Calhoun himself. For this service Scoville was made editor of the Washington (D.C.) *Spectator,* holding the position, however, for only a short time. In the middle or late 'forties he became Calhoun's private secretary, returning, after his death in 1850, to New York, where he became editor of the New York *Picayune*. From 1852 to 1855 he published *Pick,* a humorous paper, and later edited for a time the *Evening State Gazette*. Because Scoville fearlessly indulged in personalities and scandals and was of strong Southern sympathies, he was much disliked in the North. In 1864 he published *Vigor,* a novel, which is thought to have an autobiographical basis. It was received with disapproval and regarded as "indecent." *The Old Merchants of New York* is probably his most important work. In discursive fashion it tells of the commercial life of the city. His usual style of writing is spirited and simple. His wife, Caroline (Schaub) Scoville, and one daughter, whom he left financially independent as a result of his literary efforts, survived him.

PRINCIPAL WORKS: The Old Merchants of New York (5 series) 1863-66; Vigor, 1864.

ABOUT: Allibone, S. A. A Critical Dictionary of English Literature; Brainard, H. W. A Survey of the Scovils or Scovills in England and America; Atlantic Monthly December 1864; New York Commercial Advertiser June 22, 1864; New York Leader July 2, 1864; New York World June 27, 1864.

"SCRIBBLE, LOQUACIOUS, ESQ." See HAMILTON, DR. ALEXANDER

SCRIPPS, JAMES EDMUND (March 19, 1835-May 29, 1906), newspaper publisher and miscellaneous writer, was born in London, the son of James Mogg Scripps and Ellen Mary (Saunders) Scripps. His father. a bookbinder, brought his family to the United States in 1844 and settled in Rushville, Ill. James was educated in the local schools, attended a Chicago business college, and began his career in journalism on the Chicago *Daily Tribune* in 1857, two years later going to the Detroit *Daily Advertiser*. On the consolidation of the *Advertiser* and Detroit *Tribune,* Scripps became business manager and later editor. Long an advocate of a small condensed evening paper, he established the *Evening News* on August 23, 1873, to be sold at two cents. Its success was almost instantaneous and within a year it became the leading newspaper in Michigan.

In 1878, Scripps with a cousin and his two brothers, Edward and George, founded the Cleveland *Penny Press,* and later the St. Louis *Evening Chronicle* and the Cincinnati *Penny Post*. These papers, with the Detroit journals, all owned by one family, comprised the first chain of daily newspapers in the country. In 1887 he went abroad for two years, and on his return in 1891 he bought the Detroit *Tribune* and entered the morning newspaper field. Although he was a Republican, Scripps campaigned for Bryan in 1896, but returned to his party after McKinley's election; in 1902 he was elected to the state senate.

Scripps wrote several pamphlets and three books—one on travel, *Five Months Abroad*. He was one of the founders of the Detroit Museum of Art and the donor of a park to the city of Detroit. He was married in 1862 to Harriet Josephine Messinger, who bore him three daughters & one son.

Of Scripps' many services to journalism, the fostering of small, cheap, daily newspapers, progressive and independent in policy, was the most valuable and enduring, resulting in the establishment of the now powerful Scripps-Howard papers.

PRINCIPAL WORKS: Five Months Abroad, 1882; Memorials of the Scripps Family, 1891; A Genealogical History of the Scripps Family, 1903.

ABOUT: Cochran, N. D. E. W. Scripps; Gardner, G. Lusty Scripps: The Life of E. W. Scripps; McRae, M. A. Forty years in Newspaperdom; White, L. A. The Detroit News: 1873-1917; Detroit News, May 29, 1906.

SCUDDER, HORACE ELISHA (October 16, 1838-January 11, 1902), editor, biographer, and juvenile and miscellaneous writer, was born in Boston, the son of Charles Scudder, merchant and deacon in the Union Church, and Sarah Lathrop (Coit) Scudder. He prepared at the Roxbury and Boston Latin schools for Williams College, from which he was graduated in 1858; as a student he acquired a fondness for the study of Greek, and he afterwards made a practice of reading the classics and the Testament every morning before breakfast.

Scudder went to New York, became a teacher of private pupils, and a writer of juveniles; and then, returning to Boston, joined Henry O. Houghton, whose house was in the process of organization under the firm name Hurd & Houghton (later Houghton, Mifflin), as a reader of manuscripts and a general editorial assistant, which post he held for the rest of his life. With the launching of the *Riverside Magazine for Young People* Scudder found a direct outlet for his children's stories; executed a number of effective woodcut illustrations; and aided in securing Hans Christian Andersen, Jacob Abbott, Frank R. Stockton, and Sarah Orne Jewett as contributors. Moreover he found time to write a number of books of his own: biographies of Henry Oscar Houghton, Bayard Taylor,

Collection of Frederick H. Meserve
H. E. SCUDDER

George Washington, James Russell Lowell, and a pious and happy account of an older brother under the title *Life and Letters of David Coit Scudder: Missionary in Southern India*; the popular juvenile travel series of "Bodley Books"; *Men and Letters,* the best chapters of which he perhaps never surpassed; and that which is considered by many his most adequate and complete work, *Childhood in Literature and Art.*

"I have been able," he wrote in 1887, "for the most part to work out of the glare of publicity. But there is always that something in us which whispers *I* and after a while the anonymous critic becomes a little tired of listening to the whisper of his solitary cave and [comes] out into the light even at the risk of blinking a little." But the light into which Scudder emerged was not very glaring: he remained essentially an editor, planning the American Commonwealth and Riverside Literature series and taking over the reins of the *Atlantic Monthly,* 1890-98. Scudder was married in 1873 to Grace Owen, who, with one of their twin daughters, survived him.

Both directly and indirectly Scudder effected an elevation of the standards of children's literature, and his conscientious accomplishments in the capacity of editor "brought simple workmanship up into the realm of art." His influence in his time was wider than his published works would indicate.

Principal Works: Seven Little People and Their Friends, 1862; Life and Letters of David Coit Scudder: Missionary in Southern India, 1864; Dream Children, 1864; The Dwellers in Five-Sisters Court, 1876; Stories and Romances, 1880; Noah Webster, 1882; Life and Letters of Bayard Taylor, 1884; A History of the United States, 1884; Men and Letters, 1887; George Washington: An Historical Biography, 1890; Childhood in Literature and Art, 1894; Henry Oscar Houghton: A Biographical Outline, 1897; James Russell Lowell: A Biography, 1901.

About: Proceedings American Academy of Arts and Sciences: Vol. 37; Atlantic Monthly March 1902 April 1903; Boston Transcript January 13, 1902.

SEABURY, SAMUEL (June 9, 1801-October 10, 1872), Protestant Episcopal clergyman and theological writer, was born in New London, Conn., the son of the Reverend Charles Seabury, and Anne (Saltonstall) Seabury. Largely self-taught in the classics and theology, Samuel was ordained deacon in 1826 and priest in 1828. He was an instructor in the classics at Muhlenburg's school in Flushing until 1833, when he became editor of the *Churchman,* the Episcopal weekly, a position which he filled ably for sixteen years.

He was rector of the Church of the Annunciation from 1838 to 1868, and professor of Biblical Learning in the General Theological Seminary from 1862 until his death. Seabury was married three times: to Lydia Huntington Bill in 1829; to Hannah Amelia Jones, in 1835; and, in 1854, to Mary Anna Jones.

Seabury's son, William succeeded as rector of his father's parish in 1868, but the elder Seabury retained his professorship until his death, although forced by ill health to relinquish many of his duties. His reputation and influence were achieved chiefly through his editorial writings, some of which were later edited and published by his son William, under the title *Discourses Illustrative of the Nature and Work of the Holy Spirit.* A member of a distinguished Episcopal family, Seabury ably carried on the high church tradition through his work as priest, teacher and writer.

Principal Works: The Study of the Classics on Christian Principles, 1831; The Joy of the Saints, 1844; The Continuity of the Church of England, 1853; American Slavery . . . . Justified, 1861; Mary the Virgin as Commemorated in the Church of Christ, 1868; The Theory and Use of the Church Calendar, 1872; Discourses Illustrative of the Nature and Work of the Holy Spirit, and Other Papers, 1874.

About: Johnson, S. R. A Discourse . . . . in Memory of Samuel Seabury; Perry, W. S. The History of the American Episcopal Church; Historical Magazine of the Protestant Episcopal Church September 1934; Church Review July 1885; Churchman October 19, 26, 1872.

SEALSFIELD, CHARLES (Karl Anton Postl) (March 3, 1793-May 26, 1864), novelist and travel writer, was born Karl Anton Postl, in Poppitz, Moravia (then part of Austria, now of Czechoslovakia), the son of the village justice of the peace, Anton Postl, and Juliane (Rabel) Postl. He was intended for the church, and after five years, 1802-07, at the Untergymnasium at Znaim, he was sent in 1808 to the college of the Kreuzherrenstift (Knights of the Cross, a monastic order) in Prague. At twenty he became a novice in the monastery, and he was ordained as a priest. But the discipline and narrowness of the monastery galled him, and he finally escaped to Switzerland. He turned up in 1823 in New Orleans, as Charles Sealsfield. After traveling through the South and Southwest, he settled at Kittanning, Pa., and lived there for a year, but by 1826 was back in New Orleans. Then he went to France, where he published his first two books, in German and English versions. By 1827 he was in Philadelphia, working as a journalist, then he returned to Kittanning. Somewhere in his travels he acquired a plantation in Louisiana and United States citizenship. He went back to Switzerland in 1832, and remained there for the rest of his life, except for visits to the United States in 1837, 1850, and 1853, during which he traveled through Central America as well. He died at his home in Solothurn, Switzerland, unmarried and completely alone, and it was not until his will was made public that Charles Sealsfield was identified with the fugitive monk, Karl Anton Postl.

CHARLES SEALSFIELD
("Karl Anton Postl")

With the exception of his first book, published under the pseudonym of "Charles Sidons," all Sealsfield's, or Postl's, work was anonymous until 1845, when his collected works were brought out in fifteen volumes under the name of Sealsfield. Until then he had been called "the Great Unknown." He wrote for the most part in German, but nearly all his works were translated by himself or others into English, and some were written in English first. He was the inventor of the "ethnographical novel," with a whole race or nation as hero instead of an individual. Once very popular, especially for *The Viceroy and the Aristocrats* and *Tokeah,* he is now virtually forgotten.

Principal Works: (in English): The United as They Are and the Americans as They Are, 1828; Austria as It Is, 1828; Tokeah: or, The White Rose, 1828; Transatlantic Traveling Sketches, 1833; The Viceroy and the Aristocrats, 1835; The Cabin Book: or, Life in Texas, 1835; Pictures of Life in Both Hemispheres, 1837; Flirtation in America, 1842, South and North, 1843; Scenes and Adventures in Central America, 1852.

About: Faust, A. B. Charles Sealsfield; Smolle, L. Charles Sealsfield (in German); Uhlendorf, B. A. Charles Sealsfield—Ethnic Elements and National Problems in His Works; London Times June 6, 1864.

SEAMAN, ELIZABETH (COCHRANE) (May 5, 1867-January 27, 1922), journalist, better known as "Nellie Bly," was born at Cochrane Mills, a small town founded by her father, Judge Cochrane, in Pennsylvania. After early schooling at home and at Indiana, Pa., she moved to Pittsburgh. There George A. Madden, editor of the Pittsburgh *Dispatch,* became interested in her after seeing an article she had written on "girls and their sphere in life." He suggested to her the pseudonym "Nellie Bly" and asked her to write more, whereupon she set forth her views on Pittsburgh working conditions and divorce and reported theater and art news. In 1887 she traveled in Mexico with her mother, sending back travel correspondence to her paper, but when she returned and Madden offered her a raise to $15 a week she declined the offer and went on to larger fields in New York.

In New York she immediately applied to Joseph Pulitzer, editor of the *World,* and finally persuaded him that his reform crusade could benefit greatly by her sensational publicity methods. In 1888 she feigned insanity and managed to gain admittance to the asylum at Blackwell's Island, the horrible conditions of which she promptly "exposed" in the *World.* The move was successful

ELIZABETH COCHRANE SEAMAN
("Nellie Bly")

in that steps were taken to improve conditions there, and Pulitzer gave her free rein.

Further *exposés* in politics, prison conditions, and household employment followed. *Ten Days in a Mad-House,* an account of her Blackwell's Island adventure published in 1887, had a successful sale; and in 1889 came the great event of her life, her sensational voyage around the world in seventy-two days, six hours, and eleven minutes. This tour, sponsored by the *World,* really brought her into international prominence, and with the publication of *Nelly Bly's Book: Around the World in Seventy-two Days* she reached the climax of her writing career. Her later attempts at journalism were less successful, as the public appetite for sensational reform crusades decreased, but she continued to try, and was working for the New York *Journal* when she died in 1922. She had a distinctive newspaper style, writing always in the first person and in forcible terms, but the thoughts she expressed were rather commonplace. In 1895 she married Robert L. Seaman, a manufacturer who was much older than she, and after his death in 1904 she had great difficulty defending his estate from the encroachments of his dishonest employees. In fact, most of her later life was spent in disagreeable litigation.

Principal Works: Ten Days in a Mad-House, 1887; Six Months in Mexico, 1888; The Mystery of Central Park, 1889; Nelly Bly's Book: Around the World in Seventy-two Days, 1890.

About: Ross, I. Ladies of the Press; Seaman, E. C. Ten Days in a Mad-House, and Nelly Bly's Book: Around the World in Seventy-two Days; Willard, F. E. & Livermore, M. A. (eds.). A Woman of the Century; The World (N.Y.), New York Times, January 28, 1922.

SEARS, EDMUND HAMILTON (April 6, 1810-January 16, 1876), clergyman and religious writer, was born in Sandisfield, Berkshire County, Mass., the son of Joseph and Lucy (Smith) Sears. Raised on a farm in humble circumstances, he had little chance for education, but acquired a great fondness for books and at the early age of ten wrote his first poem. He was later able, through strict economy, to attend Westfield Academy, and in 1834 was graduated from Union College, Schenectady. There he had shown outstanding literary ability. He taught and studied theology at the same time, and in 1837 was graduated from Harvard Divinity School. For two years he was a missionary in Toledo, Ohio, and then, for nearly forty years, served in several small New England Unitarian churches. In 1839 he married Ellen Bacon, and became the father of three sons and a daughter. Because he was of a retiring nature and rather frail, he preferred seclusion and refused to serve many large churches which called him. Although he ministered directly only to small groups, his influence was widespread because of the popularity of his writings. They were of a deeply spiritual and devout nature that appealed to many people of his day. His prose works are no longer read, but his hymns are still sung. Two of them, "Calm on the Listening Ear of Night" and "It Came Upon a Midnight Clear," are particularly beloved. In addition to his other activities he was for many years one of the editors of the *Monthly Religious Magazine.*

Principal Works: Regeneration, 1853; Pictures of the Olden Time as Shown in the Fortunes of a Family of Pilgrims, 1857; Genealogies and Biographical Sketches of the Ancestry and Descendants of Richard Sears, 1857; Athanasia: or, Foregleams of Immortality, 1858; The Fourth Gospel: The Heart of Christ, 1872.

About: Eliot, S. A. Heralds of a Liberal Faith; In Memoriam: Edmund Hamilton Sears . . . Ellen Bacon Sears . . . Katharine Sears; Massachusetts Historical Society Proceedings: 1876, 1881; Christian Register January 2, 29, 1876; Unitarian Review February 1876; Boston Daily Advertiser January 18, 1876.

"SECONDSIGHT, SOLOMON." See McHENRY, JAMES

SEDGWICK, CATHARINE MARIA (December 28, 1789-July 31, 1867), novelist, was born at Stockbridge, Mass., the daughter of Theodore and Pamela (Dwight) Sedgwick. The Sedgwicks and the Dwights had been among the first settlers of New England, and when Catharine was growing up her family was still one of great prominence in the Berkshire region and of considerable wealth. Catharine received the best education available, studying at boarding schools in Boston and Albany, and taking private instruction in languages. Although highly intelligent and keenly interested in literature, she did not begin to write immediately; the first part of her life was given over to social pleasures.

After the death of her mother in 1807 and the remarriage of her father, Catharine left Stockbridge for a time, and lived with relatives in Albany and New York. She never married, but her brilliant and cultivated mind attracted many friends in the literary and social circles of New York and New England, among them William Cullen Bryant and Fanny Kemble Butler, the actress. Her father died in 1813 and she promptly returned to the Berkshires, making the ancestral home at Stockbridge and her brother's home at Lenox the headquarters of her social life and, incidentally, the centers of culture and hospitality of western Massachusetts. "The Sedgwicks pervaded the Berkshires," remarks Van Wyck Brooks. "Everything happened at Lenox, and everyone came there."

Miss Sedgwick's vigorous mind and her financial power to do good naturally led her to participate in philanthropic projects of her time, and she was active in the work of the Unitarian Church. The same philanthropic instincts brought her into literature. Her first novel, *A New-England Tale,* published anonymously in 1822, was written with the avowed purpose "to lend a helping hand to some of the humbler and unnoticed virtues." Realizing that all the charities and committees in the world could not arouse the individual's social conscience to justice and virtue, she determined to reach the individual through the novel and exalt the virtues of uneventful, humdrum domesticity. This moral purpose runs through almost all of her novels and stories, as the titles of some of them clearly indicate: *Home, The Poor Rich Man and the Rich Poor Man, Live and Let Live: or, Domestic Service Illustrated.* Her talent was enlisted for the moral instruction of the young, particularly for the Sunday School books, which she may be said to have "humanized."

Miss Sedgwick's literary significance, however, derives from another feature of her writing. "No one could have supposed that her work would live," Mr. Brooks observes, but "she prepared the way for the writers who followed by stimulating the interest of her readers in their own landscape and manners." She was, as Nathaniel Hawthorne said, "our most truthful novelist"; her simple domestic tales have the real flavor of New England, whether it be the New England of the early settlers, as in *Hope Leslie* (her most popular novel), or the New England of 1830, as in *Clarence.* If her plots were often artificially romanticized, her settings were nevertheless carefully and realistically drawn; and they certainly succeeded in making home life attractive, for Miss Sedgwick became the most widely-read authoress in the country, and was even translated into European languages.

After a portrait by C. Ingham
CATHERINE M. SEDGWICK

Miss Sedgwick's own life was almost as uneventful as that of her domestic heroines. Except for a short tour abroad in 1839-1840 and a tour of the West in 1854, she remained in the Berkshires and in New York during the remainder of her life. She died at seventy-seven at West Roxbury, Mass.

Principal Works: *Novels*—A New-England Tale, 1822; Redwood, 1824; Hope Leslie, 1827; Clarence: or, A Tale of Our Own Times, 1830; The Linwoods: or, 'Sixty Years Since' in America, 1835. *Biography*—Lucretia M. Davidson, 1837; Memoir of John Curtis: A Model Man, 1858.

About: Mallary, R. de W. Lenox and the Berkshire Highlands; Sedgwick, C. M. Life and Letters (edited by M. E. Dewey); Willard, F. E. & Livermore, M. A. A Woman of the Century; Boston Daily Advertiser August 1, 2, 1867.

"SELIM." See WOODWORTH, SAMUEL

SETON, WILLIAM (January 28, 1835-March 15, 1905), miscellaneous writer, was born in New York City. Descended from an ancient and distinguished Scottish family, he was the son of William Seton, a United States naval lieutenant, and Emily (Prime) Seton. After attending St. John's College, Fordham, and Mount St. Mary's College, he studied at the University of Bonn. He then took up the study of law and was admitted to the bar at the outbreak of the Civil War. He immediately joined the Union army as captain, and later was wounded twice. After the war he turned to literature, spending the next few years writing fiction. While he was in Europe around 1886 he became interested in science, to which he subsequently gave most of his time. He made yearly trips to Paris, where he came to know the scientists Albert Gaudry and Albert de Lapparent. His first published work was a novel, *Nat Gregory: or, The Old Maid's Secret,* (1867), which was followed by other novels and a single book of verse. His chief claim to literary fame, however, rests on his popularizing of the theory of evolution. His work on this subject was clearly and simply written, usually in an untechnical style. In 1884 he married Sarah Redwood Parrish of Philadelphia; their only child died in infancy. Seton, in addition to his literary activities, was well known as a philanthropist.

PRINCIPAL WORKS: Nat Gregory: or, The Old Maid's Secret, 1867; Romance of the Charter Oak, 1871; The Pride of Lexington, 1873; The Pioneer, 1874; Rachel's Fate and Other Tales, 1882; A Glimpse of Organic Life, 1897.

ABOUT: Seton, G. A History of the Family of Seton; Catholic World March 1908; New York Daily Tribune March 16, 17, 1905.

SEWALL, JONATHAN MITCHELL (1748-March 29, 1808), lawyer and occasional poet, was born in Salem, Mass., and reared in Portsmouth, N.H. He was a grandnephew of Samuel Sewall the diarist [*q.v.*]. His parents, Mitchell and Elizabeth (Prince) Sewall, died during his early childhood and he was adopted by a bachelor uncle, Stephen Sewall, chief justice of Massachusetts, who died when Jonathan was twelve years old. Young Sewall is reputed to have been a student at Harvard, although there are no official records of this or any other schooling. After clerking in a store, he studied law in a Portsmouth office, was admitted to the bar, and appointed register of probate for Grafton County, N.H., but it is not known that he ever took office.

He practiced law in Portsmouth until his death and took a prominent part in the civic and literary life of the town. He became well-known as a Revolutionary War poet, and besides achieving a local reputation for appropriate epitaphs, composed a number of laudatory poems to Washington—notably, his *Eulogy on the Late General Washington,* published in 1800.

Through his oratorical ability, he was frequently called upon to deliver patriotic speeches, but neither these nor his poems were of any permanent value. A paraphrased couplet from Sewall's "Epilogue to Cato" was a motto for Park Benjamin's *New World* and achieved momentary publicity.

PRINCIPAL WORKS: Versification of President Washington's Excellent Farewell Address, 1798; Eulogy on the Late General Washington, 1800; Miscellaneous Poems, 1801.

ABOUT: Adams, N. Annals of Portsmouth; Locke, A. H. Portsmouth and Newcastle, N.H.: Cemetery Inscriptions; Payson, A. M. & Laighton, A. The Poets of Portsmouth; Port Folio June 25, 1808.

SEWALL, SAMUEL (March 28, 1652-January 1, 1730), colonial magistrate and diarist, was born in Bishopstoke, England, the son of Henry Sewall and Jane (Dummer) Sewall. The father, a native of England, had emigrated to New England and married there; Samuel was born during a temporary visit to his father's country. When the family returned to Boston, Samuel entered Harvard and was graduated in 1671. From 1673 he was tutor at his alma mater until his marriage to Hannah Hull, daughter of John Hull, in 1675/76. His father-in-law was treasurer and mint-master, and owing no doubt to his influence and aid, Sewall was soon embarked on a political career.

He was in charge of the colony's printing press from 1681 to 1684, and for the next two years was a member of the Council. Returning to Massachusetts after a trip to England in 1688, he again served on the Council, and in 1692 was appointed one of the judges for the Salem witchcraft trials. Later convinced of the innocence of the nineteen people condemned to death, and haunted by the memory of his part in the proceedings, Sewall in 1697 had his confession of guilt read before the congregation of Old South Church, Boston.

He was a commissioner of the Society for the Propagation of the Gospel in New England in 1699, and later served as its secretary and treasurer. In 1718 he became chief justice of the superior court, holding the office until 1728, when he retired due to increasing infirmities of old age. His first wife died in 1717, and two years later he married Abigail (Melyen) Tilley who died in

From a portrait by N. Emmons
SAMUEL SEWALL
1728

1720. He was married a third time to Mary Gibbs in 1722.

Although virtually untrained in the law, Sewall's career as a judge was marked by the moderation, wisdom, and tolerance apparent in his writings. His most important and interesting work was his diary, published by the Massachusetts Historical Society a century and a half after his death in Boston. It is a valuable source of information on Puritan life and customs and contains an admirable self-portrait of one of the most eminent men of his age—a man innately conventional, of narrow views, who yet had the courage, despite political opposition, to plead the rights of slaves in his tract *The Selling of Joseph* and also to advocate education and humane treatment for the Indians.

PRINCIPAL WORKS: The Revolution in New England Justified, 1691; Phaenomena Quaedam Apocalyptica ad Aspectum Novi Orbis Configurata: or, Some Few Lies Towards a Description of the New Heaven as It Makes to Those Who Stand Upon the New Earth, 1697; The Selling of Joseph, 1700; Proposals Touching the Accomplishment of Prophecies Humbly Offered, 1713; "Diary of Samuel Sewall," (in *Massachusetts Historical Society Collections*: (1878-82).

ABOUT: Ellis, G. E. An Address on the Life and Character of Chief-Justice Samuel Sewall; Sewall, S. Diary; Washburn, E. Sketches of the Judicial History of Massachusetts; Winthrop, R. C. A Difference of Opinion Concerning the Reasons Why Katherine Winthrop Refused to Marry Chief Justice Sewall.

"SHAHCOOLEN." See KNAPP, SAMUEL LORENZO

SHAW, HENRY WHEELER (April 21, 1818-October 14, 1885), humorist, popularly known by the pseudonym "Josh Billings," was born at Lanesboro, Mass. The son of Henry Shaw, formerly a Congressman and political manager for Henry Clay in New England, and Laura (Wheeler) Shaw, this roving humorist and "cracker-box philosopher" had, according to Dr. Tandy, "a good New England ancestry and upbringing." He attended school at Lenox, Mass., and in 1832 entered Hamilton College, but he finished only one year there. "I was an indolent, trifling boy," he admitted. "I wouldn't work and I wouldn't study." In 1834 he started West, taking with him as patrimony "ten dollars and a whole lot of advice."

During his years of roving adventure and bitter experience in the West, Shaw accumulated nothing tangible, but developed a certain homely wisdom and a decided bent for practical joking. He set out first to be an explorer; then he tried to be a coal operator. After some ten years of aimless wandering he returned to Lanesboro. In 1845 he married Zilpha Bradford of Lanesboro, and for a few years remained there as a farmer, but before long the wanderlust lured him once again toward the West, and he tried his hand as a steamboat captain on the Ohio, with discouraging results.

Finally, in 1858, Shaw settled down with his wife and two children at Poughkeepsie, N.Y., and became an auctioneer and real-estate dealer. Soon afterward his first attempts at writing began to appear, in Poughkeepsie and rural Massachusetts newspapers. But success did not come immediately, and it was not until 1860, when he changed his system of spelling and brought out an *Essa on the Muel bi Josh Billings,* that his writing evoked any response from the public. Realizing that he had hit upon a popular style, Shaw began in 1863 to exploit his discovery in comic lectures, full of aphorisms and short descriptions which held the attention of audiences not because they were new but because they were in the vernacular and were delivered in a ridiculous, disorganized manner. In 1865 the publisher Carleton brought out *Josh Billings: His Sayings;* other collections followed, and by 1869 Shaw had built up enough reputation to justify publishing an annual almanac of sayings. The series of *Farmer's Allminax* which he published between 1869 and 1880, containing forecasts, rhymes, humorous paragraphs and maxims, is generally considered his best work.

The charm of his sayings derives partly from the racy, colorful language, partly from the reader's pleasure in contemplating what seems to be an unlettered mind and an extremely provincial manner, partly from Shaw's shrewd social satire. The following may illustrate his peculiar blend of humor and morality: "Most people repent ov their sins bi thanking God they aint so wicked as their nabors." "Noboddy really luvs to be cheated, but it duz seem az tho every one waz anxious to see how near they could cum to it." The morality manifests itself in repeated admonitions against atheism, hypocrisy, rum, and woman's rights fanatics—admonitions that are often familiar platitudes, but which are given life and color by Shaw's idiom and imagery. Of this imagery Max Eastman has written: "There is little in New England poetry up to that date as graphic as some of this Poughkeepsie auctioneer's metaphors—nothing quite comparable to his statement that goats 'know the way up a rock as natural as a woodbine,' which is Homeric. . . . He possessed these two gifts, the comic vision and the liberated taste for foolishness, in a degree that enabled him to create a new artistic form."

Shaw's growing fame enabled him to move from Poughkeepsie and make his headquarters in New York City during most of his lecturing career. He continued to publish his sayings, contributed regularly after 1865 to the New York *Weekly,* and even wrote for the dignified *Century Magazine,* under the pseudonym "Uncle Esek." He died at sixty-seven, a victim of apoplexy, at Monterey, Calif.

Collection of Frederick H. Meserve

HENRY WHEELER SHAW
("Josh Billings")

PRINCIPAL WORKS: Josh Billings: His Sayings, 1865; Josh Billings on Ice, 1868; Farmer's Allminax, 1869-1879.

ABOUT: Eastman, M. The Enjoyment of Laughter; Smith, C. H. The Farm and the Fireside; Smith, F. S. Life and Adventures of Josh Billings; Tandy, J. The Crackerbox Philosophers in American Humor and Satire; Nation August 17, 1918.

SHAW, JOHN (May 4, 1778-January 10, 1809), physician and poet, was born in Annapolis, Md. He attended St. John's College in Annapolis, and, after his graduation in 1796, began to study medicine under Dr. John Thomas Schaaff. In 1798, spurred by boyish desire for adventure, he sailed for Algiers as a surgeon, and during two years of his travel he acquired a knowledge of Portuguese, Spanish, Italian, and Arabic. He returned to Annapolis in 1800 but sailed in the following year to study medicine at Edinburgh. After his marriage in 1807 to Jane Selby he began to practice medicine in Baltimore, where he immediately gained recognition. In the same year he and two other men, James Cocke and John Beale Davidge, secured a charter to found the College of Medicine of America which later became the University of Maryland. As the result of a chemical experiment that he conducted at this school he acquired an attack of pleurisy, which later led to the tuberculosis from which he died. Shaw was early interested in writing poetry, publishing his first poem, "The Voice of Freedom" in 1795. He later contributed poems to Joseph Dennie's *Port Folio* under the name of "Ithacus." He had no great genius, nor even a characteristic manner in his writings, but he had a pleasing style that won him a small place in 19th century American verse.

PRINCIPAL WORKS: Poems by the Late Doctor John Shaw, 1810.

ABOUT: Duyckinck, E. A. & G. L. Cyclopaedia of American Literature; Kelly, H. A. & Burrage, W. L. American Medical Biographies; Shaw, J. Poems by the Late Dr. John Shaw (see Memoir); Annals of Medical History September 1921.

SHEA, JOHN DAWSON GILMARY (July 22, 1824-February 22, 1892), historian and editor, was born in New York City, the son of James and Mary Ann (Flannigan) Shea. He received his education in the Sisters of Charity school and the Columbia Grammar School, class of 1837. He subsequently studied law and was admitted to the bar, but devoted more time to historical studies than the pursuit of his profession. A devout Catholic, he studied for the priesthood at St. John's College, Fordham, 1848-50, and at St. Mary's College, Montreal, 1850-52, in the latter year embarking definitely on his life-work as a historian with the publication of his *Discovery and Exploration of the Mississippi Valley*.

Shea was a man of great versatility and was well informed on a variety of subjects. After his marriage to Sophie Savage in 1854, he turned out an almost continuous stream of work, beginning with his *First Book of History* and including textbooks, translations, contributions to encyclopedias, dictionaries, and periodicals. He was an accomplished classical scholar, knew several modern languages, and his knowledge of history, ancient, modern, and ecclesiastical was comprehensive and exact. His greatest work was his *History of the Catholic Church in the United States,* four volumes representing years of laborious, intricate research and an exceedingly valuable survey of the work accomplished by the church in America.

Shea was one of the founders of the United States Catholic Historical Society, serving as editor 1887-89 and as president in 1890. At the time of his death in Elizabeth, N.J., he was editor of the *Catholic News.* He never received the recognition and support that was his due as the greatest historian of the Catholic Church in America.

Principal Works: Discovery and Exploration of the Mississippi Valley, 1852; First Book of History, 1854; A General History of Modern Europe, 1854; History of the Catholic Missions Among the Indian Tribes of the United States, 1529-1854, 1854; A School History of the United States, 1855; An Elementary History of the United States, 1855; The Catholic Church in the United States: A Sketch of Its Ecclesiastical History, 1856; History and General Description of New France, 1866-72; History of the Catholic Church in the United States, 1886-92 Memorial of the First Centenary of Georgetown College, 1891.

About: Vallette, M. F. "Dr. John Gilmary Shea"; American Catholic Quarterly Review April 1913; Catholic News March 2, 1892; Catholic World April 1892; New York Freeman's Journal February 26, 1887; The Sun (New York) February 23, 1892.

SHEDD, WILLIAM GREENOUGH THAYER (June 21, 1820-November 17, 1894), theologian and miscellaneous writer, was born in Acton, Mass., the son of Marshall Shedd, Congregational pastor, and Eliza (Thayer) Shedd. William received some schooling at Westport, in upper New York State; and at fifteen he entered the University of Vermont. Upon graduating he thought first of a teaching career, and started in 1839 in a New York City school. Theological speculations had an irresistible attraction for him, however, and in 1840 he joined the Presbyterian Church. After three years of study at the Andover Theological Seminary Shedd was ordained, and from 1843 to 1845 held the pastorate of the Brandon (Vt.) Congregational Church.

Collection of Frederick H. Meserve

W. G. T. SHEDD

In 1845 Shedd was persuaded to return to teaching, and accepted the professorship of English literature at the University of Vermont. He had a notable career as a teacher, serving after 1852 as professor of sacred rhetoric at Auburn Theological Seminary and from 1854 as professor of church history at Andover. Eight years later he increased his sphere of influence by accepting the chair of sacred rhetoric at Union Theological Seminary, a great center of discussion and debate. He continued to teach there until 1893, lecturing after 1874 on systematic theology, the subject to which he made the greatest contribution.

A formidable logician and a writer of considerable talent, Shedd wrote many essays on literary and philosophical subjects, and prepared scholarly editions of St. Augustine's *Confessions* and the works of S. T. Coleridge. Highly esteemed as a teacher, he was also in demand as a public lecturer and occasional orator, for he was a man of broad culture and great personal charm.

Dogmatic Theology, his most influential and widely-read treatise, was perhaps the best American answer to the German "Higher Criticism" of the Bible, and at the time of publication (1888-1894) it was considered the greatest bulwark of Calvinistic theology. However, Shedd was defending a lost cause, and among the progressive religious thinkers at Union and the other seminaries he seemed even in his own day to be the exponent of outmoded theories.

Shedd died in New York, leaving his wife, Lucy Ann Myers Shedd, whom he had married in 1845, and four children.

PRINCIPAL WORKS: *Editions*—The Complete Works of Samuel Taylor Coleridge, 1853; The Confessions of Augustine, 1860. *Miscellaneous*—Lectures Upon the Philosophy of History, 1856; Discourses and Essays, 1856; Literary Essays, 1878; Dogmatic Theology, 1888-1894.

ABOUT: Prentiss, J. L. The Union Theological Seminary; Shedd, F. E. Daniel Shed Genealogy; New York Observer November 22, 1894; New York Tribune November 18, 1894.

SHELTON, FREDERICK WILLIAM (May 20, 1815-June 20, 1881), clergyman and miscellaneous writer, was born in Jamaica, Long Island, N.Y., the son of Dr. Nathan Shelton and Eliza (Starman) Shelton. In 1834 he was graduated from the College of New Jersey and was soon launched on a literary career. His first published work was *The Trollopiad: or, Travelling Gentleman in America,* a satire in verse in which he warmly defended American manners and character from the slanders of English travelers. In 1838 he began contributing regularly to the *Knickerbocker* a series of graceful and humorous sketches known as "The Tinnecum Papers." These included "Hans Carvel," "Rural Cemeteries," "The Country Doctor," and many others. In 1844 he entered the General Theological Seminary, New York, to study for the Protestant Episcopal ministry, and after his ordination in 1848 served in various churches in New York and New England for over thirty years. He still continued his literary work—essays, tales, a conventional romance, sermons, and several poems—but his writing became somewhat less humorous and more didactic. He was much loved as a pastor because of his gentleness, and much admired as a writer by his contemporaries. His manner was characteristic of the Irving tradition, but his usual *métier*—the kindly-humorous rural sketch—was his own. He married Rebecca Conkling, and, although they had six children, only two sons survived him.

PRINCIPAL WORKS: The Trollopiad: or, Trevelling Gentleman in America, 1837; Salander and the Dragon: A Romance of the Hartz Prison, 1850; Up the River, 1853; The Rector of St. Bardolph's, 1853; Crystalline: or, The Heiress of Fall Down Castle, 1854; Peeps From a Belfry: or, The Parish Sketch Book, 1855.

ABOUT: Duyckinck, E. A. & G. L. Cyclopaedia of American Literature; Shelton, E. N. Reunion of the Descendants of Daniel Shelton; Churchman July 23, 1881; Boston Transcript June 22, 1881.

SHEPARD, THOMAS (November 5, 1605-August 25, 1649), clergyman and theological writer, was born in Towcester, England, the son of William Shepard, a grocer's apprentice. He was educated at Cambridge University (M.A. in 1627), ordained in the established church, and silenced for non-conformity in 1630. He was married in 1632 to Margaret Tauteville, a cousin of Sir Richard Darley, in whose family he had served as tutor and chaplain.

Prevented from preaching in England, Shepard emigrated to the United States in 1635 and settled in Boston, where he became pastor of the church in Newtown (Cambridge), succeeding Thomas Hooker. A foe of the Antinomians, he was a member of the Synod at Cambridge in 1637 that silenced them. That same year he was married to Joanna Hooker, daughter of Thomas Hooker, his first wife having died shortly after their arrival in America.

Shepard was a friend of John Harvard and was active in founding Harvard College and in placing it at Cambridge. He formulated a plan whereby each family able and willing should make a small contribution toward the maintenance of needy students, in this way beginning the tradition of scholarships.

He was a vigorous and sincere writer on theological subjects, and his works among them, *Theses Sabbaticae,* with its picture of the Puritan Sabbath, are of value for their informative expositions of the life and customs of that period. His *Parable of the Ten Virgins* was used by Jonathan Edwards in his *Treatise Concerning Religious Affections.*

Shepard was married a third time, in 1647, to Margaret Boradel. He died in Cambridge.

PRINCIPAL WORKS: The Sincere Convert, 1641; New England's Lamentation for Old England's Present Errours, 1645; The Clear Sun Shine of the Gospel Breaking Forth Upon the Indians of New England, 1648; Certain Select Cases Resolved, 1648; Theses Sabbaticae, 1649; The Parable of the Ten Virgins Opened and Applied, 1660; Church Membership of Children and Their Right to Baptism, 1663; Three Valuable Pieces, Viz; Select Cases Resolved: First Principles of the Oracles of God; . . . And a Private Diary; Containing Meditations and Experiences Never Before Published, 1747; The Autobiography of Thomas Shepard (ed. by N. Adams) 1832.

ABOUT: Albro, J. A. The Life of Thomas Shepard; Morison, S. E. Builders of the Bay Colony; Whyte, A. Thomas Shepard: Pilgrim Father and Founder of Harvard; Young, A. Chronicles of the First Planters of the Colony of Massachusetts Bay.

SHERMAN, FRANK DEMPSTER (May 6, 1860-September 19, 1916), poet, architect, mathematician, and genealogist, was born in Peekskill, N.Y. The son of John Dempster Sherman, a book-dealer, and his first wife, Lucy (MacFarland) Sherman, he claimed distinguished ancestors on both sides, among them Elder William Brewster of Pilgrim days. Receiving his early education at home, he attended Peekskill Military Academy for one year, and was graduated from Columbia University in 1884, where he had specialized in architecture. He began writing at Harvard, where as a graduate student he was a contributor to undergraduate magazines—the *Harvard Advocate* and the *Harvard Lampoon*—and through his facile literary gift became an outstanding figure during his year's stay.

After managing the family book business at Peekskill for a short while, he joined the faculty of Columbia University in 1887—an important year in which he married Juliet Mersereau Durand of Peekskill, and published his first book, *Madrigals and Catches*. It was followed by a number of others which soon elevated him to a respected place among contemporary poets. A friendship with Clinton Scollard dating from Harvard days, was productive of two books, one a collaboration—*A Southern Flight* (1905)—and a posthumous volume edited by Scollard, *The Poems of Frank Dempster Sherman* (1917). Friendly association with John Kendrick Bangs, humorist, resulted in another collaboration—*New Waggings of Old Tales.*

Sherman's great personal charm sprang from a wide understanding of and sympathy for humanity and his deep interest in diversified subjects. The scholarly side of his mind revealed a brilliant mathematician, linguist, philosopher, and architect; he was endowed, too, with an unusually keen wit and warmth of nature that enabled him to write *vers de société* and delightful light verse for children, usually published under the name of "Felix Carmen." Aside from his teaching activities, the last twelve years of his life were chiefly devoted to his monumental genealogy of the Sherman family, now the property in manuscript of the New York Public Library. While Sherman can hardly be grouped with the significant American poets, his name is fixed in literary history as one of the ablest of the minor makers of verse.

Principal Works: Madrigals and Catches, 1887; New Waggings of Old Tales, 1888; Lyrics for a Lute, 1890; Little Folk Lyrics, 1892; Lyrics of Joy, 1904, A Southern Flight, 1905; The Poems of Frank Dempster Sherman, 1917.

About: Sherman, F. D. "The Sherman Genealogy," unpublished manuscript in the New York Public Library; Columbia Alumni News October 27, 1916; New York Evening Post December 3, 1904; New York Herald Tribune June 10, 1932; New York Times and Boston Transcript September 20, 1916.

SHERWOOD, MARY ELIZABETH (WILSON) (October 27, 1826-September 12, 1903), poet, novelist and miscellaneous writer, was born in Keene, N.H. Of an early American family, she was the daughter of James and Mary Lord (Richardson) Wilson, and the oldest of seven children. She attended a private school, where she was not considered a good student, and was later sent to school in Boston. About 1842 she accompanied her father to Iowa where he went as surveyor-general, and while he was in Congress, 1847-1850, she acted as his hostess. The next year she was married to John Sherwood, a New York lawyer. Soon afterward she began to contribute to Boston and New York newspapers and to various periodicals, and published a number of volumes. It was not, however, through her poetry and stories that she won popularity as a writer, but through her books on social life and etiquette. Her experience as a hostess in Washington and as a social arbiter in New York, and her life in Europe, where she was presented at many courts, made her particularly adept at this kind of writing. Her style was animated, idiomatic, and often tinged with humor. She made the acquaintance of many distinguished people of her time, she received in France the insignia of Officier d'Académie for her literary work, and she was an ardent philanthropist.

Principal Works: The Sarcasm of Destiny: or, Nina's Experience, 1878; Amenities of Home, 1881; Home Amusements, 1881; Etiquette, 1884; Manners and Social Usages, 1884; Royal Girls and Royal Courts, 1887; Sweet-Brier, 1889; The Art of Entertaining, 1892; Poems by M. E. W. S., 1892; An Epistle to Posterity: Being Rambling Recollections of Many Years of My Life, 1897; Here and There and Everywhere: Reminiscences, 1898.

About: Sherwood, M. E. W. An Epistle to Posterity; Here and There and Everywhere; Willard, F. E. & Livermore, M. A. Portraits and Biographies of Prominent American Women; New York Times September 15, 1903.

SHIELDS, GEORGE OLIVER (August 26, 1846-November 11, 1925), editor and miscellaneous writer, was born in Batavia, Ohio, the son of John F. and Eliza J. (Dawson) Shields. He attended public school for three months in Delaware County, Iowa—this being his only formal education.

In 1864 he joined the Union army and was discharged the following year after being wounded. Soon afterward he took up writing, and, despite the fact he had hunted nearly every kind of game in America, he became an ardent conservationist of wild life. Using the pseudonym "Coquina," in 1883 he published his first book, *Rustlings in the Rockies,* a series of articles and narratives of outdoor life. A later book, *The Battle of the Big Hole,* is valuable historically because it gives an account of the Nez Percé Indian battle in Montana. In 1894 he founded *Recreation,* which he published until 1905 when he was forced into bankruptcy by his printers. The New York Zoological Society then raised money to establish *Shield's Magazine,* which he published until 1912. After that he devoted his time to lecturing on conservation, influencing many states to pass game acts. He was enthusiastic and energetic in his work, but lacked tact in presenting his views, thus making many enemies in the political arena. He was married but was separated from his wife in 1892, and died in New York in comparative poverty.

PRINCIPAL WORKS: Rustlings in the Rockies, 1883; Cruisings in the Cascades, 1889; The Battle of the Big Hole, 1889; Camping and Camp Outfits, 1890; The Blanket Indian of the Northwest, 1921.

ABOUT: Hornaday, W. T. Our Vanishing Wild Life; Thirty Years' War for Wild Life; Back-Log May 1930; Outdoor Life November 1931; Shields' Magazine March 1905. New York Times November 13, 1925.

SHILLABER, BENJAMIN PENHALLOW ("Mrs. Partington") (July 12, 1814-November 25, 1890), humorist, journalist, and poet, was born at Portsmouth, N.H., the son of William and Sarah Leonard (Sawyer) Shillaber. He attended the district schools; served an apprenticeship as a printer's devil; and in 1853 became a book-compositor with Tuttle & Weeks, who issued the then popular "Peter Parley" tales and some of Whittier's anti-slavery poetry. Two years later he became a journeyman printer, but because of ill health he was shortly obliged to make a trip to the tropics. Soon after his return to Boston in July 1838 he was married to Ann Tappan de Rochemont, by whom he had eight children.

He joined the Boston *Post* and in 1847 set up a chance creation in the form of "Mrs. Partington," which very suddenly lifted him from journalistic obscurity. The characteristic vice of Frances M. Whitcher's "Widow Bedott" was the writing of bad poetry—but Mrs. Partington's was her incessant utterance of awful malapropisms, which actually

Collection of Frederick H. Meserve
B. P. SHILLABER
("Mrs. Partington")

became a part of the vernacular of the late 'forties and early 'fifties. In 1850 Shillaber was made editor of the *Pathfinder and Railway Guide,* a journal catering to railroad and steamboat traffickers; and in the year following, for the propagation of more of Mrs. Partington's wisdom, he set up, in Boston, a comic weekly, the *Carpet Bag,* widely quoted by river-town newspapers. "Mark Twain's" first printed sketch, "The Dandy Frightening the Squatter," appeared in the *Carpet Bag* on May 1, 1852, signed by one unknown "S.L.C." Charles Farrar Browne, Charles Bertrand Lewis, and other wits-to-be did their literary prospecting in this journal, which, oddly enough, flourished only about a year. Shillaber went back to the *Post* for three years and then joined the *Saturday Evening Gazette,* where he remained for ten years, and then became a lecturer-humorist on lyceum circuits. After his retirement to Chelsea, Mass., he was only indirectly connected with the press; wrote his "Ike Partington" juveniles; and continued to turn out verse in the vein of his earlier *Rhymes With Reason and Without.*

Thirty thousand copies of *The Life and Sayings of Mrs. Partington* were sold in a very short time, and the second volume had a pre-publication sale of ten thousand. Mrs. Partington and "Aunt Polly" of Mark Twain's *Tom Sawyer* (published twenty-two years later), bore a curious physical resemblance, and each was burdened with the care of an orphaned nephew. Moreover, according to Franklin J. Meine's recent discovery, a sketch presumed to be "Aunt Polly" in Mark Twain's book is the very same "Ruth Partington" portrait which provided the frontispiece for *The Life and Sayings*. . . But more significant than this scattered evidence of Shillaber's direct literary influence is the fact that for the creation of his own "Mrs. Partington" and for the wisdom of his *Carpet Bag* "scouting," the American comic tradition is very much his debtor.

PRINCIPAL WORKS: Rhymes With Reason and Without, 1853; Life and Sayings of Mrs. Partington, 1854; Knitting Work, 1859; Partingtonian Patchwork, 1872; Lines in Pleasant Places, 1874.

ABOUT: Blair, W. Native American Humor; DeVoto, B. Mark Twain's America; Bungay, G. W. Off-Hand Takings; Proceedings of the New Hampshire Press Association, 1895; New England Magazine June 1893-May 1894; Literary World December 20, 1890; New York Tribune November 26, 1890.

"SIDNEY, MARGARET." See LOTHROP, HARRIET MULFORD (STONE)

"SIDONS, CHARLES." See SEALSFIELD, CHARLES

"SIGMA." See SARGENT, LUCIUS MANLIUS

Collection of Frederick H. Meserve
LYDIA HUNTLEY SIGOURNEY

SIGOURNEY, LYDIA HOWARD (HUNTLEY) (September 1, 1791-June 10, 1865), poet, and lady of letters, was born in Norwich, Conn., the only child of Ezekiel Huntley and his second wife, Zerviah (Wentworth) Huntley. Her father, of Scotch descent, was a pious Christian and a soldier of the Revolution, but otherwise undistinguished. Her mother and Mrs. Daniel Lathrop, the elderly lady who employed Huntley as a gardener, were together responsible for Lydia's precocious intellectual attainments.

Educated in Norwich and Hartford, she wrote poetry from the age of eight, and at twenty entered on a career as school mistress in Norwich. In 1814 she opened a small school for girls in Hartford, and a year later with the encouragement of Daniel Wadsworth, an intelligent and wealthy gentleman, collected some of the genteel homilies written for the benefit of her pupils and published her first book, *Moral Pieces in Prose and Verse*.

This promising career was interrupted by her marriage in 1819 to Charles Sigourney, a well-to-do widower with three children. Precise and austere, her husband enjoyed literature but did not approve of it as a profession for his wife. Lydia wrote only for her own enjoyment until Mr. Sigourney's hardware business declined in prosperity, when she began to write in order to supplement their income. Publishing anonymously in accordance with the wishes of her husband, by 1830 she was contributing to more than twenty periodicals. Three years later, well launched on a long and successful literary career, she dropped her anonymity.

In its scope, her work never went far beyond the formulas laid down in *Moral Pieces*. She liked best to write of history, of religious sentiment, and of death; and these three themes, decorated with grace notes of elegant piety, she echoed tunefully for the next fifty years. Extremely popular, she made an excellent income from her writing and gained both respect and fame. Godey paid her $500 a year for the use of her name on the title page of his *Lady's Book*, while at the same time, against his protests, she continued her contributions to the rival *Ladies' Companion*.

In 1840 she made a trip to Europe which seems to have been primarily a literary lion hunt. Armed with letters of introduction, she met the Carlyles, the Wordsworths, and other English celebrities. She failed to meet the Southeys, but a letter from Mrs. Southey hinting at the mental breakdown of the poet laureate was included in her book, *Pleasant Memories of Pleasant Lands*, and brought a storm of recrimination. She was accused of having interpolated phrases in the letter implying a degree of intimacy quite without basis in fact. In spite of this unfortunate incident, which was never satisfactorily cleared up, she returned from Europe with added glory and a diamond bracelet presented to her by the Empress of France.

In 1850 her son Andrew died, not quite twenty years old, and was mourned by the "sweet singer of Hartford" in a lengthy memoir, *The Faded Hope*. Four years later her husband died, leaving her alone except for a married daughter. Her literary fecundity, however, suffered no decline. She continued to write poems, biographies, history, essays, juveniles, and memoirs, at the same time carrying on her many earnest philanthropies until her death at seventy-three.

Demure and energetic, kindly and shrewd, Mrs. Sigourney was loved and honored as "the most famous female bard of her country." Yet even in her own day, her writing won no real critical acclaim. The wide success of her sixty-seven published books was based largely on their unimpeachable morality and their "elegant" sentiment.

PRINCIPAL WORKS: *Poetry*—Moral Pieces in Prose and Verse, 1815; Traits of the Aborigines of America, 1822; Poems by the Author of Moral Pieces, 1827; Zinzendorff and Other Poems, 1835; Select Poems, 1841; Pocahontas and Other Poems, 1841; Poems: Religious and Elegiac, 1841; Poems, 1842; Poetry for Seamen, 1845; The Voice of Flowers, 1846; The Weeping Willow, 1847; Water-Drops, 1848; Olive Leaves, 1852; The Western Home and Other Poems, 1854; Sayings of the Little Ones and Poems for Their Mothers, 1855; The Man of Uz and Other Poems, 1862. *Sketches*—A Sketch of Connecticut Forty Years Since, 1824; Sketches, 1834; Pleasant Memories of Pleasant Lands, 1842; Scenes in My Native Land, 1845; Myrtis . . . , 1846; Gleanings, 1860. *Juveniles*—How to Be Happy, 1833; Poetry for Children, 1834; Tales and Essays, 1835; Olive Buds, 1836; The Girl's Reading Book, 1838; The Boy's Reading Book, 1839; Child's Book, 1844. *Biographies*—History of Marcus Aurelius: Emperor of Rome, 1836; Examples of Life and Death, 1852; Examples From the Eighteenth and Nineteenth Centuries, 1857. *Memoirs*—The Lovely Sisters, 1845; The Faded Hope, 1853; Memoir of Mrs. Harriet Newell Cook, 1853; Letters of Life (autobiography) 1866. *Miscellany*—Letters to Young Ladies, 1833; Letters to Mothers, 1838; Whisper to a Bride, 1850; Letters to My Pupils: With Narrative and Biographical Sketches, 1851; Past Meridian 1854; Luck Howard's Journal, 1858.

ABOUT: Griswold, R. W. The Female Poets of America; Haight, G. S. Mrs. Sigourney: The Sweet Singer of Hartford; Hart, J. S. The Female Prose Writers of America.

SILL, EDWARD ROWLAND (April 29, 1841-February 28, 1887), poet and essayist, was born in Windsor, Conn., the son of Dr. Theodore Sill and Elizabeth Newberry (Rowland) Sill. His only brother was drowned in 1847, his mother died in 1852, and his father, who had taken him to Cleveland and started practice there, died in 1853. The orphaned boy was reared by his father's brother in Cuyahoga Falls, Ohio. After a year at Phillips Exeter Academy, and another at the preparatory school of Western Reserve College, at Hudson, Ohio, he entered Yale. Though he was recognized immediately as a highly talented youth, the dull routine of college failed to hold his attention; he was "rusticated" for a year for neglecting his studies, but was nevertheless graduated with his class in 1861. His class poem was long held to be the best in the history of Yale, and he had been an editor of the *Yale Literary Magazine*.

Nevertheless, this frail hypersensitive boy did not think of literature as a career, but instead sailed around the Horn to California. There he worked in the Sacramento post office, in a bank in Folsom, played at reading law and medicine, loved the California scenery but was utterly unfitted for the robust life of the West, and returned East in 1866. Another tangent sent him to the Harvard Divinity School, the only result being a lifelong troubled agnosticism. He taught in a boys' school in Brooklyn, worked for a while as literary critic on the New York *Evening Mail*, and in 1867 married Elizabeth Newberry Sill, his first cousin. The only writing he did at this period was a translation of Rau's fictionized life of Mozart. Instead, he turned to teaching as his career, acted as principal of the high school and superintendent of schools at Cuyahoga Falls, then returned to California, and from 1871 to 1874 taught English and classics at the Oak-

Collection of Frederick H. Meserve
EDWARD ROWLAND SILL

land High School. From 1874 to 1882 Sill was professor of English at the University of California. He was an inspired teacher, but he felt more and more out of his element, and with his frail health as an excuse resigned in 1883 and went back to Cuyahoga Falls.

There he lived until his sudden death after a minor operation in a Cleveland hospital. He contributed essays anonymously to the *Atlantic,* wrote poems for various magazines under the name of "Andrew Hedbrooke," and led a shy, secluded existence, his only social contacts through letters, mostly to the college friends who, characteristically, were his dearest friends throughout life. Tall, slender, with cameo-like features only half-concealed by a full beard, Sill was always a romantic figure. With his rich, flexible voice he would have made a good actor, and in fact once played with the idea; painting and especially music were also among his talents. He was a typical minor artist of great versatility, sensitivity, and delicacy, but without power or depth. He had the playful humor of the congenitally melancholy, but his characteristic mood was one of doubt and fatigue. He himself described it:

> A clouded spirit; full of doubt
> And old misgiving, weariness of heart
> And loneliness of mind; long wearied out.

His essays are arid and trifling; but his verse has many merits—simplicity, spontaneity, subtlety, classic finish, delicate warmth—everything except creative imagination or passion. The two poems by which he is best known, "The Fool's Prayer" and "Opportunity," are in fact among his poorest, more didactic than was his wont. At his best he is reminiscent of Matthew Arnold or Arthur Clough, two poets with whom he had much in common. He might indeed have been capable of more solid work, had his health been less frail and his nature less shrinking. Even as it is, he has a small assured place in the poetic firmament.

Only one volume of Sill's poems was actually published during his lifetime. Its reception disappointed him, and his three remaining volumes (one posthumous) were privately printed for his friends. More than a decade after his death two volumes of his collected prose and verse were brought out.

Principal Works: Field Notes, The Hermitage, and Other Poems, 1868; The Venus of Milo and Other Poems (privately printed) 1883; Poems (privately printed) 1887; Hermione and Other Poems (privately printed) 1889; The Prose of Edward Rowland Sill, 1900; The Poems of Edward Rowland Sill, 1902.

About: Parker, W. B. Edward Rowland Sill: His Life and Work; Century Magazine September 1888; Cleveland Plain Dealer March 1, 1887.

SILLIMAN, BENJAMIN (August 8, 1779-November 24, 1864), educator, scientist, and scholarly writer, was born at Trumbull, Conn., the son of Gold Selleck Silliman and Mary (Fish) Silliman. Benjamin was educated at Fairfield, Conn., and at Yale College, from which he graduated in 1796. After a few indecisive years of teaching and studying the family profession of law, Benjamin was suddenly appointed in 1802 to the newly created professorship of chemistry and natural history at Yale—a surprising appointment for a youth of twenty-three, but one that later brought great credit to Yale and to American science. Silliman developed a profound knowledge of chemistry and geology through study with Robert Hare and John Maclean in this country and with Sir Humphrey Davy, John Murray, and Thomas Hope in Great Britain; and by making this knowledge available through skillful lecturing to his students at Yale he brought about great advances in scientific study in this country. He became easily the most widely respected and esteemed scientific man of his time in America.

On his return from Europe in 1806 he started writing an account of his studies and travels, and when in 1810 he published this *Journal of Travels in England, Holland, and Scotland* three editions of the work were soon sold and were widely read. By 1808 Silliman's teaching began to extend beyond the classroom; he came to be in great demand as a public lecturer throughout New England and later in the South and West as well. Tall, impressive in appearance and voice, he captivated larger and more intelligent audiences than any American scientist before him and few since. At Yale he greatly increased the opportunities for advanced scientific study by raising money, by his persuasive power over administrators, and most of all by his own example. He was the founder and first editor of the *American Journal of Science and Arts,* which became a notable vehicle for publication of research, and his own investigations in American geology had considerable value. His chief work, however, was in organizing and disseminating knowledge.

In 1809 Silliman married Harriet Trumbull, daughter of the second Governor of Connecticut, by whom he had nine children. After her death in 1850 he married Sarah

Webb. The last ten years of his life were spent in travel and retirement.

PRINCIPAL WORKS: *Travel Notes*—A Journal of Travels in England, Holland and Scotland, 1810; A Visit to Europe in 1851, 1853. *Editions*—Henry's The Elements of Experimental Chemistry, 1814; Bakewell's An Introduction to Geology, 1829. *Scientific Works*—Elements of Chemistry, 1830; Remarks Made on a Short Tour Between Hartford and Quebec in the Autumn of 1819, 1820.

ABOUT: Fisher, G. P. Life of Benjamin Silliman; Proceedings of the American Academy of Arts and Sciences: Vol. 6; Morning Journal and Courier (New Haven) November 26, 1864.

SIMMS, WILLIAM GILMORE (April 17, 1806-June 11, 1870), poet and novelist, was born in Charleston, S.C., the son of William Gilmore Simms, a poor storekeeper of northern Irish descent, and Harriet Ann Augusta (Singleton) Simms. His father became bankrupt in 1808, and, the mother dying at the same time, the boy was given to his maternal grandmother to rear, while his father went to the frontier of Tennessee and Mississippi as a volunteer under Andrew Jackson. Simms received scant schooling and while still a child was apprenticed to a druggist. He wrote verse from boyhood, however, and aspired to an education. At eighteen he went to visit his father, his only experience of the pioneer life of which so many of his books treat; a contest between the father and grandmother for his guardianship resulted in a lawsuit, which was decided (as the boy wished, but against his real interests) in his remaining in Charleston.

There he read law, was admitted to the bar (but never practiced), and in 1826 married Anna Malcolm Giles. He turned to journalism, and for two years was part owner and editor of the *City Gazette,* an anti-nullification organ. In 1832 his wife died, leaving a daughter. In the hope of furthering his literary career—he had meanwhile published several volumes of verse—Simms left the city he adored (though it constantly ignored him) and moved to New York. There he published his first novels, became a friend of Bryant's, and was more or less a member of the New York literary group. For a while he lived in New Haven. But in 1835 homesickness overcame him, and he returned permanently to South Carolina.

In 1836 he married Chevillette Roach, daughter of a wealthy and aristocratic planter, and went to live with her in her ancestral home, "Woodlands," in the southern part of the state. This was the happiest period of Simm's life, even though nine of their fourteen children died. He was able to live comfortably, to write prolifically but without strain, and to act as patron and

Collection of Frederick H. Meserve
WILLIAM GILMORE SIMMS

benefactor of young Carolinians who showed a taste for authorship. In the North he was considered the most representative Southern writer—"the Southern Cooper, the American Scott"—but in his own section of the country he was neglected and snubbed, his lower class origin outweighing his talents and culture. Politically, however, he made his way; gradually he had been weaned from his early position against nullification until he became the most ardent and sanguine of Secessionists. He served in the state legislature from 1844 to 1846 and came within one vote of being elected lieutenant-governor.

The Civil War ruined him, and the rest of his life was miserable. His wife died in 1863; "Woodlands" was burned, rebuilt, then sacked by Sherman; he took refuge in Columbia, S.C., to lose the remainder of his property when the town was destroyed; and his last years were spent in ceaseless toil to support his six remaining children, turning out "bad serials for worse magazines" (Carl Van Doren). He finally died of overwork.

Simms was a spoiled realist. He did himself a disservice by refusing to spend his formative years in the rich territory of the frontier. His best work is in his picaresque novels and in his historic romances of the South. But he wrote hastily, he had a taste for blood and thunder, and he revelled in exaggerated melodrama. Even his historical novels he ruined by introducing solid, indigestible blocks of dry factual writing. Yet he was a born story-teller—born, unfortunately, too early or too late to have found his real public. *The Yemassee* is probably the best of his novels, few of which are read today. His poetry is dreamy and sentimental; only a few of his poems, such as "The Lost Pleiad" and "The Grapevine Swing," have survived even in anthologies.

All in all, this man with the noble head of a Roman senator, who was all kindness and patriotic ardor and nobility of spirit, remained a half-failure, his life a minor tragedy, his work, which he thought of as a sort of Homeric epic of the South, a prime example of literary frustration, of misdirected effort and near-accomplishment. He was the chief "almoster" of his time.

PRINCIPAL WORKS: *Verse*—Lyrical and Other Poems, 1827; Early Lays, 1827; The Vision of Cortes, Cain, and Other Poems, 1829; The Tri-Color, 1830; Atlantis, 1832; The Book of My Lady, 1833; The City of the Silent, 1850; Poems, 1853; Areytos: or, Songs of the South, 1860. *Novels*—Martin Faber, 1833; Guy Rivers, 1834; The Yemassee, 1835; The Partisan, 1835; Mellichampe, 1836; Richard Hurdis, 1838; Pelayo: A Story of the Goth, 1838; The Damsel of the Darien, 1839; Border Beagles, 1840; The Kinsman (later The Scout), 1841; Beauchampe: or, The Kentucky Tragedy, 1842; Count Julian: or, The Last Days of the Goth, 1845; Katharine Walton, 1851; The Sword and the Distaff, 1853 (as Woodcraft, 1854); Vasconselos, 1853; The Forayers, 1855; Eutaw, 1856; The Cassique of Kiawah, 1859. *Non-Fiction*—History of South Carolina, 1840; Geography of South Carolina, 1843; Life of Francis Marion, 1844; Life of Captain John Smith, 1846; Life of the Chevalier Bayard, 1847; Life of Nathanael Greene, 1849.

ABOUT: Erskine, J. Leading American Novelists; Parrington, V. L. Main Currents in American Literature; Trent, W. P. William Gilmore Simms; Book News Monthly June 1912; Charleston Daily Courier June 13, 1870.

SIMPSON, STEPHEN (July 24, 1789-August 17, 1854), editor, political writer, and biographer, was born in Philedelphia, the son of George Simpson, banker and assistant commissary-general in the Revolution. Young Simpson was a clerk in the Bank of the United States, but resigned to join the army during the War of 1812, fighting at the Battle of New Orleans under Andrew Jackson. Returning from the war, he became editor and proprietor of the *Portico*, in Baltimore, which failed the year after its inception in 1816. In 1822, with John Conrad, he established the *Columbian Observer*, in Philadelphia, a Democratic paper supporting Jackson and featuring in its columns a series of Simpson's articles under the signature "Brutus." These able but vindictive attacks on the policies of the Bank of the United States greatly increased Simpson's popularity with the newly formed Workingmen's Party.

His political beliefs were embodied in *The Working Man's Manual* published in 1831, the year after Simpson had been defeated for Congress as a candidate of the new party. He believed that "all wealth is produced by labor" and felt that labor had earned and should receive all its production. His wish was to improve conditions through legislation and free public education. Simpson's liberal and advanced views made him a popular leader of the Workingmen's Party, until his retraction of his "Brutus" letters, in an appendix to his *Manual*, cost him some of his prestige.

His *Biography of Stephen Girard* is a curiously facetious account, probably originating in personal resentment. Simpson's political writings, however, were notable in their advanced, idealistic views of social problems.

PRINCIPAL WORKS: The Working Man's Manual: A New Theory of Political Economy on the Principle of Production the Source of Wealth, 1831; Biography of Stephen Girard, 1832; The Lives of George Washington and Thomas Jefferson: With a Parallel, 1833.

ABOUT: History of Labour in the United States; Mott, F. L. A History of American Magazines; Simpson, H. The Lives of Eminent Philadelphians; Pennsylvania (Philadelphia) August 19, 1854.

"SINGING SYBIL, THE." See VICTOR, METTA VICTORIA (FULLER)

"SINGLETON, ARTHUR, ESQ ' See KNIGHT, HENRY COGSWELL

"SINGULARITY, THOMAS." See NOTT, HENRY JUNIUS

"SIOGVOLK, PAUL." See MATHEWS, ALBERT

"SISTERS OF THE WEST, THE." See VICTOR, METTA VICTORIA (FULLER)

"SKINFLINT, OBEDIAH." See HARRIS, JOEL CHANDLER

"SLENDER, ROBERT." See FRENEAU, PHILIP

"SLICK, SAM." See Kunitz & Haycraft (eds). *British Authors of the 19th Century*

SMITH, CHARLES HENRY ("Bill Arp") (June 15, 1826-August 24, 1903), humorist, was born in Lawrenceville, Ga., the son of Asahel Reid Smith, a storekeeper, a native of Vermont, and Caroline Ann (Maguire) Smith, descendent of a good Irish

CHARLES H. SMITH
("Bill Arp")

family. He attended a manual labor school, then became a clerk in his father's store. In 1845 he was able to go to Franklin College (now the University of Georgia), but had to leave in 1848 because his father was ill and needed him to manage the store. In 1849 he married Mary Octavia Hutchins; they had thirteen children, of whom ten survived. After studying law for only two months, Smith was admitted to the bar; he moved to Rome, Ga., and practised law there until 1877, with only the Civil War as an interruption. He served in the Confederate Army throughout the war, gaining the rank of major and being judge advocate at Macon in 1864. He was state senator in 1865 and 1866, mayor of Rome in 1868 and 1869, and for a while edited the Rome *Commercial.* In 1877 he moved to a farm near Cartersville, to train his sons as farmers. In 1888, all his sons having grown up and married, he gave up the farm and moved to Cartersville, where he spent the remainder of his life.

Smith's literary reputation rests primarily on a series of letters contributed to the Atlanta *Constitution* for more than thirty years and widely reprinted; most of them were afterward published in book form. In the name and dialect of a local Rome character called "Bill Arp," Smith started writing letters to "Mr. Abe Linkhorn" in 1861. At first Arp was supposed to be a Northern sympathizer. Gradually the dialect disappeared, the topical issues grew fewer, and the letters became a series of discourses in rustic philosophy. During the dark days of the war and of Reconstruction, Smith's was the only voice of cheer and encouragement; no wonder that in later years this bald, bearded lawyer was called "the best loved man in all the Southland." In his combination of genial satire and sound common sense, Smith was a sort of precursor of Will Rogers, or a more amiable Ed Howe. He also wrote two serious historical works and a humorous autobiography.

PRINCIPAL WORKS: A Side Show of the Southern Side of the War, by Bill Arp, So Called, 1866; Bill Arp's Letters, 1868; Bill Arp's Peace Papers, 1873; Bill Arp's Scrapbook, 1884; The Farm and Fireside, 1891; A School History of Georgia as Colony and State, 1893; Stephen Decatur and the Suppression of Piracy on the Mediterranean, 1901; Bill Arp: From the Uncivil War to Date, 1903.

ABOUT: Smith, C. H. Bill Arp: From the Uncivil War to Date; Smith, M. C. I Remember; Atlanta Constitution August 25-28, 1903; New York Tribune August 30, 1903.

SMITH, ELIHU HUBBARD (September 4, 1771-September 19, 1798), physician and poet, was born at Litchfield, Conn., the son of Dr. Reuben and Abigail (Hubbard) Smith. Unusually precocious, he entered Yale College at the age of eleven. Graduated in 1786, too young to follow a profession, he took up literary and classical studies with Dr. Timothy Dwight and was soon devoting his entire time to writing. Through this association with Dr. Dwight, he took an active interest in politics and became a minor member of the clever group of writers known as the "Hartford Wits."

He later studied medicine in his father's office, received a license to practice, and established himself first in Wethersfield, Conn., and afterward in New York City, where he became highly respected in medical circles. Through his social and literary proclivities, he rose to a prominent place in metropolitan life and was one of the most popular young bachelors in the city.

In 1797, with Dr. Samuel L. Mitchill and Dr. Edward Miller, he established the *Medical Repository,* a professional journal; and was contributor and joint editor until his death. His *Letters to William Buel on the Fever Which Prevailed in New York in 1793* enhanced his professional status.

A young man of unusual charm, talents, and benevolent character, he lost his life through his unremitting labors in combating the yellow fever epidemic of 1798.

His collection of American poetry published in 1793 gave him the distinction of being the first anthologist of verse in this country, and it is through this work, more than his effusive sonnets and ballads, that he is remembered.

Principal Works: American Poems, 1793; Letters to William Buel on the Fever . . . in New York in 1795, 1795; Edwin and Angelina, 1798.

About: Bailey, M. E. A Lesser Hartford Wit; Dr. Elihu Hubbard Smith; Dexter, F. B. Biographical Sketches of Graduates of Yale College; Diary of William Dunlap; Medical Repository: Vol. 2; New York Commercial Advertiser, September 20, 1798.

SMITH, ELIZABETH OAKES (PRINCE) (August 12, 1806-November 15, 1893), miscellaneous writer, lecturer, and reformer, was born in North Yarmouth, Maine, the daughter of David and Sophia (Blanchard) Prince. Her mother remarried after her father's death and in 1814 the family moved to Portland. Although Elizabeth longed for a higher education and a career, she fell in with her mother's wishes and, in 1823, was married to Seba Smith [*q.v.*], editor of the *Eastern Argus.* They had five sons. For some years she devoted her time to her home and children but after the collapse of their fortune in the panic of 1837 she began contributing poems to several popular periodicals. The *Sinless Child,* a poem published in 1843, was commented on favorably by Poe. In addition to these she wrote seven novels, books for children, and two plays which were produced. Some of her novels, such as the *Bald Eagle,* which was very popular, show her indebtedness to James Fenimore Cooper; others, such as *The Newsboy,* show her interest in the social problems of the day. In 1851 she published *Woman and Her Needs,* a series of articles on woman suffrage, and for the next six years lectured successfully on this subject. After her husband's death in 1868, Mrs. Oakes Smith, as she was known, spent most of her time in North Carolina with her eldest son, although for one year, 1877, she was pastor of the Independent Church at Canastota, N.Y.

Principal Works: The Western Captive, 1842; The Sinless Child, 1843; The Salamander: A Legend for Christmas, 1848; Women and Her Needs, 1851; Bertha and Lily, 1854; The Newsboy, 1854; Black Hollow, 1864; Bald Eagle: or, The Last of the Ramapaughs, 1867; The Sagamore of Saco, 1868; Selections From the Autobiography of Elizabeth Oakes Smith, 1924.

About: Griswold, R. W. The Female Poets of America; Smith, E. O. P. Selections From the Autobiography of Elizabeth Oakes Smith; Appleton's Annual Cyclopaedia, 1893; Portland Daily Eastern Argus November 21, 1893.

SMITH, FRANCIS HOPKINSON (October 23, 1838-April 7, 1915), engineer, artist, and story-teller, was born in Baltimore, Md., the son of Francis and Susan (Teackle) Smith, and great-grandson of Francis Hopkinson [*q.v.*], artist-poet-musician and one of the signers of the Declaration of Independence. His father, who was to appear later as a character in the semi-autobiographical novel, *The Fortunes of Oliver Horn,* seems to have been a man of unusual gifts: a mathematician, a philosopher, and an amateur musician who invented a new musical instrument. Like his father, the younger Francis was endowed with versatility, following during his lifetime three successive careers, all of which brought him fame.

Although he prepared for college, financial difficulties made it necessary for him to go into business immediately. He began as a shipping clerk in a hardware store and became, shortly afterward, assistant superintendent in the iron foundry which belonged to his elder brother. At the close of the Civil War he moved to New York, working again in the office of a foundry until his indignation over the unfair business dealings of his employer led him to quit his job. With a partner, James Symington, he went into engineering, a career which he followed for the next thirty years. Outstanding for his courage and resourcefulness, he was responsible for several difficult feats of construction which won him deserved success: among them, the Block Island breakwater; the sea wall at Tompkinsville, Staten Island; the foundations for the Statue of Liberty; and, most difficult of all, the Race Rock Lighthouse, eight miles out to sea with a seven mile per hour rip tide.

F. HOPKINSON SMITH

During these years his hobby was painting, an occupation which he preferred to keep separate from the business of making money. He made many friends among the younger artists, and as a member of the New York Tile Club illustrated several books, including *A Book of the Tile Club,* to which he contributed anonymous sketches and stories. There followed two books of travel sketches, charming drawings to which he began to add his impressions in prose. These proved popular and brought him wide recognition as an artist. With more leisure, he devoted the greater part of his time to painting, spending his summers abroad, exhibiting, and publishing his drawings.

Almost accidentally he entered on a third career when he was more than fifty years old. Known as an excellent raconteur, he decided to put into print some of his famous after-dinner stories, and from these grew his first book of fiction, *Colonel Carter of Cartersville,* the delightful tale of an old Virginia gentleman which bore out the literary promise of his earlier descriptions. When this book proved successful he abandoned his engineering career completely and spent the rest of his life writing, lecturing, and painting.

His appearance that of a prosperous banker rather than an artist, tall and vigorous, with sweeping white mustaches, he won affection and respect, carrying on his various activities with the greatest of energy to the last days of his life. He died in New York at seventy-seven, leaving his wife, the former Josephine Van Deventer, and two sons,

His stories, and even his novels, many of which were based on his own experiences as engineer and artist, were distinguished by the special talent he had for a picturesque anecdote. With an easy colloquial style, he brought a cosmopolitan's knowledge of the world and the alert observation of an artist to these slight but engaging tales. The same sunny, hearty relish for life which marked his personality gave his prose charm and brilliance.

Principal Works: *Stories*—Colonel Carter of Carterville, 1891; A Day at Laguerre's and Other Days, 1892; A Gentleman Vagabond and Some Others, 1895; The Other Fellow, 1899; Colonel Carter's Christmas, 1903; The Under Dog, 1903; At Close Range, 1905; The Wood Fire in No. 3, 1905; The Romance of an Old Fashioned Gentleman, 1907; The Veiled Lady and Other Men and Women, 1907; Forty Minutes Late and Other Stories, 1909; The Armchair at the Inn, 1912. *Novels*—Caleb West: Master Diver, 1898; Tom Grogan, 1900; The Fortunes of Oliver Horn, 1902; The Tides of Barnegat, 1906; Peter: A Novel of Which He Is Not the Hero, 1908; Kennedy Square, 1911; Felix O'Day, 1915; Enoch Crane (left unfinished and completed by F. Berkeley Smith) 1916. *Travel*—Well Worn Roads of Spain, Holland, and Italy, 1887; A White Umbrella in Mexico, 1889; Venice of Today, 1896; Gondola Days, 1897.

About: Bookman May 1915; Literary World September 1904; Scribner's Magazine September 1915.

SMITH, JAMES (c. 1737-c. 1814), pioneer, soldier and miscellaneous writer, was born in the Conococheague settlement in Pennsylvania. He had little formal education but was well schooled in the realities of pioneer and outdoor life. In 1755, while building a military road from Shippensburg, he was captured and adopted by Indians. He lived with and followed them for four years, finally escaping near Montreal. In 1760 he returned home, took up farming, and three years later was married. He then embarked on an exciting career of Indian fighting, pioneering, and exploring. In 1769 he moved to Westmoreland County, Pa., where he served on various commissions and conventions, and in 1778 was commissioned a colonel of the militia. Ten years later he moved to Kentucky where he was a member of the constitutional convention of 1792 and for several years represented Bourbon County in the General Assembly of Kentucky. Smith was a strong churchman as well as an Indian fighter and he spent a great deal of time during his later years doing missionary work among the Indians. Upon his return from one of his missionary trips he discovered that his son, James, had become a Shaker, and after visiting the Shaker settlement near Lebanon, Ohio, Smith wrote two wrathy pamphlets against the leaders of the sect. His chief literary achievement, however, was *An Account of the Remarkable Occurrences in the Life and Travels of Col. James Smith: During His Captivity With the Indians, in the Years 1755, '56, '57, '58 & '59.* A valuable work, it has been reprinted many times and reproduced in many publications relating to Indians. Smith was reserved and reticent, of a thoughtful and meditative nature, but a man of strong convictions and unusually gifted in debate. After the death of his first wife, Anne Wilson Smith, he married a widow, Margaret (Rodgers) Irvin, whom he survived.

Principal Works: An Account of the Remarkable Occurrences in the Life and Travels of Col. James Smith: During His Captivity With the Indians, in the Years 1755, '56, '57, '58 & '59, 1799; Remarkable Occurrences Lately Discovered Among the People Called Shakers; of a Treasonous and Barbarous Nature; or Shakerism Developed, 1810; Shakerism Detected: Their Erroneous and Treasonous Proceedings . . . Exposed to Public View, 1810; Treatise on the Mode and

Manner of Indian War: Their Tactics, Discipline and Encampments, 1812.

ABOUT: Boucher, J. N. History of Westmoreland County, Pa.; Collins, Lewis & R. H. History of Kentucky; Smith, J. An Account of the . . . Travels of Col. James Smith.

SMITH, CAPTAIN JOHN (presumably January 1579 or 1580-June 21, 1631), adventurer, soldier, explorer, and chronicler, was born in the town of Willoughby, Lincolnshire, England, the elder son of three children of George Smith, sturdy yeoman, and his wife Alice. His parents had some claim to gentle blood and were people of means, but he received only an elementary education in the public schools of the nearby towns Alford and Louth, where his father had some property. At the age of fifteen, after his father's death, he was apprenticed to a merchant of Lynn. He left his master soon afterwards, however, to begin a life of adventure and travel that lasted until he was about thirty. His adventurous spirit showed itself while he was still at school. At thirteen he once sold his books and satchel to run away to sea, but his father's illness held him back. He seized, however, upon the first opportunity to get away. At first he accompanied to France a son of his father's former landlord; and then with a share of the small fortune inherited from his father, he set out for himself. He traveled about Europe, Asia, and Africa. In his aspiration towards a military career he fought as a free lance, or soldier of fortune, in the Netherlands against Spain while still in his teens, and in Hungary against the Turks at twenty-one. His military successes earned him the title of captain, a coat-of-arms, and an annual pension of 3000 ducats from the Transylvanian Prince Sigismund Bathori.

During his exploits he often suffered great hardships and danger. While sailing with a group of Catholic pilgrims to Italy, he was blamed for the turbulence of the sea and thrown overboard. A French pirate vessel rescued him, however, at an island, to which he had swum, and enriched him with a share of the booty from the plunder of a Venetian vessel. During his fight against the Turks he was once severely wounded, captured, and enslaved. He freed himself, however, by crushing his master's skull.

In 1604 he returned to England, and after a walking tour in Ireland, he became interested in the settlement of Virginia. His adventurous experiences had fitted him well for pioneering. In 1606 he sailed with the London Company. Though, because of rebellion during the crossing, he was brought to

After a portrait by S. van der Pass
CAPTAIN JOHN SMITH
1616

shore a prisoner, he advanced in 1608 to the presidency of the colony, of which he is considered virtually the founder. His accomplishments there included the exploration and discoveries of bays, rivers, and creeks of the Chesapeake. In the course of colonization he had to reckon with treachery, mutiny, and disaffection of the starving colonists, whom he saved, however, by his expeditions into Indian territory and skillful negotiations with the Indians. On one occasion he was captured by them and was to be beheaded, but his life was saved by their chief's daughter, Pocahontas. (Contrary to romantic legend, he did not wed her; so far as is known he was a lifelong bachelor.)

He had no direct share in the settlement of New England. Through his explorations, however, he was the first to see its advantages for settlement and trade and through his writings he aroused interest in it and supplied valuable information to the settlers. Hence his title "Admiral of New England."

He was nearly forty when, because of no prospects of employment, he settled down to write. Some of his writings, however, date from the years of his colonization work. He published nine books, some of them being only repetitions and enlargements of earlier ones. His works are partly autobiographical, recording his achievements, adventures, and travels; and partly historical, describing the governments, people, customs, and habits in the early settlements. He wrote also two works on sea-faring and attempted some poetry. His complete works, edited by Edward Arber, first appeared in 1884. Another edition was published in 1910. He is an unpolished but clear and forceful writer. The authenticity of his accounts of some of his exploits has been questioned by historians.

Like many natives of Lincolnshire, he was a Danish type, fair-haired and blue-eyed. His early surroundings of vast expanses of fields, hills, and woods, and sailors' tales of the nearby sea were factors in the shaping of his mind and body. He was vigorous in both, and possessed great courage, perseverance, energy, warmth, and enthusiasm. Owing to his impatient and irritable temperament and haughty bearing, he made, however, many enemies, though according to some of his contemporaries he was beloved by his comrades and the soldiers under his command. He died in London.

PRINCIPAL WORKS: *History*—A True Relation of Such Occurrences and Accidents of Noate as Hath Hapned in Virginia Since the First Planting of That Collony. . . , 1608; A Map of Virginia: With a Description of the Countrey . . . , 1612; A Description of New England, 1616; New Englands Trials, 1620; The Generall Historie of Virginia, New England, and the Summer Isles, 1624; Advertisements for the Unexperienced Planters of New England, 1631. *Miscellany*—An Accidence: or, The Path-way to Experience, 1626; The Sea-Man's Grammar, 1627. *Travel*—The True Travels, Adventures, and Observations of Captaine John Smith, 1630.

ABOUT: Armstrong, W. C. Life and Adventures of Captain John Smith; Bradley, A. G. Captain John Smith; Chatterton, E. K. Captain John Smith; Hillard, G. S. Life and Adventures of Captain John Smith; Rossiter, J. Captain John Smith; Warner, C. D. Captain John Smith: A Study of His Life and Writings; Woods, K. P. The True Story of Captain John Smith.

"SMITH, JOHNSTON." See CRANE, STEPHEN

"SMITH, MR." See LOCKWOOD, RALPH INGERSOLL

SMITH, PENN. See SMITH, RICHARD PENN

SMITH, RICHARD PENN (March 13, 1799-August 12, 1854), playwright and miscellaneous writer, was born in Philadelphia. He was the son of William Moore Smith and Ann (Rudulph) Smith, and a grandson of the Rev. William Smith, the first provost of the College of Philadelphia. Tutored at home, he afterward attended a school at Huntingdon, Pa., and in 1818 returned to Philadelphia to study law, being admitted to the bar three years later.

At this time he began his writing with a series of essays entitled "The Plagiary," published in the *Union*. He became editor and first proprietor of the Philadelphia *Aurora* in 1822 but sold it five years later to resume his law practice. He subsequently devoted much time to his writing, and fifteen of his plays were produced within the next ten years. The most successful was the tragedy *Caius Marius* which was written for Edwin Forrest and produced in 1831. Aside from his plays Smith wrote a novel, *The Forsaken,* and was the attributed author of *Col. Crockett's Exploits and Adventures in Texas.*

Smith was twice married: first in 1823, to Elinor Matilda Blodget, a cousin, who died in 1834; two years later he married Isabella Stratton Knisell. His son by first marriage collected and published a selection of his father's miscellanies with a memoir by Morton McMichael. Smith's plays were usually taken from the French and were on the whole melodramatic, complicated works. His best known play, *Caius Marius,* has been lost, probably because Forrest refused to allow plays in which he appeared to be published.

PRINCIPAL WORKS: *Plays*—The Eighth of January, 1829; The Disowned, 1829; The Sentinels, 1829; The Triumph of Plattsburgh, 1830; Caius Marius, 1831; Is She a Brigand, 1833; Quite Correct, 1835; The Actress of Padua, 1836. *Novel*—The Forsaken, 1831. *Attributed*—Col. Crockett's Exploits and Adventures in Texas, 1836.

ABOUT: Smith, H. W. Life and Correspondence of the Rev. William Smith; Smith, R. P. Miscellaneous Works (see Introduction by M. McMichael); Quinn, A. H. A History of the American Drama From the Beginning to the Civil War; Burton's Gentleman's Magazine (Philadelphia) September 1839; Daily Pennsylvanian (Philadelphia) August 14, 1854.

SMITH, SAMUEL FRANCIS (October 21, 1808-November 16, 1895), author of "America," was born in Boston, the son of Samuel and Sarah (Bryant) Smith. At the local public schools he was a pupil of high standing, and won a gold medal for an English poem. After graduating from Harvard College in 1829 Smith studied for three more years at Andover Theological Seminary, working at the same time as a translator for the *Encyclopaedia Americana* to supplement his income. After graduating, he worked as an editor until his ordination in the Baptist ministry, February 1834.

Smith held two pastorates; first in Waterville, Maine, 1834-1842, where he served at the same time as professor of modern languages and Greek at Waterville College, now Colby College, and then at Newton Center, Mass., which became his permanent home. He became more and more interested in editorial and missionary work, however,

SAMUEL FRANCIS SMITH

serving from 1842 to 1848 as editor of the *Christian Review,* and after 1854 giving all his time to the editorial secretaryship of the American Baptist Missionary Union. He married, in 1834, Mary White Smith of Haverhill, Mass., by whom he had six children.

Smith's literary reputation rests almost wholly upon his authorship of the national anthem "America." It was composed in 1832, when, at the request of Lowell Mason, Smith was going through a German school song book looking for tunes to which he might compose American hymns. Inspired by the cadence of the original music and the patriotism of the German words, Smith composed, so he affirms, "within half an hour, the verses substantially as they stand today." Published in Mason's *The Choir,* Smith's anthem was sung for the first time at a school celebration on the following Independence Day, and thereafter at all patriotic gatherings, becoming popular very rapidly. While still at Andover Smith wrote another hymn that became a great favorite, "The Morning Light is Breaking." He continued to contribute to the American hymnals, irrespective of denominations; and in fact of his 600 poems the great majority are hymns, used widely in this country and even abroad.

Smith's literary contributions in prose brought him little fame. He wrote a *History of Newton, Mass.,* and after traveling extensively with his wife through the European countries and Southern Asia in 1875 and again from 1880 to 1882, produced *Missionary Sketches* and *Rambles in Mission-Fields.* He was also co-editor of *The Psalmist,* an important nineteenth century Baptist hymnal.

Principal Works: *Poetry*—The Psalmist (ed.) 1843; Lyric Gems: A Collection of Original and Select Sacred Poetry, 1844; America, 1879; Poems of Home and Country, 1895. *Biography*—Life of the Rev. Joseph Grafton, 1849. *History*—History of Newton, Mass., 1880; Mythology and Early Greek History: or, Myths and Heroes, 1887. *Miscellaneous*—Rock of Ages, 1870; Missionary Sketches, 1879; Rambles in Mission-Fields, 1883; Poor Boys Who Became Great: or, Stories of Success, 1888; Discourse in Memory of William Hague, 1889.

About: Mason, E. A Monogram on Our National Song; Rowe, H. K. Tercentenary History of Newton; Christian Science Monitor May 15, 1930; Harvard Graduates Magazine March, 1896.

SMITH, SEBA (September 14, 1792-July 28, 1868), political satirist, journalist, editor, and poet, was born at Buckfield, Maine, the second son of Seba Smith and Aphia (Stevens) Smith, both members of Massachusetts pioneer families.

As the father's income as a post-rider was very meager, the boy had to work alternately in a grocery store, on a farm, in a brickyard, and in a cast-iron foundry, while going to school in Bridgton, where the family had moved in 1799. After he had taught, since the age of eighteen, in Bridgton and neighboring towns for several years and had supplemented his education in North Bridgton Academy, a loan from a Portland gentleman enabled him to enter Bowdoin College as a sophomore in 1815. Upon graduation with the highest honors in 1818, he taught again for a year in Portland, where he also wrote several poems that were published in the Portland paper, the *Eastern Argus.* Because of ill-health he went, however, on a journey through New England and the Atlantic States, and also crossed over to Liverpool. On his return at twenty-eight, he became connected with the *Eastern Argus,* first as an editor and then as a joint proprietor.

Shortly after he had settled in newspaper work, he married Elizabeth Oakes Prince [*q.v.*], a woman of beauty, grace, and literary gifts, who became a well-known author and editor of the day under the pen name of "Elizabeth Oaksmith."

In 1826 he sold his share in the *Eastern Argus.* For three years he devoted himself to literary work, and then in 1829 began to publish two non-partisan papers, the *Family Reader,* a weekly, and the Portland *Courier,* the first daily east and north of Boston. The success of the latter was due chiefly to the appearance in it, from 1830, of Smith's series of letters by "Major Jack Downing of Downingville." These satirical comments on political "squabbles and chicanery" in the period of Jacksonian democracy, particularly on the political disputes in the Maine legislature, brought him his first and widest recognition. They were reprinted in papers throughout the country and found many imitators. In 1833 they appeared in book form under the title *Life and Writings of Major Jack Downing of Downingville.* Some of them were republished in 1859 in his book *My Thirty Years Out of the Senate,* which embodies a series of letters started in the *National Intelligencer* in 1847.

Because of losses in land speculation in 1837, he had to sell his interest in the *Courier.* He went South as an agent for a cotton cleaning machine, invented by his brother-in-law. The device was rejected, and in 1839 he, with his wife and four sons, came to New York. At first with the help of his wife's literary work, he made a living as a contributor to a number of leading literary magazines, and from 1843 to 1845 as editor of a New York daily, *American Republican,* and of two weeklies, *Bunker Hill* and the *Rover.* In the latter, tales, sketches, and poems of eminent authors were published. About nine years later, in 1853, he was again editor of the *Budget* for one year, and after that, during 1854-1859, editor of the *United States Magazine,* a monthly, and the *United States Journal,* a bi-monthly. In 1858 he and his family undertook the editing and publishing of *Emerson's United States Magazine* and *Putnam's Monthly,* both combined into one publication. The undertaking failed, and in 1859 he started another magazine *The Great Republic* that lasted only one year. He then retired to Patchogue, Long Island, where he continued his literary work.

SEBA SMITH

His writings comprise not only humorous stories and poems but also some research studies and a volume on *New Elements of Geometry.* Next to his "Downing Letters" his best known work is *Way Down East,* a collection chiefly of realistic tales of New England life.

He is considered the first political satirist, the creator of a new type of humor in American literature and also of the Yankee type in the person of Major Downing. Many of his stories show weakness of construction, but they are realistic, original, and entertaining. His letters, says A. S. Packard, "like all writings that dwell on passing occurrences . . . have lost much of their piquancy by their lapse of time and the remoteness of those exciting scenes amid which they were produced; but there is much in them which is independent of time and circumstances, and they may still be read with pleasure and advantage."

Smith was of a retiring nature, mild and calm, and possessed great modesty and integrity of character. He spent his last years in failing health until a lingering illness brought to an end "his life of toil, not unattended by disappointment and care."

PRINCIPAL WORKS: *Humor*—The Life and Writings of Major Jack Downing of Downingville, 1833; John Smith's Letters With Picters to Match, 1839; May-Day in New York, 1845; My Thirty Years Out of the Senate, 1859. *Poems*—Powhatan: A Metrical Romance, 1841. *Science*—New Elements of Geometry, 1850. *Stories*—'Way Down East: or, Portraitures of Yankee Life, 1854. *Miscellaneous*—Dewdrops of the Nineteenth Century, 1846; Miscellanies, 1846; Speech of John Smith, Esquire: Not Delivered at Smithville, 1864.

ABOUT: Hart, J. S. Manual of American Literature; Packard, A. S. History of Bowdoin College: With Biographical Sketches of its Graduates; Smith, S. Autobiography (in manuscript, Bowdoin College); Tandy, R. J. Crackerbox Philosophers in American Humor and Satire; Trent, W. P. A History of American Literature: 1607-1865; Wyman, M. A. Selections From the Autobiography of Elizabeth Oakes Smith; Wyman, M. A. Two American Pioneers: Seba Smith and Elizabeth Oakes Smith; Pine Tree Magazine November 1906.

SMITH, WILLIAM (September 7, 1727-May 14, 1803), educator, clergyman, and miscellaneous writer, was born in Aberdeen, Scotland, the son of Thomas Smith and Elizabeth (Duncan) Smith. He was educated in the parish schools and the University of Aberdeen, class of 1747, and emigrated to America in 1751 as tutor in a Colonel Martin's family, remaining in that capacity for two years. His publication of *A General Idea of the College of Mirania* in 1753, a comprehensive plan for a college, aroused the interest of Benjamin Franklin and the Rev. Richard Peters, trustees of the Academy and Charitable School, Philadelphia, and he was invited to join that institution. He went to England in the same year, received orders in the Church of England, and on his return to Philadelphia took up his educational work as teacher of logic, rhetoric, and natural and moral philosophy. In 1754 the school received a new charter giving power to confer degrees, and Smith became provost of the College, Academy, and Charitable School of Philadelphia, which soon became under his direction one of the most important educational centers in the country.

The charter of the college was taken away by the legislature of Pennsylvania in 1779 and Smith removed to Chestertown, Md., where he became rector of Chester Parish and established Kent School, which was chartered in 1782 as Washington College, with Smith as president. He was president of every convention of the Episcopal Churches of Maryland during his residence there, and had the chief part in the alteration of the liturgy in 1786. In 1789 the charter of the College in Philadelphia was restored and Smith returned as provost. He spent the latter years of his life at his home at the Falls of the Schuylkill, engaged in secular pursuits, particularly land speculation. He died at the home of his daughter-in-law, in Philadelphia. He had married Rebecca Moore, daughter of Governor Moore in 1758.

Through Dr. Smith's activities and genius as an educator the College of Philadelphia was, even during its formative years, one of the centers of learning in the colonies. His guidance and far-sighted vision were a great factor in the early growth of what is now the University of Pennsylvania. His published works, including articles on political, religious, and educational questions were written with the logic, vigor, and forcefulness characteristic of Smith; and in his encouragement of younger writers such as Francis Hopkinson and Benjamin West he helped to forward American literature.

Principal Works: A General Idea of the College of Mirania, 1753; A Poem on Visiting the Academy of Philadelphia . . . , 1753; A Brief State of the Province of Pennsylvania, 1755; A Brief View of the Conduct of Pennsylvania in 1755, 1756; An Historical Account of the Expedition Against the Ohio Indians in 1764, 1765; Sermon on the Present Situation of American Affairs, 1775; *Attributed Works:* Plain Truth: Addressed to the Inhabitants of America . . . , 1776; Additions to Plain Truth . . . , 1776.

About: Chamberlain, J. L. Universities and Their Sons: University of Pennsylvania; Oberholtzer, E. P. The Literary History of Philadelphia; Perry, W. S. The History of the American Episcopal Church in the United States of America; Richardson, L. N. A History of Early American Magazines, 1741-1789; Smith, H. W. Life and Correspondence of the Reverend William Smith, D.D.; Stillé, C. J. A Memoir of the Reverend William Smith, D.D.

SMITH, WILLIAM (June 25, 1728-December 3, 1793), jurist and historian, was born in New York City, the son of Judge William Smith and Mary (Het) Smith. He attended Yale College, class of 1745, studied law under his father and William Livingston, and was admitted to the bar in 1750. Forming a partnership with Livingston, he soon acquired a reputation for ability and brilliance; they were appointed by the assembly to publish the first digest of the colony statutes. The first volume was completed in 1752 and the second ten years later.

In 1763 Smith became chief justice of the province, and succeeded his father as a member of the council in 1767. At the beginning of the war Smith stood between the two parties, on friendly terms with leaders on both sides, but was trusted wholly by neither Whigs nor Tories. In 1777, having refused to take the oath of allegiance to the state, he was placed on parole at Livingston Manor, and the following year was returned to New York City. He was appointed chief justice of New York in 1779, but never actually served, as the province was under military control until 1783. In that year Smith with his son, William, sailed for England, where he remained for three years before going to Canada to begin his duties as chief justice of the Dominion. Smith was joined in Quebec in 1786 by his wife Janet (Livingston) Smith, whom he had married in 1752. He lived in Quebec until his death.

Smith's literary fame rests chiefly upon his political history published in London in 1757, *The History of the Province of New York,* with its index of religious, legal, and political events of the eighteenth century. Stigmatized as dull, inaccurate, and circumstantial by his enemies, it still has value for students of the period. The unpublished part of the work, in six closely written volumes, gives a complete chronicle of the Revolution and a detailed account of colonial life.

Principal Works: Laws of New York From the Year 1691 to 1751, Inclusive, 1752; A Review of the Military Operations in North America: 1753-1756, 1757; The History of the Province of New York, from the First Discovery to the Year

MDCCXXXII, 1757; Laws of New York: 1752-1762, 1762; The History of the Late Province of New York, 1829.

About: Greene, E. B. & Morris, R. B. A Guide to the Principal Sources for Early American History (1600-1800) in the City of New York; Sabine, L. Biographical Sketches of the Loyalists of the American Revolution; Smith, W. History of the Late Province of New York; Magazine of American History June 1881.

SMYTH, ALBERT HENRY (June 18, 1863-May 4, 1907), educator and editor, was born in Philadelphia, the son of William Clarke and Adelaide (Suplee) Smyth. He was graduated from the Central High School in 1882 and in 1887 received a B. A. degree from Johns Hopkins, after studying and working there as a cataloguer for some years. In 1886 he returned to the Central High School of Philadelphia as professor of English language and literature, and he remained there for the rest of his life, serving after 1893 as head of his department. A man of cultivated tastes and wide interests, he devoted a great deal of time to lecturing outside his school and to writing. An early enthusiasm for Shakespeare led to his editorship of *Shakespeariana* for some years before 1886 and to painstaking researches on texts and translations of Shakespeare's plays. After 1886 he spent his summers abroad, studying in many libraries and gaining many friends and some prestige in scholarly circles. His interest in the American Philosophical Society, to which he was elected in 1887, led him to undertake the publication, in ten volumes, of the *Writings of Benjamin Franklin.* This work, involving long and careful examination of the Franklin papers, letters, and newspapers in the possession of the Society, was certainly the most noteworthy enterprise of Smyth's life. His sudden death in 1907 frustrated his intention to write a life of Franklin, but his excellent edition of Franklin's writings, which began to appear in 1905, was long considered a monument to Smyth's literary skill and discernment.

Principal Works: American Literature, 1889; The Philadelphia Magazines and Their Contributors, 1892; Bayard Taylor, 1896; Edmund Burke's Letter to a Noble Lord (ed.) 1898; Shakespeare's Pericles and Apollonius of Tyre, 1898; Writings of Benjamin Franklin (ed., 10 vols.) 1905-07.

About: Edmonds, F. S. The Early Life of Albert Henry Smyth: 78th Class; Winter, W. Old Friends; Barnwell Bulletin March and October 1934; Book News Monthly July 1907; Proceedings of the American Philosophical Society April 18, 1907; Philadelphia Public Ledger May 5, 1907.

SNELLING, WILLIAM JOSEPH (December 26, 1804-December 24, 1848), satirist and journalist, was born in Boston, the son of Josiah Snelling, an army officer, and Elizabeth (Bell) Snelling. After his mother's untimely death the boy was left to the care of relatives, and sent to school at Medford. In 1818 he was entered at the United States Military Academy, but he did not enjoy the life there, and after two years started Westward toward Fort Snelling, his father's army post on the Mississippi, in what is now Minnesota. Snelling lived an exciting and vagarious life in the Northwest, first among the Dakota Indians, then as a trapper. He married a French girl who died during the following winter; in 1827 he took part in subduing the Winnebago Indian revolt; finally after the death of his father in 1828 he returned to Boston.

Snelling returned to Boston in the rôle of writer. For several years he lived in obscurity, doing ill-paid literary tasks, but in 1831 he suddenly turned on his contemporary poetasters with a satire, *Truth: A New Year's Gift for Scribblers,* which caused some confusion in literary Boston at the time and which remains a notable contribution to American ironic verse. He subsequently became one of the most powerful and effective reformers among the Boston journalists, a redoubtable opponent, and a man with many enemies. As a result of his public controversies and private misfortunes, he turned to drinking, which brought him eventually to the House of Correction. Four months of confinement there ruined his health, but he emerged to triumph once more over his enemies, as editor of the *Boston Herald* in 1847. Snelling's fame rests chiefly upon his *Truth* and other satires, though his *Tales of the Northwest* still retain some interest. He was a brilliant writer, but he had not the equilibrium or the perseverance to produce any very great work.

Principal Works: Tales of the Northwest: or, Sketches of Indian Life and Character, 1830; Truth: A New Year's Gift for Scribblers, 1831; Exposé of the Vice of Gaming as It Lately Existed in New England, 1833; The Rat-Trap: or, Cogitations of a Convict in the House of Correction, 1837.

About: Perry, E. A. The Boston Herald and Its History; Woodall, A. E. William Joseph Snelling; Minnesota History June 1928; Boston Transcript December 26, 1848.

SNOW, ELIZA ROXEY (January 21, 1804-December 5, 1887), Mormon poet and hymnologist, was born in Becket, Berkshire County, Mass. When she was very young her parents, Oliver and Rosetta L. (Pettibone) Snow, moved to Mantua, Ohio, and there she received what education the frontier town could give her. In 1835, with hemother and sister, she joined the new Mormon Church, and during the next ten years followed the sect from place to place, finally arriving in Utah in 1847 under the leadership of Brigham Young. In 1855 Eliza Snow undertook the management of the women's work in the Mormon Endowment House, and in 1866 became president of the general church organization of the Women's Relief Society, continuing in this capacity until her death twenty years later.

While still a girl Eliza Snow showed some poetic talent and, as soon as she became a Mormon, began writing poems to record significant events and phases in the Church's history. These works, published under the title *Poems: Religious, Historical, and Political,* were extremely valuable to the Church in that they kept the Mormons aware of their traditions. She likewise contributed much to the Mormon hymnal, the most notable of her hymns being "O My Father, Thou that Dwellest." In 1842 she secretly married the Mormon prophet Joseph Smith, and after his death she became one of Brigham Young's wives.

Principal Works: Poems: Religious, Historical, and Political, 1856, 1877; Biography and Family Record of Lorenzo Snow, 1884.

About: Jenson, A. Latter-Day Saint Biographical Encyclopedia; Deseret Evening News December 5, 1887.

SOLEY, JAMES RUSSELL (October 1, 1850-September 11, 1911), educator, lawyer, and naval writer, was born in Roxbury, Mass., the son of James and Elvira Codman (Dégen) Soley. He was a descendant through both of his parents of Judge James Russell, the members of whose family had been prominent in the state as early as 1640. He attended Roxbury Latin School and Harvard College, graduating in 1870; became professor of ethics and English at the United States Naval Academy in 1871; and two years later was made head of the department of English studies, history, and law, a post which he held nine years. He was commissioned professor with the rank of lieutenant in the United States Navy in 1876, the year following his marriage to Mary Woolsey Howland, and was on special duty at the Paris exposition in 1878. He examined the systems of education in European naval colleges making an extensive report on his return. In 1882 Soley was transferred to Washington where he collected and arranged the Navy Department library, and superintended the publication of the naval records of the Civil War. He lectured on international law at the Naval War College from 1885 to 1889 and delivered a series of lectures at the Lowell Institute, Boston.

After resigning his commission in 1890, he was appointed Assistant Secretary of the Navy, filling the office until his resignation in 1893. That same year he moved to New York where he practiced law until his death. In 1899 Soley was one of the counsel for Venezuela before the international tribunal of arbitration in Paris. He wrote many books and articles, most of them on naval subjects, among them *The Blockade and the Cruisers* and a history of the Naval Academy. His works written from the viewpoint of an expert and specialist in naval procedure were an important addition to maritime knowledge.

Principal Works: Historical Sketch of the United States Naval Academy, 1876; Autobiography of Commodore Charles Morris, 1880; The Blockade and the Cruisers, 1883; The Rescue of Greely, 1885; The Boys of 1812, 1887; Sailor Boys of '61, 1888; Admiral Porter, 1903.

About: Tenth Report of the Class of 1870 of Harvard College, 1920; Army and Navy Journal September 16, 1911; New York Tribune September 12, 1911.

SOPHOCLES, EVANGELINUS APOSTOLIDES (c. 1805-December 17, 1883), classicist and neo-Hellenist, was born in Tsangarada, Thessaly. The exact date of his birth, and even the original form of his name are unknown. He was educated in Cairo at the monastery of St. Catherine and upon his return to Greece was persuaded by an American missionary, the Rev. Josiah Brewer, to emigrate to America. There he studied at Monson Academy in Massachusetts and entered Amherst College, soon withdrawing, however, because of ill health. He taught for some time at Mount Pleasant Classical Institute in Amherst, then at Hartford, Conn., and in 1842 became tutor in Greek at Harvard. In 1859 he was appointed assistant professor and a year later was made professor of ancient, Byzantine and modern Greek. His teaching was remarkably clear, considering his academic background, and he came to be well loved and respected at Harvard. During these years he published several textbooks on Greek, including *A Romaic Grammar* which correctly traced modern Greek to Byzantine, rather than to Aeolic-Doric. In 1848 he published a *History of the Greek Alphabet,* a work far in advance of its time. His greatest contribution, published in 1870, was a *Greek Lexicon of the Roman and Byzantine Periods.* He was of small stature, with a leonine head covered with a mass of white hair and with eyes that gleamed piercingly. Although his appearance and manner awed strangers, he was gentle and full of humor to those who knew him well. His thrifty habits enabled him to leave large sums of money to his friends, his native village, and to the Harvard Library.

PRINCIPAL WORKS: A Greek Grammar for the Use of Learners, 1835; First Lessons in Greek, 1839; Greek Exercises, 1841; A Romaic Grammar, 1842; Greek Lessons, 1843; A Catalogue of Greek Verbs, 1844; History of the Greek Alphabet, 1848; Greek Lexicon of the Roman and Byzantine Periods, 1870.

ABOUT: Hesseling, D. C. Evangelinos Apostolidis Sophoclis: Néo-Helléniste; Nation January 3, 1884; Boston Daily Advertiser and Boston Transcript December 18, 1883.

"SOULT, MARSHALL." See KNAPP, SAMUEL LORENZO

SOUTHWORTH, EMMA DOROTHY ELIZA (NEVITTE) (December 26, 1819-June 30, 1899), popular novelist, was born in Washington, D.C. Her father, Charles LeCompte Nevitte, a merchant of Alexandria, Va., died when she was an infant; and her mother, Susanna George (Wailes) Nevitte, later married Joshua L. Henshaw of Boston. Henshaw started a school in Boston around 1829, and Emma and her sister were educated there.

In 1840 Emma married Frederick H. Southworth of Utica, N.Y., and they settled on a farm near Prairie du Chien, Wisconsin. Within three years she returned to Washington, however, accompanied by an infant son, but without her husband, who is said to have deserted her. A daughter was born immediately after her return to Washington, and for some years Mrs. Southworth suffered from poor health and financial troubles.

For about six years she taught in the Washington public schools and supplemented her income by writing a novel, *Retribution,* which the *National Era* published in 1847. It achieved enough popular success to warrant Mrs. Southworth's devoting all her time to writing after 1849, and during the rest of her life she found time to write some sixty novels. Many of these, like the famous *Hidden Hand,* were written as serials for the New York *Ledger,* and they suffer from the periodic catastrophes, the sensational plots, and the other ailments that usually beset serials. *The Hidden Hand* was dramatized in England and played by John Wilkes Booth. Mrs. Southworth's audience of readers was usually confined to women, and the serials depended largely on sentimentality for this success.

Collection of Frederick H. Meserve

MRS. E. D. E. N. SOUTHWORTH

After 1862 Mrs. Southworth lived in Georgetown, Washington, D.C., receiving the adulation of visitors. Her comfortable home became for a time one of the literary *salons* of Washington, although Mrs. Southworth herself laid no claim to literary merit and admitted freely that her novels were potboilers.

Whittier's famous ballad "Barbara Frietchie" was the result of a suggestion from Mrs. Southworth, and the Quaker poet acknowledged to her that "If it is good for anything, thee deserve all the credit for it."

PRINCIPAL WORKS: Retribution, 1849; The Curse of the Clifton, 1852; The Missing Bride, 1855; The Hidden Hand, 1859; The Fatal Marriage, 1869; The Maiden Widow, 1870; Self-Raised, 1876.

ABOUT: Southworth, E. D. E. N. The Haunted Homestead; Bookman October 1916; National Magazine May 1905; Evening Star (Washington) September 6, 1890 and July 1, 1899; Washington Post December 2, 1894.

SPALDING, JAMES REED (November 15, 1821-October 10, 1872), journalist, was born at Montpelier, Vt., the son of Dr. James Spalding, an eminent physician, and Eliza (Reed) Spalding. He was graduated in 1840 from the University of Vermont, and began to study law, working at the same time in Georgia as a private tutor. Although Spalding was admitted to the bar and formed a law partnership with Joseph Prentice of Montpelier, he showed little inclination to this profession; he soon gave it up entirely and went to Europe.

During several years of travel and study in Europe and the East Spalding wrote letters to the New York *Courier and Enquirer*—letters which attracted unusual attention for their graceful style and comprehensive grasp on European politics. On his return in 1850 he joined the staff of this paper and built up an enviable reputation as a fearless, independent commentator on public issues and men. He was one of the chief founders and proprietors of the *World* in 1860, and for two years acted as editor-in-chief of that journal. Displaced in 1862 when financial troubles caused the reorganization of the *World,* he joined the editorial staff of the New York *Times,* then conducted by his old friend Henry J. Raymond. During Raymond's absence in Washington, Spalding took complete charge of the *Times;* in fact he seemed to have a promising future before him in journalism until a sudden paralytic stroke forced his retirement from active work. He died at Dover, N.H., survived by his wife Mary (Atwater) Spalding, whom he had married in 1865, and one daughter.

At his death, the *Times* expressed regret for what it termed Spalding's "incomplete life." "He accomplished little in journalism and nothing in literature," the *Times* asserted; yet, "with his ability, his judgment, his knowledge, his power with the pen, and his fearlessness, had fortune favored him, and had his health not broken down, he would have stood foremost among the honorable journalists of the day." Spalding's associates on the *World* seem to have felt that he was not truly a journalist, however. A man of reflective mind, interested in the larger moral questions, he could not produce copy fast enough; he wrote "on the topics of the time as distinguished from the topic of the day."

Principal Works: *Orations*—Our Lesson and Our Work, 1854; True Idea of Female Education, 1855.

About: University of Vermont; Obituary Record, No. 1 (1895); New York Times, New York World October 12, 1872.

Collection of Frederick H. Meserve
JARED SPARKS

SPARKS, JARED (May 10, 1789-March 14, 1866), biographer, educator, and historian, was the illegitimate son of Elinor or Eleanor Orcutt. His father may or may not have been Joseph Sparks, a farmer whom his mother married the December following his birth, and whose name he took. His mother was a natural student, his maternal grandmother a "poet and local prophetess"; his literary talent certainly came from that side of his family. At five he was taken from his birthplace, Willington, Conn., and became the little slave of a shiftless uncle at Camden, N.Y. Released at sixteen, he returned to his mother. In Willington he was a journeyman carpenter by summer, a teacher in winter; at twenty he studied Latin and mathematics with the local minister, secured a scholarship to Phillips Exeter Academy, and finally entered Harvard. Part of his way was earned by acting as tutor in Maryland, where he served against the British in the War of 1812. He was graduated from Harvard in 1815, and though he wanted to be an African explorer, he became a tutor in natural philosophy and a divinity student. For a short time he edited the *North American Review.* He received his M.A. in 1815, and having been converted from Congregationalism, he was ordained as pastor of the Unitarian church in Baltimore in 1819. From 1821 to 1823 he was chaplain of the House of Representatives, and in the same years he edited the *Unitarian Miscellany.* He resigned in 1823 and returned to New England, the first of its writers to be wholly free from the provincial viewpoint.

Sparks bought the *North American Review,* and edited it brilliantly to 1829, when he sold it at a 100 per cent profit. The next year he founded the *American Almanac.* In 1832 he married Frances Anne Allen, who died in 1835; in 1839 he married Mary Crowninshield Silsbee, an heiress and daughter of a senator, by whom he had one son and three daughters. The remainder of his life, which was spent in Cambridge except for one European trip, was given over to historical research and writing, and to Harvard. In 1838 he was made McLean professor of ancient and modern history at Harvard, the first professor of secular history in the United States, its "patriarch." In 1849 he became president of Harvard, but though he was a liberal as a professor, as president he was an extreme reactionary, disliked and unhappy. He resigned in 1853. At seventy-seven he died of pneumonia, in Cambridge.

Sparks was a handsome, kindly, simple man, gentle and winning and personally beloved. His reputation as an historian rests on his discovery and publication of the private papers of Washington, Franklin, and Gouverneur Morris, priceless material which he preserved for the use of later workers. But he was incredibly careless with these papers, giving them away to autograph collectors, "embellishing" them, altering them as he pleased, bowdlerizing them, and smoothing them off to conceal the human nature of the writers. Formal dignity and "purity" were his aim, and if they were not in the manuscripts he put them there. Hence his work, though of value, was largely negated and had to be done over. However, had it not been for his keen interest in the history of the Revolutionary period, our chief source documents would probably long ago have disappeared forever.

Principal Works: Life of John Ledyard, 1828; The Diplomatic Correspondence of the American Revolution, 1829-30; Life of Gouverneur Morris, 1832; The Writings of George Washington, 1834-37 (biography issued separately, 1839); The Works of Benjamin Franklin, 1836-40; Correspondence of the American Revolution, 1853.

About: Adams, H. B. Life and Writings of Jared Sparks; Bassett, J. S. The Middle Group of American Historians; Brooks, Van W. The Flowering of New England; Winsor, J. Narrative and Critical History of America.

SPOFFORD, HARRIET ELIZABETH (PRESCOTT) (April 3, 1835-August 14, 1921), poet and writer of romantic tales was born in Calais, Maine, the daughter of Joseph Newmarch Prescott, a merchant who was descended from a very early Massachusetts settler, and Sarah Jane (Bridges) Prescott. With her father's departure for the West, Newburyport, Mass., became her home; after three years at the Putnam Free School there, she enjoyed a brief attendance at the Pinkerton Academy in Derry, N.H. Joseph Prescott's financial ventures were failures and he returned East broken in health. Harriet, on the strength of the encouragement which Thomas Wentworth Higginson had given her when she was still a student in Newburyport, assumed a part of the domestic burden by sending small-pay contributions to newspapers and periodicals. In February 1859, the *Atlantic Monthly* only a little more than a year old but already in the sure hands of the New England intellectual aristocracy, side-stepped precedent and published her romantically frothy tale, "In a Cellar." (She was not a little conscience-stricken after accepting the one hundred and five dollars!) Entirely out of her imagination she had written some nice "descriptions" of Parisian interiors, etc.; and, in all, the piece anticipated her literary arrival. During the next few years came three volumes of rather florid stories.

In December 1865 she was married to Richard Smith Spofford, Jr., a very capable Newburyport lawyer, and for a while they lived in Washington; but not until many years later did she publish her reminiscent *Old Washington.* She made two journeys abroad, and her later years were passed in the haunts of the five-acre Deer Island, lying in the Merrimac not far from Newburyport.

Her contributions, during the 'seventies, 'eighties, and 'nineties, to outstanding literary and household journals included: serialized romances such as *The Marquis of Carabas;* critical pieces which were engulfed in superlatives and were decidedly "of the heart"; an abundance of tales afterward published under the titles *A Scarlet Poppy and Other Stories* and *Old Madame and Other Tragedies;* familiar essays, of which *Four Days of God* is representative; innumerable poems later republished in *Titian's Garden and Other Poems;* and a series of rather self-indulgent speculations on domestic

Collection of Frederick H. Meserve
HARRIET PRESCOTT SPOFFORD

assets and liabilities which were incorporated into *House and Hearth.* Besides unearthing a portion of the romantic past in *New-England Legends* she capitalized on some of the best of fictional ingredients in *The Elder's People,* published in the year before her death. Neither in poetry nor in prose was she more than a minor writer, but for a generation or more her name was virtually a household word.

Principal Works: Sir Rohan's Ghost, 1860; The Amber Gods and Other Stories, 1863; Azarian: an Episode, 1864; New England Legends, 1871; Art Decoration Applied to Furniture, 1878; In Titian's Garden and Other Poems, 1897; Old Madame and Other Tragedies, 1900; Old Washington, 1906; A Little Book of Friends, 1916.

About: Halbeisen, E. K. Harriet Prescott Spofford; Prescott, W. The Prescott Memorial: North American Review January 1865; Atlantic Monthly August 1897; Boston Transcript August 15, 1921.

SPRAGUE, ACHSA W. (c. 1828-July 6, 1862), spiritualist and poet, was born in Plymouth Notch, Vt., a daughter of Charles and Betsy Sprague. She began teaching in a country school at the early age of twelve, but after about eight years of teaching she became crippled by a scrofulous disease of the joints. She was an invalid for about six years but by 1854 she was apparently well again, cured, as she believed, by supernatural powers. After her recovery she became a medium and began to lecture extensively on spiritualism. She experimented with magnetism, hypnotism, séances, and eventually became an advocate of mental healing. She wrote voluminously, and at a tremendous rate of speed, often claiming that she was only the "mouthpiece" of a supernatural agency. Her poems expressed either great mental anguish or longing for the spiritual regeneration of mankind in a new economic order. Few of her works have been published, but her unpublished writings include essays, journals and a play, as well as a long autobiographical poem which she composed in six days. She was a woman of great charm and at the same time a militant reformer, opposed to slavery, an early advocate of women's rights and better prisons. In 1861 she became affected with her old disease again and died a year later.

Principal Works: I Still Live: A Poem for the Times, 1862; The Poet and Other Poems, 1864.

About: Smith, A. Achsa W. Sprague and Mary Clarke's Experiences in the First Ten Spheres of Spirit Life; Sprague, A. W. The Poet and Other Poems (see Biographical Sketch); Drift-Wind November 1927; National Spiritualist February 1, 1932; Rutland Weekly Herald July 24, 1862.

SPRAGUE, CHARLES (October 26, 1791 -January 22, 1875, banker and poet, was born in Boston, Mass., the son of Samuel Sprague of Hingham, who participated in the Boston Tea Party. Charles received a brief schooling at the Franklin School of Boston, and at the age of ten lost the use of his left eye in an accident. Three years later he was apprenticed to a firm of dry goods importers and by his nineteenth year he had formed a partnership with a grocer. After a subsequent business venture, he became a teller in the State Bank in 1819, and when the Globe Bank was formed in 1824 became cashier, serving for forty years as a highly respected Boston business man.

What leisure he had was devoted to reading and writing poetry, and he became well known in Boston literary circles, attracting special attention by winning prizes for each of five prologues in heroic couplet for the opening of new playhouses in New York, Philadelphia, and other cities. Over-enthusiastic critics sometimes bracketed him with William Cullen Bryant and Fitz-Greene Halleck, and one, Edwin P. Whipple, even went so far as to say, "His prologues are the best which have been written since the time of Pope. His 'Shakespeare Ode' has hardly been exceeded by anything in the same manner since Gray's 'Progress of Poesy.'" In 1829 he delivered before the Phi Beta Kappa society of Harvard his poem "Curiosity," which considerably advanced his reputation. His domestic pieces—"The Brothers" and "The Family Meeting"—definitely established him as a sincere poet ably fitted to interpret the homely American scene. His writings were collected in 1841 and brought out again in a revised edition in 1850.

Ill health troubled him in his latter years, which were spent quietly at home in the gracious company of his wife, Elizabeth Rand, whom he married in 1814. One of his four children, Charles James Sprague, inherited his father's poetic gift.

Principal Works: Prose and Poetical Writings, 1841, 1850, 1870.

About: Loring, J. S. The Hundred Boston Orators; Quincy, E. Memoir of Charles Sprague; Sprague, C. J. The Poetical and Prose Writings of Charles Sprague; Waterson, R. C. Remarks Upon the Life and Writings of Charles Sprague; Whipple, E. P. Essays and Reviews; Boston Transcript January 22, 1875.

"SPRIGGINS, WIDOW." See WHITCHER, FRANCES MIRIAM (BERRY)

"SQUIBOB." See DERBY, GEORGE HORATIO

SQUIER, EPHRAIM GEORGE (June 17, 1821-April 17, 1888), writer on archaeological subjects, journalist, and diplomat, was born in Bethlehem, N.Y., the son of Joel Squier, a Methodist minister, and Catharine (Kilmer or Külmer) Squier. Although he attended the local school, he gained his education chiefly through reading and study in leisure hours from farm-work. After a period of school teaching and the pursuit of a civil engineering course, he began writing for Albany newspapers, and established the short-lived *Poet's Magazine* in the same city in 1842. He was editor of the *Evening Journal* at Hartford, Conn., during 1844-5, and through his powerful pen was largely responsible for the state's vote in favor of Henry Clay for President. When Clay was defeated, Squier moved to Chillicothe, Ohio, where he became prominent as a journalist and politician, and served as clerk of the Ohio House of Representatives in 1847 and 1848.

During the next two years he went to Central America as chargé d'affaires, and later became secretary of the Honduras Interoceanic Railway Co. After 1860 he joined the publishing house of Frank Leslie, and served as chief editor until he went to Peru as United States commissioner between 1863 and 1865. On his return he became re-associated with the Leslie firm for a number of years until a complete mental and physical breakdown necessitated his resignation. His wife, Miriam Florence Folline [*q.v.*], of New Orleans, whom he married in 1858, divorced him in 1873 and shortly afterward married Leslie.

Diplomatic in manner, of distinguished appearance, with a ready wit, Squier became widely known as an archaeologist, as the result of studies which he began in Ohio. With Edwin Hamilton Davis, he examined the remains of the Mound Builders in that state and published an account of their observations in the first publication of the Smithsonian Institution. Further research in New York state led to another article in the same periodical.

Squier's visits to Central America resulted in a number of definitive archaeological and ethnological books, among them *Peru: Incidents of Travel and Exploration in the Land of the Incas.* He died in Brooklyn. N.Y., after a protracted illness.

Principal Works: Ancient Monuments of the Mississippi Valley (Smithsonian Contributions to Knowledge: No. 1, 1847); Aboriginal Monuments of the State of New York, 1851; Nicaragua: Its People, Scenery, Monuments and the Proposed Interoceanic Canal, 1852; The States of Central America, 1858; Peru: Incidents of Travel and Exploration in the Land of the Incas, 1877.

About: Seitz, D. C. Letters From Francis Parkman to E. G. Squier; Travis, I. D. The History of the Clayton-Bulwer Treaty; New York Times April 18, 1888.

"SQUIER, MIRIAM F." See LESLIE, MIRIAM FLORENCE (FOLLINE)

"STACY, JOEL." See DODGE, MARY (MAPES)

STANSBURY, JOSEPH (January 9, 1742?-November 9, 1809), Loyalist poet, was born in London, the son of Samuel and Sarah (Porter) Stansbury. He attended St. Paul's School until 1753, when he was withdrawn and apprenticed to a trade. Married in 1765 to Sarah Ogier, the young couple emigrated to America, where Stansbury established himself as a china merchant in Philadelphia. Here, by reason of his integrity and charm he soon became a favorite in both business and social circles. During the Revolution he satirized the colonial cause in clever verse, and during the British occupation of Philadelphia he held several offices under the crown. Apparently pacifistic by nature, he paid for substitute soldiers in the militia and signed the oath of allegiance and abjuration. He was later discovered to be a secret agent for the British, having been the courier for Benedict Arnold's messages to enemy headquarters.

He attempted to settle in Philadelphia after the close of the war, but was ousted by the persons whom he had satirized in his verses. For the next four years he traveled in Nova Scotia and England, but returned to Philadelphia in 1786. In 1793 he removed to New York, where he was for many years secretary of the United Insurance Company. He died in that city.

Stansbury's satirical political verses, edited in 1860 by Winthrop Sargent, were acclaimed as witty commentaries on a turbulent period of American history.

Principal Works: The Loyal Verses of Joseph Stansbury and Dr. Jonathan Odell (ed. by Winthrop Sargent) 1860.

About: Decker, M. Benedict Arnold; Gardiner, R. B. The Admission Registers of St. Paul's School From 1748 to 1876; Tyler, M. C. The Literary History of the American Revolution; Wines, F. H. The Descendants of John Stansbury of Leominster; New York Gazette and General Advertiser November 11, 1809.

STANTON, ELIZABETH (CADY) (November 12, 1815-October 26, 1902), reformer, was born in Johnstown, N.Y., the daughter of Judge Daniel Cady and Margaret (Livingston) Cady, daughter of a colonel on

Washington's staff. She seems to have been born a feminist, her rebellion aroused early by her parents' sternness and her own observation of the disabilities of the women who were her father's clients.

When her only brother died, she was allowed to study Latin, Greek and mathematics in his stead at the Johnstown Academy, the only girl there; but even though she won a prize in Greek she could not go to college, but had to spend two miserable years at Emma Willard's Seminary in Troy. She then studied law in her father's office, but could not take the bar examinations or practice. In 1840 she married Henry Brewster Stanton, a lawyer and Abolitionist. She went with him on their honeymoon to the Anti-Slavery Conference in London where Lucretia Mott, a delegate, was not allowed to speak.

That completed her education in feminism; in 1846 the Stantons moved from Boston to Seneca Falls, N.Y., and there, in 1848, she and Mrs. Mott called the first women's rights convention. Mrs. Stanton was the only delegate to demand equal suffrage. In the following years she wrote and spoke incessantly for suffrage, married women's property rights, and liberalized divorce. In 1851 she met Susan B. Anthony, with whom she was closely associated till her death.

In 1868 she ran for Congress, though she could not vote, and received just 24 votes. In 1869 she became president of the newly organized National Woman's Suffrage Association, and remained its president until 1890, when it became part of the National American Woman's Suffrage Association; she headed the new organization for three years more, then was honorary president until she died. Every year she spoke before Congressional committees, and for eight months annually she toured the country as a lecturer. From 1867 to 1870 she edited, with Parker Pillsbury and Miss Anthony, a suffrage weekly called *Revolution.* She wrote much for the *North American Review* and other magazines. With all this, she bore and reared five sons and two daughters, all of whom rose to distinction in some profession. She died in New York. A Rationalist, she arranged to have her funeral conducted by a Rationalist woman speaker.

Mrs. Stanton possessed charm, humor, intelligence, and courage; her style as both writer and speaker was persuasive, ingratiating, and graceful. For half a century she was the soul and heart of the woman's movement in America.

Principal Works: History of Woman Suffrage (with S. B. Anthony & M. J. Gage) 1881-86; The Woman's Bible (with others) 1895-98; Eighty Years and More, 1898.

About: Adams, E. C. Heroines of Modern Progress; Stanton, E. C. Eighty Years and More; Stanton, T. & Blatch, H. S. Elizabeth Cady Stanton as Revealed in Her Letters, Dairy, and Reminiscences; North American Review November 1915; New York Times October 27, 1902.

Collection of Frederick H. Meserve

ELIZABETH CADY STANTON

STEDMAN, EDMUND CLARENCE (October 8, 1833-January 18, 1908), banker, poet, and critic, was born in Hartford, Conn., the son of Major Edmund Burke Stedman and Elizabeth Clementine (Dodge) Stedman. His father died when he was two, and his mother remarried, becoming known as a poet and novelist under her new name of Elizabeth Kinney [*q.v.*]. The child was reared by his maternal grandfather in Plainfield, N.J., until 1839, then sent to his great uncle, a severe Puritanical lawyer in Norwich, Conn. There he attended the "Old Academy" and entered Yale in 1849, the youngest in his class. He was a troublesome student, who won poetry prizes but was suspended in his sophomore year for inattention to his studies. Instead of making up his work, he and another student started to tour New England as "traveling actors" (Stedman posing as an actress!), whereupon he was expelled from Yale. In 1871 he was restored to his class and given an honorary M.A.

After reading law for a while with his great uncle, in 1852 he bought the Norwich *Tribune* with Charles B. Platt. Both partners fell in love with Laura Hyde Woodworth, and wrote her a joint proposal, giving her her choice. She chose Stedman, and they were married in 1853; they had one son. The next year he bought the *Mountain County Herald,* of Winsted, Conn., with another partner, and edited it for a year, when he went to New York. After a year as partner in a clockmaking firm, and another in a Fourierist "Unitary Home" (one of the many experiments of the time in "Socialism in action"), Stedman suddenly found himself famous through a satirical poem in the New York *Tribune.* Others followed, and he became one of the city's literary coterie. In 1860 he joined the staff of the *World,* for which he was Washington correspondent 1861-63, resigning to work in the U.S. attorney-general's office. In 1864 he returned to New York and after a short time with a banking firm, opened his own brokerage office. For the rest of his life he was known as the "banker poet," and was equally successful in both departments.

Stedman lived in Bronxville, in an artists' colony, with a summer home in New Hampshire, giving his days to banking and his evenings to literature. With G. E. Woodberry he edited Poe; with Ellen M. Hutchinson he prepared a *Library of American Literature;* he edited Landor (with Thomas Bailey Aldrich), Austin Dobson, a Victorian and an American anthology of poetry, and a history of the New York Stock Exchange. Meanwhile his own volumes of poems and critical essays appeared regularly. A generous friend to all authors in need, he was a founder of the Authors' Club, president of the American Copyright League of the National Institute of Arts and Letters, and of the New England Society. Honorary degrees came to him from Yale, Dartmouth, Columbia. The beautifully dressed little man with delicate features and a silky beard that "parted in the middle" was the center of every literary gathering in and around New York. For many readers he was the touchstone of literary taste.

Yet his influence, though he was a conscientious scholar, was bad; his viewpoint was narrow and parochial, his literary enthusiasm stopped with Tennyson. His poems, though he had some gifts as a balladist, were "refined" and imitative. "Pan in Wall Street," the best known of them, is in its title a sort of epitome and summing up of the man himself. In one damning word, he was always "correct." American literature has gone beyond him and forgotten him. Yet there was a sparkle left in him of the rebellious youngster, a flush of the romantic youth; in occasional felicitious lines they still survive. He himself was a kindly, amiable, open-handed man; he could see no incongruity between a seat on the Stock Exchange and a seat on Parnassus—and surely there are worse avocations for a broker than the writing of verses and the editing of better poets than himself.

EDMUND CLARENCE STEDMAN

PRINCIPAL WORKS: *Poetry*—Poems Lyrical and Idyllic, 1860; Alice of Monmouth: An Idyl of the Great War, 1864; The Blameless Prince and Other Poems, 1869; Poetical Works, 1875; Hawthorne and Other Poems, 1877; Lyrics and Idyls: With Other Poems, 1879; Poems Now First Collected, 1894; Mater Corkonata, 1900. *Prose*—Victorian Poets, 1875; Poets of America, 1885; The Nature and Elements of Poetry, 1892.

ABOUT: Hay, J. Addresses; Stedman. L. & Gould, G. M. Life and Letters of Edmund Clarence Stedman; Atlantic March 1908; Bookman March 1908; Current Literature March 1908; Independent January 30, 1908; Munsey's Magazine March 1899; New York Times January 19, 1908.

STEENDAM, JACOB (1616?-1672), sometimes called "the first American poet," was born in Holland, probably in Amsterdam. He never wrote in any language but Dutch, or knew any other; but he is a part of American literature, for he was the first poet of New Amsterdam, which later became New York. Before he came to America, he had been for fifteen years in the service of the West India Company, for some time after 1641 on the coast of Guinea, in Africa. He seems, however, to have come to New Netherlands on his own initiative, as a merchant and trader, in 1650. He had paused in Holland en route and married Sara de Rosschou, by whom he had one daughter.

From an old print

JACOB STEENDAM

Steendam bought "plantations" on Long Island and houses on what are now Broadway and Pearl Street, New York. In 1660 he petitioned the authorities for permission to engage in the slave trade. In 1662 he returned to Holland, and though he retained his American property for some years, he never saw it again. Instead, in 1666 he went to Batavia, Java, in the capacity of "orphan master" and "comforter of the sick," which rather vague occupation he seems to have carried on in New Amsterdam as well. Apparently he died there; the date is not certain, but by 1673 he and his wife were both dead, and his daughter and her future husband were appointed to his position.

Steendam's writing was purely avocational. His first poems were published in Holland on his return from Africa, in two volumes. It is his second and third publications which are of interest to American readers. The former was a "complaint" of New Netherlands to its mother-country, asking for more consideration and better treatment (a plea which, if heeded, might have made the imminent English conquest less easy); the latter, an extravagant paean of praise of his new home, which he lauded as an earthly Paradise. Indeed, all Steendam's poems are characterized chiefly by extravagance and verbosity, his religious poems are sickeningly pious, and his love poems cloyingly sweet. He wrote always under the pseudonym of "Noch Vaster"—"even firmer"—a pun on his name, which means "stone dam." He was not much of a poet, except in volume of verse; but he was undoubtedly the first to sing the praises of New York City.

PRINCIPAL WORKS: Den Distelvink (The Goldfinch) 1649-50; Klacht van Nieuw Nederlandt tot Haar Moeder (Complaint of New Netherlands to Her Mother) 1659; 'T Lof van Nieuw Nederlandt (Praise of New Netherlands) 1660; Zeede-Zanger voor de Batavische Jonkheyt (Moral Songs for Batavian Youth) 1667.

ABOUT: Andrew, W. E. Jan Steendam; Murphy, H. C. Jacob Steendam: Noch Vaster; Bookman July 1904.

STERLING, JAMES (1701?-November 10, 1763), Anglican clergyman, poet, and playwright, was born at Dowrass, Kings County, Ireland, the son of James Sterling. He entered Trinity College, Dublin, and was graduated in 1720, receiving his B.A., and attaining his M.A. thirteen years later. Sterling's first play, *The Rival Generals,* was published in London in 1722 but failed to achieve production. In 1728 he issued a version of *The Loves of Hero and Leander,* from the Greek of Musaeus, but this and other poems written at the same period were not well received. *The Parricide,* his second play, was produced at Goodman's Fields in 1735 and was also unsuccessful, lasting but five performances. Sterling's journalism and pamphleteering seems likewise to have created little stir. About 1733 he was ordained and became a regimental chaplain.

He migrated to Maryland, probably in 1737, and officiated as rector of various parishes until his death. In 1752, he was appointed collector of customs at Chester, a post which Sterling himself had suggested to the treasury, and which he was politically strong enough to hold against the assaults of the Governor, the Maryland customs officials, and a group of London merchants in the Maryland trade who resented his interference.

Sterling was married three times, first to a Dublin actress, who died about 1733. His second wife was Rebecca (Hynson) Holt, a wealthy widow, whom he married in 1743; Mary Smith became his third wife in 1749.

Sterling's works during his latter years in America were more appreciated than his early efforts. His patriotic, inspirational sermon against French interests in America, *Zeal against the Enemies of Our Country Pathetically Recommended,* and a few later poems gave him a certain prestige among his colleagues but did not long outlive him.

PRINCIPAL WORKS: *Plays*—Rival Generals, 1722; The Parricide, 1736. *Poems*—The Loves of Hero and Leander, 1728; The Poetical Works of the Rev. James Sterling, 1734; An Epistle to the Hon.

Arthur Dodds, 1752; Zeal Against the Enemies of Our Country Pathetically Recommended, 1755.

ABOUT: Wroyh, L. C. James Sterling (in American Antiquarian Society Proclamation: April 1931; Burtchaell, G. D. & Sadleir, T. U. Alumni Dublinenses.

STILES, EZRA (November 29, 1727-May 12, 1795), historian and miscellaneous writer, was born in New Haven, Conn., the son of Isaac Stiles, a Congregational minister, and Kezia (Taylor) Stiles, who died when the child was five days old. The boy was always a student and was ready for Yale at twelve, but did not enter until 1742, receiving his B.A. in 1746. He then studied theology and was licensed to preach in 1749, but experiencing some religious doubts, he decided to study law instead of entering the ministry. Meanwhile he was acting as a tutor at Yale. He was admitted to the bar in 1753, and after two years of practice, his religious faith having been restored, he was ordained and became a minister of the Second Congregational Church in Newport. In 1757 he married Elizabeth Hubbard; she died in 1775, leaving two sons and six daughters, and in 1782 he married Mrs. Mary (Cranston) Checkley.

Stiles remained in Newport until the Revolution, of which he was an ardent partisan, practically evacuated the town; in 1776 he went to Bristol, then to Dighton, Mass., and the next year became minister of the First Church of Portsmouth, N.H. At Newport he had served as librarian of the Redwood Library and had built up a reputation as "the most learned man in America." A friend of Franklin's, an honorary D.D. from Edinburgh, a founder of Rhode Island College (Brown University), a member of the American Philosophical Society and later its councilor, the broad-minded friend of every religious denomination, including the Catholics and the Jews, a man who did original work in chemistry and astronomy, experimented in silk culture, and mastered several Oriental languages and French when over forty, Stiles was undoubtedly in advance of his time and an ornament to it. When late in 1777 he became president of Yale, his church in Portsmouth refused to give him up as its technical pastor until 1786.

From a portrait by G. Moulthrop
EZRA STILES

At Yale, badly disorganized by the Revolution, Stiles was chaplain as well as administrator, indeed he was practically the whole faculty, lecturing in every subject. He found time to write, though not to complete, an ecclesiastical history of New England, to make numerous speeches, and to continue his scientific and sociological interests. A short, frail, indomitable, lively man, he did the work of half a dozen. Though he wrote much, he published little, but that little was sound in scholarship and competent in style. He died at sixty-seven of a "bilious fever," full of honors but before his work was finished.

PRINCIPAL WORKS: Discourse on Christian Union, 1761; Discourse on Saving Knowledge, 1770; The United States Elevated to Glory and Honor, 1783; History of Three of the Judges of King Charles I, 1794; Literary Diary (ed. by F. B. Dexter) 1901; Extracts and . . . Miscellanies (ed. by F. B. Dexter) 1916; Letters and Papers (ed. by I. M. Calder) 1933.

ABOUT: Holmes, A. Life of Ezra Stiles; Rourke, C. Trumpets of Jubilee; Atlantic Monthly August 1844.

STILLMAN, WILLIAM JAMES (June 1, 1828-July 6, 1901), artist, journalist, diplomat, and miscellaneous writer, was born in Schenectady, N.Y., the son of Joseph and Eliza Ward (Maxson) Stillman. He was graduated from Union College in 1848, studied landscape painting under Frederick E. Church in New York, and in 1849 went to England, where he met John Ruskin and others of the Pre-Raphaelite group. Returning to America he exhibited at the National Academy 1851-59, and was elected an associate in 1854. About 1851 or 1852, after a meeting with the Hungarian patriot, Kossuth, he went to Hungary on a special mission and on his return to New York pursued his career as a painter and founded the *Crayon: A Journal Devoted to the Graphic Arts and the Literature Related to Them.* Although his journal was not a financial success, his work as editor brought

Stillman into contact with the leading literary figures of the period, among them Emerson, Lowell, and Agassiz.

In 1860 Stillman went to Europe where he renewed his friendship with Rossetti and Ruskin, serving as American consul in Rome from 1862 to 1865 and in Crete from 1865 to 1868. He resumed his journalistic work in 1870 and five years later as correspondent for the London *Times* traveled in Herzegovina, Montenegro, and Albania. His later years with the *Times* were spent chiefly in Rome as a special correspondent. He died at Surrey, England, where he had settled after his retirement in 1898. Stillman was married in 1860 to Laura Mack, who died in Greece in 1869. His second wife was Marie Spartoli, a daughter of the Greek consul general in London, whom he married in 1871.

The titles of Stillman's books indicate his wide range of interest. His works on archaeology are illustrated with his own photographs, and his two books for children are sensitive and charming stories; while his essays, articles, and critical studies are indicative of another side of an exceptionally talented mind.

PRINCIPAL WORKS: The Acropolis of Athens, 1870; The Cretan Insurrection of 1866-7-8, 1874; Poetic Localities of Cambridge, 1876; Herzegovina and the Late Uprising, 1877; Report of W. J. Stillman on the Cesnola Collection, 1885; On the Track of Ulysses, 1888; Old Italian Masters Engraved by Timothy Cole, 1892; Billy and Hans, 1897; Venus and Apollo in Paintings and Sculptures, 1897; Little Bertha, 1898; The Union of Italy, 1815-1895, 1898; The Old Rome and the New and Other Studies, 1898; Francesco Crispi: Insurgent, Exile, Revolutionist, and Statesman, 1899; The Autobiography of a Journalist, 1901.

ABOUT: Norton, C. E. Letters of James Russell Lowell; Scudder, H. E. James Russell Lowell; Stillman, W. J. The Autobiography of a Journalist; New York Evening Post July 8, 1901; London Times July 9, 1901.

STITH, WILLIAM (1707-September 19, 1755), historian, clergyman, and third president of the College of William and Mary, was born in Virginia, the son of Captain John Stith and Mary (Randolph) Stith, who was a granddaughter of William Randolph, the ancestor of Thomas Jefferson, Robert E. Lee, and John Marshall. He was educated in the grammar school of William and Mary and at Queen's College, Oxford, England, receiving his degree of B.A. in 1727-28 and his M.A. in 1730. He was ordained as a minister of the Church of England and, returning to Virginia, was elected master of the grammar school in William and Mary College and chaplain of the House of Burgesses. From 1736 to 1751 he officiated as rector of Henrico parish, and during these years wrote his history of Virginia, which was printed in Williamsburg on the only printing press in the colony. He was married on July 13, 1738, to Judith Randolph, a first cousin.

In 1752, he was appointed president of William and Mary, succeeding his brother-in-law, William Dawson, and concurrently served as minister of York-Hampton parish, York County. He died in Williamsburg two years later.

Several of Stith's sermons delivered before the House of Burgesses received publication, but his most ambitious and best known work was his *History of the First Discovery and Settlement of Virginia.* The book, though it represented arduous research on the part of Stith, who was indebted to the records of the London Company and material of his uncle, Sir John Randolph, drew divided opinion. Jefferson considered the work "inelegant and often too minute to be tolerable," and De Tocqueville objected to its "diffuseness," but various other authorities had praise for its accuracy. As a picture of the young colony of Virginia, during its founding and early years, Stith's history in its precision and exactitude has been a valuable source of research for historians.

PRINCIPAL WORKS: A Sermon Preached Before the General Assembly, 1745-46; History of the First Discovery and Settlement of Virginia, 1747; The Sinfulness and Pernicious Nature of Gaming, 1752; The Nature and Extent of Christ's Redemption, 1753.

ABOUT: Burton, L. W. Annals of Henrico Parish; Craven, W. F. Dissolution of the Virginia Company; Tyler L. G. Williamsburg.

STOCKTON, FRANK (FRANCIS) RICHARD (April 5, 1834-April 20, 1902), novelist and story writer, was born in Philadelphia into a family whose antecedents had settled in America before 1656 and included among its ranks Richard Stockton, a signer of the Declaration of Independence. He was the third son of the nine children of William Smith Stockton and his second wife, Emily (Drean) Stockton, and was educated in the common schools of Philadelphia. It was generally assumed in the family circle that he would prepare for a medical career, but he chose instead the wood-engraving by which he earned his living until 1866 in Philadelphia and New York City. Within these years he invented an engraving tool, illustrated the volume, *Poems* (1862) by his clerical half-brother, Thomas Hewlings Stockton, and published a pamphlet *A Northern Voice for the Dissolution of the United States of North America,* in 1860.

His writing ability was apparent during his school-days when he won prizes, and literature increasingly absorbed his attention so that by 1867 he was writing for the *Riverside Magazine for Young People* children's stories that later appeared under the title *Ting-a-Ling.*

In 1869 Stockton began writing for *Hearth and Home;* his assignments led to the publication in 1873 of a household handbook written in collaboration with his wife, Marian Edwards Tuttle of Amelia County, Va., whom he married in 1860.

He contributed to *Scribner's Monthly,* afterward the *Century Magazine,* and became the assistant editor of *St. Nicholas Magazine* when it was established in 1873 under the able direction of Mary Mapes Dodge. During his eight-year association with the magazine he published several children's books, among which were *A Jolly Fellowship,* and *The Floating Prince and Other Fairy Tales.* Meanwhile, in 1879, he had published the book which was to make him famous—*Rudder Grange,* enlarged from sketches which *Scribner's Magazine* had presented five years previously. In their collected form they were unsuccessfully hawked around among the publishers until Scribner's finally agreed to bring out the book. This story about a house-boat and an amusing maid-servant, Pomona, was an immediate hit and started Stockton on his career as a humorist. *Rudder Grange* was followed by two sequels, *The Rudder Grangers Abroad* and *Pomona's Travels.*

After his retirement from *St. Nicholas,* he lived in New Jersey at Nutley and at Convent Station. Here in quiet country surroundings, he wrote some of his best books. He often dictated from the comfortable depths of a hammock, and afterward revised his manuscripts with great precision, pausing at times for an hour to weigh the correctness of a single word. His originality placed him at the head of the humorists of the placid 'eighties and at this time he produced his most popular novel—*The Casting Away of Mrs. Lecks and Mrs. Aleshine,* a rollicking tale of two widows shipwrecked on an island in the Pacific.

He was a gifted short-story writer and caused a sensation by his story "The Lady or the Tiger?" It appeared in the *Century* in November 1882 and formed the title of a volume of collected stories in 1884. Stockton ingeniously set the problem of a barbaric princess under parental influence, torn between relinquishing her lover to a marriageable lady or a savage tiger. The story stirred up debates throughout the country and brought Stockton an unwelcome amount of

FRANK R. STOCKTON

publicity. It was produced as an operetta at Wallack's Theatre, May 7, 1888.

Stockton traveled extensively and was among the first American writers to sing the praises of the Bahamas. A book on European travel, *Personally Conducted,* achieved a certain popularity. A few years before his death in Washington, D.C., he lived near Harper's Ferry, W. Va., where he bought a house. Stockton's books were a faithful reflection of an unusual personality. His wit was irrepressible, his fund of good stories ever on the tip of his glib tongue. He walked with a slight limp and had the swarthy complexion, dark eyes, and hair of an Oriental, despite his long line of American ancestors. Robert Underwood Johnson, in his *Remembered Yesterdays,* describes him as a man whom "one always met with unalloyed pleasure and with a joyous expectation of wit. He had a whimsical temperament, which was also gentle and equable. I never saw him ruffled or indignant . . . He had no sharp corners or crochets to be allowed for and thus became one of the easiest of companions.

His faculty for expressing the quaint turns of a fanciful mind elevated him to a unique place among American humorists. His appeal sprang from a personal individuality and he never resorted to the props of dialect or colloquialism.

PRINCIPAL WORKS: A Northern Voice for the Dissolution of the United States of North America, 1860; Ting-a-Ling, 1870; Round About Rambles in Lands of Fact and Fancy, 1872; The Home: Where It Should Be and What to Put in It, 1873; What Might Have Been Expected, 1874; Tales

Out of School, 1875; Rudder Grange, 1879; A Jolly Fellowship, 1880; The Floating Prince and Other Fairy Tales, 1881; The Casting Away of Mrs. Lecks and Mrs. Aleshine, 1886; The Late Mrs. Null, 1886; The Man of Orn and Other Fanciful Tales, 1887; The Dusantes, 1888; Personally Conducted, 1889; The Squirrel Inn, 1891; The Rudder Grangers Abroad, 1891; Pomona's Travels, 1894; The Adventures of Captain Horn, 1895; A Chosen Few, 1895; Mrs. Cliff's Yacht, 1896; Buccaneers and Pirates of Our Coasts, 1898; Kate Bonnet: The Romance of a Pirate's Daughter, 1902; The Novels and Stories of Frank R. Stockton, 1899-1904.

ABOUT: Ellsworth, W. W. A Golden Age of Authors; Johnson, R. U. Remembered Yesterdays; Author July 15, 1891; Century July 1886.

STODDARD, CHARLES WARREN (August 7, 1843-April 23, 1909), poet, and travel writer, son of Samuel Burr Stoddard, a paper manufacturer, and his wife Harriet Abigail (Freeman), was born in Rochester, N.Y., and moved to California with his family during his twelfth year. Two years later, in 1857, he rounded Cape Horn in the clipper ship *Flying Cloud* and went back to his native state to attend an academy there until 1859. Returning to California, he remained for the following eight years, during which time he clerked in a book store, attended the College of California at Oakland and contributed widely to magazines. Under the pen-name "Pip Pepperwood" he sent verse to the *Golden Era,* edited by Mark Twain and Bret Harte. In 1867 Harte edited Stoddard's *Poems,* and this same important year marked the latter's conversion to the Roman Catholic faith.

Never robust, Stoddard for the duration of his life traveled in an effort to build up his health. Several trips to the South Sea Islands furnished him with material for his best known book, *South-Sea Idyls.* He visited Egypt, the Holy Land, and lived in Italy and England for three years. In London he met Mark Twain, who was so struck by his companionable personality and quiet humor that he engaged him as his secretary.

Stoddard was professor of English at the University of Notre Dame (1885-86) and lecturer of English literature at the Catholic University of America, at Washington, D.C., (1889-1902) until failing health necessitated his resignation. The last years of his life were spent in California, where he wrote a series of articles on California missions for *Sunset Magazine.* His death in Monterey was an irreparable loss to his many literary friends who admired him more for his charm and kindliness than for his slight writing talent.

PRINCIPAL WORKS: Poems, 1867; South-Sea Idyls, 1873 (reprinted in London as Summer Cruising in the South Seas, 1874); Mashallah! 1881; A Troubled Heart, 1885; The Lepers of Molokai, 1885; Hawaiian Life, 1894; The Wonder-Worker of Padua, 1896; A Cruise Under the Crescent, 1898; In the Footprints of the Padres, 1902; For the Pleasure of His Company, 1903; Exits and Entrances, 1903; The Island of Tranquil Delights, 1904; Poems of Charles Warren Stoddard, 1917.

ABOUT: Stoddard, C. W. Diary of a Visit to Molokai in 1884 (see 1933 ed.); Ave Maria May 15, 22, 1909; Catholic World July 1915; Harper's Monthly Magazine December 1917; Nation October 4, 1922; Overland Monthly October 1895; San Francisco Chronicle April 25, 1909.

STODDARD, ELIZABETH DREW (BARSTOW) (May 6, 1823-August, 1, 1902), novelist and poet, was born in Mattapoisett, Mass., the daughter of Wilson and Betsey (Drew) Barstow. Elizabeth attended several New England schools and, although she read widely, early showed a dislike for the academic curricula. In 1851 she married Richard Henry Stoddard, the poet [*q.v.*], and, at his encouragement, soon began to write. She contributed short stories, poems and sketches to the *Atlantic Monthly, Knickerbocker, Appletons' Journal* and other periodicals, and in 1862 published her first novel, *The Morgesons.* This was followed by two more books of fiction, a book for children, and a collection of poems. Her novels, written in a realistic style, were ahead of her time. Although they were reprinted they were never popular because, in addition to not following the romantic fashion of the day, they were poorly organized and cluttered with too many intrigues and details. Her poetry, though carelessly constructed, revealed her deepest feelings, showing her gloominess and intensity of emotion. A high strung, temperamental woman with a strong temper, she made many enemies, but she was thought of by her many friends as considerate and intelligent. She had little creative ability but was considered to have good literary taste.

PRINCIPAL WORKS: The Morgesons, 1862; Two Men, 1865; Temple House, 1867; Lolly Dink's Doings, 1874; Poems, 1895.

ABOUT: Stoddard, R. H. Recollections: Personal and Literary; Bookman November 1902; New York Times August 2, 1902.

STODDARD, RICHARD HENRY (July 2, 1825-May 12, 1903), poet, critic, and editor, was born at Hingham, Mass., the son of Reuben and Sophia (Gurney) Stoddard. Reuben Stoddard, whose forbears had all followed the sea, had risen in 1825 to the position of master and part-owner of a vessel, but he was lost in a shipwreck only a few years after the birth of his son.

Richard Henry was therefore brought up by his mother's family, the Gurneys, a vagrant tribe of mill-workers who could offer the boy no advantages whatsoever. Mrs. Stoddard took her son to Boston, tried to earn a living making clothes, and finally married another sailor, but was unable to improve their condition. From these precarious years Stoddard retained many gloomy impressions, of hunger, privation and hard work.

In 1835 the family moved to New York, and for the next five years Richard Henry was able to attend public school. Almost as soon as he had learned to read, the boy manifested an enormous appetite for literature of all kinds; and by 1840 he had formed a definite ambition to cultivate that taste to the highest degree. He continued to read from this time on his own momentum, so to speak; for he was obliged to leave school and help his family by working. During the next thirteen years he was employed, first as an errand boy, then shop boy, legal copyist, office boy, bookkeeper, and after 1843 as an iron molder; but his nights were given over to the delights of reading and writing. His love of books gained him the acquaintance of several cultured people, among them Park Benjamin, Lewis Gaylord Clark, and Nathaniel Hawthorne; these men encouraged Stoddard to write poetry, and directed his study of English literature and prosody. After 1845 his first attempts at poetry began to appear in New York magazines.

Stoddard had devoted a good deal of study to Shakespeare, Cowper, Burns—in fact to all the great masters of English poetry; but Keats was his first love. And the first volume of poems which he published, *Footprints,* followed the style of Keats with such amateurish exactness that its author repented, and burned nearly the whole edition. Certainly this discipleship did not express his whole nature, for he had brought with him from New England a vigorous, inflexible Puritanical spirit and a mind receptive to a very wide range of literary influences. Stoddard became intimate with Bayard Taylor before 1850, and the two young writers read together and wrote together on a great variety of subjects. Stoddard's next volume of poems, published in 1851, showed real promise and was favorably received in New York; and during the years that followed, while Taylor turned to Germany for inspiration and Stedman to Greece, Stoddard began to "orientalize." "The King's Bell," his longest poem, and his "Book of the East" mark the furthest limits in the realm of fantasy to which Stoddard was able to go; and it is certain that neither of them had the success of Stedman's Hellenizations or Taylor's interpretations of German literature. More to the taste of his contemporary New Yorkers were the *Songs of Summer* which he published in 1857, lyrical pieces on homely subjects, notable for their melody and transparent imagery.

Stoddard was not obliged to pursue the trade of iron-molding all his life. In 1851 he married Elizabeth Drew Barstow, a bookish lady from Mattapoisett, Mass., who later produced some sentimental novels; and two years later Nathaniel Hawthorne obtained for him an appointment as inspector of customs in New York. This position was not physically fatiguing, and it gave him a regular income, which he was able to supplement after 1860 by acting as literary reviewer for the New York *World.* From 1871 to 1874 Stoddard worked as secretary to General McClellan in the New York Department of Docks, and in 1877 he became New York City Librarian, in charge of municipal records. "In this dingy den he sat for nearly two years," wrote A. R. McDonough, "until another turn of the political wheel displaced him." The rest of his life was spent in editorial work; from 1880 to 1903 he was literary editor of the New York *Mail and Express,* carrying on at the same time the editorship of *Aldine,* a journal, and the Bric-a-Brac and Sans-Souci series of popular sketches of minor celebrities. Stoddard was highly esteemed as a critic; his writing was vigorous and he became known as an out-

RICHARD HENRY STODDARD

spoken and redoubtable opponent of literary pretense and "Bohemianism." During the last thirty years of his life, his house was a favorate rendezvous for literary men in New York. Indeed, it may be said that Stoddard's influence as a critic on younger writers, and his position as host at a *salon,* or clearing-house of letters in New York, were more valuable in the end than his own writings.

When Stoddard's complete poems were published in 1880, the critic A. R. McDonough said in extenuation of them, "There can be no such thing as originality in modern ideas. The poet does not create—he merely varies the aspects of existing thought." Later generations will hardly accept this as an excuse for Stoddard's want of originality or even individuality; for he was imitative not only in thoughts but in form. Some of his "Songs of Summer," his poetic tribute to Bryant "The Dead Master," and his "Abraham Lincoln: An Horatian Ode" still retain a certain charm, but on the whole, he it not remembered for his personal contribution to poetry.

PRINCIPAL WORKS: *Poetry*—Poems, 1851; Songs of Summer, 1857; The King's Bell, 1863; Abraham Lincoln. An Horatian Ode, 1865; The Book of the East, 1867; The Lion's Cub, 1890. *Editions*—Melodies and Madrigals From Old English Poets.

ABOUT: Stoddard, R. H. Recollections: Personal and Literary; Scribner's Monthly September 1880; New York Times May 13, 1903.

STODDARD, SOLOMON (September, 1643-February 11, 1728/29), Congregational clergyman and religious writer, was born in Boston, one of fifteen sons of Anthony and Mary (Downing) Stoddard. His mother was the sister of Sir George Downing and niece of Governor John Winthrop. He was graduated from Harvard in 1662 and from 1667 to 1674 was librarian of the college. Because of ill health he spent two years of this time as chaplain in Barbados. In 1672 he was ordained pastor of the church in Northampton, Mass., where he remained until his death. In 1670 he married Esther (Warham) Mather, a widow, who became the mother of twelve children. Stoddard was a liberal influence in the Church; he early accepted the Half-Way Covenant and introduced into his church "Stoddardeanism," or granting of church privileges to all well-meaning Christians, which doctrine he defended in a controversy with Increase Mather, publishing several works on the subject. In addition to these he published nineteen other sermons and pamphlets, all of which showed him to be a man of originality and forcefulness. He believed in more power for the clergy, was a strong advocate of preaching hellfire, and was opposed to drinking and extravagant dress. He was interested in politics and was a man of great influence in colonial Massachusetts.

PRINCIPAL WORKS: The Doctrine of Instituted Churches, 1700; The Inexcusableness of Neglecting the Worship of God: Under a Pretence of Being in an Unconverted Condition, 1708; An Appeal to the Learned, 1709; The Efficacy of the Fear of Hell to Restrain Men From Sin, 1713; A Guide to Christ, 1714; An Answer to Some Cases of Conscience Respecting the Country, 1722.

ABOUT: Sibley, J. L. Biographical Sketches of Graduates of Harvard University; Stoddard, C. & E. W. Anthony Stoddard of Boston, Massachusetts, and His Descendants: A Genealogy; Boston Weekly News Letter February 20, 1729.

STODDARD, WILLIAM OSBORN (September 24, 1835-August 29, 1925), miscellaneous writer, inventor, and secretary to President Lincoln, was born in Homer, N.Y., the son of Prentice Samuel and Sarah Ann (Osborn) Stoddard. He attended private schools, worked in his father's book and publishing shop for several years and in 1858 received an A.B. *cum laude* from the University of Rochester. He promptly became associate editor of the *Central Illinois Gazette* in West Urbana, Ill., and there met Lincoln. He was one of the first to suggest Lincoln for President and was his ardent supporter. After Lincoln became President he appointed Stoddard secretary to sign land patents and later made him an assistant private secretary. After 1866 he did journalistic work and became interested in telegraphy, manufacturing, and railways, patenting nine inventions. In addition to these activities he wrote over a hundred books, of which those for boys, numbering over seventy, were his best literary attempts. He was married to Susan Eagleson Cooper in 1870, and they had five children.

PRINCIPAL WORKS: Abraham Lincoln, 1884; The Lives of the Presidents (10 vols.) 1886-89; Inside the White House in War Times, 1890; The Table Talk of Lincoln, 1894.

ABOUT: Stoddard, E. W. Ralph Stoddard of New London and Groton, Connecticut, and His Descendants; New York Times August 30, 1925.

STONE, JOHN AUGUSTUS (December 15, 1800-May 29, 1834), actor and playwright, was born in Concord, Mass., the son of Joshua and Sarah (Avery) Stone. Very little is known of his early life and education but it is believed that his first affiliation with the theatre was at the Washington Garden Theatre, Boston, as a character actor. His first New York appearance was at the City Theatre in 1822—the year in which he was married to Mrs. Amelia (Greene) Legge, an actress.

His first play, *Restoration: or, The Diamond Cross,* was given at the new Chatham Garden Theatre in 1824, with Stone a member of the company. His best known play, *Metamora: or, The Last of the Wampanoags,* was written for a prize contest sponsored by Edwin Forrest, and provided Forrest with one of his best parts, that of the Indian King Philip.

Two years after the Forrest contest, in 1831, Stone acted in another of his own plays, *Tancred: King of Sicily,* and in the same year in April played in *The Demoniac: or, The Prophet's Bride.* There are few records of Stone's career as an actor, but according to reports he was small and rather delicate, with the talent for self-effacement of the true character actor. Most of his plays have vanished completely, among them *The Lion of the West,* which he had adapted for James Henry Hackett, and *Metamora,* only a part of which exists in manuscript, along with other mementoes of Edwin Forrest at the Forrest Home in Philadelphia.

He committed suicide May 29, 1834, by drowning in the Schuylkill River, Philadelphia, and his monument there is inscribed "Erected to the Memory of John Augustus Stone, Author of Metamora, By His Friend Edwin Forrest." Though highly regarded by his contemporaries, Stone wrote little to influence the progress of the theatre, except *Metamora* which started the fashion for Indian plays at that time.

Principal Works: Restoration: or, The Diamond Cross, 1824; Metamora: or, The Last of the Wampanoags, 1829; Tancred: King of Sicily, 1831; The Demoniac: or, The Prophet's Bride, 1831; The Lion of the West, 1831; The Ancient Briton, 1833; Fauntleroy: or, The Fatal Forgery; La Roque: The Regicide; The Knight of the Golden Fleece: or, The Yankee in Spain, 1834.

About: James, R. D. Old Drury of Philadelphia; Odell, G. C. D. Annals of the New York Stage; Rees, J. The Life of Edwin Forrest.

STONE, WILLIAM LEETE, SR. (April 20, 1792-August 15, 1844), journalist and historian, was born in New Paltz, N.Y. His parents, the Rev. William Stone and Tamson (Graves) Stone, soon moved to a farm on the upper Susquehanna, and there the boy received his only education under his father's instruction. After working for the Cooperstown (N.Y.) *Federalist,* 1809-12, he edited several papers and journals, finally becoming one of the proprietors of the New York *Commercial Advertiser.* His editorial influence then became much wider; he favored the Erie Canal, laughed at woman suffrage, and advocated freedom of slaves. His writings were mostly of a historical nature. In 1834 he published *Tales and Sketches,* which told of his own pioneer background, and these were followed by tales of New England rustic life. He was much interested in writing a history of the Iroquois Indians, and in 1838 published the first volume,*The Life of Joseph Brant-Thayendanegea. Life and Times of Red Jacket* followed three years later, and the third volume in the series, *The Life and Times of Sir William Johnson,* was completed after his death by his son, and published in 1865. In his own day Stone was known chiefly as a newspaper editor, but his most enduring contribution was the interest he aroused late in his career in preserving American historical records.

Principal Works: Matthias and His Impostures, 1833; Tales and Sketches, 1834; The Mysterious Bridal and Other Tales, 1835; Maria Monk and the Nunnery of the Hôtel Dieu, 1836; Ups and Downs in the Life of a Distressed Gentleman, 1836; Life of Joseph Brant-Thayendanegea, 1838; Life and Times of Red Jacket, 1841; Border Wars of the American Revolution, 1843; Life and Times of Sir William Johnson, 1865.

About: Stone, W. L. Life and Times of Red Jacket (see ed. of 1866); Stone, W. L., Jr. The Family of John Stone; New York Tribune August 17, 1844.

STORY, ISAAC (August 7, 1774-July 19, 1803), poet and miscellaneous writer, was born in Marblehead, Mass. He was the second son of the large family of the Rev. Isaac and Rebecca (Bradstreet) Story. After his graduation from Harvard in 1793, he studied law, but his practice was abruptly ended by his untimely death at the early age of twenty-nine. For several years before his death he contributed essays, lampoons, and verses to newspapers, but because of the custom of using pseudonyms it is hard to distinguish definitely all that he wrote. He is best remembered for a series of verses signed "Peter Quince," which were originally published in the *Political Gazette,* and later transferred to the *Farmer's Museum.* A collection of these was published in 1801 under the title, *A Parnassian Shop Opened in the Pindaric Stile: By Peter Quince, Esq.* This miscellaneous collection included satires as well as poems on patriotic and romantic subjects. Story holds only a very small place in the literary field; his verse was easy and fluent but its interest was topical rather than permanent.

Principal Works: Liberty, 1795; All the World's a Stage, 1796; An Eulogy on the Glorious Virtues of the Illustrious General George Washington, 1800; An Oration on the Anniversary of the Independence of the United States of America, 1801; A Parnassian Shop Opened in the Pindaric Stile: By Peter Quince, Esq., 1801.

ABOUT: Derby, P. & Gardner, F. A. Elisha Story of Boston; Duyckinck, E. A. & G. S. Cyclopaedia of American Literature; Salem Register July 25, 1803.

STORY, JOSEPH (September 18, 1779-September 10, 1845), juridical writer and Supreme Court Justice, was born in Marblehead, Mass., the first of eleven children of Dr. Elisha Story and his second wife Mehitable (Pedrick) Story; the doctor, a veteran of the Boston Tea Party, had already had seven children by his first marriage. The boy was educated at Marblehead Academy, but quarreled with the principal and left in 1794. In a year he had prepared himself for Harvard, where he injured his health by overstudy, taking his B.A. in 1798, the second in his class. He then read law and was admitted to the bar in 1801, starting practice in Salem, his home for many years after. In 1804 he married Mary Lynde Oliver; she died in six months, and in 1808 he married Sarah Waldo Wetmore, by whom he had seven children. Only two survived, one of whom was William Wetmore Story [*q.v.*].

In 1805 Story was elected to the Massachusetts legislature. In 1808 and 1809 he served in Congress, then returned to the state legislature, being speaker of its lower house in 1811. That year he was appointed to the United States Supreme Court, still the youngest man ever to receive such an appointment. In those days the Supreme Court justices each had his own circuit, Story's being in New England, and they met only occasionally in Washington. Therefore Story continued to live in Salem, to be president of a bank there from 1815 to 1835, to serve as Overseer and Fellow of Harvard and as Dane Professor of Law from 1829, and still to retain his position as Supreme Court Justice. Twice he served temporarily as Acting Chief Justice. When the Dane chair of law was created for him he moved to Cambridge, his home for the rest of his life.

Collection of Frederick H. Meserve
JOSEPH STORY

He found time also, not only to edit numerous legal texts, and to contribute to the serious reviews, but to publish a series of commentaries on the law that caused the Lord Chief Justice of England to call him "the greatest writer on the law since Blackstone." He was no dry-as-dust lawyer, however, but loved music, art, and poetry, and had even published—and tried to suppress—a youthful volume of poems. In his legal writing, he achieved the end which he himself recommended, in verse, to aspiring young attorneys: "Pregnant in matter, in expression brief."

PRINCIPAL WORKS: The Power of Solitude: With Fugitive Poems, 1804; Commentary on the Constitution of the United States, 1833; Commentary on the Conflict of Laws, 1834; Miscellaneous Writings, 1852.

ABOUT: Lewis, W. D. Great American Lawyers; Story, W. W. Life and Letters of Joseph Story; Sumner, C. Tribute of Friendship; The Late Joseph Story; Boston Daily Advertiser September 12, 1845.

"STORY, SYDNEY A., JR." See PIKE, MARY HAYDEN (GREEN)

STORY, WILLIAM WETMORE (February 12, 1819-October 7, 1895), sculptor, poet, and essayist, was born in Salem, Mass., the second son of Joseph Story, eminent Supreme Court justice and commentator on the Constitution, and Sarah (Wetmore) Story. The boy received the best education then available, first at Salem, then at Cambridge, where his family moved in 1829, and finally at Harvard University.

After receiving the degrees of B.A. in 1838 and LL.B. in 1840 Story gravitated naturally toward a career in law, though at this time he showed equally as much promise in letters. A dilettante at heart, he devoted most of his youth to the pleasures of friendship with James Russell Lowell, Thomas Wentworth Higginson, and other agreeable Cambridge companions, and to acquiring facility in music, painting, and writing. After 1840, however, he applied himself diligently to his law practice in Boston, and published several learned treatises on legal questions. He married Emelyn Eldredge in 1843.

Joseph Story died in 1845, and his son was nominated by the former colleagues of the great jurist to prepare a statue of him. Taking his wife and two children, Story went to Italy in 1847 to prepare himself for this great work. It was a decisive step in the young man's life, for the artistic attractions of Rome soon caused him to forsake America entirely. Returning to Boston after a period of study, he stayed only long enough to edit his father's *Life and Letters* in 1851, and submit his sketches for the statue; in 1856 he established himself permanently in Rome. According to Van Wyck Brooks, "everything in New England annoyed and bored him"; Story accepted contentedly and even eagerly the terms of his self-inflicted exile. Yet, continues the same writer, in Italy Story's mind "never found its focus."

While practicing law in Boston the young man had brought out a volume of *Poems,* standard New England verse which brought him little fame. In the more congenial Roman environment Story wrote with more vigor, but his poetic facility did not greatly increase. Soon after his arrival in Rome he had become intimate with Robert and Elizabeth Browning, and most of his poems written in Rome follow Browning's dramatic monologues with disappointing fidelity. When he tried more adventurous flights, as in the well-known poems "Cleopatra" and "Praxiteles and Phrynne," attempting to convey a feeling for sensuous beauty, his New England heritage held him in check. Perhaps his most successful, and certainly the most widely-known of his writings were the prose sketches collected under the title *Roba di Roma,* giving his first impressions of the Roman scene, the later sketch *Vallombrosa,* and the idyllic novel *Fiammetta.* Even in maturity Story was unwilling to sacrifice one pleasant activity to another; in Rome he continued to delight in singing, acting, sketching, and writing; he was most ambitious as a sculptor, and won signal honors in London for his contributions to this art.

Story's work as a sculptor brought him more European than American fame, and his literary associations after 1865 were also European. Besides the Brownings, Walter Savage Landor and Richard Monckton Milnes were frequently guests at the Palazzo Barberini, Story's magnificent dwelling in Rome. In 1861 Story's interest in the American crisis was manifested by the many influential letters he wrote to the London *Daily News* on the subject; and in 1877 he traveled for a short time in the United States and was fêted in Boston and New York as America's greatest artist. But he promptly returned to his beloved Rome, and the last two decades of his life were spent in Europe. He died at the age of seventy-six at the home of his daughter at Vallombrosa, Italy.

WILLIAM WETMORE STORY

PRINCIPAL WORKS: *Poetry*—Poems, 1845; Graffiti d'Italia, 1868. *Essays*—Roba di Roma, 1862; Vallombrosa, 1881. *Novel*—Fiammetta, 1886. *Drama*—Nero, 1875.

ABOUT: Brooks, Van W. The Flowering of New England; Browning, E. B. Letters; James, H. William Wetmore Story and His Friends; Phillips, M. E. Reminiscences of William Wetmore Story.

STOWE, CALVIN ELLIS (April 26, 1802-August 22, 1886), educator and miscellaneous writer, was born in Natick, Mass., the son of Samuel Stow, the village baker, and Hepzibah (Biglow) Stow. Samuel Stow died in 1808, leaving his wife and son in straitened circumstances. However Calvin learned early to make his way in the world; he was graduated from Bowdoin College in 1824 as valedictorian, and a year later entered Andover Theological Seminary. In 1831 he became professor of Greek at Dartmouth and two years later accepted the chair of Biblical literature in Lane Theological Seminary, Cincinnati. Because of his great interest in the common schools, he was appointed by the state of Ohio in 1836 to investigate the public school systems of Europe, the results of which commission he published in his *Report on Elementary Instruction in*

Europe. This famous report was circulated throughout Ohio and reprinted by the legislatures of several other states. In 1850 he became professor at Bowdoin, and two years later accepted the chair of sacred literature at Andover Theological Seminary. In 1864 he resigned from Andover and retired to Hartford, Conn., dividing his time between there and Mandarin, Fla. Stowe, a tall, distinguished looking man, was a scholar of many languages and a noted raconteur. He was however extremely impractical in financial matters and was usually in difficulty. After the death of his first wife, Eliza (Tyler) Stowe, he married in 1836 Harriet Elizabeth Beecher [*q.v.*], later the author of *Uncle Tom's Cabin.*

Principal Works: Introduction to the Criticism and Interpretation of the Bible, 1835; Report on Elementary Instruction in Europe, 1838; Origin and History of the Books of the Bible, 1867.

About: Stowe, C. E. Life of Harriet Beecher Stowe; Congregationalist August 26, September 2, 1886; Boston Transcript August 23, 1886.

STOWE, HARRIET ELIZABETH (BEECHER) (June 14, 1811-July 1, 1896), humanitarian and novelist, was born at Litchfield, Conn. Daughter of Lyman Beecher [*q.v.*], pastor of the Litchfield Congregational Church, Harriet grew up in an atmosphere of rigid New England Puritanism. Lyman Beecher was a follower of Jonathan Edwards and a vigorous defendant of orthodox Calvinism in the Unitarian controversy; so it was perhaps inevitable that his daughter should have received an almost wholly theological education, that her childish heroes should have been Edwards and Samuel Hopkins, and her favorite reading Cotton Mather's *Magnalia Christi Americana.* There was, however, a strain of romanticism in Harriet's nature; and even while she absorbed this thick theological atmosphere the young girl began to dramatize her struggles for salvation.

After a few years of schooling at the Litchfield Academy, Harriet went to Hartford, Conn., in 1824, to attend a school established by her elder sister Catherine. This new environment seems not to have changed her, however; she devoted her attention to such studies at Butler's *Analogy* and Baxter's *Saint's Rest,* and at the age of fourteen underwent a highly emotionalized "conversion" to the Christian faith.

In 1832 Lyman Beecher moved to Cincinnati, Ohio, to take charge of the Lane Theological Seminary, and his daughters Catherine and Harriet accompanied him. During her first years in this new home Harriet suffered much from ill-health and mental depression; and to shake off her listlessness she turned to teaching and writing. Within a year of their arrival in Cincinnati Catherine started a new school, the "Western Female Institute," and from 1833 to 1836 she employed Harriet as a teacher. In 1834 Harriet wrote, in competition for a prize, her first story, which appeared later as "Uncle Lot" in the *Western Monthly.* She continued for several years to contribute to this magazine, as well as to the *New York Evangelist,* and she also assisted her brother Henry Ward Beecher [*q.v.*] by writing for his daily newspaper the Cincinnati *Journal.* In 1836 her marriage to Professor Calvin E. Stowe [*q.v.*] of the Lane Theological Seminary put an end to her teaching; but Professor Stowe encouraged her writing and for a few years she was able to continue it. However, as household duties and the rearing of six children claimed more and more of her attention, Mrs. Stowe was obliged to put aside her career of authorship.

The years from 1836 to 1850 were by far the most difficult years of Mrs. Stowe's life. Her ill health continued, and her family suffered increasingly from poverty and hardship. In these formative years of the abolitionist controversy Cincinnati, a border city, was continually torn with conflicts; Lane Theological Seminary finally became a hotbed of abolitionist sentiment and was threatened with removal or destruction. Mrs. Stowe was not at first a "declared abolitionist," although her favorite brother Henry was early enlisted in the cause. Harriet visited a plantation in Kentucky, saw the evils of slavery at first hand, and, in 1839, even aided a runaway slave; but during the 1840's she had no ardent desire to stamp out the evil.

The fortunes of the Stowe family were greatly improved in 1850, when Professor Stowe secured the appointment to the Collins chair of Natural and Revealed Religion at Bowdoin College, Brunswick, Maine, and in 1852 when he obtained a professorship at the Andover Theological Seminary. The more congenial atmosphere of New England not only revived Mrs. Stowe's flagging health, but stimulated her to greater intellectual efforts. The passage in 1850 of the Fugitive Slave Act aroused the entire Beecher family to indignant protest: Harriet's brothers Henry and Edward began to preach aggressively against the Act from their pulpits in Brooklyn, N.Y., and Boston, and both of them incited Harriet to "use her pen . . . to make this whole nation feel what an accursed thing slavery is."

Uncle Tom's Cabin: or, Life Among the Lowly was conceived in a state of high re-

Collection of Frederick H. Meserve
HARRIET BEECHER STOWE

ligious exaltation, and inspired by indignation against the Fugitive Slave Act, the victims of which were enlisting sympathy throughout New England. It was not abolitionist propaganda, nor was it aimed directly against the Southern slaveholders, but in the uproar which resulted from its publication the abolitionists became its chief defenders and the Southerners its bitterest enemies. Mrs. Stowe was amazed at the unprecedented circulation of the novel; she had thought it "too mild" for the abolitionists; yet *Uncle Tom's Cabin* crystallized the anti-slavery sentiment of the entire North and provided the abolitionists with a most effective weapon. The novel appeared first as a serial in the Washington anti-slavery paper, the *National Era,* in 1852; later in the same year it was published by John P. Jewett of Boston, the circulation amounting to 300,000 copies within a year. Mrs. Stowe received 10 per cent royalties on these sales, but nothing for the dramatic rights, and nothing for the publication of the novel in England, where more than a million copies were sold.

If Mrs. Stowe's powerful appeal did not immediately enrich her, at least it brought her great and lasting fame, and the admiration of humanitarians throughout the world. Encouraged by the English abolitionists, she visited Europe in 1853, 1856, and 1859; and she was everywhere greeted by admiring throngs. 100,000 copies of her second anti-slavery novel *Dred,* which appeared in 1856, were sold in England in less than a month. This story, though better constructed and far more accurate in its social background than *Uncle Tom's Cabin,* met with less success because it had no striking figure, no central character on which sympathy might be lavished. However these novels brought her a large and enthusiastic circle of readers, and she was enabled to travel in Europe on the proceeds of their sales.

Mrs. Stowe's English associations had one unfortunate result. She became a friend of Lady Byron during her first visits to England, and took it upon herself to vindicate that lady in the controversy over Byron's life, by revealing in 1869 and 1870 that Byron had been guilty of incestuous relations with his sister Mrs. Leigh. The revelations were ill-received in England; people could find no justification for thus stirring the embers of a dead and forgotten scandal; yet Mrs. Stowe's stern conscience commanded her to do it.

During the 1850's Mrs. Stowe threw herself heart and soul into the agitation against slavery, arranging public meetings, assisting Negroes' schools, and distributing the money she had raised in England for aiding the cause. After the Civil War she bought a plantation at Mandarin, Fla., with a vague idea of helping the emancipated Negroes who were pouring into that State, and incidentally to help one of her sons, who had been wounded at Gettysburg, establish a business. The venture failed, but Mrs. Stowe was able to live comfortably there and at Hartford, Conn., for the rest of her life, on the proceeds of literary works which she continued to produce, in such abundance that her collected works eventually filled sixteen volumes. The anti-slavery novels were followed by *The Minister's Wooing,* an austere but revealing story reminiscent of the New England of her childhood, *The Pearl of Orr's Island,* and other sympathetic New England sketches: *Oldtown Folks* and *Poganuc People.* Besides these she produced religious poems, numerous articles for religious magazines, and housekeeping manuals. All her works are full of religious fervor and contain a great deal of abstract preaching, yet many times she caught the true tone and color of everyday New England life, and presented it vividly and artistically.

Mrs. Stowe's appearance revealed the stern daughter of Puritanism quite as much as her writings. Her conscience and moral earnestness may be seen in her face, yet there is a dreamy look about the mouth and eyes, and a whimsical expression, to make one wonder whether she were preoccupied with beauty or with salvation. "Preoccupied" she certainly was, and absent-minded; she is said to have "dreamed" through the last ten years of her life, and she was notably impractical in financial and household affairs.

Harriet Beecher Stowe's position as a writer is ably defined by Catherine Gilbertson: "Her books . . . were eagerly absorbed by millions of readers, both here and abroad, because they gave to the middle class everywhere a picture of the kind of life it believed itself to be living, and a voluble expression of the thoughts the nineteenth century believed itself to be thinking." The author of *Uncle Tom's Cabin,* herself a "composite portrait of the nineteenth-century American woman," merits serious study as a representative of her time.

PRINCIPAL WORKS: *Novels*—Uncle Tom's Cabin: or, Life Among the Lowly, 1852; Dred: A Tale of the Great Dismal Swamp, 1856; The Minister's Wooing, 1859; The Pearl of Orr's Island, 1862; Agnes of Sorrento, 1862. *Sketches*—Oldtown Folks, 1869; Sam Lawson's Oldtime Fireside Stories, 1872; Poganuc People, 1878. *Tracts*—A Key to Uncle Tom's Cabin, 1853; The True Story of Lady Byron's Life, 1869; Lady Byron Vindicated, 1870.

ABOUT: Fields, A. A. Life and Letters of Harriet Beecher Stowe; Gilbertson, C. Harriet Beecher Stowe; Rourke, C. M. Trumpets of Jubilee; Stowe, C. E. & L. B. Harriet Beecher Stowe: The Story of Her Life; Stowe, L. B. Saints, Sinners, and Beechers; Putnam's Magazine January 1853; Bookman March 1913.

STREET, ALFRED BILLINGS (December 18, 1811-June 2, 1881), poet, lawyer, and librarian, was born in Poughkeepsie, N.Y., the son of Randall Sanford and Cornelia (Billings) Street. He attended Dutchess County Academy and later read law in his father's office; he practiced for a time in Monticello, N.Y., and in 1839 moved to Albany. There he established a small practice but devoted most of his time to literary pursuits, especially poetry. In 1841 he married Elizabeth Weed, who became the mother of one son. During 1843-44 he edited and contributed to the *Northern Light,* a literary journal, and from 1848 to '62 he was director of the New York State Library, and law librarian until 1868. Street started writing poetry in his early youth, two of his poems being printed in the *Evening Post* when he was only fourteen. He was probably best known for *The Burning of Schenectady* and for *Frontenac,* a long historical poem. His poems were invariably in praise of nature, and showed keen observation and careful description. They were, however, lacking in breadth of vision and beauty of construction. He has been rated one of the first of the second-class American poets, and some of his works are deserving of a better fate than the oblivion into which they have fallen.

PRINCIPAL WORKS: The Burning of Schenectady, 1842; The Poems of Alfred B. Street, 1845; Frontenac, 1849; Our State, 1849; Knowledge and Liberty, 1849; In Memoriam: President Lincoln Dead, 1870.

ABOUT: Griswold, R. W. The Poets and Poetry of America; Street, H. A. & M. A. The Street Genealogy; Albany Argus June 3, 1881; Albany Evening Journal June 3, 1881.

STUART, MOSES (March 26, 1780-January 4, 1852), clergyman, Biblical scholar, and theological writer, was born in Wilton, Conn., the son of Isaac Stuart and Olive (Morehouse) Stuart. He was educated at an academy in Norwalk and at Yale; and after his graduation in 1799 taught for a few years in North Fairfield and Danbury. He studied law and was admitted to the bar in 1802, but did not practice, accepting instead an appointment as tutor at Yale, where he remained for two years. He devoted the next years to the study of theology and was ordained in 1806, becoming pastor of the First Church of Christ (Congregational) in New Haven where his tall slim figure, the ease and authority of his speech, made him an impressive sight in the pulpit.

In 1810 he was elected to the professorship of sacred literature at Andover Theological Seminary, Mass., where he remained for thirty-eight years and attained great fame as a teacher. Knowing little Hebrew at the time of his appointment, Stuart studied assiduously and wrote a Hebrew grammar for his students. In order to make himself thoroughly conversant with the new German theology, he also studied German, and was the first to introduce into American theology the results of the studies of Ewald, Gesonius, and others of the German Orientalists. In his diversified commentaries, particularly, he showed great progress in Biblical study, owing to German methods of philological investigation. A brilliant and gifted man, Stuart exercised a wide influence among his students during his years of teaching.

He resigned in 1848 because of infirmities due to advancing years, but continued writing until his death four years later in Andover. Stuart was married in 1806 to Abigail Clark.

His services to American theology, by his introduction of the study of Hebrew and European Biblical scholarship, were rendered in the face of opposition by his colleagues. His works, including translations, commentaries, sermons, and numerous other articles on theology, were by their brilliance, scholarship, and precision of thought to earn him the title "the father of Biblical learning in America."

PRINCIPAL WORKS: Letters to the Rev. Wm. E. Channing Containing Remarks on His Sermon Recently Preached and Published at Baltimore, 1819; Letters on the Eternal Generation of the Son of God: Addressed to the Rev. Samuel Miller, D.D. 1822; Elements of Interpretation: Translated From the Latin of J. A. Ernesti, 1822; Critical History and Defence of the Old Testament Canon, 1845; *Translations*—A Greek Grammar of the New Testament, 1825; Hebrew Grammar of Gesonius as Edited by Roediger, 1846; *Commentaries*—Hebrews, Romans, Revelation, Daniel, Ecclesiastes, and Proverbs 1827-52.

ABOUT: Adams W. A Discourse on the Life and Services of Professor Moses Stuart; Park E. A. A Discourse Delivered at the Funeral of Professor Moses Stuart; Stokes, A. P. Memorials of Eminent Yale Men; Woods, L. History of the Andover Theological Seminary; Boston Daily Evening Transcript January 5, 1852.

STUART, RUTH (McENERY) (May 21, 1849-May 6, 1917), fiction writer, was born in Marksville, Avoyelles Parish, La. Her father, James McEnery, was Irish, and her mother, Mary Routh (Stirling) McEnery, was the daughter of Sir John Stirling, a Scotchman. Ruth attended public and private schools in New Orleans and taught there for a number of years. In 1879 she married Alfred Oden Stuart, a cotton planter of Washington, Ark. After his death four years later she returned to New Orleans and began writing and contributing to several magazines. Early in the 'nineties she moved to New York and from then until her death in 1917 published over twenty books. She had an extraordinary knowledge of Southern types, including Creoles, plantation Negroes, and "poor whites," and it was these types that she put into her stories. Her ability to transcribe accurately their various dialects was unusual. Her stories were usually filled with humor and optimism. Her works as a whole were popular, one of the most outstanding successes being *Sonny*, an Arkansas "poor white" story in which are mingled gay humor, native dialect, and likable characters.

PRINCIPAL WORKS: A Golden Wedding and Other Tales, 1893; Carlotta's Intended and Other Tales, 1894; Solomon Crow's Christmas Pockets and Other Tales, 1896; Sonny, 1896; In Simpkinsville: Character Tales, 1897; Napoleon Jackson: The Gentleman of the Plush Rocker, 1902; Aunt Amity's Silver Wedding and Other Stories, 1909; The Unlived Life of Little Mary Ellen, 1910; Daddy Do-Funny's Wisdom Jingles, 1913.

ABOUT: Alderman, E. A. (ed.), Library of Southern Literature; Bookman February 1904; Harper's Bazaar December 16, 1899; New York Times Book Review May 13, 1917; Times-Picayune (New Orleans) May 8, 1917.

"SUMMERFIELD, CHARLES." See ARRINGTON, ALFRED W.

SUMNER, CHARLES (January 6, 1811-March 11, 1874), statesman and orator, was born in Boston, the son of Charles Pinckney Sumner, lawyer and sheriff, and Relief (Jacob) Sumner. After the Boston Latin School, he tried in vain for an appointment to West Point, then entered Harvard at fifteen, receiving his B.A. in 1830. From 1831 to 1833 he attended the Harvard Law School, but instead of practicing after admission to the bar, he lectured at the Law School and edited legal texts, with occasional contributions to the *American Jurist.* In 1837 he went to Europe on borrowed money for three years' intensive legal study. Gradually he came into demand as an orator, but it was not until 1845 that he became at all established, and not until 1851 that he was finally elected to the Senate, in which he served for the remainder of his life.

From the very beginning Sumner was the most outspoken and intransigent foe of slavery, brilliant, stormy, and bitter. His unrestrained invective culminated in an attack on him on the Senate floor by Representative P. S. Brooks of South Carolina, an attack which caused such serious injuries that it was three and a half years before he could resume his seat, to which he was constantly re-elected as an expression of his state's resentment of the affair. With the Civil War, Sumner's best days were over; he had outlived his cause. In Reconstruction days he was the fiercest of the "black radicals" who regarded the conquered South as a vassal state, and insisted on full

Collection of Frederick H. Meserve

CHARLES SUMNER

political rights for the newly enfranchised Negroes. Strangely, his most magnanimous act—a motion to remove the names of Civil War battles from the army register—caused a resolution of censure in the Massachusetts legislature. On the day of his death this censure was formally rescinded. That night he died of angina pectoris; he had never been well since the 1856 attack. His last years had been unhappy ones: he helped to impeach Johnson, was on terms of bitter emnity with Grant, had lost much of his influence; and at fifty-five the old bachelor married a young widow, Alice (Mason) Hooper, who soon left him and divorced him the year after.

Strictly speaking, Sumner was no writer; his published works are printed versions of his speeches. He was a storm-center always, his style full of thunder and lightning. The man and his work are both summed up in his fiery cry: "There *is* no other side!"

PRINCIPAL WORKS: Orations and Speeches, 1850; Speeches and Addresses, 1856; Works, 1870-83.

ABOUT: Haynes, G. H. Charles Sumner; Higginson, T. W. Contemporaries; Lester, C. E. Life and Services of Charles Sumner; Pierce, E. L. Memoir and Letters of Charles Sumner; Story, M. Charles Sumner; Boston Evening Transcript March 12, 1874.

SUMNER, WILLIAM GRAHAM (October 30, 1840-April 12, 1910), economist, social scientist, and educator, was born at Paterson, N.J., the son of Thomas Sumner and Sarah (Graham) Sumner. Thomas Sumner, an English mechanic who had come to America in 1836, moved soon after his son's birth to Hartford, Conn., where he worked in a railroad repair shop. An industrious and intelligent workman, he was able to send his son to the Hartford public schools and to instill in him a keen interest in economic and political questions.

Entering Yale University in 1859, Sumner distinguished himself both in scholarship and in social intercourse. For three years, after graduation, he studied theology at Geneva, Göttingen, and Oxford, aided by financial support from friends at Yale. Returning to America in 1866, he taught freshman subjects at Yale until 1869, and in that year was ordained priest in the Episcopal Church. Sumner's enthusiasm and breadth of intellectual interest well qualified him for the ministry, and his work as assistant in Calvary Church, New York City, in 1869, and as rector at Morristown, N.J., from 1870 to 1872, was very successful. While at Morristown he married Jeannie Whittemore

WILLIAM GRAHAM SUMNER

Elliott, the daughter of a New York merchant.

Perhaps because of his enormous appetite for learning, Sumner lost interest in the ministry as a career; and when in 1872 he was offered the professorship of political and social science at Yale, he accepted eagerly. This position gave him the opportunity to speak out freely his opinions on public questions, and during the next thirty years Sumner became one of the most vigorous and redoubtable controversialists on political and economic issues in America. He gained a high reputation as a teacher and lecturer; according to his pupil and disciple A. G. Keller, at Yale "he had become an institution while yet young," and "in 1895 we were given to understand by upperclassmen that no man had earned a real Yale B.A. unless he had had Old Bill." Tall, immaculately dressed, possessed of a powerful voice and a piercing eye, Sumner dealt with difficult subjects of American finance in every-day terms that compelled thought. His influence extended far beyond the University; during the 1870's and '80's he wrote and lectured throughout the country, opposing monetary inflation, protectionism, socialism, and governmental interference in business. His monumental *History of American Currency,* published in 1874, laid the foundation for his reputation in this field, but his most effective and popular pronouncements on economic questions appeared in 1883; the essay "What Social Classes Owe to Each Other," and the lecture entitled "The Forgotten Man." Sumner's "Forgotten Man" is the man who "works and votes—generally he prays—but his chief business in life is to pay;" the small capitalist who carries the burden of taxes and misgovernment and yet is slandered and victimized by the socialists, "poor men," and humanitarians. The following description of the "formula of most schemes of philanthropy" well illustrates Sumner's graphic treatment of complex problems: "A and B put their heads together to decide what C shall be made to do for D . . . C is is not allowed a voice in the matter, and his position, character, and interests . . . are entirely overlooked. I call C the Forgotten Man."

After 1890 Sumner's mind reached out once more into new fields. Careful study of Herbert Spencer had made this American pioneer begin to chafe at the restrictions of traditional economics; he branched into anthropology and a wide study of the evolution of social institutions, first known as "societology." Toward the development of this study into modern sociology, Sumner's lectures at Yale made an important contribution. His analysis of custom, which must be regarded as a central problem of social science, appeared in 1907 under the title *Folkways:* it remains today the classical work on the subject. The rest of his extensive researches in sociology, which he did not live to complete, were synthetized and revised by Professor A. G. Keller, appearing in 1927 under the title *The Science of Society.* Sumner died in 1910 at Englewood, N.J.

PRINCIPAL WORKS: Textbooks—A History of American Currency, 1874; American Finance, 1875; Folkways, 1907. *Essays and Lectures*—The Forgotten Man, 1883; What Social Classes Owe to Each Other, 1883; The Challenge of Facts and Other Essays, 1914; The Forgotten Man and Other Essays, 1919. *Biographies*—Andrew Jackson as a Public Man, 1882; Alexander Hamilton, 1890; Robert Morris, 1892.

ABOUT: Keller, A. G. Reminiscences (Mainly Personal) of William Graham Sumner; Starr, H. E. William Graham Sumner; Popular Science Monthly June 1889; New York Times April 13, 14, 1910.

SWINTON, WILLIAM (April 23, 1833-October 24, 1892), miscellaneous writer, was born in Salton, near Edinburgh, Scotland. After his parents, William and Jane (Currie) Swinton, moved to Canada in 1843 William did preparatory work at Knox College in Toronto and later attended Amherst College for a few months. He then taught for some time in North Carolina and New York City and in 1858 joined the staff of the New York *Times.* At the outbreak of the Civil War he was sent to the front as special correspondent, becoming well known (and well hated by the generals) as a critic of maneuvers, but in 1864, because of his unseemly methods of obtaining news, the War Department took away his rights as correspondent and forbade him to stay with the army. During the next few years he published several books on war subjects and in 1869 became professor of English at the University of California. Five years later he resigned because his views were too radically opposed to those of the president. He then started to write text books on practically every elementary school subject and was so successful that his royalties sometimes amounted to $25,000 a year. In 1878, because of this success, a gold medal was awarded to him at the Paris exposition. He worked hard but inconsistently, and was so unconcerned about financial matters that despite his large income he was frequently in need of money.

PRINCIPAL WORKS: The Times Review of McClellan: His Military Career Reviewed and Exposed, 1864; Campaigns of the Army of the Potomac, 1866; The Twelve Decisive Battles of the War, 1867; History of the New York Seventh Regiment During the War of the Rebellion, 1870.

ABOUT: Fletcher, R. S. & Young, M. O. Amherst College Biographical Record; Historical Magazine November 1869; New York Times October 26, 1892.

SWITZLER, WILLIAM FRANKLIN (March 16, 1819-May 24, 1906), journalist, historian and politician, was born in Fayette County, Ky., the son of Simeon and Elizabeth (Cornelius) Switzler. He studied at Mount Forrest Academy and continued his education by himself, reading widely, studying and practising law. In 1841 he became editor of one of the oldest Missouri newspapers, the *Columbia Patriot,* which he renamed the *Missouri Statesman.* He was a strong Whig, serving several terms in the Missouri legislature, and in 1862 was appointed by Lincoln as secretary of state of the provisional government in Arkansas. In 1885, when Cleveland made him chief of the bureau of statistics in the Treasury department, he gave up editing the *Statesman,* but during 1893-98 edited the *Missouri Democrat.* Switzler's greatest permanent contributions were his publications on the history of his state. He spent the last years of his life working on a history of the University of Missouri. He was interested in education and helped to found Christian and Baptist Colleges. He was popular as a public speaker, was an active temperance leader, and an outstanding editor. Shortly after his death he was recognized by the University of Missouri as the "dean of Missouri journalists."

PRINCIPAL WORKS: Early History of Missouri, 1872; Switzler's Illustrated History of Missouri, 1879; History of Boone County, Missouri, 1882; History of Statistics and Their Value, 1888.

ABOUT: Conard, H. L. Encyclopedia of the History of Missouri; Columbia Daily Tribune May 24, 1906; Kansas City Journal May 25, 1906; St. Louis Post Dispatch May 24, 1906.

TABB, FATHER. See TABB, JOHN BANISTER

TABB, JOHN BANISTER (March 22, 1845-November 19, 1909), poet, was born at Mattoax, Amelia County, Va., the son of Thomas Yelverton Tabb, a planter of old Virginia ancestry, and Marianna Bertrand (Archer) Tabb. His sight was poor from childhood, so that he was taught at home by tutors. Music was his passion, and he anticipated becoming a professional musician. When the Civil War began, Tabb, an enthusiastic Confederate, tried in vain to follow his brothers into the army; refused on account of his eyes, he became a blockade runner instead, making trips to London, Paris, and Bermuda before he was captured and imprisoned at Point Lookout in 1864. There he met his fellow prisoner Sidney Lanier, who became his steadfast friend and who first directed the young Virginian to the writing of poetry.

The war over, Tabb went to Baltimore to study music, still—as he always remained—"an unreconstructed Rebel." Support from his ruined home soon ceased, and he was obliged to teach for a living. He became a teacher at St. Paul's School for boys in Baltimore, and for a few months in 1870 at Racine College, Racine, Mich., now no longer in existence. Meanwhile, in a desultory way, he was preparing to become an Episcopal clergyman. From 1862, however, he had been more and more inclined to Roman Catholicism, and finally in 1872 he was received into the Catholic Church by Bishop (later Cardinal) Gibbons. He entered St. Charles' College, Ellicot City, Md., near Baltimore, being graduated in 1875, and then for three years taught English and Greek at St. Peter's Boys' School in Baltimore. In 1881 he went to St. Mary's Seminary to complete his theological studies, and was ordained in 1884. He never had a parish, however, returning immediately to St. Charles' College, where for the rest of his active life he was a teacher of English—a teacher long remembered by his pupils for stimulating influence, his wit, and his ardor for poetry.

In 1908 Father Tabb's long-afflicted eyes finally gave out, and he was totally blind thereafter. He continued to write, however, until the next year, when he suffered a stroke of paralysis and died before the year was out. He was buried in Hollywood, the famous cemetery in Richmond which contains the graves of so many distinguished Virginians.

As a person, Father Tabb, with his grave ascetic face whose mouth has yet a quizzical curve, gave rise to the most contradictory estimates. There were those who called him vain, ungenerous, niggling, and vindictive; and they were answered by others who said he was humility, generosity, and sympathy themselves. Certainly a study of his poetry would incline the reader to the latter conviction, if the work be a reflection of the man. Yet that poetry, too, has its contradictions. It has a deceptive simplicity which hides its polished technique. It is poetry detached from life, with a certain lack of feeling of direct contact even in the nature poems; it falls sometimes into mere quaintness, and is too much given to pedantic conceits. The humorous verses, even including some of those written for children, are frequently trivial, and like most inveterate punsters, Father Tabb cherished his weakest pun-children too much to let them die.

Yet when all this is said, we have left the only American rival to the great metaphysical poets of the 17th century. In his religious poems Father Tabb sounds a note heard only faintly elsewhere in American literature. But where his modest voice will longest remain

FATHER TABB

audible is in the brief personal lyrics and quatrains which were his characteristic expression. Believing thoroughly in the doctrine that poetry should be song, Tabb was a true lyrist. He was a disciple and defender of Poe, but in his poetic style he resembles neither Poe nor his friend Lanier of the long and rolling line, but a poet whom he probably never read—Emily Dickinson. Tabb has indeed written his own best self-criticism:

Singing my native song—
Brief to the ear, but long
To Love and Memory.

Principal Works: Poems, 1883; An Octave to Mary, 1893; Poems, 1894; Lyrics, 1897; Bone Rules: or Skeleton of English Grammar, 1897; Child Verse, 1899; Two Lyrics, 1900; Later Lyrics, 1902; The Rosary in Rhyme, 1904; Quips and Quiddits, Ques for the Qurious, 1907; Later Poems, 1910.

About: Browne, W. H. John Banister Tabb; Finn, M. P. John Banister Tabb: The Priest-Poet; Litz, F. A. Father Tabb: A Study of His Life and Works; Price, T. R. John Banister Tabb; Tabb, J. M. Father Tabb; Tabb, J. B. Poetry (see Introduction by F. A. Litz to 1928 ed); American Catholic Quarterly Review April 1910, January 1915; Ave Maria August 2, 9, 16, 1930; Borromean (St. Charles' College) December 1936; Catholic World February 1910, May 16, 1916; Independent December 17, 1908; Nation December 2, 1909; Outlook December 11, 1909; Baltimore Sun November 20, 1909.

TAILFER, PATRICK (fl. c. 1740), historian and polemicist, was a native of Georgia. As the result of a quarrel with Governor James Oglethorpe and his deputy Thomas Causton, Tailfer, Hugh Anderson, and David Douglass were forced to flee the colony; having escaped to Charleston, S.C., they published in 1740, both there and in London, a famous tract entitled *A True and Historical Narrative of the Colony of Georgia*. This work, an elaborately satirical attack on Oglethorpe's administration, is still valuable as a source book on the early history of Georgia. Although it contains many literary devices intended to make Oglethorpe's discomfiture more keenly felt, the history is well documented. Of its literary value Professor M. C. Tyler has said, "As a polemic, it is one of the most expert pieces of writing to be met with in our early literature."

About: Tyler, M. C. History of American Literature During the Colonial Period.

TALMAGE, THOMAS DE WITT (January 7, 1832-April 12, 1902), clergyman, lecturer, and editor, was born near Boundbrook, N.J., the son of David Talmage, a farmer and tollgate keeper, and Catharine (Van Nest) Talmage. He started to study law at the University of the City of New York, but before he finished, became interested in the ministry, and in 1856 was graduated from the New Brunswick Theological Seminary. He was installed the same year at the Dutch Reformed Church in Belleville, N.J. After serving in Syracuse from 1859 to 1862, he went to the conservative Second Dutch Reformed Church of Philadelphia. Because of his brilliant, unique manner of speaking and his attractive personality, tremendous crowds soon began to flock there, and Talmadge's fame spread far and wide. In 1869 he went to the Central Presbyterian Church in Brooklyn, where he drew the largest crowds in America. At that time his sermons were published each week in about 3500 papers. For a few years he served at the First Presbyterian Church of Washington, but resigned in 1899 to give all his time to the *Christian Herald* which he had edited since 1890. Prior to that he had edited *Christian at Work* from 1874-76, and *Frank Leslie's Sunday Magazine* from 1881-89. His many published works were of a evangelical nature and included several volumes of sermons. He was married three times.

Principal Works: Crumbs Swept Up, 1870; Sermons, 1872; Every-Day Religion, 1875; Twenty-five Sermons on the Holy Land, 1890; The Marriage Tie, 1890; From Manger to Throne, 1890; Fifty Short Sermons by T. De Witt Talmage, 1923.

About: Adams, C. F. The Life and Sermons of Rev. T. De Witt Talmage; Banks, C. E. Authorized and Authentic Life and Works of T. De Witt Talmage; Rusk, J. The Authentic Life of T. De Witt Talmage; Brooklyn Eagle April 13, 1902; New York Times April 13, 1902; New York Herald April 13, 1902; Washington Post April 13, 1902.

TAPPAN, HENRY PHILIP (April 18, 1805-November 15, 1881), clergyman, philosophical writer, and educator, was born at Rhinebeck, N.Y., the youngest of seven children of Peter and Ann (DeWitt) Tappan. After his graduation from Union College, Schenectady, in 1825, he studied at Auburn Theological Seminary, and in 1828 became minister of the Congregational Church in Pittsfield, Mass. He soon resigned, however, because of a throat infection, and in 1832, after a trip to the West Indies, became a professor at the University of the City of New York. Five years later he was dismissed because he had objected to the mismanagement of the school, and although he was asked to return in 1852, after acquiring a wide reputation in the meantime as philosopher, he became first president of the University of Michigan instead. There he introduced many innovations, selected brilliant professors, and built up the school in many ways. However, because of friction with the board of regents he was asked to resign in 1863. He spent his last years abroad and was buried near Lake Geneva. Tappan was deeply interested in philosophy, especially with the problem of freedom of the will, and on this subject he published several volumes, the first in 1839. His development of the problem was new and helpful; and because of this work and his *Elements of Logic,* he was recognized at home and abroad. He was, however, esteemed more for his pioneer work as an educator, than for his writings as a philosopher.

Principal Works: Review of Edwards' Inquiry Into the Freedom of the Will, 1839; Doctrine of the Will Determined by an Appeal to Consciousness, 1840; Doctrine of the Will Applied to Moral Agency and Responsibility, 1841; Elements of Logic, 1844.

About: Frieze, H. S. A Memorial Discourse, on the Life . . . of Rev. Henry Philip Tappan; Perry, C. M. Henry Philip Tappan: New York Tribune November 18, 1881.

TARBELL, FRANK BIGELOW (January 1, 1853-December 4, 1920), archaeologist and classical historian, was born in West Groton, Mass., the son of John and Sarah (Fosdick) Tarbell. Receiving his early schooling in the district school, he prepared for college at Lawrence Academy, in Groton, and was graduated from Yale in 1873, leaving behind him a distinguished scholastic record. He spent the next two years in Europe and upon his return to America taught Greek and studied for his Ph.D. at Yale. From 1882 to 1887 he was assistant professor of Greek and instructor in logic at Yale. The following year, he went to Athens as annual director of the American School of Classical Studies. Returning for two years, 1889-92, to tutor Greek at Harvard, he went back to Athens for another year as Secretary of the American School, afterward joining the faculty of the newly established University of Chicago in 1892 as associate professor of Greek. In 1893 he took the archaeology professorship, serving until 1918, when he retired to lead a quiet life at his home in Pomfret, Conn. He died in New Haven, following an operation, and left a sum to Yale for the advancement of classical archaeology. He never married.

During his years as an educator he was a frequent contributor to journals, edited *The Philippics of Desmosthenes* (1880), wrote the descriptive matter for an *Illustrated Catalogue of Carbon Prints on the Rise and Progress of Greek and Roman. Art* (1887), and in 1909 made a catalogue of the bronzes in the Field Museum, Chicago. As an outgrowth of his vast knowledge of Greek culture he wrote *A History of Greek Art,* published in 1896, a scholarly and informative volume which placed him in the front ranks of Hellenic historical writers.

Through his enthusiastic interest in archaeology, Tarbell exerted a marked influence upon his students. Stimulating them to wider research, he insisted upon accuracy, infusing them with a strength of purpose that was a high manifestation of his own forceful character.

Principal Works: The Philippics of Desmosthenes, 1880; A History of Greek Art, 1896; Illustrated Catalogue of Carbon Prints on the Rise and Progress of Greek and Roman Art, 1897.

About: History of the Yale Class of 1873; Yale University Obituary Record of Graduates, 1921; American Journal of Archaeology January-March 1921; Chicago Daily Tribune December 6, 1920.

TAYLOR, BAYARD (January 11, 1825-December 19, 1878), poet, novelist, and travel writer, was born of mixed English Quaker and German parentage in Kennett Square, Pa. Originally he signed his name J. Bayard Taylor, but in later years denied that he had been named James Bayard. His father was Joseph Taylor, his mother Rebecca Bauer (Way) Taylor.

Few men have been so completely children of their age as Bayard Taylor. The deadly quiet of a Quaker village and a Quaker family fretted him to rebellion from childhood, and from his two schools, Bolmar's and Unionville Academies, he got little but a desire for a real education which was forbidden him. When he was fourteen, Thomas Dunn English (the author of "Ben Bolt," but then practising as a combined physician-phrenologist) read young Taylor's bumps and assured him he would be a traveler and a poet. The boy deliberately bent his career in those two directions, with little more talent for one than for the other, but with enormous determination. In 1842 he was apprenticed as a printer to the West Chester (Pa.) *Record;* but already the *Saturday Evening Post* had published a poem by him, and through poetry he found the way out. R. W. Griswold, then at the height of his influence, became interested in this rebellious boy, and suggested a means of release. Through Griswold, Taylor secured an advance on services as a European correspondent from the *Saturday Evening Post,* the *United States Gazette,* and the New York

Tribune; walked to Washington for a passport; and set out for Europe in 1844. He remained two years, and returned with his path in life firmly set before him. The freshness and spontaneity of his early travel books caught the public's fancy, and he became a sort of American Marco Polo who had to keep traveling even when he tired of the task.

In 1846, however, with the profits from his first books, he bought and edited the Phoenixville (Pa.) *Gazette,* which he renamed the *Pioneer.* Before the year was out he sold it and went to New York. There for a while he taught in a girls' school, but soon became editor of the *Union Magazine and Christian Inquirer,* and went from that to a post as literary editor of the *Tribune.* In 1849 he went with the "Argonauts" to California for his paper. Meanwhile his personal life was undergoing its greatest tragedy. He had long loved and been engaged to a Quaker girl from his home town, Mary S. Agnew, but she was dying of tuberculosis. Finally in 1850 they were married, but she died two months later. Overcome by grief, Taylor lost himself in a two year trip around the world; he was with Perry as master's mate when Japan was opened to the West, in 1853. Taylor continued to travel and to write of his travels, with brief intervals back in New York, where he mingled with a mildly and self-consciously Bohemian group, including Charles F. Hoffman and N. P. Willis. In 1857 he married Marie Hansen, daughter of a Danish astronomer, and herself a writer and translator; they had one daughter. In 1858 Taylor tried to settle down; he bought a farm and built a house, "Cedarcroft," near his birthplace, only to find that Kennett Square bored him as much as ever, and also that to keep up his domestic responsibilities he was tied permanently to incessant hack writing. He kept distilling books from his travels, lectures from his books; Parke Godwin remarked that Taylor had "traveled more and seen less than any man living."

In 1862 he was appointed secretary of the legation at St. Petersburg (Leningrad), and for a while was chargé d'affaires; disappointed in not being appointed minister, he returned the next year. From 1863 to 1870 his absorbing work was his translation of *Faust,* in the original meters, which gave him a reputation in Germany almost as vast as that he enjoyed in America. From 1870 to 1877 he was non-resident professor of German literature at Cornell. Taylor's fame was like a comet—for a while it outshone the sun, but it was brief. And it did not carry

Collection of Frederick H. Meserve
BAYARD TAYLOR

prosperity with it, or else he was fated to financial misfortune; he lost all his savings and had to lease his house and return to daily slavery on the *Tribune* and weary trips abroad to produce more travel books.

At last the thing he wanted more than anything on earth was given to him—he was appointed minister to Germany in 1878. He sailed full of plans for completing his long projected biography of Goethe, which was to be his crowning achievement. But he had worn himself out. He died in Berlin in December, not yet fifty-four. His body was brought home and lay in state in the New York City Hall before it was buried in the Quaker Cemetery at Longwood, Pa.

Everything contributed to make Taylor regard himself and to make his world regard him as an authentically great writer—his fine aquiline features, his rich voice, his commanding presence, his invincible will to fame and fortune, his absolute self-assurance. But it was all hollow, hollow as his resonant poems, full of sonority and fuller of echoes. "The brilliance of his life," says Carl Van Doren, ". . . blinded men to the mediocrity of his actual achievement." The best and most recent biography well calls him the "laureate of the gilded age." He himself was gilded, not gold, and in complete accord with his era. Diffuse, commonplace, and journalistic, he was one of those writers whose supremacy is all contemporary. Nothing could hide from posterity the fact that he aspired far beyond his abilities, that his whole existence as a writer was made up artificially out of sheer will-power. What is left of him today? A few familiar rhymes —"The Song of the Camp," "The Bedouin Love Song" (which attained final apotheosis by being plagiarized in one of the worst popular songs ever written), "Proposal." His novels never had viability; his travel books are long ago forgotten. He himself remains, a pathetic figure, all the more pathetic in that he never dreamed of his own pathos. A life of Bayard Taylor is a history and indictment of America in the mid-nineteenth century.

Principal Works: *Poetry*—Ximena and Other Poems, 1844; Rhymes of Travel, Ballads, and Poems, 1849; A Book of Romances, Lyrics, and Songs, 1851; Poems of the Orient, 1854; Poems of Home and Travel, 1855; The Poet's Journal, 1862; The Picture of St. John, 1866; The Golden Wedding, 1868; Faust (translated) 1870-71; The Masque of the Gods, 1872; Lars: A Pastoral of Norway, 1873; The Prophet: A Tragedy, 1874; Home Pastorals, Ballads, and Lyrics, 1875; The Echo Club and Other Literary Diversions, 1876; Prince Duekalion, 1878. *Novels*—Hannah Thurston, 1862; John Godfrey's Fortunes, 1864; The Story of Kennett, 1866; Joseph and His Friend, 1870; Beauty and the Beast, 1872; Boys of Other Countries (juvenile) 1876. *Travel and Miscellaneous*—Views Afoot, 1846; Eldorado, 1850; A Journey to Central Africa, 1854; The Lands of the Saracen, 1854; A Visit to India, China, and Japan, 1855; Northern Travel, 1857; Travels in Greece and Russia, 1859; At Home and Abroad, 1859 and 1862; By Ways of Europe, 1869; A School History of Germany, 1874; Egypt and Iceland, 1874; Studies in German Literature, 1879; Critical Essays and Literary Notes, 1880; Unpublished Letters, 1938.

About: Beatty, R. C. Bayard Taylor: Laureate of the Gilded Age; Smyth, A. H. Bayard Taylor; Taylor, M. H. & Kiliani, L. B. T. On Two Continents; Taylor, M. H. & Scudder, H. E. Life and Letters; Vincent, L. H. American Literary Masters; Winter, W. Old Friends; American Review April 1934; Bookman March 1916; Critic October 11, 1884; North American Review June 1915; New York Times December 20, 1878.

TAYLOR, BENJAMIN FRANKLIN (July 19, 1819-February 24, 1887), poet, journalist, and lecturer, was born in Lowville, N.Y., the son of Stephen William Taylor, president of Madison (later Colgate) University, and Eunice (Scranton) Taylor. Graduated from Hamilton Literary and Theological Institute (afterward Madison University), Taylor pioneered three years in Michigan, but was unable to endure the severe life and returned to New York State where he taught school. In 1845 he went to Chicago to become literary editor of the Chicago *Daily Journal,* and served the same paper as war correspondent during the last two years of the Civil War. His vivid reports lifted him to national prominence and appeared in book form as *Mission Ridge and Lookout Mountain: With Pictures of Life in Camp and Field* (1872). Leaving the *Journal* in 1865, he engaged in free-lance writing and lecturing while living in Laporte, Ind., Syracuse, N.Y., and Cleveland, where he died. He was twice married: to Mary Elizabeth Bromley, of Norwich, Conn., in 1839, and after her death nine years later, to Lucy E. Leaming, of La Porte in 1852.

It was Taylor's rural poetry that built up his reputation and earned him the praise of Whittier and others. On the lecture platform he overcame acute shyness and charmed his audiences by his simplicity and quiet humor. His best known works are: *Old-Time Pictures and Sheaves of Rhyme* and *Songs of Yesterday.* Although these works admirably re-created the details of pioneer life, they never rose to the ranks of first-class poetry, despite the London *Times'* lavishness in calling him "the Oliver Goldsmith of America" and pronouncing his battle accounts the finest ever written in the English language.

Principal Works: *Travel Books*—The World on Wheels, 1874; Summer-Savory, 1879; Between the Gates, 1878. *Poetry*—Old-Time Pictures and Sheaves of Rhyme, 1874; Songs of Yesterday, 1875; Dulce Domum, 1884; Complete Poetrical Works, 1886. *Civil War Stories*—Mission Ridge and Lookout Mountain: With Pictures of Life in Camp and Field, 1872.

About: Bromley, V. A. The Bromley Genealogy; Scranton, E. A Genealogical Register of the Descendants of John Scranton of Guilford, Connecticut; Chicago Evening Journal, Chicago Tribune, Cleveland Plain Dealer February 25, 1887.

TAYLOR, JOHN (December 19?, 1753-August 21, 1824), political writer and agriculturalist, known as "John Taylor of Caroline," was born in Virginia, the son of James and Ann (Pollard) Taylor. His parents died very early, and he was brought up by an uncle, Edmund Pendleton, prominent lawyer, judge, patriot, and liberal. The boy was educated by tutors and at a private school, in 1770 entering William and Mary College. He read law in Pendleton's office, and in 1774 was admitted to the bar.

Except for two periods of military service —as major in the Continental Army from 1775 to 1779 and lieutenant-colonel in the state militia when Virginia was invaded in 1781—Taylor's life was spent in public service, the practice of law, at which he was highly successful, and in farming and writing. He married, in 1783, his cousin, Lucy Penn, daughter of John Penn, signer of the Declaration of Independence, and among his

JOHN TAYLOR

several estates chose "Hazelwood" in Caroline County.

He sat twice in the Virginia House of Delegates, and between 1792 and 1822 was three times elected to the United States Senate. Taylor championed democracy and decentralized government. Believing agriculturalists to be the true guardians of democracy and the land the real source of wealth, he opposed paper money, a national bank, a permanent national debt, and later the tariff as creating a "paper aristocracy" of 5,000 supported by the labor of 5,000,000.

In the United States Senate in 1792-4 Taylor was a valued member of the new Republican party, resigning to fight through his writings the strong central government policy of the Federalist party and the banking and funding policies of Alexander Hamilton. The two pamphlets published on these subjects in 1794 were expanded into the longer *Inquiry Into the Principles and Policy of the Government of the United States,* planned in 1794 but not completed till 1814, which the historian, Charles A. Beard, ranks "among the two or three really historic contributions to political science that have been produced in the United States."

In 1798 Taylor introduced into the House of Delegates the famous Virginia Resolutions against the Alien and Sedition Acts. Jefferson's candidacy in 1800 had his ardent support, and he helped in the passage of the 12th Amendment to protect the popular choice of president. He opposed the increasing power of the federal courts under the decisions of John Marshall, the War of 1812 as strengthening the central government, and the Missouri compromise. His *Tyranny Unmasked,* in 1822, was perhaps the first direct attack against a protective tariff.

Little known now, Taylor's writings, though prolix and obscure in style, were widely read in the Virginia of his day and became the Bible of later states rights spokesmen. *Arator,* a little book on agriculture in both its practical and political aspects, was his most popular work. The historian William E. Dodd has called Taylor "one of the first of the mugwumps, a prince of independents."

PRINCIPAL WORKS: A Definition of Parties, 1794; An Enquiry Into the Principles and Tendencies of Certain Public Measures, 1794; Arator, 1803; An Inquiry Into the Principles and Policy of the Government of the U. S., 1814; Construction Construed and Constitutions Vindicated, 1820; Tyranny Unmasked, 1822; New Views of the Constitution of the U. S., 1823.

ABOUT: Dodd, W. E. "John Taylor of Caroline: Prophet of Secession," (in the John P. Branch Historical Papers of Randolph-Macon College: Vol. 2); Simms, H. H. Life of John Taylor; American Political Science Review November 1928.

"TENELLA." See CLARKE, MARY BAYARD (DEVEREUX)

TENNENT, GILBERT (February 5, 1703-July 23, 1764), Presbyterian clergyman and theological writer, was born in County Armagh, Ireland, the son of William and Catharine (Kennedy) Tennent. The family emigrated to the United States when Gilbert was about fourteen and settled in Philadelphia, where the father founded a theological school, "Log College." Gilbert studied medicine for about a year, but abandoned it for divinity; was licensed by the Philadelphia Presbytery in 1726; and was ordained as pastor at New Brunswick, N.J.

Here he established a large following with his evangelical methods and remained for seventeen years. Tennent was a large man of dignified carriage, and with his fine voice and dramatic bearing must have been an impressive figure in the pulpit. At the request of George Whitefield, he made a tour of New England (1740) and had great success. The next year there was a division in the Synod, due to differences of opinion in regard to revivals; and the harshness of Tennent toward his critics was a great factor in the bitterness of the schism.

In 1743 he was called to the pastorate of the newly formed Presbyterian Church in Philadelphia, where he remained until his death, becoming in later years more gentle and conventional and less contentious. He was married three times. In 1741, after the death of his first wife, he married Cornelia

(De Peyster) Clarkson, who died in 1753. His third wife was Mrs. Sarah Spofford.

Tennent's published writings are too didactic and redolent of evangelism to have much permanent value.

PRINCIPAL WORKS: The Danger of an Unconverted Ministry. . . , 1740; Remarks Upon a Protestation Presented to the Synod of Philadelphia, 1741; The Necessity of Holding Fast the Truth Represented in Three Sermons. . .Relating to Errors Lately Vented by Some Moravians. . . , 1743; The Examiner Examined: or, Gilbert Tennent, Harmonious. . . 1743; Irenicum Ecclesiasticum: or, A Humble, Impartial Essay Upon the Peace of Jerusalem, 1749; The Late Association for Defence Encourag'd: or, The Lawfulness of a Defensive War, 1748; The Late Association for Defence Farther Encouraged: or, Defensive War Defended; and Its Consistency with True Christianity Represented, 1748.

ABOUT: Alexander, A. Biographical Sketches of the Founder and Principal Alumni of the Log College; Maxson, C. H. The Great Awakening in the Middle Colonies; Webster, R. A History of the Presbyterian Church in America; The General Assembly's Missionary Magazine May 1805.

TENNENT, JOHN (c. 1700-c. 1760), Colonial physician and writer of medical books, was born in England, and came to the colony of Virginia about 1725, settling first in Spotsylvania County and later acquiring property in Fredericksburg and Prince William County as well. About five years after his arrival, he married Dorothy Paul. He was in Williamsburg in 1735, where his *Essay on the Pleurisy* was published a year later. This small volume created a great sensation, and related Tennent's successful experience in the therapeutic use of rattlesnake-root, a plant he discovered through "a Nation of *Indians*, called the *Senekkas.*"

Returning to England in 1737 he became acquainted with prominent London physicians and attempted to win approval for his root remedy. He was in Virginia again the following year but returned to London in 1739 as a result of a controversy regarding his root treatment, in the *Virginia Gazette.* Despite the fact that the House of Burgess paid him £100 for giving his discovery to the world, he felt that the colony had not shown the proper gratitude. Nor did he meet with much better treatment in England where his theories were so little appreciated that he eventually fell in with Johsua Ward, a notorious quack, and going from bad to worse took "the foolish step in having kept one Mrs. Carey under the name of Mrs. Tennent." Inasmuch as he had married a Mrs. Hangar, "a Widow Lady from Huntingdon" in 1741, his interest in Mrs. Carey resulted in a bigamy trial at the Old Bailey. Through the timely intervention of Sir Hans Sloane, Tennent was saved from utter disgrace, and in an appreciative letter to his benefactor signified his plan to visit Jamaica, although there is no record of his doing so, nor any further details of his life.

On the medicinal uses of American herbs he published *Every Man His Own Doctor;* and he never lost faith in his snake-root theory. His writings are now little more than medical curios.

PRINCIPAL WORKS: Every Man His Own Doctor, 1724; Essay on the Pleurisy, 1736; An Epistle to Dr. Richard Mead, Concerning the Epidemical Diseases of Virginia, Particularly, a Pleurisy, and Peripneumony, 1738; A Reprieve From Death, 1741; Physical Enquiries, 1742; Detection of a Conspiracy. . . The Singular Case of John Tennent, 1743; Physical Disquitions, 1745; A Brief Account of the Case of John Tennent, M.D.

ABOUT: Blanton, W. B. Medicine in Virginia in the Eighteenth Century; American Medical Biography 1920; Journal of the House of Burgesses, Va., 1727-40, 1758-61; Va. Gazette for 1736, Nos. 6, 9, 10, 14, 31; *Ibid.* for 1737, Nos. 45, 50, 72; William and Mary Quarterly July 1923.

TENNEY, TABITHA (GILMAN) (April 7, 1762-May 2, 1837), novelist and compiler, was born in Exeter, N.H., into a family distinguished for service in New Hampshire. Daughter of Samuel Gilman and his second wife, Lydia (Robinson) Giddings (or Giddinge) Gilman, she was educated according to the prevailing fashion for young gentlewomen and was well-grounded in intellectual, artistic, and household accomplishments. Omnivorous reading ultimately led her to try a novel of her own, and in 1801 she published the book which has given her a historical place among American women novelists: *Female Quixotism: Exhibited in the Romantic Opinions and Extravagant Adventures of Dorcasina Sheldon,* a two-volume satire on contemporary literary taste and the prevalent feminine romanticism. According to a bookseller's advertisement, she had previously compiled an anthology of poetry and classical pieces in 1799 entitled *The Pleasing Instructor,* designed for the education of young women, although there is no copy extant.

In 1788 she married Samuel Tenney, and while he held office as United States Congressman (1800-07), they lived in Washington. He died in 1816 and Tabitha Gilman outlived him twenty-one years, consoling herself in charitable works. Since there is no record of further publications, she evidently gave her full attention to the needle instead of the pen, producing exquisite pieces of needlework toward the end of her life.

PRINCIPAL WORKS: The Pleasing Instructor, 1799?; Female Quixotism: Exhibited in the Romantic Opinions and Extravagant Adventures of Dorcasina Sheldon, 1801.

ABOUT: Gilman, A. The Gilman Family; Bell, C. H. History of the Town of Exeter, N. H.; Exeter News Letter May 9, 1837; New-Hampshire Statesman and State Journal (Concord) May 13, 1837.

TERHUNE, MARY VIRGINIA (HAWES) ("Marion Harland") (December 21, 1830-June 3, 1922), novelist and writer on household management, was born in Dennisville, Amelia County, Va., the daughter of Samuel Pierce and Judith Anna (Smith) Hawes. Privately tutored and under the influence of the cultured atmosphere of her home, she started writing at the age of nine and by her fourteenth year was contributing regularly to a Richmond newspaper. At the age of sixteen she wrote *Alone* (1854), over the pen-name "Marion Harland." It was the first of a long series of successes extending over sixty years, including *Nemesis* in 1860 and *The Carringtons of High Hill* in 1919.

She was married in 1856 to the Rev. Edward Payson Terhune, then pastor of a church at Charlotte Court-House, Va., and later of churches in Newark, N.J., Springfield, Mass., and Brooklyn, N.Y. These changes of scene were reflected in her books, as Mrs. Terhune avidly seized upon everything that would add interest or variety to her romances. An admirable executive, she managed to combine her duties as minister's wife, housekeeper, mother, and literary celebrity in the most praiseworthy degree. Realizing the great need for efficient manuals in the field of home economics, Mrs. Terhune wrote *Common Sense in the Household,* published in 1871. There was such a wide demand for intelligent guidance in the heretofore unappreciated but necessary department of housekeeping that Mrs. Terhune was forced to give up, except on rare occasions, her work as a fiction writer. Her articles on household management appeared in newspapers and magazines, and she published many books on the subject. Her writings were syndicated widely, she edited a magazine, *Babyhood,* for two years and had charge of a children's department in *St. Nicholas* and other magazines. Soon no well-regulated Victorian home was complete without a "Marion Harland" cookbook on its shelf.

Mrs. Terhune made two trips abroad, the second time accompanied by her son, Albert Payson Terhune, the author. They visited Egypt and the Holy Land and Mrs. Terhune published a book about this trip under the title *The Home of the Bible.*

Collection of Frederick H. Meserve

MARY VIRGINA TERHUNE
("Marion Harland")

Her autobiography, published when she was eighty years old, and the novel *The Carringtons of High Hill* were her last works. The latter she dictated, having lost her sight at the age of eighty-nine. She died in New York at ninety-one, having earned the gratitude of the women of America for the pioneer work she accomplished in the field of home economics.

PRINCIPAL WORKS: Alone, 1854; The Hidden Path, 1859; Nemises, 1860; Common Sense in the Household: A Manual of Practical Housewifery. 1871; True as Steel, 1872; Loiterings in Pleasant Paths, 1880; Judith, 1883; A Gallant Fight, 1888; His Great Self, 1892; The Home of the Bible, 1895; The National Cook Book, 1896; Where Ghosts Walk, 1898; Charlotte Brontë at Home, 1899; William Cowper, 1899; John Knox, 1900; Hannah Moore, 1900; Dr Dale, 1900; Everyday Etiquette, 1905; Marion Harland's Autobiography, 1910; The Carringtons of High Hill, 1919.

ABOUT: Willard, F. E. & Livermore, M. A. A Woman of the Century; Wright, M. H. Mary Virginia Hawes Terhune; New York Times June 4, 1922.

TEUFFEL, BARONESS VON. See HOWARD, BLANCHE WILLIS

THACHER, JAMES (February 14, 1754-May 26, 1844), physician, historian, and biographer, was born at Barnstable, Mass. His father, John Thacher, was a farmer of small means but of noteworthy ancestry, descended from the English Anthony Thacher who came to America in 1635. His mother, Content (Norton) Thacher, was the granddaughter of Gov. William Coddington of Rhode Island. Without much education he was apprenticed at sixteen to Abner Hersey, a much respected physician who in the main left the youth to gather his own instruction. The outbreak of the Revolutionary War found him with sufficient medical knowledge to gain acceptance as surgeon's mate to the military hospital at Cambridge; he was subsequently promoted to other hospitals and field services, including that of surgeon in a selected corps of light infantry. Retiring from the army in 1783 with a high reputation, he established himself as the leading physician of Plymouth. Harvard conferred on him the honorary M.A. in 1808 and M.D. in 1810. He was a member of the American Academy of Arts and Sciences, of several state medical societies, of historical and horticultural associations, and of the French society of Universal Statistics. He died at ninety.

His diary, *A Military Journal During the American Revolutionary War,* a carefully kept, detailed record of daily observations from 1775 to 1783, is a valuable historical commentary on the events and personalities of the period. It went through a number of editions. His medical writings, notably the accurate and impartial *American Medical Biography,* the first source book of its kind, greatly heightened his reputation.

Principal Works: The American New Dispensatory, 1810; Observations on Hydrophobia, 1812; American Modern Practice, 1817; The American Orchardist, 1822; A Military Journal During the American Revolutionary War, 1823; American Medical Biography, 1828; A Practical Treatise on the Management of Bees, 1829; An Essay on Demonology, Ghosts, and Apparitions, and Popular Superstititions, 1831; History of the Town of Plymouth, 1832.

About: Totten, J. R. Thacher-Thatcher Genealogy; Williams, S. W. American Medical Biography.

"THANET, OCTAVE." See FRENCH, ALICE

THAXTER, CELIA (LAIGHTON) (June 29, 1835-August 26, 1894), poet, was born at Portsmouth, N.H., the oldest of three children of Thomas Laighton and Eliza (Rymes) Laighton. Her father was a successful dealer in lumber and West Indies goods, also a newspaper editor and member of the state legislature; but, disappointed in politics, he got himself appointed lighthouse keeper on White Island, in the Isles of Shoals, nine miles off the coast of New Hampshire. There he took his family in 1839. Six years later he resigned the post and began building on Appledore, largest of the islands, what was perhaps the first summer hotel on the Atlantic coast. From the first it attracted—both as guests and as friends—artists, musicians, writers, and scholars.

As a child Celia Laighton knew and loved the life of the apparently barren islands and the many moods of the surrounding sea, and most of her writing stems from this early ecstatic, solitary experience. She and her bothers were educated by their parents, with two winters' tutoring by Levi Lincoln Thaxter, Harvard graduate, lawyer, and student of Robert Browning. In September 1851 the 27-year old scholar and the 16-year old girl were married.

For several years the Thaxters lived on Star Island, where Mr. Thaxter was lay preacher in the dying fishing village of Gosport. Three sons were born, the first a mental defective, the third to become professor of botany at Harvard. In 1860 the Thaxters moved to Newtonville, Mass., the experience producing the poem, "Land-Locked." Without the author's knowledge it was shown to James Russell Lowell, then editor of the *Atlantic Monthly,* who published it in March 1861. This success, and the advice of her friends, among them Whittier, encouraged the young woman to continue. In 1872 her first collection, *Poems,* was published, and in 1873, *Among the Isles of Shoals,* a series of prose sketches of the islands and her life there as a child.

Her father had died in 1866, and urged by her husband, she returned with her children to Appledore to be with her mother. Her brothers continued to run the hotel and built

CELIA THAXTER

a second on Star Island. After several winters at Appledore, her life subsequently consisted of winters on the mainland and summers at the Shoals. Her friends among the distinguished visitors were many, and it became a much-sought honor to attend the twice-daily meetings, for music and conversation, in her cottage living-room. Her brilliant flower garden was as famous as her "salon."

In 1877 her mother died, a great grief to her; in 1880 she made a trip abroad with one of her brothers. Mr. Thaxter died in 1884, and in 1894, at the age of fifty-nine Celia Thaxter died suddenly at Appledore, where she is buried.

"It is quite as much as a personality as a poet that Mrs. Thaxter will be remembered," read a contemporary account, and it is in her prose and her letters that her personality is most clearly revealed—courageous, vigorous, generous and sensitive. She was not a great poet, but she preserved some of the gray beauty of the New Hampshire coast.

Principal Works: *Poems*—Poems, 1872; Drift-Weed, 1879; Poems for Children, 1884; Cruise of the Mystery and Other Poems, 1886; (Appledore edition, ed. by Sarah Orne Jewett) 1896. *Miscellaneous*—Among the Isles of Shoals, 1873; An Island Garden, 1894; Letters of Celia Thaxter (ed. by Annie Adams Fields & Rose Lamb) 1895.

About: Laighton, O. (ed.). The Heavenly Guest; New England Quarterly December 1935.

THAYER, CAROLINE MATILDA (WARREN) (1787 (?) - 1844), novelist, moralist, and school teacher, was a native of New England, "tenderly educated by her parents who delighted to gratify [her] early wishes . . . caressed by . . . friends, and flattered by . . . companions." At a very early age she began to have great concern about the "hereafter," and sought diversion in the study of rhetoric, philosophy, botany, etc. Believing that the "light unthinking mind that would revolt at a moral lesson from the pulpit will seize, with avidity, the instruction offered under the similitude of a story," she wrote *The Gamesters: or, Ruins of Innocence, an Original Novel, Founded in Truth,* a book which, she hoped, might "lure one profligate from the arms of dissipation or snatch from the precipice of ruin one fair fabric of innocence." Its ultimate thesis, emerging from unwieldy figures of speech and melodramatic platitudes, was:

> When the husband can find attractions at the gaming table superior to those offered by the domestic fireside, virtue herself is eradicated from his bosom.

At the age of twenty she withdrew to an "obscure corner of New Hampshire among the people called Methodists." But she broke from this faith when she found in Swedenborgianism that which "reconciles all difficulties and apparent contradictions in the book of revelation." She was subsequently forced to withdraw as superintendent of the Female Department at Wesleyan Seminary, and in self-vindication she issued her *Letter to the Members of the Methodist Episcopal Church . . . and the Circumstances of . . . Dismission From the Wesleyan Seminary.* Her educational juvenile, *First Lessons in the History of the United States,* bringing the story of America down to the year 1820 in highly simplified and abridged form, appeared in 1823 and again in 1825. In order to "counteract the effect of infidel sentiments on the youthful mind," she prepared *Religion Recommended to Youth in a Series of Letters,* supplementing them with a few of her own "occasion" poems. She was married in her twenties, to one Mr. Thayer, by whom she had three children.

Not the "censorious hypercritic, who views with the jaundiced eyes of prejudice every production from a female pen" (him she regarded as her greatest professional enemy) but the mere passing of a few years stripped Mrs. Thayer's writings, from the point of view of the literary critic, of almost everything except a small but obvious historical interest.

Principal Works: The Gamesters: or, Ruins of Innocence, an Original Novel Founded in Truth, 1805; Letter to the Members of the Methodist Episcopal Church. . . and the Circumstances of. . . Dismission From the Wesleyan Seminary, 1821; First Lessons in the History of the United States, 1823; Religion Recommended to Youth in a Series of Letters Addressed to a Young Lady: To Which are Added Poems on Various Occasions, 1837.

About: See prefaces to the works.

THAYER, JAMES BRADLEY (January 15, 1831-February 14, 1902), legal writer, was born in Haverhill, Mass., the second son of Abijah Wyman Thayer, newspaper editor, and Susan (Bradley) Thayer. He was graduated from Harvard in 1852; entered the Law School in 1854; and two years later was admitted to the Boston bar. From 1874 until his death he was a professor in the Harvard Law School. In 1861 he married Sophia Bradford Ripley, daughter of the Rev. Samuel Ripley. Of his four children his two sons, Dr. William Snyder Thayer, a physician, and Ezra Ripley Thayer, dean of Harvard Law School, attained distinction.

An early dissertation "The Right of Eminent Domain" took a first prize at the

Harvard Law School and was published in the Boston *Monthly Law Reporter* for September and October, 1856. He published reviews of Greek and Latin translations, the letters and a biographical account of the metaphysician, Chauncey Wright, biographies of his father-in-law, the Rev. Samuel Ripley, and of John Marshall, and a reminiscence of a trip to California in 1871 with Ralph Waldo Emerson and others. His reputation, however, rests on his legal writings. His *Preliminary Treatise on Evidence at the Common Law* made him widely known as a legal scholar and jurist. This treatise was intended as an introduction to a more elaborate work which was never written, although he had collected materials for over twenty years. The need was later supplied by his pupil, J. H. Wigmore. in *A Treatise on the System of Evidence in Trials at Common Law.* Thayer also contributed to John Bouvier's *A Dictionary of Law* and, among periodicals, to the *American Law Review* and the *Harvard Law Review.* In latter years his lecturing and writing on legal subjects were almost exclusively on the phases of constitutional law and evidence. A posthumous work, *Legal Essays,* was published by his son, Ezra Ripley Thayer.

Principal Works: Letters of Chauncey Wright, 1878; A Western Journey With Mr. Emerson, 1884; Memorandum on the Legal Effect of Opinions Given by Judges to the Executive and the Legislature Under Certain American Constitutions, 1885; Select Cases on Evidence at the Common Law, 1892, 1900; Cases on Constitutional Law, 1895; Rev. Samuel Ripley of Waltham, 1897; A Preliminary Treatise on Evidence at the Common Law, 1898; John Marshall, 1901; Legal Essays, 1908.

About: Edes, G. W. Annals of the Harvard Class of 1852; American Law Review March 1902; Colonial Society of Massachusetts Transactions February 1902; Harvard Law Review April 1902.

"THOMAS, CAROLINE." See DORR, JULIA CAROLINE (RIPLEY)

THOMAS, EBENEZER SMITH (June 19, 1775-August 1844), journalist, generally known as E. Smith Thomas, was born at Cambridge, Mass., the son of Joshua Thomas, postrider for his brother Isaiah's Revolutionary journal, the *Spy.* At the age of thirteen E. Smith Thomas began a four-year apprenticeship with his uncle, Isaiah Thomas [*q.v.*], printer and bookseller, and was sometimes obliged to rise "between five and six o'clock and read proof until twelve or one at night." After three years as a bookbinder in Boston, he set out—"with decent clothes on his back, a pocket life of Franklin, and $1.50"—for Charleston, S.C. Here he set up as printer and stationer, and made, in all, four journeys to England to enhance his connections with the trade; and during one visit established a friendship with Washington Irving, then consul in London.

Following the reopening of the African slave-trade, commercial Charleston suffered a financial collapse. Thomas returned North; built a cotton factory in Providence, R.I.; and then went South again, 1804-05, to marry Ann Fonerdon. (Two of their children, Frederick William and Lewis Foulk Thomas [*qq.v.*], achieved considerable literary distinction.) He purchased the *City Gazette,* a daily dedicated to Jeffersonian republicanism; this, as well as his weekly, the *South Carolina Gazette,* became highly profitable ventures. Thomas was imprisoned on libel charges, following the publication of a bitter political letter; and on his release was escorted by a "brass band and a parade of admirers."

He afterward retired to a farm near Baltimore, Md., but with a drop in real estate values in 1827 he sold out to pay his debts and went to Cincinnati, where he set up the *Daily Commercial Advertiser;* and in 1835, the *Daily Evening Post.* Four years later he withdrew from active editorial work; interested himself in political events; and prepared his two rambling volumes of *Reminiscences of the Last Sixty-Five Years,* which, although loosely threaded and sometimes considerably muddled, has become a significant incidental footnote to a conspectus of American society in the nineteenth century.

About: Allen, H. Israfel; Marble, A. R. From 'Prentice to Patron; Thomas, E. S. Reminiscences of the Last Sixty-Five Years; United States Magazine and Democratic Review September 1840; information from R. W. G. Vail, librarian, American Antiquarian Society.

THOMAS, EDITH MATILDA (August 12, 1854-September 13, 1925), poet, was born at Chatham, Ohio, but spent her childhood at Kenton and Bowling Green, where her father, Frederick J. Thomas, was a farmer-schoolteacher. He died in 1861, and his widow, Jane Louisa (Sturges) Thomas, took Edith to Geneva, Ohio, where she attended the normal school, graduating in 1872. Here she began to write poetry which was so influenced by Greek literature that she was later called "more Greek than American."

After a brief period at Oberlin College, several months of school-teaching, and a time of free-lance writing for Geneva and Cleveland newspapers, she visited New York in 1881, where she met Anne Charlotte Lynch

Botta and Helen Hunt Jackson. This acquaintance led to the publication of her poetry in the leading periodicals. In 1885 her first book was published, *A New Year's Masque and Other Poems*. Two years later, after her mother's death, she moved to New York permanently and made her home with Dr. and Mrs. Samuel Elliott, whose guests included many distinguished persons who interested themselves in the slender little Ohio poetess. Especially helpful in advancing her success was Richard Watson Gilder.

Literary activities soon occupied her completely. Aside from her own writing, she worked on the compilation of the *Century Dictionary* and became a reader for *Harper's Magazine*, under Henry Mills Alden.

Although she made many friends and led an active social life, she was fundamentally retiring and preferred to live in her own world of imagination and poetry. This remoteness of spirit, this elusiveness, was one of the charms of her personality and was a leading characteristic of her poetry. Appreciated by a discerning few in her day, she is now grouped among the sound technicians who never captured wide public interest.

Principal Works: A New Years' Masque and Other Poems, 1885; The Round Year, 1886; Lyrics and Sonnets, 1887; The Children of the Seasons Series, 1888; The Inverted Torch, 1890; In Sunshine Land, 1885; The Dancers, and Other Legends and Lyrics, 1903; The Flower From the Ashes, 1915.

About: Rittenhouse, J. B. Selected Poems of Edith M. Thomas; Book Buyer March 1888; Dial (Chicago) November 1886.

THOMAS, FREDERICK WILLIAM (October 25, 1906-August 27, 1866), journalist and novelist, was born in Providence, R.I., the son of Ebenezer Smith Thomas [*q.v.*] and Ann (Fonerdon) Thomas. Between 1807 and 1809 the family lived on a farm near Baltimore, Md., and then moved to Charleston, S.C., where Ebenezer Thomas, who had been a bookseller there in his youth, became editor of the *City Gazette*.

Suffering two serious injuries during his childhood which permanently lamed him, Frederick grew up with relatives in Baltimore, where he was joined by his family in 1816. He studied for a legal career, was admitted to the bar in 1828 and practiced law in Baltimore until 1831 when he went to assist his father in editing the *Commercial Daily Advertiser*. At the same time he resumed his law practice and during his ten-year residence served for a time as editor of the *Democratic Intelligencer*.

After 1841 he was in Washington where he assembled a library for the Treasury Department with which he was connected. He was professor of rhetoric and English in the University of Alabama for a year, and in 1850 became a preacher in the Methodist Episcopal Church in Cincinnati. He took up his law practice again in Cambridge, Md., and in 1860 became literary editor of the Richmond *Enquirer*. Shortly before his death in Washington, D.C., he was on the editorial staff of the Columbia *South Carolinian*.

During his busy years as lawyer, professor, and editor, and despite his affliction, Thomas found time to write a number of novels which were widely read. Among these were *Clinton Bradshaw: or, The Adventures of a Lawyer* and *John Randolph of Roanoke*. Thomas' friendship and correspondence with Edgar Allan Poe will keep his memory alive long after his writings have been relegated to the shelves of lesser nineteenth century novelists.

Principal Works: Clinton Bradshaw: or The Adventures of a Lawyer, 1835; Howard Pinckney: A Novel, 1840; The Beechen Tree: A Tale Told in Rhyme, 1844; Sketches of Character and Tales Founded on Fact, 1849; An Autobiography of William Russell, 1852; John Randolph of Roanoke, 1853.

About: Coggeshall, W. T. The Poets and Poetry of the West; Harrison, J. A. The Complete Works of Edgar Allan Poe; Rusk, R. L. The Literature of the Middle Western Frontier; Thomas, E. S. Reminiscences of the Last Sixty-Five Years; Daily National Intelligencer (Washington, D.C.) August 30, 1866.

THOMAS, ISAIAH (January 19, 1749-April 4, 1831), publisher and historian, was born in Boston, the son of Moses and Fidelity (Grant) Thomas. The father, a reckless creature, died in 1852, and the mother supported her five children by keeping a small shop until she remarried in 1764. Isaiah Thomas had only six weeks' schooling in his life, though later he was made an honorary M.A. by Dartmouth and LL.D. by Allegheny College. He was a child of seven when he was apprenticed to Zechariah Fowle, a shiftless printer of chapbooks and ballads. By fourteen or so he was in charge of the business, by seventeen an excellent printer and a self-educated youth. He made two attempts to escape from his bondage to Fowle—first to Halifax, N.S., next to Charleston, S.C., each time hoping to be able to make his way to England, but having to return. Finally he secured a release from his unexpired apprenticeship, and by 1770 he was Fowle's partner and later bought him out.

Thomas was the founder of the *Massachusetts Spy*, a periodical which lived to 1904. In its early years the paper's career was an adventurous one, since it was strongly Whig.

From a portrait by E. A. Greenwood
ISAIAH THOMAS
1818

In 1775 Thomas found it expedient to move himself and his business to Worcester, his home thereafter. He, as well as Paul Revere, made the famous ride of April 18, 1775, and he was a minute man at Lexington and Concord. For two years during the Revolution he was at Salem, then returned to Worcester as the patriots' official printer. He built up an enormous publishing house, largest of its time, with branches as far away as Baltimore and Albany. His publishing experience is a series of "firsts"—the first folio Bible in English in the United States, the first Greek grammar, the first dictionary (Perry's), the first extensive printing of music, the "first American novel" (*The Power of Sympathy*), the first American juvenile books. His *New England Almanack*, with variations in title, was issued from 1771 to 1822; and between 1774 to 1796 he published three short-lived magazines. In 1802, rich, he retired in favor of his son; the son died in 1819. Thomas was also the founder of the American Antiquarian Society, and its first president; he left it his fine historical library.

For a man of his time and place, he had a curious matrimonial career. In 1769 he married Mary Dill, of Bermuda. In 1777 he divorced her for adultery and received custody of his son and daughter. (The daughter later was married four times and divorced three.) In 1779 he married Mary (Thomas) Fowle, his half cousin. They were happy for nearly forty years, until she died in 1818. The next year he married her cousin, Rebecca Armstrong, but the marriage was a failure and they were separated after 1822.

Thomas' only published work was his two-volume *History of Printing in America*. This is now 140 years old, and still the standard authority. He had a real gift for "plain English, with a dash of satire." He wrote much also for his magazines and for the *Almanac*, sometimes in rather homespun verse. Tall, slender, and strong-featured, with social charm and great business acumen, he was, as none but his intimates realized, an essentially melancholy man, and so "temperamental" that blame for the disaster of his first and third marriages cannot have been all on the side of his wives.

About: The History of Printing in America: With a Biography of Printers and an Account of Newspapers, 1810.

About: Marble, A. R. From 'Prentice to Patron: The Life Story of Isaiah Thomas; Mott, F. L. A History of American Magazines; Nichols, C. L. Isaiah Thomas: Printer, Writer, and Collector; Thomas, B. F. Memoir of Isaiah Thomas; Proceedings American Antiquarian Society: 1900, 1916, 1921; Transactions American Antiquarian Society: 1909.

THOMAS, LEWIS FOULK (November 3, 1808-December 26, 1868), poet and journalist, brother of Frederick William Thomas [*q.v*], was born near Baltimore, Md., the son of Ebenezer Smith Thomas [*q.v.*] and Ann (Fonerdon) Thomas. He spent part of his boyhood in Baltimore County and then removed to Cincinnati, Ohio, where he helped his brother conduct the *Commercial Daily Advertiser* and for a time was connected with the *Daily Evening Post* before it was discontinued in 1839. He studied law for a while and then undertook the editorship of the Louisville *Daily Herald*. In 1841 he removed to St. Louis, Mo., and subsequently to Washington, D.C., where he practiced law until the time of his death.

Thomas never enjoyed robust health and as a child had read several retrospective and rather gloomy books. One of his earliest attempts at verse writing was a kind of "stream of consciousness" poem called "A Suicide's Reflections on Death." This soliloquy was incorporated many years later, into his last ambitious undertaking, *Cortez the Conqueror*, a poetic tragedy suggested, in part, by the reading of a history of Mexico. To Col. Albert Pike, popular Arkansas poet, Thomas was indebted for corrections in the manuscript. Thomas provided the very adequate descriptive material for *The Valley of the Mississippi in a Series of Views*, with paintings and lithographs by John Cooper Wild. One critic regarded his *Inda and Other*

Poems (1842), alleged to be the first volume of poems published west of the Mississippi, as excellent evidence that the "glorious land of the Mississippi, the prairie, and the forest may be gracefully pressed by the footsteps of the muse." Some of this verse had an engaging cadence that in itself might have seemed to justify his publishing these "juvenile indiscretions" . . . (as he put it) " . . . merely to gratify [his] own whim." A lack of physical energy appears to have prevented Thomas from carrying out several contemplated literary enterprises, but his writings, though scant, have become modest landmarks in the rise of a Midwest literature.

PRINCIPAL WORKS: The Valley of the Mississippi In a Series of Views, 1841; Inda and Other Poems, 1842; Cortez the Conqueror, 1857.

ABOUT: Thomas, E. S. Reminiscences of the Last Sixty-Five Years; Thomas F. W. John Randolph of Roanoke; Southern Quarterly Review January and April 1843; Prefaces to the works; Information from R. W. G. Vail, Librarian American Antiquarian Society.

THOMES, WILLIAM HENRY (May 5, 1824-March 6, 1895), publisher and writer of adventure books, was born in Portland, Maine, the son of Job and Mary (Lewis) Thomes. The family soon moved to Boston, where both parents died. Brought up by a guardian, young Thomes took little interest in schooling and at the age of eighteen went to sea in the "Admittance" in the California hide trade. He later described his experiences in his admirable volume, *On Land and Sea* (1883), which bears a strong relationship to Richard Henry Dana's *Two Years Before the Mast*.

There is no accurate account of Thomes' early life in California but it is said that he deserted, or conveniently arranged to miss a ship's sailing. From his own writings and some biographical accounts there are indications that he was in military service during the conquest of California. In December 1846 he left the West Coast. By way of Mazatlán and England, he returned to Boston, where he served the Boston *Daily Times* as printer and reporter for a year. The gold rush of '49 was food for his adventurous spirit and he sailed for San Francisco in the "Edward Everett," as a member of the Boston and California Joint Stock Mining and Trading Co., an affiliation of short duration. After a period of mining at Bidwell's Bar, he returned to San Francisco with dissipated health and fortunes to become a ship's caretaker. During 1851 he lived in the Hawaiian Islands, visited Guam, the Philippines, China, and the gold mines of Victoria, and is said to have put himself back on his financial feet by keeping a store at Ballarat. He returned to the United States by way of the Cape of Good Hope in 1855, and went back to the Boston *Herald* as a reporter. About 1860 he became a partner of Elliott & Thomes, publishers of the *American Union,* a weekly magazine, for which he wrote a series of long and lurid adventure stories. Among these were *The Gold Hunter's Adventures: or, Life in Australia,* and *The Bushrangers.* Although he had sold over half a million copies of his books by 1895, his writing (with the exception of *On Land and Sea,* his best work) was too florid to achieve literary distinction.

Contrary to his early days of struggle, Thomes was successful at the end of his life and rose to prominence in the political and literary life of Boston. His firm became successively, Elliott, Thomes & Talbot, and Thomes & Talbot, publishers of *The Flag of Our Union,* and *Ballou's Monthly.* In 1890 Thomes led an excursion to California in connection with the Society of California Pioneers of New England, which he had founded in 1888. He was twice married, first to a daughter of Captain Peter Peterson, the master of the "Admittance," second to Frances Ullen.

PRINCIPAL WORKS: The Gold Hunters' Adventures: or, Life in Australia, 1864; The Bushrangers, 1866; The Gold Hunters in Europe, 1868; The Whaleman's Adventures, 1872; A Slaver's Adventures, 1872; Life in the East Indies, 1873; Running the Blockade, 1875; The Belle of Australia, 1883; On Land and Sea, 1883; Lewey and I, 1884; The Ocean Rovers, 1896.

ABOUT: Thomes, W. H. Lewey and I; On Land and Sea; Ball, N. The Pioneers of '49; Howe, O. T. Argonauts of '49; Boston Evening Transcript March 7, 1895.

THOMPSON, DANIEL PIERCE (October 1, 1795-June 6, 1868), novelist, was born in Charlestown, Mass., the son of Daniel and Rebecca (Parker) Thompson. In 1800 his father failed in business and moved to a farm near Berlin, Vt. The child grew up almost without schooling; at sixteen he chanced on an old volume of poetry which aroused his ambition for an education. He taught in country schools, sold some sheep he owned, and after a year at the Academy at Danville, Vt., he entered Middlebury College as a sophomore, being graduated in 1820. He then spent four years in Virginia as tutor in a wealthy family, also studying law, being admitted to the bar in 1823.

He returned to Vermont, settling in Montpelier for the rest of his life, and there began a prosperous career. He was successively registrar of probate, clerk of the legislature, judge of probabte, clerk of the county court and secretary of state for Vermont (1853-55). In 1831 he married Eunice Knight Robinson, by whom he had four sons and two daughters. He was a founder of the Vermont Historical Society and secretary of the State Education Society. From 1849 to 1856 he edited the *Green Mountain Freeman,* an anti-slavery organ. Though he had been a Jeffersonian Democrat (he interviewed Jefferson at Monticello in 1822), he became a Republican in 1856. He traveled much in New England, as a lyceum lecturer; and in his later years financial difficulties kept him at work even following several paralytic strokes, from the last of which he died.

Writing was strictly an avocation with Thompson, his attention having been turned to fiction first when he won a prize of $50 with *May Martin* in 1835. As Van Wyck Brooks says, he "never became a professional author." He never, indeed, had much reputation as a writer, being much better known in Montpelier as the town eccentric, the rawboned slovenly man who shuffled downtown in carpet slippers and went fishing with the children. He was a typical old-fashioned Yankee, shrewd, slipshod, dryly humorous, and positive. Yet, since he was "a born antiquarian," he had accumulated from casual contacts an immense fund of first-hand historical material, salty stories of old settlers and reminiscences of the great old days, and all this he wove into his Cooperesque stories, most of all into the only good one—*The Green Mountain Boys.* This Brooks calls "a border-song in prose," and it truly has more of Scott about it than of Cooper. In it Thompson displayed his narrative gift, his unstudied humor, his ability (as Flitcroft puts it) to "talk a straight story plainly and rapidly." But this novel betrays also, though not so grossly as do all his others, Thompson's poverty of imagination, his conventional characterization, his stiffness, and his dullness. His remaining novels, including the autobiographical *Locke Amsden* and the book he left unfinished at his death, *The Honest Lawyer,* are quite unreadable, but *The Green Mountain Boys* still occupies its modest niche as one of the earliest of American regional novels.

From a portrait by T. W. Wood
DANIEL PIERCE THOMPSON

PRINCIPAL WORKS: The Adventures of Timothy Peacock, Esq.: or, Freemasonry Practically Illustrated, 1835; May Martin: or, The Money-Diggers, 1835; The Green Mountain Boys, 1839; Locke Amsden: or, The Schoolmaster, 1847; The Shaker Lover, and Other Tales, 1848; Lucy Hosmer: or, The Guardian and the Ghost, 1848; The Rangers, 1851; Gaut Gurley: or, The Trappers of Umbabog, 1857; The Doomed Chief: or, 200 Years Ago, 1860; History of the Town of Montpelier, 1860; Centeola and Other Tales, 1864.

ABOUT: Brooks, Van W. The Flowering of New England; Flitcroft, J. E. The Novelist of Vermont: A Biographical and Critical Study of Daniel Pierce Thompson; Loshe, L. D. The Early American Novel; Burlington (Vt.) Times June 9, 1868.

THOMPSON, DENMAN (October 15, 1833-April 14, 1911), actor and playwright, best remembered as the author of *The Old Homestead,* was born in a log cabin near Girard, Pa., the son of Capt. Rufus Thompson and his wife, Anna Hathaway (Baxter) Thompson. At seventeen Denman went to Boston, where he worked first as a chore boy in a circus, later graduating to acting. He was with the Royal Lyceum Company, Toronto, until 1868, playing numerous parts, among them Uncle Tom in *Uncle Tom's Cabin.*

For seven years, after leaving Toronto, he led the wandering and precarious life of the not-too-successful actor, but in 1875 wrote a two-scene sketch based on his observations of the Yankee farmer, taking the leading rôle himself. The première was in Pittsburgh, February, 1875, and the sketch and his characterization were immediate hits. With success he acquired a manager, J. M. Hill, at whose suggestion the little skit was expanded into a full length play and given the title, *Joshua Whitcomb.*

The play came to the Lyceum Theatre, New York City, in 1878, and later enjoyed two seasons at the Fourteenth Street Theatre, but Thompson and his dramatic

DENMAN THOMPSON

ability actually came into their own on April 5, 1886, at the Boston Theatre, when *The Old Homestead,* an outgrowth of *Joshua Whitcomb,* now in four acts, was performed. It was an instantaneous success and a lasting one, and Thompson—Joshua Whitcomb to the life—with his round, benevolent face, white hair, and homely and unsophisticated manner played *The Old Homestead* up and down the whole country almost until his death. The play earned about $3,000,000 in its long and popular career.

Thompson died at his home in West Swanzey, N.H., having survived his wife, Maria Ballou, whom he had married in 1860, when he was a young actor in Toronto. He wrote other plays but his claim to distinction is his sturdy, down-to-earth portrait of Joshua Whitcomb in *The Old Homestead,* one of the most famous plays in the history of the American theatre.

PRINCIPAL WORKS: The Old Homestead, 1886; The Sunshine of Paradise Alley (with George W. Ryer) 1896.

ABOUT: Brady, J. J. The Life of Denman Thompson; Read, B. The History of Swanzey, N. H.; New England Magazine September 1910; Theatre May 1911; Boston Transcript April 14, 1911; New York Times April 15, 1911.

THOMPSON, HUGH MILLER (June 5, 1830-November 18, 1902), bishop of the Protestant Episcopal Church, editor, and theological writer, was born at Londonderry, Ireland, the son of John T. and Annie (Millar) Thompson. He was brought to the United States when he was six, and was educated at the Caldwell, N.J., public school, and an academy at Cleveland. At the age of nineteen, he was so determined to enter the ministry of the Protestant Episcopal Church that he walked from Cleveland to Nashotah, Wis., where he became a student at Nashotah House. He was ordained on June 6, 1852, by Bishop Kemper, and served as a missionary in Wisconsin and Illinois, later taking the pulpit of St. James's, Chicago. In 1872 he became the popular rector of Christ Church, New York, and from there proceeded to Trinity Church, New Orleans.

He became bishop coadjutor of Mississippi in 1882, and succeeded William Mercer Green as diocesan bishop four years later. He died at Jackson, Miss.

A churchman of progressive opinions, Thompson exerted a wide influence through his lucid writings for the *American Churchman,* and the *Church Journal,* which he edited. His editorials were published in book form under the title of *"Copy": Essays From an Editor's Drawer* and attracted considerable attention in America and England. Among other books were *The World and the Logos,* and *Personality and Responsibility.*

Scholarship, exceptional oratorical powers, and a profound knowledge of metaphysics, combined with a shrewd understanding of human nature, elevated Thompson to a distinguished position not only in the church but in theological literature.

He was twice married, first to Caroline Berry, in 1853; and to Anna Weatherburn Hinsdale, of Kenosha, Wis., in 1859.

PRINCIPAL WORKS: Unity and Its Restoration, 1860; First Principles, 1869; "Copy": Essays From an Editor's Drawer, 1872; Absolution, 1872; The World and the Logos, 1886; The World and the Kingdom, 1888; The World and the Man, 1890; The World and the Wrestlers: Personality and Responsibility, 1895.

ABOUT: Churchman, Living Church November 22, 1902; Weekly Clarion-Ledger (Jackson, Miss) November 20, 27, 1902.

THOMPSON, JAMES MAURICE (September 9, 1844-February 15, 1901), miscellaneous writer and editor, better known as Maurice Thompson, was born at Fairfield, Ind., where his father, the Rev. Matthew Grigg Thompson, was a Baptist minister. His mother was Diantha Jaeger, a gifted woman, who directed her son's education during the family's residence in school-less communities in Missouri, Kentucky, and Georgia, where the Rev. Mr. Thompson preached.

Thompson joined the Confederate Army when he was seventeen, serving until the end of the war. After studying law and civil engineering in Calhoun, Ga., he went to Crawfordsville, Ind., to work as a civil engineer on the construction of a new railroad, but set up a law office in Crawfordsville, Ind., three years after his marriage (1868) to Alice Lee, his employer's daughter. Meanwhile he was much occupied with literature, having as early as 1869 contributed verse and prose to Southern periodicals, such as *Scott's Monthly Magazine,* at Atlanta, Ga.

His work appeared in the *Atlantic Monthly* and other popular magazines, and he eventually became one of the Middle West's outstanding literary figures. With his brother, Will Henry Thompson, he wrote books on archery which revived wide-spread interest in the ancient sport toward the end of the nineteenth century. His first book, *Hoosier Mosaics,* a collection of dialect sketches, appeared in 1875 and was followed in rapid succession by children's books, nature sketches, and two volumes of poems. Not long before his death he wrote one of the turn-of-the century's best selling novels—*Alice of Old Vincennes,* a historical romance based on George Rogers Clark's 1779 expedition.

Throughout his life he avoided publicity, preferring the seclusion of his home and the companionship of his books and family. He died of pneumonia at Crawfordsville. During the last twelve years of his life his non-resident literary editorship of the *Independent* brought him considerable distinction as a critic.

Principal Works: *Fiction*—A Tallahassee Girl, 1881; His Second Campaign, 1883; At Love's Extremes, 1885; A Banker of Bankersville, 1886; The King of Honey Island, 1892; Alice of Old Vincennes, 1900. *Nature Studies*—By-Ways and Bird Notes, 1885; Sylvan Secrets: In Bird Songs and Books, 1887; My Winter Garden, 1900. *Poems*—Songs of Fair Weather, 1883; Poems, 1892.

About: Nicholson, M. The Hoosiers; Independent February 21, 1901; Indianapolis News February 15, 16, 1901; Indianapolis Sentinel and New York Times February 16, 1901.

THOMPSON, JOHN REUBEN (October 23, 1823-April 30, 1873), lecturer, editor, and poet, was the son of John Thompson of New Hampshire and Sarah (Dyckman) Thompson of New York. He was born in Richmond, Va., where he received his early schooling. For a time he studied at East-haven, Conn., and attended the University of Virginia from which he was graduated with the degree of Bachelor of Laws in 1845.

After a short legal practice in Richmond, in 1847 he became the editor and owner of the *Southern Literary Messenger* (formerly edited by Edgar Allan Poe), which developed under his guidance into the leading Southern publication. On the eve of the Civil War he left the *Messenger* to assume the editorship of the *Southern Field and Fireside,* published weekly at Augusta, Ga. When war was declared he returned to his native state to become assistant secretary to the Commonwealth of Virginia; to assist in editing the *Richmond Record* and *The Southern Illustrated News,* and to support the Confederacy with such facile verses as "Music in Camp," "The Burial of Latine," "Lee to the Rear," "Ashby," and others.

During the last year of the war he was a blockade-runner to England, where he was the premier writer of the *Index,* Confederate organ in England, and gained wide sympathy for the Southern cause among the distinguished writers who had befriended him on a previous visit to England—Bulwer-Lytton, Thackeray, and the Brownings. Remaining in England until 1866, he wrote for newspapers, lectured, and contributed to magazines. One of his most popular lectures was "The Genius and Character of Edgar Allan Poe," privately published in 1929. The *Memoirs of the Confederate War for Independence,* compiled from the notebook of Major Heros von Borcke, originally published in *Blackwood's Edinburgh Magazine,* was brought out in book form in 1866. The entire edition of an early publication, *Across the Atlantic,* travel sketches issued in 1856, was destroyed in a New York fire, and now exists in one copy at the University of Virginia.

In 1867 William Cullen Bryant appointed him literary editor of the New York Evening *Post,* where he remained until 1873 when tubercular symptoms took him to Colorado. He died in New York City.

Thompson's editorial ability and able pamphleteering elevated him to an influential position, in his time, among American journalists.

Principal Works: Across the Atlantic, 1856; Memoirs of the Confederate War for Independence, 1866; Collected Poems, 1920; The Genius and Character of Edgar Allan Poe, 1929.

About: Patton, J. S. Collected Poems of John Reuben Thompson; Miller, J. R., Jr. Poems of John R. Thompson; manuscripts at the University of Virginia Library; New York Evening Post May 1, 3, 1873.

THOMPSON, MAURICE. See THOMPSON, JAMES MAURICE

THOMPSON, ROBERT ELLIS (April 5, 1844-October 19, 1924), educator and economist, was born near Lurgan, County

Down, Ireland, the son of Samuel and Catherine (Ellis) Thompson. The family emigrated to the United States, settling in Philadelphia in 1857, and young Thompson attended the public schools of that city and was prepared for college at Faires' Classical Institute. Graduated from the University of Pennsylvania in 1865, he studied theology at the Reformed Presbyterian Seminary, class of 1867, receiving ordination six years later. Although he did not hold a regular pastorate, he preached until 1867-68, when he was appointed instructor in Latin and mathematics at the University of Pennsylvania. He later became professor of social science, officiated as dean of the Wharton School of Finance and Economy 1881-83, and taught political economy and the social sciences during his twenty-five years of affiliation with the school.

From 1870 to 1881 he was editor of the *Penn Monthly;* from 1880 to 1891 was on the staff of the *American,* a weekly journal of current events, and was a frequent contributor to the *Irish World* and the *Sunday School Times.* His book *Social Science and National Economy* was used as a text-book for his classes and was widely read throughout the country.

In 1894 Thompson was elected to the presidency of the Central High School of Philadelphia, which under his wise leadership became noted for its high standards of scholarship and its academic record. Thompson guided the destinies of the school until his retirement in 1920, four years before his death in Philadelphia. He was married in 1874 to Mary E. Neely who died in 1874; and in 1910 he was married a second time to Catherine Neely, a sister of his first wife.

Thompson wrote numerous articles on political economy, contributed frequently to periodicals and was a contributor to *Stoddart's Encyclopaedia.* He was a popular lecturer in schools and colleges on economics and social ethics, but his greatest service to the cause of public education was his work as president of Central High School.

PRINCIPAL WORKS: Social Science and National Economy, 1875; Hard Times and What to Learn From Them, 1877; Elements of Political Economy, 1881; Protection to Home Industry, 1886; De Civitate Dei: The Divine Order of Human Society, 1891.

ABOUT: Edmonds, F. S. History of the Central High School of Philadelphia; Harley, L. R. Confessions of a Schoolmaster and Other Essays; Montgomery, R. Robert Ellis Thompson: A Memoir; Philadelphia Public Ledger October 20, 1924.

THOMPSON, WILLIAM TAPPAN (August 31, 1812—March 24, 1882), editor and humorist, was born in Ravenna, Ohio, the son of a Virginia father and an Irish mother, David and Catherine (Kerney) Thompson, who both died in William's early youth. Educated at the district school, he went to Philadelphia where he joined the staff of the *Daily Chronicle.* Between 1830 and 1835 he was assistant to James Diament Wescott, secretary of the territory of Florida, under whom he also studied law. Resuming journalism, he next edited the *States Rights Sentinel* with Augustus Baldwin Longstreet, at Augusta, Ga. A literary journal, the *Family Companion and Ladies' Mirror,* first issued in 1842, was the outcome of a merger between the *Mirror,* which Thompson founded in 1838, and the *Macon Family Companion.* During the brief life of the new publication, his contributions, the humorous letters of "Major Jones," caught the public fancy and were collected and published in Augusta in 1843, later appearing under a Philadelphia publisher's imprint. Three additional volumes were brought out within the subsequent five years. After two years with *Miscellany,* a Madison, Ga., weekly, Thompson went to Baltimore to join Park Benjamin in editing the *Western Continent.* In 1850 he returned to Georgia, where he founded the *Savannah Morning News* and, as editor, made it one of the state's most influential newspapers.

Active in national and state political life, he threw his weight on the side of slavery before the outbreak of the Civil War, in which he served as a volunteer soldier. In 1877 he convened with a group of prominent men to draw up a new constitution for Georgia. He died in Savannah, leaving several children and his wife, Carolina A. Carrié of Augusta, whom he had married in 1837.

Some of his writings were posthumously published, among them several groups of lesser sketches.

Thompson's literary reputation rests solely on his "Major Jones" sketches, which place him in the ranks of minor American humorists.

PRINCIPAL WORKS: John's Alive, 1838; Major Jones's Courtship, 1843; Major Jones's Chronicles of Pineville, 1843; Major Jones's Sketches of Travel, 1848; The Slaveholder Abroad, 1860.

ABOUT: Clemens, W. M. Famous Funny Fellows; Tandy, J. Crackerbox Philosophers in American Humor and Satire; Thompson, W. T. John's Alive; Wade, J. D. Augustus Baldwin Longstreet; Savannah Morning News March 25, 27, 1882.

THOMPSON, ZADOCK (May 23, 1796-January 19, 1856), historian, naturalist, and mathematician, was born in Bridgewater, Vt., the son of Capt. Barnabas Thompson and Sarah (Fuller) Thompson. Forced to work his way through school, he was graduated from the University of Vermont in 1823 and two years later was appointed tutor there. From 1833 to 1837 he taught in Canada, and then, returning to Vermont, at a boys' school in Rock Point. In 1845 he was made assistant state geologist, in 1851, professor of chemistry and natural history in the University of Vermont, and in 1853, state naturalist. Although pressed for money and often ill, he was a determined and thorough worker and a prolific writer. His most outstanding work, published in 1842, was *History of Vermont: Natural, Civil, and Statistical.* It was accurately done and contains a wealth of information, not only on the early political history of Vermont but on its natural history—its birds, fishes, animals, plants, minerals, etc. It is still widely consulted today as a reference work. He published many other volumes, but only one, *The Youth's Assistant in Practical Arithmetick,* was ever widely used. He married, in 1824, Phebe Boyce, by whom he had two daughters.

Principal Works: The Youth's Assistant in Practical Arithmetick, 1825; History of the State of Vermont From Its Earliest Settlement to the Close of the Year 1832, 1833; Geography and History of Lower Canada, 1835; History of Vermont: Natural, Civil, and Statistical, 1842.

About: Crockett, W. H. Vermonters: A Book of Biographies; Thompson, C. H. A Genealogy of Descendants of John Thomson, of Plymouth, Massachusetts; History Magazine October 1858; Burlington Sentinel January 24, 1856.

THOMSON, CHARLES (November 29, 1729-August 16, 1824), secretary of the Continental Congress and theological writer, was born in County Derry, Ireland. After the death of their mother, Charles and his brothers were brought to America by their father, John Thomson, who died on the voyage over. Charles studied at the academy of Dr. Francis Alison in New London, Chester County, Pa., and on leaving became a teacher in Friends' schools in Philadelphia, where he made the acquaintance of Benjamin Franklin and other notable men.

An ardent patriot, Thomson was an active colonial leader in the years preceding the Revolution, and because of his integrity and ability was chosen secretary of the first Continental Congress in 1774. He served in this capacity until 1789, keeping the records, taking notes of the proceedings, and of the progress of the war. After the adoption of the Constitution, he helped to organize the new government, and was chosen to notify Washington of his election to the presidency. He retired in 1789 to his estate at "Harriton," near Philadelphia, where he devoted himself to a translation of the Bible, and also wrote a history of the life of Christ, *A Synopsis of the Four Evangelists.*

Thomson's translation of *The Holy Bible: Containing the Old and New Covenant,* the work of twenty years, contained the first English version of the Septuagint that had been published at the time and was considered by Biblical scholars to be an important addition to theological libraries. But it was as a patriot and "perpetual" secretary of the Congress that he attained his greatest recognition.

Principal Works: An Enquiry Into the Causes of the Alienation of the Delaware and Shawanese Indians From the British Interest, 1759; The Holy Bible: Containing the Old and New Covenant, 1808; A Synopsis of the Four Evangelists, 1815.

About: Burnett, E. C. Letters of Members of the Continental Congress; Harley, L. R. The Life of Charles Thomson; Lincoln, C. H. The Revolutionary Movement in Pennsylvania: 1760-1776; Watson, J. F. Annals of Philadelphia; Pennsylvania Magazine of History and Biography October 1891, January 1892, July 1909.

THOMSON, MORTIMER NEAL ("Q. K. Philander Doesticks, P. B.") (September 2, 1831—June 25, 1875), humorist and journalist, was born at Riga, Monroe County, N.Y., the son of Edwin and Sophia Thomson. The family moved to Ann Arbor, Mich., in 1841 and the boy entered the University of Michigan in 1849, but within the year was expelled with several other students for belonging to a secret society. Subsequently he appeared with a troupe of traveling actors, clerked in a New York store, and finally in 1854 began a career of journalism. He wrote in that year, over the signature "Q. K. Philander Doesticks, P.B." (which he later translated as meaning "Queer Critter, Philander Doesticks, Perfect Brick"), a letter entitled "Doesticks on a Bender," recounting a wild jaunt to Niagara Falls; and this letter, followed by a series of twenty-nine others reprinted by several newspapers, gained him a wide reputation as a humorist.

A year later Thomson secured a position on the staff of the New York *Tribune,* and the editors gave him free rein in making his assignments. Consequently he produced a series of sketches on the police courts and vignettes of fortune tellers, original and diverting social satire, that amused everybody and offended very few. His report to the *Tribune* of the tremendous auction of slaves

MORTIMER THOMSON
("Philander Doesticks")

at Savannah in 1859, a powerful and dramatic indictment, was translated into several foreign languages and used as a tract by the Anti-Slavery Society. Later on he developed a talent for parody, scoring a great hit with *Plu-ri-bus-tah: A Song That's-by-No-Author* (presumably aimed at Longfellow's *Hiawatha*) and another with *The Lady of the Lake* as its subject. During the war he served the *Tribune* at the front, and continued writing in 1865, remaining in New York for the rest of his life except for a short interval in Minneapolis. Thomson was married twice: first, in 1857 to Anna H. Van Cleve, who died in 1858; second, in 1861 to Grace Eldridge, the daughter of Sarah Payson Willis Parton ("Fanny Fern"), the first woman columnist.

Thomson's work, all of which was written under the same pseudonym, was replete with good-natured mockery of national follies. He left a valuable heritage for succeeding humorists in his adroit use of the native vernacular.

Principal Works: Doesticks: What He Says, 1855; The History and Records of the Elephant Club, 1856; Plu-ri-bus-tah: A Song That's-by-No-Author, 1856; Nothing to Say, 1857; The Witches of New York, 1859; The Lady of the Lake, 1860.

About: Fletcher, S. D. The Life and Letters of Mortimer Thomson; unpublished thesis in the library of Northwestern University; New York Times, New York Tribune, New York Herald June 26, 1875.

THOREAU, HENRY DAVID (July 12, 1817-May 6, 1862), naturalist and essayist, was the son of John and Cynthia (Dunbar) Thoreau. It is hardly necessary to say that he was born and died in Concord, Mass., so inseparable is the name of the town from his. The father had built up a thriving pencil manufactory, carried on at home with the assistance of all his family. The name "Thoreau" is French in origin, Henry Thoreau's grandfather having come to Massachusetts from the Isle of Jersey; his mother's people, the Dunbars, were Scotch. The boy was originally named David Henry, but reversed the order of his names in college.

Thoreau was apparently born a naturalist. When he was only twelve he was collecting specimens for Agassiz. He never had to learn the wild; all he had to do was to transmute his early instinctive feeling for nature into the finer gold of scientific observation. Meanwhile he pursued the usual course of small town, middle class boys of his day; he helped with the cows, he worked at making pencils, and he attended the Concord Academy. At sixteen he went to Harvard; between terms he taught school at Canton, Mass., boarding with the philosopher Orestes Brownson, who taught him German. He was an indifferent scholar except in the classics, already recalcitrant in respect to social observances and rules; the main thing he got from Harvard was a sound classicism, and the mystical philosophy which Jones Very fed him with his Greek. When he was graduated in 1837 he refused a diploma, having a better use for five dollars.

Thoreau's earliest journal dates from 1834; his latest goes to just before his death. This is important in chronicling the history of a man all of whose writings were made up from his journals. For the time being, however, he had to think of other things than writing. He and his brother John, with whom later he made the voyage on the Concord and Merrimac Rivers that furnished material for his first book, opened a private school together. Henry's earlier attempt at teaching in Concord had not been successful; reproached for not whipping the boys, he picked out half a dozen at random, thrashed them thoroughly, and resigned. But John was a born teacher, and the school—the first in America to take its pupils on "field trips" and teach them natural history—flourished until 1841, when it was ended because of John's fatal illness.

For the next two years Thoreau lived with Emerson. Their exact relation is difficult to define. Thoreau was Emerson's imitative disciple, his admiring younger friend, object of his rather patronizing kindness, and also his man-of-all-work, gardener, handyman, "help." At Emerson's he met Alcott, Margaret Fuller, Ripley, all the Transcendentalists—those half-mystical, half-perfectionist philosophers with their ideals drawn from India.

Thoreau was impressed; he too became a Transcendentalist. But not for him experiments in colonies, in Brook Farm or Fruitlands. His "experiment," to come a few years later, would be in self-sufficing isolated living. Now he wrote his journals and dug essays from them, he lectured at the Lyceum, and for a month, when Emerson was away, he edited the Transcendentalist organ, the *Dial.* In 1843 he went to Staten Island, N.Y., as tutor in the family of Emerson's brother William. He stayed a year, the longest time he ever spent away from Concord.

The year 1845 was Thoreau's greatest. It was the year he built himself a house for $28 on Walden Pond (there is a barbed wire fence there now, and a "No Trespassing" sign), and went to live there until September 1847. It was not a hermit existence; he came to town almost every day, he never locked his door, his visitors were many. It was an experiment in living by the rather cranky rules, expressive of a deep-seated individualistic protest, which from his boyhood Thoreau had not so much formulated as breathed out. For his bare necessaries, very simple and very few, Thoreau would farm, build fences, survey (he was a trained surveyor), or whatever, but he begrudged time or effort taken from his real business—living in communion with his kin, the animals and birds; "dusting the furniture of his mind." It was in 1845 that he spent a night in prison rather than pay his poll tax to a government that allowed slavery; much to his disgust his aunt paid it for him, as once before she had paid his church tax. Thoreau always paid his own highway tax, for he "wanted to be a good neighbor," but he refused to support "any corporation" which he had not joined voluntarily. He came out of Walden with the manuscript of *A Week on the Concord and Merrimac Rivers,* and with his mental and emotional equipment fully mature and complete; he "went in a student and came out a teacher."

For another year he lived in Emerson's house, but only as caretaker; Emerson was in Europe. The old friendship was dying; Thoreau felt that Emerson patronized him. Actually it was Thoreau's cross-grained nature that brought the rift. He hated urbanity; gentleness itself to children and animals, he was a tart apple for his friends to swallow. In 1854 *Walden,* that fascinating cross between *Robinson Crusoe* and natural history, the second and last of his books to be published in his lifetime, appeared. For the first he had paid himself, and sold only 200 of the thousand copies; with *Walden* he gained a rather wider fame. He was asked for articles, most of all by Horace Greeley; he was engaged for lectures. But he was hardly a man to be lionized. He was seldom on the popular side of any question. His abolitionism grew, until he was the first public defender of John Brown after the Harper's Ferry raid, utterly indifferent to the very real possibility of physical danger involved in his speech. For the rest, his life after *Walden* had little incident. He journeyed—on foot for the most part; he was a famous walker—to Maine, to Cape Cod, to Canada, where his anti-British sentiments crackled through his journal. He wrote voluminously, with not a motion to secure publication of anything he wrote. He contemplated a book on the Indians, and filled many notebooks; he continued to draw on the journals for his essays and lectures. His father died in 1859 and he and his sister Sophia conducted the pencil manufactory together.

From a daguerreotype
HENRY DAVID THOREAU

And then this man who had seemed as robust and tireless as an Indian or a deer, who was so hard-muscled and lean that though he was small he gave the impression of tallness, caught cold like any pale urbanite—caught cold in his own woods—and the cold grew into his hereditary curse of tuberculosis. In 1861 he made his longest journey—all the way to Minnesota, in the hope of some good from the bracing climate.

But it was useless, and too late. He came home to die in Concord, not by Walden Pond or in the forest, but in bed in his own ancestral home. He lay in bed and when he could no longer hold a pencil—he had made so many of them!—he dictated to Sophia his last germinating thoughts. A visitor asked him what his hopes were for a future life. "One world at a time!" said Thoreau. He died before his forty-fifth birthday. They buried him first in the New Burying Ground; but later they put him in Sleepy Hollow Cemetery, with his family, with Emerson and Alcott and Hawthorne and his great friend of later days, William Ellery Channing. A stone cairn marks the site of his Walden cabin.

How can one describe Henry Thoreau to a world so different from his own? He was the New England countryman raised to the *n*th degree, universalizing his parochial outlook. "I have traveled much in Concord," he said. He was a son of earth who first loved and then learned to know his mother. He was a natural rebel, an individualist to the point of simple anarchism, a Stoic, an ascetic. He could make himself as unpleasant as ascetics and Stoics usually are; he was no amiable nature-lover, no mild mystic. There was something fierce and wild about Thoreau, and there was something surly and unapproachable. Vague rumors floated around of an unrequited love in his youth; apparently he mourned the loss of the lady's brother far more than her failure to requite any emotion of his. A married Thoreau is unthinkable. Yet this man with the aggressive nose, the full or fringed brown beard, the unruly hair, and the stirring and troubling deep grey-blue eyes, was beloved by little children, and with them never ceased to be a little child. To sum him up in a phrase (Henry Seidel Canby's phrase) he was "a man who believed in doing what he wanted."

As a writer, almost unknown in his lifetime, gradually growing on the American consciousness until now he holds a place with Emerson and Hawthorne, Thoreau is almost as hard to pin down as he is difficult to appraise as a man. Canby remarks that he had three styles—the transcendental, the ecstatic, and the humorously reflective. In any of the three he is nervous, staccato, best seen in sudden vivid turns of phrase and eloquent poetic passages. His books were made from journal jottings, and they are not well organized. But, to quote Canby once more, "Thoreau's best prose is as good as any written in his century. In its directness, . . . in its curt, vigorous rhythms, its delight in racy words, its wit, it is the best American prose ever written, and as American as it is good." Of his verse, which Lowell called "worsification," not so much can be said; Van Wyck Brooks well calls it "sound and scholarly doggerel," but with occasional lines of startling beauty. He imitated, deliberately and poorly, the gnomic style of Emerson. William Sharp has noted that "though he absorbed intensely he gave off no spiritual sparks." He gave something else, however—a cleansing acid spray which clears the head of much nonsense, including his own dreamy mysticism.

Principal Works: A Week on the Concord and Merrimac Rivers, 1849; Walden: or, Life in the Woods, 1854; Excursions, 1863; The Maine Woods, 1864; Cape Cod, 1865; Letters to Various Persons, 1865; A Yankee in Canada, 1866; Early Spring in Massachusetts, 1881; Summer, 1884; Winter, 1888; Autumn, 1892; Familiar Letters, 1894; Miscellanies, 1894; Poems of Nature, 1895; First and Last Journeys, 1905; Men of Concord, 1936.

About: Atkinson, J. B. Henry Thoreau: The Cosmic Yankee; Bazalgette, L. Henry Thoreau: Bachelor of Nature; Brooks, Van W. The Flowering of New England; Canby, H. S. Classic Americans; Channing, W. E. Thoreau: The Poet-Naturalist; Christy, A. The Orient in American Transcendentalism; Emerson, E. W. Henry Thoreau as Remembered by a Young Friend; Hawthorne, J Memoirs; Jones, S. A. Pertaining to Henry Thoreau; Lowell, J. R. Literary Essays; Salt, H. S. Life and Writings of Henry David Thoreau; Sanborn, F. B. Henry D. Thoreau; Van Doren, M. The Life of Henry David Thoreau; Atlantic Monthly August 1862, June 1901, January 1905; Century Magazine July 1882; Current Opinion July 1917; Dial July 15, 1915; Outlook September 12, 1917; Saturday Review of Literature December 26, 1936, December 11, 1937.

"THORPE, KAMBA." See BELLAMY, ELIZABETH WHITFIELD (CROOM)

THORPE, THOMAS BANGS (March 1, 1815-September 20, 1878), humorist, editor, and artist, was born in Westfield, Mass., the son of the Rev. Thomas Thorpe. He attended Weslyan University, Middletown, Conn., until 1836, when ill health compelled him to move to a milder climate. Settling in Baton Rouge, La., he found the Southern scene and frontier character the inspiration for his best work, both as painter and author.

Thorpe's "Bold Dragoon," an illustration of Washington Irving's story, was exhibited at the New York Academy of Fine Arts when he was sixteen. Though he painted many pictures of the lush Louisiana country and pioneer folk, he achieved his greatest prominence with his portraits of celebrities, including Jenny Lind and Zachary Taylor.

As a publisher and editor of several newspapers, among them the Concordia Intelligencer, and the Baton Rouge *Conservative,* Thorpe met and became friendly with many of the outstanding personalities of the day. He was an astute and sincere student of politics and campaigned effectively for his good friend, Zachary Taylor.

It was in this productive period that Thorpe did his best work in another field, and laid the foundation for that lusty, robust, and exaggerated form of humor, the American tall tale. *The Big Bear of Arkansas,* the best and also the best known of his contributions to native humor was published in the New York *Spirit of the Times* in 1841. *Tom Owen: The Bee Hunter* was very well received abroad, notably in England, and was translated into several foreign languages.

His experiences with Zachary Taylor in Mexico resulted in three books, one of which was *The Taylor Anecdote Book.* After the Mexican war Thorpe returned to New York, where he was active both as publisher and politician until his death. He was married but his wife's name is not known.

Thorpe was the first of the typically native humorists, telling his tales with a native gusto and salty richness which pointed the way for a long line of similar writers.

Principal Works: *Humor*—Tom Owen: The Bee Hunter, The Big Bear of Arkansas, 1841; Mysteries of the Backwoods, 1846; The Hive of the Bee-Hunter, 1854; Colonel Thorpe's Scenes in Arkansaw, 1858. *Miscellaneous*—Our Army on the Rio Grande, 1846; Our Army at Monterey, 1847; The Taylor Anecdote Book, 1848; Lynde Weiss: An Autobiography, 1852; The Master's House, 1854; A Voice to America, 1855; Reminiscences of Charles L. Elliott, 1868.

About: DeMenil, A. N. Literature of the Louisiana Territory; Griswold, R. W. Prose Writers of America; New York Spirit of the Times July 27, 1850; New York Times September 21, 28, 1878.

TIBBLES, THOMAS HENRY (May 22, 1838-May 14, 1928), journalist, social reformer, and miscellaneous writer, was born in Washington County, Ohio, the son of William and Martha (Cooley) Tibbles. The record of his early years—which may be part legend—says that he ran away, at the age of six, from an apprenticeship on a farm; was taken west by emigrants; became a member of John Brown's company in 1856; and that just as Quantrill's men were in the act of hanging him for withholding Brown's secrets some of his own friends arrived and saved his life.

He attended Mount Union College at Alliance, Ohio, for a time, and served as scout and newspaper correspondent during the Civil War. After a period of itinerant preaching, he entered the newspaper field and was on the staff of the Omaha *Daily Herald* between 1876-79. At this time he attracted nation-wide attention through his efforts to intervene for a group of Ponca Indians, who had been arrested and returned to their reservation after an attempt to join the Omahas. Tibbles secured a court hearing for Standing Bear, the chief, and obtained their freedom. During this time his wife, Amelia Hall, of Bristol, England, died, and two years later he married Susette La Flesche, or Bright Eyes, one of the Ponca maidens, said to have been the original of Minnehaha in Longfellow's *Hiawatha.*

In the declining years of his life Tibbles took an active interest in politics, loyally supporting the National Farmer's Alliance, and the People's (Populist) Party, who chose him as candidate for vice-president in 1904.

After 1905 he became a well-known editor through his management of the *Investigator,* and also became re-associated with the *World-Herald* (the former Omaha *Daily Herald*). His Indian wife died in 1903 and four years later he married his third wife, Ida Belle Riddle.

Tibbles was a robust man with matching ideas. He was a hard worker, sincere friend and enthusiastic upholder of the principles in which he believed. An influential newspaperman, he wrote a number of books which attained a moderate degree of popularity.

Principal Works: Ponca Chiefs, 1880; Hidden Power, 1881; The American Peasant, 1892.

About: Nebraska Historical Magazine October-December 1932; New York Times, Morning World-Herald (Omaha), Nebraska State Journal (Lincoln) May 15, 1928.

TICKNOR, GEORGE (August 1, 1791-January 26, 1871), scholar, educator, biographer, essayist, and classical modern linguist, was born in Boston, the son of Elisha and Elizabeth (Billings) Ticknor. His father, before becoming a successful Boston merchant, had been a teacher, as also had his mother, and between them they undertook his early education, which was so thorough that he received a certificate of admission to Dartmouth at the age of ten. He did not actually enter college until he was fourteen.

He was graduated from Dartmouth in 1807 and was admitted to the bar in 1813. The practice of law had little attraction for Ticknor, who felt that his country would never lack good lawyers, but was urgently in need of well trained teachers and scholars. The writings of Madame de Staël influenced him in his decision to continue his study of the classics in Germany, and in 1815, in company with his brilliant friend Edward

Collection of Frederick H. Meserve
GEORGE TICKNOR

Everett, he left the United States to enroll as a student in the University of Göttingen. While in Europe he was received by Von Humboldt, Byron, Humphry Davy, Chateaubriand, Mme. de Staël, Miss Edgeworth, Goethe, Schlegel, Scott, Wordsworth, and Southey, all of whom recognized the unusual intelligence and character of this young American student. With most of these writers and poets he maintained a life-long correspondence and friendship.

In 1816 he was elected to the professorship of the Smith Chair of Modern Languages at Harvard University, and in order to equip himself for this position he left Germany to study in Spain and Portugal. At the time of his visit, Spain was in a condition of war-ravaged poverty under the rule of Ferdinand VII; the men of letters were unrecognized and were dying of starvation, and it was not difficult for Ticknor to get wholehearted cooperation in his studies from the most brilliant minds of the country. His association with these starving savants enabled him later to write his *History of Spanish Literature,* establishing himself as a world authority on Spanish letters.

He returned to the United States to take up his professorship at Harvard in 1819. Here he revolutionized higher education in America by introducing German methods of study, the severity and exactitude of which had never before been dreamed of in American universities. But his lectures, interspersed with reminiscences of the great men he knew in Europe, were an inspiration to his students, who, under his guidance, began to realize the mighty influence in modern life of the poet and the writer.

Ticknor resigned his chair at Harvard in 1835 in order to return to Spain to complete the research work necessary for his *History of Spanish Literature,* which he finally completed and published in 1849. He had married in 1821 Anna Eliot, daughter of Samuel Eliot, a prosperous Boston merchant. The considerable fortune she brought him, together with his own income, freed him from the necessity of working for a salary, and after he left Harvard he devoted the rest of his life to his own writing, contributing regularly to the *Monthly Anthology* and the *North American Review.*

He had four children, two of whom died in infancy. He was devoted to his two remaining daughters and never traveled without his wife and family. Ticknor did not allow his studies to interfere with his social life. He was a well-known and popular figure in all the great houses of both Europe and the United States.

Nathaniel Hawthorne, writing of Ticknor, says: "You recognized in him at once the man who knows the world, the scholar, too, which probably is his more distinctive character, though a little more under the surface . . . Methinks he must have spent a happy life (as happiness goes among mortals) writing his great three volumed book . . . ; writing it, not for bread, nor with any uneasy desire of fame, but only with a purpose to achieve something true and enduring."

Principal Works: Essays—Syllabus of a Course of Lectures on the History and Criticism of Spanish Literature, 1823; Remarks on Changes Lately Proposed or Adopted in Harvard University, 1825; A Lecture on the Best Methods of Teaching the Living Languages, 1833. *Biography*—Outline of Principal Events in the Life of General Lafayette, 1825; Remains of Nathaniel Appleton Haven, 1827; Remarks on the Life and Writings of Daniel Webster, 1831; Life of W. H. Prescott, 1863. *Criticism*—History of Spanish Literature, 1849.

About: Brooks, V. W. The Flowering of New England; Long, O. W. Thomas Jefferson and George Ticknor: A Chapter in American Scholarship; Northrup, G. T. George Ticknor's Travels in Spain; Lippincott's Magazine May 1876; London Quarterly Review October 1850.

"TIGER LILY." See BLAKE, LILLIE (DEVEREUX)

TILTON, THEODORE (October 2, 1835-May 25, 1907), editor, was the son of Silas and Eusebia Tilton. Born in New York City and educated at the public schools there, Tilton finally attended for three years what was afterward the College of the City of New York. A gifted youth, he secured

Collection of Frederick H. Meserve
THEODORE TILTON

immediate employment on leaving school in 1853, as a reporter for the New York *Observer*. Keenly interested in the political and religious issues of the day, he soon made friends with Henry Ward Beecher [*q.v.*], abandoned the conservative *Observer*, and became managing editor of Henry C. Bowen's Congregationalist paper the *Independent*.

In the fifteen years of his management Tilton built up this paper to a phenomenal degree, increasing its circulation, influence, and literary value tremendously. He published Beecher's sermons, secured contributions from the most influential English and American writers, and furthered the causes of emancipation and woman's suffrage. Tilton had the ability to inspire enthusiasm with the voice as well as with the pen, and after the war he made a series of very successful lyceum tours. By 1870 he had become a partner in Bowen's *Independent*, editor of Bowen's Brooklyn *Union*, and was nationally famous as an editor and speaker.

However, in the summer of 1870 began a domestic scandal which completely blighted Tilton's career. His wife Elizabeth (Richards) Tilton, whom he had married in 1855, suddenly confessed to him her intimacy—the exact degree of which was not immediately determined—with pastor Beecher. For a time both Tilton and Beecher tried to keep the affair quiet, but the scandal soon leaked out and assumed major proportions. Beecher was tried and acquitted by his own congregation; Tilton's wife had refused to testify against the great preacher. Subsequently Tilton's damage suit in the Brooklyn City Court resulted in a hung jury, extending the trial to a hundred and twelve days.

Of the trio involved he was the blameless one, but the scandal ruined him. Mrs. Tilton confirmed her husband's charges four years later, but it was too late to help him.

Tilton went abroad in 1883, after an unsuccessful attempt to salvage his editorial reputation in America, and supported himself by writing articles and poetry until his death in Paris.

PRINCIPAL WORKS: The King's Ring, 1867; The Sexton's Tale and Other Poems, 1867; Tempest Tossed, 1874; Swabian Stories, 1882; Great Tom: or, The Curfew Bell of Oxford, 1885; Heart's Ease, 1894; Sonnets to the Memory of Frederick Douglass, 1895.

ABOUT: Abbott, L. & Halliday, S. B. Life of Henry Ward Beecher; Theodore Tilton vs. Henry Ward Beecher; The Great Brooklyn Romance: All the Documents in the Famous Beecher-Tilton Case; Brockett, L. P. Men of Our Day; Evening Post (N.Y.) May 25, 1907; N.Y. Tribune and N.Y. Herald May 26, 1907.

"TIMON, JOHN." See MITCHELL, DONALD GRANT

TIMROD, HENRY (December 8, 1828-October 6, 1867), poet, was born in Charleston, S.C., the son of Capt. William Henry Timrod, a bookbinder and a bad amateur poet, and Thyrza (Prince) Timrod, a beautiful woman and a devout nature-lover. The family name was originally Dimroth; the poet's ancestry was mixed—English, Scotch-Irish, German, and Swiss.

In 1838 the father died as a result of injuries received in the Seminole War in Florida, and the widow was left in very straitened circumstances. She managed, however, to give her son a fair education, and in 1846 he went to Franklin College (now a part of the University of Georgia). He was able to stay only two years, but he cultivated two things of value—a study of the classics which formed and chastened his style, and a lifelong friendship with another Southern poet, Paul Hamilton Hayne. For a while he read law, and was even admitted to the bar, but it was soon obvious that he would never make a lawyer. He tried in vain for a professorship in some college, then, after a term at country school teaching, became a tutor on a South Carolina plantation. He began contributing poems to the *Southern Literary Messenger* and was one of the group, headed by William Gilmore Simms, which founded, edited, and filled the column's of *Russell's Magazine* from 1857 to the Civil war. As the friend of Simms and

Hayne, he was a part of a group in Charleston which was at once literary and convivial.

This placid life, shadowed only by ill health, and punctuated by publication of his early poems in 1869, was suddenly blasted by the Civil War. Timrod—short, frail, already tubercular—was all aflame with patriotic ardor. He enlisted in the Confederate Army in 1862, and was for a while clerk at regimental headquarters, but the rigors of camp life were grotesquely impossible for him, and he was soon following the army as correspondent of the Charleston *Mercury*. Even this soon proved too much for him; he was discharged from the army at the end of the year. It was a hard blow, and the harder one was the collapse of a proposed English edition of his poems.

Still a little happiness remained for him. In 1864 he went to Columbia as editor and part proprietor of the *South Carolinian,* and the same year he married Kate S. Goodwin, an English girl whom he had long loved. Their son was born the next year.

The rest of Timrod's life is painful to relate. His son died at ten months; Columbia was burned by Northern troops; in the most abject poverty, the Timrods lived by selling off their furniture or by the kindness of friends; attempts to establish a girls' school, to sell his poems, to serve as a clerk in the governor's office, came to nothing. His tuberculosis flared up again, with constant hemorrhages. He never complained except to Hayne; but he could not carry on longer. He died before he was forty. Friends saw to his burial, for Timrod was rich always—and only—in friends. In 1901 a monument was erected to his memory in Charleston.

It seems strange that this little, shy, nervous man, gentle and melancholy, should have been the war laureate of the South; yet such he was. In retrospect such passages as the ending of "The Cotton Boll," with its prediction of the ruin of New York and the triumph and generous victory of the South, seem tragically comic. When it was written, it, with "Carolina" and many others, was a battle-cry. "Ethnogenesis," the ode that hailed the new nation, the Confederate States of America, was one of the noblest of patriotic poems.

For Timrod was an artist—after Lanier, the greatest lyric artist of the pre-war South (for Poe cannot be confined to any geographical territory). He sang like a bird, but like a bird that had been trained to sing; his style was classic, limpid, crystal-clear. Sometimes he is sweetly sentimental, sometimes didactic, the twin faults of his age. But for the most part he is natural, simple, and as Hayne called him, "one of the truest and sweetest singers this country has given to the world."

Principal Works: Poems, 1860; Poems, 1873; Katie, 1884; Complete Poems, 1899.

About: Thompson, H. T. Henry Timrod: Laureate of the Confederacy; Timrod, H. Poems (see Sketch by P. H. Hayne); Complete Poems (see Memoir); Wauchope, G. A. Henry Timrod: Man and Poet; International Review July 1880; Sewanee Review October 1899; Charleston Daily Courier October 9, 1867.

Collection of Frederick H. Meserve
HENRY TIMROD

"TINTO, DICK." See GOODRICH, FRANK BOOTT

"TITCOMB, TIMOTHY." See HOLLAND, JOSIAH GILBERT

TOMPSON, BENJAMIN (July 14, 1642-April 10?, 1714), Puritan educator and poet, the youngest son of Rev. William Tompson who emigrated from England about 1637, and Abigail Tompson, was born in Quincy, Mass., then a part of Braintree. His mother died three months after his birth, and he was brought up by a neighbor, Thomas Blanchard, in Braintree and Charlestown, attending Harvard College in the class of 1662. He taught school from 1667 to 1710 in Boston, Charlestown, Braintree, and Roxbury, for thirty years, practicing also as a physician. In 1667 he married Susanna Kirtland of Lynn, by whom he had nine children. He died in Roxbury.

Tompson's chief claim to notice rests on his verse, and that by reason of the historic interest in his productions, rather than because of special merit. He was at his best in satire. His first two small volumes, *New Englands Crisis* and *New-Englands Tears for Her Present Miseries,* were based on King Philip's War. Two of his poems, *A Funeral Tribute* to Gov. John Winthrop, and *The Grammarians Funeral,* were first published as broadsides, and two others were contained in Cotton Mather's *Magnalia.* These and many more were collected and published by Howard Johnson Hall in his *Benjamin Tompson.*

PRINCIPAL WORKS: New Englands Crisis, 1676; New-Englands Tears for Her Present Miseries, 1676; A Funeral Tribute, 1676; "Upon the Very Reverend Samuel Whiting," and "Celeberrimi Cottoni Matheri" (in Mather, C. Magnalia, 1702); The Grammarians Funeral, 1708; Benjamin Tompson, 1642-1714, First Native-Born Poet of America: His Poems (ed. by H. J. Hall) 1924.

ABOUT: Green, S. A. Benjamin Tompson: A Graduate of Harvard College in the Class of 1662; Hall, H. J. Benjamin Tompson; Sibley, J. L. Biographical Sketches of Graduates of Harvard University; Tyler, M. C. A History of American Literature.

TORREY, BRADFORD (October 9, 1843-October 7, 1912), editor and ornithologist, was born at Weymouth, Mass., the son of Samuel Torrey, a shoemaker, and his wife, Sophronia (Dyer) Torrey. Educated in the local schools, he taught for two years and afterward went to Boston to enter the business world. Ornithology became his chief leisure interest and he frequently contributed articles on this subject to magazines and newspapers. In 1886, a year after the publication of his first book, *Birds in the Bush,* he joined the editorial staff of the *Youth's Companion,* remaining until 1901. His page, one of the most popular features of the magazine, was made up of miscellaneous pieces designed to appeal and to educate children, and it was never dull under his sympathetic editorship.

Despite Torrey's lack of academic ornithological training, he became widely known in his field through his accurate observations of American birds. Far removed from scientific treatises, these records were written in a charming conversational style, which placed Torrey more in the category of essayist than scientist. Among his many books, he edited the fourteen volumes of the journal of Henry David Thoreau, published in 1906.

Torrey remained a bachelor to the end of his life, which came to a close in a cabin near Santa Barbara, Calif. He lived the life of a veritable hermit during his last years in an effort to overcome poor health and to penetrate more deeply into the mysterious laws of nature. In his life, as in his writing, he was unassuming, quietly charming, and direct. Though he cultivated few friends, he was greatly beloved by those whom he admitted to his circle.

PRINCIPAL WORKS: Birds in the Bush, 1885; A Rambler's Lease, 1889; The Foot-path Way, 1892; A Florida Sketch Book, 1894; Spring Notes From Tennessee, 1896; A World of Green Hills 1898; Everyday Birds, 1901; Footing it in Franconia, 1901; The Clerk of the Woods, 1903; Nature's Invitation, 1904; Friends on the Shelf, 1906; Field Days in California, 1913.

ABOUT: Torrey, F. C. The Torrey Families and Their Children in America; Auk January 1913; Boston Transcript and New York Evening Post October 8, 1912.

TORREY, JOHN (August 15, 1796-March 10, 1873), botanist and chemist, was born in New York City, the son of Captain William Torrey and Margaret (Nichols) Torrey. He received his education in the public schools and the College of Physicians and Surgeons, from which he was graduated in 1818. The year before his graduation he was one of a group that founded the Lyceum of Natural History, one of the first contributions to that body being *A Catalogue of Plants Growing Spontaneously Within Thirty Miles of the City of New York.*

He opened an office in New York and for a time practiced medicine, but devoted a great part of his time to botany and the publication of scientific articles. In 1824 he was appointed professor of chemistry, mineralogy, and geology at the Military Academy in West Point. Three years later he returned to New York where from 1827 to 1855 he was professor of chemistry at the College of Physicians and Surgeons, and for part of that time professor of chemistry and natural history at the College of New Jersey. Torrey became assayer on the establishment of the United States Assay Office in New York in 1853, a position which he held until his death.

He was a member of the Linnean Society of London, of the American Academy of Arts and Sciences, and of the National Academy of Sciences. His famous and very valuable botanical library and herbarium were presented to Columbia College about 1860. Torrey was a man of great tolerance and understanding and as a teacher was instrumental in developing and encouraging many young men, who were later to achieve fame in science, among them Asa Gray.

His published works, including *Flora of the State of New York,* his reports on the plant collections of the Nicollet and Frémont expeditions, and his many contributions to botanical knowledge put him in the front rank of American scientists. Torrey died in

Collection of Frederick H. Meserve
JOHN TORREY

New York City six years after the founding of the Torrey Botanical Club by a group of young botanists. He was married to Eliza Shaw in 1824.

PRINCIPAL WORKS: A Catalogue of Plants Growing Spontaneously Within Thirty Miles of the City of New York, 1819; Flora of the Northern and Middle Sections of the United States, 1823; A Compendium of the Flora of the Northern and Middle States, 1826; Flora of North America (with Asa Gray), 1838-1843; Flora of the State of New York, 1843.

ABOUT: Gray, A. Scientific Papers; Torrey, F. C. The Torrey Families . . . in America; Youmans, W. J. Pioneers of Science in America; Botanical Gazette February 1883; New York Times March 11, 1873.

TOURGÉE, ALBION WINEGAR (May 2, 1838-May 21, 1905), carpet-bagger, novelist, and political-writer, was born in Williamsfield, Ohio, the son of Valentine and Louisa Emma (Winegar) Tourgée. He was educated at the Kingsville Academy and attended Rochester University from 1859 to 1861. Serving in the Union Army from 1861 to 1863, he was twice wounded, at Bull Run and Perryville, and was a prisoner of the Confederates for four months until he was exchanged. He returned to Ohio, married Emma Lodoiska in 1863. The following year he was admitted to the bar in Ohio but settled in Greensboro, N.C., where he was to have a busy and profitable career in politics.

He was an active member of the "carpet-bag" convention in 1868 and was one of the commission appointed to revise and codify the state laws. Elected judge of the superior court in 1868, he held the post until 1874, taking advantage of all its benefits, complete opportunist that he was. Several times the Ku Klux Klan planned raids for the capture of Tourgée, who was widely unpopular with the upper classes, but with his phenomenal good luck he never fell into their hands.

In 1876 Tourgée was appointed pension agent for North Carolina, and two years later he was defeated for Congress. He went to New York in 1879 and continued his prolific writing career, turning out novels and political articles and serving as editor of a magazine, *Our Continent,* from 1882 until its failure two years later. Moving to Buffalo, he tried to found a magazine *The Basis: A Journal of Citizenship,* but it lasted less than a year. During the last years of his life he was consul at Bordeaux, France, where he died.

Tourgée's works are of little value except for their subject-matter, the difficult and tragic period of Reconstruction. Among his novels, *Hot Plowshares* received a moderate degree of attention from the critics.

PRINCIPAL WORKS: *Novels*—A Fool's Errand, 1879; Figs and Thistles, 1879; Bricks Without Straw, 1880; A Royal Gentleman, 1881; John Eax and Mamelon, 1882; Hot Plowshares, 1883; *Legal*—The Code of Civil Procedure of North Carolina, 1868; A Digest of Cited Cases in the North Carolina Reports, 1879.

ABOUT: Dibble, R. F. Albion W. Tourgée; Tourgée, A. W. The Story of a Thousand; Hamilton, J. G. de R. Reconstruction in North Carolina; New York Times May 22, 1905.

TOWNSEND, ELIZA (1789-January 12, 1854), poet, was a native and resident of Boston, Mass. She was descended from an influential, early American family, and is said to have been highly esteemed, and a person of conversational felicity, culture, and mental vigor. In her latter years she lived secluded with her maiden sister in the old family mansion in Boston, the last of their blood.

Her poetry, which was published anonymously in the early part of the nineteenth century in New England periodicals, including the *Monthly Anthology,* the *Port Folio,* the *General Repository and Review,* and the *Unitarian Miscellany,* was never collected. It was of a dignified, thoughtful, and largely religious tone, and received high approbation from contemporary critics. Rufus Wilmot Griswold in *The Female Poets of America* said she was "the first native poet of her sex whose writings commanded the applause of judicious critics" and the first "whose poems evinced real inspiration or rose from the merely mechanical into the domain of art." Her outstanding poem "The Incomprehensibility of God" was favorably (if extravagantly) compared by a theologian of the day with William Cullen Bryant's "Thanatopsis." In her "Occasional Ode" she commented severely and with vigor upon Napoleon Bonaparte, then in his active career.

PRINCIPAL WORKS: "The Incomprehensibility of God" (written 1809; published in Griswold, R. W. The Female Poets of America); "Occasional Ode" (in Monthly Anthology September 1909); "Another Castle in the Air" (in Monthly Anthology November 1809); "Lines to Robert Southey" (written 1812; published in Griswold, R. W. The Female Poets of America); "The Rainbow" (in General Repository and Review January 1813).

ABOUT: Duyckinck, E. A. & G. L. Cyclopaedia of American Literature; Griswold, R. W. The Female Poets of America; Hale, S. J. Woman's Record.

TOWNSEND, GEORGE ALFRED (January 30, 1841-April 15, 1914), journalist and miscellaneous writer, was born in Georgetown, Del., the son of Stephen Townsend, a Methodist preacher, and Mary (Milbourne) Townsend, both of old Virginia and Maryland ancestry. While still at school he attracted attention by his public speaking and writings, and on being graduated from the Central High School, Philadelphia, in 1860, he became immediately associated with the Philadelphia *Inquirer,* later the *Press,* commencing a journalistic career that was to last most of his life. He was also associated with the New York *Herald* and *World,* and contributed to the Chicago *Tribune,* the Cincinnati *Daily Enquirer,* the *Cornhill Magazine* of London, and to other papers and journals aggregating nearly a hundred. He traveled widely, served as war correspondent in the Civil War and the Austro-Prussian War, and lectured and wrote in England during the years 1862-64 in support of the Northern cause. He married Bessie E. Rhodes of Philadelphia. From 1867 he resided mainly in Washington, D.C., New York City, and at his extensive country home at Crampton's Gap, South Mountain, Md. He died in New York City after ten years of invalidism.

His journalistic accounts of the final battles of the Civil War and of Lincoln's assassination gave him a reputation of almost national note. He also made frequent contributions of two to four columns under the signature of "Gath" discussing politics and topics of the day. His earlier publications were largely a revamping of his journalistic writings. *The Entailed Hat,* a novel of the kidnapping of free Negroes in Delaware and Maryland before the war, was conceded to be his best work. In some of his latter work the more careful craftsmanship and finish of his earlier writing were lacking.

PRINCIPAL WORKS: *Biography*—The Life and Battles of Garibaldi, 1867; The Real Life of Abraham Lincoln, 1867. *Dramas*—The Bohemians, 1861; President Cromwell, 1885. *Novels*—The Entailed Hat, 1884; Katy of Catoctin, 1886; Mrs. Reynolds and Hamilton, 1890. *Poetry*—Poems, 1870; Political Addresses, 1881; Poems of Men and Events, 1899. *Stories*—Tales of the Chesapeake, 1880; Bohemian Days, 1881. *Miscellaneous*—Campaigns of a Non-Combatant, 1866; The New World Compared With the Old, 1869; Lost Abroad, 1870; The Mormon Trails at Salt Lake City, 1871; Washington Outside and Inside, 1873.

ABOUT: Lippincott's Monthly Magazine November 1891; North American Review May 1900; N.Y. Times April 16, 1914.

TOWNSEND, MARY ASHLEY, (VAN VOORHIS) (September 24, 1832-June 7, 1901), poet and essayist, known as "Xariffa" and "Mary Ashley," was born in Lyons, N.Y., the daughter of James G. Van Voorhis and Catherine (Van Winkle) Van Voorhis. Educated at the neighborhood school and academy, she was married in her twenty-first year to Gideon Townsend of Fishkill, N.Y., and after a short residence in Clinton, Iowa, settled in New Orleans, where Townsend had business interests.

Mary Ashley Townsend's literary talent became apparent early in her childhood. Always a voracious reader, she wrote a number of juvenile efforts which she is said to have burned. Her first published writing appeared in the Fishkill, N.Y., *Standard* in 1850. Several years later, she contributed to the New Orleans *Delta* under the pseudonym "Xariffa," attracting notice by a series of essays called "Quillotypes," and "The Crossbones Papers," and also wrote for the New Orleans *Crescent* under the name of "Mary Ashley." A trip to Mexico in 1881 resulted in a group of letters for the *Picayune.*

Meanwhile, in 1870, her first volume of verse, *Xariffa's Poems,* including her popular "Creed," was published in Philadelphia. Four years later *The Captain's Story* appeared and stirred up considerable notice as it dealt with the subject of a supposed white man discovering that his mother was a mulatto. It was highly praised by Oliver Wendell Holmes, to whom Mrs. Townsend dedicated *Down the Bayou and Other Poems* in 1882. She died at her daughter's home in Galveston, Tex., of injuries received in a railway accident. Though her name shone with brilliance in the literary and social circles of *fin de siècle* New Orleans, it is now dimmed by later and superior work.

PRINCIPAL WORKS: *Novel*—The Brother Clerks, 1857; Xariffa's Poems, 1870; The Captain's Story,

1874; Down the Bayou and Other Poems, 1882; Distaff and Spindle, 1895.

About: Library of Southern Literature: Vol. 12; New Orleans Daily Picayune, Times-Democrat June 8, 9, 1901.

TRAIN, GEORGE FRANCIS (March 24, 1829-January 19, 1904), eccentric reformer, multi-millionaire, and miscellaneous writer, was born in Boston, the son of Oliver Train, a merchant, and Maria (Pickering) Train. In his early childhood the family moved to New Orleans, and there both parents and his three sisters died of yellow fever; his father's last act was to put the boy on a ship to Boston. He was reared by his maternal grandmother on a farm near Waltham, and educated in the public schools and for a few months at Framingham Academy. At fourteen he ran away and became a grocery clerk in Cambridge. Then he besieged the wealthy shipowner, Enoch Train, a relative, for a job, and rose in his service until in 1850 he was manager of the Liverpool office. In 1853 he went to Melbourne and started his own shipping firm. With its profits he traveled through the Orient and Europe, returning to New York in 1856. He had begun already his twin careers of pioneer moneymaking, mostly in railroads and street railways, and of wholesale espousal of numberless causes, the latter marked by innumerable pamphlets, lectures, and newspaper articles. These causes included Irish independence, woman suffrage, Free Thought (though later he believed himself possessed of psychic power), and many others; he claimed to have been a leader of the Paris Commune in 1870, and certainly was expelled from France.

Collection of Frederick H. Meserve
GEORGE FRANCIS TRAIN

He served two jail terms in America, one on a charge of obscenity (the first of the Comstock prosecutions). He declared himself an independent candidate for president in 1868, and charged for admission to his campaign talks, netting $90,000 but few votes. He made thirty millions in Omaha real estate. He claimed half a dozen inventions, including perforated postage stamps. He was declared insane by six courts, but probably was never really crazy—only an extreme eccentric who thought it amusing to shock people, to walk naked on the street or declare he was an octoroon!

In 1851 he married Wilhelmina Wilkinson Davis; she died in 1879, leaving four children. In his last years he lived at a Mills Hotel in New York, spent all his days in Madison Square talking to the children, and refused to speak to an adult except on the lecture platform. His writing had no literary value, but is of interest historically and psychologically. He was a gorgeous crank.

Principal Works: An American Merchant in Europe, Asia, and Australia, 1857; Young America in Wall Street, 1857; Young America Abroad, 1857; Spread-Eagleism, 1859; Young America on Slavery, 1860; Union Speeches, 1862; Irish Independency, 1865; Championship of Women, 1868; My Life in Many States and in Foreign Lands, 1902.

About: Seitz, D. C. Uncommon Americans; Train, G. F. An American Merchant: My Life in Many States and in Foreign Lands; Bookman March 1904; Harper's Weekly February 6, 1904; Outlook January 30, 1904; London Times January 20, 1904; New York Sun January 20, 1904.

TRESCOT, WILLIAM HENRY (November 10, 1822-May 4, 1898), historian and diplomat, was born in Charleston, S.C., the son of Henry and Sarah (McCrady) Trescot. He was educated at the College of Charleston, class of 1841, and was admitted to the bar two years later. After his marriage to Eliza Natalie Cuthbert in 1848, he supervised the management of her plantation on Barnwell Island off the Carolina coast, pursued his law practice, and wrote several political and historical works, among them *The Position and Course of the South.*

Trescot was appointed secretary of legation at London in 1852 and assistant secretary of state in 1860, but resigned the office the next year upon the secession of South Carolina. He was in the South Carolina legislature in 1862, 1864, and 1866, was on the staffs of Governor Magrath and of General Ripley and a member of the Executive Council of South Carolina. At the close of the war he went to Washington to represent the state on the recovery of lands seized during the Reconstruction. In 1877 he was appointed council for the United States on the fishing commission at Halifax, N.S.

He was one of the commissioners sent to China to revise the treaties in 1880, and the next year he concluded negotiations with the Colombian minister in reference to American rights in the Isthmus of Panama. He also served as envoy in South America and Mexico and was a delegate to the Pan-American conference of 1889 shortly before his retirement to his home in Pendleton, S.C., where he died.

Trescot's most important work, *The Diplomatic History of the Administation of Washington and Adams,* is notable for its vigor, accuracy and brilliance; and his studies of American diplomacy are the expert summations of a specialist in the field.

Principal Works: A Few Thoughts on the Foreign Policy of the United States, 1849; The Position and Course of the South, 1850; Diplomacy of the Revolution: An Historical Study, 1852; A Letter to Honor A. P. Butler . . . on the Diplomatic System of the United States, 1853; The Diplomatic History of the Administrations of Washington and Adams, 1857; Memorial of the Life of J. Johnston Pettigrew, 1870.

About: Simpson, R. W. History of Old Pendleton District; Trent, W. P. Southern Writers; American Historical Review April 1908; Charleston (S.C.) News and Courier May 5, 1898, August 30, 1903; Columbia (S.C.) State May 5, 6, 1898.

"TREVOR, ERNEST." See POWELL, THOMAS

TROWBRIDGE, JOHN TOWNSEND (September 18, 1827-February 12, 1916), story writer and poet, was born on his father's farm in Ogden Township, N.Y., the son of Windsor Stone Trowbridge and Rebecca (Willey) Trowbridge. During his early years he had bad sight and was largely self-taught, supplementing the public school with French, Latin, and Greek. For one year he attended the academy at Lockport, N.Y. He was precocious as a writer, his first poem appearing in the Rochester *Republican* when he was sixteen.

After teaching from 1845 to 1847, first in Illinois, then in Lockport, he went to New York in 1847. There Mordecai Manuel Noah befriended him and found a place for his stories in the *Dollar Magazine*. The next year he went to Boston. From 1849 to 1850 he published and edited the *Yankee Nation,* then became associate editor of the *American Sentinel,* which he killed by an ill-advised article on the fugitive slave law.

Collection of Frederick H. Meserve
J. T. TROWBRIDGE

From hack writing he turned to a higher type of journalism, being a contributor to the *Atlantic* from its beginning, and a regular contributor also to *Our Young Folks* and the *Youth's Companion.* With the former magazine for young people he was closely identified, being consulting editor from 1865 to 1870, and then managing editor to 1873.

He was twice married, in 1860 to Cornelia Warren, who died in 1864, leaving two children, and in 1873 to Sarah Adelaide Newton, by whom he had three children. His later years were spent at Arlington, Mass., near Boston, where he died. He received an honorary M.A. degree from Dartmouth in 1884, and was a close friend of Holmes and Longfellow—and also, rather surprisingly, of Whitman.

Trowbridge was known chiefly to a large and loyal audience of boys in the 'teens. John Burroughs said of him that "he knows the heart of a boy and the heart of a man, and has laid them both open." Of his works for adults, *Neighbor Jackwood* has been called the pioneer of novels of real life in New England. He himself considered his forty or more volumes of fiction as mere high-class hack-work, and depended for immortality on his didactic narrative poems, most of which are completely forgotten.

Principal Works: *Fiction*—Father Brighthopes, 1853; Martin Merrivale, 1854; Neighbor Jackwood, 1857; The Drummer Boy, 1863; Cudjo's Cave, 1864; Neighbors' Wives, 1867; Jack Hazard Series, 1871-75; Coupon Bonds and Other Stories, 1872; Fast Friends, 1874; Silver Medal Series, 1877-82; Young Joe and Other Boys, 1879; The Jolly Rover, 1882; Farnell's Folly, 1887; The Little Master,

1886; A Start in Life, 1888; The Kelp Gatherers, 1890; The Scarlet Tanager, 1891; The Fortunes of Toby Trafford, 1892; Woodie Thorpe's Pilgrimage, 1893; The Satinwood Box, 1894; The Lottery Ticket, 1895; The Prize Cup, 1896; Two Biddicut Boys, 1898; A Pair of Madcaps, 1909. *Poetry*—The Vagabonds and Other Poems, 1869; The Emigrant's Story and Other Poems, 1875; The Book of Gold and Other Poems, 1877; A Home Idyl and Other Poems, 1881; The Lost Earl and Other Poems, 1888; Poetical Works, 1903. *Miscellaneous*—The South: A Tour of Its Battlefields and Ruined Cities, 1866; My Own Story, 1903.

ABOUT: Trowbridge, J. T. My Own Story; Journal of Education March 16, 1916; Literary Digest March 18, 1916; Outlook February 23, 1916; New York Times February 13, 1916.

TRUMBULL, BENJAMIN (December 19, 1735-February 2, 1820), Congregational clergyman and historian, was born in Hebron, Conn., the son of Benjamin and Mary (Brown) Trumble. The spelling of the family name was changed in about 1768 to its present form, Trumbull. Young Trumbull attended Yale, class of 1759, and received his theological education under the Reverend Eleazer Wheelock. He was licensed in 1760 and in December of that year became pastor of the Congregational Church at North Haven, Conn. He remained in that capacity for nearly sixty years, his preaching being interrupted only by the Revolution, in which he served as a volunteer and as chaplain.

Trumbull's most famous work, *A Complete History of Connecticut,* was begun at the request of a cousin, Governor Jonathan Trumbull, and Secretary of State George Wyllys. The first volume was completed in 1797, more than twenty years later, owing to interruptions occasioned by his duites as pastor. Trumbull's other published works include a pamphlet sustaining the claim of Connecticut to the Susquehanna purchase, sermons and theological writings, and a history of the United States which was incomplete at his death. He was married to Martha Phelps in 1870. He died at North Haven, Conn., at eighty-four.

Trumbull's history of Connecticut is an accurate and painstaking account of the events from 1630 to 1713 and is one of the most important among state histories. It is a valuable source of information for scholars and a monument to his patriotism and industry.

PRINCIPAL WORKS: A Complete History of Connecticut . . . to the Year 1764, 1818; A Plea: In Vindication of the Connecticut Title to the Contested Lands Lying West of New York, 1774; An Appeal to the Public: . . With Respect to the Unlawfulness of Divorces, 1788; A General History of the United States of America: . . 1492-1792, 1810; A Compendium of the Indian Wars in New England (ed by F. B. Hartranft) 1924.

ABOUT: Johnston, H. P. Yale and Her Honor-Roll in the American Revolution; Lea, J. H. Contributions to a Trumbull Genealogy; Thorpe, S. B. North Haven Annals; Christian Spectator March 1820; Columbian Register (New Haven) February 12, 19, 1820.

TRUMBULL, JAMES HAMMOND (December 20, 1821-August 5, 1897), historian, philologist, and bibliographer, was born at Stonington, Conn., the son of Gurdon and Sarah Ann (Swan) Trumbull, and brother of Henry Clay Trumbull, well-known Sunday-School missionary. After attending Tracy's Academy, Norwich, he matriculated at Yale in 1838, remaining only two years because of ill health. Becoming assistant to James Harvey Linsley, he cataloged the mammalia, birds, reptiles, fish, and shells of Connecticut for a time, and in 1847 was appointed assistant secretary of state in Connecticut, again holding office in 1858, after a period as state librarian and registrar. Between 1861 and 1866 he served as secretary of state, after which time he became trustee and librarian of the Watkinson Library of Reference at Hartford. In 1855 he married Sarah A. Robinson of Hartford.

The long list of Trumbull's writings covers a variety of subjects including history, philological works, and biographies, but he is best remembered for his works on the North American Indian, which considerably enriched the hitherto lean material on this subject and established him as an authority on Indian dialects. Among these publications was a dictionary and vocabulary to John Eliot's Indian Bible, which, it was said, no other man had the ability to read. Other important titles were *The Composition of Indian Geographical Names, The Best Method of Studying the Indian Language,* and *Indian Names of Places in and on the Borders of Connecticut: With Interpretations.*

As a bibliographer Trumbull rose to a high place, especially with his *Catalogue of the American Library of the Late Mr. George Brinley of Hartford.*

PRINCIPAL WORKS: *History*—The Colonial Records of Connecticut, 1850-59; Historical Notes on Some Provisions of the Connecticut Statutes, 1860-61; The Defense of Stonington Against a British Squadron in 1814, 1864; Roger Williams' Key Into the Language of America, 1866; Thomas Lechford's Plain Dealing; or, Newes From New England, 1867; The Origin of McFingal, 1868. *Philological*—The Composition of Indian Geographical Names, 1870; The Best Method of Studying the Indian Languages, 1871; Some Mistaken Notions of the Algonkin Grammar, 1871; Notes on Forty Algonkin Versions of the Lord's Prayer, 1873; Indian Names of Places in and on the Borders of

Connecticut: With Interpretations, 1881. *Bibliography*—Catalogue of the American Library of Late Mr. George Brinley of Hartford . . . (5 vols.) 1878-97.

ABOUT: Wright, A. W. Biographical Memoir of James Hammond Trumbull; National Academy of Sciences, Biographical Memoirs: Vol 7; Hartford Courant August 6, 1897.

TRUMBULL, JOHN (April 13, 1750-May 11, 1831), poet and jurist, was born in Westbury (now Watertown), Conn. The son of the Rev. John Trumbull, a Congregational minister, and Sarah (Whitman) Trumbull, he was heir to a distinguished family tradition; related on his mother's side to Jonathan Edwards, and on his father's to a succession of Trumbulls famous in Connecticut history: three governors, a general, a philologist, an historian, a painter.

Almost from the cradle he followed a literary career. An extraordinarily precocious child, he learned Greek and Latin at the age of five, and at the age of seven passed the entrance examinations at Yale College. Because of his extreme youth, he did not enter Yale until six years later spending his time writing poetry and studying the classics. At thirteen he matriculated at Yale. After receiving his degree in 1767, he remained at Yale five years as fellow and tutor, while he wrote essays and verse. Although an excellent scholar, he was sharply critical of contemporary educational methods, expressing his disapproval of the curriculum in his first important literary work, *The Progress of Dullness,* a long satirical poem, the first part of which was published in 1772, additional parts in 1773.

From a portrait by his cousin, J. Trumbull
JOHN TRUMBULL
1793

Mixing Blackstone with the poets, he passed his bar examinations in 1773, and left New Haven for Boston where he began to practice law under John Adams. Here, under the influence of Adams and the stirring events preceding the Revolution, he absorbed the political views which later gave the theme to his best-known work, *M'Fingal,* a poetic burlesque of Tory politics, strongly Whiggish in sentiment.

In 1774 Adams left Boston, and Trumbull went to New Haven to practice law. In 1776, on the eve of the Revolution, he published the first two cantos of *M'Fingal,* which achieved immense popularity, selling thirty editions during his lifetime. Five years later, he published the third and fourth cantos, and moved to Hartford, where he became one of the group of poets known as the "Hartford Wits," a select circle which enjoyed a glittering reputation and made Hartford a literary center during the last two decades of the eighteenth century. Married to Sarah Hubbard, the daughter of Colonel Leveret Hubbard, he lived quietly in Hartford as the acknowledged leader of the Connecticut poets, collaborating with three others of the group in a long satirical poem, *The Anarchiad.* After the age of thirty-three, however, he wrote no poetry of major importance.

His declining creative powers were balanced by an increasing interest in law and politics. Although he had been hailed as the poet of the Revolution, he became now a Federalist, opposing the radical ideas of Jeffersonian democracy and entering on a conservative career as a jurist. By temperament, he was never a revolutionary. With his slight physique, and his elegant white periwig, he presents rather the figure of an urbane colonial gentleman, decorous, cautious, self-contained. His later years fell into the pattern of this aristocratic tradition. In 1789 he was elected state's attorney for the county of Hartford. From 1792 to 1800 he served in the state legislature. He was twice a judge: in 1801, judge of the Superior Court of Connecticut; and in 1808, judge of the Supreme Court of Errors, a position he held until 1819.

In 1820 a collection of his verse was issued in two volumes, *The Poetical Works of John Trumbull.* A monument to his earlier reputation, this work aroused little interest. He had outlived his own fame, and the last six years of his life were spent obscurely in Detroit, Mich., where he died at the age of eighty-one.

The most celebrated American poet of the eighteenth century, Trumbull remains today a minor writer. He is remembered for only one poem, *M'Fingal,* and that only because of the part it played in the Revolution. In style, he was strongly indebted to the English poetry of the period, particularly to Samuel Butler's *Hudibras.* In spite of its revolutionary subject matter, the poem is a scholarly *tour de force,* smelling of the lamp as much as of the battle. Trumbull nursed the delusion of himself as a writer of elegaic or epic poetry, but his gift was satiric and intellectual, rather than imaginative.

PRINCIPAL WORKS: *Poetry*—An Elegy on the Death of Mr. Buckingham St. John, 1771; The Progress of Dulness: Part I: The Rare Adventures of Tom Brainless, 1772; The Progress of Dulness: Part II: The Life and Character of Dick Hairbrain, 1773; The Progress of Dullness: Part III: The Adventures of Miss Harriet Simper, 1773; An Elegy On the Times, 1774; M'Fingal: Canto I (later published as Canto I and II) 1776; M'Fingal: A Modern Epic in Four Cantos, 1782; Poetical Works of John Trumbull, 1820.

ABOUT: Cowie, A. John Trumbull: Connecticut Wit; Parrington, V. L. The Colonial Mind; Tyler, M. C. The Literary History of the American Revolution; American Literature November 1931.

TUCKER, GEORGE (August 20, 1775-April 10, 1861), political economist and miscellaneous writer, was born in Bermuda, the son of Daniel Tucker, mayor of Hamilton, and Elizabeth (Tucker) Tucker. He was sent to Virginia in 1787 and was educated under the direction of St. George Tucker [*q.v.*], a distant relative. He graduated from the College of William and Mary in 1797, studied law, and practiced in Richmond and Lynchburg. He was a member of the Virginia legislature and was elected to Congress three times, serving from 1819 to 1825. On his retirement he became professor of moral philosophy at the University of Virginia, serving for twenty years until his removal to Philadelphia in 1845.

Tucker's published works include both historical and economic subjects. His *Life of Thomas Jefferson,* although slightly prejudiced in Jefferson's favor, is an important survey of an absorbing period, written from the viewpoint of a contemporary. Tucker's great interest in political economy resulted in numerous books and articles extending over many years, the best known being *The Laws of Wages, Profits, and Rent Investigated.* He was an opponent of slavery but never publicly resisted it; a book of *Letters From Virginia,* a bitterly satricial denunciation of slavery, published anonymously, has been attributed to him.

In 1869, while on a tour of the South, he met with an accident in Mobile and was brought back to Albemarle County, Va., to the home of his son-in-law, where he died. Tucker was married to Maria Ball Carter in 1801; his second wife was Mary (Byrd) Farley, and his third wife was Louisa (Bowdoin) Thompson.

PRINCIPAL WORKS: Speech of Mr. Tucker, of Virginia, on the Restriction of Slavery in Missouri . . . , 1820; Essays on Subjects of Taste, Morals, and National Policy: By a Citizen of Virginia, 1822; The Valley of Shenandoah, 1824; A Voyage to the Moon, 1827; The Life of Thomas Jefferson, 1837; The Laws of Wages, Profits and Rent Investigated, 1837; The Theory of Money and Banks Investigated, 1839; Progress of the United States in Population and Wealth in Fifty Years, 1843; The History of the United States, 1856-57; Political Economy for the People, 1859; Essays: Moral and Metaphysical, 1860.

ABOUT: Bruce, P. A. History of the University of Virginia; Emmet, T. A. An Account of the Tucker Family of Bermuda; Proceedings American Philosophical Society, 1865; Daily Richmond Enquirer April 13, 1861.

TUCKER, NATHANIEL BEVERLEY (September 6, 1784-August 26, 1851), novelist and professor of law, half-brother of John Randolph of Roanoke, son of St. George Tucker [*q.v.*], and Frances (Bland) Randolph Tucker, was born at Matoax, Chesterfield County, Va. He was educated at home and later attended the College of William and Mary, graduating in 1801. Alternating the practice of law with political pursuits, he was for a time a judge in the circuit court of Missouri.

He was married three times: first, to Mary Coalter, who died shortly after the move to Missouri; his second wife was Eliza Taylor; and after her death he married Lucy Anne Smith, 1830.

Returning to Virginia in 1833, he accepted a law professorship at his alma mater, William and Mary, a post which he filled with distinction until his death. During this time Tucker, always an ardent supporter of Southern policies, poured forth a series of political novels, letters, lectures and speeches, almost all of them presenting and defending the cause of the South.

His first novel, *George Balcombe,* appeared anonymously and was well received; Poe called it the best American novel ever written. *The Partisan Leader: A Tale of the Future,* written in 1836 under an assumed name and post-dated 1856, was a supposedly historical novel of events taking place within those years. The course of history bore out many of the prophecies made by Tucker in this book, for his predictions came not so much from intuition as through diligent study of political trends. He began a biography of John Randolph, but it was not completed.

Tucker's novels are too verbose, sentimental, and unreal to appeal to present day readers, but his writings on statecraft are of interest for their picture of the temper of the country before the Civil War, and for the light they shed on the mind of a Virginia gentleman.

PRINCIPAL WORKS: *Novels*—George Balcombe, 1836; The Partisan Leader, 1836; Gertrude (published in Southern Literary Messenger September 1844-December 1845). *Political Works*—A Discourse on the Importance of the Study of Political Science as a Branch of Academic Education in the United States, 1840; The Principles of Pleading, 1846.

ABOUT: Bruce, W. C. John Randolph of Roanoke; Findlay, H. Library of Southern Literature; Richmond College Historical Papers: Vol. 2, No. 1; Historical Magazine June 1859; International Magazine October 1851.

TUCKER, ST. GEORGE (June 29, 1752 o.s.-November 10, 1827), poet and jurist, was born at Port Royal, Bermuda, the son of Henry and Anne (Butterfield) Tucker. He came to Virginia to attend William and Mary College, was graduated in 1772, admitted to the bar and began a law practice in Williamsburg. During the Revolution, Tucker enlisted to defend the Colonies, serving with distinction and bravery through the conflict and ending his military career as lieutenant-colonel at the siege of Yorktown.

After the war he resumed his practice, was made a judge of the general court of Virginia in 1788, and in 1800 became a professor of law in the College of William and Mary. He was appointed to the Virginia supreme court of appeals in 1803, becoming judge of the United States district court of Virginia ten years later, a position which he filled with distinction until ill health forced him to resign shortly before his death.

Tucker married Frances (Bland) Randolph, widowed mother of John Randolph of Roanoke, in 1778. Their two sons, Nathaniel Beverley Tucker and Henry St. George Tucker, became prominent in Virginia affairs. Three years after his wife's death, Tucker married Lelia (Shipwith) Carter.

He was a poet as well as a jurist and wrote some dramas and several minor poems of real merit, among these *Liberty: A Poem on the Independence of America,* and *The Probationary Odes of Jonathan Pindar, Esq.*, a volume of political satires. But his most important works are his legal decisions and writings.

PRINCIPAL WORKS: Dissertation on Slavery: With a Proposal for Its Gradual Abolition in Virginia, 1796; The Probationary Odes of Jonathan Pindar, 1796; Letters on the Alien and Sedition Laws, 1799; Liberty: A Poem on the Independence of America, 1788; annotated edition of Blackstone's Commentaries, 1803.

ABOUT: Mackenzie, G. N. Colonial Families of the United States; Emmett, T. A. An Account of the Tucker Family of Bermuda; Gentleman's Magazine November 1828; Virginia Law Register March 1896; University of Pennsylvania Law Review January 1919.

TUCKERMAN, BAYARD (July 2, 1855-October 20, 1923), biographer, was born in New York City, the son of Lucius and Elizabeth Wolcott (Gibbs) Tuckerman. Through his maternal line he was the great-grandson of Oliver Wolcott, signer of the Declaration of Independence. He was prepared for college by private tutors and a two-year stay at the Pension Roulet at Neûchatel. Graduated from Harvard in 1878, he immediately returned to Europe where he settled in Paris to take up the study of English literature. *A History of English Prose Fiction From Sir Thomas Malory to George Eliot* was published in 1882 and well-received. Seven years later he produced his admirable *Life of General Lafayette* (2 vols., 1889), also publishing in the same year *The Diary of Philip Hone,* a collection of excerpts with scant notes. With the exception of his *Life of General Philip Schuyler* (1903), he produced nothing further of literary importance, although at the time of his death he had made voluminous notes for a history of chivalry.

Tuckerman's large private income enabled him to devote much time to research and writing and to lead the graceful, quiet life of his choice, with a companionable wife, Annie Osgood Smith, daughter of the Rev. John Cotton Smith, whom he married in September 1882.

From 1898 to 1907 he lectured on English literature at Princeton University. Although he was equipped with a facile pen, he never ranked as a first-class scholar.

PRINCIPAL WORKS: A History of English Prose Fiction From Sir Thomas Malory to George Eliot, 1882; Life of General Lafayette, 1889; The Diary of Philip Hone, 1889; Peter Stuyvesant, 1893; William Jay and the Constitutional Movement for the Abolition of Slavery, 1894; Life of General Philip Schuyler, 1903; Notes on the Tuckerman Family of Massachusetts, 1914; A Sketch of the Cotton Smith Family of Sharon, Connecticut, 1915.

ABOUT: Gibbs, G. The Gibbs Family of Rhode Island and Some Related Families; Tuckerman, B. Notes on the Tuckerman Family of Massachusetts; A Sketch of the Cotton Smith Family of Sharon, Connecticut; Harvard College: Class of 1878 Fiftieth Anniversary Report; Harvard Graduates' Magazine December 1923; Boston Transcript October 22, 1923.

TUCKERMAN, FREDERICK GODDARD (February 4, 1821-May 9, 1873), poet, was born in Boston, the son of Edward and Sophia (May) Tuckerman. Entered at Harvard in 1837, he was interrupted in his studies by eye trouble, but finally graduated from Harvard Law School in 1842. Although he was admitted to the bar at Suffolk in 1844 and practised for a few years, Tuckerman was primarily a lover of nature and literature, and he soon gave up the law entirely for the more congenial pursuits of astronomy, botany, and poetry. Like his brother Edward, famous professor of botany at Amherst College, he was an ardent and accomplished naturalist, and he attained considerable distinction, locally at least, in botany and astronomy.

However, Tuckerman's scientific studies must be considered valuable chiefly because they gave him that knowledge of nature, at once extensive and minute, which animates and adorns his poetry. He began writing verse at Greenfield, Mass., where he moved after his marriage in 1847 to Hannah Lucinda Jones, and where he spent the rest of his life in scholarly retirement. With the exception of two visits to Europe, during the second of which he stayed with Tennyson in England, Tuckerman lived almost as a recluse—"a life well lost," as he himself remarked, because he was not deeply interested in worldly affairs anyway. He was chiefly concerned with his own relation to the physical and metaphysical world, and this profound question occupied his mind and filled his poetry from beginning to end. Particularly after the death of his wife in childbirth only ten years after their marriage, Tuckerman showed in his sonnets a perturbed and gloomy state of mind; in Mr. Bynner's fine phrase the poet "wrote straightly to himself," and never felt a true kinship with other men or a comfortable assurance of his place in the universe.

It was perhaps only natural, then, that Tuckerman should have made only a small impression on the contemporary literary world. His poems occasionally appeared in the *Living Age* or the *Atlantic,* and a collection of them brought out in 1860 ran through one English and three American editions. But though Tennyson, Emerson, and Longfellow esteemed his poems, particularly his sonnets, rather highly, the public allowed them to be soon forgotten. Tuckerman took liberties with the sonnet form which were not always understood, and the substance of his poetry was ill-suited to the prevailing Romantic taste. At any rate, his poems fell almost completely into oblivion,

FREDERICK GODDARD TUCKERMAN

and remained unknown until Walter Pritchard Eaton resurrected them in 1909. The best of the 1860 collection, together with three unpublished sonnet sequences, were brought out in 1931 with an appreciative introduction by Mr. Witter Bynner, and in the last few years Tuckerman has been widely and sympathetically read. Mr. Bynner does not hesitate to rank the sonnets with "the noblest in the language"; he admits himself "stricken by grief" on reading Tuckerman's "sincerely felt and wrought" expressions of sadness. It has been objected by a critic in the *Bookman,* however, and Tuckerman's sonnets are certainly open to the criticism that their "grief seems both insufficiently universal and insufficiently used"; that it is, in fact, "mere gloominess, morbidity springing from private and personal sources."

PRINCIPAL WORKS: Poems, 1860; The Sonnets of Frederick Goddard Tuckerman, 1931.

ABOUT: Tuckerman, F. G. In Sonnets of Frederick Goddard Tuckerman (See Introduction by W. Bynner); Tuckerman, B. Notes on the Tuckerman Family; Bookman April 1931; Forum January 1909; Boston Daily Globe May 12, 1873.

TUCKERMAN, HENRY THEODORE (April 20, 1830-December 17, 1871), "man of letters," was born in Boston, the son of Henry Harris and Ruth (Keating) Tuckerman. He prepared at the Latin School for Harvard, where he remained only two years because of a breakdown in health. He traveled abroad, and in Italy acquired his romantic devotion to art and letters. Returning to the United States, he published *The*

Collection of Frederick H. Meserve
H. T. TUCKERMAN

Italian Sketch Book; after two more years on the Continent came his travel romance *Isabel: or, Sicily: A Pilgrimage,* which appears to have given him ample confidence in his literary ability. For a short time (1845) he edited the *Boston Miscellany of Literature and Fashion,* and two years later settled permanently in New York City, where he became a popular member of a distinguished group of writers—Washington Irving, Fitz-Greene Halleck, and other social literati.

Tuckerman wrote prolifically during the years that followed: several volumes of individual and collective biographies; familiar essays assembled under the titles *The Optimist* and *The Criterion;* a variety of Irvingesque sketches in *Leaves From the Diary of a Dreamer*; and a book of *Poems,* most of which are plainly indicative of his love of retirement, devotion to art, fascination with the glamour and tradition of Italian culture. and his over-indulgence in sentiment. One of the most sympathetic and intelligible of his critical analyses was his essay on Hazlitt, included in the second of two series of *Characteristics of Literature;* and perhaps the most durable of his books was *America and Her Commentators: With a Critical Sketch of Travel in the United States.* Tuckerman was awarded an honorary M.A. degree from Harvard in 1850, and "in recognition of his labors on behalf of Italian exiles in the United States" a special order was conferred upon him by the king of Italy.

He lamented the "want of serenity and of poetic feeling" in the national spirit of commercialism. His social poise, occasional cultural pursuits, and a sentimental effervescence that was apparently often mistaken for intellectuality, caused his contemporaries to over-estimate his literary worth.

Principal Works: *Art*—Artist Life: or, Sketches of American Painters, 1847; Book of the Artists: American Artist Life, 1867. *Biography*—The Life of Silas Talbot, 1850; Mental Portraits, 1853; The Life of John Pendleton Kennedy, 1871. *Essays*—The Optimist, 1850; Essays: Biographical and Critical, 1857; The Criterion, 1866; Leaves From the Dairy of a Dreamer, 1853. *Miscellaneous*—The Italian Sketch Book, 1835; Isabel: or, Sicily: A Pilgrimage, 1839; Poems, 1851; America and Her Commentators: With a Critical Sketch of Travel in the United States, 1864.

About: Duyckinck, E. A. A Memorial to Henry T. Tuckerman; Griswold, R. W. The Prose Writers of America; New York Evening Post December 18, 20, 1871; New York Tribune December 18, 1871.

TUDOR, WILLIAM (January 28, 1779-March 9, 1830), miscellaneous writer, was born in Boston, Mass., the son of a prominent merchant and scholar, Colonel William Tudor, and his wife Delia (Jarvis) Tudor. Graduated from Harvard in 1796, young Tudor became associated with John Codman's counting-room and was soon dispatched to Paris and Leghorn on business. These trips were not successful, but he soon established a profitable business with his brother, shipping ice from their pond at Saugus to Martinique and South America where they introduced its use in table drinks. He also served the Massachusetts legislature for many terms, and took an active interest in politics.

Deeply interested in literature from his early youth, in 1815 he founded the *North American Review,* becoming its first editor and the largest contributor to its first four volumes. Meanwhile he had founded the Anthology Society in 1805, comprising such notables as O. S. Buckminster, William Ellery Channing, President Kirkland of Harvard, John Lowell, and others. The group gathered one evening every week to go over manuscripts, and refreshed themselves with a light supper of widgeons and teal, brants or a mongrel goose, washed down with good claret. Tudor wrote much for their magazine, the *Monthly Anthology and Boston Review.* He was also one of the founders of the Boston Athenaeum, an outgrowth of the Anthology Society, and an active member of the Massachusetts Historical Society.

In 1823 he was appointed United States consul at Lima and Peru and rendered valuable service during the feud between

Peru and Columbia. Four years later he went to Rio de Janeiro as chargé d'affaires, contracted fever and died there. He never married.

Tudor published a commentary on contemporary manners in 1820 entitled *Letters on the Eastern States.* This was followed by *Miscellanies,* a group of his essays which are sufficiently light in style to be enjoyed today, but he will be best remembered for *The Life of James Otis of Massachusetts.* Although his writing does not fall within the scope of great nineteenth century literature, he had a share in the advancement of American letters. He was a person of unbounded energy who continually interested himself in civic and literary works; Daniel Webster described him as "an accomplished scholar, a distinguished writer and a most amiable man." His name was once a prop for George IV's wit, who remarked when Tudor was presented to him, "What, one of us?"

PRINCIPAL WORKS: Letters on the Eastern States, 1820; Miscellanies 1821; The Life of James Otis, 1823.

ABOUT: Loring, J. S. The Hundred Boston Orators; Quincy, J. The History of the Boston Athenaeum; Smith, C. C. Proceedings of the Massachusetts Historical Society: Vol. I; Boston Daily Advertiser May 3, May 8, 1830.

TULLEY, JOHN (c.1639-October 5, 1701), author of the earliest series of American almanacs covering any considerable span of years, was born near London, England. While still very young he was brought to this country by his widowed mother, who settled in Connecticut and married again. Tulley lived and died at Saybrook, Conn.

Tulley's almanacs, issued from 1687 to 1702, inclusive, became very well known throughout New England. They were published in Boston, and between 1693 and 1695 Benjamin Harris [*q.v.*] was the printer and may well have been a collaborator, since Tulley blamed some of the verse, which had given offence, on him. Though not so lavish of moral advice as the later almanacs, Tulley's contained an average amount of bad verse and bad spelling. The 1698 issue is notable in that it contains what is believed to be the earliest New England road guide. Tulley was one of the earliest in the country to adopt the new style of computing dates, and his almanacs are unusual in that their year begins in January.

ABOUT: Green, S. A. John Tulley's Almanacs; Page, A. B. John Tulley's Almanacks.

TURELL, JANE (COLMAN) (February 25, 1708-March 26, 1735), poet, was born in Boston, where her father, the Rev. Benjamin Colman, was pastor of the Brattle Street Church. Her mother, Jane (Clark) Colman, was his first wife. As a small child Jane absorbed a great deal of scriptural knowledge from close association with her father, and was frequently called upon by Gov. Joseph Dudley and other distinguished visitors in the home to entertain them by her precocious Bible story recitations. During her eleventh year she wrote a hymn, followed several years later by some verse-paraphrases of the Psalms that won her father's commendation, although he strictly maintained that a "Poetical Flight now and then" must not interfere with her daily reading and devotions.

In 1726, she married the Rev. Ebenezer Turell, Harvard graduate and minister at Medford. This happy alliance was fostered by a mutual interest in literature and Jane Turell was encouraged by her husband to continue her writing in verse and prose. These works were published in the year of her death at Medford under the title *Reliquiae Turellae et Lachrymae Paternae* (1735), and appeared in London as *Memoirs of the Life and Death of the Pious and Ingenious Mrs. Jane Turell . . . Collected Chiefly From Her Own Manuscripts* (1741). It is enhanced by a poetic eulogy by the Rev. John Adams, two funeral sermons delivered by her father, and a memoir by her husband, all of which reveal her as an extremely pious character. Her poetry was widely read in Boston early in the eighteenth century but in its passage down the years its claim to noteworthiness has been almost entirely extinguished.

PRINCIPAL WORKS: Reliquiae Turellae et Lachrymae Paternae, 1735.

ABOUT: Turell, E. The Life and Character of the Rev. Benjamin Turell, J. Reliquiae Turellae; Cyclopaedia of American Literature; Vol. 1.

TURNER, JOSEPH ADDISON (September 23, 1826-February 29, 1868), editor, planter, lawyer, manufacturer, and mentor of Joel Chandler Harris [*q.v.*], was born at "Turnwold," a plantation nine miles from Eatonton, Ga., to which his father, William Turner, had been the fortunate heir. He grew up in the mellow and bucolic atmosphere of Putnam County, and spent many hours in a remarkable family library gazing at the field of English letters through a very Johnsonian lens.

In 1860 Turner was a member of the Georgia state legislature; and during that same year issued his "Southern quarterly journal," the *Plantation.* The opening sentence of the first issue ("In less than twelve months this country may be deluged in blood") was a sound prophecy but hardly a reassuring preface—and the venture met an early end. He operated, at Turnwold, not only a hat factory, a tannery, and a distillery, but a printing plant, and on March 4, 1862, launched the *Countryman,* a weekly modeled after Addison's *Spectator* and Goldsmith's *Bee,* that was "independent in everything and neutral in nothing." Turner abhorred "Exchange" columns, and for "filler" he used extracts from translations of French classics; his own editorials, nevertheless, were quoted in almost every paper in the Confederacy; and the *Countryman* had, at one time, a circulation of 2,000.

Joel Chandler Harris began his apprenticeship by setting type for this paper, occasionally inserting "from the case" a few of his own literary inventions; and Turner provided him with his first workable rules for writing.

Shortly before the Civil War havoc forced Turner to suspend publication of the *Countryman* for six months, he said, in an open letter:

> As an editor I was once as bold as a lion. That was when I had a country. Now, it seems I have none. . . If I cannot edit my paper as a freeman I will edit none at all. . .

By February 1866 Turner had resumed printing and (albeit with a certain condescension) had come to regard the Negro as more than a traditional accoutrement of the "Sunny South":

> If . . . forced upon as as a citizen, we stand for educating him. . . He should receive all the aid and encouragement in the power of our people to give him.

Turner's social opinions are an interesting appendix to the literature of sectionalism, and he earned the distinction of publishing what was doubtless the only newspaper ever printed on a Southern plantation.

About: Harris, J. C. On a Plantation; Harris, J[ulia] C. Life and Letters of Joel Chandler Harris; Harris, J[ulia] C. Joel Chandler Harris: Editor and Essayist; American Review April-October 1933; files of the Countryman and of the Plantation.

"TWAIN, MARK." See CLEMENS, SAMUEL LANGHORNE

TYLER, MOSES COIT (August 2, 1835-December 28, 1900), historian and educator, was born in Griswold, Conn., the son of Elisha and Mary (Greene) Tyler. The family removed to Detroit, and Moses attended the local schools and the University of Michigan. He studied theology at Yale, class of 1857, and at Andover, and entered the Congregational ministry. He was pastor of a church in Poughkeepsie, N.Y., but remained less than two years.

Tyler was an ardent reformer and crusaded for abolition, temperance, and women's rights. In 1863 he went to England to lecture on the system of gymnastics invented by Dio Lewis. On his return to this country in 1867 he was appointed to the chair of rhetoric and English literature at the University of Michigan and remained in this capacity until 1881, with the exception of a short interlude spent on Henry Ward Beecher's *Christian Union.* In that year he was called to Cornell University as the first professor of American history in the country. That same year he was made deacon in the Episcopal Church, and in 1883 was ordained priest. He died at Ithaca, leaving his wife, Jeannette Hull (Gilbert) Tyler, whom he had married in 1859.

Tyler's *History of American Literature During the Colonial Time* and *The Literary History of the American Revolution* are the result of the methodical research and penetrating insight that made him one of the foremost American historians. Besides essays, articles, and text-books, Tyler wrote several biographies, among them *Three Men of Letters.* These, like his literary histories, were characterized by a keen critical sense and an authoritative style. In addition to his many other services to education, Tyler was one of the founders of the American Historical Association.

Principal Works: A History of American Literature During the Colonial Time: 1607-1765, 1878; Patrick Henry, 1887; Three Men of Letters, 1895; The Literary History of the American Revolution: 1763-1783, 1897; Glimpses of England, 1898.

About: Austen, J. T. Moses Coit Tyler: Selections From His Letters and Diaries; Jones, H. M. The Life of Moses Coit Tyler; Forum August 1901; New York Times December 29, 1900.

TYLER, ROYALL (July 18, 1757-August 26, 1826), jurist, soldier, playwright, novelist, and wit, was born in Boston and educated at Harvard University, but achieved renown in Vermont. He was a brilliant and attractive young man, and after his graduation from Harvard in 1776, Yale bestowed upon him the honorary degree of B.A. His interests were varied, and everything he undertook to do he did with enthusiasm and energy. After leaving college, he studied law with Francis Dana in Cambridge, but the Revolution diverted his attention from his studies, and in 1778 he joined the Independent Company of Boston, serving as aide to General Sullivan in his attack on Newport.

In spite of his digressions from serious study he was admitted to the bar in 1780. While working in the law office of John Adams, Tyler fell in love with Abigail, Adams' daughter, and they became engaged. John Adams, having no faith in Tyler's stability, removed his daughter to France and broke the engagement.

Tyler's literary career started when his play *The Contrast* was produced in New York in 1787. This play attracted a great deal of attention and enjoyed an unusually long run. The first comedy written by a native American and produced by a professional company, it is historically important as the play in which local American dialect was originally introduced for purposes of comedy. The characters in this play were the prototypes of a succession of stage Yankees, still recognizable in modern comedies—Colonel Manley, a bluff, outspoken American officer and gentleman, and Dimple, an imitator of British affectations.

Meanwhile he had joined the army and had served on General Benjamin Lincoln's staff: the suppression of Shay's Rebellion was due largely to his brilliant oratory in addressing the rioters. His military career, however, was cut short by his widowed mother, who objected strongly to her son's taking unnecessary risks, and Tyler returned to his law practice at her request.

He settled in Guildford, Vt., where he soon made a name for himself. In addition to his legal work, he continued to write plays and novels generously interspersed with his personal opinions on political and social topics of the day. In 1894 he entered into a partnership with the litterateur Joseph Dennie, and under the title of "Colon and Spondee" they became the first American columnists, contributing their topical work to *The New Hampshire Journal, Port Folio,* and the like.

After a miniature

ROYALL TYLER

Tyler did not neglect his law practice for his writing. He served as States Attorney for Windham County, and from 1807 to 1813 was Chief Justice of the Supreme Court of Vermont. He also held the professorship of jurisprudence at the University of Vermont from 1811 to 1814. In 1794 he married Mary Palmer, a childhood friend, in direct opposition to his mother's wishes. The marriage was both happy and prolific.

In addition to his political plays, several sacred dramas in blank verse are attributed to his pen, but since they were published anonymously the authorship is uncertain.

During the last few years of his life, Tyler suffered from a cancer of the face that caused blindness. He finally died of the disease in Brattleboro, Vt. Despite the painful and unpleasant nature of his illness, he remained charming, witty, high spirited, energetic and versatile until the end.

Principal Works: *Plays*—The Contrast, 1786; May Day in Town: or, New York in an Uproar, 1787; The Georgia Spec: or, Land in the Moon, 1797. *Miscellaneous*—The Algerine Captive, 1799; The Yankey in London, 1809; The Chestnut Tree, 1824 (not published until 1931); *Unpublished Plays* —The Island of Barrataria; Tantalization: or, The Governor of a Day.

About: Cabot, M. R. Annals of Brattleboro; Ellis, H. M. Joseph Dennie and His Circle; Tupper, F. Royall Tyler: Man of Law and Man of Letters; Tupper, F. & Brown, H. T. Grandmother Tyler's Book.

TYLER, WILLIAM SEYMOUR (September 2, 1810-November 19, 1897), college professor and classical editor, was born at Harford, Pa., the son of Joab and Nabby (Seymour) Tyler. Educated at home and at neighboring academies, he entered Hamilton College in 1827 but left after one term to teach school. In 1829 he joined the junior class of Amherst College, graduating in 1830. After a year of teaching at Amherst Academy, he spent two years as tutor in Amherst College, and prepared himself for the ministry under the Rev. Thomas H. Skinner of New York. Before he could leave for the West to become a home missionary, he returned to Amherst to fill a tutorship vacated by his brother, and was soon appointed to a professorship of Latin and Greek, which he filled with great distinction for fifty-six years. His religious fervor was not abated by classroom duties, and he was ordained to the Congregational ministry, October 16, 1857, taking a prominent part in the religious affairs of western Massachusetts, and preaching many memorable sermons. He was also active in educational circles and served on the boards of both Smith and Mount Holyoke Colleges.

For classroom use, he edited numerous Latin and Greek works, and contributed a number of learned articles to periodicals and encyclopedias. From his deep attachment for his alma mater grew his finest book, *The History of Amherst College During Its First Half Century,* which was later edited and continued as *Amherst College During the Administrations of Its First Five Presidents.* These two volumes are of inestimable value to research students.

Principal Works: History of Amherst College During Its First Half Century, 1873; A History of Amherst College During the Administrations of Its First Five Presidents, 1895.

About: Brigham, W. I. T. The Tyler Genealogy; Tyler, C. B. The Autobiography of William Seymour Tyler; Amherst College Biographical Record, 1927; Springfield Republican November 20, 1897.

UNDERWOOD, FRANCIS HENRY (January 12, 1825-August 7, 1894), lawyer, United States consul, and miscellaneous writer, was the son of Roswell and Phoebe (Hall) Underwood. He was born on a farm near Enfield, Mass., the town which he celebrated in his best book, *Quabbin: The Story of a Small Town.* He began his education against heavy financial odds; he entered Amherst College in 1843 but after a year of study moved to Kentucky, where he taught school and studied law. Admitted to the Kentucky bar in 1847, he married Louisa Maria Wood in 1848 and began to practice, but in 1850 he decided to return to Massachusetts.

This move was dictated partly by Underwood's aversion to slavery, which eventually changed his career completely. Surrounded by New England anti-slavery influences while practicing law at Webster, Mass., the young man conceived the idea of launching a literary magazine which should exterminate the evil, and he interested the publisher John P. Jewett in this idea. By 1857 he had gained the support of Harriet Beecher Stowe and several years of editorial experience with the firm of Phillips, Sampson & Co.; the time was ripe. Holmes, Lowell, Emerson and Longfellow promised aid; Phillips agreed to publish the magazine; and Underwood went abroad to find literary material in England. The new magazine, edited by Lowell and christened by Holmes the *Atlantic Monthly,* was launched forthwith and successfully weathered the financial panic of 1857. Underwood served as assistant editor of the magazine until 1859, when it passed into the hands of Ticknor & Fields, and then to his chagrin he was displaced on the staff of the magazine which had been to a great extent originally his own brain-child.

Underwood had a large acquaintance in Boston, and after 1859 he devoted much time to social activities and literary work. Besides writing biographical memoirs of such prominent friends as Lowell, Whittier, and Longfellow, he wrote short stories and a series of novels: *Lord of Himself, Man Proposes,* and *Doctor Gray's Quest.* His writings, however, like his work behind the scenes on the *Atlantic Monthly,* never brought him literary fame.

During Cleveland's two terms as President, Underwood was twice appointed to consulships in Scotland, first at Glasgow in 1886, then at Leith in 1893. He died at Edinburgh. He was married twice; his first wife died in 1882 and he married again in Scotland.

Principal Works: Cloud-Pictures, 1872; Lord of Himself, 1874; Man Proposes, 1885; Quabbin: The Story of a Small Town, 1893; Doctor Gray's Quest, 1895.

About: Howe, M. A. DeW. The Atlantic Monthly and Its Makers; Perry, B. Park-Street Papers; Atlantic Monthly January 1895; The Times (London) August 9, 1894.

UPHAM, CHARLES WENTWORTH (May 4, 1802-June 15, 1875), historian, clergyman and congressman, was the son of Joshua and Mary (Chandler) Upham. Born in St. John, New Brunswick, where his father was judge of the supreme court, Upham went to work in 1814 as an apothecary's apprentice, but two years later was sent to Boston to work for his cousin Phineas Upham. To this enlightened man, a prosperous merchant, Upham owed his start in life, for in 1817 Phineas sent him to Harvard, and four years later to Cambridge Divinity School. Upham was a brilliant student, graduating second in his class at Harvard, and he entered the clerical profession in 1824 well endowed with theological learning and controversial skill. During the period of his associate pastorate of the First Unitarian Church of Salem, Mass., 1824-1844, he had ample opportunity to use this erudition, for he took an active part in the struggle between the Unitarian and the orthodox Calvinist doctrines. His discourse *The*

Scripture Doctrine of Regeneration, published in 1840, claimed the triumph of Unitarianism.

Upham's ministerial career was interrupted by throat trouble in 1844, but by 1849 his health improved and he began to take an active part in politics. He served the Whig party in the Massachusetts Legislature for some years; he was elected to Congress in 1853; in 1856 he joined the new Republican party and assisted it by writing a campaign biography of John C. Frémont.

The literary work for which he is best known, however, is *Salem Witchcraft.* This historical account, an elaborate and minute record of the witchcraft scare in 1692 and the trial and punishment of the "witches," was written after Upham's withdrawal from politics in 1860. Although he seems to have supported the wrong argument in his subsequent controversy with William F. Poole, on the question of Cotton Mather's guilt in the witchcraft atrocities, Upham's work is still valuable to historians, and it has brought him considerable repute.

Upham married, in 1826, Ann Susan Holmes, sister of Oliver Wendell Holmes. He was a brilliant man and well liked by many associates; Emerson praised his "frank and attractive" demeanor. He made at least one powerful enemy, however: Nathaniel Hawthorne, whom he was instrumental in removing from the Salem Custom House, is said to have caricatured him in the character Judge Pyncheon, in *The House of the Seven Gables.*

Principal Works: Principles of the Reformation, 1826; The Scripture Doctrine of Regeneration, 1840; Salem Witchcraft, 1867; Salem Witchcraft and Cotton Mather, 1869.

About: Eliot, S. A. Heralds of a Liberal Faith; Ellis, G. E. Memoir of Charles Wentworth Upham; Upham, F. K. The Descendants of John Upham of Massachusetts; Salem Gazette June 18, 1875; Boston Transcript June 18, 1875.

VALLENTINE, BENJAMIN BENNATON (September 7, 1843-March 30, 1926), journalist and playwright, was born in London, England, the son of Benjamin Vallentine, a toy merchant, and Rosa (Nathan) Vallentine. Educated at Birmingham, he spent several early years in Sydney, Australia, as clerk in a shipping firm, studying for the English bar and contributing to the newspapers. In his late twenties he returned to England, coming to New York City in 1871, where, after a precarious partnership in a shipping firm, he turned to journalism. He studied in New York University Law School, 1907-08, and in the latter year entered the city department of finance under the civil service. He was unmarried. His last years were marked by ill health and straitened circumstances. He died at eighty-two at Bellevue Hospital.

Vallentine was one of the founders of the humorous magazine *Puck,* its managing editor for its first seven years in New York; in its initial number, March 1877, he commenced the series of colloquial, satirical paragraphs purporting to be letters of a musical-comedy Britisher, Lord Fitznoodle, which earned him the nickname "Fitznoodle" and constitutes his chief claim to remembrance. Later he was managing editor successively of *Texas Siftings* and Irving Bacheller's newspaper syndicate, 1886-88, and had editorial connection with some half-dozen New York journals, including the *Mail and Express, Evening Telegram,* and New York *Herald.* He had a wide theatrical acquaintance; wrote dramatic criticisms; and wrote, collaborated on, or adapted many plays, among which a comic opera *Fadette, A Southern Romance,* and *In Paradise* were produced in New York in 1892, 1897, and 1899 respectively, the latter being published in a one-act version.

Principal Works: *Plays*—Fadette; A Southern Romance; In Paradise; Fitznoodle; The Locksmith of Paris; The King of the world. *Miscellaneous*—Fitznoodle Papers; Fitznoodle in America.

About: New York Times September 5, 1899, March 31, 1926, April 4, 1926.

VANDENHOFF, GEORGE (1813(?)-June 16, 1885), actor, lawyer, and miscellaneous writer, was born in Liverpool, England, of Dutch extraction. His father John Vandenhoff and his sister Charlotte Elizabeth Vandenhoff both achieved distinction on the English stage. Vandenhoff received a liberal education at Stonyhurst College, studied law, and held a lucrative position as counsel for the Dock Association of Liverpool. At twenty-six he turned to the stage, making his debut at Covent Garden, London, in 1839. Three years later he came to the United States, and although the period was an unfavorable one, he quickly established himself and scored many successes, making appearances in New York and elsewhere for the next fourteen years, until his retirement in 1859 when he resumed the practice of law in New York. He acted with Charlotte Cushman, the elder Booth, and other stage personalities of note, among his characterizations being Hamlet, Macbeth, and Coriolanus, but his most pronounced success was finally attained as Captain Cozens in J. R. Planche's comedy *Knights of the Round Table.* In the intervals of and following his stage career he made a considerable reputation as a public speaker and elocutionist. He married an American actress, Mary Makeah, in 1855. His death occurred at Brighton, England, at seventy-two.

Vandenhoff published several volumes designed as textbooks for his elocutionary teaching, including *A Plain System of Elocution,* later revised and published as *The Art of Elocution,* and edited *The Clay Code: or, Text-Book of Eloquence,* a collection gathered from the public speeches of Henry Clay. Among his other published work were a social satire in verse entitled *Common Sense,* a lengthy poem *Life: or, Men, Manners, Modes, and Measures,* and a volume of anecdotes and reminiscences of the stage, *Leaves From an Actor's Note Book.*

PRINCIPAL WORKS: A Plain System of Elocution (2d ed.) 1845; Common Sense: A Dash at Doings of the Day, 1858; Leaves From an Actor's Note Book, 1860; Life: or, Men, Manners, Modes and Measures, 1861; Elocutionary Guide, 1862; The Art of Reading Aloud in Pulpit, Lecture-Room, or Private Reunions, 1878. *Editor*—The Clay Code: or, Text-Book of Eloquence, 1844.

ABOUT: Odell, G. C. D. Annals of the New York Stage; Vandenhoff, G. Leaves From an Actor's Note Book; New York Dramatic Mirror August 14, 1886.

VENABLE, WILLIAM HENRY (April 29, 1836-July 6, 1920), teacher and miscellaneous writer, was born near Waynesville Ohio, one of five children of Quaker parents, William Venable and Hannah (Baird) Venable. He commenced to teach at seventeen, later graduating from the South-Western Normal School, Lebanon, Ohio, receiving honorary degrees: M.A. DePauw University, LL.D. Ohio University, and Litt.D. University of Cincinnati, in 1864, 1886, and 1917 respectively. With the exception of about a year as principal of Jennings Academy, Vernon, Ind., 1860, his subsequent teaching was in Cincinnati where for a quarter of a century he was teacher of natural science and finally proprietor of Chickering Institute, 1862-1886, and in the English departments of the Hughes and Walnut Hills high schools, 1889-1900. After his retirement in 1900 he gave exclusive attention to literature. He married Mary Ann Vater in 1861, and among his seven children were the educator Emerson Venable and the electrician William Mayo Venable.

Venable exerted a far-reaching influence on education, was a well-known platform speaker, and contributed to the periodical press. Among his more than a score of published works were included some educational textbooks and a volume of pedagogical essays, *Let Him First Be a Man,* a few memoirs, a work on literary men and women, stories from Ohio history, and a novel of the Burr-Blennerhasset episode, *A Dream of Empire.* He wrote several volumes of verse which were posthumously collected and edited by his son. But it is on the *Beginnings of Literary Culture in the Ohio Valley*—"discursive, even desultory . . . a repository of accumulated notes" he himself called it—that his literary significance rests.

PRINCIPAL WORKS: *Essays*—Let Him First Be a Man, 1893. *History*—A School History of the United States, 1872; Footprints of the Pioneers in the Ohio Valley, 1888. *Juvenile*—Tom Tad, 1902. *Memoirs*—John Hancock, 1892. *Novels*—A Dream of Empire: or, The House of Blennerhassett, 1901. *Poetry*—June on the Miami and Other Poems, 1872; The Poems of William Henry Venable (ed. by E. Venable) 1925. *Stories*—Tales From Ohio History, 1896. *Miscellaneous*—The School Stage, 1873; Dramas and Dramatic Scenes, 1874; Beginnings of Literary Culture in the Ohio Valley, 1891.

ABOUT: Randall, E. O. History of Cincinnati and Hamilton County, Ohio; The Biographical Cyclopedia and Portrait Gallery of Ohio; Venable, E. Poets of Ohio; William Henry Venable: An Appreciation.

VERPLANCK, GULIAN CROMMELIN (August 6, 1786-March 18, 1870), miscellaneous writer, was born in New York City, the son of Daniel Crommelin Verplanck, a judge and Congressman, of Holland descent, and Elizabeth (Johnson) Verplanck. His mother died when he was three, and he was reared by his two grandmothers. He was graduated from Columbia in 1801, at less than sixteen—the youngest graduate to that date. He then studied law, and was admitted to the bar in 1807. In 1811 he married Mary Elizabeth Fenno, by whom he had two sons.

Verplanck's defense of a student during the "Columbia Commencement Riot," in 1811, made him an author, for he was fined $200 by DeWitt Clinton, the beginning of a ten-year row punctuated by pamphlets and satirical verses on both sides. From 1815 to 1817 he traveled in Europe for his wife's health (she died soon after); on his return he founded the New York *American,* with Charles King, and in this paper most of his caustic satires on Clinton appeared.

From 1821 to 1824 he was professor of the evidences of Christianity at the General Theological Seminary (Episcopal); the theological works he produced during this period have a distinctly legal tone and reveal him as a conservative deist. From 1820 to 1823 he served in the New York Assembly as a Federalist, then became a Democrat and was in Congress from 1825 to 1833. In 1831 he secured important improvements in the copy-

Collection of Frederick H. Meserve
G. C. VERPLANCK

right law. Quarreling with President Jackson, he turned Whig, and as such was barely defeated for mayor of New York in 1834, the first direct mayoralty election in the city. From 1838 to 1841 he served in the New York senate, but most of his time in later years was given to literature.

He was a close student of Shakespeare and produced a creditable edition in 1847. With his friends William Cullen Bryant and Robert C. Sands he edited an annual, the *Talisman,* from 1828 to 1830. His writing was always extraneous to his public life, and is no longer of interest to the general public.

Principal Works: A Fable for Statesmen and Politicians, 1815; The State Triumvirate (verse) 1819; The Bucktail Bards, 1819; Essays on the Nature and Uses of the Various Evidences of Revealed Religion, 1824; Essay on the Doctrine of Contracts, 1825; Discourses and Addresses on Subjects of American History, Arts, and Literature, 1833.

About: Bryant, W. C. A Discourse on the Life, Character, and Writings of Gulian Crommelin Verplanck; Hart, C. H. A Discourse on the Life and Services of the Late Gulian Crommelin Verplanck; New York Times March 19, 1870.

VERY, JONES (August 28, 1813-May 8, 1880), poet, preacher, and teacher, was born at Salem, Mass., the eldest of six children of Jones Very, a sea captain, and Lydia Very, daughter of Samuel Very. The parents were cousins, descendants of the English widow Bridget Very, American settler of about 1634. Both parents, as well as a brother and a sister, showed talent for verse making.

Very attended the public schools at Salem; in 1824 he set sail with his father for New Orleans and there spent a short term in a grammar school. At the age of fourteen he had to leave school to take a position as an errand boy, his father's death compelling him to help in the support of the family. His devotion to books and study did not cease, however, and he devoured whatever reading material he could secure from his employer or buy with his meager savings. With the help of a tutor he advanced so far that in 1832 he could take a teaching position at a private school in Salem. Offered financial assistance by an uncle, he entered Harvard College as a sophomore in 1834. During the fall after his graduation (1836) he received an appointment as tutor in freshman Greek. This enabled him to pursue further studies at the Harvard School of Divinity until 1838. He took no degree in theology, but was licensed a Unitarian preacher by the Cambridge Association in 1843.

On his return to Salem he led a retired life, occasionally engaging in genealogical research for the Essex Institute and contributing to the *Salem Gazette,* the *Christian Register,* and other papers, as representative of his denomination. When called upon, he preached, but he never held a pastorate. His love of literature, particularly of religious and ethical writings, persisted. He regularly spent a great part of his day in reading, interrupted by wanderings in the hills, where he wrote poetry.

Oblivious to the happenings of the day, he led a life of the spirit, and claimed that in all his acts he followed the inner light and heavenly guidance. He believed himself beyond earthly realities and outside the physical world. His religious ecstasy was such that at one time his sanity was questioned and he was committed, for a while in 1838, to the McLean Asylum in Somerville, Mass.

Very believed and preached that the unconditional surrender of one's will to the Will of God is the source of joy and peace. That is the keynote of all his writings, which are permeated with mysticism and aspire to the transcendental. They reflect also an intense love of nature, which he considered only a symbol of the Divine. To him all his inspirations were divine communications, which, as a passive instrument of the Divine Spirit, he had to render audible. "He valued his poems, not because they were his, but because they were not."

His earliest work was an essay on *Epic Poetry,* in which he expounds his theory of

JONES VERY

poetry and life. His *Essays and Poems*, edited by Emerson, appeared in 1839.

In spite of literary deficiencies, he was considered a poetic genius because of the depth of his sentiment and the melodious movement of his verses. Bryant, Emerson, and Dana predicted for them immortality. His sonnets received especial praise.

He never married; after the death of his mother and brother, he lived with his sisters in the family house. Because of his reserve and his fault-finding with society, which in its turn considered him erratic and morbid, he did not have many friends. He enjoyed, however, the friendship of such men as Emerson and the poet R. H. Dana. A contemporary remarked that he impressed everybody by "his quiet and dignified demeanor, his slender figure, a kind of emblem of uprightness, his sweet smile, and in general the respect and the esteem with which he inspired his companions."

Principal Works: Essays and Poems, 1839; Poems, 1883; Poems and Essays, 1886.

About: Andrews, W. P. Memoir; Bradford, G. Biography and the Human Heart; Emerson, R. W. Journals; Proudfoot, B. W. Jones Very; Essex Institute Bulletin January, February, March 1881; The Dial July 1841.

VERY, LYDIA LOUISA ANN (November 2, 1823-September 10, 1901), poet, was born in Salem, Mass., the daughter of Jones Very, a sea captain, and Lydia (Very) Very. Her family were all given to verse writing, her brother, Jones Very [*q.v.*], mystic and poet, attracting considerable attention. Throughout her life of seventy-eight years she lived in Salem, never marrying, over thirty years being given to teaching in a private school kept by her brother Washington Very, and, after his death in 1853, in the Bowditch Grammar School.

Her contributions in prose and verse appeared in Salem and Boston papers, and when she was thirty-three her first small volume, *Poems,* was published. Thirty-four years later these were reprinted, augmented with additional poetry and prose essays, as *Poems and Prose Writings.* Her verse, reflecting her best work, was marked by strong religious sentiment, naturalness, simplicity, and grace. Among her other work was a simple anecdotal record, *An Old Fashioned Garden and Walks and Musings Therein;* sixteen nature stories told with naïveté and charm appeared under the title *Sayings and Doings Among Insects and Flowers.* Her three novels were inferior to her other work. A self-taught artist, she attractively illustrated and versified *Little Red Riding-Hood* and three other books for children.

Principal Works: Poems, 1856; Poems and Prose Writings, 1890; Sayings and Doings Among Insects and Flowers, 1897; The Better Path: or, Sylph, the Organ-Grinder's Daughter (novel) 1898; A Strange Disclosure (novel) 1898; A Strange Recluse (novel) 1899; An Old-Fashioned Garden, 1900.

About: Essex Institute Historical Collections: Vols. 1, 2; Perley, S. The Poets of Essex County; Proudfoot, B. W. Jones Very.

"VETERAN OBSERVER." See MANSFIELD, EDWARD DEERING

VICTOR, FRANCES (FULLER) (May 23, 1826-November 14, 1902), poet and historian, was born in Oneida County, N.Y. Her father, reputed to have borne the distinctive name Adonijah Fuller, and her mother, Lucy (Williams) Fuller, took their family to Ohio during Frances' thirteenth year and here she spent her youth. A trial at writing for newspapers influenced her to go to New York with her sister, Metta [*q.v.*], and the two were taken under the wing of Rufus Wilmot Griswold, who edited their joint volume, *Poems of Sentiment and Imagination: With Dramatic and Descriptive Pieces* (1851). The two sisters were married to brothers—Metta, to Orville James Victor; and Frances, in 1862, to Henry Clay Victor, a naval engineer. She is said to have made an earlier marriage to a Jackson Barritt of Pontiac, Mich., in 1853.

The Victors went to California to live and Mrs. Victor became a contributor to San Francisco and Sacramento newspapers. Through indefatigable research she grew to be an authority on Pacific Northwest history, publishing a number of books on this subject, among which was her fine two-volume *History of Oregon* (1886-88).

Her husband lost his life in the tragic wreck of the "Pacific" on November 4, 1875. Penniless, she supported herself by her pen and assisted Hubert Howe Bancroft's staff in writing the *History of the Northwest Coast.* During a desperate financial struggle she was once reduced to selling toilet articles from house to house in Salem, Ore. Although the end of her life saw an improvement in her fortunes, she wrote until her last day and passed away in a Portland boarding house. A capacity for hard work and an aptitude for research, rather than any outstanding literary gift, aided her in attaining an enduring reputation as a minor historian.

PRINCIPAL WORKS: *Poems*—Poems of Sentiment and Imagination: With Dramatic and Descriptive Pieces, 1851; Poems, 1900. *History*—The River of the West, 1870; All Over Oregon and Washington, 1872; History of the Northwest Coast, 1884; History of Oregon, 1886-88; History of Washington, Idaho, and Montana, 1890; History of Nevada, Colorado, and Wyoming, 1890; History of California (Vols. 6-7) 1890. *Miscellaneous*—The New Penelope, 1877; Atlantis Arisen: or, Talks of a Tourist About Oregon and Washington, 1891; The Early Indian Wars of Oregon, 1894.

ABOUT: Bancroft, H. H. Literary Industries; Gaston, J. The Centennial History of Oregon; Powers, A. History of Oregon Literature; Quarterly Oregon Historical Society December 1903; Portland Morning Oregonian November 15, 16, 1902.

VICTOR, METTA VICTORIA (FULLER) (March 2, 1831—June 26, 1886), "dime" novelist, was born near Erie, Pa., daughter of Lucy (Williams) Fuller and her husband, whose name is variously given as Henry or Adonijah. At the age of eight she accompanied her parents to Wooster, Ohio, where she was educated at a female seminary. A precocious child, she wrote verses for newspapers at an early age and is credited with a story, *The Silver Lute,* written and published when she was thirteen. After 1844 she became a regular contributor to the *Home Journal* under the pseudonym "The Singing Sibyl." With her sister Frances Fuller she came to New York to find literary fame late in the 'forties; the two appeared often in the periodicals as "The Sisters of the West," and they produced a joint volume, *Poems of Sentiment and Imagination,* in 1851. Two years later Metta wrote *The Senator's Son,* a story designed to further the temperance crusade; the book brought her considerable fame both here and in England, where 80,000 copies of it are said to have been sold.

Metta's greatest literary activity began in 1856 when she married Orville James Victor [*q.v.*], who became editor of the famous series of "Beadle's Dime Novels." Victor was, in fact, the inventor of the dime novel; he taught his wife and many other popular story-tellers the essential requirements—simplicity of character, complexity and velocity of adventure—of the *genre* that was to have such a phenomenal success during and after the Civil War. Metta wrote *Alice Wilde: The Raftsman's Daughter,* the fourth of Beadle's series, and several others; her greatest achievement in this field was *Maum Guinea and Her Plantation Children,* published in 1862. This simple but pathetic tale of slave life sold 100,000 copies here and circulated widely in England at a time when the Unionist cause badly needed support there. Abraham Lincoln is said to have found it "as absorbing as *Uncle Tom's Cabin*"; and Henry Ward Beecher praised it as a "telling shot" for the anti-slavery cause. Mrs. Victor wrote, for circulation at the same time, an "Address to the English People" which had considerable effect.

Mrs. Victor had, at the height of her fame, an exceedingly vast audience. The New York *Weekly* is said to have paid her $25,000 for a five-year exclusive right to her serials. Late in life she turned to writing humorous sketches and stories, as the dime novel fell more and more into disrepute. She died at Hohokus, N.J., her husband's home.

PRINCIPAL WORKS: *Poetry*—Poems of Sentiment and Imagination, 1851; Fresh Leaves From Western Woods, 1853. *Novels*—The Last Days of Tul, 1846; The Senator's Son, 1853; Lives of Female Mormons, 1856; Alice Wilde: The Raftsman's Daughter, 1860; The Backwoods Bride, 1861; Maum Guinea and Her Plantation Children, 1862; The Dead Letter, 1874; The Gold Hunters, 1874; Passing the Portal, 1876.

ABOUT: Pearson, E. L. Dime Novels; Atlantic Monthly July 1907.

VICTOR, ORVILLE JAMES (October 23, 1827-March 14, 1910), editor, inventor of the dime novel, was born in Sandusky, Ohio. His parents are believed to have been Henry and Gertrude (Nash) Victor. He was graduated from the Norwalk Academy and after contributing to several periodicals, adopted journalism as a profession, becoming assistant editor of the Sandusky *Daily Register* in 1852.

In July 1856 he married Metta Victoria Fuller [*q.v.*], a writer of some reputation, who was later to achieve great popularity through the publication of several particularly successful dime novels, the most noted being *Maum Guinea and Her Plantation Children.*

Two years later they moved to New York City, where Victor edited a series of newspapers, including the *Cosmopolitan Art Journal* and the *United States Journal.* Also contributing to numerous other papers and periodicals, he turned out a surprisingly large amount of hack work. During the Civil War he published four works on the conflict, among them *The History: Civil, Political, and Military of the Southern Rebellion.* Next editing the Dime Biographical Library, he contributed sketches of Abraham Lincoln, Anthony Wayne, Giuseppe Garibaldi, and others.

It was not until 1860 that Victor was inspired by the idea that was to make publishing history. Fostering the plans, working out the formula, and tutoring his writers, he brought forth the dime novel. His authors, of whom his wife was an outstanding example, poured out the stories of Western and Southwestern adventure in quantity lots and the soldiers, surfeited with warfare, read them eagerly. They were tremendously popular, and appeared at a time when a war-torn country, tired of grim reality, avidly devoured these florid tales of romantic adventure.

Victor died at his home in Hohokus, N.J. Although he left no writing of importance, his perspicacious knowledge of the taste of the reading public influenced other popular writers.

Principal Works: The History: Civil, Political, and Military of the Southern Rebellion, 1861-68; The American Rebellion: Some Tracts and Reflections for the Consideration of the English People, 1861; Incidents and Anecdotes of the War, 1862; History of American Conspiracies, 1863.

About: Pearson, E. L. Dime Novels; Atlantic Monthly July 1907; New York Tribune March 17, 1910.

VON TEUFFEL, BARONESS. See HOWARD, BLANCHE WILLIS

VOSE, HARRIET L. See BATES, ARLO

WALCOT, CHARLES MELTON (c. 1816-May 15, 1868), dramatist and actor, was born in London, England. There are few records of his early life and education, although it is known that he trained to be an architect. His father's name was probably Thomas B. Melton. He came to America in 1837, where his beautiful singing voice and natural talent for acting led to a stage career. His début in New York City was at the Military Garden, June 28, 1842. After completing a season there, he joined the company at the Olympic where he was to remain for seven years as one of the leading players. He created many parts, among them the rôle of *Don César de Bazan,* in 1844, one of the most popular plays of that period. During his years at the Olympic, Walcot wrote many plays, including *The Imp of the Elements: or, The Lake of the Dismal Swamp,* acting the leading rôles in many of them. His wife, Anne Powell, whom he married about 1838, was also a member of the company.

In 1852, Walcot became a member of the famous Wallack Company and achieved enormous popularity with his sense of the comic, both in acting and writing. He was always most successful in comedy characterizations. He made very few appearances on the stage in the nine years that elapsed between his last appearance at Wallack's in 1859 and his death at the home of his son in Philadelphia.

The drama is indebted to Walcot, not so much for his plays themselves, outdated, now, as for their place in the rapid evolution of the theatre of the past century. Such plays as *Don Giovanni in Gotham,* and *The Don Not Done: or, Giovanni From Texas,* while crude and exaggerated in humor, contributed to the development of comedy technique and stage satire.

Principal Works: The Imp of the Elements: or, The Lake of the Dismal Swamp, 1844; Don Giovanni in Gotham; The Don Not Done: or, Giovanni From Texas, 1844; Old Friends and New Faces, 1844.

About: Brown, T. A. History of the American Stage, Ireland, J. N. Records of the New York Stage.

WALKER, AMASA (May 4, 1799-October 29, 1875), Congressman and economist, was born in Woodstock, Conn., the son of Walter and Priscilla (Carpenter) Walker. He was educated in the district school at Brookfield, Mass., where the family had moved after his birth. On leaving school he engaged in such diverse occupations as clerking, farming, and teaching, and finally moved to Boston where in 1825 he established a shoe store with the brother of Emeline Carleton, whom he was to marry the next year. His wife died in 1828, and six years later Walker married Hannah Ambrose of Concord, N.H., who bore him three children, one of whom was Francis Amasa Walker [*q.v.*].

In 1840 he retired from commercial life to devote himself to public service; two years later he went to Oberlin College, which he had helped to found, and gave lectures on political economy. In 1848 he was elected to the Massachusetts House of Representatives and the next year entered the state senate. Following his election as secretary of state in 1851 and 1852, he served as chairman of the committee on suffrage at the convention for revising the state constitution. He was one of the leaders in the formation of the Free-Soil party. From 1853 to 1860 he was an examiner in political economy at Harvard, and from 1860 to 1869 he lectured at Amherst College. In 1859 he was again elected to the legislature, assisting in the revision of the banking laws. He was a member of the House of Representatives in 1862-63, completing the unexpired term of Goldsmith F. Bailey.

Walker was vice-president of the International Peace Congress in London in 1844 and of the Paris Congress in 1849. A series of articles by him appeared in *Hunt's Merchants' Magazine and Commercial Review* in 1857 and attracted wide attention. His numerous pamphlets and publications on monetary questions, particularly *The Science of Wealth,* were received with a careful attention both in America and abroad. His natural endowments, commercial training, and lifelong study in the field of economics equipped him as an authority on questions of finance. He died at his childhood home in Brookfield, Mass.

PRINCIPAL WORKS: The Nature and Uses of Money and Mixed Currency, 1857; The Science of Wealth: A Manual of Political Economy, 1866.

ABOUT: Hurd, D. H. History of Worcester County, Massachusetts; Munroe, J. P. A Life of Francis Amasa Walker; Walker, F. A. Memoir of Hon. Amasa Walker, LL.D.; New England Historical and Genealogical Register January 1898; Boston Transcript October 29, 1875.

WALKER, FRANCIS AMASA (July 2, 1840-January 5, 1897), educator, statistician, and writer on political economy, was born in Boston, the son of Amasa Walker [*q.v.*], and Hannah (Ambrose) Walker. After graduation from Amherst College in 1860, he studied law for a year before the Civil War interrupted his career. During his military service he was wounded, confined in Libby prison, and finally mustered out with the rank of brevet brigadier-general. From 1865 to 1868 he taught Latin and Greek at Williston Seminary, Easthampton, and was soon writing editorials for the Springfield *Daily Republican.* In 1865 he married Exene Stoughton.

In 1869 he became special deputy and later chief of the Bureau of Statistics. The following year he was superintendent of the census, and in 1871 he was appointed commissioner of Indian affairs. He accepted the chair of political economy and history in the Sheffield Scientific School of Yale in 1873, remaining until 1881, when he was elected president of Massachusetts Institute of Technology, a position which he held until his death in Boston. From 1879 to 1881 he was again superintendent of census and was instrumental in bringing about many needed reforms in that mismanaged department. Walker was vice-president of the National Academy of Science from 1891 to 1897, president of the American Economic Association from 1885 to 1892, and of the American Statistical Association from 1882 to 1897.

His constant labors in the cause of education were of paramount importance in the progress achieved in the nineteenth century in the reformation and improvement of the school system. Under his far-sighted leadership and because of his exceptional executive ability, Massachusetts Institute of Technology made rapid strides toward becoming the finest technical school in the country. Besides innumerable articles and lectures, Walker's published works, among them *The Wages Question* and *Land and Its Rent,* placed him in the front rank of contemporary American writers on economics. His fund of information on economic and political issues, his vision, and his social conscience combined to make him a leader in education and economics.

PRINCIPAL WORKS: History of the Second Army Corps in the Army of the Potomac, 1886; The Indian Question, 1874; The Wages Question, 1876; Money, 1878; Money in Its Relation to Trade and Industry, 1879; Land and its Rent, 1883; Political Economy, 1883; International Bimetallism, 1896; Discussions in Economics and Statistics (ed. by D. R. Dewey) 1899; Discussions in Education (ed. by J. P. Munroe) 1899.

ABOUT: Munroe, J. P. A Life of Francis Amasa Walker; Educational Review June 1897; Journal of Political Economy March 1897; Review of Reviews February 1897; Boston Herald January 6, 1897; Springfield Daily Republican January 6, 1897.

WALLACE, HENRY (March 19, 1836-February 22, 1916, editor and agricultural writer, was born near West Newton, Pa., of farmer ancestry, the son of John Wallace who emigrated from Ireland in 1832, and Martha (Ross) Wallace. Graduated from Jefferson College (now Washington and Jefferson College) in 1859, he studied at the theological seminaries at Allegheny, Pa., and Monmouth, Ill., and in 1863 was ordained to the Presbyterian ministry, holding pastorates for the next fourteen years in Illinois and Iowa, at Rock Island, Davenport, and Morning Sun. A tendency to tuberculosis, from which other members of his family had died, then compelled him to turn to farming. At Winterset, Iowa, he soon gravitated to agricultural journalism, editing successively the *Madisonian,* and the *Winterset Chronicle,* and in 1895 he purchased with his two sons, Henry Cantwell Wallace and John P. Wallace, *Wallaces' Farm and Dairy,* later *Wallaces' Farmer*; under his long editorship it became the outstanding agricultural journal of the country. He was also influential in political and religious interests, a platform lecturer, and served in various public capacities, among others as a member of President Roosevelt's Country Life Commission in 1908, president of the National Conservation Congress in 1910, and in 1913 investigator of agricultural conditions in Great Britain. He died suddenly in the First Methodist Church, Des Moines, Ia., while chairman of a Layman's Missionary Conference. His son, Henry Cantwell Wallace, was Secretary of Agriculture in the cabinets of Presidents Harding and Coolidge; his grandson, Henry Agard Wallace, is the present (1938) Secretary of Agriculture.

In addition to being a prolific writer for his own publications, Wallace wrote many brochures and pamphlets and several volumes, chiefly on agricultural subjects. A practical idealist, he united a keen and philosophic intellect and religious background with more than three decades of preaching such doctrines as soil conservation, good farming, and other agricultural and public benefits. Three small volumes of his *Uncle Henry's Own Story of His Life* were posthumously published.

Principal Works: The Doctrines of the Plymouth Brethren, 1878; Clover Culture, 1892; Uncle Henry's Letters to the Farm Boy, 1897; Clover Farming, 1898; Trusts and How to Deal With Them, 1899; The Skim Milk Calf, 1900; Letters to the Farm Folks, 1915; Uncle Henry's Own Story of His Life, 1917-19.

About: Tributes to Henry Wallace; Wallace, H. Uncle Henry's Story of His Own Life; World To-Day November 1910.

WALLACE, LEWIS ("Lew" Wallace) (April 10, 1827-February 15, 1905), novelist, soldier, lawyer, and diplomat, was born at Brookville, Ind., the second of four sons of David Wallace, governor of Indiana, lawyer, and congressman, and of Esther French (Test) Wallace, daughter of John Test, a lawyer and first congressman from Indiana.

His systematic education ended when he was sixteen. His father turned him out into the world to earn a living, because neither severity at home nor punishment in school could restrain his truant visits to fields and woods, where he liked to read. He became a copyist in the county clerk's office. His leisure time was spent, however, in reading and studying in preparation for his literary work. He later joined his older brother in the study of law in his father's office—"pettifogging," he called it—until admitted to the bar in 1849. He settled down as a lawyer in Covington and then moved to Crawfordsville.

His studies of law as well as his practice were interrupted by his activities as soldier and diplomat. During 1846-1847 he served as volunteer in the Mexican War and during 1861-1865 in the War of the Rebellion. He distinguished himself in both wars, and left the army as major-general in 1865.

Though not very active in politics, he was elected Indiana state senator in 1856, and through presidential appointments held two diplomatic posts. He was governor of New Mexico, 1878-1881, and American minister to Turkey, 1881-1885, where he enjoyed the confidence and esteem of the Sultan, who bestowed upon him the Imperial Decoration of the Medjidie, First Class.

His literary ability began to manifest itself when he was scarcely thirteen years old. Though he wrote from the sixteenth year of his life, his literary career actually began only after his return from the Civil War, when he was nearly forty. With the publication in 1873 of his historical novel *The Fair God,* on which he had worked occasionally for twenty years, his merits as an author were at once recognized. His fame rests chiefly, however, on his novel *Ben Hur,* published in 1880, which is based on his studies of the character and doctrines of Christ. One of the "best-selling" novels of all time, it has been translated into most European languages as well as into several Oriental languages, and transcribed in braille. It was dramatized in 1900 and had a long and successful stage career. A third novel, *The Prince of India,* appeared in 1893. He wrote also an autobiography and miscellaneous works. In his youth he attempted poetry, but turned from it on advice of his critics.

Wallace never devoted his time fully to authorship. He wrote whenever the opportunity presented itself and used every occasion to gather material for his works. Thus his experiences and observations in Mexico and Turkey are embodied in his books. He

Collection of Frederick H. Meserve
GENERAL LEW WALLACE

was painstaking in his writing as well as in his preparation, his historical novels being the results of a great deal of research and careful analysis of historical facts.

Defects in his style were no deterrent to the exuberant praise of his works. According to his own statement in his *Autobiography,* he was characterized as "bold and original in conception, vigorous in handling and showing great knowledge of drawing and technical skill." His popularity as a novelist has persisted to this very day.

Though he early showed inclinations for painting and drawing, he was discouraged from an artistic career by his father because of practical considerations. Throughout his life, however, he retained his interest in art and music. The best of his pictures that have been preserved are a portrait of the Sultan and a painting of the assassination of President Lincoln.

He was considered a man of personal charm, dignified bearing, pleasant voice, democratic in his tastes and ideals. In 1852 he married Susan Elston, a woman of literary gifts and musical talent, to whose benign influence he attributed all his success. In his declining years his son relieved him of all business cares, and he enjoyed a serene and cloudless life, lecturing occasionally. He was preparing again for a novel when death claimed him. A monument in Washington commemorates his achievements.

Principal Works: *Novels*—The Fair God: A Story of the Conquest of Mexico, 1873; Ben Hur: A Tale of Christ, 1880; The Prince of India: or, Why Constantinoule Fell, 1893. *Stories*—The Boyhood of Christ, 1888. *Poems*—The Wooing of Malkatoon, 1898. *Play*—Commodus, 1877. *Miscellaneous*—The Life of Benjamin Harrison, 1888; The Story of American Heroism (with others) 1896; An Autobiography, 1906.

About: Harkins, E. F. Famous Men; Nicholson, M. Hoosiers; Wallace, L. An Autobiography; Commemorative Biographical Record of Prominent and Representative Men of Indianapolis and Vicinity; Harper's Weekly March 18, 1905; Reader Magazine April 1905.

WALLACE, WILLIAM ROSS (1819-May 5, 1881), poet, was born probably in Lexington or Paris, Ky., the son of a Presbyterian clergyman. Educated at Hanover (Ind.) College, 1833-35, he studied law at Lexington and from the age of twenty-two made his home in New York City where he engaged in the practice of his profession. He was twice married and had three children. He was a friend of the poet, Edgar Allan Poe, whom he is said to have resembled in such respects as physique, habits, temperament, and irresoluteness.

His poetry appeared in periodicals from about 1837 to the Civil War, a collection of lyrics, odes, and love songs being published about a decade before that event as *Meditations in America and Other Poems.* Some of his poems became widely popular, especially those of a lyrical nature that were set to music. His longest poem *Alban the Pirate,* a romance of New York designed "to illustrate the influence of certain prejudices of society and principles of law upon individual character and destiny," was less successful. Embodying the qualities of earnestness, imagination, and dignity, his work was highly commended by such contemporaries as the poets William Cullen Bryant and George D. Prentice, but is now mostly forgotten except for a few anthology pieces. Among his better-known poems were "The Mounds of America," "Chant of a Soul," "Hymn to the Hudson River," "Greenwood Cemetery," "The Hand That Rocks the Cradle," and patriotic productions, "The Sword of Bunker Hill," "Of Thine Own Country Sing," "Keep Step With the Music of the Union," and "The Liberty Bell."

Principal Works: The Battle of Tippecanoe, 1837; Alban the Pirate, 1848; Meditations in America and Other Poems, 1851; The Liberty Bell, 1862.

About: Griswold, R. W. The Poets and Poetry of America; United States Democratic Review December 1857.

WALLACK, LESTER (January 1, 1820-September 6, 1888), dramatist and actor-manager, son of James William Wallack.

actor-manager, and Susan (Johnstone) Wallack, was born in New York City and educated in private schools in England. With a rich theatrical heritage from his father's family who had been connected with the stage for generations, Wallack soon felt the call of the footlights. He played under the name John Wallack Lester, not wishing to trade on his father's fame. After appearing on the Dublin and London stage, he made his American début at the Broadway Theatre, New York, in 1847. From the start, Wallack was a New York favorite, acting in a wide variety of important rôles, including those of Don Cesar de Bazan, Dantes in *The Count of Monte Cristo,* and d'Artagnan in one of his own plays, *The Three Guardsmen.*

When his father opened his own theatre in 1852, Lester was an important member of the company as a leading player and stage-manager. Here in a illustrious company comprising such actors as Laura Keene, E. A. Sothern, and Wallack's father, Lester appeared in a wide variety of parts and in many of his own plays, among them *The Romance of a Poor Young Man.* Upon his father's retirement in 1861, Wallack succeeded him as manager and carried on the fine tradition by gathering around him some of the most famous actors of the period. In 1882 the third Wallack Theatre was opened and Wallack was again manager, until his withdrawal from the theatre world.

One of the most brilliant benefit performances in theatrical history was given in honor of Wallack on May 21, 1888. Actors appearing included Joseph Jefferson, Edwin Booth, Modjeska, Rose Coghlan, and Laurence Barrett. Wallack died in Stamford, Conn., leaving his wife, Emily Mary Millais, sister of Sir John Millais, the artist, whom he had married in 1848 during his first years of success in America. Wallack's plays, while they drew large audiences in their day, did not contribute so much to the theatre as his skilful work as actor-manager. His autobiography, *Memories of Fifty Years,* is a valuable commentary on an interesting period in theatre history.

Principal Works: *Plays*—The Three Guardsmen, 1849; The Four Musketeers: or, Ten Years After, 1849; Two to One, 1854; First Impressions, 1856; The Veteran; The Romance of A Poor Young Man; Central Park, 1861; Rosedale, 1863. *Autobiography*—Memories of Fifty Years, 1889.

About: Robins, E. Twelve Great Actors; Moses, M. J. Famous Actor-Families in America; Wilkes Spirit of the Times April 26, 1862; North American Review October 1888; Critic May 26, September 15, 1888; Evening Post (New York) July 23, December 17, 1910; New York Times September 7, 1888.

WALN, ROBERT (October 20, 1794-July 4, 1825), miscellaneous writer, was born in Philadelphia, the son of a Quaker merchant, manufacturer, and politician of the same name, and Phebe (Lewis) Waln. The family country seat was the stately Waln-Grove at Frankford, near Philadelphia. He was liberally educated and financially independent and could afford to apply himself to the lighter pursuit of literature. He died unmarried at Providence, R.I., at thirty-one.

He made numerous contributions to periodicals, and at twenty-five, under the pseudonym "Peter Atall, Esq.," he published his first volume, *The Hermit in America on a Visit to Philadelphia,* a satire on the fashionable life of that city. In a second volume of the *Hermit* published two years later he especially warned against the introduction of foreign vices. He produced two volumes of poetry, both written in couplets: *American Bards,* a satire in which he manifested his aptitude for critical writing in his estimates of leading personalities, and *Sisyphi Opus: or, Touches at the Times,* containing some lyric poems. His other work included a history of China, which he had visited as supercargo; the editing or writing of some fourteen lives in connection with his editorship of volumes 3 to 6 of the *Biography of the Signers to the Declaration of Independence*; and an independent life of the Marquis de La Fayette.

Principal Works: The Hermit in America on a Visit to Philadelphia, 1819; American Bards (poetry) 1820; Sisyphi Opus, 1820; The Hermit in Philadelphia: Second Series, 1821; History of China, 1823; Life of the Marquis de La Fayette, 1825; Account of the Asylum for the Insane Established by the Society of Friends, Near Frankford, in the Vicinity of Philadelphia, 1825. *Editor*—Biography of the Signers of the Declaration of Independence, 1823-24.

About: Jordan, J. W. Colonial and Revolutionary Families of Pennsylvania; Kettell, S. Specimens of American Poetry; Simpson, H. The Lives of Eminent Philadelphians.

WALSH, ROBERT (August 30, 1784-February 7, 1859), journalist and political writer, was born in Baltimore, Md., the son of Robert and Elizabeth (Steel) Walsh. He was educated at St. Mary's Academy, Baltimore, and Georgetown College, Georgetown, D.C., and was graduated in 1806. He spent three years abroad, and on his return to America settled in Philadelphia where for a time he practiced law, until his increasing preoccupation with journalism caused him to relinquish his practice.

He was editor of the *American Register* from 1809-10, and for the next two years published *The American Review of History and Politics,* the second quarterly review in America. In 1820, Walsh established the *National Gazette and Literary Register,* a liberal tri-weekly, with which he remained connected for fifteen years. He also published the *Museum of Foreign Literature and Science* and founded the *American Quarterly Review* in 1827, which he edited ably for the next ten years.

Walsh was appointed professor of English at the University of Pennsylvania in 1818, remaining in that capacity for ten years, and served as trustee for five years. He was also a manager of Rumford's Military Academy at Mount Airy. In 1837 he moved to Paris, where he contributed to French magazines and served as correspondent of the Washington *National Intelligencer* and New York *Journal of Commerce.* He was appointed consul-general in 1844 and served until 1851. He died in Paris. Walsh was married in 1810 to Anna Maria Moylan; his second wife was a Mrs. Stocker of Philadelphia.

A distinguished scholar and student of foreign affairs, Walsh was one of the first of a notable line of political commentators.

Principal Works: A Letter on the Genius and Dispositions of the French Government, 1810; Essay on the Future State of Europe, 1813: Correspondence Respecting Russia Between Robert Goodloe Harper, Esq., and Robert Walsh, Jun., 1813; An Appeal From the Judgments of Great Britain Respecting the United States of America, 1819; Didactics: Social, Literary, and Political, 1836.

About: Easby-Smith, J. S. Georgetown University; Griswold, R. W. The Prose Writers of America; Mott, F. L. A History of American Magazines; Historical Magazine May 1859; New York Tribune March 1, 1859.

"WARD, ARTEMUS." See BROWNE, CHARLES FARRAR

WARD, CYRENUS OSBORNE (October 28, 1831-March 19, 1902), editor and labor leader, was born in western New York, one of ten children of Justus Ward, a mechanic, and Silence (Rolph) Ward, and a descendant of Andrew Warde who died in Connecticut in 1659. His younger brother was the sociologist, Lester Frank Ward. When he was three his parents moved to St. Charles, Kane County, Ill. He early became skilled in mechanics, and acquired by self-study a knowledge of botany, geology, and languages. He variously traveled as violinist with a concert company, manufactured wagon hubs in partnership with his wife's brother, Edwin G. Owen, at Myersburg, Pa., served as a machinist in the Brooklyn Navy Yard during the Civil War, and, having developed deep labor sympathies, traveled extensively in America and abroad, studying conditions, lecturing, writing, and organizing. In 1884 he entered the Geological Survey, Washington, and later became a translator and librarian in the Bureau of Labor. He died in Yuma, Ariz., where he had gone for his health.

Ward contributed to the New York *Sun* and *Tribune* about 1868-69, published articles in periodicals and in bulletins of the Bureau of Labor, edited some labor journals, including the *Voice of the People,* and in 1878 was associate editor of a reform journal, *Man.* His first book *A Labor Catechism of Political Economy* met with a wide sale and gave him the means to extend his writing and lecturing. This, as well as other work, was published in his own printing office. His outstanding book, *A History of the Ancient Working People,* later published as *The Ancient Lowly,* based on the study of ancient records, inscriptions, and other sources, was of special note as an important contribution to the study of social and industrial conditions of antiquity. His views were radical for the time; he advocated a socialistic state but urged its attainment by political and non violent means.

Principal Works: A Labor Catechism of Political Economy, 1878; Our Tragedy (a dramatic poem) 1880; A History of the Ancient Working People, 1889; The Equilibration of Human Aptitudes and Powers of Adaptation, 1895.

About: Ward, G. K. Andrew Warde and His Descendants; New York Times March 21, 1902.

WARD, ELIZABETH STUART (PHELPS) (August 31, 1844-January 28, 1911), novelist, was born in Boston, the eldest child of Elizabeth (Stuart) Phelps [*q.v.*], a writer of popular religious tales, and Austin Phelps, a professor at the Andover Theological Seminary. Baptized Mary Gray, she changed her name after the death of her mother whose brilliant unstable temperament exerted a strong influence on her career.

Motherless at the age of eight, she was brought up by her father, a nervous invalid, developing under his tutelage a precocious talent for writing. After a normal girlhood, Elizabeth suffered a severe emotional shock when the boy she loved was killed in the Civil War, and she became for several years a recluse. It was after this period of brooding grief that she wrote the book which brought her fame, *The Gates Ajar,* published in 1868. Popular both in America and abroad, this religious novel brought comfort to thousands with its gentle and

Collection of Frederick H. Meserve
ELIZABETH STUART PHELPS WARD

human conception of a life after death, softening the stern theology of the time.

The many writings which followed were all motivated by the same kind of practical Christianity, a product of her preoccupation with religious and psychic matters plus a good share of Yankee common sense. Much of her work, like that of her mother, was directed by a strong sympathy with the problems of women in domestic relations and in industry. In 1888 she was married to Herbert Dickinson Ward, with whom she collaborated on several Biblical romances. Her own work, however, was much more successful than these joint efforts. Until her death at the age of sixty-six she continued to write voluminously: novels, stories, memoirs, juveniles, and verse.

The nervous disorders from which she suffered throughout her life are reflected in her work. Rooted in an extreme nervous sensibility, her style was often marred by exaggeration, yet at its best achieved fluency and clarity.

PRINCIPAL WORKS: *Novels*—The Gates Ajar, 1868; Hedged In, 1870; The Silent Partner, 1871; The Story of Avis, 1877; Friends: A Duet, 1881; Doctor Zay, 1882; Beyond the Gates, 1883; Burglars in Paradise, 1886; The Gates Between, 1887; Jack: The Fisherman, 1887; The Madonna of the Tubs, 1887; The Master of the Magicians (in collaboration with H. D. Ward) 1890; A Lost Hero (in collaboration with H. D. Ward) 1891; Come Forth, 1891; Donald Marcy, 1893; A Singular Life, 1895; The Supply at Saint Agatha's, 1896; Avery, 1902; Walled In, 1907; A Chariot of Fire, 1910; Comrades, 1911. *Stories*—Men, Women, and Ghosts, 1869; Fourteen to One, 1891; Loveliness, 1899; The Oath of Allegiance and Other Stories, 1909. *Juveniles*—Gypsy Series, 1866; The Trotty Book, 1870; Trotty's Wedding Tour, 1874. *Poetry*—Poetic Studies, 1875; Songs of the Silent World, 1885; Little Poems for Little People, 1886. *Miscellany*—What to Wear, 1873; Austin Phelps: A Memoir, 1891; Chapters From A Life, 1896; The Story of Jesus Christ, 1897.

ABOUT: Gilman, A. Poets' Homes; Ward, E. S. P. Austin Phelps: A Memoir; Ward, E. S. P. Chapters From A Life.

WARD, LESTER FRANK (June 18, 1841-April 18, 1913), sociologist, was born at Joliet, Ill., the son of Justus Ward, a mechanic, and Silence (Rolph) Ward. Educated in rural Illinois and in Iowa, where the family moved about 1848, Lester was sent in 1857 to live at Myersburg, Pa., with his elder brother Cyrenus, a manufacturer. The boy received further education at the Susquehanna Collegiate Institute, Towanda, Pa., from 1861 to 1862, but at the outbreak of the Civil War he enlisted in the Union army.

Discharged on account of wounds in 1864, Ward soon found a position in the United States Treasury at Washington. Soon after 1865 he began to devote his spare time to study of the natural sciences at Columbian College (now George Washington University). He received from this institution the degrees of B.A. in 1869 and M.A. in 1872, and acquired such proficiency in geology and botany that upon leaving the Treasury Department in 1881 he was immediately given work with the United States Geological Survey, serving as geologist from 1883 and as paleontologist from 1892. Although he traveled, collected, and observed widely, Ward was less interested in taxonomy than in the social implications of his research. By 1885 he had espoused the evolutionary doctrines, broken through the strict limits of pure science, and emerged with a treatise on *Dynamic Sociology,* the first experimental study in evolutionary sociology made in the United States. In his historical approach to the subject Ward strongly emphasized the power of the human mind and will in evolutionary development. He was a believer in perfectibility, and his popular writings provided the humanitarians with many plausible arguments against determinism. Compared with the modern objective studies, however, Ward's treatises seem excessively optimistic, like most nineteenth century sociologies.

During the last seven years of his life Ward served as professor of sociology at Brown University, and prepared his monumental work *Glimpses of the Cosmos,* a summary and restatement of his social philosophy. He acquired there a reputation comparable to that of Sumner at Yale, being a man of tireless energy and comprehensive mind (it is said that he worked almost continuously, requiring only two or three hours of sleep at night). Ward was married twice: in 1862 to Elisabeth Carolyn Vought, who died in 1872; and in 1873 to Rosamond Asenath Simons.

PRINCIPAL WORKS: Dynamic Sociology, 1883; Types of the Laramie Flora, 1887; The Psychic Factors of Civilization, 1893; Pure Sociology, 1903; Status of the Mesozoic Floras of the United States, 1905; Applied Sociology, 1906; Glimpses of the Cosmos, 1913-18.

ABOUT: Cape, E. P. Lester F. Ward: A Personal Sketch; Kimball, E. P. Sociology and Education: An Analysis of the Theories of Spencer and Ward; Odum, H. W. American Masters of Social Science; Ward, G. K. Andrew Warde and His Descendants.

WARD, NATHANIEL (?1578-October, 1652), lawyer, clergyman, and literary wit, was born in Haverhill, England, the son of John Ward, a prominent Puritan minister, and Susan Ward. Destined for the law, he entered Cambridge in 1596, being graduated in 1603, but after several years of practice he met David Pareus, the great theologian, and was persuaded to enter the ministry. He served as chaplain to the British merchants at Elbing, Prussia, for several years, and on returning to England, became, like his father and his two brothers, a Puritan clergyman.

His personal life remains obscure. Although he was married and widowed, the father of two sons and a daughter, the name of his wife is not recorded. Even the exact date of his birth is a matter of controversy. His career, however, is of great interest in its connection with American pre-Revolutionary history.

As Curate of St. James', Picadilly, London, and two years later of Stondon Massey, in Essex, he preached the Puritan doctrine. Twice he was called to answer charges of non-conformity, and finally in 1633 was dismissed from office. The following year, a man in his sixties, he emigrated to the Massachusetts Bay Colony where Puritanism had already established itself. His first parish in America was that of Aggawam, now Ipswich, a name which was to gain fame in the title of his most important literary work, *The Simple Cobler of Aggawam.*

During the years he spent in Massachusetts, he became prominent as a lawmaker, a preacher, and a caustic wit. In 1638, he was appointed by the General Court to assist in preparing a legal code for Massachusetts, the celebrated "Body of Liberties," a bill of rights which set one of the cornerstones of American constitutional history.

By 1645 he had finished *The Simple Cobler of Aggawam,* a witty dissertation on religious and political dissension in America and England. It was published first in England in 1647 under the pseudonym of "Theodore de la Guard," and later reprinted in America. Shortly after the publication of the book, he returned to England, where he spent the last four years of his life as a minister at Shenfield.

Ward's personality was an eccentric and interesting one, and though his writing impressed his own generation as political philosophy, it survives today only as a quaint example of early American satire. *The Simple Cobler of Aggawam* was an expression of his theoretical belief in religious and political freedom; yet in it, he showed himself a conservative, hating anarchy and free thought as he hated priestcraft and oppression. Although in many ways he remained essentially British, he played a part in the making of the American heritage.

PRINCIPAL WORKS: *Miscellany*—The Liberties of the Massachusetts Colony in New England, 1641; The Simple Cobler of Aggawam in America, 1647; A Religious Retreat Sounded to a Religious Army, 1647; A Sermon Preached Before the House of Commons, 1647; A Word to Mr. Peters and Two Words to the Parliament and Kingdom, 1647; The Pulpit Incendiary, 1648(?).

ABOUT: Dean, J. W. A Memoir of Nathaniel Ward; Parrington, V. S. The Colonial Mind; Phillips, S. H. Sketch of the Reverend Nathaniel Ward of Ipswich.

WARD, THOMAS (June 8, 1807-April 13, 1873), poet, playwright, and musician, was born in Newark, N.J., the son of Thomas Ward, a prominent citizen and member of Congress. Educated at the College of New Jersey, now Princeton, he presumably took a degree in 1859 at Rutgers Medical College, New York City; he traveled abroad, and afterward practiced medicine two or three years in New York. Of social prominence and ample means, he gradually withdrew to literary and musical pursuits, produced at "Land's End," Huntington, Long Island, and in a large hall, which he constructed during the Civil War, adjacent to his mansion on West Forty-seventh Street, near Fifth Avenue. Ward's entertainments given in the period 1862-1872 realized some $40,000, which was devoted to charity. He died in New York City.

Of the operettas staged, Ward was responsible for both the words and music of *Flora: or, The Gipsy's Frolic* and *The Fair Truant.* His first book, *A Month of Freedom: An American Poem,* published anonymously, was a long blank-verse account of vacation travel to Washington, Niagara, and elsewhere. Various contributions in verse to the *Knickerbocker Magazine* and the New York *American* over the pseudonym "Flaccus" attracted some attention. This signature was used also for his collection of verses *Passaic: A Group of Poems Touching That River . . .*, the second part of which included some thirty poems in various moods. Among his other published work were a pamphlet of ten war lyrics, a lyrical poem read at the two-hundredth anniversary of the founding of Newark, and a prose centennial address given before the New York Society Library in 1872.

Principal Works: A Month of Freedom, 1837; Passaic: A Group of Poems Touching That River . . . , 1842; Flora: or, The Gipsy's Frolic, 1858; War Lyrics, 1865; The Fair Truant 1869; Address Delivered Before the New York Society Library on the One-hundredth Anniversary of Its Incorporation, 1872. *Editor*—The Road Made Plain to Fortune for the Million, 1860.

About: Duyckinck, E. A. & G. L. Cyclopaedia of American Literature; Griswold, R. W. The Poets and Poetry of America; Poe, E. A. The Literati.

WARDEN, DAVID BAILIE (1772-October 9, 1845), diplomat, book collector, and historian, was born near Grey Abbey, County Down, Ireland, one of three sons of Robert Warden and Elizabeth (Bailie or Baillie) Warden. Educated at the University of Glasgow, M.A. 1797, he was licensed to preach, but his association with the United Irishmen soon led to his arrest and in 1799 he emigrated to America as an alternative to standing trial. For a few years, during which he attained American citizenship, he was principal of Columbia Academy, Kinderhook, N.Y., and principal tutor of Kingston Academy, Ulster, N.Y. In 1804 he went to Paris as secretary to the newly appointed minister to France, Gen. John Armstrong. He was associated with the American embassy until 1814, and passed virtually the whole of the latter part of his life in France, where he maintained a continuous and keen interest in America, was a correspondent of many Americans of note, including Thomas Jefferson and John Quincy Adams, and held membership in the American Philosophical Society and the Lyceum of Natural History, as well as in European societies. He died in Paris.

Ward published some works on America in French, including a ten-volume *Chronologie Historique de l'Amérique,* also published as volumes 32-41 of *L'Art de Verifier les Dates,* and published a few translations from the French, the most important being H. Grégoire's *An Enquiry Concerning the Intellectual and Moral Faculties and Literature of Negroes.* A volume on consular establishments attracted attention and was translated into several languages. He also published catalogs for two of his collections of books relating to America, one collection of 1200 volumes being subsequently presented to Harvard College by S. A. Eliot in 1823; the other of 2155 volumes, was purchased in 1840 by the New York State Library. His outstanding works were *A Chorographical and Statistical Description of the District of Columbia* and *A Statistical, Political, and Historical Account of the United States of America,* in three volumes, a work of exceptionally complete information.

Principal Works: On the Origin, Nature, Progress, and Influence of Consular Establishments, 1813; A Chorographical and Statistical Description of the District of Columbia, 1816; A Statistical, Political, and Historical Account of the United States of North America, 1819; Chronologie Historique de l'Amérique, 1826-1844.

About: Goodrich, S. A. Recollections; Maryland Historical Magazine May-September 1916; Ulster Journal of Archaeology February 1907.

WARE, EUGENE FITCH (May 29, 1841-?, 1911), poet and historian, was born in Hartford, Conn., the son of Hiram B. and Amanda M. (Holbrook) Ware. His parents and all four grandparents lived to celebrate their golden wedding anniversaries; he himself fell three years short of it. He was educated in the public schools of Hartford and of Burlington, Iowa, where his parents moved while he was a child. He served throughout the Civil War, first with the infantry then with the cavalry, being mustered out as captain of cavalry. By trade he was a harness-maker, but in 1867 he moved to Fort Scott, Kans., and under the influence of his future wife, a Vassar graduate, studied law and was admitted to the bar in 1871. In 1874 he married his fiancée, Netty P. Huntington, of Rochester, N.Y.; they had four children. He served two terms in the Kansas State Senate, became a corporation lawyer with a large practice, was twice a delegate to the National Republican Convention, and from 1902 to 1905 was United States Pension Commissioner.

Mr. Ware's verse was all written under the pseudonym of "Ironquill." William Allen White remarks that "he had unusual talent for rhyme and for lovely imagery." In addition he wrote several volumes dealing with the history of the Middle West, and translated Justinian and Castenada's *Coronado's*

March. White adds: "He was a fine fellow —one of those self-educated men whose information was accurate." He was a regular contributor to legal periodicals and also wrote frequently for literary and historical magazines.

Principal Works: Rhymes of Ironquill, 1902-04; From Court to Court, 1907; The Lyon Campaign in Missouri, 1907; Indian War of '64, 1911.

WARE, HENRY (April 1, 1764-July 12, 1845), clergyman and professor of theology, was born in Sherborn, Mass., one of ten children of John Ware, a farmer, and Martha (Prentice) Ware. His unusual promise led his brothers, after the death of his father, to give him the opportunity of a higher education, and he was graduated from Harvard as valedictorian in 1785. In 1787 he was ordained pastor at Hingham, Mass., filling that ministry for eighteen years. From 1805 he held the Hollis professorship of divinity at Harvard College until his resignation in 1840, retaining for some time longer his connection with the Divinity School, which he had organized in 1816 and concurrently taught. Of nineteen children by his first and third wives, three sons, Henry, John, and William Ware, won prominence. He died at Cambridge.

On his appointment to the Hollis professorship a memorable controversy had been instituted among the liberal and orthodox Congregationalist factions. Ware himself took little part in this until some fifteen years after his appointment when he published his *Letters Addressed to Trinitarians and Calvinists: Occasioned by Dr. Woods' Letters to Unitarians,* and after the reply of that divine issued his *Answer to Dr. Woods' Reply* and *A Postscript to the Second Series of Letters Addressed to Trinitarians and Calvinists.* He also published a number of funeral sermons and ordination discourses, among them sermons on the deaths of George Washington and John Adams. Threatened with incapacity through cataract of the eyes, he assembled a final volume of his lectures, published as *An Inquiry Into the Foundation, Evidences, and Truths of Religion.*

Principal Works: Letters Addressed to Trinitarians and Calvinists; Occasioned by Dr. Woods' Letters to Unitarians, 1820; Answer to Dr. Woods' Reply, 1822; A Postscript to the Second Series of Letters Addressed to Trinitarians and Calvinists, 1823; An Inquiry Into the Foundation, Evidences, and Truths of Religion, 1842.

About: Eliot, S. A. Heralds of a Liberal Faith; Palfrey, J. G. A Discourse on the Life and Character of the Reverend Henry Ware, D.D., A.A.S.; Sprague, W. B. Annals of the American Pulpit (Unitarian); Ware, E. F. Ware Genealogy.

WARE, HENRY, JR. (April 21, 1794-September 22, 1843), Unitarian clergyman, miscellaneous writer, the son of Henry and Mary (Clark) Ware was born in Hingham, Mass. He attended Phillips Academy, Andover, Mass., and Harvard College, class of 1812. He taught at Phillips Academy, Exeter, N.H., from 1812 to 1814, and returned to Harvard to study theology. He was ordained pastor of the Second Church (Unitarian) in Boston in 1817. His brother William was also a Unitarian minister and an author.

Ware took an active part in organizing the American Unitarian Association and was editor of its official organ, the *Christian Disciple,* from 1819 to 1823. In spite of his unprepossessing appearance and his reticence, his sincerity and fervor soon won him a large following and he became one of the leading ministers of New England. He visited Europe in 1829-30, and on his return resigned his pastorate and moved to Cambridge to devote himself to his duties as professor of pulpit eloquence and pastoral care at Harvard.

During the years at Cambridge he published numerous works, among them his best known treatise *On the Formation of the Christian Character,* inspirational work which was greatly popular at the time, went through fifteen editions, and was republished abroad. *The Life of the Saviour,* written for children, and memoirs of Joseph Priestley, Noah Worcester, and Nathan Parker were others of his works. He resigned his professorship in 1842, retiring to Framingham, Mass., where he died a year later.

Ware was married in 1817 to Elizabeth Watson Waterhouse who died in 1824, and by whom he had one son. He was married a second time to Mary Lovell Pickard in 1827, this union resulting in six children, one of whom was William Robert Ware, the architect.

Ware's works, though of slight interest today, are indicative of the sincerity and benevolence of his character; widely read in their time they were undoubtedly an inspiration and comfort to his large group of readers.

Principal Works: A Poem Pronounced . . . at the Celebration of Peace, 1815; Hints on Extemporaneous Preaching, 1824; On the Formation of the Christian Character, 1831; The Life of the Saviour, 1833; The Works of Henry Ware, Jr., D.D. (ed by C. Robbins) 1846-47.

ABOUT: Sprague, W. B. Annals of the American Unitarian Pulpit; Ware, J. Memoir of the Life of Henry Ware, Jr.; Christian Examiner November 1843, March 1846.

WARE, WILLIAM (August 3, 1797-February 19, 1852), Unitarian clergyman and miscellaneous writer, was born at Hingham, Mass., the son of Henry and Mary (Clark) Ware. His was a family of liberal churchmen, educators, and writers: his father was a prominent Massachusetts clergyman and the Hollis professor of divinity at Harvard; his brother, Henry, also became a leading minister and writer; while John Ware, another brother, was known as a physician, editor, educator, and writer.

William graduated from Harvard in 1815 and, after teaching school for several years in Hingham and Cambridge, was ordained as pastor of the first Unitarian Church in New York City. In 1823 he married Mary Waterhouse, the daughter of Dr. Benjamin Waterhouse of Cambridge, a physician who was carrying on pioneer work in vaccination. Another daughter of Dr. Waterhouse married William's brother, Henry Ware.

Always Ware had a profound interest in literature and art, and although he immersed himself in churchly duties for the next fifteen years, he felt that he was by temperament an artist. Accordingly, in 1836, plagued by ill health and increasingly oppressed by his responsibilities as a pastor, he resigned to devote himself to writing. A series of articles which appeared first in the *Knickerbocker Magazine* was published as a book in 1837, entitled *Letters of Lucius M. Piso From Palmyra to His Friend Marcus Curtius at Rome.* Describing life in the Roman Empire in the later days of Zenobia's reign, the book was widely read, appearing in subsequent editions as *Zenobia: or, The Fall of Palmyra: An Historical Romance.* The next year a sequel was published, *Probus: or, Rome in the Third Century,* later retitled *Aurelius.*

For two brief periods in his life, Ware again accepted pastorates, one in Waltham, Mass., in 1837, and one in West Cambridge seven years later; but again his ill health, which in the last years of his life appeared as epilepsy, unfitted him for the pulpit. From 1839 until 1844 he was owner and editor of the *Christian Examiner,* meanwhile finding time to write *Julian: or, Scenes in Judea,* a narrative based on incidents from the life of Jesus. This proved to be his most successful book, going through several editions both in America and England. In 1848 he went abroad for a year, spending most of his time in Italy, and on his return gave a course of lectures which were published in 1851 as *Sketches of European Capitals.* Another course, *Lectures on the Works and Genius of Washington Allston,* remained unpublished until after his death at Cambridge the next year.

WILLIAM WARE

Ware's gifts were distinguished, if not spectacular. Extremely conscientious and possessed of a vivid imagination, he was able to combine scholarship with sympathy in re-creating the classical and Biblical periods which he loved. Whether they are to be called novels or sketches, *Zenobia, Probus,* and *Julian* stand up as sound and well-wrought narratives.

PRINCIPAL WORKS: *Novels*—Letters of Lucius M. Piso From Palmyra to His Friend Marcus Curtius at Rome, 1837; Probus: or, Rome in the Third Century, 1838; Julian: or, Scenes in Judea, 1841. *Miscellany*—Memoir of Nathaniel Bacon, 1848; American Unitarian Biography (ed.) 1850-51; Sketches of European Capitals, 1851; Lectures on the Works and Genius of Washington Allston, 1852.

ABOUT: Eliot, S. A. Heralds of a Liberal Faith; Sprague, W. B. Annals of the American Unitarian Pulpit; Ware, E. F. Ware Genealogy.

WARMAN, CY (June 22, 1855-April 7, 1914), journalist, poet and story-writer, was born near Greenup, Ill., the son of John Warman, a farmer, and Nancy (Askew) Warman. After a common school education he became successively a farmer and wheat broker at Pocahontas, Ill., a railroad yard worker at Salida, Colo., and fireman and engineer for the Denver & Rio Grande Railroad. Subsequently poor health led him into journalism in Denver; in 1888 he was editing the *Western Railway,* and in 1892 he started the *Chronicle* at the new silver mines of Creede, Colo. He traveled widely, lived in Washington, D.C. for two years, and in his later years made his home in Canada, at London, Ont. He died in Chicago.

While in the West he extolled in verse the inspiring scenery of Colorado and other states, among his productions being a prize poem "The Canyon of the Grand"; a small published collection of his verse entitled *Mountain Melodies* was sold by the thousands on the Denver & Rio Grande trains. Charles A. Dana, editor of the New York *Sun,* published his verses in that journal, including "Sweet Marie," a song inspired by his second wife, Myrtle Marie Jones, whom he married in 1892. Set to music, over a million copies were sold in six months and brought him fame and wealth. He himself composed the music for some of his subsequent songs. Among his popular magazine contributions was "A Thousand-Mile Ride on the Engine of the Swiftest Train in the World." The greater part of his subsequent writing was based on the romance and adventure of the railroad and frontier.

PRINCIPAL WORKS: Mountain Melodies, 1892; Tales of an Engineer With Rhymes of the Rail, 1895; The Express Messenger and Other Tales of the Rail, 1897; Frontier Stories, 1898; The Story of the Railroad, 1898; Snow on the Headlight: A Story of the Great Burlington Strike, 1899; The Last Spike and Other Railroad Stories, 1906; Weiga of Temagami and Other Indian Tales, 1908; Songs of Cy Warman, 1911.

ABOUT: Canadian Magazine March 1902; Interludes Summer 1931; Literary Digest April 25, 1914; Overland February 1901.

WARNER, ANNA BARTLETT (August 31, 1827-January 22, 1915), novelist, juvenile and miscellaneous writer, younger sister of the novelist Susan Bogert Warner [*q.v.*], was born and spent her first ten years in New York City. Her mother, Anna (Bartlett) Warner, died shortly after her birth, and the sisters were brought up by an aunt, Frances L. Warner. Her father, Henry Whiting Warner, member of the New York bar, met with severe reverses in 1837, and they made their permanent home from that time on Constitution Island, also known as Martelaer's Rock, in the Hudson River near West Point. There they took a deep interest in the military academy, in which an uncle, Thomas Warner, was chaplain and professor, opening their home to the cadets and holding Sunday Bible classes. Anna outlived her sister by thirty years, and her wish that the island should become attached to the academy after her death was fulfilled by its purchase and presentation to the government by the philanthropist, Mrs. Russell Sage. She died at Highland Falls, N.Y., and with her sister was buried in the government cemetery at West Point.

The poverty of the home eventually led the sisters to try writing for publication, and the year after the appearance of Susan's first novel *The Wide Wide World,* Anna published her own first novel *Dollars and Cents,* under the pseudonym "Amy Lothrop." She collaborated with her sister on some fifteen published volumes, juvenile and fiction, and also produced many independent works. Her writing showed much similarity to her sister's, depicting experiences in her own life, and expressing strong pietistic and emotional feeling. A lifelong enthusiasm for gardening found expression in *Gardening by Myself,* and several religious works were produced under such titles as *The Star Out of Jacob* and *The Fourth Watch.* Among her last works were two memoirs, of James and Caroline Phelps Stokes, and of her own sister Susan.

PRINCIPAL WORKS: Dollars and Cents, 1852; My Brother's Keeper, 1855; Hymns of the Church Militant, 1858; The Star Out of Jacob, 1868; The Fourth Watch, 1872; Gardening by Myself, 1872, Stories of Vinegar Hill, 1872; Cross Corners, 1887; Some Memories of James Stokes and Caroline Phelps Stokes, 1892; Susan Warner ("Elizabeth Wetherell"), 1909. *With S. Warner*—Mr. Rutherford's Children, 1853-55; Carl Krinken, 1854; Say and Seal, 1860; Wych Hazel, 1876; The Gold of Chickaree, 1876.

ABOUT: Constitution Island Association. Constitution Island; Stokes, O. E. P. Letters and Memories of Susan and Anna Bartlett Warner; Warner, A. B. Susan Warner; Outlook August 29, 1917.

WARNER, CHARLES DUDLEY (September 12, 1829-October 20, 1900), editor, essayist, and novelist, descended from early Puritan stock, was born in Plainfield, Mass., the eldest son of Justus and Sylvia (Hitchcock) Warner. His father, a farmer, died in 1834, leaving only two bequests: a two hundred-acre farm, and the admonition that Charles must go to college.

Charles entered Hamilton College in 1847, earned most of his own schooling, and was graduated with honors. As an undergraduate he had already begun to contribute articles to the *Knickerbocker Magazine,* and in 1851 his first book, based on a commencement oration, was published under the title, *The Book of Eloquence.*

During the next nine years he found little opportunity for writing. After a year and a half as a railroad surveyor in Mis-

Collection of Frederick H. Meserve
CHARLES DUDLEY WARNER

souri, he went to Philadelphia, joining a friend in business and meanwhile studying law. In Philadelphia he was married to Susan Lee, the daughter of William Elliott Lee of New York. In 1858 he graduated from the law school of the University of Pennsylvania and was admitted to the bar. Law, however, was never to his taste, and after two years of practice in Chicago, he accepted the offer of an old college friend, Joseph R. Hawley, to come east as the assistant editor of the *Evening Press* in Hartford, Conn. From 1860 until the time of his death, he devoted himself to editorial and literary activities.

Throughout the Civil War, Hawley was engaged in military service, and Warner, too nearsighted to be a soldier, became editor in Hawley's place. He continued to carry most of the responsibility of the *Press* (later consolidated with the Hartford *Courant*), even after the war, when Hawley plunged into active politics.

A series of humorous essays written during these years was collected and published in 1871 with the aid of Henry Ward Beecher, under the title *My Summer in a Garden*. This book won him immediate recognition as an essayist of delicacy and charm. He published many volumes of essays during the next three decades: some of them travel sketches based on the five trips he made to Europe, some of them humorous, some critical; but all marked by an urbane wit which invited comparisons with Charles Lamb. He wrote also four novels, one in collaboration with his friend and neighbor, Mark Twain. This, *The Gilded Age,* was an uneven book, drawing heavily on the memories of his Missouri experience. A trilogy, written during the last years of his life, pictured the accumulation, misuse, and ruin of a great fortune, the three parts entitled: *A Little Journey in the World, The Golden House,* and *That Fortune*. In these he became a stern moralist concerning himself with the social responsibility of great wealth, quite devoid of the humor that lighted the rest of his work.

Warner himself was never a wealthy man, although his books were widely read and brought him the affectionate respect of many friends in the literary world. He received honors from several universities where he was a frequent lecturer, and became a member of various commissions of art and social reform. In poor health the last years of his life, he died of heart failure at the age of seventy-one.

Both as a writer and as a literary personality of great charm and friendliness, he made a real contribution to nineteenth century American letters. Fiction was never his field, but in the essay he was an artist of perception, wit, and taste. The *Library of The World's Best Literature* that he edited was widely sold and still remains of use in many homes and libraries.

PBINCIPAL WORKS: *Essays*—The Book of Eloquence, 1851; My Summer in a Garden, 1871; Backlog Studies, 1873; Baddeck, 1874; Being a Boy, 1878; On Horseback, 1888; As We Were Saying, 1891; As We Go, 1893; The Relation of Literature to Life, 1896; The People for Whom Shakespeare Wrote, 1897; Fashions in Literature, 1902. *Travel*—Saunterings, 1872; Mummies and Moslems, 1876; In the Levant, 1877; In the Wilderness, 1878; A Roundabout Journey, 1883; Their Pilgrimage, 1887; Studies in the South and West, 1889; Our Italy, 1891. *Novels*—The Gilded Age (with Mark Twain), 1873; A little Journey in the World, 1889; The Golden House, 1895; That Fortune, 1899. *Biographies*—Washington Irving, 1881; Captain John Smith, 1881. *Miscellany*—Library of the World's Best Literature (editor), 1896-97; Complete Writings of Charles Dudley Warner, 1904.

ABOUT: Fields, A. A. Charles Dudley Warner; Lounsbury, T. R. Biographical Sketch of Charles Dudley Warner for Complete Works; Warner, L. C. & Nichols, J. G. The Descendant of Andrew Warner.

WARNER, SUSAN BOGERT ("Elizabeth Wetherell") (July 11, 1819-March 17, 1885), novelist, was born in New York City, the daughter of Anna (Bartlett) Warner and Henry Whiting Warner, a successful lawyer and the author of several books. Her childhood was spent in New York, with summers in an historic old house at Canaan,

N.Y., which later provided the setting for several of her novels. In 1837 the family, suffering financial reverses, gave up their home in the city to live on Constitution Island, a small island in the Hudson River near West Point, which Mr. Warner had bought a year previously.

Susan grew up as a delicate, over-imaginative girl, pious and fond of books. An aunt, Frances L. Warner, who had had most of the responsibility of bringing up Susan and her younger sister, Anna, first suggested that she might write. Some years later, when she was nearly thirty, she began her first novel, writing in the hope that she could be of financial assistance to the family. In the summer of 1849 she finished *The Wide, Wide World,* which after being rejected by several publishers was accepted by George P. Putnam on the recommendation of his mother, and published under the pseudonym "Elizabeth Wetherell." The book, describing the moral and religious development of an orphan of thirteen, proved extraordinarily successful, selling thirteen editions in the United States and several in England during the next two years. Her second novel, *Queechy,* begun before the publication of *The Wide, Wide World,* achieved similar success.

This began a long series of novels and children's stories, some of them written in collaboration with Anna Bartlett Warner [*q.v.*], who also became a novelist. The two spinster sisters lived the rest of their lives on Constitution Island, writing and carrying on their pious works. Miss Susan always had a strong interest in the U.S. Military Academy at West Point, of which her uncle, Thomas Warner, was chaplain for ten years. She conducted a Sunday Bible Class for the cadets, which after her death was carried on by Miss Anna. Later, Constitution Island was attached to the Academy following the wishes of the Misses Warner, and both the sisters were buried in the government cemetery at West Point.

Like the heroines of her novels, Susan was given to an excess of "sensibility," being timid, nervous, and subject to frequent tears. Always suffering ill health, she lived for the most part in seclusion, making occasional visits to New York and Boston to see her friends, among them Julia Ward Howe and Catherine Maria Sedgwick. She died in 1885 in Highland Falls, N.Y.

The wide vogue of her books is difficult to understand today, since they are almost entirely without action or incident; but she wrote in an age when sentiment and piety were popular literary virtues. Her first

SUSAN B. WARNER
("Elizabeth Wetherell")

novel, *The Wide, Wide World,* remained the most successful of all her books, said to be second only to *Uncle Tom's Cabin* as the most popular novel written in the United States in the nineteenth century; although even in her own day, Taine, the French critic, expressed astonishment that "in America a three-volume novel is devoted to the history of the moral progress of a girl of thirteen."

PRINCIPAL WORKS: *Novels*—The Wide Wide World, 1850; Queechy, 1852; The Hills of the Shatemuc, 1856; The Old Helmet, 1863; Melbourne House, 1864; Daisy, 1868; A Story of Small Beginnings, 1872; Diana, 1877; Bread and Oranges, 1877; Pine Needles, 1877; My Desire, 1879; The End of a Coil, 1880; Nobody, 1882; The Letter of Credit, 1882; Stephen, M.D., 1883; A Red Wallflower, 1884; Daisy Plains, 1885. *Juveniles*—The House in Town, 1872; Trading: Finishing the Story of The House in Town, 1873; Willow Brook, 1874; Say and Do Series, 1875; The Flag of Truce, 1878. *Religious*—The Law and the Testimony, 1853; Walks From Eden, 1870; The Broken Walls of Jerusalem and the Rebuilding of Them, 1878; The Kingdom of Judah, 1878. *Collaborations* (with Anna Bartlett Warner)—Mr. Rutherford's Children, 1853-55; Ellen Montgomery's Bookshelf, 1853-59; Say and Seal, 1860; Books of Blessing, 1868; Wych Hazel, 1876; The Gold of Chickaree, 1876.

ABOUT: Stokes, O. E. P. Letters and Memories of Susan and Anna Bartlett Warner; Warner, A. B. Susan Warner.

WARREN, CAROLINE MATILDA. See THAYER, CAROLINE MATILDA (WARREN)

WARREN, MRS. JAMES. See WARREN, MERCY (OTIS)

WARREN, JOSIAH (c.1798-April 14, 1874), reformer, philosophical anarchist, and inventor, was born in Boston, and although little is known of his early life, any lack of special education was more than made up by his industrious and reflective habits. Soon after his marriage at the age of twenty, he taught music and led an orchestra in Cincinnati.

He took an active part in Robert Owen's communistic experiment at New Harmony, Ind., moving there with his family in 1825. After a time in the community, Warren found that he disagreed with the communal idea and sought to attain the same ends through individual sovereignty, holding that the proper reward of labor was a like amount of labor. In 1827 he returned to Cincinnati and put his theory to the test by starting an "equity store." This he conducted for two years, giving and receiving labor notes in place of money.

Warren was a successful inventor, his first venture having been a lard-burning lamp which he manufactured until his experiment with the Owenites. Later he made all of his own printing equipment, invented a cylinder press, and developed a process for making stereotype plates.

In 1850, he moved to New York, where he founded a colony called "Modern Times" on Long Island. This also proved a failure, as it lured cranks and eccentrics and did little to advance the cause of the brotherhood of man. The colony lasted until about 1862 and Warren spent his last years in Massachusetts. He died at Charlestown, Mass., after a long illness. Although small and stocky in stature, Warren was possessed of a tremendous vitality and abundant energy. His writings, although few in number, were valuable propaganda for the cause of philosophical anarchy and have left their mark on the political development of the nation.

Principal Works: Equitable Commerce, 1846; True Civilization: An Immediate Necessity, 1863; True Civilization: A Subject of Vital and Serious Interest to All People, 1875. *Miscellaneous*—Written Music Remodeled and Invested with the Simplicity of an Exact Science, 1860.

About: Bailie, W. Joseph Warren: The First American Anarchist; Conway, M. D. Autobiography; Lockwood, G. B. The New Harmony Movement; Fortnightly Review July 1, 1865; Boston Globe April 15, 1874.

WARREN, MERCY (OTIS) (September 14, 1728 o.s.-October 19, 1814), historian, poet, and dramatist, was born at Barnstable, Mass., the daughter of James and Mary (Allyne) Otis. She received some education from the village clergyman, Dr. Jonathan Russell, but undoubtedly the inspiration for her keen interest in politics and literature came from her brother James [*q.v.*] and her father, ardent liberals. She was married in 1754 to James Warren, gentleman farmer and later Revolutionary general, and their home in Plymouth became a center of anti-Royalist discussion. Through her intimacy with leaders of the Revolutionary party Mercy Otis acquired a clear understanding of political issues of the day; her advice was sought by such men as John and Samuel Adams, James Winthrop, and Thomas Jefferson, and on two notable occasions she gave valuable literary support to the American cause.

The Adulateur: A Tragedy, a satirical dramatic sketch directed against Governor Hutchinson and the Tories, was published in 1773; and two years later a more effective satire, *The Group,* proceeded from her pen. Excessively praised in her own day, perhaps because the patriot party had few strictly literary protagonists, these plays were nevertheless successful in that they helped to crystallize liberal opinion. She also composed two elaborate historical plays and several poems, but her most important contribution was her three-volume *History of the Rise, Progress, and Termination of the American Revolution,* a work that is still highly esteemed, as giving the real atmosphere of the period. It presents a clear picture of the political causes of the Revolution, but is perhaps even more highly

From a portrait by J. S. Copley
MERCY OTIS WARREN

valued for its intimate portraits of the leading figures on both sides of the conflict. The *History* caused a notable quarrel with John Adams, which was later patched up.

Mercy Warren seems to have had even stronger democratic opinions than her contemporaries, for her liberalism rather foreshadowed the "women's rights" movement of the nineteenth century. Nevertheless she found the time and inclination to raise five sons. She died in Plymouth, in her eighty-sixth year.

Principal Works: The Adulateur: A Tragedy, 1773; The Group, 1775; Poems Dramatic and Miscellaneous, 1790; History of the Rise, Progress, and Termination of the American Revolution, 1805.

About: Brown, A. Mercy Warren; Roebling, E. W. Richard Warren of the "Mayflower"; Tyler, M. C. The Literary History of the American Revolution; Warren-Adams Letters in Massachusetts Historical Society Collection: 1925; Columbian Centinel October 22, 1814.

WEBB, CHARLES HENRY (January 24, 1834-May 24, 1905) ("John Paul"), humorist and playwright, was born at Rouse's Point, N.Y., the son of Nathan and Philena King (Paddock) Webb. He was educated in schools at Champlain, N.Y., and Toronto. In 1851, he went to New York where he was an occasional contributor to the newspapers but was sidetracked from his career as a journalist by the publication of *Moby Dick,* which aroused his longing for seafaring life. He shipped for a whaling voyage, lasting three and one half years, to the South Seas and the Arctic and on his return worked with his brother in the grain and lumber business at Fulton City, Ill.

When some of his humorous poems and articles published in *Harper's Weekly* and the Chicago *Evening Journal* attracted the attention of Henry J. Raymond of the New York *Times,* he joined that paper and with the exception of a few months spent at the front as correspondent during the Civil War, was for three years a columnist and literary editor.

In 1863 Webb went to San Francisco as city editor of the *Evening Bulletin.* The next year he founded *The Californian,* a journal which numbered among its contributors two friends of Webb, Bret Harte and Mark Twain. He contributed to several other papers at this time and also wrote several plays, among them a burlesque of Boucicault's *Arrah-na-pogue.* Returning to New York in 1866, he contributed to various journals and edited and published Twain's first book, *The Celebrated Jumping Frog of Calaveras County.* After a year as banker and broker in Wall Street, 1872-73, he began the series of "John Paul" letters for the New York *Tribune,* which continued as a feature of that paper for several years, uninterrupted even by the long absence abroad of Webb and his family. He published another volume of parodies in 1876, *Sea-Weed and What We Seed,* but after that his time was given almost entirely to his inventions and the occasional writing of verse. He invented an adding machine, spending almost eight years perfecting it, only to have the company wrecked during the panic of 1893. He was married to Elizabeth W. Shipman in 1870.

A genial, witty, and warm hearted companion, Webb's work was peculiarly of its time. His parodies and satires were topical and too dependent on allusions of the moment to achieve permanent fame, while his verse is that of a competent but minor talent; but his services to American humor, particularly as editor and first publisher of Mark Twain, were distinguished.

Principal Works: *Plays*—Arrah-na-poke, 1765, Our Friend From Victoria, 1865. *Parodies*—Liffith Lank, 1866; St. Twel'mo, 1868; John Paul's Book, 1874; Sea-Weed and What We Seed, 1876; Parodies, Prose, and Verse, 1876. *Verse*—Vagrom Verses, 1889; With Lead and Line, 1901.

About: Stewart, G. R. Bret Harte; Critic March 1902; Pacific Monthly March 1908; Publishers Weekly June 3, 1905; New York Times May 25, 1905.

WEBB, JAMES WATSON (February 8, 1802-June 7, 1884), editor and diplomat, was born at Claverack, N.Y., the son of General Samuel Blachley Webb, a former aide of Washington, and Catharine (Hogeboom) Webb. His parents died while the boy was very young, leaving him in the care of a brother-in-law. Webb received some schooling at Cooperstown, N.Y., but in 1819 he ran away and became a soldier, securing through the Governor of New York a second lieutenant's commission. He was known as a rash and quarrelsome man in the army, and his only notable military exploit was a dangerous, mid-winter trek across Illinois to forestall an Indian attack on Fort Snelling, Minn., in 1822.

Leaving the army in 1827, Webb bought a New York paper, the *Morning Courier,* and in 1829 he acquired, and combined with it, Mordecai Noah's *New-York Enquirer.* He continued for more than thirty years to edit this paper, gaining wide influence as a Whig leader and exerting considerable pressure in the campaign against secession in the 'fifties. It was an era of individualism in the newspaper world, and Webb, who seems to have carried a chip on his shoulder throughout life, was one of its colorful figures. During the three years of his Jacksonian advocacy (1829-32) he secured the brilliant contributions of James Gordon Bennett, and in 1843 Henry Jarvis Raymond joined his staff. His aggressive and competitive spirit helped in the work of speeding up communications, and his vitriolic pen added spice to the journalistic controversies of the time.

Webb was sent to Vienna in 1849, as chargé d'affaires, but the Senate did not confirm his appointment. In 1861, however, he sold the *Morning Courier and New-York Enquirer,* completed a diplomatic mission to Louis Napoleon, and then went to Brazil as American minister. It is difficult to visualize this rash and contentious editor as a diplomat, yet during the eight years of his ministry in Brazil he accomplished a good deal, and in 1865 helped to secure a pledge of French withdrawal from Mexico. Webb returned from Brazil in 1869, and spent the rest of his life in travel and retirement. He was married twice: in 1823 to Helen Lispenard Stewart, who died in 1848; and in 1849 to Laura Virginia Cram.

Principal Works: *Pamphlets*—To the Officers of the Army, 1827; Slavery and Its Tendencies, 1856 (?); A National Currency, 1875. *Biography*—Reminiscences of General Samuel B. Webb, 1882.

About: Hudson, F. Journalism in the United States; Stevens, F. E. James Watson Webb's Trip Across Illinois in 1822; General J. Watson Webb . . . vs. Hamilton Fish; Webb, J. W. Reminiscences of General Samuel B. Webb.

WEBBER, CHARLES WILKINS (May 29, 1819-April 1856), journalist, explorer, naturalist, and soldier, was born in Russellville, Ky., the eldest son of Dr. Augustine Webber, a physician, and Agnes Maria (Tannehill) Webber, daughter of a Revolutionary officer. He was educated at home, and at nineteen went to Texas where he became associated with the Texas Rangers, including the Indian fighter, John Coffee Hays. Returning, he studied medicine, and in 1843 commenced a course at the Princeton Theological Seminary, but the following year took up journalism in New York. In 1849 he organized an expedition to the Colorado and Gila Rivers, which was abandoned after the Comanche Indians stole the horses of the party at Corpus Christi, Tex. Later, about 1854, he obtained from the New York legislature a charter for a camel company to cross the Western deserts. In 1855, while in Central America, he joined the party of the filibuster, William Walker, and is thought to have been killed in Nicaragua in the battle of Rivas on April 11, 1856.

While in New York he contributed to the *New World,* the *Literary World,* the *Democratic Review,* the *Sunday Dispatch,* and *Graham's Magazine* and was for two years editor and joint proprietor of the *American Review,* later the *American Whig Review.* In his writing he drew freely upon his adventures on the border life, and also upon his deep love for nature which had been fostered by a close friendship with the naturalist, John James Audubon. His *Wild Scenes and Song Birds,* constituting the second and last volume of a projected *Hunter-Naturalist* series, was illustrated by twenty colored lithographs drawn by his wife, whom he married in 1849. His first story *Old Hicks the Guide,* was followed by a sequel *The Gold Mines of the Gila.* He also wrote of the Jesuits in *"Sam,"* and included biographical sketches of Daniel Boone and other celebrated pioneers in his *Historical and Revolutionary Incidents of the Early Settlers of the United States.*

Principal Works: Old Hicks the Guide: or, Adventures in the Comanche Country, in Search of a Gold Mine, 1848; The Gold Mines of the Gila, 1849; The Hunter-Naturalist, 1851; The Wild Girl of Nebraska, 1852; Tales of the Southern Border, 1852; The Prairie Scout: or, Agatone the Renegade, 1852; The Texan Virago and Other Tales, 1852; The Romance of Forest and Prairie Life, 1853; Spiritual Vampirism, 1853; Wild Scenes and Song Birds, 1854; "Sam": or, The History of Mystery, 1855; Historical and Revolutionary Incidents of the Early Settlers of the United States, 1859.

About: Duyckinck, E. A. & G. L. Cyclopaedia of American Literature; see also his own works.

WEBSTER, DANIEL (January 18, 1782-October 24, 1852), statesman and orator, was born in Salisbury, N.H., the son of Capt. Ebenezer Webster and his second wife, Abigail (Eastman) Webster. Though almost illiterate, the captain, a Revolutionary veteran, was eager for his delicate precocious child to have a good education, and at great sacrifice sent him for an unsuccessful year to Phillips Exeter Academy, and then, in 1797, to Dartmouth. There the boy, who had already had some experience as a teacher, became known as an orator (in a florid style in marked contrast to the clipped eloquence of his later days), and contributed verse to the local newspaper. The law seemed to be his predestined profession, and though he interrupted its study to teach, he was finally admitted to the bar in Boston in 1805. He began practice, however, at Portsmouth, N.H., remaining in his native state until his father died. In 1808 he married Grace Fletcher, who died in 1828.

Collection of Frederick H. Meserve
DANIEL WEBSTER

As a conservative Federalist, the spokesman of the shipowners and merchants of New England, Webster served in Congress from 1812 to 1816. In the latter year he moved again to Boston, practiced law, and soon was involved in Massachusetts politics. He served in the legislature in 1822, then was elected to Congress again from his new state. In 1827 he became a Senator, and served until 1841, when Harrison made him Secretary of State. In 1829 he married again, his second wife being a New York heiress, Caroline Le Roy.

Webster remained in the cabinet under Tyler and Fillmore. He was the only member of Tyler's cabinet who did not resign over the Whig split with Clay on the issue of the United States bank. For this and his later compromise with Clay over the slavery question in 1850, he was considered a traitor by the abolitionists; his own attitude was that the tariff was more important than the slavery issue and the Union more important than either. He was a practical politician with no pretenses to fine-spun idealism, though there is no doubt of his sincere patriotism. Exceedingly ambitious, he never succeeded in securing the nomination for the presidency to which he approached several times; in many ways his career was a failure, though he himself considered it to have been justified by the treaty of 1842, fixing the boundaries of Canada.

It was as an orator that Webster excelled; he was perhaps the greatest orator America has ever produced, and to the stalwart New Englanders whom he represented he became a kind of godlike myth. Legends sprang up about him even before his death. They were not all political legends, either; his Gargantuan habits in drinking and eating, his extravagance and luxurious living, combined somehow with all the rugged individualism of the pioneer (and also, it must be confessed, with some very shady and suspicious business and political episodes), seemed to make him only the more beloved among those of his constituents who did not loathe his name. On his very deathbed—officially he died as the result of a fall from his carriage, actually of cirrhosis of the liver, an alcoholic complaint—he delivered one of his most grandiloquent speeches, ending, at his last breath, with the words, "I still live."

Swarthy as an Indian, and often taken for one, with "an eye as black as death and a look like a lion's" (Van Wyck Brooks), Webster fascinated and cowed his audiences. His speeches at the dedication of Bunker Hill Monument and in the Dartmouth College case are likely never to be forgotten. His published writings are all transcripts of his speeches, or letters. Though his personality gave them life, there is enough in them even in printed form to understand the tremendous reputation achieved by this disappointed politician, the debt-ridden squire of Marshfield, who Sydney Smith said was "a cathedral in himself."

Principal Works: Considerations on the Embargo Laws, 1808; Works (6 vols.) 1851; Private Correspondence (2 vols.) 1857; Letters, 1902; Works and Speeches (18 vols.) 1903.

About: Adams, S. H. The Godlike Daniel; Benson, A. L. Daniel Webster; Bradford, G. As God Made Them; Brooks, Van W. The Flowering of New England; Carey, R. L. Daniel Webster as Economist; Curtis, G. T. Life of Daniel Webster; Fisher, S. G. The True Daniel Webster; Fuess, C. M. Daniel Webster; Kennedy, E. R. The Real Daniel Webster; Lanman, C. The Private Life of Daniel Webster; Lyman, S. P. The Public and Private Life of Daniel Webster; McMaster, J. B. Daniel Webster; Ogg, F. A. Daniel Webster; Wheeler, E. P. Daniel Webster.

WEBSTER, NOAH (October 16, 1758-May 28, 1843), lexicographer, lawyer, textbook-writer, and journalist, was born in West Hartford, Conn., the fourth child of Noah and Mercy (Steele) Webster. Descended from two New England colonial governors, he was in many ways typical of the world to which he belonged: limited but original, enterprising, and stubbornly American.

Webster entered Yale in 1774, his father mortgaging the Connecticut farm to pay for his education. Two years later the outbreak of the Revolution did much to disrupt the ordinary course of academic life, at the same time, stimulating Webster's interest in politics. Determined on a law career, he earned his living by teaching and clerical work for several years after his graduation, meanwhile reading law. In 1781 he passed the bar examinations at Hartford, but was not engaged in active practice until nearly eight years later.

Teaching school at Goshen, N.Y., the Revolution and the struggle for American independence again bore an indirect influence on the future course of his career. There was a need for American textbooks, and Webster set about answering this need with the preparation of *A Grammatical Institute of the English Language,* consisting of three parts: a spelling book, a grammar, and a reader. Believing a cultural declaration of independence to be as important as the political, he made use of American subject matter, combining a patriotic with a scholarly purpose. Of these three elementary books, the speller became tremendously successful, selling approximately 75,000,000 copies in America during the nineteenth and early twentieth centuries. Together with his later work as a lexicographer, this speller and its many revised editions did much to influence the standardization of American spelling and pronunciation.

During these years he was also interested in the problem of an American copyright. Agitating for copyright legislation, he traveled throughout the country, earning his living by teaching, holding singing schools, lecturing, and writing pamphlets. Quite naturally the fight for the copyright took him into politics and he became known as an ardent Federalist, expressing his views in a pamphlet, *Sketches of American Policy,* which won the interest of Washington and Madison. In Philadelphia he met Benjamin Franklin and began with him a long correspondence on another of his pet reforms, simplified spelling.

Nor were these his only interests. His writings are a good indication of the versatility of his activities at this period: popular essays; economic treatises; medical articles, including *A Brief History of Epidemic and Pestilential Diseases;* essays in physical science, one of which, *Experiments Respecting Dew,* foreshadowed the later work of weather bureaus; statistical reports; historical and political writings. Such diversified knowledge and experience did much to lay the basis for his subsequent achievements as a lexicographer.

From a portrait by S. F. B. Morse

NOAH WEBSTER
1823

In 1789 he married Rebecca Greenleaf, the daughter of a Boston merchant, and practiced law for four years, after which he gave up law and went into active journalism, launching two Federalist newspapers, a daily, the *Minerva* (later the *Commercial Advertiser*), and a semi-weekly, the *Herald* (later the *Spectator*). For ten years he remained in journalism, until with changing politics his interest waned, and he turned at last to his real work, that of lexicography.

His three years of work on *A Compendious Dictionary of the English Language,* 1806, gave him command of the technique of lexicography; it paved the way for his larger dictionary, the result of twenty years of labor, published in 1828, *An American Dictionary of the English Language.* Recording some five thousand new words, this dictionary was the most ambitious publication up to that time in America and, in spite of the weakness of its etymologies, a scholarly achievement of the first order. Its only rival was the dictionary compiled by Joseph Emerson Worcester [*q.v.*], whom Webster accused of plagiarism, precipitating the so-called "War of the Dictionaries." Webster, it must be conceded, had little literary feeling, displaying less sense of the flavor and history of words than his rival.

After living awhile in Amherst, where he helped found Amherst College, and spending a year abroad, Webster moved back to New Haven, continuing the work on his dictionaries until he died at the age of eighty-four.

Both in his spelling reforms and in his Americanization of the usage of words, Webster has left his mark on the language, although (ironically enough) his work became later the bulwark of conservatism against newer reforms. Webster's name has been perpetuated in the title of the great standard lexicon currently published by G. & C. Merriam Co. of Springfield, Mass.

Principal Works: *Miscellany*—A Grammatical Institute of the English Language, 1784; Sketches of American Policy, 1785; The Leading Principles of the Federal Constitution, 1787; Dissertations on the English Language, 1789; The Prompter, 1791; The Revolution in France, 1794; A Brief History of Epidemic and Pestilential Diseases, 1799; The Origin and State of Banking Institutions and Insurance Offices, 1802; A Compendious Dictionary of the English Language, 1806; Philosophical and Practical Grammar of the English Language, 1807; Experiments Respecting Dew, 1809; Letters to a Young Gentleman Commencing His Education, 1825; An American Dictionary of the English Language, 1828; Manual of Useful Studies, 1832; Authorized Version of the English Bible (revised), 1833; History of the United States, 1838; A History of Animals, 1842.

About: Brooks, Van W. The Flowering of New England; Ford, E. E. F. Notes on the Life of Noah Webster; Scudder, H. E. Noah Webster; Warfel, H. R. Noah Webster: Schoolmaster to America.

WEEMS, MASON LOCKE ("Parson" (Weems) (October 11, 1759-May 23, 1825), biographer, was born in Anne Arundel County, Md., the son of David Weems, a Scottish farmer, and his second wife, Esther or Hester (Hill) Weems. He was the youngest of his father's nineteen children. His early life is obscure; he spent some time in the household of a family named Jenifer, in Charles County; perhaps studied at Kent County School, Chestertown, Md. (later Washington College); may have made two or more trips with older brothers who were sea captains; possibly, though not probably, studied medicine in London and Edinburgh from 1773 to 1776. In any event he seems to have had a knowledge of medicine and was sometimes called doctor. That he went back to England in 1781 to study theology is indubitable, also that he and a companion were the first Americans to be ordained in the Church of England after the American Revolution, the question at issue being the church's insistence that they take an oath of fealty to the king. This was in 1784, and for five or six years thereafter Weems served various parishes in Maryland, meanwhile conducting a school for girls.

In 1791 he began reprinting and publishing "improving books," gradually becoming compiler, then editor, then writer. From his personal sales of these books, he became

"PARSON" WEEMS

a regular book agent, after 1794 being employed by the famous pioneer publisher, Mathew Carey. In Carey's employ Weems traveled from New York to Savannah; he was perhaps the most successful salesman of his time. Once he interrupted his new career to preach at several Virginia churches; and again he left Carey—they quarreled frequently—and took advance orders for Marshall's projected biography of Washington. This was some time after Weems's own biography (the first to be printed) had grown from an anonymous 12-page pamphlet to a full-size book and an enormous seller. Weems found nothing inconsistent in abandoning the ministry for bookselling; he felt he was "doing God's work in a wider field." Besides, he was rather unorthodox, almost Universalist in his beliefs, and was disapproved of by his bishop for his light and easy way with sermons.

In 1795 he married Frances Ewell, and moved to her home at Dumfries, Va. There in 1806 he built his house, Bel Air, still standing. He was fond of his ten children, and apparently of his wife, but he was away from home most of the time, and from 1820 lived almost entirely at Beaufort, S.C. —possibly because of ill health. It was there that he died, but he was buried at Bel Air.

Weems was a "character." Excitable, cheerful, always full of enthusiasm and zeal, he was tolerant and charitable to a fault. Playing his fiddle, dramatizing himself in taverns as an "example" of the horrors of drunkenness, he was a sort of spiritual peddler. Quite frankly, he preferred interest to accuracy in his biographies, and made no pretense of their being more than biographical fiction. Indeed, his *Life of General Francis Marion* was actually "ghost written" and first appeared under the name of its putative author, Peter Horry, until the latter indignantly disclaimed the book because of its fictions. Weems would have been the last man on earth to have expected such anecdotes as the cherry tree episode (in his life of Washington) to be taken seriously as the fruits of scholarly research. More than most writers of his day he deserves reading, for his vigorous and racy style, his wit, his humor, and his spontaneity.

PRINCIPAL WORKS: Hymen's Recruiting Sergeant, 1799; The Philanthropist, 1799; The Life and Memorable Actions of George Washington, 1800; The Patriot, 1802; God's Revenge Against Murder, 1807; Life of General Francis Marion, 1809; God's Revenge Against Gambling, 1810; The Drunkard's Looking Glass, 1812; Life of Dr. Benjamin Franklin, 1815; God's Revenge Against Adultery, 1815; God's Revenge Against Duelling, 1820; Life of William Penn, 1822; The Bad Wife's Looking Glass, 1823.

ABOUT: Ford, P. L. & Skeel, E. E. F. Mason Locke Weems; Kellock, H. Parson Weems of the Cherry Tree; Schmalhausen, S. D. (ed.). Our Neurotic Age (see article, Alcoholism, by Maynard Shipley); Simms, W. G. Views and Reviews; Wroth, L. C. Parson Weems; Mentor February 2, 1928; National Magazine February 1910; Warrenton (N.C.) Reporter July 8, 1825.

WEEMS, "PARSON." See WEEMS, MASON LOCKE

WELBY, AMELIA BALL (COPPUCK) (February 3, 1819-May 3, 1852), poet, was born in Saint Michaels, Md., but was brought at an early age to Baltimore, where she received her education. She was the daughter of William Coppuck, a contracting mason and federal lighthouse builder, and Mary (Shield) Coppuck. When she was fourteen the family moved to Louisville, Ky., which became her home for the remainder of her life. In 1838 she married George Welby, an English merchant of that city, and the young couple soon made their home a literary center. She died at thirty-three, two months after the birth of her only child.

Before she was eighteen she was contributing verse under the pseudonym "Amelia" to the Louisville *Daily Journal,* whose editor, George D. Prentice, admired the simple melodies of her poems. Some years later her first volume of collected poems was published, fourteen editions appearing by 1855. The fluency, sweetness and naturalness of her verses won her wide popularity, the poet Edgar Allan Poe assigning her a high place among the *literati* of America. Among her more admired and anthology-quoted poems were "The Rainbow," "Twilight at Sea," "The Bereaved," "Eloquence," and "My Heart Grew Softer." In his contemporary work, *The Heart's Treasure,* J. H. Bryson published over twenty of her poems.

PRINCIPAL WORKS: Poems, 1845.

ABOUT: Coggeshall, W. T. The Poets and Poetry of the West; Read, T. B. The Female Poets of America; Kentucky State Historical Society Register 1917.

WELCH, PHILIP HENRY (March 1, 1849-February 24, 1889), journalist-wit, was the son of Joseph B. Welch and Mary (Collins) Welch. He was born in Angelica, N.Y., and there attended public school. Employed for twelve years by a New York hardware firm, much of the time "on the road"; during a stay in Oil City, Pa., he began to send petroleum reports to *Bradstreet's,* and some time later decided to devote himself to journalistic humor. A cancer, first occuring in his throat in 1886, necessitated two operations and led to his death in Brooklyn a few years later. Toward the end, when incapacitated from writing, he continued to dictate his jokes to his wife.

Welch conducted a column, "The Present Hour," in the Rochester (N.Y.) *Post-Express* in 1882, and another, "Accidentally Overheard," in the Philadelphia *Call* in 1883. From 1884 he was associated with the New York *Sun,* writing anonymously, his productions being referred to as "Queer Wrinkles." Simultaneously he contributed dialogues to *Puck, Life, Judge,* the *Epoch,* the *Times, Drake's Magazine, Harper's Bazaar,* and other periodicals. His jokes—frequently a single question and answer—were widely copied and pirated. His only life-time volume was *The Tailor-Made Girl,* a collection of twenty-six short dialogues illustrated by C. Jay Taylor, originally appearing in *Puck,* in which he satirized the friends, fashions, and follies of the fashionable girl of the day. After his death a memorial fund was collected for the education of his four children, his friends publishing as part of this effort an anthology of his more characteristic dialogues under the title *Said in Fun.*

PRINCIPAL WORKS: The Tailor-Made Girl, 1888; Said in Fun, 1889.

ABOUT: Journalist January 28, 1888.

WELD (or WELDE), THOMAS (1595-March 23, 1660/61), Puritan divine, colonial agent, and versifier, was born in Sudbury

(Suffolk), England, the son of Edmond Weld, a prosperous dealer, and Amy Weld. From Trinity College, Cambridge, he received the degrees of B.A. (1613/14) and M.A. (1618). He was ordained deacon and then priest, and held a vicarage first in Suffolk and then in Essex. Less than a year after his deposition, by the Court of High Commission, on charges of "contumacy," he arrived in Boston, June 5, 1632, and was shortly made first pastor of the church at Roxbury.

In 1638 Weld became an overseer at Harvard; and three years later he was sent to England, with Hugh Peter and William Hibbins to advance reformation within the English church, and to procure financial aid for the colony. Their early collections were most encouraging, but subsequent internal entanglements and small diplomatic fiascos led not only to their dismissal, in 1645, but to charges of embezzlement. Hibbins had returned to Boston; and in defense of himself and Peter, Weld prepared a pamphlet ("Innocency Cleared"); they were finally vindicated in 1654.

Weld served as rector at Wanlip, Leicester, and in February 1649/50 he was installed at St. Mary's, Gateshead, Durham, where he cultivated an assertively unfriendly attitude towards Quakerism, and withdrew to London only shortly before the Restoration. He was three times married: to Margaret Deresleye, by whom he had four sons; to one Judith, who died in 1656; and to one Margaret, who survived him.

With John Eliot and Richard Mather he prepared, for church singing, *The Whole Booke of Psalmes,* better known as "The Bay Psalm Book," the first *book* published in America. (Stephen Daye's early press had previously printed only the *Freeman's Oath,* believed to have been a single sheet, and an *Almanack,* made by one William Pierce, a mariner, both of which are probably no longer extant). The compilers may have felt some of that uncouthness, in their little volume, which has since brought such an onslaught of ridicule from the pens of less pious generations, for the preface states:

> If these verses are not always so smooth and elegant as some may desire . . . let them consider that God's Altar needs not our polishings . . .

The poetic poverty of the verse is apparent in:

> O blessed man, that in th'advice
> of wicked doest not walk
> Nor stand in sinners way, nor sit
> in chayre of scornful folk . . .

and

> The Lord to me a shepheard is,
> want therefore shall not I.
> He in the folds of tender-grasse
> doth cause me downe to lie.

To vindicate "those Godly and Orthodoxall Churches [of New England] from more than a hundred imputations" in an account by one William Rathband, Weld issued *An Answer to W. R. . . .* ; and *A Brief Narrative of the Practices of the Churches in New-England* was presumably written in the effort to recover favor among the English independents following the appearance of what is believed to be Weld's editing of Governor Winthrop's manuscript record of the New England Antinomian controversy, *A Short Story of the Rise, Reign, and Ruine of the Antinomians.*

Weld had a direct and indirect hand in the religious and financial affairs of the colony, and was, moreover, a joint author of America's first published volume.

PRINCIPAL WORKS: The Whole Book of Psalmes, 1640; New England's First Fruits, 1643; An Answer to W. R. . . , 1644; A Short Story of the Rise, Reign, and Ruine of the Antinomians, 1644; A Brief Narrative of the Practices of the Churches in New England, 1645.

ABOUT: Adams, C. F. Antinomianism in Massachusetts Bay; Eames, W. The Bay Psalm Book; Matthews, A. G. Calamy Revised; Records of the Colony of New Plymouth: Vol 10; Proceedings of the Massachusetts Historial Society: 1st Ser. Vols. 5, 6, 2nd Ser. Vols. 8, 42.

WELLS, DAVID AMES (June 17, 1828-November 5, 1898), economist and popularizer of science, was the son of James Wells and Rebecca (Ames) Wells, and a descendant of Governor Thomas Welles of Connecticut. Born in Spiingfield, Mass., he was educated in the schools of that city and was graduated from Williams College in 1847. After two years of experience as associate editor of the Springfield *Republican,* Wells resumed his studies, enrolling at the Lawrence Scientific School of Harvard under Louis Agassiz. Graduated in 1851, he turned his hand to writing and publishing; from 1850 he had been co-editor of *The Annual of Scientific Discovery,* and later he wrote a number of popular scientific texts and manuals. *Wells's Natural Philosophy,* issued in 1863, became widely known.

Wells' greatest contribution to our national welfare was made in the darkest period of the Civil War, when deflation of the greenback currency had shaken the entire economic structure. In 1864 appeared *Our*

Burden and Our Strength, a slender pamphlet in which Wells reassured the creditors of the United States by giving a contagiously optimistic, yet reasonable, view of our economic future. The pamphlet was influential both here and abroad, and in recognition of his services Lincoln secured Wells' appointment as special commissioner of the revenue, a post which he held from 1865 to 1870. During these years Wells became a great authority on taxation, and made important contributions to the system of taxation, such as the method of collecting liquor and tobacco revenues by stamps. He later became an influential writer on the tariff question, advocating free-trade with such eloquence that President Grant refused to reappoint him as special commissioner in 1870, and Wells went to work for the New York State tax commission. He also interested himself in railroad reorganization and the free silver issue. After 1870 he lived at Norwich, Conn., studying and writing. His first wife was Mary Sanford (Dwight) Wells, whom he had married in 1860; a second wife and a son survived him.

Wells' reputation derived from his remarkable ability to present difficult problems of economics and science in a clear style, readily comprehensible to the mass of readers. As an exponent of science in industry, and on national affairs, he made himself heard to considerable effect.

PRINCIPAL WORKS: The Science of Common Things, 1857; Wells's Natural Philosophy, 1863; Our Burden and Our Strength, 1864; The Reports of the Special Commissioner of the Revenue, 1866-69; Local Taxation, 1871; The True Story of the Leaden Statuary, 1874; Robinson Crusoe's Money, 1876; The Silver Question, 1877; Practical Economics, 1885; The Theory and Practice of Taxation, 1900.

ABOUT: Durfee, C. Williams Biographical Annals; Putnam, G. H. Memories of a Publisher; Encyclopedia of the Social Sciences: Vol. 15; New York Times November 6, 8, 1898.

WELLS, WILLIAM VINCENT (January 2, 1826-June 1, 1876), adventurer and biographer, was born in Boston, the son of Samuel Adams Wells. He spent ten of his early years at sea, was shipwrecked five times, and before twenty had become an officer in the merchant marine. In 1849 he sailed to northern California, where he led a varied career: mining, farming, engineering, business, and journalism. A visit to Honduras in 1854 as agent for the Honduras Mining and Trading Co. gave him the opportunity for intensive study of that country. Following his return to San Francisco he was appointed (1855) consul for Honduras, a post which he retained intermittently until 1874. During the Civil War he was clerk in the naval office at San Francisco, and from 1865 he was associated with the Emperor Maximilian of Mexico until his fall in 1867, part of the time conducting a propaganda office in New York City. He also passed five years as clerk in the office of the mayor of San Francisco. In 1874 his mind began to be affected, and he died in the state insane asylum at Napa.

Wells was attached to the editorial staff of the *Commercial Advertiser,* San Francisco, about 1853, and was associated with both the *Alta California* and the *Daily Times.* His first important publication, a defense of the filibuster William Walker's expedition to Nicaragua, was soon followed by his volume on Honduras, based on his daily diary and augmented by many additional facts relating to that region. His major literary effort, however, was a three-volume biography of his great-grandfather, the Revolutionary statesman, Samuel Adams, in the writing of which he had access to many basic family records.

PRINCIPAL WORKS: Walker's Expedition to Nicaragua, 1856; Explorations and Adventures in Honduras, 1857; Life and Public Services of Samuel Adams, 1865.

ABOUT: Howe, O. T. Argonauts of '49.

WEST, BENJAMIN (March ?, 1730-August 26, 1813), almanac-maker and astronomer, was born in Rehoboth, Mass., the son of John West, a farmer; his mother's maiden name is unknown. He should not be confused with Benjamin West, the painter, who was his younger contemporary.

He had only three months' schooling; for the most part he was self-educated, with some lessons in navigation from a sea captain at Bristol, R.I., where he passed his childhood. In later years, however, Brown, Harvard, and Dartmouth gave him honorary M.A. degrees, and Brown an LL.D., and he became a fellow of the American Academy of Arts and Sciences. He was a natural mathematician, and in a different environment might have become famous.

As it was, in 1858 he moved to Providence, where he opened a private school, and in the same year married Elizabeth Smith, by whom he had eight children. The school and a drygoods and book store he opened next both failed. During the Revolution he made uniforms for the army; then he started another school. Meanwhile he had begun to publish almanacs, the first appearing in 1765. So popular were they that different editions, calculated for Boston, Providence, Halifax, etc., were issued simultaneously. In 1768 he revived Swift's old pseudonym of "Isaac Bickerstaff," and under it established the first illustrated almanac in Massachusetts.

In 1786 West was appointed professor of mathematics and astronomy at Rhode Island College (Brown University). He accepted, but first taught mathematics for two years at the Protestant Episcopal Academy, Philadelphia. He remained at the college until 1799, in his last year being professor of mathematics and natural philosophy. As his salary was only $375 a year, he was obliged then to resign, and for the remainder of his life conducted a school of navigation in his own home.

West was not really an author; aside from his almanacs (many of which continued to be published under his name long after he had ceased to have anything to do with them), he published only a few astronomical articles. In the history of literature he figures only through the later development of the almanac as a literary form.

Principal Works: An Almanack for the Year of Our Lord Christ 1763, 1762; The New-England Almanack: or, Lady's and Gentleman's Diary, 1765-81; An Account of the Observation of Venus, 1769; Bickerstaff's Boston Almanac, 1768-79, 1783-93; North-American Calendar: or, Rhode Island Almanac, 1781-87; Rhode Island Almanac, 1804-05.

About: Providence Daily Journal January 22, 1881; Providence Evening Bulletin August 26, 1913.

WESTCOTT, EDWARD NOYES (September 27, 1846-March 31, 1898), banker and novelist, author of *David Harum,* was born in Syracuse, N.Y., the third child of Amos Westcott, a dentist, and his wife, Clara (Babcock) Westcott.

If it had not been for the accident of serious illness, Westcott might never have been known as a novelist. Until middle life he followed a conventional and moderately successful career as a banker. Leaving school at the age of sixteen, he went into business as junior clerk in the Mechanics' Bank of Syracuse. In 1866 he went to New York to take a position in the office of the Mutual Life Insurance Company, returning to Syracuse after two years, serving as teller in the First National Bank, and as cashier in the firm of Wilkinson & Co., bankers.

Always delicate, he appears to have had the temperament and inclinations of an artist, even while his energies were devoted largely to business. A capable amateur musician, he was a fine singer and composed several songs. He was also the author of several pamphlets issued by the Reform Club of New York, of which he was a member. Married in 1874 to Jane Dows of Buffalo, he was ambitious to give his children, two sons and a daughter, the advantages of education and culture which he had not had.

In 1880 he organized the firm of Westcott & Abbott, bankers and brokers, and was very successful until the failure of Wilkinson & Co., an allied firm. For several years following, Westcott acted as secretary to the Syracuse Water Commission, resigning his position in 1895 because of his steadily failing health.

Suffering from tuberculosis, he spent the summer of 1895 at Lake Meacham in the Adirondacks, and there began to write for his own amusement. In spite of the severe handicap of his illness, he continued through the summer and a winter spent in Naples to set down the adventures of one David Harum, a droll old rascal who practiced banking, with horse dealing on the side. The novel, *David Harum: A Story of American Life,* was completed in the latter part of 1896, and after a thorough revision began the rounds of the publishers. Like many a best-seller before and since, the manuscript of *David Harum* received no immediate recognition. Rejected by one publisher on the grounds that it was "vulgar and smelled of the stables," it was refused by six major publishing firms before Ripley Hitchcock of D. Appleton Company saw its possibilities and accepted it with a cordial letter to the author.

EDWARD NOYES WESTCOTT
1889

Westcott must have known that he could not live to see the publication of his book. At the age of fifty-two, three months after he had received the letter from Appleton's, he died of tuberculosis. A half year later the book was published, achieving immediate and lasting popularity. It went through six printings in twelve weeks; in two years it had sold over 400,000 copies, a record at that time broken only by *In His Steps* and *Trilby*. It continued to sell for the next thirty-five years, passing the million mark, and was successfully dramatized in both a stage and a motion picture version.

This tremendous popularity undoubtedly followed a current fashion in novels: stories dealing in simple emotion, sentimental or humorous. Its author was competent, modest and good-humored, but hardly distinguished. As a piece of literature, there is nothing to recommend *David Harum* except the broadly comic characterization of its central figure.

PRINCIPAL WORKS: *Novels*—David Harum: A Story of American Life, 1898. *Stories*—The Teller: With the Letters of Edward N. Westcott, 1901.

ABOUT: Westcott, E. N. The Teller (see Life by F. Hermans); Book News May 1899; Critic July 1899; New York Times Magazine July 17, 1938.

"WETHERELL, ELIZABETH." See WARNER, SUSAN BOGERT

WHEATLEY, PHILLIS (? 1753-December 5, 1784), Negro poet, was born in Africa and transported by slave ship to Boston at the age of eight, where she was bought by John Wheatley, a well-to-do tailor, as a personal servant for his wife. The Wheatleys took an interest in the girl, encouraging her to study and treating her with great kindness. Phillis, who seems to have been gifted with extraordinary sensitivity, responded to this new environment, learning English in sixteen months. Without benefit of any formal schooling, she was soon able to read the most difficult parts of the Bible and even began the study of Latin. Fond of classical literature and of poetry, she started writing verses when she was thirteen, choosing her models from the contemporary English poets, particularly Pope and Gray. Her accomplishments attracted a good deal of attention among Boston intellectuals, and through the efforts of some of these newly-acquired friends she succeeded in publishing several poems and a translation of a tale from Ovid.

In 1773, suffering poor health, she made a trip to England in the company of John

From on old print

PHILLIS WHEATLEY

Wheatley's son, Nathaniel. There she was received by Lady Huntingdon, Lord Dartmouth, and others prominent in English society, achieving immediate popularity by her wit and charm. A volume of poetry dedicated to Lady Huntingdon, *Poems on Various Subjects: Religious and Moral*, appeared in England the same year.

Soon after Phillis' return to America, Mrs. Wheatley died; the death of Mr. Wheatley followed in a few months. Thrown on her own resources, Phillis tried to support herself for a time without much success, and in 1778 married John Peters, a free Negro. Peters seems to have been a talented man with some degree of education, but the marriage was never a happy one. Both Phillis and John Peters were proud and considered themselves above menial work; he apparently, moreover, was overbearing and unprincipled, and it was largely because of him that Phillis became estranged from her former friends. The remaining years of her life were tragic ones. Two of the three children born to her died in early infancy. When her husband was imprisoned for debt, she was forced to earn a living in a Negro boarding house. Always delicate physically, she suffered many hardships and died alone and in poverty when she was thirty-one. Her third child was buried with her in an unmarked grave.

Although she has been called the "Negro Sappho," Phillis Wheatley was really a poet of minor talent. Her verses are able and imitative, strongly influenced by the English poets she admired. Yet they have considerable interest as examples of precocity, particularly in connection with the extraordinary circumstances of her life.

PRINCIPAL WORKS: *Poetry*—To the University of Cambridge in New England, 1767; To the King's Most Excellent Majesty, 1768; On the Death of Rev. Dr. Sewell, 1769; An Elegiac Poem on the Death of the Celebrated Divine . . . George Whitefield, 1770; Poems of Various Subjects: Religious and Moral, 1773; Memoir and Poems of Phillis Wheatley, 1834.

ABOUT: Brawley, B. G. Early Negro American Writers; Griswold, R. W. The Female Poets of America; Heartman, C. F. Phillis Wheatley: A Critical Attempt and a Bibliography of Her Writings.

WHEATON, HENRY (November 27, 1785-March 11, 1848), jurist, historian, diplomat, and journalist, was born in Providence, R.I., the son of Seth and Abigail (Wheaton) Wheaton, both of whom were descended from Robert Wheaton, an early Welsh emigrant to New England. He attended a Latin school before entering Brown University (then Rhode Island College), for which the admission requirements were largely "the ability to read accurately, construe, and parse Cicero's orations, Virgil's *Aeneid*, and the Greek testament . . . and to know the rules of Vulgar arithmetic." He was graduated in 1802, and ignoring his own interest in engineering he began the study of law, in compliance with his father's wishes; he wrote a number of political articles for the Rhode Island *Patriot* and the *National Intelligencer,* established in Washington, D.C., by Samuel Harrison Smith.

Shortly after his removal to New York to become editor of the *National Advocate,* Tammany organ, he was encouraged by Justice Joseph Story, then associate justice of the United States Supreme Court, in the preparation of *A Digest of the Law of Maritime Captures and Prizes.* From 1816 to 1821 Wheaton was reporter for this same high court, and into his twelve *Reports* he wrote a vast amount of his own valuable information. In 1823 he was elected to the New York Assembly; at the end of one term he ran a losing race for a United States senatorship.

Wheaton's interest in Scandinavian history and the ease with which he learned the Danish language contributed to his success as chargé d'affaires to Denmark, to which post he was appointed in 1827. He was very successful in the delicate negotiation of a treaty of indemnity by which Denmark atoned for her violation of American neutral rights. Meanwhile he was writing articles on Scandinavian law and literature, and in 1831 published his *History of the Northmen,* the purpose of which was "to seize the principal points in the progress of society and manners of this remote period . . . which have been barely glanced at . . . but which . . . illustrate the formation of the great monarchies now constituting some of [Europe's] leading states."

In March 1835, at the request of Prussia, Wheaton was appointed chargé d'affaires at Berlin; and just two years later, as an indirect outcome of the publication of his *Elements of International Law,* he was made envoy extraordinary and minister plenipotentiary to Prussia. Unfortunately the United States Senate disapproved of some of his brilliant trade and taxation measures, and in 1846 President Polk requested Wheaton's resignation; he returned to America in the year following. At his death he left his wife, Catharine (Wheaton) Wheaton, whom he had married in 1811, and two daughters and a son. From the immediate and practical point of view, there was, professionally, a certain tragedy of frustration in Wheaton's life. But his fundamental wisdom as a diplomat and his astuteness as a legal historian placed him, in his time, "confessedly at the head of American diplomacy."

PRINCIPAL WORKS: A Digest of the Law of Maritime Captures and Prizes, 1815; A Digest of the Decisions of the Supreme Court of the United States, 1821; Some Account of the Life, Writings, and Speeches of William Pinkney, 1826; History of the Northmen, 1831; History of the Law of Nations in Europe and America: From the Earliest Times to the Treaty of Washington, 1842.

ABOUT: Baker, E. F. Henry Wheaton; Kellen, W. V. Henry Wheaton: An Appreciation; Proceedings of the Massachusetts Historical Society: 1st Ser. Vol. 19; North American Review January 1856; Boston Daily Advertiser March 16, 1848.

WHEELER, CHARLES STEARNS (1816-June 13, 1843), Greek scholar, friend of Thoreau, and literary aide to Emerson, was born in Lincoln, Mass., the son of a New England farmer. He appears to have been generally known as "Stearns Wheeler." At Harvard he was a classmate (1837) of Thoreau, who, several years later, shared a straw "bunk" for six weeks in Wheeler's rough "shanty" near Flint's pond (half way between Lincoln and Concord), and was sufficiently impressed with the hut-in-the-woods procedure to make his own experiment at Walden. Wheeler was also awarded an M.A. degree from Harvard, and from 1838 to 1842 he was tutor in Greek and instructor in history at the college.

During 1838 and 1839 he volunteered his services to Emerson, who was preparing the American edition of Carlyle's *Miscellanies:* he copied *Sartor Resartus,* word for word, from *Fraser's Magazine* (British publishers had refused this book!); and he revised the bulk of the proof for the four volumes. Moreover Wheeler independently edited Tennyson's poems, and brought out the first American edition of Herodotus, in the effort to make "a famous author attractive to the eyes of American scholars," and to project him not as the "credulous, malignant, and imbecile story-teller he has been represented by Juvenal, Plutarch and Voltaire, but a careful inquirer, a judicious critic, and a conscientious man." He supplemented the text (Schweighaeuser's) with ample English notes, which the *North American Review* cited as "invaluable accompaniments."

In 1842 Wheeler sailed for Germany to study, and the *Dial,* Brook Farm literary organ, published several of his letters from Heidelberg. He died in Leipzig at the early age of twenty-seven. As a tutor he was admittedly unpopular with his students, and despite his absolute failure as a disciplinarian, John Weiss, a classmate, recalled Wheeler, in a light piece of college reminiscence, as one who held

> Duty his word, and discipline his style,
> To his own manners strictest all the while . . .

But Emerson declared that Wheeler's "too-facile and good-natured manners do some injustice to his virtues, to his great industry and his real knowledge." And Thoreau said of him: ". . . if he had lived . . . he would have been an authority on all matters of fact, and a sort of connecting link between men and scholars of different walks and tastes . . ."

About: Brooks, Van W. The Flowering of New England; Norton, C. E. (ed.). Correspondence of Thomas Carlyle and Ralph Waldo Emerson; Thoreau, H. D. Familiar Letters; Weiss, J. Poem Read at the Annual Dinner of the Class of 1837; Wheeler, C. S. Herodotus (see Introduction); Journal of Speculative Philosophy July 1885.

WHEELER, WILLIAM ADOLPHUS (November 14, 1833-October 28, 1874), lexicographer and bibliographer, was born at Leicester, Mass. His father, Amos Dean Wheeler, a Unitarian minister, was a descendant of a George Wheeler who came to Concord, Mass., from England about 1638; his mother was Louisa (Warren) Wheeler. After a boyhood spent largely at Topsham, Maine, he was graduated from Bowdoin College in 1853, receiving his M.A. degree three years later, and an honorary M.A. from Harvard in 1871. Three years of teaching were followed by his becoming assistant, at Cambridge, to Dr. Joseph Emerson Worcester in the preparation of his quarto *Dictionary of the English Language.* Subsequently he entered upon similar editorial work with the Merriam Company, supervising new editions of Noah Webster's dictionary. In 1868 he joined the staff of the Boston Public Library, shortly becoming assistant superintendent and assuming charge of the cataloging department. He died at Roxbury at forty, leaving a widow and six children.

Wheeler's work was marked by painstaking thoroughness, accuracy, and good judgment. He contributed to the Worcester dictionary an appendix entitled "Pronunciation of the Names of Distinguished Men of Modern Times," and to Webster's quarto dictionary an "Explanatory and Pronouncing Vocabulary of the Names of Noted Fictitious Persons and Places," the latter being subsequently expanded into the work for which he became best known, *An Explanatory and Pronouncing Dictionary of the Noted Names of Fiction.* To his edition of *Mother Goose's Melodies* he contributed antiquarian and philological notes and an account of the Goose or Vergoose family of Boston from one of whom the name of the book was derived. The *Dickens Dictionary,* published as "by Gilbert A. Pierce, with additions by William A. Wheeler," is said to be mostly his work, and he did much of the cataloging of the Ticknor collection of the Boston Library, published after his death by his successor. He left unfinished three works, an encyclopedia of Shakespeare which was never published, and two reference works in a more advanced stage, *Who Wrote It?* and *Familiar Allusions,* which were completed by his nephew, Charles G. Wheeler.

Principal Works: A Manual of English Pronunciation and Spelling (with Richard Soule) 1861; An Explanatory and Pronouncing Dictionary of the Noted Names of Fiction, 1865; Mother Goose's Melodies (ed.) 1869; The Dickens Dictionary (with G. A. Pierce) 1872; Who Wrote It? (with C. G. Wheeler) 1881; Familiar Allusions (with C. G. Wheeler) 1882.

About: Boston Public Library: Report of the Trustees, 1875; Bowdoin College: Class of 1853; Cleaveland, N. History of Bowdoin College.

WHIPPLE, EDWIN PERCY (March 8, 1819-June 16, 1886), lecturer and essayist, was born in Gloucester, Mass., the son of Matthew and Lydia (Gardiner) Whipple. From his mother's side came the wit, and

Collection of Frederick H. Meserve
EDWIN PERCY WHIPPLE

from his father's the blandness, which contributed to his success as a popular platform figure throughout the heydey of the lyceum movement.

His youth in Salem, where he was graduated from high school in 1834, gave only slight promise of his later career. Taking a position with a local bank, he devoted his leisure hours to literature and history, contributing occasional pieces to the newspapers from the time he was fourteen. Three years later he went to Boston to enter a brokerage firm. In this city he gained some prominence as a speaker in debates held at the Attic Nights Club, of which he was a member, and as a writer through his critical essays. An article on T. B. Macaulay written in 1843 won him wider recognition, bringing commendation from Macaulay himself.

When he was twenty-eight he married Charlotte B. Hastings, a friend of Oliver Wendell Holmes and his circle, coming now into a more intimate contact with the New England literary world. The publication of his *Essays and Reviews* in 1849, and the next year of *Lectures on Subjects Connected With Literature and Life* brought him acclaim as a keen and kindly critic.

Leaving the brokerage, he became superintendent of the newsroom of the Merchants' Exchange where, a well-known figure, he was to be seen poring over books and papers, his massive head bent to the printed pages, "a capacious dome over a capacious heart." This post he held until 1860, when he resigned to devote himself to writing and lecturing.

A man of spare build, with a blunt expressive face and large lustrous eyes, he was an excellent talker as well as a discriminating critic. For the next dozen years and more he commanded tremendous popularity as a lyceum lecturer, publishing his lectures as well as his essays in book form. At the same time his "Sunday evenings" attracted those men who were making a literary Golden Age in Boston. In 1872, at the height of his fame, he acted as literary editor of the Boston *Daily Globe*. Judged by a contemporary critic, he was "one of the most brilliant writers in the country as well as one of the most experienced reviewers." His renown, however, had begun to fade several years before his death in 1886. According to one commentator, this decline in fame is "a case for a literary autopsy." Ill health and the waning popularity of the lyceum were contributing factors, and the advent of newly popular authors helped to throw him into retirement.

Intelligent, shy, and modest, Whipple's accomplishments were not spectacular enough to spread their brilliance beyond his own time. Yet he was an important figure in the literary life of Boston at a period when that city furnished a large part of the literary life of America. His critical writing was original, keenly analytical, and enlivened with a playful wit, among his contemporaries rivaled only by the criticism of Poe and Lowell.

Principal Works: *Essays*—Essays and Reviews, 1848-49; Lectures on Subjects Connected With Literature and Life, 1850; Character and Characteristic Men, 1866; Literature of the Age of Elizabeth, 1869; Success and Its Conditions, 1871; Recollections of Eminent Men, 1887; American Literature and Other Papers, 1887; Outlooks on Society, Literature, and Politics, 1888.

About: Brooks, V. W. The Flowering of New England; Higginson, T. W. Short Studies of American Authors; Perry, B. The Early Years of the Saturday Club.

WHISTLER, JAMES ABBOTT McNEILL (July 10, 1834-July 17, 1903), painter and essayist, liked to say that he was born in Baltimore or St. Petersburg, but actually he was born in Lowell, Mass., the son of Lieut. George Washington Whistler, a civil engineer, and his second wife, Anna Mathilda (McNeill) Whistler—the "mother" of the famous portrait and the three-cent stamp. His earliest years were spent in Stonington, Conn., and Springfield, Mass.; then his father was put in charge of constructing the railroad from St. Petersburg (Leningrad) to Moscow, and in 1843 the family followed him there. "Jimmy," who had been drawing since he was four, was sent to the Imperial Academy of Fine Arts, and also to a private school. In 1847 and 1848 he was taken to England. In 1849 the father died of cholera, and though the Czar offered to make "Jimmy" and his brother imperial pages, his mother took them home to Pomfret, Conn.

In 1851 he followed his father into West Point. He lasted three years, head of his class in drawing, but was finally flunked out in mathematics and chemistry. "If silicon had been a gas," he said, "I would have been a major general." He went to Washington and demanded reinstatement from Jefferson Davis, then Secretary of War. Instead, Davis got him a job as draftsman in the Coast Survey. One year of that (it had been preceded by a few months in a Baltimore locomotive works), and he rebelled, and forced his family to send him to Paris to study art. He never saw America again.

For years he gravitated between Paris and London, until London (Chelsea) became his regular abode. In 1892 he returned to Paris, but it was in London he died. Whistler as an artist—as etcher and painter, as the daring painter of "arrangements, nocturnes, harmonies, and symphonies," as one rejected by the Academy and then made president of the Royal Society of Artists and Officer of the Legion of Honor, as the teacher of the short-lived Académie Carmen, as the apostle of Japanese art and the interior decorator who created the "Peacock Room"—does not concern us here. As a writer, Whistler was the product of his own truculent nature. All his writing was an outgrowth of his private wars—with Ruskin, with Du Maurier (who caricatured him as "Joe Sibley" in *Trilby*), with Wilde, with Eden, with many others. The "Butterfly" (for such he made his signature) was a wasp at heart; yet half his quarrelsomeness was pose, part of his romantic self-dramatization, which extended from libel suits to duels.

JAMES McNEILL WHISTLER

As a young disciple of Murger in Paris, Whistler went the whole way, from wide-brimmed hats to models as mistresses. Two of these women he lived with for a decade or more each. Finally, in 1888, at fifty-four, he married Beatrix (Philip) Godwin, widow of an architect. She died in 1896, of cancer. Whistler had had a weak heart from childhood, and never really recovered from the strain of her illness and death; he visited Africa and Corsica in a vain search for health, but in 1902 returned to London to die. He left no legitimate children, but had at least one illegitimate child who grew up.

Whistler, with Wilde, was the stock wit of his age—the person to whom all *bons mots* were ascribed, as they are today to Dorothy Parker or George S. Kaufman. Therefore how many of the epigrams attached to his name were really his, no one knows. But that he had a quick, mordant wit is liberally attested by his major work, the collection of previously published essays retitled *The Gentle Art of Making Enemies*. As Royal Cortissoz says, "he adopted originality as a career," in his writing no less than in his graphic art.

Principal Works: Whistler vs. Ruskin, 1888; Art and Art Critics, 1888; Ten O'Clock Lectures, 1888 (combined as The Gentle Art of Making Enemies, 1890); Eden vs. Whistler: The Butterfly and the Baronet, 1899; Wilde vs. Whistler, 1906.

About: Bell, N. R. E. James McNeill Whistler; Bowdoin, W. G. James McNeill Whistler: The Man and His Work; Duret, T. Histoire de Whistler; Eddy, A. J. Recollections and Impressions of James McNeill Whistler; Laver, J. Whistler; McFall, H. Whistler; Menpes, M. Whistler As I Knew Him; Pennell, E. R. Whistler, the Friend; Pennell, E. R. & J. The Life of James McNeill Whistler; The Whistler Journal; Seitz, D. C. Whistler Stories; Writings by and About James Abbott McNeill Whistler; Way, T. R. Memories of James McNeill Whistler; American Magazine of Art May and June, 1934; Atlantic Monthly December 1903, April 1908; Critic February 1906; Gazette des Beaux-Arts May-September 1905; McClure's Magazine September 1896; Munsey's Magazine October 1906; North American Review September 1903; London Times July 18, 1903.

WHITAKER, ALEXANDER (1585-March 1616/17), Anglican clergyman, son of Whitaker, master of St. John's College and Regius professor of divinity at the University of Cambridge, and maternal grandson of Nicholas Culverwell, was born in Cambridge, England. Young Whitaker was educated at Cambridge, was graduated in 1608, took orders in the Church of England, and was rector of a parish in the North of England for several years.

He emigrated to America in 1611, settling in Henrico County, Virginia, and in a year had built one church, laid the foundations of another, and "impaled a fine parsonage with a hundred acres of land, calling it Rock Hill." Here he officiated as parish priest and missionary to the Indians, becoming a man of influence in the colony; and his career, terminated six years after his arrival in America by drowning, was one of great usefulness and energy. His most famous conversion among the Indians was that of Pocahontas, whom he baptized before her marriage to John Rolfe.

His sermon, *Good News From Virginia*, was one of the first works written in the colony of Virginia, and was published by the London Company. It contained a description of the colony, urged conversion of the Indians, and set forth the problems confronting the pioneers of a new country. This sermon and two letters are the only works of his now extant. In one of the letters Whitaker expresses his surprise that more of the English clergy did not engage in missionary work.

Whitaker lived in Rock Hill until his death, earning the love and admiration of his fellow colonists by his good works, and leaving a sympathetic picture of the beginnings of a new nation.

PRINCIPAL WORK: Good News From Virginia, 1613.

ABOUT: Anderson, J. S. M. The History of the Church of England in the Colonies; Bruce, P. A. Economic History of Virginia in the Seventeenth Century; Meade, W. Old Churches, Ministers, and Families in Virginia; Stith, W. The History of the First Discovery and Settlement of Virginia; Southern Literary Messenger June 1839; William and Mary Quarterly July 1936.

WHITCHER, FRANCES MIRIAM (BERRY) (November 1, 1814-January 4, 1852), humorist, was born in Whitesboro, N.Y., the daughter of Lewis and Elizabeth (Wills) Berry. She was educated in the local schools where her talent for caricature and humorous verse made her something of a neighborhood celebrity. When a series of humorous sketches, "The Widow Spriggins," written for a Whitesboro literary club was accepted by a Rome, N.Y. newspaper, Frances was encouraged to serious literary efforts.

Her best known work, "The Widow Bedott's Table-Talk," first appeared in Joseph C. Neal's *Saturday Gazette and Lady's Literary Museum* in 1846 under the pseudonym "Frank." The sketches proved so popular that she was invited to contribute to *Godey's Lady's Book* and other periodicals. In January 1847 she was married to the Reverend B. W. Whitcher, an Episcopal clergyman, and a few months later the couple removed to his parish in Elmira, N.Y. It was here that she achieved her greatest success as a writer, but her barbed wit and sense of the ridiculous made her unpopular with her husband's parishioners, who suspected that some of Mrs. Whitcher's odd characters were drawn from life. She returned to her native town in 1850 and there continued her literary career until her death.

Besides her parodies, Mrs. Whitcher wrote a number of hymns and devotional poems that appeared in *Neal's Gazette* and the *Gospel Messenger*. After her death her prose works were collected in *The Widow Bedott Papers* and *Widow Spriggins, Mary Elmer, and Other Sketches.* In 1879 a play adapted from her work, called *Widow Bedott: or, A Hunt for a Husband,* by D. R. Locke, was successfully staged. By her ruthless parodies of the absurdities of village life, Mrs. Whitcher earned for herself a secure if minor place among native humorists.

PRINCIPAL WORKS: The Widow Bedott Papers, 1856; Widow Spriggins, Mary Elmer, and Other Sketches, 1867.

ABOUT: Whitcher, F. M. B. The Widow Bedott Papers (see Introduction by A. B. Neal); Widow Spriggins, Mary Elmer, and Other Sketches (see Memoir by Mrs. M. L. Ward Whitcher); Godey's Lady's Book July, August 1853; Gospel Messenger January 9, 1852.

WHITE, ANDREW DICKSON (November 7, 1832-November 4, 1918), educator, historian, and diplomat, was born at Homer, N.Y., the elder son of Horace White, who became a wealthy Syracuse banker, and Clara (Dickson) White. He was sent to a parish school (Episcopalian), and after a year at Geneva (now Hobart) College, he entered the class of '53 at Yale, where he acquired a strong literary bent and became an intimate friend of Daniel Coit Gilman, who afterward became an eminent college president and with whom White was soon to set sail for Europe. After a semester's study at Paris, with excellent teachers, a

Collection of Frederick H. Meserve
ANDREW D. WHITE

year's service as attaché with the American legation at St. Petersbourg; and further study at Berlin, he returned to Yale. At the end of a year's graduate work he became, at the age of twenty-five, professor of history at the University of Michigan.

Like President Henry Philip Tappan, White longed to incorporate into the American colleges some of the intellectual breadth and freedom of the continental universities, and as early as 1862 he solicited the aid of Gerrit Smith, philanthropist, reformer, and liberal, in the founding of a university that would be ". . . an asylum for *Science*," promote "a new Literature—not graceful but earnest . . ," and become a "nucleus around which liberal-minded men . . . could cluster." Receiving no sanguine response from Smith, he went abroad for his health.

With his election to the state senate in 1864 and his chairmanship of the committee on education he was guardian of the Morrill Act (1862), federal endowment for education, whereby New York received nearly a million acres of land. He shortly secured the moral and financial cooperation of the wealthy Senator Ezra Cornell and at the time of its first enrollment, in 1865, Cornell University was considerably more than a promising experiment. White was its president until 1885, devoting less of his time to disciplinary and administrative functions than to the planning and testing of new educational approaches and to that which he loved best—teaching.

Following Ezra Cornell's financial ruin in the panic of 1873, the University became virtually "land poor." Meanwhile, in the course of a few respites, White had been sent to Santo Domingo on a special commission; had observed educational conditions in the West; and in the late 'seventies was appointed minister to Germany. Returning in 1881, he found the financial prospects of the college considerably brighter. In 1884 he aided in the founding of the American Historical Association and was its first president. His first wife, Mary (Outwater) White, whom he had married in 1857, died in 1887; three years later he was married to Helen Magill, daughter of the president of Swarthmore. He was minister to Russia (1892-94); and during his second ambassadorship to Germany he aided in the establishing of the international commissions of inquiry at the Hague. White advised Andrew Carnegie in the erection of the Palace of Justice at the Hague, and in the founding of the Carnegie Institution of Washington.

White's published writings include: *The Warfare of Science,* a response to the charge that the new non-sectarian Cornell was a "godless" college, afterward expanded into two volumes of *History of the Warfare of Science With Theology in Christendom*; *Fiat Money in France,* a new version of his earlier *Paper-Money Inflation in France,* which had been the outgrowth of a series of lectures on the French Revolution; *The Autobiography of Andrew Dickson White*; and *Seven Great Statesmen, in the Warfare of Humanity With Unreason,* reflections upon modern diplomatic history and the brutalities of slavery, witch persecution, and similar evils.

White was a slender, dark-haired man; generous, reservedly buoyant, and meticulous in his dress. The best of his energies were directed toward the moulding of a culturally liberal university, and his writings, with slight exception, were only incidental to this larger purpose.

Principal Works: Outlines of a Course of Lectures on History, 1861; The Warfare of Science, 1876; Paper-Money Inflation in France, 1876; European Schools of History and Politics, 1887; My Reminiscences of Ezra Cornell, 1890; History of the Warfare of Science With Theology in Christendom, 1896; Autobiography of Andrew Dickson White, 1905; Seven Great Statesmen in the Warfare of Humanity With Unreason, 1910; Fiat Money in France, 1933 (pub. in Canada in 1896).

About: Hewett, W. T. Cornell University; White, A. D. Autobiography of Andrew Dickson White; American Historical Association Report 1918.

WHITE, HORACE (August 10, 1834-September 16, 1916), journalist, economist, and miscellaneous writer, was born in Colebrook, N.H., the son of Horace and Eliza (Moore) White. The family moved to Beloit, Wis., where Horace attended Beloit College, class of 1853. He removed to Chicago where he became city editor of the *Evening Journal*; in 1855 he was made Chicago agent of the New York Associated Press. After an interval as assistant secretary of the National Kansas Commission, he returned to Chicago and joined the *Chicago Tribune,* reporting the Lincoln-Douglas debates and becoming Washington correspondent for his paper during the Civil War. At the close of the conflict White became editor-in-chief of the *Tribune,* a position which he held until 1874.

In 1881 he was one of the editors of the *Evening Post* and the *Nation*; two years later was in complete charge of the financial and economic policies of both papers. In 1899 he succeeded Edwin L. Godkin as editor-in-chief of the *Evening Post,* continuing in that capacity until his retirement in 1903. White was married to Martha Root, who died in 1873; his second wife was Amelia Jane McDougall, whom he married in 1875.

White's published works include a translation from the Greek, *The Roman History of Appian of Alexandria,* and *The Life of Lyman Trumbull,* besides the works on finance for which he was more famous. Forty years after its first appearance, his *Money and Banking* was still a standard text-book in schools and colleges. The reticence and distinction implicit in White's own character were reflected in the policies of the *Evening Post,* which under his leadership attained an eminent position among American journals.

Principal Works: Money and Banking: Illustrated by American History, 1895; The Roman History of Appian of Alexandria, 1899; The Life of Lyman Trumbull, 1913.

About: Memoirs of Henry Villard; Nevins, A. The Evening Post: A Century of Journalism; Villard, O. G. John Brown; New York Evening Post November 16, 1901; New York Evening Post September 18, 1916.

WHITE, RICHARD GRANT (May 23, 1821-April 8, 1885), critic, essayist, and "man of letters," was born in New York City, the eldest son of Richard Mansfield White and Ann Eliza (Tousey) White. The White family was both prosperous and prominent, tracing its descent back through six generations of New England Tories to John White, one of the founders of Hartford and of Cambridge.

Educated as a scholar and a gentleman, Richard graduated from the University of the City of New York at the age of eighteen. During his student years he showed no interest in a literary career, devoting himself passionately to music. His parents, however, opposed his musical ambition, and out of respect for their wishes he began the study of medicine on his graduation in 1839, turning later to law. He was admitted to the bar in 1845, but never practiced. For several years he made excursions into the field of journalism; and when his father's fortune collapsed, leaving him with the problem of supporting a family, it was in this field he earned his living. As music critic, he joined the staff of the *Morning Courier and New York Enquirer,* rapidly achieving a distinguished reputation. He continued to write music, art, and literary criticism for the *Courier,* as well as occasional political articles, until 1859.

In 1850 he was married to Alexina Black Mease, a woman of unusual intelligence and culture. They had two sons, Richard Mansfield, and Stanford, who became famous as an architect. Although White shunned the commonplace literary and journalistic society of New York, several of the most prominent writers of the day were his close friends, among them James Russell Lowell; and his home was known as a musical and literary center.

During and after the Civil War, he accepted several public posts, the most im-

Collection of Frederick H. Meserve

RICHARD GRANT WHITE

portant as head of the Marine Revenue Bureau of the New York Custom House, a position which he held from 1861 to 1878. With an astonishing diversity of interests, he continued always to write, contributing to *Putnam's Magazine*, the *Galaxy*, and the *Atlantic Monthly*. These magazine articles, published in book form, gained him wide recognition as a scholar of English usage, and as an acute and often brilliant student of Shakespeare. From 1857 to 1866 he published his own edition of Shakespeare in twelve volumes, a scholarly text subsequently republished as the *Riverside Shakespeare*. In 1884, he wrote his first novel, *The Fate of Mansfield Humphreys*, a comic but unsuccessful literary afterthought. The next year, at the age of sixty-three, he died after a long illness at his home in New York.

Although White's critical work exhibited the prejudices of his New England Brahmin stock, during his lifetime he exerted a good deal of influence in the field of letters. Writing of him in the New York *Tribune*, a contemporary said, he "wields an intellectual battleaxe between his thumb and forefinger that will cleave its way in time through any *Front de Boeuf* castle of stupidity that he may chance to fall in with."

PRINCIPAL WORKS: *Critical Essays*—Handbook of Christian Art, 1853; Shakespeare's Scholar, 1854; The Authorship of the Three Parts of Henry VI, 1859; Memoirs of the Life of Shakespeare, 1865; Words and Their Uses, 1870; Everyday English, 1880; Studies in Shakespeare, 1886. *Miscellaneous*—Appeal From the Sentence of the Bishop of New York, 1845; The New Gospel of Peace (4 vols.) 1863-66; The Adventures of Sir Lyon Bouse, Bart., in America During the Civil War, 1867; England Without and Within, 1881. *Edited*—The Works of William Shakespeare (12 vols.) 1857-66; Poetry: Lyrical, Narrative, and Satirical of the Civil War, 1866. *Novels*—The Fate of Mansfield Humphreys, 1884.

ABOUT: Atlantic Monthly February 1882; Atlantic Monthly March 1886; New York University Quarterly, May 1881.

WHITE, WILLIAM (April 4, 1748-July 17, 1836), first Protestant Episcopal bishop of the diocese of Pennsylvania, was born in Philadelphia, the son of Col. Thomas White and his second wife Esther (Hewlings) White. He attended a dame-school until he was seven, and then entered a Latin school of the College and Academy of Philadelphia, the embryo of the University of Pennsylvania. He was graduated in 1765, the year of the passage of the Stamp Act, and in the months that followed young White appears to have shared the sentiments of the eminent Dr. William Smith, provost of the College, who regarded this levy by Parliament as a "badge of disgrace."

One of White's childhood playmates afterward declared that he had been "born a Bishop . . . he would tie his . . . apron 'round his neck for a gown . . . and he always preached . . . about being good." Of more importance, however, is the fact that White went to London, was ordained deacon in December 1770, and priest a year and a half later. Before returning White dined several times with Samuel Johnson, who, he said "told me that had he been prime minister during the then recent controversy concerning the Stamp Act, he would have sent a ship of war and levelled one of our principal cities with the ground." And during his visit with Goldsmith he experienced a "painful sensation that a man of such a genius should write for bread." He sailed from London on July 22, 1772, and, back again in Philadelphia, was made assistant minister at the Christ Church; he later became rector and retained this post until the time of his death.

What has since been known as the Protestant Episcopal Church in the United States of America emerged from White's plan for the organization, at the close of the Revolutionary War, of all the Church of England parishes in Philadelphia; White was made bishop of the diocese and in September 1786 he went to England to receive Episcopal consecration. White's subsequent religious activities were confined largely to Philadelphia and vicinity, but he succeeded in laying, there, the ground-work for effective church life. He avoided public controversies, and he was, for a long time, chaplain of Congress. He was married in 1773 to Mary Harrison, by whom he had eight children.

In addition to his early controversial pamphlet, *The Case of the Episcopal Churches in the United States Considered*, containing a kind of reorganization outline, White published the rather poorly written but factually valuable *Memoirs of the Protestant Episcopal Church* and *Commentaries Suitable to the Occasions of Ordinations*, a handbook for young clergymen; and he aided in the American revision of the Book of Common Prayer. Either because of the expense involved or the polemical nature of the book itself, his ambitious three-volume refutation of Robert Barclay's *Apology* for the Quakers remained unpublished. White's works, too often submerged in a style that was tortuous and untrimmed, were only subordinate to his very substantial achievements in the early growth of the Protestant Episcopal Church.

Principal Works: The Case of the Episcopal Churches in the United States Considered, 1782; Lectures on the Catechism, 1813; Comparative Views of the Controversy Between the Calvinists and the Arminians, 1817; Memoirs of the Protestant Episcopal Church in the United States of America, 1820; Commentaries Suited to the Occasions of Ordinations, 1833.

About: Perry, W. S. History of the American Episcopal Church; Stowe, W. H. The Life and Letters of Bishop William White; Ward, J. H. The Life and Times of Bishop White; Poulson's American Daily Advertiser (Philadelphia) July 18, 1836.

WHITMAN, ALBERY ALLSON (May 30, 1851-June 29, 1901), poet and clergyman, called the most outstanding poet of the African race between Phillis Wheatley and Paul Laurence Dunbar, was born in slavery near Mumfordsville, Hart County, Ky. He was emancipated with his father in 1863, his mother having previously died, and for a time he worked as an itinerant laborer and taught school, although his own schooling was meagre. He was finally enabled to enter Wilberforce University as a student, and although he did not graduate he was subsequently connected with it for a number of years in an official capacity. As a pastor and an elder of the African Methodist Episcopal Church, he traveled widely in the South and Southwest. He was more Caucasian than Negro in features. He died at Atlanta, Ga.

Whitman's poetry, fluent but of the imitative type, showed wide familiarity with the best English and American poets. His best known poem, *The Rape of Florida,* later published as *Twasinta's Seminoles,* suggested the influence of Byron and Tennyson; his *Leelah Misled* was reminiscent of Byron, and his *Not a Man and Yet a Man,* a lengthy poem of some two hundred and fifty pages, was of varying metrical derivation. His themes included melodramatic romances and narratives of Negro and Indian. Some of his poetry was in dialect.

Principal Works: Essays on the Ten Plagues and Miscellaneous Poems, 18—; Leelah Misled, 1873; Not a Man and Yet a Man, 1877; The Rape of Florida, 1884; An Idyl of the South, 1901.

About: Loggins, V. The Negro Author: His Development in America; Simmons, W. J. Men of Mark; Whitman, A. A. The Rape of Florida (see Dedicatory Address).

WHITMAN, SARAH HELEN (POWER) (January 19, 1803-June 27, 1878), poet and one-time *fiancée* of Edgar Allan Poe, was born in Providence, R.I., the daughter of Nicholas and Anna (Marsh) Power, and received her education in private schools in that city. Moving to Boston on her marriage in 1828 to John Winslow Whitman, an attorney, she returned to Providence after his death in 1833 and devoted herself to literature. She contributed articles on spiritualism and literary themes to numerous magazines and became well known as a writer of verse.

In 1848 Mrs. Whitman met and soon became engaged to Edgar Allan Poe, and although the engagement was broken, in a confused series of events, their friendship continued until his death. Some of her verses in *Poems* were inspired by their friendship and at times seem slightly too reminiscent of his own style. In 1860 her defense of Poe in *Edgar Poe and His Critics* appeared, and she gave generous help to his many biographers during her lifetime.

Mrs. Whitman, a small, slim attractive brunette, was a favorite in society and was greatly admired for her conversational powers. Although considering herself a delicate person, she lived to the ripe age of seventy-five. After the death of her sister, she lived at the home of a friend in Providence until her death.

Her books of verse, among them *Hours of Life,* are the work of a poet of an authentic if slight talent, and the poems are melodious and tender although not of great originality. Her defense of Poe and *The Last Letters of Edgar Allan Poe* are of more interest than her other work, giving a picture of that misunderstood genius from a friend's point of view.

Principal Works: Hours of Life and Other Poems, 1853; Edgar Poe and His Critics, 1860; Poems, 1879; The Last Letters of Edgar Allan Poe to Sarah Helen Whitman, 1909.

About: Ticknor, C. Poe's Helen; Harrison, J. A. & Dailey, C. F. (eds.). The Last Letters of Edgar Allan Poe to Sarah Helen Whitman; Providence Daily Journal July 1, 1878.

WHITMAN, WALT (May 31, 1819-March 26, 1892), poet, was born in Huntington, Long Island, N.Y., the second of the nine children of Walter Whitman, farmer and carpenter, a Hicksite Quaker, and Louisa (Van Velsor) Whitman, of mixed Holland and Welsh descent. Neither parent had any intellectual interests, and the oldest and youngest of their children were imbeciles. Like their second child, the Whitmans were large, slow, and placid. Yet in their stolidity there was a pronounced streak of hyper-sensitivity which in Walt (he called himself so from 1855 to distinguish himself from his father) amounted to genuine neuroticism.

Whitman had very little schooling, and that little in the public schools of Brooklyn, where the family moved in 1823. There he was remembered chiefly for his amiability, clumsiness, and slovenliness. His summers he spent on Long Island, then rural instead of suburban. It was a good preparation for a poet who was to be acutely aware of terrestrial and marine nature, and yet also to be essentially urban. It came to a close too soon, when at eleven the child became an office boy, first to a lawyer who let him read Scott and similar authors, then to a doctor who kept him too busy to read. The next year he was a printer's devil on the *Long Island Patriot,* and next on the *Long Island Star.* From 1833 to 1841 he alternated between printing and country school teaching, moving frequently but not far; in 1838 and 1839 he edited the *Long Islander,* in his native town. Very conventional verses began to appear in this and other newspapers. Now for the first time he began to read seriously in the classics of literature and philosophy. Now also he became interested in politics, and gained some local reputation as a stump speaker for the Democratic Party—and Tammany!

The years 1841 to 1848 were Whitman's period of inner growth. Outwardly he was both conformist and reformer. He turned up for brief periods on the staffs of at least ten New York papers and magazines, usually being discharged for inattention to his duties or else resigning in a huff—for with the Dutch amiability he also had the Dutch stubbornness and hot temper. The most important of these jobs were with the *Democratic Review* and the *Brooklyn Eagle.* For the latter he wrote, not verse, but editorials and stories, including the "temperance novel," *Franklin Evans,* which reads like a burlesque of itself. Aside from reforms of all nature, his chief journalistic interest was in the theatre, of which he was a passionate addict.

In 1848 came that curious journey to New Orleans, exaggerated in his later memories as having had great duration, though actually it lasted just three months. This is the "mystery" which is supposed to lurk in Walt Whitman's life; it is supposed to involve some hidden romance, and he himself embroidered it in later years until he confided that here lived the anonymous mother of his six apocryphal children! As a matter of cold fact, he heard in the lobby of a New York theatre of an opening on the New Orleans *Crescent,* applied for and obtained the job, went with his brother Jeff to New Orleans, worked a month, quarreled

From a daguerreotype

WALT WHITMAN
1855

with the editor, and, still with his brother, came home. It is most improbable that Whitman ever fathered any children, anywhere (though myths abound, from twins in Camden to a character actor of the silent "movies," who called himself Walt Whitman and certainly looked like his putative father); and it is unlikely that Whitman ever had a deep emotional interest in any human being except a few younger men (chiefly Peter Doyle, of Washington), and, above all, himself.

In any event, he came back to New York and to his period of dandyism, when he sported a cane, was fussy about the cut of his clothes, and haunted the theatres. This too was his Bohemian era, when he was one of the habitués of Pfaff's beer cellar. Early in the 'fifties he may have been influenced by the epilogue to George Sand's novel, *The Countess of Rudolstadt,* in which the figure of a great humanitarian poet of the common people is delineated. He worked on more papers, editing the Brooklyn *Times* from 1856 or 1857 to 1859; he may, before this, have run a book store and a printing establishment, and he certainly helped his father (who was now partially paralyzed) from 1851 to 1854, when the elder Whitman was putting up rows of cheap wooden dwellings. He had his mind set on becoming an orator: he practiced declamation and prepared lectures, few of which were ever delivered. He became a convert to phrenology, then fashionable and accredited, and believed devoutly its findings in his own case.

In the midst of this period, his most significant until the Civil War, came the central date of Walt Whitman's life, 1855. It was signalized by the appearance of the first slim edition, printed at his own expense, of *Leaves of Grass*—not as we know it now, however, for the next edition, in 1856, contained many more poems. Eleven editions appeared during his lifetime, each longer than the last. Here for the first time Whitman as we know him appears—the long, rolling, irregularly accented line, the personal refrains, the preoccupation with love and death, the celebration of self, the poet as prophet. Whitman had expected condemnation, and was prepared to defend his "naked subject-matter," but what he received in 1855 was silence. Never in all his career was he widely known to or popular with the "plain man," the democrat, the "Americano," whose voice he announced himself to be; it was always the leaders of thought and culture who hailed Whitman. Emerson was the first of these, much to his discomfiture; for his words in a private letter, "I greet you at the beginning of a great career," were quoted on the cover of the second edition, which contained poems that caused the ascetic Emerson to shrivel with dismay. This second edition loosed the whirlwind, and Whitman was viciously attacked for many years by the prurient-minded and the bigots. He had indeed given mid-nineteenth-century America a terrific dose to swallow, and that he felt this instinctively is evidenced by the gradual mellowing and "spiritualizing" of his later works, their increasing concern with a mystical democracy and a lofty religious philosophy.

The Civil War marked the next break in Whitman's life, which more than that of most men is divisible into distinct periods. He had been fired from the Brooklyn *Eagle*, back in 1848, because of an anti-slavery editorial; but after his New Orleans trip he was notably milder on the subject. Nevertheless, the Union had to him an almost mystic significance, an outgrowth of his feeling for America as the chosen land of the future; and he was one of Lincoln's earliest admirers, though there is no proof that the two men ever met. In 1862 Whitman's brother George, a Union soldier, was wounded, and Walt went to Virginia to care for him. He stayed in Washington for nine years. During the war he was an indefatigable visitor at the hospitals for wounded soldiers, both Northern and Southern; he read to them, helped to nurse them, raised funds to buy them comforts—all this purely on his own, with no official backing. His own way he earned by copying documents for the Department of the Interior. In 1865 his superior in office suddenly realized that this clerk was the author of the notorious *Leaves of Grass* and discharged him. He soon secured another clerkship in the Attorney General's office, but he was a good enough publicity man to realize the value of this very real persecution, and he made the most of it. His young disciple, John Burroughs, brought out his *Notes on Walt Whitman,* a hot defense of the "poet and person"; it was not until Burroughs' death that it was learned that Whitman himself wrote most of the book! (Similarly, in later years, he represented himself, with only partial accuracy, as poor, sick, and friendless, and started a flood of friendly articles and book orders from his English admirers.)

In 1873 Whitman suffered a light stroke of paralysis. It was a warning of inherited disease. He was obliged to leave Washington, and he came to Camden, N.J., to live with the same brother to whom he had gone in Virginia. Soon after his arrival his beloved mother died. The shock in his previously enfeebled condition combined to make him a permanent invalid. Nevertheless, until 1886 he was not confined to his room, as he was later; he traveled to Colorado, to Boston, and to Canada. He took to dressing in workmen's garb—half a pose, half a genuine instinct. In 1884 he was able to buy the little house at 328 Mickle Street, Camden, in which he died and which is preserved as a Whitman museum. Here there came to him visitors from all over America, from England, and the Continent, whose names read like a roster of the most distinguished writers of the time. He had bitter enemies, but they were overwhelmed by his adoring friends—chief among them two young men, T. B. Harned and Horace Traubel, and a woman, Mrs. Anne Gilchrist, who came from England and lived for two years in Philadelphia to be near him. He was now truly "the good gray poet," paralyzed but perhaps happier than at any other time of his life. Even his egocentricity had become lovable, and he had long outgrown the image of himself as "lusty, brawling, hirsute": now he was a reverend old man with a long white beard who purred at the idolatry of his disciples.

And yet did Whitman ever attain his own ambition? He wanted to be known, to have influence, as a seer, as a prophet of democracy. Instead he was rejected by the common people; it was the variants—the revolutionaries and the poets—who made him their standard-bearer. He was the father of free verse, with his rhythmic chants which at their best have the magnificent beat of the ocean, and at their worst read like a mail-order house catalogue interspersed with misused foreign phrases. He called himself "a child, very old," and that is what he was, with all the child's lack of taste and sentimental egotism—but a child of genius. "The most original and passionate American poet," Mark Van Doren has called him. Deep under all the "cosmic" shouts is the voice of a lonely man who felt his lack of kinship with humanity, and so all the more strenuously proclaimed his identity of feeling with it. It may be that this strain of neuroticism is the saving leaven which (more than any spurious "mysteries," more than any accidental reading or chance encounters) made of the dull, orthodox editorial writer the great poet that Walt Whitman finally became.

PRINCIPAL WORKS: *Poetry*—Leaves of Grass, 1855, 1856, 1860-61, etc.; Drum Taps, 1865; Democratic Vistas, 1871; Passage to India, 1871; As a Strong Bird on Pinions Free and Other Poems, 1872; Two Rivulets, 1876; November Boughs, 1888; Good-bye, My Fancy, 1891; Uncollected Poetry and Prose (ed. by E. Holloway) 1921. *Prose*—Specimen Days and Collect, 1882-83; Walt Whitman's Diary in Canada (ed. by W. S. Kennedy) 1904; An American Primer (ed. by Horace Traubel) 1904; Criticism: An Essay, 1913; The Letters of Anne Gilchrist and Walt Whitman (ed. by T. B. Harned) 1918; The Gathering of the Forces (ed. by C. Rogers & J. Black) 1920; Walt Whitman's Workshop (ed. by C. J. Furness) 1928; I Sit and Look Out (ed. by E. Holloway & V. Schwarz) 1932; Walt Whitman and the Civil War (ed. by C. I. Glicksberg) 1933.

ABOUT: Bailey, J. C. Walt Whitman; Barrus, C. Whitman and Burroughs; Barton, W. E. Abraham Lincoln and Walt Whitman; Bazalgette, L. Walt Whitman: L'homme et Son Oeuvre; Binns, H. B. A Life of Walt Whitman; Blodgett, H. W. Walt Whitman in England; Bucke, R. M. Walt Whitman; Burroughs, J. Notes on Walt Whitman as Poet and Person; Whitman: A Study; Carpenter, E. Days With Walt Whitman; Carpenter, G. R. Walt Whitman; Ellis, H. The New Spirit; Holloway, E. Whitman: An Interpretation in Narrative; Johnston, J. & Wallace, J. W. Visits to Walt Whitman; Long, H. Walt Whitman and the Springs of Courage; Masters, E. L. Whitman; Morris, H. S. Walt Whitman; Noyes, C. E. An Approach to Walt Whitman; O'Connor, W. D. The Good Gray Poet; Perry, B. Walt Whitman; Platt, I. H. Walt Whitman; Rogers, C. The Magnificent Idler; Shephard, E. Walt Whitman's Pose; Symonds, J. A. Walt Whitman: A Study; Thomson, J. Walt Whitman: The Man and the Poet; Traubel, H. With Walt Whitman in Camden; Triggs, O. L. Browning and Whitman; American Mercury July 1935; Atlantic June 1892, November 1903, November 1937; Bookman March 1919; New Republic May 24, 1919, May 31, 1919; Open Court July 1919; Outlook May 7, 1919; Poetry May 1919; Saturday Review of Literature July 6, 1935, May 9, 1936, May 30, 1936, March 27, 1937; Scribner's Magazine June 1919; Brooklyn Eagle March 8, 1914; New York Times March 27, 1892.

WHITNEY, ADELINE DUTTON (TRAIN) (September 15, 1824-March 20, 1906), juvenile and miscellaneous writer, was born in Watertown, Mass., the daughter of Enoch Train, a prominent Boston shipowner, and Adeline (Dutton) Train. She attended schools in Watertown and Boston, and spent one year at a boarding school in Northampton. As a student at George B. Emerson's private academy for young ladies in Boston, she became especially proficient in Latin and English composition and cultivated the deep interest in reading and writing that was never to leave her.

In 1843 she married Seth D. Whitney of Milton, Mass. Despite her four children by this marriage, she found time for writing, and in 1862 published *Boys at Chequasset,* the first of the juvenile books that were to make her name so popular among the young people of the latter nineteenth century. She continued to work until her eightieth year, and through the high moral standard of her books exercised a profound influence on her young readers. Predominant characteristics of her style were a deep belief in domesticity and woman's place in the home. Mrs. Whitney was definitely not in accord with woman's suffrage and restricted her charitable enterprises to civic causes. As a writer of juvenile books, she became prominent not only in New England but throughout America and numbered among her friends Phillips Brooks, John Greenleaf Whittier, and Lucy Larcom.

Her best known book, *Faith Gartney's Girlhood,* went into twenty editions and definitely placed Mrs. Whitney in the best-seller juvenile class of her time.

PRINCIPAL WORKS: *Fiction*—Boys at Chequasset, 1862; Faith Gartney's Girlhood, 1863; The Gayworthy's, 1865; A Summer in Leslie Goldthwaite's Life, 1866; We Girls, 1870; Real Folks, 1871; The Other Girls, 1873; Biddy's Episodes, 1904. *Verse*—Mother Goose for Grown Folks, 1860; Pansies, 1872; Holy Tides, 1886; Daffodils, 1887; White Memories, 1893.

ABOUT: Stoddard, R. H. Poets' Homes; Teele, A. K. The History of Milton, Mass.; Boston Evening Transcript March 21, 1906.

WHITNEY, WILLIAM DWIGHT (February 9, 1827-June 7, 1894), Sanskritist and college professor, was born at Northampton, Mass., the son of Josiah Dwight Whitney and Sarah (Williston) Whitney, both of rugged and distinguished New England ancestry. As a boy he loved outdoor life, and he presented to the Peabody Museum at Yale his own mounted collection of the birds of New England. He attended Northampton public schools, and was graduated valedictorian from Williams College in 1845. He began the study of medicine in October of that year, but during a convalescence from measles he occasionally thumbed through a Sanskrit grammar, by Franz Bopp, which William's brother had brought back with him from Europe. (At this time Western interest in Sanskrit was less than half a century old, and chairs of Sanskrit at Bonn and Oxford were very recent innovations.) In the summer of 1849 young Whitney took the grammar with him on a United States Geological Survey expedition into the Lake Superior region, and in the fall he began a year's study with Edward Elbridge Salisbury at Yale; there he and James Hadley, who likewise became a distinguished philologist, made amazing academic progress.

During the years 1850-53 Whitney was abroad studying in Germany, and a year after his return he was elected to what has since been called the Salisbury professorship of Sanskrit and comparative philology, which he held for forty years. At the establishment of the Sheffield Scientific School he set up and then supervised the modern language department. In 1856 he was married to Elizabeth Wooster Baldwin, daughter of Roger Sherman Baldwin, and by her had six children.

Whitney published in all about 360 titles, the most important of which might be grouped as: editings and translations from Sanskrit, including the then unpublished Atharva-Veda, a sacred and largely poetic text embodying the lore of the Atharvans and therefore belonging to a very early period in Sanskrit literature; German, French and English grammars, and his highly important *Sanskrit Grammar,* wherein by the descriptive and statistical methods he drew upon the classical and older Vedic literatures and adapted the old classifications, rules, etc., to the new framework; a number of books on the history of the study of language, including *The Life and Growth of Language* and a book of lectures delivered before the Smithsonian Institution and the Lowell Institute, *Language and the Study of Language.* Moreover he was editor-in-chief of the *Century Dictionary.*

He was a man of average build, with blue eyes, reddish hair, and a heavy beard. He was founder and first president of the American Philological Association, and received honorary degrees from various American and foreign universities. His descriptive studies in the science of language, although semi-popular, embraced the basic problems of linguistic systems. As a pure grammarian, however, he was of the very first rank, and as an independent scholar and teacher of Sanskrit he has had few peers.

Principal Works: Atharva Veda Sanhita (jt. ed. with R. Roth) (Berlin) 1856; Language and the Study of Language, 1867; Tāittirīya-Prātiçākhya, 1871; Sanskrit Grammar, 1879; The Roots, Verb-Forms, and Primary Derivatives of the Sanskrit Language (Leipzig) 1885; Max Müller and the Science of Language: A Criticism, 1892.

About: Lanman, C. R. (ed.). The Whitney Memorial Meeting; Whitney, W. D. Forty Years' Record of the Class of 1845: Williams College; American Journal of Philology October 1894; New Haven Evening Register June 7, 1894.

WHITTIER, JOHN GREENLEAF (December 17, 1807-September 7, 1892), poet, was born in Haverhill, Mass., the son of John Whittier, a Quaker farmer, and Abigail (Hussey) Whittier. His childhood was that of "the barefoot boy," whose home was in the farmhouse described in *Snow-Bound.* Tall, black-haired, with swarthy skin, he was indistinguishable from other New England farm boys of his day except that from his earliest years he had a turn for rhyme. Otherwise his aesthetic sense was blunted; he was color-blind, and slightly deaf.

What little schooling he had was in a district school held in another farmhouse. At fourteen a neighbor introduced him to Burns, whose work so entranced him that he began writing verses in Scottish dialect! He read everything he could lay his hands on—poetry, history, theology. Meanwhile he worked on the farm, so hard that at seventeen he overstrained himself, and was a semi-invalid thereafter. When he was nineteen his older sister, who herself had poetic aspirations, sent a poem of his to Henry Lloyd Garrison's Newburyport *Free Press.* It was published, and Garrison was so impressed that he made a visit to Haverhill and tried in vain to get the stubborn old farmer to agree to give his boy an education. Abijah Thayer, editor of the Haverhill *Gazette* (later the *Essex Gazette*), who also published the boy's verses, was more fortunate; he did win for Whittier a year (interrupted by teaching) at the new Haverhill Academy, in 1827.

In 1829 Whittier left home for the first time to become, through Garrison's recommendation, editor of the *American Manufacturer,* in Boston. The next year he himself became editor of Thayer's old paper. Next

Collection of Frederick H. Meserve
JOHN GREENLEAF WHITTIER
c. 1844

came the *New England Weekly Review,* in Hartford, to which he contributed stories and sketches as well as poems. His father had died now, and he was free to go where he would.

It was at this time that his distant cousin, Mary Emerson Smith, with whom he had been in love since boyhood, married another man. Whittier was all his life a mild philanderer, basking in and at the mercy of the adulation of his women admirers; and twice in later years he was involved to the point of engagement—once with Lucy Hooper, who died of tuberculosis, and once with Elizabeth Lloyd, who married somebody else, renewed her friendship with Whittier after her husband's death, and then lost the poet when she turned on their common faith, the Quaker creed. But Mary Emerson Smith was undoubtedly the real reason why Whittier remained all his life a bachelor.

In spite of his early connection with Garrison, it was not until 1833 that Whittier declared himself an abolitionist, with the fiery pamphlet, *Justice and Expediency.* Thereafter, until emancipation put an end to his cause, he never turned back. For its sake he turned politician, sat in the Massachusetts Legislature in 1835, acted as campaign manager for Charles Sumner, denounced Webster as "Ichabod" for his compromise with Clay, and ran for Congress on the Liberty ticket in 1842. For this cause he was mobbed in New Hampshire, had his office burned down in Philadelphia. Yet when a split came in the American Anti-Slavery Society, he joined the moderate faction opposed to Garrison and the extremists. He was a fighter, but he remained a non-resistant Quaker.

Meanwhile his parallel life as writer and editor continued. In 1836, after another term on the *Essex Gazette,* he sold the ancestral farm and moved to Amesbury. The next year he spent in New York, working for the anti-slavery cause, but from 1838 to 1840 he was back in editorial harness, conducting the *Pennsylvania Freeman* (formerly the *National Enquirer*), in Philadelphia. Ill health kept him quiescent for four years, except for his unsuccessful Congressional campaign; then for a year he edited the *Middlesex Standard,* in Lowell, and practically ran the *Essex Transcript,* an anti-slavery paper in Amesbury, on the side. In 1847 he became corresponding editor of the *National Era,* Washington, D.C., and in it most of his poems and articles first appeared up to 1860. All this time he was bringing out volumes of verse almost biennially, interspersed with prose, and was also continuing active in politics. He was one of the founders of the Republican party, and in 1865 he was a presidential elector.

However, after the Civil War Whittier gradually dropped the political reins, and became more and more the cloistered poet. He was at the height of his fame, probably the most quoted American author, in America, except Longfellow. In 1876, though he retained his legal residence in Amesbury, he moved permanently to the home of cousins, the Cartlands, at "Oak Knoll," Danvers. His seventieth birthday, the next year, was the occasion of a national celebration. Haverford gave him a M.A. degree, Harvard both an M.A. and an LL.D. He was bedeviled by admirers, who besieged him in his home, as they had done in Amesbury, until he never went to the door without a hat on, so that strangers might think he was about to leave the house. He complained, but he loved it. He had been a voice of prophecy, a Quaker poet of war; now he had become a sort of American Burns—if one can imagine Burns a celibate and a total abstainer.

By 1892 the old man, nearing eighty-five, was a sort of museum-piece. Longfellow, only eleven months his senior, had been dead for ten years; so had Emerson. Lowell, born twelve years after Whittier, had died the year before. Yet frail as the "Quaker poet" was, he lived abstemiously, and there was no hint of senility in him. To be sure, the black-browed half-Indian looking man had become the familiar stooped figure with its white fringe of beard. But his mind was still active, and he insisted on a summer trip to Hampton Falls, N.H. There, in September, he had a stroke, and though he longed to go back to Amesbury, or at least to Danvers, to die, it was impossible to move him. He returned to Amesbury only to be buried in its cemetery.

Whittier in his old age resented being looked upon as a gentle saint, and he was entirely justified. He was a hero, a single-minded champion of a difficult cause; but he was no angel. He was quick-tempered, he was a shrewd politician, he was a sociable man who loved to tell stories, and he was more than a bit of a miser. "Obey the Golden Rule and save your money" was his panacea for all the problems of life; and when appealed to for help he recited the benefits of poverty. He fought for the abolition of slavery, for temperance, for woman suffrage, for peace; he wrote *Songs of Labor*; but he was violently anti-union and an extreme conservative in economics.

He liked to think of himself as "the poet of human freedom." In "The Tent on the Beach" he wrote of himself as one who

Left the Muses' haunts to turn
The crank of an opinion-mill.

But the fact was that he had never done more than look in through the front door of the "Muses' haunts." He was not a poet, but a balladist. To quote Van Wyck Brooks, "his diction had no nap or freshness; it was a threadbare diction." He did not know how to stop writing, and most of his poems are far too long. He was profuse to banality. His meters were conventional, his rhymes uninspired. His mind, as Brooks says, was "sandy and thin"; he was a third-rate poet.

But when all that is said, what is left? What is left is New England. Whittier is the voice of the middle nineteenth century New England farmer and small town dweller. In loving, careful detail he speaks for the inarticulate, for the humble and the common. In vigorous, unpolished ballads he tells their traditional tales. The best of Whittier is in his most hackneyed poems—hackneyed because everybody knows them: it is in "Maud Muller," "The Barefoot Boy," "Snow-Bound" (before it grows interminably long), "Skipper Ireson's Ride," "In School-Days," even the apocryphal "Barbara Frietchie." The life he led, and the kind of people from whom he came, have vanished with homespun and linsey-woolsey. But they are a part of our national history; and so is Whittier. As time goes on, he becomes less and less the militant Quaker, less and less the impassioned foe of black slavery, and more and more the poet of the country people of Massachusetts in the days before the triumph of industrialism.

PRINCAPAL WORKS: *Poetry*—Moll Pitcher, 1832; Mogg Megone, 1836; Poems Written During the Progress of the Abolition Question in the United States, 1838; Lays of My Home and Other Poems, 1843; Voices of Freedom, 1846; Songs of Labor, 1850; The Chapel of the Hermits and Other Poems, 1853; The Panorama and Other Poems, 1856; Home Ballads, Poems, and Lyrics, 1860; In War-Time and Other Poems, 1864; Snow-Bound: A Winter Idyl, 1866; The Tent on the Beach, 1867; Among the Hills and Other Poems, 1869; Ballads of New England, 1870; Miriam and Other Poems, 1871; The Pennsylvania Pilgrim and Other Poems, 1872; Hazel-Blossoms, 1874; Mable Martin and Other Poems, 1876; Songs of Three Centuries, 1876; The Vision of Echard, 1878; The River Path, 1878; The King's Missive and Other Poems, 1881; The Bay of Seven Islands and Other Poems, 1883; Poems of Nature, 1886; St. Gregory's Guest and Recent Poems, 1886; At Sundown, 1890. *Prose*—Legends of New England in Prose and Verse, 1831; Justice and Expediency, 1833; The Stranger in Lowell, 1845; Supernaturalism in New England, 1847; Leaves From Margaret Smith's Journal (novel) 1849; Old Portraits and Modern Sketches, 1850; Literary Recreations and Miscellanics, 1851.

ABOUT: Albree, J. Whittier Correspondence; Brooks, Van W. The Flowering of New England; Carpenter, G. R. John Greenleaf Whittier; Claflin, M. B. Personal Recollections of John Greenleaf Whittier; Currier, T. F. A Bibliography of John Greenleaf Whittier; Denervaud, M. V. Whittier's Unknown Romance; Higginson, T. W. John Greenleaf Whittier; Kennedy, W. S. John Greenleaf Whittier: His Life, Genius, and Writings; Linton, W. J. Life of John Greenleaf Whittier; Mordell, A. Quaker Militant; More, P. E. Shelburne Essays; Pickard, S. T. Life and Letters of John Greenleaf Whittier, Whittier-Land; Underwood, F. H. John Greenleaf Whittier; Woodman, A. J. Reminiscences of John Greenleaf Whittier; American Literature December 1937; Book News Monthly December 1907; Dial December 16, 1907; Harper's Weekly December 21, 1907; Independent December 19, 1907; Literary World December 1877; New England Quarterly September 1933, June 1934, December 1936; North American Review December 1907; Outlook December 21, 1907, January 19, 1921.

WIGGLESWORTH, EDWARD (February 7, 1732-June 17, 1794), educator and theologian, was born in Cambridge, Mass., the son of the Rev. Edward Wigglesworth, first Hollis Professor of Divinity at Harvard, and of Rebecca (Coolidge) Wigglesworth. He was a grandson of the minister and poet, Michael Wigglesworth [*q.v.*], who came with his Puritan parents to Massachusetts in 1638. Graduated from Harvard in 1749, he remained as a resident student; fifteen years later he was made tutor, in

1765 he succeeded his father as Hollis Professor, and in 1779 he was appointed a fellow, the following year being acting president. After twenty-seven years of teaching, paralysis led to his resignation in 1791 with the title of professor emeritus.

His mathematical bent and civic interest resulted in the production of his pamphlet *Calculations on American Population,* in which he prophesied by deduction the doubling of the population in the colonies every twenty-five years and the attainment of nearly a billion and a half population by the end of the twentieth century. His two other surviving works, a Dudleian lecture on *The Authority of Tradition Considered,* in which he adduces strongly anti-Roman views, and *The Hope of Immortality,* a funeral sermon, both reflect his Puritan orthodoxy.

PRINCIPAL WORKS: Calculations on American Population, 1775; The Authority of Tradition Considered, 1778; The Hope of Immortality, 1779.

ABOUT: Paige, L. R. History of Cambridge, Mass.; Quincy, J. The History of Harvard University.

WIGGLESWORTH, MICHAEL (October 18, 1631-May 27, 1705), clergyman, physician, and poet, was born in England, probably in Yorkshire, although the exact place of his birth is unknown. His parents, Edward and Esther (?) Wigglesworth, were Puritans, emigrating to Massachusetts Bay in 1638.

During the first winter in the new land, the family suffered incredible hardships, living in a cellar with no adequate protection against the bitter weather. Young Michael started to attend school in New Haven, but his education was interrupted when his father, lame from the effects of the winter cold, needed his help at home. Too frail to be of much assistance, he was sent back to school a short time later, preparing for Harvard. He received his B.A. degree from Harvard in 1651 and remained as fellow and tutor three additional years.

As early as 1653 he began preaching, and the next year was invited to settle as minister at Malden. Always suffering poor health, he found the duties of the ministry exhausting, and with a morbid awareness of his own weaknesses, he thought often of resigning. During this period he studied and practiced medicine, becoming well-beloved as a physician as well as a preacher.

His most noted literary work, *The Day of Doom,* was published in 1662. A long poem in ballad meter, this was a terrifying piece of Puritan theology, presenting a picture of the Judgment Day in dramatic form. Eighteen hundred copies were sold within a year—which for that day indicated an extraordinary popularity. Even more extraordinary was the endurance of this popularity: the poem appeared on ballad sheets throughout colonial New England; in book form in both America and England; and no less than ten subsequent editions were published in the next century.

Still delicate, in 1663 his health was so bad that he was forced to leave his duties for a seven months' visit to Bermuda. This trip proved of little value: his health continued to be poor for the next twenty years. After 1686 his strength increased and he became more active, adding to his duties as a preacher. In 1697 he became a fellow of Harvard College, holding this position until the time of his death. According to some authorities, he was asked to consider the presidency of Harvard, an honor which he declined on the grounds of his semi-invalidism.

He was married three times. His first wife, Mary Reyner of Rowley, to whom he was married in 1655, died four years later, leaving one daughter. In 1679 he married Martha Mudge against the protest of Increase Mather and other prominent members of his congregation. The second Mrs. Wigglesworth was of lower social rank than her eminent husband, and at the time of her marriage was not even a church member; but she proved to be a good wife and left six children when she died in 1690. His third wife, Sybil (Sparhawk) Avery, a widow whom he married the next year, gave him one child and outlived him three years.

Ardently religious, conscientious, seeking always a perfect holiness, Wigglesworth wrote only "to serve God." For his writings as well as his rigorous piety, he was a figure loved and respected by his contemporaries. In spite of his feeble health and occasional fits of despondency, he was amiable, even genial. Beneath the stern theology of his *Day of Doom,* he was a kindly and humane man.

As a writer, Wigglesworth was the most widely read and the most representative poet of early New England. *The Day of Doom* has been called an "epic of New England Puritanism." Yet it remains theology rather than poetry. So zealous was his desire to edify, it is difficult to discover whether any genuine poetic gift lay stifled in the narrow Calvinistic theology. There are occasional dramatic passages emerging from the trite ballad meter, but these derive their strength of imagery from the Bible rather than from the abilities of the poet.

PRINCIPAL WORKS: *Poetry*—The Day of Doom, 1662; God's Controversy With New England, 1662; Meat out of the Eater: or, Meditations Concerning the Necessity, End, and Usefulness of Affliction Unto God's Children, 1669.

ABOUT: Dean, J. W. Memoir of Rev. Michael Wigglesworth; Sibley, J. L. Biographical Sketches of Graduates of Harvard University; New England Quarterly October 1928.

WILCOX, CARLOS (October 22, 1794-May 29, 1827), clergyman and poet, was born at Newport, N.H., the son of Ebenezer Wilcox and Thankful (Stevens) Wilcox. When he was about four his parents moved to Orwell, Vt.; several years later he injured his knee with an axe, and a violent inflammation which set in afterward was the beginning of a chronic physical ailment from which he appears never to have recovered. At Castleton (Vt.) Seminary he prepared for Middlebury College, where he excelled in languages and belles-lettres and was graduated (1813) with highest honors, delivering a valedictory "On the Reputation of Greatness in the Cause of Humanity."

At the end of a sojourn in Georgia he returned to the North, entered Andover Theological Seminary, where he completed his study in 1817, and was ordained seven years later. Meanwhile, however, he had done as much preaching as his physical strength would permit, and found himself in as sorry a financial condition as he had experienced during his undergraduate years. He was pastor of the Congregational Church in New Haven, 1823-24; and during 1824-26 he served the North Congregational Church in Hartford. He died, unmarried, in his thirty-fourth year, at Danbury, Conn.

In 1817 Wilcox had begun a 6000-line "didactic poem in the school of Young and Cowper" called *The Age of Benevolence.* It was composed of four books, and of these only the first reached publication; the response of both critic and bookseller appears to have been sufficiently bleak to discourage any further venture. This first portion, with another long poem, "Of Taste," and fourteen sermons, appeared in a volume of *Remains,* issued the year after his death. He delivered the Phi Beta Kappa poem at Yale in 1824; and a series of his articles, occasioned by a journey into the White Mountains, appeared in several contemporary journals.

Whether or not Wilcox was, as Van Wyck Brooks suggests, a victim of persecution-mania, he was undoubtedly one of those "broken reeds" [*ibid*] whose poetic promise never matured into anything more than a kind of spiritual suppleness and literary fragility.

ABOUT: Spring, G. The Discriminating Preacher; Remains of the Rev. Carlos Wilcox; Middlebury College: General Catalogue, 1800-1915.

WILCOX, ELLA (WHEELER) (November 5, 1850-October 30, 1919), poet and novelist, was born in Johnstown Center, Wis., near Madison, the daughter of Marius Hartwell Wheeler and Sarah (Pratt) Wheeler. Later in life, she was accustomed to drop three years from her age. The father was a teacher of dancing from Vermont. Both parents encouraged the child's precocity, and she was reared on such writers as "Ouida," Mrs. Mary J. Holmes, and Mrs. E. D. E. N. Southworth; proving herself an apt pupil. At nine she wrote her first "novel," at fourteen the New York *Mercury* published her first essay, and the *Waverly Magazine,* soon after, her first poem. By the time she was eighteen, what with prizes and magazine publication, she was earning a substantial income.

In 1867 her parents sent her to the University of Wisconsin, but there was nothing there she wanted or could use, and she came home at the end of the term. She kept turning out two poems a day, and the first of her forty-odd volumes (mostly of verse) appeared when she was twenty-two. For a few months she worked on a trade paper in Milwaukee. With the refusal of one publisher of *Poems of Passion* (a very treacly and innocuous passion), and its publication by another in 1876, she became nationally

Collection of Frederick H. Meserve
ELLA WHEELER WILCOX

known. She was a sensation made to order for the day; it is difficult to overestimate or to understand it.

In 1884 she married Robert Wilcox, a manufacturer of silver *objets d'art,* and moved to his home in Meriden, Conn. There their only son was born to die in a few hours. Until Mr. Wilcox's death in 1916, they lived in New York in the winter, in Short Beach, Conn., in the summer, in a house which was her pride and also an aesthetic nightmare. They traveled much, and Mrs. Wilcox, besides continuing to pour out volumes, wrote regularly for various Hearst papers and for the *Cosmopolitan Magazine.* After her husband's death she became a Spiritualist and also a Theosophist, and believed firmly that his spirit guided her minutest actions. During the World War she visited the American camps in the interest of the Red Star, the animal's Red Cross, and also lectured to the soldiers on sex problems. Exhaustion from the strain of this pilgrimage at nearly seventy brought on a fatal illness; she was taken from a nursing home in Bath, England, to Short Beach, where she died.

Mrs. Wilcox was the feminine Edgar Guest of her day. She was the high priestess of platitude, and exalted commonplaces to the stature of genius. The success of her prosy poems and her lush yet conventionally Puritanical romances is one of the mysteries of American literature.

Principal Works: *Verse*—Drops of Water, 1872; Shells, 1873; Maurine, 1876; Poems of Passion, 1876; Poems of Pleasure, 1888; Men, Women, and Emotions, 1893; Custer and Other Poems, 1895; Poems of Power, 1901; Poems of Sentiment, 1906; Pastels, 1909; Sailing Sunny Seas, 1910; Gems, 1912; Cameos, 1914; World Voices, 1916. *Prose*—Mal Moulée, 1885; Perdita and Other Stories, 1886; An Ambitious Man, 1887; A Double Life, 1890; Was It Suicide? 1891; Sweet Danger, 1892; An Erring Woman's Love, 1892; A Woman of the World, 1904; The Story of a Literary Career, 1905; The Worlds and I, 1918.

About: Wilcox, E. W. The Story of a Literary Career, The Worlds and I; American Mercury August 1934; Bookman January 1920; Cosmopolitan November 1888, August 1901; Lippincott's Monthly Magazine May 1886; Literary Digest November 22, 1919; New York Times October 31, 1919.

WILDE, RICHARD HENRY (September 24, 1789-September 10, 1847), poet, congressman, and Italian scholar, was born in Dublin, Ireland, the son of Richard and Mary (Newitt) Wilde. When Richard was eight years old, the family moved to Baltimore, where the father lost his property and died in 1802. Mrs. Wilde removed to Augusta, Ga., the next year and opened a shop in which Richard assisted her. He fitted himself for the bar and was admitted in 1809, was elected attorney-general of the state two years later, and served as a member of Congress from 1815 to 1817. He was married to Mrs. Caroline Buckle in 1819. He served four other terms in Congress but because of his opposition to President Jackson was defeated in 1834 and resigned from public affairs. Spending the next five years in Europe, he devoted himself especially to Italian literature, and in Florence brought to light some documents relating to Dante and a portrait of the poet by Giotto that had been painted on the wall of the chapel of the Bargello.

On his return to Georgia he published his work on Tasso with translations of many of his poems. He moved to New Orleans in 1843 and on the organization of the law department of the University of Louisiana became professor of constitutional law, a post which he held until his death from yellow fever. Wilde was twice reburied, the second time in the "Poet's Corner" of Augusta's City Cemetery.

Wilde left in manuscript one volume of a life of Dante, many poems, original and translated, and an epic *Hesperia,* which was published posthumously. His famous lyric, "My Life is Like the Summer Rose," became widely popular; was praised by Byron, and set to music by Sidney Lanier and Charles Thibault. His book of *Conjectures and Researches Concerning the Love, Madness and Imprisonment of Torquato Tasso* is a scholarly work, valuable chiefly for its poetical translations. Wilde was not a strikingly talented writer himself but as a translator of other poets achieved precision and elegance.

Principal Works: Conjectures and Researches Concerning the Love, Madness, and Imprisonment of Torquato Tasso, 1842; Hesperia: A Poem, 1867.

About: Jones, C. C. The Life, Literary Labors, and Neglected Grave of Richard Henry Wilde; Koch, T. W. Dante in America; Southern Literary Messenger October 1856; Daily Picayune (New Orleans) September 11, 1847.

WILKES, GEORGE (1817-September 23, 1885), journalist, was born in New York City of inconspicuous parents believed to have been named George and Helen Wilkes. After serving as a clerk in Enoch E. Camp's law office he became editor and proprietor of the *Flash, Whip* and *Subterranean,* all fleeting journals of the political and sporting underworld. In 1844, after serving a jail term for libel, he issued a pamphlet, *The Mysteries of the Tombs: A Journal of*

Thirty Days Imprisonment in the N.Y. City Prison, containing an able plea for the underdog. With Camp he founded, in 1845, the *National Police Gazette,* a blatant scandal sheet that fattened financially on its enemies' efforts to expose it.

Four years after the publication of his unauthentic *History of Oregon: Geographical and Political* (1845) Wilkes himself went west, fell heir to a fortune, and in 1853 sailed for Europe, recording his observations in *Europe in a Hurry.* In 1856 he bought the *Spirit of the Times,* with which he had been associated for several years, and remained its owner (through various changes of title) until the time of his death. For the *Spirit* he wrote some excellent eye-witness accounts of the major Civil War battles, the first of which was *The Great Battle Fought at Manassas . . . Sunday, July 21, 1861,* a chronicle of Bull Run. More than fifteen years later he wrote his last book, *Shakespeare From an American Point of View.*

Following the war, Wilkes was elected to a seat (Republican) in Congress; attempted to popularize pari-mutuel betting; and was a zealous fight promoter. He supported several charities; and although he was said to have been converted, on his death bed, from Protestantism to Catholicism, he was buried by a Baptist minister. Wilkes was a brilliant if unscrupulous editor and has been referred to as one of the three ablest writers developed by the Civil War.

Principal Works: The Mysteries of the Tombs: A Journal of Thirty Days Imprisonment in the N. Y. City Prison, 1844; History of Oregon: Geographical and Political, 1845; Europe in a Hurry, 1852; The Great Battle Fought at Manassas . . . Sunday, July 21, 1861, 1861; Shakespeare From an American Point of View, 1877.

About: Brinley, F. Life of William T. Porter; O'Meara, J. Broderick and Gwin; Washington Historical Quarterly October 1907-January 1914; Spirit of the Times September 26, 1885; New York Times September 25, 1885.

WILLARD, EMMA (HART) (February 23, 1787-April 15, 1870), educator, was born in Berlin, Conn., the daughter of Capt. Samuel and Lydia (Hinsdale) Hart. As a small girl she was exposed to the best of children's books, and at an unusually early age she became interested in the moral, religious, and political episodes in world events. She went to the district school, to Berlin Academy, and with alternate intervals of teaching, to private schools in Hartford. At the age of twenty she became the head of the Female Academy at Middlebury, Vt., resigning at the time of her marriage, two years later, to John Willard, by whom she had one son. Her later marriage to Dr. Christopher Yates was exceedingly unhappy and lasted less than a year.

Mrs. Willard had no patience with the educational tradition which placed all its higher academic facilities within the reach of men and denied the same to women. In 1814 financial reverses obliged her to turn her home into a school for young ladies, the Middlebury Female Seminary, and she replaced the curricula of the aristocratic boarding-school—harpsichord-playing, wax-modeling, embroidery, etc.—with mathematics, philosophy, etc. She prepared *An Address to the Public: Particularly to the Members of the Legislature of New York, Proposing a Plan for Improving Female Education;* sent it to Gov. DeWitt Clinton of New York in 1818; and published and presented it to the legislature in 1819. But except for a feeble expression of sympathy, the sentiments it aroused were largely ridicule and uncouth reproach. Nevertheless she set up an academy at Waterford, N.Y., for which the legislature granted a charter (1819), but appropriated no funds. The citizens of Troy, N.Y., made her a gift of a building, and she shortly founded Emma Willard's Troy Female Seminary (now the Emma Willard School), enrolling her first pupils in 1821, fifteen years before Mary Lyon's triumph with the signing of Mount Holyoke's charter. At first Mrs. Willard herself did all the teaching, devising new approaches and preparing geography and history textbooks which had a surprising general popularity. The school has had a remarkable history, and at Mrs. Willard's death was left in charge of her son and his wife.

In addition to her earlier educational publications she wrote: *The Fulfilment of a Promise,* a volume of poems the most familiar of which was "Rocked in the Cradle of the Deep"; and *Journal and Letters From France and Great Britain,* lavishly heralded by the *American Ladies' Magazine* but hotly flayed by the *American Quarterly Review.* Sales receipts from the *Journal,* however, made up the bulk of the fund for female education in Greece—a project in which Mrs. Willard was greatly interested.

She had a classic beauty of face, a dignity of bearing, and a kindly manner. Her poetry was unoriginal in idea and in phraseology and her prose writings were largely pedagogical expedients. But against tremendous odds of contrary public opinion and minimum resources she achieved for women an intellectual advancement which has undoubtedly altered the whole course of American life.

PRINCIPAL WORKS: An Address to the Public: Particularly to the Members of the Legislature of New York, Proposing a Plan for Improving Female Education, 1819; A System of Universal Geography, 1824; History of the United States or Republic of America, 1828; The Fulfilment of a Promise, 1831; Journal and Letters From France and Great Britain, 1833; A Treatise on the Motive Powers which Produce the Circulation of the Blood, 1846; Guide to the Temple of Time and Universal History for Schools, 1849; Astronography: or, Astronomical Geography, 1854.

ABOUT: Lord, J. The Life of Emma Willard; Lutz, A. Emma Willard: Daughter of Democracy; Woody, T. A History of Women's Education in the United States; Troy Daily Times April 16, 1870.

WILLARD, FRANCES ELIZABETH CAROLINE (September 28, 1839-February 18, 1898), reformer, was born at Churchville, N.Y., the daughter of Josiah Flint Willard and Mary Thompson (Hill) Willard, Vermont school teachers who migrated westward. In public affairs she was "Frances E. Willard," and to intimate friends, just "Frank." Her childhood was spent in Oberlin, Ohio, and on a homestead in the Wisconsin wilderness, where she lived until her eighteenth year. She loved to ride and to hunt, and had a bitter dislike for domestic duties. Her mother instructed her at home, encouraging her in the reading of the Bible, *Pilgrim's Progress,* Shakespeare, and travel books; her sternly religious father frowned upon Frances' fondness for novels, "Western" tales—and horses. She attended the Milwaukee Female College, and a year later entered the Northwestern Female College, from which she was graduated (1859), valedictorian of her class. About this time she experienced a kind of religious conversion, during the crisis of a fever, and afterwards became a devout Methodist.

After teaching intermittently from 1860 to 1867, she went abroad for two years, and on her return was made president of the Evanston College for Ladies, which post she maintained from 1871 to 1874. She began very shortly a series of travel lectures on her European journey, thereby schooling herself for a public speaker's career. When the temperance-crusade blast began to sweep across the country (1874), she was immediately and profoundly impressed, and kneeling on the floor of a Pittsburgh saloon, she offered her first public prayer in this new cause.

Advancing from three lesser offices, she became president, in 1879, of the National Woman's Christian Temperance Union, and twelve years later, chief executive of the world organization. Meanwhile she had taken ambitious strides in the direction of woman's suffrage, and in 1882 had aided in the organization of the Prohibition Party. But the rest of her life was devoted largely to advancing the temperance cause: providing petitions, campaign themes, emblems, and slogans gave her imagination considerable exercise and satisfied an admitted liking for politics; and the editing of official publications consumed the literary energy she had gained, in her twenties, from the books of Charlotte Brontë and Margaret Fuller. During the first few years of her intense work she had regarded the satisfaction of measurable achievement as sufficient recompense, but the lack of any independent means of support forced her, in the end, to accept a modest salary.

Collection of Frederick H. Meserve
FRANCES E. WILLARD

The bulk of her writings was in the spirit of *Woman and Temperance;* she also wrote a life of her younger sister, who died at an early age, *Nineteen Beautiful Years; Glimpses of Fifty Years; A Wheel Within a Wheel: How I Learned to Ride the Bicycle,* etc. But above all else—as pamphleteer, lecturer, and lobbyist—she was the foremost spokesman for temperance, interpreting it not as an economic but as a strongly moral issue.

PRINCIPAL WORKS: Nineteen Beautiful Years, 1864; Woman and Temperance, 1883; Glimpses of Fifty Years, 1889; A Classic Town: The Story of Evanston, 1892; A Wheel Within a Wheel: How I Learned to Ride the Bicycle, 1895; A Woman of the Century (ed. in collaboration with Mary A. Livermore) 1893.

ABOUT: Gordon, A. A. The Beautiful Life of Frances E. Willard; Strachey, R. Frances Willard: Her Life and Work; Trowbridge, L. J. Frances Willard of Evanston; New York Times February 18, 1898.

WILLIAMS, CATHARINE READ (ARNOLD) (December 31, 1787-October 11, 1872), poet and novelist, born at Providence, R.I., was descended from the Rhode Island Arnolds. Her grandfather, Oliver Arnold, was at an early age a distinguished state attorney general; her father was Alfred Arnold, a sea captain. The early death of her mother Amey R. Arnold, left her to be brought up by two maiden aunts of strict religious propensities. In 1824 she married Horatio N. Williams, a descendant of Roger Williams, residing in western New York, but the unhappy marriage was dissolved after two years and she returned to Providence. Abandoning the attempt to establish a school for the support of herself and her daughter, she was persuaded to publish by subscription a small volume of poems, many of them written between the ages of fourteen and seventeen. They were successful beyond expectation, and thereafter she devoted herself to writing. She passed some years in Brooklyn, N.Y., and Johnston, R.I., but later returned to Providence, where she died.

Her works, characterized by a vigorous and somewhat didactic style, were well received. Her one volume of poetry has been described as reflecting the "mournful spirit" of her early life. *The Neutral French,* perhaps her best work, was a historical novel based on a tour of the Canadian provinces and, in time, it was anticipatory of Longfellow's *Evangeline.* In *Biography of Revolutionary Heroes* she essayed sketches of Gen. William Barton and Capt. Stephen Olney. A satirical novel *Aristocracy,* and a story, *Fall River,* based on the sensational Avery murder case were among her other works. Five of her short stories were recently reprinted in Henrietta Palmer's *Rhode Island Tales.*

PRINCIPAL WORKS: *Biography*—Biography of Revolutionary Heroes, 1839. *Fiction and Stories*—Religion at Home, 1829; Tales: National and Revolutionary, 1830; Aristocracy: or, The Holbey Family, 1832; Fall River: An Authentic Record, 1833; The Neutral French: or, The Exiles of Nova Scotia, 1841; Annals of the Aristocracy: Being a Series of Anecdotes of Some of the Principal Families of Rhode Island, 1843, 1845. *Poetry*—Original Poems on Various Subjects, 1828.

ABOUT: Rider, S. S. Biographical Memoirs of Three Rhode Island Authors (Rhode Island Historical Tracts no. 11).

WILLIAMS, GEORGE WASHINGTON (October 16, 1849-August 4, 1891), soldier, Baptist clergyman, and Negro historian, was born in Bedford Springs, Pa., the son of Thomas Williams and Nellie (Rouse) Williams, of Welsh-Negro and German-Negro blood. He received a private and academic education; as soon as he was old enough, he enlisted in the Civil War, finally joining the staff of General N. J. Jackson. After the war, the Senate refused him a recommended appointment to the regular army. He entered Howard University, which he organized on a military plan. Graduated with the class of 1874 from the Newton Theological Institution, he was ordained a Baptist minister, entering upon pastoral duties in Boston.

His entry into journalism was initiated with his attempt to establish at Washington, D.C., a Negro journal, *The Commoner.* Later he founded the *Southwestern Review* at Cincinnati, and as "Aristides" contributed to the Cincinnati *Commercial.* Admitted to the Ohio bar, he was later appointed county auditor, served in the federal internal revenue service, was elected to the Ohio legislature, and was minister to Haiti in 1885-86. His *History of the Negro Race,* a three-volume authoritative work prepared as a result of extensive study, surveyed the place of the Negro in America between the years 1619 and 1800, and was accompanied by a philological, ethnological, cultural and historical consideration of the race in its earlier environments. It included a discussion of the status of the American Negro in relation to military service and education. He became actively interested in the problem of the Negro of the Belgian Congo, and finally entered the service of the Belgian government. While so employed he died in Blackpool, England. Williams was worthy of the highest respect for his scholarship, character, and gentlemanly qualities. A brilliant orator, he was reputed to have few equals in either race, and was invited to speak on many platforms. As a writer he was vigorous and clear-headed. He is said to have written some poetry "with grace and unction."

PRINCIPAL WORKS: History of the Negro Race in America: From 1619 to 1880, 1883; A History of the Negro Troops in the War of the Rebellion, 1888; Report Upon the Congo State and Country to the President of the Republic of the United States, n.d.; An Open Letter to . . . Leopold II, 1890.

ABOUT: Biographical Cyclopaedia and Portrait Gallery of the State of Ohio; Simmons, W. J. Men of Mark; Williams, G. W. History of the Negro Race in America (see Preface).

WILLIAMS, JOHN (April 28, 1761-October 12, 1818) ("Anthony Pasquin"), satirist, critic, and miscellaneous writer, was born in London and educated at the Merchant Taylors' School, where he started his career of defiance by the composition of an epigram directed at one of his masters. Brilliant and restless, he tried first painting and then writing, and after acting as translator for various booksellers in London, he went to Dublin, where he was connected with several journals. His denunciations of the government caused his prosecution and he fled the country. He was dramatic critic for London newspapers, where his lack of taste and tact and his envenomed pen made him most unpopular. In 1797 he instituted a suit for libel against Robert Faulder, a bookseller, and after the loss of the case came to America, where it is said he edited a newspaper in New York, the *Federalist*. He was editor of the Boston *Democrat* in 1804, but the habit of a lifetime was strong in him and he quarreled with his partners.

His whole life was a series of embroilments, quarrels, and lawsuits. He was thoroughly despised by his contemporaries and although he might have accomplished something useful with his writing, the faults of his temperament afflicted his work. The boorish, violent, and didactic qualities that kept him in a turmoil during his lifetime are an outstanding characteristic of his best-known work, his *Hamiltoniad,* written under his pseudonym. It was published in Boston in 1804 and was a vitrolic attack on the Federalists.

Principal Works: Hamiltoniad, 1804; A Life of Alexander Hamilton, 1804.

About: Ford, P. L. Bibliotheca Hamiltoniana; Gifford, W. Works; Columbian October 17, 1818; New York Advertiser October 20, 1818; New York Evening Post October 16, 1818.

WILLIAMS, ROGER (1603 or 1604-January 16 to March 15, 1683), founder of Rhode Island and theological writer, was born in London, the son of James Williams, a merchant tailor, and Alice (Honeychurch) Williams, a close relative of the powerful Pemberton family. Early in his childhood the studious boy became a protégé of the great jurist Sir Edward Coke, who employed him as a shorthand reporter and sent him to Sutton's Hospital (later the Charterhouse) in 1621 and then to Pembroke College, Cambridge. He received his B.A. degree in 1627, and remained in Cambridge for two years more, being ordained in 1629. Already, however, he was under Puritan influence and had grave doubts of the established church. He became chaplain to Sir William Masham, in Essex; the Mashams had Puritan connections and had no fault to find with Williams's theology. However, he made the mistake of falling in love with Lady Masham's niece. Chaplains were little better than servants; Williams was abruptly refused the lady's hand. After a serious illness from grief, he recovered sufficiently to marry a girl considered much more suitable, Mary Barnard (or Warnerd or Warner), a lady's maid in the household. This was in 1629; and the next year they sailed for Massachusetts.

Williams became teacher in the church at Salem. But already he was too Separatist for the Separatists. He made many enemies, and soon found it advisable to go to Plymouth, where he became assistant in the church. In 1633 he returned to Salem, as assistant to Samuel Skelton. Skelton died the next year and Williams succeeded him, in defiance of the orders of the General Court. His political democracy was as repugnant to the authorities as his religious unorthodoxy. In 1635 he was banished from the colony. An attempt to kidnap him to England was frustrated by the friendly Narragansett Indians, and he settled on a grant from them, founding Providence in 1636.

He was the Indians' friend, he learned their language, but he made no attempt to convert them. His colony was a primitive democracy, open to those of any creed, including the Quakers, whom he disliked, and a very early group of Sephardic Jews. In 1639 he was baptized and founded the first Baptist church in America; but in a few months he left it and thereafter was an Independent, or Seeker, a sort of fundamental Christian without creed. In 1644 he went back to England and returned with the first charter of "Providence Plantations in Narragansett Bay" (now Rhode Island). The colony grew and in 1646 he moved to what is now Wickford, R.I. In 1651 dissension arose. Another governor was sent from England with a charter giving him half the territory. Williams returned to England once more, but it was not until 1663 that the new charter restoring his proprietary interest was confirmed by Charles II. This charter was so admirable that it survived the Revolution and was in force until 1842. Under it Williams served three terms as president or governor of the reunited colony, and several more terms as assistant. His last years were clouded by King Philip's Wars, in which the Narragansett Indians were involved to their disaster,

ROGER WILLIAMS

and in which he, at seventy, was obliged to go out as a captain against his old Indian friends. He saw Providence and Warwick burned to the ground, and the Narragansetts enslaved. He lived until nearly eighty, still active in the colony's affairs, rather mellowed in his intransigence toward the Congregationalists. It was 1936 before the Massachusetts Legislature, in honor of Rhode Island's tercentenary, formally lifted the order of banishment against Roger Williams.

Williams was a very human person—rash, impetuous, impatient, a true democrat with a passion for liberty for others as well as for himself. His writing was all polemical tracts and pamphlets, less bitter than might have been expected from the heat of the controversy and the persecution he endured. He was a master of argument, with a genuine gift for eloquent exposition.

Principal Works: A Key Into the Language of America, 1643; The Bloudy Tenent of Persecution, 1644; Christenings Make Not Christians, 1645; The Bloudy Tenent Yet More Bloody, 1652; The Hireling Ministry None of Christs, 1652; George Fox Digg'd out of His Burrowes, 1676.

About: Carpenter, E. J. Roger Williams: A Study of the Life, Times, and Character of a Political Pioneer; Chapin, H. M. Roger Williams and the King's Colors; Dexter, H. M. As to Roger Williams; Easton, E. Roger Williams: Prophet and Pioneer; Elton, R. Life of Roger Williams; Ernst, J. The Political Thought of Roger Williams; Roger Williams: New England Firebrand; Knowles, J. D. Memoir of Roger Williams; Parrington, V. L. The Colonial Mind; Straus, O. S. Roger Williams: The Pioneer of Religious Liberty; Strickland, A. B. Roger Williams: Prophet and Pioneer of Soul Liberty; Christian Century February 12, March 4, 1936; Commonweal September 17, 1930, January 19, 1934; Forum June 1936; New York Times January 22, 26, 1936.

WILLIAMS, SAMUEL WELLS (September 22, 1812-February 16, 1884), missionary, diplomat, and Sinologue, was born in Utica, N.Y., the son of William Williams and Sophia (Wells) Williams. He was educated in the local schools and the Utica High School and attended the Rensselaer Polytechnic Institute at Troy in 1831 and 1832. In 1833 he went to China as printer for the Canton press of the American Board of Commissioners for Foreign Missions.

Williams was a natural linguist, soon learning Chinese and Portuguese and later becoming proficient enough in Japanese to translate the Gospel of Matthew into that language. In 1835 he removed to Macao, where during the next decade he was associated with Elijah Coleman Bridgman in preparing *A Chinese Chrestomathy.* In addition he published independently several works, including *Easy Lessons in Chinese,* and a Chinese *Topography,* and contributed to the *Chinese Repository.* Visiting America in 1845 he gave a series of lectures which later formed the basis of his *The Middle Kingdom.* He returned to China three years later and in 1853 and 1854 went to Japan with Commodore Perry as interpreter, serving so well in that capacity that he was appointed secretary and interpreter of the American legation to China. He held this post until 1876, among his official duties helping to negotiate the treaty of Tientsin in 1858, by which was secured the official toleration of Christianity; in 1870 he aided Sweden in securing a treaty with China.

Returning to America, he became professor of the Chinese language and literature at Yale, in 1877. It was largely an honorary office created for him and entailed no teaching. Here he devoted his time to the huge task of revising and enlarging his *Middle Kingdom* into almost encyclopedic proportions. He died in New Haven the year after its completion. Williams was married in 1847 to Sarah Walworth, who bore him five children.

Williams' work as a diplomat was of inestimable value in the opening of the East to foreigners. His books, particularly *Middle Kingdom,* interpreted and explained the Orient at a time when knowledge of that part of the world was practically nonexistent.

PRINCIPAL WORKS: A Chinese Chrestomathy in the Canton Dialect, 1841; Easy Lessons in Chinese, 1842; An English and Chinese Vocabulary in the Court Dialect, 1844; Chinese Topography, 1844; A Chinese Commercial Guide, 1844; The Middle Kingdom, 1848; A Tonic Dictionary of the Chinese Language in the Canton Dialect, 1856; A Syllabic Dictionary of the Chinese Language, 1874; Middle Kingdom, 1883.

ABOUT: Biographical Record . . . Rensselaer Polytechnic Institute; Williams, F. W. The Life and Letters of Samuel Wells Williams; Chinese Recorder May, June 1884; Missionary Herald April 1884; New York Tribune February 18, 1884.

WILLIAMSON, HUGH (December 5, 1735-May 22, 1819), statesman, scientist, and educator, was born at West Nottingham, Pa., the son of John W. Williamson and Mary (Davison) Williamson, industrious Irish emigrants. At Rev. Frances Alison's academy at New London Cross Roads and at a school in Newark he prepared for the College of Philadelphia (now the University of Pennsylvania) and was a member of the first graduating class. He studied theology, became a licensed minister, but was never ordained; and, annoyed by the discord among the Presbyterians, he accepted a post as professor of mathematics at the College of Philadelphia. He also began the study of medicine, continuing it abroad in 1764; after receiving an M.D. degree from the University of Utrecht he returned to Philadelphia to practice, but, unable to stand the nervous strain, shortly abandoned his medical career.

Just before sailing for England in 1773 Williamson witnessed the Boston Tea Party; brought first news of it to London; and before the Privy Council predicted a revolt among the colonists if the British policy was not revised. Suspecting hostility to the colonies in some of the letters of Thomas Hutchinson, Governor of Massachusetts, to members of the British cabinet, Williams got possession of a packet of them, and later gave them to Benjamin Franklin, who was, at least over a period of years, a close friend. Williamson was in Holland when Independence was declared and in the following December he set sail, with dispatches, for America; he was captured off the coast of Delaware, but escaped.

He sojourned a short time in Charleston, S.C., before setting up his West Indies mercantile trade in Edenton, N.C., where he shortly resumed his medical practice. He became surgeon-general of the state troops, and brought the small-pox death toll to an unheard-of minimum by the use of inoculation and by the introduction of bettei military diet, lodging, and the like.

He was twice elected to the House of Commons; and served in the Continental Congress from 1782 to 1785 and from 1787 until its demise. He was a curt and witty speaker and strongly advocated a stronger form of government. He sat in both the First and Second Congresses (1789-1793), and shortly afterwards moved to New York to spend his time in literary and scientific pursuits. In January 1789 he was married to Maria Apthorpe, by whom he had two sons.

One of Williamson's earliest writings (if historians are correct in ascribing it to him), was a galling epitaph "to the much esteemed memory of B— F—, the first philosopher who, contrary to any known system discovered how to maltreat his patrons without cause." *What Is Sauce for the Goose Is Also Sauce for the Gander* opens with this greeting:

Dear Children—
 I send you here a little Book
 For you to look upon
 That you may see your Pappy's Face
 When he is dead and gone.

In *The Plea of the Colonies,* an anonymous letter to Lord Mansfield in 1775, Williamson answered charges of sedition and disloyalty which had been hurled against the colonists. And in August 1787 the *American Museum* ran his "Letters of Sylvius," condemning the issue of paper money, advocating excise rather than land or poll tax, and urging the promotion of domestic manufacture. For medical and philosophical journals he wrote numerous papers, including a novel piece called "Of the Fascination of Serpents." Williamson distinguished himself, at least in a small way, as a surgeon, statesman, merchant, and educator, and his miscellaneous monographs brought him a modest recognition among general scientists.

PRINCIPAL WORKS: [What is Sauce for the Goose is Also Sauce for the Gander, 1764]; The Plea of the Colonies, 1775; Observations on the Climate in Different Parts of America, 1811; The History of North Carolina, 1812.

ABOUT: Farrand, M. The Records of the Federal Convention of 1787; Hosack, D. A Biographical Memoir of Hugh Williamson; New York Evening Post May 24 1819.

WILLIS, NATHANIEL PARKER (January 20, 1806-January 20, 1867), journalist, poet, editor, and dramatist, was born in Portland, Maine, the second child of pious New England parents. Both his father and his grandfather bore the name Nathaniel, both were journalists; but the young Willis, less pious and equipped with the charm of his mother, Hannah (Parker) Willis, became the most famous of the three.

While still an undergraduate at Yale, he acquired precocious fame as a poet, publishing his first verses in the *Boston Recorder,* a religious paper founded by his father. These versified paraphrases of Biblical themes, first printed under the pseudonym of "Roy" or "Cassius," were collected and published in book form in 1827, the year of his graduation. Making his maiden venture into journalism as editor of one of the literary annuals popular at the time, *The Legendary,* and a year later of *The Token,* he won even wider acclaim. At the age of twenty-three he established the *American Monthly Magazine* in Boston, which in spite of predicitons to the contrary, ran successfully for two and a half years. Already he had begun to build the pose of dandy and darling of society which was part of his fame, and now, as later in his life, these affectations won him a great deal of malicious criticism. Oliver Wendell Holmes described him at twenty-five as "young and already famous . . . something between a remembrance of Count D'Orsay and an anticipation of Oscar Wilde."

Quitting the narrow confines of a Puritan Boston, he went to New York, where he became associated with George Pope Morris, editor of the New York *Mirror,* an association which was to last the greater part of his life. Morris agreed to send him abroad as foreign correspondent for the *Mirror,* giving him $500 expenses and promising $10 for every weekly letter. This trip extended itself five years, young Willis penning his way across the continent and into the most brilliant drawing rooms of English society. Writing pieces for the *Mirror,* contributing to English periodicals, he met the most prominent literary and diplomatic figures of the day and put them into print.

English society adored him. Handsome in a petrified way, with delicate features and a mop of wavy light-brown hair, beautifully mannered and impeccably dressed, he was described by one English lady as "more like one of the best of our peers' sons than a rough republican." There were those who attacked him for the indiscretions of his reporting, but he succeeded nevertheless in publishing both letters and verse at the highest rate of pay. Coddled and criticized,

Collection of Frederick H. Meserve

N. P. WILLIS

he returned to America in 1836 with an English bride, Mary Stace, the daughter of General William Stace of Woolwich.

Finding that his tastes outran his finances, Willis turned now to a new field. His tragic drama, *Bianca Visconti,* was produced in New York with moderate success, and followed by *Tortesa: or, The Usurer Matched,* judged by Edgar Allan Poe as "by far the best play from the pen of an American author." Meanwhile he continued his journalistic activities. After a misunderstanding with Morris, he became for a year's period editor of a weekly magazine, *The Corsair,* and in 1840 was reconciled with Morris as editor of the *New Mirror.*

Still writing his voluminous sketches, he made two more trips to England: one in 1839, and one in 1845 after the death of his wife. During the first of these visits, he engaged Thackeray, then relatively unknown, to write for *The Corsair* at a guinea a column, "cheaper," as he wrote his associate editor, "than I ever did anything in my life." Thackeray, as well as Poe, whom he employed for the *Mirror,* was always his grateful admirer.

In 1845, he and Morris edited the *Home Journal.* Prosperous after various money troubles, he married Cornelia Grinnell, nearly twenty years his junior, and the two became leading figures in the fashionable New York society which he described for the *Journal.* As all through his career, he was tremendously popular, even while his character and work were the target of bitter critical attacks, one of the most vituperative being written by his own sister.

In 1853 he retired to his country estate, Idlewild, near Irving's home on the Hudson, where he received literary celebrities and wrote gossipy essays for the *Journal.* It was here, worn out by the burdens added to his life after Morris' death in 1864, that he died at the age of sixty-one. His funeral, held in Boston, was distinguished by the presence of such literary friends as Charles A. Dana, Holmes, Lowell, and Longfellow.

Pet of society, prince of magazinists, this Puritan dandy enjoyed a reputation which far outweighed his literary worth. With the exception of an unsuccessful novel, two plays of some merit, and several volumes of pseudo-Byronic poetry, all his books were collections of magazine chatter. Dashing and ephemeral as the fashion which it portrayed, Willis' work is the deposit of what his biographer, Professor Beers, has called the "Albuminous Age of American Literature."

PRINCIPAL WORKS: *Essays*—Pencillings by the Way, 1835; Inklings of Adventure, 1836; A l'Abri: or, The Tent Pitched, 1839; Loiterings of Travel, 1840; Dashes at Life With a Free Pencil, 1845; Complete Works of N. P. Willis, 1846; Rural Letters and Other Records of Thought at Leisure, 1849; People I Have Met, 1850; Life Here and There, 1850; Hurrygraphs, 1851; Summer Cruise in the Mediterranean, 1853; Fun Jottings: or, Laughs I Have Taken a Pen To, 1853; Health Trip to the Tropics, 1854; Ephemera, 1854; Famous Persons and Places, 1854; Outdoors at Idlewood: or, The Shaping of a Home on the Banks of the Hudson, 1855; The Rag Bag: A Collection of Ephemera, 1855; The Convalescent, 1859. *Poetry*—Sketches, 1827; Fugitive Poetry, 1829; Poem Delivered Before the Society of United Brothers at Brown University: With Other Poems, 1831; Melanie and Other Poems, 1835; Sacred Poems, 1843; Poems of Passion, 1843; The Lady Jane and Other Poems, 1844; The Poems: Sacred, Passionate, and Humorous, 1848; Poems of Early and After Years. *Plays*—Bianca Visconti: or, The Heart Overtasked, 1839; Tortest: or, The Usurer Matched, 1839. *Novels*—Paul Fane: or, Parts of a Life Else Untold, 1857.

ABOUT: Beers, H. A. Nathaniel Parker Willis; Spiller, R. E. The American in England; American Literature March 1933; Bookman September 1906.

WILSON, ALEXANDER (July 6, 1766-August 23, 1813), ornithologist, nature essayist, and poet, was born in the Seed Hills of Paisley, Renfrewshire, Scotland, and named Alexander, after his father. His mother, Mary (McNab) Wilson, died when he was a child. As one of a large working-class family, he had only the most rudimentary education. At the age of thirteen he was apprenticed to a weaver, a trade which he practiced for the next ten years.

Loving the out-of-doors, and the birds and flowers of his native countryside, he deserted his trade at twenty-three and toured Scotland as a peddler. He began writing verses, some of which, appearing anonymously, were attributed to Burns, a poet whom he greatly admired. In 1790 a small volume of his poems was published, but it was far from successful. Disappointed and embittered by a brief imprisonment for a satire which he had written, Wilson sailed for America. In 1793 he arrived in New Castle, Del., walking thence to Philadelphia.

Educating himself, he succeeded in becoming a schoolmaster, teaching for a period of ten years in small country schools of New Jersey and Pennsylvania. In 1802, teaching at Gray's Ferry near Philadelphia, he found himself a neighbor of William Bartram, the naturalist. Bartram gave him the free use of his ornithological library and encouraged him to do original work on the birds of the neighborhood. Wilson collected specimens, made extensive observations, and even learned to draw and paint. In 1807, employed as assistant editor of a new edition of Abraham Rees' *Cyclopaedia*, he succeeded in interesting Samuel F. Bradford, his employer, in financing the proposed *American Ornithology.* The first volume appeared in 1808. The same year Wilson went on a personal canvass of the country, seeking subscribers to insure further publication. He traveled by stage and on foot from Maine to Georgia, securing subscribers, correspondents, and further

From a portrait by C. W. Peale
ALEXANDER WILSON

ornithological information. It was on this trip that he met John James Audubon, who was later to supersede him in the popular mind as the greatest of American naturalists. The meeting, which took place by chance over the counter of Audubon's store in Kentucky, seems to have been hardly cordial. Audubon did not subscribe to the *Ornithology,* apparently out of jealousy, and later charged that he had given Wilson assistance which had not been acknowledged. This was to become the basis of a feud between the two, carried on chiefly by George Ord, Wilson's friend and biographer.

Seven volumes of the *Ornithology* were published by 1813. The eighth was in press when Wilson, weakened from overwork, died after an attack of dysentery. Sarah Miller, his fiancée, a sister of Daniel Miller, a Congressman from Philadelphia, erected the stone over his grave in Old Swedes' Churchyard, Philadelphia.

Wilson received a good measure of recognition before he died. He was elected to the Columbian Society of Artists, the American Philosophical Society, and the Academy of Natural Sciences of Philadelphia. Though more limited in his field than Audubon, whose *Ornithological Biography* appeared some twenty-five years after Wilson's death, he was more original and more accurate. Neither of the two men had any formal scientific training, but Audubon was often careless of veracity, letting his imagination take the place of observation, whereas Wilson confined himself strictly to the birds he had seen and studied.

His poetry was undistinguished except for its sympathetic fidelity to nature, but his *Ornithology* was an important contribution. Nothing like it in any branch of science had appeared before in America. Remarkable in its conception, it was written in clear, simple, first-hand prose of great literary charm. He has been called "the pioneer writer of the bird essay," but he was also a pioneer, both in prose and poetry, of the whole field of American nature literature.

PRINCIPAL WORKS: *Poetry*—Poems, 1790; The Foresters, 1805; The Poetical Works of Alexander Wilson, 1844. *Nature*—American Ornithology (8 vols.) 1808-13.

ABOUT: Peattie, D. C. Green Laurels; Wilson, J. S. Alexander Wilson: Poet-Naturalist; Auk April 1901 and July 1917.

WILSON, AUGUSTA JANE (EVANS). See EVANS, AUGUSTA JANE

WILSON, JAMES GRANT (April 28, 1832-February 1, 1914), editor, biographer, and soldier, was born in Edinburgh, Scotland, the son of William Wilson, a bookseller and publisher who came to America in 1833, and his second wife, Jane (Sibbald) Wilson. Educated at Poughkeepsie, N.Y., he entered into partnership with his father, and in 1855 went to Chicago where he edited and published several periodicals including the monthly *Chicago Record,* 1857-62. In the latter year he entered the Civil War as major in the 15th Illinois Cavalry, finally becoming a brevet brigadier-general of volunteers. Resigning in 1865, he engaged in literary work in New York City. He was president of the New York Genealogical and Biographical Society, 1886-1900, of the American Ethnological Society 1900-14, and of the American Authors' Guild, 1892-99. He was twice married, in 1869 to Jane Emily Searle Cogswell, by whom he had one daughter, and in 1907 to Mary (Heap) Nicholson.

His many published productions were largely biographical and included such edited works as *Appletons' Cyclopaedia of American Biography* in six volumes, later revised with a supplementary volume; *The Presidents of the United States;* and individual works on military officers and eminent soldiers, including several studies of General Ulysses S. Grant. He also produced some works of literary interest: *The Poets and Poetry of Scotland From the Earliest to the Present Time* in two volumes, *Love and Letters: Illustrated in the Correspondence of Eminent Persons,* a two-volume work including biographical sketches, and a study of the English diarist Samuel Pepys, the last two first appearing under the pseudonym "Allan Grant." He also wrote a four-volume history of New York City. He was a frequent contributor to periodicals, and among his shorter publications were a number of his public addresses on American historical and literary persons, a sketch of William Cullen Bryant which appeared in Bryant's *New Library of Poetry and Song,* an introduction to Mrs. Audubon's *Life of John James Audubon,* a memoir of Mrs. Anne Grant appearing in her *Memoirs of an American Lady,* and contributions to the *New American Cyclopaedia* and *Chambers's Encyclopaedia.*

PRINCIPAL WORKS: *Biography*—Biographical Sketches of Illinois Officers Engaged in the War Against the Rebellion of 1861, 1862; Mr. Secretary Pepys: With Extracts From His Diary, 1867; The Life and Campaigns of Ulysses Simpson Grant, 1868; The Life and Letters of Fitz-Greene Halleck, 1869; Sketches of Illustrious Soldiers, 1874; General Grant, 1897; Thackeray in the United States, 1852-53, 1855-1856, 1904. *History*—The Memorial History of the City of New York From Its First Settlement to the Year 1892, 1892-93. *Editor*—The Centennial History of the Protestant Episcopal Church in the Diocese of New York, 1785-1885, 1886; Appletons' Cyclopaedia of American Biography (with John Fiske) 1886-89, 1898-99; Personal Recollections of the War of the Rebellion (with T. M. Coan) 1891; The Presidents of the United States (by J. Fiske and others) 1894. *Miscellaneous*—Love in Letters, 1867; The Poets and Poetry of Scotland, 1876; Bryant and His Friends, 1886.

About: Fleming, H. E. Magazines of a Market-Metropolis; American Anthropologist January 1914; New York Genealogical and Biographical Record July 1914.

WILSON, ROBERT BURNS (October 30, 1850-March 31, 1916), painter, poet, and novelist, son of Thomas M. and Elizabeth (McLean) Wilson, was born at Washington, Pa., where he also received his early education. Showing both talent and a decided preference for an artistic career, he left home before his twenty-first year, joined the Hagenbeck circus, and traveled around the country sketching and painting the company animals.

Sometime between 1871 and 1875 he was in Louisville, Ky., where a crayon sketch of Henry Watterson brought him much publicity. He later moved to Frankfort and became popular in the social life of the town, but was only moderately successful as a painter despite constant hard work. In 1902 he married Anne Hendrick, eldest daughter of W. J. Hendrick, a former attorney-general of Kentucky, and a year later they moved to New York City in the hope that the metropolitan art center would improve Wilson's financial and artistic opportunities—a vain dream which reduced him to penury on several occasions.

Although he is best known as a painter of landscapes, he published several volumes of poetry and one novel which won him some recognition as a writer. These writings may be classed in the middle course between mediocrity and excellence and bear such titles as *Life and Love; Chant of a Woodland Spirit;* and *The Shadows of the Trees.*

Wilson died in Brooklyn, N.Y., and was buried in Frankfort. His handsome face and fine bearing are admirably depicted in a portrait of him owned by the Kentucky State Historical Society.

Principal Works: *Poems*—Life and Love, 1887; Chant of a Woodland Spirit, 1894; The Shadows of the Trees, 1898. *Novel*—Until the Day Break, 1900.

About: Rutherford, M. L. The South in History and Literature; Townsend, J. W. Kentucky in American Letters; Harper's New Monthly Magazine May 1887; American Art Annual, 1916; American Art News April 15, 1916; New York Times April 1, 1916.

WINSLOW, EDWARD (October 18, 1595-May 8, 1655), Plymouth colonist and historian, was born at Droitwich, Worcestershire, England, the son of Edward and Magdalene (Ollyver or Oliver) Winslow. Little is known of his early life save that he came of a good family and was well educated. In 1617 he joined John Robinson's Separatist congregation at Leyden, and there he was married the next year to Elizabeth Barker. He was a passenger on the "Mayflower" in 1620, and was one of the group landing at Plymouth in December of that year.

His abilities soon brought him into prominence in the colony, and he was chosen to treat with the Indians when Massasoit the chief visited the colony in 1621. That same year, two months after the death of his first wife, in the first marriage ceremony performed in Plymouth, he was married to Susanna (Fuller) White, a widow. In 1623 he made a trip to England to buy provisions, clothing and live-stock for the colony. Revisiting that country again the next year, he published his narrative, *Good News From New England,* a record of the first year in the colony. He was instrumental in establishing trading posts in Maine, Massachusetts, and Connecticut, thus laying the foundations of Plymouth's prosperity. He was an "assistant" in the administration of the colony nearly every year from 1624 to 1646; was governor in 1633, 1636, and 1644; and helped to organize the New England Confederation.

In 1646 he returned to England to refute the charges of Samuel Gorton against the Massachusetts Bay Co. He remained in England, where he served as chairman of a commission to adjust claims against the Dutch, arising from English shipping losses. He was appointed chief of three commissioners sent to capture the Spanish West Indies, a coup which failed in its main objective but which resulted in the acquisition by the British of Jamaica. On the return voyage Winslow died of a fever and was buried at sea.

His journals are the first accounts of the exploration and settling of the Plymouth colony; besides their great interest as historical documents they possess an honest and robust charm.

Principal Works: A Relation or Iournal of the Beginning and Proceedings of the English Plantation Setled at Plimoth in New England, 1622; Good News From New England: or, A True Relation of Things Very Remarkable at the Plantation of Plymouth in New England . . . Written by E. W., 1624; Hypocrisie Unmasked by the True Relation of the Proceedings of the Governour and Company of the Massachusetts Against Samuel Gorton . . . , 1646; New Englands Salamander Discovered by an Irreligious and Scornfull Pamphlet, 1647; The Glorious

Progress of the Gospel Among the Indians in New England.

ABOUT: Bradford, W. History of Plymouth Plantation; Goodwin, J. A. The Pilgrim Republic; Usher, R. G. The Pilgrims and Their History; Young, A. Chronicles of the Pilgrim Fathers.

WINSOR, JUSTIN (January 2, 1831-October 22, 1897), librarian and historian, was born in Boston, the son of Nathaniel Winsor, Jr., a merchant, and Ann Thomas (Howland) Winsor. He was educated in a boarding school at Sandwich, Mass., and in the Boston Latin School. From there he went to Harvard, already an historian, for his first book, a history of Duxbury, appeared in his freshman year. He could find nothing at Harvard worthy of his mettle, and left in 1852, when he was a senior, to study abroad. In 1868 Harvard conferred his B.A. on him as of the class of 1853. He studied for two years at the Universities of Paris and Heidelberg, becoming proficient in six modern languages besides English. In 1855 he married Caroline Tufts Barker; they had one daughter.

Until 1868, when he became superintendent of the Boston Public Library, he made his living by writing fiction, verse, and criticism for various magazines. As a librarian Winsor was a pioneer of modern methods; however, he found himself hamstrung by politicians, and was glad to resign in 1877 and become librarian of Harvard. That year he attended the first International Conference of Librarians, in London. He was a founder of the American Library Association, its first president from 1876 to 1885, and president again in 1897. He also gave history courses in Harvard in 1892 and 1893, and in 1897. The University of Michigan and Williams College both conferred honorary LL.D. degrees on him.

JUSTIN WINSOR

Gradually Winsor became less concerned with library methods and more engrossed in American history. Though he wrote several short historical works, he was essentially an historical editor (71 authors wrote the *Memorial History of Boston* under his direction), and above all a bibliographer and cartographer; he was perhaps the greatest cartographer of his time. His own style was lucid and pleasant, but not particularly distinguished. His avocation was the bibliography of Shakespeare.

PRINCIPAL WORKS: A History of the Town of Duxbury, 1849; Songs of Unity (ed., with G. H. Hepworth) 1859; Bibliography of the Original Quartos and Folios of Shakespeare, 1876; Reader's Handbook of the American Revolution, 1879; Memorial History of Boston (ed.) 1880-81; Narrative and Critical History of America (ed.) 1884-89; Arnold's Expedition Against Quebec, 1886; Was Shakespeare Shapleigh?, 1887; The Manuscript Sources of American History, 1887; Christopher Columbus, 1891; Cartier to Frontenac, 1894; The Mississippi Basin, 1895; The Westward Movement, 1897.

ABOUT: American Historical Review January 1898; Library Journal January 1897; Nation October 28, 1897; Boston Daily Advertiser October 23, 1897.

WINTER, WILLIAM (July 15, 1836-June 30, 1917), dramatic critic and historian, poet, and essayist, was the son of Captain Charles Winter and Louise (Wharf) Winter; he was born in Gloucester, Mass., and spent his boyhood in Boston.

Graduated from the Harvard Law School in 1857, he was admitted to the bar in Suffolk, Mass., but never practiced. From the age of eighteen when he published a volume of poems while still at Harvard, Winter was ambitious for a literary career. As a reviewer on the Boston *Transcript,* he met Longfellow, who encouraged his literary ambitions and exerted a lasting influence on his style. Finding Boston too narrow an outlet for his energies, he moved to New York in 1856 where, as an assistant to Henry Clapp Jr., editor of the satirical *Saturday Press,* he became one of the group of young writers known as "the Bohemians," numbering among them such talents as Walt Whitman, Thomas Bailey Aldrich, Fitz-James O'Brien, and Artemus Ward. Meeting in the cellar of Pfaff's cafe on Broadway near Bleecker Street, this society provided a lively center for the younger writing men of the city, giving Winter new stimulus and form-

Collection of Frederick H. Meserve
WILLIAM WINTER

ing the basis of several life-long friendships. Apparently only Whitman was not sympathetic to him, referring to him sarcastically as "a young Longfellow."

Clapp's paper was temporarily suspended, and in 1861 Winter found a place as dramatic and literary critic of the *Albion*. Four years later he became dramatic critic of Horace Greeley's *Tribune*, a position that he held for the next forty years, during which time he built up a distinguished reputation as critic and historian of the American stage.

In 1860 he married Elizabeth Campbell, a minor novelist of Scotch birth, who bore him five children. The Winters lived for the most part on Staten Island, summering in England or California. For twenty-five years or more he was an important literary figure in New York, popular as poet and essayist, and recognized as an authoritative critic of the theater. He knew intimately many of the famous actors of the day and wrote a long series of theatrical biographies, reminiscences, and critical studies. From the 'nineties on, with the advent of a new realism, his popularity declined. Unable to adjust himself to the transition from romanticism to realism, he attacked the work of Ibsen, Pinero, and Henry Arthur Jones, and in 1909 resigned his position with the *Tribune*. Although he continued for several years to write reviews for *Harper's Weekly*, his critical approach has been thoroughly outmoded, his fame surviving only as a ghost of the romantic tradition in the theater.

Winter was concerned largely with the ephemeral aspects of the theater, with performance and personalities rather than with the development of the drama; yet his writings remain a valuable repository of American theatrical history. A moralist and a romanticist, he praised in flowing sentimental phrase, reserving his gift of lively invective for the realistic theater which he was never able to understand.

Principal Works: *Essays*—The Trip to England, 1879; English Rambles and Other Fugitive Pieces, 1884; Brief Chronicles (three parts) 1889-90; The Actor and Other Speeches: Chiefly on Theatrical Subjects and Occasions, 1891; Gray Days and Gold, 1891; Old Shrines and Ivy, 1892; Shakespeare's England, 1892; Brown Heath and Blue Bells: Being Sketches of Scotland With Other Papers, 1895; Old Friends: Being Recollections of Other Days, 1909; Over the Border, 1911; Shakespeare on the Stage (3 vols.) 1911-18; Vagrant Memories, 1915. *Poetry*—The Convent and Other Poems, 1854; Poems, 1855; The Queen's Domain and Other Poems, 1858; My Witness, 1871; Thistledown, 1878; Poems, 1881; Wanderers, 1888; Poems, 1894. *Biographies*—The Jeffersons, 1881; John Brougham, 1881; Henry Irving, 1885; Ada Rehan: A Study, 1891. Life and Art of Edwin Booth, 1893; The Life and Art of Richard Mansfield, 1910; Tyrone Power, 1913 The Life of David Belasco, 1918. *Theater History*—Shadows of the Stage (3 vols.) 1892-95; Other Days: Being Chronicles and Memories of the Stage, 1908; The Wallet of Time, 1913.

About: Winter, W. Old Friends; Winter, W. Other Days; Winter, W. The Wallet of Time.

WINTHROP, JOHN (January 12, 1587/8-o.s.—March 26, 1649), first governor of the Massachusetts Bay Colony, lawyer, magistrate, and chronicler, was born in Suffolk, England, the son of Adam Winthrop, lord of the manor at Groton, and his second wife, Anne Browne.

Educated at Trinity College, Cambridge, Winthrop did not take his degree, giving up his college career at seventeen to marry Mary Forth. Within a year he had established a flourishing law practice in London, becoming subsequently a lawyer to the court, a justice of the peace, and succeeding to the lordship of Groton manor. Ten years later his wife died, leaving six children, the eldest of whom, also named John Winthrop, later became governor of Connecticut. His second wife, Thomasine Clopton, died a year after their marriage, and in 1618 Winthrop married Margaret Tyndal, a woman of remarkable character, who was to share his fortunes in the new world.

In 1629, harried by private financial burdens and deeply concerned with the political and religious confusion of the times, Winthrop interested himself in the Massachusetts Bay Co., recently chartered by Charles I, and in spite of opposition from

After a portrait attributed to Van Dyke
JOHN WINTHROP

friends and relatives, decided to emigrate to New England. Chosen as the first governor, he undertook full responsibility for the leadership of this group of settlers who were to establish a self-governing community in America.

Sailing in 1630 on the "Arbella," he began a series of writings that was to be continued throughout his career as governor. During the voyage he wrote, in *A Modell of Christian Charity,* an outline of an ideal colony and sketched the means by which it was to be achieved. The journal which he kept from this date on became a record of these developments reflecting the whole history of the colony.

Winthrop was elected governor in 1631, 1632, 1633, and again in 1637, 1638, and 1639. He was elected also to the first presidency of the Confederation of New England Colonies. For several years he served as magistrate and in 1645 was elected governor once more, holding the same office from that year until the time of his death. Throughout these years he was the center of a succession of political and religious conflicts, all of which arose from the more fundamental conflict between the aristocratic tradition in government which he represented and the rising democracy of the new world. In the Antinomian controversy, his own version of which was incorporated with Thomas Welde's *Short Story of the Rise, Reign, and Ruine of the Antinomians,* and again in the famous controversy over the "negative voice" of the magistrates, he stood sternly against democracy, of which he wrote: "there was no such government in Israel." Threatened with impeachment, 1645, for having exceeded his powers as magistrate, he made a famous speech on liberty, defining natural and civil liberty, and was vindicated.

His wife died in 1647, and he was married for the fourth time to a widow, Martha (Rainsborough) Coytmore. A little more than a year later, he died at the age of sixty-one.

As an informal historian, Winthrop may be given first rank among early writers of the kind. His *Journal of the Transactions and Occurrences in the Settlement of Massachusetts and the Other New England Colonies,* written in a fine, grave prose, stands as a valuable source book of early colonial history.

Principal Works: *Miscellany*—A Journal of the Transactions and Occurrences in the Settlement of Massachusetts and Other New England Colonies, 1790.

About: Twichell, J. H. John Winthrop; Winthrop, J. & M. Some Old Puritan Love Letters; Winthrop, R. C. Life and Letters of John Winthrop.

WINTHROP, THEODORE (September 28, 1828-June 10, 1861), miscellaneous writer, was born in New Haven, Conn., the son of Francis Bayard Winthrop and Elizabeth (Woolsey) Winthrop. The father, a lawyer and merchant, was a descendant of John Winthrop and the mother was a great-granddaughter of Jonathan Edwards and a sister of President Theodore Dwight Woolsey of Yale. Young Winthrop was privately tutored and attended Yale, class of 1848.

Following an extended tour abroad, he entered the New York office of the Pacific Mail Steamship Co., later joining the Panama Railroad. He travelled to San Francisco and Oregon; and on his return studied law and was admitted to the bar in 1855. The following year, during a vacation trip to Maine, he campaigned for John C. Frémont, but on his return to New York decided to devote his entire time to literature.

The first of his writing to appear in print was a description of a painting by his friend Frederick E. Church in *A Companion to the Heart of the Andes,* but most of his numerous works were published after his death. He enlisted at the beginning of the Civil War, and two months later was killed while leading an attack at Great Bethel.

The dramatic end of his career invested his memory and writings with a special interest, and his books *Cecil Dreeme, John Brent,* and *Edwin Brothertoft* were published in quick succession. Very favorably received at the time, they held their popularity for about forty years, going into many editions. Like most of the novels of that period Winthrop's work suffers from an overabundance of detail and mid-Victorian embroidery. The charm and high spirits that so endeared him to his friends are evident in his accounts of his wartime experiences which were published by James Russell Lowell in the *Atlantic Monthly* of June and July 1861.

Principal Works: A Companion to the Heart of the Andes, 1859; Cecil Dreeme, 1861; John Brent, 1862; Edwin Brothertoft, 1862; The Canoe and the Saddle, 1863; Life in the Open Air, 1863; Mr. Waddy's Return, 1904.

About: Colby, E. Biographical Notes on Theodore Winthrop; Johnson, L. W. The Life and Poems of Theodore Winthrop; Nation June 29, 1916; Yale Alumni Weekly January 23, 1920; New York Times June 13, 1861.

WIRT, WILLIAM (November 8, 1772-February 18, 1834), lawyer and essayist, was born in Bladensburg, Md., the son of Jacob Wirt, a Swiss, and Henrietta Wirt, a German, who kept a tavern in this little Prince George's County town. When he was two his father died; when he was eight, his mother; and he was reared by an uncle, who sent him to private schools in Maryland and the District of Columbia until 1787. He then became tutor in the family of Ninian Edwards, who later married the sister of Mrs. Abraham Lincoln. Meanwhile he studied law, and was admitted to practice in 1789, in Culpepper Courthouse, Va. In 1795

From an engraving by J. B. Longacre
WILLIAM WIRT

he married Mildred Gilmer, and lived with her father in Albemarle County. Dr. Gilmer died in 1797, Mrs. Wirt in 1799. The widower then moved to Richmond, where for three terms he was clerk of the House of Delegates.

Up to this time Wirt had shone more as a *bon vivant* and a convivial wit than as an attorney. Now, however, his serious career began. In 1802 the legislature elected him chancellor for the district, and he moved to Williamsburg, where he married Elizabeth Washington Gamble. Besides bearing twelve children, she found time to write a combined botanical dictionary and dictionary of quotations which was popular in its day. In five months Wirt gave up the chancellorship for private practice. In 1804 he moved to Norfolk. He had already "begun author"; his *Letters of the British Spy* had appeared serially in the Richmond *Argus,* and though they were anonymous everyone guessed their authorship. Wirt was always more ambitious in literature than in politics, and was always planning vainly to retire and cultivate literary pursuits.

In 1806 he returned to Richmond, and two years later served a term in the House of Delegates. For a brief time during the War of 1812 he was a captain of artillery. In 1816 Madison appointed him United States Attorney, and the next year Monroe made him Attorney General. He served until 1829, then moved to Baltimore, where he continued to practise law. In 1831 he was the presidential candidate of the anti-Masonic Party (though himself a Mason!) in the hope of uniting all forces against Andrew Jackson; he tried to withdraw but was unable to do so, and carried only Vermont. He attempted to found a colony of German immigrants on land he owned in Florida, hoping to spend his own old age there, but the colonists refused to remain and he was obliged to abandon the idea. He died in Washington, of erysipelas.

Wirt had a great reputation as an orator, in the days of florid eloquence. His written style was like his oratorical one—ornate and magniloquent. He realized the need of curbing it and made a conscious effort in his later writings to become more concise and simple. He himself considered his biography of Patrick Henry his greatest work, but if he is remembered at all as a writer, it will be by his early essays. As a man, he was sociable (sometimes too much so for his own good), lazy, imaginative, and charming; rather incongruously he was also a devout Presbyterian, and president of the

Maryland Bible Society. In appearance, he strongly resembled Goethe—a large, blonde, benign, handsome man.

PRINCIPAL WORKS: The Letters of the British Spy, 1803; The Rainbow, 1804; The Old Bachelor, 1812; Sketches of the Life and Character of Patrick Henry, 1817; Addresses to the Literary Societies of Rutgers College, 1830; Addresses on the Triumph of Liberty in France, 1830.

ABOUT: Hagan, H. H. Eight Great American Lawyers; Kennedy, J. P. Memories of the Life of William Wirt; Daily National Intelligencer February 19-21, 1834.

WISE, HENRY AUGUSTUS (May 24, 1819-April 2, 1869), naval officer and miscellaneous writer, was born at the Brooklyn (N.Y.) Navy Yard, the son of Captain George Stewart Wise of the United States Navy and Catherine (Stansberry) Wise. Orphaned at an early age, he was brought up at the home of his grandfather, George Douglas Wise, at Craney Island, near Norfolk, Va. After midshipman training, he served in the Mexican War and distinguished himself by carrying important dispatches from Mazatlán to Mexico City, a duty which was facilitated by his knowledge of Spanish and his Latin complexion. After the war his naval career progressed rapidly and he eventually rose to be a lieutenant in 1847. Meanwhile he was devoting much time to writing and produced under the pseudonym "Harry Gringo" such volumes as *Scampavias From Gibel-Tarek to Stamboul, The Story of the Gray African Parrot,* and *Captain Brand of the "Centipede."*

Although a Southerner in sympathies, he remained in the Union navy throughout the Civil War. Toward the end of his life he served as an efficiency officer in the bureau of ordnance, ultimately becoming a captain. He died in Naples, Italy, leaving his second wife, Charlotte Brooks Everett, daughter of Edward Everett, and four children.

Wise is in no way an important American writer, but his accounts of his naval experiences are valuable records in the history of American warfare, particularly *Los Gringos: or, An Inside View of Mexico and California, With Wanderings in Peru, Chile, and Polynesia.*

PRINCIPAL WORKS: Los Gringos: or, An Inside View of Mexico and California, With Wanderings in Peru, Chile, and Polynesia, 1849; Tales for the Marines, 1855; Scampavias From Gibel-Tarek to Stamboul, 1857; The Story of the Gray African Parrot, 1860; Captain Brand of the "Centipede," 1864.

ABOUT: Callahan, E. W. List of Officers of the Navy of the U.S.: 1775-1900; Wise, J. C. Col. John Wise: His Ancestors and Descendants; Army and Navy Journal May 1, July 3, 1869; New York Daily Tribune April 12, 1869.

WISE, JOHN (August 1652-April 8, 1725), Congregational clergyman, was born at Roxbury, Mass., the son of Joseph and Mary (Thompson) Wise. He went to school in Roxbury and was graduated from Harvard in 1673. Two years later he qualified for the ministry and after holding successive parishes in Connecticut and Massachusetts he began, in 1680, a life-long service at Chebacco, the newly founded parish of Ipswich. He was married, probably late in 1678, to Abigail Gardner, by whom he had seven children.

For resistance against a province tax which Sir Edmund Andros, first royal governor, had attempted to levy, Wise was tried, found guilty, and informed that he and his fellow-protesters had "no more privileges left them than not to be sold for slaves," and he himself was suspended from (and afterwards restored to) "the Ministerial Function." Wise again demonstrated his moral courage in 1692 when he signed a written appeal for one John Proctor who had been condemned for witchcraft.

Meanwhile Wise had gone as chaplain with an expedition against Quebec; and, moreover, had been sent by his own town to Boston to aid in drafting legislative reorganization. For a while after the appearance of Increase Mather's *Questions and Proposals,* a plan for the formation of associations of clergy which would absorb functions formerly delegated to the individual churches, Wise remained silent: but in 1710 he released a well-devised piece of shattering opposition, *The Churches Quarrel Espoused,* which Cotton Mather bitterly called a "foolish, cursed Libel." Wise persisted with his argument in *A Vindication of the Government of the New-England Churches.* With their dash and subtlety of humor, their dexterity of style, and foolproof earnestness of argument, these two pamphlets were far superior to the average writing of that period. Wise also published two booklets advocating the issue of paper money, *A Friendly Check From a Kind Relation . . .* (occasioned by a statement in a newspaper advertisement) and *A Word of Comfort to a Melancholy Country.*

Wise has been recorded as a man of "towering height, of great muscular power, stately and graceful in shape and movement; in his advancing years of an aspect almost venerable." His strong and rational belief in the preservation of civil liberty, his willingness to become more than a merely passive objector, and his uncommon ability as a writer have prompted some historians to call him "the first great American democrat."

PRINCIPAL WORKS: The Churches Quarrel Espoused, 1710; A Vindication of the Government of the New-England Churches, 1717; A Friendly Check From a Kind Relation, 1721; A Word of Comfort to a Melancholy Country, 1721.

ABOUT: Boas, R. & L. Cotton Mather: Keeper of the Puritan Conscience; Dexter, H. M. The Congregationalism of the Last Three Hundred Years; Sibley, J. L. Biographical Sketches of the Graduates of Harvard University; White, J. The Gospel Treasure in Earthen Vessels, A Funeral Sermon on . . . the Death of . . . John Wise.

WISTAR, CASPAR (September 13, 1761-January 22, 1818), scientific writer and literary patron, founder of the "Wistar Parties," was born in Philadelphia, the son of Richard and Sarah (Wyatt) Wistar, and grandson of the first glass manufacturer in America. He was educated at Penn Charter (Friends') School, studied medicine under Dr. John Redman, and received his B.M. at the new University of Pennsylvania in 1782. He then studied for a year in London and proceeded to Edinburgh, where he became M.D. in 1786. During this time he was president of the students' Royal Medical Society.

He returned to Philadelphia, and in 1789 succeeded Dr. Benjamin Rush as professor of chemistry in the medical school of the College of Philadelphia. In 1792 this was merged in the University of Pennsylvania, and Wistar was made first adjunct professor, then full professor, of anatomy, surgery, and midwifery. His *System of Anatomy* was the first American treatise on the subject, and long the standard textbook. He was physician at the Philadelphia Dispensary, and on the staff of the Pennsylvania Hospital. In 1787 he was president of the College of Physicians and Surgeons. In 1809 he founded a society to promote vaccination. The plant Wistaria is named for him.

Except for his anatomy textbook and a volume of essays, Wistar's only writing was in communications to the American Philosophical Society, which he joined in 1787, and of which he was president from 1815 to 1818, succeeding Jefferson. But once a week he kept open house for members of the Society and visiting celebrities with the result that his name still holds a semi-literary connotation; he was one of the few American "patrons" of literature. These "Wistar Parties," held in his house at Fourth and DeLancey Streets (still standing and

After a portrait by B. Otis

CASPAR WISTAR

occupied by members of his family) became famous, and after his death the Wistar Association was formed to continue them; they are still occasionally held.

In 1788 Wistar married Isabella Marshall. She died and in 1798 he married Elizabeth Mifflin, daughter of the governor, by whom he had two sons and a daughter. He died of angina pectoris, from which he had long been a sufferer. His anatomy collection was given to the University of Pennsylvania and later handed over to the Wistar Institute of Anatomy and Biology, founded by his grand-nephew.

PRINCIPAL WORKS: System of Anatomy for the Use of Students of Medicine, 1811; Eulogium on Dr. William Shippen, 1818.

ABOUT: Caldwell, C. An Eulogium on Casper Wistar; M.D; Hosack, D. Tribute to the Memory of the Late Caspar Wistar; Kelly, H. A. Some American Medical Botanists; Poulson's American Daily Advertiser January 23, 24, 1818.

WISTER, SARAH (July 20, 1761-April 21, 1804), diarist, was born in Philadelphia, the daughter of Daniel Wister and Lowry (Jones) Wister. Her grandfather was John Wüster, a wine merchant of German birth, and her maternal great-grandfather Dr. Edward Jones, one of the founders of the Welsh colony in Merion and Haverford townships. She was carefully educated at the school of the well-known Quaker, Anthony Benezet. She was sixteen when, during the Revolutionary War, the British threat to Philadelphia caused her to be sent with other members of the family to a retired farmhouse some fifteen miles from the city among the hills of Gwynedd, where she remained from September 1777 to the following July. While there she commenced to keep for her absent friend Deborah Norris, afterwards the wife of Dr. George Logan Stenton, "a sort of journal of the time," a vivacious record of impressions enlivened by humor and touches of the dramatic. She died unmarried at forty-two in the family home at Germantown.

Mrs. Logan is said not to have seen the diary until many years after Miss Wister's death, when it was lent to her by the author's brother, Charles J. Wister. Valuable as a social commentary as well as a human document, it was noticed by the local historian, John Fanning Watson, who included brief extracts from it in his *Annals of Philadelphia.* It was also represented in the *Historical Collections of Gwynedd,* by Howard M. Jenkins, and a private edition was published without date, together with a letter from Martha Washington. The most complete edition was, however, edited and published by Albert Cook Meyers nearly a century after the author's death. Miss Wister also wrote occasional verse, some of which was published in the *Port Folio.*

Principal Works: Sally Wister's Journal (ed. by A. C. Meyers) 1902.

About: Historical Society of Montgomery Co. Pa. Historical Sketches; Jordan, J. W. Colonial Families of Philadelphia; Wister, S. Sally Wister's Journal (see Introduction by A. C. Myers).

WITHERSPOON, JOHN (February 5, 1723-November 15, 1794), theological and political writer, was born in Yester, near Edinburgh, Scotland, the son of James Witherspoon, a Presbyterian minister, and Anne (Walker) Witherspoon. (Some authorities give his mother's name as Elizabeth Welsh, a descendant of John Knox.) He was educated at Haddington Grammar School, and at thirteen entered the University of Edinburgh (M.A. 1739, B.D. 1743). He was licensed to preach in 1743, and in 1745 was ordained at Beith, Ayrshire. The next year, through a non-combatant, he was taken prisoner by the Stuart forces in the Scottish invasion, and held for some time. In 1748 he married Elizabeth Montgomery, by whom he had ten children, of whom five survived. In 1757 he became pastor of the Low Church, Paisley, and a leader of the Popular Party, which was rigidly Calvinist. In 1759 he was moderator of the Synod of Glasgow and Ayr. In 1764 the University of St. Andrews bestowed a D.D. degree upon him.

After a portrait by C. W. Peale
JOHN WITHERSPOON

The second half of Witherspoon's life began in 1768, when he accepted the second invitation to become president of the College of New Jersey (Princeton). He did much to spread the Presbyterian doctrine in the Middle Atlantic Colonies, but his main interest was the college, where he taught theology, and of which he was an able president. He introduced the study of philosophy, history, international law, oratory, and French, and strengthened the English department.

From the beginning he was an American first, a British subject after. He was a delegate to the First Continental Congress, served with a short intermission from 1776 to 1782, and was the only clergyman to sign the Declaration of Independence. After the Revolution he devoted most of his time to rebuilding the college, though he was moderator of the first General Assembly of the Presbyterian Church in 1789; and in 1783 and again in 1789 served in the New Jersey legislature. His wife died in 1789, and two years later, at sixty-eight, he married Ann Dill, aged twenty-four. They had two daughters. His last two years were spent in blindness. He died at his farm near Princeton, and is buried in the President's Lot of the university.

Witherspoon's writings are all polemical. A master of invective and satire, he was known for his keen wit and his practical "philosophical common sense."

Principal Works: Ecclesiastical Characteristics, 1753; Essay on Justification, 1756; A Serious

Enquiry Into the Nature and Effects of the Stage, 1757; Regeneration, 1764; Sermons on Practical Subjects, 1768; Practical Discourses, 1768; Essay on Money, 1781.

About: Collins, V. L. President Witherspoon; Riley, I. W. American Philosophy: The Early Schools; Woods, D. W. John Witherspoon.

WOOD, SARAH SAYWARD (BARRELL) KEATING (October 1, 1759-January 6, 1855), the State of Maine's first fiction writer, was born in Yorke, the daughter of Nathaniel Barrell and Sarah (Sayward) Barrell. Of a wealthy and distinguished family, her education and outlook were the result of a cultured and well-bred environment. At the age of nineteen she married Richard Keating by whom she had three children. After his death in 1782, she began writing, and aside from numerous contributions to periodicals wrote four highly-colored works of fiction, the best known being *Julia and the Illuminated Baron.*

She was married a second time, on October 28, 1804, to General Abiel Wood, of Wiscasset. When he died in 1811, she lived in Portland until 1830, then removed to New York to live with her son, Capt. Richard Keating, who lost his life when his ship was destroyed by an iceberg. Mrs. Keating again returned to Maine, this time to Kennebunk, where she made her home with her granddaughter until her death.

Her works, although the first of a procession of fiction to come from Maine, were not of themselves notable, and were prevented from attaining literary distinction by their ornate and tortuous plots, their complete lack of reality. She was much influenced by the novels of Sir Walter Scott and is said to have destroyed most of the sequel to her novel, *Tales of the Night,* after reading his works.

Principal Works: Julia and the Illuminated Baron, 1800; Amelia: or, The Influence of Virtue, 1802; Ferdinand and Elmira: A Russian Story, 1804; Tales of the Night, 1827.

About: Dunnack, H. E. The Maine Book; Sayward, C. A. The Sayward Family; Spencer, W. D. Maine Immortals; Eastern Argus (Portland) January 9, 1855.

WOODBRIDGE, JOHN (1613-March 17, 1695), colonial magistrate and clergyman, was born at Stanton, Wiltshire, England, the eldest son of a minister of the same name and Sarah (Parker) Woodbridge; he was a grandson of a prominent Puritan divine, Robert Parker. Educated for the ministry at Oxford, he revolted from the oath of conformity and left without a degree, accompanying his uncle, Thomas Parker, to Newbury, Mass., in 1634. There he filled various civil offices, taught school in Boston, 1643-45, and in the latter year was ordained first pastor of the church at Andover. In 1647 he returned to England, remaining for fifteen years as minister and teacher, and on his return to America in 1663 became an assistant to his uncle, then pastor at Newbury. Strongly spiritual and generally revered, he was nevertheless dismissed from the ministry as the result of opposition from a faction under Edward Woodman. He married Mercy Dudley, the daughter of Gov. Thomas Dudley, and was the father of twelve children, three of his sons being in the ministry. He was the brother-in-law of Anne Bradstreet [*q.v.*], whose poems *The Tenth Muse* he published in London. He died at eighty-two.

While in England he had given attention to the advanced ideas on banking and currency, which he had discussed with the English writer on those subjects, William Potter. Some time after his return he endeavored to arouse interest in his theory of a bank of deposit and issue with land and commodities as collateral, presenting a proposal to the Council in 1667-68, his experimentations foreshadowing the Massachusetts land banks. Joined in 1681 by a group of merchants in "The Fund" he wrote an explanation and defense of this movement in an eight-page pamphlet, *Severals Relating to the Fund Printed for Divers Reasons, As May Appear.* Reprints of this, notable as the earliest American tract on banking and currency extant, appeared in 1902 and in the *Publications* of the Prince Society in 1910.

Principal Works: Severals Relating to the Fund . . . , 1681/82.

About: Currier, J. J. History of Newbury; Sprague, W. B. Annals of the American Pulpit; Weeden, W. B. Economic and Social History of New England; Proceedings of the American Antiquarian Society October 1884.

WOODHULL, VICTORIA (CLAFLIN) (September 23, 1838-June 10, 1927), editor and propagandist, was born in Homer, Ohio, the daughter of Reuben Buckman Claflin and Roxanna (Hummel) Claflin. The family were" poor white trash" living on both the lunatic and criminal fringe; they were finally run out of Homer on suspicion of arson and moved from town to town in Ohio, the mother giving spiritualistic and mesmeric shows in which Victoria and her sister, Tennessee Celeste (born 1846), took part. The ten children had no regular educa-

Collection of Frederick H. Meserve
VICTORIA C. WOODHULL

tion, but somewhere in her wanderings Victoria at least picked up a correct and forceful, if rather grandiloquent, style of speaking and writing.

In 1853 she married Dr. Canning Woodhull; they had two children, but she kept on traveling, the family at one time running a medicine and fortune-telling show. Then she and her sister practiced in Cincinnati and Chicago as clairvoyants. In 1864 she divorced Dr. Woodhull and afterward met Col. James H. Blood, whom she was believed to have married in 1866. In 1868 the sisters went to New York. There Tennessee, who had married a man named Bartels but had separated from him, became connected with the older Cornelius Vanderbilt, who set them up as "lady brokers." Thanks to his tips, they made a fortune. In 1870 they founded *Woodhull and Claflin's Weekly,* most of which was written by Blood and by Stephen Pearl Andrews. It advocated Socialism, woman suffrage, free love, vegetarianism, and birth control; in 1872 it created a sensation by publishing the story of Henry Ward Beecher's alleged affair with the wife of Theodore Tilton, which led to his long-drawn-out adultery trial. It also, strangely enough, published the first English translation of the *Communist Manifesto* by Marx and Engels. Meanwhile Victoria, who had beauty, charm, and, indubitably, brains, had several times almost captured the woman's rights movement, had spoken before Congress, and in 1872 had run for president on the Equal Rights Party ticket, with the Negro orator Frederick Douglass as her running-mate. The sisters were tried for uttering an obscene publication, but after two months in jail were acquitted. In 1876 Victoria divorced Blood. On Vanderbilt's death in 1877 both sisters moved to England—apparently at the expense of Vanderbilt's heirs, to get them out of the way while they tried to break his will. There they both married wealthy Englishmen of good family—Tennessee, Sir Francis Cook, Viscount Montserrat; Victoria, John Biddulph Martin, a banker who died in 1897. In 1892 Victoria founded and edited, with her daughter Zula, a magazine called the *Humanitarian.* Her later years were devoted to charity and to a successful campaign for restoration of the birthplace of Washington's ancestors, Sulgrave Manor. She died at the Martin estate, in Worcestershire, at nearly eighty-eight. Tennessee had died in 1923.

Principal Work: Origin, Tendencies, and Principles of Government, 1871; Stirpiculture: or, The Scientific Propagation of the Human Race, 1888; The Human Body the Temple of God (with T. C. Claflin) 1890; Humanitarian Money, 1892.

About: Darwin, G. S. Synopsis of the Lives of Victoria C. Woodhull and Tennessee Claflin; Legge, M. Two Noble Women; Rourke, C. M. Trumpets of Jubilee; Sachs, E. The Terrible Siren; Symes, L. & Clement, T. Rebel America; New York Times January 20, 1923; June 11, 1927.

WOODS, LEONARD (June 19, 1774-August 24, 1854), Congregational clergyman and professor of theology, was born in Princeton, Mass., the son of Samuel Woods and Abigail (Whitney) Underwood Woods. A precocious child, he entered Harvard after systematic study of only three months at Leicester Academy, and was graduated with first honors in 1796. Two years later after studying theology, in part privately, he was ordained pastor of the church at Newbury. Strongly conciliatory, he was instrumental in bringing together the Hopkinsians, or extreme Calvinists, and the Old, or more moderate, Calvinists; in promoting the consolidation of their respective organs, the *Massachusetts Missionary Magazine* and the *Panoplist,* in 1808; and also in consolidating theological seminaries proposed by the two factions into a single seminary at Andover, of which he became the first professor of theology, holding that chair for thirty-eight years. He was a founder of the American Board of Commissioners for Foreign Missions in 1810, of the American Tract Society in 1814, the Education Society in 1815, and the American Temperance Society in 1826. Of his ten children by his first wife, Abigail Wheeler, a son, Leonard

Woods, was for twenty-seven years president of Bowdoin College. He died at Andover, a second wife, widow of Dr. Ansel Ives of New York, surviving him.

In addition to publishing many pamphlets, largely sermons, and a number of books on theological subjects, Woods published some controversial productions, among them writings on doctrines of Calvinism and some pamphlets in connection with the famous "Wood'n Ware Controversy" which he carried on with Professor Henry Ware. Some of his published productions were later republished in his *Works* issued in five volumes. His last work was the writing of the history of Andover Theological Seminary, which was published, more than twenty years after his death, by his grandson.

PRINCIPAL WORKS: A Reply to Dr. Ware's Letters to Trinitarians and Calvinists, 1821; Remarks on Dr. Ware's Answer, 1822; Lectures on Infant Baptism, 1828; Lectures on the Inspiration of the Scriptures, 1829; Letters to Rev. Nathaniel W. Taylor 1830; An Examination of the Doctrine of Perfection as Held by Rev. Asa Mahan, 1841; Lectures on Church Government, 1844; Lectures on Swedenborgianism, 1846; Theology of the Puritans, 1851; The Works of Leonard Woods, D.D., 1850-51; History of the Andover Theological Seminary, 1885.

ABOUT: Rowe, H. K. History of Andover Theological Seminary; Sprague, W. B. Annals of the American Pulpit; Walker, W. Ten New England Leaders; Congregational Quarterly April 1859.

WOODWORTH, SAMUEL (January 13, 1784-December 9, 1842), poet, dramatist, and novelist, author of "The Old Oaken Bucket," was born near Scituate, Mass., the son of Benjamin Woodworth, a Revolutionary veteran and a poor farmer, and Abigail (Bryant) Woodworth. Schools were bad and almost non-existent, and he had very little education. About 1800 he went to Boston and was apprenticed to a printer until 1806; at the same time his verses, signed "Selim" (a name he liked so well he gave it later to his son), appeared in various papers.

Woodworth's whole career was that of a printer who dabbled in journalism and literature. He edited numerous magazines, nearly all of which failed. His first was the *Fly,* a juvenile periodical, in 1805 and 1806. Then he went to New Haven, and for two months in 1808 edited the *Belles-Lettres Repository.* He had little love for Connecticut (witness his satirical verse, *New Haven*) and settled finally in New York. In 1810 he married Lydia Reeder. Their large family kept his nose to the grindstone; during the War of 1812 he published the *War,* a weekly chronicle of events, from 1817 to 1818 the *Republican Chronicle,* in 1819 the *Ladies' Literary Cabinet,* in 1821 *Woodworth's Literary Casket,* and for a year from 1823 he edited the *New York Mirror.* An ardent Swedenborgian, he edited (for his customary year apiece) two magazines of that creed. His editorial efforts were consistently unsuccessful.

Woodworth's first poetical appearance in book form was as the author of verses adorning a work on hairdressing, in 1817. He had published a novel about the War of 1812, *The Champions of Freedom,* in 1816. Next he turned his attention to play-writing. His only real success was *The Forest Rose,* in which the character of "Jonathan Ploughman" caused the comedy to become a hit. *The Widow's Son,* also in 1825, had some success. But financially he was a failure (thanks partly to his over-scrupulousness, partly to his acerbity), and from 1828 on he and his family survived mostly by grace of theatrical benefits. In 1837 he was paralyzed by a stroke of apoplexy, and did no more writing.

Woodworth was little more than a topical or occasional writer. He struck a genuine chord of sentiment just once, remaining in memory as the author of that classic of domesticity, "The Old Oaken Bucket."

PRINCIPAL WORKS: The Champions of Freedom (novel) 1816; The Poems, Odes, Songs, and Other Metrical Effusions of Samuel Woodworth, 1818; The Forest Rose (play) 1825; Melodies, Duets, Trios, Songs, and Ballads: Pastoral, Amatory, Sentimental, Patriotic, Religious, and Miscellaneous, 1830.

ABOUT: Woodworth, S. Poems (see Memoir by G. P. Morris in 1861 ed.); Autograph Album April 1934; Critic January 24, March 7, 1829; New York Evening Post September 24, 1810, November 2, 1837; New York Mirror December 17, 1842; Sewanee Review April 1919.

WOOLMAN, JOHN (October 19, 1720-October 7, 1772), Quaker humanitarian and diarist, was the son of Samuel and Elizabeth (Burr) Woolman; he was born at Ancocas (afterwards Rancocas) in what was then the province of West Jersey. After attendance at a neighborhood Quaker school he was apprenticed to a tailor, and in his twenties established his own business, from which he ultimately enjoyed a somewhat (to him) alarming prosperity—"I saw," he said, "that a humble man, with the Blessing of the Lord might live on little . . . and . . . that commonly with an increase of wealth, the desire for wealth increased . . ." He was married in 1749, to Sarah Ellis.

Meanwhile he had become active in the Quaker ministry, and as an itinerant preacher he opposed military conscription and taxation, and wholeheartedly and firmly advocated the abolition of slavery, on which subject he spoke from very bitter observation. His attitude towards that "iniquitous practice of dealing in Negroes" was preserved in his *Journal* and in *Some Considerations on the Keeping of Negroes.* His social essay, *A Plea for the Poor,* first published in 1763, was later re-issued as a tract of the Fabian Society.

Woolman's lectures, writings, and personal influence bore but little fruit in his own time. But he and his Quaker associates were the very first to formulate a well-defined case for the abolition of slavery; his influence on posterity was vastly greater than on his contemporaries. Charles Lamb (whose country, incidentally, held Woolman in higher esteem than did America) said of him: "Woolman was not a bigwig in his own day, and he will never be a bigwig in history. But if there be a 'perfect witness of all judging Jove,' he may expect his meed of much fame in heaven."

PRINCIPAL WORKS: Some Considerations on the Keeping of Negroes, 1754; A Plea for the Poor, 1763; Journal, 1774.

ABOUT: Gunmere, A. M. (ed.). The Journal and Essays of John Woolman; Trevelyan, G. M. Clio: A Muse and Other Essays.

WOOLSEY, SARAH CHAUNCY (January 29, 1835-April 9, 1905), juvenile and miscellaneous writer, was born in Cleveland, Ohio, into a family prominent in the history of Yale College. Her father, John Mumford Woolsey, was the brother, nephew, and uncle of three Yale presidents: Theodore Dwight Woolsey (1801-89), Timothy Dwight (1752-1817), and Timothy Dwight (1818-1916).

Surrounded by intellectual and cultured people all her life, Sarah attained high marks for scholarship in history and literature at Cleveland private schools, and at Mrs. Hubbard's Boarding School in Hanover, N.H. Between 1855 and 1870 she lived in New Haven, Conn., after which she traveled abroad for two years, and returned to spend the remainder of her life at Newport, R.I., with her mother and sisters.

She began writing about 1870, winning favorable comment for her poems and articles in the leading periodicals under the pen-name "Susan Coolidge." Widely read, a sound critic, with a facile pen, she published many miscellaneous works during her lifetime but is chiefly remembered as a writer of popular books for girls. Among these was the well-known *What Katy Did* series, brought out at intervals between 1872 and 1886.

Her versatility and energy made her a notable figure in any group and these qualities were transmitted through her pen to influence and enliven the minds of her readers, both juvenile and adult.

PRINCIPAL WORKS: *Poetry*—Verses, 1880; A Few More Verses, 1889; Last Verses, 1906. *Miscellaneous*—Autobiography and Correspondence of Mrs. Delany, 1879; The Diary and Letters of Frances Burney, Madame d'Arblay, 1880; Letters of Jane Austen, 1892; A Short History of the City of Philadelphia, 1887. *Juvenile*—What Katy Did, 1872; What Katy Did At School, 1873; Mischief's Thankgiving, 1874; Nine Little Goslings, 1875; For Summer Afternoons, 1876; Eyebright, 1879; A Guernsey Lily, 1880; Cross Patch, 1881; A Round Dozen, 1883; A Little Country Girl, 1885; What Katy Did Next, 1886; Just Sixteen, 1889; In the High Valley, 1891; The Barberry Bush, 1893; Not Quite Eighteen, 1894; An Old Convent School in Paris and Other Papers, 1895.

ABOUT: Woolsey, S. C. Last Verses; Wickham, G. V. R. The Pioneer Families of Cleveland; Outlook April 15, 1905.

WOOLSEY, THEODORE DWIGHT (October 31, 1801-July 1, 1889), scholar and miscellaneous writer, was born in New York City, the son of William Walton Woolsey, a prosperous hardware mechant, and Elizabeth (Dwight) Woolsey, sister of Timothy Dwight [*q.v.*], the poet-president of Yale, and a granddaughter of Jonathan Edwards. In 1808 the family moved to New Haven, where he attended Hopkins Grammar School and then went to live with his uncle Theodore in Hartford. His mother died in 1813 and his father remarried. Woolsey received his B.A. at Yale in 1820, as valedictorian of his class, and his M.A. in 1823. He had meanwhile been instructed in law by his stepmother's brother in Philadelphia in 1820, and had been a student at Princeton Theological Seminary to 1823, returning to Yale both as tutor and as theological student. He was licensed to preach in the Congregational Church, but felt himself unfitted for the ministry. From 1827 to 1830 he was a student in France and Germany. The next year he became professor of Greek at Yale. Between 1834 and 1842 he edited a series of Greek texts.

In 1846 Woolsey became president of Yale; at the same time he was ordained. He served until 1871, when he was retired at the age of 70, but he remained a member of the corporation until 1885. Under his presidency Yale acquired its scientific school and its school of fine arts, and he did much

Collection of Frederick H. Meserve
THEODORE DWIGHT WOOLSEY

to raise its scholastic standard. He ceased to teach Greek, but took over the chair of political science and international law. Among his outside interests were the *Independent,* of which he was a founder, the Smithsonian Institution, of which he was a regent, and the American Committee for Revision of the English Bible. Woolsey Hall, at Yale, was named for him. He was twice married, in 1833 to Elizabeth Martha Salisbury, who died in 1852, leaving nine children, and in 1854 to Sarah Sears Prichard, by whom he had four more children.

Woolsey was a reserved, reticent man of high principles but little suavity. His books, mostly on political science or international law, are like the man—sound, scholarly, and dry.

Principal Works: Introduction to the Study of International Law, 1860; Essay on Divorce and Divorce Legislation, 1869; Religion of the Present and of the Future, 1871; Helpful Thoughts for Young Men, 1874; Political Science, 1878; Communism and Socialism, 1880.

About: Dwight, T. Theodore Dwight Woolsey; Woolsey, T. S. Theodore Dwight Woolsey: A Biographical Sketch; Atlantic Monthly October 1889; Century Magazine September 1882; Yale Review January, April, July 1912; (New Haven) Morning Journal and Courier-July 2, 1889 .

WOOLSON, ABBA LOUISA (GOOLD) (April 30, 1838-February 6, 1921), lecturer, teacher and essayist, was born in Windham, Maine, the daughter of William and Nabby Tukey (Clark) Goold. On her father's side she was descended from a Jarvice Goold who came from England in 1635 and settled in Hingham, Mass. Graduated as valedictorian from the Portland High School for Girls, she was married the same summer to its principal, Moses Woolson. They made their home successively in Portland; Concord, N.H.; and from 1868 in Boston. In the first two cities she taught in the high schools, and also for a time taught in Cincinnati, Ohio, and was principal of the Haverhill, Mass., high school. She lectured widely on English literature and, as a consequence of two visits to Spain, on historic Spanish cities. She was founder of the Castilian Club of Boston. She died childless, in Maine.

Her first published effort, a sonnet, appeared in 1856 in the New York *Home Journal,* and was soon followed by other contributions to Boston and Portland journals, a series of poems appearing anonymously from 1859 in the Portland *Transcript.* Her article on the "Present Aspect of the Byron Case" in the Boston *Journal* attracted especial attention. Several of her books, *Woman in American Society, Browsing Among Books,* and *George Eliot and Her Heroines,* were made up of collected sketches. A series of lectures on healthful dress for women was later edited by her and published as *Dress-Reform.* Her last volume was a small privately printed collection of verse.

Principal Works: Woman in American Society, 1873; Browsing Among Books, 1881; George Eliot and Her Heroines, 1886; With Garlands Green (verse) 1915. *Editor*—Dress-Reform, 1874.

About: Willard, F. E. & Livermore, M. A. A Woman of the Century; Boston Transcript Feb. 7, 1921.

WOOLSON, CONSTANCE FENIMORE (March 3, 1840-January 24, 1894), novelist, was born in Claremont, N.H., the youngest of the six daughters of Charles Jarvis Woolson, a wealthy business man, and Hannah Cooper (Pomeroy) Woolson. Other dates given for her birth, March 5, 1838, and March 5, 1848, are both incorrect. Mrs. Woolson was a niece of James Fenimore Cooper, and from him Constance inherited her middle name and perhaps her talent. In her infancy the family moved to Cleveland, where she was educated at Miss Hayden's School, and the Cleveland Young Ladies' Seminary. Then she went to New York, to Mme. Chegary's School, from which she was graduated in 1858 at the head of her class. During her vacations she took long trips with her father through what was then wilderness country in Ohio and Wisconsin, and laid the foundation of her intimate knowledge of the region and its people.

Except for a little ladylike Civil War work, Miss Woolson had no thought of any but a domestic career until her father died in 1869, and his fortune died with him. She had had a long poem published in 1862, and she determined on literature as a profession. Her early regional stories, poems, and articles appeared in the *Atlantic Monthly, Harper's, Appleton's, Lippincott's,* and all the best magazines of the period. Meanwhile, with a sister and her mother, she traveled up and down the Atlantic Coast, from New York to Florida. Always restless, she lived longer in St. Augustine, Fla., than anywhere else, and wove rural Georgia and Florida into her stories. Her mother died, and in 1879 she went to Europe, never to return. Again she traveled constantly, with Florence as her headquarters; in 1890 she went to Egypt, then for three years lived in England, chiefly at Oxford, and then returned to Italy. She died in Venice, and is buried in the English Protestant Cemetery at Rome, which contains the graves of Shelley, Keats and Trelawny.

Miss Woolson was a woman who kept her private life to herself, and except for her family devotion, and the inferences to be drawn from her constant traveling and inability to settle anywhere, little is known of her emotional history. Her picture, shows, under a cap of curls, a strong and melancholy face. Her death was both affirmed and denied to be a suicide.

Collection of Frederick H. Meserve
CONSTANCE FENIMORE WOOLSON

She was one of the pioneers of regional *genre* fiction in America. Her friend (and to some extent her master), Henry James, praised her skill in "evoking local tone" and her careful, detailed observation. Edmund Clarence Stedman called her "a realist with the transfiguring faculty of an idealist." She was a little monotonous in her favorite theme of the strong who sacrifices himself for the weak, but she remains a rewarding novelist for the fastidious and discriminating reader whose critical ear is adjusted to the quiet tone.

PRINCIPAL WORKS: Two Women (verse) 1862; Castle Nowhere: Lake County Sketches, 1875; Rodman the Keeper: Southern Sketches, 1880; For the Major, 1883; Anne, 1883; East Angels, 1886; Jupiter Lights, 1889; Horace Chase, 1894; The Front Yard, 1895; Mentone, Cario, and Corfu, 1895; Dorothy, 1896.

ABOUT: Benedict, C. Constance Feminore Woolson; James, H. Partial Portraits; Kern, J. D. Constance Fenimore Woolson: Literary Pioneer; Pattee, F. L. The Development of the American Short Story; Harper's Weekly February 3 and 10, 1894; New York Times January 25 and 26, 1904.

WORCESTER, JOSEPH EMERSON (August 24, 1784-October 27, 1865), lexicographer and geographer, was born at Bedford, N.H., the son of Jesse Worcester, a former teacher turned farmer, and himself something of an author, and Sarah (Parker) Worcester. Fourteen of the fifteen children in the family became public school teachers. The boy worked on the farm and studied long hours by himself, until in 1805 he was able to go to Phillips Academy (Andover), and in 1809 to Yale. He was graduated in 1811, and went to Salem to teach, one of his pupils being Nathaniel Hawthorne. In 1817 he moved to Andover, and two years later to Cambridge, his home for the rest of his life. He had rooms in the Craigie House when Longfellow first moved there as a young professor.

Worcester's first interest was in geography, then in history, and finally in lexicography and philology. In these subjects he was for the most part self-taught. Before issuing the first of his own dictionaries, he edited a new edition of Johnson's in 1828, and abridged Webster's in 1829. His relation with Noah Webster, however, was not a friendly one; their viewpoints were dia-

Collection of Frederick H. Meserve
JOSEPH EMERSON WORCESTER

metrically opposed, Worcester being a conservative, Webster an innovator; and Webster accused his rival of plagiarizing him. This "war of the dictionaries" lasted to the period when a more important Civil War caused it to be forgotten.

In 1830, Worcester spent eight months abroad in study, and on his return undertook the editing of the *American Almanac and Repository of Useful Knowledge,* which was his chief concern to 1842. In 1841, at the age of fifty-seven, he married for the first (and only) time; his bride, who was forty, was Amy Elizabeth McKean, daughter of a Harvard professor, and she became his chief assistant. He soon needed one, for cataracts developed on both his eyes, and after several operations he became completely blind in one eye and almost so in the other. However, he continued to bring out new editions of his *Comprehensive Dictionary,* and also published two new dictionaries; his final work in this field, the *Dictionary of the English Language,* being the first illustrated dictionary. He received honorary degrees from Yale, Brown, and Dartmouth, was elected to the Massachusetts Historical Society and the American Academy of Arts and Sciences, and—what he valued most—became a member of the Royal Geographical Society, in London.

For this dignified little man with the benign countenance was a lover of the old and well-established. He detested Webster's Americanisms in spelling and pronounciation, and he was the standby of the scholarly and fastidious, while Webster was sworn by in circles of a more pioneering cast. Worcester's dictionaries became a Boston Bible, and he had some disciples up to the end of the nineteenth century. Now, however, he belongs to the history of lexicography; Webster and his followers carried off the palm. Thirty years ago Webster and Worcester were authorities of equal weight in the schools; today his very name is unfamiliar to most high school and college students.

Principal Works: A Geographical Dictionary: or, Universal Gazetteer, Ancient and Modern, 1817; A Gazetteer of the United States, 1818; Elements of Geography, 1819; Sketches of the Earth and Its Inhabitants, 1823; Elements of History: Ancient and Modern, 1826; Comprehensive Dictionary, 1830; A Universal and Critical Dictionary of the English Language, 1846 ; A Gross Literary Fraud Exposed, 1853; A Dictionary of the English Language, 1860.

About: Abbot, E. Memoir of Joseph E. Worcester; Brooks, Van W. The Flowering of New England; Krapp, G. P. The English Language in America; Mathews, M. M. A Survey of English Dictionaries; Steger, S. A. American Dictionaries; Worcester, J. E. Dictionary of the English Language (see Biographical Sketch by G. S. Hillard in 1878 ed.); Granite Monthly April 1880; Proceedings Massachusetts Historical Society 1881; Boston Evening Transcript October 27, 1865.

WORMELEY, KATHARINE PRESCOTT (January 14, 1830-August 4, 1908), philanthropist and translator, was born in Ipswich, England. Her parents, Ralph Randolph Wormeley, Rear-Admiral in the British navy, and Caroline (Preble) Wormeley, were both of American birth and parentage. Considerable contact with French and English culture marked her early years, and when she was eighteen the family settled permanently in the United States, residing for the most part in Newport, R.I. During the Civil War she became interested in relief work for Union soldiers and for a time was superintendent of a convalescent hospital at Portsmouth Grove, R.I. She was active in philanthropic work in Newport, giving especial attention to sanitary matters and the welfare of women and girls, founding and financing for its first three years the Girls' Industrial School. She died in Jackson, N.H.

During her war work she prepared for publication an account of the purposes and work of the United States Sanitary Commission, and her letters from the headquarters of that commission were later published as *The Other Side of War.* Her most notable work was, however, her extensive translations from the French, including nearly forty works of Balzac, the works of Alphonse Daudet, several of the elder Dumas, memoirs of a number of noted people, and selections, among others, from Molière, Saint-Beuve, and Paul Bourget. The standard translations were notable for accuracy and sympathetic understanding. With her two sisters, Mrs. Mary Elizabeth Wormeley Latimer, also an author and translator, and Mrs. Ariana Randolph Curtis, author of a parlor play "The Coming Woman," she compiled the recollections of her father.

PRINCIPAL WORKS: The Other Side of War, 1889; A Memoir of Honoré de Balzac, 1892. *Compilations*—The United States Sanitary Commission, 1863; Recollections of Ralph Randolph Wormeley (with M. E. W. Latimer & A. R. Curtis) 1879.

ABOUT: Willard, F. E. & Livermore, M. A. A Woman of the Century; Dial August 16, 1908.

WRIGHT, CHAUNCEY (September 20, 1830-September 12, 1875), philosopher, was born in Northampton, Mass., the son of Ansel and Elizabeth Boleyn (or Bullen) Wright. His father was a trader and deputy sheriff, and his grandfather had been a soldier in the Revolution. Chauncey attended Harvard, concentrating on the study of philosophy, mathematics, and the natural sciences. On his graduation in 1852 he worked for the *American Ephemeris and Nautical Almanac,* devising new methods of calculation. He wrote for the *Mathematical Monthly* and other magazines, was secretary of the American Academy of Arts and Sciences from 1863 to 1870, and edited its "Proceedings." From 1864 he contributed to the *North American Review* a series of distinguished philosophical papers, and later to the *Nation.* He lectured at Harvard on the principles of psychology in 1870 and in 1874 was instructor in mathematical physics. He died in Cambridge the year after this latter appointment.

Wright was never married, and although devoted to quiet scholarly pursuits was a genial, kindly friend and a lover of children. He lived in the house known as "The Village Blacksmith's" in Cambridge.

Wright's articles and researches on the natural sciences were of great value, his essay on the law of the arrangement of leaves winning the praise of Darwin. Although influenced by Herbert Spencer and Hamilton, he adhered to no one school in philosophy and was uninfluenced by the thought of fame or money. Charles Eliot Norton ranked him "among the as yet few great thinkers of America" and his contributions to philosophy and metaphysics were the extremely valuable and important fruits of a brilliant and acute mind.

PRINCIPAL WORKS: Philosophical Discussions, 1877.

ABOUT: Fiske, J. Darwinism and Other Essays; Norton, C. E. Philosophical Discusssions; Thayer, J. B. Letters of Chauncey Wright; Boston Transcript September 14, 1875.

WRIGHT, FRANCES (September 6, 1795-December 13, 1852), reformer, freethinker, traveler, and journalist, was born in Dundee, Scotland, the daughter of James Wright, wealthy radical who aided in the publicizing of Thomas Paine's *Rights of Man.* She was scarcely two and a half years old when her parents died, leaving her heir to a large fortune. Relatives in London provided her with a conventional education in the city and saw the climax of her youthful rebelliousness in her sudden return to Scotland. At the age of eighteen Frances wrote *A Few Days in Athens,* projected as the tale of a young disciple of Epicurus; it incorporated a well-weighed theory of materialism to which she afterwards long adhered, but the *London Literary Gazette* "would only recommend kindly to this writer to lay down the pen and take up the needle. . ."

With her younger sister, Camilla, she arrived in New York in 1818; enjoyed the friendship of a number of young intellectuals; and succeeded in getting her anonymous *Altorf,* a re-enactment of the Swiss struggle for independence, produced at the Park Theatre. After an extensive journey through the Northern and Eastern states she sailed for England. The enthusiastic tone of her *Views of Society and Manners in America* eventually resulted in a friendship with Lafayette, whom she and her sister later accompanied during most of his tour through the States in 1824. The book was condemned by the *London Quarterly Review* as

> A most ridiculous and extravagant panegyric on the government and people of the United States; accompanied by the grossest and most detestable calumnies against this country . .

but from the point of view of American social history it retains considerable significance.

Both Jefferson and Madison approved of Frances Wright's plan for the gradual emancipation of the slaves. With sufficient encouragement she bought a large tract of land in Tennessee ("Nashoba"); purchased slaves, in 1825; allowed them to work off their freedom; and in 1830 colonized them in Haiti. Meanwhile in 1828 she had joined

Robert Dale Owen, the Welsh manufacturer and philanthropist, in the publication of the *New Harmony Gazette,* interpretative organ of his New Harmony (Indiana) Community. In October of that year the influence of her own socializing project occasioned a change, in series and title, to the *New Harmony and Nashoba Gazette: or, The Free Enquirer,* "devoted without fear, without reserves, without pledge to men, parties, sects or systems, to free, unbiased and universal enquiry." Beginning January 1829 it was published in New York as the *Free Enquirer.*

Frances Wright was abroad in 1831 and in July of that year was married to William Phiquepal D'Arusmont, a former associate at New Harmony, by whom she had one daughter; their marriage ended in a divorce.

Even more "unfeminine" than "Fanny" Wright's attacks on religion, defense of equal rights for women, theory of marriage in which the legal obligation is replaced by the moral obligation only, alignment with the free-thinkers, or interest in the organizing of the working-class, was, it appears, her activities as a public speaker. But Frances Wright's remarkable courage and undeniable intelligence, which occasionally combined to produce an effective piece of writing, were notable contributions to the emancipation of women.

PRINCIPAL WORKS: Altorf, 1819; Views of Society and Manners in America (London) 1821; A Few Days in Athens, 1822; Course of Popular Lectures, 1829.

ABOUT: Bradlaugh, C. Biographies of Ancient and Modern Celebrated Free Thinkers; Gilbert, A. Memoir of Frances Wright; Mott, F. L. A History of American Magazines; Waterman, W. R. Frances Wright; Cincinnati Daily Gazette December 15, 1852.

WRIGHT, JOHN STEPHEN (July 16, 1815-September 26, 1874), editor, promoter, and publicist, was born in Sheffield, Mass., the eldest son of John Wright and Huldah (Dewey) Wright. Educated under his uncle, Chester Dewey, scientist and professor in Williams College, at seventeen he went with his father to Chicago where they opened a store on the prairie at what is now Clark and Lake streets. The following year he proceeded to take a census, and in 1834 published one of the first lithographic maps of the town. He acquired extensive real estate, undertook the manufacture of a self-raking reaper, and acquired two fortunes which he lost in the successive panics of 1837 and 1856. He also variously acted as manager of the Union Agricultural Society, undertook to promote a railroad from Chicago to the Gulf of Mexico, and formed a land company. As a leader in education he built with his own funds the first public school building erected in the city. His mind gave way in his last years and he died in a Philadelphia asylum.

In 1839 he issued for the Union Agricultural Society the *Union Agriculturist,* later the *Prairie Farmer,* of which he became the owner, 1843-57. While active on the magazine he acquired wide knowledge of agricultural and industrial conditions throughout the Middle West and an enhanced conception of the importance of the city and state. His knowledge and faith in the region are embodied in his elaborate *Chicago: Past, Present and Future.*

PRINCIPAL WORKS: Citizenship Sovereignty, 1863; Illinois to Massachusetts: Greeting! 1866; Reply to Hon. Charles G. Loring Upon "Reconstruction," 1867; Chicago: Past, Present and Future, 1868.

ABOUT: Andreas, A. T. History of Chicago; Wright, A. W. In Memoriam: John S. Wright; Wright, C. Genealogical and Biographical Notices of Decendants of Sir John Wright.

WYCKOFF, WALTER AUGUSTUS (April 12, 1865-May 15, 1908), sociologist, born in Mainpuri, India, was the son of an American Presbyterian missionary of Dutch ancestry, the Rev. Benjamin DuBois Wyckoff, and Melissa Wyckoff. Sent to America for his education, he studied at the Hudson Academy, the Freehold Institute, the College of New Jersey (later Princeton), and for a year in the Princeton Theological Seminary, after which he traveled abroad. In 1891, desiring to study at first hand the conditions of the American laboring man, he made his way as an unskilled laborer from Connecticut to California, arriving in San Francisco in 1893. Later as a tutor he traveled twice around the world. In 1894 he was appointed a fellow in social science at Princeton, the following year being made lecturer of sociology, and three years later assistant professor of political economy, holding that chair until his death at forty-three. He left a wife, Leah Lucille Ehrich, who was a gifted musician, and a daughter.

Wyckoff published at account of his 1891-1893 experiences in two volumes as *The Workers: An Experiment in Reality,* and some years later recounted some further experiences of the same period as *A Day With a Tramp and Other Days. The Workers* was first published as a serial in *Scribner's Magazine,* to which he also contributed various other writings, including the "Arctic Highlanders," an outcome of his membership in the Peary Auxiliary Expedition in 1899. His labor studies were an important contribution to the realistic side of sociology, although lacking the systematic organization of a trained sociologist.

PRINCIPAL WORKS: The Workers: An Experiment in Reality—The East, 1897; The Workers: An Experiment in Reality—The West, 1898; A Day With a Tramp and Other Days, 1901.

ABOUT: Princeton Theological Seminary Necrological Report; Charities and the Commons May 30, 1908; Critic June 1903.

"XARIFFA." See TOWNSEND, MARY (ASHLEY)

YOAKUM, HENDERSON (September 6, 1810-November 30, 1856), Texas historian, was the son of a farmer, George Yoakum, and Colly (Maddy) Yoakum, of Powell's Valley, Clairborne County, Tenn. Entering the United States Military Academy at eighteen, he became on his graduation in 1832 a brevet second lieutenant in the Third Artillery, but resigned the following year to study and practice law in Murfreesboro. Re-entering military service in the Cherokee war and the war with Mexico, he served as colonel and first lieutenant. From 1845 he lived in and near Huntsville, Tex. While visiting Houston to deliver a Masonic address, he died suddenly in the old Capitol Hotel. A county in west Texas was named in his honor.

Yoakum's only published work, aside from some periodical contributions, was a history of Texas, including many important documents, in two volumes, a production which, notwithstanding some imperfections and partisanship, was accepted for half a century as a standard work. It was in 1898 republished with additional notes and chapters by Dudley G. Wooten in his *A Comprehensive History of Texas: 1685 to 1897*.

PRINCIPAL WORKS: History of Texas From Its First Settlement in 1685 to Its Annexation to the United States in 1846.

ABOUT: Bancroft, H. H. History of the Pacific States of North America; Fulmore, Z. T. The History and Geography of Texas as Told in County Names; Thrall, H. S. A Pictorial History of Texas.

"YORICK." See WARD, JAMES WARNER

YOUMANS, EDWARD LIVINGSTON (June 3, 1821-January 18, 1887), editor and writer on science, was born in Coeymans, Albany County, N.Y., the eldest son of a farmer and mechanic, Vincent Youmans, and Catherine (Scofield) Youmans. Aside from an elementary education, commenced at the age of three, he was practically self-educated. From seventeen to thirty an eye affection, aggravated by quack treatment, caused alternating periods of total and near-blindness; treatment in New York City, where he went at the age of twenty, finally gave him some measure of relief. For seventeen years (1851-1868) he was a popular lecturer on science. His sister, Eliza Ann Youmans, and later his wife, Catherine E. (Newton) Lee Youmans, whom he married in 1861, were long of material aid to him in his scientific studies, writing and promotional work. He died in New York City.

Previously anticipated in two attempts to prepare books, he finally published his first volume, *A Class-Book of Chemistry*. which had a wide sale. He later prepared a *Chemical Atlas* along similar lines, and a volume on science in the home. Among his edited works were several volumes of Herbert Spencer, whom he endeavored to popularize in America, two collections, *Correlation and Conservation of Forces,* a series of papers by well-known scientists, and *The Culture Demanded by Modern Life,* addresses on scientific education. Youmans initiated and promoted the International Scientfic Series, consisting of more than fifty volumes written by prominent scientists for the popular understanding. In 1872 he founded the *Popular Science Monthly,* later the *Scientific Monthly;* in its editing he was assisted by his brother, William Jay Youmans.

PRINCIPAL WORKS: A Class-Book of Chemistry, 1851; Alcohol and the Constitution of Man, 1854; Chemical Atlas, 1854; Hand-Book of Household Science, 1857; Herbert Spencer on the Americans and the Americans on Herbert Spencer, 1883. *Editor*—Correlation and Conservation of Forces, 1864; The Culture Demanded by Modern Life, 1867.

ABOUT: Fiske, J. Edward Livingston Youmans; Popular Science Monthly March 1887; Scientific Monthly March 1924.

"YOUNG, ANNIE." See DUPUY, ELIZA ANN

YOUNG, DAVID (January 27, 1781-February 13, 1852), astronomer, poet, teacher, lecturer, and almanac maker, the son of Amos Young, a farmer, and Sarah (Mott) Young, was a native of Pine Brook, Morris County, N.J. In early life he taught school in Elizabeth-Town and in New Providence, N.J., then known as Turkey, and in latter years in and near Hanover Neck, Morris County, where he died. A natural astronomer, of apparently wide culture and strong personality, he exerted a considerable influence through astronomical lectures and through the almanacs that he prepared annually from 1814 until his death. Among the more prominent of these were the *Citizens' & Farmers' Almanac* published at Morristown, N.J., on which he was engaged from 1814 to 1826, and the *Farmer's Almanac* of Newark. His name appeared on these as "David Young, Philom" the latter a title used by almanac makers previously, implying "love of learning."

Among his other published works were some lectures on astronomy, and two didactic Miltonian poems *The Contrast,* a religious production in blank verse comparing wisdom and folly, and *The Perusal,* a scholarly and philosophic interpretation of nature. *The Wonderful History of the Morristown Ghost* was a carefully revised production of a previously published anonymous pamphlet containing an exposé of a gold-finding hoax perpetrated in 1778-1779 by a schoolmaster, Ransford Rogers, and his confederates. In *The Astonishing Visit,* he gave a sermonic interpretation, in the light of astronomy, of the VIII Psalm.

PRINCIPAL WORKS: The Contrast, 1804; The Perusal: or, The Book of Nature Unfolded, 1818; Lectures on the Science of Astronomy, 1821; A Lecture on the Laws of Motion, 1825; The Wonderful History of the Morristown Ghost, 1826; The Astonishing Visit, 1836.

ABOUT: Proceedings of the New Jersey Historical Society October 1927.

YOUNG, JOHN RUSSELL (November 20, 1840-January 17, 1899), journalist and biographer, was born in Tyrone County, Ireland, the oldest child of George and Rebecca (Rankin) Young; both parents were Scotch, and the father was a weaver. The family emigrated while he was an infant, settling first in Downingtown, Pa., then in Philadelphia, where he attended public school. His mother died in 1851, and he was sent to New Orleans to an uncle, graduating from high school there.

In 1855 he returned to Philadelphia and was apprenticed to a cousin who was a printer. At seventeen he was a copy boy on the Philadelphia *Press.* He attracted the attention of the owner, Col. John Forney, who took him into his home and made a reporter of him. In 1861 he was a war correspondent, the first to report the battle of Bull Run. The next year he became managing editor of the *Press* and also of Forney's other paper, the *Morning Post,* which soon died.

In 1865 Jay Cooke brought Young to New York to write publicity for federal war bonds; from this job he became a columnist

Collection of Frederick H. Meserve
JOHN RUSSELL YOUNG

on the *Tribune,* under Greeley, and within a year was its managing editor. From 1870 to 1872 he published his own paper, the *Standard;* during these same years he twice went abroad on confidential trips for the State Department. In 1872 he was put in charge of the London and Paris editions of the *Herald.* When Grant reached Paris on his round-the-world trip in 1877, he struck up a friendship with Young, and took him along as companion. In China, Young, who had a genius for friendship, became the intimate of the great prime minister, Li Hung Chang; and through his and Grant's influence, President Arthur made him minister to China in 1882. He resigned on Cleveland's election in 1884, and returned to the *Herald* and to London and Paris.

In 1890 Young came back to Philadelphia, where he owned and edited the *Star.* An ardent Republican, he helped to found the Union League Club and was its president in 1892. In 1897 McKinley appointed him Librarian of Congress. In spite of lack of technical training, he filled the post efficiently, and most of the moving from the Capitol to the new library building was done during his incumbency. He died while still in office. He was married three times: in 1864 to Rose Fitzpatrick, who died soon after the death of their son and daughter; in 1882 to Julia Coleman; and in 1890 to Mrs. May (Dow) Davids, by whom he had two sons, besides adopting her two sons by her first marriage. She edited his autobiography after his death.

Young was a first-rate reporter, with a good journalistic style; but he belongs to literature less for his published books than as one of the last of the great nineteenth century dynasty of "writing editors."

PRINCIPAL WORKS: Around the World With General Grant, 1879; Men and Memories, 1901.

ABOUT: Young, J. R. Men and Memories; Washington Post January 18, 1899.

YOUNG, THOMAS (February 19, 1731/32-June 24, 1777), patriot and physician, was born in New Windsor, Ulster County, N.Y., the son of John Young who came to New York in 1729 and Mary (Crawford) Young. His education was broadened by access to the library of a kinsman, Col. Charles Clinton. In 1753 he commenced the practice of medicine at Amenia, Dutchess County, N.Y., and soon became widely known. Later he resided successively in Albany, Boston, and Philadelphia. During the Revolutionary period he was zealous in the cause of the colonies and took part in the Boston Tea Party of 1773. He assisted in the framing of the constitution of Pennsylvania and gave active encouragement to the formation of an independent state in the New Hampshire Grants, himself suggesting for it the name of Vermont, his activity in behalf of its independence being censured by the United States Congress. He died after a day's illness from a virulent fever contracted while serving as a senior surgeon in one of the Continental hospitals in Philadelphia.

Young contributed to contemporary journals on medical, political, and religious subjects. In an early epic poem of 608 lines, first published anonymously, he described the seige of Quebec by Major-General James Wolfe in 1759. Having acquired a tract of land in what is now Vermont, the long litigation over the title of which left him almost penniless, he sought to defend the claims of the Dutch trader, John Henry Lydius, from whom he had purchased it, in a pamphlet *Some Reflections on the Disputes Between New-York, New-Hampshire, and Col. John Henry Lydius,* written over the signature "Philodicaius." He is credited with collaborating with the Revolutionary soldier, Ethan Allen, in the production of *Reason the Only Oracle of Man,* most of the first edition of which was destroyed at the printer's, in part by fire, and in part by the printer, because of its alleged atheism.

PRINCIPAL WORKS: A Poem Sacred to the Memory of James Wolfe . . . Who Was Slain Upon the Plains of Abraham, 1761; Some Reflections on the Disputes Between New-York, New-Hampshire, and Col. John Henry Lydius, 1764; Reason the Only Oracle of Man: or, A Compendious System of Natural Religion (with Ethan Allen) 1784.

ABOUT: Hall, H. The History of Vermont; Hemenway, A. M. The Vermont Historical Gazetteer; Pell, J. Ethan Allen; Records of the Council of Safety . . . . of the State of Vermont; Pennsylvania Magazine of History and Biography October 1898.

ZACHOS, JOHN CELIVERGOS (December 20, 1820-March 20, 1898), educator and clergyman, was born in Constantinople, Turkey, the son of Greek parents, Nicholas and Euphrosyne Zachos. Brought to America at the age of ten by the philanthropist Dr. Samuel Gridley Howe, he studied successively at Amherst, Mass.; at Kenyon College, Gambier, Ohio, from which he was graduated with honors in 1840; and at the medical school of Miami University, Oxford, Ohio (1842-45). He became associate principal of the Cooper Female Seminary, Dayton, Ohio (1851-54), principal of the Grammar School of Antioch College, Yellow Springs, Ohio (1854-57), and during the Civil War was an assistant surgeon in the Union forces and at one time practically governor of Parris Island, Port Royal, S.C. After private study of theology he was ordained a Unitarian minister, holding pastorates at West Newton, Mass., and Meadville, Pa.; also teaching rhetoric in the Meadville Theological School. From 1871 he resided in New York City, and until his death was curator and instructor in literature and oratory in Cooper Union. He was the inventor in 1876 of the stenotype for printing at high reporting speed. He married Harriet Tomkins Canfield, by whom he had six children.

Zachos was one of the editors in 1852-53 of the *Ohio Journal of Education,* and a contributor to the *Christian Examiner.* His interest in English led to the production of several textbooks, his *Phonic Primer and Reader* being especially designed for adult evening classes and for the newly emancipated Negroes. He also prepared two publications on the life and opinions of Peter Cooper, founder of Cooper Union, and under the pseudonym "Cadmus" two pamphlets of a financial nature.

PRINCIPAL WORKS: The New American Speaker, 1851; Analytic Elocution, 1861; A New System of Phonic Reading Without Changing the Orthography, 1863; The Phonic Primer and Reader, 1864; A Sketch of the Life and Opinions of Mr. Peter Cooper, 1876; Our Financial Revolution: An Address to the Merchants and Professional Men of the Country Without Respect to Parties, 1878; The Fiscal Problem of All Civilized Nations, 1881.

ABOUT: Canfield, F. A. A History of Thomas Canfield.

ZENGER, JOHN PETER (1697-July 28, 1746), journalist and printer—the first martyr in the struggle for a free press in America—was born in southern Germany, the given names of his parents unknown. In 1710 Queen Anne sent many of the Palatine Germans to America, and the Zenger family was among them. His father died on board ship. The boy was apprenticed to William Bradford, the first printer in New York; though he was only thirteen he seems never to have gained a good command of English, and indeed Dutch was still as common a language in the former New Amsterdam.

In 1719, his indenture finished, he married Mary White and settled as a printer in Chestertown, Md.; there he printed the session laws, and was naturalized as a British subject. His wife died, leaving a son, and he moved to New York, where in 1722 he married Anna Catherina Maulin, a native of Germany, by whom he had five children. In 1725 he became a partner of his former master, Bradford; but the next year he set up in business for himself, as the second printer in New York. The books he published were mostly Dutch and English sermons, but he brought out the first arithmetic to be printed in the colony.

In 1733 Zenger was backed as publisher and nominal editor of the New York *Weekly Journal,* a paper founded to fight the administration of Gov. William Cosby. It soon fell afoul of the governor, some issues were ordered burned, and in 1734 Zenger was arrested and held in prison for ten months, while his wife brought out the paper. His trial in 1735 for criminal libel was the beginning of the struggle for a free press in America; his first attorneys were disbarred, and at the second trial the judge ordered his conviction, but the jury acquitted him. In 1737, in recognition of his martyrdom, he was named public printer of New York, and later of New Jersey also, but he was dismissed from both posts because of his poor spelling and ignorance of English idiom. He died in poverty, but his paper was continued by his widow to 1748, and by his son to 1751.

Zenger did not even write the book which appeared over his name; it was probably the work of James Alexander. But he was a courageous and freedom-loving man—"the morning star of that liberty which subsequently revolutionized America."

Principal Work: A Brief Narrative of the Case and Tryal of John Peter Zenger, 1736.

About: Hildeburn, C. R. Sketches of Printers and Printing in Colonial New York; Rutherford, L. John Peter Zenger; Thomas, I. History of Printing in America; Princeton Review January 1886; New York Evening Post August 4, 1746.